THE 2008 ANNOTATED

DIVORCE ACT

James MacDonald, Q.C.
of the Ontario and British Columbia Bars

Ann Wilton
B.A., M.A. (Oxon), LL.B., of the Ontario Bar

STATUTES OF CANADA ANNOTATED

THOMSON
CARSWELL

♾ The paper used in this publication meets the minimum requirements of American National Standard for Information Sciences — Permanence of Paper for Printed Library Materials, ANSI Z39.48–1984.

Canadian Cataloguing in Publication Data

Library and Archives Canada has catalogued this publication as follows:

MacDonald, James C., 1934–

The annotated Divorce Act / James MacDonald, Ann Wilton.

(Statutes of Canada annotated)

Annual.

ISSN 1189-8119

ISBN 978-0-7798-1222-6 (2008 Edition)

1. Canada. Divorce Act. 2. Divorce — Law and legislation — Canada.

I. Wilton, Ann, 1952– II. Carswell (Firm). III. Title: Divorce Act. IV. Series.

KE564.57.M33 346.7101'66'02632 C94-390023-9 rev
KF535.M33

The acid-free paper used in this publication meets the minimum requirements of American National Standard for Information Sciences — Permanence of Paper for Printed Library Materials, ANSI Z39.48-1984.

THOMSON
CARSWELL

One Corporate Plaza
2075 Kennedy Road
Toronto, Ontario
M1T 3V4

Customer Relations
Toronto 1-416-609-3800
Elsewhere in Canada/U.S. 1-800-387-5164
Fax 1-416-298-5082
World Wide Web: http://www.carswell.com
E-mail: carswell.orders@thomson.com

PUBLISHER'S NOTE

Legislation is current to July 25, 2007, Canada Gazette No. 141:15.

TABLE OF CONTENTS

TABLE OF CASES

DIVORCE ACT

R.S.C. 1985, c. 3 (2nd Supp.), as am. R.S.C. 1985, c. 27 (2nd Supp.), s. 10; S.C. 1990, c. 18, ss. 1, 2; 1992, c. 51, s. 46; 1993, c. 8, ss. 1–5; 1993, c. 28, s. 78 (Sched. III, items 41–43) [Amended 1998, c. 15, ss. 22, 23; 1999, c. 3, s. 12 (Sched., item 11).]; 1997, c. 1, ss. 1–15; 1998, c. 30, ss. 13(f) (Fr.), 15(f); 1999, c. 3, s. 61; 1999, c. 31, s. 74 (Fr.); 2002, c. 7, ss. 158–160; 2002, c. 8, s. 183(1)(i); 2005, c. 33, s. 8(1), (2) (Fr.); 2007, c. 14.

SHORT TITLE

1. Short title — This Act may be cited as the *Divorce Act*.

INTERPRETATION

2. (1) Definitions — In this Act,

"age of majority", in respect of a child, means the age of majority as determined by the laws of the province where the child ordinarily resides, or, if the child ordinarily resides outside of Canada, eighteen years of age;

"appellate court", in respect of an appeal from a court, means the court exercising appellate jurisdiction with respect to that appeal;

"applicable guidelines", means

(a) where both spouses or former spouses are ordinarily resident in the same province at the time an application for a child support order or a variation order in respect of a child support order is made, or the amount of a child support order is to be recalculated pursuant to section 25.1, and that province has been designated by an order made under subsection (5), the laws of the province specified in the order, and

(b) in any other case, the Federal Child Support Guidelines;

"child of the marriage" means a child of two spouses or former spouses who, at the material time,

(a) is under the age of majority and who has not withdrawn from their charge, or

(b) is the age of majority or over and under their charge but unable, by reason of illness, disability or other cause, to withdraw from their charge or to obtain the necessaries of life;

"child support order", means an order made under subsection 15.1(1);

"corollary relief proceeding" means a proceeding in a court in which either or both former spouses seek a child support order, a spousal support order or a custody order;

"court", in respect of a province, means

(a) for the Province of Ontario, the Superior Court of Justice,

(a.1) for the Province of Prince Edward Island or Newfoundland, the trial division of the Supreme Court of the Province,

(b) for the Province of Quebec, the Superior Court,

(c) for the Province of Nova Scotia and British Columbia, the Supreme Court of the Province,

(d) for the Province of New Brunswick, Manitoba, Saskatchewan or Alberta, the Court of Queen's Bench for the Province, and

(e) for Yukon or the Northwest Territories, the Supreme Court, and in Nunavut, the Nunavut Court of Justice,

and includes such other court in the province the judges of which are appointed by the Governor General as is designated by the Lieutenant Governor in Council of the province as a court for the purposes of this Act;

"custody" includes care, upbringing and any other incident of custody;

"custody order" means an order made under subsection 16(1);

"divorce proceeding" means a proceeding in a court in which either or both spouses seek a divorce alone or together with a child support order, a spousal support order or a custody order;

"Federal Child Support Guidelines" means the guidelines made under section 26.1;

"provincial child support service" means any service, agency or body designated in an agreement with a province under subsection 25.1(1);

"spousal support order" means an order made under subsection 15.2(1);

"spouse" means either of two persons who are married to each other;

"support order" means a child support order or a spousal support order;

"variation order" means an order made under subsection 17(1);

"variation proceeding" means a proceeding in a court in which either or both former spouses seek a variation order.

(2) Child of the marriage — For the purposes of the definition "child of the marriage" in subsection (1), a child of two spouses or former spouses includes

(a) any child for whom they both stand in the place of parents; and

(b) any child of whom one is the parent and for whom the other stands in the place of a parent.

(3) Term not restrictive — The use of the term "application" to describe a proceeding under this Act in a court shall not be construed as limiting the name under which and the form and manner in which that proceeding may be taken in that court, and the name, manner and form of the proceeding in that court shall be such as is provided for by the rules regulating the practice and procedure in that court.

(4) **Idem** — The use in section 21.1 of the terms "affidavit" and "pleadings" to describe documents shall not be construed as limiting the name that may be used to refer to those documents in a court and the form of those documents, and the name and form of the documents shall be such as is provided for by the rules regulating the practice and procedure in that court.

(5) **Provincial child support guidelines** — The Governor in Council may, by order, designate a province for the purposes of the definition "applicable guidelines" in subsection (1) if the laws of the province establish comprehensive guidelines for the determination of child support that deal with the matters referred to in section 26.1. The order shall specify the laws of the province that constitute the guidelines of the province.

(6) **Amendments included** — The guidelines of a province referred to in subsection (5) include any amendments made to them from time to time.

R.S.C. 1985, c. 27 (2nd Supp.), s. 10 (Sched., item 7(1), (2)); 1990, c. 18, s. 1; 1992, c. 51, s. 46; 1993, c. 28, s. 78 (Sched. III, item 41) [Repealed 1999, c. 3, s. 12 (Sched., item 11).]; 1997, c. 1, s. 1; 1998, c. 30, s. 15(f); 1999, c. 3, s. 61; 2002, c. 7, s. 158; 2005, c. 33, s. 8(1)

2§1 — "Age of majority"

The minimum age for a child of the marriage in Canada is the age of majority in the province where the child ordinarily resides (18 in Ontario) and for a child who ordinarily resides outside Canada, 18 years: *Divorce Act*, s. 2(1) "age of majority".

2§2 — "Applicable guidelines"

For the purpose of making the original child support order, or varying, or recalculating the order, the "applicable guidelines" are the provincial guidelines if they have been specified by the Governor in Council pursuant to s. 2(5) of the *Divorce Act*, or the federal guidelines if provincial guidelines have not been specified or if the federal guidelines have been adopted by a provincial or territory as its own.

Provincial guidelines of the province's own making have been specified and are in force for Quebec, Manitoba, Prince Edward Island, and New Brunswick. In these jurisdictions, their own guidelines apply both in proceedings under the *Divorce Act*, and in proceedings under provincial legislation.

Ontario, Newfoundland, British Columbia, Nova Scotia and the Northwest Territories have established their own guidelines without requesting they be specified as "applicable guidelines" for divorce matters. When Nunavut came into being (April 1, 1999), it adopted all Northwest Territories legislation and regulations, including the Northwest Territories *Child Support Guidelines*, until it could establish its own. Saskatchewan has adopted the *Federal Guidelines* as its own to make them apply to matters within its jurisdiction, as well as to matters under the *Divorce Act*. The importance of a province or territory taking the step of establishing acceptable guidelines of its own, or adopting federal guidelines as its own, is that until this occurs there are no guidelines for that province or territory which operate on a compulsory basis in proceedings under provincial legislation. The *Guidelines*, without this step, operate only under the *Divorce Act*, a federal statute. In Ontario, for instance, from May 1 to December 1, 1997, no provincial guidelines had been established. During this period, the only guidelines in force in Ontario were the *Federal Child Support Guidelines*, confined by the country's division of federal and provincial legislative powers to proceedings under the *Divorce Act*. Unless the child support relief requested invoked the *Divorce Act*, no guidelines during this period had to be followed; that is, no guidelines had to be followed where the child support relief requested was governed by provincial legislation. This changed on December 1, 1997. On that day, Ontario's *Uniform Federal and Provincial Child Support Guidelines Act, 1997*, together with the *Child Support Guidelines* (Ontario) established under it came into force. See Ontario Order in Council 200897, October 29, 1997, *Uniform Federal and Provincial Child Support Guidelines Act 1997*, s. 13 and *Child Support Guidelines* (Ontario) s. 26(1). With their coming into force, child support cases under provincial legislation were governed by guidelines also. Instead of having two sets of guidelines, it would be convenient to have one set apply both in the matters involving divorce and in matters advanced without a claim for divorce. The Ontario guidelines were drafted with this possibility in mind. They state in s. 26(2) that they "come into force with respect to cases to which the *Divorce Act* (Canada) applies on the day these guidelines are specified by order of the Governor in Council as 'applicable guidelines' within the meaning of that Act under subsection 2(5) of that Act." However, as of June 1, 1999, no order in council has been made specifying the Ontario guidelines as "applicable guidelines" with the result that there are two sets of guidelines operating in Ontario: the *Federal Child Support Guidelines* in matters under the *Divorce Act*, and the *Child Support Guidelines* (Ontario) in matters under provincial legislation.

Alberta has given royal assent to changes in its child support legislation, but has not proclaimed those changes in force. Yukon has not amended its legislation.

The *Federal Child Support Guidelines* apply in all divorce cases in two sets of circumstances: first, where the province has not had its own guidelines specified under s. 2(5) of the Act (Ontario, for example) and, secondly, where both spouses or former spouses are not "ordinarily resident in the same province at the time an application for a child support order or a variation order in respect of a child support order is made, or the amount of a child support order is to be recalculated pursuant to section 25.1": *Divorce Act*, s. 2(1) "applicable guidelines." Quebec, for instance, has had its own guidelines specified under s. 2(5) of the Act so that its courts would apply them to child support in a divorce proceeding where both spouses or former spouses are, in fact, ordinarily resident in the province at the time of the application. However, if one of them was resident in another province at the time, the operative guidelines would be the *Federal Child Support Guidelines*. See: *Divorce Act*, s. 2(1) "applicable guidelines" (a) and (b).

The *Guidelines* apply both to interim and permanent child support orders (also, to interim and confirmed provisional orders). This means one standard is to apply in all cases; not a lesser standard for interim support, for instance, and a different standard for permanent support to be determined on all the evidence at trial. This is because there is no issue to be determined on the interim hearing, or at trial of what the standard of child support should be for this particular family. the *Guidelines* remove that issue from consideration because the amounts prescribed are based on socio-economic data derived from a sampling of the larger population, and not on the particular spending habits of the individual family. The standard for measuring the level of child support is determined by the *Guidelines*, not by the standard of the individual family: *Divorce Act*, s. 15.1 (3).

The federal guidelines are more specific than the *Divorce Act*, and show that the *Guidelines* apply to

- original orders for child support,
- and "with such modifications as the circumstances require", to
    - interim orders: *Divorce Act*, ss. 15.1(2) and 19(9).

- variation orders: *Divorce Act*, s. 17(1).
- provisional orders: *Divorce Act*, s. 19(7).
- recalculations: *Divorce Act*, s. 25.1(1)(b).

The court may have a discretion with respect to its orders, but a provincial agency in making a recalculation has no discretion: *Federal Child Support Guidelines*, s. 2(5).

2§2A — "Child of the marriage" in general

In the former definition of "child of the marriage" the first branch limits the minimum parental obligation to provide for the support of a child by the sole criterion of the child's age. It read, "'child of the marriage' means a child ... who, at the material time, (a) is under the age of sixteen years." The new version amends the definition so that this minimum obligation would be limited by two criteria, not just one; age and dependency. The age would be the "age of majority" and the dependency would be such that the child "had not withdrawn from [the spouses' or former spouses'] charge."

The "age of majority," also defined in the amended section 2(1), would be the provincial age of majority in the province where the child ordinarily resides, or if the child resides outside Canada, the age of 18 years. The provincial age of majority is not uniform, but varies from province to province. (In Ontario, it is 18 years.) The description of dependency, the inability to withdraw from parental charge, is borrowed from the second branch of the definition of "child of the marriage" making this criterion the same in both branches. The effect of the amendment is that there would be no age-limited minimum for the support obligation. The obligation could terminate at any age (an age under 16, for example) where it is reasonably found that the child has withdrawn from the spouses' or former spouses' charge. However, provincial legislation could still make a parent liable for the support of a child who has withdrawn from the spouses' charge and is under provincial charge.

The second branch continues the status of a child having reached the age of majority as a child of the marriage, if the child is unable to withdraw from parental charge for reasons of "illness" and "disability" or for "other cause". Prior to the amendments, this last category was applied most frequently to obtain support for a child over the age limit of 16 (now the age limit is the age of majority) in full time attendance at an educational institution.

Divorce Act, 1985

Where the parties' 22-year-old university student daughter had entered into a stable common law relationship, she was found no longer to qualify as a "child of the marriage": *Andries v. Andries*, 38 R.F.L. (5th) 246, 2003 CarswellMan 125, 2003 MBQB 84, [2003] 7 W.W.R. 262, (sub nom. *Hrechka v. Andries*) 172 Man. R. (2d) 294 (Man. Q.B.).

In *B. (H.) v. B. (M.)*, 25 R.F.L. (5th) 239, 2002 CarswellAlta 148, 2002 A.B.Q.B. 146, 306 A.R. 380 (Alta. Q.B.), the mother was required to pay child support for her teenage son despite the fact that he had virtual no contact with her. Events themselves had alienated mother and son from each other and those events were not anyone's fault. Accordingly, the mother could not take the position that her son was no longer "a child of the marriage".

In *Nadeau v. Mitchell* (July 11, 1997), Doc. 96-MA-5290 (Ont. Gen. Div.); additional reasons at (August 21, 1997), Doc. 96-MA-5290 (Ont. Gen. Div.), the father's obligation to pay child support, recorded in a separation agreement, was to end when "(i) the child attains the age of 18 years and ceases to be in full time attendance at an educational facility approved by the husband .... (ii) the child ceases to reside with the wife; (iii) the child attains the age of twenty-one years." The child, living with her mother, was 22 years of age at the time of the hearing, and, without the knowledge of the father, had not attended school from December 1994 to November 1996. During this period the father had paid child support to the mother of $11,126.72. When the child left school, she needed three courses to complete grade eleven. The mother applied for an order varying the child support contending that the child was still a child of the marriage. The father made a cross-application for an order declaring that his obligation to pay child support ended when the child ceased to attend an educational institution on a full-time basis in 1994, and for an order that the mother repay all child support received after that date.

The court found that the child ceased to be a child of the marriage when she withdrew from school in December 1994. On this basis, the mother was ordered to reimburse the father for the $11,126.72. However, the child intended to return to school and the court found that she would be unable to withdraw from parental charge while pursuing that path. Therefore, child support was to revive and continue to be paid commencing on the child's enrolment in summer school or high school in 1997 "provided she establishes to his [the father's] satisfaction that she is enrolled in a course which, if completed successfully, will have the desired result of her obtaining the necessary credits by June 1998 to qualify her for university." See further terms of order under 2§6 Children over the age of majority, below.

Where two children, aged 19 and 21, were taking post-secondary education, and each had earnings of $7,000 a year and student loans of $7,000 a year, the children were not self-sufficient, especially where the custodial parent made up for the shortfall by contributing to the children's living and school expenses: *Westcott v. Westcott* (July 22, 1997), Doc. Barrie D363-97 (Ont. Gen. Div.). Each child, despite his age, was a "child of the marriage" for purposes of the *Divorce Act.*

In *Allison v. Allison* (June 12, 1997), Doc. D5525/94 (Ont. Gen. Div.), the court found that a 22-year-old who had completed his undergraduate degree and who had part-time jobs for a number of years and appeared to be capable of supporting himself was no longer a "child of the marriage."

Where a 23-year-old student who was working towards his Masters degree in psychology with the intent of pursuing a doctorate in the subject was found to be "a child of the marriage" and entitled to some child support: *Newman v. Thompson*, [1997] 9 W.W.R. 519, 30 R.F.L. (4th) 143, 149 D.L.R. (4th) 605, 118 Man. R. (2d) 177 (C.A.). The amount of support was small, $150, reduced from $450 per month, taking account of the student's scholarship, research assistantship and the fact that he could reduce some of his expenses.

In *Finn v. Levine* (May 27, 1997), Doc. Ottawa 23308/95 (Ont. Gen. Div.), notwithstanding a separation agreement incorporated in a divorce judgment, which provided that support ended when the child reached 21, the court ordered child support until the child had completed his undergraduate degree. The court had used the analysis of *Levesque* in determining the quantum of support as being 20 per cent of his parent's gross incomes and ordered that each party should pay his or her *pro rata* share. Part of the child's own summer employment income and some of the savings from his Bar Mitzvah fund should be used to pay the shortfall in his expenses. The child was a good student despite the fact that he suffered from a serious and rare medical disorder which had been treated with numerous surgical interventions and lengthy periods of recuperation. The gross income of both parents was $69,000.

An 18-year-old child who suffered from attention deficit disorder and oppositional deficit disorder and had stopped attending school but was taking correspondence courses to obtain high school credits so that she could enrol in a community college, was found to be a "child of the marriage" and entitled to child support: *Eyjolfson v. Eyjolfson* (May 16, 1997), Doc. Thunder Bay 97-0386 (Ont. Gen. Div.). The court was of the opinion that at this point in time the child was a person who was unable, due to her age, lack of training and education, and medical disorders from withdrawing from her parents' charge. In addition, she was unable to obtain the necessaries of life without the assistance of her parents. She would not be living with either of her parents.

Cases decided before the enactment of the Federal Child Support Guidelines:

An 18-year-old child who has quit school and is receiving unemployment insurance benefits does not qualify as a "child of the marriage": *Giorno v. Giorno* (1992), 39 R.F.L. (3d) 345 (N.S. C.A.).

In *Walsh v. Walsh* (1988), 16 R.F.L. (3d) 1 (N.B. C.A.), the parties' 20-year-old daughter, who herself had had a child, was found not to qualify as a "child of the marriage". The daughter had had ample time to complete her education but instead had chosen to work and attend school part-time.

The definition of "child of the marriage" is not one of age, but of dependence-relevant factors including full-time attendance at school or university, even where the child does not reside with the parent seeking child support: *Van de Pol v. Van de Pol* (1996), 20 R.F.L. (4th) 178, 179 A.R. 221 (Q.B.).

It is not unreasonable for a parent to contrive to support a child for a brief time after high school while the child is adjusting to the next step in his or her life, be it further studies or employment: *Bain v. Bain* (1994), 7 R.F.L. (4th) 451 (Man. Q.B.).

Where the parties' 18-year-old daughter moved out of her mother's residence and in with her boyfriend, was expelled from school, and later moved in with her father with the intention of returning to school, she was still found to qualify as a child of the marriage. The daughter's actions had not amounted to a definitive break with her parents: *N. (P.F.) v. N. (A.)* (1994), 6 R.F.L. (4th) 113 (Alta. Q.B.).

The definition of "child of the marriage" is a fluid one which, in appropriate circumstances, extends to university students. An outstanding child support order is not required to bring a child who is over the age of 16 within the provision of the Act. Furthermore, it is not necessary that the child be resident with either of the parents: *Coakwell v. Baker* (1994), 4 R.F.L. (4th) 345 (Ont. Gen. Div.).

In *Holmes v. Holmes* (1991), 305 A.P.R. 281, 96 Nfld. & P.E.I.R. 281 (P.E.I. T.D.), the parties' 18-year-old child, who had her own child out of wedlock, was found no longer to qualify as a "child of the marriage."

A 25-year-old child was found no longer to qualify as a "child of the marriage" where, although he was a full-time student, he had his own apartment and was receiving welfare benefits: *Droit de la famille — 913*, 30 R.F.L. (3d) 83, [1990] R.D.F. 642 (C.S. Qué.).

Where a child is attending university with the full financial support of the parents, the child remains a child of the marriage until his or her academic career is completed or abandoned: *Belyea v. Belyea* (1990), 30 R.F.L. (3d) 407 (N.B. Q.B.).

The phrase "other cause" in the s. 2(1) definition of "child of the marriage" should not be given a restrictive *ejusdem generis* interpretation, but rather should be broadly construed. Accordingly, since a child studying at university may be unable to support himself, the parent may be liable to pay child support: *Ramsay v. Ramsay* (1989), 73 Nfld. & P.E.I.R. 66, 229 A.P.R. 66 (T.D.).

Adult children who choose to live with one parent while attending university simply because it is more economical are not "children of the marriage" if they have the ability to live elsewhere: *Greyeyes v. Greyeyes* (1990), 24 R.F.L. (3d) 457 (Sask. Q.B.).

Where, at the time of separation, the parties' university student daughter lived with her boyfriend but later returned to live with her mother, she was found no longer to qualify as a "child of the marriage" for support purposes: *Kolsun v. Kolsun* (1989), 19 R.F.L. (3d) 306 (Man. Q.B.).

Where the parties' 19-year-old daughter boarded with her boyfriend's family and attended school in Nova Scotia after the mother's move to Ontario, the mother's application for child support was dismissed. The daughter no longer qualified as a "child of the marriage": *Botchett v. Botchett* (1989), 94 N.S.R. (2d) 339, 247 A.P.R. 339 (T.D.).

In *Jackson v. Jackson* (1988), 69 Sask. R. 148 (Q.B.) the court allowed the father's application to terminate child support for his 21-year-old son who had moved out of his mother's home and lived in his own apartment with his own child. The son had withdrawn from his mother's care and control and no longer qualified as a "child of the marriage".

In *Kidson v. Techentin* (1994), 129 N.S.R. (2d) 228, 362 A.P.R. 228 (Fam. Ct.), a 21-year-old child who was nearing the end of her university studies and had earned approximately $8,000 for each of the previous several years, was found no longer to qualify as a "child of the marriage" for support purposes.

A 19-year-old child who has a child of her own, works part-time, receives social assistance and is not in school does not qualify as a "child of the marriage": *Todd v. Todd* (1995), 144 N.S.R. (2d) 340, 416 A.P.R. 340 (S.C.).

2§3 — "Child of the marriage" at the material time

"The issue of material time arises only with respect to the age of the child". These words do not refer to the child's status "in loco parentis": per Huband J.A. in *Carignan v. Carignan* (1989), 22 R.F.L. (3d) 376 at 385–6 (Man. C.A.).

"By its use of the words 'at the material time' the definition is directed to the child's situation at the time of the hearing. If the child is at that time unable to withdraw from his or her parents charge, and the other conditions of the provision are met, then he or she qualifies as a child of the marriage": per Morder J.A. in *Harrington v. Harrington* (1981), 22 R.F.L. (2d) 40 at 50–51, 33 O.R. (2d) 150, 123 D.L.R. (3d) 689 (C.A.), finding that an adult female child who returned to her mother's home to recuperate from mental illness constituted a child of the marriage.

"The definition of 'children of the marriage' refers to the status 'at the material time'. I take this to mean at any time a child's right to maintenance is under consideration. Otherwise, Parliament would have fixed some other time, such as the date when the decree nisi was granted": per Bouck J. in *King v. King (No. 2)* (1979), 13 R.F.L. (2d) 222, 107 D.L.R. (3d) 180 (B.C. S.C.).

See also *Janzen v. Janzen* (1981), 21 R.F.L. (2d) 316, 28 B.C. L.R. 63, 123 D.L.R. (3d) 246 (C.A.), below at 2§8.

2§4 — Child of two spouses

A child legitimated by the subsequent marriage of his parents is a child of the marriage: *Mohammed v. Mohammed* (1976), 26 R.F.L. 110 (Ont. C.A.).

A child placed for adoption by its natural parents is not, with respect to them, a child of the marriage. It becomes the child of the marriage of the adopting parents: *Johnston v. Johnston*, [1969] 2 O.R. 198, 4 D.L.R. (3d) 681 (H.C.).

In order to assist in determining whether five children born to a wife after the separation of the parties should be maintained by the husband as "children of the marriage", leave was granted to the husband pursuant to the *Children's Law Reform Act*, S.O. 1977, c. 41, to obtain blood tests of himself, his wife and the five children and to submit the results in evidence in the divorce proceedings. In the event that the necessary consents were not forthcoming, the court hearing the divorce was entitled to draw such inferences as it thought appropriate: *H. v. H.* (1979), 9 R.F.L. (2d) 216 (Ont. H.C.).

2§5 — Children under the age of majority

The amount of support for a child under the age of majority is to be a basic amount plus an amount, if any, for special or extraordinary expenses: *Federal Child Support Guidelines*, s. 3(1)(a) and (b).

Divorce Act, 1985

Before the *Divorce Act* was amended in 1997, support was granted to all children under the age of sixteen and to certain specified children over the age of 16: see *Divorce Act, 1985*, s. 2, definition of "child of the marriage".

In the absence of a defence raising the change in age, a child who is under 16 years at the time the petition is presented, but who reaches 16 before the hearing, may be regarded as a child of the marriage: *Davies v. Davies* (1969), 3 D.L.R. (3d) 381 (N.W.T. S.C.).

Where a child had left school at the age of 15 and was employed, he was no longer a "child of the marriage" and was not entitled to support: *Lavoie v. Lavoie* (1991), 32 R.F.L. (3d) 77 (N.S. Fam. Ct.). (*Editorial Note*. See definition of a "child of the marriage" in the *Divorce Act*, s. 2).

2§6 — Children over the age of majority

The amount of support for a child over the age of majority is to be the amount determined in accordance with the guidelines as if the child were under the age of majority, *or* an amount in the discretion of the court having regard to the needs and means of the child and the financial ability of each spouse to contribute to the support of the child: *Federal Child Support Guidelines*, s. 3(2)(a) and (b). See also 2§8 Children continuing education — general.

As stated above, before the 1997 *Divorce Act* amendments, all children were entitled to support if they were under sixteen years of age and certain specified children over the age of sixteen were entitled to support.

Section 2(1)(b) of the *Divorce Act* does violate s. 15(1) of the *Canadian Charter of Rights and Freedoms* in as much as it imposes an obligation on divorced parents to support adult children, which obligation is not imposed on married parents. However, the violation is justified under s. 1 of the *Charter* as the legislative goal of ensuring that the children of divorced parents continue to benefit from the financial support of both parents is both pressing and substantial. The adult children of divorced parents may not receive the same financial assistance as they might if their parents were still together and the effect of the discrimination is proportionate to the benefit received: *Michie v. Michie* (1997), 36 R.F.L. (4th) 90, 48 C.R.R. (2d) 333, [1998] 4 W.W.R. 758, 162 Sask. R. 1 (Q.B.)

In *Bates v. Bates* (1995), 10 R.F.L. (4th) 261, 165 A.R. 71, 89 W.A.C. 71 (C.A.), the parties' two sons moved out of their mother's home, refused their father's offer of accommodation with him and rented an apartment while they attended university. The court ruled that the question of whether the boys in this case have removed themselves from the parents' charge in the words of s. 2(b) of the *Divorce Act* is a question of fact, with consideration of all the circumstances of the case, having due regard to the conduct of the parties, and the conditions, means and circumstances of each of them. The court took into account the fact that each boy had received $16,000 from his grandparents for education and that the mother had sold her home after the older child left for university and she no longer had accommodation for him. The appellate court affirmed the lower court's decision that child support should be ordered, but only to the extent required to support the boys during their full-time attendance at university. No support should be payable for a boy during those months when he is not attending school.

An 18-year-old child who had a poor school attendance record but was still enrolled in school and continued to receive passing grades was found still to qualify as a "child of the marriage" for support purposes: *Mathieu v. Mathieu* (1998), 38 R.F.L. (4th) 117, 127 Man. R. (2d) 150 (Q.B.).

Where the parties' 19-year-old son had left school, but intended to return, the father's application to terminate child support was dismissed. The child remained a "child of the marriage": *Corkum v. Corkum* (1998), 36 R.F.L. (4th) 367, 166 N.S.R. (2d) 329, 498 A.P.R. 329 (S.C.).

The onus rests on the person seeking maintenance for a child who is "sixteen years of age and over and under their charge" to establish the child's inability to provide: *Whitton v. Whitton* (1989), 21 R.F.L. (3d) 261, 34 O.A.C. 31 (C.A.).

Where a parent has formally undertaken to support a child who is over the age of majority and who is not enrolled in school and is not employed, that child is considered a "child of the marriage" for the purposes of an interlocutory motion: *Parsons v. Parsons* (1994), 9 R.F.L. (4th) 437 (Alta. Q.B.).

Where children over 16 years of age are making "unremarkable" progress in their studies, the court will not order support for them, but will leave the matter to their payor-father's goodwill and discretion: *Zander v. Zander* (1994), 8 R.F.L. (4th) 35 (Ont. Gen. Div.).

A child over the age of majority is not able to reinstate his or her status as a "child of the marriage", but a child under the age of majority is free to do so: *Choicoine v. Choicoine* (1992), 89 D.L.R. (4th) 604 (Ont. Gen. Div.).

2§7 — "Unable by reason of illness, disability or other cause" — disability or illness

Divorce Act, 1985

In *Scott v. Scott*, 10 R.F.L. (6th) 135, 2004 CarswellNB 587, 2004 NBCA 99, [2004] N.B.J. No. 468 (N.B. C.A.); reversing in part 265 N.B.R. (2d) 359, 695 A.P.R. 359, 2003 NBQB 345, 2003 CarswellNB 418 (N.B. Q.B.), the father successfully appealed from an order refusing his application to terminate child support for his 22-year-old son. Although it was the mother's contention that the son could not support himself because of medical issues, the only supporting evidence given at trial was her own. The wife's testimony constituted inadmissible hearsay and accordingly the son's disability had not been established.

Where the parties' disabled child had received a Bachelor of Education degree and subsequently enrolled in a Master's program, she was found to continue as a "child of the marriage" although it was found that the Master's degree was not a pre-requisite to her achieving self-sufficiency. The child suffered from spina bifida, was wheel-chair bound and profoundly deaf. As a result, her ongoing medical needs and special aid requirements precluded her from "withdrawing from her parents' charge" and the father's application to terminate support was dismissed: *Andersen v. Andersen* (1997), 32 R.F.L. (4th) 177 (B.C. S.C.).

A 19-year-old child who suffered from rheumatoid arthritis and required gold injections and physical assistance from her mother was found to be a "child of the marriage" although she had a monthly income of $400 from babysitting. Her disease rendered her unable to obtain the necessities of life for herself and she was therefore unable to withdraw from her parents' charge: *Alward v. Alward* (1994), 145 N.B.R. (2d) 299, 372 A.P.R. 299 (Q.B.).

An adult who is unable to be self-supporting because of a learning disability is entitled to ongoing child support. In quantifying such support, however, it is appropriate to consider social assistance benefits received by the child: *Magne v. Magne* (1990), 26 R.F.L. 364, 65 Man. R. (2d) 241 (Q.B.).

A mere assertion by the mother that the children had been traumatized by the father's behaviour and had accordingly left school is insufficient to classify the children as ill or disabled and thus rendered unable to withdraw from the charge of their parents: *Phillip v. Phillip (Kreger)* (1989), 76 Sask. R. 7, 60 D.L.R. (4th) 319 (Q.B.).

The court in *Andrews v. Andrews* (1995), 11 R.F.L. (4th) 117 (B.C. S.C.) ruled that a 26-year-old man who had learning disabilities and the maturity of a 16-year-old and who was thereby handicapped in obtaining employment was a "child of the marriage" until he finished his training and obtained a job or unless it was determined that he did not require training. Consequently, he was entitled to support and as there was insufficient income between the parties to support themselves and their two younger children, the parties would be required to encroach on their capital to fulfil their obligations to provide support for their children.

In *Jorden v. Jorden* (1995), 14 R.F.L. (4th) 97, 162 N.B.R. (2d) 241, 415 A.P.R. 241 (Q.B.) the parties' 25-year-old son, who suffered from schizoid personality disorder, was found no longer to qualify as a "child of the marriage". He refused to take a medication for his condition and also refused to sign the required releases allowing medical reports about his condition to go before the courts. As a result, there was insufficient evidence to establish that he was unable by reason of illness or disability to withdraw from his parents control.

In *Butler v. Butler* (1996), 19 R.F.L. (4th) 86, 148 N.S.R. (2d) 126, 429 A.P.R. 126 (S.C.) the court refused the husband's application to terminate child support for his 20-year-old daughter who had just graduated from grade 12. Although the child was no longer in school, she suffered from a lifelong impairment in her intellectual and emotional development which allowed her to work only in special programs where one on one supervision was available. She accordingly remained a "child of the marriage" as she was unable to withdraw from parental control and achieve any degree of independence.

Where the parties' 16-year-old child suffered from emotional and psychological problems which rendered it impossible for her to attend school or hold a job for an extended period of time, she remained a "child of the marriage", and her father was required to pay child support. The child was incapable of obtaining the necessaries of life, even though she had survived for an extended period of time on the streets: *James v. James* (1995), 18 R.F.L. (4th) 463 (B.C. S.C.).

2§7A — "Unable by reason of disability or other cause" — lack of available employment

Divorce Act, 1985

In *Greening v. Mills* (2006), 23 R.F.L. (6th) 165, 2006 CarswellNfld 61, 2006 NLUFC 11, 254 Nfld. & P.E.I.R. 279, 764 A.P.R. 279 (N.L. U.F.C.), the parties' 21-year-old son was found to qualify as a "child of the marriage" for support purposes. The son had never earned income from employment, had no job skills or ability to work and had serious physical and mental limitations that made it impractical for him to sustain employment. Accordingly, he was found, by reason of disability, unable to withdraw from his parents' charge or obtain the necessaries of life.

Children who are unable to obtain employment because of poor economic conditions should not be distinguished from children who are unable to provide for themselves because they are at school. Accordingly, in *Baker v. Baker* (1994), 2 R.F.L. (4th) 147, 15 Alta. L.R. (3d) 337, 147 A.R. 227, 109 D.L.R (4th) 548 (Q.B.), the husband was ordered to pay child support for his twenty-year-old daughter who was unable to find employment in the prevailing depressed economy.

In *McAdam v. McAdam* (1994), 8 R.F.L. (4th) 252, 98 Man. R. (2d) 109 (Q.B.), the parties' twenty-year-old daughter, who continued to reside with her mother, was found to be a "child of the marriage". Despite an honest, serious and diligent attempt to find employment, the daughter had been unable to do so and was accordingly unable to withdraw from the charge of her parents for "other cause" within the meaning of the s. 2(1) definition of "child of the marriage".

The words "other cause" as set forth in s. 2(1) of the *Divorce Act* should be interpreted to include the inability to obtain employment after a child has made an honest, serious, and diligent attempt to do so, if that inability renders the child unable to withdraw from the charge of the parents: *McAdam v. McAdam* (1994), 8 R.F.L. (4th) 252 (Man. Q.B.).

But see *Gartner v. Gartner* (1978), 5 R.F.L. (2d) 270, 27 N.S.R. (2d) 482 at 486, 41 A.P.R. 482 (T.D.).

2§7B — "Unable by reason of disability or other cause" — child care responsibilities

A 17-year-old daughter who is pregnant and living with her mother does not qualify as a "child of the marriage" . She cannot bring herself into the definition as a child who is unable to withdraw from her parents' charge for "other cause": *Giorno v. Giorno* (1992), 39 R.F.L. (3d) 345, 110 N.S.R. (2d) 87, 297 A.P.R. 87 (C.A.); reversing in part (1991), 103 N.S.R. (2d) 431, 282 A.P.R. 431 (T.D.).

In *Primeau v. Primeau* (1993), 47 R.F.L. (3d) 67 (Ont. Gen. Div.), the fact that the parties' 22-year-old daughter, who resided with her mother and continued to attend classes, had herself given birth, still qualified her as a "child of the marriage". If anything, the situation had made it even more difficult for her to withdraw from her mother's care and control.

In *Holmes v. Holmes* (1991), 305 A.P.R. 281, 96 Nfld. & P.E.I.R. 281 (P.E.I. T.D.), the parties' 18-year-old child, who had her own child out of wedlock, was found no longer to qualify as a "child of the marriage".

In *Walsh v. Walsh* (1988), 13 R.F.L. (3d) 168 (N.B. Q.B.), the parties' 20-year-old daughter, who was unable to withdraw herself from her mother's care because she herself had had a child, was found to be a "child of the marriage" for support purposes. On appeal at 16 R.F.L. (3d) 1, 91 N.B.R. (2d) 132, 232 A.P.R. 132 (C.A.), the court held that the daughter at age 20 was no longer a child of the marriage. The father was under no legal obligation to support his daughter or his grandchild. The daughter was attending a community college part time and was working part time. The court set aside the earlier support order for the support of the daughter and the grandchild.

2§7C — "Unable by reason of disability or other cause"

The fact that the parties' 18-year-old son trained as a member of Canada's Nordic ski team was insufficient to preserve his status as a "child of the marriage". As there was no direct evidence that the training would make him fit for an occupation, it could not be relied upon as a valid reason why he was unable to withdraw from parental charge: *Olson v. Olson* (2003), 36 R.F.L. (5th) 196, 2003 CarswellAlta 254, [2003] A.J. No. 230, 2003 ABCA 56, 320 A.R. 379, 288 W.A.C. 379, [2003] 7 W.W.R. 12, 225 D.L.R. (4th) 735, 14 Alta. L.R. (4th) 104 (Alta. C.A.)

In *Crawford v. Crawford* (1999), 45 R.F.L. (4th) 211 (N.B. C.A.), the court allowed the father's appeal from an order refusing to terminate child support for his 22-year-old adopted son. Although the trial judge had found that the child, who neither attended school nor worked, suffered from a disability, no particulars of that disability were presented. As the inability of the child to engage in some form of employment was not demonstrated, the child no longer qualified as a "child of the marriage".

An 18-year-old child who had quit school and is receiving unemployment insurance benefits does not qualify as a "child of the marriage": *Giorno v. Giorno*, above.

In *Bartkowski v. Bartkowski*, 37 R.F.L. (5th) 242, 2003 CarswellBC 712, 2003 BCSC 490 (B.C. S.C. [In Chambers]), the father's application for child support for the parties' 19-year-old daughter was refused. In the 2-year period since graduating from high school, she had worked and moved out to live with her boyfriend a number of times. Although she was again living with her father and was entertaining the possibility of returning to school, there was no compelling evidence that she was unable to withdraw from her father's charge or that she was unable to obtain the necessaries of life.

Where the parties' 18-year-old daughter was living at home while working full time to pay off debts and save money, she was found no longer to qualify as a child of the marriage. Although she had vague plans about returning to school, her remaining at home was a choice and not a necessity: *Harder v. Harder*, 41 R.F.L. (5th) 69, 2003 Carswell-Sask 454, 2003 SKQB 286 (Sask. Q.B.)

In *Buzon v. Buzon* (1999), 48 R.F.L. (4th) 263, 240 A.R. 103, 1999 CarswellAlta 547 (Q.B.), the court granted the father's application for a declaration that his mentally disabled 18-year-old son was no longer a "child of the marriage". The father's support obligation ended when the child began to receive a disability benefit upon his 18th birthday. The facts that the benefit was equal only to minimum wage and there was no evidence that the pension met the child's needs did not alter the outcome.

In *Hartikainen v. Hartikainen* (1992), 39 R.F.L. (3d) 215 (Ont. Gen. Div.), the husband was required to continue to pay child support for his 16½-year-old son who has been forced to withdraw from school because of his poor attendance record. Although the son was enrolled in a subsidized pre-employment program and earned $541 monthly, he was unable to withdraw from the custodial mother's parental support.

The phrase "other cause" in the s. 2(1) definition of "child of the marriage" should not be given a restrictive *ejusdem generis* interpretation, but rather should be broadly construed. Accordingly, since a child studying at university may be unable to support himself, the parent may be liable to pay child support: *Ramsay v. Ramsay* (1989), 73 Nfld. & P.E.I.R. 66, 229 A.P.R. 66 (T.D.).

A child with one university degree who wishes to pursue further education is not unable by reason of "other cause" to withdraw from parental control. Accordingly, such a child does not qualify as a "child of the marriage" for support purposes: *Crook v. Crook* (1992), 42 R.F.L. (3d) 297, 115 N.S.R. (2d) 258, 314 A.P.R. 258 (T.D.).

In *Strand v. Strand* (1995), 12 R.F.L. (4th) 188 (Sask. Q.B.), the court found that the parties' 18-year-old son who had been taking courses and who played in a hockey league which paid him a stipend of $120 per month during the hockey season and who was unable to take on other employment while he played competitive hockey was a "child of the marriage" and thus entitled to support for the months that he was playing hockey. However, once he completed his courses and had finished his first year of playing hockey, he could support himself during the off-season and the hockey team would provide billets for him during the playing season. If the son chose to remain at home with the concurrence of his mother, she would have to assume the additional cost of his room and board.

Where the parties' 20 year-old daughter's academic skills in arithmetic and language placed her well below the average classification and she needed one-to-one supervision for even the simplest of tasks, the court found that the daughter was unable to withdraw from her parents charge, even though she was able to acquire a modest income from minimum wage, program employment and UIC: *Butler v. Butler* (1996), 19 R.F.L. (4th) 86 (N.S. S.C.). The father's application for a declaration that the daughter was no longer a child of the marriage and for termination of child support for that child was dismissed, although the amount of support was reduced from $415 to $315 in light of the daughter's modest income.

2§8 — Children continuing education — general

In *N. (W.P.) v. N. (B.J.)* (2005), 10 R.F.L. (6th) 440, 2005 CarswellBC 10, 2005 BCCA 7, 36 B.C.L.R. (4th) 330, 249 D.L.R. (4th) 352, 207 B.C.A.C. 76, 341 W.A.C. 76 (C.A.); varying (2004), 5 R.F.L. (6th) 135, 2004 CarswellBC 1520, 2004 BCSC 880, [2004] B.C.J. No. 1351 (S.C.), it was confirmed that the parties' 22-year-old daughter, who had been accepted at medical school, continued to be a child of the marriage.

Attendance at a post secondary institution can extend dependence pursuant to the *Divorce Act*, but this is not automatic and each case is dependent on the facts relating to each child. Accordingly, the parties 21-year-old son who had moved out of his mother's home, whose education was being funded through a government programme and who only returned to his mother's home at Christmas and during the summer, was found no longer to constitute "a child of the marriage" in *Pitcher v. Pitcher* (2005), 21 R.F.L. (6th) 399, 2005 CarswellNfld 313, 2005 NLTD 191, 252 Nfld. & P.E.I.R. 156, 756 A.P.R. 156 (N.L. T.D.).

In *Bowman v. Bowman* (2005), 12 R.F.L. (6th) 258, 2005 CarswellSask 33, [2005] S.J. No. 35, 260 Sask. R. 312, 2005 SKQB 2 (Sask. Q.B.), the parties' 23-year-old daughter who was in her sixth year of post-secondary education was found no longer to qualify as a "child of marriage". The daughter had a college diploma in Recreation and subsequently had enrolled in a university Kinesiology programme. A presumption existed that the daughter could qualify for entry level employment after receiving her college diploma.

In *Arnold v. Washburn* (2000), 10 R.F.L. (5th) 1, 2000 CarswellOnt 3454 (Ont. S.C.J.); additional reasons at (2000), 13 R.F.L. (5th) 245, 2000 CarswellOnt 4721 (Ont. S.C.J.), the court found that the parties'eldest child, who rejected a job offer in favour of post-graduate university studies, was found still to qualify as a "child of the marriage". Recent case law supported the position that those children who are realizing their potential in both under-graduate and graduate university studies, are not in a position to withdraw from parental control.

In *Trottier v. Bradley* (1999), 49 R.F.L. (4th) 432, 138 Man. R. (2d) 106, 202 W.A.C. 106 (Man. C.A.); reversing (1999), 135 Man. R. (2d) 85 (Q.B.), the court, on appeal, terminated the 23-year-old child's right to support. The child was no longer residing with the custodial mother and was pursuing doctoral studies. The test for determining the ongoing support entitlement of a student child who was no longer resident with the custodial parent was a flexible one. In this case, as the information relating to the ongoing and future circumstance of the child was not before the court, support was properly terminated. Such information was critical to the central issues of entitlement and need.

In *Darlington v. Darlington* (1997), 32 R.F.L. (4th) 406, 99 B.C.A.C. 134, 162 W.A.C. 134 (C.A.), it was held that the mother's affidavit was sufficient evidence of the continuing dependency of the parties' 19-year-old university student daughter.

In *Jonasson v. Jonasson* (1997), 30 R.F.L. (4th) 20, 95 B.C.A.C. 94, 154 W.A.C. 94 (C.A.); leave to appeal refused (1998), 226 N.R. 400, 118 B.C.A.C. 320 (note), 192 W.A.C. 320 (note) (S.C.C.), the appellate court upheld the trial judge's finding that the parties' 22-year-old son, who already had one post-secondary degree and was now studying dentistry, no longer qualified as a "child of the marriage". The son could not be characterized as being "unable to withdraw from the charge" of his parents.

The entitlement to support of a child pursuing an education is not limited to a particular level of education or to a pre-set age limit. The child is not required to live with the custodial parent and the line to be drawn is flexible: *Newman v. Thompson* (1997), 30 R.F.L. (4th) 143, 149 D.L.R. (4th) 605, [1997] 9 W.W.R. 519, 118 Man. R. (2d) 177, 149 W.A.C. 177 (C.A.).

In determining whether an adult child who is attending university continues to qualify, as a "child of the marriage" the following factors should be considered: the eligibility of the child for financial assistance; the existence of reasonable career plans; the child's ability to contribute to his or her own support; parental plans for education; and whether the child has unilaterally terminated the relationship with the payor parent: *Bradley v. Zaba* (1996), 18 R.F.L. (4th) 1, 137 Sask. R. 295, 107 W.A.C. 295 (C.A.).

Where the parties' daughter had expressed her intention to move in with her boyfriend when she began university, she could no longer be considered a "child of the marriage" once such cohabitation had begun. Even though she might not be able to maintain herself totally, her decision indicated her total independence: *Vandervort v. Brettler* (1989), 22 R.F.L. (3d) 160, 70 O.R. (2d) 277 (H.C.); affirmed (April 2, 1997), Doc. CA C9864 (Ont. C.A.).

In *Bates v. Bates* (1995), 10 R.F.L. (4th) 261 (Alta. C.A.), the parties' two sons moved out of their mother's home, refused their father's offer of accommodation with him and rented an apartment while they attended university. The court ruled that the question of whether the boys in this case had removed themselves from the parents' charge in the words of s. 2(b) of the *Divorce Act* is a question of fact, with consideration of all the circumstances of the case having due regard to the conduct of the parties, and the conditions, means and circumstances of each of them. The court took into account the fact that each boy had received $16,000 from his grandparents for education and that the mother had sold her home after the older child left for university and she no longer had accommodation for him. The appellate court affirmed the lower court's decision that child support should be ordered, but only to the extent required to support the boys during their full-time attendance at university. No support should be payable for a boy during those months when he was not attending school.

In *Yaschuk v. Logan* (1992), 39 R.F.L. (3d) 417, 110 N.S.R. (2d) 278, 299 A.P.R. 278 (C.A.); affirming (1991), 33 R.F.L. (3d) 316, 103 N.S.R. (2d) 371, 282 A.P.R. 371 (T.D.), a support award in favour of the parties' 23-year-old daughter was upheld on appeal. Although she had attended university for four years and still had not obtained a degree, she continued to reside with her mother and was dependent upon her parents.

In *Taplin v. Laurie* (1992), 41 R.F.L. (3d) 197 (Man. C.A.), the court refused the father's application to terminate child support for the parties' 19-year-old son who was taking an inordinately long time to complete high school. The son had legitimate emotional and physical reasons for his slow progress and could not fulfill his genuine ambition to complete high school without financial assistance.

In *Saunders v. Saunders* (1987), 10 R.F.L. (3d) 437, 60 Sask. R. 92 (Q.B.); affirmed (1988), 14 R.F.L. (3d) 225 (Sask. C.A.), the parties' 21-year-old daughter who was attending her third year of university was found to be a "child of the marriage" for the purposes of an application for increased child support. As she was capable of benefitting from further education which would assist her future occupation, she continued to fall within the statutory definition despite her age.

In *Droit de la famille — 1451* (5 septembre 1991), Doc. C.A. Montréal 500-09-001189-901 (C.A. Qué.), the court upheld a child support order under which support payments were suspended during the summer months while the children were employed and gave part of their compensation to the custodial mother.

The transition from child to self-sustaining adult does not occur immediately upon the child's graduation. There may be a transition period during which child support is still required: *Whitcher v. Nichols* (2004), 6 R.F.L. (6th) 434, 2004 CarswellYukon 67, 2004 YKSC 35 (S.C.).

In *G. (R.W.) v. G. (S.I.)*, 26 R.F.L. (5th) 307, 2002 CarswellSask 232, 2002 SKQB 167, [2002] 6 W.W.R. 713, 218 Sask. R. 262 (Sask. Q.B.), the court found that the parties' 26-year-old university student son no longer qualified as "a child of the marriage". The son had alcohol and drug abuse problems, which he refused to deal with, and had, through his lifestyle, effectively withdrawn himself from all parental control.

In *Wolfe v. Wolfe*, 26 R.F.L. (5th) 447, 2002 CarswellNS 129, 2002 NSSF 18, 202 N.S.R. (2d) 386, 632 A.P.R. 386 (S.C.), the court found that the parties' 23-year-old daughter, who had spent 5 years obtaining her bachelor's degree, would still qualify as "a child of the marriage" were she to continue with her plans to enter a Bachelor of Education program. However, were she to decide to continue her studies in a new, unrelated field, she would no longer be eligible for parental support.

In *Kozun v. Kozun*, 18 R.F.L. (5th) 115, 2001 CarswellSask 475, 2001 SKQB 329 (Q.B.), the husband was ordered to pay child support for his daughter who attended university. The fact that the daughter was estranged from the father provided no defence, as he was himself largely responsible for the estrangement. Although tuition costs were covered by the trust fund, the daughter was still dependent upon her parents for food and shelter.

In *Symons v. Taylor* (2000), 10 R.F.L. (5th) 443, 2000 CarswellOnt 2582, [2000] O.J. No. 2703 (Ont. S.C.J.), a 20-year-old child who attended university, maintained a separate residence and chose to encroach upon an inheritance from his late mother to meet school costs and to entrench his independence, was found to have effectively withdrawn from parental control.

No indefinite obligation exists for a parent to support a child who is attending school or who is unemployed or underemployed. However, an obligation does exist for one parent to assist the other on whom such a child is dependent for a reasonable transition period: *Gamache v. Gamache* (1999), 49 R.F.L. (4th) 258, 241 A.R. 388 (Q.B.).

In *Bosse v. Bosse* (1996), 19 R.F.L. (4th) 54 (N.B. Q.B.), in earlier proceedings, the parties were divorced and as corollary relief the court had incorporated a consent order which required the respondent husband to pay for the support of two children until a specified date. The respondent had adopted these children when he had married their mother. The current hearing was an application by the mother for continuation of child support and retroactive child support. Only one child was the subject of this application. He was attending university, had received loans and/or bursaries and had worked on the side. After the parties divorced, the respondent had remarried and was now supporting his new wife and her two children.

Graser J., writing for the court held that "Support is the right of the child. The parents cannot abrogate the child's right of support by agreement. As long as an individual relies on the support of parents and is in full time attendance in post secondary education he is a dependent and comes within the definition of "child of the marriage" set out in the *Divorce Act*." The court was of the opinion that the respondent had a responsibility toward his adopted child that was certainly equal to his responsibility toward the children of his present wife. The respondent had an obligation to provide child support in question and that that obligation continued until the child completed his post-secondary education. The application was allowed in part. The mother was granted $250 each month, not retroactive for the child who attended university.

In *Droit de la famille — 2130*, [1995] R.D.F. 98 (C.S. Qué.) the parties daughter was found to continue to be a "child of the marriage" after obtaining a bachelors degree in marine biology and entering into a graduate programme. It would be very difficult for the daughter to obtain employment in her field without a Master's degree and it was legitimate for her to aspire to the same level of education as her father, who held a doctoral degree.

In *Sapergia v. Larner* (1995), 15 R.F.L. (4th) 389, 133 Sask. R. 197 (Q.B.) the parties' 22-year-old daughter who had completed her undergraduate degree but intended to return to university for further study was found no longer to qualify as a "child of the marriage". The daughter planned within a year's time to marry her live-in boyfriend and could not, therefore, be found incapable of withdrawing from parental control.

In *Fraser v. Jones* (1995), 17 R.F.L. (4th) 218 (Sask. Q.B.), the husband's application to terminate child support for his 18-year-old daughter was dismissed. As a full-time university student she continued to qualify as a "child of the marriage" although she would be expected to seek summer employment and student loans to help defray her expenses. Although she refused to speak to her father, this was a result of immaturity and was not a ground for termination of support.

In *Barber v. Barber* (1995), 18 R.F.L. (4th) 282, 137 Nfld. & P.E.I.R. 36, 428 A.P.R. 36 (Nfld. T.D.) the father was ordered to pay $150 monthly child support for his 20-year-old university student daughter until such time as she graduated. Although she shared an apartment with her boyfriend and was largely financing her education through student loans, her resources were insufficient to meet her clothing and expenses. Her father was required to provide her with the necessaries of life.

The fact that a child fails a single university course is insufficient to effect the status of a "child of the marriage": *Droit de la famille — 2112* (1994), [1995] R.D.F. 33 (C.S. Qué).

An application to terminate child support for a child over the age of majority who is in full time attendance at university will be dismissed where the child has a sincere inner conflict in regard to her father, appears not to have reached full emotional maturity and her refusal to communicate with her father is not motivated by petulance, malice or vindictiveness: *Fraser v. Jones*, above. The court was of the opinion that as a child grew older there was greater likelihood that failure to communicate with a parent who provided child support would be considered grounds for terminating support. The court held that the parties' eighteen-year-old daughter was still a "child of the marriage" and entitled to support.

Where the parties' 18-year-old daughter who moved out of her mother's residence and in with her boyfriend, was expelled from school and later moved in with her father with the intention of returning to school, she was found still to qualify as a child of the marriage. The daughter's actions had not amounted to a definitive break with her parents: *N. (P.F.) v. N. (A.)* (1994), 6 R.F.L. (4th) 113, 160 A.R. 1 (Alta. Q.B.).

The definition of "child of the marriage" is a fluid one which, in appropriate circumstances, extends to university students. An outstanding child support order is not required to bring a child who is over the age of 16 within the provisions of the Act. Furthermore, it is not necessary that the child be resident with either of the parents: *Coakwell v. Baker* (1994), 4 R.F.L. (4th) 345 (Ont. Gen. Div.).

In *Droit de la famille — 2115* (1994), [1995] R.D.F. 43 (C.S. Qué.) the court found that the parties' 23-year-old daughter no longer qualified as a "child of the marriage". She had already completed a post-secondary degree but, unable to find employment, had returned to high school to pursue another course of studies. Her return to school did not constitute "other cause" within the meaning of s. 2(1).

The fact that a child fails a single university course is insufficient to effect the status of a "child of the marriage": *Droit de la famille — 2112* (1994), [1995] R.D.F. 33 (C.S. Qué.).

In *Weise v. Weise* (1992), 44 R.F.L. (3d) 22, 12 O.R. (3d) 492, 99 D.L.R (4th) 524 (Ont. Gen. Div.), the parties' 16-year-old son was found to qualify as a "child of the marriage" despite the fact that he had attendance and behavioural problems at school and was taking a reduced course load. He still intended to complete his education.

While attendance at a post-secondary educational institution does not automatically render a child a "child of the marriage", one factor to be considered is whether or not a commitment has been made by the parent to assist the child with his or her educational expenses: *Khoury v. Khoury* (1991), 149 N.B.R. (2d) 1, 381 A.P.R. 1 (Q.B.).

In determining child support it is reasonable to inquire whether the parents would have supported a child to a certain educational level had they not separated. Accordingly, a child who would have been supported had the family stayed together, should not be punished because the marriage has broken down: *Rogge v. Rogge* (1991), 37 R.F.L. (3d) 108 (Man. Q.B.).

In *R. (L.) c. Y. (M.)* (1991), (sub nom. *Droit de la famille 1503)* [1992] R.J.Q. 63 (C.S.), the court refused support for the parties' daughter who, although she was attending university had a part-time job from which she earned $5,000 annually. The custodial wife had failed to establish that the daughter could not provide for her own needs.

In *Vokey v. Vokey* (1991), 35 R.F.L. (3d) 458, 74 Man. R. (2d) 312 (Q.B.), the parties' 18 year old daughter, who had dropped out of school and had made no real effort to find employment, was found not to be a "child of the marriage" for support purposes.

In *Droit de la famille — 1368* (1990), [1991] R.D.F. 54 (C.S. Qué.), the parties' 23-year-old daughter was found not to qualify as a child of the marriage. Although she had enrolled in a course at a cégep after quitting university, her goals were not precise and were not an extension of her recent studies.

A 21-year-old child, who, despite being enrolled full-time in university, earns $6,000 to $8,000 annually, no longer qualifies as a "child of the marriage". Such a child cannot be said to be dependent upon her parents: *Farkas v. Farkas* (1990), 85 Sask. R. 265 (Q.B.).

A 20-year-old child, who had been suicidal for an extended period of time, and who attended grade 10 under a special arrangement which allowed her to study at home and send in her assignments, was found to fall within the definition of "child of the marriage". The child intended to move on to higher grades and eventually attend Bible school. She was therefore legitimately found to be pursuing an education: *Young v. Young* (1999), 49 R.F.L. (4th) 455, 175 N.S.R. (2d) 113, 534 A.P.R. 113 (S.C.).

Where the parties' son was not attending high school on a regular basis, was employed and would be required to take adult education courses the following year to complete high school, the father's application for termination of child support was allowed. Registration in an adult education program did not qualify as a reasonable cause for the son's inability to become self-supporting or for perpetuating the father's parental obligation: *Green v. Green* (1997), 33 R.F.L. (4th) 405 (B.C. S.C.).

Where the father was required to support his daughter until she finished university, but completion of her degree was delayed because a necessary course was not available, the father's obligation continued until the degree was actually completed. The delay was not the result of any fault of the daughter: *Paterson v. Paterson* (1997), 34 R.F.L. (4th) 28 (B.C. S.C. [In Chambers]).

The fact that the parties' 19-year-old university student daughter worked part-time did not diminish the father's obligation to pay a basic level of support. However, as her income exceeded her tuition, the father was not required to finance her tuition expenses: *Glen v. Glen* (1997), 34 R.F.L. (4th) 13 (B.C. S.C.).

The fact that a 21-year-old child has been charged with a criminal offence and, as a result, has been forced to withdraw from a school program is not, of itself, sufficient grounds for a finding that the child no longer qualified as a "child of the marriage": *Cole v. Cole* (1995), 15 R.F.L. (4th) 399, 143 N.S.R. (2d) 378, 411 A.P.R. 378 (Fam. Ct.).

Where the father unilaterally ceased paying child support for his daughter on her 19th birthday, he was ordered to continue payments of a reduced amount. The fact that the father and daughter were not communicating was not relevant to her right to support although she was obliged to keep him advised of her education plans. The daughter was enrolled in university and although she had some employment income, she was not able to withdraw from her mother's control if she was to continue with her education: *Ciardullo v. Ciardullo* (1995), 15 R.F.L. (4th) 121 (B.C. S.C.).

A child is not automatically disqualified from being a child of the marriage simply because he or she already received one post-secondary school diploma. The test whether support should be continued through further studies is the reasonableness of those proposed studies: *O'Keefe v. Clarke* (1994), 7 R.F.L. (4th) 398, 122 Nfld. & P.E.I.R. 178, 379 A.P.R. 178 (Nfld. U.F.C.).

Under the *Divorce Act*, there is no absolute duty for a parent to support a child who is over the age of 16 and in attendance at a post-secondary institution. The qualification of the child as a "child of the marriage" depends upon a number of factors, including the child's eligibility for student loans, the nature of the program, the child's academic performance and relationship with the parent. Where such a child has unilaterally terminated the relationship with his or her parent, support may not be warranted: *Farden v. Farden* (1993), 48 R.F.L. (3d) 60 (B.C. Master).

Where the parties' 17-year-old child had quit school and was working, but intended to take evening classes so that he could eventually attend university, the wife's claim for child support was dismissed. As he was not currently attending school, he did not qualify as a "child of the marriage": *Kalytuk v. Kalytuk* (1992), 98 Sask. R. 311 (U.F.C.).

In *Kidson v. Techentin* (1994), 129 N.S.R. (2d) 228, 362 A.P.R. 228 (Fam. Ct.), a 21-year-old child who was nearing the end of her university studies and had earned approximately $8,000 for each of the previous several years, was found no longer to qualify as a "child of the marriage" for support purposes.

A claim for children's future education expenses should not be considered in the context of a claim for child support: *Gillespie v. Gillespie* (1988), 68 Nfld. & P.E.I.R. 255, 209 A.P.R. 255 (Nfld. U.F.C.).

2§8A — Children continuing education — part-time education

An adult child who is attending university part-time while working part-time does not qualify as a "child of the marriage": *Yaschuk v. Logan* (1991), 33 R.F.L. (3d) 316, 103 N.S.R. (2d) 371, 282 A.P.R. 371 (T.D.); affirmed on other grounds (1992), 39 R.F.L. (3d) 417, 110 N.S.R. (2d) 278, 299 A.P.R. 278 (C.A.).

See also *Walsh v. Walsh* (1988), 16 R.F.L. (3d) 1, 91 N.B.R. (2d) 132, 232 A.P.R. 132 (C.A.), above.

Where the parties' separation agreement provided that the mother was to contribute annually to the daughter's education and living expenses until she completed her university degree, she was found not responsible to help finance the daughter's post graduate degree. The evidence conclusively established that the daughter was no longer a child in need of support and the financial agreement respecting the daughter was not intended to be indefinite: *Levandusky v. Levandusky* (2003), 39 R.F.L. (5th) 134, 2003 CarswellOnt 2615 (Ont. S.C.J.); additional reasons at (2003), 2003 CarswellOnt 2613 (Ont. S.C.J.)

Where the daughter was enrolled in one college course and intended to take another which would qualify her for a teacher certification program, the court refused the father's application to terminate her child support. Although she was earning $465 monthly from babysitting, as long as she continued to pursue her long-term educational goals, she was entitled to support: *Vanderstoep v. Vanderstoep* (1998), 35 R.F.L. (4th) 385 (B.C. S.C. [In Chambers]).

Where the father had been ordered to support to his daughter until she finished university but she had elected to attend only part-time and complete her 4-year degree in 6 years, the father was only required to provide support until the end of the fourth year: *Paterson v. Paterson* (1997), 34 R.F.L. (4th) 28 (B.C. S.C. [In Chambers]).

In *Drake v. Drake* (1995), 18 R.F.L. (4th) 36 (Ont. Gen. Div.) the parties' 23-year old son who was working part-time in an apprentice program was found no longer to qualify as a "child of the marriage." The son was independent and accordingly had withdrawn from parental control.

A twenty-year-old son who was pursuing a professional hockey career and was enrolled only in two high school courses could not be found unable to withdraw from his mother's care and control because of his schooling: *Sapergia v. Larner* (1995), 15 R.F.L. (4th) 389, 133 Sask. R. 197, [1995] S.J. No. 407, 1995 CarswellSask 298 (Q.B.).

Where it is possible that a child is only attending school on a part-time basis, he would not necessarily cease to be a "child of the marriage" for purposes of the *Divorce Act*: per Fleury J. in *Hansen v. Hansen* (1995), 13 R.F.L. (4th) 335 (Ont. Gen. Div.)

Where the parties' 18-year-old daughter had failed two university correspondence courses but signed up to repeat the two courses, added a third and reduced her working time from 35 hours per week to 18, she was found to continue to qualify as a "child of the marriage." Under university regulations a student enrolled in three courses qualified as a full-time student: *Keats v. Keats*, below.

A 21-year-old child taking part time courses at university does not qualify as a "child of the marriage": *Pope v. Pope* (1995), 12 R.F.L. (4th) 391 (Nfld. U.F.C.).

The 21½-year-old daughter of the parties was not a "child of the marriage" as she was not in full-time attendance at an educational institution: *Pope v. Pope*, above. The daughter was taking three courses part-time at the University of Toronto.

A child is a "child of the marriage" if she is over 16 and taking three university courses and thus, for purposes of the university, is in full-time attendance at the university, even though there was a period where she was not a "child of the marriage" because she was not a full-time student: *Keats v. Keats* (1995), 12 R.F.L. (4th) 191 (Nfld. U.F.C.). Further, the mother was not relieved from paying support for her daughter since the evidence did not establish that the child "has unilaterally terminated contact with the payor parent."

2§8B — Children continuing education — after interruption

In *Sweeney v. Sweeney* (2004), 8 R.F.L. (6th) 424, 2004 CarswellNB 363, 2004 NBQB 267 (Q.B.), the parties' 19-year-old daughter was found to be a "child of the marriage" despite the fact that she had left the mother's home for a period to live with her boyfriend. Once she returned to the mother's home and enrolled full-time in community college, she regained her "child" status and was accordingly entitled to support.

Where the wife's 20-year-old daughter had returned to school part-time to complete grade 12 with the intention of continuing on to community college, she was found to qualify as a "child of the marriage". The concept of "withdrawal from parental control" should be narrowly construed: *Erb v. Erb* (2003), 41 R.F.L. (5th) 49, 2003 CarswellOnt 1339 (Ont. S.C.J.); additional reasons at (2003), 2003 CarswellOnt 2395 (Ont. S.C.J.)

Where the daughter had for 4 months interrupted her education and obtained a part-time job, she was found still to qualify as a "child of the marriage" during that time period. The daughter's earnings were insufficient to support her and there was no evidence that she was capable of earning more. The daughter fell within the provisions of s. 2(1)(b) of the *Divorce Act*: *Tughan v. Tughan* (2003), 39 R.F.L. (5th) 227, 2003 CarswellOnt 2398 (Ont. S.C.J.).

Where the parties' 20 year old daughter decided to leave university for one year to travel, the court allowed the father's application for termination of her child support. She had ceased to be a "child of the marriage" when she left university, but, if she decided to return, she could possibly once again be regarded as dependent: *Moore v. Moore* (1994), 121 Sask. R. 42 (Q.B.).

In *Mitchell v. Mitchell* (1992), 41 R.F.L. (3d) 443, 103 Sask. R. 278 (Q.B.), the court refused to terminate child support for a child who had interrupted her education for a brief time to work to pay off a car loan. The father had harassed the daughter to pay off the loan, which he had co-signed, and had unilaterally terminated her support upon her 18th birthday. As the child had returned to school she qualified as a child of the marriage.

A child who graduates from high school and proceeds to travel and work for a year may regain his or her status as a "child of the marriage" by returning home and enrolling in university: *Keen v. Keen* (1990), 30 R.F.L. (3d) 172, 89 Sask. R. 114 (Q.B.).

A child can reinstate entitlement to support by bringing himself or herself back within the definition of a "child of the marriage" even if at one time he or she was not a child as defined under the Act. Accordingly, where the parties' adult children had left school because of financial difficulties but had later returned, they were entitled to support as "children of the marriage": *Gray v. Gray* (1992), 39 R.F.L. (3d) 127 (Man. Q.B.).

In *Harwood v. Harwood* (1999), 45 R.F.L. (4th) 357 (B.C. S.C.), the fact that the parties' child left school temporarily to work and save funds for travel in Europe, was found not to have disqualified him as a "child of the marriage". The child had remained in the home throughout the period and remained dependent upon his mother.

Where a child is in between educational programs, he or she is entitled to be considered a "child of the marriage" for a reasonable time while he or she decides to continue with education. Accordingly, a 25-year-old child who had withdrawn from university before obtaining a degree but intended to take a community college course which was likely to lead to employment was found to continue as a "child of the marriage" for support purposes: *Cole v. Cole* (1995), 15 R.F.L. (4th) 399, 143 N.S.R. (2d) 378, 411 A.P.R. 378 (Fam. Ct.). (This case features a useful analysis of what constitutes "other cause" and a child's inability to provide him/herself with the necessaries of life).

Where the 18-year-old daughter began working as a dental assistant with the stated intention of returning to school in one year's time to study for certification as a dental hygienist, the court allowed the husband's application to terminate her child support. There was no evidence to support the wife's claim that the work experience was a pre-requisite to her acceptance into the course and as she was earning income on a full-time basis, the daughter no longer qualified as a "child of the marriage." If the daughter actually returned to school, the matter could be reconsidered: *Huisman v. Huisman* (1995), 17 R.F.L. (4th) 229 (Ont. U.F.C.).

Divorce Act, 1968

Where the 19-year-old child had left school for legitimate medical reasons and intended to return, he still qualified as a "child" for the purpose of maintenance: *Oliva v. Oliva* (1986), 2 R.F.L. (3d) 188 (Ont. H.C.); varied on other grounds (1988), 12 R.F.L. (3d) 334 (Ont. C.A.).

In *Cooper v. Cooper* (1983), 36 R.F.L. (2d) 95 (Ont. H.C.), the parties' 17½-year-old son was found not to be a child of the marriage for the purposes of interim interim support. The son had been expelled from school, and although he expressed his intent to return to school, such intent could not, on the evidence, be deemed irrevocable. If the son actually should return to school in the future, a claim for child support could then be legitimately raised.

2§8C — Children continuing education — proof of attendance

The court was of the opinion that anyone who is obligated to provide support while his or her children are in full time attendance at a school, college or university is clearly entitled to receive proof before the commencement of any new academic year of this child's continuing enrollment in an educational institution: per Fleury J. in *Hansen v. Hansen* (1995), 13 R.F.L. (4th) 335 (Ont. Gen. Div.). If this information is not provided in a timely fashion, it would be understandable for the supporting parent to pay the money into court pending receipt of satisfactory evidence of the reasons underlying the obligation to support. In Ontario, support cannot be withheld in this way, because of the mechanisms instituted for the collection of arrears of support. Mr. Justice Fleury urged the Family Support Plan to withhold the payment of any support to a recipient where time attendance at an educational institution, if the recipient fails to respond in a reasonable time to a legitimate request from the paying spouse.

2§9 — Standing "in the place of a parent" ("in loco parentis")

Divorce Act, 1985

In *Swindler v. Belanger* (2005), 22 R.F.L. (6th) 1, 2005 CarswellSask 784, 2005 SKCA 131, 261 D.L.R. (4th) 361, (sub nom. *S. (K.H.) v. S. (N.M.)*) 275 Sask. R. 129, (sub nom. *S. (K.H.) v. S. (N.M.)*) 365 W.A.C. 129, [2006] 7 W.W.R. 229 (Sask. C.A.); reversing (sub nom. *K.H.S. v. N.M.B.*) 256 Sask. R. 68, 2004 SKQB 459, 2004 CarswellSask 804 (Sask. Q.B.), it was found that the husband was not entitled to unilaterally withdraw from the in *loco parentis* relationship with the wife's child even after the wife had married the child's biological father.

In *Chartier v. Chartier* (1998), 43 R.F.L. (4th) 1, 168 D.L.R. (4th) 540, [1999] 4 W.W.R. 633, 235 N.R. 1 (S.C.C.); reversing 29 R.F.L. (4th) 96, 118 Man. R. (2d) 152, 154 D.L.R. (4th) 431, [1997] 8 W.W.R. 348 (C.A.), it was held that a spouse who had stood *in loco parentis* to a child of the other spouse is not entitled unilaterally to terminate that relationship and thus avoid child support obligations.

A person who voluntarily assumes the role of parent towards his or her spouse's children is not entitled to abandon the child. The court's jurisdiction to award child support is not lost by a step-parent's subsequent disavowal of the child: *Theriault v. Theriault* (1994), 2 R.F.L. (4th) 157, 149 A.R. 210, 63 W.A.C. 210, 113 D.L.R. (4th) 57 (C.A.).

An individual who stands *in loco parentis* to his or her spouse's children is not entitled unilaterally to terminate that status. However, where subsequent to the parties' separation, his stepchildren had rejected the husband as a parent, the *in loco parentis* relationship which existed during the marriage was severed and there was no obligation on his part to contribute to their support: *Andrews v. Andrews* (1992), 38 R.F.L. (3d) 200, [1992] 3 W.W.R. 1, 88 D.L.R. (4th) 426 (Sask. C.A.).

A person *in loco parentis* is entitled to make a unilateral withdrawal from the relationship at least up until the time that the court considers the child support application. There is no need for agreement or acquiescence in order to terminate the *in loco parentis* relationship: *Carignan v. Carignan* (1989), 22 R.F.L. (3d) 376, [1990] 1 W.W.R. 641, 61 Man. R. (2d) 66, 64 D.L.R. (4th) 119 (C.A.).

In *Lamarche c. Crevier* (2000), 4 R.F.L. (5th) 88, 2000 CarswellOnt 28 (Ont. S.C.J.); additional reasons at (2000), 2000 CarswellOnt 1142 (Ont. S.C.J.); varied (2001), 2001 CarswellOnt 3910, 151 O.A.C. 232, 22 R.F.L. (5th) 354 (Ont. C.A.), the husband was found to stand *in loco parentis* to the wife's child of a former union. The husband had attempted to adopt the child and wrote letters referring to himself as the child's father. He had made similar assertions in an application for disability benefits and on a life insurance form.

While the husband had played an active role in the life of his wife's daughter to the extent that she regarded him as her father, he was found to have a settled intention to treat the mother's child as a child of his own family in *Gregory v. Brown*, 21 R.F.L. (6th) 289, 2005 CarswellOnt 6799, [2005] O.J. No. 4565, 2005 ONCJ 284 (Ont. C.J.).

In *Johnson v. Johnson* (2005), 23 R.F.L. (6th) 46, 2005 CarswellOnt 7695, 2005 ONCJ 325 (Ont. C.J.), the husband was required to pay retroactive child support back to the date of separation for the wife's children of a previous union. The husband had sponsored the immigration of the wife and children from Russia and had executed a sponsorship agreement under which he was required to support them for 10 years. Given that the mother had given up all of her security to move to Canada, she was in immediate need from the date of separation.

Having affection for and being kind and considerate to a spouse's child from a previous union and taking part in that child's day-to-day life does not create a relationship of parent and child such as to trigger an obligation to provide child support: *Charbonneau v. Charbonneau* (2004), R.F.L. (6th) 67, 2004 CarswellOnt 5211 (S.C.J.).

Where the wife had brought her 10-month-old child into the parties' 12-year marriage, the husband was found to be primarily responsible, *vis-á-vis* the child's biological father, for the support of the child. The husband had, in every sense, stood in the place and stead of the biological father. Although the biological father was not totally exonerated from his support obligation, the husband's obligation was greater: *Vezina v. Vezina* (2004), 7 R.F.L. (6th) 435, 246 Sask. R. 139, 2004 CarswellSask 197, 2004 SKQB 134 (Q.B.).

Where the husband had consented to three earlier child support orders relating to the wife's child from a previous relationship, he could not later claim that he lacked a settled intention to treat the child as his own: *Plett v. Murphy* (2003), 38 R.F.L. (5th) 387, 2003 CarswellOnt 1629 (Ont. S.C.J.)

Once a person has made a permanent or indefinite unconditional commitment to stand in place of a parent, the court's power under the *Divorce Act* to order that person to pay support is triggered and that jurisdiction is not necessarily lost by the step-parent's subsequent disavowal of the child: *G. (K.J.) v. M. (D.M.)*, 20 R.F.L. (5th) 49, 2001 CarswellAlta 957, 2001 ABQB 617 (Alta. Q.B.).

In *Hahn v. Hahn*, 17 R.F.L. (5th) 330, 2001 CarswellAlta 559, 2001 ABQB 357 (Alta. Q.B.); additional reasons at 2001 CarswellAlta 1119, 2001 ABQB 722 (Alta. Q.B.), it was found that the fact that others may have stood *in loco parentis* to the wife's children from a previous union did not excuse or eliminate her current husband from all standing *in loco parentis*.

The determination of whether a parental relationship existed between a spouse and the child of the other spouse must be based on the relationship as it existed when the family was still together. Therefore, where the husband had intended to create such a relationship with his wife's child, but the relationship never materialized, the husband was not obliged to pay child support: *Babb v. Mantee* (1999), 49 R.F.L. (4th) 203 (Sask. Q.B.).

A parent-child relationship cannot be terminated unilaterally by either the parent or child, even one which is based upon an *in loco parentis* relationship. Accordingly, a child's refusal to visit a parent cannot, except in special circumstances, relieve the parent of the obligation of contributing towards that child's support: *Trenholm v. Trenholm* (1996), 22 R.F.L. (4th) 164 (Ont. Gen. Div.).

In *O'Hara v. O'Hara* (1995), 15 R.F.L. (4th) 408, 164 N.B.R. (2d) 295, 421 A.P.R. 295 (Q.B.) the husband was found to stand *in loco parentis* to the wife's child from a former marriage despite the fact that the child's natural father continued to pay support. Throughout the parties 8-year marriage, the husband had voluntarily assumed a parenting role toward the child and had enjoyed a close relationship with him for many years. He could not now unilaterally terminate the relationship so as to avoid support obligations.

In determining whether a spouse stands *in loco parentis* to a child, the intention of the step-parent and not that of the step-child is the governing factor: *Cote v. Cote* (1995), 12 R.F.L. (4th) 194 (Ont. Gen. Div.).

In *Droit de la famille — 2116* (1994), [1995] R.D.F. 47 (C.S. Qué.) the husband was found not to have stood in the place of a parent *vis-à-vis* the wife's daughter. The marriage had only lasted four months and, although he had contributed to the daughter's support, he treated her very differently from his own daughter and played no role in her education or discipline.

There is no distinction between "demonstrating a settled intention to treat a child as one's own" and standing "*in loco parentis*": *Cote v. Cote*, above.

The unilateral rejection of the parent/child relationship by a person who has treated a child as his own is not a public policy that should be ingrained in society: *Siddall v. Siddall* (1994), 11 R.F.L. (4th) 325 (Ont. Gen. Div.). Where a husband has treated the wife's child as his own, the child is a "child of the marriage" for purposes of the *Divorce Act* and the husband is liable to pay support for that child until he is no longer a "child of the marriage" pursuant to s. 2 of the *Divorce Act.*

Note: The *Siddall* decision has a far reaching discussion of the obligations of step-parents.

A step-parent is required to contribute to a child's support only if the biological parent is unable to meet the child's needs: *Forbes v. Forbes* (1994), 2 R.F.L. (4th) 121, 117 Sask. R. 299 (Q.B.).

A spouse cannot escape his or her parental obligations by unilaterally putting an end to an *in loco parentis* relationship which had developed during the course of a marriage: *Droit de la famille — 1369* (1991), 42 Q.A.C. 231; reversing (1990), [1991] R.D.F. 83 (C.S. Qué.).

Once a child support order has been made on the basis that the payor stands *in loco parentis* to the child and that the child qualifies as a "child of the marriage", that finding is not open to review on a variation application under s. 17 of the *Divorce Act*: *McKnight v. McKnight* (1993), 48 R.F.L. (3d) 77 (Ont. Gen. Div.). But see *Spurrill v. Spurrill* (1993), 48 R.F.L. (3d) 107, 87 Man. R. (2d) 213 (Q.B.) where the court allowed the termination of child support where the child repudiated the *in loco parentis* relationship.

A child's unilateral withdrawal from a relationship with the payor spouse may justify a denial of support. However, where the payor is unable to establish the fault for the lack of a relationship, the support obligation will continue: *Hartikainen v. Hartikainen* (1992), 39 R.F.L. (3d) 215 (Ont. Gen. Div.).

A finding that a spouse stands *in loco parentis* to a child of the other spouse requires more than the bare provision of financial assistance. Such a finding should not be made on an application for interim child support where the order unfairly prejudices the parties by predetermining the issue without the benefit of hearing their evidence: *Lopez v. Lopez* (1993), 48 R.F.L. (3d) 298 (Ont. Gen. Div.).

Generally, a person who has voluntarily assumed the role of parent to his or her spouse's child should be entitled unilaterally to withdraw from that role and terminate any relationship with the child, except in rare cases. However, this right does not include the right to put the child at any psychological or emotional risk. A spouse does not assume the role of parent simply because he or she takes on the financial responsibility, in whole or in part, for the new family unit. In a case where the husband was concerned with his spouse's child and friendly towards her, but there was no affection involved and the relationship terminated totally with the parties' separation, the husband was found to have no ongoing obligation toward the child. Any *in loco parentis* relationship which might have existed was terminated by the time of the divorce proceedings: *Slama v. Slama* (1991), 38 R.F.L. (3d) 187, 126 A.R. 210 (Q.B.).

Where it was clear after the parties' separation that the child no longer wished to see his stepfather, the stepfather was justified in unilaterally terminating his *in loco parentis* status. Accordingly, a child support order made at the time of the parties divorce was terminated: *Desjardines v. Desjardines* (1991), 31 R.F.L. (3d) 449, 113 A.R. 168 (Q.B.).

In *Gavigan v. Gavigan* (1990), 30 R.F.L. (3d) 314, 111 A.R. 62 (Q.B.); additional reasons at (1991), 30 R.F.L. (3d) at 322 (Alta. Q.B.); affirmed on other grounds (1992), 44 R.F.L. (3d) 161 (Alta. C.A.), the husband was found not to stand *in loco parrentis* to his wife's children. Although he had intended to adopt them at one point, he had not followed through and his failure to do so had contributed to the disintegration of the marriage.

A person does not stand *in loco parentis* to a child based solely on conduct which occurred when he believed he was the natural parent of the child: *Ketchum v. Ketchum* (1988), 13 R.F.L. (3d) 221 (N.B. Q.B.).

Only in exceptional cases can a stepchild terminate or refuse to accept a parental relationship with a step-parent. Generally, it is the settled intention of the step-parent to treat the stepchild as his or her own which is determinative of the issue of "*in loco parentis*": *Miller v. Miller* (1988), 13 R.F.L. (3d) 80 (Ont. H.C.).

A foster child who had lived with the parties for 12 years and who suffered from cystic fibrosis was found to be a "child of the marriage" for support purposes in *Droit de la famille — 355*, [1987] R.J.Q. 888 (C.S. Qué.).

Under the *Divorce Act*, the status of *in loco parentis* can be unilaterally terminated by the decision of the adult in question: *Ruiterman v. Ruiterman* (1994), 5 R.F.L. (4th) 192 (B.C. S.C.).

The intention of the person allegedly standing in the position of parent is the governing factor in determining whether such a relationship truly exists. Furthermore, such an individual is entitled to end the relationship before a support order is made: *Sartor v. Sartor*, 45 R.F.L. (3d) 250, [1993] N.W.T.R. 102 (S.C.).

2§9A — Child rejecting parent

Where the parties' 18 year old child had been violent towards his mother and had an unimpressive academic record, the father's application for child support was refused. By his conduct, the child had unilaterally rejected the relationship with his mother without any apparent cause. That rejection, combined with his age and poor academic record, was sufficient evidence to find that he no longer qualified as "a child of the marriage": *Pepin v. Jung* (2003), 39 R.F.L. (5th) 383, 2003 CarswellOnt 1760 (Ont. S.C.J.); additional reasons at (2003), 2003 CarswellOnt 5239 (Ont. S.C.J.)

In *Martin v. Martin*, 44 R.F.L. (5th) 164, 2003 CarswellMan 432, 179 Man. R. (2d) 35, 2003 MBQB 235 (Man. Q.B.), the court found that even if the parties' university student children had unilaterally severed their relationship with their father, he should not be relieved of the obligation to pay child support. Both children continued to live with their mother and were in full-time attendance at school pursuing undergraduate degrees.

In *Montemurro v. Shavalier* (2003), 42 R.F.L. (5th) 430, 2003 CarswellOnt 2943 (Ont. S.C.J.); additional reasons at (2003), 2003 CarswellOnt 3367 (Ont. S.C.J.), both the parties' 23-year-old son and 21-year-old daughter were found to no longer qualify as "children of the marriage". The son had completed the first year of a 2-year college course and stayed at his girlfriend's house and at his mother's house. The daughter had one more year before completing her university degree and maintained her own apartment off campus. Both children had shunned their father and, on the evidence, for no good reason.

Where the parties' 20-year-old daughter was enrolled in a 2-year post secondary Fine Arts course, she was found still to qualify as a "child of the marriage" even though she had no career plans for when she graduated and had changed her course of study several times. Although the child wanted no contact with her father, she was not found to have unilaterally terminated the relationship. Although the father had attempted over the years to contact his daughter, his efforts were sporadic: *Rosenberg v. Rosenberg* (2003), 42 R.F.L. (5th) 440, 2003 CarswellOnt 2893 (Ont. S.C.J.); additional reasons at (2003), 2003 CarswellOnt 3250 (Ont. S.C.J.).

2§10 — "Corollary relief proceeding"

Since May 1, 1997, courts and the parties have been required to distinguish between spousal and child support in orders and agreements, and to avoid combining both types of support in a single amount. If a court order or written agreement does not identify an amount as being for the support of a spouse, it will be treated as child support for tax purposes: *Income Tax Act*, s. 56(1)(b) and s. 60(b).

Prior to the 1997 amendments to s. 2(1) of the *Divorce Act* the definitions for "corollary relief proceeding," "divorce proceeding," and "support order" referred to support in a general sense without distinguishing between support for a child or children and support for a spouse. The 1997 amendments brought these definitions in line with the other reforms by qualifying support, wherever the term is used, as either child support or spousal support: *Divorce Act*, s. 2(1).

JURISDICTION

3. (1) **Jurisdiction in divorce proceedings** — A court in a province has jurisdiction to hear and determine a divorce proceeding if either spouse has been ordinarily resident in the province for at least one year immediately preceding the commencement of the proceeding.

(2) **Jurisdiction where two proceedings commenced on different days** — Where divorce proceedings between the same spouses are pending in two courts that would otherwise have jurisdiction under subsection (1) and were commenced on different days and the proceeding that was commenced first is not discontinued within thirty days after it was commenced, the court in which a divorce proceeding was commenced first has exclusive jurisdiction to hear and determine any divorce proceeding then pending between the spouses and the second divorce proceeding shall be deemed to be discontinued.

(3) **Jurisdiction where two proceedings commenced on same day** — Where divorce proceedings between the same spouses are pending in two courts that would otherwise have jurisdiction under subsection (1) and were commenced on the same day and neither proceeding is discontinued within thirty days after it was commenced, the Federal Court has exclusive jurisdiction to hear and determine any divorce proceeding then pend-

ing between the spouses and the divorce proceedings in those courts shall be transferred to the Federal Court on the direction of that Court.

2002, c. 8, s. 183(1)(i)

3 — Jurisdiction in divorce proceedings

Ordinary residence of either spouse is the sole basis for jurisdiction for divorce. Pursuant to s. 3(1), "a court in a province has jurisdiction to hear and determine a divorce proceeding if either spouse has been ordinarily resident in the province for at least one year immediately preceding the commencement of the proceeding."

The jurisdictional conflict that arises in a situation where divorce proceedings are pending in two courts is resolved by ss. 3(2) and (3). Where the proceedings were commenced on different days, the court in which a proceeding was commenced first will have exclusive jurisdiction. If the proceedings were commenced in different courts on the same day, the proceedings will be transferred to the Federal Court — Trial Division which will exercise exclusive jurisdiction.

By virtue of s. 6(1), where a divorce proceeding involves a contested claim for custody or access and the child involved is most substantially connected with another province, the court having original jurisdiction may, on application by a spouse or on its own motion, transfer the divorce proceeding to a court in that other province. The court to which the proceeding is transferred will then be vested with exclusive jurisdiction: s. 6(4).

3§1 — "Ordinarily resident"

In *Molson v. Molson* (1998), 38 R.F.L. (4th) 385, 222 A.R. 130 (Q.B.), the court rejected the husband's argument that the wife had not been "ordinarily resident" in Alberta for the required one year prior to launching a divorce action. The wife's evidence indicated that she had become "ordinarily resident" in Calgary from the date of her arrival there from her former home in Quebec. The wife had moved her furniture there and had established a residence with a friend.

In the case of conflicting affidavit evidence regarding the "ordinary residence" of the parties, an application to stay or dismiss the divorce proceeding should be granted only in a clear and obvious case. The resolution of evidentiary conflicts is best left to the trial: *Fareed v. Latif* (1991), 31 R.F.L. (3d) 354, 71 Man. R. (2d) 276 (Q.B.).

Where the wife moved from Germany to New Brunswick in May 1989 and petitioned there to divorce her German resident husband in January 1990, the petition was dismissed. As the wife had not been resident in New Brunswick for one year preceding the commencement of the proceedings, the court was without jurisdiction: *Lietz v. Leitz* (1990), 30 R.F.L. (3d) 293 (N.B. Q.B.).

The statutory residence requirements in s. 3(1) of the *Divorce Act* are substantive and not procedural in nature. Accordingly, the court is not entitled to ignore the petitioner's failure to satisfy the residency requirements even if the respondent's objections are untimely: *Droit de la famille — 360*, [1987] R.D.F. 171 (C.S. Qué.).

See also *Thomson v. M.N.R.*, [1946] S.C.R. 209 at 231–232, [1946] C.T.C. 51, [1946] 1 D.L.R. 689; *Stapleton v. Stapleton* (1977), 1 R.F.L. (2d) 190, 80 D.L.R. (3d) 562 (Man. C.A.); *MacPherson v. MacPherson* (1976), 28 R.F.L. 106 at 112–113, 13 O.R. (2d) 233, 70 D.L.R. (3d) 564 (C.A.); *Winmill v. Winmill* (1974), 47 D.L.R. (3d) 597 at 599–601, 5 N.R. 159 (Fed. C.A.); *Droit de la famille — 1006*, [1986] R.D.F. 81 (C.S. Qué.); *Byrn v.*

Mackin (1983), 32 R.F.L. (2d) 207 (Que. S.C.); *Wrixon v. Wrixon*, 30 R.F.L. (2d) 107, [1982] 6 W.W.R. 476, 22 Alta. L.R. (2d) 120 (Q.B.); *Beaton, Re* (1980), 42 N.S.R. (2d) 536, 77 A.P.R. 536 (T.D.); *Anema v. Anema* (1977), 27 R.F.L. 156 at 156–157 (Man. Q.B.); *Zawatsky v. Zawatsky* (1975), 21 R.F.L. 370 (Sask. Q.B.); *Robichaud v. Robichaud* (1974), 20 R.F.L. 14, 9 N.B.R. (2d) 662, 1 A.P.R. 662 (Q.B.); *Girardin v. Girardin* (1973), 15 R.F.L. 16 at 22, [1974] 2 W.W.R. 180, 42 D.L.R. (3d) 294 (Sask. Q.B.); *Zoldester v. Zoldester* (1973), 13 R.F.L. 398 at 400, [1974] 2 W.W.R. 572, 42 D.L.R. (3d) 316 (B.C. S.C.); *Graves v. Graves* (1973), 11 R.F.L. 112, 13 N.S.R. (2d) 262, 9 A.P.R. 262, 36 D.L.R. (3d) 367 (T.D.); *Nowlan v. Nowlan* (1971), 2 R.F.L. 67 (N.S. T.D.); *Lotoski v. Lotoski* (1970), 2 R.F.L. 64 (B.S. S.C.); *Marsellus v. Marsellus* (1970), 2 R.F.L. 53 75 W.W.R. 746, 13 D.L.R. (3d) 383 (B.C. S.C.); *Macrae v. Macrae*, [1949] P. 397, 65 T.L.R. 547, [1949] 2 All E.R. 34 (C.A.); *Cullen v. Cullen* (1969), 9 D.L.R. (3d) 610 (N.S. T.D.); *Hardy v. Hardy*, 2 R.F.L. 50, [1969] 2 O.R. 875, 7 D.L.R. (3d) 307 (H.C.)

3§2 — Concurrent applications

Section 3(2) does not apply to petitions issued in the same province: *Cavanagh v. Cavanagh* (1998) (N.S.S.C.); upholding *Cavanagh v. Cavanagh* (1999), 47 R.F.L. (4th) 271, 1999 CarswellNS 101, 175 N.S.R. (2d) 331, 534 A.P.R. 331, [1999] N.S.J. No. 100 (C.A.).

Under s. 3(2) of the *Divorce Act*, convenience of forum is not to be taken into account in determining jurisdiction: *Molson v. Molson* (1998), 38 R.F.L. (4th) 385, 222 A.R. 130 (Q.B.).

Where both spouses filed for divorce on different dates in the same judicial district, it was determined that the two petitions should be heard on the same date. As s. 5(2) [now ss. 3(2) and (3)] of the *Divorce Act* dealt only with situations where two petitions were introduced in different districts, it was inapplicable to the situation at hand: *Droit de la famille — 115* (1984), 38 R.F.L. (2d) 430 (Que. S.C.).

Where both a husband and a wife each issued a petition for divorce, but the husband wished to discontinue his action, it was held that the filing of the two separate petitions did not affect the jurisdiction of the court. The court determined that the appropriate disposition was to permit the husband to discontinue, which resulted in the disposition of the husband's proceeding permitting the court to continue with that of the wife: *H. (C.G.) v. H. (A.B.)* (1976), 22 N.S.R. (2d) 67, 31 A.P.R. 67 (T.D.).

Section 5(2)(a) [now s. 3(2)] of the *Divorce Act*, which provides that if a petition is presented in one province, 30 days after the presentation of the petition of all other later actions are "deemed to be discontinued", should be restricted to cases where one petition is commenced by one spouse and a second petition is commenced by the other spouse in another province or registry. Accordingly, where one spouse had issued petitions in Edmonton and then in Vancouver, the court in British Columbia, after the Alberta action had been discontinued, permitted the spouse to re-issue her petition. Immediately after the re-issuing of the petition, the court, with the consent of all parties, dispensed with service of the petition, set the matter down for trial, and granted a decree: *Barlow v. Barlow*, 7 R.F.L. 129, [1972] 4 W.W.R. 122, 26 D.L.R. (3d) 379 (B.C. S.C.).

"The petitions, herein, were presented to the courts of the two provinces mentioned on the same day (the husband's in British Columbia and the wife's in Ontario). Neither petition was discontinued. Therefore, the Exchequer Court of Canada, now the Federal Court of Canada, has exclusive jurisdiction to grant relief between the parties": per Cattanach J. in *Nelson v. Nelson* (1972), 31 D.L.R. (3d) 584 at 585 (Fed. T.D.).

See also *Stewart v. Stewart* (1980), 30 O.R. (2d) 63, 116 D.L.R. (3d) 383 (Master).

3§3 — Counter-petitions

A counterclaim for divorce in response to an action for separation as to bed and board is not the proper procedure for instituting an action for divorce: *Droit de la famille — 1215*, [1989] R.D.F. 3 (C.S. Qué.).

Generally, counter-petitions in divorce proceedings should be discouraged, particularly where the respondent's claim is identical to that of the petitioner. In such a case, the respondent should properly file an answer: *Penner v. Penner* (1988), 16 R.F.L. (3d) 449 (Sask. Q.B.).

3§3A — Petitioner subject to guardianship order

Where the wife petitioned for divorce in her own name while she was the subject of a guardianship order under the *Dependent Adults Act*, R.S.A. 1980, c. D-32, the court allowed the husband's appeal from the default judgment which had been entered. The guardianship order effectively deprived the wife of the right to petition in her own name and the defect could not be cured by the divorced judgment: *Piwniuk v. Piwniuk* (1992), [1993] 3 W.W.R. 242, 6 Alta. L.R. (3d) 372, 136 A.R. 157 (Q.B.).

3§3B — Third party claims

In *Burmi v. Dhiman* (2001), 18 R.F.L. (5th) 9, 2001 CarswellOnt 1812, [2001] O.J. No. 2010 (Ont. S.C.J.); additional reasons at (2001), 2001 CarswellOnt 2195 (Ont. S.C.J.), the court allowed the wife's application to amend her answer and counter-petition for divorce to add claim for general and punitive damages for deceit, slander, misrepresentation, assault and breach of fiduciary duties against her husband and to add various of his relatives subject to similar claims. The fact that the claims against the relatives were novel and unlikely to succeed was not a sufficient reason not to add them. Furthermore, as the claims against the husband and his relatives were intertwined, it was best to deal with them all in the context of one proceeding.

A third party claim is not a valid pleading within a divorce action. Family proceedings are not the proper forum for actions against individuals who are not connected to or associated with the family. Accordingly, in *Guentert v. Guentert* (1992), [1993] 7 W.W.R. 597, 87 Man. R. (2d) 1 (Q.B.), a third party notice issued by the husband against the wife's lawyer was struck on appeal.

In *Droit de la famille — 1860*, [1993] R.D.F. 598 (C.S. Qué.), the court allowed the application of the husband's new wife to have her name removed from a child support application brought by the former wife. As there was no filiation between the new wife and the daughter, she had no obligation to support.

3§3C — Setting aside unentered orders

The court has jurisdiction to rehear a matter on the basis of fresh evidence up to the time the formal order is entered. The fact that an appeal has been filed does not render the court *functus officio*: *Oppenheim v. Oppenheim* (1996), 26 R.F.L. (4th) 195, [1997] 3 W.W.R. 732, 194 A.R. 317, 46 Alta. L.R. (3d) 275 (Q.B.).

The court has inherent jurisdiction to vary or set aside an unentered divorce order, to permit additional evidence to be introduced and, if required, to vary the reasons for judgment. In exercising its jurisdiction, the court must consider whether a miscarriage of justice will occur if new evidence is not heard: *Alexa v. Alexa* (1995), 14 R.F.L. (4th) 93 (B.C. S.C.).

3§4 — Other jurisdictional issues

A wife's fear that the granting of a decree *nisi* would terminate her dower rights was not a ground for preventing the divorce action from proceeding to trial: *Schwormstede v. Schwormstede* (1993), 141 A.R. 263, 46 W.A.C. 263 (C.A.).

In *Amlani v. Hirani*, 13 R.F.L. (5th) 1, 194 D.L.R. (4th) 543, 2000 BCSC 1653, 2000 CarswellBC 2663 (B.C. S.C.), the court refused the husband's application for an order for divorce and the adjournment of all claims for corollary relief. The husband subsequently brought the same application before a different judge, disputing the policy grounds upon which his first application had been dismissed. As the husband's second application was tantamount to an appeal from the first, the court lacked jurisdiction to entertain it.

In *Wlodarczyk v. Spriggs*, 12 R.F.L. (5th) 241, 2000 SKQB 468, 200 Sask. R. 129, 2000 CarswellSask 700 (Sask. Q.B.), the court dismissed the wife's petition for divorce, recognizing an earlier decree obtained by the husband in Australia. The husband was an Australian citizen, had lived there for 15 years and, prior to filing for divorce, had moved back there with the intention of remaining. Accordingly, the husband had a real and substantial connection with Australia, sufficient to justify recognition of the Australian divorce.

Where the husband died 13 days before the divorce order was to take effect, the court allowed the wife's application to set aside the unentered order for divorce. The marriage could not be dissolved by divorce where it had already been terminated by the husband's death: *Alexa v. Alexa*, above.

Although the Northwest Territories has no legislation specifically empowering a court to issue restraining orders in family law disputes, the Supreme Court has inherent jurisdiction to grant interim injunctive relief in a divorce proceeding even though such relief was not sought in the petition: *Peterson v. MacPherson*, 32 R.F.L. (3d) 333, [1991] N.W.T.R. 178 (S.C.).

4. (1) Jurisdiction in corollary relief proceedings — A court in a province has jurisdiction to hear and determine a corollary relief proceeding if

(a) either former spouse is ordinarily resident in the province at the commencement of the proceeding; or

(b) both former spouses accept the jurisdiction of the court.

(2) Jurisdiction where two proceedings commenced on different days — Where corollary relief proceedings between the same former spouses and in respect of the same matter are pending in two courts that would otherwise have jurisdiction under subsection (1) and were commenced on different days and the proceeding that was commenced first is not discontinued within thirty days after it was commenced, the court in which a corollary relief proceeding was commenced first has exclusive jurisdiction to hear and determine any corollary relief proceeding then pending between the former spouses in respect of that matter and the second corollary relief proceeding shall be deemed to be discontinued.

(3) **Jurisdiction where two proceedings commenced on same day** — Where proceedings between the same former spouses and in respect of the same matter are pending in two courts that would otherwise have jurisdiction under subsection (1) and were commenced on the same day and neither proceeding is discontinued within thirty days after it was commenced, the Federal Court has exclusive jurisdiction to hear and determine any corollary relief proceeding then pending between the former spouses in respect of that matter and the corollary relief proceedings in those courts shall be transferred to the Federal Court on the direction of that Court.

1993, c. 8, s. 1; 2002, c. 8, s. 183(1)(i)

4 — Jurisdiction in corollary relief proceedings

Under the previous legislation [s. 4], the court that granted the divorce to either or both former spouses had exclusive jurisdiction to hear and determine claims for corollary relief. The amendment, proclaimed March 25, 1993, provides that corollary relief proceedings may be brought in any province in which either spouse is ordinarily resident at the commencement of the proceedings, or in a province in which both former spouses accept the jurisdiction of the court.

Where corollary relief proceedings are pending in two courts, the first court approached will have exclusive jurisdiction: s. 4(2). If both proceedings were commenced on the same day, both will be transferred to the Federal Court — Trial Division for hearing: s. 4(3).

The amended s. 4 mirrors the language of s. 5 of the Act.

For cases discussing "ordinarily resident", see 3§1.

Cases decided before the 1993 amendment should be read with caution.

4§1 — Jurisdiction to grant corollary relief

Divorce Act, 1985

Pursuant to s. 4 of the *Divorce Act*, a judge does not have the jurisdiction to order corollary relief under the Act in absence of a judgment of divorce: *Kalsi v. Kalsi* (1992), 41 R.F.L. (3d) 201 (Alta. C.A.).

A trial judge has discretion to grant a divorce without granting judgment on the corollary issues: *Johnson v. Johnson* (1991), 32 R.F.L. (3d) 349 (B.C. C.A.).

Where parties are in agreement as to the grounds for divorce, but disagree as to corollary relief, a court may grant the divorce and direct a trial of the corollary issues, pursuant to the *Divorce Act, 1985: Tickell v. Tickell* (1987), 10 R.F.L. 246 (Sask. C.A.).

In *Gascoyne v. Gascoyne* (1991), 94 Sask. R. 207 (Q.B.), the court refused to entertain the wife's claim for support for her daughter, raised for the first time at trial during closing argument after all evidence had been presented. It would have been unfair to allow an amendment to the petition after all evidence had been given.

Divorce Act, 1968

The power to grant an order of maintenance pursuant to s. 11 [now s. 15] of the *Divorce Act* is necessarily ancillary to jurisdiction in divorce and in that regard the Parliament of Canada was acting within its legislative competency conferred upon it by s. 91(26) of the *Constitution Act, 1867*. This principle applies equally to matters of custody, care and upbringing of children of the marriage under s. 11(c) [now s. 16], to the provisions of s. 10 [now ss. 15(3) and 16(2)], dealing with interim orders and to those of s. 12 [now ss. 15 and 16] which authorize the ordering of payments directed under s. 10 or s. 11, to be made to a trustee or administrator, and the imposition of terms, conditions and restrictions in an order made under either of those sections: *Zacks v. Zacks* (1973), 10 R.F.L. 53, [1973] S.C.R. 891, [1973] 5 W.W.R. 289, 35 D.L.R. (3d) 420.

"[T]hese intentions remain clear, namely that in the proceedings for divorce between any couple, only one court shall have jurisdiction to pronounce a decree; that as the power to grant corollary relief is given to the same court, its jurisdiction in that regard also is exclusive; that an order for corollary relief has legal effect throughout Canada; and that such an order made by any court may be registered in any other superior court in Canada and may be enforced in like manner as an order of that superior court. All these considerations lead me to the conclusion that a custody order under s. 10 [now s. 16] is paramount to any custody order theretofore or thereafter made otherwise than under the Act": per Robertson J.A. in *Hall, Re* (1976), 24 R.F.L. 6 at 11, [1976] 4 W.W.R. 634, 70 D.L.R. (3d) 493 (B.C. C.A.). See also *Rodness v. Rodness*, 23 R.F.L. 266, [1973] 3 W.W.R. 414, (sub nom. *R. v. R.)* 66 D.L.R. (3d) 746 (B.C. C.A.).

See also *Abramsen, Re*, [1977] 3 W.W.R. 764, 77 D.L.R. (3d) 103 (B.C. S.C.); *Byrn v. Mackin* (1983), 32 R.F.L. (2d) 207 (Que. S.C.); *Hudson v. Hall* (1975), 19 R.F.L. 351 (Que. S.C.); *Dimitrijevic v. Dimitrijevic*, 8 R.F.L. 368, [1972] 3 O.R. 335, 28 D.L.R. (3d) 177 (H.C.); *Muslake v. Muslake* (1987), 6 R.F.L. (3d) 280, 58 O.R. (2d) 615 (U.F.C.).

4§2 — Severance of corollary relief

In *Janz v. Harris* (1993), 84 Man. R. (2d) 251 (Q.B.); affirmed (1993), 88 Man. R. (2d) 6, 51 W.A.C. 6 (C.A.), the court granted the wife's motion to have the determination of her husband's access rights severed from the remaining divorce issues. The access issue was complex and would likely take a long time to conclude. The husband would not be prejudiced if all remaining issues proceeded to an immediate and final determination.

Where the husband wished to remarry quickly, the court allowed his application to sever the issue relating to property division from the divorce proceedings. While the divorce itself was not contested, the property issues were the cause of great dispute between the parties. The continued joining of the issues would result in prejudice and would unduly complicate the divorce: *Kornberg v. Kornberg* (1991), 74 Man. R. (2d) 179 (Q.B.); affirmed (1991), 76 Man. R. (2d) 287, 10 W.A.C. 287 (C.A.).

In divorce proceedings, corollary relief issues may be separated from the divorce and from each other and treated as separate claims: *McKenzie v. McKenzie*, 37 R.F.L. (5th) 184, 2003 CarswellAlta 196, 2003 ABQB 148, [2003] 6 W.W.R. 172, 13 Alta. L.R. (4th) 184 (Alta. Q.B.).

In *Cochran v. Cochran* (1996), 22 R.F.L. (4th) 170 (Ont. Gen. Div.) the court granted the husband's application to sever the divorce from the corollary relief proceedings which would allow him to remarry quickly. Although the husband was now resident in a different country he continued to contribute to his daughter's support voluntarily and accordingly the court rejected the wife's claim that the divorce would prejudice the making of reasonable child support provisions.

In *Wong v. Wong* (1997), 30 R.F.L. (4th) 382 (B.C. S.C.), the court allowed the husband's application to sever the divorce from corollary relief issues despite the wife's objections. Grounds for divorce clearly existed and there was no evidence that adjourning the corollary relief issue would make it difficult or expensive for the wife to maintain her claims for support and asset division.

The severance of the actual divorce decree from corollary relief proceedings generally will not prejudice a spouse's right to corollary relief. The spouse's rights crystallized on the same date regardless of when the decree actually ending the marriage is issued: *Newman v. Seaman* (1994), 140 N.S.R. (2d) 251, 399 A.P.R. 251 (S.C.).

5. (1) Jurisdiction in variation proceedings — A court in a province has jurisdiction to hear and determine a variation proceeding if

(a) either former spouse is ordinarily resident in the province at the commencement of the proceeding; or

(b) both former spouses accept the jurisdiction of the court.

(2) Jurisdiction where two proceedings commenced on different days — Where variation proceedings between the same former spouses and in respect of the same matter are pending in two courts that would otherwise have jurisdiction under subsection (1) and were commenced on different days and the proceeding that was commenced first is not discontinued within thirty days after it was commenced, the court in which a variation proceeding was commenced first has exclusive jurisdiction to hear and determine any variation proceeding then pending between the former spouses in respect of that matter and the second variation proceeding shall be deemed to be discontinued.

(3) Jurisdiction where two proceedings commenced on same day — Where variation proceedings between the same former spouses and in respect of the same matter are pending in two courts that would otherwise have jurisdiction under subsection (1) and were commenced on the same day and neither proceeding is discontinued within thirty days after it was commenced, the Federal Court has exclusive jurisdiction to hear and determine any variation proceeding then pending between the former spouses in respect of that matter and the variation proceedings in those courts shall be transferred to the Federal Court on the direction of that Court.

2002, c. 8, s. 183(1)(i)

5 — Jurisdiction in variation proceedings

Section 5(1) of the Act provides that a variation proceeding may be brought in any province in which either former spouse is ordinarily resident at the time of the commencement of the proceeding or in a province in which both spouses accept the jurisdiction of the court.

Where variation proceedings are pending in two courts, the court in which a proceeding was commenced first will have exclusive jurisdiction: s. 5(2). If the proceedings were commenced on the same day, they will be transferred to the Federal Court — Trial Division which will exercise exclusive jurisdiction: s. 5(3).

Section 6(3) provides that if a variation proceeding in respect to a custody order is opposed and the child involved is most substantially connected with another province, the court having original jurisdiction may, on application by a former spouse or on its own motion, transfer the proceeding to a court in that other province. Pursuant to s. 6(4) the court to which the variation proceeding is transferred will then have exclusive jurisdiction.

For cases discussing "ordinarily resident", see 3§1.

5§1 — General

Where the mother had taken up residence in British Columbia after leaving Alberta, it was found that the British Columbia Court had jurisdiction to vary a child support order made earlier in Alberta. As the mother was not ordinarily resident in British Columbia, the requisite jurisdiction could be found in ss. 5(1)(a) and 17(1)(a) of the *Divorce Act*: *Lavoie v. Yawrenko* (1992), 44 R.F.L. (3d) 89, 74 B.C.L.R. (2d) 321, 21 B.C.A.C. 233, 37 W.A.C. 233 (C.A.).

Section 5(2) of the *Divorce Act* is mandatory and there is nothing in the wording of that provision which gives a court a discretion to order a result other than the one specified therein: *Wolch v. Wolch* (1995), 17 R.F.L. (4th) 413 (Ont. Gen. Div.).

An Ontario court has jurisdiction to vary the custody provisions of an Ontario divorce decree, pursuant to s. 5(1)(a) of the *Divorce Act*, based upon the ordinary residence of the father in Ontario, even if Ontario is not the ordinary residence of the child: *Hiscocks v. Marshman* (1991), 34 R.F.L. (3d) 12 (Ont. Gen. Div.).

The fact that enforcement proceedings had resulted in an order under a provincial statute in relation to a divorce support order does not affect the court's jurisdiction to later vary that order under s. 17 of the *Divorce Act*: *Lamie v. Mertens* (1992), 122 N.S.R. (2d) 91, 338 A.P.R. 91 (Fam. Ct.).

6. (1) Transfer of divorce proceeding where custody application — Where an application for an order under section 16 is made in a divorce proceeding to a court in a province and is opposed and the child of the marriage in respect of whom the order is sought is most substantially connected with another province, the court may, on application by a spouse or on its own motion, transfer the divorce proceeding to a court in that other province.

(2) Transfer of corollary relief proceeding where custody application — Where an application for an order under section 16 is made in a corollary relief proceeding to a court in a province and is opposed and the child of the marriage in respect of whom the order is sought is most substantially connected with another province, the court may, on application by a former spouse or on its own motion, transfer the corollary relief proceeding to a court in that other province.

(3) Transfer of variation proceeding where custody application — Where an application for a variation order in respect of a custody order is made in a variation proceeding to a court in a province and is opposed and the child of the marriage in respect of whom the variation order is sought is most substantially connected with another province, the court may, on application by a former spouse or on its own motion, transfer the variation proceeding to a court in that other province.

(4) Exclusive jurisdiction — Notwithstanding sections 3 to 5, a court in a province to which a proceeding is transferred under this section has exclusive jurisdiction to hear and determine the proceeding.

6 — Transfer of proceedings

Section 6 provides for the transfer of proceedings to a court in another province where the proceeding involves a child of the marriage most substantially connected with that other province. For transfer of divorce proceedings, see s. 3; for transfer of corollary relief proceedings, see s. 4; and for transfer of variation proceedings, see s. 5.

6§1 — Transfer of custody proceedings

In *Shields v. Shields*, 18 R.F.L. (5th) 357, 2001 CarswellAlta 792, 2001 ABCA 140, 281 A.R. 320, 248 W.A.C. 320 (Alta. C.A.), the court allowed the mother's appeal from the dismissal of her application to have custody proceedings transferred from Alberta to Ontario. Although the children had been born in Alberta, they had to live with the mother in Ontario for several years under the parties' custody agreement. The father had refused to return the children after a visit with him in Alberta and had begun custody proceedings there. The children were ultimately returned to Ontario pursuant to a court order. The father's residence, the children's past residence and the children's visit in Alberta were not sufficient to warrant a finding that the children's most substantial connection was with Alberta. Given the children's substantial connection and ongoing residence in Ontario, it was reasonable to conclude that the bulk of the evidence at the trial would emanate from Ontario.

Where the mother moved the children from Alberta to British Columbia allegedly to get away from the oppressive and abusive father, the court refused the mother's request to transfer the Alberta custody proceedings initiated by the father to British Columbia. As the children had only been in British Columbia for eight months and the father was well-rooted in Alberta, the children continued to be "most substantially connected" with Alberta: *Ellet v. Ellet* (1994), 4 R.F.L. (4th) 358, 158 A.R. 139 (Q.B.).

Pursuant to s. 6(3) of the *Divorce Act*, custody proceedings may be transferred to another province if the subject child is more closely connected to that other province. The matter should be heard where the best evidence concerning the child's best interests is likely to be available: *Erhardt v. Erhardt* (1992), 43 R.F.L. (3d) 159, 106 Sask. R. 137 (Q.B.).

An application for the transfer of divorce proceedings under ss. 6(1) and 16(1) of the *Divorce Act* must be brought in the court where the proceedings were commenced. An Ontario court is without jurisdiction to order the transfer of proceedings commenced in Quebec: *Ruyter v. Samson* (1992), 44 R.F.L. (3d) 35, 99 D.L.R. (4th) 552 (Ont. Gen. Div.).

In *Droit de la famille — 1657*, [1992] R.J.Q. 2238 (C.S.), the court refused the wife's application for a transfer of divorce proceedings from Quebec to Ontario, where the wife had moved after separation. The parties had already litigated for over 20 months and had spent over $140,000 in relation to proceedings brought by the wife under Ontario legislation. The parties could proceed with the divorce more expeditiously in Quebec and the wife had failed to prove that it was in the parties' and their children's best interests that the divorce proceedings be transferred.

On an application under s. 6(1) of the *Divorce Act* to transfer proceedings from one province to another, the court is not restricted to transferring the specific claim but, in an appropriate case, may also transfer the entire divorce proceeding: *Mohrbutter v. Mohrbutter* (1991), 34 R.F.L. (3d) 357 (Sask. Q.B.).

Where the child resided with her father in British Columbia, but was visiting her mother in Saskatchewan, the child was found to have an insufficient connection with Saskatchewan to support the mother's custody application brought there. The court accordingly allowed the father's application for a transfer of proceedings to British Columbia: *Rempel v. Reynolds* (1991), 34 R.F.L. (3d) 82 (Sask. Q.B.).

In *Cormier v. Cormier* (1990), 26 R.F.L. (3d) 169 (N.B. Q.B.), the court refused the wife's application to have custody proceedings transferred from New Brunswick to Ontario where the wife and children were now residing. The parties had previously agreed to the jurisdiction of the New Brunswick court and the wife had removed the children to Ontario without the husband's knowledge or consent.

Where the wife left the husband in Nova Scotia and removed herself and the parties' child to Ontario ostensibly to escape the husband's abuse and harassment, the court allowed her application, in the context of the husband's Nova Scotia divorce petition, to transfer the custody proceedings to Ontario. The wife had left Nova Scotia with the child's best interests in mind and, given the age of the child, the best evidence of the circumstances surrounding the child's current condition was more readily available in Ontario than in Nova Scotia: *D. (T.W.) v. D. (Y.M.)* (1989), 20 R.F.L. (3d) 183 (N.S. T.D.).

A court is without jurisdiction to grant a divorce in one province while transferring corollary issues to another province for determination: *Tibbs v. Tibbs* (1988), 12 R.F.L. (3d) 169 (Man. Q.B.).

A parent's place of residence before a child's birth is of little consequence in determining whether a child is "most substantially connected" with that jurisdiction: *Chenkie v. Chenkie* (1987), 6 R.F.L. (3d) 371, 50 Alta. L.R. (2d) 41, 76 A.R. 224 (Q.B.).

Where the child was born and lived primarily with his mother in Alberta, but resided during the school year with his father in Saskatchewan, the father's application to transfer custody proceedings initiated by the mother from Alberta to Saskatchewan was dismissed. In the circumstances, it could not be said that the child was most substantially connected with Saskatchewan: *Astle v. Walton* (1987), 10 R.F.L. (3d) 199 (Alta. Q.B.).

Where the mother wrongfully removed the child from British Columbia to Quebec and attempted to have custody proceedings, which the husband had initiated in British Columbia, transferred to Quebec, the application was dismissed. The child's major connections continued to be with British Columbia: *Kern v. Kern* (1989), 19 R.F.L. (3d) 350 (B.C. S.C.).

Section 6(3) of the *Divorce Act, 1985* is confined to matters of custody, including access, but does not extend to the transfer of a file to deal with support: *Naylen v. Naylen* (1987), 6 R.F.L. (3d) 350 (B.C. S.C.).

To determine whether a child has "substantial connections" to a particular jurisdiction, the court should examine such factors as the child's roots, schools, homes and friends as well as where the child's support system is located: *Kermeen v. Kermeen* (1989), 93 N.S.R. (2d) 28, 242 A.P.R. 28 (Fam. Ct.). See also *Turnbull v. Turnbull* (1989), 80 Sask. R. 277 (Q.B.).

Where the wife removed the children from Sudbury to Hamilton to escape the husband's alleged abuse, the Hamilton court had jurisdiction to entertain her custody application on the basis of the children's real and substantial connection with Hamilton. It would not have been in the children's best interests to allow the husband's application to transfer the proceedings to Sudbury: *Burk v. Burk* (1991), 34 R.F.L. (3d) 27 (Ont. U.F.C.).

7. Exercise of jurisdiction by judge — The jurisdiction conferred on a court by this Act to grant a divorce shall be exercised only by a judge of the court without a jury.

7 — A judge without a jury

Section 7 provides that the jurisdiction to grant a divorce is exercisable only by a judge of the court without a jury. Section 25(2) authorized the appropriate provincial authorities to make rules respecting the conduct and disposition of any proceedings under the Act without an oral hearing.

Divorce

8. (1) Divorce — A court of competent jurisdiction may, on application by either or both spouses, grant a divorce to the spouse or spouses on the ground that there has been a breakdown of their marriage.

(2) Breakdown of marriage — Breakdown of a marriage is established only if

(a) the spouses have lived separate and apart for at least one year immediately preceding the determination of the divorce proceeding and were living separate and apart at the commencement of the proceeding; or

(b) the spouse against whom the divorce proceeding is brought has, since celebration of the marriage,

(i) committed adultery, or

(ii) treated the other spouse with physical or mental cruelty of such a kind as to render intolerable the continued cohabitation of the spouses.

(3) Calculation of period of separation — For the purposes of paragraph (2)(a),

(a) spouses shall be deemed to have lived separate and apart for any period during which they lived apart and either of them had the intention to live separate and apart from the other; and

(b) a period during which spouses have lived separate and apart shall not be considered to have been interrupted or terminated

(i) by reason only that either spouse has become incapable of forming or having an intention to continue to live separate and apart or of continuing to live separate and apart of the spouse's own volition, if it appears to the court that the separation would probably have continued if the spouse had not become so incapable, or

(ii) by reason only that the spouses have resumed cohabitation during a period of, or periods totalling, not more than ninety days with reconciliation as its primary purpose.

8 — Breakdown of the marriage — general

Under s. 8(1) of the Act, a divorce may be applied for by either or both spouses. Although joint applications for divorce are possible under the Act, spouses are not entitled to rely on their own misconduct as a basis for obtaining a divorce.

Section 8(1) provides that a divorce may be granted on the ground that there has been a breakdown of the marriage. Although marriage breakdown is the sole ground upon which a person may obtain a divorce, the fact of marriage breakdown may be established in three possible ways. The allegations involved in these three methods of proving marriage breakdown are what were previously separate grounds for divorce. Section 8(2) states that marriage breakdown will be established only if the spouses have lived separate and apart for at least one year immediately preceding the determination of the divorce proceeding, or the spouse against whom the divorce proceeding is brought has committed adultery or treated the other spouse with physical or mental cruelty of such a kind as to render intolerable the continued cohabitation of the spouses.

8A — Breakdown of the marriage — living separate and apart

The separation period required in order to establish a marriage breakdown is one year in all cases.

Where spouses are living separate and apart as a result of the unilateral intention of one spouse, *either* spouse will be entitled to a divorce after the requisite one-year period. Section 8(3) expressly provides that the spouses need not have a mutual intention to live separate and apart, but that one spouse's intention to do so is sufficient for purposes of calculating the separation period.

Section 8(2)(a) makes it possible for the spouses to commence a proceeding any time after they begin living separate and apart. The court is authorized to grant a judgment for divorce provided that at the time of the determination of the proceeding the spouses have lived separate and apart for at least one year.

In *Droit de la famille — 303*, [1986] R.D.F. 548 (C.S. Qué.), the court dismissed the wife's petition for divorce which cited only a one-month separation as the reason for the marriage breakdown. The petition was premature.

8B — Breakdown of the marriage — adultery and cruelty

Adultery and physical and mental cruelty are still bases upon which a divorce may be obtained. They are merely ways in which a spouse may establish that marriage breakdown, the sole ground for divorce, has occurred. The cases involving issues of adultery and cruelty decided under the previous Act are rendered no less relevant as a result of this change.

Divorce Act, 1970

8C — Reconciliation

The legislative policy of encouraging spouses to attempt reconciliation is found in the present Act. Pursuant to s. 9(3)(b), the spouses may make any number of attempts at reconciliation without interrupting the period of separation, provided that the total number of days for which they resume cohabitation does not exceed 90.

8§1 — Marriage validity in general

Reference re Same-Sex Marriage, S.C.C., December 9, 2004

The Governor in Council asked the Supreme Court of Canada to hear a reference respecting certain aspects of legal capacity for marriage for civil purposes. The operative sections of the government's *Proposed Act* provide as follows:

> Section 1. Marriage, for civil purposes, is the lawful union of two persons to the exclusion of all others.
>
> Section 2. Nothing in this *Act* affects the freedom of officials of religious groups to refuse to perform marriages that are not in accordance with their religious beliefs.

The reference set out four questions:

> Question 1: Is the annexed *Proposal for an Act respecting certain aspects of legal capacity for marriage for civil purposes* within the exclusive legislative authority of the Parliament of Canada? If not, in what particular or particulars, and to what extent?
>
> Question 2: If the answer to question 1 is yes, is section 1 of the proposal, which extends capacity to marry to persons of the same sex, consistent with the *Canadian Charter of Rights and Freedoms*? If not, in what particular or particulars, and to what extent?
>
> Question 3: Does the freedom of religion guaranteed by paragraph 2(a) of the *Canadian Charter of Rights and Freedoms* protect religious officials from being compelled to perform a marriage between two persons of the same sex that is contrary to their religious beliefs?
>
> Question 4: Is the opposite-sex requirement for marriage for civil purposes, as established by the common law and set out for Quebec in s. 5 of the *Federal Law-Civil Law Harmonization Act, No. 1*, consistent with the *Canadian Charter of Rights and Freedoms*? If not, in what particular or particulars and to what extent?

The court, in answering the questions put to it, held, first, that s. 1 is within the exclusive legislative competence of Parliament, while s. 2, dealing with the solemnization of marriage, is not. It held that s. 1 of the *Proposed Act*, which defines marriage as the union of two persons, is consistent with the *Canadian Charter of Rights and Freedoms*. In pith and substance the section pertains to the capacity for marriage. Section 91(26) of the *Constitution Act, 1867* confers on Parliament legislative competence with respect to the capacity to marry. Consequently the section falls within a subject-matter granted exclusively to Parliament. With regard to s. 2 of the *Proposed Act*, the court held that since legislative competence over the performance or solemnization of marriage is exclusively granted to the provinces under s. 92(12) of the *Constitution Act, 1867*, s. 2 of the *Proposed Act* is *ultra vires* Parliament. On the second question, the court held that s. 1 of the *Proposed Act* should not be impugned on the basis that it violates ss. 15(1) (equality rights) and 2(a) (guarantee of freedom of religion) in the *Charter*. The court found that the possible collision of rights raised by s. 1 of the *Proposed Act* was not shown on the reference to violate the *Charter*. It has not been shown that there are conflicts which will arise that are incapable of resolution under s. 2(a). On the third question, the court was of the opinion that unless there are unique circumstances (about which it would not speculate), the guarantee of religious freedom in s. 2(a) of the *Charter* can protect religious officials from being compelled by the state to perform civil or religious same-sex marriages that are contrary to their religious beliefs. The court declined to answer the fourth question, whether the opposite-sex requirement for marriage for civil purposes, as established by the common law and set out for Quebec in s. 5 of the *Federal-Civil Harmonization Act, No 1*, is consistent with the *Canadian Charter of Rights and Freedoms* and if not, in what particular or particulars and to what extent. The court observed that the Federal Government intended to proceed by way of legislative enactment, regardless of the court's answer to this question. Consequently, an opinion on the constitutionality of an opposite-sex requirement for marriage served no legal purpose. Further, parties to previous litigation have now relied on the finality of the judgments which they obtained. Their vested rights outweigh the benefits of answering Question 4. Lastly, answering this question may undermine the government's stated goal of reaching uniformity with regard to civil marriage across Canada. Uniformity of the law is essential as evidenced by the fact that Parliament was given legislative competence concerning marriage under s. 91(26) of the *Constitution Act, 1867*.

The common law definition of marriage as a voluntary union of one man and one woman to the exclusion of all others violates the equality provisions of s. 15(1) of the *Canadian Charter of Rights and Freedoms*. Furthermore, the definition cannot be saved under s. 1 of the *Charter*: *Halpern v. Toronto (City)* (2003), 36 R.F.L. (5th) 127, 2003 CarswellOnt 2159, (sub nom. *Halpern v. Canada (Attorney General))* [2003] O.J. No. 2268, 65 O.R. (3d) 161, 65 O.R. (3d) 201, (sub nom. *Halpern v. Canada (Attorney General))* 172 O.A.C. 276, 225 D.L.R. (4th) 529 (Ont. C.A.).

To have a valid marriage, there must be an event to which one can point which signifies that the relationship has changed from two persons who are single to two persons who are married. There must be recognition by each spouse of a change in his or her status. Finally, there must be an identifiable time and place where the change occurs and an official who is authorized by law to change the legal status of the individuals: *Yangaeva v. Kershtein* (2001), 21 R.F.L. (6th) 234, 2001 CarswellOnt 6480 (Ont. S.C.J.).

The Superior Court of Ontario has jurisdiction to annul marriages that were celebrated outside of Canada: *Bolentiru v. Radulescu* (2004), 10 R.F.L. (6th) 258, 2004 CarswellOnt 3292 (Ont. S.C.J.); additional reasons at (2004), 2004 CarswellOnt 4369 (Ont. S.C.J.).

The common law bar to same sex marriage is in contravention of s. 15 of the *Canadian Charter of Rights and Freedoms*, Part I of the *Constitution Act, 1982* being Schedule B to the *Canada Act 1982*, c. 11 and cannot be justified under s. 1 of the *Charter*: *EGALE Canada Inc. v. Canada (Attorney General)*, 38 R.F.L. (5th) 32, 2003 CarswellBC 1006, [2003] B.C.J. No. 994, 2003 BCCA 251, 13 B.C.L.R. (4th) 1, [2003] 7 W.W.R. 22, 182 B.C.A.C. 35, 300 W.A.C. 35, 225 D.L.R. (4th) 472 (B.C. C.A.); additional reasons at 2003 CarswellBC 1659, 2003 BCCA 406, 15 B.C.L.R. (4th) 226, 228 D.L.R. (4th) 416 (B.C. C.A.); reversing [2001] B.C.J. No. 1995, 2001 BCSC 1365, 19 R.F.L. (5th) 59, [2001] 11 W.W.R. 685, 95 B.C.L.R. (3d) 122, 88 C.R.R. (2d) 322, 2001 CarswellBC 2071 (B.C. S.C.)

In *Sung Estate, Re* (2003), 37 R.F.L. (5th) 441, 2003 CarswellOnt 1461, 1 E.T.R. (3d) 296 (Ont. S.C.J.); additional reasons at (2003), 2003 CarswellOnt 4002, 4 E.T.R. (3d) 137, [2003] O.J. No. 4109 (Ont. S.C.J.); affirmed (2004), 2004 CarswellOnt 4512, 11 E.T.R. (3d) 169 (Ont. C.A.) the marriage between the deceased S and one F was declared void on the application of S's children. F had been S's caregiver while he suffered from cancer and had coerced S into the marriage by threatening to discontinue caring for him when he became totally incapacitated. S had intended that there be a prenuptial agreement which F effectively thwarted. F's conduct was greedy and rapacious and, in the circumstances, the marriage was declared invalid.

In *Knight v. Knight* (1995), 16 R.F.L. (4th) 48, 1995 CarswellOnt 886, [1995] O.J. No. 3242 (Ont. Gen. Div.) the husband was precluded from attacking the validity of his second marriage on the basis that the Mexican divorce obtained to dissolve his first marriage had not been valid. The husband was estopped on the basis of both the doctrine of preclusion and insincerity.

Where a decree absolute dissolving a marriage is obtained on the basis of cruelty, the marriage no longer exists and an action for annulment on the basis of non-consummation will be dismissed: *Hillcox v. Morrow* (1986), 3 R.F.L. (3d) 45 (B.C. C.A.); leave to appeal to refused (1987), 6 R.F.L. (3d) xxviii (S.C.C.).

In *Trenholm v. Trenholm* (1989), 21 R.F.L. (3d) 223 (N.S. C.A.), the court held that non-consummation of a marriage is not, of itself, a ground for declaring a marriage a nullity. There must be an incapacity of some kind.

While a sham marriage is not valid, a marriage entered into solely for the purpose of facilitating immigration to Canada is a valid marriage, since the parties' reservations or motives in going through the ceremony are irrelevant: *Fernandez (Alarcio) v. Fernandez: Kolba v. Azevedo*, 34 R.F.L. (2d) 249, [1983] 4 W.W.R. 755, 21 Man. R. (2d) 254 (Q.B.).

Where the parties had cohabited after the marriage ceremony but, unbeknownst to the wife, no licence had been obtained and the marriage not registered, the marriage was presumed valid: *Lehoux v. Woolward* (1994), 2 R.F.L. (4th) 382 (B.C. S.C.).

In a divorce proceeding, the onus is on the petitioner to prove the marriage, the termination of which is sought. A certified copy of the marriage particulars from a provincial Department of Vital Statistics is, unless challenged by credible evidence that the parties were not qualified to marry, evidence of that marriage: *Law (Francisco) v. Francisco* (1983), 34 R.F.L. (2d) 223 (B.C. S.C.).

Where the wife had married at the age of 16 without parental consent as required by Alberta law, her petition for divorce was dismissed and a declaration of nullity was granted. As the breach of Alberta law rendered the marriage void *ab initio*, the *Divorce Act* was inapplicable: *Machaalani v. Machaalani* (1983), 144 D.L.R. (3d) 320 (B.C. S.C.).

In *Legebokoff v. Legebokoff* (1982), 28 R.F.L. (2d) 212, 136 D.L.R. (3d) 566 (B.C. S.C.), it was held that the facts that the wife had married at the age of 15 and without parental consent did not affect the validity of her marriage. As the Parliament of Canada, which had exclusive authority to legislate concerning the capacity to marry, had not prescribed a minimum age and as the wife was old enough to have capacity at common law, the marriage could not be attacked on the grounds of capacity. Similarly, as parental consent was a matter of formality rather than one of capacity and as the provincial *Marriage Act* stipulated that lack of consent or court approval did not invalidate a marriage, the marriage was held to be valid.

"The voluntary consent of both parties is necessary for a valid marriage and the marriage is void if such consent is lacking, as, for example, where it is procured by threats or duress; but mental reservations on the part of one or both of the parties to a marriage do not affect its validity": per Collingwood J. in *Silver (Kraft) v. Silver*, [1955] 1 W.L.R. 728, [1955] 2 All E.R. 614 at 615 (P.D.A.); cited with approval in *Gardner v. Gardner* (1970), 2 R.F.L. 41, 75 W.W.R. 667, 13 D.L.R. (3d) 250 (B.C. S.C.). See also *Iantsis (Papatheodorou) v. Papatheodorou*, 3 R.F.L. 158 at 164, [1971] 1 O.R. 245, 15 D.L.R. (3d) 53 (C.A.).

Where the petitioner and respondent participated in a marriage ceremony which, in accordance with provincial law, did not amount to a valid solemnization of the marriage, it was held that a divorce could not be granted as the marriage itself was invalid; *Lavery v. Lavery* (1977), 22 N.S.R. (2d) 432, 31 A.P.R. 432 (T.D.).

A marriage which is otherwise valid, but which has not been consummated, is voidable as opposed to *ab initio*, and remains valid until it is annulled by a court of competent jurisdiction at the instance of one of the parties. It is not open to the court in a divorce action to impugn any such marriage: *Hudson v. Hudson* (1976), 29 R.F.L. 257, 16 N.S.R. (2d) 122 (T.D.).

8§2 — Marriages of convenience

Where parties, having the necessary capacity to marry, went through a marriage which was duly solemnized, there was a subsisting marriage even if it was entered into for the purpose of perpetrating a fraud on the immigration authorities. This was so despite the fact that the parties had met only three days before the marriage, had lived together overnight, and had separated the day after the marriage: *Leonotion v. Leonotion* (1977), 4 R.F.L. (2d) 94 (Ont. C.A.) (where a new trial was ordered on other grounds). See also *McKenzie v. McKenzie* (1982), 26 R.F.L. (2d) 310 (Ont. C.A.); *Ciresi (Ahmad) v. Ahmad* (1983), 31 R.F.L. (2d) 326, [1983] 1 W.W.R. 710, 23 Alta. L.R. (2d) 223, 142 D.L.R. (3d) 364 (Q.B.).

Neither a fraudulent nor an innocent misrepresentation will of itself affect the validity of a marriage unless the misrepresentation induces an operative mistake such as one concerning the nature of the ceremony, or deception as to the identity of one of the persons to the marriage, as when A is induced to marry B, believing that she is marrying C. Thus a marriage will not be declared void where one or both of the parties have gone through a ceremony for a motive other than marriage, such as, to affect the immigrant status of one of the parties: *Iantsis (Papatheodorou) v. Papatheodorou*, 3 R.F.L. 158, [1971] 1 O.R. 245, 15 D.L.R. (3d) 53 (C.A.); which overruled *Johnson (Smith) v. Smith*, [1968] 2 O.R. 699, 70 D.L.R. (2d) 374 (H.C.).

Where parties go through a form of marriage, one in good faith and the other only to facilitate immigration, the marriage is void *ab initio* and the *Divorce Act* inapplicable: *Laroia v. Laroia* (1984), 47 O.R. (2d) 762 (H.C.). On appeal at (1986), 54 O.R. (2d) 762 (C.A.), however, the court reversed the earlier decision, finding that there was a subsisting marriage, the petition for divorce was allowed and the decree *nisi* was granted.

Where the respondent husband deceived the petitioner into marriage in order to obtain his Canadian landed immigrant status, the marriage was held to be valid despite the respondent's desertion of the petitioner prior to consummation: *Sattar v. Sattar* (1975), 26 R.F.L. 127 (Ont. H.C.).

A lack of intention to marry on the part of both parties may be sufficient grounds for a declaration of nullity. Therefore where a Vietnamese national married an American citizen solely to escape the turbulent political climate in Vietnam, and neither party intended to cohabit with the other and no such cohabitation had ever taken place, the marriage was held to be invalid: *Truong (Malia) v. Malia* (1975), 25 R.F.L. 256 (Ont. H.C.).

"[I]t would seem to be the law of Ontario that where persons publicly go through a form of marriage whereby they become in the eyes of the community husband and wife that marriage is perfectly valid notwithstanding any mental reservations they may have regarding the true purpose of the marriage. The refusal to declare a marriage void in these circumstances, however, is not stated to be the result of any principle of public policy. Rather the reasoning would seem to be that there is no lack of consent because the parties do intend to become man and wife for some limited purpose which can be achieved only through the status of marriage. In my view, the 'immigration cases' do not require that the court refuse to annul such marriages, but simply state that the courts will not annul the same by reason *only* of their having been entered into to achieve immigrant status. However, fear and duress vitiate consent": per VanCamp J. in *Feiner v. Demkowicz (Feiner)* (1973), 14 R.F.L. 27 at 35, 2 O.R. (2d) 121, 42 D.L.R. (3d) 165 (H.C.).

Where the defendant husband deliberately misled the plaintiff wife into going through a form of marriage with him solely for the purpose of obtaining his permanent residency in Canada, the marriage was held to be invalid. The defendant's representations to the plaintiff that he intended to make her his wife in accordance with their religious customs and to live with her as her husband clearly amounted to fraud in light of his lack of intention to enter into a real marriage: *Kalyan (Natsih) (Lal) v. Lal* (1976), 28 R.F.L. 229 (B.C. S.C.) applying, *Johnson (Smith) v. Smith*, above.

Where evidence in the course of a divorce proceeding indicated that the parties had married solely to enable the husband to enter Canada as the spouse of a Canadian citizen and that the marriage had, in accordance with the parties' intentions, never been consummated, the marriage was held to be valid. The parties had intended to create the legal status of marriage and had, by going through the necessary forms, created that status. Although the object of the marriage was not normal cohabitation, the validity of the marriage was not thereby affected: *Gardner v. Gardner* (1970), 2 R.F.L. 41, 75 W.W.R. 667, 13 D.L.R. (3d) 250 (B.C. S.C.). See also *Deol v. Deol*, 5 R.F.L. 225, [1972] 2 W.W.R. 407, 23 D.L.R. (3d) 223 (B.C. S.C.).

Where the male defendant deceived the female plaintiff going through a form of marriage solely for the purpose of obtaining his permanent residency in Canada, the marriage was held to be invalid: *Johnson (Smith) v. Smith*, [1968] 2 O.R. 699, 70 D.L.R. (2d) 374 (H.C.). But see *Iantsis (Papatheodorou) v. Papatheodorou*, above, where *Johnson (Smith) v. Smith* was overruled.

8§2A — Capacity to divorce

Where the wife: was showing early stages Alzheimer's disease, the court rejected the husband's contention that she lacked the capacity to separate and divorce. The wife understood the context of her decision, was aware of the specific choices available to her and appreciated the consequences of those choices: *Calvert (litigation Guardian of) v. Calvert* (1997), 27 R.F.L. (4th) 394, 32 O.R. (3d) 281 (Gen. Div.); affirmed (1998), 36 R.F.L. (4th) 169, 37 O.R (3d) 221 (C.A.).

8§3 — Counter-petitions

Divorce Act, 1985

Where the husband sought a divorce on the basis of a one-year separation and the wife counter-petitioned on the basis of the husband's adultery, the husband's application for summary judgment was refused. The courts should not pick which valid cause of action they will hear or not hear and granting the husband's motion would prevent the wife's action from being heard: *Gravelle v. Gravelle* (1990), 27 R.F.L. (3d) 205 (Ont. H.C.).

Divorce Act, 1968

"Generally speaking, I feel that all counter-petitions for divorce should be discouraged where the respondent admits that the grounds alleged by the petitioner are valid and are good cause for an order dissolution": per Bence C.J.Q.B. in *Mattson v. Mattson*, 4 R.F.L. 6 at 10, [1971] 3 W.W.R. 428 (Sask. Q.B.). See also *Huff v. Huff* (1971), 4 R.F.L. 258, 16 D.L.R. (3d) 584 (Man. C.A.).

"Until the petition was served, the respondent was content, apparently, with her position. Upon this event occurring, she took advice, filed an answer admitting the allegations advanced as grounds for divorce, and counter-petitioned for maintenance. In that the substantive allegations were admitted in the answer, this counter-petition, it seems to me, was hardly necessary, since maintenance is in issue in any event. I respectfully agree with what Bence C.J.Q.B. said on this point in *Mattson v. Mattson*, [1971] 3 W.W.R. 428, 4 R.F.L. 6 (Sask).": per Tyrwhitt-Drake L.J.S.C. in *Lee v. Lee*, 7 R.F.L. 140 at 144, [1972] 3 W.W.R. 214 (B.C. S.C.). See also *Johnston v. Johnston* (1973), 13 R.F.L. 181, 5 N.S.R. (2d) 403 (T.D.).

8§4 — Mutual divorces

Where the wife was found entitled to a decree *nisi* on the grounds of the husband's adultery, the court exercised its discretion against granting the husband's counter-petition based upon the wife's alleged adultery, which had occurred long after the parties' separation: *Michel v. Michel* (1982), 31 R.F.L. (2d) 350 (B.C. S.C.).

Where both parties had proved cruelty and the trial judge had found that each was entitled to a decree *nisi*, a decree which provided only that the petitioner be divorced from the respondent was emended to provide that the parties be divorced from each other: *Roschuk v. Roschuk* (1980), 15 R.F.L. (2d) 196 (Man. C.A.).

In *Bolton v. Bolton* (1976), 26 R.F.L. 284 (P.E.I. S.C.), concurrent decrees *nisi* were issued where both husband and wife established that the other had committed adultery.

8§5 — Incorporating agreements into divorce orders

See 15§150 Agreement changed according to variation provision in agreement.

Separate and Apart

Section 8, "Separate and apart", is divided into the following subsections:

8§6 — "Separate and apart" — requirement of intention

Divorce Act, 1985

Where neither party took any step to indicate a clear intention to end the marriage, the marriage continued, even though the couple lived apart physically for some long periods and for short periods over an extended period of time: *Coates v. Coates*, 2000 CarswellMan 629, 152 Man. R. (2d) 301, 2000 MBQB 197 (Q.B.). Despite these times apart, they continued to meet each other to discuss business affairs, to renovate their home, to purchase property and livestock, to maintain a joint account and to rely on one another to manage their respective businesses. It seemed clear that they wanted their marriage to continue until the wife filed a Marital Property Application.

Even if only one party has the intention to live separate and apart, this intention is sufficient for the court to find that a marriage has ended: *Mosset v. Mosset*, 2002 CarswellMan 532, 169 Man. R. (2d) 85, 2002 MBQB 278 (Man. Master). In this case, the husband had been prepared to reconcile over a 7-year period but the wife had never evinced a desire to re-establish the parties' former relationship. Events established a separation which was confirmed by the courts. The parties continued to co-operate on business matters and enjoyed some leisure activities and vacations together. However, the wife withdrew from many social functions; the husband was not included in many family events; the parties indicated on their tax returns that they were "separated"; and the husband made extensive renovations to his own separate residence. (Ed. note: The test for living separate and apart is the same under the *Divorce Act* and under the *Manitoba Property Act*).

The definition of "separate and apart" requires physical separation coupled with a recognition by only *one* of the parties that the marriage is at an end. It is not necessary that the parties form a joint intention: *Memisoglu v. Memisoglu* (1995), 18 R.F.L. (4th) 150, 170 N.B.R. (2d) 285, 435 A.P.R. 285 (C.A.); varying (1994), 154 N.B.R. (2d) 30, 395 A.P.R. 30 (Q.B.).

Where the wife was showing early stages of Alzheimer's disease, the court rejected the husband's contention that she lacked the capacity to separate and divorce. The wife understood the context of her decision, was aware of the specific choices available to her and appreciated the consequences of those choices: *Calvert (Litigation Guardian of) v. Calvert* (1997), 27 R.F.L. (4th) 394, 32 O.R. (3d) 281, 26 O.T.C 81 (Gen. Div.); affirmed (1998), 36 R.F.L. (4th) 169 (Ont. C.A.). On appeal, the court rejected the argument that s. 8(3)(b)(i) can only be relied on where there are specific findings as to when the respondent became incapable of forming an intent or as to her intent at the time of the petition and for the one year period preceding the judgment.

A spouse is entitled to commence a petition for divorce under s. 8(2)(a) before the expiry of the required one-year separation: *Mitchell v. Mitchell* (1993), 129 N.S.R. (2d) 351, 362 A.P.R. 351 (S.C.).

The words "separate and apart" are disjunctive. They mean that there must be a withdrawal from the matrimonial obligation with the intent of destroying the marital consortium, as well as physical separation. The two conditions must be met: *Rushton v. Rushton* (1968), 1 R.F.L. 215, 66 W.W.R. 764, 2 D.L.R. (3d) 25 (B.C. S.C.). See also *Dimen v. Dimen* (1974), 15 R.F.L. 322 (Sask. Q.B.).

"In determining whether a marriage exists the court must give greater weight to those matters that should be peculiar to a husband and wife relationship, i.e., sexual relations, joint social ventures, communication and discussion of family problems, etc., than to the performance or nonperformance by the wife, for example, of meal preparation and laundering, tasks that can be done by any maid or housekeeper": per Mackeigan C.J.N.S., citing MacIntosh J. (trial judgment) in *McKenna v. McKenna* (1974), 19 R.F.L. 357 at 358, 10 N.S.R. (2d) 268, 2 A.P.R. 268 (C.A.).

"Mere physical separation of the parties even if they had been so separated for the requisite period ... is not of itself sufficient to satisfy the requirements of section 4(1)(e) [now s. 8(2)(a)] of the *Divorce Act*. It must also be shown that the matrimonial association or consortium *vitae*, has been terminated": per Mifflin J. in *Devani v. Devani* (1975), 8 Nfld. & P.E.I.R. 273 at 275, 8 A.P.R. 273 (Nfld. T.D.).

"The evidence in any given case must be examined to determine upon what date the parties were not only living apart but also on what date did the matrimonial relationship cease to exist": per MacFarlane J. *Dorchester v. Dorchester*, 3 R.F.L. 396, [1971] 2 W.W.R. 634, 19 D.L.R. (3d) 126 (B.C. S.C.).

8§7 — Guidelines for determining "separate and apart"

"[The following statements can be extracted as representing the weight of judicial opinion as to what constitutes separate and apart]:

> (1) Great care must be exercised in considering the evidence and each case determined on its own circumstances.
>
> (2) There can be a physical separation within a single dwelling unit.
>
> (3) A case is not taken out of the statute just because a spouse remains in the same house for reasons of economic necessity.
>
> (4) To meet the statute there must be both (a) physical separation and (b) a withdrawal by one or both spouses from the matrimonial obligation with the intent of destroying the matrimonial consortium.
>
> (5) Cessation of sexual intercourse is not conclusive but is only one factor to be considered in determining the issue.
>
> (6) There may be an atmosphere of severe incompatibility but remain one household and one home — a distinction may be drawn between an unhappy household and a separated one":

per Stevenson J. in *Dupere v. Dupere* (1974), 19 R.F.L. 270 at 274, 9 N.B.R. (2d) 554, 1 A.P.R. 554 (Q.B.); affirmed 10 N.B.R. (2d) 148, 4 A.P.R. 148 (C.A.). See also *Burt v. Burt* (1974), 7 R.F.L. 155, 7 N.S.R. (2d) 321, 24 D.L.R. (3d) 497 (T.D.).

Where neither party took any step to indicate a clear intention to end the marriage, the marriage continued, even though the couple lived apart physically for some long periods and for short periods over an extended period of time: *Coates v. Coates*, 2000 CarswellMan 629, 152 Man. R. (2d) 301, 2000 MBQB 197 (Q.B.)

8§8 — Temporary physical separations

The fact of physical separation for the requisite time is only presumptive proof of a "permanent breakdown" of the marriage and the judge hearing a petition must ascertain whether there exists a possibility of reconciliation. The subsection [now s. 8(2)(a)] is without application while there is a mutual intention to continue the marital relationship notwithstanding a physical separation and it can only be invoked where there has been absent such an intent of at least one of the spouses throughout the prescribed period. The intention that a marriage shall continue to subsist is not consistent with physical separation for long periods: *Lachman v. Lachman*, 2 R.F.L. 207 at 211, [1970] 3 O.R. 29, 12 D.L.R. (3d) 221 (C.A.).

Where the cause of the parties' separation was the husband's incarceration, his petition on the ground of marriage breakdown was refused. In the circumstances, there was no evidence that the cessation of cohabitation was the result of a decision of either party: *Raven v. Raven* (1984), 30 Man. R. (2d) 71 (Q.B.).

"The physical separation of husband and wife is one of the factors which must be taken into consideration in cases of this kind, but there may be physical separation of the parties without there being a finding that the parties are living 'separate and apart'. For instance, a serviceman may be posted overseas and be away from his wife ... without the parties living 'separate and apart' within the meaning of the Act'": per Macfarlane J. in *Dorchester v. Dorchester*, 3 R.F.L. 396, [1971] 2 W.W.R. 634, 19 D.L.R. (3d) 126 (B.C. S.C.).

"Conceivably, there are many instances where husband and wife are physically absent from one another, even for a long duration of time. This absence may be brought about by a variety of causes, illness, nature of employment, etc. However, as long as the spouses treat the parting or absence, be it long or short, as *temporary* and *not permanent*, the couple is not living separately even though physically it is living apart. In order to come within the clear meaning of the words 'separate and apart' in the statute, there must be not only a physical absence of one from the other, but also a destruction of the consortium vitae or as the Act terms it, a marriage breakdown": per Dubinsky J. in *Herman v. Herman* (1969), 1 R.F.L. 41 at 46, 1 N.S.R. 514, 3 D.L.R. (3d) 551 (T.D.). See also *Ettinger v. Ettinger* (1974), 8 N.S.R. (2d) 293 (T.D.).

In *Compton v. Compton* (1970), 1 R.F.L. 244, 1 N.S.R. (2d) 827 (T.D.), the parties had agreed to live physically apart temporarily for an indefinite period, upon medical advice, in the hope that the health of the petitioner would improve. Since the parties, while apart, continued as between themselves many of the features of married life, it had to be concluded that although they were physically separate, they both recognized the subsistence of the marital relationship. There was no finality about their separation and thus they could not be said to be living separate and apart within the meaning of the Act. See also *Rushton v. Rushton* (1968), 1 R.F.L. 215, 66 W.W.R. 764, 2 D.L.R. (3d) 25 (B.C. S.C.).

8§9 — Separation — insanity or long-term hospitalization

In *Calvert (Litigation Guardian of) v. Calvert* (1998), 36 R.F.L. (4th) 169, 37 O.R. (3d) 221, 106 O.A.C. 299 (C.A.); affirming (1997), 27 R.F.L. (4th) 394, 32 O.R. (3d) 281, (sub nom. *Calvert v. Calvert)* 26 O.T.C. 81 (Gen. Div.); leave to appeal refused (1998), 111 O.A.C. 197 (note), 228 N.R. 98 (note) (S.C.C.), the fact that the wife became mentally incompetent after the parties' separation was found not to impact the wife's right to seek divorce based upon a one-year separation. It was clear at the time of the separation that the wife wished to divorce and that wish continued as long as she had capacity. Section 8(3)(b)(i) of the *Divorce Act*, which provided that the period of separation is not to be considered interrupted by a spouse's loss of capacity to form the intention if it appears that the separation otherwise would likely have continued, was applicable.

"I reject the suggestion that a decree may not be made merely because the separation has been caused by the insanity of one spouse. The grounds in s. 4(1)(e) [now s. 8(2)(a)] are marriage breakdown by virtue of the fact that the parties are living separate and apart ... Whatever the underlying cause of the separation, if a petitioner can show that the spouses have lived separate and apart within the meaning of the Act for the requisite time, he is entitled to a decree. ... The cause of the separation is immaterial if the time requirements are met": per McIntyre J. in *Kennedy v. Kennedy* (1968), 1 R.F.L. 217 at 220, 67 W.W.R. 91, 2 D.L.R. (3d) 405 (B.C. S.C.). See also *Smith v. Smith* (1976), 28 R.F.L. 211 (B.C. S.C.).

"[A]lthough the parties were physically apart — she at home and he in the hospital — they could not be considered as living 'separate and apart' for as long as she kept visiting him. As long as these visits continued, the marriage was still extant, just as if he were at home with her. Only from December 1968, when she resolved to having nothing more to do with him, can it be said that their marriage had broken down": per Dubinsky J. in *Hills v. Hills* (1969), 1 R.F.L. 236 at 238, 1 N.S.R. (2d) 405, 9 D.L.R (3d) 722 (T.D.).

"[I]t seems ... clear that one spouse can alter the animus so that parties who are not living separate will begin to do so. In the instant case, I consider that the parties were not living separate and apart before 1957, when the wife made her last visit to her husband in the Ontario Hospital. It is significant also that shortly after that time the wife became interested in another man and she has associated with this other man up to the present time. It may also be of some significance also that the Ontario Hospital has not for some years communicated with the wife concerning the husband but only with his mother": per Donohue J. in *Rowland v. Rowland*, 1 R.F.L. 221 at 224, [1969] 2 O.R. 615, 6 D.L.R. (3d) 292 (H.C.).

"While the mere living separate and apart of the spouses may not be conclusive of the fact that there has been a permanent breakdown of the marriage, especially in cases where the separation may have been brought about, as here, by enforced hospitalization, or, as in other cases, by service in the armed forces or in the course of other employment, all of the circumstances accompanying such separation must be considered in determining whether or not it has in fact led to a permanent marriage breakdown. In the instant case the parties could not be considered as having commenced to live separate and apart upon the wife's admission to hospital. However, in my view they did commence to live separate and apart before the beginning of 1965, by reason of the husband's discontinuance of his visits to his wife and of his deliberate abandonment of contact with her. His action in that regard amounted to a desertion by him of his wife and in my view resulted in a marriage breakdown": per Dickson J. in *McDorman v. McDorman* (1972), 11 R.F.L. 83 at 85–86, 5 N.B.R. (2d) 840 (Q.B.). See also *Lachman v. Lachman*, 2 R.F.L. 207, [1970] 3 O.R. 29, 12 D.L.R. (3d) 221 (C.A.); *Dorchester v. Dorchester*, 3 R.F.L. 396, [1971] 2 W.W.R. 634, 19 D.L.R. (3d) 126 (B.C. S.C.); *Ettinger v. Ettinger* (1974), 8 N.S.R. (2d) 293 (T.D.); *Herman v. Herman* (1969), 1 R.F.L. 41, 1 N.S.R. 514, 3 D.L.R. (3d) 551 (T.D.).

8§10 — Compassionate hospital visits

In *Norman v. Norman* (1974), 12 R.F.L. 252 at 255, 39 D.L.R. (3d) 474 (N.S. C.A.), the respondent wife was completely bedridden in a nursing home, suffering from multiple sclerosis, and evidence confirmed that she would never recover. It was held that: "The evidence of Mr. Norman, considered apart from what he said as to his visits to the nursing home when he would drop in to see Mrs. Norman, clearly established absence of intent to continue the matrimonial relationship for the requisite period. ... I cannot, with the greatest respect, accept the conclusion of the trial Judge that, because of the visits of Mr. Norman there was no 'animus' to terminate the marriage. The application of s. 4(1)(e)(i) [now s. 8(2)(a)] should not turn upon whether or not the petitioner shows compassion towards the respondent by occasional visits": per Cooper J.A.

"The fact that the petitioner during all these years did visit the respondent but a couple of times at Christmas time, to bring him some things on behalf of the children — and the further fact that more recently on being advised that he was admitted to the Victoria General Hospital in Halifax, she went there on only one occasion, together with her son to see him being prompted to do so by stories carried in the 'Halifax Herald-Chronicle' about alleged goings-on at Cole Harbour Hospital (where he is now again) do not change the situation in so far as this couple is concerned": per Dubinsky J. in *Herman v. Herman* (1969), 1 R.F.L. 41 at 46 and 47, 1 N.S.R. 514, 3 D.L.R. (3d) 551 (T.D.).

In *Eamer v. Eamer*, 5 R.F.L. 205, [1971] 5 W.W.R. 183, 21 D.L.R. (3d) 18 (Man. Q.B.), the wife had been in and out of institutions and had become increasingly disabled by multiple sclerosis, and unhappily, the affection of the petitioner had waned over these trying years. When she finally entered hospital, the husband treated the marriage as at an end, although he continued to make periodic visits, contributed to her maintenance, and encouraged their children to visit. Despite the fact that the wife never had the intention of destroying the matrimonial consortium, a decree was granted under s. 4(1)(e)(i) [now s. 8(2)(a)].

8§10A — "Separate and apart" — duration of separation

Divorce Act, 1985

A spouse is entitled to commence a petition for divorce under s. 8(2)(a) before the expiry of the required one-year separation: *Mitchell v. Mitchell* (1993), 129 N.S.R. (2d) 351, 362 A.P.R. 351 (S.C.).

In a petition for divorce on the grounds of marriage breakdown, to impose a condition that the parties be living separate and apart for at least one year prior to the commencement of proceedings is contrary to the legislative intent evident in the *Divorce Act*: *Droit de la famille — 1257*, [1989] R.D.F. 508 (C.S. Qué.).

8§11 — "Separate and apart" under same roof — general

Where factors indicated a lack of any meaningful relationship between the parties from April 1992, except for the existence of a joint bank account, the parties were deemed to have been living separate and apart from that date although the wife did not actually leave the matrimonial home until 1993: *Woolgar v. Woolgar* (1995), 10 R.F.L. (4th) 309 (Nfld. U.F.C.).

Where the husband had frequently returned home after the parties' separation for periods totalling in excess of 90 days, his petition on the basis of one-year separation was dismissed. Although the parties may not have gotten along during the periods, the evidence failed to show that the parties had lived separate and apart under the same roof: *Thorogood v. Thorogood* (1987), 11 R.F.L. (3d) 82 (Ont. U.F.C.).

See also *Lauzon v. Lauzon* (1982), 27 R.F.L. (2d) 259 (B.C. S.C.); *Galbraith v. Galbraith* (1969), 69 W.W.R. 390, 5 D.L.R. (3d) 543 (Man. C.A.); *Dick v. Dick* (1970), 2 R.F.L. 225, [1971] 2 W.W.R. 138 (B.C. S.C.); *Dimen v. Dimen* (1974), 15 R.F.L. 322 at 326 (Sask. Q.B.); *Seminuk v. Seminuk* (1969), 68 W.W.R. 249, 4 D.L.R. (3d) 253 (Q.B.); reversed (1970), 72 W.W.R. 304, 10 D.L.R. (3d) 590 (Sask. C.A.); *Bance v. Bance* (1977), 18 N.B.R. (2d) 262; *Haggarty v. Haggarty* (1972), 7 N.B.R. (2d) 182 (Q.B.); *Rushton v. Rushton* (1968), 1 R.F.L. 215 at 217, 66 W.W.R. 764, 2 D.L.R. (3d) 25 (B.C. S.C.); *Galbraith v. Galbraith* (1969), 1 R.F.L. 227, 69 W.W.R. 548, 6 D.L.R. (3d) 639 (Sask. Q.B.); *Seminuk v. Seminuk*, above; *Haggarty v. Haggarty*, above; *Smith v. Smith* (1970), 2 R.F.L. 214, 74 W.W.R. 462 (B.C. S.C.); *Rousell v. Rousell* (1969), 1 R.F.L. 227, 69 W.W.R. 568, 6 D.L.R. (3d) 639 (Sask. Q.B.); *Knight v. Knight* (1975), 20 R.F.L. 381 (Ont. H.C.); *Wells v. Wells* (1970), 2 R.F.L. 353, 75 W.W.R. 473 (B.C. S.C.); *Van Buskirk v. Van Buskirk* (1973), 14 R.F.L. 199 at 199 (Sask. Q.B.).

8§12 — "Separate and apart" under same roof — criteria

Where the spouses continued to reside under the same roof, prepared meals together (but ate separately) and attended social functions together they were found not to have been living "separate and apart." There was no economic compulsion necessitating that the parties continue to live in the same house: *Bailey v. Bailey* (1994), 119 Sask. R. 71 (Q.B.).

The intentions of the parties, or one of them, is the criteria to be regarded in determining whether parties are living separate and apart although physically they may remain under the same roof: *Droit de la famille — 841*, [1990] R.J.Q. 1571, [1990] R.D.F. 508 (headnote only) (C.S.).

Spouses who continued to live under the same roof and shared expenses, duties and social obligations were found not to have manifested an intention to live "separate and apart": *Ginter v. Ginter* (1988), 15 R.F.L. (3d) 203 (Sask. Q.B.).

See also *Cooper v. Cooper* (1974), 10 R.F.L. 184 at 187 (Ont. H.C.); *Dupere v. Dupere* (1974), 19 R.F.L. 270 at 275, 9 N.B.R. (2d) 554, 1 A.P.R. 554 (Q.B.); affirmed (1974), 10 N.B.R. (2d) 148, 4 A.P.R. 148 (C.A.).

8§13 — "Separate and apart" — cessation of intercourse

Where after the birth of the parties' child all sexual and most other contact between the parties ceased, although they continued to live under the same roof for 12 more years, it was found that the parties had lived "separate and apart" throughout that period: *Droit de la famille — 1480*, [1991] R.D.F. 630 (C.S. Qué.).

See also *Newman v. Newman* (1970), 2 R.F.L. 219 (Ont. C.A.); *Dick v. Dick* (1970), 2 R.F.L. 225 at 226, [1971] 2 W.W.R. 138 (B.C. S.C.); *Kobayashi v. Kobayashi*, 6 R.F.L. 358 at 362–363, [1972] 3 W.W.R. 221, 26 D.L.R. (3d) 119 (Man. Q.B.); *Burt v. Burt* (1972), 7 R.F.L. 155, 7 N.S.R. (2d) 321, 24 D.L.R. (3d) 497 (T.D.); *Smith v. Smith* (1970), 2 R.F.L. 214, 74 W.W.R. 462 (B.C. S.C.); *Newman v. Newman* (1970), 2 R.F.L. 219 (Ont. C.A.).

8§14 — Marriage breakdown under same roof — examples

In *Wood v. Wood* (1981), 23 R.F.L. (2d) 77 (Ont. C.A.), the court was of the view that the words "separate and apart" in the *Marital Property Act, 1978* have the same meaning as in the *Divorce Act*, R.S.C. 1970. The court held that the couple was not living "separate and apart". In the lower court decision at (1980), 6 Man. R. (2d) 36 (Q.B.), the husband and wife were found to be living separate and apart within the meaning of the *Divorce Act* although they lived under the same roof. Per Morse J. at pp. 40, 42: "In this case, the picture of the relationship between the parties which emerges for me is that of two persons merely sharing the same accommodation, each performing certain domestic services, eating certain meals together, contributing to the cost of the food they ate, and doing certain things together socially, but, in fact, living separate lives without any intention of resuming the matrimonial consortium."

In *Segal v. Qu* (2001), 17 R.F.L. (5th) 152, 2001 CarswellOnt 2304, [2001] O.J. No. 2646 (Ont. S.C.J.), the parties lived as husband and wife until the husband's lawyer sent a letter to the wife indicating that the husband was treating the marriage as over. Shortly afterwards, the wife left the country and the husband did not know for certain her whereabouts. When she returned to Canada with her daughter and lived with the husband, the marriage appeared to have been at an end. After the date that the lawyer's letter was sent to the wife, the parties were essentially living separate and apart under the same roof.

In *Smith v. Smith* (1980), 28 Nfld. & P.E.I.R. 99, 79 A.P.R. 99, 4 Fam. L. Rev. 1 (P.E.I. S.C.), where the parties had been living under the same roof for the past seven years, the wife had provided domestic services, but there had been no sexual or social life during that time and the husband had remained in his room refusing to speak, it was found that the parties had been living separate and apart within the meaning of the Act.

In *Boulos v. Boulos* (1980), 14 R.F.L. (2d) 206, 24 Nfld. & P.E.I.R. 370, 65 A.P.R. 370 (Nfld. T.D.), a couple was found to be living separate and apart, although under the same roof, where they had occupied separate bedrooms; there had been no sexual intercourse between them; there had been no shared social activities; communication, when necessary, had usually been by note; any verbal communications had been of a quarrelsome and bitter tone; no meals were shared; and the petitioner only performed household chores for the respondent where these were incidental to her doing the same chores for the children. See also *Follet v. Follet* (1984), 49 Nfld. & P.E.I.R. 58, 145 A.P.R. 58 (Nfld. U.F.C.).

A complete marriage breakdown had obviously occurred under the same roof in *Calder v. Calder* (1974), 15 R.F.L. 265 (Ont. H.C.). In 1955 the respondent husband had a nervous breakdown and moved to a bedroom of his own. Thereafter, he had his own bedroom, bathroom and recreation room. He did his own shopping for food, made his own meals and usually tried to eat when his wife was not in the house. He did his own laundry, sent his own clothes to the dry cleaners. The parties would go two weeks without speaking to each other. It was only when it was essential that they communicated with as few words as possible. The parties had not slept together since 1955 and there was no intercourse since 1966. They had not been out together since that time. The respondent would join the family approximately three times a year, on Christmas, Easter and Thanksgiving. On these occasions he would simply carve the turkey and then leave the table. A decree *nisi* was granted as there had been a permanent breakdown of the marriage within the meaning of s. 4(1)(e)(i) [now s. 8(2)(a)] of the *Divorce Act*. See also *Mayberry v. Mayberry*, 3 R.F.L. 395, [1971] 2 O.R. 378, 18 D.L.R. (3d) 45 (C.A.).

8§15 — Circumstances not amounting to marriage breakdown

In *Siller v. Siller* (1987), 6 R.F.L. (3d) 362 (B.C. S.C.), the parties had not been "separate and apart" over the last 10 years of the marriage, even though the husband had moved out of the family home to an apartment since he found the interruptions caused by his children and their friends irritating and he only returned to the family home from Saturday noon until Sunday night.

In *Hull v. Hull* (1980), 20 R.F.L. (2d) 12, 5 Man. R. (2d) 412 (Q.B.); varied (1981), 22 R.F.L. (2d) 409, 12 Man. R. (2d) 134 (C.A.), the court held that the parties were not living "separate and apart", even after the issuance of the divorce petition and service upon the husband, where the parties continued to have marital relations, ate together, took trips together, went out socially together, appeared in public together and acted as parents of a family unit. They acted as a married couple even after the husband left the matrimonial home and they bought a home together in another city.

In *Hosein v. Hosein* (1981), 6 Man. R. (2d) 255 (Q.B.), the spouses were found not to be living "separate and apart" under the same roof. Per Deniset J. at pp. 260, 261: "In the present case, although it was more economical for both to continue to live under the same roof (as it is usually for most married couples), no particular reason was advanced for continuing to live that way, if indeed there was a separation at that time. There was never from the wife any intention to separate. The husband, on the other hand, while he was extremely displeased at not having his own way and while he displayed his great dissatisfaction at the turn of events, continued nevertheless to live in the same house with his wife and children. He never gave any sign that he intended to terminate the matrimonial relationship until he petitioned for divorce in August of 1978. Until then, he was in a state of flux. ... During the years 1975 to 1978, the incompatibilities between the spouses reached a boiling point on several occasions, but there were many efforts made by both (albeit more from the wife) to perhaps reconcile eventually. It is only when the husband petitioned for divorce that then he gave a clear indication of his intention to terminate the marriage."

"Certainly there were obstacles in the way of either husband or wife moving out of the home. The house was jointly owned and there was need to provide a shelter for five children and there was a lack of money on both sides. However, the parties made no real attempt to destroy the matrimonial consortium or cause a physical separation. The circumstances in this case show no greater marriage breakdown than was apparent in the case of *Reid v. Reid*; a decision of my brother Macdonald in 1969 and reported in 1 R.F.L. 229, 71 W.W.R. 375, 9 D.L.R. (3d) 306. As his lordship said in that case, there must be proof of withdrawal from the matrimonial obligation with the intent of destroying the matrimonial consortium as well as physical separation, and the cessation of sexual intercourse is not in itself proof that the requirements of marriage breakdown within the terms of s. 4(1)(e)(i) [now s. 8(2)(a)] of the statute have been met": per Ruttan J. in *Cridge v. Cridge* (1973), 12 R.F.L. 348 at 350 (B.C. S.C.). See also *Newman v. Newman* (1970), 2 R.F.L. 219 (Ont. C.A.); *Gloude v. Gloude* (1976), 14 O.R. (2d) 571 at 573, 74 D.L.R. (3d) 405 at 406 (H.C.).

"In spite of that chasm between the parties the situation remained that of a single household in which the food eaten by the husband at breakfast was purchased by the wife, and in which she performed for him at least the service of doing his personal laundry. Unlike the spouses in the *Rushton* case the parties were not compelled by economic considerations to carry on in the half-way situation. I hold that the test of physical separation along with destruction of the matrimonial relationship has not been met": per Macdonald J. in *Reid v. Reid* (1969), 1 R.F.L. 229 at 233–234, 71 W.W.R. 375, 9 D.L.R. (3d) 306 (B.C. S.C.). See also *Cherewick v. Cherewick* (1969), 1 R.F.L. 225, 69 W.W.R. 235 (Man. Q.B.).

8§16 — Resumption of cohabitation — reconciliation attempt

A casual ongoing relationship established after separation, even one involving some degree of intimacy, does not constitute a resumption of cohabitation "with reconciliation as its main purpose": *Velisek v. Velisek*, 7 R.F.L. (5th) 192, 2000 BCSC 557, 2000 CarswellBC 928 (S.C.).

Where the parties separated but again lived together for a brief period of time, the wife's petition was struck for non-compliance with s. 8(2) of the Act. Although, when calculated from the date of the first separation the time requirements were fulfilled, the parties had resumed their ongoing marital relationship and were not living separate and apart under the same roof: *Williams v. Williams* (1990), [1991] N.W.T.R. 53 (S.C.).

"[T]he question which must be decided is whether it is sufficient, for the purposes of s. 9(3)(b) [now s. 8(3)(b)(ii)] of the *Divorce Act*, to have reconciliation in the mind of one of the parties only. In my view, for the provisions of s. 9(3)(b) [now s. 8(3)(b)(ii)] to apply, both parties must resume cohabitation with reconciliation as its primary purpose. I think it cannot properly be said that there has been a resumption of cohabitation with reconciliation as its primary purpose if one of the parties does not desire or intend to reconcile": per Morse J. in *Pfeutzenreuter v. Pfeutzenreuter* (1976), 28 R.F.L. 385 at 386 387 (Man. Q.B.). See also *Goodland v. Goodland* (1974), 15 R.F.L. 149, 30 O.R. (2d) 464, 45 D.L.R. (3d) 680 (H.C.) (neither party having view to reconciliation during period of cohabitation; petition dismissed).

8§17 — Sexual intercourse during separation

A casual ongoing relationship established after separation, even one involving some degree of intimacy, does not constitute a resumption of cohabitation "with reconciliation as its main purpose": *Velisek v. Velisek*, 7 R.F.L. (5th) 192, 2000 BCSC 557, 2000 CarswellBC 928 (S.C.).

Isolated acts of sexual intercourse between the parties which are not engaged in for the purpose of reconciliation will not interrupt the period of separation contemplated by s. 4(1)(e)(i) [now s. 8(2)(a)] of the *Divorce Act*: *Spinney v. Spinney* (1981), 33 Nfld. & P.E.I.R. 61, 93 A.P.R. 61 (P.E.I. C.A.); reversing (1980), 20 R.F.L. (2d) 378, 3 Fam. L. Rev. 49, 28 Nfld. & P.E.I.R. 78, 79 A.P.R. 78 (P.E.I. S.C.). See also *Morrow v. Morrow* (1981), 36 N.B.R. (2d) 117, 94 A.P.R. 117 (Q.B.); supplementary reasons (1981), 36 N.B.R. (2d) 117 at 128, 94 A.P.R. 117 at 128 (Q.B.).

"The issue of whether the husband and wife were living separate and apart must be determined on all the facts. Sexual intercourse is only one of the concomitants of marriage": per Fanjoy L.J.S.C. in *Rogler v. Rogler* (1978), 1 R.F.L. (2d) 398 at 400 (Ont. H.C.). See also *Richard v. Richard* (1973), 8 N.B.R. (2d) 171 (Q.B.); *H. (C.G.) v. H. (A.B.)* (1976), 22 N.S.R. (2d) 67, 31 A.P.R. 67 (T.D.).

Where the parties had frequent contact with each other in a sincere attempt to find a basis for reconciliation, took a few short vacations together and occasionally had sexual intercourse during a two and a half year period of separation, it was held that the period of separation was not terminated or interrupted by the aforesaid conduct: *McGeachy v. McGeachy* (1980), 15 R.F.L. (2d) 274 (Ont. H.C.).

"The validity, however, of a general principle that an *occasional* act of intercourse will necessarily interrupt the running of the period prescribed by s. 4(1)(e) [now s. 8(2)(a)] is open to question. For the occurrence of sexual intercourse would seem to be no more than one piece of evidence, the effect of which should be assessed in the light of the evidence as a whole": per Brooke J.A. in *Deslippe v. Deslippe* (1974), 16 R.F.L. 38 at 43–44, 4 O.R. (2d) 35, 47 D.L.R. (3d) 30 (C.A.). See also *Geransky v. Geransky* (1980), 16 R.F.L. (2d) 193 (Sask. Q.B.).

"It seems clear that a husband and wife engaging in acts of sexual intercourse are giving themselves to one another and that such is a very real form of cohabitation, wherever it may take place. Such a degree of intimacy or of reconciliation is never to be taken lightly. Moreover, such conduct is hardly consistent with a marriage that has permanently broken down.": per Sirois J. in *Boechler v. Boechler*, 30 R.F.L. 118 at 120–121, [1976] 6 W.W.R. 570 (Sask. Q.B.).

The words "separate and apart" in the *Divorce Act* mean that the parties must be completely divided and withdrawn from intercourse and each other's society. Thus where the parties to a divorce action had taken part in a casual act of intercourse during the separation period the petition was dismissed: *Foote v. Foote* (1990), 2 R.F.L. 221, [1971] 1 O.R. 338, 15 D.L.R. (3d) 292 (H.C.). See also *Dimaggio v. Dimaggio* (1971), 4 R.F.L. 3 (Ont. H.C.).

8§18 — Meaning of "deemed" — s. 8(3)(a)

The word should be construed as "deemed until the contrary is proved": per Cartwright J. in *Gray v. Kerslake* (1957), [1958] S.C.R. 3, 11 D.L.R. (2d) 225 at 239–240, discussing the meaning of the word "deemed" as used in s. 4(2) of the former Act. See also *Hickey v. Stalker* (1923), [1924] 1 D.L.R. 440, 53 O.L.R. 414 (C.A.).

8§19 — Adultery — general

In *P. (S.E.) v. P. (D.D.)*, 2005 CarswellBC 2137, 2005 BCSC 1290 (B.C. S.C.), the court held that since individuals of the same sex can now marry and divorce, the common law would be anomalous if those same-sex spouses were not bound by the same legal and social constraints against extra-marital sexual relationships that apply to heterosexual spouses. To make adultery a ground for divorce in same sex unions would make the law consistent with the *Civil Marriage Act* and harmonized with the values enunciated in the *Charter*. The traditional definition of adultery included the requirement that the sexual activity be intercourse. However, the uncertainty about precisely what would constitute adultery in a same-sex relationship is not a reasonable basis for denying spouses the ability to divorce on the basis of same-sex sexual activity. In this case, the evidence of an intimate sexual relationship outside of the parties' marriage was sufficient to grant the divorce on the grounds of adultery, notwithstanding that the act alleged was a same-sex sexual act.

The fact that the parties are living separate and apart when one of them begins a sexual relationship with another does not preclude the granting of a divorce on the grounds of adultery. *Horvath v. Fraess* (1997), 36 R.F.L. (4th) 32, 161 Sask. R. 274 (Q.B.).

Where evidence established that the respondent husband lived and slept with the person named as having committed adultery with him, but that he did not have intercourse with her, a finding of adultery was not made: *Chouinard v. Chouinard* (1969), 1 R.F.L. 101, 1 N.B.R. (2d) 941, 10 D.L.R. (3d) 263 (C.A.); affirming (1969), 1 N.B.R. 582 (Q.B.).

Where the plaintiff wife had permitted herself to be artificially inseminated without the knowledge of the husband, with the result that a child was conceived and born, the plaintiff was held to have committed adultery: *Orford v. Orford* (1921), 49 O.L.R. 15 at 22–23, 58 D.L.R. 251 (H.C.).

The matrimonial offence of adultery is possible only between persons of the opposite sex: *Droit de la famille — 1005*, [1986] R.D.F. 78 (C.S. Qué.).

A petitioner is not entitled to seek a divorce on the grounds of his or her own adultery: *Libel v. Pelletier*, [1981] C.S. 1040 (Que.).

In *Gaveronski v. Gaveronski*, 15 R.F.L. 160 at 161, [1974] 4 W.W.R. 106, 45 D.L.R. (3d) 317 (Sask. Q.B.), Macpherson J. held that the act of adultery required penetration by the male organ to some degree.

8§20 — Adultery — standard of proof

In *Low v. Robinson*, 4 R.F.L. (5th) 368, 76 Alta. L.R. (3d) 238, [2000] 4 W.W.R. 663, (sub nom. *S.E.L. v. J.M.R.)* 258 A.R. 201, 2000 CarswellAlta 68 (Q.B.); additional reasons at 7 R.F.L. (5th) 148, 79 Alta. L.R. (3d) 137, [2000] 7 W.W.R. 509, (sub nom. *S.E.L. v. J.M.R.)* 258 A.R. 201 at 235, 2000 CarswellAlta 336 (Q.B.); further additional reasons at 2000 ABQB 399, 82 Alta. L.R. (3d) 175, [2000] 10 W.W.R. 690, (sub nom. *S.E.L. v. J.M.R.)* 274 A.R. 377, 2000 CarswellAlta 574 (Q.B.), it was found that the wife had established on a balance of probabilities that the husband had committed adultery. The husband admitted that he had told the wife that he had had several affairs and that the parties' son had overheard a conversation with the woman in question. He also admitted that he had known the woman for six years and that since separation he had maintained a close exclusive relationship with her.

"The standard of proof in divorce actions is the same as in other civil actions, that is, the court must be satisfied that adultery has been committed, based on a preponderance of probability or, as it has been otherwise put, on such preponderance of evidence as to show that the conclusion sought is the most probable of the possible views of the acts": per Bull J.A. in *Adolph v. Adolph* (1964), 51 W.W.R. 42 at 44 (B.C. C.A.). The court also stated that:

> In divorce proceedings it is a fundamental rule that is not necessary to prove the direct fact of adultery but such conduct can be inferred from circumstances that lead to it by fair inference as a proper conclusion.

Per Bull J.A. at 45.

Where evidence established that a respondent husband was living in an apartment with an unmarried woman, it was held that an inference of adultery could fairly and reasonably be found: *Harrison v. Harrison* (1975), 12 N.S.R. (2d) 149, 6 A.P.R. 149 (C.A.).

"Just as a civil court will require more cogent evidence to establish an allegation of fraud than to establish negligence, so the proof of adultery must be strict proof. Where, however, as is usually the case, the evidence is circumstantial, it is not necessary that the facts should be inconsistent with any other rational conclusion than that the accused is guilty": per Harrison J. in *Bolster v. Bolster* (1952), 31 M.P.R. 175 at 188, [1953] 1 D.L.R. 18 (N.B. C.A.). See also *Furlong v. Furlong* (1963), 49 M.P.R. 377, 44 D.L.R. 594 (N.B. C.A.).

"It is now settled that the standard of proof required in a divorce action ... is the standard required in civil actions where the preponderance of probabilities determines the issues ... [i]t is sufficient if the circumstances are such as would lead the guarded discretion of a reasonable or just man to the conclusion": per Dubinsky J. citing *Power on Divorce*, 2nd ed., p. 425 in *Shaw v. Shaw* (1971), 4 R.F.L. 392 at 393, 7 N.S.R. (2d) 77 (T.D.). See also *Thompson v. Thompson* (1978), 29 R.F.L. 302 (P.E.I. S.C.); *Coates v. Coates* (1972), 16 R.F.L. 117, 8 N.B.R. (2d) 1 (Q.B.); *Paulin v. Paulin*, [1938] 1 W.W.R. 261, [1938] 1 D.L.R. 686 (Sask. C.A.); *George v. George*, [1950] O.R. 787, [1951] 1 D.L.R. 278 (C.A.).

8§21 — Adulterous acts subsequent to divorce application

In a petition for divorce based upon adultery, evidence indicating that adultery occurred four days subsequent to the date of the petition is insufficient. The cause of action must have existed at the date of the institution of the proceeding and it is not possible to amend the petition to take into account the subsequent adultery: *Nickerson v. Nickerson* (1983), 59 N.S.R. (2d) 113, 125 A.P.R. 133 (T.D.).

In *Burnett v. Burnett* (1983), 34 R.F.L. (2d) 462 (Alta. Q.B.), the petitioner's application to amend the petition for divorce to add additional grounds was refused as the facts supporting such grounds did not exist on the date on which the petition was filed.

"The date of issuance of the petition does not place a barrier to the introduction of evidence and acts which arise subsequent to the date of the issuance of the petition. It may well be that if either party wishes to introduce evidence of incidents which occurred after the issuance of the petition and takes the other side by surprise, an adjournment should be granted to enable the surprised party to consider his or her position but, surely, the extent to which the court should protect the surprised party is a different matter from the proposition that such information cannot be heard by the court in arriving at a proper adjudication on the matter": Miller L.J.S.C. in *Johnson v. Johnson* (1976), 23 R.F.L. 293 at 299 (Alta. T.D.).

Where adultery is alleged in the original petition, evidence of adulterous acts occurring after the presentment may be allowed as evidence of a continuing course of conduct. This does not mean, however, that the petitioner is relieved of demonstrating adultery prior to presentment. It is a question of evidence and not substantive procedure: *Hanser v. Hanser* (1977), 15 O.R. (2d) 631, 76 D.L.R. (3d) 422 (H.C.).

8§22 — Finding of adultery in prior proceedings

Where a divorce had been granted to the present co-respondent's wife on the ground of adultery between the present co-respondent and the respondent, such decree is a decree *in rem* and *res judicata* on the fact that such adultery had been committed. Accordingly, the proven record of the prior divorce between the co-respondent and the respondent was held to be satisfactory proof of such adultery in the present action: *Coles v. Coles* (1978), 4 R.F.L. (2d) 277 (P.E.I. S.C.) following *Love v. Love*, below.

A decree for divorce on the grounds of adultery as between petitioner A and respondents B and C is *res inter alia acta* and is not admissible in evidence, and has no probative value in a hearing for divorce on the grounds of adultery brought by petitioner D against respondents B and C: *Meshwa v. Meshwa* (1970), 2 R.F.L. 234, 75 W.W.R. 459, 13 D.L.R. (3d) 502 (B.C. S.C.).

The fact that a husband, in an undefended divorce proceeding, has been granted a divorce on the basis of his wife's adultery amounts only to *prima facie* proof of such adultery. However, the failure of the wife to deny her adultery in the course of subsequent proceedings to rescind a maintenance order, may constitute sufficient proof of the fact: *Mathews v. Mathews* (1975), 23 R.F.L. 37 (Ont. Prov. Ct.).

The finding of adultery in one case is sufficient to establish the same adultery in another case in the same court. A judgment for divorce on the grounds of adultery between two parties makes the issue of adultery *res judicata*. It is a judgment *in rem*, good as against the world because it is a judgment affecting status. Therefore, in a subsequent action for divorce, by a different plaintiff, but alleging the adultery so found in a previous action, the adultery may be proved by filing the judgment *nisi* in the previous action together with proof that the defendants named in that decree are the same as in the case at bar: *Love v. Love*, 1 R.F.L. 193, [1969] 1 O.R. 291, 2 D.L.R. (3d) 273 (H.C.). But see *Meshwa v. Meshwa*, above.

8§23 — Privilege — self-incrimination in adultery cases

In an action for divorce based on adultery where third-party evidence indicates that the respondent has committed the matrimonial offence as alleged, the refusal of the respondent to be examined or cross-examined on the issues may lend credence to what otherwise may amount to unconvincing evidence. In such a case, a finding of adultery may result: *Fogel v. Fogel* (1976), 24 R.F.L. 18 (Ont. H.C.); affirmed (1979), 9 R.F.L. (2d) 55 (Ont. C.A.).

Where a plaintiff wife in an action for alimony claims in her pleadings that the defendant husband's conduct gave rise to her "belief" of adulterous conduct on his part, the proceedings are not thereby brought into the class of actions "instituted in consequence of adultery" within the meaning of the *Evidence Act: Rayner v. Rayner (No. 2)* (1972), 7 R.F.L. 103, (sub nom. *Rayner v. Rayner)* 26 D.L.R. (3d) 169 (Ont. C.A.).

Where a wife brought an action for a divorce on the grounds of adultery and further claimed custody of the children of the marriage based upon the misconduct and immorality of the husband, it was held that the husband was not bound to answer any questions, in relation to the custody issue, which tended to prove his adultery. The entire proceeding was one "instituted in consequence of adultery", thereby entitling the husband to the protection of the *Evidence Act*, R.S.O. 1950, c. 119, s. 8: *Bradburn v. Bradburn*, [1953] 1 O.R. 882 (C.A.).

"If an answer tends to prove adultery, it is barred notwithstanding that it may tend to prove something else at the same time. The statute [the *Evidence Act*, R.S.O. 1937, c. 119, s. 7] is a protective statute and must be scrupulously observed. The onus is on the plaintiff to prove adultery without assistance from the defendant, unless that assistance is willingly given": per McRuer J.A. in *Livingstone v. Livingstone*, [1945] O.W.N. 623, [1945] 4 D.L.R. 121 (C.A.).

See also *King v. King* (1977), 25 R.F.L. 232, 20 N.S.R. (2d) 260 (T.D.); *Chandler v. Chandler* (1975), 23 R.F.L. 389 (Ont. Master); affirmed (1975), 26 R.F.L. 277 (Ont. H.C.); *Van Zant v. Van Zant* (1975), 24 R.F.L. 281 (Ont. H.C.); *MacRae v. MacRae* (1974), 15 R.F.L. 270 at 297–298, 6 Nfld. & P.E.I.R. 1 (P.E.I. S.C.); *Rosenberg v. Rosenberg* (1974), 16 R.F.L. 110, 3 O.R. (2d) 174 (H.C.); *Hunter v. Hunter*, 11 R.F.L. 94, [1973] 1 O.R. 162 (H.C.); *Anderson v. Anderson* (1973), 10 R.F.L. 27 (Ont. H.C.); *Olson v. Olson*, 4 R.F.L. 86, [1971] 3 W.W.R. 506 (Sask. Q.B.); *Zawatsky v. Zawatsky* (1975),

21 R.F.L. 370 (Sask. Q.B.); *Hirsch v. Hirsch*, 5 R.F.L. 69, [1971] 5 W.W.R. 455 (B.C. S.C.).

8§24 — Suspicious circumstances and opportunity for adultery

In *Low v. Robinson*, 4 R.F.L. (5th) 368, 76 Alta. L.R. (3d) 238, [2000] 4 W.W.R. 663, (sub nom. *S.E.L. v. J.M.R.)* 258 A.R. 201, 2000 CarswellAlta 68 (Q.B.); additional reasons at 7 R.F.L. (5th) 148, 79 Alta. L.R. (3d) 137, [2000] 7 W.W.R. 509, (sub nom. *S.E.L. v. J.M.R.)* 258 A.R. 201 at 235, 2000 CarswellAlta 336 (Q.B.); further additional reasons at 2000 ABQB 399, 82 Alta. L.R. (3d) 175, [2000] 10 W.W.R. 690, (sub nom. *S.E.L. v. J.M.R.)* 274 A.R. 377, 2000 CarswellAlta 574 (Q.B.), it was found that the wife had established on a balance of probabilities that the husband had committed adultery. The husband admitted that he had told the wife that he had had several affairs and that the parties' son had overheard a conversation with the woman in question. He also admitted that he had known the woman for six years and that since separation he had maintained a close exclusive relationship with her.

Where a petitioner wife, as the basis of a petition for divorce on the grounds of adultery, adduced evidence of observing the respondent husband driving frequently with another woman as well as observing him with that same woman at a motel, it was held that although the evidence raised suspicious circumstances, it was impossible for the court from such meagre circumstantial evidence to conclude that an adulterous act had occurred: *MacCurdy v. MacCurdy* (1971), 8 R.F.L. 125, 4 N.B.R. (2d) 10 (C.A.).

Evidence of familiarities and of opportunities for the commission of adultery which merely raises suspicions is insufficient for a finding of adultery: *Doucette v. Doucette* (1986), 73 N.B.R. (2d) 407, 184 A.P.R. 407 (Q.B.).

See also *Barbour v. Barbour* (1980), 18 R.F.L. (2d) 80, 27 Nfld. & P.E.I.R. 229, 74 A.P.R. 229 (Nfld. T.D.); *Coates v. Coates* (1974), 16 R.F.L. 117 at 199, 8 N.B.R. (2d) 1 (Q.B.); *Iachetta v. Iachetta* (1973), 11 R.F.L. 309 (Ont. H.C.); *Vogt v. Vogt* (1972), 3 N.S.R. (2d) 225 (T.D.); *Farrell v. Farrell* (1972), 4 R.F.L. 261 (Sask. Q.B.); *Nelles v. Nelles* (1971), 2 R.F.L. 153 (Ont. H.C.); *MacRae v. MacRae* (1974), 15 R.F.L. 270 at 300, 6 Nfld. & P.E.I.R. 1 (P.E.I. S.C.); *Ross v. Ellison (Ross)*, [1930] A.C. 1 at 23; *Paulin v. Paulin*, [1938] 1 W.W.R. 261, [1938] 1 D.L.R. 686 (Sask. C.A.); *Dion v. Dion*, 9 R.F.L. 276 at 278–279, [1973] 3 W.W.R. 202, 33 D.L.R. (3d) 509 (Sask. Q.B.); *Getson v. Getson* (1970), 2 R.F.L. 91, 2 N.S.R. (2d) 65, 12 D.L.R. (3d) 525 (T.D.); *Bezanger v. Bezanger* (1969), 1 R.F.L. 197 at 200, 1 N.S.R. (2d) 412 (T.D.).

8§25 — Admissions of adultery

Divorce Act, 1985

An affidavit by the respondent to a divorce petition admitting uncondoned adultery with an unnamed third party is sufficient evidence to satisfy s. 8 of the *Divorce Act*: *d'Entremont v. d'Entremont* (1992), 44 R.F.L. (3d) 224, 118 N.S.R. (2d) 51, 327 A.P.R. 51 (C.A.).

A husband and wife cannot bring a joint petition for divorce based upon the adultery of one of the parties. A divorce on the basis of adultery cannot be granted on consent: *Droit de la famille — 304*, [1986] R.J.Q. 2241, [1986] R.D.F. 589 (C.S. Qué.).

Divorce Act, 1968

See also *Morice v. Morice*, 8 R.F.L. 283, [1972] 4 W.W.R. 480, 26 D.L.R. (3d) 375 (Sask. C.A.); *Monaghan v. Monaghan*, [1931] 2 W.W.R. 1, [1931] 2 D.L.R. 933 (Sask. C.A.); *B. c. L.* (1983), R.L. 413 (C.S. Qué.); *Warman v. Warman* (1975), 20 R.F.L. 162, 54 D.L.R. (3d) 298 (B.C. S.C.); *McAdams v. McAdams* (1975), 21 R.F.L. 238 (B.C. S.C.); *Stevenson v. Stevenson* (1970), 2 R.F.L. 89 at 90 (Alta. T.D.); *Broadhead v. Broadhead* (1970), 2 R.F.L. 298 (Ont. H.C.).

8§26 — Requirement of corroboration

In *De Ross v. De Ross* (1980), 19 R.F.L. (2d) 359 (Ont. H.C.), a decree *nisi* was granted on the ground of adultery on the uncorroborated evidence of the petitioner. The respondent testified but chose to give no evidence about his relationship with the co-respondent. Per Misener L.J.S.C. at p. 367: "I simply say that I believe [the wife's] testimony as it relates to this issue [adultery] and the strength of my belief is sufficient to satisfy me, on a clear balance of probability, that the only inference to be drawn is that [the respondent and co-respondent] committed adultery as alleged. Obviously corroborative evidence is to be preferred, but it is not a legal requirement."

"The major question in issue is that of proof of adultery. The petitioner testified that he has on numerous occasions been at the residence jointed occupied by the respondent to pick up the child of the marriage, and that, to all external appearances, they were cohabiting there in an open manner as man and wife. This alone, without corroboration, I would consider insufficient to established the ground alleged": per C.R. McQuaid J. in *Coles v. Coles* (1977), 4 R.F.L. (2d) 277 at 278 (P.E.I. S.C.).

"At the conclusion of the trial I was of two minds as to whether adultery had been proven on the counterclaim. A re-reading of my notes of the evidence has not put my uncertainty to rest. On the evidence which I have the case is no higher than Mrs. Meshwa's oath against the oath of the plaintiff and the oath of Mrs. Sutton; there is no corroboration one way or the other and no evidence of circumstances sufficient to tip the scales in either direction. The case on the counterclaim is not proven on the evidence I heard": per Aikins J. in *Meshwa v. Meshwa* (1970), 2 R.F.L. 234 at 238, 75 W.W.R. 459, 13 D.L.R. (3d) 502 (B.C. S.C.).

On a petition for divorce based on adultery, the fact that the respondent does not give evidence in denial of the allegation, or call independent evidence in denial, is not necessarily corroborative of adultery. The better rule appears to be that the trial judge may conclude, once having heard the petitioner's case, that it calls for an answer. Should the respondent not call evidence in answer, it is open to the trial judge to have regard to that fact: *Lemenson v. Lemenson* (1969), 1 R.F.L. 206, 70 W.W.R. 749 (Man. Q.B.).

8§27 — Denial of adultery

Where the evidence that the wife had cohabited with another man was ambivalent and she had, at trial, waived the adultery privilege and had given plausible explanations for incidents raised by the husband, the husband's petition on the grounds of adultery was dismissed: *Kelsey v. Kelsey* (1982), 39 N.B.R. (2d) 166, 103 A.P.R. 166 (Q.B.).

Mere suspicions of a husband that his wife has committed adultery, regardless of how well founded such suspicions may be, are not a sufficient basis for a finding of adultery in the face of the wife's denial of any illicit relationship: *O'Connell v. O'Connell* (1972), 2 Nfld. & P.E.I.R. 497 (P.E.I. S.C.).

Where the respondent stated to the petitioner soon after his admission of adultery "that he had not told the truth and denied that he had committed adultery," the court held that there was no evidence of adultery which would satisfy it by an preponderance of evidence: per Barry J. in *Bustin v. Bustin* (1969), 1 N.B.R. (2d) 496 at 497–498 (Q.B.).

Although evidence may indicate the opportunity for adultery, a finding of adultery should not be made in absence of evidence of familiarity and in the face of denials by both the respondent and the co-respondent that any such familiarity occurred: *Profit v. Profit* (1971), 1 Nfld. & P.E.I.R. 431 (P.E.I. S.C.). See also *Chamberlain v. Chamberlain* (1977), 18 N.B.R. (2d) 55 (Q.B.) where in light of all the evidence the court could not believe the denials of the respondent and the party named, who had shared a motel room.

8§28 — Evidence of co-respondents

An admission of guilt made at discovery by the person named as having committed adultery with the respondent is inadmissible at trial as proof of the respondent's adultery: *Enns v. Enns* (1976), 28 R.F.L. 16 (B.C. S.C.).

As adultery is seldom a matter of public knowledge, the admissions of adultery of a co-respondent, testifying as a witness for the petitioner, may be received and acted upon, provided that the court is satisfied that there has been no collusion or connivance: *Roy v. Roy* (1976), 28 R.F.L. 179 (P.E.I. S.C.).

In a divorce action based on adultery, the sworn evidence of a co-respondent or a person named in the petition as to adultery is evidence for all purposes. Therefore, such evidence alone may form the basis of a finding of adultery against a respondent spouse: *Vickers v. Vickers* (1975), 24 R.F.L. 303 (B.C. S.C.).

8§29 — Proof of adultery — allegation of illegitimacy

A husband alleging adultery against his wife in divorce proceedings must prove the adultery beyond a reasonable doubt if the results of such proof will bastardize a child: *Loewen v. Loewen* (1969), 2 R.F.L. 230, 68 W.W.R. 767, 5 D.L.R. (3d) 95 (B.C. S.C.). See also *Hiuser v. Hiuser*, [1962] O.W.N. 220 (C.A.); *Himmelman v. Himmelman* (1959), 19 D.L.R. (2d) 291 (N.S. T.D.); *Welstead v. Brown* (1951), [1952] 1 D.L.R. 465 (S.C.C.); *Aksugyuk v. Aksugyuk* (1975), 17 R.F.L. 224, [1975] 3 W.W.R. 91, 53 D.L.R. (3d) 156 (N.W.T. S.C.).

Where the evidence being put forward in a divorce proceeding will have the effect of bastardizing a child, the adultery alleged must be proven beyond a reasonable doubt. However, the court will in such cases take judicial note of the fact that the normal human gestation period does not exceed 280 days. Therefore upon proof by a petitioner husband of the lack of intercourse with his wife for a period greatly in excess of this normal period, the evidentiary onus will be discharged: *Evans v. Evans* (1974), 15 R.F.L. 162, [1974] 3 W.W.R. 476 (N.W.T. S.C.).

Where the wife maintained that the parties had intercourse 10 months before the child in question was born, the pregnancy lasted 10 months, as did the mother's other pregnancies and evidence was introduced that a small percentage of pregnancies last 10 months, the court held that the husband had not proved that the child was not his child: *Johnston v. Johnston* (1975), 20 R.F.L. 211 (Sask. Q.B.).

"In a case of this kind [where an allegation of adultery is based exclusively on the birth of a child], the point of departure must be the presumption that the child of the marriage was and is legitimate. To rebut that presumption, an onus rests upon the petitioner to prove non- access, thus adultery, beyond a reasonable doubt. . . . The ease with which the onus may be discharged increased with the length of non-access. The length of time in issue in this case (six days) was not sufficient for the court to conclude that the petitioner was not the father of the child": per Hamilton J. in *Guevara v. Guevara* (1976), 28 R.F.L. 30 (Man. Q.B.).

In an action for divorce in which a petitioner husband argues as evidence of his wife's adultery the fact that a child born to the wife was not his issue, the failure of the wife to accede to repeated requests for a blood test and the lack of explanation for such refusal are equivalent to a refusal to testify on this vital issue and may warrant the drawing of a strong inference of adultery on the wife's part: *Loewen v. Loewen* (1969), 2 R.F.L. 230, 68 W.W.R. 767, 5 D.L.R. (3d) 95 (B.C. S.C.).

In a divorce action based upon the respondent's wife's adultery where the petitioner husband claimed that a certain child of the wife was not his issue, it was held that photographs of the child which supported a facial resemblance with the husband were admissible on the wife's behalf to disprove the husband's allegation. However in determining the weight to be attached to such evidence care must be taken: *C. v. C.* (1973), 10 R.F.L. 36 (Eng. Fam. Div.).

8§30 — Evidence of adultery — respondent taken by surprise

The fact that the evidence of adultery led by the petitioner at trial differs significantly from that indicated by the petitioner at discovery may be sufficient grounds for the ordering of a new trial by the appellate court. The element of surprise may deprive the respondent from effectively rebutting the evidence of adultery offered at trial, necessitating the intervention of the appellate court in the interest of justice: *Young v. Young*, 2 R.F.L. 239, [1970] 3 O.R. 272, 12 D.L.R. (3d) 708 (C.A.).

8§31 — Investigator's evidence

Notes recorded by a private investigator who dies prior to the hearing of a divorce petition may, in certain circumstances, be admitted as evidence of adultery. Such notes are admissible under an exception to hearsay rule as entries made in the ordinary course of business by a person who is later deceased, and to qualify as such, certain conditions must be met. First, the investigator must have been under a duty to do the very thing recorded; secondly, there must have been a duty to record or otherwise report the very thing, and thirdly, the duty must have been to record or otherwise report at the time: *Conley v. Conley*, [1968] 2 O.R. 677, 70 D.L.R. (2d) 352 (C.A.). See also *Jablonski v. Jablonski*, 8 R.F.L. 36, [1972] 3 O.R. 410, 28 D.L.R. (3d) 440 (H.C.).

8§32 — Cruelty in general

Physical cruelty towards the husband by the wife's son of a former marriage cannot constitute cruelty for the purposes of obtaining a divorce: *Burns v. Burns* (1988), 89 N.S.R. (2d) 226, 227 A.P.R. 226 (T.D.).

A joint petition for divorce on the ground of one party's mental cruelty is not allowed under the *Divorce Act*, given that s. 8(2)(b) requires one party to indicate the fault of the other and s. 11(1)(c) requires the court to satisfy itself that no condonation or connivance has occurred: *Droit de la famille — 471*, [1988] R.J.Q. 1014, [1988] R.D.F. 236 (C.S.).

See also *Austin v. Austin* (1970), 2 R.F.L. 136, 73 W.W.R. 289, 13 D.L.R. (3d) 498 (Sask. C.A.); *Zalesky v. Zalesky* (1968), 1 R.F.L. 36, 67 W.W.R. 104, 1 D.L.R. (3d) 471 (Man. Q.B.); *Pfeifer v. Pfeifer* (1982), 28 R.F.L. (2d) 236, 19 Sask. R. 15 (Q.B.); *Lacey v. Lacey*; *Winney v. Winney*; *Weiss v. Weiss*, 1 R.F.L. 84, [1970] 1 O.R. 279, 8 D.L.R. (3d) 289 (H.C.); *Fisher v. Fisher* (1970), 14 D.L.R. (3d) 482 at 487 (P.E.I. S.C.).

8§33 — Relevant time

"In my opinion the words 'of such a kind as to render intolerable the continued cohabitation of the spouses' point to the quality or degree of the physical or mental cruelty necessary to be proven. We were referred to dictionary meanings of 'continue' as including 'resuming after interruption' and 'to carry on, take up, resume from a point of suspension or interruption' and I think that they are applicable to the words 'continued cohabitation'": per Cooper J.A. in *Storr v. Storr* (1974), 14 R.F.L. 346 at 351, 44 D.L.R. (3d) 441, 8 N.S.R. (2d) 98 (C.A.). See also *N. v. N.* (1976), 24 R.F.L. 366 (Man. C.A.); *McMurdy v. McMurdy* (1975), 22 R.F.L. 312 (Ont. H.C.).

In *Feldman v. Feldman* (1970), 75 W.W.R. 715, 2 R.F.L. 173, 14 D.L.R. (3d) 222 (Alta. C.A.), counsel argued that conduct prior to marriage could not constitute cruelty on which to found a divorce. McDermid J.A. said that he thought that this was so but it was legitimate to consider such conduct in the context of what later occurred.

See also *Shannon v. Shannon* (1986), 43 Man. R. (2d) 77 (Q.B.); *Payrits v. Payrits* (1982), 26 R.F.L. (2d) 300 (B.C. S.C.); *Johnson v. Johnson* (1981), 24 R.F.L. (2d) 70 (B.C. S.C.); affirmed on other grounds (1981), 33 R.F.L. (2d) 302, [1983] 4 W.W.R. 193, 43 B.C.L.R. 173 (C.A.); *Wood v. Wood* (1977), 4 R.F.L. (2d) 182 (P.E.I. S.C.);

"The use of the words 'continued cohabitation' indicates to me a legislative intent that cruelty must occur prior to the separation the cohabitation no longer continues. Physical and mental cruelty occurring after the separation of the parties, [does] not in my view provi[d]e grounds for divorce": per Morse J. in *Saunders v. Saunders*, 22 R.F.L. 210, [1975] W.W.D. 135, 58 D.L.R. (3d) 763 (Man. Q.B.). See also *Thibodeau v. Thibodeau* (1975), 27 R.F.L. 114 (Man. Q.B.); *Pawelko v. Pawelko* (1970), 1 R.F.L. 174, 74 W.W.R. 632, 12 D.L.R. (3d) 279 (Sask. Q.B.);*Sweetapple v. Sweetapple* (1977), 15 Nfld. & P.E.I.R. 262, 38 A.P.R. 262 (Nfld. T.D.); *MacRae v. MacRae* (1974), 15 R.F.L. 270, 6 Nfld. & P.E.I.R. 1 (P.E.I. S.C.); *Greggain v. Hunter* (1984), 31 Sask. R. 311 (U.F.C.); *Barbour v. Barbour* (1980), 18 R.F.L. (2d) 80, 27 Nfld. & P.E.I.R. 229, 74 A.P.R. 229 (Nfld. T.D.); *Randell v. Randell* (1977), 1 R.F.L. (2d) 135 (Ont. H.C.).

8§34 — Both cruelty and intolerability required

"The test of cruelty is in one sense a subjective one, namely, as has been said many times, is this conduct by this man to this woman, or *vice versa*, cruelty? But that does mean that what one spouse may consider cruel is necessarily so. *Cruelty must involve serious and weighty matters, which, reasonably considered, may cause physical or mental suffering.* It must furthermore — an important additional requirement — be of such nature and kind as to render such conduct intolerable to a reasonable person": per MacKeigan C.J.N.S. in *Luther v. Luther* (1978), 5 R.F.L. (2d) 285 at 287, 26 N.S.R. (2d) 232, 40 A.P.R. 232 (C.A.). [Emphasis added.]

"One can think of many cases where continued cohabitation might be rendered intolerable even though the conduct of neither spouse could fairly be characterized as cruel. There may be cases of incompatibility, differences in lifestyle, illness, unavoidable absence, impotency. Unless there is cruelty, s. 3(d) [now s. 8(2)(b)(ii)] cannot be relied on even though there has been conduct of such a kind as to render intolerable the continued cohabitation of the spouses": per O'Sullivan J.A. in *N. v. N.* (1976), 24 R.F.L. 366 at 373 (Man. C.A.).

See also *Kulyk v. Kulyk* (1980), 5 Sask. R. 235 (Q.B.); *Randell v. Randell* (1977), 1 R.F.L. (2d) 135 (Ont. H.C.); *Turnbull v. Turnbull* (1976), 28 R.F.L. 92 (Man. Q.B.); *Fogel v. Fogel* (1976), 24 R.F.L. 18 (Ont. H.C.); affirmed (1979), 9 R.F.L. (2d) 55 (Ont. C.A.); *Thibodeau v. Thibodeau* (1975), 27 R.F.L. 114 (Man. Q.B.); *Peppard v. Peppard* (1970), 2 R.F.L. 162 (N.S. T.D.); *Goudie v. Goudie* (1969), 2 R.F.L. 128, 1 Nfld. & P.E.I.R. 34, 9 D.L.R. (3d) 90 (Nfld. T.D.).

8§35 — Definition of cruelty

"Over the years the courts have steadfastly refrained from attempting to formulate a general definition of cruelty. As used in ordinary parlance 'cruelty' signifies a disposition to inflict suffering; to delight in or exhibit indifference to the pain or misery of others; merciless or hardheartedness as exhibited in action. If in the marriage relationship one spouse by his conduct causes wanton, malicious or unnecessary infliction of pain or suffering upon the body, the feelings or emotions of the other, his conduct may well constitute cruelty which will entitle a petitioner to dissolution of the marriage, if in the court's opinion, it amounts to physical or mental cruelty 'of such a kind as to render intolerable the continued cohabitation of the spouses'": per Schroeder J.A. in *Knoll v. Knoll*, 1 R.F.L. 141, [1970] 2 O.R. 169, 10 D.L.R. (3d) 199 (C.A.).

In determining whether or not grounds of cruelty have been established, it is not necessary to establish an element of fear on the part of the petitioner: *Wales v. Wales* (1976), 2 R.F.L. 138 (Ont. C.A.).

The courts have consistently refused to attempt an inclusive definition of cruelty. Acts which one generation of women consider tolerable in order to preserve the marriage might well be considered by another generation cruel and intolerable. Too great reliance cannot be placed on former cases although many of the principles laid down therein will continue to be proper guides: *Feldman v. Feldman* (1970), 2 R.F.L. 173, 75 W.W.R. 715, 14 D.L.R. (3d) 222 (Alta. C.A.).

"The court should not grant a decree of divorce on evidence of merely distasteful or irritating conduct on the part of the offending spouse. The word 'cruelty' denotes excessive suffering, severity of pain, mercilessness; not mere displeasure, irritation, anger, or dissatisfaction": per Limerick J.A. in *Chouinard v. Chouinard* (1969), 1 R.F.L. 101, 1 N.B.R. (2d) 941, 10 D.L.R. (3d) 263 (C.A.); applied in *Storey v. Storey* (1973), 10 R.F.L. 170, 4 Nfld. & P.E.I.R. 299 (P.E.I. S.C.). See also *Baker v. Baker* (1972), 5 R.F.L. 398 (Alta. T.D.).

"Parliament, by defining cruelty as it has done in s. 3(d) [now s. 8(2)(b)(ii)], has eliminated the second safeguard mentioned *i.e.* that the cruelty must cause danger to life, limb or health, bodily or mental, or reasonable apprehension of such danger, and replaced it by the requirement that the cruel conduct, in addition to being grave and weighty, must include conduct which had the effect of rendering continued cohabitation intolerable — the key element in the definition being the intolerability of continued cohabitation due to such cruelty": per Tucker J. in *Farden v. Farden* (1970), 3 R.F.L. 315 (Sask. Q.B.); affirmed (1972), 8 R.F.L. 183 (Sask. C.A.). See also *Turnbull v. Turnbull* (1976), 28 R.F.L.

92 (Man. Q.B.); *Loh v. Loh* (1976), 24 R.F.L. 235 (Alta. T.D.); *Skovmand v. Skovmand* (1969), 1 R.F.L. 121, 2 N.B.R. (2d) 57 (Q.B.).

8§36 — Intolerability

In determining whether cruelty has been established, the standard of tolerable behaviour applied should reflect contemporary standards: *Bens v. Bens* (1983), 50 A.R. 197 (C.A.).

"The consideration of intolerable conduct arises only where it results from cruelty, mental or physical, and not from outraged principles or any other cause. The petitioner cannot be heard to contend that the physical cruelty, consisting of blows struck, was intolerable to her for she begged the respondent not to leave her": per Limerick J.A. in *Chouinard v. Chouinard* (1969), 1 N.B.R. (2d) 582 (Q.B.); affirmed (1969), 1 R.F.L. 101, 1 N.B.R. (2d) 941, 10 D.L.R. (3d) 263 (C.A.); *Barron v. Bull* (1987), 5 R.F.L. (3d) 427, 76 A.R. 120 (Q.B.); *Green v. Green* (1983), 27 Sask. R. 84 (Q.B.); *Woodward v. Woodward* (1984), 55 N.B.R. (2d) 90, 144 A.P.R. 90 (Q.B.); *Dixon v. Dixon* (1982), 37 B.C.L.R. 292 (S.C.); *Pellegrini v. Pellegrini* (1976), 30 R.F.L. 293 (Ont. H.C.); *Graham v. Graham* (1975), 25 R.F.L. 107 (B.C. S.C.); *MacDonald v. MacDonald* (1975), 23 R.F.L. 303 (Man. Q.B.); *Horne v. Horne*, [1972] 3 W.W.R. 153, 5 R.F.L. 394 (B.C. S.C.); *Durant v. Durant* (1971), 2 Nfld. & P.E.I.R. 138, 22 D.L.R. (3d) 488 (P.E.I. S.C.); *Goudie v. Goudie* (1969), 2 R.F.L. 128, 1 Nfld. & P.E.I.R. 34, 9 D.L.R. (3d) 90 (Nfld. T.D.);*Wilson v. Wilson* (1973), 13 R.F.L. 142 (B.C. S.C.).

8§37 — Injury to health

Where the wife's constant complaining to the husband of the time he spent on business eventually affected his health, the husband was granted a divorce on the grounds of cruelty: *Desmarais v. Desmarais* (1988), 13 R.F.L. (3d) 64, 84 A.R. 353 (Q.B.).

"I wish to make it clear that in considering whether there has been proof of cruelty, I have not been hampered by the definitions relating to the concepts of cruelty which are to be found in the veritable legion of decided cases which preceded and have followed *Russell v. Russell*, [1897] A.C. 395 (H.L.). There is now no need to consider whether conduct complained of caused 'danger to life, limb, or health, bodily or mentally, or a reasonable apprehension of it' or any of the variations of that definition to be found in the *Russell* case": per Tritschler C.J.Q.B. in *Zalesky v. Zalesky* (1968), 1 R.F.L. 36, 67 W.W.R. 104, 1 D.L.R. (3d) 471 (Man. Q.B.). See also *Knoll v. Knoll*, [1970] 2 O.R. 169, 1 R.F.L. 141, 10 D.L.R. (3d) 199 (C.A.); *Feldman v. Feldman* (1970), 2 R.F.L. 173, 14 D.L.R. (3d) 222, 75 W.W.R. 715 (Alta. C.A.).

"The shackles that the Russell case rivetted on the courts have only recently been struck down, and the courts will, I hope, be slow to substitute others": per Johnson J.A. in *Anderson v. Anderson* (1971), 8 R.F.L. 299 at 304, [1972] 6 W.W.R. 53, 29 D.L.R. (3d) 587 (Alta. C.A.); affirmed 10 R.F.L. 200, [1973] 2 W.W.R. 688, 32 D.L.R. (3d) 128n (S.C.C.).

See also *Delaney v. Delaney* (1968), 1 R.F.L. 29, 66 W.W.R. 275, 1 D.L.R. (3d) 303 (B.C. S.C.); *Paskiewich v. Paskiewich* (1968), 2 D.L.R. (3d) 662 (B.C. S.C.); *Lake v. Lake* (1982), 30 R.F.L. (2d) 5 (B.C. S.C.); *Augart v. Augart* (1979), 12 R.F.L. (2d) 327 (Alta. T.D.); *Lacey v. Lacey*; *Winney v. Winney*; *Weiss v. Weiss*, 1 R.F.L. 84, [1970] 1 O.R. 279, 8 D.L.R. (3d) 289 (H.C.); *Stevens v. Stevens* (1977), 17 N.B.R. (2d) 656 (Q.B.); *Zwicker v. Zwicker* (1971), 3 R.F.L. 333, 4 N.S.R. (2d) 249 (T.D.).

8§38 — Cruelty — grave and weighty conduct

In *Turner v. Turner* (1990), 85 Nfld. & P.E.I.R. 43, 266 A.P.R. 43 (Nfld. T.D.), the wife's allegations that the husband was anti-social and had attempted to separate her from her family and friends were found insufficient to support her claim of cruelty.

"Care must be exercised in applying the standard set forth in s. 3(d) [now 8.(2)(b)(ii)] that conduct relied upon to establish cruelty is not a trivial act, but one of a 'grave and weighty' nature, and not merely conduct which can be characterized as little more than a manifestation of incompatibility of temperament between the spouses. The whole matrimonial relations must be considered especially if the cruelty consists of reproaches, complaints, accusations, or constant carping criticisms. A question most relevant for consideration is the effect of the conduct complained of upon the mind of the affected spouse. The determination of what constitutes cruelty in a given case must, in the final analysis, depend upon the circumstances of the particular case, having due regard to the physical and mental condition of the parties, their character and their attitudes towards the marriage relationship": per Schroeder J.A. in *Knoll v. Knoll*, 1 R.F.L. 141 (Ont. C.A.); *Zunti v. Zunti* (1970), 15 D.L.R. (3d) 369 (B.C. C.A.); *Lacey v. Lacey*; *Winney v. Winney*; *Weiss v. Weiss*, 1 R.F.L. 84 (Ont. H.C.). See also *Ifield v. Ifield*, 24 R.F.L. 237, [1976] W.W.D. 63, 66 D.L.R. (3d) 311 (Sask. Q.B.); *Turnbull v. Turnbull* (1976), 28 R.F.L. 92 (Man. Q.B.).

See also *Bradley v. Bradley* (1984), 55 N.B.R. (2d) 189, 144 A.P.R. 189 (Q.B.); *Gilbert v. Gilbert* (1980), 18 R.F.L. (2d) 240, 39 N.S.R. (2d) 241, 71 A.P.R. 241 (T.D.); *Malkinson v. Malkinson* (1970), 2 R.F.L. 152 (B.C. S.C.); *Quinn v. Quinn* (1970), 1 R.F.L. 129, 74 W.W.R. 144, 11 D.L.R. (3d) 372 (B.C. S.C.); *Wildman v. Wildman (No. 2)* (1984), 35 Sask. R. 23 (Q.B.); *Thompson v. Thompson* (1982), 29 R.F.L. (2d) 320 (Ont. H.C.); *Elbaz v. Elbaz* (1980), 16 R.F.L. (2d) 336, 29 O.R. (2d) 207, 114 D.L.R. (3d) 116 (H.C.); *Fjermestad v. Fjermestad* (1980), 16 R.F.L. (2d) 137 (B.C. S.C.); *Rollason v. Rollason* (1978), 1 R.F.L. (2d) 97 (Ont. H.C.); *Nador v. Nador* (1977), 19 O.R. (2d) 728, 86 D.L.R. (3d) 463 (H.C.); *L. v. L.*, [1970] C.S. 222 (Que.); *Cochrane v. Cochrane* (1976), 10 Nfld. & P.E.I.R. 86 (Nfld. T.D.); *Zwicker v. Zwicker* (1971), 3 R.F.L. 333, 4 N.S.R. (2d) 249 (T.D.); *Grass v. Grass* (1976), 30 R.F.L. 363, 15 N.B.R. (2d) 709 (Q.B.); *Pavlinek v. Pavlinek* (1975), 22 R.F.L. 236 (Ont. H.C.); *P. v. P.* (1972), 7 R.F.L. 311, 4 N.B.R. (2d) 525 (Q.B.); *Hattie v. Hattie*, 3 R.F.L. 324, [1971] 2 W.W.R. 556, 18 D.L.R. (3d) 383 (B.C. S.C.); *Malkinson v. Malkinson* (1970), 2 R.F.L. 152 (B.C. S.C.); *Quinn v. Quinn* (1970), 1 R.F.L. 129, 74 W.W.R. 144, 11 D.L.R. (3d) 372 (B.C. S.C.); *B. v. R.*, [1970] C.S. 210 (Que.).

8§39 — Subjective test for cruelty

"[C]ruelty is a question of fact in determining which the circumstances of each case must be taken into consideration, including the physical and mental condition and the position in life of the parties. What has to be determined is the effect on a particular person of certain conduct or acts, rather than the nature of the acts committed and in determining such a question little help can be gained by referring to a multiplicity of cases referring to the effect of similar conduct as between other parties. The whole history of the marriage must be examined and a conclusion reached after taking into account all relevant facts — 'the question is whether *this* conduct by *this* man to *this* woman, or vice versa, is cruelty'": per Tritschler C.J.Q.B. citing *Australian Divorce Law and Practice*, by Toose,

Watson and Benjafield at pp. 171 and 174 in *Zalesky v. Zalesky* (1968), 1 R.F.L. 36, 67 W.W.R. 104, 1 D.L.R. (3d) 471 (Man. Q.B.). See also *Galbraith v. Galbraith* (1969), 1 R.F.L. 96, 70 W.W.R. 744, 8 D.L.R. (3d) 24 (Man. Q.B.); *Ashraff v. Ashraff* (1970), 1 R.F.L. 157, 73 W.W.R. 321 (Man. Q.B.); *Grandy v. Grandy* (1972), 7 R.F.L. 69, 3 N.S.R. (2d) 750, 26 D.L.R. (3d) 359 (C.A.); *Bonin v. Bonin* (1969), 1 R.F.L. 65, 1 N.S.R. 529, 5 D.L.R. (3d) 533 (T.D.); *F. v. F.* (1970), 1 R.F.L. 167, 74 W.W.R. 241, 11 D.L.R. (3d) 621 (B.C. S.C.); *Paskiewich v. Paskiewich* (1968), 2 D.L.R. (3d) 622 (B.C. S.C.); *Mark v. Mark* (1973), 15 R.F.L. 73 (Ont. H.C.); *Ebenal v. Ebenal*, [1971] 4 W.W.R. 473, 3 R.F.L. 303, 20 D.L.R. (3d) 545 (Sask. C.A.).

"Cruelty cases, more than any other class of case, depend particularly on a careful estimate of the witnesses. For in a cruelty case the question is whether *this* conduct by *this* man to *this* woman or vice versa is cruelty. How far a spouse has to depart from the normal standards of kindness and self-control that are the basis of married life and how great an effect that departure has to have on the other spouse before it constitutes cruelty is always a question of degree, depending largely on the temperament, circumstances and health of each party": Pearce J. in *Lauder v. Lauder*, [1949] P. 277, [1949] 1 All E.R. 76 (C.A.), quoted in *Knoll v. Knoll*, 1 R.F.L. 141 (Ont. C.A.); *Martin v. Martin* (1970), 1 R.F.L. 154 (B.C. S.C.); *Francescutti v. Francescutti* (1976), 24 R.F.L. 378 (B.C. S.C.); *Lacey v. Lacey*; *Winney v. Winney*; *Weiss v. Weiss*, 1 R.F.L. 84 (Ont. H.C.); *N. v. N.* (1976), 24 R.F.L. 366 (Man. C.A.).

There is no objective standard in the sense that certain conduct will constitute cruelty in every case while other conduct will not. What has to be determined is the effect on a particular person of certain conduct or acts, rather than the nature of the acts committed. It is for the court, and not the petitioner, to apply the subjective test in determining whether there has been cruelty: *Austin v. Austin* (1970), 2 R.F.L. 136, 73 W.W.R. 289, 13 D.L.R. (3d) 498 (Sask. C.A.). See also *Durant v. Durant* (1971), 2 Nfld. & P.E.I.R. 138, 22 D.L.R. (3d) 488 (P.E.I. S.C.).

See also *Chouinard v. Chouinard* (1969), 1 R.F.L. 101 (N.B. C.A.); *Eddy v. Eddy* (1984), 56 N.B.R. (2d) 26, 146 A.P.R. 26 (Q.B.); *Mes v. Mes* (1981), 24 R.F.L. (2d) 257 (Ont. H.C.); *Mark v. Mark* (1973), 15 R.F.L. 73 (Ont. H.C.); *Archibald v. Archibald* (1981), 48 N.S.R. (2d) 361, 92 A.P.R. 361 (T.D.); *Wornath v. Wornath* (1980), 19 R.F.L. (2d) 289, 3 Sask. R. 266 (Q.B.); *Turnbull v. Turnbull* (1976), 28 R.F.L. 92 (Man. Q.B.); *Emmerson v. Emmerson* (1970), 2 R.F.L. 147 (B.C. S.C.); *Graham v. Graham* (1975), 25 R.F.L. 107 (B.C. S.C.); *Goldstein v. Goldstein* (1970), 15 D.L.R. (3d) 95 (Alta. T.D.); *M. v. M.*, 3 R.F.L. 350, [1971] 2 O.R. 633, 18 D.L.R. (3d) 667 (C.A.); *Kahn v. Kahn* (1973), 13 R.F.L. 269 (Ont. H.C.); *Bramley v. Bramley* (1974), 15 R.F.L. 152, 4 O.R. (2d) 503, 48 D.L.R. (3d) 367 (H.C.); *Dumas v. Tremblay*, [1975] C.S. 501 (Que.).

8§40 — Incompatibility

"Incompatibility by itself is not recognized as a ground for divorce in the present Act": per Johnson J.A. in *Anderson v. Anderson*, 8 R.F.L. 299 at 308, [1972] 6 W.W.R. 53, 29 D.L.R. (3d) 587 (Alta. C.A.); affirmed [1973] 2 W.W.R. 668, 10 R.F.L. 200, 32 D.L.R. (3d) 128n (S.C.C.); *N. v. N.* (1976), 24 R.F.L. 366 (Man. C.A.); *Turnbull v. Turnbull* (1976), 28 R.F.L. 92 (Man. Q.B.).

See also *Knoll v. Knoll*, 1 R.F.L. 141, [1970] 2 O.R. 169, 10 D.L.R. (3d) 199 (C.A.); *Malkinson v. Malkinson* (1970), 2 R.F.L. 152 (B.C. S.C.); *Hiltz v. Hiltz* (1970), 2 R.F.L. 178, 2 N.S.R. (2d) 434 (T.D.); affirmed (1970), 11 R.F.L. 35, 4 N.S.R. (2d) 547 (C.A.);

White v. White (1970), 3 N.B.R. (2d) 357 (C.A.); *Kerr v. Kerr* (1980), 5 Sask. R. 325 (Q.B.); *Fjermestad v. Fjermestad* (1980), 16 R.F.L. (2d) 137 (B.C. S.C.); *Roschuk v. Roschuk* (1979), 12 R.F.L. (2d) 34 (Man. Q.B.); varied (1980), 15 R.F.L. (2d) 196 (Man. C.A.); *Beach v. Beach*, [1977] 3 W.W.R. 274 (Alta. T.D.); *Pellegrini v. Pellegrini* (1976), 30 R.F.L. 293 (Ont. H.C.); *Ifield v. Ifield* (1975), 24 R.F.L. 237, 66 D.L.R. (3d) 311 (Sask. Q.B.); *Jordahl v. Jordahl* (1971), 5 R.F.L. 189 (Sask. Q.B.); *Bustin v. Bustin* (1969), 1 N.B.R. (2d) 496 (Q.B.); *St. John v. St. John* (1981), 9 Sask. R. 121 at 123 (Q.B.).

8§41 — "Treated with cruelty"

"In cases of impotency or [sexual] incapacity caused by physical or psychological deficiencies, it cannot be said that such a person 'treated' his spouse with 'cruelty', for he was incapable of doing what was required of him": per Johnson J.A. in *Anderson v. Anderson*, 8 R.F.L. 299, [1972] 6 W.W.R. 53, 29 D.L.R. (3d) 587 (Alta. C.A.); affirmed 10 R.F.L. 200, [1973] 2 W.W.R. 668, 32 D.L.R. (3d) 128n (S.C.C.).

The use of the phrase "has treated the petitioner with physical or mental cruelty" does not require any particular *animus* and the words of the section are satisfied by the simple fact of cruelty having occurred: *Bugden v. Bugden* (1974), 23 R.F.L. 253, 15 N.S.R. (2d) 535, 52 D.L.R. (3d) 241 (T.D.).

"I am convinced that the word 'treated' in s. 3(d) [now s. 8(2)(b)(ii)] is an important and an operative word and in the case before me assumes, if possible even more significant importance. Beyond question, in my view, this word 'treated' implies that, whether consciously and maliciously or unconsciously and insanely (or as a result of mental illness), the respondent has *in fact* physically or mentally engaged in some form of action or conduct, whether positive or negative against, or involving, the petitioner; and it is this 'engagement', over a period of time (more or less, depending on all the circumstances), which will result in cruelty rendering intolerable the continued cohabitation of the spouses. Whatever form it may take, in my judgment, there must be a 'course of conduct'": per Washington L.J.S.C. in *Baker v. Baker* (1969), 1 R.F.L. 106, 71 W.W.R. 241, 8 D.L.R. (3d) 260 (B.C. S.C.).

"The cruelty must be exercised by the respondent actively against the petitioner and not arise from the nature of things, the human condition or the acts of third parties": per Wright J. in *Lacey v. Lacey*; *Winney v. Winney*; *Weiss v. Weiss*, *supra*. See also *Peppard v. Peppard* (1970), 2 R.F.L. 162 (N.S. T.D.); *Ells v. Ells* (1970), 2 R.F.L. 186 (N.S. T.D.).

8§42 — Course of conduct

Where, throughout their 17-year marriage, the wife was subject to mental abuse, physical violence and domination by the husband who considered her to be his property, she was granted a divorce on the basis of both mental and physical cruelty: *Thibeault v. Thibeault* (1990), 109 N.B.R. (2d) 419, 273 A.P.R. 419 (Q.B.).

In *Anthony v. Anthony* (1983), 44 Nfld. & P.E.I.R. 169, 130 A.P.R. 169 (Nfld. T.D.), the wife was granted a divorce on the grounds of physical and mental cruelty. The husband, who had a violent temper, had frequently beaten the wife and children, and had destroyed property in the matrimonial home. His conduct constituted an inexcusable pattern of cruel behaviour.

In *Cramer v. Cramer* (1981), 18 Alta. L.R. (2d) 356 (Q.B.), it was held that the husband's slapping of the wife in response to her throwing liquor in his face did not of itself constitute cruelty. However, considering the act in association with marital tensions and several post-separation incidents, the husband's conduct, taken as a whole, was found to have been cruel.

Although none of the facts alone would have been sufficient to satisfy the legal requirements of s. 3(d) [now s. 8(2)(b)(ii)], when viewed as a whole the conduct of each party in the circumstances of the case amounted to cruelty sufficient to make the marriage intolerable: *Noble v. Noble* (1974), 16 R.F.L. 368 (B.C. S.C.).

See also *Markus v. Markus*, 3 R.F.L. 306, [1971] 2 W.W.R. 35, 16 D.L.R. (3d) 520 (Sask. Q.B.); *Goudie v. Goudie* (1969), 2 R.F.L. 128, 1 Nfld. & P.E.I.R. 34, 9 D.L.R. (3d) 90 (Nfld. T.D.); *Baker v. Baker* (1969), 1 R.F.L. 106 (B.C. S.C.).

8§43 — Intention to be cruel

Mental cruelty, as a grounds for divorce, need not be intentional or malicious. The fact that it existed and that the spouse suffered from it is sufficient to justify a divorce: *Droit de la famille — 724*, [1989] R.D.F. 701 (C.S. Qué.).

'[In *Gollins v. Gollins*, [1964] A.C. 644, [1963] 2 All E.R. 966, it was] laid down that whether cruelty, as a matrimonial offence, has been established is a question of fact and degree, which should be determined by taking into account the particular individuals concerned and the particular circumstances of the case, rather than by any objective standards; that accordingly, in cases where the two spouses were of normal physical and mental health, and the conduct of the respondent spouse, so considered, was so bad that the other should not be called upon to endure it, cruelty was established, and then it did not matter what was the respondent's state of mind, *e.g.*, it was immaterial whether the defendant's conduct was 'aimed at' the other spouse or due to unwarranted indifference, attributable, perhaps, to selfishness": per Schroeder J.A. in *Knoll v. Knoll*, 1 R.F.L. 141 (Ont. C.A.). See also *Rodway v. Rodway* (1978), 3 R.F.L. (2d) 295 (Ont. H.C.); *Martin v. Martin* (1970), 1 R.F.L. 154 (B.C. S.C.); *Quinn v. Quinn* (1970), 1 R.F.L. 129, 74 W.W.R. 144, 11 D.L.R. (3d) 372 (B.C. S.C.); *White v. White* (1968), 1 R.F.L. 172, 69 D.L.R. (2d) 60 (N.S. T.D.).

See also *Wittstock v. Wittstock*, 3 R.F.L. 326, [1971] 2 O.R. 472, 18 D.L.R. (3d) 264 (C.A.); *Feldman v. Feldman* (1970), 2 R.F.L. 173, 75 W.W.R. 715, 14 D.L.R. (3d) 222 (Alta. C.A.); *King v. King*, [1953] A.C. 124, [1952] 2 All E.R. 584 (H.L.); *Krause v. Krause*, 23 R.F.L. 219, [1976] 2 W.W.R. 622, 64 D.L.R. (3d) 352 (Alta. C.A.); *Durant v. Durant* (1971), 2 Nfld. & P.E.I.R. 138, 22 D.L.R. (3d) 488 (P.E.I. S.C.); *Hattie v. Hattie*, 3 R.F.L. 324, [1971] 2 W.W.R. 556, 18 D.L.R. (3d) 383 (B.C. S.C.); *H. (A.) v. H. (A.C.)* (1971), 5 R.F.L. 185 (B.C. S.C.); *Grass v. Grass* (1976), 30 R.F.L. 363, 15 N.B.R. (2d) 709 (Q.B.); *Stevens v. Stevens* (1977), 17 N.B.R. (2d) 656 (Q.B.); *MacKay v. MacKay* (1976), 1 R.F.L. (2d) 80 (P.E.I. C.A.); *Westall v. Westall* (1949), 65 T.L.R. 337 (C.A.); *Grandy v. Grandy* (1972), 7 R.F.L. 69, 3 N.S.R. (2d) 750, 26 D.L.R. (3d) 359 (C.A.); *Rouleau v. Wells*, [1980] C.S. 915, 124 D.L.R. (3d) 766 (Qué.); *Turnbull v. Turnbull* (1976), 28 R.F.L. 92 (Man. Q.B.); *Fogel v. Fogel* (1976), 24 R.F.L. 18 (Ont. H.C.); affirmed on other grounds (1979), 9 R.F.L. (2d) 55, 24 O.R. (2d) 158 (C.A.); *Rauch v. Rauch* (1975), 22 R.F.L. 143, 9 O.R. (2d) 761, 61 D.L.R. (3d) 633 (H.C.); *Mark v. Mark* (1973), 15 R.F.L. 73 (Ont. H.C.); *McMurdy v. McMurdy* (1975), 22 R.F.L. 312 (Ont. H.C.); *Ashraff v. Ashraff* (1970), 1 R.F.L. 157, 73 W.W.R. 321 (Man. Q.B.); *Rankin v.*

Rankin (1970), 13 D.L.R. (3d) 630 (B.C. S.C.); *Francescutti v. Francescutti* (1976), 24 R.F.L. 378 (B.C. S.C.); *Dowell v. Dowell* (1976), 30 R.F.L. 278 (Man. Q.B.); *Barrios v. Barrios* (1978), 4 R.F.L. (2d) 347, 28 N.S.R. (2d) 419 (T.D.); *Goldstein v. Goldstein* (1970), 15 D.L.R. (3d) 95 (Alta. T.D.).

8§44 — Cruelty — insanity

The insanity of the respondent at the time of the alleged acts is no defence to an action for divorce based upon cruelty: *MacKay v. MacKay*, above. See also *Novak v. Novak* (1969), 1 R.F.L. 58, 68 W.W.R. 524, 4 D.L.R. (3d) 639 (B.C. S.C.); *McGrath v. McGrath* (1977), 16 N.B.R. (2d) 462 (Q.B.).

The court may grant a divorce on the ground of cruelty where a husband, who is charged with the attempted murder of his wife, suffers from a mental condition which confines him to a mental institution: *Castillo v. Castillo* (1986), 3 R.F.L. (3d) 423 (N.B. Q.B.).

In *Wlock v. Wlock* (1982), 16 Sask. R. 443 (Q.B.), it was held that the irrational conduct of the wife, caused to a large extent by mental illness, did not constitute cruelty.

In *Summerfelt v. Summerfelt* (1982), 31 R.F.L. (2d) 240 (Sask. Q.B.), it was held that although the husband's mental illness caused a breakdown of the marriage, his conduct could not be considered cruelty. The evidence described the consequences of a tragic illness more than blameworthy conduct.

The actions of the wife, who had been diagnosed as a paranoid schizophrenic and hospitalized for extensive periods both before and after the marriage, placed an ever-increasing burden on the husband which rendered continued cohabitation intolerable. The fact that her conduct was not intentional did not prevent it from constituting cruelty: *Grime v. Grime* (1980), 16 R.F.L. (2d) 365, 3 Fam. L. Rev. 75 (Ont. H.C.); *Ifield v. Ifield* (1975), 24 R.F.L. 237, 66 D.L.R (3d) 311 (Sask. Q.B.).

A respondent suffering from paranoid schizophrenia who was not violent but caused the petitioner constant mental worry, was found guilty of cruelty and his mental illness was not a bar to the granting of a decree: *LaChapelle v. LaChapelle*, 20 R.F.L. 125, [1975] 4 W.W.R. 442 (Alta. T.D.); *Bustin v. Bustin* (1969), 1 N.B.R. (2d) 496 (Q.B.); *Aubrey v. Aubrey*, [1970] 2 O.R. 206, 10 D.L.R. (3d) 311 (H.C.); *Baker v. Baker* (1969), 1 R.F.L. 106, 71 W.W.R. 241, 8 D.L.R. (3d) 260 (B.C. S.C.); *Hills v. Hills* (1969), 1 R.F.L. 236, 1 N.S.R. (2d) 405, (sub nom. *H. v. H.)* 9 D.L.R. (3d) 722 (T.D.).

8§45 — Continued cohabitation

Notwithstanding the fact that she remained in the matrimonial home with her husband until the trial, a wife succeeded in her counter-petition for divorce on the ground of cruelty where she was not a woman with substantial income, there were children at home, and she was not, in any real sense, free to move: *Krause v. Krause*, 19 R.F.L. 230, [1975] 4 W.W.R 738 (Alta. T.D.); varied on other grounds 23 R.F.L. 219, [1976] 2 W.W.R. 622, 64 D.L.R. (3d) 352 (Alta. C.A.).

See also *Boulos v. Boulos* (1979), 14 R.F.L. (2d) 206, 24 Nfld. & P.E.I.R. 370, 65 A.P.R. 370 (Nfld. T.D.); *Ifield v. Ifield*, above; *Cridge v. Cridge* (1973), 12 R.F.L. 348 (B.C. S.C.); *Horne v. Horne*, 5 R.F.L. 394, [1972] 3 W.W.R. 153 (B.C. S.C.); *Marks v. Marks* (1971), 3 R.F.L. 339 (N.S. T.D.).

8§46 — "Cruelty" not to be used for quick divorce

"The reason why the court should be alert to detect and turn back attempts to bring petitions under s. 3(d) [now s. 8(2)(a)], was aptly stated by Denning L.J. in *Kaslefsky v. Kaslefsky*, [1951] P. 38, [1950] 2 All E.R. 398, where he said at p. 403: "If the door of cruelty were opened too wide, we should soon find ourselves granting divorce for incompatibility of temperament. This is an easy path to tread, especially in undefended cases. The temptation must be resisted lest we slip into a state of affairs where the institution of marriage itself is imperilled',": per Disbery J. in *Markus v. Markus*, 3 R.F.L. 306, [1971] 2 W.W.R. 35, 16 D.L.R. (3d) 520 (Sask. Q.B.); *Hiltz v. Hiltz* (1970), 11 R.F.L. 35, 4 N.S.R. (2d) 547 (T.D.); affirming (1970), 2 R.F.L. 178, 2 N.S.R. (2d) 434 (C.A.).

The courts should not be used merely as a mechanism to extricate a petitioner from a situation in which she freely and voluntarily entered with her eyes fully open and with full foreknowledge of the same facts which now cause her to complain. For such a person who was the author of her own misfortune the Act provided the remedy set forth in s. 4(1)(e) [now s. 8(2)(a)]: *Sentner v. Sentner* (1978), 5 R.F.L. (2d) 259 (P.E.I. S.C.).

"Allegations of cruelty should not be exaggerated, nor should past hurts, real or fancied, be resurrected for the purposes of the divorce petition merely to avoid [the requisite waiting period] where the real cause of the separation is a marriage breakdown. To guard against abuses the courts should view carefully any evidence of cruelty where the parties are on the verge of separation and the alleged act of cruelty operates as a very convenient pretext for the actual separation and grounds for divorce": per MacLeod J. in *Gurski v. Gurski* (1975), 22 R.F.L. 238 (Sask. Q.B.); *Clark v. Clark* (1971), 6 R.F.L. 6 (Ont. H.C.). See also *Hasse v. Zamoyska*, [1974] C.S. 170 (Qué,); *Peppard v. Peppard* (1970), 2 R.F.L. 162 (N.S. T.D.).

8§47 — Evidence of cruelty

In cases of injury to health resulting from refusal of sexual intercourse or sexual incompatibility, the petitioner's evidence would usually need to be corroborated by a medical practitioner who had seen both parties: *Anderson v. Anderson* (1971), 8 R.F.L. 299, [1972] 6 W.W.R. 53, 29 D.L.R. (3d) 587 (Alta. C.A.); affirmed 10 R.F.L. 200, [1973] 2 W.W.R. 668, 32 D.L.R. (3d) 128n (S.C.C.).

Corroboration is not necessary to support a petition for divorce on the ground of cruelty where no issue as to credibility arises: *Thordarson v. Thordarson* (1978), 5 R.F.L. (2d) 92 (Ont. C.A.).

A respondent husband's affidavit, admitting an assault on his wife and containing a clause permitting it to be used as evidence in divorce proceedings, was held to be of no value in determining whether he had treated her with cruelty. The appeal court stated that it would not have admitted the affidavit without proof of the unavailability of the respondent to be present at the trial: *Frenette v. Frenette* (1976), 30 R.F.L. 163 (P.E.I. C.A.).

In cases where there is a sharp conflict in evidence, it is desirable that a trial judge in his reasons for judgment, after indicating the evidence that he accepts and that which he rejects, set out the facts as he finds them to be: *Spiotte v. Spiotte* (1973), 12 R.F.L. 226 (Ont. C.A.).

"The courts have in many cases stated that the judge presiding at the trial is entitled to draw inferences adverse to the litigant on whom the onus of proving his or her case rests and who fails to call obvious witnesses who, if they were of a mind to, would be in a position to support the allegations being made.": per Keith J. in *Mayberry v. Mayberry*, 2 R.F.L. 140, [1970] 2 O.R. 602, 11 D.L.R. (3d) 532 (H.C.); reversed on other grounds 3 R.F.L. 395, [1971] 2 O.R. 378, 18 D.L.R. (3d) 45 (C.A.).

The evidence of a 15-year-old child, which is crucial to a cruelty proceeding, should not be given in a private interview: *Austin v. Austin* (1970), 2 R.F.L. 136, 73 W.W.R. 289, 13 D.L.R. (3d) 498 (Sask. C.A.).

An agreement whereby the wife agreed to retract her statements alleging sexual misconduct on the part of the husband does not prevent the wife from relying upon such misconduct as evidence of cruelty in subsequent divorce proceedings: *I.M.-J.M. v. D.A.M.*; *D.A.M. v. I.M.-J.M.* (1984), 43 R.F.L. (2d) 205 (Ont. H.C.).

"It is now settled that the standard of proof required in a divorce action ... is the standard required in civil actions where the preponderance of probabilities determines the issues. ... [I]t is sufficient if the circumstances are such as would lead the guarded discretion of a reasonable or just man to that conclusion": *Thomas v. Thomas* (1976), 29 R.F.L. 181 (P.E.I. S.C.), citing *Power on Divorce*, 2d ed. (1964) at 425. See also *Paradis v. Dame Auger*, [1973] C.S. 1034 (Qué.); *Olson v. Olson*, 4 R.F.L. 86, [1971] 3 W.W.R. 506 (Sask. Q.B.); *Durant v. Durant* (1971), 2 Nfld. & P.E.I.R. 138, 22 D.L.R. (3d) 488 (P.E.I. S.C.); *Lacey v. Lacey*; *Winney v. Winney*; *Weiss v. Weiss*, 1 R.F.L. 84, [1970] 1 O.R. 279, 8 D.L.R. (3d) 289 (H.C.); *Lauder v. Lauder* (1970), 2 R.F.L. 150, 12 D.L.R. (3d) 543 (Man. C.A.). But see *Farkasch v. Farkasch* (1971), 4 R.F.L. 339, [1972] 1 W.W.R. 429 at 431, 22 D.L.R. (3d) 345 (Man. Q.B.), where the psychiatric evidence was found "lacking in authority in helping to assess the marital situation of the parties". See also *D. v. D.* (1969), 1 N.S.R. (2d) 270 (T.D.); *Fjermestad v. Fjermestad* (1980), 16 R.F.L. (2d) 137 (B.C. S.C.); *Zalesky v. Zalesky* (1968), 1 R.F.L. 36, 67 W.W.R. 104, 1 D.L.R. (3d) 471 (Man. Q.B.); *Ashraff v. Ashraff* (1970), 1 R.F.L. 157, 73 W.W.R. 321 (Man. Q.B.).

8§48 — Cruelty — provocation

In *Herring v. Williams* (1991), 103 N.S.R. (2d) 176, 282 A.P.R. 176 (T.D.), the husband's petition for divorce was granted on the grounds of the wife's mental cruelty. The parties separated after 11 days of marriage as the wife had insisted on taking her 17-year-old son along on the honeymoon, during which he exhibited bizarre behaviour.

A serious assault may constitute cruelty notwithstanding the fact that the wife had been taunting her husband as to lack of manhood: *Aucoin v. Aucoin* (1976), 28 R.F.L. 43, 15 N.S.R. (2d) 399, 72 D.L.R. (3d) 674 (C.A.).

The discovery of a wife's adultery is grave provocation and therefore an isolated assault in such circumstances may be insufficient to support a decree on the grounds of cruelty. However, where the husband, suspecting his wife of adultery, assaulted her, threatened her life and "continued to harass" her, his cruelty was not exonerated by provocation: *Feldman v. Feldman* (1970), 2 R.F.L 173, 75 W.W.R. 715, 14 D.L.R. (3d) 222 (Alta. C.A.).

See also *Barber v. Barber*, [1978] 4 W.W.R. 411 (Alta. T.D.); *Storey v. Storey* (1973), 10 R.F.L. 170, 4 Nfld. & P.E.I.R. 229 (P.E.I. S.C.); *Goudie v. Goudie* (1969), 2 R.F.L. 128, 1 Nfld. & P.E.I.R. 34, 9 D.L.R. (3d) 90 (Nfld. T.D.); *Bustin v. Bustin* (1969), 1 N.B.R. (2d) 496 (Q.B.).

Types of Cruelty

8§49 — Cruelty — abnormal sexual practices

An allegation in an affidavit that the respondent spouse is a practising homosexual is not, in itself, cruelty or grounds for divorce under the *Divorce Act*. The fact that the respondent does not contest the petition does not relieve the petitioner from the test for cruelty established under the Act: *B. (Y.) v. B. (J.).* (1989), 20 R.F.L. (3d) 154, 66 Alta. L.R. (2d) 193, [1989] 4 W.W.R. 501 (Q.B.).

"It may, perhaps, have seemed to [the respondent husband] that what he was doing was only contributing to the enjoyment of sex, but this question of mental cruelty must be considered *subjectively*, that is, from the point of view of the petitioner [wife]. His actions in turning her over and not looking at her face while having sex; the fact that he became impotent and would not have sex with her in the normal manner; his tendency to want to be struck by her and tied up by her (even though he might have thought that this was play); and the fact that he advised her that he did not think that sex was necessary anymore, all, in my opinion, amount to mental cruelty which led to the breakdown of the marriage": per Morrison J. in *Harwood v. Thomas* (1980), 21 R.F.L. (2d) 1 at 7, 43 N.S.R. (2d) 292, 81 A.P.R. 292 (T.D.); affirmed (1981), 22 R.F.L. (2d) 167, 45 N.S.R. (2d) 414, 86 A.P.R. 414 (C.A.).

A frail, sensitive, nervous petitioner, who was forced to engage in fellatio contrary to her wishes and who was obviously affected adversely by the demands made upon her by the respondent, was granted a decree on the grounds of cruelty: *M. v. M.*, 3 R.F.L. 350, [1971] 2 O.R. 663, 18 D.L.R. (3d) 667 (C.A.). See also *Sentner v. Sentner* (1978), 5 R.F.L. (2d) 259 (P.E.I. S.C.).

See also *McIntyre v. McIntyre* (1979), 9 R.F.L. (2d) 332 (Ont. H.C.); *McMurdy v. McMurdy* (1975), 22 R.F.L. 312 (Ont. H.C.); *Berger v. Berger* (1974), 17 R.F.L. 88 (B.C. S.C.); *M. v. M.* (1972), 16 R.F.L. 291, 7 N.B.R. (2d) 491 (Q.B.); *H. (A.) v. H. (A.C.)* (1971), 5 R.F.L. 185 (B.C. S.C.); *Rankin v. Rankin* (1970), 13 D.L.R. (3d) 630 (B.C. S.C.);*C. v. C.* (1969), 1 R.F.L. 127, 2 N.B.R. (2d) 187, (sub nom. *I.C. v. G.C.)* 9 D.L.R. (3d) 632 (Q.B.); *C. v. C. (No. 2)*, 2 R.F.L. 128, [1969] 2 O.R. 786, 7 D.L.R. (3d) 35 (H.C.); *Clark v. Clark*, [1969] 2 O.R. 676, 6 D.L.R. (3d) 383 (H.C.); *Hills v. Hills* (1969), 1 R.F.L. 236, 1 N.S.R. (2d) 405, 9 D.L.R. (3d) 722, (sub nom. *H. v. H.)* (T.D.).

8§50 — Cruelty — drug addiction

The respondent husband's use of heroin and his refusal to stop taking the drug amounted to cruelty where the petitioner wife had been unaware of the drug addiction prior to marriage and it induced in her a revulsion such that she could not stand to be in the same room with her husband: *Bramley v. Bramley* (1974), 15 R.F.L. 152, 4 O.R. (2d) 503, 48 D.L.R. (3d) 367 (H.C.).

"I do not suggest or imply that the use of narcotics or selling them and living a 'hippy life' from the proceeds is *automatically* mental cruelty entitling the spouse to obtain a divorce. Such a proposition or conclusion would be ridiculous. But I am satisfied beyond the degree of proof required that the actions and attitudes of *this* man to *this* (well-bred, gentle and sensitive but sensible) woman resulted in a, perhaps short, but nevertheless vivid period of exquisite mental torture for her.": per Washington L.J.S.C. in *F. v. F.* (1970), 1 R.F.L. 167, 74 W.W.R. 241, 11 D.L.R. (3d) 621 (B.C. S.C.).

8§51 — Cruelty — drunkenness

Divorce Act, 1968

A finding of physical and mental cruelty was made where the respondent had, for a long time, not accepted any responsibility for the welfare of his family and had made numerous drunken assaults on the petitioner: *Reddigan v. Reddigan* (1972), 9 R.F.L. 322 (Ont. C.A.).

The petitioner was entitled to a decree *nisi* on the ground of cruelty where the respondent did not intend to be cruel but persisted in a course of continual drinking and failure to attend to his work which caused his wife great distress and where he became angry and violent when she remonstrated with him: *Grandy v. Grandy* (1972), 7 R.F.L. 69, 3 N.S.R. (2d) 750, 26 D.L.R. (3d) 359 (C.A.).

"In the present case it is the cumulative effect of the acts of the defendant upon the petitioner which must be considered and given proper weight. The wife's return to her home after a day's work only to find her husband in an inebriated state, given to quarrelsomeness and abuse, heaping insult upon insult and indignity upon indignity, was clearly conduct amounting to mental cruelty of such a kind as to render intolerable the continued cohabitation of the spouses": per Schroeder J.A. in *Knoll v. Knoll*, 1 R.F.L. 141, [1970] 2 O.R. 169, 10 D.L.R. (3d) 199 (C.A.).

See also *Dolson v. Dolson* (1985), 67 N.B.R. (2d) 348, 172 A.P.R. 348 (Q.B.); *Phillips v. Phillips (No. 1)* (1985), 168 A.P.R. 226, 56 Nfld. & P.E.I.R. 226 (Nfld. T.D.); *Kulyk v. Kulyk* (1980), 5 Sask. R. 235 at 238 (Q.B.); *Ferguson v. Ferguson* (1980), 16 R.F.L. (2d) 207, 28 Nfld. & P.E.I.R. 498, 79 A.P.R. 498 (P.E.I. S.C.); *Ramboer v. Ramboer* (1979), 11 R.F.L. (2d) 320 (Ont. H.C.); *Rushton v. Rushton* (1976), 28 R.F.L. 204, 14 N.B.R. (2d) 338 (Q.B.); *Day v. Day*, 18 R.F.L. 56, [1975] 3 W.W.R. 563 (Alta. T.D.); *Savelieff v. Savelieff*, 10 R.F.L. 292, [1973] 2 O.R. 808, 35 D.L.R. (3d) 364 (H.C.); *Knight v. Knight* (1969), 1 R.F.L. 51, 68 W.W.R. 464, 5 D.L.R. (3d) 438 (B.C. S.C.); *Quinn v. Quinn* (1970), 1 R.F.L. 129, 74 W.W.R. 144, 11 D.L.R. (3d) 372 (B.C. S.C.).

8§52 — Cruelty — gambling

Cruelty was established where a husband inflicted on his wife continuous neglect in order to indulge his addiction to card playing. His conduct indicated a conspicuous absence of normal kindness and consideration and had caused injury to his wife's health: *Rauch v. Rauch* (1975), 22 R.F.L. 143, 9 O.R. (2d) 761, 61 D.L.R. (3d) 633 (H.C.). See also *Westall v. Westall* (1949), 65 T.L.R. 337 (C.A.); cited in *Grandy v. Grandy* (1972), 7 R.F.L. 69, 3 N.S.R. (2d) 750, 26 D.L.R. (2d) 359 (C.A.).

8§53 — Cruelty — humiliation, harassment, criticism

Where the husband constantly criticized the wife throughout the marriage, making it intolerable for her to continue living with him, her petition on the grounds of cruelty was allowed: *Balasch v. Balasch* (1986), 50 Sask. R. 225 (U.F.C.); affirmed (1988), 73 Sask. R. 71 (C.A.).

Where a husband's employment necessitated his absence from home in the evenings and resulted in constant nagging, hostility and suspicion of infidelity on the part of his wife, he was granted his petition on the ground of mental cruelty: *Krause v. Krause*, 23 R.F.L. 219, [1976] 2 W.W.R. 622, 64 D.L.R. (3d) 352 (Alta. C.A.).

A husband was entitled to a divorce owing to the mental cruelty of his wife where he had suffered a nervous breakdown as a result of her false accusations of infidelity and lack of financial support, deprecatory remarks about his family, vulgar and obscene language and lack of respect from her children: *Chorny v. Chorny* (1971), 4 R.F.L. 347, [1971] 5 W.W.R. 732 (Alta. C.A.).

"The persistent and strong advances made by the wife for the sexual act could not, in my judgment, amount to cruelty. However, she knew from what the husband had told her that he had not yet adjusted himself to her demands. Despite his pleas she continued to make her demands and her repeated conduct in ridiculing his performances and belittling them by comparing his sexual efforts with her previous experiences with 'former men' and 'one of her previous lovers' put a definite and unequivocal stamp of cruelty on that course of conduct": per Banca J.A. in *Hock v. Hock*, 3 R.F.L. 353, [1971] 4 W.W.R. 262, 20 D.L.R. (3d) 190 (B.C. C.A.).

See also *Austin v. Austin* (1986), 77 N.B.R. (2d) 79, 195 A.P.R. 79 (Q.B.); *Ingram v. Ingram* (1985), 48 Sask. R. 157 (Q.B.); *Barbour v. Barbour* (1980), 18 R.F.L. (2d) 80, 27 Nfld. & P.E.I.R. 229, 74 A.P.R. 229 (Nfld. T.D.); *Wornath v. Wornath* (1980), 19 R.F.L. (2d) 289, 3 Sask. R. 266 (Q.B.); *Whetstone v. Whetstone* (1979), 9 R.F.L. (2d) 168, 17 A.R. 17 (T.D.); *Ellis v. Ellis* (1979), 12 R.F.L. (2d) 200, 35 N.S.R. (2d) 529, 62 A.P.R. 529 (T.D.); *Rodway v. Rodway* (1978), 3 R.F.L. (2d) 295 (Ont. H.C.); *Barrios v. Barrios* (1978), 4 R.F.L. (2d) 347, 28 N.S.R. (2d) 419 (T.D.); *Brewer v. Brewer* (1978), 21 N.B.R. (2d) 154, 37 A.P.R. 154 (Q.B.); *Turnbull v. Turnbull* (1976), 28 R.F.L. 92 (Man. Q.B.); *Rowe v. Rowe* (1976), 26 R.F.L. 91 (Ont. H.C.); *Pavlinek v. Pavlinek* (1975), 22 R.F.L. 236 (Ont. H.C.); *Zwicker v. Zwicker* (1971), 3 R.F.L. 333, 4 N.S.R. (2d) 249 (T.D.); *Ivany v. Ivany* (1970), 2 R.F.L. 172 (B.C. S.C.); *Ellis v. Ellis* (1970), 2 R.F.L. 186 (N.S. T.D.).

8§54 — Cruelty — hypochondria

A respondent's hypochondria which led to cessation of communication and joint activities between the spouses and rendered cohabitation intolerable to the petitioner was held not to be of sufficiently grave and weighty nature to constitute cruelty: *Hattie v. Hattie*, 3 R.F.L. 324, [1971] 2 W.W.R. 556, 18 D.L.R. (3d) 383 (B.C. S.C.).

8§55 — Cruelty — neglect

Where the husband was content to allow the wife to support the family and also tend the house, and then deserted her after encouraging her to become pregnant, the wife was granted a divorce on the ground of cruelty: *Spurr v. Brown* (1990), 99 N.S.R. (2d) 424, 270 A.P.R. 424 (T.D.).

Where the husband's violent outbreaks towards his wife and children was followed by lengthy periods of silence on his part the wife was found entitled to a divorce on the grounds of mental cruelty: *Tramsek v. Tramsek* (1994), 6 R.F.L. (4th) 66 (B.C. S.C.).

Where the husband admitted extra-marital affairs, was for the most part unemployed and left his wife to provide the support for the family, conducted any family matters which he undertook in a cruel and callous manner, displayed an irresponsible attitude to marriage and had no regard for his wife or children, a divorce was granted on the ground of cruelty: *Thordarson v. Thordarson* (1978), 5 R.F.L. (2d) 92 (Ont. C.A.).

The husband's habit of leaving home after the evening meal and not returning until the early hours of the morning was a wilful refusal to recognize his wife's right to his society, and his persistence in this course of conduct in the face of his wife's objections was a rejection of the marriage which constituted mental cruelty: *Foley v. Foley*, 1 R.F.L. 172, [1970] 3 O.R. 226, 12 D.L.R. (3d) 589 (C.A.).

See also *Shu-Jung (Quan) v. Dick (Quan)* (1982), 38 B.C.L.R. 68 (S.C.); *Bateman v. Bateman* (1979), 10 R.F.L. (2d) 63, 102 D.L.R. (3d) 374 (B.C. S.C.); *Mark v. Mark* (1973), 15 R.F.L. 73 (Ont. H.C.); *Durant v. Durant* (1971), 2 Nfld. & P.E.I.R. 138, 22 D.L.R. (3d) 488 (P.E.I. S.C.); *Morris v. Morris* (1970), 1 R.F.L. 164 (Man. Q.B.).

8§56 — Cruelty — philandering

A husband's conduct made life intolerable for his wife where he arranged accommodation for a fellow [female] bank employee in the apartment building where he and his wife lived, drove her to work, had meals with her, and generally was solicitous of and administered to her needs: *Wereley v. Wereley* (1979), 14 R.F.L. (2d) 193 (Ont. H.C.).

A wife's "close association" with another man which was carried on near her husband's business, and mistreatment of her husband which resulted in a deterioration in his health, constituted mental cruelty: *Chelin v. Chelin* (1975), 22 R.F.L. 254 (B.C. S.C.).

8§57 — Cruelty — physical violence

An isolated but serious assault may constitute physical cruelty provided that it was not condoned by the petitioner: *Aucoin v. Aucoin* (1976), 28 R.F.L. 43, 15 N.S.R. (2d) 399, 72 D.L.R. (3d) 674 (C.A.).

Evidence of physical assaults on three occasions was sufficient to make a finding of cruelty: *Nadeau v. Nadeau* (1972), 5 N.B.R. (2d) 854 (C.A.).

See also *Archibald v. Archibald* (1981), 48 N.S.R. (2d) 361, 92 A.P.R. 361 (T.D.); *Peskett v. Peskett* (1979), 14 R.F.L. (2d) 134 (B.C. S.C.); *Whetstone v. Whetstone* (1979), 9 R.F.L. (2d) 168 (Alta. T.D.); *King v. King* (1979), 9 R.F.L. (2d) 294 (Ont. H.C.); *Nash v. Nash* (1976), 28 R.F.L. 41 (Man. Q.B.); *McLean v. McLean* (1976), 14 Nfld. & P.E.I.R. 168 (Nfld. T.D.); *McMurdy v. McMurdy* (1975), 22 R.F.L. 312 (Ont. H.C.); *Jaworski v. Jaworski*, 10 R.F.L. 190, [1973] 2 O.R. 420, 34 D.L.R. (3d) 44 (H.C.); *Curran v. Curran* (1972), 3 Nfld. & P.E.I.R. 395 (Nfld. T.D.); *Novak v. Novak* (1969), 1 R.F.L. 58, 68 W.W.R. 524, (sub nom. *N. v. N.)* 24 D.L.R. (3d) 639 (B.C. S.C.).

8§58 — Cruelty — refusal of sexual intercourse

When a spouse has done everything asked of him to overcome the physical or psychological deficiencies causing impotency or sexual incapacity, that spouse cannot be said to treat the other with cruelty if he is not successful in effecting a change: *Anderson v. Anderson* (1971), 8 R.F.L. 299, [1972] 6 W.W.R. 53, 29 D.L.R. (3d) 587 (Alta. C.A.); affirmed 10 R.F.L. 200, [1973] 2 W.W.R. 668, 32 D.L.R. (3d) 128n (S.C.C.).

A husband's persistent refusal during a year of marriage to have sexual intercourse with his young wife, resulting in a deterioration in her mental and physical health, constituted cruelty: *Delaney v. Delaney*, 5 R.F.L. 44, [1972] 1 O.R. 34, 22 D.L.R. (3d) 149 (C.A.).

"I do not find any case where any Court has yet held that the wrongful refusal of sexual intercourse without anything in addition constitutes cruelty": per Disby J. in *Cundy v. Cundy* (September 30, 1970) (Sask. Q.B.); quoted in *Ebenal v. Ebenal*, 2 R.F.L. 180,

[1971] 1 W.W.R. 473, 15 D.L.R. (3d) 242 (Sask. Q.B.); affirmed 3 R.F.L. 303, [1971] 4 W.W.R. 474, 20 D.L.R. (3d) 545 (Sask. C.A.).

See also *Lewis v. Lewis* (1982), 44 N.B.R. (2d) 268, 116 A.P.R. 268 (Q.B.);*Rouleau v. Wells*, [1980] C.S. 915, 124 D.L.R. (3d) 766 (Que.); *Langtvet v. Langtvet* (1978), 7 R.F.L. (2d) 224 (Ont. H.C.); *Grove v. Grove* (1974), 19 R.F.L. 128 (B.C. S.C.); *Perry v. Perry* (1971), 1 Nfld. & P.E.I.R. 325 (P.E.I. S.C.); *Markus v. Markus*, 3 R.F.L. 306, [1971] 2 W.W.R. 35, 16 D.L.R. (3d) 520 (Sask. Q.B.); *Pawelko v. Pawelko* (1970), 1 R.F.L. 174, 74 W.W.R. 632, 12 D.L.R. (3d) 279 (Sask. Q.B.).

8§59 — Cruelty — refusal to have children

"The matter of the abortion is at the forefront of the husband's case. The abortion without the consent or knowledge of the husband was far from a trivial act. In my judgment, it was an act of a weighty nature. No doubt it had some emotional impact on the husband but I do not think that it had a really significant effect on his physical or mental health. And I am not persuaded that the matter of the abortion, standing alone or considered in conjunction with all the other circumstances of the case, rendered intolerable his continued cohabitation": per Pennell J. in *Elbaz v. Elbaz* (1980), 16 R.F.L. (2d) 336, 114 D.L.R. (3d) 116 (H.C.).

The respondent's refusal to agree to have a family and his annoyance during discussions on the subject constituted cruelty: *Mar v. Mar* (1979), 10 R.F.L. (2d) 267 (B.C. S.C.).

The respondent's refusal to have children, when he had previously agreed to have three or four, his insistence on his wife's consent to a vasectomy, and his refusal to have normal marital relations constituted cruel behaviour: *Bravery v. Bravery*, [1954] 1 W.L.R.1169, [1954] 3 All E.R. 59 (C.A.). *Bravery* indicated that for a husband to have a vasectomy, as the respondent in this case did, without the consent of the wife, especially one who was young and childless, could constitute cruelty: *P. v. P.* (1972), 7 R.F.L. 311, 4 N.B.R. (2d) 525 (Q.B.).

8§60 — Cruelty — religious intolerance

Cruelty was established where a wife, after 12 years of tranquil marriage, reverted to the religion of her youth with uncompromising zeal and made it a matter of principle to inculcate her four children with its tenets, despite the objection of her husband who thought that the children should have some choice. In the result, there were unfortunate incidents of ugly name-calling and physical confrontation and also the children's attitude toward their father was adversely affected: *Retzer v. Retzer*, 19 R.F.L. 365, [1975] 2 S.C.R. 881, 4 N.R. 159, 52 D.L.R. (3d) 159.

The actions of the husband in objecting to his wife's lifestyle as a result of his association with the Jehovah's Witnesses and her reaction of aggressiveness and hostility towards his activities and associates constituted mental cruelty on the part of both parties: *Peskett v. Peskett* (1979), 14 R.F.L. (2d) 134 (B.C. S.C.).

The respondent's abnormal religious adherence coupled with numerous instances of physical abuse and threats of abuse towards the petitioner with their seven children, which resulted in the petitioner being kept in a state of constant terror, constituted cruelty: *Bangert v. Bangert* (1977), 18 N.B.R. (2d) 327 (Q.B.).

A wife's overzealous attempts to persuade her husband to agree with and conform to her religious views, which resulted in constant quarrels and threats, constituted cruelty: *Giesbrecht v. Giesbrecht* (1974), 16 R.F.L. 399, 47 D.L.R. (3d) 767 (Sask. Q.B.).

8§61 — Cruelty — taciturnity

The actions of the petitioner in refusing to speak to his wife or communicate with her in any way in the household except by notes or letters, which led to a breakdown in her health, amounted to cruelty: *Cook v. Cook* (1975), 20 R.F.L. 134, 19 N.S.R. (2d) 681 (T.D.). For related proceedings confined to the issue of maintenance, see *Cook v. Cook* (1975), 26 R.F.L. 101, 13 N.S.R. (2d) 125 (C.A.).

There was no justification for a finding of cruelty where a wife felt her husband was "stagnating" merely because he was a passive, undemonstrative and uncommunicative person: *Shumila v. Shumila*, 21 R.F.L. 110, [1975] 5 W.W.R. 697, 60 D.L.R. (3d) 374 (Man. C.A.).

See also *Franzen v. Franzen* (1975), 22 R.F.L. 221 (Man. Q.B.); *Cavalier v. Cavalier* (1975), 25 R.F.L. 118 (B.C. S.C.); *Joell v. Joell* (1973), 9 R.F.L. 285 (Man. Q.B.).

8§62 — Mutual cruelty

"Where there is behaviour of a cruel nature, mental or physical, moving in both directions between spouses, one does not subtract one from the other and examine the net result. The gross behaviour of the defending spouse must be examined and, if found to constitute cruelty, will entitle the petitioning spouse to the relief sought though he or she may also have been cruel": per Goodridge J. in *Boulos v. Boulos* (1979), 14 R.F.L. (2d) 206, 24 Nfld. & P.E.I.R. 370, 65 A.P.R. 370 (Nfld. T.D.).

Each party established mental and physical cruelty on the part of the other spouse where their 10-year relationship had been one of continual fighting and discord, each had developed outside relationships causing the other mental anguish and each was physically violent to the other: *Dresen v. Dresen* (1979), 13 R.F.L. (2d) 97 (B.C. S.C.).

Mutual physical assaults occurring after the separation of the parties justified the granting of a decree to both husband and wife on the ground of cruelty: *McMurdy v. McMurdy* (1975), 22 R.F.L. 312 (Ont. H.C.).

9. (1) Duty of legal advisor — It is the duty of every barrister, solicitor, lawyer or advocate who undertakes to act on behalf of a spouse in a divorce proceeding

(a) to draw to the attention of the spouse the provisions of this Act that have as their object the reconciliation of spouses, and

(b) to discuss with the spouse the possibility of the reconciliation of the spouses and to inform the spouse of the marriage counselling or guidance facilities known to him or her that might be able to assist the spouses to achieve a reconciliation,

unless the circumstances of the case are of such a nature that it would clearly not be appropriate to do so.

(2) Idem — It is the duty of every barrister, solicitor, lawyer or advocate who undertakes to act on behalf of a spouse in a divorce proceeding to discuss with the spouse the advisability of negotiating the matters that may be the subject of a support order or a custody order and to inform the spouse of the mediation facilities known to him or her that might be able to assist the spouses in negotiating those matters.

(3) **Clarification** — Every document presented to a court by a barrister, solicitor, lawyer or advocate that formally commences a divorce proceeding shall contain a statement by him or her certifying that he or she has complied with this section.

9 — Duties of legal advisor

Section 9(1) imposes a duty on lawyers to discuss with their clients the possibility of reconciliation and to inform them of marriage counselling services that might be able to assist in achieving a reconciliation. Pursuant to s. 9(2), lawyers are required to discuss with their clients the advisability of negotiation of custody and support matters and to inform them of mediation facilities that might be able to assist them in arriving at a negotiated settlement.

10. (1) Duty of court, reconciliation — In a divorce proceeding, it is the duty of the court, before considering the evidence, to satisfy itself that there is no possibility of the reconciliation of the spouses, unless the circumstances of the case are of such a nature that it would clearly not be appropriate to do so.

(2) **Adjournment** — Where at any stage in a divorce proceeding it appears to the court from the nature of the case, the evidence or the attitude of either or both spouses that there is a possibility of the reconciliation of the spouses, the court shall

(a) adjourn the proceeding to afford the spouses an opportunity to achieve a reconciliation; and

(b) with the consent of the spouses or in the discretion of the court, nominate

(i) a person with experience or training in marriage counselling or guidance, or

(ii) in special circumstances, some other suitable person, to assist the spouses to achieve a reconciliation.

(3) **Resumption** — Where fourteen days have elapsed from the date of any adjournment under subsection (2), the court shall resume the proceeding on the application of either or both spouses.

(4) **Nominee not competent or compellable** — No person nominated by a court under this section to assist spouses to achieve a reconciliation is competent or compellable in any legal proceedings to disclose any admission or communication made to that person in his or her capacity as a nominee of the court for that purpose.

(5) **Evidence not admissible** — Evidence of anything said or of any admission or communication made in the course of assisting spouses to achieve a reconciliation is not admissible in any legal proceedings.

10 — Duty of Court — reconciliation

Section 10 imposes an obligation of the court to satisfy itself, before considering the evidence, that there is no possibility of reconciliation, and to adjourn the proceeding and nominate a person to assist the spouses to achieve a reconciliation where such a possibility appears to exist. Pursuant to s. 10(4), marriage counsellors nominated by the court to help the spouses achieve a reconciliation cannot be compelled to disclose any communication made to them in their capacity as nominee of the court. Section 10(5) provides that evidence of any admission or communication made in the course of assisting the spouses to achieve a reconciliation is inadmissible in any legal proceedings.

10§1 — One spouse seeking reconciliation

In *Roadburg v. Braut* (1994), 4 R.F.L. (4th) 96, 44 B.C.A.C. 173, 71 W.A.C. 173, 96 B.C.A.C. (2d) 150 (C.A.), the court allowed the wife's application to quash the husband's appeal from the decree of divorce. The husband had based his appeal on the fact that the trial judge had not formally asked the parties whether a possibility of reconciliation existed. As the trial judge, given the circumstances of the case, would have been satisfied that reconciliation was not an option, any formal inquiry would have been meaningless.

Where one of the spouses is opposed to reconciliation, a "reasonable prospect of reconciliation" under the *Divorce Act* cannot be found: *McDermid v. McDermid* (1989), 21 R.F.L. (3d) 47 (Sask. C.A.).

See also *MacKay v. MacKay* (1976), 10 Nfld. & P.E.I.R. 22 at 33 (P.E.I. C.A.); *Derbyshire v. Derbyshire*, 16 R.F.L. 82, [1974] 6 W.W.R. 437, 46 D.L.R. (3d) 752 (Alta. T.D.); *Derbyshire v. Derbyshire*, 16 R.F.L. 82, [1974] 6 W.W.R. 437, 46 D.L.R. (3d) 752 (Alta. T.D.); *Khalifa v. Khalifa* (1971), 4 N.S.R. (2d) 576, 19 D.L.R. (3d) 460 (T.D.); *Compton v. Compton* (1970), 1 R.F.L. 244, 1 N.S.R. (2d) 827 (T.D.); *Challoner v. Challoner* (1973), 12 R.F.L. 311, 5 N.S.R. (2d) 432 (C.A.); *Matthews v. Matthews* (1969), 1 N.S.R. 397 (T.D.).

10§2 — Procedure for determining possibility of reconciliation

Divorce Act, 1968

In *Roadburg v. Braut*, above, the court allowed the wife's application to quash the husband's appeal from the decree of divorce. The husband had based his appeal on the fact that the trial judge had not formally asked the parties whether a possibility of reconciliation existed. As the trial judge, given the circumstances of the case, would have been satisfied that reconciliation was not an option, any formal inquiry would have been meaningless.

"[T]he process [inquiry to ascertain if there is any possibility of reconciliation] if inquisitorial in nature, is limited to inquiries of the parties or perhaps only one of them — persons before the court in the ordinary course of events": per McLellan L.J.S.C. in *Trites v. Trites* (1971), 1 R.F.L. 296 at 303, 9 D.L.R. (3d) 246 (N.S. T.D.).

"It may be that in the majority of cases a few perfunctory questions will satisfy the requirements of s. 8 [now s. 10], but in [some] cases ... it seems to me that the court cannot discharge its duty without a searching inquiry. Most petitioners will simply state that no possibility of reconciliation exists, else why would they be proceeding with the action? The answer to the problem I have outlined may lie in the fact that the court ought to accept that statement as final and conclusive, but such acceptance does not seem to me to be discharging the positive duty laid on the court by s. 8 [now s. 10]. In [some] cases ... counsel may have to lead evidence covering many of the matters stated on the inquiry so that it becomes evidence in the cause": per McLelland L.J.S.C. in *Rushton v. Rushton* (1971), 1 R.F.L. 357 at 362–363 (N.S. T.D.).

If the court lacks jurisdiction to entertain a divorce petition, no action may be taken under s. 8 [now s. 10] of the Act even if during the course of the proceedings the possibility of reconciliation becomes apparent: *Cullen v. Cullen* (1970), 9 D.L.R. (3d) 610 (N.S. T.D.).

In *Fleming v. Fleming* (1968), 1 R.F.L. 332 at 333–334, 66 W.W.R. 124, 69 D.L.R. (2d) 710 (N.W.T. Terr. Ct.), the respondent could not be located at the time of trial. Morrow J. stated that "if the circumstances make it clearly not appropriate [to inquire into the possibility of reconciliation] then the Court presumably can launch into the proceedings without more ado. If not, then there must be a pre-hearing of some kind. On the assumption that one must be practical and with a view to trying to avoid having to hear some evidence twice, I limited the hearing in the present case to points involving domicile, service and the marriage status first and then, when it became apparent that reconciliation was out, proceeded to hear the evidence upon which the divorce was sought."

10§3 — Resumption of proceedings

Where the divorce proceedings are adjourned to permit a marriage counsellor to assist the parties to a possible reconciliation, the court must resume the proceedings at the request of one of the parties received 14 days subsequent to the adjournment, despite the other party's allegation that the resumption is premature: *Nash v. Nash* (1976), 28 R.F.L. 41 (Man. Q.B.).

10§4 — Communications made in the course of reconciliation efforts

While s. 10(5) of the *Divorce Act* prohibits the admission into evidence "in any legal proceeding" of events that occurred during a reconciliation attempt, the provision cannot operate to prohibit the admission of evidence in a property proceeding that is governed by a provincial statute: *Piercy v. Piercy* (1990), 29 R.F.L. (3d) 18, 50 B.C.L.R. (2d) 137 (S.C.).

The privilege accorded to communications made to a marriage counsellor under s. 21 [now s. 10] of the *Divorce Act*, is applicable only to communications made to a person nominated by the court under the Act. Where persons, outside the aegis of the court, have undertaken, by virtue of their profession and/or the special confidence of people, to assist in the reconciliation of broken marriages, the court should endeavour to respect confidences made to them and may exercise a discretion not to receive such evidence, otherwise admissible. This discretion must, however, be balanced against the overpowering necessity in our society for the fair and open administration of justice: *Cronkwright v. Cronkwright*, 2 R.F.L. 241, [1970] 3 O.R. 784, 14 D.L.R. (3d) 168 (H.C.). See also *Shakotko v. Shakotko* (1976), 27 R.F.L. 1 at 10 (Ont. H.C.); refusing to follow *Cronkwright v. Cronkwright*, above; *Robson v. Robson*, [1969] 2 O.R. 857, 7 D.L.R. (3d) 289 (H.C.).

Statements made during the course of marriage counselling should not be referred to in an action for divorce: *de Araujo v. de Araujo* (1986), 11 C.P.C. (2d) 272 (Ont. Master).

Where subsequent to the commencement of divorce proceedings both parties met and communicated with a particular witness, the husband with a view toward reconciliation and the wife wishing to settle a problem regarding access, it was held that such communications were protected by privilege. Although the intentions of the parties in communicating with the witness differed, both were concerned with the attempt to settle differences relating to the litigation with the result that such communications were by implication "without prejudice": *Keizars v. Keizars* (1982), 29 R.F.L. (2d) 223 (Ont. U.F.C.).

11. (1) **Duty of court, bars** — In a divorce proceeding, it is the duty of the court

(a) to satisfy itself that there has been no collusion in relation to the application for a divorce and to dismiss the application if it finds that there was collusion in presenting it;

(b) to satisfy itself that reasonable arrangements have been made for the support of any children of the marriage, having regard to the applicable guidelines, and, if such arrangements have not been made, to stay the granting of the divorce until such arrangements are made; and

(c) where a divorce is sought in circumstances described in paragraph 8(2)(b), to satisfy itself that there has been no condonation or connivance on the part of the spouse bringing the proceeding, and to dismiss the application for a divorce if that spouse has condoned or connived at the act or conduct complained of unless, in the opinion of the court, the public interest would be better served by granting the divorce.

(2) **Revival** — Any act or conduct that has been condoned is not capable of being revived so as to constitute a circumstance described in paragraph 8(2)(b).

(3) **Condonation** — For the purposes of this section, a continuation or resumption of cohabitation during a period of, or periods totalling, not more than ninety days with reconciliation as its primary purpose shall not be considered to constitute condonation.

(4) **Definition of "collusion"** — In this section, **"collusion"** means an agreement or conspiracy to which an applicant for a divorce is either directly or indirectly a party for the purpose of subverting the administration of justice, and includes any agreement, understanding or arrangement to fabricate or suppress evidence or to deceive the court, but does not include an agreement to the extent that it provides for separation between the parties, financial support, division of property or the custody of any child of the marriage.

1997, c. 1, s. 1.1

11 — Bars to divorce

Section 11, which imposes a duty on the court to dismiss a divorce application in certain situations, in effect creates three bars to divorce. Pursuant to s. 11(1)(a), the spouses' collusion in relation to a divorce application will act as an absolute bar to divorce.

Section 11(1)(b) empowers the court to stay the granting of a divorce until such time as it is satisfied that reasonable arrangements have been made for the support of any children of the marriage and directs the court to dismiss the application if no such arrangements can be made.

The third bar to divorce arises where condonation or connivance has taken place with respect to the act or conduct relied on as the basis for establishing marriage breakdown. In that situation, the court has a duty, pursuant to s. 11(1)(c), to dismiss the application unless the public interest would be better served by granting the divorce.

The "definition" provides that a continuation or resumption of cohabitation during a period of, or periods totalling, not more than 90 days with reconciliation as the primary purpose will not constitute condonation.

In *B. (G.) v. B. (M.)* (1988), 19 R.F.L. (3d) 283 (Que. C.A.), the appellant was allowed to amend a notice of appeal in a custody action to request a declaration that s. 11(1)(c) of the *Divorce Act*, 1968 was unconstitutional as infringing the *Canadian Charter of Rights and Freedoms*.

11§1 — Reasonable arrangements for support of children

In *Orellana v. Merino* (1998), 40 R.F.L. (4th) 129 (Ont. Gen. Div.), the court refused to lift a stay of divorce proceedings which had been imposed on the basis that appropriate financial arrangements for the children had not been made. The wife continued to make no efforts to seek reasonable child support and accordingly there was no basis upon which the court could exercise its discretion to lift the stay.

The *Divorce Act*, s. 11(l)(b) requires the court "to satisfy itself that reasonable arrangements have been made for the support of any children of the marriage, having regard to the applicable guidelines, and, if such arrangements have not been made, to stay the granting of the divorce until such arrangements are made." Where the applicant cannot locate the respondent, and cannot obtain information about his income or ability to meet his child support obligations, it is in the best interests of the child to allow the applicant and the child to "get on" with their lives rather than to stay the proceedings in the hope of support the respondent might give, if found and forced to pay: *Zarebski v. Zarebski* (1997), 29 R.F.L. (4th) 93 (Sask. Q.B.). The benefit to the child of allowing the divorce to be granted outweighs the court's responsibility to oversee the creation of appropriate support arrangements between the parents. The section requires the court to "have regard" to the guidelines, not to apply them in absolutely all cases.

In *Ninham v. Ninham* (1997), 29 R.F.L. (4th) 41 (Ont. Gen. Div.), the parties, both of whom had Native status, had a split custody arrangement, with two children living with the father and one child with the mother. The father had an imputed income of $50,000 but had in the past refused to respect court orders for support. The court was not satisfied that the father would honour a child support order in this proceeding or that the mother would attempt to enforce the child support order. Accordingly, the court stayed the parties' divorce under s. 11(1)(b) of the *Divorce Act* until such arrangements could be made. Because the divorce was stayed, the court was of the opinion that support ought to be granted under the *Family Law Act* but the parties had requested that the court determine the support under the *Federal Child Support Guidelines* and an order was made requiring child support payments of $200 per month.

Cases decided before the enactment of the Federal Child Support Guidelines:

In *Reid v. Reid* (1995), 11 R.F.L. (4th) 85, 3 B.C.L.R (3d) 266, 56 B.C.A.C. 234, 92 W.A.C 234 (B.C. C.A.), the court held than an award of $100 a month payable by the husband for the maintenance of the four children of the marriage was inadequate. The court was of the opinion that this award failed to meet the duty imposed by s. 11(1)(b) of the *Divorce Act*, as the court had not satisfied itself that reasonable arrangements had been made for the support of the children. On the appeal, the court ordered that the proper amount payable by the father was $300 a month per child, which was to be charged against the husband's interest in the home.

The power to stay a divorce should not be exercised to make minor changes to a child support agreement between parents where it is evident that they have both understood and recognized the child's interest. Where the trial judge had stayed the divorce out of concern over the mother's income and the effect it might have in the future upon her ability to meet her agreed upon support obligations, the court removed the stay upon the father's appeal. The parents were responsible, reasonable and intelligent people and should the mother experience financial problems, it was not likely that the father would allow the child to suffer: *Geddert v. Geddert* (1993), 50 R.F.L. (3d) 102, 88 Man. R. (2d) 168, 51 W.A.C. 168 (C.A.).

Arrangements for support of children must be in place at the time the divorce is granted and the reasonableness of those arrangements is the proper concern of the Court. Section 11(1)(b) of the *Divorce Act*, 1985 is broader than s. 9(1)(e) of the 1968 *Divorce Act* in that it goes beyond the requirement that there be a connection between the granting of the divorce and the making of reasonable arrangements for support. In most cases where the parties have settled matters of corollary relief, having benefitted from independent legal advice, and the divorce is undefended, extensive evidence will not be required to satisfy the court that the arrangements for child support are reasonable. However, the required evidence must be primary evidence establishing the factual situation and not merely subjective opinions: *Money v. Money* (1987), 5 R.F.L. (3d) 375, 45 Man. R. (2d) 308 (C.A.).

Where no claim for child support is made in a petition for divorce and where there is an agreement providing for child support, no order for additional support should be made against a spouse unless the court is satisfied that the spouse is aware than an order for additional support is being contemplated. Even where a judge is not satisfied under s. 11(1)(b) of the Act that reasonable child support arrangements have been made, an additional order should not be made without notice to the payor: *Anderson v. Anderson* (1987), 11 R.F.L. (3d) 260 (N.B. C.A.).

The policy of the *Divorce Act*, 1985 is to encourage marital settlements. While the court possesses jurisdiction under the Act to review provisions for child support, separation agreements are not unenforceable or irrelevant in considering child support. The onus rests on the party contesting the agreement to show that the provisions for child support do not provide adequately for the children or that the agreement is not in their best interests: *Silverman v. Silverman* (1987), 7 R.F.L. (3d) 292 (N.S. C.A.).

In *Almeida v. Almeida* (1995), 11 R.F.L. (4th) 131, 166 A.R. 248 (Alta. Q.B.), the wife, in her Petition for Divorce requested child support be paid in the amount of $400 per month per child, but did not define the amount as a net or gross figure. The court ruled that the amount was a net amount. The court was of the opinion that if the court were wrong, it would take jurisdiction to amend the Petition to increase the relief claimed to $470 per month and if the court were limited by the figure of $400 a month for each child, it would be required to stay the divorce action pursuant to s. 11(1)(b) of the *Divorce Act.*

The court may stay a judgment for divorce under s. 11(1)(b) of the Act on the basis that reasonable child support arrangements have not been made if the payor spouse does not pay the amount of child support that he or she should be paying on a means and needs analysis: *Dumas v. Dumas* (1992), 43 R.F.L. (3d) 260, 134 A.R. 311 (Q.B.).

In *Tomlinson v. Tomlinson* (1992), 12 C.P.C. (3d) 8 (Ont. Gen. Div.), the court refused an application for a summary judgment of divorce and severance of corollary relief issues for separate trial. There was no evidence presented through which the court could conclude that satisfactory arrangements had been made for support of the children.

Where the wife had failed to respond either to the husband's petition for divorce or his offer of child support, the husband's petition was allowed, even though the child support offered was insufficient. As the husband wished to remarry immediately, no useful social purpose would be served by denying him the divorce. However, to protect the child, the support offer would be incorporated into an interim order only, permitting the wife to pursue full child support as she wished: *Archibald v. Archibald* (1991), 38 R.F.L. (3d) 310 (Ont. Gen. Div.).

Where the husband had quit his job under circumstances indicating his wish to avoid support payments, the court refused to grant a divorce based upon the parties' child support agreement. As the support was inadequate given the family's needs and the husband's previous income, the divorce was stayed pending the making of reasonable child support arrangements: *Eddy v. Eddy* (1992), 39 R.F.L. (3d) 339 (Alta. Q.B.).

In *McMillan v. McMillan* (1991), 126 A.R. 3 (Q.B.), the court refused to grant the wife's petition for divorce on the basis that the court was unable to make a determination that reasonable child support arrangements were in place. The mother, who was on social assistance, had accepted the husband's child support offer of $75 monthly for each of the parties' four children, but had failed to place before the court any financial information relating to the husband.

In determining the reasonableness of child support arrangements, the court should consider such factors as the impact of income tax on the support order, whether the custodial parent is receiving social assistance and whether the payment to be received constitutes an objective minimum level of contribution: *Harper v. Harper* (1991), 78 D.L.R. (4th) 548 (Ont. Gen. Div.).

The granting of a divorce will be stayed where the spouses agree that no support will be payable and where no evidence is tendered to satisfy the court that there is a "reasonable arrangement" for the support of the children. The court will not guess at the financial position of the parties: *Kenny v. Kenny* (1990), 107 N.B.R. (2d) 91, 267 A.P.R. 91 (Q.B.).

An order dispensing with the service of a petition for divorce will not be granted where children are involved and where the order would undermine the parliamentary intent of insuring that reasonable child support arrangements have been made: *L. (D.C.) v. L. (S.M.)* (1990), 108 A.R. 334 (Q.B.).

A motion for summary judgment for divorce will be dismissed where it is evident that adequate arrangements for child support have not been made: *Bourgeois v. Bourgeois* (1990), 104 N.B.R. (2d) 269, 261 A.P.R. 269 (Q.B.).

A divorce petition which fails to make reasonable arrangements for child support as required under s. 11(1)(b) of the Act may not be corrected by way of an affidavit made by the petitioner's counsel. Until the conditions of s. 11(1)(b) are met, the petition remains stayed: *Savoie v. Savoie* (1989), 101 N.B.R. (2d) 431, 254 A.P.R. 431 (Q.B.).

It is not required that the parties file statements of their financial affairs in order for the court to discharge its duty under s. 11(1) of the *Divorce Act: Palansky v. Palansky* (1989), 60 Man. R. (2d) 141 (Q.B.).

In divorce proceedings supported by affidavit evidence the petitioner must adduce evidence to allow the court to discharge its duty to ensure that reasonable arrangements for child support have been made. It is improper to simply allege that reasonable arrangements have been made without giving sufficient evidence for the court to make a decision. As well, all supporting documents should be neatly and completely filled out:

Bergman v. Bergman (1987), 8 R.F.L. 93d) 94 (N.S. T.D.). See also *Shultz v. Shultz* (1978), 8 R.F.L. (3d) 22 (Man. Q.B.); *MacKinnon v. MacKinnon* (1986), 78 N.S.R. (2d) 361, 193 A.P.R. 361 (T.D.).

The court will not "rubber stamp" a consent order dealing with child custody and support in the absence of evidence dealing with the best interests of the children: *Hayes v. Hayes* (1987), 6 R.F.L. (3d) 138 (Sask. Q.B.); *Wallace v. Wallace*, 9 R.F.L. 393 at 395–396, [1973] W.W.R. 763 (Alta. T.D.); *Secord v. Secord* (1972), 5 N.B.R. (2d) 583 (Q.B.); *Williams v. Williams* (1970), 5 R.F.L. 72, 11 D.L.R. (3d) 326 (N.S. T.D.).

The requirements of s. 11(1)(b) of the *Divorce Act* can be satisfied by a court order whereby child support issues are set down for hearing by the court and the divorce judgment granted: *Marinovic v. Marinovic* (1989), 20 R.F.L. (3d) 404 (Ont. H.C.). See also *Webb v. Webb* (1987), 11 B.C.L.R. (2d) 357 (S.C.).

Consent orders are not binding on the court in discharge of its responsibility under s. 11(1)(b) of the *Divorce Act*: *K. (L.A.) v. K. (G.N.)* (1987), 12 B.C.L.R. (2d) 9 (S.C.). See also *P. (L.W.) v. P. (T.M.)* (1987), 7 R.F.L. (3d) 110, 12 B.C.L.R. (2d) 12 (S.C.) in which the court refused to accept, without further evidence, the quantum of child support specified in the parties separation agreement; and *W. (D.M.), v. W. (H.W.)* (1987), 12 B.C.L.R. (2d) 19 (S.C.), in which the court refused to grant a desk order divorce without further evidence of the adequacy of child support agreed upon by the parties.

The requirements of s. 11(1)(b) of the *Divorce Act* are entirely for the benefit of the children, and the fact that an arrangement may artificially minimize the contribution of a non-custodial spouse in order to preserve welfare benefits for the custodial spouse will not always be considered unreasonable so as to require the granting of a divorce to be stayed. However, where the non-custodial parent can well afford to pay more, the burden should not be transferred to the state: *Simpson v. Simpson* (1987), 8 R.F.L. (3d) 216, 14 B.C.L.R. (2d) 116 (S.C.).

Where the husband and wife had agreed to the husband paying less than appropriate child support as the wife was wrongfully receiving public assistance, the husband's petition for divorce by affidavit was nevertheless granted. There was no ground to refuse the divorce on the basis that the respondent was in breach of another law and, as far as the child was con cerned, the support arrangements were reasonable and the child would be properly supported: *P. (L.W.) v. P. (T.M.)* (1987), 7 R.F.L. (3d) 110, 12 B.C.L.R. (2d) 12 (S.C.).

Under the *Divorce Act, 1985* the court has an obligation to satisfy itself that reasonable arrangements for child support have been made. The reasonableness of arrangements must be determined in the context not just of the spouses but in all the circumstances which include such items as assistance from other family members or friends, social assistance and other relevant circumstances. In such instances, the court should not simply "rubber stamp" an application for a desk order divorce: *F. (R.D.) v. F. (S.L.)* (1987), 6 R.F.L. (3d) 413, 12 B.C.L.R. (2d) 1, 34 D.L.R. (4th) 732 (S.C.).

11§2 — "Collusion"

"The appellant testified that a few months after January 1970 she wrote the respondent saying she wanted a divorce; to this communication he replied in writing. His reply according to the appellant was 'he told me to go ahead and get it'. This exchange of letters does not appear to have constituted an agreement between the parties amounting to collusion, that is, an agreement to subvert the administration of justice, or that otherwise is collusive within the meaning of the s. 2(c) [now 11(4)] of the *Divorce Act*. It is merely the not uncommon notice by one spouse to another that he or she intends to try to get a divorce and a reply by the other indicating no intention to oppose such an attempt to obtain a divorce": per Macdonald J.A. in *Burgoyne v. Burgoyne* (1974), 14 R.F.L. 92, 8 N.S.R. (2d) 142 (C.A.).

An agreement between the co-respondent and the respondent husband to commit adultery so that a divorce would be obtained against the husband is not collusive in proceedings brought by the petitioning wife who is not a party to the agreement: *Milne v. Milne*, [1970] 1 O.R. 381, 8 D.L.R. (3d) 439 (C.A.).

See also *Gillett v. Gillett* (1979), 9 R.F.L. (2d) 97 at 117, 9 Alta. L.R. (2d) 238 (T.D.); *Campbell v. Campbell* (1968), 2 R.F.L. 120, 67 W.W.R. 191, 2 D.L.R. (3d) 708 (Sask. Q.B.); *Tannis v. Tannis* (1969), [1970] 1 O.R. 323, 8 D.L.R. (3d) 333 (H.C.).

11§3 — Connivance

"There is no definition of connivance in [the Act]. ... It is therefore necessary to refer to the cases involved. See *Maddock v. Maddock*, [1958] O.R. 810 (C.A.) and *Richmond v. Richmond*, [1952] W.N. 188, [1952] 1 All E.R. 838. Discussion between the parties with reference to leading separate lives does not go far enough to be considered to be connivance": per Proudfoot J. in *Davies v. Davies* (1980), 17 R.F.L. (2d) 130 at 136 (B.C. S.C.).

"The learned trial Judge appeared to be of the opinion that at any time a petitioner becomes aware that adultery may take place it is incumbent upon the petitioner to stop it or become disentitled to any relief by reason of connivance. In our view, that is not the law": per Gale C.J.O. in *Fleet v. Fleet*, 7 R.F.L. 355 at 356, [1972] 2 O.R. 530, 26 D.L.R. (3d) 134 (C.A.).

"It will be convenient and helpful to state certain propositions or principles of law respecting connivance. ... 1. Connivance may consist of any act done with corrupt intention of a husband or wife to promote or encourage either the initiation or the continuance of adultery of his or her spouse, or it may consist of passive acquiescence in such adultery. 2. Corrupt intention of the husband or wife seeking a divorce is an essential ingredient of connivance, and the conduct of the husband or wife seeking the divorce must show that he or she, as the case may be, willingly consented to the adultery of the other spouse. 3. The issue is whether on the facts of the particular case, the husband or wife seeking the divorce was or was not guilty of the corrupt intention of promoting or encouraging either the initiation or the continuance of the adultery of the other spouse. 4. Acts done by a husband or wife seeking a divorce or by any person employed by him or her, as the case may be, to keep watch on the other spouse to see whether or not his suspicions of adultery are well-founded or unfounded, do not necessarily constitute connivance and, likewise, if one spouse does nothing without lulling into a sense of security, the other spouse about whom he or she, as the case may be, is suspicious, but merely watches her, he is not guilty of passive acquiescence amounting to connivance. 5. The Court should not allow its judgment to be affected by importing, as principles of universal application, pronouncements made with regard to wholly different circumstances and be led to a conclusion contrary to the justice of the case. ... 6. There is a presumption of law against the existence of connivance and the Court should not find a spouse guilty of connivance unless the evidence shows clearly that all the essential ingredients thereof exist in the particular facts under consideration": per Laidlaw J.A. in *Maddock v. Maddock*, [1958] O.R. 810 at 818, 16 D.L.R. (2d) 325 (C.A.).

In *Berger v. Berger* (1974), 17 R.F.L. 88 (B.C. S.C.) McKay J. dismissed the petition where the evidence disclosed beyond question that the husband connived at the wife's adultery.

11§4 — Condonation — essentials and meaning

Condonation requires a reconciliation of the spouses. Where the husband resumes cohabitation out of his desire to avoid liability for maintenance and the wife does so out of her desire for economic security, a finding of condonation is excluded, even though sexual intercourse has taken place: *Boisvert v. Marineau*, [1974] C.A. 391 (Qué.).

Three elements are necessary to constitute condonation: (1) A knowledge by the innocent spouse of the matrimonial offence committed by the other spouse; (2) an intention by the innocent spouse to forgive and remit the offence; and, (3) a reinstatement by the innocent spouse of the guilty spouse to his or her former marital position: *Leaderhouse v. Leaderhouse*, 4 R.F.L. 174, [1971] 2 W.W.R. 180, 17 D.L.R. (3d) 315 (Sask. Q.B.). See also *MacDougall v. MacDougall*, 3 R.F.L. 175, [1970] 3 O.R. 680, 13 D.L.R. (3d) 696 (C.A.); *Roschuk v. Roschuk* (1979), 12 R.F.L. (2d) 34 (Man. Q.B.); varied (1980), 15 R.F.L. (2d) 196 (Man. C.A.).

Where the husband's adultery, alleged in the divorce petition, had occurred eight years previously and the parties had continued to cohabit for six years, the wife's petition was refused on the ground of condonation: *Desrosiers v. Landry*, [1980] C.S. 356 (Qué.).

Whether or not, as a matter of fact, a matrimonial offence has been condoned is to be decided upon a consideration of all the relevant evidence. The onus is on the petitioner to establish that the adultery has not been condoned. This onus will not be discharged where it is not proven that the wife had not known that the act of adultery had taken place when she continued to cohabit with her husband as man and wife: *Seltenrich v. Seltenrich* (1977), 4 R.F.L. (2d) 169 (Sask. Q.B.).

The burden is on the petitioner to establish by a preponderance of evidence that there was no condonation. In the present case, it was held that the actions of the petitioner in continuing to live with her husband for three months after the last act of cruelty, visiting with him and accompanying him on short trips subsequent to their separation, were inconsistent with her statements that she did not forgive him and constituted condonation of the cruelty: *Sergeant v. Sergeant* (1974), 7 N.S.R. (2d) 670, 33 D.L.R. (3d) 734 (T.D.).

See also *Mackrell v. Mackrell*, [1948] 2 All E.R. 858 (C.A.); *Nielsen v. Nielsen*, 2 R.F.L. 109, [1971] 1 O.R. 393, 15 D.L.R. (3d) 423 (H.C.); *Crosby v. Crosby* (1971), 6 R.F.L. 8 (Ont. H.C.); *L'Hoir v. L'Hoir* (1978), 2 R.F.L. (2d) 23 (B.C. S.C.).

Condonation was not found where the wife went back to the husband on many occasions and attempted to arrange marriage counselling but there was no indication that she forgave him: *Horner v. Horner* (1972), 13 R.F.L. 110, 5 N.S.R. (2d) 776 (T.D.); affirmed (1973), 13 R.F.L. 110 at 117, 5 N.S.R. (2d) 757, 40 D.L.R. (3d) 685 (C.A.).

11§5 — Condonation — reconciliation requirement

In *Droit de la famille — 1382*, [1991] R.D.F. 171 (C.S. Qué.), it was found that the wife's return to the home for a period exceeding 90 days, as a result of mediation attempts in their divorce proceeding, did not constitute condonation. As nothing had changed in the husband's behaviour, the parties could not be said to have reconciled.

See also *Ingram v. Ingram* (1985), 48 Sask. R. 157 (Q.B.); *Barber v. Barber*, [1978] 4 W.W.R. 411 at 416, (sub nom. *B. v. B.)* 10 A.R. 181 (T.D.); *L'Hoir v. L'Hoir* (1978), 2 R.F.L. (2d) 23 (B.C. S.C.); *Douglas v. Douglas*, 27 R.F.L. 29, [1977] 1 W.W.R. 95 (Man. Q.B.); *McAllister v. McAllister* (1976), 14 N.B.R. (2d) 552 (Q.B.); *Henderson v. Henderson*, 29 R.F.L. 1, [1977] 3 W.W.R. 316 (B.C. Prov. Ct.); *Douglas v. Douglas*, 27 R.F.L. 29, [1977] 1 W.W.R. 95 (Man. Q.B.); *Strachan v. Strachan* (1969), 72 W.W.R. 383, 10 D.L.R. (3d) 780 (B.C. S.C.); *Goldstein v. Goldstein* (1970), 15 D.L.R. (3d) 95 (Alta. T.D.).

11§6 — Condonation — forgiveness requirement

"The nature of the forgiveness required [as a prerequisite to a finding of condonation] is forgiveness in the legal sense as implying that the legal remedy for the wrong is waived by the injured spouse": per Sirois J. in *Seltenrich v. Seltenrich* (1977), 4 R.F.L. (2d) 169 at 172 (Sask. Q.B.).

"Condonation is said to be a conclusion of fact not of law and means complete forgiveness of a matrimonial offence, followed by cohabitation, the whole being done with full knowledge of all the circumstances of the particular offence forgiven": per Nicholson J. in *Profit v. Profit* (1971), 1 Nfld. & P.E.I.R. 431 at 437 (P.E.I. S.C.).

The test for condonation must be the extent of forgiveness that the innocent spouse extends to the erring respondent. This can to some extent be measured by the reception or association that the innocent party extends to the other by word or act. ... The important consideration must be, has forgiveness been granted and confirmed by reinstatement of the erring one in the position that he occupied prior to knowledge of the offence: per Grant J. in *Tingey v. Tingey*, 2 R.F.L. 99 at 104, [1970] 3 O.R. 179, 12 D.L.R. (3d) 559 (H.C.).

11§7 — Evidence of condonation — sexual intercourse

A wife does not condone her husband's matrimonial offence by having sexual intercourse with him where there is no forgiveness or intent to forgive: *Grandy v. Grandy* (1972), 7 R.F.L. 69, 3 N.S.R. (2d) 750, 26 D.L.R. (3d) 359 (C.A.). See also *Poisson v. Poisson* (1982), 16 Man. R. (2d) 379 (Q.B.); *MacDougall v. MacDougall*, 3 R.F.L. 175, [1970] 3 O.R. 680, 13 D.L.R. (3d) 696 (C.A.); *Leaderhouse v. Leaderhouse*, 4 R.F.L. 174, [1971] 2 W.W.R. 180, 17 D.L.R. (3d) 315 (Sask. Q.B.).

"While an isolated act of cruelty would be condoned by resumption of sexual relations, acts of cruelty forming a continuing pattern when viewed in retrospect are not so condoned. The parties are duty bound to attempt to preserve the marriage and this necessarily involves resuming normal married life. The performance of this duty does not amount to condonation": per Goodridge J. in *Sheppard v. Sheppard* (1976), 15 Nfld. & P.E.I.R. 279 at 281, 38 A.P.R. 279 (Nfld. T.D.). See also *Profit v. Profit* (1971), 1 Nfld. & P.E.I.R. 431 (P.E.I. S.C.).

"[I]t is my opinion that intercourse between husband and wife in a bona fide attempt to reconcile with full knowledge of a previous matrimonial offence is merely some evidence from which a court can infer condonation. It is not conclusive": per Galligan J. in *Nielsen v. Nielsen*, 2 R.F.L. 109 at 115, [1971] 1 O.R. 393, 15 D.L.R. (3d) 423 (H.C.). See also *Tait v. Tait* (1981), 2 F.L.R.A.C. 38 (Ont. H.C.); *H. v. H.* (1976), 30 R.F.L. 122 (Ont. H.C.); *Pellegrini v. Pellegrini* (1976), 30 R.F.L. 293 (Ont. H.C.).

Condonation was established where the wife admitted that for a period of approximately one month after the alleged admissions she continued to sleep with her husband and had sexual relations with him about six times. She also agreed in cross-examination that they continued on in much the same way that they had done before: *Lalonde v. Lalonde* (1974), 15 R.F.L. 133 (Sask. Q.B.). See also *Blue v. Blue*, 5 R.F.L. 31, [1971] 2 W.W.R. 238, 17 D.L.R. (3d) 226 (Sask. Q.B.).

Where a husband and wife had previously established a life together without engaging in sexual intercourse, the wife condones her husband's adultery when she continues these same arrangements after learning of the offence. Sexual intercourse between the spouses is not a necessary element of condonation. The important question is whether forgiveness has been granted and confirmed by the reinstatement of the erring spouse to the position that he or she occupied prior to the knowledge of the offence: *Tingey v. Tingey*, 2 R.F.L. 99, [1970] 3 O.R. 179, 12 D.L.R. (3d) 559 (H.C.).

11§8 — Condonation of cruelty

Mere cohabitation or even sexual intercourse does not in law establish condonation. Where the cruelty complained of is a continuing course of conduct, such cruelty can only be condoned when it ceases to continue and is replaced by reconciliatory conduct. Repeated acts of physical cruelty without continuing mental cruelty encompassing them are in a quite different category, where only the last uncondoned act of physical cruelty has to be adjudged in granting or refusing a decree: *Aucoin v. Aucoin* (1976), 28 R.F.L. 43, 15 N.S.R. (2d) 399, 72 D.L.R. (3d) 674 (C.A.). See also *Sheppard v. Sheppard* (1976), 15 Nfld. & P.E.I.R. 279 at 280, 38 A.P.R. 279 (Nfld. T.D.); *McLean v. McLean* (1976), 14 Nfld. & P.E.I.R. 168 at 173, 33 A.P.R. 168 (Nfld. T.D.); *Boulos v. Boulos* (1979), 14 R.F.L. (2d) 206, 24 Nfld. & P.E.I.R. 370 (Nfld. T.D.).

Where the wife had no other place to reside and no money to pay for alternate accommodation, her return to the matrimonial home following an assault did not amount to condonation of her husband's previous conduct: *Khader v. Khader* (1975), 20 R.F.L. 365 (Ont. C.A.). See also *Francescutti v. Francescutti* (1976), 24 R.F.L. 378 at 388 (B.C. S.C.); *Nelles v. Nelles* (1970), 2 R.F.L. 153 (Ont. H.C.); *Wellsby v. Wellsby*, [1975] W.W.D. 160, 53 D.L.R. (3d) 476 at 477 (B.C. S.C.).

See also *Cress v. Cress* (1981), 25 R.F.L. (2d) 59 (Ont. H.C.); *Morrow v. Morrow* (1981), 36 N.B.R. (2d) 117, 94 A.P.R. 117 (Q.B.); supplementary reasons at (1981), 36 N.B.R. (2d) 117 at 128, 94 A.P.R. 117 at 128 (Q.B.); *Franzen v. Franzen* (1975), 22 R.F.L. 221 (Man. Q.B.); *Woerz v. Woerz* (1974), 17 N.S.R. (2d) 679 (T.D.); *McMurdy v. McMurdy* (1975), 22 R.F.L. 312 (Ont. H.C.); *McGowan v. McGowan* (1972), 2 Nfld. & P.E.I.R. 413 (P.E.I. S.C.); *Humphries v. Humphries* (1984), 49 Nfld. & P.E.I.R. 1, 145 A.P.R. (Nfld. U.F.C.); *H. v. H.* (1976), 30 R.F.L. 122 (Ont. H.C.).

11§9 — Condonation — burden of proof

"The burden is on the petitioner to establish, by a preponderance of evidence, that there was no condonation": per Cowan C.J.T.D. in *Sargeant v. Sargeant* (1972), 7 N.S.R. (2d) 670 at 676, 33 D.L.R. (3d) 734 (T.D.). See also *Francescutti v. Francescutti* (1976), 24 R.F.L. 378 at 388 (B.C. S.C.); *McLean v. McLean* (1976), 14 Nfld. & P.E.I.R. 168, 33 A.P.R. 168 (Nfld. T.D.); *Seltenrich v. Seltenrich* (1977), 4 R.F.L. (2d) 169 (Sask. Q.B.).

11§10 — Condonation — divorce granted in public interest

"My view is that no benefit to the public can result from keeping the parties to these proceedings bound together in marriage but that, on the contrary, the public interest requires their release from a marriage which ... has brought the parties a great measure of unhappiness ... a marriage, moreover, which has not the slightest chance of bringing benefit to anyone if it is forced to continue": per Robertson J.A. in *Allan v. Allan* (1971), 7 R.F.L. 96 at 98, 25 D.L.R. (3d) 253 (B.C. C.A.). See also *Mark v. Mark* (1973), 15 R.F.L. 73 (Ont. H.C.).

The matters to be considered by the court in determining whether or not to exercise its discretion to grant a divorce in spite of evidence of condonation include the interest of the community at large, to be judged by maintaining a true balance between respect for the binding sanctity of marriage and the social considerations which make it contrary to public policy to insist on the maintenance of a union which has utterly broken down: *Ellis v. Ellis*, [1968] 2 O.R. 843, 1 D.L.R. (3d) 46 (C.A.), applying criteria first designated in *Blunt v. Blunt*, [1943] A.C. 517, [1943] 2 All E.R. 76 (H.L.). See also *Trites v. Trites* (1969), 1 R.F.L. 296, 9 D.L.R. (3d) 246 (N.S. T.D.); *VanZoost v. VanZoost* (1969), 1 N.S.R. 390, 7 D.L.R. (3d) 373 (T.D.); *Bonin v. Bonin* (1969), 1 R.F.L. 65, 1 N.S.R. 529, 5 D.L.R. (3d) 533 (T.D.); *Croft v. Croft* (1971), 1 R.F.L. 136, 10 D.L.R. (3d) 267 (N.S. T.D.).

In *Terhorst v. Terhorst* (1986), 47 Sask. R. 102 (Sask. Q.B.), the court granted the husband a divorce on the grounds of adultery, despite the fact that he had earlier condoned the matrimonial offence. The marriage had subsequently broken down without a hope of reconciliation and accordingly the public interest was better served by the granting of the petition.

See also *Watkins v. Watkins* (1980), 14 R.F.L. (2d) 97, 25 Nfld. & P.E.I.R. 98, 68 A.P.R. 98 (Nfld. T.D.); *Ifield v. Ifield*, 24 R.F.L. 237 at 247–248, [1976] W.W.D. 63, 66 D.L.R. (3d) 311 (Sask. Q.B.).

See also *Saunders v. Saunders*, 22 R.F.L. 210 at 213, [1975] W.W.D. 135, 58 D.L.R. (3d) 763 (Man. Q.B.); *Kell v. Kell* (1969), 1 N.S.R. (2d) 307 at 309 (T.D.); *Goldstein v. Goldstein* (1970), 15 D.L.R. (3d) 95 at 98 (Alta. T.D.); *Beach v. Beach*, 2 A.R. 561, [1977] 3 W.W.R. 274 (T.D.); *Gross v. Gross* (1977), 2 A.R. 440 (T.D.); *Francescutti v. Francescutti* (1976), 24 R.F.L. 378 at 389 (B.C. S.C.); *Davidiuk v. Davidiuk* (1971), 4 R.F.L. 170 (B.C. S.C.); *Osborne v. Osborne* (1973), 14 R.F.L. 61 (Sask. Q.B.); varied (1974), 23 R.F.L. 358 (Sask. C.A.); *Nielsen v. Nielsen*, 2 R.F.L. 109, [1971] 1 O.R. 393, 15 D.L.R. (3d) 423 (H.C.). And see *Jaworski v. Jaworski*, 10 R.F.L. 190, [1973] 2 O.R. 420, 34 D.L.R. (3d) 44 (H.C.); *Getson v. Getson* (1970), 2 R.F.L. 91, 2 N.S.R. (2d) 65, 12 D.L.R. (3d) 525 (T.D); *Harasyn v. Harasyn* (1970), 2 R.F.L. 105 at 106, 13 D.L.R. (3d) 635 (Sask. Q.B.); *Bennett v. Bennett* (1968), 69 D.L.R. (2d) 341 (N.S. T.D.); *B. v. D.*, [1971] Qué. S.C. 413 at 417.

11§11 — Condonation before effective date of divorce

"I hold the view that a matrimonial offence which was the ground for a decree nisi is capable of being condoned thereafter — up to the date of the decree absolute. I can see nothing in the words or concept of the Divorce Act to justify another view": per MacPherson J. in *Brown v. Brown*, 2 R.F.L. 116 at 117, [1971] 1 W.W.R. 236, 15 D.L.R. (3d) 382 (Sask. Q.B.). See also *Einarson v. Einarson*, 4 R.F.L. 355, [1971] 5 W.W.R. 478, 20 D.L.R. (3d) 126 (B.C. S.C.).

11§12 — Doctrine of revival

Since s. 9(2) [now s. 11(2)] deals with both "act or conduct", mental cruelty can be established as the prohibition in s. 9(2) [now s. 11(2)] against revival does not apply to stop revival of each separate daily act making up the accumulation of effect. In regard to physical cruelty, only the last uncondoned act of physical cruelty is at issue in granting or refusing a decree, subject to s. 9(1)(c) [now s. 11(1)(c)]: *Aucoin v. Aucoin* (1976), 28 R.F.L. 43 at 48, 15 N.S.R. (2d) 399, 72 D.L.R. (3d) 674 (C.A.).

Although a condoned act of cruelty cannot be revived, s. 9(2) [now s. 11(2)] will not act as a bar to divorce on the ground of subsequent cruelty: *Hunt v. Hunt* (1970), 73 W.W.R. 158 (B.C. C.A.).

Condoned actions cannot be revived as a ground for an action in divorce. However, such evidence may be looked at to give a total picture of the marriage: *Storey v. Storey* (1973), 10 R.F.L. 170, 4 Nfld. & P.E.I.R. 229 (P.E.I. S.C.).

See also *Profit v. Profit* (1971), 1 Nfld. & P.E.I.R. 431 at 437 (P.E.I. S.C.); *O'Connell v. O'Connell* (1972), 2 Nfld. & P.E.I.R. 497 (P.E.I. S.C.); *Leaderhouse v. Leaderhouse*, 4 R.F.L. 174 at 177–178, [1971] 2 W.W.R. 180, 17 D.L.R. (3d) 315 (Sask. Q.B.); *Croft v. Croft* (1970), 1 R.F.L. 136, 10 D.L.R. (3d) 267 (N.S. T.D.);*Olson v. Olson* (1971), 4 R.F.L. 86, [1971] 3 W.W.R. 506 (Sask. Q.B.); *Crosby v. Crosby* (1971), 6 R.F.L. 8 at 9 (Ont. H.C.); *Jaworski v. Jaworski*, 10 R.F.L. 190 at 191, [1973] 2 O.R. 420, 34 D.L.R. (3d) 44 (H.C.); *H. v. H.* (1976), 30 R.F.L. 122 (Ont. H.C.); *Lyons v. Lyons* (1970), 1 R.F.L. 328 at 331 (N.S. T.D.).

11§13 — Stay of proceedings

Where the granting of a divorce in Canada could adversely affect the wife's ability to pursue claims for property and return of dowry in India, the divorce action was adjourned. The prejudice to the wife which would arise if the divorce was granted prior to the determination of her claims in India far outweighed any prejudice to the husband: *Bhullar v. Bhullar* (1997), 33 R.F.L. (4th) 163, 49 B.C.L.R. (3d) 147 (S.C.).

In *Battiston v. Battiston* (1986), 62 C.B.R. (N.S.) 58 (B.C. S.C.), the court dismissed an application by a trustee in bankruptcy of a company for an order staying the granting of a decree *nisi* between the company's principal and his wife and setting aside a mortgage granted by the company to the wife. The order sought would either result in the improper retrial of the action or vexatiously obstruct or prolong the true course of justice.

11§14 — Orders striking petitions for divorce

In *Jacobs v. Jacobs* (1996), 22 R.F.L. (4th) 11 (Ont. C.A.); leave to appeal refused (1996), 97 O.A.C. 238 (note), 204 N.R. 395 (note) (S.C.C.) the court dismissed the husband's appeal from on order striking the husband's petition for divorce. The husband had failed to meet interim support obligations previously ordered and allowing him a trial on the merits of the divorce would undermine the proper enforcement of those interim orders.

12. (1) Effective date generally — Subject to this section, a divorce takes effect on the thirty-first day after the day on which the judgment granting the divorce is rendered.

(2) Special circumstances — Where, on or after rendering a judgment granting a divorce,

(a) the court is of the opinion that by reason of special circumstances the divorce should take effect earlier than the thirty-first day after the day on which the judgment is rendered, and

(b) the spouses agree and undertake that no appeal from the judgment will be taken, or any appeal from the judgment that was taken has been abandoned,

the court may order that the divorce takes effect at such earlier time as it considers appropriate.

(3) Effective date where appeal — A divorce in respect of which an appeal is pending at the end of the period referred to in subsection (1), unless voided on appeal, takes effect on the expiration of the time fixed by law for instituting an appeal from the decision on that appeal or any subsequent appeal, if no appeal has been instituted within that time.

(4) Certain extensions to be counted — For the purposes of subsection (3), the time fixed by law for instituting an appeal from a decision on an appeal includes any extension thereof fixed pursuant to law before the expiration of that time or fixed thereafter on an application instituted before the expiration of that time.

(5) No late extensions of time for appeal — Notwithstanding any other law, the time fixed by law for instituting an appeal from a decision referred to in subsection (3) may not be extended after the expiration of that time, except on an application instituted before the expiration of that time.

(6) Effective date where decision of Supreme Court of Canada — A divorce in respect of which an appeal has been taken to the Supreme Court of Canada, unless voided on the appeal, takes effect on the day on which the judgment on the appeal is rendered.

(7) Certificate of divorce — Where a divorce takes effect in accordance with this section, a judge or officer of the court that rendered the judgment granting the divorce or, where that judgment has been appealed, of the appellate court that rendered the judgment on the final appeal, shall, on request, issue to any person a certificate that a divorce granted under this Act dissolved the marriage of the specified persons effective as of a specified date.

(8) Conclusive proof — A certificate referred to in subsection (7), or a certified copy thereof, is conclusive proof of the facts so certified without proof of the signature or authority of the person appearing to have signed the certificate.

12 — Effective date of divorce

Generally, a divorce granted by the court will take effect, pursuant to s. 12(1), on the 31st day after the day on which the judgment granting the divorce was rendered. At the conclusion of the prescribed waiting period, the divorce judgment becomes effective automatically, with no further steps required from the spouses.

Under s. 12(2) however, the court has jurisdiction to order that the divorce take effect at such earlier time as it considers appropriate where there are "special circumstances" and the spouses undertake not to appeal the judgment.

12§1 — Earlier effective date — special circumstances

In *Lester v. Lester* (1983), 26 Man. R. (2d) 249 (Q.B.), the wife's request that the decree absolute be issued at the hearing was granted. As the wife's parents disapproved of her living with another man while still married and accordingly refused to visit her, it was found that the parent's conduct was not in the best interests of the wife's child.

In *Baker v. Baker* (1982), 17 Sask. R. 101 (Q.B.), an immediate decree absolute was granted to permit the respondent husband to marry his paramour prior to the birth of their child.

"I have also been asked to grant an immediate absolute on the basis of the expressed desire of the [wife] to remarry at an early date, specifically on the 26th day of this month. Her intended spouse ... also expressed the desire to marry at that time, and I accept the evidence of each of them in that regard without hesitation, and I think it is in their interest specifically and the public interest generally that a decree absolute should issue forthwith": per Maloney J. in *Bowler v. Bowler* (1977), 4 R.F.L. (2d) 27 at 27 (Ont. H.C.).

Paragraphs (a) and (b) of s. 13(2) [now s. 12(2)] operate disjunctively and both the undertaking and the finding of public interest must be present before the court "may fix a shorter time after which the decree may be made absolute" [now "may order that the divorce takes effect at such earlier time as it considers appropriate"]. There is no overriding discretion to grant the decree in the absence of one of the factors: *Feigal v. Feigal* (1976), 29 R.F.L. 347 (B.C. S.C.). See also *Krawec v. Krawec* (1976), 28 R.F.L. 36 at 36 (Alta. T.D.); *Flannigan v. Flannigan* (1976), 26 R.F.L. 331 at 332 (B.C. S.C.).

The desirability of expediting and facilitating immigration is a special circumstance which the court could consider in assessing whether it would be in the public interest for a decree absolute to be made at trial: *Barba v. Barba* (1976), 30 R.F.L. 93 (B.C. S.C.).

Where an application is made under s. 13(2) [now s. 12(2)] of the *Divorce Act* to abridge the three-month period after the decree *nisi*, and where the "special circumstances" claimed involve the welfare of infant children, it is incumbent upon the court to satisfy itself by the best evidence that it is in the best interests of the children, in all respects, that an exception be made in their favour: *Hughes v. Hughes* (1975), 24 R.F.L. 265, 10 Nfld. & P.E.I.R. 170 (P.E.I. S.C.).

Where the respondent spouse is pregnant and about to give birth to a child, and the co-respondent acknowledges that he is the father of such child, and if a decree absolute is not granted immediately, the petitioner will be presumed to be the father of this child who is about to be born, these are special circumstances and it would be in the public interest for a decree absolute to be granted at this time: *Longmuir v. Longmuir* (1974), 19 R.F.L. 117 at 118 (Ont. H.C.).

"[C]ontemplated re-marriage is the normal circumstance following a divorce. It is only when there are other circumstances coupled with that intention that the case is one where special circumstances may exist. Even when special circumstances exist before relief from the three-month period can be granted those special circumstances must show that the public interest will be served": per Galligan J. in *Hansford v. Hansford* (1972), 9 R.F.L. 233 at 238, [1973] 1 O.R. 116, 30 D.L.R. (3d) 392 (H.C.). See also *Eaton v. Eaton* (1972), 8 R.F.L. 399 (Ont. H.C.), in which the court was not satisfied that the request for the immediate decree absolute arose from stated anxiety about the health of the child.

"At the conclusion of the trial both counsel joined in an application to make the decree of divorce absolute immediately, on the grounds that this protracted litigation should come to an early end and that it was in the public interest that the parties should be free to start new lives without further delay. I agree and grant the request": per Dechene J. in *Wener v. Wener* (1970), 5 R.F.L. 87 at 95, 75 W.W.R. 721 (Alta T.D.); *Barca v. Barca* (1972), 9 R.F.L. 78 at 79–80 (Alta. T.D.).

"I am of the opinion that the [fact that the petitioner planned immediately to leave the jurisdiction and that the respondent was resident in England] are not 'special circumstances', by reason of which it would be in the public interest for the decree to be made absolute before the expiration of the period of three months, referred to in s. 13(1) [now s. 12(1)] of the *Divorce Act.* While it is true that the petitioner will be away from Nova Scotia when the three-month period expires, it is necessary only for him to complete an affidavit at that time and to mail it back to Halifax, and an application can then be made to make absolute the decree *nisi* of divorce. The fact that both parties wish to have the decree made absolute at this time is not a special circumstance, as such a desire usually exists in divorce proceedings, particularly where both agree and undertake that no appeal will be taken from the decree nisi of divorce": per Cowan C.J.T.D. in *Norton v. Norton* (1970), 2 R.F.L. 59 at 63, 2 N.S.R. (2d) 358, 14 D.L.R. (3d) 489 (T.D.); *Baia v. Baia*, 1 R.F.L. 348 at 356, [1970] 3 O.R. 165, 12 D.L.R. (3d) 545 (H.C.).

Where the petitioner's wife deserted him for his own brother with whom she is now living and the petitioner wants to marry another woman and adopt her child and have the child take his name before she enters school in the fall, these are special circumstances and it would be in the public interest to allow the decree to be made absolute at once, provided the parties undertake that no appeal will be taken from the decree *nisi*: *Cooper v. Cooper* (1969), 1 R.F.L. 338 at 344, 1 N.S.R. 638, 6 D.L.R. (3d) 240 (T.D.). See also *Patterson v. Patterson* (1967), 1 N.S.R. 627 (T.D.), wherein the application for an immediate decree absolute was refused on the ground that it was made merely to suit the convenience of the parties and enable the petitioner and her intended spouse to take advantage of a Navy marriage allowance.

A special exception to s. 13(1) [now s. 12(1)] is created by s. 13(2) [now s. 12(2)], but before a case is dealt with under this exception there must be a finding of special circumstances and public interest. The mere fact that parties have been separated for six years is not by itself a special circumstance involving the public interest: *Teskey v. Teskey* (1968), 1 R.F.L. 385, 67 W.W.R. 134 (Man. Q.B.).

12§2 — Earlier effective date — undertaking not to appeal

Where the three-month period between the granting of the decrees *nisi* and absolute was ordered abridged conditional upon the wife's giving of an undertaking not to appeal, the decree absolute issued without the wife's undertaking was ordered set aside on her application. This was ordered despite the fact that the legitimacy of the husband's new marriage was thereby rendered doubtful and the fact that the husband was now able to obtain a new decree absolute immediately: *Bridgens v. Bridgens* (1984), 43 R.F.L. (2d) 432, 30 Man. R. (2d) 277 (C.A.).

Where an early decree absolute was granted without obtaining the necessary consent regarding the appeal, the decree absolute was a nullity and should be set aside. In the instant case, neither party had acted upon the decree absolute and remarried: *Dusome v. Dusome*, 10 R.F.L. 340, [1973] 3 O.R. 45, 35 D.L.R. (3d) 678 (H.C.).

12§2A — Lifting stay of divorce

Section 12(3) of the *Divorce Act* establishes that the divorce is not effective until an appeal has been determined and the time for further appeal has expired. A party cannot rely upon R. 15 of the Saskatchewan Rules of the Court of Appeal to lift the stay imposed under the *Divorce Act*: *Bast v. Bast* (1990), 30 R.F.L. (3d) 181 (Sask. C.A.).

12§3 — Finality of divorce

In *MacPherson v. MacPherson* (1976), 28 R.F.L. 106 O.R. (2d) 233, 70 D.L.R. (3d) 564 (C.A.), the court favourably entertained the husband's application to set aside a decree *nisi* upon establishing that the petitioner wife had failed to fulfil the residency requirements prescribed by the Act. Although a decree absolute had issued, the setting aside of the decree *nisi* rendered the absolute a nullity.

"In my respectful opinion the judgment of Fraser J. setting aside the decree absolute cannot stand. ... [A]s pointed out by Fraser J., a decree absolute is a judgment in rem which affects the status of the parties. In this case, unknown to Fraser J., the judgment has been acted upon. The petitioner and the present Mrs. Chadderton married in the belief that the decree absolute was valid and the present Mrs. Chadderton in particular is entitled to be protected if at all possible in her status as the lawful wife of the petitioner": per Arnup J. in *Chadderton v. Chadderton*, 8 R.F.L. 374 at 386, [1973] 1 O.R. 560, 31 D.L.R. (3d) 656 (C.A.).

12§4 — Reconciliation

The court has jurisdiction to stay a judgment of divorce as a result of the parties' reconciliation after the granting of the judgment but before it takes effect, notwithstanding the absence of an express provision in the *Divorce Act*: *Fraser v. Fraser* (1989), 23 R.F.L. (3d) 30 (Ont. H.C.).

12§5 — Notice of appeal

A motion to set aside a default judgment for divorce is not the same as an appeal. Accordingly, the time limit for filing a notice of appeal specified in s. 12(5) of the *Divorce Act* is not applicable: *Polsinelli v. Polsinelli* (1992), 11 O.R. (3d) 541 (Gen. Div.).

13. Legal effect throughout Canada — On taking effect, a divorce granted under this Act has legal effect throughout Canada.

14. Marriage dissolved — On taking effect, a divorce granted under this Act dissolves the marriage of the spouses.

14§1 — General

Where a spouse dies after the decree *nisi*, but before the decree absolute is issued, it is not necessary to issue the final decree. The marriage has, in effect, been dissolved by the death: *Droit de la famille — 1211* (1988), [1989] R.D.F. 156 (C.S. Qué.).

COROLLARY RELIEF

Interpretation

15. Definition of "spouse" — In section 15.1 to 16, **"spouse"** has the meaning assigned by subsection 2(1), and includes a former spouse.

1997, c. 1, s. 2

Child Support Orders

15.1 (1) Child support order — A court of competent jurisdiction may, on application by either or both spouses, make an order requiring a spouse to pay for the support of any or all children of the marriage.

(2) Interim order — Where an application is made under subsection (1), the court may, on application by either or both spouses, make an interim order requiring a spouse to pay for the support of any or all children of the marriage, pending the determination of the application under subsection (1).

(3) Guidelines apply — A court making an order under subsection (1) or an interim order under subsection (2) shall do so in accordance with the applicable guidelines.

(4) Terms and conditions — The court may make an order under subsection (1) or an interim order under subsection (2) for a definite or indefinite period or until a specified event occurs, and may impose terms, conditions or restrictions in connection with the order or interim order as it thinks fit and just.

(5) Court may take agreement, etc., into account — Notwithstanding subsection (3), a court may award an amount that is different from the amount that would be determined in accordance with the applicable guidelines if the court is satisfied

(a) that special provisions in an order, a judgment or a written agreement respecting the financial obligations of the spouses, or the division or transfer of their property, directly or indirectly benefit a child, or that special provisions have otherwise been made for the benefit of a child; and

(b) that the application of the applicable guidelines would result in an amount of child support that is inequitable given those special provisions.

(6) Reasons — Where the court award, pursuant to subsection (5), an amount that is different from the amount that would be determined in accordance with the applicable guidelines, the court shall record its reasons for having done so.

(7) Consent orders — Notwithstanding subsection (3), a court may award an amount that is different from the amount that would be determined in accordance with the applicable guidelines on the consent of both spouses if it is satisfied that reasonable arrangements have been made for the support of the child to whom the order relates.

(8) Reasonable arrangements — For the purposes of subsection (7), in determining whether reasonable arrangements have been made for the support of a child, the court shall have regard to the applicable guidelines. However, the court shall not consider the arrangements to be unreasonable solely because the amount of support agreed to is not the same as the amount that would otherwise have been determined in accordance with the applicable guidelines.

1997, c. 1, s. 2

Spousal Support Orders

15.2 (1) **Spousal support order** — A court of competent jurisdiction may, on application by either or both spouses, make an order requiring a spouse to secure or pay, or to secure and pay, such lump sum or periodic sums, or such lump sum and periodic sums, as the court thinks reasonable for the support of the other spouse.

(2) **Interim order** — Where an application is made under subsection (1), the court may, on application by either or both spouses, make an interim order requiring a spouse to secure or pay, or to secure and pay, such lump sum or periodic sums, or such lump sum and periodic sums, as the court thinks reasonable for the support of the other spouse, pending the determination of the application under subsection (1).

(3) **Terms and conditions** — The court may make an order under subsection (1) or an interim order under subsection (2) for a definite or indefinite period or until a specified event occurs, and may impose terms, conditions or restrictions in connection with the order as it thinks fit and just.

(4) **Factors** — In making an order under subsection (1) or an interim order under subsection (2), the court shall take into consideration the condition, means, needs and other circumstances of each spouse, including

(a) the length of time the spouses cohabited;

(b) the functions performed by each spouse during cohabitation; and

(c) any order, agreement or arrangement relating to support of either spouse.

(5) **Spousal misconduct** — In making an order under subsection (1) or an interim order under subsection (2), the court shall not take into consideration any misconduct of a spouse in relation to the marriage.

(6) **Objectives of spousal support order** — An order made under subsection (1) or an interim order under subsection (2) that provides for the support of a spouse should

(a) recognize any economic advantages or disadvantages to the spouses arising from the marriage or its breakdown;

(b) apportion between the spouses any financial consequences arising from the care of any child of the marriage over and above any obligation for the support of any child of the marriage;

(c) relieve any economic hardship of the spouses arising from the breakdown of the marriage; and

(d) in so far as practicable, promote the economic self-sufficiency of each spouse within a reasonable period of time.

1997, c. 1, s. 2

Priority

15.3 (1) Priority to child support — Where a court is considering an application for a child support order and an application for a spousal support order, the court shall give priority to child support in determining the applications.

(2) Reasons — Where, as a result of giving priority to child support, the court is unable to make a spousal support order or the court makes a spousal support order in an amount that is less than it otherwise would have been, the court shall record its reasons for having done so.

(3) Consequences of reduction or termination of child support order — Where, as a result of giving priority to child support, a spousal support order was not made, or the amount of a spousal support order is less than it otherwise would have been, any subsequent reduction or termination of that child support constitutes a change of circumstances for the purposes of applying for a spousal support order, or a variation order in respect of the spousal support order, as the case may be.

1997, c. 1, s. 2

COROLLARY RELIEF — Order for Support

15§1 — General

Corollary relief consists of child support (s. 15.1), spousal support (s. 15.2), and custody of, and access to children (s. 16). See also the definition of "corollary relief proceeding" in s. 2(1). Orders made for corollary relief are never final and may be later varied to accommodate changed circumstances: s. 17.

The law of child support was completely changed by the amendments in 1997 to the *Divorce Act* and by the establishment, at the same time, of the *Federal Child Support Guidelines*. These changes are dealt with under CHILD SUPPORT, below. Except for relatively minor procedural matters such as requiring the court to distinguish in its orders between child and spousal support, and to give priority to child support, the law of spousal support is unchanged by the amendments and the guidelines. The *Federal Child Support Guidelines* are the applicable guidelines throughout the country unless local guidelines are established by a province or a territory and specified pursuant to s. 2(5) of the *Divorce Act* for divorce purposes. As of the date of this release, Quebec is the only province or territory that has taken advantage of this provision.

Section 4(1) of the *Divorce Act*, as amended in 1993, provides that a corollary relief proceeding may be brought in any province in which either spouse is ordinarily resident at the time of the commencement of the proceedings or in a province in which both spouses accept the jurisdiction of the court. If a divorce proceeding contains a claim for an order under s. 16 (custody or access) which is contested, and the child is most substantially connected with another province, the court of original jurisdiction may on application of a spouse or on its own motion, transfer the proceeding to that other province (s. 6(2)) and that province then has exclusive jurisdiction to hear and determine the proceeding: s. 6(4).

The Act contemplates the possibility of a joint application by both spouses as well as the ordinary case of one spouse proceeding against the other: See s. 15.1(1), s. 15.2(1) and s. 16(1).

The right to corollary relief comes into existence at the time of divorce, but need not be joined with a claim for divorce and need not be heard at the time of the divorce. A corollary relief claim may be the subject of a proceeding independent of the divorce and commenced on a date after the date the divorce is obtained. It may be brought by a former spouse, as well as a spouse: s. 15.

Since, pursuant to s. 4, a court may grant corollary relief once a divorce has been granted to the spouses, generally practitioners should join with the claim for corollary relief in the petition a claim, in the alternative, for support under provincial legislation. Then, if the claim for a divorce is dismissed and the court is without corollary relief jurisdiction, it may proceed to exercise its jurisdiction under the provincial legislation on the alternative claim.

There is no time specified in the Act within which a corollary relief claim must be brought. Whether the court will hear a claim commenced long after the divorce has been granted is not a matter of jurisdiction — the jurisdiction continues indefinitely — but a question of whether defences based on that delay and other circumstances are available. Severing the claim for corollary relief from its dependence on a claim for divorce, and giving it an existence of its own, creates the possibility of three distinct proceedings under the *Divorce Act*:

1. a divorce proceeding,
2. a corollary relief proceeding, and
3. a variation proceeding.

Although the right exists, it would be a mistake on the practitioner's part to separate the proceedings of divorce and corollary relief unless there is good reason to do so. The ordinary rule of avoiding multiplicity of proceedings, if nothing else, compels the joining of the claims in one proceeding. It would be questionable strategy to think in terms of obtaining an "easy" divorce first and then, with the certificate of divorce in hand, to launch an original claim for corollary relief of support or custody. If the proceeding for divorce and the proceeding for corollary relief can reasonably be joined in one combined proceeding that is the procedure likely to be enforced through penalties in costs, or worse, in default of joinder, through some risk to the success of the second proceeding.

Parties, through their legal advisors, are encouraged to avoid litigating corollary issues and to attempt negotiated resolutions. In the document that commences a divorce proceeding, the lawyer with carriage of the proceeding must certify that he or she has discussed with the client the advisability of negotiating a settlement of the matters that may be the subject of a support order or a custody order, and must inform the client of the mediation facilities known to him or her that might assist the spouses in negotiating a settlement of those matters: s. 9(2).

The fact that the court incorporates into the decree *nisi* a provision requiring the husband to make mortgage payment does not necessarily mean that the court intended such payments to constitute support. Accordingly, where the wife obtains a judgment to enforce the payments and the husband subsequently declares bankruptcy, the order is not necessarily protected under s. 148 of the *Bankruptcy and Insolvency Act* as a liability for maintenance: *Miller, Re* (1980), 11 Alta. L.R. (2d) 376, 34 C.B.R. (N.S.) 172, 11 D.L.R. (3d) 571 (Q.B.); reversed in part (1981), 36 Alta. L.R. (3d) 29, [1996] 3 W.W.R. 421 (C.A.).

Where the payor spouse dies before expiration of a limited term support order, the divorce judgment constituted a charge against the estate because of its temporal specificity.

Open-ended orders would terminate on death, requiring the payee spouse to pursue a claim under provincial succession legislation: *Brubacher v. Brubacher Estate* (1997), 30 R.F.L. (4th) 276, 18 E.T.R. (2d) 296, 33 O.T.C. 241 (Ont. Gen. Div.).

Jurisdiction

15§2 — General

Support is awarded in corollary relief proceedings. The court "has jurisdiction to hear and determine a corollary relief proceeding if

(a) either former spouse is ordinarily resident in the province at the commencement of the proceeding; or

(b) both former spouses accept the jurisdiction of the court": *Divorce Act*, s. 4(1)(a) and (b).

Where two corollary relief proceedings are commenced on different days, the court in which the first proceeding was commenced has exclusive jurisdiction to hear and determine the matter: *Divorce Act*, s. 4(2).

Where two proceedings are commenced on the same day, the Federal Court — Trial Division has exclusive jurisdiction over the matter: *Divorce Act*, s. 4(3).

A support order may be made by a "court of competent jurisdiction": s. 15.1(1), s. 15.2(1) and s. 16(1). This is the court as defined in s. 2(1). It may make the order "if (a) either former spouse is ordinarily resident in the province at the commencement of the proceeding; or (b) both former spouses accept the jurisdiction of the court": s. 4(1). The wording of this subsection points to a further jurisdictional requirement. The support, custody or access order must be made after a divorce has been granted. This is made clear from the wording used to describe the parties; they are described not as "spouses", but as "former spouses". However, an interim order may be made before divorce, while they are still spouses. See s. 15.1(2), s. 15.2(2) and s. 16(2). The divorce may have been granted in the immediate past as where the claim for support is joined with a claim for divorce in the same proceeding and the divorce is granted first with the order for support made an instant later, or in the more distant past where the support claim is brought in an independent proceeding commenced on a date after the date of the granting of the divorce.

The jurisdiction section, s. 4(1), enables the court of a province that did not grant the divorce to award support and other corollary relief if either the elements in (a) or (b), above, are present. This is a change from where the legislation stood prior to an amendment in 1993. The old provision (now repealed) limited the right to grant corollary relief to the court of the province which granted the divorce. See JURISDICTION IN COROLLARY RELIEF PROCEEDINGS.

An order for support under s. 15(2) of the *Divorce Act* can be granted after a divorce order has been made and entered. The definition of "spouse" in s. 15(1) of the Act clearly supports such an approach: *Delaney v. Delaney*, 11 R.F.L. (4th) 155, 2 B.C.L.R. (3d) 227, [1995] 4 W.W.R. 599, 122 D.L.R. (4th) 439, 55 B.C.A.C. 258, 90 W.A.C. 258, 1995 CarswellBC 24, [1995] B.C.J. No. 307 (C.A.).

Where the original divorce decree is silent on the issue of child support, a subsequent support application should be treated as an original application and not a request for variation: *Hamonic v. Hamonic* (1992), 103 Sask. R. 29 (Q.B.).

Where a respondent claims lack of resources to pay interim support, the court is entitled to grant possession to the petitioner of a residential property owned or controlled by the respondent: *Huculak v. Huculak* (1994), 8 R.F.L. (4th) 400, 53 B.C.A.C. 170, 87 W.A.C. 170 (C.A.).

Affidavits filed in interim support proceedings should be concise and to the point and not filled with inadmissible opinions: *Weinberger v. Weinberger* (1995), 11 R.F.L. (4th) 9 (Sask. Q.B.).

15§3 — Jurisdiction to make support orders

Where the parties' settlement agreement had been incorporated into a consent order under provincial legislation but had not been incorporated in the divorce judgment, the wife was not required to prove a change of circumstances in her subsequent application for support under the *Divorce Act*: *Fraticelli v. Fraticelli* (2000), 4 R.F.L. (5th) 222, 2000 CarswellNB 19 (C.A.).

There is no jurisdiction under the *Divorce Act* to make a support order retroactive to a date prior to the commencement of divorce proceedings: *Young v. Young* (2000), 7 R.F.L. (5th) 228, 225 N.B.R. (2d) 272, 578 A.P.R. 272, 2000 CarswellNB 85 (C.A.).

Section 4 of the *Divorce Act* prevents a chambers judge from ordering corollary relief where the parties are not yet divorced: *Kalsi v. Kalsi* (1992), 41 R.F.L. (3d) 201 (Alta. C.A.).

Where the husband applied for a determination of spousal support which would have the effect of altering the support arrangements under the parties' separation agreement, he was not required to establish the "material change" required by s. 17 of the *Divorce Act*. The application was not a variation application, but an originating application. Accordingly, the variation clause in the agreement itself was properly considered: *Huszarik v. Fairfield* (2004), 9 R.F.L. (6th) 130, 2004 CarswellOnt 3962 (S.C.J.).

Under the *Divorce Act*, it is possible to make an order for spousal support following the parties' divorce. Section 15 of the *Divorce Act* includes a divorced spouse in the definition of "spouse" for the purposes of corollary relief: *Huazarik v. Fairfield* (2004), 48 R.F.L. (5th) 275, 2004 CarswellOnt 840 (Ont. S.C.J.).

Orders dispensing with spousal support are rare and orders directing that neither party shall apply for spousal support at a later date definitely require trial and hearing of surrounding issues and should not be granted in the context of a summary application for divorce: *Page v. Page*, 49 R.F.L. (5th) 157, 2003 CarswellAlta 1492, 2003 ABQB 847, 25 Alta. L.R. (4th) 321 (Alta. Q.B. [In Chambers]).

There is no authority to grant corollary relief under the Divorce Act where a divorce was granted in a foreign country. Nor is there any jurisdiction to vary that foreign order: *Jahangiri-Mavaneh v. Taheri-Zengekani* (2003), 39 R.F.L. (5th) 103, 2003 CarswellOnt 2934, 66 O.R. (3d) 272 (Ont. S.C.J.)

Corollary relief under the *Divorce Act* is not available where the parties' divorce was granted by a foreign court: *Wlodarczyk v. Spriggs*, 12 R.F.L. (5th) 241, 2000 SKQB 468, 200 Sask. R. 129, 2000 CarswellSask 700 (Q.B.).

On a reference to the Registrar of support issues, although the Registrar lacks jurisdiction to finally adjudicate the support issues, he or she does have the jurisdiction to make findings of fact on the issues of need and the ability to pay: *Larson v. Larson* (1993), 80 B.C.L.R. (2d) 303 (S.C.).

Where neither party nor the judge intended that a consent corollary relief order made during the course of proceedings was intended to be final, the wife was entitled to have the order re-opened by virtue of R. 390(1) of the Alberta Rules of Court: *Russell v. Russell* (1995), 16 R.F.L. (4th) 229, 33 Alta. L.R. (3d) 170, 175 A.R. 225 (Alta. Q.B.).

In the context of a support order, a Master has no jurisdiction under the *Divorce Act* to order a spouse to continue to make mortgage payments: *Fisher v. Fisher* (1990), 28 R.F.L. (3d) 324 (Ont. H.C.).

The court has jurisdiction to award spousal support after divorce even where the claimant had abandoned the support claim prior to the granting of the divorce: *Standing v. Standing* (1991), 37 R.F.L. (3d) 90, 96 Sask. R. 13, 85 D.L.R. (4th) 309 (Q.B.).

In *Droit de la famille — 770* (1989), [1990] R.J.Q. 581, [1990] R.D.F. 142 (C.S.), the Quebec court dismissed the wife's application for alimony where she had not sought such an award in the original New Brunswick divorce proceedings. Only the court in New Brunswick had jurisdiction to make the order requested.

In making a support order, the court lacks jurisdiction from barring the payor from seeking a variation of the order within a specified timeframe. Section 17 of the Act specifies a statutory right of review for a former spouse, and the husband could not be precluded from exercising that right in the event of a material change in circumstances: *Lidstone v. Lidstone* (1993), 46 R.F.L. (3d) 203, 121 N.S.R. (2d) 213, 335 A.P.R. 213 (C.A.).

A judge remains seized of an application for corollary relief until the final order is signed. Accordingly where the judge was dissatisfied with the draft including the introduction of new evidence, he had jurisdiction to issue an order inconsistent with the first draft: *Cromwell v. Cromwell* (1995), 14 R.F.L. (4th) 47, (sub nom. *Axent-Cromwell v. Cromwell)* 140 N.S.R. (2d) 397, 399 A.P.R. 397 (C.A.).

A court can refuse to exercise its jurisdiction to grant or refuse maintenance and may make no maintenance order at all. "There are many circumstances in which the matters of custody or maintenance are better left to the parties or to the provincial legislation": per Seaton J.A. in *Hughes v. Hughes* (1976), 30 R.F.L. 199 at 201, [1977] 1 W.W.R. 579, 1 B.C.L.R. 234, 72 D.L.R. (3d) 577 (C.A.).

15§4 — Constitutional issues

Section 10 of the *Federal Child Support Guidelines* does not violate either the right to privacy or equality rights under ss. 7 and 15 of the *Canadian Charter of Rights and Freedoms*: *Souliere v. Leclair* (1998), 38 R.F.L. (4th) 68, 52 C.R.R. (2d) 156 (Ont. Gen. Div.).

Section 6(3) of the Nova Scotia *Family Maintenance Act*, R.S.N.S. 1989, c. 160, which calls for the termination of support upon the remarriage of the payee spouse, is unconstitutional. Federal legislation in the area of divorce prevails if there is apparent conflict with provincial legislation. As the *Divorce Act* does not specifically provide for variation of spousal support on the grounds of remarriage, there is serious incompatibility between the two statutes: *Fancy v. Shephard* (1997), 35 R.F.L. (4th) 430, 51 C.R.R. (2d) 45, 155 D.L.R. (4th) 680, 164 N.S.R. (2d) 274, 491 A.P.R. 274 (S.C.)

The power to grant an order of maintenance pursuant to s. 11 [now ss. 15.1 and 15.2] of the *Divorce Act* is necessarily ancillary to jurisdiction in divorce and in that regard the Parliament of Canada was acting within its legislative competency conferred upon it by s. 91(26) of the *Constitution Act*, 1867 (U.K.), c. 3. This principle applies equally to matters of custody, care and upbringing of children of the marriage under s. 11(1)(c) [now s. 16] and to the provisions dealing with interim orders: *Zacks v. Zacks*, 10 R.F.L. 53, [1973] S.C.R. 891, [1973] 5 W.W.R. 289, 35 D.L.R. (3d) 420 (S.C.C.); *Jackson v. Jackson*, 8 R.F.L. 172, [1973] S.C.R. 205, [1972] 6 W.W.R. 419, 29 D.L.R. (3d) 641. See also *Vadeboncoeur v. Landry*, [1977] 2 S.C.R. 179, 23 R.F.L. 360, 68 D.L.R. (3d) 165, 10 N.R. 469; *Whyte v. Whyte* (1969), 69 W.W.R. 536, 7 D.L.R. (3d) 7 (Man. C.A.); *Niccolls v. Niccolls* (1969), 68 W.W.R. 307, 4 D.L.R. (3d) 209 (B.C. S.C.); *Todd v. Todd* (1969), 2 R.F.L. 303, 68 W.W.R. 315, 5 D.L.R. (3d) 92 (B.C. S.C.); *Heikel v. Heikel* (1970), 1 R.F.L. 326, 73 W.W.R. 84, 12 D.L.R. (3d) 311 (Alta. C.A.).

A "final order" of support made under a provision statute does not affect the payor's right to seek nor the court's order to grant a different order in divorce proceedings: *Delaney v. Delaney*, *supra*.

The *Charter of Rights and Freedoms* does not apply to private disputes between parties in a family law context: *Droit de la famille — 1150* (21 octobre 1993), no. 22296 (C.S.C.); affirming (1990), [1991] R.J.Q. 306, [1991] R.D.F. 112 (headnote only) (C.A.); affirming [1988] R.D.F. 40 (C.S. Qué.).

The provisions under the *Divorce Act*, 1985 relating to grounds and corollary relief are not contrary to the *Canadian Charter of Rights and Freedoms*: *Qually v. Qually*, 5 R.F.L. (3d) 365, [1987] 2 W.W.R. 553, 56 Sask. R. 165 (Q.B.); varied 18 R.F.L. (3d) 69, [1989] 2 W.W.R. 268 (C.A.).

A judicial separation granted under provincial legislation does not limit the court's power to award maintenance in a later divorce action: *Ruel v. Thomas*, [1982] C.A. 357 (Que.).

In Ontario, where there are proceedings in the Supreme Court for divorce, in which maintenance is in issue, and there is an application for maintenance in Family Court under a provincial statute, the judge of the Family Court may proceed with the application unless he or she determines after considering the circumstances of the case before him or her that actual or probable conflict of jurisdiction exists: *Tuz, Re* (1975), 25 R.F.L. 87, 11 O.R. (2d) 617, 67 D.L.R. (3d) 41 (C.A.).

"The apparent conflict between the provincial legislation and federal legislation in the area of corollary relief has been considered by a number of courts which, as far as I can ascertain, are in agreement that the federal legislation must prevail and is paramount over the provincial legislation": per Bowen J. in *Goldstein v. Goldstein*, 17 R.F.L. 346 at 348, [1975] W.W.D. 50 (Alta. T.D.); reversed on other grounds 23 R.F.L. 206, [1976] 4 W.W.R. 646, 67 D.L.R. (3d) 624 (Alta. C.A.). See also *Gillespie v. Gillespie* (1974), 13 R.F.L. 344, 6 N.B.R. (2d) 239 (C.A.).

"[When] the federal government entered the field of divorce and corollary relief by the passage of the *Divorce Act*, 1967–68 (Can.) c. 24, insofar as any provincial legislation in that field dealt with the same subject-matter as the federal legislation, it ceased to be effective. Although the provisions of the federal and provincial legislation are not exactly co-extensive, it is our opinion that any of the provincial legislation which appears to extend beyond the boundaries of the federal legislation is not effective because the federal legislation occupies the field": per Gale C.J.O. in *Richards v. Richards*, 7 R.F.L. 101 at 102, [1972] 2 O.R. 596, 26 D.L.R. (3d) 264 (C.A.).

"There can be little doubt that Parliament has power to enact provisions for maintenance and custody when these questions arise as a result of dissolution of the marriage in proceedings under the *Divorce Act*, and it also seems clear enough that the existence of such 'ancillary' jurisdiction does not oust the jurisdiction of the provincial legislatures to enact provisions conferring similar jurisdiction on the courts in other matrimonial proceedings": per Cairns J.A. in *Radke v. Radke*, 4 R.F.L. 318 at 338, [1971] 5 W.W.R. 113, 20 D.L.R. (3d) 679 (Alta. C.A.).

An order for maintenance made under provincial legislation does not survive a decree absolute. Consequently, a provisional order made after the decree purporting to vary a provincial order made before the decree is made without jurisdiction and cannot be confirmed. This is so even though the divorce decree makes no provision for maintenance: *Carson v. Carson* (1979), 9 R.F.L. (2d) 209 (P.E.I. S.C.).

15§5 — Support under provincial statutes

Paramountcy of Federal Legislation

Federal paramountcy is a doctrine of constitutional law used to resolve conflicts between orders made under federal laws and orders made under provincial laws. Conflicts in the area of support became a possibility in 1968 when corollary relief provisions were introduced in the *Divorce Act* — federal legislation. By this time, provincial support legislation of undoubted validity had already enjoyed a long history. (See Peter W. Hogg in *Constitutional Law of Canada*, 2nd edition (1985), quoted in *White v. White* (1994), [1994] 7 W.W.R. 249, 113 D.L.R. (4th) 582, 118 Sask. R. 293, 3 R.F.L. (4th) 201, 1994 CarswellSask 216 (Q.B.).

The powers of the federal Parliament to enact legislation to provide for support arises under s. 91(26) of the *Constitution Act, 1867*, which gives it the right to make laws in relation to "marriage and divorce." The provision for support "is necessarily ancillary to jurisdiction in divorce and . . . the Parliament of Canada was therefore acting within the legislative competency conferred upon it by the B.N.A. Act [now the *Constitution Act*], s. 91(26), in legislating to this end": *Jackson v. Jackson* (1972), [1973] S.C.R. 205, [1972] 6 W.W.R. 419, 29 D.L.R. (3d) 641, 8 R.F.L. 172, 1972 CarswellBC 217, 1972 CarswellBC 318 (S.C.C.) per Ritchie J. The provincial legislatures find their jurisdiction in the powers allocated to them under s. 92(13) to make laws in relation to "property and civil rights in the province." (See *White v. White*, above.)

Both parliament and the provincial legislatures have jurisdiction to enact provisions for support. "There can be little doubt that Parliament has power to enact provisions for maintenance and custody when these questions arise as a result of dissolution of the marriage in proceedings under the *Divorce Act*, and it also seems clear enough that the existence of such 'ancillary' jurisdiction does not oust the jurisdiction of the provincial legislatures to enact provisions conferring similar jurisdiction on the courts in other matrimonial proceedings": per Cairns J.A. in *Radke v. Radke* (1971), [1971] 5 W.W.R. 113, 4 R.F.L. 318, 20 D.L.R. (3d) 679, 1971 CarswellAlta 64 (C.A.).

No distinction is made between spousal support under federal (*Divorce Act*) and provincial legislation: *Bracklow v. Bracklow*, 1999 CarswellBC 532, 1999 CarswellBC 533, 169 D.L.R. (4th) 577, [1999] S.C.J. No. 14, 236 N.R. 79, 44 R.F.L. (4th) 1, 120 B.C.A.C. 211, 196 W.A.C. 211, [1999] 1 S.C.R. 420, 63 B.C.L.R. (3d) 77, [1999] 8 W.W.R. 740 (S.C.C.). For a detailed discussion of the case, see 15§6, 'General principles for determining spousal support'.

The *Divorce Act* deals with support as a matter ancillary to divorce proceedings. When it is dealt with as ancillary to divorce proceedings it comes within federal jurisdiction. Otherwise, it would fall within provincial jurisdiction as dealing with property and civil rights: *Yearley v. Yearley* (1978), 5 R.F.L. (2d) 301, 1978 CarswellSask 18 (Dist. Ct.).

Where Parliament and the legislatures under their respective heads of legislative jurisdiction enact the same, or substantially the same provisions with respect to support, the parliamentary enactments are considered to be paramount. This means that in a conflict they prevail over, and make the provincial or territorial enactments inoperative.

"The apparent conflict between the provincial legislation and federal legislation in the area of corollary relief has been considered by a number of courts which, as far as I can ascertain, are in agreement that the federal legislation must prevail and is paramount over the provincial legislation": per Bowen J. in *Goldstein v. Goldstein*, 17 R.F.L. 346 at 348, [1975] W.W.D. 50 (Alta. T.D.); reversed on other grounds 23 R.F.L. 206, [1976] 4 W.W.R. 646, 67 D.L.R. (3d) 624 (Alta. C.A.). See also *Gillespie v. Gillespie* (1974), 13 R.F.L. 344, 6 N.B.R. (2d) 239 (C.A.).

The conflict must be direct. Thus there is no conflict between an order for support under the *Divorce Act*, and an order for exclusive possession of the matrimonial home under provincial legislation. Although the order for possession is relevant to the question of support, it is not in itself a support order. Since it is not a support order, there is no conflict and no reason to resort to the doctrine of paramountcy: *Lamb v. Lamb* (1985), [1985] 1 S.C.R. 851, 20 D.L.R. (4th) 1, 59 N.R. 166, 9 O.A.C. 256, 46 R.F.L. (2d) 1, 1985 CarswellOnt 266, 1985 CarswellOnt 941 (S.C.C.).

The test to determine whether there is a conflict between the two sets of laws, and hence the circumstances in which the doctrine of paramountcy should be invoked, has evolved from an application of the 'occupied field theory' to a more narrow or specific test embraced by the 'operational conflict theory.'

Paramountcy — Occupied Field Theory

Chief Justice Gale of the Ontario Court of Appeal described what came to be known as the occupied field theory. "[When] the federal government entered the field of divorce and corollary relief by the passage of the Divorce Act, 1967-68 (Can.) c. 24, insofar as any provincial legislation in that field dealt with the same subject-matter as the federal legislation, it ceased to be effective. Although the provisions of the federal and provincial legislation are not exactly co-extensive, it is our opinion that any of the provincial legislation which appears to extend beyond the boundaries of the federal legislation is not effective because the federal legislation occupies the field": per Gale C.J.O. in *Richards v. Richards* (1972), [1972] 2 O.R. 596, 7 R.F.L. 101, 26 D.L.R. (3d) 264, 1972 CarswellOnt 126 (C.A.) at 102 [R.F.L.].

Paramountcy — Operational Conflict Theory

Justice Dickson (as he then was), in *Multiple Access Ltd. v. McCutcheon* (1982), [1982] 2 S.C.R. 161, 138 D.L.R. (3d) 1, 44 N.R. 181, 18 B.L.R. 138, 1982 CarswellOnt 128, 1982 CarswellOnt 738 (S.C.C.), is often credited with laying the foundation for the operational conflict theory, or the express contradiction theory. "In principle, there would seem to be no good reason to speak of paramountcy and preclusion except where there is actual conflict in operation as where one enactment says 'yes' and the other says 'no'; 'the same citizens are being told to do inconsistent things'; compliance with one is defiance of the other." On the basis of this theory, so long as no order has in fact been made under the *Divorce Act*, an order made under provincial law would not be deemed inconsistent (operationally in conflict) with the *Divorce Act* and would, therefore, be legally effective: *Keller v. Keller* (1987), 10 R.F.L. (3d) 268, 83 A.R. 313, 45 D.L.R. (4th) 74, 1987 CarswellAlta 339, [1987] A.J. No. 655 (Q.B.). The operational conflict theory has ousted or overruled the occupied field concept: *Keller*, above.

Accepting that the proper test for paramountcy is an express contradiction between the two legislative enactments, "a support order made pursuant to provincial legislation does not automatically lapse on the granting of a decree nisi [divorce judgment] where the judge has made no corollary relief order. While it is certainly within his prerogative to invoke federal divorce jurisdiction to make a support order, in the absence of his exercising such jurisdiction, it cannot be said that there can be a 'conflict' between federal and provincial legislation. Unless and until the federal legislation is invoked there can be no 'express conflict' or operating incompatibility. There can be no conflict until an actual order is made": *Lefebvre v. Lefebvre* (1982), 38 O.R. (2d) 683, 30 R.F.L. (2d) 184, 1982 CarswellOnt 325 (Ont. Co. Ct.).

Support under Provincial Statutes — Spousal Support

Provincial legislatures may enact provisions in their enabling statutes describing the circumstances in which a support order may be granted where there is a possibility of conflict with the exercise of jurisdiction under the *Divorce Act*. These provisions can be seen as codifying the law in the areas in which the provincial legislation operates. For instance, section 36 of the *Family Law Act* (Ontario) provides:

> **36.** — (1) When a divorce proceeding is commenced under the *Divorce Act* (Canada), an application for support under this Part [*Family Law Act*, Part III — Support Obligations] that has not been adjudicated is stayed, unless the court orders otherwise.
>
> (2) The court that deals with a divorce proceeding under the *Divorce Act* (Canada) may determine the amount of arrears owing under an order for support made under this Part and make an order respecting that amount at the same time as it makes an order under the *Divorce Act* (Canada).
>
> (3) If a marriage is terminated by a divorce or judgment of nullity and the question of support is not adjudicated in the divorce or nullity proceedings, an order for support made under this Part continues in force according to its terms.

The arrangement of the principles recorded in this section of the Ontario Act will be followed in the organization of the next part of this commentary.

Stay of claim for support in proceedings under provincial legislation

The first subsection of the Ontario provision sets out the principle of paramountcy developed in the common law that where a *Family Law Act* (Ontario) proceeding in which support is claimed has been started, and no order for support has been made in this proceeding, the mere commencement of a divorce proceeding stays the claim for support in the *Family Law Act* proceeding unless the court orders otherwise: *Family Law Act* (Ontario), s. 36(1), and see *Pope v. Pope* (1995), 12 R.F.L. (4th) 391, 1995 CarswellNfld 7 (Nfld. U.F.C.), interpreting a similar provision. "There is no jurisdiction under the *Family Law Act* [Newfoundland] to consider a claim for support once a divorce proceeding is started. Once a divorce proceeding is commenced, subs. 43(1) of the *Family Law Act* [Newfoundland] makes it clear that any application for support under that Act is stayed, except by leave of the Court." The stay is automatic. The court that is empowered to lift the stay, or in the words of the Ontario Act to order "otherwise," is the court entertaining the *Family Law Act* proceeding; that is, the provincial court. But the court has no power to order a stay where the *Family Law Act* proceeding has resulted in an order for support. The power to order a stay is operative only from the commencement of the proceeding to the time if and when a support order is granted. Once granted, the support order continues in force according to its terms and may be enforced until varied or discharged by the court that made it, notwithstanding the commencement of divorce proceedings subsequent to the order in the provincial court, or until it is superseded by an order granted by the court in the divorce proceeding. "Upon the commencement of a divorce proceeding, an application for support brought under the *Family Law Reform Act* or under the *Family Law Act* may only be stayed if it has not been determined or adjudicated by way of an interim interim or interim or a final order and then only by the court in which the application is pending": *Mongrain v. Mongrain* (1986), 1 R.F.L. (3d) 330, 1986 CarswellOnt 255, [1986] O.J. No. 2511 (H.C.).

In a divorce proceeding, court may enforce payment of arrears accumulated under provincial court order

The second provision in the codifying provision of the *Family Law Act* (Ontario) clarifies the right of the court in a proceeding under the *Divorce Act* to make an order for the payment of arrears owing under *Family Law Act* order: *Family Law Act* (Ontario), s. 36(2).

A child support order made under provincial legislation survives a divorce granted without corollary relief and continues to be enforceable with respect to arrears that may have accumulated: *Lefebvre v. Lefebvre* (1982), 38 O.R. (2d) 683, 30 R.F.L. (2d) 184, 1982 CarswellOnt 325 (Co. Ct.) on appeal from the Provincial Court (Family Division.).

The court, under the *Divorce Act*, lacks jurisdiction to deal with support arrears accumulating under an order made under a provincial statute: *Tweel v. Tweel*, 1994 CarswellPEI 16, 384 A.P.R. 40, 124 Nfld. & P.E.I.R. 40, 7 R.F.L. (4th) 204 (T.D.); additional reasons at 1995 CarswellPEI 54, 423 A.P.R. 148, 136 Nfld. & P.E.I.R. 148, 18 R.F.L. (4th) 222 (T.D.). But see *Family Law Act* (Ontario) s. 36(2).

Order under Divorce Act *supersedes provincial court order. Divorce judgment silent permits provincial court order to continue*

Lastly, the Ontario section touches on two further characteristics of the law of paramountcy in family law; first the right of the court in a proceeding under the *Divorce Act* to make an order superseding an order that has been made in a *Family Law Act* proceeding, and secondly, the fact that if this right is not exercised, and the question of support is not adjudicated in these proceedings, the *Family Law Act* support order continues in force: *Family Law Act* (Ontario), s. 36(3).

The fact that a support order has been made under a provincial family law statute does not render the issue *res judicata* in subsequent divorce proceedings: *Callison v. Callison* (1989), 39 B.C.L.R. (2d) 379, 22 R.F.L. (3d) 123, 1989 CarswellBC 171 (C.A.).

An existing order for support under the *Family Law Reform Act* does not give rise to *res judicata* in a subsequent application for interim maintenance under the *Divorce Act*: *Goodfellow v. Goodfellow* (1982), 38 O.R. (2d) 54, 28 C.P.C. 212, 1982 CarswellOnt 433 (H.C.); *Lefebvre v. Lefebvre* (1982), 38 O.R. (2d) 683, 30 R.F.L. (2d) 184, 1982 CarswellOnt 325 (Co. Ct.), affirming 1982 CarswellOnt 1432, 38 O.R. (2d) 121 (Prov. Ct.);

Ferraz v. Ferraz (1981), 16 Alta. L.R. (2d) 286, 24 R.F.L. (2d) 386, 1981 CarswellAlta 74 (Prov. Ct.).

A "final order" of support made under a provincial statute does not affect the payor's right to seek, nor the court's order to grant, a different order in divorce proceedings: *Delaney v. Delaney* (1995), 2 B.C.L.R. (3d) 227, [1995] 4 W.W.R. 599, 11 R.F.L. (4th) 155, 122 D.L.R. (4th) 439, 55 B.C.A.C. 258, 90 W.A.C. 258, 1995 CarswellBC 24, [1995] B.C.J. No. 307 (C.A.).

It is inappropriate to base a child support award solely on a previous support award made under provincial legislation. A support order made under the *Divorce Act* is grounded in constitutionally separate federal legislation and does not "continue" an order made under provincial legislation. A support order made under the *Divorce Act* must have its own evidentiary base: *Williams v. Williams*, 1999 CarswellNfld 243, 179 Nfld. & P.E.I.R. 283, 546 A.P.R. 283, 50 R.F.L. (4th) 446 (C.A.) .

Where the parties' settlement agreement had been incorporated into a consent order under provincial legislation but had not been incorporated in the divorce judgment, the wife was not required to prove a change of circumstances in her subsequent application for support under the *Divorce Act*: *Fraticelli v. Fraticelli* (2000), [2000] N.B.J. No. 22, 2000 CarswellNB 19, 4 R.F.L. (5th) 222 (C.A.).

In the case of an existing support order under provincial legislation, it is not necessary that a claimant prove a change in circumstances to bring a support claim under s. 15 of the *Divorce Act*: *Strickland v. Strickland* (1991), 32 R.F.L. (3d) 179, 107 N.S.R. (2d) 111, 290 A.P.R. 111, 1991 CarswellNS 53 (C.A.).

The court has jurisdiction to make an interim maintenance award under the *Divorce Act* which supersedes a final support order made under provincial legislation: *Strong v. Strong* (1987), 5 R.F.L. (3d) 209, 1987 CarswellOnt 280 (H.C.).

An order for support made under provincial legislation survives a decree of divorce where there is no mention of support in the decree. There is no operational incompatibility in continuing an order for support under provincial legislation where a divorce decree is silent as to support. The doctrine of paramountcy only renders the provincial order inoperative where it collides with or is repugnant to the federal legislation. Absent such conflict, the provincial support order remains in full force and effect: *Keller v. Keller* (1987), 10 R.F.L. (3d) 268, 83 A.R. 313, 45 D.L.R. (4th) 74, 1987 CarswellAlta 339, [1987] A.J. No. 655 (Alta. Q.B.).

The "divorce court" does not have exclusive jurisdiction over the issue of support. A "provincial court" under its enabling legislation may make an order for support, if the divorce court has not done so: *White v. White* (1994), [1994] 7 W.W.R. 249, 113 D.L.R. (4th) 582, 118 Sask. R. 293, 3 R.F.L. (4th) 201, 1994 CarswellSask 216 (Sask. Q.B.).

In the absence of a claim for corollary relief in a divorce petition, leave to continue an earlier support variation proceeding under provincial legislation should be granted as a matter of course: *Gow v. Gow* (1989), 18 R.F.L. (3d) 14, 67 O.R. (2d) 443, 1989 CarswellOnt 211 (Ont. H.C.).

Where the divorce decree was silent on the issue of child support, a separation agreement dealing with child support issues which had been filed with the Unified Family Court was found to continue in force. Under provincial legislation, the agreement was deemed to be an order of the court upon the filing and accordingly, the variation principles to be followed were those specified under the provincial legislation: *Coutts v. Coutts* (1995), 14 R.F.L. (4th) 234, 132 Sask. R. 288, 1995 CarswellSask 236 (Q.B.).

Where a provision for spousal support in an order under provincial legislation is suspended until a change in circumstances occurs, there is no operational conflict with proceedings under the *Divorce Act* unless the order is superseded in those proceedings through the doctrine of paramountcy. In the absence of a paramount order, the Provincial Court Family Division may vary its order pursuant to the provincial legislation: *Gaughan v. Gaughan*, 1998 CarswellOnt 5102, 45 R.F.L. (4th) 147 (Ont. Gen. Div.).

A divorce judgment which is silent on the issue of support does not affect the support obligation engrossed in an earlier separation order: *Droit de la famille — 457* (1988), EYB 1988-77647, [1988] R.D.F. 73, [1988] R.J.Q. 769, 1988 CarswellQue 1179 (S.C.).

Support under Provincial Statutes — Child Support

It is inappropriate to base a child support award solely on a previous support award made under provincial legislation. A support order made under the *Divorce Act* is grounded in constitutionally separate federal legislation and does not "continue" an order made under provincial legislation. A support order made under the *Divorce Act* must have its own evidentiary base: *Williams v. Williams*, 1999 CarswellNfld 243, 179 Nfld. & P.E.I.R. 283, 546 A.P.R. 283, 50 R.F.L. (4th) 446 (C.A.).

An operational conflict exists and the jurisdiction of the provincial court to make a support order against the father for a child on the child's own application is rendered inoperative by the doctrine of paramountcy where a prior existing child support order against the father has been made in favour of his mother (father's former wife) under the *Divorce Act*. "There is obvious conflict in operation if the father were the subject of two requirements to pay support, once to his former wife for the maintenance of the child of the marriage and again to the child himself as a dependent who has achieved relief under the provincial statue and had the quantum of that support assessed according to the criteria set out in the *Family Law Act*. The need of the child would have been determined in each assessment but that need, of necessity, would be intermingled. In my view, inconsistent determinations would yield, and subject the respondent father to inconsistent results": *Kulchyski v. Kulchyski* (1996), 22 R.F.L. (4th) 261, 1996 CarswellOnt 897, [1996] O.J. No. 992 (Gen. Div.).

There is no operational conflict between proceedings under the *Divorce Act* in which an order for child support by way of corollary relief was made against the biological mother (wife) in favour of the biological father (husband), and proceedings under the *Family Law Act* (Ontario) by the step-father against the biological father for child support. No such conflict is possible because there is no jurisdiction under the *Divorce Act* to entertain an application by the step-father for corollary relief. That jurisdiction is limited to parties who are spouses or former spouses. The step-father's claim (since he and the biological father were not spouses of one another) could only be brought under the provincial legislation. Conflict would exist only if the step-father had recourse to both the federal and provincial legistation. Since there was no operational conflict or incompatibility between two levels of legislation, there was no need to resort to the doctrine of paramountcy. The step-father (who had custody of the child) was entitled to claim child support against the biological father under the enabling provisions of the provincial legislation: *Couture v. Ferguson*, 2003 CarswellOnt 882, 37 R.F.L. (5th) 289 (Master).

Support — Discretion to Proceed under Divorce Act or under Provincial legislation

It is not possible to review maintenance awarded on judicial separation in the context of divorce proceedings: *Droit de la famille — 1117* (1987), [1987] R.D.F. 360 (S.C.).

Where the parties' divorce judgment was silent on the issue of child support, the custodial wife had the choice of pursuing a remedy under either the *Divorce Act* or provincial legislation: *French v. Mackenzie*, 2003 CarswellOnt 1748, 38 R.F.L. (5th) 81 (S.C.J.).

In Ontario, where there are proceedings in the Supreme Court for divorce, in which maintenance is in issue, and there is an application for maintenance in Family Court under a provincial statute, the judge of the Family Court may proceed with the application unless he or she determines after considering the circumstances of the case before him or her that actual or probable conflict of jurisdiction exists: *Tuz, Re* (1976), 11 O.R. (2d) 617, 67 D.L.R. (3d) 41, 25 R.F.L. 87, 1976 CarswellOnt 135 (C.A.).

The *Divorce Act* is not to be used as providing a forum to retry support issues which have been dealt with under a provincial statute: *Langner v. Langner* (1987), 11 R.F.L. (3d) 29, 1987 CarswellBC 544 (S.C.).

The court should not make an order for support under the *Divorce Act* which has the effect of varying an existing support order made under provincial legislation. The federal Act was not intended as a vehicle to frustrate the variation requirements set out by provincial legislation: *Rehn v. Rehn* (1988), 13 R.F.L. (3d) 440, 1988 CarswellOnt 236, [1988] O.J. No. 522 (U.F.C.).

Where there has been no final support order made under provincial legislation and where the prospective payee spouse intends to pursue a remedy for support, then if there is a divorce in being, the payee spouse is obligated to pursue the remedies under the *Divorce Act* if the other spouse demands it: *B. (R.) v. B. (M.)* (1989), 19 R.F.L. (3d) 92, 68 O.R. (2d) 32, 1989 CarswellOnt 221 (H.C.).

A spouse who is paying support under an order made under provincial legislation is entitled to request a support determination under the *Divorce Act*: *Clayton v. Clayton* (1989), 19 R.F.L. (3d) 430, 1989 CarswellOnt 232 (Div. Ct.).

SPOUSAL SUPPORT — Considerations

15§6 — General principles for determining spousal support

See also 17§2 Variation and rescission of support orders — general. For a consideration of the objectives of the support provisions, see 15§24 Objectives of spousal support — general. On an application by either or both spouses, the court may "make an order requiring a spouse to secure or pay, or to secure and pay, such lump sum or periodic sums, or such lump sum and periodic sums, as the court thinks reasonable for the support of the other spouse": *Divorce Act*, s. 15.2(1). The order may be made "for a definite or indefinite period or until a specified event occurs," and the court "may impose terms, conditions or restrictions in connection with the order as it thinks fit and just": *Divorce Act*, s. 15.2(3)

In exercising its discretion to award spousal support the court must be mindful of the "factors" in s. 15.2(4) and the "objectives of spousal support" in s. 15.2(6).[ep The factors are the circumstances the court should take into consideration when making a spousal support order. In making the order "the court shall take into consideration the condition, means, needs and other circumstances of each spouse, including

(a) the length of time the spouses cohabited;

(b) the functions performed by each spouse during cohabitation; and

(c) any order, agreement or arrangement relating to support of either spouse": *Divorce Act*, s. 15.2(4)

The objectives of spousal support provide further direction. The spousal support order "should

(a) recognize any economic advantages or disadvantages to the spouses arising from the marriage or its breakdown;

(b) apportion between the spouses any financial consequences arising from the care of any child of the marriage over and above any obligation for the support of any child of the marriage;

(c) relieve any economic hardship of the spouses arising from the breakdown of the marriage; and

(d) in so far as practicable, promote the economic self-sufficiency of each spouse within a reasonable period of time": *Divorce Act*, s. 15.2(6).

Where the court is considering both an application for child support and an application for spousal support, "the court shall give priority to child support in determining the applications": *Divorce Act*, s. 15.3(1). "Where, as a result of giving priority to child support, a spousal support order was not made, or the amount of a spousal support order is less than it otherwise would have been, any subsequent reduction or termination of that child support constitutes a change of circumstances for the purposes of applying for a spousal support order, or a variation order in respect of the spousal support order, as the case may be": *Divorce Act*, s. 15.3(3).

The Supreme Court of Canada in *Moge v. Moge*, 43 R.F.L. (3d) 345, [1992] 3 S.C.R. 813, changed the rules of support law in Canada. Although the issue before the court involved the circumstances under which spousal support ought to be terminated under s. 17 of the *Divorce Act*, the answer turned on "the basic philosophy of support within the Act as a whole."

The new rules, as enunciated in the *Moge* decision, are a result of an interpretation of the support provisions of the *Divorce Act*. Under this interpretation, there is a shift away from need as the basis of support to an emphasis on principles of compensation.

For a detailed discussion of the facts of the case, see 17§2 Variation and rescission of spousal support orders — general; for consideration of the objectives of the support provisions, see 15§24 Objectives of spousal support — general.

In *Bracklow v. Bracklow*, below, the Supreme Court of Canada continued the statement of the law of support that it began in *Moge v. Moge*. In this judgment, the court held:

> Entitlement to spousal support in circumstances such as where the spouse is incapacitated by illness does not depend on finding an economic disadvantage caused by the marriage. Entitlement may flow from the marriage breakdown; that is, it may flow from the fact that on breakdown the spouse no longer receives the benefits of a common household.
>
> No distinction is made between spousal support under federal (*Divorce Act*) and provincial legislation.

In assessing the duration of cohabitation, it is assumed that the time before marriage is counted and given the same weight as cohabitation after the marriage.

The words "order, agreement or arrangement" in s. 15.2(4)(c) include a contract implied from the way the spouses structure their financial affairs.

The law recognizes not one, but three, conceptual grounds for entitlement to spousal support: (1) compensatory; (2) contractual; and (3) non-compensatory: *Bracklow v. Bracklow*, 44 R.F.L. (4th) 1, [1999] 1 S.C.R. 420, 63 B.C.L.R. (3d) 77, [1999] 8 W.W.R. 740, 169 D.L.R. (4th) 577, 236 N.R. 79, 120 B.C.A.C. 211, 196 W.A.C. 211; reversing (1997), 30 R.F.L. (4th) 313, [1997] 8 W.W.R. 696, 94 B.C.A.C. 153, 152 W.A.C. 153, 37 B.C.L.R. (3d) 375 (C.A.).

Where the wife, at the time an order was made, acknowledged that she was seeing another man, the court found that it was foreseeable that they would eventually cohabit and, therefore, their cohabitation did not amount to a material change of circumstances: *B. (G.) c. G. (L.)* (1995), 1995 CarswellQue 23, 1995 CarswellQue 120, EYB 1995-67821, [1995] S.C.J. No. 72, (sub nom. *G. (L.) c. B. (G.)*) 127 D.L.R. (4th) 385, (sub nom. *G. (L.) c. B. (G.)*) 186 N.R. 201, 15 R.F.L. (4th) 201, [1995] 3 S.C.R. 370, [1995] R.D.F. 611 (S.C.C.). Consequently, the spousal support order should not be varied.

Support awards ought not to include a purely punitive component akin to aggravated or punitive damages: *Pirner v. Pirner* (2005), 22 R.F.L. (6th) 291, 2005 CarswellOnt 6878, 208 O.A.C. 147 (Ont. C.A.); additional reasons at (2006), 2006 CarswellOnt 12 (Ont. C.A.); leave to appeal refused (2006), 2006 CarswellOnt 2552, 2006 CarswellOnt 2553 (S.C.C.).

The entitlement to spousal support may be grounded on any combination of three bases, namely: contract; compensation for disadvantages arising out of the marriage or its breakdown; or support required to relieve economic hardships arising from the marriage breakdown: *Gabb v. Gabb* (2001), 13 R.F.L. (5th) 391, 153 Man. R. (2d) 157, 238 W.A.C. 157, 2001 MBCA 19, 2001 CarswellMan 68 (C.A.).

"[C]ontract law principles are not only better suited to the commercial context but it is implicit in s.15 of the 1985 [Divorce] Act that they were not intended to govern the applicability of private contractual arrangements for spousal support": *Miglin v. Miglin*, 2003 CarswellOnt 1374, 2003 CarswellOnt 1375, [2003] S.C.J. No. 21, 2003 SCC 24, 34 R.F.L. (5th) 255, 224 D.L.R. (4th) 193, 171 O.A.C. 201, 302 N.R. 201 (S.C.C.). Following the *Miglin* decision, in *Marinangeli v. Marinangeli* (2003), 2003 CarswellOnt 2691, [2003] O.J. No. 2819, 38 R.F.L. (5th) 307, 174 O.A.C. 76, 228 D.L.R. (4th) 376 (Ont. C.A.), the court held that ordinary contract law principles do not entirely govern support obligations.

A trial judge's order of a lump sum payment of $25,000 to be paid out of the husband's RRSP account should be set aside on appeal because it is a "back-door equalization" based on the parties comparative net worth, rather than on need and ability to pay. The order is also in error because it requires the payment to be made from a specified source: *Gallant v. Gallant* (1998), 42 R.F.L. (4th) 353 (Man. C.A.).

While ss. 15(7) and 17(7) enumerate certain items which the court should consider in awarding or varying support, they do not limit the court's jurisdiction to those factors: *Robson v. Robson* (1996), 20 R.F.L. (4th) 123, 178 A.R. 278, 110 W.A.C. 278 (C.A.).

It is clear that any judicial discretion that may be exercised by the Court in awarding spousal support must have regard to those factors set out in ss. 15(5) and 17(4) of the

Divorce Act and consistent with all four of the policy objectors defined in ss. 15(7) and 17(7): *Simms v. Simms* (1996), 20 R.F.L. (4th) 147, 173 N.B.R. (2d) 161, 441 A.P.R. 161 (Q.B.); affirmed (1996), 25 R.F.L. (4th) 109, 182 N.B.R. (2d) 362, 463 A.P.R. 362 (C.A.).

In an application for spousal support, the earning capacity of a couple may be regarded as a current asset giving the economically disadvantaged party, whose own economic independence was impaired in the greater interest of the dissolved marriage, a contingent proprietary interest in the earnings of a former spouse. However, the extent of that sharing or interest will depend upon the circumstances. The longer the marriage is, the more relevant is the accustomed lifestyle in framing a support award and the stronger the case for equalizing the couple's standards of living: *Waterman v. Waterman* (1995), 16 R.F.L. (4th) 10, 133 Nfld. & P.E.I.R. 310, 413 A.P.R. 310 (Nfld. C.A.).

A spouse is not entitled to deduct unilaterally from support payments payable to the other spouse, a debt which that other spouse allegedly owes to the payor: *Manuel v. Manuel* (1991), 38 R.F.L. (3d) 66, 109 N.S.R. (2d) 325, 297 A.P.R. 325 (C.A.).

A judge, in approaching a maintenance order, should continue to recognize the distinction between the traditional and the modern marriage. Upon dissolution of a modern marriage the goal should be that of placing both parties in a position of economic self-sufficiency at the earliest possible time. Although as a general rule marriage does not entitle one of the spouses to a pension for life, there may be circumstances where, due to the length of the marriage, the age of the parties and the marketability of their employment skills, permanent maintenance is required. This course should be the exception and every effort should be made to sever the relationship between the spouses to the greatest extent possible so that each spouse can pursue his or her own independent life: *Heinemann v. Heinemann* (1989), 20 R.F.L. (3d) 236, 91 N.S.R. (2d) 136, 233 A.P.R. 136 (N.S. C.A.). See also *Strang v. Strang*, 39 R.F.L. (3d) 233, [1992] 2 S.C.R. 112, at 17§1 Variation — general.

In *Jordan v. Jordan* (2005), 12 R.F.L. (6th) 382, 2005 CarswellSask 169, 260 Sask. R. 188, 2005 SKQB 129 (Sask. Q.B.), it was found that the level of family debt was properly considered in setting the quantum of the wife's interim spousal support, particularly as a large portion of the debt load related to mortgages of the family home in which the wife had possession and use.

In considering support entitlement factors under s. 15 of the *Divorce Act*, the promotion of self-sufficiency is no longer paramount. All of the factors enumerated therein are of equal importance: *Tebelmann v. Tebelmann* (1996), 186 A.R. 45 (Alta. Q.B.).

An order for support made under s. 15(2) of the *Divorce Act* is an initial order and is not to be considered as an order varying an earlier inconsistent interim support order. Accordingly, the court is not required necessarily to consider the same factors when making interim and final orders: *MacDonald v. MacDonald* (1990), 95 N.S.R. (2d) 425, 251 A.P.R. 425 (T.D.).

There is nothing in the *Divorce Act* which indicates that the purpose of support is the equalization of income. The real factors are need and the ability to pay: *Strutynski v. Strutynski* (1989), 81 Sask. R. 111 (Q.B.).

Where there are insufficient funds to meet all of the parties' needs, it is not the function of the court to prioritize them. After the needs of the children have been met, it is the parties' own responsibility to prioritize their own needs in accordance with the quantity of funds remaining available to them: *Dunn v. Dunn* (1995), 14 R.F.L. (4th) 50 (N.S. S.C.).

Even in a marriage of long duration, the court should not simply attempt to equalize incomes through an award of spousal support: *Irving v. Irving* (1988), 17 R.F.L. (3d) 318 (B.C. S.C.).

A court would not award spousal support unless there is a causal connection between the hardship being experienced by the claimant spouse and the breakdown of the marriage. It is the economic hardship created because of the marital relationship that creates entitlement: *Winterle v. Winterle* (1987), 10 R.F.L. (3d) 129 (Ont. H.C.). See 15§27 Objectives — economic advantages and disadvantages — causal connection, below.

In a long-term marriage (over 30 years), where the parties did not intend that the wife's work would be a "career" and where, in all likelihood, the wife would probably need her income supplemented to raise it above the poverty level, her need was established. As the husband had the means to pay, support was ordered at $700 per month, indexed annually and to be a charge on the husband's estate in the event he predeceases her. *Rodrigues v. Rodrigues* (1990), 30 R.F.L. (3d) 231 (Ont. Gen. Div.).

A spouse cannot avoid responsibility for the care of the other spouse during illness that arises while the marriage is continuing, even in the absence of a causal connection between the illness and the marriage: *Smith v. Smith* (1987), 11 R.F.L. (3d) 214 (Ont. H.C.). See also *Theriault v. Theriault* (1987), 10 R.F.L. (3d) 256, 81 N.S.R. (2d) 426, 203 A.P.R. 426 (Fam. Ct.); *Riley v. Riley* (1987), 11 R.F.L. (3d) 105 (N.S. Fam. Ct.).

The fact that the wife sponsored the husband's immigration to Canada was found not to have created any greater spousal support obligations on her part than those created by family law legislation in *Mbaruk v. Mbaruk* (1997), 27 R.F.L. (4th) 146 (B.C. S.C.).

Per Hinkson J.A. in *Lardner v. Lardner* (1980), 20 R.F.L. (2d) 234 at 236–237 (B.C. C.A.): "[I]n my view, the proper consideration for the court is what is the appropriate amount of maintenance having regard to the income of the husband and to the needs of the wife and children and to the other obligations of the husband, not only to live month by month, but to meet living expenses and other commitments. What is the proper apportionment to provide the wife and the children with a reasonable living allowance?"

"[P]eriodic maintenance should only be ordered to be paid to a wife or husband where there exists a demonstrable need for it. Here the award of monthly maintenance was founded not on need but rather primarily, at least, on the erroneous basis of the wife's financial contribution to the marriage": per Macdonald J.A. in *Lohnes v. Lohnes* (1980), 16 R.F.L. (2d) 57 at 62, 37 N.S.R. (2d) 629, 67 A.P.R. 629 (C.A.).

Where in a marriage the wife has contributed to the accumulation of assets, it is not improper to order a lump sum to her. In awarding periodic payments, the court should determine the length that the marriage lasted and the care given by the wife in addition, to whether or not she needs support and is able to support herself. A young wife with no children who has been briefly married and is in as good a position now as before the marriage in respect to health, material and standard of living prospects should be granted little if any periodic maintenance: *Newman v. Newman* (1977), 4 R.F.L. (2d) 97, 24 N.S.R. (2d) 12, 35 A.P.R. 12 (C.A.).

Where the husband had deliberately arranged his affairs to avoid paying support to his wife, he was ordered to readjust his financial affairs to accommodate his wife's needs and to pay to her both spousal and child maintenance: *Huth v. Huth* (1984), 43 R.F.L. (2d) 108 (Ont. H.C.).

In determining the quantum of maintenance payable to a wife, the court may consider the undesirability of allowing the husband to walk away from a marriage of several years' duration in a substantially better economic position than his wife: *Redl v. Redl* (1983), 35 R.F.L. (2d) 117 (Ont. H.C.).

In *Harpur v. Harpur* (1983), 36 R.F.L. (2d) 434 (Ont. H.C.), the wife was awarded substantial periodic payment despite the fact that the husband had taken a year's leave of absence from his job, thereby reducing his annual income from $46,000 to $13,000. The husband's sincerity of purpose in embarking on a new career which would so drastically reduce his income was dubious, and a large reduction in maintenance would be catastrophic for the wife. See also *Diamond v. Diamond* (1975), 22 R.F.L. 394 at 398 (Ont.): per Perry L.J.S.C. in *Jones v. Jones* (1978), 2 R.F.L. (2d) 345 at 363 (B.C. S.C.); *Beach v. Beach*, 2 A.R. 561 at 571, [1977] 3 W.W.R. 274 (T.D.); *Carter v. Carter* (1978), 3 R.F.L. (2d) 355 at 360, 19 Nfld. & P.E.I.R. 411, 50 A.P.R. 411 (Nfld. T.D.); *Timms v. Timms* (1976), 25 R.F.L. 23 (B.C. S.C.); *Roher v. Roher* (1976), 27 R.F.L. 218 at 223 (Ont. H.C.); *Rave v. Rave* (1975), 24 R.F.L. 306 at 310 (B.C. S.C.); *Whittke v. Whittke* (1975), 16 R.F.L. 349 at 362 (Sask. Q.B.); *Swalm v. Swalm* (1973), 12 R.F.L. 181 at 185 (Ont. H.C.); *Dyck v. Dyck* (1973), 11 R.F.L. 56 at 60 (Sask. Q.B.).

15§7 — Factors for assessing spousal support — conditions, means, needs and other circumstances — general

In making an interim or permanent spousal support order in a divorce proceeding the court is to consider "the condition, means, needs and other circumstances of each spouse, including

> "(a) the length of time the spouses cohabited;
>
> "(b) the functions performed by each spouse during cohabitation; and
>
> "(c) any order, agreement or arrangement relating to support of either spouse": *Divorce Act*, s. 15.2(4).

These elements are called "factors" taking the name from the marginal heading in the Act. Cases that deal with the general nature of the factors are annotated in this section of the commentary while specific aspects are addressed in other sections as follows:

15§17 Factors — circumstances — functions performed by the spouse during cohabitation

15§18 Factors — circumstances — any order, agreement or arrangement relating to the support of the spouse or child

15§19 Factors — circumstances — other — payor cohabiting

15§20 Factors — circumstances — other — payee cohabiting

15§21 Factors — circumstances — other — payee spouse sacrificing career

15§22 Factors — circumstances — other — payee spouse assuming custody of young children

15§23 Factors — circumstances — other — payor spouse assuming custody

The need to consider the "condition" of the spouse; the "means, needs and other circumstances" of the spouse and "the functions performed by each spouse during cohabitation," is the source in the federal legislation for both the compensatory and the non-compensatory bases for support. They invite broad consideration of all factors relating to the parties' financial positions not just the compensatory (or contractual) elements. The inquiry goes beyond compensation for what happened during the marriage and its breakdown to the actual situation of the parties at the time of the application: *Bracklow v. Bracklow* (1999), 169 D.L.R. (4th) 577 (S.C.C.). See a full summary of *Bracklow* in s. 15§6, above.

In *Taylor v. Taylor* (1998), 38 R.F.L. (4th) 408 (B.C. C.A.), the Court of Appeal in upholding the trial judge's award of periodic support to a wife incapacitated by illness observed that these cases reflect the trend to the "social obligation model" that focuses primarily on need arising as a result of the marriage breakdown, coupled with an emphasis on the condition, needs, means and other circumstances of the parties at the time the support order is made. All the disadvantages arising from the marriage and the breakdown of the marriage are to be considered, however they are caused. Both compensatory and need considerations must be applied.

Spousal support is not aimed at achieving equalization of incomes after divorce. Instead, it is based on a fair redistribution of the higher income in order to maintain as far as possible similar lifestyles for both former spouses until the effects of the marriage breakdown can be overcome. A just resolution of spousal support claims will take into account the economic effect of the marriage and its breakdown, the contribution of the spouses to the career advancement of each other, the standard of living enjoyed by each spouse during the marriage as well as the requirement that both spouses seek to achieve self-sufficiency. Both parties, nevertheless, must be able to continue with their lives, enter into new relationships and function independently of one another. A support award which does not balance a consideration of all required factors may be properly reviewed on appeal: *Ross v. Ross* (1995), 16 R.F.L. (4th) 1 (N.B. C.A.); reversing in part (1995), 157 N.B.R. (2d) 390, 404 A.P.R. 390 (Q.B.).

Where the wife suffered severe injuries in a motor vehicle accident six months prior to separation and was unable to work, she was found entitled to spousal support. Although the injury and its aftermath were not connected to the marriage, they were properly considered as "other circumstances" under s. 15 of the *Divorce Act* giving rise to an entitlement to support: *Parsons v. Parsons* (1996), 22 R.F.L. (4th) 444, 111 Man. R. (2d) 169 (Q.B.); affirmed (1996), 27 R.F.L. (4th) 11 (Man. C.A.).

In *Reid v. Reid* (1993), 99 D.L.R. (4th) 722 (Alta. Q.B.), the wife's support entitlement was determined by dividing their joint anticipated income, after taking into account their obligation to support their child, equally between them. It was deemed that this was the most equitable way to distribute the consequences of the marriage breakdown.

In situations where both spouse's economic situations are affected by heavy debt loads the quantum of support payable by one to the other should ensure that the economic hardships which both must endure are shared equally: *Nicholson v. Nicholson* (1993), 142 A.R. 254 (Q.B.); additional reasons at (May 1, 1994), Doc. Calgary 4801-72920, 9101-00325 (Alta. Q.B.).

A support award at a minimal or poverty level should not be made where the payor has sufficient means to pay more: *McKee v. McKee* (1994), 153 A.R. 8 (Q.B.).

In *Jenkins v. Jenkins* (1991), 37 R.F.L. (3d) 222, 107 N.S.R. (2d) 18, 290 A.P.R. 18 (T.D.); affirmed (1992), 40 R.F.L. (3d) 66, 112 N.S.R. (2d) 187, 307 A.P.R. 187 (C.A.), the wife, who had been steadily employed since the breakdown of the parties' 12-year marriage, was found not to be entitled to spousal support.

In *Matthews v. Matthews* (1991), 34 R.F.L. (3d) 201, 104 N.S.R. (2d) 140, 283 A.P.R. 140 (C.A.), an appeal by the wife for award of support under the *Divorce Act*, the court, considered the factors set out in s. 15 of the *Divorce Act* and particularly the respective means and needs of the parties, their circumstances and the existence of undisclosed income, and ordered that the support order must be varied upwards to provide for the children. Spousal support was extended beyond the one year cut-off date in light of the wife's difficulty in finding a job in the poor economy. If the wife were unsuccessful in finding a job at the end of that time she could apply to vary to extend the time. However, as both parties have a joint responsibility to provide for the children pursuant to s. 15(8) and a court must promote self-sufficiency where practical, pursuant to s. 15(7), the wife could not continue to be unemployed and be granted support unless she could show that it was impossible to find employment. The fact that a wife receives disability benefits arising from the husband's injury, does not displace the husband's support obligation: *Huey v. Huey* (1991), 39 R.F.L. (3d) 14 (Ont. Gen. Div.).

As a general rule, the court will not require anyone earning less than $10,000 annually to make support payments: *Burke v. Burke* (1991), 93 Nfld. & P.E.I.R. 179, 292 A.P.R. 179 (P.E.I. T.D.).

In *MacLean v. MacLean* (1991), 94 Nfld. & P.E.I.R. 265, 298 A.P.R. 265 (P.E.I. T.D.), the court, in setting the wife's spousal support entitlement, was cognizant of the fact that she had, since separation, lived rent-free and mortgage-free, while the husband had had to pay for rental accommodation. On the other hand, it was also appropriate to consider the salary of the husband's new partner in determining his ability to pay.

Where after separation there was no great disparity between the husband's and the wife's lifestyles, her application for support was refused, although the husband's income was considerably more than that of the wife: *Dyregrov v. Dyregrov* (1990), 24 R.F.L. (3d) 262, 63 Man. R. (2d) 165 (Q.B.).

In *Droit de la famille 1118*, [1987] R.D.F. 308 (C.S. Qué.), although the husband was awarded custody of the son, the wife was awarded periodic support for the sole purpose of providing for her son during his access visits. The wife had only sufficient means to support herself and the best interests and happiness of the child justified the unusual award.

Where the payee wife has need and the payor husband little ability to pay, the payor husband (where appropriate) will be ordered to reduce his expenses (for entertainment and cigarettes) and renegotiate his debts: *Lavoie v. Lavoie* (1991), 32 R.F.L. (3d) 77, 101 N.S.R. (2d) 65, 275 A.P.R. 65 (Fam. Ct.).

See also *Garratt v. Garratt*, 16 R.F.L. 168 at 170, [1974] 6 W.W.R. 659 (B.C. S.C.); *Aucoin v. Aucoin* (1976), 28 R.F.L. 43, 15 N.S.R. (2d) 399, 72 D.L.R. (3d) 674 (C.A.); *Boardman v. Boardman* (1978), 2 R.F.L. (2d) 156 (Sask. Q.B.); *Howlett v. Howlett* (1983), 34 R.F.L. (2d) 195, 48 N.B.R. (2d) 252, 126 A.P.R. 252 (Q.B.).

15§8 — Factors — means — general

"Means" includes not only actual income earned but also the ability to earn it: *Marchak v. Fleury* (1995), 15 R.F.L. (4th) 458, 102 Man. R. (2d) 121, 93 W.A.C. 121 (C.A.).

The term "means" as it is used in s. 15(5) of the *Divorce Act* includes not only what the parties are earning but also what they can "reasonably" expect to earn. The determination of what is "reasonable" is based upon the age, health and the employment prospects of the parties in the area in which they live: *Muirhead v. Muirhead* (1995), 14 R.F.L. (4th) 276 (B.C. C.A.).

The mere existence of a differential in parties' condition after marriage breakdown does not necessarily command an equalizing intervention by the court through spousal support: *Megyesi v. Megyesi* (2005), 21 R.F.L. (6th) 125, 2005 CarswellAlta 1374, [2005] A.J. No. 1261, 2005 ABQB 706, 57 Alta. L.R. (4th) 169, [2006] 7 W.W.R. 358 (Alta. Q.B.).

See also *Campbell v. Campbell* (1981), 24 R.F.L. (2d) 59 at 69 (Ont. H.C.); *Osborne v. Osborne* (1973), 14 R.F.L. 61 at 68 (Sask. Q.B.); varied (1974), 23 R.F.L. 358 (Sask. C.A.); *Raffin v. Raffin*, 5 R.F.L. 274, [1972] 1 O.R. 173, 22 D.L.R. (2d) 497 (C.A).

15§9 — Factors — means — payor's actual income and potential income — ability to pay

In *Myers v. Hawco*, 22 R.F.L. (6th) 17, 2005 CarswellNfld 342, [2005] N.J. No. 378, 2005 NLCA 74, 252 Nfld. & P.E.I.R. 121, 756 A.P.R. 121, 262 D.L.R. (4th) 719 (N.L. C.A.); reversing in part 240 Nfld. & P.E.I.R. 248, 711 A.P.R. 248, 11 R.F.L. (6th) 291, 2004 NLSCUFC 38, 243 D.L.R. (4th) 726, 2004 CarswellNfld 286 (N.L. U.F.C.), the court reversed on appeal the dismissal of the wife's claim for spousal support against the bankrupt husband. The trial judge had failed to assess the husband's attempts to earn income within the context of his support obligations.

In *Morgan v. Morgan*, 22 R.F.L. (6th) 419, 2006 CarswellNfld 9, [2006] N.J. No. 9, 2006 NLTD 6 (N.L. T.D.), the wife was denied spousal support even though entitlement was established. The husband had to spend a considerable sum of money for travel in the exercise of his access rights and accordingly lacked the ability to pay.

The income calculation provisions found in sections 15 through 19 of the Child Support Guidelines apply to the calculation of the payor spouse's income for purposes of determining spousal support as well as for determining child support: *Murray v. Murray* (2003), 2003 CarswellOnt 3258 (Ont. S.C.J.); additional reasons at (2003), 2003 CarswellOnt 3862 (Ont. S.C.J.).

In *Vitagliano v. Di Stavolo* (2001), 17 R.F.L. (5th) 194, 2001 CarswellOnt 1065, [2001] O.J. No. 1138 (Ont. S.C.J.), the wife was awarded spousal and child support based on an imputed income to the husband of $110,000 although he claimed income of only $49,000. The husband was an experienced statistician who had turned down employment offers in the range of $110,000 and, instead, established his own less than successful business. Although his decision was not intended to thwart his support obligations, he had made his career decisions recklessly and without regard to his legal obligation.

When the 60-year-old husband's job had been eliminated, she applied for and received a substantial reduction in the spousal support payable by him. The wife, whose only means of income after the dissolution of the parties' 30-year marriage was spousal support, successfully appealed. The husband, despite his age, still had marketable skills which could deliver a significant income. He had also remarried and his new wife, who was employed, could contribute to household expenses. The trial judge had erred in placing too much responsibility on the wife to obtain employment and not enough responsibility on the husband: *Wyman v. Wyman* (1999), 49 R.F.L. (4th) 447, 1999 CarswellNS 49 (N.S. C.A.).

When determining support, the court will not impute income to a payee in the absence of an evidentiary basis for such a finding: *Wong v. Wong* (1990), 27 R.F.L. (3d) 215 (Ont. C.A.).

Where a spouse who has the potential to earn income and has an obligation to support his or her spouse and children decides to stop working and sets out on another course, the courts will determine what the person's potential to earn is and require support payments commensurate with that potential: *Martens v. Martens* (1996), 22 R.F.L. (4th) 411, 109 Man. R. (2d) 189.

In *Cross v. Cross* (1994), 3 R.F.L. (4th) 276, 119 Sask. R. 241 (Q.B.); additional reasons at (1994), 4 R.F.L. (4th) 162, 119 Sask. R. 241 at 244 (Q.B.), the husband could not rely upon the fact that he had voluntarily left his employment as a means of avoiding spousal support obligations.

It is now well accepted that gross farming income cannot form the sole basis for the determination of means to pay maintenance, nor is it proper to use only net income as reported for income tax purposes. For such individuals, the court must do a calculation to determine, as near as possible, the gross income were the party employed for wages: *Moon v. Bechard* (1996), 21 R.F.L. (4th) 101, 140 Sask. R. 197 (Q.B.).

Where the wife had entered into a common law relationship which permitted her financially to remain at home with the children rather than seek employment, the court found it inappropriate to attribute to her a portion of her common law spouse's income in determining her ability to pay child support. In the circumstances, it was more appropriate to attribute to her the income she would likely earn were she to re-enter the workforce: *Lauderdale v. Lauderdale* (1996), 21 R.F.L. (4th) 17, 180 A.R. 81 (Q.B.).

Where the husband had wilfully taken a leave of absence from his job which reduced his monthly income from $4,200 to $1,000, the quantum of spousal support payable by him was set by reference to his former income. The wife after their traditional marriage of 11 years could not be expected to fill the void left by the husband's failure to maintain his income at a reasonable level: *Hildahl-Trauter v. Trauter* (1996), 140 Sask. R. 46 (Q.B.).

Where, subsequent to separation, the wife gave up her nursing job to return to university, leaving the father to care and provide for the children, her application for spousal support was dismissed. As the husband had assumed the full care and support of the children on his labourer's salary, he could not be expected to finance the wife's education as well: *Kenning v. Kenning* (1994), 11 R.F.L. (4th) 216 (B.C. S.C.).

In *Glazier v. Glazier* (1991), 36 R.F.L. (3d) 84, 5 O.R. (3d) 183 (Gen. Div.), the husband was found to have given precedence to his hobbies over pursuit of his career. Accordingly, when assessing the quantum of spousal support which should be paid by him, the court found that the amount expended on hobbies was unreasonable and assessed his ability to pay after reducing his hobby expenditures to a reasonable amount.

Where the husband was unemployed at the time of the divorce hearing but had previously enjoyed a substantial income, a spousal support order was made in the wife's favour requiring the husband to pay to the wife one-half of his gross monthly income in excess of $1,000 up to a maximum of $500: *Auger v. Auger* (1991), 77 Man. R. (2d) 196 (Q.B.).

A husband, who had retired after the parties' separation in an attempt to reduce his support obligation, was nevertheless ordered to pay support in an amount commensurate with the good employment prospectus that he still possessed: *Bellemare v. Bellemare* (1990), 28 R.F.L. (3d) 165, 98 N.S.R. 140, 263 A.P.R. 140 (T.D.).

Where the husband quit his job to defeat his wife's support order, it was continued on the basis of income attributed to him: *Titterton v. Titterton* (1990), 66 Man. R. (2d) 259 (Q.B.).

Where the husband had retired at age 67, it was not appropriate to attribute income to him for the purpose of the wife's support claim. He had reached the stage in life where he should not be forced to work and accordingly periodic support was not ordered: *Metcalf v. Metcalf* (1990), 26 R.F.L. (3d) 381 (Ont. H.C.).

As a general rule, a payor spouse should not have his or her income lowered below the poverty line by a support award. However, if the support claimant is below the poverty line, then the payor should be required to pay even if that results in the payor falling below the poverty line as well: *Younker v. Younker* (1991), 32 R.F.L. (3d) 138 (P.E.I. T.D.).

Where the payor spouse's income is based upon earnings from self-employment, the quantum of support payable should be based upon such earnings calculated over a significant period due to fluctuations in the business world: *Boult v. Boult* (1989), 62 Man. R. (2d) 161 (Q.B.).

Where the husband had lost his business and his support obligations were suspended, a provision in the order requiring the automatic reinstatement of the support payments upon the husband's finding of employment was deleted upon appeal. The husband was entitled to have his support obligation determined on the basis of actual means and needs and not on the basis of any future earnings which were unknown and speculative: *Edwards v. Edwards* (1990), 26 R.F.L. (3d) 142 (N.S. T.D.).

Where the husband's decision to maintain his income at a reduced level was taken for the sound business reason of reducing his debts, the wife's application for support was dismissed as the parties' incomes were almost equal: *Northcut v. Ruppel* (1989), 21 R.F.L. (3d) 195, 59 Man. R. (2d) 113 (Q.B.).

A court should not make an order for support if there is doubt as to the payor's ability to pay, even if the payor is willing to consent to such an order: *Day v. Day* (1988), 13 R.F.L. (3d) 313 (N.B. Q.B.).

Where the unemployed father claimed that his affluent lifestyle was supported solely by his cohabitant, but failed to call her as a witness in divorce proceedings, the court drew an adverse inference against him concerning his ability to provide child support and ordered him to pay $300 monthly: *McAfee v. McAfee* (1989), 21 R.F.L. (3d) 75 (B.C.S.C.).

Where the husband was deliberately re-arranging his affairs to avoid paying reasonable child support, the order was properly based upon a determination of his potential income: *Lisi v. Lisi* (1987), 12 R.F.L. (3d) 36 (Ont. H.C.).

A spouse's income rather than his or her state of employment is determinative of whether support should be payable: *Sagoo v. Sagoo* (1987), 6 R.F.L. (3d) 128 (Man. Q.B.).

In *Robinson v. Robinson* (1985), 49 R.F.L. (2d) 43 (Ont. C.A.), the fact that the husband had a substantial investment portfolio was taken into account in determining the quantum of maintenance he was required to pay, despite the fact that the portfolio produced little income. The husband had an obligation to arrange his affairs so that the portfolio did produce income for his family.

In *Champagne v. Morin* (1986), 30 D.L.R. (4th) 236 (Que. C.A.), an alimentary pension awarded to the wife at the trial of the parties' divorce was overturned on appeal. Although the wife had become ill and was unable to support herself at the time of the trial, she had been self-supporting for 13 years following the parties' separation and her current economic condition was not in any way related to the marriage.

See also *Hastings v. Hastings* (1984), 38 R.F.L. (2d) 462 (Sask. Q.B.); *Jaworski v. Jaworski* (1973), 10 R.F.L. 190, [1973] 2 O.R. 420, 34 D.L.R. (3d) 44 (H.C.); *Jeans v. Jeans* (1980), 44 N.S.R. (2d) 716 at 719, 83 A.P.R. 716 (T.D.); *Wener v. Wener* (1970), 5 R.F.L. 87, 75 W.W.R. 721 at 727 (Alta. T.D.); *Melanson c. Melanson* (1989), 104 N.B.R. (2d) 76, 261 A.P.R. 76 (N.B. C.A.), reversing (1989), 98 N.B.R. (2d) 357, 248 A.P.R. 357 (Q.B.); *Mitchell v. Mitchell* (1986), 74 N.S.R. (2d) 435, 180 A.P.R. 435 (T.D).

15§10 — Factors — means — payee's actual and potential income

The wife in *Butler v. Butler* (1998), 37 R.F.L. (4th) 226, 195 N.B.R. (2d) 156, 499 A.P.R. 156, 1998 CarswellNB 131 (N.B. C.A.) appealed a spousal support order of $800 per month for 8 months and $400 per month thereafter as she would then receive her share of the matrimonial home and ought to be able to increase her earnings from virtually nothing to $15,000 a year. The Court considered *Messier v. Delage*, [1983] 2 S.C.R. 401 (S.C.C.) in which the appellate court found that the trial court had erred by disregarding factors submitted for consideration and hypothesizing as to the unknown and unforeseeable future. The appellate court in the Butler decision held that the evidence disclosed that the wife had physical disabilities, mild depression and suffered from alcohol abuse, problems which made it difficult to project that her earnings would increase to $15,000 a year. The Court allowed the appeal and ordered a re-hearing of the matter.

Where the trial judge had failed to consider adequately the wife's earning capacity as a lawyer, maintenance payable to her was reduced on appeal: *Ewing v. Ewing* (1987), (sub nom. *Ewing v. Ewing (No. 2))* 56 Sask. R. 263 (C.A.); varying (1986), (sub nom. *Ewing v. Ewing (No. 2))* 51 Sask. R. 55 (U.F.C.).

Where both parties had assets of over $3,000,000, the wife's application for spousal support was dismissed. Her investments would return an annual income of $90,000 and the fact that she had stopped working during the marriage would not be particularly detrimental to her career: *Laxton v. Coglon*, 37 R.F.L. (5th) 156, 2003 CarswellBC 12, 2003 BCSC 11 (B.C. S.C.).

The courts do not require complete financial autonomy for wives who married at a time when marriage was a social contract under which women agreed to devote their working lives to raising a family: *Droit de la famille — 614*, [1989] R.J.Q. 535 (C.A.).

Where the 62-year-old husband had made no effort to find employment after marriage breakdown, he was not allowed merely to rely upon his age to support his claim for spousal support in *McGrath v. Holmes* (1995), 10 R.F.L. (4th) 161 (N.W.T. C.A.); leave to appeal to S.C.C. refused (1995), 16 R.F.L. (4th) 339 (S.C.C.).

In *Fisher v. Fisher* (2001), 12 R.F.L. (5th) 348, 190 N.S.R. (2d) 144, 594 A.P.R. 144, 2000 NSCA 18, 2001 CarswellNS 31 (C.A.), the court allowed the wife's appeal from the trial judge's dismissal of her claim for spousal support. The trial judge found that spousal support was not warranted given the wife's lack of effort to achieve self-sufficiency after the collapse of the parties' long-term traditional marriage. However, given the wife's age and background she could, at best, be expected to attain only a limited degree of self-sufficiency. Furthermore, the trial judge should have given some recognition to the change in the wife's economic circumstances resulting from the marriage breakdown.

In *Fraser v. Fraser* (2004), 8 R.F.L. (6th) 155, 2004 CarswellOnt 3433 (S.C.J.), it was held that a Northern Travel Grant provided to the husband to assist with his travel expenses to obtain medical treatment should not be characterized as "income" in determining his claim for spousal support.

In *Dillon v. Dillon* (1996), 27 R.F.L. (4th) 197, 184 N.B.R. (2d) 371, 469 A.P.R. 371 (Q.B.), the wife, who developed a debilitating mental illness after separation, was found entitled to spousal support. The wife's need and the fact that she had sacrificed her career for the sake of her husband's career during the marriage, justified the award. There was no obligation on her part to establish that her need was causally connected to the marriage.

Where the wife had a stable income, but was capable of earning more and the husband had retained custody of the children and assumed responsibility for the family debts, the wife's claim for spousal support was dismissed: *Dunn v. Dunn* (1995), 14 R.F.L. (4th) 50 (N.S. S.C.).

Where the wife had failed to present medical evidence supporting her claim that a disability prevented her from working, the court attributed income to her from employment potential in determining the quantum of support payable to her: *Labron v. Labron* (1996), 21 R.F.L. (4th) 385, 183 A.R. 251 (Q.B.).

Where the employment obtained by the wife after separation paid more than her job prior to the parties' four-year marriage, her application for support was dismissed. The marriage had not caused the wife any economic hardship: *Murray v. Murray* (1992), 98 Nfld. & P.E.I.R. 297, 311 A.P.R. 297 (Nfld. U.F.C.).

Where the husband was in poor health and was unlikely to return to work, he was ordered to pay $500 per month in maintenance until he retired: *O'Hara v. O'Hara* (1991), 34 R.F.L. (3d) 222, 104 N.S.R. (2d) 426, 283 A.P.R. 426 (T.D.).

In light of the economic disadvantage of the breakdown of the marriage of the wife and the impracticability (because of age and employability) of employment, the court awarded her $5,000 interim monthly support. The husband earned approximately $160,000 a year: *Row v. Row* (1991), 35 R.F.L. (3d) 237, 82 Alta. L.R. (2d) 173 (Q.B.).

Considering the 26-year duration of the marriage and the wife's contribution in terms of raising the parties' five children, doing farm work, her inability to find more lucrative work than babysitting, a disadvantage that clearly flowed from the marriage and keeping in mind the marital settlement she had already received, the wife had established her entitlement to maintenance. Since it was difficult to assess how long it would take her to reach self-sufficiency, the maintenance award was continued until further order of the court. *Pensaert v. Pensaert* (1990), 26 R.F.L. (3d) 378, 65 Man. R. (2d) 236 (Q.B.).

Where throughout their 30-year marriage the parties had only cohabited for two 2-year periods and had lived apart for 13 years before the divorce hearing, the court dismissed the wife's claim for support. The wife had managed to support herself for years and could not now look to the husband, who was retired: *Dezorzi v. Dezorz* (1989), 58 Man. R. (2d) 197 (Q.B.).

Where the husband had no means to pay spousal support and the wife chose to delay her re-entry into the work force at a high income position to remain at home with the parties' five-year-old child, her application for support was refused: *Storey v. Storey* (1987), 49 Man. R. (2d) 235 (Q.B.).

In *Yakimovich v. Yakimovich* (1997), 29 R.F.L. (4th) 449 (B.C. S.C.), the wife's claim for support upon dissolution of the parties' 3-month marriage was refused. The wife, after separation, had returned to her old job and had not suffered any change in lifestyle or reduction in earning capacity.

In *Grant v. Grant* (January 30, 1997), Doc. Prince George 24947 (B.C. S.C.), the court refused the wife's application for support. The wife had been given sole ownership of a family business which she proposed to wind up, mostly to better her chances of obtaining support. She had also misrepresented her resources and purposefully made it impossible to assess totally her financial situation. The allocation of assets upon separation and her income prospects did not support her claim of need.

"As maintenance is only granted for as long as it takes to acquire sufficient independence, once that independence has been acquired it follows that maintenance ceases to be necessary. A divorced spouse who is 'employable' but unemployed is in the same position as other citizens, men or women, who are unemployed. The problem is a social one and is therefore the responsibility of the government rather than the former husband. Once the spouse has been retrained, I do not see why the fact of having been married should give the new single individual any special status by comparison with any other unemployed single person". per Lamer J. in *Messier v. Delage*, 35 R.F.L. (2d) 337, [1983] 2 S.C.R. 401, 2 D.L.R. (4th) 1, 50 N.R. 14.

A maintenance award based upon the possibility that the wife could lose her job in the future is unsound. In the event of a change of circumstances, it is preferable to review the issue of maintenance when the change actually arises: *Moravcik v. Moravcik* (1983), 37 R.F.L. (2d) 102 (Alta. C.A.).

Where the wife was working and there was no evidence that she would not be able to continue to work until eligible for superannuation, she was denied maintenance, despite the fact of her arthritic condition: *Williams v. Williams* (1982), 26 R.F.L. (2d) 325 (B.C. C.A.).

In *Fuhrman v. Fuhrman* (1981), 32 R.F.L. (2d) 129 (Alta. C.A.) an award of maintenance which amounted to 40 per cent of the husband's income was substantially reduced on appeal. The trial judge, in quantifying the wife's maintenance entitlement, had neglected to consider both her existing earnings and her earning capacity.

In *Phyllis v. Phyllis* (1976), 24 R.F.L. 103, 14 O.R. (2d) 771, 74 D.L.R. (3d) 593 (C.A.), the husband had insufficient income to support two households. The wife was 40 years of age and had custody of three infant children, 15, 11 and 10. She had been working during the majority of her married life and was trained as a private secretary and it was considered reasonable to expect her to work. In those circumstances the Court of Appeal held that her potential earning capacity should be taken into account to impose on her a partial share of the responsibility to support the children. See also *Ramsay v. Ramsay* (1974), 18 R.F.L. 225 (Ont. H.C.); reversed (1976), 23 R.F.L. 147, 13 O.R. (2d) 85, 70 D.L.R. (3d) 415 (C.A.); and Lazenby v. Lazenby, 18 R.F.L. 393 at 395, [1975] W.W.D. 88 (B.C. C.A.).

"While. . .[the wife] is not employed presently, she is a relatively young woman, she is 36 years of age, and while she has had some health problems in the past, the record is silent as to whether or not these difficulties continue. Such evidence as there is indicates that she is now capable of seeking employment. In my view, this capability of seeking employment is a factor which should reduce her dependency on the husband, and, for that reason, the amount is reduced": per Zuber J.A. in *Gleza v. Gleza* (1975), 24 R.F.L. 101 at 101 (Ont. C.A.). See also *Jackson v. Jackson* (1976), 24 R.F.L. 109 (Ont. H.C.); *Sweetapple v. Sweetapple* (1978), 15 Nfld. & P.E.I.R. 262, 38 A.P.R. 262 (Nfld. T.D.); and *Barca v. Barca* (1972), 9 R.F.L. 78 at 86 (Alta. T.D.).

In *K. v. K.* (1975), 20 R.F.L. 22, [1975] 3 W.W.R. 708, 53 D.L.R. (3d) 290 (Man. C.A.), the court approved of the petitioner wife's proposal to take a degree course in nursing. Per Matas J.A. at pp. 301-302: "If petitioner's welfare only were under consideration she could not expect respondent to finance her further education. However, that is not the issue with her. It is the children's welfare that we are concerned with. It will be for the children's benefit, both in the immediate future and long-range, for petitioner to complete her nursing education. This is so, because of the additional time she will have to spend with the children and the additional money (which will benefit the children) she will be able to earn with the university degree.. . .I am also of the view that it would be in the husband's long-range interests as well as that of the wife and children, if the plan of the wife is carried out. The children will be taken care of in a much better way and the wife will be in a better position to shoulder her share of the responsibility for their financial support."

"I look then at the age of the wife, and the fact that if separation had not occurred it is most unlikely that she would have ever gone out to work. I look at the many years since she has worked and the very slight experience. I have looked at her ability to work competently, and at the intelligence and the initiative, but I have also considered the emotional problems": per Van Vamp L.J.S.C. in *Morgan v. Morgan* (1977), 1 R.F.L. (2d) 214 at 236 (Ont. H.C.). See also *Fullarton v. Fullarton*, 5 R.F.L. 356 at 358, [1972] 1 O.R. 782, 24 D.L.R. (3d) 254 (C.A.).

In *Leatherdale v. Leatherdale* (1980), 14 R.F.L. (2d) 263, 19 R.F.L. (2d) 141 (Ont. H.C.); varied 19 R.F.L. (2d) 148, (sub nom. *Re Leatherdale and Leatherdale)* 31 O.R. (2d) 141, 118 D.L.R. (3d) 72 (C.A.); varied on other grounds 30 R.F.L. (2d) 225, [1982] 2 S.C.R. 743, 142 D.L.R. (3d) 193, 45 N.R. 40, the court approached the wife's claim for support on the basis that she was capable of working full-time, even though at the time of the order, she was in fact, only working part-time. The court was not satisfied that the restricted hours of work which she was following were of any real benefit to the 15-year-old child's development in the particular circumstances. The court also took into consideration the previous division of assets.

In *Sharp v. Sharp* (1981), 22 R.F.L. (2d) 29 (Ont. H.C.), it was held that although a wife was entitled to live at substantially the same standard of living enjoyed during cohabitation, it was not unreasonable that she should supplement her income by employment, where she was in good health and the child of the marriage was 13 years old.

In *Droit de la famille — 1043*, [1986] R.D.F. 464 (C.S. Qué.), the court granted the 62-year-old wife's application for both periodic and lump sum maintenance. The wife had never worked and was entitled to live out her retirement years in accordance with her previous life style.

Where the wife was a capable business woman and was able to maintain herself and had formed a personal and business relationship with another man subsequent to the parties' separation, her application for maintenance was refused: *Loiselle v. Francis* (1984), 39 R.F.L. (2d) 355 (Que. S.C.).

Where the husband had been in an accident and was unable to work and the wife's earning potential was far greater than the husband's, no spousal maintenance was awarded: *Douglas v. Douglas* (1984), 43 R.F.L. (2d) 262 (B.C. S.C.); *Parlevliet v. Parlevliet* (1984), 39 R.F.L. (2d) 260 (Ont. Co. Ct.).

In *Stere v. Stere* (1982), 28 R.F.L. (2d) 325 (Ont. H.C.), the fact that the wife had quit her job to provide a private education for her children and was on public assistance of her own choosing led the court to a consideration of her earning capacity in her application for maintenance. As a result, maintenance was ordered for a very limited period only.

Where during the marriage the wife had left a job paying $20,000 per year in favour of one that paid half that amount, her application for maintenance in subsequent divorce proceedings was dismissed. The wife could, if she so wished, return to her former employment and, therefore, there was no reason for the husband to be called upon to support her when she did not take the opportunity to support herself: *Downes v. Downes* (1982), 29 R.F.L. (2d) 20 (Ont. H.C.).

In *Butt v. Butt* (1982), 31 R.F.L. (2d) 293 (Alta. Q.B.), the court refused to award the wife sufficient periodic maintenance to allow her to return to school to obtain a law degree. The wife had already obtained a Bachelor's degree in nursing subsequent to the parties' separation and as she had an income potential of $30,000 annually it would not have been proper to burden the husband with the support obligation requested.

In *Mero v. Mero* (1982), 32 R.F.L. (2d) 137 (Ont. H.C.), the wife was denied maintenance upon the termination of her 8-month marriage. The brevity of the marriage and the fact that the wife had already received a property settlement and had made no effort to seek gainful employment mitigated against an award of maintenance.

Where during the course of the marriage the wife had been able to develop her skills to the extent that she could support herself at a substantial level, her application for periodic maintenance was refused. As the wife had really lost nothing through the marriage, a periodic maintenance award could not be justified: *Tward v. Tward* (1982), 31 R.F.L. (2d) 251 (Ont. H.C.).

In *MacKay v. MacKay* (1981), 44 N.S.R. (2d) 361, 83 A.P.R. 361 (T.D.), the wife made reasonable efforts to find work and had had several jobs but they lasted only a short time because of "attitudinal differences". The court found that she was totally dependent on the support she received from her husband and made an order increasing periodic payments.

"I would be inclined, in these circumstances, where the petitioner [wife] has decided 'on a new career', as compared to the types of employment she was involved in while living with the respondent. . .to make no award. I think the respondent has no responsibility to assist the petitioner in her new endeavour. The petitioner has shown repeatedly during the marriage that she is enterprising, industrious and willing and that she has no difficulty in locating employment. If she chooses to go outside of her regular field of expertise, then she does so at her peril": per Dohm L.J.S.C. in *Heaps v. Heaps* (1980), 17 R.F.L. (2d) 119 at 129, 20 B.C.L.R. 382 (S.C.); *Slatten v. Slatten* (1976), 27 R.F.L. 307, 1 B.C.L.R. 349 (S.C.); *Jones v. Jones* (1977), 2 R.F.L. (2d) 345 (B.C. S.C.); *Sadowski v. Sadowski* (1975), 25 R.F.L. 240 (Ont. H.C.). See also *Vnuk v. Vnuk* (1975), 23 R.F.L. 117 at 120 (B.C. S.C.); *Carroll v. Carroll* (1974), 13 R.F.L. 357 (Ont. H.C.); *Swalm v. Swalm* (1973), 12 R.F.L. 181 at 184 (Ont. H.C.).

15§11 — Factors — means — payee's obligation to invest

Where the payee spouse receives assets on equalization in exchange for a part of her former spouse's pension entitlement, she must use those assets in a reasonable attempt to generate income at least by the time the pension starts to pay out. She cannot save the assets that she receives upon equalization and choose instead to live on the liquidation of the former spouse's pension when he retires. If she were permitted to do so, she would accumulate an estate while the former spouse's estate is liquidating. Not having invested her assets, she should be found to have an income based on what they could reasonably produce if invested: *Boston v. Boston*, [2001] S.C.J. No. 45, 201 D.L.R. (4th) 1, 17 R.F.L. (5th) 4, 271 N.R. 248, 149 O.A.C. 50, 28 C.C.P.B. 17, [2001] 2 S.C.R. 413, C.E.B. & P.G.R. 8385 (S.C.C.). Here the husband retired on his pension income and applied to reduce the support payments to his wife that were ordered in a consent judgment made before retirement. The judgment also equalized the net family properties of the parties which included the capitalized value of that part of the husband's pension earned during the marriage. In implementing the judgment the husband received net assets of approximately $385,000 ($333,329 being the capitalized value of his pension) and the wife received assets of approximately $370,000 ($213,000 of which was comprised of the matrimonial home and its contents). At the time of the proceedings the wife's assets had increased in value to approximately $493,000. The husband's assets were worth $7,000. Actuarial evidence showed that if the wife invested $250,000 in a life annuity, it would produce $18,025 per year for life. If she invested $500,000 it would produce $36,050 per year for life. The motions judge granted the application and reduced the amount of support from $3,433.12 per month (indexed annually to the cost of living) to $950 per month (not indexed) taking into account the ability of the wife to reasonably produce an income from her investments and the available income the husband would have from the part of his pension that was not equalized in the property division. The Ontario Court of Appeal changed the $950 to $2,000 a month. The Supreme Court of Canada allowed an appeal from the Court of Appeal and reinstated the judgment of the motions judge with the further order that the monthly amount be indexed and arrears, if any, of spousal support be paid to the wife.

Although the Supreme Court in the *Boston* case, above, focused on whether spousal support should be varied when the payor retires and his income is from a pension that was capitalized and included in an earlier property division, the principle that assets must be considered from the perspective of their income earning capacity has a more general application: *Corbeil v. Corbeil* (2001), 2001 CarswellAlta 1138, [2001] A.J. No. 1144, 2001 ABCA 220, 286 A.R. 330, 253 W.A.C. 330, 21 R.F.L. (5th) 1, [2002] 3 W.W.R. 60, 98 Alta. L.R. (3d) 38 (Alta. C.A.)

In *Meiklejohn v. Meiklejohn*, 2001 CarswellOnt 3480, [2001] O.J. No. 3911, 19 R.F.L. (5th) 167, 150 O.A.C. 149, C.E.B. & P.G.R. 8395 (note), [2001] O.T.C. 323(Ont. C.A.); additional reasons at (2001), 2001 CarswellOnt 4050 (Ont. C.A.), the Court of Appeal held that where most of the value in the wife's assets was reflected in the matrimonial home and RRSPs, it was not unreasonable for her to retain them. She had no entitlement to survivor benefits if the husband cancelled his life insurance and predeceased her. She was entitled to support, even if part of it came from the husband's equalized share of his pension.

The wife's application for interim support should be dismissed where she had 1.3 million dollars in income-generating assets, a house valued at $240,000, and a cottage worth $160,000: *Fields v. Fields* (2000), 6 R.F.L. (5th) 148, 2000 CarswellMan 225, 2000 MBQB 32 (Man. Q.B.). A person with substantial assets should not be allowed to organize them is such a way "as to virtually insure the need for support." This is especially the case with respect to interim support.

Although the wife had been out of the workforce for a number of years caring for the parties' children, her bank balances and R.R.S.P. had increased after separation and she had been able to purchase a house. She failed to provide adequate financial disclosure and, in the circumstances, failed to establish the need for support: *Gervasio v. Gervasio* (1999), 45 R.F.L. (4th) 342, 1999 CarswellOnt 1061 (Ont. Gen. Div.).

Where the wife had refused to make full use of the income opportunities resulting from her property award, the $765 monthly maintenance allowance granted on divorce was reduced on appeal to $450 monthly. With more effort and a more realistic management of her assets, she could realize a greater income without encroaching on her capital: *Cherney v. Cherney* (1987), 9 R.F.L. (3d) 133, 1987 CarswellSask 94, 60 Sask. R. 69 (Sask. C.A.); reversing (1986), 51 Sask. R. 158, 1986 CarswellSask 563 (Sask. Q.B.).

Each party's capital position after the division of assets must be taken into account when determining the question of spousal support: *MacIsaac v. MacIsaac* (1996), 1996 CarswellNS 177, [1996] N.S.J. No. 185, 150 N.S.R. (2d) 321, 436 A.P.R. 321, 21 R.F.L. (4th) 358 (N.S. C.A.).

Where the wife receives a substantial share of the parties' matrimonial property, her application for spousal support should be refused: *Miller v. Miller* (1996), 22 R.F.L. (4th) 103, 142 Sask. R. 149, 1996 CarswellSask 187, [1996] S.J. No. 212 (Sask. Q.B.). Given the value of the property awarded to her, it could not be said that the marriage had caused the wife to be at an economic disadvantage:

Where the income from the wife's pending property award would enable her to be self-sufficient, she should be awarded periodic support only until such time as she receives her property entitlement: *Goodfield v. Goodfield* (1989), 24 R.F.L. (3d) 429, 71 O.R. (2d) 457, 1989 CarswellOnt 332 (Ont. H.C.).

When determining the quantum of a maintenance award, the court should take into account the earning capacity of a property award made under a provincial matrimonial property statute: *Lucas v. Lucas* (1982), 35 R.F.L. (2d) 216, 1982 CarswellAlta 352 (Alta. C.A.).

In *Taylor v. Taylor* (1983), 34 R.F.L. (2d) 136, 1983 CarswellAlta 273 (Alta. Q.B.), the wife's claim for maintenance was dismissed in light of the considerable property settlement that was made in her favour.

In *Munro v. Munro* (1997), 33 R.F.L. (4th) 464, 1997 CarswellOnt 3905 (Ont. C.A.), the wife's spousal support awarded upon dissolution of the parties' 18-year marriage was reduced on appeal. Although the length of the marriage and the fact that the wife had been primary caregiver to the husband's children entitled her to support, the quantum awarded at trial was too high given the impact of the equalization payment upon the parties' incomes.

Where spousal support had been linked to equalization of net family property, a new trial ordered on the issue of equalization required that the issue of support be reconsidered, also: *Wunsche v. Wunsche* (1994), 18 O.R. (3d) 161, 1994 CarswellOnt 838, [1994] O.J. No. 816, 70 O.A.C. 380, 114 D.L.R. (4th) 314 (C.A.).

Where the assets and income of the wife are capable of providing her with a reasonable standard of living as defined by decided cases, the court will not attempt to equalize revenue between the spouses. It is the responsibility of a wife to contribute to her own support as far as she is able by arranging and investing her assets so as to manifest the best financial advantage reasonably attained. Therefore, where the wife owns a home in excess of her needs, the court may assess maintenance on the basis that the wife will replace the home with a more modest one and invest the capital so realized: *Campbell v. Campbell* (1981), 24 R.F.L. (2d) 59, 1981 CarswellOnt 280 (Ont. H.C.); *Emmett v. Emmett* (1980), 21 R.F.L. (2d) 285, 1980 CarswellOnt 337 (Ont. H.C.); *Harwood v. Thomas* (1980), 21 R.F.L. (2d) 1, 43 N.S.R. (2d) 292, 81 A.P.R. 292, 1980 CarswellNS 49 (T.D.); affirmed 22 R.F.L. (2d) 167, 45 N.S.R. (2d) 414, 86 A.P.R. 414, 1981 CarswellNS 57 (C.A.). See also *Billo v. Billo* (1982), 27 R.F.L. (2d) 150, 1982 CarswellSask 57 (Sask. Q.B.); additional reasons at 27 R.F.L. (2d) 463, 1982 CarswellSask 65 (Sask. U.F.C.); *Leask v. Leask* (1975), 24 R.F.L. 275, 1975 CarswellBC 68 (B.C. S.C.). See also *Howorko v. Howorko* (1980), 2 R.F.L. (2d) 43 at 53, [1981] 1 W.W.R. 432, 6 Sask. R. 420, 1980 CarswellSask 141 (U.F.C.).

15§12 — Factors — means — other financial factors affecting payor

Where the capitalized value of the payor's pension has been included in the division of property between the parties, it would be inequitable to continue support out of the payor's pension income. To do so would allow the payee to reap benefits from the husband's pension twice, or permit "double recovery". To avoid this result, the focus should be on the portion of the pension-holding spouse's income and assets that were not part of the equalization or division process: *Boston v. Boston*, [2001] S.C.J. No. 45, 201 D.L.R. (4th) 1, 17 R.F.L. (5th) 4, 271 N.R. 248, 149 O.A.C. 50, 28 C.C.P.B. 17, [2001] 2 S.C.R. 413, C.E.B. & P.G.R. 8385 (S.C.C.).

There is no double recovery where the pension was inadequately capitalized in the property division and it cannot be said that the pension income is from property that has already been divided. In these circumstances, the issue of double recovery simply does not arise: *Strang v. Strang*, 1992 CarswellAlta 70, 3 Alta. L.R. (3d) 1, 125 A.R. 331, 137 N.R. 203, 14 W.A.C. 331 (S.C.C.).

As a general rule, whenever practicable, the courts, for purposes of spousal support, should not resort to an asset such as a pension that has already been used in the division of property: *Chamberlain v. Chamberlain*, 36 R.F.L. (5th) 241, [2003] N.B.J. No. 168, 2003 CarswellNB 208, 2003 CarswellNB 209, 2003 NBCA 34, 226 D.L.R. (4th) 272 (N.B.C.A.); affirming 2002 NBQB 231, 252 N.B.R. (2d) 152, 658 A.P.R. 152, 2002 CarswellNB 540 (N.B. Q.B.).

In *Meiklejohn v. Meiklejohn*, 2001 CarswellOnt 3480, [2001] O.J. No. 3911, 19 R.F.L. (5th) 167, 150 O.A.C. 149, C.E.B. & P.G.R. 8395 (note), [2001] O.T.C. 323 (Ont. C.A.); additional reasons at (2001), 2001 CarswellOnt 4050 (Ont. C.A.), the Court of Appeal held that the wife was entitled to support, even if part of it came from the husband's equalized share of his pension. Most of the value in the wife's assets was reflected in the matrimonial home and RRSPs and it was not unreasonable for her to retain them in this form. She would have no entitlement to survivor benefits if the husband cancelled his life insurance and predeceased her.

The fact that a husband's pension has been divided as property between the parties does not remove the husband's pension from the consideration of his ability to pay support: *Grainger v. Grainger* (1992), 39 R.F.L. (3d) 101, 100 Sask. R. 61, 18 W.A.C. 161 (C.A.). Even though a spouse's pension value may be included in equalization proceedings, it is not improper to consider pension income received by that spouse when determining his or her ability to pay support: *Flett v. Flett* (1992), 43 R.F.L. (3d) 24 (Ont. U.F.C.).

In *Lockyer v. Lockyer*, 37 R.F.L. (5th) 174, 2003 CarswellNfld 62, 2003 NLSCUFC 7 (N.L. U.F.C.), the wife was awarded monthly support of $300, although the husband had an annual income of only $27,500. The wife was unemployable because of a debilitating disease and her monthly income was under $500. While both incomes were modest, a fundamental imbalance existed between the finances of the two and only the husband had options to restructure his affairs to maintain some liquidity.

Where the 60-year-old husband's position had been eliminated, he applied for and received a substantial reduction in the spousal support payable by him. The wife, whose only means of income after the dissolution of the parties' 30-year marriage was spousal support, successfully appealed. The husband, despite his age, still had marketable skills which could deliver a significant income. He had also remarried and his new wife, who was employed, could contribute to household expenses. The trial judge had erred in placing too much responsibility on the wife to obtain employment and not enough responsibility on the husband: *Wyman v. Wyman* (1999), 49 R.F.L. (4th) 447 (N.S. C.A.).

Currency restrictions should be considered in determining the husband's ability to pay support where he works in a country which limits the amount of money he can send to his wife out of the country: *Stebbins v. Stebbins* (1995), 14 R.F.L. (4th) 226 (N.S. S.C.).

In *Blumes v. Blumes* (1995), 174 A.R. 353, 102 W.A.C. 353 (C.A.); affirming (1995), 175 A.R. 253 (Q.B.), the court dismissed the husband's appeal from a spousal support order which he claimed, over a period of time, would place him in a deficit position. Although the order would eventually produce a deficit, it would be reduced upon the sale of the matrimonial home, the retirement of the husband's debt to his adult son and the payment of an outstanding loan.

Where only upon threats of contempt proceedings the husband revealed the existence of real estate assets in Florida, the wife's claim for spousal support was allowed. Although the husband claimed monthly income of only $475, the fact that he held American real estate indicated that he had sufficient resources to support his wife: *Droit de la famille — 2140* (1994), [1995] R.D.F. 126 (C.S. Qué).

Where the husband's income had been inflated as a result of his working overseas on a limited term contract, spousal support was ordered on the basis of that income. However, when the husband returned to Canada and resumed normal employment, the parties would have to seek a review of the order which could ultimately result in a variation or the imposition of a time limiation: *McIntyre v. McIntyre* (1995), 160 N.B.R. (2d) 81, 412 A.P.R. 81 (Q.B.).

In *Turcotte v. Turcotte* (1996), 22 R.F.L. (4th) 364, 1 O.T.C. 156 (Gen. Div.), the husband was not allowed to rely upon his heavy debt load as a reason for restricting the wife's spousal support. His situation was largely the result of deliberate choice and as he was a highly intelligent man, it was up to him to find solutions to his financial problems.

Where the only way that the husband could afford to pay child support was by selling his home or by drastically reducing his lifestyle, no order for support was made. Both alternatives would have had a detrimental effect upon the child, and the wife already enjoyed a substantial income: *DaCosta v. DaCosta* (1990), 29 R.F.L. (3d) 422, 74 D.L.R. (4th) 491 (Ont. Gen. Div.), appeal allowed in part on another issue (1992), 40 R.F.L. (3d) 216, 7 O.R. (3d) 321, 44 E.T.R. 196, 53 O.A.C. 354, 89 D.L.R. (4th) 268 (C.A.); amended (1992), 40 R.F.L. (3d) 216n (Ont. C.A.).

Where the payor spouse's draws from his dental practice are derived indirectly from bank loans, periodic support should be calculated on the basis of the payor's real or actual income without reference to its source. The payee's property entitlement had been adversely affected by the payor's bank loans for his dental practice and the payee should not be forced to suffer doubly by having her income affected adversely as well: *McGuigan v. McGuigan* (1991), 33 R.F.L. (3d) 183, 105 N.S.R. (2d) 170, 284 A.P.R. 170 (T.D.).

Where the wife was awarded $1,000 monthly child support, as well as exclusive possession of the family home, the support award was reduced to $750 on appeal. In light of the advantage accruing to the wife through the exclusive possession order, and the corresponding detriment to the husband, the support award was too high: *Francis v. Francis* (1989), 24 R.F.L. (3d) 265 (Ont. C.A.); varying (1987), 8 R.F.L. (3d) 460 (Ont. H.C.).

Where the husband had been ordered to pay spousal support based upon sizeable past income and his access to credit, the order was reversed on appeal. The husband had retained little or none of his past revenues and his wife, with some assistance from her parents, could meet her own needs: *A. (P) c. C. (S.)*, 12 Q.A.C. 278, 14 R.F.L. (3d) 246, (sub nom. *Droit de lafamille — 443)* [1988] R.J.Q. 323, [1988] R.D.F. 105 (C.A. Qué.).

An R.R.S.P. that is not generating income should not be taken into account in determining the parties' "means and needs" for support purposes: *Ellis v. Ellis* (1990), 26 R.F.L. (3d) 184 (Sask. Q.B.).

In *Robertson v. Robertson* (1974), 15 R.F.L. 379, 47 D.L.R. (3d) 159 (Man. C.A.), the court considered the effect on a maintenance order of Canada Pension benefits paid to the children due to their father's disability. Per Freedman C.J.M.: "Counsel for the wife argued that the payments under the Canada Pension Plan were a windfall which the wife should get for the benefit of her children, quite apart from the moneys payable under the decree. We do not agree. In our view Hamilton J. reached the correct decision in declaring that the husband was entitled to deduct the amount of the payments made under the Canada Pension Plan since these were being received by the children for no other reason than that they were the children of a disabled contributor".

Although the husband had squandered $20,000 of a $55,000 severance allowance after losing his job, the wife was ordered to pay periodic support to him until he found employment. Even if he had not dissipated the funds, he would have required assistance: *Jering v. Jering* (1987), 7 R.F.L. (3d) 42, 45 Man. R. (2d) 296 (Man. Q.B.).

See also *Sinclair v. Sinclair* (1984), 40 R.F.L. (2d) 95 (Man. Q.B.); *Reichel v. Reichel* (1974), 15 R.F.L. 157 at 158 (Sask. Q.B.);*Aitken v. Aitken* (1984), 38 R.F.L. (2d) 334 (Sask. Q.B.); *Tucker v. Tucker* (1982), 17 Man. R. (2d) 262 (Q.B.); *Johnson v. Johnson* (1981), 27 R.F.L. (2d) 10 (B.C. S.C.).

See also *Morgan v. Morgan* (1977), 1 R.F.L. (2d) 214 at 236 (Ont. H.C.); Schmidt v. Schmidt (1976), 26 R.F.L. 232 at 238 (B.C. S.C.); *Misener v. Misener* (1977), 3 R.F.L. (2d) 21, 26 N.S.R. (2d) 622, 40 A.P.R. 622 (T.D.); *Dixon v. Dixon* (1974), 16 R.F.L. 198, 5 Nfld. & P.E.I.R. 527 (P.E.I. S.C.); *Marshall v. Marshall* (1976), 29 R.F.L. 314 (Ont. H.C.); *Babuick v. Babuick* (1975), 17 R.F.L. 11 (Sask. Q.B.). See also *Dyck v. Dyck* (1973), 11 R.F.L. 56 at 60 (Sask. Q.B.); *Scott v. Scott*, 5 R.F.L. 231, [1972] 2 W.W.R. 456, 23 D.L.R. (3d) 689 (N.W.T. Terr. Ct.); *Cameron v. Cameron* (1970), 2 R.F.L. 339, 2 N.S.R. (2d) 50, 12 D.L.R. (3d) 378 (T.D.).

15§13 — Factors — means — one or both spouses on public assistance

See 15§24 Objectives of spousal support — general.

A spouse cannot rely on the availability of social assistance to the claimant as a means of avoiding support obligations: *Harvey v. Harvey* (1995), 14 R.F.L. (4th) 128 (B.C. C.A.).

The fact that the payor spouse is receiving welfare benefits is not an absolute bar to liability for child support: *Higgins v. Pethick* (1989), 21 R.F.L. (3d) 326 (Sask. C.A.).

The extent of a husband's obligation to pay maintenance to his wife should not be measured by the availability of social assistance to her: *Gray v. Gray* (1986), 3 R.F.L. (3d) 457, 45 Man. R. (2d) 156 (Q.B.); affirmed (1987), 8 R.F.L. (3d) 147 (Man. C.A.).

Where the wife is receiving social assistance, the fact that she will not benefit from an award that is less than this assistance is not a fact that should be taken into account when determining the issue of suuport: *Duncan v. Duncan* (1992), 40 R.F.L. (3d) 358, 128 A.R. 57 (Q.B.).

In determining the quantum of support payable by the husband, it is appropriate to consider Canada Pension Plan disability benefits which are being received by the wife: *Klassen v. Klassen* (1990), 25 R.F.L. (3d) 277, 63 Man. R. (2d) 201 (Q.B.).

Where the parties are unable to provide support for their children at a reasonable level, the court may permit the payor spouse to pay less than his share of child support so that the children will not lose welfare benefits: *F. (R.D.) v. R. (S.L.)* (1987), 6 R.F.L. (3d) 413 (B.C. S.C.).

It is contrary to public policy to allow a wife to live on social assistance where the husband has the means to pay maintenance: *Droit de la famille — 16* (1983), 34 R.F.L. (2d) 257 (Que. C.A.). The wife obtained a decree *nisi* of divorce which was silent as to maintenance. Later, when she was living on social welfare, she applied for maintenance and was successful on appeal.

An order awarding periodic maintenance to the wife was upheld on appeal although a separation agreement between the parties did not provide for spousal support. As the wife was on welfare, it was incumbent upon the court to have regard to the interest of the public as well as to that of the deserving spouse. A spouse's primary obligation and duty of maintenance should be enforced when necessary to prevent the other spouse from having to seek, or from continuing to receive, public support: *Fabian v. Fabian* (1983), 34 R.F.L. (2d) 313 (Ont. C.A.). See also *Piasta v. Piasta* (1984), 15 R.F.L. 137 (Sask. Q.B.) (compare Family Law Act, S.O. 1990, c. F.3 as amended, s. 31(4)(b), which provides that the "court may set aside a provision for support or a waiver of the right to support in a domestic contract . . . and may determine and order support . . . if the provision for support is in favour of or the waiver is by or on behalf of a dependant who qualifies for an allowance for support out of public money".).

The fact that a spouse is dependent upon welfare does not in itself justify an increase in maintenance: *Tyler v. Tyler* (1986), 2 R.F.L. (3d) 37, 41 Man. R. (2d) 112 (Man. Q.B.).

In *Droit de la famille — 1041*, [1986] R.D.F. 458 (C.S. Qué.), the wife's maintenance application, brought for the first time 6 months subsequent to the parties' divorce, was refused. Although she had lost her job and was receiving welfare, the job loss represented only a temporary set-back and the government had the resource to give assistance to those in similar situations.

Even where as a result of a spousal support order, the entire amount will be deducted from the recipient's welfare cheque, the family should, where possible, bear some responsibility for a fellow member's support: *Papaspirou v. Soussoudis* (1999), 2 R.F.L. (5th) 437 (Ont. S.C.J.). In a case such as this one where both spouses have little means, there is no point in reducing both parties to a state of impoverishment. The husband earned $23,470 a year and the wife was on welfare. The husband was ordered to pay $250 per month spousal support.

In *Smith v. Smith* (1986), 5 R.F.L. (3d) 398 (Man. Q.B.), it was held that the fact that the wife was receiving social assistance in itself did not justify an upward variation of the maintenance payable to her.

Where the wife was living on welfare both before the brief marriage and after the parties' separation and her inability to work was not attributable to the failed marriage, it was not found equitable to require the husband, who was retired and on a limited income, to contribute to his wife's maintenance: *Tomlinson v. Tomlinson* (1985), 49 R.F.L. (2d) 289 (Ont. H.C.).

In *Barrett v. Barrett* (1985), 43 R.F.L. (2d) 405 (Ont. H.C.), the court ordered an increase in spousal maintenance in excess of that specified in the separation agreement which had been incorporated into the decree *nisi*. The fact that the wife's financial position had deteriorated drastically subsequent to the decree *nisi* to the extent that she was partially dependent on public assistance justified the variation.

See also *Cassie v. Cassie* (1984), 38 R.F.L. (2d) 136 (Man. Q.B.); *Doepel v. Doepel* (1983), 36 R.F.L. (2d) 316 (Ont. H.C.); *McDougall v. McDougall* (1982), 29 R.F.L. (2d) 274 (B.C. S.C.); *Munro v. Munro* (1974), 16 R.F.L. 123 at 127 (Sask. Q.B.); *Durdle v. Durdle* (1981), 30 Nfld. & P.E.I.R. 210 at 213, 84 A.P.R. 210 (Nfld. T.D.); *Schartner v. Schartner* (1970), 72 W.W.R. 443 at 452, 10 D.L.R. (3d) 61 (Sask. Q.B.); *McLeod v. McLeod* (1970), 2 R.F.L. 386 at 387 (Man. Q.B.); *Passerino v. Passerino* (1984), 39 R.F.L. (2d) 442 (Ont. Master).

15§14 — Factors — means — capital position of spouses

In *Leskun v. Leskun*, 2006 CarswellBC 1492, 2006 SCC 25, [2006] 1 S.C.R. 25 (S.C.C.), in determining spousal support, a court can take into account a payor spouse's capital assets acquired after the marital break-up. Since the capital assets at issue did not exist at the time of the initial division, there was no question of "double dipping".

In *Munro v. Munro* (1997), 33 R.F.L. (4th) 464 (Ont. C.A.), the wife's spousal support awarded upon dissolution of the parties' 18-year marriage was reduced on appeal. Although the length of the marriage and the fact that the wife had been primary caregiver to the husband's children entitled her to support, the quantum awarded at trial was too high given the impact of an equalization payment upon the parties' incomes.

Where both parties were prohibited from working because of health issues, and the husband particularly so, the wife was nevertheless required to pay spousal support to the husband. The wife had received a substantial inheritance which would generate an annual income of approximately $35,000. Accordingly, the wife was in a financial position to pay support: *Pecore v. Pecore* (2004), 48 R.F.L. (5th) 89, [2004] O.J. No. 695, 2004 CarswellOnt 748, 6 E.T.R. (3d) 113 (Ont. S.C.J.).

In *Kowaluk v. Kowaluk* (1995), 17 R.F.L. (4th) 185 (Man. Q.B.), the husband was ordered to pay both substantial periodic and lump sum support despite the fact that he would be required to sell off farm land in order to do so.

Where the husband suffered a shortfall in the amount needed to support himself as a result of the division of matrimonial property, his need was found to be based on an economic disadvantage properly traced to the marriage breakdown. He was accordingly entitled to support: *Bracewell v. Bracewell* (1994), 4 R.F.L. (4th) 183, 152 A.R. 379 (Q.B.).

In *Melnychuk v. Melnychuk* (1995), 16 R.F.L. (4th) 366 (Sask. Q.B.), the wife's claim for spousal support was dismissed. Neither party was able to work for health reasons. Although the husband had investments in excess of $250,000, he lacked sufficient assets to support both himself and his wife without dipping into his capital. As the wife had been careless in the previous management of her resources, her claim was properly denied.

In determining the issue of spousal support, the assets of the parties are a relevant consideration regardless of whether they are matrimonial assets or assets exempt from division: *Labron v. Labron* (1996), 21 R.F.L. (4th) 385, 183 A.R. 251 (Q.B.). Where the wife received substantial assets upon dissolution of the parties' 25- year traditional marriage, her spousal support was accordingly limited to a two-year period. It was necessary that she be encouraged to become self-sufficient: *MacIsaac v. MacIsaac* (1995), 144 N.S.R. (2d) 354, 416 A.P.R. 354 (S.C.).

Where the wife received a sizable share of the parties' matrimonial property, her application for spousal support was refused. The value of her share of property was sufficient compensation for any economic disadvantage arising from the marriage: *Miller v. Miller* (1996), 22 R.F.L. (4th) 103, 142 Sask. R. 149 (Q.B.).

In *Burtnick v. Burtnick* (1995), 14 R.F.L. (4th) 158, 102 Man. R. (2d) 232 (C.A.); affirming (1994), 94 Man. R. (2d) 167 (Q.B.), the court upheld a spousal support award in the wife's favour which effectively equalized their incomes, both of which were derived solely from pensions. Considering the parties' lengthy marriage and the loss of the husband's pension if the wife survived him, the award was justified. Furthermore, the portion of the husband's pension which resulted in his higher income was not divisable.

Where the wife's main source of income was derived from her investments, she was awarded spousal support on the breakdown of the parties' 30-year marriage. The husband had a healthy income on which to draw, in addition to substantial investments, and was in a position to pay support: *Droit de la famille — 2129* (1994), [1995] R.D.F. 102 (C.S. Qué.).

The investment income earned from an accident settlement should be taken into account in determining the spouse's means and needs: *Hepp v. Hepp* (1990), 24 R.F.L. (3d) 367 (B.C. C.A.).

Where spousal support had been linked to equalization of net family property, a new trial ordered on the issue of equalization required that the issue of support also be reconsidered: *Wunsche v. Wunsche* (1994), 18 O.R. (3d) 161 (C.A.).

Where the income from the wife's pending property award would enable her to be self-sufficient, she was awarded periodic support only until such time as she received her property entitlement: *Goodfield v. Goodfield* (1989), 24 R.F.L. (3d) 429, 71 O.R. (2d) 457 (H.C.).

In *Cline v. Cline* (1988), 12 R.F.L. (3d) 289 (N.B. Q.B.), the court dismissed the wife's claims for support in divorce proceedings to end her five-year marriage. As the wife had received an equalization payment and the husband had assumed responsibility for her student loan, a support order could not be justified given the brief duration of the marriage.

Where the wife had refused to make full use of the income opportunities resulting from her property award, the $765 monthly maintenance award granted on divorce was reduced on appeal to $450 monthly. With more effort and more realistic management of her assets, the wife could realize a greater income without encroaching on her capital: *Cherney v. Cherney* (1987), 9 R.F.L. (3d) 133 (Sask. C.A.); varying (1986), 51 Sask. R. 158 (Q.B.).

Pension benefits are not a substitute for spousal support payment: *Lavoie v. Lavoie* (1991), 32 R.F.L. (3d) 77, 101 N.S.R. (2d) 65, 275 A.P.R. 65 (Fam. Ct.).

When determining the quantum of a maintenance award, the court should take into account the earning capacity of a property award made under a provincial matrimonial property statute: *Lucas v. Lucas* (1982), 35 R.F.L. (2d) 216 (Alta. C.A.).

See also *Osborne v. Osborne* (1974), 23 R.F.L. 358 (Sask. C.A.); varying (1973), 14 R.F.L. 61 (Sask. Q.B.); *Taylor v. Taylor* (1983), 34 R.F.L. (2d) 136 (Alta. Q.B.); *Passey v. Passey* (1982), 17 Man. R. (2d) 205 (Q.B.); *Campbell v. Campbell* (1981), 24 R.F.L. (2d) 59 (Ont. H.C.); Emmett v. Emmett (1980), 21 R.F.L. (2d) 285 (Ont. H.C.); *Harwood v. Thomas* (1980), 21 R.F.L. (2d) 1, 43 N.S.R. (2d) 292, 81 A.P.R. 292 (T.D.); affirmed 22 R.F.L. (2d) 167, 45 N.S.R. (2d) 414, 86 A.P.R. 414 (C.A.); *Billo v. Billo* (1982), 27 R.F.L. (2d) 150; additional reasons at 27 R.F.L. (2d) 463 (Sask. U.F.C.); *Leask v. Leask* (1975), 24 R.F.L. 275 (B.C. S.C.); *Boardman v. Boardman* (1978), 2 R.F.L. (2d) 43 at 53, [1981] 1 W.W.R. 432, 6 Sask. R. 420 (U.F.C.).

15§15 — Factors — needs

The Supreme Court of Canada in *Moge v. Moge* (1992), 43 R.F.L. (3d) 345, [1992] 3 S.C.R. 813, [1993] 1 W.W.R. 481, 145 N.R. 1, 81 Man. R. (2d) 161, 30 W.A.C. 161, 99 D.L.R. (4th) 456, held that the 1985 *Divorce Act* made a shift away from need as the basis of support to an emphasis on principles of compensation. In arriving at this opinion, the court referred to a report that the Law Reform Commission of Canada made in 1975. In this report, it recommended that "need", the traditional basis for support, be given a different interpretation. Need, in its view, should be defined in terms of the economic damage caused by the division of labour in the marriage, and the cost to repair this damage. The basis for support should be compensation for the economic loss incurred by the spouse who stays at home for the purpose of contributing non-monetary benefits to the marriage. It recommended that "the law should ascertain the extent to which the withdrawal from the labour force by the dependant spouse during the marriage (including loss of skills, seniority, work experience, continuity and so on) has adversely affected that spouse's ability to maintain himself or herself. The need upon which the right to maintenance is based therefore follows from the loss incurred by the maintained spouse in contributing to the marriage partnership." This recommendation seemed consistent with the court's understanding that the introduction of the objectives by the 1985 *Divorce Act* resulted in a shift away from "means and needs" as the exclusive test to "a much wider spectrum of considerations" defined by the objectives.

For a full summary of the *Moge* case, see 17§2 Variation and rescission of spousal support orders — general, and 15§24 Objectives of spousal support — general.

While the 1985 *Divorce Act* represent a shift away from "means and needs" to some degree "it retains the older idea that spouses may have an obligation to meet or contribute to the need of their former partners where they have the capacity to pay, even in the absence of a contractual or compensatory foundation for the obligation. Need alone may be enough.": *Bracklow v. Bracklow* (1999), 169 D.L.R. (4th) 577 (S.C.C.). For a detailed discussion of the facts of the case, see section 15§6 General principles for determining spousal support.

"In cases where need is demonstrated as a result of the marriage breakdown, the condition, needs, means and other circumstances of the parties at the time of the maintenance order must be given emphasis": *Epp v. Epp* (1998), 40 R.F.L. (4th) 137 (B.C. S.C. [In Chambers]).

Spousal support should be reduced where the quantum far exceeds the stated needs of the dependant spouse: *Turner v. Turner* (1998), 43 R.F.L. (4th) 437 (B.C. C.A.). In this case, the trial judge set an amount of support that was four times the amount requested in the wife's material, and was based in part upon her anticipated costs of living independently, even though it was not known if the wife were capable of living on her own, and the material did not provide a basis for calculating what it would cost if she were able to so do. Spousal support was reduced from $2,000 to $1,200 per month.

Need, in calculating support, varies in accordance with the circumstances of the parties and the family unit as a whole. Need does not necessarily end when the claimant spouse achieves a subsistence level of income or any level above subsistence. It is a flexible concept and is only one factor to be considered in determining whether a support award is warranted: *Myers v. Myers* (1995), 17 R.F.L. (4th) 298 (B.C. C.A.).

Although the wife had been out of the workforce for a number of years caring for the parties' children, her bank balances and R.R.S.P. account had increased after separation, and she had been able to purchase a house. She had failed to update her financial statement. In the circumstances, she was unable to establish the need for support and her claim was dismissed: *Gervasio v. Gervasio* (1999), 45 R.F.L. (4th) 342 (Ont. Gen. Div.).

Where compensation is not indicated and self-sufficiency is not possible, a support obligation may arise from the marriage relationship itself: *Bracklow v. Bracklow* (1999), 169 D.L.R. (4th) 577 (S.C.C.).

In an application for spousal support, the needs of the claimant party must be addressed, but not at the expense of impoverishing the other: *Fricker v. Fricker* (1991), 109 N.S.R. (2d) 234, 297 A.P.R. 234 (T.D.).

Where the husband suffered a shortfall in the amount needed to support himself as a result of the division of matrimonial property, his need was found to be based on an economic disadvantage properly traced to the marriage breakdown. He was accordingly entitled to support: *Bracewell v. Bracewell* (1994), 4 R.F.L. (4th) 183, 152 A.R. 379 (Q.B.). The parties had cohabited under the marriage for 32 years. At the time of the trial, the husband was unable to work because of ill-health and was dependant on a pension income and the benefit of sharing expenses with the woman with whom he lived and who operated a bed and breakfast business in her home. The wife was employed and earned an income that was higher than the husband's. His pensions were included in the property division whereby the payments were to be equally divided at source and one-half paid to the wife and one-half to the husband. The wife held the greater share of the balance of the matrimonial property and was ordered to pay the husband $22,828 as an equalization payment. A shortfall based on the husband's needs was found to be $350 a month which the wife was ordered to pay so long as she was employed and the husband was not.

Where the wife had clearly established her entitlement to spousal support but had failed to provide financial statements or information about her living expenses, the calculation of her support was adjourned to permit her to produce the required information: *R. (E.K.) v. W. (G.A.)* (1997), 32 R.F.L. (4th) 202, [1998] 1 W.W.R. 534 (Man. Q.B.); additional reasons at (January 30, 1998), Doc. Winnipeg Centre FD 93-01-33844 (Man. Q.B.).

Where the parties had lived separately for over 10 years and had maintained separate finances for several years before that, the husband's spousal support obligation was found not to extend beyond his pending retirement.Despite the fact of the wife's disability, her monthly income would still exceed that of the husband: *Phillips v. Phillips* (1998), 38 R.F.L. (4th) 31 (B.C. S.C.).

15§16 — Factors — circumstances — length of cohabitation — general

In assessing the duration of cohabitation, it is assumed that the time before marriage is counted and given the same weight as cohabitation after the marriage: *Bracklow v. Bracklow*, 169 D.L.R. (4th) 577, 236 N.R. 79, 44 R.F.L. (4th) 1, 120 B.C.A.C. 211, 196 W.A.C. 211, [1999] 1 S.C.R. 420, 63 B.C.L.R. (3d) 77, [1999] 8 W.W.R. 740, 1999 CarswellBC 532, 1999 CarswellBC 533, [1999] S.C.J. No. 14 (S.C.C.). For a detailed discussion of the facts of the case, see section 15§6 General principles for determining spousal support.

In *Anderson v. Anderson* (2000), 11 R.F.L. (5th) 1, 2000 PESCTD 79, 195 Nfld. & P.E.I.R. 150, 586 A.P.R. 150, 2000 CarswellPEI 79 (P.E.I. S.C.), although the parties, ages 25 and 27, had only been married for a very few years, in awarding the wife spousal support for a term of 1 year the court considered the fact that they had actually cohabited for a period of 6 and one-half years.

The longer a marriage lasts, the closer the economic union, and the greater the presumption of equal standards of living upon dissolution: *Moge v. Moge*, 43 R.F.L. (3d) 345, [1992] 3 S.C.R. 813, [1993] 1 W.W.R. 481, 145 N.R. 1, 81 Man. R. (2d) 161, 30 W.A.C. 161, 99 D.L.R. (4th) 456, [1993] R.D.F. 168, [1992] S.C.J. No. 107, 1992 CarswellMan 143 (Eng.), 1992 CarswellMan 222 (Fr.).

Long-term Marriage

A long-term relationship engenders long-term spousal support: *Waterman v. Waterman*, 16 R.F.L. (4th) 10, 133 Nfld. & P.E.I.R. 310, 413 A.P.R. 310, 1995 CarswellNfld 117, [1995] N.J. No. 295 (Nfld. C.A.).

The wife was entitled to spousal support to restore her to a more equitable position after the breakdown of a 31-year traditional long-term marriage: *Pearce v. Pearce* (1999), 1 R.F.L. (5th) 402, 1999 CarswellBC 2214 (B.C. S.C.).

In a long-term traditional marriage a wife who did not work for many years, but at the time of the hearing had obtained employment, was entitled to support by way of a lump sum of $39,000 for loss of economic opportunity: *DeFaveri v. Toronto Dominion Bank* (1999), 45 R.F.L. (4th) 141, 1999 CarswellOnt 773, [1999] O.J. No. 822 (Ont. C.A.). This was the same amount owing by the wife to the husband in the property division, so no exchange of funds needed to take place.

While a long relationship will create a stronger "presumptive claim to equal standards of living upon dissolution of the marriage" (see Moge at [1992] 3 S.C.R. 813 at 870) spousal support is not intended to achieve equalization of incomes after divorce: *Ross v. Ross* (1995), 16 R.F.L. (4th) 1, 168 N.B.R. (2d) 147, 430 A.P.R. 147, 1995 CarswellNB 160, [1995] N.B.J. No. 463 (N.B. C.A.). After a marriage of 30 years, support for the 47-year-old wife was reduced from $1,700 to $1,250 per month. The compensatory element of spousal support should not negate the promotion of self-sufficiency. Evidence supported the lower court's finding that the support award should be indefinite.

In *Adie v. Adie*, 7 R.F.L. (4th) 54, 134 N.S.R. (2d) 60, 383 A.P.R. 60, 1994 CarswellNS 58, [1994] N.S.J. No. 395 (N.S. S.C.), the fact that the parties had been married for over 15 years and that the separation had occurred after their retirement were found to favour the wife's claim to support. See also *Stroud v. Stroud*, 20 R.F.L. (4th) 392, 22 B.C.L.R. (3d) 183, 75 B.C.A.C. 48, 123 W.A.C. 48, 1996 CarswellBC 723 (B.C. C.A.), and *Penner v. Penner*, 24 R.F.L. (4th) 448, 82 B.C.A.C. 232, 133 W.A.C. 232, 1996 CarswellBC 2182 (B.C. C.A.). The wife was entitled to spousal support to restore her to a more equitable position after the breakdown of a 31-year traditional long-term marriage: *Pearce v. Pearce*, 1 R.F.L. (5th) 402, 1999 CarswellBC 2214 (B.C. S.C.).

In *Read v. Read*, 183 N.S.R. (2d) 181, 568 A.P.R. 181, 2000 NSCA 33, 4 R.F.L. (5th) 126, 2000 CarswellNS 52 (N.S. C.A.), the court dismissed an appeal from a judgment varying spousal support from $1,700 per month to $2,500 per month for a wife after a 28-year marriage. The husband's income had increased significantly and he would not be required to pay child support in the near future.

In *Huggins v. Huggins*, 183 N.S.R. (2d) 194, 568 A.P.R. 194, 2000 NSCA 30, 3 R.F.L. (5th) 235, 2000 CarswellNS 46 (N.S. C.A.), the husband's appeal of a variation of a spousal support award for a wife in a traditional long-term marriage of 22 years in which she was granted $400 instead of $700, but no termination date was imposed, was dismissed. There was no evidentiary basis for imposing a termination date.

Where the wife had a future need for support which arose because of her economic disadvantage suffered as a result of the long-term traditional marriage, her appeal was allowed in part and spousal support was set at $300 per month, even though she did not have a current economic need: *Savoie v. Savoie*, 49 R.F.L. (4th) 336, [1999] 9 W.W.R. 63, 175 D.L.R. (4th) 291, 138 Man. R. (2d) 128, 202 W.A.C. 128, 1999 CarswellMan 308 (Man. C.A.). This amount of $300 was half of what the wife had previously received under the parties' separation agreement and at trial. The reduction took into account her remarriage and the setting aside of the separation agreement.

In *Vint v. Vint*, 172 N.S.R. (2d) 172, 524 A.P.R. 172, 44 R.F.L. (4th) 145, 1998 CarswellNS 414 (N.S. C.A.), the court held that the evidence did not support the trial judge's finding that the respondent husband had no ability to pay spousal support. The court found that the parties had had a long-term marriage of 23 years. The wife had little education and had worked at low paying part-time jobs and the husband had provided an outdated statement of expenses. The court granted the wife's appeal and ordered a new hearing.

In *Munro v. Munro*, 33 R.F.L. (4th) 464, 1997 CarswellOnt 3905 (Ont. C.A.), the wife's spousal support awarded upon dissolution of the parties' 18-year marriage was reduced on appeal. Although the length of the marriage and the fact that the wife had been the primary caregiver to the husband's children entitled her to support, the quantum awarded at trial was too high given the impact of an equalization payment upon the parties' incomes.

After the termination of a long-term traditional marriage, the court, in determining spousal support, should not concentrate solely on identifying losses which have resulted from the marriage. The court should also recognize the social and financial effects of marriage on the claimant's ability to be self-sufficient after the termination of the marriage: *Waterman v. Waterman*, 16 R.F.L. (4th) 10, 133 Nfld. & P.E.I.R. 310, 413 A.P.R. 310, 1995 CarswellNfld 117, [1995] N.J. No. 295 (Nfld. C.A.).

In *Brace v. Brace*, 35 R.F.L. (3d) 263, 1991 CarswellOnt 318 (Ont. C.A.), the Ontario Court of Appeal upheld the trial judge's decision that the applicant was entitled to support as there was a causal connection between the wife's economic condition and the marriage. There was sufficient evidence in the medical evidence and, considering the 17-year marriage generally, to support the trial judge's conclusion.

Where the husband's abuse of the wife during the course of a long-term traditional marriage could be linked to her health problems, an award of periodic support made in the wife's favour was upheld on appeal. The wife could not work because of her health and she was entitled to have the economic disadvantage flowing from the marriage redressed: *Yaschuk v. Logan*, 39 R.F.L. (3d) 417, 110 N.S.R. (2d) 278, 299 A.P.R. 278, 1992 CarswellNS 64 (N.S. C.A.); affirming on other grounds 33 R.F.L. (3d) 316, 103 N.S.R. (2d) 371, 282 A.P.R. 371, 1991 CarswellNS 59 (N.S. T.D.).

In *Burke v. Burke*, 153 N.S.R. (2d) 1, 450 A.P.R. 1, 1996 CarswellNS 302 (N.S. S.C.), the court awarded spousal support to the wife taking into account the length of the marriage of 23 years. She had suffered economic hardship because of the marriage. Her lack of income was directly related to her assuming the role of a home making spouse and mother. By giving priority to the raising of the children she lost many of the skills required in her profession of nursing. She was awarded spousal support of $1,600 a month for the life of the parties, and a lump sum support payment of $2,500.

The court upheld an interim maintenance agreement which provided for child and spousal maintenance of $38,000 per month until further agreement or court order and the parties had acknowledged that they had had independent legal advice in *Sobey v. Sobey* (2000), 2000 CarswellNS 279 (N.S. S.C.). The parties had been married for approximately 20 years. The evidence did not disclose any ground for invalidating the contract. The mother had remained at home with the children and the father was a sophisticated and very successful businessman. The court was of the opinion that the fact that there was a maintenance agreement did not displace the court's power to award interim relief. However, in consideration of the evidence and the matters to be addressed in the context of the whole decision, the agreement should not be ignored. The negotiated amount was approximately $5,000 less than the *Guidelines* amount.

Short-term Marriage

In *Johnson v. Johnson* (2005), 23 R.F.L. (6th) 46, 2005 CarswellOnt 7695, 2005 ONCJ 325 (Ont. C.J.), the wife was awarded ongoing spousal support upon the termination of the parties' 1-month marriage. The wife had left a good career in Russia to move to Canada to marry the husband, who had executed a government sponsorship agreement under which he was obliged to support her for 10 years. The fact that the marriage was of very short duration was more than off-set by the fact that the wife had gone from a position of self-sufficiency and independence to one of reliance and dependency as a direct result of the marriage.

In the case of the relatively brief marriage, spousal support cannot be expected at the same level as upon the termination of a long-term traditional marriage. Such situations do not demand the equality of income, nor should the support applicant expect to enjoy the standard of living experienced during the marriage: *Postrasija v. Postrasija* (2002), 27 R.F.L. (5th) 148, 2002 CarswellOnt 1286 (Ont. S.C.J.).

The trial judge's decision to award maintenance for a fixed term of 5 months was affirmed on appeal, taking into account the 6 years of marriage, the fact that the wife did not significantly divert her talents to the development of the marriage, the economic advantages to the wife of the marriage, the disadvantages caused by her quitting her full-time job and the fact that the wife was now economically independent: *Grohmann v. Grohmann*, 37 R.F.L. (3d) 73, 62 B.C.L.R. (2d) 264, 5 B.C.A.C. 277, 86 D.L.R. (4th) 741, 11 W.A.C. 277, 1991 CarswellBC 321 (B.C. C.A.).

In *Baeza v. Strange-Zelaya* (2001), 18 R.F.L. (5th) 1, 2001 CarswellMan 371, 2001 MBCA 86, 156 Man. R. (2d) 166, 246 W.A.C. 166 (Man. C.A.), the court, on appeal, affirmed the award of 24 months of spousal support awarded to the wife upon the dissolution of the parties' 13-month marriage. The marriage appeared to be one of convenience, given that the husband left the wife shortly after obtaining his landed immigrant status. The wife had entered the marriage with no debt but left it with considerable debt after supporting the husband throughout. The wife had been economically disadvantaged by the marriage and was entitled to spousal support.

In *Luce v. Luce*, 30 R.F.L. (4th) 196, 188 N.B.R. (2d) 363, 480 A.P.R. 363, 1997 CarswellNB 267 (N.B. Q.B.), the wife's claim for support was dismissed upon dissolution of the parties' 3-year marriage. Since she had continued to work during the marriage and had not compromised any career aspirations or opportunities, the wife failed to prove any economic disadvantage.

In *Droit de la famille 487*, 15 R.F.L. (3d) 149, [1988] R.D.F. 205, (sub nom. *F. (F.) c. B. (R.)*) 23 Q.A.C. 323 (note), 1988 CarswellQue 44 (Que. C.A.), the appellate court ruled that the trial judge, in limiting support to a fixed term, exaggerated the importance of the short duration of the marriage. The parties were married and lived together for a little over a year and had a child. The fixed term of support should be struck from the judge's order as the wife, although young, required a reasonable time to become self-sufficient.

Where the dependant spouse was 35 and had been married for approximately 7 years, she had a duty to become self-sufficient in light of her age and the length of the marriage:

Solomon v. Solomon, 35 R.F.L. (3d) 113, 106 N.S.R. (2d) 28, 288 A.P.R. 28, 1991 CarswellNS 64 (N.S. C.A.).

Where the parties had actually lived together for only 10 weeks during their 26- month marriage, the wife's claim for spousal support was dismissed. In addition to the fact that the marriage was so brief, the wife had also reaped other financial benefits during the marriage: *Robichaud v. Harvey* (1989), 98 N.B.R. (2d) 135, 248 A.P.R. 135, 1989 CarswellNB 267 (N.B. Q.B.).

In *Abbott v. Abbott* (2001), 13 R.F.L. (5th) 233, 89 B.C.L.R. (3d) 68, 2001 BCSC 323, 2001 CarswellBC 420 (B.C. S.C.), the wife was awarded spousal support even though the parties had cohabited for less than a year. The parties had still managed to have two children and the wife bore the brunt of the marriage breakdown, having to interrupt her career to care for the children. The order was to be reviewed after 2 years or earlier in the event of a material change in circumstances.

15§17 — Factors — circumstances — functions performed by the spouse during cohabitation

In making an interim or permanent order for spousal support in divorce proceedings the court is to consider the general circumstances of each spouse including, among other things, "the functions performed by each spouse during cohabitation": s. 15.2(4)(b).

This requirement to consider the functions performed by the spouses during cohabitation is one of the provisions in the *Divorce Act* that gives rise to the compensatory basis for support. The other provisions are the need to consider the "condition" of the spouses, and the "means, needs and other circumstances" of the spouses, which may encompass lack of ability to support oneself due to foregoing career opportunities during the marriage: *Bracklow v. Bracklow* (1999), 169 D.L.R. (4th) 577 (S.C.C.).

The division of labour between the spouses in the marriage should be taken into account in determining whether there have been any economic advantages or disadvantages as a result of the marriage or its breakdown. In *Moge v. Moge*, 43 R.F.L. (3d) 465, [1992] 3 S.C.R. 813, [1993] 1 W.W.R. 481, 145 N.R. 1, 81 Man. R. (2d) 161, 30 W.A.C. 161, 99 D.L.R. (4th) 456, Madam Justice L'Heureux-Dubé stated, "In most marriages in which both partners make economic sacrifices and share domestic responsibilities, or where one spouse has suffered economic losses in order to enable the other spouse to further a career, their roles should be considered in the spousal support order".

The fact that the wife did not significantly divert her talents to the development of the marriage was a circumstance, among others, that persuaded the British Columbia Court of Appeal to affirm a support award limited to a fixed term of 5 months. Other circumstances were the duration of the marriage of 6 years, the economic advantages to the wife of the marriage, the disadvantages caused by her quitting her full-time job and the fact that, at the time of the trial, she was economically independent: *Grohmann v. Grohmann* (1991), 37 R.F.L. (3d) 73, 62 B.C.L.R. (2d) 264, 5 B.C.A.C. 277, 86 D.L.R. (4th) 741, 11 W.A.C. 277, 1991 CarswellBC 321 (B.C. C.A.).

"The award of maintenance should not be limited to the amount of maintenance which would be enough to keep her off the welfare rolls, but should be enough to take into account the contribution which the wife has made to the marriage, not only to the acquisition of the assets of the husband, but to the health and welfare of the family unit itself": per O'Sullivan J.A. in *Fedon v. Fedon* (1978), 1 R.F.L. (2d) 357 at 378, [1978] 2 W.W.R. 723 (Man. C.A.).

See also *Trifts v. Trifts* (1984), 54 N.B.R. (2d) 147, 140 A.P.R. 147 (Q.B.); *Johnson v. Johnson*, 23 R.F.L. 293 at 301, [1975] W.W.D. 167, 1975 CarswellAlta 9 (Alta. T.D.); *Hodder v. Hodder* (1976), 10 Nfld. & P.E.I.R. 82 at 84, 1976 CarswellNfld 42 (Nfld. T.D.).

15§18 — Factors — circumstances — any order, agreement or arrangement relating to the support of the spouse or child

See 15§§146–151 Effects of domestic contracts.

15§19 — Factors — circumstances — other — payor cohabiting

Where the wife had suffered a debilitating brain injury before the marriage and had been receiving interim spousal support of $650 monthly in the 6 years since the parties' separation, final spousal support in the amount of $500 monthly was awarded. While the wife had suffered economically because of the breakdown of the marriage, the award also had to recognize the financial burdens on the husband resulting from his new marriage and two new children: *Petrin v. Hahn* (2003), 47 R.F.L. (5th) 372, 2003 CarswellOnt 4108, [2003] O.J. No. 4206 (Ont. S.C.J.).

In *Underwood v. Underwood* (1994), 3 R.F.L. (4th) 457, 113 D.L.R. (4th) 571, 1994 CarswellOnt 394 (Ont. Gen. Div.), the husband's ability to pay spousal support was based on the premise that half of the husband's household expenses were being borne by his common-law wife.

The court in *MacLean v. MacLean* (1991), 94 Nfld. & P.E.I.R. 265, 298 A.P.R. 265 (P.E.I. T.D.) held it was appropriate to consider the salary of the husband's new partner in determining his ability to pay.

Support under the *Divorce Act* is based on a needs and means test. In assessing needs and means, a court should take into account a potential payor's settled, new relationship and the demands which that places upon his or her resources: *McNeilly v. McNeilly* (1987), 7 R.F.L. (3d) 385, 1987 CarswellOnt 318 (Ont. H.C.).

An annual contribution towards the maintenance of the wife and children by the wife's mother could not be expected to continue forever and was not a relevant factor in the assessment of quantum. The failure of the woman with whom the husband was living to pay a larger contribution toward their common household expenses was also not a factor, given the unstable nature of their relationship: *Gosney v. Gosney* (1980), 17 R.F.L. (2d) 28 (Nfld. T.D.); *Rathwell v. Rathwell* (1976), 16 R.F.L. 387 at 392 (Sask. Q.B.). See also *Carter v. Carter* (1978), 3 R.F.L. (2d) 355 at 363, 19 Nfld. & P.E.I.R. 411, 50 A.P.R. 411 (Nfld. T.D.); *Harris v. Harris* (1972), 8 R.F.L. 75 (Ont. H.C.); *Schartner v. Schartner* (1970), 72 W.W.R. 443 at 449, 10 D.L.R. (3d) 61 (Sask. Q.B.).

15§20 — Factors — circumstances — other — payee cohabiting

Cohabitation and remarriage do not automatically disentitle a spouse to support: *Bennett v. Bennett* (2005), 2005 CarswellAlta 1994, 2005 ABQB 984, 22 R.F.L. (6th) 399 (Alta. Q.B.). What must be considered is the need for spousal support and the effect of the cohabitation or remarriage on that need. If the cohabitation or remarriage is simply a transference to similar circumstances, there should not be an obligation to pay interim spousal support. If it is established that an applicant is living in cohabitation with another and yet refuses to provide the financial information of his partner, his application for interim spousal support should be dismissed. The wife received several economic advantages that mitigated her need for interim spousal support. She received extended health and dental benefits under her friend's Blue Cross coverage and a 50% waiver of tuition fees for her courses taken at the local college. She lived in her male friend's newly purchased home in which only the two of them resided. He earned a monthly gross income of $5,916.67 ($71,000 annually). The wife, at the time of the hearing, did not earn income as she attended college in order to gain self-sufficiency. The four children of the marriage were in the husband's care. The court did not accept that the wife's monthly expenses were an accurate reflection of her current need, as her male friend was assisting her financially. The court was of the opinion that the wife could undertake some employment in the summer months and income was imputed to her. The court found that the wife had a minimal need for spousal support and the husband had some ability to pay. The court ordered the husband to pay the wife $500 per month in interim spousal support.

The court found on the evidence that the wife and her male friend were not in a common law relationship in *Gallant v. Gallant* (2005), 2005 CarswellNS 325, 2005 NSSC 151, 234 N.S.R. (2d) 47, 745 A.P.R. 47 (N.S. S.C.). They did not hold themselves out as a common-law couple, and he had his own residence. There was no evidence of a stable relationship, a shared commitment or a financial enmeshment. The court stated that even if it were wrong in reaching this conclusion, it would not be satisfied that support should be terminated. The only relevance of the relationship would be the extent to which the male friend contributed to the household expenses thereby reducing the wife's need.

Where by the terms of a separation agreement a spouse is disentitled to spousal support if the wife remarries or other significant changes in the wife's financial circumstances occur, the court held that remarriage could not be equated with a common-law relationship: *Abbott v. Abbott* (2004), 2004 CarswellNfld 99, 236 Nfld. & P.E.I.R. 163, 700 A.P.R. 163, 2004 NLSCUFC 14 (N.L. U.F.C.). Further, the facts did not establish a finding of a common law relationship. Although the couple lived together when he was in St. John's and although there was sexual activity and the male friend assisted minimally with household expenses, by paying to the wife roughly the same amount as previous boarders, the evidence to rebut a common-law relationship was far more persuasive. Neither party had access to the other's bank accounts. The wife introduced him to family, friends and colleagues as her "boyfriend" and he referred to her, and introduced her, as his "girlfriend". In addition, there were no references, by family, friends and acquaintances, to the couple being "partners" or being in a "common-law relationship". They began dating in February 2003 and did not start living under the same roof until December 2003. Neither party had definite long term plans to stay with the other. If the male friend, a pilot, obtained employment outside of the St. John's area, the wife did not intend to move with him. Consequently, the evidence did not support the existence of a common-law relationship. In addition, the court found that there had not been a significant change in the wife's financial circumstances.

See also *McGee v. Ranson* (2003), 2003 CarswellMan 340, [2003] M.J. No. 304, 41 R.F.L. (5th) 309, 176 Man. R. (2d) 82, [2003] 11 W.W.R. 299, 2003 MBQB 182 (Man. Q.B.), where the court stated that pursuant to s. 4 of the *Family Maintenance Act*, common-law partners have a mutual obligation to contribute reasonably to each other's support and maintenance. As well, s. 6 of the Act, states: "notwithstanding section 4, a spouse or common-law partner has the obligation after separation to take all reasonable steps to become financially independent of the other spouse or common-law partner." In addition, the Act directs the court in s. 7(1) when deciding whether to make a support order to consider all the circumstances of the common-law partners, including the following:

(a) the financial needs of each;

(b) the financial means, earnings and earning capacity of each;

(c) the standard of living of the spouses or common-law partners;

(d) any obligation of either of them for the support and maintenance of a child or a person other than the other spouse or common-law partner;

(e) any contribution of a spouse or common-law partner . . .;

(f) the amount of any property settlement made between them;

(g) where one of them is financially dependent upon the other, the measures available for the dependent person to become financially independent of the other, and the length of time and cost involved in taking those measures;

(h) any impairment of the income-earning capacity and financial status of either resulting from the marriage or common-law relationship;

(i) where one of them is financially dependent upon the other, whether and to what extent the dependent spouse or common-law partner is complying with the requirements of section 6;

(j) the duration of the marriage or common-law relationship.

The court held that many of the circumstances set out in the Act had no applicability to the couple in *McGee v. Ranson*. Neither had an obligation to support anyone else. There was no property settlement between them. While the woman was financially dependent on the man during the relationship as a result of his larger income, the dependency did not arise as a result of any event other than their choice to be together. Clearly she was able to resume her prior lifestyle based on her own income, although she did not have the capacity to acquire the same lifestyle and income as he had. The relationship did not create any impairment of her income-earning ability. When the parties formed their relationship, both were pensioners. Her means were modest; his were more substantial. The parties had a relationship of 5 years. Now, her circumstances had reverted back to what they were prior to the common-law relationship. She was back to relying on her family to supplement her income, as the government pension was inadequate for her needs. The court found her entitled to support, considering all the factors set out in the Act and considering *Bracklow*. The court awarded the wife $325 per month for 12 months, with support binding on the man's estate.

In *H. (O.T.) v. H. (S.L.)* (2003), 2003 CarswellBC 2020, 2003 BCSC 1270 (B.C Master); affirmed (2003), 2003 CarswellBC 2260, 2003 BCSC 1399 (B.C. S.C.), the court held that there was insufficient evidence to establish that the wife's relationship with her male friend was a marriage-like relationship. While the male friend stayed over occasionally, he owned and maintained his own separate residence. Even if there were such a relationship, it had not as yet lasted 2 years, the time required before he might have an obligation to her. At the most, one-half of the common costs of housing and utilities might be charged to him. However, in this case, the court found that the wife and her friend were not cohabiting and an attribution of common costs could not fairly be made to the wife's friend.

Spousal Support Granted — Circumstances Affecting Quantum

Where at the time that an order was made, the wife acknowledged that she was seeing another man and the court found it was foreseeable that they would eventually cohabit, the later fact of their cohabitation did not amount to a material change of circumstances which would be sufficient to vary a prior spousal support order: *B. (G.) c. G. (L.)* (1995), 1995 CarswellQue 23, EYB 1995-67821, 1995 CarswellQue 120, [1995] S.C.J. No. 72, (sub nom. *G. (L.) c. B. (G.)*) 127 D.L.R. (4th) 385, (sub nom. *G. (L.) c. B. (G.)*) 186 N.R. 201, 15 R.F.L. (4th) 201, [1995] 3 S.C.R. 370, [1995] R.D.F. 611 (S.C.C.). Consequently, the spousal support order should not be reduced.

To establish that a spouse is in a common law relationship, it was incumbent on the husband to establish something more than the fact that the couple was having sexual relations while living together: *Alves v. Alves* (2005), 2005 CarswellAlta 1828, 2005 ABQB 911 (Alta. Q.B.). Under the terms of the parties' separation agreement, the husband was entitled to a reduction in spousal support, if the wife were in a common law relationship.

A wife's common-law relationship with another man does not automatically disentitle her to support, but is a factor properly considered in determining quantum: *Droit de la famille — 1105*, [1987] R.D.F. 293 (Que. S.C.).

In *Lockyer v. Lockyer* (2000), 10 R.F.L. (5th) 318, 2000 CarswellOnt 2805, [2000] O.J. No. 2939 (Ont. S.C.J.), the fact that the wife was enjoying a comfortable lifestyle through cohabitation with a new partner did not disentitle her to spousal support. The wife's status in her new relationship was precarious and subject to the terms of a cohabitation agreement. The wife's current lifestyle was, however, an appropriate consideration in determining the issue of quantum. The husband was ordered to pay the wife $375 per month. For a 2-year period from the date of judgment, the wife could earn $20,000 per year from employment and the husband $24,500 per year from employment without triggering a material change in circumstances. Neither party was employed at the time of judgment. The husband had retired from the Canadian army.

If a spouse suffers an economic disadvantage as a result of the breakdown of the marriage, entering into a new relationship does not change that fact: *Lauderdale v. Lauderdale* (1996), 21 R.F.L. (4th) 17, 180 A.R. 81, 1996 CarswellAlta 43, [1996] A.J. No. 53 (Q.B.); reversed (1997), 1997 CarswellAlta 448, [1997] A.J. No. 499, 200 A.R. 198, 146 W.A.C. 198, 29 R.F.L. (4th) 34 (C.A.). However, the new relationship does affect quantum. The wife was awarded a payment of $20,000 a year for four and one-half years to finance her retraining and $30,000 as an additional amount which should have been available for interim child support, with an adjustment for interest and taxes.

The fact that a spouse seeking support has entered into a common-law relationship is irrelevant to the obligation to support and is only properly considered in relation to the issue of quantum: *Squires v. Squires* (1988), 72 Nfld. & P.E.I.R. 91, 223 A.P.R. 91, 1988 CarswellNfld 241, [1988] N.J. No. 151 (Nfld. U.F.C.). The husband's payments should be reduced by the amount of the pecuniary benefits that the wife will receive from her common-law husband. The court ordered the husband to pay spousal support of $100 per month.

In *McNutt v. McNutt* (2000), 5 R.F.L. (5th) 90, 2000 CarswellOnt 847 (Ont. S.C.J.), where the parties had cohabited for 37 years in a traditional marriage, and where the wife was dependant on her husband throughout that time, support was awarded at $1000 a month ($300 less than interim support), taking into account, among other things, that she was residing with another individual and it was reasonable to assume that expenses were shared.

Where the wife was living with another man and benefiting financially from the relationship, she was nevertheless found entitled to maintenance in light of the fact that the new relationship was not yet settled: *Key v. Key* (1986), 1 R.F.L. (3d) 150, 1986 CarswellBC 509 (B.C. S.C.). The marriage had lasted 25 years and the wife was awarded $700 monthly. The court was of the opinion that the matter of support should be reviewed in the future in connection with the wife's efforts to find employment and the husband's expected retirement from the military.

In *Bell v. Bell* (1998), 42 R.F.L. (4th) 301, 1998 CarswellNfld 246 (Nfld. U.F.C.), the wife was found to have been economically disadvantaged upon the dissolution of the parties 36-year traditional marriage. Although the wife was living with another man, it was not a permanent relationship. She intended to move out on her own upon resolution of the support issues. The husband was ordered to pay the wife $5,000 as lump sum spousal support and monthly spousal support of $2,000 for an indefinite period.

Denial of Spousal Support

In *Boddington v. Boddington* (2003), 44 R.F.L. (5th) 13, 2003 CarswellOnt 3914 (Ont. S.C.J.); additional reasons at (2003), 2003 CarswellOnt 5332 (Ont. S.C.J.); further additional reasons at (2003), 2003 CarswellOnt 5333 (Ont. S.C.J.), the wife's application for spousal support was dismissed on the ground that the wife had entered into a new spousal-type relationship and had no financial need for support. Despite the wife's claim that her new relationship was a friendship only, she had moved into her male friend's house, was now shown as a co-owner on the deed to property, shared his business and had identified him as her "spouse" on her income tax return. The court stated that according to the law, a payee is not disentitled to support merely because she has a new relationship. However, in this case, the court would not order support, as the evidence did not demonstrate that the wife had a financial need that obligated the husband to pay support.

A court should deny interim spousal support where the dependant spouse fails to demonstrate, with cogent and compelling evidence, a current need for interim spousal support from the husband: *Byerley v. Byerley* (1998), 41 R.F.L. (4th) 50, 1998 CarswellOnt 3649, [1998] O.J. No. 3781 (Ont. Gen. Div.). In this case, the wife who was living in a common-law union, did not provide the court with information about her common-law spouse's income and expenses. She had been self-supporting for a year and after that lived with her common-law husband for almost a year before she sought support. At the time of the hearing the wife and her common-law husband were expecting a child.

In *Franken v. Franken* (1997), 33 R.F.L. (4th) 264, 1997 CarswellOnt 4150 (Ont. Gen. Div.), the wife's claim for spousal support was dismissed. She was living in a common law relationship with a man who earned a substantial income and contributed generously to her needs. As there was no evidence of economic hardship adduced by the wife, she did not establish the required economic disadvantage resulting from the breakdown of the marriage.

In *Carpenter v. Carpenter* (1991), 93 Nfld. & P.E.I.R. 279, 292 A.P.R. 279, 1991 CarswellNfld 146 (Nfld. T.D.), the court refused the wife's application for support because, with the training she had taken, she should be self-sufficient within a short period of time and she was already being supported by another man.

Where the wife would be able to maintain her standard of living with the income of her new partner, child support and an unequal property division in her favour, her application for periodic support was denied. She was, however, entitled to a lump sum to compensate her for the loss of a lucrative career: *Kits v. Kits* (1998), 42 R.F.L. (4th) 167, 1998 CarswellBC 2323 (B.C. S.C.).

15§20A — Factors — circumstances — payee remarrying

The court dismissed the wife's appeal of judgment claiming continued spousal support and child support in *Roberts v. Beresford* (2006), 2006 CarswellBC 337, 2006 BCCA 67, 22 R.F.L. (6th) 243 (B.C. C.A.). The parties had established the support regime by agreement and the wife had a new career, a new marriage and was financially comfortable. She had saved a significant amount of the support she received under the separation agreement. Child care responsibilities were nearly over. The husband fully complied with his obligations under the agreement. The wife could not advance any valid compensatory principle that justified an attachment to the husband's earnings. There continued to be a large income disparity between the parties as the husband at the time of the trial earned $322,607.29 and the wife $37,650. However, both parties had remarried and the husband and his second wife's net worth was approximately $847,380 and the wife and her second husband' s net worth was $1,232,500.

In *Kalaba v. Bylykbashi* (2006), 2006 CarswellOnt 749 (Ont. C.A.), the court stated that it was correct that it was not open to the motion judge to conclude that the wife's application for continued spousal support could not succeed simply because she had subsequently married and divorced. However, the court was of the opinion that the husband's full responsibility for the children and the wife's failure to exercise her access rights to them were relevant to her spousal support application. The wife's income-earning opportunities since the marriage breakdown were not curtailed by the reduced economic choices and career-diminishing responsibilities of a custodial parent, nor those of a non-custodial parent who wished to remain close to the children. The court found that the motion judge did not place great weight on the fact of the appellant's second marriage. He simply had insufficient satisfactory evidence to deal with it. In addition, the wife did not establish that need provided a non-compensatory basis for support.

Where the financial circumstances of the spouse who remarries remain essentially the same despite the remarriage, that spouse continues to be entitled to support from her first spouse: *Lee v. Lee* (2006), 2006 CarswellOnt 1093 (Ont. S.C.J.). In this case the wife and her second husband continued to maintain separate residences in different cities where they were employed. In addition, the wife attended university where she lived. The couple remained financially independent. They saw each other two times a month and there were no plans to change this arrangement due to their employment obligations and the wife's educational opportunities. The husband was ordered to continue to pay spousal support of $500 per month until such time as the wife was expected to complete her course. See also *Franz v. Wilson* (2005), 2005 CarswellOnt 3711 (Ont. S.C.J.) discussed at 15§6.

In *P. (M.F.F.A.) v. P. (F.M.A.)* (2003), 47 R.F.L. (5th) 170, 2003 CarswellBC 2447, 2003 BCSC 1502 (B.C. S.C.), the court allowed the husband's application to terminate the spousal support payable to his former wife. After the divorce, the wife had remarried, successfully completed a dental assistant's course and undertaken part-time employment. She then developed cancer and was unable to work. For the purposes of support, the wife had achieved "self sufficiency" upon completion of her course and her failure to secure full-time employment was the result of her own decision. The wife's new spouse now had primary responsibility for her support.

In *Zimmerman v. Shannon* (2004), 2004 CarswellBC 2132, 11 R.F.L. (6th) 230, 2004 BCSC 1246 (B.C. S.C.), the court held that the wife's remarriage was not a change of circumstances that was not within the reasonable contemplation of the parties, particularly since the plaintiff was aware the defendant had a relationship with her current husband when their agreement was signed. However, the husband was entitled to a declaration that his obligation to pay spousal maintenance under the parties' agreement ceased, as, through bad investments, he no longer had the asset base to make the payments.

In *Debora v. Debora* (2004), 2004 CarswellOnt 4987, 8 R.F.L. (6th) 32 (Ont. S.C.J.); additional reasons at (2005), 2005 CarswellOnt 676, 14 R.F.L. (6th) 245 (Ont. S.C.J.), the court held that the wife's remarriage in and of itself would not bar a claim for spousal support (*Harris v. Gilbert* (1997), 32 O.R. (3d) 139, 1997 CarswellOnt 115, 26 R.F.L. (4th) 199, (sub nom. *Harris v. Harris)* 97 O.A.C. 14 (Ont. C.A.); *B. (G.) c. G. (L.)* (1994), [1995] 3 S.C.R. 367, 1994 CarswellQue 130, (sub nom. *G. v. B.)* 1994 CarswellQue 130F, (sub nom. *G. (L.) v. B. (G.))* 165 N.R. 237, (sub nom. *G. (L.) v. B. (G.))* 61 Q.A.C. 179 (S.C.C.)), but it was a factor to be taken into consideration. As a result of this judgment, the wife would have sufficient assets to provide adequate support for herself. In all the circumstances, the court did not consider it appropriate to award spousal support.

15§21 — Factors — circumstances — other — payee spouse sacrificing career

See 15§24 Objectives of spousal support — general and 15§26 Objectives of spousal support — economic advantages and disadvantages — payee spouse sacrificing employment opportunities.

In *Ormerod v. Ormerod* (1990), 27 RFL (3d) 225 (Ont. U.F.C.), the issue was the quantification of the economic disadvantages suffered by the wife as a result of her interrupting her nursing career to care for the parties' children. In determining this issue, the court accepted the evidence of an economist that her future loss of earnings from the time of re-entry into the nursing field after the interruption until her retirement would be $103,000. The court awarded this amount to the wife in the form of lump sum support together with 1 month of periodic support to cover the transition period.

A similar attempt to use the opinion evidence of an economist was far less successful in the Court of Appeal in the case of *Elliot v. Elliot* (1993), 48 R.F.L. (3d) 237, 106 D.L.R. (4th) 609, 1993 CarswellOnt 348 (Ont. C.A.); leave to appeal to S.C.C. refused (1994), 3 R.F.L. (4th) 290 (note), 112 D.L.R. (4th) vii (note) (S.C.C.). Here the wife left her employment with Bell Canada in 1981 when the first child was born and remained at home to care for him and their second child until 1989. She returned to work at Bell Canada, but her prospects were not as good as when she was last there. The trial judge relying on opinion evidence offered by an economist found that the present value of the wife's income loss calculated from the date of the trial to her retirement was $158,205.90. He discounted this amount for income tax and divided the result in two holding that the husband should assume half the risk. In the result, he awarded the wife "as lump sum maintenance on her claim for lost future economic opportunity, the sum of $52,735.80." The husband appealed and the wife cross-appealed contending that the lump sum should be $236,384. The appeal was allowed and the cross-appeal dismissed. The objective in the *Divorce Act* that a spousal support order is to "recognize" an economic disadvantage, does not mean that the claimant has a right to full compensation. The objective involves compensating for an economic disadvantage as much as is reasonably possible "but, equally obviously, lack of resources may well stand in the way of full compensation." It is no answer to a lack of resources to say that the lump sum for compensation could be paid by installments at interest over a number of years. This pays no attention to the husband's means or to the principle of equitable sharing of the consequences of the marriage. It is not reasonably possible to apply these considerations where the compensation is in the form of a lump sum. Also, in ordering spousal support the court must take into account all the consequences to the parties. There should be an equal sharing of both the advantages and the disadvantages. "The basic flaw in the [economist's] approach is that it isolates one event or decision in the history of the marriage, the decision of the Elliots that Mrs. Elliot would leave the workforce to care for the children until the last of them was in school full time, and treats it as the only event on which to focus in determining the amount of the award of spousal support." And "he treated it in much the same way as if her career interruption had been caused by injuries suffered in a motor vehicle accident. He calculated all of the damages flowing from that event . . .." In so doing, he did not properly determine the full effect of the advantages and disadvantages arising from the breakdown of the marriage. In addition, the tort approach of a motor vehicle accident does not treat the means of the payor to be a relevant consideration which is contrary to the requirement in the *Divorce Act* when determining spousal support. Another problem in the economist's approach of present valuing the loss as a lump sum is that it is unnecessarily speculative when compared to periodic support which can be varied if there is a change in circumstances. In this case, an order for periodic support would be a more appropriate method of providing for the equitable sharing of the available resources. The court allowed the husband's appeal and varied the trial judgment by setting aside the orders made and substituting an order for periodic support of $2,000 a month, allocated $1,000 a month for spousal support and $500 a month for each of the two children.

Where a spouse sacrifices a career to remain in the home, the court, in assessing that spouse's entitlement to spousal support should look beyond simple loss of future earnings. Factors such as loss of seniority, missed promotions and lack of access to pension plans and insurance should also be considered: *Messer v. Messer* (1996), 26 R.F.L. (4th) 352, 150 Sask. R. 23 (Q.B.); reversed in part (1997), 33 R.F.L. (4th) 426 (Sask. C.A.).

In *Keyes v. Keyes* (1996), 17 R.F.L. (4th) 201 (N.S. S.C.), the wife was found to have been economically disadvantaged by the marriage even though she had resumed full-time employment many years prior to separation. The wife had withdrawn from the workforce for a period of 12 years to raise the children and allow the husband to complete his education from which he derived an economic advantage. Given the 24-year duration of the marriage prior to separation and the fact that, despite the wife's employment, the husband remained the primary provider, the wife was entitled to a lifestyle equal to his.

Where as a result of her assuming child care responsibilities during the marriage, the wife's earning capacity was half that of the husband, the husband was ordered to pay her $300 monthly spousal support. The amount would neither overcompensate the wife for her contributions and sacrifices, nor would it impoverish the husband: *Zanyk v. Zanyk* (1993), 46 R.F.L. (3d) 169 (Sask. Q.B.).

A wife who gives up her job to care for the parties' child with Down Syndrome is entitled to spousal support. She could not be expected to work, given her son's special needs: *Oddi v. Oddi* (2000), 7 R.F.L. (5th) 164 (Ont. S.C.J.).

Where the wife had been out of the labour force for many years during the parties' 30-year marriage and was recovering from many years of abuse, she was found to be entitled to support on both need-based and compensatory grounds: *Burnett v. Burnett* (1997), 33 R.F.L. (4th) 356 (Ont. Gen. Div.).

Where the wife moved with the husband from New York to Winnipeg to further his career with the result that she severly limited her own, she was awarded 9 months' spousal support. But for the marriage and the move, the wife would have been self-sufficient: *Weekes v. Weekes* (1998), 36 R.F.L. (4th) 323, 124 Man. R. (2d) 317 (Q.B.).

A wife, who had given up her career to move with the husband to further his career and who later developed a debilitating mental illness which prevented her from working, is entitled to spousal support: *Dillon v. Dillon* (1997), 27 R.F.L. (4th) 197, 184 N.S.R. (2d) 371, 469 A.P.R. 371 (Q.B.).

A husband who gives up his job and moves with the wife so that she could take a better paying job is entitled to spousal support: *Stefanyk v. Clancy* (1996), 26 R.F.L. (4th) 256, (sub nom. *Stefanyk v. Stefanyk)* 156 N.S.R. (2d) 161, 461 A.P.R. 161 (S.C.).

Where the wife had emigrated to Canada to improve the husband's job security and had thereby negatively affected her own career, the court found she was entitled to support with no specified termination date. During the 13-year marriage the wife had remained in the home to raise the parties' child and had always put her own needs after those of the husband and son: *Timms v. Timms* (1997), 29 R.F.L. (4th) 392 (Alta. Q.B.).

Where the wife herself had chosen to abandon her career after becoming pregnant, but was employed at the time of separation, her application for spousal support was dismissed. There was no evidence that she had been disadvantaged by the marriage or its breakdown: *Begin v. Begin* (1996), 156 N.S.R. (2d) 253, 461 A.P.R. 253 (S.C.).

Where the wife had suffered an injury upon her return to work as a nurse's assistant and could not work for some time in that field, she was awarded periodic spousal support for 30 months. She had been economically disadvantaged by the marriage in that she had been out of the job market for a number of years. The support award would allow her to complete her nursing degree and eventually achieve self-sufficiency: *McNeil v. McNeil* (1995), 16 R.F.L. (4th) 323 (Sask. Q.B.).

Where the only disadvantages suffered by the wife as a result of the marriage were the limitations placed on her social and economic opportunities resulting from her being the custodial parent, it was found that her disadvantages could be addressed exclusively through child support. There was no evidence presented which suggested that she had been denied a career or other employment opportunities: *Shackleton v. Shackleton* (1993), 46 R.F.L. (3d) 211 (Ont. Gen. Div.).

In *Lasalle v. Lasalle* (1994), 7 R.F.L. (4th) 100, 1994 CarswellAlta 387, [1994] A.J. No. 661 (Alta. C.A.), the court upheld the wife's spousal support award that was made after the divorce and the failure of the wife's business. The wife had sacrificed her own career throughout the parties' 16-year marriage and, but for this, may well have established herself financially.

In *Fejes v. Fejes* (1993), 45 R.F.L. (3d) 13, 83 Man. R. (2d) 273, 36 W.A.C. 273, 1993 CarswellMan 38 (C.A.), the court reversed the trial judge's decision which had reduced the quantum of spousal support payable to the wife. Although the wife had obtained a university degree after separation, the trial judge had placed too much emphasis upon the wife's failure to achieve self-sufficiency. The wife had given up her career aspirations to raise the children throughout the parties' 17-year marriage and the economic disadvantage to the wife resulting from the marriage continued.

In *Zander v. Zander* (1994), 8 R.F.L. (4th) 35, 1994 CarswellOnt 452 (Ont. Gen. Div.), the court refused the wife's claim for compensatory support arising from the fact that she had left a position with an airline early in the marriage to assume the role of a traditional homemaker. Structural changes occurring in the airline industry over the years would undoubtedly have impacted the wife's career and a report which ignored these changes could not be used to substantiate the considerable lump sum compensation sought.

Where the wife had given up her own career to allow the family to move several times in furtherance of the husband's career, limited term support upon termination of the parties' 22-year-marriage was deemed inappropriate: *Chaytor v. Chaytor* (1994), 6 R.F.L. (4th) 94, 133 N.S.R. (2d) 43, 380 A.P.R. 43 (S.C.).

Where the wife had remained in the home to care for the children when they were young, it was found that the husband should support her during her training as an occupational therapist. Although she could support herself through secretarial work, she should be given an opportunity to explore a new field: *Sykes v. Sykes* (1993), 46 R.F.L. (3d) 432 (B.C. S.C.).

Where the wife had given up her lucrative teaching career to spend more time with her husband and after separation became depressed and was unable to find full-time employment, she was awarded indefinite support. The wife had sustained a substantial economic disadvantage "from the marriage or its breakdown" and the economic hardship continued: *Koberlein v. Barral* (1994), 5 R.F.L. (4th) 94, 94 Man. R. (2d) 133 (Q.B.).

Where the wife had given up her teaching career during the marriage, it was found that she had suffered irremediable economic loss. Since the separation, the wife had upgraded her teaching credentials. Any decision concerning the quantum and term of her spousal support award was found to be best deferred until evidence of her progress in pursuing her career became available. Pending such determination, her interim support was to continue: *Scarlett v. Scarlett* (1993), 47 R.F.L. (3d) 130 (B.C. S.C.).

In *Reilly v. Reilly* (1994), 10 R.F.L. (4th) 6 (B.C. S.C.), although the 60-year-old wife was qualified to teach French, she was nevertheless found entitled to support because of her age and the role of homemaker she had performed throughout the parties' lengthy marriage.

In *Mears v. Mears* (1992), 82 Man. R. (2d) 156 (Q.B.); affirmed (1992), 83 Man. R. (2d) 129, 36 W.A.C. 129 (C.A.), the husband, despite his bankruptcy, was ordered to pay spousal support to the wife. Through the first half of the parties' 13-year marriage, the wife had remained in the home and cared for the children, allowing the husband to qualify as a teacher. Since separation the wife had made reasonable efforts to find employment but was hampered by her limited skills and the unfavourable economic climate. Her plans to return to school were reasonable in the circumstances.

In a long-standing traditional marriage, the court should not place too much emphasis on promoting the dependant spouse's self-sufficiency but should take into account the factors set out in s. 15(5), the economic advantages the dependant spouse derived from the marriage, and the disadvantages and hardship arising to the other from its breakdown. The husband, an orthodontist, was ordered to pay support for an indefinite period to his wife who had acquired a commerce degree during the marriage but who was working as a customer service clerk or teller, having failed to obtain management positions: *Donald v.*

Donald (1991), 33 R.F.L. (3d) 196, 103 N.S.R. (2d) 322, 282 A.P.R. 322, 81 D.L.R. (4th) 48 (C.A.).

In *Yaschuk v. Logan* (1991), 33 R.F.L. (3d) 316, 103 N.S.R. (2d) 371, 282 A.P.R. 371 (T.D.); affirmed on other grounds (1992), 39 R.F.L. (3d) 417, 110 N.S.R. (2d) 278, 299 A.P.R. 278 (C.A.), the court was of the opinion that where the wife gave up a career to marry and developed health problems, mostly attributable to the mental and physical abuse during a 27-year marriage, the spouse had an obligation to support her up to a reasonable standard of living. The wife had need and the husband had the ability to pay support. It was in his best interests to assist her to become rehabilitated into the workforce and financially self-sufficient.

In *Christian v. Christian* (1991), 37 R.F.L. (3d) 26, 7 O.R. (3d) 441 (Gen. Div.), the wife was awarded periodic support upon the breakdown of the parties' long term traditional marriage, despite the fact that she had retrained and had obtained full-time employment. The wife had, throughout the marriage, put the family first and, even with her employment, she would not be able to maintain a reasonable standard of living from her own resources.

Where it was found that the wife would likely have had a successful business career had she not given up opportunities to care for the parties' children, she was awarded periodic support for a 7-year term to enable her to educate herself and secure a position commensurate with her abilities and lifestyle: *Belliveau-Williamson v. Williamson* (1989), 21 R.F.L. (3d) 142 (N.B. Q.B.).

Where the wife forfeited a promotion in an attempt to salvage the marriage, the court awarded her support in the amount of $400 per month for 2 years: *Balcombe v. Balcombe* (1990), 30 R.F.L. (3d) 177, 42 O.A.C. 150 (Div. Ct.).

There is an entitlement to support where, as a result of the duties of a marriage, a spouse loses his or her place on the labour market ladder: *Jukosky v. Jukosky* (1990), 31 R.F.L. (3d) 117 (Ont. Gen. Div.).

Where the wife has interrupted her career for family purposes she is entitled to reasonable spousal support for 1 year until she is working full-time: *De Roo v. De Roo* (1990), 28 R.F.L. (3d) 86 (Ont. H.C.).

In *Patrick v. Patrick* (1991), 35 R.F.L. (3d) 382, 62 B.C.L.R. (2d) 188 (S.C.); affirmed (1993), 49 R.F.L. (3d) 453, 85 B.C.L.R. (2d) 303 (C.A.), the pharmacist wife was awarded spousal support upon dissolution of her 10-year marriage. Although employed, the result of the marriage breakdown and her continuing childrearing role rendered the wife financially and professionally disadvantaged in comparison with what her circumstances would have been had the marriage continued or had it never occurred. On appeal in *Patrick v. Patrick* (1993), 49 R.F.L. (3d) 453, 85 B.C.L.R. (2d) 303 (C.A.), the court found no basis for imposing a time limit on the payment of support. There was nothing to prevent the appellant from applying for a variation of maintenance if there were a change in circumstances.

In *Stunt v. Stunt* (1990), 30 R.F.L. (3d) 353 (Ont. Gen. Div.), where the failure of the couple's marriage and the wife's response to it adversely affected her career but the wife could become self-sufficient, she was entitled to reasonable support for 2 years. The wife's career lost its directness of path and stability because of the marriage and its breakdown.

Where the wife had given up her nursing career to work in her husband's office, he was ordered to pay support while she returned to school to retrain as a dental hygienist: *Tancock v. Tancock* (1990), 24 R.F.L. (3d) 389 (B.C. S.C.).

Where the wife had given up her teaching career to raise the parties' two children, she was found to have suffered a substantial economic disadvantage resulting from the marriage and was accordingly awarded decreasing support over a 7-year period: *Monaghan v. Monaghan* (1988), 14 R.F.L. (3d) 308 (Ont. H.C.).

Where the wife had left her employment to accompany the husband to the United States in furtherance of his education and later postponed her own education while the parties built a house, she was awarded support on divorce to assist her with her university studies. As the wife had contributed significantly to the parties' financial well being and the husband's educational endeavours, it was equitable that he contribute to her education: *Norris v. Norris* (1988), 13 R.F.L. (3d) 307, 70 Nfld. & P.E.I.R. 327, 215 A.P.R. 327 (Nfld. T.D.).

See also *Weichholz v. Weichholz* (1987), 81 A.R. 236 (Q.B.); *Chorny v. Chorny* (1971), 4 R.F.L. 347, [1971] 5 W.W.R. 732 (Alta. C.A.); *Langer v. Langer* (1970), 2 R.F.L. 358 at 359 (Sask. Q.B.); *Bodnar v. Bodnar* (1987), 6 R.F.L. (3d) 66 (Ont. H.C.); *Berry v. Murray*, 30 R.F.L. (2d) 310, [1983] 1 W.W.R. 561 (B.C. C.A.); *Skrlj v. Skrlj* (1986), 2 R.F.L. (3d) 305 (Ont. H.C.); *Primeau v. Primeau* (1986), 2 R.F.L. (3d) 113 (Ont. H.C.); *Balbon v. Balbon* (1984), 41 R.F.L. (2d) 218, 29 Man. R. (2d) 223 (Q.B.); *Desbiens v. Desbiens* (1981), 30 B.C.L.R. 314 (S.C.); *Tylman v. Tylman* (1980), 30 O.R. (2d) 721, 117 D.L.R. (3d) 730 (H.C.); *Spicer v. Spicer* (1980), 14 R.F.L. (2d) 180 (Nfld. T.D.); *Flannigan v. Flannigan* (1976), 26 R.F.L. 331 (B.C. S.C.); *Harding v. Harding* (1972), 8 R.F.L. 236 at 236 (B.C. S.C.); *Jackh v. Jackh*, 18 R.F.L. (2d) 310, 22 B.C.L.R. 182, [1981] 1 W.W.R. 481, 113 D.L.R. (3d) 267 (S.C.); *Von Hessert v. Von Hessert* (1982), 27 R.F.L. (2d) 197 (Sask. U.F.C.).

15§22 — Factors — circumstances — other — payee spouse assuming custody of young children

See also 15§24 Objectives of spousal support — general.

Women have tended to suffer economic disadvantages and hardships from marriage or its breakdown because of the traditional division of labour within that institution. A diminished earning capacity resulting from long interruptions in employment to take on parenting or domestic responsibilities is a fact that has been demonstrated in a number of studies. Often difficulties in returning to the work force are exacerbated by the continuing responsibility for the care of children after divorce. The spouse who has made economic sacrifices in the marriage usually becomes the custodial parent. This responsibility further reduces her economic choice by requiring her to do such things as remain within proximity to schools, refuse to work late, and to stay at home when the children are ill: *Moge v. Moge*, 43 R.F.L. (3d) 345, [1992] 3 S.C.R. 813, [1993] 1 W.W.R. 481, 145 N.R. 1, 81 Man. R. (2d) 161, 30 W.A.C. 161, 99 D.L.R. (4th) 456, [1993] R.D.F. 168, [1992] S.C.J. No. 107, 1992 CarswellMan 143 (Eng.), 1992 CarswellMan 222 (Fr.) (S.C.C.).

In *Kopelow v. Warkentin*, 21 R.F.L. (6th) 78, 2005 CarswellBC 2636, [2005] B.C.J. No. 2412, 2005 BCCA 551, 261 D.L.R. (4th) 129, 218 B.C.A.C. 209, 359 W.A.C. 209 (B.C. C.A.); additional reasons at 2006 CarswellBC 1306, 2006 BCCA 271 (B.C. C.A.); varying 2002 BCSC 1546, 2002 CarswellBC 2706, [2002] B.C.J. No. 2534 (B.C. S.C.), the wife's spousal support was increased on appeal from $1,500 monthly to $3,500. The parties had been married for 12 years during which the wife had to remain out of the workforce to care for the children, a duty which would likely last for another 6 or 7 years. The marriage was a long one and the wife was entitled to enjoy a similar status of living as the husband without having to liquidate assets.

In *Gregory v. Ball*, 9 R.F.L. (6th) 338, 2004 CarswellAlta 1450, 2004 ABQB 789 (Alta. Q.B.); reversed in part 2005 CarswellAlta 1526, 2005 ABCA 354 (Alta. C.A.), the wife was awarded spousal support for 4 years to allow her to complete her teacher's college programme. The wife had remained at home with the parties' children during the 6-year marriage and the disadvantages that she had suffered from that could best be overcome if she became financially self-sufficient.

"[T]he wife has custody of the children and not only does the husband consent to her devoting part of her time looking after them, he insists upon it. Under these circumstances, the diminution of her income makes it fit and just that the husband should contribute to her maintenance.. . .the court shall make an appropriate order for the maintenance of the wife and the children by the payment of periodic sums, having regard, inter alia, to the diminution in the income of the wife that is reasonably attributable to her caring for the children during usual working hours": per Farris C.J.B.C. in *Piller v. Piller* (1975), 17 R.F.L. 252, [1975] 4 W.W.R. 342 at 345-346, 54 D.L.R. (3d) 150 (B.C. C.A.).

In *Murphy v. Paulin*, 18 R.F.L. (5th) 339, 2001 CarswellBC 1553, 2001 BCSC 842 (B.C. S.C.), the wife was awarded periodic spousal support upon the dissolution of the parties' 15-year marriage. Their youngest child remained in the care of the wife and suffered from a serious medical condition. Although the wife did manage to work part-time, the requirement that she take time away from work to tend to the child's needs impacted on both her employment opportunities and the security of her employment.

Where the wife had to care for the parties' asthmatic son, it was not reasonable to expect her to work full-time to achieve self-sufficiency: *Droit de la famille — 1568*, [1992] R.D.F. 240 (C.S. Qué.).

In *Keane v. Keane* (1980), 17 R.F.L. (2d) 299 at 300 (Ont. H.C.), the petitioner wife sought substantial maintenance upon divorce for the parties' severely disabled child in her custody. The petitioner, who was otherwise able to work to support herself, was unable to take full-time employment because of the care this child required. Per Winter L.J.S.C. awarding $600 per month for the child: "As is usual in most cases where both partners are not gainfully employed, there is just not enough money earned to take care of the full requirements of the separated homes. This, however, is an unusual case because of the necessity of almost constant care for the infant child of the marriage. Care of the child is the first responsibility of the parents and the respondent husband and father will have to rearrange his priorities to make provision for the child.. . .The life expectancy of the child is not long and accordingly the emergency for funds will be of relatively short lived duration but must be a responsibility accepted by the father during that period."

Where the wife had custody of the children she was expected to assist herself by obtaining employment which would permit her the time to be with her children when they were not in school. Since her income earning hours would be restricted by the needs of her children she was entitled to be assisted by her husband while the children were with her: *Flannigan v. Flannigan* (1976), 26 R.F.L. 331 (B.C. S.C.).

The husband's suggestion that the wife seek gainful employment was viewed as "preposterous" where she had a full-time job on her hands in maintaining the home and looking after the children. It was a seven-day-a-week job from which there was little escape: *Schulte v. Schulte* (1972), 6 R.F.L. 164 (Ont. H.C.).

15§23 — Factors — circumstances — other — payor spouse assuming custody

See also 15§24 Objectives of spousal support — general.

The fact that the wife was unable to contribute to the support of the child in the husband's custody was found to be a relevant factor in determining the quantum of spousal support payable to her. The husband was entitled to some consideration for the child-care costs which he carried: *Reyher v. Reyher* (1993), 48 R.F.L. (3d) 111 (Man. Q.B.).

Where the husband assumed full responsibility for the support of the parties' child, a university student, the wife's claim for spousal support was dismissed. Any claim by the wife was more than offset by the husband's sole assumption of child support: *Head v. Johnson* (1989), 61 Man. R. (2d) 267 (Q.B.).

In *Fisher v. Fisher* (2000), 7 R.F.L. (5th) 45, 2000 CarswellNS 101 (N.S. S.C.), the court refused the wife's claim for support upon dissolution of the parties' 20-year marriage. After separation, the husband assumed custody of the children without support from the wife. The husband, who was 62 years of age, continued to pay off substantial matrimonial debts while the 44-year-old wife made little effort to support herself. The wife's career opportunities had not been diminished by the marriage nor had the husband's career been enhanced by the wife's contributions.

15§24 — Objectives of spousal support — general

The criteria which the court in a divorce proceeding should apply in determining a claim for spousal support are set out as factors (*Divorce Act*, s. 15.2(4)) and as objectives. For the factors, see 15§7 to 15§21, above. The objectives are set out in s. 15.2(6) of the *Divorce Act* and require that an order for the support of a spouse should recognize any economic advantages or disadvantages to the spouses, or former spouses, arising from the marriage or its breakdown; apportion between the spouses, or former spouses, any financial consequences arising from the care of any child of the marriage over and above any obligation for the support of any child of the marriage; relieve any economic hardship of the spouses, or former spouses, arising from the breakdown of the marriage; and in so far as practicable, promote the economic self-sufficiency of each spouse, or former spouse, within a reasonable time.

These objectives together with the factors in s. 15.2(4) create a new basis for spousal support: *Moge v. Moge*, 43 R.F.L. (3d) 345, [1992] 3 S.C.R. 813, [1993] 1 W.W.R. 481, 145 N.R. 1, 81 Man. R. (2d) 161, 30 W.A.C. 161, 99 D.L.R. (4th) 456, [1993] R.D.F. 168, [1992] S.C.J. No. 107, 1992 CarswellMan 143 (Eng.), 1992 CarswellMan 222 (Fr.) (S.C.C.). Their general effect is to promote an equitable sharing of the economic consequences, for both parties, of the marriage or its breakdown. This is a significant change from the 1968 *Divorce Act* constituting a shift away from "means and needs" as the exclusive test to the much wider spectrum of considerations embraced by the factors and objectives of the current Act. This shift does not ignore "means and needs" (which by s. 15.2(4) are the main items in the factors that the court must consider), but places them in the much wider context of the objectives. All four of the objectives must be taken into account. "No single objective is paramount. The fact that one of the objectives, such as economic self-sufficiency, has been attained does not necessarily dispose of the matter."

The equitable sharing of the economic consequences seeks to recognize the economic disadvantages incurred by the spouse who makes economic sacrifices and the advantages those sacrifices conferred upon the other spouse. In this sharing process, work within the home has "undeniable value and transforms the notion of equality . . . to a substantive imperative." The focus of the enquiry when assessing spousal support "must be the effect of the marriage in either impairing or improving each party's economic prospects."

The starting point in determining support is a consideration of the objectives in s. 15.2(6) of the *Divorce Act*. No single objective is paramount: all must be borne in mind: *Bracklow v. Bracklow* (1999), 169 D.L.R. (4th) 577, 236 N.R. 79, 44 R.F.L. (4th) 1, 120 B.C.A.C. 211, 196 W.A.C. 211, [1999] 1 S.C.R. 420, 63 B.C.L.R. (3d) 77, [1998] 8 W.W.R. 740, 1999 CarswellBC 532, 1999 CarswellBC 533, [1999] S.C.J. No. 14 (S.C.C.). For a detailed discussion of the facts of the case, see 15§6 General principles for determining spousal support.

The principles enunciated in the *Pelech* trilogy and applicable to an interpretation of the 1968 *Divorce Act* do not apply to the current Act. The trilogy is composed of three cases decided in the Supreme Court of Canada and reported at the same time: *Pelech v. Pelech*, 7 R.F.L. (3d) 225, [1987] 1 S.C.R. 801, 17 C.P.C. (2d) 1, 14 B.C.L.R. (2d) 145, [1987] 4 W.W.R. 481, 76 N.R. 81, 38 D.L.R. (4th) 641, 1987 CarswellBC 147 (Eng.), 1987 CarswellBC 703 (Fr.), [1987] S.C.J. No. 31 (S.C.C.); *Richardson v. Richardson*, 7 R.F.L. (3d) 304, [1987] 1 S.C.R. 857, 17 C.P.C. (2d) 104, 77 N.R. 1, 22 O.A.C. 1, 38 D.L.R. (4th) 699, 1987 CarswellOnt. 315, 1987 CarswellOnt. 963, [1987] S.C.J. No. 30 (S.C.C.); and *Caron v. Caron* (1987), 7 R.F.L. (3d) 274, [1987] 1 S.C.R. 892, 14 B.C.L.R. (2d) 186, [1987] 4 W.W.R. 522, 75 N.R. 36, 2 Y.R. 246, 38 D.L.R. (4th) 735, 1987 CarswellYukon 8, [1987] S.C.J. No. 32 (S.C.C.). These cases held that to override a support provision or waiver of support in an agreement, the court must find a causal connection between the need for support and the marriage together with a radical change in circumstances. A number of subsequent decisions of the lower courts extended the causal connection principle to the general law of support applying it in original applications for support as well as in applications to vary support orders or to override agreements.

The *Pelech* Trilogy was reviewed and limited to the 1968 Act by the Supreme Court of Canada in *Miglin v. Miglin* (2002), 34 R.F.L. (5th) 255, 224 D.L.R. (4th) 193, 2003 CarswellOnt 1374, 2003 CarswellOnt 1375, 2003 SCC 24, [2003] S.C.J. No. 21. The causal connection requirement that came to be treated as a condition precedent to the awarding of spousal support was developed in the trilogy as part of a test to determine when the court should intervene under the *Divorce Act* to override a waiver of, or a provision for spousal support contained in a pre-existing agreement. The test was based on the 1968 Act that was repealed and replaced by the 1985 *Divorce Act*, the current Act, which uses more specific and comprehensive language. The new language and judicial interpretations adopt a different approach which makes the test involving a causal connection inappropriate and not applicable where the court is considering whether to use its discretion under the current *Divorce Act* to override a support provision in an agreement. Neither causal connection nor the second element of radical change that completed the test established by the trilogy is part of the law as it now stands for this purpose.

The extension of causal connection made by some courts to a requirement for an original support order where there was no agreement to override may also have met its demise in *Miglin*. If the test is revoked for the purpose intended, should it not also be considered revoked for other purposes for which it was not intended, but to which it was made to apply? If the tree dies, does the branch live? For a detailed summary of the *Miglin* case, see 15§147.

The trilogy is not applicable to cases where spousal support has not been determined by agreement: *Moura v. Moura* (1998), 43 R.F.L. (4th) 344, 1998 CarswellOnt 4919, [1998] O.J. No. 5351 (Ont. Gen. Div.). Consequently, entitlement to support is no longer dependant on a causal connection between a spouse's need and the marriage. Instead it is governed by the 1984 *Divorce Act* and, in particular, the four objectives set out in that Act.

15§25 — Objectives of spousal support — economic advantages and disadvantages — general

See also 15§21 Factors — circumstances — other — payee spouse sacrificing career; 15§10 Factors — means — payee's actual and potential income; 15§31 Objectives of spousal support — economic advantages and disadvantages — compensatory support; 15§90 Child support — amount different from guidelines.

By clauses 15.2(6)(a) and 17(7)(a) of the Act, an order or interim order that provides for the support of a spouse, or that varies the support of a former spouse, should recognize any economic advantages or disadvantages to the spouses, or the former spouse, arising from the marriage or its breakdown.

The purpose of spousal support is to relieve economic hardship that results from the "marriage or its breakdown", and the focus of the assessment of spousal support must be on the effect of the marriage in either impairing or improving each party's economic prospects: *Moge v. Moge*, 43 R.F.L. (3d) 345, [1992] 3 S.C.R. 813, [1993] 1 W.W.R. 481, 145 N.R. 1, 81 Man. R. (2d) 161, 30 W.A.C. 161, 99 D.L.R. (4th) 456, [1993] R.D.F. 168, [1992] S.C.J. No. 107, 1992 CarswellMan 143 (Eng.), 1992 CarswellMan 222 (Fr.) (S.C.C.). Marriage is, among other things, an economic unit which generates financial benefits, and the Act reflects the fact that marriage partners should expect, and are entitled to share in those benefits. A sharing of benefits can be achieved in several ways: by child and spousal support, by the division of property, or by a combination of support and property division. The absence of accumulated assets may require that one spouse pay support to the other in order to effect an equitable distribution of resources. The Act embodies a theory of spousal support based on principles of compensation. A foundation for these principles is found in the first three of the four objectives. They deal with a broad range of economic and financial consequences. Self-sufficiency, the fourth objective, remains relevant, but is not given pre-eminence. After divorce, spouses would still have an obligation to contribute to their own support in a manner commensurate with their abilities. Compensatory spousal support would not always be awarded, or if awarded would not necessarily be granted in substantial amounts. "In cases where relatively few advantages have been conferred or disadvantages incurred, transitional support allowing for full and unimpaired reintegration back into the labour force might be all that is required to afford sufficient compensation. However, in many cases compensatory spousal support would require long-term support or an alternative settlement which provides an equivalent degree of assistance in light of all the objectives of the Act." Women have tended to suffer economic disadvantages and hardships from marriage or its breakdown because of the traditional division of labour within that institution. A diminished earning capacity resulting from long interruptions in employment to take on parenting or domestic responsibilities is a fact that has been demonstrated in a number of studies. Often difficulties in returning to the work force are exacerbated by the continuing responsibility for the care of children after divorce. The spouse who has made economic sacrifices in the marriage usually becomes the custodial parent. This responsibility further reduces her economic choice by requiring her to do such things as remain within proximity to schools, refuse to work late, and to stay at home when the children are ill. There may be some cases where, because the spouses have made economic sacrifices equally, there will be no call for compensation. But these cases will be rare. The economic consequences must be shared by both partners. The difficulty in attaining an equitable sharing of the consequences is in finding a balance between the ability of the debtor spouse to pay, and the limit to which a support order can go to achieve fair compensation for the disadvantaged spouse. The four objectives set out in the Act are an attempt to achieve an equitable sharing of the economic consequences of marriage or marriage breakdown. But the courts have an overriding discretion when ordering support which will depend on the particular facts of each case. The exercise of this discretion requires an examination of all four objectives involving a broad approach incorporating any significant element of the marriage or its termination which adversely affects the economic prospects of the disadvantaged spouse. Not all such elements will be equally important. Some of the most common compensable advantages and disadvantages which the Act envisages are:

- Loss of future earning power including such things as loss of seniority, missed promotions, lack of benefits like pension plans, and life, disability, dental and health insurance; employer-paid job-retraining and skills upgrading programs.
- Economic disadvantage from curtailing paid employment in order to care for the children. (Usually, the most significant economic consequence of marriage or marriage breakdown arises from the birth of children.)
- Other financial consequences arising from the care of a child which are not reflected in the direct costs of support.
- In a childless marriage where the couple decides that one of them is to remain at home, any economic disadvantage to that spouse flowing from their decision.
- Where both spouses work full-time and one of them incurs economic loss by declining a promotion, refusing a transfer, leaving a position to allow the other spouse to take advantage of an opportunity for advancement, or by otherwise curtailing employment opportunities in the interest of the family.
- Contributions to the other spouse's business such as the provision of secretarial, entertainment or bookkeeping services.
- Assuming increased domestic and financial responsibilities to enable the other spouse to pursue licenses, degrees or other training and education.

"To the extent that these activities have not already been compensated for pursuant to the division of assets, they are factors that should be considered in granting spousal support." In her additional comments made after concurring in the judgment of her colleague, Madame Justice McLachlin summarized her view of the first objective by saying that it is compensatory in nature allowing the judge "to compensate one spouse for sacrifices and contributions made during the marriage and benefits which the other spouse has received."

The British Columbia Court of Appeal held that where the parties executed a settlement agreement which was not challenged because of the circumstances under which it was made, but was later construed in such a way as to render it at odds with the objectives of the *Divorce Act* (including the objective that the court is to recognize any economic advantages or disadvantages to the spouses arising from the marriage or its breakdown), the court was justified in reapportioning the property division under the *Family Relations Act* (British Columbia), which permits this intervention, and awarding spousal support under the *Divorce Act. N. (D.K.) v O. (M.J.)*, 2003 CarswellBC 2290, 2003 BCCA 502 (B.C. C.A.).

In *Corbeil v. Corbeil*, 2000 ABCA 220, 2001 CarswellAlta 1138 (Alta. C.A.), the court upheld the trial judge's refusal to grant the wife spousal support, even though she sustained an economic disadvantage on account of the marriage. The fact that one party is able to prove the existence of one objective such as economic disadvantage does not establish entitlement to support. A court must consider all of the objectives of spousal support and all of the circumstances of the parties. In this case, spousal support for the wife was rejected although the marriage endured for 20 years. Other considerations were the income of the parties, the wife's superior asset position, and the wife's ability to support herself.

In determining the economic disadvantage to a party resulting from marriage, the benefits received from a matrimonial property division should also be considered: *Messer v. Messer* (1993), 47 R.F.L. (3d) 4, 108 Sask. R. 155 (Q.B.); reversed in part (1996), 22 R.F.L. (4th) 8, 141 Sask. R. 163 (C.A.).

Where the wife had moved several times during the parties' 20-year marriage to facilitate the husband's military career and had cared for the parties' two children, an economic dependence upon him had been created. She had no income and no prospect of income, and was accordingly entitled to spousal support: *Rutherford v. Rutherford* (2004), 7 R.F.L. (6th) 344, 225 N.S.R. (2d) 293, 713 A.P.R. 293, 2004 CarswellNS 301, 2004 NSSC 148 (S.C.).

Where the wife had not been financially dependent on the husband during the parties' five-year marriage and had voluntarily left her full-time employment after separation, her claim for spousal support was dismissed in *Charbonneau v. Charbonneau* (2004), 9 R.F.L. (6th) 67, 2004 CarswellOnt 5211 (S.C.J.).

Entitlement to support depends on proof of some economic disadvantage arising from marriage or its breakdown. The quantum and duration of the support should bear some relation to the extent of the economic disadvantage: *Tully v. Tully* (1994), 9 R.F.L. (4th) 131 (Ont. Gen. Div.).

Where both parties have suffered an economic disadvantage from the marriage breakdown in the form of the loss of the other spouse's income, the spouse with the smaller income is entitled to have the disadvantage addressed through a support award: *Amaral v. Amaral* (1993), 50 R.F.L. (3d) 364 (Ont. Gen. Div.); additional reasons at (1993), 50 R.F.L. (3d) 384 (Ont. Gen. Div.).

When making or varying an order for spousal maintenance, the court must consider whether the decisions made during the marriage have had the effect of economically disadvantaging one spouse or benefiting the other upon its dissolution: *Petley-Jones v. Petley-Jones* (1993), 48 R.F.L. (3d) 166 (B.C. S.C.). The court considered that the wife, a nurse, in this case had to some extent been financially disadvantaged because her commitment to her husband, her children, and their home prevented her from developing a career, particularly in the early years of the marriage. The decisions in this regard were perhaps more the wife's than the husband's but were largely for the benefit of the husband. These decisions led to an economic disadvantage but one that could not be quantified.

Where the wife was found to have suffered an economic disadvantage as a result of the marriage, it was held that she should be entitled to support that would bring her lifestyle closer to that enjoyed by the husband. Accordingly, an amount was awarded that would permit her to contribute to an R.R.S.P., purchase a car and take a vacation: *Hashem v. Hashem* (1993), 46 R.F.L. (3d) 303 (Nfld. U.F.C.).

Where as a result of the marriage breakdown the wife lost the advantage of pooled income with her husband to which she earned a right, she was found entitled to periodic support for a 3-year period. Throughout the parties' 26- year marriage both had worked and had pooled their incomes for family purposes and, absent that pooled income, the wife lacked sufficient resources to meet her needs: *Harris v. Harris* (1994), 7 R.F.L. (4th) 91 (B.C. S.C.).

In *O'Hara v. O'Hara* (1995), 15 R.F.L. (4th) 408 (N.B. Q.B.), the wife was found to have been disadvantaged by the breakdown of the parties' 8-year marriage and was awarded support for a period of 2 years, although she had worked and earned a reasonable income throughout the marriage.

Where the court found that the 57-year-old wife had been economically disadvantaged by the marriage, but found it difficult to assess the extent of the disadvantage, she was awarded spousal support based upon her current and predictable circumstances: *Best v. Best* (1993), 50 R.F.L. (3d) 120, 1 C.C.P.B. 8 (Ont. Gen. Div.).

Where the wife's income actually exceeded that of the husband, her application for spousal support was dismissed. While both parties suffered financial setbacks during marriage, neither had been more economically disadvantaged by the marriage than the other: *Voiculescu v. Voiculescu*, 42 R.F.L. (5th) 215, 2003 CarswellNS 252, 2003 NSSF 29 (N.S. S.C.).

15§26 — Objectives of spousal support — economic advantages and disadvantages — payee spouse sacrificing employment opportunities

"It is now well-settled law that spouses must compensate each other for foregone careers and missed opportunities during the marriage upon the breakdown of their union": *Bracklow v. Bracklow*, [1999] 1 S.C.R. 420, 44 R.F.L. (4th) 1, 169 D.L.R. (4th) 577, 236 N.R. 79, 120 B.C.A.C. 211, 196 W.A.C. 211, 63 B.C.L.R. (3d) 77, [1999] 8 W.W.R. 740, 1999 CarswellBC 532, 1999 CarswellBC 533, [1999] S.C.J. No. 14 (S.C.C.) at 16 (R.F.L.), McLachlin J. (as she then was).

Compensation for economic loss caused by the marriage interrupting a wife's career must be balanced against the husband's means or abililty to pay: *Elliot v. Elliot* (1993), 48 R.F.L. (3d) 237, 15 O.R. (3d) 265, 106 D.L.R. (4th) 609, 65 O.A.C. 241, 1993 CarswellOnt 348 (Ont. C.A.); leave to appeal to S.C.C. refused (1994), 3 R.F.L. (4th) 290 (note), 112 D.L.R. (4th) vii (note), 18 O.R. (3d) xvi (note), 74 O.A.C. 159 (note), 175 N.R. 324 (note) (S.C.C.).

Where the wife remained employed throughout the marriage but had moved several times to support the husband's career, she was found to have suffered an economic disadvantage and was awarded limited term support for a period of 5 years. The wife's career had suffered as she had less seniority and experience as a result of the moves and her child care responsibilities: *Kaluza v. Kaluza*, 50 R.F.L. (5th) 71, 2003 CarswellBC 3132, 2003 BCSC 1879 (B.C. S.C.).

In *Hill v. Magee*, 26 R.F.L. (5th) 95, 2002 CarswellBC 522, 2002 BCSC 353 (B.C. S.C.), the wife was awarded periodic spousal support without any time limitation upon dissolution of the parties' 23-year marriage. Although she was employed, she had been out of the workforce for 10 years when rearing the children. She had achieved the highest level of full-time employment to which she could aspire given her education and experience and her income was insufficient to meet even a modest standard of living.

Where the wife had been self-supporting throughout the parties' 8-year relationship and 4-year marriage, but was on welfare and unable to find work after separation, she was awarded periodic spousal support for a period of 18 months. The wife clearly had a need but, long term, her inability to find employment could not be attributed to the collapse of the marriage: *R. (S.M.) v. R. (P.E.)*, 25 R.F.L. (5th) 375, 2002 CarswellBC 637, 2002 BCPC 92 (B.C. Prov. Ct.).

Where the wife had worked throughout the marriage and continued to advance the career she had begun prior to the marriage, her application for spousal support was dismissed. Although she had also been the primary caregiver to the parties' children, her employment situation had never been compromised: *Roberts v. Roberts*, 42 R.F.L. (5th) 135, 2003 CarswellNS 268, 42 R.F.L. (5th) 135, 2003 NSSC 146 (N.S. S.C.).

In *Higgins v. Higgins* (2001), 19 R.F.L. (5th) 300, 2001 CarswellOnt 2729 (Ont. S.C.J.), the wife was awarded $1,000 monthly support upon the breakdown of the parties' 18-year marriage. Although the wife had failed to adduce sufficient evidence that her health prevented her from working, there was evidence that she had been economically disadvantaged by her role in the marriage and its breakdown. She would never have the same earning capacity as the husband and would never, on her own, be able to regain her pre-separation standard of living.

A spouse is clearly economically disadvantaged by the parties' traditional marital relationship where the wife had given up her job upon marriage, the marriage lasted 8 years and wife was 53 at the time of the marriage breakdown: *Gabb v. Gabb* (2001), 13 R.F.L. (5th) 391, 153 Man. R. (2d) 157, 238 W.A.C. 157, 2001 MBCA 19, 2001 CarswellMan 68 (Man. C.A.).

Where the husband had discouraged the wife from seeking employment with the same company for which he worked, he could not, after the parties' separation, claim that he had no obligation to support her, at least to some degree, until she became self-supporting. The wife would have been in a better position to become self-sufficient but for the husband's insistence that she not work and was accordingly entitled to periodic support: *West v. Marche* (2001), 17 R.F.L. (5th) 458, 2001 CarswellNfld 117, 200 Nfld. & P.E.I.R. 341, 603 A.P.R. 341 (Nfld. T.D.).

Where the wife emigrated to Canada from England for an arranged marriage, the court upheld an award of $12,500 as the wife had suffered some economic loss since she was unemployed for a short time and had to re-establish herself in the workforce: *Dyal v. Dyal* (2000), 11 R.F.L. (5th) 58, 143 B.C.A.C. 106, 235 W.A.C. 106, 2000 BCCA 527, 2000 CarswellBC 1897 (B.C. C.A.). The marriage only lasted 8 months and there were no children. The appellate court overruled the trial court finding that compensatory maintenance could not be granted on a cultural or social basis but only for economic disadvantage. The trial court had said that the wife might find it difficult to become assimilated in the East Indian community.

Where the marriage breakdown took economic security away from the wife, the appellate court upheld the lower court's decision to award the wife spousal support during the time that she attended school on a full-time basis in her effort to be self-sufficient: *Coupar v. Coupar* (1998), 43 R.F.L. (4th) 443, 114 B.C.A.C. 255, 186 W.A.C. 255, 57 B.C.L.R. (3d) 161, 1998 CarswellBC 2540 (B.C. C.A.).

Where the wife had given up her job to care for the parties' child with Down Syndrome, her application for spousal support was granted. The wife could not be expected to work, given the need to maintain the home for the children and look after her son's special needs: *Oddi v. Oddi* (2000), 7 R.F.L. (5th) 164, 2000 CarswellOnt 1772 (Ont. S.C.J.).

A wife in a traditional marriage of 17 years where her husband made financial provision and she managed the home and raised their two children is economically disadvantaged by the breakdown of the marriage and entitled to support: *Munn v. Munn* (1999), 44 R.F.L. (4th) 179, 1999 CarswellOnt 671 (Ont. C.A.).

The Court of Appeal upheld the trial judge's award of spousal support as, in the circumstances, he gave sufficient consideration to the economic advantages and disadvantages arising from the marriage: *Daoust c. Leboeuf* (1998), 35 R.F.L. (4th) 143, 107 O.A.C. 73, 1998 CarswellOnt 76 (Ont. C.A.).

The wife's award of lump sum support was upheld on appeal in *Martin v. Martin* (1998), 42 R.F.L. (4th) 251, 168 Nfld. & P.E.I.R. 181, 517 A.P.R. 181, 1998 CarswellNfld 298 (Nfld. C.A.), where she had given up a permanent job and was out of the workforce for 16 years.

Where the parties had cohabited in a traditional, long-term marriage of 22 years in which the husband advanced his career and the wife stayed at home to care for the family, time-limited spousal support would not compensate her for the economic disadvantage she suffered nor would it pay for the economic advantage it gave to the husband: *Blair v. Blair* (1997), 34 R.F.L. (4th) 370, 1997 CarswellOnt 4908, [1997] O.J. No. 4949 (Ont. Gen. Div.). Although the wife at the time of the proceedings was employed nearly full-time, she was awarded spousal support of $300 per month for an indefinite period.

Where a spouse sacrifices a career to remain in the home, the court, in assessing that spouse's entitlement to spousal support should look beyond simple loss of future earnings. Factors such as loss of seniority, missed promotions and lack of access to pension plans and insurance should also be considered: *Messer v. Messer* (1996), 26 R.F.L. (4th) 352, 150 Sask. R. 23, 1996 CarswellSask 662, [1996] S.C.J. No. 699 (Q.B.); reversed in part (1997), 33 R.F.L. (4th) 426, 163 Sask. R. 101, 165 W.A.C. 101, 1997 CarswellSask 595, [1997] S.J. No. 645 (C.A.); leave to appeal refused (1998), 227 N.R. 292 (note), 168 Sask. R. 318 (note), 173 W.A.C. 318 (note) (S.C.C.).

In *Abels v. Abels* (1995), 17 R.F.L. (4th) 154, 167 N.B.R. (2d) 32, 427 A.P.R. 32, 1995 CarswellNB 176 (C.A.), the indefinite periodic and lump sum spousal support awarded in the wife's favour upon the breakdown of the parties' 15-year traditional marriage was upheld on appeal. Factors such as the wife's contribution to the husband's career, her limited education and ability to become self-sufficient, the disparity of their incomes and the decline in her standard of living all supported a finding of economic disadvantage resulting from the marriage breakdown.

In *Lasalle v. Lasalle* (1994), 7 R.F.L. (4th) 100, 1994 CarswellAlta 387, [1994] A.J. No. 661 (Alta. C.A.), the husband's appeal from the indefinite support award granted to the wife upon dissolution of the parties' 16-year marriage was dismissed. As the wife's personal situation had not improved and her career had not developed during the marriage, her economic disadvantage could be related to the marriage.

In *Lasalle v. Lasalle* (1994), 7 R.F.L. (4th) 100, 1994 CarswellAlta 387, [1994] A.J. No. 661 (Alta. C.A.), the court upheld the wife's spousal support award that was made after the divorce and the failure of the wife's business. The wife had sacrificed her own career throughout the parties' 16-year marriage and may well otherwise have established herself financially.

In *Ross v. Ross* (1993), 45 R.F.L. (3d) 230, 62 O.A.C. 384, 12 O.R. (3d) 705, 1993 CarswellOnt 301 (Ont. C.A.), the court was of the opinion that in a long- term traditional marriage where the payee spouse has manifestly limited career skills, it is not appropriate that a spouse be given a 3-year declining support order. Such an award does not take into account the specific objectives set out in s. 15(7) of the *Divorce Act* and, in particular, does not recognize the economic disadvantages to the appellant caused by the marriage breakdown, and her 23-year absence from the paid workforce. The Court of Appeal ordered indefinite periodic support in the amount of $1,850 per month.

In *Fejes v. Fejes* (1993), 45 R.F.L. (3d) 13, 83 Man. R. (2d) 273, 36 W.A.C. 273, 103 D.L.R. (4th) 118, 1993 CarswelMan 38 (C.A.), the court reversed the trial judge's decision which had reduced the quantum of spousal support payable to the wife. Although the wife had obtained a university degree after separation, the trial judge had placed too much emphasis upon the wife's failure to achieve self-sufficiency. The wife had given up her career aspirations to raise the children throughout the parties' 17-year marrage and the economic disadvantage to the wife resulting from the marriage continued.

Where the wife had been out of the labour force for many years during the parties' 30-year marriage and was recovering from many years of abuse, she was found to be entitled to support on both need-based and compensatory grounds: *Burnett v. Burnett* (1997), 33 R.F.L. (4th) 356, 1997 CarswellOnt 3282 (Ont. Gen. Div.).

Where the wife moved with the husband from New York to Winnipeg to further his career with the result that she severely limited her own, she was awarded 9 months' spousal support. But for the marriage and the move, the wife would have been self-sufficient: *Weekes v. Weekes* (1998), 36 R.F.L. (4th) 323, 124 Man. R. (2d) 317, 1998 CarswellMan 32 (Q.B.).

Where the husband had given up his job and moved with the wife so that she could take a better paying job, the husband was found entitled to spousal support: *Stefanyk v. Clancy* (1996), 27 R.F.L. (4th) 256, (sub nom. *Stefanyk v. Stefanyk)* 156 N.S.R. (2d) 161, 461 A.P.R. 161, 1996 CarswellNS 509 (S.C.).

Where the wife had emigrated to Canada to improve the husband's job security and had thereby negatively affected her own career, she was found entitled to support with no specified termination date. During the 13-year marriage the wife had remained in the home to raise the parties' child and had always put her own needs behind those of the husband and son: *Timms v. Timms* (1997), 29 R.F.L. (4th) 392, [1997] 7 W.W.R. 392, 203 A.R. 81, 51 Alta. L.R. (3d) 99, 1997 CarswellAlta 439, [1997] A.J. No. 463 (Q.B.); additional reasons at (1997), 204 A.R. 398, 55 Alta. L.R. (3d) 138, [1998] 4 W.W.R. 458, 1997 CarswellAlta 574 (Q.B.).

Where the wife had given up her career to move with the husband to further his career and later developed a debilitating mental illness which prevented her from working, she was found entitled to spousal support. The breakdown of the marriage had resulted in economic hardship to her: *Dillon v. Dillon* (1997), 27 R.F.L. (4th) 197, 184 N.S.R. (2d) 371, 469 A.P.R. 371, 1997 CarswellNB 4 (Q.B.).

Where the wife herself had chosen to abandon her career after becoming pregnant, but was employed at the time of separation, her application for spousal support was dismissed. There was no evidence that she had been disadvantaged by the marriage or its breakdown: *Begin v. Begin* (1996), 156 N.S.R. (2d) 253, 461 A.P.R. 253, 1996 CarswellNS 521 (S.C.).

Where the wife had made sacrifices in foregoing her own career as a secretary, had suffered economic hardship because of the marriage and its breakdown, had need and the husband had the ability to pay, then the wife was entitled to spousal support: *Schmuck v. Reynolds-Schmuck* (1999), 50 R.F.L. (4th) 429, 1999 CarswellOnt 2424, [1999] O.J. No. 3104 (S.C.J.); additional reasons at (2000), 46 O.R. (3d) 72, 2000 CarswellOnt 202 (S.C.J.).

Where the husband had, with the wife's consent, left his employment, in part to attend to family concerns, he was found entitled to spousal support. The husband had suffered an economic disadvantage as a result of the marriage breakdown and he was entitled to support until he was re-established in the workforce: *Purcell v. Purcell* (1995), 11 R.F.L. (4th) 181, 1995 CarswellOnt 82 (Ont. Gen. Div.); additional reasons at (1995), 11 R.F.L. (4th) 181 at 200 (Ont. Gen. Div.); varied (1996), 26 R.F.L. (4th) 267, 1996 CarswellOnt 2305 (Ont. C.A.); additional reasons at (1996), 26 R.F.L. (4th) 272, 1996 CarswellOnt 4007 (Ont. C.A.).

In *Zander v. Zander* (1994), 8 R.F.L. (4th) 35, 1994 CarswellOnt 452 (Ont. Gen. Div.), the court refused the wife's claim for compensatory support arising from the fact that she had left a position with an airline early in the marriage to assume the role of a traditional homemaker. Structural changes occurring in the airline industry over the years would undoubtedly have impacted the wife's career and a report which ignored these changes could not be used to substantiate the considerable lump sum compensation sought.

Where the wife had given up her own career to allow the family to move several times in furtherance of the husband's career, limited term support upon termination of the parties' 22-year marriage was deemed inappropriate: *Chaytor v. Chaytor* (1994), 6 R.F.L. (4th) 94, 133 N.S.R. (2d) 43, 380 A.P.R. 43, 1994 CarswellNS 57, [1994] N.S.J. No. 342 (S.C.).

Where the wife had remained in the home to care for the children when they were young, it was found that the husband should support her during her training as an occupational therapist. Although she could support herself through secretarial work, she should be given an opportunity to explore a new field: *Sykes v. Sykes* (1993), 46 R.F.L. (3d) 432, 1993 CarswellBC 608 (B.C. S.C.); varied (July 30, 1993), Doc. Vancouver D081265 (B.C. S.C.); additional reasons at (March 21, 1994), Doc. Vancouver D081265 (B.C. S.C.); reversed (1995), 13 R.F.L. (4th) 273, 38 C.P.C. (3d) 250, 6 B.C.L.R. (3d) 296, 58 B.C.A.C. 294, 96 W.A.C. 294, 1995 CarswellBC 266 (C.A.).

Where the wife had given up her lucrative teaching career to spend more time with her husband and after separation became depressed and was unable to find full-time employment, she was awarded indefinite support. The wife had sustained a substantial economic disadvantage "from the marriage or its breakdown" and the economic hardship continued: *Koberlein v. Barral* (1994), 5 R.F.L. (4th) 94, 94 Man. R. (2d) 133, 1994 CarswellMan 37 (Q.B.).

Where the wife had given up her teaching career during the marriage it was found that she had suffered irremediable economic loss. Since the separation, the wife had upgraded her teaching credentials. Any decision concerning the quantum and term of her spousal support award was found to be best deferred until evidence of her progress in pursuing her career became available. Pending such determination, her interim support was to continue: *Scarlett v. Scarlett* (1993), 47 R.F.L. (3d) 130, 1993 CarswellBC 613 (B.C. S.C.).

In *Reilly v. Reilly* (1994), 10 R.F.L. (4th) 6, 1994 CarswellBC 645, [1994] B.C.J. No. 2482 (B.C. S.C.); additional reasons at (1994), 10 R.F.L. (4th) 6 at 23 (B.C. S.C.); additional reasons at (January 9, 1995), Doc. Vancouver D074241 (B.C. S.C.); additional reasons at (June 7, 1996), Doc. Vancouver D074241 (B.C. S.C.), although the 60-year-old wife was qualified to teach French, she was nevertheless found entitled to support because of her age and the role of homemaker she had performed throughout the parties' lengthy marriage.

In *Jenkins v. Jenkins* (1993), 47 R.F.L. (3d) 219, 81 B.C.L.R. (2d) 133, 1993 CarswellBC 171 (S.C.), the court, in considering the objectives in s. 15(7) and the *Moge* decision, was of the opinion that where the wife leaves her profession to be a homemaker, raises the parties' family, causing her qualifications to become stale and at 47 has little training for remunerative work, she has sustained a substantial economic disadvantage from the marriage and its breakdown and indefinite spousal support should be granted to supplement her own earnings.

In *Mears v. Mears* (1992), 82 Man. R. (2d) 156, 1992 CarswellMan 406 (Q.B.); affirmed (1992), 83 Man. R. (2d) 129, 36 W.A.C. 129, 1992 CarswellMan 191 (C.A.), the husband, despite his bankruptcy, was ordered to pay spousal support to the wife. Through the first half of the parties' 13-year marriage, the wife had remained in the home and cared for the children, allowing the husband to qualify as a teacher. Since separation the wife had made reasonable efforts to find employment but was hampered by her limited skills and the unfavourable economic climate. Her plans to return to school were reasonable in the circumstances.

In a long-standing traditional marriage, the court should not place too much emphasis on promoting the dependant spouse's self-sufficiency, but should take into account the factors set out in s. 15(5), the economic advantages the dependant spouse derived from the marriage, and the disadvantages and hardship arising to the other from its breakdown. The husband, an orthodontist, was ordered to pay support for an indefinite period to his wife who had acquired a commerce degree during the marriage but who was working as a customer service clerk or teller, having failed to obtain management positions: *Donald v. Donald* (1991), 33 R.F.L. (3d) 196, 103 N.S.R. (2d) 322, 282 A.P.R. 322, 81 D.L.R. (4th) 48, 1991 CarswellNS 58 (C.A.).

In *Yaschuk v. Logan* (1991), 33 R.F.L. (3d) 316, 103 N.S.R. (2d) 371, 282 A.P.R. 371, 1991 CarswellNS 59 (T.D.); affirmed on other grounds (1992), 39 R.F.L. (3d) 417, 110 N.S.R. (2d) 278, 299 A.P.R. 278, 1992 CarswellNS 64 (C.A.), the court was of the opinion that where the wife gave up a career to marry and then developed health problems, mostly attributable to the mental and physical abuse during a 27-year marriage, the spouse had an obligation to support her up to a reasonable standard of living. The wife had need and the husband had the ability to pay support. It was in his best interests to assist her to become rehabilitated into the workforce and financially self-sufficient.

Where the parties agreed that the wife would not work during the marriage, she was found entitled to spousal support. Although the wife had benefited through extensive travel and the furtherance of her education, she had also suffered adverse economic effects such as the loss of earning powers and benefits which she would have obtained if she had entered the workforce at an earlier age: *Stebbins v. Stebbins* (1995), 14 R.F.L. (4th) 226, 1995 CarswellNS 67 (N.S. S.C.).

In *Ondik v. Ondik* (1994), 1 R.F.L. (4th) 376, 118 Sask. R. 216, 1994 CarswellSask 34, [1994] S.J. No. 84 (Q.B.), the court granted the wife's application to continue her interim support order as permanent support. As she had remained in the home throughout the parties' long-term marriage, her ability to earn income had been permanently damaged.

Where the wife was employed at the time of separation, but had earlier left the workforce to care for the children, and at another time had obtained a job transfer for family purposes, she was found entitled to limited term support to allow her to complete university. The wife had been economically disadvantaged by the marriage: *Walton v. Walton* (1993), 46 R.F.L. (3d) 137, 110 Sask. R. 263, 1993 CarswellSask 47 (Q.B.), affirmed (1993), 23 C.B.R. (3d) 315, 116 Sask. R. 129, 59 W.A.C. 129, 108 D.L.R. (4th) 704, 1 R.F.L. (4th) 93, 1993 CarswellSask 33 (C.A.); amended (1993), 23 C.B.R. (3d) 315 at 320 (Sask. C.A.).

Where the parties were content that the husband remain in the home while the wife worked, with the result that he was virtually unemployable when the marriage ended, the wife was ordered to pay him periodic support. The husband had been economically disadvantaged as a result of the marriage and was entitled to support while he studied to upgrade himself: *Leek v. Lightfoot* (1993), 45 R.F.L. (3d) 364, 136 A.R. 235, 1993 CarswellAlta 438 (Q.B.).

In *Christian v. Christian* (1991), 37 R.F.L. (3d) 26, 7 O.R. (3d) 441, 1991 CarswellOnt 343 (Gen. Div.), the wife was awarded periodic support upon the breakdown of the parties' long-term traditional marriage, despite the fact that she had re-trained and had obtained full-time employment. The wife had, throughout the marriage, put the family first and, even with her employment, she would not be able to maintain a reasonable standard of living from her own resources.

In *Moura v. Moura* (1998), 43 R.F.L. (4th) 344, 1998 CarswellOnt 4919, [1998] O.J. No. 5351 (Ont. Gen. Div.), the court held that secondary-earner wives who continue to work during the marriage while assuming the responsibility of the primary child caregiver, but whose employment is subordinated to that of their husbands, are disadvantaged in terms of career advancement and should be entitled to spousal support. The wife in this case was awarded $400 monthly support for an indeterminate period.

Where it was found that the wife would likely have had a successful business career had she not given up opportunities to care for the parties' children, she was awarded periodic support for a 7-year term to enable her to educate herself and secure a position commensurate with her abilities and lifestyle: *Belliveau-Williamson v. Williamson* (1989), 21 R.F.L. (3d) 142, 97 N.B.R. (2d) 186, 245 A.P.R. 186, 1989 CarswellNB 22 (N.B. Q.B.).

Where the wife forfeited a promotion in an attempt to salvage the marriage, the court awarded her support in the amount of $400 per month for 2 years: *Balcombe v. Balcombe* (1990), 30 R.F.L. (3d) 177, 42 O.A.C. 150, 1990 CarswellOnt 322 (Div. Ct.).

There is an entitlement to support where, as a result of the duties of a marriage, a spouse loses his or her place on the labour market ladder: *Jukosky v. Jukosky* (1990), 31 R.F.L. (3d) 117, 1990 CarswellOnt 336 (Ont. Gen. Div.).

Where the wife has interrupted her career for family purposes she is entitled to reasonable spousal support for 1 year until she is working full-time: *De Roo v. De Roo* (1990), 28 R.F.L. (3d) 86, 1990 CarswellOnt 281 (Ont. H.C.).

In *Patrick v. Patrick* (1991), 35 R.F.L. (3d) 382, 62 B.C.L.R. (2d) 188, 1991 CarswellBC 315 (S.C.); additional reasons at (December 6, 1991), Doc. Vancouver D076591 (B.C. S.C.), the pharmacist wife was awarded spousal support upon dissolution of her 10-year marriage. Although employed, the result of the marriage breakdown and her continuing childrearing role rendered the wife financially and professionally disadvantaged in comparison with what her circumstances would have been had the marriage continued or had it never occurred. On appeal in *Patrick v. Patrick* (1993), 49 R.F.L. (3d) 453, 85 B.C.L.R. (2d) 303, 1993 CarswellBC 320 (C.A.) the court found no basis for imposing a time limit on the payment of support. There was nothing to prevent the appellant from applying for a variation of maintenance if there were a change in circumstances.

In *Stunt v. Stunt* (1990), 30 R.F.L. (3d) 353, 1990 CarswellOnt 329 (Ont. Gen. Div.), where the failure of the couple's marriage and the wife's response to it adversely affected her career but the wife could become self-sufficient, she was entitled to reasonable support for 2 years. The wife's career lost its directness of path and stability because of the marriage and its breakdown.

Where the wife had given up her nursing career to work in her husband's office, he was ordered to pay support while she returned to school to retrain as a dental hygienist: *Tancock v. Tancock* (1990), 24 R.F.L. (3d) 389, 1990 CarswellBC 436 (B.C. S.C.).

Where the wife had given up her teaching career to raise the parties' two children she was found, in divorce proceedings, to have suffered a substantial economic disadvantage resulting from the marriage and was accordingly awarded decreasing support over a 5-year period: *Monaghan v. Monaghan* (1988), 14 R.F.L. (3d) 308, 1988 CarswellOnt 248 (Ont. H.C.).

Where the wife had left her employment to accompany the husband to the United States in furtherance of his education and later postponed her own education while the parties built a house, she was awarded support on divorce to assist her with her university studies. As the wife had contributed significantly to the parties' financial well-being and the husband's educational endeavours, it was equitable that he contribute to her education: *Norris v. Norris* (1988), 13 R.F.L. (3d) 307, 70 Nfld. & P.E.I.R. 327, 215 A.P.R. 327, 1988 CarswellNfld 12 (Nfld. T.D.).

Where a 66-year-old Canadian man convinced his 35-year-old Polish niece to come to Canada and marry him, the wife was awarded periodic support although the couple separated only weeks after marrying. The wife spoke no English, had left a good paying job in Poland and was in failing health: *Weichholz v. Weichholz* (1987), 81 A.R. 236, [1987] A.J. No. 331, 1987 CarswellAlta 472 (Q.B.).

A wife who forsakes her pre-marital career for marriage may prejudice her future prospects for earning a living. If she is absent too long, she may find it impossible to resume her occupation, or if she does return she may find her absence has decreased her likelihood of success. Marriage does not entail such a hazard for the husband. This consideration should not be an unsubstantial item in fixing maintenance for a wife: *Chorny v. Chorny*, 4 R.F.L. 347, [1971] 5 W.W.R. 732, 1971 CarswellAlta 87 (Alta. C.A.). See also Langer v. Langer (1970), 2 R.F.L. 358 at 359, 1970 CarswellSask 16 (Sask. Q.B.).

Although a spouse may be entitled to support in recognition of the fact that she contributed to her husband's support while he attended university, this will not be the case where it was unlikely that the husband's degree would provide him with more employment income than he would have earned without it: *Bodnar v. Bodnar* (1987), 6 R.F.L. (3d) 66, 1987 CarswellOnt 289 (Ont. H.C.).

In *Berry v. Murray*, 30 R.F.L. (2d) 310, [1983] 1 W.W.R. 561, 1982 CarswellBC 665 (B.C. C.A.), the husband's appeal against an order requiring him to pay monthly maintenance of $900 to his wife was dismissed. As the wife had supported her husband through medical school, she could not be expected to be self-sufficient when she had sacrificed her own development to further his ability to earn a substantial income.

Where the wife had, during the parties' 16-year marriage, removed herself from the work force for 6 years because of family duties, she was accordingly awarded periodic maintenance. Her absence from the work force had adversely affected her pension and seniority rights as well as creating a significant disparity between her salary and that of her husband: *Skrlj v. Skrlj* (1986), 2 R.F.L. (3d) 305, 1986 CarswellOnt 276 (Ont. H.C.).

Where, as a result of her role in the marriage, the wife had lost some degree of competitiveness in the job market and her subsequent efforts to become self- sufficient had been fruitless, she was found to be entitled to periodic maintenance: *Primeau v. Primeau* (1986), 2 R.F.L. (3d) 113, 1986 CarswellOnt 267 (Ont. H.C.).

See also *Balbon v. Balbon* (1984), 41 R.F.L. (2d) 218, 29 Man. R. (2d) 223, 1984 CarswellMan 55 (Q.B.); varied (1984), 34 Man. R. (2d) 162, 1985 CarswellMan 391 (Man. C.A.); *Desbiens v. Desbiens* (1981), 30 B.C.L.R. 314, 1981 CarswellBC 217 (S.C.); *Tylman v. Tylman* (1980), 30 O.R. (2d) 721, 117 D.L.R. (3d) 730 (H.C.); *Spicer v. Spicer* (1980), 14 R.F.L. (2d) 180, 25 Nfld. & P.E.I.R. 133, 68 A.P.R. 133, 1980 CarswellNfld 9 (Nfld. T.D.); *Flannigan v. Flannigan* (1976), 26 R.F.L. 331, 1976 CarswellBC 88 (B.C. S.C.); *Harding v. Harding* (1972), 8 R.F.L. 236 at 236-237, 1972 CarswellBC 34 (B.C. S.C.); *Jackh v. Jackh*, 18 R.F.L. (2d) 310, 22 B.C.L.R. 182, [1981] 1 W.W.R. 481, 113 D.L.R. (3d) 267, 1980 CarswellBC 574 (S.C.); additional reasons at (1981), 22 R.F.L. (2d) 455, 124 D.L.R. (3d) 179, 1981 CarswellBC 525 (B.C. S.C.), ; *Von Hessert v. Von Hessert* (1982), 27 R.F.L. (2d) 197, 1982 CarswellSask 58 (Sask. U.F.C.).

15§27 — Objectives of spousal support — economic advantages and disadvantages — illness suffered by payee

A spouse who is unable to work because of a debilitating illness may be entitled to support on the "social obligation model" where there are no compensatory or contractual elements present. The social obligation model gives rise to non-compensatory support, which is the third conceptual basis for spousal support; the other two being the compensatory and the contractual basis. Non-compensatory support predicated on this model may be awarded on establishing only the fact of marriage and need: *Bracklow v. Bracklow*, 1999 CarswellBC 532 (S.C.C.), 1999 CarswellBC 2978 (quantum assessment on referral to the trial judge). The parties cohabited for 7 years: 4 years before marriage and 3 years after. For the first 2 years, the wife paid two-thirds of their living expenses because she was earning more than her husband and because her two children were living with them. After this initial period, they shared expenses equally. About a year before the separation, the wife suffered from health problems causing her to quit her employment, and she was unable to work from that time on. The marriage breakdown caused the wife to be in a state of economic hardship as contemplated by s. 15.2(6)(c) of the *Divorce Act*, that is, an "economic hardship of the spouses arising from the breakdown of the marriage." The wife was eligible for support on the basis of this hardship, the length of cohabitation, her need and the husband's financial ability to pay. Although a potential for a lifelong obligation was involved in the serious commitment of marriage, full payment for the indefinite future, in the circumstances of this case, may be unfair. The determination of the quantum and duration of support was referred back to the trial judge. All relevant statutory factors were to be considered, together with the amount of support already paid. The trial judge's determination on this referral, reported at 1999 CarswellBC 2978, was that the husband should continue to pay support of $400 a month for a period of 5 years from when support was first ordered. This determination created arrears of $16,000 for payments that should have been made in this period. To satisfy the arrears, the husband was ordered to pay a further $400 a month starting at the end of the 5-year period and continuing until the full amount of the arrears had been paid.

Where a person is ordered to make payments pursuant to s. 15.2 of the *Divorce Act* to a former spouse who, as a result of having developed a devastating physical illness during the marriage, was unable to be gainfully employed, the amount and duration of support varies with the circumstances and practical and policy issues affecting the particular case. While the payor should not be obligated to pay in perpetuity, a time limit may not be appropriate either: *Rayvals v. Rayvals*, 11 R.F.L. (6th) 125, 2004 CarswellBC 2870, 205 B.C.A.C. 267, 337 W.A.C. 267, 248 D.L.R. (4th) 262, 37 B.C.L.R. (4th) 374, 2004 BCCA 630 (B.C. C.A.); reversing in part 25 R.F.L. (5th) 399, 2002 CarswellBC 304, 2002 BCSC 128, [2002] B.C.J. No. 201 (B.C. S.C.).

Where the wife suffered from clinical depression resulting from the breakdown of the marriage, her spousal support award was upheld on appeal. Although the wife had worked throughout the marriage her health problems now prevented her from doing so. As there was a link between the wife's depression, her economic disadvantage and the marriage breakdown, spousal support was appropriate: *Haldone v. Haldone* (1999), 45 R.F.L. (4th) 285, 122 B.C.A.C. 280, 200 W.A.C. 280, 1999 CarswellBC 735 (C.A.).

A wife who is disadvantaged by the marriage in circumstances where her husband is advantaged, and who, because of illness is disadvantaged by the breakdown of the marriage, may be awarded support for an indefinite period: *Taylor v. Taylor* (1998), 38 R.F.L. (4th) 408, 157 D.L.R. (4th) 701, 104 B.C.A.C. 217, 170 W.A.C. 217, 50 B.C.L.R. (3d) 212, 1998 CarswellBC 547, [1998] B.C.J. No. 586 (C.A.). The husband and wife cohabited for 3 years and were married for 6 years. With the consent of the husband, the wife did not seek employment outside the marriage. She cared for the husband's daughter and supported him in his business by entertaining customers and associates, and by traveling with him. She began to develop medical problems during cohabitation and after separation became permanently disabled. The trial judge ordered the husband to pay support of $3,000 a month to her for an indefinite period. An appeal to the British Columbia Court of Appeal was dismissed. The trial judge's findings based on compensatory principles that the wife had been economically disadvantaged, and the husband economically advantaged as a result of the marriage, should not be disturbed. Nor should his finding that the wife was economically disadvantaged by the marriage breakdown, principally because her illness had intervened to render her unemployable. The husband did not suffer a similar disadvantage arising from the marriage breakdown, having survived a bankruptcy, paid down his debt to his employer, and set up a new beginning for himself in California, with the advantage of ongoing, remunerative employment. In addition to applying compensatory principles, the trial judge viewed this as a case in which the wife's need for support, and the husband's corresponding ability to meet that need without undue hardship. The need in this case arose largely, but not solely, as a result of the wife's illness, which was not causally connected to the marriage. However, the fact that a spouse's illness and consequent inability to become self-sufficient was not causally connected to the marriage does not necessarily justify the denial of support, or the limitation of support. In any event, the nine-year period of cohabitation and the specific findings of economic disadvantage to the wife arising from the marriage and its breakdown fully justified the trial judge's conclusion that the husband should continue to pay support to her at the rate of $3,000 a month.

Where, throughout the marriage, the wife had been an equal and, at times, the primary breadwinner, her claim for spousal support was denied despite the fact that she was at the time of trial unemployed. The wife's current difficulty was the result of illness and industry changes and was not related to any economic disadvantage suffered as a result of the marriage: *Woloshyn v. Woloshyn* (1996), 22 R.F.L. (4th) 129, 109 Man. R. (2d) 35, 1996 CarswellMan 170, [1996] M.J. No. 153 (Q.B.); affirmed (1997), 28 R.F.L. (4th) 70, 115 Man. R. (2d) 225, 139 W.A.C. 225, 1997 CarswellMan 116 (C.A.).

A wife's multiple sclerosis, in remission during the marriage, which resurfaces after separation preventing her from working is a "condition" or one of the "other circumstances" within s. 15(5) [now 15.2(4)] that justifies an order for support for an indefinite period: *Kloos v. Kloos* (1996), 21 R.F.L. (4th) 1, [1996] 5 W.W.R. 553, 110 Man. R. (2d) 129, 118 W.A.C. 129, 1996 CarswellMan 126, [1996] M.J. No. 146 (Man. C.A.). There is no inconsistency between the general principles that govern an award of "compensation" and the principles applicable where a spouse has a continuing illness following the break-up of the marriage. "The relevance of the medical circumstances of the spouse seeking support is mandated by an analysis of the factors to be taken into account pursuant to sec. 15(5) of the Act, namely, the "condition" and the "other circumstances" of the parties." When dealing with a sick or disabled spouse, a court should consider all the circumstances and hardships that result from the breakdown of the marriage, however caused.

Where the husband was diagnosed with leukemia after separation and was unable to work, he was found to have suffered an economic disadvantage from the breakdown of the marriage and was awarded spousal support in *Fraser v. Fraser* (2004), 8 R.F.L. (6th) 125, 2004 CarswellOnt 3343 (S.C.J.).

Where the breakdown of the marriage compounded with the wife's numerous physical ailments severely curtailed her ability to work, she was awarded periodic support, subject to review in four year's time: *Leonard v. Leonard* (2002), 26 R.F.L. (5th) 146, 2002 CarswellOnt 367 (Ont. S.C.J.).

In *Stang v. Stang*, 19 R.F.L. (5th) 187, 2001 CarswellBC 1526, 2001 BCSC 975 (B.C. S.C.), the wife's economic disadvantage was found to have arisen partially from injuries suffered in a post separation automobile accident for which she had recovered damages. However, as a substantial difference existed between the allocated income to the wife in the damage award and the husband's income, she was entitled to the ongoing spousal support. The disparity between her income and the husband's was a direct result of the marriage and its breakdown.

In *Riberdy v. Riberdy* (2001), 18 R.F.L. (5th) 161, 2001 CarswellOnt 2400 (Ont. S.C.J.); additional reasons at (2001), 2001 CarswellOnt 2920 (Ont. S.C.J.), the wife was awarded spousal support on the basis of the need arising from injuries she had suffered in two post-separation accidents.

Where the wife developed a debilitating mental condition 5 years into the parties' marriage with the result that the husband supported her throughout the remaining 17 years of marriage, she was awarded periodic support subject to review in1 year's time. Although the wife's economic circumstances were the result of her illness and not the marriage, the effect of the marriage breakdown was to deprive her of her sole means of support:

Cherkewich v. Cherkewich, 18 R.F.L. (5th) 17, 2001 CarswellAlta 666, 2001 ABQB 419 (Alta. Q.B.); additional reasons at 2001 CarswellAlta 851, 2001 ABQB 540 (Alta. Q.B.).

In *Kennedy v. Kennedy* (2000), 11 R.F.L. (5th) 150, 2000 CarswellOnt 3622, [2000] O.J. No. 3742 (Ont. S.C.J.), where the wife's stress-related illnesses, which prevented her from working, were the result of emotional and psychological abuse by the husband, the court found she suffered an economic disadvantage related to the marriage and was entitled to interim spousal support.

In *Epp v. Epp* (1998), 40 R.F.L. (4th) 137, 1998 CarswellBC 1346 (B.C. S.C. [In Chambers]), the wife was awarded periodic spousal support reviewable upon her attaining age 45. She had worked as a nurse throughout most of the marriage, but had developed a disability caused in part by the husband's conduct. Her disability pension amounted to half her former income and, as she had been economically disadvantaged by the marriage, she was entitled to support.

A wife in a marriage of 30 years who had multiple sclerosis was found to have suffered economic disadvantages as a result of the end of the marriage: *Winfield v Winfield* (1998), 35 R.F.L. (4th) 393, 1998 CarswellOnt 134, [1998] O.J. No. 175 (Ont. Gen. Div.); additional reasons at (February 6, 1998), Doc. Peterborough D17840/96. Because of the marriage break-up, she was required to spend money for services that she was unable to perform and which her husband would have undertaken if the parties had remained married. She was awarded periodic support for an indefinite term.

Where the wife had developed fibromyalgia 6 years before the parties separated, her condition was found to be a factor in determining spousal support to alleviate the economic disadvantages caused by the marriage: *Stuart v. Stuart* (1997), 30 R.F.L. (4th) 204, 1997 CarswellNB 265 (N.B. Q.B.).

A wife who had given up her career to move with the husband to further his career, and later developed a debilitating mental illness which prevented her from working, is entitled to spousal support. The breakdown of the marriage resulted in her suffering economic hardship: *Dillon v. Dillon* (1997), 27 R.F.L. (4th) 197, 184 N.B.R. (2d) 371, 469 A.P.R. 371, 1997 CarswellNB 4 (Q.B.).

Where the wife's economic problems were largely the result of a neurological disorder which existed before the marriage, but her post-separation depression could be traced in part to the marriage breakdown, she was found entitled to limited term support: *Morrison v. Morrison* (November 16, 1995), Doc. No. New Westminster D034379 (B.C. S.C.).

Where the wife's poor health was not related to the marriage, but her economic hardship could be traced to the marriage breakdown, she was awarded spousal support until further order of the court: *Clifford v. Clifford* (1995), 13 R.F.L. (4th) 374, 1995 CarswellSask 15 (Sask. Q.B.).

Where the parties married in their later years and the wife's health had deteriorated during the marriage so that she could not work, she was found to have suffered economic hardship as a result of the marriage breakdown: *Sand v. Sand* (1994), 2 R.F.L. (4th) 136, 1994 CarswellBC 651 (B.C. S.C.).

Where the wife's illness, which limited her working ability, was not directly related to the marriage but was aggravated as a result of the marriage breakdown, she was found entitled to indefinite periodic support: *Roy v. Roy* (1993), 1 R.F.L. (4th) 170, 1993 CarswellOnt 282 (Ont. Gen. Div.).

Where the wife was prevented from working as a result of an illness which she developed after separation, she was nevertheless found entitled to support. If it had not been for the marriage breakdown, the illness from which she suffered would not have resulted in her economic disadvantage: *Snyder v. Snyder* (1993), 47 R.F.L. (3d) 13, 138 A.R. 255, 1993 CarswellAlta 441 (Q.B.); affirmed (September 23, 1994), Foisy J.A., Irving J.A., Lieberman J.A. (Alta. C.A.); leave to appeal refused (1995), 188 N.R. 239 (note), 178 A.R. 77 (note), 110 W.A.C. 77 (note) (S.C.C.).

A spouse cannot avoid responsibility for the care of the other spouse during illness that arises while the marriage is continuing, even in the absence of a causal connection between the illness and the marriage: *Smith v. Smith* (1987), 11 R.F.L. (3d) 214 (Ont. H.C.). See also *Theriault v. Theriault* (1987), 10 R.F.L. (3d) 256, 81 N.S.R. (2d) 426, 203 A.P.R. 426 (Fam. Ct.); *Riley v. Riley* (1987), 11 R.F.L. (3d) 105 (N.S. Fam. Ct.).

15§28 — Objectives of spousal support — economic advantages and disadvantages — application for spousal support dismissed

In *Caron v. Caron*, 9 R.F.L. (6th) 268, 2004 CarswellSask 745, 2004 SKQB 424 (Sask. Q.B.); additional reasons at 2005 CarswellSask 145, 261 Sask. R. 141, 2005 SKQB 120 (Sask. Q.B.), the wife's claim for spousal support was dismissed upon the dissolution of the parties' 16-year marriage. The wife had been employed throughout most of the marriage and was capable of supporting herself at a fairly decent wage, although had chosen not to do so. Her plans to upgrade her education were doubtful.

In *Lambton v. Lambton*, 9 R.F.L. (6th) 400, 2004 CarswellBC 2606, 2004 BCSC 1400 (B.C. S.C.); additional reasons at 2004 CarswellBC 3062, 2004 BCSC 1725 (B.C. S.C.), the wife's claim for spousal support was dismissed upon the termination of the parties' 5-year marriage. Although unemployed at the time of the proceedings, the 48-year-old wife had worked throughout the marriage and had not suffered any economic disadvantage as a result of the marriage or its breakdown.

In *Jorgensen v. Jorgensen*, 43 R.F.L. (5th) 386, 2003 NSSF 32, 2003 CarswellNS 312 (N.S. S.C.), the 56-year-old wife's claim for spousal support was dismissed upon the dissolution of her 10-year marriage. The wife was not financially disadvantaged by the marriage and had always found work when she wanted it. She could not expect the husband to subsidize her in her wish to remain home to care for her mentally challenged adult child.

In *Leet v. Leet* (2002), 25 R.F.L. (5th) 302, 2002 CarswellNB 98, 2002 NBQB 87 (N.B. Q.B.), the court refused the wife's application for spousal support upon the dissolution of the parties' 15-year marriage. The wife's career had not been prejudiced by the marriage. She continued to work throughout the relationship and had enjoyed advancement to a responsible management position. Although the husband's income was larger than the wife's, her employment was more secure and the husband would be paying a significant amount in child support.

In *M. (D.G.) v. M. (K.M.)* (2002), 26 R.F.L. (5th) 152, 2002 CarswellAlta 289, 2002 ABQB 225 (Alta. Q.B.), the fact that the husband had a substantially larger income than the wife was not, in itself, evidence that the wife suffered career inequalities as a result of the marriage or its breakdown. The wife's annual income had more than doubled since the date of the marriage and there was no evidence that her living standard had declined. Accordingly, her claim for spousal support was dismissed.

In *Prince v. Prince* (1995), 16 R.F.L. (4th) 236, 144 N.S.R. (2d) 47, 416 A.P.R. 47, 1995 CarswellNS 201 (N.S. S.C.); additional reasons at (1996), 153 N.S.R. (2d) 356, 450 A.P.R. 356, 1996 CarswellNS 329 (N.S.S.C.); appeal allowed in part on other grounds; cross-appeal dismissed (1997), 163 N.S.R. (2d) 28, 487 A.P.R. 28, 35 R.F.L. (4th) 328, 1997 CarswellNS 444, [1997] N.S.J. No. 433 (N.S.C.A.), the wife's claim for lump sum support for "lost opportunity" because of an interruption of her career was dismissed in light of the finding that she had not suffered an economic disadvantage from the marriage in terms of her career. Although she had been forced to give up well-paying employment to move with the husband, she had located another lucrative position and her claim that had she stayed in her original job her salary would be higher was purely speculative. There was no compensable loss as a result of the wife leaving her employment. (However, she was awarded a lump sum of $8,000 as compensation for the economic disadvantage she suffered as a result of the marriage breakdown. After the separation, she encroached on her capital as a result of the husband's inadequate payment of child support for a period of 6 months.).

In *Huisman v. Huisman* (1996), 21 R.F.L. (4th) 341, 91 O.A.C. 293, 137 D.L.R. (4th) 41, 30 O.R. (3d) 155, 1996 CarswellOnt 2470 (Ont. C.A.); varying (1994), 8 R.F.L. (4th) 145, 1994 CarswellOnt 456 (Ont. U.F.C.), the court allowed the appeal from the wife's award of indefinite spousal support and imposed a 6-year limitation. The trial judge had failed to consider that throughout the parties' 8-year marriage a number of economic advantages had also accrued to the wife.

In *Fisher v. Fisher* (2000), 7 R.F.L. (5th) 45, 2000 CarswellNS 101 (N.S. S.C.); varied 2001 NSCA 18, 12 R.F.L. (5th) 348, 190 N.S.R. (2d) 144, 594 A.P.R. 144, 2001 CarswellNS 31 (C.A.), the court refused the wife's claim for support upon dissolution of the parties' 20-year marriage. After separation, the husband assumed custody of the children without any support from the wife. The husband, who was 62 years old, continued to pay off substantial matrimonial debts while the 44-year-old wife made little effort to support herself. The wife's career opportunities had not been diminished by the marriage nor had the husband's career been enhanced by the wife's contributions.

In *Stewart v. Stewart* (2000), 12 R.F.L. (5th) 218, 2000 CarswellNS 316 (N.S. S.C.), the court refused the husband's application for spousal support upon dissolution of the parties' 38-year marriage. The husband had retired from the military and his health impeded his ability to work, while the wife continued to be employed as a nurse. Although the wife could afford to pay, the husband could not point to any economic loss or hardship resulting from the marriage, which justified his claim.

In *Mason v. Mason* (1995), 10 R.F.L. (4th) 249, 104 Man. R. (2d) 81, 1995 CarswellMan 3 (Man. Q.B.); affirmed (1995), 18 R.F.L. (4th) 134, 102 Man. R. (2d) 239, 93 W.A.C. 239, 1995 CarswellMan 498 (Man. C.A.), although the wife had given up her career to raise the children, her claim for spousal support was dismissed on the ground that the advantages flowing to her from the marriage outweighed the disadvantages. She had received substantial assets and cash which would provide her with sufficient income to support herself.

In *Hoskins v. Hoskins* (1998), 36 R.F.L. (4th) 44, 1998 CarswellSask 38 (Sask. Q.B.), the fact that the wife, who had inherited a large estate from her first marriage, had expended considerable sums which had benefitted both herself and her current husband did not give rise to an economic disadvantage resulting from the marriage. The wife had made the expenditure voluntarily and she maintained the bulk of the exempt property with which she had entered the marriage. Her application for support upon termination of the parties' 5-year marriage was dismissed.

Where both the parties were physicians, but the wife worked only part time, to some degree because of illness and an addiction to prescription drugs, her application for support was refused. The wife's claims of debilitating pain were already exaggerated so as to ensure her supply of prescription drugs. Her dependency was not related to the marriage and her limited practice was largely the result of her own choice: *MacDonald v. Rasmussen* (1997), 29 R.F.L. (4th) 310, 1997 CarswellSask 362 (Sask. Q.B.).

Where the wife had given up her full-time job upon marriage but had resumed full-time work after separation, her claim for spousal support was dismissed. Although somewhat disadvantaged by the marriage, she had trained and gained experience while married and would soon achieve financial independence: *Kyle v. Kyle* (February 9, 1996), Doc. Saskatoon U.F.C. 775/94 (Sask. Q.B.).

Where the wife's income, both before and after marriage, was relatively equal and her asset base had increased in value during the parties' relationship, her claim for spousal support was dismissed: *Kessel v. Kessel* (1993), 1 R.F.L. (4th) 324, 1993 CarswellOnt 286 (Ont. Gen. Div.); additional reasons at (January 18, 1994), Doc. D21601/90, 1994 CarswellOnt 3069 (Ont. Gen. Div.).

Compensatory support is only justified on the basis of recognizing any economic advantages or disadvantages caused by the marriage. Where the wife was actually in a better position than the husband at the end of the marriage and any decrease in her earnings was the result of her own decision not to return to her more lucrative earlier career, her application for support was dismissed: *Stich v. Stich* (1995), 17 R.F.L. (4th) 178, 1995 CarswellBC 1094 (B.C. S.C.).

The fact that the parties had mutually decided that the wife should only pursue her nursing career part-time during the parties' 6-year marriage was found insufficient to establish that she had been economically disadvantaged. She was a trained and self-sufficient professional and she was only entitled to interim periodic support for a 6- month period to assist her in re-entering the workforce: *Mullins v. Mullins* (1995), 12 R.F.L. (4th) 461, 1995 CarswellNfld 8 (Nfld. U.F.C.).

Where the wife had withdrawn from nursing school shortly before the marriage, contrary to the husband's wishes, her claim for support was refused. The wife was unable to prove that the marriage prevented her from returning to nursing school; accordingly, no economic disadvantage had been established: *Ho v. Ho* (1993), 1 R.F.L. (4th) 340, 1993 CarswellOnt 287, [1993] O.J. No. 2919 (Ont. Gen. Div.).

In *Bakken v. Bakken* (1992), 132 A.R. 356, 1992 CarswellAlta 520 (Q.B.), the husband's application for support was dismissed. The husband had lost his job and between working sporadically and receiving social assistance, had maintained a monthly income of $1,500. Although the wife had a substantial income as a medical doctor, the husband had not suffered any economic disadvantage as a result of the marriage. The marriage had not restricted his ability to work or to maintain and upgrade his qualifications.

In *Pope v. Pope* (1995), 12 R.F.L. (4th) 391, 1995 CarswellNfld 7 (Nfld. U.F.C.), the court rejected the wife's claim for support based upon her assertion that her business had faltered as a result of the trauma from the marriage breakdown. The husband had co-signed the wife's business loans and had suffered more post-separation economic hardship than had she.

Where after her early years as a homemaker, the wife qualified as a registered nurse, obtained a good paying job and, subsequent to separation, left that job to return to university, her application for spousal support was dismissed. Whereas the wife had improved her station considerably throughout the 21-year marriage, the husband had been confined to his job as a labourer and had assumed full responsibility for the children after the separation. The wife had suffered no economic disadvantage from the marriage or its breakdown and was capable of caring for herself: *Kenning v. Kenning* (1994), 11 R.F.L. (4th) 216, 1995 CarswellBC 83 (B.C. S.C.).

In *Gawley v. Gawley* (1993), 48 R.F.L. (3d) 104, 86 Man. R. (2d) 317, 1993 CarswellMan 52 (Q.B.), the husband's application for interim support was refused although the wife had throughout the parties' brief marriage supported the alcoholic husband and paid his debts. As the husband's financial position was about the same as it had been before the marriage, he could not point to any economic disadvantage suffered.

In *Noseworthy v. Noseworthy* (1995), 17 R.F.L. (4th) 21, 136 Nfld. & P.E.I.R. 64, 423 A.P.R. 64, 1995 CarswellNfld 128, [1995] N.J. No. 360 (Nfld. U.F.C.), the husband's claim for spousal support was dismissed upon termination of the parties' 2-year marriage. Although he was no longer able to work because of a medical condition and could not achieve self-sufficiency, he had suffered no economic disadvantage from the marriage or its breakdown.

15§29 — Objectives of spousal support — economic advantages and disadvantages — miscellaneous

An order for partial spousal support confirms that the dependant spouse had suffered economic disadvantage from the marriage or its breakdown: *Baldwin v. Ward* (1999), 2 R.F.L. (5th) 56, 180 Sask. R. 124, 205 W.A.C. 124, 1999 CarswellSask 355 (Sask. C.A.). On appeal, the duration of spousal support was lengthened from 10 months to 3 years to permit the wife to continue with her studies. The parties separated after 18 years of marriage.

In considering the disadvantages to a spouse arising from the marriage or its breakdown, a court may consider a spouse's potential liability for debts, particularly if the other spouse will have funds available to him in the near future: *Cantwell v. Cantwell* (2000), 12 R.F.L. (5th) 33, 2000 CarswellOnt 4391 (Ont. S.C.J.).

Where, throughout the parties' 21-year marriage, the wife had performed the bulk of household and family duties while continuing to work full-time, she was awarded both lump sum and limited term periodic support, which together would promote her eventual self-sufficiency. The wife's efforts had freed the husband to pursue more lucrative career and business opportunities: *Weir v. Weir* (2000), 11 R.F.L. (5th) 223, 2000 BCSC 1391, 80 B.C.L.R. (3d) 342, 2000 CarswellBC 1892, [2000] B.C.J. No. 1900 (B.C. S.C.).

The fact that a spouse may remarry is not a relevant consideration in determining whether or not that spouse suffered an economic disadvantage as a result of the marriage. Such a possibility can, however, be relevant in determining whether support should be restricted to a limited term: *Lauderdale v. Lauderdale* (1999), 50 R.F.L. (4th) 411, 241 A.R. 355, 1999 CarswellAlta 296 (Q.B.).

Where the husband stopped paying spousal support under the parties' separation agreement after the wife remarried, the court refused the wife's application to re-instate support after her second marriage failed. The agreement specifically called for termination of spousal support if the wife remarried and any economic hardship suffered by the wife was the result of the failure of her second marriage and not the first one: *Scheel v. Henkelman* (1999), 45 R.F.L. (4th) 419, 1999 CarswellOnt 1156 (Ont. Gen. Div.).

Where some of the wife's current problems were attributable to her first marriage, this did not remove from her second husband the responsibility for the continued and exacerbated economic disenfranchisement which she experienced as a result of the second marriage. The wife was accordingly entitled to support: *Morison v. Morison* (1993), 47 R.F.L. (3d) 34, 139 A.R. 124, 1993 CarswellAlta 442, [1993] A.J. No. 334 (Q.B.).

15§30 — Objectives of spousal support — economic advantages and disadvantages — causal connection

See also 15§27 — Objectives of spousal support — economic advantages and disadvantages — illness suffered by payee

The principle that there must be a causal connection between the marriage and the need for support is no longer part of the law. The notion that there must be such a connection has its origins in the *Pelech* Trilogy, three cases decided in the Supreme Court of Canada under the 1968 *Divorce Act* (repealed). The Trilogy did not deal with issues relating to spousal support arising for the first time, but with respect to the issue of when, after the parties have either waived or provided for support in their separation agreement, the court should override their agreement. The answer given by the court was that it should override a waiver or provision for support in a separation agreement only where the applicant was able to establish a radical and unforseen change in circumstances that was causally connected to the marriage: *Pelech v. Pelech*, 7 R.F.L. (3d) 225, [1987] 1 S.C.R. 801, 17 C.P.C. (2d) 1, 14 B.C.L.R. (2d) 145, [1987] 4 W.W.R. 481, 76 N.R. 81, 38 D.L.R. (4th) 641 (S.C.C.); *Richardson v. Richardson*, 7 R.F.L. (3d) 304, [1987] 1 S.C.R. 857, 17 C.P.C. (2d) 104, 77 N.R. 1, 22 O.A.C. 1, 38 D.L.R. (4th) 699 (S.C.C.); *Caron v. Caron*, 7 R.F.L. (3d) 274, [1987] 1 S.C.R. 892, 14 B.C.L.R. (2d) 186, [1987] 4 W.W.R. 522, 75 N.R. 36, 2 Y.R. 246, 38 D.L.R. (4th) 735 (S.C.C.).

The last part of this test, that the change must be "causally connected to the marriage," was taken out of the context of applications to override agreements and, by many courts, more generally applied to original claims for spousal support where no previous agreement was in existence. This extension was held by the Supreme Court of Canada in *Moge v. Moge*, 43 R.F.L. (3d) 345, [1992] 3 S.C.R. 813, [1993] 1 W.W.R. 481, 145 N.R. 1, 81 Man. R. (2d) 161, 30 W.A.C. 161, 99 D.L.R. (4th) 456 (discussed in detail at 15§24 Objectives for spousal support — general) to be unwarranted. The court in its enunciation of the law of spousal support under the 1985 *Divorce Act* (the successor to the 1968 Act) held that the causal connection test did not apply to non-consensual dispositions under the new Act.

But *Moge* left open the question of whether the Trilogy test — which included causal connection as an element — should apply to final agreements under the 1985 Act. The question was determined, and finally answered, by the Supreme Court of Canada in *Miglin v. Miglin*, 2003 CarswellOnt 1374 (S.C.C.), which held that the Trilogy test does not apply to cases under the current *Divorce Act*. The test was based on the predecessor of the 1985 Act, the current *Divorce Act*. The current Act uses more specific and comprehensive language. This new language and the judicial interpretations of the language adopt a different approach which makes the test involving a causal connection inappropriate and not applicable where the court is considering whether to use its discretion to override a support waiver or provision in an agreement. Neither causal connection nor the second element of radical change that completed the test established by the trilogy is part of the law as it now stands for this purpose. Instead, in determining whether to override a support disposition in an agreement, the court is to consider the agreement broadly in light of the objectives of the Act as a whole which include policy goals of certainty, autonomy and finality. None of the elements of the *Pelech* trilogy are included in this approach. The approach is taken in two stages. The first stage involves determining whether the agreement was unimpeachably negotiated and, at the time, whether it was settled in substantial compliance with the general objectives of the Act. In the second stage, the court assesses the extent to which the agreement still reflects the original intention of the parties, and the extent to which it is still in substantial compliance with the objectives of the Act. If the agreement survives this two-stage scrutiny, it should be given great weight and not be overridden. For a detailed summary of the *Miglin* case, see section 15§147. Causal connection in the sense used in the *Pelech* trilogy is not part of the law of spousal support under the current *Divorce Act*: *Moge v. Moge*, above, and *Miglin v. Miglin*, above. Cases decided before these cases were reported should be read with caution

Entitlement to spousal support in curcumstances such as where the spouse is incapacitated by illness does not depend on finding an economic disadvantage caused by the marriage. Entitlement may flow from the marriage breakdown; that is, it may flow from the fact that on breakdown the spouse no longer receives the benefits of a common household: *Bracklow v. Bracklow*, 169 D.L.R. (4th) 577, 236 N.R. 79, 44 R.F.L. (4th) 1, 120 B.C.A.C. 211, 196 W.A.C. 211, [1999] 1 S.C.R. 420, 63 B.C.L.R. (3d) 77, [1998] 8 W.W.R. 740, 1999 CarswellBC 532, 1999 CarswellBC 533, [1999] S.C.J. No. 14. For a detailed discussion of the facts of the case, see section 15§6 General principles for determining spousal support.

In *Moge v. Moge* (1992), [1992] 3 S.C.R. 813, 43 R.F.L. (3d) 345, [1993] 1 W.W.R. 481, 99 D.L.R. (4th) 456, 81 Man. R. (2d) 161, 30 W.A.C. 161, 145 N.R. 1, [1993] R.D.F. 168, [1992] S.C.J. No. 107, 1992 CarswellMan 143, 1992 CarswellMan 222 (discussed in detail at 15§24 Objectives of spousal support — general), the court considered the question of the extent to which the causal connection test articulated in *Pelech* decided under the 1968 *Divorce Act* applied to non-consensual dispositions under the 1985 *Divorce Act* and was of the opinion that the test should not be extended to non-consensual dispositions under the current Act. It left open the question of whether or not the causal connection test as discussed in the trilogy in the context of a final settlement would apply to final agreements under the 1985 Act.

In light of *Moge v. Moge* (1992), [1992] 3 S.C.R. 813, 43 R.F.L. (3d) 345, [1992] S.C.J. No. 107, 1992 CarswellMan 143, 1992 CarswellMan 222, [1993] 1 W.W.R. 481, 99 D.L.R. (4th) 456, 81 Man. R. (2d) 161, 30 W.A.C. 161, 145 N.R. 1, [1993] R.D.F. 168; the *Pelech* trilogy, [*Pelech v. Pelech*, 7 R.F.L. (3d) 225, [1987] 1 S.C.R. 801, 17 C.P.C. (2d) 1, 14 B.C.L.R. (2d) 145, [1987] 4 W.W.R. 481, 76 N.R. 81, 38 D.L.R. (4th) 641, 1987 CarswellBC 147, 1987 CarswellBC 703, [1987] S.C.J. No. 31; *Richardson v. Richardson*, 7 R.F.L. (3d) 304, [1987] 1 S.C.R. 857, 17 C.P.C. (2d) 104, 77 N. 1, 22 O.A.C. 1, 38 D.L.R. (4th) 699, 1987 CarswellOnt 315, 1987 CarswellOnt 963, [1987] S.C.J. No. 30; *Caron v. Caron*, 7 R.F.L. (3d) 274, [1987] 1 S.C.R. 892, 14 B.C.L.R. (2d) 186, [1987] 4 W.W.R. 522, 75 N.R. 36, 2 Y.R. 246, 38 D.L.R. (4th) 735, 1987 CarswellYukon 8, [1987] S.C.J. No. 32, 1987 CarswellYukon 43] is not applicable to cases where spousal support has not been determined by agreement: *Moura v. Moura* (1998), 43 R.F.L. (4th) 344, 1998 CarswellOnt 4919, [1998] O.J. No. 5351 (Gen. Div.). Consequently, entitlement to support is no longer dependant on a causal connection between a spouse's need and the marriage. Instead it is governed by legislation and in particular the four objectives contained within the legislation.

The causal connection requirement was developed in the trilogy as part of a test to determine when the court should intervene under the *Divorce Act* to override a waiver of, or a provision for spousal support contained in a pre-existing agreement. The test was based on the Act that was replaced by the 1985 Act, the current *Divorce Act*, which uses more specific and comprehensive language. The new language and judicial interpretations adopt a different approach which makes the test involving a causal connection inappropriate and not applicable where the court is considering whether to use discretion under the current *Divorce Act* to override a support provision in an agreement. Neither causal connection nor the second element of radical change that completed the test established by the trilogy is part of the law as it now stands for this purpose: *Miglin v. Miglin* (2001), 16 R.F.L. (5th) 185, 144 O.A.C. 155, 53 O.R. (3d) 641, 198 D.L.R. (4th) 385, 2001 CarswellOnt 1404 (C.A.); leave to appeal allowed (2001), 2001 CarswellOnt 3484, 283 N.R. 395 (note), 157 O.A.C. 400 (note) (S.C.C.). The extension of causal connection made by some courts to a requirement for an original support order where there was no agreement to override also have met its demise in *Miglin*. If the test is revoked for the purpose intended, should it not also be considered revoked for other purposes for which intended, but to which it was extended? It the tree dies, does the branch live? For a detailed summary of the *Miglin* case, see 15§147.

Where the need for support results from an illness or disability the fact that the illness of disability is not casually connected to the marriage should not be a factor in denying or limiting support: *Taylor v. Taylor* (1998), 38 R.F.L. (4th) 408, 1998 CarswellBC 547, [1998] B.C.J. No. 586157 D.L.R. (4th) 701, 104 B.C.A.C. 217, 170 W.A.C. 217, 50 B.C.L.R. (3d) 212 (C.A.). These cases reflect the trend to the "social obligation model" that focuses primarily on need arising as a result of the marriage breakdown, coupled with an emphasis on the condition, needs, means and other circumstances of the time the support order is made. All the disadvantages arising from the marriage breakdown have to be considered, however they are caused. Both compensatory and need considerations must be applied.

Where the wife developed a medical condition after separation which prevented her from working, she was found entitled to spousal support despite the fact that there were no economic disadvantages to the wife from the marriage itself or its breakdown. The wife was not obliged to establish a causal connection between her economic disadvantage arising from her illness and the marriage or its breakdown, just the reasonable expectation of support arising from the marriage: *Sheldon v. Sheldon* (1996), 21 R.F.L. (4th) 422, 182 A.R. 131, 1996 CarswellAlta 291 (Q.B.).

Pre Moge v. Moge Cases

The Supreme Court of Canada, in three appeals heard together, defined the test to be used in resolving the conflict between the use of the court's overriding jurisdiction to make support orders, on the one hand, and upholding agreements dealing with support on the other: *Pelech v. Pelech*, 7 R.F.L. 225, [1987] 1 S.C.R. 801, 17 C.P.C. (2d) 1, 14 B.C.L.R. (2d) 145, [1987] 4 W.W.R. 481, 76 N.R. 81, 38 D.L.R. (4th) 641, 1987 CarswellBC 147, 1987 CarswellBC 703, [1987] S.C.J. No. 31; *Caron v. Caron*, 7 R.F.L. (3d) 274, [1987] 1 S.C.R. 892, 14 B.C.L.R. (2d) 186, [1987] 4 W.W.R. 522, 75 N.R. 36, 2 Y.R. 246, 38 D.L.R. (4th) 735, 1987 CarswellYukon 8, [1987] S.C.J. No. 32, 1987 CarswellYukon 43;

and *Richardson v. Richardson*, 7 R.F.L. (3d) 304, [1987] 1 S.C.R. 857, 17 C.P.C. (2d) 104, 77 N.R. 1, 22 O.A.C. 1, 38 D.L.R. (4th) 699, 1987 CarswellOnt 315, 1987 CarswellOnt 963, [1987] S.C.J. No. 30.

The *Pelech* case came from the court on an appeal by the wife from the Court of Appeal of British Columbia. Fifteen years after the divorce, the former wife applied to vary an order in the divorce decree. This order had incorporated the terms of an agreement providing for her maintenance in a lump sum of approximately $29,000 payable by installments over thirteen months. These funds had long since been de and the former wife was reduced to relying on social assistance. In the meantime, the circumstances of her former husband had improved to the point where his net worth had increased from $128,000 at the time of the divorce $1,800,000 at the time she brought the application to vary the maintenance order. Since the order was based on an agreement, the court, in being asked to vary the order, was being asked to override the support provisions in the agreement.

A statement that derives from this case is that, where the parties have entered an agreement that was intended as a final settlement of their affairs, the should exercise its jurisdiction to ignore a waiver or limitation in the agreement, and award support or further support only where there is (a) a radical change in circumstances; and (b) a causal connection between the changed circumstances and the marriage. The second condition is new to our law of support.

In *Richardson v. Richardson* the second of the three appeals, the issue before the court was whether it was "fit and just" to make an original order for spousal maintenance under the *Divorce Act*, R.S.C. 1970, c. D-8, in an amount different from that agreed upon by the parties in a settlement agreement.

The Supreme Court of Canada dismissed the wife's appeal for spousal maintenance. It relied on the *Pelech* decision and held at 7 R.F.L. (3d) 225 at 310 that "a court should vary a settlement agreement only where there has been a radical change in the circumstances of a former spouse and that change is the result of a pattern of economic dependency generated by the marriage relationship." It stressed the importance of finality in the financial affairs of former spouses and the right and responsibility of individuals to make their own decisions. The appellant's financial difficulties had not occurred because of a pattern of economic dependency generated from the marriage. There was not a great gap in time from her last period of employment to the time of the separation so that it could not be said that the marriage atrophied her skills. In the circumstances, it was the state's responsibility and not the husband's to support the applicant.

Indirect deprivation of the child in her care was held not to be a basis for awarding support to the wife.

The court rejected the applicant's argument of a failed common expectation. The wife argued that, at the time she and her husband entered into the settlement agreement, they expected she would be employed within the Supreme Court of Canada found no evidence of such a common expectation and held that the possibility that the applicant would not be employed at the end pf the year was reasonably foreseeable by the parties.

In *Caron v. Caron* the court refused to vary the order in the decree (based on the settlement agreement) to restore the maintenance payments lost when the wife cohabited with a man for more than 90 days, contrary to the settlement agreement. The right to vary maintenance under the agreement was limited to a power to vary quantum and did not include a power of reinstatement where the right to maintenance had been validly terminated.

Wilson J., following the *Pelech* decision, stated at 7 R.F.L. (3d) 225 at 277 that, under the *Divorce Act*, in order for courts to interfere with a settlement entered into by former spouse, applicant must satisfy the court that there has been a radical change in circumstances related to a pattern of economic dependency generated by the marriage relationship. In the case before her, there was no evidence of such a change in the circumstances. The only change was that the respondent had ceased to make maintenance payments as he was entitled to under the agreement. Accordingly, the appeal was dismissed.

Some recent cases influenced by this trilogy in the Supreme Court of Canada have extended the concept of causal connection to a general support principle applicable on any support application, including original applications. According to these cases, in order to obtain, the claimant must not only establish need, but also that the need is causally connected to the marriage. However, this connection arises, it seems, only where the marriage has prevented the claimant from becoming financially self-sufficient after the breakdown.

Assessment of the Pelech Trilogy

The *Pelech*, *Richardson*, and *Caron* decisions were cases under the *Divorce Act, 1968* were the parties had entered into agreements disposing of the support claims and where subsequently one of the parties sought to resurrect her right to support by applying to vary the decree when her circumstances had changed. It may be that the "causal connection test" should be confined to similar cases and not extended to a general support principle. Or it may be that, as *Linton v. Linton* (1990), 30 R.F.L. (3d) 1, 1 O.R. (3d) 1, 42 O.A.C. 328, 75 D.L.R. (4th) 637, 1990 CarswellOnt 316, [1990] O.J. No. 2267, 41 E.T.R. 85 (C.A.), has suggested, the causal connection test is of significant in the law today only to the extent that a causal connection requirement emerges from the *Divorce Act*. See *Moge v. Moge* above. See *Miglin* above.

Connection — An Applicable Test — Under the *Divorce Act, 1985*

The Ontario Court of Appeal in *Linton v. Linton* above, held that the causal connection principles are relevant only to the extent that a causal connection requirement or objective may be taken to emerge from the *Divorce Act, 1985*. Osborne J.A., writing for the court, found that the specific references to a causal connection in s. 17(10) and to elements of causal connection in s.15 indicate some relevancy and that to a limited extent the causal connection requirement is applicable both on original support claims and on applications to vary support orders.

In *Willms v. Willms* (1988), 14 R.F.L. (3d) 162, 65 O.R. (2d) 151, 27 O.A.C. 316, 51 D.L.R. (4th) 757, 1988 CarswellOnt 244 (C.A.), the court was of the opinion that the causal connection test is not limited to variation applications made after the parties have entered into a separation agreement, but should be considered and applied in cases where the facts warrant its application. In this case, the court terminated support for a chronically disabled spouse with paranoid schizophrenia who was unlikely to function adequately outside an institutional setting. The husband had supported his former spouse for twelve years. The illness had begun during the marriage.

McEachern C.J.B.C., writing for the majority in the British Columbia Court of Appeal in *Story v. Story* (1989), 23 R.F.L. (3d) 225 at 235, 42 B.C.L.R. (2d) 21, 65 D.L.R. (4th) 549, 1989 CarswellBC 237, [1989] B.C.J. No. 2238 (C.A.), was of the opinion that, "the concept of causal relation only app when one is considering an application to vary a support order after rights have been finally determined either by agreement or order, or when a support order falls within the description contained in *Divorce Act*, s. 17(10) . . .. In all other cases . . . applications under s. 17 for a variation of a support order should be determined in accordance with the principles specifically prescribed for such purpose by the *Divorce Act*, but without re to the question of causal relation." For a detailed discussion of this case see 17$2A Variation — causal connection with marriage.

In *Brody v. Brody* (1990), 25 R.F.L. (3d) 319, 105 A.R. 41, 1990 CarswellAlta 268 (Q.B.) the court was of the opinion that the causal connection principles applied in spousal support cases generally and not only in cases where the courts were to vary separation agreements. On the wife's application, brought fifteen years after the parties' divorce, the court rejected the wife's claim for increased support, finding that the evidence did not establish that her need arose from the marriage or its breakdown: instead, the need arose from her illness (high blood pressure).

In *Droit de la famille — 382*, 16 R.F.L. (3d) 379, [1988] R.J.Q. 2408, [1988] R.D.F. 482, 1988 CarswellQue 46 (C.A.), it was held that the causal connection test is applicable on a claim at first instance where there has been no agreement the parties. The wife's claim for support was denied because her inability to work was caused by the head injuries she sustained in a car accident after the marriage.

The court, in *Fisher v. Fisher* (1987), 11 R.F.L. (3d) 42, 1987 CarswellOnt 254 (Dist. Ct.), held that if the *Pelech* support system was appropriate under the 1968 *Divorce Act*, it was more appropriate under the 1985 Act because of the language of the later Act. However, this case was reversed on appeal at (1989), 22 R.F.L. (3d) 225, 70 O.R. (2d) 336, 39 O.A.C. 154, 62 D.L.R. (4th) 544, 1989 CarswellOnt 288 (Div. Ct.); leave to appeal to Ont. C.A. refused (1989), 23 R.F.L. (3d) xli, 70 O.R. (2d) 336 (note) (C.A.).

Causal Connection Test — Not an Applicable Test Under the Divorce Act, 1985

The absence of a "causal connection" between the applicant spouse's need and the marriage itself does not bar a court from exercising its discretionary power to award support in the first instance under s. 15: *per* Mitchell J.A. in *Currie v. Currie* (1991), 32 R.F.L. (3d) 67, 278 A.P.R. 44, 89 Nfld. & P.E.I.R. 44, 1991 CarswellPEI 15 (C.A.).

There have been several cases which have taken the position that the causal connection test is not applicable under the *Divorce Act*, 1985. In *Fenwick v. Fenwick* (1988), 15 R.F.L. (3d) 18, 1988 CarswellAlta 334, [1988] A.J. No. 542, 89 A.R. 373 (Q.B.), the Supreme Court of Canada trilogy restricting the court's power to award or alter support in the face of a final settlement agreement was held not to apply to cases under the *Divorce Act*, 1985. The court questioned whether the trilogy applied where the wife's maintenance had been set by a pre-1985 divorce settlement and decree: *Troughton v. Troughton* (1988), 18 R.F.L. (3d) 113, 64 Alta. L.R. (2d) 157, 93 A.R. 23, 55 D.L.R. (4th) 761, 1988 CarswellAlta 250 (C.A.).

The factors and objectives to be considered in granting spousal maintenance in an initial application are those set forth in the *Divorce Act* and not those found in the *Pelech* test, which are applicable only where one of the parties to a contract wants support on different terms than those set out in the contract: *Finch v. Finch* (1990), 24 R.F.L. (3d) 335, 103 A.R. 228, 1990 CarswellAlta 265 (Q.B.). The applicability of pre-*Divorce Act*, 1985 jurisprudence must be tested against the new legislation. In the *Finch* decision, the wife in a 21-year marriage had psychological problems which restricted her employment. She was found to suffer economic hardship on the breakdown of the marriage. The court, without applying the causal connection test, awarded spousal support of $500 a month for two years.

In the Saskatchewan Queen's Bench case of *Trainor v. Trainor* (1988), 16 R.F.L. (3d) 349, 1988 CarswellSask 66 (Q.B.); affirmed (1989), 23 R.F.L. (3d) 39, 80 Sask. R. 1, 1989 CarswellSask 77 (C.A.), the court was of the opinion that the Supreme Court trilogy did not apply in circumstances where there was no existing settlement agreement. *Feehan v. Feehan* (1989), 24 R.F.L. (3d) 185, 79 Nfld. & P.E.I.R. 54, 246 A.P.R. 54, 64 D.L.R. (4th) 557, 1989 CarswellPEI 31 (T.D.), categorically rejects the application of the test under the *Divorce Act*, stating that the causal connection doctrine is not applicable to support proceedings under the *Divorce Act*, 1985. The Act itself outlines the criteria for determining whether support should be awarded.

In *Hunkin v. Hunkin* (1988), 14 R.F.L. (3d) 157, 54 Man. R. (2d) 44, 1988 CarswellMan 48 (Q.B.), the court questioned whether the trilogy should be limited to cases under the 1968 *Divorce Act* and should not be extended to cases under the 1985 *Divorce Act*.

Where the parties signed a separation agreement which provided support for the wife for one year and any continuing support according to a further agreement between the spouses, or according to a court order. Such and agreement is not final and conclusive regarding support and the court could make an originating order under s. 15 and not a variation order under s. 17. The order was not then subject to the provisions set out in the *Pelech* trilogy: *Vaandering v. Vaandering* (1990), 25 R.F.L. (3d) 310, 1990 CarswellBC 449 (S.C.).

Distinction Between Traditional and Modern Marriages

In *Moge v. Moge* (1992), 43 R.F.L. (3d) 345, [1992] 3 S.C.R. 813, [1993] 1 W.W.R. 481, 145 N.R. 1, 81 Man. R. (2d) 161, 30 W.A.C. 161, 99 D.L.R. (4th) 456, [1992] S.C.J. No. 107, 1992 CarswellMan 143, 1992 CarswellMan 222, [1993] R.D.F. 168, the Supreme Court of Canada was of the opinion that the distinction between "traditional" and "modern" marriages was not as useful as some lower courts have indicated. In the traditional marriage, where the wife remains at home and takes responsibility for the domestic aspects of marital life, courts have frequently been more amenable to awarding support. But this same dichotomy has also inspired decisions to deny support. In addition, there are many cases in which the distinction is not helpful either way. In some "modern" marriages the wife is disadvantaged financially as a result of the breakdown of the marriage and should be compensated by receiving support. And in "traditional" marriages in circumstances, for example, where the wife does have prospects of resuming full-time employment, support may still be in order because of a need created by the wife placing the good of the family ahead of her own career during the years of the marriage.

Where the wife had remained in the home to care for the children during the early part of the marriage and had only a modest income at the time of separation, she was found to be entitled to spousal support. The wife had suffered an economic disadvantage from the homemaker role she had adopted through much of the parties' 25-year traditional marriage: *Crook v. Crook* (1992), 42 R.F.L. (3d) 297, 1992 CarswellNS 75, 115 N.S.R. (2d) 258, 314 A.P.R. 258 (T.D.).

The court considered the distinction between traditional and modern marriages in the Appeal Division of the Nova Scotia Supreme Court in *Heinemann v. Heinemann* (1989), 20 R.F.L. (3d) 236, 91 N.S.R. (2d) 136, 233 A.P.R. 136, 60 D.L.R. (4th) 648, 1989 CarswellNS 56, [1989] N.S.J. No. 231 (C.A.), Hart J.A. noted that the courts have recognized a substantial change in the nature of marriages and in the roles played by the parties. He contrasted traditional and modern marriages. In the traditional marriage, one spouse is the main financial provider and the other the primary childcare giver. In the modern marriage, both spouses participate in the economic advancement of the family unit. In the traditional marriage, the dependent spouse is often entitled to support for life. In the modern marriage, the temporary economic disadvantage for one spouse can be balanced at the end of the marriage by provisions promoting self-sufficiency of that spouse. Many other marital arrangements exist between these extremes of the spectrum.

The court was of the opinion that, where the parties had a traditional marriage, although the attainment of self-sufficiency should be emphasized, this goal might not be practical. In such situations, the courts should award permanent maintenance in certain circumstances, considering the length of the marriage, the age of the parties, and the marketability of employment skills. In the *Heinemann* decision, the wife's support order of $1,500 per month was upheld on appeal. See also *Ripley v. Ripley* (1991), 30 R.F.L. (3d) 41, 1991 CarswellBC 2, 52 B.C.L.R. (2d) 362 (C.A.).

Where the wife was unaware of her right to seek permanent support at the time of the parties' divorce, her subsequent claim for support was not barred by the fact that 20 years had elapsed since the date of the divorce. Her continuing need was still causally connected to the parties' long-term traditional marriage: *Hillhouse v. Hillhouse* (1992), 43 R.F.L. (3d) 266, 74 B.C.L.R. (2d) 230, 20 B.C.A.C. 28, 35 W.A.C. 28, 1992 CarswellBC 359, [1992] B.C.J. No. 2409 (C.A.); additional reasons at (1994), 1994 CarswellBC 1743, 52 B.C.A.C. 42, 86 W.A.C. 42 (C.A.); reversing (November 27, 1990), Doc. Vancouver 5936/D06332 (B.C. S.C.).

Types of Changes That Can Be Causally Connected to the Marriage Relationship

Several cases have suggested the greater likelihood of establishing a causal connection between the economic disadvantages of the spouse claiming support and the marriage relationship, when the marriage has been a long-term traditional marriage in which the husband has been the chief financial provider and the wife has performed child care and household duties. Conversely, a causal connection is less likely to be found and a clean break philosophy is more likely to be adopted where there has been a short "modern marriage" with each party pursuing his or her own career objectives, especially of the parties have not had children.

In *Pelech v. Pelech*, 7 R.F.L. (3d) 225 at 270, [1987] 1 S.C.R. 801, 17 C.P.C. (2d) 1, 14 B.C.L.R. (2d) 145, [1987] 4 W.W.R. 481, 76 N.R. 81, 38 D.L.R. (4th) 641, 1987 CarswellBC 147, 1987 CarswellBC 703, [1987] S.C.J. No. 31, Wilson J. stated, "In the case of a wife who has devoted herself exclusively to home and children and has acquired no working skills outside the home, this relationship between the change and the marriage is readily established. The former spouse in these circumstances should have a responsibility for a radical change in his ex-wife's circumstances."

Where the wife has remained in the home for 23 years during the marriage to tend to the household, her economic need was found to be causally connected to the marriage. Accordingly, she was found entitled to periodic support without any time limitation: *G. (L.) c. P. (G)*, (sub nom. *Droit de la famille — 1566)* [1992] R.D.F. 222 (C.A. Qué.).

Osborne J.A., in *Linton v. Linton* (1990), 30 R.F.L. (3d) 1, 1 O.R. (3d) 1, 41 E.T.R. 85, 42 O.A.C. 328, 75 D.L.R. (4th) 637, 1990 CarswellOnt 316, [1990] O.J. No. 2267 (C.A.), was of the opinion that courts were likely to find a causal connection between a spouse's economic need and the marriage where the parties had had a long traditional marriage.

Where the wife had worked throughout the parties' lengthy marriage, with the result that she had no opprtunity to upgrade her limited education and skills, her economic need was found to be causally connected to the marriage, and support for an indefinite term was ordered: *Brace v. Brace* (1988), 16 R.F.L. (3d) 287, 1988 CarswellOnt 286 (H.C.); varied (1991), 35 R.F.L. (3d) 263, 1991 CarswellOnt 318 (C.A.). See also *McMillan v. McMillan* (1990), 27 R.F.L. (3d) 409, 107 A.R. 254, 1990 CarswellAlta 280, [1990] A.J. No. 527 (Q.B.).

In *Droit de la famille — 1321*, [1990] R.D.F. 233 (C.S. Qué.), the court refused the husband's claim that the wife be denied spousal support. Although the parties had been separated for 18 years, the wife had carried the burden of raising the children herself, which, combined with her health problems, had impeded her opportunity to become self-sufficient.

The court in *Bast v. Bast* (1988), 13 R.F.L. (3d) 98, 1988 CarswellOnt 216 (H.C.), found that the wife's 21 years outside the work-force created a causal connection between the marriage and the wife's dependency. The trial judge continued the wife' support of $500 per month for two years even though she was working at the time. See also *Faint v. Faint* (1989), 21 R.F.L. (3d) 65, 1989 CarswellBC 408 (S.C.), which concerned a long-term marriage, this time one of approximately 17 years. The court followed the Bast decision and added at p. 71 that "where a wife is employed during the marriage there should be taken into account the limitations on the equality of the employment necessarily brought about by the demands of the marriage, and family duties."

Similarly in *Klassen v. Klassen* (1990), 25 R.F.L. (3d) 277, 63 Man. R. (2d) 201, 1990 CarswellMan 38 (Q.B.), the wife's economic plight was seen as being causally connected to the marriage. She has failed to become self-sufficient as a direct result of the many years she had devoted to being a homemaker and primary child care giver. The wife, who had rheumatoid arthritis which restricted her ability to work, was awarded $250 bi-weekly for an indefinite term.

The wife was entitled to support where she had an economic need, established in her evidence, as a result of her inability to earn any more than she was presently earning. The inability was caused by her long-standing withdrawal from the workforce due to the marriage relationship: *Le Breton v. Le Breton* (1989), 21 R.F.L. (3d) 254, 60 Man. R. (2d) 234, 1989 CarswellMan 49 (Q.B.).

Support was also granted in *Payne v. Payne* (1988), 16 R.F.L. (3d) 8, 1988 CarswellOnt 278 (H.C.), to the wife who performed a traditional role in a 27-year marriage. Although entitlement to support is dependent upon proof of a causal connection between the claimant spouse's need and the marriage, once entitlement has been established, the support order need not be limited to redressing economic loss. After a causal connection is determined under s. 11 of the *Divorce Act, 1968* or under s. 15 of the *Divorce Act, 1985*, then s. 11 or s. 15, respectively, is the only guide to determine the contents of the order.

In *Alexander v. Alexander* (1988), 15 R.F.L. (3d) 422, 85 N.S.R. (2d) 443, 216 A.P.R. 443, 1988 CarswellNS 54 (T.D.), the court also found that the wife's need was causally connected to the marriage. After paying some debts, the wife invested money from the sale of the matrimonial home in an unsuccessful business venture.

Where the wife had moved several times in furtherance of the husband's career and had assumed the majority of child care responsibilities, a sufficient causal connection was found to justify an award of spousal support to her. However, as she had worked in the past, she was obliged to contribute to some extent to her own support, despite her frequent bouts with depression: *Vokey v. Vokey* (1991), 35 R.F.L. (3d) 458, 74 Man. R. (2d) 312, 1991 CarswellMan 47 (Q.B.).

Where the wife was unable to cope independently and where her poor health and financial difficulties were caused by the marriage, there was a relationship between the marriage and her present need. The respondent was ordered to pay the applicant $500 per month periodic maintenance until further order of the court. As an aside, it is interesting to note that in the *Pelech* decision Wilson J. stated in *obiter dictum* that a spouse will not be held financially responsible for his or her former spouse's unwise investments.

In *Droit de la famille — 1486*, [1991] R.D.F. 592 (C.S. Qué.), the court granted support to the 61-year old wife on the basis that the husband had acquiesced in her not working throughout the parties' 30-year marriage and that it was unlikely, at her age, that she would find full-time employment.

Where there has been a short-term marriage and where the parties have a child, the courts may find a causal connection between one spouse's need and the marriage, as was the case in *Wagener v. Wagener* (1988), 17 R.F.L. (3d) 308, 55 Man. R. (2d) 91, 1988 CarswellMan 65 (Q.B.). In this decision, the wife had remained in the home and cared for the parties' child. Support for three years was awarded despite the fact that the marriage had lasted for only one year.

Where the wife was found, following separation, to have suffered an economic downturn that flowed from a pattern of economic dependency created by the marriage she was awarded support until such time as the parties' matrimonial property was distributed: *Mailhot v. Mailhot* (1989), 19 R.F.L. (3d) 140, 1989 CarswellBC 381 (S.C.). The parties in this case had experienced a long marriage lasting 16 years.

Where the wife voluntarily gave up her career to attempt a reconciliation between the parties, she was awarded periodic support for a period of two years to allow her to re-establish herself: *Stunt v. Stunt* (1990), 30 R.F.L. (3d) 353, 1990 CarswellOnt 329 (Gen. Div.).

Types of Changes that Cannot be Causally Connected to the Marriage Relationship

Generally, the courts consider that there should be any responsibility for spousal support in a marriage of short duration, especially where both spouses have been employed and where there are no children. In such situations, there is no causal connection between economic need and the marriage relationship. For support applications following the dissolution of these relationships, the principle of self-sufficiency rather that the principle of causal connection should be given priority: *Linton v. Linton* (1990), 30 R.F.L. (3d) 1, 1 O.R. (3d) 1, 42 O.A.C. 328, 75 D.L.R. (4th) 637, 41 E.T.R. 85, 1990 CarswellOnt 316, [1990] O.J. No. 2267 (C.A.); and *Heinemann v. Heinemann* (1989), 20 R.F.L. (3d) 236, 91 N.S.R. (2d) 136, 233 A.P.R. 136, 60 D.L.R. (4th) 648, 1989 CarswellNS 56, [1989] N.S.J. No. 231 (C.A.).

Support is awarded to redress an economic disadvantage attributable to the marriage and not to guarantee a continuation of the marital lifestyle. Accordingly, where the wife could not establish that her inability to maintain her pre-separation lifestyle was causally connected to the marriage, she was found not to have any general right to support: *Caspick v. Caspick* (1988), 17 R.F.L. (3d) 295, 93 N.B.R. (2d) 63, 238 A.P.R. 63, 1988 CarswellNB 50 (Q.B.); varied (1990), 27 R.F.L. (3d) 337, 106 N.B.R. (2d) 249, 265 A.P.R. 249, 71 D.L.R. (4th) 411, 1990 CarswellNB 24 (C.A.); application for reconsideration refused (1990), 27 R.F.L. (3d) 337n, 1990 CarswellNB 439, 110 N.B.R. (2d) 278, 276 A.P.R. 278 (C.A.); leave to appeal to S.C.C. refused (1991), 29 R.F.L. (3d) xxxvi, 110 N.B.R. (2d) 270 (note), 276 A.P.R. 270 (note), 129 N.R. 238 (note) (S.C.C.). In that case, the parties had been married for nine years and the wife had worked part-time as a book-keeper in the husband's business. There was no evidence that the marriage diminished her earning potential. At the time of the divorce hearing, the wife was earning, $1,500 per month.

Where, during the course of the parties' brief marriage, the wife quit her job of her own accord and did not assume the role of homemaker, her application for support was refused. She was capable of full-time employment and her need was not causally connected to the marriage: *Green v. Green (La Montagne)* (1989), 23 R.F.L. (3d) 386, 1989 CarswellNS 65 (T.D.); affirmed (1989), 23 R.F.L. (3d) 398, 1989 CarswellNS 66 (C.A.).

The Nova Scotia Court of Appeal restricted support to a wife in *Snyder v. Snyder* (1987), 10 R.F.L. (3d) 144, 80 N.S.R. (2d) 257, 200 A.P.R. 257, 1987 CarswellNS 53 (C.A.), where the parties had both worked throughout their seven-year marriage and were capable of being self-sustaining. The husband was 39 and the wife was 40, and they had not had any children. The court, in allowing the husband's appeal from a maintenance order, ruled that the trial judge had not given due consideration to the provision in the Divorce Act for the spouses to achieve self-sufficiency and to the fact that there was nothing in the marriage which gave rise to a condition of economic dependency. The wife was awarded $600 per month for a period of two years.

Where the parties had executed a valid settlement agreement that is incorporated in an order of the court, the agreement will only be overturned where there is a radical change in circumstances flowing from a pattern of economic dependency engendered by the marriage: *Fyffe v. Fyffe* (1988), 12 R.F.L. (3d) 196, 63 O.R. (2d) 783, 25 O.A.C. 219, 48 D.L.R. (4th) 759, 1988 CarswellOnt 205 (C.A.). A very large decline in interest rates did not constitute such as change, as the decline was reasonably foreseeable and was not related to the marriage.

In *Soyland v. Soyland* (1992), 128 A.R. 89, 1992 CarswellAlta 629 (Q.B.), the court refused the husband's application for spousal support. Although he had failed at a number of various employment and business ventures, he had proved his ability o be self-sufficient should he choose to work and could not point to any economic hardship arising from the marriage or its breakdown.

Where the wife returned to work after the birth of the parties' child, but lived beyond her means, her application for support was dismissed. There was no causal connection between the wife's perceived need and the marriage: *Ryan v. Ryan* (1989), 18 R.F.L. (3d) 435, 1989 CarswellOnt 217 (H.C.).

The wife's claim for support for a period while she completes her doctorate was dismissed in *Oswell v. Oswell* (1990), 28 R.F.L. (3d) 10, 74 O.R. (2d) 15, 1990 CarswellOnt 278 (H.C.); affirmed (1992), 43 R.F.L. (3d) 180, 1992 CarswellOnt 306, 12 O.R. (3d) 95 (C.A.). Since the wife had followed her academic aspirations during the marriage and had thereby attained a degree of self-sufficiency, it could not be said that due to the marriage she was in a worse position to earn a living than if she had never married her husband.

The court ordered support for six months from the date o trial so that the former wife could find employment or make the adjustment to pursue her doctorate.

The husband was denied support in *Mogard v. Mogard* (1988), 15 R.F.L. (3d) 415, 1988 CarswellNB 44 (Q.B.), where his pathetic economic condition was caused, not by the marriage, but by his failure to work for more than two years while he cared for his mother.

Where the wife had worked both before and during the marriage, he application for spousal support was dismissed. She had not suffered an economic disadvantage because of the marriage and should be encouraged to be self-sufficient: *Lewis v. Lewis* (1989), 23 R.F.L. (3d) 252, 1989 CarswellNfld 15 (T.D.).

Where the wife was unemployed not as a result of her marriage relationship, but as a result of her own lack of effort to retain or find suitable employment, her application for support was refused: *Garner v. Garner* (1988), 16 R.F.L. (3d) 242, 1988 CarswellOnt 285 (U.F.C.).

Illness or Disability and the Causal Connection Test

A great number of cases in which the causal connection test has been applied involve circumstances where the claimant spouse has an illness or disability that prevents him or her from being self-supporting. On a straightforward needs and means analysis, such spouses would be entitled to permanent support. However, once the causal connection test is introduced, the issue arises whether the illness (and therefore the need) was caused by the marriage or whether the illness was innate to that individual or caused by circumstances unrelated to the marriage.

The illness and disability cases have been divided into three categories. These are (a) cases where spousal support has been awarded without applying the causal connection test; (b) cases where support has been awarded on the basis of causal connection; and (c) cases where support has been denied since a causal connection was found to exist between the claimant spouse's need and the marriage relationship.

Illness of Disability — Spousal Support Without Applying The Causal Connection Test

The concept of causal relation only applies upon an application to vary a support order when the parties' rights have been finally decided by agreement or order or when a support order falls within the description contained in s. 17(10) of the *Divorce Act*. In all other cases, variation of support should be considered under the principles in the Divorce Act, but without considering the issue of causal relation: *Story v. Story* (1989), 23 R.F.L. (3d) 225, 42 B.C.L.R. (2d) 21, 65 D.L.R. (4th) 549, 1989 CarswellBC 237, [1989] B.C.J. No. 2238 (C.A.). The court found that the wife's mental illness, lack of experience and training, and long absence from the work-force would not enable her to become self-sufficient. The husband had the ability to pay support and the wife was entitled to support without a time limitation.

In proceedings for originating support under the *Divorce Act*, there is no need for the claimant to prove a causal connection between a medical condition that makes the claimant unemployable and the marriage in order to establish entitlement: *Dumais v. Dumais* (1988), 14 R.F.L. (3d) 337, 54 Man. R. (2d) 13, 1988 CarswellMan 51 (C.A.). Section 15 of the *Divorce Act* applies.

Where the wife's ability to work was affected by her alcoholism it was found that proof of a causal connection between her alcoholism and the marriage was not a prerequisite to the granting of her claim for spousal support: *Day v. Day* (1994), 129 N.S.R. (2d) 169, 362 A.P.R. 169, 1994 CarswellNS 133 (S.C.); additional reasons at 3 R.F.L. (4th) 432, 129 N.S.R. (2d) 186, 362 A.P.R. 186, 1994 CarswellNS 48, [1994] G.S.T.C. 26 (S.C.).

Where the husband's continuing health problems prevented him from being self-sufficient, the wife, who had the ability to pay, was ordered to contribute to his support. The fact that the husband's need was not related to the marriage did not disentitle him to support: *Parish v. Parish* (1993), 46 R.F.L. (3d) 117, 1993 CarswellOnt 316 (Gen. Div.).

There is no requirement of a causal connection between a spouse's need and the marriage where the wife has developed an illness that restricts her ability to work. She has a need for support and the husband has the ability to pay for this support: *Finch v. Finch* (1990), 24 R.F.L. (3d) 355, 103 A.R. 228, 1990 CarswellAlta 265 (Q.B.).

Where the wife had developed health problems during the course of a long traditional marriage and was accordingly unable to support herself, the husband was ordered to pay support. Although the wife's illness was not caused by the marriage, the husband could not thereby evade his support responsibility to his wife: *Klassen v. Klassen* (1990), 25 R.F.L. (3d) 277, 63 Man. R. (2d) 201, 1990 CarswellMan 38 (Q.B.). The wife's rheumatoid arthritis had caused her to leave several jobs over the years.

Where the husband had support his disabled wife during the marriage, he could not rely upon her disability and a reason disentitling her support upon divorce: *Henton v. Henton* (1990), 28 R.F.L. (3d) 383, 1990 CarswellBC 483 (S.C.).

A spouse is responsible for the care of the other spouse where an illness develops during the parties' marriage, irrespective of any causal connection between the illness and the marriage: *Smith v. Smith* (1987), 11 R.F.L. (3d) 214, 63 O.R. (2d) 146, 1987 CarswellOnt 268 (H.C.). The wife had ulcerative colitis and was unable to work. The husband was of substantial means. See also *White v. White* (1989), 18 R.F.L. (3d) 216, 1989 CarswellOnt 215 (H.C.), which followed *Smith v. Smith* in holding that the husband was responsible for the wife's support, since her illness, rheumatoid arthritis, developed during the marriage, even if there was no causal connection between the illness and the marriage.

In *Deane v. Deane* (1989), 81 Sask. R. 171, 1989 CarswellSask 572 (Q.B.), the wife's prospects of becoming self-sufficient were hampered by bouts of depression. Although her condition was not causally connected to the marriage, the husband was aware of it before he married her. The husband was ordered to pay support to the wife for a two-year period.

Where the husband was aware at the time of the marriage of the serious ailments which the wife suffered, it was inappropriate to set any time limit upon her spousal support entitlement: *Droit de la famille — 1420*, [1991] R.D.F. 293 (C.S. Qué.).

Where there was no formal separation agreement, but where the parties had negotiated the terms of settlement that were incorporated into the decree *nisi*, the settlement was binding: *Tremblay v. Tremblay* (1988), 18 R.F.L. (3d) 337, 67 O.R. (2d) 76, 32 E.T.R. 110, 1988 CarswellOnt 325 (H.C.). The former wife's misfortune, caused by her illness (bursitis) and the loss of her job after separation, was not related to the marriage or to any dependency arising out of the marriage, but was related to the economic climate and lack of employment opportunities. The former wife's application to increase the support order was dismissed.

See also *Enns v. Enns* (1989), 68 O.R. (2d) 345, 1989 CarswellOnt 1431 (U.F.C.).

In the absence of a settlement agreement, a spouse who suffers a physical illness is entitled to claim spousal support, particularly where the illness arose during the parties' cohabitation: *Melnychuk v. Melnychuk*, 16 R.F.L. (4th) 366, 1995 CarswellSask 224, [1995] 9 W.W.R. 764, 133 Sask. R. 299 (Sask. Q.B.).

Illness or Disability — Causal Connection to the Marriage Relationship

There was no requirement that a spouse established a causal link between a debilitating illness and the marriage as a prerequisite to support. Such an illness can properly constitute a "condition" or "other circumstance" that affect the spouse's economic prospects: *Ashworth v. Ashworth* (1995), 15 R.F.L. (4th) 379, 1995 CarswellOnt 489, [1995] O.J. No. 2112 (Gen. Div.); additional reasons at (October 19, 1995), Doc. 91-DV-23050 (Ont. Gen. Div.).

Where the 45-year-old wife had not been employed outside the home for 19 years and had severe psychiatric problems, the court refused to place a time limit on her support award: *Lenner v. Lenner* (1991), 118 A.R. 99, 1991 CarswellAlta 508 (Q.B.); affirmed (1991), 125 A.R. 231, 14 W.A.C. 231 (C.A.); leave to appeal to S.C.C. refused (1992), 145 N.R. 391 (note), 141 A.R. 316 (note), 46 W.A.C. 316 (note) (S.C.C.).

A spouse is not disqualified from support under the *Divorce Act* because his or hr need arises from physical or emotional disabilities, at least where the condition arose during the marriage: *McKean v. McKean* (1992), 38 R.F.L. (3d) 172, Man. R. (2d) 318, 6 W.A.C. 318, 1992 CarswellMan 28 (C.A.).

Where the wife had suffered her epilepsy, which prevented her from working full-time, the husband was obliged to par spousal support. The wife's inability to achieve self-sufficiency was related to the marriage in as much as the husband was aware of the wife's condition at the time of the marriage and had accepted it: *Droit de la famille — 803*, [1990] R.J.Q. 957, [1990] R.D.F. 317 headnote only) (C.A. Qué.).

A causal connection between the economic hardship of the wife and the dependent relationship arising from the marriage was found in *Marshall v. Marshall* (1988), 13 R.F.L. (3d) 337, 1988 CarswellOnt 228 (Ont. C.A.); leave to appeal to S.C.C. refused (1988), 31 O.A.C. 160n (S.C.C.), in that decision, the majority of the court was of the opinion that inflation and the wife's decline in income, which was aggravated by her fragile health, had created a radical change in circumstances, justifying an increase in support from that provided in the parties' separation agreement. The parties had separated in 1970 after 23-year marriage. The wife had developed cancer in 1977 and was in financial need. The husband had the ability to pay. The Court of Appeal dismissed the husband's appeal from an increase in maintenance from $728 per month to $1,228 per month.

Where it was unclear whether the wife's debilitating psychiatric disorder was related to the marriage, the husband was ordered to pay spousal support. The wife was in desperate need of support and the husband had the ability to pay: *Ivans v. Ivans* (1992), 42 R.F.L. (3d) 270, 1992 CarswellMan 51, 82 Man. R. (2d) 101 (Q.B.).

Where the wife's inability to be economically self-sufficient could be directly traced to the husband's aggressive conduct and its detrimental effect upon the wife's self-esteem and mental health, her need was found to have been causally connected to the marriage: *Anderson v. Anderson* (1990), 27 R.F.L. (3d) 358, 66 Man. R. (2d) 248, 1990 CarswellMan 50 (Q.B.); affirmed (1991), 1991 CarswellMan 43, 35 R.F.L. (3d) 223, 75 Man. R. (2d) 235, 6 W.A.C. 235 (C.A.).

On an application to vary a support order under the *Divorce Act*, support was extended to relieve economic hardship resulting form the marriage in *Alexander v. Alexander* (1988), 15 R.F.L. (3d) 422, 85 N.S.R. (2d) 443, 216 A.P.R. 443, 1988 CarswellNS 54 (T.D.). The court considered that the wife's health problems and the failure of her investment to generate sufficient income were both results of the marriage.

Where the wife had had an aneurism that caused her to be unable to live independently, the court found that she was entitled to support in *Henton v. Henton* (1990), 28 R.F.L. (3d) 383, 1990 CarswellBC 483 (S.C.). During the marriage, the husband had absorbed the wife's disadvantages and the resulting hardship; since the end of the marriage she was more vulnerable, a direct result of the marriage breakdown.

Where the wife's health problems and her resulting inability to work were related to complications that arose during the pregnancy, her need upon the parties' separation was found to be causally connected to the marriage and she was found to be entitled to support: *McAfee v. McAfee* (1989), 21 R.F.L. (3d) 75, 1989 CarswellBC 409, [1989] B.C.J. No. 1134 (S.C.). Since the husband claimed to have no assets and no income, he was ordered to pay the wife maintenance of $1 annually until there was a material change in the circumstances of either of the parties as contemplated by s. 17 of the *Divorce Act, 1985*.

Where the 51-year-old wife had been out of the workforce throughout the parties' 20-year marriage and where health problems prevented her from working full-time, she was found to be entitled to support. As some of her health problems, particularly her emotional instability and lack of confidence, were causally connected to her treatment by the husband, her entitlement to support was established: *Vogel v. Vogel* (1988), 18 R.F.L. (3d) 445, 1988 CarswellOnt 329 (H.C.).

Where the wife had assumed the role of a traditional homemaker during the marriage and had developed serious physical and emotional problems that prevented her from seeking employment, her economic need was found to be causally connected to the marriage and indeterminate support was ordered: *Brace v. Brace* (1988), 16 R.F.L. (3d) 287, 1988 CarswellOnt 286 (H.C.); varied (1991), 35 R.F.L. (3d) 263, 1991 CarswellOnt 318 (C.A.).

In *Fairall v. Fairall* (1989), 20 R.F.L. (3d) 107, 93 A.R. 224, 1989 CarswellAlta 378 (Q.B.); additional reasons at (1990), 26 R.F.L. (3d) 128, 106 A.R. 277, 1990 CarswellAlta 272 (Q.B.), the wife's health problems could be traced in part to the birth of the parties' children; consequently, her economic needs were found to be related to the marriage. The husband was ordered to pay $200 per month to the wife for three years.

In *Stevens v. Stevens* (1992), 41 R.F.L. (3d) 212, 93 D.L.R. (4th) 311, 1992 CarswellOnt 275 (U.F.C.); affirmed (November 16, 1993), Doc. Hamilton-Wentworth V-428/91 (Ont. U.F.C.), it was held that the lack of causal connection between the wife's illness, which inhibited her from becoming self-sufficient, and the marriage did not justify a time limitation on her support award. As the parties' marriage was a long-term traditional one, the wife had suffered economic disadvantage justifying ongoing support even without taking her illness into account.

It is improper to limit spousal support after the breakdown of a long-term traditional marriage where the wife's inability to support herself has been complicated by health problems which she developed during the marriage: *Devernichuk v. Devernichuk* (1993), 45 R.F.L. (3d) 328, 1993 CarswellSask 43, 109 Sask. R. 297, 42 W.A.C. 297 (C.A.).

Illness or Disability — No Causal Connection to the Marriage

In the leading case of *Pelech v. Pelech*, 7 R.F.L. (3d) 225, [1987] 1 S.C.R. 801, 17 C.P.C. (2d) 1, 14 B.C.L.R. (2d) 145, [1987] 4 W.W.R. 481, 76 N.R. 81, 38 D.L.R. (4th) 641, 1987 CarswellBC 147, 1987 CarswellBC 703, [1987] S.C.J. No. 31, the Supreme Court of Canada dismissed the wife's appeal to vary the divorce support order to provide for additional support. Before and during the marriage, the wife had serious psychological problems which, after the divorce, worsened and were compounded by several physical problems. At the time of the variation application she was receiving social assistance.

In denying the motion for variation of maintenance, Wilson J. stated that, where the parties have negotiated their own agreement with independent legal advice, it should only be overridden if there is a radical change in the dependent spouses' circumstances and if there is a causal connection between the changed circumstances and the marriage. On the facts of the *Pelech* decision, no such link existed between the former wife's changed circumstances and the marriage. On the contrary, the trial judge had found that the wife's psychological problems, which resulted in her inability to care for herself, pre-dated the marriage and contributed to its end.

Where the wife had released support claims in a separation agreement, but was later prevented from working because of further aggravation of existing health problems, her claim for support was disallowed on appeal. The wife's economic dependency flowed from her illness and did not have its genesis in the marriage: *Pilon v. Pilon* (1988), 16 R.F.L. (3d) 225, 66 O.R. (2d) 1, 29 O.A.C. 306, 53 D.L.R. (4th) 130, 1988 CarswellOnt 284 (C.A.); leave to appeal to S.C.C. refused (1989), 19 R.F.L. (3d) xxxv, 66 O.R. (2d) xi, 34 O.A.C. 400n, 100 N.R. 237n (S.C.C.).

In another Ontario Court of Appeal decision, *Willms v. Willms* (1988), 14 R.F.L. (3d) 162, 65 O.R. (2d) 151, 27 O.A.C. 316, 51 D.L.R. (4th) 757, 1988 CarswellOnt 244 (C.A.), the court was of the opinion that an individual should not be responsible indefinitely for the support of a chronically disabled former spouse when the disability had no causal relation to the marriage. The causal connection test is not limited to circumstances where the parties have signed a separation agreement, the court held, but should be considered wherever the facts warrant.

Where the wife became ill after separation and was unable to work, it was held that the husband was not responsible for any economic disadvantage flowing from this post-separation disability. Accordingly, the support otherwise ordered payable was reduced by an amount which the wife could have earned had she not been ill: *Jerowsky v. Jerowsky* (1990), 32 R.F.L. (3d) 188, 114 A.R. 381, 1990 CarswellAlta 292 (Q.B.).

In *Brody v. Brody* (1990), 25 R.F.L. (3d) 319, 105 A.R. 41, 1990 CarswellAlta 268 (Q.B.), the former wife was in financial need because she was suffering from high blood pressure which prevented her from earning a living. The husband, a dentist, had the ability to pay support.

In the *Brody* decision, the court found that the marriage was not a particular time of stress for the wife, but acknowledged that the rather sudden termination of the marriage was, for her, traumatic. The evidence did not disclose a causal connection between the nedd and the marriage in this case. While the absence of such a causal connection was not the only matter that a court should take into account in reviewing a support order for an ex-spouse, it was determinative in cases such as the one under consideration, particularly where a considerable period of time (15 years) had passed since the marriage had ended, where the children had for all practical purposes become independent of the claimant, and where the court had been gradually reducing the amount of support payments to the former wife, signalling to her that she should become economically independent of her former spouse.

The wife, who was suffering from multiple sclerosis diagnosed during the marriage and who was unable to work, was denied support in *Schroeder v. Schroeder* (1987), 11 R.F.L. (3d) 413, 52 Man. R. (2d) 219, 45 D.L.R. (4th) 632, 1987 CarswellMan 89 (Q.B.). The court was of the opinion that, where the economic hardship of a spouse has its genesis in the disabling effects of a disease which affects him or her and which has nothing to do with the marriage or its breakdown, the support obligation becomes the communal responsibility of the state and not that of the other spouse. The wife granted support for six months to adjust to her new situation.

In *Williams v. Williams* (1988), 13 R.F.L. (3d) 321, 70 Nfld. & P.E.I.R. 331, 215 A.P.R. 331, 1988 CarswellNfld 13 (T.D.), the court held that where, after separation, the wife had developed Parkinson's disease and was therefore unable to work, her application for support was dismissed. The wife's economic hardship was not connected to the marriage; it resulted from the disease.

The court also denied support to a former husband on the basis of an absence of causal connection between his need and the marriage in *Winterle v. Winterle* (1987), 10 R.F.L. (3d) 129, 1987 CarswellOnt 236 (H.C.). In this case, the parties had cohabited for nine years and the husband suffered from manic depression and chronic schizophrenia diagnosed during the marriage.

See also *Miller v. Miller* (1988), 15 R.F.L. (3d) 366, 1988 CarswellOnt 272 (H.C.), where the wife was injured in a car accident after the marriage and was denied support.

In *Garbutt v. Garbutt* (1993), 84 Man. R. (2d) 237, 1993 CarswellMan 172 (Q.B.), the court found, in assuming the wife's support, that her economic disability could not be totally attributed to the marriage. The wife had been blind and the date of the marriage and her disability would have affected her functioning in a work environment whether or not she had married.

Where the wife's severe hypertension together with her anginal syndrome and consequent inability to work might have had its genesis in the marriage, she mut prove this link or otherwise become self-supporting within a reasonable time which, in this case, would be six years from the date of separation: *Francis v. Francis* (1988), 16 R.F.L. (3d) 149, 1988 CarswellOnt 280 (H.C.). The parties had been married for 23 years, had two children, and were in their mid-forties.

The wife in *Goering v. Goering* (1988), 13 R.F.L. (3d) 383, 1988 CarswellOnt 231 (H.C.), suffered from high blood pressure and asthma and was undergoing psychiatric treatment. She was on welfare prior to the marriage, did not work during cohabitation, and had not sought employment after she lost custody of the parties' child. The husband applied to vary the wife's support order. The husband discharged the burden of proof to establish that the connection between the wife's economic dependency and her marriage no longer existed. In light of the wife's past employment history, the standard of living to which she had been accustomed prior to marriage, her lack of formal education, and the short duration of the marriage, the wife was entitled to two years' support from the date of the divorce in order to retain for employment.

In *Smithson v. Smithson* (1988), 15 R.F.L. (3d) 393, 32 B.C.L.R. (2d) 241, 53 D.L.R. (4th) 136, 1988 CarswellBC 403 (S.C.), the wife's need, which arose out of the health problems that existed before the marriage and that eventually disabled her, was found not to be causally connected to the marriage. Accordingly, although the husband was not required to pay support, the bulk of the parties' property was awarded to the wife.

In *Rice v. Rice (MacGlashen)* (1992), 113 N.S.R. (2d) 444, 309 A.P.R. 444, 1992 CarswellNS 541 (T.D.), a three-year limitation was placed upon the wife's right to spousal support upon termination of the parties 16-year marriage. Although the wife suffered from serious psychological problems which prevented her from working, the condition arose after separation and there was no evidence that it was related to the marriage.

In the case of *Droit de la famille — 1194*, [1988] R.D.F. 406 (C.S. Qué.), the court terminated the wife's support after 17 years since the wife's poor health, which prevented her from working, had developed long after separation and was not related to the marriage.

If a dependent spouse's illness exists prior to the marriage, it may also be seen as unrelated to the marriage. Consequently, support may be terminated, as in the decision of *Droit de la famille — 1170*, [1988] R.D.F. 180 (C.S. Qué.); *Huber v. Huber* (1987), 11 R.F.L. (3d) 208, 63 O.R. (2d) 201, 1987 CarswellOnt 267 (U.F.C.).

Where the wife's failure to become self-sufficient after the parties' divorce was largely the result of personal and emotional problems that were not related to the marriage, the court ordered that her spousal support payments were to cease two years after the last of her child support payments. Although it was not reasonable to expect the husband to support her for life, he had benefited from her home and child care responsibilities and should support her for a further limited time: *Rouleau v. Rouleau* (1992), 111 N.S.R. (2d) 162, 303 A.P.R. 162, 1992 CarswellNS 505 (Fam. Ct.).

In refusing the applicant husband's claim for spousal support, the court was of the opinion, in *Golini v. Golini* (1991), 31 R.F.L. (3d) 289, 82 D.L.R. (4th) 255, 1991 CarswellOnt 246 (U.F.C.), that the husband's mental illness was not caused by the wife. The illness had not prevented him from achieving significant academic success and there ws no reason why he could not be self-sufficient.

Evidence of Economic Hardship

In practice, the quantum of support had generally been determined by looking at both spouses' present needs and means. In the recent decision of *Ormerod v. Ormerod* (1990), 27 R.F.L. (3d) 225, 1990 CarswellOnt 270 (U.F.C.), the court, in determining the quantum of support, took evidence into account of the wife's future economic losses, attributable to the fact that she had interrupted her nursing career in order to look after the parties' children and home. She had no present need for support. Implicit in this approach is the idea that the wife should be compensated for losses that are causally connected to the marriage.

The evidence the court received was a report, prepared by an economist, that addressed future economic loss in earnings by the wife because of the interruption of her career, and a second report, prepared by an actuary, that responded to the first report.

The wife was awarded $103,000 lump sum support to compensate her for future economic loss from the time of her return to nursing until her retirement. She did not receive compensation for her losses between the date of separation and the date of the trial. The court concluded that there was a mutual aspect to this loss for the husband and wife.

While the wife retrained, she did without the income she would have received if she had instead returned to work. At the same time, the husband paid support and did not receive occupational rent for the matrimonial home.

15§31 — Objectives of spousal support — economic advantages and disadvantages — compensatory support

See also15§6 General principles for determining spousal support, and 15§24 Objectives of spousal support — general.

General

One of the three "conceptual grounds" or "models" for entitlement to spousal support is compensatory. The other two are contractual and non-compensatory: *Bracklow v. Bracklow*, 1999 CarswellBC 532, 1999 CarswellBC 533, [1999] S.C.J. No. 14, 169 D.L.R. (4th) 577, 236 N.R. 79, 44 R.F.L. (4th) 1, 120 B.C.A.C. 211, 196 W.A.C. 211, [1999] 1 S.C.R. 420, 63 B.C.L.R. (3d) 77, [1999] 8 W.W.R. 740 (S.C.C.) (S.C.C. on appeal from the B.C. C.A.). Compensatory support should be awarded where it would be just to compensate a spouse for his or her contributions to the marriage or for sacrifices made or hardships suffered as a result of the marriage — for contributions to the marriage and for losses sustained as a consequence of the marriage:

> The compensatory basis for support finds its source in a number of factors mentioned in the statutes. In the British Columbia *Family Relations Act*, these include [certain described factors]. '[T]he role of each spouse in their family' embraces the contributions made by the spouses to the family for which compensation may be appropriate on the collapse of the marriage. Similarly, 'the ability and capacity of . . . either or both spouses to support themselves' permits a court to examine whether spouses have foregone opportunities to develop the ability to support themselves because of the marriage, or have been rendered less able to support themselves by adverse effects of the marriage or the marriage breakdown. '[C]ustodial obligations respecting a child' . . . may relate to compensation. While spousal support is distinct from child support, the need to care for children has an impact on factors relevant to spousal support. Under the *Divorce Act*, compensation arguments can be grounded in the need to consider the 'condition' of the spouse; the 'means, needs and other circumstances' of the spouse, which may encompass lack of ability to support oneself due to foregoing career opportunities during the marriage; and 'the functions performed by each spouse during cohabitation', which may support the same argument. In sum, these compensatory statutory provisions can be seen to embrace the independent, clean-break model of marriage and marriage breakdown.

The emphasis on self-sufficiency in *Pelech v. Pelech*, [1987] 1 S.C.R. 801, 7 R.F.L. (3d) 225, 17 C.P.C. (2d) 1, 14 B.C.L.R. (2d) 145, [1987] 4 W.W.R. 481, 76 N.R. 81, 38 D.L.R. (4th) 641, 1987 CarswellBC 147, 1987 CarswellBC 703, [1987] S.C.J. No. 31, REJB 1987-80055 (S.C.C.) is inconsistent with both the compensatory model of support developed in *Moge v. Moge* (1992), [1992] 3 S.C.R. 813, [1993] 1 W.W.R. 481, 43 R.F.L. (3d) 345, 145 N.R. 1, 81 Man. R. (2d) 161, 30 W.A.C. 161, 99 D.L.R. (4th) 456, REJB 1992-67141, [1992] S.C.J. No. 107, 1992 CarswellMan 143, 1992 CarswellMan 222, [1993] R.D.F. 168 (S.C.C.), and the non-compensatory model of support developed in *Bracklow v. Bracklow*, [1999] 1 S.C.R. 420, 44 R.F.L. (4th) 1, 169 D.L.R. (4th) 577236 N.R. 79, 120 B.C.A.C. 211, 196 W.A.C. 211, 63 B.C.L.R. (3d) 77, [1999] 8 W.W.R. 740, 1999 CarswellBC 532, 1999 CarswellBC 533, [1999] S.C.J. No. 14 (S.C.C.). It is also inconsistent with the point in both cases that no single objective in s. 15.2(6) is paramount: *Bracklow*, at para. 35; Moge, at p. 852 (S.C.R.): *Miglin v. Miglin*,

[2003] 1 S.C.R. 303, 34 R.F.L. (5th) 255, 224 D.L.R. (4th) 193, 2003 CarswellOnt 1374, 2003 CarswellOnt 1375, 2003 SCC 24, [2003] S.C.J. No. 21, REJB 2003-40012, 66 O.R. (3d) 736 (note), 171 O.A.C. 201, 302 N.R. 201 (S.C.C.). For a discussion of *Bracklow* and *Moge* and compensatory support, see 15§6 General principles for determining spousal support.

The first two objectives in s. 15.2(6) of the *Divorce Act* are primarily related to compensation: *Bracklow v. Bracklow*, 169 D.L.R. (4th) 577, [1999] 1 S.C.R. 420, 44 R.F.L. (4th) 1, 236 N.R. 79, 120 B.C.A.C. 211, 196 W.A.C. 211, 63 B.C.L.R. (3d) 77, [1999] 8 W.W.R. 740, 1999 CarswellBC 532, 1999 CarswellBC 533, [1999] S.C.J. No. 14 (S.C.C.). For a detailed discussion of the facts of the case, see section 15§6 General principles for determining spousal support.

Section 15(7)(a) [now s. 15.2(6)(a)] of the *Divorce Act* does not provide a right to full compensation through spousal support for the economic disadvantage that arises from a marriage or its breakdown, and any recovery is limited by the payor's ability to pay: *Elliot v. Elliot* (1993), 48 R.F.L. (3d) 237, 15 O.R. (3d) 265, 1993 CarswellOnt 348, [1993] O.J. No. 2308, 106 D.L.R. (4th) 609, 65 O.A.C. 241 (Ont. C.A.); reversing in part (1992), 42 R.F.L. (3d) 7, 95 D.L.R. (4th) 614, 1992 CarswellOnt 284 (Ont. U.F.C.); leave to appeal to S.C.C. refused (1994), 3 R.F.L. (4th) 290 (note), 18 O.R. (3d) xvi (note), 112 D.L.R. (4th) vii (note) (S.C.C.).

In cases where support is mainly compensation-based and not primarily based on needs, care should be taken to avoid double recovery: *Boston v. Boston*, [2001] 2 S.C.R. 413, 17 R.F.L. (5th) 4, 2001 CarswellOnt 2432, 2001 CarswellOnt 2433, [2001] S.C.J. No. 45, 2001 SCC 43, 201 D.L.R. (4th) 1, 271 N.R. 248, 149 O.A.C. 50, 28 C.C.P.B. 17, REJB 2001-25002, C.E.B. & P.G.R. 8385 (headnote only) (S.C.C.). Where a pension is involved, double recovery occurs where the pension, equalized as property, is also treated as income from which the pension-holding spouse makes spousal support payments. However, sometimes double recovery cannot be avoided. In certain circumstances, a pension which has been equalized previously can also be viewed as a maintenance asset. Double recovery may be permitted where the payor spouse has the ability to pay, and where the payee-spouse has made a reasonable effort to use the equalized assets in an income-producing way but, despite this, an economic hardship from the marriage or its breakdown persists. Double recovery may also be permitted in spousal support orders/agreements based mainly on need as opposed to compensation, which was not the case in this appeal (at para. 65).

A reapportionment of the matrimonial home under the *Family Relations Act* (British Columbia) in favour of the wife is not an order for a lump sum or compensatory support. Therefore, an order for periodic support that comes close to equalizing the parties' incomes and that is made in addition to the reapportionment is not double recovery: *Penner v. Penner* (1996), 1996 CarswellBC 2182, 24 R.F.L. (4th) 448, 82 B.C.A.C. 232, 133 W.A.C. 232 (B.C. C.A.).

In compensatory support cases, where spouses have been out of the workforce and have on-going childcare responsibilities, limited term spousal support orders should be an exception: *Phinney v. Phinney*, 33 R.F.L. (5th) 211, 2002 CarswellNS 525, 2002 NSCA 168, 211 N.S.R. (2d) 135, 662 A.P.R. 135, [2002] N.S.J. No. 540 (N.S. C.A.). But an exception was made in this case where the dependant spouse in such a relationship had suffered economic disadvantage and hardship resulting from the marriage breakdown (s.

15.2(6)(a), (b) and (c)). The court awarded spousal support of $750 monthly for a year and then declining amounts for 3 years.

There is no separate head of relief in the *Divorce Act* for compensatory spousal support: *Stuart v. Stuart* (1996), 22 R.F.L. (4th) 26, 21 B.C.L.R. (3d) 65, 73 B.C.A.C. 30, 120 W.A.C. 30, 1996 CarswellBC 517, [1996] B.C.J. No. 526 (B.C. C.A.). See also *Zammit v. Zammit* (1999), 1999 CarswellOnt 3357 (Ont. Div. Ct.); and *Marinangeli v. Marinangeli* (2001), 16 R.F.L. (5th) 326, 15 O.R. (3d) 179, 2001 CarswellOnt 1591, [2001] O.J. No. 1765 (Ont. S.C.J.); varied (2003), 38 R.F.L. (5th) 307, [2003] O.J. No. 2819, 2003 CarswellOnt 2691, 66 O.R. (3d) 40, 174 O.A.C. 76, 228 D.L.R. (4th) 376 (Ont. C.A.).

A support award under the *Divorce Act* should reflect any assistance given by a dependant to his or her spouse's education or professional advancement, despite the fact that the dependant may have shared in the increased income that resulted for some considerable time: *Colletta v. Colletta* (1993), 50 R.F.L. (3d) 1, 1993 CarswellOnt 359, [1993] O.J. No. 2537 (Ont. C.A.).

In determining entitlement to spousal support, the court is required to take into account advantages and disadvantages resulting from the marriage and to weigh whether there is a net loss or gain which should be compensated by a support order. The court need not calculate with precision the financial contributions of each party and award support to offset any inequality of contribution to living costs and expenses: *McGrath v. Holmes* (1995), 10 R.F.L. (4th) 161, 1995 CarswellNWT 1 (N.W.T. C.A.); leave to appeal refused (1995), 16 R.F.L. (4th) 339 (note), (sub nom. *Holmes v. McGrath)* 196 N.R. 79 (note) (S.C.C.).

Where the wife had contributed to her husband's career at the expense of her own, she was found entitled to a compensatory allowance: *Caratun v. Caratun* (1992), 42 R.F.L. (3d) 113, 10 O.R. (3d) 385, 96 D.L.R. (4th) 404, 1992 CarswellOnt 287, 47 E.T.R. 234, 58 O.A.C. 140 (Ont. C.A.); leave to appeal to S.C.C. refused (1993), 46 R.F.L. (3d) 314 (note), 13 O.R. (3d) xvi (note), 101 D.L.R. (4th) vii (note), 157 N.R. 317 (note), 64 O.A.C. 273 (note) (S.C.C.).

Where the husband had dissipated the wife's assets to pay off his debts and the wife, because of her age, lack of education and the depression resulting from the marriage breakdown, was unable to find full-time employment for a number of years, the wife was found entitled to lump sum compensatory support. The marriage had left her at an economic disadvantage and had given the husband an advantage at her expense: *Henderson v. Sharma-Henderson* (1993), 47 R.F.L. (3d) 388, 1993 CarswellOnt 338 (Ont. Gen. Div.); affirmed (1994), 7 R.F.L. (4th) 317, 1994 CarswellOnt 444 (Ont. C.A.).

Where one spouse is entitled to compensatory support, and the other is entitled to non-compensatory support, the entitlement to compensatory support acts as a shield or set-off to the other spouse's entitlement to non-compensatory support: *Kennedy v. Kennedy* (2004), 2004 CarswellOnt 3192, [2004] O.J. No. 3222, 8 R.F.L. (6th) 155 (Ont. S.C.J.). The wife was entitled to compensatory support since she dropped out of high school to be a full-time wife and mother. She stayed at home for the first 7 years of the marriage. Even after she began working outside the home in 1967, she remained primarily responsible for the care of the children during their dependency. The husband frittered away tens of thousands of dollars on farming operations in the years 1995 to 2002 and was able to exclude from sharing with his wife $30,000 that he loaned their daughter and son-in-law. The wife's inherited funds were entirely shared with the husband in the net family property equalization. The wife was the only breadwinner in the family from 1999 to 2002. At the time of the application, the wife earned $45,000 to $50,000. The husband had pension income of about $17,000. Given the length of marriage and disparity in income at the time of separation, the husband was entitled to at least transitional spousal support. The husband's need for additional money was not the result of any role he played in the marriage but the result of voluntary decisions he made independent of his marital role and responsibilities, notably his decision to become a farmer. The wife had paid interim spousal support of $500 per month since the order of July 2002. The court ordered that she continue to pay this amount until the end of 2004. The court stated: "She is not an insurer of his self-created need."

Where the husband refused to list the family home for sale and it was subsequently lost in a forced sale by the mortgagee at a reduced price, the wife was found entitled to some level of compensatory support: *Taylor v. Taylor* (2004), 10 R.F.L. (6th) 202, 2004 CarswellOnt 4851, [2004] O.J. No. 4802 (S.C.J.).

Where compensatory grounds of support do not exist or have been satisfied, a support obligation may still exist because one of the parties has an economic need: *Stier v. Stier*, 2004 CarswellBC 2615, 2004 BCSC 1458 (B.C. S.C. [In Chambers]). The court found that 14 years of support payments satisfied any obligation the husband may have had to provide compensatory support, but that the wife was entitled to non-compensatory support.

In terms of spousal support compensatory objectives, a long-term traditional marriage is certain to involve some form of economic disadvantage and resulting hardships. Even if both parties remain in the workplace, decisions made by the family may result in some form of economic disadvantage: *Thomas v. Thomas*, 50 R.F.L. (5th) 226, 2004 CarswellAlta 41, 2004 ABQB 27, 22 Alta. L.R. (4th) 46, 350 A.R. 58 (Alta. Q.B.); affirmed 2005 CarswellAlta 97, [2005] A.J. No. 61, 14 R.F.L. (6th) 170, 2005 ABCA 24, 37 Alta. L.R. (4th) 4, (sub nom. *Abel v. Abel)* 363 A.R. 159, (sub nom. *Abel v. Abel)* 343 W.A.C. 159 (Alta. C.A.).

In assessing a claim for compensatory spousal support, the court must consider all existing financial realities as well as all that might befall the parties: *Lacharite v. Lacharite* (2003), 39 R.F.L. (5th) 119, 2003 CarswellOnt 939, [2003] O.J. No. 1027 (Ont. S.C.J.).

A claim for compensatory support for an unmarried cohabitee is not made out under the *Family Law Act* where the applicant contributed materially to the relationship, but she also derived economic benefits from it: *Peter v. Eichler* (2003), 2003 CarswellOnt 5095, [2003] O.J. No. 5141, 49 R.F.L. (5th) 162 (Ont. S.C.J.). The applicant maintained the family home for the respondent, bought household items and some clothes for him, cared for some of the gardens, and helped out in the marketing and the selling of blueberries (for which she was paid). Once she lost her job, he paid for most of the household expenses, which enabled her to maintain and slightly increase her small capital fund.

A spouse is entitled to compensatory support where she was a stay-at-home mother caring for young children for 11 years: *N. (T.A.) v. N. (R.G.)*, 2003 CarswellAlta 1622, 2003 ABQB 920, 3 R.F.L. (6th) 121 (Alta. Q.B.); additional reasons at 2003 CarswellAlta 1722, 2003 ABQB 988, 3 R.F.L. (6th) 129 (Alta. Q.B.); additional reasons at 2004 CarswellAlta 66, 2004 ABQB 48, 3 R.F.L. (6th) 131 (Alta. Q.B.). Although there was no evidence of any opportunities which actually existed that were foregone by the wife during the course of their marriage, the court acknowledged that the husband did gain as a result of the wife being at home looking after the children. The court held that the wife was entitled to some compensatory support following the separation given her limited financial means, and the problems she faced in the transition after a long-term marriage, many of the debts of which she was still paying at the time of the hearing. The court awarded compensatory support of $750 per month for the first year following the parties' separation, after which the court concluded that the wife became sufficiently self-supporting.

In *Snjaric v. Snjaric* (2003), 2003 CarswellOnt 4033, 48 R.F.L. (5th) 193 (Ont. S.C.J.), the court held that notwithstanding a long marriage of 27 years and an entitlement to compensatory and non-compensatory support, it was equitable to leave the payor spouse with more of the parties' combined net disposable income. In this case, the husband had to work full-time; twice the number of actual and imputed hours that the wife would work. In the equalization of property, he was required to include the capitalized value of his future pension, affording the wife the ability to use those funds right away towards the purchase of a home, and thus a smaller mortgage payment. The original order made the wife's support conditional upon her making her best efforts to develop her proficiency in English. Her diligence in this matter was questionable. Spousal support was varied from $1,200 monthly to $1,000 monthly. She would continue to have 43 percent of the combined net disposable income of the parties and the husband 57 percent.

No distinction is to be made between marital and common law relationships in applying the models of spousal support established in *Bracklow*. In that case, the court clearly stated that it was the relationship that is established, not marriage *per se*, that gives rise to the obligation of support. Moreover, the decisions of both the Supreme Court of Canada and the British Columbia court relied in part on the spousal support provisions of the *Family Relations Act*, which apply equally to common law partners. Finally, the judgments in *Walsh v. Bona*, REJB 2002-36303, 2002 CarswellNS 511, 2002 CarswellNS 512, (sub nom. *Nova Scotia (Attorney General) v. Walsh)*) [2002] S.C.J. No. 84, [2002] 4 S.C.R. 325, 2002 SCC 83, (sub nom. *Nova Scotia (Attorney General) v. Walsh)* 32 R.F.L. (5th) 81, 221 D.L.R. (4th) 1, 297 N.R. 203, 211 N.S.R. (2d) 273, 659 A.P.R. 273, 102 C.R.R. (2d) 1 (S.C.C.) clearly distinguished between the effect of a common law relationship with respect to matrimonial assets, as opposed to spousal support: *S. (M.A.) v. M. (F.K.)*, 2003 CarswellBC 1315, 2003 BCSC 849 (B.C. S.C.).

A claim for compensatory support arises when one spouse confers on the other a benefit that would unjustly enrich the other, if he or she were allowed to retain the benefit without some form of accounting made to the conferring spouse. Generally, there must be something more than the assumption of household management and child-care to justify an award of compensatory support. There should be evidence of an exceptional contribution: *DeCicco v. DeCicco* (2003), 2003 CarswellOnt 4364, 45 R.F.L. (5th) 147 (Ont. S.C.J.); additional reasons at (2003), 2003 CarswellOnt 4937, 47 R.F.L. (5th) 312 (Ont. S.C.J.).

In cases where support is awarded to compensate a spouse for advantages he or she conferred on a partner during their relationship, the fact that the spouse remarries or cohabits with another person should be irrelevant. Support in such cases is in the nature of relief against unjust enrichment and the second relationship is irrelevant to the benefit conferred on the prior partner. Accordingly, a payee in such cases should receive the same amount of support regardless of whether he or she remarries or cohabits with another person: *Uens v. Uens* (2000), 2000 CarswellOnt 4478, 11 R.F.L. (5th) 202 (Ont. S.C.J.).

A lump sum "compensatory disposition" may be made where a clean break is called for: *Baranec v. Baranec* (1998), 1998 CarswellOnt 2350 (Ont. Gen. Div.).

Where the wife had been out of the labour force for several years and was still recovering from a long-term abusive relationship, she was entitled to both needs-based and compensatory support: *Burnett v. Burnett* (1997), 1997 CarswellOnt 3282, 33 R.F.L. (4th) 356 (Ont. Gen. Div.). Until the equalization payment was made and the wife's share of joint assets was purchased, her only income was from rent which provided her with little income. She was not ready to go back into the work force for about a year. The court granted the wife's modest request for spousal support of $100 a month.

An order requiring the defendant to pay compensatory support based on the plaintiff's contributions to the support of the family, the realization of the defendant's career potential as well as his substantial earning capacity which significantly exceeded the plaintiff's capacity, constituted a debt or liability under a support order within the meaning of s. 178(1)(c) of the *Bankruptcy and Insolvency Act*: *Bronson v. Bronson* (1997), 1997 CarswellOnt 2411, 47 C.B.R. (3d) 142, 31 O.T.C. 312 (Ont. Gen. Div.). Accordingly, the defendant was not released from this debt as a result of his bankruptcy. An order was made declaring that subsequent to his discharge from bankruptcy, the sum of $10,400 remained owing by the defendant to the plaintiff as a debt or liability under a support order together with post-judgment interest and costs.

When determining whether an award of compensatory support should be made, the court must also examine the economic advantages flowing to the claimant as a result of the marriage. Compensatory support should not be awarded unless the economic disadvantages resulting from the marriage outweigh the economic advantages and non-economic rewards of the relationship: *Rosin v. Rosin* (1993), 46 R.F.L. (3d) 242, 1993 CarswellAlta 439 (Alta. Q.B.).

The support provisions in the *Divorce Act*, pursuant to *Moge v. Moge* (1992), 43 R.F.L. (3d) 345, REJB 1992-67141, [1992] S.C.J. No. 107, 1992 CarswellMan 143, 1992 CarswellMan 222, [1993] 1 W.W.R. 481, 99 D.L.R. (4th) 456, [1992] 3 S.C.R. 813, 81 Man. R. (2d) 161, 30 W.A.C. 161, 145 N.R. 1, [1993] R.D.F. 168 (S.C.C.) are to be seen as having a compensatory aspect where there is evidence of economic disadvantage arising from the marital relationship: *Zanyk v. Zanyk* (1993), 46 R.F.L. (3d) 169, 1993 CarswellSask 48, 110 Sask. R. 112 (Sask. Q.B.).

According to the compensatory support model established by the Supreme Court of Canada in *Moge*, spousal support is intended to relieve economic hardship resulting from the marriage or its breakdown. In determining the appropriate support, the effect of any property divisions should also be taken into account: *Sneddon v. Sneddon* (1993), 46 R.F.L. (3d) 373, 9 Alta. L.R. (3d) 311, 139 A.R. 167, 1993 CarswellAlta 342 (Alta. Q.B.).

In *Kernahan v. Skworoda* (November 30, 1995), Doc. Vancouver D092932 (B.C. S.C.) it was held that the wife's loss of the financial security created by the marriage was not a factor to be considered in determining her entitlement to compensatory support.

Courts may only grant compensatory support orders based on need. The orders should take into account one spouse's contribution to the other's career enhancement as an element of such orders: *Baker v. Baker* (1989), 22 R.F.L. (3d) 346, 1989 CarswellOnt 291 (Ont. U.F.C.).

Cases Where Compensatory Support Awarded

A party is entitled to compensatory support for economic disadvantage suffered on the breakdown of a marriage: *Brophy v. Brophy* (2004), 2004 CarswellOnt 23, 45 R.F.L. (5th) 56, 180 O.A.C. 389, [2004] O.J. No. 17 (Ont. C.A.); additional reasons at (2004), 2004 CarswellOnt 584 (Ont. C.A.). The parties separated after 23 years of marriage. At the time of separation, the husband was 52 and the wife was 57 years old. They had three adult sons who all had special needs. This was a marriage of long duration and the wife had been out of the workforce for many years while caring for the children and managing the household. The wife was not working at the time of the appeal. The trial judge also took into account the wife's imputed investment income of $8,000 to $10,000 annually. The amount the trial judge ordered properly reflected a relatively equal sharing of the decline in the parties' lifestyles. The court upheld the lower court's award of $8,000 per month based on the husband's income of $242,000 annually.

In *W. (M.R.) v. W. (C.M.U.)*, 2004 CarswellBC 2695, 7 R.F.L. (6th) 187, 2004 BCCA 577 (B.C. C.A.), the appellate court upheld the lower court's decision to award compensatory and non — compensatory support on the basis that the wife stayed home as homemaker and primary caregiver to the children during the marriage. The court concluded that the wife required, and that the husband was able to pay $600 per month in spousal maintenance.

The wife was entitled to compensatory support to recognize her lost economic opportunity through a joint decision for many years that she not work full-time so she could care for the children: *Skrivanek v. Pow*, 2004 CarswellBC 2949, 2004 BCSC 1609 (B.C. S.C.).

Where the wife had supported the husband through his completion of two university degrees, her compensatory support award was upheld on appeal. The fact that she had to postpone her own secondary education resulted in a permanent economic detriment to her: *Allaire v. Allaire* (2003), 35 R.F.L. (5th) 256, 2003 CarswellOnt 1002, 170 O.A.C. 72, [2003] O.J. No. 1069 (Ont. C.A.). In situations such as in the present case where a former spouse will continue to suffer financial disadvantages of the marriage and its breakdown and the other spouse will continue to obtain financial advantages, long-term compensatory support is appropriate, even if the disadvantaged spouse is self-sufficient. In the 3 years prior to the trial, the husband earned between $207,721 and $176,689. The wife was presently enrolled in a Masters programme and anticipated that with the completion of this degree, her income would increase to $68,793. The appellate court upheld a spousal award of $2,500 per month without time limitation.

Where a spouse is in need because the marriage, parenting responsibilities and the breakdown of the marriage have impaired her earning capacity, the court will uphold a decision to provide lump sum spousal support in order to enhance the spouse's economic self-sufficiency and operate as a one-time form of compensation to enable her to provide a permanent home for herself and child which would better approximate the lifestyle the child enjoyed while living with both parents, a lifestyle to which the father has the means to contribute: *Tauber v. Tauber* (2003), 34 R.F.L. (5th) 450, 2003 CarswellOnt 1009, 64 O.R. (3d) 229, 170 O.A.C. 1, 225 D.L.R. (4th) 186 (Ont. C.A.). The wife's award of $500,000 lump sum spousal support after a 3-year marriage was affirmed.

In *T. (J.G.) v. N. (T.)*, 42 R.F.L. (5th) 208, 2003 CarswellAlta 868, 330 A.R. 187, 299 W.A.C. 187, 2003 ABCA 195, [2003] A.J. No. 786 (Alta. C.A.), the mere fact that the mother was able to return to the same type of employment she had before assuming primary responsibility for the parties' children was no reason not to award her compensatory support. To adopt a contrary approach would be to ignore the reality of career progression and advancement.

Entitlement to spousal support may be established on any combination of three bases, contract, compensation for the disadvantages arising out of the marriage or its breakdown, or support required to relieve the economic hardships arising from the marriage breakdown: *Gabb v. Gabb*, 2001 CarswellMan 68, [2001] M.J. No. 55, 2001 MBCA 19, 153 Man. R. (2d) 157, 238 W.A.C. 157, 13 R.F.L. (5th) 391 (Man. C.A.). In the *Gabb* case, given the duration (9 years) and circumstances of the marriage combined with the age of the wife at the time of the marriage breakdown (53), the wife was undoubtedly economically disadvantaged as a result of the nature of the relationship itself. The court, in upholding the trial court's spousal support award of $500 per month, stated that the support award was justifiable in all of the circumstances, on the ground of relieving economic hardship alone. In the year following separation the wife's income was just over $10,000 and the husband's income remained between $40,000 and $45,000. The wife was debt-free and the husband owed $75,000 in income tax. The court dismissed the husband's appeal.

The payee is clearly entitled to compensatory support where she changed her work to respond to the career plans and goals of her husband and to the needs of the children: *Hunt v. Smolis-Hunt*, 2001 CarswellAlta 1357, 2001 ABCA 229, [2001] 11 W.W.R. 233, 286 A.R. 248, 253 W.A.C. 248, 205 D.L.R. (4th) 712, 20 R.F.L. (5th) 409, 97 Alta. L.R. (3d) 238, [2001] A.J. No. 1170 (Alta. C.A.). Her sacrifices were made in order for him to achieve his goal of becoming a lawyer. By assisting her husband with his goals, she bestowed a great economic advantage on him and a disadvantage on herself and an economic hardship, both short and long-term. The court held that the trial judge complied with the requirements of s. 15.3 (terms and conditions of spousal support orders) of the *Divorce Act* by giving reasons why she could not quantify the award. She did not do so because she found that the payor would be unable to pay any periodic or lump sum other than through his equity in the matrimonial assets which had been extinguished by the child support awards.

A spouse who consents to moves initiated by the other spouse which necessitate her changing to comparable jobs, is disadvantaged but only to a small extent and is thereby entitled to a small amount of compensatory support: *Leitch v. Leitch* (1999), 1999 CarswellOnt 3942 (Ont. S.C.J.); affirmed (2001), 2001 CarswellOnt 3289 (Ont. C.A.). Although the wife was not, at the time of the appellate hearing, working as a qualified nurse, a position for which she was qualified, she was working in an associated field at the top of her pay scale. She had not shared her earnings with the family over the course of the marriage, but had enjoyed the lifestyle provided by the husband. She had also upgraded her skills by taking a 2-year full-time university programme during the marriage.

Where a spouse has shouldered the primary responsibility for the care of the children and maintained the marital home, retiring the mortgage in the process, and has been required to survive on minimal earnings due to her lack of education and the fact that she has been out of the work force for 14 years, she is entitled to lump sum compensatory support of $11,621: *Craplewe v. Craplewe* (2001), 2001 CarswellMan 635, 2002 MBCA 3, 22 R.F.L. (5th) 39, 163 Man. R. (2d) 65, 269 W.A.C. 65 (Man. C.A.). The husband had failed to provide the wife with the required financial disclosure, and if she were not granted spousal support, the husband would be rewarded for failure to meet his legal and financial responsibilities to the wife over a period of years.

A spouse is entitled to compensatory support where she has been economically disadvantaged by the marriage through giving up her career in order to stay home with the children, and where she has been economically disadvantaged by the marriage breakdown by no longer being able to benefit from her husband's significant income, and where the other spouse has received economic advantages as a result of the marriage: *Schnell v. Schnell*, 2001 CarswellSask 744, 2001 SKCA 123, 21 R.F.L. (5th) 197, 213 Sask. R. 174, 260 W.A.C. 174, [2001] S.J. No. 704 (Sask. C.A.). The husband had an average income of $191,472 for 1996 to 1998. The appellate court upheld the trial judge's award of $2,500 per month in spousal support. The order was made for a 9-month period and was reviewable at the end of that time on the application by either party.

Support may be awarded to compensate an economic disadvantage arising from the breakdown of the marriage: *Rea v. Rea* (1998), 42 R.F.L. (4th) 92, 1998 CarswellMan 440, 166 D.L.R. (4th) 443, 131 Man. R. (2d) 95, 187 W.A.C. 95 (Man. C.A.). The wife in a traditional marriage of 36 years assumed the role of homemaker, raised their three children, and assisted her husband in his career. She was a qualified teacher, but because of her domestic duties, taught only in the first year of the marriage and for 7 years after the birth of their first child. The trial judge ordered the husband to pay support to the wife of $1,000 a month until his retirement and $850 a month thereafter. On appeal, the amount payable on retirement was reduced to $500 a month. In making the reduction the Court of Appeal observed that the original order would have given the husband less disposable income on retirement than the wife would have. However, she was entitled to compensation for economic disadvantage, and the husband was able to continue paying that compensation into his retirement. Although the wife may not have suffered an economic disadvantage as a result of the marriage, she did suffer an economic disadvantage as a result of the martial breakdown.

Where the trial judge's findings that the marriage had not interfered with the wife's finding of employment and that she had not furthered the husband's career were both reasonable, the appellate court upheld the dismissal of the wife's claim for compensatory support: *Jonasson v. Jonasson* (1997), 30 R.F.L. (4th) 20, [1997] B.C.J. No. 1704, 1997 CarswellBC 1505, 95 B.C.A.C. 94, 154 W.A.C. 94 (B.C. C.A.); leave to appeal refused (1998), [1997] S.C.C.A. No. 519, 226 N.R. 400, 118 B.C.A.C. 320 (note), 192 W.A.C. 320 (note) (S.C.C.).

There are three different thresholds for compensatory support found in clauses 15.2(6)(a), (b) and (c) of the *Divorce Act*: (1) an "economic disadvantage" to a spouse which arises from "the marriage or its breakdown" (clause 15.2(6)(a)); or (2) "financial consequences [to a spouse] arising from the care of any child of the marriage" that needs apportioning (clause 15.2(6)(b)); or (3) some "economic hardship" to a spouse flowing from "the breakdown of the marriage" (clause 15.2(6)(c)): *Taylor v. Taylor*, 2004 CarswellOnt 4851, [2004] O.J. No. 4802, 10 R.F.L. (6th) 202 (S.C.J.). Although subsection 15.2(6) is phrased conjunctively, a party need only cross one of the thresholds to be entitled to compensatory support. Under clause 15.2(6)(a), fairness is a test that may be used. In other words, the court should act on a proven economic disadvantage where the disadvantage is of such a degree that it would be unfair to ignore. In this case, the wife sought compensatory support to reflect her share of "the financial losses" sustained as a consequence of the marriage, the separation and the conduct of the husband. The husband had become extremely depressed after his daughter's murder and eventually he had a mental breakdown and declared bankruptcy. The court held that the wife had suffered an unfavourable condition and therefore an economic disadvantage arising from the marriage or its breakdown and was entitled to specific compensatory support in the sum of $10,517.

Compensatory support addresses the economic advantage or disadvantage arising from the marriage, the roles adopted in marriage, and the breakdown of the marriage. Non-compensatory support is based on needs and means, and a pattern of economic dependence that developed during the marriage: *McLean v. McLean*, 2004 CarswellOnt 4234, [2004] O.J. No. 4621 (S.C.J.); additional reasons at 2004 CarswellOnt 4412 (S.C.J.). Compensatory and non-compensatory components of spousal support to be paid to the wife were assessed equally at $350 monthly. Grossed up for the income tax the wife would be required to pay, the court found that the appropriate monthly award was $1,000. The parties cohabited under the marriage for 20 years. They had two children. The wife earned approximately $72,300 a year and the husband earned $160,000. The wife's ability to earn a good income while looking after home and children allowed the husband time and flexibility to change careers and to succeed in what he chose to do. Also, she was placed in a position of some financial dependency during the marriage by the husband's contribution of his income to the whole of the family unit.

In *Collins v. Collins*, 2003 CarswellNfld 168, [2003] N.J. No. 169, 42 R.F.L. (5th) 273, 229 Nfld. & P.E.I.R. 1, 679 A.P.R. 1, 2003 NLSCTD 102 (N.L. T.D.), the husband agreed to provide his wife with employment for a certain period and was ordered to pay $1,000 as compensatory support for failure to do so.

Where a spouse lost the opportunity to have a successful career at an earlier age as a result of her assumed role of mother and traditional wife, the economic disadvantage continued even though at a later period, she became available for work: *Juvatopolos v. Juvatopolos* (2004), 2004 CarswellOnt 4423, 9 R.F.L. (6th) 147 (Ont. S.C.J.); affirmed (2005), 2005 CarswellOnt 4774, 19 R.F.L. (6th) 76 (Ont. C.A.). Where, as in this case, the wife had formed a new relationship, the onus lay with her to establish, that notwithstanding this new relationship, the economic loss resulting from the first relationship remained. The court found that from the perspective of compensatory support, the wife had discharged that onus. Since she offered very little by way of genuine effort to become self-sufficient, the quantum of spousal support was reduced substantially. In addition, her failure to invest at least some of her inheritance of $56,000 as a continuing source of income was an exacerbating factor in reducing support. At the present time she was receiving approximately $31,000 per year with the contribution received from her partner. The court held that the order should be varied and the spousal support should be reduced to from $1,200 to $400 per month.

The purpose of compensatory support is to compensate a spouse who has given up his or her own economic security for the purpose of caring for children and supporting his or her spouse's career: *Walkden v. Walkden*, 2004 CarswellAlta 1799, 2004 ABQB 823 (Alta. Q.B.). In this case, the wife was working full time and had her own career before marriage. After the parties' marriage, she followed the husband to Saudi Arabia where, as a woman, she was technically not able to work. However, she did work from time to time in order to keep herself busy rather than to earn an income. When her first child was born in 1980, she left the work force entirely to stay at home with the children. Since returning to Canada she had taken additional upgrading courses and was now working full time. She would never be able to replace the income and positions she would have received had they not gone to Saudi Arabia. She was the classic case for which compensatory spousal support was intended. The court awarded her a lump sum of $300,000 in compensatory support.

In order to establish entitlement to spousal support based on compensatory grounds, it is not essential that the court find that the applicant was economically disadvantaged by the role she played in the relationship. The objectives of the *Divorce Act* speak of "economic advantages or disadvantages to the spouses". Even if the applicant did not experience a disadvantage, the fact that her spouse experienced an advantage gives rise to an entitlement to spousal support. In this case, the wife who worked full time was found to be the mainstay of the household during much of the marriage, relieving the childcare provider and managing the childcare needs. Her assumption of responsibility for those two aspects of household management relieved the husband of those responsibilities and allowed him to make his career his priority. It followed that applicant established on the balance of probabilities that she was entitled to compensatory spousal support: *Shaw v. Shaw* (2002), 2002 CarswellOnt 2333, [2002] O.J. No. 2782 (Ont. S.C.J.). For the first 2 years of their marriage, the wife made more money than the husband. After that time, his income significantly increased and thereafter the gap between their incomes widened dramatically. While the wife's ability to contribute to a R.R.S.P. was interrupted by her maternity leaves and her change of jobs, the husband's contribution to a spousal R.R.S.P. compensated for this disadvantage. The wife became less career oriented once she had children. The court found that there was no evidence that the wife refused any opportunities or declined to pursue any educational programmes which would have enhanced her marketability. There was no independent evidence from the wife's superiors at her former employer's as to her value as an employee and whether her commitment to her family undermined or precluded promotion. Nor was there any evidence whether her innate abilities would have limited her prospects of advancement. The court was not prepared to find that the disadvantage which the wife experienced as a result of her role in the relationship was significant. However, the fact that the husband did receive an advantage led to the wife's entitlement to compensatory support.

In *Koch v. Koch* (2001), 2001 CarswellOnt 3460, 22 R.F.L. (5th) 114 (Ont. S.C.J.), the court awarded the wife compensatory spousal support where she had suffered *some* economic disadvantage as a result of the marriage breakdown. She was the main caretaker of the children, looked after her mother and father in their failing health and experienced the emotional wear and tear of the lawsuit which contributed to part of her loss of her earnings for some of the years following separation. The court did find, however, that another, perhaps larger, component of the decrease in income in the later years was the availability of the children's trust money into which the wife dipped. This lessened her motivation to work as hard as she had previously. The court accepted the wife's evidence that the disadvantage would be removed after the conclusion of the parties' litigation and awarded her lump sum support of $25,000, which was not taxable and which would bring some final resolution to the case. The marriage, while of a reasonably lengthy duration, enabled the wife to become qualified and able to support herself. She had some significant assets and would have more liquid capital from the disposition of the jointly-held property. Importantly, she had no demonstrable need, even if there was no particular emphasis placed on the monetary assistance from her boyfriend who had helped her for the prior 2 years.

A spouse was entitled to compensatory support where there was a lengthy 28-year marriage and she had health problems. Additional factors in making such an award were her involvement in the husband's education and his consulting business, as well as the time she devoted to child care and the care of his parents: *Rothenburg v. Rothenburg*, 2003 CarswellOnt 1380, [2003] O.J. No. 1551, 40 R.F.L. (5th) 363, [2003] O.T.C. 327 (Ont. S.C.J.). Further, given the ages of the parties, there must be some consideration to allowing the wife to save for retirement given the likelihood of a support variation on his retirement. The court awarded the wife support in the monthly sum of $4,500 which was $500 a month more than the strictly needs based model provided.

The *Divorce Act* allows the court, through compensatory support, to apportion between the spouses financial consequences arising from the care of a child over and above the obligation for child support. Accordingly, the husband was ordered to contribute to the doctor-ordered respite case for the mother which had been the result of the stress relating to her care of the parties' emotionally challenged child: *Y. (A.L.) v. Y. (L.M.)*, 17 R.F.L. (5th) 233, 2001 CarswellAlta 491, 2001 ABQB 311, [2001] 9 W.W.R. 141, 92 Alta. L.R. (3d) 347, 294 A.R. 274 (Alta. Q.B.).

In *Halloran v. Hotte* (2000), 12 R.F.L. (5th) 57, 2000 CarswellOnt 3997 (Ont. S.C.J.), the wife was granted spousal support for 3 years upon dissolution of the parties' 9-year marriage. The wife had left her civil service job during the marriage to care for the parties' children. Although she was once again employed as a civil servant, her salary was much lower than it could have been if she had not given up her job. The wife was 33 years old and her salary would likely increase over time, eliminating her need for spousal support.

Where after the separation, the parties negotiated a settlement which formed the basis of an order and, at that time, the equalization and spousal and child support settlement arrangements addressed all of the objectives of the *Divorce Act*, including compensatory support that recognized the economic realities of the family partnership, the wife, after 26 years of commitment to her first husband and family, remained entitled to some continued compensatory spousal support, despite the fact that she was living with a third party: *Levandusky v. Levandusky* (2003), 2003 CarswellOnt 2615, 39 R.F.L. (5th) 134 (Ont. S.C.J.); additional reasons at (2003), 2003 CarswellOnt 2613 (Ont. S.C.J.). Spousal support was reduced by two-thirds to $460 per month, plus $80 for one-half of that portion of the wife's pension not previously equalized, for a monthly support total of $540 from and including January 4, 2003 until the husband attained age 65 or until the wife's mother died, whichever event first occurred. Thereafter, compensatory spousal support would continue monthly, in an amount representing one-half of that portion of the husband's unequalized pension, namely $18,6,50.. The court in determining support took into account that the wife would be entitled to one-half of her elderly mother's estate, which was presently valued at between $430,000 to $440,000 and perhaps an additional $118,000 for the value of the cottage which the wife's brother did not want, nor use.

In *Beaton v. Beaton*, 2001 CarswellNS 419, 2001 NSSF 30, 20 R.F.L. (5th) 252, 199 N.S.R. (2d) 271, 623 A.P.R. 271 (N.S. S.C.), the wife was granted very limited compensatory support where she was absent from the workforce for approximately 4 years and the court had little or no evidence quantifying her "loss of seniority, promotion opportunities, training and pension contributions". She had received $1,100 per month for 13 months and was entitled to a further $1,000 per month for a period of 1 year and $725 per month in spousal support for an additional year.

Where there is a short marriage of 5 years, a spouse is still entitled to compensatory support, where she left her business which she co-owned and helped to build, and relocated to another province to be with her husband: *Tabata v. Smith*, 2001 CarswellAlta 1294, 2001 ABQB 776, 21 R.F.L. (5th) 451, 297 A.R. 168 (Alta. Q.B.). As a result of her leaving, the company experienced financial difficulties and eventually failed. The parties did not have children. Both were employed at the time of the hearing and the wife was becoming self sufficient. The court found that had the wife not married, she would have stayed in the province where her business was located and would have continued to run her business which would have been a successful enterprise. She was required to forgo this business opportunity because of the marriage and therefore was entitled to compensatory support. In light of the circumstances, and because of the very short term during which periodic spousal support payments would be warranted, the means of the husband to pay a lump sum award, and the clear need for these parties to put this process behind them and move on, the court found that it was an appropriate case for a lump sum spousal support award.

Where the wife had given up her career and had relocated several times when her husband, who was in the armed forces, was transferred, she was found to be entitled to support to compensate her for lost economic advantages. Although the wife was employed, she had lost the opportunities for advancement which would have arisen had she not given up her career: *Lee v. Lee* (1992), 42 R.F.L. (3d) 445, 1992 CarswellOnt 298 (Ont. Gen. Div.).

In *Kits v. Kits* (1998), 42 R.F.L. (4th) 167, 1998 CarswellBC 2323 (B.C. S.C.), the wife was awarded lump sum compensatory support upon dissolution of the parties' 14-year marriage. The wife had forfeited a lucrative career to remain in the home to care for the children and was accordingly entitled to compensation. However, given her sizable property entitlement and the fact that she had entered into a relationship with a man who had considerable resources to support her, she had no need for ongoing support.

In *Lanctot v. Lanctot* (1996), 1996 CarswellOnt 2518, 6 O.T.C. 161 (Ont. Gen. Div.), the court held that because of the marriage and its breakdown, the wife was cast out on her own with no work experience. She was entitled to compensatory support sufficient to enable her to re-train. The husband had been a chaplain in the military and had taken various postings in Canada and Europe. The military terminated the husband's employment. He eventually obtained employment on a contract basis. Shortly after the husband told the wife that he wished to end their marriage, she was admitted to hospital, depressed and suicidal and she continued to suffer from depression at the time of the proceedings.

Where a spouse has "lost opportunity" for advancement in the marketplace due to her marriage, some compensation is appropriate pursuant to s. 51 of the B.C. *Family Relations Act*: *Napper v. Napper* (1995), 1995 CarswellBC 1176, 18 R.F.L. (4th) 309 (B.C. S.C.); additional reasons at (1997), 1997 CarswellBC 822, 28 R.F.L. (4th) 378 (B.C. S.C.). The wife at the time of the proceedings earned less than her husband and, given the evidence, had no ability to increase her income significantly. This was to be contrasted with her future at her previous employment where, but for the marriage, she would have been earning considerably more, perhaps equal to, or greater than the husband's income.

Support should be ordered to compensate a spouse for loss of income for the time (6 months) that he was prevented from carrying on his old law practice and to provide some assistance in financing the start-up costs of a new practice: *Dunn v. Menear* (2000), 2000 CarswellOnt 4778, 14 R.F.L. (5th) 293 (Ont. S.C.J.). The husband was unable to carry on his old law practice, as he was convicted of assaulting his wife and spent some time in jail, followed by time on probation where he was forbidden from being in the city where his old practice was situated. The wife was required to pay a lump sum payment of support based upon the husband's average monthly billings in a total amount of $9,000. That sum was reduced to allow for the fact that the lump sum payment would not be deductible to the applicant and would not be taxable in the hands of the respondent. The husband had given up his job in Toronto to work in Orillia where the wife was employed.

In *Osmar v. Osmar* (2000), 2000 CarswellOnt 1927, [2000] O.J. No. 2060, 8 R.F.L. (5th) 375 (Ont. S.C.J.); additional reasons at 2000 CarswellOnt 2343, [2000] O.J. No. 2504, 8 R.F.L. (5th) 387, [2000] O.T.C. 979 (Ont. S.C.J.), the court held that while the wife's day-to-day financial needs were significantly reduced because she cohabited with a man who earned approximately $75,000 per annum, the spousal support provisions of the separation agreement clearly must have contemplated compensatory support for the roles adopted by the spouses during the marriage and the economic consequences of those roles. The marriage was a traditional one with the husband in the paid work force and the wife staying at home with the children. The court considered the factors and circumstances identified in ss. 33(8) and (9) of the Family Law Act and concluded that it was not appropriate to vary the spousal support provision of the separation agreement. The wife had lost ground financially by converting the child support to a tax neutral award under the *Guidelines*. The husband had made extravagant purchases, leasing a new $65,000 vehicle and committing himself to the purchase of a 4,000 square foot, $400,000 home during the currency of the litigation. Compensatory spousal support ought to be paid in priority to R.R.S.P. contributions and the husband's other lifestyle choices. Although the agreement contemplated future variation of spousal support, it did not refer to the wife's remarriage or cohabitation as specific factors that would trigger a variation. Such a clause is often found in such agreements. Its absence fortified the court's conclusion that the spousal support was primarily, if not exclusively, compensatory in nature. It was premature to vary it.

In a long-term traditional marriage where the wife did not work for many years but at the time of the hearing had obtained employment, she was entitled to a lump sum of $39,000 for loss of economic opportunity and support: *DeFaveri v. Toronto Dominion Bank* (1999), 45 R.F.L. (4th) 141, (sub nom. *Babij v. DeFaveri)* 1999 CarswellOnt 773, [1999] O.J. No. 822 (Ont. C.A.); additional reasons at (1999), 1999 CarswellOnt 1828 (Ont. C.A.). This was the same amount owing by the wife to the husband in the property calculation, so no exchange of funds needed to take place.

The appellate Court in *De Beeld v. De Beeld* (1999), 2 R.F.L. (5th) 162, 1999 CarswellBC 2084, 179 D.L.R. (4th) 186, 129 B.C.A.C. 101, 210 W.A.C. 101, 1999 BCCA 515 (B.C. C.A.), in affirming the lower court decision, awarded the wife $40,000 lump sum compensatory support. During the marriage, the wife had supported her husband through university and during the time he qualified as a *charter*ed accountant and she had later suffered a serious injury in a car accident, which prevented her from working full-time.

Where the wife had left her native United States to marry the husband in Canada, and the marriage lasted barely a year, she was awarded modest periodic support for a 1-year period. The husband was obliged to contribute since he had asked the wife to leave the U.S. knowing that she would be financially dependent on him: *Millward v. Millward* (2003), 48 R.F.L. (5th) 294, 2003 CarswellOnt 1403 (Ont. S.C.J.).

Where the wife forfeited a promotion in an attempt to salvage the parties' marriage, she was entitled to $400 per month for 2 years as a compensatory award: *Balcombe v. Balcombe* (1990), 30 R.F.L. (3d) 177, 42 O.A.C. 150, 1990 CarswellOnt 322 (Ont. Div. Ct.).

See *Romaniuk v. Romaniuk* (2005), 2005 CarswellOnt 1779, 17 R.F.L. (6th) 272 (Ont. S.C.J.); additional reasons at (2005), 2005 CarswellOnt 1780 (Ont. S.C.J.), below.

Cases Where Compensatory Support Not Awarded

There is no basis for awarding support on compensatory principles where the wife's career potential had not suffered as a result of the marriage or the traditional role she played in it. However, non-compensatory support may be awarded on the ground that she suffered economic disadvantage as a result of the breakdown of the marriage: *Fisher v. Fisher*, 2001 CarswellNS 31, [2001] N.S.J. No. 32, 2001 NSCA 18, 12 R.F.L. (5th) 348, 190 N.S.R. (2d) 144, 594 A.P.R. 144 (N.S. C.A.).

Compensatory support should not be awarded where a spouse in a relatively short marriage claims to be economically disadvantaged because she did not make R.R.S.P. and pension contributions during 3 years of the marriage. She did not have regular employment outside the home during that time: *Roseneck v. Gowling* (2002), 35 R.F.L. (5th) 177, 2002 CarswellOnt 4396, 167 O.A.C. 203, 62 O.R. (3d) 789, 223 D.L.R. (4th) 210 (Ont. C.A.); additional reasons at (2003), 2003 CarswellOnt 159, 223 D.L.R. (4th) 229 (Ont. C.A.); further additional reasons at (2003), 38 R.F.L. (5th) 180, 2003 CarswellOnt 649 (Ont. C.A.). Fair distribution does not require a minute accounting of the financial details of the parties. In terms of compensatory support, the courts should be looking at a wide view of the advantages and disadvantages of the spouses caused by their roles in the marriage. In this case, both parties had a relatively equal earning power before and after the marriage.

"Compensatory support, premised on marriage being a joint endeavour, seeks to alleviate economic disadvantage by taking into account all the circumstances of the parties, including the advantages conferred on either spouse during the marriage. It is concerned with an equitable sharing of the benefits of the marriage . . . In practical terms, the issue will generally revolve around whether one spouse has gained an advantage in his or her ability to earn income or acquire assets that should be shared, for at least some period of time": *Corbeil v. Corbeil* (2001), 2001 CarswellAlta 1138, [2001] A.J. No. 1144, 2001 ABCA 220, 286 A.R. 330, 253 W.A.C. 330, 21 R.F.L. (5th) 1, [2002] 3 W.W.R. 60, 98 Alta. L.R. (3d) 38 (Alta. C.A.). The appellate court held that the trial judge was wrong in not taking into account the wife's care of the children in considering spousal support. However, taking all the objectives and the circumstances into consideration, the wife's income after imputing some income, her potential for income growth, the fact that she works only part time, the fact that the husband also raised the children for a period of time when she left the home without significant contribution from her, their ages and the security of their positions and her asset advantage and the rejection of her evidence by the trial judge on relevant issues, and that significantly more of the assets received on the distribution are subject to tax as income, the court held that it would uphold the trial court's decision not to provide spousal support.

Compensatory support will not be awarded on the basis that a party contributed to the development of a spouse's ability which enabled the spouse to earn income: *Crandall v. Crandall* (1996), 1996 CarswellNB 233, 23 R.F.L. (4th) 387, 179 N.B.R. (2d) 59, 455 A.P.R. 59 (N.B. C.A.). The court held that there was no possibility of fixing a value on the development of an ability, or of finding any merit in the notion that each ability developed should be valued as a distinct asset. The compensatory aspect of a support award is related to the economic hardship resulting from the lack of opportunity of a party to develop his or her own potential during the marriage. The fact that the husband was able to pursue a career and to develop other skills is evidence of the fact that the wife was in a less advantageous position, and has a right to claim compensatory support. It does not form the basis for a distinct claim.

The court in *Romaniuk v. Romaniuk*, 2005 CarswellOnt 1779, 17 R.F.L. (6th) 272 (S.C.J.); additional reasons at 2005 CarswellOnt 1780 (S.C.J.); dismissed the wife's claim for compensatory support where, after being laid off by her employer, she voluntarily moved from the city in which she lived to another city to pursue a relationship with the respondent. She later moved to yet another city to pursue her career and the respondent followed her. Subsequently, she left that employment and moved to Ottawa with the respondent. She had had employment in a number of different fields, and was pursuing a career as a dispatcher. She was, in fact, unemployed when she finally did move to Ottawa. The facts of the case do not support a compensatory order for support in terms of any loss of career opportunity on the part of the applicant. However, the applicant was entitled to compensatory support on account of her debt which arose from his declaration of bankruptcy.

A court will not award compensatory support to a party whose spouse induced her to take early retirement so that they could purchase and run a business together where, at the time of the hearing, the party was earning close to her previous income and had a significant net worth ($500,000) and did not require support: *Launchbury v. Launchbury* (2001), 2001 CarswellOnt 1384, 15 R.F.L. (5th) 106 (Ont. S.C.J.); affirmed (2005), 2005 CarswellOnt 1335, 12 R.F.L. (6th) 393 (Ont. C.A.).

In *Sibbet v. Sibbet*, 17 R.F.L. (5th) 424, 2001 CarswellMan 204, [2001] M.J. No. 181, 2001 MBQB 40, 157 Man. R. (2d) 33, [2001] 10 W.W.R. 241 (Man. Q.B.), the court rejected the wife's claim for compensatory support. The wife, who suffered from a number of emotional problems, had maliciously and deliberately set out on a course of conduct designed to undermine the husband's business interests. The businesses were, in the end, destroyed and her claim for compensatory support was lost as a result of her economic misconduct.

In *Janakowski v. Janakowski* (2000), 2000 CarswellOnt 2478, 7 R.F.L. (5th) 117 (Ont. S.C.J.), the court denied the wife's claim for lump sum spousal support because such an award would be inequitable having regard to the relevant circumstances of the relationship of the parties, the choices made by the wife after the separation, and a consent order whereby the husband provided support to the wife for 3 years. At separation, the wife was not employed and, therefore, was dependent upon the husband. The separation clearly disadvantaged her, since she could no longer rely on the husband's income from employment to cover her living expenses. The consent order helped to address this economic disadvantage. There was no evidence to indicate that the wife gave up any employment or educational opportunities as a result of her role in the household. She made minimal efforts to secure employment since separation as she preferred not to work. The court held that the present inability of the wife to be self-sufficient was unrelated to the marriage or its breakdown. She had sporadic part-time employment, which indicated that she was physically capable of performing some type of work. She could not simply expect the husband to support her indefinitely because she had a need for support.

In *Worst v. Worst* (1997), 1997 CarswellBC 1985 (B.C. S.C.), the court denied a claim for compensatory spousal support in the following circumstances: (1) There had already been an equitable sharing of the economic consequences of the marriage and its breakdown with the reapportionment of the matrimonial home. (2) The wife had not suffered an economic disadvantage in the relationship such as to trigger a right to compensatory support. (3) The husband did not continue to reap economic advantages from the relationship. (4) The wife had chosen not to pursue employment with her existing qualifications but, instead, decided to attend retraining courses. A court should not place responsibility for that economic decision on the respondent. The court stated that of the two, upon completing her studies, the wife likely faced the more secure future.

The court dismissed a claim for lump sum compensatory support in *R. (W.H.) v. R. (J.M.)* (1997), 1997 CarswellOnt 3178, [1997] O.J. No. 2795 (Ont. Gen. Div.), based primarily on the loss to the wife arising from the fact she gave up her teaching career when the family moved from Quebec to Ontario in 1983. The court held that the Ontario Court of Appeal has been critical of lump sum compensatory support to redress alleged economic loss claimed to be caused by one decision made during the marriage. Considering an order for support compensatory or otherwise the *Divorce Act* directed that consideration of the *condition, means, needs and other circumstances of each spouse* be taken into account. Financially the parties were relatively equal. Each had property of approximately $100,000 and earning power of $45,000 per annum. The wife had a better education including musical talent. She had superior living skills, resiliency, and health and was clearly the stronger person. The husband had had an unfortunate life experience and except for finances, had less than his wife in every category. The court held that the compensatory lump sum and child support claims were more than satisfied by the value the wife had enjoyed in the use of the equalization payment ($100,500) for the last 7 years.

Where a party undertakes work and expense to assist his or her spouse through training and helps in a business, no compensatory support is payable where the business is based almost entirely on the spouse's ability and will probably only be a hobby, depending a great deal on the respondent's incentive and interest in doing the work involved: *French v. French*, 1996 CarswellNB 385, [1996] N.B.J. No. 386, [1996] N.B.R. (2d) (Supp.) No. 39 (N.B. Q.B.). In this case, the spouse did return to his former employment where he worked until retirement. The applicant wife was not entitled to compensatory support.

In *Johnson v. Johnson* (1988), 16 R.F.L. (3d) 113, 29 B.C.L.R. (2d) 359, 1988 CarswellBC 301 (B.C. C.A.), compensatory maintenance was not granted where the wife's claim was founded on the ground that she gave up her goals in order to support the appellant in becoming an ophthalmologist, and that the his ability to earn a substantial income was due in part to her contribution. The wife did receive benefits from her husband's training, and during the marriage she had a higher standard of living and, afterwards, higher maintenance. Most of the husband's present income was attributable to his hard work, some to his qualifications.

Where the wife claimed compensatory support based solely on her decision to turn down a teaching job during her engagement believing it would be detrimental to her future family life, her claim was dismissed. That approach was found to be flawed as it isolated one event in the parties' marriage and treated it as the only one to be determined by the court in determining the issue of spousal support: *Cerget v. Cerget* (1994), 7 R.F.L. (4th) 322, 1994 CarswellOnt 445 (Ont. Gen. Div.); additional reasons at (1994), 7 R.F.L. (4th) 343, 1994 CarswellOnt 446 (Ont. Gen. Div.); affirmed (1994), 1994 CarswellOnt 3496 (Ont. Gen. Div.).

Where the wife's contribution to the husband's career was helpful, but not crucial, and the husband would have no doubt succeeded on his own and the wife did not delay or give up her career ambitions so as to advance his career, there was no factual or legal basis for an award of compensatory maintenance: *McDonell v. McDonell* (1988), 16 R.F.L. (3d) 174, 1988 CarswellBC 596 (B.C. S.C.).

15§32 — Objectives of spousal support — consequences of child care

The second objective to be recognized by an order, interim order, or variation order for the support of a spouse or former spouse, is that any financial consequences arising from the care of any child of the marriage over and above any child support obligation, is to be apportioned between the spouses or former spouses: *Divorce Act*, ss. 15.2(6)(b) and 17(7)(b)

The first two objectives in s. 15.2(6) of the *Divorce Act* are primarily related to compensation: *Bracklow v. Bracklow* (1999), 169 D.L.R. (4th) 577, 44 R.F.L. (4th) 1, [1999] 1 S.C.R. 420, 63 B.C.L.R. (3d) 77, [1998] 8 W.W.R. 740, 1999 CarswellBC 532, 1999 CarswellBC 533, [1999] S.C.J. No. 14 (S.C.C.). For a detailed discussion of the facts of the case, see section 15§6 General principles for determining spousal support

In *Moge v. Moge*, 43 R.F.L. (3d) 345, [1992] 3 S.C.R. 813, [1993] 1 W.W.R. 481, 145 N.R. 1, 81 Man. R. (2d) 161, 30 W.A.C. 161, 99 D.L.R. (4th) 456, the Supreme Court of Canada found that Mrs. *Moge* should be compensated by way of spousal support, in part, because her ability to earn income had been diminished by assuming responsibility for the care of the children. Madame Justice L'Heureux-Dube writing for the majority was of the view that compensation may be indicated if "due to childcare responsibilities one spouse declines a promotion, refuses a transfer, leaves a position to allow the other spouse to take advantage of an opportunity for advancement or otherwise curtails employment opportunities and thereby incurs economic loss." If child care responsibilities continue after divorce, the disadvantages attached to those responsibilities also continue. To be a custodial parent involves adopting a lifestyle which places many limitations upon that parent. She must find accommodation suited to the needs of the child, including play space, closeness to daycare, schools and recreational facilities. She is seldom free to accept shift work, is restricted in any overtime work by the daycare arrangements available, and must be prepared to give priority to the needs of a sick child over the demands of an employer. After a full day's work, the custodial parent faces a full range of homemaking responsibilities including cooking, cleaning and laundry, as well as the demands of the child himself for the parent's attention. Madame Justice McLachlin (as she then was) concurred with Madame Justice L'Heureux-Dubé in holding that the *Divorce Act* raised compensatory considerations. She stated that "if a spouse either before or after separation, has or continues to incur financial disadvantages as a result of caring for a child of the marriage, he or she should be compensated

In *Kowalewich v. Kowalewich* (1998), 38 R.F.L. (4th) 282, 108 B.C.A.C. 12, 176 W.A.C. 12, 50 B.C.L.R. (3d) 12 (B.C. C.A.), both the issues of child and spousal support were deferred and to be considered afresh after the property arrangements between the spouses had been finalized and paid out.

In *Loiselle v. Loiselle* (2000), 12 R.F.L. (5th) 400, 2000 CarswellOnt 3488 (Ont. S.C.J.) the wife was awarded monthly periodic spousal support of $1,500, which was to reduce to $900 once she had received her equalization entitlement.

In *N. (D.K.) v. O. (M.J.)* (2003), 41 R.F.L. (5th) 142, 2003 CarswellBC 2290, 18 B.C.L.R. (4th) 247, 232 D.L.R. (4th) 323, 187 B.C.A.C. 129, 307 W.A.C. 129, 2003 BCCA 502 (B.C. C.A.), the wife was awarded spousal support despite the fact that she had waived her support rights by agreement. Although the reapportionment of family assets under the agreement went someway towards meeting the wife's needs, spousal support was also needed in the short term.

As a general rule, whenever practicable, the courts, for purposes of spousal support, should not resort to an asset such as a pension that has already been used in the division of property: *Chamberlain v. Chamberlain*, 36 R.F.L. (5th) 241, [2003] N.B.J. No. 168, 2003 CarswellNB 208, 2003 CarswellNB 209, 2003 NBCA 34, 226 D.L.R. (4th) 272 (N.B. C.A.); affirming 2002 NBQB 231, 252 N.B.R. (2d) 152, 658 A.P.R. 152, 2002 CarswellNB 540 (N.B. Q.B.)

Allowing a spouse to reap benefits from the other spouse's pension twice, once through the division of matrimonial assets and secondly through spousal support, would be inequitable. To avoid double recovery, the focus for spousal support purposes, the focus should be on the position of the pension- holding spouse's income and assets that were not part of the equalization or division of matrimonial assets: *Boston v. Boston* (2001), 17 R.F.L. (5th) 4, 2001 CarswellOnt 2432, 2001 CarswellOnt 2433, [2001] S.C.J. No. 45, 2001 SCC 43, 201 D.L.R. (4th) 1, 271 N.R. 248, 149 O.A.C. 50, 28 C.C.P.B. 17 (S.C.C.); reversing (1999), 126 O.A.C. 296, [1999] O.J. No. 4140, 1999 CarswellOnt 3472 (Ont. C.A.).

In order to avoid double-dipping in cases where a spouse is awarded a share in the other's pension plan and proceeds from that plan are also used to determine the other spouse's ability to pay spousal support, the portion of the pension that has not been equalized or compensated for should be considered for support purposes: *Shadbolt v. Shadbolt* (1997), 32 R.F.L.(4th) 253 (Ont. Gen. Div.).

Where it was assumed that the husband would retire with full pension within 3 years, the wife's spousal support was to be subject to review at that time. The wife would receive a substantial lump sum when the pension was divided and it would be unfair to require the husband to continue to pay support from the half pension remaining to him: *Pacheco v. Pacheco* (2001), 13 R.F.L. (5th) 442, 2001 CarswellOnt 798 (Ont. S.C.J.).

Where the husband's only income was from his pension the court was required, in determining the quantum of the wife's spousal support, to consider the fact that the husband's pension had been included in calculating the equalization payment payable by him: *Dolman v. Dolman* (1998), 38 R.F.L. (4th) 362 (Ont. Gen. Div.); additional reasons at (June 18, 1998), Doc. D/630/97 (Ont. Gen. Div.). While ordering the payment of spousal support from funds previously equalized property could be considered "double dipping", such payment may be justified where the payor's assets have increased in value since separation: *Caldwell v. Caldwell* (1999), 46 R.F.L. (4th) 446 (Ont. Gen. Div)

15§33 — Objectives of spousal support — relieve economic hardship

The third objective to be recognized by an order, interim order, or variation order for the support of a spouse or former spouse, is that the order should relieve any economic hardship of the spouses, or of the former spouses, arising from the breakdown of the marriage: *Divorce Act*, ss. 15.2(6)(c) and 17(c).

This objective, "economic hardship . . . arising from the breakdown of the marriage," encompasses not only compensatory subject matter, but also non- compensatory subject matter such as the fact that a person who formerly enjoyed entitlement to support during cohabitation now finds herself or himself without it. This is to say that the breakdown of the marriage may cause economic hardship in a larger sense (non-compensatory) than can be realized by asking what loss the marriage or marriage breakup caused that would not have been suffered but for the marriage (compensatory sense). Economic hardship arising from the breakdown of the marriage, as distinct from the marriage itself, is a recognition of non- compensatory support: *Bracklow v. Bracklow* (1999), 169 D.L.R. (4th) 577 (S.C.C.). For a detailed discussion of the facts of the case, see section 15§6 General principles for determining spousal support.

In *Moge v. Moge* (1993), 43 R.F.L. (3d) 345, [1992] 3 S.C.R. 813, [1993] 1 W.W.R. 481, 145 N.R. 1, 81 Man. R. (2d) 161, 30 W.A.C. 161, 99 D.L.R. (4th) 456, [1993] R.D.F. 168, [1992] S.C.J. No. 107, 1992 CarswellMan 143 (Eng.), 1992 CarswellMan 222 (Fr.) (S.C.C.), the Supreme Court of Canada found in the majority judgment of Madame Justice L'Herureux-Dubé that Mrs. *Moge* continued to suffer economic hardship as a result of the "breakdown of the marriage" within the meaning of s. 17(7)(c) of the Act, and should be compensated for it. Madame Justice McLachlin, in her concurring reasons, held that in the considering the question of economic hardship arising from the breakdown of the marriage the focus was "not on compensation for what the spouses have contributed to or gained from the marriage but rather on post-marital need." She states that "if the breakdown of the marriage has created economic hardship for one or the other, the judge must attempt to grant relief from that hardship." The principles embodied in the current *Divorce Act* engage the courts in a different type of analysis than that which was required under the 1970 *Divorce Act* when considering the question of support. The most significant change is a shift away from "means and needs" as the exclusive test to a set of objectives which require the courts to accommodate a much wider spectrum of considerations. This change recognizes that the economic variables of marriage breakdown do not lend themselves to the application of only one objective. "All four of the objectives defined in the Act must be taken into account when spousal support is claimed or an order for spousal support is sought to be varied. No single objective is paramount."

Where the wife suffered from economic hardship that resulted from the breakdown of the traditional marriage between the parties, she was entitled to spousal support: *Greener v. Greener* (1997), 35 R.F.L. (4th) 179 (N.B. C.A.). The trial judge properly considered the wife's employment history, her present circumstances, and her attempts at self-sufficiency. The order was upheld on appeal.

Where the 60-year-old dependant spouse in a traditional 34-year marriage gave birth to 11 children, she was economically disadvantaged as a result of the breakdown of the marriage and suffered economic hardship. She was entitled to spousal support and was awarded $500 a month: *Tracey v. Tracey* (1998), 41 R.F.L. (4th) 278 (Ont. Gen. Div.).

The wife was entitled to non-compensatory spousal support to assist her to adjust to the marriage breakdown and to reorganize her financial affairs in *Hoxford v. Hoxford* (1999), 2 R.F.L. (5th) 257 (Ont. S.C.J.). The parties had a modern marriage in which both of them worked and they were not dependent upon each other. The only disadvantage that the wife suffered was that she would have to return to a reasonable lifestyle by herself, with the necessary changes to achieve self-sufficiency without the advantages of both parties pooling their resources. The husband was ordered to pay lump sum spousal support of $10,800, payable in the amount of $450 a month over 24 months.

15§34 — Objectives of spousal support — promotion of economic self-sufficiency

See *Moge v. Moge* at 15§24 Objectives of spousal support — general

Similarly, the fourth objective — to promote economic self-sufficiency — is not necessarily tied to compensation for disadvantages caused by the marriage or its breakup. A spouse's lack of self-sufficiency may arise from sources that have nothing to do with the marriage and are non-compensatory like the disappearance of the kind of work the spouse was trained to do, or ill-health: *Bracklow v. Bracklow, supra.*

In *Leskun v. Leskun*, 2006 CarswellBC 1492, 2006 SCC 25, [2006] 1 S.C.R. 25 (S.C.C.), the court held that failure to achieve self-sufficiency is not a breach of duty. Self-sufficiency is simply one factor amongst others to be taken into account. Where incapacity to support oneself is alleged, independent evidence is highly desirable, but not essential.

While the wife was able to contribute to her support, she was unable to be self-sufficient as she was not capable of earning anything resembling the income which would permit her to live in accordance with the standard of living of the parties during marriage. Consequently, a time-limited order was inappropriate: *Tedham v. Tedham*, 2005 CarswellBC 2346, 20 R.F.L. (6th) 217, 47 B.C.L.R. (4th) 254, 2005 BCCA 502 (B.C. C.A.); additional reasons at 2005 CarswellBC 2699, 2005 BCCA 553, 47 B.C.L.R. (4th) 276 (B.C. C.A.). With a time-limited order, the other objectives of a support order, which were significant were overshadowed by the objective of self-sufficiency and the failure to recognize fully that the objective of self-sufficiency is qualified by the words, "in so far as is practicable". The court considered the appropriate order for spousal support where there was a 16-year marriage and the court was utilizing the "without child support formula" which would yield a support order in the range of $6,300 to $8,500 per month with a duration of between 8 and 16 years, assuming the husband's income was in the range of $343,000 per year and the wife's was in the range of $30,000 per year. The court ordered indefinite spousal support of $6,000 per month. The previous time-limited order which was under appeal did not address the compensatory factors arising from the marriage, her need in relation to the standard of living enjoyed by the parties during the marriage, or her contribution to his income.

In *Fisher v. Fisher* (2001), 12 R.F.L. (5th) 348, 190 N.S.R. (2d) 144, 594 A.P.R. 144, 2000 NSCA 18, 2001 CarswellNS 31, [2001] N.S.J. No. 32 (C.A.); reversing in part (2000), 7 R.F.L. (5th) 45, 2000 CarswellNS 101 (N.S. S.C.), the court allowed the wife's appeal from the dismissal of her claim for spousal support. The trial judge found that spousal support was not warranted given the wife's lack of effort to achieve self-sufficiency after the collapse of the parties' long-term traditional marriage. Given the wife's age and background she could at best, be expected only to attain a limited degree of self-sufficiency. Furthermore, there should have been some recognition of the change in the wife's economic circumstances resulting from the marriage breakdown.

An order awarding a wife a lump sum of $10,000 for retraining should not be interfered with on appeal merely because she changes her mind about retraining and saves the money instead: *Martin v. Martin* (1998), 42 R.F.L. (4th) 251 (Nfld. C.A.).

Where the marriage breakdown took economic security away from the wife, the appellate court upheld the lower court's decision to award the wife spousal support during the time that she attended school on a full-time basis in her effort to be self-sufficient: *Coupar v. Coupar* (1998), 43 R.F.L. (4th) 443 (B.C. C.A.).

In *Giraud v. Giraud* (1997), 34 R.F.L. (4th) 255 (B.C. C.A.) the court found that the trial judge gave inappropriate emphasis to the promotion of economic self-sufficiency as an objective of an order for spousal support. The wife had a disability before marriage and that disability worsened during marriage. She had cancelled her disability insurance when, according to the parties' agreement, she quit her job upon her marriage to the respondent. The court held that the appropriate order would have guaranteed that the appellant could maintain a lifestyle equivalent to that which she would have enjoyed had she not accepted the respondent's promises to provide financial security for her when she married him. The court ordered that the appellant should receive $2,500 per month as support during the parties' joint lives. The appellant was 57 and the respondent 76 years of age.

Where the wife had previously been self-sufficient, but at the time of separation was unemployed, her application for support was dismissed. The wife's economic difficulties were not related to the breakdown of the marriage but rather to the recession: *B. (N.) v. C. (N.)* (1993), 57 Q.A.C. 1 (C.A. Qué.).

In terms of non-compensatory spousal support objectives, after a long-term marriage involving economic dependency, economic self-sufficiency may never be possible, especially where a large disparity in standard of living exists between the parties: *Thomas v. Thomas*, 50 R.F.L. (5th) 226, 2004 CarswellAlta 41, 2004 ABQB 27, 22 Alta. L.R. (4th) 46 (Alta. Q.B.).

Where the time limited spousal support payable to the wife pursuant to the parties' separation agreement expired, the wife's application for spousal support was refused. Since the parties' separation, the wife did not assume responsibility for becoming self-supporting and it was her lack of serious effort that left her financially needy. The wife had failed to fulfill her obligation to make concrete plans and serious efforts to re-enter the workplace, particularly in the face of a time-limited spousal support provision. The wife's current circumstances were reasonably foreseeable when the parties executed the agreement: *Lyster v. Lyster* (2003), 49 R.F.L. (5th) 139, 2003 CarswellOnt 5008 (Ont. S.C.J.).

Where the dependant spouse in a traditional 34 year marriage had had 11 children and was 60 years old, it was unrealistic to expect that she could become self-sufficient and she was awarded spousal support of $500: *Tracey v. Tracey* (1998), 41 R.F.L. (4th) 278 (Ont. Gen. Div.).

In *Dorey v. Snyder* (1999), 48 R.F.L. (4th) 67 (Ont. Gen. Div.), the wife was awarded limited term support upon dissolution of the parties' 16-year marriage. At the outset of the marriage the parties shared the same educational background and were both employed in thriving careers. However, after the wife had taken 4 years off to raise the parties' children, she returned to the workforce earning less than half of the husband's salary. The wife had proven herself capable of earning income and by gradually reducing support over four years, she would have the opportunity to re-establish herself.

In *Nock v. Nock* (1998), 43 R.F.L. (4th) 110 (Ont. Gen. Div.), the husband was found to be entitled to spousal support. After separation the husband lost his job and decided that retraining would be his best chance for re-entering the workforce. The husband suffered from a learning disability and would require tutorial assistance to complete his studies. The husband's inability to access the wife's income to cover living expenses while retraining constituted an economic hardship flowing directly from the marriage breakdown. The husband was entitled to periodic support reviewable in 18 months' time.

The promotion of self-sufficiency is but one factor to be considered in assessing a spouse's entitlement to support and may not be persuasive in the context of a long-term traditional marriage: *Prothman v. Prothman* (1993), 137 A.R. 241 (Q.B.).

Where the wife had earned $20,000 annually after separation, she was nevertheless found entitled to "top up" support. In the current economy, and considering the fact that the wife was resident in a large city, her current income amounted to subsistence and not self-sufficiency: *Morison v. Morison* (1993), 47 R.F.L. (3d) 34, 139 A.R. 124 (Q.B.).

In *Au v. Au* (1993), 47 R.F.L. (3d) 342 (Alta. Q.B.), the husband was ordered to pay to the wife indefinite periodic support upon termination of their 20-year traditional marriage. Given the wife's difficulty with English and the disadvantages resulting from the marriage, it was not reasonable to expect her to achieve any form of self-sufficiency within the foreseeable future.

Where the wife had returned to school and had obtained a part-time job, her application for support was dismissed. Given her part-time employment and her access to interest-free student loans, she was self-sufficient and could prove no need for support: *Huppe v. Huppe* (1990), 28 R.F.L. (3d) 70, 66 Man. R. (2d) 241 (Q.B.).

Pre Moge v. Moge Cases

The fact of marriage itself does not give rise to a spouse's right to support. Support is intended to return a spouse to the position in life that he or she would have enjoyed had his or her talents not been diverted by the marriage. Frequently, this end can be accomplished through retraining and re-entry into the workforce and by placing a time limit on the time needed, based on the facts of the case, to attain self-sufficiency: *Blais c. Blais* (1992), 38 R.F.L. (3d) 337 (N.B. C.A.). The objective of self-sufficiency is clearly qualified by Parliament's expression "insofar as practicable": *Linton v. Linton* (1988), 11 R.F.L. (3d) 444, 64 O.R. (2d) 18, 29 E.T.R. 14, 49 D.L.R. (4th) 278 (H.C.); affirmed (1990), 30 R.F.L. (3d) 1, 1 O.R. (3d) 1, 41 E.T.R. 85, 42 O.A.C. 328, 75 D.L.R. (4th) 637 (C.A.). See also *Row v. Row* (1991), 35 R.F.L. (3d) 237, 82 Alta. L.R. (2d) 173 (Q.B.).

In *Brace v. Brace* (1991), 35 R.F.L. (3d) 263, the Ontario Court of Appeal in upholding the High Court decision granting support for an indefinite term noted that "the wife's efforts to become self-sufficient should not impact negatively on her claim for support."

In *Matthews v. Matthews* (1991), 34 R.F.L. (3d) 201, 104 N.S.R. (2d) 140, 283 A.P.R. 140 (C.A.), the court was of the opinion that, considering the factors set out in s. 15 of the *Divorce Act* and, particularly, the respective means and needs of the parties, their circumstances and the existence of undisclosed income, the support order must be varied upwards to provide for the children. Spousal support was extended beyond the one year cut-off date in light of the difficulty of finding a job in the poor economy. If the wife remained unsuccessful in finding a job at the end of that time she could apply to vary to extend the time. However, as both parties have a joint responsibility to provide for the children pursuant to s. 15(8) and a court must promote self-sufficiency where practical, pursuant to s. 15(7), the wife could not continue to be unemployed and be granted support unless she could show that it was impossible to find employment.

In *Solomon v. Solomon* (1991), 35 R.F.L. (3d) 113, 106 N.S.R. (2d) 28, 288 A.P.R. 28 (C.A.), the wife was 35 and worked part-time in a day-care centre since a back injury prevented her from returning to her nursing career. She had custody of the parties' two children. The parties were married for approximately seven years. The wife had a duty to become self-sufficient in light of her age and the length of the marriage. The court, considering all the circumstances, upheld the decision that the husband should pay $1,400 per month for spousal and child support payments for two years and thereafter $1,800 per month.

Where the wife was in need after the parties' lengthy marriage but was not making best use of her talents, a modest support award made at trial was upheld on appeal: *Robinson v. Robinson* (1988), 13 R.F.L. (3d) 90, 82 N.S.R. (2d) 424, 207 A.P.R. 424 (C.A.).

See *Grohmann v. Grohmann* (1991), 37 R.F.L. 73 (B.C. C.A.), discussed at 15§8 Length of cohabitation.

Where the parties had separated after 25 years of marriage and the wife had devoted most of that time to maintaining the household and raising the children, her economic need was found to be causally connected to the marriage. Although the 48-year-old wife had retrained and secured full-time employment as a receptionist/secretary, it was unreasonable at this stage to expect her to become fully self-supporting: *LeMoine v. LeMoine* (1991), 118 N.B.R. (2d) 53, 296 A.P.R. 53 (Q.B.).

In *Rose v. Rose* (1990), 27 R.F.L. (3d) 267 (Alta. Q.B.), where the evidence indicated that the payee spouse would be able to complete her studies in two years, but that such a regime would be intellectually and emotionally draining, and make efforts to parent the child in her custody difficult, and so discouraging and disruptive to the wife's life as to make hope of self-sufficiency an unrealistic goal, the court ordered spousal support for three years.

In *Stunt v. Stunt* (1990), 30 R.F.L. (3d) 353 (Ont. Gen. Div.), the court awarded the wife reasonable support for two years where the failure of the parties' marriage and the wife's response to that failure adversely effected her career but she could become self-sufficient.

Where the husband's convincing of the wife to move had cost her over $22,000 in lost seniority benefits, her application for support was refused in subsequent divorce proceedings. As the wife had re-established a stable career and was now earning more than the husband, there was no basis for an award: *Jukosky v. Jukosky* (1990), 31 R.F.L. (3d) 117 (Ont. Gen. Div.).

The principle of spousal self-sufficiency should be given a restrictive interpretation in cases of long-term traditional marriages where a spouse is unable to achieve financial independence. In such cases, it cannot be relied upon as a ground for reducing or terminating spousal support: *Matthews v. Matthews* (1990), 29 R.F.L. (3d) 381 (B.C.C.A.).

Where the wife was not self-sufficient despite the fact that she had worked throughout the marriage, the husband was ordered to pay support to her for two years to permit her to complete a nursing course. The *Divorce Act* recognizes spousal responsibility to promote economic self-sufficiency of the other spouse: *Giddings v. Giddings* (1989), 100 N.B.R. (2d) 224, 252 A.P.R. 224 (Q.B.).

Where the wife's nursing skills had not been eroded by the marriage and where she could expect shortly to be self-sufficient through upgrading and a substantial property settlement, her application for support was refused: *Motz v. Motz* (1989), 22 R.F.L. (3d) 238, 99 A.R. 339 (Q.B.).

Where the wife had been employed as a secretary throughout the marriage, it was found not to be reasonable to expect the husband to finance her retraining as a nurse after the parties' separation. The wife was accordingly allowed spousal support for a period of five months only: *Droit de la famille — 1236*, [1989] R.D.F. 241 (C.S. Qué.).

In *Droit de la famille — 1229*, [1989] R.D.F. 152 (C.S. Qué.), the court awarded support to the wife despite the fact that the parties had been separated for over 10 years. The wife had attempted self-sufficiency but a decline in her health had prevented her from working, with the result that the court was unable to conclude that she could be self-sufficient.

Where the wife wished to resume her education and retrain, but the husband earned insufficient funds to support two households, it was held that the wife was required for the time being to forego retraining and seek work: *Norlander v. Norlander* (1989), 21 R.F.L. (3d) 317 (Sask. Q.B.).

Where the wife had incurred debts after separation to upgrade her skills and had achieved self-sufficiency, it was held that the husband should contribute to her self-sufficiency expenses through a limited term support order, despite her current lack of need: *Scobie v. Scobie* (1989), 21 R.F.L. (3d) 447 (Sask. Q.B.).

In *Longmuir v. Longmuir* (1989), 21 R.F.L. (3d) 151, 59 Man. R. (2d) 122 (Q.B.), the fact that the 48-year-old wife lacked work experience did not excuse her from attempting to achieve self-sufficiency. Accordingly, she was awarded periodic support which was subject to review by the court in one year's time.

Where during the three years after the parties' separation the wife made no real effort to re-enter the work force but was content to live on the proceeds of an interim support award, her application for support in divorce proceedings was refused. Her conduct was not consistent with her argument that she was unable to support herself: *Picciano v. Picciano* (1989), 22 R.F.L. (3d) 196 (Man. Q.B.).

Where the wife's lifestyle and income were consistent with those enjoyed prior to marriage, her application for support was dismissed. Further, as the husband lacked the means to pay and as the wife had previously released her support rights in an agreement prior to a brief reconciliation, support was not appropriate: *Mueller v. Mueller* (1992), 39 R.F.L. (3d) 328 (B.C. S.C.)

Where the wife had moved from Czechoslovakia to Canada to marry, but the marriage disintegrated very quickly, she was awarded support for a six-month period only. Although the wife had made no effort to achieve self-sufficiency in Canada, there was employment for her in Czechoslovakia. The six-month period would allow the wife to plan for her future and to make the appropriate arrangements: *Sadilkova v. Sadilkova* (1991), 38 R.F.L. (3d) 441 (B.C. S.C.).

In *Hayes v. Hayes* (1991), 34 R.F.L. (3d) 274 (B.C. S.C.), the court was of the opinion that in order to be entitled to spousal support, an applicant must satisfy the court that she is taking reasonable steps to achieve financial independence. Where the wife wished to give up her present job to complete her educational qualifications to become a teacher and the evidence showed that she was likely to obtain this type of employment, she met the onus and was awarded support during her retraining period. In the event that she did not obtain employment when her course ended, the spousal support would be continued. The wife's use of the proceeds from her share of the family assets to purchase a smaller home for herself and the parties' two children was reasonable as she had reduced accommodation costs. The proceeds need not be used to finance her retraining program.

In *Rodrigues v. Rodrigues* (1990), 30 R.F.L. (3d) 231 (Ont. Gen. Div.), the wife was awarded periodic support despite the fact that she had been employed throughout the marriage. The wife could not be viewed as a "career woman" and realistically required support.

In *Elsom v. Elsom* (1987), 10 R.F.L. (3d) 234 (B.C. S.C.), it was found that the wife had no obligation to become self-supporting given her husband's considerable assets and the fact that she had remained in the home during the marriage to raise the parties' child.

The duty of a spouse to become self-sufficient must be considered in the context of each individual case. The duty is extinguished only in the face of clear evidence of a spouse's inability to become self-supporting: *Rednall v. Rednall* (1986), 4 R.F.L. (3d) 337 (B.C. S.C.).

The principle of spousal self-sufficiency is to be given a restrictive interpretation in the case of traditional long-term marriages where the spouse in need has sacrificed a career for the family and is unlikely ever to achieve full economic independence: *Harris v. Harris* (1992), 40 R.F.L. (3d) 253 (B.C. S.C.).

In *Fogel v. Fogel* (1976), 24 R.F.L. 18 (Ont. H.C.); affirmed (1979), 9 R.F.L. (2d) 55 (Ont. C.A.), the wife's claim for maintenance was denied as the husband had been awarded custody of the children, the marriage had been of brief duration and the evidence established that the wife was able to support herself adequately. See also *Biscutti v. Biscutti* (1977), 4 R.F.L. (2d) 60 (Ont. H.C.).

In *Fahr v. Fahr* (1986), 50 Sask. R. 55 (Q.B.), the wife's claim for maintenance was refused in light of the substantial capital assets she had received upon the division of the matrimonial property and because her training as a registered nurse would allow her to become self-sufficient.

In *Cherney v. Cherney* (1986), 51 Sask. R. 158 (Q.B.), the petitioner wife was ordered, in the course of quantifying her support entitlement, to deregister her R.R.S.P. in order to increase her income.

Where the mother had supported her son for eight years after the parties' separation without any contribution from the father and at the hearing of the divorce petition she had refused to disclose her assets, no order for child support was made: *Basarowich (Bouchard) v. Basarowich* (1985), 49 R.F.L. (2d) 59 (Man. Q.B.).

See also *Gillis v. Gillis* (1984), 40 R.F.L. (2d) 145 (Man. Q.B.); *Hanuse v. Hanuse* (1984), 40 R.F.L. (2d) 250 (B.C. S.C.); *Singleton v. Singleton* (1982), 28 R.F.L. (2d) 39 (B.C. S.C.); *Forster v. Forster* (1981), 24 R.F.L. (2d) 99, 31 B.C.L.R. 105 (S.C.); *Bozyk v. Bozyk* (1980), 18 R.F.L. (2d) 329, 6 Sask. R. 36 (Q.B.); *Isailovic v. Isailovic* (1976), 25 R.F.L. 391 at 394 (B.C. S.C.); *Siemieniuk v. Siemieniuk* (1975), 24 R.F.L. 263 (Ont. H.C.).

15§35 — Economist's reports

In *Elliot v. Elliot* (1993), 48 R.F.L. (3d) 237, 15 O.R. (3d) 265 (C.A.); reversing in part (1992), 42 R.F.L. (3d) 7, 95 D.L.R. (4th) 614 (Ont. U.F.C.); leave to appeal refused (1994), 3 R.F.L. (4th) 290 (note), 18 O.R. (3d) xvi (note), 112 D.L.R. (4th) vii (note) (S.C.C.), the court struck on appeal an order requiring the husband to pay lump sum support as compensation to the wife for surrendering her career during the marriage. The order had been based solely on an economist's report which specified the wife's loss of future income because of the marriage but totally disregarded the husband's lack of ability to pay. Further, the report considered the effect of only one decision made during the marriage, instead of balancing the advantages and disadvantages accruing to both parties as a result of the marriage relationship. See also *Petley-Jones v. Petley-Jones* (1993), 48 R.F.L. (3d) 166 (B.C. S.C.) in which the court also refused to award lump sum support based upon an economist's report, citing the number of contingencies inherent in the statistical analysis.

In *Picard v. Picard* (2001), 18 R.F.L. (5th) 352, 2001 CarswellOnt 2111, [2001] O.J. No. 2299 (S.C.J.), the court dismissed the husband's application to strike an affidavit prepared by the wife's accountant estimating the husband's income for the purposes of a temporary spousal and child support application. The accountant had carefully set out in detail his assumptions and the factual background he relied upon as well as the source of information. Accordingly, the court could determine the appropriate weight to be given to this piece of evidence without abdicating its responsibility to make findings of fact. The accountant's opinion amounted to evidence, it decided nothing and ultimately the court could accept or reject it, in whole or in part.

15§36 — Tax consequences of support orders

It is the responsibility of counsel to place before the court the information necessary to calculate the tax implications to both parties of a particular support award: *Millar v. Millar* (1996), 22 R.F.L. (4th) 238, 139 Nfld. & P.E.I.R. 91, 433 A.P.R. 91 (P.E.I. C.A.).

An unsigned draft separation agreement is insufficient to support an alimony deduction under the *Income Tax Act*: *McIntosh v. R.*, 5 R.F.L. (5th) 417, [2000] 2 C.T.C. 2423, 2000 CarswellNat 221 (T.C.C. [Informal Procedure]).

Section 60.1 (2) of the *Income Tax Act*, R.S.C. 1985, c. 1 (5th Supp.) creates a presumption that payments made by one spouse to a third party on behalf of the other spouse constitute a periodic payment to be used at the beneficiary's discretion, and is therefore properly characterized as a "support amount": *Veilleux c. R.*, 27 R.F.L. (5th) 450, 2002 CarswellNat 1083, 2002 CarswellNat 2577, 2002 CAF 201, 2002 FCA 201 (Fed. C.A.).

Where the husband had been ordered to pay interim spousal support in the form of monthly mortgage payments, subsequent amending orders that deemed the payments retroactively to be "maintenance" for the income tax purposes were found to render the amounts deductible by the husband in *Larsson v. R.*, 25 R.F.L. (4th) 384, [1996] 3 C.T.C. 2430 (T.C.C.); affirmed (1997), 216 N.R. 315, 35 R.F.L. (4th) 62 (Fed. C.A.).

In *Low v. Robinson* (2000), 7 R.F.L. (5th) 148, 79 Alta. L.R. (3d) 137, [2000] 7 W.W.R. 509 (Alta. Q.B.); additional reasons to (2000), 4 R.F.L. (5th) 368, 76 Alta. L.R. (3d) 238, [2000] 4 W.W.R. 663 (Alta. Q.B.), the spousal support paid by the husband was found not to be tax deductible in his hands. Although the husband was ordered to pay periodic support for 9 months, the court further ordered that he pay it in a lump sum given his limited cash flow. Revenue Canada, in its interpretation of "periodic payments" had stated that an amount paid as a single lump sum in place of several periodic payments not yet due did not qualify for deduction.

In *Simpson v. R.*, 25 R.F.L. (4th) 443, [1996] 2 C.T.C. 2687 (T.C.C.), a jointly signed letter of instruction to the wife's solicitor to prepare the parties' separation agreement was found to constitute "a written agreement" within the meaning of the *Income Tax Act*. The fact that the wife had written "without prejudice" on the document did not change its character. Accordingly, support paid by the husband pursuant to the letter was properly deducted by him.

Spouses are entitled to enter into arrangements between themselves which effectively set aside the application of ss. 56(1)(b) and 60(b) of the *Income Tax Act*, R.S.C. 1985, c. 1 (5th Supp): *Pelletier c. R.* (1994), 4 R.F.L. (4th) 287, [1995] 1 C.T.C. 2327 (T.C.C.).

In *Godinek v. Godinek* (1992), 40 R.F.L. (3d) 78 (Ont. Gen. Div.), it was ordered that any money that the husband was to give to the wife over and above his required support obligation should also qualify as tax deductible support.

Where in anticipation of separation and divorce, the husband had deposited funds in a joint bank account and the wife, over four months, had withdrawn in excess of $4,000, the husband was not allowed for tax purposes to treat the funds withdrawn as support. At the time, the husband's support obligation was moral rather than legal and absent an agreement or court order he could not properly deduct the amount: *Teevens v. R.*, 3 R.F.L. (4th) 212, [1994] 1 C.T.C. 2848 (T.C.C.).

A transfer of property in settlement of support arrears may be properly deducted from the transferor's income pursuant to ss. 60(b) or (c) of the *Income Tax Act*. Cash payment is not required provided that an agreement or binding determination of the cash value of the transferred property exists: *Gibson v. R.* (1994), 5 R.F.L. (4th) 209, 95 D.T.C. 749, [1996] 1 C.T.C. 2105 (T.C.C.).

Where the husband, pursuant to an amending separation agreement, conveyed the family home to the wife and agreed to pay half of the mortgage payments until the children completed their education, the payments were properly treated as child support and should be included in the wife's income for tax purposes: *Jasper v. Minister of National Revenue* (1994), 7 R.F.L. (4th) 187, 81 F.T.R. 258, [1994] 2 C.T.C. 309 (Fed. T.D.).

In *Nelson v. R.* (1993), 1 R.F.L. (4th) 1, 94 D.T.C. 1003, (sub nom. *Nelson v. Canada)* [1994] 1 C.T.C. 2031, a letter from the wife's solicitor to the husband specifying a proposed settlement of all outstanding issues between the parties, including spousal support, was found to constitute a "separation agreement" for the purposes of the *Income Tax Act*. The husband, who was not represented, had written his acceptance of the proposed settlement and had signed and returned it to the wife's solicitor, evidencing the parties' mutual intention to live separate and apart and to be bound by the terms of the agreement.

A support order in which the amount payable was stipulated as "excluding tax" does not prevent the Minister of National Revenue from treating as taxable the amount received by the payee spouse. If the intent of the order was that the specified amount was to be received after taxes, the base amount should have been grossed up accordingly: *Arshinoff v. R.* (1994), 3 R.F.L. (4th) 221, [1994] 1 C.T.C. 2850 (T.C.C.).

In *Low v. Robinson*, 7 R.F.L. (5th) 148, 79 Alta. L.R. (3d) 137, [2000] 7 W.W.R. 509, (sub nom. *S.E.L. v. J.M.R.)* 258 A.R. 201 at 235, 2000 CarswellAlta 336 (Q.B.); additional reasons to 4 R.F.L. (5th) 368, 76 Alta. L.R. (3d) 238, [2000] 4 W.W.R. 663, (sub nom. *S.E.L. v. J.M.R.)* 258 A.R. 201, 2000 CarswellAlta 68 (Q.B.), the spousal support paid by the husband was found not to be tax deductible in his hands. Although the husband was ordered to pay periodic support for nine months, the court further ordered that he pay it in a lump sum given his limited cash flow. Revenue Canada, in its interpretation of "periodic payments" had stated that an amount paid as a single lump sum in place of several periodic payments not yet due did not qualify for deduction.

Where the parties' incomes are roughly equivalent, each should bear one-half of the costs of child rearing and claim the benefit of one-half of the equivalent-to-married and child tax credit and deductions: *Almeida v. Almeida* (1995), 14 R.F.L. (4th) 88, 170 A.R. 244 (Alta. Q.B.).

If a court intends to invoke the remedial power in s. 60(1)(3) of the *Income Tax Act*, it should follow the wording of the provision as closely as possible and should indicate the amount paid in the taxation year or the immediately preceding taxation year. In addition, it should clearly provide that these amounts are to be considered as having been paid and received pursuant to the order or written agreement: *Pallotto v. R.* (1993), 48 R.F.L. (3d) 116 (T.C.C.). See also: *Family Law Act of Ontario*, vol. 2, Income Tax Aspects of Income and Property Sharing: $1, Alimony and Maintenance.

Money spent on legal fees to establish a support right under the *Divorce Act* is not deductible by the payee in calculating his or her income for tax purposes: *Meisels v. R.*, 50 R.F.L. (3d) 45, [1993] 2 C.T.C. 3108 (T.C.C.).

The Court, in a divorce action, lacks jurisdiction to make an order granting retroactive tax deductibility under the *Income Tax Act* for support payments. Furthermore, retroactivity of tax treatment under the *Divorce Act* can extend only back to the date of the divorce petition: *Short v. Short* (1996), 21 R.F.L. (4th) 429 (B.C. S.C.).

In *Dunn v. Dunn* (1995), 14 R.F.L. (4th) 50 (N.S. S.C.), the wife was ordered to pay child support to the custodial husband in the form of a housing allowance which was to be used for accommodation of the husband and the children. The allowance was to go towards rent or a mortgage, depending on the home in which the children resided, and was to be neither tax-deductible for the wife nor taxable for the husband.

The court lacks jurisdiction to declare that a support order is not subject to tax consequences. The court may, however, decline to make an interim support order for a brief time to allow the payor the opportunity to make voluntary payments that will not attract tax consequences: *Green v. Green* (1993), 1 R.F.L. (4th) 130 (B.C. S.C.).

15§37 — Standard of living

Insofar as economic circumstances permit, the Act seeks to put the remainder of the family in as close a position as possible to the household before the marriage breakdown: per Madame Justice L'Heureux-Dubé in *Moge v. Moge*, [1992] 3 S.C.R. 813, 43 R.F.L. (3d) 345 at 385–386, [1993] 1 W.W.R. 481, 145 N.R. 1, 81 Man. R. (2d) 161, 99 D.L.R. (4th) 456. She continues at p. 390 (R.F.L.):

> Although the doctrine of spousal support which focuses on equitable sharing does not guarantee to either party the standard of living enjoyed during the marriage, this standard is far from irrelevant to support entitlement. Furthermore, great disparities in the standard of living that would be experienced by spouses in the absence of support are often a revealing indication of the economic disadvantages inherent in the role assumed by one party. As marriage should be regarded as a joint endeavour, the longer the relationship endures, the closer the economic union, the greater will be the presumptive claim to equal standards of living upon its dissolution.

In *Tauber v Tauber* (2003), 2003 CarswellOnt 1009, 34 R.F.L. (5th) 450, 64 O.R. (3d) 229, 170 O.A.C. 1, 225 D.L.R. (4th) 186 (C.A.), the appellate court upheld a lump sum payment of $500,000 for spousal support. The payment would assist the wife to provide a lifestyle comparable to the one which the child had enjoyed when he lived with the parents, a lifestyle to which the husband was readily able to contribute. The payment would enable the wife to enhance her self-sufficiency and help her to purchase a permanent home for herself and the parties' child. While the amount was a substantial one, it should be seen in the context of the husband's assets which were worth between $19 and $20 million, his undisputed ability to pay, and the parties' lifestyle during th marriage.

It is inconsistent with the overall scheme of the *Divorce Act* that economic hardship should be equated with a subsistence standard of living: *Giraud v. Giraud* (1997), 34

R.F.L. (4th) 255 (B.C. C.A.). According to dictionary definitions what is economic hardship, like what is need, will vary with the circumstances of the parties.

Support at such a level as to support the marital lifestyle should only be ordered where the means are clearly available: *Escaravage v. Escaravage* (1995), 14 R.F.L. (4th) 256, 59 B.C.A.C. 113, 98 W.A.C. 113 (C.A.).

The appropriate standard of living for a dependent spouse in a traditional marriage is, according to the court in *Heinemann v. Heinemann* (1989), 20 R.F.L. (3d) 236, 91 N.S.R. (2d) 136, 233 A.P.R. 136, 60 D.L.R. (4th) 648 (C.A.), the approximate standard she would have had if she had followed her own career objectives rather than those of the marriage. However, it should not be wholly unrelated to that which she enjoyed prior to the dissolution of the marriage.

In a more traditional decision concerning a marriage of 46 years, the appellate division of the Nova Scotia Supreme Court decided in *Lynk v. Lynk* (1989), 21 R.F.L. (3d) 337, 92 N.S.R. (2d) 1, 237 A.P.R. 1 (C.A.), that the standard of living to which the wife was entitled, having regard to the husband's ability to pay, was equal to that which she would have enjoyed had this long-lasting marriage continued through the husband's retirement years.

In *Reinhardt v. Reinhardt* (2004), 8 R.F.L. (6th) 340, 2004 CarswellOnt 3275 (S.C.J.), the wife was awarded periodic spousal support although she was employed full-time. The husband's annual salary was considerably greater than the wife's, who accordingly had suffered an economic disadvantage because of the loss to the standard of living she enjoyed as a beneficiary of combined incomes. See also *Sweeney v. Sweeney* (2004), 8 R.F.L. (6th) 424, 2004 CarswellNB 363, 2004 NBQB 267 (Q.B.) in which the loss of a standard of living was also a factor in awarding spousal support to the wife.

Where the wife chose to remain in a large, five-bedroom home and eat all of her meals in restaurants, she could not realistically expect the husband to subsidize the same through spousal support, despite the affluence of both parties and lavish lifestyle that they enjoyed together: *Cook v. Cook*, 27 R.F.L. (5th) 12, 2002 CarswellNS 198, 2002 NSSC 124, 204 N.S.R. (2d) 167, 639 A.P.R. 167 (S.C.).

Where as a result of the husband's car business the wife had habitually had the use of a luxury car, the court rejected the husband's application to replace the vehicle currently in the wife's possession with one of significantly less value. The husband could not attempt, through court orders, to create a "new, less lavish reality" for the wife, especially when his own would significantly increase if he was not required to maintain hers: *Bennett v. Bennett* (2001), 13 R.F.L. (5th) 325, 2001 CarswellOnt 168, O.J. No. 224 (S.C.J.).

In a long-term traditional marriage where the wife has generally fulfilled the role of caregiver for the family while the husband has developed a career, there is a strong presumption that both parties should share an equal standard of living upon dissolution of the marriage: *Labron v. Labron* (1996), 21 R.F.L. (4th) 385, 183 A.R. 251 (Q.B.).

Where the wife had sufficient income to support herself in a style which would have been sufficient for most Canadians, she had been used throughout the parties' 25-year marriage to a lavish lifestyle. She was therefore found entitled to periodic support up until the husband's retirement: *Droit de la famille — 2132*, [1995] R.D.F. 116, 11 C.C.P.B 272 (C.S. Qué).

Where the husband had, throughout the parties' 23-year traditional marriage, imposed a frugal lifestyle on the family in order to accumulate savings, the quantum of spousal support to which the wife was entitled was not limited to a continuation of that lifestyle: *Katay v. Katay* (1995), 168 A.R. 31 (Q.B.).

Support is awarded to redress economic disadvantages attributable to the marriage and not to guarantee a continuation of the marital lifestyle: *Caspick v. Caspick* (1990), 27 R.F.L. (3d) 337, 106 N.B.R. (2d) 249, 265 A.P.R. 249, 71 D.L.R. (4th) 411 (C.A.); application for reconsideration refused (1990), 27 R.F.L. (3d) 337n (N.B. C.A.); leave to appeal refused (1991), 29 R.F.L. (3d) xxxvi (note) (S.C.C.).

In *Linton v. Linton* (1990), 30 R.F.L. (3d) 1, 1 O.R. (3d) 1, 42 O.A.C. 328, 75 D.L.R. (4th) 637 (C.A.), the court was of the view that the appropriate standard of living is a reasonable standard of living, having in mind the circumstances of the marriage. Where there is a long marriage and an ability to pay support according to this standard, reasonable standard of living should be assessed in the context of the marital standard of living. The amount to be awarded should take into account the effect of the property disposition. See also *Row v. Row* (1991), 35 R.F.L. (3d) 237 (Atla. Q.B.).

The Ontario Court of Appeal in *Marshall v. Marshall* (1988), 13 R.F.L. (3d) 337 (Ont. C.A.); leave to appeal refused (1988), 31 O.A.C. 160 (note) (S.C.C.), affirmed a decision which had stated that, while the wife was not expected to retain the standard of living which she had had before separation, she was intended to have a reasonable and adequate standard of living. The majority of the Court of Appeal was of the opinion that because of inflation, which resulted in a decline in the value of money between the date of the separation and the date of the trial, the consequent decline in the wife's own income was a radical change in her circumstances generated by her previous pattern of dependency and aggravated by her fragile health. The required causal connection between the hardship experienced by the wife and the dependent relationship arising from the marriage was established. There was no error in principle in increasing the wife's support from $728 per month to $1,228 per month.

In *Bast v. Bast* (1988), 13 R.F.L. (3d) 98 (Ont. H.C.), the court commented that the wife, who was in her mid-fifties and who had been married for 21 years, was unlikely to achieve, through her own economic efforts, the kind of lifestyle she had enjoyed during the marriage. Salhany L.J.S.C. stated that this fact was not the husband's fault. The court was of the view that an order for support should attempt to promote self-sufficiency and, at the same time, recognize that the wife would need a period of time to gear down from her former standard of living. Support was continued for another two years; support would therefore end three years after the divorce.

15§38 — Equalization of incomes

In *Martin v. Martin* (2004), 12 R.F.L. (6th) 415, 2004 CarswellOnt 5438 (Ont. S.C.J.); additional reasons at (2005), 2005 CarswellOnt 1437 (Ont. S.C.J.); affirmed (2006), 2006 CarswellOnt 4876 (Ont. C.A.), the court dismissed the wife's claim for an almost equal share in the husband's income for spousal support. The husband had earned a substantial income as a professional hockey coach and equating the parties contribution to the marriage to earned income ignored the husband's talent.

Economic disadvantage or the sacrifice of a career by one spouse, in conjunction with the advancement of the other's career, will not justify the equalization of the parties' incomes through a support award: *Chalmers v. Chalmers* (1994), 2 R.F.L. (4th) 446 (B.C. S.C.).

The *Divorce Act* does not require that spouses' incomes be equalized to alleviate economic disadvantage arising out of roles adopted by the parties in the marriage. The quantum of support should be determined by reference to the factors specified in the Act: *Chalmers v. Chalmers*, above.

15§39 — Relationship of spousal support to child support

Subsections 15.3(1) and (2) of the *Divorce Act* give express priority to an application for child support over an application for spousal support. In keeping with the general tenor of the amendments, the *Guidelines* amount would be ordered for child support even if the amount left over would be inadequate for spousal support. There would be no *pro rata* allocation of the available fund between the two applicants with both receiving less than they need. The child would receive full share, and the spouse less than full share in the allocation.

Voluntary payments to children cannot take precedence over spousal support in circumstances where the children are living independently and earning income: *Tedham v. Tedham*, 2005 CarswellBC 2346, 20 R.F.L. (6th) 217, 47 B.C.L.R. (4th) 254, 2005 BCCA 502 (B.C. C.A.); additional reasons at 2005 CarswellBC 2699, 2005 BCCA 553, 47 B.C.L.R. (4th) 276 (B.C. C.A.).

In *Peters v. Peters*, 2002 CarswellNS 389, 2002 NSSF 40 (N.S. S.C.), the husband was ordered to pay an amount of spousal support that was less than that to which the payee spouse was entitled, because of the husband's obligations to pay child support. Under section 15.3 of the *Divorce Act*, the priority of the child support payments requires the court to make an order for spousal support "less than it otherwise would have been". In the *Peters* case, if the husband paid the full amount of child and spousal support, he would be in a deficit position. The wife was disabled. She was awarded $1,500 per month, rather than the $2,500 to which she was entitled. The wife could revisit the issue of spousal support, if the husband's obligation to pay child support was decreased or terminated.

In *Y. (H.) v. Y. (D.)* (1999), 49 R.F.L. (4th) 450, 1999 CarswellPEI 43, 175 Nfld. & P.E.I.R. 85, 537 A.P.R. 85 (P.E.I. T.D. [In Chambers]), the husband was not allowed to set-off his monthly child support obligation against a spousal support over-payment owed by the wife. Child support and spousal support obligations should not be intermingled. It is unfair to the child and contrary to the spirit of the legislation to excuse a parent from paying child support on the basis of dealings between the spouses.

In *Kaderly v. Kaderly* (1997), 1997 CarswellPEI 85, [1997] P.E.I.J. No. 74 (P.E.I. T.D.), Jenkins J. stated that while section 15.3(1) of the *Divorce Act* stated that child support is to take priority over spousal support, Parliament did not intend this to operate so as to provide everything a child may need or which may benefit a child and leave the mother, who is a spouse, destitute. For purposes of the *Guidelines*, the payor earned $111,000. He was ordered to pay $850 per month in spousal support until October 31, 2007, subject to specific conditions for variation and $1 per year from November 2007 to October 2012. He was also ordered to pay child support to the mother of $1,800 per month and upon the child enrolling in university, the father was instead required to pay the portion of child support applicable to that child, i.e., $450 per month for the 8-month period from September to May, directly to that child or to the university in which the child was enrolled.

In *Bourque v. Phillips* (2000), 2000 CarswellNB 17, (sub nom. *R.B. v. J.P.)* 223 N.B.R. (2d) 242, 572 A.P.R. 242 (N.B. Q.B.), an application for child support by the child's grandmother against his biological parents was successfully opposed by the father. The father pleaded undue hardship resulting from his obligations under a separation agreement for the support of his spouse and two children of his second marriage. The court was satisfied that the payment of support for three children (total combined child and spousal support payments of approximately $24,000 per year) on an income of $34,000 per year was "excessive" or "disproportionate" and consequently permitted the father to succeed on his claim up to and inclusive of the date when he was no longer required to pay spousal support for his second wife.

Where the husband lacked sufficient funds to pay both child and spousal support, it was held that the needs of the child must take priority: *Hiller v. Hiller* (1995), 167 A.R. 81, 1995 CarswellAlta 618 (Alta. Q.B.).

In determining child support, the children's needs should be given priority over those of the parents: *King v. King* (1990), 25 R.F.L. (3d) 338, 95 N.S.R. (2d) 409, 251 A.P.R. 409, 1990 CarswellNS 39 (N.S. T.D.). In this case, the children's needs were paramount to those of the father, the payor parent. The wife had not made out any case for lump sum maintenance. The application of the husband for reduced periodic maintenance was refused. The court held that the husband could elect either to continue as he had in the past to pay the amount of $750 per month tax-free to his wife, or to pay an equivalent amount with respect to which the wife would pay the income tax.

In *R. v. R.* (2000), 10 R.F.L. (5th) 88, 2000 CarswellOnt 2744, [2000] O.J. No. 2830 (Ont. S.C.J.); additional reasons at (January 30, 2001), Doc. Hamilton D752/98, 2001 CarswellOnt 797 (Ont. S.C.J.), the court took into account that the wife would benefit indirectly from substantial child support payments in quantifying her own spousal support entitlement

In *Merali v. Merali* (2002), 27 R.F.L. (5th) 363, 2002 CarswellBC 989, 2002 BCSC 529 (B.C. S.C.), the court, in quantifying the wife's spousal support entitlement, considered the fact that the custodial husband's childcare expenses were likely to reduce considerably over the next 5 years, given the ages of the children.

15§40 — Conduct

Section 15.2(5) provides that in making an order, or an interim order for spousal support, "the court shall not take into consideration any misconduct of a spouse in relation to the marriage."

In *Leskun v. Leskun*, 2006 CarswellBC 1492, 2006 SCC 25, [2006] 1 S.C.R. 25 (S.C.C.), the court held that while misconduct is not a relevant consideration in determining support, the consequences of misconduct are relevant considerations. The matter of misconduct cannot be viewed in isolation. The lower court judgment to continue spousal support should be sustained on the basis of factors other than misconduct. In this particular case, the wife had various family difficulties. In addition, she and her family had medical problems, all of which were exacerbated by the breakdown of the marriage. Further, the narrowness of the wife's work experience and the difficulty for someone approaching 60 years of age to re-enter the work force after a lengthy absence with few marketable skills outside of her former job, which had been eliminated, were factors in determining whether she could support herself.

Mr. Justice Binnie delivered the unanimous judgment of a seven-member panel of the Supreme Court of Canada, which affirmed the Court of Appeal decision to continue the wife's spousal support. The parties had been married for 20 years. The wife worked most of the marriage and assisted the husband financially in obtaining his education. She had a serious back surgery. Shortly before separation, she learned that her employment would be terminated. The wife had expected to move with the husband to Chicago, but he informed her that she would not be going, and that he wanted a divorce, as he wished to marry someone else. Southin J.A., in the British Columbia Court of Appeal, described the wife as "bitter to the point of obsession with [the husband's] misconduct and in consequence [she] has been unable to make a new life. Her life [was] this litigation."

In *Imani v. Imani* (1999), 48 R.F.L. (4th) 118, 1999 CarswellBC 1369 (B.C. S.C.), the wife's application for spousal support upon termination of her 2-year marriage was dismissed. Although it appeared that the husband entered the marriage solely to facilitate his immigration to Canada and left the wife for no reason when his status allowed him to work, the wife's income still exceeded that of the husband. The husband's apparent misconduct could not be considered

Although a judge may not properly consider marital fault in fixing support, he or she is entitled to take into account the economic effects of one spouse's conduct on the other: *Martin v. Martin* (1993), 50 R.F.L. (3d) 77, 113 Sask. R. 316, 52 W.A.C. 316, 1999 CarswellSask 57 (C.A.)

Where a spouse repudiates the spousal relationship to live with someone else, that fact alone does not disentitle that spouse to support if need is established: *Robichaud v. Robichaud* (1988), 17 R.F.L. (3d) 285, 1988 CarswellBC 608 (B.C. C.A.)

In determining support, s. 5(6) [now s. 15.2(5)] prevents a trial judge from taking into account the conduct of the parties (such as finding on the basis of their conduct that the marriage from the outset was doomed to failure) in determining the amount of support: *Droit de la famille — 487* (1988), 15 R.F.L. (3d) 149 (Que. C.A.)

While according to s. 15(6) [now s. 15.2(5)], moral misconduct no longer results in financial punishment *per se*, nevertheless, where duplicitous conduct by one spouse to save his own ends leads to a quantifiable financial loss by the other spouse, a spousal support order should roughly compensate the wife for her loss of income: *Jukosky v. Jukosky* (1990), 31 R.F.L. (3d) 117, 1990 CarswellOnt 336 (Ont. Gen. Div.). However, spousal support was not awarded because the wife's career was stable and her disclosed income was higher than her husband's

In *Cole v. Cole* (1991), 91 Nfld. & P.E.I.R. 301, 286 A.P.R. 301, 1991 CarswellNfld 175 (Nfld. T.D.), the court refused the wife's application for support upon the failure of their 5-year marriage. She had made little effort to provide for herself since the separation and, furthermore, her lack of commitment had been largely responsible for the dissolution of the parties' relationship.

15§41 — Effects of property awards

Authors' Note: The *Advisory Guidelines* set out exceptions to the "with" and "without" child support formulas for calculating spousal support. These exceptions are:

1. the compensatory exception;
2. illness and disability;
3. debt payment;
4. prior support obligation; and
5. interim support — compelling financial circumstances.

The payment of an equalization payment is not one of the enumerated exceptions to the formula. However, in an article "The Advisory Guidelines One Year Later: Cases, Criticisms and Responses, Revisions" by Rollie Thompson and Carol Rogerson, the authors write that an additional exception to the formula might be found in situations where the spouse had significant assets or an unequal division of property. They write:

> A good example of [a] flexible approach would be our approach to the issue of an "exception" for high asset cases or cases where there is an unequal division of property. We say that there should not be an "automatic" exception for such cases, as the current case law is not clear whether spousal support should be reduced or refused just because of the property division (apart from any income issues). But it is clear that the property division may lead to a departure from the formula outcomes in any particular case. If both parties have high assets, a court may find no entitlement, as both parties are seen as self-sufficient. Or, if there is an unequal division of property based upon compensatory considerations, as occurs in B.C., again there may be a reduction or even elimination of spousal support in some cases. Most often, adjustments for property division can occur in locating the amount or duration within the ranges.

Where a property award has compensated the other spouse to some extent for the disadvantages she suffered as a result of the marriage and its breakdown, an award of spousal support, whether the *Advisory Guidelines* are taken into account or not, should be lower than it otherwise would have been: *Tedham v. Tedham*, 2005 CarswellBC 2346, 20 R.F.L. (6th) 217, 47 B.C.L.R. (4th) 254, 2005 BCCA 502 (B.C. C.A.); additional reasons at 2005 CarswellBC 2699, 2005 BCCA 553, 47 B.C.L.R. (4th) 276 (B.C. C.A.). The court considered the appropriate order for spousal support where there was a 16-year marriage and the court was utilizing the "without child support formula" which would yield a support order in the range of $6,300 to $8,500 per month with a duration of between 8 and 16 years, assuming the husband's income was in the range of $343,000 per year and the wife's was in the range of $30,000 per year. The court ordered indefinite spousal support of $6,000 per month, less than amounts provided in the range in the Advisory Guidelines since it held that an award must take into account the reapportionment of property ordered by the court.

The fact that a court has reapportioned property under section 65 of the *Family Relations Act* does not mean that there should not be an award of spousal support. That matter will be determined on the extent to which the reapportionment has adequately compensated for the economic dislocation caused to a spouse flowing from the marriage or its breakdown, and any continuing need the spouse may have for support: *Tedham v. Tedham*, 2005 CarswellBC 2346, 20 R.F.L. (6th) 217, 47 B.C.L.R. (4th) 254, 2005 BCCA 502 (B.C. C.A.); additional reasons at 2005 CarswellBC 2699, 2005 BCCA 553, 47 B.C.L.R. (4th) 276 (B.C. C.A.).

Allowing a spouse to reap benefits from the other spouse's pension twice, once through the division of matrimonial assets and secondly through spousal support, would be inequitable. To avoid double recovery, the focus for spousal support purposes, the focus should be on the position of the pension-holding spouse's income and assets that were not part of the equalization or division of matrimonial assets: *Boston v. Boston*, 17 R.F.L. (5th) 4, 2001 CarswellOnt 2432, 2001 CarswellOnt 2433, [2001] S.C.J. No. 45, 2001 SCC 43, 201 D.L.R. (4th) 1, 271 N.R. 248, 149 O.A.C. 50, 28 C.C.P.B. 17, REJB 2001-25002, C.E.B. & P.G.R. 8385 (headnote only), [2001] 2 S.C.R. 413 (S.C.C.).

In *Gregory v. Ball*, 9 R.F.L. (6th) 338, 2004 CarswellAlta 1450, 2004 ABQB 789 (Alta. Q.B.); reversed in part 2005 CarswellAlta 1526, 2005 ABCA 354 (Alta. C.A.) in part, the court refused the wife's application for unlimited spousal support upon the dissolution of the parties' 16-year marriage. Although the wife was not expected to earn income during the marriage, the husband did not discourage the wife from pursuing a career. Furthermore, the wife had received over $4 million on division of the parties' assets and was in a position to generate income.

In *N. (D.K.) v. O. (M.J.)*, 41 R.F.L. (5th) 142, 2003 CarswellBC 2290, 18 B.C.L.R. (4th) 247, 232 D.L.R. (4th) 323, 187 B.C.A.C. 129, 307 W.A.C. 129, 2003 BCCA 502 (B.C. C.A.), the wife was awarded spousal support despite the fact that she had waived her support rights by agreement. Although the reapportionment of family assets under the agreement went someway towards meeting the wife's needs, spousal support was also needed in the short term.

As a general rule, whenever practicable, the courts, for purposes of spousal support, should not resort to an asset such as a pension that has already been used in the division of property: *Chamberlain v. Chamberlain*, 36 R.F.L. (5th) 241, [2003] N.B.J. No. 168, 2003 CarswellNB 208, 2003 CarswellNB 209, 2003 NBCA 34, 226 D.L.R. (4th) 272 (N.B. C.A.).

Where the wife, as a result of a motor vehicle accident, had negotiated a settlement which guaranteed her a lifetime income indexed for inflation, she was found not to qualify for support. The settlement, combined with a property award weighted in her favour rendered support unnecessary: *Boel v. Boel* (1994), 4 R.F.L. (4th) 266, 95 B.C.L.R. (2d) 375, 45 B.C.A.C. 261, 72 W.A.C. 261, 1994 CarswellBC 387 (B.C. C.A.).

Where the wife had released all interest in the husband's pension, his continuing obligation to provide spousal support after his retirement did not offend the principle of "double dipping". The wife continued to experience economic hardship as the result of the marriage or its breakdown and she had a continuing need for support. Furthermore, the husband had the ability to pay and the wife had been responsible with her finances: *Bertrim v. Bertrim* (2004), 49 R.F.L. (5th) 1, 2004 CarswellOnt 10, 180 O.A.C. 372 (Ont. Div. Ct.).

Property and support issues should be dealt with separately in making orders in respect of either issue. First, property rights should be determined and then spousal and child support: *Hanna v. Hanna* (1994), 4 R.F.L. (4th) 148, 1994 CarswellNS 51 (N.S. C.A.).

In *Droit de la famille — 1990*, [1994] R.D.F. 463, EYB 1994-73357, 1994 CarswellQue 2062 (Que. S.C.), the wife was granted only limited term spousal support as the parties' marriage had lasted only 8 years, and was childless. Furthermore, the wife's share of family assets was sufficient to allow her time to find suitable employment.

In *Rosenau v. Rosenau*, 6 R.F.L. (6th) 372, 2004 CarswellSask 462, 2004 SKQB 275, 267 Sask. R. 1 (Sask. Q.B.), the husband was ordered to pay periodic spousal support decreasing over time in accordance with the percentage of the property judgment that was also payable over time to the wife.

Where the 44-year-old wife had received over $3,000,000 after division of the parties' assets, her claim for spousal support was dismissed. At the time of marriage the wife's assets had been minimal and she had benefited considerably from the marriage in terms of property acquisition. The wife, although she had not worked during the 9-year marriage, had marketable skills and her potential employment income, in combination with her investment income, was sufficient to meet her needs: *Hodgkinson v. Hodgkinson*, 44 R.F.L. (5th) 82, 2003 CarswellBC 2461, 2003 BCSC 1538, [2003] B.C.J. No. 2296 (B.C. S.C.).

In *Spiers v. Spiers* (2003), 48 R.F.L. (5th) 198, [2003] A.J. No. 1223, 2003 CarswellAlta 1413, 25 Alta. L.R. (4th) 131, 2003 ABQB 830, [2004] 9 W.W.R. 371 (Alta. Q.B.), it was held that the disadvantage suffered by the wife as a result of the breakdown of the marriage did not obligate the husband to ensure that the wife's matrimonial property package retain its purchasing power.

Where it was assumed that the husband would retire with full pension within 3 years, the wife's spousal support was to be subject to review at that time. The wife would receive a substantial lump sum when the pension was divided and it would be unfair to require the husband to continue to pay support from the half pension remaining to him: *Pacheco v. Pacheco* (2001), 13 R.F.L. (5th) 442, 2001 CarswellOnt 798, [2001] O.J. No. 1122 (Ont. S.C.J.).

On an application for review of spousal support payable to the wife in *Metzner v. Metzner* (2001), 2001 CarswellBC 1923, 2001 BCSC 1288, 22 R.F.L. (5th) 149 (B.C. S.C. [In Chambers]), the court awarded the wife additional spousal support of $5,000 a month for a further 2 years to complete her law degree in order to assuage continuing need and to reflect the husband's ability to pay, even though the wife had received $7,000 in spousal support for 7 years, which, according to the order, was to cease after the 7-year period. She had also left the marriage with substantial assets worth $817,000. The husband's income had increased from $250,000 at the time of separation to over $1,700,000 for purposes of the Child Support Guidelines at the time of the application.

In *Loiselle v. Loiselle* (2000), 12 R.F.L. (5th) 400, 2000 CarswellOnt 3488 (Ont. S.C.J.), the wife was awarded monthly periodic spousal support of $1,500, which was to reduce to $900 once she had received her equalization entitlement.

In *Bailey v. Plaxton*, 2000 CarswellOnt 1194, [2000] O.J. No. 1187, 47 O.R. (3d) 593, 6 R.F.L. (5th) 29, [2000] O.T.C. 243 (Ont. S.C.J.), the court, on an interim application ordered the husband to pay increased spousal support of $5,000, in the face of a separation agreement, which provided for spousal support for 3 years ending in 1990, and despite the fact that the wife had received a large capital payment. The husband had argued that the wife's current financial problems were the direct result of poor investment decisions on her part and that she had made "some lifestyle decisions that were profligate." The court held that it could not decide this matter at an interim stage. However, it did decide to award her interim spousal support, pending the determination of an application under section 15.2(1) of the *Divorce Act*. The court was satisfied that the wife was in severe financial circumstances. She was in need. The husband's net worth had greatly increased since separation and was now over $5 million dollars. He had the ability to pay support.

In *Cavanagh v. Cassidy* (2000), 2000 CarswellOnt 1658, 7 R.F.L. (5th) 282, [2000] O.J. No. 1658 (Ont. S.C.J.), the husband had provided the wife with a fully paid home, all of the household furniture and a van, by using assets which were "excluded" assets under the *Family Law Act*, namely his inheritance from his mother and the insurance proceeds from the parties' child's death to pay off credit card debt, the van and the mortgage on the home, for a value of approximately $135,000. He had paid support to the wife for 6 years, and he had abandoned any claim for equalization. In light of the husband's provisions for the wife, the court held that he had discharged his obligations to the wife for "non-compensatory" factors. Any need on the part of the wife would be nominal. Further, the court doubted if the husband had the ability to continue to pay spousal support, based on his income and budget and in light of his responsibilities to the parties' other child and to the husband's new family. The court considered that the wife must contribute to her own support. The parties' union lasted 5 years, three of which occurred when they were married. The husband was required to pay the wife $750 for a 3-month period, $500 for a 4-month period and $300 for a 5-month period.

While ordering the payment of spousal support from funds previously equalized property could be considered "double dipping", such payment may be justified where the payor's assets have increased in value since separation: *Caldwell v. Caldwell* (1999), 46 R.F.L. (4th) 446, 1999 CarswellOnt 1491 (Ont. Gen. Div.).

Where the husband's only income was from his pension, the court was required, in determining the quantum of the wife's spousal support, to consider the fact that the husband's pension had been included in calculating the equalization payment payable by him: *Dolman v. Dolman* (1998), 38 R.F.L. (4th) 362, 1998 CarswellOnt 2082 (Ont. Gen. Div.); additional reasons at (1998), 1998 CarswellOnt 2884 (Ont. Gen. Div.).

In order to avoid double-dipping in cases where a spouse is awarded a share in the other's pension plan and proceeds from that plan are also used to determine the other spouse's ability to pay spousal support, the portion of the pension that has not been equalized or compensated for should be considered for support purposes: *Shadbolt v. Shadbolt* (1997), 32 R.F.L. (4th) 253, 1997 CarswellOnt 3544, [1997] O.J. No. 3666, 45 O.T.C. 124 (Ont. Gen. Div.).

Where the husband was totally and permanently disabled and in receipt of long-term disability benefits, the wife's claim for support was denied. In matrimonial property proceedings, the wife had already been awarded the entire proceeds from the ordered sale of the matrimonial home, which would provide her with funds with which to support herself: *Rains v. Rains* (1994), 9 R.F.L. (4th) 141, 1994 CarswellNS 61, 5 C.C.P.B. 258, 137 N.S.R. (2d) 250, 391 A.P.R. 250 (N.S. S.C.).

It is not improper to divide a payor's pension as property and to include pension income in calculating the payor's ability to pay spousal support upon retirement: *Rivers v. Rivers* (1993), 47 R.F.L. (3d) 90, 1993 CarswellOnt 330 (Ont. Gen. Div.).

Although a party's pension may have already been divided in matrimonial property proceedings, it may still be considered in determining the pensioner's ability to pay support: *Inverarity v. Inverarity* (1993), 50 R.F.L. (3d) 251, 146 A.R. 389, 1993 CarswellAlta 456 (Alta. Q.B.); varied (1996), 1996 CarswellAlta 51, 182 A.R. 1 (Alta. Q.B.).

In determining entitlement to support, the court should strive to promote the equitable sharing of the economic consequences of marital separation. This can be achieved, however, through the division of marital assets in which case a support order may not be required: *Newson v. Newson* (1993), 45 R.F.L. (3d) 115, 78 B.C.L.R. (2d) 35, 1993 CarswellBC 84, [1993] B.C.J. No. 438, 25 B.C.A.C. 24, 43 W.A.C. 24 (B.C. C.A.).

Periodic payments received by a spouse as a share of the other spouse's pension are properly characterized as property and not as support: *Lavoie v. Lavoie* (1991), 32 R.F.L. (3d) 77, 101 N.S.R. (2d) 65, 275 A.P.R. 65, 1991 CarswellNS 51 (N.S. Fam. Ct.).

Where the court has divided family assets, including the husband's pension, before determining the amount of spousal support payable by him, he has no cause to complain of "double dipping". The husband has suffered no injustice from having his pension income treated as "means" for support purposes: *Vennels v. Vennels* (1993), 45 R.F.L. (3d) 165, 76 B.C.L.R. (2d) 69, 1993 CarswellBC 17, [1993] B.C.J. No. 378 (B.C. S.C.).

Where a trial court fixes support subsequent to dividing matrimonial property, an appellate court is entitled to revisit the support issue if the division of property was altered on appeal: *Tibbetts v. Tibbetts* (1992), 44 R.F.L. (3d) 281, 119 N.S.R. (2d) 26, 330 A.P.R. 26, 98 D.L.R. (4th) 609, 1992 CarswellNS 85 (N.S. C.A.); additional reasons at (1993), 1993 CarswellNS 475, 102 D.L.R. (4th) 767 (N.S. C.A.).

In *Kowalewich v. Kowalewich* (1998), 38 R.F.L. (4th) 282, 108 B.C.A.C. 12, 176 W.A.C. 12, 50 B.C.L.R. (3d) 12, 1998 CarswellBC 767, [1998] B.C.J. No. 8 (B.C. C.A.); additional reasons at (1998), 1998 CarswellBC 2438 (B.C. C.A.); reconsideration granted (1998), 1998 CarswellBC 2630 (B.C. C.A.); varied 2001 CarswellBC 1418, 2001 BCCA 451, 92 B.C.L.R. (3d) 56, [2001] 9 W.W.R. 644, 19 R.F.L. (5th) 348 (B.C. C.A.), both the issues of child and spousal support were deferred and to be considered afresh after the property arrangements between the spouses had been finalized and paid out.

In determining a spouse's need for support, the court should not take into consideration an equalization payment ordered under a provincial property division statute where such payment is required by the spouse to purchase or replace assets necessary for daily life: *Anderson v. Anderson* (1990), 27 R.F.L. (3d) 358, 66 Man. R. (2d) 248, 1990 CarswellMan 50 (Man. Q.B.); affirmed (1991), 1991 CarswellMan 43, 35 R.F.L. (3d) 223, 75 Man. R. (2d) 235, 6 W.A.C. 235 (Man. C.A.).

In *Mitchell v. Mitchell* (1988), 72 Sask. R. 255, 1988 CarswellSask 413 (Sask. Q.B.); varied (1992), 1992 CarswellSask 58, 41 R.F.L. (3d) 220, 100 Sask. R. 149, 18 W.A.C. 149 (Sask. C.A.), the wife was awarded periodic support pending an improvement in her health and the settlement of the parties' property division.

Where the wife had potential investment income and was also to share in the husband's pension income, her application for support was refused: *Grieve v. Grieve* (1990), 29 R.F.L. (3d) 8, 1990 CarswellNB 28, 109 N.B.R. (2d) 304, 273 A.P.R. 304 (N.B. Q.B.).

In *Kremp v. Kremp* (1988), 92 A.R. 188, 1988 CarswellAlta 463 (Alta. Q.B.); varied (1989), 1989 CarswellAlta 394, 100 A.R. 6, 23 R.F.L. (3d) 164 (Alta. C.A.) the wife's application for support was refused in light of the $300,000 worth of assets which she had received upon division of the matrimonial property.

Following an equalization of property, the court is not then also to equalize income through an award of support. The purpose of matrimonial property legislation is to alleviate, at least partially, the need for support: *Veres v. Veres* (1987), 9 R.F.L. (3d) 447, 1987 CarswellOnt 353 (Ont. H.C.).

Where the wife was to receive $534,000 after equalization of family property, her anticipated capital position was found to have disentitled her from spousal support: *Saeglitz v. Saeglitz* (1994), 3 R.F.L. (4th) 244, 1994 CarswellOnt 389 (Ont. U.F.C.).

A court should only award compensatory support based upon the usual requirement of need. Such an award should not be used to effect a division of property: *Baker v. Baker* (1989), 22 R.F.L. (3d) 346, 1989 CarswellOnt 291 (Ont. U.F.C.).

15§41A — Payor spouse's post-separation increase in income

In *Francis v. Baker* (1997), 1997 CarswellOnt 1774, [1997] O.J. No. 2196, 28 R.F.L. (4th) 437, 150 D.L.R. (4th) 547, 30 O.T.C. 369 (Ont. Gen. Div.); additional reasons at (1997), 1997 CarswellOnt 3187 (Gen. Div.); affirmed (1998), 1998 CarswellOnt 931, [1998] O.J. No. 924, 157 D.L.R. (4th) 1, 34 R.F.L. (4th) 317, 107 O.A.C. 161, 38 O.R. (3d) 481 (Eng.), 38 O.R. (3d) 509 (Fr.) (C.A.); leave to appeal allowed (1998), [1998]

S.C.C.A. No. 191, 230 N.R. 396 (note), 117 O.A.C. 398 (note) (S.C.C.); affirmed 1999 CarswellOnt 2734, [1999] S.C.J. No. 52, 1999 CarswellOnt 2948, [1999] 3 S.C.R. 250, 44 O.R. (3d) 736 (headnote only), 177 D.L.R. (4th) 1, 246 N.R. 45, 50 R.F.L. (4th) 228, 125 O.A.C. 201 (S.C.C.), the wife, 1 year after a separation agreement had been signed, commenced an action to have it set aside and to claim spousal support, among other things. The case did not reach trial until 9 years later (12 years after the separation). Although the evidence failed to establish that the agreement should be set aside, the court held that with the clear discrepancy existing between the incomes of the spouses very shortly after the separation, the wife would have been entitled to "top up" support. The separation agreement made provision for support for "herself and the children" and the court found that far from releasing spousal support, the agreement contemplated ongoing support "for herself". In any event, the agreement was only one of many factors that must be considered in determining the right to, and the amount and duration of spousal support. All four of the objectives of spousal support orders under subsection 15(7) of the *Divorce Act* must be considered. There was no evidence that the agreement sought to address these objectives. The wife had not received adequate support during the 12 years she had been separated. At the time of trial, she earned $63,000 a year as a teacher. The husband had a net worth of about 78 million dollars and an annual income of nearly $1,000,000. In the circumstances, the wife was awarded lump sum support. Her child-raising responsibilities clearly affected her career-earning potential and her career path would have been entirely different and more lucrative but for the children. Lump sum support was advisable as there would be no prejudice to the husband given his net worth; it would reduce the financial connection between the parties, recognize the economic disadvantages to the wife arising from her marriage and its breakdown, relieve her economic hardship and promote her self-sufficiency. Recognizing that a lump sum would not be taxable to the wife, the spousal support claims were assessed at $500,000 payable as a lump sum to satisfy her entitlement to past support and future support. (The main thrust of the case, especially on appeal, was whether the Table Amount of child support was "inappropriate". Spousal support was only a secondary consideration. For child support, the current income of the payor — that is, his post-separation income — was the relevant income. However, the court made no distinction between post-separation income and income at the time of the separation in awarding the lump sum to the wife. The husband's circumstances at the time of trial were the determining circumstances for both child and spousal support.)

In *Horner v. Horner* (2004), 6 R.F.L. (6th) 140, [2004] O.J. No. 4268, 2004 CarswellOnt 4246, 245 D.L.R. (4th) 410, 191 O.A.C. 28, 72 O.R. (3d) 561 (Ont. C.A.), the wife brought a corollary relief application under the *Divorce Act* for spousal support for an indefinite period of time. As part of her application she sought to set aside the time-limited support provision in her separation agreement and claimed support in a higher amount. She also applied to vary a prior order for child support. Based on the husband's increased post-separation income, the applications judge awarded spousal support for more than the amount set out in the separation agreement, made the increase retroactive to 1 month after she had requested it, but did not extend the duration of payment beyond the limited period. The Court of Appeal awarded a further increase in spousal support finding that the applications judge had used too low an amount for the husband's income, did not reflect in his award the contribution the wife had made to her husband's career advancement during the marriage, although he noted the fact of this contribution, and notwithstanding that the wife's budget was reasonable and not criticized, he did not award the amount requested to maintain this budget. The Court of Appeal also found that the amount awarded was below the median of awards made in cases involving similar circumstances. After the separation, the husband obtained an engineering degree and "advanced rapidly in his career to become Vice-President of Engineering" in his company. His income increased accordingly. The applications judge connected the husband's advance in his career to the marriage saying: "while Mr. Horner has undeniably improved his educational skills since the separation, and thereby enhanced his job and salary within his company, nevertheless, his upward progress clearly started well back in the 1980's and cannot be separated from the marriage and arrangements made with his wife as to how their marriage would be structured."

Post-separation income from an asset that is subject to sharing is not part of the accounting and equalization regime of the Manitoba legislation: *Ramantanis v. Ramantanis*, 2004 CarswellMan 371, 187 Man. R. (2d) 190, 330 W.A.C. 190, 8 R.F.L. (6th) 326, 2004 MBCA 122 (C.A.). An award of $10,000 to the wife for her share of post-separation rental from a condominium owned by the husband was set aside on appeal. The value of condominium, itself, had properly been included in the accounting and division of the parties' assets.

In *Marinangeli v. Marinangeli*, 2003 CarswellOnt 2691, [2003] O.J. No. 2819, 66 O.R. (3d) 40, 38 R.F.L. (5th) 307, 174 O.A.C. 76, 228 D.L.R. (4th) 376 (C.A.), the Court of Appeal dealt with the wife's application to vary her support on the assumption, which was not articulated, that she was entitled to share in the husband's post-separation increase in income.

In *Mosher v. Mosher*, 1995 CarswellNS 11, 13 R.F.L. (4th) 385, 140 N.S.R. (2d) 40, 399 A.P.R. 40 (C.A.), the court viewed the wife's claim for support "to a significant degree" in light of the husband's post separation income. It came to this conclusion because of her contribution to the marriage and the upbringing of the children, her willingness to share in a compromise of the family's standard of living in order to purchase rental properties and to invest in the stock market. The court found that it would be inequitable if her claim was affected as a consequence of the reduction of her husband's income for the 2 years after he left his previous position, and not by the spectacular increases thereafter.

On an application to vary, the fact that the husband's ability to pay may have increased since the settlement does not, in itself, constitute a basis for an increase in spousal support: *Dextraze v. Dextraze*, 2004 CarswellBC 287, 2004 BCSC 215 (S.C.).

In *Fitzpatrick v. Fitzpatrick*, 2004 CarswellOnt 2606, [2004] O.J. No. 2695, 3 R.F.L. (6th) 325 (S.C.J.), the husband's income increased significantly after the separation. In considering the question of spousal support the court observed that the husband's income had "taken off" and that the process began at least a year before the parties separated. The husband's interests in the business from which his income was derived "were directly related to the roles of the spouses within the marriage, their joint decision to sacrifice salary for equity eight years earlier when he joined [the company], and their mutual plan to adopt a modest lifestyle, emphasizing financial security for their retirement. When the parties separated . . . [the company] seemed poised for takeoff. Mrs. Fitzpatrick was on that plane until it left the ground." The award for her support was assessed against the husband's greatly increased post-separation income.

In *Giguere v. Giguere* (2003), 2003 CarswellOnt 5006, [2003] O.J. No. 5102, 46 R.F.L. (5th) 184 (Ont. S.C.J.); additional reasons at (2004), 2004 CarswellOnt 273, [2004] O.J. No. 444 (Ont. S.C.J.), the issue was whether the wife should be relegated to a standard of living enjoyed during the marriage in circumstances where the husband currently had a much higher standard of living. His standard of living resulted from a substantial raise in salary which he received less than a year after the separation. The court held that she should not be obliged to stay at the standard of living established by the marriage. She had clearly suffered a disadvantage as a result of the separation. Not only did she lose the benefit of residing in a two-income household, she also lost the benefit of the enjoyment of the husband's vastly increased salary which came so soon after the separation. The raise was attributable to the tremendous effort the husband had put into his work from the outset, when the parties were still residing together. They had been together for 26 years. Cases decided more than 10 years earlier may be read as holding that the standard of living of the wife ought to be that enjoyed during the marriage. These should be distinguished from recent cases. "More recent cases have entitled a wife in a long-term marriage to increased support flowing from the husband's post-separation increased income. One such case is *Francis v. Baker* (1997), 150 D.L.R. (4th) 547, 28 R.F.L. (4th) 437 (Ont. Gen. Div.), *Francis v. Baker* (1998), 38 O.R. (3d) 481 . . . (Ont. C.A.) where the Court of Appeal upheld an award of lump sum spousal support of $500,000 made 12 years after the separation. At trial, the judge had found that Mr. Baker's wealth 'seems to have erupted when he became C.E.O. of Seven-Up Canada Inc.', an event which occurred a few years after separation."

In *Giguere* the case of *Rozen v. Rozen* (2003), 2003 CarswellBC 1564, [2003] B.C.J. No. 1486, 2003 BCSC 973, 37 R.F.L. (5th) 205 (B.C. S.C.), where the judge refused to increase a wife's support on the basis of the husband's substantial increase in income following separation, can be distinguished on the basis of the court's finding "that the substantial increase in income occurred 'by reason of a re-organization of [the husband's] accounting firm and additional work being required of him'. The additional income was not, in the judge's view, related to the breakdown of the marriage or the sacrifice made by the wife during marriage." Having done this analysis, the court in *Giguere* found that the wife was entitled to compensatory and needs-based support. Her current income was $34,372 a year. The husband's income, including the free use of a car, was $140,000. The court rejected the wife's argument that their incomes should be "almost equalized". The support order must take into account the substantial effort the husband made to earn his income. A support award of $3,000 per month was found to be appropriate in the circumstances. This gave the wife approximately 42 percent and the husband approximately 58 percent of the net disposable incomes of the parties. The parties had one child who was now independant. The wife performed the vast majority of childcare and household management functions during cohabitation. Both parties worked throughout the marriage. There was no evidence that the wife was disadvantaged to the extent that she might have had a more lucrative career, had she not assumed the child and household responsibilities. However, by undertaking those responsibilities, she lost any opportunity she might have had.

In *Rozen v. Rozen*, 2003 CarswellBC 1564, 37 R.F.L. (5th) 205, [2003] B.C.J. No. 1486, 2003 BCSC 973 (S.C.), the court held that the wife was not entitled to share in the husband's increase in income after separation. The best indicator of the amount that the wife should receive in spousal support was the amount that would provide her with a lifestyle similar to that enjoyed by her during the 20-year marriage. Spousal support was based on the husband's income ($200,000) at the time of the parties' settlement in 1997, and not on his income ($425,000) at the time of the spousal maintenance review in 2005. The wife currently had part-time income of $30,500. She had health problems that interfered with her obtaining full-time employment. The court determined that the spousal support based on the income of $200,000, combined with the return on the wife's investments and her employment income would yield close to $100,000, which was roughly half of what the husband earned in 1996, the amount upon which spousal support was calculated in the minutes of settlement. The wife had worked while the husband continued his education and later worked part-time so that she could attend to child care responsibilities. One of the reasons for the review was to consider the extent of the wife's share in her father's estate which still was not determined at the time of the review hearing. (See comment on this case in *Giguere*, above.)

In *Fletcher v. Fletcher*, 2003 CarswellAlta 1534, [2003] A.J. No. 1333, 2003 ABQB 890 (Q.B.), the court considered the husband's post-separation income on his wife's claim for interim spousal support. The Court held that he was able to earn this increased income as a result of developing his managerial ability, including obtaining an M.B.A. during cohabitation, and because of his close relationship to the Cosco family. "As his economic partner for 26 years, [the wife was] entitled to share equally with her husband in the income stream which represented his development during the marriage."

In assessing spousal support for the wife in *Rothenburg v. Rothenburg*, 2003 CarswellOnt 1380, [2003] O.J. No. 1551, 40 R.F.L. (5th) 363, [2003] O.T.C. 327 (S.C.J.), the court considered the husband's post-separation increase in income finding that "her involvement in the husband's education and his consulting business, as well as the time devoted to child care and care of his parents, require the wife share in some of the financial gain received by the husband." She was not entitled to an equalization of incomes, but her relationship with her husband in a 28-year marriage entitled her to "more than just her actual need". And given their ages and the likelihood of a support variation on the husband's retirement, she should be allowed an amount from which she could save for her own retirement.

In *Keast v. Keast*, 1986 CarswellOnt 257, 1 R.F.L. (3d) 401 (Dist. Ct.), the court determined the quantum of support in two amounts, $600 monthly in permanent support for the wife's lifetime and a quasi-restitutionary or compensatory support sum would be paid to her for her contributions to the husband's career potential, fixed at $1,000 monthly but commencing in 1990, when he was expected to have established his practice and be earning the average amount for a physician and continuing for 10 years thereafter.

15§41B — Effect of delay

Mere delay as with the equitable doctrine of laches is not a defence to a claim for spousal support. In addition, there must be acquiescence on the part of the plaintiff, or the plaintiff's conduct must have either caused the defendant to alter his position in reasonable reliance on the appellant's acceptance of the *status quo* or permitted a situation which it would be unjust to disturb. Ultimately, the issue of delay or laches is a matter of justice as between the parties: *C. (Y.J.) v. C. (Y.D.)* (2001), 2001 CarswellOnt 3514, 56 O.R. (3d) 150, 150 O.A.C. 247 (Ont. C.A.); *M. (K.) v. M. (H.)*, [1992] 3 S.C.R. 6, 1992 CarswellOnt 841, 1992 CarswellOnt 998, [1992] S.C.J. No. 85, EYB 1992-67549, 142 N.R. 321, 96 D.L.R. (4th) 289, 57 O.A.C. 321, 14 C.C.L.T. (2d) 1 (S.C.C.).

A relevant consideration is whether the delay is prejudicial to the payor: *Marinangeli v. Marinangeli* (2003), 2003 CarswellOnt 2691, [2003] O.J. No. 2819, 66 O.R. (3d) 40, 38 R.F.L. (5th) 307, 174 O.A.C. 76, 228 D.L.R. (4th) 376 (Ont. C.A.). While there was some delay on the part of the respondent in requesting increased spousal support once she became aware of the appellant's income, this delay occasioned no prejudice. The major portion of the delay after the Minutes were signed arose prior to the respondent becoming aware of the appellant's circumstances and was due to his non-disclosure.

In *Brown v. Brown* (1996), 1996 CarswellAlta 651, [1996] A.J. No. 658, 127 W.A.C. 156, 187 A.R. 156 (Alta. C.A.), the Chambers Judge, without giving reasons, awarded the wife spousal support, despite the fact that the parties had been divorced for approximately 18 years and despite the fact that at that time the former wife had received legal advice that she was entitled to seek support. When the parties were divorced, spousal support was reserved. The wife cared for the parties' severely disabled child and prior to seeking support, developed various illnesses. The former husband agreed that spousal support was payable, but disputed the amount. The wife had assisted the husband with his education and had suffered much of the economic hardship arising from the breakdown of the marriage. It was unlikely that she would ever be able to achieve economic self-sufficiency. The Chambers Judge ordered the appellant to pay the respondent $1500/month by way of spousal support, a lump sum of $3,700, and costs. The appellant court granted the appeal and substituted an award of $500 a month in place of the award granted by the Chambers Judge. Hunt J.A. stated at paragraph 17:

> There is nothing in the very unusual facts of this case that provide a method of setting the quantum of spousal support with any degree of mathematical certainty. However, the long delay in seeking spousal support and the short duration of the marriage are key factors militating against the amount awarded by the chambers judge. In our view, that award was excessive. The respondent's circumstances make it unlikely that she will ever enjoy a comfortable level of income. On the other hand, although the appellant is more economically secure than she is, he is not wealthy and he has a new child to support. In this situation, all that can be accomplished with a spousal award is a modest alleviation of the impoverished circumstances of the respondent.

In *Lautermilch v. Lautermilch*, 2005 CarswellNB 294, 2005 CarswellNB 295, 2005 NBCA 59, 286 N.B.R. (2d) 46, 748 A.P.R. 46 (N.B. C.A.), the court quoted from the judgment of the trial judge who considered the reasonableness of the former wife's eight and a half year delay in seeking spousal support. The judge stated:

> Delay is not a concept that is evaluated in a vacuum. All of the circumstances of the case require consideration. I have taken into consideration the case law outlined by [Mr. Lautermilch] in his brief, as well as the case law outlined in the brief submitted on behalf of [Mrs. Lautermilch]. Of importance in this case are [Mrs. Lautermilch's] financial circumstances throughout rendering her incapable of seeking legal advice, her emotional condition, of living with her physical limitations, her use of medication and the emotional trauma of living with a very sick child and coping with her untimely death. Taking all of those circumstances into consideration, I am satisfied that the pursuit of her legal rights was the bottom end of priorities throughout. She should not be deprived of pursuing her claim in all of the circumstances of this case. I therefore conclude that the delay in this case was both adequately explained and in my view justified.

The former husband asserted that in the circumstances "there was an agreement between the parties that no spousal support would be claimed." In the alternative, he sought a reduction of the $700 per month support payment and a limited term for payment of it. Further, he claimed that the trial judge erred "in determining that the former wife was able to work only thirty five hours per week in the absence of medical evidence." The appellate court held that there was no basis in law on which to interfere with the trial judge's decision; deference must be accorded. The appeal was dismissed.

Where the wife did not seek spousal support for 11 months after the parties' separation, the delay was explained by two agreements, a pre-nuptial agreement and a separation agreement, which precluded the wife from seeking spousal support unless she moved to set them aside. *B. (B.A.) v. B. (S.S.)*, 2005 CarswellBC 945, [2005] B.C.J. No. 882, 15 R.F.L. (6th) 247, 2005 BCSC 593 (B.C. S.C.). The court found that there was no evidence that a retroactive lump sum award would impose an unfair burden on the husband at this time. The award would have the effect of redistributing capital, but that would not be its purpose. Its purpose would be to compensate the wife for the extent to which she depleted her resources during a time in which she should have been receiving spousal support. The wife had received social assistance for 11 months after separation, but was currently employed and earning $51,000 per year. The court found that the separation agreement was negotiated in a rush and should be somewhat discounted. The husband was ordered to pay the wife lump sum spousal support of $17,500.

In a determination of whether spousal support should be granted, the *Divorce Act* and the case law support the conclusion that a delay is an important circumstance to be considered, but it can, in certain exceptional circumstances, be superseded by putting forth a reasonable explanation for the delay, so that that a court can exercise its discretion to allow a consideration of entitlement to spousal support: *Gearin v. Gearin* (1999), 1999 CarswellNfld 87, [1999] N.J. No. 97, 45 R.F.L. (4th) 333, 176 Nfld. & P.E.I.R. 76, 540 A.P.R. 76 (Nfld. U.F.C.). The court considered that delay was *one* critical circumstance in the determination but that it was generally accepted that a court does have discretion to permit a party to make a claim for permanent maintenance years after a divorce was granted without an original order. It cited *Provost v. Provost* (1997), 27 R.F.L. (4th) 184, 1997 CarswellBC 159 (B.C. S.C.) for this proposition and also stated that the delay is not an "unexplained delay". See *K. (H.J.) v. B. (J.E.)* (1997), 33 R.F.L. (4th) 409, 1997 CarswellBC 2558, 100 B.C.A.C. 1, 163 W.A.C. 1, 44 B.C.L.R. (3d) 77 (B.C. C.A.). In the *Gearin* case, the parties were divorced in 1990 and there was a consent order, without reference to spousal support in 1992. The wife brought an application for interim spousal support in 1998. Although she sought support in her divorce counter petition, it was not dealt with in the consent order following the divorce. She considered that the $990 monthly payments of child support to her supplemented her own income. She believed that it would have been pointless to attempt to also get spousal support from the husband at that time because he did not have the resources to pay spousal support in addition to $990 in monthly child support. She also considered that if she were denied spousal support in 1992, and she subsequently applied, this could prove detrimental because her entitlement to spousal support *could* then be deemed to be *res judicata*.

The court quoted with approval from *Janes v. Janes* (1985), 54 Nfld. & P.E.I.R. 310, 1985 CarswellNfld 32, 47 R.F.L. (2d) 378, 160 A.P.R. 310 (Nfld. U.F.C.), where Cameron, J. stated at p. 313 (Nfld. & P.E.I.R.):

> . . .time lags are appropriate factors for consideration in determining if maintenance should be awarded.. . . The applicant must demonstrate exceptional circumstances to satisfy the court that the marriage having been dissolved and issues having been resolved between the parties, the court should disturb that arrangement and grant an order for maintenance. One critical circumstance to be considered is the delay in bringing the application.

The court found that the wife had provided reasonable explanations for her long delay in seeking spousal support. It exercised its discretion and allowed the wife to have her entitlement to interim spousal support considered at this time.

For purposes of interim relief the court found that a delay in applying for support eight and one-half years after support had ended was sufficiently explained by the efforts the wife made to become self-supporting and to live off her capital in order to avoid bringing the application: *Bailey v. Plaxton*, 2000 CarswellOnt 1194, [2000] O.J. No. 1187, 47 O.R. (3d) 593, 6 R.F.L. (5th) 29, [2000] O.T.C. 243 (Ont. S.C.J.).

SPOUSAL SUPPORT — Nominal Awards

15§42 — Nominal awards in general

The husband in *Mannarelli v. Mannarelli* (1998), 41 R.F.L. (4th) 117 (Ont. Gen. Div.) was ordered to pay $1.00 per year nominal spousal support where the parties had been married for 25 years, had had three children and the wife had a full-time job as a bus driver.

As the *Divorce Act* permits a subsequent support application, there is no need for a nominal order: *Folga v. Folga* (1986), 2 R.F.L. (3d) 358 (Ont. H.C.).

Future entitlement to maintenance is not foreclosed by the absence of a protective order. Accordingly, it is preferable to avoid the use of a nominal maintenance order when it is clearly unnecessary: *Filbert v. Filbert* (1985), 48 R.F.L. (2d) 101, 35 Man. R. (2d) 294 (C.A.).

The failure to make a nominal maintenance award at the time of a divorce does not bar a subsequent application for maintenance. Therefore a nominal award made only to preserve a spouse's right to maintenance in the future is not proper: *Nelson v. Nelson* (1984), 65 N.S.R. (2d) 210, 147 A.P.R. 219 (C.A.); reversing (1984), 64 N.S.R. (2d) 30, 143 A.P.R. 30 (T.D.).

15§43 — Circumstances — justifying nominal awards

When there was no evidence that the wife had ever been financially dependent on the husband, a nominal support award made in her favour was struck on appeal: *Vickers v. Vickers*, 18 R.F.L. (5th) 431, 2001 CarswellNS 194, 2001 NSCA 96, 201 D.L.R. (4th) 65, 194 N.S.R. (2d) 268, 606 A.P.R. 268 (N.S. C.A.).

Where the trial judge dismissed the wife's claim for spousal support, despite the fact that it was unclear whether she would be able to achieve self-sufficiency once the children were grown, a nominal support order was made in her favour on appeal: *Dobranski v. Dobranski* (1998), 35 R.F.L. (4th) 403, 103 B.C.A.C. 214, 169 W.A.C. 214 (C.A.).

In *Dababneh v. Dababneh* (2003), 48 R.F.L. (5th) 55, 2003 CarswellOnt 5004 (Ont. S.C.J.); additional reasons at (2004), 2004 CarswellOnt 654 (Ont. S.C.J.), the wife was awarded nominal support of $1.00 per year. The husband had health and alcohol-related problems which inhibited him from working and he could not be ordered to work just to create income for support. The nominal order left open the possibility of variation in the future.

In *Wolfe v. Wolfe*, 26 R.F.L. (5th) 447, 2002 CarswellNS 129, 2002 NSSF 18, 202 N.S.R. (2d) 386, 632 A.P.R. 386 (S.C.), the court awarded the wife nominal spousal support. The wife acknowledged that she would have financial difficulty if child support were awarded in accordance with guideline amounts. However her concern about her financial status should she no longer qualify for support was legitimate.

Where the wife's dependency on the marriage had increased over the parties' 16-year marriage, but the husband's resources were limited, she was awarded nominal spousal support of one dollar per year: *Young v. Young* (1999), 49 R.F.L. (4th) 455, 175 N.S.R. (2d) 113, 534 A.P.R. 113, 1999 CarswellNS 24 (S.C.).

In *Davies v. Davies* (1999), 50 R.F.L. (4th) 353, 1999 CarswellBC 1505, [1999] B.C.J. No. 1578 (B.C. S.C.), the wife was awarded annual spousal support of $1.00 following the dissolution of the parties' 35-year traditional marriage. Although the wife was entitled to more, the husband had retired at age 55, had no source of income other than his pension and was unable to locate employment. The order could be reviewed should either parties' circumstances change.

In *Davidson v. Davidson* (1998), 42 R.F.L. (4th) 154, 230 A.R. 151 (Q.B.), the wife was granted only nominal interim support. The wife had substantial assets, considerable rental income and had obtained two university degrees during the marriage. The parties had amassed a sizable fortune and the wife had actually been economically advantaged by the marriage by her entitlement to a share in these assets.

In *Davis v. Davis* (1994), 6 R.F.L. (4th) 121, 94 Man. R. (2d) 175 (Q.B.) the wife was awarded nominal support to protect her right to apply for greater support in the future. Although at the time of the trial she had sufficient resources to meet her own needs, she was legally blind and suffered from emotional and psychiatric problems which could impact her in the future.

Where the wife would require retraining to achieve self-sufficiency but the husband was without means, the wife was nevertheless awarded nominal support: *Peer v. Peer* (1989), 19 R.F.L. (3d) 388 (Ont. H.C.).

Where the husband, who had limited means, was required to pay the wife a substantial equalization payment over a ten-year period, he was required to pay spousal support of only $50 monthly, despite the wife's unquestionable need for support: *McTaggart v. McTaggart* (1993), 50 R.F.L. (3d) 110 (Ont. Gen. Div.).

Where the husband had lost his career and business but had prospects of a career revival, the wife was awarded nominal support: *McAfee v. McAfee* (1989), 21 R.F.L. (3d) 75 (B.C. S.C.).

Where the wife lacked current economic need but was likely to have need in the future given her inability to set aside funds for future security, she was awarded nominal support: *Johnston v. Johnston* (1989), 21 R.F.L. (3d) 399 (Ont. H.C.).

Where the wife's dependency on the marriage had increased over the parties' 16-year marriage, but the husband's resources were limited, she was awarded nominal spousal support of one dollar per year: *Young v. Young* (1999), 49 R.F.L. (4th) 455, 175 N.S.R. (2d) 113, 534 A.P.R. 113 (S.C.).

In *Davies v. Davies* (1999), 50 R.F.L. (4th) 353 (B.C. S.C.), the wife was awarded annual spousal support of $1.00 following the dissolution of the parties 35-year traditional marriage. Although the wife was entitled to more, the husband had retired at age 55, had no source of income other than his pension and was unable to locate employment. The order could be reviewed should either parties' circumstances change.

Where the 52-year-old wife had done contract work from her home throughout the marriage but was in poor health and could lose the ability to work in the future, she was granted nominal support which would allow her to seek a variation should her circumstances deteriorate. The husband's pension income was insufficient to allow payment of spousal support at the time of the order: *Bosomworth v. Bosomworth* (1997), 34 R.F.L. (4th) 71 (B.C. S.C.); additional reasons at (December 12, 1997), Doc. Vancouver D102977 (B.C. S.C.).

Where at the time of the hearing the wife was working and self-sufficient, but had the potential of developing serious health problems, the court ordered support of $1 to preserve her support rights should a future need arise: *Ghidoni v. Ghidoni* (1992), 40 R.F.L. (3d) 184 (B.C. S.C.).

SPOUSAL SUPPORT — Terms and Conditions

15§44 — Date of commencement of support

In *Martin v. Martin* (2004), 12 R.F.L. (6th) 415, 2004 CarswellOnt 5438 (Ont. S.C.J.); additional reasons at (2005), 2005 CarswellOnt 1437 (Ont. S.C.J.); affirmed (2006), 2006 CarswellOnt 4876 (Ont. C.A.), the wife's claim for retroactive spousal support was refused. Not only did the wife lack an explanation as to why she had failed to seek interim support, she had continued to live very well after separation. There was no evidence of hardship, nor had the husband participated in any blameworthy conduct.

In *Allaire v. Allaire* (2003), 35 R.F.L. (5th) 256, 2003 CarswellOnt 1002, 170 O.A.C. 72 (Ont. C.A.), the wife's lump sum retroactive spousal support award was upheld on appeal. The lump sum compensated the wife for the expenses she incurred between the parties' separation and the trial, and there was no basis to interfere with the award.

A lump sum for past support should only be awarded in exceptional circumstances as it is really a windfall and is not really used for past support. Accordingly, where the wife's spousal support order was increased substantially on appeal, the court refused her request for a lump sum equivalent to the differential over time between the appellate amount and the original amount. The wife had delayed in bringing the appeal forward, such delay resulting in a substantial differential for which the husband had no opportunity to plan: *Messer v. Messer* (1996), 26 R.F.L. (4th) 352, 150 Sask. R. 23 (Q.B.); reversed in part (1997), 33 R.F.L. (4th) 426 (Sask. C.A.); leave to appeal dismissed (1998), 227 N.R. 292 (note), 168 Sask. R. 318 (note), 173 W.A.C. 318 (note) (S.C.C.).

The power to award spousal support retroactively back to the date of separation should be exercised sparingly. Where after separation the wife had delayed bringing her support claim on the chance that the parties had incurred no debt and she had no immediate pressing need then for funds, her spousal support was made retroactive only to the date of her claim: *Giguere v. Giguere* (2003), 46 R.F.L. (5th) 184, 2003 CarswellOnt 5006 (Ont. S.C.J.); additional reasons at (2004), 2004 CarswellOnt 273 (Ont. S.C.J.).

Where the only purpose of an award of retroactive spousal support would be to redistribute capital, the wife's claim for such an award was refused in *MacKinnon v. MacKinnon* (2003), 47 R.F.L. (5th) 338, 2004 CarswellOnt 534, [2004] O.J. No. 374 (Ont. S.C.J.); additional reasons at (2004), 2004 CarswellOnt 2227 (Ont. S.C.J.).

In *Leeder v. Leeder* (2002), 25 R.F.L. (5th) 291, 2002 CarswellOnt 80 (Ont. S.C.J.), the husband was ordered to pay combined retroactive spousal and child support of $10,000 monthly, although his annual income was only $125,000. The husband had previously owned a business which generated an annual income of close to $500,000 but had sold it for a considerable amount of money. Reduction of his income was the husband's own doing and he had realized a substantial profit on the sale.

In *Terris v. Terris* (2003), 41 R.F.L. (5th) 433, 2003 CarswellOnt 2685 (Ont. S.C.J.), the court ordered that the issue of the wife's entitlement to spousal support be deferred for one year. The wife, while capable of some employment, had apparently decided to put off working pending the completion of the parties' divorce proceedings. The husband had also lost his job and had taken one at less than a third of his former salary. The wife had an obligation to work and the husband should also seek out a better paying job. The year deferral should accommodate the resolution of these issues.

In *Vitagliano v. Di Stavolo* (2001), 17 R.F.L. (5th) 194, 2001 CarswellOnt 1065, [2001] O.J. No. 1138 (Ont. S.C.J.), the wife was awarded retroactive lump sum spousal and child support. Whereas the interim support orders had been based on the husband's forecast income of $115,000, his actual income throughout the duration of the interim order had been in excess of $200,000. His contribution towards his children's support had, therefore, clearly been unreasonable.

There is no jurisdiction under the *Divorce Act* to make a support order retroactive to a date prior to the commencement of divorce proceedings: *Young v. Young* (2000), 7 R.F.L. (5th) 228, 225 N.B.R. (2d) 272, 578 A.P.R. 272, 2000 CarswellNB 85 (C.A.).

The trial judge's order that the wife pay spousal support to the husband for a two year period was upheld on appeal where the husband suffered from depression and chronic anxiety but the parties had been married for a short time: *Olstead v. Olstead* (1999), 45 R.F.L. (4th) 46, 124 B.C.A.C. 315, 203 W.A.C. 315 (C.A.).

In *Hopkinson v. Hopkinson* (1997), 34 R.F.L. (4th) 137 (B.C. C.A.), the court refused the wife's appeal from the time limitation placed upon her spousal support award. As she had already obtained employment and a degree of self-sufficiency, the limitation was warranted.

Where the wife had been unemployed and forced to encroach upon her capital to support herself and her child, a lump sum retroactive spousal support order made in her favour was upheld on appeal in *Prince v. Prince* (1997), 35 R.F.L. (4th) 328, 163 N.S.R. (2d) 28, 487 A.P.R. 28 (C.A.).

Where the wife had not claimed support immediately upon separation but had maintained herself by drawing upon capital resources, the award of retroactive support back to the date of separation was upheld on appeal: *Kloos v. Kloos* (1996), 20 R.F.L. (4th) 1 (Man. C.A.).

The *Divorce Act* permits, in the proper circumstances, for the making of a support order which includes payment for a period which predates the petition: *Lidstone v. Lidstone* (1993), 46 R.F.L. (3d) 203, 121 N.S.R. (2d) 213, 335 A.P.R. 213 (C.A.).

The court is entitled to award lump sum spousal support to compensate a spouse retroactively for the interim support which could have been awarded for the period between separation and trial: *Kowaluk v. Kowaluk* (1995), 17 R.F.L. (4th) 185 (Man. Q.B.); reversed in part (1996), 110 Man. R. (2d) 184, 118 W.A.C. 184, 24 R.F.L. (4th) 261 (C.A.). On appeal, the court found that lump sum support, which is the exception and not the rule, was not justified on the facts of the case. The wife never made any attempt to obtain interim maintenance, nor was there any evidence that she maintained her right to such interim maintenance during the proceedings.

In *Leeder v. Leeder* (2002), 25 R.F.L. (5th) 291, 2002 CarswellOnt 80 (S.C.J.), the husband was ordered to pay combined retroactive spousal and child support of $10,000 monthly, although his annual income was only $125,000. The husband had previously owned a business which generated an annual income of close to $500,000 but had sold it for a considerable amount of money. Reduction of his income was the husband's own doing and he had realized a substantial profit on the sale.

A retroactive support order is not intended as a contribution to daily expenses but rather is a creation of a debt obligation. Retroactive orders are appropriate where the payor should have been paying support: *Schmuck v. Reynolds-Schmuck* (1999), 50 R.F.L. (4th) 429 (Ont. S.C.J.); additional reasons at (2000), 46 O.R. (3d) 702, 2000 CarswellOnt 202 (S.C.J.).

The wife in *Balcerzak v. Balcerzak* (1998), 41 R.F.L. (4th) 13 (Ont. Gen. Div.); additional reasons at (1998), 42 R.F.L. (4th) 297 (Ont. Gen. Div.) was awarded $600 monthly until she obtained full-time employment as a teacher. The wife had stayed home with the children during a 16 year marriage and had resumed her teaching career as a supply teacher after the separation.

In *Motyl v. Motyl* (1998), 36 R.F.L. (4th) 268 (Sask. Q.B.), the husband, who had been employed at the outset of the marriage worked for the wife during the latter part of the marriage, and lost his job when the relationship ended. The court held that the husband was entitled to spousal support, as he suffered economic hardship as a result of the breakdown of the marriage. The wife had paid seven monthly payments to the husband before discontinuing them. As the husband was capable, the court was of the opinion that with due diligence he could have re-established himself within the seven months. Spousal support was awarded only in the amount already paid.

The court has jurisdiction under s. 15 of the *Divorce Act* to award retroactive spousal support. It should be made retroactive where the applicant expresses an intention to seek support, immediately begins sincere negotiations, conducts them expeditiously, and promptly brings the application when negotiations break down. The date for the beginning of the retroactive period should be the date when the intention to seek support was made known: *Moro v. Miletich*, 40 R.F.L. (4th) 115, 1998 CarswellOnt 1194 (Gen. Div.).

In *Moro v. Miletich* (1998), 40 R.F.L. (4th) 115 (Ont. Gen. Div.), the wife was awarded retroactive spousal support for a 13-month period during which she had legitimate need, had actively sought support and had negotiated toward that end.

Section 15 of the *Divorce Act* appears to be concerned with providing support for only the present and the future. It does not appear to authorize a retroactive support order: *Cerget v. Cerget* (1994), 7 R.F.L. (4th) 322 (Ont. Gen. Div.); additional reasons at (1994), 7 R.F.L. (4th) 343 (Ont. Gen. Div.); further additional reasons at (November 23, 1994), Doc. Windsor 19940/89 (Ont. Gen. Div.).

In *Fiacco v. Fiacco* (1995), 11 R.F.L. (4th) 240 (Sask. Q.B.), the wife's application for retroactive spousal support upon the breakdown of the parties' two year marriage was dismissed. Although she had no job and no immediate prospects there was no justification, after such a brief marriage, for retroactive support. She was, however, entitled to periodic support to assist her in getting back on the path she was on prior to the marriage.

Section 15 of the *Divorce Act* is broad enough to entitle a judge to award support for a period predating the date of the divorce: *Donald v. Donald* (1991), 33 R.F.L. (3d) 196, 103 N.S.R. (2d) 322, 282 A.P.R. 322, 81 D.L.R. (4th) 48 (C.A.).

A judge has jurisdiction to make a retroactive child support order to cover support which a payor should have paid in the past: *Ambrose v. Ambrose* (1990), 24 R.F.L. (3d) 353 (Man. C.A.).

Section 15 of the *Divorce Act* does not authorize the court to set maintenance retroactively. The issue of retroactive maintenance is only properly addressed in the case of an existing maintenance order for which a variation is sought pursuant to s. 17: *Mannett v. Mannett* (1992), 111 N.S.R. (2d) 327, 303 A.P.R. 327 (T.D.).

In *Novotny v. Novotny* (1991), 31 R.F.L. (3d) 306 (B.C. S.C.), the court allowed the husband's application to characterize retroactively as child support certain child counselling and household expenses which the husband had earlier been ordered to pay. The payments were indeed support-related and the husband was entitled to benefit from the tax relief flowing from the retroactive order.

Where a maintenance award was increased on appeal, the substituted award was made retroactive to the date of the original order: *Chegwin v. Chegwin* (1976), 28 R.F.L. 28 (Man. C.A.). See also *Keddy v. Keddy* (1974), 8 N.S.R. (2d) 158 at 166, 167, 45 D.L.R. (3d) 609 (C.A.); *Tassou v. Tassou* (1976), 23 R.F.L. 351 (Alta. T.D.).

Where the wife fails to claim interim maintenance, the court is without jurisdiction to award maintenance retroactively to a time prior to the petition under the guise of lump sum maintenance: *Chadderton v. Chadderton*, 8 R.F.L. 374, [1973] 1 O.R. 560, 31 D.L.R. (3d) 656 (C.A.).

Where a husband's violent conduct justified the plaintiff-wife's reasonable apprehension of danger to her health and safety, the wife was awarded alimony from the date of the last separation: *Wall v. Wall* (1974), 15 R.F.L. 154 (Ont. H.C.); reversed on other grounds 26 R.F.L. 257 (Ont. C.A.).

The court has jurisdiction under s. 11(1) [now s. 15(1)] of the *Divorce Act* to make retroactive orders: *Nightingale v. Nightingale* (1986), 5 R.F.L. (3d) 175 (Nfld. T.D.).

The court has no jurisdiction to grant retrospective maintenance orders as a method of enforcing arrears owing under a separation agreement: *Richardson v. Richardson* (1984), 43 R.F.L. (2d) 132 (Sask. Q.B.); *Willinsky v. Willinsky* (1976), 30 R.F.L. 330, 14 O.R. (2d) 569 at 569–71, 74 D.L.R. (3d) 402 (H.C.). See also *Goerzen v. Goerzen* (1975), 24 R.F.L. 271, 11 O.R. (2d) 401 at 404, 66 D.L.R. (3d) 217 (H.C.); *Diamond v. Diamond* (1975), 22 R.F.L. 394 (Ont. H.C.); *Ratcliff v. Ratcliff* (1976), 27 R.F.L. 227 (B.C. S.C.).

15§45 — Support for a definite period

Divorce Act, 1985

In *Archer v. Archer* (2005), 12 R.F.L. (6th) 247, 2005 CarswellOnt 1515 (Ont. C.A.); reversing (2004), 10 R.F.L. (6th) 229, 2004 CarswellOnt 4957 (Ont. Div. Ct.), the court, on appeal, reinstated a trial judgement limiting the wife's spousal support to a 3-year term. Although the wife was borderline mentally retarded, the trial judge's findings was supportable based upon the lack of medical evidence and the fact that the wife's application for disability benefits had been rejected.

In *Gregory v. Ball*, 9 R.F.L. (6th) 338, 2004 CarswellAlta 1450, 2004 ABQB 789 (Alta. Q.B.); reversed in part 2005 CarswellAlta 1526, 2005 ABCA 354 (Alta. C.A.), the court refused the wife's application for unlimited spousal support upon the dissolution of the parties' 16-year marriage. Although the wife was not expected to earn income during the marriage, the husband did not discourage the wife from pursuing a career. Furthermore, the wife had received over $4 million on division of the parties' assets and was in a position to generate income.

Where the wife had been out of the workforce for part of the marriage, but was employed full-time at the time of the parties' separation, the court dismissed her appeal from the time limitation placed upon her spousal support award. The trial judge had properly characterized the marriage as a "hybrid" one rather than a "traditional" one, and that the prospect of her achieving self-sufficiency was a realistic one: *Spencer v. Spencer* (2002), 27 R.F.L. (5th) 431, 2002 CarswellBC 1081, 2002 BCCA 265, 212 D.L.R. (4th) 323 (B.C. C.A.); affirming 8 R.F.L. (5th) 419, 2000 CarswellBC 1391, 2000 BCSC 965 (B.C. S.C.).

In *Arvai v. Arvai* (2000), 12 R.F.L. (5th) 1, 1999 CarswellOnt 4848 (Ont. S.C.J.); additional reasons at (September 20, 1999), Doc. London 5855, 1997, 1999 CarswellOnt4847 (Ont. S.C.J.); varied (February 20, 2001), Doc. CA C32629, 2001 CarswellOnt 432 (Ont. C.A.), the wife was granted spousal support reviewable after a 9-month period. Given that her only experience throughout the parties' 17-year marriage was helping the husband farm, she was entitled to support during a period of retraining and while seeking employment. The marriage had caused the wife to lose the ability to support herself, as it was not reasonable to expect that she could find employment in farming.

Where a spouse has been out of the workforce and has on-going childcare responsibilities, limited term spousal support orders should not be the norm: *Phinney v. Phinney* (2002), 33 R.F.L. (5th) 211, 2002 CarswellNS 525, 211 N.S.R. (2d) 135, 662 A.P.R. 135 (N.S.C.A.). However, the court in the *Phinney* case awarded spousal support of $750 monthly for a year and then declining amounts for 3 years

The trial judge's order that the wife pay spousal support to the husband for a two-year period was upheld on appeal where the husband suffered from depression and chronic anxiety but the parties had been married for a short time: *Olstead v. Olstead* (1999), 45 R.F.L. (4th) 46, 124 B.C.A.C. 315, 203 W.A.C. 315, 1999 CarswellBC 895 (C.A.).

In *Juretic v. Ruiz* (1999), 49 R.F.L. (4th) 299, 126 B.C.A.C. 196, 206 W.A.C. 196 (C.A.), the court, on appeal, upheld a three-year limited term spousal support order after the dissolution of the parties' five-month marriage. The husband had advertised for a wife in Guatemala, and had brought her to Canada where she was taking English language training to improve her job prospects. At the time of the marriage, the husband must have been aware that the wife would need time to integrate into the language and social customs of Canada.

In *Mason v. Blatt* (2004), 12 R.F.L. (6th) 115, 2004 CarswellOnt 5440 (Ont. Div. Ct.), the time limitation placed upon the spousal support awarded to the husband was upheld on appeal. Although the husband suffered from depression, the evidence supported the finding that the husband's inability to support himself was more related to his abuse of prescription medication. The husband had done nothing to rehabilitate himself while receiving interim support and an unlimited permanent order could actually do him a disservice.

Where the wife had no real prospect of obtaining work other than in retail sales, no time limit was placed on her spousal support. The wife was emotionally and economically dependant on the husband, lacked self-confidence and self-reliance and had a severely diminished capacity to earn income: *Huck v. Huck* (2004), 9 R.F.L. (6th) 362, 2004 CarswellOnt 3607 (Ont. S.C.J.).

The wife in *Balcerzak v. Balcerzak* (1998), 41 R.F.L. (4th) 13, 1998 CarswellOnt 3785 (Gen. Div.); additional reasons at 42 R.F.L. (4th) 297, 1998 CarswellOnt 4256 (Gen. Div.) was awarded $600 monthly until she obtains full time employment as a teacher.

The wife had stayed home with the children during a 16-year marriage and had resumed her teaching career as a supply teacher, after the separation.

In *St. Germaine v. St. Germaine* (1996), 21 R.F.L. (4th) 244 (Alta. C.A.); additional reasons at (1996), 22 R.F.L. (4th) 292 (Alta. C.A.), the court allowed the husband's appeal from an indefinite support award in the wife's favour and imposed a six month limit on his further obligations. Although the wife had suffered an economic disadvantage from the marriage, the husband had supported the wife during a retraining program which gave her the potential to be self-sufficient and it was now time for her to realize that potential.

In *Crawford v. Crawford* (1997), 33 R.F.L. (4th) 381 (Ont. C.A.), the court dismissed the wife's appeal from a limitation upon her spousal support award that would see it terminate when she reached 65. Although the parties' 41-year marriage had been a traditional one, the limitation was appropriate given that the wife at age 65 would receive pension income that would replace the support income.

Where the wife had given up her waitress job and her plans to start a catering business in order to move with her husband to Italy so that he could take a job there, she was found entitled to five years of spousal support on dissolution of the parties' brief marriage. Although the wife had failed to prove that she had lost a definite business opportunity, she would have difficulties for many years in re-establishing herself: *Roberts v. Shotton* (1996), 22 R.F.L. (4th) 342, 149 N.S.R. (2d) 371, 432 A.P.R. 371 (S.C.); appeal allowed, cross-appeal dismissed (1997), 156 N.S.R. (2d) 47, 461 A.P.R. 47 (C.A.). The appellate court found that the shortfall in the wife's monthly budget arose from her low earnings as a waitress and not from the breakdown of her one-year marriage. As the marriage was brief, the wife was not entitled to support solely because the marriage ended. For the same reason, she was not entitled to periodic support and was granted a $5,000 lump sum.

Where the wife had entered the marriage with some university education and job experience and since separation was close to achieving self-sufficiency, she was awarded support for a period of 30 months to allow her to adapt to a life without the income and other benefits that formerly flowed into the household she had maintained with her husband: *Hopkinson v. Hopkinson* (1996), 21 R.F.L. (4th) 285, 20 B.C.L.R. (3d) 254 (S.C.); affirmed (1997), 34 R.F.L. (4th) 137, 43 B.C.L.R. (3d) 232, 101 B.C.A.C. 41, 164 W.A.C. 41 (C.A.).

Where two years prior to the termination of the parties' 15-year marriage the homemaker wife had returned to school and was earning $4,000 as a part-time supply teacher, her spousal support was limited to a 20-month period. Given her training, the wife was well positioned to obtain full-time employment within that timeframe: *Kent v. Frolick* (1996), 19 R.F.L. (4th) 152, 1996 CarswellOnt 91 (Gen. Div.); varied (1996), 23 R.F.L. (4th) 1, 1996 CarswellOnt 3580 (C.A.). The court varied the order as the appellant at time of trial had only achieved part-time employment and it was not reasonable to limit her support. The time limitation was deleted.

In *Walton v. Walton* (1993), 1 R.F.L. (4th) 93, 23 C.B.R. (3d) 315, 116 Sask. R. 129, 59 W.A.C. 129, 108 D.L.R. (4th) 704 (C.A.); affirming on other grounds (1993), 46 R.F.L. (3d) 137, 110 Sask. R. 263 (Q.B.), a fixed-term spousal support award in favour of the wife was upheld on appeal. During the marriage both parties had worked and pooled their resources until the time the wife had returned to school. In light of their pooling arrangement and the fact that the husband's income had substantially exceeded that of the wife, it was not unreasonable to expect the husband to support the wife for the brief period required for her to improve her ability to be self-supporting.

In *Westersund v. Westersund* (1993), 48 R.F.L. (3d) 416 (Alta. C.A.), the court allowed the wife's appeal from an order which granted her spousal support only until the date on which the wife surmised that she would obtain full-time employment. It was unreasonable for the trial judge to assume that the wife would definitely achieve full-time employment within the time period specified. Furthermore, even if the wife did obtain the position, this would not necessarily remove all economic risks associated with the marriage. The proper course would be to review the support order at the time the wife's circumstances actually changed.

In *Ross v. Ross* (1993), 45 R.F.L. (3d) 230, 12 O.R. (3d) 705 (C.A.), the court deleted on appeal a time limit placed by the trial judge on the wife's spousal support. It was inappropriate to impose such a limitation upon the breakdown of a 23-year traditional marriage. Such an order did not address the economic disadvantage suffered by the wife as a result of the marriage breakdown and her lengthy absence from the workforce.

Where the wife's ability to achieve self-sufficiency had been affected by her health and the role she had assumed during the marriage, the court refused on the husband's appeal to place a time limit on her support award: *Laurence v. Laurence* (1993), 50 R.F.L. (3d) 26, 85 B.C.L.R. (2d) 378, 33 B.C.A.C. 81, 54 W.A.C. 81 (C.A.).

In *C. (L.) c. D. (R.)* (7 janvier 1993), Doc. CA Québec 200-09-000508-926 (C.A. Qué.), the two-year limitation period placed upon the wife's support was deleted on appeal given that she was making every effort to achieve self-sufficiency and eliminate any economic dependency upon her husband.

In *Colletta v. Colletta* (1993), 50 R.F.L. (3d) 1 (Ont. C.A.), the court removed, on appeal, a time limit imposed upon the wife's support. In fixing the term, the trial judge had improperly speculated concerning an improvement in the wife's existing poor health.

Where the wife refused to take medication which would alleviate the symptoms of her manic depressive condition and allow her to live a normal life, her spousal support was limited to a one-year period. The wife had to accept the consequences of her own choice: *Droit de la famille — 1696*, [1992] R.D.F. 686 (Que. S.C.); affirmed (20 May 1993), Doc. Montreal 500-09-001916-923 (Que. C.A.).

In *Boyd v. Boyd* (1992), 41 R.F.L. (3d) 182, 68 B.C.L.R. (2d) 201 (C.A.), the court overturned a support award requiring the husband to pay spousal support to his wife until she had discharged the student loans incurred while she was retraining. The correct principle to be applied was that spousal support should terminate within six months to a year after the spouse has completed retraining.

Where the wife already had the ability to support herself but wished to obtain her Ph.D., she was awarded support for a brief time only to permit her to decide on her future plans and to readjust. As the wife could not prove a need causally connected to the marriage, the husband had no obligation to support her while she obtained her doctorate: *Oswell v. Oswell* (1990), 28 R.F.L. (3d) 10, 74 O.R. (2d) 15 (H.C.); affirmed (1992), 43 R.F.L. (3d) 180 (Ont. C.A.).

Where the wife, over the parties' nine-year marriage, had contributed to the husband's success and had suffered a decrease in her standard of living since separation, she was found entitled to four years' support to assist her with retraining or in finding more remunerative employment: *Caspick v. Caspick* (1988), 17 R.F.L. (3d) 295, 93 N.B.R. (2d) 63,

238 A.P.R. 63 (Q.B.); varied on other grounds 27 R.F.L. (3d) 337, 106 N.B.R. (2d) 249, 265 A.P.R. 249, 71 D.L.R. (4th) 411 (C.A.); application for reconsideration refused (1990), 27 R.F.L. (3d) 337n (N.B. C.A.); leave to appeal refused (1991), 29 R.F.L. (3d) xxxvi (S.C.C.).

It is inappropriate to limit the duration of a support order in the absence of evidence establishing the probability of future self-sufficiency on the part of the payee spouse: *Trainor v. Trainor* (1988), 16 R.F.L. (3d) 349 (Sask. Q.B.); affirmed (1989), 23 R.F.L. (3d) 39, 80 Sask. R. 1 (C.A.).

Where there was no indication that the wife could become self-sufficient within the time limit imposed upon her support award, given her age and the role she had adopted during the parties' long-term traditional marriage, the limitation was struck on appeal: *Stutely v. Stutely* (1992), 41 R.F.L. (3d) 312, 92 D.L.R. (4th) 603 (N.S. C.A.).

In determining whether a temporal limitation on a support order is warranted, the court should give due consideration to the issue of whether the marriage has interfered with the payee's ability to achieve self-sufficiency: *Snyder v. Snyder* (1987), 10 R.F.L. (3d) 144, 80 N.S.R. (2d) 257, 200 A.P.R. 257 (C.A.).

Where the wife had been economically self-sufficient for much of the marriage but would require some time to build up her medical practice, she was awarded spousal support for a period of 9 months: *Low v. Robinson*, 4 R.F.L. (5th) 368, 76 Alta. L.R. (3d) 238, [2000] 4 W.W.R. 663, 2000 CarswellAlta 68, 258 A.R. 201 (Alta. Q.B.); additional reasons at 7 R.F.L. (5th) 148, 79 Alta. L.R. (3d) 137, [2000] 7 W.W.R. 509, 2000 CarswellAlta 336, 258 A.R. 201 at 235 (Alta. Q.B.); further additional reasons at 2000 CarswellAlta 574, 2000 ABQB 399, 82 Alta. L.R. (3d) 175, [2000] 10 W.W.R. 690, 274 A.R. 377 (Alta. Q.B.).

An appeal court may intervene and impose a temporal limitation upon a support order where the trial judge had not given sufficient weight to the payee's income and relative lifestyle in the community where he or she resides: *Czepa v. Czepa* (1990), 26 R.F.L. (3d) 118 (Ont. C.A.); varying (1989), 16 R.F.L. (3d) 191 (Ont. H.C.).

Where the wife had been a nurse prior to the parties' 23-year marriage, but gave up nursing 5 years into the marriage when the parties' first child was born, she was nevertheless required to seek self-sufficiency through nursing and was awarded only limited-term support: *Hedley v. Hedley* (1989), 22 R.F.L. (3d) 309 (B.C. C.A.).

Where the wife had not made a reasonable effort to find employment, an order extending the period of her limited term support was reversed on appeal: *Mroz v. Mroz* (1988), 18 R.F.L. (3d) 331 (Alta. C.A.).

Where two years prior to the termination of the parties' 15-year marriage the homemaker wife had returned to school and was earning $4,000 as a part-time supply teacher, her spousal support was limited to a 20-month period. Given her training, the wife was well positioned to obtain full time employment within that timeframe: *Kent v. Frolick* (1996), 19 R.F.L. (4th) 152 (Ont. Gen. Div.); additional reasons (1996), 3 O.T.C. 122 (Gen. Div.); further additional reasons (July 3, 1996), Doc. 93-ND-199927 (Ont. Gen. Div.); varied (1996), 23 R.F.L. (4th) 1 (Ont. C.A.). On appeal, the judgment was varied to delete the time limitation for spousal support. Otherwise, the wife's appeal and the husband's cross-appeal were dismissed.

Where the wife had not suffered any economic disadvantages from the marriage, the court refused her application for five or six years of spousal support which would allow her to complete her doctorate. The wife would be economically self-sufficient upon completion of her Master's degree in nine months' time and should she wish to continue her education beyond that, both scholarships and part-time employment were available to her. Accordingly, her spousal support was limited to a term of nine months: *Baldwin v. Ward* (1998), 36 R.F.L. (4th) 193, 164 Sask. R. 81 (Q.B.); On appeal at (1999), 2 R.F.L. (5th) 56, 180 Sask. R. 124, 205 W.A.C. 124, 1999 CarswellSask 355 (C.A.), the court held that there was no basis on which the trial judge could have reached his conclusion. The appellate court extended the period of support to three years, such support to be retroactive to January 1, 1999.

In *Perron v. Perron* (2000), 13 R.F.L. (5th) 162, 151 Man. R. (2d) 161, 2000 MBQB 166, 2000 CarswellMan 524, [2000] M.J. No. 476 (Q.B.), the 49-year-old wife was granted a spousal support order, which was reviewable in 3 years, upon the dissolution of the parties' 18-year marriage. The wife had worked continuously throughout the marriage and, in fact, had acquired considerable economic advantage from it. However, a pattern of economic dependence had developed and the wife would require some time to establish a financial plan that would maximize her investment income.

In *Jefferson v. Jefferson*, 26 R.F.L. (5th) 129, 2002 CarswellBC 298, 2002 BCSC 151 (S.C.), the wife was awarded periodic spousal support for a period of 1 year upon the dissolution of the parties' 10-year marriage. Except for the immediate periods surrounding the birth of the children the wife continued to work and there was no evidence that her career aspirations had been adversely affected by the marriage. Her child rearing responsibilities had, to a small degree, impacted her economically.

In *Rush v. Rush*, 27 R.F.L. (5th) 151, 2002 CarswellPEI 28, 2002 PESCTD 22, 211 Nfld. & P.E.I.R. 198, 633 A.P.R. 198 (P.E.I. T.D.), the wife was awarded spousal support for a period of 7 years. Although she was young and employable, she had the care of four young children and she would be required to provide them with full-time care for some time

Where the wife had been economically self-sufficient for much of the marriage but would require some time to build up her medical practice, she was awarded spousal support for a period of 9 months: *Low v. Robinson* (2000), 4 R.F.L. (5th) 368, 76 Alta. L.R. (3d) 238, [2000] 4 W.W.R. 663 (Alta. Q.B.); additional reasons at (2000), 7 R.F.L. (5th) 148, 79 Alta. L.R. (3d) 137, [2000] 7 W.W.R. 509 (Alta. Q.B.); further additional reasons at (June 13, 2000), Doc. Edmonton 4803-110822 (Alta. Q.B.)

Where the husband had ended the marriage in a sudden and unconscionable way, the wife was found to be entitled to limited term support to help her cope with the hardships caused and to ease her through the transition: *Millar v. Homenuik*, 41 R.F.L. (5th) 322, 2003 CarswellAlta 963, 2003 ABQB 570 (Alta. Q.B.)

Where the wife felt obliged to leave her employment with her husband's family business after separation, she was granted limited term spousal support. The wife had suffered a disadvantage from the breakdown of the marriage because of the practical necessity of leaving the business: *Erb v. Erb* (2003), 41 R.F.L. (5th) 49, 2003 CarswellOnt 1339 (Ont. S.C.J.); additional reasons at (2003), 2003 CarswellOnt 2395 (Ont. S.C.J.).

Where the wife remained employed throughout the marriage but had moved several times to support the husband's career, she was found to have suffered an economic disadvantage and was awarded limited term support for a period of 5 years. The wife's career had suffered as she had less seniority and experience as a result of the moves and her child care responsibilities: *Kaluza v. Kaluza*, 50 R.F.L. (5th) 71, 2003 CarswellBC 3132, 2003 BCSC 1879 (B.C. S.C.).

The fact that a spouse may remarry is not a relevant consideration in determining whether or not that spouse suffered an economic disadvantage as a result of the marriage. Such a possibility can, however, be relevant in determining whether support should be restricted to a limited term: *Lauderdale v. Lauderdale* (1999), 50 R.F.L. (4th) 411, 241 A.R. 355 (Q.B.).

In *Dorey v. Snyder* (1999), 48 R.F.L. (4th) 67 (Ont. Gen. Div.), the wife was awarded limited term support upon dissolution of the parties' 16-year marriage. At the outset of the marriage the parties shared the same educational background and were both employed in thriving careers. However, after the wife had taken four years off to raise the parties' children, she returned to the workforce earning less than half of the husband's salary. The wife had proven herself capable of earning income and by gradually reducing support over 4 years, she would have the opportunity to re-establish herself.

In *Motyl v. Motyl* (1998), 36 R.F.L. (4th) 268, 162 Sask. R. 310, 1998 CarswellSask 11 (Q.B.), the husband, who had been employed at the outset of the marriage worked for the wife during the latter part of the marriage, and lost his job when the relationship ended. The court held that the husband was entitled to spousal support, as he suffered economic hardship as a result of the breakdown of the marriage. The wife had paid seven monthly payments to the husband before discontinuing them. As the husband was capable, the court was of the opinion that with due diligence he could have re-established himself within the seven months. Spousal support was awarded only in the amount already paid.

Where the wife had not suffered any economic disadvantages from the marriage, the court refused her application for five or six years of spousal support which would allow her to complete her doctorate. The wife would be economically self-sufficient upon completion of her Master's degree in nine months' time and should she wish to continue her education beyond that, both scholarships and part-time employment were available to her. Accordingly, her spousal support was limited to a term of nine months: *Baldwin v. Ward* (1998), 36 R.F.L. (4th) 193, 164 Sask. R. 81 (Q.B.); varied (1999), 2 R.F.L. (5th) 56, 180 Sask. R. 124, 205 W.A.C. 124, 1999 CarswellSask 355 (C.A.).

Where the wife had limited her employment opportunities by moving with the husband from New York to Winnipeg, she was found to be entitled to support. However, as the parties had only been married for two years and the wife had unduly restricted her job search, she was found entitled to only nine additional months' of support: *Weekes v. Weekes* (1998), 36 R.F.L. (4th) 323, 124 Man. R. (2d) 317 (Q.B.).

Where the parties had no children and the wife had a grade 12 education and job skills, she was granted limited term support, upon dissolution of the 22-year marriage. As the wife had suffered no economic disadvantage from the marriage, termination of her support was linked into the payment to her of her equalization entitlement: *Russell v. Russell* (1997), 29 R.F.L. (4th) 370, 155 Sask. R. 213, [1997] 7 W.W.R. 443 (Q.B.).

Where the wife had been unable, during the parties' troubled 12-year marriage, to establish any long-term employment as a result of frequent moves required by the husband's military career, she was awarded periodic support for a period of two years: *Burns v. Burns* (1997), 33 R.F.L. (4th) 446, 194 N.B.R. (2d) 195, 496 A.P.R. 195 (Q.B.).

In *Horvath v. Fraess* (1997), 36 R.F.L. (4th) 32, 161 Sask. R. 274 (Q.B.), the court refused the wife's request for a three and a half-year spousal support award which would have allowed her to remain in the home until the parties' child began school. The award was limited to a year as the postponement of the wife's re-entry into the workforce for three and a half-years would not promote her economic self-sufficiency and would make it very difficult for the husband to establish an independent life.

In *Bellman v. Bellman* (1999), 46 R.F.L. (4th) 414, 1999 CarswellBC 1122 (S.C.); additional reasons at (1999), 1999 CarswellBC 1749 (S.C.), the wife was awarded spousal support for a period of three years. The parties had a traditional marriage for fifteen years during which the wife agreed to stay in the home with the children. In the seven years since separation the wife had achieved a certain degree of self-sufficiency and given that the husband was now sixty and the wife only fifty, three-years' worth of support was appropriate.

Where the wife had left her employment on several occasions during the parties' 4-year marriage and vast discrepancies existed between the parties' incomes, the wife was found to have suffered an adverse financial consequence from the marriage and was found entitled to support for a period of 30 months: *Turcotte v. Turcotte* (1996), 22 R.F.L. (4th) 364, 1 O.T.C. 156 (Gen. Div.).

In *Scott v. Scott* (1996), 21 R.F.L. (4th) 436, 183 A.R. 103 (Q.B.) the court imposed a one year limitation on the wife's spousal support award upon the termination of the parties' 16-year marriage. As the wife had left her employment to move with the husband to further his career the wife had been economically disadvantaged by the marriage and its breakdown. However, in the three years since the parties had separated the wife had not taken any steps towards upgrading her education or obtaining full-time employment. The one year's worth of support would allow her the opportunity to do so.

Where the mother had given up full-time employment in favour of part-time employment in order to raise the parties' children, one of the factors considered in setting her 24-month spousal support entitlement was the difference between what she had earned part-time during the marriage and what she could have earned full-time: *Bascello v. Bascello* (1995), 18 R.F.L. (4th) 362 (Ont. Gen. Div.); additional reasons to (1995), 26 O.R. (3d) 342 (Gen. Div.); further additional reasons at (1996), 9 O.T.C. 384 (Gen. Div.).

Where the husband's unemployment was due in part to the marriage, he was awarded spousal support for a two-year period. It was probable that the husband would be able to find employment within two years, failing which he could seek an extension of the support order: *Purcell v. Purcell* (1995), 11 R.F.L. (4th) 181 (Ont. Gen. Div.); additional reasons (1995), 11 R.F.L. (4th) 181 at 200 (Ont. Gen. Div.); varied (1996), 26 R.F.L. (4th) 267 (Ont. C.A.); additional reasons (1996), 26 R.F.L. (4th) 272 (Ont. C.A.). On appeal, the court reduced the husband's support from $1,350 to $900 per month.

In *Droit de la famille — 1990*, [1994] R.D.F. 463 (C.S. Qué.) the wife was granted only limited term spousal support as the parties' marriage had lasted only 8 years, and was childless. Furthermore, the wife's share of family assets was sufficient to allow her time to find suitable employment.

Where the wife's diabetic condition, which hampered her ability to work, was aggravated as a result of the marriage breakdown, the husband's requested limitation for her support rights was refused as inappropriate: *Roy v. Roy* (1993), 1 R.F.L. (4th) 170 (Ont. Gen. Div.).

Where the wife had given up a secretarial position to raise the parties' children and remained in the home throughout their lengthy marriage she was awarded spousal support for a period of two years. The wife's economic hardship was, at least in part, directly attributable to the marriage breakdown: *Cerget v. Cerget*, above.

Where the wife continued to be disadvantaged from having given up her career at the time of marriage and by the husband's mismanagement of family finances, limited term support was found not to be appropriate. Although the wife was attempting to re-educate herself, she was not likely to achieve self-sufficiency in the near future: *Wood v. Wood* (1993), 45 R.F.L. (3d) 85 (Ont. Gen. Div.).

In *Robichaud v. Robichaud* (1992), 124 N.B.R. (2d) 332, 312 A.P.R. 332 (Q.B.), the court imposed a two-year limit on the wife's support entitlement upon dissolution of the parties' six-year marriage. The limitation was appropriate given the brevity of the marriage, the parties' means, the effect of the matrimonial property division and the wife's promising prospects for future employment.

Where the wife had been a homemaker throughout the parties' 20-year marriage and had limited job skills and training, she was nevertheless found to have an obligation to attempt self-sufficiency. She was accordingly awarded support for a period of one year to allow her to retrain, after which the order was subject to review: *Romanoff v. Romanoff* (1992), 41 R.F.L. (3d) 433 (Man. Q.B.).

Where the wife had not become totally dependent upon the husband during the parties' 17-year marriage, she was awarded periodic support for a four year period only: *Duncan v. Duncan* (1992), 40 R.F.L. (3d) 358, 128 A.R. 57 (Q.B.).

Where the wife would be unable to meet her needs until she received her property entitlement, the husband was ordered to pay periodic support until that time: *Miller v. Miller* (1992), 40 R.F.L. (3d) 428 (Sask. Q.B.).

In *Droit de la famille — 1412*, [1991] R.J.Q. 1911 (C.S.), the wife was awarded limited-term support pending the division of family assets.

Where the wife was not employed, but would have the same income potential as the husband once she received her share of the matrimonial property, the husband should pay support until payment of the judgment and transfer to the wife of her land: *Metz v. Metz* (1991), 34 R.F.L. (3d) 255 (Sask. Q.B.).

When the breakdown of the parties' marriage and the wife's reaction to the breakdown detrimentally affected her career, but she could eventually become self-sufficient, she was entitled to reasonable support for two years: *Stunt v. Stunt* (1990), 30 R.F.L. (3d) 353 (Ont. Gen. Div.).

Where the wife's lack of job skills and economic dependency could be directly traced to the marriage, she was found to be entitled to support. However, as she had not taken sufficient steps to upgrade her skills or gain employment since the parties' separation, her support entitlement was limited to two years: *Magne v. Magne* (1990), 26 R.F.L. (3d) 364, 65 Man. R. (2d) 241 (Q.B.).

Where it was inappropriate to restrict the wife's support entitlement to a specified period because of the unpredictability of her mental condition, the court nevertheless ordered that either party could seek a review in three years' time without the need to prove a material change in circumstances: *Anderson v. Anderson* (1990), 27 R.F.L. (3d) 358, 66 Man. R. (2d) 248 (Q.B.).

Where the wife during the marriage had developed mental problems which affected her ability to work, the husband was ordered to pay spousal support for a two-year period. Thereafter she would have to survive on her own or with social assistance: *Finch v. Finch* (1990), 24 R.F.L. (3d) 355, 103 A.R. 228 (Q.B.).

A support order should recognize the pattern of financial interdependence in a marriage and allow each spouse to get on with his life. As a general rule, however inter-spousal financial obligation should not continue indefinitely in the future. Support payments should be designed to promote self-sufficiency and give the payee spouse time to gear down from a former standard of living: *Fairall v. Fairall* (1989), 20 R.F.L. (3d) 107, 93 A.R. 224 (Q.B.).

In *Gavigan v. Gavigan* (1990), 30 R.F.L. (3d) 314, 111 A.R. 62 (Q.B.); additional reasons at (1991), 30 R.F.L. (3d) 314 at 322 (Alta. Q.B.), the wife was awarded periodic support for a period of 18 months upon termination of the parties' two-year marriage. Although the wife's current employment offered no future security, she had demonstrated a proven ability to be self-sufficient.

In determining a custodial mother's entitlement to spousal support, her responsibility to the children must be balanced against her obligation to work towards self-sufficiency. In such instances, limited term support may be appropriate: *Kofoed v. Fichter* (1990), 29 R.F.L. (3d) 312, 87 Sask. R. 143 (Q.B.).

In *Power v. Power* (1987), 65 Nfld. & P.E.I.R. 1, 199 A.P.R. 1 (Nfld. T.D.), the wife was awarded periodic maintenance for a three-year period, which coincided with the completion of her university studies.

Where the wife had made no real effort to become self-sufficient and her plans for the future were vague, she was awarded decreasing support for three years only: *Joyce v. Joyce* (1987), 8 R.F.L. (3d) 164, 79 N.B.R. (2d) 100, 201 A.P.R. 100 (Q.B.).

Where the wife had resigned from her job because of health reasons she was awarded support for one year only at which time her entitlement would be reviewed. The wife could apply for a disability pension which would provide economic self-sufficiency, and further, her need was not causally connected to the marriage: *White v. White* (1989), 18 R.F.L. (3d) 216 (Ont. H.C.).

In *Nicol v. Nicol* (1989), 21 R.F.L. (3d) 236 (Ont. H.C.), the wife was awarded spousal support for a three year term. Although she had the same career at separation that she had when she married, the roles adopted in marriage had removed her from the workplace and had prevented her from progressing as she would have otherwise done.

Where the 45-year-old wife had assumed responsibility for the home and child care during the 21-year marriage, she was awarded support for a two-year period. Although a causal connection was established between the wife's need and the marriage, the support order was to promote self-sufficiency and was not intended to guarantee the marital standard of living: *Bast v. Bast* (1988), 13 R.F.L. (3d) 98 (Ont. H.C.).

Where the wife was found to have suffered some economic disadvantage because of the marriage breakdown, she was awarded periodic support for a one-year period to assist in respect of the disadvantage: *Matthews v. Matthews* (1988), 11 R.F.L. (3d) 431, 68 Nfld. & P.E.I.R. 91, 209 A.P.R. 91 (Nfld. T.D.).

Where the wife's economic difficulties stemmed not from the marriage but rather from illness, she was found not to be entitled to an order for permanent support and was granted only seven months' periodic support to allow her to adjust to her new situation: *Schroeder v. Schroeder* (1987), 11 R.F.L. (3d) 413 (Man. Q.B.).

Where the long-term marriage and the roles adopted during marriage interfered with the wife's ability to provide for her future security, she was awarded limited term spousal support to allow her to upgrade her skills on a part-time basis: *Roberts v. Roberts* (1987), 9 R.F.L. (3d) 220, 66 Nfld. & P.E.I.R. 97, 204 A.P.R. 97 (Nfld. T.D.).

In *Pincock v. Pincock* (1986), 73 N.S.R. (2d) 381, 176 A.P.R. 381, 29 D.L.R. (4th) 515 (T.D.), the wife was granted limited term periodic maintenance only to enable her to take a refresher nursing course and meet her obligation to support herself.

In *Gresham v. Gresham* (1987), 8 R.F.L. (3d) 102 (Sask. Q.B.), the wife, who had been absent from the work force for a number of years, was granted periodic support for two years to permit her to retrain.

In *Epstein v. Epstein* (1988), 86 N.B.R. (2d) 326, 219 A.P.R. 326 (Q.B.), as a condition of her periodic support award, the wife was ordered to deliver to the husband in two years' time an affidavit outlining her efforts to find employment and details of possible inheritances. Such information would permit the court to analyze the pattern of financial interdependence and to minimize the economic consequences of the marriage breakdown.

Where the wife had come to Canada to marry the husband and at the time of the divorce she was studying, but spoke little English, she was awarded $600 monthly maintenance until the parties' property award was settled and thereafter $400 until 1988. It was anticipated that at that time her English would be sufficient to allow her to find employment and that the issue of maintenance should be again reviewed: *Lee v. Lee* (1986), 3 R.F.L. (3d) 172 (Alta. Q.B.).

In *Bellman v. Bellman* (1999), 46 R.F.L. (4th) 414 (B.C. S.C.); additional reasons at (July 13, 1999), Doc. Penticton 6612 (B.C. S.C.), the wife was awarded spousal support for a period of three years. The parties had a traditional marriage for fifteen years during which the wife agreed to stay in the home with the children. In the seven years since separation the wife had achieved a certain degree of self-sufficiency and since the husband was now sixty and the wife only fifty, three years' worth of support was appropriate.

In *Gosset v. Gosset* (1997), 30 R.F.L. (4th) 221, 38 B.C.L.R (3d) 289 (B.C. S.C.), the wife's support was limited to two years upon the dissolution of the parties' 21-year traditional marriage. The order was intended to promote economic independence on the wife's part and to give her an opportunity to retrain to achieve that end.

Where the parties marriage had been troubled for several years it was found that limited term not indefinite, support as appropriate: *Harris v. Harris* (1994), 7 R.F.L. (4th) 91 (B.C. S.C.).

In *Andersen v. Carter* (1994), 6 R.F.L. (4th) 90 (B.C. S.C.) the wife's support was limited to two years to permit her to re-establish herself. Rather than suffer economic hardship as a result of the marriage, she had actually benefited from it. Neither her problems resulting from a medical condition and her frequent job losses could be traced to the marriage.

Where the wife had an ability over time to improve her employment position, she was awarded decreasing term support which would promote self-sufficiency. Her support would terminate upon her husband's retirement at which time she would share in his pension income: *Hashem v. Hashem* (1993), 46 R.F.L. (3d) 303 (Nfld. U.F.C.).

Where after the breakdown of the parties' 28-year marriage the wife quit her nursing position because of stress associated with the divorce, she was awarded spousal support in declining amounts over a three-year period. It was highly likely that within that timeframe she would be able to regain employment as a nurse: *Woolgar v. Woolgar* (1995), 10 R.F.L. (4th) 309 (Nfld. U.F.C.).

Where the wife had worked throughout the marriage, but had left her job as a result of the emotional stress resulting from the marriage breakdown, she was awarded periodic support for a period of nine months. By the date of trial, the wife was able to once again seek employment. The limited term support would give her the opportunity to re-establish herself to her former income level: *Swirhun v. Swirhun* (1993), 1 R.F.L. (4th) 53 (B.C. S.C.).

In *McDonnell v. McDonnell* (1988), 16 R.F.L. (3d) 174 (B.C. S.C.), five years from the date of separation, the wife was awarded limited term spousal support until she was self-sufficient. The court was of the opinion that the payee spouse (wife) should not be criticized or penalized simply because her efforts to become financially independent had not been completely successful. The costs of an unsuccessful career should not lie with the payor spouse except to the extent that it is reasonable and just to do so in promoting the wife's economic self-sufficiency within a reasonable period of time.

In determining whether a time limit should be placed on a maintenance award, several factors should be considered, such as: the ages of the spouses and their children; the length of time that the payee spouse has been out of the work force; and the skills, education, health and capabilities of both of the parties: *Lashley v. Lashley* (1985), 47 R.F.L. (2d) 371, 10 O.A.C. 283 (C.A.).

See also *R. (S.M.) v. R. (P.E.)*, 25 R.F.L. (5th) 375, 2002 CarswellBC 637, 2002 BCPC 92 (Prov. Ct.).

15§46 — Support for an indefinite period

In *Allaire v. Allaire* (2003), 35 R.F.L. (5th) 256, 2003 CarswellOnt 1002, 170 O.A.C. 72 (Ont. C.A.), the trial judge's refusal to put a time limitation on the wife's spousal support award was upheld on appeal. The wife had supported the husband through two university degrees and therefore the marriage had a long- term impact on her career advancement and earning capacity.

In *Allaire v. Allaire* (2003), 2003 CarswellOnt 1002, 170 O.A.C. 72, 35 R.F.L. (5th) 256 (C.A.), the court was of the opinion that a trial judge is within his or her discretion to award indefinite support to compensate a spouse for the long-term impact of the marriage on the spouse's career advancement and earning capacity, even if at the time of the hearing the spouse was self-sufficient within the meaning of the *Divorce Act*. In this case, the wife postponed her ambitions in the early part of the marriage, so that she could finance the appellant's 6 years of university education. The parties' decision to have a family further delayed her university studies. The court held that it was inappropriate to consider the wife's annual income of $68,000 "sufficient" without considering whether the husband could financially assist her to live a lifestyle closer to that which they had enjoyed as a couple. The amount of $2,500 in monthly spousal support for an indefinite period was upheld on appeal.

Where the wife, after separation, had been unable to seek employment because of depression relating to the marriage breakdown, the court allowed her appeal from a limited term spousal support order. The wife, throughout the parties' 30-year marriage, had periodically pursued studies and some part-time employment. Given the wife's personality and life experiences it was unlikely that she would be able to achieve self-sufficiency during the term of the 18-month spousal support order. Accordingly, a permanent support order was substituted, requiring the wife periodically to provide the husband with copies of job applications and responses, reports on her health and copies of her income tax returns:

Sitwell v. Sitwell (1998), 38 R.F.L. (4th) 401, 108 B.C.A.C. 278, 176 W.A.C. 278, 50 B.C.L.R. (3d) 205 (C.A.).

In *Choquette v. Choquette* (1998), 39 R.F.L. (4th) 384 (Ont. C.A.), the court dismissed the husband's appeal from an indefinite support award in the wife's favour. The husband sought either reduction in support on a defined schedule or review at a specified time out of concern that the wife would not attempt self-sufficiency. It was held that these circumstances would be better dealt with in a variation application after they occurred rather than anticipating them in the current order.

In *Schmidt v. Schmidt* (1998), 36 R.F.L. (4th) 1, 44 B.C.L.R. (3d) 223, [1998] 6 W.W.R. 624, 156 D.L.R. (4th) 94, 102 B.C.A.C. 124, 166 W.A.C. 124 (C.A.), the court, on appeal, removed a time limitation imposed in the wife's application for a variation of spousal support which would have terminated her support payments upon the husband's retirement. The wife would continue to be in need after the husband's retirement and although his income would be reduced it would still significantly exceed that of the wife. The husband's pension income should have properly been considered in the wife's variation application although the fact of the pension had been a factor in the parties' earlier property division.

Spousal support orders made for an indefinite period of time do not need to contain dates by which a review is to take place, nor must they contain financial disclosure requirements on the part of the spouse receiving support: *Flewwelling v. Flewwelling* (1997), 33 R.F.L. (4th) 390, 194 N.B.R. (2d) 100, 496 A.P.R. 100 (C.A.).

Where a spouse is employable, a permanent order for support in that spouse's favour will generally not provide incentive to seek self-sufficiency or gainful employment. A limited term order is appropriate in such circumstances: *Messer v. Messer* (1993), 47 R.F.L. (3d) 4, 108 Sask. R. 155 (Q.B.). Given the large discrepancy between the incomes of the two parties and the fact that they had been married for 22 years, the court allowed the wife's appeal of a time-limited spousal support order and ordered the matter remitted to a lower court for a determination of quantum. On a further appeal at (1997), 33 R.F.L. (4th) 426 (Sask. C.A.), the husband's appeal was allowed in part as spousal support was reduced from $3,000 to $1,500 per month. The trial judge correctly decided that spousal support should not be time limited. Leave to appeal to the Supreme Court of Canada was dismissed at (1998), 227 N.R. 292 (note), 173 W.A.C. 318 (note) (S.C.C.).

The wife successfully appealed a time-limited spousal support award of three months duration and granted the wife periodic support of $800 per month for an indefinite period in *Clarke v. Clarke* (1997), 34 R.F.L. (4th) 382, 101 B.C.A.C. 225, 164 B.C.A.C. 225, 46 B.C.L.R. (3d) 37 (C.A.). The division of assets in this case was not of such a nature that the need for periodic support was eliminated. The parties had had a traditional marriage and the wife had been out of the workforce for many years. However she did acquire full-time employment, but her future earning prospects were limited. The trial judge recognized that she had suffered an economic disadvantage because of the role she assumed in the marriage. She was 50 years of age at the time of trial.

The court should not impose a limitation on spousal support simply because the need arose from health problems which predated the marriage: *Kloos v. Kloos* (1996), 20 R.F.L. (4th) 1, [1996] 5 W.W.R. 553, 110 Man. R. (2d) 129, 118 W.A.C. 129 (C.A.).

In *Rozen v. Rozen* (2003), 37 R.F.L. (5th) 205, 2003 CarswellBC 1564, 2003 BCSC 973 (B.C. S.C.), the court refused to put a time limitation on the wife's support following the breakdown of the parties' 20-year marriage. The wife had, in the early stages of the marriage, entered into the workplace to allow the husband to continue his studies full time. She had also, throughout the marriage, been the primary caregiver to the parties' children. Taking into account the wife's contribution to the marriage, the economic advantages obtained by the husband as a result of the marriage, and the economic hardships which befell her in not being able to pursue her own professional aspirations, permanent support was appropriate.

In *Doherty v. Doherty* (2001), 19 R.F.L. (5th) 46, 2001 CarswellOnt 2238 (Ont. S.C.J.), the court refused to place a time limitation on the wife's spousal support upon the dissolution of the parties' 23-year marriage. The wife had supported the husband through the first five years of marriage as he completed medical studies and thereafter had remained at home to raise the parties' children. Now 46 years of age, she suffered from osteo–arthritis. The wife was found to have sacrificed her own career and had experienced a serious economic disadvantage from the breakdown of the marriage. Given her age, the time out of the workplace and, to some extent, her health, her prospects for employment and self-sufficiency were quite limited.

In *Johnston v. Johnston*, 19 R.F.L. (5th) 154, 2001 CarswellNB 235, 2001 NBQB 52, [2001] N.B.J. No. 251 (Q.B.), the court refused to put a time limitation on the spousal support awarded to the wife, despite the fact that she had maintained her professional status as a nurse throughout the marriage and worked on a part-time basis.

In *Schmuck v. Reynolds-Schmuck* (1999), 50 R.F.L. (4th) 429 (Ont. S.C.J.); additional reasons at (2000), 46 O.R. (3d) 702, 2000 CarswellOnt 202 (S.C.J.), the court refused to place a time limitation on the wife's spousal support award. The wife had left her secretarial job two years into the parties' 12-year marriage to care for the parties' child. Although she had attempted to upgrade her skills during the marriage, she could never aspire to employment beyond a relatively low paid clerical position.

Where the wife was suffering from multiple sclerosis at the time of the parties' separation and was likely never to return to work, the court found it to be an inappropriate case for imposing a time limit on the wife's spousal support: *Winfield v. Winfield*, 35 R.F.L. (4th) 393, 1998 CarswellOnt 134, [1998] O.J. No. 175 (Gen. Div.); additional reasons at 1998 CarswellOnt 855 (Ont. Gen. Div.)

The wife was awarded spousal support for three years as the parties had only been married for five years and she had a university degree and should pursue more remunerative employment prospects than as an administrative clerk with the government: *Hunter v. Hunter* (1998), 37 R.F.L. (4th) 453 (Man. Q.B.).

Where the wife was suffering from multiple sclerosis at the time of the parties' separation and was likely never to return to work, the court found it to be an inappropriate case for imposing a time limit on the wife's spousal support: *Winfield v. Winfield* (1998), 35 R.F.L. (4th) 393 (Ont. Gen. Div.).

In *Stretch v. Stretch* (1996), 186 A.R. 26 (Q.B.) the wife was found entitled to indefinite spousal support upon the breakdown of the parties' 15-year traditional marriage. There were six children of the marriage, ranging from ages six to 17 and the youngest, who suffered from cerebral palsy required the mother to provide 24-hour care. As a result, the wife's ability to return to the workforce after a 20-year absence would have to be delayed.

In *Fontaine v. Fontaine* (1995), 14 R.F.L. (4th) 16 (Ont. Gen. Div.) the court refused to put a temporal limitation on the wife's support upon the breakdown of the parties' 24-year traditional marriage. Given her age, her grade nine education, her lack of work experience and back problems which she suffered, it was unreasonable to expect her to achieve self-sufficiency.

Where the wife had given up her career to remain in the home during the parties' 22-year marriage she was granted unlimited spousal support. Although the wife had been earning some income from caring for children in her home, the husband's allegation that her failure to take courses to upgrade her skills in that area should bar her support was not well founded: *Drake v. Drake* (1995), 18 R.F.L. (4th) 36 (Ont. Gen. Div.).

Where the wife had abandoned her career as a dental assistant to raise the parties' children throughout the parties' 14-year marriage, she was found to have suffered an economic disadvantage from the marriage entitling her to support without time limitation. The wife's lack of job experience, seniority and opportunity for advancement made it unlikely that she would ever become self-sufficient: *Horvath v. Horvath* (1996), 22 R.F.L. (4th) 279, 109 Man. R. (2d) 20 (Q.B.).

In *Fox v. Fox* (1994), 8 R.F.L. (4th) 257, 153 N.B.R. (2d) 1, 392 A.P.R. 1 (N.B. C.A.); reversing in part (1993), 133 N.B.R. (2d) 361, 341 A.P.R. 361 (Q.B.), it was found that it would be inappropriate to limit the support of the 42-year-old wife, who had returned to university, to the period up to her graduation. She had no previous employment experience and it was premature to determine that her need would not extend beyond graduation.

In *Reilly v. Reilly* (1994), 10 R.F.L. (4th) 6 (B.C. S.C.); additional reasons (1994), 10 R.F.L. (4th) 6 at 23 (B.C. S.C.); further additional reasons (January 9, 1995), Doc. Vancouver D074241 (B.C. S.C.); further additional reasons (June 7, 1996), Doc. Vancouver D074241 (B.C. S.C.) the husband's request that his spousal support obligations end at the time of his future retirement was denied. Given the speculative nature of the husband's retirement income and the fact that it was unrealistic to expect his 60-year-old wife to enter the workforce, a temporal limitation on the wife's support was not justified.

Where the wife's ongoing health problems made it difficult to determine whether she would be able to obtain full-time employment, the husband's request for limited term spousal support was found inappropriate: *Borys v. Borys* (1994), 3 R.F.L. (4th) 139 (Alta. Q.B.).

Where the 53-year-old wife suffered from poor health and self-sufficiency was not a likely scenario within the foreseeable future the court refused to place a time limitation on her spousal support in *Clifford v. Clifford* (1995), 13 R.F.L. (4th) 374 (Sask. Q.B.).

Where the wife had given up her lucrative teaching career to spend more time with her husband and after separation became depressed and was unable to find full-time employment, she was awarded indefinite support. The wife had sustained a substantial economic disadvantage "from the marriage or its breakdown" and the economic hardship continued: *Koberlein v. Barral* (1994), 5 R.F.L. (4th) 94, 94 Man. R. (2d) 133 (Q.B.).

Where the mother had been forced to give up her job as a result of a move occasioned by the husband's employment and she assumed the role of primary care giver to the parties' children, she was awarded indefinite periodic support: *Scullion v. Scullion* (1995), 12 R.F.L. (4th) 421, 158 N.B.R. (2d) 259, 406 A.P.R. 259 (Q.B.).

Where the wife's health problems and lack of education had rendered her unemployable upon the breakdown of the parties' 21-year traditional marriage, she was awarded support without any time limitation. The wife had been fully committed to the marriage in the traditional sense and had suffered economic disadvantage as a result. The court refused to speculate as to what life might have held for the wife had she not been committed to the marriage: *Rossiter-Forrest v. Forrest* (1994), 129 N.S.R. (2d) 130, 362 A.P.R. 130 (S.C.).

In *Laurence v. Laurence* (1993), 50 R.F.L. (3d) 26, 85 B.C.L.R. (2d) 378, 33 B.C.A.C. 81, 54 W.A.C. 81 (C.A.), an indefinite award of spousal support made in favour of the 48-year-old wife, who suffered from muscular dystrophy and was unable to work, was upheld on appeal.

A time limited spousal support order is inappropriate where the payee spouse is incapable of employment because of a psychiatric disorder. If the payee eventually were to become capable of employment, the payor is free to seek variation: *Laue v. Laue* (1995), 17 R.F.L. (4th) 53, 86 O.A.C. 75 (Gen. Div.).

Where the wife had remained in the home during the parties' 18-year traditional marriage and was a recovering alcoholic, the court refused to place a time limit on her spousal support. There was real uncertainty as to whether or not and to what extent the wife would be able to approach self-sufficiency in the foreseeable future: *Day v. Day* (1994), 129 N.S.R. (2d) 169, 362 A.P.R. 169 (S.C.); additional reasons at (1994), 3 R.F.L. (4th) 432, 129 N.S.R. (2d) 186, 362 A.P.R. 186, [1994] G.S.T.C. 26 (S.C.).

In *Chalmers v. Chalmers* (1994), 2 R.F.L. (4th) 446 (B.C. S.C.), the court refused the husband's request that spousal support be ordered only until his retirement. The court should not, in setting support, anticipate the future. Variation proceedings are available to allow for later adjustments should circumstances warrant.

Where the wife had been employed by the husband's business throughout much of the parties' 22-year-marriage and her employment had ceased upon the parties' separation, she was awarded unlimited periodic support. The ending of the marriage had resulted in the wife's economic hardship: *Droit de la famille — 1968*, [1994] R.D.F. 301 (C.S. Qué.).

Where the husband's sole means of support was his pension, which had already been found to be his major entitlement in property division proceedings, it was held to be unfair to order indefinite support at the end of the parties' long term traditional marriage. Accordingly, the wife's support was limited to a 30-month period: *Keyes v. Keyes* (1995), 17 R.F.L. (4th) 201 (N.S. S.C.).

In *Ripley v. Ripley* (1991), 30 R.F.L. (3d) 41, 52 B.C.L.R. (2d) 362 (C.A.), the three-year limitation imposed upon the wife's support order was removed on appeal. The wife was required to care for the parties' sick child and it did not appear that the wife could achieve self-sufficiency within the three-year period.

Where the wife had foregone a career and had assumed home and child care responsibilities over the parties' 24-year marriage, it was inappropriate to impose a limited term support order: *Linton v. Linton* (1988), 11 R.F.L. (3d) 444 (Ont. H.C.); affirmed (1990), 30 R.F.L. (3d) 1 (Ont. C.A.).

Where the 50-year-old wife had required psychiatric assistance both before and after separation and had no prospect of full-time employment, the two-year time limit imposed upon her support order at trial was removed upon appeal: *Hudson v. Hudson* (1989), 19 R.F.L. (3d) 409 (B.C. C.A.).

Where it was doubtful whether the wife would ever be able to work due to her health problems, limited term support was deemed inappropriate: *Trainor v. Trainor* (1989), 23 R.F.L. (3d) 39, 80 Sask. R. 1 (C.A.).

It is improper to apply "clean break analysis" and to award decreasing support in the case of a traditional long-term marriage: *Lynk v. Lynk* (1989), 21 R.F.L. (3d) 337, 92 N.S.R. (2d) 1, 237 A.P.R. 1 (C.A.).

Where at the time of trial the wife was recovering from surgery and was therefore unable to work the court refused to place a time limit on her support award. The husband's appeal from the award was refused, the court holding that it was impossible for the trial judge to determine the time needed before the wife would be well enough to return to work: *Droit de la famille — 683*, [1989] R.D.F. 390 (C.A. Qué.).

Where the wife's opportunity for career advancement had been significantly curtailed because of her home and child care responsibilities, and the husband's career had thereby been advanced, it was inappropriate to place a time limit on the wife's periodic support: *Dick v. Dick* (1993), 46 R.F.L. (3d) 219 (Ont. Gen. Div.); additional reasons at (May 27, 1993), Doc. Ottawa 40021/90 (Ont. Gen. Div.).

A limited term support order intended to promote self-sufficiency is not appropriate where the dependant spouse is in her mid-50's, has uncertain health, is without marketable skills and has been part of a lengthy traditional marriage: *White v. White* (1988), 13 R.F.L. (3d) 458 (N.B. C.A.); reversing in part (1987), 8 R.F.L. (3d) 388, 80 N.B.R. (2d) 221, 202 A.P.R. 221 (Q.B.).

In *Landry v. Landry* (1991), 117 N.B.R. (2d) 200, 295 A.P.R. 200 (Q.B.), the court refused to place a time limit on the wife's spousal support in deference to the parties' separation agreement which required the husband to pay periodic support as long as the wife worked less than 32 hours per week. The wife, upon the termination of the parties' long term traditional marriage, was unable to find full-time employment and the court rejected the husband's assertion that he intended the separation agreement provision to apply for a short time until the wife had readjusted.

An open-ended support order is appropriate where, as a result of a long, traditional marriage, it is unlikely that a wife will achieve self-sufficiency given her age and her lengthy absence from the work force: *Wedgwood v. Wedgwood* (1989), 74 Nfld. & P.E.I.R. 198, 231 A.P.R. 198 (Nfld. T.D.).

Where the wife had few job skills and little work experience but was making an effort to find employment, it was held that placing a temporal limitation upon the award of spousal support was inappropriate. It was open to the husband to have the matter reviewed in the future if the wife's efforts were insufficient: *Fejes v. Fejes* (1988), 13 R.F.L. (3d) 267, 51 Man. R. (2d) 132 (Q.B.).

Section 15(7) of the *Divorce Act*, which requires support to be limited to promote the economic self-sufficiency of the claimant, should be applied only where practical. Where the age and abilities of the claimant render self-sufficiency unlikely, a time limit should not be imposed on a support award: *Gautreau v. Gautreau* (1988), 92 N.B.R. (2d) 178, 236 A.P.R. 178 (Q.B.).

In *Butler v. Butler* (1987), 9 R.F.L. (3d) 70, 66 Nfld. & P.E.I.R. 42, 204 A.P.R. 42 (Nfld. T.D.), limited term support was found not to be suitable in the case of a wife who had not worked outside of the home for 34 years and who had no job skills or experience.

In *Messier v. Delage*, 35 R.F.L. (2d) 337, [1983] 2 S.C.R. 401, 2 D.L.R. (4th) 1, 50 N.R. 14, the Supreme Court held that the trial judge had erred in awarding the wife maintenance for a limited term because he had disregarded the actual factors submitted for consideration and hypothesized as to the unknown and then unforeseeable future. The majority of the court, affirming the Court of Appeal decision deleting the temporal limitation, stated that the parties could always bring an application for variation if their circumstances changed.

In *Sproule v. Sproule* (1986), 2 R.F.L. (3d) 54, 176 A.P.R. 131, 73 N.S.R. (2d) 131 (C.A.), it was held that limited term maintenance was inappropriate for a wife with limited skills who had been out of the job market for 20 years.

Where the 50-year-old wife was a qualified nurse but she had not worked for 23 years the trial judge's decision refusing fixed term maintenance was upheld on appeal: *Jensen v. Jensen* (1986), 5 R.F.L. (3d) 346, 43 Man. R. (2d) 241 (C.A.).

It is an error to limit a wife's support to a term of two years when there is no evidence that she is likely to find full-time employment within that period: *Chadder v. Chadder* (1986), 2 R.F.L. (3d) 433 (Ont. C.A.).

15§47 — Support after termination of support order

A prior termination of support rights does not prevent the court from reviewing the issue of support at a later time: *Droit de la famille — 382*, 16 R.F.L. (3d) 379, [1988] R.J.Q. 2408 (C.A.).

An application for support upon the expiration of the support obligations in the parties' separation agreement should be treated as an original application for support under s. 15 of the *Divorce Act* and not an application to vary under s. 17(10) of the Act: *Vaandering v. Vaandering* (1990), 25 R.F.L. (3d) 310 (B.C. S.C.).

15§48 — Terms and conditions — general

An order for spousal support may be made "for a definite or indefinite period or until a specified event" occurs, and the court "may impose terms, conditions or restrictions in connection with the order as it thinks fit and just": *Divorce Act*, s. 15.2(3).

The court has no jurisdiction to order that a payor spouse's bank accounts be frozen until that spouse honours his or her spousal support obligation. Enforcement mechanisms are available to the payee spouse if required: *Poitras c. Poitras* (1994), 3 R.F.L. (4th) 111, 149 N.B.R. (2d) 211, 381 A.P.R. 211 (N.B. C.A.).

In determining support, the court lacks the jurisdiction to order the payor to advise his former spouse and the court of any changes in his or her financial situation. Before an obligation to disclose arises, it is necessary for the payee to commence proceedings for variation: *Poitras c. Poitras*, above.

A decree *nisi* was altered, on appeal, to delete conditions limiting the wife's entitlement to maintenance which were included when the husband's solicitor prepared the decree *nisi* but were not imposed in the reasons for judgment: *Roschuk v. Roschuk* (1980), 15 R.F.L. (2d) 196 (Man. C.A.).

In *Tennant v. Tennant* (2001), 20 R.F.L. (5th) 195, 2001 CarswellOnt 3297 (S.C.J.); reversed (2002), 2002 CarswellOnt 3865, 62 O.R. (3d) 185, 166 O.A.C. 99, 222 D.L.R. (4th) 51, 39 R.F.L. (5th) 167, 43 C.C.L.I. (3d) 191 (C.A.), the husband had purchased two annuity policies, under which his former wife was named as beneficiary, to fund the wife's spousal support payments. When the husband left Canada and discontinued support, the wife was successful in obtaining an order requiring the insurance company which had issued the annuity policies to remit all future payments under them to her and to vest in her the husband's interests and policies. As the parties' divorce had been finalized before the policies were issued, the wife's claim was not barred by s. 196(2) of the *Insurance Act*, R.S.O. 1990, c. I.8.

Upon payment of a lump sum the husband was entitled to have the wife's share in his company transferred to him: *Denton v. Denton* (1978), 22 N.B.R. (2d) 525, 39 A.P.R. 525 (C.A.).

It is doubtful whether the power under s. 12(6) [now s. 15(4)] to impose terms and conditions includes a power to order a transfer of property: *K. v. K.*, 20 R.F.L. 22, [1975] 3 W.W.R. 708, 53 D.L.R. (3d) 290 (Man. C.A.).

An award of a lump sum and periodic maintenance may be subject to such conditions as the equal division of furniture and surrender of shares by one spouse in the other spouse's corporations: *Krause v. Krause*, 19 R.F.L. 230, [1975] 4 W.W.R. 738 (Alta. T.D.); varied 23 R.F.L. 219, [1976] 2 W.W.R. 622, 64 D.L.R. (3d) 352 (Alta. C.A.).

An award to the wife may be ordered to be reduced three years subsequent to the divorce decree in the expectation that she will require the time to educate herself for an appropriate occupation: *Lazenby v. Lazenby* (1974), 15 R.F.L. 343 (B.C. S.C.); varied 18 R.F.L. 393, [1975] W.W.D. 88 (B.C. C.A.); *G. v. G.* (1970), 2 R.F.L. 243, 3 N.S.R. (2d) 630, 16 D.L.R. (3d) 107 (T.D.); *Hlady v. Hlady* (1978), 11 A.R. 446 (T.D.); *Profitt v. Profitt* (1978), 23 N.B.R. (2d) 249, 44 A.P.R. 249 (Q.B.); *McGrath v. McGrath* (1977), 16 N.B.R. (2d) 462 (Q.B.); *Felix v. Felix*, 10 R.F.L. 313, [1973] 2 O.R. 424, 34 D.L.R. (3d) 48 (H.C.); *Johnstone v. Johnstone*, 1 R.F.L. 363, [1969] 2 O.R. 765, 7 D.L.R. (3d) 114 (H.C.); *Perrin v. Perrin* (1968), 3 D.L.R. (3d) 139 at 142 (Sask. Q.B.).

15§49 — Terms and conditions — specified event

A term in a separation agreement providing for the cessation of maintenance payments upon remarriage or cohabitation by the wife is a valid term. The non obstante language in another paragraph of the agreement does not empower the court to reinstate maintenance for the former wife where it has been validly discontinued as a result of the wife's cohabitation: *Caron v. Caron*, 7 R.F.L. (3d) 274, [1987] 1 S.C.R. 892.

In *Motyl v. Motyl* (1998), 36 R.F.L. (4th) 268, 1998 CarswellSask 11, 162 Sask. R. 310 (Q.B.), the husband, who had been employed at the outset of the marriage worked for the wife during the latter part of the marriage, and lost his job when the relationship ended. The court held that the husband was entitled to spousal support, as he suffered economic hardship as a result of the breakdown of the marriage. The wife had paid seven monthly payments to the husband before discontinuing them. As the husband was capable, the court was of the opinion that with due diligence he could have re-established himself within the seven months. Spousal support was awarded only in the amount already paid.

The wife in *Balcerzak v. Balcerzak*, 41 R.F.L. (4th) 13, 1998 CarswellOnt 3785 (Gen. Div.); additional reasons at 42 R.F.L. (4th) 297, 1998 CarswellOnt 4256 (Gen. Div.) was awarded $600 monthly until she obtained full-time employment as a teacher. The wife had stayed home with the children during a 16-year marriage and had resumed her teaching career as a supply teacher, after the separation.

Where the wife was required to pay off $14,000 resulting from courses she had taken, the husband was barred from seeking a variation of spousal support until such time as he had paid her that amount in periodic support: *Armstrong v. Armstrong* (1997), 34 R.F.L. (4th) 38 (Ont. Gen. Div.); additional reasons at (November 12, 1997), Doc. Ottawa 23545/96 (Ont. Gen. Div.).

15§50 — Terms and conditions — support orders specifying review

In *Leskun v. Leskun*, 2006 CarswellBC 1492, 2006 SCC 25, [2006] 1 S.C.R. 25 (S.C.C.), the court held that review orders under s. 15.2 have a useful but very limited role. Common examples of where they are useful are: the need to establish a new residence, start a program of education, train or upgrade skills, or obtain employment. Where possible, courts should resolve the controversies before them and make an order which is permanent, subject to change only under s. 17 on proof of a change of circumstances. If, as in this case, the s. 15.2 court considers it essential to identify an issue for future review, the issue should be tightly circumscribed in the s. 15.2 order. This should be done because on a "review", neither party bears an onus to show changed circumstances. If the issue is not tightly limited, one of the parties will see the hearing as an opportunity to reargue its case. On the facts of this case, whether the application was treated as brought under s. 15.2 (review application) or under s. 17 (variation application), it made no difference to the outcome. The application was not decided on the matter of the onus. The lower court had made a review order, which was justified by serious doubt at the time of the trial as to the true financial situation and prospects of the wife and what support would be needed.

The difficulty with review orders is that if they are made as a matter of course, they have the potential for unduly increasing the expense of litigation and suspending the ability of the parties from getting on with their lives. However, in this case, since the husband's problems with his eyesight might seriously affect his income-earning ability and/or work-related expenses and this was a foreseeable event which may not meet the test for a variation under s. 17(1) of the Act, the spousal support order should be subject to review: *Tedham v. Tedham*, 2005 CarswellBC 2346, 20 R.F.L. (6th) 217, 47 B.C.L.R. (4th) 254, 2005 BCCA 502 (B.C. C.A.); additional reasons at 2005 CarswellBC 2699, 2005 BCCA 553, 47 B.C.L.R. (4th) 276 (B.C. C.A).

A review hearing for spousal support, as distinct from an application to vary, does not require a demonstration of a change in circumstances: *Phinney v. Phinney* (2002), 33 R.F.L. (5th) 211, 211 N.S.R. (2d) 135, 662 A.P.R. 135, 2002 CarswellNS 525 (N.S. C.A.). Thus, the governing section of the *Divorce Act* is s. 15.2.

In *Arvai v. Arvai*, 12 R.F.L. (5th) 1, 1999 CarswellOnt 4848 (S.C.J.); additional reasons at 1999 CarswellOnt 4847 (S.C.J.); varied (2001), 14 R.F.L. (5th) 223, 52 O.R. (3d) 481, 141 O.A.C. 343, 2001 CarswellOnt 432, [2001] O.J. No. 561 (C.A.), the wife was granted spousal support reviewable after a nine-month period. Given that her only experience throughout the parties' 17-year marriage was helping the husband farm, she was entitled to support during a period of retraining and while seeking employment. The marriage had caused the wife to lose the ability to support herself, as it was not reasonable to expect that she could find employment in farming.

When a review order is made the quantum of support on the review is to be determined in light of all of the circumstances then existing, and with regard to the factors and objectives for spousal support orders contained in the *Divorce Act*: *Munn v. Munn* (1999), 44 R.F.L. (4th) 179 (Ont. C.A.). The parties were in a traditional marriage of 17 years where the husband made financial provision and the wife managed the home and raised their two children. On appeal from order of trial judge that husband pay spousal support of $700 a month for 18 months, the Court of Appeal increased the order to $1,100 a month for five years with the provision that on or before the end of the five years, either party could apply to the court to reconsider the wife's entitlement and any continuation of support.

In *Bildy v. Bildy* (1999), 44 R.F.L. (4th) 81 (Ont. C.A.), the parties separated after 13 years of marriage. The wife was a full-time mother of their two children and a home-maker. She had not worked outside the home for eight years. She was experienced in secretarial work and the highest income she had earned was $27,000 a year. Her husband was a lawyer with an income of $240,000 a year. She owed an equalization payment to him of $43,165 which was to be paid by installments of $500 a month. By agreement made prior to May 1, 1997, her husband was paying $60,000 a year for the support of the two children and $30,000 a year for her support for total support payments of $90,000 a year. Because the agreement was made before May 1, 1997, the full $90,000 was deductible from the husband's income for tax purposes, and includible in the wife's. The issue was whether the spousal support under the agreement should be time limited. The trial judge found that it should be, and ordered that the payments terminate after five years. On appeal, the court held that the spousal support should be paid for a further two years giving a term of seven years with the right of either party at the end of that term to reconsider the wife's entitlement to support for herself and any continuation of it. "The quantum of support, if any, should be decided in light of all of the circumstances as may then exist and upon the application of ss. 15(5) [factors] and (7) [objectives] of the *Divorce Act*..."

A support order specifying a review after a certain period of time is not a limited-term order and the review hearing is not a variation proceeding to which s. 17(10) of the *Divorce Act* applies: *Haigh v. Haigh* (1991), 33 R.F.L. (3d) 161 (B.C. C.A.).

Spousal support orders made for an indefinite period of time do not need to contain dates by which a review is to take place, nor must they contain financial disclosure requirements on the part of the spouse receiving support: *Flewwelling v. Flewwelling* (1997), 33 R.F.L. (4th) 390, 194 N.B.R. (2d) 100, 496 A.P.R. 100 (C.A.).

In *Kozun v. Kozun*, 18 R.F.L. (5th) 115, 2001 CarswellSask 475, 2001 SKQB 329 (Sask. Q.B.), the husband was ordered to pay periodic spousal support, the order to be reviewed in three years' time. The wife, as a result of family duties, had been out of the workforce for 20 years and, although she had found some part-time employment, the extent of the wife's ability to become self-sufficient was unknown.

In *Low v. Henderson*, 17 R.F.L. (5th) 111, 2001 CarswellBC 482, 2001 BCSC 357 (B.C. S.C. [In Chambers]), the parties, in the context of their divorce, signed an agreement which required that the wife's spousal support provided therein be reviewed by the court in two years' time. At that time the parties were both resident in British Columbia and the specified review was to be conducted by a British Columbia court. The wife had moved to Ontario shortly after the divorce and had registered the agreement there. After the husband had commenced review proceedings in British Columbia, the wife sought an order that the British Columbia court decline jurisdiction in favour of an Ontario court. The court refused the wife's request as all factors favoured British Columbia as the forum. The parties had lived there, the agreement was signed there and British Columbia law was to be applicable.

A review order under s. 15.2 of the *Divorce Act*, in contrast to a variation order under s. 17 of the *Divorce Act*, is a determination of support in the first instance and does not require proof of a material change in circumstances: *Bergeron v. Bergeron* (1999), 2 R.F.L. (5th) 57 (Ont. S.C.J.). In situations where a dependant spouse needs time to re-educate, upgrade skills or otherwise find suitable employment, a review order is especially appropriate. In the *Bergeron* decision, the court ordered an additional review in order that there would be a time limit on the wife's efforts to re-educate or re-train.

In *Nock v. Nock* (1998), 43 R.F.L. (4th) 110 (Ont. Gen. Div.), the husband was found to be entitled to spousal support. After separation the husband lost his job and decided that retraining would be his best chance for re-entering the workforce. The husband suffered from a learning disability and would require tutorial assistance to complete his studies. The husband's inability to access the wife's income to cover living expenses while re-training constituted an economic hardship flowing directly from the marriage breakdown. The husband was entitled to periodic support reviewable in 18 months' time.

Where the wife had put her career on hold to care for the children but intended to return to full-time work when the youngest child began school in less than a year, the husband was ordered to pay $950 in monthly spousal support, subject to review when the wife's financial situation became clearer: *Harman v. Harman* (1997), 34 R.F.L. (4th) 121 (B.C. S.C.); additional reasons at (April 29, 1998), Doc. Vancouver D102109 (B.C. S.C.).

The court's jurisdiction to grant support orders which are subject to review in a specified time are supported by the broad language of s. 15(4) of the *Divorce Act* concerning terms and conditions of support orders: *Baggs v. Baggs* (1997), 28 R.F.L. (4th) 185 (Ont. Gen. Div.).

Where the court was not satisfied that the wife was doing all that she could do to become self-sufficient, it made "a review order," granting spousal support for two years and then requiring a review of the order: *Magne v. Magne* (1990), 26 R.F.L. (3d) 364, 65 Man. R. (2d) 241 (Q.B.).

A wife who, during the marriage, became unable to work because of illness was awarded $800 a month to be reviewed at age 45 on the strength of a reasonable prospect that she would attain greater self-sufficiency by that time: *Epp v. Epp* (1998), 40 R.F.L. (4th) 137 (B.C. S.C. in Chambers).

15§51 — Terms and conditions — fluctuating awards

In *Champion v. Champion* (1994), 2 R.F.L. (4th) 455, 115 Nfld. & P.E.I.R. 175, 360 A.P.R. 175 (P.E.I. T.D.), where it was anticipated that the father would experience future periods of unemployment, he was ordered to pay $400 monthly child support while working and only $200 when not.

15§52 — Terms and conditions — indexed awards

Where the spousal support payable to the wife pursuant to the parties' agreement was not indexed, her application for increased spousal support based on retroactive indexing brought 20 years later against the husband's estate was dismissed. The parties, at the time of the settlement, had carefully contemplated the wife's future needs and the failure to index was not unreasonable given the other advantages achieved by the wife in the settlement. The wife had failed to apply for a variation for decades and, in light of all the circumstances, it was inappropriate now to reopen the settlement. Indexing on an ongoing basis was, however, granted: *Misumi v. Misumi Estate* (2003), 39 R.F.L. (5th) 150, 2003 CarswellOnt 957 (Ont. S.C.J.); additional reasons at (2003), 2003 CarswellOnt 3085, 42 R.F.L. (5th) 428 (Ont. S.C.J.).

The language of s. 15(4) of the *Divorce Act*, (1985) is sufficiently broad to provide jurisdiction to index a support order: *Linton v. Linton* (1990), 30 R.F.L. (3d) 1 (Ont. C.A.).

Where both of the parties earned their income from publicly funded institutions, the court refused to order indexation of the spousal and child support payable by the husband. Given the economic climate, it was inappropriate for the support orders to be indexed: *Kent v. Frolick* (1996), 19 R.F.L. (4th) 152 (Ont. Gen. Div.); additional reasons at (1996), 3 O.T.C. 122 (Gen. Div.); further additional reasons at (July 3, 1996), Doc. 93-ND-199927 (Ont. Gen. Div.); varied (1996), 23 R.F.L. (4th) 1 (Ont. C.A.). On appeal, the judgment was varied to delete the time limitation for spousal support. Otherwise, the wife's appeal and the husband's cross-appeal were dismissed.

In *Smith v. Smith* (1998), 36 R.F.L. (4th) 419 (Ont. Gen. Div.); additional reasons at (March 31, 1998), Doc. Barrie 513/97 (Ont. Gen. Div.); further additional reasons at (June 22, 1998), Doc. Barrie 513/97 (Ont. Gen. Div.), the spousal support payable by the husband was ordered to be indexed. Although there is no specific authority for indexing in the *Divorce Act*, jurisdiction was found under s. 15.2(4) and the criteria applied in determining the order was borrowed from s. 38 of the *Family Law Act*, R.S.O. 1990, c. F.3.

In *Simms v. Simms* (1996), 20 R.F.L. (4th) 147, 173 N.B.R. (2d) 161, 441 A.P.R. 161 (Q.B.) the court declined to index the wife's spousal support order until such time as a freeze on the husband's income was lifted.

The court has the authority to index support obligations in divorce proceedings notwithstanding the lack of express authority to do so in the *Divorce Act*: *Payne v. Short* (1995), 10 R.F.L. (4th) 257 (Ont. Gen. Div.).

Where the 57-year-old wife had been away from the workforce during the parties' 21-year marriage, the 61-year-old husband was ordered to pay spousal support. Such order was to be indexed and subject to review upon the parties' retirement: *Yamniuk v. Yamniuk* (1991), 33 R.F.L. (3d) 86 (B.C. S.C.).

Under the broad "terms and conditions" language of s. 15(4) of the *Divorce Act*, the court has power to include in an order for support a clause for automatic increase or decrease based upon the Consumer Price Index: *Kerr v. Kerr* (1989), 22 R.F.L. (3d) 221, [1990] 1 W.W.R. 93, 62 D.L.R. (4th) 694, 79 Sask. R. 52 (C.A.).

Where it was determined that the wife would likely require support indefinitely, the support order was indexed to the lesser of the Consumer Price Index or the percentage increase in the husband's income: *Vogel v. Vogel* (1988), 18 R.F.L. (3d) 445 (Ont. H.C.).

In *Rice v. Pask*, [1983] 2 W.W.R. 302 (Sask. Q.B.), a separation agreement providing for cost of living increases was incorporated into the decree *nisi* to avoid the necessity of repeated variance applications.

See *Richardson v. Richardson* (1987), 7 R.F.L. (3d) 305 (S.C.C.), where the court was of the opinion that where the parties do not have an escalator clause in their settlement agreement, a trial judge cannot insert one in the decree *nisi* where there is no change in circumstances of the kind required to justify a variation of the minutes of settlement.

15§53 — Terms and conditions — matrimonial home

Where the husband's income was insufficient to meet the wife's and children's interim spousal support needs, but he had inherited $170,000, the husband was ordered to pay that amount to discharge the mortgage on the family home and thus considerably reduce the wife's expenses. When the house was eventually resold, the proceeds were to be used to repay the husband: *Polson v. Polson* (1998), 38 R.F.L. (4th) 449 (Ont. Gen. Div.).

In awarding maintenance, a court has power to impose terms and conditions even if the terms and conditions are intended as an inducement to the owner of a matrimonial home to allow his wife and children to continue to reside in the home; an order directing the payment of $400 maintenance for the wife with such payment being satisfied to the extent of $300 by the husband owner making the mortgage, tax and insurance payments on the house so long as the wife and children remain in the house, is not a division of property: *Van Zyderveld v. Van Zyderveld*, 23 R.F.L. 200, [1977] 1 S.C.R. 714, 1 A.R. 14, [1976] 4 W.W.R. 734, 68 D.L.R. (3d) 364, 9 N.R. 413.

It is improper for a trial judge to order the husband to pay an amount representing the weekly value of the wife's interest in the matrimonial home as long as he remains there. The wife has the same right as the husband to occupy and to obtain an order for partition and sale of the property: *Richards v. Richards* (1978), 22 N.B.R. (2d) 107, 39 A.P.R. 107 (C.A.).

"In the event of the petitioner [wife] and/or her minor children being deprived of the exclusive occupancy of the matrimonial home at any time because of any act, omission or failure on the part of the appellant [husband] the petitioner shall be at liberty to apply for an increase in the amount of the periodic payments hereby confirmed or as subsequently may be ordered": per Limerick J.A. in *McConnell v. McConnell* (1975), 57 D.L.R. (3d) 268 at 271, 11 N.B.R. (2d) 19, 7 A.P.R. 19 (C.A.). See also *Storm v. Storm* (1977), 19 N.B.R. (2d) 359 at 360, 30 A.P.R. 359 (C.A.).

The husband was ordered to pay maintenance in the sum of $60 a week for the wife and children on the condition that he allow them to have exclusive occupation of the matrimonial home. If he refused to allow them to occupy the matrimonial home exclusively he would have to pay maintenance of $500 a month: *Chamberlain v. Chamberlain* (1977), 18 N.B.R. (2d) 55 (Q.B.).

"While s. 12(b) [now s. 15(4)] is broad enough to encompass a term or condition that [the wife] be permitted the use of the dwelling (see *Huff v. Huff* (1971), 4 R.F.L. 258, 16 D.L.R. (3d) 584 (Man. C.A.)). I cannot conclude that conveyance of the property can be made a term or condition": per Seaton J. in *Gomes v. Gomes*, 6 R.F.L. 398 at 400, [1972] 3 W.W.R. 151, 24 D.L.R. (3d) 112 (B.C. S.C.).

15§54 — Terms and conditions — remarriage

"This payment [$2,500 per month] of course, continues so long as the wife remains unmarried or is not living in circumstances similar to a state of marriage, and the maintenance payments will be made by the male respondent to the petitioner": per Morand J. in *Gelgoot v. Gelgoot* (1977), 1 R.F.L. (2d) 204 at 207 (Ont. H.C.).

In *Taylor v. Taylor* (1971), 4 N.B.R. (2d) 227 (Q.B.), the husband was ordered to pay maintenance for the wife and children in the sum of $90 a week. In the event of the wife remarrying, payments would be limited to $20 maintenance for each child still attending school or university.

"The wife shall receive her [maintenance of] $150 per month so long as she leads a chaste life and remains unmarried": per Sirois J. in *Upson v. Upson* (1970), 2 R.F.L. 405 at 407 (Sask. Q.B.).

"The usual *dum casta* provision shall apply to this [maintenance] order: and the order shall, of course, terminate upon remarriage": per Davis J. in *Perrin v. Perrin* (1968), 3 D.L.R. (3d) 139 at 142 (Sask. Q.B.).

"Whether a *dum sola et casta vixerit* clause is to be inserted into a maintenance order is a matter of discretion for the court ... However, notwithstanding this discretion, there has been a marked change in judicial attitude towards such clauses and there is a certain reluctance to include them in an order." See *Martin v. Martin* (1965), 51 W.W.R. 318 at 319 (B.C.); *Seeman v. Seeman* (1976), 28 R.F.L. 275 at 278–279, 13 O.R. (2d) 414, 71 D.L.R. (3d) 204 (H.C.).

15§55 — Support — payment to third parties

In *Tennant v. Tennant* (2001), 20 R.F.L. (5th) 195, 2001 CarswellOnt 3297 (S.C.J.); reversed (2002), 34 R.F.L. (5th) 167, 2002 CarswellOnt 3865, C.E.B. & P.G.R. 8483 (note), 62 O.R. (3d) 185, 166 O.A.C. 99, 222 D.L.R. (4th) 51, 43 C.C.L.I. (3d) 191, [2003] I.L.R. I-4192 (C.A.), the husband had purchased two annuity policies, under which his former wife was named as beneficiary, to fund the wife's spousal support payments. When the husband left Canada and discontinued support, the wife was successful in obtaining an order requiring the insurance company which had issued the annuity policies to remit all future payments under them to her to vest in her husband's interests and policies. As the parties' divorce had been finalized before the policies were issued, the wife's claim was not barred by s. 196(2) of the *Insurance Act*, R.S.O. 1990, c. 1.8.

Section 60.1 (20 of the *Income Tax Act*, R.S.C. 1985, c. 1 (5th Supp.) creates a presumption that payments made by one spouse to a third party on behalf of the other spouse constitute a periodic payment to be used at the beneficiary's discretion, and is therefore properly characterized as a "support amount": *Veilleux c. R.* (2002), 27 R.F.L. (5e) 450, 2002 CarswellNat 1083, 2002 CarswellNat 2577, 2002 CAF 201, 2002 FCA 201, [2002] F.C.J. No. 737, 294 N.R. 323, [2003] 1 C.T.C. 138 (C.F.A.).

The court has jurisdiction to order a husband to make maintenance payments to a government welfare agency. The *Divorce Act* does not require that maintenance payments be made to a party to the marriage: *Hamelin v. Ladouceur* (1985), 43 R.F.L. (2d) 420 (Alta. Q.B.).

A lump sum payment was awarded to the respondent wife but the trial judge was doubtful of her ability to manage or administer a relatively large sum of money without assistance. Accordingly, he ordered that her husband pay the sum of $5,000 to the Public Trustee to be disbursed by him for the benefit of the respondent: *Raffin v. Raffin*, 5 R.F.L. 274, [1972] 1 O.R. 173, 22 D.L.R. (3d) 497 (C.A.).

The court may order that child maintenance payments be made to the registrar of the Supreme Court, Family Division: *MacKenzie v. MacKenzie* (1975), 25 R.F.L. 354, 9 Nfld. & P.E.I.R. 176 (P.E.I. S.C.). See also *Proctor v. Proctor* (1975), 22 R.F.L. 217, 57 D.L.R. (3d) 766 (Man. Q.B.), where payment of child maintenance was through the Family Court.

"While it is not necessary that the decree nisi itself so provide I direct that payment of the lump sum aforesaid shall be made to the petitioner and her solicitor jointly. I have full confidence in the latter's ability to see that the moneys are, at least initially, properly invested and that some appropriate scheme is set up for their management to ensure, as far as possible, that they will be of enduring value to the petitioner": per Dickson J. in *Bates v. Bates* (1971), 7 R.F.L. 344 at 349, 4 N.B.R. (2d) 174 (Q.B.).

15§56 — Terms and conditions — support orders binding against estates

In *Reilly v. Reilly* (1999), 50 R.F.L. (4th) 424 (B.C. S.C.); varied 5 R.F.L. (5th) 116, 2000 BCCA 130, 137 B.C.A.C. 151, 223 W.A.C. 151, 2000 CarswellBC 361 (C.A.) the court refused the wife's request to have her spousal support award made binding on the husband's estate. The wife was not in extremely necessitous circumstances, nor was the husband in relatively affluent circumstances.

It is unclear whether the court has any power to make a divorce support order binding on the payor's estate. In any case, such an order is inappropriate where the payor has limited means and a likely modest estate: *Hillhouse v. Hillhouse* (1992), 43 R.F.L. (3d) 266, 74 B.C.L.R. (2d) 230 (C.A.). See also *Carmichael v. Carmichael* (1992), 43 R.F.L. (3d) 145, 115 N.S.R. (2d) 45, 314 A.P.R. 45, 96 D.L.R. (4th) 685 (C.A.), where the court held that it was without jurisdiction to make a support order binding the payor's estate.

It takes clear, specific and unequivocal language before a spousal support order will be construed as surviving the death of the payor spouse. An award which is stated to be "for an indefinite period" does not meet the test and is insufficient to bind the estate of the payor spouse: *Schwartz Estate v. Schwartz* (1998), 36 R.F.L. (4th) 110, 21 E.T.R. (2d) 9 (Ont. Gen. Div.).

15§57 — Terms and conditions — designating beneficiary

Where the husband had previously cancelled certain life insurance policies which had named his wife as beneficiary, he was ordered to secure his wife's spousal support by designating her irrevocably as beneficiary of all supplementary death benefits accruing to him under the Canadian Forces Superannuation Act: *Parsons v. Parsons* (1995), 17 R.F.L. (4th) 267 (Ont. Gen. Div.); additional reasons (1995), 17 R.F.L. (4th) 267 (note) (Ont. Gen. Div.).

15§58 — Terms and conditions — interest on support award

In *Kopunovic v. Cukotic-Kopunovic* (1996), 19 R.F.L. (4th) 137 (Ont. Gen. Div.); additional reasons at (March 22, 1996), Doc. 35506905/92 (Ont. Gen. Div.), the wife was awarded substantial prejudgment interest on a lump sum spousal support claim brought eight years after the parties' separation. The interest was not properly reduced despite the wife's delay, as it was the result of her psychological problems and a dependency which had been fostered by the husband. Furthermore, the husband had continued to benefit from the wife after separation and had not altered his financial position in reliance upon the absence of a claim.

There is nothing in the *Divorce Act* nor in the Civil Code of Quebec on alimentary obligations that suggests that interest is automatically payable on arrears of support. The requirement to pay interest must accordingly be explicit in the case of an alimentary order: *G. (L.) v. B. (G.)* (1996), 21 R.F.L. (4th) 234, [1996] R.J.Q. 381, [1996] R.D.F. 187 (C.S. Qué.).

15§58A — Terms and conditions — maintaining benefits

Where the wife's inability to find meaningful employment flowed directly out of the marriage, the husband was ordered to maintain for the benefit of the wife all extended health, dental and medical benefits available to him through his employment, or alternatively to pay costs of a similar plan for the wife until she was covered herself by a future employer: *Eccles v. Eccles* (2002), 27 R.F.L. (5th) 47, 2002 CarswellOnt 1284 (S.C.J.); reversed (2003), 2003 CarswellOnt 3235 (C.A.).

15§58B — Terms and conditions — provisional awards

In *Noel v. Noel*, 39 R.F.L. (4th) 214, 1998 CarswellAlta 409, 217 A.R. 201, [1998] 10 W.W.R. 605, 62 Alta. L.R. (3d) 376 (Alta. Q.B.), the husband won a prize of $5.47 million in a lottery 14 months after the parties' final separation but before their divorce. At the time of the hearing there were approximately $8 million of lottery winnings and earnings. The parties had been married for over 15 years and the wife was in poor health. The Court ordered that the husband pay the wife approximately $2 million and in the event that order was set aside, provisional spousal support in a lump sum to be calculated at the rate of $2,500 per month for 20 years, beginning on the date of this judgment using a discount rate of 5%. Support was ordered on the basis of the economic interdependency of the parties, the lengthy duration of the marriage, the functions each spouse performed during cohabitation, the wife's present condition, means and needs and, most significantly, the husband's vast financial resources.

SPOUSAL SUPPORT — Method of Payment

15§59 — Spousal support order — general

In awarding support the court may "make an order requiring a spouse to secure or pay, or to secure and pay, such lump sum or periodic sums, or such lump sum and periodic sums, as the court thinks reasonable for the support of the other spouse": *Divorce Act*, s. 15.2(1). The term "spouse" in this subsection includes a former spouse: *Divorce Act*, s. 15.

In assessing a claim for compensatory spousal support, the court must consider all existing financial realities as well as all that might befall the parties: *Lacharite v. Lacharite* (2003), 39 R.F.L. (5th) 119, 2003 CarswellOnt 939 (Ont. S.C.J.)

In *T. (J.G.) v. N. (T.)* (2003), 42 R.F.L. (5th) 208, 2003 CarswellAlta 868, 330 A.R. 187, 299 W.A.C. 187, 2003 ABCA 195 (Alta. C.A.), the mere fact that the mother was able to return to the same type of employment she had before assuming primary responsibility for the parties' children was no reason not to award her compensatory support. To adopt a contrary approach would be to ignore the reality of career progression and advancement.

15§60 — Spousal support order — to secure lump sum or periodic sums

The power to "secure" support has two meanings: to post an income producing security with the income to be used as support, and, secondly, to post security as a guarantee of payment. The two meanings come from the two similar phrases used in the subsection — "to secure or pay" and "to secure and pay" [emphasis added]. If the subsection contained only the first phrase, to secure or pay, the court would have no jurisdiction to order payment of support and the posting of security to be realized in default of payment. This, in fact, was the case with the 1968 *Divorce Act*. The comparable subsection in this early version of the Act contained only the power to "secure or pay" the support amount, and the judicial interpretation of this phrase at the Supreme Court of Canada level clarified the distinction between the two meanings.

The requirement that a spouse name the other one as an irrevocable beneficiary under a life insurance policy is not fulfilled by naming that spouse as a beneficiary under an accidental death policy: *Collins v. Collins* (2005), 12 R.F.L. (6th) 272, 2005 CarswellAlta 265, 2005 ABCA 98, 363 A.R. 229, 343 W.A.C. 229 (Alta. C.A.).

In *Nash v. Nash*, 16 R.F.L. 295, [1975] 2 S.C.R. 507, 47 D.L.R. (3d) 558, 2 N.R. 271 and *Van Zyderveld v. Van Zyderveld*, 23 R.F.L. 200, [1977] 1 S.C.R. 714, [1976] 4 W.W.R. 734, 9 N.R. 413 the Supreme Court held that the phrase "secure or pay" was not broad enough to permit the court to make both an order to pay periodic sums and concurrently to order the posting of security which could be realized if there were default under the order to pay. The court had no power under this single phrase, it was held, to order security to stand as a guarantee of payment. An order to pay and an order to secure are two distinct and independent orders. An order to pay periodic support creates a personal obligation and a debtor creditor relationship. Under the Act of 1968 an order to secure, on the other hand, did not impose such an obligation. If ordered to secure periodic payments, the only obligation of the spouse against whom the order was made, was to provide the security and nothing more. There was no personal obligation to pay, and the spouse never became a debtor in respect of the payments. The other spouse had the benefit of the security and was required to look to it alone. If it did not yield the expected payments, the spouse putting up the security could not be called upon to make good the deficiency: *Nash v. Nash, supra*.

"The wording in [s. 11 of the *Divorce Act*, 1969] ... is the court may make an order 'requiring the husband to secure'. The section to my mind contemplates that the court shall direct the husband to do the things that are necessary to make the security effective and may order him to execute an instrument whereby the sum ordered to be paid is effectively secured on the property. The husband, however, is not personally liable to pay the periodic sums where he has been ordered to secure such sums. In respect of any sum ordered to be paid by the court but not secured he is, of course, personally liable to pay such sums": per McDermid J.A. in *Switzer v. Switzer* (1969), 1 R.F.L. 262, 70 W.W.R. 161, 7 D.L.R. (3d) 638 (Alta. C.A.). See also *Dexter v. Dexter* (1975), 11 N.B.R. (2d) 11 at 13, 7 A.P.R. 11 (C.A.).

The court, when ordering periodic payments or a lump sum amount and at the same time providing for security of payment, must direct that the payments be paid out of the security. Therefore, where the maintenance is ordered to be secured against a house which is further ordered to be sold, the order must show that it is the proceeds of any sale from which payment of the lump sum is to be made without attaching additional conditions for the time of sale: *Van Zyderveld v. Van Zyderveld*, above. See also *Law v. Law* (1978), 23 N.B.R. (2d) 114, 44 A.P.R. 114 (C.A.); and *Foy v. Foy* (1979), 14 R.F.L. (2d) 12 (Ont. C.A.).

"I have considered the possibility of requiring a personal guarantee from the respondent as well but the decision in the *Nash* case above makes it clear that, when a sum for maintenance is secured, the party providing the security is free from any further obligation in respect of the sum secured so long as the security remains in force without variation": per Stevenson J. in *Bastarache v. Bastarache* (1975), 25 R.F.L. 72 at 74, 11 N.B.R. (2d) 564, 7 A.P.R. 564 (Q.B.).

The subsequent addition of the second phrase "to secure *and* pay" (emphasis added) solves the problem seen under the old wording and allows the court to order a spouse to pay support, and at the same time order the spouse to post security to guarantee payment in the sense that if the spouse defaults in the obligation to pay, the security could be realized, at least to the extent of the deficiency.

The combination of the two phrases in the present Act: "to secure *or* pay, or to secure *and* pay" (emphasis added) leads to the possibility of three kinds of orders, and not merely two as existed under the old statute:

(i) order to pay support;

(ii) order to secure support where the security yields periodic payments such as interest payments and the benefitting spouse is entitled to these payments and nothing more; and

(iii) order to secure payment of support where the order is collateral to a concurrent order to pay support and the security can be realized if there is default in payment.

A court has no jurisdiction to secure maintenance payments against the interest in property of a trustee in bankruptcy as neither a claim for maintenance nor a claim for arrears of maintenance is provable in bankruptcy proceedings: *Kutschenreiter v. Kutschenreiter* (1983), 46 C.B.R. (N.S.) 1 (Ont. H.C.); *Switzer v. Switzer* (1970), 1 R.F.L. 262, 70 W.W.R. 161, 7 D.L.R. (3d) 638 (Alta.); *J. v. J.* (1969), 8 D.L.R. (3d) 760 (Sask.); *Pugh v. Pugh* (1970), 4 R.F.L. 213 at 221, 2 N.S.R. (2d) 409, 16 D.L.R. (3d) 318 (T.D.).

15§61 — Periodic — payment secured against payor's property

Where the husband had demonstrated a disinclination to make child support payments in a timely manner, an order securing those payments was upheld on appeal: *Koyama v. Leigh* (1998), 36 R.F.L. (4th) 64, 103 B.C.A.C. 168, 169 W.A.C. 168, 46 B.C.L.R. (3d) 299 (C.A.).

Where the father was an alcoholic and had a poor past record of paying support, his child support obligation was ordered secured against his share of the proceeds from the sale of the family home. Furthermore, in the event that he died while the child support order remained in force, it was further ordered that the support payments should bind his estate: *Nicklason v. Nicklason* (1989), 22 R.F.L. (3d) 185 (B.C. S.C.).

Where the husband had expressed his intention never to pay spousal or child support, the wife was awarded lump sum support as well as periodic child support, 15 months of which were ordered secured from the proceeds of sale of the husband's property: *Sukhram v. Sukhram* (1987), 7 R.F.L. (3d) 453, 47 Man. R. (2d) 126 (Q.B.).

In *Gilbert v. Gilbert* (1972), 7 R.F.L. 188 (Ont. H.C.), the evidence indicated that the respondent husband had not supported his wife. Her health, as indicated by a doctor's report and the petitioner's own evidence was such that she had suffered more than one heart attack. The petitioner was 59 years of age. The respondent lived in Florida and had disposed of all assets within the jurisdiction of the court save and except a one-third interest as a tenant-in-common in a farm having an estimated value of between $500,000 and $600,000. The respondent had refused to pay any alimony or support to the petitioner because of the petitioner's refusal to bar her dower in the aforementioned farm. Periodic payments of $650 per month were secured against the husband's interest in this property. See also *Harasyn v. Harasyn* (1970), 2 R.F.L. 105, 13 D.L.R. (3d) 635 (Sask. Q.B.); *Grypiuk v. Grypiuk* (1970), 2 R.F.L. 280 (Sask. Q.B.); *Bangert v. Bangert* (1977), 18 N.B.R. (2d) 327 (Q.B.); *Sullivan v. Sullivan* (1973), 18 R.F.L. 298 at 300, 8 N.B.R. (2d) 690 (Q.B.); *Vickers v. Vickers* (1973), 18 R.F.L. 338 at 339, 9 N.B.R. (2d) 96, 1 A.P.R. 96 (Q.B.); *Golightly v. Golightly* (1973), 9 R.F.L. 212 (Ont. H.C.); *Calder v. Calder* (1974), 15 R.F.L. 265 at 267 (Ont. H.C.); *Lyman v. Lyman* (1973), 18 R.F.L. 326, 9 N.B.R. (2d) 89, 1 A.P.R. 89 (Q.B.); and *J. v. J.* (1970), 8 D.L.R. (3d) 760 (Sask. Q.B.).

In *Neville v. Neville* (1980), 30 Nfld. & P.E.I.R. 176, 84 A.P.R. 176 (Nfld. U.F.C.), the petitioner sought an order of maintenance for herself and her children, who were receiving social assistance. The respondent gave evidence, under oath, which in effect amounted to his having no income, no savings, no prospects of work, nor was he in a position to provide any maintenance to his wife and children. However, in view of the fact that the respondent husband had a $4000 equity in some parcels of land, periodic payments were secured by a mortgage on the equity of redemption in the husband's lands.

15§61A — Transfer of pension

An order requiring that the entirety of the husband's pension be transferred to the wife, 50 per cent to be paid as registered retirement savings and the other 50 per cent as pension in pay on a monthly basis does not contravene the *Pension Benefits Act*, R.S.O. 1990, c. P.8: *Nicholas v. Nicholas* (1998), 37 R.F.L. (4th) 13, 17 C.C.P.B. 130 (Ont. Gen. Div.).

15§61B — Forced sale of property

In *Knoth v. Knoth*, 38 R.F.L. (5th) 123, 2003 CarswellBC 579, 2003 BCSC 417 (B.C. S.C.), the court refused the wife's application for an order compelling the husband to sell his farm to make funds available for the payment of spousal support. The farm was the only source of the husband's income and the sale would prevent him from earning anything in the traditional way he had.

15§62 — Lump sum — jurisdiction

Divorce Act, 1985

A lump sum order blending pension entitlement, spousal and child support should not be made without clear apportionment: *Hanna v. Hanna* (1994), 4 R.F.L. (4th) 148 (N.S. C.A.).

A trial judge is entitled to consider and award lump sum support where the claimant asserts the claims orally during trial but the documents contain only a general claim for support: *Mosher v. Mosher* (1995), 13 R.F.L. (4th) 385, 140 N.S.R. (2d) 40, 399 A.P.R. 40 (C.A.); reversing in part (1993), 126 N.S.R. (2d) 367, 352 A.P.R. 367 (S.C.).

Divorce Act, 1968

"Section 11(1) [now s. 15.2(1)] does not authorize the court to enter into the area of divisions of property for any purpose. The reason is plain. The *B.N.A. Act*, 1867, c. 3, s. 92(13), gives exclusive jurisdiction to the provinces in the realm of 'property and civil rights in the Province'. It is only when the court grants a divorce that s. 11 [now s. 15] empowers the court to make an order for maintenance, and such is then made solely as consequential relief accompanying the divorce itself. When a divorce is refused no order can be made under said s. 11 [now s. 15.2(1)], because such would not be relief corollary to a divorce but would be an order affecting the property and civil rights of a husband and wife, inter se, and such an order would be outside the legislative authority of the Parliament of Canada: see *Zacks v. Zacks*, [1973] S.C.R. 891, 10 R.F.L. 53, [1973] 5 W.W.R. 289, 35 D.L.R. (3d) 420": per Disbery J. in *Rathwell v. Rathwell* (1974), 16 R.F.L. 387 at 390–91 (Sask. Q.B.).

Although the court lacks jurisdiction to order the transfer of the matrimonial home from the husband to the wife in a divorce proceeding, an order awarding lump sum maintenance to the wife, which sum could be satisfied by the husband's transfer of the home, is within the court's jurisdiction: *Widrig v. Widrig* (1981), 24 R.F.L. (2d) 379, 48 N.S.R. (2d) 269, 92 A.P.R. 269 (T.D.).

In *Hoyer v. Hoyer* (1981), 24 R.F.L. (2d) 444, 32 B.C.L.R. 41 (S.C.), the wife's one-half interest in the matrimonial home was ordered to be transferred to the husband by way of lump sum maintenance for the child of the marriage.

"In my opinion Parliament has a jurisdiction to authorize a maintenance order as an incident to a decree of divorce. Parliament may not have the power to redistribute capital assets acquired during the marriage. It is only when a lump sum is a proper way to provide maintenance or when a lump sum is necessary to put a person in a particular position that a lump sum award should be made. Granting a lump sum to reduce periodic maintenance — because capital will produce income — is really redistributing capital. Maintenance has always had a particular meaning in the law — as is shown by the English and Australian decisions — as well as our own. It does not mean a sharing of capital assets. It is doubtful that Parliament could legislate such a division": per Moir J.A. in *Krause v. Krause*, 23 R.F.L. 219 at 227, [1976] 2 W.W.R. 622, 64 D.L.R. (3d) 352 (Alta. C.A.).

Wide as the court's discretion is on applications for maintenance, including the power to order payment of a lump sum, the court's discretion must be exercised for the attainment of one purpose only, namely, the provision of proper maintenance. In arriving at the amount of such a lump sum, care must be taken not to do so on any basis of working out what might be an equitable division of assets between the husband and the wife, having regard to their respective contributions to its accumulation, and then to fix a lump sum arrived at on that basis: *Osborne v. Osborne* (1973), 14 R.F.L. 61 (Sask. Q.B.); varied (1974), 23 R.F.L. 358 (Sask. C.A.).

15§63 — Lump sum — general objectives

In *Tauber v. Tauber* (2003), 2003 CarswellOnt 1009, 34 R.F.L. (5th) 450, 64 O.R. (3d) 229, 170 O.A.C. 1, 225 D.L.R. (4th) 186 (C.A.), the appellate court upheld a lump sum payment of $500,000 for spousal support. The payment would assist the wife to provide a lifestyle comparable to the one which the child had enjoyed when he lived with both parents, a lifestyle to which the husband was readily able to contribute. The payment would enable the wife to enhance her self-sufficiency and help her to purchase a permanent home for herself and the parties' child. While the amount was substantial, it should be seen in the context on the husband's assets which were worth between $19 and $20 million, his undisputed ability to pay, and the parties' lifestyle during the marriage.

In *Topolnitsky v. Topolnitsky* (1997), 32 R.F.L. (4th) 196, 118 Man. R. (2d) 276, 149 W.A.C. 276 (C.A.), a lump sum spousal support in favour of the wife was found to be justified by the following factors: the wife's inability to work because of her health; the resistance of the husband in the past to provide any support for the wife; the parties' advancing years; the husband's interest in a successful company; the lack of any real chance of improvement in the wife's financial circumstances; and the existence of a financial pool from which the husband could draw to pay the lump sum.

As a general rule, lump sum support as a method of paying retroactive support should only be made in the exceptional case. A lump sum in satisfaction of prior support obligations is simply a windfall for the claimant in reimbursement for funds notionally spent: *Hovorka v. Hovorka* (1996), 140 Sask. R. 36 (Q.B.).

Lump sum support is appropriate in cases where it is needed to fund retraining and to meet immediate needs. It should not be awarded to cover legal fees nor is it appropriate to provide for future security where the claimant is also receiving periodic support: *Mosher v. Mosher* (1995), 13 R.F.L. (4th) 385, 140 N.S.R. (2d) 40, 399 A.P.R. 40 (C.A.); reversing in part (1993), 126 N.S.R. (2d) 367, 352 A.P.R. 367 (S.C.).

The discretion to award lump sum spousal support under s. 15 of the *Divorce Act* should not be used to redistribute property or to compensate a spouse for contingent liabilities: *Graham v. Platt* (1996), 19 R.F.L. (4th) 32, 108 Man. R. (2d) 62 (Q.B.).

Where a spouse has an immediate or specific need, such as paying the extraordinary expenses of furthering her education, a court will award lump sum support: *McGuigan v. McGuigan* (1991), 33 R.F.L. (3d) 183, 105 N.S.R. (2d) 170, 284 A.P.R. 170 (T.D.).

A lump sum award should only be awarded in exceptional circumstances where economic need is demonstrated: *Leblond v. Grenier* (12 février 1992), C.A. Québec 200-09-00369-907 (C.A. Qué.).

Lump sum interim support should be awarded only in the most exceptional of circumstances: *Droit de la famille — 1613*, [1992] R.D.F. 404 (C.S. Qué.).

Lump sum support is not an appropriate remedy where the claimant wishes only to avoid future possible harassment from the payor spouse: *D. (D.) c. B. (J.)* (1991), 43 Q.A.C. 105.

In *McDonald v. McDonald* (1988), 15 R.F.L. (3d) 268, 216 A.P.R. 118, 85 N.S.R. (2d) 118 (T.D.), the court awarded the wife periodic and lump sum maintenance to promote her self-sufficiency, providing her with funds for a car, driving lessons and possibly for training to return to the work force. The lump sum payment could be satisfied by the husband conveying to the wife his interest in the matrimonial home.

In *Magne v. Magne* (1990), 26 R.F.L. (3d) 364, 65 Man. R. (2d) 241 (Q.B.), the wife was granted a lump sum award of $7000 which represented the payments that should have been made under the parties' voluntary agreement and which the husband unilaterally stopped.

"In my opinion, when the court finds that a petitioner is entitled to a maintenance order the court should first order periodic payments, and then, when it is necessary to provide proper maintenance, to order a lump-sum payment in addition to the periodic payments. There will be, of course, special cases where in their circumstances a lump sum in lieu of periodic payments would be justified": per Disbery J. in *Osborne v. Osborne* (1973), 14 R.F.L. 61 at 70–71 (Sask. Q.B.); varied (1974), 23 R.F.L. 358 (Sask. C.A.).

The purpose of lump sum maintenance is to provide for some particular purpose, such as the purchase of a home or to guarantee maintenance payments in an unstable situation. The award is not to be used to affect a division of family assets: *Droit de la famille — 49*, [1983] C.S. 996 (C.S. Que.). See also *Dieser v. Dieser* (1977), 6 A.R. 298 (T.D.).

In *Laflamme v. Laplante*, [1981] C.S. 1031 (Que.), it was held that the wife was not entitled to an award of lump sum maintenance on the sole basis that the husband had accrued sizeable assets during the course of the marriage. The purpose of lump sum maintenance is not to divide or redistribute the husband's capital. See also *Rathwell v. Rathwell* (1974), 16 R.F.L. 387 (Sask. Q.B.); *Ferguson v. Ferguson* (1974), 19 R.F.L. 331 at 334–35 (B.C. S.C.).

Lump sum support should generally be granted only to cover costs and expenses which are of an alimentary nature: *Droit de la famille — 1229*, [1989] R.D.F. 152 (C.S. Qué.).

In *Daly v. Daly*, 19 R.F.L. (2d) 247, [1980] 6 W.W.R. 680, 4 Man. R. (2d) 63, 114 D.L.R. (3d) 435 (C.A.), a lump sum award was reduced on appeal where the trial judge appeared to have used it as a mechanism to effect a division of assets, the wife's means were greater than the husband's and her needs were met by her own earnings.

The court does not have the authority to effect a division of property acquired by one or the other of the parties during the marriage, under the separation of property regime. A lump sum payment cannot be ordered to enrich one party at the expense of the other. The matter of re-adjusting the patrimonies of the spouses is not within the jurisdiction of the court granting the divorce but is left to the Civil Code and the matrimonial regime into which the parties contracted. The judge is entitled to order a lump sum payment on top of periodic payments, provided it is for the support of the person to whom it is awarded: *Levesque v. Faguy*, 14 R.F.L. (2d) 370, [1978] C.A. 376 (Que.). See also *Lebrun v. Rodier*, 14 R.F.L. (2d) 378, [1978] C.A. 380 (Que.).

A court should not give a lump sum support award a "property" appearance by setting it off against a property entitlement unless no other reasonable alternative exists: *Glazier v. Glazier* (1991), 36 R.F.L. (3d) 84, 5 O.R. (3d) 183 (Gen. Div.).

A lump sum is commonly given to permit current needs to be met in a more satisfactory way than by periodic payments, usually by giving the wife and children a roof over their heads. This may be done by giving the wife a lump sum which induces the husband to turn over a house or his interest in a house, or which, with her own funds, may permit her to buy a house: *Dupuis v. Dupuis* (1978), 3 R.F.L. (2d) 272, 25 N.S.R. (2d) 444, 36 A.P.R. 444 (C.A.).

15§64 — Lump sum — circumstances justifying — general

The Court of Appeal in *Nahatchewitz v. Nahatchewitz* (1999), 1 R.F.L. (5th) 395 (Ont. C.A.) upheld the award of $15,000 in lump sum spousal support following the reasoning in *Hickey v. Hickey* (1999), 46 R.F.L. (4th) 1 (S.C.C.) that great deference must be given to trial judges in matters of support. Unless there is an error in principle, the significant misapprehension of the evidence, or unless the award is clearly wrong, it should stand. In this case the trial judge considered all the circumstances of the case including the husband's Undertaking of Assistance given to Immigration Canada.

In a long term traditional marriage where the wife did not work for many years but at the time of the hearing had obtained employment, the wife was entitled to a lump sum of $39,000 on account of loss of economic opportunity and support: *DeFaveri v. Toronto Dominion Bank* (1999), 45 R.F.L. (4th) 141 (Ont. C.A.); additional reasons at (June 14, 1999), Doc. CA C29199, C30283 (Ont. C.A.). This was the same amount owing by the wife to the husband in the property calculation, so no exchange of funds needed to take place.

The appellate court in *De Beeld v. De Beeld* (1999), 2 R.F.L. (5th) 162 (B.C. C.A.), in affirming the lower court decision, awarded the wife $40,000 lump sum compensatory support. During the marriage, the wife had supported her husband through university and during the time he qualified as a chartered accountant. She had later suffered a serious injury in a car accident which prevented her from working full-time.

Where a dependant spouse is forced to encroach upon capital for her own needs because of the payor spouse's inadequate child support, the defendant spouse is not employed and the family's practice has been that the payor's income went to the support of the family, it is appropriate that the trial judge awarded the dependant spouse lump sum spousal maintenance: *Prince v. Prince* (1997), 35 R.F.L. (4th) 328 (N.S. C.A.). The dependant received $8,000 lump sum maintenance for the period from the time of separation until the first interim support order, a period of approximately six months.

In awarding lump sum maintenance, the court is entitled to consider the lifestyle enjoyed by the claimant during a period of cohabitation prior to marriage: *Droit de la famille — 805* (1990), 26 R.F.L. (3d) 198 (Qué. C.A.).

Where the husband's means did not permit payment to his wife of sufficient periodic maintenance, a lump sum was awarded to her in an amount equal to the husband's interest in the matrimonial home: *Pennington v. Pennington* (1985), 49 R.F.L. (2d) 113 (B.C. C.A.).

In *Noel v. Noel* (1998), 39 R.F.L. (4th) 214 (Alta. Q.B.), the husband won a prize of 5.47 million dollars in a lottery 14 months after the parties' final separation but before their divorce. At the time of the hearing there were approximately eight million dollars of lottery winnings and earnings. The parties had been married for over 15 years and the wife was in poor health. The court ordered that the husband pay the wife approximately two million dollars, under the Alberta *Matrimonial Property Act*, and in the event that that order was set aside, spousal support in a lump sum to be calculated at the rate of $2,500 per month for 20 years, beginning on the date of this judgment using a discount rate of 5%. Support was ordered on the basis of the economic interdependency of the parties, the lengthy duration of the marriage, the functions each spouse performed during cohabitation, the wife's present condition, means and needs and, most significantly, the husband's vast financial resources.

The wife was entitled to non-compensatory spousal support to assist her to adjust to the marriage breakdown and to reorganize her financial affairs in *Hoxford v. Hoxford* (1999), 2 R.F.L. (5th) 257 (Ont. S.C.J.). The parties had had a modern marriage in which both of them worked and they were not dependant on each other. The only disadvantage that the wife suffered as a result of the breakdown of the marriage was that she would have to return to a lifestyle by herself, with the necessary changes to achieve self-sufficiency without the advantages of both parties pooling their resources. The husband was ordered to pay lump sum spousal support of $10,800, payable in the amount of $450 a month over 24 months.

"There is clearly bitter hostility on the part of the husband towards his wife. As I say he seems quite determined to pay her no maintenance and this in spite of court orders. In all the circumstances, this case is one in which, in my view, it is appropriate to award by way of maintenance for the wife a lump sum together with periodic payments": per Catliffe L.J.S.C. in *Ratcliffe v. Ratcliffe* (1976), 27 R.F.L. 227 at 232 (B.C. S.C.). See also *Helfrich v. Helfrich* (1977), 1 A.R. 595 at 596 (C.A.).

"The usual method of providing for the maintenance of the wife is by periodic payments. There are cases where it is appropriate to provide for the maintenance of the wife by a lump sum settlement, for example: (1) Where a lump sum is necessary to provide a home for the wife. (2) Where the history of the relations of the parties shows that the husband has failed to meet periodic payments, and the only way to assure that she will be maintained is by a lump sum settlement": per Farris C.J.B.C. in *Carmichael v. Carmichael*

(1976), 27 R.F.L. 325 at 330, 69 D.L.R. (3d) 297 (B.C. C.A.). See also *Gray v. Gray* (1978), 28 N.S.R. (2d) 491, 43 A.P.R. 491 (T.D.).

"In my opinion, there are many cases where lump sum awards should be made. Where the wife has a particular skill and needs capital to earn her own way or to complete her education or training so as to reduce the periodic maintenance that would otherwise be payable by the husband is an example. Where the husband is likely to fritter away the capital is another. However, the provision for lump sum awards is the exception and not the rule": per Moir J.A. in *Krause v. Krause*, 23 R.F.L. 219 at 228, [1976] 2 W.W.R. 622, 64 D.L.R. (3d) 352 (Alta. C.A.).

Where because of the husband's age and inclination it appeared that he would not long continue to be employed, it was held that an award of lump sum maintenance to the wife was appropriate: *Weir v. Weir* (1976), 26 R.F.L. 345, 14 N.S.R. (2d) 539 (C.A.). See also *Green v. Green* (1977), 6 A.R. 485 (T.D.) and *MacDonald v. MacDonald* (1974), 14 R.F.L. 125, 8 N.S.R. (2d) 678 (C.A.).

"Unless there are sufficient assets to warrant a lump-sum payment being made the court will not order one, but what constitutes sufficient assets will depend on the financial position of the parties as it is affected by consideration of their socio-economic position. The phrase 'sufficient capital assets' is a relative one and is not absolute in its terms. The relationship of the value of the capital assets to the style of living of the parties is of importance and what may not appear to be a very large capital asset to one person may loom very large in the eyes of another. The *Divorce Act* does not contain any qualifying words in respect of dollar amounts": per Matas J. in *Hutchinson v. Hutchinson*, 6 R.F.L. 353 at 355, [1972] 3 W.W.R. 59, 25 D.L.R. (3d) 23 (Man. Q.B.). See also *Hunter v. Hunter* (1974), 15 R.F.L. 336 (Alta. T.D.) and *MacDonald v. MacDonald* (1973), 14 R.F.L. 125, 8 N.S.R. (2d) 678 (C.A.).

The use of the lump-sum payment is not confined to cases of large estates or large estates and special circumstances. If anything, it may well be more applicable to safeguard the needs of members of a family entitled to maintenance where the people are of modest means: *Raffin v. Ruffin*, 5 R.F.L. 274, [1972] 1 O.R. 173, 22 D.L.R. (3d) 497 (C.A.)

In *Carter v. Carter* (1978), 3 R.F.L. (2d) 355, 19 Nfld. & P.E.I.R. 411, 50 A.P.R. 411 (Nfld. T.D.), the court listed some of the circumstances in which lump sum payments should be ordered: 1. Where the husband's assets are in liquid form and permit a painless separation of a lump sum: *Zelko v. Zelko* (1973), 11 R.F.L. 123 (Sask. Q.B.); 2. Where the husband is of an advanced age (idem); 3. Where the wife has demonstrated an ability to deal with a lump sum property (idem); 4. Where the parties are anxious to bring their relationship to a complete end (idem); 5. Where the imposition of an obligation to pay periodic sums would create further conflict between the parties: *Hayre v. Hayre* (1973), 11 R.F.L. 188 (B.C. S.C.); 6. Where a lump sum is necessary to provide a home for the wife: *Carmichael v. Carmichael* (1976), 27 R.F.L. 325, 69 D.L.R. (3d) 297 (B.C. C.A.); 7. Where the history of the relations of the parties shows that the husband has failed to meet periodic payments and the only way to assure that the wife will be maintained is a lump sum payment (idem); 8. To provide a nest-egg against the contingencies of life: *Lazenby v. Lazenby*, 18 R.F.L. 393, [1975] W.W.D. 88 (B.C. C.A.); and 9. To recognize the contribution of the wife to the marriage: *Feldman v. Feldman* (1970), 2 R.F.L. 173, 75 W.W.R. 715, 14 D.L.R. (3d) 222 (Alta. C.A.).

"[O]ther examples of where such [a lump sum] award has been held acceptable are: (1) Where a lump sum is necessary to provide a home for the wife: *Davis v. Davis (No. 2)*,

[1967] 1 All E.R. 123 (C.A.); (2) Where the husband has in the past failed to make periodic payments for maintenance; *Ottho v. Ottho*, 20 R.F.L. 1, [1975] W.W.D. 37 (B.C.); (3) Where the husband has assets but does not have a sufficient income to make periodic payments: *Lawson v. Lawson* (1973), 9 R.F.L. 294 (Ont.); (4) Where the marriage has subsisted for a number of years and as compensation for the sacrifice of the wife during the marriage: *Chorny v. Chorny*, 4 R.F.L. 347, [1971] 5 W.W.R. 732 (Alta. C.A.); *Maillet v. Maillet* (1975), 13 N.B.R. (2d) 330, 25 R.F.L. 126; (5) Where the award is for the purpose of securing a family home for the wife: *MacDonald v. MacDonald* (1974), 8 N.S.R. (2d) 678, 14 R.F.L. 125 (C.A.); *Johnson v. Johnson* (1974), 10 N.S.R. (2d) 624, 20 R.F.L. 12 (C.A.)": per MacDonald J. in *Secord v. Secord* (1978), 2 R.F.L. (2d) 97 at 100 (P.E.I. S.C.). See also *Pruden v. Pruden* (1976), 28 R.F.L. 83 (B.C. S.C.).

Where the husband, who was an alcoholic and living on welfare, had failed to make periodic support payments under an earlier order, the arrears were cancelled on the parties' divorce and the wife awarded lump sum support payable from the husband's interest in the family home: *Wiseman v. Wiseman* (1987), 8 R.F.L. (3d) 447, 18 B.C.L.R. (2d) 19 (S.C.).

Lump sum maintenance should not be awarded merely to equalize earnings between the parties. In an application for lump sum maintenance, the following factors should be considered: the duration of the marriage; the conduct of the parties during marriage; the division of responsibilities both during marriage and after separation; the assets of each party; and the means of each party: *Kiesman v. Kiesman* (1986), 42 Man. R. (2d) 78 (Q.B.).

See also *MacGregor v. MacGregor* (1984), 65 N.S.R. (2d) 113, 147 A.P.R. 113 (T.D.); *Caslake v. Caslake* (1982), 29 R.F.L. (2d) 168 (N.S. T.D.); *Rees v. Rees* (1980), 21 B.C.L.R. 188 (S.C.); *Mackenzie v. Mackenzie* (1977), 19 N.S.R. (2d) 96 at 103 (T.D.); *Riddell v. Riddell* (1978), 10 A.R. 111 (T.D.); *Roy v. Roy* (1977), 2 A.R. 494 at 498 (T.D.)); *Schroeder v. Schroeder* (1977), 6 A.R. 480 (T.D.); *Brocklebank v. Brocklebank* (1976), 25 R.F.L. 53 at 67–68 (B.C. S.C.); *Blackham v. Blackham* (1977), 1 R.F.L. (2d) 160 at 168–69, 3 B.C.L.R. 277 (S.C.); *Sheppard v. Sheppard* (1976), 15 Nfld. & P.E.I.R. 279, 38 A.P.R. 279 (Nfld. T.D.); *Rauch v. Rauch* (1975), 22 R.F.L. 143, 9 O.R. (2d) 761, 61 D.L.R. (3d) 663 (H.C.); *Zelko v. Zelko* (1973), 11 R.F.L. 123 at 123–24 (Sask. Q.B.).

15§65 — Lump sum — recognition of contribution to marriage and accumulation of assets

Where the husband had enriched his assets at the wife's expense and where the wife had never received a salary for all the years she had worked in the family business, a compensatory lump sum payment to her of $90,000 was upheld on appeal: *Droit de la famille — 873*, [1990] R.D.F. 616 (C.A. Qué.).

Where the wife's current level of self-support and provisions for her retirement were affected by the interruption of her career as a registered nurse to raise the children, she was awarded lump sum compensatory support in *Jorden v. Jorden* (1995), 14 R.F.L. (4th) 97, 162 N.B.R. (2d) 241, 415 A.P.R. 241 (Q.B.).

Where the wife's career advancement had been impeded by a move designed to enhance her husband's career, she was awarded a lump sum compensatory allowance of $8,000: *Monks v. Monks* (1993), 44 R.F.L. (3d) 459 (Man. Q.B.).

Where the wife had remained in the home to care for the parties' four children and had helped to finance the husband's education, she was found entitled to lump sum support.

Thanks to the wife, the husband had been able to pursue his education and career unfettered by family constraints: *Smithson v. Smithson* (1991), 72 Man. R. (2d) 174 (Q.B.).

Where the wife had supported the husband and the family during the husband's medical studies, the wife was awarded a $10,000 compensatory allowance: *Droit de la famille — 1327*, [1990] R.D.F. 347 (C.S.).

Where evidence established that the wife had assisted the husband in accumulating $240,000 in assets, the wife was awarded a compensatory lump sum of $30,000: *Droit de la famille — 859*, [1990] R.J.Q. 1891, [1990] R.D.F. 498 (headnote only) (C.S.).

Where the wife had assisted the husband in his business and had borne household and child care responsibilities by herself, she was granted lump sum support of $5,000 as compensation for her contribution: *Droit de la famille — 1349*, [1990] R.D.F. 562 (C.S. Qué.).

Where the wife had foregone her own education to finance the husband's dentistry studies, she was awarded $6,000 lump sum support upon divorce together with a further $6,000 should she enroll in an educational course: *Cole v. Cole* (1989), 88 N.S.R. (2d) 432, 225 A.P.R. 432 (T.D.).

Where the wife had raised the parties' four children and had worked for the husband during the marriage without salary, she was awarded lump sum maintenance. The wife had contributed to the enrichment of the husband's patrimony as he would have been unable to tend to his medical practice and to take care of his personal assets without the wife's assistance: *Droit de la famille — 1013*, [1986] R.D.F. 109 (C.S. Qué.). See also *Droit de la famille — 1009*, [1986] R.D.F. 91 (C.S. Qué.).

Where the wife had given up career opportunities during the parties' six year marriage in order to allow the husband to get ahead, she was granted lump sum support to enable her to establish herself in her new career as an interior decorator: *MacLean v. MacLean* (1990), 28 R.F.L. (3d) 103 (B.C. S.C.).

Where the parties' marriage was only of a short duration and subsequent to the separation the husband had assumed responsibility for a $13,000 family debt, the wife was found entitled to lump sum maintenance of only $600 to compensate her for her expenditures on the family home: *Morrison v. Morrison* (1984), 41 R.F.L. (2d) 215 (Man. Q.B.).

15§66 — Lump sum — to provide home

In *Tauber v. Tauber* (2003), 2003 CarswellOnt 1009, 34 R.F.L. (5th) 450, 64 O.R. (3d) 229, 170 O.A.C. 1, 225 D.L.R. (4th) 186 (C.A.), the appellate court upheld a lump sum payment of $500,000 for spousal support, which would enable the wife to enhance her self-sufficiency and help her to purchase a permanent home for herself and the parties' child. The payment would assist her to provide a lifestyle comparable to the one which the child had enjoyed when he lived with both parents, a lifestyle to which the husband was readily able to contribute. While the amount was substantial, it should be seen in the context on the husband's assets which were worth between $19 and $20 million, his undisputed ability to pay, and the parties' lifestyle during the marriage.

While lump sum spousal support payments may be made to provide funds towards the purchase of a house in certain circumstances, it is an error in law to make a lump sum award without specifics required to determine the amount and without an immediate need being shown: *Vermeulen v. Vermeulen* (1999), 2 R.F.L. (5th) 140 (N.S. C.A.).

A lump sum award is justifiable to meet expenses involved from moving to a new residence and to pay for tuition at a post-secondary institution: *MacDonald v. MacDonald* (1990), 98 N.S.R. (2d) 229, 263 A.P.R. 229 (T.D.).

In *Evans v. Evans* (1988), 16 R.F.L. (3d) 437 (Ont. H.C.), the wife was awarded lump sum support to give her some security and to enable her to purchase the husband's share of the matrimonial home. Lump sum was preferable to periodic support given the facts that a disability prevented the wife from working and the husband's health was also precarious.

A lump sum was ordered to be secured against the matrimonial home that could be satisfied by conveying the payor's interest in the matrimonial home so as to bring about a clean break between the parties and enable them to get on with their lives. It would allow the payee, if she augmented her income by taking in boarders, to upgrade her education at a pace consistent with her disability. Where the payor has a continuing deficit position, to order any periodic support is a useless exercise and not justified when the lump sum support is taken into consideration: *Snell v. Snell* (1987), 10 R.F.L. (3d) 30 (Ont. H.C.).

Having regard to the respondent's substantial means and to the fact that the three youngest children were respectively only 14, 13 and 9 years of age and were being cared for by the petitioner, reasonable maintenance for the petitioner included the provision of a house where she could establish a home for herself and her children: *Osborne v. Osborne* (1973), 14 R.F.L. 61 at 71 (Sask. Q.B.); varied (1974), 23 R.F.L. 358 (Sask. C.A.).

Where the wife established a need for a home, car and future security, a lump sum payment of $50,000 was ordered: *Starrs v. Kost* (1986), 2 R.F.L. (3d) 368 (Que. S.C.).

15§67 — Lump sum — for real and immediate needs

A lump sum spousal support award should not be made in relation to the claimant's retirement needs which are still many years in the future. An immediate and specific need must be established before a lump sum will be awarded: *Coady v. Coady* (1995), 144 N.S.R. (2d) 106, 416 A.P.R. 106 (S.C.).

Lump sum support is justifiable in the case of immediate needs such as home repairs and professional upgrading: *MacNaughton v. MacNaughton* (1991), R.F.L. (3d) 312, 103 N.S.R. (2d) 356, 282 A.P.R. 356 (C.A.). See also *Matthews v. Matthews* (1991), 34 R.F.L. (3d) 201 (N.S. C.A.), below at 15§80 Refusal of lump sum awards.

A lump sum maintenance award may be struck on appeal where it does not appear that the trial judge made the award upon a finding on the evidence of a specific or immediate need of the payee spouse: *Moore v. Moore* (1987), 6 R.F.L. (3d) 438, 77 N.S.R. (2d) 267, 191 A.P.R. 267 (C.A.).

"I do not consider that the mortgage debt, per se, is a changed circumstance which requires a lump sum payment at this time. However, when one looks at the capital requirements of the wife, who had the care and custody of the children to consider, these were clearly not fulfilled by the wife's receipts from the matrimonial home and the lump sum payment of $16,500 can readily be justified on this basis": per Carrothers J. in *Ciarniello v. Ciarniello*, 21 R.F.L. (2d) 410 at 414–415, [1981] 3 W.W.R. 146 (B.C. C.A.).

"In addition, and on the authority of *Raffin v. Raffin*, [1972] 1 O.R. 173, 5 R.F.L. 274, 22 D.L.R. (3d) 497 (C.A.), I do order the husband to pay to the wife the sum of $1,533.33 with which to pay the unpaid 1972 taxes of $449.33 and the unpaid fuel account of $84 and to provide her with $1,000 for her future security against any emergency": per Vannini Local Master in *Whalen v. Whalen* (1972), 8 R.F.L. 332 at 341 (Ont. Master).

"It would appear from the husband's earnings and his assets that he is financially able to handle the lump sum payment imposed on him. We are of the opinion that in light of the circumstances the lump sum award was fully justified and should not be disturbed. This cannot be regarded as a distribution of capital as in the case of *Krause v. Krause*, 23 R.F.L. 219, [1976] 2 W.W.R. 622, 64 D.L.R. (3d) 352 (Alta. C.A.), where a lump sum award was given at trial in addition to payments of periodic maintenance with the idea that part of the lump sum award would have an income earning potential to supplement the monthly award. At p. 630 Mr. Justice Moir said: It is only when a lump sum is a proper way to provide maintenance or where a lump sum is necessary to put a person in a particular position that a lump sum award should be made. He gives examples of particular positions at p. 631 of the report. That statement sets out two prime tests and in our view the lump sum award in this case meets both of them. Firstly, the lump sum award was not made in addition to periodic payments but was given in lieu thereof and is therefore a proper way to provide maintenance. Secondly, the award was to assist the wife for the particular purposes pointed to by the learned trial judge": per Haddad J.A. in *Schubert v. Schubert* (1978), 6 Alta. L.R. (2d) 364, 10 A.R. 305 at 310 (C.A.).

"[The petitioner wife] has indicated that she has found the marital home too expensive to keep up and has moved into another home with her three daughters for which she is paying rent. There will be some expense involved in getting set up in the new home and in getting established in their new life-style. In my opinion, the wife should receive a lump sum payment from her husband to assist her in the re-establishment of her new life-pattern over the next couple of years": per Morrison J. in *Lawrence v. Lawrence* (1981), 20 R.F.L. (2d) 414 at 419, 45 N.S.R. (2d) 541, 86 A.P.R. 541 (T.D.); *Mesrobian v. Mesrobian* (1978), 4 R.F.L. (2d) 341 at 346 (Ont. H.C.). See also *Eisenhauer v. Eisenhauer* (1975), 14 N.S.R. (2d) 164 at 167 (C.A.); *Glave v. Glave* (1977), 4 R.F.L. (2d) 358 (B.C. S.C.); *Schmidt v. Schmidt* (1976), 26 R.F.L. 232 at 238 (B.C. S.C.). See also *Monastersky v. Monastersky* (1978), 12 A.R. 492 at 502 (T.D.).

15§68 — Lump sum — future needs

In *Theberge v. Theberge* (1995), 17 R.F.L. (4th) 196 (Ont. C.A.) the court upheld on appeal the wife's lump sum support order which was granted in anticipation of her future needs. Evidence clearly established the likelihood of a decline in the wife's income given her poor health and the order therefore fell within the broad ambit of the trial judge's discretion.

15§69 — Lump sum — to retire payee's debts

In *M. (F.) v. G. (S.)*, [1994] R.D.F. 625 (Que. C.A.) a $1,000,000 lump sum support award made in favour of the wife was upheld on appeal where the court was satisfied that it was needed by the wife to maintain her standard of living and to pay off accumulated debts.

In *Droit de la famille — 1633*, [1992] R.D.F. 657 (C.S. Qué.), the wife was awarded lump sum support to assist her in retiring some post-separation debts and to compensate her for the fact that she had no pension funds.

In *Droit de la famille — 840*, [1990] R.J.Q. 1565, [1990] R.D.F. 510 (headnote only) (C.S.), the wife was awarded lump sum support to allow her to purchase a new car and discharge her legal fees and to provide her with some financial stability.

In *T. (M.) v. G. (G.)*, [1989] R.L. 614 (C.A. Qué.), the wife, after 22 years of marriage, was granted a lump sum award of $10,000 to assist her with legal fees and other predictable and unpredictable expenses related to her change in lifestyle. In awarding that sum, her age, earning capacity, and the length of the marriage were all considered.

In *Bedgood v. Bedgood* (1982), 28 R.F.L. (2d) 113, 52 N.S.R. (2d) 42, 106 A.P.R. 42 (C.A.); varying 26 R.F.L. (2d) 256, 50 N.S.R. (2d) 157, 98 A.P.R. 157 (T.D.), the husband was ordered to pay lump sum maintenance to his wife to cover outstanding property taxes owing on the matrimonial home in which she continued to reside.

In the application for divorce, it may be proper to order a lump sum payment where the wife has outstanding debts. The wife should be put in a position such that she can begin afresh without major indebtedness where the husband has income and assets of sufficient value that he does not find it difficult to make a lump sum payment: *Skinner v. Skinner* (1977), 2 R.F.L. (2d) 67 (B.C. S.C.). See also *Carroll v. Carroll* (1974), 13 R.F.L. 357 at 364 (Ont. H.C.); *Day v. Day*, 18 R.F.L. 56 at 62, [1975] 3 W.W.R. 563 (Alta. T.D.); and *Brody v. Brody* (1976), 1 A.R. 470 at 488 (T.D.).

"I propose firstly to deal with the question of the lump sum. The evidence before me indicates that the wife is indebted to her parents in the sum of approximately $5,000. It is true that the parents probably have not been pressing her for it, but there is no reason, on the other hand, that the parents should be required to pay that sum of money. That responsibility is the responsibility of the male respondent, the husband in this particular action": per Morand J. in *Gelgoot v. Gelgoot* (1977), 1 R.F.L. (2d) 204 at 206 (Ont. H.C.). See also *Evans v. Evans* (1976), 4 A.R. 263 at 265 (T.D.).

15§70 — Lump sum — as conclusive settlement

In *Stricker v. Stricker* (1994), 4 R.F.L. (4th) 29 (Alta. C.A.); additional reasons (1994), 4 R.F.L. (4th) 29 at 31 (Alta. C.A.), an award of lump sum child support was confirmed on appeal in light of the payor father's past history of evasion and non-cooperation.

Where the husband had a history of failing to comply with court orders as well as a history of violence towards the wife it was determined that a clean break between the parties was the best. Accordingly, lump sum spousal support was appropriate: *Kennedy v. Sinclair* (2001), 18 R.F.L. (5th) 91, 2001 CarswellOnt 1634 (Ont. S.C.J.); affirmed (2003), 42 R.F.L. (5th) 46, 2003 CarswellOnt 2507 (Ont. C.A.).

In *Sagl v. Sagl* (1997), 31 R.F.L. 405 (Ont. Gen. Div.); additional reasons at (1997), 35 R.F.L. (4th) 107 (Ont. Gen. Div.), the wife was granted lump sum spousal support in order to facilitate a clean break between the parties. The relationship between the parties was a bitter one and the husband had a history of ignoring previous periodic support orders.

In *Droit de la famille — 1955*, [1994] R.D.F. 247 (C.S. Qué.); reversed (1995), 67 Q.A.C. 224 (Que. C.A.), the wife was awarded $50,000 lump sum support to facilitate a clean break and to allow the wife to relocate. As the husband had recently declared bankruptcy, his inability to pay would not allow an additional award of compensatory support to the wife, although she had contributed significantly to his career.

In *Droit de la famille — 2123* (1994), [1995] R.D.F. 90 (C.S. Qué.), the wife was awarded lump sum support to facilitate a clean break after the parties' 15-year marriage. The wife had given up her career to care for the parties' children and was therefore economically disadvantaged. However, her decision not to return to her former teaching career somewhat compromised her claim and resulted in a smaller lump sum than claimed.

In *Droit de la famille — 1532* (1991), [1992] R.D.F. 89 (C.S. Qué.), the wife was awarded lump sum support where it was found that the future frequent contact between the parties which would result from periodic support was not advisable.

Where periodic support was not practical because of ongoing friction between the parties, the wife was ordered to pay the needy husband a small lump sum: *Parish v. Parish* (1993), 46 R.F.L. (3d) 117 (Ont. Gen. Div.).

In *Droit de la famille — 1352*, [1990] R.D.F. 576 (C.S. Qué.), the wife was awarded a $5,000 lump sum above, alone and beyond the periodic support provided for in the parties' separation agreement. The sum would allow her to retire some of her debts and would facilitate a clean break between the parties. See also *Droit de la famille — 1326*, [1990] R.D.F. 602 (C.S. Qué.).

In *Duff v. Duff* (1989), 91 N.S.R. (2d) 375, 233 A.P.R. 375 (T.D.), the wife was awarded lump sum support to enable the parties to sever ties with one another once and for all.

In *Currie v. Currie* (1986), 5 R.F.L. (3d) 192, 75 N.S.R. (2d) 439, 186 A.P.R. 439 (C.A.) the wife was awarded lump sum maintenance based upon the animosity between the parties, the likelihood that the husband would default in the payment of periodic maintenance and the wife's need. It was held that maintenance awards should be as final as possible to reduce conflict and to discourage multiplicity of proceedings.

Where the wife had made no request for support for the four years subsequent to the parties separation, she was nevertheless awarded $3,000 by way of lump sum in divorce proceedings. The award would allow the parties to make a clean break and would permit the wife to work towards financial independence: *Godin v. Godin* (1986), 74 N.B.R. (2d) 85, 187 A.P.R. 85 (Q.B.).

Lump sum maintenance is appropriate where an acrimonious relationship exists between the parties and where assets available to satisfy maintenance are liable to disappear should a periodic award be made: *Braithwaite v. Braithwaite* (1984), 40 R.F.L. (2d) 415 (Ont. H.C.). See also *Ottho v. Ottho*, 20 R.F.L. 1 at 2, [1975] W.W.D. 37 (B.C. S.C.).

In *Ferniuk v. Ferniuk*, [1983] 5 W.W.R. 406, 22 Man. R. (2d) 135 (Q.B.), the wife was awarded $15,000 by way of lump-sum maintenance as it was found that lump-sum rather than periodic maintenance would better assist the wife in becoming financially independent.

See also *Shewchuk v. Shewchuk* (1981), 25 R.F.L. (2d) 95 (Alta. Q.B.); *Hayre v. Hayre* (1973), 11 R.F.L. 188 at 193–94 (B.C. S.C.); *Cameron v. Cameron* (1970), 2 R.F.L. 339 at 349, 2 N.S.R. (2d) 50, 12 D.L.R. (3d) 378 (T.D.); *Covey v. Covey* (1980), 20 R.F.L. (2d) 368 at 376, 42 N.S.R. (2d) 612, 77 A.P.R. 612 (T.D.); *Saxton v. Saxton*, 12 R.F.L. 135 at 165–166, [1973] 3 W.W.R. 219 (B.C. S.C.); *Hunter v. Hunter* (1974), 15 R.F.L. 336 at 339 (Alta. T.D.); *Kearley v. Kearley* (1991), 94 Nfld. & P.E.I.R. 171, 298 A.P.R. 171 (Nfld. U.F.C.).

15§71 — Lump sum — other reasons justifying award

A lump sum award of support was upheld on appeal where support has not been paid even though ordered, except under compulsion, and support was substantially in arrears: *McClure v. McClure* (1999), 45 R.F.L. (4th) 31, 123 B.C.A.C. 231, 201 W.A.C. 231 (C.A.).

Considering all the assets of the parties — their acquisition, disposal of some of these assets, their income, the respondent's interest in the matrimonial home which the appellant brought into the marriage, and the need for both parties to become economically independent, the trial judge awarded the respondent $60,000 as lump sum support and her interest in the matrimonial home, a decision which was upheld in *Richardson v. Richardson* (1998), 41 R.F.L. (4th) 137 (B.C. C.A.).

Where the evidence indicated that the husband had failed to make timely interim spousal support payments and that he had attempted to make off with and conceal assets because of his animosity towards his wife, the wife was granted lump sum spousal support on appeal: *Gray v. Gray* (1998), 35 R.F.L. (4th) 456 (Alta. C.A.).

Where the wife had given up her waitressing job and also speculative plans to start a catering business to move with her husband to Italy for his work, she was found entitled to a lump sum payment of $5,000 in spousal support on dissolution of the parties' brief marriage, less the gross amount of periodic support, if any, paid by the husband between the trial and the judgment. This payment was made out of an abundance of caution and in order to allow the wife to adjust to her post-marital situation: *Roberts v. Shotton* (1997), 156 N.S.R. (2d) 47, 461 A.P.R. 47 (N.S. C.A.).

In *Droit de la famille — 974*, [1991] R.L. 278 (C.A. Qué.), the 60-year-old wife received lump sum support of $10,000 upon dissolution of the parties' 32-year marriage. The wife had need and limited earning capacity and, although the husband was retired, he had accumulated significant pension assets.

In *Waterman v. Waterman* (1995), 16 R.F.L. (4th) 10, 133 Nfld. & P.E.I.R. 310, 413 A.P.R. 310 (Nfld. C.A.) the dismissal of the wife's claim for retroactive lump sum support was reversed on appeal. The wife had delayed in seeking support primarily because of her health problems. Further, the husband had not paid any support after separation with the result that he acquired additional assets while the wife was forced to seek welfare.

In *Tauber v. Tauber* (2003), 2003 CarswellOnt 1009, 34 R.F.L. (5th) 450, 64 O.R. (3d) 229, 170 O.A.C. 1, 225 D.L.R. (4th) 186 (C.A.), the appellate court upheld a lump sum payment of $500,000 for spousal support, which would enable the wife to enhance her self-sufficiency and help her to purchase a permanent home for herself and the parties' child. The payment would assist her to provide a lifestyle comparable to the one which the child had enjoyed when he lived with both parents, a lifestyle to which the husband was readily able to contribute. While the amount was a substantial one, it should be seen in the context on the husband's assets which were worth between $19 and $20 million, him undisputed ability to pay, and the parties' lifestyle during the marriage.

In *McKay v. McKay*, 12 R.F.L. (6th) 118, 2004 CarswellAlta 1801, 2004 ABQB 974 (Alta. Q.B.); additional reasons at 12 R.F.L. (6th) 125, 2005 CarswellAlta 43, 2005 ABQB 25 (Alta. Q.B.), the wife was awarded lump sum support of $5,000 to compensate her retroactively for the brief period after the marriage breakdown during which she was getting back on her feet in terms of employment and living circumstances.

In *Aunger v. Aunger* (2004), 9 R.F.L. (6th) 29, 2004 CarswellOnt 4677 (S.C.J.), the wife was awarded lump sum spousal support of $200,000 upon her divorce from her wealthy husband. As the husband lived abroad and had no assets in Ontario, the wife was not going to receive any equalization payment to assist her in her financial adjustment because of the marriage breakdown. The lump sum was reflective of the limited-term support to which she would otherwise be entitled.

See also *Tauber v. Tauber* (2001), 18 R.F.L. (5th) 384, 2001 CarswellOnt 2842, [2001] O.J. No. 3259, 203 D.L.R. (4th) 168 (Ont. S.C.J.), the wife was awarded lump sum support of $500,000 upon the breakdown of the parties' 18-month marriage. The husband was extremely wealthy and his conditions, means, needs and circmstances had not changed since the time of the marriage. The wife on the other hand had given birth to the parties' child. Accordingly her needs were greater than before the marriage, particularly as the child was now entitled to a lifestyle commensurate with being the son of a wealthy father. Although the wife had already been paid $100,000 pursuant to the parties' marriage contract, the payment was in the nature of a property settlement and not in satisfaction of the husband's spousal support obligation.

In *Noel v. Noel*, 39 R.F.L. (4th) 214, [1998] 10 W.W.R. 605, 62 Alta. L.R. (3d) 376, 217 A.R. 201 (Q.B.), the wife was awarded lump sum support in light of the facts that she was in ill health and had not worked outside the home during the parties' 15-year marriage and that the husband was 70 years old and possessed significant assets.

In *Kits v. Kits* (1998), 42 R.F.L. (4th) 167 (B.C. S.C.), the wife was awarded lump sum compensatory support upon dissolution of the parties' 14-year marriage. The wife had forfeited a lucrative career to remain in the home to care for the children and was accordingly entitled to compensation. However, given her sizable property entitlement and the fact that she had entered into a relationship with a man who had considerable resources to support her, she had no need for ongoing support.

In *Droit de la famille — 2123* (1994), [1995] R.D.F. 90 (C.S. Qué.) the wife was awarded lump sum support to facilitate a clean break after the parties' 15-year marriage. The wife had given up her career to care for the parties' children and was therefore economically disadvantaged. However, her decision not to return to her former teaching career somewhat compromised her claim and resulted in a smaller lump sum than claimed.

Where the husband's income was limited and a periodic spousal support award would strain his ability to support himself and meet his child support obligations, a modest lump sum was awarded to the wife which would allow both parties to become self-sufficient within a reasonable time: *Amaral v. Amaral* (1993), 50 R.F.L. (3d) 364 (Ont. Gen. Div.); additional reasons at (1993), 50 R.F.L. (3d) 384 (Ont. Gen. Div.).

Where it was likely that the wife would be self-sufficient upon completion of a training course, she was awarded lump sum support to assist her throughout her training and in re-establishing herself: *Leek v. Leek* (1994), 3 R.F.L. (4th) 63 (B.C. S.C.).

Where the husband has neglected both his wife and children for a period of 7 years, the wife was awarded a lump sum spousal and child support award reflecting the amount the husband should have paid during that period. As the husband had a history of failing to support his family, a periodic support order was not appropriate: *Battaglini v. Battaglini* (1994), 4 R.F.L. (4th) 235 (Ont. Gen. Div.).

Where the marriage had delayed the wife's development of employment skills and the marriage breakdown had impaired her ability to pursue a career because of a diminished psychological capacity, she was awarded a lump sum as a compensatory allowance:

Kopunovic v. Cukotic-Kopunovic (1996), 19 R.F.L. (4th) 137 (Ont. Gen. Div.); additional reasons at (March 22, 1996), Doc. 35506905/92 (Ont. Gen. Div.).

Where an award of periodic support to the unemployed husband would possibly discourage him from actively seeking employment, lump sum support was found to be appropriate: *Andrews v. Andrews* (1995), 11 R.F.L. (4th) 117 (B.C. S.C.).

In *Droit de la famille — 1206*, [1990] R.D.F. 354 (C.A. Qué.); reversing in part [1988] R.D.F. 435 (C.S. Qué.), the $25,000 lump sum awarded to the 60-year-old wife at trial was increased to $75,000 on appeal. Although the husband had always fulfilled his obligations toward his wife in the past, she was entitled to a certain degree of security for the future.

In *Guemili v. Guemili* (1989), 19 R.F.L. (3d) 347 (Man. C.A.), the wife had waived the right to support and the husband had agreed to pay $815 towards a family debt. When the husband declared bankruptcy and the debt was unpaid, the wife successfully obtained in divorce proceedings, a lump sum support order for $815. The husband's appeal from the order was allowed, given that the payment could not be properly characterized as support.

Where it was feared that the husband's alcoholism could interfere with his payment of periodic support, the wife was awarded a lump sum on appeal: *Droit de la famille — 467*, [1988] R.J.Q. 633, [1988] R.D.F. 73 (C.A.).

Where the wife had given up her own aspirations to assist her husband through his medical training she was found entitled, upon divorce, to lump sum support to allow her to pursue her educational goals: *Morris v. Morris* (1988), 85 N.S.R. (2d) 307, 216 A.P.R. 307 (T.D.); affirmed (1988), 17 R.F.L. (3d) 179, 86 N.S.R. (2d) 378, 218 A.P.R. 378 (C.A.). See also *Drummond v. Smith* (1988), 18 R.F.L. (3d) 120 (Alta. Q.B.).

A court may make a lump sum award from assets for child and spousal support where the husband is likely to fritter away the capital. The case follows *Pelech v. Pelech*, above, at 15§12. Because of the possibility of unfairness to a non-custodial parent who may have considered property and support issues globally in arriving at an earlier agreement, a lump sum support award should be carefully considered before it is granted. The court noted that the wording of s. 15(2) makes it clear that the court has jurisdiction to make awards which "secure and pay." *Stricker v. Stricker* (1991), 33 R.F.L. (3d) 367, 118 A.R. 138 (Q.B.).

Where the mother's circumstances made it unlikely that she would be able to contribute in the near future to her children's support, she was ordered to pay lump sum support out of a capital sum she had received in property division proceedings: *Dawe v. Dawe* (1988), 18 R.F.L. (3d) 95 (Nfld. T.D.).

Where the husband had unilaterally terminated voluntary support payments prior to the divorce hearing, the wife was awarded lump sum support to compensate for the periodic payments not received: *Magne v. Magne* (1990), 26 R.F.L. (3d) 364, 65 Man. R. (2d) 241 (Q.B.).

In *Bhatthal v. Bhatthal* (1990), 28 R.F.L. (3d) 152, 74 Alta. L.R. (2d) 307, 107 A.R. 70 (Q.B.), the wife was awarded lump sum support even though her income exceeded that of the husband. The husband had forced her to give up her teaching job in India and move to Canada, where he proceeded to dissipate her property. As a result, the wife had been severely economically disadvantaged by the marriage.

Where there was little likelihood of the 50-year-old wife achieving self-sufficiency and where the husband had a poor past record of paying periodic support, the wife was awarded $60,000 by way of lump sum: *Morrissette v. Morrissette* (1987), 47 Man. R. (2d) 138 (Q.B.).

In *Horner v. Horner* (1992), 132 A.R. 106 (Q.B.); additional reasons at (1992), 136 A.R. 241 (Q.B.), the wife was awarded lump sum support to be paid out of the husband's share of the proceeds of sale of the matrimonial home. The sum would assist the wife in upgrading her skills in her efforts to achieve self-sufficiency.

Where the wife was employed but required training to become proficient in English she was awarded a lump sum of $7,500 upon termination of her 30-year marriage: *Bhatti v. Bhatti* (1992), 40 R.F.L. (3d) 161 (B.C. S.C.).

Where the wife had left her career in India to come to Canada to marry the husband, she was awarded, in divorce proceedings, lump sum support which would allow her to retrain: *Thind v. Thind* (1988), 14 R.F.L. (3d) 165 (B.C. S.C.).

Where the wife gave up a secure job to marry the husband, she was found entitled to lump sum support upon the termination of the parties' brief marriage. Her need could be causally connected to the marriage: *Mogard v. Mogard* (1988), 15 R.F.L. (3d) 415 (N.B. Q.B.).

Where the wife had given up secure employment and accommodation in Hungary to immigrate to Canada to marry the husband, she was found entitled to $20,000 by way of lump sum support, although the marriage had only lasted a month: *Babek v. Babek* (1988), 15 R.F.L. (3d) 168 (Ont. H.C.).

Where the wife had remained in the home for five years after the parties' separation in order to care for the parties' five children, she was awarded $5,000 by way of lump sum support in order to upgrade her skills. The wife's inability to enter the workforce could be attributed directly to the marriage: *Simms v. Simms* (1988), 68 Nfld. & P.E.I.R. 341, 209 A.P.R. 341, (sub nom. *Simms v. Simms (No. 1)*) (Nfld. T.D.).

Where the wife had given up her job to remain in the home during the parties' three-year marriage, she was awarded lump sum support of $5,000 to permit her to retrain: *Brookes v. Strohschein* (1987), 11 R.F.L. (3d) 163 (Alta. Q.B.).

Where because of her family responsibilities, the wife interrupted her nursing career for a number of years, the husband was ordered to pay her a lump sum of $103,000 as compensation for her loss of future income resulting from the interruption. The lump sum was based upon the report of an economist and his projection of the wife's loss of future income, which was both relevant and probative to the issues at hand: *Ormerod v. Ormerod* (1990), 27 R.F.L. (3d) 225 (Ont. U.F.C.).

Where the wife had given up her career as a pharmacist to care for the children, but was able after separation to resume her career at a salary between $25,000 and $50,000, she was awarded a lump sum of $15,000 to assist her with the adjustment: *Katz v. Katz* (1989), 21 R.F.L. (3d) 167 (Ont. U.F.C.).

Where the husband had brought his wife to join him from Poland simply because he wished to be reunited with his son who had been in the wife's care, the wife was awarded lump sum maintenance on appeal. The sum was required to permit the wife to requalify as a doctor in Canada: *Mroz v. Mroz* (1987), 7 R.F.L. (3d) 66, 77 A.R. 159 (C.A.).

See also *Kudlowich v. Kudlowich* (1984), 44 R.F.L. (2d) 111 (Man. C.A.); *Palahitski v. Palahitski* (1982), 18 Man. R. (2d) 374 (C.A.); *Droit de la famille — 42*, [1983] C.A. 96 (Que.); *Lowe v. Lowe* (1974), 15 R.F.L. 244 at 247, 8 N.S.R. (2d) 529 (C.A.); *Hommel v. Hommel* (1985), 171 A.P.R. 85, 71 N.S.R. (2d) 85 (T.D.); *Murdoch v. Murdoch*, 26

R.F.L. 1 at 11–12, 1 Alta. L.R. (2d) 135, [1977] 1 W.W.R. 16, 1 A.R. 378 (T.D.); *McCrea v. Berman*; *Berman v. McCrea* (1984), 30 Man. R. (2d) 41 (Q.B.); *McManus v. McManus* (1984), 37 R.F.L. (2d) 407 (Ont. H.C.); *Matheson v. Matheson* (1984), 43 R.F.L. (2d) 16 (P.E.I.S.C.); *Bonke v. Bonke* (1984), 42 R.F.L. (2d) 72 (B.C. S.C.); *Buytendorp v. Buytendorp* (1983), 24 Man. R. (2d) 81 (Q.B.); *Grossman v. Grossman* (1982), 29 R.F.L. (2d) 300 (Ont. H.C.); *Hutchinson v. Hutchinson* (1982), 20 Man. R. (2d) 1 (Q.B.); *Johnson v. Johnson*, [1981] 6 W.W.R. 316, 30 B.C.L.R. 115 (S.C.); affirmed on other grounds 33 R.F.L. (2d) 302, [1983] 4 W.W.R. 193, 43 B.C.L.R. 173 (C.A.); *Byzruki v. Byzruki* (1981), 26 R.F.L. (2d) 243, 131 D.L.R. (3d) 82 (Ont. H.C.); *Wright v. Wright* (1976), 26 R.F.L. 103 at 105, 13 N.B.R. (2d) 354 (Q.B.); *Sidorski v. Sidorski* (1984), 30 Man. R. (2d) 4 (Q.B.); *Howlett v. Howlett* (1983), 34 R.F.L. (2d) 195 (N.B. Q.B.); *Mason v. Mason* (1981), 21 R.F.L. (2d) 233 at 251 (Ont. H.C.); *Hull v. Hull* (1980), 20 R.F.L. (2d) 12, 5 Man. R. (2d) 412 (Q.B.); *Fisher v. Fisher* (1978), 11 A.R. 359 at 360 (T.D.); *Sullivan v. Sullivan* (1973), 18 R.F.L. 298 at 300, 8 N.B.R. (2d) 690 (Q.B.); *Kress v. Kress* (1971), 8 R.F.L. 264 (Sask. Q.B.); *Fisher v. Giles* (1986), 75 N.S.R. (2d) 395 (Fam. Ct.); *Rowe v. Rowe* (1987), 63 Nfld. & P.E.I.R. 185, 195 A.P.R. 185 (Nfld. U.F.C.).

15§72 — Lump sum — reservation of award

"As the respondent [husband] has no assets now, nor did he have any after he transferred virtually all that he had to the petitioner pursuant to the agreement between them, I am less certain as to her right to lump sum maintenance. I reserve to her the right to apply for lump sum maintenance, but this is not to be taken as a finding that she is so entitled. That will have to be decided then": per Mahoney J. in *Stack v. Stack* (1978), 4 R.F.L. (2d) 215 at 224 (Nfld. T.D.).

Where there was no satisfactory evidence before the court as to whether payment by the Armed Forces for the wife's retraining would cease upon divorce, nor was there adequate evidence of the actual cost of retraining, the court reserved the question of a lump sum award: *Gross v. Gross* (1977), 2 A.R. 440 at 445 (T.D.).

"If all of the information was available to the court, it may have been possible to determine whether or not the respondent [wife] was entitled to receive an award of a lump sum by way of maintenance. A great deal more information is required to determine this issue. In the result, the matter of the lump sum award is reserved, the respondent to have the right to make an application to the court for the determination of this issue as and when she may be advised, upon proper notice to the petitioner": per Greschuk J. in *Elligott v. Elligott* (1977), 3 R.F.L. (2d) 61 at 66, 6 A.R. 282 (T.D.).

15§73 — Lump sum — in addition to periodic sums

Where the husband was ordered to pay the wife periodic maintenance from the date of petition, the court, on an appeal of the maintenance provision, varied the decree *nisi* to provide for periodic payments payable from the date of hearing and a lump sum payable in lieu of arrears of interim maintenance accruing from the date of petition: *Wolch v. Wolch* (1981), 20 R.F.L. (2d) 325 (Man. C.A.).

"The monthly sum agreed to be paid by the husband could not in any way be considered adequate even for the maintenance of the children, although it would not appear desirable for practical purposes to fix that amount any higher. I am satisfied that these are proper circumstances in which to require the respondent to pay to the petitioner, in addition to the periodical payments for the maintenance of the children, a lump sum in respect of the future maintenance of the wife": per Dickson J. in *Maillet v. Maillet* (1976), 25 R.F.L. 126 at 127–128, 13 N.B.R. (2d) 330 (Q.B.). See also *Van Snick v. Van Snick* (1978), 27 N.S.R. (2d) 127, 41 A.P.R. 127 (C.A.).

When a lump sum is awarded as maintenance, the monthly allowance which otherwise would be granted must be appropriately reduced or even eliminated: *Eisenhauer v. Eisenhauer* (1975), 14 N.S.R. (2d) 164 (C.A.). See also *Dexter v. Dexter* (1975), 11 N.B.R. (2d) 11, 7 A.P.R. 11 (C.A.), where the wife was awarded two lump sums in lieu of a single lump sum and periodic maintenance.

"Lump-sum payments are given when such are necessary in order to provide reasonable maintenance in the light of the particular circumstances, because the giving of periodic payments alone would not result in providing such maintenance. ... Generally reasonable maintenance can be provided by ordering periodic payments alone, and by so doing the court maintains the power to vary its order from time to time in order to do justice to both parties whenever a change in circumstances requires that such be done .... when the court finds that a petitioner is entitled to a maintenance order the court should, generally speaking, first order periodic payments, and then, when it is necessary in order to provide proper maintenance, to order a lump-sum payment in addition to the periodic payments": per Disbery J. in *Rathwell v. Rathwell* (1974), 16 R.F.L. 387 at 394–395 (Sask. Q.B.). See also *Juby v. Juby* (1977), 3 R.F.L. (2d) 323 (Ont. H.C.). See also *Lawrence v. Lawrence* (1981), 20 R.F.L. (2d) 414 at 418–419, 45 N.S.R. (2d) 541, 86 A.P.R. 541 (T.D.), where the circumstances warranted both a lump sum award and periodic payments. See also *Van Mehren v. Van Mehren*, [1970] 1 W.W.R. 56, [1970] 1 All E.R. 153; *Hutchinson v. Hutchinson*, 6 R.F.L. 353 at 357, [1972] 3 W.W.R. 59, 25 D.L.R. (3d) 23 (Man. Q.B.).

15§74 — Lump sum — calculation

Where the husband was unemployed because of health reasons, but the wife required financial support, the court ordered him to pay lump sum support. The lump sum was calculated on the assumption that the husband would return to work and the gross sum determined by calculating the periodic support which would otherwise be payable until the date of the husband's retirement. The amount was discounted to reflect the tax payable on the funds, the present value of the funds and for negative contingencies such as remarriage or loss of employment: *Poisson v. Poisson* (1993), 46 R.F.L. (3d) 105 (Ont. Gen. Div.).

15§75 — Lump sum — set-off

In *Newstone v. Newstone* (1994), 2 R.F.L. (4th) 129, 91 B.C.L.R. (2d) 246, 39 B.C.A.C. 223, 64 W.A.C. 223 (C.A.), it was held that the court could properly award lump sum support to a wife by setting the sum off against funds which the wife would otherwise be required to pay to the husband. Such an order does not amount to an improper redistribution of capital.

15§76 — Lump sum — jurisdiction to secure awards

The court lacks jurisdiction to order a husband's property to be registered in the wife's name under the guise of securing maintenance to the wife: *Morrison v. Morrison* (1972), 4 R.F.L. 399 (B.C. S.C.). See also *Olynyk v. Olynyk*, [1932] 1 W.W.R. 825, 26 Alta. L.R.

485, [1932] 2 D.L.R. 785 (C.A.). See also *Brickman v. Brickman* (1982), 27 R.F.L. (2d) 391 (Ont. C.A.).

Where the parties have sold the jointly owned matrimonial home, there is no jurisdiction in a District Court judge to order the husband to pay his share of the proceeds into court as security for a possible maintenance order in favour of the wife in a future divorce hearing: *Hind v. Hind* (1975), 20 R.F.L. 331 (Ont. Div. Ct.).

15§77 — Lump sum — corporate property not subject to charge

In *Adams v. Adams* (1970), 3 N.B.R. (2d) 451 (C.A.), the husband transferred two properties, which constituted his main assets, to a holding company in order to put them out of the reach of the wife who was claiming maintenance. The court held that there was no authority to support an order securing maintenance payments by making them a charge upon property not belonging to the husband but to a company which the husband owns or controls. See also *Minty v. Minty* (1977), 4 R.F.L. (2d) 1 at 2, 5 B.C.L.R. 119 (S.C.); *Re Lister and Lister*, 3 R.F.L. 194, 14 D.L.R. (3d) 641, [1971] 1 O.R. 149 (H.C.).

15§78 — Lump sum — secured on matrimonial home

Where the father had a nominal income but was the joint owner of the encumbrance-free matrimonial home valued at $275,000, the child support ordered to be paid by him was charged against his interest in the home: *Reid v. Reid* (1995), 11 R.F.L. (4th) 85, 3 B.C.L.R. (3d) 266, 56 B.C.A.C. 234, 92 W.A.C. 234 (C.A.).

Where the relationship between the parties was acrimonious and where the wife feared that the husband would abandon the family and return to India, the lump sum child and spousal support that the husband was ordered to pay was further ordered to be secured against the husband's interest in the family home: *Bhatthal v. Bhatthal* (1990), 28 R.F.L. (3d) 152, 74 Alta. L.R. (2d) 307, 107 A.R. 70 (Q.B.).

A judge has no power under the *Divorce Act* to direct the sale of a matrimonial home. However, a trial judge may order that one spouse secure payment to the other of a lump sum, charged together with interest on the payor's share of the matrimonial home. Consequently, upon the sale of the home, all maintenance arrears would be a charge upon the payor's share of the proceeds: *Andrews v. Andrews* (1980), 21 R.F.L. (2d) 348 (Ont. C.A.).

"There have been many cases ... where a husband has been ordered to pay a lump sum equivalent to the value of his equity in the family home. But the amount to be paid should be specified. It is often provided that a husband may satisfy payment by transferring his equity or an appropriate part of it to the wife. Here, payment was to be deferred until the property would be sold. There is no way of knowing now what the value of the equity would be when that event occurs. In our view, this is not an order for payment of a lump sum. In our opinion, an appropriate order, under all the circumstances here, would be to require a lump sum payment of $5,000 to be secured against the husband's equity in the home, the lump sum to be payable when the property is sold": per Monnin J.A. in *Lachance v. Lachance* (1976), 28 R.F.L. 186 at 187 (Man. C.A.).

"With this in mind I would vary the order of the trial Judge and set aside the lump sum payment of $25,000.00 as creating too great a hardship on the appellant [husband] which could affect his ability to make the periodic payments. In lieu thereof I would order the appellant to secure to the petitioner, the payment of $25,000.00 by way of a mortgage on the matrimonial home, and one acre of land including that on which the house is situate and access to the highway road and a chattel mortgage on the household effects, furniture and fixtures in the matrimonial home subject to any mortgage or mortgages now in effect thereon, without interest and without recourse against the appellant, payable in two years from the date of this judgment": per Limerick J.A. in *McConnell v. McConnell* (1975), 11 N.B.R. (2d) 19 at 22, 7 A.P.R. 19, 57 D.L.R. (3d) 268 (C.A.).

In *Chadderton v. Chadderton*, [1973] 1 O.R. 560, 31 D.L.R. (3d) 656, 8 R.F.L. 374, the Court of Appeal held that a judge in Ontario has no authority under the *Divorce Act* to order one spouse to transfer real estate or specific assets to the other spouse, although Arnup J.A., said he thought there ought to be such a provision. It seems clear, then, that I have no authority to order directly the result which I think would be fair in this case. I think that I can accomplish that result indirectly, however, by varying the form of the order made in the *Chadderton* case. There will be an order requiring the husband to secure in favour of the wife the lump sum of $36,000, upon certain conditions: *Gloude v. Gloude* (1976), 14 O.R. (2d) 571, 74 D.L.R. (3d) 405 at 407–408 (H.C.); *Schell v. Schell* (1978), 29 R.F.L. 349 at 351 (B.C. S.C.). See also *Davis v. Davis* (1979), 23 A.R. 440 (Q.B.); and *Vosper v. Vosper* (1981), 7 Man. R. (2d) 92 (Q.B.); *Leitch v. Leitch* (1978), 12 A.R. 65 at 72 (T.D.). See also *Stevens v. Stevens* (1977), 17 N.B.R. (2d) 656 at 662 (Q.B.); *Ottho v. Ottho*, 20 R.F.L. 1 at 2, [1975] W.W.D. 37 (B.C. S.C.). See also *Johnson v. Johnson* (1976), 23 R.F.L. 293 at 302, [1975] W.W.D. 167 (Alta. T.D.); *Bandura v. Bandura* (1977), 6 A.R. 478 at 484 (T.D.); *Wagner v. Wagner* (1970), 73 W.W.R. 474 (Alta. T.D.); and *Schulte v. Schulte* (1972), 6 R.F.L. 164 (Ont. H.C.); *Secord v. Secord* (1978), 2 R.F.L. (2d) 97 (P.E.I. S.C.); *Kinshella v. Kinshella* (1976), 30 R.F.L. 297 (Alta. T.D.).

15§79 — Lump sum — grounds for securing or refusing to secure awards

Generally it is inappropriate to link security for maintenance to custody and access matters: *D. (B.) v. B. (L.D.)*, 37 R.F.L. (5th) 318, 2003 CarswellBC 719, 2003 BCCA 189, 181 B.C.A.C. 33, 298 W.A.C. 33 (B.C.C.A.).

"On the issue of the appellant [husband] providing security, I am unable to find any evidence or real or apprehended concern that the appellant will not comply with the maintenance order. It is true that the respondent has taken up residence in California and that the appellant's business interests are in Manitoba and Canada, but that is her choice. ... Should the circumstances change, making the provision of security essential, that can be appropriately obtained": per Hall J.A. in *Guberman v. Guberman*, 27 R.F.L. 15 at 21, [1977] 2 W.W.R. 1 (Man. C.A.).

"The evidence is clear that the respondent ... [husband] deserted the petitioner in 1959, leaving her with two daughters. From that time until the present, the petitioner supported not only herself, but the two daughters without any assistance from the respondent. There was an order in the Family Court for payment, but it appears that this order was not productive. ... The petitioner now wishes a lump sum award to be made, and that lump sum to be secured against the property. The end product of this sought-after lump sum award is to, in effect, make the petitioner the sole owner of the property. In our opinion, this is a fit case for the making of such an order in view of the efforts expended by the petitioner in the past. The decree nisi will be varied by adding an order that the respondent pay the petitioner a lump sum in the amount of $25,000, this lump sum award to be secured against the property in question": per Zuber J.A. in *Bradshaw v. Bradshaw* (1976), 24 R.F.L. 200 at 200–1 (Ont. C.A.).

"[The husband] is unwilling to pay his former wife anything. He left his salaried job last July and took work as a commission salesman for a building supply company. At the time of the second hearing he was out of work. He has established a relationship with another woman and she and her two children live with him. ... [The wife] is working at two jobs and has had to carry the burden of the support of the children. The Registrar has recommended that the respondent pay $50 per month for each of the three children, and I confirmed that part of the recommendation on 17th April 1974. With respect, I think that the Registrar has come to the correct conclusion on the maintenance for the petitioner in his recommendation that the respondent pay a lump sum of $10,000 which, when paid, will end the obligations of the respondent for the maintenance and support of the petitioner. I propose to adopt the procedure that was followed by the Court of Appeal of Ontario in *Chadderton v. Chadderton*, [1973] 1 O.R. 560, 8 R.F.L. 374, 31 D.L.R. (3d) 656, to require the respondent to secure in favour of the petitioner the lump sum of $10,000": per Hutcheon L.J.S.C. in *Garratt v. Garratt*, 16 R.F.L. 168 at 171, [1974] 6 W.W.R. 659 (B.C. S.C.). See also *Redding v. Redding* (1976), 13 Nfld. & P.E.I.R. 214 at 216, 29 A.P.R. 214 (Nfld. T.D.).

In *Sundholm v. Sundholm* (1980), 17 R.F.L. (2d) 365 (Ont. H.C.), a trustee in bankruptcy obtained title to the husband's interest in the matrimonial home by virtue of the operation of a court order, which was registered on title after the petition was issued but before the matter came on for trial. It was held that the wife could not claim a charge against the half interest registered in the name of the trustee in bankruptcy in an application for maintenance. See also *Kutschenreiter v. Kutschenreiter* (1983), 46 C.B.R. (N.S.) 1 (Ont. H.C.); *Brocklebank v. Brocklebank*, 25 R.F.L. 53 at 70, [1976] W.W.D. 15 (B.C. S.C.). See also *Mesrobian v. Mesrobian* (1978), 4 R.F.L. (2d) 341 at 346 (Ont. H.C.); and *Jacyk v. Jacyk* (1970), 1 R.F.L. 274 at 275 (Ont. H.C.); reversed 2 R.F.L. 412 (Ont. C.A.); *Jackson v. Jackson* (1976), 24 R.F.L. 109 at 118 (Ont. H.C.); *Dart v. Dart* (1974), 14 R.F.L. 97 at 100–101 (Ont. H.C.); *J. v. J.* (1969), 8 D.L.R. (3d) 760 at 763 (Sask. Q.B.). See also *Holewa v. Holewa* (1977), 6 A.R. 476, 3 Alta. L.R. (2d) 253 (T.D.).

15§80 — Lump sum — refusal of awards

In *Russell v. Russell* (1995), 16 R.F.L. (4th) 229, 33 Alta. L.R. 3(d) 170, 175 A.R. 225 (Q.B.) the court rejected the wife's claim for lump sum support. The wife's claim was to redress the perceived deficiency resulting from the parties' property division order and, as a veiled attempt to redistribute property, was not a proper basis for a lump sum order.

In *Gallant v. Gallant* (1998), 42 R.F.L. (2d) 353, 166 D.L.R. (4th) 79, 131 Man. R. (2d) 15, 187 W.A.C. 15 (C.A.), the court allowed the husband's appeal from an order requiring him to transfer $25,000 from his R.R.S.P. to the wife as lump sum support. By specifying the payment from a particular source the order amounted to "back-door equalization" rather than spousal support.

Lump sum support is not properly used to compensate a spouse for a perceived inadequacy of interim support earlier ordered: *Hauff v. Hauff* (1994), 5 R.F.L. (4th) 419, 95 Man. R. (2d) 83, 70 W.A.C. 83 (C.A.).

Lump-sum spousal support was not awarded where the effect of the order would primarily amount to a shifting of assets: *Dababneh v. Dababneh* (2003), 48 R.F.L. (5th) 55, 2003 CarswellOnt 5004 (Ont. S.C.J.); additional reasons at (2004), 2004 CarswellOnt 654 (Ont. S.C.J.).

In *Mondino v. Mondino* (2004), 9 R.F.L. (6th) 170, 2004 CarswellOnt 3513 (S.C.J.), the court refused the wife's claim for lump sum spousal support in the form of allowing her to keep all the proceeds from the sale of the family home. Although there was evidence that the husband might be inclined to put his own financial interests before those of the family, the order requested would be a disguised form of property transfer and, accordingly, unfair.

In *Laflamme v. Laflamme* (1998), 38 R.F.L. (4th) 335 (Alta. Q.B.), the court rejected the wife's claim for lump sum spousal support based upon her temporary loss of Indian treaty status during the parties' one-year marriage. The marriage was of very short duration and the wife had been aware of the status loss during marriage.

Where the husband had taken early retirement as a result of illness and lacked the capital to pay lump sum spousal support, the wife's claim for lump sum was dismissed. Although the wife had left her employment to care for the parties' child, this one factor could not be considered in isolation as a rationale for ordering lump sum spousal support: *Deane v. Deane* (1995), 14 R.F.L. (4th) 55 (Ont. Gen. Div.).

In *Sword v. Sword* (1994), 118 Nfld. & P.E.I.R. 69, 369 A.P.R. 69 (Nfld. U.F.C.) the wife's claim for lump sum support was dismissed in the absence of evidence that she had suffered an economic disadvantage of a type warranting lump sum compensatory support. The disadvantage resulting from her remaining in the home with the children could be adequately addressed through periodic support.

In *Graham v. Platt* (1996), 19 R.F.L. (4th) 32 (Man. Q.B.), the wife's request for lump sum support was refused. The wife had cosigned a business loan for the husband, whose business subsequently failed and the loan had been called against him. Any economic hardship as a result of the loan remained only a possibility for the wife and as such could not be the basis for a spousal support award.

Lump sum support is appropriate in cases where it is needed to fund retraining and to meet immediate needs. It should not be awarded to cover legal fees nor is it appropriate to provide for future security where the claimant is also receiving periodic support: *Mosher v. Mosher* (1995), 13 R.F.L. (4th) 385 (N.S. C.A.); reversing in part (1993), 126 N.S.R. (2d) 367, 352 A.P.R. 67 (S.C.).

To be entitled to support a party must show she has an immediate need: *Matthews v. Matthews* (1991), 34 R.F.L. (3d) 201 (N.S. C.A.) citing *Hemming v. Hemming* (1983), 33 R.F.L. (2d) 157, 58 N.S.R. (2d) 65, 123 A.P.R. 65, 145 D.L.R. (3d) 699 (C.A.). Where a party seeks a lump sum in order to obtain a division of assets in the guise of a support payment, it will not be granted. In the *Matthews* case the court was of the opinion that there was no immediate need justifying an order for lump sum support.

In *MacNeil v. MacNeil* (1994), 2 R.F.L. (4th) 432, 129 N.S.R. (2d) 284, 362 A.P.R. 284, 113 D.L.R. (4th) 218 (C.A.), the court allowed the husband's appeal from an award of lump sum support made in the wife's favour. Although she had at one time during the marriage put her nursing career on hold to care for the family, she had returned full-time prior to separation and was earning at the top of the pay scale. Accordingly, she had not established that she was economically disadvantaged and the order amounted more to an improper redistribution of capital between the spouses.

In *Droit de la famille — 1661*, [1992] R.J.Q. 2479 (S.C.), the husband's claim for lump sum support to allow him to set up a pension fund for himself was dismissed. The husband could not claim a lump sum to compensate for that which the division of family assets did not give him.

In *DaCosta v. DaCosta* (1990), 29 R.F.L. (3d) 422, 74 D.L.R. (4th) 491 (Ont. Gen. Div.); affirmed (1992), 40 R.F.L. (3d) 216, 7 O.R. (3d) 321, 44 E.T.R. 196, 53 O.A.C. 354, 89 D.L.R. (4th) 268 (C.A.); amended (1992), 40 R.F.L. (3d) 216n (Ont. C.A.), the court refused the wife's claim for compensatory support based upon her contributions to her husband's political campaign. She had not expected to be compensated for her political contributions and he had not been financially enriched thereby.

Where the unemployed husband's only asset was his equity in the family home, a lump sum support award in the wife's favour was found not to be appropriate: *Auger v. Auger* (1991), 77 Man. R. (2d) 196 (Q.B.).

Where the wife had use of $40,000 more than her share of matrimonial property after separation and had been re-instated to the same employment position that she had held prior to marriage, her claim for lump sum support was dismissed. Having an annual income of $63,000, the wife was unable to establish any need: *McWilliam v. McWilliam* (1989), 23 R.F.L. (3d) 265, 100 A.R. 65 (Q.B.).

Where the wife had quit her job to return to school, her claim for lump sum support to discharge her debts accumulated during her schooling was dismissed. She had voluntarily taken on the debts by not consulting her husband before quitting her job, and further, the husband had no assets beyond the family home out of which to pay a lump sum: *Krohn v. Krohn* (1987), 47 Man. R. (2d) 58 (Q.B.).

Where the husband had previously ignored a child support order, the court nevertheless refused the wife's request for $60,000 lump sum child support. The request was excessive given the parties' means and the children's needs and would have the effect of stripping the husband of his assets. The children's needs could better be met through the income from a trust imposed upon the husband's share of a revenue-producing property: *Ling v. Ting* (1990), 25 R.F.L. (3d) 214 (B.C. S.C.).

In *Zabiegalowski v. Zabiegalowski* (1992), 40 R.F.L. (3d) 321 (Ont. U.F.C.), the court refused the wife's application for lump sum support upon the collapse of a marriage in which the parties had cohabited for only 14 months. The lump sum would have depleted the 57-year-old husband's only asset and would have amounted to an unequal division of property.

A court ought not to award support based upon speculation on possibility. Accordingly, a wife's claim for lump sum support to finance the parties' son's university education was dismissed as it was based on the presumption that the son would complete school: *Riley v. Riley* (1987), 11 R.F.L. (3d) 105 (N.S. Fam. Ct.).

15§81 — Set-off

See *Kent v. Frolick* (1996), 19 R.F.L. (4th) 152 (Ont. Gen. Div.); additional reasons at (1996), 3 O.T.C. 122 (Gen. Div.); further additional reasons at (July 3, 1996), Doc. 93-ND-199927 (Ont. Gen. Div.); varied (1996), 23 R.F.L. (4th) 1 (Ont. C.A.).

SPOUSAL SUPPORT — Disclosure

15§82 — Disclosure of financial information

In *Hum v. Man* (1998), 42 R.F.L. (2d) 382 (Ont. C.A.), the court allowed the wife's appeal from her spousal support award and ordered a new trial. The trial judge had rejected the wife's claim that the husband falsified financial records and participated in questionable business practices to conceal income. The husband's lifestyle simply was not consistent with his claimed income which was below the poverty level.

In *Lamarche c. Crevier* (2000), 4 R.F.L. (5th) 88, 2000 CarswellOnt 28 (S.C.J.); additional reasons at (2000), 2000 CarswellOnt 1142 (S.C.J.); varied in part, on other grounds (2001), 2001 CarswellOnt 3910, 151 O.A.C. 22, 22 R.F.L. (5th) 354 (C.A.), neither party was awarded costs at the conclusion of their divorce proceedings. Both had demonstrated a lack of co-operation in producing the documents required to reach conclusions about each party's rights.

Improper conduct regarding timely disclosure of improvements to a payor's financial position may, in certain circumstances, give rise to retroactive spousal support despite the parties' agreement to the contrary: *Leinburd v. Leinburd*, 10 R.F.L. (6th) 398, 2004 CarswellMan 194, 185 Man. R. (2d) 215, [2004] 9 W.W.R. 635, 2004 MBQB 113 (Man. Q.B.).

Where the wife had clearly established her entitlement to spousal support but had failed to provide financial statements or information about her living expenses, the calculation of her support was adjourned to permit her to produce the required information: *R. (E.K.) v. W. (G.A.)* (1997), 32 R.F.L. (4th) 202, [1998] 1 W.W.R. 534, 122 Man. R. (2d) 120 (Q.B.); additional reasons (1998), 124 Man. R. (2d) 258 (Q.B.).

Spousal support is not to be awarded as a means of punishing one spouse and rewarding another. Accordingly, where a spouse misled the court concerning assets, the court's reproval is more appropriately expressed through a cost award and not through an enhanced support award: *Chisholm v. Chisholm* (1997), 32 B.C.L.R. (3d) 20 (S.C.).

Where the evidence in an interim support application indicates that the husband's income exceeds that specified in his declaration, the court is not bound by such declaration in quantifying the support payable: *Droit de la famille — 1231*, [1989] R.D.F. 189 (C.S. Qué.).

In *Bodman v. Bodman* (1998), 38 R.F.L. (4th) 210, 127 Man. R. (2d) 1 (Master), the court rejected the wife's application to compel the husband provide financial disclosure of the affairs of his common law wife. The application for disclosure had not been served on the common law wife and there was no evidence that the husband had access to her financial information.

In proceedings for support, the parties have an obligation to make full disclosure and to produce all relevant documents. In the absence of such disclosure the court may, *inter alia*, draw adverse inference or order disclosure: *Ewing v. Ewing* (1987), 7 R.F.L. (3d) 168, 56 Sask. R. 260 (C.A.). Even where a settlement is negotiated by the parties it is desirable that the means of the payor be disclosed so that the court can satisfy itself of the propriety of the settlement: *Cumisky v. Cumisky*, 18 R.F.L. 182, [1974] 5 W.W.R. 544 (Sask. Q.B.).

A record of three years of financial disclosure on the part of a claimant is generally sufficient in a claim for spousal support: *Forbes v. Forbes* (1994), 99 Man. R. (2d) 280 (Master).

Where the father, in his application for child support, refused to disclose his income as sole beneficial owner of a corporation, his claim was dismissed. In the circumstances no apportionment of the child care expenses could be calculated and it was likely that the father, in his earlier offer of spousal support to the wife, had already made adjustments for his ongoing support of the children: *Woolgar v. Woolgar* (1995), 10 R.F.L. (4th) 309 (Nfld. U.F.C.).

In *N. v. N.* (1976), 24 R.F.L. 366 (Man. C.A.), where there was no evidence of the parties' expenses and minimal evidence of their assets and liabilities, the court struck out the reference to maintenance in the petition, reserving the petitioner's right to apply to the Court of the Queen's Bench for an appropriate order. See also *LeRoux v. LeRoux*, 19 R.F.L. 14 at 17, [1975] W.W.D. 3, 50 D.L.R. (3d) 765 (B.C. S.C.); *Uhryn v.Uhryn* (1975), 23 R.F.L. 28 (Sask. Q.B.). See also *McKay v. McKay*, 2 R.F.L. 398, [1971] 1 W.W.R. 487, 16 D.L.R. (3d) 344 (Man. Q.B.); *Morrow v. Morrow* (1974), 44 D.L.R. (3d) 711, 8 N.S.R. (2d) 149 (C.A.); *Green v. Green* (1977), 6 A.R. 485 (T.D.).

Where the husband claimed that full disclosure of his financial position would hurt his company's financial position and he indicated his ability and willingness to pay any reasonable increase in spousal support ordered, the requirement that he make full financial disclosure was waived. The finding would only have added unnecessarily to the length and cost of the proceedings: *Zwingenberger v. Zwingenberger* (1995), 17 R.F.L. (4th) 239 (Ont. Gen. Div.).

CHILD SUPPORT — Jurisdiction

15§83 — General — status of parties and jurisdiction of the court

At the time the child support order is made under the *Divorce Act*, the parties must be "former" married spouses. However, a support claim may be joined as corollary relief in a proceeding with a claim for divorce; that is, support may be claimed in a proceeding commenced when the parties are still married, as long as one of the claims is for a divorce. At the hearing, jurisdiction is established by granting the divorce first in time. The parties are then former spouses when the court turns to the support claim.

Although the support claim may be joined with a claim for divorce in the same proceeding, this joinder is not a necessary prerequisite for the court having jurisdiction to deal with it. Child support may be claimed separately in a corollary relief proceeding, after the proceeding for divorce has been commenced or determined: *Divorce Act*, s. 2(1) "corollary relief proceeding" and "spouse"; *Federal Child Support Guidelines*, s. 2(1) "spouse".

A court in a province has jurisdiction to hear and determine a corollary relief proceeding if

> "(a) either former spouse is ordinarily resident in the province at the commencement of the proceeding; or
>
> (b) both former spouses accept the jurisdiction of the court:" *Divorce Act*, s. 4(1).

Where each spouse commences a separate proceeding with one of them in a different province, the Act sets out a procedure for determining which court is to have jurisdiction. See subsections 4(2) and (3) of the Act.

Unless complementary legislation and regulations are enacted and established in the provincial sphere, the guidelines are restricted in their operation to the federal jurisdiction of divorce and corollary relief.

As of June 1, 2002, Quebec, Prince Edward Island, Manitoba, and New Brunswick have created their own guidelines which have been accepted and designated by the Governor in Council as "applicable guidelines" for each respective province. Where a proceeding under the *Divorce Act* concerns two parents who both reside in one of these four provinces, that province's guidelines will apply to that proceeding.

Saskatchewan has adopted the *Federal Guidelines* as its own; therefore, they apply to provincial matters as well as to matters under the *Divorce Act.*

British Columbia, Newfoundland, Nova Scotia, Northwest Territories, Nunavut, and Yukon have all adopted the *Federal Child Support Guidelines* (with minor amendments in each case) under their respective statutes governing child support obligations.

In Ontario, two sets of guidelines operate: one, the federal guidelines when child support is corollary relief in a divorce proceeding, and the other, the provincial guidelines, where provincial legislation is invoked. However, the content of the tables is the same in both sets.

Alberta has given royal assent to changes in its child support legislation, but has not proclaimed those changes in force.

Where a province or territory has not established its own guidelines and had them designated or specified under s. 2(5) of the *Divorce Act*, in matters involving divorce, the *Federal Child Support Guidelines* will apply.

The parties must be married spouses or former spouses: *Divorce Act*, s. 2(1) "spouse," *Federal Child Support Guidelines, s. 2(1) "spouse."*

Where the father had a long-term relationship with a woman whom he eventually married, the court allowed the mother's application to amend pleadings and add the new wife as a party to the mother's child support application. The parties had a joint custody arrangement and it was arguable that the new wife stood *in loco parentis* to the child: *Johnson v. Johnson* (1998), 38 R.F.L. (4th) 279 (Ont. Gen. Div.).

There is no authorization under either the *Divorce Act* or the *Federal Child Support Guidelines* for a payor spouse to join individuals standing *in loco parentis* to the children in order to claim a support contribution from them: *Robinson v. Domin* (1998), 39 R.F.L. (4th) 92 (B.C. S.C.).

Where a child support order is granted in the Provincial Court, the Supreme Court of British Columbia does not have jurisdiction to review or vary that order: *Schaff v. Schaff* (1997), 30 R.F.L. (4th) 63, 93 B.C.A.C. 248, 151 W.A.C. 248, 38 B.C.L.R. (3d) 89 (C.A.). The Supreme Court of British Columbia has concurrent jurisdiction under the *Divorce Act* to order child support, even where the Provincial Court has already made such orders under the *Family Relations Act*: *Schaff v. Schaff, supra.* In this case, however, the father had sought to vary a provincial court child support order in the British Columbia Supreme Court.

In *Thomas v. Thomas* (November 4, 1997), Doc. Sault Ste. Marie 17037/97 (Ont. Gen. Div.), the mother brought an originating application for support after the parties had been divorced. Counsel for the father contended that, because of the divorce, there was no jurisdiction to grant support pursuant to the *Divorce Act*. The *Family Law Act* governs, it was submitted, and since the provincial guidelines were not then in force, the provision for child support in the separation agreement should be enforced except for a modification made necessary by a change in the child's living arrangements. The court observed that an original order for support is no longer limited to being made "upon the granting of a divorce," and held that it had jurisdiction to deal with the application.

Cases decided before the enactment of the Federal Child Support Guidelines:

A custody applicant should raise the issue of child support at the time of the custody application, failing which a change of circumstances must occur before a support order can be made. An applicant will not be allowed to divide a case in two by waiting until after custody is obtained to claim support: *Dewar v. Dewar* (1992), 41 R.F.L. (3d) 420 (N.B. C.A.).

It is improper to award retroactive child support for a period which predates the proceedings. Child support is awarded to meet present and future needs and not for past obligations for which no claim was ever made: *Sartor v. Sartor* (1993), 45 R.F.L. (3d) 250, [1993] N.W.T.R. 102 (S.C.).

Under the *Divorce Act*, the court is not empowered to make a retrospective award of child support: *Orlando v. Orlando* (1987), 11 R.F.L. (3d) 418 (B.C. S.C.).

The court has discretion as to what amount, if any, should be payable from moneys held in trust for an infant towards her maintenance: *Houle v. Ritcht*, [1977] 6 W.W.R. 486 (Man. Q.B.).

The court has jurisdiction to order child maintenance commencing on a date prior to pronouncement of the decree *nisi*: *Ratcliffe v. Ratcliffe* (1976), 27 R.F.L. 227 (B.C. S.C.). See also *Campbell v. Campbell*, 27 R.F.L. 40, [1976] 5 W.W.R. 513 (Sask. Q.B.), where the court ordered an immediate lump sum payment where the husband had not been making payments as previously awarded and ordered periodic maintenance payments thereafter.

Where the petition for divorce is dismissed, the court has no jurisdiction to grant corollary relief, but it may have jurisdiction to grant child maintenance under the *Family Relations Act, 1972* (B.C.), c. 20 even after the child has attained the age of majority: *Visscher v. Visscher*, 24 R.F.L. 65, [1976] 4 W.W.R. 359 (B.C. S.C.).

Even though the *Family Relations Act* of British Columbia was enacted subsequent in time to the *Divorce Act*, the federal legislation with respect to maintenance remains paramount; and, consequently, no question of electing remedies could ever arise: *Traill v. Traill*, 21 R.F.L. 183 at 186–187, [1975] W.W.D. 113, 55 D.L.R. (3d) 760 (B.C. S.C.).

"Although I am of opinion that this Court is not deprived of jurisdiction over infants by the terms of a decree issued under the *Divorce Act* in another province, this is for powerful reasons, related to the welfare of the children involved. Thus it is not a jurisdiction to be lightly exercised, without regard to what has already been determined after trial elsewhere, nor is it to be exercised to adjust minor matters of convenience or administration. Those who invoke it must satisfy the Court that its order is needed for the welfare of the child": per Wright J. dealing with an application for maintenance in *Emerson v. Emerson*, 8 R.F.L. 30 at 36, [1976] 3 O.R. 5, 27 D.L.R. (3d) 278 (H.C.).

15§84 — The *Divorce Act* and provincial statutes

Child support and the division of matrimonial property are distinct issues and should be dealt with separately. *Zaparaniuk v. Wagar*, 27 R.F.L (5th) 223, 2002 CarswellSask 250, 2002 SKQB 158, 281 Sask. R. 224 (Sask. Q.B.).

The court has jurisdiction to make an interim child support order under the *Divorce Act* superseding an earlier final order made under provincial legislation: *Lewkoski v. Lewkoski* (1998), 40 R.F.L. (4th) 86 (Ont. Gen. Div.).

A consent child support order under provincial legislation does not prevent the court from assessing support under the guidelines in the context of an originating application for corollary relief under the *Divorce Act*: *Young v. Young* (1998), 39 R.F.L. (4th) 110, 51 B.C.L.R. (3d) 299 (S.C. [In Chambers]); additional reasons at (1998), 51 B.C.L.R. (3d) 310 (S.C.).

"The Supreme Court, under the *Divorce Act*, has undoubted jurisdiction to deal with custody and maintenance of children of divorced parents. Until, however, it exercised that jurisdiction in any particular case, the provincial Act continues in full effect as to children and confers on the appropriate magistrate or Family Court Judge the power and duty to deal with maintenance": per MacKeigan C.J.N.S. in *Toole v. Toole* (1976), 27 R.F.L. 63 at 63–64, 14 N.S.R. (2d) 537 (C.A.).

Where a nominal child-maintenance award was made under the *Divorce Act*, but the parties later consented to an increased child-maintenance award under a provincial statute, the court favourably entertained the husband's application to quash the provincial order. As the maintenance issue had been dealt with by a superior court under the *Divorce Act*, a provincial judge acting under the authority of a provincial statute lacked jurisdiction to make a conflicting order: *Caves v. Caves* (1983), 34 R.F.L. (2d) 116, [1983] 4 W.W.R. 592, 146 D.L.R. (3d) 553 (Man. Q.B.).

Where the spouses had agreed that the petitioner would not claim either maintenance for herself or their child on the understanding, expressed in writing in minutes of settlement, that a pre-existing Family Court order for the wife and child would continue, it was held that as a matter of law the Family Court order became null and void, *with regards to the petitioner*, at the time the decree absolute was issued: *Izewski v. Izewski* (1976), 30 R.F.L. 257, 15 O.R. (2d) 53 (H.C.).

In *Scott v. Scott* (1972), 10 R.F.L. 8 (Ont. Co. Ct.), the court held that the jurisdiction of a Family Court to require the father of children to pay for their support is not destroyed because of the divorce of the parents because it does not depend on the husband and wife relationship. The court added that it was desirable not to have concurrent orders for the maintenance of the children of a marriage in two different courts. See also *McFadyen v. McFadyen* (1975), 22 R.F.L. 140 at 142 (Alta. T.D.).

The fact that a child may not qualify for support under the *Divorce Act* does not affect any support rights which may exist under the *Family Relations Act*, R.S.B.C. 1979, c. 121, s. 1. There is no operational incompatibility between the statutes: *Slattery v. Slattery* (1993), 48 R.F.L. (3d) 38 (B.C. S.C.).

A child cannot seek support under provincial legislation where a child support order under the *Divorce Act* remains in force: *Kulchyski v. Kulchyski* (1996), 22 R.F.L. (4th) 261 (Ont. Gen. Div.).

15§85 — Constitutional issues

In *Zeyha v. Canada (Attorney General)*, 11 R.F.L. (6th) 465, 2004 CarswellSask 786, 2004 SKCA 157, 246 D.L.R. (4th) 631 (Sask. C.A.), it was found that the two divorced fathers lacked public interest standing to challenge the validity of the *Guidelines* on constitutional grounds. Neither had sought to impugn the *Guidelines* in the context of their now completed matrimonial actions. It could hardly be said that there was no other reasonable and effective means to bring the issue before the court.

Section 2(1)(b) of the *Divorce Act* does violate s. 15(1) of the *Canadian Charter of Rights and Freedoms* in as much as it imposes an obligation on divorced parents to support adult children, which obligation is not imposed on married parents. However, the violation is justified under s. 1 of the *Charter* as the legislative goal of ensuring that the children of divorced parents continue to benefit from the financial support of both parents is both pressing and substantial. The adult children of divorced parents may not receive the same financial assistance as they might if their parents were still together and the effect of the discrimination is proportionate to the benefit received: *Michie v. Michie* (1997), 36 R.F.L. (4th) 90, 48 C.R.R. (2d) 333, [1998] 4 W.W.R. 758, 162 Sask. R. 1 (Q.B.).

Section 7 of the *Federal Child Support Guidelines* does not violate s. 15 of the *Canadian Charter of Rights and Freedoms* by discriminating against separated parents in as much as it requires a contribution to a child's post-secondary education: *Souliere v. Leclair* (1998), 38 R.F.L. (4th) 68, 52 C.R.R. (2d) 156 (Ont. Gen. Div.).

The household income test under the undue hardship provisions in s. 10 of the *Federal Child Support Guidelines* do not violate the right to privacy guaranteed in s. 7 of the *Canadian Charter of Rights and Freedoms*. The right of children to support is paramount over an individual's right to privacy: *Souliere v. Leclair* (1998), 38 R.F.L. (4th) 68, 52 C.R.R. (2d) 156 (Ont. Gen. Div.).

In *Dyck v. Highton*, 45 R.F.L. (5th) 322, 2003 CarswellSask 619, 111 C.R.R. (2d) 137, 239 Sask. R. 38, 2003 SKQB 396 (Sask. Q.B.), the court rejected the claim that the Child Support *Guidelines* were unconstitutional under s. 15 of the Charter as discriminatory against disabled parents. The fact that the Table Amounts were based on data relating to "average" persons did not mean that the *Guidelines* failed to consider the disadvantaged position of disabled persons. Additional expenses incurred by disabled persons could be accommodated by the "undue hardship" provisions of the *Guidelines*.

See also *Brandt v. Brandt*, 42 R.F.L. (5th) 257, 2003 CarswellNfld 166, 2003 NLCA 34, 227 Nfld. & P.E.I.R. 75, 677 A.P.R. 75 (N.L. C.A.); *Fitzell v. Weisbrod* (2005), 11 R.F.L. (6th) 239, 2005 CarswellOnt 805 (Ont. S.C.J.).

CHILD SUPPORT — Consideration

15§86 — Entitlement in general

A temporary child support order can be made where a child has relocated his residence from one parent to the other for a defined period of time: *Tynan v. Moses*, 25 R.F.L. (5th) 445, 2002 CarswellBC 283, 2002 BCSC 100 (B.C. S.C.).

In *Walgren v. Walgren*, 26 R.F.L. (5th) 226, 2002 CarswellBC 884, 2002 BCSC 432 (B.C. S.C.), a separate benefit received by the child pursuant to the father's CPP disability benefits, was not deducted from the father's income. Under the *Guidelines* the child's benefit was not a factor in absence of circumstances calling for a comparison of the standard of living in both households.

Where a child meets the definition of "child of the marriage" set out in s. 2(1) of the Act, he or she is entitled to child support. See the cases under s. 2(1).

Since the right to child support is the child's right, the fact that child support will indirectly benefit the payee spouse cannot be used as a justification for decreasing the quantum awarded to the child: *Leopold v. Leopold* (2000), 12 R.F.L. (5th) 118, 195 D.L.R. (4th) 717, 2000 CarswellOnt 4707, 51 O.R. (3d) 275, [2000] O.J. No. 4604 (S.C.J.).

The fact that the husband had not wanted the wife to become pregnant does not provide a defence to a child support claim: *Miller v. Ufoegbune* (2000), 11 R.F.L. (5th) 347, 2000 CarswellOnt 3760 (Ont. S.C.J.).

Where the parties' 20-year-old child had moved into her own apartment from the wife's home, the court refused the wife's application for child support. The husband paid for all of the child's living and school expenses and had reimbursed the wife for some of the child's expenses that she had paid. Accordingly, there was no need for a formal child support order: *Krill v. Krill* (2000), 4 R.F.L. (5th) 249, 2000 CarswellAlta 136, [2000] A.J. No. 163 (Q.B.).

The use of the word "may" in ss. 15.1(1) and (4) of the *Divorce Act* gives discretion to the court to ignore the *Federal Child Support Guidelines* and not to award child support where the custodial parent so requested. Where there is a possibility that support could lead to harassment and interference with the custodial parent the absence of a child support order can actually be in both the child's and the custodial parent's best interests: *Close v. Close* (1999), 50 R.F.L. (4th) 342, (sub nom. *T.C. v. L.C.)* 215 N.B.R. (2d) 383, 551 A.P.R. 383, 1999 CarswellNB 265 (Q.B.).

The fact that children moved from the care of the custodial mother to foster care does not automatically relieve the father of the obligation to support them: *Pawliuk v. Pawliuk* (1999), 48 R.F.L. (4th) 188 (Sask. Q.B.).

The length of the parties' marriage is not a relevant factor in the determination of child support: *Fibke v. Fibke* (1999), 48 R.F.L. (4th) 288, 240 A.R. 17 (Q.B.).

One of the objectives of the guidelines is that after separation the children are to continue to benefit from the financial means of the spouses: *Johnson v. Checkowy* (1997), 157 Sask. R. 71 (Q.B.).

In the absence of evidence of an 18 year old child's ability or efforts to support himself, there is no presumption as to support: *Viswalingam v. Viswalingam* (1996), 22 R.F.L. (4th) 372, [1996] N.W.T.R. 342 (S.C.).

In *Scullion v. Scullion* (1995), 12 R.F.L. (4th) 421, 158 N.B.R. (2d) 259, 406 A.P.R. 259, the husband's allegations of spousal misconduct on the part of the wife were found to be irrelevant in the context of the wife's child support claim. The paramount concern was the needs of the children.

A regular deposit into a child's savings account cannot properly be classified as an expense for the purpose of calculating child support: *Savage v. Savage* (1994), 98 Man. R. (2d) 241 (Q.B.).

A parent's primary obligation is to support his or her children. Such responsibility takes precedence over car payments, high mortgage payments, entertainment, tobacco, alcohol, recreation, vacation savings and debts: *Murray v. Murray* (1991), 35 R.F.L. (3d) 449, 82 Alta. L.R. (2d) 260, [1992] 1 W.W.R. 183, 123 A.R. 68 (Q.B.).

The obligation to support children takes priority over a parent's obligation to creditors: *Malcolm v. Malcolm* (1995), 10 R.F.L. (4th) 242 (Ont. Gen. Div.).

The cost of supporting children is a debt and a payor spouse's obligation to pay his or her share of that debt, regardless of ability to pay, until death and thereafter as a charge on the estate. The obligation takes precedence over ability to pay, which should only be considered in deferring the debt as opposed to cancelling it: *Gosnell v. Gosnell* (1993), 138 A.R. 205 (Q.B.).

The joint obligation between parents to contribute to the support of their children is not frozen in time. Accordingly, the remarriage of the payor spouse did nothing to deflect, postpone or lessen his obligation to his child in *Jardine v. Jardine* (1992), 119 N.S.R. (2d) 361, 330 A.P.R. 361 (T.D.).

Unless a legally recognized parental or guardian's obligation arises as between a parent's new spouse or common law spouse, no obligation of support exists on the part of the new cohabitant: *Levesque v. Levesque* (1994), 4 R.F.L. (4th) 375, 116 D.L.R. (4th) 314, 20 Alta. L.R. (3d) 429, [1994] 8 W.W.R. 589, 155 A.R. 26, 73 W.A.C. 26 (C.A.); additional reasons at (1995), 165 A.R. 319, 89 W.A.C. 319 (C.A.).

Generally, the conduct of a custodial parent is not relevant to the determination of child support. Such conduct may be the reason for removing the child from the custody of the offending parent, but it cannot be the basis for causing the child to suffer financially. Under some circumstances a misbehaving custodial parent who deprives the other parent of access rights can be deprived of child support, but not in circumstances where the withholding of the support would interfere with the proper maintenance of the child: *Welstead v. Bainbridge* (1995), 10 R.F.L. (4th) 410 (Ont. Gen. Div.).

15§87 — Approaches to determining child support

Since May 1, 1997, an order under the *Divorce Act* for the support of any or all children of the marriage (a child support order), or an interim child support order must be made in accordance with the applicable guidelines: s. 15.1(3). The "applicable guidelines" are the guidelines of the province where both spouses or former spouses ordinarily reside. If that province has not established guidelines, or if both spouses do not ordinarily reside in the province (e.g., one of them ordinarily resides elsewhere), then the applicable guidelines are the *Federal Child Support Guidelines*. See the *Divorce Act*, s. 2(1) "applicable guidelines."

The exercise of judicial discretion under the *Guidelines* must be shaped by *Guidelines* goals and objectives consistent with the child-focused approach mandated by the Supreme Court of Canada and the *United Nations Convention on the Rights of the Child*: *S (D.B.) v. G (S.R.)* (2005), 7 R.F.L. (6th) 373, 249 D.L.R. (4th) 72, 38 Alta. L.R. (4th) 199, 361 A.R. 60, 339 W.A.C. 60, [2005] 5 W.W.R. 229, 2005 CarswellAlta 18, 2005 ABCA 2 (C.A.); leave to appeal to S.C.C. granted (August 18, 2005), Doc. 30808 (S.C.C.).

Prior to the May 1997 amendments, the courts were indicating the need for better and more consistent approaches to the determination of child support.

The Supreme Court of Canada, in *Moge v. Moge* (1992), 43 R.F.L. (3d) 345, [1992] 3 S.C.R. 813, [1993] 1 W.W.R. 481, 81 Man. R. (2d) 161, 145 N.R. 1, 99 D.L.R. (4th) 456, a case dealing with spousal support, drew attention to the fact that many divorced wives and their children are living below the poverty line. The Court was of the opinion that support awards in general, both for spouses and for children, have been too low.

The same court in *Thibaudeau v. Thibaudeau* (1995), 12 R.F.L. (4th) 1, [1995] 1 C.T.C. 382, 124 D.L.R. (4th) 449, 29 C.R.R. (2d) 1, 182 N.R. 1 (S.C.C.), during public debate over the issue dealt with the question of whether a custodial parent receiving child support payments pursuant to an order or written agreement must continue to include these payments in income for tax purposes. It held that the payments should be included in income, but the attention brought to bear on the issue led to government sponsored legislation changing the deduction/[hmp.1]inclusion rule for child support and, at the same time, implementing a more general reform in the guise of the child support guidelines.

The way to acceptance of the guideline approach was prepared by the courts struggling for standards and consistency in support awards. In 1994, the Alberta Court of Appeal laid down a number of principles developed from the case law that later appeared in a revised and much expanded form in the guidelines. (See, below.) In *Levesque v. Levesque* (1994), 4 R.F.L. (4th) 375 (Alta. C.A.); additional reasons at (1995), 165 A.R. 319, 80 W.A.C. 319 (C.A.), the Court held that in determining the level of child support, it should first determine what the obligation of each parent for payment of the support would be without adjustment for the parent's needs, and then consider whether the parent can meet the obligation. If the parent should seek to pay an amount at a reduced level because of his or her own subsistence would be affected, the adjustment should not be permitted if it would drive the child support award so low that the subsistence level of the other parent, or the child, falls below that of the parent seeking the adjustment. The "cost-to-the-child" approach, based upon a reasonable shared-use valuation, is the correct starting point for calculation of "soft" costs, that is the costs of items which are shared with others, such as shelter which is shared with the custodial parent. In deciding what expenses are incurred to earn income, judges should not necessarily use the tests employed by the *Income Tax Act* for the calculation of expenses. The approach to be followed in determining child support awards for two-income families is the following:

1. Calculate the combined gross income of the parents.
2. Calculate a reasonable cost for the upbringing of the child.
3. Apportion that cost between the parents.
4. Recalculate the adjusted assigned share for tax consequences, and make an award.
5. Make adjustments to the assigned share for the special circumstances of any parent.

In *Parsons v. Parsons* (1994), 9 R.F.L. (4th) 137 (Alta. Q.B.), the court was of the opinion that the Levesque "litmus test" may be used where there is a claim for spousal support in addition to the claim for child support, and that the award for child support should be made first. Once the child support award is made, the court will take that award into account in determining what, if any, spousal support will be awarded.

Similar principles expressed in other cases can be seen, also, as precursors to provisions in the guidelines.

Where the parties' incomes are roughly equivalent, each should bear one-half of the costs of child rearing and claim the benefit of one-half of the equivalent-to-married and child tax credit and deduction: *Almeida v. Almeida* (1995), 14 R.F.L. (4th) 88, 170 A.R. 244 (Q.B.)

In determing child support where it is clear that the total of family resourses will not allow either party or the children to maintain their pre-separation standard of living, the Court must seek proportionality and attempt to be fair to all family members: *Matheson v. Matheson* (1995), 15 R.F.L. (4th) 418 (P.E.I. S.C.).

The fact that the husband paid $400 monthly to support a child from a previous marriage had no bearing on the quantum of child support for the children of his second marriage. The child of the first marriage was an adult with a disability who had an income of

$9,000 annually and, in such circumstances, it was inappropriate to treat both children as the same: *Deane v. Deane* (1995), 14 R.F.L. (4th) 55 (Ont. Gen. Div.).

The May 1997 amendments completely change the approach to child support. Part of the change is the elimination of the "deduction/inclusion" rule for child support (but not spousal support) from the income tax system. See 15§110 Tax consequences of agreement or order, below.

Another major aspect of the change is the use of tables of average family spending for determining child support, instead of relying on evidence of individual need and financial ability. The averages in the tables give the basic amount (see 15§88 Child Support — table amount, below) to which may be added "special or extraordinary" expenses (see 15§89 Child support — special or extraordinary expenses, below) for the total support amount. In the vast majority of cases, this is the amount which must be paid unless "undue hardship" can be shown (see 15§97 Child support — undue hardship, below).

Special or extraordinary expenses, and undue hardship are considerations which do not lend themselves to a table or strict formula approach, and are dealt with by a combination of criteria, rules and judicial discretion.

Judicial discretion may be employed, also, to modify the table amounts in those less frequent cases where the child to be supported is of the age of majority or over (see 15§94 Child support — age of majority or over, below), the child is under a shared custody arrangement (see 15§96 Child support — shared custody, below), or where the payor's income exceeds $150,000 a year (see 15§93 Child support — payor income more than $150,000, below).

Under the guidelines the former spouses may still agree on the child support amounts to be paid and other terms for support. These amounts need not be in strict conformity with the guidelines, but as a minimum should be a close approximation. See 15§98 Child support — consent orders, below.

The table amount is based on the average percentage of income which families in the population spend on raising their children. Only the income of the payor is considered on the understanding that the contribution of the payee is in the direct care of the children, and if the payee earns an income the amount of that income spent on the children will be in the same proportion (statistically speaking) as the payor's support payment bears to his or her income; that is, in a two-income family, after the table amount is in place, both the custodial spouse and the non-custodial spouse are presumed to spend the same proportion of their incomes on the children.

The basic amount for child support is determined from the table by matching the income of the payor with the number of children for whom support is to be paid.

Special or extraordinary expenses are tested by "necessity" and "reasonableness" and are shared by the spouses in proportion to their incomes.

The *Divorce Act* provides the broad framework for this approach to the determination of child support, and leaves the detail to the regulatory process. This process has produced the *Federal Child Support Guidelines*.

The following is a summary of the 1997 amendments, together with the provincial and territorial position regarding child support guidelines as of June 1, 1999:

- In matters involving divorce, child support guidelines always apply, but they may be either the federal or the provincial guidelines. They will be the federal guidelines unless the province has established guidelines of its own, and has had them designated or specified under s. 2(5) of the *Divorce Act*. However, where the matter does not involve divorce, guidelines will only apply if the province has established them (whether or not they have been designated to apply in divorce matters). If the province has not enacted guidelines, then no guidelines apply at all on claims for child support in proceedings not involving a claim for divorce.

- Provinces may either establish guidelines of their own, or adopt the federal guidelines. If they establish guidelines of their own, they will apply to all child support matters within the provincial jurisdiction, but will only apply in divorce matters if designated or specified under s. 2(5) of the *Divorce Act* as "applicable guidelines". In order to be so designated or specified, the provincial guidelines must be "comprehensive" and "deal with the matters referred to in section 26.1" of the Act. As of June 1, 1999, the provinces which have requested the designation, and met this test, are Manitoba, New Brunswick, Prince Edward Island, and Quebec. If a province adopts the federal guidelines, they become the province's own guidelines for all child support matters within the provincial jurisdiction. Only Saskatchewan, as of June 1, 1999, has adopted the *Federal Guidelines*.
- Ontario, British Columbia, Newfoundland, Nova Scotia and the Northwest Territories have established their own guidelines without requesting they be specified as "applicable guidelines" for divorce matters. Therefore, in Ontario, for example, two sets of guidelines operate: one, the federal guidelines when child support is corollary relief in a divorce proceeding, and the other, the provincial guidelines, where provincial legislation is invoked. However, the content of the tables is the same in each set. When Nunavut came into being, April 1, 1999, it adopted all Northwest Territories' legislation and regulations, including the Northwest Territories *Child Support Guidelines*, until Nunavut could establish its own laws. Saskatchewan has adopted the federal guidelines as its own to make them apply to matters within its jurisdiction, as well as to matters under the *Divorce Act*.
- Alberta has given royal assent to changes in its child support legislation, but has not proclaimed those changes in force. Yukon has not amended its legislation. Where a province or territory has not established its own guidelines and had them designated or specified under s. 2(5) of the *Divorce Act*, in matters involving divorce, the *Federal Child Support Guidelines* will apply. The parties must be married spouses or former spouses: *Divorce Act*, s. 2(1) "spouse," *Federal Child Support Guidelines*, s. 2(1) "spouse."

The following is a summary of child support provisions in divorce proceedings:

- The minimum age for a child of the marriage in Canada is the age of majority in the province where the child ordinarily resides (18 in Ontario) and for a child who ordinarily resides outside Canada, 18 years: *Divorce Act*, s. 2(1) "age of majority."
- Instead of referring to undifferentiated support, the amendments distinguish, throughout the Act, between spousal support and child support: *Divorce Act*, ss. 2(1) "corollary relief proceeding" and "support order," 15.1(1), 15.2(1), 34(1.1) and 35.1(2).
- Child support is given priority over spousal support: *Divorce Act*, s. 15.3(1).
- Child support, interim and permanent, is to be awarded according to the applicable guidelines with one exception: *Divorce Act*, ss. 2(1) "applicable guidelines" and s. 15.1(3).

- The exception is where the child is already receiving a financial benefit and the application of the guidelines would result in an "inequitable" amount: *Divorce Act*, s. 15.1(5).
- The applicable guidelines are the provincial guidelines if both spouses are ordinarily resident in the same province and the province is a designated prov ince under section 2(5) of the *Divorce Act*. It is the *Federal Child Support Guidelines* in all other cases: *Divorce Act*, s. 2(1) "applicable guidelines" (a) and (b), s. 2(5), and s. 15.1(3).
- The guidelines include a table showing the basic amount payable depending upon the payor's income (payee's income not considered) and the number of children: *Federal Child Support Guidelines*, s. 3(1)(a).
- The table amounts are calculated on the basis that they are not subject to tax in the hands of the recipient.
- The amount of support for a child under the age of majority is to be a basic amount plus an amount, if any, for special or extraordinary expenses: *Federal Child Support Guidelines*, s. 3(1)(a) and (b).
- Income for guidelines purposes is the total taxable income adjusted by making the deductions and additions described in Schedule III.
- Where the payor's income is $150,000 or less a year, the basic amount for child support is the table amount regardless of the income of the payee: *Federal Child Support Guidelines*, s. 3(1)(a).
- Where the payor's income is over $150,000 a year, the basic amount for child support is the table amount plus a fixed percentage of the amount in excess of $150,000, or the table amount for the first $150,000 plus an amount determined in the discretion of the court after taking into consideration the needs of the child and the financial ability of both payor and payee spouses: *Federal Child Support Guidelines*, s. 3(4)(a) and (b).
- Where the spouse stands in the place of a parent (is not a biological or adoptive parent), the amount of child support is in the discretion of the court having regard to the *Guidelines* and any other parent's legal duty to support the child: *Federal Child Support Guidelines*, s. 5.
- A spouse may be ordered to acquire or continue medical or dental insurance coverage for a child where that coverage is available: *Federal Child Support Guidelines*, s. 6.
- Special or extraordinary expenses are limited to expenses in the following categories: (1) child care expenses, (2) medical and dental insurance premiums attributable to the child, (3) health- related expenses that exceed insurance reimbursement by at least $100 annually, (4) extraordinary expenses for primary and secondary school, (5) expenses for post-secondary education, and (6) extraordinary expenses for extracurricular activities: *Federal Child Support Guide lines*, s. 7(1).
- Special or extraordinary expenses are determined in the discretion of the court after considering the necessity and reasonableness of the expense "having regard to the means of the spouses and those of the child and the family's pattern of spending prior to the separation": *Federal Child Support Guidelines*, s. 7(1).

- Special or extraordinary expenses are to be "shared by the spouses in proportion to their respective incomes after deducting from the expenses, the contribution, if any, of the child": *Federal Child Support Guidelines*, s. 7(2).
- The amount of support for a child over the age of majority is to be the amount determined in accordance with the guidelines as if the child were under the age of majority, or an amount in the discretion of the court having regard to the needs and means of the child and the financial ability of each spouse: *Federal Child Support Guidelines*, s. 3(2)(a) and (b).
- Where custody is "split" between the spouses with each spouse having the custody of one or more children, the amount of support is to be the difference between the amount that each spouse would otherwise pay if a child support order were made against each of the spouses: *Federal Child Support Guidelines*, s. 8.
- Where both spouses care for a child in such a way that one spouse has a right of access to, or has physical custody of a child not less than forty percent of the time during the year, the amount of the child support order is determined by taking into account (1) the amounts set out in the applicable tables for each of the spouses, (2) the increased costs of shared custody arrangements, and (3) the needs and means of each spouse and of any child of the marriage for whom support is sought: *Federal Child Support Guidelines*, s. 9.
- Where undue hardship results from applying the guidelines amount, the court may order a different amount: *Federal Child Support Guidelines*, s. 10(1). Some of the circumstances which the court may consider in determining whether the guidelines amount should be adjusted for hardship are high family debts, unusually high costs of exercising access, and obligations to support other persons: *Federal Child Support Guidelines*, s. 10(2). The provision for adjusting the order because of undue hardship does not apply if, without adjustment, the household of the spouse pleading undue hardship would have a higher standard of living than the household of the other spouse: *Federal Child Support Guidelines*, s. 10(3) and (4).
- A method for comparing the standards of living which the court may use, is set out in a schedule to the guidelines: *Federal Child Support Guidelines*, s. 10(3) and (4), and Schedule II.
- In the ordinary case child support in agreements or orders made after April 1997 will not be deductible by the payor nor included in the income of the recipient for tax purposes: *Income Tax Act*, s. 60(b) and s. 56(1)(b).
- Where both spousal and child support are payable, and there is a shortfall in the payments, amounts paid are credited first to child support for tax purposes: *Income Tax Act*, s. 56(1)(b) and s. 60(b).
- Provincial Child Support Services may be authorized to assist the court in determining the amount of child support and, in light of new income information, recalculating the amount "at regular intervals." An order may be issued in the recalculated amount, subject to the right of the parties to apply within 30 days to vary the order as recalculated: *Divorce Act*, s. 25.1.
- Where spousal support is awarded in a reduced amount to allow for appropriate child support, the termination of child support would operate as a change in circumstances permitting an application to vary the spousal support: *Divorce Act*, s. 15.3(3).

- The court may make a support order on consent and in determining whether the order requested is reasonable the guidelines are advisory, and not presumptive, enabling the court to approve an amount that is different from the guidelines amount: *Divorce Act*, s. 15.1(7).
- An application to vary a global amount awarded for both a spouse and children will be treated as two separate applications for support; an application for spousal support, and a second application for child support: *Divorce Act*, ss. 34(1.1) and 35.1(2).
- A change of circumstances for the purpose of allowing the court to entertain an application to vary a child support order occurs (1) where the amount of child support in the order includes a determination made in accordance with the applicable table, and the change in circumstance would result in a different amount or provision; (2) where the amount does not include such a determination, any change in the condition, means, needs or other circumstances of either spouse or of any child entitled to support; and (3) in the case of an order made before May 1, 1997, the coming into force of the 1997 amendments to the *Divorce Act* (May 1, 1997): *Federal Child Support Guidelines*, s. 14(a) to (c).
- Unless, before May 1, 1997, the parties filed a joint election to have the new tax rule apply, or unless the order or agreement provided for the new tax rule to come into effect after May 1, 1997, payees receiving child-support under pre-guidelines orders or agreements must continue to include the support payments in their income for tax purposes until the order is varied or, in the case of an agreement, an order supersedes the agreement or the terms of the agreement are re- negotiated.
- The guidelines set out a procedure for determining the income of the party through adjustments to be made to income for income tax purposes: *Federal Child Support Guidelines*, ss. 15-20 and Schedule III.
- Once a child support order is made, the recipient spouse may obtain, on request, income documents and information from the other spouse every year: *Federal Child Support Guidelines*, s. 25(1).
- Where a spouse receives child support and his or her income is used to determine the amount of support, that spouse, on request, must produce to the other spouse income documents and information not more than once a year: *Federal Child Support Guidelines*, s. 25(3).
- Where the parties consent in an agreement or order to include prior payments on the conditions described in section 56.1(3) of the *Income Tax Act*, the payments are deemed to be made pursuant to the agreement or order, and the date of the agreement or order is deemed to be the date of the first prior payment.
- A spouse may apply to vary an order as often as there is a change in circumstances.
- In cases where the other spouse is out of the jurisdiction, any provisional order for child support must be made according to the federal guidelines, and any order confirming a provisional order must be according to the federal guidelines: *Divorce Act*, s. 19(7.1) and (9) to (11).
- Child support orders that are corollary to divorce may be assigned to a federal or provincial ministry or agency: *Divorce Act*, s. 20.1.

- The information bank of the Department of National Revenue may be searched for address information of a spouse indebted under a child support order: *Family Orders and Agreements Enforcement Assistance Act*, s. 2.
- Federally granted passports, specified licences, privileges and certificates of a debtor spouse in persistent arrears of support may be suspended, refused on an application for renewal, or refused on an original application: *Family Orders and Agreements Enforcement Assistance Act*, s. 67.
- Garnishment attachment proceedings to collect support have been streamlined and made more effective: *Garnishment, Attachment and Pension Diversion Act*, ss. 2, 6, 8 to 11, 18, 20 to 23, 32, 35 to 36, 38 to 40, 46.
- A receiving spouse may apply to a court for an order preventing a debtor from deferring his or her public service pension where there is an extended pattern of non-payment of family support obligations, and reasonable steps have been taken to enforce the obligation by other means: *Garnishment, Attachment and Pension Diversion Act*, s. 35.1.
- The applicant for diversion of public service pension benefits no longer needs to reside in Canada: *Garnishment, Attachment and Pension Diversion Act*, s. 36. * When a financial support order is in arrears and where no provincial law applies, the amount to be diverted may exceed 50% of the debtor's net pension benefit: *Garnishment, Attachment and Pension Diversion Act*, s. 40.1.

Section 7(1) of the *Federal Child Support Guidelines* requires the consideration of the "means" of the parties and not just income. A consideration of a parent's family income can be appropriate in assessing that parent's "means": *Baum v. Baum* (2000), 13 R.F.L. (5th) 258, 2000 BCSC1835, 2000 CarswellBC 2604 (B.C. S.C.)

Where the trial judge had quantified child support using the *Federal Child Support Guidelines* prior to the proclamation, the payor father was successful in appealing the order. The issue of child support should properly have been determined using the Levesque formula. *Reid v. Reid* (1997), 33 R.F.L.(4th) 308 (Alta. C.A.)

A *Guidelines* approach may not be appropriate for determining the quantum of child support for a child attending university. A better approach is to apportion the cost of support between the parents, after deducting from their respective income a reasonable component for self-sufficiency: *Kapogiannes v. Kapogiannes* (2000), 10 R.F.L. (5th) 63, 2000 CarswellOnt 2374 (Ont. S.C.J.)

The fact that child support was payable pursuant to the terms of a separation agreement does not constitute the making of "special provisions" allowing for deviation from *Guidelines* amounts: *Duffield v. Duffield* (1998), 36 R.F.L. (4th) 374 (B.C. S.C.).

An unequal division of matrimonial property in the custodial wife's favour does not in and of itself constitute a special provision directly or indirectly benefitting a child, making the application of the *Guidelines* inequitable: *Grexton v. Grexton* (1999), 4 R.F.L. (5th) 72, 182 D.L.R. (4th) 728 (B.C. S.C. [In Chambers]).

Where rather than make a child support order under the *Guidelines* the trial judge required the parties to submit quarterly declarations of their incomes as a basis for ongoing support calculations, an order for support under the *Guidelines* was substituted on appeal. It was doubtful whether the trial judge had jurisdiction to make such an order and, even if he did, the order was unworkable: *Rust v. Rust* (2003), 42 R.F.L. (5th) 161, 2003 CarswellSask 410, 2003 SKCA 55, 232 Sask. R. 242, 294 W.A.C. 242 (Sask. C.A.)

Where the father, from time to time, deducted amounts paid by him on behalf of the children from the child support paid by him, he was ordered not to do so in the future without the written consent of the wife. Each parent should always expect to participate in additional expenses that arise from time to time when the children are with them without expectation of credit or contribution from the other parent: *Hewat v. Hewat* (2003), 43 R.F.L. (5th) 370, 2003 CarswellOnt 2280 (Ont. S.C.J.).

15§88 — Child support — table amount

The heart of the federal or provincial guidelines is the provision of standardized tables to use in the calculation of the basic amount for child support. By matching the number of children with the payor's income, the tables themselves determine the amount of support where the payee's income is $150,000 a year or less.

Where the income is more than this, another method is used to decide the incremental support. Basic support is found by starting with the table amount for $150,000, and then adding a further amount determined either by multiplying the excess over $150,000 times the percentage given by the table, *or* having the court assess the additional amount having regard to the needs of the child or children and the means of the parents: *Federal Child Support Guidelines*, s. 3(4)(a) and (b).

The amounts in the tables are set according to the payor's income without reference to the income of the custodial parent. They "are fixed by a formula that calculates the appropriate amount of support in light of economic data of average expenditures on children across different income levels. The formula reserves a basic amount of income for the payor's self-support, and adjusts for the impact of federal and provincial income taxes. There are separate tables for each province to take differences in provincial income tax rates into account": *The New Child Support Package*, March 6, 1996, p. 12, and *Federal Child Support Guidelines*, Sch. I, Notes 1 and 4. Accordingly, new tables will be published in the *Canada Gazette* as and when the income tax rates, federal or provincial, are changed.

The formula was developed from economic studies of average spending on children in families at different income levels in Canada: *Federal Child Support Guidelines*, Sch. I, Note 5. "The formula . . . sets support amounts to reflect average expenditures on children by a spouse with a particular number of children and level of income. The calculation is based on the support payor's income. The formula uses the basic personal amount for non-refundable tax credits to recognize personal expenses, and takes other federal and provincial income taxes and credits into account. Federal Child Tax benefits and Goods and Services Tax credits for children are excluded from the calculation. At lower income levels, the formula sets the amount to take into account the combined impact of taxes and child support payments on the support payor's limited disposable income": *Federal Child Support Guidelines*, Sch. I, Note 6.

A threshold level of income below which no amount of child support is payable is shown at the beginning of each provincial table: *Federal Child Support Guidelines*, Sch. I, Note 2.

The tables are annexed as schedules to the guidelines. The *Federal Child Support Guidelines* provide that the applicable table depends on the pace of residence of the payor spouse. If the payor spouse resides in Canada, the applicable table is the table for the province in which that spouse ordinarily resides at the time the application is made, or, if a move is contemplated "in the near future," the province where that spouse is planning to reside. Where the payor spouse resides outside Canada, or the place of residence is unknown, the applicable table is the table of the province where the payee spouse resides: *Federal Child Support Guidelines*, s. 3(3)(a) and (b) as amended.

Where the mother had custody of the parties' two children, but one child lived with the father approximately 40% of the time, the father's child support obligation was assessed at an amount which fell between the table support amounts of one child and two children in the *Federal Child Support Guidelines*: *Brodland v. Brodland* (1997), 34 R.F.L. (4th) 79, 160 Sask. R. 311 (Q.B.).

In *Holtby v. Holtby* (1997), 30 R.F.L. (4th) 70 (Ont. Prov. Ct.), the court dealt with a situation where the payee was below a threshold. Each of the parties had two of their children in his or her care. The payment of monthly support for the children in the mother's custody was increased slightly above the table amount to $400 because the mother was living at a subsistence level.

15§88A — Section 3 — Presumptive Rule

Presumptive Rule: S. 3(1)

Components of Support

The amount of support to be paid for a child under the age of majority is made up of two components: a basic (table) amount, and an amount, if any, for special or extraordinary expenses. See discussion under 15§89 Child Support — special or extraordinary expenses, and 15§93 Child Support — payor income more than $150,000.

The amount of support where the child is at, or over, the age of majority may be determined in the same way; that is by applying the *Guidelines* as if the child were under the age of majority, or, if that approach is inappropriate, by assessing an amount "having regard to the condition, means, needs and other circumstances of the child and the financial ability of each spouse to contribute to the support of the child": *Federal Child Support Guidelines*, s. 3(2)(a) and (b). See *Support Where Child is Age of Majority or Over*, below.

In *Martin v. Martin* (2004), 12 R.F.L. (6th) 415, 2004 CarswellOnt 5438 (Ont. S.C.J.); additional reasons at (2005), 2005 CarswellOnt 1437 (Ont. S.C.J.); affirmed (2006), 2006 CarswellOnt 4876 (Ont. C.A.), the court refused to apply *Guideline* amounts in determining support for the parties' 21-year-old daughter. The father was already paying $1,000 monthly in child support under the terms of an interim separation agreement as well as contributing significantly towards her living expenses while she was away at school. In the circumstance, there was no good reason to simply apply the presumption under s. 3 of the *Guidelines* that the amount of support should be the Table Amount.

Table Amount

The heart of the Federal and *provincial Guidelines* is a set of standardized tables for the calculation of the basic amount for child support. By matching the number of children with the payor's income, the tables show the amount of support to be paid where the payee's income is $150,000 a year or less.

Where the income is more than this, another method is used to decide the additional support applicable to that part of the income over $150,000. The total amount of basic support payable is the amount for the first $150,000 as derived from the applicable table together with a further amount determined either by multiplying the excess over $150,000 by the percentage given by the table, or instead of applying a percentage, assessing the further amount having regard to the needs of the child or children and the means of the parents: *Federal Child Support Guidelines*, s. 4(a) and (b).

The amounts in the tables are set according to the payor's income without reference to the income of the custodial parent. They "are fixed by a formula that calculates the appropriate amount of support in light of economic data on average expenditures on children across different income levels. The formula reserves a basic amount of income for the payor's self-support, and adjusts for the impact of federal and provincial income taxes. There are separate tables for each province to take differences in provincial income tax rates into account": *The New Child Support Package*, March 6, 1996, at 12, and *Federal Child Support Guidelines*, Sch. I, Notes 1 and 4. Accordingly, new tables will be published in the *Canada Gazette* as and when the income tax rates, federal or provincial, are changed.

The formula was developed from economic studies of average spending on children in families at different income levels in Canada: *Federal Child Support Guidelines*, Sch. I, Note 5. "The formula . . . sets support amounts to reflect average expenditures on children by a spouse with a particular number of children and level of income. The calculation is based on the support payor's income. The formula uses the basic personal amount for non-refundable tax credits to recognize personal expenses, and takes other federal and provincial income taxes and credits into account. Federal Child Tax benefits and Goods and Services Tax credits for children are excluded from the calculation. At lower income levels, the formula sets the amount to take into account the combined impact of taxes and child support payments on the support payor's limited disposable income": *Federal Child Support Guidelines*, Sch. I, Note 6.

The tables are annexed as schedules to the *Guidelines*. The *Federal Child Support Guidelines* provide that the applicable table depends on the place of residence of the payor spouse. If the payor spouse resides in Canada, the applicable table is the table for the province in which that spouse ordinarily resides at the time the application is made, or, if a move is contemplated "in the near future", the province where that spouse is planning to reside. Where the payor spouse resides outside Canada, or the place of residence is unknown, the applicable table is the table of the province where the payee spouse resides: *Federal Child Support Guidelines*, s. 3(3)(a) and (b) as amended.

Income Below the Threshold Amount

A threshold level of income below which no amount of child support is payable is shown at the beginning of each provincial table: *Federal Child Support Guidelines*, Sch. I, Note 2. For example, in *Turner v. Turner* (1998), 1998 CarswellBC 2434, 43 R.F.L. (4th) 437 (C.A.), the court observed that s. 15.1(1) and (3) of the *Divorce Act* create the obligation for a parent to pay child support according to the *Guidelines*. The tables for British Columbia indicate that no obligation to pay child support is to be imposed on a parent earning less than $6,730 a year. Therefore, the trial judge's reapportionment of property was granted on a non-existent obligation to the extent that it was based on the wife's supposed obligation to pay child support in circumstances where she was earning no income and, because of her condition, was in no position to earn an income.

Support Where Sole Custody and the Income of the Non-Custodial Spouse is $150,000 or Less

The *Guidelines* tables reach a cut-off point at incomes of $150,000. For incomes greater than this, a combination of approaches is used. See 15§93 Child support — payor income more than $150,000.

However, the upper level in the table is sufficiently high so that the vast majority of cases fall below it, and it is for this majority that the *Guidelines* were especially designed.

In this section assume the payor is the biological or adoptive parent (as distinct from a parent standing in the place of a parent — see above), income is $150,000 or less, the payee has sole custody of the child or children (for other arrangements, see 15§ 95 Child support — split custody, and 15§ 96 Child support — shared custody) and the child or children are 18 years of age or under. (For children over the age of 18, see *Support Where Child is Age of Majority or Over*, below.)

Child Support on Consent

The *Guidelines* provide an exception for some consent arrangements that differ from the Table Amounts. The consent arrangements will be incorporated in an order if the court is satisfied that the arrangements are reasonable. When the court is considering the reasonableness of the arrangements, it will consider what amount of support the tables would produce but is not bound to adopt this amount. The *Guidelines* in this instance are advisory only, and not presumptive: *Divorce Act*, s. 15.1(8).

The court may, for example, find that since the arrangements include the custodial parent having exclusive possession of the matrimonial home, the support should be less than the Table Amount.

Support Where Child is Age of Majority or Over: S. 3(2)

The court has jurisdiction to make an order "for the support of any or all children of the marriage": *Divorce Act*, s. 15.1(1). The definition of "children of the marriage" extends this jurisdiction to the making of support orders for children who have attained the age of majority, or who are over that age: *Divorce Act*, s. 2(1) "child of the marriage" cl. (b).

In deciding whether a child is under or over the age of majority, under the *Divorce Act* the age of majority is determined by the "laws of the province where the child ordinarily resides" (see: s. 2(1) of the *Divorce Act*).

Department of Justice Recommendation for changes to S. 3(2) of the Federal Child Support Guidelines:

In *Children Come First: A Report to Parliament Reviewing the Provisions and Operation of the Federal Child Support Guidelines* (Ottawa, 2002), Vol. 2 at 33, it was recommended that the *Guidelines* should be amended to require recipients of support for a child the age of majority or older to disclose information relevant to the child's ongoing eligibility for support. The commentary for this recommendation states:

> Many people have argued that older children getting support should be accountable and provide financial and other information to demonstrate that they are still entitled to support. Others say this is an unnecessary breach of the older child's privacy that, effectively, involved the child in the parents' litigation.

The recommendation proposes to address these concerns by requiring the recipient parent, not the child, to provide the information on the written request of the paying parent, thus insulating the child from direct involvement in the litigation.

Table Amount

Where the payor spouse earns $150,000 a year or less, the *Guidelines* are "presumptive" as distinct from "advisory"; that is, the court must apply the table and the provision for special or extraordinary expenses (if either party has requested them), as opposed to the case, for example, where it is considering the reasonableness of a consent arrangement. Where there is a consent arrangement, the *Guidelines* are advisory in that the court shall have regard to the applicable guidelines. However, the court shall not consider the arrangements to be unreasonable solely because the amount of support agreed to is not the same as the amount that would otherwise have been determined in accordance with the applicable guidelines: *Divorce Act*, ss. 15.1(7) and (8), and 17(6.4) and (6.5).

Unless a case of hardship can be made out or a contribution to special expenses is claimed where the annual income of the payor spouse is $150,000 a year or less, the court is not concerned with the income of the payee spouse in determining the amount of support. The payee spouse, that is the custodial parent, can be earning no income at all, or $100,000 a year, and the Table Amount would be the same in each case. The amount is determined without reference to the payee's income.

The Table Amounts have been calculated on the understanding that the deduction/inclusion rule for income tax has been eliminated for child support, and that the payments are not included in the income of the payee.

Assume there are two children of the marriage and that they are in the father's sole custody. He is a real estate agent with an average income of $80,000 each year. The mother is a physician with an annual income of $135,500. Both spouses are ordinarily resident in Ontario. The amount of child support she should pay is found by finding the Federal Child Support Tables for Ontario and locating the sheet for two children. Ignore the custodial spouse's income of $80,000, and look for the place on the two-children table where the payor spouse's income of $135,500 a year fits in. This is between $135,000 and $136,000. The lower level at $135,000 gives the basic amount. Reading from the table, this is $1,604. In addition to this basic amount, add a percentage for the income which exceeds the lower level of $135,000. The percentage is read from the Plus (per cent) column and is 1.04 per cent for amounts between $135,000 and $136,000. This percentage is applied against the amount by which the payor's income of $135,500 exceeds the lower level, that is, $135,500 - $135,000 or $500. The percentage of 1.04 per cent times $500 is $1.04/100 \times 500$ or $5.20. Adding this amount to the basic amount, $5.20 + $1,604, the total of $1,609.20 is the amount to be paid each month to the custodial spouse for the support of the two children. Note again that the calculation of the support is without reference to the custodial spouse's income of $80,000.

In another example, the determination of the support award may be more difficult. Where there are two children under the age of majority and one child over the age of majority, the support award would be the Table Amount for two children plus a separate award for the third child.

Special or Extraordinary Expenses

In the first example, immediately above, assume the older child is enrolled in post-secondary education where the tuition is $3,000 a year. The total family income is $80,000 plus $135,500 for a total of $215,500. The father's share of the tuition would be $80,000 divided by $215,500 times 100 for 37.1 per cent. The tuition of $3,000 times 37 per cent is $1,110. The mother's share is $3,000 less the father's share of $1,110 or $1,890. The same result is obtained when we find the mother's percentage ($135,500/ $215,500 × 100 or 62.87 per cent round to 63 per cent) and multiply the $3,000 tuition by this percentage ($3,000 × 63 per cent is $1,890).

Where Guidelines *"provide otherwise"*

The Table Amount plus the amount for special or extraordinary expenses give the total of the child support payable for children under the age of majority (18 in Ontario) "unless otherwise provided under these *Guidelines*": *Federal Child Support Guidelines*, s. 3(1)(a) and (b). Where the child is the age of majority or over, "unless otherwise provided" the amount of child support is determined by applying the *Guidelines* as if the child were under the age of majority; or, if this approach is considered inappropriate, by resort to the court's discretion "having regard to the condition, means, needs and other circumstances of the child and the financial ability of each spouse to contribute to the support of the child": *Federal Child Support Guidelines*, s. 3(2)(a) and (b).

The *Guidelines* provide otherwise on applications for original orders and on applications to vary existing orders (whether for children under, at, or over the age of majority) in cases where:

(a) The payor is not a biological or adoptive parent of the child or children to be supported, but stands in place of a parent. (See *Guidelines*, s. 5, SPOUSE IN PLACE OF A PARENT.)

(b) The payor's income is over $150,000 a year. (See *Guidelines*, s. 4, SUPPORT WHERE PAYOR INCOME IS MORE THAN $150,000, below.)

(c) The making of a child support order in the basic amount would cause undue hardship. (See *Guidelines*, s. 10, UNDUE HARDSHIP, below.)

(d) Custody of the children is split between the spouses. (See *Guidelines*, s. 8, SPLIT CUSTODY, below.)

(e) Custody of the children is shared by the spouses. (See *Guidelines*, s. 9, SHARED CUSTODY, below.)

(f) Child support orders are made on consent. (See *Child Support on Consent*, above.)

(g) An application is made for child support and an existing order or agreement provides for direct or indirect benefits for the child: *Divorce Act*, s. 15.1 (5).

With respect to (f), the court has a general discretion to award an amount that is different from the amount which would be determined under the *Guidelines*, if the court is satisfied

(1) first,

(a) that special provisions in an order, a judgment or a written agreement respecting the spouses' financial obligations, or the division of their property, directly or indirectly benefit a child, or

(b) that special provisions have otherwise been made for the benefit of a child; and

(2) secondly, that the application of the applicable guidelines would result in an amount of child support that is inequitable given those special provisions: *Divorce Act*, s. 15.1(5).

An example of the first type of special provision would be a provision in an agreement whereby a payee spouse was given a lower than average child support amount but had the right to exclusive possession of the matrimonial home until the youngest child was 18 years of age. An example of the second type of special provision which has "otherwise been made for the benefit of a child" would be where a child is a beneficiary of a family trust. The special provisions test is two-pronged. An educational trust providing for a private school and post-secondary education would qualify as a special provision. However, it would not always meet the second part of the test (inequitable result), because the education costs do not affect the day-to-day costs of raising a child, with the exception of a child who is in residence at the school. Consequently, it would still be equitable to apply the *Guidelines* amount.

Case Law

Presumptive Rule

The court held that an increase in child care expenses constituted a sufficient change in circumstances to warrant a variation of child support and that there was no discretion to depart from the Table Amount under s. 3, where the father had not claimed undue hardship in *Montalbetti v. Montalbetti*, [2000] B.C.J. No. 1834, 235 W.A.C. 140, 143 B.C.A.C. 140, 10 R.F.L. (5th) 377, 2000 CarswellBC 1902, 2000 BCCA 504 (B.C. C.A.).

There must be "clear and compelling evidence" for departing from the *Guidelines* figures, (*i.e.* the Table Amounts): *Francis v. Baker* (1997), 50 R.F.L. (4th) 228, 1999 CarswellOnt 2734, 1999 CarswellOnt 2948 (S.C.C.).

Where one of the parents has shown that his circumstances fall within one of the exceptions in the *Guidelines*, in this case, s. 9 (shared parenting), the presumption of the Table Amount, in this case, in s. 3, no longer applies: *Contino v. Leonelli-Contino* (2003), 42 R.F.L. (5th) 295, 2003 CarswellOnt 4099 (C.A.); leave to appeal to S.C.C. granted (2004), 2004 CarswellOnt 1319, 2004 CarswellOnt 1320 (S.C.C.).

In *Pelletier v. Pelletier* (2003), 2003 CarswellOnt 422 (S.C.J.), the court held that there should not be an automatic deviation from the *Guidelines* amount, (presumably under s. 3), just because there is an issue of shared custody. Both parties had physical custody of the child for no less than 40 per cent of the time over the course of the year. The court was satisfied that it had been established on clear and compelling evidence that it was in the child's best interests to deviate from the *Guidelines* amounts. Considering the Respondent father's income of $49,956 and the Applicant's income of $16,800, the Respondent was ordered to pay the Applicant support of $296.59 per month.

A basic child support payment is designed to address the basic needs of housing, clothing, food, basic transportation, etc., for children. When a child goes to university, most of these expenses continue, although since some duplication between basic and extra expenses would occur, it is appropriate to reduce the payor's contribution by a small amount for the period of the school year: *Bruce v. Kelly* (2002), 2002 CarswellPEI 43, 30 R.F.L. (5th) 42 (T.D.). Section 7 of the *Guidelines* provides for sharing "expenses for post-secondary education". It does not describe those expenses as "extraordinary" as it does, for example, with respect to expenses for extra-curricular activities.

Section 3 of the *Guidelines* provides that the amount of child support payable is the amount set out in the applicable table and the amount, if any, determined under s. 7, thereby giving the court discretion to make provision for medical and dental expenses. As the father in this case agreed in a consent judgment under provincial legislation to pay the medical and dental expenses, he cannot be relieved of this obligation by requiring the mother to pay these expenses out of support payments in an interim order for support under the *Divorce Act*: *Lewkoski v. Lewkoski* (1998), 40 R.F.L. (4th) 86, 1998 CarswellOnt 1775 (Gen. Div.). The court found that the expenses were reasonable and necessary and the father's refusal to pay any of these expenses was unreasonable. The interim child order under the *Divorce Act* superceded the child support provisions of the Ontario *Family Law Act*.

Support for Children the Age of Majority or Over: S. 3(2)

Approach to Determining Support

The court may approach the support for children over the age of majority in four steps:

(1) Determine whether the child is a "child of the marriage" as defined in the *Divorce Act*. If not, that ends the matter.

(2) Determine whether applying the *Guidelines* as if the child were under the age of majority ("the usual *Guidelines* approach") is challenged. If that approach is not challenged, determine the amount payable based on the usual *Guidelines* approach.

(3) If the usual *Guidelines* approach is challenged, decide whether the challenger has proven that the usual *Guidelines* approach is inappropriate. If not, the usual *Guidelines* amount applies.

(4) If the usual *Guidelines* approach is inappropriate, decide what amount is appropriate, having regard to the condition, means, needs and other circumstances of the child and the financial ability of each spouse to contribute to the support of the child: *Wesemann v. Wesemann* (1999), 1999 CarswellBC 1347, 49 R.F.L. (4th) 435, [1999] B.C.J. No. 1387 (S.C.).

Whether the usual *Guidelines* approach is inappropriate (step 3) requires a judicial determination of inappropriateness. The court may move away from the *Guidelines* amount if either the usual amount in s. 3(2)(a) or the approach of s. 3(2)(a) is inappropriate. The usual *Guidelines* approach is based on factors that normally apply to a child under the age of majority; that is the child resides with one or both parents, is not earning an income and is dependent on his or her parents. It is also based on the understanding that, though only the income of the person paying is used to calculate the amount payable, the other parent makes a significant contribution to the costs of that child's care because the child is residing with him or her. The closer the circumstances of the child are to those upon which the usual *Guidelines* approach is based, the less likely it is that the usual *Guidelines* calculation will be inappropriate. The opposite is also true. Children over the age of majority may reside away from home and earn a significant income. If a child is not residing at home, the nature of the contribution towards the child's expenses may be quite different. After finding that the usual *Guidelines* approach is inappropriate, the next step is to determine what approach or amount is appropriate. At this stage, it is helpful to consider:

(1) the reasonable needs of the child;

(2) the ability and opportunity of the child to contribute to those needs; and

(3) the ability of the parents to contribute to those needs.

Where the child is a child of the marriage by reason of attendance at a post-secondary educational institution, his or her reasonable needs have two aspects to it. First, there are the child's needs for accommodation, food, clothing, and other miscellaneous expenses. Second, there are the child's actual post-secondary educational expenses. Post-secondary education is a privilege, not a right. Children have an obligation to make a reasonable contribution to their education. However, just because a child is earning income, it does not follow that all of that income must be applied to the child's education. The desirability of allowing the child to experience some personal benefit from the fruits of his or her labours should also be considered.

It may not be appropriate to require a child to work part-time during the school year in addition to summer employment as that might interfere with the child's studies. Nor should the availability of student loans automatically require the child to obtain a loan. A student loan delays payment of certain expenses, rather than defraying them. The ability to contribute to the needs of the child involves a consideration of the ability to pay of both parents. The court may choose to apportion the amount payable on a proportionate basis as contemplated by s. 7 of the *Guidelines*: *Wesemann v. Wesemann*, above.

Whether child is a "child of the marriage" — See Guidelines, s. 2 *DEFINITION OF CHILD*

"The trial judge's discretion under s. 3(2) should focus . . . not on the payor's income but on the amount of support and its appropriateness having regard to the needs and condition of the children and the financial ability of the spouses to contribute to the children's support": *Arnold v. Washburn* (2001), 2001 CarswellOnt 4439, 20 R.F.L. (5th) 236, 152 O.A.C. 364, 57 O.R. (3d) 287 (C.A.); leave to appeal refused (2002), 2002 CarswellOnt 4386, 2002 CarswellOnt 4387, [2002] S.C.C.A. No. 82.

Usually, where a child attends university away from home the courts resort, not to the *Guidelines* Table Amounts, but to the means and needs consideration set out in s. 3(2)(b) of the *Guidelines*: *Krueger v. Tunison* (1999), 183 Sask. R. 255, 1999 CarswellSask 482, [1999] S.J. No. 482 (Q.B.).

Where the party having the primary residence for the parties' adult children must maintain her home so that the children can return there when not attending college or university, and when they finish their education, child support payments are properly paid directly from the payor parent to the recipient parent and not to the children or a third party: *Monaghan v. Monaghan* (2002), 2002 CarswellOnt 3629 (S.C.J.).

When a child is over the age of majority, the child's situation and not the relative means of the parents is the proper factor for consideration in applying the *Guidelines*: *Oswald v. Oswald*, 17 R.F.L. (5th) 127, 2001 CarswellMan 64, 2001 MBQB 47, [2001] M.J. No. 73 (Q.B.).

In *Higgins v. Higgins* (2001), 19 R.F.L. (5th) 300, 2001 CarswellOnt 2729 (S.C.J.), the mother was ordered to pay the child support for the parties' child who was attending university while continuing to live with the father. As the child had a monthly income of

$800, many of the expenses generally covered by child support were already being met. Accordingly, the conventional application of the *Guidelines* was not appropriate. Instead it made more sense to require the husband and wife to share in the child's proven expenses in proportion to their respective incomes, after taking into account the child's income.

Where a child is 17 years of age, the court has no jurisdiction to make a "step-down" order to a lower amount when the child reaches 18, the age of majority. Such a two-stage order would be different from the order mandated by s. 3(1), and for that reason the court has no authority to make it. Also, the amount may not be lower. The *Guidelines* do not provide that the amount of child support *should* be different because a child is 18 years old. On the contrary, the presumptive order is the Table Amount. It is only where the payor, who has the onus of proof, convinces the court that the Table Amount is inappropriate, that a different amount may be ordered: *Merritt v. Merritt* (1999), 1999 CarswellOnt 1471, [1999] O.J. No. 1732, 98 O.T.C. 321 (S.C.J.).

In *Glen v. Glen* (1997), 1997 CarswellBC 2644, [1997] B.C.J. No. 2806, 34 R.F.L. (4th) 13 (S.C.), the mother claimed support for her 19-year-old daughter who was attending university and living at home with her. The *Federal Child Support Guidelines* require the parents to pay the same level of support to adult children as to minor children unless the parent can show this approach is inappropriate. The fact that the daughter worked part-time did not diminish the father's obligation to pay the basic level of support. The father was not required to make any contribution to the daughter's university tuition because her income exceeded the tuition amount. The father was ordered to pay $542 per month in child support.

The court must determine how much the adult child needs to maintain a reasonable lifestyle, and how much the child can reasonably contribute from his or her own resources. The shortfall can then be compared to the *Guidelines* amount to determine if the *Guidelines* are inappropriate. If inappropriate, the court can apportion the shortfall between the parties according to their respective incomes. Where the adult children are residing with the custodial parent, and attending post-secondary educational institutions, the basic amount under the *Guidelines* may be awarded plus a proportional share of the educational expenses, after taking into account a reasonable contribution from the child: *Sherlow v. Zubko* (1999), 1999 CarswellAlta 472, [1999] A.J. No. 644, 1999 ABQB 435, 50 R.F.L. (4th) 160, [2000] 1 W.W.R. 699, 247 A.R. 66, 76 Alta. L.R. (3d) 202 (Q.B.).

The most common approach is to seek basic child support for those over the age of majority pursuant to s. 3(2)(a), as well as a contribution towards post-secondary educational expenses pursuant to s. 7(1)(e). See *Kavanagh v. Kavanagh* (1999), 1999 CarswellNfld 358, 185 Nfld. & P.E.I.R. 247, 562 A.P.R. 247, 3 R.F.L. (5th) 96 (U.F.C.); and *Bowering v. Bowering* (1998), 1998 CarswellNfld 314, 171 Nfld. & P.E.I.R. 50, 525 A.P.R. 50 (U.F.C.).

Duration of Support for Adult Children

In *McGowan v. McGowan* (2002), 2002 CarswellOnt 1951 (S.C.J.), the court held that child support for an adult child taking post-secondary education where the parents' means are limited should be restricted to the Table Amount. In this case, the child was able to earn a significant sum, ($8,000), during the summer and the school year which could be applied towards his college expenses. The remainder should be borne by his parents, in proportion to their respective incomes.

An adult child is neither automatically entitled to support for one 4-year degree, nor to child support for as long as he or she decides to remain in post-secondary education: *Monaghan v. Monaghan* (2002), 2002 CarswellOnt 3629 (S.C.J.). The circumstances of the parties and the child must be considered at the time that support is sought.

Child support for an adult child attending university should continue for 4 months after graduation as this is a reasonable time for the child to become independent: *Erickson v. Erickson* (1999), 175 N.S.R. (2d) 185, 534 A.P.R. 185, 47 R.F.L. (4th) 326, 1999 CarswellNS 137 (S.C.).

The entitlement to support of a child pursuing an education is not limited to a particular level of education or to a pre-set age limit. The child is not required to live with the custodial parent and the line to be drawn is flexible: *Newman v. Thompson*, 30 R.F.L. (4th) 143, 149 D.L.R. (4th) 605, [1997] 9 W.W.R. 519, 118 Man. R. (2d) 177, 149 W.A.C. 177, 1997 CarswellMan 385, [1997] M.J. No. 447 (C.A.).

Allocation of Funds Between Children Over and Under the Age of Majority

In *Waese v. Bojman* (2001), 2001 CarswellOnt 1813, 19 R.F.L. (5th) 220 (S.C.J.), the court was of the opinion that where there is one child over the age of majority living away from home at university and one under the age of majority living at home, the custodial parent does not have the benefit of economies of scale while the one child is away from home. The payor spouse should pay the Table Amount for one child during the months the older child is at university, and the Table Amount for two children when both are at home.

In *Seburn v. Seburn* (2001), 2001 CarswellOnt 1339 (S.C.J.), two of the parties' four children were away at university for two-thirds of the year. The court deducted a notional amount per month that they were away for groceries not spent by the mother. The court ordered that the Table Amount for the four children minus the deduction for groceries for 8 months should be paid to the mother directly.

Where one child is over the age of majority and pursuing post-secondary education and another is under the age of majority, s. 3 provides the possibility of two separate orders that can be made in isolation from each other, with a possible inequitable result to the payor: *Foster v. Foster* (2000), 13 R.F.L. (5th) 61, 2000 CarswellOnt 4082 (S.C.J.). The proper approach is to apportion the support amount due to two children under legislation or to reduce the father's income by the amount of the first payment when calculating the second payment. The result should be the same notwithstanding which approach is used. Child support was varied from $487 for each of two children to $300 for the older child and $398 for the younger child.

For a child over the age of majority, the presumptive rule for the amount of the child support is the same as the amount would be if the child were under the age of majority. But if the court considered that approach to be inappropriate, the amount is to be the amount the court considered appropriate having regard to the condition, means, needs and other circumstances of the child and the financial ability of each spouse to contribute to the support of the child. The parties, in the circumstances of this case, were of limited means. The Table Amount was $2,100 a month for four children. An agreed amount of $300 was deducted for an insurance contribution leaving a balance of $1,800 a month owing for support. The father was ordered to pay child support to the mother for each of the four children of the marriage in the aggregate amount of $1,800 per month. Upon a child enrolling in university, the father was to pay, instead, the portion of child support applicable to that child, that is, $450 per month (one-fourth of $1,800) for the 8-month period from September to May, directly to that child or to the university in which the child is enrolled: *Kaderly v. Kaderly* (1997), 1997 CarswellPEI 85, [1997] P.E.I.J. No. 74 (T.D.).

There is no guidance as to how the tables are to be used where one child is under the age of majority, and another child is over that age. One approach is to take the Table Amount for two children, and then deduct the Table Amount for the one child who is under age. The difference represents the Table Amount for the other child who is over the age of majority. Where the Table Amount for two children is $2,954 per month and the Table Amount for one child is $1,876 per month, the difference of $1,078 per month would represent the Table Amount of child support for the child over the age of majority. That approach is reasonable where both children reside at home with the custodial parent. However, where a child attends university away from home, the courts normally resort not to the Table Amounts, but to the means and needs considerations set out in s. 3(2)(b) of the *Guidelines*. This is because there is an implicit assumption in the tables that the children are residing in the same household as the recipient parent. The assumption is implied from the fact that the tables reflect economies of scale. The amount payable for two children is less than twice the amount payable for one, because feeding and sheltering two children in the same household does not cost twice as much as feeding and sheltering one. Where, however, a child is residing in another residence for the bulk of the year, it is inappropriate to apply tables that are not designed with that living arrangement in mind. Furthermore, the table approach assumes that the recipient parent discharges her obligation by being physically in the same household and providing the home and other amenities for the child. Where a child is at college, this assumption does not hold true. It is, therefore, more appropriate to calculate the actual costs of providing for the needs of the child in his other residence, factoring in a contribution toward the cost of maintaining the home to return to on weekends and school breaks where appropriate, and apportion that between the spouses after considering the child's own ability to contribute. In the circumstances of this case, after deducting the amount available from a trust, an amount of $1,375 per month was required to meet the needs of the university student. To determine the contribution of the payor husband, both the incomes of the husband and wife should be considered. The wife's income, including $4,000 a month for her support, was $73,000 per year. The husband's income, net of spousal support, amounted to $216,701. The court allowed each of them a self-sufficiency allowance of $20,000 per year, leaving net figures of $53,000 and $196,701 respectively. On this analysis, the husband was required to contribute 79 per cent of the adult child's costs, or $1,086 per month ($1,375 × 79 per cent = $1,086.25 rounded to $1,086). This amount when compared to the wife's budget for the child included a component for maintaining the home for the child when he returned on weekends and holidays. This was an appropriate item. The child support should be payable to the wife as she would be responsible for providing for the child's needs: *Merritt v. Merritt* (1999), 1999 CarswellOnt 1471, [1999] O.J. No. 1732, 98 O.T.C. 321 (S.C.J.).

On a strict interpretation of s. 3, where there is one child under the age of majority and a second child over that age, the basic Table Amount could be awarded to the first child and the same amount to the second. If that were done in the circumstances of this case, the amount would be $413 for each child or a total of $826 a month. The court declined to use this interpretation and awarded $677 a month, the Table Amount for two children:

Marshall v. Marshall (1998), 1998 CarswellNS 295, 169 N.S.R. (2d) 151, 508 A.P.R. 151 (S.C.).

In *Blair v. Blair* (1997), 1997 CarswellOnt 4908, [1997] O.J. No. 4949, 34 R.F.L. (4th) 370 (Gen. Div.), the younger of two children lived at home with the mother and the older child attended university in another city. The husband earned $75,192 *per annum* and the wife $44,345. Because the younger child was in another city while attending university, he did not share in the economies of the mother's home. The wife was awarded child support for both children under the *Guidelines* as if each were an only child.

In *Pitt v. Pitt* (1997), 1997 CarswellBC 1622 (S.C.); additional reasons at (1997), 1997 CarswellBC 1947, [1997] B.C.J. No. 1949 (S.C.), a 16-year-old child and a 21-year-old were in the joint custody of their parents living with their mother. The payor father's income was $79,472 annually. The mother's income was $29,000 annually. Support for the 16-year-old was fixed at the Table Amount for the payor's income and came to $630 a month. The 21-year-old (over the age of majority) was continuing his education, and earned approximately $280 a month from part-time employment. After taking into consideration the matters set out in s. 3(2)(b) of the *Guidelines*, the court fixed his support at the Table Amount for a single child less $200; that is, $630 less $200 or $430. This made a total amount of $1,060 a month for child support.

Where one of two children is under the age of the majority and the other is over, the Table Amount for the adult child can be calculated as the difference between the Table Amount for two children and the Table Amount for one child. Where the Table Amount for two children was $2,260 a month and for one child was $1,430, the court ordered support for the adult child in the amount of $830 monthly (the difference between $2,260 and $1,430) and support for the younger child at $1,430 monthly. The $830 monthly child support was to remain payable to the mother in the expectation that the child would be residing in her home when not away at school. The father was also ordered to pay $600 directly to the older child. The $830 amount and the $600 amount total $1,430 a month, the Table Amount payable for one child. There is no evidence to suggest the application of the *Child Support Guidelines* to the older child's situation was "inappropriate": *Garrison v. Garrison* (1998), 1998 CarswellOnt 2086, 38 R.F.L. (4th) 435 (Gen. Div.).

In *Cornborough v. Cornborough* (1997), 1997 CarswellBC 1926, [1997] B.C.J. No. 1981 (S.C.); affirmed (1998), 1998 CarswellBC 1975 (C.A.), there were two children under the age of majority and one child over. The child over the age of majority was 20-years of age, had completed 2 years of college, and was entering university away from home. He worked part-time earning $9,000 a year and had investments of his own of $8,300. The payor father's income was imputed to be $34,900 a year. The court found that the 20-year-old was 50 per cent self-supportive. The court observed that where the child is at the age of majority or over, it is not bound to implement the amount set out in the *Guidelines* tables if that approach is considered inappropriate. On the basis of the 20-year-old's circumstances, support for the three children was set "by interpolating the Table Amounts as if there were 2.5 children of the marriage." The result was a child support order of $583 a month to be paid "so long as three children remain children of the marriage, or until further order."

Presumptive Order Not Inappropriate: S. 3(2)(a)

Where the payor parent has an income close to the poverty line, he is still presumed to have the ability to pay support for an adult child in accordance with his income, unless it is below the amount covered by the *Guidelines*: *Nolte v. Nolte* (2001), 2001 CarswellSask 402, 2001 SKQB 268, 208 Sask. R. 88, [2002] 1 W.W.R. 156 (Q.B.).

In *Livingstone v. Buskard*, 2002 CarswellBC 2799, 2002 BCSC 1602 (S.C.); additional reasons at 2003 CarswellBC 163, 2003 BCSC 154 (S.C.), an adult child received $33,865, comprised of $26,980 from a family trust and $6,885 from her employment. The mother was the sole contributor to the trust and used the father's child support payments and her own funds to pay the child's expenses through the trust. The court found that the child was unable to withdraw from her parents' charge and was still a "child of the marriage", despite the fact that she worked and would only be attending college part-time. Although the child would pay for some of her own expenses, the mother would be required to provide for the daughter's basic living expenses. As the daughter had not been taking academic courses for 2 years, her planned gradual re-entry to academic work was reasonable. The parents, both doctors, had substantial academic and professional qualifications of their own and had made scholarship investments, planning that their daughter would pursue post-secondary academic training. The father's income was $259,000 and the mother's $92,000. The father had the means to contribute to his daughter's basic living expenses. Consequently, the father had not met the onus of proving that the application of the usual *Guidelines* amount would be inappropriate. The father was required to pay the Table Amount for three children, even though one of them was an adult child.

Where the children had demonstrated an ability to obtain reasonable remunerative summer employment so that they were not dependent upon their parents during the summer months and they had the ability to contribute adequately to their food, shelter and related expenses when not at university, the father was ordered to pay support of $1,153 per month during the academic year pursuant to ss. 3(2)(a) and 3(1)(a) of the *Guidelines*: *McConnell v. McConnell*, 25 R.F.L. (5th) 341, 2002 CarswellSask 118, 2002 SKQB 72, [2002] 5 W.W.R. 180, 215 Sask. R. 195 (Q.B.). The father's income was $96,300 per year and the mother's imputed income was $24,000, including spousal support. In terms of s. 7 expenses, the respondent father was ordered to pay his proportionate share, which was 80 per cent of the expenses.

The presumptive amount under s. 3(2)(a) should be applied to a child over the age of majority unless there is a challenge to this amount and the court decides to apply s. 3(2) instead: *Thompson v. Ducharme* (2001), 2001 CarswellMan 545, 159 Man. R. (2d) 246, [2001] M.J. No. 493, 2001 MBQB 161 (Q.B.). Without a challenge, the court shall apply the same criteria as those applicable to children under the age of majority. The court applied the same criteria as those applicable to children under the age of majority. In the present case, the father failed to challenge the approach of applying the *Guidelines* as if the child were under the age of majority. He submitted that she be treated as if she were still under the age of majority and that the amount of child support for her be determined pursuant to s. 3(2)(a) of the *Guidelines*. The court relied on the case of *Wesemann v. Wesemann* (1999), 49 R.F.L. (4th) 435, 1999 CarswellBC 1347, [1999] B.C.J. No. 1387 (S.C.).

Where a child has funds, in this case trust funds, to cover his or her tuition and earnings to cover personal expenditures, but the child is still dependent upon parents for shelter and sustenance and is therefore unable to withdraw from parental charge, it is not inappropriate for the payor to pay the Table Amount: *Kozun v. Kozun*, 2001 CarswellSask 475, 2001 SKQB 329, 18 R.F.L. (5th) 115 (Q.B.). The father was ordered to pay $509 per month in child support for his adult daughter, a university student.

Where the parties had three adult children who attended university away from home and lived with their mother during the summer, the court found that the presumptive rule in s. 3(2) of *Guidelines* applied. The father was ordered to pay the Table Amount during the summer for his children in university. The father was also ordered to pay his proportionate share of university expenses as extraordinary expenses. The children had to make a more determined effort at obtaining meaningful summer employment in the future to contribute in an appropriate measure to the cost of their education, and it was recommended that they apply for student loans. The court stated that the circumstances may well vary in future years depending on whether or not one or more of the university students live at home during the summer months: *Simpson v. Palma* (1998), 171 Sask. R. 89, 1998 CarswellSask 556, [1998] S.J. No. 581 (Q.B.).

In *Mathieu v. Mathieu* (1998), 1998 CarswellMan 202, 127 Man. R. (2d) 150, 38 R.F.L. (4th) 117 (Q.B.), the father paid monthly child support of $250 pursuant to a separation agreement and an order in the divorce judgment. He stopped making payments when the child reached the age of 18 on grounds that the child was no longer in full-time attendance at school. The mother brought a motion for variation of the child support order. In granting the motion the court held that the child support payable was to be assessed under the *Federal Child Support Guidelines* as though the child were under the age of majority. The father's annual income for *Guidelines* purposes was $39,734. He was to pay monthly child support of $319.43 until the child completed Grade 12, provided that the child remained a full-time student and continued to achieve a passing grade in three courses each semester.

Presumptive Order Inappropriate: S. 3(2)(b)

In principle, support for an adult child who is entitled to child support because of attendance at a post-secondary institution generally should be determined under s. 3(2)(b) of the *Guidelines*. Child support determined under that provision does not preclude a specific award for special and extraordinary expenses under s. 7: *N. (W.P.) v. N. (B.J.)*, 10 R.F.L. (6th) 440, 2005 CarswellBC 10, 2005 BCCA 7, 36 B.C.L.R. (4th) 330, 249 D.L.R. (4th) 352, 207 B.C.A.C. 76, 341 W.A.C. 76 (B.C. C.A.); varying 5 R.F.L. (6th) 135, 2004 CarswellBC 1520, 2004 BCSC 880, [2004] B.C.J. No. 1351 (B.C. S.C.).

In *Arnold v. Washburn* (2001), 2001 CarswellOnt 4439, 20 R.F.L. (5th) 236, 152 O.A.C. 364, 57 O.R. (3d) 287 (C.A.); leave to appeal refused (2002), 2002 CarswellOnt 4386, 2002 CarswellOnt 4387, [2002] S.C.C.A. No. 82, the court payor held that factors relevant to determining an appropriate amount of support under s. 3(2)(b) are the conditions, means, needs and other circumstances of the children. The court held that the appropriate amount, taking into account the father's increased ability to pay from his exercise of his stock options and considering the children's needs as indicated in the latest budget for them was an additional $1,000 per month or a total of $5,121.80 per month for the two adult children under s. 3(2)(b) of the *Guidelines*.

The court in *R. (M.T.) v. R. (I.S.)*, 34 R.F.L. (5th) 123, 2003 CarswellBC 518, 2003 BCSC 384 (S.C.); reversed in part 2004 CarswellBC 489, 2004 BCCA 131 (C.A.), held that the usual *Guidelines* approach was inappropriate for the child support of a disabled adult child, where the child had sufficient assets and income to meet his needs. The child was a joint tenant of a rental property with an assessed value of $617,000. He also had savings, mutual funds and R.R.S.P.s totaling $22,109.95, an annual income of at least $8,403.62 and the petitioner received $2,250 every month from the province to offset the costs of extra care for him. The application for child support for this child was dismissed.

The court held that the Table Amount was inappropriate for a child over the age of majority attending post-secondary school where there was a shortfall in the child's expenses after taking the child's earnings and student loans into account in *Molloy v. Molloy*, 23 R.F.L. (5th) 307, 2001 CarswellYukon 141, 2001 YKSC 548, [2001] Y.J. No. 142 (S.C.). The shortfall with respect to the older child's attendance at school was $7,385. Employing a ratio between the parents of 75/25, the appropriate amount under the *Guidelines* was a payment by the father of $553.87. The father was ordered to pay child support of $560 per month to the older child.

The Appellate Court upheld the trial judge's decision to refuse to apply the *Child Support Guidelines* and instead applied the terms of the parties' separation agreement in *Graves v. Eager* (2002), 2002 CarswellOnt 3347, 29 R.F.L. (5th) 313 (C.A.); varying (2001), 2001 CarswellOnt 4395 (S.C.J.)(2001), 2001 CarswellOnt 4395 (S.C.J.). The trial judge had a narrow discretion to do so, founded on s. 3(2) of the *Guidelines*.

Under s. 3(2)(b) of the *Guidelines*, it is not necessary to apportion expenses according to the respective income of the parents as must be done under s. 7 of the *Guidelines*: *Cole v. McNeil* (2001), 2001 CarswellNB 42, [2001] N.B.J. No. 37 (Q.B.).

Where a child has returned to post-secondary school after an absence, has fathered a child, and is able to provide in part for his own maintenance and education, the child is nonetheless a "child of the marriage" and entitled to child support under s. 3(2) of the *Guidelines*: *Lacey v. Lacey*, 2000 BCSC 529, 2000 CarswellBC 691 (S.C.).

A *Guidelines* approach may not be appropriate for determining the quantum of child support for a child attending university. A better approach is to apportion the cost of support between the parents, after deducting from their respective income a reasonable component for self-sufficiency: *Kapogiannes v. Kapogiannes* (2000), 2000 CarswellOnt 2374, 10 R.F.L. (5th) 63 (S.C.J.).

In *Gore-Hickman v. Gore-Hickman* (1999), 177 D.L.R. (4th) 222, 187 Sask. R. 45, 1999 CarswellSask 550, [1999] S.J. No. 503 (Q.B.), the court rejected the father's request that the mother pay him child support on the basis of the presumptive rule set out in s. 3 of the *Guidelines*. He did not request a contribution for extra expenses. He also requested an order eliminating his payment of child support to the mother as the access parent. The mother's income was $28,881 and the father's income was over $500,000. The court held that it has the power to refuse to apply the *Guidelines* if the conditions set out in s. 17(6.1) and (6.2) of the *Divorce Act* are met. Section 17(6.1) and (6.2) of the *Act* state as follows:

> 17. (6.1) A court making a variation order in respect of a child support order shall do so in accordance with the applicable guidelines.
>
> (6.2) Notwithstanding subsection (6.1), in making a variation order in respect of a child support order, a court may award an amount that is different from the amount that would be determined in accordance with the applicable guidelines *if* the court is satisfied
>
> > (a) that special provisions in an order, *a judgment* or a written agreement *respecting the financial obligations of the spouses*, or the division or transfer of their property, *directly or indirectly benefit a child*, or that special provisions have otherwise been made for the benefit of a child; and

(b) that the application of the applicable guidelines would result in an amount of child support that is inequitable given those special provisions. [Emphasis added]

Section 17(6.2) provides an enabling discretion to the courts when the criteria set out in the section are met. The court held that s. 17(6.2) extends to a refusal to vary altogether. The original order made special provision respecting financial obligations of the spouses by recognizing the vast disparity in their incomes. That order was for the benefit of the children. The original order provided for child maintenance to be paid by the father, the primary residence parent in favour of the access parent. The court ruled that the application of the *Guidelines* would be inequitable because the mother would be unable to afford access. The court held that the award of child maintenance to the mother was a special provision at the time and is a special provision within the meaning of s. 17(6.2).

Where a child over the age of majority leaves home to undertake post-secondary education, it is inappropriate to apply the presumptive Table Amount under s. 3(1) of the *Guidelines*: *Wilkins v. Wilkins* (1998), 204 N.B.R. (2d) 70, 520 A.P.R. 70, 1998 CarswellNB 297 (Q.B.). Section 3(2)(b) applies which requires the court to consider the: ". . . conditions, means, needs . . . of the child and the financial ability of each spouse to contribute." As the mother had an onerous debt burden, she was of limited means at the time of the hearing. Although the mother was aware of the father's increased income, because of legal fees and other reasons, she never made an application to increase support, which application would certainly have been successful. Given these "other circumstances", the court held that it was only right, proper and appropriate that for the next year, the respondent should assume the full extra cost of assisting the child until the completion of her course. He was ordered to pay $424 per month.

Section 3(2)(b) does not necessarily require that the parents contribution to the support of a child over the age of majority be shared in proportion to his or her respective income, although clearly each parent must contribute to the extent of his or her financial ability to do so. This provision differs from s. 7(2) where the expense is prorated in proportion to the parents' respective incomes after deducting any contribution from the child: *Michie v. Michie* (1997), 1997 CarswellSask 608, [1997] S.J. No. 668, 48 C.R.R. (2d) 333, [1998] 4 W.W.R. 758, 162 Sask. R. 1, 36 R.F.L. (4th) 90 (Q.B.). Here the court ordered the father to contribute to the daughter's expenses during the 8 months she was in attendance at school. The mother had limited financial means and her contribution, in these circumstances, was to shoulder the costs of providing a home for the child when she was not at school.

What is appropriate or inappropriate must be determined on a case-by-case basis. The onus of proof lies on the party claiming that the *Guidelines* are inappropriate.

The court must determine how much the adult child needs to maintain a reasonable lifestyle, and how much the child can reasonably contribute from his or her own resources. The shortfall can then be compared to the *Guidelines* amount to determine if the *Guidelines* are inappropriate. If inappropriate, the court can apportion the shortfall between the parties according to their respective incomes. Where the adult children are residing with the custodial parent, and attending post-secondary educational institutions, the basic amount under the *Guidelines* may be awarded plus a proportional share of the educational expenses, after taking into account a reasonable contribution from the child: *Sherlow v. Zubko* (1999), 1999 CarswellAlta 472, [1999] A.J. No. 644, 1999 ABQB 435, 50 R.F.L. (4th) 160, [2000] 1 W.W.R. 699, 247 A.R. 66, 76 Alta. L.R. (3d) 202 (Q.B.).

No Order for Support

Where there was no evidence as to the 20-year-old child's attendance at school, dependency or income, a claim for child support for the older child was dismissed as he was no longer a child of the marriage: *Passarello v. Passarello* (1998), 64 O.T.C. 118, 1998 CarswellOnt 2983, [1998] O.J. No. 2792 (Gen. Div.); additional reasons at (1998), 1998 CarswellOnt 3131 (Gen. Div.). There was little evidence of the father's needs with respect to the son's support and the father's financial ability to support him.

Condition, Means, Needs and Circumstances of the Child and the Financial Ability of Each Spouse

Child's Means

Child support for the parties' 20-year-old child who lived on her own while attending college, and lived with her mother during summer vacations was awarded pursuant to s. 3(2)(b) where the child had low paying summer employment which made her dependent on her parents. However, her summer employment could further her eventual career and afforded a reasonable income level for a university student. She remained a child of the marriage. Her costs for 12 months would be $18,000 and the shortfall, taking into consideration her income from employment and savings, was $9,500. The parents were to bear their proportionate share of the shortfall, based on their respective incomes: *Farrus v. Farrus*, 267 A.R. 103, 82 Alta. L.R. (3d) 315, 2000 CarswellAlta 562, 2000 ABQB 389, [2000] A.J. No. 680 (Q.B.); varied on other grounds 28 R.F.L. (5th) 37, 100 Alta. L.R. (3d) 255, 266 W.A.C. 382, 299 A.R. 382, 2002 CarswellAlta 549, 2002 ABCA 100 (C.A.).

The Appellate Court held that the presumption in s. 3(1) of the amount of child support for children under the age of majority being the amount set out in the applicable table is rebuttable taking into account s. 3(2)(b) of the *Guidelines* having regard to the actual needs of the children: *Hagen v. Rankin*, 24 R.F.L. (5th) 38, 260 W.A.C. 257, 213 Sask. R. 257, 2002 CarswellSask 20, 2002 SKCA 13, [2002] S.J. No. 15 (C.A.). The son's income served to reduce the extent of legal obligation of the parents and rebutted the presumption that the Table Amount was the appropriate amount. When the Chambers Judge ordered the Table Amount of support, he misapplied the *Guidelines* since this amount was determined presumptively, irrespective of the son's actual needs. At best, the son needed some assistance with room and board. Accordingly, the father was ordered to pay $200 per month and the mother pay $100 per month, each being about one third of the Table Amount for their respective incomes.

In *Livingstone v. Buskard*, 2002 CarswellBC 2799, 2002 BCSC 1602 (S.C.); additional reasons at 2003 CarswellBC 163, 2003 BCSC 154 (S.C.), an adult daughter received $33,865, comprised of $26,980 from a family trust and $6,885 from her employment. The mother was the sole contributor to the trust and used the father's child support payments and her own funds to pay the child's expenses through the trust. The court found that the child was unable to withdraw from her parents' charge and was still a "child of the marriage", despite the fact that she worked and would only be attending college part-time. Although the child would pay for some of her own expenses, the mother would be required to provide for the daughter's basic living expenses. As the daughter had not been taking academic courses for two years, her planned gradual re-entry to academic work was reasonable. The parents, both doctors, had substantial academic and professional qualifications of their own and had made scholarship investments, planning that their daughter would pursue post-secondary academic training. The father's income was $259,000 and the mother's $92,000. The father had the means to contribute to his daughter's basic living expenses. Consequently, the father had not met the onus of proving that the application of the usual *Guidelines* amount would be inappropriate. The father was required to pay the Table Amount for three children, even though one of them was an adult child.

Where the children had demonstrated an ability to obtain reasonable remunerative summer employment so that they were not dependent upon their parents during the summer months and they had the ability to contribute adequately to their food, shelter and related expenses when not at university, the father was ordered to pay support of $1,153 per month during the academic year pursuant to ss. 3(2)(a) and 3(1)(a) of the *Guidelines*: *McConnell v. McConnell*, 25 R.F.L. (5th) 341, 2002 CarswellSask 118, 2002 SKQB 72, [2002] 5 W.W.R. 180, 215 Sask. R. 195 (Q.B.). The father's income was $96,300 per year and the mother's imputed income was $24,000, including spousal support.

The daughter, who was working part-time was expected to contribute to her expenses with her father paying support only for the months that she was in school: *Leier v. Leier*, 2001 CarswellSask 120, 2001 SKQB 81, 202 Sask. R. 169 (Q.B.). During the summer months, it was assumed that she would work full-time, with her earnings covering her personal expenses.

Even though a child attending university makes a reasonable contribution towards his or her education, she may nonetheless have an ongoing need for support: *Hamilton v. Pearce*, 11 R.F.L. (5th) 114, 2000 BCSC 1432, 80 B.C.L.R. (3d) 326, 2000 CarswellBC 1921, [2000] B.C.J. No. 1953 (S.C.). The father was ordered to pay $920 per month in child support for his daughter.

Where a child receives a Canada Pension Plan benefit payment, it is triggered by the parent's disability, but the benefit belongs to the child and is payable directly to the child or, where the child is a minor, to the person having custody of the child: *Malbeuf v. Malbeuf* (1999), 185 Sask. R. 267, 1999 CarswellSask 637, [1999] S.J. No. 635, 1999 SKQB 74 (Q.B.). A benefit that is payable to the child is independent of any order for child support. The *Child Support Guidelines* do not direct the court to take a child's resources into account in reduction of the Table Amount except in a few limited circumstances which include apportioning the cost of special expenses (s. 7) and determining support for adult children (s. 3(1)(b)). In this case, the children were under the age of majority.

No indefinite obligation exists for a parent to support a child who is attending school or who is unemployed or underemployed. However, an obligation does exist for one parent to assist the other on whom such a child is dependent for a reasonable transition period: *Gamache v. Gamache*, 49 R.F.L. (4th) 258, 241 A.R. 388, 1999 CarswellAlta 369, [1999] A.J. No. 474, 1999 ABQB 313 (Q.B.).

In *Harwood v. Harwood* (1999), 45 R.F.L. (4th) 357, 1999 CarswellBC 921, [1999] B.C.J. No. 975 (S.C.), the fact that the parties' child left school temporarily to work and save funds for travel in Europe, was found not to have disqualified him as a "child of the marriage". The child remained in the home throughout the period and remained dependent upon his mother.

On an application for interim child support, the court held that the presumptive order was inappropriate. It was inferred that one child, who was over the age of majority was physically fit and capable of contributing to his own support and the younger child who was under the age of majority spent equal time with each parent: *Gordon v. Gordon* (1998), 36 R.F.L. (4th) 443, 1998 CarswellOnt 966 (Gen. Div.). The court also stated that the material filed did not permit it to determine whether the older child was in fact a "child of the marriage" and thus entitled to support. This issue should be left to the trial judge. The court did not make an order for interim child support.

Children have a very real and substantial responsibility (quite irrespective of the means or financial position of their parents) to make earnest and concerted efforts to obtain the best employment which they can in order to earn income and contribute in an appropriate measure to the cost of their education. The same is also true of the Canada Student Loan Program if children may be eligible to receive support from it: *Simpson v. Palma* (1998), 171 Sask. R. 89, 1998 CarswellSask 556, [1998] S.J. No. 581 (Q.B.). (See Sask. R., para. 64).

Where the daughter was enrolled in one college course and intended to take another which would qualify her for a teacher certification program, the court refused the father's application to terminate her child support. Although she was earning $465 monthly from babysitting, as long as she continued to pursue her long-term educational goals, she was entitled to support: *Vanderstoep v. Vanderstoep* (1998), 35 R.F.L. (4th) 385, 1998 CarswellBC 167 (S.C. [In Chambers]).

Where an adult child is pregnant and not attending school, but she plans to return to full-time educational studies after her child's birth, the court found that she was a "child of the marriage" and entitled to support for 9 months, at which time child support would be terminated if she failed to be enrolled as a full-time student in a post-secondary institution: *Bragg v. Bragg* (2000), 2 R.F.L. (5th) 344, 2000 CarswellNfld 22, [2000] N.J. No. 14, 188 Nfld. & P.E.I.R. 202, 569 A.P.R. 202 (U.F.C.).

In *Glen v. Glen* (1997), 1997 CarswellBC 2644, [1997] B.C.J. No. 2806, 34 R.F.L. (4th) 13 (S.C.), the mother claimed support for her 19-year-old daughter who was attending university and living at home with her. The *Federal Child Support Guidelines* require the parents to pay the same level of support to adult children as to minor children unless the parent can show this approach is inappropriate. The fact that the daughter worked part-time did not diminish the father's obligation to pay the basic level of support. The father was not required to make any contribution to the daughter's university tuition because her income exceeded the tuition amount. The father was ordered to pay $542 per month in child support.

In *Nadeau v. Mitchell* (1997), [1997] O.J. No. 2833, 1997 CarswellOnt 3107, 36 O.T.C. 34 (Gen. Div.); additional reasons at (1997), 1997 CarswellOnt 3275, [1997] O.J. No. 3440, 36 O.T.C. 34 at 34 (Gen. Div.), child support was reduced to take into account the child's financial contribution.

In *Wesemann v. Wesemann* (1999), 1999 CarswellBC 1347, [1999] B.C.J. No. 1387, 49 R.F.L. (4th) 435 (S.C.), the court in determining the quantum of child support under the *Guidelines* for a child attending university, held that both scholarships received by the child and summer earnings may properly be taken into account in assessing the child's needs. On this basis an amount other than the regular *Guidelines* amount may be found to be appropriate.

In *Wahl v. Wahl*, 2000 CarswellAlta 13, [2000] A.J. No. 29, 2 R.F.L. (5th) 307, 2000 ABQB 10, 257 A.R. 212 (Q.B.), the court was of the opinion that an adult child was expected to contribute to the cost of his or her education wherever possible through bursaries, scholarships, student loans, or summer employment. Courts will also consider the reasonableness of a course of studies. Usually courts will require a student to contribute to the cost of his or her maintenance with summer employment and weekends during the school year.

Where a child over the age of majority works part-time during the school year and earns a substantial amount, in this case, $300 per month, the *Guidelines* amount under s. 3(2)(a) would be inappropriate: *Meyers v. Meyers* (1998), 1998 CarswellSask 216, [1998] S.J. No. 265 (Q.B.). The amount of the child's contribution should be deducted from the cost of paying his expenses and the remainder apportioned between the parents in accordance with their proportionate share of combined total income. The father earned approximately $30,700 per year.

In *Khoee-Solomonescu v. Solomonescu* (1997), 1997 CarswellOnt 5286, [1997] O.J. No. 5396 (Gen. Div.); additional reasons at (1998), 1998 CarswellOnt 1796 (Gen. Div.); considered in *Clarke v. Clarke* (1999), 1999 CarswellOnt 4096 (S.C.J.), the court held where a child is over the age of majority and has resources to contribute to her own support, including scholarships, student loans, employment income, and savings, the non-custodial parent should pay the Table Amount of support minus the child's contribution to her own support. See also *Amaral v. Amaral* (1993), 1993 CarswellOnt 372, 50 R.F.L. (3d) 364 (Gen. Div.); additional reasons at (1993), 1993 CarswellOnt 373, 50 R.F.L. (3d) 384 (Gen. Div.).

Where an adult child is a student and also works part-time with substantial earnings ($7,800 a year), the Table Amount is inappropriate and support should be determined under s. 3(2)(b) of the *Guidelines*: *Leier v. Leier*, 2001 CarswellSask 120, 2001 SKQB 81, 202 Sask. R. 169 (Q.B.).

In *Evans v. Evans* (1998), 1998 CarswellSask 65, [1998] S.J. No. 91, 164 Sask. R. 101, 35 R.F.L. (4th) 158 (Q.B.), the court was of the opinion that where a child is contributing to his own support and the child is living away from the home of the payee parent in order to pursue his education, it is inappropriate to apply the *Guidelines* in order to determine the amount payable. Instead, the costs other than those paid for by the child, should "be apportioned in accordance with the parties' respective abilities to pay." The court ordered that the father pay to the mother his proportionate share, being 55 per cent of the deficit remaining after deducting the child's contribution until the end of the academic year. Subsequently the amount would be reduced to $550 per month. There was no separate payment to the son.

Child's Needs — At Educational Institution Away From Home

Where adult children are attending university away from home, child support is not usually based on the Table Amount but on an amount in the court's discretion "having regard to the condition, means and needs and other circumstances of the child and the financial ability of each spouse to contribute to the support of the child": s. 3(2).

In *Corsano v. Simms*, 33 R.F.L. (5th) 301, 2002 CarswellNS 420, 2002 NSCA 125, 209 N.S.R. (2d) 242, 656 A.P.R. 242 (C.A.), the mother appealed from an order regarding the amount of the father's contribution to the child's post-secondary educational expenses. The court in upholding the lower court decision was of the opinion that the expenses of over $12,000 for university were not reasonable in the circumstances. The parties' son could have significantly reduced those expenses by living at home and attending a university in a city where one of his parents resided. In the circumstances of the case, a reasonable amount for university expenses was $4,698, limited to tuition, books and fees.

The applications judge reduced the amount by the amount of the child's summer savings ($600) and the educational savings plan contribution ($3,019). This left a shortfall of approximately $1,000. Since it was reasonable to infer that the tax savings from the educational credit would exceed the shortfall in expenses, there were no reasonable expenses to be shared.

In *Bitterman v. Weaver*, 2002 CarswellNB 206, 2002 NBQB 9 (Q.B.), the court, in an *obiter* remark, stated that where adult children have not established that it was reasonable to attend university outside their hometown; the children have not supplied the court with the necessary expense evidence; the parent from whom payment is sought, (the mother) has no ability to pay support; and one child has little contact with the mother, no child support should be ordered. The court decided the case on the basis that the adult children were no longer "children of the marriage".

Normally when a child is not residing at home while attending university, the courts do not establish child support based upon the *Guidelines* amount but rather the condition, means and needs consideration set forth in s. 3(2)(b) of the *Guidelines*. However, in this case, the parties by agreement, as recently as December of 1997, agreed to the *Guidelines* applying and had the court sanction that agreement. Given the currency of the agreement, and the fact that the Petitioner was only asking for the *Guidelines* to continue up to and including April of 1999, it was found that the request was reasonable and fair under these unique circumstances: *Pollard v. Pollard*, 75 Alta. L.R. (3d) 350, [2000] 3 W.W.R. 322, 257 A.R. 36, (sub nom. *C.M.P. v. P.E.P.)* 1999 CarswellAlta 1189, [1999] A.J. No. 1478, 1999 ABQB 976 (Q.B.).

The *Guidelines* amount of child support is inappropriate where an adult child was living apart from the custodial parent to pursue post-secondary education and the expenses attributable to her were greater than if she were living at home. In such a case, none of the living expenses, such as shelter and utilities are common to and shared with the custodial parent. Accordingly, in such circumstances it is more appropriate to apply s. 3(2)(b) of the *Guidelines* and have regard to ". . . the condition, means, needs and other circumstances of the child and the financial ability of each spouse to contribute to the support of the child" in calculating the ongoing support: *Krueger v. Tunison* (1999), 183 Sask. R. 255, 1999 CarswellSask 482, [1999] S.J. No. 482 (Q.B.). In this decision, the court was satisfied that it was in the child's best interests to pursue a particular curriculum and career path for which the university away from home offered the best program. The court ordered that the father pay a proportionate share of the costs for the child during the school year. The court did not require the father to contribute to the child's costs during the summer months when she was employed and living away from home. The balance of the child's costs during the school year, her summer costs and her extra-curricular expenses must be met by the child through her employment earnings, by student loans or by accessing the mother's trust fund established for her post-secondary education. Similarly, the father was ordered to pay his proportionate share of the expenses for another adult child who was living away from home to pursue athletic interests and who was enrolled in a secondary school program. This child was a world class level competitor and his expenses were not unreasonable having regard to the necessity of the expenses in relation to his best interests and the means of the parties.

The reason for avoiding the tables and using the court's discretion for children of the marriage living away from home is that some of the underlying assumptions of the *Guidelines* are not applicable or valid in this situation: *Brockman v. Ofukany* (1998), 1998 CarswellSask 638, [1998] S.J. No. 650, 173 Sask. R. 233, 41 R.F.L. (4th) 426

(Q.B.). "The economies of scale are reflected in the Table Amounts of the *Guidelines* where the child is residing in the same household as the recipient parent" and these economies are not present where the child is living away from the household: *Wahl v. Wahl*, 2000 CarswellAlta 13, [2000] A.J. No. 29, 2000 ABQB 10, 257 A.R. 212, 2 R.F.L. (5th) 307 (Q.B.). The Ontario General Division held that where a child over the age of majority is studying far away from the payee's residence, the payee is not entitled to receive the Table Amount for his notional care: *Van Wynsberghe v. Van Wynsberghe* (1997), 1997 CarswellOnt 2240, [1997] O.J. No. 2566 (Gen. Div.).

In this case, the parties' son was taking an intensive 10-month film course in Vancouver and a daughter was living at home with her mother in Ontario. The Table Amount ($553 a month) was awarded to the mother for the support of the daughter, and no amount was awarded for the son. Money from a trust fund was available to assist in the education costs. The father was ordered to provide for the son's air travel and $300 per month for living expenses. There was no evidence of any expense to be incurred by the mother for the son's primary residential care when he was in Vancouver. In the circumstances, "her receipt of the Table Amount for his notional care [would be] completely illogical."

Another case along the same line is *Evans v. Evans* (1998), 1998 CarswellSask 65, [1998] S.J. No. 91, 164 Sask. R. 101, 35 R.F.L. (4th) 158 (Q.B.). The Saskatchewan Court was of the opinion that where a child is making a contribution to his own support, and is living away from the home of the payee parent in order to pursue his education, it is inappropriate to apply the *Guidelines* in order to determine the amount payable. Instead, the costs other than those paid for by the child, should "be apportioned in accordance with the parties' respective abilities to pay."

When a child for whose benefit child support is paid ceases to live with the custodial parent, the obligation to pay child support does not automatically end: *McKay v. Collins* (1999), 1999 CarswellBC 893, 48 R.F.L. (4th) 422, 125 B.C.A.C. 293, 204 W.A.C. 293 (C.A.). In this case, the children were still financially dependent upon their parents. The children moved for educational and employment opportunities. The older child moved to his maternal grandparents and the younger child moved to a different city.

In *Seburn v. Seburn* (2001), 2001 CarswellOnt 1339 (S.C.J.), two of the parties' four children were away at university for one-third of the year. The court deducted a notional amount per month for groceries not spent by the mother. The court ordered that the Table Amount for the four children minus the deduction for groceries for 8 months should be paid to the mother directly.

Where an older child is living away from home, the custodial parent is not entitled to both the basic monthly child support pursuant to the *Guidelines*, and to an order for a proportionate share of the child's special expenses, which include 8 months of food, accommodation, and expenses for the child while she is in Vancouver attending university. In the circumstances, the court ordered the father, the non-custodial parent, to pay to the mother child support pursuant to the *Guidelines* for the four summer months if the child lived with her for those months. During the months the child was away at university the father was ordered to pay his two-thirds proportionate share of her special expenses directly to the child: *Bellman v. Bellman* (1999), 1999 CarswellBC 1122, 46 R.F.L. (4th) 414 (S.C.); additional reasons at (1999), 1999 CarswellBC 1749 (S.C.).

Where support for older children away from home at university has been awarded as special expenses, another award under the *Guidelines* for those same months would lead to double counting and be inappropriate. This may mean that the custodial parent is not supported for any marginal fixed costs that she incurs because of the need to maintain accommodation for six children (in the circumstances of this case), rather than four children. However, in the absence of evidence on this issue, it is reasonable to conclude that any such marginal costs would be minimal. For the five months when the children are living at home, support should be awarded in the *Guidelines* amount: *Moss v. Moss* (1997), 1997 CarswellNfld 308, [1997] N.J. No. 299, 159 Nfld. & P.E.I.R. 1, 492 A.P.R. 1 (T.D.).

Where the child, a university student, is earning an income which provides for many of his expenses, it is not appropriate to apply the *Guidelines* in the usual manner: *Higgins v. Higgins* (2001), 2001 CarswellOnt 2729, 19 R.F.L. (5th) 300 (S.C.J.). Instead the parents should share the child's expenses in proportion to their respective incomes, after deducting the child's income.

The court, in *MacDonald v. Rasmussen*, 2000 CarswellSask 659, 2000 SKQB 494, 198 Sask. R. 1 (Q.B.); additional reasons at 2002 CarswellSask 486, 2002 SKQB 307, 221 Sask. R. 305 (Q.B.), held that to determine that it would be inappropriate to apply s. 3(2)(a), there is a two-step process. First, there should be a determination of the applicable Table Amount and then a calculation of the amounts payable under s. 7. In this case with three out of four children living away from home much of the year, the Table Amount would be inappropriate. In calculating the correct amount of child support under s. 3(2)(b), the court took into account the amount the father would have paid under the *Guidelines* tables, his debt load, and his present wife's ability to pay expenses.

Where a father was paying 80 per cent of the expenses of an older child living away from home at university for 8 months of the year, the court refused the mother's request for an additional one-half the Table Amount (being $294 a month) to compensate her for maintaining the home for the child. The child would be home earning an income for the other 4 months of the year and could pay her own expenses: *H. (A.S.) v. H. (S.L.)* (1999), 1999 CarswellAlta 1214, 253 A.R. 392 (Q.B.); additional reasons at (2000), 2000 CarswellAlta 377, [2000] A.J. No. 424, 7 R.F.L. (5th) 94, 263 A.R. 150 (Q.B.).

Where adult children are attending university away from home, child support is not usually based on the *Guidelines* amount but rather the courts consider the condition, means and needs criteria set out in s. 3(2)(b) of the *Guidelines*. The reason for this position is that "the economies of scale are reflected in the Table Amounts of the *Guidelines* where the child is residing in the same household as the recipient parent": *Wahl v. Wahl*, 2000 CarswellAlta 13, [2000] A.J. No. 29, 2000 ABQB 10, 257 A.R. 212, 2 R.F.L. (5th) 307 (Q.B.). Support, which the father had stopped when the child was 18, was reinstated. The father was ordered to pay $1,188.52 per month, provided, *inter alia*, that there would be no support payable during the summer months. The child was required to obtain summer employment.

Applying s. 3(2)(a) is inappropriate where a child is living away from home pursuing a post-secondary education and spends little time at her mother's home: *Power v. Hunt* (2000), 2000 CarswellNfld 328, 196 Nfld. & P.E.I.R. 149, 589 A.P.R. 149 (U.F.C.). In this case, the parties' daughter was home two weekends a month and on holidays. The father was ordered to pay $50 to compensate the mother for out-of-pocket and intangible expenses, as the child's visits were regular but infrequent. The court found it significant that the mother had to provide food and shelter for the child's visits. The father was also ordered to pay two-thirds of the daughter's monthly shortfall of $311, after student loans, as the father's income was approximately twice as much as the mother's. The court followed a principle of proportionate sharing although this approach was not required by s. 3(2)(b). All payments, which were of $257 monthly and were $38 more than the Table Amounts, were to be made to the Support Enforcement Agency. (The case does not say whether the Support Enforcement Agency paid the mother or daughter for the contribution for the shortfall.)

In *McLean v. McLean*, 2000 CarswellBC 550, 2000 BCSC 433 (S.C. [In Chambers]), the court was of the opinion that when a court is deciding whether s. 3(2)(b) should apply rather than s. 3(2)(a), circumstances such as whether the child resides at home and whether the child is earning income are significant. In this case the child had been living away from home, was currently home but was likely to be away from home in the coming years. The child contributed substantially to his educational cost. The court decided the issue of child support under s. 3(2)(b). The court considered the child's costs for the months he attended university, deducted the child's contribution from employment and using the expense sharing principle of s.7(2) of the *Guidelines* allocated the remaining 77 per cent to the father, representing his proportionate share of the incomes of the father and the mother. The child had a shortfall of $6,500 for the 8-month school year. It was considered a possibility that he would reside with his mother in the summer. The father was ordered to pay the mother $425 per month. There was no specific amount paid to the mother for maintaining the home for the child. There was also no difference made between the months when the child lived at home and was at university.

In *Michie v. Michie* (1997), 1997 CarswellSask 608, [1997] S.J. No. 668, 48 C.R.R. (2d) 333, [1998] 4 W.W.R. 758, 162 Sask. R. 1, 36 R.F.L. (4th) 90 (Q.B.), the court determined that it would be inappropriate to determine support under s. 3(2)(a) for an adult child pursuing post-secondary education and living at home. Instead, it should be determined under s. 3(2)(b). The court held (at para. 45) "that s. 3(2)(b) does not necessarily require that the parent's contribution be shared in proportion to their respective incomes although clearly each parent must contribute to the extent of their financial ability to do so." The father had an income of $54,844.39 and the mother had lost her full-time position and had an income of $15,300. The father was ordered to pay the Table Amount for two children living at home and the amount of $375 per month for each month that the child is in attendance at school. The court decided "on the basis of what the parents could reasonable be expected to contribute to their daughter's post-secondary education." A reasonable amount would be $3,000.

Where adult children are studying full-time away from home some cases had held that support should be determined under s. 3(2)(b) and others under s. 3(2)(a). In this case the determination was made under s. 3(2)(b) as the child would not be spending much time with his mother, would probably work in the summer, and a significant amount of money was available to him in a trust fund for his education: *Cole v. McNeil* (2001), 2001 CarswellNB 42, [2001] N.B.J. No. 37 (Q.B.). The university costs for a year were approximately $12,200. The court held that an amount of $4,000 per year to cover tuition costs should be paid from the trust fund and that the parents divide the remaining costs after deducting a reasonable contribution ($2,000) by the child. The father was ordered to pay the mother $517 per month. The father's income was $62,600 and the mother's income was almost the same.

Financial Ability of Each Spouse

In *Watts v. Enns*, 2000 CarswellSask 830, 2000 SKQB 586, 13 R.F.L. (5th) 210 (Q.B.), the court found that the father could not afford to pay the Table Amount for the parties' younger adult son who had moved with his mother to the United States. The son was at university in Ontario. In making the decisions to move to the United States without the father's approval, the child could not qualify for Canadian student loans. Also the decision to go to university away from either parent increased the son's costs. Further, the mother who had had at separation an income comparable to the father's no longer worked, as her second husband's income was sufficient for the second family. The court ordered that the father continue to pay child support of $300 per month and $3,700 toward the child's university tuition, a sum approximately equal to the amount he paid for the older son who had largely lived with the father. If this arrangement did not work out for the younger son, he could return to Regina, attend university there, qualify for Canadian student loans, and live with his father or brother.

In *Michie v. Michie* (1997), 1997 CarswellSask 608, [1997] S.J. No. 668, 48 C.R.R. (2d) 333, [1998] 4 W.W.R. 758, 162 Sask. R. 1, 36 R.F.L. (4th) 90 (Q.B.), the court determined that it would be inappropriate to determine support under s. 3(2)(a) for an adult child pursuing post-secondary education and living at home. Instead, it should be determined under s. 3(2)(b). The court held (at para. 45) "that s. 3(2)(b) does not necessarily require that the parent's contribution be shared in proportion to their respective incomes although clearly each parent must contribute to the extent of their financial ability to do so." The father had an income of $54,844.39 and the mother had lost her full-time position and had an income of $15,300. The father was ordered to pay the Table Amount for two children living at home and the amount of $375 per month for each month that the child is in attendance at school. The court decided "on the basis of what the parents could reasonably be expected to contribute to their daughter's post-secondary education." A reasonable amount would be $3,000.

Where a parent has no financial ability to contribute to the support of children, nor to their university costs, the court pursuant to s. 3(2)(b) may hold that the parent should not be required to pay child support: *Simmons v. Wilcox* (2001), 2001 CarswellOnt 2612, 21 R.F.L. (5th) 218 (S.C.J.).

Where *Guidelines* Provide Otherwise

The Appellate Court upheld the trial judge's decision to refuse to apply the *Child Support Guidelines* and instead apply the terms of the parties' separation agreement in *Graves v. Eager* (2002), 2002 CarswellOnt 3347, 29 R.F.L. (5th) 313 (C.A.); varying (2001), 2001 CarswellOnt 4395 (S.C.J.). The trial judge had a narrow discretion to do so, founded on s. 3(2) of *Guidelines*.

In assessing child support under the *Federal Child Support Guidelines*, the court should properly consider the evidentiary value of a separation agreement with respect to the determination of the children's needs: *Dergousoff v. Dergousoff*, 48 R.F.L. (4th) 1, [1999] 10 W.W.R. 633, 1999 CarswellSask 231 (C.A.).

There is no reason in principle why a party cannot successfully apply for an original child support order simply because there is a written separation agreement in force. Such an agreement may lead to an order not strictly in accordance with the *Federal Child Support Guidelines* if the parties' circumstances can be brought within s. 15.1(5) of the *Divorce Act*: *Fung-Sunter v. Fabian* (1999), 48 R.F.L. (4th) 95, 1999 CarswellBC 1204 (C.A.); reversing (1998), 38 R.F.L. (4th) 266, 53 B.C.L.R. (3d) 75, 1998 CarswellBC 824 (S.C.).

Where the wife forfeited child support in exchange for the husband's forfeiture of his interest in the matrimonial home, the court nevertheless allowed the wife's later application for child support, citing the parties' agreement as unreasonable on its face. On appeal, the court set aside the support order. It was not sufficient for the trial court to conclude that the child support provision was inadequate "on the face" on no other basis than the existence of the *Child Support Guidelines*. The court was required to consider whether the support provisions met or failed to meet the needs of the child having regard to other relevant provisions, such as the transfer of property. The trial judge had failed to do so and therefore the order could not stand: *Spencer v. Irvine* (1999), 45 R.F.L. (4th) 434, 1999 CarswellOnt 1365 (S.C.J.).

In *Davidson v. Davidson* (1998), 42 R.F.L. (4th) 154, 230 A.R. 151, 1998 CarswellAlta 879 (Q.B.), the father's obligation to pay support was reduced from the *Guidelines* amount as a result of the fact that the children received an income from an irrevocable family trust under which they were the exclusive beneficiaries. The family trust qualified under s. 15.1 of the *Divorce Act* as a "special provision made for the benefit of the children."

In *Armstrong v. Armstrong* (1997), 34 R.F.L. (4th) 38, 1997 CarswellOnt 4268 (Gen. Div.); additional reasons at (1997), 1997 CarswellOnt 5551 (Gen. Div.), a consent order made prior to trial granted the mother, among other things, support in the global amount of $3,000 per month for herself and the two children of the marriage. Although the father stated his income was about $57,000, his real income was closer to $85,000 or $90,000 and was even higher, given that he received corporate benefits free of tax liability. The mother, after the separation, earned a diploma in computer programming, but was unemployed at the time of the trial. Given the means and circumstances of parties and needs of children, the husband was ordered to continue to pay $3,000 per month in support for the wife and children according to the consent order. Of the $3,000 per month, $1,621.20 was reserved for child support. It would be inappropriate to apply *Child Support Guidelines* to the husband's income as it was impossible to ascertain his true income. Material filed by parties indicated that it was advantageous for both of them to continue to treat support payments as taxable.

Where the parties have made an agreement for child support that is different from that provided in the *Guidelines*, the court must have financial disclosure if it is to compare the agreement with the amounts provided in the *Federal Guidelines*: *McCrum v. McCrum* (1997), 1997 CarswellNB 372 (Q.B.). The court also held that if the payee (wife) is unable to swear as to the income level of her husband, he will have to provide 3 years' income tax returns and the court stated that it would be reassuring if both parties submitted affidavits as to their agreement in order to satisfy it that the arrangements are at least as good as those provided by the *Guidelines*.

In *Thomas v. Thomas* (1997), 1997 CarswellOnt 4368 (Gen. Div.), the Table Amount calculated on the payor's income of $59,400 a year would be $503 a month. The amount under the separation agreement with a modification proposed by the payor increasing the amount would be approximately $295 a month. Section 15.1(5) of the *Divorce Act* provides that the court may award an amount that is different from the *Guidelines* if satisfied that special provisions have been made in an agreement, and that the application of the *Guidelines* would be inequitable given those special provisions. The court held that the agreement amount was inadequate having regard to the father's annual income, the mother's income of $40,000 a year, "and the means and needs of each of the parties." In addition, the apportionment of the child's costs under the agreement had led to conflict, and the change in the child's living arrangements required a change in support. The application of the *Guidelines* would not result in an amount of child support that is inequitable, and the objectives of the *Child Support Guidelines* set out in s. 1 can best be met by requiring the payor to pay child support according to the Table Amount of $503 a month.

In *Haggith v. Trader* (1997), 1997 CarswellOnt 1995 (Gen. Div.), the mother sought under provincial legislation to vary the terms of child support set out in a separation agreement in which the children had received a low amount of child support in exchange for the father's equity in the matrimonial home, said to be $40,000. In the 4 years since the agreement, the father's income had increased approximately 12 per cent from $32,539 to $36,400 *per annum*. Under the *Federal Guidelines*, the children would have been entitled to approximately $523. In light of the father's increased income, but keeping in mind that the transfer of the husband's interest in the home was the equivalent of a $25,000 lump sum amount of child support and that the father would no longer receive a tax deduction for child support, the court modestly increased the support from $200 to $225 for the two children.

In *Harwood v. Harwood* (1999), 45 R.F.L. (4th) 357, 1999 CarswellBC 921 (S.C.), the court refused the wife's increase in child support from the amount specified in the parties' separation agreement. Although the husband's income had risen by $6,000, the support called for in the agreement was reasonable and exceeded that required under the *Federal Child Support Guidelines*.

Where the parties purchased a home 2 years after the divorce and the wife and children lived upstairs and her former husband lived downstairs, the situation was found not to constitute "a special provision for the benefit of the children" within the meaning of the *Federal Child Support Guidelines*: *Chan v. Chan* (1999), 46 R.F.L. (4th) 339, 1999 CarswellBC 1137 (S.C.).

In *Jaworsky v. Jaworsky* (1997), 32 R.F.L. (4th) 59, 1997 CarswellBC 2094 (S.C. [In Chambers]), with the agreement of the mother, the father made direct payments for various expenses of the children instead of making payments to the mother required under the support order. These payments included the purchase of a home in his name, in which the mother and children resided. The court dismissed the mother's application for payment of arrears under the order, and also dismissed the father's application to evict the mother and children from the home so that he could sell it. Under the circumstances, it would be unjust to grant the father's application in that it would have allowed him to both avoid enforcement of the arrears and be released from one of his principal obligations relating to support.

In *Jaworsky v. Jaworsky* (1997), 32 R.F.L. (4th) 59, 1997 CarswellBC 2094 (S.C. [In Chambers]), an order made in 1987 required the father to pay support of $250 monthly for each child. The evidence established an agreement in which the father made payments of expenses on behalf of the children in lieu of the support order. These payments exceeded the amount to which the children were entitled under the order. As such, the father had a reasonable expectation that the wife would not seek to enforce the order. A court is not bound to enforce arrears where it would be inequitable to do so or where special circumstances existed. Accordingly, the mother's application for payment of arrears of support was dismissed.

Where the parties' separation agreement required the husband to pay $400 monthly child support, the fact that his pension plan paid $160 monthly directly to the child was found not to warrant a downward variation. The agreement itself did not specifically allow for the deduction: *Corkum v. Corkum* (1998), 36 R.F.L. (4th) 367, 166 N.S.R. (2d) 329, 498 A.P.R. 329, 1998 CarswellNS 57 (S.C. [In Chambers]).

In *Anderson-Devine v. Anderson* (2002), 33 R.F.L. (5th) 29, 2002 CarswellMan 514, 2002 MBCA 166, [2003] 3 W.W.R. 409, 170 Man. R. (2d) 85, 285 W.A.C. 85 (C.A.), the court held that an assumption of debt by a payor can amount to a special provision pursuant to s. 17(6.2) of the *Divorce Act*. In this case, the parties had entered into written minutes of settlement. The terms of the Minutes of Settlement regarding child support were incorporated in a consent divorce judgment, which provided for child support for the two adult children of the marriage in the amount of $1,300 per month. According to the consent judgment, the wife would receive no support for herself, nor would she seek any share of the husband's partnership assets, but she would receive the husband's equity in the family home, valued at $20,000. The husband assumed responsibility for the family debts, which were valued at approximately $239,000. The court found that the agreement contained in the Minutes of Settlement did contain special provisions respecting the financial obligations of the spouses or the division or transfer of their property. It found that there were an indirect benefit to the children because of the size of the imbalance in the financial position between the parties and that it would be inequitable, if the husband were required to pay child support as set out in the Manitoba *Guidelines*. It would be inequitable to unravel the element of child support while leaving the distribution of the debt as is, from the parties' comprehensive and integrated settlement of their affairs when they concluded their Minutes of Settlement. Both parties had independent legal advice. The payments would no longer be tax deductible to the father.

The court, in allowing the father's appeal, varied the child support payment from the Table Amount of $1,600 per month for two children to $1,000 per month, payable in two equal installments. This amount reflected the father's increase in income, the special provisions of the agreement and the fact that the support payments for the children were no longer tax deductible.

In *Evans v. Gravely* (2000), 2000 CarswellOnt 4781, [2000] O.J. No. 4748, 14 R.F.L. (5th) 74 (S.C.J.), before Benotto J., the parties had signed Minutes of Settlement, which were incorporated into an order in1995. The order provided for a shared parenting plan and there was no provision for the payment of child support by one parent to the other. The court held that where there is a parenting plan and no provision for child support, there is no special provision that benefits the child which would cause the court to exercise its discretion not to apply the *Guidelines*. Provisions found in the order do not overcome the presumptive rule in the *Guidelines*.

In *May-Rutter v. Crisp* (2002), 29 R.F.L. (5th) 402, 2002 CarswellOnt 2239 (Div. Ct.), the parties consented to an order declared to be a final judgment after trial that amounts payable to the children as disability benefits would be deductible by the husband from the child support he was otherwise required to pay. In subsequent proceedings by the wife, the issue was found to be *res judicata*. Furthermore, where the parties had consented, the exception regarding the deduction arrangement was supportable under s. 33(14) and (15) of the *Family Law Act*.

Even where parents in relatively equal bargaining positions, with independent legal advice, have bargained for payment of no child support, the court is entitled to review the agreement to ensure that it meets the child's best interests. An assessment of whether special provisions under s. 33(12) of the *Family Law Act* exist must be objective and with a child-centred focus: *Deiter v. Sampson* (2002), 31 R.F.L. (5th) 296, 2002 CarswellOnt 3603 (S.C.J.); affirmed (2004), 2004 CarswellOnt 934 (C.A.).

Child Support — Retroactive Orders

[*Authors' Note*: *D.B.S. v. S.R.G.*; *T.A.R. v. L.J.W.*; *Henry v. Henry*; *Hiemstra v. Hiemstra*, 2006 CarswellAlta 976, [2006] S.C.J. No. 37, 2006 CarswellAlta 977, 61 Alta. L.R. (4th) 1, 2006 SCC 37 was recently decided by the Supreme Court of Canada. Cases in this section decided before *D.B.S. v. S.R.G.*; *T.A.R. v. L.J.W.*; *Henry v. Henry*; *Hiemstra v. Hiemstra* (S.C.C.) should be relied on with caution in light of this decision.]

This section is organized into the following parts:

1. *D.B.S. v. S.R.G.*; *T.A.R. v. L.J.W.*; *Henry v. Henry*; *Hiemstra v. Hiemstra* (S.C.C.)
2. Meaning of Retroactive
3. Availability of Retroactive Orders
4. Objectives
5. Factors
6. The Commencement Date for Retroactive Child Support
7. Period of Retroactive Child Support — Is there a Limitation Period?
8. Jurisdiction Under Both the *Divorce Act* and Provincial Legislation
9. Whether Same Principles Apply Federally and Provincially
10. Guideline Formulas or Court's Discretion
11. Retroactive Child Support Ordered
12. No Retroactive Child Support When Payor Fulfilled His Support Obligation
13. General

1. — *D.B.S. v. S.R.G.*; *T.A.R. v. L.J.W.*; *Henry v. Henry*; *Hiemstra v. Hiemstra* (S.C.C.)

D.B.S. v. S.R.G.; *T.A.R. v. L.J.W.*; *Henry v. Henry*; *Hiemstra v. Hiemstra*, 2006 CarswellAlta 976, [2006] S.C.J. No. 37, 2006 CarswellAlta 977, 61 Alta. L.R. (4th) 1, 2006 SCC 37 (S.C.C.). These four Alberta cases were heard by a panel of seven judges. Bastarche J. with McLachlin C.J., LeBel and Deschamps JJ., wrote the majority judgement, and Abella J., with Fish and Charron JJ., wrote concurring reasons. The issue before the Court was the nature of parents' obligations to make child support payments for periods of time when the responsibility to do so was never identified, mush less enforced. This situation arises when the parent receiving support decides that he or she should have been paid more support than he or she received, even though there was no court order or separation agreement which provided for these higher payments. While the Court termed these awards retroactive awards, it pointed out that they were "retroactive" only in the sense that they were not dealing with future payments. The parents who were ordered to make these payments, were being ordered to do so, because, in hindsight, it was determined that the parents should have made these payments before.

Two of the appeals before the Court dealt with retroactive awards under the federal *Divorce Act* and two appeals were brought under the Alberta *Parentage and Maintenance Act*, R.S.A. 2000, c. P-1, now repealed. The parties in those cases accepted that that their cases would essentially be decided as if they fell under the federal system. Two cases dealt with claims where no support payments had ever been made and two asked for original awards to be increased. All of these cases concerned parents who failed to ask for increases in child support in a timely fashion. In each of the cases, the children lived prolonged periods without the support that they were entitled to have. Bastarache J. stated that whatever the outcome in these particular cases, the ultimate objective must be to make certain that children benefit from the support which they are owed, at the time they are owed it.

Mr. Justice Bastarache set out the particular legal principles to be considered in granting or refusing to grant retroactive child support. They are:

1. Retroactive awards are not truly retroactive. They do not hold parents to a legal standard that did not exist at the relevant time.

2. Retroactive awards should not be seen as exceptional orders to be made in exceptional circumstances. While such an order should not be presumed, it will not only be found in rare circumstances.

3. In exercising their discretion, courts should award retroactive support where fairness dictated it, but should keep in mind that certainty for payor parents was also an important principle.

4. A payor parent under the federal legislation has the obligation to increase his or her child support payments when his or her income rises.

5. Where the payor parent's income rises and the amount of child support does not, there will be an unfulfilled obligation that could later be enforced by a court.

6. An application is necessary to trigger the court's jurisdiction to make a retroactive award of child support.

7. It will not always be appropriate for a court to make a retroactive child support order. Such awards will not always conform to the purposes behind the child support regime. Such awards may cause hardship to a payor parent where prospective awards would not.

8. A court should strive for a holistic view of the matter and decide each case on the basis of its particular facts.

9. Parents have an obligation to support their children in a way commensurate with their incomes.

10. Bastarache J., at paragraph 50, held that "in exercising their own power to legislate matters concerning child support, the provinces need not conform to the paradigm espoused by the *Divorce Act* and the *Guidelines*." In this decision, the parties in the *D.B.S. v. S.R.G.* and *T.A.R. v. L.J.W.* cases, which proceeded under Alberta's now repealed *Parentage and Maintenance Act*, accepted that their cases would be decided substantially as if they fell under the federal system.

11. Delay in seeking child support is not presumptively justifiable.

12. Where the delay is caused by the recipient parent's unreasonableness and not by the payor parent's blameworthy conduct, the principle of certainty will be compelling. Nonetheless, unreasonable delay by the recipient parent does not have the effect of eliminating the payor parent's obligation. Child support is the right of the child and cannot be waived by the parent.

13. Recipient parents must act promptly and responsibly in monitoring the amount of child support paid. From the child's point of view, a retroactive award is a poor substitute for past obligations not met.

14. A payor parent who knowingly avoids or diminishes his/her support obligation to his or her children should not be allowed to benefit from such conduct.

15. The conduct of the payor parent could militate against a retroactive award where the payor parent's conduct has had the effect of fulfilling his or her support obligation.

16. Courts should consider the present circumstances of the child, as a child who is currently enjoying a relatively high standard of living may benefit less from a retroactive award than a child who is currently in need. Need is an important factor when courts consider retroactive awards. It is significant to consider the child's needs at the time that the support should have been paid. A child who experienced hardship in the past may be compensated for this experience with a retroactive award. A child, who had all the advantages, is less likely to receive retroactive support.

17. Courts should try to craft retroactive awards in a way that minimizes the payor parent and his other dependants' hardship.

18. A retroactive award should be retroactive to the date when effective notice was give to the payor parent that support should be paid or that the amount being paid is inadequate.

19. It will usually be inappropriate to make a support award retroactive to a date more than 3 years before formal notice was given to the payor parent.

20. The date when increased support should have been paid will be a more appropriate date from which retroactive support should begin, when the payor parent engages in blameworthy conduct such as when he or she intimidates and lies to the recipient parent, but also when he or she withholds information. When a payor parent does not disclose a material change in circumstances, including an increase in income, the presumptive date may be moved to the time that the circumstances changed materially.

21. Undue hardship arguments under s. 10 are available in determinations of retroactive child support awards and will generally be easier to show in such cases than in determinations of prospective awards.

22. In summary, on an application for retroactive support, a court must consider:

(a) whether the recipient parent has supplied a reasonable excuse for the delay;

(b) the conduct of the payor parent;

(c) the circumstances of the children; and

(d) the hardship the retroactive award might entail.

Abella J. (with Fish, Charron JJ.) concurred in the results of the appeals, but differed in respect to Bastarache J.'s views about the presumptive starting date for the calculation of child support arrears, about the relevance of blameworthy conduct, and about the desirability of a 3-year limitation period. Abella J.'s justification for her different view was based on the underlying premise that parents have a free-standing joint obligation to support their children based on their ability to do so.

She agreed with Bastarache J. that these awards are not in fact "retroactive" awards, as they are instead compensation for what is legally owed.

She added that since only the payor parent knows when there has been a change in income that would justify an increase in child support, he or she should have the major responsibility for ensuring that a child benefits from the change as soon as is reasonably possible. To require the recipient parent to ensure that the payor parent is paying a fair amount is impractical and unrealistic. The presumptive starting point for payment of an increased amount of support should be when the change occurred, not when the change was disclosed or discovered. The need for certainty for payor parents and a child's entitlement to support in accordance with parental ability to pay are not inconsistent propositions.

There should be no role for "blameworthy conduct" in determining the date at which children can recover the support to which they are entitled. The amount of support should fluctuate with the amount of income, regardless of parental misconduct.

The recipient parent should not be required to demonstrate that the payor parent's failure to pay increased support resulted in hardship for the child. The debt remains nonetheless. Having a presumptive date of entitlement to increased child support, does not eliminate judicial discretion.

If a recipient parent has delayed in seeking increased support, it should not usually affect child support awards.

There should not be any automatic time limit on the amount of retroactive support. However, undue hardship could militate against a retroactive order being made as of the date of the change of circumstances. The 3-year rule is an unnecessary fettering of judicial discretion.

2. — Meaning of Retroactive

Retroactive awards are not truly retroactive. They do not hold parents to a legal standard that did not exist at the relevant time: *D.B.S. v. S.R.G.*; *T.A.R. v. L. J.W.*; *Henry v. Henry*; *Hiemstra v. Hiemstra*, 2006 CarswellAlta 976, [2006] S.C.J. No. 37, 2006 CarswellAlta 977, 61 Alta. L.R. (4th) 1, 2006 SCC 37 (S.C.C.).

Strictly speaking, it is incorrect to characterize child support awarded for a period of time that passed prior to the making of the order as "retroactive" support. It is not retroactive in the sense that the order creates an obligation to pay support for this period where no such obligation existed before. Unlike the case in some other areas of the law, a retroactive order for child support does not impose an obligation that did not exist at first instance. The obligation comes into existence at the moment of the birth of the child and persists whether or not an action for support is commenced: *MacMinn v. MacMinn* (1995), 17 R.F.L. (4th) 88, 174 A.R. 261, 102 W.A.C. 261, 1995 CarswellAlta 813 (Alta. C.A.); additional reasons at (1997), 29 R.F.L. (4th) 206, 209 A.R. 58, 160 W.A.C. 58, 1997 CarswellAlta 697 (Alta. C.A.); *S. (L.) v. P. (E.)*, 50 R.F.L. (4th) 302, 175 D.L.R. (4th) 423, 126 B.C.A.C. 28, 206 W.A.C. 28, 67 B.C.L.R. (3d) 254, [1999] 12 W.W.R. 718, 1999 CarswellBC 1402 (B.C. C.A.); leave to appeal refused (1999), 252 N.R. 194 (note), 135 B.C.A.C. 160 (note), 221 W.A.C. 160 (note), [1999] 3 S.C.R. xii, 179 D.L.R. (4th) vii (S.C.C.).

3. — Availability of Retroactive Orders

Retroactive awards should not be seen as exceptional orders to be made in exceptional circumstances. While such an order should not be presumed, it will not only be found in rare circumstances: *D.B.S. v. S.R.G.*; *T.A.R. v. L. J.W.*; *Henry v. Henry*; *Hiemstra v. Hiemstra*, 2006 CarswellAlta 976, [2006] S.C.J. No. 37, 2006 CarswellAlta 977, 61 Alta. L.R. (4th) 1, 2006 SCC 37 (S.C.C.).

An order for the payment of child support should generally be made retroactive to the date upon which the application was filed. Retroactive awards to a date prior to the filing of the application should be made only in exceptional circumstances, taking into account any blame on the part of the payor and reasonable diligence on the part of the claimant to pursue a remedy: *Ennis v. Ennis*, 2000 CarswellAlta 79, [2000] A.J. No. 75, 281 A.R. 161, 248 W.A.C. 161, 5 R.F.L. (5th) 302, 77 Alta. L.R. (3d) 289, 2000 ABCA 33 (Alta. C.A.); *MacNeal v. MacNeal* (1993), 50 R.F.L. (3d) 235, 1993 CarswellOnt 369 (Ont. Gen. Div.); additional reasons at (1994), 1994 CarswellOnt 4344 (Ont. Gen. Div.). In *MacNeal*, the court held where need is shown, support should be retroactive to at least the date the spouse obtaining the order made known his or her intention to seek support. Retroactive support was ordered from the date of the statement of claim to the date of the interim support order, in the form of a lump sum of $4,500.

Only in special or exceptional circumstances: Retroactive support should only be ordered in special or exceptional circumstances: *Andries v. Andries*, 1998 CarswellMan 180, [1998] M.J. No. 196, 36 R.F.L. (4th) 175, 159 D.L.R. (4th) 665, 126 Man. R. (2d) 189, 167 W.A.C. 189, [1998] 7 W.W.R. 536 (Man. C.A.); *Trick v. Trick* (2003), 2003 CarswellOnt 1103, 39 R.F.L. (5th) 418 (Ont. S.C.J.). [But see *D.B.S. v. S.R.G.*; *T.A.R. v. L. J.W.*; *Henry v. Henry*; *Hiemstra v. Hiemstra*, above.]

Presumption against retroactive orders: The "norm" is to restrict the extension of the order backward in time to the date of the application. The concern about any farther backward extension is that payors, who reasonably thought there would be no support liability for this period, would be unfairly treated: *S. (L.) v. P. (E.)*, 50 R.F.L. (4th) 302, 175 D.L.R. (4th) 423, 126 B.C.A.C. 28, 206 W.A.C. 28, 67 B.C.L.R. (3d) 254, [1999] 12 W.W.R. 718, 1999 CarswellBC 1402 (B.C. C.A.); leave to appeal refused 252 N.R. 194 (note), 135 B.C.A.C. 160 (note), 221 W.A.C. 160 (note), [1999] 3 S.C.R. xii, 179 D.L.R. (4th) vii (S.C.C.).

The decision to award retroactive support should be exercised sparingly: *Marinangeli v. Marinangeli* (2003), 2003 CarswellOnt 2691, 38 R.F.L. (5th) 307, 174 O.A.C. 76, 228 D.L.R. (4th) 376, 66 O.R. (3d) 40 (Ont. C.A.).

Retroactive variation orders, whether they impose new obligations or grant relief from old obligations, are inherently unfair and should only be made where exceptional circumstances are shown to exist: *Colbert v. Andersen* (2003), 2003 CarswellMan 29, 171 Man. R. (2d) 97, 2003 MBQB 13 (Q.B.). [But see *D.B.S. v. S.R.G.*; *Henry v. Henry*; and *Hiemstra v. Hiemstra*, above].

4. — Objectives

Courts should award retroactive support where fairness dictates it, but should keep in mind that certainty for payor parents is also an important principle: *D.B.S. v. S.R.G.*; *T.A.R. v. L.J.W.*; *Henry v. Henry*; *Hiemstra v. Hiemstra*, 2006 CarswellAlta 976, [2006] S.C.J. No. 37, 2006 CarswellAlta 977, 61 Alta. L.R. (4th) 1, 2006 SCC 37 (S.C.C.).

Parents have an obligation to support their children in a way commensurate with their incomes: *D.B.S. v. S.R.G.*; *T.A.R. v. L. J.W.*; *Henry v. Henry*; *Hiemstra v. Hiemstra*, above.

A court should strive for a holistic view in determining retroactive child support and decide each case on the basis of its particular facts: *D.B.S. v. S.R.G.*; *T.A.R. v. L.J.W.*; *Henry v. Henry*; *Hiemstra v. Hiemstra*, above.

"In considering retroactive child support, it is important to keep in mind that the overall purpose of the Guidelines requires a parent to put the interests of the child first in terms of financial support. . .[If] the child is a 'child of the marriage' within the meaning of the Act, putting the interests of the child first requires a parent not to act in his or her own self-interest at the expense of the child. . .. [P]utting the interests of the child first also requires a parent to ensure that a divorce from his or her spouse affects the child as little as possible:" *Horner v. Horner* (2004), 6 R.F.L. (6th) 140, 2004 CarswellOnt 4246, 245 D.L.R. (4th) 410, 191 O.A.C. 28, 72 O.R. (3d) 561 (Ont. C.A.).

Support should not be limited to current needs. The consequences of endorsing the contrary approach "would be punitive for children and the custodial parent": *MacMinn v. MacMinn* (1995), 17 R.F.L. (4th) 88, 174 A.R. 261, 102 W.A.C. 261, 1995 CarswellAlta 813 (Alta. C.A.); additional reasons at (1997), 29 R.F.L. (4th) 206, 209 A.R. 58, 160 W.A.C. 58, 1997 CarswellAlta 697 (Alta. C.A.).

Parents are jointly responsible for child support: In recognition of this principle, the courts have ordered retroactive support where the custodial parent has borne a disproportionate share of child expenses, and fairness and justice require that the parent be compensated for these expenses: *S. (L.) v. P. (E.)*, 50 R.F.L. (4th) 302, 175 D.L.R. (4th) 423, 126 B.C.A.C. 28, 206 W.A.C. 28, 67 B.C.L.R. (3d) 254, [1999] 12 W.W.R. 718, 1999 CarswellBC 1402 (B.C. C.A.); leave to appeal refused 252 N.R. 194 (note), 135 B.C.A.C. 160 (note), 221 W.A.C. 160 (note), [1999] 3 S.C.R. xii, 179 D.L.R. (4th) vii (S.C.C.).

Retroactive support may be regarded as a "compensatory" payment. The element of compensation may have aspects similar to compensation in a claim for unjust enrichment. In *Denesi v. Neves* (1998), 36 R.F.L. (4th) 154, [1998] O.J. No. 736, 1998 CarswellOnt 1074 (Ont. Prov. Div.), the court found that by not paying the support he should have paid, "the father has managed to live a highly comfortable lifestyle by *intentionally* depriving his own children out of almost $200,000 in support over the past decade." The father "profited handsomely to the tune of some $200,000". The court made an order for $199,272 for retroactive support ("arrears") for 9 years by determining the difference between what the father actually paid during this time and what he should have paid.

5. — Factors

In *D.B.S. v. S.R.G.*; *T.A.R. v. L. J.W.*; *Henry v. Henry*; *Hiemstra v. Hiemstra*, 2006 CarswellAlta 976, [2006] S.C.J. No. 37, 2006 CarswellAlta 977, 61 Alta. L.R. (4th) 1, 2006 SCC 37 (S.C.C.), the court set our four factors which should be considered on an application for child support. These are:

(a) whether the recipient parent has supplied a reasonable excuse for the delay;

(b) the conduct of the payor parent;

(c) the circumstances of the children; and

(d) the hardship the retroactive award might entail.

These factors were very similar to those set out in *Horner v. Horner* (2004), 6 R.F.L. (6th) 140, 2004 CarswellOnt 4246, 245 D.L.R. (4th) 410, 191 O.A.C. 28, 72 O.R. (3d) 561 (Ont. C.A.). Weiler J., in the *Horner* case set out the considerations in determining whether retroactive child support should be ordered. They are:

(a) the need on the part of the child and ability to pay of the payor parent;

(b) whether the payor parent had engaged in "blameworthy" conduct;

(c) whether a retroactive order would cause an unreasonable or unfair burden on the payor; and

(d) the delay in seeking increased child support and any explanation for the delay.

Weiler J. distinguished the *Horner* case (above) from the *Walsh* case, below, since in *Walsh* the court was dealing with an appeal from an interim order that in effect granted a final order by awarding retroactive child support to four years before the applicant began her application. The judge who heard the application did not make a finding of a "change of circumstances" and did not find that the needs of the children required a retroactive increase. The increase in *Walsh* was based on the fact that the *Guidelines* gave the judge an inherent discretion to vary the order. In the *Horner* case, there was no disagreement that the father's increase in income resulted in a change in circumstances pursuant to the parties' separation agreement. Further, the parties' amended agreement was a domestic contract pursuant to s. 56(4) of the Ontario *Family Law Act*. Under that provision there was a statutory duty to make disclosure when the amendment to the agreement was signed. The husband had failed to make full disclosure.

(a) — Delay

Whether the recipient parent has supplied a reasonable excuse for the delay is one of the four factors to be considered on an application for retroactive child support: *D.B.S. v. S.R.G.*; *T.A.R. v. L. J.W.*; *Henry v. Henry*; *Hiemstra v. Hiemstra*, above.

Delay in seeking child support is not presumptively justifiable: *D.B.S. v. S.R.G.*; *T.A.R. v. L. J.W.*; *Henry v. Henry*; *Hiemstra v. Hiemstra*, above.

Where the delay is caused by the recipient parent's unreasonableness and not by the payor parent's blameworthy conduct, the principle of certainty will be compelling. Nonetheless, unreasonable delay by the recipient parent does not have the effect of eliminating the payor parent's obligation. Child support is the right of the child and cannot be waived by the parent: *D.B.S. v. S.R.G.*; *T.A.R. v. L. J.W.*; *Henry v. Henry*; *Hiemstra v. Hiemstra*, above.

Recipient parents must act promptly and responsibly in monitoring the amount of child support paid. From the child's point of view, a retroactive award is a poor substitute for past obligations not met: *D.B.S. v. S.R.G.*; *T.A.R. v. L. J.W.*; *Henry v. Henry*; *Hiemstra v. Hiemstra*, above.

Child support is the right of the child, not of the parent: A fundamental tenet of the law is that the right to child support is the right belonging to the child, not the parent. "As the right belongs to the child it cannot be waived or bargained away by the custodial parent or lost due to that parent's neglect, delay, or lack of diligence in enforcing the right:" *S. (L.) v. P. (E.)*, 50 R.F.L. (4th) 302, 175 D.L.R. (4th) 423, 126 B.C.A.C. 28, 206 W.A.C. 28, 67 B.C.L.R. (3d) 254, [1999] 12 W.W.R. 718, 1999 CarswellBC 1402 (B.C. C.A.); leave to appeal refused 252 N.R. 194 (note), 135 B.C.A.C. 160 (note), 221 W.A.C. 160 (note), [1999] 3 S.C.R. xii, 179 D.L.R. (4th) vii (S.C.C.); *Richardson v. Richardson*, 7 R.F.L. (3d) 304, 17 C.P.C. (2d) 104, 38 D.L.R. (4th) 699, 77 N.R. 1, 22 O.A.C. 1, [1987] 1 S.C.R. 857, 1987 CarswellOnt 315, [1987] S.C.J. No. 30, EYB 1987-67464 (S.C.C.).

In *Morgan v. Morgan* (2006), 2006 CarswellBC 1940, 2006 BCSC 1197 (B.C. S.C.), the court rejected the application for retroactive child support where the husband did not inform the wife of his increased income. The court could not conclude that her delay was reasonable, as there was no evidence that she tried to find out whether the husband was meeting his child support obligations. However, as the husband contributed to the delay in failing to disclose his income and increase his support payments, the court did not consider this factor significant. After considering the four factors set out in *D.B.S. v.*

S.R.G.; *T.A.R. v. L. J.W.*; *Henry v. Henry*; *Hiemstra v. Hiemstra*, above, the court held that retroactive child support should not be granted. The fact that the husband failed to disclose his increased income and pay increased child support did not outweigh the fact that the child did not need a retroactive award.

The court in *Park v. Thompson* (2005), 2005 CarswellOnt 1632, [2005] O.J. No. 1695, 252 D.L.R. (4th) 730, 13 R.F.L. (6th) 415, 77 O.R. (3d) 601, 197 O.A.C. 158 (Ont. C.A.), set aside the part of the order concerning retroactivity and directed a trial of that issue and other issues where the Appellate Court held that the Application judge erred in his application of the factors adopted in *Walsh v. Walsh* (2004), 2004 CarswellOnt 356, 69 O.R. (3d) 577, 183 O.A.C. 179, 46 R.F.L. (5th) 455 (Ont. C.A.); additional reasons at (2004), 2004 CarswellOnt 1389, 6 R.F.L. (6th) 432 (Ont. C.A.). Contrary to the evidence, the trial judge had found that the mother's delay in pursuing support was not unreasonable because the father knew from the date that he stopped paying child support in November 2002, that a claim for child support would be pursued. The Appellate Court found that while there was an exchange of correspondence concerning the daughter's relationship with her father, there was nothing at that time to indicate that the mother intended to pursue child support. Also, the fact that the child was attending a private school and that the father had a pre-existing contractual agreement to pay child support were important factors relating to the question of need. The application judge did not consider any other relevant factors in *Walsh*, including whether the mother had been required to encroach on capital or incur debt, or, most importantly, whether the father presently had the ability to pay in light of his obligations to his new family. While it is not necessary to refer expressly to all of the factors in *Walsh*, the judge should refer to those factors clearly raised by the circumstances of the case and that are not clearly neutral in their application.

A court is more likely to order retroactive payments where there is a clear and compelling explanation to excuse the custodial parent's delay in pursuing child support: *S. (L.) v. P. (E.)*, above.

In *Maloney v. Maloney* (1998), 1998 CarswellNfld 347, 171 Nfld. & P.E.I.R. 38, 525 A.P.R. 38 (Nfld. U.F.C.), the father knew that his daughter was no longer attending university, but he did not apply to vary support for another year. He unilaterally stopped paying support for his two children, the younger of whom was attending university. His decision adversely affected the mother financially. The court decided to eliminate support from the time of the father's application to vary. The arrears were set at $6,345 and were to be paid in monthly payments of $100.

The determining factor for a retroactive variation of child support is the actual cost of raising and caring for the children. It is incumbent upon the custodial spouse not to delay in seeking a legal remedy: *Macbeth v. Macbeth* (1998), 1998 CarswellAlta 136, [1998] A.J. No. 195, 36 R.F.L. (4th) 390, 214 A.R. 104 (Alta. Q.B.).

A court should not order retroactive support where the applicant has failed to show reasonable diligence to pursue an increase in child support, where the applicant is a family law practitioner who should be held to a higher standard than the average applicant and where, most importantly, it is not in the best interests of the children: *Pollard v. Pollard* (1999), 1999 CarswellAlta 1189, 257 A.R. 36, 1999 ABQB 976, 75 Alta. L.R. (3d) 350, [2000] 3 W.W.R. 322, (sub nom. *C.M.P. v. P.E.P.)* [1999] A.J. No. 1478 (Alta. Q.B.). As the children were currently residing with their father, the payor for most of the period since the parties' separation, if the court awarded retroactive support, it would be taking money away from the home in which the children were currently residing. Such an award would enrich the non-custodial parent which is not the purpose of a retroactive support award. Consequently, the application for retroactive support was denied.

In *Budyk v. Sol* (1998), 40 R.F.L. (4th) 348, (sub nom. *Budyk v. Budyk)* 126 Man. R. (2d) 305, (sub nom. *Budyk v. Budyk)* 167 W.A.C. 305, 1998 CarswellMan 224, [1998] M.J. No. 252 (Man. C.A.), a retroactive child support order was upheld on appeal on the basis that the father had delayed the original proceedings by failing to provide financial information promptly.

(b) — The Conduct of the Parent

The conduct of the parent is one of the four factors which should be considered on an application for child support: *D.B.S. v. S.R.G.*; *T.A.R. v. L.J.W.*; *Henry v. Henry*; *Hiemstra v. Hiemstra*, above.

A payor parent who knowingly avoids or diminishes his/her support obligation to his or her children should not be allowed to benefit from such conduct: *D.B.S. v. S.R.G.*; *T.A.R. v. L.J.W.*; *Henry v. Henry*; *Hiemstra v. Hiemstra*, above.

"Courts should not hesitate to take into account a payor parent's blameworthy conduct in considering the propriety of a retroactive award... . [C]ourts should take an expansive view of what constitutes blameworthy conduct in this context. I would characterize as blameworthy conduct anything that privileges the payor parent's own interests over his/her children's right to an appropriate amount of support": *D.B.S. v. S.R.G.*; *T.A.R. v. L.J.W.*; *Henry v. Henry*; *Hiemstra v. Hiemstra*, above, per Bastarache J.

In *Morgan v. Morgan*, above, the court rejected the application for retroactive child support where the husband's conduct was blameworthy, as he failed to disclose his increase in income and pay greater child support. However, he did pay $150 per child per month more support than he was required under court order to pay. He also paid for one child's health, clothing and extracurricular expenses. There is no evidence that her standard of living departed from the means of her parents as a result of the husband's failure to disclose his income and increase his support payments. The court held that the husband's failure to disclose his increased income and pay increased child support did not outweigh the fact that the child did not need a retroactive award.

A court will order retroactive child support where a payor parent, the step-father in this case, had a substantial increase in income but failed to report it as ordered by the court: *H. (U.V.) v. H. (M.W.)* (2006), 2006 CarswellBC 2008, 2006 BCSC 1160 (B.C. S.C.). The step-father sought to excuse his conduct because he delivered the support cheques directly to the plaintiff's counsel's office, and her lawyer failed to enquire about his income. The court held that there was no duty imposed upon the plaintiff or her counsel to enquire; the duty rested with the defendant stepfather.

While the court did order retroactive child support, it did not do so for the full period requested, as the defendant's failure to provide financial information due to lack of preparation of financial statements and income tax returns was innocent rather than blameworthy: *Ladd v. Ladd* (2006), 2006 CarswellBC 2088, 2006 BCSC 1280 (B.C. S.C.). In other circumstances, such conduct could be found to be blameworthy.

In circumstances where the payor husband was well aware of his obligation to make full and complete disclosure upon which support payments were to be calculated and did not do so, and he knew of the children's need for support, the court found that he both failed to recognize an obvious need for support and failed to disclose a greatly increased income from at least 1998 to 2001: *Burke v. Burke*, 2 Alta. L.R. (4th) 67, 26 R.F.L. (5th) 1, [2002] A.J. No. 385, [2002] 6 W.W.R. 670, 2002 CarswellAlta 380, 2002 ABQB 281 (Alta. Q.B.). It was insufficient that the payor made expenditures on the children's behalf unilaterally when he was not contributing to maintenance payable on a continual basis. The court ordered retroactive child support for 2 of the 4 years when the payor had an enhanced income in the amount of the difference between the child support which should have been paid, and that which was paid.

Without a contractual duty to disclose an increase in income, failure to disclose an increase does not permit a court to award a retroactive increase in child support. The payee must in fact, determine the payor's change in income, apply for a variation, establish a change of circumstances, and if seeking a retroactive order, establish ability to pay and need during the relevant period: *Walsh v. Walsh*, above.

The court would not interfere with a settlement and order retroactive support, even though the payor's income had increased since execution of the agreement where the applicant had legal advice and there was no evidence of coercion and no evidence that the amount agreed upon was insufficient for the support of the children: *Norris v. Norris*, 2005 CarswellNWT 10, 14 R.F.L. (6th) 49, 2005 NWTSC 18 (N.W.T. S.C.). Although retroactive support was not referred to in the settlement proposal made by the respondent and accepted by the applicant, it was clear from the parties' e-mails that there had been discussion of it. The applicant did not pursue it at the time the corollary relief order was sought. The court inferred that it was considered to be part of the settlement since no other explanation for why she did not pursue the claim at that time arises from the material before the court.

Retroactive support is only obtainable from the date that paternity is established: *G. (E.) v. D. (R.)* (2003), 2003 CarswellAlta 1451, 2003 ABQB 695, 45 R.F.L. (5th) 203 (Alta. Q.B.). Before that time, in this case, there was no blameworthy conduct on the part of the father in not providing support. The father promptly complied with requests for disclosure of income. However, it was reasonable that the father should be liable for child support from the time that he was certain that he was the father.

Where the father had deceived the mother about his income at the time of settlement of child support, she was later awarded retroactive child support in her application under the *Guidelines* to vary the support payable: *Brans v. Brans* (2000), 2000 CarswellOnt 4897, 13 R.F.L. (5th) 335 (Ont. S.C.J.); additional reasons at (2001), 2001 CarswellOnt 1096 (Ont. S.C.J.).

Orders for retroactive child support should only be made in situations where the payor parent avoided the obligation to pay child support for a period in the past without justification: *Ackland v. Brooks* (2001), 19 R.F.L. (5th) 7, 2001 CarswellBC 1568, 2001 BCSC 877 (B.C. S.C.).

(c) — The Circumstances of the Children

The circumstances of the children is one of the four factors which should be considered on an application for child support: *D.B.S. v. S.R.G.*; *T.A.R. v. L.J.W.*; *Henry v. Henry*; *Hiemstra v. Hiemstra*, above.

In *D.B.S. v. S.R.G.*; *T.A.R. v. L.J.W.*; *Henry v. Henry*; *Hiemstra v. Hiemstra*, above, the court held that courts should consider the present circumstances of the child, since a child who is currently enjoying a relatively high standard of living may benefit less from a retroactive award than a child who is currently in need. Need is an important factor when courts consider retroactive awards. It is significant to consider the child's needs at the time that the support should have been paid. A child who experienced hardship in the past may be compensated for this experience with a retroactive award. A child, who had all the advantages, is less likely to receive retroactive support.

In *Morgan v. Morgan* (2006), 2006 CarswellBC 1940, 2006 BCSC 1197 (B.C. S.C.), above, the court rejected the application for retroactive child support. While the husband failed to disclose his increased income and pay increased child support, that failure did not outweigh the fact that the child did not need a retroactive award.

Where a woman has a child who is not the child of her husband and she does not bring parentage proceedings against the biological father for many years (until the child was eight years old), the court will not award retroactive child support where the child was not in need: *P. (N.J.) v. H. (D.W.)* (2006), 2006 CarswellAlta 586, 2006 ABQB 352 (Alta. Q.B.); additional reasons at (2006), 2006 CarswellAlta 945, 2006 ABQB 548 (Alta. Q.B.). While the benefit to the child is the primary consideration, in this case, retroactive child support was denied. The biological father was not given any opportunity to parent this child. The mother's delay acted against her, as it is very difficult for a biological parent to answer a claim that has been so long delayed, to assess its fairness or the necessity of it. It is highly likely that the expenses for which payment is sought have been covered by the husband, who probably acted in *loco parentis*. Further, the evidence is not clear on major matters. While laches is generally not to be raised in cases of child support, in this case, where the child has been apparently provided for in a marriage situation, there was a basis to deny a retroactive order.

Before ordering retroactive support the court should be satisfied that during the period in question the child was in need of support and the non-custodial parent had the ability to pay support: *S. (L.) v. P. (E.)*, above.

(d) — The Hardship the Retroactive Award Might Entail

The hardship the retroactive award might entail is one of the four factors which should be considered on an application for child support: *D.B.S. v. S.R.G.*; *T.A.R. v. L. J.W.*, *Henry v. Henry*; *Hiemstra v. Hiemstra*, above.

It will not always be appropriate for a court to make a retroactive child support order. Such awards will not always conform to the purposes behind the child support regime. Such awards may cause hardship to a payor parent where prospective awards would not: *D.B.S. v. S.R.G.*; *T.A.R. v. L. J.W.*, *Henry v. Henry*; *Hiemstra v. Hiemstra*, above.

Courts should try to craft retroactive awards in a way that minimizes the payor parent and his other dependants' hardship: *D.B.S. v. S.R.G.*; *T.A.R. v. L. J.W.*; *Henry v. Henry*; *Hiemstra v. Hiemstra*, above.

Undue hardship arguments under s. 10 are available in determinations of retroactive child support awards and will generally be easier to show in such cases than in determinations of prospective awards: *D.B.S. v. S.R.G.*; *T.A.R. v. L. J.W.*; *Henry v. Henry*; *Hiemstra v. Hiemstra*, above.

In *Morgan v. Morgan*, above, the court rejected the application for retroactive child support, even though the payor parent's payment of retroactive child support would not cause him to suffer hardship. He had assets with which he could satisfy such an award.

Unreasonable burden for the non-custodial parent: The court is less likely to award retroactive support in cases where the order would place an unreasonable burden on the non-custodial parent, and especially where it would prejudice that parent's ability to pay ongoing support: *S. (L.) v. P. (E.)*, above.

No unreasonable burden on the payor spouse: The court in *Marinangeli v. Marinangeli* (2003), 2003 CarswellOnt 2691, 38 R.F.L. (5th) 307, [2003] O.J. No. 2819, 174 O.A.C. 76, 228 D.L.R. (4th) 376, 66 O.R. (3d) 40 (Ont. C.A.) added the factor, "no unreasonable burden on the payor spouse" to those set out in *S. (L.) v. P. (E.)*, above. In the *Marinangeli* case, the appeal by the appellant from a judgement ordering him to pay retroactive child and spousal support to the mother was dismissed, except for child support awarded in accordance with the *Guidelines* for a period prior to their coming into force. Support prior to the *Guidelines* must be based on evidence of need as might be shown in a budget. Since no budget had been submitted for this period, the Appellate Court refused to allow the retroactive order to extend that far back.

The determining factor for a retroactive variation of child support is the actual cost of raising and caring for the children. It is incumbent upon the custodial spouse not to delay in seeking a legal remedy: *Macbeth v. Macbeth* (1998), 1998 CarswellAlta 136, [1998] A.J. No. 195, 36 R.F.L. (4th) 390, 214 A.R. 104 (Alta. Q.B.).

Retroactive child support will not be awarded where to do so would create an unreasonable and unfair burden on the child's step-father while at the same time provide a windfall for the mother. There would be no real benefit for the child who was working to support himself and to contribute to the support of his mother. Any support from the step-father could not compensate the child for his lost adolescence: *Deimuth v. Fortin*, 37 R.F.L. (5th) 69, 2003 CarswellMan 55, 2003 MBQB 36, [2003] M.J. No. 60, 171 Man. R. (2d) 143, [2003] 5 W.W.R. 711 (Man. Q.B.).

(e) — Other Factors

General

In *Conrad v. Rafuse*, 2002 CarswellNS 181, 2002 NSCA 60, 212 D.L.R. (4th) 236, 27 R.F.L. (5th) 315, 205 N.S.R. (2d) 46, 643 A.P.R. 46, [2002] N.S.J. No. 208 (N.S. C.A.), the court specifically approved *S. (L.) v. P. (E.)*, 50 R.F.L. (4th) 302, 175 D.L.R. (4th) 423, 126 B.C.A.C. 28, 206 W.A.C. 28, 67 B.C.L.R. (3d) 254, [1999] 12 W.W.R. 718, 1999 CarswellBC 1402 (B.C. C.A.); leave to appeal refused 252 N.R. 194 (note), 135 B.C.A.C. 160 (note), 221 W.A.C. 160 (note), [1999] 3 S.C.R. xii, 179 D.L.R. (4th) vii (S.C.C.). The court agreed with the analysis in the *S. (L.) v. P. (E.)* case and adopted the policy considerations and factors as listed in that case as relevant to the review of the exercise of discretion in the case. The court was satisfied that the trial judge properly considered and weighed each of the possibly relevant factors, and, given the scarcity of evidence, drew permissible inferences where appropriate, in finding that:

- a retroactive order would benefit the child;
- the appellant had an ability to pay towards a retroactive award;
- there was no bad faith on behalf of the respondent;
- the respondent must have subsidized the child support shortfall;
- the appellant did not make any contribution outside the amount ordered; and,
- the mother's relatively short delay in proceeding and the father's absence of financial disclosure ought not to affect the child adversely.

At common law, the court is always able to intervene and to determine the appropriate level of support: *Richardson v. Richardson*, [1987] 1 S.C.R. 857, 1987 CarswellOnt 315, 1987 CarswellOnt 963, 17 C.P.C. (2d) 104, 38 D.L.R. (4th) 699, 77 N.R. 1, 22 O.A.C. 1, 7 R.F.L. (3d) 304, [1987] S.C.J. No. 30, EYB 1987-67464 (S.C.C.); *Horner v. Horner* (2004), 6 R.F.L. (6th) 140, 2004 CarswellOnt 4246, 245 D.L.R. (4th) 410, 191 O.A.C. 28, 72 O.R. (3d) 561 (Ont. C.A.).

Using capital or incurring debt: "If. . .it appears that too little was paid by the non-custodial parent to the principal custodial parent to support the children and the result is that the custodial parent has had to call on resources such as capital or debt that should not have had to be used, then it is appropriate for an award of retroactive child support to be made to restore the capital fund or pay off the debt which should not have had to be called on. Similarly, if the children go short of necessaries such as clothing in the interim period, a retroactive award can make that up by an amount sufficient to meet the shortfall. And if, as in this case, the award of permanent child support is designed not only to provide appropriate current support but also to create a fund for major intermittent future expenditures, then the trial judge has a discretion to enhance that fund from a retroactive award. But there is no absolute entitlement to a retroactive award embodying such an enhancement. And. . .to the extent that an award of retroactive child support is properly seen as a redistribution of capital or an award of spousal support in the guise of child support, such a retroactive award should not be made": *Macdonald v. Macdonald*, 2005 CarswellBC 48, 2005 BCCA 23, 10 R.F.L. (6th) 423 at 438, 37 B.C.L.R. (4th) 121, [2005] 4 W.W.R. 622, 207 B.C.A.C. 201, 341 W.A.C. 201, [2005] B.C.J. No. 38, ¶33 (B.C. C.A). In the *Macdonald* case, the Court of Appeal upheld the trial judge's decision granting partial retroactive child support. The court had ordered retroactive child support to September 2000, the effective date of an earlier order for child support, not from October 2002, the date of his judgement but also not back to June 1999, the time of service of the child support application. Consequently, the retroactivity was partial only and was calculated to balance the application of the relevant principles set out in *S. (L.) v. P. (E.)*.

See also *Skrivanek v. Pow* (2006), 2006 CarswellBC 1167, 2006 BCCA 239 (B.C. C.A.) which considered the factors identified in *S. (L.) v. P. (E.)* in awarding retroactive child support. The Appellate Court upheld the trial judge's award of $3,250 in retroactive child support which was approximately one-half of the debt that the appellant had incurred for property taxes after the separation. The court declined to consider the factors set out by the Alberta Court of Appeal in *S. (D.B.) v. G. (S.R.)* (2005), 2005 CarswellAlta 18, [2005] A.J. No. 2, 7 R.F.L. (6th) 373, 249 D.L.R. (4th) 72, 38 Alta. L.R. (4th) 199, 361 A.R. 60, 339 W.A.C. 60, [2005] 5 W.W.R. 229, 2005 ABCA 2 (Alta. C.A.), which at the time was under appeal to the Supreme Court of Canada, a case, which if followed, the appellant argued, would lead to a different result. However, the law of British Columbia and Alberta at the time of the hearing was different and the court held that the law of British Columbia must be followed. Subject to an adjournment of the hearing of this appeal, which was not sought, the appeal must be decided on the basis of the law of British Columbia as it now stands. It could not be said that the judge made any error in principle in the factors she considered in arriving at the award she determined to be appropriate.

Redistributing capital or awarding disguised spousal support: Courts have declined to award retroactive child support where to do so would amount to a redistribution of capital, or the awarding of spousal support in the guise of child support (no order for retroactive support should be made where the only purpose is to redistribute capital between the parties.): *S. (L.) v. P. (E.)*, above; *Hoar v. Hoar* (1993), 45 R.F.L. (3d) 105, 62 O.A.C. 50, 1993 CarswellOnt 29, [1993] O.J. No. 605 (Ont. C.A.).

Where the effect of awarding retroactive interim child support would actually amount to an award of additional spousal support, the application was refused in *Volken v. Volken* (2001), 19 R.F.L. (5th) 205, 2001 CarswellBC 1401, 2001 BCSC 970 (B.C. S.C. [In Chambers]).

Retroactive child support will not be awarded where to do so would create an unreasonable and unfair burden on the child's step-father while at the same time provide a windfall for the mother. There would be no real benefit for the child who was working to support himself and to contribute to the support of his mother. Any support from the step-father could not compensate the child for his lost adolescence: *Deimuth v. Fortin*, 37 R.F.L. (5th) 69, 2003 CarswellMan 55, 2003 MBQB 36, [2003] M.J. No. 60, 171 Man. R. (2d) 143, [2003] 5 W.W.R. 711 (Man. Q.B.).

Lump sum payment: In determining whether or not a retroactive child support order is appropriate, the court must ensure, should such a lump sum order be made, that the children will benefit first and foremost and not the custodial parent: *Hunt v. Smolis-Hunt*, 39 R.F.L. (4th) 143, 1998 CarswellAlta 427, [1998] 10 W.W.R. 1, 61 Alta. L.R. (3d) 279, 224 A.R. 68, [1998] A.J. No. 514 (Alta. Q.B.); reversed in part 2001 CarswellAlta 1357, [2001] A.J. No. 1170, 286 A.R. 248, 253 W.A.C. 248, [2001] 11 W.W.R. 233, 205 D.L.R. (4th) 712, 2001 ABCA 229, 20 R.F.L. (5th) 409, 97 Alta. L.R. (3d) 238 (Alta. C.A.).

Determination of income — 3-year averaging: In *Pawliuk v. Pawliuk* (1999), 48 R.F.L. (4th) 188, (sub nom. *E.J.P. v. P.M.P.)* 181 Sask. R. 212, 1999 CarswellSask 261 (Sask. Q.B.), the court dismissed the father's application for a retroactive variation of child support. The father claimed that his income had been incorrectly determined on an interim child support application. The interim determination of his income, calculated by using a 3-year average, was not a matter reviewable by the court or one that warranted retroactive consideration.

Disparity in incomes: Where the child left the custody of the mother to live with the father, the court, on appeal, allowed the father's application both to terminate the wife's child support order and to require her to pay child support to him in accordance with *Guideline* amounts. As the father's income was considerably larger than that of the mother, the court deemed it inequitable to require the mother to pay support retroactively to the date when the child actually moved out: *Birss v. Birss* (2000), 12 R.F.L. (5th) 9, 2000 CarswellOnt 5057, [2000] O.J. No. 3692 (Ont. Div. Ct.).

Presumption that a previous order is to be respected: A previous court order is assumed to be correct and should be respected unless it is reversed on appeal or varied: *S. (L.) v. P. (E.)*, 50 R.F.L. (4th) 302, 175 D.L.R. (4th) 423, 126 B.C.A.C. 28, 206 W.A.C. 28, 67 B.C.L.R. (3d) 254, [1999] 12 W.W.R. 718, 1999 CarswellBC 1402 (B.C. C.A.); leave to appeal refused 252 N.R. 194 (note), 135 B.C.A.C. 160 (note), 221 W.A.C. 160 (note), [1999] 3 S.C.R. xii, 179 D.L.R. (4th) vii (S.C.C.).

Encourage negotiated settlement: There is a strong policy interest in family law to encourage negotiated settlements to avoid the acrimonious, costly, and often destructive process of litigation. But the reach given to the policy of encouraging negotiated settlements must be constrained in light of the fundamental principle that child support is the right of the child and cannot be bargained away by either parent: *S. (L.) v. P. (E.)*, above.

6. — The Commencement Date for Retroactive Child Support

A payor parent under the federal legislation has the obligation to increase his or her child support payments when his or her income rises: *D.B.S. v. S.R.G.*; *T.A.R. v. L.J.W.*; *Henry v. Henry*; *Hiemstra v. Hiemstra*, 2006 CarswellAlta 976, [2006] S.C.J. No. 37, 2006 CarswellAlta 977, 61 Alta. L.R. (4th) 1, 2006 SCC 37 (S.C.C.).

A retroactive award should be retroactive to the date when effective notice was given to the payor parent that support should be paid or that the amount being paid is inadequate. "By 'effective notice' [to the payor parent, in determining the date to which a child support order should be retroactive], I am referring to any indication by the recipient parent that child support should be paid, or if it is, that the current amount of child support needs to be re-negotiated. Thus, effective notice does not require the recipient parent to take any legal action; all that is required is that the topic be broached:" *D.B.S. v. S.R.G.*; *T.A.R. v. L. J.W.*; *Henry v. Henry*; *Hiemstra v. Hiemstra*, above, per Bastarache J.

It will usually be inappropriate to make a support award retroactive to a date more than 3 years before formal notice was given to the payor parent: *D.B.S. v. S.R.G.*; *T.A.R. v. L. J.W.*; *Henry v. Henry*; *Hiemstra v. Hiemstra*, above.

The date when increased support should have been paid will be a more appropriate date from which retroactive support should begin, when the payor parent engages in blameworthy conduct such as when he or she intimidates and lies to the recipient parent, but also when he or she withholds information. When a payor parent does not disclose a material change in circumstances, including an increase in income, the presumptive date may be moved to the time that the circumstances changed materially: *S. (D.B.) v. G. (S.R.) [D.B.S. v. S.R.G.*; *T.A.R. v. L. J.W.*; *Henry v. Henry*; *Hiemstra v. Hiemstra]* (2006), 2006 CarswellAlta 976 (S.C.C.).

Where the parties execute an agreement whereby an unemployed father provides lump sum child support in lieu of future support payments, the court can order retroactive child support from the time that the father becomes employed: *B. (J.M.) v. B. (A.C.)*, 2006 CarswellAlta 533, [2006] A.J. No. 487, 27 R.F.L. (6th) 9, 2006 ABCA 150 (Alta. C.A.). Waivers of child support are not binding on a court. In this case, the new employment was a change in circumstances not contemplated by the parties at the time the agreement was made.

Child support should be retroactive to the date when the payor receives a promotion and thereby a significant increase in income, where it is appropriate in light of the overall purpose of the *Guidelines* to promote the interests of children first and applying the criteria for awarding retroactive child support: *Horner v. Horner* (2004), 6 R.F.L. (6th) 140, 2004 CarswellOnt 4246, 245 D.L.R. (4th) 410, 191 O.A.C. 28, 72 O.R. (3d) 561 (Ont. C.A.).

An increase in income triggers an increased obligation to pay child support: *S. (A.M.) v. I. (J.)* (2005), 2005 CarswellAlta 459, 366 A.R. 179, 2005 ABQB 255 (Alta. C.A.). While the payor contended that his employer would be eliminating any further overtime, the court held that until there had been an actual decrease in the amount of earnings from employment, it could not prospectively consider overtime as being eliminated in terms of the payor's income, and discount his income in advance. The payor in the past made the same argument and overtime was not eliminated. If overtime is eliminated, the payor can re-apply 12 months after the fact based on his reduced or non-existent overtime earnings.

The court in *Lahaye v. Dyck*, 2005 CarswellSask 414, [2005] S.J. No. 385, 18 R.F.L. (6th) 186, 2005 SKQB 267 (Sask. Q.B) held that the presumptive date for the commencement of a retroactive order is the date of an increase in the payor's income. The court did not accept the trilogy analysis which it considered reduced the discretion of the court and established a presumptive or automatic date for the commencement of a retroactive order. The court gave its reasons as follows:

(a) Parliament, in considering the *Divorce Act* and the *Guidelines*, could have mandated the regular interval exchange of financial information. Similarly, Parliament could have imposed an automatic increase in support payments when a payor's income increased. Parliament chose not to follow these options and the courts should not create an obligation that does not exist in the legislation.

(b) Since neither the *Divorce Act* nor the *Guidelines* detail any principles to be applied by the court in considering the issue of retroactive orders, it can be inferred that Parliament left that matter for judicial interpretation.

(c) The factual circumstances in cases concerning retroactive support are almost inevitably case-specific.

Where there is a court order for child support and the provision of medical benefits and the recipient spouse finds that medical benefits are denied, contacts the payor spouse to address the loss of medical benefits, and the payor spouse's income has increased substantially, but he merely informs the recipient spouse that he has changed jobs, a duty to disclose an increase in income is triggered at that time: *Critch v. Critch* (2005), 2005 CarswellOnt 295, 12 R.F.L. (6th) 283, [2005] O.J. No. 235 (Ont. S.C.J.); additional reasons at (2005), 2005 CarswellOnt 1985 (Ont. S.C.J.). The court was satisfied that the father had consistently understated his income. As a result of his underpayment, the children's needs went unmet or were paid for disproportionately by the mother and her new partner from their income and capital. There was little delay in her taking action after the loss of benefits. She never acquiesced in the dispute about loss of benefits. The modest variation sought would not be an unfair burden if well timed and did not result in a redistribution of capital. Since the father had more income available to him than at the time of the original order and no longer had a spousal support obligation the court did not consider retroactivity as an unfair extra burden.

An order for the payment of child support should generally be made retroactive to the date upon which the application was filed. Retroactive awards to a date prior to the filing of the application should be made only in exceptional circumstances: *Ennis v. Ennis*, 2000 CarswellAlta 79, [2000] A.J. No. 75, 281 A.R. 161, 248 W.A.C. 161, 5 R.F.L. (5th) 302, 77 Alta. L.R. (3d) 289, 2000 ABCA 33 (Alta. C.A.).

In *MacNeal v. MacNeal* (1993), 50 R.F.L. (3d) 235, 1993 CarswellOnt 369 (Ont. Gen. Div.); additional reasons at (1994), 1994 CarswellOnt 4344 (Ont. Gen. Div.). Where need is shown support should be retroactive to, at least, the date the spouse obtaining the order made known his or her intention to seek support. Retroactive support was ordered from the date of the statement of claim to the date of the interim support order, in the form of a lump sum of $4,500.

In *C. (K.) v. B. (S.)*, 36 R.F.L. (5th) 22, [2003] O.T.C. 227, 2003 CarswellOnt 988, [2003] O.J. No. 1124 (Ont. S.C.J.), the mother brought a motion for interim child support from the child's biological father. The child was born shortly after the relationship between the child's parents ended. The mother married and the mother's husband treated the child as his own. The biological father paid no support. The mother and her husband separated and the mother and her husband were at the time of this hearing engaged in divorce proceedings which included claims for child support. The husband agreed to pay child support according to the *Child Support Guidelines* on the basis that the child was a child of the marriage. The mother sought support from the biological father, retroactive to the date of the first official request set out in her solicitor's letter in September, 2001. The father submitted that it should be retroactive only to the month following the date of the application, September, 2002. The court accepted the father's submission, as the court held that the divorce proceedings against the husband created some confusion and raised some legitimate questions on the part of the father. While the father had the ability to pay, an extra year of support would create immediate and sizeable arrears. Also, the child had been well looked after by his mother and her husband.

On a motion for interim child support for the *Guideline* amount, the court in *Pakka v. Nygard* (2002), 61 O.R. (3d) 328, 2002 CarswellOnt 3403, [2002] O.J. No. 3858 (Ont. S.C.J.) ordered that the payment of child support should be made retroactive to the date after the request for leave to appeal the dismissal of his motion for an order setting aside service of the originating process in the Bahamas was dismissed. This was the time when the defendant, who lived outside the jurisdiction, knew he had no alternative but to deal with the matter in Ontario.

When the non-custodial parent had been willing to contribute to the child's support pending hearing of the support application and had voluntarily made some payments pending trial, the custodial parent's application for retroactive child support was dismissed in *Adler v. Jonas* (1999), 48 R.F.L. (4th) 228, 1999 CarswellBC 311, [1999] B.C.J. No. 358 (B.C. S.C.).

Retroactive support is only obtainable from the date that paternity is established: *G. (E.) v. D. (R.)*, 2003 CarswellAlta 1451, [2003] A.J. No. 1269, 2003 ABQB 695, 45 R.F.L. (5th) 203 (Alta. Q.B.). Before that time, in this case, there was no blameworthy conduct on the part of the father in not providing support. The father promptly complied with requests for disclosure of income. However, it was reasonable that the father should be liable for child support from the time that he was certain that he was the father.

Where a court has found that a parent's provision of child care satisfied his child support obligation for a specified period of time, child support cannot be awarded retroactively for a portion of that period: *Drygala v. Pauli* (2002), 29 R.F.L. (5th) 293, 2002 CarswellOnt 3228, 61 O.R. (3d) 711, 219 D.L.R. (4th) 319, 164 O.A.C. 241, (sub nom. *A.M.D. v. A.J.P.)* [2002] O.J. No. 3731 (Ont. C.A.); additional reasons at (2003), 2003 CarswellOnt 17, 35 R.F.L. (5th) 323, [2003] O.J. No. 3, 167 O.A.C. 274 (Ont. C.A.). In this case, the Appellate Court held that the commencement date for retroactive support would be at the time when the father's provision of child care ceased.

Support should be retroactive to the first month following the commencement of an application for support, so that the children could have the earliest benefit of s. 3 of the *Federal Child Support Guidelines*: *Scotcher v. Hampson* (1998), 41 R.F.L. (4th) 271, 1998 CarswellOnt 3651, [1998] O.J. No. 3700 (Ont. Gen. Div.); additional reasons at (1998), 1998 CarswellOnt 3913, 43 R.F.L. (4th) 132 (Ont. Gen. Div.).

If need be, retroactive support pre-dating a petition can and should be awarded on fairness principles: *Chubey v. Chubey* (2005), 2005 CarswellMan 183, 194 Man. R. (2d) 237, 2005 MBQB 121 (Man. Q.B.). There is nothing in the *Family Maintenance Act* itself which would deny a spouse's claim or limit a court's jurisdiction in respect of retroactive support: *Chubey v. Chubey*, above. In this case, the husband did not provide financial disclosure from the outset. He made every effort to avoid paying fair and equitable child support for the benefit of himself and to the detriment of his wife and children. The court found it fair and reasonable that the husband pay retroactive child support from the date of separation to the date the wife's petition was launched.

Where appropriate, the court has jurisdiction to order the payment of child support for a period pre-dating the commencement of the proceedings. But this jurisdiction is not to be exercised as a matter of course: The norm is to make the order run from the date of service (and filing) of the application, and to have it begin earlier than this date requires exceptional circumstances: *Ennis v. Ennis*, above.

One of the reasons exceptional circumstances should exist before the court extends the date prior to the date of service and filing of the application, is that it would be unfair to the payor to have him or her suddenly faced with a demand for support for a period which had been reasonably thought to have passed without support liability: *Ennis v. Ennis*, above.

Retroactive child support starting before the date on which the child support application was filed should only be awarded when necessitated by the child's best interests and where extraordinary expenses exist: *Gamache v. Gamache*, 49 R.F.L. (4th) 258, 241 A.R. 388, 1999 CarswellAlta 369, [1999] A.J. No. 474, 1999 ABQB 313 (Alta. Q.B.).

The court should be cautious about making a child support order retroactive to a date prior to the commencement of the proceedings: *Young v. Young* (2000), 2000 CarswellNB 85, 7 R.F.L. (5th) 228, [2000] N.B.J. No. 93, 225 N.B.R. (2d) 272, 578 A.P.R. 272 (N.B. C.A.).

In *Wishlow v. Bingham*, 10 R.F.L. (5th) 229, 2000 ABCA 198, 188 D.L.R. (4th) 588, 82 Alta. L.R. (3d) 226, 261 A.R. 299, 225 W.A.C. 299, 2000 CarswellAlta 681, [2000] A.J. No. 809 (Alta. C.A.), the wife, on appeal, was awarded a retroactive variation of child support back to May 1997, the date on which the *Federal Child Support Guidelines* came into force. The wife had informed the husband of the *Guidelines* as early as February 1997 and had repeatedly, to no avail, requested that the husband voluntarily agree to an increase in child support. Furthermore, the wife was delayed in bringing her formal variation application because of surgery. Although it was the norm to make a support order retroactive only to the date of the initial application, the blameworthiness of the husband and the reasonably diligent attempts by the wife to pursue her remedies justified the departure from the norm.

For a consideration of notice to the non-custodial parent of an intention to pursue child support followed by negotiations to that end: see *S. (L.) v. P. (E.)*, 50 R.F.L. (4th) 302, 175 D.L.R. (4th) 423, 126 B.C.A.C. 28, 206 W.A.C. 28, 67 B.C.L.R. (3d) 254, [1999] 12 W.W.R. 718, 1999 CarswellBC 1402 (B.C. C.A.); leave to appeal refused 252 N.R. 194 (note), 135 B.C.A.C. 160 (note), 221 W.A.C. 160 (note), [1999] 3 S.C.R. xii, 179 D.L.R. (4th) vii (S.C.C.).

The court may award retroactive support which predates the bringing of the application where there is evidence that the custodial parent manifested an intention to engage in sincere negotiations toward settlement or reconciliation: *S. (L.) v. P. (E.)*, 50 R.F.L. (4th) 302, 175 D.L.R. (4th) 423, 126 B.C.A.C. 28, 206 W.A.C. 28, 67 B.C.L.R. (3d) 254, [1999] 12 W.W.R. 718, 1999 CarswellBC 1402 (B.C. C.A.); leave to appeal refused 252 N.R. 194 (note), 135 B.C.A.C. 160 (note), 221 W.A.C. 160 (note), [1999] 3 S.C.R. xii, 179 D.L.R. (4th) vii (S.C.C.).

There are policy considerations tending to encourage the making of orders that reach back to an earlier date. To refuse jurisdiction to award retroactive child support for a period that predates the commencement of the action would discourage attempts at reconciliation: *Celi v. Eagle* (1996), 23 O.T.C. 89, 1996 CarswellOnt 4780, [1996] O.J. No. 4429 (Ont. Gen. Div.). Also, such a policy would discourage spouses from attempting to resolve their differences through negotiation: *MacNeal v. MacNeal* (1993), 50 R.F.L. (3d) 235, 1993 CarswellOnt 369 (Ont. Gen. Div.); additional reasons at (1994), 1994 CarswellOnt 4344 (Ont. Gen. Div.).

Retroactive support is available in some situations since it is in furtherance of the principles embodied in the legislation. Reconciliation between parties is to be encouraged and, to facilitate this objective, parties should be allowed a certain period of time to negotiate the issue of support rather than being compelled to apply immediately to the court for a support order. Disallowing claims for retroactive support as a general rule would also penalize those individuals who make reasonable efforts to negotiate support with their spouses. Without the availability of such orders, if negotiations failed, the period during negotiations would not be taken into account when an application for support was finally determined by the court: *Moro v. Miletich* (1998), 40 R.F.L. (4th) 115, 1998 CarswellOnt 1194, [1998] O.J. No. 1799 (Ont. Gen. Div.).

In *Smith v. Smith* (1999), 1999 CarswellOnt 137 (Ont. Gen. Div.), the issue was whether the arrears that had accumulated under support orders for three children should be varied or should be paid. There had been an 18-year delay and the payor father took the position that it was now too late to enforce the obligation. The orders had been made in 1973 and 1974 and attempts to enforce them from 1973 to 1976 were unsuccessful. No further attempts at enforcement were made until 1995. By the time the application for variation was heard, one of the children had died, one had graduated as a registered nurse, and the third had graduated as a registered health aid. Arrears were fixed for the period of the children's dependency including the child who had died. This child was mentally challenged and died when he was 28. The total arrears came to approximately $18,400. The period of dependency was found to have ended for the child who died, on the date of death, and for the other children upon their graduation. The two living children were 32 and 26 years of age when the order was made. In relation to enforcing the arrears, Justice Thompson, who heard the matter, made observations that are relevant to the exercise of the discretion to make retroactive orders. He said:

> Every parent has the moral and legal duty to ensure that the children they bring into this world are given every opportunity to flourish. This necessitates that the parent's personal material well-being is secondary to that of their children, subject to the realities of the parent's economic situation.
>
> Any parent who has the means to financially support their children but declines to do so, cannot later protest the inequities when their debt to their children is called due. Where a payer parent is fully aware of their child support obligations, the mere passage of time, even if significant, will not act as a bar to the collection of child support arrears provided that it is open to the payer parent to show that they did not have, during the relevant times, the financial resources to honour their support obligations. The onus to prove financial inability rests on the payer parent.
>
> The sole issue should be whether the payer spouse had the resources to honour their support obligations during the relevant time period. It is irrelevant that no efforts were made to enforce the support order. The obligation imposed as the result of court-ordered child support is the honouring of that court order. The onus should not be diverted to the enforcer of that order. Their actions cannot, and should not, affect the basic obligation of a parent to their child.
>
> In this case Mr. Smith has failed to show that he did not have the financial resources to honour his child support obligations. In fact the evidence discloses that Mr. Smith had

ample financial resources to contribute to his children's well-being in excess of the court-ordered child support.

In *Willson v. Willson* (1997), 1997 CarswellBC 2696, 34 R.F.L. (4th) 242 (B.C. S.C. [In Chambers]), the court was persuaded to order retroactive support to a date prior to the date of the application. The mother applied to vary an order for child support for two children that had been made in a nominal amount when the father was unemployed. At the time of the application the father had become employed as an accountant at $55,200 a year. In ordering a variation retroactive to a date occurring before the date of the application, the court held that the father ought to have paid more child support when he became employed. Support was increased to $800 a month for the two children for a retroactive period before May 1, 1997 (when the *Guidelines* came into effect) and $722 a month based on the *Guidelines* from May 1st forward. The father was given credit for certain family debts that he paid by starting the retroactive period on a date 6 months after he secured his employment.

7. — Period of Retroactive Child Support — Is there a Limitation Period?

In *D.B.S. v. S.R.G.*; *T.A.R. v. L.J.W.*; *Henry v. Henry*; *Hiemstra v. Hiemstra*, 2006 CarswellAlta 976, [2006] S.C.J. No. 37, 2006 CarswellAlta 977, 61 Alta. L.R. (4th) 1, 2006 SCC 37 (S.C.C.), the Court stated that it will usually be inappropriate to make a support award retroactive to a date more than 3 years before formal notice was given to the payor parent. (See above, "6. The Commencement Date for Retroactive Child Support").

A party will be ordered to pay arrears of child support where he has promised to pay the shortfall of payments under a separation agreement when he is financially able to do so, but has failed to keep his undertaking: *Graves v. Eager* (2002), 2002 CarswellOnt 3347, 29 R.F.L. (5th) 313 (Ont. C.A.); varying (2001), 2001 CarswellOnt 4395 (Ont. S.C.J.). The court held that neither the *Limitations Act* nor the alleged delay in making the claim for arrears barred the order made by the trial judge. In enforcing the arrears going back 12 years, the trial judge was giving effect to the father's promise to the mother made on many occasions.

There is no rule that after a particular number of years a claim for child support would be extinguished: *Brett v. Brett* (1999), 46 R.F.L. (4th) 433, 119 O.A.C. 94, 173 D.L.R. (4th) 684, 44 O.R. (3d) 61, 1999 CarswellOnt 1090, [1999] O.J. No. 1384 (Ont. C.A.).

There is nothing in the *Family Maintenance Act* itself which would deny a spouse's claim or limit a court's jurisdiction in respect of retroactive support: *Chubey v. Chubey*, 2005 CarswellMan 183, 2005 MBQB 121, 194 Man. R. (2d) 237 (Man. Q.B.). In this case, the husband did not provide financial disclosure from the outset. He made every effort to avoid paying fair and equitable child support to the benefit of himself and to the detriment of his wife and children. The court found it fair and reasonable that the husband pay retroactive child support from the date of separation to the date the wife's petition was launched.

8. — Jurisdiction Under Both the *Divorce Act* and Provincial Legislation

In *D.B.S. v. S.R.G.*; *T.A.R. v. L.J.W.*; *Henry v. Henry*; *Hiemstra v. Hiemstra*, 2006 CarswellAlta 976, [2006] S.C.J. No. 37, 2006 CarswellAlta 977, 61 Alta. L.R. (4th) 1, 2006 SCC 37 (S.C.C.), Bastarache J. at paragraph 50, held that "in exercising their own power to legislate matters concerning child support, the provinces need not conform to the paradigm espoused by the *Divorce Act* and the *Guidelines*." In this decision, the parties in the *D.B.S. v. S.R.G.* and *T.A.R. v. L.J.W.* cases which proceeded under Alberta's now repealed *Parentage and Maintenance Act*, accepted that their cases would be decided substantially as if they fell under the federal system.

In *D.B.S. v. S.R.G.*; *T.A.R. v. L.J.W.*; *Henry v. Henry*; *Hiemstra v. Hiemstra*, above, the Court held that there are three situations where the courts have jurisdiction to award retroactive child support awards.

1. Retroactive child support may be awarded where there has already been a court order for child support, but the amount has been insufficient for some time. There is always the possibility that such orders may be varied when the underlying circumstances at the time of the making of the order change. (See s. 17 of the *Divorce Act*; s. 18(2) of the *Parentage and Maintenance Act*).

2. Retroactive child support may be granted where child support obligations have previously been set out in an agreement between the parents. Courts may award retroactive child support where circumstances have changed or were never as they first appeared and the payor parent's actual support obligations have not been met. Courts may order a retroactive award so long as the applicable statutory regime permits it.

3. The courts may also award retroactive support where there has not already been a court order for child support to be paid. Jurisdiction to award retroactive support in this situation is found in s. 15.1 of the *Divorce Act* and in the relevant provincial legislation.

The court has jurisdiction under both the *Divorce Act* and provincial legislation (the *Family Relations Act* in British Columbia) to award child support retroactively, that is, for a period of time predating the date of the judgement: *S. (L.) v. P. (E.)*, 50 R.F.L. (4th) 302, 175 D.L.R. (4th) 423, 126 B.C.A.C. 28, 206 W.A.C. 28, 67 B.C.L.R. (3d) 254, [1999] 12 W.W.R. 718, 1999 CarswellBC 1402 (B.C. C.A.); leave to appeal refused 252 N.R. 194 (note), 135 B.C.A.C. 160 (note), 221 W.A.C. 160 (note), [1999] 3 S.C.R. xii, 179 D.L.R. (4th) vii (S.C.C.); *Moro v. Miletich* (1998), 40 R.F.L. (4th) 115, 1998 CarswellOnt 1194, [1998] O.J. No. 1799 (Ont. Gen. Div.).

As the *Federal Child Support Guidelines* make no provision for retroactive child support, any lump sum ordered for this purpose should be determined in accordance with principles previously applicable under the *Divorce Act*: *Andries v. Andries*, 36 R.F.L. (4th) 175, [1998] 7 W.W.R. 536, 159 D.L.R. (4th) 665, 126 Man. R. (2d) 189, 167 W.A.C. 189, 1998 CarswellMan 180, [1998] M.J. No. 196 (Man. C.A.); varying (1997), 119 Man. R. (2d) 224, 1997 CarswellMan 324, [1997] M.J. No. 301 (Man. Q.B.).

The *Divorce Act* contains neither authority for, nor prohibition against, making a retroactive interim child support order. The absence of such a prohibition indicates that such an order is permitted: *Dickie v. Dickie* (2001), 17 R.F.L. (5th) 304, 2001 CarswellOnt 2551, [2001] O.J. No. 2885 (Ont. S.C.J.); additional reasons at (2001), 2001 CarswellOnt 2768, 20 R.F.L. (5th) 343 (Ont. S.C.J.).

The jurisdiction to make a retroactive child support award is a discretionary jurisdiction to be exercised on a case-by-case basis: *Perrett v. Perrett*, 1999 CarswellSask 938, 1999 SKQB 277 (Sask. Q.B.).

9. — Whether Same Principles Apply Federally and Provincially

In *D.B.S. v. S.R.G.*; *T.A.R. v. L.J.W.*; *Henry v. Henry*; *Hiemstra v. Hiemstra*, 2006 CarswellAlta 976, [2006] S.C.J. No. 37, 2006 CarswellAlta 977, 61 Alta. L.R. (4th) 1, 2006 SCC 37 (S.C.C.), Bastarache J. at paragraph 50, held that "in exercising their own power to legislate matters concerning child support, the provinces need not conform to the paradigm espoused by the *Divorce Act* and the *Guidelines*." In this decision, the parties in the *D.B.S. v. S.R.G.* and *T.A.R. v. L.J.W.*, cases which proceeded under Alberta's now repealed *Parentage and Maintenance Act*, accepted that their cases would be decided substantially as if they fell under the federal system. While it is desirable that children of married and unmarried parents are treated the same by federal and provincial governments, the *Guidelines* should not take precedence over the legislative will of the provinces.

The same principles govern the award of retroactive support whether the application is made under the *Divorce Act* or under provincial legislation. In British Columbia, the *Family Relations Act* (as distinct from the *Divorce Act*) would apply if the parents were not married: *S. (L.) v. P. (E.)*, 50 R.F.L. (4th) 302, 175 D.L.R. (4th) 423, 126 B.C.A.C. 28, 206 W.A.C. 28, 67 B.C.L.R. (3d) 254, [1999] 12 W.W.R. 718, 1999 CarswellBC 1402 (B.C. C.A.); leave to appeal refused 252 N.R. 194 (note), 135 B.C.A.C. 160 (note), 221 W.A.C. 160 (note), [1999] 3 S.C.R. xii, 179 D.L.R. (4th) vii (S.C.C.). The court stated:

> Legislative reforms in the various provinces have attempted to remove the historical legal disadvantage and stigma resulting from the fact that a child is born of unmarried parents. Where those attempts have failed to do so fully, the courts have completed the task under s. 15 of the *Charter*. . . .To ensure that a child's right to support is not a function of the marital status of his or her parents, the right to retroactive maintenance should not be a function of whether the proceedings are brought under the *Divorce Act* or the *Family Relations Act*. For that reason, there is a strong policy interest in ensuring that the same principles and factors structure a judge's discretion in awarding or refusing to award retroactive maintenance, regardless of which act is applicable.

Where the father has the ability to pay child support but provided woefully inadequate support for his child both before and after the *Guidelines* came into force, the court should award additional retroactive support for the entire period in an amount deemed appropriate by the legislative authorities: *C. (S.E.) v. G. (D.C.)* (2003), 43 R.F.L. (5th) 41, [2003] B.C.J. No. 1359, 2003 CarswellBC 1414, 2003 BCSC 896 (B.C. S.C.).The quantum of support for the period from 1986 to 1997, consisting of a compensation order and a further amount based on the application of the *Guidelines* adjusted for notional tax and inflation considerations less the amount already paid was $250,000. For the period between 1997 and 2001, the court determined the amount based on the *Guidelines*, less all amounts actually paid by the father during that period, resulting in an amount of $505,112. The court set the starting date as the first of January, 1997 because of the proximity in time to the new *Guideline* regime and the fact that at the time the mother made her application in 1996 for an increase in child support the enactment of the Federal *Guidelines* was imminent and the Table Amounts were being widely used.

Equal treatment under the Divorce Act and provincial legislation: The right to retroactive support should not be a function of whether the proceedings are brought under the *Divorce Act* or under provincial legislation. The same principles and factors should govern the court's discretion regardless of which legislation applies: *S. (L.) v. P. (E.)*, above.

10. — Guideline Formulas or Court's Discretion

In exercising their discretion, courts should award retroactive support where fairness dictates it, but should keep in mind that certainty for payor parents is also an important principle: *D.B.S. v. S.R.G.*; *T.A.R. v. L.J.W.*; *Henry v. Henry*; *Hiemstra v. Hiemstra*, 2006 CarswellAlta 976, [2006] S.C.J. No. 37, 2006 CarswellAlta 977, 61 Alta. L.R. (4th) 1, 2006 SCC 37 (S.C.C.); (2006), 2006 CarswellAlta 976 (S.C.C.).

The *Guidelines* do not apply to a period earlier than May 1, 1997, the date on which they came into force: *Andries v. Andries*, 36 R.F.L. (4th) 175, [1998] 7 W.W.R. 536, 159 D.L.R. (4th) 665, 126 Man. R. (2d) 189, 167 W.A.C. 189, 1998 CarswellMan 180, [1998] M.J. No. 196 (Man. C.A.). On an application to vary a child support order the court must apply the *Guidelines* "when varying prospectively or retroactively for periods after 1 May 1997": *Razutis v. Garrett* (1999), 48 R.F.L. (4th) 452, 126 B.C.A.C. 249, 206 W.A.C. 249, 175 D.L.R. (4th) 730, 1999 CarswellBC 142, [1999] B.C.J. No. 1505 (B.C. C.A.), disapproving *Shankland v. Harper*, 43 R.F.L. (4th) 379, 119 B.C.A.C. 13, 194 W.A.C. 13, 60 B.C.L.R. (3d) 242, 1999 CarswellBC 105, 1999 BCCA 45, [1999] B.C.J. No. 97 (B.C. C.A.).

Pre-*Guideline* principles would be applied in cases of retroactive orders that extend backward in time from May 1, 1997 to earlier periods. However, *Cuddy v. Cuddy* (1999), 45 R.F.L. (4th) 131, 1999 CarswellOnt 1092, [1999] O.J. No. 1399 (Ont. S.C.J.), raised the question of whether the *Guidelines* have any application to retroactive orders whether made retrospectively back to, or beyond May 1, 1997. In that case the court held that the formulas in the *Guidelines* are prospective in their application and do not apply to retroactive support. In determining the amount to be paid for the retroactive period the court should use its discretion and make a determination that is "fair". "[T]he court should be guided in its deliberations by the principle of the fair and equitable sharing of moneys *actually* spent during the period, based on a ratio of the parents' respective incomes."

11. — Retroactive Child Support Ordered

In respect to the *Henry* case, determined in *D.B.S. v. S.R.G.*; *T.A.R. v. L.J.W.*; *Henry v. Henry*; *Hiemstra v. Hiemstra*, 2006 CarswellAlta 976, [2006] S.C.J. No. 37, 2006 CarswellAlta 977, 61 Alta. L.R. (4th) 1, 2006 SCC 37 (S.C.C.), the Supreme Court of Canada held that the appeal should be dismissed and that retroactive child support should be granted. The father acted in a blameworthy manner as he was aware of the children's needs, but excused himself on the basis that the recipient parent had not asked for disclosure. In addition, he insinuated that he did not have great financial means and that the mother's financial management was to blame. He was aware of his substantial increase in income and that his children were living at a standard commensurate with their mother's low income. The children deserved compensation for the unfulfilled obligation of their father. The children would benefit from an award given at the present time. The award of retroactive support would not impose too great a burden upon the father.

In respect to the *Hiemstra* case, determined in *D.B.S. v. S.R.G.*; *T.A.R. v. L.J.W.*; *Henry v. Henry*; *Hiemstra v. Hiemstra*, above, the Supreme Court of Canada held that it was appropriate to uphold the lower court decision to grant retroactive child support as there was a reasonable explanation for the mother's delay in applying for retroactive support — she was reticent to resume litigation, as previous litigation had been overwhelming and had strained her relationship with her daughter. Further, given the father's substantial income, almost $100,000 per year, he could not be considered blameless in not paying child support. The fact that the father could afford child support but the mother provided all of the support meant that the father's conduct could not readily be excused.

Retroactive child support will be ordered where the payor fails to make a serious effort to seek employment; he has had the benefit of most of the matrimonial assets; and may receive additional funds from the sale of the matrimonial home: *Stutz v. Stutz*, 2006 CarswellNS 320, 2006 NSSC 228 (N.S. S.C.). Planning to be a magician on a cruise boat does not constitute a financial plan.

In *Lu v. Sun*, 2005 CarswellNS 338, [2005] N.S.J. No. 314, 2005 NSCA 112, 235 N.S.R. (2d) 353, 747 A.P.R. 353, 17 R.F.L. (6th) 57 (N.S. C.A.); leave to appeal refused (2005), 2005 CarswellNS 580, 2005 CarswellNS 581, 349 N.R. 400 (note) (S.C.C.), the court held that retroactive child support was payable, even where the payor parent paid $8,688 more child support in the years prior to the mother's application to vary than he would have paid if he had paid the Table Amounts of child support based on his income. While this overpayment was an important consideration, it was not the only consideration. Considering all the facts of this case, this factor did not rule out an award of retroactive child support for the following reasons:

- The Table Amounts do not take into account s. 7 expenses that may have been payable by the father if his child support had been determined by court order.
- In 1993, the father consented to pay $550 per month as child and spousal support. Under the 1997 Corollary Relief Judgement spousal support was reduced to $1 and child support was agreed to at $550 per month.
- The father consented to pay $550 per month child support when the Corollary Relief Judgement was issued, at a time when the Table Amount of child support based on his income of $41,200 (Cdn.) would have been $344 per month;
- The father never applied to reduce child support. Such an application would have required him to disclose his income. Such disclosure may have prompted the mother to apply for increased spousal support, since entitlement to spousal support had been established by the Corollary Relief Judgement.
- The father did not file a statement of property so the court did not know what his present assets and liabilities were to allow it to assess the effect, if any, the payment of the $550 per month child support has had on him and his family's financial situation. His affidavit indicated he increased the balance on his credit card at one time because of his need to pay $550 per month child support. On the other hand his filed Statement of Financial Information indicated he currently owns a mortgaged home and owes money on his automobile, but otherwise has no debts.

The court further held that regardless which approach is taken on the facts of this appeal, payment of 13-months retroactive child support was not an error considering:

- the need of the daughter;
- the unique relationship between the daughter and her father which required him to put her interests ahead of his and the mother's;
- the father's ability to pay, taking into account his income, Statement of Financial Information and his obligation to his new family;

- the father's failure to report the significant increase in his income despite the provision in the Corollary Relief Judgement that he report "significant changes in his financial situation";
- the mother's past and present debt as a result of doing what was necessary to support her daughter over the years;
- the fact the mother brought the application for retroactive child support as soon as she was aware of the father's significantly improved financial situation; and
- the relatively short period of retroactive support ordered, so there would not be an unreasonable or unfair burden on the father.

In *MacDougall v. MacDougall*, 2005 CarswellNS 144, [2005] N.S.J. No. 129, 19 R.F.L. (6th) 103, 2005 NSSF 23, 231 N.S.R. (2d) 270, 733 A.P.R. 270 (N.S. S.C.); additional reasons at 2005 CarswellNS 574, 2005 NSSC 326, 239 N.S.R. (2d) 76, 760 A.P.R. 76 (N.S. S.C.), the court ordered retroactive child support where the children were dependent. The father, given his imputed income, was in a much better position than the mother to meet the ongoing cost of rearing children. The father concealed income consistently over the years for which there was income tax information available, and the mother encroached on her share of the parties' assets to support the children. Consequently, it was necessary that this capital be, in effect, returned to her. An order for retroactive child support would not be unfair to the father, nor would it place an unreasonable burden on him.

In *Olhmann v. Olhmann* (2005), 2005 CarswellAlta 177, 14 R.F.L. (6th) 64, 2005 ABQB 98 (Alta. Q.B.), the court held that the father must pay retroactive child support even though when he reduced his payments, from $862 to $600 per month, he informed the mother his financial situation would not allow him to meet his obligations fully as required by a strict application of the *Guidelines*. While the father claimed that he reduced his payments as a result of "a slow period" in his work, there was no evidence of any reduction in his actual income for the year, so as to justify a reduction in his obligations. The evidence did not establish any undue hardship within the meaning of s. 10 of the *Guidelines*. The fact that the father, at the time he reduced his payments, sent a letter to the mother indicating that her failure to respond to the reduction previously left him to "assume" that she had agreed to it and a failure to respond again would leave him to "continue to assume" that she agreed to and accepted the new arrangement, did not mean that she acquiesced to the change and was estopped from claiming the difference between what he should have paid and what he did pay, or that she had waived her right to do so. The court held that without even considering the issue of whether the defences of estoppel or waiver could be asserted in a claim by a parent for child support, as it is the child, and not the parent, who is entitled to it, the elements had not been made out. The one who asserts the defence of estoppel must establish that the other party has made an unambiguous representation which was relied upon to the detriment of the one asserting it. In this case, there was no evidence of the mother's unequivocal conduct which showed an intention on her part to waive her right to claim the full child support that the father was obligated to pay.

Retroactive child support was awarded where the recipient spouse made inquires of the payor spouse about the loss of court ordered medical benefits, the payor did not mention the increase in his income, the needs of the children were not met or were addressed disproportionately by the mother and her new partner from their income and capital:

Critch v. Critch (2005), 2005 CarswellOnt 295, 12 R.F.L. (6th) 283, [2005] O.J. No. 235 (Ont. S.C.J.); additional reasons at (2005), 2005 CarswellOnt 1985 (Ont. S.C.J.).

In *LePage v. LePage* (2005), 2005 CarswellNS 332, 2005 NSSC 200 (N.S. S.C.), the court granted the wife retroactive child support from the date of separation since she had almost single-handedly borne the financial burden of providing for the parties' child since that time. While the father had submitted that he was off work for a period of time, his income tax information indicated his income was the equivalent of his current salary. The payment of retroactive support would not be an unreasonable or unfair burden to the father, but it could complicate ongoing support obligations. The mother did not delay in seeking support. The court ordered the father to pay retroactive child support in the amount of $226 per month for three months payable one-half approximately nine months after the date of judgement and one-half payable approximately 18 months after the date of judgement.

In *Tedham v. Tedham*, 2003 CarswellBC 2742, [2003] B.C.J. No. 2554, 44 R.F.L. (5th) 204, 20 B.C.L.R. (4th) 56, 2003 BCCA 600, 188 B.C.A.C. 297, 308 W.A.C. 297 (B.C. C.A.); additional reasons at 2004 CarswellBC 377, 2004 BCCA 101, 5 R.F.L. (6th) 218 (B.C. C.A.); leave to appeal refused 2004 CarswellBC 1483, 2004 CarswellBC 1484, [2004] S.C.C.A. No. 4, 210 B.C.A.C. 320 (note), 348 W.A.C. 320 (note), 331 N.R. 397 (note), [2004] 2 S.C.R. vii (S.C.C.), the father's actual income was considerably greater than anticipated at the time of an interim child support order. The Appellate Court considered whether child support should be made retroactive to the date of the first payment required under an interim order based on the payor's actual income. The trial judge had refused to grant retroactive support based on his finding that the father had not deliberately misled the court as to his income at the time of the interim order and the fact that the mother had failed to seek further financial information from the payor/father and to apply for a variation of the interim order prior to trial. The Appellate Court held that neither ground constituted a valid basis for refusing the order. Interim orders are by their nature made at a time when all the facts are not known to the court. Children should not be deprived of their rightful amount of support because the judicial officer was not in possession of all the facts and custodial parents should not be made to pay more than their proportionate share because the payor does not have, or has not produced, all of the information required to make a final determination of the quantum of child support. Further, the custodial parent was not required to go to the expense of a variation hearing, the cost of which might have erased any increase in support that she might have obtained. Where there are payors whose base income is significantly different from their actual income, interim awards should be subject to adjustment at the time of the trial or final order so that the children are adequately supported and their support is fairly shared between the parties. The delay between the time of the interim order and trial did not prejudice the payor and make a retroactive order inappropriate. The court had not found any blameworthy conduct on the payor/father's part in regard to his anticipated earnings. While blameworthy conduct may be a reason for awarding retroactive child support, its absence does not preclude the making of such an order. The Court of Appeal ordered retroactive child support for the period covered by the interim order.

Where the father was deliberately underemployed and he did not provide ongoing financial disclosure, as required by the earlier order, the payment of arrears was ordered retroactive to the date of the application: *Thompson v. Ducharme*, 2001 CarswellMan 545, 159 Man. R. (2d) 246, [2001] M.J. No. 493, 2001 MBQB 161 (Man. Q.B.).

In *Carty v. Jones* (1995), 15 R.F.L. (4th) 367, 1995 CarswellOnt 488, [1995] O.J. No. 1827 (Ont. Prov. Div.), the mother was awarded retroactive support of $30,000 and ongoing support in a varied amount of $400 a month. Prior to this trial the father failed to disclose his true income. From April, 1988 to May 1993, he paid $30,970 for child support, which represented 8.5 per cent of his true income. The court found that he should have paid 17 per cent of his income for child support. At 17 per cent, the father would owe $30,000 in retroactive support.

In *Mohr v. Hall* (1995), 1995 CarswellOnt 2268 (Ont. Gen. Div.), where the payor had been unable to meet his child support obligations in the past because he did not have adequate means, but subsequently received a large windfall from a lottery, the court awarded retroactive child support. The amount awarded was one-half of the amount the payor would probably have paid for the child, namely $300 per month for five years for a total of $18,000. The court also awarded ongoing child support of $1000 per month based on the payor's present assets and income.

12. — No Retroactive Child Support When Payor Fulfilled His Support Obligation

The conduct of the payor parent could militate against a retroactive award where the payor parent's conduct has had the effect of fulfilling his or her support obligation: *D.B.S. v. S.R.G.*; *T.A.R. v. L.J.W.*; *Henry v. Henry*; *Hiemstra v. Hiemstra*, 2006 CarswellAlta 976, [2006] S.C.J. No. 37, 2006 CarswellAlta 977, 61 Alta. L.R. (4th) 1, 2006 SCC 37 (S.C.C.).

In *Hodgkinson v. Hodgkinson* (2006), 2006 CarswellBC 767, 2006 BCCA 158, 267 D.L.R. (4th) 357, 25 R.F.L. (6th) 235, 53 B.C.L.R. (4th) 52 (B.C. C.A.), the Appellate Court upheld the trial judge's refusal of a retroactive child support order where the payor paid support without a court order to the appellant and their child pending the outcome of the trial.

Where the payor has not paid child support to the payee since separation, other than an early payment of $400, but she has made substantial payments on behalf of the children, to them and to third parties, she is not liable for retroactive child support from the time of separation at least until the mother's solicitor was advised by the father's solicitor that the father would be claiming retroactive child support. Up until that time, the court found that the parties had an understanding that the mother would pay for the children's expenses in this way. From the undisputed evidence it is clear that she probably paid to the children or third parties more than she would have been required to pay under the Guidelines for child support during this period of time in any event: *C. (J.T.) v. C. (S.L.)* (2006), 2006 CarswellAlta 94, 2006 ABQB 27 (Alta. Q.B.).

When the non-custodial parent had been willing to contribute to the child's support pending hearing of the support application and had voluntarily made some payments pending trial, the custodial parent's application for retroactive child support was dismissed in *Adler v. Jonas* (1999), 48 R.F.L. (4th) 228, 1999 CarswellBC 311, [1999] B.C.J. No. 358 (B.C. S.C.).

Where a court has found that a parent's provision of child care satisfied his child support obligation for a specified period of time, child support cannot be awarded retroactively for a portion of that period: *Drygala v. Pauli* (2002), 29 R.F.L. (5th) 293, 2002 CarswellOnt 3228, 61 O.R. (3d) 711, 219 D.L.R. (4th) 319, 164 O.A.C. 241, (sub nom. *A.M.D. v. A.J.P.)* [2002] O.J. No. 3731 (Ont. C.A.); additional reasons at (2003), 2003 CarswellOnt

17, 35 R.F.L. (5th) 323, [2003] O.J. No. 3, 167 O.A.C. 274 (Ont. C.A.). In this case, the Appellate Court held that the commencement date for retroactive support would be at the time when the father's provision of child care ceased.

A spouse is not entitled to receive retroactive child support where the other spouse after separation paid for monthly bills having to do with the matrimonial home; the children benefited from the father's contribution to accommodation costs; there was no evidence that any of the mother's debt was attributable to lack of a formal order for child support, and there was no evidence of any delay, obstruction, non-disclosure or other misconduct on the part of the husband: *Koch v. Koch* (2001), 22 R.F.L. (5th) 114, 2001 CarswellOnt 3460 (Ont. S.C.J.). The children were able to work for the husband's employer as summer and part-time workers during the period of their post-secondary education. An order for retroactive child support would have ignored the children's contribution to their own education. Fairness did not demand a retroactive award to ameliorate past dependency demonstrated by the adult children.

However, in *Denesi v. Neves* (1998), 36 R.F.L. (4th) 154, [1998] O.J. No. 736, 1998 CarswellOnt 1074 (Ont. Prov. Div.), the court considered and rejected the argument that the father should not be burdened with paying substantial retroactive support to the mother because she had demonstrated that she could survive all that time.

13. — General

The Ontario Court of Appeal held in *McGouran v. Connelly* (2006), 2006 CarswellOnt 1540, 207 O.A.C. 368, [2006] O.J. No. 993 that the issue regarding the proper test for ordering the payment of retroactive child support, including the effect of the payor spouse's failure to disclose income increases, the failure of the payee spouse to apply to court in a timely manner, and the onus of proof of the effect of a retroactive order should be reserved until the Supreme Court of Canada had released its decision in the four Alberta cases above. See *D.B.S. v. S.R.G.*; *T.A.R. v. L.J.W.*; *Henry v. Henry*; *Hiemstra v. Hiemstra*, 2006 CarswellAlta 976, [2006] S.C.J. No. 37, 2006 CarswellAlta 977, 61 Alta. L.R. (4th) 1, 2006 SCC 37 (S.C.C.).

In *Stebner v. Stebner* (2005), 2005 CarswellAlta 465, 2005 ABQB 266, 17 R.F.L. (6th) 363 (Alta. Q.B.), the court held that the father was entitled to a retroactive adjustment to his child support obligations for the period 2002, 2003 and 2004, as his child support obligations would be recalculated according to his income from employment as disclosed on his tax assessments.

Any calculation of the retroactive child support should be made on the net amount of a bonus: *Laflamme v. Laflamme* (2006), 2006 CarswellBC 1767, 2006 BCSC 1081 (B.C. Master). Normally this would not be done as child support would be calculated first and then spousal support, but it appears the parties had in contemplation a greater deductibility for the defendant by paying the spousal support as set out in the order. The plaintiff sought retroactive child support based on the defendant's bonus of $55,000 for 2005. The defendant has to pay the plaintiff 25% of the gross amount of the bonus. The court was of the opinion that the calculation of the retroactive child support based on the gross amount of the bonus is akin to double dipping.

Where the children spent 3 days per week in the care of their mother, the court held that it would factor this matter into the spousal support order rather than deal with it as a separate claim for retroactive child support, as suggested by the wife: *Korwin v. Potworowski* (2006), 2006 CarswellOnt 3436 (Ont. S.C.J.). The court came to this decision as it found that while the children were with the wife three days per week, this arrangement was against their best interests. The court had concluded, among other things, that the wife interfered with the husband's role as sole custodial parent, undermined him as the custodial parent, and contributed largely to the intense parental conflict. To order retroactive child support now would provide the wife with an inappropriate windfall and reward her for unreasonable behaviour since the separation. However, the fact remained that for the period in question, the wife had no income.

The court refused to award retroactive child support where the payee parent dissipated matrimonial property and apparently spent the proceeds on living expenses for herself and her children: *Hennesey v. Hennesey*, 2005 CarswellAlta 1812, [2005] A.J. No. 1703, 2005 ABQB 883 (Alta. Q.B.).

Where a payor makes payments which do not benefit the parties' children or the payee spouse, then the payor cannot receive credit for them as a substitute for retroactive child support: *W. (S.L.) v. W. (W.N.)* (2006), 2006 CarswellAlta 791, 2006 ABQB 447 (Alta. Q.B.).

15§89 — Child Support — special or extraordinary expenses

General

[See amendment to s. 7 of the *Guidelines* which came into force May 1, 2006. Cases under this section, decided before the amendment, should be read with caution.]

Section 7 of the *Federal Child Support Guidelines* defines special or extraordinary expenses, and provides that on the application of either spouse the court may, in its discretion, make an order for their payment in whole or in part.

The special or extraordinary expenses are defined by way of a list which describes expenses of specific kinds. The list is exhaustive of the kind that can be considered. This is made clear in s. 7(1) which, in introducing the list, empowers the court to provide in a child support order "an amount to cover the *following* expenses, or any portion of those expenses." (Emphasis added.) If the expense is of a kind not described in the list, it is not a special or extraordinary expense within the meaning of the section. There is no catch-all description of an expense.

In arriving at the amount, the court must take "into account the necessity of the expense in relation to the child's best interests and the reasonableness of the expense, having regard to the means of the spouses and those of the child and to the family's spending pattern prior to the separation": s. 7(1).

The guiding principle to be followed by the court in determining the amount of an expense is that it should be shared by the spouses in proportion to their respective incomes after deducting from the expense, the contribution, if any, from the child: *Federal Child Support Guidelines*, s. 7(2).

In assessing the amount to be paid, the court must take into account any subsidies, benefits or income tax deductions or credits relating to the expense or any eligibility to claim a subsidy, benefit or income tax deduction or credit relating to the expense: *Federal Child Support Guidelines*, s. 7(3).

The expenses which may be claimed as special or extraordinary expenses are:

(a) child care expenses incurred as a result of the custodial parent's employment, illness, disability or education or training for employment;

(b) that portion of the medical and dental insurance premiums attributable to the child;

(c) health-related expenses that exceed insurance reimbursement by at least $100 annually, including orthodontic treatment, professional counselling provided by a psychologist, social worker, psychiatrist or any other person, physiotherapy, occupational therapy, speech therapy and prescription drugs, hearing aids, glasses and contact lenses;

(d) extraordinary expenses for primary or secondary school education or for any other educational programs that meet the child's particular needs;

(e) expenses for post-secondary education; and

(f) extraordinary expenses for extracurricular activities: s. 7(1).

The description of the expenses in s. 7(1) is taken from the marginal heading of the subsection which uses the terms, Special or extraordinary expenses. (Apart from this heading there is no reference to "special" expenses in s. 7 or elsewhere in the *Guidelines.*)

The "extraordinary" expenses are singled out in (d) and (f) so by this elimination all other categories of expense described in the list are "special" expenses; that is, expenses, or the portion of those expenses that relate to the child, for day-care (a), medical and dental insurance premiums (b), certain kinds of health-related expenses (c), and costs of post-secondary education (e), are special expenses. There is no ambiguity about special expenses — they mean what they say — and no definition of them is necessary. However, that is not the case with extraordinary expenses. There has been difficulty with determining their meaning and a definition has been added by the following amendment to s. 7(1) in the *Federal Child Support Guidelines*:

> (1.1) Definition of "extraordinary expenses" — For the purposes of paragraphs (1)(d) and (f), the term "extraordinary expenses" means
>
> (a) expenses that exceed those that the spouse requesting an amount for the extraordinary expenses can reasonably cover, taking into account that spouse's income and the amount that the spouse would receive under the applicable table or, where the court has determined that the table amount is inappropriate, the amount that the court has otherwise determined is appropriate; or
>
> (b) where paragraph (a) is not applicable, expenses that the court considers are extraordinary taking into account
>
> (i) the amount of the expense in relation to the income of the spouse requesting the amount, including the amount that the spouse would receive under the applicable table or, where the court has determined that the table amount is inappropriate, the amount that the court has otherwise determined is appropriate,
>
> (ii) the nature and number of the educational programs and extracurricular activities,
>
> (iii) any special needs and talents of the child or children,
>
> (iv) the overall cost of the programs and activities, and
>
> (v) any other similar factor that the court considers relevant.

Referring to "extraordinary" expenses for educational programmes in s. 7(1)(d) and "extraordinary" expenses for extracurricular activities in (f) implies that ordinary expenses for these programmes and activities do not count toward an additional payment. The difficulty is in determining when the program or activity is over and above the ordinary and is, therefore, in the realm of an extraordinary expense that should be considered as a possibility for additional payment.

A request for an extraordinary expense calls for the application of the two paragraphs, 7(1) and 7(1.1). However, the order of application is reversed. Before looking at the necessity and reasonableness of the expense as required by 7(1), one has to first consider whether the request fits the definition of extraordinary expenses contained in the second paragraph, 7(1.1); that is, one must jump to (1.1) and then go back to (1). The important point to remember is that meeting the requirements of the definition in (1.1) is only going half the distance. Satisfying the necessity and reasonableness of the expense required by (1) (as is done with special expenses, also) is the other half.

The main problem seen in the cases prior to the amendment was to decide whether a subjective or an objective approach should be used in giving meaning to "extraordinary."

The definition of "extraordinary" invites a comparison to what is usual, but there is no standard of what is usual that cuts across all income levels. A relatively modest expense for a child's extracurricular activity may be "extraordinary" for parents who are living at a very low income level, but trivial for those with generous incomes. This must be some attempt by the court to measure "extraordinary" in accordance with a norm. An income base and a presumptive capacity to pay is the foundation of the *Guidelines*. The amounts for support are to this extent, subjective not objective. All payors with equivalent incomes do not necessarily have the same ability to pay support. Section 7 recognizes this by linking ability to pay not just to income, but to the broader concept of "financial means." Accordingly, it is most consistent with the structure of the *Guidelines* to assess the "extraordinary" nature of the expense, subjectively. For this purpose, the parents' joint incomes should be used. If, in this assessment, the court determines that the expense is extraordinary, it then moves on to consider the reasonableness of the expense. The court only considers the reasonableness of the expense, if it is first found to be extraordinary. If it is not extraordinary, the matter ends there: Bateman J.A., concurring with the majority, but delivering separate reasons in *Raftus v. Raftus* (1998), 37 R.F.L. (4th) 59 at 69–70, 166 N.S.R. (2d) 179, 159 D.L.R. (4th) 264 (C.A.)

The difference in using the subjective approach is that whether or not the expense is extraordinary is determined by considering the expense in relation to the financial circumstances of the particular family in question. Applying the objective standard, on the other hand, requires the court to consider whether the expense is disproportionately high in relation to an assumed general standard for all families at the particular level of the payor's income. The amendment is intended to solve the problem. The Department of Justice gives this explanation on its website, http://www.justice.gc.ca:

> The definition has been added to clarify the meaning of "extraordinary expenses," which various courts across the country have interpreted differently.
>
> Under this amendment, an expense is considered extraordinary if it is higher than the parent requesting the amount can reasonably cover. The requesting parent's income, as well as any child support the requesting parent would receive, is considered to determine if the expense is extraordinary.
>
> Or, if the requesting parent can reasonably cover the expense, the expense may still be considered extraordinary when taking into account:
>
> - the income of the parent requesting the amount (including the child support amount);
> - the nature and number of the educational programs and extracurricular activities;

- any special needs and talents of the child;
- the overall costs of the programs and activities;
- and any other similar factor that is relevant.

According to this explanation, the expenses for educational programs (d) or extracurricular activities (f), are extraordinary if the requesting spouse or parent cannot afford them, or alternatively, if while affordable, they are extraordinary in light of the circumstances mentioned in the second part of the definition.

The amendment seems to have a provincial origin. Except for interchanging the word "spouse" for "parent" and "paragraph" for "clause", the wording of s. 7(1.1) is identical to the wording of the amendment to the Manitoba *Child Support Guidelines Regulation* which came into force 5 years earlier on July 1, 2001. Therefore, cases decided in Manitoba on applying the section as amended are useful in applying the federal amendment. Some of these cases are annotated in the section on Cases that follow this Commentary. (Cases under s. 7 of the *Guidelines* decided before May 1, 2006, the in-force date of amendment 7(1.1), are retained here but should be read with caution.)

Expenses described in s. 7(1)(a) (child care), (b) (medical and dental insurance), (c) (excess health care) and (e) (post-secondary education) expenses, are not included in the table amount, but an average amount for s. 7(d) (extraordinary school) and (f) (extraordinary extracurricular) expenses is included in the table: Bateman J.A., concurring with the majority, but delivering separate reasons in *Raftus v. Raftus* (1998), 37 R.F.L. (4th) 59, 166 N.S.R. (2d) 179, 159 D.L.R. (4th) 264 (C.A.).

The Manitoba and Federal legislative amendments were prompted by the discussion of the meaning of "'extraordinary expenses' which various courts across the country have interpreted differently." As mentioned, the discussion was over whether a subjective or an objective approach should be followed. The leading case for the subjective side is *McLaughlin v. McLaughlin* (1998), 44 R.F.L. (4th) 148, [1998] B.C J. No. 2514, 1998 CarswellBC 2327, 113 B.C.A.C. 224, 184 W.A.C. 224, 167 D.L.R. (4th) 39, 57 B.C.L.R. (3d) 186, [1999] 7 W W.R. 415 (B.C. C.A.); additional reasons at 1999 CarswellBC 471, 44 R.F.L. (4th) 176, 172 D.L.R. (4th) 70, 1999 BCCA 135 (B.C. C.A.). This is a judgement of the British Columbia Court of Appeal which came down firmly in favour of a subjective approach. This decision and the language in the judgement inspired the wording of first, the Manitoba amendment, and then the Federal.

The difference between the approaches to the interpretation of the expenses, according to the *McLaughlin* judgement, is that the subjective approach "takes into consideration the joint incomes of the parties" whereas the objective approach does not. Working with the joint incomes is consistent with the concept of sharing expenses according to a formula that factors in both incomes, as distinct from a formula that uses only the payor's income as is the case when calculating the basic or Table Amount. "[W]here both parties are expected to share additional expenses, as under s. 7, it is reasonable to utilize their joint incomes in determining whether an expense is extraordinary." The use of "extraordinary" in paragraphs 7(1)(d) (extraordinary expenses for primary or secondary education) and 7(1)(f)(extraordinary expenses for extracurricular activities) "implies that 'ordinary' expenses are included within the table amounts. The problem, the judgement continues, "has been the difficulty of ascertaining the nature and extent of the extracurricular activities [and educational expenses]" that are extraordinary and separating them from expenses "which are 'ordinary' and, thus, included in the basic table amounts." The judgement solves the problem and, in doing so, suggests the wording for the amendment, in the following passages:

> 81 ... [I]n deciding whether an expense, or the totality of expenses claimed on behalf of children under s. 7(1)(f) are extraordinary, the court should take into consideration the combined income of the parties, as well as the nature and amount of the individual expense, the nature and number of the activities, any special needs or talents of the children, and the overall cost of the activities. This list is not intended to be exhaustive, as considerations may arise in other cases which may also be relevant. ...
>
> 82 ... [O]nce an expense or expenses are found to be extraordinary it is necessary for the court to proceed to determine whether the expenses are necessary in relation to the children's best interests and reasonable, having regard to the means of the spouses and those of the child, and to the family's spending pattern prior to separation. ... [T]hose questions do not need to be addressed until the expense or expenses in question have been found to be extraordinary. That would also be true of "extraordinary" educational expenses under s. 7(1)(d). With respect to the other expenses included under s. 7(1), which fit under the rubric of "special" expenses as that word is used in the heading of the section, the expenses need not be extraordinary, but they must meet the tests of necessity and reasonableness.

Where a payor is concerned about whether the special or extraordinary expense to which he is ordered to contribute a payment is actually being incurred, once a year he may request under the *Federal Child Support Guidelines*, s. 25(1)(b) current information in writing about the status of the expense and the payee spouse is obliged to provide that information: s. 25(3): *McLaughlin v. McLaughlin* (1998), 113 B.C.A.C. 224, 184 W.A.C. 224, 1998 CarswellBC 2327, 57 B.C.L.R. (3d) 186, 44 R.F.L. (4th) 148, [1999] 7 W.W.R. 415, [1998] B.C.J. No. 2514, 167 D.L.R. (4th) 39 (B.C. C.A.); additional reasons at (1999), 1999 CarswellBC 471, 44 R.F.L. (4th) 176, 172 D.L.R. (4th) 70, 1999 BCCA 135 (B.C. C.A.).

An award for special expenses is discretionary under s. 7 of the *Federal Child Support Guidelines* and the claimant must provide the court with the necessary supporting details: *Young v. Young* (2000), 7 R.F.L. (5th) 228 (N.B. C.A.).

Payments for extraordinary expenses are not deductible from the payor's income for tax purposes and are not includible in the income of the recipient. Sections 56(1)(b), 56.1, 60(b) and 60.1 of the *Income Tax Act* govern the tax treatment of payments for extraordinary expenses: *Fung-Sunter v. Fabian* (1998), 38 R.F.L. (4th) 266, 53 B.C.L.R. (3d) 75, 1998 CarswellBC 824 (B.C. S.C.); reversed on other grounds 69 B.C.L.R. (3d) 18, 1999 CarswellBC 1204, 1999 BCCA 346, [1999] B.C.J. No. 1263, 125 B.C.A.C. 268, 204 W.A.C. 268, [1999] 10 W.W.R. 592, 48 R.F.L. (4th) 95 (B.C. C.A.).

In assessing support under the *Federal Child Support Guidelines*, the determination of special or extraordinary expenses should be determined independently of basic child support: *Dergousoff v. Dergousoff* (1999), 48 R.F.L. (4th) 1, [1999] 10 W.W.R. 633, 177 Sask. R. 64, 199 W.A.C. 64 (Sask. C.A.); varying (1998), 167 Sask R. 66 (Q.B.).

In *Sanders v. Sanders* (1998), 42 R.F.L. (4th) 239 (Alta. C.A.), s. 7 claims for basketball registration, school registration, school supplies, and camp expenses cannot be categorized as extraordinary expenses, given the total income of the parties and using the approach followed in *Middleton v. MacPherson* (1997), 29 R.F.L. (4th) 334, 204 A.R. 37, 150 D.L.R. (4th) 519 (Q.B.). The father had an imputed income of $96,500. The mother's income was not stated.

The similarity in language between *McLaughlin* and paragraphs 7(1) and (1.1) is such that the principles described in *McLaughlin* continue to be applicable to a determination of a request for extraordinary expenses: *Milette v. Milette* (2006), 2006 BCSC 982, 2006 CarswellBC 1569, 29 R.F.L. (6th) 358 (B.C. S.C.).

"Merely describing an expense as 'extraordinary' will not automatically entitle a claimant to the amount sought. The court must still consider whether the expense is reasonably necessary for the benefit of the child, whether the expense is reasonable relative to the parties' joint income post-separation, and the court must consider the family's spending pattern prior to the separation": *Albo v. Albo* (2006), 2006 CarswellAlta 1383, 65 Alta. L.R. (4th) 340, 2006 ABQB 785, [2006] A.J. No. 1330 (Alta. Q.B.).

The test of necessity relates to the best interests of the child, but the child does not require any special talent for an activity's expenses to qualify as necessary. They will be deemed necessary when they relate to activities such as sports that aid in the development of a child's character and health to their full potential: *Earles v. Earles* (2006), 2006 CarswellBC 362, 2006 BCSC 221, [2006] B.C.J. No. 346 (B.C. S.C.).

In *Earles v. Earles* (2006), 2006 CarswellBC 362, 2006 BCSC 221, [2006] B.C.J. No. 346 (B.C. S.C.), the court held that the "means" of a parent should be interpreted broadly to include not just income but other sources of revenue available to the parent, including family income and, most notably, the income of a new spouse. The income of this third party is not taken into account in calculating the proportionate amount of each parent's contribution, but the court looks at the necessity of the expense and the reasonableness of the expense in relation to the means of the spouses to afford that expense. "So, the reasonableness of the expense may be affected by the totality of the income accruing in the two households notwithstanding that the proportionate sharing will only be calculated on the basis of the two parent's income."

Section 7(1) orders should only be granted where they would be declaratory of existing rights and obligations of the parties and should not be granted where such rights and obligations are merely speculative: *Myke v. Myke* (2000), 2000 CarswellOnt 1945, [2000] O.J. No. 2056 (Ont. S.C.J.).

In deciding if expenses are necessary, the test is whether they are necessary "in relation to the best interests of the child" and not one of strict necessity: *Omah-Maharajh v. Howard* (1998), 58 Alta. L.R. (3d) 236, [1998] 7 W.W.R.. 342, [1998] A.J. No. 173, 1998 ABQB 81, 1998 CarswellAlta 158, 215 A.R. 159 (Alta. Q.B. [In Chambers]).

An extracurricular expense relating to a child's custody may or may not be an "extraordinary expense" depending on the family's circumstances. An ordinary expense for a family with a substantial income may not be ordinary for one with less income: *Campbell v. Martijn* (1998), 40 R.F.L. (4th) 41, 163 Nfld. & P.E.I.R. 126, 503 A.P.R. 126 (P.E.I. T.D. [In Chambers]).

The word "extraordinary" means activities for which the cost is disproportionately high in relation to the payor's income, which would not be included in the usual allowance for recreation which is part of the Table Amount": *Rains v. Rains* (June 16, 1997), Doc. Sault Ste. Marie 16655/197 (Ont. Gen. Div.).

Dawson J., in *Miller v. McClement* (1997), 35 R.F.L. (4th) 83, 160 Sask. R. 232 (Sask. Q.B.) was of the opinion that "the expression 'extraordinary' implies that the expenses must be exceptional or out of the ordinary, either in their nature or in their amount, when compared to the expenses ordinarily incurred by a typical household with a similar income". As well as being extraordinary, an expense must be necessary in regard to the child's best interests and reasonable having regard to the means of the spouses, the child and the family's spending pattern. In this case, the court rejected the claim that school fees, supplies and a bus pass are extraordinary expenses under s. 7(1)(d) of the *Guidelines*. The cost of swimming lessons, voice lessons and piano lessons are extraordinary expenses, both in nature and in their amount considering the means of the parties and their spending patterns, and a s. 7 order was made for these expenses.

In *Andries v. Andries* (1998), 36 R.F.L. (4th) 175, 126 Man. R. (2d) 189, 159 D.L.R. (4th) 536 (C.A.), the court was of the opinion that special expenses provided for under s. 7(1)(a), (b), (c) and (e) are expenses which are not covered in the tables. Extraordinary expenses provided for in s. 7(1)(d) and (f) are expenses for "specified purpose which are out of the ordinary." Consequently, ordinary expenses of education below the post-secondary level and ordinary expenses for extracurricular activities are not covered by s. 7. In other words, "an expense for an extracurricular activity is extraordinary only where it is out of proportion to the usual costs associated with that particular activity." The court held that the word "extraordinary" in s. 7(1)(d) and (f) qualifies expense rather than activity. All the expenses in s. 7(1) are determined without reference to the means of the parties but are then subject to same tests of necessity and reasonableness. This approach allows for regional differences within a province and the particular needs of special-needs children.

An agreement by parents to share equally the children's "extraordinary expense" does not oust the jurisdiction of the court under the *Guidelines* to make a different order: *Walsh v. Walsh* (2006), 23 R.F.L. (6th) 447, 2006 CarswellNfld 37, 2006 NLUFC 7, 254 Nfld. & P.E.I.R. 338, 764 A.P.R. 338 (N.L. U.F.C.).

The $7,725.84 that the applicant received in federal Child Tax Benefits and B.C. Family Bonus payments is not part of her income for the purposes of determining the proportion of extraordinary expenses to be paid by each party. Income is a defined term under the *Guidelines* and is to be calculated "using the sources of income set out under the heading 'Total income' in the T1 General [tax] form." Amounts received under Child Tax Benefit and the B.C. Family Bonus are not included under the heading "Total Income" on the form, and therefore, should not be included in the applicant's income when determining the parties' proportionate share of extraordinary expenses: *Gold v. Romhanyi* (2006), 2006 CarswellBC 658, 2006 BCSC 443 (B.C. S.C.); additional reasons at 2006 BCSC 443, 2006 CarswellBC 1265 (B.C. S.C.).

In order to qualify as a special or extraordinary expense under s. 7 of the *Guidelines* an expense must be out of the ordinary or normal expenses incurred from time to time for children: *Ewart v. Miller* (1997), 34 R.F.L. (4th) 408, 160 Sask. R. 151 (Q.B.). Most children participate in some extracurricular activities and the costs for these activities are not necessarily "extraordinary expenses." In this decision, the payment for hockey registration and camp did not qualify as "extraordinary expenses" where the father was earning approximately $55,000, the mother $34,000 and her second husband with whom she shared expenses had a very substantial income.

In keeping with the concern for predictability and certainty in child support matters, s. 7 orders should be the exception not the rule: *Hansvall v. Hansvall* (1997), 160 Sask. R. 201, [1998] 4 W.W.R. 202 (Q.B.). When expenses are greater than would have been the norm for a family at a particular income level or, alternatively when they involve unusual expenditures such as those required by a child with a disability, these expenses are "special" or "extraordinary."

Special expenses are expenses out of the usual course: *Stanbridge v. Stanbridge* (January 30, 1998), Doc. Vancouver D102899 (B.C. S.C.). In that decision, the court awarded

$1,800 *per annum* for special expenses. The court eliminated such items as saxophone lessons, karate lessons, hot lunches and field trips.

In *Ellis v. Ellis* (1997), 158 Nfld. & P.E.I.R. 193, 490 A.P.R. 193 (P.E.I. T.D. [In Chambers]), the court commented that the norm for what is an "ordinary" expense likely changes as incomes increase. In order to determine what is extraordinary, a court should decide what would be extraordinary for the custodial parent and thus decide what would be expected to be absorbed by that spouse as ordinary for the family's income level. Anything beyond that would be extraordinary. In determining the custodial parent's income for purposes of special and extraordinary expenses, the court should include child support payable under the *Guidelines*.

In *Krislock v. Krislock* (1997), 34 R.F.L. (4th) 420, 160 Sask. R. 212, [1998] 4 W.W.R. 230 (Q.B.), the court held that in deciding whether an extracurricular expense is an extraordinary expense in particular circumstances, the court must do so in the context of the means of the spouses. In the *Krislock* case, the custodial parent had no financial resources other than spousal and child support. The non-custodial parent earned a reasonable income. The court found that for the custodial parent, payment for hockey would be an extraordinary expense and unlikely to occur without a contribution from the non-custodial parent. The court ordered that the custodial parent contribute to the expenses for hockey.

It is the current "means of the spouses and those of the child," not the means prior to the separation, that must be taken into account in deciding the "reasonableness of the expense." The phrase "prior to the separation" is separate from and does not modify or in any way limit the phrase "means of the spouses" as used in s. 7: *Greenwood v. Greenwood* (1998), 37 R.F.L. (4th) 422, [1998] B.C.J. No. 729, 1998 CarswellBC 632 (B.C. S.C. [In Chambers]).

"The word 'means' should be interpreted broadly to include not just the income of the spouse, but other sources of revenue available to that spouse. The court can look at the economic well-being of the spouses and this includes a consideration of family income": *Baum v. Baum* (2000), 2000 BCSC 1835, 13 R.F.L. (5th) 258, 2000 CarswellBC 2604, [2000] B.C.J. No. 2565 (B.C. S.C.).

In *Raftus v. Raftus* (1998), 37 R.F.L. (4th) 59, 166 N.S.R. (2d) 179, 159 D.L.R. (4th) 264, 498 A.P.R. 179, 1998 CarswellNS 167, [1998] N.S.J. No. 119 (N.S. C.A.), the court noted that when assessing the reasonableness of the "extraordinary" expense taking into account the means of the parties, the judge will consider factors such as capital, income distribution, debt load, third party resources which impact upon a parent's ability to pay, access costs, obligations to pay spousal or other child support orders, spousal support received and any other relevant factors. The exercise is akin to the conventional "ability to pay" approach.

The "means of the spouses" is more than income earning capacity and "includes all of a person's pecuniary resources, capital assets, income from employment or earning capacity and any other source from which the person receives gains or benefits, together with, in certain circumstances, moneys which the person does not have in possession but which are available to such person": *Cornelius v. Andres* (1998), 36 R.F.L. (4th) 436, 125 Man. R. (2d) 144, 1998 CarswellMan 93 (Man. Q.B.); varied 170 D.L.R. (4th) 254, 1999 CarswellMan 86, 134 Man. R. (2d) 140, 193 W.A.C. 140, [1999] M.J. No. 103, 45 R.F.L. (4th) 200, [1999] 6 W.W.R. 317 (Man. C.A.); reconsideration refused (1999), 1999 CarswellMan 273 (Man. C.A.). Where the income generated from the respondent's assets is used almost entirely in paying debts, and the income from employment is below the threshold for the payment of the Table Amount (so that no Table Amount is owing), no order should be made for the payment of special or extraordinary expenses.

In addition, in considering the means of the spouses the court may consider the income of a spouse's partner: *Simpson v. Trowsdale* (2007), 2007 CarswellPEI 5, 2007 PESCTD 3 (P.E.I. T.D.). The income of new partners should be considered when reasonableness is an issue: *K. (D.J.) v. K. (C.J.)* (2006), 2006 CarswellBC 1715, 27 R.F.L. (6th) 196, 2006 BCPC 326 (B.C. Prov. Ct.).

Most expenses covered under s. 7 are commonplace, even though the *Guidelines* describe such expenses as special or extraordinary: *Fisher v. Heron* (1997), 157 Nfld. & P.E.I.R. 42, 486 A.P.R. 42 (P.E.I. T.D. [In Chambers]).

Child Care Expenses (s. 7(1)(a))

Expenses Allowed

In *MacKinnon v. MacKinnon* (2005), 2005 CarswellOnt 1536, [2005] O.J. No. 1552, 199 O.A.C. 353, 75 O.R. (3d) 175, 13 R.F.L. (6th) 221, 256 D.L.R. (4th) 385 (Ont. C.A.), the court held that it is an error to hold that a child care expense must be significant or extraordinary before it is shared by the parties in proportion to their incomes. No such requirement is set out in s. 7. The section only requires that such an expense be necessary and reasonable. If it is, absent any other reason to order otherwise, the payor spouse is required to share the expense proportionately with the other spouse.

That portion of nanny expense consisting of a special expense under s. 7 need not be extraordinary to be included in a child support order. Where the expense is reasonably incurred as result of the mother's employment, there is no basis on which the court could interfere with it on appeal: *Barker v. Barker* (2005), 2005 CarswellBC 717, 15 R.F.L. (6th) 43, 45 B.C.L.R. (4th) 43, 210 B.C.A.C. 199, 348 W.A.C. 199, 2005 BCCA 177 (B.C. C.A.).

In *McLaughlin v. McLaughlin* (1998), 44 R.F.L. (4th) 148, 57 B.C.L.R. (3d) 186, 167 D.L.R. (4th) 39, 113 B.C.A.C. 224 (C.A.), the court held that child care for the time that a child is not in school is a necessary expense even though there are older children capable of providing this care where the payor's portion is $225 a month and the parents' combined income is $120,000. The provision of consistent, reliable care on a regular basis is in the best interests of the child, and making the older children responsible for the care would not permit them to pursue their own activities, including sports, social and volunteer activities.

In *Rebak v. Rebak* (1998), 43 R.F.L. (4th) 123, 169 D.L.R. (4th) 184, 115 B.C.A.C. 100, 189 W.A.C. 100 (B.C. C.A.), an order denying the mother child care expenses under the *guidelines* was reversed on appeal. Prior to the separation the children had a live-in nanny and continued to be involved in numerous beneficial activities which required supervision. Furthermore, the custodial mother's employment required long hours and extensive travel, rendering the award of child care expenses reasonable.

Where there was no evidence that a nanny employed by the wife performed any personal services for the wife, the entire cost of the nanny was allowed as a child care expense in *Low v. Robinson* (2000), 4 R.F.L. (5th) 368, 76 Alta. L.R. (3d) 238, [2000] 4 W.W.R. 663 (Alta. Q.B.); additional reasons at (2000), 7 R.F.L. (5th) 148, 79 Alta. L.R. (3d) 137,

[2000] 7 W.W.R. 509 (Alta. Q.B.); further additional reasons at (June 13, 2000), Doc. Edmonton 4803-110822 (Alta. Q.B.).

Child care expenses incurred when the mother was working were found to be extraordinary expenses which were necessary and reasonable. The family income was $280,000: *McCrea v. McCrea* (1999), 1 R.F.L. (5th) 320, 1999 CarswellBC 1476, [1999] B.C J. No. 1514 (B.C. S.C.); additional reasons at 2000 CarswellBC 1998, 2000 BCSC 1437 (B.C. S.C.).

In *Williams v. Williams* (1997), 32 R.F.L. (4th) 23, [1997] N.W.T.R. 303, 1997 CarswellNWT 30, [1997] N.W.T.J. No. 49 (N.W.T. S.C.), the custodial father's new employment required him to do shift work, which necessitated overnight child care at times. The increase in child care costs constituted a special expense, and the non-custodial mother was ordered to pay a proportionate amount of this expense in addition to the basic amount under the *Guidelines*.

In *Bially v. Bially* (1997), 28 R.F.L. (4th) 418 (Sask. Q.B.) on an application for interim relief the court considered questions relating to support for the parties' three children in the custody of the wife. The husband had an annual gross income of $43,450 and the wife, $23,435. Child care expenses were $400 a month. The court found that the child care expenses were necessary in order for the wife to maintain her employment, and were in the best overall interests of the children. Based on their respective incomes, the husband's share would be 65% or $191. This amount was added to the table income of $767 for a total of $958 each month.

In *Brown v. Brown* (July 4, 1997), Doc. FDSJ-75-97 (N.B. Q.B.), the court held that baby-sitting expenses of $4,680 a year, additional medical insurance coverage of $286, and registration for swimming of $208 totaling $5,174 a year were special or extraordinary expenses. On a monthly basis, these expenses were $215. The payor husband, whose income was $33,600 a year, was ordered to pay one-half of these expenses or $2,587 at a monthly rate of $215. This amount was added to the Table Amount under the *Guidelines* of $280 a month for a total monthly payment of $495.

Where the father earned $35,200, the mother earned $29,113, and the parties lived in a common law relationship for a few months, the court found that it was in the best interests of the child that the mother continue to be employed and that a child care expense was reasonable in the circumstance and was to be shared by the parties in accordance with their relative incomes: *Gee v. Ng* (May 22, 1997), Regina F.L.D. 145/97 (Sask. Q.B.). This case was decided under the Saskatchewan *Family Maintenance Act*.

Child care: *Rains v. Rains* (June 16, 1997), Doc. Sault Ste. Marie 16655/197 (Ont. Gen. Div.). The court allowed the child care expense as it was incurred substantially as a result of the mother's unemployment and was not an unreasonable expense having regard to the mother's earnings, her part-time work and the children's needs.

Child care: *Herman v. Rathbone* (August 27, 1997), Doc. Hamilton D2023/196 (Ont. Gen. Div.), additional reasons at (November 20, 1997), Doc. Hamilton D2023/196 (Ont. Gen. Div.). Where the mother was about to start medical school in the United States, the court allowed this expense prospectively.

Annual child care: *Hedderson v. Kearsey* (1998), 162 Nfld. & P.E.I.R. 271, 500 A.P.R. 271 (Nfld. U.F.C.).

Child care: *Raynor v. Raynor* (1997), 163 N.S.R. (2d) 117, 487 A.P.R. 117 (N.S. S.C.). Where the mother intended to return to university to improve her qualifications, the court awarded her $1,000 per month for child care.

Net day care: *Yaremchuk v. Yaremchuk* (1998), 38 R.F.L. (4th) 312, 218 A.R. 153, 158 D.L.R. (4th) 180 (Alta. Q.B. [In Chambers]).

Nanny services: Defendant to contribute $250 a month toward the salary of a nanny preferred by the plaintiff over day care. Amount assessed without reference to proportion of incomes: *Loewen v. Traill* (1998), 36 R.F.L. (4th) 231 (B.C. S.C.) before Boyle J.

Child care expenses of $247 a month and disposable underwear of $40 a month with non-custodial father's proportion being 57.4%: *Doege v. Doege* (1998), 37 R.F.L. (4th) 52, 162 Sask. R. 145 (Q.B.) *per* Zarzeczny J.

Payor's proportionate share in amount of $173.70 a month for child care costs: *Kyle v. Kyle* (1998), 37 R.F.L. (4th) 286, 164 Sask. R. 52 (Q.B.) *per* Wilkinson J., additional reasons (1998), 169 Sask. R. 111 (Q.B.).

Special child care expenses for a child with Down's syndrome: *Husfeldt v. Husfeldt* (January 9, 1998), Doc. Thunder Bay 011932 (Ont. Gen. Div.). The wife sought interim child support according to the child support guidelines. She maintained that the special care expenses were $5,000 annually, for which the Province of Ontario contributed $1,680. The court made an interim order allowing $100 for special child care expenses, leaving it to the trial judge to determine the exact amount for the final order, once supporting material had been provided.

In *S. (N.) v. M. (M.)* (2006), 2006 BCPC 381, 2006 CarswellBC 1997 (B.C. Prov. Ct.), the father of two children planned to attend university for 1 year and to work part time during this period. He had been an engineer in Egypt, but could not find employment in this area, so he planned to qualify as a high school teacher. His income would be $27,000 for the year. The mother attended school for 2 hours a day and worked as a playground supervisor for 1 hour a day. The father was ordered to pay 95% of day care costs during his year at school because he would not be available to look after the youngest child for part of the time as he had been doing. He was not ordered to pay for retroactive day care fees because full-time day care was not necessary when mother worked only 1 hour per day. He was not ordered to contribute to private school fees. The decision for one of the children to attend private school was not necessary and was not within the income of family.

In *Marshall v. Marshall* (1999), 4 R.F.L. (5th) 115 (B.C. Master), the husband was required to contribute to the children's extraordinary child care expenses despite the fact that the wife had lost the total subsidy for those expenses when she began to cohabit with another man.

Expenses Disallowed

In *Aukstuolyte v. Balchun* (2005), 2005 CarswellOnt 3482 (Ont. S.C.J.), the court held that child care, when provided by a live-in family member, is deemed to be "free" child care and not subject to payment from the separated parent, even for "room and board." Further, in such situations, the live-in family member is receiving benefits from other members of the household which compensate for the performance of child care functions.

Day care expenses: *Omah-Maharajh v. Howard* (1998), 58 Alta. L.R. (3d) 236, [1998] 7 W.W.R. 342, 215 A.R. 159 (Q.B. [In Chambers]). The father, a doctor, had a guideline income of $219,384 and the mother an income of $43,300. The parties had two children who were 9 and 12. Both parties had remarried and the mother had an infant child from the second marriage. The court rejected the mother's claim for day care expenses, as the majority, if not all, of the child care expenses were attributable to the infant child of the mother and her current husband. The court had no material before it to show what the child care expenses would be, if any, for only the two older children.

In *Woode v. Woode*, 26 R.F.L. (5th) 232, 2002 CarswellSask 49, 2002 SKQB 33, 216 Sask. R. 1 (Sask. Q.B.), the husband was not required to contribute to the wife's child care expenses. The father had offered to care for the children himself until the wife was finished work. Although the wife was not compelled to accept this viable alternative, she would be required to bear the entire cost if she continued with her existing paid arrangement.

The cost of the mother's own respite care resulting from the stress of caring for the parties' emotionally challenged child does not qualify as a child care expense under s. 7 of the *Guidelines*: *Y. (A.L.) v. Y. (L.M.)*, 17 R.F.L. (5th) 233, 2001 CarswellAlta 491, 2001 ABQB 311, [2001] 9 W.W.R. 141, 92 Alta. L.R. (3d) 347 (Alta. Q.B.).

A request for payment of day care expenses were not allowed because of the absence of particulars. It was not clear how the wife arrived at the cost of day care. She had not specified who the caregiver would be and what days and hours were involved. She did not lead evidence under s. 7(3) regarding the tax implications of support paid under s. 7(1)(a): *Myke v. Myke* (2000), 2000 CarswellOnt 1945, [2000] O.J. No. 2056 (Ont. S.C.J.).

In *S. (N.) v. M. (M.)* (2006), 2006 BCPC 381, 2006 CarswellBC 1997 (B.C. Prov. Ct.), the father of two children planned to attend university for 1 year and to work part time during this period. He had been an engineer in Egypt, but could not find employment in this area, so he planned to qualify as a high school teacher. His income would be $27,000 for the year. The mother attended school for 2 hours a day and worked as a playground supervisor for 1 hour a day. The father was ordered to pay 95% of day care costs during his year at school because he would not be available to look after the youngest child for part of the time as he had been doing. He was not ordered to pay for retroactive day care fees because full-time day care was not necessary when mother worked only 1 hour per day. He was not ordered to contribute to private school fees. The decision for one of the children to attend private school was not necessary and was not within the income of family.

Child's Portion of Medical and Dental Insurance (s. 7(1)(b))

Expenses Allowed

In *Wolfe v. Wolfe*, 26 R.F.L. (5th) 447, 2002 CarswellNS 129, 2002 NSSF 18, 202 N.S.R. (2d) 386, 632 A.P.R. 386 (N.S. S.C.), it was held that the father was required to contribute to the cost of the children's medical and dental care that was beyond the limit of his insurance coverage. However, the father was first to be given the opportunity to participate in the decision that the expenses were necessary.

In *Bradley v. Kallstrom* (2006), 2006 CarswellSask 397, 2006 SKQB 289, 286 Sask. R. 246 (Sask. Q.B.), the father's dental plan paid up to $2,000 in coverage per year. The estimate for completing the daughter's dental work was $6,000. The court ordered that any amounts not covered by the plan were to be shared by the parents on a 50/50 basis.

They would normally be shared on a pro-rata basis. However, even though the parties shared parenting of the children, the father agreed to pay the full Table Amount of basic child support in recognition of his significantly higher income. It was therefore appropriate that there be an equal sharing of extraordinary expenses.

Medical insurance: *Herman v. Rathbone* (August 27, 1997), Doc. Hamilton D2023/1 96 (Ont. Gen. Div.); additional reasons at (November 20, 1997), Doc. Hamilton D2023/196 (Ont. Gen. Div.). Where the mother was about to start medical school in the United States, the court allowed extraordinary expenses for medical insurance prospectively.

In *Dodd v. Dodd* (May 14, 1997), Brampton 010400/95 (Ont. Gen. Div.), the court permitted extraordinary expenses for orthodontic and medical coverage. The combined family income was $84,000.

In *Rains v. Rains* (June 16, 1997), Sault Ste. Marie 16655/97 (Ont. Gen. Div.), an interim motion for child support, the court was of the opinion that the payor spouse should pay 60% of the children's health coverage, dental insurance, and child care under s. 7 of the *Guidelines.*

See *Brown v. Brown* (July 4, 1997), Doc. FDSJ-75-97 (N.B. Q.B.), under "Child Care Expenses (s. 7(1)(a)" above, where a claim for additional medical insurance coverage was allowed as one of the special expenses.

Medical and dental insurance coverage. Father ordered to maintain medical and dental insurance coverage for the three children of the marriage on his plan. The father's plan did not cover 100% of the costs, and the mother had claimed the greater premium costs attributable to the children under her plan which did cover 100% of the cost. The court refused to order payment of the cost of the premiums under the mother's plan because most families get by without 100% coverage, and the additional expense was found to be not necessary or reasonable having regard to the means of the spouses, the needs of the children, and the family's spending patterns prior to the separation: *White v. Rushton* (1998), 37 R.F.L. (4th) 373 (B.C. Master); reversed in part (1998), 38 R.F.L. (4th) 454 (B.C. S.C.), *per* Master Horn.

Hansvall v. Hansvall (1997), 160 Sask. R. 201, [1998] 4 W.W.R. 202, [1997] S.J. No. 782, 1997 CarswellSask 709 (Sask. Q.B.): Section 6 of the *Guidelines* provides that, "In making an order for the support of a child, where medical or dental insurance coverage for the child is available to either parent or spouse through his or her employer or otherwise at a reasonable rate, the court may order that coverage be acquired or continued." This section should be utilized whenever possible before resorting to s. 7(1)(b). The court, pursuant to s. 6, ordered the father, at his own expense, to maintain dental and health insurance for the two children.

Krislock v. Krislock (1997), 34 R.F.L. (4th) 420, 160 Sask. R. 212, [1998] 4 W.W.R. 230, 1997 CarswellSask 679 (Sask. Q.B.): Where there is no evidence as to the portion of the medical and dental insurance premiums attributable to the children, the court will not make an order under s. 7(1)(b). However, the court in this case, did make an order pursuant to s. 6 of the *Guidelines.*

In *Murphy v. Murphy* (2000), 2000 CarswellBC 1974, 2000 BCSC 1476 (B.C. S.C.), it was held that medical and dental premiums and health-related expenses for the children are special expenses that should be allowed. The father's income was $105,000 and the mother's, $37,000. There were four children.

Dental insurance coverage. Father ordered to continue his dental plan coverage for the children. Mother to submit dental expenses to the father, for reimbursement from his plan. Any amount not reimbursed by the plan to be shared proportionately with the father paying to the mother 75% of such an amount not reimbursed within 15 days of receiving the invoice from her: *Carnall v. Carnall* (1998), 1998 CarswellSask 179, 165 Sask. R. 305, 37 R.F.L. (4th) 392 (Sask. Q.B.); varied on reconsideration (June 30, 1998), Doc. Regina Q.B. 015251 (Sask. Q.B.), *per* Dawson J.

Expenses Disallowed

Section 6 of the *Guidelines* provides that, "In making an order for the support of a child, where medical or dental insurance coverage for the child is available to either parent or spouse through his or her employer or otherwise at a reasonable rate, the court may order that coverage be acquired or continued." In *Hansvall v. Hansvall* (1997), 160 Sask. R. 201, [1998] 4 W.W.R. 202, [1997] S.J. No. 782, 1997 CarswellSask 709 (Sask. Q.B.), the court held that this section should be utilized whenever possible before resorting to s. 7(1)(b). Following this principle, the court avoided s. 7(1)(b) and pursuant to s. 6 ordered the father, at his own expense, to maintain dental and health insurance for the parties' two children.

In *Krislock v. Krislock* (1997), 34 R.F.L. (4th) 420, 160 Sask. R. 212, [1998] 4 W.W.R. 230, 1997 CarswellSask 67 (Sask. Q.B.), the court held that where there is no evidence as to the portion of the medical and dental insurance premiums attributable to the children, it will not make an order under s. 7(1)(b). However, the court in this case did make an order pursuant to s. 6 of the *Guidelines.*

Future orthodontic treatment was not found to be an expense under s. 7 as the evidence relating to the treatment was wholly insufficient. But the court observed that it would not have made an order in any event as the expenses might not be incurred for another 6 years: *Myke v. Myke* (2000), 2000 CarswellOnt 1945, [2000] O.J. No. 2056 (Ont. S.C.J.).

In *White v. Rushton* (1998), 37 R.F.L. (4th) 373, 1998 CarswellBC 443, [1998] B.C.J. No. 422 (B.C. Master); reversed in part (1998), 38 R.F.L. (4th) 454, 1998 CarswellBC 1125 (B.C. S.C.), the father was ordered to maintain medical and dental insurance coverage on his plan for the three children of the marriage, but his plan did not cover 100% of the costs. The mother's plan did cover 100% of the cost and she claimed the greater premium costs attributable to the children under her plan. The court refused to order payment of the cost of the premiums under the mother's plan because most families get by without 100% coverage, and the additional expense was found to be not necessary or reasonable having regard to the means of the spouses, the needs of the children, and the family's spending patterns prior to the separation.

Apportionment of medical and dental insurance premiums under s. 7(1)(b) is not appropriate where the insured spouse is not incurring an extra expense in maintaining the child of the marriage on his company's plan: *Middleton v. MacPherson* (1997), 29 R.F.L. (4th) 334, 150 D.L.R. (4th) 519, 204 A.R. 37 (Alta. Q.B.).

In *Barnett v. Barnett*, 20 R.F.L. (5th) 8, 2001 CarswellPEI 71, 2001 PESCTD 60 (P.E.I. T.D.), the fact that the mother paid a very modest sum under her group medical plan to cover the children's medical needs did not justify an award of "extraordinary expenses" in that regard.

Health-related Expenses (s. 7(1)(c))

Expenses Allowed

Where the mother was receiving funds from a third party to assist in meeting a child's special needs, only the amount above and beyond that assistance should be used in calculating "special needs" under *Guidelines*: *Giles v. Villeneuve* (1998), 43 R.F.L. (4th) 61, 1998 CarswellOnt 4260 (Ont. Gen. Div.); affirmed (1999), 125 O.A.C. 135, 1999 CarswellOnt 3124 (Ont. C.A.).

Medical expenses are not included in the basic *Guideline* amount. They are expenses that come within s. 7(1)(c) of the *Guidelines* and should be shared proportionately between the parties. Physiotherapy for treatment of a medical problem is an allowable expense within this provision: *Earles v. Earles* (2006), 2006 CarswellBC 362, 2006 BCSC 221, [2006] B.C.J. No. 346 (B.C. S.C.).

In *Frass v. Frass* (2006), 2006 CarswellSask 276, 2006 SKQB 189 (Sask. Q.B.), child care costs and asthma medication costs were of sufficient amount and peculiar to the child as to be extraordinary or not expected to be reasonably covered from the Table Amount of child support and the custodial parent's income. The non-custodial parent was ordered to pay 71% of those costs amounting to a monthly sum of $125. If the payor's health plan covered the residual cost of the asthma medication not paid for by the recipient's plan, the payor's payment was to decrease by $67.45 per month.

In *Gold v. Romhanyi* (2006), 2006 CarswellBC 1265, 2006 BCSC 443 (B.C. S.C.), *per* Maczko J., additional reasons to 2006 CarswellBC 658, 2006 BCSC 443 (B.C. S.C.), the mother's dental plan paid for one-half of orthodontic expenses. These expenses were estimated at $1,000 per month. The father was required to pay his proportionate share (42%) of the amount not covered by the mother's plan.

Orthodontic expenses represent required expenses and the net costs, after the application of all dental insurance proceeds, should be apportioned between the parties: *Earles v. Earles* (2006), 2006 CarswellBC 362, 2006 BCSC 221, [2006] B.C.J. No. 346 (B.C. S.C.).

In *H. (L.M.) v. H. (G.D.)* (2006), 2006 CarswellBC 1684, 2006 BCSC 1035 (B.C. S.C.), the father was ordered to pay his share (80%) of orthodontic expenses estimated at an initial cost of $1,300 and $160 per month thereafter for a total of 20 months. The order provided that he could pay his portion of these expenses directly to the orthodontist as and when it was required.

Orthodontic work: *Seiferling v. Langmaier* (1998), 36 R.F.L. (4th) 296 (Sask. Q.B.), *per* Dawson J. The father was ordered to pay 86%, his proportionate share, of the cost of his child's orthodontic work ($1,950) even though the mother's new spouse had a dental plan which would pay for one-half of the expense.

In *Tapper v. Connolly* (2002), 26 R.F.L. (5th) 199, 2002 CarswellNfld 81, [2002] N.J. No. 83 (Nfld. U.F.C.), the child's orthodontic expenses were deemed to be "extraordinary" for *Guideline* purposes.

In *McCrea v. McCrea* (1999), 1 R.F.L. (5th) 320, 1999 CarswellBC 1476, [1999] B.C.J. No. 1514 (B.C. S.C.); additional reasons at (2000), 2000 CarswellBC 1998, 2000 BCSC 1437 (B.C. S.C.), orthodontic expenses were considered necessary and reasonable. The family income was $280,000.

In *Husfeldt v. Husfeldt* (1998), 1998 CarswellOnt 378 (Ont. Gen. Div.), the wife sought interim child support and requested special child care expenses for a child with Down's Syndrome. She contended that the special care expenses were $5,000 annually, for which the Province of Ontario contributed $1,680. The court made an interim order allowing $100 for special child care expenses, leaving it to the trial judge to determine the exact amount for the final order, once supporting material had been provided.

Cost of orthodontic work consisting of an initial fee of $1,300 and a monthly charge of $160. The father to pay the full $1,300 which was to apply against arrears of child support that had accumulated. He was to pay his proportionate share of the monthly expense which was 69.61% of $160. This share was added to the Table Amount of $239 for a total payment of $350 a month: *Schroder v. Schroder* (1998), 38 R.F.L. (4th) 395, 221 A.R. 395 (Q.B.) *per* Sanderman J.

Ritalin medication of $10 a month and cost of eyeglasses when incurred, with non-custodial father's proportion being 57.4%: *Doege v. Doege* (1998), 37 R.F.L. (4th) 52, 162 Sask. R. 145 (Q.B.) *per* Zarzeczny J.

In *McAllister v. Chishti* (September 3, 1997), Docs. FDF-573-95, Registrar's File 1301-037840 (N.B. Q.B.), the court found that orthodontic treatment (and music and dance lessons) came within the definition of s. 7 as special expenses. The father's income was $60,500 and he was ordered to pay one-half of the cost of orthodontic treatment (and two-thirds of the cost of the music and dance lessons).

Medical treatment of asthma: *Fisher v. Heron* (1997), 157 Nfld. & P.E.I.R. 42, 486 A.P.R. 42 (P.E.I. T.D. [In Chambers]). The parties' twin sons had developed asthma after the parties had separated. The father's contribution was less than his purported share as he did not have the means to pay. The order as granted, consumed 48% of his after-tax income and he had a second family to support.

In *Dodd v. Dodd* (May 14, 1997), Brampton 010400/95 (Ont. Gen. Div.), the court permitted extraordinary expenses for prescription drugs. The combined family income was $84,000.

Orthodontic treatment qualifies as a special expense: *Bell v. Griffin* (1997), 155 Nfld. & P.E.I.R. 87 (P.E.I. T.D.). This case was decided under the Prince Edward Island *Family Law Act*, but before that province's guidelines had come into effect. The *Federal Child Support Guidelines* were used as a guide in this decision. The total family income was $34,560 and the father was ordered to pay $96 per month for the orthodontic treatment. The parties had had a relationship but had never lived together and never married.

If dental expenses for the parties' child should exceed the amount payable under the dental plan by more than $100 per year, then the father should pay his proportionate share: *Walkeden v. Zemlak* (1997), 33 R.F.L. (4th) 52, 160 Sask. R. 1 (Q.B.).

McMahon v. Hodgson (2002), 2002 CarswellOnt 620, 25 R.F.L. (5th) 102, [2002] O.J. No. 555, [2002] O.T.C. 145 (Ont. S.C.J.). The court found a disabled adult child entitled to expenses under s. 7 for the costs of leasing and operating a motor vehicle as these costs were extraordinary expenses that were necessary in relation to the child's best interests.

In *Kohlfurst v. de Oliveira* (1999), 1999 CarswellOnt 2938 (Ont. C.J.), the father of a disabled child was required to contribute to the payment of expenses not covered by the child's handicap benefits. The child support order included an amount under s. 7 for expenses such as speech and language therapy, special equipment and toys for learning, private swimming lessons, therapeutic horseback riding and some costs towards camp.

In *Cabernel v. Cabernel* (1997), 1997 CarswellMan 348 (Man. Q.B.), the child required prescription drugs at a cost of $100 a month, and, within the foreseeable future, orthodontic treatment of at least $2,500 for the cost of braces. One hundred dollars monthly should be set aside immediately for the braces. The payor husband's income was "considerably higher" than the $7,500 a year he reported from self-employment, because of the personal expenses he was able to write off; and the wife's income was negligible. The expenses were necessary in relation to the child's best interests, and reasonable having regard to the means of the spouses and the spending pattern prior to the separation. The court held that the wife was unable to contribute to the payment of these expenses, and ordered the husband to pay $200 a month for the drugs and orthodontic treatment, in addition to the $200 a month basic support agreed upon by the parties.

Eyeglasses are a special expense: *Acorn v. DeRoche* (1997), (sub nom. *Acorn v. Deroche)* 155 Nfld. & P.E.I.R. 325, (sub nom. *Acorn v. Deroche)* 481 A.P.R. 325, 1997 CarswellPEI 79 (P.E.I. T.D.).

In *G. (J.) v. L. (F.)* (2006), 2006 CarswellBC 2204, 2006 BCPC 420 (B.C. Prov. Ct.), the father had an extended health care plan through his employment, which covered himself and his common-law spouse and her children. It also covered the parties' three children. His monthly premium did not change based on the number of persons on the plan. It was found to be appropriate that the parties share any medical, dental or health related expenses for the three children which exceeded those covered or reimbursed by any insurance plan that they had. The father's proportionate share of those expenses would be 69% and the mother's 31%.

Expenses Disallowed

In *LaForce v. Bassendowski* (2006), 2006 CarswellAlta 667, 2006 ABQB 397, [2006] A.J. No. 638 (Alta. Q.B.), *per* Veit J., the mother requested a sharing of the costs of a psychological intervention to improve the relationship between the mother and their 12-year-old daughter who refused to see her. The court found that while it was in the child's best interest to have a relationship with each of her parents, the breakdown of the relationship between the child and her mother was due to the mother's own actions, both in the way she chose to discipline the child and in failing to sufficiently nurture the parent-child relationship. In these circumstances, it was appropriate for the mother to pay for the intervention that was required to attempt to restore a healthy relationship with her daughter without contribution from the father.

The cost of non-prescription vitamins are not health-related expenses that qualify as "extraordinary expenses": *C. (D.B.) v. W. (R.M.)*, 12 R.F.L. (6th) 14, 2004 CarswellAlta 1810, 2004 ABQB 954 (Alta. Q.B.).

An annual expense for the children's eyeglasses which, after insurance reimbursement, required the wife to pay less that $100 per child did not constitute an "extraordinary" or special health care expense. It is expected that such minor expenses would already be covered under the base *Guideline* amounts: *Woode v. Woode*, 26 R.F.L. (5th) 232, 2002 CarswellSask 49, 2002 SKQB 33, 216 Sask. R. 1 (Sask. Q.B.).

In *Barnett v. Barnett* (2001), 20 R.F.L. (5th) 8, 2001 CarswellPEI 71, 2001 PESCTD 60 (P.E.I. T.D.), the fact that the mother paid a very modest sum under her group medical plan to cover the children's medical needs did not justify an award of "extraordinary expenses" in that regard.

In *Tallman v. Tomke* (1997), 204 A.R. 119 (Q.B.), the parties who had never married and never lived together had a special needs child. The child had required surgery for the placement of a shunt and she needed monitoring for this condition. She was also legally blind. The mother's claim for special day care costs for a special caregiver, rather than a regular babysitter, on the basis that the child did not handle change well, was rejected by the court as being too costly. The mother's claim for her expenses when she stayed with the child for adjustments to her shunt was rejected as not being within the contemplation of s. 7(1)(c) of the *Guidelines*. The mother had claimed her travel expenses to the hospital, parking charges and meals while at the hospital.

Braces for the teeth do not constitute special expenses under the *Guidelines*: *Knill v. Knill* (July 8, 1997), Williams Lake 5940/00955 (B.C. S.C.). The parties had a combined family income of $79,033.09.

A $100 deductible from a health plan (which must be paid out-of-pocket) does not come within the provisions of the section. "If ever there is a usual or expected expense for a child, a deductible of an extended health benefit plan is just such an expense. This usual cost is clearly intended to be included within the guideline amount for support and is NOT an 'extraordinary' or 'special' expense. Section 7 of the *Guidelines* is not intended to offer full indemnification of a custodial parent of all of her out-of-pocket monthly expenses for a child": *Thomson v. Howard* (1997), 33 R.F.L. (4th) 45 (Ont. Gen. Div.).

Cost of medication for child's thyroid condition: *Muir-Halliday v. Halliday* (1998), 37 R.F.L. (4th) 312 (Ont. Prov. Div.) *per* Foran Prov. J.

Where the mother is receiving funds from a third party to assist in meeting a child's special needs, only the amount above and beyond that assistance should be use din calculating "special needs" under the *Guidelines*: *Giles v. Villeneuve* (1998), 43 R.F.L. (4th) 61 (Ont. Gen. Div.).

Ongoing expenses for contact lenses: *Krislock v. Krislock* (1997), 34 R.F.L. (4th) 420, 160 Sask. R. 212, [1998] 4 W.W.R. 230 (Q.B.). The court disallowed claims for ongoing expenses for contact lenses, where the petitioner did not identify the nature of those expenses or when they were likely to occur.

In *Acorn v. Deroche* (1997), 155 Nfld. & P.E.I.R. 325, 481 A.P.R. 325 (P.E.I. T.D.), the court held that eyeglasses were a special expense.

Extraordinary Expenses for Primary or Secondary School (s. 7(1)(d))

Meaning of "Extraordinary"

Author's Note: Cases dealing with "extraordinary expenses" under the *Federal Child Support Guidelines* that were decided before May 1, 2006 should be read with caution. Prior to this date the courts differed on whether a subjective or an objective approach should be taken to determining the meaning of "extraordinary." In the subjective approach the expense is determined to be extraordinary, or not, by considering the expense in relation to the financial circumstances of the particular family in question. The objective approach, on the other hand, requires the court to consider whether the expense is disproportionately high in relation to an assumed general standard for all families at the particular level of the payor's income. The amendment to s. 7, which came into force on May 1, 2006 as s. 7(1.1) resolved the issue in favour of the subjective approach. By the amendment the expenses for educational programs, s. 7(1)(d), or extracurricular activities, s. 7(1)(f), are extraordinary if the requesting spouse or parent cannot afford them, or alternatively, if while affordable, they are extraordinary in light of the "income of the parent requesting the amount (including the child support amount)," "the nature and number of the educational programs and extracurricular activities," "any special needs and talents of the child," "the overall costs of the programs and activities," "and any other similar factor that is relevant." A request for extraordinary expenses calls for the application of both subsections 7(1) and (1.1). However, the order of application is reversed. Before looking at the necessity and reasonableness of the expense as required by s. 7(1), one has to first consider whether the request fits the definition of "extraordinary expenses" contained in the second paragraph, 7(1.1); that is, one must jump to (1.1) and then go back to (1). The important point to remember is that meeting the requirements of the definition in (1.1) is only going half the distance. Satisfying the necessity and reasonableness of the expense required by (1) (as is done with special expenses, also) is the other half.

Cases decided prior to the in-force date of the amendment are included subject to the caveat noted above.

Manitoba Cases Dealing with Meaning of Extraordinary in Manitoba Provision

The Manitoba cases annotated here deal with s. 7(1.1) of the Manitoba *Child Support Guidelines Regulation*. The subsection was added by an amendment which came into force in Manitoba on July 1, 2001. It is substantially the same as the Federal amendment and reads:

> 7. (1.1) In clauses 1(c) and (e), "extraordinary expenses" means
>
> (a) expenses that exceed those that the parent requesting an amount for the extraordinary expenses can reasonably cover, taking into account that parent's income and the amount that the parent would receive under the applicable table or, where the court has determined that the table amount is inappropriate, the amount that the court has otherwise determined is appropriate; or (b) where clause (a) is not applicable, expenses that the court considers are extraordinary taking into account
>
> (i) the amount of the expense in relation to the income of the parent requesting the amount, including the amount that the parent would receive under the applicable table or, where the court has determined that the table amount is inappropriate, the amount that the court has otherwise determined is appropriate,
>
> (ii) the nature and number of the educational programs and extracurricular activities,
>
> (iii) any special needs and talents of the child or children,
>
> (iv) the overall cost of the programs and activities, and
>
> (v) any other similar factor the court considers relevant. (Man. Reg. 87/2001, s. 2(4).)

In *Correia v. Correia* (2002), 2002 CarswellMan 269, 2002 MBQB 172, 165 Man. R. (2d) 134, 29 R.F.L. (5th) 28 (Man. Q.B.), the court held that a claim for extraordinary expenses under the Manitoba regulation should be analyzed as follows. Determine whether the expenses exceed those which the claimant parent can reasonably cover taking into account the parent's own income and the child support received. If they do, they are "extraordinary," and the following must be considered: the necessity of the expense in relation to the child's best interests, and the reasonableness of the expense in relation to, first, the means of the parents and those of the child, and secondly, the family's spending patterns prior to the separation. In considering the reasonableness of the expense in relation to the parents' means and the family's spending patterns, the court should take into account the combined income of the parents; the fact that two households must be maintained; the extent of the expense in relation to the parents' combined level of income; the debt position of the parents; any prospects of a decline or increase in the parents' means in the near future; and, whether the non-custodial parent was consulted regarding the expenditure prior to the expense being incurred. Examining the family's spending pattern prior to the separation "helps to see if the activity was one which would have been likely to be supported by the parents when together and thus considered by both to be in the child's best interests."

The court in *Laurie v. Laurie* (2004), 2004 CarswellMan 120, 2004 MBQB 59 (Man. Q.B.) noted that s. 7(1.1) modifies the objective test regarding extraordinary expense as previously held by the Manitoba Court of Appeal. According to the objective test, an expense for an extracurricular activity is only extraordinary when it is out of proportion to the usual costs associated with that particular activity. As a result of the amendment, the court is now required, as a first step, to determine whether the expenses of the extracurricular activities exceed those which the custodial parent can reasonably cover with his/her own income together with the child support. A finding that the custodial parent is unable to meet the extracurricular expenses on her own places them within the definition of "extraordinary." The second step of the test is to examine the necessity of the expense in relation to the child's best interests, and the reasonableness of the expense in relation to the means of the parents and those of the child, and the family's spending patterns prior to the separation. If this second step is not met, the expenses are not extraordinary as defined by s. 7(1) of the Manitoba *Child Support Guidelines Regulation*.

Chambers v. Chambers (2004), 2004 CarswellMan 456, 2004 MBQB 239, 9 R.F.L. (6th) 62, 188 Man. R. (2d) 283, [2004] M.J. No. 397 (Man. Q.B.) discussed the definition of "extraordinary" found in s. 7(1.1), to which a court must look before considering whether a parent ought to be ordered to contribute to a s. 7(1)(c) or (e) expense. In determining whether an expense meets the definition of "extraordinary," a court is not to look at the finances of both spouses. Rather the court must consider the income, including child support, of the *claimant* parent. The payor's financial circumstances, for the purposes of s. 7(1.1) are irrelevant. Once the court concludes that an expense is "extraordinary", *and only if such a conclusion is reached*, the court is then to turn its attention to s. 7(1). Even if all of the requirements of the two sections are met, the court need not order that an expense be paid/shared. The order is discretionary: "the court *may* provide for an amount...". In coming to its decision under s. 7, the court *must* take into account the necessity of the expense in relation to the child's best interests, and the reasonableness of the expense in relation to the means of *both* parents and those of the child; and where the parents cohabited after the birth of the child, regard must be had to the family's spending pattern prior to the separation.

Fong v. Charbonneau (2005), 2005 CarswellMan 129, 2005 MBQB 92, 194 Man. R. (2d) 45, [2005] M.J. No. 124 (Man. Q.B.), case followed the analysis of a claim for extraordinary expenses set out in *Chambers v. Chambers*, above.

The court in *Holeman v. Holeman* (2006), 2006 CarswellMan 430, 2006 MBQB 278 (Man. Q.B.), noted that in analyzing a claim for an "extraordinary" expense the court is first required to consider whether the expense is indeed "extraordinary". Somewhat oddly, the analysis is commenced by examining s. 7(1.1) first. This section directs the court to determine whether the claimed expense is one which exceeds an amount that the spouse can "reasonably cover," considering the spouse's own income and child support. Once the court concludes that the expense is extraordinary, the balance of s. 7 must be considered. Section 7.1 directs the court to "take into account" three factors that are intertwined. Each must be examined. The factors are the necessity of the expense in relation to the child's best interests; the reasonableness of the expense in relation to the means of the parents and the child; and, the family's spending pattern pre-separation. The second factor, the reasonableness of the expense in relation to the means of both parents and the children, can be assessed by looking at the combined income of the parties; the fact that two households must be maintained; the extent of the expense in relation to the parties' combined level of income; the debt of the parties; any prospect for a decline or increase in the parties' means in the near future; and whether the non-custodial parent was consulted regarding the expense prior to the expense being incurred.

Cases Dealing with Meaning of Extraordinary in Federal Provision

One area the amendments sought to clarify is what constitutes an extraordinary expense as distinct from one that is ordinary. The Table Amount encompasses those expenditures that are ordinary. Section 7 focuses upon expenditures which are extraordinary and therefore over and above the Table Amount: *Frass v. Frass* (2006), 2006 CarswellSask 276, 2006 SKQB 189 (Sask. Q.B.).

In *Laflamme v. Laflamme* (2006), 2006 CarswellBC 1767, 2006 BCSC 1081 (B.C. Master), the court applied s. 7(1.1)(a) and found that the expenses claimed were "expenses that exceed those that the plaintiff/payee can reasonably cover," where she had no income except for spousal and child support under the court order. The husband's annual income was $192,000. Spousal support was $2,600 per month plus 25% of the husband's annual bonus. (Twenty-five percent of the last year's bonus was $13,750.) Child support for two children was $2,575 per month.

In considering what would be the "ordinary" amount of an expense for extracurricular activities and hence covered by the Table Amount, the court looked to government Social Service benefits as a standard and estimated that 1% of the applicant's income would be the amount of the ordinary portion. "[T]he applicant's total income is $65,921. One percent of the latter figure is $659. The "extraordinary expenses" being claimed are $4,622, which exceeds the cutoff of $659. Consequently, the applicant is considered to have "extraordinary expenses" in the amount of $3,963 ($4,622 less $659 = $3,963)": *Simpson v. Trowsdale* (2007), 2007 CarswellPEI 5, 2007 PESCTD 3 (P.E.I. T.D.).

Additional Cases

In *Slade v. Slade* (2001), 2001 CarswellNfld 12, 13 R.F.L. (5th) 187, 197 Nfld. & P.E.I.R. 4, 591 A.P.R. 4, 2001 NFCA 2, 195 D.L.R. (4th) 108, [2001] N.J. No. 5 (Nfld. C.A.), the court held that the cost of care for family pets and the costs related to the children's computer do not qualify as "extraordinary expenses."

In *Abbott v. Abbott* (2001), 2001 CarswellBC 420, 89 B.C.L.R. (3d) 68, [2001] B.C.J. No. 371, 2001 BCSC 323, 13 R.F.L. (5th) 233 (B.C. S.C.), expenses related to diapers and baby formula were found not to constitute "extraordinary expenses."

Expenses Allowed

Private school: The father was ordered to pay child support for three children. In addition, he was to pay the tuition for one of the children attending private school and, as well, his proportionate share of the other special and extraordinary expenses. The father's income for these purposes was $66,650 and the mother's $52,480: *Bolt v. Bolt* (2006), 2006 CarswellOnt 1490 (Ont. S.C.J.); additional reasons at (2006), 2006 CarswellOnt 1734 (Ont. S.C.J.).

Additional Cases

Driving expenses incurred and to be incurred for the daughter to obtain her driver's licence were held to fall within s. 7 in *Earles v. Earles* (2006), 2006CarswellBC 362, [2006] B.C.J. No. 346, 2006 BCSC 221 (B.C. S.C.). Taking driving lessons is conducive to learning safe driving habits and thus necessary to a child's health and education. The parties had combined income of some $80,000 and the income in the father's family unit was approximately the same as what was earned between him and the mother. "The reasonableness of the driving expenses already incurred and to be incurred must be looked at, not only relative to the family income, but also as being a one time expense. The fact is that the ability to work part-time often requires the ability to drive oneself to the place of employment, and in some cases the actual employment requires the ability to drive. Applying this criteria, I am of the view that ... the expense of a child's driving lessons and associated costs fall within s. 7 of the *Federal Child Support Guidelines* where the family incomes are as indicated. I therefore order that the expenses relating to Candace obtaining her driver's licence fall within s. 7 and must be proportionately paid for by Mr. and Ms. Earles in the percentages indicated."

In *Hartshorne v. Hartshorne* (1999), 1999 CarswellBC 2778, [1999] B.C.J. No. 2861 (B.C. S.C.); additional reasons at (2001), 2001 CarswellBC 431, 89 B.C.L.R. (3d) 110, 2001 BCSC 325 (B.C. S.C.); further additional reasons at (2001), 2001 CarswellBC 2622, 2001 BCSC 749 (B.C. S.C.); affirmed on other grounds (2002), 2002 CarswellBC 2592, [2002] B.C.J. No. 2416, 174 B.C.A.C. 129, 286 W.A.C. 129, 6 B.C.L.R. (4th) 250, 2002 BCCA 587, 31 R.F.L. (5th) 312, 220 D.L.R. (4th) 655 (B.C. C.A.); leave to appeal allowed (2003), 2003 CarswellBC 700, 2003 CarswellBC 701, [2002] S.C.C.A. No. 536, 313 N.R. 192 (note), 192 B.C.A.C. 160 (note), 315 W.A.C. 160 (note) (S.C.C.); reversed (2004), 2004 CarswellBC 603, 2004 CarswellBC 604, [2004] S.C.J. No. 20, REJB 2004-55588, 236 D.L.R. (4th) 193, 47 R.F.L. (5th) 5, 25 B.C.L.R. (4th) 1, 318 N.R. 1, 2004 SCC 22, [2004] 6 W.W.R. 1, 194 B.C.A.C. 161, 317 W.A.C. 161, [2004] 1 S.C.R. 550 (S.C.C.), the parties were the parents of two children in the custody of the wife. The husband's annual income for purposes of the *Guidelines* was approximately $175,000 for a Table Amount of $1,972.31 per month. The father was also ordered to pay all the costs related to the children's private schooling and counseling until such time as the mother obtained employment. Upon her obtaining employment these costs were to be shared in proportion to the parties' respective incomes.

Pursuant to an order made in 1997, the father in *Millard v. Cargoe* (2004), 2004 CarswellOnt 962 (Ont. S.C.J.) paid support for the parties' two children in the *Guidelines* amount of $700 per month based on an agreed income of $50,000 a year. The order did not contemplate payment of special or extraordinary expenses. By the time of the application in 2004, child support arrears had accumulated to $2,700. The mother applied to vary the support order claiming, among other things, payment of private school fees and orthodontic expenses. The father's assertions that his income in the last 3 years did not exceed $30,000 a year was not tenable, and the court imputed the same income that had been originally agreed upon; that is, $50,000 a year. The court found that the children's needs for private school and orthodontic expenses constituted a material change of circumstance warranting a variation. The father was ordered to pay 50% of the ongoing and 50% of the retroactive orthodontic expenses and private school fees.

In *Fitzgerald v. Gerlich* (2003), 2003 CarswellOnt 1816, 40 R.F.L. (5th) 84, [2003] O.J. No. 1946 (Ont. S.C.J.). the child had attended a Catholic school since kindergarten. In British Columbia, where she lived with her mother, Catholic schools were private institutions. The tuition cost for the child was $3,500 per year. An annual income of $25,000 was imputed to the mother. For the last 3 years the father earned between $62,332 and $73,404 per year. On the issue relating to the payment for the child's school tuition, the father was ordered to contribute 70%. The cost for school tuition was extraordinary. In most situations, parents incur no expense for the cost of secondary school and the expense is not reflected in the basic or Table Amount for child support. Attendance at a Catholic school was in the child's best interests.

The failure of the defendant to acknowledge that he was the child's father and to provide care and example expected of a father led the court to consider that the child had special or extraordinary needs. The defendant continued to deny paternity, even though in a proceeding under the *Child Paternity and Support Act*, the defendant was declared to be the father of the plaintiff's child. The court held that the provision should be made for the child to continue his education at a private school and to participate in some recreational activities beyond those associated with his schooling: *S. (L.) v. P. (E.)* (1997), 1997 CarswellBC 2083, [1997] B.C.J. No. 2206, 41 B.C.L.R. (3d) 14, 32 R.F.L. (4th) 75 (B.C. S.C.); varied *S. (L.) v. P. (E.)* (1999), 67 B.C.L.R. (3d) 254, 50 R.F.L. (4th) 302, [1999] 12 W.W.R. 718, [1999] B.C.J. No. 1451, 1999 BCCA 393, 1999 CarswellBC 1402, 126 B.C.A.C. 28, 206 W.A.C. 28, 175 D.L.R. (4th) 423 (B.C. C.A.); leave to appeal refused *S. (L.) v. P. (E.)* (1999), 135 B.C.A.C. 160 (note), 221 W.A.C. 160 (note), [1999] S.C.C.A. No. 444, 252 N.R. 194 (note), [1999] 3 S.C.R. xii, 179 D.L.R. (4th) vii (S.C.C.).

Where the parties had no prior spending pattern in relation to particular costs because the children were too young to incur such costs, such as educational trips to Europe, the court in *Waese v. Bojman* (2001), 2001 CarswellOnt 1813, 19 R.F.L. (5th) 220, [2001] O.J. No. 2009 (Ont. S.C.J.), acknowledged the fact that the mother had financed such a trip for the older of two children. Consequently, the court found that there was a parenting decision that such trips were in the best interests of these children and allowable under s. 7.

In *Davies v. Jenkin* (2001), 2001 CarswellOnt 4959, [2001] O.J. No. 5711 (Ont. S.C.J.), the court allowed transportation costs for a disabled adult child as part of her educational expense.

Where there is no evidence that it is in the best interests of a child to attend private rather than public school, the court will not grant an application for support to cover extraordinary expenses for primary or secondary education: *Demarchi v. Selwyn* (2002), 2002 CarswellOnt 3217, 32 R.F.L. (5th) 20 (Ont. S.C.J.); leave to appeal refused 2004 CarswellOnt 3874, 7 R.F.L. (6th) 243 (Ont. C.A.).

The cost of school books is not considered an "extraordinary expense" for *Guideline* purposes. *Walsh v. Walsh* (2006), 23 R.F.L. (6th) 447, 2006 CarswellNfld 37, 2006 NLUFC 7, 254 Nfld. & P.E.I.R. 338, 764 A.P.R. 338 (N.L. U.F.C.).

In *S. (N.) v. M. (M.)* (2006), 2006 CarswellBC 1997, 2006 BCPC 381 (B.C. Prov. Ct.), the father of two children planned to attend university for 1 year and to work part time during this period. He had been an engineer in Egypt, but could not find employment in this area, so he planned to qualify as a high school teacher. His income would be $27,000 for the year. The mother attended school for 2 hours a day and worked as a playground supervisor for one hour a day. The father was ordered to pay 95% of day care costs during his year at school because he would not be available to look after the youngest child for part of the time as he had been doing. He was not ordered to pay for retroactive day care fees because full-time day care was not necessary when the mother worked only 1 hour per day. He was not ordered to contribute to private school fees. The decision for one of the children to attend private school was not necessary and was not within the income of family.

In *Aamodt v. Aamodt* (2000), 2000 CarswellBC 1914, 2000 BCSC 1411, [2000] B.C.J. No. 1912 (B.C. S.C.), the husband and wife were married for 4 years and lived together with the wife's two children from her previous marriage. They separated while continuing to live in the same home. The wife had custody of children and the husband did not seek access. The children's natural father was divorced from the wife, lived out of the country, and did not pay child support. The wife brought an application against the husband for child support which was allowed. He stood in place of the father to the children. The children had continuing home contact with him and it was unlikely that the natural father would assume support obligations. The husband was ordered to pay the Table Amount of child support. He was not required to contribute to payment for the children's private schooling, but was ordered to pay his proportionate share of child care costs during the summer months and the fees for orthodontic treatment.

Where the court does not consider that the expense of sending a child to a religious elementary school is necessary in relation to the child's best interests and the reasonableness of the expense having regard to the means of the parents, the court will dismiss an application for payment of private school costs. The primary purpose in sending the child to a private school was to satisfy the interests of the mother and step-father in seeing the child raised in the Catholic religion. The father had a gross annual income of approximately $50,000: *Byrne v. Byrne* (1999), 1999 CarswellBC 1039, [1999] B.C.J. No. 1087 (B.C. S.C. [In Chambers]).

Where the mother did not make an effort to enroll the child in the regular school system within the prescribed deadlines and she decided to enroll the child in private school at the cost of $18,648 per year, without consulting the father in a timely way, the court held that the expense of private school was not extraordinary and the father was not obligated to contribute to the cost: *Steiger v. Steiger* (1999), 1999 CarswellAlta 551 (Alta. Q.B.).

In *Vallis v. Vallis* (1998), 1998 CarswellNS 319, 170 N.S.R. (2d) 116, 515 A.P.R. 116, [1998] N.S.J. No. 342 (N.S. S.C. [In Chambers]), the husband lost his job with the Coast Guard and then worked for $200 per month plus commission as the harbourmaster. His son was enrolled at college. The husband, who was paying $500 bi-weekly for spousal and child support, applied to vary child support. The son's need for tuition was uncertain, and there was no evidence to indicate that the daughter's skating lessons were the responsibility of the father. The court made no order for payment of extraordinary expenses — that is, no order for payment for the lessons or tuition.

In *McCoy v. Hucker* (1998), 1998 CarswellOnt 2919, 75 O.T.C. 12, [1998] O.J. No. 2831 (Ont. Gen. Div.); additional reasons at (1999), 1999 CarswellOnt 10, [1999] O.J. No. 19 (Ont. Gen. Div.), the husband earned an annual income of $181,000 and the wife earned $64,000. The husband was to pay child support for two children in the Table Amount of $2,711 per month. The wife's claim under s. 7 for contribution from the husband to the cost of private schools was denied. The wife had not demonstrated that private school was necessarily in the best interests of the children. There was no evidence concerning the particular needs of each child and what private school had to offer in terms of these needs. The means of the parents would not support, reasonably, the expense of private school.

The cost of a pre-school program for one of the parties' children was not proven to be necessary or reasonable: *Casey v. Casey* (2000), 2000 CarswellNB 91 (N.B. Q.B.).

Expenses for Post-secondary Education (s. 7(1)(e))

Expenses Allowed

In *N. (W.P.) v. N. (B.J.)* (2005), 2005 CarswellBC 10, 2005 BCCA 7, 10 R.F.L. (6th) 440, 249 D.L.R. (4th) 352, 36 B.C.L.R. (4th) 330, [2005] B.C.J. No. 12, 207 B.C.A.C. 76, 341 W.A.C. 76 (B.C. C.A.); varying (2004), 2004 CarswellBC 1520, [2004] B.C.J. No. 1351, 2004 BCSC 880, 5 R.F.L. (6th) 135 (B.C. S.C.), the father agreed to pay the Table Amount and that "all costs of education" would be "special and extraordinary expenses" to be shared equally with the mother. He appealed the order of the trial judge that he pay support for their 22-year-old daughter and contribute to her medical school expenses on the ground that she was no longer a child of the marriage. The Court of Appeal rejected this ground and dismissed the father's appeal. The father was required to pay the daughter's support (according to the Table Amount as provided in the separation agreement and the judgement of the trial judge, although the preferred approach for the support of adult children attending university away from home is to exercise the discretion found in s. 3(2)(b)), and that the father pay either directly or from the family trust, the sum of $11,000 to the daughter on July 1 and January 1 of each year that she attended medical school as his 50% share of her "special and extraordinary expenses" (per the separation agreement and the consent of the mother).

In *Scott v. Scott* (2004), 2004 CarswellNB 588, 278 N.B.R. (2d) 61, 728 A.P.R. 61, 2004 CarswellNB 587, 2004 NBCA 99, [2004] N.B.J. No. 468, 10 R.F.L. (6th) 135 (N.B. C.A.); reversing in part (2003), 2003 CarswellNB 418, 2003 NBQB 345, 265 N.B.R. (2d) 359, 695 A.P.R. 359 (N.B. Q.B.), the Court of Appeal upheld an order requiring the husband to pay his proportional share of a $17,000 yearly educational budget for his 20-year-old daughter at university, plus $1,400 per month from May to August inclusive when she was not in school and living with her mother. The motions judge found that the husband had an income at time of the proceeding, of $259,000 a year. The daughter was a gifted and talented musician whose specialties were the flute and the piccolo. She intended to pursue her studies in the United States after obtaining her first degree. She was employed during the summer months earning approximately $3,000. However, her need to practice made it impossible for her to work part-time during the academic year. (The motions judge considered the factors set out in s. 3(2)(b) of the *Guidelines* and concluded that an appropriate amount for her support was "$1,400 per month for those months when room and board are not being covered through the post-secondary educational expense claim.") The daughter's expenses at university were found to be $19,500. From this, the motions judge deducted $2,500, which she expected that the daughter could reasonably contribute from her summer employment earnings, thereby reducing the cost to $17,000.

In *Farrus v. Farrus* (2000), 2000 CarswellAlta 562, [2000] A.J. No. 680, 2000 ABQB 389, 82 Alta. L.R. (3d) 315, 267 A.R. 103 (Q.B.); varied (2002), 2002 CarswellAlta 549, 299 A.R. 382, 266 W.A.C. 382, 100 Alta. L.R. (3d) 255, 2002 ABCA 100, 28 R.F.L. (5th) 37 (Alta. C.A.), the parties' 20-year-old child lived on her own while attending college, and stayed with the wife during summer vacations. She had a further 3 years of post- secondary education to complete. She turned down a lucrative offer of factory shift work, and accepted a summer job in a day care centre in order to have time to devote to Ukrainian dancing. She was expected to earn approximately $5,000. She had savings of $10,000, and could have supported herself entirely from her own savings and summer employment income had she accepted the factory job. However, her choice of summer employment could further her eventual career, and did afford a reasonable income level for a university student. Her decision to forego more lucrative summer employment in order to have time for dancing was reasonable in light of the amount of time she had invested in developing her dancing skills. Her decision to pursue summer employment which left her financially dependent on her parents was reasonable. She remained a child of the marriage. Her expenses for 12 months would be $18,000. The shortfall, taking into consideration income from employment and savings, was $9,500. An income of $18,000 was imputed to the mother. Each of the father and mother were to bear his or her proportionate share of the shortfall.

An order was made against the father to pay the mother monthly child support for their son and daughter in an amount based on the *Guidelines* table. Shortly after turning 19, the son graduated from high school, moved out of his mother's residence and worked for 15 months. He then began studies at a computer college. The daughter, 17-years of age, graduated from high school, moved out of her mother's residence, began working, and enrolled in a cosmetology program. The father's annual income increased from $32,800 to $44,475. The father applied for an order reducing the amount of child support payable and the mother brought a cross-application seeking an increase in child support and an order for special expenses. In the result, the father was ordered to pay retroactive child support for daughter in amount of $359 per month, child support for both children in amount of $594 per month, and 80% of the daughter's unfunded tuition fees for her cosmetology program, plus 80% of her unfunded living expenses. The court found that the daughter continued to be a child of marriage as a consequence of her age, her dependence on her mother for financial assistance, and her intention to continue her studies. While the son ceased being a child of the marriage during the 15 months when he was over the age of 19, self-supporting, and not living with his mother, he requalified as a child of the marriage as a consequence of his attendance at the computer college. The *Guidelines*' Table Amount was appropriate support for both son and daughter. Costs of the cosmetology program were expenses for the daughter's post-secondary education under s. 7(1)(e) of Act. She was to contribute $300 a month from her part-time earnings: *Newman v. Tibbetts* (2004), 2004 CarswellNB 80, 2004 NBQB 81, 272 N.B.R. (2d) 337, 715 A.P.R. 337, [2004] N.B.J. No. 72 (N.B. Q.B.); appeal allowed (2005), 283 N.B.R. (2d) 63, 740 A.P.R. 63, 2005 CarswellNB 181, 2005 CarswellNB 182, 2005 NBCA 37, 16 R.F.L. (6th) 318 (N.B. C.A.)

In *Bertram v. Murdock* (2006), 2006 CarswellOnt 1394, 2006 ONCJ 69 (Ont. C.J.), the applicant mother's income was $61,188 for the year and the father's $63,180. Their son was attending university on a full-time basis while living in residence. The cost of his schooling totalled $15,446.84 for the current year and included tuition: $5,346.84; Residency and Meal Plan: $7,100.00; Books: $1,000.00; and Laptop Computer: $2,000.00. (A laptop computer is a reasonable and necessary expense in the furtherance of a child's post-secondary education.) The son contributed $7,709 to the payment of these expenses through an Ontario Student Assistance Plan loan. He used $6,347 of the loan to pay his tuition fees and books, and the remainder of $1,362 for unspecified incidental costs. The amount remaining on account of his post-secondary education was $9,100, representing the cost of his residency, meal plan and computer. Both parents are responsible for contributing to their son's university costs in accordance with their respective incomes. Clause 7(1)(e) of the *Guidelines* imposes an absolute requirement for the non-custodial parent to contribute his or her proportionate share towards reasonable post-secondary educational expenses after the contribution by the child, if any. Furthermore, there is no ability to vary, adjust or avoid the obligation to contribute to the parent's proportionate share of the s. 7 expenses on the basis that it would cause undue hardship, even if the undue hardship threshold has been met, (which was not met in this case). Recognizing that the mother's and father's incomes were relatively equal, the court ordered the father to pay the mother 50% of the post-secondary educational costs of the child after his contribution, fixed in the amount of $4,550 for the current academic year. In each subsequent academic year during which the child attended university, the father was to pay to the applicant 50% of the post-secondary educational costs of the child after the child's contribution of 80% of his OSAP loans and/or net summer employment income.

Under s. 7(e) of the *Guidelines*, the costs of post-secondary education are an expense to which a parent obliged to pay child support can be required to contribute, taking into account the best interests of the child and the reasonableness of the expense. In *Stewart v. Stewart* (2006), 2006 ABQB 668, 2006 CarswellAlta 1222 (Alta. Q.B.), the child, a daughter, was alienated from her father, but his obligation did not depend on there being a healthy relationship between them. The father should contribute his proportionate share of the daughter's university expenses. The amount of the contribution should be determined on the assumption that the daughter herself would contribute to the cost. The total cost was estimated to be $7,500, which included tuition, books and $1,500 for a computer. The court did not accept that a computer was a necessary expense, and reduced the estimate to $6,000. The court assumed that the daughter would be able to contribute $1,000 of that expense from her savings and from a scholarship she had earned. It therefore ordered the father to pay his proportionate share of $5,000 a year in respect of the cost of the older post-secondary education costs, so long as she remained a child of the marriage.

In *Hitchens v. Hitchens* (2004), 2004 CarswellOnt 1932, 2 R.F.L. (6th) 63 (Ont. S.C.J.), the father and mother were married for 24 years and had one dependant child who was a full-time community college student living at home. The father was a tool and die maker who ran his own design business. The business was forced into bankruptcy following his return to England at the time of separation. He petitioned for divorce and the mother brought a counterpetition in which she joined with the claim for divorce a claim for child support as well as other claims. Despite the fact that he earned only $8,000 in 2003, the court on the evidence imputed an income to the father of $45,000. Tuition fees and art supply expenses for the child were almost $10,000 per year. At the time of the trial, the child had incurred over $18,000 in outstanding student loans. During the year of the trial, she had been able to secure bursaries of approximately $6,000. She had no other means of support, and her father was not prepared to volunteer support. The court found that he could and would have been working had he been in Canada. He chose not to remain in Canada and, as a result, he was intentionally under-employed. Accordingly, the court ordered him to pay the Table Amount of child support of $387 per month based on his imputed income of $45,000. These payments were made retroactive to the date of separation of December 6, 2001.

In *Hyatt v. Whitney* (2002), 28 R.F.L. (5th) 366, 2002 CarswellOnt 1467 (Ont. S.C.J.), the mother and father both remarried. The father earned $69,700 a year and his second wife earned $24,000. The mother earned $22,000 a year and her husband earned $46,000. They had two children. The mother and the father had a 19-year-old son who was enrolled in the first year of a 7-year pre-law and law program in the United States. The mother applied for payment of the expenses for tuition, rowing fees, equipment and related items. The court ordered the father to pay special or extraordinary expenses of $250 per month commencing on the date the son entered college and continuing for so long as the father was under an obligation to provide basic child support. The son had experienced little contact with the father for 15 years and the mother's husband had acted in *loco parentis*. The husband had an obligation to assist in the financial upbringing of his son. But the son had moved from a less expensive educational regime to a substantially more expensive one. The father should not have to pay for much of the special expenses resulting from the son's decisions. The evidence did not establish that the son had any unique ability in law or rowing to justify an education in the United States.

In *Fraser v. Fraser* (2001), 2001 CarswellOnt 3378 (Ont. S.C.J.), the parties' twins were attending university and another younger child was expected to follow them. The mother's father had settled two trust funds for the children; one was for education purposes that had a current balance of $11,000 (which was one-third of the original balance) and the second was for the general benefit of the children with a balance of $55,000. The parents were required to pay the basic child support under the *Guidelines*. A university education for all children and ballet classes for the youngest child were valid "special" or "extraordinary expenses". The court allocated the balance of the education trust to the youngest child as she had not yet benefited from it. One twin was self-supporting so was not entitled to a further amount for special or extraordinary expenses. Half of these expenses for the other twin and the youngest child were to be paid from the second trust. The mother and the father were required to pay the other half in proportion to their incomes.

In *Holizki v. Reeves* (1997), 1997 CarswellSask 647, 34 R.F.L. (4th) 414, [1997] S.J. No. 746, 161 Sask. R. 76 (Sask. Q.B.), the mother applied for ongoing child support for her 18-year-old son and a further order pursuant to s. 7 to provide for the expenses of his post-secondary education. The son lived with his mother, was attending college and worked part-time. He was unable to withdraw from his mother's charge. Obtaining a college education was in his best interests, and the costs were reasonable. The father's annual income was $61,442 and the mother's was $61,093.56. Both parents were able to bear the costs of a college education. Having regard to their means and their son's limited ability to contribute to the payment of the costs, the father was ordered to pay child support in the Table Amount of $487 plus 50% of the costs of the son's tuition, books and transportation pursuant to s. 7. Nominal income earned by the son was to be used for his lunch expenses. The mother was ordered to reimburse to the father his proportionate share of any tax benefit she received for the son's tuition, credit and education credit.

Section 7(1)(e) of the *Guidelines* does not require that the court find that a child's post-secondary education expenses be "extraordinary" in order to be considered as an add-on expense: *Cavanaugh v. Glass* (2001), 14 R.F.L. (5th) 251, 2001 CarswellOnt 423, [2001] O.J. No. 457 (Ont. S.C.J.).

In *Budyk v. Sol* (1998), 1998 CarswellMan 224, 40 R.F.L. (4th) 348, [1998] M.J. No. 252, (sub nom. *Budyk v. Budyk*) 126 Man. R. (2d) 305, (sub nom. *Budyk v. Budyk*) 167 W.A.C. 305 (Man. C.A.), the appellant father had an annual income of $78,174.15 and the respondent an income of $76,728. Child support had been varied in accordance with the *Child Support Guidelines* resulting in an order of $978 per month. The father was ordered, also, to pay one-half of the children's special expenses consisting of university tuition, book and other supplies. These expenses amounted to $5,973.28 for the current year.

In *Pollard v. Pollard* (1999), 1999 CarswellAlta 1189, 257 A.R. 36, (sub nom. *C.M.P. v. P.E.P.)* [1999] A.J. No. 1478, 1999 ABQB 976, 75 Alta. L.R. (3d) 350, [2000] 3 W.W.R. 322 (Alta. Q.B.), the court held that an agreement between the parents to provide for a child's post-secondary education coupled with an intention to support her until she turned 21, should be enforced.

The father was ordered to pay child support and extraordinary expenses of $55 per month, and contribute to Registered Education Savings Plan (RESP) in the amount of $80 per month: *Cook v. McManus* (2006), 301 N.B.R. (2d) 372, 783 A.P.R. 372, 2006 CarswellNB 442, 2006 NBQB 138 (N.B. Q.B.).

The court allocated 43% of the payment for the shortfall in the daughter's education expense to the father, his proportionate share, after deducting the child's Canada and Saskatchewan student loans and 50% of her employment earnings: *Cyrenne v. Costache* (2003), 2003 CarswellSask 112, 2003 SKQB 81, 230 Sask. R. 228 (Sask. Q.B.).

In *T. (D.J.W.) v. T. (S.E.M.)* (2002), 2002 CarswellAlta 1565, 2002 ABQB 1053, 333 A.R. 170 (Alta. Q.B.), the court noted that the parent providing the primary residence for an adult child attending a post-secondary institution must take steps to ensure that the child makes every reasonable effort to provide for his or her own financial needs. If an adult child fails to make a sufficient contribution to his or her post-secondary expenses through employment, the parent providing the primary residence for the child must assume financial responsibility for the shortfall.

Where the parties are of considerable means with a combined income of $122,000, it is not reasonable that their child should graduate with a crushing student loan debt. As the child was able to earn over $5,000 each summer, she should be able to cover 50% of her university expenses by earnings from employment, student loans, tax credits or other income. The balance of $5,170 was apportioned between the parties: *McMahon v. Hodgson* (2002), 2002 CarswellOnt 620, 25 R.F.L. (5th) 102, [2002] O.J. No. 555, [2002] O.T.C. 145 (Ont. S.C.J.).

A computer and printer are necessary parts of an adult child's university education and therefore are proper expenses under s. 7 of the *Child Support Guidelines*: *Waese v. Bojman* (2001), 19 R.F.L. (5th) 220, 2001 CarswellOnt 1813, [2001] O.J. No. 2009 (Ont. S.C.J.).

In *Davies v. Jenkin* (2001), 2001 CarswellOnt 4959, [2001] O.J. No. 5711 (Ont. S.C.J.), the court held that special expenses relating to schooling for an adult child attending university for 8 months a year are ongoing expenses and the father's contributions should be averaged and spread over the entire year.

In *Kozun v. Kozun* (2001), 18 R.F.L. (5th) 115, 2001 CarswellSask 475, 2001 SKQB 329, [2001] S.J. No. 441 (Sask. Q.B.), the husband was ordered to pay child support for his daughter who was attending university. The fact that the daughter was estranged from the father provided no defence, as he was himself largely responsible for the estrangement. Although tuition costs were covered by a trust fund, the daughter was still dependent upon her parents for food and shelter.

The following were to be deducted from the post secondary school expenses before determining the proportionate shares of the parties: (a) any scholarships, bursaries, awards or grants; (b) any amount payable under a Registered Education Savings Plan; (c) 50% of the net earnings of each child: *da Silva v. da Silva* (2004), 2004 CarswellOnt 1890, 5 R.F.L. (6th) 274 (Ont. S.C.J.).

On the mother's application for child support, among other things, the husband was ordered to contribute a different amount to extraordinary expenses for two children in each of the last 3 years because of his fluctuating income. He was ordered to pay 66% of "extraordinary expenses" in 1998, 45.5% in 1999, 65% in 2000, and 53% in 2001. The daughter was to be responsible for 20% of her own university tuition with the mother and father to share responsibility for the balance in proportion to their incomes: *Mellway v. Mellway* (2002), 2002 CarswellMan 72, 162 Man. R. (2d) 104, 2002 MBQB 29, [2002] M.J. No. 59 (Man. Q.B.); reversed in part (2004), 2004 CarswellMan 332, [2004] M.J. No. 300, 241 D.L.R. (4th) 623, 2004 MBCA 119, 4 R.F.L. (6th) 70, 187 Man. R. (2d) 247, 330 W.A.C. 247, [2005] 3 W.W.R. 608 (Man. C.A.).

Where the mother was unemployed and unlikely to obtain meaningful remunerative employment in the future, the father was ordered to pay child support of $823 per month for two children, with various terms attached to the order concerning educational expenses. The father had a present income of $60,000: *Ghazal v. Ghazal* (2000), 2000 CarswellOnt 728 (Ont. S.C.J.).

In *Jaasma v. Jaasma* (1999), 3 R.F.L. (5th) 74, 249 A.R. 357, 1999 CarswellAlta 927, [1999] A.J. No. 1186 (Alta. Q.B.), the court held that the s. 7 expenses for post-secondary education of $3,400 per year should be payable with the child contributing one-half the amount, and the remaining half being apportioned between the parties.

In *Achkewich v. Achkewich* (1998), 220 A.R. 385, 1998 CarswellAlta 1275, [1998] A.J. No. 383, 1998 ABQB 280 (Alta. Q.B.), child support was ordered on the basis that there is a presumption of parental support for a child's first degree lasting up to 4 years, unless there are other contrary considerations.

Where a consent order provided that the father was to pay child support in the amount of $500 per month until the child reached the age of 18, and the mother was to be responsible for all other costs for the maintenance of the child, the support order could be varied requiring the father to contribute to the child's post-secondary education expenses. The threshold requirement of material change of circumstances was met, as the likelihood of post-secondary education was not contemplated by the parties at the time of the support order, and the order was made before the coming into force of s. 15.1 of the *Divorce Act*: *Kembi v. Kembi* (1999), 1999 CarswellBC 1052, [1999] B.C.J. No. 165 (B.C. S.C.).

In *Cook v. Cook* (1998), 1998 CarswellBC 1638 (B.C. S.C.); additional reasons at (1998), 1998 CarswellBC 3124 (B.C. S.C.), the wife applied for child support for the parties' 19-year-old son who lived with her. He quit school to work in a restaurant, and then left this job to take a 3-month course to be a ferry deck hand. The court held that the wife was entitled to child support until the son completed the course and obtained work. The husband was ordered to pay the Table Amount of $567 a month until the son earned an income equivalent to what he earned when last in the work force. Also, the husband was ordered to reimburse the wife for 75% of the cost of the son's course as a "special" expense.

The mother had custody of the parties' two teenage children. The husband's annual income for *Guidelines* purposes was $49,607. The wife's annual income for these purposes was $17,000. The father was ordered to pay child support in an amount of $695 per month. The son was attending private school as he had not been performing well in public school. The daughter had been doing well in public school, but was attending private school, also, as her parents wanted her to attend the same school as their son. The son's enrollment in private school was in his best interests. However, the daughter should attend public school as private school was not necessary for her. The father was ordered to pay his proportionate share of the son's private school expenses as an extraordinary expense under s. 7 of *Guidelines*: *Ostlund v. Ostlund* (2000), 2000 CarswellBC 1241, 2000 BCSC 842 (B.C. S.C.).

Expenses Disallowed

Instead of ordering a monthly amount for the eldest child's schooling and no Table Amount, the trial judge ought to have ordered the Table Amount and no additional amount for her expenses at school. The monthly amount ordered was more properly classified as basic support, and not as an "extraordinary expense": *Pollock v. Rioux* (2004), 2004 CarswellNB 599, 2004 CarswellNB 600, [2004] N.B.J. No. 467, (sub nom. *J.P. v. R.R.)* 278 N.B.R. (2d) 351, (sub nom. *J.P. v. R.R.)* 728 A.P.R. 351, 2004 NBCA 98, 11 R.F.L. (6th) 330 (N.B. C.A.).

The court held that where children are too young to attend university, there are no current "extraordinary expenses" for post-secondary education, and there is no obligation for a party to contribute to an R.E.S.P. The court stated that the contribution to the educational plan could perhaps be characterized as the making of provisions for an anticipated expense in the future: *Luedke v. Luedke* (2004), 2004 CarswellBC 1565, 2004 BCCA 327, [2004] B.C.J. No. 1157, 198 B.C.A.C. 293, 10 R.F.L. (6th) 74, 44 B.C.L.R. (4th) 35 (B.C. C.A.).

In *Corsano v. Simms* (2002), 2002 CarswellNS 420, 33 R.F.L. (5th) 301, 2002 NSCA 125, 209 N.S.R. (2d) 242, 656 A.P.R. 242 (N.S. C.A.), the mother appealed from an order dealing with post-secondary educational expenses. The court in upholding the lower court decision was of the opinion that the expenses of over $12,000 for the parties' son to attend university were not reasonable in the circumstances. He could have significantly reduced those expenses by living at home and attending a university in a city where one of his parents resided. In the circumstances of the case, a reasonable amount for university expenses was $4,698, limited to tuition, books and fees. The applications judge reduced this sum by the amount of the child's summer savings ($600) and the educational savings plan contribution ($3,019). This left a shortfall of approximately $1,000. Since it was reasonable to infer that the tax savings from an educational credit would exceed the shortfall in expenses, there were no reasonable expenses to be shared.

In *Moss v. Moss* (2004), 2004 CarswellNfld 125, 2004 NLSCTD 83, 2 R.F.L. (6th) 121, 237 Nfld. & P.E.I.R. 223, 709 A.P.R. 223, [2004] N.J. No. 164 (N.L. T.D.), all of the parties' children qualified as children of the marriage at the time of separation. At the time of the application, the three eldest children were adults attending post-secondary education at various levels. A. was 26 years of age and had completed a Bachelor of Science degree in Environmental Science. L. was 24 years of age and had been a full-time student for the period under review. B. was 21 and enrolled in a flight instructor's course full-time which he was due to complete in 6 months. The mother asked the court to review the expenses she had incurred with the children and requested a year-by-year adjustment from 1998 to date of these special expenses, the large portion of which included the cost of post-secondary education for four of the older children. First the court considered whether the three eldest children, were "children of the marriage" within the meaning of the *Divorce Act.* On the basis of his choices, and the fact that he was employable after graduation, A. ceased to be child of the marriage 6 months after he obtained his degree. L.'s status as child of the marriage ended 4 months after she entered university for commencement of her Masters of Science program. At that point, she was making her own decisions concerning what areas she wished to pursue, whom she would be living with, where she was going to school and whether she wished to continue her formal education. B. was no longer a child of the marriage 6 months after he completed his flight training program. The program and his increased maturity should make him employable and thus independent. The father was required to pay child support for as long as each of these three children was considered a child of the marriage.

An RESP (which is a plan directed to saving for the future costs of post-secondary education) taken out for children at a young age whose post secondary education is many years ahead, does not fit into the principles of claiming for actual and ongoing expenses as set out in the *Guidelines*. Also, while the RESP may be desirable, it is not necessary. The father was not required to contribute to the cost of $65 a month: *LaRosa v. LaRosa* (2003), 2003 CarswellMan 236, 2003 MBQB 138, 175 Man. R. (2d) 72 (Man. Q.B.)

Where a 21-year-old child was away from school and held a full-time job for approximately 3 1/2 half years, resigned from her job where she earned $23,000 a year, purchased a vehicle for $16,000, financed a foreign holiday for herself, and did not have any savings, she was not a child of the marriage and was not entitled to basic child support or s. 7 post-secondary educational expenses, even though she planned to attend college: *Harrison v. Vargek* (2002), 2002 CarswellMan 162, 164 Man. R. (2d) 74, 2002 MBQB 97, 28 R.F.L. (5th) 176, [2002] M.J. No. 155 (Man. Q.B.).

Where an adult child continues to hold a part-time job while attending university and fails to dedicate his time and energy to his educational pursuits, he should assume financial responsibility for the program from income earned from his employment: *Nikita v. Nikita* (2002), 2002 CarswellOnt 1673, [2002] O.J. No. 1893 (Ont. C.J.).

In *McCrea v. McCrea* (1999), 1999 CarswellBC 1476, [1999] B.C.J. No. 1514, 1 R.F.L. (5th) 320 (B.C. S.C.); additional reasons at (2000), 2000 CarswellBC 1998, 2000 BCSC 1437 (B.C. S.C.), a post-secondary school reserve for a 10-year-old child did not qualify as an extraordinary expense. However the court ordered that the father set up an educational fund for the child in question and contribute $3,000 a year to the fund.

Extraordinary Expenses for Extracurricular Activities (s. 7(1)(f))

Meaning of "Extracurricular" — Expenses Allowed

Special sports training camps: extracurricular activities of the family's two teenage sons included football and basketball. They would be participating in special training camps for those sports and there would be "extraordinary expenses" associated with playing at an elevated level. The father was ordered to pay to the mother $100 per month with $50 to be attributed to each son. Expenses incurred for extracurricular activities over and above this amount were to be shared by the parties in proportion to their respective incomes: *Kloosterman v. Kloosterman* (2006), 2006 CarswellOnt 1951 (Ont. S.C.J.), *per* Turnbull J.

Expenses associated with the child's cheerleading activities estimated at $2,000 per year or $167 per month were found to be extracurricular activities important to the child. And it was in her best interests to be able to participate in these activities. The father was ordered to pay his proportionate share: *H. (L.M.) v. H. (G.D.)* (2006), 2006 CarswellBC 1684, 2006 BCSC 1035 (B.C. S.C.).

In *Simpson v. Trowsdale* (2007), 2007 CarswellPEI 5, 2007 PESCTD 3 (P.E.I. T.D.), the father's income was $62,828 and that of the mother was $51,989, for a combined total of $114,817. Expenses claimed under s. 7(1)(d) and (f) were for the daughter's figure skating, in which she had been involved since she was 3 years old, at a cost of $1,962 a year made up of a registration fee $355, spring school registration $290, private skating lessons $517, and the cost of new skates at $800. One son had guitar lessons costing $500. The other son had hockey expenses of $1,200 made up of hockey school registration $135, hockey registration $175, tryout fee $50, rep team fee $140, and hockey equipment estimated at $700, and a Spell Read education program, falling under (d), costing $960 for a yearly total of $2,160. The aggregate of these extraordinary expenses was $4,622. The court deducted 1% of the mother's income including child support ($65,921) as being attributable to the "ordinary" portion of the extracurricular and educational expenses (1% of $65,921 or $659) leaving "extraordinary expenses" of $3,963 ($4,622 less $659 = $3,963) to be apportioned between the parents. The father's share was 55% of $3,963 amounting to $2,180, or $182 per month.

In response to the parents' request for an amount of ongoing "extraordinary expenses" to be fixed for the father to pay, the court in *K. (D.J.) v. K. (C.J.)* (2006), 2006 CarswellBC 1715, 27 R.F.L. (6th) 196, 2006 BCPC 326 (B.C. Prov. Ct.), was of the view that "the question is what might be reasonable." The combined income of the separated parents was $95,000. The incomes of their new spouses were not stated in the reasons. The court considered the incomes of the new spouses as well as previous spending patterns in concluding that approximately $7,800 per year was reasonable for the extraordinary expenses. The parents had agreed that the father's proportional share would be two-thirds of the expenses. His two-thirds share, based on current incomes, would be $5400 per year, or $450 per month. If the mother chose to spend an amount greater than $7,800 per year she could do so, but the father's contribution was limited to $450 per month until further court order.

Dance costs for the daughter of $7,000 a year, which were a necessary expense in relation to the child's best interests and a reasonable expense in relation to the means of the spouses and the family's spending pattern prior to separation, should continue to be supported after she reached her majority. However, her ability to contribute to the expense should be taken into account and the father's obligation should decline over time. Accordingly, for the current year only two-thirds of the total dance costs were to be an "extraordinary expense". The total dance costs to be covered were limited to $7,000. The father was required to pay his proportionate share of two-thirds of that amount. If $7,000 was expended, he would be required to pay his proportionate share of $4,666. If less than $7,000 was expended, he would be required to pay his proportionate share of two-thirds of the amount spent. For the next year only one-half of the total dance costs would be an "extraordinary expense" and for the year after that, only one third would qualify for the parents' contribution. For the following year no payment for this expense would be required. The cap of $7,000 would remain throughout these years. A condition of the arrangement was that the daughter remain a child of the marriage: *Stewart v. Stewart* (2006), 2006 ABQB 668, 2006 CarswellAlta 1222 (Alta. Q.B.).

In *G. (J.) v. L. (F.)* (2006), 2006 CarswellBC 2204, 2006 BCPC 420 (B.C. Prov. Ct.), the mother sought, among other relief, an increase in the amount that the father should pay for their daughter's dance classes as an "extraordinary extracurricular expense". The total of the mother's income and the child support she would receive was $50,704 per year. The father's income at the time of signing their separation agreement was $52,000 per year and at the time of the proceeding was over $74,000. The daughter's dance competition and costuming fees were $265 per month. The mother included in her budget $5,000 as expenses for activities and lessons for the daughter (and her two siblings). There was a shortfall between her income and her expenses of $5,036 per year. The court found that the mother could not reasonably cover the expense of her daughter's dance activities after taking into account her income and the amount she would receive under the *Guideline* table. The expenses related to her daughter's dance classes and dance activities were, therefore, "extraordinary expenses" within the meaning of s. 7(1.1)(a). The court next considered the necessity of the expense in relation to the child's best interests and the reasonableness of the expense having regard to the means of the parents and the child, and the spending pattern of the parents prior to separation. The daughter had been in dance for 8 to 9 years (since she was 6 or 7 years old). She had a job dancing at the Pacific National Exhibition in the current year. She wanted to make a career of dancing. Her father agreed that she was both good at dancing and that she enjoyed it, but indicated he would rather see her involved in other activities, such as sports, and that her dancing took her away from that. He stated he only agreed to pay one half of one dance class when he signed the separation agreement and he should not be required to pay for any more than that. Against this objection, the court found the daughter had committed herself to her dancing; that she not only enjoyed it, but she was good at it and had the ability to earn some income from it. It was in her best interests to continue with the dance classes and competitions. The father's income was $74,000 a year and he had expenses of $58,816. He had no rent or mortgage expense. His common-law spouse paid the rent/mortgage and he paid all other living expenses of the household. On the basis of this and other evidence, the court found that the parents had the means to pay the expenses relating to their daughter's dance activities. At the time that the separation agreement was signed, it was contemplated that she would be in dance. She was 9 years old at the time. She had progressed in her dance and was more involved in it than she was before. When the father agreed to pay for one dance class, he supported her being involved in dance as an extracurricular activity. The parents obviously were of the view that they should contribute to their children's activities. At the time of the agreement, the father's income was $52,000 per year. At the time of the proceeding, it had increased to over $74,000 per year. The court found that there was a pattern on the part of both parents before and at the time of their separation of contributing to the extracurricular activities of the children, including dance classes for the daughter. They agreed to devote at least a part of their incomes to those extracurricular activities. Accordingly, the court ordered the father to pay to the mother a portion of the costs of any dance activities, which for the current year were $265 per month. His proportionate share was 69% or $182.85 per month.

In *Fong v. Charbonneau* (2005), 2005 CarswellMan 129, 2005 MBQB 92, 194 Man. R. (2d) 45, [2005] M.J. No. 124 (Man. Q.B.), at issue was whether or not the daughter's expenses for figure skating were "extraordinary expenses." The custdial mother's income including basic child support for 2004 would be $50,489. The amount of the figure skating expense was approximately $11,000 for the year or $916 per month. The skating expenses represented the only s. 7 expense incurred by the mother for which contribution was sought. The daughter was a competitive figure skater who needed to train and required coaching, both in her home community and, during the summer months, away from that community. The mother's evidence was that the daughter was "extremely talented." The father disputed this saying "she has not progressed very far despite all the money spent on coaching". Moreover, the figure skating interfered with his ability to spend time with her. The court found that the expenses were "extraordinary expenses" within the meaning of s. 7(1.1)(b) of the Manitoba *Guidelines*. "In making this determination I accept that Rebecca has some talents in this area and that they are being fostered by additional practice and coaching. In my view, it is not necessary that a child, in order to qualify for contribution from a non-custodial parent for such an expense be a regional, provincial, national or world-class athlete or champion. To hold otherwise would be to deprive the vast majority of children from the possibility of having expenses for their particular extracurricular activity considered under this section. In my view, this was not the intent of the legislature in enacting the *Guidelines*." There was no evidence that the skating activities were detracting from, or interfering with her school performance or overall development notwithstanding that the activity was quite time consuming. She had been involved in this activity in a substantial way for about 5 years. It would not be in her best interests to be withdrawn from this activity against her wishes. The physical activity and sport contribute to the health and well-being of children. Accordingly, the criteria associated with the necessity of the expense in relation to the child's best interests were satisfied. The parents had combined means of $138,178 per annum, $96,495 of which was income of the father. The court found that the expense was reasonable having regard to their means. As the daughter was still a toddler when her parents separated, the pattern of spending within the family unit on extracurricular activities of the child had not yet been established. The extracurricular figure skating expense should be shared, and the amount to which the father should be required to contribute was $10,800 per year or $900 per month. The required contribution of the father to this expense was 72% or $648 per month.

Expenses Disallowed

In *McLaughlin v. McLaughlin* (1998), 1998 CarswellBC 2327, 57 B.C.L.R. (3d) 186, 44 R.F.L. (4th) 148, [1999] 7 W.W.R. 415, [1998] B.C.J. No. 2514, 167 D.L.R. (4th) 39, 113 B.C.A.C. 224, 184 W.A.C. 224 (B.C. C.A.); additional reasons at (1999), 1999 CarswellBC 471, 44 R.F.L. (4th) 176, 172 D.L.R. (4th) 70, 1999 BCCA 135 (B.C. C.A.), the mother of two children requested payment of expenses for soccer, softball, outdoor school, swimming and hockey/skating totalling $965. The father's annual income was $70,000 and the mother's was $50,000 for a combined income of $120,000. In that decision, Madam Justice Prowse, speaking for the court, said:

> In my view, none of these expenses, individually, can be viewed as extraordinary expenses. The activities are common extracurricular activities for children of these ages and there are not, as there are in some cases, additional fees for such things as camps, trips, or expensive equipment. Nor is the total monthly amount associated with these expenses high, either in absolute terms or in relation to the joint incomes of the parties. In my view, Mr. McLaughlin's proportionate share of these expenses ($70 per month) must be treated as being included within the amount of maintenance he is paying under the basic table.

Not all expenses for extracurricular activities will qualify for sharing between former spouses. The expenses must be "extraordinary." Basic expenses, such as the costs of registration in a community sports league, or normal costs commonly associated with sport, such as the purchase of ordinary equipment and minimal travel costs, are not "extraordinary expenses." And where there are no special abilities that would make the expenses "extraordinary," badminton lessons are not "extraordinary expenses." They are recreational or sporting expenses that are included within the basic child support mandated by the *Guidelines*. It is to be expected that a child will have sporting expenses and the badminton expenses are expenses that are contemplated in the basic amount: *Earles v. Earles* (2006), 2006 CarswellBC 362, 2006 BCSC 221, [2006] B.C.J. No. 346 (B.C. S.C.).

In *K. (D.J.) v. K. (C.J.)* (2006), 2006 CarswellBC 1715, 27 R.F.L. (6th) 196, 2006 BCPC 326 (B.C. Prov. Ct.), the mother requested, among other things, that the father pay arrears of skating-related "extraordinary expenses." In denying the request the court found that the expenses were not "reasonable" and necessary in regard to the child's best interests. It is not reasonable for parents with a total income of $97,145 to spend $23,107 (after tax) for "extraordinary expenses." It is equally unreasonable for the same parents to spend $15,866 (after tax). Regardless of the child's talent and prospects, the family could not afford this level of spending. If the parents were still cohabiting, it is unlikely they could pay these expenses without incurring debt. When they are divorced, it is not reasonable for one parent to incur significant expenses and expect the other to shoulder a share, without advance discussion about the level of spending and whether it is necessary or prudent. Ms. D. and the father were living together during the year. When reasonableness is an issue the income of new partners should be considered. In this case, even if Ms. D.'s income of $29,500 for that year were included in "family income," the "extraordinary expenses" incurred in that year would still not be reasonable. The skating-related expenses were not reasonable and necessary having regard to the child's best interests. Given this finding, the father was not required to pay any arrears of "extraordinary expenses" incurred during the year.

In response to the parents' request in K.(D.J) for an amount of ongoing "extraordinary expenses" to be fixed for the father to pay, the court was of the view that, "Again the question is what might be reasonable." It considered the incomes of the new spouses as well as previous spending patterns in concluding that approximately $7,800 per year was reasonable for extraordinary expenses. The parents had agreed that the father's proportional share would be two-thirds of the expense. His two-thirds share, based on current incomes, would be $5,400 per year, or $450 per month. If the mother chose to spend an amount greater than $7,800 per year she could do so, but the father's contribution was limited to $450 per month until further court order.

In *Hendrickson v. Hendrickson* (2005), 2005 CarswellNS 430, 237 N.S.R. (2d) 89, 754 A.P.R. 89, 2005 NSSC 272 (N.S. S.C.), the mother claimed "extraordinary expenses" for extracurricular activities consisting of school lunches at $500 per year, gymnastics at $600 per year and swimming lessons and tennis at $400 per year. The court in disallowing the claim found that these expenses were not extraordinary, whether viewed considering nature of activities or in light of income of each parent. The father's income was $140,000 and mother's income as $43,000 for total income of $183,000.

Sharing Expenses (s. 7(2))

In *Lewi v. Lewi* (2006), 2006 CarswellOnt 2892, 80 O.R. (3d) 321, 267 D.L.R. (4th) 193, [2006] O.J. No. 1847, 28 R.F.L. (6th) 250, 209 O.A.C. 344 (Ont. C.A.); additional reasons at (2006), 2006 CarswellOnt 3214 (Ont. C.A.), the parties' two children, B and D, lived with their mother. The father's income was $180,000 a year. The mother was unemployed, and her sole income was spousal support of $3,500 a month. The children each had capital assets of almost $42,000 resulting from funds gifted by their grandfather for their education. D, who had reached his majority, began attending university while continuing to live with the mother. B planned to attend university out of town upon attaining his majority. The mother brought a motion to vary child support that had been ordered, and sought increased contributions for university education expenses. On the issue of the education expenses, the motions judge ordered the children to contribute a minimum of $10,000 each from their summer employment earnings, and ordered the parties to pay the balance of university expenses in proportion to their incomes. The father appealed, and on this issue requested an order that the children be required to exhaust their capital assets before obtaining a contribution from the parties. On the appeal, the order requiring the children to contribute summer employment earnings was set aside. D was required to pay all of his undergraduate expenses, estimated at $24,167.57, and B was to pay one-half of his undergraduate expenses, estimated at $64,000. The motions judge had erred in failing to include the children's capital assets in her analysis. The *Guidelines* require the court to consider whether children of majority age are able to contribute to post-secondary education expenses. The *Guidelines* do not imply that the children are required to contribute all of their capital assets, or that they should not have to make any contribution out of capital. The extent of the contribution expected depends on the circumstances of each case. In the case at bar, the children's capital assets had been gifted for their education. Although prior to separation, the parties had not intended that these assets be used for educational expenses, their financial circumstances had changed. The father was now the sole income earner, and the university expenses would be a significant burden on the parties. The new amount of support ordered would leave the children with substantial capital assets on graduation.

In *Bertram v. Murdock* (2006), 2006 CarswellOnt 1394, 2006 ONCJ 69 (Ont. C.J.), the applicant mother's income was $61,188 for the year and the father's income was $63,180. Their son was attending university on a full-time basis while living in residence. The cost of his schooling totaled $15,446.84 for the current year and included Tuition: $5,346.84; Residency and Meal Plan: $7,100; Books: $1,000; and Laptop Computer: $2,000. (A laptop computer is a reasonable and necessary expense in the furtherance of a child's post-secondary education.) The son contributed $7,709 to the payment of these expenses through an Ontario Student Assistance Plan loan. He used $6,347 of the loan to pay his tuition fees and books, and the remainder of $1,362 for unspecified incidental costs. The amount remaining on account of his post-secondary education was $9,100, representing the cost of his residency, meal plan and computer. Both parents were responsible for contributing to payment of this amount in accordance with their respective incomes. Recognizing that the mother's and father's incomes were relatively equal, the court ordered to father to pay the mother 50% of the post-secondary educational costs of the child after his contribution, fixed in the amount of $4,550 for the current academic year. In each subsequent academic year during which the child attended university, the father was to pay to the applicant 50% of the post-secondary educational costs of the child after the child's contribution of 80% of his OSAP loans and/or net summer employment income.

In *Albo v. Albo* (2006), 2006 CarswellAlta 1383, 65 Alta. L.R. (4th) 340, 2006 ABQB 785, [2006] A.J. No. 1330 (Alta. Q.B.), each of the parents had low, but similar incomes. Their daughter was enrolled in a post secondary educational institution. She had obtained a student loan of $14,365 for the academic year, and through her summer and part-time employment earned approximately $10,000 per year. Annual tuition was approximately $6,800 and annual expenses for books were approximately $1,000. The daughter was able to cover these and most of her other school and living expenses herself. The applicant requested contribution from the respondent for some other expenses she paid for the daughter's benefit: tuition deposit ($300 - $500), Blue Cross premiums, dental fees, and premiums for AMA insurance. These expenses paid by the applicant benefited the daughter directly and allowed her to continue pursuing her post secondary education. Given the combined financial resources of the parties, they were "extraordinary expenses." The parties had little income between the two of them. However, the expenses were minimal compared to what the daughter provided for herself. They were therefore reasonable. Since the parties had similar incomes, the expenses were ordered to be divided between them on a 50-50 basis.

In *L. (W.) v. W. (R.)* (2005), 2005 CarswellNB 640, 2005 NBQB 405, 290 N.B.R. (2d) 306, 755 A.P.R. 306 (N.B. Q.B.), a mother claimed $1,000 for tuition for two courses at university and $100 for books paid on behalf of her son. However, he earned in excess of $5,000 in the year and was held, therefore, to be responsible for his own university costs.

According to s. 7(2) of the *Guidelines*, the court should first take into account the child's contribution to the s. 7(1) expenses which are found to be necessary and reasonable: *Thomson v. Howard* (1997), 33 R.F.L. (4th) 45, 1997 CarswellOnt 4454, [1997] O.J. No. 4431 (Ont. Gen. Div.).

The court in *Reyes v. Rollo* (2000), 2001 CarswellOnt 4541, 24 R.F.L. (5th) 120, [2001] O.J. No. 5110 (Ont. S.C.J.), held that any scholarships which the child obtained in the past or would obtain in the future, should not be considered contributions to expenses for post-secondary education within the meaning of s. 7(1)(e). However, since the child had earned significant amounts from her employment, she should be expected to contribute toward payment of her expenses, but not a large part because her father could readily pay a larger share.

When a child is able to obtain a student loan, parents are not, pursuant to s. 7(2), relieved of the obligation of contributing to their children's post-secondary education: *Young v. Young* (2000), 2000 CarswellOnt 488, [2000] O.J. No. 556 (Ont. S.C.J.).

Mascarenhas v. Mascarenhas (1999), 1999 CarswellOnt 12, 44 R.F.L. (4th) 131, [1999] O.J No. 37 (Gen. Div.); affirmed (2000), 2000 CarswellOnt 3887, 18 R.F.L. (5th) 148 (Ont. Div. Ct.), showed that student loans should be considered as a "contribution" from the child for his or her educational expenses.

Benefits and Deductions (s. 7(3))

In *Myers v. Myers* (2000), 189 N.S.R. (2d) 214, 590 A.P.R. 214, 2000 CarswellNS 347, [2000] N.S.J. No. 367 (N.S. S.C.), the father was ordered to pay 73% of his daughter's expenses at university. She was entitled to an income tax credit made up of her actual tuition expense plus $200 per month for the months she was enrolled as a full-time student. The court, observing that under s. 7(3) it "must take into account any subsidies, benefits or income tax deductions or credits relating to the expense, and any eligibility to claim a subsidy, benefit or income tax deductions or credit relating to the expense" ordered that the credit, to the extent it was transferable, was to be transferred to the husband. He, in turn, was to provide the wife with 27% of any tax deduction he received as a result of the credit.

In *Holizki v. Reeves* (1997), 1997 CarswellSask 647, [1997] S.J. No. 746, 161 Sask. R. 76, 34 R.F.L. (4th) 414 (Sask. Q.B.), a mother was ordered to reimburse to the father his proportionate share of any tax benefit she received for the son's tuition, credit and education credit.

15§90 — Child Support — amount different from guidelines

The amount in the table plus the amount for special or extraordinary expenses produce the total amount for child support "unless otherwise provided under these Guidelines": *Federal Child Support Guidelines*, s. 3(1)(a) and (b) (children under the age of majority), and s. 3(2)(a) and (b) (children the age of majority or over).

The *Guidelines* provide otherwise on applications for original orders and on applications to vary existing orders (whether for children under, at, or over the age of majority) in cases where:

(1) The payor is not a biological or adoptive parent of the child or children to be supported, but stands in place of a parent. (See *Child Support — Payor Stands in Place of a Parent*, below.)

(2) The payor's income is over $150,000 a year and an award in the amount in the table plus an amount for special or extraordinary expenses would be inappropriate. (See *Amount Where Payor's Income is More Than $150,000*, below.)

(3) The making of a child support order in the basic amount would cause undue hardship. (See *Undue Hardship*, below.)

(4) Custody of the children is split between the spouses. (See *Split Custody*, below.)

(5) Custody of the child or children is shared by the spouses. (See *Shared Custody*, below.)

(6) Custody order is made on consent. (See *Child Support on Consent*, below.)

In addition to these specific exceptions, the court has a general discretion to award an amount that is different from the amount which would be determined under the guidelines, if the court is satisfied

(1) first,

(a) that special provisions in an order, a judgment or a written agreement respecting the spouses' financial obligations, or the division of their property, directly or indirectly benefit a child, or

(b) that special provisions have otherwise been made for the benefit of a child; and

(2) secondly, that the application of the applicable guidelines would result in an amount of child support that is inequitable given those special provisions: *Divorce Act*, s. 15.1(5).

Where the mother had debts in excess of her income and a lifestyle profoundly inferior to that of the custodial father, a child support order below *Guidelines* levels was made in *Eccles v. Eccles* (2002), 27 R.F.L. (5th) 47, 2002 CarswellOnt 1284 (Ont. S.C.J.); reversed (2003), 2003 CarswellOnt 3235 (C.A.).

Where the parties purchased a home 2 years after the divorce and the wife and children lived upstairs and the former husband downstairs the situation was found not to constitute "a special provision for the benefit of the children" within the meaning of the *Federal Child Support Guidelines*: *Chan v. Chan* (1999), 46 R.F.L. (4th) 339, 1999 CarswellBC 1137 (S.C.).

In *Davidson v. Davidson* (1998), 42 R.F.L. (4th) 154, 230 A.R. 157 (Q.B.), the father's obligation to pay support was reduced from the *Guidelines* amount as a result of the fact that the children received an income from an irrevocable family trust under which they were the exclusive beneficiaries. The family trust qualified under s. 15.1 of the *Divorce Act* as a "special provision made for the benefit of the children".

In *Campbell v. Martijn* (1998), 40 R.F.L. (4th) 41, 163 Nfld. & P.E.I.R. 126, 503 A.P.R. 126 (P.E.I. T.D. [In Chambers]), the court awarded child support at guideline levels for a child over the age of 18 who was attending school despite the fact that the parties' separation agreement called for a reduction in child support upon that child's eighteenth birthday. The agreement provision should not be strictly applied given that the parties clearly wished to encourage their children to pursue post-secondary education as, without it, financial independence was more difficult.

Where the parties purchased a home two years after the divorce and the wife and children lived upstairs and the former husband downstairs the situation was found not to constitute "a special provision for the benefit of the children" within the meaning of the *Federal Support Guidelines*: *Chan v. Chan* (1999), 46 R.F.L. (3d) 339 (B.C. S.C.).

A release clause in a separation agreement cannot bar the application of the *Federal Child Support Guidelines*: *Duffield v. Duffield* (1998), 36 R.F.L. (4th) 374 (B.C. S.C.).

Although the *Divorce Act* allows for a deviation from the *Federal Child Support Guidelines*, if a separation agreement contains "special provisions" respecting division of property, the mere fact of an unequal division does not in itself constitute a "special provision": *Wallace v. Wallace* (1998), 36 R.F.L. (4th) 428, 156 D.L.R. (4th) 762 (B.C. S.C.).

Where the mother was prepared to share in the costs of the children's extracurricular activities, the fact that the father paid them, himself did not warrant a reduction in the child support payable by him: *Soderberg v. Soderberg* (1998), 42 R.F.L. (4th) 403 (N.W.T. S.C.).

In *Young v. Young* (1998), 39 R.F.L. (4th) 110, 51 B.C.L.R. (3d) 299 (S.C. [In Chambers]); additional reasons at (1998), 51 B.C.L.R. (3d) 310 (S.C.), the fact that the parties had a separation agreement containing child support requirements below *Guidelines* levels did not constitute a "special provision" justifying a departure from *Guidelines* amounts.

Where the husband had, after separation, given the family car to the wife for the benefit of the children and had to purchase another car for his own use, child support was ordered payable by him at lower than *Guidelines* amounts. The situation qualified under s. 37(2.3) of the *Guidelines* as a special provision made in respect of a division of property which benefitted the children: *Muir-Halliday v. Halliday* (1998), 37 R.F.L. (4th) 312 (Ont. Prov. Div.).

Where the parties have made an agreement for child support that is different from that provided in the guidelines, the court must have financial disclosure if it is to compare the agreement with the amounts provided in the federal guidelines: *McCrum v. McCrum* (1997), 192 N.B.R. (2d) 249, 489 A.P.R. 249 (Q.B.).

The court also held that if the payee (wife) is unable to swear as to the income level of her husband, he will have to provide three years' income tax returns and the court stated that it would be reassuring if both parties submitted affidavits as to their agreement in order to satisfy it that the arrangements are at least as good as those provided by the guidelines.

In *Thomas v. Thomas* (November 4, 1997), Doc. Sault Ste. Marie 17037/97 (Ont. Gen. Div.), the table amount calculated on the payor's income of $59,400 a year would be $503 a month. The amount under the separation agreement with a modification proposed by the payor increasing the amount would be approximately $295 a month. Section 15.1(5) of the *Divorce Act* provides that the court may award an amount that is different from the guidelines if satisfied that special provisions have been made in an agreement, and that the application of the guidelines would be inequitable given those special provisions. The court held that the agreement amount was inadequate having regard to the father's annual income, the mother's income of $40,000 a year, "and the means and needs of each of the parties." In addition, the apportionment of the child's costs under the agreement had led to conflict, and the change in the child's living arrangements required a change in support. The application of the guidelines would not result in an amount of child support that is inequitable, and the objectives of the *Child Support Guidelines* set out in s. 1 can best be met by requiring the payor to pay child support according to the table amount of $503 a month.

In *Haggith v. Trader* (June 5, 1997), Doc. London F1278/95 (Ont. Gen. Div.), the mother sought under provincial legislation to vary the terms of child support set out in a separation agreement in which the children had received a low amount of child support in exchange for the father's equity in the matrimonial home, said to be $40,000. In the four years since the agreement, the father's income had increased approximately 12 percent from $32,539 to $36,400 per annum. Under the federal guidelines, the children would have been entitled to approximately $523. In light of the father's increased income, but keeping in mind that the transfer of the husband's interest in the home was the equivalent of a $25,000 lump-sum amount of child support and that the father would no longer receive a tax deduction for child support, the court modestly increased the support from $200 to $225 for the two children.

Cases decided before the enactment of the Federal Child Support Guidelines:

Where the arrears of child support owing by the father were wiped out in light of an agreement with the mother relieving him from child support obligations if he did not see the children, the order was reversed on appeal. Support was the right of the children and was not to be bartered away by the parents: *Black v. Black* (1995), 19 R.F.L. (4th) 442, 71 B.C.A.C. 233, 117 W.A.C. 233 (C.A.).

In *Bakes v. Kelly* (1995), 15 R.F.L. (4th) 361 (B.C. C.A.), the fact the the wife had filed a petition for divorce claiming claiming child support was not a repudiation of her right to enforce the child support provisions under the parties' separation agreement. Although the agreement contained a waiver of the right to support, the wife had, prior to filing the petition, commenced an action to enforce the agreement under which the husband was delinquent. Only if the wife had obtained the divorce order would the issue of electing between inconsistent remedies arise.

In *Chalmers v. Simpson* (1994), 3 R.F.L. (4th) 407, 92 B.C.L.R. (2d) 258 (C.A.), the Court of Appeal affirmed the trial judge's refusal to interfere with child support provisions which had originally been set by the parties' agreement. The agreement had specified that support was to continue until the children were 19 and the mother had requested that it be extended until such time as the children no longer qualified as "children of the marriage". The trial judge dismissed the application on the grounds that the mother's expense claims were excessive, the changes were foreseeable at the time of the agreement, the children had part-time income and the mother's new husband could contribute to household expenses.

The courts are extremely reluctant to interfere with judicial separation agreements which include provisions for child support. Consequently, the parties ought, pending trial, to be held to the amount they set out in their agreement: *Bacon v. Bacon* (1991), 33 R.F.L. (3d) 170 (Sask. C.A.).

Although the parties' agreement may act to bar a claim for extended spousal support, the court is still competent, notwithstanding the agreement, to award an increase in child support: *Droit de la famille — 927* (1990), [1991] R.D.F. 21 (C.A. Qué.).

A court should not lightly vary the terms, including the child support terms, of a settlement agreement: *Droit de la famille — 646* (1989), 20 R.F.L. (3d) 432 (C.A. Qué.).

In *Day v. Day* (1989), 20 R.F.L. (3d) 113 (B.C. C.A.), a settlement agreement whereby the husband conveyed this equity in the family home to the wife in exchange for her waiver for spousal and child support was found to have adequately addressed the needs of the children.

A court may override settlements dealing with child support where it is appropriate having regard to the child's needs. Since child support is the right of the child, the fact that an increase in child support will indirectly benefit the custodial spouse cannot make any difference: *Dickson v. Dickson*, 11 R.F.L. (3d) 337, 21 B.C.L.R. (2d) 69, [1988] 2 W.W.R. 117 (C.A.).

The obligation of the non-custodial parent to contribute to child support is owed to the child and not to the other parent, and cannot be bargained away by an agreement between the parties. However, the court will generally respect agreements settling child support where the agreement provides the same level of financial support which the children could reasonably have expected if the family had remained united. The situation is different, however, where the financial arrangements made by the parents for the children are such that the custodial parent is unable, for financial reasons, to provide the children with the lifestyle they might have enjoyed, in reasonable terms, if the parents had stayed together. It may then be incumbent on the court to review the agreement as to the parties' respective contributions to raising the children, given the parties' incomes: *Currie v. Currie*, 10 R.F.L. (3d) 207, [1988] 1 W.W.R. 361, 49 Man. R. (2d) 129 (C.A.).

A court should be cautious about overriding the child support provisions of a comprehensive and interrelated separation agreement: *McKillop v. McKillop* (1988), 17 R.F.L. (3d) 1 (B.C. C.A.).

Where the mother had debts in excess of her income and a lifestyle profoundly inferior to that of the custodial father, a child support order before *Guidelines* levels was made in *Eccles v. Eccles* (2002), 27 R.F.L. (5th) 47, 2002 CarswellOnt 1284 (Ont. S.C.J.); reversed in part (2003), 43 R.F.L. (5th) 321, 2003 CarswellOnt 3235, (sub nom. *T.A.E. v. M.E.E.)* 175 O.A.C. 394 (Ont. C.A.); additional reasons at (2003), 47 R.F.L. (5th) 4, 2003 CarswellOnt 4098 (Ont. C.A.).

In *Hansen v. Hansen* (1995), 13 R.F.L. (4th) 335 (Ont. Gen. Div.), before Fleury J., the court noted that the Ontario General Division has repeatedly stated that agreements between the parties as to child support are not enforceable where to enforce them might operate against the best interests of the child in question.

In *Bosse v. Bosse* (1996), 19 R.F.L. (4th) 54 (N.B. Q.B.), the court refused to abide by an agreement between the former spouses which limited the husband's child support obligation to a specified time period. The parties could not abrogate the child's right to support by agreement where that child would otherwise qualify for support.

A separation agreement which provides for insufficient child support does not restrict the court from increasing the quantum of support: *Larson v. Larson* (1994), 8 R.F.L. (4th) 333 (Ont. Gen. Div.).

Where the custodial mother had signed a separation agreement setting the child support payable by the father under threat that her failure to do so would result in a custody application by the father, the court disregarded the agreement in subsequently setting child support. The agreed upon amount was totally inadequate and the mother had been coerced into signing the document: *Alward v. Alward* (1994), 145 N.B.R. (2d) 299, 372 A.P.R. 299 (Q.B.).

The fact that a separation agreement is silent on the issue of child support does not amount to a waiver of the right to child support: *Droit de la famille — 1993*, [1993] R.D.F. 381 (C.S. Qué.).

Where the provisions for child support contained in a separation agreement are incorporated into a divorce order and no reference is made to the particular Act under which support is being awarded, it results in a presumption that the order was made under the paramount legislation which, in this case, is the *Divorce Act*: *Varey v. Varey* (July 4, 1995), Doc. New Westminster D011020 (B.C. S.C.).

In *Varey v. Varey*, above, the court was of the opinion that the parties, by agreement, not spoken to in court, could not limit an obligation to pay child support. The paramount concern, in respect to child maintenance, is the best interests of the child.

In *Wilson v. Wilson* (1995), 13 R.F.L. (4th) 260; additional reasons at (1995), 13 R.F.L. (4th) 260n (N.W.T. S.C.), the court allowed the mother's application for an upward variation of the child support specified in the parties' separation agreement despite the fact that the wife had unilaterally moved the children from Yellowknife to Edmonton without informing the husband. The mother had been paying a disproportionately large share of the child support and the father was able to pay more.

In *Trider v. Trider* (1994), 131 N.S.R. (2d) 152, 371 A.P.R. 152 (S.C.), an informal arrangement whereby the non-custodial parent had paid for the purchase of some of the children's clothing and sports equipment and had contributed to their dental expenses was found not to be a substitute for a formal support order. The *Divorce Act* plainly calls for a monetary contribution to satisfy the obligation to contribute to the support of one's children, absent an express agreement to the contrary.

Where the mother had not achieved self-sufficiency as had been anticipated at the time when the parties agreed upon their respective child support obligation, the court allowed the mother's application for increased child support. The original agreement had been based upon one child residing with each parent whereas, in actuality, both children rotated between parents on a regular basis. The resultant increase in the mother's expenses constituted a sufficient change in circumstances to warrant a variation: *Debacker v. Debacker* (1993), 49 R.F.L. (3d) 106, 143 A.R. 228 (Q.B.).

Courts are not bound by the parties' settlement agreements as far as child support is concerned: *Mosher v. Turner* (1990), 26 R.F.L. (3d) 230, 96 N.S.R. (2d) 267, 253 A.P.R. 267 (T.D.).

A drastic or unforeseen change in circumstances is required before the court will vary a child support award that is based on the parties' separation agreement: *McKenzie v. McKenzie* (1989), 81 Sask. R. 108 (Q.B.). See also *Czerniak v. Czerniak* (1989), 81 Sask. R. 96 (Q.B.).

The general rule restricting the court's jurisdiction to override the spousal support provisions of a settlement agreement does not apply to child support applications: *Conley v. Conley* (1988), 12 R.F.L. (3d) 202 (N.S. T.D.).

The court is bound by the terms of a settlement agreement where child support is in issue, even if the result of awarding additional child support is to benefit the custodial parent. However, the court should not award additional support too easily to a spouse who has agreed to and accepted lump sum support: *Carruthers v. Carruthers* (1988), 15 R.F.L. (3d) 321 (P.E.I. T.D.).

In *Kelley v. Kelley* (1988), 16 R.F.L. (3d) 238 (B.C. S.C.), the court found that the $225 monthly child support payable by the father pursuant to the parties' separation agreement was insufficient to maintain the 19-year-old son who suffered from reflex neurovascular dystrophy, and increased the monthly amount to $750. The court was free to reassess the adequacy of the child support irrespective of the parties' agreement. See also *Yaholnitsky v. Yaholnitsky* (1988), 16 R.F.L. (3d) 283 (Sask. Q.B.) in which the court reiterated the principle that parents cannot barter away their children's right to support.

An agreement by a wife to waive child support is unconscionable, unenforceable and contrary to public policy. Likewise, laches on the part of a wife is not a proper principle to be applied to a claim for child support: *Aken v. Aken* (1988), 15 R.F.L. (3d) 156 (B.C. S.C.). See also *Decker v. Decker* (1987), 70 Nfld. & P.E.I.R. 29, 215 A.P.R. 29 (Nfld. T.D.); *Hayes v. Hayes* (1988), 73 Nfld. & P.E.I.R. 157, 229 A.P.R. 157 (Nfld. U.F.C.).

Waiver of child support is an interim agreement not determinative of the issue: *Kamimura v. Squibb* (1988), 13 R.F.L. (3d) 31 (B.C. S.C.).

"Child maintenance, like access, is the right of the child: *Cartlidge Re*, [1973] 3 O.R. 801, 11 R.F.L. 384 (Prov. Ct.). For this reason, a spouse cannot barter away his or her child's right to support in a settlement agreement": per Wilson J. in *Richardson v. Richardson* (1987), 7 R.F.L. (3d) 304 (S.C.C.).

In *de Leeuw v. de Leeuw* (1982), 38 B.C.L.R. 117 (Co. Ct.), it was held that the wife was entitled to enforce child maintenance provisions in a separation agreement although the decree *nisi*, obtained subsequent to the agreement, entitled the wife to monthly child maintenance of $1. It had been agreed by the parties at the time of executing the agreement that the maintenance provisions therein would prevail and that the wife would only seek nominal child maintenance in the divorce proceedings.

"While I have said that the terms of a separation agreement will not be lightly disturbed, the Court cannot, of course, permit the parties to fix maintenance of the children at a fixed figure without regard to the interests of the children": per Anderson J. in *Dal Santo v. Dal Santo* (1975), 21 R.F.L. 117 at 121 (B.C. S.C.).

"It is trite to say that the separation agreement regarding the maintenance of children is of no binding effect either upon this court or the children. In such circumstances the court in considering what maintenance ought to be ordered for a child should not be fettered in any way by terms of the agreement save only as to whether or not they provide adequately for the child in respect of the circumstances then existent at trial": *Makins v. Makins* (1978), 2 R.F.L. (2d) 104 at 118–119 (Ont. U.F.C.), Steinberg U.F.C.J.

A separation agreement which, although silent on the issue of child support, has been incorporated into the decree *nisi* does not affect the court's jurisdiction later to consider an application for child support: *Chalifour v. Chalifour* (1990), 25 R.F.L. (3d) 455, 82 Nfld. & P.E.I.R. 345, 257 A.P.R. 345 (Nfld. U.F.C.).

The court is not bound by a separation agreement with respect to maintenance for a child: *Peacey v. Peacey* (1980), 17 R.F.L. (2d) 91 (B.C. S.C.). See also *Armstrong v. Armstrong* (1980), 5 Sask. R. 435 (Q.B.); *Kravetsky v. Kravetsky*, 21 R.F.L. 211, [1976] 2 W.W.R. 470, 63 D.L.R. (3d) 733 (Man. C.A.).

"The court, of its own motion, may consider the position of the children and their need for maintenance from one parent or another. I do not consider it a breach of the agreement by the wife to put before the court the matter of maintenance for the children whether or not the parties had dealt with the matter in a separation agreement": *Krueger v. Taubner* (1974), 17 R.F.L. 86 at 88 (Man. Q.B.); affirmed 17 R.F.L. 267, [1975] W.W.D. 40, 50 D.L.R. (3d) 159 (Man. C.A.), Hamilton J.

A decree *nisi* may provide for child maintenance in accordance with the terms of an existing separation agreement: *Seminuk v. Seminuk* (1970), 10 D.L.R. (3d) 590, 72 W.W.R. 304 (Sask. C.A.).

See also *Day v. Day* (1988), 15 R.F.L. (3d) 70 (B.C. S.C.); *Moore v. Moore* (1986), 49 R.F.L. (2d) 160 (Ont. H.C.); *Colpitts v. Colpitts* (1970), 3 N.B.R. (2d) 743 (Q.B.); *MacKenzie v. MacKenzie* (1975), 25 R.F.L. 354 at 355–356, 9 Nfld. & P.E.I.R. 176 (P.E.I. S.C.); *R. v. MacDonald* (1976), 26 R.F.L. 204 at 229, 14 O.R. (2d) 409, 74 D.L.R. (3d) 57 (H.C.); *Irwin v. Irwin* (1972), 8 R.F.L. 237 at 239 (B.C. S.C.); *Spridgeon v. Spridgeon* (1980), 20 C.P.C. 272 (Master).

See also 15§146–151 Effects of domestic contracts, below.

The *Federal Child Support Guidelines* require the child support order, itself, to contain a number of specific facts relating to the determination of the amount and terms of payment. The *Guidelines* state in s. 13:

> 13. A child support order must include the following information:
>
> (a) the name and birth date of each child to whom the order relates;
>
> (b) the income of any spouse whose income is used to determine the amount of the child support order;
>
> (c) the amount determined under paragraph 3(1)(a) for the number of children to whom the order relates;
>
> (d) the amount determined under paragraph 3(2)(b) for a child the age of majority or over;
>
> (e) the particulars of any expense described in subsection 7(1), the child to whom the expense relates, and the amount of the expense or, where that amount cannot be determined, the proportion to be paid in relation to the expense; and
>
> (f) the date on which the lump sum or first payment is payable and the day of the month or other time period on which all subsequent payments are to be made.

15§91 — Child support — payor standing in place of a parent

A spouse who is not a biological or adoptive parent of the child to be supported, but stands in place of a parent (see *Divorce Act*, s. 2(1) "child of the marriage") has an obligation to the child which rests entirely in the discretion of the court. The amount of child support in respect of that spouse is such amount as the court considers appropriate, having regard to the guidelines and any other parent's legal duty to support the child: *Federal Child Support Guidelines*, s. 5.

In determining whether a person stands in the place of a parent, a court must take into account all relevant factors, such as expressed intention, intention inferred from conduct, and the actual fact of forming a new family: *Chartier v. Chartier* (1998), 1998 CarswellMan 533, 1998 CarswellMan 534, [1998] S.C.J. No. 79 (S.C.C.); additional reasons at (1999), 43 R.F.L. (4th) 1, 168 D.L.R. (4th) 540, [1999] 4 W.W.R. 633, 235 N.R. 1, [1998] S.C.J. No. 79, 1999 CarswellMan 25, 1999 CarswellMan 26, 134 Man. R. (2d) 19, 193 W.A.C. 19, [1999] 1 S.C.R. 242 (S.C.C.).

In *Chartier v. Chartier* (1998), 1998 CarswellMan 533, 1998 CarswellMan 534, [1998] S.C.J. No. 79 (S.C.C.); additional reasons at (1999), 43 R.F.L. (4th) 1, 168 D.L.R. (4th) 540, [1999] 4 W.W.R. 633, 235 N.R. 1, [1998] S.C.J. No. 79, 1999 CarswellMan 25, 1999 CarswellMan 26, 134 Man. R. (2d) 19, 193 W.A.C. 19, [1999] 1 S.C.R. 242 (S.C.C.); reversing 29 R.F.L. (4th) 96, 118 Man. R. (2d) 152, 154 D.L.R. (4th) 431, [1997] 8 W.W.R. 348, 1997 CarswellMan 335, [1997] M.J. No. 371, 149 W.A.C. 152 (Man. C.A.), it was held that a spouse who had stood in the place of a parent to a child is not entitled unilaterally to terminate that relationship and thus avoid child support obligations. Once it is decided that a child is a "child of the marriage" within the *Divorce Act*, the child must be treated as if born of the marriage.

The obligations to provide child support should be assessed independently of the contributions required to be paid by the stepparent: *Chartier v. Chartier* (1998), 1998 CarswellMan 533, 1998 CarswellMan 534, [1998] S.C.J. No. 79 (S.C.C.); additional reasons at (1999), 43 R.F.L. (4th) 1, 168 D.L.R. (4th) 540, [1999] 4 W.W.R. 633, 235 N.R. 1, [1998] S.C.J. No. 79, 1999 CarswellMan 25, 1999 CarswellMan 26, 134 Man. R. (2d) 19, 193 W.A.C. 19, [1999] 1 S.C.R. 242 (S.C.C.); reversing 29 R.F.L. (4th) 96, 118 Man. R. (2d) 152, 154 D.L.R. (4th) 431, [1997] 8 W.W.R. 348, 1997 CarswellMan 335, [1997] M.J. No. 371, 149 W.A.C. 152 (Man. C.A.). The obligations of parents to a child are joint and severable. If a parent seeks contribution from another parent, he must in the meantime pay child support. The case was remanded to the Manitoba Queen's Bench for the determination of the quantum of child support.

In *Millward v. Millward* (2003), 48 R.F.L. (5th) 294, 2003 CarswellOnt 1403 (Ont. S.C.J.), the husband was found to have a settled intention, after a one-year marriage, to treat his wife's son as his own. The wife and son had moved from the U.S. at the husband's urging and the husband had encouraged the wife to indicate on her immigration forms that they had formed a family unit. The husband provided necessities for the son and participated in activities with him and engaged in disciplining. Support was ordered for a 12-month period which would allow the wife time to re-establish support from the natural father which had been discontinued at the time of her immigration.

Having affection for and being kind and considerate to a spouse's child from a previous union and taking part in that child's day-to-day life does not create a relationship of parent and child such as to trigger an obligation to provide child support: *Charbonneau v. Charbonneau* (2004), R.F.L. (6th) 67, 2004 CarswellOnt 5211 (S.C.J.).

Where the wife had brought her 10-month-old child into the parties' 12-year marriage, the husband was found to be primarily responsible, vis-á-vis the child's biological father, for the support of the child. The husband had, in every sense, stood in the place and stead of the biological father. Although the biological father was not totally exonerated from his support obligation, the husband's obligation was greater: *Vezina v. Vezina* (2004), 7 R.F.L. (6th) 435, 246 Sask. R. 139, 2004 CarswellSask 197, 2004 SKQB 134 (Q.B.).

Section 5 of the *Guidelines* directs that a child support order against a person standing in the place of a parent is to be in such an amount as the court considers appropriate. In enacting the *Guidelines*, the legislature intended that there be a presumption in favour of awarding the Table Amount. The onus is on the step-parent to rebut the presumption, even in circumstances when the natural parent is also required to contribute toward child support: *Kobe v. Kobe* (2002), 30 R.F.L. (5th) 135, 2002 CarswellOnt 1139 (Ont. S.C.J.).

Section 5 of the *Guidelines* permits a court to order a person *in loco parentis* to pay child support in the amount that the court considers appropriate, having regard to the *Guidelines* and any other parent's legal duty to support the child. However, it is not necessary that the other parent's legal duty to support the child does not have to be established and quantified before the court can take it into account under s. 5: *Cook v. Kilduff* (2000), 11 R.F.L. (5th) 48, 2000 SKQB 347, [2001] 1 W.W.R. 597, 196 Sask. R. 314, 2000 CarswellSask 497, [2000] S.J. No. 482 (Q.B.).

A child support order against a party "*in loco parentis*" is a matter of discretion and the amount payable by that party is not limited by the duty of the natural parent to support the child: *Dumais v. Lupul*, 10 R.F.L. (5th) 265, 2000 BCSC 1309, 2000 CarswellBC 1881, [2000] B.C.J. No. 1907 (S.C.).

In *Symons v. Taylor* (2000), 10 R.F.L. (5th) 443, 2000 CarswellOnt 2582, [2000] O.J. No. 2703 (S.C.J.), the natural father of two children was successful in a child support application against the mother's second husband. The children had moved back in with their father subsequent to their mother's death. As the second husband continued in a parental relationship with the children he was obligated, under the *Guidelines*, to contribute to their support.

In *Lamarche c. Crevier* (2000), 4 R.F.L. (5th) 88, 2000 CarswellOnt 28 (S.C.J.); additional reasons at (2000), 2000 CarswellOnt 1142 (S.C.J.); varied (2001), 2001 CarswellOnt 3910, 151 O.A.C. 232, 22 R.F.L. (5th) 354 (C.A.), the child's biological father was ordered to pay child support, while the step-father, who was found to be *in loco parentis* to the child, was required to contribute towards the child's extraordinary expenses.

Where the payor believed himself to be the father of a child until blood tests were taken and he treated the child as his own, the court ordered him to pay $30 per month for the child, having regards to the *Guidelines* and any other parent's legal duty to support the child: *Hautala v. Morgan* (July 28, 1997), Doc. Thunder Bay 97-0419 (Ont. Gen. Div.). The court also ordered the payor to pay support for two children of the common-law union of the parties and the payor father also had a legal duty to provide support for another child of a prior relationship.

Where the payor had supported his wife's child from a previous marriage and treated him as his own but the relationship between the child and his stepfather had deteriorated after the parties' separation, and the child had a natural father who was employed, the court ordered the stepfather to pay child support for the child in the amount of one-half of the *Guidelines* amount for one year: *Irwin v. Irwin* (September 22, 1997), Doc. Cornwall 7224/95 (Ont. Gen. Div.).

In *Bevand v. Bevand* (June 20, 1997), Doc. Barrie 1422/96 (Ont. Gen. Div.), the payor had lived with a woman for seven years and had demonstrated a settled intention to treat her daughter as his own child. At the time when an order was made against the payor, the child's biological father had disappeared leaving behind him a total of $57,000 in child support arrears. The payor was the only "father" whom the child knew. The order against the payor was for $650 a month. Later, the payor located the biological father and added him as a respondent to an application to vary the order. The biological father launched a variation application of his own to rescind or reduce the arrears.

The payor's income was between $44,000 and $46,000 annually, and the father's approximately $15,400 annually. The mother's income aside from support was about $23,000. Both the payor and the father had cut off all contact with the child.

It was held that the obligation to provide support is the obligation of every parent under s. 31 of the *Family Law Act*, and the obligation of one particular parent should be a reasonable one in all the circumstances of the case. The payor, stepfather, cannot eliminate his obligation to pay child support by cutting off all contact with the child. The provincial legislation, then pending, would repeal clause 33(7)(b) of the Act and substitute a new clause (b): "(b) apportion the obligation according to the child support guidelines." Thus, since the provincial legislation has been in force, there is no predominance given to the obligation of a 'natural' father. Indeed, it appears that the child support payable by another parent is generally irrelevant."

Section 5 of the *Federal Child Support Guidelines* provides that the guidelines are not binding where the payor is not the child's natural parent. "That section directs the court to make the order that it deems 'appropriate' in light of the guidelines and 'any other parent's legal duty to support the child.'" The *Guidelines* amount for the payor's income of $45,000 annually would be $387 on a non-deductible, non-taxable basis. This amount, in the circumstances, would be the appropriate amount. The payor has the greatest means of the three "parents", and is the only father whom the child has known. The obligation should not be time-limited. To require the payor to continue support for the length of time he lived with the mother and the child would take the obligation almost to the normal termination point of 18 years.

15§92 — Child support — payor income $150,000 or less

See 15§88A — Section 3 — Presumptive Rule

15§93 — Child support — payor income more than $150,000

The amount of child support payable by non-custodial spouses with annual incomes over $150,000 is:

(a) the amount derived from the applicable table as in cases where the income is $150,000 a year or less, together with an amount, if any, for special or extraordinary expenses; or

(b) if that amount is inappropriate,

(i) in respect of the first $150,000 of the spouse's income, the amount derived from the applicable table;

(ii) in respect of the balance of the spouse's income, the amount that the court considers appropriate, having regard to the condition, means, needs and other circumstances of the children who are entitled to support and the financial ability of each spouse to contribute to the support of the children;

(iii) the amount, if any, for special or extraordinary expenses: *Federal Child Support Guidelines*, s. 4.

(See *Special or Extraordinary Expenses*, above.)

The category of special or extraordinary expenses is defined for certain items and no others. Where the income is over $150,000 an expense may not come within the category of Special or Extraordinary Expenses, but be allowed in the different category of "needs" according to the test of "condition, means, needs and other circumstances of the children" in section 4(b)(ii) of the *Federal Child Support Guidelines.*

In *Francis v. Baker* (1999), 177 D.L.R. (4th) 1, 50 R.F.L. (4th) 228 (S.C.C.), the father had an income of approximately one million dollars a year and a net worth of 78 million dollars. The Supreme Court of Canada considered two issues: 1) Was the Ontario Court of Appeal correct in its interpretation of s. 4 of the *Federal Child Support Guidelines*? and 2) Did the Ontario Court of Appeal err in upholding the discretion of the trial judge to award the Table amount of child support applicable to the applicant's income?

Mr. Justice Bastarache was of the opinion that there is only one principle or approach of statutory interpretation, namely, the words of an Act are to be read in their entire context and in their grammatical and ordinary sense harmoniously with the scheme of the Act, the object of the Act, and the intention of Parliament. Taking this approach into account, the word "inappropriate" in s. 4 means "unsuitable" and not "inadequate" as interpreted by the Court of Appeal. Consequently, in cases where the payor parent has an annual income greater than $150,000, courts have the discretion either to increase or decrease the amount of child support set out in the *Guidelines*. The appellant failed to demonstrate that the trial judge erred in refusing to exercise her discretion to decrease the amount of the child support award and the appeal was dismissed.

The explicit wording of s. 4(b)(i) does not permit a departure from the set amount in the Table based on the first $150,000 of the payor parent's income. For the portion of the support award attributable to income over $150,000, the amount can be increased or decreased at the discretion of the court.

"Parliament intended that there be a presumption in favour of the Table amounts (set amount for $150,000 of income and percentage amount for balance of income) ... the *Guidelines* figures can only be increased or reduced under s. 4 if the party seeking such a deviation has rebutted the presumption that the applicable Table amount is appropriate": *Francis v. Baker*, above *per* Bastarache J. at p. 13.

The closer the payor parent's income is to $150,000, the more likely that the Table amount will be awarded: *Francis v. Baker*, above.

Courts may decide that the applicable *Guidelines* amount is so much in excess of a child's reasonable needs as to be functional wealth transfer to a parent or *de facto* spousal support which is not the objective of the *Divorce Act*: *Francis v. Baker*, above. However, courts should not readily assume that the *Guidelines* figures constitute wealth transfers or spousal support. In determining whether a child support award under s. 4 is inappropriate, need is only one of the factors the courts must consider.

In contested cases, child expense budgets will often be required since children's needs are one of the factors to be considered in assessing appropriateness under s. 4: *Francis v. Baker*, above. However, unlike forms of financial disclosure, the requirement for child support budgets is left to the discretion and experience of trial judges on an individual case basis. But trial judges are not required to adjust child support orders to be in line with submitted budgets. The *Guidelines* give judges a wide discretion to consider a range of factors, of which the children's needs are only one.

The court dismissed the argument that where there is a very large child support award amount flowing from the set amount and the percentage in the table, it is *prima facie* inappropriate: *Francis v. Baker*, above. The plain wording of s. 4, its context in the child support scheme, as well as the purposes of the *Guidelines*, indicate that the legislature intended that there be a presumption in favour of the amount determined by the table and the applicable percentage. In addition, while the legislature differentiated between those earning above and below $150,000, the legislature did not specify a category, that was to be treated differently for high income earners where child support awards are extremely large. The court was not prepared to create such a category on its own. Finally, if children do have actual needs equal *to* or greater than the applicable *Guidelines* amount, the payment should not be disallowed simply because it involves a large amount of money. The court dismissed the argument that the trial judge abused her discretion in awarding the amount determined by using the prescribed percentage as part of the calculation.

Where the trial judge awarded the respondent discretionary expenses above the figures listed in her budget, the child support award should not be disallowed on the basis that there is not a proper evidentiary foundation *for the award*. The respondent's budgets were prepared without the appellant's financial information, and they did not include the level of discretionary expenses possibly appropriate for children of an exceptionally wealthy father. Therefore, the trial judge's decision to increase these expenses is not an abuse of her discretion: *Francis v. Baker*, above.

In *R. v. R.* (2002), 2002 CarswellOnt 902, [2002] O.J. No. 1095, 24 R.F.L. (5th) 96, 211 D.L.R. (4th) 403, 58 O.R. (3d) 656, 159 O.A.C. 46 (C.A.), before Catzman, Doherty and Laskin JJ.A, it was found that the father's income after separation doubled from approximately $2,000,000 a year to approximately $4,000,000.

In reviewing the trial judge's order for the support of four children, the Court of Appeal upheld the finding that the Table Amount based on the increased income — over $65,000 a month — was inappropriate. However, the court disagreed with the trial judge's assessment of an appropriate amount and increased his award of $20,000 to $36,000 a month. The trial judge had erred in two respects. First, he measured the amount of child support against the parties' standard of living as it existed before the separation, thereby failing to take into account the very significant increase in the husband's post-separation income. Secondly, he failed to consider whether the wife's budget of $80,750 a month was reasonable in light of the new income. In justifying its variation of the trial judge's award, the Court of Appeal held that the children should benefit from the increase in income after the separation, and that as children of a wealthy parent they were entitled to an amount that contained a significant element of discretionary spending. After applying these principles, the court found $36,000 a month to be appropriate. It was made up of $12,000 for basic expenses and $4,000 for special expenses, together with discretionary expenses of $6,000 for a family cottage, $3,000 for skiing and golf expenses, $1,000 for vacation and travel, $2,000 for miscellaneous recreational and activity expenses, and $8,000 for savings for the children.

The needs of children of very wealthy families are different from those of ordinary middle class families when determining child support. The fact that a custodial mother had managed a budget in the context of pre-*Guidelines* child support order does not justify a departure from the Table Amount: *Hollenbach v. Hollenbach*, 10 R.F.L. (5th) 280, 2000 BCCA 620, 82 B.C.L.R. (3d) 228, 194 D.L.R. (4th) 151, 144 B.C.A.C. 193, 236 W.A.C. 193, 2000 CarswellBC 2282, [2000] B.C.J. No. 2316 (B.C. C.A.); varying (1999), 47 R.F.L. (4th) 39, 67 B.C.L.R. (3d) 192, 1999 CarswellBC 990, [1999] B.C.J. No. 1063 (B.C. S.C.).

In *Tauber v. Tauber* (2001), 18 R.F.L. (5th) 384, 2001 CarswellOnt 2842, [2001] O.J. No. 3259, 203 D.L.R. (4th) 168 (S.C.J.); affirmed (2003), 2003 CarswellOnt 1009, 34 R.F.L. (5th) 450, 64 O.R. (3d) 229, 170 O.A.C. 1, 225 D.L.R. (4th) 186 (C.A.), the parties' four-year-old child was awarded the Table Amount of support, namely $11,171 per month. Despite the child's young age, his needs and circumstances had to be viewed in the context of his father's affluence. The father earned millions of dollars and enjoyed a luxurious lifestyle, in which the child was entitled to share. Although the budget presented by the mother was high and contained a significant element of discretionary expenses, it was not so excessive as to constitute either a transfer of wealth to the child or *de facto* spousal support.

Metzner v. Metzner (January 27, 2000), Doc. 27529 (S.C.C.); referred for consideration from (1999), 1999 CarswellBC 1539, 175 D.L.R. (4th) 587, 127 B.C.A.C. 9, 207 W.A.C. 9, 69 B.C.L.R. (3d) 39, 1999 BCCA 434 (C.A.) is a case determined prior to the enactment of the *Federal Child Support Guidelines*. The mother, after the *Guidelines* were in force, successfully sought an increase in child support from $1,276 per month per child to $12,800 per month for both children. This increase was partially based on the fact that the father's annual income had increased by over $500,000 since the date of the previous order. There were several court orders and eventually the mother applied for leave to appeal to the Supreme Court of Canada on the issue of child support. The Supreme Court of Canada, in response to the mother's application, gave a direction stating that the British Columbia Court of Appeal had rendered its decision on the basis of the impact on custodial arrangements occasioned by the application of the *Federal Child Support Guidelines*, and under s. 17(6.2) of the *Divorce Act*, without the benefit of *Francis v. Baker*, 50 R.F.L. (4th) 228, [1999] 3 S.C.R. 250, 177 D.L.R. (4th) 1, 246 N.R. 45, 125 O.A.C. 201, 44 O.R. (3d) 736 (headnote only), [1999] S.C.J. No. 52, 1999 CarswellOnt 2734, 1999 CarswellOnt 2948, which provides for support corresponding to the actual living conditions of the children. The Supreme Court of Canada remanded the matter to the Court of Appeal to be disposed of in accordance with the decision in *Francis v. Baker*.

In *Metzner v. Metzner*, 2000 BCCA 474, [2000] 9 W.W.R. 379, 80 B.C.L.R. (3d) 133, 9 R.F.L. (5th) 162, 190 D.L.R. (4th) 366, 141 B.C.A.C. 84, 231 W.A.C. 84, 2000 CarswellBC 1696, [2000] B.C.J. No. 1693 (C.A.); leave to appeal refused (2000), 2000 CarswellBC 2504, 2000 CarswellBC 2505, 266 N.R. 199 (note), 153 B.C.A.C. 60 (note) (S.C.C.); affirming (1997), 46 B.C.L.R. (3d) 149, 1997 CarswellBC 2730, [1997] B.C.J. No. 2903 (S.C. [In Chambers]), with a minor variation, the court ordered child support payments of the Table amount of $12,800 per month for two children, as it observed that there is a presumption in favour of the Table amounts being payable in all cases, and the presumption can only be rebutted by clear and compelling evidence. Such evidence was not adduced in this case. The father had sole custody of the children, but the children's primary residence was with their mother.

In *Bates v. Bates* (2000), 5 R.F.L. (5th) 259, 49 O.R. (3d) 1, 188 D.L.R. (4th) 642, 133 O.A.C. 319, 2000 CarswellOnt 2091, [2000] O.J. No. 2269 (C.A.), a variation of child support case, the court considered when it has discretion to order an amount of child support that differs from the Table amount under the *Guidelines*. The appellate court held that the court may depart from the Table amounts only under subsections 17(6.2) to 17(6.5) of the *Divorce Act* or under ss. 4, 5, 7, 8, 9, or 10 of the *Guidelines*. Section 4 applies to high-income payers like the husband in this case. If the court considers the Table amount "inappropriate" under s. 4(b), it has the discretion to order a different amount. The Court of Appeal held that because of the case of *Sherman v. Sherman* (1999), 45 R.F.L. (4th) 424, 44 O.R. (3d) 411, 119 O.A.C. 88, 1999 CarswellOnt 1463 (C.A.) which decided that the courts maintain a discretion not to vary child support, despite the coming into force of the *Guidelines* and because the jurisprudence on the court's discretion under s. 4(b) of the *Guidelines* changed between the hearing of the application and the hearing of the appeal, the fair result was a new hearing. At the new hearing, the wife would have the chance to establish a material change in circumstances justifying a change in the amount of child support, and the husband would have the chance to convince the court that the amount under the *Guidelines* was inappropriate. Both parties were lawyers working in downtown Toronto law firms. At the time of the original child support order in 1993, the husband's gross income was $233,750. When the order under appeal was made in October 1998, his 1997 income tax return showed an income of $543,596.

In *Simon v. Simon* (1999), 1 R.F.L. (5th) 119, 182 D.L.R. (4th) 670, 46 O.R. (3d) 349, 127 O.A.C. 17, 1999 CarswellOnt 3863, [1999] O.J. No. 4492 (C.A.); leave to appeal refused (2000), 255 N.R. 198 (note), 135 O.A.C. 196 (note), 2000 CarswellOnt 1203, 2000 CarswellOnt 1204 (S.C.C.), the mother appealed from a lower court's refusal to apply the amount set out in the *Federal Child Support Guidelines* in the mother's application for increased child support based upon the father's professional hockey contract which guaranteed him a $1,000,000 salary for two years. The lower court found that it was not in the child's best interests to provide him with the luxury of large monthly support payments where such payments could not be guaranteed over the course of the child's dependency, as it was unknown how long the father's professional hockey career would last.

On appeal, the court was of the opinion that the lower court judge made a crucial error in imposing a heavy burden on the mother to justify her child care budget. This position was inconsistent with *Francis v. Baker*, above, which established that the burden is on the paying spouse to demonstrate that the Table amount is inappropriate. Factors such as a sudden increase in salary or uncertainty about the father's future salary are irrelevant. The child's needs and the paying spouse's income and ability to pay, are the only factors relevant to an analysis under s. 4 of the *Guidelines*. The Table amounts are determined by the income of the paying spouse. If the income changes in the future, then the child support order can be varied. The fact that the father in this case has a modest lifestyle is of no significance. It is only his income that matters. *Francis v. Baker* established that "in all cases Parliament intended that there be a presumption in favour of the Table amounts". The father in the *Simon* case did not rebut the presumption.

The appellate court was of the opinion that a court should not impose a trust to secure a child's care and education, unless there were a good reason for doing so, such as the misuse of support payments by the custodial parent. The presumption is that the custodial parent will provide both for the child's immediate and future needs. The appeal was allowed and the father was ordered to pay child support of $9,215 per month dating from May 1, 1997. The provisions varying the trust provisions of the separation agreement and subsequent divorce judgment were deleted and the original provisions regarding the trust were restored. (See *M. (O.) v. K. (A.)*, below)

In *Bailey v. Bailey* (1999), 47 R.F.L. (4th) 35, 1999 CarswellAlta 442 (C.A.), the court affirmed the lower court's application of the *Guidelines* for income over $150,000 on a straight mathematical basis of 1.17 percent of any income over $150,000, on the basis that whatever the correct interpretation of the exercise of a court's discretion under s. 4 of the *Guidelines*, the amounts set by the Chambers Judge were justified, in light of the evidence. The father had been ordered to pay child support of $3,811 for four months and then $4,834 onward, based on an income for *Guidelines* purposes of $315,191 and

$402,691 for each of these periods respectively. The father had also received $1.9 million in 1997, a fact which the mother said was not known to her at the time of its receipt.

In *R. v. R.* (2002), 24 R.F.L. (5th) 96, 2002 CarswellOnt 902, [2002] O.J. No. 1095, 211 D.L.R. (4th) 403, 58 O.R. (3d) 656, 159 O.A.C. 46 (C.A.), before Catzman, Doherty and Laskin JJ.A., the father's income after separation rose from approximately $2,000,000 to approximately $4,000,000 annually. The court upheld the trial judge's ruling that the table amount of child support, over $65,000 for the parties' four children, was inappropriate. However, it did interfere with the order as granted. The Court of Appeal was of the opinion that there were two material and consequently reviewable errors in the trial judgment. The trial judge determined the amount of child support on the parties' lifestyle and their pattern of expenditure during the time that they cohabited and therefore did not take into account sufficiently the very significant increase in the husband's income after the parties' separation. Also, the trial judge failed to consider whether the wife's budget was reasonable considering the substantial increase in the husband's income. The Appellate Court varied the amount of support from $20,000 to $36,000 per month. The monthly expenses were for the following: amount $12,000 for basic expenses for the children, and the $20,000 for discretionary expenses. In addition, the Appellate Court allowed the trial judge's order of $4,000 per month under s. 7 to stand. At trial, the court had dismissed the wife's budget since she had included items, which were not previously considered by the parties, and he set out an "arbitrary" amount of $4,000 for discretionary expenses without any explanation as to why that was a reasonable amount. As the husband's income had increased dramatically, the Appellate Court was of the opinion that the wife could include items, which were not previously acquired or considered by the parties. (See paras. 60–61.)

In *Ruel v. Juodis* (2004), 10 R.F.L. (6th) 129, 2004 CarswellOnt 3371 (S.C.J.), the court refused to reduce the Table Amount of child support payable by the father. The father, whose income exceeded $450,000 annually, was seeking an independent medical assessment of the mother, who claimed to be disabled as a result of an injury and had accordingly experienced a reduction in her income. Given the father's substantial income, it was irrelevant if another $25,000 annually was imputed to the mother.

In *Pakka v. Nygard* (2002), 61 O.R. (3d) 328, 2002 CarswellOnt 3403, [2002] O.J. No. 3858 (S.C.J.), the defendant was the father of seven children with four different mothers. On a motion for interim support, the court rejected his argument that it would be "inappropriate" for him to pay the Table Amount for a child who lived with his mother in Ontario, on the basis that he treated all his children the same. He paid each mother $3,000 per month, net after tax for each child in her custody. The court held that it would not be inappropriate to require the defendant to pay the Table Amount to the applicant. The approach submitted by the father did not comply with the laws of Ontario. It would allow payers, rather than the *Guidelines*, to determine the amount of support payable. It would undermine the *Guidelines* and be inconsistent with the principles of the Supreme Court of Canada and Ontario Court of Appeal which emphasize the actual situation of the child. It would not take account of the circumstances of the child and the financial ability of the parents as required by s. 4(b)(ii) of the *Guidelines*. The court ordered interim child support in the amount of $15,091.54 per month, based on an income of $2.2 million per year.

The sheer size of Table Amount, $15,091.54 per month, (which was $8,000) per month higher that monthly budget), was not in itself an "articulable reason" for departing from the Table Amount: *Pakka v. Nygard* (2002), 61 O.R. (3d) 328, 2002 CarswellOnt 3403,

[2002] O.J. No. 3858 (S.C.J.). In a schedule to his affidavit, the defendant's income was said to be $2,237,096.

Although the husband's income for one of the three years before the hearing was $222,559.59, the court did not average his income to determine child support, as he had been terminated from his employment two years before the hearing: *Walker v. Walker* (1999), 1 R.F.L. (5th) 180, 1999 CarswellAlta 641 (Q.B.). However, he did receive a severance package from his employment. The husband's current support obligations were based on his income from the previous year, which was after his termination.

In *Dergousoff v. Dergousoff*, 48 R.F.L. (4th) 1, [1999] 10 W.W.R. 633, 177 Sask. R. 64, 199 W.A.C. 64, [1999] S.J. No. 192, 1999 CarswellSask 231 (C.A.), the parties had executed a separation agreement that was incorporated in an order providing that the father would pay $3,500 towards the support of the parties' four children who resided with their mother. Subsequent to the enactment of the *Federal Child Support Guidelines*, the mother applied successfully for an order varying the amount of support. The court found that the introduction of the *Guidelines* constituted a material change in circumstances in relation to the support of the children and varied the amount of support from $3,500 to $3,735 per month. The father appealed and the appeal was allowed.

The court held in the *Dergousoff* decision that the coming into force of s. 15.1 of the *Divorce Act* in the case of an order made before the passage of the *Guidelines* must be regarded as a change in circumstances and thus a court must consider an application for variation. Consideration of special or extraordinary expenses was a separate determination. Where, as in the *Dergousoff* decision, the payor earned more than $150,000 annually the court must, under s. 4(b), determine whether a Table amount is "inappropriate". The court must consider the condition, means, needs and other circumstances of the children, together with the abilities of each of the spouses to contribute to their maintenance. If the court decides that the Table amount is inappropriate, it must determine an appropriate amount. The presumption of s. 3 of the *Guidelines* is that the amount of money in the Table amount is the amount that the payor spouse is obliged to pay for the parties' children for their ordinary needs. (Their extraordinary needs are covered under s. 7.) "An appropriate amount may be less than the sum of the fixed and proportionate amounts specified by the table, but not less than the fixed amount attributable to the first $150,000 earned by the spouse against whom the order is sought": para. 80. In the *Dergousoff* decision, the court, on appeal, found that the increased amount was inappropriate, given the actual needs of the children and the means of both parties. (The court was critical of the fact that there was no evidence of the current needs of the children.) The court awarded support of $3,000 a month, which was an increase for the children from the amount under the agreement and an increase of $15,000 a year for the father, in light of the tax changes to child support payments.

In *MacDonald v. MacDonald* (1997), 57 Alta. L.R. (3d) 195, [1998] 6 W.W.R. 86, 209 A.R. 178, 160 W.A.C. 178, 1997 CarswellAlta 1062, [1997] A.J. No. 1262 (C.A.); additional reasons at (1998), 40 R.F.L. (4th) 397, [1999] 2 W.W.R. 277, 64 Alta. L.R. (3d) 125, 216 A.R. 340, 175 W.A.C. 340, 1998 CarswellAlta 506, [1998] A.J. No. 630 (C.A.); leave to appeal refused (1998), 227 N.R. 399 (note), 237 A.R. 135 (note), 197 W.A.C. 135 (note) (S.C.C.), the court held that the amount of child support would be based on the father's deemed gross annual income made up of $96,000 salary and $114,000 severance. Thus, his income should be considered to be over $150,000. The multiplier used in the *Federal Child Support Guidelines* for incomes over $150,000 would determine any additional income in excess of $96,000 gross income. The father should pay his proportionate share of the special or extraordinary expenses provided for in the *Guidelines*.

In *M. (O.) v. K. (A.)*, 9 R.F.L. (5th) 111, (sub nom. *Droit de la famille — 3148)* [2000] R.J.Q. 2339, (sub nom. *Droit de la famille — 3148)* [2000] R.D.F. 761, 2000 CarswellQue 1709 (S.C.), the father/payor was a professional hockey player who earned $1,940,400 (Cdn.) a year from his National Hockey League team, as well as any earnings he might receive from the Russian National Team. The parties had triplet daughters who were approximately six years of age at the time of judgment. Child support would amount to over $300,000 per year under the federal *Guidelines* and the Table for Quebec. The court found at paragraph 86 that the application of the Table amounts would be inappropriate for the following reasons:

(a) The applicant mother in 1998 was still admitting that an award of $40,000 after taxes, as was agreed upon in 1995, would meet the needs of the children.

(b) The parties, while they were living together, never had a lifestyle commensurate with that which would result from an order for $300,000 per year in child support.

(c) The substantial increase in the father's earnings would have constituted a change in circumstances which would justify a significant increase in support, if the needs of the children had not been completely satisfied by the initial support award.

(d) The applicant mother, even in her latest statement of income and expenses, stated that the needs of the children and of herself amounted to $15,550 net per month or $186,600 per year, which included some non-recurring expenses, which when deducted, reduced the mother and children's needs to $107,400 per year.

(e) The court held that where the support debtor's capacity to pay is not an issue, current needs should be met as established. Anticipated needs should be met as they occur.

(f) There was no evidence that the father had a contract for the coming year but the parties agreed that the court could render its decision assuming that the father's income would be similar to his income for the past year.

The court, in the *M. (O.) v. K. (A.)* case, relying on *Willick v. Willick*, [1994] 3 S.C.R. 670, 6 R.F.L. (4th) 161, 119 D.L.R. (4th) 405, 173 N.R. 321, 125 Sask. R. 81, 81 W.A.C. 81, [1994] R.D.F. 617, [1994] S.C.J. No. 94, 1994 CarswellSask 48, 1994 CarswellSask 450 and *Francis v. Baker*, [1999] 3 S.C.R. 250, 177 D.L.R. (4th) 1, 246 N.R. 45, 50 R.F.L. (4th) 228, 125 O.A.C. 201, [1999] S.C.J. No. 52, 1999 CarswellOnt 2734, 1999 CarswellOnt 2948, was of the opinion at paragraph 87 that since the children's needs could be met without hardship with less than $55,000 per year, any order which was substantially greater than that would result in the former wife sharing in her former husband's income by means of receiving excessive child support. It was held that a court should consider as actual needs of the children their future education and other benefits normally given to privileged children, particularly in situations where the payor parent has a short-lived high earning power. Where, as in this case, both parents had shown a manifest immaturity in managing their financial affairs, the court should set up a trust for the benefit of the children without encroaching upon any portion of the support required for their daily needs. The court ordered that the father pay $4,600 per month ($55,200 per year) in child support and $5,400 per month ($64,800 per year) into a trust to be established for the joint benefit of the three children.

In *Greenwood v. Greenwood*, 2 R.F.L. (5th) 190, [1999] B.C.J. No. 2093, 1999 CarswellBC 2039 (S.C. [In Chambers]), the court granted the father's application for a reduction in child support where the father's income had dropped from $995,819.61 to an estimated $210,670 per year. However, as the father had been particularly poor at predicting his future income, the court set his income at $389,327.14 for *Guidelines* purposes. The court found that the drop in child support from the original amount to that for an income of $210,670 would not meet the child's needs. Given the condition, means, and other circumstances of the child and the financial ability of each of the parties to contribute to the child's support, the amount would not meet his needs and would be inappropriate. Even the father stated in his affidavit that the child would need approximately $3,000 per month. Lastly, there should be some stability to the widely fluctuating support amounts produced by the father's widely fluctuating income.

In *Turner v. Turner* (1999), 2 R.F.L. (5th) 286, 1999 CarswellOnt 3662 (S.C.J.), the court rejected the husband's argument that the amount of child support was "inappropriate". He had maintained that the amount was excessive, as it would exceed the "reasonable needs" of the two children who were living with their mother. The court found that the father was earning approximately $350,000 and that his income had been increasing each year. In addition, his second wife had a gross income of $62,500 as his employee and her income was not required to pay household expenses. The father and his second wife could benefit from income-splitting for tax purposes and could invest in R.R.S.P.'s and thereby not pay tax on the money invested in the R.R.S.P.'s. In the mother's household, until this judgment, she received $45,000 annually in child support, plus $15,000 in spousal support. She had had to pay tax on the whole amount. Income splitting was not a possibility. Pursuant to the *Guidelines*, the court held that the amount of child support payable was $4,940.43 per month for three children or $3,823.50 per month for two children. Out of this amount of child support, the court permitted the father to make some direct payments to the children for their allowances, to Blue Cross for medical insurance and to the Canadian Scholarship Trust Foundation, so that the father could know that these payments were being used for the purposes intended.

In *R. v. R.* (2000), 10 R.F.L. (5th) 88, 2000 CarswellOnt 2744, [2000] O.J. No. 2830 (S.C.J.); additional reasons at (2001), 15 R.F.L. (5th) 163, 2001 CarswellOnt 797 (S.C.J.); varied (2002), 2002 CarswellOnt 902, [2002] O.J. No. 1095, 24 R.F.L. (5th) 96, 211 D.L.R. (4th) 403, 58 O.R. (3d) 656, 159 O.A.C. 46 (C.A.), the father had an annual income of $4,143,186 and the *Guidelines* or Table amount for each of the four children in this case was $16,398 per month. There is a presumption in favour of the Table amounts. While there cannot be any deviation from the Table amounts for the first $150,000 of the payor's income, for amounts above $150,000, the strict *Guidelines* amount is immediately open to review. The payor need not testify or call evidence. In fact, in this case, the husband did testify and the wife was cross-examined extensively on her child expense budget. The court was of the view that the children's needs should be assessed in the context of the parties' background and family history. Despite their wealth, the parties had a conservative and modest pattern of expenditure. In the circumstances, the court concluded that the Table amount of child support would be inappropriate. The father had demonstrated that budgeted child expenses were so high as to "*exceed the generous ambit within which reasonable disagreement is possible*". The court was of the opinion that the family's previous expenditures were equally relevant to the determination of an appropriate award of child support under s. 4(b)(ii), as it is to determining the reasonableness of a proposed special or extraordinary expense under s. 7. The husband was ordered to pay $20,000 per month in child support.

In *Sarafinchin v. Sarafinchin* (2000), 189 D.L.R. (4th) 741, 2000 CarswellOnt 2640, [2000] O.J. No. 2855 (S.C.J.), the husband was found to have an average income for child support purposes over the three years from 1997 to 1999 of $384,505. The court held that the onus was on the payor to provide clear and compelling evidence why it was inappropriate to award the Table amount for child support. Where, as in this case, no such evidence was provided, nor were the needs of the children as set out in the Financial Statement filed seriously challenged, then it was not inappropriate to award the Table amount. The husband was ordered to pay child support of $4,217 per month, retroactive to May 1, 1997. The support was made retroactive, as the wife had demanded increased support almost immediately after May 1, 1997, the husband had the ability to pay the increased amount since May 1, 1997, and the children's needs during that time made the amount an appropriate one. To refrain from granting retroactive support would reward the husband for the period it took to resolve matters, thereby rewarding him for his lack of forthrightness in providing information needed for a fair assessment.

The court upheld an interim maintenance agreement which provided for child and spousal maintenance of $38,000 per month until further agreement or court order, and the parties had acknowledged that they had had independent legal advice in *Sobey v. Sobey* (2000), 11 R.F.L. (5th) 401, 2000 CarswellNS 279 (S.C.). The evidence did not disclose any ground for invalidating the contract. The mother had remained at home with the children and the father was a sophisticated and very successful businessman. The court was of the opinion that the fact that there was a maintenance agreement did not displace the court's power to award interim relief. However, in consideration of the evidence and the matters to be addressed in the context of the whole decision, the agreement should not be ignored. The negotiated amount was approximately $5,000 less than the *Guidelines* amount.

In *Dickinson v. Dickinson* (1998), 1998 CarswellOnt 4501 (Gen. Div.), Perkins J. held that if the court had the discretion to reduce the Table amount for an income over $150,000, it would not do so in this case, as the father had been in substantial default under an interim order for almost a year and a half and provided no substantial assistance for the year and a half before that time. In the opinion of the court, where, as in this case, the father's income was approximately $200,000, it was not so great that it could be argued that the quantum of child support was out of all proportion to the needs of the child.

In *MacDougall v. MacDougall* (1997), 191 N.B.R. (2d) 254, 488 A.P.R. 254, 1997 CarswellNB 363 (Q.B.), the court held that it had the discretion under ss. 3 and 4 of the *Guidelines* to decide an appropriate amount of support where the children in question were over the age of majority and the payor spouse, the father, earned over $150,000 a year. In this case, the court found that the parties' existing arrangement was appropriate whereby the father put money in an account managed by the eldest child and he, in turn, paid the university and living expenses of the children. Each child in full-time attendance at university was to receive approximately $10,000 annually.

There are additional cases where the payor's income is relatively close to $150,000 per year. These cases are the following: *Orszak v. Orszak* (2000), 8 R.F.L. (5th) 350, 2000 CarswellOnt 1574 (S.C.J.); *Murphy v. Murphy*, 8 R.F.L. (5th) 338, 2000 BCSC 974, 2000 CarswellBC 1304, [2000] B.C.J. No. 1253 (S.C.); *Adams v. Adams* (2000), 4 R.F.L. (5th)

1, 2000 CarswellOnt 273 (S.C.J.); reversed (2001), 15 R.F.L. (5th) 1, 2001 CarswellOnt 1492, [2001] O.J. No. 1575, 145 O.A.C. 388 (Ont. C.A.); *Leger v. Leger* (2000), 2000 CarswellNB 53 (Q.B.); *Armaz v. van Erp* (2000), 7 R.F.L. (5th) 1, 2000 CarswellOnt 1461, [2000] O.J. No. 1544 (S.C.J.); *Schmid v. Smith* (1999), 1 R.F.L. (5th) 447, 1999 CarswellOnt 2390 (S.C.J); *Schnarr v. Schnarr* (1999), 49 R.F.L. (4th) 384, 1999 CarswellBC 238, [1999] B.C.J. No. 303 (S.C.); *Andrews v. Andrews* (1999), 50 R.F.L. (4th) 1, 124 O.A.C. 259, 45 O.R. (3d) 577, 1999 CarswellOnt 3019, [1999] O.J. No. 3578 (C.A.); *McCrea v. McCrea* (1999), 1 R.F.L. (5th) 320, 1999 CarswellBC 1476, [1999] B.C.J. No. 1514 (S.C.); additional reasons at 2000 BCSC 1437, 2000 CarswellBC 1998 (S.C.); *Pearce v. Pearce* (1999), 1 R.F.L. (5th) 402, 1999 CarswellBC 2214 (S.C.); *Currie v. Currie* (1999), 2 R.F.L. (5th) 153, 1999 CarswellOnt 3615 (S.C.J.); *Hama v. Werbes*, 2 R.F.L. (5th) 203, 1999 CarswellBC 2515 (S.C. [In Chambers]).

In *Macdougall v. Macdougall* (September 2, 1997), Doc. FOF-620-94 (N.B. Q.B.), the court held that it had the discretion under ss. 3 and 4 of the *Guidelines* to decide an appropriate amount of support where the children in question were over the age of majority and the payor spouse, the father, earned over $150,000 a year. In this case, the court found that the parties' existing arrangement was appropriate whereby the father put money in an account managed by the eldest child and he, in turn, paid the university and living expenses of the children. Each child in full-time attendance at university was to receive approximately $10,000 annually.

15§94 — Child support — age of majority or over

See 15§88A — Section 3 — Presumptive Rule

15§95 — Child support — split custody

Split custody is an arrangement where each spouse has sole custody of one or more children.

In these arrangements the amount of a child support order is the difference between the amount that each spouse would otherwise pay if a child support order were sought against each of the spouses: *Federal Child Support Guidelines*, s. 8.

The steps in determining the difference that should be paid by one of the spouses to the other, are:

(1) Wife or former Wife applies the table matching the number of children in her custody with her husband's income and arrives at an amount owing to her.

(2) Husband or former Husband does the same, viewing the arrangement from the perspective of his situation. He applies the table matching the number of children in his custody with his wife's income and arrives at an amount owing to him.

(3) The lesser amount is subtracted from the greater amount, and this difference is the basic amount of support payable to the spouse having the greater amount owing to him or to her.

(4) The Wife calculates the share, if any, of the special or extraordinary expenses owing to her.

(5) The Husband does the same with respect to the share, if any, of the special or extraordinary expenses owing to him.

(6) The lesser share is subtracted from the greater share and the difference is the amount for special or extraordinary expenses payable to the spouse having the greater amount owing to her or to him.

(7) If both the difference in the basic amounts and the difference in the special expenses are owing to the same spouse, the total is the amount of child support payable to that spouse.

(8) If one amount is owing to one spouse, and the second amount is owing to the other spouse, one amount would be set off against the other and the excess would be the support payable.

In *Anderson v. Anderson*, 5 R.F.L. (5th) 235, 2000 BCSC 359, 2000 CarswellBC 530 (S.C.), child support was calculated under s. 8 of the *Guidelines*, despite the fact that custody was shared and not split. The calculation of child support based on the percentage of time children spent with each parent and setting off of the amounts was not appropriate and would be unfair to the receiving spouse. If that method were used in this case, the mother would receive less child support than the receiving spouse in a split custody arrangement.

Where each parent had custody of one child and both parents were employed, the mother was nevertheless not required to pay child support. Such an order would result in undue hardship to the mother as the child living with her had health and emotional problems and the mother could not afford to provide the child with any ordinary activities. As the mother's living standard was below that of the father's, the court was justified in departing from the *Guidelines*: *Scharf v. Scharf* (1998), 40 R.F.L. (4th) 422 (Ont. Gen. Div.).

In *R. (W.H.) v. R. (J.M.)* (July 3, 1997), Doc. 45563/93 (Ont. Gen. Div.), one child who was to some degree self-sufficient, lived with the father, and two children resided with the mother. The husband was returning to work after an illness. Both parties were anticipating earning $45,000. The father was ordered to pay $500 per month (rather than the *Guidelines* amount of $387) because the daughter living with the father was not fully dependent on him so as to merit the father's suggestion that he pay for only one child. The mother was allowed to withhold $12,000 from the equalization payment from which she could take any of the father's unpaid support obligations.

In *Calderisi v. Brothers* (October 10, 1997), Doc. Vancouver D096959 (B.C. S.C.); additional reasons (March 19, 1998), Doc. Vancouver D096959 (B.C. S.C.), the father was a medical doctor and the mother a registered nurse. One of the children of the marriage lived with the father, and the other with the mother. The father's income was $240,000 a year. The mother worked half-time and was studying to complete her Bachelor of Science degree in nursing. Her income was $26,200 a year. According to the guidelines, the father was required to pay support of $1,355 a month for the child in the mother's care, and the mother obliged to pay $233 a month for the child in the father's care. After setting off one amount against the other, the father was ordered to pay child support of $1,122 a month.

15§96 — Child support — shared custody

For a more detailed account of this subject, see MacDonald and Wilton, *Child Support Guidelines: Law and Practice*.

Where both spouses share physical custody of a child in such a way that one spouse has a right of access to, or has physical custody of a child for not less than 40 percent of the time during the year, the amount of the child support order shall be determined by taking into account:

(a) the amounts set out in the applicable tables for each of the spouses;

(b) the increased costs of shared custody arrangements; and

(c) the conditions, means, needs and other circumstances of each spouse and of any child of the marriage for whom support is sought: *Federal Child Support Guidelines*, s. 9.

Not all joint custody arrangements would fall under this provision since often what is called joint custody does not amount to sharing physical custody of the child. All that is shared to a substantial degree is the responsibility for decision making. This is enough under present practice to label the arrangement as one of joint custody. The physical custody that actually occurs in these situations is often close in terms of actual time with the child to sole custody subject to access, but instead of using these terms the arrangements describe the child as having a permanent home with one parent and spending time with the other parent. The time spent with this parent is usually much less than the 40 percent required by the section.

Where the spouses do share actual physical custody at least in a 60/40 ratio, any sense of a mechanical calculation of child support is abandoned. The table amount is only one element of the assessment with costs and the old "means and needs" test being equally important and possibly overriding the table determination.

Contino v. Leonelli-Contino (2005), 204 O.A.C. 311, 341 N.R. 1, 80 O.R. (3d) 480 (note), [2005] S.C.J. No. 65, 2005 SCC 63, 2005 CarswellOnt 6281, 2005 CarswellOnt 6282, 19 R.F.L. (6th) 272, 259 D.L.R. (4th) 388, [2005] 3 S.C.R. 217 (S.C.C.), was an appeal from the Court of Appeal for Ontario heard by a panel of nine judges who decided (8:1) how the amount of support should be determined for shared custody arrangements under s. 9 of the *Child Support Guidelines*.

By agreement, the father and mother assumed joint custody of their son who was 9½-years-old at the time of the appeal. His daily residence was with his mother subject to free and liberal access by his father. The father was to pay child support of $500 a month subject to adjustments according to the cost of living index. He did not adjust the amount and, in any event, instead of enforcing the agreement the mother applied for a variation according to the *Guidelines*, which she settled for $563 a month. The mother moved into a new home and incurred other expenses for the child in the expectation that she would continue to receive child support of $563 or more. After the son's time with him increased to 50%, and 3 years after the settlement, the father applied for a reduction in support pursuant to s. 9 of the *Guidelines* on the ground that the arrangements had changed from sole custody to shared custody. On the application, the mother's annual income was found to be $68,082 for a Table Amount of $560 a month, and the father's $87,315 for a Table Amount of $688. The set-off amount was $128. The ratio between the father's and mother's income calculated against their combined income was 56:44 ($87,315/($87,315+$68,082) × 100 = 56, and $68,082/($87.315+ $68,082) × 100 = 44). Both parents attributed one-half of their fixed and variable expenses such as the mortgage, taxes and groceries to the son, and both claimed additional expenses for him. The total expenses came to $1,814 a month for the father and $1,916.95 a month for the mother. The father's net worth was $255,750 and the mother's $190,651 for a difference of $65,099.

The motions judge at first instance reduced the support amount from $563 a month to $100 per month. The Divisional Court ordered the father to pay the full Table amount of $688 per month. The Court of Appeal reduced the amount to $399.61. "It used the simple set-off amount as a starting point for determining the support amount (s. 9(a)), and adjusted the set-off amount by applying a multiplier of 67.6% to account for the mother's fixed costs (s. 9(b)) and by taking the actual situation of the parents and the child into account (s. 9(c))."

The Supreme Court of Canada allowed the appeal (Fish J. dissenting) awarding child support to the mother of $500 a month. Bastarache J. wrote the judgement for the majority.

There was no dispute that at the time of the proceedings the child spent more than 40% of his time with the father and was, therefore, in a shared custody arrangement under s. 9 of the *Child Support Guidelines*. The issue related to how the amount of the support in such an arrangement should be determined.

The wording of s. 9 is imperative. Once the 40% threshold is met, the court "must" determine the amount of child support in accordance with the three listed factors. The regime for determining the amount of support under s. 9 is different from the formula approach used in ss. 3 (presumptive rule) and 8 (split custody). A new category of custodial arrangements was created under s. 9. It is not a variation of the general regime, but is a complete regime or system of its own. The presumption specifically prescribed in ss. 3(2) and 4 for determining support — that the amount in the *Guidelines* is mandatory unless the court finds it is inappropriate — is not found in s. 9. There are no presumptions in s. 9. On the contrary, the amount of child support "must" be determined in accordance with the three listed factors in 9(a), (b) and (c) and this can only be done on the basis of evidence without resorting to artificial multipliers or assumptions about costs.

Some of the realities that should be recognized when addressing the problems created by s. 9 are that more time spent with the child may not involve increased spending by the parent or significant savings for the other parent; that a significant disparity of incomes may exacerbate the differences in standard of living in the two households; and that shared custody may entail more costs in the duplication of services and leave less money for support.

The amount of support under s. 9 is in the discretion of the court. The exercise of this discretion is structured by the three factors in s. 9. No one factor prevails. The weight given to each factor will vary according to the particular facts of each case. The costs of the overall arrangement of shared custody should be considered paying attention to the needs, resources and situation of the parents and any child. The emphasis is on flexibility and fairness to ensure that the economic reality and particular circumstances of each family are properly accounted for, and to ensure a fair level of child support. "Parliament, in adopting s. 9, deliberately chose to emphasize the objectives of fairness, flexibility and recognition of the actual conditions, means, needs and other circumstances of each spouse and of any child for whom support is sought, even if to the detriment of predictability consistency and efficiency to some degree." There is an automatic deviation from the method in s. 3, but not necessarily from the amount. It is possible that after a review of the factors in s. 9, the court will find that the *Guidelines* amount is the proper amount. Thus, not only is there no presumption in favour of awarding at least the *Guidelines* amount under s. 3, there is no presumption in favour of reducing the *Guidelines* amount.

The Table does not take into account expenses incurred by the non-custodial parent. The formula used to establish the Table Amounts assumed that all of the expenditures for the children are met by the recipient parent and none by the other parent.

Section 9(a) Table Amount for each Parent: Section 9(a) requires the court to take the financial situations of both parties into account, and not just the income of the parent against whom the order is sought as in s. 3. (It refers to the Table Amounts, not the *Guidelines* amounts, precluding consideration under the paragraph of all of the discretionary factors in the *Guidelines* for departure from the Table Amounts. This restriction makes paragraph (a) too narrow in scope to form the exclusive basis for a s. 9 award and, therefore, paragraphs (b) and (c) must be considered, also.) The section does not state how the Table Amounts are to be considered or taken into account. A simple set-off as used for split custody under s. 8 of the *Guidelines* is the preferred starting point for a s. 9 analysis. But a rigid application of a set-off should be cautioned against especially in variation applications where it could result in a drastic change in support because of the "cliff effect." (A sole-custody parent receiving the Table Amount without set-off, by a small change in time with the child may become a shared-custody parent with support reduced by a set-off and no corresponding savings in child care costs. The cliff edge is located at the point where the time of the child with other parent increases from 39% to 40%.) Such a change may not be warranted when the financial situation of the parents and the standard of living in both households is considered. A court will depart from the set-off amount or make adjustments to it, if it is inappropriate in light of the factors considered under ss. 9(b) and 9(c). Considering these factors involves an examination of the continuing ability of the recipient parent to meet the needs of the child — especially in light of the fact that many costs are fixed. "What is important is that the set-off does not take into account actual spending patterns as they relate to variable costs or the fact that fixed costs of the recipient parent are not reduced by the increased spending of the payor parent." The value of the set-off "is in bringing the court to focus first on the fact that both parents must make a contribution and that fixed and variable costs of each of them have to be measured before making adjustments to take into account increased costs attributable to joint custody and further adjustments needed to ensure that the final outcome is fair in light of the conditions, means, needs and other circumstances of each spouse and child for whom support is sought."

The Table Amounts are an estimate of the amount being paid by the non-custodial parent. Where both parents are contributing to the child's support, it is necessary to examine how their actual contributions compare to the Table Amount calculated as if they were each non-custodial payor parents. Adjustments to the set-off amount may be based on the actual sharing of child-related expenses. The court also retains the discretion to modify the set-off amount where it would lead to a significant variation in the standard of living experienced by the children as they move from one household to the other. As far as possible, the child should not suffer a noticeable decline in his or her standard of living from what the child experienced when the family lived under one roof.

Section 9(b) Increased Costs of Shared Custody Arrangements: The increased costs referred to in (b) are not merely the expenses assumed by the payor parent resulting from the increase in access time from less than 40% to more than 40%. They are the total costs of raising the child and paragraph (b) recognizes that these costs may be greater in shared custody than in sole custody arrangements. The court will determine whether shared custody has resulted in increased costs globally by examining the budgets and actual expenditures of both parents made to address the needs of the child. Increased costs would normally result from duplication because the child now lives in two homes. A change in time will give rise to an inquiry under (b) to determine the increased costs of the shared custody arrangement, but the time may not, in itself, lead to increased costs. "One parent can simply assume a larger share of responsibilities, for school supplies or sports activities for example. For these reasons, the court will be called upon to examine the budgets and actual child care expenses of each parent." The actual expenses, when determined, will be apportioned between the parents according to their respective incomes.

Section 9(c) Condition, Means, Needs and Other Circumstances of Each Parent and the Child: Not every dollar spent by a parent exercising access over the 40% threshold results in a dollar saved by the recipient parent. It is possible that the recipient parent's fixed costs remain unchanged by the increased access and that his or her variable costs have been reduced only modestly. The court must examine these costs and use the broad discretion vested in it by (c) to analyse the resources and needs of both the parents and the children. Here again, it is important to keep in mind that the objectives of the *Guidelines* require a fair standard of support for the child and fair contributions from both parents. The court will be especially concerned with the standard of living of the child in each household and the ability of each parent to pay the costs required to maintain the appropriate standard of living. Financial statements and child expense budgets are necessary for a proper evaluation of these costs. Since the court has full discretion under (c) to consider "other circumstances,"there is no need to resort to s. 10 (hardship) or s. 7 (special or extraordinary expenses) to increase or reduce support. (Although the court's discretion, properly exercised, should not result in hardship, s. 10 might be applied in an extraordinary situation.)

Application of s. 9 to the Facts: Given that the Table Amount for the father was $688 a month and that of the mother was $560, the set-off amount was $128 ($688 - $560 – $128). The expenditures for the child were not the same for both parents ($1,814 a month for the father and $1,916.95 for the mother), and there was "a large amount of duplication" in the budgets for fixed costs. The difference in the expenditures for the child and the duplication in fixed costs were factors that pointed to the need for significant adjustments to the set-off amounts. With the ratio of income of the parents being 56:44, the father ought to be responsible for 56% of the total child related costs and the mother for 44%. The total costs were $3,730.95 a month ($1,814 + $1,916.95 = $3,730.95) and at 56% the father's share was $2,089.33 a month and the mother's at 44% was $1,641.62. Based only this ratio, the father, already paying $1,814 a month, would be required to pay the mother $275.33 a month ($2,089.33 less $1,814 = $275.33). The mother's fixed or variable costs did not decrease following the shared custody arrangement. Nor did the father's actual expenses increase because of it. Since the application under s. 9 represented a variation from a long-standing financial status quo upon which the mother incurred valid expenses on behalf of the child, including moving into a new home, the fact that shared custody created no change in costs on either side was an important consideration. Also, the means and conditions test in (c) required that the court consider the difference in net worth between the parties, which was $65,099 in favour of the father, and the general ability of each parent to absorb increased costs. With these circumstances in mind, the court turned to a consideration of the impact of a new support order on the standard of living of the child. Central to this consideration, was the fact that the mother purchased a new home believing it to be in the child's best interests, in the expectation that the support she had been receiving from the father would continue at the same or a higher level. The father knew and "could not have ignored that." The court summarized its conclusions by saying that no formula will "recognize the reality of various families" in shared custody arrangements and that a "contextual approach which takes into account all three factors enunciated by Parliament in s. 9 of the *Guidelines* must be applied." The appeal was allowed and the amount of support to be paid by the father to the mother was set at $500 a month. Both parties were to bear their own costs throughout the proceedings.

Authors' Note: Cases decided before *Contino v. Leonelli-Contino*, 204 O.A.C. 311, 341 N.R. 1, 80 O.R. (3d) 480 (note), [2005] S.C.J. No. 65, 2005 SCC 63, 2005 CarswellOnt 6281, 2005 CarswellOnt 6282, 19 R.F.L. (6th) 272, 259 D.L.R. (4th) 388, [2005] 3 S.C.R. 217 (S.C.C.), should be read with caution.

In an appeal by the father from an interim order granting joint custody with primary care and control to the mother in *Skinner v. Skinner* (1999), 47 R.F.L. (4th) 394, 134 Man. R. (2d) 313, 193 W.A.C. 313, 1999 CarswellMan 229 (Man. C.A.), the father argued that the terms of the interim order kept the father's custody at less than 40 percent to ensure that the maximum amount of child support would be payable under the Guidelines. The Appellate court held that the issue of the amount of access should be determined at trial, following the general policy of the Court of Appeal which is not to interfere with interim orders.

Under s. 9(b), the court took into account the fact that the father was incurring additional expenses because the children spent more than 40 percent of their time with him: *Green v. Green* (2000), 6 R.F.L. (5th) 197, 2000 CarswellBC 1048, [2000] B.C.J. No. 1001, 2000 BCCA 310, 75 B.C.L.R. (3d) 306, [2000] 6 W.W.R. 130, 187 D.L.R. (4th) 37, 138 B.C.A.C. 121, 226 W.A.C. 121 (B.C. C.A.). Specifically, he had increased costs for food, housing, transportation, recreation and "miscellaneous" expenses.

In *Green v. Green* (2000), 6 R.F.L. (5th) 197, 2000 CarswellBC 1048, [2000] B.C.J. No. 1001, 2000 BCCA 310, 75 B.C.L.R. (3d) 306, [2000] 6 W.W.R. 130, 187 D.L.R. (4th) 37, 138 B.C.A.C. 121, 226 W.A.C. 121 (B.C. C.A.), Madam Justice Prowse, after reviewing various decisions based on "formula" for shared custody situations, was of the opinion that there was no "one size fits all" solution. In this case, Mr. Green's basic child support payment under the *Guidelines* was reduced from $1040 per month to $790 per month. The wife earned $35,000 and the husband $82,000 a year. The children spent at least 40 percent of their time with their father.

In *Elliott v. MacAskill* (2005), 21 R.F.L. (6th) 270, 2005 CarswellNS 508, 2005 NSFC 20, 238 N.S.R. (2d) 180, 757 A.P.R. 180 (N.S. Fam. Ct.), the father's application to terminate child support was refused. Under the parties' shared custody arrangement, the father's custody time had increased to between 43 and 60.5% on a weekly basis. However, the extra time spent by the father was not significant in terms of increasing his actual expenses.

Whether father did not keep any log or record to support his assertion that he parented his sons at least 40% of the time, his application for a decrease in child support under s. 9 of the *Guidelines* failed: *Walsh v. Walsh* (2006), 23 R.F.L. (6th) 447, 2006 CarswellNfld 37, 2006 NLUFC 7, 254 Nfld. & P.E.I.R. 338, 764 A.P.R. 338 (N.L. U.F.C.).

The court has a broad discretion in addressing child support under s. 9 of the *Guidelines* in the case of shared parenting. There is no overriding presumption in favour of a direct set-off: *Young v. Young* (2005), 20 R.F.L. (6th) 461, 2005 CarswellSask 601, 2005 SKQB 378, 276 Sask. R. 178 (Sask. Q.B.).

To determine whether a parent has had access to or physical custody of the parties' children for over 40% of the time over the course of a year, the custodial parent should receive credit for hours where responsibility cannot be determined in the evidence. In absence of evidence to the contrary, the custodial parent was deemed to have custody over the children during school hours in *Ferguson v. Ferguson* (2005), 12 R.F.L. (6th) 304, 2005 CarswellPEI 22, 2005 PESCTD 16, 246 Nfld. & P.E.I.R. 204, 731 A.P.R. 204 (P.E.I. T.D.).

Where the children spent six of every 14 nights with the father, it was held that s. 9 of the *Guidelines* Tables were not to be strictly applied: *Nitsopoulos v. Alousis* (2000), 5 R.F.L. (5th) 430, 2000 CarswellOnt 1150 (Ont. S.C.J.).

No formula exists in the *Guidelines* to provide for every situation in which the parties' share custody. Section 9 of the *Guidelines* requires the court to assess the specific facts of each case and exercise its discretion accordingly: *Morrison v. Morrison*, 10 R.F.L. (5th) 384, 2000 BCSC 1101, 2000 CarswellBC 1533 (S.C.).

In *Anderson v. Anderson*, 5 R.F.L. (5th) 235, 2000 BCSC 359, 2000 CarswellBC 530 (S.C.), child support was calculated under s. 8 of the *Guidelines*, despite the fact that custody was shared and not split. The calculation of child support based on the percentage of time children spent with each parent and setting off of the amounts was not appropriate and would be unfair to the receiving spouse. If that method were used in this case, the mother would receive less child support than the receiving spouse in a split custody arrangement.

In *Yaremchuk v. Yaremchuk* (1998), 38 R.F.L. (4th) 312, 218 A.R. 153, 158 D.L.R. (4th) 180 (Q.B. [In Chambers]), the court rejected the father's argument that the 40 percent calculation referenced in s. 9 of the *Federal Child Support Guidelines* should be based upon the total time spent under the care and direction of parents and should not include time when children were in the direct care of others, such as during school or daycare. The presumption is that the custodial parent starts with 100 percent of the time.

In *MacNaught v. MacNaught* (1998), 37 R.F.L. (4th) 79, 169 Nfld. & P.E.I.R. 153, 521 A.P.R. 153 (P.E.I. T.D.), the fact that the father, under the parties' joint custody arrangement, had physical custody of the children 40 percent of the time was considered in setting the child support payable by him under s. 9 of the *Federal Child Support Guidelines*.

In calculating whether a parent has custody of a child for 40 percent of the time, each parent is entitled to include in the calculation the time the child spent in school and sleeping while in that parent's control: *Cross v. Cross* (1998), 40 R.F.L. (4th) 242 (B.C. S.C.).

By s. 9 of the *Guidelines*, the non-custodial parent's access or physical custody of the child must be at least 40 percent of "the time over the course of a year" before his or her access costs and other child-care expenses are taken into account. The section "requires the non-custodial parent to exercise access or physical custody 40 percent of the total custodial time, presuming that the custodial parent starts with 100 percent of that time." The non-custodial spouse must show that he or she has this time with the child over the course of the year. The fact that because the child is away at school during the week and only at home on holidays and weekends, the non-custodial parent has more or less the same amount of actual time with the child as the custodial parent is not sufficient to satisfy the 40 percent requirement. It is not the amount of time that each parent spends with the child that is relevant; it is the time that the non-custodial parent spends with the child. The usual access of every second weekend and part of the holidays does not amount to 40 percent of the year. "To interpret s. 9 otherwise, then for the *support payor* to have physical custody of the child for 40 percent of the total time that the child is available, would place the courts in a situation of counting hours when the child is not in the actual presence of the custodial parent. This could not have been the intention of the legislature, that when the child is in school, away on holidays, with friends, or with grandparents, that this mandated a consideration by the courts as to whether the non-custodial parent was with the child 40 percent of the relative time each of the parents spent with the child": *Meloche v. Kales* (1997), 35 R.F.L. (4th) 297, 35 O.R. (3d) 688 (Gen. Div.).

In *Dempsey v. Dempsey* (July 14, 1997), Doc. 1201-48886/94, 95-109501/94 (N.S. S.C.), the court held that the payor was not entitled to a reduction in the amount of child support payable as he did not exercise access to the children 146 days/nights over the course of the year, even including the after school care so as to come within the 40 percent requirement in s. 9.

In *Hubic v. Hubic* (1997), 157 Sask. R. 150 (Q.B.), the father, who had the children for 11 out of 28 days during the regular weeks of the year and half of the holiday time, had the children for over 40 percent of the time. The parties consequently had shared custody and child support was to be determined in accordance with s. 9.

In this decision, the court was of the opinion that in interpreting s. 9(c), the consideration of any extraordinary expenses incurred by either party or other circumstances which are relevant, s. 9(c) contemplates a broad discretion which should be viewed in light of s. 26.1(2) of the *Divorce Act* — that is, that parents have a joint responsibility to support their children. The total cost of raising the children should be allocated between the parents having regard to the costs each parent incurs, and their relative incomes.

In *Irwin v. Irwin* (September 22, 1997), Doc. Cornwall 7224/95 (Ont. Gen. Div.), the court was not satisfied that the husband had the children more than 40 percent of the time. The court was of the opinion that even if the husband met such a threshold, the court would not, in the circumstances of the case, order support payments below the level suggested by the *Guidelines*. The husband was a surgeon whose annual income was determined to be $210,000 for purposes of support.

In calculating whether a parent has custody of a child for 40 percent of the time, each parent is entitled to include in the calculation the time the child spent in school and sleeping while in that parent's control: *Cross v. Cross* (1998), 40 R.F.L. (4th) 242 (B.C. S.C.).

Where a party claims to spend at least 40 percent of the time with a child and consequently to have a shared parenting arrangement, the other party is not required to make financial disclosure until a shared parenting arrangement is found by the court: *Cross v. Cross*, above.

Where the parties have shared custody of their child but the mother has no income, the court in setting support should take into account the cost to the payee spouse of maintaining his home for the child: *Josdal v. Josdal* (1997), 157 Sask. R. 135 (Q.B.).

In determining the amount of child support in shared custody situations, the court is required by s. 9 of the *Guidelines* to weigh each of the items in subsections (a), (b) and (c): *Middleton v. MacPherson*, 29 R.F.L. (4th) 334, 150 D.L.R. (4th) 519, [1997] 7 W.W.R. 601, 51 Alta. L.R. (3d) 152 (Q.B.). It cannot simply consider subsection(a), "the amounts set out in the applicable tables for each of the spouses," and perform the calculation referred to in s. 8. But it could use a s. 8 type calculation as the starting point. In the present case, the table amount that the husband would owe the wife would be $278 per month in child support, while the wife would owe the husband $120 per month. The difference between the amounts is $158.

The allowable special or extraordinary expenses (net of subsidies, benefits, income tax deductions or credits) are $1,264 a year for professional counselling of the child (s. 7(1)(c)), $1,584 a year for extraordinary expenses made up of $252 in extraordinary school expenses plus $1,332 per year for viola lessons and rental (s. 7(1)(d)), and $615 a year in extraordinary expenses for extracurricular activities consisting of ballet or other lessons (s. 7(1)(f)), for a total of $3,463 a year or $289 a month. The special and extraordinary expenses in this total amount should be paid by the wife with the monthly child support adjusted upward to cover the payor husband's proportionate share of the cost. Based on their incomes, his proportionate share is 68.25 percent or $197 a month. The difference in the table amounts ($158) and the husband's proportionate share of the special and extraordinary expenses ($197) is a total of $355 a month. There was no evidence of the extra costs associated with shared custody as contemplated by s. 9(b).

In showing "the conditions, means, needs and other circumstances" of each spouse and of the child pursuant to s. 9(c), the parties relied on childcare budgets they put in evidence. They showed that the total child-related expenses were $1,263 a month, and found on the basis of computer calculations that "the husband would owe the wife $215 net per month. ... Neither party has sufficient assets. Both have debts in the range of $10,000 to $20,000." The budgets were "very modest and may not have addressed all 'soft costs' associated with raising a child."

The court concluded that it should exercise its "discretion in favour of awarding the difference between the table amounts that each spouse would pay to the other plus the amount determined under s. 7. The husband will therefore pay child support to the wife in the amount of $355 per month. The wife will from this monthly amount pay the husband's proportionate share of the s. 7 expenses relating to the child's schooling, extracurricular activities and psychological therapy."

15§97 — Child support — undue hardship

Introduction

At the request of either spouse, where the court is satisfied that the spouse or child would suffer undue hardship from the application of the *Guidelines*, it may make an order which is different from the amount payable under s. 3 (incomes of $150,000 or less), s. 4 (incomes of more than $150,000), s. 5 (spouse in place of a parent), under s. 8 (split custody) and s. 9 (shared custody): *Federal Child Support Guidelines*, s. 10.

Either the payor or the payee spouse may resort to s. 10 of the *Guidelines* to set the amount of child support at a higher or lower level than the Table Amount on the ground of undue hardship: *Middleton v. MacPherson* (1997), 29 R.F.L. (4th) 334, 204 A.R. 37, 150 D.L.R. (4th) 519, 1997 CarswellAlta 512, [1997] A.J. No. 614, [1997] 7 W.W.R. 601, 51 Alta. L.R. (3d) 152 (Alta. Q.B.).

The "undue hardship" provisions of the *Federal Child Support Guidelines* are available, in appropriate circumstances, to both the payor and the payee spouse: *Racette v. Gamauf* (1997), 35 R.F.L. (4th) 357, 158 Nfld. & P.E.I.R. 38, 490 A.P.R. 38, 1997 CarswellPEI 118, [1997] 2 P.E.I.R. 333 (P.E.I. T.D. [In Chambers]); additional reasons at (1998), 176 Nfld. & P.E.I.R. 359, 540 A.P.R. 359, 1998 CarswellPEI 1 (P.E.I. T.D. [In Chambers]).

Circumstances that May Cause Undue Hardship

The circumstances that a court may consider on a question of hardship are not defined exhaustively in the *Guidelines*, but are described to "include" circumstances where:

(a) the spouse has responsibility for an unusually high level of debts reasonably incurred to support the spouses and their children prior to the separation or to earn a living;

(b) the spouse has unusually high expenses in relation to the exercise of access to a child;

(c) the spouse has a legal duty under a judgement, order or written separation agreement to support any person;

(d) the spouse has a legal duty to support a child, other than a child of the marriage, who is

(i) under the age of majority, or

(ii) the age of majority or over but is unable, by reason of illness, disability or any other cause, to obtain the necessaries of life; and

(e) the spouse has a legal duty to support any person who is unable to obtain the necessaries of life due to an illness or disability: Child Support *Guidelines*, s. 10(2).

In determining whether "undue hardship" has been established, the court is not limited to the circumstances enumerated in s. 10(2)(a) to (e) of the *Guidelines*, but in the circumstances in the absence of full disclosure of the payor's household income and household expenses, the court was unable to find undue hardship: *Cross v. Cross* (1997), 1997 CarswellBC 1523, [1997] B.C.J. No. 1741 (B.C. S.C. [In Chambers]).

High Level of Debt: s. 10(2)(a)

Where an adjustment in the amount is made because of debts causing hardship, the court may establish a reasonable time for the repayment of the debts and specify in the child support order the amount payable at the expiration of that time: *Federal Child Support Guidelines*, s. 10(5).

For a finding of "undue hardship" based on a parent's debt, the debt load must be unusually high and reasonably incurred either to support the spouse and children before the separation or to earn a living: *Dyck v. Highton*, 45 R.F.L. (5th) 322, 2003 CarswellSask 619, 111 C.R.R. (2d) 137, 239 Sask. R. 38, 2003 SKQB 396 (Sask. Q.B.).

In *Samson v. Samson*, 49 R.F.L. (5th) 202, 2003 CarswellNfld 259, 2003 NLSCUFC 25, 232 Nfld. & P.E.I.R. 148, 690 A.P.R. 148 (N.L. T.D.), the court rejected the husband's "undue hardship" defence to his wife's claim for child support. His expenses were not adequately documented to meet the threshold of excessive, extreme, unreasonable or unjustified which was required to support an undue hardship claim.

In assessing "undue hardship" on the basis of a parent's debt load under the *Federal Child Support Guidelines*, only debts reasonably incurred to support spouses and children prior to separation or to earn a living may properly be considered: *Ellis v. Ellis* (1999), 45 R.F.L. (4th) 234, 175 N.S.R. (2d) 268, [1999] N.S.J. No. 78, 1999 CarswellNS 124, 534 A.P.R. 268 (N.S. C.A.); varying (1998), 167 N.S.R. (2d) 248, 502 A.P.R. 248, 1998 CarswellNS 87, [1998] N.S.J. No. 84 (N.S. S.C. [In Chambers]).

The court in *Kennedy-Dowell v. Dowell* (2002), 28 R.F.L. (5th) 187, 2002 CarswellNS 111, [2002] N.S.J. No. 123, 203 N.S.R. (2d) 130, 635 A.P.R. 130, 2002 NSSF 13 (N.S.

S.C.); additional reasons at 2002 CarswellNS 487, [2002] N.S.J. No. 499, 2002 NSSF 50, 209 N.S.R. (2d) 392, 656 A.P.R. 392 (N.S. S.C.), took into account an unusually high level of debts, some of which were reasonably incurred in determining that the father would suffer undue hardship in paying the Table Amount of child support.

In *MacNeil v. MacNeil*, 4 R.F.L. (5th) 273, 2000 NWTSC 6, 2000 CarswellNWT 4 (N.W.T. S.C. [In Chambers]), the father's application for a reduction from the *Guidelines* Table Amount on the basis of undue hardship was refused. Although the father owed matrimonial debts of over $45,000, given his $100,000 annual income and his ability to earn more through overtime, the debt load was not excessively high.

In *Jackson v. Holloway* (1997), 35 R.F.L. (4th) 272, [1998] 5 W.W.R. 556, 161 Sask. R. 31, 1997 CarswellSask 668, [1997] S.J. No. 691 (Sask. Q.B.), the fact that the husband had purchased a new house and therefore had increased monthly expenses was not found to constitute an "undue hardship" justifying an exemption from application of the *Federal Child Support Guidelines*.

In *Pilotte v. Pilotte* (February 24, 1998), Doc. Kenora 97-075(1998), 1998 CarswellOnt 759 (Ont. Prov. Div.), the court rejected the husband's assertion that payment of child support at table levels under the *Federal Child Support Guidelines* would result in undue hardship to him. The husband argued that the hardship was the result of an unequal apportionment of family liabilities and expenses following separation. As the arrangement was the result of an agreement between the parties, the husband could not now claim undue hardship as a result of the arrangement.

In *Arcinas v. Stanley* (1999), 49 R.F.L. (4th) 157, 1999 CarswellBC 1319 (B.C. S.C.), the court refused the father's application for reduced child support launched on the basis of undue hardship. The father relied upon debts such as income tax arrears, court costs and car payments as the basis for his argument. The tax arrears were not excessive, the car debt could be extinguished by selling the car and none of the debts had been incurred to support either his wife or his children. Furthermore, despite his claims of poverty, the father had managed to take numerous overseas holidays.

High Expenses of Exercising Access: s. 10(2)(b)

In *Morgan v. Morgan*, 22 R.F.L. (6th) 419, 2006 CarswellNfld 9, [2006] N.J. No. 9, 2006 NLTD 6 (N.L. T.D.), the fact the father had to spend a considerable sum in travelling in order to exercise his access rights was found not to constitute "undue hardship" under the *Guidelines*.

Since travel for access from Florida to Ontario and long-distance telephone communication are expensive, the court reduced the amount of child support payable from the guideline amount of $572 monthly to $400 monthly in *Mallia v. Wellman* (2003), 2003 CarswellOnt 586 (Ont. C.J.).

Where the custodial parent has the much greater income, and the non-custodial parent would suffer undue hardship in paying high access costs, the court made a finding of undue hardship, and held that there would be no child support payable either prospectively or retroactively: *Kennedy-Dowell v. Dowell* (2002), 28 R.F.L. (5th) 187, 2002 CarswellNS 111, [2002] N.S.J. No. 123, 203 N.S.R. (2d) 130, 635 A.P.R. 130, 2002 NSSF 13 (N.S. S.C.); additional reasons at 2002 CarswellNS 487, [2002] N.S.J. No. 499, 2002 NSSF 50, 209 N.S.R. (2d) 392, 656 A.P.R. 392 (N.S. S.C.).

Where a lower court has rejected the argument that the exercise of access amounts to undue hardship under section 10(2) of the *Guidelines*, the court cannot then order the appellant to pay one-half of the airfare incurred in exercising access: *Holtskog v. Holtskog* (1999), 47 R.F.L. (4th) 162, 177 Sask. R. 273, 199 W.A.C. 273, 1999 CarswellSask 313, [1999] S.J. No. 304 (Sask. C.A.). The mother's appeal from a decision requiring her to pay half the cost of children's airfare for visits to the father was allowed.

Where the mother had found employment subsequent to a mental breakdown, the court allowed the custodial husband's application for child support. The payment of child support would reinforce the mother's parental role and input. However, as payment of support at *Guidelines* levels would interfere with the mother's ability to provide adequately for the children during access visits and would cause her financial hardship, support was set below *Guidelines* levels: *Petrocco v. von Michalofski* (1998), 36 R.F.L. (4th) 278, 1998 CarswellOnt 336, [1998] O.J. No. 200 (Ont. Gen. Div.); affirmed (1998), 43 R.F.L. (4th) 372, 1998 CarswellOnt 4813, (sub nom. *Petrocco v. Michalofski)* 120 O.A.C. 193 (Ont. Div. Ct.).

Travel costs in exercising access rights in a province such as Saskatchewan do not constitute "undue hardship" under the *Federal Child Support Guidelines* as travel distance between communities is a reasonably common fact of life: *Beeler v. Beeler* (1997), 32 R.F.L. (4th) 397, 161 Sask. R. 167, 1997 CarswellSask 503, [1997] S.J. No. 612 (Sask. Q.B.).

In *Martin v. Girard* (June 16, 1997), Doc. Thunder Bay 97-0367, 1997 CarswellOnt 2286, [1997] O.J. No. 2517 (Ont. Gen. Div.), the former husband applied for a variation of child support as his former wife, since the time of the support order, had become employed and was earning $26,000 a year. The former wife pleaded undue hardship as, among other things, she would incur significant access costs. The court was of the opinion that the parties should equally share the costs of access whereas previously the father had paid the entire amount. The father was no longer required to pay the mother $1,000 during summer access.

The court in *Anderson v. Anderson* (1997), 1997 CarswellOnt 3644, [1997] O.J. No. 3219, 42 O.T.C. 313 (Ont. Gen. Div.), rejected the father's argument that child support should be reduced because of increased access costs occasioned by the mother's move with the children from Barrie, where the father lived, to Newmarket. The court found that the father's reasons did not meet the requirement of the Federal *Guidelines* and many of his access visits were organized when he was passing by Newmarket to and from work.

In *Demonte v. Demonte* (1998), 40 R.F.L. (4th) 57, 1998 CarswellBC 939, [1998] B.C.J. No. 1041 (B.C. S.C.), the husband was required to pay support at *Guidelines* levels even though the effect of the order would be that he could no longer afford the travel costs associated with his access visits.

In *Williams v. Williams*, 32 R.F.L. (4th) 23, [1997] N.W.T.R. 303, 1997 CarswellNWT 30, [1997] N.W.T.J. No. 49 (N.W.T. S.C.), the mother made a bona fide choice to move from Northwest Territories to Nova Scotia after the parties' divorce leaving her son in the custody of his father. She applied to eliminate her support obligation, claiming that high access costs resulted in undue hardship. The court held that her undue hardship claim should be rejected. It is not mere hardship that must be established for a claim under section10 of the *Guidelines* but undue hardship. There was nothing unusual about the high costs of travelling between Nova Scotia and the Northwest Territories. She could not say, on the one hand, that she had made a bona fide choice in moving to Nova Scotia, and then ask to be relieved from the costs that would clearly have been foreseeable. Furthermore, the mother had provided very little evidence to substantiate her claim of undue hardship. Her new partner contributed to her household expenses, she had an income and business assets, and she had an obligation to support her child. Finally, there was a danger in using undue hardship claims as a means of redistributing income.

In *Uhrich-Cormier v. Cormier*, 11 R.F.L. (5th) 434, 2000 SKQB 410, 198 Sask. R. 34, 2000 CarswellSask 581 (Sask. Q.B.), the husband, a New Brunswick resident, sought a reduction in child support on the basis of undue hardship in exercising access to his children in Saskatchewan. Although the father failed to meet the specific requirements of the undue hardship test, there was justification to give him some relief from access costs in order to promote maximum contact between him and the children.

Legal Duty Under Judgment, Order or Written Separation to Support Person: s. 10(2(c)

In *Bourque v. Phillips*, 2000 CarswellNB 17, (sub nom. *R.B. v. J.P.*) 223 N.B.R. (2d) 242, (sub nom. *R.B. v. J.P.*) 572 A.P.R. 242 (N.B. Q.B.), the maternal grandparents, had sole custody of the child and applied for an order for child support against the child's biological parents. The father opposed the application or alternatively he pleaded undue hardship resulting from his financial obligations for the support of his spouse and two children from his second marriage. Paragraph 10(2)(c) of the *Child Support Guidelines* provides that a legal obligation to support another person pursuant to a written separation agreement is one of the circumstances that justifies a plea of undue hardship. The court was satisfied that the payment of spousal support at the rate of $1,200 per month as well as payment of support for three children (total combined child and spousal support payments of approximately $24,000 per year) on an income of $34,000 per year was "excessive" or "disproportionate" and consequently permitted the father to succeed on his claim of undue hardship up to and inclusive of the date when he was no longer required to pay spousal support for his second wife. From that time forward, he would be required to pay support for the children of both his unions. The obligation to support three children would no longer be considered as a hardship that is either "excessive", "exceptional" or "disproportionate".

Legal Duty to Support a Child, Other than the Child of the Marriage: s. 10(2)(d)

In *Schenkeveld v. Schenkeveld* (2002), 23 R.F.L. (5th) 352, 2002 CarswellMan 87, 2002 MBCA 9, 163 Man. R. (2d) 243, 269 W.A.C. 243 (Man. C.A.), the court was of the opinion that in order for hardship to be considered "undue", the hardship must be exceptional or excessive and not just the natural consequence of dividing modest resources between two households. In this case, the husband and his first wife had two children. On appeal, the husband contended that the motions court judge failed to consider that he had three additional children from his second marriage to support on an income of $42,136 with overtime. The first wife had an income of $44,609 per year. The court held that the decision of the motions judge was discretionary and dismissed the appeal from his refusal to find undue hardship.

The fact that the husband had entered into a new relationship and had more children did not establish "undue hardship" in relation to his child support obligations for a child born in an earlier union: *Reid v. Nelson* (2002), 30 R.F.L. (5th) 153, 2002 CarswellOnt 2257

(Ont. S.C.J.). In a second-family situation, the court expects clear and cogent evidence, not conjecture or speculation, from which an inference could reasonably be made that the children in the second family would suffer from some significant deprivation, if the Table Amount of support is ordered for the child of the first relationship. By this is meant food, clothing, shelter or some medical or other health need. In this case, there was no evidence of this nature and the claim of undue hardship was rejected.

In *L. (K.H.) v. G. (B.)*, 2000 CarswellAlta 1654, [2000] A.J. No. 457, 263 A.R. 80, 2000 ABQB 243 (Q.B.), the father's income had been reduced from $51,000.00 when the order was made to approximately $28,000.00 at the time of the hearing. At the time that the order was made, the natural mother of the child was on social assistance. Her monthly income, including GST, child tax credit and social assistance was $1,122.00 per month. The court found that the father had not met the test of undue hardship. He had argued that in supporting his second family, in paying for his house and loans, he spent all that he earned. The court was of the opinion that the father's circumstances seemed to have improved since the initial order and as the children of his second family were now 5 and 7, the payor's wife could more readily enter the workforce. Alternatively, the payor might need to consider returning to his former more lucrative career. The payor has been benefiting from a pre-*Guidelines* order. On the evidence presented, his household standard of living was higher than the mother's. The father had not met the test of undue hardship. His application to vary his current order was dismissed.

The court may reduce the Table Amount of support for the parties' child on the basis that to do so would create undue hardship for the payor's child of his second union: *Frechette v. Chiasson* (2000), 13 R.F.L. (5th) 68, 2000 CarswellPEI 106, 2000 PESCTD 98, 197 Nfld. & P.E.I.R. 149, 591 A.P.R. 149 (P.E.I. S.C.). In this case, the mother of the child in question worked and the mother of the child of the second union did not. There was no evidence of the job skills or likelihood of employment for the mother in the second union. The total household income of the applicant mother's family was $25,968 for three people compared to the respondent father's household income of $17,343 for a family of three. Any payment by the father to the applicant mother would increase the disparity between the two households. The father was ordered to pay a nominal amount of $40 per month in child support.

The financial hardships caused by having to support a second family is not by itself "undue hardship" under the *Federal Child Support Guidelines*: *Walkeden v. Zemlak*, 33 R.F.L. (4th) 52, 160 Sask. R. 1, 1997 CarswellSask 548, [1997] S.J. No. 601 (Sask. Q.B.).

In *Miller v. Ufoegbune*, 11 R.F.L. (5th) 347, 2000 CarswellOnt 3760 (Ont. S.C.J.), the father's obligation to his three children from his second marriage was found to constitute undue hardship in respect to paying the full *Guidelines* amount to support the child of his first marriage. The father's household had an income of $58,581 less $3,429 a year for child maintenance payments. The mother's household income was $50, 409. The father was ordered to pay child support of $200 per month, rather than the Table Amount of $285.75. The order was made retroactive to 1966. The "undue hardship" test applied to retroactive child support as well. Ordinarily the father would be assessed for retroactive child support at $12,774 using the appropriate tables. However, the court ordered him to pay $7,000.

The coming into force of the *Guidelines* constitutes a material change in circumstances under s. 17(4) of the *Divorce Act* and s. 14 (3) of the *Guidelines*: *Giroux v. Giroux*

(1999), 3 R.F.L. (5th) 61, 1999 CarswellOnt 4382, [1999] O.J. No. 4999 (Ont. S.C.J.); additional reasons at (2000), 2000 CarswellOnt 518 (Ont. S.C.J.). In this case, the father's earnings did not increase as anticipated at the time of the signing of the minutes of settlement, later incorporated into the divorce judgment. He was forced to leave his employment due to a disability and subsequently required surgery. He remarried and had two more children. For approximately six months one of the parties' two children lived with the payor. The court ordered rescission of child support arrears. The payor suffered undue hardship in relation to the arrears. He was responsible for an unusually high level of debts reasonably incurred to earn a living; he had unusually high expenses in relation to exercising access; and he had a legal duty to support a child who was under the age of majority. The standard of living of the payee's household would have been significantly higher than that of the payor during the period that arrears accumulated.

In *Knill v. Knill* (July 11, 1997), Doc. Williams Lake 5940/00955, 1997 CarswellBC 1639 (B.C. S.C. [In Chambers]), the court rejected the father's argument that he should not be required to pay the *Guidelines* amount on the basis of undue hardship where he and his second wife had just purchased a home and the custodial parent and child had just purchased a mobile home. The court was not convinced that the payor would be living at a lower standard of living than that of the first wife and child.

The fact that the husband supported his common-law spouse and her child would not lead to "undue hardship" if the existing child support order were increased to *Guidelines* level: *Dancak v. Dancak* (1998), 38 R.F.L. (4th) 227, 1998 CarswellBC 486 (B.C. S.C.); additional reasons at (1998), 1998 CarswellBC 1122 (B.C. S.C.).

To qualify as "hardship" under s. 10 of the *Guidelines*, the hardship must be "exceptional", "excessive", or "disproportionate". A father, who is aware of his child support obligations, cannot take on new second family responsibilities and live beyond his substantial means and then claim undue hardship: *Ryan v. McGunigal*, 48 R.F.L. (5th) 147, 2003 CarswellSask 656, [2003] S.J. No. 632, 2003 SKQB 428, 239 Sask. R. 257 (Sask. Q.B.).

Legal Duty to Support Person With Illness or Disability: s. 10(2)(E)

Other Circumstances: Reduction in Recipient's Income

In *Saby v. MacIntosh* (2002), 31 R.F.L. (5th) 142, 2002 CarswellBC 1848, 2002 BCSC 1144 (B.C. S.C. [In Chambers]), the court held that the worsening of the recipient's spouse's circumstances could not justify a finding of undue hardship and a variation of child support. At a date after the making of the child support order, the mother's disabilities had prevented her from working and she had separated from her second husband. The court decided that it would be contrary to the underlying principles of the *Guidelines* to make an order in this case. s. 10(2) sets out in a non-exhaustive list, circumstances which may cause a spouse or child to suffer undue hardship. The enumerated list suggests circumstances where the payor lacks the financial ability to pay the Table Amount of child support. The section should not become a means for the payment of spousal support. Undue hardship should be the exception rather than the norm. Generally it should be used defensively by the payor and not offensively by the recipient. In comparing the two households in this case, the court found that the payor's household had the higher standard of living than the recipient's. However, this was due not to the payor, but to his second wife, who was the main provider for the husband's second family. At the present time the payor was paying the Table Amount based on his imputed income. If the court ordered a higher amount, it would be imputing a higher income or transferring the obligation for support to the second wife. The court dismissed the undue hardship application.

Children's Income

The court in *Kennedy-Dowell v. Dowell*, 28 R.F.L. (5th) 187, 2002 CarswellNS 111, [2002] N.S.J. No. 123, 203 N.S.R. (2d) 130, 635 A.P.R. 130, 2002 NSSF 13 (N.S. S.C.); additional reasons at 2002 CarswellNS 487, [2002] N.S.J. No. 499, 2002 NSSF 50, 209 N.S.R. (2d) 392, 656 A.P.R. 392 (N.S. S.C.), took into account the children's substantial income of approximately $15,000 each per year in determining that the father would suffer undue hardship in paying the Table Amount of child support.

Higher Costs — Split Custody

Where the parties' daughter had left the custodial mother's home and had begun living with the father, the father's application for a reduction in child support was refused. Although normally the father would be entitled to a set-off under the *Guidelines*, the mother successfully made a claim for undue hardship. The mother had purchased a home to provide a suitable residence for her daughter and son and was faced with the expenses relating to that home even though the daughter had moved out: *Inglis v. Birkbeck*, 7 R.F.L. (5th) 114, 2000 SKQB 165, 2000 CarswellSask 236 (Sask. Q.B.); affirmed 2000 SKCA 144, 2000 CarswellSask 798 (Sask. C.A.).

Where each parent had custody of one child and both parents were employed, the mother was nevertheless not required to pay child support. Such an order would result in undue hardship to the mother as the child living with her had health and emotional problems and the mother could not afford to provide the child with any ordinary activities. As the mother's living standard was below that of the father's, the court was justified in departing from the *Guidelines*: *Scharf v. Scharf* (1998), 40 R.F.L. (4th) 422, 1998 CarswellOnt 371, [1998] O.J. No. 199 (Ont. Gen. Div.).

Higher Costs — Special Needs Child

Where the court had found that a special needs child was entitled to special expenses for tuition, schooling and sports, the father's claim for undue hardship was dismissed as the father had the means to provide for two children, the one from his first marriage and the child whom his wife was expecting, even with the father's debt and living expenses: *Tallman v. Tomke* (1997), 204 A.R. 119, 1997 CarswellAlta 595, [1997] A.J. No. 682 (Alta. Q.B.). The father earned $49,800 and the mother $20,000 per year. The father was required to pay $428 a month, plus 71 percent of the special needs which were allowed.

Effect of Other Children No Longer Being Dependant

Where a judgment incorporating the parties' separation agreement provided that the payor was to pay $1,000 a month in child support for three children, his application for variation was granted, as there was only one dependant child: *Block v. Baltimore*, 5 R.F.L. (5th) 18, 2000 CarswellMan 139, 2000 MBQB 5, 149 Man. R. (2d) 137 (Man. Q.B.); additional reasons at 2000 CarswellMan 316, 2000 MBQB 83 (Man. Q.B.). Support was reduced to $428 a month. The court ruled that the loss of the additional child support would objectively create hardship for the remaining child but that the hardship was not "undue" which was defined as "exceptional", "excessive", or "unreasonable".

The court was of the opinion that s. 10 should be given a narrow interpretation and that the onus of proof is on the party who asserts and that the standard of proof is strict. Living in an apartment, which many people do, could not be considered an undue hardship and the fact that there would be less money available to give the remaining child certain amenities was not accepted. There was no evidence to support the assertion that the payor's alleged failure to exercise more access than he did increased costs of custody.

Restructuring Finances

In *Chan v. Chan* (1999), 46 R.F.L. (4th) 339, 1999 CarswellBC 1137 (B.C. S.C.), the court allowed the mother's application for an increase in child support to bring it up to *Guidelines* levels. The fact that the husband would have to restructure his affairs to pay the increased amount was not found to be inequitable.

Where the husband's financial difficulties were more likely due to poor money management and priorities rather than a true inability to meet expenses, the court refused his request that child support be awarded at a level lower than Table Amounts specified in the *Federal Child Support Guidelines*: *T. (C.M.) v. S. (L.A.)* (1997), [1998] N.W.T.R. 139, 1997 CarswellNWT 39 (N.W.T. S.C.).

General

A substantial difference in household income does not in itself constitute "undue hardship": *Demarchi v. Selwyn* (2002), 32 R.F.L. (5th) 20, 2002 CarswellOnt 3217 (Ont. S.C.J.); leave to appeal refused (2004), 7 R.F.L. (6th) 243, 2004 CarswellOnt 3874 (Ont. C.A.).

A party may be on a tight budget but still not suffer "undue hardship": *Ness v. Ness*, 43 R.F.L. (4th) 363, 118 B.C.A.C. 292, 192 W.A.C. 292, 1999 CarswellBC 261, [1999] B.C.J. No. 262, 1999 BCCA 51 (B.C. C.A.).

In *Montalbetti v. Montalbetti*, 10 R.F.L. (5th) 377, 2000 BCCA 504, 143 B.C.A.C. 140, 235 W.A.C. 140, 2000 CarswellBC 1902, [2000] B.C.J. No. 1834 (B.C. C.A.), the court found on appeal that the trial judge had erred in departing from the *Guidelines* Table Amount where the father had not claimed undue hardship.

The objectives of the *Federal Child Support Guidelines* are defeated if "undue hardship" is given too broad an interpretation and therefore it is appropriate that the burden of establishing undue hardship is a heavy one. The hardship to be established must be exceptional, excessive or disproportionate and not merely awkward or inconvenient: *Hanmore v. Hanmore*, 4 R.F.L. (5th) 348, 255 A.R. 163, 220 W.A.C. 163, 2000 ABCA 57, [2000] A.J. No. 171, 2000 CarswellAlta 144 (Alta. C.A.); additional reasons at 2000 ABCA 128, 2000 CarswellAlta 400 (Alta. C.A.); leave to appeal refused 264 N.R. 392 (note), 277 A.R. 187 (note), 242 W.A.C. 187 (note), 2000 CarswellAlta 1274, 2000 CarswellAlta 1275, [2000] S.C.C.A. No. 182 (S.C.C.); varying 47 R.F.L. (4th) 157, 243 A.R. 195, 1999 CarswellAlta 554 (Alta. Q.B.).

The fact that some support orders would be reduced as a result of the application of the *Guidelines* must have been foreseen by Parliament and cannot be equated with "undue hardship": *Hoover v. Hoover* (1997), [1998] N.W.T.R. 209, 1997 CarswellNWT 16, [1997] N.W.T.J. No. 43 (N.W.T. S.C.); additional reasons at (1997), 1997 CarswellNWT 62 (N.W.T. S.C.).

Under the *Federal Child Support Guidelines*, there is no provision compelling disclosure of financial information by a new spouse of one of the litigants. The overall means of the family only comes into play if an "undue hardship" application is brought: *Desjardins v. Desjardins*, 49 R.F.L. (4th) 242, 1999 CarswellBC 1283 (B.C. Master).

Mere inconvenience caused by a lower standard of living is insufficient to establish undue hardship under the *Guidelines*: *Jeans v. Jeans*, 5 R.F.L. (5th) 398, 187 Nfld. & P.E.I.R. 112, 566 A.P.R. 112, 2000 CarswellNfld 37, [2000] N.J. No. 42 (Nfld. U.F.C.).

Comparison of Households

A finding that paying the *Guidelines* amount would impose an undue hardship on the applicant does not, by itself, entitle him or her to relief. The applicant must prove two things:

(1) an award of child support in the *Guidelines* amount would cause undue hardship; and

2) that if the *Guidelines* amount were awarded, the standard of living in his or her present household would be lower than the standard of living in the other spouse's household: *Federal Child Support Guidelines*, s. 10(3).

The combination of these two requirements turns hardship into a comparative concept. The applicant must not only show that his or her household is badly off, but must go further and show that if the *Guidelines* amount were to be awarded, the applicant's household would be worse off than the household of the other spouse. Unlike the procedure to determine the amount of child support, the incomes of all members of the household are relevant, not simply the incomes of one or both spouses.

While Schedule II of the *Guidelines* provides one method of comparing the standards of living of the parties, it is not the only method: *Kennedy-Dowell v. Dowell*, 28 R.F.L. (5th) 187, 2002 CarswellNS 111, [2002] N.S.J. No. 123, 203 N.S.R. (2d) 130, 635 A.P.R. 130, 2002 NSSF 13 (N.S. S.C.); additional reasons at 2002 CarswellNS 487, [2002] N.S.J. No. 499, 2002 NSSF 50, 209 N.S.R. (2d) 392, 656 A.P.R. 392 (N.S. S.C.). The court held that the disparity between the parties' incomes was sufficient for the court to reach the conclusion that the husband had the lower household standard of living. The father earned approximately $20,000 but was deemed to have an income of $35,000 and would have very large costs for exercising access to his children, as he lives in Nova Scotia and they live in Ontario. The mother has an adjusted annual income over $82,000 and the parties' children have a combined annual tax-free income of $24,500 from trust funds. The wife is a trustee of the children's funds and has complete discretion over how their money is invested or spent. She consequently had a household income equivalent of approximately $112,000. The court found that the father has the lower income of the two parties and that his application need not be denied on the basis of s. 10(3) of the *Guidelines*, which provides that an application should be denied if the applicant claiming undue hardship would have, after determining the amount of child support, a higher standard of living than the household of the other spouse.

In *L. (K.H.) v. G. (B.)*, 2000 CarswellAlta 1654, [2000] A.J. No. 457, 263 A.R. 80, 2000 ABQB 243 (Alta. Q.B.), counsel did not provide a comparison of household standards of living, but the Child Support Centre confirmed that the father would have a higher standard of living after payment of support. The father had failed to meet the test of undue hardship and his application to vary his current order was dismissed.

The court must first determine if there are circumstances which may cause undue hardship and if such circumstances are found, the court must consider the standards of living of the payor and recipient spouses under s. 10(3) of the *Guidelines*: *Frechette v. Chaisson*, 13 R.F.L. (5th) 68, 2000 CarswellPEI 106, 2000 PESCTD 98, 197 Nfld. & P.E.I.R. 149, 591 A.P.R. 149 (P.E.I. T.D.). If the payor has a higher standard of living than the recipient, the claim of undue hardship would be denied.

Comparison of Household Standards of Living Test

In comparing the households, the court may "use the comparison of household standards of living test set out in Schedule II [of the *Guidelines*]": *Federal Child Support Guidelines*, s. 10(4). The word "may" in prescribing the test indicates that its use is optional. However, it is expected that the test will be used in all cases except where it would be clearly inappropriate.

A household consists of a spouse and any person who is a dependant or a provider living with the spouse. The definition reads:

> "household" means a spouse and any of the following persons residing with the spouse
>
> (a) any person who has a legal duty to support the spouse or whom the spouse has a legal duty to support;
>
> (b) any person who shares living expenses with the spouse or from whom the spouse otherwise receives an economic benefit as a result of living with that person, if the court considers it reasonable for that person to be considered part of the household, and
>
> (c) any child whom the spouse or the person described in paragraph (a) or (b) has a legal duty to support; *Federal Child Support Guidelines*, Schedule II, section "household", as amended.

An amendment to the *Federal Child Support Guidelines* on December 9, 1997, added to the definition of "household" any child of the spouse or person residing with the spouse.

The comparison is between the total household incomes. The incomes that make up the totals are the "adjusted annual income for all the persons in each household": *Federal Child Support Guidelines*, Schedule II, s. 2, Step 3. The significance of comparing household incomes in this fashion, rather than parties' incomes, is, of course, that the incomes of new spouses or partners, and other persons who share the living expenses, are included in the comparison.

The annual incomes of the persons in each household are determined in the same way as the spouse's income is determined for calculating support — that is, by making the adjustments called for by sections 15 to 20 of the *Guidelines* and Schedule III — but unlike the support calculation, two further sets of adjustments are made:

> (1) the income of each person in the household is adjusted by making it net of income tax: *Federal Child Support Guidelines*, Schedule II, s. 2, Step 1; and,
>
> (2) the income of each person is adjusted by taking into account three other items:
>
> > (1) "any amount relied on by the court as a factor that resulted in a determination of undue hardship,"
> >
> > (2) the amount of child support that would be payable under the *Guidelines* in the absence of hardship, and
> >
> > (3) any other support actually paid or received: *Federal Child Support Guidelines*, Schedule II, s. 2, Step 2.

The calculation used in the comparison of standards of living test is designed to produce a Household Income Ratio for each household, and it is these ratios which are then actually compared to determine which household has the higher standard of living. The ratio for each household is the actual total income in the spouse's household, divided by the "low-income" level for that household. The low-income level is found by consulting the "low-income measures" table in Schedule II, Step 4, which gives this level for households of various sizes. The low-income level for a household consisting of one adult and two children, for example, is $17,649 a year.

A ratio of 1 would show that the standard of living in the household is the same as the low level standard. A ratio of 1.5 is a household that is 11/2 times better in terms of income than the low level. A ratio of 2 says that the income in the household is twice the low level measure.

The ratio is calculated for the household of each spouse, and the two are then compared to see which is higher. The household with the higher ratio has the higher standard of living. If the household of the spouse who claims undue hardship has the higher ratio, the application to be relieved from paying the guideline amount must be denied: *Federal Child Support Guidelines*, s. 10(3).

There are six steps involved in calculating and comparing the household income ratios using "the comparison of household standards of living test." These steps are set out in Schedule II, s. 2.

Step 1: Calculate the annual income for comparison purposes of each person in each household:

(a) Establish the real annual income of each person (not the taxable income) by taking the total taxable income as shown on the T1 General form and adjusting it according to Schedule III and sections 15 to 20 of the *Guidelines*. (These adjustments include the adding back in to income such items as certain employment expenses, support payments, non-taxable portions of dividends and capital gains, non-arm's length payments. See Schedule III.)

(b) Deduct "the federal and provincial taxes payable on the person's taxable income" to make the annual income net of income tax.

Step 2: "Adjust the annual income of each person in each household by:

"(a) deducting the following amounts, calculated on an annual basis:

(i) any amount relied on by the court as a factor that resulted in a determination of undue hardship, except any amount attributable to the support of a member of the household that is not incurred due to a disability or serious illness of that member,

(ii) the amount that would otherwise be payable by the person in respect of a child to whom the order relates, if the pleading of undue hardship was not made,

(A) under the applicable table, or

(B) as is considered by the court to be appropriate, where the court considers the Table Amount to be inappropriate,

(iii) any amount of support that is paid by the person under a judgment, order or written separation agreement, except

(A) an amount already deducted under subparagraph (i), and

(B) an amount paid by the person in respect of a child to whom the order referred to in subparagraph (ii) relates; and

(b) adding the following amounts calculated on an annual basis:

(i) any amount that would otherwise be receivable by the person in respect of a child to whom the order relates, if the pleading of undue hardship was not made,

(A) under the applicable table, or

(B) as is considered by the court to be appropriate, where the court considers the Table Amount to be inappropriate,

(ii) any amount of child support that the person has received for any child under a judgment, order or written separation agreement": *Federal Child Support Guidelines*, Schedule II, s. 2, Step 2.

Step 3: Determine the total household income for each household by adding together the amounts of adjusted net income for all the persons in each household.

Step 4: Consult the table in Schedule II which gives the low-income measures for households according to the number of adults and children in the household, and choose the low-income measures amount which corresponds to the size of the applicant's household, and the amount for the size of the other spouse's household.

Step 5: Divide the total household income amount by the low-income measures amount to get a household income ratio for each household.

Step 6: "Compare the household income ratios. The household that has the higher ratio has the higher standard of living."

The court is not limited to circumstances enumerated in s. 10(2) of the *Guidelines* in making a finding of undue hardship. Undue hardship may arise from substantial relative disparities between the custodial and non-custodial households. However, the income disparity must still be filtered through the standard of living test contained in s. 10(3) of the *Guidelines*: *Guetz v. Guetz*, 11 R.F.L. (5th) 80, 186 N.S.R. (2d) 237, 581 A.P.R. 237, 2000 CarswellNS 226, [2000] N.S.J. No. 250 (N.S. S.C.); varied 2001 NSCA 57, 2001 CarswellNS 127, 15 R.F.L. (5th) 73, 193 N.S.R. (2d) 143, 602 A.P.R. 143, [2001] N.S.J. No. 131 (N.S. C.A.).

Before departing from *Guidelines* amounts on the basis of a disparity between the parties' standard of living, the court must first address the issue of "undue hardship" as outlined in s. 10(2): *Ross v. Mathieu*, 17 R.F.L. (5th) 422, 2001 CarswellNS 170, 2001 NSCA 85, 194 N.S.R. (2d) 62, 606 A.P.R. 62 (C.A.).

In *Dean v. Friesen* (1999), 50 R.F.L. (4th) 363, 185 Sask. R. 208, 1999 CarswellSask 428, [1999] S.J. No. 424 (Sask. Q.B.), the facts that the husband had remarried and had three more children and that his household had a lower standard of living than the wife's, justified a finding of "undue hardship" within the meaning of the *Federal Child Support Guidelines*.

The household income test under the undue hardship provisions in s. 10 of the *Federal Child Support Guidelines* does not violate the right to privacy guaranteed in s. 7 of the *Canadian Charter of Rights and Freedoms*. The right of children to support is paramount over an individual's right to privacy: *Souliere v. Leclair* (1998), 38 R.F.L. (4th) 68, 52 C.R.R. (2d) 156, 1998 CarswellOnt 1318, [1998] O.J. No. 1393, 59 O.T.C. 293 (Ont. Gen. Div.).

In *Middleton v. MacPherson*, 29 R.F.L. (4th) 334, 204 A.R. 37, 150 D.L.R. (4th) 519, 1997 CarswellAlta 512, [1997] A.J. No. 614, [1997] 7 W.W.R. 601, 51 Alta. L.R. (3d) 152 (Alta. Q.B.), only a spouse who is a party to the application may claim undue hardship under s. 10. Other members of the household such as the payor's common-law partner or the payee's mother living with her, cannot claim undue hardship. The adjustment of income referred to in Schedule II, Step 2(a)(1) is restricted to spouses. "However, the circumstances in which undue hardship can be claimed under s. 10(2) are not closed. It may be that in a particular case, a spouse can establish that his or her share of the household expenses are unusually high due to the presence of other persons in the household, such as children of a common-law spouse. In such a case, the court should exercise circumspection in determining those circumstances which should properly derogate from a spouse's primary obligation to his or her own children."

In applying the comparison of household standards of living test set out in Schedule II of the *Guidelines* a child of the marriage in a shared custody arrangement should be considered as part of the household of each party: *Middleton v. MacPherson*, 29 R.F.L. (4th) 334, 204 A.R. 37, 150 D.L.R. (4th) 519, 1997 CarswellAlta 512, [1997] A.J. No. 614, [1997] 7 W.W.R. 601, 51 Alta. L.R. (3d) 152 (Alta. Q.B.).

A child of a spouse's common-law partner to whom the spouse owes no legal duty of support is not considered to be a person in the household for the comparison of household standards of living pursuant to the test set out in Schedule II. "However, if a court determined that the presence of the children of a common-law partner (whom the payor or payee spouse owes no legal duty of support) did cause that spouse to incur extra costs that resulted in undue hardship under s. 10(2) of the *Guidelines* . . . that spouse may be entitled to claim an adjustment to his or her annual income by that cost under Schedule II, Step 2(a)(1), as a circumstance of undue hardship."

The court is not bound to determine the issue of undue hardship in accordance with Schedule II. Other case-specific considerations may be used to determine whether to allow or deny an application under s. 10(1). There is no requirement that the court, in comparing standards of living, use the test set out in Schedule II. The court, in its discretion, may use it.

The husband based his claim of undue hardship on the fact that there were three children in his household while the wife had only one in hers. The husband did not argue that he stood in *loco parentis* to the children of his common-law spouse such that he had a legal duty to support them. If the husband was suffering financial hardship because of these children, it might be held that this was a hardship circumstance under s. 10(2). But the court should exercise caution in entertaining such claims, and, in any event, the evidence fell short of establishing that the presence of the extra children in the husband's household imposed an undue financial burden upon him. There was no hardship resulting to the husband, and consequently, there was no need to apply the standards of living test.

In applying the Standards of Living Test in Schedule II of the *Guidelines*, the obligation of the payor's common-law partner to pay child and spousal support should be deducted when calculating her income as a member of the household: *Middleton v. MacPherson*, 29 R.F.L. (4th) 334, 204 A.R. 37, 150 D.L.R. (4th) 519, 1997 CarswellAlta 512, [1997] A.J. No. 614, [1997] 7 W.W.R. 601, 51 Alta. L.R. (3d) 152 (Alta. Q.B.). In the present case, the court should "take into account in the calculation of the income of the husband's common-law spouse the fact that she pays tax deductible spousal support of $400 per month and non-tax deductible child support in the amount of $600 per month."

In *Cook v. Hare* (1999), 46 R.F.L. (4th) 343, 1999 CarswellBC 988, [1999] B.C.J. No. 1065 (B.C. S.C.), the court dismissed the payor mother's application for a reduction in child support based upon undue hardship. While the mother's obligation to support another child of a different union did create an undue hardship, a comparison of the standard of living in both households indicated that the support amount was reasonable. To be successful, the mother was required to satisfy both aspects of the two-part test for undue hardship.

Reasons Recorded Where Hardship Adjustment: s.10(6)

A court making a child support order adjusted for hardship must record the reasons for doing so: *Federal Child Support Guidelines*, s. 10(6).

15§98 — Child support — consent orders

As under the law before the coming into force of the *Guidelines*, the spouse or former spouses are at liberty to agree, under the *Guidelines* regime, on an amount and ask the court to make an order on consent. The order will be made if the court is satisfied that the support arrangements are reasonable. When the court is considering the reasonableness of the arrangements, it will refer to guidelines but is not bound to adopt the *Guidelines* amount. The guidelines in this instance are advisory only, and not presumptive: *Divorce Act*, s. 15.1 (8).

The court may, for example, find that since the arrangements include the custodial parent having exclusive possession of the matrimonial home, the support should be less than the table amount

15§99 — Child support — priority over other obligations

Since May 1, 1997, courts and the parties have been required to distinguish between spousal and child support in orders and agreements, and to avoid combining both types of support in a single amount. If a court order or written agreement does not identify an amount as being for the support of a spouse, it will be treated as child support for tax purposes: *Income Tax Act*, s. 56(1)(b) and s. 60(b). See Chapter 2, Income Tax, above.

Prior to the 1997 amendments to section 2(1) of the *Divorce Act* the definitions for "corollary relief proceeding," "divorce proceeding," "support order" referred to support in a general sense without distinguishing between support for a child or children and support for a spouse. The 1997 amendments brought these definitions in line with the other reforms by qualifying support, wherever the term is used, as either child support or spousal support: *Divorce Act*, s. 2(1).

Subsections 15.3(1) and (2) of the *Divorce Act* gives express priority to an application for child support over an application for spousal support. In keeping with the general tenor of the amendments, the Guidelines amount would be ordered for child support even if the amount left over would be inadequate for spousal support. There would be no *pro rata* allocation of the available fund between the two applicants with both receiving less than they need. The child would receive full share, and the spouse less than full share in the allocation. But since the spouse making the application is also the custodial spouse, the total amount of child and spousal support goes to the same household where no accounting is expected to take place. The support received is spent from day to day on living expenses without thought as to which expense is for the child and which for the spouse.

In the end, it is the total amount of support which matters. See, however, *Kaderly v. Kaderly*, below.

The possibility of a shortfall for the spouse where there is also a child support application is contemplated by the legislation. In this case, any subsequent reduction or termination of child support is deemed to be a change of circumstances entitling the spouse to apply for a variation of the spousal amount if an order has been made, or to apply for an original order if there is no previous spousal support order: *Divorce Act*, s. 15.3(3).

The priority of child support over other obligations was well established in the case law before the introduction of guidelines.

In *Kaderly v. Kaderly* (August 1, 1997), Doc. 1101/3954 (P.E.I. T.D.), Jenkins J. stated that while s. 15.3(1) of the *Divorce Act* states the child support is to take priority over spousal support, Parliament did not intend this to operate so as to provide everything a child may need or which may benefit a child and leave the mother, who is a spouse, destitute. For purposes of the guidelines, the payor earned $111,000. He was ordered to pay $850 per month in spousal support until October 31, 2007, subject to specific conditions for variation and $1 per year from November 2007 to October 2012. He was also ordered to pay child support to the mother of $1,800 per month and upon a child enrolling in university, the father was instead required to pay the portion of child support applicable to that child, *i.e.*, $450 per month for the eight month period from September to May, directly to that child or to the university in which the child was enrolled.

Where the husband had quit two jobs, was unemployed, failed to remove his wife's name from the mortgages on income properties and failed to manage those properties profitably, spousal support was suspended but could be reviewed when the payor husband obtained employment: *Monette v. Jordan* (1997), 163 N.S.R. (2d) 70, 487 A.P.R. 70 (S.C.), before Glube C.J.

Cases decided before the enactment of the Federal Child Support Guidelines:

Child support is a parent's first obligation and takes precedence over the payment of legal fees: *Martin v. Martin* (1994), 10 R.F.L. (4th) 51, 136 N.S.R. (2d) 207, 388 A.P.R. 207 (C.A.). There was no reference to the governing statute in this decision.

In an application to terminate child support, the support obligations should properly take precedence over claims by other creditors and over the payor's wish to preserve capital assets such as an R.R.S.P.: *Blake v. Blake* (1994), 121 Nfld. & P.E.I.R. 263, 377 A.P.R. 263 (Nfld. T.D.).

In *Tweel v. Tweel* (1994), 7 R.F.L. (4th) 204 (P.E.I. T.D.); additional reasons at (1995), 18 R.F.L. (4th) 222 (P.E.I. T.D.), it was held that the father's financial obligations toward his children took precedence over this other financial obligations. Accordingly, child support was set without consideration for the substantial tax arrears owed by the husband.

A parent's primary obligation is to support his or her children. Such responsibility takes precedence over car payments, high mortgage payments, entertainment, tobacco, alcohol, recreation, vacation, savings and debts: *Murray v. Murray* (1991), 35 R.F.L. (3d) 449, 82 Alta. L.R. (2d) 260, [1992] 1 W.W.R. 183, 123 A.R. 68 (Q.B.).

A husband's business financial commitments should not be allowed to override his obligation to contribute to the support of his children: *Cook v. Cook* (1990), 81 Nfld. & P.E.I.R. 231, 255 A.P.R. 231 (Nfld. T.D.).

Where the husband lacked sufficient funds to pay both child and spousal support, it was held that the needs of the child must take priority: *Hiller v. Hiller* (1995), 167 A.R. 81 (Q.B.).

In determining child support, the children's needs should be given priority over those of the parents: *King v. King* (1990), 25 R.F.L. (3d) 338, 95 N.S.R. (2d) 409, 251 A.P.R. 409 (T.D.).

A parent is not entitled to sit back, maintain a modest income, and ignore a substantial equity in property in order to reduce his or her child support obligations: *Wishart v. Wishart* (1990), 29 R.F.L. (3d) 68 (B.C. S.C.).

15§100 — Calculating income for purposes of determining child support — calculation of annual income

With certain exceptions, the annual income of the former spouse or former spouses, whose income is necessary for the determination of the guidelines amount for child support is to be determined using the sources of income, subject to adjustments, listed under the heading "Total income" in the T1 General form issued by Revenue Canada. The required adjustments to the sources of income are described in Schedule III attached to the *Guidelines*: *Federal Child Support Guidelines*, s. 16.

The exceptions to using these sources adjusted in accordance with Schedule III are those instances where the procedure does not lead to a fair determination of the income. These exceptions are spelled out in the *Guidelines* and are described under paragraph headings below: 15§101 Pattern of income; 15§102 Non-recurring losses; 15§103 Shareholder, director or officer; 15§104 Adjustment to corporation's pre-tax income; 15§105 Imputing income; Reasonableness of expenses and 15§106 Income of non-resident.

The sources of income shown on the T1 General form as the sources which make up the total income are:

(a) Employment income

(b) Commissions

(c) Old Age Security Pension

(d) Canada or Quebec Pension Plan benefits

(e) Disability benefits

(f) Other pensions or superannuation

(g) Unemployment Insurance benefits

(h) Dividends

(i) Interest and other investment income

(j) Partnership income

(k) Rental income

(l) Capital gains

(m) Registered retirement savings plan income

(n) Other income

(o) Business income

(p) Professional income

(q) Commission income

(r) Farming income

(s) Fishing income

(t) Workers' Compensation payments

(u) Social Assistance payments

(v) Net federal supplements.

The payor spouse must use the most recent information available for each source of income: *Federal Child Support Guidelines*, s. 2(3).

In calculating the father's income for child support purposes in *Johnson v. Johnson* (2005), 23 R.F.L. (6th) 46, 2005 CarswellOnt 7695, 2005 ONCJ 325 (Ont. C.J.), the court rejected the father's assertion that the income should be reduced in light of his pending retirement. It is inappropriate that a support order presume reduction in income, as that type of speculation is too tenuous and could result in an incorrect order.

But see *Johnson v. Checkowy* (1997), 157 Sask. R. 71 (Q.B.) in which the court held that it was not appropriate to average income of past taxation years where the income is likely to remain at the current level, or increase. The court is to use the most current information available, and it is only where that information would not provide the fairest determination of the annual income that the court may resort to the provisions of s. 17.

The adjustments that are to be made to the income from the various sources which are described in Schedule III of the *Guidelines* consist of both deductions from the income as produced by the source, and additions to that income.

The deductions to be taken from income produced by particular sources are:

- employment expenses defined in the *Income Tax Act*, clauses 8(1)(c)–(j),(l), (n)–(q), relating to a clergyman's residence, a teacher's exchange fund contribution, railway employees, commission sales persons, transport employees, travel, dues and other expenses of performing duties, motor vehicle and aircraft costs, *Canada Pension Plan* contributions and *Employment Insurance Act* premiums paid in respect of another employee who acts as an assistant or substitute for the spouse, salary reimbursement, forfeited amounts, musical instrument costs, and artists' employment expenses: Schedule III, s. 1;
- any child support that has been received and has been reported to determine total income: Schedule III, s. 2;
- for the purpose of determining the *table* amount, deduct from the total income reported in the return, spousal support that has been included in the return as part of the total income; that is, support that has been *received* from the other spouse: Schedule III, s. 3(1). (For the purpose of determining the table amount, do not deduct the amount of support *paid* to the other spouse.);
- for the purpose of determining the contribution to *special or extraordinary expenses* to be paid pursuant to s. 7 of the *Guidelines* (not for the purpose of determining the table amount) deduct from the total income reported in the return, the spousal support *paid* to the other spouse: Schedule III, s. 3(2);
- social assistance payments attributable to any person other than the spouse: Schedule III, s. 4;

- the taxable amount of dividends received from taxable Canadian corporations, and substitute the actual amount of those dividends received by the spouse: Schedule III, s. 5;
- the taxable capital gains realized, and substitute the actual amount of capital gains realized by the spouse during the year in excess of the spouse's actual capital losses: Schedule III, s. 6;
- the actual amount of business investment losses suffered during the year: Schedule III, s. 7;
- carrying charges and interest expenses paid and that would be deductible under the *Income Tax Act*: Schedule III, s. 8;
- self-employment income, net of reserves reported as part of the total income, that is in excess of the self-employment income for the 12 months ending on December 31 of the reporting year: Schedule III, s. 10;
- portion of partnership or sole proprietorship income that has been included in income and is required by the partnership or sole proprietorship for purposes of capitalization: Schedule III, s. 12; and,
- where the spouse has disposed of shares of a Canadian controlled private corporation which were purchased on an option to purchase received as an employee benefit, deduct the value of the shares at the time the options were exercised less (1) the amount paid by the spouse for the shares and (2) any amount paid to acquire the option to purchase: Schedule III, s. 13(2).

The additions to be made to the income from particular sources are:

- salaries, benefits, wages, management fees or other payments, paid to non-arm's length persons, that have been deducted from self-employment income: Schedule III, s. 9;
- allowable capital cost allowance with respect to real property that has been deducted: Schedule III, s. 11; and
- where during the year reported the spouse has exercised options to purchase shares of a Canadian controlled private corporation which were received as an employee benefit, add the value of the shares at the time the options were exercised less (1) the amount paid by the spouse for the shares and (2) any amount paid to acquire the option to purchase: Schedule III, s. 13(1).

Where the father was enrolled in a plan whereby 20 per cent of his annual salary was deferred for five years and paid out to him during a "sabbatical" year, it was found that the deferral should not be deducted in determining his annual income for *Guidelines* purposes. The fairest course was to calculate child support on 100 per cent of his earnings through the "saving" years and then wait and see what he did on his sabbatical: *Watts v. Willie* (2004), 8 R.F.L. (6th) 456, 247 D.L.R. (4th) 54, 206 B.C.A.C. 192, 338 W.A.C. 192, 2004 CarswellBC 2795, 2004 BCCA 600 (C.A.).

In calculating the parties' income for *Guidelines* purposes, it is not proper to deduct the child support payable from the payor's income and add it to that of the payee: *Ostapchuk v. Ostapchuk* (2003), 38 R.F.L. (5th) 172, 2003 CarswellOnt 1661, 171 O.A.C. 132, 64 O.R. (3d) 496, 226 D.L.R. (4th) 385 (Ont. C.A.).

The receipt of payment when stock options are exercised is the taking of deferred income at that time and the value should be brought into income in the year in which the options are exercised: *Marinangeli v. Marinangeli* (2003), 2003 CarswellOnt 2691, [2003] O.J. No. 2819, 38 R.F.L. (5th) 307, 174 O.A.C. 76, 228 D.L.R. (4th) 376 (Ont. C.A.). The value of the options that have been exercised is an appropriate factor for the trial judge to consider in making an order for child support.

Where the father had inadvertently neglected to file financial material on the mother's application for increased child support, the Chambers judge nevertheless imputed a level of income to him and increased the support payable. The father successfully appealed from the order on the basis that the Chambers judge lacked appropriate information to vary the support order and had arbitrarily attributed income: *Wood v. Wood*, 39 R.F.L. (5th) 238, 2003 CarswellSask 110, 2003 SKCA 16, 227 Sask. R. 314, 287 W.A.C. 314 (Sask. C.A.).

Where information relating to the father's obligation to pay union dues and expenses had not been presented at trial, his obligation was reduced on appeal in accordance with the proper *Guidelines* amount: *Budyk v. Sol* (1998), 40 R.F.L. (4th) 348, (sub nom. *Budyk v. Budyk)* 126 Man. R. (2d) 305, 167 W.A.C. 305, 1998 CarswellMan 224, [1998] M.J. No. 252 (C.A.).

A monthly payment from the payor's firm for a R.R.S.P. contribution and a housing loan repayment contribution are additional benefits which are income to the payor and should be included in his income for the purposes of applying the *Child Support Guidelines*: *Wooldridge v. Wooldridge* (1999), 45 R.F.L. (4th) 308, 172 D.L.R. (4th) 637, 237 A.R. 64, 197 W.A.C. 64 (C.A.); additional reasons (1999), 49 R.F.L. (4th) 445, 250 A.R. 168, 213 W.A.C. 168 (C.A.).

Section 16 of the *Guidelines* points to s.6(1)(a)(i) of the Income Tax Act for the determination of income. Section 6(1)(a)(i) makes it evident that pension contributions by an employer are not to be considered as income. The court does, however, retain the discretion to include such an amount in income for *Guidelines* purposes in the appropriate case: *Ennis v. Ennis*, 5 R.F.L. (5th) 302, 77 Alta. L.R. (3d) 289, 2000 CarswellAlta 79, [2000] A.J. No. 75, 2000 ABCA 33, 281 A.R. 161, 248 W.A.C. 161 (C.A.); affirming on this point (1998), 45 R.F.L. (4th) 323, 1998 CarswellAlta 1284, [1998] A.J. No. 352 (Alta. Q.B.).

The determination of income for *Guidelines* purposes is essentially a factual matter that is within the province of a trial judge. Accordingly, if the trial judge has not made a manifest error, has not ignored evidence, has not misunderstood evidence, and has not drawn erroneous conclusions from it, an appellate court will not intervene: *Wedsworth v. Wedsworth*, 12 R.F.L. (5th) 232, 2000 NSCA 108, 188 N.S.R. (2d) 252, 587 A.P.R. 252, 2000 CarswellNS 280 (N.S. C.A.); varying on other grounds (2000), 185 N.S.R. (2d) 215, 575 A.P.R. 215, 2000 CarswellNS 194 (N.S. Fam. Ct.).

Workers' compensation benefits should be considered as income for the purposes of child support, even if these payments are not treated as income for income tax purposes: *Dahlgren v. Hodgson* (1998), 43 R.F.L. (4th) 176, 228 A.R. 332, 188 W.A.C. 332 (C.A.).

In *Salzmann v. Salzmann* (2004), 50 R.F.L. (5th) 181, 2004 CarswellOnt 169 (Ont. S.C.J.), expenses that the husband had claimed through his business that could be attributed to his personal expenses were added back to his income for *Guidelines* purposes.

The reasonableness of a deduction from a parent's income under the *Guidelines* is not solely governed by the acceptance of the deduction for income tax purposes: *McGowan v. McGowan*, 42 R.F.L. (5th) 420, 2003 CarswellSask 527, 236 Sask. R. 137, 2003 SKQB 343 (Sask. Q.B.).

In *Roby v. Roby* (2003), 48 R.F.L. (5th) 389, 2003 CarswellOnt 4581 (Ont. S.C.J.), a lump sum of $15,000 withdrawn by the father from his R.R.S.P. was properly not included in the father's annual income calculation for child support purposes. The RRSP was "family property" that had been subject to equalization. Including the amount in his income would constitute "double dipping".

A payment made by the trustee in bankruptcy subsequent to the father's bankruptcy was not required to be included in his income calculation for child support purposes. The payment did not represent ongoing income, nor was it a lump sum income replacement: *Roby v. Roby* (2003), 48 R.F.L. (5th) 389, 2003 CarswellOnt 4581 (Ont. S.C.J.).

Where the father had numerous sources of income and there was ample evidence to support the conclusion that he used his family operation to deduct personal expenses and income split with his new spouse, such deductions were not allowed in calculating his income for *Guidelines* purposes. While the husband's approach was acceptable from a taxation perspective, the *Guidelines* precluded such artificial deductions to operate as a detriment to the child: *Nichol v. Johnson*, 49 R.F.L. (5th) 385, 2003 CarswellSask 760, 2003 SKQB 486, 240 Sask. R. 275 (Sask. Q.B.).

In *Waese v. Bojman* (2001), 19 R.F.L. (5th) 220, 2001 CarswellOnt 1813 (Ont. S.C.J.), the court had to determine the mother's income for *Guidelines* purposes, a great deal of which came from family trusts and her father's estate. Given her close relationship to the trustee, it was appropriate to consider the maximum potentially available to the mother under the trusts and the estate. Averaging the income paid over several years would not produce a fair estimation.

A housing allowance received by a parent for working in a remote part of the country is properly included in that parent's income calculation under the *Federal Child Support Guidelines*: *Esligar v. Esligar* (1999), 45 R.F.L. (4th) 258, 211 N.B.R. (2d) 188, 539 A.P.R. 188, 1999 CarswellNB 132, [1999] N.B.J. No. 150 (C.A.).

In *Stafford v. Stafford*, 38 R.F.L. (5th) 211, 2003 CarswellAlta 339, [2003] A.J. No. 351, 2003 ABQB 245 (Alta. Q.B.), the husband, for the purpose of calculating his income for Guidelines purposes, was entitled to deduct the interest by him on a loan taken out to satisfy the wife's property entitlement.

In determining a parent's income for *Guidelines* purposes, deductions will be allowed for carrying charges, interest expenses and professional dues, all of which are deductible under the *Income Tax Act*: *Tynan v. Moses*, 25 R.F.L. (5th) 445, 2002 CarswellBC 283, 2002 BCSC 100 (B.C. S.C.).

In *West v. West* (2001), 18 R.F.L. (5th) 440, 2001 CarswellOnt 1936 (Ont. S.C.J.), the husband, for the purposes of calculating his income for *Guidelines* purposes, was not allowed to deduct from his income wages he had paid to his sons for some summer work.

The reference in s. 16 of the *Guidelines* to determining a spouse's annual income by looking at amounts in the spouse's T1 General Form under the heading "Total Income" means looking to sources of income in the form and not historical amounts: *Dickie v. Dickie* (2001), 17 R.F.L. (5th) 304, 2001 CarswellOnt 2551 (Ont. S.C.J.); additional reasons at (2001), 2001 CarswellOnt 2768, 20 R.F.L. (5th) 343 (Ont. S.C.J.).

In determining the income of the retired father for *Guidelines* purposes in *Stevens v. Boulerice* (1999), 49 R.F.L. (4th) 425 (Ont. S.C.), it was found that his pension income was properly included but most non-recurring amounts for severance pay, vacation pay and team award were not included.

Where the payor spouse was a trucker who worked mainly in the United States, the court was of the opinion that it was appropriate to deduct only the amount allowed by the *Income Tax Act* for meal expenses: *O'Dell v. Kragh*, [1999] 2 C.T.C. 289 (Sask. Q.B.). The court did not accept the payor's argument that it should take into account the actual expenses incurred or at least adjust upwards the deductible allowance based upon the U.S./Canadian dollar exchange rates. Revenue Canada places a limit upon the maximum allowable deductions on amount of meal expenses as being 50% of $11.00 (Canadian) per meal, unless receipts are provided.

Where part of the spouse's income was made up of payment for work in lieu of holiday time, and with separation he intended to use that holiday time to exercise access to his children, the spouse's most recent tax return did not represent the fairest determination of income for the purposes of determining child support payments for the 1998 year and thereafter: *Good v. Good* (September 24, 1998), Doc. Kelowna 28106 (B.C. S.C.). The court was of the opinion that it would be appropriate to consider the holiday pay to be non-recurring, at least for the two-week holiday the spouse would take with his children, and to consider the past four years of his earnings in order to take account of the fluctuations in his income.

Where a payor has received repayment of shareholder's loans, he may have a far greater cash flow than would be reflected in his employment income alone, but these payments would not be income within the meaning of the *Income Tax Act*, nor within the meaning of the *Guidelines*: *Rudachyk v. Rudachyk* (May 29, 1997), Doc. Yorkton Q.B. 01164 (Sask. Q.B.).

Where the husband was a lawyer, the determination of income should take into account his deferred income which, because of changes in the *Income Tax Act*, must be brought into current income over a period of time: *Brady v. Watson* (March 27, 1998), Doc. Vancouver D54618 (B.C. S.C.).

Interest payments relating to the respondent's law practice should be taken into account in calculating the respondent's income: *Brady v. Watson* (March 27, 1998), Doc. Vancouver D54618 (B.C. S.C.).

In determining the income of the respondent's spouse, her childcare expenses should be taken into account: *Brady v. Watson* (March 27, 1998), Doc. Vancouver D54618 (B.C. S.C.).

Section 16 of the *Guidelines* does not mean that in all cases income is to be determined by reference to the last income tax return. "What is required, in the first instance is to determine the actual income at the date of the application from all 'sources of income' falling within the categories of income which a respondent is required to report in T1 General tax return. That may be the same amount as actually recorded on the most recent return or it may not be, where, for example, the paying spouse has not filed a recent return, has failed to file a proper return, or has lost or changed employment between the date of the last filing and the date of the application": *Fahel v. Fahel* (July 14, 1997), Doc. New Westminister D38400 (B.C. Master).

In *Thomas v. Thomas* (November 4, 1997), Doc. Sault Ste. Marie 17037/97 (Ont. Gen. Div.), in 1996, the father had no income for five weeks while he was on strike; but if his income for 47 weeks were applied at the same rate for 52 weeks, his income would have been $62,603.27. Earnings projected for 1997 from the rate of pay shown on his June pay slip would be $60,511.88. The court concluded that "the most equitable manner" of determining his income was to take the average of his 1995 actual earnings, the 1996 adjusted income and the 1997 projected income for a gross annual income of $62,288.99. The court then found that after deducting employment insurance premiums to be paid in 1997 estimated at $1,200, union dues he would likely pay at $790, and the Canada Pension contributions at $900, his net income would be $59,400 annually.

In *Nadeau v. Mitchell* (July 11, 1997), Doc. 96-MA-5290 (Ont. Gen. Div.); additional reasons at (August 21, 1997), Doc. 96-MA-5290 (Ont. Gen. Div.), the father received a base salary or $106,000 and a discretionary bonus. The bonus in 1996 was $14,000. "While that bonus was discretionary and in no way certain for 1997, I consider it equitable and appropriate to use $120,000 as the father's income for the purposes of calculating child support."

In *Schick v. Schick*, Sask. Q.B. (Fam. Law Div.), the court held that in determining child support, spousal support should not be added to employment income of the payor spouse. While s. 16 of the *Guidelines* provides that subject to ss. 17 to 20 a spouse's annual income is determined using the sources of income set out under the heading "total income" in the T1 General form issued by Revenue Canada as adjusted in accordance with Schedule 1, and spousal support received is a source of income under the heading "total income" in the T1 General form, s. 3 provides in calculating income for purposes of determining an amount of child support under an applicable table, spousal support received from the other spouse should be deducted.

The projected annual income, not historical income, is the income figure to be used for the Table amount in the Federal Guidelines: *Holtby v. Holtby* (1997), 30 R.F.L. (4th) 70 (Ont. Prov. Div.).

In *Westcott v. Westcott* (July 11, 1997), Doc. Barrie D363-97 (Ont. Gen. Div.), the father was the owner of a real estate brokerage and was also a real estate agent in his firm. Thus, he received an income from the brokerage as well as his own commissions. In regard to the father's real estate commission income, the court was of the opinion that in the absence of evidence to explain the father's claim of a decrease in income from 1996 to 1997, and in light of the fact that it was general knowledge that the economy and the real estate market were generally performing at least as well in 1997 as in 1996, the court used the father's 1996 income as the basis for assessing his means. The court also used the father's 1996 brokerage income as the basis for his income for 1997, that income being approximately $100,000. However, as the mother was making a motion for interim support, the income base used was $75,000.

The mother had no means of gaining her own income at the time of the hearing. The father was ordered to pay child support for the one child in the wife's care and the wife was not required to pay any support for the three children in the husband's care.

The *Federal Child Support Guidelines* do not specifically provide for bringing Capital Cost Allowances for business expenses into income. The issue of whether CCA expenditure should be imputed back into income is dependent upon the merits of each case: *Cornelius v. Andres* (1999), 45 R.F.L. (4th) 220, [1999] 6 W.W.R. 317, 170 D.L.R. (4th) 254, 134 Man. R. (2d) 140, 193 W.A.C. 140 (C.A.); varying (1998), 36 R.F.L. (4th) 436, 125 Man. R. (2d) 144 (Q.B.).

Where the mother had won a lottery, her income for *Guidelines* purposes was determined by adding her income from employment to the imputed income that could be derived from the lottery winnings: *Wilson v. Eronchi*, 4 R.F.L. (5th) 146, 2000 NWTSC 5, 2000 CarswellNWT 3 (S.C. [In Chambers]).

In *MacNeil v. MacNeil*, 4 R.F.L. (5th) 273, 2000 NWTSC 6, 2000 CarswellNWT 4 (S.C.), the husband's bonus was taken into account when determining his income for *Guidelines*' purposes. It formed part of his employment income and there was no indication that it was likely to be discontinued in the future.

A student loan received by a parent does not constitute a "benefit" under s. 7(3) of the *Federal Child Support Guidelines* and accordingly that parent is not required to include the loan amount in the income calculation. A loan which requires repayment with interest cannot be classified as a "benefit": *Maynard v. Maynard* (1999), 45 R.F.L. (4th) 395, 1999 CarswellBC 333, [1999] B.C.J. No. 325 (S.C.).

Section 16 of the *Federal Child Support Guidelines* clearly directs that a parent's income should be determined without reference to any spousal support that parent might receive: *Mabbett v. Mabbett* (1999), 48 R.F.L. (4th) 157, 1999 CarswellNS 87 (S.C. [In Chambers]).

The receipt of student loans does not constitute income for the purposes of calculating a parent's income under the *Federal Child Support Guidelines*: *Bhandal v. Bhandal* (1999), 48 R.F.L. (4th) 39 (Ont. Gen. Div.).

In *Gervasio v. Gervasio* (1999), 45 R.F.L. (4th) 342 (Ont. Gen. Div.), it was held that the husband's decision to tax shelter part of an employment severance package was irrelevant to the calculation of his income for the purposes of the *Federal Child Support Guidelines*.

Section 16 of the *Guidelines* points to s. 6(1)(a)(i) of the *Income Tax Act* for the determination of income. Section 6(1)(a)(i) makes it evident that pension contributions by an employer are not to be considered as income. The court does, however, retain the discretion to include such an amount in income for *Guidelines* purposes in the appropriate case: *Ennis v. Ennis*, 5 R.F.L. (5th) 302, 77 Alta. L.R. (3d) 289, 2000 CarswellAlta 79, [2000] A.J. No. 75, 2000 ABCA 33, 281 A.R. 161, 248 W.A.C. 161 (Alta. C.A.); affirming on this point (1998), 45 R.F.L. (4th) 323 (Alta. Q.B.).

Where the husband had, for income tax purposes, set off losses from a part-time business against his income from employment, the court refused to allow the deduction in calculating his income for the purposes of the *Federal Child Support Guidelines*. The business operated at a loss and it was inappropriate to subsidize his self-employment efforts with funds that could properly be used for child support: *Cooke v. Colomy* (1998), 38 R.F.L. (4th) 342, 128 Man. R. (2d) 219 (Q.B.).

In calculating lawyer's income for the purpose of the *Federal Child Support Guidelines*, it was held that his end of year work-in-progress was properly included: *Augaitis v. Augaitis* (1998), 40 R.F.L. (4th) 341 (Ont. Gen. Div.).

Where it was impossible to ascertain the father's true annual income because of a number of variables, it was held to be an inappropriate case for application of the *Federal Child Support Guidelines*. Accordingly, an existing interim child support order was to continue: *Armstrong v. Armstrong* (1997), 34 R.F.L. (4th) 38 (Ont. Gen. Div.); additional reasons at (November 12, 1997), Doc. Ottawa 23545/96 (Ont. Gen. Div.).

Where the father had not yet started a new job which paid considerably more than his current one, his income for the purposes of the *Federal Child Support Guidelines* was assessed at his new salary. The expected income was not speculative in that he had already accepted the job and negotiated the salary. Additional income from potential bonuses and stock option was, however, speculative and not properly considered: *Fibiger v. Fibiger* (1998), 38 R.F.L. (4th) 258 (B.C. S.C.).

Where, in calculating the husband's share of s. 7 expenses under the *Federal Child Support Guidelines*, the Master had subtracted the taxes payable by the husband from his taxable income instead of his total income, the wife's appeal was allowed and the matter remitted for recalculation: *White v. Rushton* (1998), 38 R.F.L. (4th) 454, 1998 CarswellBC 1125 (B.C. S.C.); reversing in part (1998), 37 R.F.L. (4th) 373, 1998 CarswellBC 443, [1998] B.C.J. No. 422 (B.C. Master).

In calculating income under the *Federal Child Support Guidelines*, a spouse is not permitted to deduct Canada Pension Plan contributions or Employment Insurance premiums paid by that spouse: *Phillips v. Phillips* (1997), 32 R.F.L. (4th) 218, 42 B.C.L.R. (3d) 218 (B.C. S.C.).

Where the mother was entitled to rental income but had not, in fact, received her share, she was nevertheless required to include it in her income for purposes of the *Federal Child Support Guidelines*. Section 16 of the *Guidelines* required income to be calculated by using the same source identified by Revenue Canada in tax returns, which included rental income: *Bergman-Illnik v. Illnik* (1997), [1998] N.W.T.R. 131 (S.C.).

Capital Cost Allowance

The *Federal Child Support Guidelines* do not specifically provide for bringing Capital Cost Allowances for business expenses into income. The issue of whether CCA expenditure should be imputed back into income is dependent upon the merits of each case: *Cornelius v. Andres* (1999), 45 R.F.L. (4th) 200, [1999] 6 W.W.R. 317, 170 D.L.R. (4th) 254, 134 Man. R. (2d) 140, 193 W.A.C. 140 (Man. C.A.); varying (1998), 36 R.F.L. (4th) 436, 125 Man. R. (2d) 144 (Q.B.).

In *R. (P.C.J.) v. R. (D.C.)*, 38 R.F.L. (5th) 408, 2003 CarswellBC 788, 2003 BCCA 207, 12 B.C.L.R. (4th) 142, 181 B.C.A.C. 95, 298 W.A.C. 95 (B.C. C.A.), the capital cost allowance deducted by the husband relating to his vessel and equipment used in his commercial fishing business was found not to be a proper deduction for determining his income for *Guidelines* purposes.

In *Egan v. Egan*, 26 R.F.L. (5th) 288, 2002 CarswellBC 905, 2002 BCCA 275, 100 B.C.L.R. (3d) 252, 2002 D.T.C. 7050, 214 D.L.R. (4th) 687, 169 B.C.A.C. 14, 276 W.A.C. 14 (B.C. C.A.), in determining his income for *Guidelines* purposes, the father was allowed to deduct capital cost allowance for his truck.

There is no exemption under the *Guidelines* in calculating income for public service income or income from a second job: *Young v. Young* (1998), 39 R.F.L. (4th) 110, 51 B.C.L.R. (3d) 299 (S.C. [In Chambers]); additional reasons at (1998), 51 B.C.L.R. (3d) 310 (S.C.).

In calculating income under the *Federal Child Support Guidelines*, a spouse is not permitted to deduct Canada Pension Plan contributions or Employment Insurance premiums paid by that spouse: *Phillips v. Phillips* (1997), 32 R.F.L. (4th) 218, 42 B.C.L.R. (3d) 218 (B.C. S.C.).

Where the mother had won a lottery, her income for *Guidelines* purposes was determined by adding her income from employment to the imputed income that could be derived from the lottery winnings: *Wilson v. Eronchi* (2000), 4 R.F.L. (5th) 146 (N.W.T. S.C.).

In *MacNeil v. MacNeil* (2000), 4 R.F.L. (5th) 273 (N.W.T. S.C. [In Chambers]), the husband's bonus was taken into account when determining his income for *Guidelines* purposes. It formed part of his employment income and there was no indication that it was likely to be discontinued in the future.

A student loan received by a parent does not constitute a "benefit" under s. 7(3) of the *Federal Child Support Guidelines* and accordingly that parent is not required to include the loan amount in the income calculation. A loan which requires repayment with interest cannot be classified as a "benefit": *Maynard v. Maynard* (1999), 45 R.F.L. (4th) 395 (B.C. S.C.).

Where information relating to the father's obligation to pay union dues and expenses had not been presented at trial, his obligation was reduced on appeal in accordance with the proper *Guidelines* amount: *Budyk v. Sol* (1998), 40 R.F.L. (4th) 348, (sub nom. *Budyk v. Budyk)* 126 Man. R. (2d) 305, 167 W.A.C. 305 (C.A.).

In *Stafford v. Stafford*, 38 R.F.L. (5th) 211, 2003 CarswellAlta 339, [2003] A.J. No. 351, 2003 ABQB 245 (Alta. Q.B.), the husband, for the purpose of calculating his income for *Guidelines* purposes, was entitled to deduct the interest by him on a loan taken out to satisfy the wife's property entitlement.

In calculating a lawyer's income for the purpose of the *Federal Child Support Guidelines*, it was held that his end of year work-in-progress was properly included: *Augaitis v. Augaitis* (1998), 40 R.F.L. (4th) 341 (Ont. Gen. Div.).

The receipt of student loans does not constitute income for the purposes of calculating a parent's income under the *Federal Child Support Guidelines*: *Bhandal v. Bhandal* (1999), 48 R.F.L. (4th) 39 (Ont. Gen. Div.).

In calculating a parent's income under the *Federal Child Support Guidelines*, an annual bonus which may or may not be paid, should not be included: *Jackson v. Holloway* (1997), 35 R.F.L. (4th) 272, [1998] 5 W.W.R. 556, 161 Sask. R. 31 (Q.B.).

A housing allowance received by a parent for working in a remote part of the country is properly included in that parent's income calculation under the *Federal Child Support Guidelines*: *Esligar v. Esligar* (1999), 45 R.F.L. (4th) 258, 211 N.B.R. (2d) 188, 539 A.P.R. 188 (N.B. C.A.).

Section 16 of the *Guidelines* points to s. 6(1)(a)(i) of the *Income Tax Act* for the determination of income. Section 6(1)(a)(i) makes it evident that pension contributions by an employer are not to be considered as income. The court does, however, retain the discretion to include such an amount in income for *Guidelines* purposes in the appropriate case: *Ennis v. Ennis* (2000), 5 R.F.L. (5th) 302, 77 Alta. L.R. (3d) 289 (Alta. C.A.); affirming on this point (1998), 45 R.F.L. (4th) 323 (Alta. Q.B.).

Where the father had not yet started a new job which paid considerably more than his current one, his income for the purposes of the *Federal Child Support Guidelines* was assessed at his new salary. The expected income was not speculative in that he had already accepted the job and negotiated the salary. Additional income from potential bonuses and stock option was, however, speculative and not properly considered: *Fibiger v. Fibiger* (1998), 38 R.F.L. (4th) 258 (B.C. S.C.).

Where it was impossible to ascertain the father's true annual income because of a number of variables, it was held to be an inappropriate case for application of the *Federal Child Support Guidelines*. Accordingly, an existing interim child support order was to continue: *Armstrong v. Armstrong* (1997), 34 R.F.L. (4th) 38 (Ont. Gen. Div.); additional reasons at (November 12, 1997), Doc. Ottawa 23545/96 (Ont. Gen. Div.).

Where, in calculating the husband's share of s. 7 expenses under the *Federal Child Support Guidelines*, the Master had subtracted the taxes payable by the husband from his taxable income instead of his total income, the wife's appeal was allowed and the matter remitted for recalculation: *White v. Rushton* (1998), 38 R.F.L. (4th) 454 (B.C. S.C.); reversing in part (1998), 37 R.F.L. (4th) 373 (B.C. Master).

In *Gervasio v. Gervasio* (1999), 45 R.F.L. (4th) 342 (Ont. Gen. Div.), it was held that the husband's decision to tax shelter part of an employment severance package was irrelevant to the calculation of his income for the purposes of the *Federal Child Support Guidelines*.

Where the husband had, for income tax purposes, set off losses from a part-time business against his income from employment, the court refused to allow the deduction in calculating his income for the purposes of the *Federal Child Support Guidelines*. The business operated at a loss and it was inappropriate to subsidize his self-employment efforts with funds that could properly be used for child support: *Cooke v. Colomy* (1998), 38 R.F.L. (4th) 342 (Man. Q.B.).

In *Waese v. Bojman* (2001), 19 R.F.L. (5th) 220, 2001 CarswellOnt 1813 (Ont. S.C.J.), the court had to determine the mother's income for *Guidelines* purposes, a great deal of which came from family trusts and her father's estate. Given her close relationship to the trustee, it was appropriate to consider the maximum potentially available to the mother under the trusts and the estate. Averaging the income paid over several years would not produce a fair estimation.

Where the mother was entitled to rental income but had not, in fact, received it, she was nevertheless required to include it in her income for purposes of the *Federal Child Support Guidelines*. Section 16 of the *Guidelines* required income to be calculated by using the same source identified by Revenue Canada in tax returns, which included rental income: *Bergman-Illnik v. Illnik* (1997), [1998] N.W.T.R. 131 (S.C.).

Section 16 of the *Federal Child Support Guidelines* clearly directs that a parent's income should be determined without reference to any spousal support that parent might receive: *Mabbett v. Mabbett* (1999), 48 R.F.L. (4th) 157 (N.S. S.C. [In Chambers]).

In calculating the parties' income for *Guidelines* purposes, it is not proper to deduct the child support payable from the payor's income and add it to that of the payee: *Ostapchuk v. Ostapchuk* (2003), 38 R.F.L. (5th) 172, 2003 CarswellOnt 1661, 171 O.A.C. 132, 64 O.R. (3d) 496, 226 D.L.R. (4th) 385 (Ont. C.A.).

15§101 — Calculating income for purposes of determining child support — pattern of income

Where adjusting a source of income in accordance with Schedule III would not provide the fairest determination of the annual income from that source, "the court may determine the annual income from that source

(a) where the amount in respect of the source of income has increased in each of the three most recent taxation years or has decreased in each of those three years, to be the amount from that source of income in the spouse's most recent taxation year;

(b) where the amount in respect of the source of income has not increased or decreased as described in paragraph (a), to be the average of the amount received by the spouse from that source of income in the three most recent taxation years, or such other amount, if any, that the court considers appropriate; or

(c) where the spouse has received a non-recurring amount in any of the three most recent taxation years, to be such portion of the amount as the court considers appropriate, if any." *Federal Child Support Guidelines*, s. 17(1).

Where the father had discontinued his own farming operation and accepted employment as a farm labourer, his income for *Guidelines* purposes was determined by projected income rather than by looking at his historical income. This approach was appropriate and likely more accurate given the father's employment change: *Arvai v. Arvai* (1999), 12 R.F.L. (5th) 1, 1999 CarswellOnt 4848 (S.C.J.); additional reasons at (1999), 1999 CarswellOnt 4847 (S.C.J.); varied (2001), 14 R.F.L. (5th) 223, 52 O.R. (3d) 481, 141 O.A.C. 343, 2001 CarswellOnt 432, [2001] O.J. No. 561 (C.A.).

Using a parent's last income tax return to determine income for *Guidelines* purposes may not be appropriate where the bulk of that income is derived from investments, the values of which can fluctuate dramatically. The better approach is to examine current factors in order to best project current income: *Hollenbach v. Hollenbach*, 10 R.F.L. (5th) 280, 2000 BCCA 620, 82 B.C.L.R. (3d) 228, 194 D.L.R. (4th) 151, 144 B.C.A.C. 193, 236 W.A.C. 193, 2000 CarswellBC 2282, [2000] B.C.J. No. 2316 (C.A.); varying (1999), 47 R.F.L. (4th) 39, 67 B.C.L.R. (3d) 192, 1999 CarswellBC 990, [1999] B.C.J. No. 1063 (S.C.).

In *Arnold v. Washburn* (2000), 10 R.F.L. (5th) 1, 2000 CarswellOnt 3454, [2000] O.J. No. 3653 (S.C.J.); additional reasons at (2000), 13 R.F.L. (5th) 245, 2000 CarswellOnt 4721 (S.C.J.), the court found it inappropriate to include in the husband's income for *Guidelines* purposes monies realized in the past and potentially in the future from the exercising of stock options that he held. Options already realized did not form a pattern of income and to include future options would be tantamount to treating property as income.

Where the father's income could vary dramatically depending on the amount of overtime he worked, the court recognized that the father may have to seek variations several times throughout the year to adjust the child support payable by him in accordance with the *Guidelines*: *Leet v. Leet*, 25 R.F.L. (5th) 302, 2002 CarswellNB 98, 2002 NBQB 87 (N.B. Q.B.).

Where part of the father's remuneration was in the form of a bonus and stock options, the decision by the father's employer not to issue stock option for 2003 would not have the effect of making a three-year average of his income artificially high for *Guidelines* purposes: *Paslawski v. Paslawski*, 49 R.F.L. (5th) 392, 2003 CarswellSask 755, 2003 SKQB 462 (Sask. Q.B.).

Where the father's substantial professional income from the practice of law fluctuated from year to year and he had been less than truthful in disclosing financial information to the wife, his last 3 years' income were averaged for *Guidelines* purposes: *Brans v. Brans* (2000), 13 R.F.L. (5th) 335, 2000 CarswellOnt 4897 (Ont. S.C.J.); additional reasons at (2001), 2001 CarswellOnt 1096 (Ont. S.C.J.).

Income derived from stock options is indicative of a pattern of income that is to be taken into account in assessing sustainable income for the purpose of the *Federal Child Support Guidelines*. Such income is required by law to be considered on an application for review of child support: *Schnarr v. Schnarr* (1999), 49 R.F.L. (4th) 384 (B.C. S.C.).

In determining the income of the retired father for *Guidelines* purposes in *Stevens v. Boulerice* (1999), 49 R.F.L. (4th) 425 (Ont. S.C.J.), it was found that his pension income was properly included but non-recurring amounts for severance pay, vacation pay and team award were not included.

Where the father ceased working overtime and premium shifts at the commencement of child support proceedings, additional income was attributed to him for calculation purposes. Prior to the proceedings, the father had a consistent pattern of working such shifts: *Odendahl v. Brule* (1999), 45 R.F.L. (4th) 37 (Ont. Gen. Div.).

Where the non-custodial mother had not yet been employed for a year and her income fluctuated dramatically from month to month, the father's application for child support was adjourned. It was appropriate to fix the level of the mother's support contribution at a later date when actual income for a 12-month period was known: *Adler v. Jonas* (1998), 48 R.F.L. (4th) 218 (B.C. S.C.); additional reasons (1999), 48 R.F.L. (4th) 228 (B.C. S.C.).

Where the father did not have a fixed monthly income upon which to calculate child support payments he was ordered to pay 23 percent of his gross monthly income as child support: *Voros v. Voros* (April 19, 1999), Doc. Edmonton 4803-109517 (Alta. Q.B.).

In *Nkwazi v. Nkwazi* (1998), 171 Sask. R. 120 (Q.B.), while the father had a fixed employment contract of $110,000 U.S. a year as affirmed by his current financial statement, he maintained his income was considerably less and was declining each year, although no explanation was given for this decrease. The court accepted the mother's argument that a three-year average of earnings would provide a fair determination of his income but would grant leave to the father to apply to the court to explain the inconsistencies in his material and supporting evidence.

Generally, in determining a farmer's income, the best approach is to average the most recent three years of income information available: *Wilson v. Wilson* (1998), 165 Sask. R. 241, [1998] 8 W.W.R. 493 (Q.B.). The father's average income was $35,887 and he was required to pay child support of $494 per month for two children.

While s. 17(1)(a) of the *Guidelines* provides that in determining the payor's income, the income from the most recent taxation year should be given, this provision is permissive and not mandatory: *Wilson v. Wilson*, above.

In *Fisher v. Gerrard* (1998), 174 Sask. R. 163 (Q.B.), the father worked in a mine and also had his own farming business. In 1997 the farming business was significantly better than in 1998, while his income from mining increased in 1998 over 1997. The court considered it fair and reasonable to take the average of the 1997 and projected 1998 income. The preceding years were not relevant because the father only began work at the time in 1997.

Where a party whose income is to be determined for purposes of calculating child support obligations asserts that his or her income will be substantially different from previous years, there is an onus on that party to provide information in sufficient detail to explain why the change has occurred: *MacDonald v. Rasmussen* (1997), 34 R.F.L. (4th) 451, 161 Sask. R. 103, [1998] 4 W.W.R. 588 (Q.B.); further considered at (1998), 38 R.F.L. (4th) 294, 161 Sask. R. 1 (Q.B.). In this case, the applicant, a doctor, failed to provide sufficient particulars. The court determined that as the applicant had provided details of his income over the first seven months of 1997, it would calculate his income as the average of his 1996 income and his extrapolated 1997 income. His 1994 and 1995 income could not be used because he and the respondent, also a doctor, split income to minimize tax payable.

The methods provided in s. 17(1)(a) and (b) of the *Federal Guidelines* are directory and not mandatory: *MacDonald v. Rasmussen*, above.

Where a parent has a remarkable financial year and is not anticipated to have such a successful year in the future, the anticipated income is properly considered under the *Guidelines*: *Chambers v. Chambers*, 40 R.F.L. (4th) 351, [1998] N.W.T.R. 252 (S.C.).

Where the father's income fluctuated in accordance with stock market conditions, the average of his three previous years' income was used to determine the amount of child support payable by him under the *Guidelines*: *Kits v. Kits* (1998), 42 R.F.L. (4th) 167 (B.C. S.C.).

In determining the income of the farmer husband for the purposes of the *Federal Child Support Guidelines*, the average of the last 5 years of farming income was used in *Klaver v. Klaver* (1997), 32 R.F.L. (4th) 223 (Ont. Gen. Div.).

In *Magnes v. Magnes* (July 22, 1997), Doc. Regina Q.B. 0159664/94 (Sask. Q.B.), the husband was a self-employed farmer and because his income in one particular year may not be representative, it was necessary to examine the pattern of income over time. "It is permissible under the guidelines to fix the income at the average earned in the three most recent taxation years." His income in each of the three most recent taxation years was $28,490, $14,359 and $30,144. Adjustments to be made to income were the addition of $2,150 which had been deducted over the period for real property capital cost allowance, as well as a $5,000 deduction made in the last year for the purchase of fertilizer for use in the following year. The total then becomes $80,143, or an average of $26,714. The basic amount payable for the two children of the marriage on this income was $384 a month.

It is not appropriate to average income of past taxation years where the income is likely to remain at the current level, or increase. The court is to use the most current information available, and it is only where that information would not provide the fairest determination of the annual income that the court may resort to the provisions of s. 17: *Johnson v. Checkowy* (1997), 157 Sask. R. 71 (Q.B.).

Where the petitioner has been employed for a relatively short time in a new job (21 months) the fairest approach in determining his annual income is to consider the total number of months worked at the new job and the total income from those months of work: *Crick v. Crick* (1997), 43 B.C.L.R. (3d) 251 (S.C.).

See also *Lee v. Lee* (1998), 43 R.F.L. (4th) 339, 165 D.L.R. (4th) 619, 167 Nfld. & P.E.I.R. 176, 513 A.P.R. 176 (Nfld. C.A.).

In *Sagl v. Sagl* (1997), 31 R.F.L. (4th) 405 (Ont. Gen. Div.); (1997), 35 R.F.L. (4th) 107 (Ont. Gen. Div.), before Macdonald J., the court was concerned that the payor/father deliberately withheld his tax returns so as to make it more difficult for the court to calculate his income and to make an informed application of the guidelines. The court held that it could impute income to the father under s. 18(1)(a) and s. 19(1)(f) of the *Guidelines*. As the father had said at trial that he would have an annual income of U.S. $200,000 (Can. $274,680), the court set the amount of support for the parties' only child at $1,725 (the base table amount and an additional sum for the income difference between $150,000 and $274,680).

In an *obiter* remark, the court noted that s. 17 of the *Federal Guidelines* addresses fluctuations in a source of income, not fluctuations in total income under the *Federal Child Support Guidelines*: *Holtby v. Holtby* (1997), 30 R.F.L. (4th) 70 (Ont. Prov. Div.).

15§102 — Calculating income for purposes of determining child support — non-recurring losses

Where a spouse has suffered a non-recurring capital or business loss, and adjustments in accordance with Schedule III would not provide the fairest determination of the annual income, the court may choose not to substitute the actual amount of capital gains realized in excess of the spouse's actual capital losses as directed by s. 6 of the schedule, or deduct the actual amount of business investment losses suffered during the year as directed by s. 7, and may instead "adjust the amount of the loss, including related expenses and carrying charges and interest expenses, to arrive at such amount as the court considers appropriate:" *Federal Child Support Guidelines*, s. 17(2).

In *Aitken v. Aitken* (2003), 42 R.F.L. (5th) 1, 2003 CarswellOnt 2561 (Ont. S.C.J.), it was found that the husband should include in his income for *Guidelines* purposes one-half of the substantial losses he had incurred from day trading on the stock market.

In *Hill v. Hill* (1999), 48 R.F.L. (4th) 110 (Sask. Q.B.), it was held that farm losses relating to a hobby farm were not an appropriate deduction in determining a parent's income under the *Federal Child Support Guidelines*.

15§103 — Calculating income for purposes of determining child support — shareholder, director or officer

Where the spouse is a shareholder, director or officer of a corporation and the amount of the spouse's annual income as adjusted in accordance with Schedule III does not fairly reflect all the money available to the spouse for the payment of child support the court may consider the situations described under 15§101 Pattern of income and 15§102 Non-recurring losses, above (*Federal Child Support Guidelines*, s. 17), and determine the spouse's annual income to include

(a) all or part of the pre-tax income of the corporation, and of any corporation that is related to that corporation, for the most recent taxation year; or

(b) an amount commensurate with the services that the spouse provides to the corporation, provided that the amount does not exceed the corporation's pre-tax income. (*Federal Child Support Guidelines*, s. 18(1).)

In determining a spouse's income for *Guidelines* purposes, prior retained earnings of a company owned by that spouse should not be available as income in a year in which they were not earned: *Grossi v. Grossi* (2005), 10 R.F.L. (6th) 28, 2005 CarswellBC 146, [2005] 6 W.W.R. 607, 2005 BCCA 47, 249 D.L.R. (4th) 317, 207 B.C.A.C. 266, 341 W.A.C. 266, 38 B.C.L.R. (4th) 247 (C.A.).

In *Scott v. Scott* (2004), 10 R.F.L. (6th) 135, 2004 CarswellNB 587, 2004 NBCA 99, [2004] N.B.J. No. 468 (C.A.), the fact that the husband had not included the retained earnings of his company in his income for *Guidelines* purposes was upheld on appeal. The motions judge was entitled to accept the husband's evidence that the retained earnings were necessary for the viability of the business.

In *Barker v. Barker*, 27 R.F.L. (5th) 231, 2002 CarswellBC 1243, 2002 BCCA 345, 2 B.C.L.R. (4th) 149, 214 D.L.R. (4th) 452, [2002] B.C.J. No. 1193, 169 B.C.A.C. 299, 276 W.A.C. 299 (C.A.), it was held that an amount which the husband's company had recorded as an amortization expense was not properly included in the husband's income for *Guidelines* purposes.

In *Kowalewich v. Kowalewich*, 19 R.F.L. (5th) 330, 2001 CarswellBC 1417, [2001] B.C.J. No. 1406, 2001 BCCA 450, 92 B.C.L.R. (3d) 38, [2001] 9 W.W.R. 626, 155 B.C.A.C. 143, 254 W.A.C. 143 (B.C. C.A.), the court reduced, on appeal, the amount determined as the father's income for child support purposes. The husband's income was derived solely from a number of businesses he owned and his income had originally been set as a portion of the pre-tax income of these businesses. While the appellate court found this overall approach to be appropriate, the trial judge had not properly taken into account the contingencies affecting the businesses and the need for capital reserves.

Where the paying spouse is the sole shareholder of a company, the court may, pursuant to s. 18(1)(a) of the *Guidelines*, add the company's pre-tax income to the payor's salary to determine his income: *Rudachyk v. Rudachyk*, 47 R.F.L. (4th) 363, [1999] 10 W.W.R. 321, 180 Sask. R. 73, 205 W.A.C. 73, 1999 CarswellSask 317, [1999] S.J. No. 312 (C.A.). In this case the trial judge had added the payor's construction company's pre-tax income to his income.

In *Nesbitt v. Nesbitt*, 19 R.F.L. (5th) 359, 2001 CarswellMan 308, [2001] M.J. No. 271, 2001 MBCA 113, [2001] 8 W.W.R. 635, 156 Man. R. (2d) 238, 246 W.A.C. 238 (C.A.), the court held that the appropriate method of determining the husband's *Guidelines* income from a wholly-owned corporation was to attribute to the husband the average of three years of the corporation's income. Fairness, equity and common sense mandated using a three-year average rather than the actual income in the preceding year. Thus the risk of a variation application due to reliance on an unusual year was reduced.

A T1 income tax form may not provide a fair determination of a parent's annual income where it includes funds that are actually not available to that parent: *Rosenau v. Rosenau* (2004), 6 R.F.L. (6th) 372, 2004 CarswellSask 462, 2004 SKQB 275 (Q.B.).

Where the father owned three companies and controlled the amount of income flowing to himself, income was imputed for child support purposes. The father's reported income was not truly indicative of his ability to pay: *Hendrickson v. Hendrickson* (2004), 7 R.F.L. (6th) 245, 225 N.S.R. (2d) 205, 713 A.P.R. 205, 2004 CarswellNS 315, 2004 NSSF 73 (S.C.)

Where the father's income, derived from numerous companies he owned, was based on tax considerations rather than services rendered, the corporate income method was used to determine his income for *Guidelines* purposes. This method was appropriate given that the father had complete control over the companies and allocated salary depending on the circumstances: *Hodgkinson v. Hodgkinson* (2003), 44 R.F.L. (5th) 82, 2003 CarswellBC 2461, 2003 BCSC 1538 (S.C.).

In *Sevier v. Sevier*, 42 R.F.L. (5th) 174, 2003 CarswellBC 1627, 2003 BCSC 1022 (B.C. S.C.), it was held that the tax shelter loss deducted by the husband's personal corporation should be included in his income for *Guidelines* purposes.

Where the father continually re-invested his income back into his business it was found, for the purposes of determining his income for child support purposes, that he could deduct amounts that the business legitimately needed to operate, but that he must provide compelling evidence of that need: *Bartkowski v. Bartkowski*, 37 R.F.L. (5th) 242, 2003 CarswellBC 712, 2003 BCSC 490 (B.C. S.C. [In Chambers]).

In *Kowalewich v. Kowalewich*, 19 R.F.L. (5th) 330, 2001 CarswellBC 1417, [2001] B.C.J. No. 1406, 2001 BCCA 450, 92 B.C.L.R. (3d) 38, [2001] 9 W.W.R. 626, 155 B.C.A.C. 143, 254 W.A.C. 143 (B.C. C.A.), the court reduced, on appeal, the amount determined as the father's income for child support purposes. The husband's income was derived solely from a number of businesses he owned and his income had originally been set as a portion of the pre-tax income of these businesses. While the appellate court found this overall approach to be appropriate, the trial judge had not properly taken into account the contingencies affecting the businesses and the need for capital reserves.

Where the father continually re-invested his income back into his business it was found, for the purposes of determining his income for child support purposes, that he could deduct amounts that the business legitimately needed to operate, but that he must provide compelling evidence of that need: *Bartkowski v. Bartkowski*, 37 R.F.L. (5th) 242, 2003 CarswellBC 712, 2003 BCSC 490 (B.C. S.C. [In Chambers]).

Where the father had chosen to retain all pre-tax income of his company inside the corporation and had deferred payment of his own salary and benefits, one-half of that deferred income was imputed to him for *Guidelines* purposes: *Boser v. Boser*, 47 R.F.L. (5th) 259, 2003 CarswellSask 752, 2003 SKQB 477, 240 Sask. R. 66 (Sask. Q.B.).

Where there were legitimate business concerns prompting the retention of earnings within the husband's company, those earnings were not imputed into the husband's income for *Guidelines* purposes: *Koester v. Koester* (2003), 50 R.F.L. (5th) 78, 2003 CarswellOnt 5372 (Ont. S.C.J.)

Where the husband was a sole owner and operator of a successful corporation and therefore could directly affect the direction of the corporate finances, the court found it an appropriate case for the application of s. 18 of the *Guidelines* in determining the husband's income. His income was very substantial, having regard to the value of the service the husband continued to provide, which permitted the lifting of the corporate veil to determine all funds available to him for child support: *Volken v. Volken*, 19 R.F.L. (5th) 205, 2001 CarswellBC 1401, 2001 BCSC 970 (S.C. [In Chambers]).

A marriage contract which specifically excluded certain shares and information relating to the issuing corporation from equalization proceedings had no bearing on a child support application under the *Federal Child Support Guidelines*. Section 18 of the *Guidelines* permits consideration of factors included in s. 17, and the determination of a spouse's annual income is to include all or part of the pre-tax income of a corporation in which the spouse was a shareholder: *Pastway v. Pastway* (1999), 49 R.F.L. (4th) 375 (Ont. Gen. Div.).

In *Morley v. Morley* (1999), 44 R.F.L. (4th) 442, 176 Sask. R. 287 (Q.B.), the court considered whether a portion of a corporation's retained earnings could be included in the income of the respondent. However, as it is only the pre-tax income of a corporation, or a related corporation, for the most recent taxation year that may be included in a spouse's income and the corporation in question showed a net income loss, there was no pre-tax income of the corporation to be included in the respondent's income for the purpose of paying child support. The court also observed that there were many sound business reasons for accumulating net income in a corporation as retained earnings, not least of which may be to offset net income losses in the future or to satisfy the requirements of lending institutions.

In *Desjardins v. Desjardins* (1998), 1998 CarswellBC 1101, [1998] B.C.J. No. 1173 (S.C.), the father had his own computer consulting business of which he was the sole shareholder. He controlled payments out of the company. The capital requirements of the company were minimal, as the company was not in the business of buying products for re-sale. The court was of the opinion that it could, pursuant to s. 18(1)(a), incorporate all of the pre-tax income of the corporation ($45,189), in the income of the father for *Guide-*

lines purposes. However, it determined that $25,189 would be added to the father's income. The rest of the corporation's pre-tax income, combined with other amounts would remain available for payment of corporate income taxes, the cash needs of the company and as a base for his income if the company's income dropped in the future.

The payor in *Jess v. Strong* (1998), 169 N.S.R. (2d) 271, 508 A.P.R. 271, 1998 CarswellNS 296 (S.C) was one of three shareholder/director/employees of an offshore oil company and had a one-half interest in a holding company which owned all the shares of his corporate employer and 90% of a new company that dealt with industrial environmental cleaning services. The payor could determine the exact amount of his taxable income through a corporate structure which paid him a combination of salary, bonus and dividends, taking into account his needs, tax implications for himself and the companies, and the amount of retained earnings for the companies. The court held that the payor could arrange payment to himself of his share of the net profit of both operating companies without seriously undermining the financial health of those companies and accordingly additional income was imputed to him for purposes of the *Child Support Guidelines*.

The purpose of s. 18 is to prevent a paying spouse from using a corporation to hide personal income. Its purpose is not to have the court direct how an individual is to operate his or her business: *Lyttle v. Bourget* (1999), 1999 CarswellNS 273, 178 N.S.R. (2d) 1, 549 A.P.R. 1, [1999] N.S.J. No. 298 (S.C.). In this case, the court relied on the evidence of a specialist in taxation and a certified valuator. Among other matters, the court found that the paying spouse's retention of over $200,000 in retained earnings from his dentistry practice to be legitimate.

In *Giene v. Giene* (1998), 234 A.R. 355 (Q.B.) the father owned 51% of the common shares of a company and the husband's second wife owned 49% of the shares. The court was satisfied that the second wife's interest was purchased at fair market value and considered only the portion of the corporation's pre-tax income which was attributable to the father, namely 51%. The court was of the opinion that the father's annual income as determined under s. 16 did not fairly reflect all the money available to him for the payment of child support. The corporation had a pre-tax profit in 1996, 1997, 1998 and the father projected a loss of $100,000 in 1999. In order to determine the father's corporate pre-tax income, the court attributed 51% of the average of the last three years' earnings before income tax, together with the projected loss in 1999. The court calculated that the father's guideline income was $126,754 made up of his personal income of $77,691 and the sum of $49,063 which has been determined pursuant to s. 18(1)(a) of the *Guidelines*.

Where the father owned 50 percent of the corporation he managed, the court rejected the wife's claim that the father had arranged to minimize his income through the corporation. The father's income derived from the corporation was steady for years and the corporation appeared to be managed reasonably and in good faith with respect to retained earnings. Income was accordingly not attributed to the father for *Guidelines* purposes: *Beeching v. Beeching* (1998), 40 R.F.L. (4th) 15, 169 Sask. R. 18 (Q.B.).

In *Sagl v. Sagl* (1997), 31 R.F.L. (4th) 405, 1997 CarswellOnt 2144, [1997] O.J. No. 2837 (Gen. Div.); additional reasons at (1997), 35 R.F.L. (4th) 107, 1997 CarswellOnt 4984 (Gen. Div.) before Macdonald J., the court was concerned that the payor/father deliberately withheld his tax returns so as to make it more difficult for the court to calculate his income and to make an informed application of the *Guidelines*. The court held that it could impute income to the father under s. 18(1)(a) and s. 19(1)(f) of the *Guidelines*. As the father had said at trial that he would have an annual income of U.S. $200,000 (Can.

$274,680), the court set the amount of support for the parties' only child at $1,725 (the base table amount and an additional sum for the income difference between $150,000 and $274,680).

Section 18 of the *Guidelines* does not require that in every case, a corporate entity should pay out all net income as dividends and that the retained earnings should be restricted, particularly, as in the instant case, a significant portion of the net income was paid out as dividend income: *Kelly v. Kelly* (1997), 33 R.F.L. (4th) 16, 162 Sask. R. 74, 1997 CarswellSask 558, [1997] S.J. No. 604 (Q.B.). In this case, the respondent was an optometrist who was a shareholder in two companies. The first company was wholly owned by the respondent and his associate. The respondent's share was 40 percent. The second company owned the respondent's shares in the first company and was wholly owned by the respondent.

Where the payor was a dentist who carried on his practice through his company with his professional services as the sole source of income for the company, the court should consider the pre-tax income of the company in order to determine the true value of the services of the payor: *Blackburn v. Elmitt* (1997), 34 R.F.L. (4th) 183, 1997 CarswellBC 2491, [1997] B.C.J. No. 2569 (S.C. [In Chambers]). The court was of the opinion that the payor's annual income for child support purposes should be determined by adding the corporation's pre-tax income and the payor's employment income.

Sections 17 and 18 of the *Guidelines* should not be applied so as to "dictate the economic decisions which must be made in relation to the operation of the business including the investment and re-investment of capital as opposed to its distribution to principals": *S. (L.) v. P. (E.)* (1997), 32 R.F.L. (4th) 75, 41 B.C.L.R. (3d) 14, 1997 CarswellBC 2083, [1997] B.C.J. No. 2206 (S.C.); appeal dismissed on other grounds but appropriate ongoing child support ordered in *S. (L.) v. P. (E.)*, 175 D.L.R. (4th) 423, 126 B.C.A.C. 28, 206 W.A.C. 28, 67 B.C.L.R. (3d) 254, [1999] 12 W.W.R. 718, 50 R.F.L. (4th) 302, 1999 CarswellBC 1402, [1999] B.C.J. No. 1451 (C.A.); leave to appeal refused 252 N.R. 194 (note), 135 B.C.A.C. 160 (note), 221 W.A.C. 160 (note), [1999] S.C.C.A. No. 444 (S.C.C.). The lower court was of the opinion that adjustments set out in ss. 17 and 18 should only be used sparingly when it may be inferred that the payor has intended to avoid his or her obligations under the *Guidelines*. In this case, there was no evidence that the defendant could have received a larger income without affecting business operations and the companies' investments in properties. There was no evidence that the defendant's standard of living was being subsidized by corporate funding. The court found that the defendant's total income for tax purposes fairly reflects his ability to pay child support at the time of the hearing.

15§104 — Calculating income for purposes of determining child support — adjustment to corporation's pre-tax income

(2) In determining the pre-tax income of a corporation for the purposes of subsection (1), all amounts paid by the corporation as salaries, wages or management fees, or other payments or benefits, to or on behalf of persons with whom the corporation does not deal at arm's length must be added to the pre-tax income, unless the spouse establishes that the payments were reasonable in the circumstances. *Federal Child Support Guidelines*, s. 18(2).

In *S. (L.) v. P. (E.)* (1997), 32 R.F.L. (4th) 75, 41 B.C.L.R. (3d) 14 (S.C.); varied on other grounds 50 R.F.L. (4th) 302, 175 D.L.R. (4th) 423, 126 B.C.A.C. 28, 206 W.A.C. 28, 67

B.C.L.R. (3d) 254, [1999] 12 W.W.R. 718, 1999 BCCA 393 (C.A.); leave to appeal refused (1999), 252 N.R. 194 (note), 135 B.C.A.C. 160 (note), 221 W.A.C. 160 (note) (S.C.C.), the court considered the onus in s. 18(2) of the *Federal Guidelines*. The court was of the opinion that the onus resting with the defendant to prove the reasonableness of salaries paid to non-arms length's recipients arises after the plaintiff has made out a *prima facie* case of reasonableness. In this decision the court found that there was evidence of considerable active involvement of the defendant's spouse in the corporate business operations.

15§105 — Calculating income for purposes of determining child support — imputing income

19. (1) The court may impute such amount of income to a spouse as it considers appropriate in the circumstances, which circumstances include the following:

(a) the spouse is intentionally under-employed or unemployed, other than where the under-employed or unemployed is required by the needs of a child of the marriage or any child under the age of majority or by the reasonable educational or health needs of the spouse;

(b) the spouse is exempt from paying federal or provincial income tax;

(c) the spouse lives in a country that has effective rates of income tax that are significantly lower than those in Canada;

(d) it appears that income has been diverted which would affect the level of child support to be determined under these Guidelines;

(e) the spouse's property is not reasonably utilized to generate income;

(f) the spouse has failed to provide income information when under a legal obligation to do so;

(g) the spouse unreasonably deducts expenses from income;

(h) the spouse derives a significant portion of income from dividends, capital gains or other sources that are taxed at a lower rate than employment or business income; and

(i) the spouse is a beneficiary under a trust and is or will be in receipt of income or other benefits from the trust.

Reasonableness of expenses

(2) For the purpose of paragraph (1)(g), the reasonableness of an expense deduction is not solely governed by whether the deduction is permitted under the *Income Tax Act*.

Imputing Income — Spouse is intentionally under-employed or unemployed — s. 19(1)(a)

In *Ladisa v. Ladisa* (2005), 11 R.F.L. (6th) 50, 2005 CarswellOnt 268, 193 O.A.C. 336, [2005] O.J. No. 276 (C.A.), it was found, on appeal, that the trial judge had erred in failing to impute income to the father, beyond his disability pension, for *Guidelines* purposes. The father could and did work up to 90 days at a time without impacting his pension entitlement.

In *D. (D.R.) v. M. (J.)* (2004), 6 R.F.L. (6th) 240, 2004 CarswellAlta 1580, 247 D.L.R. (4th) 569, 36 Alta. L.R. (4th) 221, 361 A.R. 214, 339 W.A.C. 214, 2004 ABCA 380, [2004] A.J. No. 1331 (C.A.), income imputed to the wife for *Guidelines* purposes was struck on appeal. The fact that the wife's unemployment was necessitated by the needs of her two youngest children was adequately supported by evidence.

Where the father wound down his own independent electrical contracting company and went to work for someone else at a much lower salary, income was imputed to him for *Guidelines* purposes. There was no reason justifying the abandonment of his very successful business and, accordingly, the father was found to be intentionally underemployed: *Reil v. Holland* (2003), 42 R.F.L. (5th) 120, 2003 CarswellOnt 3828, 232 D.L.R. (4th) 265, 177 O.A.C. 162 (Ont. C.A.).

In *White v. White*, 27 R.F.L. (5th) 462, 2002 CarswellNS 224, 2002 NSCA 66, 206 N.S.R. (2d) 122, 645 A.P.R. 122, [2002] N.S.J. No. 248 (C.A.), it was held that a parent cannot avoid child support obligations on the basis of an unreasonable decisions to leave a secure job for the prospect of pursuing other career goals.

In *Stanghi v. Stanghi* (2001), 19 R.F.L. (5th) 392, 2001 CarswellOnt 1726 (Ont. C.A.), the court dismissed the husband's appeal from a judgment dismissing his application to eliminate his spousal and child support obligation. The husband, in the original consent application, had agreed to an imputed income of $40,000 annually. As the husband's evidence supported the conclusion that he was in the same physical and financial condition as at the time of the original order, the trial judge could not properly impute the same level of income to him.

Where the father had quit a second job after separation, the court refused to impute additional income to him for *Guidelines* purposes. The father had not left the job in order to defeat his child support obligations and he was not under-employed: *M. (S.A.J.) v. M. (D.D.)* (1998), 40 R.F.L. (4th) 95, 127 Man. R. (2d) 78 (Q.B.); reversed on other grounds (1999), 45 R.F.L. (4th) 301, 134 Man. R. (2d) 242, 193 W.A.C. 242 (C.A.).

In *Gray v. Gray* (November 30, 1998), Doc. 2996 (Sask. C.A.), the court held that the trial judge erred in determining the payor/father's income at $50,000, where the evidence was that his income was $43,402 and there was no evidence of the husband voluntarily reducing his income in order to reduce his child support payments. The court granted the payor's appeal and awarded child support in the amount of $915 per month based on an income of $43,402.

In *Furlong v. Furlong* (1998), 42 R.F.L. (4th) 350 (Alta. C.A.), the court refused to impute income to the husband for child support payments when he had left the armed forces upon closure of his home base and refused transfer to another. The husband had elected to return to school and his decision to refuse the transfer was reasonable, given his desire to remain in the community where the children lived.

In *Melzack v. Germain* (June 11, 1998) (Ont. C.A.), the appellate court upheld the trial court's finding under s. 19(1)(a) of the *Guidelines* that the appellant's decision to move to Hawaii demonstrated an intention to be under-employed and that he was capable of earning a substantial income. The Court of Appeal found no error in principle in imputing income to the appellant in light of his past work history, his business activities and experience and the level of income he had earned prior to his bankruptcy. The appellant's evidence that he would not be able to find employment in Canada or reestablish himself in business here was not accepted by the trial court which also commented adversely on the *bona fides* of the appellant and the merits of his application.

In *MacDonald v. Underhay* (2005), 21 R.F.L. (6th) 114, 2005 CarswellPEI 80, 2005 PESCTD 56 (P.E.I. T.D. [In Chambers]), the court refused to impute income to the unemployed husband where he had lost employment through no fault of his own.

Where the father's overtime work had declined from 1998 in 2000 to 110 in 2004, the court refused to impute additional overtime income to him beyond 110 hours. The amount of overtime was simply not available as it once was, nor was it reasonable to require the husband to work all overtime available to him: *S. (R.) v. S. (T.)* (2005), 21 R.F.L. (6th) 411, 2005 CarswellNB 614, 2005 NBQB 357, 293 N.B.R. (2d) 313, 762 A.P.R. 313 (N.B. Q.B.).

In *Caron v. Caron* (2004), 9 R.F.L. (6th) 268, 2004 CarswellSask 745, 2004 SKQB 424 (Q.B.); additional reasons at 2005 CarswellSask 145, 261 Sask. R. 141, 2005 SKQB 120 (Sask. Q.B.), the court refused to impute income to the mother for *Guidelines* purposes after she had lost her employment largely due to her own conduct.

In *Stephen v. Stephen* (2004), 10 R.F.L. (6th) 183, 2004 CarswellSask 618, 253 Sask. R. 228, 2004 SKQB 386 (Q.B.), an additional income of $15,000 was imputed to the father who had voluntarily retired at age 47 and taken an equivalent reduction in his income. Although the father's decision was reasonably motivated by workplace stress, he could work in another capacity and earn at least $15,000 in an entry-level job.

Where the husband had executed a limited-term "no compete" agreement which prevented him from working in his usual field and earning his usual income, the court refused to impute income to him for *Guidelines* purposes. However, the husband was required to provide continuing disclosure of changes in his income: *Mondino v. Mondino* (2004), 9 R.F.L. (6th) 170, 2004 CarswellOnt 3513 (S.C.J.).

In *Stringer v. Stringer* (2003), 48 R.F.L. (5th) 422, 2003 CarswellBC 2824, 2003 BCSC 1739 (B.C. S.C.), full-time employment income was imputed to the father for *Guidelines* purposes although he had only been working part time. The father had an obligation to work full time in order to support his family.

Where the father derived a frugal income from farming, a further sum of $1,200 was imputed to his income for *Guidelines* purposes to reflect work that he did from time to time as a casual labourer in *Knoth v. Knoth* (2003), 38 R.F.L. (5th) 123, 2003 CarswellBC 579, 2003 BCSC 417 (B.C. S.C.).

Where the father retired at age 65, his application for a reduction in child support in keeping with his reduced income was allowed. Imputation of income to him for *Guidelines* purposes was inappropriate as his retirement was not unreasonable: *Buenten v. Harrhy* (2003), 43 R.F.L. (5th) 259, 2003 CarswellBC 2025, 2003 BCSC 1287 (B.C. S.C.).

Where the wife was remaining at home to raise her youngest child and an existing consent order for spousal support contemplated that it would take her 8 years to achieve self-sufficiency, it was inappropriate to impute income to her for *Guidelines* purposes: *Sevier v. Sevier* (2003), 42 R.F.L. (5th) 174, 2003 CarswellBC 1627, 2003 BCSC 1022 (B.C. S.C.).

In *Lay v. Lay*, 38 R.F.L. (5th) 285, 2003 CarswellNWT 12, 2003 NWTSC 11 (N.W.T. S.C.); additional reasons at 2003 CarswellNWT 20, 2003 NWTSC 23 (N.W.T. S.C.), the custodial father was successful in his application for child support against the unemployed mother. There was no evidence that the mother was unable to work and a minimum wage income was imputed to her.

The court may find the payor spouse intentionally underemployed when he or she has obtained professional training but does not obtain employment in his field of study: *Egan v. Egan*, 2003 CarswellBC 1, 2003 BCSC 2 (B.C. S.C. [In Chambers]). In this case, the father had obtained a law degree, but had not sought a career in law.

Where the father had discontinued participation in lucrative lecture tours after separation, income was imputed to him for *Guidelines* purposes. The father had no good reason justifying his actions and was accordingly found to be "intentionally underemployed": *West v. West* (2001), 18 R.F.L. (5th) 440, 2001 CarswellOnt 1936 (Ont. S.C.J.).

Where the father left his job to work full time at a store he had purchased, he was found to be "intentionally underemployed" within the meaning of the *Guidelines* and income was imputed to him for child support purposes. His annual income, as a result of his actions, had decreased from $85,000 to $24,000. The father had not been motivated by a sound business decision but primarily by the fact that he disliked his job: *Weir v. Therrien* (2001), 20 R.F.L. (5th) 199, 2001 CarswellOnt 2327 (Ont. S.C.J.).

In *Vitagliano v. Di Stavolo* (2001), 17 R.F.L. (5th) 194, 2001 CarswellOnt 1065, [2001] O.J. No. 1138 (Ont. S.C.J.), the wife was awarded spousal and child support based on an imputed income to the husband of $110,000 although he claimed income of only $49,000. The husband was an experienced statistician who had turned down employment offers in the range of $110,000 and, instead, established his own less than successful business. Although his decidion was not intended to thwart his support obligations, he had made his career decisions recklessly and without regard to his legal obligation.

Where the father had worked significant overtime during the marriage to support the family, his desire post-separation to cut down on the overtime in order to spend more time with the children was reasonable. Accordingly, for the purposes of determining income under the *Guidelines*, it was not appropriate that additional income be imputed to him: *Uens v. Uens* (2000), 11 R.F.L. (5th) 202, 2000 CarswellOnt 4478 (S.C.J.).

Where the wife had lost her job for cause as a result of her behaviour, an annual income of $18,000 was attributed to her for the purposes of calculating her spousal support: *Faflak v. Faflak* (1999), 4 R.F.L. (5th) 216, 1999 CarswellOnt 3598 (Div. Ct.).

In *Neisz v. Spagrud* (1998), 42 R.F.L. (4th) 393, 174 Sask. R. 174, 1998 CarswellSask 661 (Q.B.), the court allowed the husband's application for a reduction in child support after he left his $63,000 per year job to enter into a partnership with his father, yielding an annual income of only $24,000. However, as he had unilaterally made the decision to leave his job without considering the consequences for his children, an additional annual income of $12,000 was imputed to him for *Guidelines* purposes.

In *Necemer v. Necemer* (1999), 4 R.F.L. (5th) 409, 1999 CarswellBC 2953 (B.C. S.C.), the 52-year-old father who lived on pension income of approximately $24,000 per annum had an income of $50,000 imputed to him for *Guidelines* purposes. He was able to work and the $50,000 reflected his earning ability.

Where the father ceased working overtime and premium shifts at the commencement of child support proceedings, additional income was attributed to him for calculation purposes. Prior to the proceedings, the father had a consistent pattern of working such shifts: *Odendahl v. Brule* (1999), 45 R.F.L. (4th) 37 (Ont. Gen. Div.).

Before income will be imputed to a parent on the basis of "intentional under-employment" that situation must be proven to be the result of an intention to undermine or avoid a child support obligation: *Yaremchuk v. Yaremchuk* (1998), 38 R.F.L. (4th) 312, 158 D.L.R. (4th) 180, 218 A.R. 153 (Alta. Q.B.).

Where the mother quit her job to work on her new husband's farm, she could not rely upon her drop in income as a reason to avoid her child support obligations. She could not voluntarily change her lifestyle and expect to pass the consequences along to her children. The mother was accordingly ordered to pay child support based upon the income she had forfeited: *Wiebe v. Oviatt* (1998), 40 R.F.L. (4th) 338, 167 Sask. R. 165 (Q.B.).

Where the father was attending law school but working during the summer months, the court imputed income to him for *Guidelines* purposes. The lack of summer employment constituted intentional unemployment or under-employment on the father's part: *Carson v. Buziak* (1998), 40 R.F.L. (4th) 50, 166 Sask. R. 8 (Q.B.).

In *Laflamme v. Laflamme* (1998), 38 R.F.L. (4th) 335 (Alta. Q.B.), although the husband's expenditures compared to his income raised a strong suspicion, there was no basis on which to impute income under s. 19 of the *Federal Child Support Guidelines*.

Where a payor parent stubbornly continues to follow a career path that permits him or her to pay a level of support demonstrably inadequate to meet the children's needs, when he or she has the proven ability to earn more, then he or she will be found to be "intentionally under-employed" within the meaning of s. 19(1)(a) of the *Guidelines*: *Hunt v. Smolis-Hunt*, 39 R.F.L. (4th) 143, [1998] 10 W.W.R. 1, 61 Alta. L.R. (3d) 279, 224 A.R. 68 (Q.B.).

Where the father had diverted assets to his son, was unemployed and let the son support him, an annual income of $10,000 was imputed to him for the purposes of determining his child support obligation toward his daughter. A parent who is without income and is supported by relatives is still obliged to pay child support: *Arsenault v. Mann* (1998), 42 R.F.L. (4th) 294, 171 Nfld. & P.E.I.R. 136, 525 A.P.R. 136 (P.E.I. T.D. [In Chambers]).

The payor father in *Krawczyk v. Krawczyk* (June 11, 1998), Doc. Brampton D31852/96 (Ont. Gen. Div.) was a police officer who was required to attend at court in the course of his employment. For these "court days", he was given the option of receiving $200 a day or taking time off. The court viewed the fact that during the marriage the payor took time off in lieu of pay for court days was irrelevant to a consideration of any practice or handling of "court days" after separation and divorce. The court did not accept the payor's contention that the payor needed to take time off instead of pay for "court days" in order to exercise access. The court attributed additional income of $2000 to the payor per year based on ten "court days" at a value of $200 per day for those days which he had taken time off when he could otherwise have been working.

Where the father had lost his job for cause after deliberately continuing with a course of behaviour which he knew would ultimately result in his dismissal, the husband was found to be "deliberately under-employed" within the meaning of the *Federal Child Support Guidelines*. Accordingly, income equivalent to his former employment income was attributed to him for the purposes of quantifying his child support obligation: *Baldini v. Baldini* (1999), 46 R.F.L. (4th) 407 (B.C. S.C.).

Where an employer has provided subsidized accommodation for a spouse, it may be treated as additional or imputed income of the beneficiary, but where, as in this case, there is no evidence as to the cost if the spouse rented such accommodation, the evidentiary base has not been established and no amount would be imputed to the spouse for the accommodation: *Adler v. Jonas* (1999), 48 R.F.L. (4th) 228 (B.C. S.C.); additional reasons to (1998), 48 R.F.L. (4th) 218 (B.C. S.C.). The mother was provided with rent free accommodation while she taught in Korea but was required to pay an "apartment management fee" equal to $81 (Canadian) per month and $6 (Canadian) for the cost of heating.

The court in *Halley v. Hannon* (1998), 40 R.F.L. (4th) 60, 162 Nfld. & P.E.I.R. 315, 500 A.P.R. 315 (Nfld. U.F.C.) considered whether, on an application to vary child support, it should impute income to an unemployed father who had R.R.S.P.'s and an investment from proceeds of a personal injury settlement. The father had an engineering consulting firm but had only secured one small contract since the date of the order and had no income with which to pay support. The court used its discretion under s. 19(1) of the *Guidelines* to impute income for 1998 based upon what the father may reasonably be expected to earn during the year, including the potential revenue from his basement apartment. In addition, the court ruled that the court may consider capital as well as income in deciding whether to impute income. However, in this case, it declined to do so. The court took into account that the father's personal injury settlement was based in part upon his probable future need for medical treatment, including the possibility of surgery. As the father faced unemployment and an uncertain financial future, it was reasonable that he would not draw down capital at any faster rate than he was currently doing. The court also considered the rental income available to him from his basement apartment. The consent order was varied retroactively to reduce payments and as of January 1, 1998 based upon an income of $16,500 (formerly projected at $40,000), he was required to pay $300 monthly (formerly $1050 monthly) for three children.

In *Neisz v. Spagrud* (1998), 42 R.F.L. (4th) 393, 174 Sask. R. 174 (Q.B.), the court allowed the husband's application for a reduction in child support after he left his $63,000 per year job to enter into a partnership with his father, yielding an annual income of only $24,000. However, as he had unilaterally made the decision to leave his job without considering the consequence for his children, an additional annual income of $12,000 was imputed to him for *Guidelines* purposes.

In *Clements v. Clements* (July 17, 1997), Doc. Whitehorse 95-D2617 (Y.T. S.C.), the payor father sought to vary the consent corollary relief order made before May 1, 1997 reducing the child support payment from $300 to $50 per month, the latter being the amount set out in the *Federal Child Support Guidelines*. Although the payor was a full-time student studying social work, the court was not satisfied that he was making all reasonable efforts to fulfil his obligations towards his children, as he could try to find at least part-time or summer employment. The court imputed an income of $13,000 to $15,000 which was compatible with his income history over the past few years. The court took into account that before May 1, 1997, the payor had sought to reduce child support to $125 per month and also observed that child support was no longer taxable (in the hands of the payee or deductible in the hands of the payor). The court set child support at $125 per month.

Where the father had quit two jobs, was unemployed, failed to remove his wife's name from the mortgages on income properties and failed to manage those properties profitably, the court imputed an income of $19,500 per year to him: *Monette v. Jordan* (1997), 163 N.S.R. (2d) 70, 487 A.P.R. 70 (S.C. [In Chambers]), before Glube C.J.

The court refused to impute a higher income to the father on an interim motion, where the father had taken a lower paid job after a review had recommended that his position be eliminated, but no final decision based on this recommendation had been made: *Rains v. Rains* (June 16, 1997), Doc. Sault Ste. Marie 16655/97 (Ont. Gen. Div.). The court would not conclude that the father was intentionally under-employed, or that his decision to seek other less remunerative employment before termination of his employment was so imprudent as to justify imputing his former level of income to him.

Overtime income should not be imputed where the evidence indicates that overtime is no longer available to the parent: *Abudulai v. Abudulai* (2003), 41 R.F.L. (5th) 1, 2003 CarswellNS 250 (N.S. Fam. Ct.).

Where the husband legitimately had sought out less strenuous and less lucrative work as a result of health issues, the court refused to impute income to him for *Guidelines* purposes: *Tapper v. Connolly* (2002), 26 R.F.L. (5th) 199, 2002 CarswellNfld 81, [2002] N.J. No. 83 (U.F.C.).

The payor husband was without an income, because he had quit the business where he had been self-employed, and was occupied taking a business administration and computer course. On an application for interim child support, the court attributed an annual income to him of $30,000 on the basis that he had been earning approximately that amount after personal expenses charged to the business were taken into account. He had "chosen an inopportune time to re-educate himself": *Fahel v. Fahel* (June 30, 1997), Doc. New Westminister D38400 (B.C. Master).

In *Goudie v. Buchanan* (2001), 19 R.F.L. (5th) 280, 2001 CarswellNfld 185, 203 Nfld. & P.E.I.R. 34, 610 A.P.R. 34, [2001] N.J. No. 187 (U.F.C.), the court accepted the husband's claim of undue hardship in varying the child support payable by him to a level below that specified in the *Guidelines*. The father had returned to school after work in his field had all but disappeared. As his monthly expenses greatly exceeded his income, payment of the Table Amountts would have caused the father undue hardship. As the father's primary goal in returning to school rather than working was not to lower his child support payments, it was not appropriate to input income to him.

Imputing Income — Spouse is exempt from paying federal or provincial income tax — s. 19(1)(b)

Where the father's only income was from a $3,000 monthly tax free disability payment, he was still required to pay child support. The benefit was equivalent to a taxable annual income of $47,000 and that amount was imputed to the husband for *Guidelines* purposes: *Walgren v. Walgren*, 26 R.F.L. (5th) 226, 2002 CarswellBC 884, 2002 BCSC 432 (S.C.).

As the formulas to determine child support under the *Guidelines* take into account the payment of tax, special procedure must be used where a parent is in receipt of non-taxable income. The amount should be grossed up to take into account what it would have been if taxed: *Belisle v. Belisle* (2000), 13 R.F.L. (5th) 262, 2000 CarswellOnt 4735, [2000] O.J. No. 4744 (Ont. S.C.J.).

Where the husband was a status Indian who did not pay income tax, his income for the purposes of the *Federal Child Support Guidelines* was grossed up to reflect that fact. The *Guidelines* require that the children benefit from the financial means of both parents and ignoring the husband's tax situation would thwart that intention: *Le Bourdais v. Le Bourdais*, 36 R.F.L. (4th) 387, [1998] 8 W.W.R. 563, 49 B.C.L.R. (3d) 373 (S.C.).

Where the payor has Native status and consequently does not pay federal or provincial income tax, his income should be adjusted to reflect that fact, and under s. 19(1)(b), the court may impute additional income to him: *Ninham v. Ninham* (1997), 29 R.F.L. (4th) 41 (Ont. Gen. Div.). In this case, the payor father's income was adjusted from $35,000 to $50,000, to take account of his non-payment of tax.

Pursuant to s. 19(1)(b) of the *Federal Child Support Guidelines* income may be imputed where the payor is exempt from paying income tax: *Hoover v. Hoover* (1997), [1998]

N.W.T.R. 209 (S.C.). In this decision, the father's sole source of income was a Workers' Compensation Board pension benefit of $22,900, which was exempt from income tax. The grossed up amount for national income tax was calculated as $29,565.

Imputing Income — Spouse lives in a country that has effective rates of income tax that are significantly lower than those in Canada — s. 19(1)(c)

In *Nkwazi v. Nkwazi* (1998), 171 Sask. R. 120 (Q.B.), the father, a doctor, had moved to the United States and was paid in American dollars. The court imputed an income of $177,700 to the father, which was his average income in equivalent Canadian dollars for the past three years. On the evidence before the court, it was not prepared to accept the father's argument that the benefits of lower taxation in the United States were offset by higher living expenses.

Imputing Income — It appears that income has been diverted which would affect the level of child support to be determined under the *Guidelines* — s. 19(1)(d)

No cases to report at this time.

Imputing Income — Spouse's property is not reasonably utilized to generate income — s. 19(1)(e)

In *Motyka v. Motyka*, 12 R.F.L. (5th) 421, 83 B.C.L.R. (3d) 339, 147 B.C.A.C. 233, 241 W.A.C. 233, 2001 BCCA 18, 2001 CarswellBC 38, [2001] B.C.J. No. 52 (B.C. C.A.), an annual income of $60,000 was imputed to the father for *Guidelines* purposes. The father managed his real estate development business in a way that deferred his income. Regardless, it was necessary that he contribute to his children's current needs and expenses.

Where the paying spouse had a shareholder loan to his company and the loan bore no interest, the court did not impute income interest on this loan as it was not of the view that the income as determined by the chamber judge and increased by appellate court was unrealistically low. *Rudachyk v. Rudachyk*, 47 R.F.L. (4th) 363, [1999] 10 W.W.R. 321, 180 Sask. R. 73, 205 W.A.C. 73, 1999 CarswellSask 317, [1999] S.J. No. 312 (C.A.). The father's income was determined to be $62,883 and support payments were $807 for each of two children.

Only where the payor spouse has control over the corporation and has caused the corporation to retain an excessive amount of retained earnings would s. 19(1)(e) of the *Guidelines* apply to the retained earnings of the corporation: *Blaine v. Sanders*, 2000 CarswellMan 177, 2000 MBQB 13, 144 Man. R. (2d) 300 (Q.B.). While in this case, the payor spouse controls the corporation in question, he has not caused the corporation to retain earnings unduly. The payor spouse had a 51 percent interest in a numbered company and his second wife has a 49 percent interest in the company.

The court in *H. (P.) v. H. (D.)* (1998), 40 R.F.L. (4th) 60, 162 Nfld. & P.E.I.R. 315, 500 A.P.R. 315, 1998 CarswellNfld 75 (U.F.C.) considered whether, on an application to vary child support, it should impute income to an unemployed father who had Registered Savings Plan and investments from proceeds of a personal injury settlement. The father had an engineering consulting firm but had only secured one small contract since the date of the order and had no income with which to pay support. The court used its discretion under s. 19(1) of the *Guidelines* to impute income for 1998 based upon what the father may reasonably be expected to earn during the year, including the potential revenue from his basement apartment. In addition, the court ruled that the court might consider capital as well as income in deciding whether to impute income. However, in this case, it declined to do so. The court took into account that the father's personal injury settlement was based in part upon his probable future need for medical treatment, including the possibility of surgery. As the father faced unemployment and an uncertain financial future, it was reasonable that he would not draw down capital at any faster rate than he was currently doing. The court also considered the rental income available to reduce payments and as of January 1, 1998, based upon an income of $16,500 (formerly projected at $40,000), he was required to pay $300 monthly (formerly $1050 monthly) for three children.

The payor's average income over the last three years after adjustments came to $28,000. But his net worth had increased from approximately $100,000 to $485,000 since the original order for support was made. In the circumstances, the court imputed an annual income of $56,000 after finding that his "assets are not being reasonably utilized to generate income": *Marshall v. Marshall* (July 25, 1997), Doc. Weyburn D.I.V. 886/93 (Sask. Q.B.).

Where the mother had won a lottery, her income for *Guidelines* purposes was determined by adding her income from employment to the imputed income that could be derived from the lottery winnings: *Wilson v. Eronchi*, 4 R.F.L. (5th) 146, 2000 NWTSC 5, 2000 CarswellNWT 3 (S.C. [In Chambers]).

Imputing Income — Failure to provide income information — s. 19(1)(f)

In *Cornelius v. Andres*, 45 R.F.L. (4th) 200, [1999] 6 W.W.R. 317, 170 D.L.R. (4th) 254, 134 Man. R. (2d) 140, 193 W.A.C. 140 (C.A.); reconsideration refused (May 31, 1999), Doc. AF 98-30-03713 (Man. C.A.), the husband was in breach of his disclosure obligations under the *Guidelines* as he had only provided incomplete tax records, and for one of his businesses, some financial statements, monthly income and expenses for one year and various other records. The court held that in determining income from rental property, a party can deduct interest payments but not principal on loans for capital expenditures. However, as the husband had not provided full financial disclosure, it was difficult to break down the current mortgage payments as between principal and interest. The court fixed the husband's rental income expenses at $813.20 per month and thus raised his net monthly income from this source to $1,824.80 per month or $21,897.60 per year.

In *Friedt v. Fraser*, 26 R.F.L. (5th) 80, 2002 CarswellSask 169, [2002] S.J. No. 150, 2002 SKQB 79, 216 Sask. R. 300 (Q.B.), income was imputed to the husband for *Guidelines* purposes. The father had been evasive in addressing the issue of expenses and failed to produce any receipts verifying his claims. Accordingly, the court was entitled to infer that the receipts would not have supported the father's claim and income was appropriately imputed.

In *O'Brien v. O'Brien* (2003), 39 R.F.L. (5th) 161, 2003 CarswellOnt 1712, [2003] O.J. No. 1787 (Ont. S.C.J.), greater income was attributed to the father than the amount he had disclosed. The father's capacity to borrow large sums in a short time and repay those loans using undisclosed sources of income justified imputing income to him.

In *Harari v. Harari*, 20 R.F.L. (5th) 59, 2001 CarswellBC 1645, 2001 BCSC 1068 (B.C. S.C. [In Chambers]), the court imputed an annual income to the husband far in excess of that declared in his tax returns. His spending habits supported the conclusion that his income was significantly higher than that declared.

Where the husband's income was difficult to ascertain for child support purposes because of his history of providing misleading and contradictory information, it was appropriate to impute an income to him at the high end of the range for his job: *Kapogiannes v. Kapogiannes* (2000), 10 R.F.L. (5th) 63, 2000 CarswellOnt 2374 (S.C.J.).

Where the husband claimed to make no money from his restaurant business, despite the fact that the parties had led an extravagant lifestyle, the court imputed an annual income of $50,000 to him for the purpose of determining his child support obligation. The court accepted the wife's evidence that the husband actually derived a substantial amount of money from the business which he did not declare: *Biamonte v. Biamonte* (1998), 36 R.F.L. (4th) 349 (Ont. Gen. Div.).

Where the father lived in the United States and had failed to file an income statement, the court imputed income to him for purposes of the *Federal Child Support Guidelines*. As a basis the court used the husband's 1993 American income tax return and utilized the current exchange rate to translate his income into Canadian dollars: *Garrison v. Garrison* (1998), 38 R.F.L. (4th) 435 (Ont. Gen. Div.).

In *Vivier v. Vivier* (1997), 120 Man. R. (2d) 231 (Man. Q.B.), the court, under s. 19(1) of the *Guidelines*, imputed income to a father payor who was employed as a construction worker for 26 weeks of the year and received unemployment insurance benefits for the remaining 26 weeks of the year. He had failed to make the financial disclosure ordered by the court.

The court in *Holtby v. Holtby* (1997), 30 R.F.L. (4th) 70 (Ont. Prov. Div.), imputed an income of $40,000 to the husband, relying on figures from a loan application setting out a projected income and the husband's tax returns.

Taking into account the pre-tax income of the husband's corporation, the services provided by the husband to that corporation and related corporations, the benefits paid by corporate entities on behalf of the husband, and the pre-separation lifestyle, the court attributed income of $150,000 to the husband for the purpose of determining interim support: *Shelleby v. Shelleby* (June 20, 1997), Doc. Sault Ste. Marie 010829/97 (Ont. Gen. Div.).

In *Sagl v. Sagl* (1997), 31 R.F.L. (4th) 405 (Ont. Gen. Div.); additional reasons at (1997), 35 R.F.L. (4th) 107 (Ont. Gen. Div.), before Macdonald J., the court was concerned that the payor/father deliberately withheld his tax returns so as to make it more difficult for the court to calculate his income and to make informed application of the *Guidelines*. The court held that it could impute income to the father under s. 18(1)(a) and s. 19(1)(f) of the *Guidelines*. As the father had said at trial that he would have an annual income of U.S. $200,000 (Can. $274,680), the court set the amount of support for the parties' only child at $1,725 (the base table amount and an additional sum for the income difference between $150,000 and $274,680).

Imputing Income — Spouse unreasonably deducts expenses from income — s. 19(1)(g)

In *Myketiak v. Myketiak* (2001), 13 R.F.L. (5th) 431, 203 Sask. R. 90, 240 W.A.C. 90, 2001 SKCA 17, 2001 CarswellSask 84 (C.A); affirming (1999), 185 Sask. R. 231, 1999 CarswellSask 693 (Sask. Q.B.), the court rejected the father's appeal from a finding that disallowed his deduction of farm losses from his employment income for *Guidelines* purposes. The manner in which he managed the farm would likely continually result in such losses year after year. If he chose to operate his farm at a loss over an extended period, he could not expect his wife and children to subsidize the operation when reasonable alternatives were open to him.

In *Cornelius v. Andres*, 45 R.F.L. (4th) 200, [1999] 6 W.W.R. 317, 170 D.L.R. (4th) 254, 134 Man. R. (2d) 140, 193 W.A.C. 140 (C.A.); reconsideration refused (May 31, 1999), Doc. AF 98-30-03713 (Man. C.A.), the court considered whether s. 19(2) could be relied on to impute income where capital cost allowance had been taken for business expenses. The court held that the husband could not deduct from his trucking revenue all of his capital cost allowance or the amortized payment as defined by the motions court judge, especially taking into account the husband's lack of financial disclosure. The court imputed into income from his trucking business 75 percent of the amount claimed as an amortized payment or capital cost allowance.

In *Cavanaugh v. Ziegler* (1999), 43 R.F.L. (4th) 40, 228 A.R. 283, 188 W.A.C. 283 (C.A.); additional reasons at (1999), 237 A.R. 396, 197 W.A.C. 396 (C.A.), the court upheld the trial judge's ruling which imputed income of $27,000 to the father. The court applied the *Federal Child Support Guidelines* even though the parties were unmarried. The trial judge indicated his overall dissatisfaction with the financial picture presented by the father at trial. The father had farming income and the appellate court was of the opinion that deductions relating to farming have received extensive treatment in the case law, specifically in relation to the question of whether to impute income. Inventory elections and capital cost allowance on equipment in particular have often been found to be unreasonable deductions for the purposes of s. 19 of the *Guidelines*.

In *Jang v. Jang*, 17 R.F.L. (5th) 370, 2001 CarswellAlta 555, 2001 ABQB 351, 300 A.R. 387 (Q.B.), the court increased the child support payable by the husband after varying upward the income imputed to the husband from the parties' motel business. The husband had improperly deducted in total his legal, car and travel expenses from the motel profile and the fact that he enjoyed "free" room and board also had to be considered.

In *Hill v. Ilnicki* (2000), 13 R.F.L. (5th) 73, 273 A.R. 131, 2000 CarswellAlta 1153, [2000] A.J. No. 1219 (Alta. Q.B.), the father had an additional $7,500 imputed to his income for *Guidelines* purposes. The father had deducted $15,000 from his income in relation to research work purportedly subcontracted out to his common law spouse. The payment was deemed excessive.

Where the lawyer father made large deductions from his professional fees for travel, meals and entertainment and also paid his new wife $40,000 annually for doing very litle work, income was imputed to the father for *Guidelines* purposes, negating a significant amount of the questionable deductions: *Brans v. Brans* (2000), 13 R.F.L. (5th) 335, 2000 CarswellOnt 4897 (Ont. S.C.J.); additional reasons at (2001), 2001 CarswellOnt 1096 (Ont. S.C.J.).

In *Morley v. Morley* (1999), 44 R.F.L. (4th) 442 (Sask. Q.B.), the court also considered whether a portion of the capital cost allowance deducted by the corporation should be included in the respondent's income and found that it should not. The court followed the reasons in *Beeching v. Beeching* (1998), 169 Sask. R. 18 (Q.B.) which provides as follows:

> Section 19(1)(g) of the *Guidelines* which permits the court to impute income where expenses are unreasonably deducted makes specific reference to the spouse only. If the court has the ability to adjust the corporation's income for capital cost allowance, it must be derived from the court's entitlement to include "all or part of the pre-tax income of the corporation" as set out in s. 18(1)(a).

In *Sackney v. Ficko* (1999), 182 Sask. R. 299, 1999 CarswellSask 27 (Q.B.), the applicant sought interim child support for two children of a common law relationship with the respondent and for a third child of a former relationship to whom the respondent stood *in loco parentis*. The respondent worked full-time as a welder at a potash mine and the parties also operated a sole proprietorship in which they maintained a greenhouse and raised pheasants and peacocks. The respondent declared all the income and expenses from the business in his tax returns, even though the applicant retained the income from the business. There was a loss for each year of the operation of the business but the respondent was limited to a deduction of restricted farm losses as determined under s. 31 of the *Income Tax Act*, since farming was not the respondent's chief source of business.

The court was of the opinion that while the reasonableness of a deduction is not solely governed by whether it is permissible under the *Income Tax Act*, it is of some assistance to understand the criteria which the tax department uses to determine whether a business is being operated with a reasonable expectation of profit. The court considered that in the *Sackney v. Ficko* case that there appeared to be a genuine attempt to earn a profit from the business. While there were substantial expenses incurred, the parties were attempting to establish the business and the gross income increased steadily. The court held that the business might in the long term be successful and that the losses sustained to date did not constitute an unreasonable deduction.

On an interim child support application, no part of the father's capital cost allowance claims should be added to his income pursuant to s. 19 and particularly s. 19(2) of the *Guidelines* having regard to the actual capital expenditures undertaken in comparison to the allowances claimed: *Doege v. Doege* (1998), 37 R.F.L. (4th) 52, 162 Sask. R. 145 (Q.B.).

The court in *Kyle v. Kyle* (1998), 37 R.F.L. (4th) 286, 164 Sask. R. 52 (Q.B.); additional reasons at (1998), 169 Sask. R. 111 (Q.B.), rejected the mother's argument that the father, an oil field worker, was unreasonably deducting expenses from income by deducting the entire amount of his living allowance of $21,840 per annum to compensate him for travel, meals and accommodation in the course of his employment while working in Alberta. The mother had argued that the father should only be able to deduct one-half of the living allowance. The court ruled that the father met the requirements of s. 6(6) of the *Income Tax Act* which permits certain specified benefits relating to special work sites or remote work locations to be excluded from income. The court was of the opinion that considering the distances involved and the fact that the allowance covered all expenditures for hotel, meals and travel, the court was not prepared, in the absence of specific proof, to deem the deduction of the entire amount of the living allowance unreasonable.

Where the husband practiced medicine exclusively in the United States, for the purposes of calculating his income under the *Federal Child Support Guidelines*, he was not permitted to deduct his Saskatchewan licencing and malpractice insurance costs: *Marshall v. McNeil*, 36 R.F.L. (4th) 264, (sub nom. *McNeil v. McNeil)* 164 Sask. R. 91 (Q.B.).

Even though s. 11 of Schedule 111 requires that allowable capital cost allowance with respect to real property be added back into income, this does not mean that all or a portion of capital cost allowance claimed on non-real property must be added back into income: *Wilson v. Wilson*, 165 Sask. R. 241, [1998] 8 W.W.R. 493 (Q.B.). Section 19(1)(g) of the *Guidelines* specifically provides expenses deducted for income tax purposes may be added back into income when: "The spouse unreasonably deducts expenses from income." Reasonableness of an expense deduction is not solely governed by whether the deduction is permitted under the *Income Tax Act*: s. 19(2). For child support purposes, the issue is whether or not the full deduction, as permitted by the *Income Tax Act*, provides a fair recognition of the actual income that is available to the spouse from that income source. In the *Wilson* decision, the court was of the opinion that one-half of the capital cost allowance claimed on property other than real property should be added back into income. In addition, the court added back into income the proceeds of cattle sales in 1997 which the payor was not required to report on his 1997 tax return.

In *Dunham v. Dunham* (November 18, 1998), Doc. D3234.96 (Ont. Gen. Div.), the court, in deciding what should be deducted from the husband's bus company's revenues when determining the husband's income for support purposes, held that a rental loss should not be included, as the property was unnecessary for the operation of the business. Further, gas and oil for recreational vehicles and payments of $1,250 monthly to the wife as a dividend to redeem her shares in the company should also not be included, the latter as the payments were a form of capital acquisition for the husband, whereby he became the sole owner of the bus line.

In *Sackney v. Ficko* (1999), 182 Sask. R. 299 (Q.B.), the applicant sought interim child support for two children of a common-law relationship with the respondent and for a third child of a former relationship to whom the respondent stood *in loco parentis*. The respondent worked full-time as a welder at a potash mine and the parties also operated a sole proprietorship in which they maintained a greenhouse and raised pheasants and peacocks. The respondent declared all the income and expenses from the business in his tax returns, even though the applicant retained the income from the business. There was a loss for each year of the operation of the business, but the respondent was limited to a deduction of restricted farm losses as determined under s. 31 of the *Income Tax Act*, since farming was not the respondent's chief source of business.

The court was of the opinion that while the reasonableness of a deduction is not solely governed by whether it is permissible under the *Income Tax Act*, it is of some assistance to understand the criteria which the tax department uses to determine whether a business is being operated with a reasonable expectation of profit. The court considered that in the *Sackney v. Ficko* case that there appeared to be a genuine attempt to earn a profit from the business. While there were substantial expenses incurred, the parties were attempting to establish the business and the gross income increased steadily. The court held that the business might in the long term be successful and that the losses sustained to date did not constitute an unreasonable deduction.

Where the father's deduction of all of his capital cost allowance on personal property resulted in the understatement of his income from which he could pay child support, 15 percent of that capital cost allowance was imputed to him as income under s. 19 of the *Guidelines*: *Seiferling v. Langmaier* (1998), 36 R.F.L. (4th) 296 (Sask. Q.B.).

In *Needham v. Needham* (1998), 36 R.F.L. (4th) 395 (B.C. S.C.), the court refused the husband's appeal from a child support order. The Master had imputed an annual income of $75,000 to the husband although his tax return showed only $40,000. Although the deductions reducing the husband's income may have been allowed for income tax purposes, they were not found to be reasonable under the *Federal Child Support Guidelines*.

Where the husband practiced medicine exclusively in the United States, for the purposes of calculating his income under the *Federal Child Support Guidelines*, he was not permitted to deduct his Saskatchewan licencing and malpractice insurance costs: *Marshall v. McNeil* (1998), 36 R.F.L. (4th) 264, 164 Sask. R. 91 (Q.B.).

In *Shaw v. Shaw* (1997), 120 Man. R. (2d) 310, [1998] 3 C.T.C. 202 (Man. Q.B.), the court, under s. 19, included $24,257.94 in the father's income for *Guidelines* purposes which he had claimed as a cost allowance for farm machinery. The court was of the opinion that this amount might not be an actual expense in the year claimed.

The court in *Wedge v. McKenna* (1997), 155 Nfld. & P.E.I.R. 294, 481 A.P.R. 294 (P.E.I. T.D.), dismissed the mother's application for variation of child support. She had argued that the court should impute income to the father but the court was of the opinion that changes in his income did not materially affect his ability to pay support. The father was entitled to deduct expenses incurred to produce rental income. The father's proportionate share of his law firm's payment toward long-term debt should not be added back into his income, and his proportionate share of the firm's capital cost allowance, a non-cash item, should not be deducted from his share of the expenses. These practices were consistent with the financial evidence, particularly the law firm's financial statements, generally accepted accounting principles, and business reality. Long-term debt is not an income and expense item. Capital cost allowance is a real and allowable expense which addresses amortization of the firm's assets.

Imputing Income — Income from dividends, capital gains or other sources taxed at a lower rate — s. 19(1)(h)

"Pursuant to s. 5 of Schedule III, the taxable amount of dividends from taxable Canadian corporations is to be replaced by the actual amount of dividends received. This is achieved by multiplying the taxable amount of dividends as reported on line 120 of the tax return by 4/5. Section 6 of Schedule III requires that taxable capital gains realized in a year be replaced by the actual amount of capital gains realized in excess of capital losses. Taxable capital gains are multiplied by 4/3 to determine the actual amount of capital gains realized": *Johnson v. Checkowy* (1997), 157 Sask. R. 71 (Q.B.).

In *Pitt v. Pitt* (June 23, 1997), Doc. Victoria 1591/97 (B.C. S.C.); additional reasons at (August 20, 1997), Doc. Victoria 1591/97 (B.C. S.C.), the mother contended that the court should impute an income of 12 percent of the $100,000 that the father held in mutual funds. The 12 percent was based on the historical growth of the fund, and would add $12,000 a year to the father's income. At the time of the hearing, he did not derive any income from these savings. They were invested in stocks with only the possibility of a future gain, and the possibility of a future loss. The court declined to impute an income from the mutual funds, finding that it would be "artificial in the extreme to ascribe the character of income to the possibility of a future capital gain."

Where the father wound down his own independent electrical contracting company and went to work for someone else at a much lower salary, income was imputed to him for *Guidelines* purposes. There was no reason justifying the abandonment of his very successful business and, accordingly, the father was found to be intentionally underemployed: *Reil v. Holland* (2003), 42 R.F.L. (5th) 120, 2003 CarswellOnt 3828, 232 D.L.R. (4th) 265, 177 O.A.C. 162 (Ont. C.A.).

Where possible income from the husband's inheritance from his mother was not known at the time of trial nor at the time of the subsequent appeal it was improper to impute any income to him on that basis: *O. (E.M.) v. O. (W.R.)* (2003), 37 R.F.L. (5th) 401, 2003 CarswellBC 660, 2003 BCCA 191, 181 B.C.A.C. 49, 298 W.A.C. 49 (B.C. C.A.)

Imputing Income — General

In *Sanders v. Sanders* (1998), 42 R.F.L. (4th) 239 (Alta. C.A.), the court imputed an income of $96,500 per year to the payor/father, which was the average of what he stated he made and the amount shown by the corporate records. The father, a veterinarian, had claimed that his income had dropped to $38,037 in 1996 and was $7,200 for the first half of 1997. However, on a brokerage form, he had stated his income to be $100,00 and he had given no valid reason for any drop in his income.

The father was ordered to pay $1,254 each month for 2 children and pursuant to s. 6 of the *Guidelines*, to provide Alberta Health Care for the children by including them under his registration, which gave them extended medical benefits insurance, optometric services, and dental insurance.

An appeal from an order made increasing the amount of child support payable was dismissed in *Benvie v. Mills* (1997), 34 R.F.L. (4th) 313, 163 N.S.R. (2d) 238, 487 A.P.R. 238 (C.A.). The Court of Appeal found that while the trial judge had imputed a greater amount of income to the appellant than that disclosed in his income tax return, the compromise figure of $25,000 was not reasonable as there was evidence before the trial judge supporting a much higher figure which could have been reached.

The court in *MacDonald v. MacDonald* (1997), 57 Alta. L.R. (3d) 195, 209 A.R. 178, 160 W.A.C. 178, [1998] 6 W.W.R. 86 (C.A.); additional reasons at (1998), 40 R.F.L. (4th) 397, 216 A.R. 340, 175 W.A.C. 340, [1999] 2 W.W.R. 277, 64 Alta. L.R. (3d) 125 (C.A.); leave to appeal refused (1998), 227 N.R. 399 (note) (S.C.C.), held that a bonus of $20,000, a severance package, and an employee stock option should be deemed to be income. The court was of the opinion that all these items increased the payor's ability to pay child support. Bonuses, severance monies, and taxable capital gains from the disposition of employee stock options are items which are considered income on a tax return. While the bonus was discretionary, the payor had received bonuses in the past, and there was an expectation that the bonus would be paid and it was therefore in some way a predictable form of compensation. The court was of the opinion that the severance package was an acceleration of income which would have been earned by the payor over the termination period. The stock options were paid on a regular and consistent basis. Monies received from the disposition of stock options in the form of taxable capital gains should be considered income.

In *Penner v. Penner* (1997), 38 R.F.L. (4th) 25, 212 A.R. 217, 168 W.A.C. 217 (C.A.), before Conrad, Medhurst, Veit JJ. (ad hoc), the court heard an appeal from an interlocutory maintenance order for spousal and child maintenance. The husband owned some land, which he farmed, and he rented other property. He also assisted in his own father's farming operation. Income of the father, the non-custodial parent, varied from year to year. The court found it extremely difficult to assess the father's income accurately for the purpose of establishing child support under the *Federal Child Support Guidelines*. The court was satisfied that in looking at the income tax returns and supporting documents for two years and considering the only evidence relating to the current year, it was necessary to select an arbitrary figure and chose $35,000. The court directed that the *Child Support Guidelines* be applied assuming that level of income.

In *Andries v. Andries* (1997), 119 Man. R. (2d) 224 (Q.B.); varied on other grounds (1998), 36 R.F.L. (4th) 175, 159 D.L.R. (4th) 665, 126 Man. R. (2d) 189, 167 W.A.C. 189, [1998] 7 W.W.R. 536 (C.A.), the payor husband was a long-time employee of Manitoba Hydro and had worked overtime in every year he had been there. Lately, the opportunities for overtime had increased. The husband argued, however, that since his overtime hours were not guaranteed to him in any particular year, overtime payments should not be included in his income for *Guidelines* purposes. The court rejected this argument and found that his income for these purposes was his income in the previous year which included payments for overtime hours.

In *Mylrea v. Benoit* (2003), 42 R.F.L. (5th) 82, 2003 CarswellOnt 2760 (Ont. S.C.J.), an additional $500 was imputed to the husband's income to reflect the fact that his business absorbed most of his transportation costs.

In *Fantin v. Fantin* (2003), 37 R.F.L. (5th) 327, 2003 CarswellOnt 1294 (Ont. S.C.J.); additional reasons at (2003), 2003 CarswellOnt 2070 (Ont. S.C.J.), income was imputed to the father for *Guidelines* purposes to reflect the fact that his company paid his gas, car maintenance and car insurance.

Where it was virtually impossible, because of the complexity of the husband's financial dealings, to determine his income accurately, an annual income of $350,000 was imputed to him for child support purposes: *Laxton v. Coglon*, 37 R.F.L. (5th) 156, 2003 CarswellBC 12, 2003 BCSC 11 (B.C. S.C.).

In *Jefferson v. Jefferson*, 26 R.F.L. (5th) 129, 2002 CarswellBC 298, 2002 BCSC 151 (S.C.), quantum of the truck payments made by the father's company on his behalf were imputed to him as income for *Guidelines* purposes.

Where the husband had been unemployed for 17 months but was caring for his elderly father, the court refused to impute income to him for the purposes of the *Federal Child Support Guidelines*. Imputing income would likely only have the effect of penalizing the husband's father. The preferable approach was to wait for the husband to start earning income and then review the issue of support: *Chown v. Chown* (1999), 50 R.F.L. (4th) 335, 214 N.B.R. (2d) 98, 547 A.P.R. 98 (Q.B.).

In a situation where the court would be justified in arbitrarily deeming income under s. 19(1)(e) of the *Federal Child Support Guidelines*, the preferable route is to deem the income that the father's own accountants consider appropriate in the circumstances: *Dean v. Friesen* (1999), 50 R.F.L. (4th) 363, 185 Sask. R. 208, 1999 CarswellSask 428, [1999] S.J. No. 424 (Q.B.).

In *Maynard v. Maynard*, 45 R.F.L. (4th) 395, 1999 CarswellBC 333, [1999] B.C.J. No. 325 (S.C.), it was held on appeal that the failure by the Master to impute income to the wife, under the *Federal Child Support Guidelines*, in relation to a student loan received by her, was not a "clearly wrong" decision which required reversal. On matters involving an exercise of discretion, as did the imputing of income, an appellate court can only intervene upon proof that the Master was "clearly wrong."

In *Lobo v. Lobo* (1999), 45 R.F.L. (4th) 366, 240 A.R. 257, 1999 CarswellAlta 114, [1999] A.J. No. 113 (Q.B.), the court imputed income to the husband for the purposes of the *Federal Child Support Guidelines*. The husband was trained as an architect and was self-employed as he found that situation allowed him the greatest creative freedom. However, as a result, he was not earning income commensurate with his education ability and experience and had placed the expression of his creativity before the interests of his children.

Where the father's lifestyle could not possibly be supported on his reported annual income of $17,314, an income of $40,000 was imputed to him in *Stamp v. McIntosh* (1998), 49 R.F.L. (4th) 416, 221 A.R. 133, 1998 CarswellAlta 1296, [1998] A.J. No. 429

(Q.B.); reconsideration refused (1998), 225 A.R. 76, 1998 CarswellAlta 1309, [1998] A.J. No. 706 (Q.B.).

Where an employer has provided subsidized accommodation for a spouse, it may be treated as additional or imputed income of the beneficiary, but where, as in this case, there is no evidence as to the cost if the spouse rented such accommodation, the evidentiary base has not been established and no amount would be imputed to the spouse for the accommodation: *Adler v. Jonas* (1999), 48 R.F.L. (4th) 228 (B.C. S.C.). The mother was provided with rent free accommodation while she taught in Korea but was required to pay an "apartment management fee" equal to $81 (Canadian) per month and $6 (Canadian) for the cost of heating.

When imputing income for a child support order in the case of a parent resident in a foreign country, the court must adjust income from the other jurisdiction by considering exchange rates and different income tax rates: *R. (E.K.) v. W. (G.A.)* (1997), 32 R.F.L. (4th) 202, [1998] 3 W.W.R. 554, 122 Man. R. (2d) 120 (Q.B.); additional reasons at (1998), 124 Man. R. (2d) 258 (Q.B.).

Where the father's average annual income was $130,000 but he was suffering from a reactive depression which was expected to improve once the litigation had been completed, the court imputed an annual income of $104,000 to take into account his reduced workload and determined child support based on that income: *Josdal v. Josdal* (1997), 157 Sask. R. 135 (Q.B.).

In *D. (L.M.) v. D. (G.S.)* (June 24, 1997), Doc. Battleford Q.B. 3319/95 (Sask. Q.B.), the husband was a truck driver. Because he was so troubled by the breakdown of his marriage he had "thrown himself into his work" and derived much of his income from working extra days. The court held that it "would be unfair to determine an annual income on the basis that someone is working extra hours at a particular stage of his life" and imputed a lower annual income.

Where the wife, a trained chartered accountant, had been out of the workforce for some years and her return could be impeded by ongoing health problems, it was necessary to impute income to her for determination of her child support contribution under the *Federal Child Support Guidelines*. Given the $2,000,000 property settlement to which she was entitled, half of which could be used to produce income and the likelihood that she would be capable of some remunerative work, an annual income of $75,000 was imputed: *Forzley v. Forzley* (1997), 34 R.F.L. (4th) 105 (B.C. S.C.); additional reasons at (March 20, 1998), Doc. Vancouver D100167 (B.C. S.C.).

The fact that the father owned several vehicles was sufficient grounds upon which to conclude that his lifestyle exceeded his stated income. The father produced evidence proving that the total value of the vehicles was only $11,000. Accordingly, no additional income was imputed to him for *Guidelines* purposes: *Tapper v. Connolly* (2002), 26 R.F.L. (5th) 199, 2002 CarswellNfld 81, [2002] N.J. No. 83 (U.F.C.).

In assessing a parent's ability to pay child support under s. 15(8) of the *Divorce Act*, the court should consider not only the parents' incomes but also their assets, their ability to earn income, and their future incomes and assets. A person's income is what he or she can generate by personal effort and the prudent use of existing assets. In assessing ability to contribute, the judge should first assess each parent's income–earning ability. Ability to pay should be based on gross income: *Levesque v. Levesque* (1994), 4 R.F.L. (4th) 375 (Alta. C.A.); additional reasons (1995), 165 A.R. 319 (Alta. C.A.); reversing (1991), 38 R.F.L. (3d) 273 (Alta. Q.B.).

15§106 — Calculating income for purposes of determining child support — income of non-resident

> 20. Where a spouse is a non-resident of Canada, the spouse's annual income is determined as though the spouse were a resident of Canada.

See *Pakka v. Nygard* (2002), 61 O.R. (3d) 328, 2002 CarswellOnt 3403, [2002] O.J. No. 3858 (Ont. S.C.J.), where the payor was resident in the Bahamas and the child in question lived in Ontario. For Canadian tax purposes, a portion of the payor's income was taxed in Canada, so assumptions were made to which resulted in imputing income to the payor under ss. 19(1)(c), 19(1)(h) and 20 of the *Child Support Guidelines*.

In *Ward v. Ward*, 19 R.F.L. (5th) 232, 2001 CarswellBC 1550, [2001] B.C.J. No. 1206, 2001 BCSC 847 (B.C. S.C.), the mother lived and worked in the United States. To determine her income for *Guidelines* purposes, the court used a rate of exchange based upon the average rate for the preceding year. This approach was consistent with the general approach in determining income under the *Guidelines* and could avoid variation applications when frequent fluctuations in the exchange rate occurred.

When imputing income for a child support order in the case of a parent resident in a foreign country, the court must adjust income from the foreign jurisdiction by considering exchange rates and different income tax rates: *R. v. (E.K.) v. W. (G.A.)* (1997), 32 R.F.L. (4th) 202, [1998] 3 W.W.R. 534, 122 Man. R. (2d) 120 (Q.B.); additional reasons at (1998), 124 Man. R. (2d) 258 (Q.B.).

Where the father lived in the United States and had failed to file an income statement, the court imputed income to him for purposes of the *Federal Child Support Guidelines*. As a basis the court used the husband's 1993 American income tax return and utilized the current exchange rate to translate his income into Canadian dollars: *Garrison v. Garrison* (1998), 38 R.F.L. (4th) 435 (Ont. Gen. Div.).

15§107 — Child support — relation to spousal support

Where applications are made for both child and spousal support, the court must give priority to the application for child support. If, by giving this priority, a spousal support order cannot be made, or is made in an amount that is less than it otherwise would have been, a procedural requirement and a substantive right follows.

The procedural requirement is that the court must record reasons for its disposition of the application for spousal support.

The substantive right is that any subsequent reduction or termination of child support constitutes a change of circumstances for the purposes of applying for a spousal support order, or a variation order in respect of the spousal support order, as the case may be. See *Divorce Act*, s. 15.3(1), (2) and (3).

15§108 — Duty to disclose financial circumstances

The guidelines not only reinforce the obligation to disclose financial information, but go further to identify the specific documents which should be produced to discharge this obligation.

In an application for child support, or for the variation of a child support order, each party for whom income is to be determined is to produce: (1) Copies of the spouse's personal income tax returns for each of the previous three years. (2) Copies of the notice of assessment or re-assessment for each of the three years. (3) For an employed spouse, the most recent statement of earnings indicating the total earnings paid in the year to date, including overtime or, where such a statement is not provided by the employer, a letter from the spouse's employer setting out that information including the spouse's rate of annual salary or remuneration. (4) For a self-employed spouse, for the three most recent taxation years, financial statements of his or her business or professional practice, other than a partnership, and a statement showing a breakdown of all salaries, wages, management fees or other payments or benefits paid to, or on behalf of, persons or corporations with whom the spouse does not deal at arm's length. (5) For a spouse who is a partner, confirmation of the spouse's income and draw from, and capital in, the partnership for its three most recent taxation years. (6) For a spouse who controls a corporation, for its three most recent taxation years the financial statements of the corporation and its subsidiaries, and a statement showing a breakdown of all salaries, wages, management fees or other payments or benefits paid to, or on behalf of, persons or corporations with whom the spouse does not deal at arm's length. (7) Where a spouse is a beneficiary under a trust, a copy of the trust settlement agreement and copies of the trust's three most recent financial statements: *Federal Child Support Guidelines*, s. 21(1)(a) to (g) and s. 21(2).

The obligations of the respondent, who is served with an application for a child support order or a variation order and whose income information is necessary to determine the amount of the order, has a certain time after the application is served in which to produce the information and documents listed above. The time after service of the support application in which the respondent must produce the information and documents is 30 days if he or she lives in Canada or the United States, and 60 days if he or she lives elsewhere: *Federal Child Support Guidelines*, s. 19(2).

Where there is a request for special expenses (see discussion under Special or Extraordinary Expenses, below) or a pleading of undue hardship (see discussion under Undue Hardship, below) the spouse who would be receiving the amount of child support as well as the payor spouse, must produce the documentation listed above. If the recipient spouse resides in Canada or the United States, the production must be within 30 days after the expenses are sought or the hardship is pleaded, and if he or she resides elsewhere the period is 60 days: *Federal Child Support Guidelines*, s. 21(3).

If, in an application for child support or the variation of child support order, the spouse who would be making child support payments has income that is greater than $150,000, the other spouse has 30 days if resident in Canada or the United States, and 60 days if resident elsewhere, to produce the documents listed above: *Federal Child Support Guidelines*, s. 21(4).

Where a spouse fails to produce income information, the other spouse may (a) apply to have the application for a child support or a variation order in respect of a child support order set down for a hearing or move for judgment; or (b) apply for an order requiring the spouse who failed to comply with the obligation to provide the court with the documents: *Federal Child Support Guidelines*, s. 22.

Pursuant to section 22, an adverse inference can be drawn by the court against the spouse who failed to provide income information.

Where a spouse fails to comply with an order to provide the court with income information documents, the court may (a) strike out any of the spouse's pleadings; (b) make a contempt order against the spouse; (c) proceed to a hearing, draw an adverse inference against the spouse and impute income to that spouse in such amount as the court considers appropriate; and (d) award costs in favour of the other spouse up to an amount that fully compensates the other spouse for all costs and disbursements incurred in the proceedings.

Section 25(1) initiates the greatest change in practice. This is a requirement for continuing disclosure of income information. On request, no more than once a year, every spouse against whom a child support order has been made must produce the income information documents, listed above, for any of the previous three taxation years for which they have not been produced. This same annual requirement, on request, applies as well to a spouse who is excused from paying support because of his or her low income level: *Federal Child Support Guidelines*, s. 25(2).

Where income information of the receiving spouse is used to determine any part of the support amount, he or she is under the same obligation as the payor spouse to provide income documents and information on a continuing basis no more than once a year at the request of the payor: *Federal Child Support Guidelines*, s. 25(3).

Where a spouse or the order assignee of the spouse requests income information and documents from the other spouse, and the income information of that spouse is used to determine the amount of child support, that spouse or assignee must include the request the documents and information referred to in s. 25(1): *Federal Child Support Guidelines*, s. 25(4) as amended.

Where a child support order is made against a spouse whose income is over $150,000, the payee spouse shall, not more than once a year after the order was made, on request of the payor spouse, provide the payor spouse with the income information documents, listed above, in respect of any of the previous three taxation years for which the spouse has not previously provided the documents: *Federal Child Support Guidelines*, s. 21(4).

Where either spouse fails to comply with the continuing obligation to provide income information as required under section 25(1) to (3), the court may deal with the non-compliance as a contempt of court, and the other spouse may be entitled to the payment of costs up to an amount that fully compensates the applicant for all costs and disbursements incurred in the proceedings: *Federal Child Support Guidelines*, s. 25(7).

A provision in an agreement, judgment or order purporting to limit a spouse's obligation to provide documents pursuant to section 25 is unenforceable: *Federal Child Support Guidelines*, s. 25(8).

Where, for *Guidelines* purposes, the father had unintentionally misled the court concerning his income, the wife successfully appealed the child support order. The husband could not be allowed to benefit from honest ignorance concerning his financial situation where the effect was to penalize the children: *Tedham v. Tedham*, 44 R.F.L. (5th) 204, 2003 CarswellBC 2742, 2003 BCCA 600, 20 B.C.L.R. (4th) 56, 188 B.C.A.C. 297, 308 W.A.C. 297 (B.C. C.A.); additional reasons at 2004 CarswellBC 377, 2004 BCCA 101 (B.C. C.A.).

Where the husband failed to provide additional financial information in the context of the wife's uncontested divorce, his appeal from the resulting child support order was dismissed. The court had accepted the wife's evidence that the husband's actual income exceeded that claimed and had ordered child support accordingly. The appeal court refused to admit as fresh evidence the financial information that the husband had failed to provide when earlier requested. The appeal was not an opportunity for a second trial and to admit such evidence now would condone the husband's disregard of his legal obligation to provide information at the trial stage: *MacKenzie v. MacKenzie*, 47 R.F.L. (5th)

104, 2003 CarswellNS 391, 2003 NSCA 120, 218 N.S.R. (2d) 306, 687 A.P.R. 306 (N.S. C.A.).

Where an agreement contemplates a variation in child and spousal support in the event of a material increase in a party's income, there is an implied duty on the party to disclose that increase at the time it is received. Failure to make the disclosure is a ground for making the variation retroactive to the time of the increase: *Marinangeli v. Marinangeli* (2003), 2003 CarswellOnt 2691, [2003] O.J. No. 2819, 38 R.F.L. (5th) 307, 174 O.A.C. 76, 228 D.L.R. (4th) 376 (Ont. C.A.). Where, in minutes of settlement, there is a clear intention that spousal and child support could be varied if there were a material changes in the circumstances of the parties, and a material change does occur, the party whose circumstances have changed has an implicit obligation to disclose to the other party an increase or decrease in income at least during the period before the other party would first have access to the income tax returns of the party whose circumstances have changed. The trial judge did not err in finding that the husband had an implicit duty to disclose to the wife changes in his financial circumstances. In this case, the payor spouse's representations and the almost immediate improvement in the payor's finances were the factual basis upon which to ground such a duty. The appellant had an implicit obligation to disclose his change in circumstances so as to give business efficacy to the agreement. It was reasonable and equitable to imply a term relating to disclosure. The implication of the implied term was capable of clear expression and was not contrary to any express term in the agreement. Thus, the implication by the trial judge of a term relating to disclosure met the requirements for implying a term in an agreement on ordinary contract principles. See 15§155B Non-disclosure, for a detailed discussion of the case.

The fact that the mother waived the father's obligation for financial disclosure in the parties' separation agreement did not relieve him from the mandatory disclosure obligation contained in the *Guidelines*: *Quinn v. Keiper* (2005), 23 R.F.L. (6th) 226, 2005 CarswellOnt 6764 (Ont. S.C.J.).

The Court has no jurisdiction to grant relief from the financial disclosure requirements under the *Guidelines*: *Mylrea v. Benoit* (2003), 42 R.F.L. (5th) 82, 2003 CarswellOnt 2760 (Ont. S.C.J.).

In *Murray v. Murrray* (2003), 2003 CarswellOnt 3258 (Ont. S.C.J.); additional reasons at (2003), 2003 CarswellOnt 3862 (Ont. S.C.J.), the parties entered into a separation agreement which included a release of spousal support and provided for a lump sum payment for child support. A provision in the agreement stated that if the husband's income increased by a material amount, the husband's obligation for child support could be recalculated. Although there was a material change in the husband's income, he took no steps to recalculate his child support. The wife applied to have the agreement set aside. The court held that the provision imposed a positive obligation on the husband to inform the wife of the material change in his income and to recalculate his child support obligations. The wife's spousal support was contingent on the husband meeting his child support obligations, including disclosure of changes in his income. The court set aside the spousal release in the agreement. The wife did not seek an award of child support as all the children had moved in with their father, but instead, sought spousal support. In light of the overall objectives of the *Divorce Act*, including the fair and equitable sharing of the economic consequences of the marriage and its breakdown, the court found the wife entitled to lump sum spousal support, in the amount of $233, 911 retroactive to the date of separation, together with pre-judgement interest and periodic support for an indefinite period.

Any attempt to limit financial disclosure by agreement is unenforceable under the *Guidelines*: *Leinburd v. Leinburd*, 49 R.F.L. (5th) 102, 2003 CarswellMan 510, 2003 MBQB 283, 179 Man. R. (2d) 232 (Man. Q.B.).

There is no jurisdiction under the *Guidelines* to order financial disclosure from anyone other than a parent. Although a parent's common law spouse cannot be ordered to disclose its financial situation, that parent runs the risk of having income imputed to him or her as a result: *Cecotka v. Cecotka* (2001), 13 R.F.L. (5th) 358, 2001 ABQB 3, 2001 CarswellAlta 21 (Alta. Q.B.).

Where the mother had failed to provide the financial disclosure required under the *Guidelines*, the court rejected her claim for extraordinary expenses relating to the child's recreational expenses: *Ordano v. Moore* (2003), 39 R.F.L. (5th) 361, 2003 CarswellAlta 576, 2003 ABQB 362 (Alta. Q.B.).

Under the *Federal Child Support Guidelines*, there is no provision compelling disclosure of financial information by a new spouse of one of the litigants. Over-all family means only come into play if an "undue hardship" application is brought: *Desjardins v. Desjardins* (1999), 49 R.F.L. (4th) 242 (B.C. Master).

Where, in child support proceedings, the husband failed to produce satisfactory evidence of his income, the court was entitled to draw an adverse inference that his income was equal to that of the wife: *Almeida v. Almeida* (1995), 11 R.F.L. (4th) 131, 166 A.R. 248 (Q.B.).

A motion to vary an existing support order, in this case a child support order, must be filed before a notice to disclose can be issued: *Rosin v. Rosin* (1994), 7 R.F.L. (4th) 402 (Alta. Q.B.). On the facts of the case, it would be an abuse of process to hear the motion to disclose financial information before the Court of Appeal has issued its decision on the trial decision awarding spousal support. The motion was adjourned. In supplementary reasons to this judgment, reported at (1994), 8 R.F.L. (4th) 315 (Alta. Q.B.), the court was of the opinion that a litigant who has filed a notice of motion to vary child or spousal support does not have to establish a prima facie entitlement to a variation before being authorized to issue a notice to disclose.

A failure to inform the payor spouse of a child's receipt of substantial benefits as the result of an accident is a clear violation of the obligation to provide continuing disclosure pursuant to the Rules of Civil Procedure: *Hansen v. Hansen* (1995), 13 R.F.L. (4th) 335 (Ont. Gen. Div.), before Fleury J.

Where the former wife received too much in child support, because of her failure to disclose that one of the parties' children no longer attended school and that the child was receiving benefits as a result of a personal injury, she was ordered to reimburse the Ontario Family Support Plan for its overpayments to her: *Hansen v. Hansen* (1995), 13 R.F.L. (4th) 335 (Ont. Gen. Div.), before Fleury J. The court ordered that if repayment was not made in a lump sum within 30 days, all support payments would be temporarily suspended, until the payor recovered the amount of overpayment.

Where the father supplied incomplete and unreliable financial information to the court in the context of the wife's claim for child support, the court drew on adverse inference against him and calculated his income at a level above his proven income: *Plowman v. Plowman* (1995), 16 R.F.L. (4th) 82 (Ont. Gen. Div.).

Where a party in receipt of child support failed to provide information about his or her child's attendance at educational institutions, such conduct is unconscionable and cost consequences should follow the event: *Hansen v. Hansen* (1995), 13 R.F.L. (4th) 335 (Ont. Gen. Div.), before Fleury J.

15§109 — Death of the payor or payee

See 15§145 Support obligation binding against estate of deceased payor, below.

15§110 — Tax consequences of agreement or order

The May 1997 amendments made a fundamental change in the taxation of child support. They eliminated the "deduction/inclusion" rule from the calculation of income tax for child support (but not spousal support) so that child support paid under orders or agreements made after April 1997 is no longer taxable in the hands of the payee, nor deductible in the hands of the payor. (A limited exemption is made with respect to prior payments. See 15§116 Income tax considerations — prior payments where no variation and 15§117 Income tax considerations — prior payments with variation, below.)

The Supreme Court of Canada in the case of *Thibaudeau v. Thibaudeau, (*sub nom. *R. v. Thibaudeau)* 12 R.F.L. (4th) 1, [1995] 1 C.T.C. 382, 124 D.L.R. (4th) 449, 29 C.R.R. (2d) 1, 182 N.R. 1, [1995] 2 S.C.R. 627 by its declaration of the law as it then existed, encouraged the reform that resulted in the 1997 tax amendments and the establishment of the Guidelines. When Ms. Thibaudeau and her former husband Mr. Chainé were divorced in 1987, the divorce judgment contained an order that Mr. Chainé pay maintenance for the two children of the marriage in the amount of $1,150 a month. The inclusion/deduction system created by s. 56(1) and s. 60(b) of the *Income Tax Act* made the maintenance payments received by Ms. Thibaudeau, the custodial parent, subject to tax in her hands. Ms. Thibaudeau appealed her assessment to the Tax Court of Canada, (reported at 92 D.T.C. 2111, [1992] 2 C.T.C. 2497, claiming that she should not be required to pay the tax because the inclusion/deduction system violated her equality rights as guaranteed by subsection 15(1) of the *Charter of Rights and Freedoms*. The Tax Court dismissed her appeal. At the Federal Court of Appeal level, (reported at [1994] 2 F.C. 189, 94 D.T.C. 6230, 2 C.T.C. 4, 167 N.R. 161, 114 D.L.R. (4th) 261, 21 C.R.R. (2d) 35, 3 R.F.L. (4th) 153), Ms. Thibaudeau's application for judicial review was allowed and the Tax Court of Canada's decision set aside. In the Supreme Court of Canada, the majority (5:2) allowed the appeal and held that s. 56(1)(b) of the *Income Tax Act* did not infringe her equality rights. Consequently, custodial parents receiving child support payments pursuant to an order or a written agreement were to continue to include those payments in income for tax purposes. Although Ms. Thibaudeau lost at this final level in the courts, her cause was taken up by Parliament resulting in the 1997 reforms.

15§111 — Income tax considerations — deduction/inclusion rules

The deduction/inclusion rules for income tax were designed to shift the tax burden on support in situations where the payments were made pursuant to a written agreement or a court order and certain other conditions were satisfied. Before May 1997, the deduction/inclusion rules for income tax applied to both spousal and child support. Since that date, the rules continue to apply with respect to spousal support, but only in severely limited circumstances with respect to child support.

The support provisions are divided into two categories under the *Income Tax Act*; receipts (included in income of recipient), and deductions (from income of payor). These provisions are mirror images of each other. A payment that is deductible by the payor is required to be included in income by the recipient.

Prior to May 1997, support payments were deductible from the income of the payor for tax purposes and included in the income of the recipient both for spousal and child support, if the parties were separated, the payments were periodic and made pursuant to an agreement or order.

The deduction/inclusion provisions or rules, still applicable to spousal support, are found in sections 60(b) (deduction) and 56(1)(b) (inclusion) of the *Income Tax Act*. These rules can be used to effect substantial tax savings where there is a significant difference between the marginal rates of the payor and recipient. For example, assume a husband or former husband with a marginal tax rate of 50 percent pays $12,000 in support to his wife. Under the deduction/inclusion rules (where the payment obligation is in an agreement or order), he receives a deduction that is worth $6,000 in tax savings; that is, 50 percent on the $12,000 he would have to pay if the $12,000 were part of his taxable income. This means that the net cost of his support payments is only $6,000. If his wife or former wife has a marginal rate of 20 percent, her tax cost is only $2,400. The gain in savings to the family is the difference in the tax that would be paid; that is, instead of the family (through the husband) paying $6,000 in tax, the family (through the wife) pays only $2,400 for a saving of $6,000 - $2,400 or $3,600.

This example illustrates the tax treatment for support, whether spousal or child support, as it existed before May 1997, and for *spousal* support after April 1997. The tax treatment for child support, generally speaking, has been changed.

15§112 — Income tax considerations — elimination of deduction/inclusion rule for child support

New tax rules affecting the deduction/inclusion rule for child support came into effect on May 1, 1997. In the ordinary case, as of May 1, 1997, child support paid pursuant to a written agreement or court order made on or after that day will *not* be deductible to the payor nor included in the income of the recipient for tax purposes. The two exceptions involve agreements or orders made before May 1997, and prior payments recited in agreements or orders made after April 1997. See 15§114 Income tax considerations — agreements or orders made before May 1997; 15§116 Income tax considerations — prior payments where no variation; and 15§117 Income tax considerations — prior payments with variation, below.

Because spousal support will continue to be included in the income of the recipient and deductible from the income of the payor, child support amounts must be distinguished from any other support amounts that are to be paid.

The distinction between child support and other support amounts, and the conditions which must be met to come within the formulae regulating deductibility, are contained in the definitions "support amount" and "child support amount" in subsection 56.1(4).

The definition of "support amount" sets up the conditions under which payments, whether they be for spousal or child support, qualify for use in the formulae. The payments must be:

- allowances paid on a periodic basis;
- for the maintenance of the recipient or children;
- at the discretionary use of the recipient;

- paid to a spouse or former spouse who is living separate and apart from the payor because of a breakdown of their marriage or paid in respect of a natural child of the payor; and
- paid under an order of a competent tribunal or a written agreement.

Although the amendments to the *Income Tax Act* came into force at the same time as the amendments to the *Divorce Act* and the *Federal Child Support Guidelines*, they are not limited to divorce situations. The tax treatment in its amended form applies to orders of any competent tribunal made in any proceeding whether or not a claim for divorce is involved. A provincial court making a child support order meets the requirements of the formulae provided the other conditions mentioned above are met. Similarly, the written agreement that is required can be any agreement — not only a separation agreement — that creates a legal obligation to pay the support.

A "child support amount" is defined as a support amount that is not identified as being solely for the support of a spouse or former spouse or the parent of the payor's child. Therefore, for example, if a written agreement provides for a global amount of support to be paid in respect of a spouse and child, the amount will be considered, for the purposes of the income tax rules, to be a child support amount.

In *O'Neill v. R.*, 19 R.F.L. (5th) 179, 2001 CarswellNat 1500, [2001] T.C.J. No. 429, [2001] 3 C.T.C. 2644 (T.C.C. [Informal Procedure]), the court disallowed the husband's deduction of child support payments made pursuant to an amendment to an agreement between the parties in January 1998. The parties had been aware of an amendment to the *Income Tax Act* disallowing the deduction of child support paid pursuant to an agreement made or amended after April 1997. The fact that the husband and wife did not intend to modify the tax treatment of the child support payments was irrelevant.

15§113 — Income tax considerations — determining the support amount to be included in income

Where both child and spousal support are paid, or where child support alone is paid, but part falls under the deduction/inclusion rule, the portion to be included in the income of the recipient for income tax purposes is found by applying the formula in section 56(1)(b). The formula is

$$A - (B + C)$$

where

A is the total of all amounts each of which is a support amount received after 1996 and before the end of the year by the taxpayer from a particular person where the taxpayer and the particular person were living separate and apart at the time the amount was received;

B is the total of all amounts each of which is a child support amount that became receivable by the taxpayer from the particular person under an agreement or order on or after its commencement day and before the end of the year in respect of a period that began after its commencement day; and

C is the total of all amounts each of which is a support amount received after 1996 by the taxpayer from the particular person and included in the taxpayer's income for a preceding taxation year.

See the *Income Tax Act, 1996* sections 56(1), 56.1, 60(b), and 60.1(1) to (4), for the circumstances in which the deduction/inclusion rule operates.

15§114 — Income tax considerations — agreements or orders made before May 1997

Child support paid pursuant to an existing agreement or order that was made before May 1997 and has not been varied since April 1997, will continue to be deductible to the payor and included in the income of the recipient with the following exceptions contained in the definition of "commencement day" in subsection 56.1(4)(b):

- where the payor and recipient file a joint election with Revenue Canada that the payor will not, for income tax purposes, deduct from income and the recipient will not include in income, payments in respect of child support obligations that arise on or after a specified date (which cannot be earlier than May 1, 1997);
- where the agreement or order is varied after April 30, 1997 to change the amount of child support;
- where an agreement or order provides that the payor will not, for income tax purposes, deduct from income and the recipient will not include in income, payments in respect of child support obligations that arise on or after a specified date (which cannot be earlier than May 1, 1997).

Once the tax treatment of the child support payments has been changed by the filing of a joint election (as in (a) above) or by an agreement or order made after April 1997, spouses will not be permitted to return to the old tax rules for support that becomes payable after the new rules apply.

In *Suian v. Suian* (November 3, 1997), Doc. Victoria 95 1777 (B.C. S.C.), a consent order for interim child support of $825 a month was made before May 1, 1997 which was more than the amount prescribed by the *Federal Child Support Guidelines*. The court observed that the deduction of this amount in the hands of the payor and the deductibility in the hands of the payee was favourable to both parties. The court ruled that the interim order remain in force in order to give the parties the present tax advantage. However, if in fact the present tax treatment were lost, the quantum of child support could be reviewed by the court, failing agreement of the parties.

15§115 — Income tax considerations — commencement day

The definition "commencement day" provides that an agreement or order will have a date fixed as its commencement day in certain circumstances. The commencement day of an agreement or order is used in the formulae contained in revised paragraphs 56(1)(b) and 60(b) to determine whether payments are to be included in the income of the recipient and deductible from the income of the payor. Payments are deductible/includible only to the extent that they exceed all child support payments that are required to be made to the recipient by the payor under agreements or orders on or after their commencement days. See subsection 56.1(4).

The commencement day of an agreement or order cannot be a day that is before May 1997. As a result, when the formulae in sections 56(1)(b) and 60(b) are applied to payments made under an order or agreement that predates May 1997, amounts will continue to be included in the recipient's income and deducted from the payor's income.

15§116 — Income tax considerations — prior payments where no variation

Subsection 56.1(3) makes two assumptions of fact for tax purposes. It deems

(1) that amounts paid before the agreement or order was made were received under the agreement or order; and

(2) that the agreement or order was made on the day on which the first amount was received.

These assumptions are necessary for purposes of determining the agreement or order's commencement day, if there is one, as defined by subsection 56.1(4), which, in turn, will determine the treatment of support payments under the formulae in paragraphs 56(1)(b) and 60(b).

For example, a husband and wife separate January 1, 1997, with the husband voluntarily paying $300 a month for the support of their child starting on that date. On June 1, 1997, the husband and wife enter into a written separation agreement which provides that the amounts received before that time and in the year are to be considered to have been paid and received under the agreement. By subsection 56.1(3), the agreement will be deemed to have been made on the day the first payment was received, January 1, 1997. Because this date is before April 1997, there is no "commencement day" within the meaning of the definition in section 56.1(4), and when the formulae in paragraphs 56(1)(b) and 60(b) are applied, all payments made under the agreement will be deductible from the husband's income and included in the wife's.

Another way of expressing the central notion of these provisions is to say that support paid before an order or agreement is made will be deemed to be paid pursuant to the order or agreement, and the order or agreement will be deemed to be made on the date of the first payment, if

(a) the amount is paid at any time in the period beginning on January 1st of the previous taxation year; and

(b) the order or agreement provides that the amount is to be considered to have been paid and received under the order or agreement: *Income Tax Act, 1996*, s. 56.1 (3).

15§117 — Income tax considerations — prior payments with variation

Where an agreement or order is made after April 1997, and varies a voluntary amount paid to the recipient before April 1997, the varied amount is deemed to have been receivable under an agreement or order made on the date the first varied payment is due. In this case, the child support would not be included in the income of the recipient for tax purposes, nor deductible in the hands of the payor: *Income Tax Act, 1996*, s. 56.1(3).

The following example illustrates the effect of varying the prior payments:

(1) In January 1997, the Husband and Wife separate and enter into a separation agreement which provides for child support in the amount of $400 a month commencing February 1, 1997.

(2) In the summer of that year, the Wife commences a legal proceeding and obtains an order for child support in the amount of $500 a month starting August 1, 1997.

(3) This amount is paid to the end of 1997.

(4) The calculation of the income inclusion and deduction amounts for the year is illustrated in the following paragraphs.

(5) The commencement day for the order is August 1, 1997.

(6) The value of A in the formula in paragraph 56(1)(b) and 60(b) is the total support amounts received after 1996 and before the end of 1997; i.e., support for 11 months with 6 months at $400 a month for $2,400, and 5 months at $500 a month for $2,500 giving an 11-month total of $4,900.

(7) The value of B in the formula is the total child support amounts that became payable after the commencement day and before the end of the year in respect of periods that began after commencement day; i.e., $2,500 (the amounts that became receivable in the five months of August through December).

(8) The value of C is the amount received in 1997 and included in income in the preceding year which, in this example, is nil.

Substituting these values in the formula,

$$A - (B + C)$$

results in $4,900 - $2,500 or $2,400 as the amount for income inclusion and deduction.

15§118 — Income tax considerations — third party payments

Payments made to third parties for the benefit of a spouse or former spouse are deductible by the payor and are included in the recipient's income for tax purposes if they are periodic and made pursuant to a written agreement or a court order. In the same way that global amounts which do not distinguish between spousal and child support will be considered as child support when paid to a spouse,global payments to third parties, considered to be support amounts by the provisions of subsection 56.1 (2), will be treated as child support. Accordingly, to be deductible by the payor and included in income by the recipient, the agreement or order under which the payments are made should clearly identify the payments as being solely for the support of a spouse, former spouse or parent of the payor's child.

15§119 — Income tax considerations — effect of the formulae

The effect of the formulae in paragraphs 56(1)(b) and 60(b) is that if there is a shortfall in the payment of support, any amounts that are paid will be first credited to child support and hence will not be deductible by the payor (or included in the income of the recipient) for tax purposes. This is because the formulae provide that in any year the amount included or deductible will be only that support amount actually paid that exceeds the child support amounts that should have been paid in the period beginning on or after the commencement day of the agreement or order.

For example, assume the wife is under an obligation to pay $200 a month for child support and $300 a month for the support of her spouse. The total support amounts are $6,000 a year. However, during the course of the year, she falls behind in making the payments and only pays a total of $5,000. To work out the amount she is entitled to deduct for spousal support, she applies the formula in section 56(1)(b). The value for A is $5,000, the total support paid during the year. The value for B is $2,400, the amount she is required to pay under the agreement or order containing the support obligation. The value for C is zero because no support paid or received this year was included in income for last year, or any preceding taxation year. Applying the formula,

$$A - (B + C)$$

we obtain $5,000 - $2,400 for $2,600. This last amount, $2,600, is the amount she is entitled to deduct in calculating her income for tax purposes. The formula takes the deficiency from the spousal entitlement, not from the child support.

15§120 — Income tax considerations — Spouse is exempt from paying federal or provincial income tax

Where the payor has Native status and consequently does not pay federal or provincial income tax, his income should be adjusted to reflect that fact and, under s. 19(1)(b), the court may impute income to him: *Ninham v. Ninham* (1997), 29 R.F.L. (4th) 41 (Ont. Gen. Div.). In this case, the payor father's income was adjusted from $35,000 to $50,000, to take account of his non-payment of tax.

Pursuant to s. 19(1)(b) of the *Federal Child Support Guidelines*, income may be imputed where the payor is exempt from paying income tax: *Hoover v. Hoover, supra*. In this decision, the father's sole source of income was a Workers' Compensation Board pension benefit of $22,900, which was exempt from income tax. The grossed up amount for national income tax was calculated as $29,565.00.

Cases decided before the enactment of the Federal Support Guidelines:

The parties had two dependent children who were living with the mother. At trial, the father ordered to pay $700/week in child support. The father appealed on the grounds that the trial judge set the amount of support based on tax implications; however, both parents were native Indians, and were not subject to income tax. Support payments were reduced to $103/week: *R. (M.) v. D. (G.)* (October 24, 1994), no C.A. 200-09-000088-945 (C.A. Que.).

15§121 — Child support — delay in application

In *Miller v. Ufoegbune* (2000), 11 R.F.L. (5th) 347, 2000 CarswellOnt 3760 (S.C.J.), child support was granted for the parties' 19-year-old child who had been born subsequent to the parties' divorce. There had been no reference in the decree *nisi* or the minutes of settlement to child support.

Cases decided before the enactment of the Federal Child Support Guidelines:

In *Graefer v. Petty* (1992), 107 Sask. R. 119 (Q.B.), the court allowed the mother's application for child support brought 4 years after the parties' divorce. The mother had been injured in an automobile accident and could no longer support the child on her own. In the circumstances, both a lump sum and periodic support were appropriate.

In the *Graefer v. Petty* case, the court held an application for child support brought several years after the divorce is a corollary relief proceeding and not a variation proceeding. There is no order to be varied.

Delay by a mother in seeking child support is not fatal to an application where the child is in need and the father has the ability to pay: *Young v. Young* (1987), 10 R.F.L. (3d) 337 (B.C. C.A.).

Claims involving maintenance for children of the marriage ought not to be considered on the same basis as that of their parents. A child is under a disability and, accordingly, in divorce proceedings, whether by failure to make a claim, or by waiver, a parent cannot forfeit the right of a child to maintenance under the *Divorce Act* should such become necessary for his or her welfare at any stage. Also, the dismissal by a judge of the claim of a parent to maintenance brought on behalf of a child in the course of a divorce hearing cannot irrevocably foreclose the child's rights. Such an application may be made on behalf of a child of a marriage at any time it is in its best interest to do so: *Goldstein v. Goldstein*, 23 R.F.L. 206, [1976] 4 W.W.R. 646, 67 D.L.R. (3d) 624 (Alta. C.A.). See also *McCutcheon v. McCutcheon* (1977), 2 Alta. L.R. (2d) 121, 2 A.R. 387, 74 D.L.R. (3d) 317 (C.A.).

The *Divorce Act* requires a consideration of the arrangement for children of the marriage and thus it may be that child maintenance need not be pleaded to be put in issue. Be that as it may, even if maintenance had been a pleaded issue, orders in that regard are never final and thus could be raised on subsequent applications in new circumstances: *Ginter v. Ginter*, [1953] O.R. 688 (H.C.); affirmed [1953] O.W.N. 917 (C.A.); *Holland v. Holland*, [1961] 1 W.L.R. 194, [1961] I All E.R. 226 (C.A.). To decline jurisdiction may leave a child who took no part in earlier proceedings without the proper financial resources to which he or she may be entitled so that his or her full potential may be realized: *Lipman v. Lipman* (1978), 3 R.F.L. (2d) 49, 19 O.R. (2d) 486, 85 D.L.R. (3d) 558 (H.C.).

15§122 — Child's repudiation of parent-child relationship — child's rejection of parent — no support

In the following cases the parent has not been required to support a child when the child has unilaterally terminated the relationship.

In *Fernquist v. Garland*, 10 R.F.L. (6th) 332, 2004 CarswellSask 648, 2004 SKCA 123 (Sask. C.A.); reversing 46 R.F.L. (5th) 388, 2003 CarswellSask 753, 2003 SKQB 460 (Sask. Q.B.), the court allowed the mother's appeal from an order dismissing her application to lift a temporary suspension of the father's obligation to pay child support. The order had originally been imposed as a result of the children's refusal to allow their father access and was intended to encourage access. The order had failed to achieve its purpose and that fact alone constituted a sufficient change of circumstances to warrant a review of the father's support obligations.

In *Johnson v. Johnson* (2004), 9 R.F.L. (6th) 380, 2004 CarswellOnt 3512 (Ont. S.C.J.), it was found that the intensity of the rejection of their father by his two university student sons was properly a factor in determining the extent of their ongoing support. The father's actions had not justified the bitter and absolute rejection to which he had been subjected.

In *Fahandezh v. Sadi* (2002), 2002 CarswellOnt 4217, 33 R.F.L. (5th) 327 (Ont. S.C.J.), the father claimed for extraordinary expenses on behalf of his son who had repudiated his relationship with his mother. The son had been incarcerated for assaulting her and no longer communicated with her. The son had taken three and a half years to complete 2 years of high school, did not work even part time, and did not have any physical or mental disabilities. Harris J. held that having a sensible discussion with the payor parent is the least that a child seeking financial support should do. The son was not a "child of the marriage" and the mother had no obligation to provide support.

In *Frankum v. Frankum*, 2001 CarswellBC 1898, 2001 BCSC 1250 (B.C. S.C. [In Chambers]), for 6 months since the 18-year-old son and the mother's boyfriend had been involved in a struggle, the mother and son had not been in communication with each other, despite her many attempts to re-establish the relationship. The court was of the opinion that there was sufficient evidence that the son would be returning to high school to repeat Grade 12 and would thus continue to be a "child of the marriage". The mother would be required to pay child support for him.

Mere attendance at an educational institution does not automatically make a mature child a "child of the marriage". Where the daughter, now nineteen and a half years old, had unilaterally completely rejected her father from the time that she was 11 years of age, the court found that she was no longer a child of the marriage and the mother's application for child support on behalf of the child was dismissed: *Marsland v. Gibb*, 2000 CarswellBC 574, 2000 BCSC 471, 5 R.F.L. (5th) 406 (B.C. S.C.). The daughter had never given any evidence to explain her attitude to her father.

Where a mature child unilaterally terminates a relationship with one of the parents for no apparent reason that becomes a factor in determining whether it is fit and just to provide support. A child who expects to receive support should entertain some type of relationship with the payor parent in the absence of misconduct: *Law v. Law* (1986), 2 R.F.L. (3d) 458, 1986 CarswellOnt 284 (Ont. H.C.). The court found that the mature child was no longer a child of the marriage and terminated the father's support obligation, as of her 21st birthday.

15§123 — Child support — effect of prior orders, judgments and written agreements

Prior orders, judgments, or written agreements may allow a court to use its discretion to make a child support order in an amount that is different from the guideline amount. To do so, the court must be satisfied" (a) that special provisions in an order a judgment or a written agreement respecting the financial obligations of the spouses, or the division or transfer of their property, directly or indirectly benefit a child, or that special provisions have otherwise been made for the benefit of a child; and (b) that the application of the applicable guidelines would result in an amount of child support that is inequitable given those special provisions": *Divorce Act*, s. 15.1(5).

In *Demarchi v. Selwyn* (2004), 7 R.F.L. (6th) 243, 2004 CarswellOnt 3874 (C.A.), the lump sum child support paid by the husband under the parties' settlement was subsequently taken into account in reducing the periodic child support payable by the husband under the *Guidelines*.

Where a global spousal and child support order was made pre-dating the *Guidelines*, the appropriate method of determining the respective support amounts is to identify child support obligations pursuant to *Guidelines* amounts and assign the balance of after-tax benefit of global support paid to spousal support: *Rondeau v. Kirby*, 49 R.F.L. (5th) 189, 2003 CarswellNS 414, [2003] N.S.J. No. 436, 2003 NSSF 49 (N.S. S.C.); affirmed 2004 CarswellNS 140, 2004 NSCA 54 (N.S. C.A.).

There is no reason in principle why a party cannot successfully apply for an original child support order simply because there is a written separation agreement in force. Such an agreement may lead to an order not strictly in accordance with the *Federal Child Support Guidelines* if the parties' circumstances can be brought within s. 15.1(5) of the Divorce Act: *Fung-Sunter v. Fabian* (1999), 48 R.F.L. (4th) 95, [1999] 10 W.W.R. 592, 125 B.C.A.C. 268, 204 W.A.C. 268 (C.A.), reversing (1998), 38 R.F.L. (4th) 266, 53 B.C.L.R. (3d) 75 (S.C.).

In assessing child support under the *Federal Child Support Guidelines*, the court should properly consider the evidentiary value of a separation agreement with respect to the determination of the children's needs: *Dergousoff v. Dergousoff* (1999), 48 R.F.L. (4th) 1, [1999] 10 W.W.R. 633, 177 Sask. R. 64, 199 W.A.C. 64 (C.A.); varying (1998), 167 Sask. R. 66 (Q.B.).

A release clause in a separation agreement cannot bar the application of the *Federal Child Support Guidelines*: *Duffield v. Duffield* (1998), 36 R.F.L. (4th) 374 (B.C. S.C.).

Although the *Divorce Act* allows for a deviation from the *Federal Child Support Guidelines*, if a separation agreement contains "special provisions" respecting division of property, the mere fact of an unequal division does not in itself constitute a "special provision": *Wallace v. Wallace* (1998), 36 R.F.L. (4th) 428, 156 D.L.R. (4th) 762 (B.C. S.C.).

In *Campbell v. Martijn* (1998), 40 R.F.L. (4th) 41, 163 Nfld. & P.E.I.R. 126, 503 A.P.R. 126 (P.E.I. T.D. [In Chambers]), the Court awarded child support at guideline levels for a child over the age of 18 who was attending school despite the fact that the parties' separation agreement called for a reduction in child support upon that child's eighteenth birthday. The agreement provision should not be strictly applied given that the parties clearly wished to encourage their children to pursue post-secondary education as, without it, financial independence was more difficult.

Where the wife forfeited child support in exchange for the husband's forfeiture of his interest in the matrimonial home, the court nevertheless allowed the wife's later application for child support citing the parties' agreement as unreasonable on its face. On appeal, the court set aside the support order. It was not sufficient for the trial court to conclude that the child support provision was inadequate "on the face" on no other basis than the existence of the *Child Support Guidelines*. The court was required to consider whether the support provision met or failed to meet the needs of the child having regard to other relevant provisions, such as the transfer of property. The trial judge had failed to do so and therefore the order could not stand: *Spencer v. Irvine* (1999), 45 R.F.L. (4th) 434 (Ont. S.C.J.).

In *Harwood v. Harwood* (1999), 45 R.F.L. (4th) 357 (B.C. S.C.), the court refused the wife's increase in child support from the amount specified in the parties' separation agreement. Although the husband's income had risen by $6,000, the support called for in the agreement was reasonable and exceeded that required under the *Federal Child Support Guidelines*.

On an original application for child support, where there is a prior interspousal agreement dealing with the issue, there is no need that the applicant establish a change of circumstances since the date of the agreement: *Crosby v. Crosby*, 26 R.F.L. (5th) 20, 2002 CarswellSask 174, 216 Sask. R. 181, 2002 SKQB 106 (Sask. Q.B.).

Parents cannot make an enforceable agreement reducing or ignoring the child support obligation established by a court order. However, if the parents mutually establish a reasonable alternative arrangement to the order, the court may consider any such arrangement as one factor in assessing whether arrears owing under the order should be reduced or cancelled: *D'Ambrosio v. D'Ambrosio* (2000), 11 R.F.L. (5th) 284, 2000 BCSC 1252, 2000 CarswellBC 1719 (B.C.S.C.).

15§123A — Child Support — children receiving social assistance

Where a child receives a direct payment from the *Canada Pension Plan* of a monthly amount resulting from a parent's disability, that payment, for child support purposes, should not be characterized as having been made on behalf of the disabled parent. The benefit, under the *Canada Pension Plan Act*, clearly belongs to the child, even if the parent's disability is the triggering event: *Vickers v. Vickers*, 18 R.F.L. (5th) 431, 2001 CarswellNS 194, 2001 NSCA 96, 201 D.L.R. (4th) 65, 194 N.S.R. (2d) 268, 606 A.P.R. 268 (N.S. C.A.).

In *Giles v. Villeneuve* (1998), 43 R.F.L. (4th) 61 (Ont. Gen. Div.), the trial judge exceeded his jurisdiction when he ordered that the child support payable to the mother was not to be used to reduce the benefits payable to her under the *Family Benefits Act*, R.S.O. 1990, c. F.2.

15§123B — Child support — children's own income

Where the parties' daughter had part-time earnings during a brief interruption of her education, those earnings were taken into account in determining the child support arrears owed by the father in *Tughan v. Tughan* (2003), 39 R.F.L. (5th) 227, 2003 CarswellOnt 2398 (Ont. S.C.J.)

15§123C — Child support — child receiving support from other sources

Step-parents are exempt from the mandatory application of the *Guidelines* Table Amounts and therefore the court has broad discretion regarding such awards. However, the obligation of a biological parent does not necessarily displace that of a step-parent: *Mancuso v. Weinrath* (2005), 22 R.F.L. (6th) 165, 2005 CarswellBC 2757, 2005 BCSC 1606 (B.C. S.C.).

In *Cowie v. Makin* (2004), 8 R.F.L. (6th) 1, 2004 CarswellOnt 3062 (S.C.J.), the court refused to order the husband to pay the full *Guidelines* amount in respect of the wife's children from an earlier marriage. Primary responsibility for child support remained with the biological parents and the biological father was still paying more than his required *Guidelines* contribution. The parties had a separation agreement which dealt with the issue of child support and neither party had ever contemplated that the husband pay the full *Guidelines* amount. However, as the husband had manipulated the wife in signing the agreement, it was not unfair that he be required to pay the agreed upon amount plus an additional amount to make up for a child support shortfall.

In *Willson v. Willson* (2003), 39 R.F.L. (5th) 464, 2003 CarswellOnt 2233 (Ont. S.C.J.), the wife, after the parties' separation, was granted custody of both the parties' child as well as the husband's child from a previous union. The fact that the wife received a support amount from the one child's natural mother was found not to constitute grounds for relieving the father from paying the full Table Amount.

In *Samson v. Samson*, 49 R.F.L. (5th) 202, 2003 CarswellNfld 259, 2003 NLSCUFC 25, 232 Nfld. & P.E.I.R. 148, 690 A.P.R. 148 (N.L. T.D.), it was found that the normal Table Amount of child support that the father should have been paying in respect of his stepson should be reduced by an amount that should have been paid by the child's natural father.

15§123D — Child support — adoption orders

Although an adoption order does not terminate pre-adoption arrears of child support owing by a natural parent, it may be considered by the court as a factor in enforcement proceedings: *Catalano v. Ontario (Family Responsibility Office)* (2004), 6 R.F.L. (6th) 235, 2004 CarswellOnt 2304 (S.C.J.).

15§124 — Agreements involving child support

There is no legislative support in either the *Divorce Act* or the *Guidelines* for interference with the child support provisions of the parties' agreement simply because the support amount therein specified was excessive: *Kuling v. Kuling* (2004), 10 R.F.L. (6th) 391, 2004 CarswellSask 552, 252 Sask. R. 128, 2004 SKQB 328 (Q.B.).

In *Ennis v. Ennis* (2000), 5 R.F.L. (5th) 302, 77 Alta. L.R. (3d) 289 (Alta. C.A.), affirming on this point (1998), 45 R.F.L. (4th) 323 (Alta. Q.B.), the husband was ordered on appeal to pay 80 percent of any medical and dental costs incurred by the children above and beyond what the husband's insurance covered. The order was made despite a settlement agreement in which the parties agreed to share such expenses equally. While settlement agreements were not to be generally ignored by the court, the gross disparity in the parties' income warranted the departure from the general rule.

In *Hutchings v. Hutchings* (1999), 4 R.F.L. (5th) 79, 72 B.C.L.R. (3d) 73, 133 B.C.A.C. 12, 217 W.A.C. 12 (B.C. C.A.), the mother, in the parties' separation agreement, had agreed to pay a lump sum of $12,000 to the father as final settlement of all child support relating to the two children in his custody. When one child subsequently moved in with the mother, the mother sought child support and an order was made taking into account her obligation to contribute towards the support of the one child remaining in the father's care. On the mother's appeal, the requirement was struck on the basis that the lump sum payment had totally discharged her support obligation towards that child.

An informal child support agreement is not binding and does not affect a parent seeking an order under the *Guidelines*: *Gabriel v. Robinson* (2005), 23 R.F.L. (6th) 132, 2005 CarswellOnt 7476, 2005 ONCJ 327 (Ont. C.J.).

In *Reinhardt v. Reinhardt* (2004), 8 R.F.L. (6th) 340, 2004 CarswellOnt 3275 (S.C.J.), the child support provisions contained in the parties' separation agreement were both inadequate and illegal. Not only was the support provided well below the *Guidelines* level, but the agreement bargained away the child's support rights.

In *Cowle v. Makin* (2004), 8 R.F.L. (6th) 1, 2004 CarswellOnt 3062 (S.C.J.), the court refused to allow the husband to rely strictly on the terms of the parties' separation agreement to prohibit the wife's applications for increased child support. Both parents were in breach of the agreement, and to require the wife to relitigate would harm the children. Accordingly, the court invoked its *parens patriae* jurisdiction to deny literal compliance with the agreement.

Where the parties had reached an agreement on the issue of child support on the eve of trial, the court allowed the agreement to stand as an interim order until further information was available to the court pursuant to the *Guidelines*: *Leopold v. Leopold* (2000), 12 R.F.L. (5th) 118, 195 D.L.R. (4th) 717, 2000 CarswellOnt 4707 (Ont. S.C.J.).

Where the parties' final order was silent on the issue of child support, it was found that the interim child support order survived the final one. Any misunderstandings of the state of the law may be relevant where it affects the parties' intent to enter into the consent order. The parties had been under the misapprehension that in exchange for the father's agreement to forego access, he could be relieved of his child support obligation: *Smood v. Smood*, 50 R.F.L. (5th) 197, 2004 CarswellBC 215, 2004 BCSC 166 (B.C. S.C.).

Where the mother's income rose from $27,000 to $43,000 after the parties' divorce, the husband sought to vary the provision in the parties' separation agreement requiring him to pay all of the children's post secondary school expenses. As the wife had waived her right to spousal support, it was foreseeable that her income would rise, given her need to support herself. The agreement represented a thorough resolution of the parties' issues in a package deal consistent with the *Divorce Act* and could not be dismantled: *Brown v. Brown*, 47 R.F.L. (5th) 272, 2003 CarswellOnt 4932 (Ont. S.C.J.).

In *Collins v. Collins*, 42 R.F.L. (5th) 273, 2003 NLSCTD 102, 2003 CarswellNfld 168, [2003] N.J. No. 169 (N.L. T.D.), the court enforced the child support terms in the parties' separation agreement even though they required the father to pay virtually twice the *Guidelines* Table Amount. The agreement had been unimpeachably negotiated and both parties had access to counsel. The father's claim that he was unaware of how badly his business was doing at the time lacked credibility. There was no suggestion of mistake, coercion or vulnerability and the father was well aware when executing the agreement of the required *Guidelines* amount.

Where the parties' separation agreement provided that the mother was to contribute annually to the daughter's education and living expenses until she completed her university degree, she was found not responsible to help finance the daughter's post graduate degree. The evidence conclusively established that the daughter was no longer a child in need of support and the financial agreement respecting the daughter was not intended to be indefinite: *Levandusky v. Levandusky* (2003), 39 R.F.L. (5th) 134, 2003 CarswellOnt 2615 (Ont. S.C.J.); additional reasons at (2003), 2003 CarswellOnt 2613 (Ont. S.C.J.).

Even where parents in relatively equal bargaining positions, with independent legal advice, have bargained for payment of no child support, the court is entitled to review the agreement to ensure that it meets the child's best interests. An assessment of whether special provisions under s. 33(12) of the *Family Law Act* exist must be objective and with a child-centred focus: *Deiter v. Sampson* (2002), 31 R.F.L. (5th) 296, 2002 CarswellOnt 3603 (Ont. S.C.J.).

In *Pruss v. Pruss* (2000), 12 R.F.L. (5th) 188, 2000 CarswellOnt 3548, [2000] O.J. 3662 (Ont. S.C.J.), the court rejected the child support called for in the parties' separation agreement and awarded the higher amount called for under the *Guidelines*.

At the time of the parties' separation agreement, the husband had anticipated the continuation of his income at existing levels, and the wife's spousal and child support were set at a corresponding level. Subsequently, when the husband's income fell dramatically, his application for a reduction in the spousal and child support payable by him was allowed and upheld on appeal. The failure to earn as much as anticipated amounted to a material change in circumstances, even if it was foreseeable: *Kehler v. Kehler*, 39 R.F.L. (5th) 299, 2003 CarswellMan 270, 177 Man. R. (2d) 135, 304 W.A.C. 135, 2003 MBCA 88, [2003] 8 W.W.R. 429 (Man. C.A.).

Irrespective of the terms of any agreement between the parties, a judge has jurisdiction in a motion for corollary relief to deal with all issues of custody and child support. While the agreement may be one factor to be taken into consideration when deciding a child's best interests, it is not necessary that a change in material provisions, as specified in the agreement's variation provisions, be established: *Jay v. Jay*, 41 R.F.L. (5th) 306, 2003 CarswellPEI 71, 2003 PESCAD 19 (P.E.I. C.A.).

Cases decided before the enactment of the *Federal Child Support Guidelines*: *Divorce Act*, 1985.

Where the arrears of child support owing by the father were wiped out in light of an agreement with the mother relieving him from child support obligations if he did not see the children, the order was reversed on appeal. Support was the right of the children and was not to be bartered away by the parents: *Black v. Black* (1995), 19 R.F.L. (4th) 442, 71 B.C.A.C. 233, 117 W.A.C. 233 (C.A.).

In *Hansen v. Hansen* (1995), 13 R.F.L. (4th) 335 (Ont. Gen. Div.), before Fleury J., the court noted that the Ontario General Division has repeatedly stated that agreements between the parties as to child support are not enforceable where to enforce them might operate against the best interests of the child in question.

In *Bakes v. Kelly* (1995), 15 R.F.L. (4th) 361 (B.C. C.A.), the fact that the wife had filed a petition for divorce claiming child support was not a repudiation of her right to enforce the child support provisions under the parties' separation agreement. Although the agreement contained a waiver of the right to support, the wife had, prior to filing the petition, commenced an action to enforce the agreement under which the husband was delinquent. Only if the wife had obtained the divorce order would the issue of electing between inconsistent remedies arise.

In *Chalmers v. Simpson* (1994), 3 R.F.L. (4th) 407, 92 B.C.L.R. (2d) 258 (C.A.), the Court of Appeal affirmed the trial judge's refusal to interfere with child support provisions which had originally been set by the parties' agreement. The agreement had specified that support was to continue until the children were 19 and the mother had requested that it be extended until such time as the children no longer qualified as "children of the marriage". The trial judge dismissed the application on the grounds that the mother's expense claims were excessive, the changes were foreseeable at the time of the agreement, the children had part-time income and the mother's new husband could contribute to household expenses.

The courts are extremely reluctant to interfere with judicial separation agreements which include provisions for child support. Consequently, the parties ought, pending trial, to be held to the amount they set out in their agreement: *Bacon v. Bacon* (1991), 33 R.F.L. (3d) 170 (Sask. C.A.).

Although the parties' agreement may act to bar a claim for extended spousal support, the court is still competent, notwithstanding the agreement, to award an increase in child support: *Droit de la famille — 927* (1990), [1991] R.D.F. 21 (C.A. Qué.).

A court should not lightly vary the terms, including the child support terms, of a settlement agreement: *Droit de la famille — 646* (1989), 20 R.F.L. (3d) 432 (C.A. Qué.).

"There will be an order for the payment by the husband of maintenance for his daughter in the amount of $75 per month commencing 1st August 1976. I am not confident that the wife would receive those maintenance payments for the daughter if they are not secured. [The husband] has been in arrears with respect to the child's maintenance for a considerable time. . . . The child's maintenance payments will be secured by the payment into court of $4,000": per MacDonald J. in *Fernandes v. Fernandes* (1976), 28 R.F.L. 266 at 267-268 (B.C. S.C.).

An order that child support payments be deducted directly from the payor's employment income at source is a form of "charging order" available under the *Divorce Act*: *Long v. Long* (1993), 1 R.F.L. (4th) 110, 147 A.R. 108 (Q.B.).

In *Pritchett v. Pritchett* (December 16, 1996), Doc. New Westminster D026544 (B.C. S.C.); additional reasons to (October 2, 1996), Doc. New Westminster D026544 (B.C. S.C.), the husband was ordered to secure the sum of $20,000 to be held in trust for the child's post-secondary education.

15§124A — Costs

Where the father was unsuccessful in having his child support obligation reduced from the *Guidelines* amount, the mother was entitled to costs. It was the father's insistence that certain unilateral payments made on the children's behalf entitled him to a reduction that had led to the proceedings in the first place: *Soderberg v. Soderberg* (1998), 42 R.F.L. (4th) 403 (N.W.T. S.C.).

15§125 — Child support — lump sum

The *Federal Child Support Guidelines* provide that, the court may require in the child support order that the amount payable under the order be paid in periodic payments, in a lump sum or in a lump sum and periodic payments.

In *Andries v. Andries* (1997), 119 Man. R. (2d) 224 (Q.B.); varied (1998), 36 R.F.L. (4th) 175 (Man. C.A.), child support was not paid for several months after the separation, and then in the amount of $300 a month. The court ordered the payment of a lump sum "to compensate for the insufficiency of the past payments." The court found that the support should have been $629.50 a month, and ordered a lump sum of $4,754 after giving the payor husband credit for part of the payments for maintenance that were allocated to the child, and credit for the actual support payments made.

In *Pearce v. Murphy* (2004), 47 R.F.L. (5th) 192, 2004 CarswellOnt 334 (Ont. S.C.J.); additional reasons at (2004), 47 R.F.L. (5th) 237, 2004 CarswellOnt 673 (Ont. S.C.J.); additional reasons (2004), 2004 CarswellOnt 2145, 3 R.F.L. (6th) 173 (S.C.J.), the wife was awarded lump sum retroactive child support under the *Guidelines* back to the date of the parties' separation agreement which had been executed in 1992, years prior to the enactment of the *Guidelines*.

In *Lambton v. Lambton* (2004), 9 R.F.L. (6th) 400, 2004 CarswellBC 2606, 2004 BCSC 1400 (S.C.); additional reasons at 2004 CarswellBC 3062, 2004 BCSC 1725 (S.C.), the court awarded the father's step-son lump sum child support in the amount of $20,000. Although there had been no contact since the parties' separation, if the parties' marriage had not failed it was probable that the father would have made a contribution towards the child's post-secondary education.

An order for lump sum child or spousal support should not be a disguise attempt to distribute matrimonial property: *Hunt v. Smolis-Hunt* (1998), 39 R.F.L. (4th) 143, [1998] 10 W.W.R. 1, 61 Alta. L.R. (3d) 279, 224 A.R. 68 (Q.B.).

Cases decided before the enactment of the *Federal Child Support Guidelines*:

The court may consider retroactive child support in the form of a lump sum as compensation for a shortfall in an interim support order: *Phillips v. Phillips* (1995), 14 R.F.L. (4th) 113, 174 A.R. 11, 102 W.A.C. 11 (C.A.).

A lump sum child support award may be appropriate to compensate a custodial parent retroactively for child expenses incurred after separation and the commencement of formal proceedings: *MacMinn v. MacMinn* (1995), 17 R.F.L. (4th) 88 (Alta. C.A.).

A judge can properly award lump sum child support even if it has not been specificially claimed and should consider whether to make a retroactive award to compensate for a shortfall all an interim award: *Phillips v. Phillips* (1995), 14 R.F.L. (4th) 113, 174 A.R. 11, 102 W.A.C. 11.

In *Sequeira v. Sequeira* (1992), 44 R.F.L. (3d) 95, 74 B.C.L.R. (2d) 246 (C.A.), a lump sum child support order made in favour of the parties' 20-year-old student daughter was rescinded on an appeal brought by the payor father. As the trial judge had concluded that the father had been unable to work for the eight years preceding the divorce hearing, the award was inappropriate.

Where the evidence indicated the husband was disinclined to work on a regular basis and he had recently enjoyed a windfall of cash, lump sum child support was awarded on appeal: *Droit de la famille -946*, [1991] R.D.F. 91 (C.A. Qué.).

A court may award lump sum child support where a parent has sufficient capital to make a lump sum payment but limited ongoing capability to pay periodic support: *Dimitry v. Dimitry* (1990), 26 R.F.L. (3d) 418 (Ont. C.A.).

In *Macedo v. Macedo* (1996), 19 R.F.L. (4th) 65 (Ont. Gen. Div.), the court quantified the sum payable by the father as lump sum child support by capitalizing what would otherwise have been probable future periodic child support payments.

Where the mother had received $43,000 after selling the matrimonial home and settling her debts, the court allowed the custodial father's application for lump sum child support. The mother had problems with both drugs and alcohol and might otherwise squander the money: *McIntosh v. McIntosh* (1996), 19 R.F.L. (4th) 46 (Man. Q.B.).

In *Rosas v. Rosas* (1995), 15 R.F.L. (4th) 61, 103 Man. R. (2d) 137 (Q.B.), the court rejected the wife's claim for lump sum child support. Lump sum should be awarded in only exceptional cases and the wife's claim, based on her assertion that the husband should have been paying more in the past, was insufficient justification.

Where at trial the amount of interim child support was found to have been grossly inadequate, an additional lump sum of retroactive child support was awarded: *Hess v. Hess* (1994), 2 R.F.L. (4th) 22 (Ont. Gen. Div.), additional reasons at (1994), 2 R.F.L. (4th) 40 (Ont. Gen. Div.).

Where the husband had contributed nothing to the children's support for the 15 months following separation, the wife was awarded lump sum child support in compensation: *Mondoux v. Mondoux* (1994), 152 N.B.R. (2d) 259, 390 A.P.R. 259 (Q.B.).

Where the husband had verbally agreed to assist the children with their education costs, but had failed to do so, he was ordered to pay lump sum child support. His past conduct had raised serious questions about whether he would honour an ongoing periodic support award: *Taylor v. Taylor* (1992), 38 R.F.L. (3d) 313, 111 N.S.R. (2d) 91, 303 A.P.R. 91 (T.D.).

Where the husband had abandoned his family and had not contributed to their support, lump sum child support was awarded in divorce proceedings after the husband had won a lottery. The lump sum was to compensate for past expenses only whereas periodic support was found appropriate for future needs: *Gray v. Gray* (1992), 39 R.F.L. (3d) 127 (Man. Q.B.).

In *Binczak v. Binczak* (1992), 44 R.F.L. (3d) 122 (Ont. Gen. Div.), the court refused ther husband's lump sum child support claim under which he sought the transfer to him of the wife's interest in the matrimonial home. The order would not serve any true support purpose as the husband would not gain any immediate relief in meeting the children's expenses. The more appropriate order was granting of a long-term exclusive possession order in favour of the husband and the forfeiture by the wife of an equalization payment due her.

In *Mannett v. Mannett* (1992), 111 N.S.R. (2d) 327, 303 A.P.R. 327 (T.D.), the court refused to grant an order for lump sum child support. Although the order could be justified, it would have had the inappropriate effect of depriving the payor of a vehicle which he required for his employment.

Lump sum child support was refused where it appeared that the applicant's main motivation was to use the money for the purchase of a new home. The child's needs could be adequately met through periodic support which would not interfere with the equity realized by the respondent upon the sale of the matrimonial home: *Healy v. Healy* (1991), 115 N.B.R. (2d) 327, 291 A.P.R. 327 (Q.B.).

A lump sum child support order cannot be based on future needs which are purely hypothetical: *Droit de la famille -1377* (1990), [1991] R.D.F. 42 (C.S. Qué.).

Where the wife, who had been diagnosed as paranoid, had failed in the past to contribute to child support despite her substantial assets and investment income, she was ordered to pay lump sum child support: *Grieve v. Grieve* (1990), 29 R.F.L. (3d) 8 (N.B. Q.B.).

Where the husband had failed to make reasonable attempts to find employment and had failed to honour an existing child support order, he was ordered to pay lump sum child support, such sum to be set off against the equalization debt due to the husband from the custodial wife: *Jukosky v. Jukosky* (1990), 31 R.F.L. (3d) 117 (Ont. Gen. Div.).

Where the husband left his $40,000 per year job to start his own business, the wife's application for lump sum child support was allowed. It was possible that the husband's new venture would eventually diminish his ability to provide for his children on a periodic basis: *Droit de la famille - 1241*, [1989] R.D.F. 266 (C.S. Qué.).

A past underpayment of child support can be compensated through an award of lump sum support: *Barr v. Barr* (1990), 28 R.F.L. (3d) 403 (Man. Q.B.).

Where a wife is ordered by a divorce decree to pay a sum of money to be held in trust by the husband as her contribution to the children's education, the husband has no beneficial interest in such fund. Therefore, if they money proves not to be required for educational purposes, the fund properly reverts to the wife, since the money originally belonged to her: *MacDonald v. MacDonald* (1989), 100 N.B.R. (2d) 121, 252 A.P.R. 121 (Q.B.).

Where the father had shown no interest in the children since the parties' separation and was unlikely to observe a periodic child support order, the wife was awarded lump sum child support in the form of the husband's half interest in the matrimonial home: *Droit de la famille -1086*, [1987] R.D.F. 123 (C.S. Qué.).

In *Edwards v. Edwards* (1994), 7 R.F.L. (4th) 105, 97 B.C.L.R. (2d) 177 (S.C.), the mother was awarded lump sum retroactive child support back to the date of the expiration of an earlier child support order made under provincial legislation. The parties' decree *nisi* had been silent on the issue of child support as the provincial order was still in force as of that date.

Lump sum child support should not be used as a vehicle for redistributing capital between the parties. Where the wife did not qualify for an unequal division of the family home provincial legislation, child support could not be properly used as a means of affecting the same end: *Reid v. Reid* (1993), 48 R.F.L. (3d) 441 (B.C. S.C.).

In *Donovan v. Donovan* (1986), 7 B.C.L.R. (2d) 221, 5 R.F.L. (3d) 1 (S.C.), the wife was found obligated to contribute to the maintenance of the children who were in the custody of the father. Given the mother's income and debts, periodic maintenance was not feasible or practical; however, the property award made in her favour justified a lump sum order of $10,000.

Where the husband had refused to disclose his assets and income and had failed to honour previous orders for disclosure and child support, a lump sum child support award was deemed appropriate: *Fletcher v. Fletcher* (1993), 1 R.F.L. (4th) 117 (Ont. U.F.C.).

In *Mount v. Doucette* (1995), 18 R.F.L. (4th) 90 (N.S. Fam. Ct.) the mother's application for lump sum child support was dismissed. The father's current source of income was unemployment insurance benefits and there was no evidence that he could be able to obtain a loan to pay the lump sum.

A lump sum award should not have the effect of establishing an estate for a child and accordingly, provision should be made for contingencies, such as the possibility of the child's death prior to the exhaustion of the sum awarded. In determining whether a lump sum is appropriate the main consideration should be the welfare of the child and a secondary consideration, the effect on the paying parent. If depriving a parent of the sum would harm his or her ability to make a living, such an award should not be made: *Zielke v. Zielke*, 30 R.F.L. (2d) 113, [1983] 1 W.W.R. 152, 22 Alta. L.R. (2d) 319, 40 A.R. 299 (C.A.).

In *Gibson v. Gibson* (1980), 5 Man. R. (2d) 320 (Q.B.), a lump sum of $16,000 was awarded for the maintenance of five children where the husband no longer resided in the jurisdiction and had refused to give assistance to children not in his custody in the past. See also *Krawec v. Krawec* (1976), 28 R.F.L. 36 at 38 (Alta. T.D.); *Johnson v. Johnson*, 23 R.F.L. 293, [1975] W.W.D. 167 (Alta. T.D.); *Dart v. Dart* (1974), 14 R.F.L. 97 at 99-100 (Ont. H.C.).

See also *Gamester v. Gamester* (1980), 18 R.F.L. (2d) 103 (P.E.I. S.C.).

15§126 — Child support — orders to secure payment

Under the *Divorce Act*, s.15.1(4) the court "may impose terms, conditions or restrictions in connection with the [child support] order or interim order as it thinks fit and just." The *Federal Child Support Guidelines* add to these powers, a specific provision for securing the amount payable:

> 12. The court may require in the child support order that the amount payable under the order be paid or secured, or paid and secured, in the manner specified in the order.

This combination of powers now divided between the Act and the *Guidelines* existed before the establishment of the *Guidelines*, in the Act, alone. They permit the court, among other things, to secure payment of the amount specified in the order by charging property with this obligation so that the payment could be taken out of the property if the payor was in default. Whether this form of security is what is intended by s. 12 of the *Guidelines* is not of great practical importance. If it is not, the power exists in the right to impose terms or conditions given by s. 15.1(4) of the Act.

In *Roby v. Roby* (2003), 48 R.F.L. (5th) 389, 2003 CarswellOnt 4581 (Ont. S.C.J.), the court refused the wife's request to have the husband's child support obligation secured against the husband's pension. Although the husband had been delinquent in his payments in the past, this had been the result of his poor financial situation resulting from a disability. In addition, the obligation could not be secured against the pension.

Cases decided before the enactment of the Federal Child Support Guidelines:

In *Reid v. Reid* (1995), 11 R.F.L. (4th) 85 (B.C. C.A.), the court allowed the wife's appeal of an award of $100 a month payable by the husband for the maintenance of the four children of the marriage. The proper amount payable by the father was $300 a month per child, which was to be charged against the husband's interest in the home.

In *English v. English* (1995), 16 R.F.L. (4th) 250, 133 Sask. R. 274 (Q.B.); additional reasons (July 27, 1995), Doc. Regina Q.B. 015530/93 (Sask. Q.B.); appeal dismissed, cross-appeal allowed (1996), 21 R.F.L. (4th) 85, 141 Sask. R. 171, 114 W.A.C. 171 (C.A.); additional reasons (1996), 22 R.F.L. (4th) 312 (Sask. C.A.) the court refused the wife's application that the children's support order be varied to require the husband to post security for future payments. Although the husband had left his employment to further his education, he had always made regular payments and there was nothing to indicate that he would not continue to do so. The appellate court found at (1996), 21 R.F.L. (4th) 85, that while the trial decision was in reserve, the older of two children had finished her education and was no longer a "child of the marriage". Consequently, the father was not required to pay further child support for her. The court remitted the wife's cross-appeal from the judgment dismissing her application for variation of child support. The court stated, although it expressed no opinion on the matter, that a sufficient change of circumstances might have occurred to warrant the making of a lump sum order to secure the father's obligation to contribute toward the support of the parties' younger child.

"Because of the husband's past performance on the matter of support, his share [of the proceeds of sale of matrimonial home] is to remain in court until further order of this court, and the payments for the support of the children are to be made against that amount. If the husband fails to make the said monthly payments, the wife may apply to the Official Guardian to have the sum of $400 per month released to her for the support of the children. If the husband makes the payments as ordered and satisfies the court by his conduct that he intends to continue to support his children, he may apply for payment out of court": per Labrosse J. in *Rollason v. Rollason* (1978), 1 R.F.L. (2d) 97 at 107 (Ont. H.C.).

"There will be an order for the payment by the husband of maintenance for his daughter in the amount of $75 per month commencing 1st August 1976. I am not confident that the wife would receive those maintenance payments for the daughter if they are not secured. [The husband] has been in arrears with respect to the child's maintenance for a considerable time... The child's maintenance payments will be secured by the payment into court of $4,000": per MacDonald J. in *Fernandes v. Fernandes* (1976), 28 R.F.L. 266 at 267–268 (B.C. S.C.).

An order that child support payments be deducted directly from the payor's employment income at source is a form of "charging order" available under the *Divorce Act*: *Long v. Long* (1993), 1 R.F.L. (4th) 110, 147 A.R. 108 (Q.B.).

In *Pritchett v. Pritchett* (December 16, 1996), Doc. New Westminster D026544 (B.C. S.C.); additional reasons to (October 2, 1996), Doc. New Westminster D026544 (B.C. S.C.), the husband was ordered to secure the sum of $20,000 to be held in trust for the child's post-secondary education.

15§127 — Child support — duration of orders

The *Divorce Act*, s. 15.1(4) allows the court to make a child support "order ... or an interim order ... for a definite or indefinite period or until a specified event occurs, and may impose terms, conditions or restrictions in connection with the order or interim order as it thinks fit and just."

Cases decided before the enactment of the Federal Child Support Guidelines:

While the court has jurisdiction to impose a termination date on child support, generally it should not do so. An order should simply provide for termination when the child ceases to be a child of the marriage: *Corkum v. Corkum* (1988), 14 R.F.L. (3d) 275 (Ont. H.C.).

The court did not favour setting a time limit on support for a child attending university on a full-time basis: *Jamieson v. Jamieson* (1995), 14 R.F.L. (4th) 354, 163 N.B.R. (2d) 178, 419 A.P.R. 178 (C.A.).

Section 15(4) of the *Divorce Act* gives the Court the power to place a time limitation on a child support order where it considers it fit and just to do so. However, where the limitation is set to expire long before the child ceases to be a child of the marriage, it is not a proper case for the exercise of the discretion: *Lutz v. Lutz* (1995), 80 O.A.C. 293 (C.A.).

Where the parties' 20-year-old daughter was unable to find employment because of the economy and her lack of job skills, her support entitlement was restricted to six months: *Smith v. Smith* (1987), 12 R.F.L. (3d) 50 (B.C. S.C.).

"The order or maintenance should also be varied to provide that the husband shall pay to the wife for the maintenance of each of the children the sum of $25 per week until such child reaches the age of 16, and thereafter the payments shall continue for such child who is in full-time attendance at an educational institution, or by reason of illness, disability or other cause is unable to withdraw from the charge of the mother or to provide for the necessaries of life": per Dubin J.A. in *Wallin v. Wallin* (1975), 18 R.F.L. 122 at 126–127, 6 O.R. (2d) 33, 51 D.L.R. (3d) 677 (C.A.). See also *Brower v. Brower* (1974), 18 R.F.L. 348 at 350, 8 O.R. (2d) 144, 57 D.L.R. (3d) 336 (H.C.); *Martyn v. Martyn* (1975), 23 R.F.L. 14 at 17 (Ont. H.C.).

"The allowance for the children is to continue until they respectively attain the age of 18 years and thereafter until they respectively attain the age of 21 years, providing that they or either of them are still residing with their mother and are in full-time attendance at school, college or university": per Keith J. in *Jackson v. Jackson* (1976), 24 R.F.L. 109 at 121 (Ont. H.C.). See also *Pongor v. Pongor* (1976), 27 R.F.L. 109 (Ont. C.A.).

Where the custodial mother remarried and her second husband support her child it was held that the father's obligation to pay child maintenance was suspended during the period of the second marriage. However, upon the termination of that marriage, the original child maintenance order was once again of full force and effect: *Gray v. Gray* (1983), 32 R.F.L. (2d) 438 (Ont. H.C.).

See also *Fisher v. Epton* (1980), 19 R.F.L. (2d) 211 (Alta. Q.B.); *Elligott v. Elligott* (1977), 3 R.F.L. (2d) 61 at 69, 6 A.R. 282 (T.D.); *Schmidt v. Schmidt* (1976), 26 R.F.L. 232 at 239 (B.C. S.C.); *McAllister v. McAllister* (1976), 14 N.B.R. (2d) 552 at 555 (Q.B.); *MacPhee v. MacPhee* (1973), 18 R.F.L. 331 at 333, 9 N.B.R. (2d) 115, 1 A.P.R. 115 (Q.B.); *Stein v. Stein* (1975), 10 Nfld. & P.E.I.R. 358 (Nfld. T.D.); *Star v. Star* (1973), 17 R.F.L. 15, 8 N.B.R. (2d) 162 (Q.B.); *Ferrari v. Ferrari* (1974), 9 N.B.R. (2d)

602, 1 A.P.R. 602 (Q.B.); *Wright v. Wright* (1975), 26 R.F.L. 103, 13 N.B.R. (2d) 354 (Q.B.); *Wrightsell v. Wrightsell*, 11 R.F.L. 271 at 274, [1973] 1 O.R. 649 (H.C.).

15§128 — Child support — terms and conditions — general

In making a child support order or interim order, the court "may impose terms, conditions or restrictions in connection with the order or interim order as it thinks fit and just": *Divorce Act*, s. 15.1 (4).

15§129 — Child support — payment to child

Custodial parents are presumed to manage child support in the children's best interests and, accordingly, compelling reasons must exist to permit payment, in whole or in part, directly to the children: *Mylrea v. Benoit* (2003), 42 R.F.L. (5th) 82, 2003 CarswellOnt 2760 (Ont. S.C.J.).

In *Armaz v. van Erp* (2000), 7 R.F.L. (5th) 1, 2000 CarswellOnt 1461, [2000] O.J. No. 1544 (Ont. S.C.J.), the father's application to pay child support directly to his daughter was refused. The 20-year-old university student lived in residence during the school term and with her mother for the balance of the year. One of the purposes of child support is to maintain a child's permanent home and to cover the incidentals that the custodial parent provides to the child, whether at home or in residence.

Where a portion of the child support payable by the father would be claimed back by the government which was paying the disabled child an income support allowance, the court ordered that an amount equivalent to the clawback be paid to the mother in trust. The impact of the clawback would accordingly be avoided: *Greening v. Mills* (2006), 23 R.F.L. (6th) 165, 2006 CarswellNfld 61, 2006 NLUFC 11, 254 Nfld. & P.E.I.R. 279, 764 A.P.R. 279 (N.L. U.F.C.).

Cases decided before the enactment of the Federal Child Support Guidelines:

In *Lilley v. Lilley* (1993), 50 R.F.L. (3d) 329 (B.C. S.C.); additional reasons at (1994), 50 R.F.L. (3d) 341 (B.C. S.C.), an order was made permitting the father to pay child support directly to his 19-year-old daughter. See also *Adam v. Adam* (1993), 50 R.F.L. (3d) 216, 89 Man. R. (2d) 275 (Q.B.), in which it was held that the *Divorce Act* allowed for the direct payment of child support to a child even without an express provision in the Act to that effect.

When one spouse is ordered to pay to the other spouse a periodic sum for a child's maintenance, the payment cannot be made directly to the child if the child is of mature years unless the custodial parent knows and consents to payment being made in that fashion: *Shachter v. Shachter* (1980), 17 R.F.L. (2d) 36 (Man. Q.B.). See also *Fennell v. Fennell* (1989), 92 N.S.R. (2d) 266, 237 A.P.R. 266 (Fam. Ct.), where the court stated that moneys paid directly to a child cannot be set off against child support owing to the custodial parent.

15§129A — Third party payments

Where the parties' separation agreement required the husband to pay $400 monthly child support, the fact that his pension plan paid $160 monthly directly to the child was found not to warrant a downward variation. The agreement itself did not specifically allow for the deduction: *Corkum v. Corkum* (1998), 36 R.F.L. (4th) 367, 166 N.S.R. (2d) 329, 498 A.P.R. 329 (S.C.).

15§129B — Set-off

In *Low v. Robinson*, 7 R.F.L. (5th) 148, 79 Alta. L.R. (3d) 137, [2000] 7 W.W.R. 509, (sub nom. *S.E.L. v. J.M.R.)* 258 A.R. 201 at 235, 2000 CarswellAlta 336 (Q.B.); additional reasons to 4 R.F.L. (5th) 368, 76 Alta. L.R. (3d) 238, [2000] 4 W.W.R. 663, (sub nom. *S.E.L. v. J.M.R.)* 258 A.R. 201, 2000 CarswellAlta 68 (Q.B.), the husband was entitled to set-off against retroactive child support ordered for the sum that he had paid towards the children's hockey and soccer expenses. The parties had believed that the husband was, in essence, contributing towards s. 7 expenses. When it was later determined that he was not obliged to make such a contribution, it would be unjust if he was not to be given credit for the payments.

In *Y. (H.) v. Y. (D.)* (1999), 49 R.F.L. (4th) 450, 175 Nfld. & P.E.I.R. 85, 537 A.P.R. 85 (P.E.I. T.D. [In Chambers]), the husband was not allowed to set off his monthly child support obligation against a spousal support over-payment owed by the wife. Child support and spousal support obligations should not be intermingled. It is unfair to the child and contrary to the spirit of the legislation to excuse a parent from paying child support on the basis of dealings between the spouse.

Interim Support

15§130 — General

Like the case of permanent support, the principles governing the award of interim support depend on whether the support is for the support of a child or a spouse.

On an application for child support the court may make an interim order "requiring a spouse to pay for the support of any or all children of the marriage, pending the determination of the application": *Divorce Act*, s. 15.1(2). The order must be in accordance with the applicable guidelines unless it would be inequitable in light of special provisions in an existing order, judgment or written agreement directly or indirectly benefitting the child or children: *Divorce Act*, s. 15.1(3) and (5). The "applicable guidelines" are the guidelines of the province where both spouses or former spouses ordinarily reside. If that province has not established guidelines, or if both spouses do not ordinarily reside in the province (e.g., one of them ordinarily resides elsewhere), then the applicable guidelines are the *Federal Child Support Guidelines*. See the *Divorce Act*, s. 2(1) "applicable guidelines."

The obligation under the order may be "for a definite or indefinite period or until a specified event occurs" and the court "may impose terms, conditions or restrictions in connection with the ... interim order as it thinks fit and just": *Divorce Act*, s. 15.1(3) and (4).

On an application for spousal support the court may "make an interim order requiring a spouse to secure or pay, or to secure and pay, such lump sum or periodic sums, or such lump sum and periodic sums, as the court thinks reasonable for the support of the other spouse, pending the determination of the application": *Divorce Act*, s. 15.2(2). The order may be made "for a definite or indefinite period or until a specified event occurs," and the court "may impose terms, conditions or restrictions in connection with the order as it thinks fit and just" : *Divorce Act*, s. 15.2(3). In making the order "the court shall take into consideration the condition, means, needs and other circumstances of each spouse, including

(a) the length of time the spouses cohabited;

(b) the functions performed by each spouse during cohabitation; and

(c) any order, agreement or arrangement relating to support of either spouse": *Divorce Act*, s. 15.2(4).

The spousal support order should

(a) recognize any economic advantages or disadvantages to the spouses arising from the marriage or its breakdown;

(b) apportion between the spouses any financial consequences arising from the care of any child of the marriage over and above any obligation for the support of any child of the marriage;

(c) relieve any economic hardship of the spouses arising from the breakdown of the marriage; and

(d) in so far as practicable, promote the economic self-sufficiency of each spouse within a reasonable period of time": *Divorce Act*, s. 15.2(6).

Where the court is considering both an application for child support and an application for spousal support, "the court shall give priority to child support in determining the applications": *Divorce Act*, s. 15.3(1).

Divorce Act, 1985

The traditional approach to interim support based on established need and the ability to pay is not always an approach that is fair and just in the circumstances. Where the ability to pay is not an issue, the parties should have the financial ability to enjoy a similar lifestyle, regardless of whether they did in fact choose to enjoy such a lifestyle: *Lakhani v. Lakhani* (2003), 43 R.F.L. (5th) 125, 2003 CarswellOnt 3928 (Ont. S.C.J.); additional reasons at (2003), 2003 CarswellOnt 3927 (Ont. S.C.J.).

An order for interim support to be paid out of capital should only be made where the recipient requires the funds to maintain a minimal standard of living: *Plaxton v. Plaxton* (2002), 27 R.F.L. (5th) 135, 2002 CarswellOnt 1343 (S.C.J.).

In *Moschuk v. Moschuk* (1999), 1999 CarswellOnt 3193 (S.C.J.), the court was of the opinion that "The purpose of an interim motion in family breakdown situations is to maintain, as far as it is possible, the status quo until such time as the matters at issue can be fully explored at trial."

In *Suian v. Suian* (November 3, 1997), Doc. Victoria 95 1777 (B.C. S.C.), a consent order for interim child support of $825 a month was made before May 1, 1997 which was more than the amount prescribed by the *Federal Child Support Guidelines*. The court observed that the deduction of this amount in the hands of the payor and the deductibility in the hands of the payee was favourable to both parties. The court ruled that the interim order remain in force in order to give the parties the present tax advantage. However, if in fact the present tax treatment were lost, the quantum of child support could be reviewed by the court, failing agreement of the parties.

See also *Rains v. Rains* (June 16, 1997), Doc. Sault Ste. Marie 16655/97 (Ont.Gen. Div.); *Miller v. Miller* (May 30, 1997), Doc. Victoria 97/1015 (B.C. Master); and *Shelleby v. Shelleby* (June 20, 1997), Doc. Sault Ste. Marie 010829/97 (Ont. Gen. Div.).

In *Parsan v. Parsan* (September 26, 1997), Doc. Brampton D30331/95 (Ont. Gen.Div.), the father's motion to vary an interim order of support was denied even though the father was earning substantially less per year than when the order was made. He could claim a substantial tax deduction and, consequently, there was really no significant difference in the amount he was paying under the existing order (with tax deduction) and the amount he would be paying under the *Federal Guidelines*, sufficient to justify a variation at this time.

In *Sobey v. Sobey* (2000), 11 R.F.L. (5th) 401, 2000 CarswellNS 279 (S.C.), the court allowed the wife's application to incorporate the spousal and child support provisions of the parties' maintenance agreement into an interim support order. Both parties had been represented by experienced counsel and the agreement had actually been drafted by the husband's counsel. No change of circumstances had occurred since the signing of the agreement and it should not be ignored.

Cases decided before the enactment of the Federal Child Support Guidelines:

Typically, an interim support award is made without benefit of discoveries, production of documents, evidence and the general safeguards which are found in a trial. It is intended to be made quickly to meet the immediate needs of the claimant based on the best evidence before the court. However, at trial, where full evidence has been adduced it is proper for the trial judge to make adjustments to the interim order based on that evidence: *MacMinn v. MacMinn* (1995), 17 R.F.L. (4th) 88 (Alta. C.A.).

The purpose of interim support is to permit the recipient spouse to maintain an acceptable standard of living until trial. Absent evidence of need, the award should not be made: *Eder v. Eder* (1995), 18 R.F.L. (4th) 454 (N.W.T. S.C.).

In an application for interim support, it is not sufficient merely to consider the factors of need and ability to pay. The presumptive claim to an equal standard of living, subject to the equitable sharing of the consequences of the marriage breakdown, should also be considered: *Carr v. Carr* (1993), 46 R.F.L. (3d) 326 (B.C. S.C.).

Where the husband, who was awarded custody of the parties' daughter, could no longer work overtime because of his child care responsibilities, the decrease in his income was considered in determining the quantum of interim spousal support to be paid by him: *Laue v. Laue* (1996), 19 R.F.L. (4th) 168 (Ont. Gen. Div.).

The determination of whether either party suffered an economic disadvantage as a result of the marriage or its breakdown is not a proper issue on an application for interim support. Such a determination is best left for the judge at trial: *Cafik v. Cafik* (1993), 46 R.F.L. (3d) 321 (Ont. Gen. Div.).

In awarding interim support, the court should give as much care as when awarding final support, as the interim amount frequently becomes the final amount. Accordingly, courts should be cautious in changing interim awards prior to trial: *Murray v. Murray* (1991), 35 R.F.L. (3d) 449, 82 Alta. L.R. (2d) 260, [1992] 1 W.W.R. 183, 123 A.R. 68 (Q.B.).

By its very nature, an interim support order is not a final order. It does not in any way limit the trial judge's discretion in determining any issue as to final maintenance: *De Grandis v. De Grandis* (1990), 28 R.F.L. (3d) 45, 48 B.C.L.R. (2d) 53 (S.C.).

On an interim support application, the court is entitled to consider the prospect of denial of a permanent support order: *Polgari v. Polgari* (1991), 36 R.F.L. (3d) 369 (B.C. Master).

On an application for interim support, a full inquiry concerning support issues is not necessary. The applicant must, however, establish a *prima facie* case for entitlement: *Theriault v. Theriault* (1994), 2 R.F.L. (4th) 157 (Alta. C.A.).

Interim support orders are temporary by nature and their purpose is to ensure the welfare of the parties, and any children, until the case can be heard on its merits. Such orders are not binding on the judge who rules on the merits: *Miller c. Cameau* (12 décembre 1991), C.A. Montréal 500-09-000496-912 (C.A. Qué.).

On an interim support application the court was of the opinion that support money to a wife need not be payable solely from income, as the word in the statute is "means", which would include both income and capital. The court also ruled that entertainment is not an allowable expense in the consideration of interim matters: *Manning v. Manning* (1990), 26 R.F.L. (3d) 151 (B.C. S.C.).

Where there was sufficient concern as to whether the mother was seeking spousal support trader the guise of child support and thereby abrogating her responsibility to contribute to the children's needs, her application for interim child support was dismissed: *Chutter v. Chutter* (1989), 23 R.F.L. (3d) 22 (B.C. S.C.); affirmed (1990), 26 R.F.L. (3d) 463 (B.C. C.A.).

The court must be cautious on interim applications for support because, if it transpires at trial that the evidence fails to support a finding of entitlement, it is not usually practical to order that the money be paid back: *Segal v. Segal* (1988), 14 R.F.L. (3d) 453, 54 Man. R. (2d) 142 (Q.B.).

Interim maintenance should only be awarded in cases where maintenance is likely to be awarded at trial: *Potschka v. Potschka* (1987), 5 R.F.L. (3d) 225 (Man. Q.B.).

The effect granting interim relief to a spouse would have at the subsequent trial is not a proper consideration in determining that spouse's right to interim support: *Lila v. Lila* (1986), 3 R.F.L. (3d) 226 (Ont. C.A.).

Under the *Divorce Act* of 1968, the court had the power to make interim orders for spousal support "as the court thinks reasonable having regard to the means and needs of each spouse", and for child support: *Divorce Act*, R.S.C. 1970, c. D-8, s. 10(a) and (b). No mention was made of the right to award lump sums or to secure support. In this respect the power of the court under the old statute was differently described for interim support than for permanent support. This difference led the court to hold that lump sums could not be awarded on interim applications. See *Forsythe v. Forsythe* (1980), 20 R.F.L. (2d) 295, 43 N.S.R. (2d) 707, 81 A.P.R. 707 (C.A.); *Wierzbicki v. Wierzbicki* (1982), 138 D.L.R. (3d) 673 (Ont. H.C.).

"I strongly incline to the view that under the *Divorce Act* an order can be made under s. 10 [now s. 15], where the party against whom it is sought to enforce the order is beyond the provincial boundaries": per Arnup J.A. in *Johnson v. Johnson*, 6 R.F.L. 171 at 175, [1972] 1 O.R. 212 (C.A.).

Where the wife's grounds for divorce are very tenuous but not impossible, the action is not clearly frivolous and vexatious. However, an interim maintenance award in such circumstances that goes beyond what is required to enable the wife to live modestly and in retirement may be reduced: *Nishikawa v. Nishikawa* (1971), 6 R.F.L. 191 (Ont. C.A.).

In *Wilson v. Wilson* (1984), 35 Sask. R. 238 (Q.B.), the wife was awarded interim maintenance on the basis that any moneys paid to her by the husband constituted an advance on the wife's share of matrimonial property.

Although the wife had accepted the transfer of the husband's interest in the matrimonial home in exchange for releasing him from all future claims, her application for interim maintenance was held not to be barred. The wife's health had deteriorated subsequent to the agreement, to the point that she was incapable of working, whereas the husband continued to enjoy a substantial income: *Pilon v. Pilon* (1983), 33 R.F.L. (2d) 239 (Ont. H.C.).

The fact that the petitioner wife may, at the trial of a pending divorce action, have difficulty proving her case because of a possible finding of condonation does not constitute a valid reason for refusing her interim corollary relief: *Barrett v. Barrett* (1982), 29 R.F.L. (2d) 13 (Ont. H.C.).

Where the likelihood of a permanent award is in substantial doubt, and where the applicant does not need assistance to maintain the standard to which she is accustomed, it is not "fit and just" to make an award of interim maintenance: *St. Clair-Hughes v. St. Clair-Hughes* (1980), 16 R.F.L. (2d) 189 (Ont. H.C.); *Sugar v. Sugar* (1974), 15 R.F.L. 145 at 148 (Ont. H.C.); *Mercer v. Mercer* (1972), 9 R.F.L. 356, [1973] 1 O.R. 84, 30 D.L.R. (3d) 284 (H.C.). See also *Windsor v. Windsor* (1975), 22 R.F.L. 296, 10 O.R. (2d) 653 (H.C.); *Davis v. Davis*, 4 R.F.L. 160 at 161–162, [1971] 2 O.R. 780 (H.C.). See also *H. (I) v. H. (H)*, 5 R.F.L. 214, [1971] 3 O.R. 222, 20 D.L.R. (3d) 62 (Master); *Tischler v. Tischler* (1970), 3 R.F.L. 193 (Ont. H.C.).

15§131 — Relationship to permanent support

In determining the quantum of permanent spousal support, significance should not be attached in all cases to the size of an interim support award: *Mosher v. Mosher* (1995), 13 R.F.L. (4th) 385, 140 N.S.R. (2d) 40, 339 A.P.R. 40 (C.A.); reversing in part (1993), 126 N.S.R. (2d) 67, 352 A.P.R. 367 (S.C.).

In *Pawliuk v. Pawliuk* (1999), 48 R.F.L. (4th) 188 (Sask. Q.B.), the court dismissed the father's application for a retroactive variation of child support. The father claimed that his income had been incorrectly determined on an interim child support application. The interim determination of his income, calculated by using a 3-year average, was not a matter reviewable by the court or one that warranted retroactive consideration.

Where the wife had developed alcoholism during the period of cohabitation which impaired her ability to work, her application for interim support was granted. It was reasonable to award support on an interim basis although the larger issue of whether the husband should be ordered to assist in the rehabilitation of the wife would require determination at trial: *Sencza v. Donohue* (1995), 18 R.F.L. (4th) 115 (Ont. Gen. Div.).

A detailed examination of an unequal property division in the wife's favour and her failure to seek retraining were found not to be appropriate in the case of an interim spousal support application in which the wife had established a *prima facie* case for support: *Gearin v. Gearin* (1999), 45 R.F.L. (4th) 333, 176 Nfld. & P.E.I.R. 76, 540 A.P.R. 76 (Nfld. U.F.C.)

In *Gearin v. Gearin* (1999), 45 R.F.L. (4th) 333, 176 Nfld. & P.E.I.R. 76, 540 A.P.R. 76 (Nfld. U.F.C.), the court accepted the wife's explanation for her nine-year delay in seeking interim support and granted her application. The wife admitted that she had benefitted from a consent child support order throughout the years and genuinely believed, given the husband's income, that spousal support would not have been granted.

15§132 — Jurisdiction to grant interim relief

Section 17 of the *Divorce Act* cannot be used as authority for granting interim spousal support in the context of an application to vary and extend limited term spousal support. The provision does not expressly authorize interim support on variation applications: *Y. (H.) v. Y. (D.)* (1998), 42 R.F.L. (4th) 418, 170 Nfld. & P.E.I.R. 44, 522 A.P.R. 44 (P.E.I. C.A.).

Cases decided before the enactment of the Federal Child Support Guidelines:

A court should not make an interim support order under the *Divorce Act* where the petition has been brought prematurely and the divorce itself cannot be granted: *Zemliak v. Zemliak* (1992), 40 R.F.L. (3d) 181, 78 Man. R. (2d) 104, 16 W.A.C. 104 (C.A.).

A Master has jurisdiction to grant interim relief in a divorce action despite the existence of a final support order made under a provincial statute: *Pantry v. Pantry* (1986), 50 R.F.L. (2d) 240, 53 O.R. (2d) 667, 25 D.L.R. (4th) 636, 13 O.A.C. 48 (C.A.).

The court is without jurisdiction to order interim support where the petition for divorce has been filed prematurely. An order made in such circumstances is properly stayed: *Zemliak v. Zemliak*, above.

Where the wife's claim for permanent maintenance is referred to the registrar contemporaneously with the granting of the decree *nisi*, the pronouncement of the decree does not deprive the trial judge of jurisdiction to make an interim order for maintenance under the *Divorce Act* pending the registrar's report: *Vedovato v. Vedovato*, 25 R.F.L. (2d) 297, [1982] 1 W.W.R. 752, 32 B.C.L.R. 360 (C.A.).

Where there is no final order for support under provincial legislation and the payee or prospective payee spouse intends to pursue a remedy for support or custody, if a divorce proceeding is initiated, support must be sought under the *Divorce Act*, if the other spouse demands it. The issue of spousal and child support should be determined as an interim motion under the *Divorce Act*, rather than as a variation of an interim order under the *Family Law Act*. The wife would not be disadvantaged by having the matter dealt with as an interim application under the *Divorce Act* either because the husband gains a right to argue causal connection or she loses her right to demand proof of change of circumstances. The advantages of consolidation in one action take precedence: *B. (R.) v. B. (M.)* (1989), 19 R.F.L. (3d) 92, 68 O.R. (2d) 32 (H.C.).

Where maintenance has been granted in a previous order, it is incorrect for a court, at a later date, to make an order of interim maintenance, pending a recommendation from the registrar. The proper course is to order a variation of the original maintenance order until such time as the reference to the registrar is made an order of the court: *Burton v. Burton* (1982), 27 R.F.L. (2d) 170, 36 B.C.L.R. 169 (C.A.). See also *Simpson v. Simpson* (1982), 27 R.F.L. (2d) 130, 134 D.L.R. (3d) 209 (Ont. H.C.) where it was held that there is no jurisdiction granted by the *Divorce Act* or other legislation to make interim maintenance orders pending cross-examination in an application to vary a maintenance order engrossed in a decree *nisi*.

Where the corollary relief in a decree *nisi* provides for joint custody, care and control but there is no provision for child maintenance to be paid by either parent to the other, the court may make an interim order for support under s. 15(2) of the *Divorce Act*. The court also was of the opinion that while the second wife of the payor cannot be expected to finance her husband's children from his first marriage, her income is a factor to be considered where the father claims, that on his salary, he cannot afford to contribute cash to his two children from his first marriage. The father was ordered to pay $500 per month for a child who spent one night a week with him and $250 per week for a child who spent 3 or 4 nights a week with him: *House v. Tunney (House)* (1991), 35 R.F.L. (3d) 68, 95 Sask. R. 73 (Q.B.).

"If the divorce judgment is silent on spousal or child support, the application to provide for support by the judgment may be brought under s. 15(2), *i.e.*, as in the action for divorce, and the court may then make an interim order under s. 15(3) and there is no need to invoke the parens patriae powers of the court in respect of child support": per Vannini D.C.J. in *Vipond v. Vipond* (1990), 25 R.F.L. (3d) 128 at 133, 72 O.R. (2d) 82 (S.C.).

In an application for increased maintenance, the court is without jurisdiction to make an interim order pending the variation hearing. In such an instance, however, the court can make a final order which itself can be subsequently varied: *McKillop v. McKillop* (1985), 44 R.F.L. (2d) 221 (Ont. H.C.).

"[T]here are exceptional or compelling circumstances where it is within the jurisdiction of the court to make an interim or interim interim order for maintenance for a former spouse ... and where the court should exercise its discretion to grant that relief pending the hearing of the motion to vary a decree nisi ... There is a heavy onus on the applicant to cause the court to exercise its discretion in this way": *Southgate v. Southgate* (1984), 41 R.F.L. (2d) 246 at 250 (Ont. H.C.).

Where the wife had already obtained an interim interim support order under the *Family Law Reform Act*, her subsequent application for interim maintenance under the *Divorce Act* was struck. As both parties considered the first order to continue in effect and as the two applications were essentially identical as far as the relief sought, it was held that the wife's application had been effectively dealt with in the earlier proceeding: *Bombier v. Bombier* (1984), 42 R.F.L. (2d) 93 (Ont. Master).

There is no statutory power authorizing the court to grant any interim relief once a decree *nisi* has been granted. Therefore, in an application to vary the maintenance provisions of a decree *nisi*, the court is without jurisdiction to grant interim maintenance pending the hearing of the variation application: *MacNeil v. MacNeil* (1982), 134 D.L.R. (3d) 115 (Ont. H.C.).

A court making an interim order for corollary relief must also have jurisdiction to grant the actual divorce. Therefore, where a court on an application for interim relief adjourns a challenge to its jurisdiction until the trial of the divorce, such court lacks jurisdiction to make an interim order: *Bickerton v. Bickerton* (1983), 31 R.F.L. (2d) 323, 45 N.B.R. (2d) 112, 118 A.P.R. 112 (T.D.).

Where the wife, in response to her husband's petition for divorce, applied for interim maintenance prior to delivering an answer or counter-petition, her application was adjourned pending her delivery of pleadings. The court was without jurisdiction at that stage of the proceedings to grant the relief requested: *Collis v. Collis* (1983), 35 R.F.L. (2d) 8 (Ont. H.C.); *Mudrinic v. Mudrinic* (1978), 6 R.F.L. (2d) 326 (Ont. Masters); *Cisecki v. Cisecki* (1972), 8 R.F.L. 232 (B.C. S.C.).

15§133 — Interim spousal support

On an application for spousal support the court may "make an interim order requiring a spouse to secure or pay, or to secure and pay, such lump sum or periodic sums, or such lump sum and periodic sums, as the court thinks reasonable for the support of the other spouse, pending the determination of the application": *Divorce Act*, s. 15.2(2). The order may be made "for a definite or indefinite period or until a specified event occurs," and the court "may impose terms, conditions or restrictions in connection with the order as it thinks fit and just": *Divorce Act*, s. 15.2(3). In making the order "the court shall take into consideration the condition, means, needs and other circumstances of each spouse, including

(a) the length of time the spouses cohabited;

(b) the functions performed by each spouse during cohabitation; and

(c) any order, agreement or arrangement relating to support of either spouse": *Divorce Act*, s. 15.2(4).

The spousal support order "should

(a) recognize any economic advantages or disadvantages to the spouses arising from the marriage or its breakdown;

(b) apportion between the spouses any financial consequences arising from the care of any child of the marriage over and above any obligation for the support of any child of the marriage;

(c) relieve any economic hardship of the spouses arising from the breakdown of the marriage; and

(d) in so far as practicable, promote the economic self-sufficiency of each spouse within a reasonable period of time": *Divorce Act*, s. 15.2(6).

Where the court is considering both an application for child support and an application for spousal support, "the court shall give priority to child support in determining the applications": *Divorce Act*, s. 15.3(1).

The court in *Glass v. Glass* (1997), 34 R.F.L. (4th) 411, 1997 CarswellMan 632, 123 Man. R. (2d) 239, 159 W.A.C. 239 (Man. C.A.), allowed in part the appeal by the husband from an interim spousal support order. The provision in the motions judge's order that the husband make mortgage and utility payments on the marital home was deleted, as was the court's provision for an arbitrary amount of maintenance of $2,200 per month if the wife left the marital home, without having evidence to determine the wife's needs in other accomodation.

A judge has jurisdiction to make an interim support order finite in time even where counsel had agreed that the order should be open-ended: *Gidora v. Gidora* (1997), 27 R.F.L. (4th) 292, 85 B.C.A.C. 311, 138 W.A.C. 311, 1997 CarswellBC 273 (B.C. C.A.).

The court held in *Hennig v. Hennig* (1995), 18 R.F.L. (4th) 87, 1995 CarswellAlta 840, 178 A.R. 114, 110 W.A.C. 114 (Alta. C.A.) that under s. 16(2) of the *Domestic Relations Act*, if the plaintiff has sufficient means of support independent of her husband from any source, then an interim order for support cannot be made. The court was of the opinion that the legislation was anachronistic and inconsistent with the current theories of spousal support and possibly *Charter* values. In this case, there was also an application pending for spousal support under the *Divorce Act*. In that hearing, the chambers judge would determine what spousal support, if any, should be payable by the husband. The appellate court invited the chambers judge to consider the retroactive provisions of the *Divorce Act* in deciding what spousal support should be payable and the duration of the order. If there has been an overpayment, then the husband would be entitled to be repaid the difference or credited with the extra amount, if any.

In *Novak v. Bingle* (11 décembre 1991), nº C.A. Montréal 500-09-000988-907 (C.A. Qué.), an interim support award granted to the wife to permit her to perform urgent repairs on the family home was upheld on appeal.

An order for interim spousal support should reflect the amount of income required by one spouse in order to allow that spouse to maintain a reasonable standard of living, having regards to the means of both parties. It should cover only those needs that will arise from the time of an application until litigation is complete: *Bennett v. Bennett* (2005), 22 R.F.L. (6th) 399, 2005 CarswellAlta 1994, 2005 ABQB 984, 57 Alta. L.R. (4th) 380 (Alta. Q.B.).

In a claim for interim spousal support, the fact that the husband has the expense of defending charges for an alleged assault of the wife was irrelevant. The wife should not have to fund the defence by a reduction in her support entitlement: *Sharf v. Sharf* (2004), 10 R.F.L. (6th) 167, 2004 CarswellOnt 4858 (S.C.J.).

Although an in-depth analysis of entitlement is not required on an application for interim spousal support, it is necessary that the claimant establish a *prima facie* case of entitlement: *Charbonneau v. Charbonneau* (2004), 9 R.F.L. (6th) 67, 2004 CarswellOnt 5211 (S.C.J.)

Where the wife had significant assets upon which she could draw to support herself until trial, her application for interim support was dismissed. The fact that the equalization payment owing to her was outstanding did not automatically entitle her to support: *Tout v. Bennett* (2003), 38 R.F.L. (5th) 223, 2003 CarswellOnt 1625 (Ont. S.C.J.)

In *Cherneski v. Cherneski* (2003), 49 R.F.L. (5th) 299, 2003 CarswellOnt 4896 (Ont. S.C.J.), the court refused the wife's claim for interim spousal support brought after the expiration of the limited term support provided for in the parties' separation agreement. The wife's allegations that she had been pressured to sign the agreement were not determinative of the issue and she was not financially desperate. Also the possibility existed that permanent support could be awarded at trial and enforced retroactively.

Expenses such as R.R.S.P. contributions, R.E.S.P. contributions and charitable donations are inappropriate claims on an application for interim support: *Titchener v. Titchener*, 42 R.F.L. (5th) 461, 2003 CarswellBC 1771, 2003 BCSC 1120 (B.C. S.C. [In Chambers]).

Where the wife had given up her nursing career to raise the parties' children and had enjoyed a high standard of living throughout the marriage, her application for interim support was allowed. The parties' high standard of living was relevant in establishing the wife's needs: *Vandale v. Vandale* (2003), 39 R.F.L. (5th) 445, 2003 CarswellAlta 724, 2003 ABQB 407 (Alta. Q.B.).

At the time of the marriage breakdown, the wife held a well-paying job and was economically self-sufficient. She lost this job and found work at a lower salary that did not meet her needs. Her claim for support in a *Family Law Act* proceeding was dismissed on the ground that her need for support did not result from an economic disadvantage caused by the marriage. In subsequent divorce proceedings taken four years after the marriage breakdown, she claimed support again and moved for interim support. In allowing her motion, and granting interim support of $800 a month, the court held that the fact that she had achieved economic self-sufficiency at the time of the marriage breakdown did not extinguish the support obligation founded on the marriage relationship. This obligation remained dormant for four years — which was not an unreasonable period considering that cohabitation under the marriage lasted 27 years — until the need for support arose. The loss of the job that gave rise to the need was not too remote. Her claim for support was neither tenuous nor uncertain, and there was no reason for not making an interim support order: *Radcliff v. Radcliff* (2001), 2001 CarswellOnt 1141, 15 R.F.L. (5th) 423 (Ont. S.C.J.); additional reasons at (2001), 2001 CarswellOnt 1928, 17 R.F.L. (5th) 417 (Ont. S.C.J.).

In *Volken v. Volken*, 2001 CarswellBC 1401, 2001 BCSC 970, 19 R.F.L. (5th) 205 (B.C. S.C. [In Chambers]), the husband's annual income was found to be $2,000,000. The wife was not employed outside the home and had no income of her own. After the separation the husband made voluntary payments of $5,000 a month which reflected the relatively frugal lifestyle of the family before the separation. The wife's expenses after the separation exceeded these payments. She supplemented them by taking out a mortgage on her equity in the family home. She applied for interim child support for three children and spousal support for herself. The *Guidelines* Table amount of $25,723 per month in child support was awarded retroactive to the 1st of January, the month in which her application for interim support was made. For herself, the wife sought interim spousal support of $18,000 per month plus a lump sum of $10,000 to pay for repairs to the home and an automobile, $50,000 for payment of the services of a business valuator and $100,000 for a legal retainer. The husband's monthly expenses were about $9,000. The court found that after taking into account the child support obligation, the husband's after tax earnings would meet the needs of the wife and still leave him with more than enough for his own expenses. Exercising its discretion on the basis of the condition, means, needs, and other circumstances of each spouse in light of the objectives of spousal support orders described in s. 15.2 of the *Divorce Act*, the court ordered interim monthly spousal support of $15,000 plus a lump sum payment of $10,000. The court refused to make the spousal support payments retroactive. The husband could not be faulted for his delay in making financial disclosure because of the complexities of his holdings. Any deficiencies in child support were made up by the retroactivity of that order, and the high amount compared to the "relatively frugal" lifestyle before separation. Also, any shortfall experienced by the wife was met by her borrowing against the equity in the family home. And any order that might be made as to retroactivity would have the undesirable effect of redistributing capital, or awarding additional spousal support, under the guise of child support. With respect to the claim for an amount to cover the payment of fees, the husband consented to an interim advance of $50,000 against the wife's entitlement on property division to fund equal retainers for the business valuator and counsel. Because it was on consent the court made an order in those terms, but in doing so expressed the opinion that the weight of authority is against ordering an interim distribution of assets to meet past, and, in particular, future legal expenses except to fund unusual disbursements relating specifically to the valuation of assets.

Interim spousal support will be refused where the marriage or its breakdown have not caused any diminution in a spouse's ability to earn income as a result of the roles adopted in the marriage: *Burmi v. Dhiman* (2001), 18 R.F.L. (5th) 9, 2001 CarswellOnt 1812, [2001] O.J. No. 2010 (Ont. S.C.J.); additional reasons at (2001), 2001 CarswellOnt 2195 (Ont. S.C.J.). In this case, the parties had married in India in an arranged marriage and had cohabited for seven weeks. The wife claimed that her husband's repudiation of the marriage had led to her ostracism and ridicule within her religious community and her inability to remarry well. The court was of the opinion that the wife had not suffered any economic loss as contemplated by the *Divorce Act*.

The trend in law is to ensure that each party's household enjoys a similar standard of living. The financial circumstances of each parent should not be so divergent that a child is tempted to make the more affluent household the primary residence. The *Divorce Act* requires a fair and equitable distribution of resources to alleviate the consequences of marriage breakdown. This principle is as applicable to interim situations as it is to final situations. Taking into account the fact that the applicant earned $20,000 a year and the respondent earned $99,000 a year, that the respondent would be paying child support and, possibly, a payment for extraordinary expenses, the court ordered interim spousal support of $2,400 a month: *Harrison v. Harrison* (2001), 2001 CarswellOnt 420, 14 R.F.L. (5th) 321 (Ont. S.C.J.).

Legal costs are not appropriate expenses for consideration on an interim support motion: *Burmi v. Dhiman* (2001), 18 R.F.L. (5th) 9, 2001 CarswellOnt 1812, [2001] O.J. No. 2010 (Ont. S.C.J.); additional reasons at (2001), 2001 CarswellOnt 2195 (Ont. S.C.J.).

The wife's unilateral action to leave secure employment in India to move to join her husband in Ontario, when she knew or ought to have known that the relationship was over, cannot create economic disadvantage contemplated by the *Divorce Act*: *Burmi v. Dhiman* (2001), 18 R.F.L. (5th) 9, 2001 CarswellOnt 1812, [2001] O.J. No. 2010 (Ont. S.C.J.); additional reasons at (2001), 2001 CarswellOnt 2195 (Ont. S.C.J.). The wife's application for interim spousal support was rejected. The court was of the opinion that it must perform a rigorous analysis of all the factors in s. 15.1 of the *Divorce Act* in determining support, both on an application for interim support and for final support.

Interim spousal support will be granted, even though access visits to children will be less frequent, since to receive support is in the children's best interests: *Hahn v. Hahn*, 17 R.F.L. (5th) 330, 2001 CarswellAlta 559, 2001 ABQB 357 (Alta. Q.B.); additional reasons at 2001 CarswellAlta 1119, 2001 ABQB 722 (Alta. Q.B.).

The effective date for the commencement of interim support should be the date of the issue of the petition, when there are no special circumstances to favour an earlier date and where the divorce action is commenced a month after the separation began: *Radcliff v. Radcliff* (2001), 17 R.F.L. (5th) 417, 2001 CarswellOnt 1928 (Ont. S.C.J.).

In determining quantum of support, after a long term traditional marriage, it is reasonable for the parties to have a similar after-tax income available to them: *Haroun v. Haroun* (2001), 20 R.F.L. (5th) 64, 2001 CarswellOnt 2253 (Ont. S.C.J.); additional reasons at (2001), 2001 CarswellOnt 2450 (Ont. S.C.J.).

Where a lavish and opulent lifestyle has been enjoyed by the spouse over several decades, the traditional "living modestly in retirement" approach to interim spousal support is inadequate and inappropriate: *Bennett v. Bennett* (2001), 13 R.F.L. (5th) 325, 2001 CarswellOnt 168, [2001] O.J. No. 224 (S.C.J.).

In *Bailey v. Plaxton*, 6 R.F.L. (5th) 29, 47 O.R. (3d) 593, 2000 CarswellOnt 1194, [2000] O.J. No. 1187 (Ont. S.C.J.), the court held that the former wife was entitled to interim spousal support pursuant to s. 15.2 of the *Divorce Act* despite a separation agreement which provided for spousal support for three years ending 10 years before the judgment. The court considered all factors required pursuant to s. 15.2, including the separation agreement, and concluded that in the circumstances it was warranted and reasonable to make an interim support order, in the amount of $5,000 per month pending the determination of the application under s. 15.2(1).

The court, in *Fritze v. Day*, 15 R.F.L. (5th) 60, 2001 CarswellAlta 282, 2001 ABQB 172 (Alta. Q.B.), ordered interim spousal support for a limited term of three months where the wife, an intelligent, capable and university-educated woman without children had done nothing to obtain a job for 14 months. She was found to be capable of supporting herself.

A lower income parent who is required to make child support payments under the *Guidelines* to the higher income custodial parent is not automatically precluded from receiving spousal support: *Richter v. Vahamaki* (2000), 8 R.F.L. (5th) 194, 2000 CarswellOnt 2440 (Ont. S.C.J.). The father was ordered to pay the mother $1,000 per month in interim spousal support.

In *Andrews v. Andrews*, 8 R.F.L. (5th) 1, 2000 CarswellAlta 564, 2000 ABQB 384 (Alta. Q.B.), interim spousal support for six months was granted to the husband where he suffered a disability. However, the court did not accept that the husband was incapable of doing any work and he might receive increased disability payments from the government.

In *Kennedy v. Kennedy* (2000), 11 R.F.L. (5th) 150, 2000 CarswellOnt 3622, [2000] O.J. No. 3742 (Ont. S.C.J.), the court accepted the wife's evidence that her stress-related illnesses which prevented her from working were the result of emotional and psychological abuse imposed by the husband. Accordingly, the wife had established an economic disadvantage related to the marriage and she was awarded interim spousal support.

A claim for interim spousal support will be rejected where the wife had been recently employed at occupations which met her modest needs and there was no explanation for her decision not to return to work when it appeared that workers' compensation authorities had apparently deemed her fit to work: *Harris v. Harris* (1999), 48 R.F.L. (4th) 341, 1999 CarswellAlta 558, 242 A.R. 382 (Alta. Q.B.). Moreover, the wife had not shown that her move outside the jurisdiction was made with some reasonable assessment of employment opportunities available or with the welfare of the children in mind. The husband ought not to be required to subsidize the wife's personal choice. Lastly, the husband's assumption of all matrimonial debt should be taken into account as this action provided the wife with some financial benefit.

In *Y. (H.) v. Y. (D.)* (1999), 49 R.F.L. (4th) 450, 175 Nfld. & P.E.I.R. 85, 537 A.P.R. 85, 1999 CarswellPEI 43 (P.E.I. T.D. [In Chambers]), the husband was not allowed to set off his monthly child support obligation against an interim spousal support overpayment owed by the wife. Child support and spousal support obligations should not be intermingled. It is unfair to the child and contrary to the spirit of the legislation to excuse a parent from paying child support on the basis of dealings between the spouses.

In an application for interim spousal support, the parties must generally take each other as they find them. Accordingly, a husband's allegations that his unemployed wife was able to work and support herself may be appropriate in an application for long-term support, but it should not be adjudicated upon in an interim/interim application: *Ridgeway-Firman v. Firman* (1999), 1999 CarswellOnt 1201 (Ont. Gen. Div.).

Even though any amounts received as interim spousal support will reduce payments from social assistance, where the wife is at an economic disadvantage caused by the birth of the parties' child, the primary financial responsibility for her support should be with the husband, rather than the state: *Cluett v. Cluett* (1998), 1998 CarswellNWT 38 (N.W.T. S.C.).

In *Mahoney v. King* (1998), 39 R.F.L. (4th) 361, 1998 CarswellOnt 2348, [1998] O.J. No. 2296 (Ont. Gen. Div.), an application for interim spousal support was refused where the parties had cohabitated in a five or six-year relationship while one of the parties had been married to another person. The court ruled that if support were ordered at trial, the award would be retroactive to at least the date of the application.

If a party is dissatisfied with an interim interim support order the proper procedure is to arrange for cross-examinations as quickly as possible and return a motion for a hearing on the interim application. Appealing from the order is not the appropriate approach: *Jessome v. Jessome* (1998), 43 R.F.L. (4th) 196, 1998 CarswellOnt 5161 (Ont. Gen. Div.).

In *Gordon v. Gordon* (1998), 36 R.F.L. (4th) 443, 1998 CarswellOnt 966 (Ont. Gen. Div.), the wife who was unemployed and heavily indebted was able to make out a *prima facie* case for interim support, even though the husband also had serious debt obligations. The court took into account only the most basic needs of the parties. It assessed the wife's basic needs, deducted the amount the wife would receive in unemployment benefits and the remainder was the amount of the wife's interim support.

A court should deny interim spousal support where the dependant spouse fails to demonstrate, with cogent and compelling evidence, a current need for interim spousal support from the husband: *Byerley v. Byerley* (1998), 41 R.F.L. (4th) 50, 1998 CarswellOnt 3649 (Ont. Gen. Div.). In this case, the wife who was living in a common-law union did not provide the court with her common-law spouse's income and expenses. The wife had been self-supporting for a year and then her common-law husband had supported her for almost a year before she sought support. At the time of the hearing the wife and her common-law spouse were expecting a child.

An award of interim spousal support requires need on the part of the claimant and the ability to pay on the part of the payor and is not to be based solely on the income of the payor: *Warford v. Warford* (1998), 1998 CarswellOnt 781 (Ont. Gen. Div.).

An interim spousal order, which is subject to review after a set period of time, is not truly a "time limited" award. Accordingly, such an award is properly open to review under s. 15.2 of the *Divorce Act*, even after it has expired: *Chambers v. Chambers*, 40 R.F.L. (4th) 351, [1998] N.W.T.R. 252, 1998 CarswellNWT 100 (N.W.T. S.C.).

In *Modry v. Modry*, 42 R.F.L. (4th) 387, 1998 CarswellAlta 949, [1998] A.J. No. 1162, 231 A.R. 110, 1998 ABQB 868 (Alta. Q.B.), the wife was granted $15,000 monthly interim support despite the fact that the husband's accountant gave evidence that the husband's liabilities exceeded his assets. The husband showed no evidence indicating any demand for loan repayments nor had he reduced his own lifestyle. The husband could liquidate assets to reduce his debt load, which had ballooned since separation, while paying support and maintaining his own lifestyle.

Where both the husband and the wife had monthly incomes in deficit positions, the wife's needs for interim spousal support purposes were properly determined by taking into account only her most basic requirements for sustenance: *Gordon v. Gordon* (1998), 36 R.F.L. (4th) 443, 1998 CarswellOnt 966 (Ont. Gen. Div.).

In *Davidson v. Davidson* (1998), 42 R.F.L. (4th) 154, 230 A.R. 151, 1998 CarswellAlta 879, [1998] A.J. No. 1040 (Alta. Q.B.), the wife was granted only nominal interim support. The wife had substantial assets, considerable rental income and had obtained two university degrees during the marriage. The parties had amassed a sizable fortune and the wife had actually been economically advantaged by the marriage by her entitlement to a share in these assets.

Where there has been a fairly lengthy marriage and a substantial history of the use of capital to support a joint lifestyle, a spouse should not be required to have a lifestyle based on income alone, rather than the other means available to the spouse, at least on an interim basis: *Jackson v. Jackson* (1997), 35 R.F.L. (4th) 194, 1997 CarswellOnt 4717, [1997] O.J. No. 4790 (Ont. Gen. Div.).

On an interim interim support motion pending the return of an interim support motion, it is appropriate to modify the claimed needs of the petitioner and consequently, the court ordered support of $45,000 per month and not the $60,000 per month claimed: *Webster v. Webster* (1997), 37 R.F.L. (4th) 347, 1997 CarswellOnt 815, 32 O.R. (3d) 679, 28 O.T.C. 81 (Ont. Gen. Div.).

Where there were two options for calculating interim child and spousal support depending on whether the husband's pension plan benefits were included as part of the wife's income, the parties were ordered to choose an option: *Thompson v. Thompson* (1997), 30 R.F.L. (4th) 376, 1997 CarswellPEI 23, 150 Nfld. & P.E.I.R. 86, 470 A.P.R. 86 (P.E.I. T.D. [In Chambers]).

In *Haddad-Hashem v. Hashem* (1997), 1997 CarswellPEI 32, 28 R.F.L. (4th) 225 (P.E.I. T.D. [In Chambers]), the husband since separation had been paying all expenses for the matrimonial home, including taxes, oil, electricity and upkeep and had permitted the wife to live in the house. Title to the home was in the name of the husband and his father. The court, in refusing the wife's application for interim spousal support, held that the husband was providing sufficient spousal support by paying the expenses and the arrangement should continue. If the wife had sought support at the time of separation, she probably would have received a support order in a specific amount. The wife claimed that the parties had separated in 1988. The husband claimed that the date was 1976.

The matters, which are to be considered on interim or interim interim support orders, are the means and needs of the parties. Such orders are to provide a reasonably acceptable solution to problems until trial: *Peel v. Griffin* (1996), 19 R.F.L. (4th) 94, 1996 CarswellOnt 292 (Ont. Gen. Div.). Although the parties were married for only two years, the wife relied on the relationship to her detriment and the court awarded the wife $2,000 per month in interim interim support. A different result may be obtained at trial.

On an application for interim support, while the needs and means of the parties should not take a predominant position in the deliberations, they are considerations which provide greater certainty when all the information is not available and before the court has determined whether there is economic advantage or disadvantage or economic hardship arising from the marriage or its breakdown: *Short v. Short* (1996), 21 R.F.L. (4th) 429, 1996 CarswellBC 893, [1996] B.C.J. No. 910 (B.C. S.C.). It would seem that the court decided to grant the petitioner $700 per month in interim spousal support primarily on the basis of considerations of the needs and means and needs of the parties.

In *Robertson v. Hotte* (1996), 1996 CarswellOnt 1506, 2 O.T.C. 1, 21 R.F.L. (4th) 452 (Ont. Gen. Div.), the court was of the opinion that on an interim or interim interim application for support, the cases support a four-step analysis that concentrates on the parties' needs and means:

(1) Does the Applicant have standing to claim support?

(2) Is the Applicant entitled to the support?

(3) What are the dependent's needs?

(4) Does the payor have the ability to pay?

In *Robertson v. Hotte* (1996), 1996 CarswellOnt 1506, 2 O.T.C. 1, 21 R.F.L. (4th) 452 (Ont. Gen. Div.), because of the nature of the proceedings, the court will not conduct an in-depth analysis of the first two issues, standing and entitlement. If the applicant is able to make out an arguable case for standing and entitlement the court will assess support on the basis of the parties' needs and means. The parties had lived together off and on for over 20 years. They had entered into a domestic contract that contained a provision releasing support, and the respondent contended that the applicant did not qualify as a spouse. The motions judge awarded interim support finding that the domestic contract was ambiguous and that it would be unconscionable if it provided for no support. The applicant was unemployed. The respondent's appeal to the General Division was dismissed. There was a triable issue with respect to the domestic contract, and the fact that the parties had three children provided a good argument that the applicant was a spouse within the meaning of the *Family Law Act*.

The applicant was granted interim spousal support where her current difficulty in obtaining employment was largely attributable to her eight-year relationship with the respondent who encouraged her to remain on the farm and not seek work elsewhere: *Thorvaldson v. Vanin* (1996), 25 R.F.L. (4th) 273, 1996 CarswellSask 617, 149 Sask. R. 231 (Sask. Q.B.).

Where the applicant has demonstrated a need for spousal support and the respondent has the means, interim support will be granted: *Cote v. Cote* (1995), 12 R.F.L. (4th) 194, 1995 CarswellOnt 91 (Ont. Gen. Div.).

On an application for interim support, the court is to take into account any benefit to the parties from use of family property as well as the cost of paying family debts. The court, through the award, should attempt an equitable distribution of the parties' resources although a fair reorganization of wealth is not automatically achieved through the equalizing of incomes: *Bettles v. Bettles* (1994), 7 R.F.L. (4th) 153, 122 Nfld. & P.E.I.R. 341, 379 A.P.R. 341, 1994 CarswellPEI 15 (P.E.I. T.D.).

Where the spouses had used all of their resources to meet their living expenses, interim support should be determined by considering all available resources and not the parties' estimated expenses. After the children's reasonable needs have been met, the remaining resources should be distributed equitably between the parties: *Forbes v. Forbes* (1994), 2 R.F.L. (4th) 121, 117 Sask. R. 299, 1994 CarswellSask 36 (Sask. Q.B.).

On an application for interim support, it is not necessary, appropriate or possible for the court to make the in depth type of inquiry contemplated in *Moge v. Moge* (1992), 43 R.F.L. (3d) 345, [1992] S.C.J. No. 107, 1992 CarswellMan 143 (Eng.), 1992 CarswellMan 222 (Fr.), [1993] 1 W.W.R. 481, 99 D.L.R. (4th) 456, [1992] 3 S.C.R. 813, 81 Man. R. (2d) 161, 30 W.A.C. 161, 145 N.R. 1 (S.C.C.). Interim orders are, by their nature, "holding orders" and whereas the support objectives outlined in the *Divorce Act* are, strictly speaking, applicable on an interim hearing, common sense dictates that the depth of the inquiry at that stage of the proceedings is quite different from that expected at trial: *Labelle v. Labelle* (1993), 46 R.F.L. (3d) 341, 1993 CarswellMan 48, 87 Man. R. (2d) 207 (Man. Q.B.).

The support objectives set out in s. 15(7) [now s. 15.2(6)] of the *Divorce Act* are relevant to a claim for interim spousal support. Where the limited evidence presented by a wife on an interim support application indicated her need for funds to complete her education and to assist her in becoming self-sufficient, she was found entitled to interim support. If at the final hearing the wife was found to be disentitled from support, an order requiring the repayment of the interim funds could be made: *Kendell v. Kendell* (1993), 48 R.F.L. (3d) 146, 1993 CarswellNfld 25, 110 Nfld. & P.E.I.R. 213, 346 A.P.R. 213 (Nfld. T.D.).

Where the wife is unemployed, the quantum of interim spousal support is likely to exceed that finally awarded at trial to ease the transition between her non-working status and her return to the workforce. The issue of her ability to achieve self-sufficiency is a matter for determination by the trial judge: *Offet v. Offet* (1993), 1 R.F.L. (4th) 203, 1993 Carswell-Alta 435, [1993] A.J. No. 1029, 150 A.R. 11 (Alta. Q.B.).

The fact that the wife left the husband for another man was found not to disentitle her from interim spousal support in *Kendell v. Kendell* (1993), 48 R.F.L. (3d) 146, 1993 CarswellNfld 25, 110 Nfld. & P.E.I.R. 213, 346 A.P.R. 213 (Nfld. T.D.). Her conduct was not relevant to her claim.

The prevalent view of interim support is that the dependent spouse should be allowed to maintain his or her existing lifestyle pending resolution: *Weil v. Weil* (1993), 143 N.B.R. (2d) 108, 366 A.P.R. 108, 1993 CarswellNB 281, [1993] N.B.J. No. 560 (N.B. Q.B.).

Where the wife claimed both interim spousal and child support, and the child support claim was dismissed, it was held that the wife's spousal support claim was not limited to the amount specified in her application. The wife had anticipated that the child support order would also help to defray her costs. As that claim had been dismissed, it was not proper to hold her to the quantum of spousal support outlined in her pleading: *Lopez v. Lopez* (1993), 48 R.F.L. (3d) 298, 1993 CarswellOnt 350 (Ont. Gen. Div.).

Where the wife planned to quit her part-time career shortly after separation to pursue upgrading for long-term career plans, she was found entitled to interim support. Given her age (46) and her position, she was under no obligation to defer her career plans until trial, particularly as the husband had not established that her plan was unreasonable: *Davison v. Davison* (1992), 42 R.F.L. (3d) 341, 1992 CarswellNS 76 (N.S. T.D.).

An award of interim support or interim interim support should not be made if there is no possibility of the claimant's success at trial. The onus is on the claimant to plead the facts necessary to support the case, the entitlement principles being the same for an interim disposition as for a final disposition: *Smith v. Smith* (1987), 11 R.F.L. (3d) 214, 1987 CarswellOnt 268, 63 O.R. (2d) 146 (Ont. H.C.).

The fact that a spouse might be found entitled to support at trial does not justify an interim support award where that spouse could not establish any immediate pressing need: *Viswalingam v. Viswalingam* (1992), 41 R.F.L. (3d) 155, 1992 CarswellNWT 6 (N.W.T. S.C.).

The requirement that a spouse seek self-sufficiency should not be scrutinized as closely on an interim application as it might be on a final hearing: *Titchener v. Titchener* (1991), 31 R.F.L. (3d) 173, 1991 CarswellBC 509 (B.C. Master).

An application for interim spousal support should be refused where the claimant's earning capacity has not been altered or impaired during the course of the marriage: *Horne v. Horne* (1989), 19 R.F.L. (3d) 399, 1989 CarswellBC 390 (B.C. S.C.).

Where the wife had $20,000 remaining from an interim distribution of matrimonial property, her application for interim support was refused. Given her resources, she did not require the husband's assistance to live comfortably until trial: *Kujawa v. Kujawa* (1990), 28 R.F.L. (3d) 386, 1990 CarswellSask 71, 87 Sask. R. 101 (Sask. Q.B.).

In *Fabian v. Fabian* (1987), 65 Sask. R. 271, 1987 CarswellSask 593 (Sask. Q.B.), the wife was awarded $780 monthly as interim support in recognition of her at-home contribution during the parties' 25-year marriage. The wife had been employed as a medical technician but since losing her job had attempted to sell real estate with little success. The court rejected the husband's assertion that the wife's claim should be denied because of her refusal to attempt to find alternative employment as a medical technician.

In order to prove entitlement to interim support, as well as permanent support, a claimant must be able to prove a causal connection between the need and the marriage: *Miller v. Miller* (1988), 15 R.F.L. (3d) 366, 1988 CarswellOnt 272 (Ont. H.C.). See also *Weppler v. Weppler* (1988), 15 R.F.L. (3d) 279, 1988 CarswellOnt 265 (Ont. H.C.).

Where the wife had an annual salary of $41,200 her application for interim maintenance was dismissed. Although she would probably be entitled to maintenance at trial, she would be able to maintain a reasonable standard of living pending trial using her own resources: *Koulack v. Saifer* (1986), 43 Man. R. (2d) 70, 1986 CarswellMan 269 (Man. Q.B.).

In *Lemmon v. Lemmon* (1984), 43 R.F.L. (2d) 186, [1985] 2 W.W.R. 574, 1984 CarswellMan 193, 33 Man. R. (2d) 176 (Man. Q.B.); additional reasons at (1984), 43 R.F.L. (2d) 436, 33 Man. R. (2d) 174 (Man. Q.B.), the wife's application for interim maintenance was refused in light of the fact that the wife was not in financial difficulty and an immediate trial date was available.

Where the parties had only been married for four months, the wife's application for interim maintenance was refused. The marriage had in no way affected the wife's lifestyle or her ability to maintain herself and as no application for permanent maintenance was contemplated, interim maintenance would not be "fit and just". *MacKenzie v. MacKenzie* (1984), 38 R.F.L. (2d) 14, 1984 CarswellSask 43, 32 Sask. R. 84 (Sask. Q.B.). See also *Alexander v. Alexander* (1977), 3 R.F.L. (2d) 47, 1977 CarswellBC 269 (B.C. S.C.); *Selmes v. Selmes* (1975), 25 R.F.L. 396, 1975 CarswellBC 81 (B.C. S.C.) at 397 [R.F.L.]; *Fehr v. Fehr* (1973), 10 R.F.L. 399, 1973 CarswellSask 12 (Sask. Q.B.); *Millard v. Millard* (1987), 11 R.F.L. (3d) 119, 1987 CarswellOnt 260 (Ont. U.F.C.); *Goldberg v. Goldberg* (1982), 39 O.R. (2d) 637, 1982 CarswellOnt 818 (Ont. Master); *Bayer v. Bayer* (1985), 49 R.F.L. (2d) 75, 1985 CarswellOnt 336 (Ont. Master).

Where both parties worked during most of the marriage and the wife only became dependant after she left her employment, perhaps unreasonably, she should be entitled to some interim support to help her to contribute to her own support and to relieve her current economic hardship: *Marshall v. Marshall* (2001), 16 R.F.L. (5th) 347, 2001 CarswellNfld 111, 200 Nfld. & P.E.I.R. 120, 603 A.P.R. 120 (Nfld. U.F.C.). The interim support was primarily needs-based or non-compensatory.

A detailed examination of an unequal property division in the wife's favour and her failure to seek retraining were found not to be appropriate in the case of an interim spousal support application in which the wife had established a *prima facie* case for support: *Gearin v. Gearin* (1999), 45 R.F.L. (4th) 333, 176 Nfld. & P.E.I.R. 76, 540 A.P.R. 76, 1999 CarswellNfld 87 (Nfld. U.F.C.).

Where the wife stayed at home to raise the parties' four children and was definitely economically disadvantaged and currently has health problems, she should be granted interim spousal support to help her attain the objectives set out in s. 15(7): *Bell v. Bell* (1998), 42 R.F.L. (4th) 301, 1998 CarswellNfld 246 (Nfld. U.F.C.).

Where a spouse has formed a relationship with a third party but the relationship is transient only with no contemplation of a long-term commitment, the applican'ts entitlement to interim spousal support should not be eliminated nor reduced: *Bell v. Bell* (1998), 42 R.F.L. (4th) 301, 1998 CarswellNfld 246 (Nfld. U.F.C.)

Where the parties, after divorcing, resumed cohabitation for a period of six months, they were found to be "spouses" within the meaning of the *Family Law Act*. During the six-month period, there was an economic component to the relationship and the parties again, together with their children, considered themselves to be a faimly unit. As the parties intended the arrangement to be permanent, the relationship could properly be characterized as one of "some permanence". Furthermore, the reference in s. 29 of the Act to "children" would include those born prior to the new period of cohabitation. Accordingly, the female plaintiff's claim for interim spousal support under the Act was sustainable: *DeSouza v. DeSouza* (1999), 48 R.F.L. (4th) 63, 1999 CarswellOnt 1550 (Ont. Prov. Div.).

The husband's income was $158,000 a year and the wife earned $39,000 a year. Their son was in the wife's custody. On an application by the wife for interim child and spousal support, the court held the husband should pay child support including s. 7 expenses of $1,888 each month and interim spousal support of $750 each month on the ground that the wife's income was considerably short of the income enjoyed by the husband, and it could not be said that she had achieved a level of self-sufficiency that would preclude spousal support. The amount awarded would enable each of the parties to enjoy comparable lifestyles and permit their son to continue to enjoy a lifestyle similar to that to which they have made him accustomed: *Nataros v. Nataros* (1998), 1998 CarswellBC 944, 40 R.F.L. (4th) 308, [1998] B.C.J. No. 1417 (B.C. Master).

15§134 — Interim spousal support for husband

The husband, a lawyer, had left a good position with a firm to start a practice on his own. At the time of the separation his billings were only $1,500 a month. His wife was earning $90,000 a year. On a motion by the husband for interim support, the court held that the test on the issue of spousal support at this stage is the need of the spouse seeking support and the ability to pay of the other spouse. While the husband had suffered an economic loss as a result of the separation, the low monthly billings prior to separation meant that the amount of that loss was not a great one. In addition, his proven ability to earn significant income had not been adversely affected by the separation on a permanent basis. Therefore, support should be provided to compensate directly for loss of income for the six months that he was prevented, for one reason or another, from carrying on his old practice and, at the same time, to provide some assistance in financing the start up costs of a new practice. To achieve these objectives, the wife was ordered to pay the husband compensatory interim support by way of a lump sum of $7,500. This was calculated using the average billings of the husband's practice prior to the separation for a period of six months (which was $1,500 times six or $9,000) less a reduction of $1,500 to allow for the fact that the lump sum payment would not be deductible to the wife and would not be taxable in the hands of the husband: *Dunn v. Menear* (2000), 2000 CarswellOnt 4778, 14 R.F.L. (5th) 293 (Ont. S.C.J.).

A husband sought support on the basis that he was economically disadvantaged as a result of assuming the role of a "house husband" during part of the marriage, and moved for interim support. He contended that in this role he helped the wife advance her career to the detriment of his own career opportunities. In dismissing his motion for interim support, the court held, in the circumstances, that the mere fact of marriage did not entitle the husband to support, and the evidence did not show that his efforts at home advanced his wife's career or was the cause of his unemployment: *Cuzzocrea v. Swain* (1995), 1995 CarswellOnt 485, 15 R.F.L. (4th) 300, [1995] O.J. No. 2824 (Ont. Gen. Div.); additional reasons at (1995), 1995 CarswellOnt 1085, 17 R.F.L. (4th) 245 (Ont. Gen. Div.).

In *Stefanyk v. Stefanyk* (1994), 1 R.F.L. (4th) 432, 128 N.S.R. (2d) 335, 359 A.P.R. 335, 1994 CarswellNS 38 (S.C.), the wife was ordered to pay interim support to the husband. The husband had given up his job to allow the family to move to Nova Scotia so that the wife could pursue a career opportunity. As a result, the husband had proven an economic disadvantage arising from the marriage.

In *Mitchell v. Mitchell* (1993), 129 N.S.R. (2d) 351, 362 A.P.R. 351, 1993 CarswellNB 143 (S.C.), the court granted the 62-year-old husband's claim for interim support against the 67-year-old wife. The wife's income greatly exceeded that of the husband and in the later years of the parties' 12-year marriage, the husband had depended upon the wife's superior income. In the interim period, there was a need for a more equitable distribution of the parties income.

15§135 — Interim child support

On an application for child support the court may make an interim order "requiring a spouse to pay for the support of any or all children of the marriage, pending the determination of the application": *Divorce Act*, s. 15.1(2). The order must be in accordance with the applicable guidelines unless it would be inequitable in light of special provisions in an existing order, judgment or written agreement directly or indirectly benefitting the child or children: *Divorce Act*, s. 15.1(3) and (5). The obligation under the order may be "for a definite or indefinite period or until a specified event occurs" and the court "may impose terms, conditions or restrictions in connection with the ... interim order as it thinks fit and just": *Divorce Act*, s. 15.1(3) and (4).

In *Fernquist v. Garland* (2005), 12 R.F.L. (6th) 315, 2005 CarswellSask 34, 2005 SKQB 41 (Sask. Q.B.), the mother was granted an interim child support award despite the existence of an earlier consent order that allowed the father to suspend child support if the mother continued to frustrate his access rights. Although the frustration continued, it was found that the children should not be further penalized financially as a result of their parents' actions.

In a motion for interim child support in accordance with the Ontario Child Support Guidelines, in *Pakka v. Nygard* (2002), 61 O.R. (3d) 328, 2002 CarswellOnt 3403, [2002] O.J. No. 3858 (Ont. S.C.J.), the court ordered that the arrears of child support should commence on the date after the request for leave to appeal the interim support order was dismissed, which was the time when the defendant, who lived outside the jurisdiction, had no alternative but to deal with the matter in Ontario.

On an interim child support proceeding, it is appropriate not to pursue expenses such as housing, car and savings, which are within the domain of the trial judge: *Pakka v. Nygard* (2002), 61 O.R. (3d) 328, 2002 CarswellOnt 3404, [2002] O.J. No. 3858 (S.C.J.).

In *O. (J.D.) v. O. (S.K.)*, 27 R.F.L. (5th) 394, 2002 CarswellAlta 501, 2002 ABQB 365, 313 A.R. 116 (Q.B.); additional reasons at 2002 CarswellAlta 571, 2002 ABQB 419 (Q.B.), the husband was ordered to pay retroactive interim child support. Although after separation the husband had continued to pay the matrimonial debts, the wife's income was far less and much less stable than the husband's.

In *Ogden v. Ogden* (1998), 42 R.F.L. (4th) 83, 216 A.R. 197, 175 W.A.C. 197 (C.A.), the lower court in making an interim child support order had indicated that the mother had the primary care of the children and refused to make a finding of shared custody. On appeal, the court was of the opinion that in the circumstances, a finding of shared custody could only be made at trial, and on an interim application, the court must apply the guidelines as though the mother had sole custody.

In *Letourneau v. Letourneau* (1998), 131 Man. R. (2d) 123, 187 W.A.C. 123 (C.A.), the motions court was of the opinion that the husband was not earning income at a level commensurate with his potential as a result of his own misconduct and consequently the periodic payments, calculated in accordance with the guidelines were woefully short of what was required and what the husband could have paid prior to his job loss. The appellate court found that these facts did not amount to extraordinary circumstances justifying an interim lump sum award of child support. A parent should only be ordered to pay a lump sum amount for child support on an interim basis if there has been a failure to recognize an obvious obligation or an attempt to avoid it. Claims for lump sums should only be considered once marital property division has been finalized and all material facts known.

Where the effect of awarding retroactive interim child support would actually amount to an award of additional spousal support, the application was refused in *Volken v. Volken*, 19 R.F.L. (5th) 205, 2001 CarswellBC 1401, 2001 BCSC 970 (B.C. S.C. [In Chambers]).

In determining the ability of a parent to pay interim child support, the court is entitled to look at the current financial circumstances of the payor and is not required to simply rely on the amount specified in the payor's most recent income tax return: *Muir v. Muir* (February 20, 1998), Doc. Thunder Bay 3535011973-98 (Ont. Gen. Div.).

Where, on an interim child support application, there is a general triable issue as to whether a party stood *in loco parentis* to the child of the other party, the issue is best left to the trial judge. However, if the *in loco parentis* relationship is established at trial, retroactive child support may be awarded: *Warford v. Warford* (February 9, 1998), Doc. Thunder Bay 97-1047 (Ont. Gen. Div.).

Although a paying spouse was definitely underemployed and had significant assets which could generate income if liquidated, the court would not attribute income to him on a motion for interim spousal and child support: *Jackson v. Jackson* (1997), 35 R.F.L. (4th) 194, 1997 CarswellOnt 4717, [1997] O.J. No. 4790 (Gen. Div.). The husband's assets included real properties, mortgages receivable, a boat worth an estimated $150,000, various investments and bank accounts, as well as an interest in a trust, his share of which was valued at approximately $690,000.

15§136 — Interim support and the causal connection test

There is no common law impediment to considering an interim order for spousal support without reference to the trilogy of *Pelech v. Pelech*, 7 R.F.L. (3d) 225, [1987] 1 S.C.R. 801, 17 C.P.C. (2d) 1, 14 B.C.L.R. (2d) 145, [1987] 4 W.W.R. 481, 76 N.R. 81, 38 D.L.R. (4th) 641, 1987 CarswellBC 147, 1987 CarswellBC 703, [1987] S.C.J. No. 31; *Caron v. Caron*, 7 R.F.L. (3d) 274, [1987] 1 S.C.R. 892, 14 B.C.L.R. (2d) 186, [1987] 4 W.W.R. 522, 75 N.R. 36, 38 D.L.R. (4th) 735, 2 Y.R. 246, 1987 CarswellYukon 8, [1987] S.C.J. No. 32, 1987 CarswellYukon 43; and *Richardson v. Richardson*, 7 R.F.L. (3d) 304, [1987] 1 S.C.R. 857, 17 C.P.C. (2d) 104, 77 N.R. 1, 22 O.A.C. 1, 38 D.L.R. (4th) 699, 1987 CarswellOnt 315, 1987 CarswellOnt 963, [1987] S.C.J. No. 30; *Bailey v.*

Plaxton, 47 O.R. (3d) 593, 2000 CarswellOnt 1194, [2000] O.J. No. 1187, 6 R.F.L. (5th) 29, [2000] O.T.C. 243, S.C.J.. There is every reason to depart from the trilogy, considering the statutory changes to the Divorce Act since the time that the trilogy of cases was decided. In the *Bailey v. Plaxton* decision, the court held that the former wife was entitled to interim spousal support pursuant to s. 15.2 of the Divorce Act despite a separation agreement which provided for spousal support for three years ending 10 years before the judgment.

The Supreme Court of Canada enunciated a new support principle of causal connection in three decisions involving support applications where the parties had agreed to the terms either by written agreement, by minutes of settlement, or by consent order: *Pelech v. Pelech*, 7 R.F.L. (3d) 225, [1987] 1 S.C.R. 801, 17 C.P.C. (2d) 1, 14 B.C.L.R. (2d) 145, [1987] 4 W.W.R. 481, 76 N.R. 81, 38 D.L.R. (4th) 641, 1987 CarswellBC 147, 1987 CarswellBC 703, [1987] S.C.J. No. 31; *Richardson v. Richardson*, 7 R.F.L. (3d) 304, [1987] 1 S.C.R. 857, 17 C.P.C. (2d) 104, 77 N.R. 1, 22 O.A.C. 1, 38 D.L.R. (4th) 699, 1987 CarswellOnt 315, 1987 CarswellOnt 963, [1987] S.C.J. No. 30; and *Caron v. Caron*, 7 R.F.L. (3d) 274, [1987] 1 S.C.R. 892, 14 B.C.L.R. (2d) 186, [1987] 4 W.W.R. 522, 75 N.R. 36, 2 Y.R. 246, 38 D.L.R. (4th) 735, 1987 CarswellYukon 8, [1987] S.C.J. No. 32, 1987 CarswellYukon 43, all involved support applications where there was a prior agreement determining the issue of support. The question whether the causal connection test enunciated by the court is applicable on an interim application has been discussed in several cases. However, see a consideration of *Moge v. Moge* (1992), 43 R.F.L. (3d) 345, [1992] 3 S.C.R. 813, [1993] 1 W.W.R. 481, 145 N.R. 1, 81 Man. R. (2d) 161, 30 W.A.C. 161, 99 D.L.R. (4th) 456, [1992] S.C.J. No. 107, 1992 CarswellMan 143, 1992 CarswellMan 222, [1993] R.D.F. 168, for limitations upon the causal connection test at 15§27 regarding support law under the Divorce Act.

The Pelech trilogy was decided under the 1968 Divorce Act, but the decisions in the three cases were released after the 1985 Act came into force causing confusion about their applicability to the new legislation. After extensive debate in the cases and in legal and academic circules the question came squarely before the Supreme Court of Canada in the case of *Miglin v. Miglin* (2001), 16 R.F.L. (5th) 185, 53 O.R. (3d) 641, 198 D.L.R. (4th) 385, 144 O.A.C. 155, 2001 CarswllOnt 1404 (C.A.); leave to appeal allowed (2001), 2001 CarswellOnt 3484, 283 N.R. 395 (note), 157 O.A.C. 400 (note) (S.C.C.); reversed 2003 CarswellOnt 1374, 2003 CarswellOnt 1375, [2003] S.C.J. No. 21, 2003 S.C.C. 24, 34 R.F.L. (5th) 255, 224 D.L.R. (4th) 193, 171 O.A.C. 201, 302 N.R. 201 (S.C.C.). Here the court resolved the confusion by holding in a seven to two majority that the trilogy test (which was established to determine when the court should use its discretion to make a spousal support order that overrides provisions in a pre-existing agreement) was not valid or applicable under the new Act. The language of the section in the new Act is more comprehensive and specific than was used in the 1968 Act and points to a different interpretation. It rejects the causal connection requirement developed in the trilogy together with the radical change component that completed the test. Neither causal connection nor radical change is part of the law as it now stands for the purpose of determining when the court's discretion should be used to override a support agreement. The question is whether this decision also means that causal connection can no longer be considered a necessary ingredient for an original support order where there is no agreement to override. If the language of the new Act and judicial interpretations reject the test that embodies causal connection as an instrument to use for the purpose intended — that is, to determine when the courts discretion should be used to override agreements — should it not also be considered as rejected for other purposes for which it was not intended — that is, as a ground for original support orders where there is no agreement to override — but to which it was extended? This extended purpose has no more legislative backing than the intended purpose. If the tree dies, does the branch live? For a detailed summary of the *Miglin* case, see 15§147 Overriding jurisdictions of the courts.

The "causal connection" rule cannot be applied to applications for interim support as a condition to be met before relief can be given. Although there must be a balance between the need for economic assistance and the right of the other spouse not to be unduly burdened for something that was not caused by the marriage, the judge must first look to the source of his power under s. 15 of the Divorce Act, and at the factors to be considered as well as the objectives to be achieved, which are stated in the section. Unlike s. 17(10)(a) of the Act, s. 15 does not require a causal connection between the marriage and the disability as a precondition to payment of support. However, under s. 15, the judge has the obligation to take into account all the circumstances of the parties, including any lack of causal connection between the marriage and the disability, and to give it appropriate weight in the result in order to avoid, as much as possible, harshness or injustice to either party. As the possible factual variations from case to case are infinite, so must the discretion of the judge be broad enough to meet the needs of the case within theparameters of s. 15; *Doncaster v. Doncaster*, 21 R.F.L. (3d) 357, [1989] 5 W.W.R. 723, 76 Sask. R. 81, 1989 CarswellSask 281 (C.A.). In this case, the wife suffered from a mental illness (multiple personality disorder) which prevented her from supporting herself. The illness existed before the marriage, but her health deteriorated during the marriage and after the seperation.

As a general rule, important issues such as "causal connection" should not be determined on an application for interim support: *B. (R.) v. B. (M.)* (1989), 19 R.F.L. (3d) 92, 68 O.R. (2d) 32, 1989 CarswellOnt 221 (H.C.).

Although a claimant on an interim support application has an onus to establish a causal connection between the need and the relationship, the onus is not as exacting as at trial. In the case of a long-term relationship, the court should err on the side of the claimant where evidence conflicts: *Iwan v. Iwan* (1989), 22 R.F.L. (3d) 306, 1989 CarswellOnt 290 (H.C.).

In an interim application for support, the court should consider the causal connection test in addition to the needs and means of the parties: *Weppler v. Weppler* (1988), 15 R.F.L. (3d) 279, 1988 CarswellOnt 265 (H.C.). The court must be satisfied that the spouse's need had its genesis in the marriage in order to award spousal support. In the Weppler decision, the court in dismissing the wife's application for interim support stated that the wife, a stockbroker, was in need and that the husband had the ability to pay. However, the wife was not entitled to support since her hardship stemmed directly from the stockmarket collapse, and had no connection to the marriage or to its breakdown.

Similarly, in *Miller v. Miller* (1988), 15 R.F.L. (3d) 366, 1988 CarswellOnt 272 (H.C.), the court was of the opinion that, on an interim application for support as well as on an application for permanent support, there must be some evidence of a causal connection between the needs of the party seeking support and the marriage. In the Miller case, the wife's injury to her hand, which occurred after the parties' separation and which prevented her from obtaining employment for the first time being, was not causally connected to the marriage. The application for interim support was dismissed.

Where the wife was temporarily disabled by a ski accident which occurred after separation, her application for interim support was dismissed on the basis that her need was not causally connected to the marriage. Prior to the accident, the wife had not taken part in the husband's divorce proceedings because both parties had agreed to live out their respective lives financially independent from one another: *Bouchard v. Quesnel* (1989), 97 N.B.R. (2d) 273, 245 A.P.R. 273, 1989 CarswellNB 368 (Q.B.).

Interim support, like permanent support, should address the economic disadvantage or hardship arising from a marriage while promoting the economic self-sufficiency of each spouse within a reasonable period of time. Where a spouse has been economically self-sufficient throughout the marriage, it is not a proper case for interim support, even if that spouse is unable to continue the lifestyle enjoyed during the marriage: *Pidgeon v. Pidgeon* (1992), 39 R.F.L. (3d) 209, 1992 CarswellBC 552 (S.C.).

In considering an interim order for spousal support, the court is not bound by the trilogy of *Pelech v. Pelech*, *Caron v. Caron* and *Richardson v. Richardson* (*Pelech v. Pelech*, [1987] 1 S.C.R. 801, 7 R.F.L. (3d) 225, 17 C.P.C. (2d) 1, 14 B.C.L.R. (2d) 145, [1987] 4 W.W.R. 481, 76 N.R. 81, 38 D.L.R. (4th) 641, 1987 CarswellBC 147, 1987 CarswellBC 703, [1987] S.C.J. No. 31; *Caron v. Caron*, [1987] 1 S.C.R. 892, 7 R.F.L. (3d) 274, [1987] 1 S.C.R. 892, 14 B.C.L.R. (2d) 186, [1987] 4 W.W.R. 522, 75 N.R. 36, 2 Y.R. 246, 38 D.L.R. (4th) 735, 1987 CarswellYukon 8, [1987] S.C.J. No. 32, 1987 CarswellYukon 43; *Richardson v. Richardson*, [1987] 1 S.C.R. 857, 1987 CarswellOnt 315, 1987 CarswellOnt 963, [1987] S.C.J. No. 30, 17 C.P.C. (2d) 104, 38 D.L.R. (4th) 699, 77 N.R. 1, 22 O.A.C. 1, 7 R.F.L. (3d) 304; *Bailey v. Plaxton*, 6 R.F.L. (5th) 29, 47 O.R. (3d) 593, 2000 CarswellOnt 1194, [2000] O.J. No. 1187, [2000] O.T.C. 243 (Ont. S.C.J.). There is every reason to depart from the trilogy, because of the statutory changes to the Divorce Act since the time that the trilogy was decided. In the *Bailey v. Plaxton* decision, the court held that the former wife was entitled to interim spousal support pursuant to s. 15.2 of the Divorce Act despite a separation agreement which provided for spousal support for 3 years ending 10 years before the judgment.

15§137 — Defences — delay in application for interim support

The *Divorce Act* does not prescribe a time limit within which to bring a claim for interim spousal support. Interim support was denied on the basis of delay in *Byerley v. Byerley* (1998), 41 R.F.L. (4th) 50 (Ont. Gen. Div.) and *Bouchard v. Quesnel* (1989), 97 N.B.R. (2d) 273, 245 A.P.R. 273 (Q.B.).

In the *Byerley* case, the parties lived together in a common law relationship for three years and were married for eight years. The parties separated in 1996. A year after the parties' separation, the wife began to live in a common law relationship with another man. She quit her job and became pregnant. In the fall of 1998, almost two years from the date of separation, the wife sought interim spousal support. The court in dismissing the motion, held that the wife was self-supporting from the time of separation to the time of the hearing, first from her own earnings and latterly because of the support of her common law partner. The court was of the opinion that at the preliminary stage of awarding interim relief, the function of the court was to determine if the applicant had current needs during the period of the order, decide if the applicant required interim relief and whether the responding party had the means to provide interim support. In this case, the wife did not provide the court with material as to her common-law spouse's income and expenses and the details of their joint expenses. The wife, according to the court, at page

52, "failed to demonstrate, with cogent and compelling evidence, a current need for interim spousal support from the husband."

In *Gearin v. Gearin* (1999), 45 R.F.L. (4th) 333 (Nfld. U.F.C.), the wife was awarded interim spousal support seven years after a consent order that provided maintenance for the children only. The court was of the opinion that the wife had an honest belief that she obtained some benefits from the reasonably generous child support payments, benefits which, at the time of the hearing had ceased as child support was no longer payable. Further, the court considered that at the time of the consent order, it would have been unlikely that the husband would have been ordered to pay spousal support above the amount he was already paying for child support.

Where the wife first brought an application for interim maintenance three and a half years after the parties' separation, it was held that the delay was not fatal to the application. As the wife had been living on the capital realized upon the sale of the matrimonial home, the delay in seeking maintenance could not be interpreted as a lack of financial need on her part: *Williams v. Williams* (1984), 42 R.F.L. (2d) 110 (B.C. C.A.).

Although a long delay in making application for alimony may raise a presumption that the wife is able to take care of herself and needs no interim alimony, this may be rebutted by evidence of injury or incapacity demonstrating that she is in necessitous circumstances: *Deeton v. Deeton* (1970), 4 R.F.L. 120 (Ont. C.A.); *Bate v. Bate* (1977), 16 O.R. (2d) 763 at 763–4 (Master); *Daly v. Daly* (1973), 11 R.F.L. 307 at 308–9 (Ont. H.C.).

Where the wife was temporarily disabled by a ski accident which occurred after separation, her application for interim support was dismissed on the basis that her need was not causally connected to the marriage. Prior to the accident, the wife had not taken part in the husband's divorce proceedings because both parties had agreed to live out their respective lives financially independent from one another: *Bouchard v. Quesnel*, above.

15§138 — Defences — interim support and domestic contracts

In *Walmsley v. Moore* (2002), 25 R.F.L. (5th) 462, 2002 CarswellOnt 584 (S.C.J.); additional reasons at (2002), 2002 CarswellOnt 1865 (S.C.J.); reversed (2002), 2002 CarswellOnt 4428, 167 O.A.C. 14, 34 R.F.L. (5th) 206 (Div. Ct.), the wife executed a separation agreement releasing her support rights in exchange for continuing employment with the husband's company. When her employment was terminated 1 year later, her application for interim spousal support was granted. In the circumstances, the release clause was not a bar to her claim for interim support pending determination of the issue of entitlement at trial.

In *Rodrigues v. Rodrigues* (2004), 6 R.F.L. (6th) 365, 2004 CarswellBC 1503, 2004 BCSC 855 (S.C.), the court refused the wife's application for interim support pending her challenge to the waiver of spousal support contained in the parties' separation agreement. Although it was not certain that the wife's action would be unsuccessful, the status quo established by the agreement should govern until the final disposition.

In *Camp v. Camp* (2004), 9 R.F.L. (6th) 54, 2004 CarswellBC 1900, 2004 BCSC 1096 (S.C. [In Chambers]), the wife's claim for interim spousal support was refused. Under the parties' separation agreement, the wife continued to have a capital fund to draw upon. Furthermore, there was no evidence indicating an economic disadvantage to the wife and it was uncertain whether her support claim would be successful at trial.

In *Woode v. Woode*, 26 R.F.L. (5th) 232, 2002 CarswellSask 49, 2002 SKQB 33, 216 Sask. R. 1 (Q.B.), the court refused the wife's application for interim nominal support. The wife already had such support pursuant to the parties' separation agreement and a formal order was not required.

Although the court pays great heed to agreements made between parties regarding maintenance, less weight is to be accorded such agreements in the case of interim matters: *Ziniuk v. Ziniuk* (1986), 2 R.F.L. (3d) 398, 1986 CarswellBC 524 (C.A.).

An award of interim maintenance should not be made in the face of a separation agreement which makes reasonable provision for dependants, unless failure to make such an award would work hardship on the parties: *Macy v. Macy* (1984), 40 R.F.L. (2d) 11, 1984 CarswellOnt 238, 3 O.A.C. 369 (C.A.). See also *Macy v. Macy* (1983), 36 R.F.L. (2d) 89, 43 O.R. (2d) 385, 1983 CarswellOnt 320, 1 D.L.R. (4th) 718 (C.A.), where the husband successfully appealed an award for interim maintenance.

In *Trinchan v. Trinchan* (1983), 34 R.F.L. (2d) 331, 1983 CarswellOnt 287, 43 O.R. (2d) 360, 1 D.L.R. (4th) 102 (C.A.), the court allowed the husband's appeal from an award of interim maintenance to the wife which was in excess of the maintenance payable to her under the parties' separation agreement. Although the court's jurisdiction under the *Divorce Act* was not displaced by the separation agreement, the court was obliged to give considerable weight to it, especially in an application for interim maintenance. Furthermore, there was nothing to suggest the agreement was harsh or unfair or to justify altering the maintenance provisions. See also *Macy v. Macy* (1984), 40 R.F.L. (2d) 11, 1984 CarswellOnt 238, 3 O.A.C. 369 (C.A.).

In *Salzmann v. Salzmann* (2004), 50 R.F.L. (5th) 181, 2004 CarswellOnt 169 (Ont. S.C.J.), the wife was awarded interim spousal support despite the existence of a cohabitation agreement in which she had waived her right to support. The wife had raised arguable issues on each element of the test for determining if the terms of the agreement were unconscionable. If she was unsuccessful in challenging the agreement at trial, payments made by the husband could be addressed through an unequal diversion of property.

Where the wife had signed a separation agreement waiving her right to support after a specified date, her subsequent application for interim spousal support was refused. Although the wife challenged the validity of the agreement, the trial judge would be in the best position to assess that issue: *Palmer v. Palmer*, 45 R.F.L. (5th) 447, 2003 CarswellSask 690, 2003 SKQB 438, 240 Sask. R. 25 (Sask. Q.B.).

A separation agreement is a defence to a claim to interim support but not necessarity to a claim for permanent support: *Bedard v. Huard* (2000), 5 R.F.L. (5th) 282, 2000 CarswellOnt 1129, [2000] O.J. No. 969 (S.C.J.); additional reasons at (2000), 2000 CarswellOnt 1226 (S.C.J.).

Where the separation agreement contains a waiver of spousal support, the onus is on the applicant to satisfy the trial judge that he or she should invoke the inherent jurisdiction of the court to override the agreement: *Allen v. Allen* (1999), [2000] 3 W.W.R. 271, 256 A.R. 121, 1999 CarswellAlta 1210, 2 R.F.L. (5th) 1, 75 Alta. L.R. (3d) 305 (Q.B.).

In *Kennedy v. Kennedy* (2000), 11 R.F.L. (5th) 150, 2000 CarswellOnt 3622, [2000] O.J. No. 3742 (S.C.J.), an agreement signed by the wife in which she purportedly waived her right to spousal support was found to have been improperly executed and was entered into without independent legal advice or financial disclosure. Accordingly, the agreement was not a bar to the wife's application for interim spousal support.

While a contract is an important factor to consider in determining whether spousal support should be granted, there are other factors which a court must take into account. If the terms of the contract do not promote or cease to promote the objectives of the Divorce Act, a court should intervene to protect those objectives and policies: *Bailey v. Plaxton*, 6 R.F.L. (5th) 29, 47 O.R. (3d) 593, 2000 CarswellOnt 1194, [2000] O.J. No. 1187, [2000] O.T.C. 243 (S.C.J.). In that decision, the court held that the former wife was entitled to interim spousal support pursuant to s. 15.2 of the Divorce Act, despite a separation agreement which provided for spousal support for three years ending 10 years before the judgment.

In *Scheel v. Henkelman* (1999), 45 R.F.L. (4th) 419, 1999 CarswellOnt 1156, [1999] O.J. No. 1372 (Gen. Div.), the husband was not allowed to rely upon a mutual support waiver contained in the parties' cohabitation agreement as a defence to the wife's claim for interim spousal support. There were triable issues relating to the validity of the agrement arising out of issues of unconscionability and the husband's alledged breaches of the agreement.

In *Lees v. Lees* (1998), 1998 CarswellOnt 1329 (Gen. Div.), the wife had signed a separation agreement dealing with spousal support among other matters, against the advice of independent legal counsel. When the wife learned that the husband was cohabiting with his lawyer, she attempted suicide and injured herself so that she was not in a wheel chair. The wife moved for interim relief including spousal support. She sought to set aside the agreement on the grounds that it was improvident and unconscionable. The husband moved for an adjournment of the wife's motion. The court granted an adjournment since it considered that there was no urgency to the matter; the final separation agreement was in place and needed to be carefully examined. Further, the husband was looking after the children well.

Where an agreement provides for a combined monthly amount of spousal and child support, and the husband had been paying the amount until recently, the court will not interfere with the agreement on an interim basis other than to specify the amounts for spousal and child support separately: *Beeching v. Beeching* (1998), 40 R.F.L. (4th) 15, 1998 CarswellSask 432, [1998] S.J. No. 355, 169 Sask. R. 18 (Q.B.).

Where a party is receiving social assistance, and the other party has the means to pay support, interim spousal support will be granted despite the provisions of marriage contract in which support rights were given up: *Burton v. Burton* (1998), 42 R.F.L. (4th) 310, 1998 CarswellOnt 5186 (Gen. Div.); additional reasons at (1998), 1998 CarswellOnt 5988 (Gen. Div.). The validity of the agreement was an issue for trial but for the purposes of the interim spousal support application, the contract was considered valid.

Hay v. Hay (1997), 1997 CarswellOnt 2123 (Gen. Div.), the parties had signed a separation agreement and the wife had paid the husband $2,000 in full and final settlement of all support obligations as a result of the marriage relationship. The busband and wife worked for the same company and after separation the wife resigned from her position, alleging a history of her husband's violent conduct. The wife attempted to establish a business of her own, but to date had little success. The court was of the opinion that where there was a separation agreement in place, the party seeking interim spousal support could sustain himself or herself and where there was a serious issue of credibility, the terms of the separation agreement should prevail on an interim basis until the trial judge made a determination.

Where the wife released any claim for spousal support in the separation agreement if she obtained two years of full time employment and her full time employment was reduced to half time, the court could award interim spousal support because she was in need: *Munn v. Munn* (1996), 23 R.F.L. (4th) 115, 1996 CarswellOnt 1240, [1996] O.J. No. 1188 (Gen. Div.).

Where the husband's obligation, under the parties' separation agreement, to pay spousal support had expired, but the wife had an arguable case on the validity of the agreement, she was granted interim support pending the hearing of the issue in the parties' divorce action. The quantum of interim support, however, recognized the fact that if the agreement were upheld, the funds would not be repaid: *Carlsen v. Carlsen* (1990), 25 R.F.L. (3d) 461, 1990 CarswellOnt 243 (H.C.).

Where the wife was attempting to set aside some of the provisions of the parties' separation agreement at trial, it was held that the agreement, which limited her support rights, did not act to bar her claim for interim support: *Desimone v. Desimone* (1993), 48 R.F.L. (3d) 161, 1993 CarswellBC 620, [1993] B.C.J. No. 1480 (S.C.).

In *Pineault v. Pineault* (1993), 49 R.F.L. (3d) 411, 1993 CarswellOnt 358 (Gen. Div.), the court considered whether the wife was entitled to interim support, even though she had signed a marriage contract after the wedding and before the reception whereby she waived any right to spousal support. The court noted that in light of the *Moge* decision, it was questionable whether *Pelech v. Pelech*, 1987 CarswellBC 147, 1987 CarswellBC 703, [1987] S.C.J. No. 31, [1987] 1 S.C.R. 801, [1987] 4 W.W.R. 481, 38 D.L.R. (4th) 641, 76 N.R. 81, 14 B.C.L.R. (2d) 145, 17 C.P.C. (2d) 1, 7 R.F.L. (3d) 225, above, now represents the law with respect to overriding support provisions in a valid and enforceable settlement agreement. However, the court in the *Pineault* case noted that *Moge v. Moge* did not deal with the issue of overriding a valid and enforceable settlement agreement. The court exercised its discretion and awarded interim support. (*Pelech* decided under the 1968 Divorce Act does not apply to the exercise of discretion under the current Act to override support provisions in agreements. See *Miglin v. Miglin* (2001), 16 R.F.L. (5th) 185, 53 O.R. (3d) 641, 198 D.L.R. (4th) 385, 144 O.A.C. 155, 2001 CarswllOnt 1404 (C.A.); leave to appeal allowed (2001), 2001 CarswellOnt 3484, 283 N.R. 395 (note), 157 O.A.C. 400 (note) (S.C.C.); reversed 2003 CarswellOnt 1374, 2003 CarswellOnt 1375, [2003] S.C.J. No. 21, 2003 S.C.C. 24, 34 R.F.L. (5th) 255, 224 D.L.R. (4th) 193, 171 O.A.C. 201, 302 N.R. 201 (S.C.C.) discussed in 15§147 Overriding jurisdiction of the courts.)

In *Legg v. Legg* (1991), 38 R.F.L. (3d) 23, 1991 CarswellBC 574 (S.C.), the wife's claim for interim support was dismissed on the basis of a variation to the parties' separation agreement whereby the wife had agreed to forgo spousal support. Although agreed to without legal advice, the variation was intended by the parties to result in a final agreement and could only be varied by proof of a radical change in circumstances. The wife could not establish any change and the final determination of the validity of the agreement was best left to the trial judge.

In *Droit de la famille — 1222* (1988), [1989] R.D.F. 168 (C.S. Qué.), the court refused the wife's application for interim support where the application would have required it to override a provision in the parties' separation agreement whereby the wife waived all claims against the husband. Although the wife had spent all of the money she received under the agreement, the court could not override the agreement absent proof of a radical change in circumstances that resulted from the marriage.

A settlement agreement which is orally varied by the parties is not a "final" settlement and in no way restricts the court's jurisdiction to award interim support which is inconsistent with a consent support award based upon the agreement: *Hunkin v. Hunkin* (1988), 14 R.F.L. (3d) 157, 1988 CarswellMan 48, 54 Man. R. (2d) 44 (Q.B.).

In an application for interim maintenance, a separation agreement may only be considered as evidence to establish the appropriate alimony and maintenance which should be paid: *Conley v. Conley* (1987), 7 R.F.L. (3d) 372, 54 Sask. R. 17, 1987 CarswellSask 86 (C.A.); affirming (1986), 54 Sask. R. 21, 1986 CarswellSask 570 (Q.B.).

Where the wife claimed maintenance in divorce proceedings and received an interim maintenance award in the same amount as that provided in an earlier agreement, it was held that the support provisions of the agreement had been suspended by the subsequent maintenance order. The court was, therefore, without jurisdiction to grant the wife judgment for arrears which had accumulated undew the agreement: *Winger v. Winger* (1984), 42 R.F.L. (2d) 414, 1984 CarswellOnt 303 (H.C.).

Where there is an agreement which provides for interim spousal support and a subsequent agreement that deals only with property, the obligation to pay interim spousal support is not terminated by the second agreement: *Johnston v. Johnston* (1997), 35 R.F.L. (4th) 37, 1997 CarswellBC 2403, [1997] B.C.J. No. 2597 (Master). The second agreement specifically stated that it did not settle spousal support.

In *Lodjn v. Lodjn* (1997), 34 R.F.L. (4th) 147, 43 B.C.L.R. (3d) 271, 1997 CarswellBC 2716, [1997] B.C.J. No. 2834 (Master), the wife was awarded interim spousal support despite the fact that she had executed a prenuptial agreement waiving her right to claim support. The agreement was entered into two years prior to the marriage and indicated the parties' intention not to have children. As they did in fact have a child which required the wife to be primary carefiver and had created an economic dependency, it was possible that the trial judge could find a radical change in circumstances justifying that the agreement be set aside.

In an application for interim maintenance, a separation agreement may only be considered as evidence to establish the appropriate alimony and maintenance which should be paid: *Conley v. Conley* (1987), 7 R.F.L. (3d) 372, 54 Sask. R. 17 (C.A.); affirming (1986), 54 Sask. R. 21 (Q.B.).

15§139 — Interim support securing payment

Where, in response to the wife's claim for interim spousal and child support, the husband, who was not a Canadian citizen, threatened to leave the country, the court required him to guarantee one year s interim support by way of a bank note or suretyship in the amount of $10,000: *Droit de la famille — 1231*, [1989] R.D.F. 189 (C.S. Qué.).

15§140 — Duration of interim support order

Generally, a time limit should not placed upon an interim spousal support order. By definition, such an order is already limited until the trial: *Vauclair v. Vauclair* (1998), 39 R.F.L. (4th) 124, 126 Man. R. (2d) 136, 167 W.A.C. 136 (C.A.).

Time-limited support awards are not appropriate in interim proceedings: *D. (L.) c. D. (J.-P.)* (9 juin 1993), Doc. C.A. Québec 200-09-000044-930 (C.A. Qué.).

Where the parties disputed the amount of the husband's earnings on the wife's interim support application, the award was made subject to a review in six months' time: *Watson v. Watson* (1992), 107 Sask. R. 127 (Q.B.).

In *Nord v. Nord* (1986), 42 Man. R. (2d) 50 (Q.B.), the wife's award of interim maintenance was stated to continue only until such time as she obtained employment.

An order for interim maintenance is to be effective from the date of the application and not from the date of the order: *Ferguson v. Ferguson* (1980), 16 R.F.L. (2d) 207, 38 Nfld. & P.E.I.R. 498, 78 A.P.R. 498 (P.E.I. S.C.).

The trial judge may order that the interim maintenance award stand following pronouncement of the decree *nisi* where there has been a reference to the Master regarding quantum of permanent maintenance: *Rice v. Rice* (1977), 27 R.F.L. 11, 16 O.R. (2d) 8, 77 D.L.R. (3d) 39 (H.C.).

The decree *nisi* ends the interim order for alimony and the husband's obligation to pay it. To protect the wife, the decree *nisi* should provide for maintenance in the amount ordered as interim alimony until the reference to the registrar has been made an order of the court: *Blanchard v. Blanchard* (1978), 7 B.C.L.R. 252 (S.C.), dealing with a husband's application to have funds attached by his wife paid out of court. See also *Peacock v. Peacock* (1975), 20 R.F.L. 207 at 208 (B.C. S.C.).

"The interim [maintenance] order made by McIntyre J. prevails, as it in fact provides 'pending and hearing and determination of these proceedings'. The determination of these proceedings is when the judgment of the court has been rendered. There is ample authority, already established, indicating that the judgment of the court is the decree *nisi*": per Wootten J. in *Favor v. Favor* (1971), 4 R.F.L. 352 at 354, [1971] 5 W.W.R. 573 (B.C. S.C.).

15§141 — Retrospective payment of interim support

In *Yaholnitsky v. Yaholnitsky* (1992), 105 Sask. R. 255, 32 W.A.C. 255 (C.A.), an interim support award made on July 3, 1992 granting support from July 1, 1992 was found not to constitute an improper retroactive award. The award was merely intended as payment for the month of July and all subsequent months.

Where, in the 3 years since the parties' separation, the husband had managed to increase his asset base substantially while the wife had been forced to liquidate investments to support herself and the children, retroactive interim spousal and child support was awarded: *Lakhani v. Lakhani* (2003), 43 R.F.L. (5th) 125, 2003 CarswellOnt 3928 (Ont. S.C.J.); additional reasons at (2003), 2003 CarswellOnt 3927 (Ont. S.C.J.).

Where the mother had started but had not pursued a claim for interim child support, her subsequent claim for retroactive child support was dismissed. The mother had no reasonable excuse for abandoning the interim application, and had not incurred any debt or decrease in capital in supporting the children. The father was in no way blameworthy for the delay and a retroactive order would be tantamount to additional payment of capital or spousal support to the mother: *Hodgkinson v. Hodgkinson*, 44 R.F.L. (5th) 82, 2003 CarswellBC 2461, 2003 BCSC 1538 (B.C. S.C.).

In *Volken v. Volken*, 2001 CarswellBC 1401, 2001 BCSC 970, 19 R.F.L. (5th) 205 (B.C. S.C. [In Chambers]), the husband's annual income was found to be $2,000,000. The wife was not employed outside the home and had no income of her own. After separation the husband made voluntary payments of $5,000 a month which reflected the relatively frugal lifestyle of the family before the separation. The wife's expenses after the separation exceeded these payments. She supplemented them by taking out a mortgage on her equity in the family home. She applied for interim child support for three children and spousal support for herself. The *Guidelines* Table amount of $25,723 per month in child support was awarded retroactive to the 1st of January, the month in which her application for interim support was made. For herself, the wife sought interim spousal support of $18,000 per month plus a lump sum of $10,000 to pay for repairs to the home and an automobile, $50,000 for payment of the services of a business valuator and $100,000 for a legal retainer. The husband's monthly expenses were about $9,000. The court found that after taking into account the child support obligation, the husband's after tax earnings would meet the needs of the wife and still leave him with more than enough for his own expenses. Exercising its discretion on the basis of the condition, means, needs, and other circumstances of each spouse in light of the objectives of spousal support orders described in s. 15.2 of the *Divorce Act*, the court ordered interim monthly spousal support of $15,000 plus a lump sum payment of $10,000. The court refused to make the spousal support payments retroactive. The husband could not be faulted for his delay in making financial disclosure because of the complexities of his holdings. Any deficiencies in child support were made up by the retroactivity of that order, and the high amount compared to the "relatively frugal" lifestyle before separation. Also, any shortfall experienced by the wife was met by her borrowing against the equity in the family home. And any order that might be made as to retroactivity would have the undesirable effect of redistributing capital, or awarding additional spousal support, under the guise of child support. With respect to the claim for an amount to cover the payment of fees, the husband consented to an interim advance of $50,000 against the wife's entitlement on property division to fund equal retainers for the business valuator and counsel. Because it was on consent the court made an order in those terms, but in doing so expressed the opinion that the weight of authority is against ordering an interim distribution of assets to meet past, and, in particular, future legal expenses except to fund unusual disbursements relating specifically to the valuation of assets.

In *Walters v. Walters* (1997), 1997 CarswellOnt 1369, 28 R.F.L. (4th) 94, 29 O.T.C. 132, [1997] O.J. No. 1808 (Ont. Gen. Div.), the court, on an application for interim support under the *Family Law Act*, held that there was no basis for an interim order because of a lack of entitlement to permanent support, but made an order requiring the husband to pay to the wife a monthly sum of $500 as a pre-payment of his obligation with respect to the equalization of their net family property. In making this order, the court observed that if the applicant satisfied a trial judge that she was entitled to support, a retroactive award could be made under s. 34(1)(f) of the *Family Law Act*.

In *Volken v. Volken*, 19 R.F.L. (5th) 205, 2001 CarswellBC 1401, 2001 BCSC 970 (B.C. S.C. [In Chambers]), the court refused to award retroactive interim spousal support where the effect of such an order would really amount to a redistribution of capital between the parties.

In *Zander v. Zander* (1994), 8 R.F.L. (4th) 35 (Ont. Gen. Div.), the court refused the wife's request for retroactive interim support to reimburse her for the fact that her interim support award had not been indexed to the cost of living. As she had not previously appealed or sought a variation of the award, an adjustment at the trial stage would be gratuitous.

Where an applicant had not sought interim child support, retroactive child maintenance should not be granted: *Fraser v. Fraser* (1991), 34 R.F.L. (3d) 284, 94 Sask. R. 253 (Q.B.).

"To insist that in all cases interim maintenance could not be obtained until an application therefor had been brought, might precipitate the early launching of motions which would seriously interfere with the possibilities of reconciliation. As a general rule I would feel that where there has been an unequivocal expression of intention by one party, in this case the wife, to seek maintenance and that intention had not been followed immediately by the launching of a motion but rather had been followed by sincere negotiations between solicitors which were carried on promptly and expeditiously and where a successful application for an order of maintenance has been made promptly after the negotiations broke down, justice to the infants would require that the maintenance become effective from the date when the demand for maintenance had been made or the successful parent had made known to the other his or her intention to seek maintenance": per Kelly J.A. in *Steinhuebl v. Steinhuebl*, 2 R.F.L. 317 at 318–319, [1970] 2 O.R. 683, 11 D.L.R. (3d) 669 (C.A.).

Apart from any special circumstances to support an earlier date, and where the dates of separation, of the commencement of proceedings and of the interim orders are all proximate, interim maintenance awards should be payable from the date of commencement of the action, not the date of the separation: *Headrick v. Headrick*, [1970] 1 O.R. 405, 8 D.L.R. (3d) 519 (C.A.). See also *H. (I.) v. H. (H.)*, 5 R.F.L. 214, [1971] 3 O.R. 222, 20 D.L.R. (3d) 62 (Master).

Where the wife's application for interim alimony was made after pronouncement of the decree absolute, the resulting order was made effective as of the date of service of the wife's counter-petition: *Royal v. Royal* (1975), 21 R.F.L. 389, 8 O.R. (2d) 241, 57 D.L.R. (3d) 529 (H.C.).

The court has a discretion as to the appropriate date from which interim alimony should be paid. This will often be the date of filing of the original petition, but may be earlier: *Leask v. Leask* (1975), 24 R.F.L. 275 (B.C. S.C.).

In *Soucy v. Soucy* (1981), 36 N.B.R. (2d) 80, 94 A.P.R. 80 (Q.B.), the wife was granted interim alimony retroactively to the date on which the divorce action was commenced.

15§142 — Interim support pending appeal

An order for interim support pending an appeal to the Supreme Court of Canada on a support issue will only be made in exceptional circumstances: *B. (G.) c. G. (L.)* (1994), 165 N.R. 237, 61 Q.A.C. 179, [1995] 3 S.C.R. 367.

An application by the wife for a stay of an order which varied an interim support order pending appeal of the order was refused as the court was of the opinion that any damage which might result from the variation order was not irreparable: *Armstrong v. Armstrong* (1998), 1998 CarswellBC 2172, 112 B.C.A.C. 186, 182 W.A.C. 186, [1998] B.C.J. No. 2309 (C.A. [In Chambers]).

The Ontario Court of Appeal held that the interlocutory order allowing the motion for interim support to proceed should be stayed pending the determination of a constitutional issue under appeal, since if the applicant were successful in her appeal, there would be no basis in law for proceeding with the interim support hearing: *M. v. H.* (1996), 20 R.F.L. (4th) 278, 1996 CarswellOnt 595 (Ont. C.A. [In Chambers]). It would be wasteful to proceed if the process were unnecessary and it is not certain that the applicant would be able to recover the costs if she were successful on appeal. The potential prejudice to the applicant outweighs any potential benefit to the respondent if the interim support hearing proceeded.

15§142A — Interim support pending re-hearing

Where the appellate court determined that the issues at trial on an application to vary spousal support had not been satisfactorily adjudicated, a new hearing was ordered pending which the husband was required to pay $1,000 monthly as interim spousal support: *Sadler v. Sadler* (1999), 46 R.F.L. (4th) 368, 1999 CarswellBC 1069 (C.A.)

15§143 — Interim disbursements

A claim for suit money is different from a claim for interim support and should be granted where the evidence establishes that the claimant does not have sufficient independent funds to pay his or her lawyer in the divorce proceedings: *Poirier v. Poirier* (1989), 23 R.F.L. (3d) 109, 93 N.S.R. (2d) 33, 242 A.P.R. 33 (C.A.).

In Ontario, the awarding of interim disbursements, which are in the nature of an additional allowance for interim maintenance of the wife, is based on the traditional notion that a wife, considered to have no resources of her own, would be precluded from obtaining relief if her disbursements, as distinguished from her costs, were not made available to her. Interim disbursements were not warranted where the husband was an undischarged bankrupt who had to live from day to day on his earnings and the wife was on legal aid and would not be prevented through poverty from proceeding with the action: *Saberi v. Saberi* (1979), 10 R.F.L. (2d) 381, 30 C.B.R. (N.S.) 314 (Ont. C.A.).

The making of an "interim interim" maintenance order is a by-product of the congestion of the courts and related offices, including that of the special examiner. The purpose of such an order is to prevent hardship to a wife until the necessary material upon which the court can act can be procured, including cross-examinations and transcripts. "Interim interim" procedures are not to be invoked as a matter of course. An order for interim disbursements in an "interim interim" application, where the disbursements are ordered to be paid as part of the conditions of obtaining an adjournment, should not be made unless it is clearly shown that without the disbursements the wife cannot proceed to the stage when the actual motion for interim maintenance is to be heard: *Elliston v. Elliston* (1979), 3 Fam. L. Rev. 154 (Ont. C.A.).

The fact that a party has a Legal Aid certificate is irrelevant on an application for interim disbursements. A legally aided person stands before the court in exactly the same position as any other litigant: *Cropper v. Cropper* (1974), 16 R.F.L. 113 at 115–116 (Ont. C.A.).

Legal expenses are not appropriate expenses to be considered on a motion for interim support: *Burmi v. Dhiman* (2001), 18 R.F.L. (5th) 9, 2001 CarswellOnt 1812, [2001] O.J. No. 2010 (S.C.J.); additional reasons at (2001), 2001 CarswellOnt 2195 (S.C.J.).

In setting suit costs, the court is to encourage the minimization of proceedings and of disbursements: *Doolittle v. Doolittle* (1991), 109 N.S.R. (2d) 400, 297 A.P.R. 400 (T.D.).

An application for interim disbursements should not include solicitor's fees but only cash disbursements properly made or projected up to the time of trial: *Nathani v. Nathani* (1983), 48 N.B.R. (2d) 410, 126 A.P.R. 410 (Q.B.).

In *Graat v. Graat* (1982), 29 R.F.L. (2d) 312 (Ont. H.C.), it was held that the master lacked jurisdiction to award the wife interim disbursements to cover the costs of her lawyer's fees. It was also held that although the Master had jurisdiction to award interim disbursements to cover a wife's accounting expenses involved in unravelling her husband's complex financial affairs, such an award should not be made merely as a matter of course in every case.

There is a distinction between costs and interim disbursements. Where there was no evidence that the solicitors of record intended to retain counsel outside the firm, an anticipated counsel fee sought was not properly an interim disbursement: *Jenkins v. Jenkins* (1979), 12 R.F.L. (2d) 376, 26 O.R. (2d) 365, 14 C.P.C. 210, 102 D.L.R. (3d) 713 (H.C.).

15§144 — Advance against equalization payment

The court in *Glass v. Glass* (1997), 34 R.F.L. (4th) 411, 1997 CarswellMan 632, 123 Man. R. (2d) 239, 159 W.A.C. 239 (Man. C.A.), allowed in part the appeal by the husband from an interim spousal support order. The evidence did not establish that the husband should make an $8,000 payment for interim disbursements. However, the wife could apply under the *Marital Property Act* for an interim equalization payment if proper evidence were provided in support of the application.

In *Tollestrup v. Tollestrup* (1995), 1995 CarswellAlta 1016, [1995] A.J. No. 443 (Alta. C.A.), the court held that the respondent pay the appellant $20,000, as an advance toward her interim expenses in relation to the matrimonial litigation. The trial judge was directed to take this amount into consideration.

In *Walters v. Walters* (1997), 1997 CarswellOnt 1369, 28 R.F.L. (4th) 94, 29 O.T.C. 132, [1997] O.J. No. 1808 (Ont. Gen. Div.), the court, on an application for interim support under the *Family Law Act*, held that there was no basis for an interim order because of a lack of entitlement to permanent support, but made an order requiring the husband to pay to the wife a monthly sum of $500 as a pre-payment of his obligation with respect to the equalization of their net family property. In making this order, the court observed that if the applicant satisfied a trial judge that she was entitled to support, a retroactive award could be made under s. 34(1)(f) of the *Family Law Act*.

15§144A — Costs

Where the wife was successful on an application for interim support she was successful in recovering her costs only on a party-and-party basis and not on a solicitor and client basis as claimed under R. 49. Rule 49 was not applicable to motions and, despite the wife's settlement offers, there was no reason to justify the extraordinary cost award sought: *Cuzzocrea v. Swain* (1995), 17 R.F.L. (4th) 245 (Ont. Gen. Div.); additional reasons to (1995), 15 R.F.L. (4th) 300 (Ont. Gen. Div.).

Estate of Deceased Payor

15§145 — Support obligation binding against estate of deceased payor

"In a traditional marriage, making a support order binding on the payor's estate is consistent with s. 15(7)(a) of the *Divorce Act*. It recognizes, in the particular circumstances, the economic disadvantages arising from the marriage and its breakdown": per Osborne J.A. in *Linton v. Linton* (1990), 30 R.F.L. (3d) 1 (Ont. C.A.) at p. 39. He also writes at page 38: "Although the *Divorce Act* has no specific provision making a support order an obligation of the payor's estate, there is ample authority to support the conclusion that [a] trial Judge [has] jurisdiction to make the support order an obligation of the husband's estate: see *Snively v. Snively*, [1971] 3 O.R. 132, 6 R.F.L. 75, 19 D.L.R. (3d) 628 (H.C.); *Connelly v. Connelly* (1974), 47 D.L.R. (3d) 535, 9 N.S.R. (2d) 48 (C.A.); *Katz v. Katz* (1983), 33 R.F.L. (2d) 412, 21 Man. R. (2d) 1 (C.A.); additional reasons at (1983), 25 Man. R. (2d) 57 (C.A.); *Chadderton v. Chadderton* (1972), [1973] 1 O.R. 560, 8 R.F.L. 374, 31 D.L.R. (3d) 656 (C.A.); *Krause v. Krause* (1975), 23 R.F.L. 219, [1976] 2 W.W.R. 622, 64 D.L.R. (3d) 352 (Alta. C.A.) and *Huff v. Huff* (1971), 4 R.F.L. 258, 16 D.L.R. (3d) 584 (Man. C.A.); *Hemming v. Hemming* (1983), 33 R.F.L. (2d) 157, 145 D.L.R. (3d) 699, 58 N.S.R. (2d) 65, 123 A.P.R. 65; leave to appeal refused (1983), 145 D.L.R. (3d) 699n, 57 N.S.R. (2d) 346 (note); *Lesser v. Lesser* (1985), 49 O.R. (2d) 794, 44 R.F.L. (2d) 255, 16 D.L.R. (4th) 312 (H.C.); affirmed (1985), 51 O.R. (2d) 100 (C.A.); *Swalm v. Swalm* (1973), 12 R.F.L. 181 (Ont. H.C.); *Burns v. Burns*, [1981] 6 W.W.R. 685, 17 Alta. L.R. (2d) 30, 129 D.L.R. (3d) 178, 32 A.R. 367 (Q.B.)."

In *Despot v. Despot Estate* (1992), 42 R.F.L. (3d) 218, 46 E.T.R. 169, 95 D.L.R. (4th) 62 (B.C. S.C.), the wife was not entitled to continued support against her late husband's estate although a term in the parties' separation agreement had entitled her to support for life or until she remarried. Although the financial terms of the agreement had been incorporated into the decree *nisi*, the decree was silent concerning the duration of the order. Accordingly, the support order terminated upon the husband's death and, as she had elected to take support under the *Divorce Act*, the wife could not revive the agreement.

In *Van de Sande v. Van de Sande* (1994), 148 A.R. 30 (Q.B.), the court refused the wife's application that her spousal support be secured against the husband's estate. It was held that if the wife, who was incapacitated, wished security, she was free to take out an insurance policy on his life.

Assuming that a spousal support order can be made binding the payor's estate, it is inappropriate to do so where the estate is likely to be only a modest one: *Hillhouse v. Hillhouse* (1992), 43 R.F.L. (3d) 266 (C.A.); additional reasons (1994), 52 B.C.A.C. 42, 86 W.A.C. 42 (B.C. C.A.); reversing (November 27, 1990), Doc. Vancouver 5936/D06332 (B.C. S.C.).

The court has never recognized the jurisdiction to make an order under the *Divorce Act* whereby child support payments are binding upon the payor's estate. Nor does it recognize the constitutional jurisdiction of parliament to provide for such an order: *Carmichael v. Carmichael* (1992), 43 R.F.L. (3d) 145, 115 N.S.R. (2d) 45, 314 A.P.R. 45, 96 D.L.R. (4th) 685 (C.A.); reversing in part (1991), 110 N.S.R. (2d) 21, 299 A.P.R. 21 (T.D.).

The court refused to make an order for support binding on the estate of the payor spouse in *Ripley v. Ripley* (1991), 30 R.F.L. (3d) 41 (B.C. C.A.), where, although the wife was in necessitous circumstances, they were not extreme and the husband was not a wealthy man and had other financial obligations.

An originating order for support under s. 15 of the Act cannot be made after the potential payor has died: *B.C. (Public Trustee) v. Price*, 25 R.F.L. (3d) 113, 43 B.C.L.R. (2d) 368, [1990] 4 W.W.R. 52, (sub nom. *Price Estate v. Price)* 67 D.L.R. (4th) 481 (C.A.).

An order for child support survives the death of the payee spouse. Such an order is subject to variation on the application of the personal representative of the deceased spouse: *Chalmers Estate v. Chalmers* (1990), 29 R.F.L. (3d) 54 (Alta. Q.B.).

Where the payee spouse required support from the payor in order to supplement her income and to raise it above the poverty level, a support order will be a charge on the husband's estate in the event that he predeceases her: *Rodrigues v. Rodrigues* (1990), 30 R.F.L. (3d) 231 (Ont. Gen. Div.).

Where it was held on the wife's application for an upward variation of maintenance that the amount was still adequate but may not be so in the future, a variation was granted rendering the wife's maintenance a permanent obligation of the husband's estate: *Katz v. Katz* (1983), 33 R.F.L. (2d) 412, 21 Man. R. (2d) 1 (C.A.); reversing in part 15 Man. R. (2d) 435 (Q.B.).

Where the 67-year-old husband was ordered to pay $12,000 maintenance to his wife in $250 monthly instalments, it was further ordered that the husband's estate be fixed with the payment of any unpaid balance should the husband die before the full award was satisfied: *Buydens v. Buydens* (1983), 33 R.F.L. (2d) 134, 20 Man. R. (2d) 344 (Q.B.).

Also in *Rice v. Pask*, a separation agreement containing a provision that maintenance under the agreement was to be binding upon the husband's estate was incorporated into the decree *nisi*. The provision reflected the parties' intention that the husband's maintenance obligation was not to terminate should he die before the child of the marriage attained the age of majority; see also *Machum v. Machum* (1976), 14 N.B.R. (2d) 79 (Q.B.); *McClelland v. McClelland*, 6 R.F.L. 91 at 95, [1972] 1 O.R. 236, 22 D.L.R. (3d) 624 (H.C.); *Burkett v. Burkett* (1970), 71 W.W.R. 479 at 480 (B.C. S.C.); *Warnock v. Warnock* (1968), 63 W.W.R. 529 (B.C. S.C.); *Baker v. Baker* (1972), 5 R.F.L. 398 (Alta. T.D.).

In *Swalm v. Swalm* (1973), 12 R.F.L. 181 (Ont. H.C.), Galligan J. made an order charging the husband's estate with periodic monthly payments and therefore did not include in the order an amount to enable the wife to set aside money to secure herself in the case of the husband's early death. See also *Krause v. Krause*, 19 R.F.L. 230, [1975] 4 W.W.R. 738 (Alta. T.D.); varied 23 R.F.L. 219 at 230, [1976] 2 W.W.R. 622, 64 D.L.R. (3d) 352 (Alta. C.A.).

The court cannot make an order fixing the husband's estate with a liability not imposed during the husband's lifetime. Unless the decree or an agreement between the parties extended the husband's maintenance obligation beyond his death, the obligation to pay is extinguished on the death of the payor unless the order states otherwise, except with respect to arrears: *Ducharme v. Ducharme*, 21 R.F.L. (2d) 309, [1981] 3 W.W.R. 336, 6 Man. R. (2d) 367, 119 D.L.R. (3d) 478 (Q.B.).

"I am satisfied that if an order survives the death of the payor, it, in the proper circumstances may be varied": per Gagne J., allowing the wife's application for a variation of maintenance subsequent to the payor husband's death in *Wells v. Davidson* (1981), 24 R.F.L. (2d) 358, (sub nom. *Wells v. Wells)* 12 Sask. R. 115 (U.F.C.). See also *Burns v. Burns*, [1981] 6 W.W.R. 685, 17 Alta. L.R. (2d) 30, 32 A.R. 367, 129 D.L.R. (3d) 178 (Q.B.), where the wife's application to vary maintenance was allowed subsequent to the death of the payor husband.

Where the husband is not a wealthy man it is not appropriate to make an order for maintenance extending beyond his lifetime because it would unduly encumber what is likely to be a relatively modest estate: *Jackh v. Jackh*, 18 R.F.L. (2d) 310, 22 B.C.L.R. 182, [1981] 1 W.W.R. 481, 113 D.L.R. (3d) 267 (S.C.).

"The fact that the Legislature did not provide for the continuation of the payments [beyond the death of the payor] suggests to me that the sole question which we are called upon to consider is what the order itself says and to concern ourselves wholly with the construction of that order": per Furlong C.J.T.D. in *Hall v. Hall* (1975), 7 Nfld. & P.E.I.R. 265 at 266, 3 A.P.R. 265 (Nfld. T.D.).

An award of maintenance was made to continue for the lifetime of the wife or until her remarriage where she did not have much in the way of capital and would continue to need support should she survive the husband: *Roher v. Roher* (1976), 27 R.F.L. 218 at 224 (Ont. H.C.). See also *Chadderton v. Chadderton*, 8 R.F.L. 374, [1973] 1 O.R. 560, 31 D.L.R. (3d) 656 (C.A.); *MacNeil v. MacNeil* (1975), 25 R.F.L. 82 at 84, 13 N.S.R. (2d) 118, 9 A.P.R. 118 (C.A.); *Elligott v. Elligott* (1977), 3 R.F.L. (2d) 61 at 69, 6 A.R. 282 at 290 (T.D.).

Where no "special circumstances" were shown to exist, the court exercised its discretion in limiting the maintenance order for the joint lives of the parties: *Armel v. Armel* (1974), 17 R.F.L. 71 (Ont. H.C.).

"[N]o case has been cited to me, nor have I been able to find any, which holds that an order for maintenance for a wife in the bare words of X dollars per month, with no qualifying words to the effect 'during her lifetime' can mean during her lifetime and therefore payable by the former husband's estate should he die leaving his former wife surviving": per Gould J. in *Re Whitelock*, 22 R.F.L. 179 at 186, [1975] 6 W.W.R. 86, 58 D.L.R. (3d) 632 (B.C. S.C.).

On the issue of the liability of a spouse's estate under a separation agreement, the crucial inquiry must be as to the parties' intention at the time the agreement was made: *Re Whitelock*, above.

An order for maintenance under the Act need not be limited to the joint lives of the parties: *Horne v. Roberts* (1971), 20 D.L.R. (3d) 719 (B.C. S.C.).

Effects of Domestic Contracts

See also 15§90 Child support — amount different from guidelines.

15§146 — Introduction

One of the factors the court must take into account in making a support order is "any ... agreement ... relating to support of either spouse": s. 15.2(4)(c). A separation agreement is usually such an agreement. However, as a "factor" to be considered by the court, it runs the risk of having its provisions for support supplanted by a court order for a different amount, or for different terms of payment. This power to override the support provisions of an agreement gives the court a choice. It may, in its discretion, find that it should not interfere in the arrangement made and dismiss the claim for support, or that it should ignore the agreement and make a support order on other terms.

The exercise of discretion calls for a balancing of two conflicting policies. On the one hand, the court has a responsibility to see that support arrangements are made according to the principles in the *Divorce Act*. On the other, the parties have a right to make their own arrangement. How should the conflict in these two policies be resolved? How can the court give weight to the agreement and, at the same time, discharge its responsibility to consider the other factors and implement the support objectives set out in the *Act*? What is the proper balance between freedom of contract and the duty of the court in support matters? To refuse jurisdiction whenever there is a valid and enforceable agreement settling support matters is to give full weight to the agreement, but may be a dereliction of judicial responsibility. On the other hand, to assess support in every case and then, if the agreement falls short, make an order in the amount assessed, gives no weight to the agreement. Nor would such a policy be practicable. The courts simply could not handle all the cases. Although an administrative concern should not determine the issue, it does put pressure on the courts to be sure of their ground when ignoring agreements.

Some restricting principle or test must be applied "so that all final separation agreements are not the subject of application to the court to ascertain the extent to which the agreement reflects the objectives of the *Divorce Act*." Some principle or test must be found to cut between the two conflicting policies, and to control the flood of litigation. The "threshold test" is such a device. If the test is not met, the court does not exercise its overriding jurisdiction and the support provisions in the agreement are allowed to stand; if it is met, the jurisdiction is exercised and support is assessed according to the principles in the *Divorce Act*. See *Santosuosso v. Santosuosso* (1997), 27 R.F.L. (4th) 234, 32 O.R. (3d) 143, 97 O.A.C. 42, 1997 CarswellOnt 369, [1997] O.J. No. 501 (Div. Ct.).

15§147 — Overriding jurisdiction of the courts

The power to "override" an agreement for support should be distinguished from the power to "vary" a previous order. When a court exercises its power to override an agreement, it does not amend the agreement itself but, instead, makes an original support order that stands apart from the agreement. When a court varies an order, on the other hand, it does amend the actual order.

The power to override an agreement has a respected history at common law. The House of Lords in *Hyman v. Hyman*, [1929] A.C. 601, [1929] All E.R. Rep. 245 (U.K. H.L.), held that the existence of a covenant in a deed of separation does not preclude a wife from making an application to the court for maintenance. The parties cannot agree not to invoke the jurisdiction of the court, or to control the powers of the court, once its jurisdiction is invoked. The power to provide for a wife on the dissolution of her marriage is a necessary incident of the power to decree such a dissolution, an action which is done not only in the interests of the wife but also in the interests of the public.

Madam Justice Wilson in *Pelech v. Pelech*, 7 R.F.L. (3d) 225 at 269, [1987] 1 S.C.R. 801, 17 C.P.C. (2d) 1, 14 B.C.L.R. (2d) 145, [1987] 4 W.W.R. 481, 76 N.R. 81, 38 D.L.R. (4th) 641, 1987 CarswellBC 147, 1987 CarswellBC 703, [1987] S.C.J. No. 31, stated the position in Canada: ". . . [The] Hyman principle that parties cannot by contract oust the jurisdiction of the court in matters of spousal maintenance, is an established tenet of Canadian law . . . where the parties have negotiated their own agreement, freely and on the advice of independent legal counsel, as to how their financial affairs should be settled on the breakdown of their marriage, and the agreement is not unconscionable in the substantive law sense it should be respected".

The common law position has been carried forward to the *Divorce Act*, 1985, s. 15.2(4)(c). The effect of this position and the legislation is that an agreement providing for support is entitled to weight, but does not preclude the court from dealing with an inadequate support provision by making an order on better terms.

Where the negotiations are unimpeachable, the court should exercise its discretion to set aside an agreement only when it fails to be in substantial compliance with the objectives of the *Divorce Act*. The objectives set out in s. 15.2(a) to (d) of the Act are to "recognize any economic advantages or disadvantages to the spouses arising from the marriage or its breakdown;" to "apportion between the spouses any financial consequences arising from the care of any child of the marriage over and above any obligation for the support of any child of the marriage;" to "relieve any economic hardship of the spouses arising from the breakdown of the marriage; and . . . in so far as practicable, [to] promote the economic self-sufficiency of each spouse within a reasonable period of time." In addition to these express objectives, the objectives of certainty, finality and autonomy implied from the language of the Act and found in the cases interpreting the Act are to be considered. Substantial compliance, rather than strict compliance with the other objectives, is permitted by the objective of autonomy. In commenting on this objective, the court held that in exercising their autonomy, separating or divorcing parties must be allowed some latitude to pursue their own objectives and need only be in substantial compliance with the law's objectives as reasonably understood by them in a subjective sense: *Miglin v. Miglin*, 34 R.F.L. (5th) 255, 224 D.L.R. (4th) 193, 2003 CarswellOnt 1374, 2003 CarswellOnt 1375, 2003 SCC 24, [2003] S.C.J. No. 21, 66 O.R. (3d) 736 (note), [2003] 1 S.C.R. 303, 171 O.A.C. 201, 302 N.R. 201 (S.C.C.). In determining whether it should override an agreement, the court should take a two-stage approach; the first relating to the time of the negotiation and execution of the agreement, and the second, to the time of the application for spousal support. In the first stage, the court must satisfy itself that the negotiation of the agreement was unimpeachable and that the agreement itself, at this time, was in substantial compliance with the overall objectives of the *Divorce Act*. In reviewing the negotiations, the court should consider the duration of cohabitation and the functions performed by each spouse during cohabitation (s. 15.2(4)(a) and (b)) the circumstances existing at the time of the negotiations and the conditions affecting the parties, including whether there was oppression, pressure, or other vulnerabilities that were taken advantage of, the conditions of the negotiations themselves such as the time over which they extended and whether they were conducted with the assistance of lawyers working on their own or with other professionals. It is not necessary to "look for 'unconscionability' as it is understood in the common law of contract . . . . There may be persuasive evidence brought before the court that one party took advantage of the vulnerability of the other party in separation or divorce negotiations that would fall short of evidence of the power imbalance necessary to demonstrate unconscionability in a commercial context between, say, a consumer and a large financial institution." But the court should not "presume that the apparently stronger party took advantage of any vulnerability on the part of the other. Rather, there must be evidence to warrant the court's finding that the agreement should not stand on the basis of a fundamental flaw in the negotiation process." It must be recognized that the emotional stress generally associated with separation and divorce does not give rise to a presumption that the parties are incapable of making agreements that it would be fair to enforce. In the same vein, vulnerabilities in and of themselves do not justify the court's intervention as professional assistance can often overcome "any systemic imbalances between the parties." However, "where the power imbalance did vitiate the bargaining process, the agreement should not be read as expressing the parties' notion of equitable sharing in their circumstances and the agreement will merit little weight."

In this first stage, after determining that the agreement was negotiated under satisfactory conditions the court must next consider the substance of the agreement. It "must determine the extent to which the agreement takes into account the factors and objectives listed in the Act, thereby reflecting an equitable sharing of the economic consequences of marriage and its breakdown. Only a significant departure from the general objectives of the Act will warrant the court's intervention on the basis that there is not substantial compliance with the Act." The agreement must be scrutinized in its totality, but the whole agreement will not necessarily be set aside if intervention is necessary. Setting aside part of it way serve to address the inequity.

At the second stage, relating to the time of the application, the court should assess the extent to which the agreement remains in substantial compliance with the overall objectives. Not all changes in circumstances since the execution of the agreement will result in the agreement, or part of it, being set aside. Changes that will not affect the enforceability of the agreement are such things as changes in the job market, more onerous parenting responsibilities than were contemplated, and a challenging transition to the workforce. Moreover, "negotiating parties should know that each person's health cannot be guaranteed as a constant" and that values of assets distributed in a property division could change. Housing prices and business prospects may fluctuate. A spouse may decide not to work. On the other hand, a judge is not required to follow the high *Pelech* standard to set aside a support provision only when a change is shown to be "radical". Similarly, it is unnecessary for the spouse claiming support to demonstrate that the change in circumstances from the time of the execution of the agreement is causally connected to the marriage or its breakdown. The test is not foreseeability but rather "the extent to which the unimpeachably negotiated agreement can be said to have contemplated the situation before the court at the time of the application". The court should focus on the "agreement's continued correspondence to the parties' original intentions as to their relative positions and the overall objectives of the Act, not on whether a change occurred per se." The court must be convinced that the intervention of the court and the degree of intervention are warranted before the agreement, or a provision in it, is set aside.

Parties must take responsibility for their contracts, as well as for their own lives. The court should give their agreement little weight only when the parties' circumstances at the time of the application depart significantly from the range of reasonable outcomes anticipated by the parties in a manner that puts them at odds with the objectives of the Act.

On the facts of the case, the court found that the evidence did not show that the circumstance at the time of the negotiation and execution of the agreement contained vulnerabilities. The parties negotiated their agreement over a 15- month period and were assisted by several professionals including experienced and expert counsel. The parties received sophisticated advice in tax planning and income projections. As to the substance of the agreement, there was nothing to indicate that there was a significant departure from the overall objectives of the *Divorce Act*. The assets that the parties received were of equal value. The wife received $60,000 in child support per year and indicated that it was her preference to release the husband from spousal support, provided her economic needs were met through child support. The wife as also provided with a 5-year contract in the consulting agreement. Accordingly, the court found that the separation agreement was in substantial compliance with the *Divorce Act* at the time of its formation.

The court found that the only real changes in circumstances at the time of the application from the time of formation of the agreement were that the eldest child now resided with the father and the variation of the child support award was now in accordance with the *Guidelines*. The wife did not intend to work at the time she executed the agreement. She contemplated a drop in income when the consulting agreement ended. The change in her child care obligations did not take her current position beyond the reasonable range of circumstances that the parties anticipated at the time that the agreement was signed.

The court, in granting the husband's appeal, held that the wife's "evidence and argument regarding her circumstances at the time of her support application fail to demonstrate that the agreement fairly negotiated and substantially compliant with the objectives of the

1985 Act at its formation should not continue to govern the parties' post-divorce obligations towards each other."

However, the Supreme Court in *Hartshorne v. Hartshorne*, 2004 SCC 22, 2004 CarswellBC 603, 2004 CarswellBC 604, [2004] 6 W.W.R. 1, 194 B.C.A.C. 161, 317 W.A.C. 161, 236 D.L.R. (4th) 193, 47 R.F.L. (5th) 5, 25 B.C.L.R. (4th) 1, 318 N.R. 1, [2004] S.C.J. No. 20 (S.C.C.), held that the court should not establish a "hard and fast" rule regarding the deference to be afforded to marriage agreements as compared with separation agreements. But, the court would not wish to interfere with an agreement unless it was convinced that the agreement did not substantially comply with the overall objectives of the Act in question, such as the *Family Relations Act* (British Columbia). It would be unlikely that a court would disregard an agreement in its entirety, unless there was a significant change in the parties' circumstances from what could reasonably have been anticipated at the time of negotiation. The change would be that the terms of the agreement no longer reflected the parties' intentions at the time of execution and did not comply with the objectives of the Act. To have the agreement set aside, it would be necessary to establish that these new circumstances were not reasonably anticipated by the parties, and that they led to a situation which could not be condoned. The test is not strict forseeability. Instead, the question is the extent to which the unimpeachably negotiated agreement can be said to have contemplated the situation before the court at the time of the application: *Hartshorne v. Hartshorne*, above. Although this case was decided under the British Columbia *Family Relations Act*, it has important implications for cases determined under the federal *Divorce Act*. Here the parties entered into a marriage agreement on their wedding day. The husband had arranged for the preparation of the agreement. It provided that the parties would not share their property, but that the wife would be entitled to a 3 percent interest in the family home for each year of the marriage to a maximum of 49 percent. The husband brought assets valued at approximately $1.6 million into the marriage. The wife had no assets on the date of the marriage and was, in fact, heavily in debt. Both parties obtained independent legal advice. The wife's lawyer advised her that the agreement was unfair and that the courts would likely set it aside if the parties separated. The parties cohabited for twelve and a half years, nine of which were under the marriage. They had two children. While both parents were lawyers, the wife left her law practice to take maternity leave and remained at home to look after the children. After the separation, she obtained a position as an associate in a law firm at a salary of $52,000 a year. The main policy objective guiding the courts' role in a division of property on marital breakdown in British Columbia is fairness. This is derived from the *Family Relations Act* (British Columbia) which provides that to be enforceable, any agreement to govern a division of property upon the dissolution of marriage must operate fairly at the time of distribution of the property. If it does not, the court may reapportion the property.

To determine whether a marriage agreement in British Columbia operates fairly the court in *Hartshorne*, above, held that as a first step, it must consider the financial entitlements under the agreement, and all other entitlements for the spouses outside the agreement including spousal and child support. Second, the court must consider the factors listed in s. 65(1) of the FRA. These factors are (a) the duration of the marriage; (b) the duration of the period during which the spouses have lived separate and apart; (c) the date when property was acquired or disposed of; (d) the extent to which property was acquired by one spouse through inheritance or gift; (e) the needs of each spouse to become or remain economically independent and self sufficient; and (f) any other circumstances relating to the acquisition, preservation, maintenance, improvement or use of property or the capacity or liabilities of a spouse. In order for the agreement to be set aside, a court must find that by reason of these factors, taken together, the economic consequences of the marriage breakdown as found in the first step were not shared equitably in all of the circumstances. What matters is whether the agreement was unfair in the circumstances present at the time of distribution. In the present case, the marriage agreement, at the wife's insistence, expressly preserved a right to spousal support which gave rise to an understanding on her part that, in light of the provisions with respect to property, her future needs could be met through support. Only if her needs could not be met, and self-sufficiency could not be attained through an order of spousal support, should it be concluded that an agreement operated unfairly. The Supreme Court of Canada reversed the trial judge's reapportionment of the division of property, which gave the wife a 40 percent share or all the assets, on the understanding that she had the right to apply for spousal support. Any economic disadvantage that the respondent suffered could be addressed on such an application. Considering the provisions of the *Family Relations Act*, the provisions of the agreement, and the circumstances of the parties at the time of separation, the agreement was fair at the time of the distribution under the agreement, and it should be left intact. Courts should not conclude that agreements are unfair only because they deviate from the statutory matrimonial property regime. Fairness must be considered in light of the realistic contemplation of the parties, the attention they give to changes in circumstances or unrealized implications, their true circumstances, and whether the discrepancy is such, given the s. 65 factors, a different apportionment should be made. (The court also held that where a party has been advised that an agreement is "grossly unfair" and that a court would "easily find" that a provision could be set aside, the party should not be allowed to avoid his or her contractual obligations on the basis that he or she believed from the outset that the contract was void or unenforceable.)

Where the husband's real estate business had suffered an uncharacteristic "bad year", the court, on appeal, reserved a judgment reducing the husband's spousal support obligation under the parties' separation agreement. While the income reduction was not insignificant, the real estate market was known to be cyclical and the husband had sought the variation within a matter of a few months after executing the agreement: *Hanna v. Hanna* (2004), 9 R.F.L. (6th) 114, 2004 CarswellOnt 4099 (C.A.).

The determination of an application to override an agreement for spousal support where the spouses have executed a final agreement that purports to address all matters respecting their separation involves a two-step approach. Stage one relates to the circumstance of the agreement's execution and its substance. The second stage involves an inquiry into the extent to which enforcement of the agreement reflects the original intention of the parties and the extent to which it is still in compliance with the objectives of the *Divorce Act*: *L. (H.) v. L. (M.H.)*, 44 R.F.L. (5th) 388, [2003] B.C.J. No. 2098, 2003 CarswellBC 2206, 232 D.L.R. (4th) 52, 19 B.C.L.R. (4th) 327, 186 B.C.A.C. 264, 306 W.A.C. 264, 2003 BCCA 484 (B.C. C.A.).

A party will not obtain spousal support that is inconsistent with the terms of a pre-existing separation agreement which meets the tests set out in *Miglin v. Miglin*, 34 R.F.L. (5th) 255, 224 D.L.R. (4th) 193, 2003 CarswellOnt 1374, 2003 CarswellOnt 1375, 2003 SCC 24, 66 O.R. (3d) 736 (note), [2003] 1 S.C.R. 303, 171 O.A.C. 201, 302 N.R. 201, [2003] S.C.J. No. 21 (S.C.C.); *Marks v. Tokarewicz* (2004), 2004 CarswellOnt 97, 181 O.A.C. 11, [2004] O.J. No. 92 (Ont. C.A.); leave to appeal refused (2004), 2004 CarswellOnt 1949, 2004 CarswellOnt 1950 (S.C.C.). Although the trial judge decided the case before the *Miglin* decision at the Supreme Court of Canada, the Court of Appeal in the *Marks v. Tokarewicz* case held that her findings were dispositive of the issues on appeal. After the parties' separation, the husband paid interim spousal support to the wife pursuant to a consent order to enable her to study medicine outside the country. After completing her degree, she returned to Canada and entered into a separation agreement, whereby the husband agreed to continue paying spousal support for over a year and a half and the wife released all claims to further support. The wife did not qualify to practice medicine in Canada and, when she became destitute and was relying on social assistance, applied for spousal support under the *Divorce Act*. As the husband was earning between $500,000 and $550,000 a year, there was no question that the he had the ability to pay. The appellate court, following the procedure described in the *Miglin* decision, found that the agreement was negotiated and executed in satisfactory circumstances and that at the time when the parties entered into the agreement, it was in substantial compliance with the considerations in s. 15.2 *Divorce Act*, and with the Act's more general objectives of certainty, finality and autonomy. Both parties had independent legal advice, exchanged sworn financial statements, and the major assets were independently valued. Each party had full disclosure of the other's financial circumstances. The court considered whether the agreement still reflected the original intention of the parties and the extent to which it was still in substantial compliance with the objectives of the act. The trial judge had considered that a material change in circumstances had occurred, as the parties had anticipated that the wife would qualify to practise medicine in Canada, which she did not do. The appellate court upheld that trial court's ruling that despite the change of circumstances, a support order should not be made. The trial judge had properly assessed the parties conflicting objectives of autonomy, finality and certainty versus a plan for the equitable resolution of the financial and property issues arising from the marriage and its breakdown, in the context of the intervening events.

According to the *Miglin* case, general principles of contract are not intended to govern the applicability of private contractual arrangements for spousal support: *Katz v. Katz*, 2004 CarswellMan 226, 2004 MBCA 85 (Man. C.A.). In this case, the husband appealed and the wife cross-appealed from an order varying a consent judgment. The judgment provided that spousal support would be terminated if the wife were in default for more than 10 days of her obligation to pay one-half of her monthly portion of the couple's debt. The wife missed making a payment, but the husband did not give the wife notice that support would be terminated if the default were not remedied. "Had such notice been given by the husband, it is a reasonable inference to draw from the evidence that the wife would promptly have remedied the default, so as to avoid the disproportionate and disastrous consequences of the complete termination of her spousal support. Indeed, the wife argued that such a result would be so disproportionate as to constitute a penalty and thus be unenforceable, but that argument need not be resolved on these facts." The court agreed with the motions judge that spousal support did not terminate as a result of the missed payment and it dismissed the husband's appeal. The wife's cross-appeal was allowed in part with the court holding that she was entitled to apply for an increase in spousal support, as the husband had declared bankruptcy and there was a change of circumstances. The motions judge erred when he limited that increase to the amount required to permit the wife to service the debt payment. The words of the separation agreement and the objectives of s. 17 of the Act did not support such a limited consideration. The appellate court ordered a greater quantum of spousal support, with the increase to take effect on the same date as the increase ordered by the motions court.

Although spousal support payments and the provision of other financial arrangements in a separation agreement may be in substantial compliance with the general objectives of the Act at the time of execution, expected self-sufficiency and a time-limited award may not be in compliance with those objectives at the time of execution of the agreement: *Lang v. Lang*, 46 R.F.L. (5th) 200, 2003 CarswellMan 527, 2003 MBCA 158, [2004] 6 W.W.R. 454, 180 Man. R. (2d) 223, 310 W.A.C. 223, 234 D.L.R. (4th) 525 (Man. C.A.). At the time of execution of the agreement, the wife had primary care of all of the children, two of whom had special needs requiring an extraordinary amount of her time. Considering these circumstances and the fact that she had stayed home with her children and had limited marketable skills, it was unreasonable to anticipate that she would be self-sufficient in 5 years time as contemplated by the agreement. While it is important to consider that certainty, finality and autonomy are significant objectives of the Act, they must be balanced with other objectives. The 5-year limit for spousal support did not take into account the "condition, means, needs and other circumstances" (*Divorce Act*, s. 15.2(4)) of the wife as the primary caregiver to the children and the effect her responsibilities would have on her ability to become self-sufficient. Nor did it take into account the objective to "apportion between the spouses any financial consequences arising from the care of any child of the marriage over and above any obligation for the support of any child" (s. 15.2 (b)). It also disregarded the "reasonable period of time" aspect in the objective that a spousal support order should "in so far as practicable, promote the economic self-sufficiency of each spouse within a reasonable period of time" (s. 15.296)(d)). Since the 5-year limit did not comply substantially with the overall objectives of the Act at the time the agreement was executed, the weight given to the agreement should be significantly discounted. The same reasons for deciding that the 5-year limit on spousal support was not in compliance with the overall objectives of the Act at the time of the execution of the agreement also applied with equal force at the time of the trial. Accordingly, the provision in the agreement to limit spousal support to 5 years could not stand.

A wife's waiver of spousal support in a separation agreement was enforced in *McGeachy v. McGeachy* (2003), 42 R.F.L. (5th) 415, 2003 CarswellOnt 3793, [2003] O.J. No. 3881 (Ont. C.A.) where the court found that in the circumstances surrounding the signing of the agreement, there was no basis for ignoring it. The wife had received independent legal advice; she was aware of her right to seek spousal support; she provided a full and final release of that support; and the original agreement at the time of the execution was in general compliance with the objectives of the *Divorce Act*. The court further found that the agreement remained in compliance with the objectives of the Act and that there had been no significant change in the parties' circumstances from what could reasonably have been anticipated at the time they negotiated the agreement. (The court did not comment on the matters which made the agreement in compliance with the objectives of the Act). The court set aside the lower court's order for spousal support and ordered that the funds paid into court were to be paid to the husband. In addition, the wife was to reimburse the husband (without interest) for spousal support that had been paid to her pursuant to an earlier order.

On a motion for summary judgment in *Kelly v. Kelly* (2003), 2003 CarswellOnt 3521, 45 R.F.L. (5th) 403 (Ont. S.C.J.); reversed (2004), 2004 CarswellOnt 3074 (Ont. C.A.), the court found that in view of the level of professional legal advice involved and the principles as set out by the Supreme Court of Canada in *Miglin v. Miglin*, the husband had discharged the onus of establishing that there was no genuine issue to be tried and dismissed the wife's action for support. Two separation agreements had been entered into with the wife receiving independent legal advice at the time of the first agreement. Both agreements contained a waiver of spousal support. At the appellate level, the court held that a motion for summary judgment is poorly suited to dispose of claims that must be resolved by applying the detailed analysis in *Miglin*, which typically requires the court to draw inferences, determine credibility, and find facts in the face of disputed evidence. In this case, the Court of Appeal set aside the order of the motions judge and dismissed the husband's motion for summary judgment.

In *Gauthier v. Gauthier* (2004), 9 R.F.L. (6th) 312, 2004 CarswellOnt 4747 (S.C.J.), the court gave no weight to the spousal support terms of the parties' separation agreement, which allowed for very modest limited-term support for the wife. At the time of execution, the wife had no income, was receiving public assistance, was in poor health, had no education and had been totally dependant upon the husband throughout the parties' 22-year traditional marriage.

In *Girard v. Girard*, 2004 CarswellBC 756, 2004 BCSC 467 (B.C. S.C.), the court held that the provisions of the parties' separation agreement were within the objectives set out in s. 15.2(6) of the *Divorce Act* and in substantial compliance with the overall objectives of the Act, which included certainty, finality and autonomy. The court observed that the parties had received independent legal advice and acknowledged there had been full and complete disclosure of each of their financial circumstances; the agreement took into account that the marriage was for a long term in which the husband was the primary breadwinner and the wife, the primary caregiver and homemaker. The provision for the acquisition of a house by the wife, time-limited spousal support for her for 5 years, and a continuing contribution towards the mortgage for another 5 years recognized her dependency. This provision together with a commitment that she would make reasonable efforts to find employment to become self-supporting, and the provision that spousal support could be reduced in the event of a material reduction in the husband's yearly income, demonstrated the context within which the agreement was made. The change since the execution of the agreement was the sudden and substantial decrease in the husband's income, which was a risk that the parties understood and accepted at the time of the execution of the agreement and for which they provided a right to adjust spousal support. Since the agreement substantially complied with the objectives of the Act when it was made and continued to reflect the original intention of the parties and remained in substantial compliance with the objectives of the Act, and since the current circumstances were not a significant departure from the range of prospective circumstances that the parties could expect, the court should give the agreement significant weight. The effect in doing so was that the agreement "must be interpreted and, if appropriate, applied including the provision that spousal support may be reduced in the event of a material reduction in the plaintiff's yearly income." However, in applying these principles to the evidence, the court declined to reduce the husband's support obligation as requested because he had not produced his last income tax return, nor the banking documents or financial statements concerning the company for which he was an officer. "In order for the plaintiff to rely upon the separation agreement to reduce his obligation to pay the defendant spousal support, he must offer proof that his annual income has been materially reduced. Similarly, the plaintiff has the same obligation of putting forward a body of evidence when he asks the court to enforce the agreement." He was given leave to bring an application to vary, supported by evidence consisting at least of his personal income tax returns for the last 2 years, as well as the corporate tax returns for the same years.

A separation agreement will be given no weight where at the time of its execution the dependant spouse does not receive legal advice, was not aware of her legal entitlements and received almost nothing under the agreement after a lengthy marriage (17 years), which involved raising two children: *Rogerson v. Rogerson*, 2004 CarswellNS 154, 222 N.S.R. (2d) 324, 701 A.P.R. 324, 2004 NSSF 37 (N.S. S.C.). The wife could not afford to retain counsel and did not know that Legal Aid was available to her. Although the stress that she was under at the time of the signing of the agreement may not have been severe enough, in itself, to amount to sufficient circumstances of oppression or vulnerabilities to invalidate the agreement under the first stage of the test set out in *Miglin*, this stress combined with the other circumstances at the time, principally her lack of independent legal advice, her limited education and low-paying employment, did invalidate the agreement. In view of this finding, it was unnecessary to proceed further with the *Miglin* analysis. However, the court held that if it were wrong in its assessment of the circumstances at the time of execution, the agreement was invalid on the ground that it was not in substantial compliance with the *Divorce Act*. The court observed that *Miglin* was a situation where the principal issue related to spousal support, whereas in the case at bar spousal support was an issue, but the principal issues related to matrimonial property, particularly the husband's military pension.

A separation agreement will be set aside after applying the tests set out in the *Miglin* decision, where the circumstances surrounding the execution of the agreement are suspect and the agreement does not meet the objectives of the *Divorce Act*: *Slipak v. Slipak* (2004), 2004 CarswellOnt 13 (Ont. S.C.J.). The husband made inadequate disclosure to his wife, a person not involved in the business aspects of the marriage, and informed her that unless she signed the agreement, she would receive nothing whatsoever. The wife knew of the contentious nature of the husband's litigation with his first wife and that he had been taking a course on separation for several weeks. She saw no alternative but to sign the agreement. Although there was independent legal advice, there was no evidence as to the quality of that advice. The agreement was not fair at the time it was made and did not meet the objectives of the *Divorce Act*. On the question of fairness, the court stated, "The Agreement provided for no spousal support whatsoever. There had been an eight-year marriage where the wife was the primary caregiver for the children and held a limited part-time job during that time period. The parties had actually resided together for two years before that. Accordingly, spousal support should have been payable under the Agreement in the circumstances."

A cohabitation agreement is subject to the same tests that *Miglin* provides for separation agreements: *Salzmann v. Salzmann* (2004), 2004 CarswellOnt 169, 50 R.F.L. (5th) 181 (Ont. S.C.J.). On an interim application for spousal support, the court following the tests set out in *Miglin*, found that with respect to the first stage, the applicant raised an arguable case that the negotiations of the parties' cohabitation agreement were not unimpeachable While the parties acknowledged in the agreement that the respondent was providing support to the applicant and that she was not able to provide for her own support, the period for support was "only during the relationship." Support after that was waived. There was no provision for a review of support or a possible variation if the parties married and had children. They did, in fact, marry and had one child. It appeared that the applicant was "taken advantage of" by the respondent and did not have a proper understanding of what she was "waiving" or 'releasing". In addition, there were serious doubts about whether she received adequate professional assistance before she executed the agreement. Following the *Miglin* analysis, the court found that the agreement totally failed to be in compliance with the spousal support objectives of the *Divorce Act*. The spousal support provision, once the parties married became a provision in a marriage contract by operation of the *Family Law Act* (Ontario) and constituted a factor to be considered in a claim for support under the *Divorce Act*. The waiver attempted to exclude the applicant's claim for spousal support regardless of any change in the parties' situation. The wife was not working, as the husband had terminated her employment with his company. He was found to have an imputed income of $225,000 a year. The court held that in the circumstances, and in light of the *Divorce Act* objectives, the applicant was entitled to interim spousal support. There were new circumstances that the parties had not anticipated. Consequently, the court was to give little weight, if any, to the agreement on the spousal support issue.

There is no requirement for a finding of a material change in circumstances as a condition precedent for setting aside the spousal support provisions in an agreement: *Fitzgerald v. Gerlich* (2003), 2003 CarswellOnt 1816, 40 R.F.L. (5th) 84 (Ont. S.C.J.). The court quoted from the *Miglin* decision, stating ". . . it is not the existence of change per se that matters but whether, at the time of the application, all the circumstances render continued reliance on the pre-existing agreement unacceptable."

In *Collins v. Collins*, 2003 CarswellNfld 168, 2003 NLSCTD 102, 42 R.F.L. (5th) 273, 229 Nfld. & P.E.I.R. 1, 679 A.P.R. 1, [2003] N.J. No. 169 (N.L. T.D.), the court upheld the parties' agreement as it had been negotiated in good faith. It was a fair and equitable division of their matrimonial and business assets and liabilities and corollary relief issues had been determined reasonably. The agreement continued to deal with all issues between the parties and there had been no changes in the parties' circumstances since the separation agreement so it could still govern the parties' post-divorce obligations to each other.

The court held that the general rule from the *Miglin* decision is that a court should be loathe to interfere with a separation agreement that shows a mutual intent to finalize the terms of the parties' separation agreement, and indicates their substantive intentions: *Wigle v. Wigle* (2003), 2003 CarswellOnt 1672, 39 R.F.L. (5th) 233 (Ont. S.C.J.). The court found that the Wigle case fell within the general rule in *Miglin*. Each party was represented by counsel. The former wife's self-sufficiency is outweighed by the aspects of finality and autonomy. The agreement was substantially in compliance with the support provisions of the Act, and the philosophy of the Act that the parties settle their affairs. There were no new circumstances which indicate that the agreement no longer reflects the parties' intentions at the time the agreement was executed. It still reflects the philosophy of the *Divorce Act*. The agreement was upheld.

Where the parties' separation agreement provided for a review of spousal support if there was a substantial increase in the husband's income, the application should be dismissed when the increase in income is caused by a transaction referred to in the agreement and consequently contemplated by the parties: *Bellingham v. Bellingham*, 44 R.F.L. (5th) 357, 2003 CarswellMan 396, 178 Man. R. (2d) 60, 2003 MBQB 221 (Man. Q.B.); additional reasons at 2004 CarswellMan 100, 1 R.F.L. (6th) 11, 2004 MBQB 75 (Man. Q.B.); further additional reasons at 2004 CarswellMan 191, 2004 MBQB 115 (Man. Q.B.). Pursuant to the terms of the parties' agreement, the husband purchased the wife's shares in a company and subsequently received all the company dividends. At the time the agreement was executed, the parties assumed that the entire company income, which had been split between the parties during the marriage, would be attributable to the husband following the share purchase transaction.

A provision in a separation agreement that support will terminate if the wife cohabited in a conjugal relationship may be enforced against the wife: *Bakes v. Bakes*, 40 R.F.L. (5th) 1, 2003 CarswellNS 220, 2003 NSSC 130, 215 N.S.R. (2d) 1, 675 A.P.R. 1 (N.S. S.C.). The separation agreement provided that spousal support would be terminated if the wife were living in a common law relationship. She entered into such a relationship and applied for a continuation of spousal support. At the first stage, as set out in the *Miglin* decision, the court found that any concerns about oppression at the time of the execution of the agreement were on the side of the husband in that an unduly heavy financial burden had been placed on him. He was however, prepared to live with it. The negotiation of the agreement did not lead to an unduly harsh or oppressive agreement for the wife. At the second stage, following the procedure in *Miglin*, the court assessed the substance of the agreement and held that an application of the terms of the agreement did not represent a significant departure from the range of reasonable expectations as anticipated by the parties so as to put them out of step with the objectives of the act. Both parties had developed health problems. The *Miglin* case specifically stated that "Negotiating parties should know that each persons (sic) health cannot be guaranteed as a constant . . ." The husband's illness stemmed from his increased work load in fulfilling his obligations under the agreement. The wife received very generous support immediately after the marriage breakdown. The court held that it was appropriate that the terms of the separation agreement be respected and that support should be terminated as of the date when the court found that the wife was living in a common law relationship.

The same principles applied in *Miglin* to separation agreements apply equally to prenuptial agreements: *Culen v. Culen*, 37 R.F.L. (5th) 300, 2003 CarswellAlta 716, 2003 ABQB 480, 338 A.R. 308 (Alta. Q.B.). Here, with respect to the first stage, there was no evidence to indicate that the agreement should be discounted. The fact that the plaintiff was pregnant and therefore vulnerable is undermined by the fact that the agreement was negotiated at her insistence. Both parties had previous experience with separation and divorce and each was represented by counsel. The agreement was in substantial compliance with the overall objectives of the *Divorce Act*. At the second stage, the court found that the current circumstances of the parties did not represent a significant departure from the range of the reasonable outcomes which the parties would have anticipated. The prenuptial agreement continued to reflect the parties' original intentions with respect to their finances and provided certainty and finality. There was evidence throughout the 9-year cohabitation of the intention of the parties to be self-sufficient or autonomous and the court should take this factor into account. The court must take into account the objectives of spousal support. There was no evidence of any economic disadvantage to the plaintiff arising from the marriage or its breakdown. While the plaintiff received disability payments at the time of the hearing, as she was epileptic, she began receiving these payments prior to separation. There was no evidence that the parties established an interdependent relationship at any point in time. The parties were not in circumstances that they did not contemplate would occur. The court dismissed the plaintiff's application for spousal support.

Where there is no reason to discount the weight of the agreement because of the circumstances surrounding the negotiation and execution of an agreement, and the substance of the agreement takes into account the factors and objectives in s. 15.2 of the *Divorce Act*, the court should then assess the extent to which the agreement still reflects the original intention of the parties, and the extent to which it is still in substantial compliance with the objectives of the Act: *Deneweth v. Deneweth*, 2003 CarswellMan 431, 44 R.F.L. (5th)

368, 179 Man. R. (2d) 4, 2003 MBQB 236 (Man. Q.B.); additional reasons at 2004 CarswellMan 101, 50 R.F.L. (5th) 341, 183 Man. R. (2d) 67, 2004 MBQB 60 (Man. Q.B.). In this case, the parties' original intention was that the spousal support provisions could be varied if either party had a material change in his or her circumstances. The court found that there had been a material change in the parties' circumstances, as the husband's income had decreased from $59,992 per annum to an expected income of $49,500. The wife's income from employment increased from $3,000 to $11,900. The court held that a reduction in spousal support must be limited in recognition of the factors and objectives set out in s. 15.2 of the *Divorce Act*. The reduction in the husband's income reduced his obligation for child support, which in turn placed further stress on the wife. In all the circumstances, the court ordered spousal support reduced from $800 to $700 per month.

A time-limited provision for spousal support may be enforced even though the spouse develops health problems and, at the time of the application, is on welfare: *Lyster v. Lyster* (2003), 2003 CarswellOnt 5008, 49 R.F.L. (5th) 139 (Ont. S.C.J.). The wife had developed knee problems and was on welfare at the time of her application for support beyond the 3-year provision in the agreement. She submitted that, at its formation, the substance of the agreement represented a significant departure from the *Divorce Act's* general objective of autonomy, and also from all of the s. 15.2 objectives. The court held that, as the spousal support amounted to 30% of the husband's gross annual income for 3 years, it was a generous amount that recognized her economic vulnerability and relative lack of work experience and extra childcare responsibilities. They would have considered that their marriage was relatively short, that their one child would be enrolled full-time in daycare and/or school, and that there was no reason that the wife could not be fully employed. At the time that it was signed, the agreement reflected the general objectives of the Act and, consequently, it should be given great weight.

An agreement that released each party from claims to support from the other was upheld in *Merke v. Merke*, 2003 BCSC 1070, 2003 CarswellBC 1708, 39 R.F.L. (5th) 339 (B.C. S.C.). The court found nothing in the circumstances of the negotiation and execution of the agreement to discount it, and at that time it was in substantial compliance with the principles in the *Divorce Act*. In assessing the extent to which enforcement of the agreement at the time of the hearing still reflected the original intention of the parties and the extent to which the agreement was still in substantial compliance with the objectives of the Act, the court considered whether the parties' circumstances had changed. The main change was the liquidation of the wife's business. The court found that although the wife had liquidated her restaurant business for substantially less than she had expected, the agreement had anticipated its sale or liquidation. The agreement continued to reflect the intention of the parties when they originally made the agreement. It was in substantial compliance with both the *Divorce Act* and the *Family Relations Act*.

15§148 — Unimpeachable negotiations

A court should consider evidence of lack of disclosure as part of the overall vulnerability issue when determining whether an agreement met all of the objectives of the *Divorce Act* at the time of its formation: *Leinburd v. Leinburd*, 2004 CarswellMan 194, 2004 MBQB 113 (Man. Q.B.). In its assessment, a court would weigh many factors, including the taking of professional advice. If the agreement is not set aside at this formation stage, the court must proceed to the second stage to decide whether the applicant has established that the agreement no longer reflects the parties' intention or is no longer in substantial compliance with the objectives of the *Divorce Act*. The court held that the issue of whether the wife's position was vulnerable because of inadequacies in the husband's disclosure could not be determined on a motion for summary judgment and would have to be resolved at a trial.

Whether a party has legal counsel throughout the negotiation and execution of a separation agreement is relevant to determining the weight that should be given to an agreement: *Lang v. Lang* (2003), 2003 CarswellMan 527, 46 R.F.L. (5th) 200, 2003 MBCA 158, [2004] 6 W.W.R. 454, 180 Man. R. (2d) 223, 310 W.A.C. 223, 234 D.L.R. (4th) 525 (Man. C.A.). However, there is no requirement that a party to a separation agreement must have legal counsel.

One of the circumstances considered by the court in upholding the parties' separation agreement in *McGeachy v. McGeachy* (2003), 42 R.F.L. (5th) 415, 2003 CarswellOnt 3793, [2003] O.J. No. 3881 (Ont. C.A.) was that the respondent had independent legal advice.

Absence of independent legal advice is not a ground in itself to set aside a contract at common law: *Phillips-Renwick v. Renwick Estate* (2003), 41 R.F.L. (5th) 337, 2003 CarswellOnt 3107, 229 D.L.R. (4th) 158, [2003] O.J. No. 3156 (Ont. S.C.J.). Although a lawyer gave the wife a general summary of the nature and consequences of the cohabitation agreement, which became a marriage contract upon the parties' marriage, and ascertained that she understood the terms, this procedure did not amount to independent legal advice as to the wisdom of the contract, nor provide any recommendation to the client that she should sign it or refrain from doing so. Lack of independent legal advice may be relevant to one or more of the common law grounds available to set aside the contract. However, the wife was not able to establish the existence of any such ground. Further, she initiated the agreement and understood its nature and effect. Consequently, she was bound by the agreement.

An agreement may not be negotiated in unimpeachable circumstances where, among other concerns, there are serious doubts regarding whether the applicant received adequate professional assistance before she signed the agreement: *Salzmann v. Salzmann* (2004), 2004 CarswellOnt 169, 50 R.F.L. (5th) 181 (Ont. S.C.J.).

A separation agreement may be found to be unenforceable where at the time of its execution, among other circumstances, one spouse does not receive legal advice: *Rogerson v. Rogerson*, 2004 CarswellNS 154, 222 N.S.R. (2d) 324, 701 A.P.R. 324, 2004 NSSC 37 (N.S. S.C.).

The court in *Slipak v. Slipak* (2004), 2004 CarswellOnt 13 (Ont. S.C.J.) held that a separation agreement should be set aside where, among other considerations, there was no evidence as to the quality of the independent legal advice that was given.

Where it was evident that the wife had had the benefit of legal counsel on numerous occasions throughout the parties' matrimonial proceedings, the court refused an appeal from an order that upheld the parties' separation agreement, despite the wife's allegations that she had lacked independent legal advice. It appeared that the wife's true intentions were merely to aggravate her husband: *Massé c. Poirier*, 19 mai 1992, no C.A. Montréal 500-09-000567-909 (C.A. Qué.).

In *Durocher v. Durocher* (1991), 106 N.S.R. (2d) 215, 288 A.P.R. 215, 1991 CarswellNS 559 (N.S. T.D.), the court refused to set aside the support provisions of the parties' separation agreement executed upon the dissolution of their 29-year marriage. The parties had obtained independent legal advice before signing the agreement, and the wife's allegations of undue influence, duress and unconscionability were not supported by the evidence. Furthermore, the wife had experience in handling the parties' financial affairs and, considering the property provisions of the agreement, the arrangement as a whole was not unfair.

In *Dubin v. Dubin* (2003), 34 R.F.L. (5th) 227, 2003 CarswellOnt 534, [2003] O.J. No. 547 (Ont. S.C.J.), the court set aside the parties' marriage contract under which the wife had forfeited her right to spousal support. Although the agreement made reference to financial disclosure, the wife had been misled about the husband's true financial circumstances and had no realistic understanding of his assets and liabilities as of the date of the agreement.

Where a signatory to a separation agreement has been advised of the right to independent legal advice but chooses not to pursue it, that party cannot later rely upon the inequality of bargaining power as a reason for setting aside the agreement: *Sartor v. Sartor*, 45 R.F.L. (3d) 250, [1993] N.W.T.R. 102, 1993 CarswellNWT 6, [1993] N.W.T.J. No. 18 (N.W.T. S.C.).

A single instance of one party telling the other that he would cut off support payments if she did not sign a separation agreement does not constitute duress: *Roberts v. Roberts*, 6 R.F.L. (5th) 407, 2000 BCSC 611, 2000 CarswellBC 784 (B.C. S.C.). The agreement was comprehensive and, in the opinion of the court, fair. The wife was represented by counsel throughout the negotiations and preparation of the agreement and had independent legal advice. The wife had accepted benefits under the agreement for at least 2 years before challenging the validity of the agreement.

In *Chandra v. Chandra* (1999), 45 R.F.L. (4th) 181, 174 Nfld. & P.E.I.R. 136, 533 A.P.R. 136, 1999 CarswellNfld 99, [1999] N.J. No. 101 (Nfld. C.A.); affirming (1997), 27 R.F.L. (4th) 114, 150 Nfld. & P.E.I.R. 333, 470 A.P.R. 333, 1997 CarswellNfld 27 (Nfld. U.F.C.), the court refused the husband's appeal from an order setting aside the parties' marriage agreement. The husband had drafted the agreement without consultation with the wife who signed the document without understanding its contents and without benefit of independent legal advice.

Where parties enter into an agreement through counsel, the courts tend to uphold the agreements except in the clearest of cases, and in exceptional circumstances: *P. (M.L.) v. P. (G.W.)* (2000), 12 R.F.L. (5th) 434, 2000 CarswellOnt 3937, [2000] O.J. No. 4059 (Ont. S.C.J.). This case did not meet the requirements for such exceptional circumstances and the wife's motion for judgment in accordance with the settlement was granted. The case did involve stressful litigation but the issues raised were not gratuitously or tactically created. The husband negotiated actively up to the signing of the agreement and after it was finalized. These circumstances make it difficult to find that he lacked free will in his conduct. The allegation of false accusations of sexual abuse was not a new issue at the time of execution of the settlement agreement. Another forum could deal with this issue rather than in the context of a hearing for divorce. To enforce the agreement would not prejudice either party; rather, it would benefit both by ending the litigation, providing emotional and financial relief.

Where the husband, during settlement negotiations, had failed to advise the wife that his financial circumstances had recently improved, the portion of the agreement under which the wife had waived her right to support was set aside and her support claim was allowed to go forward: *Underwood v. Underwood* (1994), 3 R.F.L. (4th) 457, 113 D.L.R. (4th)

571, 1994 CarswellOnt 394 (Ont. Gen. Div.); varied (1995), 11 R.F.L. (4th) 361, 1995 CarswellOnt 88 (Ont. Div. Ct.).

In *Droit de la famille — 1532* (1991), [1992] R.D.F. 89 (C.S.), (sub nom. *B. (P.) v. N. (R.))* 59 O.A.C. 151, 59 Q.A.C. 151, [1993] R.D.F. 720 (C.S. Qué.); reversed in part [1993] R.J.Q. 2712, (sub nom. *B. (P.) v. N. (R.))* 59 O.A.C. 151, 59 Q.A.C. 151, [1993] R.D.F. 720, 1993 CarswellQue 335 (C.A. Qué.), the court, in the context of a divorce proceeding, set aside a separation agreement on the grounds that the lawyer who prepared it had done so in a conflict of interest situation. The lawyer worked for a firm that had represented the husband for a number of years and therefore the wife had lacked independent legal advice. The agreement was clearly unreasonable and had to be annulled.

Where the wife, inexperienced in business matters, had agreed to child and spousal support which resulted in living at the poverty line, the agreement was overridden in subsequent divorce proceedings. The agreement was bordering on improvidence and failed to meet the criteria set out in s. 15 of the *Divorce Act*, 1985: *Brockie v. Brockie* (1987), 5 R.F.L. (3d) 440, 46 Man. R. (2d) 33, 1987 CarswellMan 93, [1987] M.J. No. 56 (Man. Q.B.); affirmed (1987), 8 R.F.L. (3d) 302, 1987 CarswellMan 115, [1987] M.J. No. 295 (Man. C.A.).

In *McVeetors v. McVeetors* (1985), 43 R.F.L. (2d) 113, 49 O.R. (2d) 225, 7 O.A.C. 1, 1985 CarswellOnt 227 (Ont. C.A.); leave to appeal to the Supreme Court of Canada refused (1985), 49 O.R. (2d) 225 (note), 15 D.L.R. (4th) 105 (note), 8 O.A.C. 320 (note) (S.C.C.), it was held that a separation agreement did not bar an award of lump sum maintenance to the wife where the husband had himself breached the agreement and the agreement itself was unconscionable. The agreement was found to be unconscionable on the evidence that the wife had executed the agreement while under great stress, the husband had failed to disclose material facts prior to its execution and the wife's standard of living had deteriorated drastically since the separation. See also *Straiton v. Straiton* (1972), 9 R.F.L. 21, 30 D.L.R. (3d) 102, 1970 CarswellBC 35 (B.C. S.C.) at 28 [R.F.L.].

Where the wife obtained independent legal advice prior to settling the issue of support, it was held that she could not later challenge the competence of that advice in seeking increased support in a subsequent divorce action: *Brosseau v. Brosseau* (1988), 1988 CarswellAlta 387, 85 A.R. 385 (Alta. Q.B.); varied (1989), 1989 CarswellAlta 162, 63 D.L.R. (4th) 111, 23 R.F.L. (3d) 42, 100 A.R. 15, 70 Alta. L.R. (2d) 247, [1990] 2 W.W.R. 34 (Alta. C.A.); leave to appeal refused (1990), 70 Alta. L.R. (2d) lii (note), 23 R.F.L. (3d) xli (note), 65 D.L.R. (4th) vii (note) (S.C.C.).

In *Macdonald v. Macdonald* (1986), 4 R.F.L. (3d) 463, 79 N.S.R. (2d) 58, 196 A.P.R. 58, 1986 CarswellNS 71 (N.S. T.D.), the court refused to hold the wife to a divorce settlement to which she had agreed the previous day. The wife had been under considerable strain during the negotiations and the husband would not be prejudiced by the repudiation.

In *Helmes v. Helmes* (1984), 40 R.F.L. (2d) 319, 1984 CarswellOnt 253 (Ont. H.C.), the wife was awarded monthly maintenance of $1,000 despite the fact that under earlier minutes of settlement she had agreed to accept the monthly sum of only $600. Although the husband had not exerted any pressure on the wife at the time of the settlement, she had been under psychiatric care and was in no condition to understand fully the future implications of the agreement she signed

Where, in negotiating a separation agreement, the husband consulted his brother and the wife consulted her husband's niece, who was an associate of the husband's brother, the court set aside a clause whereby the wife agreed not to pursue support. There had been a clear conflict of interest which had not been dispelled by a cursory review of the agreement on the wife's behalf by a second solicitor: *Brosseau v. Brosseau* (1989), 23 R.F.L. (3d) 42, 70 Alta. L.R. (2d) 247, [1990] 2 W.W.R. 34, 100 A.R. 15, 63 D.L.R. (4th) 111, 1989 CarswellAlta 162 (Alta. C.A.); leave to appeal to the S.C.C. refused (1990), 23 R.F.L. (3d) xli (note), 70 Alta. L.R. (2d) lii (note), 65 D.L.R. (4th) vii (note) (S.C.C.).

The presence of a separation agreement is an important circumstance for the court to take into account in awarding maintenance. However, in a case where there exists an unfair and unbalanced settlement arrived at in circumstances where the wife was subject to intimidation by the husband and where her independent legal advisor did not anticipate enforcement difficulties, judicial intervention is justified: *Ross v. Ross* (1984), 39 R.F.L. (2d) 51, 6 D.L.R. (4th) 385, 26 Man. R. (2d) 122, 1984 CarswellMan 35 (Man. C.A.); leave to appeal refused (1984), 6 D.L.R. (4th) 385n, 39 R.F.L. (2d) xxxviii, 55 N.R. 238n (S.C.C.).

In *Grossmann v. Grossmann* (1982), 29 R.F.L. (2d) 300, 1982 CarswellOnt 309 (Ont. H.C.), the court set aside a separation agreement upon which the husband relied in defence to his wife's maintenance claim. The agreement had been entered into at the instigation of the husband who had represented that it was for tax purposes only and was not intended otherwise to affect their relationship. As the wife had not had legal advice and as the agreement was not fair to her, it was ordered set aside in its entirety and transactions arranged under it were ordered unwound. See also *Bengston v. Bengston* (1976), 28 R.F.L. 208, 1976 CarswellBC 106 (B.C. S.C.); *Beach v. Beach*, [1977] 3 W.W.R. 274, 2 A.R. 561, 1977 CarswellAlta 203 (Alta. T.D.) at 282-283 [W.W.R.]; *Woods v. Woods* (1975), 22 R.F.L. 370, 1975 CarswellOnt 217 (Ont. H.C.) at 377 [R.F.L.]; *Nador v. Nador* (1977), 19 O.R. (2d) 728, 86 D.L.R. (3d) 463, 1977 CarswellOnt 1169 (Ont. H.C.) at 735 [O.R.], affirmed (1977), 22 O.R. (2d) 685, 97 D.L.R. (3d) 161, 1977 CarswellOnt 587 (Ont. C.A.); *Thompson v. Thompson* (1974), 16 R.F.L. 158, 1974 CarswellSask 23 (Sask. Q.B.).

A separation agreement will be set aside when there has been material misrepresentation of a party's assets: *Souder v. Wereschuk*, 2003 CarswellAlta 358, 2003 ABQB 258, 38 R.F.L. (5th) 185 (Alta. Q.B.). In this case, the parties married in 1989 and separated in 1994. In 1995, the husband won $500,000 in the lottery and did not disclose his win to his wife. The parties executed a separation agreement in 1997 and were divorced in 2001. In the agreement, the wife, who was disabled, waived her claim for spousal support. The court found that the husband had materially misrepresented his assets at the time that the agreement was being negotiated. The wife claimed a matrimonial property order reflecting all the assets of the husband and spousal support. The court considered that the 5-year length of the marriage was a factor. As the lottery prize was acquired 10 months after the parties' separation, there was not a significant degree of separation. The parties were nearly 2 years short of entering into a separation agreement and the plaintiff began receiving interim spousal maintenance a few months later. The court awarded the wife one quarter of the lottery proceeds but she did not receive any spousal support. The court considered the three different models of marriages set out in *Bracklow v. Bracklow*, [1999] 1 S.C.R. 420, 1999 CarswellBC 532, 1999 CarswellBC 533, [1999] S.C.J. No. 14, 169 D.L.R. (4th) 577, 236 N.R. 79, 44 R.F.L. (4th) 1, 120 B.C.A.C. 211, 196 W.A.C. 211, 63 B.C.L.R. (3d) 77, [1999] 8 W.W.R. 740 (S.C.C.) and held that the wife had not established entitlement for support under any of the models.

Where the petitioner wife executed a separation agreement without first obtaining legal advice, she was nevertheless estopped from denying its validity in her application for maintenance in an action for divorce. The wife was highly intelligent and had accepted benefits under the agreement and had not been deceived into accepting the terms: *Sherren v. Sherren* (1981), 33 Nfld. & P.E.I.R. 526, 93 A.P.R. 526, 1981 CarswellNfld 88 (Nfld. T.D.); *Armstrong v. Armstrong* (1980), 5 Sask. R. 435, 1980 CarswellSask 278 (Sask. Q.B.) at 436 [Sask. R.]; *Acorn v. Acorn* (1980), 15 R.F.L. (2d) 257, 1980 CarswellBC 480 (B.C. S.C.); *Methe v. Methe* (1973), 9 R.F.L. 320, 1973 CarswellOnt 217 (Ont. H.C.); *Curtin v. Curtin* (1975), 20 R.F.L. 140, 1976 CarswellOnt 143 (Ont. H.C.); *Dempster v. Dempster* (1976), 26 R.F.L. 337, 1976 CarswellBC 89 (B.C. S.C.) at 338-339 [R.F.L.]; *Divinsky v. Divinsky* (1970), 2 R.F.L. 372, [1971] 1 W.W.R. 389, 13 D.L.R. (3d) 717, 1970 CarswellBC 53 (B.C. S.C.) at 375-376 [R.F.L.].

In *Biscutti v. Biscutti* (1977), 4 R.F.L. (2d) 60, 1977 CarswellOnt 161 (Ont. H.C.), the fact that the wife entered into the separation agreement without any independent legal advice did not preclude the husband from utilizing the agreement as a defence to her claim for maintenance where she understood the agreement and no undue influence was brought to bear. Upon a consideration of the conduct of the parties and the terms of the agreement, it was the intention of the parties that there was to be a division of the property and the wife was to be on her own.

In *Marinangeli v. Marinangeli* (2003), 2003 CarswellOnt 2691, [2003] O.J. No. 2819, 38 R.F.L. (5th) 307, 174 O.A.C. 76, 228 D.L.R. (4th) 376, 66 O.R. (3d) 40 (Ont. C.A.), prior to the signing of the parties' settlement agreement, the husband indicated at a pre-trial conference that he anticipated a decrease in his income. In fact, he received over a million dollars when he exercised stock options within 14 months of signing the parties' settlement agreement. The case centered on the issue of whether or not the increase in the appellant's income was a change in circumstances. The wife sought to enforce the provision in the agreement that support could be revised where there had been a material change of circumstances. The appellant argued that there had not been a change in circumstances as described in *Miglin v. Miglin*, 34 R.F.L. (5th) 255, 224 D.L.R. (4th) 193, 2003 CarswellOnt 1374, 2003 CarswellOnt 1375, 2003 SCC 24, [2003] S.C.J. No. 21, 66 O.R. (3d) 736 (note), [2003] 1 S.C.R. 303, 171 O.A.C. 201, 302 N.R. 201 (S.C.C.), meaning a change that was not foreseeable as part of the ordinary course of living at the time the settlement agreement was signed.

In the *Marinangeli* case, Madam Justice Weiler wrote at paragraph 50:

> The comments of the Supreme Court in *Miglin*, supra were intended to address the situation where the parties chose to release one another from all future support obligations by a one-time payment of lump sum support. Since no future adjustments were envisaged, the parties were expected to consider such foreseeable future changes in the ordinary course of living as an increase or decrease in income before arriving at the amount of the one time payment.

She distinguished the *Marinangeli* case from *Miglin*, since in *Marinangeli*, the parties envisaged that the amount of support would change, if there were a material change in circumstances in a party's income. The court held that the provision in the separation agreement relating to a material change in circumstances, read in its context and as a whole, did not exclude foreseeable events such as an increase or decrease in income, but the opposite.

The appellant was unsuccessful in arguing that the exercise of his options was not a material change in circumstances as defined in *Willick v. Willick*, 1994 CarswellSask 48, 1994 CarswellSask 450, 6 R.F.L. (4th) 161, 119 D.L.R. (4th) 405, 173 N.R. 321, 125 Sask. R.

81, 81 W.A.C. 81, [1994] 3 S.C.R. 670, [1994] R.D.F. 617, [1994] S.C.J. No. 94 (S.C.C.) that is, had the alleged change been known, the support provision would not likely have been different. As the appellant did not know the value of his options at the time the agreement was signed, the respondent could not be assumed to know their value at that time. In addition, the respondent was not told the parameters for the exercise of the options and consequently she had no way of ascertaining the value of the options in relation to the price of the underlying stock. The respondent was dependant upon the appellant for information about the value of the options.

A change in circumstances must be something that has some measure of continuity. The court did not accept the appellant's argument that the exercise of the options was not a material change in circumstances because their exercise lacked continuity. There is continuity in the frequency with which the options are awarded and continuity in that the options may be exercised over a period of time.

The increase in a payor's salary and bonus by nearly 20 per cent over the previous year is a material change in circumstances that entitled the trial judge to consider the profit from the options in determining the quantum of support.

Where a separation agreement provides that the payor spouse was to recalculate his support obligations, if there were a material change in his income and such a change occurred and he did not inform his spouse of this change, nor recalculate his support obligations, the court held that there was an implied disclosure obligation on the payor spouse arising from the agreement: *Murray v. Murray* (2003), 2003 CarswellOnt 3258, 40 R.F.L. (5th) 244, 66 O.R. (3d) 540, [2003] O.J. No. 3350 (Ont. S.C.J.); additional reasons at (2003), 2003 CarswellOnt 3862 (Ont. S.C.J.). Following *Miglin* and Marinangelli, the court was of the opinion that in light of the payor's non-disclosure of his increased income as well as other factors, it should set aside the agreement. It held that the wife could no longer be considered bound by the release of spousal support in the agreement.

Following *Miglin*, the court held that where a payee spouse is suffering stress and anxiety at the time of the execution of a separation agreement, there is no presumption that the parties are incapable of assenting to a binding agreement: *McGregor v. Van Tilborg*, 2003 CarswellBC 1488, 2003 BCSC 918, [2003] B.C.J. No. 1427 (B.C. S.C. [In Chambers]). In this case, the wife claimed to be suffering from a mental condition and under psychiatric care when she negotiated a separation agreement. The mental problems were related to some form of historical sexual abuse and did not appear to be related to the divorce.

In upholding the parties' agreement in *Merke v. Merke*, 2003 BCSC 1070, 2003 CarswellBC 1708, 39 R.F.L. (5th) 339 (B.C. S.C.), the court found nothing in the circumstances of the negotiation and execution of the agreement to discount it. The objectives of finality, certainty, and the general interest of the parties determining their own affairs were important factors in upholding the agreement, especially where, as here, the parties both had a history of misrepresenting their incomes in order to live essentially on a tax-free basis.

15§149 — Law prior to *Miglin* (S.C.C.)

AUTHORS' NOTE: The law in this section is included for its historical interest. It may be read to see the Supreme Court of Canada's decision in *Miglin v. Miglin* (2001), 198 D.L.R. (4th) 385, 2001 CarswellOnt 1404, (sub nom. *M. (L.S.) v. M. (E.J.)*) 16 R.F.L. (5th) 185, 144 O.A.C. 155, 53 O.R. (3d) 641, [2001] O.J. No. 1510 (Ont. C.A.); leave to appeal allowed (2001), 2001 CarswellOnt 3484, 2001 CarswellOnt 3485, [2001] S.C.C.A. No. 328, 283 N.R. 395 (note), 157 O.A.C. 400 (note) (S.C.C.), in context, but any attempt to apply this law to current situations should be made with caution.

15§150 — Agreement changed according to variation provision in agreement

Where a separation agreement provides that spousal support is payable when there is a material change of circumstances, the court held that it would be payable when there were changes in the spouses' incomes: *Innes v. Innes* (2003), 44 R.F.L. (5th) 113, 2003 CarswellOnt 2884 (Ont. S.C.J.). Specifically, the court held that termination of child support constituted a material change in circumstances, as set out in the separation agreement. Further, the decline in the wife's standard of living from the time of marriage and in particular from the time that child support ceased, as well as maintenance or improvement in the husband's standard of living and in his income, constituted material changes. The parties were married for 26 years and had four children who were adults at the time of the trial. The wife did not work for 12 years. For a further 7 years, she worked part-time and started working full time only 2 years before separation. The separation agreement provided for child support of $1,647 per month based on the husband's 1999 income of $101,914.44. At that time, the wife was earning $56,900. In the separation agreement, the parties agreed to pay each other $1.00 per year with the right to claim further support based on a material change of circumstance. The husband had ceased to pay child support and the wife applied for spousal support. At the time of trial, the husband was expected to have an income of $138,000 a year and the wife an income of $63,500. The husband's new wife had an income of $99,000 a year, but that amount was unchanged since the execution of the parties' separation agreement. The court stated that a difference of incomes of the spouses should not automatically lead to an order of spousal support. However, that difference should not exist, where there is a significant disparity in the standards of living between two spouses after a long marriage and in particular if a short time has transpired since the execution of the agreement. The court held that as it should encourage self-sufficiency and also recognize the husband's new family commitments, spousal support should be less than a 50/50 equalization of incomes, and it should be based on the husband's base salary of $128,000. The court did not take the husband's yearly bonuses into account, as the wife had started to upgrade her qualifications which would result in her moving to a higher salary level. The wife was awarded spousal support of $2,000 per month retroactive to the date when the husband stopped paying child support, secured by an insurance policy, considering the husband's history of terminating child support and resisting spousal support.

Where spousal support provisions in a separation agreement allow for variation if there is any change in circumstances, material or not, the parties should be bound by the agreement if the respondent did not have the means to provide support unless he were to encroach upon his capital: *Burroughs v. Burroughs* (2004), 2004 CarswellBC 17, 2004 BCSC 7 (B.C. S.C.). In the Burroughs case, the parties separated, an interim order was granted and then the parties entered into a separation agreement. The court held that the support set out in the interim order, in accordance with the separation agreement, be terminated. Although the petitioner was in need of support, the respondent could not pay it unless he encroached upon his capital. The parties' assets had already been divided and the wife had not used her assets or income prudently to plan for her retirement and consequently had declared bankruptcy.

If there were no reason to discount the circumstances of negotiation and execution of an agreement, and the substance of the agreement takes into account the factors and objectives in s. 15.2 of the *Divorce Act*, the court should assess the extent to which the enforcement of the agreement still reflects the original intention of the parties, and the extent to which it is still in substantial compliance with the objectives of the act: *Deneweth v. Deneweth* (2003), 44 R.F.L. (5th) 368, 179 Man. R. (2d) 4, 2003 CarswellMan 431 (Man. Q.B.); additional reasons at (2004), 2004 CarswellMan 101, 2004 MBQB 60. In this case, the parties' original intention was that the spousal support provisions could be varied if either party had a material change in his or her circumstances. The court found that there had been a material change in the parties' circumstances, as the husband's income had decreased from $59,992 per annum to an expected income of $49,500. The wife's income from employment increased from $3,000 to $11,900. The court held that a reduction in spousal support must be limited in recognition of the factors and objectives set out in s. 15.2 of the Divorce Act. The reduction in the husband's income reduced his obligation for child support, which in turn placed further stress on the wife. In all the circumstances, the court ordered spousal support reduced from $800 to $700 per month.

Where the quantum of spousal and child support payable by the husband pursuant to the parties' agreement was based on his income level, the court allowed the husband's application for a reduction in support when, upon his change of careers, his income decreased substantially. Both parties intended the obligation to be based upon the husband's ability to pay, and there was no suggestion that the career change was motivated by a desire to frustrate the wife's support rights: *Bucher v. Bucher* (1990), 67 Man. R. (2d) 233, 1990 CarswellMan 339 (Q.B.).

In *Kemick v. Kemick* (1990), 85 Sask. R. 189 (Q.B.), the court allowed the husband's application for termination of support payable pursuant to the terms of the parties' separation agreements. The husband had suffered serious financial setbacks, owing creditors in excess of $100,000, while the wife had an income of $2,500 monthly.

Where a final settlement agreement includes a clause permitting variation in the event of a material change in circumstances, the court can vary the agreed amount of support whenever it would be able to vary under s. 17 of the *Divorce Act*: *Corkum v. Corkum* (1988), 14 R.F.L. (3d) 275, 1988 CarswellOnt 247 (Ont. H.C.).

15§151 — Overriding agreements — Interim applications

A marriage contract in which both spouses waive the right to spousal support is not necessarily a bar to an application for interim support. If serious issues to be tried have been raised with respect to the circumstances under which the contract was negotiated and executed, it will not act as a bar to an interim application: *Chaitas v. Christopoulos* (2004), 12 R.F.L. (6th) 43, 2004 CarswellOnt 4956, [2004] O.J. No. 907 (S.C.J.).

In *Bailey v. Paxton*, 6 R.F.L. (5th) 29, 47 O.R. (3d) 593, 2000 CarswellOnt 1194, [2000] O.J. No. 1187, [2000] O.T.C. 243 (S.C.J.), the court held that the former wife was entitled to interim spousal support pursuant to s. 15.2 of the *Divorce Act* despite a separation agreement which provided for spousal support for 3 years ending 10 years before the judgment. The court considered all factors required pursuant to s. 15.2, including the separation agreement, and concluded that in the circumstances it was warranted and reasonable to make an interim support order in the amount of $5000 per month pending the determination of the application under s. 15.2(1). See also *Taimoori v. Fanaian* (2000), 2000 CarswellOnt 2847, [2000] O.J. No. 2997 (S.C.J.).

A court may award interim spousal support despite a written separation agreement where the waiver of support provision does not meet the objectives of the spousal support provisions of the Divorce Act: *Kennedy v. Kennedy* (2000), 11 R.F.L. (5th) 150, 2000 CarswellOnt 3622, [2000] O.J. No. 3742 (S.C.J.).

A court may award interim spousal support under the *Divorce Act* notwithstanding a full contractual release, where significant changes have occurred since the agreement was made and where it is in the public interest for the court to exercise its inherent jurisdiction to override the agreement: *Pineault v. Pineault* (1993), 49 R.F.L. (3d) 411, 1993 CarswellOnt 358 (Gen. Div.).

Where the interim agreement under which the husband paid support to the wife was stated to be "without prejudice", the court was nevertheless required to consider the agreement under s. 15(5)(c) of the *Divorce Act* in order to determine final support: *Tancock v. Tancock* (1990), 24 R.F.L. (3d) 389, 1990 CarswellBC 436 (S.C.).

An interim draft separation agreement may properly be considered in a support application as an indication of the parties' intentions: *Fejes v. Fejes* (1988), 13 R.F.L. (3d) 267, 51 Man. R. (2d) 132, 1988 CarswellMan 44 (Q.B.).

15§152 — Agreements involving child support

See 15§124 Agreements involving child support

15§153 — What constitutes an agreement

Where the parties reached an agreement concerning custody and access through mediation but later disagreed on the wording of the consent order, the husband successfully applied for a stay of the proceedings which the wife was attempting to re-institute. The agreement reached through mediation was sufficiently certain to constitute an enforceable contract. The inability of the parties to agree on wording did not impact the formation of the agreement: *E. (C.R.) v. E. (K.L.)*, 44 R.F.L. (5th) 65, 2003 CarswellBC 2585, 2003 BCSC 1570 (B.C. S.C.); additional reasons at 44 R.F.L. (5th) 65, 2003 CarswellBC 2585, 2003 BCSC 1570 (B.C. S.C.).

Where, in the course of negotiations to settle a variation of support dispute, the wife rejected the husband's offer to settle and made an unacceptable counter-offer, it was held that it was subsequently no longer open to her to accept the husband's original offer: *Leslie v. Leslie* (1988), 55 Man. R. (2d) 215, 1988 CarswellMan 354 (Q.B.).

In *Butler v. Butler* (1987), 9 R.F.L. (3d) 70, 66 Nfld. & P.E.I.R. 42, 204 A.P.R. 42, 1987 CarswellNfld 31 (U.F.C.); additional reasons at 18 R.F.L. (3d) 180, 1988 CarswellNfld 17 (U.F.C.), the court refused to allow the wife to rely upon a document which she had her husband sign whereby he purportedly agreed to share his disability pension equally with her. As the husband did not remember signing the document, it was not witnessed and no legal advice had been sought, it was found not to be the type of document usually protected by the courts.

Where the interim agreement under which the husband paid support to the wife was stated to be "without prejudice", the court was nevertheless required to consider the agreement under s. 15(5)(c) of the *Divorce Act* in order to determine final support: *Tancock v. Tancock* (1990), 24 R.F.L. (3d) 389, 1990 CarswellBC 436 (S.C.).

An interim draft separation agreement may properly be considered in a support application as an indication of the parties' intentions: *Fejes v. Fejes* (1988), 13 R.F.L. (3d) 267, 51 Man. R. (2d) 132, 1988 CarswellMan 44 (Q.B.).

15§154 — Validity of agreements

Divorce Act, 1985

A pre-nuptial contract in *Mucha v. Mucha* (2001), 212 Sask. R. 1, 2001 CarswellSask 712 (Sask. Q.B.); reversed in part on other grounds (2003), 232 Sask. R. 78, 294 W.A.C. 78, 2003 CarswellSask 264 (Sask. C.A.) was found to be valid where there was no evidence that the husband dominated the wife. His precondition for marriage that she sign the agreement was reasonable, given his experience of an earlier divorce. There was no urgency to meet a deadline and no evidence that he took advantage of her or that there were stressful circumstances. The husband was the more powerful of the two parties, but the wife was not under his power because of need or distress and she fully understood his financial circumstances. She had competent legal advice. Further, the contract was not grossly unfair at the time that it was made between the parties. However, the spousal support provision in which the parties waived the right to seek support was severed from the rest of the agreement and was declared unenforceable, as there had been a radical change of circumstances since the execution of the contract. The parties had lived together for 16 years; they had two sons; they moved and sold the husband's business. Further, the contract was focused on property, not support. The court ordered spousal support of $1,000 monthly for 8 months to assist the wife in her transition from part-time to full-time employment.

In *Chandra v. Chandra* (1999), 45 R.F.L. (4th) 181, 174 Nfld. & P.E.I.R. 136, 533 A.P.R. 136, 1999 CarswellNfld 99 (Nfld. C.A.); affirming 27 R.F.L. (4th) 114, 150 Nfld. & P.E.I.R. 333, 470 A.P.R. 333, 1997 CarswellNfld 27 (Nfld. U.F.C., the court refused the husband's appeal from an order setting aside the parties' marriage agreement. The husband had drafted the agreement without consultation with the wife who signed the document without understanding its contents and without benefit of independent legal advice.

Where it was evident that the wife had had the benefit of legal counsel on numerous occasions throughout the parties' matrimonial proceedings, the court refused an appeal from an order that upheld the parties' separation agreement, despite the wife's allegations that she had lacked independent legal advice. It appeared that the wife's true intentions were merely to aggravate her husband: *Massé c. Poirier* (19 mai 1992), C.A. Montréal 500-09-000567-909 (C.A. Qué.).

In *Johnson v. Johnson* (2005), 23 R.F.L. (6th) 46, 2005 CarswellOnt 7695, 2005 ONCJ 325 (Ont. C.J.), the court declared the parties' marriage contract, under which the wife purportedly waived her right to spousal support, to be invalid. The wife had resigned a good position in Russia and had moved with her children to Canada, to marry the husband. His insistence that her executing the contract was a prerequisite to the marriage was, giving her vulnerable position, a misuse of his far stronger bargaining position.

Where the husband had signed a separation agreement under the threat that the wife withdraw her immigration sponsorship of him if he failed to do so, the agreement was nevertheless upheld. The husband had been advised not to sign by both his brother and immigration counsel and had the opportunity to seek further legal advice. The evidence fell short of establishing an unconscionable use of power by the wife over the husband:

Gregory v. Brown, 21 R.F.L. (6th) 289, 2005 CarswellOnt 6799, [2005] O.J. No. 4565, 2005 ONCJ 284 (Ont. C.J.).

In *Myers v. Hawco* (2004), 11 R.F.L. (6th) 291, 2004 CarswellNfld 286, 240 Nfld. & P.E.I.R. 248, 711 A.P.R. 248, 2004 NLSCUFC 38, 243 D.L.R. (4th) 726 (U.F.C.), the court refused to enforce the substantial arrears owing under the parties' separation agreement. The intent of the parties in drafting the agreement was to gain priority over the husband's creditors and therefore the agreement was found to be contrary to public policy.

In *Davis v. Davis* (2003), 44 R.F.L. (5th) 56, 2003 CarswellOnt 2800, [2003] O.J. No. 2938 (Ont. S.C.J.), the court found that the parties' separation agreement was invalid and allowed the wife's claim for spousal support to proceed. While the husband had been receiving legal advice, the wife signed the document without benefit of counsel. The husband had failed to disclose his financial information and the separation date clearly favoured the husband over the evidence. Ultimately, the agreement reflected neither the parties' intentions nor the objectives of the *Divorce Act* as relating to the wife's economic disadvantage.

A separation agreement will be set aside when there has been material misrepresentation of a party's assets: *Souder v. Wereschuk* (2003), 38 R.F.L. (5th) 185, 2003 CarswellAlta 358 (Alta. Q.B.). In this case, the parties married in 1989 and separated in 1994. In 1995, the husband won $500,000 in the lottery and did not disclose his win to his wife. The parties executed a separation agreement in 1997 and were divorced in 2001. In the agreement, the wife, who was disabled, waived her claim for spousal support. The court found that the husband had materially misrepresented his assets at the time that the agreement was being negotiated. The wife claimed a matrimonial property order reflecting all the assets of the husband and spousal support. The court considered that the 5-year length of the marriage was a factor. As the lottery prize was acquired 10 months after the parties' separation, there was not a significant degree of separation, The parties were nearly 2 years short of entering into a separation agreement and the plaintiff began receiving interim spousal maintenance a few months later. The court awarded the wife one quarter of the lottery proceeds but she did not receive any spousal support. The court considered the three different models of marriages set out in *Bracklow v. Bracklow*, [1999] S.C.R. 420, 44 R.F.L. (4th) 1, 169 D.L.R. (4th) 577, 236 N.R. 79, 120 B.C.A.C. 211, 196 W.A.C. 211, 63 B.C.L.R. (3d) 77, [1999] 8 W.W.R. 740, 1999 CarswellBC 532, 1999 CarswellBC 533, [1999] S.C.J. No. 14 (S.C.C.), and held that the wife had not established entitlement for support under any of the models.

Where at the wife's insistence the parties had executed a prenuptial agreement containing mutual releases from support applications, the wife's subsequent claim for spousal support was dismissed. At the time of the agreement, both parties had experience with divorce, were represented by counsel and had been fully advised of their rights and liabilities. There was no basis to justify setting aside the agreement: *Culen v. Culen*, 37 R.F.L. (5th) 300, 2003 CarswellAlta 716, 2003 ABQB 480 (Alta. Q.B.).

In *Dubin v. Dubin* (2003), 34 R.F.L. (5th) 227, 2003 CarswellOnt 534 (Ont. S.C.J.), the court set aside the parties' marriage contract under which the wife had forfeited her right to spousal support. Although the agreement made reference to financial disclosure, the wife had been misled about the husband's true financial circumstances and had no realistic understanding of his assets and liabilities as of the date of the agreement.

In *Durocher v. Durocher* (1991), 106 N.S.R. (2d) 215, 288 A.P.R. 215 (T.D.), the court refused to set aside the support provisions of the parties' separation agreement executed upon the dissolution of their 29-year marriage. The parties had obtained independent legal advice before signing the agreement, and the wife's allegations of undue influence, duress and unconscionability were not supported by the evidence. Furthermore, the wife had experience in handling the parties' financial affairs and, considering the property provisions of the agreement, the arrangement as a whole was not unfair.

Where the wife had executed a letter, without the advice of her solicitor, which allowed for the variation of the support terms in the parties' separation agreement, the letter was found to be a valid collateral agreement. The separation agreement was, in fact, executed later by the wife in the presence of her solicitor, thereby giving her the opportunity of discussing the significance of the letter with him and thereby curing any defect in its execution: *Remillard v. Remillard* (1990), 24 R.F.L. (3d) 156, 103 A.R. 110, 1990 CarswellAlta 263 (Q.B.).

A settlement reached during trial under the pressure of the proceedings, without the time being taken to reduce the agreement to writing, to consider and revise it and so formally execute it, is not a final settlement agreement sufficient to restrict the court's override power to fact situations involving radical unforeseen changes: *Huot v. Huot* (1989), 19 R.F.L. (3d) 85, 58 Man. R. (2d) 116, 1989 CarswellMan 38 (Q.B.).

Where the wife had consented on the basis of a misunderstanding to an amendment to the support provisions of the decree *nisi* but refused to sign the consent upon discovery of the mistake, the court refused to incorporate the amendment. The wife's mistake was an honest one and not a factor to be considered on the husband's variation application: *Hennessey v. Hennessey* (1993), 122 N.S.R. (2d) 220, 338 A.P.R. 220, 1993 CarswellNS 326 (Fam. Ct.).

In *Droit de la famille — 1560*, [1992] R.D.F. 186 (C.S. Qué.), the court awarded the wife lump sum support, in addition to a lump sum to which the parties had earlier agreed, upon proof by the wife that the agreement had been disadvantageous to her interests.

Where a signatory to a separation agreement has been advised of the right to independent legal advice but chooses not to pursue it, that party cannot later rely upon the inequality of bargaining power as a reason for setting aside the agreement: *Sartor v. Sartor* (1993), 45 R.F.L. (3d) 250, [1993] N.W.T.R. 102, 1993 CarswellNWT 6 (S.C.).

An informal agreement between the parties whereby the husband was to support the wife through her studies after she had done the same for him was not analogous to a contractual obligation which should be considered when determining the wife's maintenance: *Botterill v. Botterill* (1986), 1 R.F.L. (3d) 267, 48 Sask. R. 49, 1986 CarswellSask 51 (Q.B.).

In *Bailey v. Plaxton* (2001), 15 R.F.L. (5th) 16, 2001 CarswellOnt 925, [2001] O.J. No. 1111 (S.C.J.), the court found that all the requirements existed to constitute an enforceable settlement. There was both an offer and an acceptance, which were clear and unambiguous as to their terms. They represented a complete agreement, without any other terms to be concluded. The plaintiff's lawyer had clear authority and instructions to make the offer, as the plaintiff signed it. The court should not exercise its discretion and refuse to grant judgment in accordance with the accepted offer where, as in this case, the plaintiff asserts a mistaken impression that she made the offer because she believed that she had to.

A single instance of one party telling the other that he would cut off support payments if she did not sign a separation agreement does not constitute duress: *Roberts v. Roberts*, 6 R.F.L. (5th) 407, 2000 BCSC 611, 2000 CarswellBC 784 (S.C.). The agreement was comprehensive and in the opinion of the court, fair. The wife was represented by counsel throughout the negotiations and preparation of the agreement and had independent legal advice. The wife had accepted benefits under the agreement for at least two years before challenging the validity of the agreement.

Where parties enter into an agreement through counsel, the courts tend to uphold the agreements except in the clearest of cases, and in exceptional circumstances: *P. (M.L.) v. P. (G.W.)* (2000), 12 R.F.L. (5th) 434, 2000 CarswellOnt 3937 (S.C.J.). This case did not meet the requirements for such exceptional circumstances and the wife's motion for judgment in accordance with the settlement was granted. The case did involve stressful litigation but the issues raised were not gratuitously or tactically created. The husband negotiated actively up to the signing of the agreement and after it was finalized. These circumstances make it difficult to find that he lacked free will in his conduct. The allegation of false accusations of sexual abuse was not a new issue at the time of execution of the settlement agreement. Another forum could deal with this issue rather than in the context of a hearing for divorce. To enforce the agreement would not prejudice either party; rather, it would benefit both by ending the litigation, providing emotional and financial relief.

Where the husband, during settlement negotiations, had failed to advise the wife that his financial circumstances had recently improved, the portion of the agreement under which the wife had waived her right to support was set aside and her support claim was allowed to go forward: *Underwood v. Underwood* (1994), 3 R.F.L. (4th) 457, 113 D.L.R. (4th) 571, 1994 CarswellOnt 394 (Gen. Div.); varied (1995), 11 R.F.L. (4th) 361, 1995 CarswellOnt 88 (Div. Ct.).

In *Droit de la famille — 1532* (1991), [1992] R.D.F. 89 (C.S. Qué.); reversed in part [1993] R.J.Q. 2712, (sub nom. *B. (P.) v. N. (R.)*) 59 O.A.C. 151, 59 Q.A.C. 151, [1993] R.D.F. 720, 1993 CarswellQue 135 (C.A.), the court, in the context of a divorce proceeding, set aside a separation agreement on the grounds that the lawyer who prepared it had done so in a conflict of interest situation. The lawyer worked for a firm that had represented the husband for a number of years and therefore the wife had lacked independent legal advice. The agreement was clearly unreasonable and had to be annulled.

Where the inexperienced wife had agreed to child and spousal support which resulted in living at the poverty line, the agreement was overridden in subsequent divorce proceedings. The agreement was bordering on improvident and failed to meet the criteria set out in s. 15 of the *Divorce Act, 1985*: *Brockie v. Brockie* (1987), 5 R.F.L. (3d) 440, 46 Man. R. (2d) 33, 1987 CarswellMan 93 (Q.B.); affirmed (1987), 8 R.F.L. (3d) 302, 1987 CarswellMan 115 (C.A.).

In *McVeetors v. McVeetors* (1985), 43 R.F.L. (2d) 113, 49 O.R. (2d) 225, 7 O.A.C. 1, 1985 CarswellOnt 227 (C.A.); leave to appeal refused 49 O.R. (2d) 225n, 15 D.L.R. (4th) 105n, 8 O.A.C. 320, it was held that a separation agreement did not bar an award of lump sum maintenance to the wife where the husband had himself breached the agreement and the agreement itself was unconscionable. The agreement was found to be unconscionable on the evidence that the wife had executed the agreement while under great stress, the husband had failed to disclose material facts prior to its execution and the wife's standard of living had deteriorated drastically since the separation. See also *Straiton v. Straiton* (1970), 9 R.F.L. 21 at 28, 30 D.L.R. (3d) 102, 1970 CarswellBC 35 (S.C.).

In the absence of unconscionability, duress, undue influence or a defence of *non est factum*, the parties should be held to the support provisions of a separation agreement. Where the payor spouse understands the settlement, the lack of independent legal advice and the perceived unfairness of the agreement would not justify setting it aside: *Harker v. Harker* (1990), 26 R.F.L. (3d) 165, 1990 CarswellBC 458 (S.C.); affirmed (May 16, 1991), Doc. CA012446 (B.C. C.A.).

Where the husband agreed to pay two-thirds of his salary as spousal support, the court, on appeal, refused to set aside the agreement. Although the husband may have miscalculated the fiscal impact of the settlement, he had entered into the agreement freely with benefit of counsel and without any undue pressure from the wife: *Droit de la famille — 799*, [1994] R.D.F. 436 (C.A. Qué.); affirming [1990] R.J.Q. 1053 (C.S.).

Where the wife obtained independent legal advice prior to settling the issue of support, it was held that she could not later challenge the competence of that advice in seeking increased support in a subsequent divorce action: *Brosseau v. Brosseau* (1988), 85 A.R. 385, 1988 CarswellAlta 387 (Q.B.); varied 63 D.L.R. (4th) 111, 23 R.F.L. (3d) 42, 100 A.R. 15, 70 Alta. L.R. (2d) 247, [1990] 2 W.W.R. 34, 1989 CarswellAlta 162 (C.A.); leave to appeal refused (1990), 70 Alta. L.R. (2d) lii, 23 R.F.L. (3d) xli, 65 D.L.R. (4th) vii (S.C.C.).

In *Macdonald v. Macdonald* (1986), 4 R.F.L. (3d) 463, 79 N.S.R. (2d) 58, 196 A.P.R. 58, 1986 CarswellNS 71 (T.D.), the court refused to hold the wife to a divorce settlement to which she had agreed the previous day. The wife had been under considerable strain during the negotiations and the husband would not be prejudiced by the repudiation.

In *Helmes v. Helmes* (1984), 40 R.F.L. (2d) 319, 1984 CarswellOnt 253 (H.C.), the wife was awarded monthly maintenance of $1,000 despite the fact that under earlier minutes of settlement she had agreed to accept the monthly sum of only $600. Although the husband had not exerted any pressure on the wife at the time of the settlement, she had been under psychiatric care and was in no condition to understand fully the future implications of the agreement she signed.

Where, in negotiating a separation agreement, the husband consulted his brother and the wife consulted her husband's niece, who was an associate of the husband's brother, the court set aside a clause whereby the wife agreed not to pursue support. There had been a clear conflict of interest which had not been dispelled by a cursory review of the agreement on the wife's behalf by a second solicitor: *Brosseau v. Brosseau* (1989), 23 R.F.L. (3d) 42, 70 Alta. L.R. (2d) 247, [1990] 2 W.W.R. 34, 100 A.R. 15, 63 D.L.R. (4th) 111, 1989 CarswellAlta 162 (C.A.); leave to appeal refused (1989), 23 R.F.L. (3d) xli, 70 Alta. L.R. (2d) lii, 65 D.L.R. (4th) vii (S.C.C.).

15§155 — Not a final agreement

The "radical change in circumstances" test does not apply to the variation of the support provisions of a separation agreement which states that a specific amount is payable "until further order". Such an agreement envisages variation and cannot be characterized as a "conclusive and final" agreement: *Zarowny v. Zarowny* (1991), 33 R.F.L. (3d) 345, 1991 CarswellAlta 331 (C.A.). However, see *Lagimodiere v. Lagimodiere* (1991), 33 R.F.L. (3d) 285, 75 Man. R. (2d) 72, 6 W.A.C. 72, 1991 CarswellMan 39 (C.A.) where an agreement was, on the basis of the parties' intentions, found to be "final and conclusive" despite containing the words "until further order".

The Supreme Court of Canada decisions restricting exercise of jurisdiction in the case of final settlement agreements do not apply to an agreement, the terms of which clearly contemplate variation on proof of a material change: *Shepard v. Shepard* (1989), 19 R.F.L. (3d) 40, 1989 CarswellMan 37 (Q.B.).

15§155A — Upholding agreements

In *Hartshorne v. Hartshorne* (2004), 2004 CarswellBC 603, 2004 CarswellBC 604, 2004 SCC 22, the court considered the following issues:

1. whether a marriage agreement respecting the division of property, entered into with independent legal advice without duress, coercion or undue influence, can subsequently be found to be unfair and set aside because it failed to compensate the wife for sacrificing her career and her career development, even though the agreement preserved her right to spousal support;

2. whether a marriage agreement entered into before marriage should be subject to the same review as a separation agreement; and

3. where provisions for the division of property in a marriage agreement are found to be unfair at the time of distribution, whether the whole agreement should be ignored.

Although this case was decided under the British Columbia *Family Relations Act*, it has important implications for the *Divorce Act*. This summary will concentrate on the effect of an agreement on spousal support.

The facts of the case are as follows. The parties entered a marriage contract on their wedding day. The appellant husband had arranged for an agreement to be drawn up. The agreement stipulated that the parties would be separate as to property. However the respondent wife would be entitled to a 3 percent interest in the family home for each year the parties were married, up to a maximum of 49 percent. The appellant brought assets valued at approximately $1.6 million into the marriage. The respondent did not bring any assets into the marriage and was in fact heavily in debt. Both parties obtained independent legal advice. The respondent's lawyer informed her that the agreement was unfair and that the courts would likely set it aside if the parties separated. The parties cohabited for 12-1/2 years, nine of which while they were married. They had two children. While both parents were lawyers, the respondent left her law practice to take maternity leave and remained at home to look after the parties' children. The respondent, after separation obtained a position as an associate in a law firm at a salary of $52,000 a year, at the time of distribution.

The court held that it should not establish a "hard and fast" rule regarding the deference to be afforded to marriage agreements as compared to separation agreements. The court accepted the general legal proposition that some weight should be given to marriage agreements. The court would not wish to interfere with an agreement unless it were convinced that the agreement did not substantially comply with the overall objectives of the act in question. It would be unlikely that a court would disregard an agreement in its entirety, unless there was a significant change in the parties' circumstances from what could reasonably have been anticipated at the time of negotiation. The change would be that "the terms of the agreement no longer reflect[ed] the parties' intentions at the time of execution and the objectives of the act". To have the agreement set aside, it would be necessary to establish that these new circumstances were not reasonably anticipated by the parties, and have led to a situation that cannot be condoned. The test is not strict forseeability. Instead the question is the extent to which the unimpeachably negotiated agreement can be said to have contemplated the situation before the court at the time of the application.

The main policy objective guiding the courts' role in a division of property on marital breakdown in British Columbia is fairness. The *Family Relations Act* (FRA) provides that to be enforceable, any agreement to govern a division of property upon the dissolution of marriage, to be enforceable, must operate fairly at the time of distribution. If it does not, the court can reapportion property to achieve fairness.

The court set out the process for determining whether a marriage agreement operates unfairly. First, the court must apply the agreement and in particular, the court must determine and award those financial entitlements provided to each spouse under the agreement, and other entitlement from all other sources including spousal and child support. Second, the court must consider the factors listed in s. 65 of the FRA to make a determination as to whether the contract operates fairly. At this stage, the court must consider the parties' personal and financial circumstances and the manner in which these circumstances evolved over time. In order for the agreement to be set aside, a court would have to find that in a consideration of the factors listed in s. 65(1) of the FRA, taken together, the economic consequences of the marriage breakdown were not shared equitably in all of the circumstances.

The court held that before deciding that the agreement operated unfairly, the court should consider the impact of any financial awards to which the spouse was entitled under the agreement or otherwise, including spousal and child support. In the present case, the explicit preservation of a right to spousal support which was an amendment to the draft agreement at the respondent's insistence supported an understanding by the wife that, in light of the provisions in respect to property, her future needs and self-sufficiency could be met through support. Only if self-sufficiency and need could not be met through an order of spousal support, should it be concluded that an agreement operated unfairly. The Supreme Court of Canada reversed the trial judge's reapportionment of the division of property, a 60/40 split in favour of the appellant, with the understanding that the respondent's entitlement to spousal support was reopened. The court also held that even where a party has been advised that an agreement is "grossly unfair" and that a court would "easily find" a provision could be set aside, that party could never be allowed to avoid his or her contractual obligations on the basis that he or she believed from the outset that the contract was void or unenforceable.

The court decided that the law practice which had not increased in value since the marriage was not a family asset.

The court held that any economic disadvantage that the respondent suffered could be addressed through spousal support. What matters is whether the agreement is unfair in the circumstances present at the time of distribution. The court held that considering the provisions of the FRA, and after examining all of the provisions of the agreement and the circumstances of the parties at the time of separation, the agreement was fair at the time of the triggering event. The agreement should be left intact.

Courts should not conclude that agreements are unfair only because they deviate from the statutory matrimonial property regime. Fairness must be considered in light of the realistic contemplation of the parties, the attention they gave to changes in circumstances or unrealized implications, their true circumstances, and whether the discrepancy is such, given the s. 65 factors, whether a different apportionment should be made.

Where the parties' separation agreement provided that either party could apply for review of spousal support where there was a substantial increase in the husband's income, the application should be dismissed when the increase in income was caused by a transaction referred to in the agreement and consequently contemplated by the parties: *Bellingham v. Bellingham* (2003), 44 R.F.L. (5th) 357, 2003 CarswellMan 396, 178 Man. R. (2d) 60 (Man. Q.B.); additional reasons at (2004), 2004 CarswellMan 100 (Man. Q.B.). Pursuant to the terms of the parties' agreement, the husband purchased the wife's shares in a company and subsequently he received all the company dividends. At the time the agreement was executed, the parties assumed that the entire company income, which had been split between the parties during the marriage, would be attributable to the husband following the share purchase transaction.

A party will not obtain spousal support where to do so would be inconsistent with the terms of a pre-existing separation agreement which meets the tests set out in *Miglin v. Miglin*, [2003] 1 S.C.R. 303, 2003 CarswellOnt 1374, 34 R.F.L. (5th) 255, 224 D.L.R. (4th) 193, 171 O.A.C. 201, 302 N.R. 201 (S.C.C.): *Marks v. Tokarewicz* (2004), 181 O.A.C. 11, [2004] O.J. No. 92, 2004 CarswellOnt 97 (Ont. C.A.). After the parties' separation, the husband paid interim spousal support to the wife, pursuant to a consent order to enable her to study medicine outside the country. After completing her degree, the wife returned to Canada and entered a separation agreement, whereby the husband agreed to continue paying spousal support for over a year and a half and the wife released all claims to further support. The wife never qualified to practice medicine in Canada and applied for spousal support under s. 15.2(1) of the *Divorce Act*, when she became destitute and was relying on social assistance for support. As the husband was earning between $500,000 and $550,000 a year, there was no question that he had the ability to pay. Although the trial judge decided the case before the *Miglin* decision at the Supreme Court of Canada, the Court of Appeal in the *Marks v. Tokarewicz* case held that her findings were dispositive of the issues on appeal. The appellate court, following the process set out in the Miglin decision held that the agreement was negotiated and executed in satisfactory circumstances and that at the time that the parties entered the agreement, it was in substantial compliance with the considerations in s. 15.2 of the *Divorce Act*, and also with the Act's more general objectives of certainty, finality and autonomy. Both parties had independent legal advice, sworn financial statements, and major assets evaluated. Each party had full disclosure of the other's financial circumstances. The court considered whether the agreement still reflected the original intention of the parties and the extent to which it was still in substantial compliance with the objectives of the act. The trial judge had considered that a material change in circum stances had occurred, as the parties had anticipated that the wife would qualify to practise medicine in Canada, which she did not do. The appellate court upheld that trial court's ruling that despite the change of circumstances, a support order should not be made. The trial judge had assessed the parties conflicting objectives of autonomy, finality and certainty versus a plan for the equitable resolution of the financial and property issues arising from the marriage and its breakdown, in the context of the intervening events.

While a pre-nuptial contract was upheld in *Mucha v. Mucha* (2001), 212 Sask. R. 1, 2001 CarswellSask 712, 2001 SKQB 505 (Sask. Q.B.); reversed in part on other grounds (2003), 232 Sask. R. 78, 294 W.A.C. 78, 2003 CarswellSask 264 (Sask. C.A.), the spousal support provision in which the parties waived the right to seek support was severed from the rest of the agreement and was declared unenforceable, as there had been a radical change of circumstances since the execution of the contract. The parties had lived together for 16 years; their two sons were born; they moved and sold the husband's business. Further, the contract was focused on property, not support. The court ordered spousal support of $1,000 monthly for 8 months to assist the wife in her transition from part to full-time employment.

In *Marinangeli v. Marinangeli* (2003), 2003 CarswellOnt 2691, [2003] O.J. No. 2819, 38 R.F.L. (5th) 307, 174 O.A.C. 76, 228 D.L.R. (4th) 376 (Ont. C.A.), prior to the signing of the parties' settlement agreement, the husband indicated at a pre-trial conference that he anticipated a decrease in his income. In fact, he received over a million dollars when he exercised stock options within 14 months of signing the parties' settlement agreement. The case centered on the issue of whether or not the increase in the appellant's income was a change in circumstances. The wife sought to enforce the provision in the agreement that support could be revised where there had been a material change of circumstances. The appellant argued that there had not been a change in circumstances as described in *Miglin v. Miglin*, 2003 CarswellOnt 1374, 2003 CarswellOnt 1375, [2003] S.C.J. No. 21, 2003 SCC 24, 34 R.F.L. (5th) 255, 224 D.L.R. (4th) 193, 171 O.A.C. 201, 302 N.R. 201 (S.C.C.), meaning a change that was not foreseeable as part of the ordinary course of living at the time the settlement agreement was signed.

In the *Marinangeli* case, Madam Justice Weiler wrote at paragraph 50:

> The comments of the Supreme Court in *Miglin*, supra were intended to address the situation where the parties chose to release one another from all future support obligations by a one-time payment of lump sum support. Since no future adjustments were envisaged, the parties were expected to consider such foreseeable future changes in the ordinary course of living as an increase or decrease in income before arriving at the amount of the one time payment. She distinguished the *Marinangeli* case from *Miglin*, since in *Marinangeli*, the parties envisaged that the amount of support would change, if there were a material change in circumstances in a party's income. The court held that the provision in the separation agreement relating to a material change in circumstances, read in its context and as a whole, did not exclude foreseeable events such as an increase or decrease in income, but the opposite.

The appellant was unsuccessful in arguing that the exercise of his options was not a material change in circumstances as defined in *Willick v. Willick*, [1994] S.C.J. No. 94, 1994 CarswellSask 48, 1994 CarswellSask 450, 6 R.F.L. (4th) 161, 119 D.L.R. (4th) 405, 173 N.R. 321, 125 Sask. R. 81, 81 W.A.C. 81, [1994] 3 S.C.R. 670, [1994] R.D.F. 617 (S.C.C.), that is, had the alleged change been known, the support provision would not likely have been different. As the appellant did not know the value of his options at the time the agreement was signed, the respondent could not be assumed to know their value at that time. In addition, the respondent was not told the parameters for the exercise of the options and consequently she had no way of ascertaining the value of the options in relation to the price of the underlying stock. The respondent was dependant upon the appellant for information about the value of the options.

A change in circumstances must be something that has some measure of continuity. The court did not accept the appellant's argument that the exercise of the options was not a material change in circumstances because their exercise lacked continuity. There is continuity in the frequency with which the options are awarded and continuity in that the options may be exercised over a period of time.

The increase in a payor's salary and bonus by nearly 20 per cent over the previous year is a material change in circumstances that entitled the trial judge to consider the profit from the options in determining the quantum of support.

A material change in circumstances with respect to child support occurred when the *Guidelines* came into force that entitled the trial judge to consider the profit from the options in determining the quantum of support.

The court held that 10 per cent more or less in income from what a party anticipates at the time of signing a separation agreement, is not a material change in circumstances justifying setting aside a separation agreement: *Slaughter v. McCormick*, 2003 CarswellBC 1029, 2003 BCSC 692 (B.C. S.C.).

A separation agreement will not be set aside where the payee spouse has health concerns that predated the agreement and were in the parties' minds when they reached their agreement on spousal support: *Hambuch v. Hambuch*, 2003 CarswellBC 1584, 2003 BCSC 1001 (B.C. S.C.).

Following *Miglin*, the court held that where a payee spouse is suffering stress and anxiety at the time of the execution of a separation agreement, there is no presumption that the parties are incapable of assenting to a binding agreement: *McGregor v. Van Tilborg*, 2003 CarswellBC 1488, 2003 BCSC 918 (B.C. S.C. [In Chambers]). In this case, the wife claimed to be suffering from a mental condition and under psychiatric care when she negotiated a separation agreement. The mental problems were related to some form of historical sexual abuse and did not appear to be related to the divorce.

In upholding the parties' agreement in *Merke v. Merke*, 2003 BCSC 1070, 2003 CarswellBC 1708, 39 R.F.L. (5th) 339 (B.C. S.C.), the court found nothing in the circumstances of the negotiation and execution of the agreement to discount it. The objectives of finality, certainty, and the general interest of the parties determining their own affairs were important factors in upholding the agreement, especially where, as here, the parties both had a history of misrepresenting their incomes in order to live essentially on a tax-free basis.

See also *Collins v. Collins*, 2003 CarswellNfld 168, 2003 NLSCTD 102 (N.L. T.D.), where the court upheld the parties' agreement as it had been negotiated in good faith. It was a fair and equitable division of their matrimonial and business assets and liabilities and corollary relief issues had been determined reasonably. The agreement continued to deal with all issues between the parties and there had been no changes in the parties' circumstances since the Separation Agreement so it could still govern the parties' post-divorce obligations to each other.

The court held that the general rule from the *Miglin* decision is that a court should be loathe to interfere with a separation agreement that shows a mutual intent to finalize the terms of the parties' separation agreement, and indicates their substantive intentions: *Wigle v. Wigle* (2003), 2003 CarswellOnt 1672, 39 R.F.L. (5th) 233 (Ont. S.C.J.).The court found that the *Wigle* case fell within the general rule in *Miglin*. Each party was represented by counsel. The former wife's self-sufficiency is outweighed by the aspects of finality and autonomy. The agreement was substantially in compliance with the support provisions of the Act, and the philosophy of the Act that the parties settle their affairs. There were no new circumstances which indicate that the agreement no longer reflects the parties' intentions at the time the agreement was executed. It still reflects the philosophy of the *Divorce Act*. The agreement was upheld.

Where the parties, in their separation agreement, stipulated that neither was entitled to spousal support, the court subsequently refused the wife's support application. Although, subsequent to the agreement, the wife liquidated her restaurant business for substantially less than she had anticipated, the agreement had anticipated the liquidation. The agreement was in substantial compliance with the principles in the *Divorce Act* and there was nothing in the circumstances surrounding the negotiation of the agreement suggesting any reason to discount it: *Merke v. Merke*, 39 R.F.L. (5th) 339, 2003 CarswellBC 1708, 2003 BCSC 1070 (B.C. S.C.).

15§155B — Non-disclosure

Where an agreement contemplates a variation in child and spousal support in the event of a material increase in a party's income, there is an implied duty on the party to disclose that increase at the time it is received. Failure to disclose is a ground for making the variation retroactive to the time of the increase: *Marinangeli v. Marinangeli* (2003), 2003 CarswellOnt 2691, [2003] O.J. No. 2819, 38 R.F.L. (5th) 307, 174 O.A.C. 76, 228 D.L.R. (4th) 376 (Ont. C.A.). Here, the parties married in 1973 and separated in 1992 after a 19-year marriage. The wife, employed as a secretary, supported the husband in the early years of the marriage, while he attended university. He completed his B.A., M.B.A. and obtained his C.A. designation. The wife stopped working outside the home after 10 years of marriage and the following year the parties' only child was born. The parties separated in 1992 and began litigation in 1993. At a pre-trial conference in May, 1996, the husband maintained that he expected a decrease in his income. In October, 1996, just prior to trial, the parties signed minutes of settlement. They provided that spousal and child support could be varied if there were a material change in circumstances. A financial statement sworn immediately prior to execution of the minutes disclosed the husband's income and showed that his property included stock options and phantom stock units, that is, notional units of stock taxed at full rates based on underlying stock performance. Although certain terms were incorporated in a judgement, the provisions for spousal support, child support and life insurance were not, with the parties relying on the minutes, or their agreement as evidenced in the minutes, to record their rights and obligations with respect to them.

The day after the minutes were signed, the husband cashed in $27,850 worth of stock options, and in the 14 months from the time of the execution of the agreement, he realized a gain from his options of over $1,000,000. He also received a substantial increase in his compensation. He did not inform his wife of these changes in his financial circumstances. After the *Guidelines* came into force, the wife's lawyer contacted the husband's lawyer with respect to the effect the *Guidelines* might have on the husband's child support obligations. Eventually the parties exchanged tax returns and the wife claimed an increase in spousal and child support on the basis of the increase in the husband's income.

The trial judge ordered increased spousal and child support retroactive to the year in which the agreement came into force. He found that the profit the husband realized on his options and the substantial increase in his employment income were material changes in circumstances, and that the husband had an implied duty to disclose them to his wife. The variation was made retroactive, because he failed to disclose the changes at the time they were effective. The husband appealed.

The Court of Appeal held that the profit realized from the exercise of his stock options was income to the husband, and found that it amounted to a material change in circumstances within the meaning of the minutes. The *Miglin* case was distinguished on the ground that there the parties executed a separation agreement intending it to be a full and final release of all future obligations, whereas here the parties agreed in the minutes of settlement that if there were a change in circumstances, spousal and child support could be varied. It was within the trial judge's discretion to award retroactive support since the criteria for making such an award was met. The court did allow the appeal with respect to the award of retroactive child support at the *Guidelines* level for the period prior to the enactment of the *Guidelines*.

The Court of Appeal held that where an agreement states that spousal and child support could be varied in the event of a material change in circumstances, the payor husband, whose income had increased, had an obligation to disclose the exercise of his options and increase in salary. (See paragraphs 4 and 57.) The court also held that where, in minutes of settlement, there is a clear intention that spousal and child support could be varied if there were a material changes in the circumstances of the parties, and a material change in income occurs, the party whose income changes has an implicit obligation to disclose the change to the other party at the time it occurs. (See paragraphs 59 and 60.) The trial judge did not err in finding that the husband had an implied duty to disclose to the wife changes in his financial circumstances. In this case, the payor spouse's representations and the almost immediate improvement in his finances were the factual basis upon which to ground such a duty. The appellant had an implicit obligation to disclose his change in circumstances so as to give business efficacy to the agreement. It was reasonable and equitable to imply a term relating to disclosure. The implication of the implied term was capable of clear expression and was not contrary to any express term in the agreement. Thus, the implication by the trial judge of a term relating to disclosure met the requirements for implying a term in an agreement on ordinary contract principles.

The respondent in *Marinangeli v. Marinangeli* (2003), 2003 CarswellOnt 2691, [2003] O.J. No. 2819, 38 R.F.L. (5th) 307, 174 O.A.C. 76, 228 D.L.R. (4th) 376 (Ont. C.A.) met the criteria set out in *S. (L.) v. P. (E.)*, 1999 CarswellBC 1402, [1999] B.C.J. No. 1451, 175 D.L.R. (4th) 423, 126 B.C.A.C. 28, 206 W.A.C. 28, 67 B.C.L.R. (3d) 254, [1999] 12 W.W.R. 718, 50 R.F.L. (4th) 302, 1999 BCCA 393 (B.C. C.A.), leave to appeal refused (1999), [1999] S.C.C.A. No. 444, 252 N.R. 194 (note), 135 B.C.A.C. 160 (note), 221 W.A.C. 160 (note) (S.C.C.), for awarding retroactive spousal and child support under the *Divorce Act* which are as follows: (a) need and a corresponding ability to pay; (b) improper conduct by the payor spouse; (c) need to encroach on capital or incur debt; (d) excuse for delay in bringing the application; (e) notice to the payor spouse of an intention to pursue support; and an unreasonable burden on the payor spouse. The appeal by the father from a judgement ordering him to pay retroactive child and spousal support to the mother, was dismissed, except with respect to the awarding of child support in accordance with the *Guidelines* amount for a period prior to the coming into force of the *Guidelines*. It is an error in principle to extend the *Guidelines* amounts to a time period prior to the enactment of the legislation. Prior to the *Guidelines* being in force, the payee spouse usually prepared and introduced into evidence a proposed budget for the child's needs and no budget was filed relating to the pre-*Guidelines* period. Consequently, the appellate court refused to award any retroactive support for that period.

The general rule against double dipping does not apply to phantom stock bonuses where a significant portion of the profit from the phantom stock arose after separation: *Marinangeli v. Marinangeli* (2003), 2003 CarswellOnt 2691, [2003] O.J. No. 2819, 38 R.F.L. (5th) 307, 174 O.A.C. 76, 228 D.L.R. (4th) 376 (Ont. C.A.). The appellant's income had increased. The respondent was not hoarding her capital at the expense of the appellant. Most of what she received in the equalization process was the matrimonial home which is not an income-producing asset. The respondent was not able to contribute to her own support in a significant way and she was in debt. She demonstrated need and suffered economic hardship from the marriage or its breakdown. There was no error on the part of the trial judge in including a phantom stock bonus in the appellant's income.

The receipt of payment when stock options are exercised is the taking of deferred income at a particular time and the value should be brought into income in the year that the options are exercised: *Marinangeli v. Marinangeli* (2003), 2003 CarswellOnt 2691, [2003] O.J. No. 2819, 38 R.F.L. (5th) 307, 174 O.A.C. 76, 228 D.L.R. (4th) 376 (Ont. C.A.). The value of the options which have been exercised are an appropriate factor for the trial judge to consider in making an order for spousal support.

In the *Marinangeli* case, Madam Justice Weiler wrote at paragraph 50:

> The comments of the Supreme Court in *Miglin*, supra were intended to address the situation where the parties chose to release one another from all future support obligations by a one-time payment of lump sum support. Since no future adjustments were envisaged, the parties were expected to consider such foreseeable future changes in the ordinary course of living as an increase or decrease in income before arriving at the amount of the one time payment. She distinguished the *Marinangeli* case from *Miglin*, since in *Marinangeli*, the parties envisaged that the amount of support would change, if there were a material change in circumstances in a party's income, meaning if a party's income increased or decreased. The court held that the provision in the separation agreement relating to a material change in circumstances, read in its context and as a whole, did not exclude foreseeable events such as an increase or decrease in income, but rather the opposite.

The appellant was unsuccessful in arguing that the exercise of his options was not a material change in circumstances as defined in *Willick v. Willick*, [1994] S.C.J. No. 94, 1994 CarswellSask 48, 1994 CarswellSask 450, 6 R.F.L. (4th) 161, 119 D.L.R. (4th) 405, 173 N.R. 321, 125 Sask. R. 81, 81 W.A.C. 81, [1994] 3 S.C.R. 670, [1994] R.D.F. 617 (S.C.C.) — that is, had the alleged change been known, the support provision would not likely have been different. As the appellant did not know the value of his options at the time the agreement was signed, the respondent could not be assumed to know their value at that time. In addition, the respondent was not told the parameters for the exercise of the options and consequently she had no way of ascertaining the value of the options in relation to the price of the underlying stock. The respondent was dependant upon the appellant for information about the value of the options.

A change in circumstances must be something that has some measure of continuity. The court did not accept the appellant's argument that the exercise of the options was not a material change in circumstances because their exercise lacked continuity. There was continuity in the frequency with which the options were awarded and continuity in that the options could be exercised over a period of time.

The increase in a payor's salary and bonus by nearly 20 per cent over the previous year is a material change in circumstances that entitled the trial judge to consider the profit from the options in determining the quantum of support.

A material change in circumstances with respect to child support occurred when the *Guidelines* came into force that entitled the trial judge to consider the profit from the options in determining the quantum of support.

The court, relying on the *Miglin* decision, held that where there is a separation agreement in which spousal support provisions are included, and the issue of spousal support is to be decided under s. 15.2 of the *Divorce Act*, it is raised by an application of first instance, not a variation application: *Fitzgerald v. Gerlich* (2003), 2003 CarswellOnt 1816 (Ont. S.C.J.). Before a court can set aside the spousal support provisions in an agreement, there is no requirement for a finding of a material change in circumstances. The court quoted from the *Miglin* decision, stating ". . ..it is not the existence of change per se that matters but whether, at the time of the application, all the circumstances render continued reliance on the pre-existing agreement unacceptable."

Where a separation agreement provides that the payor spouse was to recalculate his support obligations, if there were a material change in his income and such a change occurred and he did not inform his spouse of this change, nor recalculate his support obligations, the court held that there was an implied disclosure obligation on the payor spouse arising from the agreement: *Murray v. Murray* (2003), 2003 CarswellOnt 3258 (Ont. S.C.J.); additional reasons at (2003), 2003 CarswellOnt 3862 (Ont. S.C.J.). Following *Miglin* and *Marinangelli*, the court was of the opinion that in light of the payor's non-disclosure of his increased income as well as other factors, it should set aside the agreement. It held that the wife could no longer be considered bound by the release of spousal support in the agreement.

A separation agreement will not be set aside on the basis of failure to disclose where there is no evidence at trial to verify the value or the extent of a respondent's assets either at the date of marriage or at the time the contract was executed. It is therefore not possible to conclude that the respondent failed to disclose significant assets existing when the contract was made: *Trick v. Trick* (2003), 2003 CarswellOnt 1103, 39 R.F.L. (5th) 418 (Ont. S.C.J.). At the time the agreement was entered into, the husband did not provide any formal financial disclosure. There was no valuation of his pension, nor were any documents produced to disclose his investments, bank accounts or RRSP's. In 1991, the parties signed the separation agreement which was incorporated into a divorce judgment in 1992, with the exception that the judgement was silent as to spousal support.

In *Coady v. Boyle* (2003), 47 R.F.L. (5th) 283, 2003 CarswellOnt 5074 (Ont. S.C.J.); additional reasons at (2004), 2004 CarswellOnt 938 (Ont. S.C.J.), the wife's application to set aside the parties' settlement agreement based upon the husband's alleged fraud was dismissed. The wife was basing her claim on the inadequacy of the husband's disclosure, an issue which had been decided against her in numerous earlier proceedings. Accordingly, further proceedings in respect of the issue were barred on the basis of *res judicata*.

15§156 — General

Where the parties' minutes of settlement were silent on responsibility for the taxes on the matrimonial home occupied by the wife and the children, it was confirmed on appeal that the husband was liable for half of the taxes. The parties were joint owners of the home, and in absence of a clear indication in the minutes of settlement and existing court orders, the taxes should be the equal responsibility of both parties: *Ostapchuk v. Ostapchuk* (2003), 38 R.F.L. (5th) 172, 2003 CarswellOnt 1661, 171 O.A.C. 132, 64 O.R. (3d) 496, 226 D.L.R. (4th) 385 (Ont. C.A.).

In Quebec, a provision in an agreement whereby support would terminate when the payee began to live with someone else is invalid since spouses cannot renounce a future right to support: *Cohn v. Leboff*, 11 R.F.L. (3d) 379, (sub nom. *Droit de la famille — 1135)* [1987] R.D.F. 449, 1987 CarswellQue 30 (C.A.).

Where the husband unilaterally stopped paying spousal support to the wife after losing his job, he could not rely upon an arbitration clause in the parties' separation agreement to stay the wife's application to enforce arrears. Under the agreement, the scope of matters available for arbitration was clear and limited to the narrow issue of where a change in the husband's circumstances limited his ability to pay support. The husband had stopped paying support arbitrarily and that was outside the scope of the arbitration clause: *Range v. Bremner*, 47 R.F.L. (5th) 394, 2003 CarswellBC 3099, 2003 BCCA 675, 192 B.C.A.C. 186, 315 W.A.C. 186 (B.C. C.A.).

Where the husband had unilaterally reduced the spousal support payable by him under the parties' separation agreement because of a reduction in his income, the reduction was subsequently ordered to be paid to the wife as arrears: *Sloss v. Forget* (2004), 8 R.F.L. (6th) 388, 2004 CarswellOnt 3923 (S.C.J.).

A court cannot override the support provisions of a final settlement agreement in the absence of a radical change in circumstances that is causally related to the marriage. This rule applies to variation applications by the payor as well as by the payee: *Fetterley v. Fetterley* (1988), 14 R.F.L. (3d) 47, 89 A.R. 350, 1988 CarswellAlta 331 (Q.B.); affirmed 24 R.F.L. (3d) 61, (sub nom. *Fetterly v. Fetterly)* 102 A.R. 131, 1989 CarswellAlta 396 (C.A.).

Where the wife had agreed to the termination of her spousal support entitlement upon entering into a new cohabitation arrangement, she could not rely upon the ending of her common law relationship as a "change of circumstances" warranting an award of spousal support: *Svarckopf v. Svarckopf* (2002), 27 R.F.L. (5th) 193, 2002 CarswellOnt 1342 (S.C.J.).

The fact that the support provisions in a separation agreement contain a no "change of circumstances" clause does not prevent the court from entertaining an application for variation of support: *Wilkinson v. Wilkinson* (1996), 22 R.F.L. (4th) 46, 1996 CarswellOnt 693 (Gen. Div.).

Where the limited term spousal support provided for in the parties' separation agreement was based upon a premise that the wife would achieve self-sufficiency, she was later granted an upward variation and extension of support in view of her deteriorating financial circumstances. Changes in the economy which had negatively impacted the wife's prospects had not been contemplated when the agreement was signed and given that the wife continued to suffer economic hardship as a result of the marriage, she was entitled to the variation: *Baker v. Baker* (1996), 22 R.F.L. (4th) 13, 182 A.R. 41, 1996 CarswellAlta 188 (Q.B.).

Where the quantum of spousal support payable by the husband had been tied in the parties' agreement to issues such as custody, access, matrimonial property and the negative economic effects of the marriage upon the wife, the court refused the husband's application for a reduction of spousal support, although his annual income had declined from $150,000 to $46,000. To make any changes would likely have resulted in inequities and would have required the reopening of the entire agreement: *Rondeau v. Rondeau* (1995), 157 N.B.R. (2d) 142, 404 A.P.R. 142 (Q.B.).

Where a separation agreement provides for future variation, an applicant need only prove a material change in circumstances, as opposed to a radical change, in order to support a variation application: *Doole v. Doole* (1991), 32 R.F.L. (3d) 283, 115 A.R. 1, 1991 CarswellAlta 326 (Q.B.).

Where the parties' separation agreement specified termination of the wife's support upon remarriage only, the husband could not rely upon her finding full-time employment as a basis upon which to terminate her support: *Wohlfahrt v. Wohlfahrt* (1990), 26 R.F.L. (3d) 181, 1990 CarswellOnt 251 (H.C.).

Any radical change in circumstances of the payor which is caused by, attributable to, results from or relates to the obligation to pay support will permit a court to reduce support entered into under a final settlement agreement. It need not be specifically proved that the change was causally connected to the marriage: *Osterkampf v. Osterkampf* (1989), 22 R.F.L. (3d) 153, 99 A.R. 286, 1989 CarswellAlta 383 (Q.B.). See also *Byers v. Byers* (1989), 23 R.F.L. (3d) 280, 1989 CarswellOnt 312 (H.C.).

A separation agreement negotiated when the wife was unemployed and the parties' children were living with her is no longer valid after the children achieve economic independence and the wife finds employment: *Matthews v. Matthews* (1988), 11 R.F.L. (3d) 431, 68 Nfld. & P.E.I.R. 91, 209 A.P.R. 91, 1988 CarswellNfld 10 (T.D.).

Changes in circumstances which were in the contemplation of the parties at the time a support agreement was entered into cannot later be used as the basis for a variation of spousal support: *MacMillan v. MacMillan* (1988), 18 R.F.L. (3d) 149, 88 N.S.R. (2d) 368, 225 A.P.R. 368, 1998 CarswellNS 65 (T.D.).

In order to override the support terms of a final settlement agreement, an applicant must prove a radical change in circumstances that was both unforeseen at the time of the agreement and related to the marriage: *Cook v. Cook* (1988), 17 R.F.L. (3d) 35, 87 N.S.R. (2d) 232, 222 A.P.R. 232, 1988 CarswellNS 60 (Fam. Ct.).

Custody Orders

16. (1) Order for custody — A court of competent jurisdiction may, on application by either or both spouses or by any other person, make an order respecting the custody of or the access to, or the custody of and access to, any or all children of the marriage.

(2) Interim order for custody — Where an application is made under subsection (1), the court may, on application by either or both spouses or by any other person, make an interim order respecting the custody of or the access to, or the custody of and access to, any or all children of the marriage pending determination of the application under subsection (1).

(3) Application by other person — A person, other than a spouse, may not make an application under subsection (1) or (2) without leave of the court.

(4) Joint custody or access — The court may make an order under this section granting custody of, or access to, any or all children of the marriage to any one or more persons.

(5) Access — Unless the court orders otherwise, a spouse who is granted access to a child of the marriage has the right to make inquiries, and to be given information, as to the health, education and welfare of the child.

(6) Terms and conditions — The court may make an order under this section for a definite or indefinite period or until the happening of a specified event and may impose such other terms, conditions or restrictions in connection therewith as it thinks fit and just.

(7) Order respecting change of residence — Without limiting the generality of subsection (6), the court may include in an order under this section a term requiring any person who has custody of a child of the marriage and who intends to change the place of residence of that child to notify, at least thirty days before the change or within such other period before the change as the court may specify, any person who is granted access to that child of the change, the time at which the change will be made and the new place of residence of the child.

(8) Factors — In making an order under this section, the court shall take into consideration only the best interests of the child of the marriage as determined by reference to the condition, means, needs and other circumstances of the child.

(9) Past conduct — In making an order under this section, the court shall not take into consideration the past conduct of any person unless the conduct is relevant to the ability of that person to act as a parent of a child.

(10) Maximum contact — In making an order under this section, the court shall give effect to the principle that a child of the marriage should have as much contact with each spouse as is consistent with the best interests of the child and, for that purpose, shall take into consideration the willingness of the person for whom custody is sought to facilitate such contact.

16 — Custody and access — general considerations

"Custody" is defined in s. 2 of the *Divorce Act, 1985*, as including "care, upbringing and any other incident of custody." "Access" is not defined specifically but it would at least include the right of the spouse with access to obtain information about the health, education and welfare of the child: s. 16(5). The spouse with access may also request an order that he or she be notified of anticipated changes in the child's residence: s 16(7) is viewed as "contact" with the child: s. 16(10).

One of the major features of the provisions relating to custody and access is that joint custody is recognized by giving the court the power to award custody or access to more than one person: s. 16(4). This person need not be one of the spouses, but a person who is not a spouse may only apply for the custody or access order if given leave of the court: s. 16(1) and (3). Once a spouse has made an application for custody, the court is not limited to awarding custody to either of the spouses. It could award custody to a non-spouse or joint custody to a spouse and a non-spouse. On an application for leave to apply for a custody or access order the court would likely require evidence of a relationship to the child which would qualify the application as a reasonable candidate to parent the child.

Instead of a requirement to review "the conduct of the parties and the condition, means and other circumstances of each of them", the present Act has moved to the approach developed in provincial legislation and in the case law generally that "the court shall take into consideration only the best interests of the child": s. 16(8). However, the best interests are qualified by reference to the condition, means, needs and other circumstances of the child: s. 16(8). The Information Paper issued by the Minister of Justice in May, 1985 at the time of first reading of the Bill to create the *Divorce Act* commented:

> [I]t is widely accepted that the law should ensure that all arrangements regarding children are made solely according to their best interests having regard to all circumstances. The ... Act contains such a provision. (p.8)

Evidence relating to conduct has been restricted in custody and access applications. Such evidence may not be considered unless it is relevant to the ability of a party to act as a parent: s. 16(9). Contact of the child with both spouses is emphasized and one of the criteria for determining which placement would be in the best interests of the child is the willingness of the person seeking custody to facilitate contact with the other spouse: s. 16(10).

An order providing for custody or access may be made for a definite period or until the happening of a specified event, a power not previously expressed in the statute: s. 16(6). This might invite the court to state that custody, for instance, is to continue until the child reaches a certain age or a certain education level.

16A — Jurisdiction

A custody or access order may be made by a "court of competent jurisdiction": s. 16(1). This is the court as defined in s. 2(1) (superior court or designated court) that "has granted a divorce to either or both former spouses": s. 4.

If an application for a custody or an access order is made in a divorce proceeding and the child is most substantially connected with another province, the court on the application of the other spouse or on its own motion may transfer the whole proceeding (both custody or access and divorce) to the other province: s. 6(1).

Similarly, if an application for a custody or an access order is made in a corollary relief proceeding or for a variation order in respect of a custody order in a variation proceeding and the child is most substantially connected with another province, the court on the application of the former spouse, or on its own motion, may transfer the whole proceeding (both custody or access and corollary relief or both custody and variation) to the other province: ss. 6(2) and (3).

Where a child is most substantially connected with another province, a divorce proceeding in which an application for custody or access has been joined, or a corollary relief or variation proceeding involving custody or access, may be transferred to that province on application by a party or by a court on its own motion: ss 6(1), (2) and (3). The court to which the proceeding is transferred has exclusive jurisdiction to hear and determine the proceeding notwithstanding that the jurisdictional requirements in ss. 3,4 or 5 that would otherwise be applicable have not been met: s. 6(4)

As a prerequisite to the initiation of divorce proceedings, every lawyer undertaking to act for a spouse must discuss with the spouse the advisability of negotiation a custody (or support) settlement and to inform the spouse of mediation facilities known to him or her which might help the spouses in their negotiations: s. 9(2). Note that this section applies only to custody, and not access matters, and that it applies to original proceedings, but not to variation proceedings. Also, it applies only to spouses, although non-spouses with the leave of the court may apply for custody.

16B — Parties

Under the *Divorce Act, 1985*, former spouses, as well as spouses, can apply for a custody order. Previously, only spouses could make such an application, since, in prior legislation, corollary relief was incidental to a claim for divorce and could not be maintained independently from such a claim. Under the 1985 Act, a corollary relief proceeding has an independent status and can be heard separately from the claim for divorce and may be brought at some time later than the time of divorce: s. 4.

The new Act also envisages a proceeding that is brought "by either or both spouses" for a custody order: ss. 16(1) and (2).

16§1 — Custody under the *Divorce Act* — constitutional issues

Divorce Act, 1985

The test in the *Divorce Act*, requiring that custody and access be determined solely on the basis of the child's best interests, does not violate the *Charter of Rights and Freedoms*. The Charter will not protect conduct which violates the best interests test: *Young v. Young*, 49 R.F.L. (3d) 117, [1993] 4 S.C.R. 3, [1993] 8 W.W.R. 513, 84 B.C.L.R. (2d) 1, 160 N.R. 1, 34 B.C.A.C. 161, 108 D.L.R. (4th) 193; affirming (1990), 29 R.F.L. (3d) 113, 50 B.C.L.R. (2d) 1, 75 D.L.R. (4th) 46 (C.A.); reversing in part (1989), 24 R.F.L. (3d) 193 (B.C. S.C.).

Divorce Act, 1968

The power to grant an order of maintenance pursuant to s. 11 [now s. 15] of the *Divorce Act* is necessarily ancillary to jurisdiction in divorce and in that regard the Parliament of Canada was acting within its legislative competency conferred upon it by s. 91(26) of the *Constitution Act, 1867* (U.K.), c. 3. This principle applies equally to matters of custody, care and upbringing of children of the marriage under s. 11(1)(c) [now s. 16] and to the provisions dealing with interim orders: *Zacks v. Zacks*, 10 R.F.L. 53, [1973] S.C.R. 891, [1973] 5 W.W.R. 289, 35 D.L.R. (3d) 420; *Jackson v. Jackson* (1970), 8 R.F.L. 172, [1973] S.C.R. 205, [1972] 6 W.W.R. 419, 29 D.L.R. (3d) 641. See also *Vadeboncoeur v. Landry*, 23 R.F.L. 360, [1977] 2 S.C.R. 179, 68 D.L.R. (3d) 165, 10 N.R. 469; *Whyte v. Whyte* (1969), 69 W.W.R. 536, 7 D.L.R. (3d) 7 (Man. C.A.); *Niccolls v. Niccolls* (1969), 68 W.W.R. 307, 4 D.L.R. (3d) 209 (B.C. S.C.); *Todd v. Todd* (1969), 2 R.F.L. 303, 68 W.W.R. 315, 5 D.L.R. (3d) 92 (B.C. S.C.); *Heikel v. Heikel* (1970), 1 R.F.L. 326, 23 W.W.R. 84, 12 D.L.R. (3d) 311 (Alta. C.A.).

"The apparent conflict between the provincial legislation and federal legislation in the area of corollary relief has been considered by a number of courts which, as far as I can ascertain, are in agreement that the federal legislation must prevail and is paramount over the provincial legislation": per Bowen J. in *Goldstein v. Goldstein*, 17 R.F.L. 346 at 348, [1975] W.W.D. 50 (Alta. T.D.); reversed on other grounds 23 R.F.L. 206, [1976] 4 W.W.R. 646, 67 D.L.R. (3d) 624 (Alta. C.A.). See also *Gillespie v. Gillespie* (1973), 13 R.F.L. 344 at 349, 6 N.B.R. (2d) 239 (C.A.).

"There can be little doubt that Parliament has power to enact provisions for maintenance and custody when these questions arise as a result of dissolution of the marriage in proceedings under the *Divorce Act*, and it also seems clear enough that the existence of such 'ancillary' jurisdiction does not oust the jurisdiction of the provincial legislatures to enact provisions conferring similar jurisdiction on the courts in other matrimonial proceedings": *Radke v. Radke*, 4 R.F.L. 318 at 338, [1971] 5 W.W.R. 113, 20 D.L.R. (3d) 679 (Alta. C.A.), Cairns J.A.

"[When] the federal government entered the field of divorce and corollary relief by the passage of the *Divorce Act*, 1967–68 (Can.) c. 24, insofar as any provincial legislation in that field dealt with the same subject-matter as the federal legislation, it ceased to be effective. Although the provisions of the federal and provincial legislation are not exactly co-extensive, it is our opinion that any of the provincial legislation which appears to extend beyond the boundaries of the federal legislation is not effective because the federal legislation occupies the field": *Richards v. Richards*, 7 R.F.L. 101 at 102, [1972] 2 O.R. 596, 26 D.L.R. (3d) 264 (C.A.), Gale C.J.O.

"On the view I have taken of the restricted nature of the custody jurisdiction under the Canadian *Divorce Act*, I hold that its provision as to custody are valid enactments under the federal power in relation to marriage and divorce. To me, they are bound up with the direct consequences of marriage and its dissolution as much as is alimony and maintenance; and, much more importantly than those it is so bound up by reason of the physical and human relationships of parents and their children. The fact that these can exist outside of formal marriage does not affect the matter where it is dealt with in terms of marriage and its dissolution. The very concept of divorce where there are dependent children of the marriage makes the question of their custody a complementary one to divorce itself": *Papp v. Papp*, [1970] 1 O.R. 331 at 338, 8 D.L.R. (3d) 389 (C.A.), Laskin J.A. See also *Hutchings, Re* (1976), 24 R.F.L. 328, 9 Nfld. & P.E.I.R. 438, (sub nom. *Re Clarke and Hutchings)* 71 D.L.R. (3d) 356 (Nfld. C.A.); *Bray v. Bray* (1970), 2 R.F.L. 282, [1971] 1 O.R. 232, 15 D.L.R. (3d) 40 (H.C.).

The exclusive jurisdiction of provincially constituted courts in child welfare matters remains intact and it has not been supplanted by the powers given to the federally constituted courts under the *Divorce Act*. When they are involved in custody matters it is only corollary to the main action, *i.e.*, divorce. It is between the parties only and the state is not brought into the decision-making process: *Children's Aid Society of Halifax v. McIlveen* (1980), 20 R.F.L. (2d) 302 (N.S. Fam. Ct.), following *Fortowsky and Essex R.C.C.A. Society Re*, [1960] O.W.N. 235, 23 D.L.R. (2d) 569 (C.A.); *Kredl v. Quebec (Attorney General)*, [1966] S.C.R. 320, 56 D.L.R. (2d) 437; *Natural Parents v. Supt. of Child Welfare* (1975), 21 R.F.L. 267, [1976] 2 S.C.R. 571, [1976] 1 W.W.R. 699, 60 D.L.R. (3d) 148, 6 N.R. 491.

The limited nature of the custody jurisdiction bestowed by the *Divorce Act* must be noted. There is a limitation beyond the confinement to corollary relief in relation to divorce. the "children of the marriage" alone are brought within the Act, not children generally of the one spouse or the other Moreover, within this limitation the definition of "children of the marriage" refers to dependent children, either those under age 16, or those age 16 or over in the charge of the spouses but unable by reason of illness, disability or other cause to maintain themselves.

16§2 — Custody — the *Divorce Act* and provincial custody provisions

Divorce Act, 1985

Where the mother's claim for custody had cited both the *Divorce Act* and provincial legislation, but the actual order was silent as to which legislation it was made under, the doctrine of paramountcy deemed the order to have been made under the federal legislation. Accordingly, the Provincial Court was without jurisdiction to entertain the father's subsequent claim for access: *Spiers v. Spiers* (1995), 18 R.F.L. (4th) 246, 15 B.C.L.R. (3d) 148 (S.C.).

Any custody order in a divorce proceeding is paramount over a custody order made under provincial legislation, and a claim for custody within divorce proceedings may only be struck if it is frivolous and vexatious and an abuse of process. Such circumstances must be very clear and uncontroverted: *Husband v. Husband* (1987), 7 R.F.L. (3d) 380 (B.C. S.C.).

A superior court in a divorce action has jurisdiction to make a custody order inconsistent with an earlier order made by a provincial court under provincial legislation: *Manj v. Manj*, 27 R.F.L. (5th) 121, 2002 CarswellBC 767, 2002 BCSC 450 (Master).

Divorce Act, 1968

A judge of the Nova Scotia Family Court has jurisdiction to entertain a mother's application for custody despite the fact that the father has initiated divorce proceedings, which include a claim for custody, in another province. Such jurisdiction continues until such time as a custody order is actually made in the divorce action: *Lor v. Lor* (1978), 5 R.F.L. (2d) 138, 25 N.S.R. (2d) 243, 36 A.P.R. 243, 85 D.L.R. (3d) 362 (C.A.).

"The Supreme Court, under the *Divorce Act*, has undoubted jurisdiction to deal with custody and maintenance of children of divorced parents. Until, however, it exercises that jurisdiction in any particular case, the provincial Act continues in full effect as to children and confers on the appropriate magistrate or Family Court Judge the power and duty to deal with maintenance": *Toole v. Toole* (1976), 27 R.F.L. 63 at 63–64, 14 N.S.R. (2d) 537 (C.A.), MacKeigan C.J.N.S. It should be noted, however that the court further stated that once a custody awarded had been made pursuant to the *Divorce Act*, the custody jurisdiction under the provincial Act is ousted.

The effect of a custody order made under the *Divorce Act* is to supersede any other custody order made in respect of the child in any province in Canada. Thus an interim custody order made in Quebec under the Act will be paramount to a custody order made in British Columbia under provincial legislation. Under such circumstances it is not open for the British Columbia court to invoke its *parens patriae* jurisdiction so as to make a custody order in respect of the child: *Hall, Re*, 24 R.F.L. 6, [1976] 4 W.W.R. 634, 70 D.L.R. (3d) 493 (B.C. C.A.).

Where a decree *nisi* granted in Ontario contains a custody award relating to a child of the marriage, the *parens patriae* jurisdiction of the Newfoundland Supreme Court to award custody of the child to an uncle is not thereby ousted when, at the time of application, the child is physically present in Newfoundland: *Hutchings, Re* (1976), 24 R.F.L. 328, 9 Nfld. & P.E.I.R. 438, (sub nom. *Re Clarke and Hutchings)* 71 D.L.R. (3d) 356 (Nfld. C.A.).

In *Gillespie v. Gillespie* (1972), 13 R.F.L. 344 at 349, N.B.R. (2d) 227, 36 D.L.R. (3d) 421 (C.A.), the court stated: (1) It was the intent of the *Divorce Act* to empower the court having jurisdiction over an action for divorce, to adjudicate with respect to the custody of the children of the marriage wherever they may be. (2) When Parliament enacted the corollary provisions respecting custody of children of a marriage, it carried out of the general jurisdiction in custody matters, theretofore administered solely by courts deriving their powers through provincial legislation, a segment of that jurisdiction limited to the children of a marriage sought to be dissolved, and empowered the courts exercising divorce jurisdiction to make orders applicable to any children of such marriage. Since in the present case provincial legislation and federal legislation covered the same subject-matter, the federal legislation must prevail and supersede that enacted by the province. It followed that any custody order made by a divorce court under s. 10 or 11 [now s. 46] of the *Divorce Act* superseded any previous order made under provincial legislation with respect to the same child.

Where children who are within the *Divorce Act* are equally within the terms of a provincial Act, the former Act alone must be taken to apply to any claim for corollary relief in respect of those children, when such relief is sought in association with a petition for divorce brought under the federal enactment: *Tapson v. Tapson*, 2 R.F.L. 305 at 306–307, [1970] 1 O.R. 521, 8 D.L.R. (3d) 727 (C.A.); *Robinson, Re*; *Robinson v. Robinson* (1974), 14 R.F.L. 120 (Ont. H.C.). See also *Eccles v. Van Duin* (1978), 2 R.F.L. (2d) 375, 19 O.R. (2d) 37, 84 D.L.R. (3d) 406 (H.C.).

In *McKay v. McKay* (1982), 30 R.F.L. (2d) 463 (Ont. H.C.), it was held that the court, in the context of an action for divorce, had jurisdiction to entertain the wife's application for interim custody despite the continuing existence of an earlier interim custody order granted to the father under the *Family Law Reform Act*. Per Blair L.J.S.C. at p. 464: "[I]t is clear that the legislation of the federal Parliament giving jurisdiction to deal with [custody] matters under s. 10 [now s. 16] of the *Divorce Act* is paramount and the exercise of it cannot be prevented by the fact that orders with respect to the same subject matters have been made under a provincial statute."

The court, in an action for divorce, has the power to make a custody order regarding a child who is residing in another province and is subject to a custody order made under provincial legislation by a court of that province: *Kyle v. Kyle* (1985), 44 R.F.L. (2d) 200 (Sask. Q.B.).

See also *Saulnier v. Saulnier* (1980), 17 C.P.C. 303 (Ont. H.C.); *Lachner v. Lachner* (1980), 18 R.F.L. (2d) 366 at 373–374, 29 O.R. (2d) 123 (H.C.); *Hilborn v. Hilborn* (1977), 2 R.F.L. (2d) 5, 7 A.R. 62, 4 Alta. L.R. 52 (T.D.); *Ambramsen, Re*, [1977] 3 W.W.R. 764, 77 D.L.R. (3d) 103 (B.C. S.C.); *Kuehn, Re* (1976), 29 R.F.L. 72, 1 B.C.L.R. 192, 71 D.L.R. (3d) 433 (S.C.); varied on other grounds (1976), 30 R.F.L. 94, 1 B.C.L.R. 193, 71 D.L.R. (3d) 433 (S.C.); *Abbey v. Abbey* (1976), 28 R.F.L. 222 (Ont. H.C.); *Miller v. Miller* (1976), 27 R.F.L. 189 (B.C. S.C.); *Renouf v. Renouf* (1975), 23 R.F.L. 66 (Ont. H.C.); *Bray v. Bray* (1970), 2 R.F.L. 282, [1971] 1 O.R. 232, 15 D.L.R. (3d) 40 (H.C.).

16§3 — Custody — child outside the jurisdiction

Section 6(1) provides that where an application for custody (or access) is made in a divorce proceeding and the child is most substantially connected with another province, the court may, on an application by a spouse or on its own motion, transfer the divorce proceeding to a court in that other province. In similar circumstances where there is an application for custody or access in a corollary relief proceeding, or an application for a variation order in respect of a custody order in a variation proceeding, the court may, on application by a former spouse or on its own motion, transfer the corollary relief proceeding to the province with which the child is most substantially connected: s. 16(2).

Thus, if a child in a province other than the one where the divorce is being sought, or where the divorce has been granted, is most substantially connected with that other province, all the proceedings must be transferred to the other jurisdiction with which the child is more closely associated. Thus the ties of the child to another jurisdiction may be determinative of the jurisdiction of the divorce, corollary relief and variation proceedings as well as the custody proceedings.

Divorce Act, 1985

A Canadian court has no jurisdiction to grant custody or to enforce access in respect of children resident in another country: *C. (T.S.) v. N. (D.L.)* (1990), 28 R.F.L. (3d) 353 (N.B. C.A.).

Divorce Act, 1968

It was the intent of the *Divorce Act* to empower the court having jurisdiction over an action for divorce to adjudicate with respect to the custody of the children of the marriage wherever they may be: *Gillespie v. Gillespie* (1972), 13 R.F.L. 344 at 349, 6 N.B.R. (2d) 227, 36 D.L.R. (3d) 421 (C.A.).

The court which grants a decree *nisi* providing for the custody of children may continue to possess jurisdiction to vary those custody provisions, regardless of the fact that at the time of the application for variance, the subject children are resident in a different province: *Skjonsby v. Skjonsby*, 18 R.F.L. 95, [1975] 4 W.W.R. 319, 53 D.L.R. (3d) 602 (Alta. C.A.).

The courts of the place of ordinary residence of the children have jurisdiction to determine the welfare of those children, *i.e.*, to determine their custody even though the courts of the place where they are physically present also have such jurisdiction. If this were not so, an unscrupulous person could move children from jurisdiction to jurisdiction preventing the effective adjudication upon their welfare by due process of the law. Unless in exceptional circumstances the court is satisfied beyond reasonable doubt that serious harm could result to the child, the courts of the jurisdiction where the child is physically present should recognize and give effect to the orders of the courts of the place in which the child is ordinarily resident. Further, the ordinary residence of a child cannot be changed by the surreptitious removal of the child from the place of its ordinary residence: *Nielsen v. Nielsen*, 5 R.F.L. 313, [1971] 1 O.R. 541, 16 D.L.R. (3d) 133 (H.C.). See also *Ritchie v. Ritchie* (1975), 20 R.F.L. 225, 5 O.R. (2d) 520 (C.A.), a further case dealing with the ordinary residency of children.

Where the father sought custody of his children who were ordinarily resident in Ontario but prior to the hearing the mother had removed the children to Massachusetts, it was held that the Supreme Court of Ontario continued to possess jurisdiction. It was found that in cases of custody, the court had jurisdiction over an infant who was ordinarily resident within its jurisdiction. In this case, the children's ordinary Ontario residence could not be defeated by the mother's kidnap-like actions, in absence of the father's acquiescence to the arrangement: *Walker v. Walker*, 3 R.F.L. 78, [1970] 3 O.R. 771, 14 D.L.R. (3d) 155 (H.C.).

In assessing with which jurisdiction a child has the most substantial connection for the purposes of a custody proceeding, the court should consider the reason for the removal of the child to a different jurisdiction, the strength of the child's links with each jurisdiction, the *forum conveniens* and where the child might finally live: *Chenkie v. Chenkie* (1987), 6 R.F.L. (3d) 371, 50 Alta. L.R. (2d) 41, 76 A.R. 224 (Q.B.).

Where the husband petitioned for divorce in Prince Edward Island and sought custody of the child of the marriage who, since birth, had always been resident in Ontario, the Supreme Court of Prince Edward Island declined jurisdiction on the custody issue. Although no custody proceedings had been initiated in Ontario, the significant contacts of the child with that province better favoured the Ontario courts in making a full inquiry into the issue: *Furjan v. Furjan* (1977), 28 R.F.L. 319 (P.E.I. S.C.).

Where the child of the marriage was resident in Singapore and in the custody of the mother pursuant both to custody orders granted in Singapore and British Columbia, the British Columbia Supreme Court declined jurisdiction with respect to the father's application to vacate the existing custody order in favour of one vesting custody in him. Although the court found that it possessed jurisdiction to make a custody order in respect of children outside the province where the parties are domiciled in British Columbia, the court was free to decline to exercise it in light of the child's ordinary residence in Singapore: *Jonasson v. Jonasson* (1977), 2 R.F.L. (2d) 311 (B.C. S.C.).

"The modern approach to the question of jurisdiction to make orders for the custody of children of separated parents is to prefer the test of 'ordinary residence' over the more artificial concept of 'domicile'. On the material before me, the children are not only temporarily out of the jurisdiction. The wife has bought a house in England and there is no indication of any intention to come back. ... In the circumstances, the authorities appear clear that the husband [or the wife] could not succeed before this court on an application for custody of the children of the marriage": *Cotter v. Cotter* (1976), 29 R.F.L. 197 at 199 (Ont. H.C.), Labrosse J.

Where the child of the marriage had been taken to Germany prior to the hearing of divorce proceedings, it was held that no order as to custody could be granted in Ontario by way of corollary relief: *Jablonowski v. Jablonowski*, 8 R.F.L. 36, [1972] 3 O.R. 410, 28 D.L.R. (3d) 440 (H.C.). See also *Paschke v. Paschke* (1975), 26 R.F.L. 324 (Alta. T.D.).

Where the mother and child were resident in British Columbia and an order under the *Equal Guardianship of Infants Act*, R.S.B.C. 1990, c. 130, vesting custody of the child in the mother had been made, the Master in Ontario declined to entertain the husband's application for interim access under the *Divorce Act*, stating that the matter could be more conveniently dealt with in British Columbia under the provincial statute: *Craddock v. Craddock* (1974), 20 R.F.L. 61, 5 O.R. (2d) 657 (H.C.); *Knowles, Re*; *Knowles v. Knowles* (1973), 13 R.F.L. 76 (B.C. S.C.); *Hudson v. Hall* (1974), 19 R.F.L. 351 (Que. S.C.); *Adams v. Adams* (1971), 7 R.F.L. 203, 4 N.B.R. (2d) 275 (Q.B.). See also *Hilborn v. Hilborn* (1977), 2 R.F.L. (2d) 5, 7 A.R. 62, 4 Alta. L.R. 52 (T.D.).

16§4 — "Child of the marriage"

This definition formerly included a child who was "unable to ... provide himself with necessities of life." The current definition includes a child who is "unable ... to obtain the necessities of life" and it may impose less of an obligation upon the child to provide for himself or herself.

When the parties to the action are the parents of the child involved, an order for custody may be made with respect to a child who is over the age of 16. The child's age alone does not nullify the power of the court to make an order for the interim custody, or custody, of one coming within the definition of "children of the marriage": *Gelbloom v. Gelbloom*, 10 R.F.L. 274 at 276, [1973] 3 O.R. 289, 36 D.L.R. (3d) 517 (C.A.).

"The child referred to in the petition attained the age of sixteen shortly after institution of the action and apparently chooses to remain with her mother. She still attends school and will undoubtedly continue to be a dependent for several years yet. In the circumstances it hardly appears necessary to make an order in respect of her custody": *McAllister v. McAllister* (1976), 14 N.B.R. (2d) 552 at 553 (Q.B.), Dickson J.

"James Meyer, the son in respect of whom the claim for custody is asserted, is 25 years of age, retarded and an epileptic. The epilepsy is controllable but will not improve. Since leaving the farm to live in Morden with his mother he has had some employment for which he received nominal remuneration in a sheltered workshop type of situation. However, he can be described as unemployable and unable by reason of disability to withdraw himself from the charge of a parent or to provide himself with necessaries of life. His father appears to have no interest in him. I find James Meyer to be a child within the meaning of the *Divorce Act*, R.S.C. 1970, c. D-8, and regard it as proper that he be placed in the wife's custody": *Meyer v. Meyer* (1974), 18 R.F.L. 105 at 107–108 (Man. Q.B.), Dewar C.J.Q.B.

"Under the *Divorce Act*, R.S.C. 1970, c. D-8, in theory at least, courts can deal with custody until the children are 18. In practice it is recognized that there is no point in making custody orders when children get to be about 15 or 16 because they will simply make their own choice and obviously courts cannot supervise these custody orders in the case of older children, with any real degree of effectiveness": per Zuber J. in *Sharpe v. Sharpe* (1974), 14 R.F.L. 151 at 151 (Ont. H.C.).

The courts should not grant custody of a young man almost 19 except in the most exceptional cases. There should be very few such cases, limited generally to those covered by a restrictive *ejusdem generis* interpretation of the definition of "children of the marriage": *Clark v. Clark*, 4 R.F.L. 27 at 31, [1971] 1 O.R. 674, 16 D.L.R. (3d) 376 (H.C.). See also *Kralik v. Kralik* (1974), 17 R.F.L. 244, 4 O.R. (2d) 171, 47 D.L.R. (3d) 359 (C.A.).

16§4A — Custody — procedure

The fact that a father had failed to pay costs as agreed upon in a consent judgment dealing with the divorce, matrimonial property and costs, did not thereby prohibit him from bringing the custody issue into court for determination. The custody issue was outside of the issues settled in the consent judgment and was not thereby affected: *Yakimyshyn v. Yakimyshyn* (1994), 9 R.F.L. (4th) 41, 163 A.R. 75 (Alta. Q.B.).

16§5 — Custody — general considerations

Divorce Act, 1985

All custody awards have a provisional element in them since the paramount concern is the children's best interest: *Lorenz v. Lorenz* (1998), 38 R.F.L. (4th) 291 (B.C. C.A.).

An order awarding custody to one parent does not prevent the non-custodial parent from carrying out his or her responsibilities of playing a meaningful role in the child's life: *N. v. N.* (1994), 3 R.F.L. (4th) 133 (B.C. C.A.).

In determining a child's "best interests" in custody/access matters, the court should be aware of the child's need for space, time, and opportunity to pursue social interests with friends as well as to engage in extracurricular activities. These needs will increase as the child grows older: *Milleker v. Milleker*, 21 R.F.L. (6th) 381, 2005 CarswellSask 761, [2005] S.J. No. 697, 2005 SKQB 455, 272 Sask. R. 223 (Sask. Q.B.).

In *Clayton v. Clayton* (1998), 38 R.F.L. (4th) 320, 40 O.R. (3d) 24 (Gen. Div.), the court found it inappropriate to make a custody order in relation to a 17-year-old child.

Where the custodial mother had agreed to consult the father regarding the children's education, but the parties were unable to resolve a conflict over private versus public schooling the mother as custodial parent was found to have the ultimate decision-making power: *Ducas v. Varkony* (1995), 16 R.F.L. (4th) 91, 104 Man. R. (2d) 110 (Q.B.); additional reasons at (1995), 16 R.F.L. (4th) 91 (note), 105 Man. R. (2d) 214 (Q.B.).

Where after separation, the custodial mother began to use the surname of both parents in a hyphenated fashion for the child, the husband's application for an order requiring the wife to use his name alone was refused. The hyphenated name connected the child with the custodial mother and was therefore in the child's best interests: *Ducas v. Varkony*, above.

The only ground upon which to challenge in court a child-rearing decision of a custodial parent is to show that the decision was contrary to a child's best interests: *Scanlan v. Tootoo* (1994), 152 N.B.R. (2d) 304, 390 A.P.R. 304 (Q.B.).

There are no hard and fast rules that must apply when the court is considering the custody of children. In each case the sex, the age, and the environment of the children are all factors that must be considered along with many other factors in determining custody, so that what is done is done in the best interests of the children: *Dykes v. Dykes* (1977), 24 N.S.R. (2d) 527 at 536, 35 A.P.R. 527 at 536 (T.D.).

"In dealing with the matter of custody, the welfare of the child is of paramount importance and takes priority over all other considerations. The legal rights of the parents are equal but the courts generally, in the case of children of tender year, which term usually applies to children under six, lean towards the mother as being the proper person to have custody and also, in a case of girls, the courts tend to lean towards the mother because of a more suitable relationship for a mother in bringing up a little girl than a father. Now, those are just basic principles that always have to be borne in mind in deciding the matter of custody": *Banks v. Banks* (1977), 2 R.F.L. (2d) 179 at 180, 6 A.R. 421 (T.D.), Kirby J.; *D. v. D.* (1978), 3 R.F.L. (2d) 327 at 331, 2 O.R. (2d) 722, 88 D.L.R. (3d) 578 (Co. Ct.); *Martens v. Martens* (1981), 31 O.R. (2d) 313 (U.F.C.).

16§5A — Non-parental custody claims

In a custody contest between a biological parent and a legal stranger (such as a sibling of the other parent), the "best interests" assessment requires that the importance of maintaining a relationship with the natural parent be considered. The biological parent relationship should not be disturbed, absent factors requiring interference in order to ensure the children's best interests: *J. (K.E.) v. J. (D.L.)*, 26 R.F.L. (5th) 105, 2002 CarswellAlta 282, 2002 ABQB 188, [2002] 6 W.W.R. 124, 3 Alta. L.R. (4th) 353 (Q.B.); additional reasons at 2002 CarswellAlta 850, 2002 ABQB 608, [2002] 10 W.W.R. 306, 3 Alta. L.R. (4th) 377 (Q.B.).

In *Droit de la famille — 1529* (1991), [1992] R.D.F. 1 (C.S. Qué.), the children's aunt and uncle were granted leave to seek variation of a custody order in favour of the children's father, provided that the family's counsel was first consulted.

In *C. (E.S.) v. C. (D.A.)* (1990), 26 R.F.L. (3d) 101 (Man. Q.B.), the maternal grandparents were granted joint custody of the children together with the mother. The father had abandoned his custody claim and the grandparents had long been involved in the children's lives, given the allegations of child sexual abuse made against the mother's boyfriend.

In divorce proceedings between the natural parents of a child, leave to apply for custody should be granted to a non-parent where the claim is obviously not frivolous or vexatious. The application for leave should be decided on the basis of the information contained in the affidavit in support of the application and a prior bearing on the merits is not necessary: *M. (R). v. B. (G.)* (1987), 6 R.F.L. (3d) 441 (Nfld. T.D.).

In *Smith v. Smith* (1986), 75 A.R. 99 (Q.B.), the mother was granted custody of her infant child in the face of a guardianship application brought by the paternal grandparents. Although the child had, pursuant to the decree *nisi*, been in the joint care of the father and his parents, the mother had matured into a responsible custodian and the grandparents had attempted to poison the relationship between the mother and child contrary to a court order. The integrity of the natural parental relationship outweighed the advantage of the grandparent's superior station in life and greater experience.

In *Fisher v. Fisher* (1985), 166 A.P.R. 206, 70 N.S.R. (2d) 206 (T.D.), the court refused the application of the paternal grandparents to be included in the determination of the custody of their grandchildren. As the grandparents were not seeking custody themselves, their participation was not necessary to ensure full and effectual adjudication of the custody matter.

16§5B — Custody — changing child's name

Generally, changing a child's last name after a divorce is an emotional flashpoint which should be avoided if at all possible: *Lyon v. Lyon* (2004), 49 R.F.L. (5th) 122, 2004 CarswellOnt 1571 (Ont. S.C.J.).

16§6 — Right to custody

The law does not presume that the father or the mother has a greater right than the other to the custody of their child. Which parent is awarded custody is determined solely on the basis of "best interests" of the child. See *Divorce Act, 1985*, s. 16(8). Cases decided under the previous statute should be read with caution.

Divorce Act, 1985

In *Young v. Young*, [1993] 4 S.C.R. 3, 49 R.F.L. (3d) 117, 84 B.C.L.R. (2d) 1, [1993] 8 W.W.R. 513, 108 D.L.R. (4th) 193, the court held that the express wording of s. 16(8) of the *Divorce Act* requires the court to look *only* at the "best interests of the child" in making orders of custody and access. Consequently, no consideration should be given to parental preferences and "rights".

In *Gordon v. Goertz*, 19 R.F.L. (4th) 177, [1996] 2 S.C.R. 27, [1996] 5 W.W.R. 457, 196 N.R. 321, 134 D.L.R. (4th) 321, 141 Sask. R. 241, 114 W.A.C. 241, the Supreme Court of Canada held that where a non-custodial parent applies for a variation of a custody order to prevent the custodial parent from moving to another jurisdiction with the child, there is no legal presumption in favour of the custodial parent, although the custodial parent's views are entitled to great respect. The only test is the best interests of the child.

Custody should not be approached from the perspective of the mother's entitlement: *Gunn v. Gunn* (1994), 10 R.F.L. (4th) 197 (Man. C.A.).

Divorce Act, 1968

"[The husband] was not the father of the child. He never adopted the child. He is no longer married to the child's mother. His claim is advanced as one who stands in loco parentis to the child. The claim of the husband to custody of the child, based on so tenuous a relationship, must yield to the claim of the natural mother unless, by conduct, the natural mother has forfeited those rights which would normally accrue to her": *Gelfant v. Gelfant* (1980), 20 R.F.L. (2d) 337, 7 Man. R. (2d) 157 (C.A.), Huband J.A.

"If a Court is of the view that the scales are evenly balanced as to whether it is in the interests of the child to be with the father or mother, custody should be awarded to the former": per Bridges C.J.N.B. in *Re Hudson v. Hudson* (1968), 68 D.L.R. (2d) 191 at 193

(N.B. C.A.). See also *Bolster v. Bolster* (1953), 32 M.P.R. 143 (N.B. C.A.), where the principle relating to a father's common law right to custody was also applied.

Both parents have an equal right to the custody of their children, the determining factor being the children's welfare: *Nieforth v. Nieforth* (1974), 11 N.S.R. (2d) 10 at 14, 5 A.P.R. 10 at 14 (C.A.).

The principle that a father has a paramount right to the custody of his child has been weakened considerably: *Re Parks* (1976), 15 N.B.R. (2d) 43 (Q.B.).

In the determination of custody, the best interests of the children will prevail over a father's common law claim to a right to custody: *Richards v. Richards* (1978), 22 N.B.R. (2d) 107, 39 A.P.R. 107 (C.A.). See also *Boucher v. Boucher* (1975), 11 N.B.R. (2d) 697, 7 A.P.R. 697 (Q.B.).

16§7 — "Best interests (welfare) of the child"

Pursuant to s. 16(8), custody and access orders are to be made on the sole basis of the best interests of the child of the marriage, qualified by the conditions, means, needs and other circumstances of the child. The best interests of the child is further qualified by the provision in s. 16(10) which states that "a child of a marriage should have as much contact with each spouse as is consistent with the best interests of the child and, for that purpose, [the court] should take into consideration the willingness of a person for whom custody is sought to facilitate such contact."

Under the *Divorce Act, 1968*, there appeared to be different tests for interim and final applications concerning custody. In applications for interim custody, the court would make a determination based on what was "fit and just" (s. 10), and for final applications, the court decided on the basis of what was "fit and just ... having regard to the conduct of the parties and condition, means and other circumstances of the spouses" (s. 11(1)). Effectively, there would seem to be little change in the test in determining custody of or access to a child, as the previous case law indicated that the best interests of the child was generally considered the paramount consideration. However, the new act emphasizes the best interests of the child as the *sole* criterion, as qualified in the Act.

Many of the provinces have statutory definitions of "best interests". For instance, see s. 24(2) of the Ontario *Children's Law Reform Act*, R.S.O. 1990, c. C-12. Further there is extensive case law interpreting the phrase "best interests".

Divorce Act, 1985

In *Gordon v. Goertz*, *supra*, the court held that where a non-custodial parent applies for a variation of a custody order to prevent the custodial parent from moving to another jurisdiction with the child, there is no legal presumption in favour of the custodial parent, although the custodial parent's views are entitled to great respect. The only test is the best interests of the child.

In *Young v. Young*, [1993] 4 S.C.R. 3, 49 R.F.L. (3d) 117, 84 B.C.L.R. (2d) 1, [1993] 8 W.W.R. 513, 108 D.L.R. (4th) 193, the court held that the express wording of s. 16(8) of the *Divorce Act* requires the court to look *only* at the "best interests of the child" in making orders of custody and access. Consequently, no consideration should be given to parental preferences and "rights".

Where the children had a close emotional bond with their mother but where the father was in a better position financially to meet their needs, custody was awarded to the mother. The children's psychological needs were more important than financial concerns: *K. (M.M.) v. K. (U.)* (1990), 28 R.F.L. (3d) 189, 76 Alta. L.R. (2d) 216, 109 A.R. 241 (C.A.); reversing (1990), 105 A.R. 102 (Q.B.); additional reasons at (1990), 106 A.R. 314 (Q.B.); leave to appeal refused (1991), 31 R.F.L. (3d) 366 (note), 78 Alta. L.R. (2d) 1x (note), 114 A.R. 80 (note), 131 N.R. 160 (note) (S.C.C.).

Where the mother had a gambling addiction, had removed the children from the matrimonial home and had earlier thwarted the father's access rights, the court dismissed her appeal from an order whereby the father was to be primary caregiver for 8 months of the year: *O'Quinn v. O'Quinn* (1998), 39 R.F.L. (4th) 414, 171 N.S.R. (2d) 122, 519 A.P.R. 122 (C.A.); affirming (1997), 165 N.S.R. (2d) 330, 495 A.P.R. 330 (S.C.).

Where the husband was bitter over a relationship that the wife had formed and was not likely to foster a positive relationship between the children and their mother, custody was awarded to the wife: *Carmichael v. Carmichael* (1991), 110 N.S.R. (2d) 21, 299 A.P.R. 21 (T.D.); reversed in part (1992), 43 R.F.L. (3d) 145, 115 N.S.R. (2d) 45, 314 A.P.R. 45 (C.A.).

In *Bérubé c. Massicotte* (15 mai 1992), C.A. Montréal 500-09-001650-910 (C.A. Qué), the court refused the husband's request that a transfer of custody from himself to his wife, which had been confirmed by court order, be delayed. The husband had made the request for income tax reasons, whereas the best interests of the child were the only criteria which the court could consider.

Where the father had suffered a brain injury which made him overly aggressive with the mother, primary care of the children was awarded to the mother. The father was not aggressive with the children and a parallel parenting scheme was accordingly ordered: *Brocker v. Brocker* (1998), 42 R.F.L. (4th) 143 (Alta. Q.B.).

Where the mother had always played the dominant role in the children's lives, she was granted custody. Although the father obviously loved the children he had no plans as to how he would care for them were he granted custody and had put his own interests ahead of those of the children soon after separation: *Jarrett v. Jarrett* (1994), 10 R.F.L. (4th) 24 (Ont. Gen. Div.); additional reasons (December 13, 1994), Doc. Cobourg D3871/93 (Ont. Gen. Div.); further additional reasons (February 1, 1995), Doc. Cobourg D3871/93 (Ont. Gen. Div.).

Where in the year following the parties' separation the wife had lived with three different men and had a number of other affairs, custody of the children was awarded to the husband upon divorce. The wife's search for romantic relationships did not provide the secure and constant environment required by the children: *Doucet v. Doucet* (1990), 105 N.B.R. (2d) 172, 264 A.P.R. 172 (Q.B.).

In *Williams v. Williams* (1988), 13 R.F.L. (3d) 321, 70 Nfld. & P.E.I.R. 331, 215 A.P.R. 331 (Nfld. T.D.), the mother was awarded custody of the parties' five-year-old child despite the fact that the mother suffered from bouts of depression and had been diagnosed as having Parkinson's disease. Although she had health problems, the mother had managed to care for the child and the child's interests were best served by remaining with the mother.

Divorce Act, 1968

"It is the duty, the primary duty, of a tribunal to seek to determine what will be best for the child. In order to reach a decision conditions and circumstances as they exist are of prime importance. In the final analysis one engages in an exercise of prophecy. The decision in the case should be based upon the Court's considered answer to the question, with which of the contestants will she be happier and most likely to attain her highest potential as a person. The word 'potential' is used, of course, in its broadest sense. This I believe to be the meaning of the expression 'welfare of the child'": per Clunis Co. Ct. J. in *Re G.* (1973), 14 R.F.L. 201 at 210–211, 1 O.R. (2d) 318, 40 D.L.R. (3d) 198 (Co. Ct.). But see the appeal judgment (1974), (sub nom. *Smith v. Goulet)* 19 R.F.L. 45, 5 O.R. (2d) 337, 50 D.L.R. (3d) 321 (C.A.), where a new trial was ordered citing, *inter alia*, the failure of Clunis Co. Ct. J. to deal fully with the child's welfare in determining custody.

"The welfare of children must not be measured by money only, or by physical comfort only. The word 'welfare' must be taken in its widest sense. The moral and religious welfare of the child must be considered as well as its physical well-being": per Richards C.J.Q.B. in *Re Phillips* (1954), 36 M.P.R. 97 at 101–102 (N.B. Q.B.), quoted with approval in *Re Arbeau* (1970), 3 R.F.L. 102, 3 N.B.R. (2d) 286 (Co. Ct.). See also *Houston v. Houston* (1975), 21 R.F.L. 65 (Ont. H.C.); *Layton v. Layton* (1973), 11 R.F.L. 79, 6 N.B.R. (2d) 68 (C.A.).

The age and sex of the child, the claims of affection of the respective parents, and the social and moral upbringing of the child are factors which relate to the welfare of the child: *Re Peddle* (1975), 7 Nfld. & P.E.I.R. 362 at 365–366, 3 A.P.R. 362 (Nfld. T.D.).

When considering the "welfare" of the children in a custody dispute, the court is not to restrict itself to the issues of love and affection. It is welfare in its largest sense that must be considered. The broad and long-range view of the interests and well-being of the children is the one to be taken, and not only whether the children would be happier in one place than another. Therefore where the father is able to provide for his children and the mother is dependent solely upon the generosity of another man, the welfare of the children will be better served by having the father as custodial parent: *MacEachern, Re* (1973), 4 Nfld. & P.E.I.R. 130 (Nfld. T.D.).

In *Barca v. Barca* (1972), 9 R.F.L. 78 at 85 (Alta. T.D.), Cullen J., made the following remarks in awarding the custody of an infant girl to her mother: "While one might wish for a happier life for Bonnie Mae than what she may have if continued in the custody of her mother, I must reject the hedonistic philosophy that happiness is of primary importance. I rather feel that the question of the welfare of the child is linked more to the child's development, and the engendered sense of creativity and fulfillment."

See also *Re Naugle* (1968), 2 N.S.R. 493 at 496 (T.D.).

16§8 — Children of tender years

Divorce Act, 1985

In *Struck v. Struck*, 47 R.F.L. (5th) 405, 2003 CarswellBC 2813, 2003 BCCA 623, 20 B.C.L.R. (4th) 242, 189 B.C.A.C. 291, 309 W.A.C. 291 (B.C. C.A.), the court, on appeal, reinstated one order granting custody of the parties' 17- month-old child to the father. The mother had a violent temper and the evidence supported the finding that the father had a more stable lifestyle and that he would facilitate access more readily than the mother.

In *Langtry v. Langtry* (1997), 27 R.F.L. (4th) 340, 85 B.C.A.C. 284 (C.A.), the mother was awarded custody of the parties' child, as well as of two older children born to her during a previous marriage. The father appealed and sought custody of the parties' child, who was six at the time of the trial. The appellate court, in dismissing the appeal, did not rely on any presumption in favour of the mother as primary caregiver.

The "tender years" doctrine is merely a factor to be considered in custody cases. It is not a rule of law: *Lancaster v. Lancaster* (1992), 38 R.F.L. (3d) 373, 109 N.S.R. (2d) 88, 297 A.P.R. 88 (C.A.).

Neither the "tender years" doctrine nor the argument that the needs of female children are best met by their mother are of any validity today: *Williams v. Williams* (1989), 24 R.F.L. (3d) 86 (B.C. C.A.).

In *Donnelly v. Donnelly* (1988), 85 N.S.R. (2d) 257, 216 A.P.R. 257 (T.D.), the "tender years" doctrine was applied in awarding custody of the parties' four-year-old daughter to the mother. A joint custody arrangement was not feasible as it was opposed by the mother and would require both parents to co-operate in discharging their parental responsibilities.

The custody of even young children is to be determined on the basis of the children's best interests and not on any gender bias relating to the parents: *Tyabji v. Sandana* (1994), 2 R.F.L. (4th) 265, 112 D.L.R (4th) 641 (B.C. S.C.).

Divorce Act, 1968

It is not part of the law of Saskatchewan that a female, by virtue of her sex alone, is inherently superior as a custodial parent, in the case of a child of tender years, to her husband: *Harden v. Harden* (1987), 6 R.F.L. (3d) 147, 54 Sask. R. 155 (C.A.).

The "tender years" principle should not be given much weight in custody applications, considering the substantial changes in society's attitude toward the ideal family situation. For many families, the idea that a mother is intrinsically better suited to care for a young child is anathema. In light of changing attitudes, each custody case must be decided on its own merits: *R. v. R.*, 34 R.F.L. (2d) 277, 26 Alta. L.R. (2d) 289, [1983] 5 W.W.R. 385 (C.A.).

In *Ferjan v. Ferjan* (1980), 19 R.F.L. (2d) 113, 4 Man. R. (2d) 346 (C.A.), custody of a six-year-old female child was awarded to her father, on appeal, where it was found in the circumstances that the trial judge had placed unwarranted emphasis on the factor of children of tender years being awarded to the mother. The mother's plans for the child were extremely vague and unstable while the father offered a reasonable plan to the court. The evidence did not support the trial judge's finding that the parties were evenly matched in all important respects.

It is now well-established that there is equality in the claims of the father and mother as to the custody of their infants. There is no principle of law that the mother is *prima facie* entitled to the custody of children of tender years. This is particularly so in the case where both parents work. The rule that children of tender years belong with their mother is a rule of human sense rather than a rule of law. It is only one factor to be considered with all the circumstances: *Desilets v. Desilets* (1975), 22 R.F.L. 87, 60 D.L.R. (3d) 546 (Man. C.A.). See also *Nieforth v. Nieforth* (1974), 11 N.S.R. (2d) 10 at 14, 5 A.P.R. 10 at 14 (C.A.).

In *Hurley v. Hurley* (1982), 29 R.F.L. (2d) 145, 38 Nfld. & P.E.I.R. 29, 108 A.P.R. 29 (T.D.), custody of a young child was awarded to the father despite the court's consideration of the "tender years" doctrine. As the child had remained in the custody of the father in a highly stable environment prior to and throughout the proceedings, it was held that the existing satisfactory arrangements should not be disturbed. Further, the facts that the father had more available time to spend with the child and that the mother was living with another man favoured the father as custodial parent.

There must be a very strong case before children of tender years will be ordered removed from the custody of their mother. This is not a rule or presumption of law so much as a rule of human sense. Therefore, where the children are in the custody of the father, but their care is largely in the hands of the paternal grandmother or a stepmother, it would be preferable, all things being equal, that the natural mother be granted custody: *Bratland v. Bratland* (1976), 29 R.F.L. 34 (B.C. S.C.). See also *Cress v. Cress* (1981), 25 R.F.L. (2d) 59 (Ont. H.C.); *Talsky v. Talsky* (1975), 21 R.F.L. 27, [1976] 2 S.C.R. 292, 7 N.R. 246, 62 D.L.R. (3d) 267; *Re Taylor* (1976), 14 N.B.R. (2d) 578 (Q.B.); *Conrad v. Conrad* (1973), 7 N.S.R. (2d) 684 (T.D.); *Haughn v. Haughn* (1974), 8 N.B.R. (2d) 428 (C.A.).

Henderson v. Henderson, 29 R.F.L. 1 at 29, [1977] 3 W.W.R. 316 (B.C. Prov. Ct.), citing *Re Orr*, [1933] O.R. 212, [1933] 2 D.L.R. 77 (C.A.). See also *Peter v. Peter* (1974), 17 R.F.L. 80 (B.C. S.C.).

In *Mes v. Mes* (1981), 24 R.F.L. (2d) 257 (Ont. H.C.), custody of the children of the marriage, aged five and seven, was awarded to the father. It was held that in this case the rule of common sense that the custody of children of tender years should be awarded to the mother had to give way to more pressing considerations, one such consideration being the father's superior capability to deal with the emotional problems of the eldest child.

Where children are females of tender years and the mother is available to look after them and there is no evidence that she is not a fit and proper person to do so, the welfare and happiness of the children will best be served by ordering custody to the mother: *Sayre v. Sayre* (1980), 6 Sask. R. 31 (Q.B.); *Miron v. Miron* (1978), 10 A.R. 550 at 553 (T.D.).

See also *Vosper v. Vosper* (1981), 28 B.C.L.R. 252 (S.C.); *Skubovius v. Skubovius* (1977), 1 R.F.L. (2d) 284 (Man. Q.B.); *Andrew v. Andrew* (1980), 16 R.F.L. (2d) 129 (B.C. S.C.); *Barrios v. Barrios* (1978), 4 R.F.L. (2d) 347, 28 N.S.R. (2d) 419, 43 A.P.R. 419 (T.D.); *MacKinnon v. MacKinnon* (1978), 28 N.S.R. (2d) 541, 43 A.P.R. 541 (T.D.); *Somers v. Somers* (1976), 15 N.B.R. (2d) 311 at 312–313 (Q.B.); *Re Thorne* (1976), 29 R.F.L. 384, 16 N.B.R. (2d) 254 (Q.B.), *Ward v. Ward* (1975), 21 R.F.L. 387, 12 N.B.R. (2d) 163 (Q.B.); *Goerzen v. Goerzen* (1975), 24 R.F.L. 271 at 273–274, 11 O.R. (2d) 401, 66 D.L.R. (3d) 217 (H.C.); *Berger v. Berger* (1974), 17 R.F.L. 216 (Ont. S.C.).

"Ordinarily with a child of nine, I would incline, all other things being equal, towards the mother when considering the infant's custody. This case, however, presents difficulties": *Hayre v. Hayre* (1973), 11 R.F.L. 188 at 190 (B.C. S.C); affirmed (1976), 21 R.F.L. 191 (B.C. C.A.), McIntyre J., awarding custody to father to enable son to be reared as a Sikh; *Gauci v. Gauci* (1972), 9 R.F.L. 189, [1973] 1 O.R. 393, 31 D.L.R. (3d) 257 (H.C.); *Farkasch v. Farkasch* (1971), 4 R.F.L. 339, [1972] 1 W.W.R. 429, 22 D.L.R. (3d) 345 (Man. Q.B.); *Torresan v. Torresan* (1971), 6 R.F.L. 16 at 17 (B.C. S.C.).

16§9 — Custody awarded to father

Divorce Act, 1985

In *Struck v. Struck*, 47 R.F.L. (5th) 405, 2003 CarswellBC 2813, 2003 BCCA 623, 20 B.C.L.R. (4th) 242, 189 B.C.A.C. 291, 309 W.A.C. 291 (B.C. C.A.), the court, on appeal, reinstated one order granting custody of the parties' 17- month-old child to the father. The mother had a violent temper and the evidence supported the finding that the father had a more stable lifestyle and that he would facilitate access more readily than the mother.

The appellate court in *Circelli v. Circelli* (1999), 47 R.F.L. (4th) 121, 120 O.A.C. 189 (C.A.), held that it is an error to grant an order of permanent custody on affidavit evidence, that is, without conducting a trial of that issue. The parties had provided affidavit evidence and an assessor had recommended in a report that the children be placed in the father's day-to-day care. It would have been appropriate for the motions judge to award interim custody to the father, as he found that it would have been in the children's best interests to have the predictability and reliability of the father's care. The appeal was allowed and the father was granted interim custody of the two children.

Where a court awards sole custody to the father, when such relief has not been requested but instead both parties have asked for joint custody, the trial judge will not have exceeded his jurisdiction in making a sole custody order: *Brundrett v. Brundrett* (1998), 35 R.F.L. (4th) 131, 212 A.R. 11, 168 W.A.C. 11, 1998 CarswellAlta 48 (C.A.). While it would be preferable for a trial judge in these circumstances to inform counsel that he is contemplating a sole custody order, sole custody was one of the options open to the trial judge. The judge's conduct amounted, at most, to a procedural error.

In *Brooke v. Grandin*, 37 R.F.L. (5th) 23, 2003 CarswellBC 476, 2003 BCSC 344 (B.C. S.C.), the father was awarded custody of the parties' 3-year-old child with supervised access to the mother. The mother had made a number of unsubstantiated abuse claims against the father and, on more than one occasion, had removed the child from the country surreptitiously. Many of the mother's decisions had been impulsive and not in the child's best interests and called into question her psychological stability.

In *Savidis v. Savidis* (2003), 49 R.F.L. (5th) 219, 2003 CarswellOnt 4042 (Ont. S.C.J.), custody of the parties' three children was awarded to the father. The mother was challenged to meet her own needs, let alone those of the children. In addition she had made unsubstantiated claims of child abuse against the father, was unable to control the children, was repeatedly relocating with the children and interfered with the father's access rights.

In *C. (B.A.) v. C. (D.L.)*, 48 R.F.L. (5th) 15, 2003 CarswellBC 3143, 2003 BCCA 672 (B.C. C.A.), the court upheld on appeal an order awarding the custody of the parties' children to the father. The mother had made unfounded allegations of child abuse against the father and had seriously distorted facts so as to denigrate him. Were the wife to have custody, she would likely disregard the children's interests in having a meaningful relationship with their father.

Where the mother had a history of depression and had twice attempted suicide and was also on medication for depression, bulimia and obsessive/compulsive disorder, the best interests of the child favoured the father as interim custodial parent in *Flegel v. Mazoka* (1999), 48 R.F.L. (4th) 90, 1999 CarswellSask 258 (Q.B.); reversed (1999), 180 Sask. R. 128, 205 W.A.C. 128, 1999 CarswellSask 459 (C.A.).

In *Dinelle v. Sametz* (1994), 7 R.F.L. (4th) 277 (Ont. Gen. Div.) custody of the parties' 4 children was awarded to the father. The mother was under treatment for a psychiatric disorder and the children would be better off with the father who, although he was a recovering alcoholic, had demonstrated that he was a caring and concerned parent.

Where the evidence supported the husband's allegation that the wife had suffered both alcohol and drug problems and that she had previously depleted the family's bank account to support her addiction, custody of the parties' two children was awarded to the father. The mother's parenting abilities had been marred by her substance abuse, and the home environment that she had created would pose a risk to the children: *Curr v. Curr* (1993), 50 R.F.L. (3d) 84, 13 Alta. L.R. (3d) 289, 144 A.R. 16 (Q.B.).

Where the mother's behaviour towards her children had been unstable and erratic, including harsh physical punishment and verbal abuse, custody was awarded to the father: *Hill v. Hill* (1993), 114 Sask. R. 29 (Q.B.).

Where the mother had dismissed the children's allegations that they had been molested by a maternal uncle, dismissed her daughter's contemplation of suicide as unimportant and had discouraged the children's relationship with the father, custody was awarded to the father. Whereas the mother had failed to provide proper parenting, the father could provide a stable, caring environment: *F. (C.) v. F. (R.)* (1992), 82 Man. R. (2d) 225 (Q.B.).

Where both the mother and her common law boyfriend had criminal records, the mother's application for custody was dismissed. The child had been primarily in her father's care where she enjoyed a stable environment. It was not in her best interests to expose her to the instability and potential harm of her mother and her companion: *Simpson v. Simpson* (1992), 99 Sask. R. 266 (Q.B.).

In *Carpenter v. Carpenter* (1991), 93 Nfld. & P.E.I.R. 279, 292 A.P.R. 279 (Nfld. T.D.), custody of the parties' child was awarded to the husband. The wife had left the child with the husband at the time of separation and he had provided a stable environment. The wife, on the other hand, had limited financial ability to care for the child and was currently living with a married man who had not commenced divorce proceedings.

In *Roy v. Roy* (1991), 118 N.B.R. (2d) 347, 296 A.P.R. 347 (Q.B.), custody of the parties' child was awarded to the husband. The husband had provided a stable home for the child since the parties' separation and, as the wife could not cope with her own psychological problems, the child's best interests would be served with the husband.

Where the mother had left the children in the husband's care at the time of separation and had virtually no contact with them for the following three years, her application for custody of the two youngest children was dismissed. The husband and his new partner had provided a loving, stable environment for the children and their interests would not be served by disrupting their lives. Furthermore, the wife had been hospitalized with psychiatric problems four times since the parties' separation: *Dodeman v. Dodeman* (1991), 107 N.S.R. (2d) 113, 290 A.P.R. 113 (T.D.).

Where the mother's allegations the father had sexually abused the child were not supported by evidence and given the fact that the husband was better able to provide structure, direction and consistency in the home environment, custody of the six-year-old child was awarded to the husband: *Whyte v. Whyte* (1991), 101 N.S.R. (2d) 249, 275 A.P.R. 249 (T.D.).

Where the parties' five-year-old daughter had been in the father's care for the past three years, during which the mother had not exercised full access rights, the father's application for custody was granted. Although both parties' had stable relationships, the child was doing well in a stable and caring home and any disruption of that was not justified: *Roberts v. Roberts* (1991), 104 N.S.R. (2d) 27, 283 A.P.R. 27 (T.D.).

Where the mother had already perjured herself in the course of the custody hearings and evidence indicated that, as a result of psychological problems, she would do anything to achieve her goals, regardless of the children's best interests, custody was awarded to the father: *Hanson v. Hanson* (1989), 97 A.R. 228 (Q.B.).

In *Basha v. Basha* (1988), 74 Nfld. & P.E.I.R. 92, 231 A.P.R. 92 (Nfld. T.D.), custody of the parties' five-year-old daughter was granted to the father. The child's interests would be thereby best served as the father retained possession of the family home and as his workday ended at 3:30 p.m., whereas the mother's ended at 7:30 p.m.

Where the mother suffered from paranoid psychosis and often refused to take her medication and to visit her regular psychiatrist, an order granting custody of the children to the father was confirmed on divorce proceedings: *MacDonald v. MacDonald* (1986), 75 N.B.R. (2d) 318, 188 A.P.R. 318 (Q.B.).

In *Gagne v. Gagne* (1986), 42 Man. R. (2d) 231 (Q.B.), the father was granted custody of the children despite the fact that the mother was considered to be better qualified to act as custodial parent. The mother exhibited exaggerated fear of the father which was not in the children's best interests and, if she were made custodial parent, would likely become an obstacle to continued access by the father.

Where the mother indicated that if granted custody she would not allow the children any contact with the father, the father was granted custody. Although the mother's concerns over the father's fitness as a parent were genuine in her own mind, they were without foundation, and it was in the children's best interests to maintain contact with both parents: *Hayes v. Hayes* (1990), 82 Nfld. & P.E.I.R. 299, 257 A.P.R. 299 (Nfld. U.F.C.).

Where the father had been very involved in his children's lives and could provide them with a stable home in familiar surroundings, he was awarded custody of the three children, all of whom were under the age of six. The father's calm personality better suited the children's interests than their mother's ambitious temperament: *Tyabji v. Sandana, supra*.

Where the father was able to offer a more stable environment for the children and the mother tended to put her interests first and had previously made false accusations against the father, custody was awarded to the father: *Dupont v. Dupont* (1993), 47 R.F.L. (3d) 273 (B.C. S.C.).

In *Alain v. Alain* (1993), 119 N.S.R. (2d) 435, 330 A.P.R. 435 (S.C.), custody of the parties' 10-year-old son was granted to the father despite the fact that in the past the father had been abusive, had shown little interest in the child and had been content to leave the child with the mother at the time of separation. The child had a history of behavioural problems at school and the mother could not provide him with the guidance, structure and stimulation which he required. The child would have a better chance of breaking his past behavioural pattern if he remained in the father's care.

Divorce Act, 1968

Where the mother suffered from multiple sclerosis and was not really capable of looking after both herself and her daughter, custody of the daughter was awarded to the father: *Cronkhite v. Cronkhite* (1978), 20 N.B.R. (2d) 447, 34 A.P.R. (Q.B.); varied on other grounds (1978), 22 N.B.R. (2d) 510, 39 A.P.R. 510 (C.A.).

In *Tyndale v. Tyndale* (1985), 48 R.F.L. (2d) 426 (Sask. Q.B.), custody of the parties' three children was awarded to the father who was self-employed and had more flexible hours than the wife. The children were more likely to remain in contact with both parents if custody was awarded to the father.

Where the mother, who was a cocktail waitress, often stayed out late after working hours and was frequently intoxicated and neglectful of her children, custody was awarded to the father, who exhibited a better attitude toward the children: *Kitchen v. Kitchen* (1983), 26 Sask. R. 7 (Q.B.).

Until the marriage breakdown, the husband was always with the children when the wife was absent from the home because of work commitments. Now she would have to bring in somebody as a substitute mother during these periods of travel. As I have already indicated, the father can organize his hours of work so that there would be relatively little interference with his day-to-day personal care of the children. They will have the advantage of continuity if they remain with their father. In my view, their total welfare would be best served by awarding custody to the husband": per Pennell J. *Elbaz v. Elbaz* (1980), 16 R.F.L. (2d) 336, 29 O.R. (2d) 207, 114 D.L.R. (3d) 116 (H.C.).

See also *Peskett v. Peskett* (1979), 14 R.F.L. (2d) 134 (B.C. S.C.); *Smith v. Smith* (1978), 3 R.F.L. (2d) 13 (B.C. S.C.); *Gabriel v. Gabriel* (1977), 13 Nfld. & P.E.I.R. 104, 29 A.P.R. 104 (Nfld. T.D.); *Ellis v. Ellis* (1976), 27 R.F.L. 199 (B.C. S.C.); *Boone v. Boone* (1976), 15 Nfld. & P.E.I.R. 349 at 353, 38 A.P.R. 349 at 353 (Nfld. T.D.); *Ploughman v. Ploughman* (1972), 3 Nfld. & P.E.I.R. 489 at 493–494 (Nfld. T.D.), awarding custody to the father.

16§10 — Custody — child's preference

The expressed wish of children of tender years to stay in a particular location is only one circumstance to be weighed in an application by the custodial parent to relocate in another jurisdiction: *Myketiak v. Myketiak*, 13 R.F.L. (5th) 431, 203 Sask. R. 90, 240 W.A.C. 90, 2001 SKCA 17, 2001 CarswellSask 84 (C.A.), affirming (1999), 185 Sask. R. 231, 1999 CarswellSask 693 (Sask. Q.B.).

Divorce Act, 1985

The wishes of a 12-year-old child cannot be the sole basis for determining the question of custody: *Leblue v. Leblue* (1997), 33 R.F.L. (4th) 118, 209 A.R. 227, 160 W.A.C. 227 (C.A.). Generally, a contested permanent change of custody should only occur after a *vive voce* hearing.

Where the trial judge, in awarding custody of the parties' children to the father, had accepted the findings of the assessing psychologist that these children had no clear preference of one parent over the other, the court rejected the mother's appeal from the order. The judge had not erred in determining that the children's views had been adequately investigated and there was no application requesting the preparation of an Official Guardian's report. If prepared at the court's own request, the litigation would continue and would subject the children to pressures inconsistent with their best interests: *Lougheed v. Sillett* (1994), 6 R.F.L. (4th) 10 (Ont. C.A.).

Where the child's preference as to the custody had been inconsistent, a custody award based largely on the child's statements of preference was overturned on appeal in *Docherty v. Beckett* (1989), 21 R.F.L. (3d) 92 (Ont. C.A.).

Although a child's wishes are not necessarily determinative of custody, there comes a point when at near-adult years a child, capable of responsible thought, must be deemed to be able to settle his or her own future. In *Alexander v. Alexander* (1988), 15 R.F.L. (3d) 363 (B.C. C.A.), a 14-year-old child was found to have reached such a point.

The views of the child in a custody dispute were given no weight where it was clear that they had not been arrived at independently: *Boukema v. Boukema* (1997), 31 R.F.L. (4th) 329 (Ont. Gen. Div.); additional reasons at (December 19, 1997), Doc. 94-ND-212384 (Ont. Gen. Div.).

The wishes of the children is not the basis upon which a custody award to either parent should be made. The test is the welfare and best interests of the children: *Demeter v. Demeter* (1996), 21 R.F.L. (4th) 54, 133 D.L.R. (4th) 746 (Ont. Gen. Div.).

The court is entitled to admit hearsay evidence of a child's wishes in a custody case where such evidence appears reliable and relevant. The weight to be accorded such evidence, however, is a matter for the judge to determine: *Lapierre v. Lapierre* (1991), 34 R.F.L. (3d) 129 (Sask. Q.B.).

It is inappropriate to make a custody order in respect of children aged 13 and 15. Children of those ages are able to decide their own living arrangements: *House v. Tunney (House)* (1991), 35 R.F.L. (3d) 68 (Sask. Q.B.).

The wishes of a 12-year-old child should be seriously considered in a custody dispute: *Smith v. Smith* (1991), 34 R.F.L. (3d) 367, 117 N.B.R. (2d) 81, 295 A.P.R. 81 (Q.B.). See also *Metz v. Metz* (1991), 34 R.F.L. (3d) 255 (Sask. Q.B.); additional reasons at (1991), 36 R.F.L. (3d) 419 (Sask. Q.B.), in which custody was awarded in accordance with the wishes of children aged 13 and 11.

In *Power v. Power* (1987), 65 Nfld. & P.E.I.R. 1, 199 A.P.R. 1 (Nfld. T.D.), the husband was granted custody of the children, ages 19, 12, and 10 based upon the children's wishes and the fact that the wife had a volatile temper.

In *Young v. Young* (1989), 19 R.F.L. (3d) 227 (Ont. H.C.), the wishes of the children, aged 13 and 11, to be placed in the custody of their father was overridden by the fact that the father's abuse of their mother raised serious concerns as to his parenting ability. Accordingly, the children's best interests required that they be placed with their mother.

It is inappropriate for the court to interview a 12-year-old child concerning his custody preferences, given the child's age, lack of maturity and the possible trauma which may result: *Mamchur v. Mamchur* (1987), 11 R.F.L. (3d) 66 (B.C. S.C.).

Divorce Act, 1968

Although the wishes of a child are properly considered in determining custody, the best interests of the child do not necessarily correspond with those wishes: *Jespersen v. Jespersen* (1985), 48 R.F.L. (2d) 193 (B.C .C.A.).

"Children must not write their own order of custody nor dictate their wishes to the court. ... The sole duty of the court [in a review of custody] is to ascertain that there have been material changes such as to warrant the court disturbing a prior order. I repeat that custody is always open but prior decisions must carry great weight and be disturbed only when new evidence or undisclosed circumstances are such that, if proven, they warrant disturbing the prior order": *Jandrisch v. Jandrisch* (1980), 16 R.F.L. (2d) 239, 3 Man. R. (2d) 135 (Man. C.A.), Monnin J.A.

"The infants were represented by counsel who informed the court that the children were willing to be examined. The learned judge, in his discretion, decided not to examine them, however. This is a matter within his discretion. The evidence presented what he described as a shameful situation with the entire family torn apart and sharply divided. In his view no good could come of bringing the young children into the bitter conflict and he had the right to so decide": *Wakaluk v. Wakaluk* (1976), 25 R.F.L. 292 at 293 (Sask. C.A.), Woods J.A.

In *Shapiro v. Shapiro* (1973), 33 D.L.R. (3d) 764 (B.C. C.A.), the Court of Appeal awarded custody to the father despite the trial judge's finding that he turned his daughter against the mother and secured her confidence by manipulation and maneuvering. Per Branca J.A.: "No matter how that feeling on the part of the daughter was induced, it is present and real, and the daughter now honestly wishes to be with her father. I cannot conceive in ordinary circumstances why the wishes of a girl of 15 years of age, who, without necessarily any fault on the part of the mother, has turned against her should be ignored by a Court. In other circumstances not present here, the result might be otherwise."

"I am in agreement with the reasoning in the decision in *Stevenson v. Florant*, [1925] S.C.R. 532, [1925] 4 D.L.R. 530, where it was laid down that the welfare of the child is not to be confused with the wishes of the child and it is the duty of the Court to decide what is best for the child, even though the child expresses a strong preference for one parent": per Tuckern J. in *Farden v. Farden* (1970), 3 R.F.L. 315 at 322–323 (Sask. Q.B.); affirmed (1972), 8 R.F.L. 183 (Sask. C.A.).

The preferences of the children should be taken into account in a custody dispute even where the non-custodial parent may possibly have manoeuvred and manipulated the children: *Bechard v. Bechard* (1985), 45 Sask. R. 63 (Q.B.).

The burden of deciding whether to live with his father or mother should not be placed upon a 10-year-old child: *McCartney v. McCartney* (1985), 49 R.F.L. (2d) 69, 36 Man. R. (2d) 238 (Q.B.).

See also *Camick v. Camick* (1975), 26 R.F.L. 98, 12 N.B.R. (2d) 463 (Q.B.); *Loewen v. Loewen* (1982), 29 R.F.L. (2d) 25 (B.C. S.C.); *Thatcher v. Thatcher* (1980), 16 R.F.L. (2d) 263, 7 Sask. R. 95 (Q.B.); *Re Kuehn* (1976), 29 R.F.L. 72 at 85, 2 B.C.L.R. 97 (S.C.); *Grass v. Grass* (1977), 17 N.B.R. (2d) 4 at 7 (Q.B.); *Hatzioannidis v. Hatzioannidis (Hadson)* (1976), 29 R.F.L. 200 at 201–202, (sub nom. *H. v. H.)* 13 O.R. (2d) 371, 71 D.L.R. (3d) 161 (H.C.); *Sharpe v. Sharpe* (1974), 14 R.F.L. 151 (Ont. H.C.); *Makins v. Makins* (1978), 2 R.F.L. (2d) 104 (Ont. U.F.C.); *Martin v. Martin* (1976), 15 Nfld. & P.E.I.R. 317 at 335, 38 A.P.R. 317 (Nfld. T.D.); *Copithorne v. Copithorne* (1976), 2 A.R. 431 at 434 (T.D.); *Saxon v. Saxon*, 17 R.F.L. 257, [1974] 6 W.W.R. 731 (B.C. S.C.); *Rudd v. Rudd* (1972), 10 R.F.L. 22 at 26 (Ont. H.C.); *Dominix v. Dominix* (1972), 7 N.S.R. (2d) 270 (T.D.).

16§11 — Disruption of child's environment

Divorce Act, 1985

In custody and access matters, if the court is unable to decide which of the parent's plans better favours the child's best interests, the result must be in accord with the legal status quo: *Carter v. Brooks* (1990), 30 R.F.L. (3d) 53, 2 O.R. (3d) 321, 41 O.A.C. 389, 77 D.L.R. (4th) 45 (C.A.).

Where the children, immediately after the parties' separation, had moved with the mother and settled in a new community, the father's application for custody was dismissed. The children had adjusted well to their new community and school and the situation did not warrant a change in custody: *Woloshyn v. Woloshyn* (1996), 22 R.F.L. (4th) 129, 109

Man. R. (2d) 35 (Q.B.); affirmed (1997), 28 R.F.L. (4th) 70, 115 Man. R. (2d) 225, 139 W.A.C. 225 (C.A.).

Where the custodial mother threatened to move for personal reasons regardless of the children's wishes, it was ordered, in the context of the parties' divorce proceedings, that the father be given notice of any such move to permit him to act to protect the children's interests: *Katz v. Katz* (1989), 21 R.F.L. (3d) 167 (Ont. U.F.C.).

Divorce Act, 1968

The "status quo" rule is relevant only in an application for interim custody, and not one where permanent custody is sought: *R. v. R.*, 34 R.F.L. (2d) 277, [1983] 5 W.W.R. 385 (Alta. C.A.).

After being in the custody of their grandparents in Winnipeg for five years, the court refused the custody application of the father, who proposed to remove the children to their native Trinidad. Considering the time in which the children had lived in their present environment, the possible trauma occasioned by their exposure to a different culture, civilization and religion necessitated that the status quo be preserved: *Delvenne v. Nabbie*, 4 R.F.L. (2d) 21, [1978] 2 W.W.R. 439 (Man. C.A.).

"It seems to me that to uproot the children from this environment at this time and award custody to their father would have a traumatic effect on the children. Surely, where children are healthy and happy and doing well at their school work it would be gambling with their future to suggest that they would be better off by moving them to a totally new and different environment with different custodial care": *Dykes v. Dykes* (1977), 24 N.S.R. (2d) 527 at 536, 35 A.P.R. 527 (T.D.), Morrison J. See also *Spencer v. Spencer* (1980), 20 R.F.L. (2d) 91 (B.C. C.A.).

"The respondent [husband], in his argument, has suggested that I should take judicial notice of the detrimental effect upon the child of moving from the G. home to the S. home. There was no evidence in this regard. The child's doctor was called as a witness, but he was not asked for his opinion and gave none. I should think that one must recognize that a move of this kind will have an effect on a child. I realize this is a factor to be considered. In the absence of evidence, it must bear limited weight. In her seven-and-a-half years this little girl has had her home life disturbed four times. The most recent move was to the home where she has lived for two months. There was no evidence of ill effects and I observed none when I spoke with her. In any event, the child's welfare is not to be thought of as extending over a short span. It must be regarded in terms of the next 10 to 12 years or longer": per Clunis Co. Ct. J. in *Re G.* (1973), 14 R.F.L. 210 at 211, 1 O.R. (2d) 318, 40 D.L.R. (3d) 198 (Co. Ct.); reversed on other grounds (1974), (sub nom. *Smith v. Goulet)* 19 R.F.L. 45, 5 O.R. (2d) 337, 50 D.L.R. (3d) 321 (C.A.).

In *McPherson v. McPherson* (1982), 31 R.F.L. (2d) 380 (Sask. Q.B.), the wife's application for custody of the children, age seven and 11, was dismissed. The children had been placed in the father's custody pursuant to the terms of a separation agreement and as both parties were equally suitable as parents there was no reason justifying the disruption of the status quo.

Custody of children aged five and one-and-a-half was awarded to the father where it was established that he was providing them with a familiar and stable environment, whereas the wife had recently entered into an unstable relationship with another man; *Re Howe* (1981), 38 N.B.R. (2d) 123, 100 A.P.R. 123 (Q.B.).

See also *Elias v. Elias* (1980), 14 R.F.L. (2d) 288, 8 Man. R. (2d) 114 (Q.B.); *Lawrence v. Lawrence* (1975), 24 R.F.L. 300 at 302, 13 N.B.R. (2d) 637 (Q.B.); *Skubovius v. Skubovius* (1977), 1 R.F.L. (2d) 284 (Man. Q.B.); *Smith v. Smith* (1978), 22 N.B.R. (2d) 418 at 420, 39 A.P.R. 418 (Q.B.); *Sutherland v. Sutherland* (1977), 4 R.F.L. (2d) 335 at 340 (Ont. H.C.); *Maloney v. LeBlanc*, 12 R.F.L. 368, [1974] 1 W.W.R. 443, 41 D.L.R. (3d) 463 (Alta. T.D.).

16§12 — Custody — financial resources of parents

"The paramount consideration [in determining the issue of custody] is the welfare of the children; subsidiary to this and as a means of arriving at the best answer to that question are ... the pecuniary circumstances of the father and the mother — not for the purpose of giving the custody to the parent in the better financial position to maintain and educate the children, but for the purpose of fixing the amount to be paid by one or both parents for the maintenance of the children": per Beck J.A. in *Leboeuf v. Leboeuf*, [1928] 1 W.W.R. 423 at 425, 23 Alta. L.R. 328, [1928] 2 D.L.R. 23 (C.A.).

Where the father was financially stable but had an alcohol problem and the mother, who would be irreproachable as custodial parent, earned an income below the poverty level, it was held that the best interests of the child necessitated that he remain in the custody of the father: *Re Goupil* (1972), 9 R.F.L. 87, 4 N.B.R. (2d) 602 (C.A.).

Where the wife removed the children from the rural matrimonial home to an apartment in an urban area, the court ordered that the children be returned to the custody of their father. The husband was able to support his wife and his children in a modest environment but his financial resources were not capable of keeping another home on the sophisticated basis required of urban living: *Skubovius v. Skubovius* (1977), 1 R.F.L. (2d) 284 at 285–286 (Man. Q.B.).

The fact that the father is possessed of insufficient funds to maintain a separate household for his wife and the younger children of the marriage may be a consideration in awarding custody to the father: *Barrios v. Barrios* (1978), 4 R.F.L. (2d) 347, 28 N.S.R. (2d) 419, 43 A.P.R. 419 (T.D.). See also *Re Reid* (1975), 25 R.F.L. 209 at 212, 11 O.R. (2d) 622, 67 D.L.R. (3d) 46 (Div. Ct.).

Where the petitioner husband lived in a beautiful home, had plenty of money and employed the services of a full-time housekeeper, while the respondent wife lived in an apartment, lacked adequate accommodation and had limited resources, it was held that the interests of the children would be better served if the father acted as custodial parent: *Grant v. Grant* (1975), 9 Nfld. & P.E.I.R. 33 (P.E.I. S.C.).

16§13 — Custody and religion

Divorce Act, 1985

In *S. (L.) v. S. (C.)*, [1997] 3 S.C.R. 1003, 37 R.F.L. (4th) 344, the trial judge had ordered that the mother be awarded custody of the child on the following conditions: 1. The mother could not bring the child with her for door-to-door preaching; 2. The child was not to attend religious reunions; 3. The mother was not to indoctrinate the child with the values of her religion in a continuous way. The Court of Appeal dismissed the mother's appeal, as if found that the mother's constitutional rights were not violated by the order. However, at the Supreme Court of Canada, the court allowing the appeal in part, held that the best interests of the child were not jeopardized by the mother's practices and the restrictions imposed upon the mother regarding her religious practices were removed.

The *Charter of Rights and Freedoms* does not protect religious expression which is not in the best interests of the child: *Young v. Young*, [1993] 4 S.C.R. 3, 49 R.F.L. (3d) 117, 84 B.C.L.R. (2d) 1, [1993] 8 W.W.R. 513, 108 D.L.R. (4th) 193. The court held that ss. 16(8) and 17(5) of the *Divorce Act*, 1985, which provide that judicial decisions regarding custody and access be made "in the best interests of the child," do not deny the rights and freedoms guaranteed in s. 2(a), (b) and (d) of the *Canadian Charter of Rights and Freedoms*. In the *Young* decision, however, the court held that the order forbidding the father, a Jehovah's Witness, from discussing religion with his children was not valid. Any perceived harm to the children could not be said to outweigh the benefits of unrestricted access.

In *Ligate v. Richardson* (1997), 34 O.R. (3d) 423 (C.A.), the mother, the custodial parent, on appeal, was allowed to move from Toronto to Cambridge with her child contrary to the parties' separation agreement and despite the fact the father had been the parent who was more active in looking after the child's religious training.

See *Voortman v. Voortman* (1994), 4 R.F.L. (4th) 250, 72 O.A.C. 252 (C.A.), a case decided under the *Children's Law Reform Act*, where the court held that in custody matters it was not for the court to decide as between two religions.

See also *Fruitman v. Fruitman* (1998), 37 R.F.L. (4th) 416 (Ont. Gen. Div.), where the mother's action for restriction of the father's access in order to conform to the children's upbringing of Orthodox Jewery was dismissed. The father, at the time of the hearing, was prepared to comply with the practices of Orthodox Jewery, but he did not want to commit to these practices in the future because of uncertainty regarding his employment. The court held that absent "harm" to the children, an access parent ought to be able to exercise access without restrictions. No harm to the children would likely occur if the father's access plan were followed.

In *Moseley v. Moseley* (1990), 25 R.F.L. (3d) 110, 102 A.R. 293 (Q.B.), the mother's application for custody was denied after the custodial father had been severely injured in an accident and had passed the care of the children along to his brother. The father had originally been granted custody because of concerns about the effects of the mother's religious beliefs upon the children, and these concerns continued.

Where neither party to a custody dispute actively practised his or her religion, the husband's claim based upon ensuring the child's religious upbringing was not persuasive: *White v. White* (1990), 28 R.F.L. (3d) 439 (B.C. S.C.).

In *McNeil v. McNeil* (1989), 20 R.F.L. (3d) 52 (B.C. S.C.), the wife's deep involvement with her fundamentalist religion was not a factor in her custody claim given that her religious practice did not pose serious parenting problems.

In the absence of evidence of actual or potential harm to the children, the fact that the children's religious beliefs differ from the parent seeking custody is not material to deciding which parent will best afford the future welfare of the children: *Barrett v. Barrett* (1988), 18 R.F.L. (3d) 186 (Nfld. T.D.).

In a custody dispute, the court is not to determine whether one parent's religion is better than the other's. It is only the effect of the religious involvement on the children that is relevant: *Harvey v. Lapointe* (1988), 13 R.F.L. (3d) 134 (Que. S.C.).

Divorce Act, 1968

The courts should support the reasonable right of a custodial parent to determine the religion of the children. Accordingly, where the non-custodial father was attempting to persuade the children to adopt a faith different from their mother's, an order was made prohibiting him from continuing to do so: *Fougère v. Fougère* (1987), 6 R.F.L. (3d) 314 (N.B. C.A.).

Although the court has no right to deny custody to a parent because of his or her religious beliefs, it is required to consider the effect of such beliefs on the welfare of the children: *Brown v. Brown* (1983), 39 R.F.L. (2d) 396, 29 Sask. R. 265, 3 D.L.R. (4th) 283 (C.A.).

In *Singh v. Singh* (1981), 26 R.F.L. (2d) 75 (Alta. C.A.), a custody order in favour of the wife was confirmed on appeal despite the fact that the children were to be raised in the father's Sikh religion and mother was not of that faith.

"In my view, the boy's interests require that the father have custody. This boy is a Sikh; he will always be regarded as a Sikh in this country. It will be well for him to be brought up as a Sikh, to preserve his existing knowledge of the Punjabi language, to be schooled in the religion and traditions of the people with whom he will always be associated. It will, in my view be possible for him to find a secure personal identity only in the Sikh community. It is the only identity our society will permit him. Let him, then, be a Sikh and be proud of the tradition and accomplishments of a proud and worthy race. No matter how much she loves him, his mother cannot accomplish this. I direct that custody of the boy be given to his father": per McIntyre J. in *Hayre v. Hayre* (1974), 11 R.F.L. 188 at 190–192 (B.C. S.C.); affirmed (1976), 21 R.F.L. 191 (B.C. C.A.).

In *Benoit v. Benoit* (1973), 10 R.F.L. 282 at 284 (Ont. C.A.), the father appealed the terms of an access order whereby he was prohibited from discussing with his children matters dealing with his religious beliefs or related subjects. In allowing the appeal, which was later confirmed by the Ontario Court of Appeal, Beardall Co. Ct. J. stated: "I do not think that any court has the right to decide that one form of religious instruction and belief is the true religion and that some other one is false, or to say that one is better than the other, but that all men are free to select their own religious belief and to practise it without interference by someone else thrusting upon them a religion that they do not care for. I have therefore come to the conclusion that the restriction as to the religious discussion contained in the learned Provincial Judge's order should be overruled."

In *Irmert v. Irmert* (1984), 64 A.R. 342 (C.A.); reversing in part (1983), 36 R.F.L. (2d) 260 (Alta. Q.B.), the court allowed the husband's appeal in part and granted custody of an older child to the husband, an active Jehovah Witness. The court made this order, considering it to be in the best interests of the child, keeping in mind this was the recommendation of the Amicus Curiae at trial and that the law is clear that the court must be neutral on religious disputes and that a parent cannot be found unfit for custody simply because of his or her religious beliefs and practice. However, it is also the duty of a parent to a child to refrain from the insensitive assertion of religious beliefs in circumstances where the child otherwise would suffer serious psychological harm. Other cases which consider custody and religion are *Brown v. Brown* (1978), 2 R.F.L. (2d) 165 (Sask. Q.B.); *Robb v. Robb* (1977), 2 R.F.L. (2d) 172, 27 N.S.R. (2d) 15, 41 A.P.R. 15 (Q.B.); *Re Murphy* (1976), 29 R.F.L. 161 at 170–171 (P.E.I. S.C.); *Gunn v. Gunn* (1975), 24 R.F.L. 182, 10 Nfld. & P.E.I.R. 159 (P.E.I. S.C.); *Re Pamela A., (an infant)* (1969), 1 N.S.R. (2d) 232 at 238–239 (T.D.); *Cortan v. Dessler* (1977), 4 R.F.L. (2d) 111 at 119 (Ont. Surr. Ct.).

16§14 — Custody and separation agreements

Irrespective of the terms of any agreement between the parties, a judge has jurisdiction in a motion for corollary relief to deal with all issues of custody and child support. While the agreement may be one factor to be taken into consideration when deciding a child's best interests, it is not necessary that a change in material provisions, as specified in the agreement's variation provisions, be established: *Jay v. Jay*, 41 R.F.L. (5th) 306, 2003 CarswellPEI 71, 2003 PESCAD 19 (P.E.I. C.A.).

Divorce Act, 1985

Although the jurisdiction to deal with the custody of children may be based in the *Divorce Act*, the obligation owed by the Ontario Court of Justice to ensure that any settlement or proposed order is in the best interest of the children remains: *Nickerson v. Nickerson* (1991), 34 R.F.L. (3d) 341, 4 O.R. (3d) 447 (Gen. Div.).

A separation agreement in itself cannot vest jurisdiction in a court to deal with custody or child support under the *Divorce Act*: *Cattani v. Mihalich* (1989), 22 R.F.L. (3d) 84 (Ont. Dist. Ct.).

Divorce Act, 1968

"It is the court's position that the agreements ... may well be a reflection of the thinking of the parties and to that end are instructive to the court in considering the issue of custody of the infant children, but that is no sense is the court bound by whatever the parties may have heretofore agreed to themselves when dealing with the custody of the infant children: per Green Prov. J. in *Henderson v. Henderson*, 29 R.F.L. 1, [1977] 3 W.W.R. 316 at 342–343 (B.C. Prov. Ct.): *Bickley v. Bickley*, [1957] S.C.R. 329, 7 D.L.R. (2d) 465, a decision of the Supreme Court of Canada".

An agreement between the parents as to the custody of their child is not binding on the court if the court in its discretion is of the opinion that it is not in the best interests of the child's physical, moral, emotional and spiritual welfare: *Clark v. Clark*, [1952] O.W.N. 671 (H.C.). See also *Re Allan and Allan* (1958), 16 D.L.R. (2d) 172 (B.C. C.A.); *Vienneau v. Vienneau* (1983), 52 N.B.R. (2d) 1, 137 A.P.R. 1 (Q.B.).

The court was unable to subscribe to a custody agreement which gave the wife access for three months of the year. It was not in the best interests of the children to provide her with custody during all school holiday periods. The court made its own custody order for the benefit of the children which did as much justice as possible to the agreement of the parents: *Watkins v. Watkins* (1980), 14 R.F.L. (2d) 97, 25 Nfld. & P.E.I.R. 98, 68 A.P.R. 98 (Nfld. T.D.).

"The separation and custody agreement is part of the evidence to be considered in determining the question of custody": per Nicholson J. in *Grant v. Grant* (1975), 9 Nfld. & P.E.I.R. 33 at 78 (P.E.I. S.C.).

16§15 — Separating siblings

Divorce Act, 1985

It may be appropriate to separate siblings where there is a successful *de facto* situation and the children have stable homes: *Poole v. Poole* (1999), 45 R.F.L. (4th) 56, 173 D.L.R. (4th) 299, 64 B.C.L.R. (3d) 70, 123 B.C.A.C. 272, 201 W.A.C. 272 (C.A.).

In *Langtry v. Langtry* (1997), 27 R.F.L. (4th) 340, 85 B.C.A.C. 284 (C.A.), the mother was awarded custody of the parties' child, as well as of two older children born to her during a previous marriage. The father appealed and sought custody of the parties' child, who was six at the time of the trial. The appellant court, in dismissing the appeal, emphasized the family unit of the mother, child and half-siblings remaining together.

Where the elder of the parties' two children wished to remain in the custody of his father, and the younger child was very close to his older brother, the court refused the mother's claim for custody of the younger child. The father appeared better able to care for the children and simply to ensure contact between the younger child and his mother did not justify separating the children: *Clark v. Clark* (1995), 18 R.F.L. (4th) 234, 139 Sask. R. 114 (Q.B.).

In *Lynch v. Lynch* (1995), 12 R.F.L. (4th) 367 (Ont. Gen. Div.); additional reasons (June 22, 1995), Doc. Barrie G3454 (Ont. Gen. Div.), the court rejected the mother's plan that one of the four children remain in her day to day control while the remaining three stay in the custody of the father. Although the child had experienced some behavioural problems it was not in his best interests that the children be divided.

Where the father had had interim custody of one child and the mother of the other two, custody of all three children was granted to the mother. The father had sought custody of only the child in his care while the mother wanted all three. In general, it is desirable that siblings remain together so that they may share their childhood together, show their affection for one another and support one another: *White v. White* (1994), 7 R.F.L. (4th) 414, 151 N.B.R. (2d) 10, 387 A.P.R. 10 (Q.B.).

Keeping siblings together is an important but not determining factor in custody applications, particularly where the children are not close in age. Accordingly, the husband was awarded custody of the 15-year-old son and the mother custody of the nine-year-old daughter where the son was extremely bitter towards his mother and the daughter required special care which the mother was better able to provide: *Jones v. Jones* (1994), 4 R.F.L. (4th) 293, 122 Sask. R. 114 (Q.B.).

A court, whether on a interim motion or at trial, should strive to ensure that siblings are raised together. Compelling evidence is required before a custody order will be made which has the effect of separating siblings in their formative years: *Hurdle v. Hurdle* (1991), 31 R.F.L. (3d) 349 (Ont. Gen. Div.).

In awarding custody, the court should only separate siblings under the most exceptional of circumstances: *Taylor v. Taylor* (1987), 83 N.B.R. (2d) 145, 212 A.P.R. 145 (Q.B.).

Divorce Act, 1968

It is a serious error in principle to award custody of some of the children of the marriage to the father on the basis that the birth of twins would reduce the wife's ability to meet the needs of her other children: *Sherrett v. Sherrett* (1987), 6 R.F.L. (3d) 172 (Ont. C.A.).

Where it is in the best interests of younger children to remain with their mother, the separation of siblings may be justified: *MacKenzie v. MacKenzie*, 9 R.F.L. (3d) 1, [1987] 5 W.W.R. 481 (Man. C.A.); varying on other grounds (1986), 42 Man. R. (2d) 73 (Q.B.).

Where it was feared that the separation of the two children of the marriage could only act to aggravate their difficulties, created by the misconduct and bitterness of the parents, custody of both was awarded to the father, despite the fact that he had deliberately attempted to turn the children against their mother: *Shapiro v. Shapiro* (1973), 33 D.L.R. (3d) 764 (B.C. C.A.).

The proposition that children should not be separated from each other unless "absolutely necessary" should not be elevated to a principle or rule of law. It is desirable, if it can be accomplished, to keep the children of a family together so that they may share the affection and support of each other and grow up with a sense of family solidarity. However, this is only one factor of the many that must be balanced and considered in determining what is in the best interest of the individual children respectively: *Zinck v. Zinck* (1973), 14 R.F.L. 106, 6 N.S.R. (2d) 622, 43 D.L.R. (3d) 157 (C.A.). See also *Barrios v. Barrios* (1978), 4 R.F.L. (2d) 347, 28 N.S.R. (2d) 419, 43 A.P.R. 419 (T.D.).

In *McCabe v. Ramsay* (1980), 19 R.F.L. (2d) 70, 31 Nfld. & P.E.I.R. 481, 87 A.P.R. 481 (P.E.I. S.C.), divided custody was awarded where a joint custody arrangement, which had been granted on a decree *nisi*, failed because of conflict between the parties. The children had been in the physical custody of their father and it was in the best interests of the two boys to remain with him as they had adjusted well to their home, school and neighbourhood. On the other hand, custody of the daughter, who had rejected the father and gone back to live with her mother, was awarded to the mother: *Wereley v. Wereley* (1979), 14 R.F.L. (2d) 193 (Ont. H.C.); *Knowles v. Knowles* (1977), 2 R.F.L. (2d) 396 (B.C. S.C.); *MacDonald v. MacDonald* (1977), 4 R.F.L. (2d) 368 (P.E.I. S.C.); *Foley v. Foley* (1976), 14 Nfld. & P.E.I.R. 26, 33 A.P.R. 26 (Nfld. T.D.). See also *Woerz v. Woerz* (1974), 17 N.S.R. (2d) 679 (T.D.); *Grant v. Grant* (1975), 9 Nfld. & P.E.I.R. 33 at 81 (P.E.I. S.C.); *MacDonald v. MacDonald* (1975), 10 Nfld. & P.E.I.R. 267 (P.E.I. S.C.); *Case v. Case* (1974), 18 R.F.L. 132 (Sask. Q.B.).

16§15A — Custody and evidence of abuse

The court has jurisdiction to find that a child has not been sexually abused at the hands of the father, but lacks the jurisdiction to make a declaration to that effect: *Nickerson v. Nickerson* (1991), 34 R.F.L. (3d) 341, 4 O.R. (3d) 447 (Gen. Div.).

In dealing with allegations of child abuse in custody disputes, the court should err on the side of caution. A professional's evidence, even if based upon hearsay, should not be easily rejected where the children's safety is at stake: *Migliore v. Migliore* (1989), 23 R.F.L. (3d) 131 (B.C. S.C.).

16§16 — Custody — spouse's past conduct

Pursuant to s. 16(9), a court in making the custody or access order is not entitled to take into account past conduct of any person "unless the conduct is relevant to the ability of that person to act as a parent of a child." Under the previous legislation the court was entitled to take into account the conduct of parties as well the condition, means and other circumstances of each of them before making a custody order: s. 11(1). Presumably, the current legislation is intended to eliminate evidence of past misconduct between the parties where it is not relevant to the parents' relationship to the child for whom custody or access is sought.

Note that there is no provision in the *Divorce Act, 1985*, prohibiting taking into account present conduct or future plans of the person seeking access or custody. Section 16(10) in emphasizing the importance of the willingness of the person for whom custody is sought in facilitating access to the non-custodial parent seems to take into account anticipated conduct of the prospective custodial parent.

Divorce Act, 1985

Where the husband was involved in a stable relationship at the time of the hearing of his custody claim, his past adultery was found to be irrelevant to the issue: *McNeil v. McNeil* (1989), 20 R.F.L. (3d) 52 (B.C. S.C.).

Where the husband had shown great animosity to the wife and had involved the children in the dispute, his application for custody was refused. Although the children had lived with their father most of the time pursuant to a joint custody agreement, their best interests now favoured the wife as custodial parent: *Nelson v. Nelson* (1990), 86 Sask. R. 10 (Q.B.).

In *Badakhshan v. Moradi* (1993), 120 N.S.R. (2d) 405, 332 A.P.R. 405 (Fam. Ct.), the fact that the mother had secretly removed the children from Nova Scotia to Ontario after the parties' separation was not a sufficient ground on which to deny her custody. The parties had married in Iran and the mother feared that the husband would take the children back there.

A parent's conduct is only relevant in custody proceedings insomuch as it affects the children's best interests and demonstrates a parent's willingness or lack of willingness to put those interests before his or her own: *Tyabji v. Sandana* (1994), 2 R.F.L. (4th) 265, 112 D.L.R. (4th) 641 (B.C. S.C.).

Divorce Act, 1968

"[A] wife who is 'well nigh impossible' as a wife may nevertheless be a wonderful mother": per Grandpré J. in *Talsky v. Talsky* (1975), 21 R.F.L. 27 at 29, [1976] 2 S.C.R. 292, 7 N.R. 246, 62 D.L.R. (3d) 301.

Where the Court of Appeal admitted new evidence indicating that the custodial mother had used her five-year-old child in the commission of a theft, subsequent to the dismissal of the husband's application for a variation of the custody provisions in the decree *nisi*, the husband's appeal from the dismissal was allowed and he was granted custody: *Nayar v. Nayar* (1981), 24 R.F.L. (2d) 400 (B.C. C.A.).

Where the father was living with another woman and the mother drank heavily and had been involved in several extra-marital affairs, custody of the children was awarded to the mother, the court having characterized the mother as a weak but honest person, as opposed to the father who was described as self-centred and occasionally dishonourable: *Re Miechkota* (1977), 19 N.B.R. (2d) 191, 30 A.P.R. 191 (Q.B.); affirmed (1978), 21 N.B.R. (2d) 373, 37 A.P.R. 373 (C.A.).

In reversing an earlier custody award, and thereby awarding custody of the children to their mother, the court made the following comments regarding the husband's conduct: "In the petition for divorce proceedings, the learned trial Judge found specific acts of cruelty on the part of the husband towards the wife. He found that the husband had committed acts of violence upon his wife, which the evidence disclosed was upon occasion inflicted in the presence of the children. He further found on four occasions that the husband had left the family household leaving the children with his wife, and on one occasion he was absent for a period of approximately two months. He further characterized the husband's attitude towards his wife as 'unloving and inconsiderate and harsh', and that his cruelty has rendered continued co-habitation intolerable for her. The husband has encouraged the children to reject and ignore their mother and has sought to destroy their love for her. All these factors, in my opinion, throw some light on his character and disposition. They are relevant in assessing his probable behaviour as a parent in the future and cast doubt upon his fitness as a father. In my opinion, the learned trial Judge erred in failing to take into consideration the conduct of the father as a relevant consideration in determining the issue of custody": *Wallin v. Wallin* (1974), 18 R.F.L. 122 at 126, 6 O.R. (2d) 33, 51 D.L.R. (3d) 677 (C.A.), Dubin J.A.; *Richardson v. Richardson* (1971), 4 R.F.L. 150, 17 D.L.R. (3d) 481 (Sask. Q.B.). See also *Dunne v. Dunne* (1973), 12 R.F.L. 210 at 211, 5 Nfld. & P.E.I.R. 335 (Nfld. T.D.).

While there may be cases in which consideration should be given to the question as to which spouse was responsible for the break-up of the marriage, such considerations should not detract from the primary concern: the welfare of the child or children. Thus, the consideration, if any, to be given to this factor depends entirely on the circumstances in each case. If this factor should be considered, any reliance thereon should never be punitive in character. In the instant case, little weight was given to the fact that the respondent [wife] was responsible for the break-up of the marriage. She was a good mother and a fit person to have the custody of the children, and in the circumstances the association which led to the marital break-up had been finally and completely ended: *Francis v. Francis* (1972), 8 R.F.L. 209 (Sask. C.A.).

In *Schreiner v. Schreiner* (1986), 49 Sask. R. 119 (Q.B.), custody of the parties' young daughter was awarded to the husband in light of evidence indicating that the wife placed her own desires before the child's welfare. During the marriage the wife frequently left the child with the husband when she was out late drinking and on one occasion, when the husband had moved with the child to another town, the wife made no effort to visit her for eight months.

Where the 31-year-old mother's relationship had led to the breakdown of the marriage, custody of the parties' four-and-a-half and two-year-old daughters was awarded to the father. Whereas the mother's continuation of the relationship indicated that it was unlikely she would put the children's needs ahead of her own, the father had adjusted his life-style to accommodate the children and had sought parenting advice: *Bosch v. Bosch* (1985), 49 R.F.L. (2d) 157, 45 Sask. R. 189 (Q.B.).

In *Cormier v. Cormier* (1983), 49 A.R. 232 (Q.B.), the husband was granted custody of the son despite a history of occasional alcohol abuse and wife battering. The husband had provided satisfactory care to the child in the three years after the separation and a special bond had developed between them. The husband was ordered, however, to seek counselling as a condition of the custody award.

Where the husband had difficulty controlling his drinking, custody of the children of the marriage was awarded to the wife, in spite of the fact that she was on social assistance. Considering all factors, the wife presented the better potential for stability: *Saboe v. Saboe* (1981), 26 R.F.L. (2d) 284 (Sask. Q.B.); affirmed in regard to custody and reversed in part on another issue (1981), 20 R.F.L. (2d) 284 (Sask. Q.B.); *Simms v. Simms* (1976), 5 Nfld. &. P.E.I.R. 238, 38 A.P.R. 238 (Nfld. T.D.). See also *Ferguson v. Ferguson* (1980), 16 R.F.L. (2d) 207, 28 Nfld. & P.E.I.R. 498, 79 A.P.R. 498 (P.E.I. S.C.); *Banda v. Banda*, 6 R.F.L. (2d) 261, [1978] 6 W.W.R. 130 (Sask. Q.B.); *D. v. D.* (1978), 3 R.F.L. (2d) 327, 20 O.R. (2d) 722, 88 D.L.R. (3d) 578 (Co. Ct.); *Rollason v. Rollason* (1978), 1 R.F.L. (2d) 97 (Ont. H.C.); *Adams v. Adams* (1971), 7 R.F.L. 203, 4 N.B.R. (2d) 275 (Q.B.); *Schaber v. Schaber* (1977), 3 A.R. 76 at 77 (T.D.); *Skubovius v. Skubovius* (1977), 1 R.F.L. (2d) 284 at 285 (Man. Q.B.); *Bolton v. Bolton* (1976), 26 R.F.L. 284 (P.E.I. S.C.); *Ellis v. Ellis* (1976), 27 R.F.L. 199 (B.C. S.C.); *Bowyer v. Bow-*

yer (1976), 27 R.F.L. 131 (Sask. Q.B.); *Smith v. Smith* (1975), 23 R.F.L. 126 (Ont. Div. Ct.); *Sinclair v. Sinclair* (1974), 17 R.F.L. 202 (Ont. H.C.); *Gauci v. Gauci* (1972), 9 R.F.L. 189 at 194, [1973] 1 O.R. 393, 31 D.L.R. (3d) 257 (H.C.); *Re Lessard* (1971), 3 R.F.L. 107 at 114 (Ont. Surr. Ct.).

16§17 — Custody and homosexuality

Divorce Act, 1985

The same-sex preference of a parent is merely one of many factors which the court should consider in determining the best interests of the children in a custody dispute: *Boots v. Sharrow*, 49 R.F.L. (5th) 260, 2004 CarswellOnt 25, (sub nom. *J.S.B. v. D.L.S.)* [2004] 3 C.N.L.R. 110 (Ont. S.C.J.).

Where the mother's homosexual relationship was found not to have a detrimental effect upon her child, the mother's custody was confirmed: *Daller v. Daller* (1988), 18 R.F.L. (3d) 53 (Ont. H.C.); reversed in part on other grounds (1989), 22 R.F.L. (3d) 96 (Ont. C.A.).

Divorce Act, 1968

Homosexuality, either as a tendency, a proclivity or a practised way of life, is not in itself a ground for refusing custody to the parent with respect to whom such evidence is given. The question is and must always be what effect upon the welfare of the children that aspect of the parent's make-up and lifestyle has, and it will therefore be a question of evidence in that very case as to whether what has been shown to exist has or may tend to have effects adverse to the welfare of the children: *Bezaire v. Bezaire* (1980), 20 R.F.L. (2d) 358 (Ont. C.A.).

In *Worby v. Worby* (1985), 48 R.F.L. (2d) 369 (Sask. Q.B.), the homosexual father was granted general access but denied overnight access as his living arrangements with another man could potentially be harmful to the children.

In *Droit de la famille — 31* (1983), 34 R.F.L. (2d) 127 (Que. S.C.), custody of the parties' three- and six-year-old daughters was granted to the husband. Although homosexuality itself was not an obstacle to custody, the parties lived in a small town, and the possibility existed that the wife's lifestyle could become public knowledge and the children hurt as a result of public reprobation. Furthermore, it was preferable that the children's custody be granted to their father to be brought up in a heterosexual milieu, thus guarding against the possibility that by living in a homosexual home with their mother, the two girls could form a proclivity later on in their lives to imitate their mother's sexual orientation. See also *Case v. Case* (1974), 18 R.F.L. 132 at 136 (Sask. Q.B.); *K. v. K.*, 23 R.F.L. 58 at 64–65, [1976] 2 W.W.R. 462 (Alta. Prov. Ct.).

16§18 — Removal of children to another jurisdiction

Divorce Act, 1985

In *Gordon v. Goertz* (1996), 19 R.F.L. (4th) 177, [1996] 2 S.C.R. 27, the Supreme Court of Canada considered the issue of whether or not the trial and appeal courts erred in permitting a child to move away from her home in Saskatchewan to Australia with her mother, the custodial parent. The non-custodial parent who had exercised access regularly when the child was in Saskatchewan had been ordered to exercise access only in Australia once the child had moved there. The court held that where a parent applies for a variation of a custody order, there is no legal presumption in favour of the custodial parent, although the custodial parent's views are entitled to great respect. The only real test is the best interests of the child.

At the Supreme Court of Canada, the court was of the opinion that where, as in this case, the custody order sets out terms of access based on the assumption that the child's principal residence would be near the access parent, the relocation of the custodial parent and the child could not have been within the reasonable contemplation of the judge who issued the original permanent custody order. The move constituted a material change and the trial judge was required to make a fresh inquiry as to the best interests of the child. Where, as in this case, the judge did not do so, it was appropriate that the Supreme Court of Canada should review the decision.

Madam Justice McLachlin held that the fact that the child had been in her mother's custody for several years, that the reasons for granting the mother custody in the first place had substantially changed, and that a change in custody would probably be difficult for the child, were reasons for granting custody to the mother. On the other hand, the move had greatly diminished the child's contact with her father, her extended family and her community in Canada. However, the fact that the father has the means to visit the child in Australia, had helped to reduce the detrimental effect of the move on his relationship with her.

The Supreme Court of Canada ruled that the trial judge did not err in continuing the mother's custody of the child, even though she intended to move to Australia. However, the court could see no reason to restrict the father's access to Australia. Access in Canada would permit the child to maintain contact with friends and family. Thus the court affirmed the custody order and allowed the appeal in part, to permit the father to exercise access in Canada.

In an *obiter* remark in *Young v. Young*, [1993] 4 S.C.R. 3, 49 R.F.L. (3d) 117, 84 B.C.L.R. (2d) 1, [1993] 8 W.W.R. 513, 108 D.L.R. (4th) 193, the court stated at 151 (R.F.L.) of the judgement that a judge might be of the opinion that it is in the best interests of a child that he or she move with the custodial parent to a distant location, even though this action would limit the access of the other parent.

A court should consider the issue of custody first and the issue of the child's mobility second: *Bjornson v. Creighton* (2002), 31 R.F.L. (5th) 242, 2002 CarswellOnt 3866, [2002] O.J. No. 4364, 62 O.R. (3d) 236, (sub nom. *C.B. v. E.C.C.)* 166 O.A.C. 44, 221 D.L.R. (4th) 489 (C.A.); leave to appeal refused (2003), 2003 CarswellOnt 1387, 2003 CarswellOnt 1388 (S.C.C.). This case was not decided under the Divorce Act.

While there is no legal presumption in favour of the views of the custodial parent on the issue of mobility, the custodial parent's views remain a very important consideration in any analysis of the best interests of the child: *Bjornson v. Creighton* (2002), 31 R.F.L. (5th) 242, 2002 CarswellOnt 3866, [2002] O.J. No. 4364, 62 O.R. (3d) 236, (sub nom. *C.B. v. E.C.C.)* 166 O.A.C. 44, 221 D.L.R. (4th) 489 (C.A.); leave to appeal refused (2003), 2003 CarswellOnt 1387, 2003 CarswellOnt 1388 (S.C.C.). In this case, the father's controlling behavior and the improvement in the mother's terms of employment indicated that it would be in the best interests of the child, if he moved with the mother from Waterloo, Ontario to Calgary, Alberta.

In *Singer v. Singer* (2002), 35 R.F.L. (5th) 208, 2002 CarswellOnt 4473 (Ont. S.C.J.); affirmed (2003), 42 R.F.L. (5th) 202, 2003 CarswellOnt 3113, 175 O.A.C. 1 (Ont. C.A.); leave to appeal refused (2004), 2004 CarswellOnt 51, 2004 CarswellOnt 52 (S.C.C.), the court allowed the application of the custodial mother to relocate to Germany to live with her new spouse. Although the move would have an impact on the children's relationship with their father, the loss of their primary caregiver would have even a greater impact.

In *Rushinko v. Rushinko* (2002), 29 R.F.L. (5th) 173, 2002 CarswellOnt 1997, 161 O.A.C. 85 (C.A.), the court held that in determining whether a move with a custodial parent to a different city would adversely affect the children's best interests, the court should seriously consider the views of the custodial parent, the wishes of the children, and whether the move might enhance the custodial parent's ability to care for the children. The trial judge had given undue emphasis to the effect on the children of leaving the community and on the children's relationship with their father in making an order requiring the mother to move back to the city where the father resided or surrender custody. In addition, the judge gave little or no consideration to the harm that the children would suffer, if the mother were no longer the custodial parent. The order was overturned on appeal.

In *Sodhi v. Sodhi* (2002), 25 R.F.L. (5th) 420, 2002 CarswellOnt 1050, 158 O.A.C. 83 (C.A.); additional reasons at (2002), 2002 CarswellOnt 1943 (C.A.), the court, on appeal, struck a provision from the mother's custody award which would have required the transfer of custody to the father in the event that the mother refused to relocate to the community in which the father lived. Custody had been awarded to the mother in the children's best interests and the default provision in the order was inconsistent with those best interests.

In *Delaire v. Delaire*, 27 R.F.L. (5th) 335, 2002 CarswellSask 369, 2002 SKCA 71, [2002] S.J. No. 341, 223 Sask. R. 229, 277 W.A.C. 229 (C.A.), the court, on appeal, deleted a condition of the mother's custody order which required her to move with the children back to the city where the father resided. A parent's relocation is only relevant in respect of his or her ability to meet the needs of the children. The mother was capable of meeting those needs in a new city.

The expressed wish of children of tender years to stay in a particular location is only one circumstance to be weighed in an application by the custodial parent to relocate to another jurisdiction: *Myketiak v. Myketiak*, 13 R.F.L. (5th) 431, 203 Sask. R. 90, 240 W.A.C. 90, 2001 SKCA 17, 2001 CarswellSask 84 (C.A.); affirming (1999), 185 Sask. R. 231, 1999 CarswellSask 693 (Q.B.). The court, on appeal, deleted a condition of the mother's custody order which required her to move with the children back to the city where the father resided. A parent's relocation is only relevant in respect of his or her ability to meet the children's needs. The mother was capable of meeting those needs in a new city.

In *Johnson v. Cleroux* (2002), 23 R.F.L. (5th) 176, 2002 CarswellOnt 787, (sub nom. *J. (M.) v. C. (P.)*) 156 O.A.C. 197 (C.A.); additional reasons at (2002), 2002 CarswellOnt 1559, [2002] O.J. No. 1801, 24 R.F.L. (5th) 422, (sub nom. *J. (M.) v. C. (P.)*) 159 O.A.C. 346 (C.A.); additional reasons at (2003), 2003 CarswellOnt 896 (C.A.), a lower court had dismissed the mother's motion to move from Ottawa to Oakville with the parties' 5-year-old daughter. The court had observed that a move would disrupt the child's relationship with her father and would affect her association with grandparents, extended family and her exposure to the Francophone culture. However, the court had refused to hear important fresh evidence that the mother and her husband were expecting a child, evidence which was directly relevant to determining the best interests of the parties' child. The appelate court in allowing the appeal was of the opinion that the trial judge had erred in refusing to admit such important evidence of the pregnancy and its effect on the family unit. In light of the pregnancy, the husband had decided that he should not leave his secure employment in Oakville. If the parties' child were required to remain in Ottawa, the mother would stay with her in Ottawa during the week and travel to Oakville on weekends. The new family could not function as a unit on an everyday basis. If the parties' child moved to Oakville there would be better employment prospects for the mother and she should be able to spend more time with the parties' child. The appelate court allowed the mother's appeal. She was named the legal custodial parent and the child was ordered to reside with her. This case was not decided under the *Divorce Act*.

In *Chan v. Chow* (2001), 15 R.F.L. (5th) 274, 199 D.L.R. (4th) 478, 90 B.C.L.R. (3d) 222, [2001] 8 W.W.R. 63, 152 B.C.A.C. 176, 250 W.A.C. 176, 2004 CarswellBC 868, 2001 BCCA 276 (C.A.), the mother's joint custody rights were clearly breached when the father removed the child without the mother's approval.

In determining whether or not a custodial parent should be permitted to move with children, the court should consider the economic impact of the proposed move on the children and give adequate weight and respect to the custodial parent's views. It should not make findings without evidence in respect to the probable traumatic effect of a move and not place undue emphasis on reduction in access: *Burns v. Burns*, 3 R.F.L. (5th) 189, [2000] N.S.J. No. 2, 2000 CarswellNS 2, 183 D.L.R. (4th) 66, 2000 NSCA 1, 182 N.S.R. (2d) 101, 563 A.P.R. 101 (C.A.).

The Manitoba Court of Appeal in *Zeaton v. Zeaton* (1999), 3 R.F.L. (5th) 320, 1999 CarswellMan 561, [1999] M.J. No. 501, 180 D.L.R. (4th) 609, 142 Man. R. (2d) 36, 212 W.A.C. 36 (C.A.), granted the father's appeal from an order which allowed the mother to remove children from the jurisdiction to Saskatoon where she planned to remarry. The parties had joint custody of their two sons. The court found that the trial judge had failed to apply the relevant factors to the evidence in the case. The only certain fact was that the children were doing well in their present location. The move was not in the best interests of the children, considering the unnecessary stress for them, the disruption of continuity in their relationship with both parents, and the upheaval in their current living arrangements. The children's residence during past moves was not a certain indicator of their resilience in regard to the proposed move. The appelate court held that the children were to continue to live in Winnipeg.

In deciding whether a custodial parent should be allowed to continue to have custody and to move with the children away from the residence of the non-custodial parent, the court should give sufficient weight to the wishes of the children, the way in which each parent meets the needs of the children, including facilitating contact with the other parent, and the children's relationship with their father and his family: *Irwin v. Irwin* (1998), 1998 CarswellOnt 3510 (C.A.). The appellate court upheld the decision of the lower court and permitted the mother and children to relocate from Cornwall, Ontario to Hamilton, Ontario. While the court acknowledged that access would change, it was of the opinion that alternative terms could ensure meaningful contact with the father and his extended family.

In *Linehan v. Linehan* (1998), 1998 CarswellAlta 989 (Q.B.); affirmed 1998 CarswellAlta 923, [1998] A.J. No. 1126, 228 A.R. 85, 188 W.A.C. 85, 1998 ABCA 329 (C.A.), the court held that where the father, the custodial parent, was in a stable common-law relationship and the children were thriving within the new family unit, the parties' children should be permitted to move with their father from Calgary to Victoria, as the father wished to accompany his common law wife, who was required to move for work-related reasons.

In considering the best interests of the children, the court was of the opinion in *Brown v. Brown* (1997), 1997 CarswellMan 21, 116 Man. R. (2d) 229 (Q.B.); affirmed (1997), 1997 CarswellMan 629, 123 Man. R. (2d) 166, 159 W.A.C. 166 (C.A.), that where the mother wanted to remove the children from the jurisdiction in which the father resided, the determining factor in the case was the location where the custodial parent would be most settled and secure psychologically and economically and best able to provide and care for the children. The court concluded that the best interests of the children would be served if the mother were to be permitted to move with the children from Manitoba to New Mexico where the mother's parents lived and where she could obtain a better paying job than in Manitoba.

In *Johnson v. Johnson* (1997), 28 R.F.L. (4th) 25, 196 A.R. 233, 141 W.A.C. 233, 1997 CarswellAlta 208 (C.A.), the mother, the custodial parent, had, on a temporary basis, with the approval of the court, moved from Edmonton to Regina with the parties' child. Subsequently, the court ordered that the child's primary residence would be with the mother, but that the mother was to live in Edmonton, where the father resided, as it would be in the child's best interests to live in the same city as both of his parents. The court allowed the mother's appeal on the basis that the trial judge had disregarded the importance of financial security to the interests of the child, a security which was more likely to be found by allowing the mother and child to stay in Regina where the mother had steady employment and the cost of living was considerably lower than in Edmonton. The appeal was allowed and the matter referred back to the trial level for rehearing.

The expressed wish of children of tender years to stay in a particular location is only one circumstance to be weighed in an application by the custodial parent to relocate in another jurisdiction: *Myketiak v. Myketiak* (2001), 13 R.F.L. (5th) 431, 203 Sask. R. 90, 240 W.A.C. 90, 2001 SKCA 17, 2001 CarswellSask 84 (C.A.); affirming (1999), 185 Sask. R. 231, 1999 CarswellSask 693 (Sask. Q.B.).

In *Nunweiler v. Nunweiler*, 5 R.F.L. (5th) 442, 186 D.L.R. (4th) 323, 78 B.C.L.R. (3d) 1, [2000] 8 W.W.R. 30, 2000 BCCA 300, 137 B.C.A.C. 1, 223 W.A.C. 1, 2000 CarswellBC 958, [2000] B.C.J. No. 935 (C.A.), a condition whereby the mother would lose custody of the child if she did not relocate to within 20 miles of the city in which the father was resident was struck on appeal. The mother's move away, which frustrated the father's access, appeared to be based on sound financial reasons and not merely to frustrate the father's rights. The trial judge had focused more on the father's economic interests and insufficiently on the mother's financial situation and the probable impact of the change on the child.

Where the trial judge is of the opinion that a move outside the jurisdiction is in the children's best interests, even though there will be access difficulties for the non-custodial parent, the judgment should be allowed to stand: *Appiah v. Appiah* (1999), 45 R.F.L. (4th) 172, 118 O.A.C. 189 (C.A.).

The petitioner mother in *Hurst v. Hurst* (1998), 39 R.F.L. (4th) 406, 219 A.R. 105, 179 W.A.C. 105 (C.A.), appealed from an order of a chambers judge directing the return of children from Seattle to Calgary. The mother gave notice that she was moving to Seattle where her family lived. The mother had had custody of the children in Calgary and the father had had specified access. The court was of the opinion that failure to provide access was not a sufficient ground upon which to base a decision to change custody. It was necessary to consider the best interests of the children. The appeal was granted.

In determining interim custody, where the mother had moved the children to another city without advance notice to the father but the move was not made to frustrate access, the court found that the determining factor was the children's closer emotional ties with the community in which they had grown up: *Grant v. Grant*, 2001 CarswellBC 1944, 2001 BCSC 1289, [2001] B.C.J. No. 1907 (Master). Interim custody was the weight to be placed upon the wish or decision of the custodial parent having temporary custody of a child involved in a disputed custody matter may be less than in regard to a parent with final custody who is wishing to move: *Hunt v. Hunt* (2001), 21 R.F.L. (5th) 309, 2001 CarswellOnt 4549 (S.C.J.); additional reasons at (2001), 2001 CarswellOnt 4548, [2001] O.J. No. 5111 (S.C.J.).

In *Van Goozen v. Van Goozen* (1993), 47 R.F.L. (3d) 1 (Ont. C.A.), the court upheld on appeal an order which permitted the custodial mother to remove the children to another jurisdiction. The order was in the children's best interests and, although some adjustments would be required to the father's access rights, the move had not totally frustrated them.

In *Levesque v. Lapointe* (1993), 44 R.F.L. (3d) 316, 75 B.C.L.R. (2d) 1, 99 D.L.R. (4th) 667 (C.A.), the court, on the mother's appeal, reversed an order refusing permission for her to move with the children from British Columbia to Alberta where she had a better job opportunity. Although the move would disrupt the parties' joint custody arrangement, which had previously worked well, it would not be in the children's best interests to remove them from their mother's daily care, which they had enjoyed since birth.

In deciding whether to permit a custodial parent to remove a child to another jurisdiction, the court should consider any existing custody order, the nature of the relationship between the child and the access parent, the reason for the move, the distance of the move, the possible effect upon the resources of the access parent, and the child's view: *Carter v. Brooks* (1990), 30 R.F.L. (3d) 53, 2 O.R. (3d) 321, 41 O.A.C. 389, 77 D.L.R. (4th) 45 (C.A.).

In *Rosenau v. Rosenau* (2004), 6 R.F.L. (6th) 372, 2004 CarswellSask 462, 2004 SKQB 275 (Q.B.), the court allowed the father's application for joint custody and rejected the mother's planned move with the children from Saskatchewan to Ontario. The child's best interests would be served by a joint custody arrangement that ensured regular, frequent and consistent contact with both parents.

In *Johnstone v. Brighton* (2004), 6 R.F.L. (6th) 294, 2004 CarswellOnt 3420 (S.C.J.), the court allowed the mother's application to relocate with the child from Ontario to Pennsylvania to allow her to live with her fiancé. Despite the parties' joint custody order, approval of the proposal was more beneficial to the child's interests than would be a refusal. Further, the mother allowed for generous access which she agreed to finance by foregoing a portion of her spousal support.

In *Liberati v. Liberati* (2004), 10 R.F.L. (6th) 410, 2004 CarswellOnt 3718 (S.C.J.), the mother was granted sole custody of the children despite the fact that she had unilaterally moved them to France. The father's custodial plan was not sufficient and was a disorganized patchwork of help from various relatives. The father was granted access for 7 weeks annually.

The best interests of children are not served by the court sanctioning the unilateral acts of a parent who relocates a child contrary to a court order. In *McMurray v. Gerow* (2004), 9

R.F.L. (6th) 431, 2004 CarswellOnt 3199 (Ont. S.C.J.), the court refused the mother's leave to appeal application requiring her to return the children when she had relocated to Connecticut in breach of a court order.

Where the parties had joint custody, the court refused the mother's application to relocate with the children in Australia. The move would effectively cut off the children's relationship with their father as the cost of access travel would be prohibitive. Furthermore the children were too young for any meaningful telephone and email contact: *Terris v. Terris* (2003), 41 R.F.L. (5th) 433, 2003 CarswellOnt 2685 (Ont. S.C.J.).

In *Karol v. Karol* (2003), 49 R.F.L. (5th) 346, 2003 CarswellOnt 4832 (Ont. S.C.J.), the court allowed the mother's application to travel with the children to Israel to visit with her extended family after the father had withheld his consent over concerns of terrorism. There was no general travel ban to Israel, only warnings about travel to specific areas to which the mother had no intention of taking the children. It was in the children's best interests that they be able to travel to Israel which would connect them with their heritage.

In *Cameron v. Cameron*, 41 R.F.L. (5th) 30, 2003 CarswellMan 268, 2003 MBQB 149 (Man. Q.B.), the court allowed the mother's application to remove the children from their father's home in Manitoba and relocate with them to her new home in Alberta. The father used physical punishment on the children and the care provided to them while in his home was unsatisfactory.

In *Stringer v. Stringer*, 48 R.F.L. (5th) 422, 2003 CarswellBC 2824, 2003 BCSC 1739 (B.C. S.C.), the court rejected the mother's plan to relocate with the children from Vancouver to Quebec. The mother's plan to become self-sufficient in Quebec was unrealistic and would reduce the father's important role in his children's lives to that of occasional visitor.

In *T. (J.S.) v. M. (G.W.)*, 42 R.F.L. (5th) 211, 2003 CarswellAlta 964, 2003 ABQB 578 (Alta Q.B.), the court allowed the mother's application to take the parties' child with her to England prior to the determination of custody. The mother had a fully funded Ph.D. education opportunity there and she should be allowed to pursue it. She was, however, required to post a $50,000 bond to ensure both that she return to Canada for the custody trial and that she granted the father access in England.

In *Singer v. Singer* (2002), 35 R.F.L. (5th) 208, 2002 CarswellOnt 4473 (Ont. S.C.J.); affirmed (2003), 42 R.F.L. (5th) 202, 2003 CarswellOnt 3113, 175 O.A.C. 1 (Ont. C.A.); leave to appeal refused (2004), 2004 CarswellOnt 51, 2004 CarswellOnt 52 (S.C.C.), the court allowed the application of the custodial mother to relocate to Germany to live with her new spouse. Although the move would have an impact on the children's relationship with their father, the loss of their primary caregiver would have even a greater impact.

In *Oddi v. Oddi* (2000), 7 R.F.L. (5th) 164, 2000 CarswellOnt 1772 (S.C.J.), the court refused the husband's request for an order prohibiting the custodial mother from removing the children from the jurisdiction until the eldest child completed high school in five years. The wife had no intention to move and no reason existed to restrict her mobility rights. Should the wife wish to move in the future, she was to give the husband 90 days' advance notice which would give the husband the opportunity to object to the proposed relocation.

Where the mother justified her unilateral decision to move the children from their home in Alberta to Saskatchewan, the court allowed the husband's application for an order compelling her to return the children to Alberta where custody would be determined. The mother's allegation that she moved as a result of physical abuse at the hands of the husband was not supported by any evidence and was raised for the first time only in response to the husband's application: *M. (T.K.) v. M. (P.S.)* (1999), 48 R.F.L. (4th) 393 (Alta. Q.B.).

Kits v. Kits (1998), 42 R.F.L. (4th) 167 (B.C. S.C.), the mother was granted custody of the children and would be allowed to move with them to the United States to reside with her new partner. Although the children were comfortable with both parents and their respective partners, their primary attachment was to their mother.

In *Elliott v. Elliott* (1998), 42 R.F.L. (4th) 341 (Ont. Gen. Div.) the court allowed the custodial mother to move with the child from Barrie, Ontario to Toronto where she was employed. The mother had secured housing in Toronto and that was where her extended family lived. The father had physically assaulted the mother in the child's presence and any benefit to the child from daily contact with the father was outweighed by the father's abuse of the mother.

In *Hayward v. Hayward* (1994), 8 R.F.L. (4th) 66 (Alta. Q.B.), the court refused the mother's request for an interim sole custody award which would have allowed her to move with the child from Alberta to British Columbia for employment reasons. The parties had earlier agreed to joint custody and to an Albertan residence for the child. As serious factual disputes were involved, a trial of the issue was best directed and the status quo arrangements continued pending the outcome.

Where the determination of final custody remains outstanding, the court should be cautious in allowing an interim custodial parent to move with the child to another jurisdiction: *Scott v. Scott* (1993), 49 R.F.L. (3d) 405, 111 Nfld. & P.E.I.R. 122, 348 A.P.R. 122 (P.E.I. T.D.).

Where the father had vague future plans of relocating to another province with the child in his care, the court granted the mother's request for an order that the child not be removed from the province without the mother's consent or a court order. The court could not, in the absence of particulars, assess the effect of such a move on the child's best interests: *Hines v. Hines* (1992), 40 R.F.L. (3d) 274, 111 N.S.R. (2d) 281, 303 A.P.R. 281 (T.D.).

Where the mother had intended to remove the children to another jurisdiction, the court affirmed an earlier joint custody award and added a provision that the child were not to be removed from the jurisdiction without a specific order of the court: *H. (M.A.) v. H. (R.V.)* (1990), 108 N.B.R. (2d) 448, 269 A.P.R. 448 (Q.B.).

Where the children's best interests would be served if custody was awarded to the mother, but her planned move to California would be to their detriment, the mother was awarded custody on condition that she not remove the children from Ontario: *Appleby v. Appleby* (1989), 21 R.F.L. (3d) 307 (Ont. H.C.).

Where the custodial mother was unable to afford a home in the municipality where the father lived, the custody order provided that she would be able to relocate elsewhere failing the father's assistance in obtaining a house in that municipality: *Monaghan v. Monaghan* (1988), 14 R.F.L. (3d) 308 (Ont. H.C.).

In *Droit de la famille — 1322*, [1990] R.D.F. 409 (S.C. Qué.), the court rejected the husband's action for custody brought after the custodial mother announced her intention to move with the children to her native Denmark. The children wished to make the move, had lived in Denmark previously, and spoke and read Danish fluently. Although both parties were good parents, the children's needs would be better met by the mother.

In *MacInnis v. MacInnis* (1992), 40 R.F.L. (3d) 345 (Ont. U.F.C.), the court granted the father's application for an order enjoining the mother from moving the children from Ontario to Alberta. The mother had already unduly influenced the children against their father and it was in everyone's best interest if the former loving relationship between the father and children be restored. This would not be possible if the move were allowed.

In *Butler v. Koch* (February 6, 1991), Doc. London D555/88 (Ont. Prov. Div.), the court refused the husband's application for an interim order restraining the custodial wife from removing the children to another province, despite the existence of a joint custody order. The wife planned to move with her new husband and, as the children were very attached to both the mother and their new stepfather, it was in the children's best interests to allow the move.

Where the custodial mother wished to relocate with her children to British Columbia for no particular reason, the court allowed the father's application for an order restraining the mother from removing the children from the jurisdiction. As the move would disrupt the children's lives and interfere with their relationship with their father and their family, it was clearly not in their best interest: *T (K.A.) v. T. (J.)* (1989), 23 R.F.L. (3d) 214 (Ont. U.F.C.).

Where the child was not even aware of the existence of his biological father and considered his mother's second husband to be his father, the court allowed the mother's application for a variation of the existing custody order to allow her to remove the child with her new family to Hawaii. Although, at the time of the custody order, the court had ordered that a plan for reintroduction of the child to his biological father be prepared prior to the ordering of access, no such plan had ever been acted upon. Accordingly, there was no need even to order a termination of access. The child's interests were best served through preservation of the new family unit of which he was a part: *Sulit v. Sulit* (1993), 47 R.F.L. (3d) 148 (Ont. U.F.C.).

In *Brigante v. Brigante* (1991), 32 R.F.L. (3d) 299 (Ont. U.F.C.), the mother's application to remove the child from Hamilton to Ottawa to permit the mother to live with her new partner was refused. As the mother's new relationship was of a short duration and as the child enjoyed a close relationship with his father and his extended family in Hamilton, the move would not be in the child's best interests.

Generally, a custodial spouse has the right to remove the child from the jurisdiction unless he or she does so for unreasonable purposes or there is an agreement to the contrary. Such agreements are to be honoured by the courts unless the welfare of the child requires otherwise: *Chisholm (Bower) v. Bower* (1987), 11 R.F.L. (3d) 293 (N.S. Fam. Ct.).

Divorce Act, 1968

In *Beairsto v. Beairsto* (1982), 30 R.F.L. (2d) 459 (Alta. C.A.), the court enforced on appeal a Prince Edward Island order awarding custody to the father despite the fact that the wife had obtained an interim custody order from the Alberta Court of Queen's Bench in the course of a divorce proceeding. As the wife had surreptitiously removed the child to Alberta from the father's home in Prince Edward Island, the Alberta order was vacated. Per Kerons J.A. at p. 461, applying *Read v. Read*, [1982] 2 W.W.R. 25, 17 Alta. L.R. (2d) 273 (C.A.): "[The Alberta Court of] Queen's Bench should not give aid and comfort to those who would breach a custody order by exercising its admitted jurisdiction, a jurisdiction which arises whenever a child is actually in Alberta, in a case where the child is here as a result of transportation which is unlawful under a valid and existing custody order, where adequate relief is available elsewhere, and where the child otherwise has no substantial connection with Alberta. All these criteria here obtain."

In a case in which a non-resident is applying for custody of a child, a greater than usual preponderance of evidence in favour of the non-resident should be demonstrated before the court makes an award which, by its very nature, will be final and put an end to its effective control over and ability to act in the interest of the infant: *Smith v. Goulet* (1974), 19 R.F.L. 45, 5 O.R. (2d) 337, 50 D.L.R. (3d) 321 (C.A.).

Where the mother had removed the child of the marriage from Scotland to Manitoba, in breach of her undertaking given to the Scottish court whereby she had agreed not to remove the child from the jurisdiction, an order obtained by the father that the child be returned to Scotland was overturned on appeal. The paramount consideration of the child's welfare was held to outweigh those factors related to the surreptitious removal and the existence of an interim custody award of the Scottish court in the father's favour: *Stalder v. Wood* (1975), 20 R.F.L. 214 (Man. C.A.).

Absenting all consideration of unreasonableness, the parent who has custody of the children has the right to remove the children without the permission of the other parent in the absence of some specific agreement to the contrary or in the absence of such specific terms with respect to access as would clearly indicate that the parties must have intended that the children remain in close proximity if the specified right of access provided in the agreement was to be an effective right. If, for example, the agreement provided that the parent who did not have custody should have a right of access to the children for a period of several hours on Sunday, the court could imply a term that the parties intended that the children should reside within such proximity to the parent having access that the specific right of access granted might be implemented without undue inconvenience to such parent: *Wright v. Wright* (1973), 12 R.F.L. 200, 1 O.R. (2d) 337, 40 D.L.R. (3d) 321 (C.A.). See also *Re Ritchie* (1974), 20 R.F.L. 225, 5 O.R. (2d) 520 (C.A.), where the mother, in a separation agreement, agreed that the father should act as custodial parent, but later surreptitiously removed the children to another jurisdiction, and the court in that new jurisdiction declined to entertain her application for custody.

In *Ridderstroem v. Ridderstroem*, 6 R.F.L. 18 at 19, [1972] 2 O.R. 113, 25 D.L.R. (3d) 29 (C.A.), the court declined jurisdiction to deal with the custody of a child who had been hastily removed from his home in Denmark by the applicant father. Aylesworth J.A. stated: "It has been made abundantly clear before this in recent decisions, particularly in England, that in these days of quick transportation by air, including the facilities for hasty removal of children from one country to another, that the courts of the English countries operating under the common-law system will look with great disfavour on any attempt to flout the invoked jurisdiction of a proper court in a foreign country unless the paramount interests of the child demand that such be done — and such paramount interest of the child is to be demonstrated by cogent, convincing proof, that to leave the child with the parent who had custody in the country of original jurisdiction, or the parent to whom the foreign jurisdiction has awarded custody, will seriously endanger the child's welfare." See also *Loughran v. Loughran*, 9 R.F.L. 255 at 256, [1973] 1 O.R. 109, 30 D.L.R. (3d) 385 (C.A.).

Where the mother removed the children from Alberta to Manitoba in order to avoid the father's custody application which was pending in Alberta, it was held on appeal that the

Manitoba court had properly declined jurisdiction to entertain the mother's custody application. As the children had grown up in Alberta and were totally unknown in Manitoba, their welfare could best be determined by the Alberta courts which were already properly seized of the matter: *Leatherdale v. Ferguson* (1964), 50 W.W.R. 700, 50 D.L.R. (2d) 182 (Man. C.A.).

The court may, in the custody provisions contained in a decree *nisi*, engross a condition that the children are to remain within the jurisdiction of the court unless permission is granted to remove them: *Ashraff v. Ashraff* (1970), 1 R.F.L. 157, 73 W.W.R. 321 (Man. Q.B.). See also *Wittstock v. Wittstock*, 3 R.F.L. 326, [1971] 2 O.R. 472, 18 D.L.R. (3d) 264 (C.A.); *Wallace v. Wallace* (1975), 20 R.F.L. 324 (Sask. Q.B.); *Tardif v. Tardif* (1975), 25 R.F.L. 283 (Sask. Q.B.); *Roberts v. Roberts* (1977), 19 N.B.R. (2d) 700, 30 A.P.R. 700 (Q.B.).

In *Publicover v. R.* (1981), 22 R.F.L. (2d) 1, 120 D.L.R. (3d) 310 (Fed. T.D.), after the wife was granted interim custody of the children under the *Divorce Act*, one child went to visit the husband, a member of the Canadian Armed Forces stationed in Germany, and never returned. Since the wife's attempts to recover the child in the Manitoba Queen's Bench were futile, as the husband could not be served, she brought an application for relief to the Federal Court. However, it was held that the Federal Court had no jurisdiction to intervene to compel the Minister of Defence to have the custody order enforced. Therefore, her application was dismissed: *Re Ohm* (1976), 25 R.F.L. 376 (B.C. S.C.); *Hilborn v. Hilborn* (1977), 2 R.F.L. (2d) 5 at 14, 7 A.R. 62, 4 Alta. L.R. 52 (T.D.); *Prossor-Jones v. Prossor-Jones* (1972), 7 R.F.L. 150 (Man. Q.B.); *Lussier v. Lussier* (1977), 3 R.F.L. (2d) 335 at 336–337 (Ont. Div. Ct.); *Cobel v. Cobel* (1975), 21 R.F.L. 343 (Sask. Q.B.); *Mandel v. Mandel* (1971), 5 R.F.L. 50 (Man. Q.B.).

16§18A — Custody — jurisdiction to override agreements

In *Tumino v. Tumino* (2002), 2002 CarswellOnt 3089, 29 R.F.L. (5th) 427 (S.C.J.), the court was of the opinion that while parenting agreements should be encouraged, a court can look at the matter of custody afresh where there has been a material change in circumstances. In this case, the parties executed a parenting agreement, later incorporated in a separation agreement, in which they agreed to remain in the Greater Toronto Area for a minimum of 5 years. Approximately 8 months later, the mother applied to the court for permission to move with the children North Bay to reside with and eventually marry a friend. There was no evidence that the mother had an improper motive in seeking to move. The court held that the court must not consider the current trend in mobility cases but instead focus on children and family appearing before it. The proposed move was too soon for the children. They were just beginning to experience a new form of family life. To move them at the present time would put their relationship with their father, the access parent, at risk. Perhaps at some point in the future it would be in the children's best interests to move to North Bay.

In *Ligate v. Richardson* (1997), 34 O.R. (3d) 423, 1997 CarswellOnt 2185, [1997] O.J. No. 2519, 101 O.A.C. 161 (C.A.), the mother, the custodial parent, on appeal, was allowed to take the parties' child with her from Toronto to Cambridge, contrary to the parties' separation agreement. The appellate court was of the opinion that a lower court should not take the lack of a compelling reason to move into account in assessing the child's best interests. In light of *Gordon v. Goertz*, [1996] 2 S.C.R. 27, 19 R.F.L. (4th) 177, 134 D.L.R. (4th) 321, [1996] 5 W.W.R. 457, 196 N.R. 321, 141 Sask. R. 241, 114 W.A.C. 241, 1996 CarswellSask 199, [1996] S.C.J. No. 52, 1996 CarswellSask 199F, (sub nom. *Goertz c. Gordon)* [1996] R.D.F. 209, the reason for the move is irrelevant, except in exceptional circumstances where the reason for the move can reflect adversely on the parent's ability to meet the needs of the child. The mother was not attempting to frustrate access. The trial judge had fled to give the custodial parent's views the respect that they deserved.

In *Woodhouse v. Woodhouse* (1996), 20 R.F.L. (4th) 337, 1996 CarswellOnt 1906, [1996] O.J. No. 1975, 136 D.L.R. (4th) 577, 91 O.A.C. 91, 29 O.R. (3d) 417 (C.A.); leave to appeal refused (1997), [1996] S.C.C.A. No. 402, 99 O.A.C. 80 (note), 209 N.R. 80 (note) (S.C.C.), an order restricting the parties' children's residence to the Hamilton area was the subject of the appeal. The mother had remarried and wished to move with the children to Scotland. The parties had executed a separation agreement which provided that the mother was the custodial parent and the father was to have reasonable access. The agreement was not incorporated into the divorce judgment and, strictly speaking, the *Children's Law Reform Act* applied, but both it and the *Divorce Act* state that the best interests of the child is the governing test. The appellate court upheld the trial court's decision, which found that the mother's view as to the best interests of the children did not take into account an important matter. Her plan of access both in Canada and Scotland would not preserve the quality of relationship that the children had with their father. Although the trial judge had taken into consideration the positive effects of a happy custodial parent, he had concluded that such a benefit would not outweigh the detriment that the move would cause. He had decided that the best interests of the children would be realized if the children maintained their relationship with their father and their community in Ontario. The reasons of the trial judge, taken as a whole, did not indicate any error and the appeal as to the residence restrictions of the children was dismissed.

16§19 — Custody — parental role models

Young children, and in particular, young girls should be in the care of their mother if it is feasible: *Barrios v. Barrios* (1978), 4 R.F.L. (2d) 347 at 357, 28 N.S.R. (2d) 419, 43 A.P.R. 419 (T.D.).

Where an 11 ½-year-old girl expressed a desire to live with her mother rather than remain with her brothers in the custody of her father, custody of the girl was awarded to the mother, the court citing, *inter alia*, the absence of a mother figure in the father's home: *Currie v. Currie* (1975), 18 R.F.L. 47 (Alta. T.D.).

In *Saunders v. Saunders*, 22 R.F.L. 210, [1975] W.W.D. 135, 58 D.L.R. (3d) 763 (Man. Q.B.), the custody of the son was awarded to the father, the court citing, *inter alia*, the benefits which a male child can derive from his father.

Where custody of the three young male children of the marriage was awarded to the mother, the father was provided with generous access so as to allow him to provide such discipline as would provide a desirable balance in the raising of the children: *Tassou v. Tassou* (1975), 23 R.F.L. 351 (Alta. T.D.). See also *MacDonald v. MacDonald* (1975), 23 R.F.L. 303 at 308 (Man. Q.B.).

Everything else being equal, young girls are better off being brought up by their mother than their father, the converse is not necessarily true: *Ploughman v. Ploughman* (1974), 5 Nfld. & P.E.I.R. 431 at 433 (Nfld. T.D.).

16§19A — Custody and change of children's names

In *Hubley v. Hubley* (1987), 83 N.S.R. (2d) 2, 210 A.P.R. 2, 45 D.L.R. (4th) 758 (T.D.); affirmed (1988), 13 R.F.L. (3d) 407, (sub nom. *Hubley v. Hubley (Boyd))* 84 N.S.R. (2d) 225, 213 A.P.R. 225 (C.A.), the court refused the husband's application to vary the decree *nisi* to prevent the custodial mother from changing the children's names. The welfare of the children was best served by not denying the custodial parent her common law right to add a new surname to the children's names.

16§20 — Temporary custody

In *Grinde v. Grinde* (1977), 5 A.R. 561, 3 Alta. L.R. (2d) 280 (T.D.), prior to the making of a final custody order under the *Divorce Act*, a home study was ordered by the court, pending the preparation of which interim custody was awarded to the mother. See also *Schmidt v. Schmidt* (1976), 26 R.F.L. 232 at 239–240 (B.C. S.C.).

"The [custody] order I propose to make is admittedly an unusual one. If the wife was in a position to devote herself entirely to looking after the children, as she is doing at the moment, I would be slow to remove them from their present environment. But I am unable to judge with any clearness the lines of her future. In these circumstances I have decided to postpone the final decision for a period of four months. It is desirable, however, that someone [in this case, the father] should have the formal custody pending that decision": per Pennell J. in *Houston v. Houston* (1975), 21 R.F.L. 65 at 86 (Ont. H.C.).

Where the court expressed concern over the correctness of awarding the custody of an 11½-year-old girl to her mother, it was ordered that the custody arrangement would be for four months only, after which the matter would be reviewed with the participation of an *amicus curiae* acting on the child's behalf: *Currie v. Currie* (1975), 18 R.F.L. 47 (Alta. T.D.).

Where the children had been in the *de facto* custody of the father, the father was awarded custody of the children subject, however, to a review of the matter by the court upon the expiration of a six-month period: *Marks v. Marks* (1974), 15 N.S.R. (2d) 13 (T.D.).

In *Peter v. Peter* (1974), 17 R.F.L. 80 (B.C. S.C.), the court refused to make a custody order that could be reviewed in 12 months' time because it would create a continuous unsettled problem between the parents and the children would suffer as a consequence. Instead the court awarded custody and stated that, "if, in the future, circumstances change, or events create a different situation on either side, the other parent may make an application then on proper grounds to alter the present decision."

In *Profit v. Profit* (1971), 1 Nfld. & P.E.I.R. 431 (P.E.I. S.C.), the custody order engrossed in the decree *nisi* was expressly stated to be subject to review by the court upon the expiration of one year.

16§21 — Conditional orders for custody

Divorce Act, 1985

In *Amaral v. Amaral* (1993), 50 R.F.L. (3d) 384 (Ont. Gen. Div.); additional reasons to (1993), 50 R.F.L. (3d) 364 (Ont. Gen. Div.), the custodial mother was ordered to provide the husband with notification of any serious medical problems experienced by the children. The husband was also entitled to receive, at his own expense, reports from the children's schools of their academic progress.

Divorce Act, 1968

The court has jurisdiction to impose conditions on custody orders under both the *Divorce Act* and its *parens patriae* jurisdiction: *Card v. Card* (1984), 43 R.F.L. (2d) 74, 65 N.S.R. (2d) 368, 147 A.P.R. 368 (C.A.).

Although there is a risk in trusting the custody of children to a woman suffering from a manic-depressive illness, the evidence of a competent psychiatrist can support such a granting of custody. In such a case it is not important for the trial judge to insert in the order, with the consent of the wife, provision for her to continue psychiatric care and abstain from the use of alcohol: *J. v. J.*, 4 R.F.L. (2d) 157, [1978] 1 W.W.R. 8 (Man. C.A.).

In *Parker v. Parker* (1975), 20 R.F.L. 232 (Man. C.A.), a joint custody award, whereby the mother was prohibited in the absence of the father's consent from committing the children to a certain religious organization of which she was a member, was confirmed on appeal.

Where the children had a violent antipathy toward their father due to their mother's influence, custody was granted to her on condition that the children receive therapy to improve their relationship with the father: *El-Sohemy v. El-Sohemy* (1980), 17 R.F.L. (2d) 1 (Ont. H.C.). See also *Lawrence v. Lawrence* (1975), 24 R.F.L. 300 at 302, 13 N.B.R. (2d) 637 (Q.B.); *MacRae v. MacRae* (1974), 15 R.F.L. 270 at 305, 6 Nfld. & P.E.I.R. 1 (P.E.I. S.C.); *Zwicker v. Zwicker* (1971), 3 R.F.L. 333, 4 N.S.R. (2d) 249 (T.D.); *Armstrong v. Armstrong*, 5 R.F.L. 165 at 173, [1971] 3 O.R. 544, 21 D.L.R. (3d) 140 (H.C.); *Nielsen v. Nielsen*, 5 R.F.L. 313 at 328–329, [1971] 1 O.R. 541, 16 D.L.R. (3d) 33 (H.C.).

16§22 — Joint Custody

The *Divorce Act* allows the court to award custody of the children of the marriage to any one or more persons: s. 16(4). This has been interpreted as authorizing orders for joint custody. However, it is far from enacting a presumption of joint custody. No presumption as to either joint or sole custody has been created. The court must decide the question on the basis of what is in the best interests of the child, without the guidance of any legislated policy preferring "joint custody" over "sole" custody, or vice versa. In this respect, the marginal note to the subsection setting out custody options, (s. 16(4)), may be misleading in its reference to "joint custody or access". The body of the section goes beyond this limited authority by providing that custody may be awarded to one [sole custody] or more [joint custody] persons. Clearly, joint custody is not given a preference.

The wording of s. 16(4) of the *Divorce Act*, closely parallels s. 28(a) of the Children's Law Reform Act (Ontario) which states that the court "by order, may grant the custody of or access to the child to one or more persons." This provision has not given rise to a presumption of joint custody.

As the following case notes show, joint custody can take a variety of forms. The most common form involves separating decision-making from the bundle of custody rights so that three elements are considered: (1) physical custody, (2) access, and (3) decision-making. The first two elements are reframed as (1) primary residence, (2) time with the other parent, and the third is left without change as (3) decision-making. In a typical situation, the order incorporating these elements would provide that the child has her or his primary residence with one parent, would spend certain specified times with the other parent, and that both parents jointly would be involved in major decisions affecting the child's health, education, religion, and general well being. Variations on this form involve dividing the primary residence of the child between the parents in equal or some other proportions (shared parenting), or allocating decision-making on all child-related questions to one or other of the parents, or dividing the questions giving some to one parent for decision and the rest to the other. A more recent variation on the form of joint custody is called parallel parenting. In this form, the parents are given equal status, but each exercises the rights and responsibilities associated with custody independently of the other. For a detailed discussion, see 16§22C Parallel custody.

Divorce Act, 1985

In *Kaplanis v. Kaplanis* (2005), 2005 CarswellOnt 266 (Ont. C.A.), the court held that an order of joint custody should be set aside (a) where there was no evidence of historical co-operation and appropriate communication between the parents, and (b) the order for joint custody was made in the hope that it would improve the parenting skills of the parties. Further, the court held that the trial judge had exceeded her jurisdiction by ordering that the parties attend counselling, and by imposing a requirement that, if they could not agree, a counselor was to decide the matter for them. In the result, the court set aside the award of joint custody and ordered that the mother be awarded sole custody of the child.

In *Lawson v. Lawson*, 2006 CarswellOnt 4789 (C.A.), the court refused to order joint custody where the trial judge had found that the parties were genuinely unable to cooperate and communicate effectively. The court acknowledged that it owed considerable deference to the trial judge's finding of fact. Clearly, by awarding sole custody to the mother the trial judge preferred her testimony and accepted her explanation of her behaviour. The trial judge acted in the children's best interests. The appellate court relied on *Kaplanis v Kaplanis*, above, which held that joint custody is not appropriate where parents are unable to cooperate or communicate effectively. The father had argued that rather than being a high-conflict situation, it was an "angry mother situation," and that her behaviour and general hostility towards him was not a reason to deny him joint custody of the children. He was more than willing to cooperate with her and claimed that she had denied him access to the children as a way to punish him. In the *Lawson* case, the respondent admitted that she had been emotional after the separation and had on occasion behaved in inappropriate ways. The appellant pointed to occasions in which he had called the police as a result of the respondent's behaviour, incidents which occurred in front of the children. He testified that the respondent had sworn at him in front of the children and called his new wife disparaging names.

The appellate court upheld the trial judge's decision to award sole custody to the mother rather than joint custody to the parties in *Coyle v. Danylkiw*, 2006 CarswellOnt 3158 (C.A.), since there was a body of evidence to support the trial judge's conclusion that granting the father sole custody would not have been in the child's best interests. There were a number of incidents which showed that the father exercised poor judgment and that some of his decisions were not in the child's best interests. Joint custody was not an option, given the relationship between the parties and the fact that the trial judge ruled that the mother could move with the child to Montreal. The court held that the move would be in the child's best interests, even though it meant a different and probably more limited access regime.

Joint custody should not be ordered where virtually the entire record established that a foundation for a joint or parallel custody order, namely cooperation and effective communication, was and continued to be entirely missing: *Roy v. Roy* (2006), 27 R.F.L. (6th)

44, 2006 CarswellOnt 2898 (C.A.). The court-appointed mediator testified that the parties had a "horrendous mistrust of each other." The trial judgment referred to "the enormous antipathy and mistrust that pervades [the parties'] relationship." However the Court of Appeal found that the record amply supported the trial judge's conclusion that it was in the child's best interest to spend approximately equal time with each parent.

The fact that each parent acknowledges that the other is a fit parent does not mean that it is in the children's best interests for a joint custody order to be made, particularly where the parents have communication issues: *Kaplanis v. Kaplanis* (2005), 10 R.F.L. (6th) 373, 2005 CarswellOnt 266, 249 D.L.R. (4th) 620, 194 O.A.C. 106, [2005] O.J. No. 275 (C.A.).

Separated parents in conflict but able to cooperate where the interests of the children are concerned should have joint custody of a son, 16, and a daughter, 9. However, a daughter almost 17 who quit school, was out of control, and lived with whichever parent she pleased, should not be subject to a joint custody order. No order with respect to custody should be made for her: *Ladisa v. Ladisa* (2005), 2005 CarswellOnt 268 (Ont. C.A.).

In *Gregory v. Ball* (2004), 9 R.F.L. (6th) 338, 2004 CarswellAlta 1450, 2004 ABQB 789 (Q.B.); reversed in part 2005 CarswellAlta 1526, 2005 ABCA 354 (C.A.), the court granted joint custody of the children to both parties, but the children were to live with the father on a day-to-day basis. The mother had returned to school while the father was well established. The mother's situation was accordingly not as settled as the father's and given that the parties lived 50 miles apart, shared parenting was impractical.

The general rule in situations of joint custody is that the parent with primary care and control also has the final decision-making authority with respect to the children in his or her care: *Lamont-Daneault v. Daneault* (2003), 2003 CarswellMan 369, [2003] M.J. No. 318, [2004] 6 W.W.R. 505, 177 Man. R. (2d) 235, 304 W.A.C. 235, 44 R.F.L. (5th) 412, 2003 MBCA 111 (Man. C.A.). The mother and father of two boys separated after 9 years of marriage. They agreed to joint custody, but disagreed on which of them should have primary care and control and which should have final decision-making authority. The trial judge gave primary care and control to the mother but final decision making authority to the father. The father appealed from the part of the judgment giving primary care and control of the boys to the mother and the mother cross-appealed from the part of the judgment giving final decision-making authority to the father. The father's appeal was dismissed and the mother's cross-appeal was allowed. The result gave the mother, who had primary care of the children, final decision-making authority, as well.

Mr. Justice Twaddle, in giving his reasons in the *Daneault* case (concurred in by Mr. Justice Steel) reviewed the introduction of joint custody into our law. He observed that not long ago, on separation or divorce the custody of a child of a marriage would be granted usually to one parent with access by the other:

> As time went by, the grant of sole custody to one parent became less routine. Courts began to realize that it was not in the best interests of a child to exclude one parent from the responsibility of bringing up the child and participating in the making of decisions with respect to him or her. As a result, it is now common to award custody to the parents jointly. Care and control is split between them for such periods as circumstances dictate. Thus, instead of one parent having custody and the other access, both participate in the child's upbringing and in the making of decisions respecting the child.
>
> For both practical reasons and the child's best interests, it is seldom that care and control is split evenly. It is thus customary to grant primary care and control to one parent and speci-

fied periods of care and control to the other. As long as custody is joint, however, the decision-making authority for the child is shared.

The sharing of custody works well in the case of mature parents who are able to recognize that, as parents, their role is to make decisions which are in the best interest of the child. Unfortunately, not all separated parents are able to do this. It is therefore not uncommon for a judge, seeing a potential for future discord, to designate one of the parties as the one with the final decision-making authority with respect to the child generally or with respect to certain major issues, e.g., schooling, medical treatment.

The choice of party on whom the final decision-making power should be conferred will depend on many factors. As a general rule, however, the decision-making power should, in my opinion, be conferred on the party with primary care and control.

In *Marginson v. Deveau*, 2004 CarswellNS 391, 9 R.F.L. (6th) 411, 2004 NSCA 119 (N.S.C.A.), the children's grandmother appealed from a decision granting joint custody to the grandchildren's parents and day-to-day care to their father. The grandmother had been the primary caregiver of the children for at least 2 years while the mother was unwell and unable to care for the children. Prior to the hearing, the parents had agreed to joint custody, day-to-day care and access. In light of this agreement, the onus was on the grandmother to demonstrate that it was in the best interests of the children that she, rather than the parents, have custody and day-to-day care. This onus was not discharged and the trial judge ordered custody and day-to-day care in accordance with the parents' agreement except for a slight variation that gave the grandmother additional access. The appellate court dismissed the grandmother's appeal on the ground that she had accepted the custody and day-to-day care arrangements the parents had agreed to, and that the additional access she received was more-or-less what she sought.

In *T. (T.E.) v. L. (J.D.)* (2003), 2003 CarswellSask 801, [2003] S.J. No. 778, 2003 SKQB 517 (Sask. Q.B.); additional reasons at 2003 CarswellSask 807, 2003 SKQB 517 (Sask. Q.B.); additional reasons at (2004), 2004 CarswellSask 136, [2004] S.J. No. 127 (Sask. Q.B.); affirmed 2004 CarswellSask 392, 2004 SKCA 75 (Sask. C.A.), the court distinguished between joint custody and shared parenting by making the following definitions:

"Joint custody" means an arrangement whereby the parents share responsibility in making major decisions concerning their child's welfare, be it the welfare of a long- or short-term nature. Whether the child resides only with one parent or spends an equal amount of time with each parent is of secondary importance to the arrangement.

"Shared parenting" means the parents jointly exercise normal parenting authority with the child dividing his or her time between their respective homes, usually on a rotating basis, sometimes referred to as "divided custody".

The court added:

It is well established that the ability of the parents to communicate in a reasonable and dispassionate manner regarding the welfare of their child is a fundamental requirement for a joint custody arrangement. In the absence of such ability, a joint custody arrangement should not be entertained by the court.

In arriving at its decision, the court observed that where a shared parenting arrangement is proposed in addition to the requirement that the parents are to have the ability to communicate with each other in a reasonable manner regarding major issues concerning their children's welfare, the court should be satisfied that the children do not need the security of one residence, one set of rules and expectations, and one set of primary friends. In the circumstances, the court found that a joint custody arrangement with the children residing with their father subject to access by the mother was appropriate for the long-term welfare and development of the children, which welfare and development included their education, health, religious instruction and city of residence. The joint custody arrangement would also enable the mother to play a significant role in the children's future.

In *R. (J.B.) v. R. (A.M.)*, 36 R.F.L. (5th) 210, 2003 CarswellBC 498, 2003 BCCA 135, 11 B.C.L.R. (4th) 310, 180 B.C.A.C. 37, 297 W.A.C. 37 (B.C. C.A.), the mother appealed from a judgment which varied an order for joint custody and guardianship of the children. The trial judge had given the father the authority to determine the manner in which the children would share their time between the parents and to determine the amount of time each parent spent with the children. The court held that to give the father sole control of access was a delegation of the key issue before the court for determination. The trial judge was required to provide the parties with a schedule of access, and there should be a rehearing for this purpose.

In ordering a new trial in *Segal v. Segal* (2002), 2002 CarswellOnt 2228, 26 R.F.L. (5th) 433, 162 O.A.C. 119 (Ont. C.A.), the Court of Appeal found the trial judge erred in ordering joint custody, which changed the existing custody arrangement, after finding that a change in custody would traumatize the children; that he further erred in focusing on the interests of the parents rather than on the best interests of the children; that he erred in giving no explanation of how the joint custody order served the best interests of the children where, in the circumstances of this case, the parents found communication between themselves almost impossible and there were no mechanisms in place to cope with this inability to communicate; he gave no explanation why he gave the mother final decision-making power on "any significant matter relating to the children's health, education or religion" when the lack of clarity and the conflict to which this would inevitably lead was contrary to the best interests of the children; and that he further erred by ordering access to the children by the father without making reference to the evidence of a court appointed therapist who recommended that to permit them to have a period of emotional stability and security the father should not have access to the children for a period of at least two years.

Where there is a joint custody order, but a child is in the primary care of one of the parents, it is incorrect to treat the primary care parent as a custodial parent and the other parent as an access parent: *Young v. Young*, 2003 CarswellOnt 63, [2003] O.J. No. 67, 223 D.L.R. (4th) 113, 168 O.A.C. 186, 34 R.F.L. (5th) 214, 63 O.R. (3d) 112 (Ont. C.A.). The failure of the court to comprehend the joint custody parenting arrangement was one of the reasons that the appellate court set aside the judge's order and instead ordered a new hearing, if the primary care parent wished, to decide whether she could, for employment reasons, move away with the children from their present community.

In a joint custody situation, the court may award primary care and control of the children to one parent and divide between the parents the children's matters on which each is to have decision-making responsibility: *Sawatzky v. Sherris*, 2002 CarswellMan 465, 2002 MBCA 143, [2003] 2 W.W.R. 22, 32 R.F.L. (5th) 450, 170 Man. R. (2d) 51, 285 W.A.C. 51 (Man. C.A.). The two children of the marriage were in the sole custody of the mother with reasonable access by the father. The mother wished to move with the children to another province to accompany her common-law husband. On a variation application by the father, the trial judge made an order prohibiting the move and granted joint custody of the children to the mother and the father. Under this order, primary care and control remained with the mother but final decision-making in all matters rested with the father because the mother had made inappropriate decisions respecting daycare and medical care of children. On the mother's appeal, the court observed that although the mother made poor decisions respecting daycare and medical care, there was no evidence of inappropriate decisions regarding education, religious studies or dental care. Accordingly, the father was granted final decision-making power respecting daycare, extra-curricular activities and medical care, and the mother given final decision-making power in other areas.

Conflict and lack of co-operation, whatever the source, are an impediment to an effective joint-parenting arrangement. A "worsening conflict between the parties" justifies a trial judge in varying a joint custody award to sole custody: *Wreggitt v. Belanger*, 2001 CarswellOnt 4297, [2001] O.J. No. 4777, 23 R.F.L. (5th) 457 (Ont. C.A.). In *L. (V.) v. L. (D.)*, 2001 CarswellAlta 1282, [2001] A.J. No. 1259, 2001 ABCA 241, [2002] 1 W.W.R. 651, 206 D.L.R. (4th) 325, 293 A.R. 104, 257 W.A.C. 104, 97 Alta. L.R. (3d) 51 (Alta. C.A.); additional reasons at 2002 CarswellAlta 465, 2002 ABCA 43, 211 D.L.R. (4th) 191, [2002] 6 W.W.R. 620, 1 Alta. L.R. (4th) 12, 303 A.R. 122, 273 W.A.C. 122 (Alta. C.A.), a corollary relief judgment in a divorce action gave sole custody of two children to the mother with reasonable access to the father — which he never exercised. After he remarried, and his job no longer required as much traveling, he brought a successful variation application resulting in an award of joint custody. An appeal by the mother was dismissed. On the appeal, the court observed that joint custody orders take many forms ranging from those which intend shared physical custody to those in which one parent has little physical contact with the child. The father's intent, in this case, was not to seek physical custody of either child, but to secure an ongoing role in their lives, including a right to be kept informed of and consulted about major decisions affecting them and a joint custody order was an appropriate way of accomplishing this intent. The court also observed that unless a parent is declared unfit, the children are entitled to an ongoing relationship with both parents even after their separation or divorce. The chambers judge, the court emphasized, was not persuaded that the parents were unwilling or unable to cooperate. But in any event, the mere unwillingness of one parent to share custody should not preclude an order of joint custody. The effect of an order for joint custody is to confirm the father's status as a joint guardian of the children.

In *Johnson v. Cleroux*, 2002 CarswellOnt 1559, [2002] O.J. No. 1801, 24 R.F.L. (5th) 422, (sub nom. *J. (M.) v. C. (P.)*) 159 O.A.C. 346 (Ont. C.A.), the court stated that joint custody "requires a high degree of co-operation between the parents and ought only to be awarded where the parents have demonstrated the ability to co-operate." It held that in this case the requisite degree of co-operation was not apparent on the record. Instead, the evidence suggested continuing conflict around parenting issues. Sole custody to the mother as ordered by the trial judge was confirmed.

In *Bachor v. Lehmann-Bachor*, 2001 CarswellAlta 247, [2001] A.J. No. 222, 2001 ABCA 53, 14 R.F.L. (5th) 238, 277 A.R. 269, 242 W.A.C. 269 (Alta. C.A.), the Court of Appeal held, in the circumstances, that the mother's move to another locality did not affect the child or the parents' ability to meet the child's needs in any significant way. Therefore, the move did not constitute a material change in circumstances such that a variation from sole to joint custody was warranted. (However, the move could be a material change in circumstances justifying a variation in the terms of access.) But even if a material change in circumstances affecting custody were demonstrated by the father, joint custody would not be appropriate in this case. Joint custody requires a willingness by both parents to work together and is not something that can be imposed by a court. There must be an ability on the part of each parent to put aside personal differences to make co-operative decisions about their children; a demonstrated ability to co-operate and communicate openly and freely about the child's needs and situation. In the case at bar, communications problems existed between the parties, and they had difficulty reaching agreement on child-related issues. Accordingly, the chambers judge made no error in his decision not to vary custody from sole to joint custody.

In *Tauber v. Tauber* (2000), 2000 CarswellOnt 2019, [2000] O.J. No. 2133, 48 O.R. (3d) 577, 6 R.F.L. (5th) 442, 187 D.L.R. (4th) 1, 133 O.A.C. 66 (Ont. C.A.); additional reasons at (2000), 2000 CarswellOnt 3097, [2000] O.J. No. 3355, 8 R.F.L. (5th) 441, 190 D.L.R. (4th) 509, 51 O.R. (3d) 81 (Ont. C.A.), the father appealed from the trial judge's ruling on joint custody. The father agreed that the child should have his primary residence with his mother, but contended that this should be in the context of an order for joint custody. The trial judge ruled against the father stating: "Joint custody, which is rarely imposed without consent, requires a mutual commitment between parents to cooperate fully on all matters pertaining to the nurturing of their child, and an ability for the parents to put their own interests behind those of the child. It of necessity requires that each parent trust the other and be able to communicate fully, freely, and easily with the other. Sadly, I have no confidence that at the present time these parents can deal with each other in the manner required of joint custodians." The father submitted that the trial judge took an unnecessarily conservative approach to joint custody, as courts were tending to impose joint custody without the consent of the other party. He argued that once the litigation was over, the parties would be able to reach decisions in the best interests of the children. The appellate court held that the trial judge was in the best position to rule on the suitability of joint custody. The judge was aware that he could make an award of joint custody even though the mother was opposed to such an order. On the evidence, the Court of Appeal was not persuaded that the trial judge had erred in refusing joint custody.

In *Heittola v. Heittola* (1990), 1990 CarswellOnt 1815 (Ont. C.A.), the court held that a joint custody order should not be made in the absence of a reasonable prospect that the parties will co-operate with each other. In this case, there was ample evidence on which the trial judge could find against the appellant on this issue and there was no proper basis on which the court could interfere with his decision.

In *Halloran v. Hotte* (2000), 12 R.F.L. (5th) 57, 2000 CarswellOnt 3997 (Ont. C.A.), the husband was granted joint custody with the wife to continue as primary caregiver. This enabled the husband to play a decision-making role in the children's lives. Although there had been difficulties between the parties in the past concerning the children, these had arisen because of the wife's refusal to grant the husband reasonable access and this issue had now been resolved.

The father's special appeal from an order for joint custody, and his application for sole custody were dismissed by the appellate court on the ground that the trial judge had the advantage of observing the witnesses, including the psychologist that conducted an assessment, and that the judge must have had a basis for determining that the parties could set aside their differences in the best interests of the children: *Daoust c. Leboeuf* (1998), 35 R.F.L. (4th) 143, 107 O.A.C. 73, 1998 CarswellOnt 76 (C.A.).

Where both parties claim joint custody, the trial judge does not exceed his jurisdiction by awarding sole custody to one of them: *Brundrett v. Brundrett* (1998), 35 R.F.L. (4th) 131, 1998 CarswellAlta 48, 212 A.R. 11, 168 W.A.C. 11 (C.A.). While it would be preferable for a trial judge in these circumstances to inform counsel that he is contemplating a sole custody order, sole custody is one of the options open to him. The judge's conduct of the case amounted, at most, to a procedural error.

Where the parents were granted interim joint custody with primary care and control to the mother, the father's appeal on the basis that the mother would try to limit his access to less than 40 percent in order to receive the maximum child support under the *Guidelines*, was considered to have some possible merit, but the court, in dismissing the appeal, found that the issue would be dealt with at trial: *Skinner v. Skinner* (1999), 47 R.F.L. (4th) 394, 193 W.A.C. 313, 1999 CarswellMan 229, 134 Man. R. (2d) 313 (C.A.).

The mother's appeal was dismissed where the judgement granted joint custody of the children to both parents with day-to-day care and control to the father. Their principal place of residence was with the father for two-thirds of the year when he was at home, with generous access to the mother. The mother was to have the day-to-day care and control of the children for the other one-third of the year while the father was serving in his employment at sea: *O'Quinn v. O'Quinn* (1998), 39 R.F.L. (4th) 414, 171 N.S.R. (2d) 122, 519 A.P.R. 122, 1998 CarswellNS 219, [1998] N.S.J. No. 243 (C.A.).

Where the parties' constant recourse to the courts had exacerbated the relationship of the parties, it was found that a joint custody order would have little prospect of success: *Langtry v. Langtry* (1997), 27 R.F.L. (4th) 340, 85 B.C.A.C. 284, 138 W.A.C. 284, 138 W.A.C. 284, 1997 CarswellBC 287 (C.A.).

In *Gorham v. Gorham* (1994), 3 R.F.L. (4th) 88, 131 N.S.R. (2d) 7, 371 A.P.R. 7, 1994 CarswellNS 44 (C.A.), the trial judge's refusal to award joint custody was upheld on appeal. The trial judge had properly concluded that the parties' differences in lifestyle and parenting methods precluded a joint custody order which would not have been in the child's best interests.

In *Welton v. Welton* (1992), 42 R.F.L. (3d) 233, 96 D.L.R. (4th) 767, [1992] A.J. No. 879, 1992 CarswellAlta 322 (Alta. C.A.), the parties' joint custody arrangement vested day-to-day decision-making regarding the child with the parent who had the care and control of the child at the moment. During such periods it was within the rights of this parent to remove the child from the jurisdiction to attend a funeral without the consent of the other parent.

Where the parties' shared-parenting arrangement had worked since the time of separation, it was held that a formal custody order was not required: *DaCosta v. DaCosta* (1990), 29 R.F.L. (3d) 422, 74 D.L.R. (4th) 491, 1990 CarswellOnt 314 (Ont. Gen. Div.); affirmed (1992), 40 R.F.L. (3d) 216, 7 O.R. (3d) 321, 44 E.T.R. 196, 53 O.A.C. 354, 89 D.L.R. (4th) 268, 1992 CarswellOnt 257 (Ont. C.A.); amended (1992), 40 R.F.L. (3d) 216n, 1992 CarswellOnt 3786 (Ont. C.A.).

A joint custody order is inappropriate where the parties are unable to communicate with one another: *Simmchen v. Potter* (1991), 33 R.F.L. (3d) 430, 119 N.B.R. (2d) 325, 300 A.P.R. 325, 1991 CarswellNB 35 (N.B. Q.B.); affirmed (1992), 39 R.F.L. (3d) 149, 120 N.B.R. (2d) 447, 302 A.P.R. 447, 1992 CarswellNB 41 (N.B. C.A.).

Where a joint custody order had been made, the wife had no right to decide unilaterally to enroll the child in a private school and to expect the husband to bear the cost through increased child support payments: *Lennox v. Frender*, 27 R.F.L. (3d) 181, 47 B.C.L.R. (2d) 394, [1990] 6 W.W.R. 282, 1990 CarswellBC 165 (C.A.).

Where the parents are in conflict but both have something to offer the child and the child would benefit from both parties' active parenting, a joint custody order with structured terms concerning physical custody and access can be made: *Johnston v. Johnston*, 49 R.F.L. (5th) 82, 2004 CarswellAlta 336, 2004 ABQB 221, [2004] A.J. No. 333 (Alta. Q.B.).

Where the parties agreed ultimately on joint custody but the father was better equipped to provide the necessary firm parenting, the children's needs would best be served by living with the father: *Moro v. Miletich* (1998), 40 R.F.L. (4th) 115, 1998 CarswellOnt 1194, [1998] O.J. No. 1799 (Ont. Gen. Div.).

In *Stringer v. Stringer*, 48 R.F.L. (5th) 422, 2003 CarswellBC 2824, 2003 BCSC 1739 (B.C. S.C.), a joint custody order was made with respect to the parties' two young children. The parties were capable of putting aside their personal animosity to promote the best interests of the children who had a right to the equal involvement of both parents in their lives.

In *Ardizzone v. Ardizzone*, 42 R.F.L. (5th) 239, 2003 ABQB 536, 2003 CarswellAlta 865, [2003] A.J. No. 784 (Alta. Q.B.), both parents' applications for sole custody of their 5-year-old child were dismissed and an order for joint custody made. Although both parents loved the child, their conduct had resulted in a less than ideal atmosphere for raising the child. Accordingly, an order of joint custody was made, a parenting plan was established and both parties ordered to participate in counselling.

In *P. (N.S.) v. P. (M.A.)*, 42 R.F.L. (5th) 106, 2003 CarswellAlta 1055, 2003 ABQB 629 (Alta. Q.B.), the court granted the wife's application to enroll the parties' child in French immersion kindergarten despite the objections of the joint custodial father. The fact that the child was of Portuguese descent should not preclude the child's attendance at a French/English bilingual school.

Where the mother lacked an appreciation of the father's role in the children's lives, as evidenced by the fact that she unilaterally extended an out of country trip with the children from 3 weeks to 4 months, an order for joint custody was made. Although the mother was preferred as the day-to-day caregiver, it was necessary to protect the father's position as a parent: *Terris v. Terris* (2003), 41 R.F.L. (5th) 433, 2003 CarswellOnt 2685, [2003] O.J. No. 2829 (Ont. S.C.J.).

In *Vitagliano v. Di Stavolo* (2001), 17 R.F.L. (5th) 194, 2001 CarswellOnt 1065, [2001] O.J. No. 1138 (Ont. S.C.J.), the court refused the father's application for joint custody and granted sole custody to the mother. The children had lived with the mother for over 3 years since the parties' separation and she had, during that time, had de facto sole custody. Also, given the parents' inability to communicate effectively, it was unrealistic to expect them to consult and reach a consensus regarding the children's affairs.

Where the parents are not together for a sufficiently long time to develop a common approach to raising children, joint custody may not be appropriate. Capacity for agreement is an essential pre-condition to joint custody: *Abbott v. Abbott* (2001), 13 R.F.L. (5th) 233, 89 B.C.L.R. (3d) 68, 2001 BCSC 323, 2001 CarswellBC 420, [2001] B.C.J. No. 371 (B.C. S.C.).

In *Dagg v. Pereiva* (2000), 12 R.F.L. (5th) 325, 2000 CarswellOnt 4390, [2000] O.J. No. 4450 (Ont. S.C.J.), the husband's application for joint custody was allowed, despite the acrimony that existed between him and his wife. Both parents loved the children but the wife was a deeply troubled woman who hated the husband and rejected the advice of health care and other professionals. A joint custody arrangement ensured that neither parent was alienated from the children and preserved the children's contact with both as much as was consistent with the children's best interests.

An order for joint custody is inappropriate where the parties are incapable of communicating or working together to the extent necessary for joint custody to work: *Oddi v. Oddi* (2000), 7 R.F.L. (5th) 164, 2000 CarswellOnt 1772, [2000] O.J. No. 1778 (Ont. S.C.J.).

Where both parents would be fit as custodial parents, but an antagonism and bitterness which existed between them to such an extent that they would be unable to communicate or cooperate in such a way that would permit a joint custody arrangement to work in the child's best interests, the father's application for joint custody was refused and sole custody was awarded to the mother: *Close v. Close* (1997), 33 R.F.L. (4th) 210, [1997] O.J. No. 3288, 1997 CarswellOnt 3638, 37 O.T.C. 98 (Ont. Gen. Div.).

Where both parties had deficiencies as parents, joint custody was awarded with the father's home as the primary residence. The father was incapable of acting as sole custodial parent and despite their history of acrimony, both parents wanted the continuing involvement of the other in the children's lives: *Mbaruk v. Mbaruk* (1997), 27 R.F.L. (4th) 146, 1997 CarswellBC 362, [1997] B.C.J. No. 125 (B.C. S.C.).

Where the mother repudiated a joint custody agreement shortly after it was signed but evidence supported the view that the mother was rigid in her views and bitter about the divorce and was therefore likely to put her dislike of the father ahead of the child's interests, her application for sole custody was dismissed. The child had a better chance of maintaining a relationship with both parents if she remained in the father's custody. A sole custody order in the father's favour was accordingly substituted, the acrimony between the parties rendering joint custody no longer tenable: *Boukema v. Boukema* (1997), 31 R.F.L. (4th) 329, 1997 CarswellOnt 3115, [1997] O.J. No. 2903, 33 O.T.C. 190 (Ont. Gen. Div.); additional reasons at (1997), 1997 CarswellOnt 5151 (Ont. Gen. Div.).

In *Armstrong v. Armstrong* (1997), 34 R.F.L. (4th) 38, 1997 CarswellOnt 4268, [1997] O.J. No. 4137, 46 O.T.C. 274 (Ont. Gen. Div.); additional reasons at (1997), 1997 CarswellOnt 5551 (Ont. Gen. Div.), the father's application for joint custody, whereby the children would alternate residences weekly, was refused. The parties had worked out a generous access arrangement in the 2 years since separation and it would not be in the children's best interests to disrupt their now stable environment.

In *T. (C.M.) v. S. (L.A.)*, [1998] N.W.T.R. 139, 1997 CarswellNWT 39 (N.W.T. S.C.), the court rejected the husband's suggestion that the children, in the context of a joint custody arrangement, alternate their primary residence from the wife's to the husband's on a yearly basis. The evidence indicated that the children were at a stage where structure and certainty were important and that they would find it difficult to adapt to a major disruption in their lives. Accordingly, their best interests were served by maintaining primary residency with their mother.

In *Corrigan v. Corrigan* (1998), 43 R.F.L. (4th) 48, 1998 CarswellOnt 4123 (Ont. Gen. Div.), the court made an order of joint custody awarding daily care and control to the father. The mother had previously entered a substance abuse programme and moved the children out of town, both without advising the father. The father had moved back into the matrimonial home and adjusted his work schedule to maximize his time with the children, thus restoring stability to the children's lives.

Where the parties' joint interim custody arrangement had worked to the children's benefit in spite of the parties' animosity, a final joint custody order was made in *Lichter v. Lichter* (1997), 30 R.F.L. (4th) 33, 1997 CarswellOnt 2323, [1997] O.J. No. 2558 (Ont. Gen. Div.).

In *Tweel v. Tweel* (1994), 7 R.F.L. (4th) 204, 124 Nfld. & P.E.I.R. 40, 384 A.P.R. 40, 1994 CarswellPEI 16 (P.E.I. T.D.); additional reasons at (1995), 18 R.F.L. (4th) 222, 136 Nfld. & P.E.I.R. 148, 423 A.P.R. 148, 1995 CarswellPEI 54 (P.E.I. T.D.), an award of joint custody was made but without the delineation of specific blocks of time requested by the father. The parties were already effectively sharing de facto care and control and the elaborate 14-day schedule suggested by the father would be confusing to the children and cause emotional upset.

Where both parents had demonstrated patience, cooperation and the ability to effectively communicate on all matters relating to the child, their separate claims for sole custody were dismissed and a joint custody order alternating the child's residence on a 2-week basis was made: *Woodington v. Woodington* (1994), 154 N.B.R. (2d) 117, 395 A.P.R. 117, 1994 CarswellNB 365 (Q.B.).

Where the children's emotional bonds were stronger with the mother than the father, an order of joint custody was made with the mother having primary care and control. Although the mother had sought sole custody, the joint order was found to be in the children's best interests: *Hussein v. Hussein* (1994), 3 R.F.L. (4th) 375, 146 N.B.R. (2d) 87, 374 A.P.R. 87, 3 C.C.P.B. 252, 1994 CarswellNB 271 (Q.B.).

Where both parents were loving and brought special skills to the care of their dysfunctional child, an order of joint custody was made. It was essential that bothparties' parenting skills be made available to the child: *Ysebaert v. Ysebaert* (1993), 47 R.F.L. (3d) 69, 1993 CarswellOnt 327 (Ont. Gen. Div.).

There is no presumption favouring joint custody under the *Divorce Act* or in the case law. The onus rests on the party requesting joint custody to make out a case justifying it. Joint custody may be granted in the absence of the consent of one parent, provided it is in the best interests of the children to do so. Only where the parents have displayed an ability to co-operate and communicate about decisions relating to the children, notwithstanding personal differences, and where each has maintained an ongoing and meaningful relationship with the children through the separation period, should such an order be made: *Colwell v. Colwell* (1992), 38 R.F.L. (3d) 345, 1992 CarswellAlta 307, [1992] A.J. No. 145, 128 A.R. 4 (Alta. Q.B.).

In *Surka v. Surka* (1992), 40 R.F.L. (3d) 208, 1992 CarswellMan 42, Man. R. (2d) 243 (Man. Q.B.), an award of joint custody was made although the parties were experiencing some difficulty in communicating. It appeared that the parties couldco-operate to meet the children's needs and there was no reason why the father should not be allowed to participate in decisions affecting the children's development, although daily care would remain with the mother.

In *Crawford v. Crawford* (1991), 36 R.F.L. (3d) 337, 1991 CarswellOnt 339, [1991] O.J. No. 1656 (Ont. Gen. Div.), an award of joint custody was made although both parties had claimed individual custody. Despite the fact that evidence favoured the husband were a single custodian to be chosen, both parents had an important role to play in the children's lives.

Where the husband had displayed a propensity for violence, but was not a "bad person", an order for joint custody of the children was made, with primary care and control to be exercised by the wife. The husband's lifestyle was not a good example to the children, while the wife offered a better parenting plan and greater stability: *Rezansoff v. Rezansoff* (1991), 32 R.F.L. (3d) 443, 1991 CarswellMan 34 (Man. Q.B.).

Joint custody was found to be inappropriate where one of the parties opposed it, and where one lived in Newfoundland and the other in the Northwest Territories: *Smith v. Smith* (1990), 84 Nfld. & P.E.I.R. 149, 262 A.P.R. 149, 1990 CarswellNfld 197 (Nfld. T.D.).

Where the mother lived in Quebec and the father in France, the father's request for joint custody was refused. The distance between the parties would render joint decisions on necessities and everyday life of the children too difficult: *Droit de la famille — 1219* (1988), [1989] R.D.F. 112 (C.S. Qué.). See also *Jones v. Jaworski* (1989), 18 R.F.L. (3d) 385, 93 A.R. 378, 1989 CarswellAlta 373 (Alta. Q.B.); *Sichmann v. Sichmann* (1988), 15 R.F.L. (3d) 307, 1988 CarswellAlta 335, 88 A.R. 270 (Alta. Q.B.); *Demchuk v. Demchuk* (1988), 13 R.F.L. (3d) 348, 1988 CarswellAlta 330, [1988] A.J. No. 121, 84 A.R. 206 (Alta. Q.B.); *Anderson v. Anderson* (1989), 24 R.F.L. (3d) 119, 62 Man. R. (2d) 163, 1989 CarswellMan 62 (Man. Q.B.).

Joint custody is not an appropriate order where there is hostility betweenthe parties and a lack of communication: *Hume v. Hume* (1989), 79 Nfld. & P.E.I.R. 114, 246 A.P.R. 114, 1989 CarswellPEI 65, [1989] 2 P.E.I.R. G12 (P.E.I. T.D.).

In *Heyman v. Heyman* (1990), 24 R.F.L. (3d) 402, 1990 CarswellBC 437, [1990] B.C.J. No. 484 (B.C. S.C.), an award of joint custody was made despite the fact that both parties had requested sole custody. Although the parents had differing parenting philosophies, the children's interests would still be best served through a joint custody award.

Where the parties had agreed to joint custody on an interim basis and they had been able to cooperate regarding the children, a joint custody order with shared care and control was made: *Kamimura v. Squibb* (1988), 13 R.F.L. (3d) 31, 1988 CarswellBC 570 (B.C. S.C.).

Joint custody involves a joint exercise of parental authority with both parents participating in decision-making but with one parent having physical custody of the children. Shared custody, on the other hand, includes not only joint decision-making but also a sharing of physical custody. The recognition in the *Divorce Act*, 1985 of joint custody shows that the concept is acceptable and should be considered where it is in the best interests of the child, even if one spouse does not request it: *Droit de la famille — 361*, 8 R.F.L. (3d) 272, [1987] R.J.Q. 1094, 1987 CarswellQue 33 (Qué. S.C.).

Where the spouses have a history indicating an inability to co-operate, a joint custody order is inappropriate: *Adams v. Adams* (1987), 6 R.F.L. (3d) 299, 1987 CarswellNS 65, 78 N.S.R. (2d) 437, 193 A.P.R. 437 (N.S. T.D.). See also *Menage v. Hedges* (1987), 8 R.F.L. (3d) 225, [1987] O.J. No. 1512, 1987 CarswellOnt 2397 (Ont. U.F.C.).

Where the parties held disparate views on the religion, education and recreational activities of their children, it was held that a joint custody order was inappropriate: *McNeil v. McNeil* (1989), 20 R.F.L. (3d) 52, 1989 CarswellBC 394 (B.C. S.C.).

Divorce Act, 1968

"'Joint custody is shared parental responsibility. A joint custody award gives legal custody to both parents, with care and control to one and liberal access to the other. Although a joint custody order, as opposed to the more common custody and access order, has been infrequently used by Canadian courts, in my respectful view, there is nothing unusual or startling about such an order, as it merely continues the status enjoyed by the spouses during their marriage. Joint custody orders are lauded by experts in the field of child study, are used in consent and interim situations in our courts and are recognized in other jurisdictions. Parents with joint custody have the right to continue to act as parents, as well as the responsibility of sharing in such important decisions as the child's health, education and spiritual and general welfare. Such an order retains for both parents participation and influence in the child's life, which does not occur when one parent has custody and the other has access, as the granting of even the most liberal access does not confer the right to participate in the upbringing of the child. Joint custody should be considered in cases where there are two parents who are well qualified to give affection and guidance to the child and where it can be reasonably contemplated that they are capable of co-operating with each other in the best interests of the child.' Before giving determinate consideration to joint custody, it should be established that there is no overriding case made out in favour of one parent, upon the consideration of all of the factors which enter into the determination of what is in the best interests of the child": per Carter L.J.S.C., citing *Baker v. Baker*, infra, in *Rodway v. Rodway* (1978), 3 R.F.L. (2d) 295 at 314, 1978 CarswellOnt 255 (Ont. H.C.).

A shared custody arrangement does not deprive the mother of the right to maintenance for the cost of accommodation for the children merely because the husband chooses to duplicate accommodation: *Oldham v. King* (1986), 5 R.F.L. (3d) 220, 1986 CarswellMan 114, 44 Man. R. (2d) 90 (Man. C.A.).

In *Parsons v. Parsons* (1985), 48 R.F.L. (2d) 83, 162 A.P.R. 226, 55 Nfld. & P.E.I.R. 226, 1985 CarswellNfld 33, [1985] N.J. No. 101 (Nfld. T.D.), an order of joint custody was made in accordance with the children's wishes, despite the fact that both parties had asserted a claim for individual custody.

The concept of joint custody is only viable in a situation where there is an agreement between all parties who are to share custody under such an arrangement: *Donnelly v. Donnelly* (1976), 30 R.F.L. 318, 16 N.B.R. (2d) 547, 1976 CarswellNB 20 (Q.B.).

In *Baker v. Baker* (1979), 8 R.F.L. (2d) 236, 23 O.R. (2d) 391, 1979 CarswellOnt 367, 2 Fam. L. Rev. 69, 95 D.L.R. (3d) 529 (Ont. C.A.), an order for joint custody was struck down on appeal. It was held that joint custody is an exceptional disposition which should be reserved for a limited category of separated parents. As there was no evidence to support the trial judge's conclusion that the parents were able and willing to cooperate with respect to the child, the order was inappropriate.

In *Carruthers v. Carruthers* (1982), 30 R.F.L. (2d) 215, 1982 CarswellNS 62, 55 N.S.R. (2d) 88, 114 A.P.R. 88 (N.S. T.D.), the husband's application for a joint interim custody order was denied in light of evidence that the relationship between the husband and wife was poor and that they were incapable of co-operating together in matters which affected the children.

The husband's request for joint custody was refused on the basis that the total lack of communication between the parties would render such an arrangement unworkable: *Hintze v. Hintze* (1984), 42 R.F.L. (2d) 380, 1984 CarswellAlta 279 (Alta. Q.B.).

In *Collison v. Collison* (1983), 22 Man. R. (2d) 256, 1983 CarswellMan 271 (Q.B.), the decree *nisi* which provided for joint custody was amended to vest custody in the husband alone. In light of the parties' bitter relationship, a joint-custody arrangement was not in the children's best interests.

"My judgment here is based on the very strong feeling that divided custody is inherently a bad thing. A child must know where its home is and to whom it must look for guidance and admonition and the person having custody and having that responsibility must have the opportunity to exercise it without any feeling by the infant that it can look elsewhere. It may be an unfortunate thing for the spouse who does not have custody that he or she does lose a great deal of the authority and indeed to some extent the love and affection of the child that might otherwise be gained, but this is one of the things which is inherent in separation and divorce. The parents cannot have it both ways": per Weatherston J. in

McCahill v. Robertson (1974), 17 R.F.L. 23 at 23-24, 1974 CarswellOnt 148, [1974] O.J. No. 664 (Ont. H.C.).

Where each parent fervently advocated a different form of religion and would take the opportunity to uphold their individual religious beliefs, it was held that joint custody would not be in the best interests of their children: *Brown v. Brown* (1978), 2 R.F.L. (2d) 165, 1978 CarswellSask 11 (Sask. Q.B.).

In *Fontaine v. Fontaine* (1980), 18 R.F.L. (2d) 235, 1980 CarswellMan 37 (Man. C.A.), on an application for custody, the trial judge ordered that legal custody would continue to be jointly exercised by both parents, with each having physical custody for part of every week. On appeal, per Huband J.A.: "The parents are both mature and sensible people and seem to be able to cooperate with each other concerning custody matters and the proper care of the child. The father has a stable job providing a modest but adequate income. He has overcome an alcohol problem which afflicted him in the past. He is a good provider and has demonstrated a conscientious attitude toward the care of his daughter. Because the mother is pursuing university studies, the task has fallen to the father to pick up his daughter after school and see to it that she engages in those supplementary activities which are a desirable part of every child's experience — swimming lessons, choir practice, community club activities, piano lessons. The mother is intellectually active and is pursuing university studies. As a consequence, she is not able to spend as much time with her daughter as she might wish, but she has not been distracted from a continuing genuine interest in the care and upbringing of the child. In short, we have those rare circumstances where an order of joint custody is appropriate, and the arrangements as to physical custody are realistic given the activities and availability of the parents."

Per Solomon J. in *Babyak v. Babyak* (1980), 7 Man. R. (2d) 98, 1980 CarswellMan 279 (Q.B.): "[D]uring her visitations with the girls, and during seven months of custody, the wife won the girls completely and the girls do not want to go back to live with their father. The girls are 11 and 13 years of age and they have decided they would rather live with their mother in a more permissive environment than with their father, who believes in a more strict upbringing. I am satisfied that the two girls should live together. I am also satisfied that even if this court would make an order of custody in favour of the husband, such order would not be observed because the girls, particularly the older one, would refuse to live with the father. The petitioner is living with a reformed drug addict in a common-law relationship and he has no intention of getting married. I have some serious doubts about the stability of this relationship. I am, therefore, granting joint custody of the two girls to the husband and wife, with physical custody to the wife. The husband shall have generous, reasonable access and if the parties cannot agree on the terms of visitations, they can see me in my chambers."

In *Parker v. Parker* (1975), 20 R.F.L. 232, 1975 CarswellMan 7 (Man. C.A.), a joint custody award where the children were to be in the actual care and control of the mother from September through June and in the care and control of the father during July and August was confirmed on appeal.

Where the child had particularly strong links with the father's family, an order was affirmed, within the context of the parties' joint-custody arrangement, that the child's interest were best served by having his primary residence with the father: *Cormier v. Bell* (2003), 43 R.F.L. (5th) 307, 2003 CarswellOnt 3259 (Ont. C.A.); additional reasons at (2003), 2003 CarswellOnt 4593 (Ont. C.A.).

In *Goslin v. Goslin* (1986), 4 R.F.L. (3d) 223, 1986 CarswellOnt 320, [1986] O.J. No. 743 (Ont. C.A.), the court allowed an appeal from a joint-custody order whereby the residence of the children alternated between the parents from year to year. Neither party had requested this form of joint custody and there was no evidence that such an order was in the children's best interests.

Where the husband was resident in New Brunswick and the wife in Nova Scotia, custody of the parties' child was granted to the father to permit the child to continue his schooling there. However, if the mother re-established residency in New Brunswick, the order was to change to one of joint custody: *Doucette v. Doucette* (1986), 73 N.B.R. (2d) 407, 184 A.P.R. 407, 1986 CarswellNB 523 (Q.B.).

Where the children of the marriage were two-and-a-half and four-and-a-half years of age and therefore required the care of their mother, but the father was also capable and very much interested in the rearing and training of his children, it was held that a "split custody" order was appropriate. Whereas custody of the children was vested in the father, their actual care and control was left in the hands of the mother: *Huber v. Huber* (1975), 18 R.F.L. 378, 1975 CarswellSask 8 (Sask. Q.B.).

16§22A — Divided custody

A mother was granted a stay of judgment granting custody of the parties' children to their father where the father agreed that it was in the children's best interests that they live with their mother: *Fergus v. Fergus* (1997), 33 R.F.L. (4th) 63, 104 O.A.C. 254 (C.A.). The court did not accept the father's argument that legal custody should remain with him, whilst *de facto* custody should be transferred to the mother. The court was of the opinion that there was nothing to be gained for the children by having a clear inconsistency between the court's custody order and *de facto* custody.

In *Metzner v. Metzner* (1997), 28 R.F.L. (4th) 166, 91 B.C.A.C 241, 148 W.A.C. 241, 34 B.C.L.R. (3d) 314 (C.A.), an order giving the father custody, but day-to-day control of the children to the mother, was upheld on appeal. The trial judge had found the father to be the more likely of the two to promote successful child relationships with both parents and as the children appeared to be prospering under the arrangement, there was no reason to interfere.

In *Zenner v. Zenner* (1990), 87 Nfld. & P.E.I.R. 190, 271 A.P.R. 190 (P.E.I. T.D.), the court refused the husband's application for a "divided" custody order that would have given him full parental rights during the children's periods of visitation with him. It was in the child's best interests that the custodial mother retain parental rights at all times. On appeal at ; (1991), 37 R.F.L. (3d) 313, 96 Nfld. & P.E.I.R. 337, 305 A.P.R. 337 (P.E.I. C.A.), the court affirmed the order of the trial judge with respect to custody, except it added a provision giving the respondent the right to consent to any emergency medical treatment the children might need and varied the access provision regarding telephone calls so that the father would have the right to make additional telephone calls to his children on certain holidays and other special occasions.

16§22B — Shared custody

In *Stewart v. Stewart*, 38 R.F.L. (5th) 215, 2003 CarswellPEI 58, 2003 PESCTD 41 (P.E.I. T.D.), the father's application for shared custody was denied. There had been incidents in the father's home which rendered the atmosphere unsuitable for young children.

Furthermore, the parents lacked the degree of mutual deference and respect that was necessary for shared custody to create a harmonious situation for the children.

Where the mother followed an intentional course of conduct to frustrate the father's participation in the parties' joint custody arrangement, an order for shared custody placing the final say about children-related issues in the hands of the father was made in the context of the parties' divorce. The factor tipping the balance against the mother was the impact of her past conduct on the children: *S. (C.) v. L. (T.)*, 48 R.F.L. (5th) 155, 2003 CarswellAlta 1806, [2003] A.J. No. 1561, 2003 ABQB 1013 (Alta. Q.B.).

In *Rutherford v. Rutherford* (2004), 7 R.F.L. (6th) 344, 225 N.S.R. (2d) 293, 713 A.P.R. 293, 2004 CarswellNS 301, 2004 NSSC 148 (S.C.), shared custody was ordered in respect of the parties' 10-year-old son, despite the animosity between the parents. The child had the right to as much contact with both parents as was in his best interests. If the son were to remain in the custody of his father alone, the father would continue to interfere in the child's relationship with his mother.

In *Hamlyn v. Hamlyn* (1999), 50 R.F.L. (4th) 398, 180 Nfld. & P.E.I.R. 262, 518 A.P.R. 262 (Nfld. U.F.C.), the court awarded shared custody of the children despite an agreement between the parties which designated the mother's home as principal residence. An assessment report recommended shared custody and it was also the wish of the children to live with both parents. Neither the status quo of the agreement nor the wishes of the mother could be used to subvert the children's best interests.

In *Zenner v. Zenner* (1990), 87 Nfld. & P.E.I.R. 190, 271 A.P.R. 190 (P.E.I. T.D.), the court refused the husband's application for a "divided" custody order that would have given him full parental rights during the children's periods of visitation with him. It was in the children's best interests that the custodial mother retain parental rights at all times.

On appeal, *Zenner v. Zenner* (1991), 37 R.F.L. (3d) 313, 96 Nfld. & P.E.I.R. 337, 305 A.P.R. 337 (P.E.I. C.A.), the court affirmed the order of the trial judge with respect to custody, except it added a provision giving the respondent the right to consent to any emergency medical treatment the children might need and varied the access provision regarding telephone calls so that the father would have the right to make additional calls to his children on certain holidays and other special occasions.

16§22C — Parallel custody

In parallel parenting, the parents are given equal status, but exercise the rights and responsibilities associated with custody independently of one another: *Lefebvre v. Lefebvre* (2002), 2002 CarswellOnt 4325, [2002] O.J. No. 4885, 167 O.A.C. 85 (Ont. C.A. [In Chambers]). See *Dagg v. Pereira* (2000), 2000 CarswellOnt 4390, [2000] O.J. No. 4450, 12 R.F.L. (5th) 325 (Ont. S.C.J.); *Mol v. Mol*, 1997 CarswellOnt 3693, [1997] O.J. No. 4060, 40 O.T.C. 1 (Ont. Gen. Div.); *Cox v. Stephen* (2002), 2002 CarswellOnt 2321, [2002] O.J. No. 2762, 30 R.F.L. (5th) 54, [2002] O.T.C. 499 (Ont. S.C.J.); affirmed (2003), 2003 CarswellOnt 4554, [2003] O.J. No. 4371, 47 R.F.L. (5th) 1, 179 O.A.C. 45 (Ont. C.A.).

"Under a parallel parenting regime decision-making responsibility on major matters affecting a child's welfare is divided between the parents." *Hildinger v. Carroll* (2004), 2004 CarswellOnt 444, [2004] O.J. No. 291, 2 R.F.L. (6th) 331 (Ont. C.A.); additional reasons at (2004), 2004 CarswellOnt 1334 (Ont. C.A.); leave to appeal refused (2005), 2004 CarswellOnt 4951, 2004 CarswellOnt 4952 (S.C.C.).

Joint custody with the child's primary residence to remain with the mother may be ordered on a "parallel parenting" model where the parents are to have equal status, but are to exercise the rights and responsibilities associated with custody independent of one another: *Cox v. Stephen* (2003), 2003 CarswellOnt 4554, [2003] O.J. No. 4371, 47 R.F.L. (5th) 1, 179 O.A.C. 45 (Ont. C.A.). The child, 7 years of age at the time of trial, was born of a relationship between his father and mother, who was already the mother of two children. She remarried and had a fourth child. The child involved in the legal proceeding had always lived with his mother, her husband and the other children. The mother had interfered with the father's right of access and had attempted to minimize his significance in the child's life. The parallel parenting model of joint custody took appropriate account of the risk of alienation between the father and the child, yet protected the child's sense of stability by not requiring him to leave his lifelong home and family.

In *Meyer v. Meyer*, 2002 CarswellOnt 2524, [2002] O.J. No. 3013 (Ont. S.C.J.), the father applied for joint custody of children on a parallel-parenting model with the children to be in each parent's home on alternate weeks. The mother made a cross-application, among other things, for sole custody of the children. A report by a social worker in the Office of the Children's Lawyer recommended that the children be in the joint custody of their parents because of the close relationship they had with both of them. However, the court found that there was hostility between the parents and that the most prominent feature of their relationship was their lack of effective communication. Their conflict had caused difficulty with access. They held very different views on parenting. After many court appearances there was still an unresolved legal issue. The court held, in the circumstances, that it was unable to find that a parallel parenting arrangement would be in the best interests of the children. The father's application was dismissed and custody of the children was to remain with the mother.

In *M. (T.J.) v. M. (P.G.)*, 2002 CarswellOnt 356, [2002] O.J. No. 398, 25 R.F.L. (5th) 78 (Ont. S.C.J.), Mr. Justice Aston made an order for joint custody where there was poor communication between the parents. In doing so, he reviewed the history of joint custody and its offshoot of parallel parenting. He is worth quoting at length:

> In this case, counsel for the mother argues that to impose joint custody on these particular acrimonious parents will only increase the conflict to which the children are exposed. I fail to see why that is necessarily so. A critical factual issue in any case is whether a joint custody order will expose a child to parental conflict and negatively affect the child. The focus in any particular case is not the parental hostility in a vacuum, but rather the consequence for the child. As recently as last month, the Court of Appeal in *Wreggitt v. Belanger* (2001), 2001 CarswellOnt 4297, [2001] O.J. No. 4777, 23 R.F.L. (5th) 457 (Ont. C.A.) confirmed that worsening conflict between the parents found to be a source of stress for the children precluded continuation of a 3-year-old joint custody order and justified a sole custody order in favour of the mother. In this case, the evidence does not reveal any adverse effect on any of the three children from the parental conflict. The M. children are thriving, notwithstanding the fact the parents do not communicate or co-operate very well.
>
> The evolution of the case-law on joint custody orders in Ontario, starting with the foundation case of *Baker v. Baker* (1979), 23 O.R. (2d) 391, 1979 CarswellOnt 367, 2 Fam. L. Rev. 69, 8 R.F.L. (2d) 236, 95 D.L.R. (3d) 529 (Ont. C.A.), decided more than 20 years ago by our Court of Appeal, is nicely summarized by Bellamy J. in *Dagg v. Pereira* (2000), 12 R.F.L. (5th) 325, 2000 CarswellOnt 4390, [2000] O.J. No. 4450 (Ont. S.C.J.) at paras. 39-45. She identifies *Mol v. Mol*, [1997] O.J. No. 4060, 1997 CarswellOnt 3693, 40 O.T.C. 1 (Ont. Gen. Div.) as a significant turning point. In that case, Kruzick J. reviewed a substantial number of cases from across Canada to conclude that "joint custody" can be an appropriate disposition even in cases where parents are openly hostile and uncooperative if

crafted as "parallel parenting" instead of "co-operative parenting". Consequently, "parallel-parenting" orders have become a form of joint custody, a sub-category if you will, which does not depend upon co-operative working relationships or even good communication between the parents. The concept (consistent with subsection 20(1) of the Children's Law Reform Act) is that the parents have equal status but exercise the rights and responsibilities associated with "custody" independently of one another. Section 20(7) of the Children's Law Reform Act, R.S.O. 1990, c. C.12 provides clear authority for the court to deal separately and specifically with "incidents of custody". The form of a "parallel-parenting" order addresses specific incidents of custody beyond a mere residential schedule for where children will reside on a day-to-day basis. For example, in *South v. Tichelaar*, [2001] O.J. No. 2823, 2001 CarswellOnt 2447, 20 R.F.L. (5th) 175 (Ont. S.C.J.), the court granted "joint custody" but then went on to give the father sole decision-making authority over the children's sporting activities and the mother sole decision-making authority over the dental health of the children.

The words 'custody' and 'joint custody' are often used as shorthand descriptors. However, I am convinced that many custody and access trials could be avoided if parents had to first describe, without using the words 'custody' or 'joint custody', what specific rights and responsibilities they wish to have, or are willing to share with the other parent. The phrase 'joint custody' is emotionally charged. The parent who does not have the child on a day-to-day basis, still typically the father, pursues the Holy Grail of joint custody to avoid being reduced to the status of a mere visitor to the child. This case is typical. Inevitably, the issue is framed as a question of parental rights rather than an allocation of parental responsibilities.

Before Mr. and Mrs. M. separated, she assumed responsibility for the children to a far greater extent than he did, including decision-making, not just day-to-day care. She is resentful of his position today, in part because it is inconsistent with his attitude when they were together. She attributes an ulterior motive to his claim for joint custody. She understands he has a right of access, though she believes that is all he has.

Mrs. M. already has legal custody under the Separation Agreement. The court encourages parents to settle custody and access issues. Such encouragement must include curial deference to those agreements unless they are demonstrably no longer in the best interests of the children or the person relying on the agreement has breached it in a fundamental way. Mrs. M. does not forfeit her custodial rights as a matter of censure or punishment for the type of conduct identified in paragraph 10 of these reasons. She has made good decisions for the children in areas of education, health and dental care. To her credit, she has not actively undermined the relationship between the children and their father, nor is there any pattern of resisting his access rights. If she were obstructing or refusing access or otherwise undermining Mr. M.'s relationship with the children, this would be a different case.

On the other hand, paragraph 6(B) of the Separation Agreement in this case specifically requires Mrs. M. to keep Mr. M. 'fully informed of all matters touching the interests of the children' and to 'confer' with him. Mr. M. had been seeking joint custody in the negotiation of the agreement. It is reasonable to infer paragraph 6(b) was fundamental to his concession of custody which was 'entrusted' to Mrs. M. Her subsequent conduct and attitude, reducing him to the role of a visitor to the children and most dramatically epitomized when S. was apprehended by the Children's Aid Society, substantially undermines the Separation Agreement as a factor to consider.

In my view, this is an appropriate case for a joint custody order using the 'parallel parenting' model.

The parties shall have joint custody, exercising their rights and responsibilities as set out in this order and in the best interests of the children.

The children shall be in the care and control of the applicant father as follows:

1. Every second weekend, from Friday at 3:30 p.m. to Monday at 7:30 a.m., or Tuesday at 7:30 a.m. if the Monday is a statutory holiday, except as otherwise provided herein;

2. From Wednesday at 3:30 p.m. until Thursday at 7:30 a.m. each week, except as otherwise provided herein;

3. For two weeks out of every six weeks, from 3:30 p.m. on weeknights until 7:30 a.m. the following morning, such weeks to coincide, if possible, with the weeks the mother is working an afternoon shift;

4. For two weeks each summer, on the basis that

(a) the applicant is to have the choice of those two weeks, provided he gives notice on or before June 1st each year,

(b) if he fails to do so, the respondent is to advise him by June 15th of a two-week period when she wants to have the children exclusively, and his two weeks will be subject to her wishes in that regard, and

(c) in any event, the applicant and respondent will each have the children in his or her exclusive care and control for two weeks each summer;

5. At Christmas, from 2:00 p.m. December 24th to 8:00 p.m. December 25th in "odd numbered" years and from December 25th at 8:00 p.m. to December 27th at 8:00 p.m. in "even numbered" years;

6. Father's Day each year, provided Mother's Day will be with the respondent each year;

7. Such further or other times as the parties agree.

The children shall, otherwise, be in the care and control of the respondent mother. The parties are each entitled to obtain directly from any teacher, school, health practitioner, counsellor or other person, hospital, company, institution or agency information and documents relating to the children, or any of them. All such documentation shall be shared forthwith with the other parent.

Medical appointments will be scheduled by the mother after consultation with the father, so as to enable him to attend if he wishes. If the mother resumes midnight shifts, the babysitter will be instructed to call the father in the event of any emergency relating to the children. Either parent has the authority to deal with any medical or dental emergency.

The parents are jointly appointed as guardians of the property of the children, including any passports, health cards or other documents.

Neither parent shall remove any of the children from the Province of Ontario without the written permission of the other, such permission not to be unreasonably withheld.

If either parent wishes to move from Mitchell, he or she will first give the other parent 60 days written notice, together with a proposal for any variation of the terms of this order.

Each parent is entitled to reasonable telephone contact with the children when they are with the other parent.

Each parent is entitled to attend all public events and school activities involving the children, even when they occur while the child is in the care of the other parent.

The parties will confer with one another before making any decision concerning the health or dental care, education or religious instruction of any child. In the event the parties disagree on a medical or dental decision, the mother will have the final say. Either may apply to the court by Notice of Application for a summary disposition of any other matter upon which they disagree.

Where the father had suffered a brain injury which made him overly aggressive with the mother, primary care of the children was awarded to the mother. The father was not aggressive with the children and a parallel-parenting scheme was accordingly ordered:

Broder v. Broder (1998), 42 R.F.L. (4th) 143, 1998 CarswellAlta 878, [1998] A.J. No. 1046, (sub nom. *J.E.B. v. C.B.)* 238 A.R. 187 (Alta. Q.B.).

16§23 — Death of custodial parent

Where the mother had been awarded custody of the child of the marriage, had remarried and was subsequently killed in an automobile accident, custody of the child was awarded to the natural father against the claim of the mother's new husband. Although the father had in the past been delinquent in making child maintenance payments, it was held that *prima facie* the natural father was entitled to custody absent some act, condition or circumstance requiring the natural relation be severed in deference to the child's welfare: *Meikle v. Authenac* (1970), 3 R.F.L. 84, 74 W.W.R. 699 (Alta. C.A.).

Upon the death of a court-ordered custodial parent the other parent's rights to custody of the children are not to be considered as exclusive, but are subject to the paramount consideration of the welfare of the children: *Gordon v. Gordon* (1975), 20 R.F.L. 355 (Ont. Prov. Ct.).

In *Kociuba v. Children's Aid Society of Halton* (1971), 18 R.F.L. 286 (Ont. H.C.), custody of the child of the marriage was awarded to the father upon the death of the custodial mother, despite the deceased mother's wishes that the child be raised by members of her family.

An order for custody under the *Divorce Act* is an order *in personam* as between the parties. That being the case, the very nature of a custody order mandates its automatic termination upon the death of the custodial parent: *Re Cowles* (1981), 21 R.F.L. (2d) 337, 32 O.R. (2d) 114 (U.F.C.).

16§24 — Official Guardian and Superintendent of Child Welfare

Divorce Act, 1985

There is no jurisdiction in the court to dispense with the filing of the Official Guardian's report prior to the granting of a decree *nisi*. Accordingly, a decree issued without the filing of the report may be set aside: *Lorentz v. Lorentz* (1987), 60 O.R. (2d) 383 (H.C.).

Divorce Act, 1968

The practice whereby the Superintendent of Child Welfare is represented by counsel before the court in relation to child custody issues and assumes a role akin to that of an *amicus curiae*, is a commendable one: *Re Hall* (1975), 20 R.F.L. 142, [1975] W.W.D. 96, 53 D.L.R. (3d) 710 (B.C. S.C.); reversed on other grounds 24 R.F.L. 6, [1976] 4 W.W.R. 634, 70 D.L.R. (3d) 493 (B.C. C.A.).

Neither the Official Guardian nor the infants whose interests he represents are, in any sense, normal parties to the proceedings under a divorce petition. The Official Guardian is an officer of the court, has specific rights of audience, and may always have the ear of the court when infants are concerned. He is there to help the court. It is the court in whose care the interests of the infants lie, and no default by anyone can relieve the court of its duty to discharge the high prerogative right and duty of the Crown towards infants as *parens patriae*, nor permit the court, in any final way, to disregard the clear commands of the rules designed to protect infants: *Wallin v. Wallin*, 13 R.F.L. 305, [1973] 2 O.R. 870 (H.C.); reversed on other grounds (1974), 18 R.F.L. 122, 6 O.R. (2d) 33, 51 D.L.R. (3d) 677 (C.A.).

"Although there was a Queen's Proctor appointed to protect the interests of the children, and to advise the court as to custody, I have not called upon him to perform his usual functions. Normally this would have entailed an investigation, usually undertaken by a member of the Department of Social Services, into the background situation of the respective households. Such investigation would necessarily have been undertaken both here and in Winnipeg. Because of the exclusive nature of the evidence adduced, giving the court a pretty clear picture of both situations, counsel agreed, and I concurred, that it would not be necessary to follow that procedure in this instance. Not only would it cause a further delay in the disposition of a matter which should not be unduly delayed, but would do little more than cover ground already a matter of court record": per McQuaid J. in *Bolton v. Bolton* (1976), 26 R.F.L. 284 at 295 (P.E.I. S.C.).

In *Whitehead v. Ziegler (Whitehead)* (1974), 18 R.F.L. 357, 50 D.L.R. (3d) 145 (Sask. Q.B.), a father's application to vary the custody provisions contained in a decree of nullity, it was ordered that the Official Guardian represent the children throughout the proceedings with full right of participation as if the children themselves had been named parties.

The court may, in the course of divorce proceedings, direct that the Department of Social Welfare conduct a full investigation and report its findings to the court concerning the suitability of the parties as custodial parents: *Csicsiri v. Csicsiri* (1973), 13 R.F.L. 263 (Alta. T.D.); varied on other grounds (1974), 17 R.F.L. 31 (Alta. T.D.).

Children are still children of the marriage notwithstanding their committal to the Minister. Furthermore, the parents, in the absence of an adoption, have contingent future statutory guardianship rights to them, which rights vary depending on whether the committal was voluntary or otherwise. Accordingly, a petition for divorce must include particulars of such children and an Official Guardian investigation is still mandatory: *Martens v. Martens* (1981), 31 O.R. (2d) 313 (U.F.C.).

16§25 — Custody and child's right to counsel

Divorce Act, 1985

Where the father brought a motion for custody of the parties' adult, mentally disabled son against the custodial mother, the son was granted intervenor status. The son was entitled to be represented as he had a direct interest in the outcome of the proceedings and could bring a different and useful perspective to the proceedings. *R. (M.T.) v. R. (I.S.)*, 48 R.F.L. (5th) 385, 2003 CarswellBC 2345, 187 B.C.A.C. 240, 307 W.A.C. 240, 2003 BCCA 513 (B.C. C.A.).

In *Strobridge v. Strobridge* (1994), 4 R.F.L. (4th) 169, 18 O.R. (3d) 735, 115 D.L.R. (4th) 489, 4 R.F.L. (4th) 169, 72 O.A.C. 379 (C.A.); reversing in part (1992), 42 R.F.L. (3d) 154, 10 O.R. (3d) 540, 95 D.L.R. (4th) 503 (Gen. Div.), the court was of the opinion that counsel appointed by the Official Guardian to represent the children in a custody dispute was entitled to file or call evidence and make submissions on all of the evidence. Mr. Justice Osborne was of the view that counsel was not entitled to express his or her personal opinion on any issue, including the children's best interests. Counsel was not entitled to become a witness and advise the court what the children's access-related preferences were. If those preferences should be before the court, the appropriate evidentiary means must be used. Without consent, counsel could not be both an advocate and a witness on an important issue.

Divorce Act, 1968

In *J. v. J.*, 4 R.F.L. (2d) 157 at 161, [1978] 1 W.W.R. 8 (Man. C.A.), the husband argued on an appeal from an order denying him custody that the failure of the trial judge to require independent legal representation for the children necessitated the direction of a new trial. O'Sullivan J.A., in rejecting the argument, stated: "There may indeed be cases where it is desirable that children should have separate representation, but we do not think the case before us is such a one. Where it is thought desirable, however, there is ample scope in the rules and practice of the courts to allow for appropriate representation to be supplied. An infant may at any time make application by a next friend. Such an application may be made through counsel acting for a next friend. Alternatively, there is provision in the rules for the appointment of a guardian ad litem, either the public trustee or a guardian appointed for that purpose by the court. A guardian ad litem has the right to instruct counsel. A guardian ad litem might be appointed on the application of a next friend or either of the parties in litigation or on the motion of the court in appropriate cases. We do not think it would be sound to give illustrations of those rare cases when separate representation might be useful. The question should be resolved by a trial judge in the exercise of his discretion. We demur, however, from the suggestion that such separate representation should be a matter of course because we are of the view that it is not desirable, in the usual case, to involve children in choosing between parents who might exert pressure on them in making a difficult and traumatic selection of one against the other."

"I also believe that the court must recognize growing public support for the view that children are entitled to independent representation in custody cases, at least where it is clear that their true interests will not be served by an adversarial contest between parents or other parties. An important recommendation for such independent representation should not be allowed to languish unacted upon, as was the case in these proceedings, for a period of well over six months": *More v. Primeau* (1978), 2 R.F.L. (2d) 254 at 260 (Ont. C.A.), per Blair J.A.

In the context of a custody dispute, the *amicus curiae* is not entitled to call hearsay evidence on fundamental issues relating to custody. The appointment of an *amicus* by the court does not relieve the *amicus* from ordinary evidentiary restrictions relating to expert evidence. The expert's qualifications must be established and his opinion expressed within the expertise so established. An expert cannot testify as to matters of "common sense". The role of the *amicus* is to provide assistance to the court in arriving at a custody decision. The *amicus* does not necessarily represent the child. It is useful, then, when applying for the appointment of an *amicus*, to inform the court of the specific role the *amicus* is to perform. If the *amicus* is a resource person appointed to provide an expert opinion, he or she should not be considered a party or have the right to cross-examine. Where the *amicus* acts as a "party", his or her conduct should be regulated by the same rules and provisions which govern other parties. The *amicus* should make every effort to be and appear to be even-handed and impartial: *Young v. Young*, 48 R.F.L. (2d) 390, 41 Alta. L.R. (2d) 66, [1986] 1 W.W.R. 555, 65 A.R. 347 (Q.B.).

In *Bonenfant v. Bonenfant* (1981), 21 R.F.L. (2d) 173 (Ont. H.C.), an application by the Official Guardian to represent children of the marriage in divorce and custody proceedings was refused. Per Fitzgerald L.J.S.C.: "I have found nothing in this material of a nature that is not encountered in one form or another in virtually every contested custody matter. There is nothing to indicate that the children are being pressured by either parent or that they are being abused by either parent or that they are afraid or reluctant to speak their minds. There is nothing in this case to indicate that the court could not discover from the children what their feelings are in the matter. There is nothing in this case that indicates that the children require the intervention of a champion to present their plight to the court in order to enable the court to decide what is in the best interest of the children. There is no reason to suppose that an independent solicitor will be better able than the court to discover either the true feelings of the children or to resolve, in his advocacy, the possible conflict between what the children may think they want and what may be in their best interests. Nor is there any indication that the solicitor would need to call witnesses who would not be called in any event ... as a practical matter, the cost of the intervention in this case outweighs the probability of the intervention being of any substantial assistance to the court or to the children." See also *Rowe v. Rowe* (1976), 26 R.F.L. 91 at 96 (Ont. H.C.); *Re Reid* (1975), 25 R.F.L. 209 at 217, 11 O.R. (2d) 622, 67 D.L.R. (3d) 46 (Div. Ct.).

In *Currie v. Currie* (1975), 18 R.F.L. 47 (Alta. T.D.), the court directed that an *amicus curiae* be appointed to represent the interests of an 11½-year-old child who was the subject of a custody dispute.

16§25A — Custody assessments

In *Walsh v. Walsh* (1998), 39 R.F.L. (4th) 416, 111 O.A.C. 118 (C.A.); affirming (1996), 20 O.T.C. 77 (Gen. Div.), the wife appealed from a custody order on the grounds that the trial judge had abdicated his responsibility by placing undue weight on a psychologist's report. As it was evident that the trial judge had analyzed the report critically and had refused to follow the ultimate recommendations contained therein, the appeal was dismissed.

Where the father had been awarded interim custody after the assessment officer had testified before the case management judge who had not allowed cross-examination or the introduction of other evidence, the mother's appeal was allowed. The procedure had been contrary to the basic principles of fundamental justice as the parties had lacked any knowledge of the content of the report and had been given no opportunity to challenge it: *LeClair v. LeClair* (1997), 31 R.F.L. (4th) 378, 200 A.R. 373, 146 W.A.C. 373 (C.A.).

In *Z. (M.J.) v. Z. (A.M.)* (1997), 31 R.F.L. (4th) 446 (Ont. C.A.), the wife had appealed an order granting access to the child of the marriage, although acknowledging that the trial judge did not err in granting access, but submitting that in making certain of the terms of access, the trial judge had failed to consider evidence concerning the husband's character and disregarded expert psychiatric evidence. The court was of the opinion that the trial judge gave his reason for rejecting the expert evidence of a psychiatrist retained by the mother, who did a history and psychological profile of the mother, but never saw or tested the father. The trial judge had rejected the expert evidence because of the methodology employed and the fact that he had not assessed the father. The appeal was allowed in part on other issues.

In *Elliott v. Elliott* (1996), 27 R.F.L. (4th) 23, 193 A.R. 177, 135 W.A.C. 177 (C.A.), the trial judge relied on bilateral medical expert opinion that the father harboured a negative attitude to the mother which could become an alienation syndrome. This syndrome would have a detrimental effect upon the child. Consequently, the trial judge changed the custody order from day-to-day custody with the father and access to the mother to joint custody, with day-to-day care and control to the mother. The trial judge's solution was not a fundamental error.

Where, in a custody dispute, an assessment report prepared under the direction of the children's lawyer was both incomplete and contained errors and was therefore largely disregarded by the trial judge, an order of costs against the children's lawyer was refused. The lawyer was not a party and did not represent a party in the action. Furthermore, there was no evidence that showed that any costs were incurred as a result of the report: *Takis v. Takis* (2003), 38 R.F.L. (5th) 422, 2003 CarswellOnt 2358 (Ont. S.C.J.)

Where the husband contended that the expert giving evidence in the parties' custody dispute was biased in the wife's favour, the court ordered that a second assessment be done by a different qualified psychologist. There was a great deal of conflicting evidence and the court required further professional advice: *O. (J.D.) v. O. (S.K.)*, 27 R.F.L. (5th) 394, 2002 CarswellAlta 501, 2002 ABQB 365, 313 A.R. 116 (Q.B.); additional reasons at 2002 CarswellAlta 571, 2002 ABQB 419 (Q.B.).

A home study/assessment is not a mandatory component of every custody and access dispute. Such inquiries are expensive and relatively invasive and should only be awarded when grounds exist for taking such a unique step: *G. (K.J.) v. M. (D.M.)*, 20 R.F.L. (5th) 49, 2001 CarswellAlta 957, 2001 ABQB 617 (Alta. Q.B.).

A psychologist's report prepared at the request of both parties to a custody dispute was found not to be privileged and therefore admissible in evidence. The report was not produced solely for the purposes of settlement negotiation and accordingly privilege did not apply: *Fairbairn v. Hoenig* (1999), 4 R.F.L. (5th) 66, 1999 CarswellOnt 3410 (Ont. Master).

Where a custody assessment was ordered in the context of a custody dispute the mother was prohibited from removing the children to another community as she had planned to do. It was better that the status quo be maintained so as not to interfere with the neutrality of the assessment process: *Gallant v. Jackson* (1994), 7 R.F.L. (4th) 391 (Ont. Gen. Div.).

The evidentiary role of a custody assessment ordered in the context of an interim custody application is questionable: *Genovesi v. Genovesi* (1992), 41 R.F.L. (3d) 27, 93 D.L.R. (4th) 262 (Ont. Gen. Div.).

Although a judge, and not an assessor, must make the decision in a custody case, a judge is entitled to rely upon a thorough, impartial assessment report in making the decision: *Lapierre v. Lapierre* (1991), 34 R.F.L. (3d) 129 (Sask. Q.B.).

Although experts have a role in custody cases, it is ultimately the court's responsibility to decide who is best able to meet a child's needs. Accordingly custody assessments should not be ordered as of right in all cases: *Saffin v. Saffin* (1991), 35 R.F.L. (3d) 250 (Alta. Q.B.).

In custody and access assessments, the assessor is not an arbitrator and is not bound by the rules regulating decision-making tribunals. The assessor may set the rules of procedure and decide about conveying information received between the parties. Any such information is not privileged and production may later be compelled in the court proceeding: *Hunka v. Hunka* (1991), 35 R.F.L. (3d) 176 (Alta. Q.B.).

An expert witness' opinions in a child custody and access dispute are entitled to substantial weight only if based upon personal observations. An expert's report which is based solely on interviews of some of the witnesses in the case does not meet these requirements: *Sherry v. Sherry* (1993), 1 R.F.L. (4th) 146, 114 Nfld. & P.E.I.R. 67, 356 A.P.R. 67 (P.E.I. S.C.).

Expert assessments in custody proceedings are useful to the court but are only one factor to consider in awarding custody. Accordingly, in *Tyabji v. Sandana* (1994), 2 R.F.L. (4th) 265, 112 D.L.R. (4th) 641 (B.C. S.C.), the court found that the children's best interests favoured the father as custodial parent despite two assessment reports which recommended that the mother be granted custody.

A psychologist's report prepared at the request of both parties to a custody dispute was found not to be privileged and therefore admissible in evidence. The report was not produced solely for the purposes of settlement negotiation and accordingly privilege did not apply: *Fairbairn v. Hoenig* (1999), 4 R.F.L. (5th) 66, 1999 CarswellOnt 3410 (Master).

In *Rawlek v. Rawlek*, 39 R.F.L. (5th) 201, 2003 CarswellBC 1276, 2003 BCSC 1466 (B.C. S.C.), the court refused to allow into evidence in a custody dispute telephone conversations which the mother had secretly taped involving herself, the father and the children. The evidence was one-sided and was surreptitiously obtained, the transcripts were edited and inaccurate, and the tapes could give a distorted picture of the father's parenting skills.

16§26 — Evidence in custody matters

Divorce Act, 1985

In *Segal v. Segal* (2002), 26 R.F.L. (5th) 433, 2002 CarswellOnt 2228, 162 O.A.C. 119 (C.A.), the court allowed the mother's appeal from an order granting the father access to the children. Therapist's evidence presented at the trial recommended a 2-year moratorium be placed on the father's access. The evidence was germane to the issue of the children's best interest, and the court should have given reasons for departing from the recommendation.

In *Rockwell v. Rockwell* (1988), 43 R.F.L. (4th) 450, 167 D.L.R. (4th) 293, 114 B.C.A.C. 189, 186 W.A.C. 189, 59 B.C.L.R. (3d) 380 (C.A.), a trial, the mother was permitted to move out of the jurisdiction to Edmonton in order to live with her new partner. The court was of the opinion that the trial judge's dismissal of the father's motion to adjourn the trial until the psychologist could attend was within the discretion of the trial judge. The psychologist did not not interview the new partner and it was the evidence of the respondent and the new partner in particular that led to the trial judge's decision regarding custody and the move to Edmonton.

In family law matters, the courts are reluctant to dismiss motions for new evidence on the basis of due diligence where that evidence is central to the issue before the court and prohibiting the admission of such evidence could lead to an injustice in regard to the best interests of the children: Rockwell v. Rockewell, above. In this decision, contradictory affidavit evidence as to the events between the parties after oral reasons were given did not have a bearing on the outcome of the case and thus their admission was rejected as fresh evidence.

In a custody case, the advisability of a judge holding a private interview with a child is an issue within the trial judge's discretion. However, the use of such interviews should be limited and not perceived as an opportunity to obtain valuable information shielded from the knowledge of and the challenge by the litigants: *Hamilton v. Hamilton* (1989), 20 R.F.L. (3d) 152 (Sask. C.A.).

In determining the issue of a child's best interests in a custody case, the issue is to be decided by the judge and not by expert witnesses: *Lambright v. Lambright* (June 5, 1990), Doc. Edmonton Appeal 9003-0129-AC (Alta. C.A.).

Evidence of a psychologist in a custody case which was based on hypothetical questions and not actual interviews with the parties was found to be inadmissible in *Johnstone v. Brighton* (2004), 6 R.F.L. (6th) 288, 2004 CarswellOnt 3229 (S.C.J.).

In *Rawlek v. Rawlek*, 39 R.F.L. (5th) 201, 2003 CarswellBC 1276, 2003 BCSC 1466 (B.C. S.C.), the court refused to allow into evidence in a custody dispute telephone conversations which the mother had secretly taped involving herself, the father and the children. The evidence was one-sided and was surreptitiously obtained, the transcripts were edited and inaccurate, and the tapes could give a distorted picture of the father's parenting skills.

Where the child's social worker had improperly played the role of both investigator and therapist in substantiating the child's allegations that the father had sexually abused her, the trial judge's findings of sexual misconduct could not be allowed to stand. However, as the child was afraid of the father, the sole custody award in the mother's favour was not disturbed on appeal: *T. (M.) v. T. (J.)* (1997), 33 R.F.L. (4th) 430 (Ont. Gen. Div.).

Where a judge personally interviews the children involved in a custody dispute to learn their preferences and views, it is the prerogative of the judge as to whether to describe the results of the interview. Although the results may be revealed in general terms, specifics are properly withheld if they could embarrass the children or potentially damage their future relationship with either parent: *Demeter v. Demeter* (1996), 21 R.F.L. (4th) 54, 133 D.L.R. (4th) 746 (Ont. Gen. Div.).

In *Roberts v. Roberts* (1991), 104 N.S.R. (2d) 27, 283 A.P.R. 27 (T.D.), the court refused to allow into evidence, at a custody trial, a videotape of the wife's residence contrasted with that of her husband. Such evidence was highly prejudicial, not objective, and ripe for tampering.

Where the motions judge refused the custodial mother's application for an adjournment in the father's application for an order allowing him to remove the child from the country for a vacation, the order in the father's favour was reversed on appeal. The purpose of the adjournment was to allow the mother time to file affidavit evidence and, as the judge's decision was to be based upon the child's best interests, he required all available information to perform his duty: *Bajzat v. Bajzat* (1991), 35 R.F.L. (3d) 59, 52 O.A.C. 25 (Div. Ct.); additional reasons at (September 30, 1991), Doc. 075D (Ont. Div. Ct.).

Divorce Act, 1968

Where the trial judge, in determining custody, had rejected expert evidence called by the parties for legally incorrect reasons and had called his own expert despite an abundance of available evidence, an appeal from the custody award was allowed and a new trial ordered: *Bzdel v. Bzdel* (1987), 8 R.F.L. (3d) 1, 57 Sask. R. 81 (C.A.).

Expert evidence is of great value in determining the issue of custody, but the decision must be made by the court. It is a responsibility that cannot be delegated: *More v. Primeau*, above.

Although there have been instances in which an infant has been called to give evidence as a witness in a custody proceeding and has been subjected to examination and cross-examination, such a procedure, except in the case of a very stable and mature child, should only be resorted to in the most exceptional circumstances: *Re Miechkota* (1978), 21 N.B.R. (2d) 373, 37 A.P.R. 373 (C.A.), citing Mendes da Costa, *Studies in Canadian Family Law* (Butterworths, 1972).

"If the trial judge should decide to allow a child to express his wishes, the judge should then decide upon the procedure he should use in the particular instance for the expression of those wishes. A certain procedure may be appropriate for one case but not another. To call the child as a witness and ask direct questions to establish his preferences is a procedure that should be discouraged. It is generally, but not always, inappropriate. In the present case the learned trial judge was right, in my respectful view, to decline to hear the children as witnesses, even though they were represented by independent counsel. The procedure involving a judge speaking to a child, informally, in his chambers, also is not a particularly satisfactory one. To expect a child in such a short period and abnormal atmosphere (from the child's point of view) to choose between parents, and to expect to obtain from that child an accurate insight into the reasons for the child's feelings and preferences is ordinarily to expect too much. ... A procedure involving a trained and competent third party, independent of the parents, charged with the responsibility of ascertaining the child's opinions and preferences using such techniques as are most likely to yield genuine feelings and wishes, and be least harmful to the child, over such period of time as may be necessary, and thereafter reporting to the court, by giving testimony or otherwise, is the procedure to be looked upon with the most favour": per Bayda J.A. in *Wakaluk v. Wakaluk* (1976), 25 R.F.L. 292 at 304 (Sask. C.A.).

Where the father had continually denigrated the mother in the child's presence, it was held that the case was not a proper one in which to have the child privately interviewed by the trial judge, due to the inability of the mother to rebut or cross-examine on the evidence privately given: *Austin v. Austin* (1970), 2 R.F.L. 136, 73 W.W.R. 289, 13 D.L.R. (3d) 498 (Sask. C.A.).

In custody matters, the court must always treat expert evidence in the same manner as other evidence and assess and decide the outcome on the whole of the evidence. Therefore, the court may award access to the children's father on the basis of the total evidence, despite the opinion of a psychiatrist that the father be denied access: *Tassou v. Tassou* (1975), 23 R.F.L. 351 (Alta. T.D.).

In a custody dispute in which the report of an eminently qualified doctor has been filed in evidence, the court may feel bound to give effect to the expert testimony should the reported views of the doctor not be challenged: *Kahn v. Kahn* (1973), 13 R.F.L. 269 (Ont. H.C.).

See also *Taberner v. Taberner* (1971), 5 R.F.L. 14 at 15 (Ont. H.C.); *Ansley v. Ansley*, 12 R.F.L. 93 at 96, [1973] 5 W.W.R. 181 (B.C. S.C.); *Henderson v. Henderson*, 29 R.F.L. 1, [1977] 3 W.W.R. 316 (B.C. Prov. Ct.).

16§27 — Access — general

The term access is not defined under the current Act. Under the current legislation, access must at least include the right to make inquiries, and to obtain information about the health, education, and welfare of the child: s. 16(5).

The sole criterion in awarding access is the best interests of the child as determined by reference to the condition, means, needs and other circumstances of the child: s. 16(8), taking into account s. 16(10).

Section 16(10) suggests that access is for the benefit of the child and not for the benefit of the parent. It provides that a child of the marriage should have as much contact with each spouse as is consistent with the best interests of that child. Further, the subsection indicates the importance to the child of a cooperative attitude in the custodial parent toward access by the other parent. It follows from this provision that where two parents are otherwise equal, the one more willing to encourage access may be awarded custody.

The court may make access orders for a definite or indefinite period, or until the happenings of a specified event, and may in its discretion impose terms and conditions.

Divorce Act, 1985

In *Gordon v. Goertz*, 19 R.F.L. (4th) 177, [1996] 2 S.C.R. 27, the Supreme Court of Canada held, inter alia, that the father's access to his daughter who had moved to Australia with her mother, the custodial parent, should not be restricted to Australia. While the mother should continue to have custody, the father should be permitted to exercise access in Canada. Access in Canada would permit the child to maintain contact with friends and family. The court affirmed the custody order but allowed the appeal in part, to permit the father to exercise access in Canada.

Although the decision to place responsibility for ongoing access in the hands of the custodial parent may be unusual, it is not, in and of itself, improper: *McGrath v. Thomsen*, 11 R.F.L. (5th) 174, 2000 BCCA 640, 2000 CarswellBC 2383, 147 B.C.A.C. 195, 241 W.A.C. 195 (B.C. C.A.).

The court in *Henderson v. Henderson* (1998), 43 R.F.L. (4th) 317 (Alta. C.A.), dismissed the father's appeal from a decision requiring that an assessment be conducted for determination of access to children. The father, a Scientologist, said that he did not believe in psychologists or psychiatrists, would not expose his children to them and could not afford to pay for such a study. The court ruled that such an assessment, in the view of the trial judge, was important in providing an independent, objective and professional viewpoint and the appellate court could see no error in so doing.

The costs to an access parent of arranging and carrying out his or her visitation rights are properly considered in determining that parent's ability to pay child support: *Armstrong v. Armstrong* (1993), 49 R.F.L. (3d) 456, 88 Man. R. (2d) 109, 51 W.A.C. 109 (C.A.).

Where the father, who had been a substance abuser, had been denied access to the children for almost 2- 1/2 years, the court ordered that access was to be gradually introduced. There was evidence supporting the husband's claims to be drug-free and the mother's claims that access was harmful for the children were unfounded: *Sawyers v. McKechnie* (2003), 42 R.F.L. (5th) 165, 2003 CarswellOnt 2650 (Ont. S.C.J.).

The facts that the father was homosexual and was involved in a relationship were found not to be reasons to restrict his access to his children: *Droit de la famille — 663*, [1989] R.J.Q. 1550, [1989] R.D.F. 544 (C.S.).

In *Droit de la famille — 663*, above, the court rejected the wife's application that the husband, who had AIDS, be granted supervised access only. There was no evidence indicating that the children were likely to contract the virus and it was in their best interest to have regular contact with their father.

In *B. (G.) v. B. (M.)* (1988), 19 R.F.L. (3d) 283 (Que. C.A.), the appellant was allowed to amend a notice of appeal in a custody action to request a declaration that s. 11(1)(c) of the *Divorce Act, 1968* was unconstitutional as infringing the *Canadian Charter of Rights and Freedoms*.

Where the father, who had been a substance abuser, had been denied access to the children for almost 2 1/2 years, the court ordered that access was to be gradually introduced. There was evidence supporting the husband's claims to be drug-free and the mother's claims that access was harmful for the children were unfounded: *Sawyers v. McKechnie* (2003), 42 R.F.L. (5th) 165, 2003 CarswellOnt 2650 (Ont. S.C.J.).

A 16-year-old child is sufficiently old enough to make personal choices regarding access by the non-custodial parent: *Paslawski v. Paslawski*, 49 R.F.L. (5th) 392, 2003 CarswellSask 755, 2003 SKQB 462 (Sask. Q.B.).

Where the parties' three children, ranging in age from 13 to 17 years, refused to see their father after separation despite professional evidence that contact with their father was in their best interests, the court had no realistic option to bring about contact. The father was accordingly allowed reasonable access provided the children wished to have contact with him: *Lampron v. Lampron* (2003), 50 R.F.L. (5th) 98, 2003 CarswellOnt 5062 (Ont. S.C.J.); additional reasons at (2004), 2004 CarswellOnt 2517 (Ont. S.C.J.).

It is contrary to family law practice to permit an 11-year-old child to refuse to see her father, absent any logical explanation on her part: *Kuntz v. Kaytor* (1995), 10 R.F.L. (4th) 246 (Sask. Q.B.).

In *Strobridge v. Strobridge* (1992), 42 R.F.L. (3d) 154, 10 O.R. (3d) 540, 95 D.L.R. (4th) 540 (Gen. Div.), the father was granted supervised access to the children despite their wishes not to see him. It was still in the children's best interests to know their father and to develop a relationship with him. The mother's appeal regarding access was allowed at (1994), 4 R.F.L. (4th) 169 (C.A.). The court ruled that it would not be in the children's best interests to be forced to see their father in supervised or unsupervised conditions. In reaching this conclusion, the court took into account the clearly expressed preferences of the children.

In *Droit de la famille — 1144*, [1988] R.D.F. 50 (C.S. Qué.), the wife's application to deny child access rights to her homosexual husband was refused. Contact with their father had not and would not harm the children and it was in their best interests that normal visitation rights be granted.

Where the parties have established access provisions in a separation agreement, these should be followed. The court will not make an access order where reasonable arrangements are already in place: *Crowe v. Crowe* (1988), 16 R.F.L. (3d) 420, 66 O.R. (2d) 157 (H.C.).

In the absence of compelling evidence that the sharing of religious practices by the access parent with the child or that exposure to two religions is contrary to the child's best interests, an access parent ought to be allowed to share his or her religious beliefs with the children: *Hockey v. Hockey* (1989), 21 R.F.L. (3d) 105, 69 O.R. (2d) 338, 60 D.L.R. (4th) 765 (Div. Ct.).

Where a party in an access dispute alleges sexual abuse of the children by the spouse seeking access, the standard of proof, although not required to be beyond a reasonable doubt, is required to be on a strong balance of probabilities or a strong preponderance of evidence commensurate with the gravity of the conduct alleged: *Sullivan v. Sullivan* (1993), 122 N.S.R. (2d) 167, 338 A.P.R. 167 (S.C.).

The rights of an access parent are limited to the right to access; the right to information concerning the health, education, and welfare of the children; and the right to be informed by the custodial parent in writing of the children's medical concerns and problems. The access parent's consent is not required for the children's participation in school activities, even when such activities interfere with regular access visits: *Moss v. Boisvert* (1990), 74 Alta. L.R. (2d) 344, 107 A.R. 385 (Master).

16§28 — Aims of access

Section 16(10) indicates that the right to access is for the benefit of the child and not that of the parent. It also suggests than an aim of access is to provide as much contact between the child and each spouse as is consistent with the best interests of the child. Maximum contact, where suitable, is the objective.

A spouse who is granted access is entitled to make inquiries, and to be given information, as to the health, education and welfare of the child: s. 16(5). The source of the information is not specified. It might be that the source is the prime source, such as the child's doctor or teacher, or it might be that the information must come by way of the custodial parent.

It is uncertain, at this point, whether s. 16(5) enables the access parent to obtain information by subjecting the child to medical, educational or other tests.

The court may require the person with custody to give the person or persons with access 30 days' notice (or some other specified period of notice) of any change of residence: s. 16(7).

Divorce Act, 1985

In *Gordon v. Goertz*, 19 R.F.L. (4th) 177, [1996] 2 S.C.R. 27, the access parent applied for an order preventing the custodial parent from moving with the child to a distant jurisdiction. McLachlin J., writing for the majority, was of the opinion that, "The reduction of beneficial contact between the child and the access parent does not always dictate a change of custody or an order which restricts moving the child. If the child's needs are likely to be best served by remaining with the custodial parent, and this consideration offsets the loss or reduction in contact with the access parent, then the judge should not vary custody and permit the move. This said, the reviewing judge must bear in mind that Parliament has indicated that maximum contact with both parents is generally in the best interests of the child." The court held that the principle of having "maximum contact" with the access parent was mandatory but not absolute.

Although a judge, when determining access, should consider the desirability of maximizing contact between the child and both parents, circumstances may exist which render such contact undesirable: *F. (R.J.) v. F. (K.E.)* (1997), 33 R.F.L. (4th) 241, 209 A.R. 204, 160 W.A.C. 204 (C.A.).

Section 16(10) provides that in making a custody or access order, the court shall give effect "to the principle that a child of the marriage should have as much contact with each spouse as is consistent with the best interests of the child." In *Young v. Young*, [1993] 4 S.C.R. 3, 49 R.F.L. (3d) 117, 84 B.C.L.R. (2d) 1, [1993] 8 W.W.R. 513, 108 D.L.R. (4th) 193, the court stated that "the modifying phrase 'as is consistent with the best interests of the child' means that the goal of maximum contact of each parent with the child is not absolute. To the extent that contact conflicts with the best interests of the child, it may be restricted. But *only* to that extent" (*per* McLachlin J. at 150 (R.F.L.)). A court must consider "whether the conduct in question poses a risk of harm to the child which outweighs the benefits of a free and open relationship, which permits the child to know the access parent as he or she is" (at 152). In the *Young* decision, the court held that an order forbidding the father, a Jehovah's Witness, from discussing religion with his children was not valid. Any perceived harm to the children could not be said to outweigh the benefits of unrestricted access.

Although a judge when determining access should consider the desirability of maximizing contact between the child and both parents, circumstances may exist which render such contact undesirable: *F. (R.J.) v. F. (K.E.)* (1997), 33 R.F.L. (4th) 241 (Alta. C.A.).

It is the child's right of access to a parent which is to be considered in respect of access to a non-custodial parent. The best interests of a child have been held to be constituted by a loving relationship with both parents and such a relationship should be interfered with only in demonstrated circumstances of danger to the child's physical or mental well being: *Pastway v. Pastway* (1999), 49 R.F.L. (4th) 375 (Ont. Gen. Div.).

Where the mother opposed the father's application for Christmas access on the basis that he had become a Jehovah's Witness, the application was allowed. The mother was unfairly prejudicing the children against their father and thereby undermining the benefits which would result from regular contact with their father: *Friesen v. Friesen* (1988), 56 Man. R. (2d) 303 (Q.B.).

Where the parties' teenaged children found it difficult to communicate with their father, access was granted only at their discretion. It was not in the children's best interests to force access: *Katz v. Katz* (1989), 21 R.F.L. (3d) 167 (Ont. U.F.C.).

16§29 — Access — extra-provincial effect

Divorce Act, 1985

The court of a province in which the petitioner is resident has jurisdiction to deal with access issues under the *Divorce Act* regardless of where the children reside and the fact that there is an outstanding order for access made under the legislation of another province: *Migliore v. Migliore* (1989), 21 R.F.L. (3d) 412 (B.C. S.C.).

Divorce Act, 1968

In *Kibble v. Kahn* (1975), 20 R.F.L. 228 (B.C. S.C.), after a divorce hearing in Ontario in which the issue of access to a child was thoroughly reviewed and a detailed order made in that regard, the applicant mother moved to British Columbia and brought an application there to deny the respondent father access. The applicant, while acknowledging her contempt of the Ontario order, asked the court to disregard that as unimportant in light of the court's obligation to enter into a new hearing to review again the evidence considered by the Ontario court and any other evidence that the parties might wish to adduce. The court substantially confirmed the order of the Ontario court without a fresh hearing. To say that the British Columbia court could not hold the applicant in contempt of the Ontario order as to access was not to say that the order had no standing in British Columbia. The order commanded from the British Columbia court the utmost respect, and from the parties to whom it was directed meticulous performance.

16§30 — Determination of access terms

Divorce Act, 1985

In *R. (J.B.) v. R. (A.M.)*, 36 R.F.L. (5th) 210, 2003 CarswellBC 498, 2003 BCCA 135, 11 B.C.L.R. (4th) 310, 180 B.C.A.C. 37, 297 W.A.C. 37 (B.C. C.A.), the mother appealed from a judgement which varied an order for joint custody and guardianship of the children and the father cross-appealed from an order of child support. The trial judge had given the father the authority to determine the manner in which the children would share their time between the parents and to determine the proportions of time each parent spent with the children. The court held that to give the father sole control of access was a delegation of the key issue before the court for determination. The trial judge was required to provide the parties with a schedule of access. The appellate court ordered a rehearing in the Supreme Court. The father's cross- appeal was dismissed.

Where the trial judge had vested control in the custodial father to determine the mother's access, the condition was struck on appeal and a new hearing ordered. Giving the father sole control of the schedule of access was a complete delegation of the very issue that was before the court for determination: *R. (J.B.) v. R. (A.M.)*, 36 R.F.L. (5th) 210, 2003 CarswellBC 498, 2003 BCCA 135, 11 B.C.L.R. (4th) 310, 180 B.C.A.C. 37, 297 W.A.C. 37 (B.C. C.A.).

Although the decision to place responsibility for ongoing access in the hands of the custodial parent may be unusual, it is not, in and of itself, improper: *McGrath v. Thomsen*, 11 R.F.L. (5th) 174, 2000 BCCA 640, 2000 CarswellBC 2383, 147 B.C.A.C. 195, 241 W.A.C. 195 (C.A.).

Where animosity between the parents would complicate the exercise of access rights by the non-custodial parent, such access should be carefully structured: *K. (M.M.) v. K. (U.)* (1990), 28 R.F.L. (3d) 189, 76 Alta. L.R. 216, 109 A.R. 241 (C.A.); reversing (1990), 105 A.R. 102 (Q.B.); additional reasons at (1990), 106 A.R. 314 (Q.B.); leave to appeal refused (1991), 31 R.F.L. (3d) 366 (note), 78 Alta. L.R. (2d) 1x (note), 114 A.R. 80 (note), 131 N.R. 160 (note) (S.C.C.).

A custodial parent does not have the right to determine whether limitations should be placed upon the other parent's access. His or her right to make basic child-rearing decisions does not mean that an access parent of a different faith should not share his or her religion with the child. Even if the child is not inclined to receive such religious instruction, this does not mean that the teachings are not in the child's best interest: *Young v. Young*, 49 R.F.L. (3d) 117, [1993] 4 S.C.R. 3, [1993] 8 W.W.R. 513, 84 B.C.L.R. (2d) 1, 160 N.R. 1, 34 B.C.A.C. 161, 108 D.L.R. (4th) 193; affirming (1990), 29 R.F.L. (3d) 113, 50 B.C.L.R. (2d) 1, 75 D.L.R. (4th) 46 (B.C. C.A.); which reversed in part (1989), 24 R.F.L. (3d) 193 (B.C. S.C.).

Although the decision to place responsibility for ongoing access in the hands of the custodial parent may be unusual, it is not, in and of itself, improper: *McGrath v. Thomsen*, 11 R.F.L. (5th) 174, 2000 BCCA 640, 147 B.C.A.C. 195, 241 W.A.C. 195, 2000 CarswellBC 2383 (C.A.).

In *F. (E.) v. S. (J.S.)* (1995), 16 R.F.L. (4th) 415, 32 Alta. L.R. (3d) 414, 174 A.R. 296, 102 W.A.C. 296 (C.A.) the Court dismissed the wife's application for a stay of an order granting the husband unsupervised access to the parties' son. Although a social worker's report recommended that the husband be denied all access, the social worker had never interviewed the husband nor made any mention that the father had had custody of the child for a three-month period without any adverse incident. Accordingly, the wife's evidence had failed to demonstrate that there would be irreparable harm to the child if the order was not stayed. The limited relationship between the father and son was best encouraged. See also *F. (E.) v. S. (J.S.)* (1995), 17 R.F.L. (4th) 283, 34 Alta. L.R. (3d) 158 (C.A.) in which the court dismissed the wife's appeal from the access order on the grounds that there was no evidence suggesting that the attempt to rehabilitate the relationship between the husband and child placed the child at unreasonable risk.

While the court was of the opinion in *VandenElsen v. Merkley* (2003), 36 R.F.L. (5th) 215, 2003 CarswellOnt 656 (Ont. S.C.J.) the custody matters are concerned with the best interests of the children, not the rights or needs of the parents, it held that any access order that did not take into account the mother's desperate need to be parent was doomed to fail. The court ordered that the parties' triplets would spend alternate weekends with their mother and each of them individually would spend one week day night with the mother. The mother had abducted the children 2 years prior to the hearing and taken them to Mexico. At the time of the hearing, the children wished to spend a significant amount of time with their mother.

Where the mother had frustrated the father's access to the parties' son for almost 10 years, he was granted telephone, email and written access, with the goal of eventually re-introducing personal contact. A gradual re-introduction of the father into the son's life was in the child's best interest: *Rosenberg v. Rosenberg* (2003), 42 R.F.L. (5th) 440, 2003 CarswellOnt 2893 (Ont. S.C.J.); additional reasons at (2003), 2003 CarswellOnt 3250 (Ont. S.C.J.).

In *Beaumont v. Beaumont* (2003), 39 R.F.L. (5th) 23, 2003 CarswellOnt 954 (Ont. S.C.J.), the court refused to put all decisions about access to their father into the hands of the children, ages 10 and 17. To leave the issue completely to the children would be to put the responsibility of adult decisions about adult behavior solely on them. Accordingly, the court specified the father's access terms.

In *Stubbert v. Ferrare* (2002), 25 R.F.L. (5th) 428, 2002 CarswellOnt 189 (S.C.J.); additional reasons at (2002), 2002 CarswellOnt 625 (S.C.J.), the father, as a condition of his access, was prohibited from taking the child to attend his church and from attempting to persuade the child to subscribe to the teachings and observances of his church. Although there was no evidence that the beliefs promoted by the church were contrary to contemporary Canadian thinking, the mother's belief that exposure to these beliefs could prove to be detrimental to the child was not unreasonable.

In the case of very young children, appropriate access would consist of frequent contact for shorter periods in time and in the context of a predictable and stable routine: *Abbott v. Abbott* (2001), 13 R.F.L. (5th) 233, 89 B.C.L.R. (3d) 68, 2001 BCSC 323, 2001 CarswellBC 420 (S.C.).

Where the mother feared the possibility that the father could flee the country with their child during his access visits, the father was, as a condition of access, required to deposit his passport with his counsel: *Harari v. Harari*, 20 R.F.L. (5th) 59, 2001 CarswellBC 1645, 2001 BCSC 1068 (B.C. S.C. [In Chambers]).

Allowing 12- and 13-year-old children to dictate when they would allow their father access to them would be a very unusual access condition. Young children should not be placed in the difficult situation of having to negotiate access for themselves: *Chubay v. Chubay*, 20 R.F.L. (5th) 29, 2001 CarswellAlta 1030, 2001 ABQB 639 (Alta. Q.B.).

Where the mother was granted custody and the right to move the children to the United States, a strict access schedule allowing monthly visits with their father was set up to preserve their relationship with him: *Kits v. Kits* (1998), 42 R.F.L. (4th) 167 (B.C. S.C.).

Where the father's long working hours complicated access to the children and led to friction between the parties, the father's right to access was confirmed with the suggestion that a family counsellor become involved to facilitate access: *Davidson v. Davidson* (1998), 42 R.F.L. (4th) 154, 230 A.R. 151 (Q.B.).

In *Jarrett v. Jarrett* (1994), 10 R.F.L. (4th) 24 (Ont. Gen. Div.); additional reasons (December 13, 1994), Doc. Cobourg D3871/93 (Ont. Gen. Div.); further additional reasons (February 1, 1995), Doc. Cobourg D3871/93 (Ont. Gen. Div.) the court rejected the suggestion of an Official Guardian social worker that the court devise a structure for access by the father with a view to reassessment in the future. The parties had chosen the adversarial forum of the court over counselling, mediation or alternate dispute resolution and after an expensive and divisive ten day trial, it would have been irresponsible for the court to provide a tentative rather than a final decision.

There is no need for the court to specify access where there is no history of access problems between parties. In such cases, an order granting "reasonable access" to the non-custodial parent is appropriate: *Colwell v. Colwell* (1992), 38 R.F.L. (3d) 345 (Alta. Q.B.).

Where the mother behaved in a bizarre manner during access visits, with the result that the child would return frightened, tired, anxious and withdrawn, her access was ordered to be supervised. The mother was required to confirm to the court that she was receiving psychiatric treatment: *Starko v. Starko* (1990), 74 Alta. L.R. (2d) 168, 106 A.R. 62 (Q.B.).

In determining access rights, the court should consider the child's best interests as well as the child's age and the parents respective roles in the child's education: *Droit de la famille — 1326*, [1990] R.D.F. 401 (C.S. Qué.).

In *Smith v. Smith* (1989), 92 N.S.R. (2d) 204, 237 A.P.R. 204 (T.D.), the court refused to add conditions to the father's access order prohibiting him from exposing the children to his Jehovah's Witness faith. There was no evidence that exposure to their father's church had caused the children any harm.

Where the husband's employment required him to deal with emergency situations during his access visits, his access was made expressly conditional upon his leaving the children with his parents when such emergency situations arose: *Deroo v. Deroo* (1990), 28 R.F.L. (3d) 86 (Ont. H.C.).

In *Nicol v. Nicol* (1989), 21 R.F.L. (3d) 236 (Ont. H.C.), the husband was awarded overnight access with the children, aged 10 and 14, despite their contrary wishes. It was in the children's best interests to spend time with their father.

In determining issues of access around vacation and school holidays, the welfare of the children should be the paramount consideration: *Innes v. Van Den Ende* (1995), 15 R.F.L. (4th) 452 (B.C. S.C.).

In *Samila v. Samila* (1988), 32 B.C.L.R. (2d) 25 (S.C.), the mother's request that a rigid schedule be set for the exercise of the father's access rights to the parties' four children was refused. "Reasonable access" was preferable given that the children led hectic lives and were of an age when they needed free time to themselves and no further scheduled activities.

A custodial parent who requests that the child's right to cultivate a relationship with the access parent be restricted is required to prove that the child's best interests would be served by the imposition of restrictions. The fact that the parents' relationship was marred by the access parent's aggression and inability to communicate will not justify access restrictions where these difficulties did not relate directly to the children: *Sherry v. Sherry* (1993), 1 R.F.L. (4th) 146, 114 Nfld. & P.E.I.R. 67, 356 A.P.R. 67 (P.E.I. S.C.).

Where the father's mental problems, for which he refused to seek treatment, frightened the parties' child, his access visits were at the wife's discretion: *Golini v. Golini* (1991), 31 R.F.L. (3d) 289 (Ont. U.F.C.).

Where the mother was emotionally and psychologically traumatized by the divorce and was bent upon destroying the relationship between the children and the custodial father, her access visits were ordered to be supervised until a change in her emotional circumstances would permit otherwise: *Hayes v. Hayes* (1990), 82 Nfld. & P.E.I.R. 299, 257 A.P.R. 299 (Nfld. U.F.C.).

In *Prince v. Prince* (1995), 16 R.F.L. (4th) 236 (N.S. S.C.); additional reasons at (1996), 153 N.S.R. (2d) 356, 450 A.P.R. 356 (S.C.), it was held that although the access times requested by the father should be respected, the custodial mother had the right to change the times if they were not in the child's best interests.

16§30A — Costs of exercising access

Where the mother had been awarded $90,000 in annual spousal support, the court allowed the custodial father's appeal requiring him to pay half the cost of transporting the child from Saskatchewan to British Columbia to facilitate the mother's access. The mother did not require any financial assistance: *Rice v. Rice* (1996), 19 R.F.L. (4th) 26, 137 Sask. R. 285, 107 W.A.C. 285 (C.A.).

In order to calculate joint gross income, where access costs are appropriate, they should be added to the cost of child care rather than deducted from the income of the non-custodial parent: *Levesque v. Levesque*, 4 R.F.L. (4th) 375 (Alta. C.A.); additional reasons (1995), 165 A.R. 319 (Alta. C.A.).

Where the children had accumulated frequent flyer points as a result of travelling to be with their father during access visits, the father applied successfully to have the frequent flyer points applied against the costs of access: *Clegg v. Clegg* (1990), [1991] N.W.T.R. 63 (S.C.); affirmed (1991), [1992] N.W.T.R. 114 (C.A.).

An order requiring the custodial mother to pay the father's increased access costs occasioned by the mother's move from Toronto to Ottawa was reversed on appeal. The order created a financial hardship for both mother and child: *Daller v. Daller* (1989), 22 R.F.L. (3d) 96 (Ont. C.A.); reversing in part (1988), 18 R.F.L. (3d) 53 (Ont. H.C.).

Need is central to an application for maintenance. The *Divorce Act* does not provide a category which permits an award to be made to a parent to help defray the costs of exercising access even where provision for the same is contained in minutes of the settlement: *Wood v. Kuchurean* (1986), 4 R.F.L. (3d) 160, 75 N.S.R. (2d) 370, 186 A.P.R. 370 (C.A.).

The non-custodial parent's pro rata share of child care costs may be reduced to take into account increased access costs where the custodial parent moves away with the child: *Marinovic v. Marinovic* (1989), 20 R.F.L. (3d) 404 (Ont. H.C.).

16§31 — Denial of access

Divorce Act, 1985

In *Segal v. Segal* (2002), 26 R.F.L. (5th) 433, 2002 CarswellOnt 2228, 162 O.A.C. 119 (C.A.), the court allowed the mother's appeal from an order granting the father access to the children. Therapist's evidence presented at trial recommended 2-year moratorium be placed on the father's access. The evidence was germane to the issue of the children's best interest, and the court should have given reasons for departing from the recommendation.

The fact that the father had failed to return his children at the end of an access visit corroborated the view of the family therapist and the trial judge that the father was incapable of a positive relationship between the children and their mother and would instead sabotage their relationship: *Cavanaugh v. Cavanaugh* (1999), 47 R.F.L. (4th) 271, 175 N.S.R. (2d) 331, 534 A.P.R. 331 (C.A.). The father's application for custody was dismissed and termination of access was upheld.

In *N. (D.) v. K. (B.)* (1999), 48 R.F.L. (4th) 400 (Ont. S.C.J.), the father's application for access to the child brought six years after custody had been ordered transferred from him to the custodial mother was adjourned as premature. In the application to vary custody, the trial judge had found that the developmentally delayed child had suffered sexual abuse at the hands of the father. The child was progressing under the care of a psychiatrist who expressed concern that the child could regress if the father re-entered her life prematurely. Accordingly, the father was ordered to undergo examination to determine his suitability as an access parent and the psychiatrist was ordered to begin preparing the child for access while monitoring possible signs of regression.

The court should be reluctant to grant access to a non-custodial parent where no possible benefit will accrue to the children, and that reluctance should be even stronger where there is evidence that access might negatively impact the children: *R. (M.) v. S.(K.)* (1998), 35 R.F.L. (4th) 346, 195 N.B.R. (2d) 368, 499 A.P.R. 368 (Q.B.).

Access should not be awarded if it is not in the child's best interests even where the child's hatred of the non-custodial parent is the result of the custodial parent's attitude and conduct: *P. (J.E.) v. W. (H.J.)* (1987), 11 R.F.L. (3d) 136 (Sask. Q.B.).

Where the father had not seen the children in the seven years since separation and the children had no interest in seeing their father, his claim for access was refused. The youngest of the parties' three children was now 14 and it was found that making an access order contrary to the wishes of children of that age would be futile. However, the father was allowed to correspond with the children and the mother was ordered to assist with access should the children's wishes change: *Bellman v. Bellman* (1999), 46 R.F.L. (4th) 414 (B.C. S.C.).

In *Johnson v. Johnson* (1987), 12 R.F.L. (3d) 352 (B.C. S.C.), the husband was denied access to his child. The husband had been imprisoned for having caused the death of another of his wife's children and the subject child had no knowledge of him but regarded the wife's current cohabitant as his father. Although the father posed no physical threat to the child, it was not in the child's best interests to re-introduce the father into his life at this date.

16§32 — Conditional access orders

Divorce Act, 1985

Restrictions on access should be imposed only in accordance with the best interests of the child. "Best interests", however, is not the equivalent to "absence of harm". A perceived harm may not, on the facts of a case, outweigh the benefits of unrestricted access: *Young v. Young*, 49 R.F.L. (3d) 117, [1993] 4 S.C.R. 3, [1993] 8 W.W.R. 513, 84 B.C.L.R. (2d) 1, 160 N.R.1, 34 B.C.A.C. 161, 108 D.L.R. (4th) 193; affirming (1990), 29 R.F.L. (3d) 113, 50 B.C.L.R. (2D) 1, 75 D.L.R. (4th) 46 (B.C. C.A.); which reversed in part (1989), 24 R.F.L. (3d) 193 (B.C. S.C.).

Where the non-custodial mother refused to seek treatment for her drug abuse, and had engaged in a vendetta against the custodial father and his wife, which had a disturbing effect on the child, the dismissal of her application for further and unsupervised access was dismissed on appeal: *McGrath v. Thomsen*, 11 R.F.L. (5th) 174, 2000 BCCA 640, 147 B.C.A.C. 195, 241 W.A.C. 195, 2000 CarswellBC 2383 (C.A.).

In *Brooke v. Grandin*, 37 R.F.L. (5th) 23, 2003 CarswellBC 476, 2003 BCSC 344 (B.C. S.C.), the father was awarded custody of the parties' 3-year-old child with supervised access to the mother. The mother had made a number of unsubstantiated abuse claims against the father and, on more than one occasion, had removed the child from the country surreptitiously. Many of the mother's decisions had been impulsive and not in the child's best interests and called into question her psychological stability.

In *Fruitman v. Fruitman* (1998), 37 R.F.L. (4th) 416 (Ont. Gen. Div.), the mother's action for restriction of the father's access in order to conform to the children's upbringing of Orthodox Jewery was dismissed. The father at the time of the hearing was prepared to comply with the practices of Orthodox Jewery, but did not want to commit to these practices in the future because of uncertainty regarding his employment. The court held that absent "harm" to the children, an access parent ought to be able to exercise access without restrictions. No harm to the children would likely occur if the father's access plan was followed.

In *Forzley v. Forzley* (1997), 34 R.F.L. (4th) 105 (B.C. S.C.); additional reasons at (March 20, 1998), Doc. Vancouver D100167 (B.C. S.C.), the court refused to fit restrictions applicable to the mother's exercise of her access rights. The mother continued to have an extreme animosity towards the father which resulted in inappropriate behaviour with respect to the children.

In *Dinelle v. Sametz* (1994), 7 R.F.L. (4th) 277 (Ont. Gen. Div.) the wife, who was undergoing treatment for a psychiatric disorder, was granted supervised access to the children providing her condition remained stable and she continued to follow her psychiatrist's treatment.

Where the father's behaviour suggested the possible truth of the children's allegations that he had sexually abused them, but did not amount to conclusive proof, only supervised access was ordered: *D. (D.L.) v. W. (R.J.)* (1994), 10 R.F.L. (4th) 130 (Sask. Q.B.).

In *Fullarton v. Fullarton* (1994), 7 R.F.L. (4th) 272, 152 N.B.R. (2d) 321, 390 A.P.R. 321 (Q.B.), strict conditions were attached to the husband's access rights to ensure that there was no further direct contact between the parents. The parties had a history of violence but it was still not in the children's best interests to deny all contact with their father.

Where the father had a history of violence brought on by his temper and the excessive use of alcohol, the court allowed the wife's application for an order restricting the husband's access to the youngest child to daytime hours: *Horner v. Horner* (1992), 132 A.R. 106 (Q.B.); additional reasons at (1992), 136 A.R. 241 (Q.B.).

In *Rodger v. Rodger*, [1988] N.W.T.R. 163 (S.C.), the husband's access to the children was made conditional upon his payment of child support.

16§33 — Interference with access rights

Divorce Act, 1985

The *Charter of Rights and Freedoms* does not protect religious expression which is not in the best interests of the child: *Young v. Young*, [1993] 4 S.C.R. 3, 49 R.F.L. (3d) 117, [1993] 8 W.W.R. 513, 108 D.L.R. (4th) 193, 18 C.R.R. (2d) 41, 84 B.C.L.R. (2d) 1, 160 N.R. 1. The court held that ss. 16(8) and 17(5) of the *Divorce Act, 1985*, which provide that judicial decisions regarding custody and access be made "in the best interests of the child," do not deny the rights and freedoms guaranteed in s. 2(a), (b) and (d) of the Canadian *Charter of Rights and Freedoms*. In the *Young* decision, however, the court held that the order forbidding the father, a Jehovah's Witness, from discussing religion with his children was not valid. Any perceived harm to the children could not be said to outweigh the benefits of unrestricted access.

In *Martin v. Martin* (1998), 42 R.F.L. (4th) 251, 168 Nfld. & P.E.I.R. 181, 517 A.P.R. 181 (Nfld. C.A.), the court refused to suspend the father's child support payments as a means of enforcing his access rights. The children themselves resisted access and there was no evidence that the mother had refused to facilitate access. The husband did not acknowledge his own contribution to the strained relationship with his children.

Numerous acts of wrongdoing are not a prerequisite to find a custodial parent in contempt for intentionally frustrating the access right of the other parent: *Kassay v. Kassay* (2000), 11 R.F.L. (5th) 308, [2000] O.J. No. 3373, 2000 CarswellOnt 3262 (S.C.J.).

In family law situations, such as where a custodial parent encourages a child to refuse access, contempt should be found reluctantly, and only where there is unequivocal evidence. If a custodial parent acts in the child's best interests, and not with an intent to disobey an access order out of self-interest, contempt should generally not be found. Denial of access must generally be wilful and persistent before finding the custodial parent in contempt: *Paton v. Shymkiw* (1996), 26 R.F.L. (4th) 22, [1997] 2 W.W.R. 667, 3 C.P.C. (4th) 176, 114 Man. R. (2d) 303 (Q.B.); additional reasons (1997), 117 Man. R. (2d) 78, 8 C.P.C. (4th) 214 (Q.B.).

Where the mother encouraged her son to become an active participant on her side in her efforts to limit the father's access rights, the father was granted generous access: *Lindsay v. Lindsay* (1995), 19 R.F.L. (4th) 103 (Ont. Gen. Div.).

The reluctance of a child to participate in access visits is not a sufficient reason for the custodial parent to obstruct access: *Hume v. Hume* (1989), 79 Nfld. & P.E.I.R. 114, 246 A.P.R. 114 (P.E.I. T.D.).

Where the mother failed to advise the father of her removal of the child from Manitoba to Ontario, thereby frustrating his court ordered access, the mother was found to be in contempt of court: *Green v. Beaulieu* (1988), 54 Man. R. (2d) 74 (Q.B.).

The fact that the wife had removed the child from the jurisdiction contrary to the terms of the parties' separation agreement did not justify termination or a reduction of the husband's child support obligations. However, the husband's increased costs in exercising access which resulted from the move did justify a support reduction: *Gillies v. Gillies* (1990), 27 R.F.L. (3d) 53 (B.C. S.C.).

Divorce Act, 1968

Absenting all consideration of unreasonableness, the parent who has custody of children pursuant to a separation agreement has the right to remove the children without the permission of the other parent in the absence of such specific agreement to the contrary or in the absence of such specific terms with respect to access as would clearly indicate that the parties must have intended that the children remain in close proximity if the specified right of access provided in the agreement was to be an effective right. If, for example, the agreement provided that the parent who did not have custody should have a right of access to the children for a period of several hours on Sunday, the court could imply a term that the parties intended that the children should reside within such proximity to the parent having access that the specific right of access granted might be implemented without undue inconvenience to such parent. However, where the access provisions are general in nature, granting the non-custodial parent access at "reasonable" times, such provisions do not fetter the custodial parent's right to remove the children to a new dwelling in a distant locale: *Wright v. Wright* (1973), 12 R.F.L. 200, 1 O.R. (2d) 337, 40 D.L.R. (3d) 321 (C.A.).

16§34 — Adoption and termination of access rights

In *W. v. H.* (1981), 25 R.F.L. (2d) 337, 17 Alta. L.R. (2d) 139, (sub nom. *Williams v. Hillier)* 33 A.R. 613, 130 D.L.R. (3d) 492, [1982] 1 W.W.R. 397 (C.A.), the rights of access obtained by a father under a divorce decree were terminated by a provincial adoption order. It was held that in enacting the *Divorce Act,* Parliament did not purport to assert jurisdiction in the provincial fields of adoption, child welfare or guardianship. Accordingly, no issue of paramountcy arose, even though the adoption order might incidentally affect an order made in a divorce action.

Where the husband was found in the course of divorce proceedings to stand *in loco parentis* to his wife's child of a former marriage and was accordingly granted access, it was held that an adoption order in favour of the wife and her new husband, which was silent as to custody and access, did not have the effect of terminating the former husband's access rights: *Kerr v. McWhannel*, 16 R.F.L. 185, [1974] 6 W.W.R. 543, 46 D.L.R. (3d) 624 (B.C. C.A.).

An adoption order made under provincial legislation does not terminate the rights of access granted to a non-custodial parent by a prior decree *nisi: North v. North*, 6 R.F.L. (2d) 217, [1978] 6 W.W.R. 75, 89 D.L.R. (3d) 714 (B.C. S.C.).

16§35 — Access — procedure

Divorce Act, 1985

A judge is not entitled to delegate his access jurisdiction under the *Divorce Act* to a third party, including an expert child care worker: *Lake v. Lake* (1988), 11 R.F.L. (3d) 234 (N.S. C.A.).

Where the parties disagree over the issue of access and have little ability to co-operate, access should be specified: *Ingbrigtson v. Ingbrigtson* (1990), 27 R.F.L. (3d) 188, 85 Sask. R. 153 (Q.B.).

Divorce Act, 1968

Where the wife had been granted custody of the children of the marriage in divorce proceedings, it was held that for the husband to seek access, the proper course of action was an application in the divorce proceedings themselves and not one under the provincial statute: *West, Re* (1973), 10 R.F.L. 395, 36 D.L.R. (3d) 319 (B.C. S.C.).

Where the wife's action for alimony and custody was pending before the court, the husband's separate proceedings in which he sought access were dismissed. The proper course was for the husband to launch a motion within the wife's proceedings: *Bockner, Re* (1971), 6 R.F.L. 34 (Ont. H.C.).

16§36 — Appeal of custody and access awards

Divorce Act, 1985

In *P. (J.E.) v. W. (H.J.)* (1987), 56 Sask. R. 256 (C.A.); varying (1985), 41 Sask. R. 221 (Q.B.), the father successfully appealed from an order whereby he was to be allowed access to this child only upon the written consent of the custodial mother. The order was ambiguous as to the mother's right to deny access, and particularly so as the trial judge had not found as fact the mother's allegation that the father had sexually abused the child.

Where an 11-year-old child did not want to visit with her father, the children's lawyer had recommended the suspension of access. The trial judge suspended access and the appellate court upheld the ruling on appeal: *Lidkea v. Jarrell* (1999), 49 R.F.L. (4th) 324 (Ont. C.A.).

Divorce Act, 1968

"On reading and rereading the reasons of the learned trial judge in the light of all the evidence in the record we find it impossible to say that he did not make full judicial use of the opportunity given to him, and denied to the appellate Courts, of seeing and hearing the parties; the advantage thus afforded to the trial judge is always great but peculiarly so in a case of this sort where so much depends upon the character of the parents whose claims are in conflict. It is not suggested that the learned judge misdirected himself on any question of law; and, in our respectful opinion, the Court of Appeal were not warranted in setting aside his decision that it was in the best interest of the children that they should be given into the custody of their father": per Cartwright J. in *Bickley v. Bickley*, [1957] S.C.R. 329 at 333, 7 D.L.R. (2d) 465, (sub nom. *Bickley v. Blatchley*). See also *Shanks v. Shanks* (1971), 15 R.F.L. 399 (Sask. C.A.); *Rennie v. Rennie* (1973), 11 R.F.L. 278 at 281, 38 D.L.R. (3d) 401 (P.E.I. C.A.) and, *Praught, Re* (1973), 13 R.F.L. 302 (P.E.I. C.A.).

It is important that bitterly contested custody disputes be brought to an end at the trial level as in most cases the expense of bringing an appeal is prejudicial to the children's best interests: *deVerteuil v. deVerteuil* (1986), 5 R.F.L. (3d) 294 (B.C. C.A.).

In *Bezaire v. Bezaire* (1980), 20 R.F.L. (2d) 358 (Ont. C.A.), a complicated custody dispute, it was decided that the strict rule regarding the admissibility of new evidence on appeal ought not to be applied. Accordingly, new evidence in the form of psychiatric reports, psychologist's reports, children's aid society reports, and evidence with respect to a party's new living arrangements were admitted, reserving the right of counsel to make submissions regarding the weight to be attached to such evidence.

The trial judge's decision should not be disturbed unless he has clearly acted on some wrong principle or disregarded material evidence. This is true even where credibility is not an issue and inferences are to be drawn from established facts. An appellant court is not in as good a position as the trial judge to draw those inferences. The issues are so intensely personal that the trial judge is able to draw the inferences and does far more than merely assigning credibility: *Tower v. Newsome* (1981), 34 N.B.R. (2d) 413, 85 A.P.R. 413 (C.A.), following *Adams v. McLeod* (1976), 20 N.R. 212 (Alta. Surr. Ct.); reversed (1977), 20 N.R. 210 (Alta. C.A.); reversed 1 R.F.L. (2d) 330, [1978] 2 S.C.R. 621, 5 Alta. L.R. (2d) 391, 9 A.R. 1, 20 N.R. 203, 84 D.L.R. (3d) 440.

Since the question of custody of an infant is a matter which lies within the discretion of the trial judge, his decision should not be overturned merely because the appellate court judge may have been tempted to decide otherwise, but only if it is clear that he acted on some wrong principle or disregarded material evidence: *Dupuis v. Dupuis* (1978), 3 R.F.L. (2d) 272, 25 N.S.R. (2d) 444, 36 A.P.R. 444 (C.A.).

In a custody application where both parents requested the custody of their four children it was held that an appeal court will not interfere with the decision of a trial judge in custody matters unless it clearly appears that there is a manifest error in what the trial judge has done: *J. v. J.*, 4 R.F.L. (2d) 157, [1978] 1 W.W.R. 8 (Man. C.A.).

Where the appellate court found that the trial judge had misdirected himself in determining a custody issue, but a great deal of time had elapsed since the trial date, a new trial was directed. As many of the relevant circumstances had changed since the date of trial, an entirely fresh assessment of the circumstances of the parties was required: *Smith v. Goulet* (1974), 19 R.F.L. 45, 5 O.R. (2d) 337, 50 D.L.R. (3d) 321 (C.A.).

In *Barnes v. Barnes* (1974), 16 R.F.L. 196 (Ont. C.A.), in dealing with an appeal of a custody award, the Court of Appeal accepted into evidence affidavit material dealing with events which had occurred subsequent to the trial judgment.

As the decision of whether to obtain a report from the Director of Child Welfare for use in a custody trial is a matter within the discretion of the trial judge, the appellate court may refuse to interfere with this discretion, even if it is felt that the report may have been of some use: *Dimock v. Dimock* (1973), 5 N.S.R. (2d) 414 (C.A.).

"In the instant case, it does not appear that the order was founded on any wrong principle or that the trial Judge appealed from failed to give due effect to all the relevant factors in evidence or that an injustice was done. Therefore, I feel it is not open to this Court to interfere with the order": per Bugold J.A. in *Layton v. Layton* (1973), 11 R.F.L. 79 at 83, 6 N.B.R. (2d) 68 (C.A.).

A court of appeal should be reluctant, without the most impelling reasons, to interfere with a considered judgment of a trial judge in a matter relating to the custody of children. The advantage to the trial judge in seeing and hearing the parties is always great, but particularly so in custody matters where so much depends upon the character of the parents whose claims are in conflict: *Genest v. Genest* (1970), 3 R.F.L. 97, 73 W.W.R. 81, 11 D.L.R. (3d) 254 (B.C. C.A.). See also *Francis v. Francis* (1972), 8 R.F.L. 209 (Sask. C.A.).

16§37 — Interim custody

Divorce Act, 1985

Interim joint custody and shared parenting should not be ordered where there is substantial conflict between the parents, and certainly not before trial where there is significant disagreement on evidence: *Ritcher v. Ritcher* (2005), 20 R.F.L. (6th) 396, 2005 CarswellAlta 1530, [2006] A.J. No. 616, 2005 ABCA 165, 371 A.R. 1, 354 W.A.C. 1 (Alta. C.A.).

Where an 11-year-old child did not want to visit with her father, the children's lawyer had recommended the suspension of access. The trial judge suspended access and the appellate court upheld the ruling on appeal: *Lidkea v. Jarrell*, 49 R.F.L. (4th) 324, 1999 CarswellOnt 1906 (C.A.).

Where the father had been awarded interim custody after the assessment officer had testified before the case management judge who had not allowed cross-examination or the introduction of other evidence, the mother's appeal was allowed. The procedure had been contrary to the basic principles of fundamental justice as the parties had lacked any knowledge of the content of the report and had been given no opportunity to challenge it: *LeClair v. LeClair* (1997), 31 R.F.L. (4th) 378, 200 A.R. 373, 146 W.A.C. 373 (C.A.).

In *Raugust v. Steeves* (1996), 22 R.F.L. (4th) 101, 181 A.R. 269, 116 W.A.C. 269 (C.A.) the court allowed the mother's appeal from an interim custody order which rotated custody from one parent to the other every four weeks. The parents now lived 600 miles apart and a month away from her mother at such a young age created difficulty for the child and was not in her best interests. The order was amended to allow the father physical care only two weeks out of every two months.

The mother was granted interim custody of the child despite her plans to move from Alberta to Connecticut to accept a new teaching position. The mother had been primary caregiver to the child since birth and although the move would complicate the parties' joint custody arrangement, it would ultimately prove to be less disruptive for the child: *Trueman v. Nicholson* (1995), 15 R.F.L. (4th) 320 (Alta. C.A.).

Interim custody and access applications, and appeals from the same, are meant to have a temporary effect and are not the proper forum for resolving, on a permanent basis, issues such as the religious upbringing of the children: *Young v. Young* (1989), 21 R.F.L. (3d) 57 (B.C. C.A.), appeal on other grounds dismissed, but the Court of Appeal's order regarding other issues was varied and the order of the trial judge returned.

Where, on an interim custody application, there are serious allegations of misconduct between the parties and serious differences on the facts, a trial to determine final custody and not an appeal from the interim order, is the appropriate forum for a resolution of the dispute: *P. (D.P.) v. P. (L.E.)* (1992), 39 R.F.L. (3d) 302 (Sask. C.A.).

On applications for interim custody, the court should maintain the status quo in the absence of reasons to the contrary: *Prost v. Prost* (1990), 30 R.F.L. (3d) 80 (B.C. C.A.).

Generally, the status quo should be maintained on interim custody orders: *Hultman v. Hultman* (1990), 28 R.F.L. (3d) 185, 68 Man. R. (2d) 228 (C.A.).

A joint custody order made in favour of parties who live some distance apart is not desirable on an interim basis: *Hultman v. Hultman* (1990), 28 R.F.L. (3d) 185, 68 Man. R. (2d) 228 (C.A.).

In *Woode v. Woode*, 26 R.F.L. (5th) 232, 2002 CarswellSask 49, 2002 SKQB 33, 216 Sask. R. 1 (Q.B.), the court refused the wife's application for an interim custody order.

The wife already had secure custody entitlement under the parties' separation agreement and an order was not necessary.

The weight to be placed on the wish or decision the custodial parent having temporary custody of a child involved in a disputed custody matter may be less than the weight given to the plans of a parent with final custody who wishes to move: *Hunt v. Hunt* (2001), 21 R.F.L. (5th) 309, 2001 CarswellOnt 4549 (S.C.J.); additional reasons at (2001), 2001 CarswellOnt 4548, [2001] O.J. No. 5111 (S.C.J.).

On an application for interim custody, the children's situation should remain as stable as possible absent a good reason to change: *MacNeil v. MacNeil*, 4 R.F.L. (5th) 273, 2000 CarswellNWT 4, 2000 NWTSC 6 (S.C.).

On an application for interim custody, the children's situation should remain as stable as possible absent a good reason to change: *MacNeil v. MacNeil*, 4 R.F.L. (5th) 273, 2000 NWTSC 6, 2000 CarswellNWT 4 (S.C.).

In *Elliott v. Elliott* (1998), 42 R.F.L. (4th) 341 (Ont. Gen. Div.), the husband's application for interim custody was refused. He had assaulted the mother in the child's presence, had taken the child for an extended access period without the mother's consent or knowledge of the child's whereabouts and had continually attempted to undermine the mother's ability as a parent.

Where the mother had been the primary caregiver to the parties' two children aged 3 and 5, the father's application for interim custody was dismissed. Despite the father's concerns over the mother's Jehovah Witness faith and his claim that she over-medicated the children, there was no evidence demonstrating that removing them from their mother's home was consistent with their best interests: *Fattali v. Fattali* (1996), 22 R.F.L. (4th) 159 (Ont. Gen. Div.).

As a general rule, the status quo with respect to custody should not be changed on an interim basis in the absence of evidence that the existing arrangement was harmful to the children. The wishes of young children to live with the other parent is no basis on which to interfere with an interim custody order: *McEachern v. McEachern* (1994), 5 R.F.L. (4th) 115 (Ont. Gen. Div.).

Where both parties have made allegations as to the other's fitness as a parent, the issues cannot be settled in the course of an interlocutory application for sole custody: *Woodside v. Woodside* (1994), 8 R.F.L. (4th) 430, 158 A.R. 42 (Q.B.).

Where the child remained with the father in the matrimonial home after the parties' separation, and the home was subsequently sold, it was held that the change in residence alone was insufficient to support the wife's claim for interim custody. The child's best interests continued to be served by leaving custody with the father: *Labelle v. Labelle* (1993), 46 R.F.L. (3d) 341 (Man. Q.B.).

In *Brewer v. MacIntosh* (1993), 45 R.F.L. (3d) 437 (N.B. Q.B.), the court refused the husband's application for an interim order requiring the custodial mother to return the children to New Brunswick from British Columbia where she had moved with them. The mother, both under the custody order and the parties' agreement, was not prohibited from moving the children and her decision appeared to be reasonable. In any event, the children should not be ordered returned without the benefit of a full hearing.

Although s. 26 of the *Children's Law Reform Act*, requiring prompt trials of custody matters, does not apply to the *Divorce Act*, the philosophy of the provision is equally applicable. Accordingly, interim custody proceedings should not be prolonged where the trial of the matter can be expedited: *Hurdle v. Hurdle* (1991), 31 R.F.L. (3d) 349 (Ont. Gen. Div.).

Where the parents' maturity enabled a truly shared parenting relationship, a joint interim custody award was made whereby the younger children would reside part of the week with one parent and the balance with the other: *Matheson v. Matheson* (1995), 15 R.F.L. (4th) 418 (P.E.I. S.C.).

Where the father had some concerns about the child's health, but where the child had lived with the mother since birth, the father's application for interim custody was dismissed and the mother's granted. It was in the child's best interests that the status quo be maintained. However, as a term of the order, the mother was required to keep the father informed of all matters relating to the child's health: *McMillan v. Cavanagh* (1990), 28 R.F.L. (3d) 218 (B.C. S.C.).

The main concerns on an interim custody determination concerning a very young child are the provision of love, warmth, and nurturing and the ability to meet the child's needs, coupled with the preservation of parental bonding: *White v. White* (1990), 28 R.F.L. (3d) 439 (B.C. S.C.).

Where the parties continued to reside under the same roof, both of their claims for interim custody of their children were dismissed. It was not in the children's best interests to be under the care and control of one parent given that the parties had been able to share parenting and could continue to do so pending trial: *Perrier v. Perrier* (1989), 20 R.F.L. (3d) 388 (Ont. H.C.).

Where the parties disagreed on the date of separation and on the involvement of each in parenting during separation, and the court could not readily resolve the conflicts, an award of joint interim custody was found to be appropriate: *Cruzventura v. Cruzventura* (1989), 19 R.F.L. (3d) 444 (Ont. H.C.).

Where both parties were actively involved in the care of the children and both sought interim custody, the order was made in the mother's favour given her superior understanding of the children's needs. The father was, however, granted generous access including the daily care of the children when the mother was working: *Stefanyk v. Stefanyk* (1994), 1 R.F.L. (4th) 432, 128 N.S.R. (2d) 335, 359 A.P.R. 335 (S.C.).

Where a custody order had been made in the mother's favour during divorce proceedings, the husband could not later properly seek an order for interim custody. Since a final order for custody had been made under the *Divorce Act*, the father's remedy was to seek a variation order: *Wile v. Wile* (1990), 29 R.F.L. (3d) 32 (Ont. Master).

Divorce Act, 1968

The Master has jurisdiction to entertain an application for interim custody despite the existence of a final custody order made under a provincial statute: *Pantry v. Pantry* (1986), 50 R.F.L. (2d) 240, 53 O.R. (2d) 667, 25 D.L.R. (4th) 636, 13 O.A.C. 48 (C.A.).

An order whereby a child rotates between the residences of the father and mother is not practical on an interim basis: *Robinson v. Robinson* (1985), 49 R.F.L. (2d) 43 (Ont. C.A.).

In *Serruys v. Serruys* (1982), 29 R.F.L. (2d) 215 (Ont. C.A.); reversing (1982), 28 R.F.L. (2d) 452 (Ont. Master), an interim interim order awarding custody of the children to the husband was varied in favour of the wife where it was established that the order would have to be in force for several months and that the husband, who worked full time, would have to arrange for child care whereas the wife would not.

Where an order is sought for what might be called an "interim interim" order for custody pending the determination by the Master, in the absence of material evidence that the welfare of the children demands an immediate change, it is not in the interests of the children to be tossed back and forth pending the determination of an application for interim custody: *Niel v. Niel* (1976), 28 R.F.L. 257 (Ont. C.A.).

"As I have observed, the children have now been with their father for six months. The separation agreement, which the parties had entered into, provides access to the mother. There is no reason why these proceedings cannot be brought to trial very shortly, and, in the interim, with the access provided, the mother will have the opportunity of being with the children on many occasions before trial. I do not think that it is in the welfare of the children to change their present environment pending trial": *Hubert v. Hubert* (1976), 28 R.F.L. 273 at 274 (Ont. C.A.), Dubin J.A.

Where the appellant appeared to be living in an adulterous relationship and had custody of two children, aged 10 years and 12 years, but there was no evidence to support a conclusion the children would fare badly in their material or moral upbringing if they remained with their mother until trial, and it appeared the trial would be held within three months, an appeal from an earlier order granting interim custody to the husband was allowed and the children were returned to the mother: *Thorgerson v. Thorgerson*, 22 R.F.L. 389, [1975] W.W.D. 162 (Sask. C.A.).

In most cases where a trial is close at hand and where the child is being well taken care of, it is preferable not to disturb the *de facto* custody. However, in *Cropper v. Cropper* (1974), 16 R.F.L. 113 (Ont. C.A.), an order of interim custody in favour of the wife was confirmed where: the father had the child looked after by a stranger; there was no evidence of where the child was residing; and there was no evidence as to any of the circumstances in which the child was being cared for.

Where the husband, an Ontario resident, petitioned for divorce in Ontario and removed the child of the marriage from the province immediately before his wife was granted interim custody, it was held that the Senior Master possessed the jurisdiction to make the interim award despite the child's absence: *Johnson v. Johnson* (1970), [1971] 2 O.R. 516 (Master); affirmed (1970), 6 R.F.L. 171, [1972] 1 O.R. 212 (C.A.).

"It may be taken as a working rule that evidence to warrant an order for interim custody must more cogently support disturbance of the *de facto* situation than evidence to support an order for custody after trial on the merits. But, as in custody after trial so in respect of interim custody, the welfare of the children is the paramount consideration; and any difference in the required weight of evidence is a matter of degree and not of kind. The conduct of the parties *inter se* may not as such have any bearing on custody, let alone interim custody; but if it offers any assistance on how the children are likely to fare in their material and moral upbringing in the hands of the one parent or the other, it has relevancy": *Papp v. Papp*, [1970] 1 O.R. 331 at 344–45, 8 D.L.R. (3d) 389 (C.A.), Laskin J.A.

"The reconciliation policy of the [*Divorce*] *Act* does not, in my opinion, have any bearing on interim custody. Merely because the husband wishes to reconcile and to have the wife return to the matrimonial home with the children is not a ground for preferring him as an interim custodian against a wife who refuses to reconcile, and between whom and her husband there are alleged differences, forming the very basis of the divorce action, on which no helpful findings are possible at this stage of the proceedings. ... [T]o permit reliance upon the reconciliation policy of the Act on interlocutory applications would be to turn it into an instrument of pressure by one spouse upon another on issues to which it is extraneous. However laudable be the desire of one spouse for a reunion, it is not his best interests or the best interests of the family as he sees them that are controlling upon an application for interim custody": per Laskin J.A. in *Dyment v. Dyment*, [1969] 2 O.R. 748 at 751 (C.A.).

In *Procyshen v. Procyshen* (1983), 36 R.F.L. (2d) 223 (Sask. Q.B.), interim custody of the children of the marriage was awarded to the husband despite the fact that he had unilaterally terminated a joint custody arrangement by keeping the children. Although the court could not condone the husband's actions, the interest of the children would nevertheless best be served were they left in his custody pending the trial.

The court rejected the husband's interim custody proposal of having the children spend one week with himself and one with his wife on an alternating basis, as to approve such a scheme would unduly disturb the status quo whereby the children were in the constant care of their mother: *Kuyek v. Kuyek* (1981), 13 Sask. R. 215 (Q.B.); *Dolecki v. Dolecki* (1976), 28 R.F.L. 270 at 271 (Ont. H.C.); *Wine v. Wine* (1976), 27 R.F.L. 129 (Ont. H.C.). See also *Sobanski v. Sobanski* (1973), 9 R.F.L. 318 (Ont. H.C.); *Copithorne v. Copithorne* (1976), 2 A.R. 431 (T.D.); *Skjonsby v. Skjonsby* (1973), 13 R.F.L. 135 at 136 (Sask. Q.B.); *Hanson v. Hanson* (1974), 18 R.F.L. 301 at 302 (Sask. Q.B.); *Stephens v. Stephens* (1986), 4 R.F.L. (3d) 200 (B.C. S.C.); *Turner v. Turner* (1982), 30 R.F.L. (2d) 412 (B.C. S.C.).

16§38 — Interim access

In *MacDonald v. Finkelman* (1976), 26 R.F.L. 302 at 302–303 (Ont. H.C.), the mother was allowed interim access to the child only upon the posting of a monetary bond in the sum of $200, giving her undertaking under seal that while exercising her interim access pending trial she will not remove the infant from the province of Ontario and that if she does remove the child from the province, while exercising her interim access or at any other time, the said $200 will be cashed and credited to the consolidated revenue fund of the province.

In *Sinclair v. Sinclair* (1972), 8 R.F.L. 286 at 288 (Ont. C.A.), the court dismissed the mother's appeal from an interim access order whereby the father was to be permitted to take the children, in the company of his girlfriend, to Prince Edward Island for a vacation.

"The husband's alternative claim to custody was that, the access be enlarged and in particular he would like a period of time during the summer. He suggests three weeks, whereas counsel for the wife feels this is too long a period of time in view of the tender years of the infant. There has not, to my mind, been demonstrated any reason why the husband ought not to have a reasonable length of time with his son during summer vacation and I think a period of two weeks is such a reasonable time and I would so order": per Master Davidson in *I.H. v. H.H.*, 5 R.F.L. 214 at 215, [1971] 3 O.R. 222, 20 D.L.R. (3d) 62 (Master).

16§39 — Restraining orders

Where the father had threatened the mother's life in the presence of the child and had further abused the child physically, verbally and emotionally, both mother and child were granted a restraining order in *Armstrong v. Khan* (1997), 33 R.F.L. (4th) 438 (Ont. Gen. Div.).

16§40 — Costs in custody disputes

Where the parties settled their custody dispute after the trial had begun, the husband's subsequent application for a court award against the wife was refused. The integrity of the settlement process would be compromised if the court were to countenance an application for costs after the parties had arrived at a good faith settlement in which no claim for costs had been advanced: *Groenveld v. Groenveld*, 38 R.F.L. (5th) 271, 2003 CarswellAlta 441, 2003 ABQB 281, 13 Alta. L.R. (4th) 70 (Alta. Q.B.).

Where the Ontario Provincial Police refused to execute a B.C. order requiring them to apprehend and return to him his children with whom the mother had absconded, the additional costs incurred by the father as a result of the refusal were awarded against the O.P.P. The B.C. order had been properly registered in Ontario and the O.P.P. were obliged to enforce it. The conduct of the O.P.P. was inexcusable and had caused needless concerns and legal expense to the father: *Spurgeon v. Spurgeon* (2003), 48 R.F.L. (5th) 219, 2003 CarswellOnt 4345 (Ont. S.C.J.).

Costs in a custody dispute in which the Director of Child and Family Services was involved should generally not be awarded against the Director about evidence of improper conduct or other special circumstances warranting such an order: *D. (G.) v. M. (G.)* (1999), 49 R.F.L. (4th) 237 (N.W.T. S.C.).

Variation, Rescission or Suspension of Orders

17. (1) **Order for variation, rescission or suspension** — A court of competent jurisdiction may make an order varying, rescinding or suspending, prospectively or retroactively,

(a) a support order or any provision thereof on application by either or both former spouses; or

(b) a custody order or any provision thereof on application by either or both former spouses or by any other person.

(2) **Application by other person** — A person, other than a former spouse, may not make an application under paragraph (1)(b) without leave of the court.

(3) **Terms and conditions** — The court may include in a variation order any provision that under this Act could have been included in the order in respect of which the variation order is sought.

(4) **Factors for child support order** — Before the court makes a variation order in respect of a child support order, the court shall satisfy itself that a change of circumstances as provided for in the applicable guidelines has occurred since the making of the child support order or the last variation order made in respect of that order.

(4.1) **Factors for spousal support order** — Before the court makes a variation order in respect of a spousal support order, the court shall satisfy itself that a change in the condition, means, needs or other circumstances of either former spouse has occurred since the making of the spousal support order or the last variation order made in respect of that order, and, in making the variation order, the court shall take that change into consideration.

(5) **Factors for custody order** — Before the court makes a variation order in respect of a custody order, the court shall satisfy itself that there has been a change in the condition, means, needs or other circumstances of the child of the marriage occurring since the making of the custody order or the last variation order made in respect of that order, as the case may be, and, in making the variation order, the court shall take into consideration only the best interests of the child as determined by reference to that change.

(5.1) **Variation order** — For the purposes of subsection (5), a former spouse's terminal illness or critical condition shall be considered a change of circumstances of the child of the marriage, and the court shall make a variation order in respect of access that is in the best interests of the child.

(6) **Conduct** — In making a variation order, the court shall not take into consideration any conduct that under this Act could not have been considered in making the order in respect of which the variation order is sought.

(6.1) **Guidelines apply** — A court making a variation order in respect of a child support order shall do so in accordance with the applicable guidelines.

(6.2) **Court may take agreement, etc., into account** — Notwithstanding subsection (6.1), in making a variation order in respect of a child support order, a court may award an amount that is different from the amount that would be determined in accordance with the applicable guidelines if the court is satisfied

(a) that special provisions in an order, a judgment or a written agreement respecting the financial obligations of the spouses, or the division or transfer of their property, directly or indirectly benefit a child, or that special provisions have otherwise been made for the benefit of a child; and

(b) that the application of the applicable guidelines would result in an amount of child support that is inequitable given those special provisions.

(6.3) **Reasons** — Where the court awards, pursuant to subsection (6.2), an amount that is different from the amount that would be determined in accordance with the applicable guidelines, the court shall record its reasons for having done so.

(6.4) **Consent orders** — Notwithstanding subsection (6.1), a court may award an amount that is different from the amount that would be determined in accordance with the applicable guidelines on the consent of both spouses if it is satisfied that reasonable arrangements have been made for the support of the child to whom the order relates.

(6.5) **Reasonable arrangements** — For the purposes of subsection (6.4), in determining whether reasonable arrangements have been made for the support of a child, the court shall have regard to the applicable guidelines. However, the court shall not consider the arrangements to be unreasonable solely because the amount of support agreed to is not the same as the amount that would otherwise have been determined in accordance with the applicable guidelines.

(7) Objectives of variation order varying spousal support order — A variation order varying a spousal support order should

(a) recognize any economic advantages or disadvantages to the former spouse arising from the marriage or its breakdown;

(b) apportion between the former spouses any financial consequences arising from the care of any child of the marriage over and above any obligation for the support of any child of the marriage;

(c) relieve any economic hardship of the former spouses arising from the breakdown of the marriage; and

(d) in so far as practicable, promote the economic self-sufficiency of each former spouse within a reasonable period of time.

(8) [Repealed 1997, c. 1, s. 5(5).]

(9) Maximum contact — In making a variation order varying a custody order, the court shall give effect to the principle that a child of the marriage should have as much contact with each former spouse as is consistent with the best interests of the child and, for that purpose, where the variation order would grant custody of the child to a person who does not currently have custody, the court shall take into consideration the willingness of that person to facilitate such contact.

(10) Limitation — Notwithstanding subsection (1), where a spousal support order provides for support for a definite period or until a specified event occurs, a court may not, on an application instituted after the expiration of that period or the occurrence of the event, make a variation order for the purpose of resuming that support unless the court is satisfied that

(a) a variation order is necessary to relieve economic hardship arising from a change described in subsection (4.1) that is related to the marriage; and

(b) the changed circumstances, had they existed at the time of the making of the spousal support order or the last variation order made in respect of that order, as the case may be, would likely have resulted in a different order.

(11) Copy of order — Where a court makes a variation order in respect of a support order or a custody order made by another court, it shall send a copy of the variation order, certified by a judge or officer of the court, to that other court.

1997, c. 1, ss. 4, 5; 2007, c. 14, s. 1

17§1 — Variation proceeding

When the child support reforms came into force on May 1, 1997, spousal support remained virtually unchanged with only comparatively minor procedural changes such as requiring the court to distinguish in its orders between child and spousal support, and giving child support priority over spousal support. For a consideration of the variation of child support orders, see 17§46.

A variation order is an application to vary, rescind or suspend, prospectively or retroactively, any provision in an order previously made in a corollary relief proceeding for support or custody: s. 2(1) definitions of "variation order" and "variation proceeding", and s. 17(1).

A variation proceeding is a proceeding in a court in which either or both former spouses seek a variation order.

The express power to vary retroactively confirms the right to have arrears as well as ongoing future payments adjusted to meet new circumstances.

The proceeding may be taken in any province in which either former spouse is at the time of the proceeding ordinarily resident, or in a province where both former spouses accept the jurisdiction of the court: ss. 5(1)(a) and (b). Allowing jurisdiction on the ground of ordinary residence overcomes the hardship occurring when both spouses move after the divorce and cannot bring the application in the original court without incurring the expense of travel for themselves, and the additional expense of producing evidence from a distance. The alternative branch of jurisdiction based on the fact that the parties "accept" the jurisdiction departs from the principle that jurisdiction cannot be based on consent.

A limitation imposed on the choice of jurisdiction arises in the case of a variation proceeding involving the variation of a custody order. If the proceeding is opposed and the child involved is most substantially connected with another province, the court having original jurisdiction may, on application by the former spouse or on its own motion, transfer the entire proceeding to the court in that other province (s. 6(3)) and that court will then have exclusive jurisdiction: s. 6(4).

Where, because the parties have re-established themselves in different provinces and one of them would either have to travel or conduct the proceeding from afar, the alternative is to proceed by way of a provisional order: ss. 18 and 19.

A further feature, following the precedent established with respect to original orders discussed above at 15§1 Corollary relief — order for support — general, and using the same terms, is to declare the objectives of a variation order: s. 17(7). The objectives section seems to take into account circumstances arising from the marriage or its breakdown, whereas s. 17(4) and s. 17(4.1) direct the court to consider circumstances occurring *since* the making of the support order or the last variation of it: s. 17(7). If ss. 17(4.1) and (7) are read together, it might be argued that the circumstances arising out of the marriage or its breakdown must have affected the spouse in a different way since the making of the last order than at the time of the making of that order, if a variation is to be granted.

An important limitation contained in the Act is that where spousal support has been ordered for a definite period and has terminated because that period has expired, no variation can be made unless economic hardship is shown and the change relied upon is related to the marriage: s. 17(10).

Parties — either or both former spouses. Either or both former spouses may apply for variation of support or custody orders. The procedure whereby the parties may make an application together is discussed under the support provision at s. 15 Parties.

A person other than a former spouse cannot make an application for a variation of a custody order without leave of the court.

Note that an application can, it would appear, only be made by a former spouse. Consequently, until the divorce is final, an application for variation of either an interim or a permanent order cannot be made. This procedure would appear to apply to variations of custody orders as well as variations of support orders.

Where a party is a social assistance recipient, a support order may be assigned. In this way, the assignee becomes the support creditor and has the right to take part in proceedings affecting the support order: see *Divorce Act*, s. 20.1(2). Consequently, if a client or a client's former spouse has assigned a support order, this fact will have to be taken into account before a variation proceeding begins.

Canadian courts do not have jurisdiction under the *Divorce Act* to vary a support order incorporated in a divorce judgment of another country. Variations of foreign support orders can only be addressed by Canadian courts under the provincial legislation respecting reciprocal enforcement of support orders: *Rothgiesser v. Rothgiesser* (2000), 2 R.F.L. (5th) 266, 183 D.L.R. (4th) 310, 46 O.R. (3d) 577, 128 O.A.C. 302, 2000 CarswellOnt 50 (C.A.). The parties were divorced by the Supreme Court of South Africa. The Final Order of Divorce incorporated terms of settlement including a provision for spousal support. After the divorce, the wife made her home in California and the husband in Ontario. The husband applied in the Ontario courts to terminate the spousal support contending that the wife had consented to the court having jurisdiction. In allowing an appeal from an order terminating the support, the Court of Appeal held that the Ontario courts do not have jurisdiction to vary a foreign support order, and that the parties cannot confer such jurisdiction on them: *Rothgiesser*, above.

The fact that an original order is made on consent does not bar an application for variation: *Benoit v. Reid* (1995), 18 R.F.L. (4th) 136, 131 D.L.R. (4th) 346, 171 N.B.R. (2d) 161, 437 A.P.R. 161 (C.A.).

A party's rights under the *Divorce Act* in respect of support, custody and access are determined at the time the order is made. Such orders are not final and a court may make an order under the *Divorce Act*, provincial legislation or its *parens patriae* jurisdiction to supplant an earlier order if circumstances change as was done in: *Kunkel v. Kunkel* (1994), 2 R.F.L. (4th) 1, 111 D.L.R. (4th) 457, 162 A.R. 81, 83 W.A.C. 81 (C.A.); additional reasons (1994), 8 R.F.L. (4th) 225, 162 A.R. 81 at 97, 83 W.A.C. 81 at 97 (C.A.).

Where a support order is specifically stated to be subject to review after a specified period of time, a change of circumstances need not be proven to trigger that review: *Vincent v. Vincent* (1994), 5 R.F.L. (4th) 368, 123 Nfld. & P.E.I.R. 295, 382 A.P.R. 295 (Nfld. U.F.C.); affirmed (1995), 132 Nfld. & P.E.I.R. 181, 410 A.P.R. 181, 15 R.F.L. (4th) 273 (Nfld. C.A.).

Where the husband petitioned for divorce, the wife was permitted to seek a variation under the *Divorce Act* of child and spousal support orders made originally under provincial legislation. There was no evidence that the wife was attempting to avoid the substantive provisions of the provincial legislation and the order made would be in the nature of an original order under the *Divorce Act*: *Smith v. Smith* (1998), 36 R.F.L. (4th) 419 (Ont. Gen. Div.); additional reasons at (March 31, 1998), Doc. Barrie 513/97 (Ont. Gen. Div.); further additional reasons at (June 22, 1998), Doc. Barrie 513/97 (Ont. Gen. Div.).

17§2 — Variation and rescission of spousal support orders — general

Divorce Act, 1985

Moge v. Moge, 43 R.F.L. (3d) 345, [1992] 3 S.C.R. 813.

Moge v. Moge is the most important decision in the law of variation of spousal support and is in fact the most significant decision in the general law of spousal support.

The decision rejects a strict "needs" and "means" approach in favour of one based on compensation for a wide range of "economic disadvantages" arising out of the marriage or its breakdown. It attacks the "self-sufficiency model" of spousal support and calls, instead, for an equitable sharing of economic consequences. In using this new approach, the court is to consider all four policy objectives in the Act and exercise an overriding discretion, if necessary, to adjust the result.

The parties in the case were persons of modest means and they came before the court on an appeal from an order made on an application to vary their support award. However, in dealing with the case, the court defined the philosophy of support in general terms so that its decision applies equally to persons of all economic levels, and to original applications for support as well as to variation applications.

In the case before the court, the main question raised by the former husband as the appellant, was whether the obligation to pay support should be terminated because of the passage of time, or whether it should be allowed to continue indefinitely.

It is important to note that *Moge v. Moge* should be borne in mind when reading cases which predate this decision.

In the *Moge* decision, Madame Justice L'Heureux-Dubé, writing for the court, stated that the question to be determined involved the circumstances under which spousal support ought to be varied or terminated under s. 17 of the *Divorce Act*. However, the answer to this question turned on the meaning of "the basic philosophy of support within the Act as a whole."

At the time of the appeal, Mrs. Moge was 55 years of age. She and her husband had married in 1955 or 1957, and separated in 1973 for a period of cohabitation under the marriage of approximately 16 years. They had three children, none of whom, by the time this appeal was heard, was eligible for support.

Mrs. Moge's formal education ended at grade seven. During the marriage she assumed responsibility for the day-to-day care of the children and for all of the housework. She was also employed in the evenings from 5:00 p.m. until 11:00 p.m. cleaning offices, except for a brief period when she worked as a seamstress. Her employment supplemented the family income without her husband counter-balancing these efforts by taking on extra responsibilities at home.

When the parties separated in 1973, Mr. Moge was ordered to pay $150 each month for spousal and child support.

Mrs. Moge continued to work at her cleaning job for six hours in the evenings and remained responsible for the care of the children.

In 1980, Mr. Moge issued a petition for divorce which Mrs. Moge did not oppose. The payments of $150 per month were continued for her support and that of the remaining dependent child. Mr. Moge remarried in 1984.

Mrs. Moge lost her job in 1987 and applied to vary the $150 to a higher amount. She had been earning approximately $795 each month, and when her employment ended, she began to receive $593 a month in unemployment insurance benefits. Mr. Moge was earning approximately $2,000 a month and also received a small amount from investments. He and his second wife had purchased a home.

On the application, the support order of $150 was increased to a total of $400 a month: $200 of this amount was for child support and the balance of $200 for spousal support. Later in the year, Mrs. Moge returned to work at another part-time cleaning job.

In 1989, Mr. Moge applied to vary both the child and spousal support orders. At that time, Mrs. Moge was receiving approximately $800 a month from her part-time job. Mr. Moge was earning about $2,200 a month and his second wife was also employed.

On this application, the Court of Queen's Bench terminated the child support and ordered that the spousal support should cease at the end of the year. The child no longer qualified for support, and, the court found, there had been a change of circumstances sufficient to warrant a termination of the spousal obligation. Mrs. Moge was earning more than she had earned when the last order was made, two years previously. She was working only four hours a day at her cleaning job and should have been able, in the court's view, to find additional part-time cleaning work. She should not expect to receive support forever. Enough time had gone by since the separation to enable her to become financially independent, and Mr. Moge had supported her as long as he could be required to provide support.

Mrs. Moge appealed from this decision, which was allowed in part by the Manitoba Court of Appeal. It held that she should receive spousal support in the amount of $150 each month for an indefinite period. In making this order, the court observed that Mr. Moge's case for terminating his obligation was Mrs. Moge's failure to attain self-sufficiency. While agreeing that self-sufficiency was now the rule, it was a rule that did not merit universal application. It should not be applied to a wife who has spent her entire married life in a traditional relationship with her husband and is economically disadvantaged when divorced. In the result, the court found that Mrs. Moge's earning potential had been diminished by the marriage and that in the interests of true equality, she was entitled to a subsidy by way of support. The amount was fixed, in the circumstances, at $150 each month.

Mr. Moge appealed that decision to the Supreme Court of Canada. Mr. Moge responded to the appeal, but did not cross-appeal to contest the amount awarded.

Mr. Moge's submission on the threshold question of whether there had been a material change in circumstances was not seriously contested. The court quickly dealt with the question by agreeing with the trial judge and the Court of Appeal that a material change in circumstances had occurred. Mrs. Moge was earning more than she had been at the time of the last variation order two years ago, and since then had not secured full-time employment.

In her reasons, Madame Justice L'Heureux-Dubé was of the view that the principles embodied in the current *Divorce Act* engage the courts in a different type of analysis than that which was required under the 1970 *Divorce Act* when considering the question of support. The most significant change is a shift away from "means and needs" as the exclusive test to a set of objective which require the courts to accommodate a much wider spectrum of considerations. This change recognizes that the economic variables of marriage breakdown do not lend themselves to the application of only one objective. "All four of the objectives defined in the Act must be taken into account when spousal support is claimed or an order for spousal support is sought to be varied. No single objective is paramount. The fact that one of the objectives, such as economic self-sufficiency, has been attained does not necessarily dispose of the matter.

The objectives set out in ss. 15 and 17 require that an order for the support of a spouse, or an order that varies the support of a former spouse, should:

1. recognize any economic advantages or disadvantages to the spouses arising from the marriage or its breakdown;

2. apportion between the spouses any financial consequences arising from the care of any child of the marriage over and above the obligation apportioned between the spouses for direct support;

3. relieve any economic hardship of the spouses arising from the breakdown of the marriage; and

4. in so far as practicable, promote the economic self-sufficiency of each spouse within a reasonable time.

The court noted there is a growing body of doctrine which expresses dissatisfaction with the current norms by which spousal support is assessed, especially those solely based on self-sufficiency, and which proposes, instead, a scheme on principles of compensation.

Legislative support for applying the principles of compensation may be found in the objectives stated in the Act which are extremely broad in scope. "As a matter of statutory interpretation, it is precisely the manner in which compensatory spousal support is able to respond to the diversity of objectives the Act contains that makes it superior to the strict self-sufficiency model."

In the *Moge* decision, in finding that there had been a change of circumstances of the parties since the last support order was made, and in holding that an order terminating support should not be granted, Madame Justice L'Heureux-Dubé made the following specific findings:

1. Mrs. Moge had sustained a substantial economic disadvantage "from the marriage or its breakdown" within the meaning of s. 17(7)(a) of the Act.

2. Mrs. Moge's long-term responsibility for the upbringing of the children of the marriage after the spousal separation in 1973 had an impact on her ability to earn an income so as to trigger the application of s. 17(7)(b) of the Act.

3. Mrs. Moge continued to suffer economic hardship as a result of the "breakdown of the marriage" within the meaning of s. 17(7)(c) of the Act.

4. Mrs. Moge had failed to become economically self-sufficient notwithstanding her conscientious efforts.

There was no error in the majority judgment of the Court of Appeal and the further appeal to the Supreme Court should be dismissed.

See 17§38 Variation — objectives — general, for discussion of objectives considered in *Moge v. Moge*, above.

In *Strang v. Strang*, [1992] 2 S.C.R. 112, 39 R.F.L. (3d) 233, 3 Alta. L.R. (3d) 1, 125 A.R. 331, 92 D.L.R. (4th) 762, the court was of the opinion that the chambers judge was correct in finding that it was impractical, in light of the respondent's age, which was 59, and her lack of training to require her to become more self-sufficient. Also, he found that the wife's present employment status, as a bookkeeper, was causally connected to the marriage. However, he recognized that the husband's forced retirement reduced his capacity to continue to support his wife. This change was a valid change in circumstances justifying reduction in maintenance from $1000 to $500 per month. The parties had been married for 29 years.

There is no conflict between s. 140 of the *Courts of Justice Act*, R.S.O. 1990, c. C.43 and s. 17 of the *Divorce Act*, R.S.C. 1985, c. 3 (2nd Supp.) as the statutes have different purposes. Section 17 of the *Divorce Act* provides statutory authority to a judge to vary, rescind or suspend support and custody orders. In contrast, s. 140 of the Courts of Justice Act does not deal in pith and substance with divorce, support or custody and is intended to prevent abuses of the court's processes: *Ballentine v. Ballentine* (2003), 37 R.F.L. (5th) 9, 2003 CarswellOnt 2492, 228 D.L.R. (4th) 570 (Ont. C.A.).

See *Rothgiesser v. Rothgiesser* (2000), 2 R.F.L. (5th) 266, 183 D.L.R. (4th) 310, 46 O.R. (3d) 577, 128 O.A.C. 302, 2000 CarswellOnt 50 (C.A.).

Where the husband was ordered to make monthly payments to the wife to replace pension benefits lost on the dissolution of the marriage, it was held that such payments could properly by characterized as "support payments" which could be varied under s. 17 of the *Divorce Act*: *McCowan v. McCowan* (1995), 14 R.F.L. (4th) 325, 24 O.R. (3d) 707, 84 O.A.C. 125 (C.A.).

In *Kosendiak v. Kosendiak* (October 19, 1992), Doc. CA013867 (B.C. C.A.), it was held that the trial judge, in the context of divorce proceedings, was without jurisdiction to vary orders made earlier under provincial legislation.

The fact that a payee spouse has managed to make ends meet does not necessarily equate with having achieved financial independence, so as to justify the termination of a support award: *Droit de la famille — 901*, [1990] R.J.Q. 2771 (C.A.).

The fact that the parties resumed cohabitation prior to the granting of the decree absolute does not remove from a spouse the right to seek variation of corollary relief granted at the time of the decree *nisi: Droit de la famille — 665*, [1989] R.D.F. 429 (C.A. Qué.).

Where the husband agreed to purchase, through instalments, the wife's share of the family business, such payments could not be characterized as support payments and accordingly could not be varied as such. The fact that the payment had been classified as support payments in the husband's bankruptcy proceedings did not render the issue *res judicata: Craig v. Craig* (1989), 24 R.F.L. (3d) 341, 78 C.B.R. (N.S.) 97, 65 D.L.R. (4th) 106 (N.S. C.A.).

An order for support made under the *Divorce Act* is not properly reduced under provincial enforcement legislation: *Newfoundland v. Reid* (1989), 19 R.F.L. (3d) 385 (Nfld. C.A.).

Section 17(7)(d) of the *Divorce Act, 1985* indicates a policy which will, in many cases, require spousal support to be cut off at some point. The court must decide when that point in time is reached: *Martin v. Martin* (1988), 14 R.F.L. (3d) 388, 26 B.C.L.R. (2d) 390 (C.A.).

An order pursuant to s. 17(7) of the *Divorce Act* varying an order for support is intended to encourage self-sufficiency as far as practicable. However, the provision was not intended to impose an obligation on a spouse to become self-sufficient: *Gray v. Gray* (1986), 3 R.F.L. (3d) 457, 45 Man. R. (2d) 156 (Q.B.); affirmed (1987), 8 R.F.L. (3d) 147 (Man. C.A.).

Provincial legislation restricting the jurisdiction to cancel support arrears is not applicable on divorce. In the case of a conflict, the federal law is paramount: *Droit de la famille — 356*, 8 R.F.L. (3d) 349, 8 Q.A.C. 142, [1987] R.J.Q. 764 (C.A. Qué.).

Where the husband on a variation application shows that the wife does not require support on the basis of need, she may still be entitled to it on the basis of a compensation approach: *Provost v. Provost* (1999), 2 R.F.L. (5th) 442, 1999 CarswellAlta 1067 (Q.B.). The wife received $4,000 a month in support for four years with a provision that it be reviewed at the end of that period. At the time of the review, the husband applied to extinguish or reduce the support. The wife, because of her own assets, a disability and a small annuity payment, was not entitled to continued support on a needs-based approach. However, as a result of the breakdown of the marriage she lost the benefit of the income stream generated by her husband. On a needs-based approach the support would be reduced to $1,800 a month. However, the husband was earning an income of $300,000 a year, and so long as he was earning a substantial income, the reduction should be less to reflect a support amount of $2,500 a month taking into account an increase in her assets since the original order was made and an income of $850 a month that she did not have at that time.

It is not the intention of the support variation provisions of the *Divorce Act* to reduce a payee spouse's lifestyle immediately to one which is as modest as possible as soon as that spouse makes significant efforts at achieving self-sufficiency: *Petrocco v. von Michalofski* (1998), 36 R.F.L. (4th) 278 (Ont. Gen. Div.); affirmed (1998), 43 R.F.L. (4th) 372, 120 O.A.C. 193 (Div. Ct.).

A court in one province may vary a support order made in another province only after the divorce is in effect. Section 17 of the *Divorce Act*, which deal with the jurisdiction to vary, clearly specifies jurisdiction only in the case of an application by either or both *former* spouses: *Jackson v. Jackson* (1997), 32 R.F.L. (4th) 243 (Ont. Gen. Div.).

The court has no jurisdiction to vary spousal support provisions after the death of the payor spouse, as a claim for support or variation must be made against a living spouse: *Brubacher v. Brubacher Estate* (1997), 30 R.F.L. (4th) 276, 18 E.T.R. (2d) 296 (Ont. Gen. Div.).

A court, in divorce proceedings, lacks the jurisdiction under s. 17 to vary support if the original order was made pursuant to provincial legislation or if the parties had entered into a separation agreement: *Champion v. Champion* (1994), 2 R.F.L. (4th) 455, 115 Nfld. & P.E.I.R. 175, 360 A.P.R. 175 (P.E.I. T.D.).

In a variation application, the court stated that, in general, a person paying support should not have his or her income lowered to the extent that he or she is forced below the poverty line. However, if the person being supported is below the poverty line, then the supporting person should be required to pay support even if that results in the supporting person being placed below the poverty line: *Younker v. Younker* (1991), 32 R.F.L. (3d) 138 (P.E.I. T.D.).

Dismissal of a prior application to vary a support order does not render the variation issues *res judicata*. The *Divorce Act* expressly allows for variation applications to be brought when and as often as the specified pre-conditions for the applications exist: *Gessner v. Gessner* (1990), 24 R.F.L. (3d) 308 (Sask. Q.B.).

Where a spouse's claim for support is refused in divorce proceedings, the claim can only be revisited through a motion brought within the same proceedings. The bringing of a new claim under s. 15 of the Act is improper: *Booth v. Arnott* (1991), 90 Sask. R. 172 (Q.B.).

Where the divorce decree is silent on the issue of support, a party who subsequently seeks such an order should bring an original application for corollary relief and not a variation application. In such a circumstance, the court has jurisdiction to grant interim relief: *House v. Tunney (House)* (1991), 35 R.F.L. (3d) 68 (Sask. Q.B.).

The fact that a Saskatchewan child support order had been confirmed in Alberta for enforcement purposes did not affect the jurisdiction of the Saskatchewan court to vary the original order: *Daniels v. La Plante* (1990), 83 Sask. R. 7 (Q.B.).

Where the parties' divorce granted in one province made no reference to support or to the parties' separation agreement, the wife's application to vary support in another province was dismissed. As the application was essentially an original application for corollary relief, only the original divorce court had the jurisdiction to entertain it: *Puersten v. Puersten* (1988), 55 Man. R. (2d) 172 (Q.B.).

Where the husband's business was cyclical in nature, a temporary decline was found insufficient ground on which to base an application for reduced support: *Gresham v. Gresham* (1988), 16 R.F.L. (3d) 108 (Sask. Q.B.).

A variation proceeding is only appropriate where the party is seeking to vary an order that specifically provides for support. Where a decree *nisi* is silent on the issue, the application should be classed as a corollary relief proceeding and proof of a change of circumstances since the time of the decree is accordingly not required: *Currie v. Currie*, 6 R.F.L. (3d) 40, [1987] 3 W.W.R. 374, 45 Man. R. (2d) 289 (Q.B.). See also *Evans v. Evans* (1987), 6 R.F.L. (3d) 166 (B.C. S.C.). But see *Thompson v. Thompson* (1987), 6 R.F.L. (3d) 372 (Ont. Div. Ct.), where the court entertained a variation application although the decree *nisi* was silent on the issue of support.

Once a *bona fide* reconciliation has occurred, any existing support order is of no force and effect. The onus of proving that a reconciliation is not *bona fide* rests on the person so alleging: *Smith v. Smith* (1989), 22 R.F.L. (3d) 393 (Ont. H.C.).

A payor is not entitled to have support arrears rescinded simply because the amount is substantial. In the absence of proof of prior inability to pay, unreasonable delay in enforcement or laches, arrears should not be reduced: *Greve v. Greve* (1987), 11 R.F.L. (3d) 180 (Ont. H.C.).

Section 11(5) of the *Maintenance Enforcement Act* R.S.P.E.I. 1988, c. M-1, does not authorize variation of a *Divorce Act* support order in enforcement proceedings under the *Maintenance Enforcement Act*. Variation must be sought under the *Divorce Act* itself: *Director of Maintenance Enforcement v. Callaghan* (1991), 32 R.FL. (3d) 117 (P.E.I. S.C.).

Where the husband sought a variation of the custody, access, and support provisions under s. 17 of the Act only to the extent of changing the court in which the issues would be considered, the application was dismissed. As he did not propose changing the actual terms of the order, it was not a proper case for variation under s. 17: *Grunewald v. Grunewald* (1990), 27 R.F.L. (3d) 101 (B.C. S.C.).

Section 17 of the *Divorce Act* allows the court to make a permanent variation order. The power is discretionary, however, and even where the required conditions are established the court may decline to act having regard to considerations of procedural fairness. In addition to procedural fairness, a court may find that in the absence of the respondent it simply does not have the information to satisfy the requirements and duties placed on it by ss. 17(4), (7), (8) and (10) of the Act: *Adams v. Adams* (1986), 3 R.F.L. (3d) 157, 4 B.C.L.R. (2d) 330 (S.C.).

Where the wife had managed to spend or dissipate $183,000 subsequent to the divorce, her application for increased maintenance was refused. The husband could not be expected to subsidize her bad judgment: *Caufield v. Caufield* (1986), 4 R.F.L. (3d) 312 (Ont. H.C.).

Reconciliation does not, in itself, terminate an order for support. With the concept of fault having been effectively removed from family law, it would be anachronistic if the existence of a valid support order depended upon marital conduct: *Norris v. Norris* (1991), 32 R.F.L. (3d) 103 (Ont. U.F.C.).

The variation provisions of the *Divorce Act, 1985* merely codify the principles that have developed through the case law as it relates to the obligation of a former spouse to become self-supporting: *Single v. Single* (1986), 5 R.F.L. (3d) 287 (N.S. Fam. Ct.).

Where, having received support payments for two years after the parties' divorce, the wife had achieved self-sufficiency and had emerged from the marriage free from any related economic disadvantage, the support order was terminated: *Sookocheff v. Sookocheff* (1988), 15 R.F.L. (3d) 303 (Sask. U.F.C.).

Divorce Act, 1968

The payor spouse may not set-off overpayments of a spousal maintenance against underpayment of child maintenance since the obligations are independent: *Richardson v. Richardson* (1985), 1 R.F.L. (3d) 67 (Ont. C.A.); affirmed 7 R.F.L. (3d) 304, [1987] 1 S.C.R. 857.

17§3 — Variation and delay in enforcement

Where the wife, four years after the termination of an eight-year common law relationship, attempted to enforce 12 years of support arrears against her former husband, the court found that her claim for that period was barred by the doctrine of laches: *McMullen v. McMullen* (1994), 5 R.F.L. (4th) 444, 150 N.B.R. (2d) 277, 385 A.P.R. 277 (C.A.); reversing (1993), 141 N.B.R. (2d) 297, 361 A.P.R. 297 (Q.B.).

In *Richardson v. Normand*, 8 R.F.L. (5th) 185, [2000] 9 W.W.R. 360, 2000 MBQB 110, 151 Man. R. (2d) 12, 2000 CarswellMan 420 (Q.B.), the wife was granted spousal support 17 years after the parties' uncontested divorce, since the court found that there was a change in circumstances as the wife's cancer had reoccurred, thus preventing her from continuing her employment. At the time of the divorce, the wife was granted nominal spousal support of $1.00 per year, and that award, according to the court, kept the door open for support. While the court found the wife's delay troubling, it accepted her argument that the illness left her without the strength or will to pursue her legal rights. Her explanation for the delay was credible and the application for variation was granted.

17§4 — Variation of interim support orders

Divorce Act, 1985

Where a court has made an interim order for spousal support and the court rescinds the support arrears without the party seeking rescission making full disclosure, the order should be set aside and the arrears fixed: *Vaandering v. Vaandering*, 2002 CarswellBC 48, 2002 BCCA 34, 162 B.C.A.C. 199, 264 W.A.C. 199, 24 R.F.L. (5th) 192 (B.C. C.A.).

In *Davignon v. Davignon* (2000), 5 R.F.L. (5th) 37, 129 O.A.C. 322, 2000 CarswellOnt 468 (C.A.), the husband paid $3,500 per month in spousal support on consent from the date of separation until it was reduced to $2,500, on motion, to the time of trial. At trial, the judge failed to give any reasons for his award of support. The husband sought a reduction in the outstanding interim award. While the court would normally order a new trial, the appellate court, in light of the parties' limited resources, determined the issues on the record before it. The court found that the proper amount of support was $2,500 per month.

The husband's appeal from a dismissal of an application for variation of spousal support paid to him by his wife was dismissed, as there was no evidence of a material change in circumstances properly before the court and the courts are reluctant to interfere with a discretionary order at the interlocutory level: *Parsons v. Guevremont* (1999), 1999 CarswellNS 199, 48 R.F.L. (4th) 437 (N.S. C.A.).

The doctrine of *res judicata* does not apply to interim orders in family law proceedings: *White v. White*, 45 R.F.L. (4th) 100, 172 Nfld. & P.E.I.R. 233, 528 A.P.R. 233, 1999 CarswellNfld 67 (C.A.). While there is no specific provision allowing variation of interim support orders, there are numerous cases where the courts have permitted such variations. In addition, interim orders are interlocutory and consequently are always open to review by the court that made them.

The court is very reluctant to interfere with interim maintenance orders unless, as here, there is an obvious error which must be corrected and where the matter is not immediately going to trial: *Kennedy v. Dutchak* (1998), 172 Sask. R. 312, 1998 CarswellSask 756, 185 W.A.C. 312 (Sask. C.A.). In this case the chambers judge, without having found a change in circumstances sufficient to warrant a review of the child support, ordered a variation and did not relate his award to the guidelines.

Where, since the date of the original interim spousal support order, the husband had transferred considerable assets to the wife, the court granted the husband's application to terminate the order. As the assets transferred would generate income in excess of the order, a change in circumstances had accrued of such a nature and magnitude as to make the original order no longer appropriate: *O. (C.) v. C. (O.N.)* (2005), 11 R.F.L. (6th) 309, 2005 CarswellNfld 16, 2005 NLTD 12 (T.D.).

In *West v. West* (2001), 18 R.F.L. (5th) 440, 2001 CarswellOnt 1936 (Ont. S.C.J.), the court refused the husband's application for a retroactive downward variation of the interim child and spousal support payable by him. The matter was best left to the trial judge where the court would have the best and most complete evidence available. If any inequity had resulted from the interim order, it could be redressed at trial.

Where the husband, a chiropractor, experienced a decline in income on account of his suspension from the College of Chiropractors, but he did continue to work at a reduced income level, the court granted his motion for reduced support in part by reducing the amount payable for child support. However, the court ordered that spousal support be maintained at the same level as in the interim order: *Robertson v. Oake* (2000), 2000 CarswellOnt 1393 (S.C.J.). Both parties knew of the upcoming disciplinary proceedings against the husband at the time the settlement was negotiated.

Where an application for interim support is dismissed, the court lacks jurisdiction to entertain an application for a variation of that order: *France v. France* (1996), 22 R.F.L. (4th) 203 (Ont. Gen. Div.).

In *Renpenning v. Renpenning* (1992), 107 Sask. R. 23 (Q.B.), the court allowed the husband's application for a 50 percent reduction in interim spousal support payable where he suffered a drastic decline in income, owed substantial tax arrears, had assumed responsibility for the marital debts and had developed Parkinson's disease.

The court lacks jurisdiction under s. 17(1) of the *Divorce Act* to vary a spousal or child support order in a divorce judgment on an interim basis. The court can, however, make such a variation of a child support order in a proper case through an exercise of its *parens patriae* jurisdiction: *Hannon v. Sherrett* (1992), 44 R.F.L. (3d) 134 (Ont. Gen. Div.).

An interim order for support under s. 15 of the Act may be varied under s. 17, notwithstanding that the order incorporates a settlement agreement: *Nein v. Nein* (1991), 36 R.F.L. (3d) 417 (Sask. Q.B.).

The court has jurisdiction to vary an interim support order in the face of a substantial change in circumstances: *Stannard v. Stannard* (1991), 34 R.F.L. (3d) 249 (Alta. Q.B.).

Variation of an interim support order is not a remedy available to a party dissatisfied with the order, except where the order is obtained fraudulently or where material information is withheld or where there is a material and unanticipated change of circumstances. Otherwise a dissatisfied party should proceed to trial as soon as possible: *Kolter v. Kolter* (1990), Sask. R. 127 (Q.B.).

A court lacks jurisdiction to vary an interim support order before a divorce is granted, unless the order contains terms and conditions under s. 15(4) of the *Divorce Act* permitting the variation. In such a case, the individual seeking the variation bears a heavy onus: *Validen v. Validen* (1990), 30 R.F.L. (3d) 163, 71 Man. R. (2d) 213 (Q.B.).

Although the *Divorce Act* is silent on the issue, the court has jurisdiction to vary interim support orders where warranted. The court is entitled to use its inherent jurisdiction to do justice between the parties and the absence of an express statutory authority does not deprive the court of this jurisdiction: *Dumont v. Dumont* (1987), 86 N.B.R. (2d) 183, 219 A.P.R. 183 (Q.B.).

In *Saeglitz v. Saeglitz* (1994), 3 R.F.L. (4th) 244 (Ont. U.F.C.), the court enforced substantial arrears owing under an interim support order which had been accumulating over seven years. Although the wife had not vigorously pursued them during the seven-year period, the husband, given his substantial means, was not allowed to argue that he interpreted non-enforcement as an indication that he need not pay them.

Where the parties were divorced, but no final support order was made, it was found that an earlier interim support order continued in force. Given its interim nature, such an order is not subject to variation under s. 17 of the *Divorce Act*: *Boznik v. Boznik* (1993), 45 R.F.L. (3d) 354, 76 B.C.L.R. (2d) 202 (S.C.). But see *Dupont v. Dupont* (1993), 47 R.F.L. (3d) 273 (B.C. S.C.), in which the court entertains an application under s. 17 for variation of an interim support order.

The absence of an express power to vary an interim support order under the *Divorce Act* does not mean that interim orders cannot be varied. An interim support order under the *Divorce Act* is always subject to review, alteration, or variation. Specifically, the Nova Scotia Supreme Court has the authority to vary an interim order. A Family Court judge, on the other hand, has the jurisdiction to make recommendations to the Supreme Court with respect to variations of interim orders under r. 57.30 of the Nova Scotia *Civil Procedure Rules*. In general, though, interim orders should be brought back directly to the Supreme Court. Interim orders are intended to be temporary, and any change in circumstances warranting a variation should be addressed at trial. Exceptions to this general rule occur when there are lengthy delays in getting the matter on for trial and enforcement proceedings of support, custody, or access order have already been commenced in the Family Court: *McLeod v. McLeod* (1993), 45 R.F.L. (3d) 181 (N.S. Fam. Ct.).

Where the wife's interim support order contemplated that she would reside with her mother and therefore have minimal shelter costs, she was granted an increase in support when circumstances required that she find her own apartment. To deny the wife a reasonable and necessary allowance for shelter would be absurd: *Spolenti v. Spolenti* (1996), 22 R.F.L. (4th) 330 (B.C. S.C.).

17§5 — Practice

The court should have regard to the objectives and factors underlying a consent judgment when considering an application to vary the judgment. Accordingly, in the appropriate case, the negotiations leading up to the consent judgment may properly be considered as evidence in the variation application: *Comrie v. Comrie*, 17 R.F.L. (5th) 271, 2001 CarswellSask 130, [2001] 7 W.W.R. 294, 2001 SKCA 33, 197 D.L.R. (4th) 223, 203 Sask. R. 164, 240 W.A.C. 164 (Sask. C.A.).

In *Davignon v. Davignon* (2000), 5 R.F.L. (5th) 37, 129 O.A.C. 322, 2000 CarswellOnt 468 (C.A.), the husband paid $3,500 per month in spousal support on consent from the date of separation until it was reduced to $2,500, on motion, to the time of trial. At trial, the judge failed to give any reasons for his award of support. The husband sought a reduction in the outstanding interim award. While the court would normally order a new trial, the appellate court, in light of the parties' limited resources, determined the issues on the record before it. The court found that the proper amount of support was $2,500 per month.

Where the husband was in substantial arrears of spousal support, his application to vary his ongoing obligation was stayed pending the payment of arrears and the continued meeting of his obligation. The husband had, in previous proceedings involving support, demonstrated bad faith: *P. (M.L.) v. P. (G.W.)* (2003), 42 R.F.L. (5th) 100, 2003 CarswellOnt 1278 (Ont. S.C.J.).

In *Andrews v. Andrews* (2000), 4 R.F.L. (5th) 161, 2000 CarswellOnt 311, [2000] O.J. No. 324 (S.C.J.), the husband's application for a variation of spousal and child support was ordered stayed. The father had largely ignored both interim and final support orders as well as a substantial cost award against him. He engaged in litigation without any regard for the consequences of his actions, and his conduct in disobeying the court orders and acting in an unreasonable fashion was not in his favour.

A motion to vary an existing support order must be filed before a notice to disclose can be issued: *Rosin v. Rosin* (1994), 7 R.F.L. (4th) 402, 158 A.R. 14 (Q.B.); additional reasons at (1994), 8 R.F.L. (4th) 315, 158 A.R. 14 at 19 (Q.B.); further additional reasons (1994), 158 A.R. 14 at 19 (Q.B.). See also *Mumby v. Mumby* (1993), 158 A.R. 21 (Q.B.), in which it was determined that a notice to disclose is not to be used only to determine whether grounds exist to bring a corollary relief application.

17§6 — Interim orders pending variation

Divorce Act, 1985

In *Stevens v. Stevens* (2004), 8 R.F.L. (6th) 223, 252 Sask. R. 166, 2004 CarswellSask 544, 2004 SKQB 332 (Q.B.), the husband was granted an interim variation of the spousal support payable by him. While the wife had played a "traditional" role during the parties' 19-year marriage, in the 7 years since separation she had earned two university degrees and enjoyed an annual income in excess of $40,000.

The court has jurisdiction to make an interim variation of a final spousal support order in clear cases of hardship or where continuation of the order would be incongruous or absurd: *Carter v. Carter* (1998), 42 R.F.L. (4th) 310 (Ont. Gen. Div.).

The court has jurisdiction to vary an interim support order in the face of a substantial change in circumstances: *Stannard v. Stannard* (1991), 34 R.F.L. (3d) 249 (Alta. Q.B.).

A court has no jurisdiction under s. 17 of the *Divorce Act* to make an interim order varying child support. However, in cases of pressing and immediate urgency, a court may invoke extraordinary jurisdiction to make a variation order that can itself be varied on the full hearing of the issue on *viva voce* evidence: *Vipond v. Vipond* (1990), 25 R.F.L. (3d) 128, 72 O.R. (2d) 82 (H.C.).

There is no statutory power authorizing the court to grant any interim relief once a decree *nisi* has been granted. Therefore, in an application to vary the maintenance provisions of a decree *nisi*, the court is without jurisdiction to grant interim maintenance pending the hearing of the variation application: *MacNeil v. MacNeil* (1982), 134 D.L.R. (3d) 115 (Ont. H.C.).

17§7 — Application to vary by person other than spouse

In *Droit de la famille — 1655* (27 août 1992), C.S. Terrebonne 700-12-000584-755 (C.S. Qué.), the court allowed a second wife to proceed with an application to terminate the first wife's spousal support. The husband had insufficient funds to make support payments to both of his ex-wives and as he appeared to be acting in bad faith, the second wife was justified in seeking termination of the first wife's support.

A child has no standing to seek a variation of a child support order. Section 17 of the *Divorce Act* permits variation applications to be brought only by either or both former spouses: *Garbers v. Garbers* (1993), 48 R.F.L. (3d) 217 (Ont. U.F.C.).

17§8 — Change of circumstances — general

Pursuant to s. 17(4), the court, before making a variation order in relation to spousal support, must determine whether there has been a change in the condition, means, needs or other circumstances of either former spouse since the making of the support order or the last variation of that order. Similarly, pursuant to s. 17(5), the court, before making a variation order in respect of custody, must determine whether there has been a change in the "condition, means, needs or other circumstances" of the child of the marriage since the making of the custody order or the last variation of it.

Note that there is the limitation upon the court where spousal support has been ordered for a definite period and has terminated because that time has expired, and a variation cannot be made unless hardship has resulted and the change is related to the marriage and the changed circumstances, if they had existed at the time of making the support order or the last variation of it, would likely have resulted in a different order: s. 17(10).

Note also that the limitation in s. 17(10) appears to apply only to applications made *after* the definite period for support has expired or after the happening of a specified event. If an application were made *before* the definite period had expired or *before* the specified event occurred, it would appear that the additional requirements in s. 17(10) would not have to be met.

On an application for a variation of an order for spousal support, the court must first find, under s. 17(4) of the *Divorce Act*, that there has been a material change in the conditions, means, needs or circumstances of either spouse, and in making the order in the variation application, the court must take that change into consideration. The change must be material, and cannot be trivial or insignificant. Once this threshold is passed, the court must consider all four of the objectives of spousal support described in s. 17(7). In applying the objectives, neither the compensatory model nor the needs and means model is the sole model to be followed. Where it is not possible to use one, the other may be used. The objectives take into account the nature of the marriage, its economic consequences, the consequences of the breakdown, and the situation of the parties before the court: *Hickey v. Hickey* (1999), 46 R.F.L. (4th) 1 (S.C.C.). In this case, the motions judge on the wife's application increased the amount of support from $1,000 a month to $1,300 concluding that a change of circumstances had occurred because of the increase in the cost of living. The Supreme Court of Canada restored this order on the ground that the adjustment for inflation continued, in part, to compensate the wife for the financial disadvantage she suffered as a result of the parties decision that she would leave the workforce to care for their children.

In determining the proper interpretation of s. 17(4) of the *Divorce Act*, a contextual approach to the interpretation of the statutory material is not appropriate: *Willick v. Willick*, [1994] 3 S.C.R. 670, 6 R.F.L. (4th) 161, 125 Sask. R. 81, 81 W.A.C. 81, 173 N.R. 321, 119 D.L.R. (4th) 405. Where, as in this decision, there is a narrow focus in a case, an examination of the broad policy grounds for a decision is not required. In particular, it is not appropriate to consider the *Canadian Charter of Rights and Freedoms* as an interpretive tool where the parties have not relied on the *Charter* and other rules of construction make the intention of the legislature plain.

Material and Substantial Change. As under the 1968 *Divorce Act*, the 1985 Act does not specify the magnitude of the change required in order to justify a variation of the order in question. See *B. (G.) c. G. (L.)*, 15 R.F.L. (4th) 201, 127 D.L.R. (4th) 385, 186 N.R. 201, [1995] 3 S.C.R. 370, [1995] R.D.F. 611.

In *Willick v. Willick*, above, the court considered the proper interpretation of s. 17(4) of the *Divorce Act*. The court was of the opinion that an order for child support is made by assessing the needs of the children having regard to the means of the parents. Pursuant to s. 17(4), the court may vary a support order when the relationship between those factors changes in a material way. A significant change in one of the factors, that is, a change in the circumstances of either former spouse *or* of any child of the marriage could cause a material change in the relation of the factors. In the *Willick* decision, the court held that the fact alone that a payor's income had increased significantly did constitute a material change in circumstances justifying an increase of child support.

The fact that the 57-year-old wife had managed to find modest employment 6 years after the parties' divorce was not found to constitute a sufficient change in circumstances to justify a reduction in her spousal support: *Haigh v. Haigh* (1997), 31 R.F.L. (4th) 435 (B.C. C.A.).

In *Mullin v. Mullin* (1993), 48 R.F.L. (3d) 322, 108 Nfld. & P.E.I.R. 61, 339 A.P.R. 61 (P.E.I. C.A.), the court started at p. 326 (R.F.L.) that it was now settled law that there must be a material and substantive change in the circumstances before a variation order will be granted under the provisions of s. 17(4) of the Act: per Carruthers C.J.P.E.I.

In variation applications, s. 17(4) of the *Divorce Act, 1985* does not contemplate consideration by the court of every little change in a party's financial circumstances. Changes must be significant for a finding that a variation is warranted: *Oldham v. King* (1987), 11 R.F.L. (3d) 75 (Man. Q.B.).

A court on a support variation application, should not respond by minor or temporary changes or changes which were within the contemplation of the judge at the original hearing: *Michel v. Michel* (1988), 18 R.F.L. (3d) 182 (Ont. H.C.).

Under the former Act, the courts considered that the change must be material: *Kostyna v. Kostyna*, [1979] 4 W.W.R. 191, 5 Sask. R. 185 (C.A.); or significant and substantial:

Vance v. Vance (1974), 13 R.F.L. 378 at 382–83, 2 O.R. (2d) 537, 43 D.L.R. (3d) 481 (C.A.); or a sufficient change to justify the variation: *Bolger v. Bolger* (1983), 36 R.F.L. (2d) 184, 50 N.B.R. (2d) 3, 131 A.P.R. 3 (C.A.); *Landry v. Landry* (1981), 36 N.B.R. (2d) 209, 94 A.P.R. 209 (Q.B.); *Bussey v. Bussey* (1975), 8 Nfld. & P.E.I.R. 504 at 507–508, 8 A.P.R. 504 (Nfld. T.D.). A change in circumstances had to be something which had some measure of continuity: *Lafferty, Re* (1975), 12 R.F.L. 345 at 346 (Ont. C.A.). Presumably, under the new Act, the change must also be material, that is, significant and substantial.

The court must satisfy itself that the change has occurred. It would do so on the basis of the usual civil standard on the balance of probabilities.

Changes in Circumstances — Differences From the 1968 Act. There are several important differences in the nature of the change in circumstances required to justify a variation order in support and custody matters under the current Act. The word "needs" is included where previously it was not. There is a specific reference to the circumstances of the child in s. 17(4) and (5) whereas under s. 11(2) there was no such reference. Further, concerning the variation of a custody order, there is a provision stating that the court shall take into consideration only the best interests of the child as determined by reference to that change. In addition, in making a variation order the court is expressly prohibited from considering any conduct that could not have been considered in making the order in respect of which the variation is sought: s. 17(6). In making an original order for support, the court is prevented by the statute from taking into consideration any misconduct of a spouse in relation to the marriage: s. 15(6). In making an original order for custody the court is prevented from considering the past conduct of any person unless the conduct is relevant to the ability of that person to act as a parent of a child. Thus on a variation application, the court is restricted to considering only that conduct allowed under s. 17(6) and s. 15(6).

A determination of "condition, means, needs" in regard to variation support orders or other circumstances is further qualified in light of the objectives of variation orders set out in s. 17(7) and (8). Considerations in applications to vary custody orders are qualified by the principle of achieving maximum contact between the child and the non-custodial parent with the best interests of the child: s. 17(9). This provision reflects the same objective stipulated in an original application for custody in s. 16(10).

A further important change in the legislation is the limitation upon the court where support has been ordered for a definite period and has terminated because that time has expired, a variation cannot be made unless hardship has resulted and the change is related to the marriage and the changed circumstances, if they had existed at the time of making the support order or the last variation of it, would likely have resulted in a different order: s. 17(10).

Under the old Act, courts had held that support orders could be varied at any time even after the expiration of a limited term award. Section 17(10) prohibits the making of a variation order after the term expires except in exceptional circumstances. The obvious purpose is to introduce some finality into the support process. If limited term orders could be generally varied or revived indefinitely, the limitation would be meaningless and no one could rely on them to reorganize their affairs. This restriction was explained in the Information Paper issued by the Minister of Justice in May, 1985 on the first reading of the Bill for the Act.

"While the (*Divorce Act, 1985*) gives the court the express right to make fixed-term maintenance orders in appropriate cases, having regard to all the circumstances of a specific case, it follows that such awards should not be varied or revived indefinitely. Otherwise, such orders would be meaningless. However, the Act provides for certain exceptions in order to alleviate injustices that certain situations would create. That is not to say that all conditions arising after the expiration of a fixed-term maintenance award, and the need for support which could thereby be incurred by an ex-spouse, should be the responsibility of the other spouse. In situations where it could be proved that economic hardship has arisen through changed circumstances *related to the marriage*, which would have resulted in a different original order if they had existed at the time of the original order, an application to change the conditions of the order will be received. This, for example, will encompass the incapacity of an ex-spouse to become economically self-sufficient after the expiration of a fixed-term maintenance award because of changing circumstances related to child care."[p. 8.]

Divorce Act, 1985

A "material" change in circumstances is one which likely would have resulted in different terms if known at the time of the original orders: *Hayes v. Hayes* (1995), 14 R.F.L. (4th) 296, 166 N.S.R. (2d) 1, 425 A.P.R. 1 (C.A.); leave to appeal refused (1996), 18 R.F.L. (4th) 89 (note) (S.C.C.).

When determining whether a change of circumstances exists, on which to base a variation of a spousal support order, the guiding principle is the determination of whether, if known at the time of the original order, the change would have resulted in a different order: *Read v. Read*, 4 R.F.L. (5th) 126, 183 N.S.R. (2d) 181, 568 A.P.R. 181, 2000 NSCA 33, 2000 CarswellNS 52, [2000] N.S.J. No. 54 (C.A.).

Change of Circumstances — General — Cases. The fact that the 57-year-old wife had managed to find modest employment six years after the parties' divorce was not found to constitute a sufficient change circumstances to justify a reduction in her spousal support: *Haigh v. Haigh* (1997), 31 R.F.L. (4th) 435, 94 B.C.A.C. 263, 152 W.A.C. 263, 41 B.C.L.R. (3d) 139 (C.A.).

Although a spouse's concerns over his or her economic future may be justified, they cannot support an application for increased support. Issues may only be dealt with as they arise: *Murphy v. Murphy* (1994), 10 R.F.L. (4th) 102 (Man. C.A.).

In *Kerwood v. Kerwood* (1999), 48 R.F.L. (4th) 127, 1999 CarswellBC 780 (S.C. [In Chambers]), the court allowed the 83-year-old wife's application for an increase to her 30-year-old spousal support order. The wife's health had declined as she grew older and she required near-daily home care. The fact that declining health with age is foreseeable did not alter that the wife had experienced a change in circumstances. As the husband's income had actually increased over the years, he was in a position to pay the increased amount.

The mere passing of time in itself does not constitute a "change in circumstances" justifying a variation in support: *Droit de la famille — 1187*, [1988] R.D.F. 290 (C.S. Qué.). See also *Droit de la famille — 1230* (1988), [1989] R.D.F. 193 (C.S. Qué.); *Vigneault v. Cloutier* (1989), 65 D.L.R. (4th) 598, (sub nom. *Droit de la famille — 716)* [1989] R.D.F. 686 (C.A. Qué.).

Changes in circumstances which must have been contemplated by the parties at the time a support order was made cannot later be relied upon as a basis for varying that order:

Gaudet v. Gaudet (1988), 15 R.F.L. (3d) 65, 70 Nfld. & P.E.I.R. 107, 215 A.P.R. 107 (P.E.I. C.A.).

To justify a variation of a support order, a material change in circumstances must be proven to be of such a nature that if known at the time of the original order would likely have resulted in different terms: *Machum v. Machum* (1995), 14 R.F.L. (4th) 35, 162 N.B.R. (2d) 187, 415 A.P.R. 187 (Q.B.).

In *Machum v. Machum*, above, the court allowed the husband's application for a reduction in spousal support 20 years after the parties' divorce. Material changes in circumstances resulted from the fact that the husband's health had forced him to retire and accept a drastically reduced income; the wife had completed a university degree and for a while had operated a moderately successful business; the parties' children were grown and had become independent; and the wife had managed to accumulate significant assets.

The change in circumstances required to be proved as a condition precedent to a variation of a support order need not arise from the marriage or its breakdown: *Tully v. Tully* (1994), 9 R.F.L. (4th) 131 (Ont. Gen. Div.); additional reasons (December 22, 1994), Lambton SCO 35/38/01126/73 (Ont. Gen. Div.).

Where a support order itself provides for periodic review by the court, it is not necessary to find a change in circumstances in order to vary the order: *Brody v. Brody* (1990), 25 R.F.L. (3d) 319, 105 A.R. 41 (Q.B.).

While s. 17 of the *Divorce Act, 1985* requires that there be a change in circumstances before a court can make a variation order, once that change is established s. 17(7) introduces far-reaching criteria that almost give the court a curative power in varying a prior order. The court can attempt to encourage self-sufficiency by refusing to award support or limiting the order: *Oldfield v. Oldfield* (1987), 8 R.F.L. (3d) 297 (Man. Q.B.), in which the court refused to increase the support payable to the wife, who was alcoholic and refused treatment, and in fact limited her future entitlement to two years to encourage self-sufficiency.

In *Brickman v. Brickman* (1987), 8 R.F.L. (3d) 318 (Man. Q.B.), the court increased the support payable to the wife although she had maintained a $35,000 capital fund intact since the time of the divorce. It was held that, particularly in the case of a "traditional" marriage, the payee spouse should not be required to render herself penniless before seeking increased support based on changed circumstances.

The coming into force of the *Divorce Act, 1985*, and in particular the provisions regarding spousal support, was not in itself a "change of circumstances" justifying a variation of the maintenance provisions contained in a decree *nisi* granted under the *Divorce Act, 1970: Derkach v. Derkach* (1986), 5 R.F.L. (3d) 335 (Sask. Q.B.).

A change in the law cannot, for the purposes of an application to vary support, be relied upon as a "change in circumstances". Accordingly, in *Enns v. Enns* (1989), 68 O.R. (2d) 345 (U.F.C.), the husband was not permitted to rely upon the "causal connection" line of authority as a grounds to vary a support award which predated the "causal connection" case law.

On an application to vary support, the court is restricted to considering changes in circumstances occurring subsequent to the date of the order and is not entitled to consider events occurring between the time when minutes of settlement were executed and the order made: *Thombs v. Thombs* (1988), 15 R.F.L. (3d) 83 (Ont. U.F.C.).

Divorce Act, 1968

"It is not the intention of the *Divorce Act*, R.S.C. 1970, c. D-8, that every temporary change in the circumstances of one order to pay maintenance should be the occasion for an application to vary the order. A change of circumstances must be something which has some measure of continuity": per Kelly J.A. in *Lafferty, Re, supra.*

In an application for an upward variation of maintenance, the test is not that the claiming spouse be enduring hardship but rather what is reasonable in the circumstances: *Katz v. Katz* (1983), 33 R.F.L. (2d) 412, 21 Man. R. (2d) 1 (C.A.); additional reasons at (1983), 25 Man. R. (2d) 57 (C.A.); reversing in part (1982), 15 Man. R. (2d) 435 (Q.B.).

The mere passage of time from the date of a decree *nisi* is not in itself sufficient justification for a decrease in spousal maintenance: *Lawson v. Kroitor* (1984), 43 R.F.L. (2d) 326, 37 Sask. R. 306 (Q.B.).

In *Dunham v. Dunham* (1984), 40 R.F.L. (2d) 126 (Alta. Q.B.), the sum of $6,200 owed by the husband by way of maintenance arrears was ordered to be reduced to $2,300 in light of evidence that as a result of injuries he was unable to support even himself. The sum was ordered to be paid out of the husband's share of assets as determined on an application for property division.

"Where the parties stand beyond mere necessity and ability to pay, any adjustment must be made with due regard for and in harmony with the arrangements that have already been prescribed": *Taylor v. Taylor* (1981), 44 N.S.R. (2d) 367, 83 A.P.R. 367 (T.D.), Burchell J.

"I can vary that award at this stage in light of changed circumstances but I do not concede that a change in circumstances necessarily reopens the entire issue. In other words, the change that is to be made or the variation in the decree *nisi*, should reflect the changed circumstances. A changed circumstance is not the key that unlocks the door to a reconsideration of the whole matter from the very beginning. To a certain extent, this is what the petitioner invites me to do — to say now that circumstances have changed somewhat, let us go back to the starting line and reconsider the whole matter: I decline to do that": per Zuber J. in *Tobin v. Tobin* (1974), 19 R.F.L. 18 at 20 (Ont. H.C.).

"It is neither possible nor desirable to approach the resolution of an application ... [for variation of maintenance] on the basis of any mathematical formula related either to the husband's income or by applying to the present time and facts ratio extracted from the maintenance and income amounts at the time of the decree *nisi*": *Wilson v. Wilson* (1982), 27 R.F.L. (2d) 424 (B.C. C.S.).

17§9 — Change of circumstances — onus of proving change

Divorce Act, 1985

On a variation application, the onus of showing that the circumstances have changed lies with the applicant: *Walker v. Walker* (1992), 39 R.F.L. (3d) 305, 68 B.C.L.R. (2d) 92, 12 B.C.A.C. 137, 23 W.A.C. 137 (C.A.).

"When a support order is made where there is no reason to expect that it will be reviewed upon certain events occurring or facts becoming known, as upon the hearing of a trial, there will be a heavier onus upon a party seeking a variance to establish a substantial economic change in the circumstances of at least one of the parties which, even if recognized as a possibility, was not taken into account at the trial, and which results in serious economic disadvantage to one party which can be accommodated without serious disadvantage to the other": *Story v. Story* (1989), 23 R.F.L. (3d) 225, 42 B.C.L.R. (2d) 21, 65 D.L.R. (4th) 549 (C.A.), McEachern C.J.B.C.

Where the husband had failed to make a complete and frank disclosure of his assets on his application to terminate his wife's spousal support, he was not found to have established the required material change in circumstances: *Alexander v. Alexander* (1997), 31 R.F.L. (4th) 131, 25 O.T.C. 103 (Gen. Div.); additional reasons at (July 10, 1998), Doc. 88620/95, 92FL20193/TT (Ont. Gen. Div.); further additional reasons at (1998), 43 R.F.L. (4th) 166 (Ont. Gen. Div.).

The onus is on a party seeking variation of a support order to satisfy the court that the "change" specified in s. 17(4) of the *Divorce Act* is a material and substantive break with the past situation of the parties. The altered circumstances must render the existing order of support irreconcilable with the current conditions, means, needs and other circumstances of either former spouse or child: *Pardy v. Pardy* (1986), 3 R.F.L. (3d) 317, 73 N.B.R. (2d) 340, 184 A.P.R. 340 (Q.B.).

The onus is on an applicant to show that the change in circumstances is such that it warrants a variation of the original support order: *Harris v. Harris* (1992), 40 R.F.L. (3d) 253 (B.C. S.C.).

Divorce Act, 1968

In an application to vary the terms of a maintenance agreement which have been incorporated into a decree *nisi*, the applicant must establish a change in circumstances of a sufficient degree to render continued enforcement of the original order unfair, unjust or unreasonable: *Loveless v. Loveless* (1986), 59 Nfld. & P.E.I.R. 139, 178 A.P.R. 139 (Nfld. T.D.).

"I must start with the proposition that the amount awarded in 1969 by the Court of Appeal was correct: *Fenn v. Fenn* (1973), 13 R.F.L. 147 (Man.); *Tobin v. Tobin* (1974), 19 R.F.L. 18 (Ont.). In order to succeed the burden is on the plaintiff to show a "change in the condition, means, or other circumstances" of either of the parties. In my view, the plaintiff has succeeded": *Roher v. Roher* (1976), 27 R.F.L. 218 at 222–223 (Ont. H.C.), Holland J.

"The onus to show such change or rescission lies on the applicant on the balance of probabilities": *Bucholtz v. Bucholtz* (1977), 1 R.F.L. (2d) 289 at 290 (B.C. S.C.), McTaggart L.J.S.C.

See also *Meszaros v. Meszaros* (1972), 8 R.F.L. 323 at 326 (Ont. Prov. Ct.).

17§10 — Change of circumstances — facts known at time of order

In *L. (H.) v. L. (M.H.)*, 2003 CarswellBC 2206, 2003 BCCA 484 (B.C. C.A.), the parties entered into a separation agreement which included terms relating to spousal support, giving the wife $3,000 per month for 2 years. These terms were incorporated into an order for divorce. Before the end of the 2 years, the wife brought an application to extend the payment of spousal support indefinitely. The wife had developed significant health problems. Support was extended for another 10 months. At a second variation hearing, the wife was granted further support, retroactive to when support under the first variation ceased and that order was reviewable after 3 years. The husband appealed from this order. Since the original order, as varied, had expired, s. 17(10) of the *Divorce Act*, applied. Section 17(10) provides that where a spousal support order is for a definite period or until a specified event occurs, a court cannot make a variation order resuming support on an application after the expiration of the period or occur rence of the event, unless the court is satisfied that a variation order is needed to relieve economic hardship related to the marriage and the changed circumstances since the making of the order or last variation order would have resulted in a different order.

The court held in a two to one decision, that the chambers judge, not having the benefit of the Miglin judgement, erred in her overall approach to the problem of variation. The court must look at the objectives of support set out in the Act as a whole, including the policy goals of certainty, autonomy and finality. The fact that the wife was not able to obtain work was not sufficient reason to find that the agreement should no longer continue to govern the parties' post-divorce obligations towards each other. The court noted that the first variation was based on a delay in seeking employment because of illness, whereas the second variation was based on the inability to find employment. The reason for the inability was not disclosed to the court. The court was of the opinion that the absence of evidence connecting the inability to find work with something that occurred in the marriage was fatal to the wife's claim for further support. The alleged change in circumstances was not related to the marriage. There was no reason to interfere with the agreement between the parties. The husband's appeal was allowed.

Facts which are known at the time a support order is made cannot later be relied upon to prove a change of circumstances justifying a variation of the order. Accordingly where the court at the time the wife's support order was made acknowledged that she was seeing another man and it was foreseeable that they could eventually cohabit, the later fact of that cohabitation did not justify a reduction in support: *B. (G.) c. G. (L.)* (1995), 15 R.F.L. (4th) 201, [1995] 3 S.C.R. 370.

When determining whether a change of circumstances exists, on which to base a variation of a spousal support order, the guiding principle is the determination of whether, if known at the time of the original order, the change would have resulted in a different order: *Read v. Read*, 4 R.F.L. (5th) 126, 183 N.S.R. (2d) 181, 568 A.P.R. 181, 2000 NSCA 33, 2000 CarswellNS 52, [2000] N.S.J. No. 54 (C.A.).

Where the wife's limited term support order was based on an assumption that she would complete a nursing course, the removal of the limitation upon her failure to complete the course was upheld on appeal. The wife's changed circumstances, had they existed at the time of the original order, would have resulted in a different support order: *Therrien-Cliche v. Cliche* (1997), 30 R.F.L. (4th) 97, 99 O.A.C. 202 (C.A.).

In *Poohkay v. Poohkay* (1997), 30 R.F.L. (4th) 9, 200 A.R. 211, 146 W.A.C. 211 (C.A.); additional reasons (1997), 33 R.F.L. (4th) 140 (Alta. C.A.) the wife successfully appealed from an order dismissing her application for a lifting of the time limitation on her spousal support order. At the time of the original order, the parties had not anticipated the extent to which the mother's duties as a custodial parent would interfere with her educational upgrading efforts. Had the parties known that their assumptions were incorrect at the time the original order was made, a different order would likely have resulted. As the wife would likely be able to enter the workforce in the near future, a lump sum award was preferable to an indefinite periodic one.

A 20 percent increase in the husband's salary 4 years after the parties' divorce constituted a sufficient change in circumstances to warrant an increase in the wife's spousal support. If the pending increase had been known at the time of the original order, it would likely have resulted in an award of support to be increased at the time the salary change was anticipated: *MacDonald v. MacDonald* (1997), 30 R.F.L. (4th) 1, 200 A.R. 193, 146 W.A.C. 193 (C.A.).

An application to vary a spousal support award was refused when the bulk of the wife's arguments centred around the unfairness of the original order, which had already been the basis for an unsuccessful appeal: *Cosper v. Cosper* (1997), 32 R.F.L. (4th) 241 (N.S. C.A.).

Where subsequent to the divorce, the wife's existing multiple sclerosis condition deteriorated to the extent that she could no longer work, the court extended her limited term support award. But for the marriage breakdown, she would not have to bear the economic consequence which flowed from her disability. If the total disability had existed at the time of the original order, it would likely have resulted in an in determinate order for a higher amount: *Tees v. Tees* (1997), 31 R.F.L. (4th) 290, [1997] N.W.T.R. 315 (S.C.).

17§11 — Change of circumstances — inflation

Divorce Act, 1985

In *Cymbalisty v. Cymbalisty* (2002), 35 R.F.L. (5th) 31, 2002 CarswellMan 561, [2002] M.J. No. 526, 2002 MBQB 324 169 Man. R. (2d) 265 (Man. Q.B.); affirmed (2003), 44 R.F.L. (5th) 27, 2003 CarswellMan 458, 232 D.L.R. (4th) 718, 180 Man. R. (2d) 112 (Man. C.A.), it was found that the fact that the wife's spousal support order had never been reviewed in the 13 years since it was made was in itself a material change in circumstances which supported her claim for an upward variation.

In *Marshall v. Marshall* (1992), 43 R.F.L. (3d) 303, 81 Man. R. (2d) 156 (C.A.), an increase in the cost of living and the greater costs involved in raising an older child were found to be sufficient material changes in circumstances to warrant an increase in child support.

The increased child care expenses resulting from inflation and the aging of the children may constitute a "material change in circumstances" justifying an increase in support: *Will v. Thauberger Estate* (1991), 34 R.F.L. (3d) 432 (Sask. Q.B.); varied (1991), 38 R.F.L. (3d) 68 (Sask. C.A.).

In *Leblanc v. Leblanc* (1995), 14 R.F.L. (4th) 414, 163 N.B.R. (2d) 192, 419 A.P.R. 192 (Q.B.); affirmed (1995), 14 R.F.L. (4th) 414 (note), 167 N.B.R. (2d) 375, 427 A.P.R. 375 (C.A.), the wife's application for an increase in spousal support was allowed. Although she had $81,000 in savings and R.R.S.P.'s valued at $15,900, she should not be required to use her assets to achieve an acceptable level of self-sufficiency. Over the years her means had been depleted through inflation while the husband's income had increased dramatically.

In *Duplak v. Duplak* (1988), 54 Man. R. (2d) 70 (Q.B.), the inflation which had occurred in the 12 years since the parties' support order was made was found in itself to be a sufficient change in circumstances justifying an upward variation.

Although inflation by itself may constitute a "change in circumstances" within the meaning of the *Divorce Act*, there must be evidence that the inflation has brought about a need for additional support before the court will grant an application for increased support: *Basque v. Basque* (1988), 89 N.B.R. (2d) 214, 226 A.P.R. 214 (Q.B.).

Where the effect of inflation has been relatively equal on both parties, the payee spouse cannot rely upon that factor as a grounds for an upward variation in maintenance: *Single v. Single* (1986), 5 R.F.L. (3d) 287 (N.S. Fam. Ct.).

In *Horn v. Horn* (1987), 48 Man. R. (2d) 142 (Q.B.); affirmed (1987), 11 R.F.L. (3d) 23, 49 Man. R. (2d) 301 (C.A.), the adverse influence of inflation upon the wife's circumstances was sufficient to justify a variation in support.

In *MacKean v. MacKean* (1993), 119 N.S.R. (2d) 252, 330 A.P.R. 252 (Fam. Ct.), the wife's claim for increased support was dismissed. The income which she had begun to receive from Old Age Security and Canada Pension more than off-set any inflationary erosion which had taken place since the original support award.

Divorce Act, 1968

In *Lardner v. Lardner* (1980), 20 R.F.L. (2d) 234 (B.C. C.A.), an order by the trial judge directing that a periodic maintenance award be tied to the cost of living index and be adjusted accordingly on the 1st of January each year subsequent thereto was upheld on appeal.

"[The] judgment provided that the weekly maintenance for the wife and each of the children 'shall be increased by the percentage shown in the annual cost of living index of Statistics Canada'. ... Generally an order for maintenance must be varied by an order made upon a motion for that relief. This order cannot stand. In the circumstances of this case it was not appropriate": *Ursini v. Ursini* (1975), 24 R.F.L. 261 at 263 (Ont. C.A.), Brooke J.A.

Inflation over a long period of time may warrant an increase in spousal maintenance payable: *France v. France* (1986), 42 Man. R. (2d) 315 (Q.B.); varied on other grounds (1987), 6 R.F.L. (3d) 354 (Man. C.A.).

In *Katz v. Katz* (1982), 15 Man. R. (2d) 435 (Q.B.), the court dismissed the wife's application for increased maintenance which had been based upon the argument that inflation in the ten years' subsequent to the award had eroded it. As the original order had incorporated into it the terms of a separation agreement about which the wife had been fully informed and competently advised and which had not been undermined by fraud or misrepresentation, inflation alone did not constitute sufficient economic hardship to justify judicial interference with the agreement.

See also *Galbraith v. Galbraith*, 2 R.F.L. (2d) 278 at 283, [1977] 6 W.W.R. 236 (Man. Q.B.); *Campbell v. Campbell* (1983), 34 R.F.L. (2d) 397, 22 Man. R. (2d) 130, [1983] 6 W.W.R. 333 (Q.B.); *Peters v. Peters* (1975), 21 R.F.L. 237 at 238, 10 N.B.R. (2d) 526, 4 A.P.R. 526 (Q.B.); *Carter v. Carter* (1982), 39 N.B.R. (2d) 506, 103 A.P.R. 506 (Q.B.); *Carroll v. Carroll* (1974), 13 R.F.L. 357 at 364 (Ont. H.C.); *Armel v. Armel* (1974), 17 R.F.L. 71 at 75 (Ont. H.C.).

17§12 — Change of circumstances — payee cohabiting

Divorce Act, 1985

Where at the time that a support order was made, the wife acknowledged that she was seeing another man and the court found that it was foreseeable they would cohabit, their eventual cohabitation did not amount to a material change of circumstances that would be sufficient to vary the order: *B. (G.) c. G. (L.)*, 1995 CarswellQue 23, 1995 CarswellQue 120, EYB 1995-67821, [1995] S.C.J. No. 72, (sub nom. *G. (L.) c. B. (G.)*) 127 D.L.R. (4th) 385, (sub nom. *G. (L.) c. B. (G.)*) 186 N.R. 201, 15 R.F.L. (4th) 201, [1995] 3 S.C.R. 370, [1995] R.D.F. 611 (S.C.C.). Consequently, the spousal support order should not be reduced.

See *Bracklow v. Bracklow* (1999), 44 R.F.L. (4th) 1, 169 D.L.R. (4th) 577, 236 N.R. 79, 120 B.C.A.C. 211, 196 W.A.C. 211, [1999] 1 S.C.R. 420, 63 B.C.L.R. (3d) 77, [1999] 8 W.W.R. 740, 1999 CarswellBC 532, 1999 CarswellBC 533, [1999] S.C.J. No. 14, (sub nom. *B. (G.) v. G. (L.))* [1995] 3 S.C.R. 370 (S.C.C.).

In *Juvatopolos v. Juvatopolos* (2004), 9 R.F.L. (6th) 147, 2004 CarswellOnt 4423 (S.C.J.); affirmed (2005), 2005 CarswellOnt 4774, 19 R.F.L. (6th) 76, 202 O.A.C. 1 (C.A.), the husband's support obligation toward his wife was reduced in light of her new relationship. The relationship appeared to be one of some permanence and her new partner was providing for her financially in a significant way. He was giving her $1,200 per month for living expenses, the amount the husband was required to pay under the existing spousal support order. The application judge had ordered that the quantum of support be reduced to $400 per month. The appellate court held that it should not interfere with the decision of the application judge as that decision was entitled to deference on appeal. It did not exceed the generous ambit within which reasonable disagreement was possible and was not plainly wrong.

Where the husband had stopped paying support to the wife for 12 years after she had entered into a common-law relationship, the court, on appeal, reversed an order compelling the husband to recommence payments. The onus was on the wife to demonstrate that the economic loss resulting from the marriage or its breakdown continued. She had failed to do so: *McMullen v. McMullen* (1994), 5 R.F.L. (4th) 444, 150 N.B.R. (2d) 277, 385 A.P.R. 277, 1994 CarswellNB 26, [1994] N.B.J. No. 308 (C.A.); reversing (1993), 141 N.B.R. (2d) 297, 361 A.P.R. 297, 1993 CarswellNB 378 (Q.B.).

While the payee's establishment of a common-law relationship can constitute a substantial change in circumstances for the purposes of s. 17 of the *Divorce Act* in certain cases, where the evidence indicates a relationship which is a matter of financial convenience and there is no evidence that the third party contributes more on significantly less than his individual share of expenses, no such material change in circumstances warranting a variation of support will be found: *Walker v. Walker* (1992), 39 R.F.L. (3d) 305, 68 B.C.L.R. (2d) 92, 12 B.C.A.C. 137, 23 W.A.C. 137, 1992 CarswellBC 156 (C.A.).

Living in a common-law relationship or remarriage is not an automatic bar to the receipt of spousal support from a previous partner. This is, however, a material consideration: *Ryan v. Hardy*, 2004 CarswellNS 505, 2004 NSSF 111 (S.C.). In this case, support would terminate within 2 years as the wife's circumstances had changed. She had been in a common-law relationship for over a year. She had marketable skills and could re-train to achieve self-sufficiency.

In *Hatchard v. Hatchard* (2003), 45 R.F.L. (5th) 357, 2003 NSCA 100, 2003 CarswellNS 352 (C.A.), the court, on appeal, affirmed the trial judge's finding that the wife had entered into a common-law relationship. Although the wife lived on a separate floor in her new partner's house and paid rent to him, they socialized and vacationed together and partook in sexual relations.

In *Gillham v. Gillham* (1993), 48 R.F.L. (3d) 156, 11 Alta. L.R. (3d) 153, 1993 Carswell-Alta 56, [1993] A.J. No. 527 (C.A.), the court reversed on appeal an order reducing the wife's spousal support. The husband claimed that the wife had entered into a common-law relationship which, under the terms of the parties' separation agreement, entitled him to a reduction in the spousal support payable. The evidence of the wife's relationship presented at the hearing was vague and ambiguous and did not discharge the husband's onus of proving the relationship. To discharge the onus, it was incumbent on the husband to establish something more than the fact that the couple was having sexual relations while living together.

A wife's entry into a common-law relationship does not automatically justify a termination of her spousal support. The statutory objectives of s. 17(7) of the *Divorce Act* must still be considered: *Gallant v. Gallant* (1999), 50 R.F.L. (4th) 389, 214 N.B.R. (2d) 86, 547 A.P.R. 86, 1999 CarswellNB 263 (Q.B.).

Where the emphasis in the original spousal support order was on the wife's need and the order was arguably compensatory in nature, the court refused to terminate the wife's support on the basis that she had entered into a common-law relationship. The original order had been based upon the parties' agreement and although the relationship constituted a change in the wife's circumstances, it was not of a sufficient magnitude to warrant a variation in support, particularly in light of the fact that the attainment of self-sufficiency on the part of the wife was entirely illusory: *Tabel v. Tabel* (1997), 35 R.F.L. (4th) 379, 162 Sask. R. 49, 1997 CarswellSask 746 (Q.B.).

Where the wife had entered into a common-law relationship and it was expected that, with her new partner's assistance, she would soon be self-supporting, the court, on appeal, allowed the husband's application for termination of spousal support: *M. (P.) c. R. (R.)* (1991), (sub nom. *Droit de la famille — 1490)* [1992] R.D.F. 20 (Que. C.A.).

Cohabitation by a payee with another individual does not in itself provide the basis for cancellation of a maintenance order. The relevant test continues to be the payee's need and cohabitation does not necessarily decrease these needs: *F. (J.) v. H. (B.)* (1987), 6 Q.A.C. 221, 1987 CarswellQue 380 (C.A.).

In *Gallagher v. Hogg* (1993), 45 R.F.L. (3d) 337, 1993 CarswellMan 43 (Man. Q.B.), it was held that the wife's living arrangement with a male friend and her modest inheritance of $20,000 were not in themselves sufficient changes in circumstances to warrant a variation of a court order which incorporated the support provisions of a final settlement agreement. The husband had to prove a radical unforseen change in circumstances before a variation would be granted. The reduction in the husband's income met the criterion and support was consequently reduced.

The fact that a payee spouse cohabits with another person is not a ground to terminate or vary support under the *Divorce Act*: *MacDougall v. MacRae* (1989), 19 R.F.L. (3d) 329, 95 N.B.R. (2d) 200, 241 A.P.R. 200, 1989 CarswellNB 17 (Q.B.).

Where the wife entered into a common-law relationship in which all of her economic needs were being met, her order for support, which was based upon the parties' separation agreement, was terminated. As the agreement contemplated variation, the court's jurisdiction was in no way affected. Support is based on need, and if no need exists, a support order should be terminated: *Babington v. Babington* (1993), 47 R.F.L. (3d) 296, 134 N.B.R. (2d) 271, 342 A.P.R. 271, 1993 CarswellNB 20 (Q.B.).

Where the wife entered into a common-law relationship with a man who employed her, shared accommodation with her, and provided her with a car and trips, the husband's application for a decrease in spousal support was allowed. The parties' separation agreement allowed for support variation based upon a "material change in circumstances" and such a material change had occurred when the wife's relationship substantially reduced what she would have had to pay to maintain a similar lifestyle: *Trueman v. Trueman* (1989), 100 N.B.R. (2d) 281, 252 A.P.R. 281, 1989 CarswellNB 217 (Q.B.).

A court has jurisdiction to vary an order for corollary support where the financial circumstances of the parties have not changed significantly from the time of the order but other circumstances have changed. A financial contribution by a cohabitee to a payee and the efforts of the payee in respect of self-sufficiency are relevant circumstances on an application to vary support: *Dubois v. Dubois* (1987), 8 R.F.L. (3d) 48, 50 Man. R. (2d) 174, 1987 CarswellMan 104 (Q.B.); additional reasons at 1987 CarswellMan 410, 50 Man. R. (2d) 174 at 176 (Q.B.).

Where, subsequent to the divorce, the wife's annual income had increased from $11,000 to $36,000 and she began sharing living expenses with a new common-law partner, the husband's application to reduce the support payable to her was allowed: *Manson v. Manson* (1990), 101 N.S.R. (2d) 83, 275 A.P.R. 83, 1990 CarswellNS 514 (Fam. Ct.).

Where the children's needs increased because of the breakdown of the mother's common-law relationship, the court overrode the parties' settlement agreement and ordered increased child support: *Comeau v. Comeau* (1990), 27 R.F.L. (3d) 173, 97 N.S.R. (2d) 42, 258 A.P.R. 42, 1990 CarswellNS 46 (Fam. Ct.).

It is contrary to public policy for a woman after a divorce to live with another man, enjoy all of the amenities of marriage and continue to receive support from her former husband: *Cann v. Huxley* (1987), 7 R.F.L. (3d) 430, 78 N.S.R. (2d) 422, 193 A.P.R. 422, 1987 CarswellNS 73 (Fam. Ct.).

The fact that a payee spouse has begun to cohabit does not automatically disentitle that spouse to continued support. However, the impact of the living arrangement on the spouse's need is valid consideration in determining the continued right to support: *Thombs v. Thombs* (1988), 15 R.F.L. (3d) 83, 1988 CarswellOnt 256 (U.F.C.).

A spouse who enters into a new relationship has the burden of demonstrating a continuing need for support: *Rideout v. Rideout* (1995), 13 R.F.L. (4th) 191, 1995 CarswellBC 87, [1995] B.C.J. No. 571 (S.C.); additional reasons at [1995] B.C.J. No. 1213, 13 R.F.L. (4th) 191n (S.C.).

Divorce Act, 1968

The cases generally suggest that unless there is an explicit provision in a separation agreement dealing with the effect of remarriage or cohabitation on a spouse's right to maintenance, cohabitation in itself does not disentitle a spouse to maintenance. However, cohabitation is a relevant factor on a support application or variation: see *Caron v. Caron*, [1987] 1 S.C.R. 892, 7 R.F.L. (3d) 274, [1987] 4 W.W.R. 522, 14 B.C.L.R. (2d) 186, 75 N.R. 36, 38 D.L.R. (4th) 735, 2 Y.R. 246, EYB 1987-67973, 1987 CarswellYukon 8, 1987 CarswellYukon 43, [1987] S.C.J. No. 32 (S.C.C.) at 280 [R.F.L.].

Where the wife began to live in a common-law relationship with a disabled man, the court allowed the husband's application for a reduction in the maintenance payable to her. The husband was not obliged to support the common-law couple simply because they were unable to support themselves: *Droit de la famille 1000*, [1986] R.D.F. 58 (Que. C.S.). See *Eddy v. Eddy* (1986), 5 R.F.L. (3d) 418, 1986 CarswellBC 568 (C.A.), discussed at 17§25 Change of circumstances — involuntary loss or reduction of payor's income. See also *Gallant v. Gallant* (1984), 42 R.F.L. (2d) 132, 51 Nfld. & P.E.I.R. 192, 150 A.P.R. 192, 1984 CarswellNfld 15 (Nfld. T.D.) discussed at 17§12 Change of circumstances — payee cohabiting.

The fact that a wife lives in a common-law relationship does not disentitle her to support under an existing maintenance order. It is merely a factor to consider in determining whether it is fit and just to vary the order. However, the onus is on the wife to establish that the economic loss resulting from the marriage remains in spite of the second relationship: *Vine v. Vine* (1986), 1 R.F.L. (3d) 425, 54 O.R. (2d) 580, 1986 CarswellOnt 258 (H.C.).

The mere fact that a former wife lives in a common law relationship with another man does not, by itself, disentitle her to continued maintenance. When a former wife enters into a new relationship, however, she bears the burden of demonstrating that despite her new relationship she has a continuing need for maintenance from her former husband: *Lowther v. Lowther* (1986), 12 B.C.L.R. (2d) 158, 1986 CarswellBC 35 (S.C.).

See also *Moul v. Moul* (1982), 36 B.C.L.R. 291, 1982 CarswellBC 104 (S.C.); *Morrow v. Morrow* (1980), 18 R.F.L. (2d) 374, 1980 CarswellBC 500 (S.C.).

17§13 — Change of circumstances — remarriage of payee

Divorce Act, 1985

Where the wife had a new career, a new marriage and was financially comfortable, the termination of her spousal support was upheld on appeal in *Roberts v. Beresford* (2006), 22 R.F.L. (6th) 243, 2006 CarswellBC 337, 2006 BCCA 67, 222 B.C.A.C. 234, 368 W.A.C. 234, 50 B.C.L.R. (4th) 276 (B.C. C.A.).

In *Peloquin v. Peloquin* (2005), 22 R.F.L. (6th) 47, 2005 CarswellMan 424, 2005 MBCA 133, 201 Man. R. (2d) 93, 366 W.A.C. 93 (Man. C.A.); affirming (2004), 186 Man. R. (2d) 308, 11 R.F.L. (6th) 111, 2004 MBQB 193, 2004 CarswellMan 344, [2006] 2 W.W.R. 165 (Man. Q.B.), the fact that the wife had remarried four and an half years after the parties' divorce was found not to be a sufficient ground to justify termination of her spousal support. Her income had increased only marginally, and the first husband's income had increased substantially, and the reduction in her living costs upon remarriage was not significant.

In *Peloquin v. Peloquin* (2004), 11 R.F.L. (6th) 111, 2004 CarswellMan 344, 186 Man. R. (2d) 308, 2004 MBQB 193, [2006] 2 W.W.R. 165 (Q.B.); affirmed on appeal (2005), 2005 CarswellMan 424, 2005 MBCA 133, 22 R.F.L. (6th) 47 (C.A.), the court refused the husband's application to terminate spousal support upon the remarriage of the wife. The wife's financial situation had not dramatically improved with her remarriage. She and her husband had been together for 24 years in a traditional marriage and as only 4½ years had elapsed since their separation, there had been insufficient time for the wife to overcome the financial disadvantage she had suffered.

In *Ennis v. Ennis* (2000), 5 R.F.L. (5th) 302, 77 Alta. L.R. (3d) 289, 2000 ABCA 33, 281 A.R. 161, 248 W.A.C. 161, 2000 CarswellAlta 79, [2000] A.J. No. 75 (C.A.); affirming on this point (1998), 45 R.F.L. (4th) 323, 1998 CarswellAlta 1284, [1998] A.J. No. 352 (Q.B.), the appellate court refused to reinstate the wife's original support award after the failure of her second marriage. Although more attention should have been paid to ss. 17(4.1) and 17(10) of the *Divorce Act*, the trial judge reached the correct conclusion in finding that the wife's economic difficulties related more to the failure of her second marriage than to the first one.

In *Savoie v. Savoie* (1999), 49 R.F.L. (4th) 336, [1999] 9 W.W.R. 63, 175 D.L.R. (4th) 291, 138 Man. R. (2d) 128, 202 W.A.C. 128, 1999 CarswellMan 308, [1999] M.J. No.

298 (C.A.), the court was of the opinion that remarriage in and of itself does not necessarily justify termination of a spousal support order. However, in that decision, spousal support was reduced from $600 to $300, reflecting the wife's remarriage and the setting aside of the parties' separation agreement. The wife had a future need for support, which arose because of her economic disadvantage suffered as a result of the long-term traditional marriage.

In *Plotz v. Boehmer-Plotz* (2004), 2004 CarswellOnt 613 (Ont. S.C.J.); additonal reasons at (2004), 2004 CarswellOnt 1196 (Ont. S.C.J.), the wife accepted a variation based on the material change in circumstances resulting from her remarriage. The court held that it would be inappropriate to terminate spousal support from her first husband as it might jeopardize her in the event that her second marriage ended. The spousal support provision was varied to be a nominal annual payment of $1.00.

On a variation application where the payee spouse has remarried, the financial contribution of the new spouse, or what his contribution should be, is of great significance: *Millen v. Millen*, 2004 CarswellOnt 2594 (S.C.J.); additional reasons at (2004), 2004 CarswellOnt 2571 (S.C.J.). The former husband and the wife had been in a long-term marriage. The court held that the wife remained entitled to a support award against the former husband, although at a reduced rate, to redress the economic consequences of their marriage. Support was reduced to $900 monthly.

Where the wife's new husband died within months of remarriage it was held that the fact of the marriage did not effect her former husband's support obligations towards her: *Droit de la famille — 941*, (sub nom. *M. (P.) c. G. (G.)*) [1991] R.D.F. 502, (sub nom. *M. (P.) c. G. (G.)*) 41 Q.A.C. 278, 1991 CarswellQue 200 (C.A.); reversing in part (1990), [1991] R.J.Q. 412, [1991] R.D.F. 107 (S.C.).

The decisions of the Supreme Court of Canada in *Moge v. Moge* (1992), [1992] 3 S.C.R. 813, 99 D.L.R. (4th) 456, EYB 1992-67141, [1992] S.C.J. No. 107, 1992 CarswellMan 143, 1992 CarswellMan 222, [1993] 1 W.W.R. 481, 81 Man. R. (2d) 161, 30 W.A.C. 161, 43 R.F.L. (3d) 345, 145 N.R. 1, [1993] R.D.F. 168 (S.C.C.), and *B. (G.) c. G. (L.)*, [1995] 3 S.C.R. 370, 15 R.F.L. (4th) 201, EYB 1995-67821, 1995 CarswellQue 23, 1995 CarswellQue 120, [1995] S.C.J. No. 72, (sub nom. *G. (L.) c. B. (G.)*) 127 D.L.R. (4th) 385, (sub nom. *G. (L.) c. B. (G.)*) 186 N.R. 201, [1995] R.D.F. 611 (S.C.C.), indicate that remarriage is not a bar to continuance of spousal support and that on an application to vary, the court must take into account all the factors in s. 17(7), not merely need. See also *Harris v. Gilbert* (1997), 32 O.R. (3d) 139, 26 R.F.L. (4th) 199, (sub nom. *Harris v. Harris*) 97 O.A.C. 14, 1997 CarswellOnt 115 (C.A.).

Where the spousal support agreed to by the parties was intricately tied in to the parties' property settlement, the court refused the husband's application to vary the wife's spousal support after her remarriage. The original support order had been compensatory in nature and reflected the fact that the wife had agreed not to seek a portion of the husband's employment pension. In the circumstances, rescinding or reducing the wife's support would be unfair: *McKay v. McKay* (2000), 11 R.F.L. (5th) 179, 2000 BCSC 1393, 2000 CarswellBC 1983 (S.C.).

Remarriage does not itself end a spouse's entitlement to support, but it does constitute a change in circumstances as contemplated under s. 17(4.1): *Friesen v. Friesen*, 2004 CarswellBC 2454, 2004 BCSC 1344 (S.C.). The wife bears the burden of demonstrating that despite her remarriage she has a continuing need for spousal support. A variation of the existing order should meet the objectives set out in s. 17(4). The court considered the following matters:

1. the length of the parties' marriage was 25 years;

2. the five children of the marriage continued to reside with the wife;

3. the wife was not permitted to undertake employment in Canada at the time of the hearing;

4. the parties have been separated for 4 years, but the wife has not achieved economic self-sufficiency;

5. the wife's new husband was self-employed and earned income in 2002 of $58,687;

6. the new husband had the care of two children from his first marriage who reside with him and the wife; and

7. the parties have not yet resolved their respective claims to family assets.

The court reduced spousal support from $3500 per month to $2500 per month.

Remarriage usually constitutes a material change in circumstances sufficient to trigger a variation application. However, the remarriage of a spouse who is the recipient of spousal support does not automatically mean that support should be terminated: *Franz v. Wilson*, 2005 CarswellOnt 3711 (S.C.J.). In this case, the court considered the article "Glass Ceilings in Spousal Support", Syrtach Collection of Family Law Articles, SFLRP/1998-2001 at pp. 33–34, where the author provides a list of issues that the court must consider in making a determination of whether support should be terminated. That list includes the following:

1. Does the spouse still need support in view of her new relationship and the income of her new partner?

2. Is there a way to terminate the periodic obligation while acknowledging an ongoing entitlement? (ie., by way of a final lump sum payment).

3. Did the parties specify the reason(s) why support was being paid when they signed their agreement?

4. Was it foreseeable at the time of the agreement that the spouse would remarry/cohabit?

5. Can it be said with any degree of certainty that the new relationship will last? Is it an enduring relationship, or is it short-lived?

6. What efforts is the spouse making to achieve self-sufficiency? Is the spouse staying out of the workforce to maintain a new home for the new relationship?

7. Will the new relationship ever compensate her for the economic consequences of the first marriage?

The court held that the wife continued to have need of spousal support but not at the same level as before her remarriage. Considering all the factors involved, the court ordered spousal support of $1500 per month, (reduced from $2,000 per month).

The remarriage of the applicant can no longer be a bar to continued support, but merely a factor in determining if there ought to be a change to the quantum: *Kennedy v. Kennedy*, 2005 CarswellOnt 2296, [2005] O.J. No. 2334 (S.C.J.).

Despite the fact that the interspousal agreement and consent order provided that the wife's remarriage would result in a reduction of spousal support, the court held in *Wright v. Wright*, 2005 CarswellSask 626, 2005 SKQB 138, 261 Sask. R. 227 (Q.B.) that the wife's remarriage and the modest consequent change in her standard of living did not constitute a material change in circumstance sufficient to justify a variation in the spousal support order rendered 3 years previously. The parties had been married for 21 years and the wife was primarily a homemaker, responsible for caring for the home and family. She was only employed part-time during the marriage. She was 51 years old at the time of the order. The husband was retired at the time the order was made and was in receipt of his pension. The fact that the wife was not employed at the time of the hearing and had not become self-sufficient was not a material change sufficient to warrant variation.

In *Moore v. Moore* (1992), 137 A.R. 211, 1992 CarswellAlta 576, [1992] A.J. No. 1140 (Q.B.), the fact that the wife had remarried was found not to constitute a sufficient radical unforeseen change in circumstances to justify the termination of her support payable under a final settlement agreement.

As the purpose of support is to compensate a spouse for what he or she may have given up by reason of the marriage, it is not improper, in some cases, to require a payor spouse to continue spousal support notwithstanding the fact that the payee has remarried: *Rosario v. Rosario* (1991), 37 R.F.L. (3d) 24, 120 A.R. 331, 8 W.A.C. 331, 1991 CarswellAlta 344 (C.A.); reversing (1989), 24 R.F.L. (3d) 168, 102 A.R. 234, 1989 CarswellAlta 398 (Q.B.).

Where the payee had re-married and she was healthier and working part-time, the court reduced spousal support in *Prince v. Prince* (2000), 8 R.F.L. (5th) 165, 2000 Carswell-Alta 557, 2000 ABQB 371 (Alta. Q.B.). Support was not eliminated in light of the 27-year marriage and the fact that her illnesses seemed to flow from the parties' marriage.

Where the remarriage of the wife had not redressed the economic disadvantage to her as a result of the breakdown of her first marriage, the court refused the husband's application for a reduction in the spousal support payable by him: *Bettles v. Wright* (1997), 30 R.F.L. (4th) 256, 1997 CarswellPEI 56, (sub nom. *Bettles v. Bettles)* 153 Nfld. & P.E.I.R. 350, (sub nom. *Bettles v. Bettles)* 475 A.P.R. 350, [1997] 1 P.E.I.R. 222 (T.D. [In Chambers]).

More than a determination of self-sufficiency is required to reduce or terminate a spousal support award. Accordingly, where the wife had remarried and achieved a degree of self-sufficiency, her spousal support was reduced, but not terminated as the husband had requested. The wife had been a homemaker throughout the parties' 29-year traditional marriage and had foregone the accumulation of her own pension so that her husband could accumulate his own. Without continuing to pay support, the husband would have reaped all the benefits from that pension: *Lamey v. Lamey* (1996), 19 R.F.L. (4th) 172, 138 Nfld. & P.E.I.R. 53, 431 A.P.R. 53, 1996 CarswellPEI 9 (T.D.).

The fact that a former spouse is entitled to support benefits from a second relationship does not relieve the first spouse from the obligation to continue to pay spousal support if need is continuing: *Nantais v. Nantais* (1995), 16 R.F.L. (4th) 201, 26 O.R. (3d) 453, 1995 CarswellOnt 891 (Gen. Div.).

Remarriage does not automatically disentitle a spouse from support where that spouse continues to suffer an economic disadvantage resulting from the marriage and is in need: *Campbell v. Rooney* (1994), 10 R.F.L. (4th) 351, (sub nom. *Campbell v. Campbell)* 129 Nfld. & P.E.I.R. 294, (sub nom. *Campbell v. Campbell)* 402 A.P.R. 294, 1995 CarswellPEI 1 (T.D.).

In *Wrobel v. Wrobel* (1994), 8 R.F.L. (4th) 403, 160 A.R. 241, 1994 CarswellAlta 401, [1994] A.J. No. 688 (Q.B.), it was found that the remarriage of the wife to an individual with a good income justified the termination of her spousal support order and the cancellation of arrears owing from the date of the marriage.

It is no longer correct to hold that a former spouse, who has entered into a new relationship, must prove that he or she still has a continuing need to receive support. Self-sufficiency is only one factor for the court to consider in establishing the quantum of an award. In an application to vary support, the court must deal with all of the statutory objectives of support as specified in the *Divorce Act*: *May v. May* (1993), 48 R.F.L. (3d) 432, 1993 CarswellOnt 354 (Gen. Div.).

In the *May* case, the court was of the opinion that the wife in her second marriage continued to be economically disadvantaged by her first marriage and its dissolution. The husband had also remarried and had three step-children. The court granted an order reducing the support payments.

Where the wife attempted to enforce a support order against her first husband after the failure of her second marriage, the court allowed the husband's application to terminate the order. The wife's remarriage and failure to enforce support was tantamount to an agreement whereby the parties severed their prior ties and went their own ways: *Bush v. Bush* (1989), 21 R.F.L. (3d) 298, 1989 CarswellOnt 266 (Ont. U.F.C.). See also *Underwood v. Underwood* (1987), 7 R.F.L. (3d) 447, 1987 CarswellNS 74 (N.S. Fam. Ct.) discussed at 17§22 Change of circumstances — remarriage of payor.

The remarriage of a payee spouse does not, of itself, constitute a change of substantial circumstances justifying a reduction in the child support paid to that spouse: *Lever v. Lever* (1991), 90 Nfld. & P.E.I.R. 266, 280 A.P.R. 266, 1991 CarswellNfld 48 (U.F.C.).

Although remarriage does not automatically terminate a spouse's right to support, it does shift the onus to that spouse of proving why the second marriage does not meet his or her needs. Where the wife and her second husband maintained two homes and were short of funds to meet their needs, the first husband's application for termination of spousal support was allowed. The burden of maintaining the second home should not properly be passed on to the husband: *Range v. Range* (1995), 14 R.F.L. (4th) 11, 1995 CarswellBC 416, [1995] B.C.J. No. 1248 (S.C.).

17§14 — Change of circumstances — payee no longer has primary responsibility for children

Divorce Act, 1985

The fact that the wife no longer had to support one of the children was not a ground for reduction of her own spousal support in *P. (F.) c. T. (Y.)* (16 septembre 1993), no C.A. Montréal 500-09-001863-927 (C.A. Qué.).

While there may be instances where a material change in circumstances results from the fact that the payee no longer has primary responsibility for the parties' children, where there is a modest amount of spousal maintenance in issue, such a variation could not be supported on this basis: *Walker v. Walker* (1992), 39 R.F.L. (3d) 305, 12 B.C.A.C. 137, 23 W.A.C. 137 (C.A.).

Where the husband had been paying $250 directly to the wife as child support for the parties' 22-year-old son, it was held that when the child no longer qualified for support, the amount was to continue to be paid to the wife as spousal support. The support had been used by the wife for her own benefit as well as that of the child and her need would continue: *Smith v. Smith* (1998), 36 R.F.L. (4th) 419 (Ont. Gen. Div.); additional reasons (March 31, 1998), Doc. Barrie 513/97 (Ont. Gen. Div.); further additional reasons (June 22, 1998), Doc. Barrie 513/97 (Ont. Gen. Div.).

Spousal support payable to a custodial parent should not be reduced simply because the children have left home and become self-sufficient. If spousal need continues, there is no reason to justify a reduction in support: *Gillis v. Gillis* (1994), 3 R.F.L. (4th) 128, 130 N.S.R. (2d) 112, 367 A.P.R. 112 (S.C.).

17§15 — Change of circumstances — property awards to payee

In *Hickey v. Hickey* (1997), 32 R.F.L. (4th) 193, 123 Man. R. (2d) 139, 159 W.A.C. 139 (C.A.), the court allowed the husband's appeal from an order increasing the wife's spousal support. Although the husband's income had doubled in the 10 years since the parties separation, the wife was still of an age where she was capable of earning income and had been equipped by education and training to do so. Also, she had been provided with an equitable share of marriage assets which had increased in value over the years. The wife's appeal at 46 R.F.L. (4th) 1, 172 D.L.R. (4th) 577, 240 N.R. 312, [1999] 8 W.W.R. 485, 138 Man. R. (2d) 40, 202 W.A.C. 40, [1999] 2 S.C.R. 518, was allowed and the reasons of the motions judge restored. The Supreme Court of Canada was of the opinion that the objectives of s. 17(7) were reflected in the reasons and that he took account of the material changes in circumstances and also considered the separation agreement. The property award to the payee was not specifically considered.

Where the spousal support agreed to by the parties was intricately tied in to the parties' property settlement, the court refused the husband's application to vary the wife's spousal support after her remarriage. The original support order had been compensatory in nature and reflected the fact that the wife had agreed not to seek a portion of the husband's employment pension. In the circumstances, rescinding or reducing the wife's support would be unfair: *McKay v. McKay*, 11 R.F.L. (5th) 179, 2000 BCSC 1393, 2000 CarswellBC 1983 (S.C.).

In *Adams v. Adams* (1998), 42 R.F.L. (4th) 285 (Ont. Gen. Div.), the court allowed the husband's application for a reduction in the spousal support payable by him pursuant to the parties' settlement. After the settlement, the wife had succeeded in an application for division of the husband's pension. The husband was accordingly entitled to a reduction equal to the monthly pension benefit received by the wife.

Where the wife was awarded a substantial property settlement subsequent to the parties' divorce, the earlier maintenance order made in the divorce proceeding was reduced to the nominal sum of $1. The property award constituted a material change in circumstances which, if properly invested, would allow the wife to become self-sufficient: *Weicker v. Weicker* (1986), 4 R.F.L. (3d) 397, 74 A.R. 16 (Q.B.).

In *Hansen v. Hansen* (1997), 31 R.F.L. (4th) 384 (N.S. S.C.), the wife's spousal support was ordered reduced in light of her ownership of substantial income producing assets.

17§16 — Change of circumstances — payee disabled

Where the husband had sought a downward variation of spousal support payable by him on the basis of a disability, the variation was refused. His appeal was likewise dismissed on the basis that the trial judge was entitled to find that the husband had failed to prove that he lacked the means to make the support payments: *Kollinger v. Kollinger* (1995), 14 R.F.L. (4th) 363, 102 Man. R. (2d) 296, 93 W.A.C. 296 (C.A.).

In *Richardson v. Normand*, 8 R.F.L. (5th) 185, [2000] 9 W.W.R. 360, 2000 MBQB 110, 151 Man. R. (2d) 12, 2000 CarswellMan 420 (Q.B.), the wife was granted spousal support 17 years after the parties' uncontested divorce, since the court found that there was a change in circumstances as the wife's cancer had reoccurred, thus preventing her from continuing her employment. The parties had no contact for 20 years. At the time of the divorce, the wife was granted nominal spousal support of $1.00 per year, and that award acknowledged that the wife was entitled to support but at the time of the divorce did not need it. The wife had been disadvantaged by the breakdown of the marriage as she had lost the financial assistance she would have received if the parties had remained together. She had suffered economic hardship, as she was no longer economically self-sufficient. Considering the factors for spousal support and the objectives of a variation order, the court ordered support of $250 per month.

In *Kerwood v. Kerwood* (1999), 48 R.F.L. (4th) 127, 1999 CarswellBC 780 (S.C. [In Chambers]), the court allowed the 83-year-old wife's application for an increase to her 30-year-old spousal support order. The wife's health had declined as she grew older and she required near-daily home care. The fact that declining health with age is foreseeable did not alter that the wife had experienced a change in circumstances. As the husband's income had actually increased over the years, he was in a position to pay the increased amount.

In *Boudreau v. Bradbury* (1998), 38 R.F.L. (4th) 1 (B.C. S.C.), the court allowed the wife's application for an upward variation of a nominal support award 17 years after the parties' divorce. The wife had developed severe medical problems which constituted the required "changed in circumstances" and, although she had remarried, this fact alone did not disqualify her from support. At the time of the divorce, the husband's pension had not been a divisible asset and he had been receiving a pension benefit now for a number of years.

In *Elaschuk v. Elaschuk* (1997), 31 R.F.L. (4th) 119, 28 O.T.C. 392 (Gen. Div.); affirmed (June 30, 1999), Doc. 581/97 (Ont. Div. Ct.), the wife's total disability 26 years after the end of the parties' 6-year marriage was found to be a change in circumstances warranting an increase in her spousal support.

In *Pace v. Pace* (1992), 116 N.S.R. (2d) 205, 320 A.P.R. 205 (T.D.), the court refused the wife's application for an upward variation of her nominal maintenance award. The wife claimed that the strain of the relationship with her former husband had forced her to seek medical care and had impaired her earning ability. It was found, however, that her medical condition could hardly be characterized as a radical change resulting from a pattern of economic dependency generated by the marriage relationship.

Where the wife, even with support, was not likely ever to achieve self-sufficiency because of health problems, the court allowed the husband's application to terminate her spousal support four years after the divorce. The husband had fulfilled his obligations toward the wife: *Droit de la famille — 1638*, [1992] R.D.F. 458 (C.S. Qué.).

Where the husband had suffered a stroke, but was in receipt of disability benefits, his application to reduce spousal and child support was dismissed. As the husband's new wife was also employed, the means currently available to the husband were equal to those available when the order had originally been made: *Kearney v. Kearney* (1988), 54 Man. R. (2d) 42 (Q.B.).

Where the wife was injured and unable to work two years after her support award had terminated, the court refused to reinstate her support. There was no casual link between the wife's economic difficulties and her former marriage: *Droit de la famille — 382*, [1987] R.J.Q. 1748 (C.S. Qué.).

17§17 — Change of circumstances — payee on welfare

Divorce Act, 1985

Where the wife would otherwise be forced on public assistance, the court refused to grant the husband's application for termination of spousal support payable to her, despite the fact that she had remarried. Her new husband had died within a month of the marriage and, therefore, an annulment of the support obligation could not be justified: *Droit de la famille — 941* (1990), [1991] R.J.Q. 412 (C.S.); reversed in part [1991] R.D.F. 502, 41 Q.A.C. 278 (C.A. Qué.).

The fact that a payee spouse may become a public charge if the payor's application for reduced support is granted is not grounds to add the state as a party to the variation application: *Pearson v. Pearson* (1990), 25 R.F.L. (3d) 79 (N.B. Q.B.).

The receipt by a payee spouse of old age pension and supplement may amount to a material change in circumstances warranting a variation of support. The supplement does not have the same connotation as welfare and does not preclude the termination of support: *Miles v. Miles* (1990), 25 R.F.L. (3d) 348, 80 Nfld. & P.E.I.R. 333, 249 A.P.R. 333 (Nfld. T.D.).

Where the effect of an application to increase child support would require the husband to make larger payments to welfare authorities, the application was dismissed. An increase would only worsen the husband's financial position without improving the children's position: *Gaudet v. Gaudet* (1988), 18 R.F.L. (3d) 142 (Sask. Q.B.).

Where the wife had executed a separation agreement releasing the husband from all obligations, the fact that she was on welfare both before and after the agreement was insufficient to warrant a variation to provide support for the wife: *Droit de la famille — 390*, [1987] R.D.F. 506 (C.S. Qué.).

In *Harding v. Harding* (1991), 109 N.S.R. (2d) 268, 297 A.P.R. 268 (Fam. Ct.), the court allowed the husband's application to terminate his wife's support although she was living on unemployment insurance and had little prospect of employment after the end of the parties' 24-year traditional marriage. The husband was also destitute, suffering from depression and alcoholism, and was living on welfare. Severing the tie between the parties was the best and possibly only change to promote the economic self-sufficiency of each.

Divorce Act, 1968

The fact that a former spouse has been forced onto the welfare rolls is not of itself grounds for the variation of a spousal support order. In absence of a significant change in circumstances tied to economic dependency resulting from the marriage, the obligation to support a former spouse in need becomes the responsibility of the state: *Richardson v. Richardson*, 7 R.F.L. (3d) 304, [1987] 1 S.C.R. 857. See also *Pelech v. Pelech*, 7 R.F.L. (3d) 225, [1987] 1 S.C.R. 801.

17§18 — Change of circumstances — payee squandering assets

Divorce Act, 1985

In *Droit de la famille — 783*, [1990] R.D.F. 220 (C.A. Qué.), the court allowed the husband's application to annul the wife's alimony award on the basis that she had administered her income badly and had shown no determination to become financially independent.

In *Gullens v. Gullens* (1990), 26 R.F.L. (3d) 121, 97 N.S.R. (2d) 30, 258 A.P.R. 30 (Fam. Ct.), the fact that the wife had squandered the settlement she had received in a personal injury action was found insufficient to justify a variation to the husband's support obligations contained in a final separation agreement. The funds were intended as special and general damage for personal injuries and the wife was not accountable to the husband for their expenditure.

Where it would have been more reasonable for the wife to have used her property settlement funds for her own retraining, rather than to purchase a new home, the court allowed the husband's application to reduce her spousal support and to place a time limit on her future entitlement: *L. (D.L.) v. L. (D.J.)* (1991), 34 R.F.L. (3d) 163 (B.C. S.C.).

The fact that the wife had made a bad investment and lost a significant amount of money was held not to be sufficient reason to justify the termination of her support: *Shabaga v. Shabaga* (1987), 6 R.F.L. (3d) 357 (B.C. S.C.).

Divorce Act, 1968

Where the wife squandered the property awarded to her under a provincial statute, her subsequent claim for greater maintenance on divorce was dismissed despite the fact that the husband's means had increased significantly. The husband could not be expected to subsidize the wife's mistakes: *Kitson v. Kitson* (1986), 1 R.F.L. (3d) 103 (Ont. H.C.).

17§19 — Change of circumstances — payee — other

Divorce Act, 1985

The fact that the income differential between the parties had changed does not necessarily mean that an order varying spousal support should issue. Accordingly, when the wife began to receive disability benefits subsequent to her spousal support order it was found not to constitute a sufficient material change to justify a variation of her spousal support: *LeClair v. LeClair*, 22 R.F.L. (6th) 123, 2005 CarswellNB 704, 2005 CarswellNB 705, [2005] N.B.J. No. 502, 2005 NBCA 107, (sub nom. *Leclair v. Leclair)* 293 N.B.R. (2d) 137, (sub nom. *Leclair v. Leclair)* 762 A.P.R. 137 (N.B. C.A.).

In an appeal by the wife from a judgment ordering the termination of spousal support and the reduction of child support, the court, in *Wooldridge v. Wooldridge* (1999), 45 R.F.L. (4th) 308, 172 D.L.R. (4th) 637, 237 A.R. 64, 197 W.A.C. 64, 1999 CarswellAlta 320 (C.A.); additional reasons at (1999), 49 R.F.L (4th) 455, 250 A.R. 168, 213 W.A.C. 168, 1999 CarswellAlta 620 (C.A.) granted her appeal. In considering that the wife had not fulfilled her undertaking in the parties' separation agreement to retrain "as soon as possible", the chambers judge had given too narrow an interpretation of the phrase. A proper interpretation of the phrase must take into account all of the circumstances of the wife, not just her own poor health since separation, but also the fact she had taken care of two severely psychologically ill children and that she had not worked outside the home for 20 years. Under these circumstances, self-sufficiency for the wife might not be possible for some time, if ever. The husband was ordered to pay $2,500 per month in spousal support. Once the husband has ceased to pay child support, the spousal support, if necessary, could be increased.

Where the payee gives a large sum of money to a relative and then seeks an increase in support to cover expenses which, without her gift, could have been covered by the payee, there is no material change in circumstances to warrant a variation: *Murta v. Murta* (1997), 33 R.F.L. (4th) 429, 123 Man. R. (2d) 155, 159 W.A.C. 155, 1997 CarswellMan 561, [1997] M.J. No. 547 (C.A.).

In *Canuel v. Canuel* (1997), 33 R.F.L. (4th) 195, 94 B.C.A.C. 188, 39 B.C.L.R. (3d) 358, 152 W.A.C. 188, 1997 CarswellBC 1335, [1997] B.C.J. No. 1654 (C.A.), the court held that where the children had left the father's home and one, who was not a child of the marriage within the meaning of the *Divorce Act*, had moved in with the mother and the other child now lived on his own, it was appropriate to increase spousal maintenance. However, doubling the amount was excessive. The appeal was allowed and spousal support, which had been $700, then doubled to $1400, was set at $1,000 a month. The lower court had not given due consideration to the fact that the payor had resigned from his employment resulting in a reduction in income, and that the family home was now in the sole possession of the payor.

Where subsequent to the divorce, the wife discovered that she had lost the right to the widow's benefit under the husband's pension, it was held that this alone did not constitute a change of circumstances warranting an upward variation of her spousal support: *Murphy v. Murphy* (1994), 10 R.F.L. (4th) 102 (Man. C.A.).

Where the court had based a wife's spousal support on the assumption that she would become self-sufficient, the fact that she did not, despite her efforts, itself constituted a change in circumstances sufficient to support a variation application: *Wilson v. Wilson* (1994), 5 R.F.L. (4th) 75, 95 Man. R. (2d) 253, 70 W.A.C. 253 (C.A.).

In *Rogers v. Rogers* (1997), 28 R.F.L. (4th) 265 (B.C. S.C.), the court allowed the husband's application for a downward variation of the wife's spousal support. At the time of the original order the wife implied to the husband that her use of her qualifications as a real estate sales person would eventually minimize her support needs. However, in the 4 years since the order, she had made virtually no efforts to achieve self-sufficiency.

Where the wife had re-entered the workforce following the termination of a long-term traditional marriage, an order ending her spousal support was upheld on appeal. Although it was unlikely that the wife would ever be as successful in her career as she would have been had the parties not married, there was insufficient evidence to justify an indefinite support award: *McGregor v. McGregor* (1994), 3 R.F.L. (4th) 343, 148 N.B.R. (2d) 176, 378 A.P.R. 176 (C.A.); reversing in part (1993), 49 R.F.L. (3d) 17, 139 N.B.R. (2d) 296, 357 A.P.R. 296 (Q.B.).

Where the parties' pension benefits had been settled in the course of matrimonial property proceedings, the husband could not later rely upon the fact that the wife had begun to share in his pension benefits as a reason to justify a reduction in the spousal support payable to her: *Grainger v. Grainger* (1991), 37 R.F.L. (3d) 139 (Sask. Q.B.); affirmed (1992), 39 R.F.L. (3d) 101, 100 Sask. R. 61, 18 W.A.C. 161 (C.A.).

A 400 percent increase in the payee's annual income is a change of circumstances warranting a reduction in support payable: *Mullin v. Mullin* (1990), 87 Nfld. & P.E.I.R. 1,

271 A.P.R. 1 (P.E.I. T.D.); varied (1991), 37 R.F.L. (3d) 142, 95 Nfld. & P.E.I.R. 73, 301 A.P.R. 73 (C.A.).

Where the mother unilaterally made the decision to enroll the child in private school, her application for increased support to cover the cost was refused. The child did not require private schooling: *Lennox v. Frender*, 27 R.F.L. (3d) 181, 47 B.C.L.R. (2d) 394, [1990] 6 W.W.R. 282 (C.A.).

The fact that the wife received CPP benefits had no impact upon her spousal support order which specified a reduction should she find "employment". CPP benefits could not be characterized as "employment income": *Crawford v. Kelly* (2004), 9 R.F.L. (6th) 299, 2004 CarswellBC 1972, 2004 BCSC 1000 (S.C.).

In *Young v. Young* (1999), 47 R.F.L. (4th) 214, 1999 CarswellOnt 1332 (S.C.J.), the court reduced the husband's spousal support payments from $2,000 to $500 per month for a time-limited period, since, subsequent to minutes of settlement, the husband's ill health had prompted him to work part-time as a lawyer which greatly reduced his income and at the same time, the wife's income from employment and investments had increased. The parties had been married for 34 years and the court was of the opinion that the parties should be placed on an equal financial basis, as much as possible. There had been no "material" change in the parties' net worth since the time of settlement.

In *Andrew v. Andrew* (1999), 1999 CarswellOnt 2056 (Gen. Div.), the court held that it would be unfair to require the former husband to continue to pay support to his former wife when she had achieved a practical level of self-sufficiency and spousal support was terminated. The parties had had a 13-year marriage and the applicant had paid spousal support for 19 years. The applicant was near retirement age but his net worth would not realistically permit retirement at an appropriate standard. The respondent had chosen to retire and had factored her support payments into her decision to do so. However, her earnings from a new post retirement job would offset her loss of support.

Where the wife died subsequent to an order fixing the husband's substantial support arrears, the court granted the husband's application to vacate the arrears. The purpose of spousal support is to meet the ongoing expenses of the payee, a purpose which had disappeared with the wife's death: *King Estate v. King* (1994), 8 R.F.L. (4th) 380, 153 N.B.R. (2d) 20, 392 A.P.R. 20 (Q.B.).

In *Sittmann v. Sittmann* (1987), 6 R.F.L. (3d) 268 (Nfld. T.D.), it was held that the husband was not to be relieved of, or have diminished, his liability to pay support for his wife and their children because of gratuitous financial assistance provided by the wife's father which enabled them to enjoy a higher standard of living than they would ordinarily enjoy.

In *Stonestreet v. Stonestreet* (1989), 19 R.F.L. (3d) 314 (B.C. S.C.), where the wife had been awarded support because of her inability to work due to illness, the court refused the husband's application to reduce her support after she began working part-time. As she continued to have health problems and her employment was not secure, there was no significant change of circumstances upon which to base the variation requested.

17§20 — Change of circumstances — payor's bankruptcy

In *Richards v. Richards* (1986), 48 Sask. R. 131 (C.A.), the court dismissed the husband's appeal from an order refusing to cancel arrears and reduce maintenance payable after his assignment in bankruptcy. The husband was a young, able-bodied man who continued to operate a business in spite of the bankruptcy.

Where the parties' decree *nisi* incorporated a settlement whereby the wife released her interest in the husband's business in exchange for money to be paid in instalments, the wife's right to those funds was not affected by the husband's subsequent bankruptcy. The money owing to the wife was basically for her support and was accordingly protected by s. 148 of the *Bankruptcy Act: Craig v. Bassett* (1988), 15 R.F.L. (3d) 461 (N.S. T.D.); affirmed (1988), 17 R.F.L. (3d) 71 C.B.R. (N.S.) 82, 87 N.S.R. (2d) 218, 222 A.P.R. 216 (C.A.).

Where the husband was unexpectedly assessed a sizable tax debt and had to declare bankruptcy to clear it, his application to cancel the spousal support payable to his former wife was allowed. The assignment into bankruptcy constituted a material change justifying the cancellation. Furthermore, the wife had sizable assets and was not entitled to further support: *Bargh v. Bargh*, 37 R.F.L. (5th) 235, 2003 CarswellBC 740, 2003 BCSC 489 (B.C. S.C.).

17§21 — Change of circumstances — payor cohabiting

Cohabiting with another either in a common-law relationship or in a marriage does not automatically give rise to a material change in circumstances sufficient to vary or terminate spousal support. Particularly in long-term marriages, support is composed of a number of elements. One of them is the result of dealing with the economic disadvantages of the marriage. Being a homemaker, caregiver, meal maker, not having a job or a career, pension entitlements, higher education, and other assets often leave the payee with little to show for years of dedication and sacrifice. Support covers not only living expenses, but also compensation for abandoning personal advancement or development for the general welfare of the family unit. In each case, the court must look at the length of the previous marriage and the consequences of the dissolution; the current living standards of each of the former spouses; the nature and permanence of subsequent relationships; and the economic benefits flowing to the payee as a result of the new relationships. On a variation application, all the objectives of s. 17(7) of the *Divorce Act* must be considered: *Gallant v. Gallant* (1999), 50 R.F.L. (4th) 389, 214 N.B.R. (2d) 86, 547 A.P.R. 86, 1999 CarswellNB 263 (Q.B.)

In *Chevalier v. Chevalier* (1993), 128 N.S.R. (2D) 112, 359 A.P.R. 112 (S.C.), the father's ability to pay, on an application by the mother for increased child support, was calculated on the premise that the father's common-law spouse contributed one-half of the couple's rent and utilities.

Where the former husband is living with another woman who is employed, that woman is expected to help pay his household expenses, thereby freeing more of his funds for the payment of maintenance: *McLean v. McLean* (1975), 26 R.F.L. 115, 14 N.B.R. (2d) 64 (Q.B.).

17§22 — Change of circumstances — remarriage of payor

Where the husband had separated from his second wife and would likely face a substantial support claim, his support obligation toward his first wife was terminated. Combined with other factors, the husband's circumstances had been significantly changed: *Harvey v. Harvey* (1995), 14 R.F.L. (4th) 128 (B.C. C.A.).

In *Foster v. Foster* (2000), 13 R.F.L. (5th) 61, 2000 CarswellOnt 4082 (Ont. S.C.J.), the court rejected the husband's application to terminate the wife's spousal support and allowed her application for an increase. The wife's medical conditions resulted in her classification as "disabled" under the *Canada Pension Plan*. The husband could afford to pay more, given an increase in his salary and the fact that he had remarried and had a new wife with whom to share expenses.

While the income of a child support payor's new spouse cannot be used directly to support the payor's children, it is properly taken into account in determining the income available to meet the payor's household expenses: *Hersey v. Hersey* (1993), 47 R.F.L. (3d) 117 (N.B. C.A.).

In *Hachey v. Hachey* (1994), 9 R.F.L. (4th) 71 (N.B. Q.B.), the husband's application for a reduction in the spousal support payable by him to a nine month old consent order was dismissed. The husband was splitting the income from a catering business with his common law wife, whose income was also properly considered in determining his ability to pay. Although the common law wife was not obligated to contribute towards support of the first wife, it did affect the husband's funds.

Where a father has remarried and started a new family but has not made any effort to adjust his lifestyle to accommodate the child support made in relation to the children of his first marriage, the court may refuse the application to completely expunge the arrears owing under a court order for support of the children of the first marriage: *Kerr v. Kerr* (1992), 41 R.F.L. (3d) 264 (Ont. Gen. Div.).

In *Droit de la famille — 1672*, [1992] R.D.F. 566 (C.S. Qué.), the court refused the husband's application to terminate spousal support three years after the termination of their 23-year marriage. Although the husband had considerable debts and new family obligations, his financial problems could be attributable largely to his mismanagement of his sizeable income. The wife had made genuine efforts to achieve self-sufficiency and, given the lavish lifestyle the parties had enjoyed, she could not be expected to do just anything to earn a living.

Where a payor has insufficient income and resources to maintain two families, the support payable to his first family should be reduced, thereby giving the new family unit the opportunity to flourish: *Burt v. Burt* (1990), 25 R.F.L. (3d) 92 (Nfld. T.D.).

The remarriage of the payor spouse in itself will not justify a reduction in support payable absent proof of actual economic effect: *Jacobs v. Jacobs* (1990), 29 R.F.L. (3d) 320 (Ont. Gen. Div.).

A payor spouse who remarries is not permitted to rely upon obligation to the second family as justification of an inability to pay support for a child from the first family. Second family obligations are undertaken with full knowledge of the first family obligations: *Greco v. Levin* (1991), 33 R.F.L. (3d) 405 (Ont. Gen. Div.).

Where at the time the parties' spousal support order was made the husband was supporting his cohabitant, his subsequent marriage to the cohabitant could not be relied upon as a change in circumstances warranting a variation of the support order: *Smith v. Smith* (1989), 23 R.F.L. (3d) 89 (Man. Q.B.).

In *Mense v. Mense* (1988), 54 Man. R. (2d) 228 (Q.B.), the husband was ordered to disclose financial information about his new wife in the context of an application for variation of support brought by his former wife. See also *Kearney v. Kearney* (1988), 54 Man. R. (2d) 42 (Q.B.) at 17§13 Change of circumstances — payee disabled.

In *Wolfe v. Wolfe* (1995), 15 R.F.L. (4th) 86 (B.C. S.C.), the court allowed the husband's application to terminate the spousal support payable to the wife. Although the award had been a modest one and did little to redress the economic imbalance which flowed from the marriage, it was a substantial burden to the husband. The continuation of the award threatened the continued economic viability of the husband's second family and, given the imminent ability of the wife to rejoin the workforce, the termination was justifiable.

Where the husband was only employed seasonally, was reliant on social assistance and had a second family to support, his application to terminate spousal support was allowed: *Wolfe v. Wolfe* (1995), 15 R.F.L. (4th) 86 (B.C. S.C.).

Where, as a result of remarriage and the sharing of expenses, the husband had more disposable income, the quantum of child support which he was required to pay was increased: *Watson v. Watson* (1991), 35 R.F.L. (3d) 169 (B.C. S.C.).

It is difficult, if not impossible, to develop a set of rules governing the effect of second families on first family support obligations that will apply in all cases. In many instances, the court can do little more than try to make life liveable where there is not enough money to go around: *Smith (Arseneault) v. Smith* (1992), 40 R.F.L. (3d) 316, 113 N.S.R. (2d) 226, 309 A.P.R. 226 (Fam. Ct.).

Where both parties had remarried and the husband had, since the divorce, parented twins, his application to rescind spousal support was allowed: *Underwood v. Underwood* (1987), 7 R.F.L. (3d) 447 (N.S. Fam. Ct.).

17§23 — Change of circumstances — payor's future contingencies

Where a support order has been based upon the husband's anticipated income, the husband's failure to reach such anticipated income was found to be a sufficient change of circumstances to justify a variation of the support order: *August v. August* (1989), 21 R.F.L. (3d) 1, 57 Man. R. (2d) 128, 58 D.L.R. (4th) 459 (C.A.).

The fact that a trial judge, in setting maintenance recognized that a dependant spouse might in the future receive income from employment does not preclude that income, when received, from being recognized as a change of circumstances justifying a variation: *Benson v. Benson* (1987), 8 R.F.L. (3d) 43, 63 Nfld. & P.E.I.R. 35, 194 A.P.R. 35 (Nfld. C.A.).

The fact that a payor spouse may be contemplating retirement should not be considered on the payee's application for increased support. The payor is free to raise the issue in future variation applications after the retirement has actually taken place: *Tatomir v. Tatomir* (1989), 78 Sask. R. 49 (Q.B.).

17§24 — Change of circumstances — payor's retirement

Divorce Act, 1985

The forced retirement of a payor spouse is a "change of circumstances" within the meaning of s. 17 of the *Divorce Act* which may justify a reduction in support: *Strang v. Strang* (1990), 26 R.F.L. (3d) 113 (Alta. C.A.); affirmed 39 R.F.L. (3d) 233, [1992] 2 S.C.R. 112.

In *Bishop v. LaCroix* (2004), 12 R.F.L. (6th) 1, 2004 CarswellNB 563, 2004 NBQB 401, 276 N.B.R. (2d) 75, 724 A.P.R. 75 (Q.B.), the fact that the husband had taken early retirement as a result of a disability was found to warrant a reduction in the spousal support payable to the wife. The decision to retire was reasonable in the circumstances and as the wife had voluntarily consented to a reduction in child support as a result of the retirement, she could not reasonably expect a different treatment for spousal support.

In *Meiklejohn v. Meiklejohn* (2001), 19 R.F.L. (5th) 167, 2001 CarswellOnt 3480, 150 O.A.C. 149 (Ont. C.A.); additional reasons at (2001), 2001 CarswellOnt 4050 (Ont. C.A.); reversing (2000), 6 R.F.L. (5th) 360, 2000 CarswellOnt 1190 (Ont. S.C.J.), the court allowed the husband's appeal from the dismissal of his application to reduce the quantum of spousal support payable by him. The 40% reduction in his income that occurred upon his early retirement was significant and had to be acknowledged. Although he had remarried and his new wife was employed, the trial court had placed too much emphasis on the new wife's income, disregarding the fact that the combined resources of the husband and his wife had to support a household of four people.

The husband's retirement no longer enabled him to support the wife and consequently the appeal court upheld the trial judgment terminating spousal support: *Cramer v. Cramer*, 6 R.F.L. (5th) 107, 75 B.C.L.R. (3d) 125, [2000] 6 W.W.R. 47, 186 D.L.R. (4th) 704, 2000 CarswellBC 908, 2000 BCCA 272, 139 B.C.A.C. 34, 227 W.A.C. 34 (C.A.). At trial, the parties' assets had been split slightly in the wife's favour and a generous award of maintenance had been granted to enable her to pursue her educational and vocational objectives. To continue support at the present time would be effectively redistributing the parties' assets. Like her husband, the wife should realize on her remaining capital asset and live on the resulting income until she is eligible for an old age pension.

Where the payor takes early retirement contrary to his intention at the time of a property settlement made between the parties, and the court finds that the early retirement is for the purpose of avoiding the payment of spousal support, the court may impute an income to the payor in an amount that is more than his retirement income: *Teeple v. Teeple* (1999), 2 R.F.L. (5th) 464, 124 O.A.C. 294, 1999 CarswellOnt 2958 (C.A.). Here, the payor's income was $80,000 a year prior to retirement and $27,000 a year afterwards. By reasons of the early retirement, his pension increased in value from $51,000 to $145,000. The wife was 53 years of age and he was 50. In the circumstances, the court, without stating the amount, imputed an income that was less than he was earning before he retired. Monthy support of $1,000 a month "represents a fair compromise and we so order." The $1,000 a month to be indexed in accordance with the Consumer Price Index and made binding on the payor's estate.

The court should refuse to consider a reduced income resulting from retirement to be a material change in circumstances where it is apparent that the payor spouse has intentionally organized his financial affairs to frustrate a support obligation: *Doe v. Doe* (1999), 44 R.F.L. (4th) 105, 90 O.T.C. 297, 1999 CarswellOnt 679 (Gen. Div.); reversed (1999), 126 O.A.C. 168, 1999 CarswellOnt 2111 (C.A.).

In *Doe v. Doe* (1999), 126 O.A.C. 168, 1999 CarswellOnt 2111 (C.A.), the husband appealed from a judgment dismissing his application to vary spousal support. The parties had been married for 20 years, separated in 1977 and divorced in 1981. On a variation application in 1987, spousal support had been increased from $3000 to $4,500 per month and the appellant acknowledged that he would have to support the respondent after his retirement. In 1999, the former husband withdrew from his law practice and took a lump sum payment and two years of salary before retiring at age 65. The appellant had remarried. The respondent's net worth was $550,000. The court was of the opinion that the appeal should be allowed and spousal support reduced. The appellant's retirement gave rise to a material change of circumstances, which warranted a reduction in spousal support from $4,500 to $2,500 per month. Further, support payments were ordered to be a first charge on the appellant's estate for the rest of the respondent's life.

In *Bullock v. Bullock* (2003), 48 R.F.L. (5th) 253, 2004 CarswellOnt 919 (Ont. S.C.J.), the court refused the husband's application to terminate spousal support. Despite the claim that the 62-year-old husband had been forced to close down his business as a result of a downturn in business, the evidence supported the view that he had voluntarily retired and was living comfortably on his second wife's income.

Where the husband had agreed to pay spousal support annually of $28,800 until he retired at age 65 but had unilaterally reduced the support to $12,000 annually when he had unexpectedly taken early retirement at 55, the court awarded the wife monthly support of $600 until she was 65. The wife's anticipated support was significantly reduced by the husband's early retirement and, despite his reduced income, she was still entitled to support that addressed her need for financial security: *Sisk v. Sisk*, 41 R.F.L. (5th) 409, 2003 CarswellNS 245, 216 N.S.R. (2d) 144, 680 A.P.R. 144, 2003 NSSF 28 (N.S. S.C.)

Where the wife had been awarded a share in the husband's pension, her spousal support was reduced to $1 per month subsequent to his retirement. While his pension income was now his only source of revenue, the wife continued to be employed earning $13,000 per annum. As the wife's income was now higher than the husband's and considering the fact that she shared in his pension, the reduction was appropriate. Given her age, tenuous health, her job security and the fact that she could not yet access the husband's pension, her right to spousal support should not be completely eliminated: *Stone v. Stone*, 37 R.F.L. (5th) 435, 2003 CarswellNS 27, 2003 NSSC 131 (N.S. S.C.).

The retirement of one of the parties and the consequent reduction of income are reasonably foreseeable circumstances at the time that parties execute a separation agreement: *Pearson v. Pearson*, 8 R.F.L. (5th) 396, 2000 SKQB 232, 194 Sask. R. 284, 2000 CarswellSask 378 (Sask. Q.B.). The husband's application for a variation of spousal support pursuant to a separation agreement signed 25 years before, which was incorporated in the divorce decree, was dismissed.

Where physical problems necessitated a decision by the husband to take early retirement, it was found that a change in circumstances had occurred sufficient to warrant a downward variation of the spousal support payable by him. There was nothing in the husband's decision which, in the circumstances, would make a variation unreasonable. Furthermore, the prospect of the husband's early retirement was neither known or contemplated when the order had been made ten years earlier: *Gowan v. Gowan* (2000), 11 R.F.L. (5th) 101, 2000 CarswellOnt 3567 (S.C.J.).

In *Andrew v. Andrew* (1999), 1999 CarswellOnt 2056 (Gen. Div.), the court held that it would be unfair to require the former husband to continue to pay support to his former wife when she had achieved a practical level of self-sufficiency and spousal support was terminated. The parties had had a 13-year marriage and the applicant had paid spousal support for 19 years. The applicant was near retirement age but his net worth would not realistically permit retirement at an appropriate standard. The respondent had chosen to retire and had factored her support payments into her decision to do so. However, her earnings from a new post retirement job would offset her loss of support.

However, in *Allen v. Allen* (1999), 47 R.F.L. (4th) 218, 1999 CarswellBC 876 (S.C.), the court refused to vary support where there had been a traditional marriage and the husband had retired. The court held that a spouse is not entitled to a variation based solely on the fact of retirement. The parties had been married for 24 years, had had four children and the wife had not worked outside the home during the marriage. The husband had remarried and his second wife was employed. The husband had a long-standing obligation to pay spousal support and could afford to do so. Until recently, the first wife, who was presently employed at substantially less than her husband's pre-retirement earnings, had suffered significant economic hardship as a result of the breakdown of the marriage.

Retirement of one of the parties would be a material change in circumstances if the retirement was not known at the relevant time and not taken into account by the trial judge: *Allen v. Allen* (1999), 47 R.F.L. (4th) 218, 1999 CarswellBC 876 (S.C.). In this decision, the husband's retirement was foreseen and considered at the time of the support order. The wife's economic disadvantage was not addressed by reapportionment of the main family asset, but was specifically to be addressed by spousal support. The husband's application to vary spousal support was dismissed.

In *Kerwood v. Kerwood* (1999), 1999 CarswellBC 780, 48 R.F.L. (4th) 127 (S.C. [In Chambers]), the former wife, aged 83, was successful in increasing her support from her 82-year-old husband where she had health problems due to aging. It was immaterial that her physical decline was foreseeable. The former husband had reduced his work-load as a doctor but this reduction was not considered significant as he continued to see patients and had a considerable investment fund. The parties married in 1942, separated in 1964 and divorced in 1976.

Where the payor spouse has retired from employment and double recovery of the payor's pension in property division and support cannot be proved, spousal support will be reduced on the basis of the of the parties' changed financial circumstances: *MacLeod v. MacLeod*, 3 R.F.L. (5th) 401, 190 Sask. R. 90, 1999 CarswellSask 931, [1999] S.J. No. 891, 1999 SKQB 267 (Q.B.). The husband had separated from his second wife and the first wife's capital and income positions had improved.

If there is no change in circumstances, the passage of time does not end a spousal support obligation. Where a payor's income has dropped significantly (44%) from the date of the order, there is a significant change of circumstances and spousal support should be terminated: *Roller v. Roller* (1997), 35 R.F.L. (4th) 373, 161 Sask R. 149, 1997 CarswellSask 732 (Q.B.). The husband had supported his wife for 27 years, from the time she was stricken with multiple sclerosis. The court also took into account the fact that the husband had an obligation to support a dependant common-law spouse of 25 years, who was also ill.

In *Hutchison v. Hutchison* (1998), 38 R.F.L. (4th) 377, 1998 CarswellOnt 2867, [1998] O.J. No. 3027 (Gen. Div.), the court allowed the husband's application for a reduction in the spousal support payable by him after his retirement. A substantial portion of the husband's income was derived from his pension, an asset which had already been equalized in the wife's favour. The retirement represented a material change in circumstances justifying a reduction in support.

Early retirement voluntarily taken without justification cannot be relied upon as a reason to reduce support obligations. However, retirement is justified where the applicant pays the agreed spousal support for 13 years, retires at age 58 from a strenuous job in a company which is downsizing, and, as an incentive, receives severence pay at two and one-half times the normal amount together with a substantial pension supplement: *Haramis v. Haramis* (1997), 44 R.F.L. (4th) 207, 28 O.T.C. 203, 1997 CarswellOnt 5837, [1997] O.J. No. 518 (Gen. Div.). The court, on the husband's application, terminated the support obligation, but ordered him to pay to the wife a lump sum amount of 14 percent of his severance pay.

In *Pick v. Pick* (1991), 92 Sask. R. 171 (Q.B.); affirmed (September 5, 1991), Vancise, Wakeling, Gerwing JJ.A. (Sask. C.A.); leave to appeal refused (1992), 138 N.R. 407 (note), 113 Sask. R. 160 (note), 52 W.A.C. 160 (note) (S.C.C.), the court refused the husband's application for an order terminating his spousal support obligations under a separation agreement. Although his financial condition had changed because of his forced retirement at age 65, the change was not related to the marriage.

In *Capuska v. Capusaka* (1993), 46 R.F.L. (3d) 37 (Man. C.A.), the husband appealed from an order which had reduced support from $500 to $150 per month. On appeal, the court eliminated maintenance since, as a practical reality, the husband, who since trial had taken early retirement, had barely sufficient funds to meet his own needs.

In determining an application for a reduction in spousal support the fact that the payee spouse has begun to receive old age pension may properly be considered: *R. (M.) c. L. (R.)* (14 janvier 1993), no C.A. Québec 200-09-000693-918 (C.A. Qué.).

In *Hodgert v. Hodgert* (1993), 47 R.F.L. (3d) 216 (Alta. C.A.), in light of the wife's continuing need, the fact that the husband had retired was insufficient to justify a termination of the spousal support payable by him.

In *C. (J.R.) c. L. (L.)*, [1992] 48 Q.A.C. 239 (C.A. Qué.), the wife's spousal support was reduced in light of the facts that the husband's income had been reduced significantly upon his retirement and that the parties' child, who had been living with the wife, had achieved self-sufficiency.

In *Droit de la famille — 1138*, [1990] R.D.F. 216 (C.A. Qué.); affirming (1987), [1988] R.D.F. 29 (C.S. Qué.), the court refused, after the husband's retirement, to reduce significantly the alimony payable to the wife. The trial judge, at the time of the divorce, had considered the husband's retirement when establishing the quantum of alimony payable.

In *Leblanc v. Leblanc* (1995), 14 R.F.L. (4th) 414 (Q.B.); affirmed (1995), 14 R.F.L. (4th) 414 (note), 167 N.B.R. (2d) 375, 427 A.P.R. 375 (C.A.), the husband's application for termination of the wife's spousal support brought in anticipation of his retirement was dismissed. The husband had not yet suffered a reduction in income and, in fact, since the date of the last variation his income had increased substantially.

Mandatory retirement with a concurrent significant drop in income constitutes a change in circumstances justifying a review of spousal support obligation: *Smyth v. Smyth* (1993), 48 R.F.L. (3d) 280, 142 A.R. 132 (Q.B.).

In *Allen v. Allen* (1992), 127 N.B.R. (2d) 390, 319 A.P.R. 390 (Q.B.), the court allowed the husband's application for a termination of the support contained in the parties' 1984 divorce decree. As the husband had recently retired and his pension income was now less than the wife's employment income, a clean break was appropriate. Considering the wife's employment income at the time of the divorce, it was arguable that, had the present *Divorce Act* been in force then, she would not have received any support.

Where the husband's income had decreased upon his retirement and his former wife's had increased as a result of pension benefits, the spousal support payable by him was reduced. Although he sought termination of all support payable, this was not possible as long as the wife's need and the husband's ability to pay remained: *Petersen v. Petersen* (1989), 59 Man. R. (2d) 119 (Q.B.).

Where the husband had voluntarily taken early retirement and could no longer afford to pay the $350 monthly spousal support required, the support order was reduced by a minimum amount only on his variation application: *Tatomir v. Tatomir* (1989), 24 R.F.L. (3d) 282 (Sask. Q.B.). Where a payor has taken voluntary early retirement, the court should assess the facts of the case carefully to ensure that the retirement was not motivated by a desire to defeat the payor's support obligations: *Vennels v. Vennels* (1993), 45 R.F.L. (3d) 165, 76 B.C.L.R. (2d) 69 (S.C.).

Where the husband had chosen early retirement and had thus reduced his ability to pay spousal support, the court allowed his application to terminate periodic support payments provided he pay $18,000 to his wife by way of lump sum. While the choice of early retirement is not a change of circumstances to consider in reducing support, the fact the husband could no longer pay required resolution: *Levesque v. Levesque (No. 2)* (1992), 99 Sask. R. 11 (Q.B.).

In *Droit de la famille — 1446*, [1991] R.D.F. 370 (C.S. Qué.), the husband was not allowed to rely upon his voluntary early retirement as a ground for terminating the spousal support specified in the parties' agreement. The wife, who had been a homemaker throughout the parties' 25-year marriage, continued to suffer from the economic consequences of the marriage.

Where the husband's early retirement at age 51 was justified for medical reasons, his application for termination of spousal support to his former wife was allowed. His sole income was derived from a pension, the monthly amount of which was equalled by the former wife's employment income: *Molnar v. Molnar* (1991), 35 R.F.L. (3d) 424 (Sask. Q.B.).

Where the wife had been awarded sizeable assets upon the dissolution of the parties' marriage, the court allowed the husband's application to set a termination date for the wife's spousal support five years hence. The husband planned to retire at that time and sought the order to facilitate his financial planning: *Epstein v. Epstein* (1991), 115 N.B.R. (2d) 418, 291 A.P.R. 418 (Q.B.).

In *Droit de la famille — 1526* (1991), [1992] R.D.F. 81 (C.S. Qué.), the court allowed the husband's application for termination of spousal support after his retirement at age 61. The husband's decision was reasonable and it would not be proper to require the husband to draw upon his assets to support his former wife when her own assets remained untouched.

Where the husband's income had been reduced drastically upon his retirement, the court allowed his application to terminate spousal support. Although the wife would have to sell her home and continue to work part-time after turning 65, she could, on the basis of these occurrences, be said to have achieved financial independence: *Droit de la famille — 1344*, [1990] R.D.F. 529 (C.S. Qué.).

In *Campbell v. Campbell* (1991), 36 R.F.L. (3d) 284 (Ont. U.F.C.), the court dismissed the husband's application for termination of spousal support to his wife based upon the fact that he had taken early retirement. The husband had earlier confirmed to the wife in writing his intention not to retire for several more years. As the wife had arranged her affairs accordingly, the doctrine of promissory estoppel applied and the husband was estopped from adducing evidence of changed circumstances until the indicated retirement date.

In *Morse (Rand) v. Morse* (1991), 108 N.S.R. (2d) 133, 294 A.P.R. 133 (Fam. Ct.), the court refused the husband's application for reduced spousal support which he based upon a reduction of income resulting from his early retirement and the illness of his second wife. Both changes cited by the husband had been taken on voluntarily and could not be relied upon by him as changes in circumstances.

See also *Strang v. Strang*, [1992] 2 S.C.R. 112, 39 R.F.L. (3d) 233, 3 Alta. L.R. (3d) 1, 125 A.R. 331, 92 D.L.R. (4th) 762 at 17§2.

In *Hannon v. Brennan* (1995), 18 R.F.L. (4th) 407, 138 Nfld. & P.E.I.R. 62, 431 A.P.R. 62 (Nfld. U.F.C.), the court refused the husband's application for a decrease in the spousal support payable by him. Although the husband had retired, he continued to have the means of paying the support ordered. Furthermore, the wife's economic disadvantage resulting from the marriage was continuing.

The imposition of an obligation to pay support requires an ability to meet the order by a reasonable apportionment of available means. The nature or source of those means, whether salary, pension, other income or salary is not material. Accordingly, the court refused the husband's application for a decrease in the spousal support payable based on the fact that he had retired and his salary was replaced by pension income: *Bartlett v. Bartlett* (1994), 2 R.F.L. (4th) 202, 115 Nfld. & P.E.I.R. 245, 360 A.P.R. 245 (Nfld. U.F.C.).

Where the husband's annual income was reduced upon his retirement from $422,000 annually to under $120,000 the court allowed his application for a downward variation of the $6,300 monthly spousal support payable by him. The retirement constituted a change of circumstances which would have a substantial and continuing effect. Furthermore, it had not been foreseen at the original trial as the trial judge had not considered the effect of the husband's pending retirement when setting the quantum of support: *Rousseau v. Rousseau* (1995), 18 R.F.L. (4th) 292 (B.C. S.C.).

17§25 — Change of circumstances — involuntary loss or reduction of payor's income

A non-voluntary loss of employment by the payor is a change in circumstances sufficient to warrant a variation of a support order: *Strang v. Strang* (1989), 23 R.F.L. (3d) 17, 100 A.R. 208 at 210 (Q.B.); affirmed (1990), 26 R.F.L. (3d) 113, 107 A.R. 111 (C.A.); affirmed 39 R.F.L. (3d) 233, [1992] 2 S.C.R. 112, 3 Alta. L.R. (3d) 1, 125 A.R. 331, 14 W.A.C. 331, 137 N.R. 203.

Where a trial judge found that the payor's evidence that his income from his law practice had been reduced from $200,000 to $150,000 and then to almost nil was "incomprehensible and not believable", the appellate court was of the opinion that this reduction constituted a change of circumstances that would justify a reduction in the amount of support from $3,000 to $2,000 a month: *Reilly v. Reilly*, 5 R.F.L. (5th) 116, 137 B.C.A.C. 151, 223 W.A.C. 151, 2000 BCCA 130, 2000 CarswellBC 361 (C.A.).

Where a trial court has varied the amount of spousal support downwards so that both former spouses have approximately the same income, taking into account the reduction in the payor's income, an appellate court will not interfere in the quantum of support: *LeBlanc v. LeBlanc* (2000), 5 R.F.L. (5th) 76, 225 N.B.R. (2d) 235, 578 A.P.R. 235, [2000] N.B.J. No. 61, 2000 CarswellNB 45 (C.A.). In this case, the parties, who were both in their seventies, had been divorced for 23 years. The wife was not self-sufficient and the husband had a diminished capacity to earn his livelihood as a lawyer. He had spent all his RRSP's and RIF's to try to meet his expenses.

In *Harris v. Harris* (2000), 2000 CarswellOnt 2703, 10 R.F.L. (5th) 45, 135 O.A.C. 312 (C.A.), the court dismissed an appeal by the husband from a lower court judgment dismissing his application to vary spousal support in a divorce judgment. The court was of the opinion that the applicant did not meet the threshold test that there had been a change in circumstances because the circumstances were known when the minutes of settlement were signed. The husband sought to reduce spousal support on the basis of his own reduced income owing to the substantial drop in activity in the international construction business in which he worked. The husband claimed to have no business income in 1998. The court relied on *B. (G.) v. G. (L.)*, 15 R.F.L. (4th) 201, 127 D.L.R. (4th) 385, 186 N.R. 201, [1995] 3 S.C.R. 370, [1995] R.D.F. 611, 1995 CarswellQue 23, 1995 CarswellQue 120, [1995] S.C.J. No. 72 at 271 [R.F.L.] in stating that a material change is a change which, if known at the time, would likely have resulted in different terms. The court was of the view that the swings in the economy, particularly in the construction industry, were foreseeable. It was also foreseeable that the husband would at some point no longer be employed. He would have believed that he could find support from other sources than income. The husband was an accountant and businessman and was assumed to have considered these possibilities.

A trial judge erred in placing the onus on a wife to seek employment while the husband should also be employable and seek work: *Wyman v. Wyman* (1999), 49 R.F.L. (4th) 447, 1999 CarswellNS 49 (C.A.). The appellate court granted the wife's appeal from a decision reducing the amount of spousal support paid by the husband after his job was eliminated. The spousal support, which had been reduced from $1000 to $500 per month, was increased to $700 per month.

Where the payor's income is considerable, little weight should be placed on the decline in the payor's income since he is clearly in a position to pay increased monthly maintenance for the children if an increase is otherwise justified in the circumstances: *Oyen v. Oyen* (1994), 9 R.F.L. (4th) 454, 2 B.C.L.R. (3d) 166, 52 B.C.A.C. 277, 86 W.A.C. 277 (C.A.).

In *Mullin v. Mullin* (1992), 100 Nfld.& P.E.I.R. 161, 318 A.P.R. 161 (P.E.I. T.D.), the court refused the husband's application for a termination of his wife's support based, inter alia, on his decline in income. There was no evidence that the husband's income decline was a permanent situation and, in all likelihood, it was a temporary aberration. See additional decisions in this case listed in *Mullin v. Mullin* (1993), 48 R.F.L. (3d) 322, 108 Nfld. & P.E.I.R. 61, 339 A.P.R. 61 (P.E.I. C.A.).

In *Brassard c. Beaulieu* (3 juin 1992), no C.A. Québec 200-09-000121-928 (C.A. Qué.), a reduction in the husband's annual income from $38,000 to $32,000 was found to be a sufficient change in circumstances to warrant a downward variation of his wife's support from $100 weekly to $250 monthly.

In *B. (G.) v. D. (S.)*, [1990] R.L. 167, 33 Q.A.C. 87 (C.A.), the court allowed the husband's appeal from an order refusing to annul his ongoing spousal support obligations. The husband had experienced an economic downturn, having to sell off some of his assets to discharge support arrears, whereas the wife had practically achieved financial independence.

Where as a result of losing his job it appeared that the husband would have to liquidate his assets to provide for his own needs, his application to terminate spousal support over a period of time was allowed: *Droit de la famille — 600*, [1989] R.D.F. 58 (C.A. Qué.).

Where subsequent to the maintenance award the husband had lost his job, the wife had moved in with another man and the parties shared custody of their child despite a custody award in the wife's favour, the husband's application for a reduction in the quantum of maintenance payable by him was granted: *Eddy v. Eddy* (1986), 5 R.F.L. (3d) 418 (B.C.C.A.).

In *Hollenbach v. Hollenbach* (2005), 12 R.F.L. (6th) 323, 2005 CarswellBC 167, 2005 BCSC 81 (B.C. S.C.), the court refused the father's application for a lowered variation of child support. The father's income derived solely from his substantial investment portfolio, the income from which varied depending upon the use annually of capital assets and tax strategies. It was appropriate to impute income to him at a 5% return rate on his $9.4 million capital base, an income which justified the correct level of child support.

Where the husband's hearing deteriorated to the point that he was compelled to close his medical practice, his application for a reduction in the spousal support payable by him was granted. In addition, the wife had also proven herself capable of generating revenue: *Hanson v. Hanson*, 43 R.F.L. (5th) 119, 2003 CarswellSask 573, 2003 SKQB 370 (Sask. Q.B.).

In a case under the Ontario *Family Law Act*, the court held that where a payor has been terminated but receives salary under a severance package and also receives consulting contract payments, his plea of reduced income relates only to the future: *Sasonow v. Sasanow* (2000), 6 R.F.L. (5th) 415, 2000 CarswellOnt 1085 (S.C.J.). The husband's application to vary spousal support was dismissed.

In *Loiselle v. Loiselle* (2000), 12 R.F.L. (5th) 400, 2000 CarswellOnt 3488 (S.C.J.), the court reduced spousal support from $2,500 to $1,500 per month, and $900 per month upon equalization, as the husband's business had declined. The court made its determination after taking into account the monies that are available to the wife from assisting her elderly mother and from selling Avon products. The court did not take into account the interest on the wife's RRSPs, which were unrealized.

In *Fleury v. Fleury* (2000), 2000 CarswellOnt 2833, 11 R.F.L. (5th) 71 (C.J.), the court reduced the amount of support payable from $722 to $350 per month where the husband's projected gross annual income for 2000 was $33,200 down from his 1999 gross annual income of $64,196.

In *Young v. Young* (1999), 47 R.F.L. (4th) 214, 1999 CarswellOnt 1332 (S.C.J.), the court reduced the husband's spousal support payments from $2,000 to $500 per month for a time-limited period, since, subsequent to minutes of settlement, the husband's ill health had prompted him to work part-time as a lawyer which greatly reduced his income and at the same time, the wife's income from employment and investments had increased. The parties had been married for 34 years and the court was of the opinion that the parties should be placed on an equal financial basis, as much as possible. There had been no "material" change in the parties' net worth since the time of settlement.

Where the payor spouse loses his job because of a wrong-doing, there is a change of circumstance which would permit a court to vary or rescind a support order: *Pavlicevic v. Pavlicevic* (1998), 37 R.F.L. (4th) 107 (B.C. S.C.). However, the payor had not met the onus to show that, because of this change, a variation of periodic permanent maintenance should be made. The payor had not made full disclosure on his means and financial circumstances.

In *Bettles v. Wright* (1997), 30 R.F.L. (4th) 256, 153 Nfld. & P.E.I.R. 350, 475 A.P.R. 350 (P.E.I. T.D. [In Chambers]), the husband's application for a reduction in spousal support payable to the wife was refused. There had been no real change in the husband's income since his last successful application for a reduction and any financial difficulties he was suffering were the result of poor financial management and not a lack of funds.

In *Williams v. Williams* (1997), 35 R.F.L. (4th) 387, 165 N.S.R. (2d) 188, 495 A.P.R. 188 (S.C.), the court refused the husband's application to terminate the spousal support payable to his disabled wife. Since the husband had previously experienced periods of unemployment, there had been no radical change in circumstances. The wife's need was continuing and would likely never abate. The order was, however, amended to allow the husband to reduce spousal support payments to $1.00 when he was unemployed.

Where the husband had been forced to retire from full time employment, but kept working part time to meet his spousal support obligations, although it adversely affected his health, his application to terminate spousal support was allowed. The husband had suffered undue hardship and the wife, who had remarried, actually enjoyed a higher standard of living than the husband: *Ferrigan v. Ferrigan* (1998), 36 R.F.L. (4th) 206 (Ont. Gen. Div.).

Where the husband's income had decreased by 24 percent since the making of a spousal support order, the court allowed his application to reduce the arrears owing under that order by the same 24 percent in *Kurbegovich v. Kurbegovich* (1998), 36 R.F.L. (4th) 220 (Ont. Gen. Div.).

In *Gillard v. Gillard* (1998), 36 R.F.L. (4th) 209 (Alta. Q.B.), the court refused the husband's application to terminate the spousal support payable by him after he had lost his employment. The husband had received a substantial severance package and was not likely to remain unemployed for long.

In *Garner v. Garner* (1997), 35 R.F.L. (4th) 262, [1998] 5 W.W.R. 443, 160 Sask. R. 95 (Q.B.), it was held that the husband's loss of employment was an insufficient change in circumstances to relieve him from his spousal support obligations contained in minutes of settlement to which both parties had agreed. Although payment under the minutes was qualified specifically by the condition that the husband remain employed, the 72-week severance package received by him resulted in no immediate change to his financial position. As the 72-week period had not expired, the husband could conceivably still find alternate employment before his financial situation truly changed.

In *Roller v. Roller* (1997), 35 R.F.L. (4th) 373, 161 Sask. R. 149 (Q.B.), the court allowed the husband's application to terminate spousal support for his wife who had permanently entered a nursing home 13 years into their 31-year marriage. The husband had entered into a common law relationship that had endured for over 25 years and with a 44% reduction in his income after a health-induced forced retirement, the husband could not meet the needs of both his former wife and his common law wife. This was an appropriate case in which the public purse should take up the support burden as it related to the former wife.

Where the husband had lost his job but received a one year severance package, the job loss was found not to constitute a sufficient change in circumstances justifying a variation of the support payable by the husband. The severance award still enabled the husband to pay: *Kattler v. Kattler* (1996), 22 R.F.L. (4th) 274, 145 Sask. R. 5 (Q.B.).

Where the husband was still receiving severance payments relating to his job loss, his application for a decrease in his support obligation resulting from that job loss was dismissed as premature in *Wilkinson v. Wilkinson* (1996), 22 R.F.L. (4th) 46 (Ont. Gen. Div.).

Where the husband owned his own company and set his own salary, his application for reduced spousal support based upon the effect of the recession on his business was dismissed. If he chose not to reduce further the retained earnings in his company, he had ample additional resources which he could draw upon to meet his support obligations: *Peters v. Karr* (1994), 93 Man. R. (2d) 222 (Q.B.).

In *Tingley v. Tingley* (1993), 49 R.F.L. (3d) 87 (N.B. Q.B.), the court granted the husband's application for a termination of spousal support 12 years after the parties time. In the intervening time, the husband's financial situation had deteriorated and the wife's had improved. Furthermore, the wife failed to adduce any evidence that she had suffered any economic disadvantages arising from the marriage or its breakdown.

In *Wood v. Wood* (1993), 45 R.F.L. (3d) 85 (Ont. Gen. Div.), the reduction in the husband's annual income from $500,000 to $75,000 justified a reduction in the spousal support payable to the wife from $7,000 to $2,500. Limiting the term of spousal support could not be justified given the wife's continuing economic disadvantage which resulted from the marriage.

Where the husband who had been earning $88,000 at the time of the support order lost his job, the court allowed his application and reduced his spousal support obligation from $1,000 to $400 monthly with a limit of one-year. The change in the husband's financial circumstances was dramatic and justified a variation: *Johnston v. Johnston* (1992), 84 Man. R. (2d) 12 (Q.B.).

Where the husband's income had been reduced by 22 percent since the date of the decree *nisi* and the wife had since found employment, the payor husband's application for a reduction in the spousal support payable was allowed: *Ewert v. Ewert* (1991), 91 Sask. R. 311 (Q.B.).

Where the husband's reduced resources were the result of a business failure for which he was 50 percent responsible, his application for a variation of his spousal support obligation was only allowed in part. Support was reduced by 50 percent, being the amount inversely proportional to the degree that the business failure could be attributed to the husband: *Craig v. Craig* (1989), 30 R.F.L. (3d) 66 (N.S. T.D.).

In *Smith v. Smith* (1989), 23 R.F.L. (3d) 89 (Man. Q.B.), the husband's application for a decrease in the support payable to his wife was dismissed. Although he had lost his employment because of health problems and was living on disability benefits, he could continue to make his support payments by rationalizing his expenses and his debts.

Where the husband was involuntarily unemployed and consequently decided to return to school, the wife's application for an upward variation in maintenance was refused: *Hasting v. Hastings* (1986), 42 Man. R. (2d) 215 (Q.B.).

In *Leet v. Leet* (1994), 131 N.S.R. (2d) 19, 371 A.P.R. 19 (S.C.), the court allowed the husband's application to terminate support to his former wife of 19 years in light of the fact that he had lost his job and had an uncertain future and that she had made little effort to achieve self-sufficiency. A lump sum award equivalent to two years' support was substituted in recognition of the wife's continuing need.

17§26 — Change of circumstances — payor voluntarily reducing own income

The husband's claim of impecuniosity following the transfer of all of his assets to his new wife could not be relied upon as a change in circumstances justifying a reduction in the spousal support payable by him: *Reilly v. Reilly* (1999), 50 R.F.L. (4th) 424 (B.C. S.C.); varied 5 R.F.L. (5th) 116, 137 B.C.A.C. 151, 223 W.A.C. 151, 2000 BCCA 130, 2000 CarswellBC 361 (C.A.).

Where the payor spouse's decline in income is the result of his or her own deliberate actions, it cannot be relied upon as a basis for an application to reduce the amount of support payable: *Hildebrandt v. Hildebrandt* (1991), 34 R.F.L. (3d) 373, 94 Sask. R. 215 (Q.B.).

If a person's circumstances change through choice or by voluntary conduct, an applicant spouse cannot take advantage of those circumstances and hope to seek a variance of the original support order: *Harris v. Harris* (1992), 40 R.F.L. (3d) 253 (B.C. S.C.).

The court may deny a variation in support where the payor spouse has failed to honour commitments that he or she has the capacity to fulfill. If a payor's reduced ability to pay are the result of circumstances which are self-induced, it would be unfair to the payee to reduce support: *Callison v. Callison* (1992), 40 R.F.L. (3d) 451 (B.C. S.C.).

17§27 — Change of circumstances — payor deceased

The court has jurisdiction to vary a maintenance award, even though the payor spouse has died: *Banks v. Banks* (1985), 47 R.F.L. (2d) 450 (Y.T. S.C.).

In *Droit de la famille — 324*, [1987] R.J.Q. 149, [1987] R.D.F. 48 (C.S. Qué.), the court allowed an application by the executors of the late husband's estate to terminate the wife's maintenance. During the 20 years since the parties' separation the wife had sufficient time to achieve financial independence and had managed to improve her financial position considerably.

17§28 — Change of circumstances — payor — other changes

Divorce Act, 1985

The fact alone that a payor's income had increased did not constitute a material change in circumstances justifying an increase of child support:. *Willick v. Willick*, [1994] 3 S.C.R. 670, 6 R.F.L. (4th) 161, 125 Sask. R. 81, 81 W.A.C. 81, 173 N.R. 321, 119 D.L.R. (4th) 405.

The fact that a payee spouse's income has been reduced because of risky financial ventures is no reason to reduce that spouse's child support obligations: *Jensen v. Jensen (Binns)* (1992), 39 R.F.L. (3d) 118, 109 N.S.R. (2d) 106, 297 A.P.R. 106 (C.A.); affirming (1991), 106 N.S.R. (2d) 247, 288 A.P.R. 247 (T.D.); leave to appeal refused (1992), 114 N.S.R. (2d) 90 (note), 313 A.P.R. 90 (note), 143 N.R. 392 (note) (S.C.C.).

The increased debt load of the payor does not constitute a change in the condition, means, needs or other circumstances which justify reduction in the amount of monthly spousal support payments: *Stordy v. Stordy*, 6 R.F.L. (5th) 436, 186 Nfld. & P.E.I.R. 142, 564 A.P.R. 142, 2000 PESCAD 7, 2000 CarswellPEI 34 (C.A.). The wife's appeal from a variation order to decrease spousal support payments made to her by her husband was granted.

Where the wife by her conduct frustrated the order of the court on access, spousal support was terminated after reasonable notice: *McGregor v. McGregor* (1993), 49 R.F.L. (3d) 17 (N.B. Q.B.); reversed in part on other grounds (1994), 3 R.F.L. (4th) 343 (N.B. C.A.). Support for the children was continued for a limited time period.

Where the intended state of affairs upon which an interim maintenance order has been made does not materialize, an order should be made cancelling the arrears: *Martin v. Martin* (1993), 50 R.F.L. (3d) 77, 113 Sask. R. 316, 52 W.A.C. 316 (C.A.). In the *Martin* decision, the wife had expected to live independently, but, in fact, moved in with her parents and thus reduced expenses.

Where one party was just about to move at the time of trial and was only estimating her budget, once she had become settled in her new home, her circumstances will have changed, and the other party may apply at any time to vary the maintenance order made by the trial judge on the ground of a change in circumstances: *MacDonald v. MacDonald* (1993), 10 Alta. L.R. (3d) 20, 46 R.F.L. (3d) 1 (C.A.).

In a modern marriage in which the parties cohabited for five years, and the wife planned to remain at home with the parties' child until the child was approximately three years old, and that time has come, support should be terminated in five months to give the wife the opportunity to enter a retraining program or to enter the job market and make child care arrangements: *South v. South* (1992), 40 R.F.L. (3d) 179, 76 Man. R. (2d) 256, 10 W.A.C. 256 (C.A.).

The absence of full financial disclosure by the payor spouse may not in itself constitute a change of circumstances justifying the variation of an order setting the quantum of spousal arrears owing: *Miller v. Miller* (1992), 42 R.F.L. (3d) 278 (Sask. C.A.).

The fact that a spouse misrepresented the value of assets and liabilities where maintenance was originally determined may justify a later variation of maintenance payable: *Psaila v. Psaila* (1987), 6 R.F.L. (3d) 141, 10 B.C.L.R. (2d) 336 (C.A.).

In *Jang v. Jang*, 17 R.F.L. (5th) 370, 2001 CarswellAlta 555, 2001 ABQB 351, 303 A.R. 387 (Alta. Q.B.), the wife was granted an upward variation of spousal support. The husband had arbitrarily renegotiated the mortgage on the matrimonial home by reducing the amortization period and thus increasing the monthly payments. The wife had actually requested that the husband extend the amortization, thus freeing up more money on a monthly basis. Given the negative impact of the husband's actions on the wife's cash flow and the fact that the husband's income had increased, the upward variation of spousal support was justified.

The fact that the husband, as a result of an *Income Tax Act* ruling, was required to bring certain income tax reserves into his income, did not justify a reduction in the spousal support payable by him pursuant to the parties' separation agreement. The assessment did not constitute a material change in circumstances: *Ravka v. Ravka* (2001), 18 R.F.L. (5th) 155, 2001 CarswellOnt 1642 (Ont. S.C.J.); reversed (2002), 2002 CarswellOnt 3081, 165 O.A.C. 44, 35 R.F.L. (5th) 176 (C.A.).

Where, since the date of the spousal support order, the husband had become unemployed, had lost his home to fire and had had a child with his common law partner, the court allowed his application for variation and made a provisional order terminating his obligation to pay spousal support: *Ralph v. Ralph* (1994), 7 R.F.L. (4th) 238, 122 Nfld. & P.E.I.R. 153, 379 A.P.R. 153 (Nfld. T.D.).

The deterioration of a payor's health amounts to a substantial change in circumstances warranting a variation of a spousal support order only where a concomitant impairment in the payor's income has also occurred: *Tait v. Tait* (1994), 8 R.F.L. (4th) 18 (Ont. Gen. Div.).

In *Brewer v. MacIntosh* (1993), 45 R.F.L. (3d) 437, 134 N.B.R. (2d) 137, 342 A.P.R. 137 (Q.B.), the father's application for reduced child support was refused. Although after the mother's move with the children from New Brunswick to British Columbia his access costs would certainly be higher, the father had ignored the fact that his income had doubled since the time of the original order.

The fact that the wife was unable to complete her degree as she missed one course and would not be able to graduate until several months later than expected and that she had been unable to obtain employment constituted changes of the nature contemplated by s. 17(4) of the Act: *Debacker v. Debacker* (1993), 49 R.F.L. (3d) 106, 143 A.R. 228 (Q.B.). However, where as in this case, the division of property and the maintenance paid until the end of the fixed term recognized the economic advantages and disadvantages arising from the marriage or its breakdown, no further maintenance would be granted.

Where the result of the custodial mother's move to another city would be to increase the father's access costs, the amount of support payable to the wife was ordered decreased: *Heintz v. Heintz* (1992), 101 Sask. R. 119 (Q.B.).

A payor's child support obligations take priority over the payor's creditors. Such debts cannot be relied upon as a reason for a downward variation of child support: *Kerr v. Kerr* (1992), 41 R.F.L. (3d) 264 (Ont. Gen. Div.).

In circumstances where the husband erroneously believed, on the advice of his lawyer, that his ongoing spousal support obligation had been settled through the payment of a lump sum, it was found that this alone was insufficient to justify a termination of his wife's periodic support: *Douthwright v. Douthwright* (1991), 38 R.F.L. (3d) 48 (N.B. Q.B.).

In *Droit de la famille — 1643*, [1992] R.D.F. 449 (C.S. Qué.), the court refused the husband's application to terminate spousal support on the basis that the wife had left secure employment to pursue studies in journalism. After 25 years of marriage, the wife was entitled to start afresh and seemed likely to achieve her goals. As the wife was not yet self-supporting the termination application was premature, although a reduction in support was justified.

In *McGuire v. McGuire* (1989), 20 R.F.L. (3d) 45 (N.S. T.D.), the court refused the application of the mentally ill and institutionalized husband for a reduction of child and spousal support, which would have permitted him to transfer to a residential from an institutional setting. The potential benefit to the husband from the transfer would not offset the detriment resulting to the wife and child caused by the drastic reduction in support.

Where the wife's decision to return to school was reasonable, given that it would enhance her prospects of becoming self-sufficient, her application for increased support was allowed: *Hayes v. Hayes* (1991), 34 R.F.L. (3d) 274 (B.C. S.C.).

Where the husband sought to terminate the support payable to the wife in order to allow him to take a sabbatical and finish his Ph.D., his application was dismissed. As the wife was still in the home caring for the parties' child, her need for support continued: *Egan v. Egan* (1990), 100 N.S.R. (2d) 49, 272 A.P.R. 49 (Fam. Ct.).

The fact that a husband has adopted a "back-to-earth" stress-free lifestyle does not relieve him of the obligation to support his children: *Anderson v. Anderson* (1989), 92 N.S.R. (2d) 333, 237 A.P.R. 333 (Fam. Ct.).

Divorce Act, 1968

In *Barnes v. Barnes* (1986), 50 R.F.L. (2d) 163, 38 Man. R. (2d) 131 (C.A.) the husband's appeal from an order dismissing his application for a reduction in maintenance payable was allowed. The fact that the husband was undergoing heart surgery with the result that his income would be reduced was a sufficient change in circumstances to justify the variation.

Where the ordered sale of the marital home brought less than anticipated, with the result that the husband was left to pay family debts out of his own resources rather than out of the proceeds of sale, it was held that a sufficient change of circumstances had occurred to justify a reduction in the quantum of maintenance payable by him to his wife: *Bolger v. Bolger* (1983), 36 R.F.L. (2d) 184, 50 N.B.R. (2d) 3, 131 A.P.R. 3 (C.A.).

Where the husband was working over 80 hours per week, his application for a reduction in the maintenance payable to his former spouse was allowed. As he was working far in excess of the norm, it was fitting that he be allowed to enjoy some benefit from his extraordinary effort: *Clarke v. Clarke* (1986), 62 Nfld. & P.E.I.R. 264, 190 A.P.R. 264 (Nfld. T.D.).

Where the wife's $50 maintenance entitlement was determined at the time when her husband was in full-time attendance at university she was granted substantially greater maintenance after he graduated and obtained a job paying $35,000 annually: *Graves v. Graves (No. 1)* (1986), 74 N.B.R. (2d) 136, 187 A.P.R. 136 (Q.B.).

See also *Kadziora v. Kadziora* (1984), 42 R.F.L. (2d) 328 (Ont. H.C.); *Willhoft v. Willhoft* (1976), 27 R.F.L. 309 at 311 (Sask. Q.B.); *Brown v. Brown* (1986), 73 N.S.R. (2d) 197, 176 A.P.R. 197 (Fam. Ct.), *Dukin v. Dakin* (1982), 56 N.S.R. (2d) 356, 117 A.P.R. 356 (Fam. Ct.); *Ryan v. Ryan* (1984), 41 R.F.L. (2d) 126 (Nfld. U.F.C.).

17§29 — Variation ordered — change of mode of payment

Divorce Act, 1985

Where the wife had a propensity to spend freely, the court allowed the husband's appeal whereby periodic support was substituted for the earlier order of a substantial lump sum: *Droit de la famille — 874*, [1990] R.D.F. 623 (C.A. Qué.); leave to appeal refused (28 février 1991), no 22155 (S.C.C.).

Where the husband had been ordered to pay periodic support, as well as lump sum support. The lump sum support was to be derived from the sale of certain assets for which the husband was to use his best efforts to sell. The wife's application to vary was allowed and an immediate lump sum ordered. The husband had not used his best efforts to dispose of the assets and had been continually delinquent in his periodic support obligations: *Tottrup v. Tottrup* (1991), 32 R.F.L. (3d) 361, 115 A.R. 311 (C.A.).

Where the parties' agreement at the time of divorce called for periodic support, the court refused to interfere with that agreement to grant the wife's later request for a considerable lump sum: *Droit de la famille — 402*, [1990] R.D.F. 184 (C.A. Qué.); affirming [1987] R.D.F. 492 (C.S. Qué.).

In *Kulcheski v. Kulcheski* (1990), 66 Man. R. (2d) 32 (Q.B.), the wife's nominal support order was varied and a $6,500 lump sum granted after the husband had inherited $99,000.

Where, despite her reasonable efforts to achieve self-sufficiency, the wife had been unable to do so, her periodic support was varied to a lump sum so as to bring about a clean break between the parties: *Droit de la famille — 913*, 30 R.F.L. (3d) 83, [1990] R.D.F. 642 (C.S. Qué.).

Where, during the 20 years after the parties' divorce, the husband had paid the weekly support ordered only twice, the court allowed the wife's application for a lump sum equivalent to the husband's interest in the family home which the wife continued to occupy. Since the husband, an alcoholic, could not assist the wife in any other way, it would not have been fair if the wife were to lose the house and be forced to look to her children for support: *Droit de la famille — 918*, [1990] R.J.Q. 2927 (C.S.).

In an application for the variation of a child support order, the effect of ordering that such payments be made directly to the child would be to render such payments non-tax deductible to the payor. Therefore, the order was not changed: *Johnson v. Johnson* (1990), 91 Sask. R. 190 (Q.B.).

The *Divorce Act, 1985* gives the court the jurisdiction to convert an order for periodic support into one lump sum support: *Sagoo v. Sagoo* (1987), 6 R.F.L. (3d) 128 (Man. Q.B.).

In *Henderson v. Henderson* (1987), 7 R.F.L. (3d) 153 (B.C. S.C.), the husband had been ordered to pay periodic child support as well as lump sum child support at the time when the parties' home was sold. The wife's application to vary the order, to provide only lump sum child support to be satisfied by conveyance to the wife of the husband's interest in the home, was dismissed. As well as being inappropriate to transfer property under the guise of support, the lump sum was not justified given the ages of the children, the uncertainty of the duration of their entitlement and the lack of evidence that the husband would not honour his support obligations.

Where after the parties' divorce, the wife had acted unreasonably in pursuing an unsuccessful real estate career, the court allowed the husband's application to vary her periodic spousal support. She was awarded a lump sum to allow her to retrain and periodic support for only one year further to allow her to readjust: *Boucher v. Boucher* (1991), 36 R.F.L. (3d) 179, 108 N.S.R. (2d) 96, 294 A.P.R. 96 (Fam. Ct.).

Divorce Act, 1968

"On a motion to vary under s. 11(2) [now s. 17], the court's jurisdiction is a jurisdiction to vary the maintenance, and it is not restricted to the particular mode of payment that the original order called for": per Berger J. in *Hayre v. Hayre (No. 2)* (1978), 5 R.F.L. (2d) 85, 6 B.C.L.R. 390 at 392 (S.C.); affirmed 8 B.C.L.R. 161, 93 D.L.R. (3d) 766 (C.A.). See also *Smith v. Smith*, 29 R.F.L. 91, [1976] 6 W.W.R. 510 at 517 (Alta. T.D.); and *Van Snick v. Van Snick* (1978), 27 N.S.R. (2d) 127, 41 A.P.R. 127 (C.A.).

An order providing for the payment of periodic maintenance may be varied so as to provide for the substitution or addition of a lump sum payment: *Vance v. Vance* (1974), 13 R.F.L. 378 at 381–82, 2 O.R. (2d) 537, 43 D.L.R. (3d) 481 (C.A.); approved in *Sangha v. Sangha*, 19 R.F.L. 342, [1975] 5 W.W.R. 191 (B.C. C.A.). See also *Veinotte v. Veinotte* (1977), 23 N.S.R. (2d) 84, 32 A.P.R. 84 (C.A.).

In *Hastings v. Hastings* (1986), 42 Man. R. (2d) 215 (Q.B.), a nominal periodic maintenance award was varied to permit a lump sum award where the husband had demonstrated an unwillingness to volunteer support and his future earnings were precarious.

The court has jurisdiction to include lump sum child support upon an application to vary child maintenance. Such an order should not be made, however, simply to allow a child to acquire capital assets: *Goncalves v. Goncalves* (1986), 49 R.F.L. (2d) 376 (B.C. S.C.).

In *Rumbolt v. Rumbolt* (1980), 28 Nfld. & P.E.I.R. 532, 79 A.P.R. 532 (Nfld. T.D.), a periodic award was varied to provide for a lump sum instead, where the unemployed husband had made no payments on the periodic order but was expecting insurance proceeds and owned the matrimonial home. The arrears of periodic payments owing were not affected by the lump sum award.

"In a case such as this where: (a) there are no children involved; (b) both parties were represented by legal counsel throughout all the proceedings; and (c) the parties agreed that the lump sum settlement would be a "full and complete discharge of any and all obligations", it seems to me that a court should be most reluctant to re-open the matter and make an award for periodic maintenance": per Richard J. in *Ritcey v. Ritcey* (1980), 14 R.F.L. (2d) 284, 37 N.S.R. (2d) 120, 67 A.P.R. 120 (T.D.).

See also *Tobin v. Tobin* (1974), 19 R.F.L. 18 at 20 (Ont. H.C.); *Pruden v. Pruden* (1976), 28 R.F.L. 83 (B.C. S.C.); *Fernandes v. Fernandes* (1976), 28 R.F.L. 266 at 267 (B.C. S.C.).

17§30 — Variation ordered — gradual phasing out

Where the objectives of the *Divorce Act* may be better served by giving the spousal support recipient a "softer landing" then would flow from a stark and sudden termination of support, termination after further specified period may be appropriate: *de Gobeo v. de Gobeo*, 22 R.F.L. (6th) 228, 2005 CarswellMan 157, [2005] M.J. No. 441, 2005 MBQB 261, 197 Man. R. (2d) 229 (Man. Q.B.).

In *Boucher v. Boucher* (2006), 23 R.F.L. (6th) 432, 2006 CarswellNS 141, 242 N.S.R. (2d) 286, 770 A.P.R. 286, 2006 NSSC 88 (N.S. S.C.), the court allowed the father's application for termination of the wife's spousal support by ordering decreasing payments over a period of time. Since the parties' divorce, the children had matured and no longer required the wife's constant care and she had made no efforts towards self-sufficiency.

In *MacKenzie v. MacKenzie* (1988), 17 R.F.L. (3d) 99 (N.B. Q.B.), the court granted the husband's application to terminate spousal support eight years after the parties' divorce. Although the wife had been economically disadvantaged because of her role as a wife and mother, the children had now grown up and become independent. It was time to conclude the matter and therefore the wife's support would continue only for one and a quarter years more.

Where in the seven years subsequent to the parties' divorce the wife had made no effort to achieve self-sufficiency, the court granted the husband's application to phase out spousal support. The wife had been previously instructed by the court to seek employment and could not rely upon child care duties as an excuse for not having done so: *Droit de la famille — 1177*, [1988] R.D.F. 320 (C.S. Qué.).

Where the wife failed to make an effort to obtain available employment, an order was made gradually phasing out the support payable to her pursuant to the parties' decree *nisi*: *Deering v. Deering* (1986), 60 Nfld. & P.E.I.R. 230, 181 A.P.R. 230 (Nfld. T.D.).

17§31 — Variation ordered — variation of lump sum awards

Divorce Act, 1985

In *Lavoie v. Yawrenko* (1992), 44 R.F.L. (3d) 89, 74 B.C.L.R. (2d) 321, 21 B.C.A.C. 233, 37 W.A.C. 233 (C.A.), the court entertained the wife's application to restore periodic child support where the mother had spent a portion of an earlier lump sum child support award on an unsuccessful business venture.

The court may vary a lump sum support award that has not yet been paid: *Hiscock v. Hiscock* (1987), 7 R.F.L. (3d) 418, 62 Nfld. & P.E.I.R. 336, 190 A.P.R. 336 (Nfld. T.D.).

Where the parties agreed to a lump sum payable in instalments, representing the father's past and future child support obligations, the court refused the father's application to reduce the sum. Any reduction would allow the father to bargain his way out of arrears and then on default of the bargain to escape responsibility for obligations he had acknowledged: *Connellan v. Galbraith* (1988), 17 R.F.L. (3d) 351 (N.S. Fam. Ct.).

Divorce Act, 1968

An order granting maintenance, lump sum or otherwise, must be based on a need which the respondent should meet. The need must exist at the time the grant of maintenance is made or varied. In the instant case, by virtue of the wife remarrying and moving out of the house, there was no longer any need which the respondent had to meet. Therefore a lump sum award in favour of the wife and secured against the matrimonial home was properly rescinded: *Pattie v. Richardson* (1976), 30 R.F.L. 144, 17 N.S.R. (2d) 508 (C.A.).

"If the petitioner does not within one year from the date of the payment of the lump sum to her purchase a house for this purpose, then the respondent has leave to apply to this court to vary this order, having regard to the petitioner's receipt of said lump sum and her failure to purchase and occupy a home": per Disbery J. in *Osborne v. Osborne* (1973), 14 R.F.L. 61 at 71 (Sask. Q.B.); varied (1976), 23 R.F.L. 358 (C.A.).

Where the wife had been awarded lump sum maintenance to cover future needs, her subsequent application for further periodic and lump sum maintenance was found to be res judicata: *Droit de la famille — 287*, [1987] R.D.F. 37 (C.S. Qué.).

The court has jurisdiction to vary a maintenance order even after a lump sum previously awarded has been paid and spent: *Wyatt v. Wyatt* (1986), 1 R.F.L. (3d) 252, 59 Nfld. & P.E.I.R. 124, 178 A.P.R. 124 (Nfld. T.D.).

See also *Howard v. Howard* (1982), 41 N.B.R. (2d) 171, 107 A.P.R. 171 (Q.B.); *Jones v. Jones* (1980), 20 R.F.L. (2d) 191, 27 A.R. 503 (Q.B.); *Collins v. Collins* (1978), 2 R.F.L. (2d) 385, 5 Alta. L.R. (2d) 315, 10 A.R. 214 (T.D.); *Holewa v. Holewa* (1977), 3 Alta. L.R. (2d) 253, 6 A.R. 476 (T.D.); *Gomes v. Gomes*, 6 R.F.L. 398, [1972] 3 W.W.R. 151, 24 D.L.R. (3d) 112 (B.C. S.C.); applied in *Lloyd v. Lloyd*, 18 R.F.L. 179, [1974] 5 W.W.R. 667 (B.C. S.C.).

17§32 — Variation ordered — variation to add lump sum awards

Divorce Act, 1985

Where the wife was unable to find employment during the four-year period following the parties' divorce the husband was ordered, on a variation application, to pay a lump sum of $12,000 to the wife to permit her to retrain. A causal connection existed between the marriage and the wife's inability to find employment: *Peckford v. Peckford* (1989), 78 Nfld. & P.E.I.R. 167, 244 A.P.R. 167 (Nfld. U.F.C.).

17§33 — Variation ordered — discharge of security

Divorce Act, 1985

The registration of an earlier support order against property does not prevent the court from later varying support or cancelling arrears in a proceeding for divorce: *Wiseman v. Wiseman* (1987), 8 R.F.L. (3d) 447, 18 B.C.L.R. (2d) 19 (S.C.).

Divorce Act, 1968

"What [the husband] is asking, in effect, is permission to sell what he himself describes as his "only remaining asset", the home in which his first wife and family are living, and wish to continue to live, so that the proceeds of this security can replace, for two years or so, his personal obligation under the maintenance order. Given this breathing space, he says, he should be in a position to make the requisite payments thereafter. These being the facts, what are the applicable legal principles? I start from the proposition that a maintenance order registered in the Land Registry Office: ... is, by its very nature, a charge on the lands until all provisions of the judgment have been fully satisfied. Such a charge is not satisfied and discharged merely by keeping payments up to date. It is a charge by way of security for future payments": per Wilson J. in *Harvey v. Gould* (1959), 28 W.W.R. 329 at 332, 18 D.L.R. (2d) 590 (B.C. S.C.).

"This security, it goes without saying, is the respondent's; and the fact that the security, in addition, provided her and the children with a roof over their heads was, I think, a very real factor in assessing the quantum of money payable by the applicant for monthly maintenance;": per Kirke Smith J. in *Re Campbell* (1972), 9 R.F.L. 323 at 324 (B.C. S.C.).

"I would be prepared to make an order that the judgment [registered against the matrimonial home] be cancelled upon payment into Court of the sum of $20,000 which I understand to be equivalent, approximately, to the present value of the payments ordered by the decree nisi. If that sum is paid into Court consideration can then be given to its use for the maintenance payments": per Hutcheon L.J.S.C. in *MacHale v. MacHale* (1974), 15 R.F.L. 380 at 381–382 (B.C. S.C.).

17§34 — Variation ordered — support order binding payor's estate

Divorce Act, 1985

Where the wife was likely to survive the husband and the husband owed a continuing obligation to the wife given the long-term traditional nature of the marriage, the support order was varied so as to be binding upon his estate: *Brickman v. Brickman* (1987), 8 R.F.L. (3d) 318 (Man. Q.B.).

17§35 — Effect of default in payment in variation application

Divorce Act, 1968

"It is the unanimous decision of this court that the respondent should either have paid the arrears or given some explanation as to why he had not done so before his application for reduction of the monthly payments was entertained": per Coffin J.A. in *Young v. Young* (1976), 29 R.F.L. 391 at 391, 17 N.S.R. (2d) 375 (C.A.).

In *Berman v. Berman* (1981), 22 R.F.L. (2d) 109 (Ont. H.C.), the court granted the husband's application to vary retroactively a decree absolute by incorporating therein the terms of the separation agreement between the parties. The husband was not required to pay the arrears accumulated to the time of his application, in view of the fact that the wife was not in urgent need, there had been a substantial change in circumstances, and both parties should have an equal right to apply for a variation.

"I think that the *Parkinson* decision ([1973] 3 O.R. 293, 11 R.F.L. 128) is also authority for the proposition that the matter of varying the existing quantum of support should not be entertained until such time as the respondent Mr. Carter had demonstrated to the court that he is acting in good faith, and that can be demonstrated by payment of the arrears which are presently outstanding": per McDermid L.J.S.C. in *Carter v. Carter* (1977), 4 R.F.L. (2d) 396 at 400 (Ont. H.C.).

In *Hayes v. Hayes* (1981), 43 N.S.R. (2d) 349, 81 A.P.R. 349 (T.D.), a husband was refused a variation in periodic payments under a decree *nisi* where he had overstated his budgetary expenses, failed to establish grounds for variation and was still in arrears on the original order.

In *Sinclair v. Sinclair* (1984), 43 R.F.L. (2d) 153, 32 Man. R. (2d) 108 (Q.B.), it was held that the court could properly hear the husband's application for a reduction in child maintenance even though the husband was in contempt for failure to pay support and an appeal from the contempt order was pending.

"I think it is also relevant that the applicant husband was two months in arrears in his alimony payments on the date on which the motion was argued. His resources clearly were such that he could have continued to make the alimony payments while the motion was pending and I can only infer that he chose to put economic pressure on the respondent by ignoring his obligations under the decree *nisi*, in hopes that she would thereby be compelled to agree to a settlement under which the alimony payments would be reduced. The court is most reluctant to grant relief to an applicant who will resort to such tactics and will scrutinize his claim with great care": per Southey J. in *Baker v. Baker* (1977), 25 R.F.L. 328 at 331 (Ont. H.C.).

In *Gray v. Gray* (1983), 32 R.F.L. (2d) 438 (Ont. H.C.), the court refused to entertain the husband's application for a downward variation of child maintenance until such time as accrued maintenance arrears were discharged or satisfactory arrangements to do so were made.

17§35A — Retroactive variation of support orders — general

The *Divorce Act* explicitly provides for a retroactive variation of a support order:

> 17. (1) A Court of competent jurisdiction may make an order varying, rescinding or suspending, prospectively or retroactively,
>
> > (a) a support order or any provision thereof on application by either or both former spouses: *Divorce Act*, s. 17(1)(a).

An application to cancel arrears under a support order made after a divorce has been granted is an application to vary, rescind or suspend the order under s. 17 of the *Divorce Act*. Under this section, the onus is on the payor to show that a material change of circumstances has occurred, which is a change that, if known at the time of the original order, would likely have resulted in different terms: *Plett v. Plett*, 2002 CarswellBC

2083, 2002 BCSC 1308 (B.C. S.C. [In Chambers]). In the case, no such change of circumstances was found.

In *Marinangeli v. Marinangeli* (2003), 2003 CarswellOnt 2691, 66 O.R. (3d) 40, 38 R.F.L. (5th) 307, 174 O.A.C. 76, 228 D.L.R. (4th) 376, [2003] O.J. No. 2819 (Ont. C.A.), the Court of Appeal sets out the criteria for making or declining to make an award of retroactive support, quoting from Rowles J.A. in *S. (L.) v. P. (E.)*, 67 B.C.L.R. (3d) 254, 1999 CarswellBC 1402, 175 D.L.R. (4th) 423, 126 B.C.A.C. 28, 206 W.A.C. 28, [1999] 12 W.W.R. 718, 50 R.F.L. (4th) 302, 1999 BCCA 393, [1999] B.C.J. No. 1451 (B.C. C.A.); leave to appeal to S.C.C. refused 252 N.R. 194 (note), 135 B.C.A.C. 160 (note), 221 W.A.C. 160 (note), [1999] 3 S.C.R. xii, 179 D.L.R. (4th) vii, [1999] S.C.C.A. No. 444 (S.C.C.). While these criteria in the *L.S. v. E.P.* decision were applied only to child support orders, Weiler J.A., in the *Marinangeli* case, stated that they apply both to child and spousal support orders. Rowles J.A. states,

> A review of the case law reveals that there are a number of factors which have been regarded as significant in determining whether to order or not to order retroactive child maintenance. Factors militating in favour of ordering retroactive maintenance include: (1) the need on the part of the child and a corresponding ability to pay on the part of the non-custodial parent; (2) some blameworthy conduct on the part of the non-custodial parent such as incomplete or misleading financial disclosure at the time of the original order; (3) necessity on the part of the custodial parent to encroach on his or her capital or incur debt to meet child rearing expenses; (4) an excuse for a delay in bringing the application where the delay is significant; and (5) notice to the non-custodial parent of an intention to pursue maintenance followed by negotiations to that end.
>
> Factors which have militated against ordering retroactive maintenance include: (1) the order would cause an unreasonable or unfair burden to the non-custodial parent, especially to the extent that such a burden would interfere with ongoing support obligations; (2) the only purpose of the award would be to redistribute capital or award spousal support in the guise of child support; and (3) a significant, unexplained delay in bringing the application.

Retroactive support should only be ordered in special or exceptional circumstances: *Andries v. Andries*, 36 R.F.L. (4th) 175, 1998 CarswellMan 180, 159 D.L.R. (4th) 665, 126 Man. R. (2d) 189, 167 W.A.C. 189, [1998] 7 W.W.R. 536, [1998] M.J. No. 196 (Man. C.A.); *Trick v. Trick* (2003), 2003 CarswellOnt 1103, 39 R.F.L. (5th) 418, [2003] O.J. No. 1263 (Ont. S.C.J.).

The decision to award retroactive support should be exercised sparingly: see *Marinangeli*, above.

Retroactive variation orders, whether they impose new obligations or grant relief from old obligations, are inherently unfair and should only be made where exceptional circumstances are shown to exist: *Colbert v. Andersen*, 2003 CarswellMan 29, 2003 MBQB 13, 171 Man. R. (2d) 97 (Man. Q.B.). Here, where arrears under a support order had accumulated over a number of years, fairness to the payor required that the order be varied with respect to 2 years when his income was far less than the support to be paid.

Notwithstanding the substantial increase in the husband's income from $50,000 at the time of separation to an average of $258,966 in the 3 years prior to trial, the appellate court in *Scott v. Scott*, 2004 CarswellNB 587, 2004 CarswellNB 588, 2004 NBCA 99 (N.B. C.A.) held that "while there was some evidence in the . . . case which might have justified the exercise of discretion in favour of a retroactive variation, and while it would have been helpful to have the benefit of the motions judge's reasons for refusing a retroactive award,[it was] unable to conclude that the refusal was the result of either a palpable and overriding error in the motions judge's findings or an error in principle. Considering the deference owed to the motions judge,[it] would not interfere with the manner in which she exercised her discretion."

A husband with substantial assets who unilaterally terminated spousal support requiring the wife to borrow funds to maintain the standard of living for the children was ordered to pay interest on a relatively small amount of spousal support arrears at a credit card rate of 18;pc per year: *Lawson v. Lawson*, 2004 CarswellAlta 780, 7 R.F.L. (6th) 72, 2004 ABQB 415 (Alta. Q.B.); additional reasons at 2004 ABQB 922 (Alta. Q.B.).

Where a divorce judgment is silent on support — that is, it contains no order for support — a variation is not available and a motion to vary the divorce judgment to provide support must be dismissed. However, the request for support may be pursued in a corollary relief proceeding: *Bekarkhanchi v. Bozchelouei* (2004), 2004 CarswellOnt 2161 (Ont. S.C.J.); additional reasons at (2004), 2004 CarswellOnt 3338 (Ont. S.C.J.).

Support payable to the wife was terminated in the circumstances, but the termination was not made retroactive since a retroactive variation (and an obligation to repay an amount to the husband) would force her to sell RRSP's which would reduce one of her future sources of income at retirement: *E. (R.G.) v. B. (J.)*, 2004 CarswellQue 1358, [2004] R.D.F. 461 (Que. S.C.).

Where the husband who suffered from leukemia and was unable to work because of his ill health had need that was not addressed by spousal support payable by the wife, his claim for retroactive variation of spousal support was dismissed where the wife did not have sufficient income to look after his need: *Fraser v. Fraser* (2004), 2004 CarswellOnt 3343 (Ont. S.C.J.).

If the evidence established a finding of incomplete or misleading financial disclosure on the part of either or both parties, but such a finding would not be determinative of the case, the court would not order retroactive variation of the interim support orders in question: *Fotheringham v. Fotheringham* (2004), 2004 CarswellOnt 67, R.F.L. (6th) 288 (Ont. S.C.J.).

In *Kumar (Litigation Guardian of) v. McKenna* (2003), 2003 CarswellOnt 5450 (Ont. S.C.J.), the court held that there was no basis for retroactive variation of spousal support as the husband's income had varied very little over the years, but generally had remained in the $30,000 range.

In *Fitzgerald v. Gerlich* (2003), 2003 CarswellOnt 1816, 40 R.F.L. (5th) 84 (Ont. S.C.J.), the former husband sought, among other things, a review and variation of the provisions for spousal support contained in a separation agreement which he had entered into with his former spouse. The husband had unilaterally reduced spousal support from $1,750 per month as set out in the agreement to $1,000 per month. Under the agreement, support provisions were subject to variation in the event of a material change in circumstances. The agreement also provided for a review of support after the wife had completed her education. The husband sought to reduce the wife's spousal support to $250 per month from May 2001 and to cease making payments in June 2005. According to the separation agreement either party was entitled to a review of support after April 2001, and the husband argued that he was entitled to a variation of support based on his former wife's changes in circumstances, her remarriage and her move from Ontario to British Columbia. The court imputed an annual income to the former wife from September 2001 forward of $25,000 annually after the completion of her course and her move to British Columbia. It ordered an increase in child support over the amount stipulated in the agreement, noting that under the *Child Support Guidelines*, child support must be given precedence to spousal support, and it retroactively varied spousal support providing the wife with $400 per month until May 2003 after which she was entitled to $600 per month as the husband was no longer required to pay child support for one of the parties' children. The former wife's financial circumstances improved in 2001 and 2002 but she suffered economic disadvantages that flowed from her role in the family. The former husband's income increased; he had stable secure employment, and he was sharing expenses with a partner who earned as much as he did. The court held that the termination of spousal support was not consistent with objectives under the *Divorce Act*.

In *Trick v. Trick* (2003), 2003 CarswellOnt 1103, 39 R.F.L. (5th) 418, [2003] O.J. No. 1263 (Ont. S.C.J.), the court held that there were in this case special and exceptional circumstances which justified a retroactive order of spousal support. The husband did not disclose to the wife the dramatic increase in his income which occurred shortly after the execution of the parties' separation agreement. The wife delayed in pursuing her claim for increased support but did not know the extent of the husband's improved financial circumstances. In order to live, the applicant had completely depleted the capital she received on separation and had borrowed money from friends and family for living expenses and to provide a decent place to live for herself and her children. As the court found that the husband had misled the court throughout in the proceedings regarding his financial position, and had failed to inform his former wife of his improved financial circumstances, at trial the court found that he had financial resources and was able to make up the proper financial support for his former wife and children to make their lives reasonably comfortable. The fact that his new wife was the sole titled owner of their home, despite his significant financial contributions over the years to the equity in the home, constituted a transfer made with the intention of defeating the support claims of his former wife. The change in the method of holding title, while these proceedings were pending, was clearly an attempt to put his assets out of the first wife's reach in the event that she secured a judgment for retroactive support. The court imputed a current and prospective income of $120,000 (Can.) to him, which included the $31,000 (Can.) pension. Having regard to all of the factors and objectives noted in s. 15.2 of the *Divorce Act*, the court ordered that the husband pay the sum of $800 per month towards the wife's spousal support for a period of 3 years or until the entire retroactive child and spousal support had been paid, whichever was sooner.

Where the change in circumstances resulting in a reduction in the husband's income was wholly within his control and was not necessary nor sufficient to support a change in his support obligations, the court declined to grant retroactive variation of the interim spousal award in *Coolen v. Coolen*, 2002 CarswellNS 300, 2002 NSSF 34 (N.S. S.C.).

In *Harder v. Harder*, 2001 CarswellBC 1811, 2001 BCSC 919 (B.C. S.C.), the court rejected the wife's argument that the court should make an order increasing the quantum of support retroactive to the time of an interim support hearing on the ground that at that time the defendant misled the court and understated his income when he applied to reduce the quantum of support. It held that at the time of the hearing the defendant provided his most current income information including a recent pay stub that clearly indicated some overtime. The court was not satisfied the defendant intentionally misled the court, nor was it satisfied that the circumstances established a degree of misconduct on the part of the defendant that would justify a retroactive variation of the amount of support that was ordered on an interim basis.

Where the husband has received huge increases in income since the granting of the Corollary Relief Judgment which was subsequently approved by the Court of Appeal, and consequently he received a large benefit by paying less child and spousal support than he would otherwise have been required to pay, the court ordered a retroactive adjustment by way of a lump sum spousal support order: *Mosher v. Mosher* (1999), 47 R.F.L. (4th) 445, 177 N.S.R. (2d) 236, 542 A.P.R. 236, 1999 CarswellNS 182, [1999] N.S.J. No. 202 (N.S. S.C.). The court estimated that the husband had received a $100,000 advantage as a result of paying inadequate child support that effected the wife's spousal support, some of which she used to assist the children. The court awarded the wife $50,000, after taking into account the wife's delay in pursuing the matter and the fact that none of the children at the time of the hearing lived with their mother.

A support order may be varied retroactively where circumstances do not transpire as anticipated at the time of the order: *Brown v. Brown* (1999), 2 R.F.L. (5th) 65, 45 O.R. (3d) 308, 1999 CarswellOnt 2245 (Ont. S.C.J.). Husband's income was reduced to $66,000 a year when he returned to Canada from Saudi Arabia where he earned $200,000 a year tax-free. This was a material change in circumstances that was not forseeable entitling him to a reduction in the support obligation of $3,500 a month he had agreed to in divorce proceedings. Support was reduced to $1,250 a month giving the parties equivalent standards of living. The reduction was retroactive for a period of 15 months which would require the wife to repay $33,750. But on a basis of the competing needs and equities of the parties, it would be unfair to require a repayment in this amount. The wife was ordered to repay $17,000, the amount she had saved in this period.

17§36 — Retroactive variation of support orders — arrears

In s. 17(1) of the Act the explicit power to vary support orders retroactively confirms the right to have arrears as well as ongoing future payments adjusted to meet changed circumstances.

Divorce Act, 1985

In *Miller v. Miller*, 2001 CarswellNS 54, 2001 NSCA 31, 196 D.L.R. (4th) 689, 14 R.F.L. (5th) 139, 193 N.S.R. (2d) 371, 602 A.P.R. 371 (N.S. C.A.), the appellate court allowed the wife's appeal of an order which had forgiven the husband's payment of arrears of spousal support. At the time that the arrears accrued, the husband had an obligation to make payments and had the ability to do so. The fact that paying the arrears in monthly periodic payments would make it difficult for the husband to pay spousal support from the time of the hearing forward, was not a valid reason for completely forgiving the arrears. While he did not have sufficient employment income to pay a lump sum of $5,500 owing in arrears, he had an RRSP which could be cashed in and he could thereby make a significant payment on the arrears. The wife had a need for support. The court held that the husband was required to pay the sum of $3,000 in full satisfaction of arrears of $5,500 of spousal support.

In *Thompson v. Dorn*, 2000 CarswellBC 334, 2000 BCSC 265, [2000] B.C.J. No. 315 (B.C. Master), the master, in an obiter remark, stated that if the child were adopted by the mother's fiancé with the father's consent, it might be appropriate for the father to apply to cancel all his arrears of spousal maintenance. He would then be in a better position to support his new family. With the prospect of such an arrangement, the master suspended the enforcement of payment of arrears of spousal support for 6 months, after which they would become payable at $500 per month. The total amount of arrears was $8,387. The father had had little contact with the child after the separation. The child was just over 3 years of age and the mother's fiancé was prepared to adopt her.

Where the husband had transferred his assets into the name of a third party, ceased paying spousal support and went to live abroad, the court refused his application to discharge the spousal support arrears owing. The husband's actions were designed to defeat the wife's claims and it would be inequitable and morally repugnant to cancel the arrears: *Johnson v. Johnson* (1995), 66 B.C.A.C. 239, 108 W.A.C. 239, 1995 CarswellBC 858 (C.A.).

Where the payor's inability to pay spousal support was found to predate a debilitating injury, arrears were properly remitted back to the date of the inability to pay and not merely back to the date of the injury: *Klassen v. Klassen* (1993), 44 R.F.L. (3d) 433, 1993 CarswellMan 34, 83 Man. R. (2d) 214, 36 W.A.C. 214 (Man. C.A.).

Where the husband had, without a good reason, unilaterally stopped paying spousal support the annulment of the arrears was reversed on appeal: *Québec (Procureur général) c. Champagne*, 3 juin 1992, No. C.A. Québec 200-09- 000166-923 (C.A. Qué.).

Where the husband was unemployed and accordingly unable to pay support arrears owing, he was nevertheless not totally relieved of the obligation for the arrears. He had not made payments when he had been financially able to do so and accordingly a total cancellation of arrears would be unfair: *Galan v. Galan* (1990), 25 R.F.L. (3d) 225, 64 Man. R. (2d) 203, 66 D.L.R. (4th) 259, 1990 CarswellMan 37 (C.A.).

Arrears accruing under a support order made pursuant to provincial legislation are beyond the court's discretion on a variation application brought under s. 17 of the *Divorce Act*: *August v. August* (1989), 21 R.F.L. (3d) 1, 57 Man. R. (2d) 128, 58 D.L.R. (4th) 459, 1989 CarswellMan 43, [1989] M.J. No. 1 (C.A.).

The court rejected the Public Guardian and Trustee's argument to forgive the support arrears owed by the husband as, at the time in question, the husband had the ability to pay and no compelling reason not to do so: *Kumar (Litigation Guardian of) v. McKenna* (2003), 2003 CarswellOnt 5450 (Ont. S.C.J.); additional reasons at (2004), 2004 CarswellOnt 842 (Ont. S.C.J.). Despite an ability to pay, the husband, almost from the beginning, failed to provide the support as ordered. His conduct resulted in his wife's inability to sell the matrimonial home which tied her to a house which she could not afford. When the Public Guardian and Trustee took control of the husband's affairs, it determined that his estate could not afford to pay global support but continued to pay for expenses in relation to the matrimonial home, expenses which had not been ordered to be paid. The court rejected the Public Guardian and Trustee's request that these expenses be considered support and applied against arrears. The wife was in need of support during these years, circumstances which the husband and his representatives were in a position to alleviate. The claim to forgive arrears was dismissed.

The fact that the husband found that paying required spousal support was "difficult" did not meet the heavy burden required for the cancellation of support arrears in *Newton v. Newton*, 37 R.F.L. (5th) 391, 2003 CarswellBC 497, 2003 BCSC 333 (B.C. S.C.).

In *Greco v. Greco* (2000), 11 R.F.L. (5th) 109, 2000 CarswellOnt 3431 (Ont. S.C.J.), the court ordered both the spousal and child support arrears owing by the husband to be substantially reduced, provided that the husband regularly paid the amount of on-going support specified.

Where payor's income was insufficient to sustain spousal support obligations, arrears were extinguished: *Balaski v. Balaski* (1999), 45 R.F.L. 114, 178 Sask. R. 313, 1999 CarswellSask 250, [1999] S.J. No. 259 (Q.B.).

In *Adam v. Adam* (1993), 50 R.F.L. (3d) 216, 89 Man. R. (2d) 275 (Q.B.), the husband had unilaterally reduced the child support payable to his wife when one of the children had left home for university. As the husband had then commenced paying some support directly to the daughter, the arrears were calculated in subsequent variation proceedings as if the variation application had been brought at the time the child started university.

In proceedings to cancel child support arrears, the ability to pay is to be determined over the life of the obligation and not merely by reference to the time immediately before or after the court proceedings: *Haisman v. Haisman* (1993), 7 Alta. L.R. (3d) 157, 137 A.R. 245, 1993 CarswellAlta 256, [1993] A.J. No. 42 (Alta. Q.B.); reversed in part (1994), 7 R.F.L. (4th) 1, 22 Alta. L.R. (3d) 56, 116 D.L.R. (4th) 671, 157 A.R. 47, 77 W.A.C. 47, [1994] A.J. No. 553 (Alta. C.A.); leave to appeal refused 15 R.F.L. (4th) 51 (note), 32 Alta. L.R. (3d) xliv, 181 A.R. 79 (note), 116 W.A.C. 79 (note), 195 N.R. 159 (note), [1995] 3 S.C.R. vi, [1995] S.C.C.A. No. 86 (S.C.C.).

Where the husband had quit his employment and later accepted a lower-paying job in an effort to undermine his wife's and children's support entitlement, his application to cancel arrears and spousal support and reduce child support was dismissed. Any change in the husband's circumstances was self-induced and mala fides: *Irvine v. Irvine* (1990), 27 R.F.L. (3d) 199, 1990 CarswellMan 49, 67 Man. R. (2d) 205, [1990] M.J. No. 392 (Man. Q.B.).

Where as a result of the wife's inaction to enforce a support order, arrears had accumulated in the sum of $30,000, the arrears were ordered reduced to $5,000. As the husband had also not acted reasonably in failing to bring a variation application earlier, both parties were required to assume some responsibility for their inaction: *Newman v. Newman* (1990), 26 R.F.L. (3d) 313, 1990 CarswellMan 42, 65 Man. R. (2d) 294 (Man. Q.B.).

Where the mother had made no effort to enforce a child support order for the 9- year period after it was first made, all arrears were ordered cancelled because of the delay: *Campbell v. Campbell* (1989), 79 Nfld. & P.E.I.R. 179, 246 A.P.R. 179, 1989 CarswellPEI 67 (P.E.I. T.D.). See also *Strowbridge v. Strowbridge* (1989), 80 Nfld. & P.E.I.R. 111, 249 A.P.R. 111, 1989 CarswellNfld 203, [1989] N.J. No. 252 (Nfld. T.D.), where arrears that had been accumulating for 6 years were ordered cancelled because of the payee's failure to seek enforcement.

The mere fact of delay in the enforcement of support does not justify the cancellation of arrears, particularly where the payor had the means to pay support and also the means to discharge the arrears: *Martin v. Martin* (1989), 24 R.F.L. (3d) 150, 81 Sask. R. 98, 1989 CarswellSask 82 (U.F.C.).

Where the husband had met his support obligations for only one year out of the seven since the parties' divorce, his application to vary support and cancel arrears was dismissed. The wife and the two children in her care were living near the poverty level while the husband enjoyed substantial cash flow from farming: *Nykoliation v. Nykoliation* (1989), 60 Man. R. (2d) 307, 1989 CarswellMan 287 (Q.B.).

If respect for a negotiated final support settlement is to be given full accord and the support payments thereunder are to be sustained, then, absent delay amounting to laches, the arrears of such payments should be left intact and should not be subject to reduction or cancellation: *Fetterley v. Fetterley* (1988), 14 R.F.L. (3d) 47, 1988 CarswellAlta 331, 89

A.R. 350 (Alta. Q.B.); affirmed (1989), 1989 CarswellAlta 396, 24 R.F.L. (3d) 61, (sub nom. *Fetterly v. Fetterly)* 102 A.R. 131 (Alta. C.A.).

Where the wife had for many years accepted less support than that specified in the divorce decree, the court allowed the husband's application for an order rescinding the arrears. The wife had not incurred debt from not receiving the arrears and to allow enforcement would constitute a windfall: *Seward v. Seward* (1988), 12 R.F.L. (3d) 54, 1988 CarswellNS 35, 85 N.S.R. (2d) 30, 216 A.P.R. 30 (N.S. Fam. Ct.).

Where the husband had suffered a heart attack in 1982 and had advised the wife of his inability to pay her spousal support as ordered, the court allowed the husband's 1995 application to rescind all arrears and terminate the order. The wife had never attempted in 13 years to enforce the order and the husband's heart attack, had a variation been sought at the time, would have constituted a change in circumstances: *Fawcett v. Fawcett* (1995), 18 R.F.L. (4th) 450, 1995 CarswellBC 1178 (B.C. S.C.).

Divorce Act, 1968

An appeal from a decision reducing child maintenance payments but requiring all maintenance arrears to be paid in full was allowed and a new hearing ordered where evidence that the applicant spouse had become employed 4 days prior to the hearing had not been available to the trial judge: *Levinsky v. Levinsky; Levinsky v. MacNeil* (1986), 4 R.F.L. (3d) 361, 1986 CarswellNB 32, (sub nom. *Levinsky v. MacNeil)* 76 N.B.R. (2d) 410, (sub nom. *Levinsky v. MacNeil)* 192 A.P.R. 410 (N.B. C.A.).

The court has jurisdiction to deal with arrears of maintenance. A practice has grown up under which the court will generally not enforce arrears of maintenance beyond a period of one year: *Septon v. Septon* (1978), 3 R.F.L. (2d) 26, 1978 CarswellMan 12 (Man. C.A.). For a thorough review of the authorities dealing with the variation of maintenance arrears see *R. v. MacDonald* (1976), 26 R.F.L. 204, 14 O.R. (2d) 409, 74 D.L.R. (3d) 57, 1976 CarswellOnt 146 (H.C.).

The court has power to cancel or reduce arrears of maintenance ordered to be paid under a decree *nisi* and, where necessary, to give directions as to how the remaining arrears shall be paid: *Englar v. Englar* (1978), 2 R.F.L. (2d) 237 at 247, 19 O.R. (2d) 561, 85 D.L.R. (3d) 609, 1978 CarswellOnt 225 (C.A.).

See also *Hotchkiss v. Hotchkiss* (1987), 7 R.F.L. (3d) 51, 1987 CarswellOnt 305 (Ont. H.C.); *Remillard v. Remillard*, 2 R.F.L. (3d) 215, [1986] 4 W.W.R. 721, 42 Man. R. (2d) 151, 1986 CarswellMan 328 (Q.B.); *Coghill v. Coghill* (1975), 21 R.F.L. 353, 1975 CarswellSask 26 (Sask. Q.B.); *Olsen v. Olsen* (1973), 12 R.F.L. 326, 1973 CarswellSask 24 (Sask. Dist. Ct.); *Thomas v. Thomas* (1982), 28 R.F.L. (2d) 90, 1982 CarswellPEI 19 (P.E.I. Fam. Ct.); *Faulkner v. Faulkner* (1982), 28 R.F.L. (2d) 162, 1982 CarswellOnt 285 (Ont. U.F.C.); *Beaumont v. Beaumont* (1981), 10 Sask. R. 292, 1981 CarswellSask 340 (Q.B.).

17§37 — Delay inducing belief arrears would not be enforced

The parties in *Ballentine v. Ballentine* (1999), 50 R.F.L. (4th) 211, 45 O.R. (3d) 706, 1999 CarswellOnt 2591 (Ont. S.C.J.); affirmed (2000), 2000 CarswellOnt 2768, 10 R.F.L. (5th) 11, 135 O.A.C. 276 (Ont. C.A.) divorced in 1976 after a 20-year marriage. The husband was ordered to make spousal support payments of $1,447.31 per month, subject to the cost-of-living adjustments. After 1995, the husband began to default on support obligations. The wife applied for a writ of seizure and sale against the husband's property to enforce the arrears, more than 3 years after the default began. Pursuant to rule 60.07(2) of the Rules of Civil Procedure, leave was required. The application for leave was granted. There is no "one-year" rule for enforcement of support arrears. The one-year rule is compatible with neither the provisions nor the spirit of family law legislation. Delay in enforcement is only a factor to be considered where, and to the extent that, it support a finding of waiver or acquiescence or a finding that it would otherwise be inequitable to enforce the claim. Delay is only a factor to be considered along with others including evidence of detrimental reliance or change of position. Enquiry into the application of the provisions of s. 17 of the *Divorce Act* is not automatically called for whenever an application for leave is made under r. 60.07(2). Such an enquiry should be made only when the obligor has moved to cancel arrears and has the onus of proving that the factual conditions for rescinding or varying an order have satisfied. The evidence in this case did not show that the husband reasonably believed that the wife was abandoning her right to support or that he was misled in any way or to any extent. The wife's conduct was consistent with her continuing intention to enforce the right to support.

After a 12-year marriage, the parties divorced in 1979. The husband was ordered to pay the wife monthly spousal support. The husband unilaterally stopped paying spousal support in 1981 after becoming aware that the wife had entered into a common-law relationship. The wife's common-law relationship ended in 1989. Subsequently, the wife had full-time employment until she was disabled in an automobile accident in 1991. As the injuries prevented her from working, the wife began receiving social assistance benefits. In early 1993, following a dispute with the husband concerning their child, the wife applied to have the spousal support resumed and to collect the arrears. The husband applied to have the support terminated and the arrears eliminated. Citing the delay on the part of both parties, the trial judge eliminated the arrears but refused to terminate the support. Arguing that the wife had achieved self-sufficiency and was no longer entitled to support, the husband appealed. The court was of the opinion that, considering the length of the wife's common-law relationship, her failure to enforce the support obligation for 12 years and the circumstances which eventually led her to attempt to enforce it, the trial judge should have placed the onus on the wife to establish that the economic loss resulting from the marriage continued. As that onus was never placed on the wife, the husband's appeal was allowed: *McMullen v. McMullen* (1994), 5 R.F.L. (4th) 444, 150 N.B.R. (2d) 277, 385 A.P.R. 277, 1994 CarswellNB 26, [1994] N.B.J. No. 308 (N.B. C.A.).

Where the husband no longer paid combined child and spousal support after a child had become 19 but the wife did not try to enforce the order until approximately 12 years after the payment had stopped, the court found that the doctrine of laches and the "hoarding" principle barred the wife from retroactively collecting payments for spousal support: *Delaney v. Elkins*, 2004 CarswellNS 269, 224 N.S.R. (2d) 168, 2004 NSSF 63 (N.S. S.C.).

In *Delorme v. Woodham* (1993), 89 Man. R. (2d) 16, 1993 CarswellMan 275 (Man. Q.B.), the husband had been ordered to pay $150 per month support for his wife and their son. The wife subsequently remarried and, on his own initiative, the husband ceased making the support payments. The wife took no steps to claim payment of arrears for a lengthy period of time, during which period the husband suffered business losses culminating in bankruptcy. The husband owed support arrears of $15,000. On application for the cancellation of arrears, the husband's arrears were reduced to $4,000 which was to be repaid at the rate of $25 per month. The court found that there had been a change in the condition, means, needs and other circumstances of the parties. It was inferred that if the husband had brought an application to vary the maintenance based on his wife's remarriage, or based on his business difficulties, his obligation to pay would likely have been reduced.

In *McGean v. McGean* (1992), 42 R.F.L. (3d) 251, 116 N.S.R. (2d) 209, 320 A.P.R. 209, 1992 CarswellNS 74 (N.S. T.D.), the court retroactively rescinded spousal support back to when the last support order was made in August, 1987 on the basis of changed circumstances of both parties. In the alternative, the court stated that if it were necessary, it would have found that any arrears of support which had accumulated to date should be terminated by virtue of the doctrine of laches. The court rejected the former wife's explanation that the reason for her delay in enforcing support was discomfort or reluctance to pursue the instant litigation and the "stress" of pursuing her former husband. While there is no general rule of a one-year limit on the enforcement of spousal arrears, the court stated that it had the discretion to decline to enforce all or a portion of the amount owing in order to relieve against hoarding or because of laches.

The application of the so-called "one-year rule" was held to be appropriate in *Cormier v. Cormier* (1988), 90 N.B.R. (2d) 431, 228 A.P.R. 431, 1988 CarswellNB 169 (N.B. Q.B.); reversed in part on other grounds (1989), 102 N.B.R. (2d) 13, 256 A.P.R. 213, 1989 CarswellNB 335 (N.B. C.A.). In that case, the former wife sought to enforce maintenance arrears which had accumulated under a 1958 divorce order. She had attempted to enforce the order once in 1968. The youngest of the four beneficiaries under the order was now 37 years of age, and the oldest was 44. The court held that the support order should not be enforced beyond one year given that the applicant had sat idly by and had taken no steps to enforce her rights, given the paucity of evidence in general, and given that the children were now all adults.

Where, in order to receive social assistance, the creditor spouse has assigned the support order to a government department, that department must act in a timely manner to enforce any arrears accumulating under the order: *Barnesky v. Barnesky* (1988), 16 R.F.L. (3d) 450, 53 Man. R. (2d) 212, 1988 CarswellMan 60, [1988] M.J. No. 357 (Man. Q.B.). In the *Barnesky* decision, where the Department of Employment Services and Economic Security sat on its rights to enforce the support order for 5 or 6 years and offered no explanation as to why no efforts were made to enforce the order, the court granted the husband's application to rescind all of the arrears. Prompt action by the Department would have alerted the husband that the support order, which he and his spouse believed was no longer in effect because they had reconciled briefly after the order was made, was still existing and in effect. The unexplained laches was alone sufficient to justify the remission of arrears, although the court also noted that the husband had no ability to pay during the period when the arrears were accumulating.

If respect for a negotiated final support settlement is to be given full accord and the support payments thereunder are to be sustained, then, absent delay amounting to laches, the arrears of such payments should be left intact and should not be subject to reduction or cancellation: *Fetterley v. Fetterley* (1988), 14 R.F.L. (3d) 47, 1988 CarswellAlta 331, 89 A.R. 350 (Alta. Q.B.); affirmed (1989), 1989 CarswellAlta 396, 24 R.F.L. (3d) 61, (sub nom. *Fetterly v. Fetterly)* 102 A.R. 131 (Alta. C.A.).

In *Grimwood v. Grimwood* (1988), 68 Sask. R. 179, 1988 CarswellSask 487 (Sask. Q.B.), a provisional order pursuant to s. 8(8) of the Saskatchewan *Reciprocal Enforcement of Maintenance Orders Act* was made substantially reducing the arrears under a registered British Columbia order. The court considered the fact that the wife had made no efforts to enforce the order from the time it was made in 1978 to 1986 when she registered the order in Saskatchewan even though she knew of the husband's whereabouts. Similarly, in *Caissie v. Caissie* (1988), 89 N.B.R. (2d) 313, 226 A.P.R. 313, 1988 CarswellNB 159 (N.B. Q.B.), a factor militating against full recovery of the arrears was the wife's inability to offer a satisfactory explanation for her delay in enforcing the support provisions of an Ontario decree *nisi* when she knew the whereabouts of her former husband and his financial circumstances.

The failure of the wife to do anything about the arrears that had accumulated since 1980 was taken by the court to be strong evidence of a lack of need on her part: *Vine v. Vine* (1986), 1 R.F.L. (3d) 425, 54 O.R. (2d) 580, 1986 CarswellOnt 258 (Ont. H.C.). However, arrears for a period of 12 months were ordered paid, as the husband had unilaterally ceased paying support without first obtaining an order to vary the decree *nisi*. Such conduct was not to be condoned nor encouraged by the court.

The fact that the delay in some cases has caused debtors to be lulled into believing falsely that the creditor would not enforce the order has also been considered by the courts as a reason why the full amount of the arrears should not be enforced: *Tremblett v. Tremblett* (1988), 75 Nfld. & P.E.I.R. 175, 234 A.P.R. 175, 1988 CarswellNfld 251 (Nfld. U.F.C.). Thus, where the amount of the debtor's wages being attached, on consent, was less than the amount of support set out in the court order, and where no action was taken by the wife for 5 years to recover the balance, it was not unreasonable for the debtor to be lulled into a certain sense of security that the wife was prepared to accept the lesser amount. Similarly, in *Spedding v. Spedding* (1989), 19 R.F.L. (3d) 368, 1989 CarswellBC 389, [1989] B.C.J. No. 153 (B.C. S.C.), the court held that it was reasonable for the respondent to expect that the petitioner would never enforce a 1979 support order.

Leave to issue an order for seizure and sale in respect of arrears of child support, which had become due more than 12 months before the proceedings, was refused to a wife where she had made no effort to enforce payment, had by her conduct led her husband to believe she would not enforce her rights, and had been able to meet all her obligations during the period in question: *Wood v. Wood* (1986), 68 N.B.R. (2d) 219, 175 A.P.R. 219, 1986 CarswellNB 130 (N.B. Q.B.). These arrears were cancelled.

Where the wife failed for 6 years to enforce arrears of child support ordered pursuant to a decree *nisi*, and the husband had, in fact, been forbidden by the wife's second husband to pay, the court applied the "one-year rule." The conduct of the wife had misled the husband into believing that she was not going to require payment: *Rollins v. Kutash* (1982), 26 R.F.L. (2d) 444, 18 Alta. L.R. (2d) 322, 1982 CarswellAlta 35 (Alta. Prov. Ct.).

Where both parties' actions had contributed to the accumulation of arrears over a 23-month period and the husband's circumstances had changed so that he was no longer in as good a financial position to pay, the Nova Scotia Family Court ordered him to pay maintenance for only 12 of the 23 months' worth of arrears: *Beauchemin v. Beauchemin* (1981), 47 N.S.R. (2d) 594, 90 A.P.R. 594, 1981 CarswellNS 168 (N.S. Fam. Ct.).

The court limited recovery of arrears to a period of one year only, where the wife had allowed the arrears to accrue for 5 years before she sought to enforce payment. The court ruled that the wife had waited too long to bring her action: *Ruth v. Ruth* (1981), 47 N.S.R. (2d) 357, 90 A.P.R. 357, 1981 CarswellNS 165 (N.S. Fam. Ct.). See also *Foley v. Foley* (1981), 46 N.S.R. (2d) 475, 89 A.P.R. 475, 1981 CarswellNS 152 (N.S. Fam. Ct.), in which the court dismissed the wife's application to enforce a foreign maintenance order where she had agreed not to enforce the order and had abided by this agreement for 6 years.

The enforcement order must be one which the debtor is able to perform. Thus, the debtor should not be put in a position where it would be impossible to meet his obligations in respect of ongoing maintenance as well as the arrears: *Grimwood v. Grimwood* (1988), 68 Sask. R. 179, 1988 CarswellSask 487 (Sask. Q.B.): *Tremblett v. Tremblett* (1988), 75 Nfld. & P.E.I.R. 175, 234 A.P.R. 175, 1988 CarswellNfld 251 (Nfld. U.F.C.).

In many cases dealing with the "one-year rule", not only is there a delay by the creditor spouse in enforcing the support order, but the evidence often reveals that the debtor spouse has no reasonable prospect of ever being able to pay the accumulated arrears. For instance, in *Spedding v. Spedding* (1989), 19 R.F.L. (3d) 368, 1989 CarswellBC 389, [1989] B.C.J. No. 153 (B.C. S.C.), the wife delayed 9 years in enforcing the order, and the husband was lulled into believing she would never enforce the order, with the result that he made no provision for maintenance payments in his budget and saved nothing. However, the evidence also indicated that the husband never had much money and certainly did not now have any prospect of earning sufficient moneys to pay ongoing maintenance as well as the full amount of arrears. See also *August v. August* (1989), 21 R.F.L. (3d) 1, 57 Man. R. (2d) 128, 58 D.L.R. (4th) 459, 1989 CarswellMan 43, [1989] M.J. No. 184 (Man. C.A.), wherein the terms of the variation order made by the trial judge reduced the arrears of $79,000 to $22,000 upon the transfer by the husband of his interest in the family home to the wife. The Court of Appeal, in allowing the appeal and rescinding the arrears, held that the provisions of the variation order were not supported by the evidence and that the terms were beyond the husband's means and abilities to meet. For other cases where the debtor's inability to ever be able to pay the accumulated arrears was as important as the delay by the creditor spouse in enforcing the arrears, see *Barnesky v. Barnesky* (1988), 16 R.F.L. (3d) 450, 53 Man. R. (2d) 212, 1988 CarswellMan 60, [1988] M.J. No. 357 (Man. Q.B.); and *Steeves v. Steeves* (1988), 87 N.B.R. (2d) 400, 221 A.P.R. 400, 1988 CarswellNB 248 (N.B. Q.B.).

The doctrine of laches was held to apply to maintenance payments under the Nova Scotia *Children of Unmarried Parents Act*, R.S.N.S. 1967, c. 32. Accordingly, where the claimant mother had commenced enforcement proceedings but did nothing until seven years later when she instituted fresh proceedings to enforce the arrears, the court ordered the respondent to pay approximately one year's maintenance. The court held that the laches of the claimant had misled the respondent into thinking that she would not pursue the claim: *C. v. P.* (1980), 13 R.F.L. (2d) 340, 1980 CarswellNS 36 (N.S. Fam. Ct.).

However, the more prevalent view is that the defence of laches is not available in a proceeding to enforce child support: *Collister v. Renaud* (1987), 80 N.S.R. (2d) 205, 200 A.P.R. 205, 1987 CarswellNS 171 (N.S. Fam. Ct.); *Daniels v. Lakes* (1987), 11 R.F.L. (3d) 159, 22 B.C.L.R. (2d) 208, 1987 CarswellBC 438 (B.C. C.A.); *Lefebvre v. Lefebvre* (1982), 38 O.R. (2d) 121, 1982 CarswellOnt 1432 (Ont. Prov. Ct.); affirmed (1982), 30 R.F.L. (2d) 184, 38 O.R. (2d) 683, 1982 CarswellOnt 325 (Ont. Co. Ct.). But see *Seward v. Seward* and *Maximitch v. Maximitch*, below and *C. v. P.*, above.

Although the plaintiff had not taken steps to enforce the arrears of child support that had accumulated under the terms of a separation agreement until 10 years had passed, her delay was not unreasonable or unexplained since she feared non-payment if she took proceedings or that the defendant would involve the children in the dispute: *Balzer v. Balzer* (1989), 24 R.F.L. (3d) 110, 1989 CarswellBC 441 (B.C. S.C.). The court noted, however, that the plaintiff's recovery of arrears could be limited to a 6-year period because it appeared that s. 3(4) of the British Columbia *Limitations Act*, R.S.B.C. 1979, c. 236, was applicable.

Where the support obligation in the order exists for the benefit of the children of the marriage, the arrears which had accumulated thereunder were enforced even though there was no explanation for the delay: *Basque v. Basque* (1988), 89 N.B.R. (2d) 214, 226 A.P.R. 214, 1988 CarswellNB 157 (N.B. Q.B.).

17§37A — Hoarding — the "one-year rule"

The so-called "one-year rule" is raised almost invariably whenever a creditor spouse seeks to enforce arrears of support which have accumulated over a period exceeding one year, or when the defaulting spouse seeks a reduction or rescission of those arrears. The existence of this "rule" as a rule of law has been disavowed in some cases, while others state that it is not a rule of law but a guideline. In most instances the courts tend to use the policy reasons underlying the "one-year rule" to limit the recovery of arrears, although the limitation may be more or less than one year depending upon the circumstances of a particular case. Also, in addition to considering such factors as the creditor spouse's delay in enforcing the arrears, courts have frequently made a finding that the accumulation of arrears is so great that the debtor spouse can never reasonably be expected to have the means or the ability to satisfy the arrears.

Rule of Law or Guideline

"One-Year Rule" Not a Rule of Law

The Ontario Divisional Court has disavowed the practice of limiting the enforcement of arrears to one year as a rule of law. See *Johannes v. Johannes* (1981), 24 R.F.L. (2d) 412, 34 O.R. (2d) 548, 127 D.L.R. (3d) 88, 1981 CarswellOnt 299 (Ont. Div. Ct.) (a decision concerning an application to vary a support order). The ruling in the Johannes case supports the opinion expressed earlier by some enforcement courts in Ontario that the so-called "one-year rule" did not apply in Ontario. See *Re Gurney* (1975), 22 R.F.L. 172, 1975 CarswellOnt 199 (Ont. Prov. Ct.) and *Snyder v. Snyder* (1973), 12 R.F.L. 335, 1973 CarswellOnt 158 (Ont. Prov. Ct.). The notion that there is a one-year rule that exists to prevent a payee from collecting more than one year of accumulated support arrears is not part of the law of Ontario: *Hennings v. Hennings Estate* (1999), 48 R.F.L. (4th) 346, 27 E.T.R. (2d) 251, 1999 CarswellOnt 1541, [1999] O.J. No. 1740 (Ont. S.C.J.); additional reasons at (1999), 49 R.F.L. (4th) 295, 1999 CarswellOnt 1780 (Ont. S.C.J.).

Similarly, the Nova Scotia Supreme Court (Appeal Division) in *Lake v. Lake* (1988), 11 R.F.L. (3d) 234, 82 N.S.R. (2d) 357, 207 A.P.R. 357, 1988 CarswellNS 34 (N.S. C.A.), held that the "one-year rule" was not a rule of law and should be considered merely as a guide.

Because spousal-support orders are made to satisfy the financial need of the payee spouse there is good reason for the court to be vigilant against hoarding. But this should be accomplished on a case-by-case basis and not through the application of a rigid rule, such as the "one-year" rule. Justice prevails if the court uses simple fairness (or unfairness) as the test in determining whether arrears of spousal support should be varied: *MacKinnon v. Duffy* (2000), 2000 CarswellOnt 2752, 10 R.F.L. (5th) 336 (Ont. S.C.J.). The husband was ordered to pay the wife $750 a month for spousal support and the same amount for child support. He immediately fell into arrears. His lawyer wrote to the wife setting out his understanding that she was remarrying and moving to the United States and that, therefore, the husband would no longer be under an obligation to pay support. Thirteen years later, without any contact in the meantime, the wife filed the support orders with Family Responsibility Office for enforcement. The arrears at that time were $241,500. The husband applied to vary the orders retroactively. The court granted the application in part finding on the facts, that it was fair to allow the wife to enforce $25,000 of the arrears of spousal support. The balance should be rescinded. Too much time had passed to allow post judgment interest. The husband's income had decreased and the wife, who was unemployed at the time of the orders, was earning income, a situation which satisfied the requisite test of a material change in circumstances. The wife did not adequately explain her delay in enforcing the orders. The husband was not guilty of bad faith, and his belief that his obligation had ceased was not unreasonable.

In *Belcourt v. Belcourt* (1987), 6 R.F.L. (3d) 396, 77 A.R. 347, 1987 CarswellAlta 349 (Alta. Q.B.), it was held that it is no longer the law in Alberta to prevent enforcement of arrears beyond a one-year period.

As the "one-year rule" was found to be too arbitrary, the court declined to apply this rule in abating maintenance arrears in *Tulik v. Tulik* (1983), 28 Sask. R. 150, 1983 CarswellSask 407 (Sask. Q.B.).

However, in *August v. August* (1989), 21 R.F.L. (3d) 1, 57 Man. R. (2d) 128, 58 D.L.R. (4th) 459, 1989 CarswellMan 43 (Man. C.A.), it was held that the "one-year rule" was still applicable to variation proceedings under the *Divorce Act*.

In 1988, the husband in *Hennings v. Hennings Estate* (1999), 48 R.F.L. (4th) 346, 27 E.T.R. (2d) 251, 1999 CarswellOnt 1541, [1999] O.J. No. 1740 (Ont. S.C.J.); additional reasons at (1999), 49 R.F.L. (4th) 295, 1999 CarswellOnt 1780 (Ont. S.C.J.) was ordered to pay $250 monthly in spousal support. At the time of the wife's death in 1997, the husband had paid only $611.60 through garnishments by the Family Responsibility Office and arrears of $44,000 had accumulated. The husband's application for an order extinguishing the arrears on the basis of material change in circumstances was dismissed. Support arrears constituted a valid judgment debt enforceable by the recipient's estate. The failure by the applicant to make support payments contributed significantly to the depletion of assets in the wife's estate. There was no "one-year" rule which limited enforcement of arrears to one year especially in light of provincial schemes of governmental enforcement of support orders. There has been no material change in circumstances. A mere accumulation of arrears, without reliable evidence of a past inability to pay, is neither a change of circumstances under the statutes, nor a special circumstance.

"One-Year Rule" Not a Hard and Fast Rule

In several cases, the courts, while not rejecting the existence of the rule completely, have taken the position that the "one-year rule" is not a hard and fast rule to be applied in all cases, but rather a guideline designed to assist the court in its determination of how much, if anything, the payor spouse should pay: *Hamelin v. Ladouceur (No. 2)* (1985), 46 R.F.L. (2d) 419, 61 A.R. 244, 1985 CarswellAlta 340 (Alta. Q.B.); *Ruth v. Ruth* (1981), 47 N.S.R. (2d) 357, 90 A.P.R. 357, 1981 CarswellNS 165 (N.S. Fam. Ct.); *Harris v. Harris* (1980), 21 B.C.L.R. 145, 110 D.L.R. (3d) 483, 1980 CarswellBC 136 (B.C. S.C.); *Dufresne v. Chew* (1979), 1 F.L.R.A.C. 287, 1979 CarswellOnt 98 (Ont. Co. Ct.); *R. v. MacDonald* (1976), 26 R.F.L. 204, 14 O.R. (2d) 409, 74 D.L.R. (3d) 57, 1976 Carswell-

Ont 146 (Ont. H.C.); *Patry v. Patry* (1974), 16 R.F.L. 332, 1974 CarswellOnt 143 (Ont. Fam. Ct.).

The Divisional Court in the *Johannes* case, above, did make it clear that the reasoning on which the "one-year rule" was based could be relevant in determining what relief should be granted. Thus the "rule" could continue to serve as a guideline. See also *Belcourt v. Belcourt*, above, where it was stated that a court, in exercising its discretion to allow a retrospective variation, should consider the following questions:

1. Is there a reasonable explanation for the delay?
2. Has the debtor tried to comply with the order?
3. Does the debtor have the ability to pay?
4. Will a denial of variation result in "windfall hoarding"?

The Provincial Court ordered the father to pay $350 per month in child support, later reducing child support to $50 per month. At the time of the variation, however, a divorce judgment had been issued which confirmed the original child support order of $350. The mother commenced enforcement proceedings and the original order was confirmed and arrears were fixed. The father was ordered to pay $150 per month toward arrears until they were paid in full. The child had stayed with the father for considerable periods of time. The father's application for retroactive suspension of arrears of child support was allowed in part. In the circumstances, it was held to be just to enforce the arrears from July 1, 1992 to the present. The one-year rule of enforcement of arrears was only a rule of thumb and not an established principle: *Moriarty v. Hood* (1993), 142 N.B.R. (2d) 334, 364 A.P.R. 334, 1993 CarswellNB 448 (N.B. Q.B.).

"One-Year Rule" Overridden by Statutory Enactment

Saskatchewan

The "one-year rule," whereby payment of arrears is not enforceable beyond a one-year period, is not a binding limitation in Saskatchewan. The *Enforcement of Maintenance Orders Act*, S.S. 1984-85-86, c. E-9.2, provides that 15 arrears owing for up to 10 years are enforceable: *Perrault (Unger) v. Unger* (1986), 52 Sask. R. 70, 1986 CarswellSask 432 (Sask. Q.B.).

Section 53 of the *Enforcement of Maintenance Orders Act* applies to "final" foreign orders registered in Saskatchewan for the purposes of enforcement under the *Reciprocal Enforcement of Maintenance Orders Act*, S.S. 1983, c. R.-4.1: *Jungaro v. Wannamaker* (1990), 26 R.F.L. (3d) 292, 84 Sask. R. 64, 68 D.L.R. (4th) 636, 1990 CarswellSask 63 (Sask. C.A.); varying (1989), 23 R.F.L. (3d) 50, 79 Sask. R. 56, 63 D.L.R. (4th) 497, 1989 CarswellSask 78 (Sask. Q.B.).

The parties were married in 1984 and separated in 1989. There were three children of the marriage and one child of the wife's prior to the marriage. The husband was a farmer whose income had increased over the past 3 years. Spousal and child support were ordered following divorce proceedings, but the husband accumulated $8,400 in arrears, although paying legal expenses of $20,000. The husband's application to extinguish payment of arrears was refused. Given the husband's payment of legal fees over his support obligations, and in view of his vastly improved financial situation, there was no justification for extinguishing the arrears: *Duncan v. Duncan* (1994), 117 Sask. R. 274, 1994 CarswellSask 560 (Sask. Q.B.).

In 1980, the father was ordered to pay the mother $150 per month in child support and $100 per month in spousal support. Nothing was paid until the mother registered her order with the Maintenance Enforcement Office 11 years later. The father's income was then garnished to pay arrears of $35,550. The father brought an application for a reduction in child support payable and a cancellation of arrears, asserting that he was unable to pay because he had been living in poverty. Arrears of child support were to be forgiven only if the court was satisfied that the payor could not have paid and there was no possibility that he would ever be able to pay. The father should have detailed his situation and the steps he took to remedy his alleged decrease in income. The court was left to conclude that he could have paid his modest obligation but chose not to, and there was no doubt that he presently had the ability to pay. The application was therefore dismissed: *Bulych v. Bulych* (1993), 117 Sask. R. 157, 1993 CarswellSask 502 (Sask. Q.B.).

Manitoba

The "one-year rule" no longer restricts enforcement of maintenance arrears under the Manitoba *Family Maintenance Act*, S.M. 1978, c. 25: *Flamand v. Flamand* (1987), 8 R.F.L. (3d) 51, 48 Man. R. (2d) 33, 1987 CarswellMan 105 (Man. C.A.). Such arrears are held to be a vested debt subject to divestment pursuant to s. 31.3(4) of the Act where it can be shown that it would be "grossly unfair and inequitable not to do so" and that such divestment is justified having regard to the interests of the payee. The onus is on the payor to establish the conditions set out in s. 31.3(4), on the balance of probabilities. See also *Kent v. Kent* (1985), 44 R.F.L. (2d) 263, 31 Man. R. (2d) 244, 16 D.L.R. (4th) 712, 1985 CarswellMan 38 (Man. C.A.); leave to appeal to S.C.C. granted (1985), 46 R.F.L. (2d) xxxv (note), 35 Man. R. (2d) 238 (note), 62 N.R. 322 (note), 21 R.F.L. (3d) xxxiv (note) (S.C.C.). In this case, the court held that when the Legislature, in 1980, enacted provisions in the *Family Maintenance Act*, specifying that no limitation as to time existed for the recovery of maintenance arrears (subject to the power of the court to relieve the debtor of the obligation to pay the arrears for the reasons set out in s. 31.3(4) of the Act), the so-called "one year rule" or "2-year rule" was no longer relevant.

Where a debtor seeks relief from an obligation to pay arrears of support which have accumulated under an order made pursuant to the provisions of the Manitoba *Family Maintenance Act*, R.S.M. 1987, c. F.20, the applicable section is s. 64(1) of that Act rather than s. 54 of the *Court of Queen's Bench Act*, S.M. 1988-89, c. 4: *Galan v. Galan* (1990), 25 R.F.L. (3d) 225, 66 D.L.R. (4th) 259, 64 Man. R. (2d) 203, 1990 CarswellMan 37 (Man. C.A.). Subsection 61(4) of the *Family Maintenance Act* sets out a two-pronged test for the court to apply in determining whether a debtor should be relieved from having to pay all or some of the arrears. Under the first branch of the test in s. 61(4), a court must be satisfied that, having regard to the interests of the debtor or the debtor's estate, it would be grossly unfair and inequitable not to rescind or reduce the arrears. If, and only if, the court is satisfied that the first branch of the test has been met is it then required to consider the second branch of the test in s. 61(4) of the Act. Under the second branch of the test, the court must determine whether rescission or reduction of arrears is justified, having regard to the "interests of the person entitled to the payments or the estate of that person." In the case at bar, there had been no formal assignment of the support order by the wife to the Director, and words "interests of the person" in s. 61(4)(b) referred to the wife's interest and not to the Director's.

The husband paid child and spousal support until his death in 1982. The wife then took title to the matrimonial home, which was subject to a $15,020 lien. On the death of the wife, her executors sought to cancel the debt as not being part of the husband's estate, as the matrimonial home was acquired by right of survivorship. It did not matter whether the lien formed part of the husband's estate. The court refused to remove the lien under s. 61(4) of the Family Maintenance Act, R.S.M. 1987, c. F20, as it would not be grossly unfair and inequitable not to relieve the estate from the obligation to pay the arrears: *Stopchycki Estate v. Stopchycki Estate* (1992), 82 Man. R. (2d) 77, 1992 CarswellMan 190 (Man. Q.B.).

After the parties separated in 1988, the father had been paying $600 per month in child support, which fell into arrears. Under a consent variation order in 1990, the parties agreed to set arrears at $6,500 and child support at $300 per month for one year. The father failed to pay as agreed and he was currently unemployed. The father had entered a new relationship in 1988 and had two additional children. His new partner was employed and supporting him. The mother alleged that the father had unreported business income. The mother relied on her parents and had taken out $10,000 in loans. The mother had attended law school and had recently found employment as a lawyer. The father brought a motion to have child support reduced and arrears remitted. The court held it was equitable and just to remit all arrears, except for the $6,500 under the consent order, considering the father's situation, particularly both parties' continued expectation of him being able to pay, and the mother's improved prospects. The arrears under the 1990 consent order were the subject of an agreement between the parties which the court was not to vary. Payment on the arrears was ordered at $50 per month. Having considered the respective incomes of the parties, the court set ongoing child support at $200 per month: *Seon v. Molgat* (1993), 89 Man. R. (2d) 317, 1993 CarswellMan 286 (Man. Q.B.).

In *Remillard v. Remillard*, 2 R.F.L. (3d) 215, [1986] 4 W.W.R. 721, 42 Man. R. (2d) 151, 1986 CarswellMan 328 (Man. Q.B.), the court declined to apply the judge-made "one-year rule" in respect of an order made under the *Divorce Act*. Since it had been held that the rule was inapplicable in respect of orders made under provincial statutes, it would be incongruous for a debtor spouse to be in a better position should his arrears happen to be "federal".

However, the disinclination of the court in the *Remillard* case to apply the "one-year rule" to "federal arrears" was questioned in *August v. August* (1989), 21 R.F.L. (3d) 1, 57 Man. R. (2d) 128, 58 D.L.R. (4th) 459, 1989 CarswellMan 43, [1989] M.J. No. 184 (Man. C.A.). Philp J.A. (Monnin C.J.M. concurring) expressed the view at (R.F.L.) p. 11 that although the "one-year rule" was a development of the common law, "its abrogation ought to be found in direct statutory enactment, if for no other reason than the fact that the [*Divorce Act*] is national in its application." The court further stated that it was beyond the jurisdiction of a provincial superior court to say that the broad discretion permitted under the *Divorce Act* was to be restricted in that particular province.

British Columbia

In British Columbia, when an application is brought under the *Family Relations Act* for an order cancelling arrears of maintenance, the court may do so "only if it is satisfied that it would be grossly unfair not to do so": ss. 62(1.1) and (1.2); *C. (L.K.) v. C. (M.I.)* (1993), 44 R.F.L. (3d) 229, 77 B.C.L.R. (2d) 52, (sub nom. *C. v. C.)* 22 B.C.A.C. 53, (sub nom. *C. v. C.)* 38 W.A.C. 53, 100 D.L.R. (4th) 68, 1993 CarswellBC 46, [1993] B.C.J. No. 155 (B.C. C.A.); *Longstaff v. Longstaff* (1993), 49 R.F.L. (3d) 1, 86 B.C.L.R. (2d) 1, 30 B.C.A.C. 306, 49 W.A.C. 306, 1993 CarswellBC 333, [1993] B.C.J. No. 1911 (B.C. C.A.). "[T]he onus is on the applicant to show that it would be grossly unfair for his or her application not to be granted. Furthermore, when determining whether refusal of the order would be grossly unfair, the court is directed to focus on the reasons why the applicant did not comply with or seek variation of the order, with further provision for the court to consider any 'special circumstances.' Except in the case of special circumstances then, the statute focuses on the circumstances of the applicant, not the circumstances of the recipient": per Boyd J., in *Weinstein v. Weinstein* (1994), 8 R.F.L. (4th) 354, 1 B.C.L.R. (3d) 174, 1994 CarswellBC 37 (B.C. S.C.); reversed (1995), 1995 CarswellBC 304, 8 B.C.L.R. (3d) 23, 61 B.C.A.C. 314, 100 W.A.C. 314, 15 R.F.L. (4th) 353 (B.C. C.A.). "beyond fettering judicial discretion, the subs. (1.1) *grossly unfair* test cannot be said to alter the impact of settled case law on laches and hoarding . . . With respect, what the grossly unfair test does is to simply impose a more onerous burden upon the person applying for reduction or cancellation of arrears. It obviously does not affect the position of a party seeking enforcement, and I think the learned Provincial Court judge was bound to consider the authorities cited, among other things, that the mother's delay was not satisfactorily explained": *British Columbia (Director of Maintenance Enforcement) v. Wiebe* (1992), 39 R.F.L. (3d) 220, 1992 CarswellBC 553, [1992] B.C.J. No. 3044 (B.C. S.C.). In *Wiebe*, the court, in allowing the appeal in part, held that the mother's perceived lack of diligence in seeking enforcement, combined with the father's impression that maintenance was not welcome (after discussion relating to the adoption of the children) did not justify cancelling arrears of maintenance that the parties' children may need to draw upon in the future.

The father was required to pay child maintenance of $125 per moth commencing October 1988. The father had been periodically unemployed and was on welfare. The court fixed the arrears at $1,575 to be paid at $10 per month. The father was a young man who should be able to earn money to meet his maintenance payments. It would not be grossly unfair to him not to cancel his maintenance payments: *Ryley v. Gooding* (1992), 1992 CarswellBC 1273 (B.C. Prov. Ct.).

Policy Reasons Underlying the "One-Year Rule"

The policy rationale underlying the practice of not enforcing arrears of maintenance beyond one year was succinctly stated by Krever J. in *R. v. MacDonald* (1976), 26 R.F.L. 204, 14 O.R. (2d) 409, 74 D.L.R. (3d) 57, 1976 CarswellOnt 146 (Ont. H.C.), at p. 223 [R.F.L.], as follows:

> The policy reasons for limited enforcement are: (1) to prevent hoarding; (2) to prevent the husband being induced by the delay of the wife in enforcement to believe he will not be required to pay; and (3) to obtain some money from the husband rather than insisting on the entire amount and having him go to jail, paying nothing.

See also *Patry v. Patry* (1974), 16 R.F.L. 332, 1974 CarswellOnt 143 (Ont. Fam. Ct.).

"One-Year Rule" a Means of Establishing Onus of Proof

The one-year limit, while not to be considered a hard and fast rule, is a means by which the onus of proof may be assigned in enforcement proceedings; the onus to show why the court might enforce more than one year's arrears would be upon the wife or child or other recipient seeking to enforce the order: *Patry v. Patry* (1974), 16 R.F.L. 332, 1974 CarswellOnt 143 (Ont. Fam. Ct.). See also *Mihalic v. Mihalic* (1973), 11 R.F.L. 102, 1973 CarswellOnt 121 (Ont. H.C.), where the court expressed the view that the effect of the "one-year rule" was one of onus. Accordingly, where a person was attempting to enforce arrears beyond one year, there was an onus on that person to satisfy the court that such discretion should be exercised in his or her favour.

However, in *Jans v. Page* (1976), 29 R.F.L. 210 at 213, 1976 CarswellOnt 216 (Ont. Prov. Ct.), the court stated that, insofar as the enforcement proceedings related to arrears of child support, it was prepared to hold not only that an order for child support should not be subject to the same constrictions of the "one-year rule", but that the onus of showing why the whole of the arrears should not be enforced lay squarely on the shoulders of the payor, the father, and not on those of the payee, the mother of the child.

Policy Against Hoarding

In *Hampton v. Carrier* (1994), 1994 CarswellOnt 2020 (Ont. Gen. Div.), the court opined that in all but very exceptional circumstances, arrears, particularly when not pursued in a timely fashion, should not reach backward in time beyond one year. Child support, like spousal support, is intended to provide for monthly present needs. No exceptional circumstances existed here, and accordingly, all the arrears that had accumulated during the last 4 years were to be stayed except for those arrears which had accrued in the past year, less the amount that the payor had voluntarily paid and less the amount which he had likely spent on the children while they were in his care.

In *D. (S.) v. R. (G.)* (February 17, 1994), Doc. C.A. Montreal 500-09-001107- 929 (Que. C.A.), in 1988, a divorce decree ratified the parties' agreement, which provided that the wife would have custody of the children and the husband would pay her $1,100 in monthly support. The parties had also agreed that, should the wife move to Vancouver, child support would be reduced to $1,000 per month. After the divorce, the wife moved to Vancouver but, in 1989, she returned to Montreal. After her return, the husband continued to pay her $1,000 per month. In 1991, the wife moved for variation of support and claimed the arrears for the period after she came back to Montreal. The motion was allowed in part on other grounds. The trial judge concluded that the wife had waived her right to arrears. The wife's appeal of the trial judge's decision on the motion was allowed in part on other grounds. The wife received the reduced amount of support during 3 years without protest which amounted to a waiver of her right to claim arrears.

In *Young v. Konkle* (1993), 1 R.F.L. (4th) 211, 1993 CarswellAlta 436 (Alta. Q.B.), the parties married in 1975, separated in 1980 and divorced in 1982. The father was ordered to pay child support of $50 a month for each of the two children of the marriage. He rarely paid. Both parties remarried and the father had three more children. He was unemployed from 1980 to 1984 and occasionally employed until 1989, after which he had a full-time job. The mother left the province in 1984, returning in 1988. While away, she had no contact with the father and made no demands for support. The parties' older child was no longer a child of the marriage and the younger child would only be so for a few more months. The court held that the father's liability for supporting the older child was to cease immediately. The arrears of $10,650 were reduced to $4,500, and the father was ordered to pay reduced arrears and support of $100 per month in respect of the younger child, while he remained a child of the marriage. After child support ended, the father was to pay the mother $100 a month towards the reduced arrears. In exercising its discretion regarding the cancellation or reduction of arrears, the court had to consider the reality of the payor's present financial circumstances, including the right of a second family to support. In this case, the father had little means to pay support until 1989. It was unfair of the mother to wait until the children were almost independent to demand child support.

In 1978, in Quebec, pursuant to a divorce order, the husband was ordered to pay child and spousal support of $50 a week. In 1991, the wife applied to enforce the order reciprocally in New Brunswick. Arrears were approximately $37,000. As the children were now adults and the wife had not previously attempted to enforce the arrears, arrears of one year were ordered, together with a lump sum of $3,000 in satisfaction of all further spousal support obligations: *Labrecque c. Dupuis* (1992), 1992 CarswellNB 345 (B.R. N.B.).

Where the wife accepted funds diverted to her from the Canadian Armed Services for seven years, without pursuing any of the legal remedies available to her to enforce the difference in amount between what she received and what she was entitled to receive under the order, the court concluded that all outstanding arrears should be cancelled: *Seward v. Seward* (1988), 12 R.F.L. (3d) 54, 85 N.S.R. (2d) 30, 216 A.P.R. 30, 1988 CarswellNS 35 (N.S. Fam. Ct.). There was no justification for applying the "one-year rule" since the former wife was obviously satisfied with the amount that was being diverted to her, as evidenced by her having done nothing about the arrears. The court was of the opinion that laches applied to arrears that were for the benefit of the children as well as the spouse. Moreover, the former wife had no debts arising from not having received the arrears. Accordingly, to enforce the payment of arrears now would result in a windfall for the wife. A windfall was against public policy, as maintenance was to maintain a person and was not to be hoarded.

Similarly, in *Maximitch v. Maximitch* (1987), 8 R.F.L. (3d) 54, 48 Man. R. (2d) 302, 1987 CarswellMan 106 (Man. Q.B.), the court rescinded arrears of child support where the wife had taken no steps for 9 years to enforce the order. The court ruled that it was not the intent of the *Divorce Act* to permit a parent to accumulate child support.

See also *Steeves v. Steeves* (1988), 87 N.B.R. (2d) 400, 221 A.P.R. 400, 1988 CarswellNB 248 (N.B. Q.B.), in which the court held that the arrears of child maintenance which had accumulated under a 1979 divorce decree should not be enforced because of laches and because it was contrary to public policy against hoarding beyond one year.

Delay Inducing Belief Arrears Would not be Enforced

See 17§37.

Facts Not Warranting Application of "One-Year Rule"

The "rule against hoarding" should be considered along with the provisions of s. 17 of the *Divorce Act*, and in this context the court may exercise its discretion and not enforce arrears of over one year: Section 17, although not specifically mentioning the right to cancel arrears, should be approached in the same way as provincial legislation, which expressly grants this right: *Lewis v. Lewis* (1999), 2 R.F.L. (5th) 417, 1999 CarswellBC 2468 (B.C. S.C.). The parties entered into a separation agreement and had the support provision incorporated in their divorce judgment. At a time when the obligation was to pay $500, a month the former husband unilaterally reduced his payments to $250 a month. Eleven years later he applied to cancel the arrears under the judgment which were in excess of $34,000, and to vary retroactively the support order to $250 a month. In the meantime, he had remarried and both he and his second wife had retired. He had a retirement income and some registered retirement savings plans. His former wife had sold her home, used the proceeds for her living expenses until they ran out, and then relied on social assistance. In dismissing the former husband's application, the court exercised its discretion and enforced payment of the arrears for a 10-year period, the parties having agreed that by reason of the *Limitation Act*, R.C.B.C. arrears of spousal support over 10 years cannot be collected. The former wife was not hoarding because she was emotionally incapable of confronting her former husband about the default. Although this lack of dissent and her subsequent silence induced the husband to believe he would not be required to pay and was free to plan his retirement accordingly, the prejudice involved was offset by the fact that his substantially superior financial position was based in part upon the financial deprivation that she suffered. The recovery of arrears is important not only to compensate the recipient for what was improperly withheld, but also to demonstrate that the orders of the court are to be obeyed. The arrears were fixed at $30,000 for the 10 years payable with interest under the *Court Order Interest Act*.

Pursuant to a divorce in 1988, the father was required to pay child support and fell into arrears. In 1990, the mother filed a statement of arrears with the Director of Support and Custody Enforcement. By the time the father applied to rescind the arrears in 1994, no arrears had yet been paid. The father argued that the mother was guilty of laches in her pursuit of the arrears. The court did not rescind the arrears. While the mother might have been more vigorous in pursuing enforcement, her conduct fell short of what was necessary to establish laches. She had placed the matter in the hands of the Director and was entitled to rely on him or her to carry out his or her statutory obligations: *Coakwell v. Baker* (1994), 4 R.F.L. (4th) 345, 1994 CarswellOnt 404, [1994] O.J. No. 1217 (Ont. Gen. Div.).

In *Saeglitz v. Saeglitz* (1994), 3 R.F.L. (4th) 244, 1994 CarswellOnt 389 (Ont. U.F.C.), the husband was ordered to pay $300 per week interim support to his wife. Subsequently, arrears of $45,400 accumulated. Upon separation, the wife had commenced an action in the Supreme Court which was transferred to the Unified Family Court 2 years later but did not find its way into that court's administration until 4 years after that. Both parties had not pursued their claims. The wife's action included a claim for arrears of support with prejudgment interest. The court found that the husband's argument that he was induced by the delay in enforcement into believing that he would not be required to pay had no merit, and that he had the ability to pay the arrears. In determining that prejudgment interest was allowed from the date at which the case was transferred to the United Family Court, the court considered that s. 140 of the *Courts of Justice Act*, 1984, S.O. 1984, c. 11 permitted consideration of the parties' conduct when determining the appropriate rate of interest. While neither party moved this case along, the bulk of the delay was attributed to the wife, whose responsibility it was to move the case forward in a timely fashion. The court found that if the wife had pursued her rights expeditiously, she would not have been deprived of her funds for such a long time. While interest was not to be awarded as punishment, it was appropriate to account for the wife's conduct and to consider the unfairness that would arise to the husband if he were made responsible for prejudgment interest from the date of separation.

The parties divorced in 1975. The husband was ordered to pay 14 percent of his salary as child support. He paid the initial amount for 17 years, but did not increase the amount as his salary increased. The children were no longer children of the marriage. The wife sued for 14 percent of the salary increase. As she was in need, although she had waited so long to bring the action, the court granted her part of the arrears owing in the amount of $11,200: *Morrison v. Morrison (Shaw)* (1992), 1992 CarswellNS 445 (N.S. T.D. [In Chambers]).

Where the husband interpreted the maintenance provisions of the minutes of settlement to mean that he did not have to pay child maintenance, and the wife did not apply to enforce the maintenance provisions for 2 years, the court ordered maintenance paid, including arrears: *McKinnon v. McKinnon* (1991), 1991 CarswellNS 515 (N.S. T.D.).

The wife had failed to claim increases in arrears of maintenance arising from a cost of living index provision in the maintenance agreement. She was permitted to claim the additional amounts as the provision regarding the cost of living adjustment was mandatory: *Hunt v. Hunt* (1992), 1992 CarswellOnt 1657 (Ont. Gen. Div.).

In *Martin v. Martin* (1989), 24 R.F.L. (3d) 150, 81 Sask. R. 98, 1989 CarswellSask 82 (Sask. Q.B.), the husband's application to rescind arrears was dismissed in circumstances where he relied not only on an inability to pay but on the wife's failure to enforce the arrears for 6 years even though she knew of his whereabouts. A cancellation of arrears under the *Divorce Act* requires a change of circumstances. A delay in enforcement did not warrant cancellation of the arrears. In any event, the court found that there had not been any unreasonable and unexplained delay by the former wife since she was unable to pursue her husband, who lived in another province, until 1987 when interprovincial enforcement services were made available to her and she could garnishee his salary.

Neither the fact that the wife failed to enforce the order for child maintenance nor the husband's new family obligations could be used by the husband to avoid his moral and financial obligations to support his children. The one-year guide respecting enforcement of support did not apply to child maintenance: *Brubacher v. Brubacher* (1988), 84 N.S.R. (2d) 343, 213 A.P.R. 343, 1988 CarswellNS 132 (N.S. Fam. Ct.); affirmed (June 23, 1988), Doc. S.P. 01597/88, F.N.G. 780-A (N.S. T.D.).

Where a husband applied to cancel arrears of maintenance accumulated over several years, in circumstances where he had had a realistic ability to pay during that time, the court dismissed his application. There was no general rule of a one-year limit on the enforcement of arrears although the court did have a discretion to not enforce the full amount owing in order to relieve against hoarding or because of laches. In the present case, the community was entitled to be reimbursed for assuming the husband's child support duties and therefore none of the arrears were cancelled. A payment schedule was imposed: *Hamelin v. Ladouceur (No. 2)* (1985), 46 R.F.L. (2d) 419, 61 A.R. 244, 1985 CarswellAlta 340 (Alta. Q.B.).

In *McDonald v. McDonald* (1983), 61 N.S.R. (2d) 341, 133 A.P.R. 341, 1983 CarswellNS 404 (N.S. Fam. Ct.), the "one-year rule" was not applied. The wife's delay in seeking enforcement was not motivated by a desire to hoard 3 years' worth of maintenance arrears; rather, the delay arose from the wife's misunderstanding of a previous verbal instruction from the court that no further maintenance applications were to be made until the husband's income had increased.

Where there was no suggestion that the enforcement remedies were not actively pursued and there was no hoarding, the court held that there was no justification for applying the "one-year rule" even if such a rule did exist: *Cassidy v. Cassidy* (1985), 47 R.F.L. (2d) 106, 1985 CarswellOnt 298 (Ont. Fam. Ct.).

Where the respondent's wife had been faced with many expenses during the period in which the arrears had accumulated, an order for payment of the arrears was held not to constitute hoarding. Moreover, the respondent had diligently pursued her claim and the petitioner had sufficient assets to pay the accumulated arrears: *Harris v. Harris* (1980), 21 B.C.L.R. 145, 110 D.L.R. (3d) 483, 1980 CarswellBC 1 (B.C. S.C.).

Where a husband was substantially in arrears of maintenance pursuant to an Illinois maintenance order, the Alberta court awarded the wife arrears going back approximately 6 years. The Alberta court also dismissed the husband's appeal of the award, stating that it was not against public policy to enforce a foreign maintenance award for arrears past one year, and that the Illinois judgment was final and conclusive under Illinois law: *Stark v. Stark*, 8 R.F.L. (2d) 254, [1979] 1 W.W.R. 748, 13 A.R. 339, 94 D.L.R. (3d) 556, 1978 CarswellAlta 288 (C.A.).

The applicant was allowed to enforce arrears which had accumulated under a support order in a decree *nisi* for a period beyond one year in circumstances where (a) the applicant had left the collection of maintenance with the Family Court which did not deal expeditiously with the matter, and (b) the respondent husband had notified the applicant that he would be going to university for a number of years and that it would be impossible for him to pay any substantial sums for maintenance: *S. v. S.* (1974), 18 R.F.L. 373, 1974 CarswellSask 37 (Sask. Q.B.).

17§37B — Retroactive variation of support orders — tax credits

Divorce Act, 1985

In *Meltzer v. Meltzer* (1992), 41 R.F.L. (3d) 257, 1992 CarswellMan 48, 78 Man. R. (2d) 299, 16 W.A.C. 299, 93 D.L.R. (4th) 435 (Man. C.A.), the court overturned on appeal a retroactive variation of a support award intended to give tax relief to the payor husband. A purported agreement between the spouses that monies paid voluntarily by the husband to the wife would attract tax consequences in the wife's hands should be enforced by suit, and not by varying a prior support order.

The court has, in the proper case, jurisdiction to make an order varying an earlier support order or rectifying a separation agreement to allow for retroactive income tax creditors for payments made: *Gallo v. Gallo* (1990), 26 R.F.L. (3d) 217, 1990 CarswellAlta 273 (Alta. Q.B.).

17§37C — Retroactive variation of support orders — other

Where the husband has received huge increases in income since the granting of the Corollary Relief Judgment which was subsequently approved by the Court of Appeal, and consequently he received a large benefit by paying less child and spousal support than he would otherwise have been required to pay, the court ordered a retroactive adjustment by way of a lump sum spousal support order: *Mosher v. Mosher* (1999), 47 R.F.L. (4th) 445, 177 N.S.R. (2d) 236, 542 A.P.R. 236, 1999 CarswellNS 182 (S.C.). The court estimated that the husband had received a $100,000 advantage as a result of paying inadequate child support that effected the wife's spousal support, some of which she used to assist the children. The court awarded the wife $50,000, after taking into account the wife's delay in pursuing the matter and the fact that none of the children at the time of the hearing lived with their mother.

17§38 — Variation — objectives — general

Objectives of spousal support

The objectives set out in s. 17 (as in s. 15 of the Act) require that an order for the support of a spouse, or an order that varies the support of a former spouse, should

1. recognize any economic advantages or disadvantages to the spouses arising from the marriage or its breakdown;

2. apportion between the spouses any financial consequences arising from the care of any child of the marriage over and above the obligation apportioned between the spouses for direct support;

3. relieve any economic hardship of the spouses arising from the breakdown of the marriage; and

4. in so far as practicable, promote the economic self-sufficiency of each spouse within a reasonable time.

Annotations of objectives

(1) *Economic Consequences*, s. 17(7)(a):

> An order that provides for the support of a spouse, or that varies the support of a former spouse, should
>
> > (a) recognize any economic advantages or disadvantages to the spouses arising from the marriage or its breakdown.

The Supreme Court of Canada, in reasons delivered by Madame Justice L'Heureux-Dubé in the case of *Moge v. Moge* (discussed at 17§2 Variation and rescission of support orders — general) observed that the purpose of spousal support is to relieve economic hardship that results from "marriage or its breakdown", and that the focus of the enquiry when assessing spousal support must be on the effect of the marriage in either impairing or improving each party's economic prospects. Marriage is, among other things, an economic unit which generates financial benefits, and the Act reflects the fact that marriage partners should expect, and are entitled to share in those benefits. A sharing of benefits can be achieved in several ways: by child and spousal support, by the division of property, or by a combination of support and property division. The absence of accumulated assets, as in the case at bar, may require that one spouse pay support to the other in order to effect an equitable distribution of resources.

The Act embodies a theory of spousal support based on principles of compensation. This is not a new theory. The Law Reform Commission of Canada in its working paper, *Maintenance on Divorce* (1975), recommended that the economic disabilities due to the marriage and the care of children be treated as matters for compensation. The working paper states in part:

> The spouse who stops working in order to care for children and manage a household usually requires financial provision from the other. *On divorce, the law should ascertain the extent to which the withdrawal from the labour force by the dependent spouse during the marriage (including loss of skills, seniority, work experience, continuity and so on) has adversely affected that spouse's ability to maintain himself or herself. The need upon which the right to maintenance is based therefore follows from the loss incurred by the maintained spouse in contributing to the marriage partnership.* (Emphasis added by L'Heureux-Dubé J.).

Legislative support for applying the principles of compensation may be found in the first three of the four objectives stated in the Act. These objectives deal with a broad range of economic and financial consequences and it is the ability of compensatory spousal support to respond to the diversity of these objectives that, as a matter of statutory interpretation, makes it superior to the strict self-sufficiency model.

Self-sufficiency, the fourth objective, remains relevant under this view of spousal support, but is not given pre-eminence. After divorce, spouses would still have an obligation to contribute to their own support in a manner commensurate with their abilities.

Compensatory spousal support would not always be awarded. "In cases where relatively few advantages have been conferred or disadvantages incurred, transitional support allowing for full and unimpaired reintegration back into the labour force might be all that is required to afford sufficient compensation. However, in many cases compensatory spousal support would require long-term support or an alternative settlement which provides an equivalent degree of assistance in light of all the objectives of the Act."

The four objectives set out in the Act are an attempt to achieve an equitable sharing of the economic consequences of marriage or marriage breakdown. But the courts have an overriding discretion when ordering support which will depend on the particular facts of each case. The exercise of this discretion requires an examination of all four objectives in order to achieve an equitable sharing of the economic consequences of the marriage or marriage breakdown. This involves a broad approach incorporating any significant element of the marriage or its termination which adversely affects the economic prospects of the disadvantaged spouse. Not all such elements will be equally important, and it may be useful to consider some examples which the courts may consider in the exercise of their discretion.

In her additional comments made after concurring in the judgment of her colleague, Madame Justice McLachlin summarized her view of the first objective by saying that it is compensatory in nature allowing the judge "to compensate one spouse for sacrifices and contributions made during the marriage and benefits which the other spouse has received."

See 17§39 Variation objectives — economic advantages and disadvantages.

(2) *Burden of Child Support*, s. 17(7)(b):

> An order that provides for the support of a spouse, or that varies the support of a former spouse, should
>
> > (b) apportion between the spouses any financial consequences arising from the care of any child of the marriage over and above the obligation apportioned between the spouses pursuant to subsection (8).

In the *Moge* case, the Supreme Court of Canada was of the opinion that Mrs. Moge should be compensated, in part, because her ability to earn income had been diminished by the fact that she had been left with the care of the children.

Madame Justice L'Heureux-Dubé discussed the effect of responsibility for child care in the context of the economic consequences of marriage or marriage breakdown. She noted that the most significant consequences usually arises from the birth of children. To care for children, women usually cut back on their paid work and thereby jeopardize their income security and independent economic well-being. Spousal support might be a means of compensating for these economic disadvantages.

If childcare responsibilities continue after divorce, the existing disadvantages also continue. To describe this situation, Madame Justice L'Heureux-Dubé adopted the words of Bowman J. in *Brockie v. Brockie* of the Manitoba Court of Appeal. He said that to be a custodial parent involves adopting a lifestyle which places many limitations upon that parent. The parent must find accommodation suited to the needs of the child, including play space, closeness to daycare, schools and recreational facilities. She is seldom free to accept shift work, is restricted in any overtime work by the daycare arrangements available, and must be prepared to give priority to the needs of a sick child over the demands of an employer. After a full day's work, the custodial parent faces a full range of homemaking responsibilities including cooking, cleaning and laundry, as well as the demands of the child himself for the parent's attention.

Even where both parties work full-time, a spouse may be entitled to compensation if "due to childcare responsibilities one spouse declines a promotion, refuses a transfer, leaves a position to allow the other spouse to take advantage of an opportunity for advancement or otherwise curtails employment opportunities and thereby incurs economic loss."

Madame Justice McLachlin concurred with Madame Justice L' Heureux-Dubé in holding that section 17(7)(b) of the *Divorce Act* raised compensatory considerations. She stated that "if a spouse either before or after separation, has or continues to incur financial disadvantages as a result of caring for a child of the marriage, he or she should be compensated." She was in agreement with the Court of Appeal judgment in finding that Mrs. Moge should be compensated for, among other things, her contribution as a homemaker and mother during the marriage and the permanent economic disadvantages she suffered as a consequence.

(3) *Economic Hardship*, s. 17(c):

> An order for the support of a spouse, or an order that varies the support of a former spouse, should
>
> > (c) relieve any economic hardship of the spouses arising from the breakdown of the marriage.

In the *Moge* case Madame Justice L'Heureux-Dubé found that Mrs. Moge continued to suffer economic hardship as a result of the "breakdown of the marriage" within the meaning of s. 17(7)(c) of the Act, and should be compensated for it.

(See annotation under *Economic Consequences*, above.)

Madame Justice McLachlin held that the focus in the consideration of economic hardship arising from the breakdown of the marriage was "not on compensation for what the spouses have contributed to or gained from the marriage but rather on post-marital need." She states that "if the breakdown of the marriage has created economic hardship for one or the other, the judge must attempt to grant relief from that hardship."

(4) *Economic Self-sufficiency*, s. 17(7)(d):

> An order that provides for the support of a spouse, or that varies the support of a former spouse, should
>
> > (d) in so far as practicable, promote the economic self-sufficiency of each spouse within a reasonable period of time.

The Supreme Court of Canada held that compared with the other objectives, the objective of economic self-sufficiency has been given too much emphasis in the decided cases. In *Moge*, the former husband contended that support under the *Divorce Act* was based on a self-sufficiency model. This model, he argued, had been established by the court in the trilogy of *Pelech*, *Richardson* and *Caron* as a model for support in all applications, not simply those involving a final agreement. As an alternative argument, he submitted that the *Divorce Act*, itself, proposed a self-sufficiency model.

The court rejected the former husband's submissions and accepted those advanced by counsel for Mrs. Moge.

Madame Justice L'Heureux-Dubé, delivering the opinion of the court, stated that the trilogy did not establish a new model for support. The principles described in the trilogy were derived in the context of a final settlement. They do not determine the basis on which entitlement, or continuing entitlement, to spousal support rests in the absence of a settlement agreement intended by the parties to be final.

The principles embodied in the current *Divorce Act* engage the courts in a different type of analysis than that which was required under the 1970 *Divorce Act* when considering the question of support. The most significant change is a shift away from "means and needs" as the exclusive test to a set of objectives which require the courts to accommodate a much wider spectrum of considerations. This change recognizes that the economic variables of marriage breakdown do not lend themselves to the application of only one objective. "All four of the objectives defined in the Act must be taken into account when spousal support is claimed or an order for spousal support is sought to be varied. No single objective is paramount. The fact that one of the objectives, such as economic self-sufficiency, has been attained does not necessarily dispose of the matter."

In commenting on her concurrence in the decision of the court, Madame Justice McLachlin was of the opinion that the trial judge erred by giving no weight to the first three factors, and by imposing a categorical requirement of self-sufficiency. With respect to self-sufficiency, "the judge's order must", in so far as is practicable, "promote the economic self-sufficiency of each former spouse within a reasonable period of time." However, this factor, unlike the other three, is stated in qualified language, using the conditional phrase "in so far as practicable." Economic self-sufficiency is to be promoted, meaning that it is not be required or assumed. Parliament, in the language used, acknowledges that self-sufficiency may not be feasible.

Madame Justice McLachlin endorsed the Court of Appeal's view that there is no absolute obligation for a spouse to become self-sufficient, and that there is no time limit after which one spouse is no longer required to support another.

See 17§40 Variation — objectives — failure of payee to become self-sufficient.

17§39 — Variation — objectives — economic advantages and disadvantages

Divorce Act, 1985

See *Moge v. Moge*, [1992] 3 S.C.R. 813, [1993] 1 W.W.R. 481, 81 Man. R. (2d) 161, 145 N.R. 1, 99 D.L.R. (4th) 456, 43 R.F.L. (3d) 345, discussed at 17§35 Variation — Objectives — general ((1) Economic Consequences and (3) Economic Hardship). For a consideration of the facts in the *Moge* decision, see 17§2 Variation and rescission of support orders — general.

Where the wife had a future need for support which arose because of her economic disadvantage suffered as a result of the long-term traditional marriage, her appeal was allowed in part and spousal support was set at $300 per month, even though she did not have any current economic need: *Savoie v. Savoie*, 49 R.F.L. (4th) 336, [1999] 9 W.W.R. 63, 175

D.L.R. (4th) 291, 138 Man. R. (2d) 128, 202 W.A.C. 128, 1999 CarswellMan 308 (C.A.). This amount of $300 was half of what the wife had previously received under the parties' separation agreement and at trial. The reduction took into account her remarriage and the setting aside of the separation agreement.

In *Wooldridge v. Wooldridge* (1999), 45 R.F.L. (4th) 308, 172 D.L.R. (4th) 637, 237 A.R. 64, 197 W.A.C. 64, 1999 CarswellAlta 320 (C.A.); additional reasons at (1999), 49 R.F.L. (4th) 445, 250 A.R. 168, 213 W.A.C. 168, 1999 CarswellAlta 620 (C.A.) the court held that where the wife has not worked outside the home for 20 years and she and two of her four children have suffered severe psychological difficulties since separation, there have been economic disadvantages to the wife as a result of the marriage and its breakdown, spousal support should not be terminated. Under these circumstances, self-sufficiency for the wife might not be possible for some time, if ever. The husband was ordered to pay $2,500 per month in spousal support. Once the husband has ceased to pay child support, the spousal support, if necessary, could be increased.

On an application for termination of spousal support, the court should examine the economic consequences resulting from the breakdown of the marriage: *C. (N.) c. L. (Y.), (*sub nom. *Droit de la famille — 1932)* [1994] R.D.F. 205 (C.A. Qué).

It is appropriate for a court to take into account the detrimental economic consequences that one spouse's abusive conduct has created for the other spouse: *Martin v. Martin* (1993), 50 R.F.L. (3d) 77, 113 Sask. R. 316, 52 W.A.C. 316 (C.A.). On this basis, the appellate court would not interfere with the trial judge's award of spousal maintenance.

In *Walker v. Walker* (1992), 39 R.F.L. (3d) 305, 68 B.C.L.R. (2d) 92, 12 B.C.A.C. 137, 23 W.A.C. 137 (C.A.), where the wife has been economically disadvantaged by the marriage by remaining at home and she has not overcome those disadvantages, the trial court did not err in respect to the recognition of the promotion of self-sufficiency. She was still in need and support should not be reduced.

In *Eccles v. Eccles* (2002), 27 R.F.L. (5th) 47, 2002 CarswellOnt 1284 (Ont. S.C.J.); reversed (2003), 2003 CarswellOnt 3235 (C.A.), the wife had, for 10-years during the parties' marital cohabitation, sublimated her own career development and for 10 years following separation had devoted herself to the care of the children. Eventually custody was transferred to the husband, which further aggravated the wife's fragile mental state and limited her employment opportunities. The court dismissed the husband's application to terminate her spousal support and upwardly adjusted the support payable and included a lump sum award. There was a wide disparity between the employment abilities of the parties resulting directly from the marriage and the wife's financial dependence on the marriage was a complete one.

In *Krill v. Krill* (2000), 4 R.F.L. (5th) 249, 2000 CarswellAlta 136, [2000] A.J. No. 163 (Q.B.), the court refused the husband's application for a downward variation of the spousal support payable by him. At the time of the divorce, the wife had been enrolled in university with the intent of upgrading her skills. She had, however, voluntarily dropped out and was unemployed, although attempting to start a career. Given the parties' long-term traditional marriage, it was found that it was not unreasonable for the wife to remain economically dependent on the husband $2^1/_2$ years subsequent to the divorce and $5^1/_2$ years after the parties' separation. Accordingly, the wife's support was extended for a further two years.

The loss on marriage breakdown of an income stream generated by her husband is an economic disadvantage to the wife which should be considered in favour of the wife on the husband's application to reduce spousal support where there is a great disparity in their incomes: *Provost v. Provost* (1999), 2 R.F.L. (5th) 442, 1999 CarswellAlta 1067 (Alta. Q.B.).

In *Kurbegovich v. Kurbegovich* (1998), 36 R.F.L. (4th) 220 (Ont. Gen. Div.), the court allowed the husband's application to terminate the wife's spousal support seven years after the parties' divorce. The parties had separated frequently through their marriage with the result that the wife's need did not flow from a pattern of dependency created by the marriage. In addition, the 39-year-old wife could have returned to employment similar to that held prior to marriage, but had failed to do so.

Where income the wife derives from a job is not less than it would have been had she not been married, the wife has not suffered any economic disadvantage because of the marriage or its breakdown and support should not be granted on the basis of economic disadvantage: *Tingley v. Tingley* (1993), 49 R.F.L. (3d) 87, 141 N.B.R. (2d) 86, 361 A.P.R. 86 (Q.B.). On a motion to vary or terminate support, the court ordered that spousal support should be terminated.

Although under s. 17(7)(a) of the *Divorce Act* the court should recognize the economic disadvantages of a spouse which have resulted from the failure of the marriage, the Act does not require the court to eliminate those disadvantages through a support award: *Droit de la famille — 341*, [1987] R.J.Q. 416 (C.S. Qué.).

In *Burmeister v. Burmeister* (1993), 47 R.F.L. (3d) 186 (Man. Q.B.), the court refused the husband's application to terminate the spousal support which had been awarded at the end of the parties' 28-year traditional marriage. The wife had never been self-supporting and, given her health problems, was never likely to be. The economic disadvantage suffered by her as a result of the marriage continued and was likely to continue. Accordingly, the case was one in which support should be considered permanent.

In order to vary downward a compensatory support order, the payor must establish that not only had there been a significant change in financial circumstances but also that the factors which resulted in economic disadvantage no longer existed and that the lost advantage had been recovered: *Patrick v. Patrick*, 92 B.C.L.R. (2d) 50, [1994] 7 W.W.R. 441 (S.C.); additional reasons at (April 19, 1994), Doc. Vancouver D076591 (B.C. S.C.).

17§39A — Variation — objectives — financial consequences of child care

The appellate court granted the father's appeal from an order increasing spousal support in *Imrie v. Imrie*, 1 R.F.L. (5th) 65, 1999 CarswellOnt 3266 (C.A.). The Court of Appeal presumed that the motions court decision was based on the fact that the appellant's income from the time of the initial order was sufficient to constitute a change in the appellant's "means" within s. 17(4) of the *Divorce Act*. The Court of Appeal was of the opinion that the motions judge did not give appropriate weight to all the objectives in s. 17(7) of the *Act*, specifically s. 17(7)(b), as the appellant was the sole financial support for three teenage daughters.

In *Wooldridge v. Wooldridge* (1999), 45 R.F.L. (4th) 308, 172 D.L.R. (4th) 637, 237 A.R. 64, 197 W.A.C. 64, 1999 CarswellAlta 320 (C.A.); additional reasons at (1999), 250 A.R. 168, 49 R.F.L. (4th) 445, 213 W.A.C. 168, 1999 CarswellAlta 620 (C.A.) the court held that where the wife has not worked outside the home for 20 years and two of her four children have suffered severe psychological difficulties since separation, there had been financial consequences to the wife of caring for the children of the marriage, and spousal support should not be terminated. Considering all of the circumstances, self-sufficiency for the wife might not be possible for some time, if ever. The husband was ordered to pay $2,500 per month in spousal support. Once the husband has ceased to pay child support, the spousal support, if necessary, could be increased.

17§40 — Variation — objectives — failure of payee to become self-sufficient

Divorce Act, 1985

In *Moge v. Moge*, 43 R.F.L. (3d) 345, [1992] 3 S.C.R. 813, discussed at 17§35 Variation — objectives — general ((4) Economic Self-sufficiency), the Supreme Court of Canada considered that self-sufficiency was a relevant objective in making variation orders together with the other objectives set out in s. 17(7). Self-sufficiency, however, should not be given pre-eminence. After divorce, parties should contribute to their own support according to their abilities. For a consideration of the facts in the Moge decision, see 17§2 Variation and rescission of support orders — general.

Where a spouse is unable to work at the time of the variation hearing, but such inability is the result of her intentional failure to return to her employer, and is not related to the marriage, the court will not require the payor spouse to continue to pay spousal support: *Teeple v. Teeple* (1998), 43 R.F.L. (4th) 251, 1998 CarswellOnt 5165 (Gen. Div.); reversed (1999), 2 R.F.L. (5th) 464, 124 O.A.C. 294, 90 O.T.C. 80 (note), 1999 CarswellOnt 2958 (C.A.). This is so, even though the payor spouse takes early retirement to reduce his income substantially so that he could decrease the amount of anticipated spousal support.

Where a payee spouse among other reasons, refuses to take any active steps to become employed, spousal support should cease: *Ungerer v. Ungerer*, 37 R.F.L. (4th) 41, 158 D.L.R. (4th) 37, 105 B.C.A.C. 250, 171 W.A.C. 250, [1998] 7 W.W.R. 469, 48 B.C.L.R. (3d) 188, 1998 CarswellBC 670 (C.A.).

In *Reid v. Reid* (1997), 33 R.F.L. (4th) 145, 192 N.B.R. (2d) 156, 489 A.P.R. 156 (C.A.), it was held that the wife's voluntary relocation to an area where she could not readily find employment was not a sufficient reason to allow the husband's application to terminate her support. The wife's move to be closer to her family was reasonable and her employment at the time of separation had paid only minimum wages and had no prospect for advancement.

Where the wife was unable to justify her failure to upgrade her education as was anticipated in her original spousal support order, the dismissal of her application for increased support was upheld on appeal. Her educational goals should have improved as her children became older and less dependant upon her as the primary care-giver: *Lilley v. Lilley* (1994), 9 R.F.L. (4th) 434 (B.C. C.A.); affirming (1993), 50 R.F.L. (3d) 329 (B.C. S.C.); additional reasons at (1994), 50 R.F.L. (3d) 341 (B.C. S.C.).

In determining an application for termination of spousal support, self-sufficiency of the payee spouse is a goal only insofar as it is practical. Where the payee continues to suffer an economic disadvantage as a result of the marriage, support should not be terminated: *Droit de la famille — 1675*, 46 R.F.L. (3d) 131, [1993] R.D.F. 218 (C.A. Qué.).

The fact that a spouse should be able to become self-sufficient in the future is not an adequate ground for revoking the support payable to that spouse: *Helston v. Helston* (1992), 39 R.F.L. (3d) 168 (Sask. C.A.).

In *Lapointe c. Lavoie* (3 juin 1992), no C.A. Québec 200-09-000102-928 (C.A. Qué.), the court on appeal allowed the husband's application to terminate the wife's spousal support. Although she had not worked during the parties' 18-year marriage, the 52-year-old wife had made no effort in the five years following the divorce to become self-sufficient despite the fact that she was in good health and had some education.

In *Baker v. Baker* (2005), 22 R.F.L. (6th) 209, 2005 CarswellOnt 7067 (Ont. S.C.J.), the court allowed the husband's application for termination of his former wife's spousal support 4 years after the parties' divorce. The husband's burden of child support was substantial and would be even more so when the two youngest joined the older ones at university. The wife had not been qualified as a teacher subsequent to divorce and had not been diligent in exploring further income opportunities.

In *Gosnell v. Gosnell* (1993), 138 A.R. 205 (Q.B.), the court allowed the husband's application to suspend the spousal support arrears owing. The parties had separated after only five years of marriage. In the 13 years since separation, the wife had made no attempt to achieve self-sufficiency.

On an application to vary spousal support, the court must consider all of the factors outlined in s. 17(7) of the Act and not just s. 17(7)(d): *Jayatilaka c. Roussel* (1991), 36 R.F.L. (3d) 447 (N.B. C.A.).

Where the wife had made no effort to achieve self-sufficiency during the 25 years which she received spousal support, the court, on the husband's appeal from an order increasing her support, placed a one-year limit on her future support entitlement. The marriage had not been a traditional one and the parties had only actually cohabited for a three-year period: *Douthwright v. Douthwright* (1992), 42 R.F.L. (3d) 1, 95 D.L.R. (4th) 188 (N.B. C.A.).

Where the 46-year-old wife had failed to achieve complete self-sufficiency seven years after separation, the husband's application for reduced support was granted and her monthly support was reduced by half: *L. (G.) c. T. (N.)*, [1990] R.L. 504 (C.A. Qué.).

In *Droit de la famille — 978*, [1991] R.D.F. 220 (C.A. Qué.), the court terminated the wife's support, which had been based upon the parties' agreement, 13 years after the parties' divorce. The wife had never made an effort to seek self-sufficiency and as a result her needs were caused by her own inactivity and not the failure of the marriage.

In *P. (M.F.F.A.) v. P. (F.M.A.)*, 47 R.F.L. (5th) 170, 2003 CarswellBC 2447, 2003 BCSC 1502 (B.C. S.C.), the court allowed the husband's application to terminate the spousal support payable to his former wife. After the divorce, the wife had remarried, successfully completed a dental assistant's course and undertaken part-time employment. The wife then developed cancer and was unable to work. For the purposes of support, the wife had achieved "self sufficiency" upon completion of her course and her failure to secure full-time employment was the result of her own decision. The wife's new spouse now had primary responsibility for her support.

In *Janakowski v. Janakowski* (2000), 7 R.F.L. (5th) 117, 2000 CarswellOnt 2478 (S.C.J.), the court refused to extend the wife's spousal support entitlement beyond the period called for in the parties' consent order. The wife had been employed throughout the relationship and neither of the parties had realized any economic advantage from the marriage. The wife had preferred to remain unemployed after the parties' separation with the result that her need was not truly related to the marriage or its breakdown.

A clause in minutes of settlement signed by the parties in which the wife agreed to "diligently seek full-time employment" and also acknowledged "her intention to make her best efforts to secure full-time employment" does not bar her from support if she is unable to find full-time work: *Erickson v. Erickson* (1999), 47 R.F.L. (4th) 326, 175 N.S.R. (2d) 185, 534 A.P.R. 185, 1999 CarswellNS 137 (S.C.). The court found, following *Moge v. Moge*, [1992] 3 S.C.R. 813, that the court must look at all four objectives under s. 17(7) of the *Divorce Act* and not just self-sufficiency. In any event, the court also found that the wife had used her best efforts to secure full-time employment and at 56 it was unrealistic to expect her to become economically self-sufficient.

The court held in *Dorey v. Dorey* (1998), 44 R.F.L. (4th) 383, 172 N.S.R. (2d) 75, 524 A.P.R. 75, 1998 CarswellNS 493 (S.C.) that where the husband had paid spousal support for three years and the court ordered further support for a year, as well as payment of the wife's home-care course, the husband's spousal support obligations had been met. The parties had been in a relatively short marriage (eight years) and the wife's career path had not been hindered by the marriage; rather, during the marriage, the wife had improved herself by obtaining her Grade 12.

In *Garrison v. Garrison* (1998), 38 R.F.L. (4th) 435 (Ont. Gen. Div.), the wife was allowed to rely upon the fact that her expectation that she would be able to re-train and become self-sufficient had not materialized as a change in circumstances warranting an increase in her spousal support.

In an application for a variation of spousal support, the factors set out in s. 17(7) of the *Divorce Act* should be reviewed not only from the date of the original order but from the inception of the marriage. Applying this principle in *Adam v. Adam* (1993), 50 R.F.L. (3d) 216, 89 Man. R. (2d) 275 (Q.B.), a wife was found entitled to compensation from the husband for support that she had needed but not received in the past.

In *Furlong v. Furlong* (1992), 111 N.S.R. (2d) 391, 303 A.P.R. 391 (T.D.), the court allowed the husband's application to terminate the wife's support brought four years after the parties' divorce. The wife was only working part-time and had failed to prove that she had made every reasonable effort to achieve self-sufficiency.

In *Gillam v. Gillam* (1991), 89 Nfld. & P.E.I.R. 89, 278 A.P.R. 89 (Nfld. T.D.), the husband's application to terminate spousal support and the wife's application for increased support were both set aside pending a review of the parties' situation in six months' time. Although the wife had attempted to become self-sufficient she had not yet succeeded and a better picture of her prospects would be obtained after a further six months.

In *Stevens v. Stevens* (1991), 102 N.S.R. (2d) 262, 279 A.P.R. 262 (T.D.), the court refused the husband's application to terminate spousal support despite the fact that the wife had made minimal efforts to achieve self-sufficiency. Under the decree, the wife was only entitled to support for seven more months, which would give her a final opportunity to acquire marketable skills.

Where the wife was required, under the terms of the decree *nisi*, to raise the children in an economically depressed area, the husband could not rely upon the wife's failure to become self-sufficient as a grounds for reducing spousal support: *Rebelo v. Rebelo* (1991), 104 N.S.R. (2d) 172, 283 A.P.R. 172 (T.D.).

In *Ryan v. Ryan* (1992), 114 N.S.R. (2d) 255, 313 A.P.R. 255 (T.D.), the court refused the husband's application to terminate the wife's spousal support. Although the wife continued to live in the matrimonial home in which there was over $70,000 in equity, it was impracticable to require her to sell it to increase her self-sufficiency.

Where the wife claimed that ill health had prevented her from achieving self-sufficiency in the 11 years since the parties' divorce, the husband was ordered to continue paying spousal support only for a further two-year period. If the wife had failed to achieve financial independence during that period, she would be required to seek social assistance to meet her needs: *Droit de la famille — 886*, [1990] R.D.F. 550 (C.S. Qué.).

Where the wife had been through several pregnancies and 13 moves during the parties' 23-year marriage, the husband could not rely upon the failure to achieve self-sufficiency as grounds for terminating her spousal support. The wife's economic hardships had resulted directly from the marriage and its failure, since her total lack of experience and training throughout the marriage prevented her from finding suitable employment: *Droit de la famille — 1354*, [1990] R.D.F. 582 (C.S. Qué.).

Where the wife's decision to work only part-time was motivated solely out of a dislike of her career or a lack of ambition, the court allowed the husband's application to terminate spousal support. As she was fully capable of becoming economically self-sufficient, it was appropriate that the husband's support obligations be brought to an end: *MacAllister v. MacAllister* (1990), 101 N.B.R. (2d) 422, 254 A.P.R. 422 (Q.B.).

Where, subsequent to the termination of the parties' long term traditional marriage, the wife had shown little ambition and had made only spotty efforts to find full-time employment, the husband's application to terminate her support after a further six-month period was allowed. The husband had supported her for five years after the divorce and should be allowed to get on with his life: *Klaudi v. Klaudi* (1990), 25 R.F.L. (3d) 134 (Ont. H.C.).

Where the wife had difficulty adjusting to the breakdown of the parties' traditional marriage and had accordingly not made a reasonable attempt to achieve self-sufficiency during the seven years since the divorce, her support was ordered terminated: *Derkach v. Derkach* (1989), 22 R.F.L. (3d) 423, 60 Man. R. (2d) 278 (Q.B.).

Where subsequent to the parties' divorce the wife realized significant assets from the sale of the family home, had entered into a stable conjugal relationship with another man and had failed to seek employment despite her ability to do so, the court allowed the husband's application to terminate her support: *Schofield v. Schofield* (1989), 19 R.F.L. (3d) 165, 65 Alta. L.R. (2d) 258, [1989] 4 W.W.R. 84, 98 A.R. 150 (Q.B.).

Where the wife had solely provided for the needs of the parties' children during the 11 years following the parties' divorce, her failure to become self-sufficient could not be cited as a ground for terminating her support: *Droit de la famille — 1240*, [1989] R.D.F. 262 (C.S. Qué.).

The principle of spousal self-sufficiency should be given a restrictive interpretation in cases of long-term marriages where a spouse is unable to achieve self-sufficiency: *Harris v. Harris* (1992), 40 R.F.L. (3d) 253 (B.C. S.C.). In the Harris decision, the wife had achieved a measure of self-sufficiency but her standard of living had fallen drastically as a result of the dissolution of the marriage. The husband's income had declined significantly since trial. Consequently, the wife was awarded permanent maintenance at a reduced amount.

Where the wife was unemployed, had limited education and was without job skills, the husband's application to terminate his support obligation on a date two years after the parties' divorce was allowed. It was held that support could only be continued where there was a causal connection between the dependent's inability to achieve self-sufficiency and the marriage relationship. Given that the marriage had only lasted four years, the wife had not taken any concrete steps to achieve self-sufficiency and the husband had additional financial demands resulting from his remarriage, the variation was warranted: *Goering v. Goering* (1988), 13 R.F.L. (3d) 383 (Ont. H.C.).

The husband's application for termination of spousal support brought 16 years after the parties' divorce was allowed. The wife had had ample time to become self-sufficient: *Hudson v. Hudson* (1989), 102 N.B.R. (2d) 199, 256 A.P.R. 199 (Q.B.).

Where the wife, who was educated and capable of self-sufficiency, failed to seek employment during the five years subsequent to the parties' divorce, the husband's application to terminate spousal support was allowed. Her failure to seek self-sufficiency was a material change in circumstances justifying a variation of the support order: *Smith v. Smith* (1989), 20 R.F.L. (3d) 38 (Ont. H.C.).

In *Droit de la famille — 1238*, [1989] R.D.F. 251 (C.S. Qué.), the court granted the husband's application to phase out gradually the support payable to his 49-year-old former wife. The wife was in good health, had a university degree and her children were grown. Accordingly, her claim that it was impossible for her to find a job was not credible.

Where the wife left a well-paying job to commence a five-year post-graduate programme, the husband's application to terminate spousal support was allowed. The obligation did not encompass the financing of his wife's studies after having paid generous support for a 4-year period: *Droit de la famille — 473*, [1988] R.J.Q. 1034, [1988] R.D.F. 240 (C.S.).

In *Hawker v. Hawker* (1992), 103 Sask. R. 247 (Q.B.), the court made a provisional order terminating the wife's support two years after the parties' divorce. At the time of the divorce it was anticipated that it would take the wife two years to complete a rehabilitation programme relating to her drug, alcohol and depression problems. The court accepted the husband's uncontested evidence that the recovery time had passed and that the wife should now take responsibility for her own self-sufficiency.

In *Droit de la famille — 1104*, [1987] R.D.F. 266 (C.S. Qué.), the court allowed the husband's application to terminate the 11-year-old spousal support order. Although the wife was unemployed, she had extensive employment experience and her current difficulties were not related to the marriage.

Where the wife's need for continuing support was based upon an alcohol problem which the wife developed after divorce, the husband's application to terminate spousal support was allowed. The wife's problem was not related to the marriage and the husband had already paid support for 16 years in relation to a marriage which had only lasted 11 years: *Droit de la famille — 399*, [1987] R.D.F. 509 (C.S. Qué.).

Where after the parties' divorce the wife had quit her job to continue schooling and had later left yet another job, the court dismissed the husband's application to terminate her support. Although the wife's need could no longer be traced to the marriage, she should be allowed one false start and her support rights be continued for a defined period of time: *Merrell v. Merrell* (1987), 11 R.F.L. (3d) 18 (B.C. S.C.).

Where the wife was not able to achieve self-sufficiency because of the role she adopted during the marriage, the husband's application to reduce the amount of support payable to her was dismissed: *Hickey v. Hickey* (1987), 8 R.F.L. (3d) 416, 65 Nfld. & P.E.I.R. 38, 199 A.P.R. 38 (Nfld. T.D.).

In *Droit de la famille — 1091*, [1987] R.D.F. 174 (C.S. Qué.), the court refused to grant the husband's application to terminate his 54-year-old wife's support. The wife had, throughout the 26-year marriage, devoted herself to raising the partner's five children and it was not reasonable to expect her now to achieve self-sufficiency.

In *Droit de la famille — 318*, [1986] R.J.Q. 2911, [1986] R.D.F. 591 (C.S.); affirmed [1990] R.D.F. 178 (C.A. Qué.), the court ordered the termination of the wife's maintenance 10 years after the parties' divorce. Although the wife had since the divorce completed her Master's degree in translation, her refusal to accept work outside of the medical area greatly reduced the possibility of her achieving economic independence.

Where the wife refused to take medication which would control a psychotic condition from which she suffered, the court allowed the husband's application to terminate her support upon the expiration of three years time. In the five years since the parties' divorce the wife had had ample time to achieve self-sufficiency and her unemployability resulting from her condition could not be traced back to the marriage: *Potter v. Smith* (1989), 93 N.S.R. (2d) 389, 242 A.P.R. 389 (Fam. Ct.).

In *Droit de la famille — 1007*, [1986] R.D.F. 84 (C.S. Qué.), the court allowed the husband's application for termination of the maintenance payable to the wife brought 8 years after the parties' separation. Although the wife was not working full-time, she had placed herself in a situation where finding employment was difficult and the husband could not be held responsible for her problems.

Even in the case of a traditional marriage, a wife may still be required to take reasonable steps to retrain and to decide on a suitable career. Accordingly, where in the seven years subsequent to the end of the parties' traditional marriage, the wife had not acted reasonably in pursuing self-sufficiency, the court allowed the husband's application for a variation of spousal support. The wife was granted a $4,000 lump sum to permit her to retrain together with continued periodic support for one more year only: *Boucher v. Boucher* (1991), 36 R.F.L. (3d) 179, 108 N.S.R. (2d) 96, 294 A.P.R. 96 (Fam. Ct.).

Where the wife deliberately failed to meet the stated goal of self-sufficiency, the husband's application to terminate support was allowed: *Langille v. Langille* (1988), 88 N.S.R. (2d) 445, 225 A.P.R. 445 (Fam. Ct.).

17§41 — Variation — standard of living

In *Moge v. Moge, supra*, a case concerning the circumstances under which spousal support should be terminated under s. 17, the court also considered the issue of the parties' standards of living. Madame Justice L'Heureux-Dubé, writing at page 390, was of the opinion that since marriage should be regarded as a joint enterprise, the longer the relationship, the greater the presumption of equal standards of living upon dissolution. Note that in her reasons, Madame Justice L' Heureux-Dubé referred to *Mullin v. Mullin* (1991), 37 R.F.L. (3d) 142, 95 Nfld. & P.E.I.R. 73, 301 A.P.R. 73 (P.E.I. C.A.) and *Linton v. Linton* (1990), 1 O.R. (3d) 1, 30 R.F.L. (3d) 1, 75 D.L.R. (4th) 637, 42 O.A.C. 328, 41 E.T.R. 85 (Ont. C.A.).

In *Smyth v. Smyth* (1993), 48 R.F.L. (3d) 280, 142 A.R. 132 (Q.B.), Mr. Justice O'Leary stated that it was essential, especially in long-term marriages to consider the relative standards of living of the spouses following divorce. He wrote: "equitable sharing can only be considered in the light of the economic circumstances of the parties as they existed during the marriage, as they are at the time of the application for support, or for variation, and as they may reasonably be expected to emerge in the future."

"I have no doubt that cases will arise in the exercise of the discretion given under s. 11(2) [now s. 17] of the *Divorce Act* where it will be fit and just to order additional maintenance so a divorced wife may share in the increased standard of living of her former husband. I do not say that such cases will be limited only to those where need can be shown. Without doubt many cases will arise where, because of the wife's limited means, her health, the existence of dependent children, past contributions made by the wife or other circumstances, an increase in the fortune or income of the husband occurring after the divorce will justify an order enlarging maintenance payments to the wife. I reject, however, the argument that such a result must follow automatically in all cases": per McIntyre J.A. in *Marcus v. Marcus*, [1977] 4 W.W.R. 458 at 463–64 (B.C. C.A.).

There is no authority for the proposition that a decree of divorce which incorporates an agreement for maintenance already entered into between the parties may only be varied if the wife demonstrates need; the discretion vested in the court by s. 11(2) [now s. 17] of the *Divorce Act* is not so limited. Where the earnings of the husband substantially increase in the years following the decree the wife may, in a proper case, be granted increased maintenance even though she cannot prove actual need; she is entitled to an increase in her standard of living commensurate with the increase in the means of the husband: *Clark v. Clark*, 16 R.F.L. 214, [1974] 6 W.W.R. 424, 47 D.L.R. (3d) 149 (B.C. S.C.).

17§41A — Variation — interference with access rights

Where the wife had, for over five years, thwarted the husband's access to their child, even after having been imprisoned for contempt, the court ordered the termination of her spousal support. The wife's breach of the access order in itself was sufficiently reprehensible to justify termination and her further refusal to seek employment was also inexcusable: *Ungerer v. Ungerer*, 37 R.F.L. (4th) 41, [1998] 7 W.W.R. 469, 158 D.L.R. (4th) 47, 105 B.C.A.C. 250, 171 W.A.C. 250, 48 B.C.L.R. (3d) 188 (C.A.).

17§42 — Variation and rescission of support orders — practice — evidence

In *Moge v. Moge* (1992), 43 R.F.L. (3d) 345, [1992] 3 S.C.R. 813, [1993] 1 W.W.R. 481, 81 Man. R. (2d) 161, 145 N.R. 1, 99 D.L.R. (4th) 456, the court considered the evidence required for a court's determination of spousal support. Madame Justice L'Heureux-Dubé noted the difficulty of the analysis, but stated at p. 390 (R.F.L.) that "this complexity does not excuse judges from hearing relevant evidence or from fully applying the law. There are no easy recipes, nor are there neat compartments on which to rely, as families and family relationships are not simple. But there are few matters more important before the courts, given the repercussions on the future of the parties themselves and in particular, their children."

She added at p. 391 (R.F.L.) that "in some cases, such evidence might come in the form of highly specific expert evidence which enables parties to present an accurate picture of the economic consequences of marriage breakdown in their particular circumstances. ... Although of great assistance in assessing the economic consequences of marriage breakdown in a particular marriage, such evidence will not be required, nor will it be possible, in most cases. For most divorcing couples, both the cost of obtaining such evidence and the amount of assets involved are practical considerations which would prohibit or at least discourage its use. Therefore, to require expert evidence as a sine qua non to the recovery of compensation would not be practical for many parties, not to mention the use of court time which might be involved. It would be my hope, therefore, that different alternatives be examined."

Where expert evidence was not given, Madame Justice L'Heureux-Dubé considered a proposal of legislative guidelines for support, but seemed to prefer the use of the doctrine of judicial notice in determining spousal support. The court was of the opinion at p. 393 (R.F.L.) that "the general economic impact of divorce on women is a phenomenon, the existence of which cannot reasonably be questioned and should be amenable to judicial notice."

However, where a party wishes to give evidence on the issue of spousal support, the court should ensure that his or her evidence is heard, no matter if it is lengthy. Madame Justice L Heureux-Dubé writes at p. 394 (R.F.L.): "This being said, even if a major portion of the time of the civil courts in this country is taken by family law matters, and the efficient and speedy disposition of affairs before the court is a valuable goal, the paramount goal is to render justice to the parties in accordance with the Act."

17§43 — Variation and recission of support orders — practice — miscellaneous

Divorce Act, 1985

Arrears accumulating under a *Divorce Act* order cannot be cancelled or reduced in an application under a provincial statute: *Weinstein v. Weinstein* (1995), 15 R.F.L. (4th) 353, 8 B.C.L.R. (3d) 23, 61 B.C.A.C. 314, 100 W.A.C. 314 (C.A.); reversing (1994), 8 R.F.L. (4th) 354, 1 B.C.L.R. (3d) 174 (S.C.).

Where an order for support provides for a fixed period and then states that at the end of that period, the payor may apply for a review, a former spouse is not precluded at any time from exercising his statutory right of review of support under s. 17(1), in the event of a material change in circumstances: *Lidstone v. Lidstone* (1993), 46 R.F.L. (3d) 203, 121 N.S.R. (2d) 213, 335 A.P.R. 213 (C.A.).

In allowing a motion for a reduction in support payable, the court has jurisdiction to set a payment formula which takes into account the contingency that the payor's circumstances may improve, thus eliminating the need for the payee to seek a further variation: *Klassen v. Klassen* (1993), 44 R.F.L. (3d) 433, 83 Man. R. (2d) 214, 36 W.A.C. 214 (C.A.).

Where the evidence on entitlement in the wife's application for increased support would take only half a day or less, the husband's application to sever the determination of entitlement from quantum was dismissed in *Zwingenberger v. Zwingenberger* (1995), 17 R.F.L. (4th) 239 (Ont. Gen. Div.).

A party seeking variation of a support order is not required to establish a prima facie entitlement to variation before being authorized to issue to the other party, a notice to disclose: *Rosin v. Rosin* (1994), 8 R.F.L. (4th) 315, 158 A.R. 14 (Q.B.); additional reasons (1994), 158 A.R. 14 at 19 (Q.B.).

In *Van de Sande v. Van de Sande* (1994), 148 A.R. 30 (Q.B.), the court allowed a variation to her spousal support award whereby her support payments were to be increased annually by the actual percentage for any cost of living increase granted to the husband.

In spite of the absence of statutory jurisdiction under the *Divorce Act*, 1985 to make an interim variation of a prior support order, the superior court retains its parens patriae jurisdiction to make an interim variation of a child support order. Although no generalized power to make an interim variation order exists, where the child has an urgent need for support, the parens patriae jurisdiction affords a basis to a superior court of record, in making an interim order, to provide for the child: *Parr v. Lavallee* (1992), 42 R.F.L. (3d) 58 (Ont. Gen. Div.).

The Nova Scotia Family Court lacks jurisdiction under rr. 35 and 57.30 to order a variation of a divorce decree or a corollary relief judgment. The court is restricted to making variation recommendations for consideration by the Supreme Court: *Lewin v. Lewin* (1992), 115 N.S.R. (2d) 145, 314 A.P.R. 145 (T.D.).

Although the Civil Code restricts cost awards to divorce proceedings and does not include subsequent variation proceedings, the *Divorce Act* itself permits the court to determine cost issue on variation applications: *Droit de la famille — 605*, [1989] R.J.Q. 505, (sub nom. *L.(L.) v. D.(R.))* 28 Q.A.C. 106 (C.A.).

Where variation proceedings are commenced in two different provinces, exclusive jurisdiction belongs to the province where such proceedings were first commenced: *Droit de la famille — 541*, [1988] R.J.Q. 2386, [1988] R.D.F. 484, (sub nom. *R. v. S.)* 25 Q.A.C. 284.

In *Wilson v. Wilson* (1987), 11 R.F.L. (3d) 244 (B.C. C.A.), the court dismissed the wife's appeal from an order in which her maintenance had been reduced in the course of enforcement proceedings which she had initiated. Although there had been no application for variation, the judge's actions were realistic and his conclusion supportable in the circumstances.

A husband's petition for termination of spousal support cannot be disposed of through the wife's mere motion for dismissal. The matter must be dealt with at trial: *Droit de la famille — 1265*, [1989] R.D.F. 501 (C.S. Qué.).

It is impossible for a party to present an application to vary an original award where an appeal from that award has not yet been decided: *Droit de la famille — 338*, [1987] R.J.Q. 126, [1987] R.D.F. 28 (C.S. Qué.).

A party is still entitled to seek variation of a support order under the *Divorce Act* even after the order has been filed with the Director under the *Family Maintenance Enforcement Act* (B.C.): *McKinney v. Polston* (1992), 42 R.F.L. (3d) 141 (B.C. S.C.).

Where the decree *nisi* is silent on the issue of support, only the court which granted the decree has jurisdiction to entertain a subsequent support application. Such a proceeding is an application for corollary relief and cannot be characterized as a variation application: *Evans v. Evans* (1987), 6 R.F.L. (3d) 166 (B.C. S.C.).

17§44 — Variation — consent orders for support

Divorce Act, 1985

See *Willick v. Willick*, [1994] 3 S.C.R. 670, 17§48 Variation — order incorporating spousal support provisions of agreements

In *D. (B.G.) v. D. (R.W.)*, 35 R.F.L. (5th) 315, 2003 CarswellBC 1192, 2003 BCCA 259181 B.C.A.C. 312, 298 W.A.C. 312, 226 D.L.R. (4th) 378 (B.C. C.A.), the parties separated, signed a separation agreement, whereby they agreed that the husband would pay spousal support for 2 years and either party could apply for continued support or termination of support. After 2 years, the wife applied for spousal support. The parties reached an agreement which was incorporated into a consent order, whereby the wife was awarded support which was duly paid. The wife subsequently applied to vary the consent order to provide support. The doctrines of res judicata and issue estoppel do not apply to an agreement which is incorporated into an order for spousal maintenance made under the *Divorce Act*. The jurisdiction of the court has not been ousted.

In an obiter remark in *Kehler v. Kehler*, 2003 CarswellMan 270, 2003 MBCA 88, [2003] 8 W.W.R. 429, 39 R.F.L. (5th) 299 (Man. C.A.), the court was of the opinion that in some circumstances involving consent orders based on a separation agreement, Miglin would be applicable in variation proceedings. The court referred to paragraph 91 of that decision which stated "it would be inconsistent if a different test applied to change an agreement in the form of an initial order under s. 15.2 and to a variation of an agreement incorporated into an order under s. 17." The Supreme Court held that the *Divorce Act* does not create such inconsistency.

In family law, the courts, for obvious policy reasons, encourage parties to settle their affairs in order to prevent unnecessary litigation and the unnecessary dissipation of assets and, consequently, courts are reluctant to later interfere with consensual arrangements reached between the parties, except where substantial grounds are demonstrated: *Huculak v. Huculak*, 12 R.F.L. (5th) 107, 2000 BCCA 662, 2000 CarswellBC 2546 (B.C. C.A.). Such substantial grounds were not found. There was not a proper evidentiary basis for the variation sought by the appellant. In this case, a spousal support order was made following a settlement conference.

"A consent order is similar to a separation agreement; principles analogous to those set out by the Supreme Court of Canada in Miglin apply to determine whether a person who has consented to an order should be allowed to ask for relief which is inconsistent with the terms of the existing consent order:" *Ordano v. Moore*, 2003 CarswellAlta 576, 2003 ABQB 362, 39 R.F.L. (5th) 361 (Alta. Q.B.). This case dealt with access.

In *Lee v. Lee* (1998), 41 R.F.L. (4th) 303, (sub nom. *1998)* 1998 CarswellBC 2031, [1998] B.C.J. No. (S.C.), the husband in a consent decree had been ordered to pay spousal support payments until he retired, at which time the wife would receive an interest in her husband's pension. The legislation changed and the wife elected to receive a lump sum payment of the pension. The husband stopped making spousal support payments. A lower court set aside the spousal support order but on appeal at (1997), 35 R.F.L. (4th) 200, 1997 CarswellBC 2845, [1997] B.C.J. No. 2947 (C.A.), the court referred the matter of spousal support back to the court below. The lower court, at (1998), 41 R.F.L. (4th) 303, 1998 CarswellBC 2031, [1998] B.C.J. No. 2201 (S.C.), ruled that a material change had occurred and the consent order was inapplicable. The court was of the opinion that the husband no longer had an obligation to pay support once the wife had obtained her lump sum pension, but since the husband had delayed in applying for maintenance and as a result the wife had incurred debts, the husband should be required to pay an additional six months of support from the time that the wife received her share of the pension.

Where the wife, in a consent judgment, agreed to forego spousal support in exchange for payments by the husband to replace pension benefits lost on the dissolution of the marriage, it was held that the wife could properly seek variation of the payments under s. 17 despite the dismissal of the wife's support claim in the consent judgment. The pension payments could properly be characterized as support: *McCowan v. McCowan* (1995), 14 R.F.L. (4th) 325, 24 O.R. (3d) 707, 84 O.A.C. 125 (C.A.).

Where a settlement agreement provides evidence that adequate provision has been made for the support of the children, the agreement should not be disturbed on a variation application absent proof of a change in circumstances: *Ryan v. Ryan* (1990), 29 R.F.L. (3d) 278, 110 N.B.R. (2d) 176, 276 A.P.R. 176, 1990 CarswellNB 30 (C.A.).

On an application to vary support, the court should take the amount originally ordered as correct and consider the extent of any changes since that order. In particular, consent orders made with legal advice ought not to be lightly disturbed: *Friedman v. Friedman* (1987), 8 R.F.L. (3d) 83 (B.C. S.C.).

In *Mason v. Mason* (1989), 93 N.S.R. (2d) 428, 242 A.P.R. 428 (Fam. Ct.), the husband's application for a reduction in support, brought two months after the parties had agreed to a consent support order, was dismissed. The factors upon which the husband based the claim, namely his poor health and failing real estate business, were neither radical changes nor unforeseen at the time of the consent order.

17§45 — Variation — suspension of support payments

Divorce Act, 1985

In *Freund v. Dent* (1995), 14 R.F.L. (4th) 251, 102 Man. R. (2d) 316, 93 W.A.C. 316 (C.A.), the court allowed the husband's appeal and ordered that enforcement proceedings respecting the support arrears owed by him be suspended for four months. The husband was attempting to overcome a drug problem and find steady employment. The four-month suspension would permit him to find employment without risk of losing it because of enforcement proceedings.

Although the court may temporarily reduce a support award based upon a settlement agreement where the payor is out of work, such an order should not be interpreted as meaning that the original settlement will not be upheld once the payor is again employed: *Sobstyl v. Sobstyl* (1989), 100 A.R. 178, 1989 CarswellAlta 443 (Q.B.).

Where the husband lost his employment and the evidence indicted that the wife had not made sufficient efforts to find employment since the divorce, the wife's spousal support order was suspended. Although there had been a change in circumstances, it was not sufficient to warrant rescission of the order. The wife was, therefore, free to seek re-instatement when the husband found employment: *Sequens v. Sequens* (1999), 48 R.F.L. (4th) 53, 1999 CarswellBC 1114 (S.C.).

Where the husband had lost his job, the court ordered a temporary reduction in the child support payments he was required to make, until such time as he was again employed: *Hamilton v. Hamilton* (1992), 101 Sask. R. 222 (Q.B.).

In *Dupont v. Dupont* (1993), 47 R.F.L. (3d) 273 (B.C. S.C.), it was found that an accident suffered by a payor spouse justified a suspension of child support obligations pending settlement of the accident claim, but did not justify a cancellation of the order.

Where the wife lost her employment because of her unreasonable refusal to seek assistance for alcohol dependency, the husband's obligation to pay spousal support was suspended until the wife completed certain drug dependency programmes: *Robertson v. Robertson* (1988), 84 N.S.R. (2d) 303, 213 A.P.R. 303 (Fam. Ct.).

17§46 — Variation — extension of limited term support orders

In *Wedsworth v. Wedsworth*, 19 R.F.L. (5th) 455, 2001 CarswellNS 218, 2001 NSCA 102, 194 N.S.R. (2d) 198, 606 A.P.R. 198 (N.S. C.A.), the court, on appeal, upheld the dismissal of the wife's application for an interim order extending the period of her limited term spousal support. Although the trial judge had misstated the threshold test for variation of a consent order, the evidence still supported the correct test as set out in s. 17(4.1) of the *Divorce Act*.

In *McKinney v. McKinney* (2004), 9 R.F.L. (6th) 418, 2004 CarswellAlta 1344, 2004 ABQB 717 (Q.B.), the wife's support was ordered extended to a date 6 months after the anticipated completion of her training as a teaching assistant. The wife was entitled to support for a reasonable time after graduation as security against the possibility that she may not find employment immediately.

Section 17 of the *Divorce Act* provides clear rules when spousal support is sought after the expiration of time-limited support. The provision, however, is not applicable to a case in which the parties executed a full and final release as part of their separation agreement: *Leopold v. Leopold* (2000), 12 R.F.L. (5th) 118, 195 D.L.R. (4th) 717, 2000 CarswellOnt 4707, [2000] O.J. No. 4604, 51 O.R. (3d) 275 (S.C.J.).

In an application to vary and extend a limited term spousal support award, the court cannot rely upon its *parens patriae* jurisdiction to grant interim support pending the hearing. *Parens patriae* can only be invoked in the case of adult dependents if they are mentally incompetent: *Y. (H.) v. Y. (D.)* (1998), 42 R.F.L. (4th) 418, 170 Nfld. & P.E.I.R. 44, 522 A.P.R. 44 (P.E.I. C.A.).

In *Rizzo v. Rizzo* (2000), 12 R.F.L. (5th) 445, 2000 CarswellOnt 4983 (Ont. S.C.J.), the wife's application for spousal support, brought after the expiration of the 4-year support period called for in the parties' separation agreement, was dismissed. The wife had fallen and permanently injured herself and her resulting depression inhibited her employment opportunities. Although the wife's injuries were found to be a radical unforeseen change in her circumstance, her situation was not the result of the marriage or its breakdown. The marriage had not been a long one, nor had the wife given up career opportunities as a result. She had been given adequate time to achieve self-sufficiency.

In *Seymour v. Seymour*, 20 R.F.L. (5th) 139, 2001 CarswellBC 1564, 2001 BCSC 777 (B.C. S.C.), the court refused the wife's application to extend her spousal support entitlement in a court ordered review of the original support order. The wife had realized significant assets upon the parties' divorce but had quit her job to move thousands of miles away to live with a man. The relationship failed after the wife had dissipated much of her money. It was held that the wife's need was largely related to events occurring after the parties' divorce and that her choices had unreasonably limited her ability to become self-sufficient. An order of permanent spousal support would have been tantamount to a redistribution of the parties' assets.

The fact that the wife could not find employment after the completion of her degree and intended to pursue further education were insufficient to warrant an extension of her time-limited support in *Duplisea v. Duplisea* (1995), 15 R.F.L. (4th) 1, 164 N.B.R. (2d) 170, 421 A.P.R. 170 (C.A.).

Section 17 of the *Divorce Act* provides clear rules when spousal support is sought after the expiration of time-limited support. The provision, however, is not applicable to a case in which the parties executed a full and final release as part of their separation agreement: *Leopold v. Leopold* (2000), 12 R.F.L. (5th) 118, 195 D.L.R. (4th) 717, 2000 CarswellOnt 4707, 51 O.R. (3d) 275, [2000] O.J. No. 4604 (S.C.J.).

In *Janakowski v. Janakowski* (2000), 7 R.F.L. (5th) 117, 2000 CarswellOnt 2478 (S.C.J.), the court refused to extend the wife's spousal support entitlement beyond the period called for in the parties' consent order. The wife had been employed throughout the relationship and neither of the parties had realized any economic advantage from the marriage. The wife had preferred to remain unemployed after the parties' separation with the result that her need was not truly related to the marriage or its breakdown.

In *Marshall v. McNeil* (1998), 36 R.F.L. (4th) 264, (sub nom. *McNeil v. McNeil)* 164 Sask. R. 91, 1998 CarswellSask 100 (Q.B.), the court extended the 30-month limitation on the wife's spousal support after she suffered a back injury which would temporarily thwart her efforts toward self-sufficiency.

Where subsequent to the divorce, the wife's existing multiple sclerosis condition deteriorated to the extent that she could no longer work, the court extended her limited term support award. But for the marriage breakdown, she would not have to bear the economic consequence which flowed from her disability. If the total disability had existed at the time of the original order, it would likely have resulted in an indeterminate order for a higher amount: *Tees v. Tees*, 31 R.F.L. (4th) 290, [1997] N.W.T.R. 315, 1997 CarswellNWT 29 (S.C.).

Where the wife was unable to justify her failure to upgrade her education as was anticipated in her original spousal support award, the dismissal of her application for an extension of her limited term support was upheld on appeal: *Lilley v. Lilley, supra.*

In *Marshall v. McNeil* (1998), 36 R.F.L. (4th) 264, 164 Sask. R. 91 (Q.B.), the court extended the 30-month limitation on the wife's spousal support after she suffered a back injury which would temporarily thwart her efforts toward self-sufficiency.

In *Schroder v. Schroder* (1998), 38 R.F.L. (4th) 395, 221 A.R. 395 (Q.B.), the court dismissed the wife's application to vary spousal support 8 years after the expiry of her limited term support. The wife had upgraded her education and found employment but had been forced to quit because of a back injury. As the wife's current financial difficulty was not connected to the marriage, the variation was not appropriate.

In *Frederickson v. Frederickson* (1993), 48 R.F.L. (3d) 18, 111 Sask. R. 219 (Q.B.), the court allowed the wife's application for an extension of her spousal support beyond the term specified in the parties' separation agreement. The time frame contemplated in the agreement was based upon the wife's completion of her education and her resulting self-sufficiency. As the parties could not have anticipated the recession which frustrated the wife's ability to find employment after obtaining her teaching qualifications, it would be unfair not to provide her with additional time to make the adjustments.

In *Hiscock v. Dickie* (1994), 6 R.F.L. (4th) 149 (N.B. Q.B.), the court refused to extend the wife's support period as called for in the parties' consent order. Although she had been unable to find employment despite retraining she was unable to demonstrate that her economic hardship arose from a change that was related to the marriage.

In *Droit de la famille — 1786*, [1993] R.D.F. 185 (C.S. Qué.), the court refused to extend the wife's limited term support order. Although her psychiatric problems prevented her from working, she could not establish that the disease was causally connected to the marriage.

Where the wife had agreed to limited term support and a substantial property settlement, her subsequent application for an extension of support was refused. The wife had the resources to achieve self-sufficiency and any benefits to the husband and disadvantages to the wife from the relationship had already been compensated through the property and support settlement: *Debacker v. Debacker* (1993), 49 R.F.L. (3d) 106, 143 A.R. 228 (Q.B.).

In *Droit de la famille — 1645*, [1992] R.D.F. 460 (C.S. Qué.), the court refused to set aside a provision in the parties' agreement whereby the wife's support entitlement was to end on a specified date. The wife had had legal advice at the time of the agreement and her current financial problems were more related to her own mismanagement of funds than to the marriage.

Where the wife's efforts at job hunting had been hindered by her need to care for the parties' autistic child, who had recently been placed in a residential school, her support award was extended for a further six-month period: *Hack v. Hack* (1991), 72 Man. R. (2d) 131 (Q.B.).

In *Ehlers v. Ehlers* (1991), 38 R.F.L. (3d) 41 (Sask. Q.B.), the court refused the wife's application to extend her spousal support beyond its specified expiration date. The wife refused to use any of the property settlement to support herself and as the husband drew upon his pension to pay support, a pension which had also been divided with the wife, the ongoing support order was effectively a derogation from the proceeds of his share of the matrimonial property. Support was accordingly ordered to continue for only three more months.

An application to extend support after the expiration of an existing support order is properly considered as a variation application, rather than as an original application for support: *Matas v. Matas* (1990), 26 R.F.L. (3d) 349 (Man. Q.B.).

Where the wife had failed to find employment within the six-month period during which the parties had agreed that the husband would pay spousal support, the court refused to extend her support. The wife's financial dependency could no longer be related to the marriage and did not justify a modification of the parties' agreement: *Droit de la famille — 1350*, [1990] R.D.F. 558 (C.S. Qué.).

The *Divorce Act* does not provide for variation of fixed term support prior to the expiration of the term: *Droit de la famille — 1243*, [1989] R.D.F. 298 (C.S. Qué.).

A separation agreement which provides for limited term spousal support does not oust the court's jurisdiction to extend the term of support absent clear and concise language evidencing that intention: *Ellis v. Ellis* (1988), 15 R.F.L. (3d) 252 (Sask. Q.B.).

Where the result of the expiry of a time-limited spousal support award would require the wife to encroach upon capital for her living expenses, her application for an extension was allowed: *Tees v. Tees* (1997), 31 R.F.L. (4th) 290, [1997] N.W.T.R. 315 (S.C.).

Where subsequent to the divorce, the wife's existing multiple sclerosis condition deteriorated to the extent that she could no longer work, the court extended her limited term support award. But for the marriage breakdown, she would not have to bear the economic consequence which flowed from her disability. If the total disability had existed at the time of the original order, it would likely have resulted in an indeterminate order for a higher amount: *Tees v. Tees*, above.

In *Isaacson v. Isaacson* (1987), 10 R.F.L. (3d) 121 (B.C. S.C.), the court granted the wife an extension of spousal support beyond the period specified in the parties' settlement agreement which had been incorporated into the decree *nisi*. As the wife had miscalculated the remaining duration of her studies, the agreement had been based upon the parties' mutual mistake.

17§47 — Jurisdiction to override domestic contracts

See 15§147 — Overriding jurisdiction of the courts.

Since the decision of the Supreme Court of Canada in *Miglin v. Miglin* (2001), 16 R.F.L. (5th) 185, 53 O.R. (3d) 641, 198 D.L.R. (4th) 385, 144 O.A.C. 155, 2001 CarswllOnt 1404 (C.A.); leave to appeal allowed (2001), 2001 CarswellOnt 3484, 283 N.R. 395

(note), 157 O.A.C. 400 (note) (S.C.C.); reversed 2003 CarswellOnt 1374, 2003 CarswellOnt 1375, [2003] S.C.J. No. 21, 2003 S.C.C. 24, 34 R.F.L. (5th) 255, 224 D.L.R. (4th) 193, 171 O.A.C. 201, 302 N.R. 201 (S.C.C.) the trilogy of *Pelech*, *Richardson* and *Caron* discussed below and referred to in cases in this section, cannot be considered as applying to the exercise of the court's discretion under the *Divorce Act* 1985 to override support agreements. See discussion of the *Miglin* case in 15§147.

In *Moge v. Moge* (1992), 43 R.F.L. (3d) 345, [1993] 1 W.W.R. 481, 145 N.R. 1, [1992] 3 S.C.R. 813, 81 Man. R. (2d) 161, 30 W.A.C. 161, 99 D.L.R. (4th) 456, [1992] S.C.J. No. 107, 1992 CarswellMan 143, 1992 CarswellMan 222, [1993] R.D.F. 168, discussed in detail at 17§2, 35. The Supreme Court Canada, ended the idea of causal connection as a general support principle. In that decision, the court clearly indicated that the *Pelech*, *Richardson* and *Caron* trilogy, discussed below, was restricted to applications to vary support where the parties have entered into a settlement agreement intended to be final. The court left the question open as to whether the trilogy applied only to such cases under the 1968 *Divorce Act* or whether it would be extended to final settlement cases under the 1985 *Divorce Act*.

The court the *Moge* decision stated that instead of relying on a causal connection as a general support principle in determining support under the 1985 *Divorce Act*, judges should consider the four statutory objectives set out in ss. 15(7) and 17(7) of the *Divorce Act*.

See also *B. (G.) c. G. (L.)*, [1995] 3 R.C.S. 370, 15 R.F.L. (4e) 201, 127 D.L.R. (4e) 385, 186 N.R. 201, [1995] R.D.F. 611, 1995 CarswellQue 23, 1995 CarswellQue 120, [1995] S.C.J. No. 72.

In the trilogy of cases *Pelech*, *Richardson*, and *Caron*, below, the Supreme Court of Canada held that, where the parties have entered into an agreement that was intended to settle their affairs in a final and conclusive manner, the court should exercise its jurisdiction to ignore a waiver or limitation in the agreement and award support or further support only after there has been a radical change in circumstances and if there is a causal connection between the changes circumstances and the marriage. See *Pelech v. Pelech*, 7 R.F.L. (3d) 225, [1987] 1 S.C.R. 801, 17 C.P.C. (2d) 1, 14 B.C.L.R. (2d) 145, [1987] 4 W.W.R. 481, 76 N.R. 81, 38 D.L.R. (4th) 641, 1987 CarswellBC 147, 1987 CarswellBC 703, [1987] S.C.J. No. 31; *Richardson v. Richardson*, 7 R.F.L. (3d) 304, [1987] 1 S.C.R. 857, 17 C.P.C. (2d) 104, 77 N.R. 1, 22 O.A.C. 1, 38 D.L.R. (4th) 699, 1987 CarswellOnt 315, 1987 CarswellOnt 963, [1987] S.C.J. 30; and *Caron v. Caron*, [1987] 1 S.C.R. 892, 14 B.C.L.R. (2d) 186, [1987] 4 W.W.R. 522, 7 R.F.L. (3d) 274, 75 N.R. 36, 38 D.L.R. (4th) 735, 2 Y.R. 246, 1987 CarswellYukon 8, 1987 CarswellYukon 43, [1987] S.C.J. No. 32. It is difficult to determine what radical changes in circumstances flowing from an economic pattern of dependency engendered by the marriage could occur between the date of the initial support order and the date of the variation application. Most often, the cases to date indicate that the causal connection test is a means of terminating support upon a variation application.

In *Strang v. Strang*, 39 R.F.L. (3d) 233, [1992] 2 S.C.R. 112, 3 Alta. L.R. (3d) 1, 125 A.R. 331, 92 D.L.R. (4th) 762, 1992 CarswellAlta 70, 1992 CarswellAlta 468, 14 W.A.C. 331, 137 N.R. 203, the court found that the wife's present low employment status, as a bookkeeper, was causally connected to the marriage. The parties had a traditional marriage which had lasted 29 years. However, the court reduced the maintenance payments in light of the husband's forced retirement.

The requirement that a change in circumstances be related to the marriage is found only in s. 17(10) of the *Divorce Act*, with respect to orders which defined a time when maintenance would cease. In support variation applications where s. 17(10) is not applicable, a causal connection need not be established: *Carter v. Carter* (1991), 34 R.F.L. (3d) 1, 58 B.C.L.R. (2d) 45, 1991 CarswellBC 170, 2 B.C.A.C. 241, 5 W.A.C. 241 (C.A.).

The concept of causal connection applies under the *Divorce Act* on an application to vary a support order only to determine whether the courts' overriding jurisdiction should be exercised contrary to what has been settled either by agreement or by order, or when the application is to vary a support order which falls within the description contained in s. 17(10) of the Act. In all other cases, applications for a variation should be determined in accordance with the principles specifically prescribed by the *Divorce Act* but without regard to the issue for causal connection: *Story v. Story* (1989), 23 R.F.L. (3d) 225, 42 B.C.L.R. (2d) 21, 65 D.L.R. (4th) 549, 1989 CarswellBC 237, [1989] B.C.J. No. 2238 (C.A.).

In the *Story* judgment, McEachern C.J.B.C., writing for the majority, stated that there was a substantial economic hardship accruing to the wife, by reason of the breakdown of the marriage, that would continue indefinitely. The parties separated after a marriage of 18 years. The wife suffered from a mental illness that predated the marriage. By the time of the variation of the application, she was considered by the court to be unemployable. The husband's appeal from an order refusing to terminate support was dismissed.

Spousal maintenance cannot be varied except in respect of catastrophic, radical, and unforeseen changes causally connected to the marriage: *Dickson v. Dickson* (1987), 11 R.F.L. (3d) 337, 21 B.C.L.R. (2d) 69, [1988] 2 W.W.R. 117, 46 D.L.R. (4th) 280, 1987 CarswellBC 412 (C.A.). In the *Dickson* case, the court was of the opinion that the wife had failed to meet the causal connection test. The parties had made an agreement that the court found to be a final settlement of their affairs. However, the court may override the provisions of an agreement dealing with child support where deemed appropriate having regard to the needs of the children and to the payor's ability to pay. Consequently, in the circumstances, support for the children was increased.

In an *obiter* remark in *Linton v. Linton* (1990), 30 R.F.L. (3d) 1, 1 O.R. (3d) 1, 42 O.A.C. 328, 75 D.L.R. (4th) 637, 41 E.T.R. 85, 1990 CarswellOnt 316, [1990] O.J. No. 2267 (C.A.), Osborne J.A. commented on the courts' jurisdiction to vary a support order under s. 17 of the *Divorce Act*. He noted that the reference in s. 17(10) to economic hardship arising from a change related to the marriage is the only specific reference in the *Divorce Act* support scheme to a specific causal connection requirement. However, he held that it may be implied under s. 15 of the *Divorce Act*. The court ruled that the causal connection principles were only relevant to the extent that a causal connection requirement or objective may be taken to emerge from the *Divorce Act*, 1985.

In *MacDonald v. MacDonald* (2004), 6 R.F.L. (6th) 348, 2004 CarswellOnt 2305 (S.C.J.), the court considered the husband's application for a reduction in spousal support under the parties' separation agreement. At the time the agreement was executed, the husband earned additional monthly income through a small contracting business. As the husband was now 64 years old and was no longer able to do the physical labour which generated the income, the required material change in circumstances had been established.

In *Zimmerman v. Shannon* (2004), 11 R.F.L. (6th) 230, 2004 CarswellBC 2132, 2004 BCSC 1246 (S.C.), the court terminated the husband's obligation to pay spousal support under an agreement in which the wife had waived any interest in the husband's pension in exchange for spousal support payable for life. The husband no longer had the means to make payments to the wife and to support himself. The agreement had ceased to achieve the objectives of the *Divorce Act.*

In *Myers v. Hawco* (2004), 11 R.F.L. (6th) 291, 2004 CarswellNfld 286, 240 Nfld. & P.E.I.R. 248, 711 A.P.R. 248, 2004 NLSCUFC 38, 243 D.L.R. (4th) 726 (U.F.C.), the court allowed the husband's application to set aside the spousal support provisions of the parties' separation agreement under which the husband was $300,000 in arrears. Although the wife had supported the husband through his law school education, he had been suspended from practice for a period of 5 years and had great difficulty in gaining reinstatement. Although the wife was entitled to support, the husband, through no fault of his own, lacked the ability to pay.

In *Debacker v. Debacker* (1993), 49 R.F.L. (3d) 106, 143 A.R. 228, 1993 CarswellAlta 453 (Q.B.), the court was of the opinion that the trilogy does not have a place under the 1985 *Divorce Act.* The causal connection element has been removed by the difference between s. 17(4) and its predecessor, and that there need only be a change in circumstances and not a radical change in order to obtain a variation. The proper approach in determining wherther a variation order should be made is to consider the interplay of the relevant sections of s.17. Also, note that s. 17(4) makes no mention of a change that is related to the marriage as was done in s. 17(10) of the Act. Further, Ritter J. was of the opinion that the threshold test contained in s. 17(4) is the same for both spousal and child support and it would be inconsistent to interpret s. 17(4) as retaining jurisdiction respecting child support but precluding spousal support in the same or similar circumstances.

Where a settlement agreement is ambiguous as to whether or not it is subject to variation, it would not constitute a final agreement as contemplated by the trilogy: *Debacker v. Debacker* (1993), 49 R.F.L. (3d) 106, 143 A.R. 228, 1993 CarswellAlta 453 (Q.B.). Such final agreements are only factors to be considered with respect to variation of proceedings under the 1985 *Divorce Act.*

In *Smyth v. Smyth* (1993), 48 R.F.L. (3d) 280, 142 A.R. 132, 1993 CarswellAlta 449 (Q.B.), in minutes of settlement confirmed in the decree *nisi*, the applicant had agreed to pay spousal support to the respondent in the amount of $3,000 per month with no mention as to the rights of the parties to have the level of support reviewed and varied. The applicant required to take early retirement. As the parties would have anticipated that the applicant's income over time would diminish and ultimately cease, they would have anticipated that support would eventually be reduced.

The court was of the opinion that the minutes of settlement were not intended to be final and conclusive in regard to spousal support, and the applicant did not have to show a radical change in his circumstances which was unforeseen by the parties at the time the document was executed. He need only show "a change in the condition, means, needs or other circumstances of either former spouse." Spousal support was reduced.

Since the Supreme Court of Canada in the *Moge* decision has not expressly overruled the *Pelech* trilogy regarding the effect of a final separation agreement on spousal support, the trilogy, on this issue, remains binding authority on all courts, except the Supreme Court of Canada: *Tully v. Tully* (1993), 49 R.F.L. (3d) 31, 1993 CarswellOnt 356 (Gen. Div.).

A final agreement is one intended by the parties to govern fully their future economic relationship, and the fact that it might contemplate changes in quantum does not deprive it of finality: *Tully v. Tully* (1993), 49 R.F.L. (3d) 31, 1993 CarswellOnt 356 (Gen. Div.).

Where an agreement is not final, the *Pelech* decision does not apply, and the court may exercise its discretion pursuant to s. 17 of the *Divorce Act.*

Where the parties, at the time of their divorce, agreed upon limited-term spousal support for the wife, she could not rely on health problems which developed subsequent to the divorce as a basis for the extension of her support. As the wife's need could no longer be causally connected to the marriage, she had failed to bring her case within s. 17(10) of the *Divorce Act* and the variation sought could not, therefore, be granted: *Paredes v. Paredes* (1992), 38 R.F.L. (3d) 267, 1992 CarswellBC 550 (S.C.).

There is no need to prove a causal connection between a spouse's need and the marriage in order for a support order to be continued. A support order will not be automatically terminated under the *Divorce Act* because there is no causal connection between the spouse's need and the marriage: *Bush v. Bush* (1989), 21 R.F.L. (3d) 298, 1989 CarswellOnt 266 (U.F.C.).

An application to terminate support payments was dismissed in *Enns v. Enns* (1989), 68 O.R. (2d) 345, 1989 CarswellOnt 1431 (U.F.C.), where the court was of the opinion that the *Divorce Act*, 1985 does not require that the change in circumstances in s. 17(4) be causally connected or have its genesis in the marriage. The case law developments in the *Pelech* trilogy do not constitute a material change in circumstances. Causal connection is only applicable after a finding of a material change in circumstances.

Change in Circumstances of Payee — Causal Connection — Increase in Support. Where the wife's child care responsibilities following separation had restricted her emplohyment opportunities, and where inflation had eroded the spousal support under an earlier order, her support was ordered increased in recognition of a continuing disadvantage that was attributable to the marriage: *Swift v. Swift* (1989), 23 R.F.L. (3d) 140, 93 N.S.R. (2d) 124, 242 A.P.R. 124, 1989 CarswellNS 64 (Fam. Ct.).

In *MacDonald v. MacDonald* (1991), 107 N.S.R. (2d) 165, 290 A.P.R. 165, 1991 CarswellNS 262 (Fam. Ct.), the wife's nominal support order made at the time of the parties' divorce was increased 12 years later, after the children had grown and left the wife's care. Although the wife's current lack of employment could not be causally connected to the marriage, she had given up some productive economic years to raise the parties' children and had thereby forfeited a build-up of long-term pension equity: *MacDonald v. MacDonald* (1991), 107 N.S.R. (2d) 165, 290 A.P.R. 165, 1991 CarswellNS 262 (Fam. Ct.).

No Change in Circumstances of Payee — Causal Connection — Support Continued. Where the wife suffered from a nervous illness which prevented her from working, and the condition had been aggravated by her pregnancies during the parties' 17-year marriage, the court, on the wife's appeal, restored the monthly support order which had been reduced on the husband's application for variation: *Alexander c. David* (16 avril 1992), nº C.A. Montréal 500-09-001846-914 (C.A. Qué.).

In *De Montigny c. Morin* (30 avril 1992), nº C.A. Québec 200-09-000038-916 (C.A. Qué.), the court upheld the dismissal of the husband's application to reduce support for his 59-year-old wife. The wife had left her employment, at the husband's suggestion, to care for the parties' children and her continuing state of dependency was a result of the marriage.

In *G. (R.) v. B. (E.)* (1992), 53 Q.A.C. 241, (sub nom. *Droit de la famille — 1728)* [1993] R.D.F. 71, 1992 CarswellQue 331 (C.A.), a time limit attached to the wife's support entitlement in the course of a variation application was stricken on appeal. Although the parties had been divorced for over 15 years, the wife had not achieved self-sufficiency because of health problems which had forced her to leave her employment. However, as the wife had remained in the home throughout the parties' 15-year traditional marriage to raise the children and continued to do so after the divorce, her lack of self-sufficiency could be causally connected to the marriage. A time limit upon her support was accordingly inappropriate.

A variation which placed a time limitation on the spousal support of a 60-year-old wife who had remained in the home throughout a lengthy traditional marriage was found to be justified in *Droit de la famille — 1458*, [1991] R.D.F. 686, 39 C.A.Q. 234, 1991 CarswellQue 161 (C.A.).

In *Droit de la famille — 778*, [1990] R.D.F. 169 (C.A. Qué.), the court refused the husband's request for the termination of the wife's spousal support 20 years after the parties' separation. The 57-year-old wife had not worked for 25 years and had a Grade VI education. Her economic condition was a direct result of the marriage, which had placed her in an impoverished position.

In *Droit de la famille — 843*, [1990] R.D.F. 356 (C.A. Qué.) the court affirmed on appeal the dismissal of the husband's application for a reduction in the support payable to the wife. Although the wife had had a promising musical career early in life, the responsibilities resulting from the marriage had made the continuation or resumption of that career impossible. The husband's musical career, on the other hand, had flourished.

Where the wife was 19 years of age with little education at the time of the wedding, and where the husband forbade her to work throughout a long marriage, his application to terminate support 16 years after the parties' divorce was dismissed. The wife's continuing inability to achieve autonomy had been caused by the marriage and its failure, and was likely to continue for the foreseeable future: *Droit de la famille — 664*, [1989] R.D.F. 426, 1989 CarswellQue 233, (sub nom. *sub nom. C. (G.) c. S. (H.))* 29 C.A.Q. 193 (C.A.).

Where the wife developed health problems and lost her employment after the divorce, her application for an increase in support was dismissed. The parties had negotiated the quantum of support, and as the wife's increased need was not causally connected to the marriage, her entitlement to increase support had not been established: *Tremblay v. Tremblay* (1988), 18 R.F.L. (3d) 337, 67 O.R. (2d) 76, 32 E.T.R. 110, 1988 CarswellOnt 325 (H.C.).

Where the health of the wife was such that she was unable to earn a living either before or after the marriage, the court refused the husband's application to terminate support 12 years after the parties' divorce. The support obligation was difficult to terminate given that the wife was unable to provide for her own needs and that the marriage had lasted for may years: *Droit de la famille — 1235*, [1989] R.D.F. 235 (C.S. Qué.).

Where the wife had originally left the work force to care for the parties' children at the husband's request, and where she was 50 years old at the time of the separation and unemployable because of health problems, the husband's application to terminate spousal support was dismissed: *G. (R.) c. L. (Y.)*, [1990] R.L. 47 (C.A. Qué.).

In *Smith v. Smith* (1990), 25 R.F.L. (3d) 256, 1990 CarswellBC 446 (S.C.), the court refused to confirm a provisional order, obtained by the husband six years after the parties' divorce, that would have terminated the wife's support. The wife had supported the family while the husband had completed his education, and her inability to achieve self-sufficiency could still be traced to the emotional effects resulting from the marriage breakdown.

Where the parties' support agreement had been incorporated into the decree *nisi*, the fact that the husband had remarried and that the wife was living in a common-law relationship were insufficient to justify a reduction in the support payable by him. There was no causal connection between the changed circumstances and the marriage, and the agreement had not imposed any obligation on the wife to re-establish herself financially: *Lerette v. Wheaton* (1988), 95 N.B.R. (2d) 350, 241 A.P.R. 350, 1988 CarswellNB 313 (Q.B.).

Change in Circumstances of Payee — Causal Connection No Longer Exists — Support Terminated. Where the wife had developed a debilitating heart problem after the expiration of her limited term support, her application for further support was refused, and the refusal was affirmed on appeal. The wife's incapacity to support herself was in no way related to the marriage: *D. (G.) c. V. (C.)*, [1990] R.L. 272 (C.A. Qué.).

In *McGean v. McGean* (1992), 42 R.F.L. (3d) 251, 1992 CarswellNS 74, 116 N.S.R. (2d) 209, 320 A.P.R. 209 (T.D.), the court retroactively terminated the wife's support order. Following the parties' separation, the wife began to develop an illness which eventually prevented her from working. As the illness was not connected to the marriage and she had made no effort for a number of years to enforce outstanding arrears, her economic dependency could no longer be related to the marriage.

In *Kirby v. Kirby* (1991), 31 R.F.L. (3d) 162, 101 N.S.R. (2d) 226, 275 A.P.R. 226, 1991 CarswellNS 48 (T.D.), the wife, who could not work full-time because of health problems that predated the marriage, had been awarded support upon her divorce, such award being varied to a time-limited one when her health improved. Her application for an extension of the order after her health again deteriorated was refused as her need could no longer be found to be causally connected to the marriage.

Where the husband had been ordered to pay periodic support to his wife, who suffered from an incurable psychiatric illness which required her to be constantly cared for, the court allowed the husband's application to terminate her support. Neither the wife's illness nor her inability to support herself were related to the marriage: *Droit de la famille — 1498,*, [1991] R.D.F. 559 (C.S. Qué.).

In *Wilson v. Wilson* (1990), 104 N.B.R. (2d) 261, 261 A.P.R. 261, 1990 CarswellNB 120 (Q.B.), the court allowed the husband's application to terminate spousal support that had been awarded after 14 years of marriage. The wife had begun full-time employment and there was no evidence that she was earning less than she would have been had she not been married for 14 years.

In *Klaudi v. Klaudi* (1990), 25 R.F.L. (3d) 134, 1990 CarswellOnt 227 (H.C.), the court was of the opinion that the question that underlies a variation application is what is fit and just in the circumstances of the case, having regard to the objectives and considerations set out in the *Divorce Act*. The presence of a causal connection between the need and the marriage does not guarantee support. Where the dependent spouse has not become self-sufficient partly because she was out of the work-force, but also because of an innate shortage of skills and a shortfall in ambition and motivation, the payor spouse should not be required to support the former spouse. The wife had been supported for five years and the support would be terminated in six months. The parties had separated after 20 years of marriage. After the separation, the wife had obtained part-time employment but was not self-sufficient.

Where the wife had worked both during and after the marriage, but had developed debilitating health problems 15 years after the parties' divorce, she was found to be no longer entitled to support, and the support obligation was terminated. The combination of the lapse of time since the divorce and the fact that her health problems were not causally connected to the marriage justified the termination: *Brody v. Brody* (1990), 25 R.F.L. (3d) 319, 105 A.R. 41, 1990 CarswellAlta 268 (Q.B.).

Where the husband had supported the wife for 17 years after separation, the court allowed the husband's application for an order to terminate support. Although the wife was unable to work because of her health, these problems had arisen long after separation and were not related to the marriage: *Droit de la famille — 1194*, [1988] R.D.F. 406 (C.S. Qué.).

In *Beaumont v. Beaumont* (1988), 19 R.F.L. (3d) 33, 95 N.B.R. (2d) 258, 241 A.P.R. 258, 1988 CarswellNB 53 (Q.B.), the 41-year-old unemployed wife had been awarded support upon the dissolution of the parties' seven-year marriage. After the wife obtained employment at a minimum wage, the court granted the husband's application terminating support in two years, citing the facts that it was not the wife's first marriage and that her limited means could not be causally connected to the marriage.

In *Droit de la famille — 1170*, [1988] R.D.F. 180 (C.S. Qué.), the court allowed the husband's application to terminate spousal support nine years after the parties' divorce. The parties had been married for only 18 months and the mental and physical incapacities that prevented the wife from working had existed prior to the marriage.

A Change in Circumstances of payor. In *Jensen v. Jensen (Binns)* (1991), 106 N.S.R. (2d) 247, 288 A.P.R. 247, 1991 CarswellNS 561 (T.D.); affirmed (1992), 39 R.F.L. (3d) 118, 109 N.S.R. (2d) 106, 297 A.P.R. 106, 1992 CarswellNS 59 (C.A.); leave to appeal to S.C.C. refused (1992), 114 N.S.R. (2d) 90, 313 A.P.R. 90, 143 N.R. 392 (S.C.C.), the court refused to vary the child support provision in the parties' separation agreement despite the fact that the payor husband had experienced serious business difficulties. Although the husband had undergone a radical change in circumstances, it was in no way connected to the parties' marriage.

In *Fetterley v. Fetterley* (1988), 14 R.F.L. (3d) 47, 89 A.R. 350, 1988 CarswellAlta 331 (Q.B.); affirmed (1989), 24 R.F.L. (3d) 161, 102 A.R. 131, 1989 CarswellAlta 396 (C.A.), the court rejected the husband's application to terminate maintenance where he had ceased his own employment in order to help his second wife with her business without remuneration. The court held that the reasoning in the *Pelech* decision applied to paying spouses on applications for reduction of maintenance. The court unfortunately did not explain how the *Pelech* test applied in these situations.

In *Francis v. Francis* (1988), 16 R.F.L. (3d) 149, 1988 CarswellOnt 280 (H.C.), the court ruled that deterioration in the husband's mental health since the divorce justified termination of the wife's support unless she could produce evidence of a causal connection between the parties' marriage and her physical misfortune. She suffered from severe hypertension and anginal syndrome and consequently was unable to work. Despite the husband's mental illness, there was no indication that his salary had been reduced, although there appeared to be no hope of career advancement for him. The parties had been married for 25 years and had four children.

Where a payor is seeking a variation of a spousal support order, it is not necessary that a causal connection between the change and the marriage be established: *Savoy v. Savoy* (1989), 23 R.F.L. (3d) 32, 98 N.B.R. (2d) 259, 248 A.P.R. 259, 1989 CarswellNB 23 (Q.B). See also *Swan v. Swan* (1988), 14 R.F.L. (3d) 385, 89 N.B.R. (2d) 111, 226 A.P.R.

111, 1988 CarswellNB 41 (Q.B.); *Ritchie v. Ritchie* (1988), 16 R.F.L. (3d) 163, 1988 CarswellBC 595 (S.C.).

In *Swiderski v. Swiderski* (1988), 15 R.F.L. (3d) 295, 70 Sask. R. 97, 1988 CarswellSask 58 (Q.B.), the husband's decline in income was found to be an insufficient basis on which to lower the amount of child and spousal support set by the parties agreement. As the income decline was not causally connected to the marriage there was no basis for the requested variation.

A payor spouse who seeks to vary a support order and to override the support provisions of a settlement agreement because of a change in his or her circumstances need not prove that the change is causally connected to the marriage: *R. (L.D.) v. R. (H.D.)* (1988), 18 R.F.L. (3d) 280, 1988 CarswellNS 66 (Fam. Ct.).

Burden of Proof— Causal Connection. On a variation application, the burden of proof is upon the payor spouse to establish that the connection no longer exists between the dependent spouse's economic dependency and the marriage: *Goering v. Goering* (1988), 13 R.F.L. (3d) 383, 1988 CarswellOnt 231 (H.C.).

Although remarriage does not automatically disentitle a payee to support, in order for support to continue, the onus is on the payee to establish that, notwithstanding the new relationship, the economic loss resulting from the first relationship remains: *Rosario v. Rosario* (1989), 24 R.F.L. (3d) 168, 102 A.R. 234, 1989 CarswellAlta 398 (Q.B.); reversed on other grounds (1991), 37 R.F.L. (3d) 24, 120 A.R. 331, 1991 CarswellAlta 344, 8 W.A.C. 331 (C.A.).

The *Pelech*, *Richardson* and *Caron* trilogy (*Pelech v. Pelech*, [1987] 1 S.C.R. 801, 7 R.F.L. (3d) 225, 17 C.P.C. (2d) 1, 14 B.C.L.R. (2d) 145, [1987] 4 W.W.R. 481, 76 N.R. 81, 38 D.L.R. (4th) 641, 1987 CarswellBC 147, 1987 CarswellBC 703, [1987] S.C.J. No. 31; *Richardson v. Richardson*, [1987] 1 S.C.R. 857, 7 R.F.L. (3d) 304, 17 C.P.C. (2d) 104, 38 D.L.R. (4th) 699, 77 N.R. 1, 22 O.A.C. 1, 1987 CarswellOnt 315, 1987 CarswellOnt 963, [1987] S.C.J. 30; *Caron v. Caron*, [1987] 1 S.C.R. 892, 7 R.F.L. (3d) 274, [1987] 1 S.C.R. 892, 14 B.C.L.R. (2d) 186, [1987] 4 W.W.R. 522, 75 N.R. 36, 2 Y.R. 246, 38 D.L.R. (4th) 735, 1987 CarswellYukon 8, 1987 CarswellYukon 43, [1987] S.C.J. No. 32) still applies: *Y. (D.) v. Y. (H.)* (1998), 43 R.F.L. (4th) 408, 170 Nfld. & P.E.I.R. 298, 522 A.P.R. 298, 1998 CarswellPEI 113 (T.D. [In Chambers]). Consequently, where the parties have executed a separation agreement intended to be final, and the parties have executed a separation agreement intended to be final, and the agreement was incorporated in the original support order, a court should give considerable weight to the agreement. In this case, the agreement provided that after the limited term support came to an end, no change in the parties' respective financial circumstances that might create a dependency, including by reason of their health or employment, would give the other spouse the right to claim spousal support. The wife experienced symptoms of fatigue before the date of the divorce judgment. The court held that where a spouse has not established that a radical unforeseen change in his or her circumstances has occurred since the date of a final agreement and the change in circumstances is not causally connected to the marriage, a court should not vary the provisions of a divorce judgment whose provisions flow from the parties' separation agreement.

17§48 — Variation — order incorporating spousal support provisions of agreements

In *Miglin v. Miglin* (2003), 34 R.F.L. (5th) 255 (S.C.C.), discussed in detail at 15§147 Overriding jurisdiction of the courts, Bastarache Arbour JJ., writing for the majority, said at paragraph 91,

> . . . it would be inconsistent if a different test applied to change an agreement in the form of an initial order under s. 15.2 and to variation of an agreement incorporated into an order under s. 17. In our view the Act does not create such an inconsistency. . ..The objectives of finality and certainty noted above caution against too broad a discretion in varying an order that the parties have been relying on in arranging their affairs. Consideration of the overall objectives of the Act is consistent with the non-exhaustive direction in s. 17(7) that variation order "should" consider the four objectives listed there. More generally, a contextual approach to interpretation, reading the entire Act, should indicate that the court would apply those objectives in light of the entire statute. Where the order at issue incorporated the mutually acceptable agreement of the parties, that order reflected the parties' understanding of what constituted an equitable sharing of the economic consequences of the marriage. In our view, whether acting under s. 15.2 or under s. 17, the Court should take that into consideration.

A court will vary a spousal support order based on an agreement when there is a change in circumstances of a certain kind. That change is the same change that the court requires to enable it to override an agreement and make an original support order under s. 15: *Richardson v. Richardson*, [1987] 1 S.C.R. 857, 7 R.F.L. (3d) 304, 17 C.P.C. (2d) 104, 38 D.L.R. (4th) 699, 77 N.R. 1; *Santosuosso v. Santosuosso* (1997), 27 R.F.L. (4th) 234, 32 O.R. (3d) 143, 97 O.A.C. 42 (Div. Ct.); and *Large v. Large* (1997), 29 R.F.L. (4th) 188 (B.C. S.C.). The nature of this change has been the subject of several decisions discussed under 15§146.

In *Harris v. Harris* (2000), 10 R.F.L. (5th) 45, 135 O.A.C. 312, 2000 CarswellOnt 2703 (C.A.), the court refused, on appeal, to interfere with the dismissal of the husband's application to vary the spousal support payable by him. The original support order was based upon the parties' settlement agreement in which the husband specifically agreed not to seek a variation. Although the husband had experienced a reduction in income from his construction business, he was well aware when he agreed to the support terms that the construction industry was sensitive to swings in the economy. The husband was an astute businessman and when he entered into the agreement he obviously believed that changes in his ability to earn income were not material to his support obligations.

Where a final separation is incorporated into the decree *nisi*, the wording of the decree providing for the payment of spousal support "until further order" cannot alter the final effect of the agreement for the purposes of a variation application: *Masters v. Masters* (1991), 34 R.F.L. (3d) 34, 84 D.L.R. (4th) 253, 93 Sask. R. 241, 4 W.A.C. 241 (C.A.); affirming (1990), 24 R.F.L. (3d) 374, 82 Sask. R. 190 (Q.B.); affirmed 4 R.F.L. (4th) 1, [1994] 1 S.C.R. 883, 168 N.R. 11, 120 Sask. R. 318, 68 W.A.C. 318, 114 D.L.R. (4th) 575.

A court may vary a support order based upon a final settlement agreement where there is a radical unforeseen reduction in the payor's ability to pay. A reduction in the payor's ability caused by a stroke qualifies as valid grounds for variation: *Smith v. Smith* (1990),

27 R.F.L. (3d) 32, 71 D.L.R. (4th) 612, 66 Man. R. (2d) 181 (C.A.); leave to appeal refused (1991), 32 R.F.L. (3d) 159 (note), 79 D.L.R. (4th) vii (note) (S.C.C.).

The incorporation of a spousal support agreement into a divorce judgment implies that the parties recognize that variation of the amount of support is possible if there is compliance with the variation provisions of the *Divorce Act*: *MacDonald v. MacDonald* (1997), 30 R.F.L. (4th) 1, 200 A.R. 193, 146 W.A.C. 193 (C.A.).

Minutes of settlement, which provide for spousal support "until further order of the court", contemplate a future variation and, accordingly, are not subject to the principles outlined in the Supreme Court trilogy of *Pelech*, [1987] 1 S.C.R. 801, *Caron*, [1987] 1 S.C.R. 892, and *Richardson*, above: *Colp (Silmarie) v. Colp* (1994), 1 R.F.L. (4th) 161, (sub nom. *Colp v. Colp)* 128 N.S.R. (2d) 132, 359 A.P.R. 132, 111 D.L.R. (4th) 252 (C.A.).

A support order which incorporates the provisions of a separation agreement may be varied under s. 17 of the Act where such agreement contemplates future variation: *Barrington v. Barrington* (1991), 38 R.F.L. (3d) 77 (Sask. C.A.).

Where the husband was forced to cease work for a six-month period because of hip surgery, the court, on appeal, reversed an order reducing his monthly support obligation from $4,000 to $3,000. The quantum of support had been settled by the parties, and the husband's decline in income was not substantial in any permanent sense and could have been anticipated at the time of the parties' agreement: *Chant v. Chant* (1990), 30 R.F.L. (3d) 271 (B.C. C.A.).

Where the husband had voluntarily changed jobs and accepted a lower salary, his application to vary support was refused. The order had been based upon the parties' minutes of settlement and the change in the husband's circumstances could not be characterized as material, let alone radical and unforeseen as required by the Supreme Court of Canada trilogy for varying an award based upon a final settlement: *Fetterly v. Fetterly* (1989), 24 R.F.L. (3d) 61, 102 A.R. 131 (C.A.).

Where the husband was unable to comply with a support order because of business reversals from which he was not likely to recover quickly, the court allowed on appeal his application to reduce support, despite the fact that the order had incorporated the parties' agreement: *Kalavrouziotis v. Kalavrouziotis* (1988), 14 R.F.L. (3d) 376 (N.S. C.A.).

Generally, the court will not vary a court order incorporating the spousal support terms of a settlement agreement: *Wiley v. Wiley* (1987), 7 R.F.L. (3d) 68 (B.C. S.C.). See also *Buri v. Dila* (1987), 11 R.F.L. (3d) 373 (Qué. C.A.); *B. (A.) v. M. (C.)* (1987), 11 R.F.L. (3d) 386, (sub nom. *M. v. B.)* 10 Q.A.C. 118, [1988] R.J.Q. 72, (sub nom. *Droit de la famille — 424)* [1988] R.D.F. 72 (C.A.).

In *Meiklejohn v. Meiklejohn* (2001), 2001 CarswellOnt 3480, 19 R.F.L. (5th) 167, 150 O.A.C. 149, C.E.B. & P.G.R. 8395 (note) (Ont. C.A.); additional reasons at (2001), 2001 CarswellOnt 4050 (Ont. C.A.), spousal support was reduced where the payor spouse's income declined when he took earlier than expected retirement from his teaching position. There had been a material change in circumstances from the time of the signing of the parties' separation agreement and there had been a serious reduction in his income.

Where spousal support provisions in a separation agreement allow for variation if there is any change in circumstances, material or not, the parties should be bound by the agreement when the payor could not make the support payments: *Burroughs v. Burroughs* (2004), 2004 CarswellBC 17, 2004 BCSC 7 (B.C. S.C.). In the *Burroughs* case, the parties separated, an interim order was granted and then the parties entered into a separation agreement. The court held that the support set out in the interim order in accordance with the separation agreement be terminated. The petitioner was in need of support but the respondent did not have the means to provide that support unless he were to encroach upon his capital. Their assets had already been divided and the wife had not used her assets or income prudently to plan for her retirement and had therefore had to declare bankruptcy.

Where the husband had retired and the wife had begun to live with a new partner, the husband was successful in reducing the amount of spousal support payable to her pursuant to the parties' earlier minutes of settlement: *Levandusky v. Levandusky* (2003), 39 R.F.L. (5th) 134, 2003 CarswellOnt 2615 (Ont. S.C.J.); additional reasons at (2003), 2003 CarswellOnt 2613 (Ont. S.C.J.).

In *Y. (D.) v. Y. (H.)* (1998), 170 Nfld. & P.E.I.R. 298, 522 A.P.R. 298, 43 R.F.L. (4th) 408 (P.E.I. T.D. [In Chambers]), the parties signed a separation agreement, some of the terms of which were incorporated into a divorce judgment. The wife sought to have spousal support re-instituted, as the agreement had provided for time-limited support. She alleged that the necessary change was her development of chronic fatigue syndrome, a condition that made it impossible for her to be gainfully employed. The court held that it was bound to apply the *Pelech* trilogy as it was without direction from a higher court to do otherwise. It was of the opinion that a court should give considerable weight to a separation agreement which the parties intended to be final and ratified by the original support order. The court in dismissing the wife's claim for a variation of support stated that she had not established that a radical unforeseen change in her circumstances had occurred and any changes that had happened were not causally connected to the marriage.

Where the payor spouse develops a terminal illness which necessitates substantial health costs after the separation agreement has been executed and a consent order at the time of divorce has reduced the amount of support, the court in *Carson v. Carson* (April 8, 1998), Doc. FDSJ-2079-92 (N.B. Q.B.) found that a "radical change in circumstances" which was not foreseen at the time of divorce had occurred. In varying the order and reducing spousal support from $350 to $200 per month, the court found that the fact that the husband was seriously ill with cancer constituted a material change in circumstances as required for a variation under s. 17(1) of the *Divorce Act*.

In *Mendelssohn v. Anderson* (August 17, 1998), Doc. Brampton A5138/97 (Ont. Gen. Div.), the parties had entered into a separation agreement which had been incorporated into a divorce judgment. The husband had ceased making support payments. The husband sought a variation or termination of support. At the time of the separation, the husband had an income of $250,000. Four years later, his employment was terminated and he received $1,000,000 as a settlement. At the time of the variation application, he had an imputed income of $65,000. The former husband had remarried. The court found that there had been a change in the applicant's circumstances and reduced support to $2,000 a month. Arrears of spousal support could be satisfied by redeeming R.R.S.P. savings.

In *Barber v. Barber* (September 25, 1998), Doc. Ottawa 24905/98 (Ont. Gen. Div.), the parties signed a comprehensive separation agreement in which they agreed that spousal support would be reviewed in the court if necessary. No material change in circumstances was required to be demonstrated. In its review, the court held that while the wife might have earned more in another field rather than as a library technician, self-sufficiency was not the only objective of s. 17(7) of the *Divorce Act* and spousal support was still payable at least until the child of the marriage had reached the age of majority. As the former wife was now earning $25,000 more per year than originally, support was reduced from $1,000 to $500 monthly.

In *Fraser v. Fraser* (1998), 227 A.R. 389 (Q.B.), the court considered whether the threshold test set out in s. 17(4.1) of the *Divorce Act* had been met and considered that the appropriate standard is that the court must be satisfied that there has been a material change in circumstances between the time of the prior order and the time of the application before the court. The change would be some unknown matter that arises or changes to a known matter that the parties were unable to anticipate with a requisite degree of certainty. In this case, the parties knew that the wife had developed multiple sclerosis but they did not know the degree to which the disease would affect her in the future. The wife's application was allowed and her support increased to $1,200 per month.

Where the payor spouse develops a terminal illness which necessitates substantial health costs after the separation agreement has been executed and a consent order at the time of divorce has reduced the amount of support, the court in *Carson v. Carson* (April 8, 1998), Doc. FDSJ-2079-92 (N.B. Q.B.) found that a "radical change in circumstances" which was not foreseen at the time of divorce had occurred. In varying the order and reducing spousal support from $350 to $200 per month, the court found that the fact that the husband was seriously ill with cancer constituted a material change in circumstances as required for a variation under s. 17(1) of the *Divorce Act*.

In *Bradley v. Bradley* (1997), 29 R.F.L. (4th) 151 (Ont. Gen. Div.), the parties signed a separation agreement which precluded variation proceedings except for a catastrophic change in either party's circumstances. At the time the agreement was signed the parties knew that the applicant wife was suffering from multiple sclerosis. The court was of the opinion that even though the parties knew of the wife's illness, the court was not prevented from considering her illness on an application to vary. The court held that where, as in this case, the parties had agreed to a provision permitting an application to the courts based on a change in circumstances, the prerequisite test of unforseeability did not apply. The wife proved that her deterioration in health in the two years before the application amounted to a "catastrophic change". The court in determining spousal support considered the appropriate amount based on the respondent's ability to pay. In balancing the interests of the first wife with those of the respondent's second family, particularly to those of his children who were 12 and 14, the court was of the opinion that the respondent could not meet all of the first wife's financial needs and she might be required to look to government and community resources to assist her with her remaining medical expenses. Spousal support was increased by a further $393 per month.

In *Robinson v. Robinson* (1997), 33 O.T.C. 297, 1997 CarswellOnt 2437 (Gen. Div.), the court upheld a divorce judgment which incorporated minutes of settlement whereby the husband was required to pay $1,300 monthly for the support of the wife. The court relied on *Willick v. Willick*, 6 R.F.L. (4th) 161, [1994] 3 S.C.R. 670, 119 D.L.R. (4th) 405, 125 Sask. R. 81, 173 N.R. 321, [1994] R.D.F. 617 in holding that in order to grant a variation, there must be a change in circumstances which, if known at the time, would have resulted in different terms. Conversely, if a matter were known at the relevant time, it could not be relied on as a basis for variation. The parties' incomes had both increased since the divorce judgment but those increases were clearly anticipated at the time of separation. The parties were aware of the wife's impending inheritance at the time they executed the minutes of settlement. Further, the wife's present income of $64,851.22 did not render her self-sufficient within the meaning of s. 17(7) of the *Divorce Act*. The wife's employment was uncertain, given her health and lack of education and skills.

In *Wilson v. Pollard* (1997), 31 O.T.C. 206, 1997 CarswellOnt 757, [1997] O.J. No. 1017 (Gen. Div.), the parties had executed a separation agreement in which each released the other from any claims against his or her respective pension or retirement savings plans and subsequently they signed a consent order for spousal support which was indexed to the applicant's net employment income. The former husband was forced to retire from his employment and claimed that he was no longer required to pay spousal support. The court found that the separation agreement was a valid binding agreement and that the consent order was a final order which expressed the real intention of the parties. When the former husband was forced to retire, his employment income was reduced to zero and his pension income was not available to the wife as she had released her interest in his pension by signing the separation agreement. The husband was no longer required to pay spousal support.

In *Garner v. Garner* (1997), 35 R.F.L. (4th) 262, [1998] 5 W.W.R. 443, 160 Sask. R. 95 (Q.B.), it was held that the husband's loss of employment was an insufficient change in circumstances to relieve him from his spousal support obligations contained in minutes of settlement to which both parties had agreed. Although payment under the minutes was qualified specifically by the condition that the husband remain employed, the 72-week severance package received by him resulted in no immediate change to his financial position. As the 72-week period had not expired, the husband could conceivably still find alternate employment before his financial situation truly changed.

The husband's application for termination of spousal support and the wife's cross-application for an increase in spousal support were both dismissed in *Sneideman v. Sneideman* (1998), 125 Man. R. (2d) 214 (Q.B.). The parties entered into a separation agreement in which the husband agreed to pay the wife spousal support of the difference between her earnings and $1,000 per month. The parties agreed that all of the terms of the agreement would survive divorce. The parties had one daughter whom the husband supported. The decree *nisi* provided that the husband pay the wife $1,000 per month. The husband had remarried and had two very young children. The first wife developed mental illness during the marriage and continued to suffer from this disability. The court was of the opinion that all of the changes in the parties' circumstances were not sufficient to warrant a variation of spousal support as required by s. 17(4)(1) of the *Divorce Act*. The court considered s. 17(7) of the *Divorce Act* and found that the first wife had been economically disadvantaged both by the marriage and its breakdown. Further, because of her mental illness she had, so far as was practicable, done all she could to become economically self-sufficient. Following *Moge v. Moge* (1992), 43 R.F.L. (3d) 345, [1992] 3 S.C.R. 813, [1993] 1 W.W.R. 481, 99 D.L.R. (4th) 456, 145 N.R. 1, 81 Man. R. (2d) 161, 30 W.A.C. 161 and *Kloos v. Kloos*, [1996] 5 W.W.R. 553, 20 R.F.L. (4th) 1, 110 Man. R. (2d) 129, 118 W.A.C. 129 (C.A.), the court was of the opinion that the model for support under the *Divorce Act* was compensatory in nature, providing an equitable sharing of economic consequences of the marriage and its break-up.

Where the parties sign a comprehensive separation agreement which is incorporated in a consent order, the person seeking to vary the order must demonstrate a radical and unforeseen change in circumstances: *Knechtel v. Knechtel* (August 15, 1997), Doc. Prince George 30594/95 (B.C. S.C.). The fact that the former wife had remarried did not constitute such a change. Her remarriage ought to have been in the contemplation of both parties as they negotiated a final settlement of their own marriage. Further, while the wife's current husband had a significant income, marriages do not necessarily represent life-long security. The wife's remarriage is neither radical nor unforeseen and she does not have income on which she may rely as a matter arising from her own capacity. The parties' agreement that the respondent was to provide the petitioner with a university education falls squarely within the statutory objectives of a spousal support award, as a means of providing the spouse with a new career.

The husband's application to rescind spousal support and the wife's cross-application to vary spousal maintenance upwards were both dismissed in *Shephard v. Fancy* (March 20, 1998), Doc. S.H. 1201-43005/89 (N.S. S.C. [In Chambers]) where the court held that as the payor spouse's financial circumstances had deteriorated an the payee spouse's mental and physical condition had also deteriorated, there would be no change in the amount of support from that amount set out in the parties' separation agreement which was subsequently incorporated in a corollary relief judgment. The parties' changes in circumstances had cancelled each other out. The court considered the factors set out in s. 17(7) and found that it did not assist the wife but at the same time the husband could not eliminate his obligation to support the wife as set out in the agreement.

In *Lipschitz v. Lipschitz* (1998), 41 R.F.L. (4th) 108 (B.C. S.C.), the court held that where the parties have entered into a final separation agreement in which they agreed that no spousal maintenance would be payable beyond a limited period and the parties signed a consent order, a variation will only be granted when the test of a change of circumstances within the meaning of s. 17 of the *Divorce Act* has been met. The change must be a material change which is substantial, unforeseen and of a continuing nature. In this decision, the parties at the time of signing the separation agreement knew that their daughter needed counselling. Therefore, the test, if applied to the daughter, would have indicated that no such change could be said to have occurred. However, there were changes in a different sense. The wife upgraded her education, but with the deterioration in the health of her daughter, she left her employment and cared for the daughter for two years. The court found that the wife was justified in making her decisions relating to her daughter. The change in the wife's plans from re-introduction into the work force to remaining at home to care for a sick child was a material change and one not known or foreseen at the time of entering into the separation agreement. It was substantial and unforeseen and of a continuing nature as it caused the wife to be economically dependent. The court awarded an additional year of support but reduced the amount from $3,000 provided in the separation agreement to $2,000 per month.

In *Hansen v. Hansen* (1997), 31 R.F.L. (4th) 384 (N.S. S.C.), the parties signed a separation agreement which was incorporated in the decree *nisi* with certain modifications and was amended again after divorce. The parties had been married for 35 years and the wife had been a traditional stay-at-home wife and mother for the first 16 years. She later upgraded her education and obtained employment. According to the agreement amended after divorce, the wife was to receive spousal support until she was economically self-sufficient. The wife had inherited rental property, her share of which was valued at between $127,000 and $137,000.

In the *Hansen* decision, the court was of the opinion that where a spouse remains economically dependent on the spousal support provided by their separation agreement, the spouse is entitled to such support. Where, however, as in this decision, the spouse has valuable assets, such as registered retirement savings plans and an interest in the real property from her mother's estate, both of which are income producing assets which could provide her with income which would approximately equal her present income including support, her spousal support should not necessarily be continued. The agreement provided for a review of maintenance and to consider "... any change in the conditions, means or other circumstances of ... the parties." The court found that the wife was in some measure dependent on the husband but reduced spousal maintenance from $1,230 monthly under the agreement to $410 monthly.

Where, as in *Verbrugge v. Verbrugge* (1997), 28 R.F.L. (4th) 35 (B.C. S.C.), the parties had executed a separation agreement which provided for spousal support for one year and thereafter $1 each year and either party could apply to change the quantum of support if there were a material change in his or her circumstances, the court held that the wife had met the threshold test for which the parties had contracted as well as the test as to whether or not the parties' changes were material and also the test of a change of a substantial, unforeseen and a continuing nature as set out in *Carter v. Carter* (1991), 34 R.F.L. (3d) 1, 58 B.C.L.R. (2d) 45, 2 B.C.A.C. 241, 5 W.A.C. 241 (C.A.).

Where the parties' separation agreement allowed the husband to vary the quantum of spousal support payable in accordance with fluctuations in his income, he was required to include severance pay received on termination of his position as income. The husband had reduced the amount paid to his wife after receiving severance and finding new employment. He was accordingly ordered to pay increased support as well as support arrears: *Richard v. Richard* (1994), 2 R.F.L. (4th) 395, 145 N.B.R. (2d) 383, 372 A.P.R. 383 (Q.B.).

Where a support provision of a separation agreement is incorporated into a decree *nisi*, an application to vary support relates to the decree and not to the original agreement: *King Estate v. King* (1994), 8 R.F.L. (4th) 380, 153 N.B.R. (2d) 20, 392 A.P.R. 20 (Q.B.).

In *Smyth v. Smyth* (1993), 48 R.F.L. (3d) 280, 142 A.R. 132 (Q.B.), the court allowed for a reduction in the quantum of spousal support payable to the wife pursuant to minutes of settlement. The agreement had been predicated on the understanding that the husband would work to his normal retirement age and that the wife would obtain employment. The husband's forced early retirement was a radical unforeseen change in circumstances which permitted the variation, even in the absence of a specific clause in the minutes allowing for variation. In setting the new support payable, the failure of the wife to seek employment commensurate with her education and experience was also properly considered.

The radical unforeseen change in circumstances standard is not applicable to an application for variation of support based upon the incorporation of a separation agreement into a decree *nisi* where the agreement specifically allowed for variation: *Winsor v. Winsor* (1992), 39 R.F.L. (3d) 8, 8 O.R. (2d) 433 (C.A.); reversing (1992), 39 R.F.L. (3d) 1 (Ont. Gen. Div.).

In *Coskey v. Coskey* (1992), 39 R.F.L. (3d) 449 (Alta. Q.B.), the court refused to vary the quantum of spousal support payable by the husband pursuant to earlier *minutes of settlement*. Although the wife had found full-time employment, the settlement had contemplated that she would do so. Furthermore, the husband was unable to meet the radical unforeseen change standard required to override the settlement agreement.

The radical unforeseen change standard does not apply to the variation of support orders based upon minutes of settlement, where the minutes and order contemplate future variation: *Harris v. Gilbert* (1992), 39 R.F.L. (3d) 458 (Ont. Gen. Div.).

In *Gallagher v. Hogg* (1993), 45 R.F.L. (3d) 337 (Man. Q.B.), the facts that the payee wife had commenced to live with another man, had received a modest inheritance and an increase in salary were not sufficient grounds to vary a support order based upon the parties' final settlement agreement. However, a drastic decrease in the husband's salary did meet the "unforeseen change in circumstances" test and a reduction in spousal support was justified.

Where the support provisions of the parties' agreement are incorporated into a decree *nisi*, a party seeking a variation of support needs to prove a change in circumstances from the date of the order and not from the date of the agreement: *Huey v. Huey* (1991), 39 R.F.L. (3d) 14 (Ont. Gen. Div.).

Where the husband had lost his job and suffered a decline in income, his application to vary the agreement-based spousal support was refused. The husband's circumstances were not connected to the marriage and could properly be considered as part of the normal "ups and downs" of life that the parties had in mind when they negotiated the settlement: *Smith v. Smith* (1991), 32 R.F.L. (3d) 353 (Ont. Gen. Div.).

In a variation application dealing with a consent order based upon the support provision of the parties' separation agreement, the court must be guided by the relevant provisions of the *Divorce Act* and by the nature of the parties' bargain. However, if the agreement is found to have been unfair to the payee spouse from its inception, the court's decision on the variation application is not fettered by the agreement: *Davies v. Davies* (1991), 32 R.F.L. (3d) 14 (Ont. Gen. Div.).

Where the parties' minutes of settlement anticipate a future variation of support, the radical unforeseen change of circumstances onus is not applicable: *Jerowsky v. Jerowsky* (1990), 32 R.F.L. (3d) 188, 114 A.R. 381 (Q.B.).

Where by minutes of settlement the husband had agreed to pay specified maintenance to his wife, his subsequent application to vary the sum was dismissed. The husband had freely entered into the agreement and no change of circumstances had occurred: *Carrigan v. Carrigan* (1987), 80 N.S.R. (2d) 276, 200 A.P.R. 276 (T.D.).

A court should only override the support provisions of a settlement agreement that has been incorporated into a court order where there has been a radical change in the parties' circumstances since the granting of the decree. Changes which were contemplated by the parties at the time of the agreement, such as remarriage of the payee spouse, do not constitute radical change: *Tomlin v. Christie* (1987), 10 R.F.L. (3d) 292 (Sask. Q.B.).

Where five years after the divorce the wife agreed to accept a lump sum in exchange for renouncing the periodic support payable to her under the parties' decree, it was held that she could not bring an application to vary the support provisions of the decree. The award no longer existed and therefore could not be varied: *Droit de la famille — 1052*, [1986] R.D.F. 553 (C.S. Qué).

Even where a separation agreement reflects the parties' intention that the spousal support payable thereunder was intended as a pension for life, the court has, in appropriate circumstances, the power to vary an order based upon such an agreement. To vary the order, the payor must prove a radical change in circumstances and that such change was outside the reasonable contemplation of the parties at the time of the agreement: *Byers v. Byers* (1989), 23 R.F.L. (3d) 280 (Ont. H.C.).

Where the parties had entered into minutes of settlement calling for payment of only nominal support by the unemployed husband to his ill wife, such agreement was found not to constitute a final agreement for variation purposes. Accordingly the agreement was variable upon proof by the wife of a "material change in circumstances" rather than proof of a "radical change": *Basciano v. Basciano* (1989), 23 R.F.L. (3d) 246 (Ont. H.C.).

Where the husband was forced to retire early because of health reasons, the court allowed his application to reduce the support payable pursuant to the parties' separation agreement. The reduction in the husband's income was not reasonably foreseeable when the agreement was executed: *Sheahan v. Sheahan* (1989), 21 R.F.L. (3d) 206 (Ont. H.C.).

Where the husband had agreed to pay spousal support by minutes of settlement, his obligation was later terminated in the face of his retirement and the wife's confinement to a nursing home. The husband's ability to pay was limited and as the wife was able to cover her living arrangements from her own resources, she no longer had need of support: *Goddard v. Goddard* (1988), 16 R.F.L. (3d) 453 (Ont. H.C.).

In *Leman v. Leman* (1988), 14 R.F.L. (3d) 122 (Ont. H.C.), the court refused to vary a spousal support order which was based upon the parties' written agreement, although the husband's income had decreased and the wife had found employment since the date of the agreement. The changes in the parties' financial positions were foreseeable at the time of the agreement and the decrease in the husband's income was not a change related to the marriage.

The *Divorce Act, 1985* does not change the principles governing variations of a decree based upon a separation agreement. Such a decree should not be disturbed in the absence of a drastic change in circumstances: *Neufeld v. Neufeld* (1986), 3 R.F.L. (3d) 435 (Ont. H.C.).

Where the husband had, through minutes of settlement, agreed to the quantum of spousal support payable, his subsequent retirement was found not to constitute sufficient grounds for a reduction of the amount. As the minutes of settlement were intended to be final, they could only be varied in the face of a radical change in circumstances. As the parties must have contemplated the husband's eventual retirement, the radical change threshold had not been met: *LaPierre v. LaPierre* (1995), 10 R.F.L. (4th) 327, 137 N.S.R. (2d) 189, 391 A.P.R. 189 (S.C.).

The court has jurisdiction to incorporate a separation agreement into a divorce judgment and to vary it retroactively. There is no general principle that a party seeking such incorporation or variation must first pay all arrears outstanding under the agreement: *Pousette v. Pousette* (1993), 46 R.F.L. (3d) 152 (B.C. S.C.).

In *Cooper v. Cooper* (1998), 42 R.F.L. (4th) 317, 168 Nfld. & P.E.I.R. 58, 517 A.P.R. 58 (Nfld. U.F.C.), the husband was not allowed to rely upon a cohabitation clause in the parties' separation agreement to justify termination of the wife's spousal support. The agreement allowed for termination if the wife lived with another man as husband and wife. Although the wife shared a home with her boyfriend in Florida for several months of the year, she maintained separate financial arrangements and paid for her own food. She also maintained a separate residence during the balance of the year.

Where the parties, by consent order, ended the wife's spousal support in 1985, the court refused the wife's application for re-instatement in 1992. The parties had consented to the termination with benefit of counsel and the granting of such an application would allow any divorce order to be reinstated in the face of a valid agreement: *Shaw v. Rhude* (1993), 129 N.S.R. (2d) 234, 362 A.P.R. 234 (Fam. Ct.).

The court's discretion in variation applications involving separation agreements which have been engrossed in a decree *nisi*, should not be restricted to circumstances where there have been radical changes related to the marriage unless the parties have entered into a final agreement. If an agreement lacks the element of finality then the higher test is not justified: *Publicover v. Publicover* (1987), 9 R.F.L. (3d) 308 (N.S. Fam. Ct.).

Where the former husband has not met the onus on him of establishing that his current circumstances represent a significant departure from the range of reasonable outcomes anticipated by the parties at the time their support order was made, which incorporated their separation agreement, a court is unable to proceed to the next step and examine whether the circumstances place the parties at odds with the objectives of the act, so that the agreement should be given little weight: *Venables v. Venables* (2004), 2004 CarswellSask 85, 2004 SKQB 29 (Sask. U.F.C.).

17§49 — Variation of child support orders — *Federal Child Support Guidelines*

The law governing the award of child support and the variation of child support orders was radically changed by the amendments to the *Divorce Act* and the establishment of *Federal Child Support Guidelines*, both of which became effective on May 1, 1997. (The law for the determination and variation of *spousal* support was not changed.)

Under the amendments to the *Divorce Act*, the courts retain the same wide power that they had before the amendments to deal with the amount and terms of support on an application to vary a support order. A court "may make an order varying, rescinding or suspending, prospectively or retroactively, ... a support order or any provision thereof on application by either or both former spouses": *Divorce Act*, s. 17(1)(a). A condition precedent to the making of the order (same condition as before the amendments) is that the court must satisfy itself that a change of circumstances has occurred since the order was made or varied: *Divorce Act*, s. 17(4). What is radically new with the amendments is the way the amount of support is to be determined (see, s. 15, above), and the additional events that constitute a change in circumstances.

The change of circumstances which must occur is a change of circumstances as defined in the guidelines: *Divorce Act*, s. 17(4). The federal guidelines provide that a change of circumstances is:

- in the case of an order made before May 1, 1997, the mere fact that the law of child support changed on May 1, 1997: *Federal Child Support Guidelines*: s. 14(c) and *Divorce Act*, s. 17(4);
- in the case where an amount in an order was determined in accordance with the applicable table, any change in circumstance that would result in a different child support order: *Federal Child Support Guidelines*, s. 14(a) and *Divorce Act*, s. 17(4); and
- in the case where the amount does not include a determination in accordance with the applicable table, any change in the condition, means, needs or other circumstances of either spouse or of any child who is entitled to support: *Federal Child Support Guidelines*, s. 14(b) and *Divorce Act*, s. 17(4).

After finding that a change in circumstances has occurred, the court may then make a variation order. The order must be in accordance with the guidelines: *Divorce Act*, s. 17(6.1) and *Federal Child Support Guidelines*, s. 2(4)(b). See commentary under s. 15, above.

Because different approaches are used to determine child support and spousal support, and because different tax treatment follows from whether the order is for child support or spousal support, a special provision was enacted for dealing with global orders. Sections 34(1.1) and 35.1(2) of the *Divorce Act* now provide that where the order to be varied is a global award for the combined support of both spouse and child or children, the court must rescind the award and treat the application to vary as two separate original applications; an original application for spousal support and a second original application for child support.

The discretion to vary a child support order must include the discretion not to vary. Only if a court determines that child support should be varied does the application of the *Guidelines* become mandatory under s. 17(6.1) and subject to the exception in s. 17(6.2): *Wang v. Wang* (1998), 39 R.F.L. (4th) 426, 164 D.L.R. (4th) 146, 58 B.C.L.R. (3d) 159, [1999] 4 W.W.R. 752, 110 B.C.A.C. 302, 178 W.A.C. 302 (C.A.); affirming (1997), 41 B.C.L.R. (3d) 375 (S.C. [In Chambers]).

The Court has discretion under the *Guidelines* as to whether a variation of child support should be granted, even if one of the listed criteria for such variation is satisfied: *Hogan v. Hogan* (2004), 8 R.F.L. (6th) 250, 2004 CarswellOnt 3896 (S.C.J.).

The *Federal Child Support Guidelines* are determinative of the amount of support whether the court is hearing an initial application for support or an application to vary an existing order: *Katzer v. Egeland* (1997), 33 R.F.L. (4th) 416 (Sask. Q.B.).

17§50 — Child support — change in circumstances — orders before May 1997

The change of circumstances which must occur is a change of circumstances as defined in the guidelines: *Divorce Act*, s. 17(4). In the case of an order made before May 1, 1997, there are two circumstances which fall within the definition. One is the mere fact that the law of child support changed on May 1, 1997: *Federal Child Support Guidelines*, s. 14(c) and *Divorce Act*, s. 17(4). The second is any new circumstance amounting to the familiar "change in the condition, means, needs or other circumstances of either spouse or of any child who is entitled to support": *Federal Child Support Guidelines*, s. 14(b) and *Divorce Act*, s. 17(4). (See 17§52 Child support — change in circumstances — change in condition, means, needs or other circumstances — general, below).

On December 9, 1997, the introduction to s. 14 of the *Federal Child Support Guidelines* was amended to clarify that only one of the listed circumstances was sufficient to invoke the court's jurisdiction to consider making a variation order. The amendment replaced the words, "a change of circumstances is", which introduced the list, with the words, "any one of the following constitutes a change of circumstances".

Section 14(c) of the *Federal Child Support Guidelines* is a decree by Parliament that the coming into force of the *Guidelines* constitutes a change in circumstances which will support an application for variation of child support. Furthermore, a strong presumption exists in favour of such a variation: *Lister v. Gould*, 11 R.F.L. (5th) 167, 231 N.B.R. (2d) 161, 597 A.P.R. 161, 2000 NBCA 33, 2000 CarswellNB 425 (C.A.).

Where the parties' consent divorce judgment was silent on the issue of child support, it was found that the intention by both parties to incorporate the terms of the interim child support order had not been sufficiently established. The interim order had been made one day before the *Federal Child Support Guidelines* came into force. The court therefore allowed the father's appeal from the dismissal of his application to vary the interim order to bring it into line with *Guidelines* amounts and ordered a hearing on the issue: *Rist v. Rist*, 13 R.F.L. (5th) 179, 199 Sask. R. 204, 232 W.A.C. 204, 2000 SKCA 115, 2000 CarswellSask 821 (Sask. C.A.).

Parliament did not intend to make a variation of every existing child support agreement and order to comply with the *Guidelines* mandatory upon application by either party. The court still retains a discretion not to vary an agreement flowing from s. 17(1) of the *Divorce Act* which provides that a court "may" make a variation order: *Fullerton v. Fullerton* (1999), 49 R.F.L. (4th) 255 (B.C. C.A.).

The coming into force of the *Federal Child Support Guidelines* does not automatically result in a downward variation of an earlier child support award which is greater than the *Guidelines* amount. The court is also required to consider a variety of other factors in determining whether an order should be varied. A material change in the circumstances of some family member is still required: *Baker v. Baker* (1999), 49 R.F.L. (4th) 162, 127 B.C.A.C. 1, 207 W.A.C. 1 (C.A.).

In *Wang v. Wang* (1998), 39 R.F.L. (4th) 426, 164 D.L.R. (4th) 146, 58 B.C.L.R. (3d) 159, [1999] 4 W.W.R. 752, 110 B.C.A.C. 302, 178 W.A.C. 302 (C.A.), it was held that, although the implementation, by itself, of the *Federal Child Support Guidelines* on May 1, 1997 gives the court a discretion to vary a prior child support order made in divorce proceedings, it is not required to exercise that discretion simply because the amount is different from the amount in the *Guidelines*. The discretion includes a right not to vary.

In *Klain v. Klain* (1998), 36 R.F.L. (4th) 214, 165 N.S.R. (2d) 58, 495 A.P.R. 58 (C.A.). the mother applied for leave to appeal from a decision refusing to grant leave to the appellant to appeal from a variation of an interim child support order in a pending divorce proceeding. The interim order was made before the enactment of the *Federal Child Support Guidelines*. The coming into force of the *Guidelines*, in combination with the amendments to the *Divorce Act* and *Income Tax Act* changed the law in regard to calculating child support and the associated income tax consequences. Section 14(c) of the *Guidelines* provides that for the purposes of s. 17(4) of the *Divorce Act* with respect to variation orders made before May 1st, 1997, the change in the law is a "change of circumstances". As a result, a court hearing a variation application has a discretion to order a variation by reason of that fact alone. The court in dismissing the appeal held that the judge who had heard the interim custody and child support application took into consideration the tax consequences in the order he made, and there was no evidence of exceptional circumstances that would have warranted the judge hearing the variation application granting leave to the appellant to apply for an upward variation in the support order. The trial is the proper place to remedy the situation if any remedy is needed.

In *Lee v. Lee* (1998), 43 R.F.L. (4th) 339, 165 D.L.R. (4th) 619, 167 Nfld. & P.E.I.R. 176, 513 A.P.R. 176 (Nfld. C.A.), the wife appealed a child support order which had originally been made before the guidelines were adopted and which had been varied after the *Guidelines* were in force. The father's work situation had changed since the making of the original order, as his guaranteed wage plan benefit had expired and he maintained that for the foreseeable future, his income would be based solely on employment insurance. The wife argued that even though the husband had lost a component of his previous income, the judge ought to have fixed his income for the purpose of the application of the *Guidelines* on the basis of the husband's gross taxable income for the previous three years. The court, in dismissing the appeal held that past financial information will not be a reliable predictor of the payor-spouse's ability to pay, where the evidence indicates that income is and for the foreseeable future will be substantially different from historical income levels. Section 2(3) of the *Guidelines* supports this analysis since it requires the use of "the most current information".

In *Daoust c. Leboeuf* (1998), 35 R.F.L. (4th) 143, 107 O.A.C. 73 (C.A.), the trial judge made his judgment in light of the proposed *Federal Child Support Guidelines*. The evidence before the court did not allow proper evaluation of child support. Any change in child support should be made in light of the guidelines and in the context of a variation request in accordance with ss. 17(4) and 17(6.1) of the *Divorce Act*.

A retroactive application of the *Federal Child Support Guidelines* is not appropriate according to *Andries v. Andries*, 36 R.F.L. (4th) 175, [1998] 7 W.W.R. 536, 159 D.L.R. (4th) 665, 126 Man. R. (2d) 189 (C.A.). An interim order was made for support in 1995, with the understanding that the husband would pay certain expenses until the matrimonial home was sold. Once the house was sold the husband paid the same amount of support. The wife at trial sought a retroactive lump sum award of child support to compensate her for the period before trial when she was receiving nothing or only the amount in the interim order. The appellate court was of the opinion that a lump sum payment for child support that a spouse was entitled to receive for a period prior to trial before the guidelines were enacted should be assessed on principles applicable at that time and not on the basis of the guidelines which had only come into force by the time of trial.

In *Porcari v. Porcari* (1997), 34 R.F.L. (4th) 156 (Ont. C.A.), the trial occurred prior to the enactment of the guidelines and the appeal after their enactment. The appellate court found that as the husband's income was minimal, under the *Federal Child Support Guidelines* he would not be required to pay child support. There was no basis for a lump sum payment. The court ordered support in the amount equal to eight percent of net proceeds to the husband from the sale of the matrimonial home, after the husband made an equalization payment ordered by the trial judge and paid half the realty tax arrears.

In *Dennis v. Wilson* (1997), 35 R.F.L. (4th) 146, 104 O.A.C. 250 (C.A.); additional reasons at (1998), 42 R.F.L. (4th) 131, 115 O.A.C. 370, [1999] 2 C.T.C. 175 (C.A.), the court was of the opinion that as the *Federal Child Support Guidelines* were not in force at the time of the original application for support, they did not govern the determination of child support on appeal after the guidelines were in force. They were, however, instructive. In this case, the trial judge had based his decision on quantum of child support upon the father's affidavit as to expenses when the parties had joint custody of their child and were paying the upkeep of two households. By the date of trial, the child resided primarily with the mother. The trial judge ordered the father to pay $3,900 a month in child support. On appeal, the court considered what the quantum would be if the *Guidelines* were applied, taking into account among other matters the mother's decision to change her occupation which resulted in a lower income. The court allowed the appeal and reduced the father's child support to $2,400 a month which was grossed up for tax purposes.

In *Prince v. Prince* (1997), 35 R.F.L. (4th) 328, 163 N.S.R. (2d) 28, 487 A.P.R. 28 (C.A.), the appellate court was of the view that it would be inappropriate for the court of appeal to assess child support according to the *Guidelines* since those guidelines had not come into effect when the original award was made and were not considered by the trial judge.

In *Hughes v. Hughes* (1997), 35 R.F.L. (4th) 185, 164 N.S.R. (2d) 323, 491 A.P.R. 323 (C.A.), the court was of the opinion that the *Federal Child Support Guidelines* have no impact upon an appeal from a variation made before the guidelines became effective.

Provisions dealing with the special expenses of children found in a separation agreement that predates the *Guidelines* are subject to variation as a result of the passing of the legislation: *Roy v. Hart* (2003), 48 R.F.L. (5th) 112, 2003 CarswellOnt 4882 (Ont. S.C.J.).

Although the coming into force of the *Guidelines* constitutes a "change of circumstances" entitling a spouse to seek a variation of child support, the court retains the discretion to refuse the variation: *Turner v. Turner* (2000), 11 R.F.L. (5th) 411, 2000 ABQB 683, [2001] 3 W.W.R. 465, 274 A.R. 124, 87 Alta. L.R. (3d) 193, 2000 CarswellAlta 1135 (Q.B.); additional reasons at (2000), 11 R.F.L. (5th) 432, [2001] 3 W.W.R. 486, 247 A.R. 124 at 143, 87 Alta. L.R. (3d) 214, 2000 CarswellAlta 1136 (Q.B.); additional reasons at 2001 CarswellAlta 769, 2001 ABQB 479, 289 A.R. 352 (Alta. Q.B.); additional reasons at 2001 CarswellAlta 1614, 2001 ABQB 1010 (Alta. Q.B.).

Where the amount of child support payable by the father under the parties' agreement contemplated the sale by the mother of her business, the mother's application for increased child support was allowed when the sale failed to materialize. In addition to that significant change, the fact that the parties agreement predated the coming into force of s. 15.1 of the *Divorce Act* triggered an automatic change of circumstances under s. 14(c) of the *Federal Child Support Guidelines*: *Todd v. Morine* (1999), 46 R.F.L. (4th) 391 (N.B. Q.B.).

In *Burns v. Burns* (1998), 40 R.F.L. (4th) 32 (Ont. Gen. Div.), the wife applied successfully to vary the parties' child support order 13 months after their divorce. The *Federal Child Support Guidelines* had come into force in the interim and there was no "special" provision in the parties' settlement that would benefit the children and justify a departure from the *Guidelines*.

The enactment of the *Federal Child Support Guidelines* constitutes a material change in circumstances potentially justifying a variation in child support: *Rivett v. Bylund* (1998), 40 R.F.L. (4th) 416 (Ont. Gen. Div.).

In *Ireland v. McMillan* (1997), 36 R.F.L. (4th) 48, 124 Man. R. (2d) 114 (Q.B.), the court refused the wife's application to have an earlier child support order reassessed under the *Federal Child Support Guidelines*. Application of the *Guidelines* would actually have resulted in a lower support award and an inequity to the child.

A court is not compelled to a vary a child support order made before the proclamation of the *Federal Child Support Guidelines* simply because it was made prior to the *Guidelines*. Proof of changed circumstances is still required: *Vanderstoep v. Vanderstoep* (1998), 35 R.F.L. (4th) 385 (B.C. S.C. [In Chambers]).

In *Laroque v. Allooloo* (1999), 48 R.F.L. (4th) 381 (N.W.T. S.C.), the court allowed the father's application for a reduction of child support payable by him to *Guidelines* amounts after the *Guidelines* come into force.

In *Goudie v. Buchanan* (2001), 19 R.F.L. (5th) 280, 2001 CarswellNfld 185, 203 Nfld. & P.E.I.R. 34, 610 A.P.R. 34 (Nfld. U.F.C.), the court accepted the husband's claim of undue hardship in varying the child support payable by him to a level below that specified in the *Guidelines*. The father had returned to school after work in his field had all but dried up. As his monthly expenses greatly exceeded his income, payment of the Table Amounts would have caused the father undue hardship. As the father's primary goal in returning to school rather than working was not to lower his child support payments, it was not an appropriate case for imputing income to him.

17§50A — Applicable table

A court making a variation order in respect of a child support order must do so in accordance with the applicable guidelines: *Divorce Act*, s. 17(6.2). The applicable guidelines are defined in s. 2 of the Act.

17§51 — Child support — change in circumstances — change which would produce different order

In the case where an amount in an order was determined in accordance with the applicable table, one type of change that amounts to a change of circumstances enabling the court to consider making a variation order is "any change in circumstances that would result in a different child support order or any provision thereof": *Divorce Act*, s. 17(4) and *Federal Child Support Guidelines*, s. 14(a). A second type of change is any new circumstance amounting to the more familiar "change in the condition, means, needs or other circumstances of either spouse or of any child who is entitled to support": *Federal Child Support Guidelines*, s. 14(b) and *Divorce Act*, s. 17(4). (See 17§52 Child support — change in circumstances — change in condition, means, needs or other circumstances — general, below).

In *Gorgichuk v. Gorgichuk* (1999), 50 R.F.L. (4th) 395, 180 Sask. R. 126, 205 W.A.C. 126 (C.A.), the court refused the husband's appeal from an order granting the wife a substantial upward variation of child support. Since the original order, the child had increased expenses relating to his sports activities and increased medical expenses relating to health problems, both of which constituted changed circumstances warranting the variation.

While the court will usually comply with a request to bring a support obligation made prior to May 1, 1997 into line with the *Guidelines*, it should not do so where the parties deliberately agreed to avoid the *Guidelines* as part of a comprehensive settlement of their matrimonial affairs. Complying with the request would allow one party to invoke the court process to unfairly renegotiate one part of their agreement: *Strand v. Strand* (1999), 50 R.F.L. (4th) 174, 246 A.R. 70, 1999 CarswellAlta 420, [1999] A.J. No. 545 (Q.B.).

Where the original order for child support was based on an average income of $996,000 and the actual income for the year prior to the application was only 38% of this amount, there is "change of circumstances that would result in a different order for the support of the child" within the meaning of s. 14 of the *Guidelines*: *Greenwood v. Greenwood* (1999), 2 R.F.L. (5th) 190, [1999] B.C.J. No. 2093, 1999 CarswellBC 2039 (S.C. [In Chambers]).

17§52 — Child support — change in circumstances — change in condition, means, needs or other circumstances — general

Where the amount in the child support order does not include a determination in accordance with the applicable table, a change in circumstances which would enable the court to consider making a variation order is "any change in the condition, means, needs or other circumstances of either spouse or of any child who is entitled to support": *Federal Child Support Guidelines*, s. 14(b) and *Divorce Act*, s. 17(4).

The most obvious instance of a child support order where the amount "does not include a determination made in accordance with a table" is the case where the order is made before the guidelines came into force, that is, before May 1, 1997. However, in such a case, it is not necessary to prove a change in the personal situation of the parties or the children. It is sufficient to point out that the order was made under the old law. The new law, itself, can be the required change in circumstances. See 17§50 Child support — change in circumstances — orders before May, 1997, above.

Orders for child support made after May 1, 1997, where the amount "does not include a determination made in accordance with a table" may be orders:

- for the support of a child over the age of majority made under the alternative provision in s. 3(2)(b) of the *Federal Child Support Guidelines*;
- against a spouse in place of a parent made under s. 5 of the *Federal Child Support Guidelines*;
- for special or extraordinary expenses made under s. 7 of the *Federal Child Support Guidelines*;
- for the support of a child or children in a shared custody arrangement made under s. 9 of the *Federal Child Support Guidelines*;
- for a different amount in cases of undue hardship made under s. 10 of the *Federal Child Support Guidelines*;
- where special provisions in an order, a judgment or a written agreement directly or indirectly benefit the child or children, for a different amount made under s. 15.1(5) of the *Divorce Act*; or,
- for a different amount made on consent under s. 15.1(6) of the *Divorce Act*.

In *Hickey v. Hickey* (1997), 32 R.F.L. (4th) 193, 123 Man. R. (2d) 139, 159 W.A.C. 139, 1997 CarswellMan 526, [1997] M.J. No. 536 (C.A.); reversed 46 R.F.L. (4th) 1, 172 D.L.R. (4th) 577, 240 N.R. 312, [1999] 8 W.W.R. 485, 138 Man. R. (2d) 40, 202 W.A.C. 40, [1999] 2 S.C.R. 518, [1999] S.C.J. No. 9, 1999 CarswellMan 254, 1999 CarswellMan 255, the Court of Appeal reduced a variation order which had doubled the child support payable under the parties' separation agreement. The trial judge had largely based the increase upon the factor of inflation since the agreement had been executed 11 years previous. As inflation during that period was somewhat less than 100%, the doubling of the support payment was not justified. The Supreme Court of Canada at (1999), 46 R.F.L. (4th) 1 (S.C.C.) allowed the appeal, set aside the judgment of the Manitoba Court of Appeal and restored the trial judgment. See 17§38 Change of Circumstances — general.

In *Wedsworth v. Wedsworth*, 12 R.F.L. (5th) 232, 2000 NSCA 108, 188 N.S.R. (2d) 252, 587 A.P.R. 252, 2000 CarswellNS 280 (C.A.); varying (2000), 185 N.S.R. (2d) 215, 575 A.P.R. 215, 2000 CarswellNS 194 (Fam. Ct.), the court, on appeal, restored an order requiring the husband to contribute towards the children's daycare expenses. The husband had not claimed a change in circumstances which prevented him from paying, but had simply responded to the wife's application for an increased contribution with the assertion that he could not pay more. Accordingly, absent proof of changed circumstances, the trial judge lacked jurisdiction to discharge the husband from the ongoing obligation.

In *Wang v. Wang* (1998), 39 R.F.L. (4th) 426, 164 D.L.R. (4th) 146, 58 B.C.L.R. (3d) 159, [1999] 4 W.W.R. 752 (B.C. C.A.), it was held that, although the implementation, by itself, of the *Federal Child Support Guidelines* on May 1, 1997 gives the court a discretion to vary a prior child support order made in divorce proceedings, it is not required to exercise that discretion simply because the amount is different from the amount in the *Guidelines*. The discretion includes a right not to vary. And that right goes beyond cases of "special provisions" within s. 17(6.2) of the *Divorce Act* or reasonable consent arrangements within s. 17(6.4) where it is expressly recognized. The court should exercise its discretion not to vary an order that differs from the *Guidelines* amount unless, in addition to a change in circumstances brought about by the implementation of the *Guidelines* (*Guidelines*, s. 14(c)), there is a material change "in the condition, means, needs or other circumstances" of a family member within the meaning of s. 14(b) of the *Guidelines*. Only then does the application of the *Guidelines* become mandatory under s. 17(6.1) of the *Divorce Act* subject to the exceptions for cases of special provisions in 17(6.2) and reasonable consent arrangements in s. 17(6.4). The court dismissed the appeal of a father from a consent order to pay $1,000 a month for each of three children for a total of $3,000 a month where it was found that the only change in circumstances was the implementation of the *Guidelines*. The *Guidelines* amount, depending on the father's income, would have been $1,181 or $1,202 in total.

In *Hill v. Hill* (1997), 34 R.F.L. (4th) 18 (N.S. C.A.), the husband had been served with a notice of petition and petition for divorce, but did not respond, nor file a Statement of Financial Information, and the divorce proceeded on an uncontested basis. Included in the corollary relief was child support determined in accordance with the federal *Guidelines*. The appellate court held that the appellant's concerns about the quantum of child support could be addressed in an Application to Vary, if his financial situation were to be other than that assumed by the judge granting the Corollary Relief Judgement.

In *Jantzen v Jantzen* (1998), 35 R.F.L. 282, 155 D.L.R. (4th) 656, 126 Man. R. (2d) 71 (C.A.), the trial court had awarded the wife $1000 in monthly spousal support which was varied on appeal to $800 spousal support and $200 child support. The husband's contribution towards his daughter's tuition, books and other university-related costs was confirmed. The appellate court was of the opinion that the spousal support had been on the high side and that the parties had neglected to take into account that the child was still mainly residing with the wife.

In *MacDonald v. MacDonald* (1998), 40 R.F.L. (4th) 397, 216 A.R. 340, 64 Alta. L.R. (3d) 125, [1999] 2 W.W.R. 277 (C.A.), the court, on appeal, increased the amounts of child and spousal support from May 1, 1998. The child support was to be based on the *Federal Child Support Guidelines*. The appellate court did not accept the respondent's argument that the appellant ought to have reapplied to the court of Queen's Bench to vary the terms of maintenance according to the *Federal Child Support Guidelines* as this was a simpler and less expensive remedy than appealing the matter.

In *Budyk v. Sol* (1998), 40 R.F.L. (4th) 348, (sub nom. *Budyk v. Budyk)* 126 Man. R. (2d) 305 (C.A.) the father appealed from a variation order under the *Divorce Act* in which the appellant was found to have an annual income of $78,174.15 and the respondent an income of $76,728. Child support had been varied in accordance with the *Child Support Guidelines* resulting in maintenance of $978 per month, retroactive to September 1, 1997 and the appellant was ordered to pay one-half of the children's special expenses, being university tuition, book and supply expenses. For the 1997-1998 academic year, this amounted to $5,973.28.

The appellant's appeal was dismissed with the exception of the finding that the appellant's income should be reduced to take account of union dues of $1000 and travel expenses related to his work. The court did not accept the argument that the older child, 20 years of age at the time of the appeal, was not a child of the marriage because his marks were not exemplary. Further there was no evidence that the trial judge failed to apply s. 3(2)(b) or that if she applied it, she did so incorrectly. Based on the financial circumstances of the parties, it is not surprising that the motions court judge declined to deviate from the *Guidelines* amount for the appellant's income. Since the husband delayed in providing the wife with financial information that she was entitled to demand and receive under the *Guidelines*, the motions court was correct in making the child support order retroactive.

In *Wedsworth v. Wedsworth*, 12 R.F.L. (5th) 232, 2000 NSCA 108, 188 N.S.R. (2d) 252, 587 A.P.R. 252, 2000 CarswellNS 280 (C.A.); varying (2000), 185 N.S.R. (2d) 215, 575 A.P.R. 215, 2000 CarswellNS 194, [2000] N.S.J. No. 209 (Fam. Ct.), the court, on appeal, restored an order requiring the husband to contribute towards the children's daycare expenses. The husband had not claimed a change in circumstances which prevented him from paying, but had simply responded to the wife's application for an increased contribution with the assertion that he could not pay more. Accordingly, absent proof of changed circumstances, the trial judge lacked jurisdiction to discharge the husband from the ongoing obligation.

Where the father obtained a provisional order in New Brunswick rescinding all child support arrears owing by him and reducing his on-going child support obligation under an original Saskatchewan order, the court in Saskatchewan refused to comer. While the father had claimed a substantial reduction in his income, he had not been forthcoming in disclosing his most recent tax return. Income was accordingly imputed to him and, in the basis, the arrears were not properly discharged: *Uhrich-Cormier v. Cormier*, 11 R.F.L. (5th) 434, 2000 SKQB 410, 198 Sask. R. 34, 2000 CarswellSask 581 (Q.B).

In *Hill v. Ilnicki* (2000), 13 R.F.L. (5th) 73, 273 A.R. 13, 2000 CarswellAlta 1153, [2000] A.J. No. 1219 (Q.B.); affirmed 31 R.F.L. (5th) 335, 2002 CarswellAlta 1217, 2002 ABCA 209, 317 A.R. 389, 284 W.A.C. 389 (C.A.); leave to appeal refused (2003), 2003 CarswellAlta 410, 2003 CarswellAlta 411 (S.C.C.), the court allowed the husband's application for a downward variation of the child support payable under the parties' separation agreement to the level calculated in accordance with the Guidelines. Since the agreement was made, the husband's income had decreased, the wife had relocated with the children to Alberta and the wife unexpectedly continued to receive disability benefits. A material change in circumstance had accordingly occurred.

Where the father's annual income was reduced from $37,000 annually to $11,000 a reduction in child support payable by him was warranted. The fact that he might obtain more lucrative employment in the near future was not a sufficient reason to deny him relief: *Wolkowski v. Doroshenko*, 27 R.F.L. (5th) 214, 2002 CarswellSask 186, 216 Sask. R. 237, 2002 SKQB 114 (Q.B.).

In *Dick v. Dick* (1999), 4 R.F.L. (5th) 54, 1999 CarswellOnt 3243 (S.C.J.); additional reasons at (2000), 2000 CarswellOnt 1551 (S.C.J.), the court allowed the husband's application for a reduction in child support payable after his retirement. As the husband had made an equalization payment based upon the capitalization of his pension, that portion of his pension that had been capitalized was not properly included in his income after retirement.

Paragraph 14(c) of the *Federal Child Support Guidelines* provides that, for child support determined before May 1, 1997, the coming into force of the *Guidelines* is, in and of itself, deemed to be the required "change in circumstances" that opens the door to a variation under s. 17 of the *Divorce Act*: *Holtby v. Holtby* (1997), 30 R.F.L. (4th) 70 (Ont. Prov. Div.).

In *Claridge-Skof v. Skof* (July 11, 1997), Doc. Peterborough 3550 11494/96 (Ont. Gen. Div.), the court was of the opinion that according to s. 14(c) of the *Guidelines*, the coming into force of s. 15.1 of the *Divorce Act* does constitute a change in circumstance. However, the court is still required to review the condition, means and needs of the children and if a variation order is made, if it would be made under the new *Federal Guidelines*. Where the children would suffer a significant loss if the child support payment was required to be made pursuant to the new *Federal Guidelines* and the payor spouse would receive only a nominal benefit, the variation is not in the best interests of the children and the court will not order a variation.

On an application to "rescind" a child support order made before May 1, 1997 (the date when the *Guidelines* came into force), the court is not obliged to amend the order to conform with the *Guidelines*. Subsections 17(1) and (4) of the *Divorce Act* gives either or both parties the right to institute an application to vary an order if there is a change of circumstances as provided for in the *Guidelines*. One of the circumstances provided for is the coming into force of the *Guidelines* themselves. By s. 14(c) of the *Guidelines*, the fact of the *Guidelines* coming into force is deemed to be a change of circumstances. Although this deemed change permits the review of child support awarded prior to May 1, 1997, the court should employ the traditional test involving its discretion to determine whether there should be a variation as a result of the change. Where no change to an order made before May 1, 1997 is warranted, then the guideline tables are not mandated. It is not necessary to implement the *Guidelines* where the court makes a determination that the order of child support need not be altered. It is only if a variation is ordered that the tables for child support must be applied: *Meloche v. Kales* (1997), 35 R.F.L. (4th) 297, 35 O.R. (3d) 688 (Gen. Div.).

Where the amount of child support payable by the father under the parties' agreement contemplated the sale by the mother of her business, the mother's application for increased child support was allowed when that sale failed to materialize. In addition to that significant change, the fact that the parties' agreement predated the coming into force of s. 15.1 of the *Divorce Act* triggered an automatic change of circumstances under s. 14(c) of the *Federal Child Support Guidelines: Todd v. Morine* (1999), 46 R.F.L. (4th) 391 (N.B. Q.B.).

In *A. (T.) v. A. (R.C.)* (1999), 48 R.F.L. (4th) 205 (B.C. S.C. [In Chambers]), the husband was successful in his application to terminate child support years after the parties' divorce when he learned that he was not the biological father of the child as the wife had earlier represented to him. The husband could not have a properly informed intention to place himself in a parent-child relationship with a child he knew was fathered by another.

In *Mayo v. O'Connell* (1998), 42 R.F.L. (4th) 193, 170 Nfld. & P.E.I.R. 157, 522 A.P.R. 157, 1998 CarswellNfld 205 (U.F.C.), the court dismissed the mother's application for a reduction of child support payable by her. The evidence did not support the mother's "undue hardship" argument. Although the cost of access by her was high given the children lived in Newfoundland and she in Florida, she had not in fact exercised her access rights in over two years. Also, although another ex-husband was in arrears of child support payable to her, the resulting hardship was not "undue" given her income and expenses.

Cases decided before the enactment of the Federal Child Support Guidelines

Divorce Act, 1985

In *English v. English* (1996), 21 R.F.L. (4th) 85 (C.A.), the father appealed and the mother cross-appealed from a judgment dismissing applications for variation of child support. The court ordered that the father's appeal should fail as it was incumbent upon him, in making an application to vary, to demonstrate that there had been a material change in circumstances since the making of the order he sought to have varied.

After a change of circumstances has been established in an application to vary child support, the children's needs must be reassessed in light of the change of circumstances: *Jamieson v. Jamieson* (1995), 14 R.F.L. (4th) 354, 163 N.B.R. (2d) 178, 419 A.P.R. 178 (C.A.).

Where the husband did not respond to the wife's petition for divorce with the result that child support was awarded as claimed, the court reversed on appeal the dismissal of the husband's application for a reduction. The amount of the award almost equalled the husband's total income and the failure of the husband to earn what the trial judge assumed he did amounted to a material change in circumstances: *Pelley v. Pelley* (1995), 14 R.F.L. (4th) 1, 59 B.C.A.C. 249, 98 W.A.C. 249 (C.A.).

Where a material change in circumstances has been established in an application for reduced child support, the court is entitled to consider all of the facts of the case and is not restricted to considering the extent of the change: *Edwards (Pereira) v. Edwards* (1994), 5 R.F.L. (4th) 321, 133 N.S.R. (2d) 8, 380 A.P.R. 8, 118 D.L.R. (4th) 217 (C,A.); affirming (1994), 126 N.S.R. (2d) 341, 352 A.P.R. 341 (S.C.); additional reasons at (1994), 127 N.S.R. (2d) 379, 355 A.P.R. 379 (S.C.).

Under s. 17(5) of the *Divorce Act*, a court must find a change in circumstances has occurred before granting a variation. Variation proceedings cannot be used as a mechanism for merely correcting perceived errors in an earlier support award: *King v. King* (1994), 2 R.F.L. (4th) 407, 115 Nfld. & P.E.I.R. 56, 360 A.P.R. 56 (Nfld. C.A.).

Increases resulting from inflation, the changing needs of children as they grow older and the fact that the custodial parent has an increased tax burden are changes of circumstances which could justify an increase in child support: *Noble v. Noble* (1994), 3 R.F.L. (4th) 25 (Ont. C.A.); affirming (October 7, 1993), Doc. 92-PF-1919 (Ont. Gen. Div.).

Where the custodial mother had enrolled the child in private school without consulting the father, it was held that the father should not be responsible for the resulting increase in expense: *Sperker v. Sperker* (1994), 2 R.F.L. (4th) 243, 131 N.S.R. (2d) 1, 371 A.P.R. 1 (N.S. C.A.). Although the mother's request for increased child support was granted on other grounds.

The words "the condition, means, needs or other circumstances" of the parties referred to in s. 17(4) and s. 15(5) are so wide that they confer a substantial discretion on the judge at first instance. The criteria requires a balancing of the defined interests of the children with those of their parents. The statute provides that priority is to be given to the needs of the children: *Vincent v. Vincent* (1995), 15 R.F.L. (4th) 273, 132 Nfld. & P.E.I.R. 181, 410 A.P.R. 181 (Nfld. C.A.).

The court in *Gunn v. Gunn* (1994), 10 R.F.L. (4th) 197 (Man. C.A.), reduced the payor-father's support payment from $750 to $600 per month for the parties' three children, in recognition of the fact that the father had very modest means and a person cannot pay more than is reasonably available out of his or her income and assets. There was no reference to the governing statute in this decision.

In reviewing the quantum of child support in the *Gunn* decision, the court was of the opinion that the payor's first obligation was to his own children and not to the woman with whom he was currently living and to her children.

The decision of the Alberta Court of Appeal in *Levesque v. Levesque* (1994), 4 R.F.L. (4th) 375, 155 A.R. 26 (C.A.); additional reasons at (1995), 165 A.R. 319 (C.A.), was a reserved decision of the Court of Appeal, intended by the court to change the law as it related to child support. Where there has been such a marked change in the law of child support, a custodial parent should be entitled to apply for an increase based upon it. The new law entitles custodial parents who are receiving less than the application of the Levesque standards to apply for an increase in child support, so long as the increase is in excess of 10 percent: *Hennessey v. Hennessey*, 20 R.F.L. (4th) 79, 36 Alta. L.R. (3d) 250, [1996] 4 W.W.R. 507, 177 A.R. 335 (Q.B.).

In *J. (A.) v. T. (M.)* (15 janvier 1993), Doc. C.A. Montreal 500-09-001076-918 (C.A. Qué.), it was held that in determining an application for increased child support the husband's ability to pay properly involved not only a consideration of his income, which had declined in the recession, but also of his considerable assets.

In *Boucher c. Bombardier* (8 mai 1992), C.A. Québec 200-09-000045-929 (C.A. Qué.), the court found that the fact that an inheritance received by the children was used to construct a swimming pool was not a reason justifying a reduction in child support. Since the children were the ones using the pool, the inheritance could not be said to have been spent extravagantly.

In *Willick v. Willick* (1994), 6 R.F.L. (4th) 161 (S.C.C), the court considered the proper interpretation of s. 17(4) of the *Divorce Act*. The court was of the opinion that an order for child support is made by assessing the needs of the children having regard to the means of the parents. Pursuant to s. 17(4), the court may vary a support order when the relationship between those factors changes in a material way. A significant change in one of the factors, that is, a change in circumstances of either former spouse or of any child of the marriage could cause a material change in the relation of the factors. In the Willick decision, the court held that the fact alone that a payor's income had increased significantly did constitute a material change in circumstances justifying an increase of child support.

In determining the proper interpretation of s. 17(4) of the *Divorce Act*, a contextual approach to the interpretation of the statutory material is not appropriate: *Willick v. Willick*, above. Where, as in this decision, there is a narrow focus in a case, an examination of the broad policy grounds for a decision is not required. In particular, it is not appropriate to consider the *Canadian Charter of Rights and Freedoms* as an interpretative tool where the parties have not relied on the *Charter* and other rules of construction make the intention of the legislature plain.

In today's economy, $200 monthly child support must be seen as a minimal requirement for support. Only the most extraordinary circumstances could justify a reduction of such a minimal award: *Wundele v. Wundele* (1994), 8 R.F.L. (4th) 325, 99 B.C.L.R. (2d) 1, 52 B.C.A.C. 116, 86 W.A.C. 116 (C.A.).

Where the husband, who was a doctor, terminated his general practice and began to specialize in psychiatry, with the result that his income was halved from $62,000 to $30,000 annually, the court upheld on appeal an order reducing his child support obligation from $1,500 monthly to $1,000. Although considering his income alone, the order could be characterized as being high, he had remarried and his wife, although not employed, was employable. The court could properly consider the ability of the father's new wife to earn income: *Hynes v. Tierney-Hynes* (1993), 50 R.F.L. (3d) 279, 88 Man. R. (2d) 134, 51 W.A.C. 134 (C.A.).

On an application for variation of child support, once a parent has established a material change in circumstances, the reasonable childcare costs should be apportioned between the parents in the same manner as an originating application: *Pawsey v. Pawsey* (1992), 38 R.F.L. (3d) 371 (Man. C.A.).

A party will not be relieved of his financial obligation to provide child support because he has engaged in risky financial ventures and thereby incurred extensive debts: *Jensen v. Jensen (Binns)* (1992), 39 R.F.L. (3d) 118, 109 N.S.R. (2d) 106, 297 A.P.R. 106 (C.A.).

In *Jayatilaka c. Roussel* (1991), 36 R.F.L. (3d) 447 (N.B. C.A.), the appellate court held that on a variation application the court must take into consideration all the factors in s. 17(7), and not only s. 17(d), the promotion of self-sufficiency of each spouse. Where the wife's full-time earnings would not be enough to pay for a baby-sitter and the children were too young to be left on their own, it was impractical for the wife to work full-time. There was no reason to interfere with the trial judge's award of increased support, based on the greater ages of the children and the effects of inflation. The trial court had held that these developments had amounted to a material change in circumstances.

Where the father appeared irresponsible and neglectful of his child support obligations and failed to disclose his assets or living expenses, the court upheld the dismissal of his application to reduce child support: *Jensen v. Jensen* (1990), 28 R.F.L. (3d) 350, 86 Sask. R. 257 (C.A.).

Where the father did not raise the issue of paternity in divorce proceedings, he was found to be estopped from raising it in a subsequent application by the mother for increased child support: *Young v. Young* (1987), 10 R.F.L. (3d) 337 (B.C. C.A.).

17§53 — Change in circumstances — children's post-secondary education

Divorce Act, 1985

In *Budyk v. Sol* (1998), 40 R.F.L. (4th) 348, 126 Man. R. (2d) 305, 167 W.A.C. 305 (C.A.), the father appealed from a variation order under the *Divorce Act* in which the appellant was found to have an annual income of $78,174.15 and the respondent an income of $76,728. Child support had been varied in accordance with the Child Support Guidelines resulting in maintenance of $978 per month, retroactive to September 1, 1997 and the appellant was ordered to pay one-half of the children's special expenses, being university tuition, book and supply expenses. For the 1997–1998 academic year, this amounted to $5,973.28.

The appellant's appeal was dismissed with the exception of the finding that the appellant's income should be reduced to take account of union dues of $1000 and travel expenses related to his work. The court did not accept the argument that the older child, 20 years of age at the time of the appeal and a full-time university student residing with his mother, was not a child of the marriage because his marks were not exemplary. Further there was no evidence that the trial judge failed to apply s. 3(2)(b) or that if she applied it, she did so incorrectly. Based on the financial circumstances of the parties, it is not surprising that the motions court judge declined to deviate from the guidelines amount for the appellant's income. Since the husband delayed in providing the wife with financial information that she was entitled to demand and receive under the guidelines, the motions court was correct in making the child support order retroactive.

Evans v. Turner, 37 R.F.L (5th) 84, 2003 CarswellPEI 36, 2003 PESCTD 23, 224 Nfld. & P.E.I.R. 120, 669 A.P.R. 120 (P.E.I. T.D.), the father's application to be relieved of child support obligations for a 6- month period during which the parties' 19-year-old daughter was not at school was dismissed. The daughter had some outstanding credits towards the completion of her grade 12 and by the time she decided to return to finish them, she was too late to register for the upcoming semester. Accordingly, she had to wait 6 months for the following semester to begin. The daughter did not have the ability to contribute to her own support and had not terminated her dependency on either parent.

Cases decided before the enactment of the Federal Child Support Guidelines

Under the *Divorce Act*, there is no age at which child support may be automatically terminated. A child of any age may be a "child of the marriage" while seriously pursuing his or her education. The fact that both the custodial parent and the children have failed to keep the payor informed of the children's educational achievements may be a factor in determining the payor's ongoing support obligation: *McGregor v. McGregor* (1994), 3 R.F.L. (4th) 343 (N.B. C.A.); reversing in part (1993), 49 R.F.L. (3d) 17 (N.B. Q.B.).

As a general rule, where a child is over the age of 16, the parents remain responsible for his or her support if the child is a *bona fide* student. The period of dependency will continue until the child reaches a level of education, commensurate with his or her abilities, that will enable him or her to join the workforce at least at an entry level position in an appropriate field. Whether that period has ended is a question of fact in each case, but judges should make their decisions in light of the prevailing social and economic conditions. A bachelor's degree no longer ensures that the holder will become self-sufficient. Although no automatic age or scholastic cut-off point exists, as the child ages or augments his or her education, the onus on the claimant to prove dependency becomes greater: *Martell v. Height* (1994), 3 R.F.L. (4th) 104, 130 N.S.R. (2d) 318, 367 A.P.R. 318, 113 D.L.R. (4th) 54 (C.A.).

Where the parties' 20-year-old twin sons were both attending an American college on football scholarships, the husband's application to terminate child support was allowed. As the emphasis at the college was on football, the husband could not be expected to contribute where the future advantages and benefits of the children's studies were highly speculative: *Pink v. Pink* (1991), 31 R.F.L. (3d) 233, 71 Man. R. (2d) 48 (C.A.).

Where the children who were over 18 had not been serious with their studies with the result that their educations had already been prolonged two years longer than they should have been, the court allowed the father's application to terminate child support: *Droit de la famille — 1204*, [1988] R.D.F. 430 (C.A. Qué.).

In *Fraser v. Jones* (1995), 17 R.F.L. (4th) 218 (Sask. Q.B.), the court refused the mother's application for increased child support based upon the child's enrollment in university. Although the child's expenses would undoubtedly increase, these could be off-set through summer employment, student loans and scholarships.

In *Golder v. Green* (1994), 8 R.F.L. (4th) 455 (Ont. Gen. Div.), the court refused the mother's application for an extension of child support beyond her daughter's twenty-first birthday. Although the child continued to attend school, she had purchased a car without any consultation with her father, a fact which weighed against any claim of economic hardship.

In *I. (E.) c. L. (R.)* (1994), 1 R.F.L. (4th) 364 (C.S. Qué.), the husband's application to terminate child support for his son who had completed a bachelor's degree and wished to pursue his master's was dismissed. The husband had the ability to pay and an obligation to contribute to his children's intellectual development.

In *Auld v. Auld* (1994), 5 R.F.L. (4th) 132, 123 Nfld. & P.E.I.R. 43, 382 A.P.R. 43 (P.E.I. T.D.), the fact that the daughter's boyfriend had moved into the custodial mother's home did not release the father from his child support obligations. The father had agreed to pay all post-secondary education costs of the children and his daughter, who was a university student, could not afford to withdraw from her mother's care. Her boyfriend had moved into the mother's residence largely as a paying boarder and had no effect upon the daughter's status as a "child of the marriage".

Children who were in their final years of university studies, had received student loans and were fully employed in the summer were found to no longer qualify as "children of the marriage" in *Picard v. Picard* (1990), 110 N.B.R. (2d) 419, 276 A.P.R. 419 (Q.B.).

If a child does not complete a post-secondary education programme in the usual time period, the parent should not be obligated to continue to support the child during the additional period of study needed: *O'Keefe v. O'Keefe* (1990), 88 Sask. R. 202 (Q.B.).

In *Tracy v. DeWitt* (1988), 89 N.B.R. (2d) 381, 226 A.P.R. 381 (Q.B.), the court refused the mother's application to extend the father's obligation to support the child through a period of post-graduate studies when the decree nisis called for support while the child was attending a post-secondary institution.

Parents who are responsible for the support of adult children are not excused from their support obligations merely because the child can borrow from the government to pursue further education: *Thompson v. Thompson* (1988), 13 R.F.L. (3d) 372 (Ont. Div. Ct.); reversing (1987), 6 R.F.L. (3d) 161 (Ont. H.C.).

17§54 — Change in circumstances — children earning income

The children's earnings (means) are relevant under the May 1997 amendments and the *Federal Child Support Guidelines* only when considering:

- special or extraordinary expenses incurred on behalf of the child: *Federal Child Support Guidelines*, s. 7(1);
- the alternative option for determining support for a child of the age of majority or over who is still under the parents' charge: *Divorce Act*, s. 2 "child of the marriage", *Federal Child Support Guidelines*, s. 3(2)(b); or
- support for a child under the age of majority where the payor's income is over $150,000 a year and the support amount out of the balance in excess of $150,000 is determined according to the discretion of the court instead of the percentage in the table: *Federal Child Support Guidelines*, s. 4(b)(ii).

The child support payable pursuant to the *Guidelines* is based upon the means of the payor and not benefits received by the child from a third party source. Accordingly, a father was not entitled to a reduction in child support payable after the child began to receive Canada Pension Plan benefits after the death of his step-father in *Blain-Hughes v. Blain* (1998), 39 R.F.L. (4th) 327 (Ont. Gen. Div.).

Cases decided before the enactment of the Federal Child Support Guidelines

Divorce Act, 1985

Where the parties' university-age children moved out of their mother's home and into an apartment while attending university, and had refused their father's offer of accommodation, the consent order for their support was varied requiring the father only to pay support for those months when the children were actually attending classes: *Bates v. Bates* (1995), 10 R.F.L. (4th) 261, 165 A.R. 71, 89 W.A.C. 71 (C.A.).

In *English v. English* (1995), 16 R.F.L. (4th) 250, 133 Sask. R. 274 (Q.B.); additional reasons at (July 27, 1995), Doc. Regina Q.B. 015530/93 (Sask. Q.B.); reversed in part (1996), 21 R.F.L. (4th) 85, 141 Sask. R. 171, 114 W.A.C. 171 (C.A.); additional reasons at (1996), 22 R.F.L. (4th) 312 (Sask. C.A.), the father could not rely upon his children's trust fund as a grounds for reducing the child support payable by him. The trust fund had existed when the parties settled the issue of child support and therefore a change in circumstances had not been established.

In *Guillemette v. Horne* (1993), 48 R.F.L. (3d) 229, 88 Man. R. (2d) 15, 51 W.A.C. 15 (C.A.), the court reduced on the husband's appeal the increase in child support ordered for the parties' daughter. Part of the increase had been based upon the cost to the daughter of a separate apartment, based upon her claim that she could not study properly while living with her mother. The claim was unfounded and the husband should not be required to shoulder the economic consequences of the child's decision to remove herself voluntarily from her mother's control. Further, the trial judge had erred in failing to consider the child's ability to contribute to her own support.

In *Currie v. Currie* (1989), 18 R.F.L. (3d) 20 (Sask. C.A.), the court allowed the husband's application to terminate support for his disabled sons, ages 23 and 29. As both children were receiving disability pensions and as the husband's own income had been reduced significantly, a sufficient change in circumstances had been established.

Child support was varied where the child, as a result of a motor vehicle injury, was receiving considerable financial benefits for 2 years and was, at the date of the variation application, no longer enrolled in school: *Hansen v. Hansen* (1995), 13 R.F.L. (4th) 335 (Ont. Gen. Div.).

In *Auld v. Auld* (1994), *supra*, the court allowed the husband's application to vary a child support provision requiring him to finance his daughter's post-secondary education. Since the date of the agreement, the daughter had demonstrated an ability to contribute somewhat to her own keep and the income of the custodial mother, who paid nothing towards the daughter's support, had increased. Given the change of circumstances, it was fair that the father's responsibility be restricted to his daughter's book and tuition costs.

In *Droit de la famille — 1530*, [1992] R.D.F. 3 (C.S. Qué.), it was found that the fact that the parties' daughter had obtained a part-time job did not justify a reduction in child support.

In *Crawford v. Crawford* (1993), 114 Sask. R. 232 (Q.B.), the court allowed the husband's application for a reduction in the child support payable for his college student daughter who had begun to benefit under an educational trust fund which had been set up by her grandmother.

In *Torrens v. Torrens* (1991), 94 Sask. R. 246 (Q.B.), the court allowed the husband's application to terminate child support for the parties' 20-year-old son, despite the fact that he was enrolled full-time in university and continued to live with his mother. As he had earned $8,000 from his last summer job and had inherited $20,000 from his grandparents, the financial position of the son required that he no longer be considered as a child of the marriage.

Where the parties 18-year-old son left school and took a job, the court allowed the husband's application for termination of child support. Although the son's job was about to end and the mother alleged his intention to return to school, the son had proven that he could make his own decisions and support himself: *Pritchard v. Pritchard (Zinck)* (1991), 38 R.F.L. (3d) 45, 110 N.S.R. (2d) 390, 299 A.P.R. 390 (Fam. Ct.).

Where the parties' 20-year-old child suffered from an emotional and mental impairment which prevented her from achieving independence, the father's application for termination of child support was refused. However, as she did earn some income from employment in special programs, the father's support was reduced accordingly: *Butler v. Butler* (1996), 19 R.F.L. (4th) 86, 148 N.S.R. (2d) 126, 429 A.P.R. 126 (S.C.).

Divorce Act, 1968

Where one of the two children of the marriage had become financially independent, it was held, in the course of the father's application to vary child maintenance, that it was inappropriate merely to divide the existing order in half. The needs of the youngest child required examination in the context of existing circumstances: *Swidzinsky v. Swidzinsky* (1984), 43 R.F.L. (2d) 456, 32 Man. R. (2d) 144 (Q.B.).

Where the child of the marriage had commenced work in a government programme whereby he received room, board and $3,000 on completion, the court granted the father's application for a reduction in child maintenance payable until such time as the child had completed the programme: *Sinclair v. Sinclair* (1984), 13 R.F.L. (2d) 153, 32 Man. R. (2d) 108 (Q.B.).

17§55 — Change in circumstances — access provisions not followed

In *Hollenbach v. Hollenbach* (2005), 12 R.F.L. (6th) 323, 2005 CarswellBC 167, 2005 BCSC 81 (B.C. S.C.), the court rejected the father's application to terminate his daughter's child support. Although the daughter wanted nothing to do with her father, their relationship had been strained at the time the original child support order was made and he had done little since then to remedy the situation.

The non-custodial parent of a child who is not yet recognized as being mature should not be allowed to terminate the child support on the ground that the child refuses to maintain the desired relationship with the parent: *Pohlod v. Bielajew* (1998), 38 R.F.L. (4th) 35 (Ont. Gen. Div.); additional reasons at (May 6, 1998), Doc. 23309/95 (Ont. Gen. Div.).

The fact that the father's child support obligation would rise by over $500 monthly upon application of *Guidelines* amounts 13 years after the parties' divorce was not found to be an "undue" hardship. The fact that the father had no contact with the children also did not justify a departure from the *Guidelines*: *Robinson v. Domin* (1998), 39 R.F.L. (4th) 92 (B.C. S.C.).

The *Federal Child Support Guidelines* do not provide for a reduction in *Guidelines* amounts on the basis that the custodial parent denies access to the payor parent: *Robinson v. Domin*, above.

Cases decided before the enactment of the Federal Child Support Guidelines

Divorce Act, 1985

In *Al-Maghazachi v. Dueck* (1995), 17 R.F.L. (4th) 132, 107 Man. R. (2d) 47, 109 W.A.C. 47 (C.A.), the court refused the husband's application for a rescission in child support owed by him based on the wife's refusal to allow him access as specified. Despite the wife's actions, the husband's refusal to pay was not justified.

In *Kuntz v. Kaytor* (1995), 10 R.F.L. (4th) 246 (Sask. Q.B.), the interim child support payable by the father was ordered suspended until regular access between the father and his daughter had been established.

Although the court may properly direct that child support be terminated if the custodial parent has denied or restricted the payor's access rights, such an order should not be made where harm would result to the children: *McGregor v. McGregor* (1994), 3 R.F.L. (4th) 343, 148 N.B.R. (2d) 176, 378 A.P.R. 176 (C.A.); reversing in part (1993), 49 R.F.L. (3d) 17, 139 N.B.R. (2d) 206, 357 A.P.R. 296 (Q.B.).

Child support is the right of the child and may not be eroded or qualified by reason of parental misconduct. Accordingly, the fact that the custodial spouse interferes with the payor's access rights cannot be relied upon as a reason for terminating child support: *Lee v. Lee* (1990), 29 R.F.L. (3d) 417 (B.C. C.A.).

Where the mother had frustrated the father's access rights to the point that his relationship with his children was destroyed, the court granted the father's application for termination of child support. The mother's interference with the father's maintaining contact with his children constituted a substantial change in circumstances justifying the variation of the support order: *Wilbur v. MacMurray* (1991), 38 R.F.L. (3d) 74 (N.B. Q.B.).

Where the father had failed to exercise his access rights, which would have regularly relieved the mother of some of the child care costs, the court allowed the mother's application for an upward variation of the child support arrangements which had originally been outlined in the parties' minutes of settlement: *Vervoorst v. Vervoorst* (1991), 37 R.F.L. (3d) 178, 85 Alta. L.R. (2d) 244, [1992] 3 W.W.R. 221, 122 A.R. 280 (Q.B.).

Where the mother, by her conduct has frustrated the court's order regarding access, support for the children will be continued for a limited time period until each child reaches 19 years of age: *McGregor v. McGregor* (1993), 49 R.F.L. (3d) 17, 139 N.B.R. (2d) 296, 357 A.P.R. 296 (Q.B.); reversed in part on other grounds (1994), 3 R.F.L. (4th) 343 (N.B. C.A.). The court held that after each child reached the age of 19 years, if she was pursuing her education, support would be on a basis worked out between the father and the child.

Where a custodial parent interferes with the access rights of the other parent, an order suspending the payment of child support to the custodial parent is not an appropriate remedy. Such a penalty would simply punish the child for the conduct of the parent: *G. (M.G.) v. T. (C.)* (1992), 42 R.F.L. (3d) 284 (B.C. S.C.).

Where the husband's unilateral termination of his access rights increased the custodial mother's child care costs, she was found entitled to an increase in child support: *Russo v. Russo* (1988), 15 R.F.L. (3d) 243 (Ont. H.C.).

17§56 — Change in circumstances — decrease in payor's income

Under the May 1997 amendments to the *Divorce Act* and the *Federal Child Support Guidelines*, a decrease in the payor spouse's income may be a change of circumstances within any or all of the defined sets of circumstances giving the court jurisdiction to consider making a variation order. These sets of circumstances are:

- in the case of an order made before May 1, 1997, the mere fact that the law of child support changed on May 1, 1997: *Federal Child Support Guidelines*, s. 14(c) and *Divorce Act*, s. 17(4);
- in the case where an amount in an order was determined in accordance with the applicable table, any change in circumstance that would result in a different child support order: *Federal Child Support Guidelines*, s. 14(a) and *Divorce Act*, s. 17(4); and
- in the case where the amount does not include a determination in accordance with the applicable table, any change in the condition, means, needs or other circumstances of either spouse or of any child who is entitled to support: *Federal Child Support Guidelines*, s. 14(b) and *Divorce Act*, s. 17(4).

Divorce Act, 1985

Where the husband left employment which paid him $175,000 to take on less lucrative consulting contracts, the dismissal of his application for reduced child support was upheld on appeal. It was appropriate that an income of $175,000 continue to be imputed to the husband as he was not justified in abandoning his employment and persistently minimizing his income to avoid support obligations: *Pirner v. Pirner* (2005), 22 R.F.L. (6th) 291, 2005 CarswellOnt 6878, 208 O.A.C. 147 (Ont. C.A.); additional reasons at (2006), 2006 CarswellOnt 12 (Ont. C.A.); leave to appeal refused (2006), 2006 CarswellOnt 2552, 2006 CarswellOnt 2553 (S.C.C.).

In *Furlong v. Furlong* (1998), 42 R.F.L. (4th) 350 (Alta C.A.), pursuant to an order in a divorce judgment granted in June 1996, the respondent was required to pay to the appellant child support in the amount of $275 per month for each of two children of the marriage. The respondent was granted a variation of the order as he had left his job with the Canadian military and was working part-time while attending school and full-time when not in school. The court held that the previous child support order did not constitute a special provision within s. 17.6(2) of the *Divorce Act* which would shield the order from variation.

In *Tapping v. Hetherington* (1998), 42 R.F.L. (4th) 411, 115 B.C.A.C. 127, 189 W.A.C. 127 (C.A.) the husband's application to reduce child support was dismissed despite the fact that the evidence indicated that his income was insufficient to make the payments. The husband had sold a business for $1.5 million and had failed to produce evidence that his capital had been depleted. When the order had originally been made, it had been contemplated that the payments would be paid out of his capital for some time.

Temporary unemployment, especially when it occurs with some regularity, cannot be relied upon as a circumstance justifying a reduction in the child support payable by a parent: *Harder v. Harder*, 41 R.F.L. (5th) 69, 2003 CarswellSask 454, 2003 SKQB 286 (Sask. Q.B.).

Where the father's annual income was reduced from $37,000 annually to $11,000 a reduction in child support payable by him was warranted. The fact that he might obtain more lucrative employment in the near future was not a sufficient reason to deny him relief: *Wolkowski v. Wolkowski*, 27 R.F.L. (5th) 214, 2002 CarswellSask 186, 216 Sask. R. 237, 2002 SKQB 114 (Sask. Q.B.).

In *Hill v. Ilnicki* (2000), 13 R.F.L. (5th) 73, 273 A.R. 131, 2000 CarswellAlta 1153, [2000] A.J. No. 1219 (Alta. Q.B.), the court allowed the husband's application for a downward variation of the child support payable under the parties' separation agreement to the level calculated in accordance with the *Guidelines*. Since the agreement was made, the husband's income had decreased, the wife had relocated with the children to Alberta and the wife unexpectedly continued to receive disability benefits. A material change in circumstance had accordingly occurred.

A parent should make adequate provisions for the support of his or her children before investing in speculative business ventures. The failure of such a venture should not be relied upon as a justification for reduction in child support: *Blais v. Blais*, 20 R.F.L. (5th) 17, 2001 CarswellSask 513, 2001 SKQB 357, 210 Sask. R. 123 (Sask. Q.B.); affirmed 27 R.F.L. (5th) 263, 2002 CarswellSask 368, 2002 SKCA 70 (Sask. C.A.).

Where a parent seeks reduction in child support as a result of a career change that negatively impacts income, it is incumbent upon that parent to demonstrate that the decision to change careers was reasoned, thoughtful and highly practical: *Hagner v. Hawkins* (2005), 21 R.F.L. (6th) 315, 2005 CarswellOnt 6701, [2005] O.J. No. 4975 (Ont. S.C.J.).

Temporary unemployment, especially when it occurs with some regularity, cannot be relied upon as a circumstance justifying a reduction in the child support payable by a parent: *Harder v. Harder*, 41 R.F.L. (5th) 69, 2003 CarswellSask 454, 2003 SKQB 286 (Sask. Q.B.)

Where the father obtained a provisional order in New Brunswick rescinding all child support arrears owing by him and reducing his on-going child support obligation under an original Saskatchewan order, the court in Saskatchewan refused to confirm the order. While the father had claimed a substantial reduction in his income, he had not been forthcoming in disclosing his most recent tax return. Income was accordingly imputed to him and, on that basis, the arrears were not properly discharged: *Uhrich-Cormier v. Cormier*, 11 R.F.L. (5th) 434, 2000 SKQB 410, 198 Sask. R. 34, 2000 CarswellSask 581 (Q.B.).

In *Feuchter v. Feuchter*, 4 R.F.L. (5th) 345, 2000 BCSC 203, 2000 CarswellBC 280 (S.C.), the father based his application for a reduction in child support on the fact that he had lost his business and a subsequent job and then used shares and his Registered Retirement Savings Plan ("RRSP") to purchase another business that was still not producing much income. It was inappropriate that the father be allowed to finance his business at the expense of his children, particularly when he could have used both shares and his RRSP to pay child support. Accordingly, the variation was refused, but payments were suspended to allow the business time to generate income.

Where the father had lost his job by pursuing a course of conduct that he knew would result in his dismissal, he could not rely on his unemployment as justification for reduction in child support arrears owing by him: *Baldini v. Baldini* (1999), 46 R.F.L. (4th) 407, 1999 CarswellBC 1370 (S.C.).

In *Poyntz Estate v. Poyntz* (1998), 37 R.F.L. (4th) 134, 157 D.L.R. (4th) 552 (Ont. Gen. Div.), the court refused the husband's application to expunge child support arrears owing by him. Although he had experienced some impecunious years, he had failed during that period to seek a variation of child support and a subsequent inheritance from his mother now gave him the means to pay.

The fact that the husband had developed an addiction to gambling was found to be an insufficient ground upon which to reduce his child support payments. The court could not sanction gambling as a justification for not meeting child support obligations: *Scanlon v. Scanlon* (1998), 42 R.F.L. (4th) 397, [1999] 3 W.W.R. 151, 132 Man. R. (2d) 79 (Q.B.).

In *Ferrigan v. Ferrigan* (1998), 36 R.F.L. (4th) 206 (Ont. Gen. Div.), the court allowed the husband's application for a reduction in child support from the amount specified in the parties' separation agreement. When the agreement was signed, the husband was fully employed as a teacher but was forced to take early retirement for health reasons. The husband had suffered real hardship and the wife, who had remarried and had not returned to employment, was actually in a better financial position than the husband.

In *Cornelius v. Andres* (1998), 36 R.F.L. (4th) 436, 125 Man. R. (2d) 144 (Q.B.), the court allowed the husband's application to terminate the payment of child support. The husband's business was in serious financial difficulty with the result that his annual income had been reduced to $3,382. As the husband could not even afford to pay the base amount under the *Federal Child Support Guidelines*, he could not additionally be expected to pay extraordinary and dental expenses. On appeal at (1999), 45 R.F.L. (4th) 200, 170 D.L.R. (4th) 254, 134 Man. R. (2d) 140, 193 W.A.C. 140, [1999] 6 W.W.R. 317, [1999] M.J. No. 103, 1999 CarswellMan 86 (C.A.); reconsideration refused (1999), 1999 CarswellMan 273 (Man. C.A.), the court allowed the wife's appeal on the issue of the calculation of income.

The fact alone that the payor parent is bankrupt and that child support arrears are accordingly unenforceable does not of itself justify the cancellation, suspension or variation of child support obligations: *Kerton v. Kerton* (1997), 33 R.F.L. (4th) 285 (Ont. Gen. Div.).

Where the father had lost his job by pursuing a course of conduct that he knew would result in his dismissal, he could not rely on his unemployment as justification for reduction in child support arrears owing by him: *Baldini v. Baldini* (1999), 46 R.F.L. (4th) 407 (B.C. S.C.).

A short-term inability to pay child support will generally not justify a variation of the support order: *Smith v. Smith* (1998), 39 R.F.L. (4th) 88, 55 B.C.L.R. (3d) 99 (S.C. [In Chambers]).

In *Finney v. Finney* (1998), 40 R.F.L. (4th) 249 (B.C. S.C.), the court allowed the father's application for a decrease in child support from an amount previously agreed upon by the parties. The father's income had not reached the amount anticipated when the agreement was signed. Furthermore, the support level sought by the father still exceeded the amount which would have been calculated under the *Guidelines*. Finally, as the agreement had also provided the wife with a lump sum to house the children, the agreement was found to contain "special provisions" pursuant to s. 17(6.2)(a) of the *Divorce Act* for direct and indirect benefit of the children.

Cases decided before the enactment of the Federal Child Support Guidelines

The reasonable expectations of children for future support are not frozen as of the date of the parent's separation. If, subsequent to the ordering of support provisions, there is a significant change in the economic circumstances of one of the parents, the reasonable expectations of the children could be affected. For example, a significant increase in the means of the payor parent might require that the needs of the children include benefits that were previously not included, justifying an increase in the child support payable: *Willick v. Willick* (1994), 6 R.F.L. (4th) 161, 173 N.R. 321 (S.C.C.); reversing (1992), 41 R.F.L. (3d) 107, 100 Sask. R. 211, 18 W.A.C. 211 (C.A.); varying (1992), 98 Sask. R. 239 (Q.B.).

Where the husband, who was a doctor, terminated his general practice and began to specialize in psychiatry, with the result that his income was halved from $62,000 to $30,000 annually, the court upheld on appeal an order reducing his child support obligation from $1,500 monthly to $1,000. Although considering his income alone, the order could be characterized as being high, he had remarried and his wife, although not employed, was employable. The court could properly consider the ability of the father's new wife to earn income: *Hynes v. Tierney-Hynes* (1993), 50 R.F.L. (3d) 279, 88 Man. R. (2d) 134, 51 W.A.C. 134 (C.A.); leave to appeal refused (1994), 2 R.F.L. (4th) 431 (note) (S.C.C.).

17§56A — Change in circumstances — undue hardship

The change of residence of one of two children of the marriage from one parent to the other is a change of circumstances that permits the court to order a reduction in child support payments: *Inglis v. Birkbeck*, 7 R.F.L. (5th) 114, 2000 SKQB 165, 2000 CarswellSask 236 (Q.B.); affirmed 2000 SKCA 144, 2000 CarswellSask 798 (C.A.). However, where the court finds that the child remaining with the first parent would suffer undue hardship under the *Guidelines* amount, the court may award an amount greater than the Table Amount for the child remaining with the first parent.

Where the father could not pursue gainful employment because of his poor health, his application for variation of child support was granted in *Dixon v. Fleming*, 6 R.F.L. (5th) 124, 2000 CarswellOnt 1189 (S.C.J.). But since the *Guidelines* amount of child support would result in undue hardship to the father, as he was already adversely affected by high access costs, child support was set at a nominal level far below this amount.

The mother's application for an upward variation of child support was dismissed where the combination of the father's increased access costs and his financial obligations to his new household constituted undue hardship: *Deveau v. Groskopf*, 10 R.F.L. (5th) 24, 2000 SKQB 186, [2000] 7 W.W.R. 757, 192 Sask. R. 227, 2000 CarswellSask 305 (Q.B.).

Where a judgment incorporating the parties' separation agreement provided that the non-custodial parent was to pay $1,000 in child support for three children, and only one child remained at home as a dependant, the father's application for variation was granted: *Block v. Baltimore* (2000), 5 R.F.L. (5th) 18, 2000 MBQB 5, 149 Man. R. (2d) 137, 2000 CarswellMan 139 (Q.B.); additional reasons at 2000 MBQB 83, 2000 CarswellMan 316 (Q.B.). Support was reduced to $428 a month. The court found that the loss of additional child support would objectively create hardship for the remaining child, but that the hardship was not "undue" which was defined as "exceptional", "excessive", or "unreasonable". The court was of the opinion that s. 10 (the hardship section) should be given a narrow interpretation and that the onus of proof was on the party who asserts the hardship and that the standard of proof is high. Living in an apartment, which many people do, could not be considered an undue hardship and the fact that there would be less money available to give the remaining child certain amenities was not accepted. There was no evidence to support the assertion that the payor's alleged failure to exercise more access than he did, increased costs of custody. Accordingly, the Table Amount was ordered without any reduction for undue hardship.

The fact that the father's child support obligation would rise by over $500 monthly upon application of *Guidelines* amounts 13 years after the parties' divorce was not found to be an "undue" hardship. The fact that the father had no contact with the children also did not justify a departure from the *Guidelines*: *Robinson v. Domin*, 39 R.F.L. (4th) 92, [1998] B.C.J. No. 1145, 1998 CarswellBC 1103 (S.C.).

In *Giroux v. Giroux*, 3 R.F.L. (5th) 61, [1999] O.J. No. 4999, 1999 CarswellOnt 4382 (S.C.J.); additional reasons at (February 15, 2000), Doc. 40096/90, 2000 CarswellOnt 518 (S.C.J.), the father's earnings did not increase as anticipated at the time of signing the minutes of settlement, later incorporated into the divorce judgment. He was forced to leave his employment due to a disability and subsequently required surgery. He remarried and had two more children. For approximately six months one of the parties' two children lived with the payor. The court ordered rescission of child support arrears. The payor suffered undue hardship in relation to the arrears. He was responsible for an unusually high level of debts reasonably incurred to earn a living; he had unusually high expenses in relation to exercising access and he had a legal duty to support a child who was under the age of majority. The standard of living of the payee's household would have been significantly higher than that of the payor.

In *Ferrigan v. Ferrigan* (1998), 36 R.F.L. (4th) 206, 1998 CarswellOnt 901 (Gen. Div.), the court allowed the husband's application for a reduction in child support from the amount specified in the parties' separation agreement. When the agreement was signed, the husband was fully employed as a teacher but was forced to take early retirement for health reasons. The husband had suffered real hardship and, the wife, who had remarried and had not returned to employment, was actually in a better financial position than the husband.

In *Claridge-Skof v. Skof* (July 11, 1997), [1997] O.J. No. 3112, 1997 CarswellOnt 3203, Doc. Peterborough 3550 11494/96 (Gen. Div.), the court was of the opinion that where the children would suffer a significant loss if the child support payment was required to be made pursuant to the new guidelines and the payor spouse would receive only a nominal benefit, the variation was not in the best interests of the children and the court would not order a variation.

In *Olah v. Olah*, 7 R.F.L. (5th) 173, 2000 CarswellOnt 1691 (S.C.J.), the court deleted the requirement for the father to pay extraordinary expenses of $156 per month where the father had left the jurisdiction and his income had been reduced from $58,000 per annum to $2,400 per annum. The father was still required to pay the *Guidelines* base amount of $492 per month as the child support award was made in the context of an overall settlement. The court reduced the amount for extraordinary expenses because there was no evidence before the court of the actual extraordinary expenses at the time of the appellate hearing and because, in the view of the court, there is some additional leniency built into the discretion to be applied in calculating s. 7 expenses and the relative obligations with respect to them.

In *Mayo v. O'Connell*, 42 R.F.L. (4th) 193, 170 Nfld. & P.E.I.R. 157522 A.P.R. 157, 1998 CarswellNfld 205 (U.F.C.), the court dismissed the mother's application for a reduction of child support payable by her. The evidence did not support the mother's "undue hardship" argument. Although the cost of access by her was high, given that the children lived in Newfoundland and she in Florida, she had not in fact exercised her access rights in over two years. Also, although another ex-husband was in arrears of child support payable to her, the resulting hardship was not "undue" given her income and expenses.

17§57 — Change in circumstances — increase in payor's income

Under the May 1997 amendments to the *Divorce Act* and the *Federal Child Support Guidelines*, an increase in the payor spouse's income is similar to a decrease in the sense that it is a change of income that may be a change of circumstances within any one, or all of the defined sets of circumstances which trigger the jurisdiction allowing the court to make a variation order. These sets of circumstances are:

- in the case of an order made before May 1, 1997, the mere fact that the law of child support changed on May 1, 1997: *Federal Child Support Guidelines*, s. 14(c) and *Divorce Act*, s. 17(4);
- in the case where an amount in an order was determined in accordance with the applicable table, any change in circumstance that would result in a different child support order: *Federal Child Support Guidelines*, s. 14(a) and *Divorce Act*, s. 17(4); and
- in the case where the amount does not include a determination in accordance with the applicable table, any change in the condition, means, needs or other circumstances of either spouse or of any child who is entitled to support: *Federal Child Support Guidelines*, s. 14(b) and *Divorce Act*, s. 17(4).

Divorce Act, 1985

In *Simon v. Simon* (1997), 33 R.F.L. (4th) 310, 1997 CarswellOnt 4269, [1997] O.J. No. 4145 (Gen. Div.); varied (1999), 1 R.F.L. (5th) 119, 182 D.L.R. (4th) 670, 127 O.A.C. 17, 46 O.R. (3d) 349, 1999 CarswellOnt 3863, [1999] O.J. No. 4492 (C.A.); leave to appeal refused (2000), 255 N.R. 198 (note), 135 O.A.C. 196 (note), [2000] S.C.C.A. No. 36, 2000 CarswellOnt 1203, 2000 CarswellOnt 1204 (S.C.C.) the court refused to apply the amount set out in the *Federal Child Support Guidelines* in the mother's application for increased child support based upon the father's professional hockey contract which guaranteed him a $1,000,000 salary for two years. It was not in the child's best interests to provide him with the luxury of large monthly support payments where such payments could not be guaranteed over the course of the child's dependency as it was unknown how long the father's professional hockey career would last.

Where the mother had lost her medical benefits and the husband had failed for sometime to advise her of an increase in his income, she was found entitled to a retroactive increase in child support: *Critch v. Critch* (2005), 12 R.F.L. (6th) 283, 2005 CarswellOnt 295, [2005] O.J. No. 235 (Ont. S.C.J.); additional reasons at (2005), 2005 CarswellOnt 1985 (Ont. S.C.J.).

Cases decided before the enactment of the Federal Child Support Guidelines

The reasonable expectations of children for future support are not frozen as of the date of the parent's separation. If, subsequent to the ordering of support provisions, there is a significant change in the economic circumstances of one of the parents, the reasonable expectations of the children could be affected. For example, a significant increase in the means of the payor parent might require that the needs of the children include benefits that were previously not included, justifying an increase in the child support payable: *Willick v. Willick* (1994), 6 R.F.L. (4th) 161, 173 N.R. 321 (S.C.C.); reversing (1992), 41 R.F.L. (3d) 107, 100 Sask. R. 211, 18 W.A.C. 211 (C.A.); varying (1992), 98 Sask. R. 239 (Q.B.)

In *Dahl v. Dahl* (1995), 18 R.F.L. (4th) 122 (Alta. C.A.), on a variation application, the court had increased child support from $250 each month gross to $1,295 each month net as the payor father's income had greatly increased. The order was made retroactive to October 1, 1994. The court also awarded the mother $36,000 as retroactive child support. The court was of the opinion that section 17 of the *Divorce Act* enables a court in the appropriate circumstances to vary a child support order retroactively both ways, either by increasing or decreasing the award. In this case, the father did not disclose to the mother the dramatic increases in his income which had incurred in recent years.

In *Pion v. Pion* (1992), 45 R.F.L. (3d) 40, 83 Man R. (2d) 303, 36 W.A.C. 303 (C.A.), the court allowed the custodial mother's application for an increase in child support. The facts that the parties' income had risen by more than 30 percent since the original support order and that the children's expenses had risen with the passage of time and their parents' adoption of a more affluent lifestyle, were sufficient changes in circumstances to warrant the variation.

Where the father, in a previous application by the mother for increased child support, had failed to disclose an increase in his income, his failure was considered in setting a higher child support payment in subsequent variation proceedings: *Williams v. Berridge* (1996), 21 R.F.L. (4th) 157 (Ont. Gen. Div.).

The fact that the formerly unemployed husband had found a job subsequent to the granting of a consent child support order was held to constitute a change in circumstances justifying an upward variation: *Russell v. Russell* (1995), 16 R.F.L. (4th) 229, 33 Alta. L.R. (3d) 170, 175 A.R. 225 (Q.B.).

Child support was increased considering the increase in the respondent father's income and the direct costs associated with the care of the child in *Fraser v. Fraser* (1995), 17 R.F.L. (4th) 347 (P.E.I. T.D.). The court affirmed that the amount of child support should be indexed to reflect costs of living increases.

Where the disparity between the parties' financial circumstances had grown significantly in the husband's favour since their divorce, the court found a sufficient change in circumstances to justify an upward variation of the parties' child support order: *Larson v. Larson* (1994), 8 R.F.L. (4th) 333 (Ont. Gen. Div.).

The parties were married in 1984 and separated in 1989. There were three children of the marriage and one child of the wife's prior to the marriage. The husband was a farmer whose income had increased over the past three years. Spousal and child support were ordered following divorce proceedings, but the husband accumulated $8,400 in arrears, although paying legal expenses of $20,000. The husband's application to extinguish payment of the arrears was refused. Given the husband's payment of legal fees over his support obligations, and in view of his vastly improved financial situation, there was no justification for extinguishing the arrears: *Duncan v. Duncan* (1994), 117 Sask. R. 274 (Q.B.).

17§58 — Change in circumstances — change in payee's income

In determining the amount of a child support order the income of the payee, that is, the custodial parent, is ignored whether it be $100,000 a year or zero, except where

- special or extraordinary expenses are claimed: *Federal Child Support Guidelines*, ss. 7(1) and (2), 21(3);
- the child is the age of majority or over and the alternative determination of the support amount is used: *Federal Child Support Guidelines*, s. 3(2)(b);
- the payor spouse's income is more than $150,000 a year and instead of using the percentage set out in the table to calculate the part of the amount to come from the balance of the income over $150,000, the court chooses to exercise its discretion: *Federal Child Support Guidelines*, ss. 4(b)(ii), 21(4);
- the children are in a split or shared custody arrangement: *Federal Child Support Guidelines*, ss. 8 and 9; or
- undue hardship is claimed: *Federal Child Support Guidelines*, ss. 10 and 21(3).

Unless the order which is to be varied involved one or more of these exceptions when it was made, a change in the income of the payee spouse will not entitle either spouse to a variation order. Since in all other cases, the payee's income is ignored on the making of the original order, it must be ignored when considering the making of a variation order.

Cases decided before the enactment of the Federal Child Support Guidelines

Divorce Act, 1985

In *Al-Maghazachi v. Dueck* (1995), 17 R.F.L. (4th) 132 (Man. C.A.), the appellant (the husband) applied to vary a Quebec consent judgment in which the husband was *inter alia* required to pay support for his children and the respondent (the wife) in the total amount of $1,200 a month. The wife also applied to vary, seeking among other things an increase in spousal and child support. At trial, the judge increased the husband's total support to $1,900 each month, with $600 per child and $700 for the wife and ordered the payment of arrears. Both parties appealed the order.

The court also held that based on an income of $70,000, the quantum of $500 per child is too low. While the spouses have a joint financial obligation to maintain a child, and one of the spouses has failed to provide for a child according to that spouse's ability, that failure should not result in an order which will victimize the children and require them to live at poverty level if the other spouse's means can provide them with adequate support. The court made a child support award of $750 per month per child.

On a variation application, the father was ordered to pay increased support where: the mother's income had decreased as a result of her inability to work at the same rate due to cancer; the child's expenses had increased with his age; the payor's income had increased and he was no longer supporting the parties' older son: *Lenic v. Lenic* (1995), 12 R.F.L. (4th) 406 (Sask. Q.B.).

In *Adam v. Adam* (1993), 50 R.F.L. (3d) 216, 89 Man. R. (2d) 275 (Q.B.), the parties were married in 1968 and separated in 1982. After separation, the wife remained in the home with the four children of the family. The husband was ordered to pay spousal and child support of $350 per month in divorce proceedings in 1988, by which time the two oldest children had left the home. When the parties' third child left home for university, the husband unilaterally reduced support for the wife and fourth child to $150 per month and financially assisted the third child directly. The husband currently earned $1,200 per month and the wife had improved her position and was earning $18,000 per year. The husband applied to reduce support retroactively and to cancel arrears of $1,906. Allowing the application in part, the court ordered the husband to pay $100 per month directly to the child and $250 per month to the wife for herself and the youngest child. Arrears were to be calculated from the date the husband started paying the third child directly, which reduced the arrears to $906. The increase in the wife's income was a material change in circumstances sufficient to vary the previous order, however the wife was still not self-sufficient and required assistance. She had been economically disadvantaged by the marriage. The factors set out in s. 17(7) of the *Divorce Act* were to be reviewed not just from the date of the last order but from the date of the marriage.

In *Wilson v. Wilson* (1995), 13 R.F.L. (4th) 260 (N.W.T. S.C.) in the original child support order, the father was required to pay $150 a month for each of two children. Four years later, the support was increased to $600 per month. After this second order the mother, the custodial parent unilaterally decided to leave a well-paid job to attend a two-year technical school program and had a much reduced income compared to what she received at the time of the original order and at the time of the variation four years later. The father's income had increased but he had also incurred significant debts, including a mortgage on his home.

The court held that even if the mother had remained in her job, child support should have been increased. It set out an amount of $450 for the support of each child each month and an additional amount of $150 each month for each child to cover the shortfall which the mother would have paid, if she had remained in her job. This additional amount was to be considered as an advance on support payments which may become payable when the mother finishes her course.

Where a spouse has remarried and the court has rescinded spousal support, the court will not increase child support where there is nothing in the material to show a change of circumstances of the respondent or the children which would justify an order increasing child support: *Range v. Range* (1995), 14 R.F.L. (4th) 11 (B.C. S.C.).

17§59 — Change in circumstances — payor spouse remarrying or entering common law relationship

Under the May 1997 amendments to the *Divorce Act* and the *Federal Child Support Guidelines*, remarriage of the payor spouse or the acquiring of a common law marriage partner will not entitle that spouse to a variation order unless there is undue hardship which works in his or her favour: *Federal Child Support Guidelines*, s. 10. See 15§97 Undue Hardship, above.

An increase in child support to a child of a first marriage is a sufficient change of circumstances to warrant a variation in the child support payable to the children of a second marriage. In *Meuser v. Meuser* (1998), 43 R.F.L. (4th) 140, 58 B.C.L.R. (3d) 131, [1999] 4 W.W.R. 739, 168 D.L.R. (4th) 387, 115 B.C.A.C. 135, 189 W.A.C. 135 (C.A.); additional reasons at (1999), 44 R.F.L. (4th) 262 (B.C. C.A.); varying (1998), 40 R.F.L. (4th) 295 (B.C. S.C.) the child support for children of a second marriage was reduced through application of the *Guidelines*.

In *A. (J.A.) v. A. (S.R.)* (1999), 45 R.F.L. (4th) 165, 64 B.C.L.R. (3d) 154, 120 B.C.A.C. 142, 196 W.A.C. 142 (C.A.), the fact that the father had remarried and taken on second family obligation could not justify a reduction in the child support payable to the children of his first marriage. Even after payment of the *Guidelines* amounts, the second family could enjoy a higher standard of living than the first. In the circumstances, there was no jurisdiction to order an amount less than that specified in the *Guidelines*.

In *Cook v. Hare* (1999), 46 R.F.L. (4th) 343 (B.C. S.C.), the court dismissed the payor mother's application for a reduction in child support based upon undue hardship. While the mother's obligation to support another child of a different union did create an undue hardship, a comparison of the standard of living in both households indicated that the support amount was reasonable. To be successful, the mother was required to satisfy both aspects of the two-part test for undue hardship.

Divorce Act, 1985

On an application for a reduction in child support, where the payor has new obligations, the court must consider the needs of both the first and the second families, and the financial resources available to fulfill those needs: *Dubois v. Dubois* (1993), 48 R.F.L. (3d) 419 (Man. C.A.).

A payor father is not entitled to seek a reduction in child support based upon his second family obligations when his new wife has not assumed a reasonable share of the costs of that second family: *Edwards (Pereira) v. Edwards* (1994), 5 R.F.L. (4th) 321, 133 N.S.R. (2d) 8, 390 A.P.R. 8, 118 D.L.R. (4th) 217 (C.A.); affirming (1994), 126 N.S.R. (2d) 341, 352 A.P.R. 341 (S.C.); additional reasons at (1994), 127 N.S.R. (2d) 379, 355 A.P.R. 379 (S.C.).

Children are entitled to a lifestyle commensurate with the joint income of their parents. A payor father is not entitled to maintain a lifestyle better than the custodial wife and children and then rely upon the existence of his second family as a justification for a reduction in the child support payable by him: *Edwards (Pereira) v. Edwards* (1994), 5 R.F.L. (4th) 321, 133 N.S.R. (2d) 8, 390 A.P.R. 8, 118 D.L.R. (4th) 217 (C.A.); affirming (1994), 126 N.S.R. (2d) 341, 352 A.P.R. 341 (S.C.); additional reasons at (1994), 127 N.S.R. (2d) 379, 355 A.P.R. 379 (S.C.).

In *Parsons v. Parsons* (1995), 17 R.F.L. (4th) 267 (Ont. Gen. Div.); additional reasons at (1995), 17 R.F.L. (4th) 267 (note) (Ont. Gen. Div.), it was held that the husband's second family arrangements could not be used as a means of diluting his child support obligations towards his first family.

Where a non-custodial spouse remarries, the income of his or her new partner is properly considered as a factor in determining the spouse's continuing ability to contribute to the children's support: *Taylor v. Le Boubon* (1994), 8 R.F.L. (4th) 348 (Ont. Gen. Div.) (in which the non-custodial mother's application for a downward variation of child support payable by her was dismissed subsequent to her remarriage despite a decrease in her annual income).

The parties married in 1975, separated in 1980 and divorced in 1982. The father was ordered to pay child support of $50 a month for each of the two children of the marriage.

He rarely paid. Both parties remarried and the father had three more children. He was unemployed from 1980 to 1984 and occasionally employed until 1989, after which he had a full-time job. The mother left the province in 1984, returning in 1988. While away, she had no contact with the father and made no demands for support. The parties' older child was no longer a child of the marriage and the younger child would only be so for a few more months. The court held that the father's liability for supporting the older child was to cease immediately. The arrears of $10,650 were reduced to $4,500, and the father was ordered to pay reduced arrears and support of $100 per month in respect of the younger child, while he remained a child of the marriage. After child support ended, the father was to pay the mother $100 a month towards the reduced arrears. In exercising its discretion regarding the cancellation or reduction of arrears, the court had to consider the reality of the payor's present financial circumstances, including the right of a second family to support. In this case, the father had little means to pay support until 1989. It was unfair of the mother to wait until the children were almost independent to demand child support: *Young v. Konkle* (1993), 1 R.F.L. (4th) 211 (Alta. Q.B.).

In *Greco v. Levin* (1991), 33 R.F.L. (3d) 405 (Ont. Gen. Div.), the court held that a payor spouse's obligations to his second family are not a reason to relieve him of his duty to support a child from his first family. The husband had undertaken his obligations to his second family with knowledge of his pre-existing responsibility for his first child.

In assessing the parties' second family obligation in an application for variation of child support, the idea that a new spouse bears no responsibility to his or her partner's children from a previous union is outdated. A new spouse's income is a resource which a custodial or non-custodial parent can draw upon, diectly or indirectly. The law can and should impose upon those who marry a parent, a duty and obligation to his or her children which would, in turn, be balanced against the primary duty of the parents: *Snelgrove-Fowler v. Fowler* (1993), 46 R.F.L. (3d) 353, 138 A.R. 192 (Q.B.).

Where the father had remarried and taken on new family obligations, the court allowed his application for a reduction in child support. Although an individual should not generally be allowed to escape support obligations through the formation of new relationships, in this instance the mother had also entered into a common-law relationship with a man who was assisting her financially: *Kelly v. Kelly* (1992), 44 R.F.L. (3d) 214 (P.E.I. T.D.); additional reasons at (1992), 44 R.F.L. (3d) 214 at 217 (P.E.I. T.D.).

Where the father had married twice since his divorce and was supporting children from both subsequent unions, his application to reduce support for the children of his first marriage was allowed. Although his income had increased substantially, he had new family responsibilities and his ability to pay support for the children of his first marriage was therefore reduced considerably: *Strowbridge v. Strowbridge* (1989), 80 Nfld. & P.E.I.R. 111, 249 A.P.R. 111 (Nfld. T.D.).

The fact that both parties had entered into new family arrangements was found to be insufficient to disturb child support arrangements which had been established through minutes of settlement in: *Potter v. Bragg* (1988), 16 R.F.L. (3d) 323, 86 N.S.R. (2d) 363, 218 A.P.R. 363 (T.D.).

A payor cannot avoid a contractual obligation to pay child support by assuming new family obligations: *Storer v. Storer* (1988), 17 R.F.L. (3d) 222 (Sask. Q.B.).

See also *Burton v. Burton* (1994), 9 R.F.L. (4th) 108 (Ont. Gen. Div.).

The father was ordered to pay $400 per month combined spousal and child support. The divorce order varied support to $266 per month child support, to be increased annually.

At that time, the father earning $22,000 per year and his common-law wife was earning $17,000. They had one child and were expecting another. The father was also ordered to pay $50 per month towards arrears, in addition to the regular order. He had been jailed for one month for failure to do so. The mother's application for enforcement of arrears was allowed. A variation could not be made where there were unexplained arrears and the father's payment record did not justify an exception to the general rule, particularly since his combined household income had increased. The father's maintenance obligation probably represented less than 10 percent of his household's gross income. The maintenance payment was tax deductible and the payment considerably less than he paid for the children of his new family. In addition, the amount was not unrealistic, given the father's means, nor was it unfair to his second family. The father's application to reduce the arrears was dismissed except to the extent that arrears for the month he had no income, due to an unemployment insurance waiting period, were not enforced: *L. (G.M.) v. L. (V.A.)* (1993), 127 N.S.R. (2d) 66, 355 A.P.R. 66 (Fam. Ct.).

17§60 — Change in circumstances — payee spouse remarrying or entering common law relationship

Under the May 1997 amendments to the *Divorce Act* and the *Federal Child Support Guidelines*, the remarriage of the payee spouse or that spouse acquiring of a common law marriage partner will not entitle the other spouse to a variation order unless there is undue hardship which works in his or her favour: *Federal Child Support Guidelines*, s. 10. See 15§97 Undue Hardship, above.

17§61 — Change in circumstances — child withdrawing from parental control

In *Racicot v. Racicot* (2003), 47 R.F.L. (5th) 384, 2003 CarswellOnt 4615 (Ont. S.C.J.), the fact that the parties' 20-year-old daughter had her own child was, in and of itself, insufficient to justify a termination of her father's child support obligation. The child had a severe learning disability that impaired her ability to work and she could not therefore withdraw from her mother's charge.

Where the parties' daughter battled with depression and had temporarily dropped out of school subsequent to multiple suicide attempts, the court rejected the father's application to terminate her child support. Although she only attended school sporadically and worked part-time, she was clearly unable to withdraw from her mother's charge because of her mental illness: *Dodd v. Dodd* (2003), 49 R.F.L. (5th) 20, 2003 CarswellOnt 5126 (Ont. S.C.J.).

The question of whether children have removed themselves from parental control is one of fact. In determining the issue, the court may have regard to the conduct of the parties and the conditions, means and circumstances of each of them: *Bates v. Bates* (1995), 10 R.F.L. (4th) 261, 165 A.R. 71 (C.A.).

Where the parties' 19-year-old son moved out of the custodial mother's residence after deterioration of their relationship, the husband's application for termination of child support was allowed. As the son had voluntarily withdrawn from parental control, he no longer qualified as a child of the marriage. The fact that he continued to eat meals at his mother's out of economic necessity did not alter the withdrawal: *Wieland v. Wieland* (1994), 3 R.F.L. (4th) 56 (Ont. Gen. Div.).

The refusal of a 16-year-old child to speak with the payor mother was not found to be a sufficient reason to justify a termination of child support in *Filice v. Lepore* (1995), 16 R.F.L. (4th) 42 (Ont. Gen. Div.).

An application to terminate child support for a child over the age of majority who is in full time attendance at university will be dismissed where the child has a sincere inner conflict in regard to her father, appears not to have reached full emotional maturity and her refusal to communicate with her father is not motivated by petulance, malice or vindictiveness: *Fraser v. Jones* (1995), 17 R.F.L. (4th) 218 (Sask. Q.B.). The court was of the opinion that as a child grew older there was greater likelihood that failure to communicate with a parent who provided child support would be considered grounds to terminating support. The court held that the parties' 18-year-old daughter was still a "child of the marriage" and entitled to support.

In *Keats v. Keats* (1995), 12 R.F.L. (4th) 191 (Nfld. U.F.C.), the court rejected the wife's application for termination of child support. Although the wife contended that her daughter had unilaterally terminated her relationship with her, the claim was not supported by the evidence.

17§62 — Jurisdiction to override separation agreements

Where a child support obligation is contained in an agreement, such as a separation agreement, and not in a court order, leaving no order to vary, the remedy where the guidelines amount is sought, is to apply by way of an original application under the *Divorce Act* for the corollary relief of child support. The order obtained on the application would supersede the amount in the agreement.

Unless the terms of the agreement reach or surpass what a court would include in an order made under the guidelines, or the terms are reasonable within the meaning of section 15.1(5) of the *Divorce Act*, a court would likely make an order superseding the agreement. This would be so notwithstanding that in the agreement the applicant waived all rights to further support and released the payor or intended payor from all claims for this relief. See, for example, *Santosuosso v. Santosuosso* (1997), 27 R.F.L. (4th) 234, 32 O.R. (3d) 143, 97 O.A.C. 42 (Gen. Div.), where the court had no difficulty in overriding releases of spousal support in an agreement to substitute a different order of its own. For a detailed discussion of this decision, see 15§146 Effects of Domestic Contracts — Introduction.

Where the father unilaterally cut off child support payments for his 18-year-old daughter, the court agreed to enforce the parties' agreement under which the father was obligated to pay until his daughter was 19. At the time the agreement had been negotiated, the father had hoped that his daughter would pursue a post-secondary education and had been disappointed when she chose not to do so. The father's changed expectations were not sufficient to qualify as a changed circumstance weighty enough to warrant a variation of the parties' agreement: *Jordan v. Bolt* (2004), 10 R.F.L. (6th) 54, 2004 CarswellNfld 370, 2004 NLTD 226 (T.D.).

In *Finney v. Finney* (1998), 40 R.F.L. (4th) 249 (B.C. S.C.), the court allowed the father's application for a decrease in child support from an amount previously agreed upon by the parties. The father's income had not reached the amount anticipated when the agreement was signed. Furthermore, the support level sought by the father still exceeded the amount which would have been calculated under the *Guidelines*. Finally, as the agreement had also provided the wife with a lump sum to house the children, the agreement was found to contain "special provisions" pursuant to s. 17(6.2)(a) of the *Divorce Act* for direct and indirect benefit of the children.

In *Vaillancourt v. Vaillancourt* (1998), 43 R.F.L. (4th) 135, 174 Nfld. & P.E.I.R. 18, 533 A.P.R. 18 (P.E.I. S.C.[In Chambers]), the court refused to reduce the child support payable under the parties' separation agreement through the application of the *Guidelines*. The father had competent counsel when negotiating the agreement and the amount specified therein was the actual amount required by the mother and child to live. Application of the *Guidelines* would be inequitable in these circumstances.

In *Wedge v. McKenna* (1997), 155 Nfld. & P.E.I.R. 294, 481 A.P.R. 294 (P.E.I. T.D.), the parties had signed a separation agreement which had been incorporated into a divorce judgment in 1995, whereby each party stated his or her inability to pay child support to the other for their three children. The agreement provided that child support could be reviewed upon the father's total income from his law practice reaching a certain level. The court held that s. 17(6.2)(a) and (b) applied, that is, that the court could apply an amount for child support different from the *Guidelines* amount since there were special provisions in a written agreement benefitting the children and that the application of the *Guidelines* would lead to an inequitable amount of child support, given those special provisions.

Cases decided before the enactment of the Federal Child Support Guidelines

In *Willick v. Willick*, [1994] 3 S.C.R. 670, 6 R.F.L. (4th) 161, 125 Sask. R. 81, 81 W.A.C. 81, 173 N.R. 321, 119 D.L.R. (4th) 405, the court considered the extent of the powers of the court, under the *Divorce Act*, to vary child support which has been agreed to by the parties in a separation agreement and which has subsequently been incorporated into the decree *nisi*. The court was of the opinion that, as between the parties, the agreement was strong evidence that, at the time of the signing of the agreement, the parties accepted its terms as providing for the needs of the children. In a variation proceeding, where, as in this case, the agreement was embodied in a court judgment, the original child support order or the previous variation order was assumed to have properly taken into account the needs of the children having regard to the means of the parents. The correctness of the previous order would not be reviewed and would only be varied if the requirements of s. 17(4) of the *Divorce Act* were properly satisfied.

In the *Willick* decision, the court set aside the judgment of the Court of Appeal and restored the judgment of the trial court which increased the child support award, based on the substantial increase in the income of the non-custodial parent.

Where the parties' consent child support order anticipated the children's commencement of post-secondary education, the father could not rely upon the beginning of that education as a change in circumstances warranting a variation of child support: *MacDonald v. MacDonald* (1996), 22 R.F.L. (4th) 314 (N.B. C.A.).

A child support agreement should be given heavy weight in an application for increased support but should be overridden where the children's circumstances have change adversely or where support is below the proper range: *Paquette v. Dingwell* (1996), 22 R.F.L. (4th) 87 (Alta. C.A.).

The mother's appeal in *Black v. Black* (1995), 19 R.F.L. (4th) 442 (B.C. C.A.), was granted where the chambers judge had cancelled the father's arrears of child support on the basis of an oral agreement to waive the support payments by the respondent if he would refrain from visiting or making contact with the children. The court, relying on *Richardson v. Richardson*, [1987] 1 S.C.R. 857, held that child maintenance is the right of the child and a spouse cannot barter away his or her child's right to support in a settlement agreement. The court may always intervene and determine the correct level of support for a child.

In *Brans v. Brans* (1996), 20 R.F.L. (4th) 429 (Ont. Gen. Div.), the court held while a child has a right to share in a parent's increased standard of living, that right is not without limits and if an agreement is sufficient to meet the children's reasonable needs and the costs are fairly apportioned between the parents, the court will not override or vary the order that incorporates it. In this case, there was a very significant increase in the respondent's income for one year, but the court did not find the change, seen in the entire context of the parties' circumstances including the applicant's management of her own affairs, warranted a reallocation of the proportionate responsibilities of the parents.

In *Staple v. Tucker* (1995), 132 Nfld. & P.E.I.R. 60, 410 A.P.R. 60 (Nfld. T.D.), the court refused the mother's application for an increase in child support from the amount specified in the parties' separation agreement. The mother's unsubstantiated claim of an increase in one of the children's expenses did not constitute a material change in circumstances let alone the radical change needed to override the separation agreement which had been incorporated into the parties' decree *nisi*.

In *Payne v. Short* (1995), 10 R.F.L. (4th) 257 (Ont. Gen. Div.), the applicant, the former wife, sought to vary a judgment under the *Divorce Act* which awarded custody and child maintenance to include either the indexing provision in the separation agreement or an indexing clause pursuant to s. 38 of the *Family Law Act*. Mr. Justice Rutherford held that a court does not have jurisdiction to amend or vary a separation agreement and a judgment granted after a separation agreement exhaustively supercedes anything in the separation agreement. Further, the court was of the opinion that where support is ordered under the *Divorce Act*, that support order cannot be indexed pursuant to the *Family Law Act*. In the interests of finalizing the matter without additional expense, the court decided to terminate the earlier court decision and ordered child support of $400 per month per child to be indexed in accordance with the cost of living.

In *Auld v. Auld* (1994), 5 R.F.L. (4th) 132, 123 Nfld. & P.E.I.R. 43, 382 A.P.R. 43 (P.E.I. T.D.), the court allowed the husband's application to vary a child support provision requiring him to finance his daughter's post-secondary education. Since the date of the agreement, the daughter had demonstrated an ability to contribute somewhat to her own keep and the income of the custodial mother, who paid nothing towards the daughter's support, had increased. Given the change of circumstances, it was fair that the father's responsibility be restricted to his daughter's book and tuition costs.

Where the parties' separation agreement had placed an undue burden on the wife regarding child support, the court allowed the wife's application to vary the decree incorporating the agreement by providing for increased support: *Thomson v. Thomson* (1988), 14 R.F.L. (3d) 347 (Sask. C.A.).

A court is not bound by the terms of a separation agreement as regards child support: *Tosky v. Taphorn* (1991), 36 R.F.L. (3d) 457, 77 Man. R. (2d) 218 (Q.B.). Where the child's circumstances have changed, making his needs more costly because of ageing and because of inflation, the court may increase support.

A court will vary a child support award based upon an agreement between the parties only where the needs of the children so demand or the circumstances of the parties have changed substantially. A general increase in the cost of living does not constitute such a change: *Krasnesky v. Krasnesky* (1989), 62 Man. R. (2d) 237 (Q.B.).

Where the parties had entered into a separation agreement containing child support provisions with a variation formula on the happening of certain specified contingencies, it was held that the omission of variation on other contingencies was intentional. Accordingly an application for increased support based upon increased child care costs was dismissed, as such a ground was both foreseeable and not specifically provided for in the agreement: *Crowe v. Crowe* (1988), 16 R.F.L. (3d) 420, 66 O.R. (2d) 157 (H.C.).

Where a child support provision, incorporated as part of a judgment in a divorce decree provides for the termination of support when a child becomes 19 years of age, the court may still find that the child is a "child of the marriage" requiring support after the child is 19 where the child is unable by reason of "other cause to withdraw from their parent(s) charge or to obtain the necessaries of life": *Varey v. Varey* (July 4, 1995), Doc. New Westminister D011020 (B.C. S.C.).

In *Rudelier v. Cunningham* (1995), 18 R.F.L. (4th) 430 (B.C. S.C.), the mother's claim for an increase in the child support provided for in the parties' separation agreement was dismissed. The mother had failed to prove any change in circumstances since the date of the agreement and her claims that the settlement was unfair were refuted by the facts that she herself was a lawyer and had obtained legal advice before signing the agreement.

17§63 — Variation of a global amount for spousal and child support, awarded prior to May 1, 1997

An application to vary a global amount previously awarded for the support of both spouse and children or a child, will be treated as two separate original applications for support; one for spousal support to be determined under the criteria set out in the Act, and one for child support to be determined under the guidelines: *Divorce Act*, s. 34(1.1) and s. 35.1. The court may include in a variation order any provision that under the Act could have been included in the order in respect of which the variation order is sought: *Divorce Act*, s. 17(3).

17§64 — Variation of child support orders on consent

A court may make a variation order in respect of a child support order on the consent of the spouses if it is satisfied that reasonable arrangements have been made for the support of the child to whom the order relates. In determining whether the arrangements are reasonable, the court is to refer to the guidelines. However, the guidelines are advisory only, and the court is not to consider the arrangements to be unreasonable solely because the amount of support is not the same as the amount that would otherwise have been determined in accordance with the guidelines: *Federal Child Support Guidelines*, s. 17(6.4).

17§65 — Retrospective variation and variation of arrears

Divorce Act, 1985

In *S. (L.) v. P. (E.)* (1997), 32 R.F.L. (4th) 75, 41 B.C.L.R. (3d) 14 (B.C. S.C.); varied 1999 CarswellBC 1402, [1999] B.C.J. No. 1451, 175 D.L.R. (4th) 423, 126 B.C.A.C. 28, 206 W.A.C. 28, 67 B.C.L.R. (3d) 254, [1999] 12 W.W.R. 718, 50 R.F.L. (4th) 302, 1999 BCCA 393 (B.C. C.A.); leave to appeal refused [1999] S.C.C.A. No. 444, 252 N.R. 194 (note), 135 B.C.A.C. 160 (note), 221 W.A.C. 160 (note) (S.C.C.), the court held that there are a number of factors which militate in favour of ordering retroactive support. These include:

(1) the need on the part of the child and a corresponding ability to pay on the part of the non- custodial parent;

(2) some blameworthy conduct on the part of the non-custodial parent such as incomplete or misleading financial disclosure at the time of the original order;

(3) necessity on the part of the custodial parent to encroach on his or her capital or incur debt to meet child rearing expenses;

(4) an excuse for a delay in bringing the application where the delay is significant; and

(5) notice by the non-custodial parent of an intention to pursue maintenance followed by negotiations to that end.

Factors which have militated against ordering retroactive maintenance include:

1) the order would cause an unreasonable or unfair burden to the non-custodial parent, especially to the extent that such a burden would interfere with ongoing support obligations;

2) the only purpose of the award would be to redistribute capital or award spousal support in the guise of child support; and

3) a significant, unexplained delay in bringing the application.

In this case, the parties who had never married had one child. The mother had obtained a paternity order but originally had not applied for support. Support was set at $1 per year. The mother successfully applied to increase the award and the father was ordered to pay $3,000 per month in child support. The mother unsuccessfully applied for retroactive variation of the child-support order. Because of the contribution of the wife and her family, the child had not been at a disadvantage during the period for which support was sought. The court set aside the support order made by the trial judge, including the provision for payment of school fees and extracurricular activities, and substituted an order of $1,700 per month, effective 1 October 1997.

In *Llewellyn v. Llewellyn*, 26 R.F.L. (5th) 389, 2002 CarswellBC 529, 2002 BCCA 182, 99 B.C.L.R. (3d) 361, 212 D.L.R. (4th) 153, 165 B.C.A.C. 268, 270 W.A.C. 268 (C.A.), child support arrears payable to the mother were reduced in accordance with *Guidelines* amounts for the period of time in which one of the children lived intermittently with the father.

Where the mother had for a number of years financed the bulk of the children's extracurricular activities, the court allowed her application for a partial retroactive increase in child support. While the mother had a plausible explanation for her delay in seeking a variation earlier, she had to bear some of the responsibility: *Dodd v. Dodd* (2003), 49 R.F.L. (5th) 20, 2003 CarswellOnt 5126 (Ont. S.C.J.).

Where the husband had failed to disclose significant increases in his income, the wife was successful in her application for a retroactive upward variation of child support: *Burke v. Burke*, 26 R.F.L. (5th) 1, 2002 CarswellAlta 380, 2002 ABQB 281, [2002] 6 W.W.R. 670, 2 Alta. L.R. (4th) 67 (Q.B.).

Where the father had used his severance package to pay off personal debts, he could not relay on the loss of his job as justification for rescinding his child support arrears:

Wolkowski v. Doroshenko, 27 R.F.L. (5th) 214, 2002 CarswellSask 186, 216 Sask. R. 237, 2002 SKQB 114 (Q.B.).

See *Razutis v. Garrett*, 48 R.F.L. (4th) 452, 126 B.C.A.C. 249, 206 W.A.C. 249, 175 D.L.R. (4th) 730, 1999 BCCA 410 (C.A.).

Although the best interests of the children is the overriding consideration awarding retroactive child support, exceptional circumstances must exist to order support for a period that commenced prior to the date on which the application to vary was made: *Sherlow v. Zubko* (1999), 50 R.F.L. (4th) 160, [2000] 1 W.W.R. 699, 247 A.R. 66, 76 Alta. L.R. (3d) 202, 1999 CarswellAlta 472, [1999] A.J. No. 644 (Q.B.).

The determining factor for a retroactive variation of child support is the actual cost of raising and caring for the children. It is incumbent upon the custodial spouse not to delay in seeking a legal remedy: *Macbeth v. Macbeth* (1998), 36 R.F.L. (4th) 390, 214 A.R. 104 (Q.B.).

Caution should be exercised in relieving a parent of the obligation to pay child support arrears, particularly when it is uncertain that a current inability to pay will extend into the future: *Smith v. Smith* (1998), 39 R.F.L. (4th) 88, 55 B.C.L.R. (3d) 99 (S.C. [In Chambers]).

The fact that the father had voluntarily left a job to take another lower paying one and then returned to school were insufficient grounds upon which to forgive his child support arrears owing. The father was well aware when he made his employment decisions of the negative impact on his ability to pay support: *Vaillancourt v. Vaillancourt* (1998), 43 R.F.L. (4th) 135, 174 Nfld. & P.E.I.R. 18, 533 A.P.R. 18 (P.E.I. S.C. [In Chambers]).

After the father of two children obtained a position as an accountant at $55,200 a year, the mother applied to vary an order for child support that had been made in a nominal amount when the father was unemployed. In ordering a variation, the court held that it had jurisdiction to make a retroactive order beyond the date of the application. The father ought to have paid more child support when he secured the position as an accountant, and the delay by the mother in bringing the application should not be allowed to adversely affect the children. Child support was increased to $800 a month for the two children for a retroactive period before May 1, 1997 (when the *Guidelines* came into effect) and $722 a month based on the *Guidelines* from May 1st forward. The father was given credit for certain family debts that he paid by starting the first retroactive period six months after his income increased with his position as an accountant: *Willson v. Willson* (1997), 34 R.F.L. (4th) 242 (B.C. S.C. [In Chambers]).

Cases decided before the enactment of the Federal Child Support Guidelines

Where the wife had consented to a three month downward variation of the child and spousal support payable by the husband, who subsequently continued to pay at the reduced level for nine years, the Court of Appeal upheld an order calling for a retroactive increase in the support payable: *Cawker v. Cawker* (1995), 18 R.F.L. (4th) 268, 17 B.C.L.R. (3d) 160, 67 B.C.A.C. 305, 111 W.A.C. 305 (C.A.); affirming (1994), 7 R.F.L. (4th) 282 (B.C. S.C.).

Section 17 of the *Divorce Act* authorizes the Court, in the appropriate circumstances, to retroactively vary a child support in both ways, by either increasing or decreasing the award: *Dahl v. Dahl* (1995), 18 R.F.L. (4th) 122, 178 A.R. 119, 110 W.A.C. 119 (C.A.).

Where a court orders support for more than one child, without specifying the amount for each child, and one of the children is found to be no longer a "child of the marriage", thus requiring support, it cannot be assumed that each child is entitled to receive the same amount of support: *Hansen v. Hansen* (1995), 13 R.F.L. (4th) 335 (Ont. Gen. Div.) before Fleury J. There is no authority in the Rules of Civil Procedure to justify such a proposition. However, in such a case, the court would have jurisdiction to vary support retroactively based on a material change in circumstances, where for instance, one child no longer attended any educational institution.

In *Stacey v. Hacking* (1993), 142 N.B.R. (2d) 99, 364 A.P.R. 99 (Q.B.), the court refused the husband's application to vary retroactively back until 1980 the child support he had been required to pay. Although the custodial mother had remarried that year and moved to another jurisdiction, the husband had failed to prove a material change in circumstances. However, as he lacked the ability to pay the arrears owing, they were forgiven.

In *Al-Maghazachi v. Dueck* (1995), 17 R.F.L. (4th) 132 (Man. C.A.), the appellant (the husband) applied to vary a Quebec consent judgment in which the husband was *inter alia* required to pay support for his children and the respondent (the wife) in the total amount of $1,200 a month. The wife also applied to vary, seeking among other things an increase in spousal and child support. At trial, the judge increased the husband's total support to $1,900 each month, with $600 per child and $700 for the wife and ordered the payment of arrears. Both parties appealed the order.

The appellate court held that where as in this case the majority of the arrears represented child support and the evidence did not suggest that the failure to remit or reduce the arrears would be grossly unfair or inequitable for the husband, the husband was required to pay the arrears.

In *Heiden v. British Columbia (Director of Maintenance Enforcement)* (1995), 19 R.F.L. (4th) 320 (C.A.), the Director of Maintenance Enforcement appealed from an order reducing child-support arrears owed by the father. The ex-wife did not try to enforce her 1978 child-support order until 1994, when she enlisted in the Family Maintenance Enforcement Program. The court followed *Meyers v. Meyers* (1995), 12 R.F.L. (4th) 170 (B.C. C.A.), in holding that where a parent fails to enforce a child support order, this fact is not, in most instances, a reason to penalize the child or parent, as is not in itself evidence of any waiver of the support obligation on the child's behalf. However once a change of circumstances has been shown, the consequences of delay, such as the amount of accrued arrears and the reduced or increased means of the parents may well be relevant in determining the appropriate results in a given case.

The ex-wife had not known the whereabouts of her former husband when his payments fell into arrears and believed that legal fees for enforcement would be too costly. When she eventually discovered where her former husband was living and learned of the availability of the free services of the Director, she undertook enforcement proceedings. Consequently, the ex-wife's "delay" was not a factor in barring her application for child support.

The appellate court allowed the Director's appeal of the reduction of child support arrears where the evidence before the court did not meet the onus on the father to show the significance and extent of change in his circumstances in relation to his ability to pay — past, present and future: *Heiden v. British Columbia (Director of Maintenance Enforcement)* (1995), 19 R.F.L. (4th) 320 (B.C. C.A.). The father had argued that the failure of his business some years before, his current income, and his obligation to support the three children of his second marriage constituted a material change in circumstances. The Court of Appeal held that the Chambers judge fell into error in ordering cancellation of part of the arrears, based perhaps on an overall impression of reasonableness in all the circumstances.

Where the father claimed that he was unemployed and trying to overcome a drug problem, the court allowed the father's appeal in part and ordered a suspension of arrears of child support for four months to enable him to find employment without the risk of losing his employment because of immediate enforcement proceedings in *Freund v. Dent* (1995), 14 R.F.L. (4th) 251, 102 Man. R. (2d) 316 (C.A.). During the four month period, the father was required to pay ongoing monthly maintenance.

A parent who fails to file an answer in divorce proceedings in which a claim for child support is made cannot succeed in an application to rescind support arrears on the ground that he or she was not notified of the support order: *Meyers v. Meyers* (1995), 12 R.F.L. (4th) 170 (B.C. C.A.).

Where the husband had incrementally over a period of time reduced the quantum of spousal and child support payable pursuant to the parties' separation agreement, he could not later characterize his wife as having consented to the reduction and thus eliminating arrears owing. The husband could not point to any specific agreement which would have supported his position: *Cawker v. Cawker* (1994), 7 R.F.L. (4th) 282 (B.C. S.C.); affirmed (1995), 18 R.F.L. (4th) 268, 17 B.C.L.R. (3d) 160 (C.A.).

In *Vincent v. Vincent* (1995), 15 R.F.L. 273 (Nfld. C.A.), the parties were divorced in 1992 and included in the divorce judgment was a direction that the father pay lump sum child support equivalent to $300 each month for each of two children, subject to review after two years. The court was of the opinion that where there is a provision in a child support order stating that the order would be reviewed after a specified term, then a party who seeks to change the quantum of support does not need to establish material change and any application for child support can be treated as an original order. However, in this case, the court held that if it were required to treat the application as a variation application, then there had been a sufficient change of circumstances to justify a variation.

Where the failure of the husband to disclose all his financial circumstances was found to be inadvertent and the injury occasioned by the non-disclosure was remedied by the award of lump sum maintenance, special costs were not justifiable: *Oyen v. Oyen* (1994), 9 R.F.L. (4th) 454 (B.C. C.A.).

In 1988, a divorce decree ratified the parties' agreement, which provided that the wife would have custody of the children and the husband would pay her $1,100 in monthly support. The parties had also agreed that should the wife move to Vancouver, child support would be reduced to $1,000 per month. After the divorce, the wife moved to Vancouver but, in 1989, she returned to Montreal. After her return, the husband continued to pay her $1,000 per month. In 1991, the wife moved for variation of support and claimed the arrears for the period after she came back to Montreal. The motion was allowed in part on other grounds. The trial judge concluded that the wife had waived her right to arrears. The wife's appeal of the trial judge's decision on the motion was allowed in part on other grounds. The wife received the reduced amount of support during three years without protest which amounted to a waiver of her right to claim arrears: *D. (S.) v. R. (G.)* (February 17, 1994), Doc. C.A. Montreal 500-09-001107-929 (Que. C.A.).

Neither the "one year rule" nor the "rule against hoarding" have any application in proceedings to vary child support arrears: *Haisman v. Haisman* (1994), 7 R.F.L. (4th) 1, 22

Alta. L.R. (3d) 56, 116 D.L.R. (4th) 671, 157 A.R. 47, 77 W.A.C. 47 (C.A.); reversing in part (1993), 7 Alta. L.R. (3d) 157, 137 A.R. 245 (Q.B.).

The amount paid by the father to purchase things for his daughter while his child support payments were in arrears was not properly deducted in calculating those arrears: *Haisman v. Haisman* (1994), 7 R.F.L. (4th) 1, 22 Alta. L.R. (3d) 56, 116 D.L.R. (4th) 671, 157 A.R. 47, 77 W.A.C. 47 (C.A.); reversing in part (1993), 7 Alta. L.R. (3d) 157, 137 A.R. 245 (Q.B.).

In *Québec (Procureur général) c. Dion* (9 août 1993), no C.A. Québec 200-09-000226-933 (C.A. Qué.), the Court of Appeal reinstated the husband's support arrears obligation despite the fact that payment of them would require him to borrow money. The husband had merely been negligent and there had been no real change in his financial circumstances.

Where the mother removed the child from the jurisdiction in order to frustrate the father's access with the result that he refused to pay child support for 6 years, the dismissal of her application to enforce payment of arrears was upheld on appeal. As the mother had assumed the burden of the child's expenses solely to frustrate the access order, it was not now reasonable to relieve her of those costs. However, the mother's conduct did not relieve the father from his ongoing child support obligations and he was ordered to pay increased support: *Turecki v. Turecki* (1989), 19 R.F.L. (3d) 127, 35 B.C.L.R. (2d) 51 (C.A.).

Where the father sought cancellation of child support arrears on the basis of an accident which prevented him from working, his application was refused in light of a pending damage settlement which included a component for lost wages: *Higgins v. Pethick* (1989), 21 R.F.L. (3d) 326 (Sask. C.A.).

In *Finn v. Finn* (1988), 14 R.F.L. (3d) 462, 60 Alta. L.R. (2d) 255 (C.A.), arrears of child support owing by the husband were ordered reduced in light of the wife's failure to explain her delay in enforcing the order and the loss sustained by the parties because of the wife's refusal to co-operate in a property deal relating to the matrimonial home. As a company owned by the wife's mother benefited from the deal it was appropriate that the arrears be reduced.

Arrears of child support should not be reduced where the evidence discloses that the payor spouse had the ability to pay during the period when the arrears were accruing. It would be unfair to the custodial spouse to thus allow the payor spouse to avoid all obligations toward the children: *Lake v. Lake* (1988), 11 R.F.L. (3d) 234 (N.S. C.A.).

In *Moon v. Bechard* (1996), 21 R.F.L. (4th) 101 (Q.B.), the court found the cost of living adjustment provision in the order applied cumulatively. The husband had made maintenance payments, adjusted to the cost of living, but had not made the adjustments cumulative. The court was of the opinion that the arrears caused by the husband's interpretation of the cost of living adjustment should be extinguished as the wife's inaction and failure to substantiate her position that the cost of living adjustments should be cumulative suggested that she acquiesced in her husband's interpretation of the provision. The court did increase child maintenance, based on the change in the needs of the child and the fact that the original order was inadequate. Taking into account the Federal/Provincial/Territorial Guidelines, and the parties' financial circumstances and income tax implications, the father should pay $600 each month.

The fact that a wife has not attempted to enforce child support arrears does not amount to an abandonment of a right to collect them. The child support belonged to the children and not the wife who could not abandon that which was not hers: *Droit de la famille — 2131*, [1995] R.D.F. 114 (C.S. Qué.).

Where the father had quit his job to start a business which ultimately failed he was not allowed to rely upon his financial problems as a grounds for reducing child support arrears owing. The children should not suffer as a result of the father's decision. Enforcement of the arrears was nevertheless suspended pending the father's reemployment: *Bakken v. Bakken* (1995), 11 R.F.L. (4th) 246 (Sask. Q.B.).

Where the unemployed father had been ordered to pay minimal child support but later had obtained employment paying $14,000 annually, his application to vacate child support arrears was dismissed. The mother had been forced to take on extra work to meet the children's needs and the accumulated arrears were properly owed to her: *D. (G.A.) v. D. (G.)* (1995), 11 R.F.L. (4th) 270, 168 A.R. 169 (Q.B.).

Where subsequent to the divorce the husband had been unemployed for some time and then remarried and assumed support responsibility for his new wife and her two children, his application to reduce child support arrears was allowed. It was necessary to adjust for the change in circumstances: *Cass v. Cass* (1995), 15 R.F.L. (4th) 436, 131 Nfld. & P.E.I.R. 347, 408 A.P.R. 347 (T.D.)

In *Pearson v. Pearson* (1995), 16 R.F.L. (4th) 75, 104 Man. R. (2d) 210 (Q.B.), the child support arrears owing by the husband were mitigated by the fact of his direct contributions to the children over the years and the fact that the wife had moved with the children without notice to the husband, resulting in a lack of contact for a six year period.

Where the wife had made no effort between 1982 and 1991 to enforce arrears of spousal and child support owing by the husband, the court allowed the husband's application to reduce drastically the arrears owing. The wife could offer no explanation for her delay in seeking enforcement and the husband had exhibited a genuine effort to abide by the orders although he had no resources to pay the considerable arrears: *Ralph v. Ralph* (1994), 7 R.F.L. (4th) 238, 122 Nfld. & P.E.I.R. 153, 379 A.P.R. 153 (Nfld. T.D.).

Where the mother had over several years failed to provide the husband with the calculation of the children's educational expenses as required under the parties' separation agreement, the court refused the mother's application to enforce arrears owing in respect of those expenses. The father had informally agreed with the children concerning their educational expenses and his payment of those had discharged his obligation: *Tait v. Tait* (1994), 8 R.F.L. (4th) 18 (Ont. Gen. Div.).

In *Wrobel v. Wrobel* (1994), 8 R.F.L. (4th) 403, 160 A.R. 241 (Q.B.), the court refused the husband's application for cancellation of considerable child support arrears despite the fact that he had made an assignment in bankruptcy. Although he could not currently pay, this had not been the case while the arrears had been accumulating and it was therefore right that the debt owed to his children be allowed to stand.

In *Coakwell v. Baker* (1994), 4 R.F.L. (4th) 345 (Ont. Gen. Div.), the court refused to rescind the child support arrears owing by the father in respect of his university student daughter. The enforcement of the arrears would not amount to a windfall to the mother who had herself gone into substantial debt to assist in financing her daughter's education.

Where the payor spouse had made child support payments directly to a child, and he has further on-going costs in relation to that child, it is justifiable to reduce arrears for the period in which such payments were made: *Adam v. Adam* (1993), 50 R.F.L. (3d) 216, 89 Man. R. (2d) 275 (Q.B.).

In 1980, the father was ordered to pay the mother $150 per month in child support and $100 per month in spousal support. Nothing was paid until the mother registered her order with the Maintenance Enforcement Office 11 years later. The father's income was then garnished to pay arrears of $35,550. The father brought an application for a reduction in child support payable and a cancellation of arrears, asserting that he was unable to pay because he had been living in poverty. Arrears of child support were to be forgiven only if the court was satisfied that the payor could not have paid and there was no possibility that he would ever be able to pay. The father should have detailed his situation and the steps he took to remedy his alleged decrease in income. The court was left to conclude that he could have paid his modest obligation but chose not to, and there was no doubt that he presently had the ability to pay. The application was therefore dismissed: *Bulych v. Bulych* (1993), 117 Sask. R. 157 (Q.B.).

It is unfair for a payee spouse to wait until the children are no longer dependent and then try to seek enforcement of a child support order long in arrears. This is particularly so where the payor has remarried and assumed additional financial responsibilities. In such a case, the court is entitled to exercise its discretion and order the arrears reduced: *Young v. Konkle* (1993), 1 R.F.L. (4th) 211 (Alta. Q.B.).

On an application to cancel child support arrears, the court should consider the nature of the support order, the ongoing financial capability of the payor, the ongoing needs of the child, any unexplained delay by the recipient in enforcing and/or the payor seeking relief from the arrears and whether enforcement would result in hardship to the payor. The one-year limitation on the enforcement of support arrears is not applicable to child support: *Loshney v. Hankins* (1993), 48 R.F.L. (3d) 67 (Sask. Q.B.).

Where the husband had accumulated child support arrears while unemployed, such arrears were later reduced to a level in accordance with his ability to pay while unemployed: *Doole v. Doole* (1991), 32 R.F.L. (3d) 283, 115 A.R. 1 (Q.B.).

Where the payor spouse had made child support payments directly to a child, and he has further on-going costs in relation to that child, it is justifiable to reduce arrears for the period in which such payments were made: *Adam v. Adam* (1993), 50 R.F.L. (3d) 216, 89 Man. R. (2d) 275 (Q.B.).

Arrears of child support should be remitted in part where the means of the payor are such that it would be impossible for him to pay the full amount owing and would perhaps force him and his second family to seek social assistance: *Greco v. Levin* (1991), 33 R.F.L. (3d) 405 (Ont. Gen. Div.). However, some portion of the arrears should be paid as otherwise the mother would be required to carry the whole financial burden of child support and the father's financial irresponsibility would be rewarded. The father was ordered to pay $10,000 together with interest on arrears which totalled $38,000.

In *Steeves v. Steeves* (1988), 87 N.B.R. (2d) 400, 221 A.P.R. 400 (Q.B.), the court forgave $17,000 in support arrears which had accumulated over eight years. The wife had delayed inordinately in enforcing the arrears and since the date of the original order, at which time the husband had earned $600 every two weeks, the husband had worked only 10 weeks yearly and lived on unemployment insurance for the balance of the time.

Where the husband had unilaterally reduced monthly child support from $65 to $20 for a period of 12 years, his application to reduce the arrears owing was allowed. The wife had not challenged the reduction and the children had not been prejudiced as they had been adequately provided for by the wife and her new spouse: *S. (D.E.) v. S. (S.L.)* (1988), 92 A.R. 101 (Q.B.).

The parties were married in 1980 and their child was born later that year. Shortly thereafter, the parties separated and executed a separation agreement requiring the husband to pay child maintenance of $100 per month. In 1984, in divorce proceedings brought by the wife, the court ordered child maintenance of $100 per month. By October 1993, the husband was in arrears under the agreement and the order in the amount of $12,697. The husband's application under s. 17 of the *Divorce Act*, to vary the order and to reduce or cancel the arrears, was dismissed. There was no basis for ordering cancellation of any part of the arrears and all of it remained payable without reference to any limitation period. The right to bring an action for the enforcement of child maintenance was within the meaning of s. 7 of the *Limitations Act*, R.S.B.C. 1979, c. 236 and the running of time was postponed during the child's minority: *Schmitke v. Schmitke* (1993), 87 B.C.L.R. (2d) 377 (S.C.).

Where the father had experienced a $30,000 decrease in annual income and had incurred considerable expense in his motion to suspend enforcement of the existing child support order due to numerous adjournments granted to the wife, his motion was granted. Further, all arrears owing under the order was rescinded: *McCurdy v. McCurdy* (1994), 8 R.F.L. (4th) 284 (Ont. U.F.C.).

Where the husband claimed that child support arrears had accrued during a period in which he was unable to work, but he could prove a disability for only part of that time, he was only entitled to remission of arrears for that shorter period: *Beaudoin v. Beaudoin* (1993), 45 R.F.L. (3d) 412 (B.C. S.C.).

Where the wife had not attempted to enforce child support arrears for nine years and the husband had left his employment and had few assets, his application to cancel support arrears was allowed. The husband had a reasonable expectation that he would not be required to pay arrears given the lack of enforcement over the years: *Spedding v. Spedding* (1989), 19 R.F.L. (3d) 368 (B.C. S.C.).

The father in *Wilson v. Wilson* (1995), 16 R.F.L. (4th) 192 (Ont. Prov. Div.), applied on the basis of his temporary loss of employment followed by a lower level of income than at the time of the original child support order to vary a child support order made on consent of both parties and to rescind arrears. The wife's income has greatly increased since the time that the original order was made. The father had remarried and had another child with his second wife. He had incurred significant debts in trying unsuccessfully to establish a business.

The court held that it is generally not appropriate to rescind arrears that have accumulated during a period of unemployment or reduced income, where there is evidence that the payor has the ability to return to a level of income equivalent to, or close to, his prior income. It is more appropriate to suspend enforcement of arrears. At the time of the variation hearing the mother had the greater ability to assume financial responsibility for the child, relative to that of the father.

The court varied the order by rescinding some of the arrears and suspending the enforcement of the balance for some period of time. In addition, the amount of ongoing support was reduced from $375 to $200 each month.

17§65A — Variation of periodic award to lump sum

Where the father had, subsequent to the parties' divorce, returned to his native Vietnam, remarried and started a new family, the mother's application to vary the periodic child support award to a lump sum award was granted. The father had not made a payment since his departure and the award was not enforceable in Vietnam: *Tu v. Tu* (2000), 7 R.F.L. (5th) 178, 2000 CarswellOnt 1297 (S.C.J.).

17§66 — Variation of child support orders — practice

Divorce Act, 1985

In *Marchak v. Fleury* (1995), 15 R.F.L (4th) 458 (C.A.), that part of a child support order which provided for the automatic accrual of arrears could not stand. Arrears can only accrue where there has been a failure to meet a current obligation.

Where the failure of the husband to disclose all his financial circumstances was found to be inadvertent and the injury occasioned by the non-disclosure was remedied by the award of lump sum maintenance, special costs were not justifiable: *Oyen v. Oyen* (1994), 9 R.F.L. (4th) 454 (B.C. C.A.).

Where a Supreme Court judge in a child support variation proceeding adopted the family court judge's recommendation without a copy of the lower judge's ruling or a copy of the transcript, the payor's appeal against the increased order was allowed. The supreme court judge did not have before him sufficient information upon which to exercise his jurisdiction properly: *Gorman v. Gorman* (1994), 2 R.F.L. (4th) 190 (N.S. C.A.). See also *Sperker v. Sperker* (1994), 2 R.F.L. (4th) 243 (N.S. C.A.), in which an appeal was allowed in similar circumstances where the supreme court judge adopted the family court judge's recommendation without hearing evidence from the husband who had filed notice of objection to the family court recommendation.

A custodial parent's delay in enforcing a child support order is irrelevant to an application to vary a child support order: *Haisman v. Haisman* (1994), 7 R.F.L. (4th) 1, 22 Alta. L.R. (3d) 56, 116 D.L.R. (4th) 671, 157 A.R. 47, 77 W.A.C. 47 (C.A.); reversing in part (1993), 7 Alta. L.R. (3d) 157, 137 A.R. 245 (Q.B.).

Where the father's legal tactics resulted in the delay in hearing the mother's application to increase child support, the ultimate order included a lump sum to compensate retroactively for the result of the delay: *Jackson v. Halloway* (1997), 35 R.F.L. (4th) 272, [1998] 5 W.W.R. 556, 161 Sask. R. 31 (Q.B.).

The New Brunswick Court of Queen's Bench has jurisdiction to hear a motion for variation of a child support order contained in an Ontario divorce judgment where the payor resided in New Brunswick and the custodial parent and child continued to reside in Ontario: *Hennigar v. Knight* (1996), 21 R.F.L. (4th) 411 (N.B. Q.B.).

There is no jurisdiction under the *Divorce Act* to make an interim order on an application under s. 17(1) to vary child support: *Vipond v. Vipond* (1990), 25 R.F.L. (3d) 128, 72 O.R. (2d) 82 (H.C.).

An order reserving the issue of child support in a variation application does not act to terminate the original support order. The original order remains in existence and can be the subject of future variation applications: *Young v. Young* (1987), above.

In *Huisman v. Huisman* (1995), 17 R.F.L. (4th) 229 (Ont. U.F.C.), the court held that it had jurisdiction to entertain a motion to vary child support even though the respondent father had appealed the divorce judgment. Once the father abandoned claims related to termination or reduction of child support, based on changes after the trial and the date of the pending motion, the court had jurisdiction.

17§67 — Variation of interim child support orders

In *Klain v. Klain* (1998), 36 R.F.L. (4th) 214, 165 N.S.R. (2d) 58, 495 A.P.R. 58 (C.A.) the mother applied for leave to appeal from a decision refusing to grant leave to the appellant to appeal from a variation of an interim child support order in a pending divorce proceeding. The interim order was made before the enactment of the *Federal Child Support Guidelines*. The coming into force of the *Guidelines*, in combination with the amendments to the *Divorce Act* and *Income Tax Act* changed the law in regard to calculating child support and the associated income tax consequences. Section 14(c) of the *Guidelines* provides that for the purposes of s. 17(4) of the *Divorce Act* with respect to variation orders made before May 1st, 1997, the change in the law is a "change of circumstances". As a result, a court hearing a variation application has a discretion to order a variation by reason of that fact alone. The court in dismissing the appeal held that the judge who had heard the interim custody and child support application took into consideration the tax consequences in the order he made, and there was no evidence of exceptional circumstances that would have warranted the judge hearing the variation application granting leave to the appellant to apply for an upward variation in the support order. The trial is the proper place to remedy the situation if any remedy is needed.

In *West v. West* (2001), 18 R.F.L. (5th) 440, 2001 CarswellOnt 1936 (Ont. S.C.J.), the court refused the husband's application for a retroactive downward variation of the interim child and spousal support payable by him. The matter was best left to the trial judge where the court would have the best and most complete evidence available. If any inequity had resulted from the interim order, it could be redressed at trial.

Cases decided before the enactment of the Child Support Guidelines

If, at the time an interim child support order is made, it is apparent that the parties did not intend that a variation of that order be subject to the "material change in circumstances" test, a judge can properly vary the order without regard to any change: *Ryment v. Ryment* (1995), 17 R.F.L. (4th) 163, 175 A.R. 131 (Q.B.).

In *Dixon v. Dixon* (1995), 13 R.F.L. (4th) 160, 170 A.R. 336 (Q.B.), the Alberta court held that it had jurisdiction to entertain an application to vary an interim child support order made in British Columbia, particularly when it has full jurisdiction to vary a support order.

17§68 — Review and variation

Where a lump sum child support order provided for a review in two years' time, it is not necessary for the custodial parent to establish a change of circumstances at the review hearing. The Court is to determine support issues on the basis of the facts as they exist at the date of the review hearing: *Vincent v. Vincent* (1995), 15 R.F.L. (4th) 273, 132 Nfld. & P.E.I.R. 181, 410 A.P.R. 181 (C.A.).

17§68A — Delay in enforcement

In *Poyntz Estate v. Poyntz* (1998), 37 R.F.L. (4th) 134, 157 D.L.R. (4th) 552 (Ont. Gen. Div.), the wife's delay in enforcing child support owing by the father was not found to constitute a waiver. The wife could not implicitly bargain away the rights of the children.

In *Goudie v. Buchanan* (2001), 19 R.F.L. (5th) 280, 2001 CarswellNfld 185, 203 Nfld. & P.E.I.R. 34, 610 A.P.R. 34 (Nfld. U.F.C.), the mother was estopped from claiming arrears in child support. The father had unilaterally reduced the support payable to the wife after one of the children had left the wife's residence, although the parties had not formally agreed to the arrangement. However, the wife had accepted the reduced payments for 25 months without seeking redress. As a result, the husband had reasonably understood the mother's conduct as a suspension of her strict legal rights.

17§68B — Suspension of order

Where the father had been suspended from his employment without pay and his financial future was uncertain, the court ordered the suspension of a portion of his child support obligations for a four-month period. As he had savings and other resources available to him, the suspension rather than a reduction was appropriate: *Smith v. Smith* (1998), 39 R.F.L. (4th) 88 (B.C. S.C. [In Chambers]).

In *Martin v. Martin* (1998), 42 R.F.L. (4th) 251, 168 Nfld. & P.E.I.R. 181, 517 A.P.R. 181 (Nfld. C.A.), the court refused to suspend the father's child support payments as a means of enforcing his access rights. The children themselves resisted access and there was no evidence that the mother had interfered. The husband did not acknowledge his own contribution to the strained relationship with his children.

Where the husband was imprisoned for robbery the court suspended his obligation to pay child support for the duration of his sentence in *Scanlon v. Scanlon* (1998), 42 R.F.L. (4th) 397, [1999] 3 W.W.R. 151, 132 Man. R. (2d) 79 (Q.B.).

17§69 — Jurisdiction to vary custody and access awards

The court has jurisdiction to make an interim order varying an existing custody order, despite the fact that such jurisdiction is not expressly provided under s. 17 of the *Divorce Act*: *Dorval v. Dorval*, 22 R.F.L. (6th) 305, 2006 CarswellSask 92, [2006] 8 W.W.R. 430, 2006 SKCA 21, 264 D.L.R. (4th) 512 (Sask. C.A.).

Where a custody order had been made in the parties' divorce proceedings, the wife could not seek in essence to vary that order through an application under provincial legislation: *French v. Mackenzie* (2003), 38 R.F.L. (5th) 81, 2003 CarswellOnt 1748 (Ont. S.C.J.).

Divorce Act, 1985

In *Anderson v. Sullivan* (1996), 22 R.F.L. (4th) 115 (B.C. C.A.), the British Columbia Court of Appeal allowed an appeal from the trial court's refusal to entertain her application to vary an Ontario custody order. The custodial mother and the children were now permanent residents of British Columbia and, despite the fact that the father was also seeking a variation in Ontario, British Columbia was the most convenient and appropriate jurisdiction in which to determine questions relating to the children.

In *Holt v. Lippert* (1996), 21 R.F.L. (4th) 241, 107 Man. R. (2d) 302, 109 W.A.C. 302 (C.A.), the court allowed the mother's appeal from an order requiring that variation of custody terms be dealt with by an Ontario court and not by a Manitoba court where the wife and children were not resident. Despite an original agreement between the parties that disputes be settled in accordance with Ontario laws, the parties had executed an amending agreement after the mother's move from Ontario to Manitoba allowing disputes to be dealt with by a court of competent jurisdiction. The children were now more substantially connected to Manitoba and to require the people with whom they had developed social, educational and professional relationships to travel to Ontario to give evidence was not in the children's best interests.

Under the former *Divorce Act*, jurisdiction to vary a corollary relief order lay only with the court of the province which granted the order: s. 11(2): *Rodness v. Rodness*, 23 R.F.L. 266, [1976] 3 W.W.R. 414, 66 D.L.R. (3d) 746 (B.C. C.A.); *Ramsay v. Ramsay* (1976), 23 R.F.L. 147, 13 O.R. (2d) 85, 70 D.L.R. (3d) 415 (C.A.). Under the *Divorce Act, 1985*, an application can be brought in a province other than the province which made the original order. The following courts have jurisdiction: the court in the province in which either former spouse is ordinarily resident at the commencement of the proceeding: s. 5(1)(a); the court in any province that both former spouses accept as having jurisdiction: s. 5(1)(b); if the proceeding includes a claim for variation of a custody award, and this claim is opposed, the court in the province most substantially connected with a child: s. 6(3); and if two proceedings are commenced in different provinces on the same day, the Federal Court: s. 5(3).

In *Keyuk v. Keyuk* (1993), 114 Sask. R. 222 (Q.B.), the court varied a joint custody order moving the child's principle residence from his mother's home to his father's. Although both parties were good parents, the father was the stronger personality of the two and the stricter disciplinarian. As the child appeared to thrive in his father's care, the child's best interests warranted the change.

In a variation application for custody, pursuant to s. 17(1)(b) of the *Divorce Act*, the place of trial should be the county in which the child resides: *Kerr v. Irvine* (1989), 22 R.F.L. (3d) 462, 70 O.R. (2d) 275 (H.C.).

On an application to vary a custody order, a court must be satisfied that there has been a change in the condition, means, needs or other circumstances of the children since the making of the original order: *Watson v. Watson* (1991), 35 R.F.L. (3d) 169 (B.C. S.C.). Where the changes in circumstances are changes in the lives of the parents which do not fundamentally affect the best interests of the children, there should not be any change in custody. In the Watson decision, the changes which the father relied upon were his remarriage and by implication, the greater financial resources which he could thereby provide. The court did increase child support payments so as to remedy many of the deficiencies in the children's lifestyle.

In Ontario, a motion to vary an order of a High Court judge must be made before a High Court judge and cannot be made to the master pursuant to R. 37. 14: *Blitstein v. Blitstein* (1989), 21 R.F.L. (3d) 26 (Ont. Master).

17§70 — Variation of custody and access — general

In determining whether a change in a custody order should be made, the court must consider the conditions, means, needs or other circumstances of the child since the making of the order or the last variation of it and must consider only the best interests of the child as determined by reference to that change. Note that the best interests test is explicit. In addition, the court must focus on the child's circumstances rather than the circumstances of the parties as in the 1968 Act. Also a factor in varying custody is the willingness of the person seeking a change in custody to facilitate the maximum contact between the child and the other parent as is consistent with the best interests of the child: s. 17(9). In making a variation order the court is prohibited from considering any conduct that could not have been considered in making the order in respect of which the variation is sought: s. 17(6). In making an original order for custody, the court is prevented from considering the past conduct of any person unless the conduct is relevant to the ability of that person to act as a parent of a child: s. 16(9).

Divorce Act, 1985

A parent applying to change a custody or access order under the *Divorce Act* must establish a material change in circumstances affecting the child. If such a threshold is met, the judge must embark on a fresh inquiry into the best interests of the child having regard to all of the relevant circumstances of the case. The focus of the inquiry is the child's interests and not the parents' interests and rights. The inquiry based on the findings of the judge who made the original order as well as the evidence of the new circumstances does not begin with a legal presumption in favour of the custodial parent, although the custodial parent's views are entitled to great respect. Once an applicant has discharged the burden of showing a material change in circumstances, both parents should bear an evidentiary burden in establishing the best interests of the child. In assessing the best interests of the child, where the custodial parent wishes to relocate with the child, the judge should consider, *inter alia*, a) the existing custody relationship and relationship between the child and custodial parent; b) the existing access arrangement and the relationship between the child and the access parent; c) the desirability of maximizing contact between the child and both parents; d) the views of the child; e) the custodial parent's reason for moving only in the exceptional case where is relevant to that parent's ability to meet the children's needs; f) disruption to the child of a change in custody; and g) disruption to the child from removal from family, friends and community. The maximum contact principle in s. 16(10) and s. 17(9) of the *Divorce Act* is not absolute and is subject to the child's best interests. In the end, the importance of the child remaining with the custodial parent must be weighed against the continuance of full contact with the access parent, its extended family and community: *Gordon v. Goertz*, [1996] 2 S.C.R. 27, 19 R.F.L. (4th) 177, 134 D.L.R. (4th) 321, [1996] 5 W.W.R. 457, 196 N.R. 321, 141 Sask. R. 241, 114 W.A.C. 241; affirming (1995), 128 Sask. R. 156, 85 W.A.C. 156 (C.A.).

In *Gordon v. Goertz*, 19 R.F.L. (4th) 177, [1996] 2 S.C.R. 27, [1996] 5 W.W.R. 457. McLachlin J., in her reasons stated that an application for a variation order relating to custody and access under the *Divorce Act* requires a two-stage inquiry. First the party seeking a variation must show a material change in the circumstances of the child. If this is shown, the judge must consider the merits and make an order that provides for the best interests of the child in the new circumstances.

The court must be satisfied that there has been a material change in the circumstances of the child since the last custody or access order was made. A material change is one that "must have altered the child's needs or the ability of the parents to meet those needs in a fundamental way." The change must either not have been foreseen or could not have been reasonably contemplated by the judge at first instance.

A move does not necessarily constitute a material change. Where, as in the case at bar, a move would seriously restrict the child's frequent and meaningful contact with her access parent, there is a necessary connection between the change and the needs and circumstances of the child. Where as in this case, the custody order sets out terms of access based on the assumption that the child's principal residence would be near the access parent, the relocation of the custodial parent and the child from Saskatchewan to Australia could not have been within the reasonable contemplation of the judge who issued the previous order. All the requirements for a material change have been met.

The *Charter of Rights and Freedoms* does not protect religious expression which is not in the best interests of the child: *Young v. Young*, [1993] 4 S.C.R. 3, 49 R.F.L. (3d) 117, [1993] 8 W.W.R. 513, 108 D.L.R. (4th) 193, 18 C.R.R. (2d) 41, 84 B.C.L.R. (2d) 1, 160 N.R. 1. The court held that ss. 16(8) and 17(5) of the *Divorce Act, 1985*, which provide that judicial decisions regarding custody and access be made "in the best interests of the child" do not deny the rights and freedoms guaranteed in s. 2(a), (b) and (d) of the Canadian *Charter of Rights and Freedoms*. In the *Young* decision, however, the court held that the order forbidding the father, a Jehovah's Witness, from discussing religion with his children was not valid. Any perceived harm to the children could not be said to outweigh the benefits of unrestricted access.

In the face of conflicting affidavits and an obvious level of animosity between the parties, a chambers judge should not make an order drastically altering a custody arrangement. Even the parties' mutual wish to avoid a retrial does not give a chambers judge the authority to make a dramatic change in a child's living arrangements: *Werrell v. Schultz*, 18 R.F.L. (5th) 243, 2001 CarswellSask 123, 2001 SKCA 26, 203 Sask. R. 300, 240 W.A.C. 300 (Sask. C.A.).

In *Hannant v. Christie* (1999), 189 Sask. R. 168, 216 W.A.C. 168 (C.A.), the court was of the opinion that on a variation of a custody application, where custody was contested, there should be a *viva voce* hearing with witnesses under oath and subject to cross-examination. The chambers judge had relied heavily on a home-study report, which was not comprehensive, and adopted portions of the report as the foundation of his findings and conclusion. The mother's appeal of the custody order, which varied custody from sole custody to the mother to the joint custody, with primary residence shifted to the father who lived outside the jurisdiction, was granted.

In *Rosenke v. Rosenke* (1998), 36 R.F.L. (4th) 288 (Alta. C.A.), the father appealed from a decision dismissing his application to vary custody. The father had overcome his drinking problem, had obtained reasonable access under the divorce judgement, but the parents were not able to work together to establish access. The mother's inability to forgive the father was contrary to the best interests of the children, as made clear by the *Divorce Act*. The court held that the children ought to be assisted and encouraged to have some contact with their father and their extended paternal family. The father's appeal was allowed and the case was referred back to the Court of Queen's Bench and made subject to the case management.

In *Dhaliwal v. Beloud* (1998), 38 R.F.L. (4th) 345, 107 B.C.A.C. 249, 174 W.A.C. 249 (C.A.), the court dismissed the father's appeal from an order refusing his application for an order varying custody from the matter to himself. The only change in circumstances cited by the father was difficulty in implementing access arrangements and the father's appeal appeared to be no more than an attempt to relitigate custody and access.

In *Wilson v. Grassick* (1994), 2 R.F.L. (4th) 291, [1994] 6 W.W.R. 570, 120 Sask. R. 1, 68 W.A.C. 1 (C.A.); leave to appeal refused (1994), 7 R.F.L. (4th) 254 (note) (S.C.C.), the court was of the opinion that in an application for variation of a custody order, a two-step inquiry is required. Before the court can consider whether the child's interests would be best served by a transfer of custody from one parent to the other, a change in circumstances must first be established. Absent the finding of changed circumstances, the inquiry can proceed no further.

In *Fantin v. Fantin* (2003), 37 R.F.L. (5th) 327, 2003 CarswellOnt 1294 (Ont. S.C.J.); additional reasons at (2003), 2003 CarswellOnt 2070 (Ont. S.C.J.), the court refused the father's application to vary the mother's sole custody arrangement to one of joint custody. The child had been in the mother's care for 5 years and had done well. The parties themselves did not have a good working relationship. In those circumstances, the child's interests would be best served by maintaining the *status quo*.

In *Dean v. Dean* (1997), 33 R.F.L. (4th) 451 (Ont. Gen. Div.), the wife could not rely upon her own unilateral breach of the parties custody and support agreement as a "change in circumstances" warranting a variation of that agreement.

The *Divorce Act* directs a two-stage inquiry in custody variation cases: (1) the reviewing judge must determine whether there has been a change in the condition, means, needs or other circumstances of the children — the party seeking to vary the order bears the onus of proof; (2) if a material change is proven, the court must decide whether the change requires a variation of the custody order based upon the child's best interest. Accordingly, if a change of custody is ordered without the required proof of changed circumstances, the variation should be overturned: *Talbot v. Henry*, 25 R.F.L. (3d) 415, [1990] 5 W.W.R. 251 (Sask. C.A.).

Where the father's principal reason for seeking a retroactive joint custody order was to prevent the custodial mother from legally changing the child's last name to that of her new husband, the application was refused. Nevertheless, the mother would be required to obtain the father's consent to any legal change of name until such time as the child turned 16: *Belisle v. Poole* (1994), 2 R.F.L. (4th) 165, 111 D.L.R. (4th) 717 (Ont. Gen. Div.).

There is a significant difference between the provisions respecting variation of custody orders under the former *Divorce Act* and the new Act. Under the new legislation, the applicant is required to show a change in the condition, means, needs or other circumstances of the child, as well as showing that the variation requested would be in the child's best interest. The new Act contemplates that the child should have as much contact with each parent as is in his or her best interests: *Perry v. Perry*, 52 Alta. L.R. (2d) 321, (sub nom. *Perry (Smith) v. Perry)* [1987] 5 W.W.R. 86, 79 A.R. 71 (Q.B.).

17§71 — Variation of joint custody

Where the husband had sought to vary a joint custody award to one granting him sole custody on the basis that the wife had abused the child, the court upheld, on appeal, an order vesting sole custody in the wife. The husband's allegations were found to have been without basis and the parental co-operation necessary for a successful joint custody arrangement had now been eroded: *Lucken v. Hopkins* (1994), 8 R.F.L. (4th) 226 (B.C. C.A.).

In *Winton v. Lofranco* (2004), 7 R.F.L. (6th) 444, 2004 CarswellOnt 3346 (S.C.J.), the court refused the father's emergency application to alter the parties' joint custody arrangement and to name him sole custodian. Although the mother had both a cocaine and alcohol abuse problem, the evidence indicated that she had been in a successful treatment program for some time. A custody assessment was underway, and it would be best to wait until it was completed before making any changes.

In *Grierson v. Brunton* (2004), 8 R.F.L. (6th) 146, 2004 CarswellOnt 2944 (S.C.J.), the court refused to vary the parties' long-standing joint custody arrangement after the mother had relocated to Florida, leaving the children to reside with the applicant father. The arrangement had worked for many years despite the parties' acrimonious relationship, and as the children were now teenagers and able to make many decisions themselves, their best interests were served by leaving the arrangement undisturbed.

Where the mother had entered into a new relationship and relocated with the child to a different city to pursue that relationship, the father was successful in his application requiring the mother to return the child to the father's day-to-day care. The parties had joint custody and the mother's course of conduct had real potential for producing unknown and unsettling consequences for the child. The father and his extended family would offer a far more stable environment: *Hoff v. Hoff*, 41 R.F.L. (5th) 90, 2003 CarswellAlta 988, 2003 ABQB 560 (Alta. Q.B.).

In *Belisle v. Belisle* (2000), 13 R.F.L. (5th) 262, 2000 CarswellOnt 4735, [2000] O.J. No. 4744 (Ont. S.C.J.), the court allowed the mother's application for a variation of custody from a joint custody arrangement to sole custody in her favour. Cooperation and communication between the parties had broken down rendering the existing joint arrangement unworkable. Although both parents were capable, the wife's lead role in parenting favoured her as custodial parent.

In *Tu v. Tu* (2000), 7 R.F.L. (5th) 178, 2000 CarswellOnt 1297 (S.C.J.), the court allowed the mother's application to vary a joint custody order to a sole custody arrangement. The father had returned to his native Vietnam three years earlier and had, since then, neither seen the child nor contributed towards the child's support.

In *MacNaught v. MacNaught* (1998), 37 R.F.L. (4th) 79 (P.E.I. T.D.), the court refused the wife's application to vary the parties' joint custody arrangement to one in which both parties had equal weekend time with the children. The existing arrangement, which had been in place for eight months, allowed the husband physical custody for three days out of eight, those three days having been timed to coincide with his days off in his four days on/four days off work schedule. As the existing arrangement was working well, a change in the *status quo* would not be in the children's best interests.

Where the mother repudiated a joint custody agreement shortly after it was signed but evidence supported the view that the mother was rigid in her views and bitter about the divorce and was therefore likely to put her dislike of the father ahead of the child's interest, her application for sole custody was dismissed. The child had a better chance of maintaining a relationship with both parents if she remained in the father's custody. A sole custody order in the father's favour was accordingly substituted, the acrimony between the parties rendering joint custody no longer tenable: *Boukema v. Boukema* (1997), 31 R.F.L. 329 (Ont. Gen. Div.); additional reasons at (December 19, 1997), Doc. 94-ND-212384 (Ont. Gen Div.).

17§72 — Variation of interim custody orders

Prior to divorce, there is no jurisdiction under s. 17 of the *Divorce Act* to vary an interim custody order. The variation powers under s. 17 are available only in the context of a "final" order: *Brooks v. Brooks* (1998), 39 R.F.L. (4th) 187, 22 C.P.C. (4th) 209, 111 O.A.C. 177, 163 D.L.R. (4th) 715 (C.A.).

In *Sider v. Sider* (2004), 10 R.F.L. (6th) 171, 2004 CarswellOnt 3421 (S.C.J.), the court ordered a variation of a temporary custody order so that the parties' 12½-year-old daughter could relocate to the father's residence prior to the commencement of the new school year. The trial of the issue had been postponed and could not be rescheduled before school started. The daughter had expressed her wish to live with her father, rendering the mother's success at trial less likely.

In *Lindsay v. Lindsay* (2002), 35 R.F.L. (5th) 105, 2002 CarswellOnt 4291 (Ont. S.C.J.); additional reasons at (2003), 2003 CarswellOnt 1334 (Ont. S.C.J.), the court allowed the wife's application to vary the parties' joint custody order to allow her to relocate with the children and her new husband to Kansas City. The wife's circumstances would allow her to remain in the home on a full-time basis and care for the children. The father's plan was unrealistic on a number of fronts, including his intention to leave the children for part of the time in the care of a woman with whom he had only interacted over the internet. The children's best interests favoured the mother's plan.

In *Warner v. Warner*, 27 R.F.L. (5th) 202, 2002 CarswellBC 878, 2002 BCSC 619 (S.C.), the court refused the mother's application to vary an interim joint custody award to award her sole custody. Although the parents were unable to communicate with one another, the circumstances did not favour altering the *status quo*.

Interim orders, such as those for access, once made should be varied only when a compelling change in circumstances occurs that would have the effect of seriously prejudicing one or both parties by waiting for trial: *Randhawa v. Randhawa* (1999), 49 R.F.L. (4th) 144 (B.C. S.C.).

In *Droit de la famille — 2119* (1994), [1995] R.D.F. 81 (C.S. Qué.), the parties' interim custody award was varied and the custody of the child transferred from the wife to the husband. The original order gave the husband very generous access rights which were seriously disrupted when the wife moved with the child some 225 km away from the husband's residence. The mother's move had gone against the spirit of the custody order and she was no longer able to fulfill the obligations under it.

17§73 — Change in circumstances — general

Divorce Act, 1985

In determining an application for variation of custody, the court should consider the material change of circumstances occurring since the making of the last significant custody or variation order and not the whole history of the marriage and its breakdown: *Kubel v. Kubel* (1995), 15 R.F.L. (4th) 356, 169 A.R. 295, 97 W.A.C. 295 (C.A.).

In *Fahlman v. Fahlman* (1994), 4 R.F.L. (4th) 353 (Sask. Q.B.), the father's application for a variation of custody from his wife to himself was dismissed. He had failed to meet the burden of proof to establish that such a material change in circumstances had occurred that the children's interests were no longer best served by the existing order. Nor was there a change in either parent's circumstances which could be relevant in determining a change in the children's circumstances.

In *Drake v. Drake* (1992), 99 Sask. R. 176 (Q.B.), the court found the fact that the husband had remarried and established a more stable home life was not a sufficient reason to justify a change of custody from the wife to him.

In *Courtney v. Courtney* (1992), 42 R.F.L. (3d) 450 (Ont. Gen. Div.), the court dismissed the husband's application to vary custody so that the children, who lived with their mother, would spend every second week with him. The father was concerned because the children's increased involvement with outside activities interfered with his specified access. This was, however, a natural development in the children's lives and could not be relied upon as a "material change in circumstances".

Where the wife had consented to the husband having custody of the parties' child, her later application to vary the custody arrangement was dismissed, despite the fact that she had entered into a stable relationship. The existing arrangements were working well for the child and there was no need to alter them simply to satisfy the wife's wishes: *Allen v. Allen* (1988), 72 Nfld. & P.E.I.R. 138, 223 A.P.R. 138 (Nfld. T.D.).

17§73A — Change in circumstances — child's wishes

Where an 11-year-old child did not want to visit her father, the children's lawyer had recommended the suspension of access. The trial judge suspended access and the appellate court upheld the ruling on appeal: *Lidkea v. Jarrell* (1999), 49 R.F.L. (4th) 324 (Ont. C.A.).

An order varying custody should not be made solely on the basis of affidavit evidence of a 12-year-old child: *Leblue v. Leblue* (1997), 33 R.F.L. (4th) 118, 209 A.R. 227, 160 W.A.C. 227 (C.A.).

In *Di Liberatore v. Fabrizi* (2005), 23 R.F.L. (6th) 147, 2005 CarswellNS 576, 2005 NSSC 321 (N.S. S.C.), the parties' 14-year-old son's expressed desire to move from his father's to his mother's home was a sufficient "change in circumstances" to support a custody variation application.

An expressed wish of a child to move from the custodial parent's home to the other parent's home does not constitute a change in circumstances justifying a variation of custody unless it is clear and unequivocal: *Beeler v. Beeler* (1997), 32 R.F.L. (4th) 397, 161 Sask. R. 167 (Q.B.)

17§74 — Change in circumstances — children moving

Divorce Act, 1985

A parent applying to change a custody or access order under the *Divorce Act* must establish a material change in circumstances affecting the child. If such a threshold is met, the judge must embark on a fresh inquiry into the best interests of the child having regard to all of the relevant circumstances of the case. The focus of the inquiry is the child's interests and not the parents' interests and rights. The inquiry based on the findings of the judge who made the original order as well as the evidence of the new circumstances does not begin with a legal presumption in favour of the custodial parent, although the custodial parent's views are entitled to great respect. Once an applicant has discharged the burden of showing a material change in circumstances, both parents should bear an evidentiary burden in establishing the best interests of the child. In assessing the best interests of the child, where the custodial parent wishes to relocate with the child, the judge should consider, *inter alia*, a) the existing custody relationship and relationship between the child and custodial parent; b) the existing access arrangement and the relationship between the child and the access parent; c) the desirability of maximizing contact between the child and both parents; d) the views of the child; e) the custodial parent's reason for moving only in the exceptional case where is relevant to that parent's ability to meet the children's needs; f) disruption to the child of a change in custody; and g) disruption to the child from removal from family, friends and community. The maximum contact principle in s. 16(10) and s. 17(9) of the *Divorce Act* is not absolute and is subject to the child's best interests. In the end, the importance of the child remaining with the custodial parent must be weighed against the continuance of full contact with the access parent, its extended family and community: *Gordon v. Goertz*, [1996] 2 S.C.R. 27, 19 R.F.L. (4th) 177, 134 D.L.R. (4th) 321, [1996] 5 W.W.R. 457, 196 N.R. 321, 141 Sask. R. 241, 114 W.A.C. 241; affirming (1995), 128 Sask. R. 156, 85 W.A.C. 156 (C.A.).

In *Gordon v. Goertz*, above, the court held that a move does not necessarily constitute a material change in circumstances. Where, as in the case at bar, a move from Saskatchewan to Australia seriously restricted the child's frequent and meaningful contact with her access parent, there was a necessary connection between the change and the needs and circumstances of the child. In this case, where the custody order set out terms of access based on the assumption that the child's principal residence would be near the access parent, the relocation of the custodial parent and the child from Saskatchewan to Australia could not have been within the reasonable contemplation of the judge who issued the previous order and all the requirements for a material change had been met.

The Supreme Court of Canada ruled that the trial judge did not err in continuing the mother's custody of the child, even though she intended to move to Australia. However, there was no reason to restrict the father's access to Australia. Access in Canada would permit the child to maintain contact with friends and family. The court affirmed the custody order but allowed the appeal in part, to permit the father to exercise access in Canada.

Where the mother had removed the child from Quebec to live in France contrary to the terms of the parties' settlement agreement, the Supreme Court of Canada affirmed a Quebec Court of Appeal order which transferred custody from the wife to the husband. As the wife had been represented by counsel but had not actually participated in the original trial, the only evidence which the Supreme Court had before it was the fact of the wife's conduct and evidence supporting the husband's parenting activities: *P. (M.) c. L. (G.)* (1995), 18 R.F.L. (4th) 185, 1995 CarswellQue 188, (sub nom. *P. (M.) v. L.B. (G.)*) 130 D.L.R. (4th) 382, (sub nom. *P.M. v. L.B. (G.)*) [1985] 4 S.C.R. 592, (sub nom. *P. (M.) v. B. (G.L.)*) 190 N.R. 183 (S.C.C.); affirming 1993 CarswellQue 277, (sub nom. *Droit de la famille — 1826)* [1993] R.J.Q. 1728, [1993] R.D.F. 544, (sub nom. *P. (M.) c. B. (G.L.)*) 57 Q.A.C. 241 (Que. C.A.); affirmed [1995] 4 S.C.R. 592, 18 R.F.L. (4th) 185, 130 D.L.R. (4th) 382, 190 N.R. 182.

In *Young v. Young*, 2003 CarswellOnt 63 (Ont. C.A.), the father appealed from an order permitting the mother to move with the parties' three young children to a location 100 kilometres from the father's residence. The court was of the opinion that where parties have joint custody, the two-stage test in *Gordon v. Goertz*, above, applies, whether the provision sought to be varied is in a court order or in minutes of settlement, as in this case. The two-stage test is, first, the parent who wishes to relocate must show that there has been a material change in the circumstances affecting the child, which was either not foreseen or could not have been reasonably contemplated by the court which made the original order. The second stage is to undertake a fresh inquiry into the best interests of the child.

The appellate court in the *Young* decision found that relocating for an employment opportunity was a typical material change in circumstances. The lower court had concluded that following *Gordon v. Goertz*, above, it was in the best interests of the children to relocate with their mother. The appellate court decided that these reasons were conclusory reasons and not reasoned reasons. It was desirable in family law cases that courts give reasoned reasons to engender public confidence in the administration of the justice system, give the losing party the reasons for having lost, and making the right of appeal meaningful. There were several errors in the lower court decision. First, the lower court judge had focused almost entirely on the mother's employment and failed to undertake a "full and sensitive inquiry" into the best interests of the children, as required by *Gordon v. Goertz*. Second, he had failed to take into account the disruption to the children. Third, he had misapprehended the parenting arrangement as he mistook an earlier agreement as being the existing parenting agreement. The earlier agreement had been superceded by partial minutes of settlement in which the father was not the access parent but instead a joint custodial parent. Fourth, the lower court should have taken into account the report of an independent assessor regarding the children's best interests. The court set aside the order and ordered a new hearing.

In an appeal by the father from the dismissal of an application to vary a consent order respecting custody and access, the court allowed the appeal in *Larose v. Larose* (2002), 27 R.F.L. (5th) 347, 2002 CarswellBC 1389, 2002 BCCA 366, 1 B.C.L.R. (4th) 262, 171 B.C.A.C. 27, 280 W.A.C. 27 (C.A.). The court held that where a custodial parent seeks to move with the children to a different city, the central question to be determined is the best interest of the children and not parental rights.

In the *Larose* case, the parties, in the consent order, had agreed that the father would have custody of the children; the mother would have specified access and the father would not move his residence from West or North Vancouver without the written agreement of the mother. When the father's application to move was refused, he and the children nonetheless moved to Nanaimo. Following *Gordon v. Goertz*, [1996] 2 S.C.R. 27, 19 R.F.L. (4th) 177, 134 D.L.R. (4th) 321, [1996] 5 W.W.R. 457, 196 N.R. 321, 141 Sask. R. 241, 114 W.A.C. 241, 1996 CarswellSask 199, [1996] S.C.J. No. 52, 1996 CarswellSask 199F, (sub nom. *Goertz v. Gordon)* [1996] R.D.F. 209 (S.C.C.), the court was of the opinion that once the threshold of a material change in circumstances was met, (the father's consideration that he should seek further education and greater employment income elsewhere), the court could make a fresh inquiry regarding the best interests of the children. The custodial parent's reason for relocating was of significance only in an exceptional case where it was relevant to the parent's capability to meet the child's needs. The appellate court found that the father's decision that the move would be in the best interests of the children should be allowed to prevail. Both counsel conceded that the chambers judge had erred in law by placing the onus on the custodial parent, the father, to justify his plan to move from Vancouver to Nanaimo. Since their move, the children were well settled in their new community. The disruption to access would be minimal and could be lessened by increased summer and holiday access. The move would not adversely affect the relationship each child had with his mother. It may be that in the case of one child, some distance might in fact help the mother and son's relationship.

In *Brink v. Brink*, 24 R.F.L. (5th) 1, 2002 CarswellPEI 9, 2002 PESCAD 2, (sub nom. *W.J.B. v. B.S.B.)* 208 Nfld. & P.E.I.R. 315, (sub nom. *W.J.B. v. B.S.B.)* 624 A.P.R. 315 (P.E.I. C.A.), the court was of the opinion that where the custodial parent, without notice to the access parent, removes the child from the jurisdiction in order to be near her sick relative and a court grants a variation order with new access provisions set out, but without indicating where such access will take place or at whose expense, these omissions constitute an error by the trial judge. The matter was ordered referred back to the Trial Division for a determination of where access was to take place and who would pay for access expenses.

The mother, the custodial parent, appealed from an order denying her permission to remove the parties' child from Alberta and take him to Scotland for two years in *Pisko v. Pisko* (1997), 151 D.L.R. (4th) 189, 200 A.R. 330, 146 W.A.C. 330 (C.A.). Under the terms of the divorce judgement, the parties had joint custody of their child, with primary care and control to the mother and reasonable access to the father. The mother's second husband was transferred to Scotland and she wished to accompany him there with the child. The appellate court held that the Chambers Judge failed to balance the disadvantages and the advantages of the proposal to take the child to Scotland. The advantages outweighed the disadvantages, particularly as the mother would not be working in Scotland and would have more time to devote to the child's welfare.

Where a custodial parent wishes to relocate with the children there is no automatic presumption that the wishes of the custodial parent automatically served the children's best interests: *Manore v. Manore* (1995), 20 R.F.L. (4th) 68, 16 B.C.L.R. (3d) 364, 67 B.C.A.C. 259, 111 W.A.C. 259, 1995 CarswellBC 1081, [1995] B.C.J. No. 2719 (C.A.).

In determining the issue of whether a custodial parent should be allowed to relocate the children in another jurisdiction, it is not incumbent upon the custodial parent to prove that the move is justified, but only that it is reasonable. The real issue is the best interests of the children which could well be sensed if the most favourable environment for their development is in the proposed new location, given the custodial parent's preference: *Lapointe v. Lapointe*, 17 R.F.L. (4th) 1, [1995] 10 W.W.R. 609, 107 Man. R. (2d) 1, 109 W.A.C. 1, 1995 CarswellMan 21 (C.A.).

In an application by a custodial parent to relocate with the child to another jurisdiction, the best interests of the child should be assessed from a perspective of the child. The proper test is whether there is any reason to believe that the move would not be in the best interests of the child: *Benoit v. Reid* (1995), 18 R.F.L. (4th) 136, 131 D.L.R. (4th) 346, 171 N.B.R. (2d) 161, 437 A.P.R. 161 (C.A.).

In *Foreman v. Foreman* (2005), 23 R.F.L. (6th) 273, 2005 CarswellAlta 621, 2005 ABQB 343, [2006] 2 W.W.R. 560, 53 Alta. L.R. (4th) 319 (Alta. Q.B.), the court refused to award the custody provisions agreed to in the parties divorce to allow the mother to relocate with the children. The parties' had negotiated a comprehensive settlement agreement which allowed for a court application when reduction under the terms of the agreement failed. However, the court application brought the matter under the terms of the *Divorce Act*, requiring the mother to prove a change in circumstances. She had failed to do so.

In *Norris v. Norris* (2004), 9 R.F.L. (6th) 446, 2004 CarswellOnt 3298, [2004] O.J. No. 3336 (S.C.J.); additional reasons at 2004 CarswellOnt 4372 (S.C.J.), the court dismissed the husband's application for custody brought in response to the wife's plans to relocate with the children from Ontario to California. The mother had been the children's primary caregiver since birth and there was no evidence that the relocation would be clearly disruptive or damaging to them.

In *Sloss v. Forget* (2004), 8 R.F.L. (6th) 380, 2004 CarswellOnt 3923 (S.C.), the court rejected the mother's application to vary the terms of the custody provisions of the parties' separation agreement to allow her to relocate the children to another municipality. All of the grounds argued by the mother had existed at the time the agreement was signed.

Where the custodial parent wished to move to a location in another country with which she had no present connection or history and a very questionable future, the court found that a material change of circumstances had occurred and varied the previous order of sole custody to the mother to joint legal custody of the child, with the primary residence of the child remaining with her mother: *Lipscombe v. Lipscombe* (2002), 2002 CarswellOnt 2657 (Ont. S.C.J.). Neither party was permitted to change the child's residence from the city in which she lived. The court had determined that the effects of the proposed move would be catastrophic. The 35-year-old mother had met a 22-year-old man, an apprentice undertaker, on the internet and proposed moving to Kentucky to be in closer proximity to him. The young man was not prepared to provide for the mother or her child.

In *Hood v. Hood* (2001), 20 R.F.L. (5th) 78, 2001 CarswellOnt 2613, [2001] O.J. No. 2918 (S.C.J.), the court refused the custodial mother's application to abridge the 120-day notice that she was required to provide the husband prior to moving more than 30 kilometers from the city in which both parties resided. The notice contemplated the mother's employment situation but the nature of her application was not within the "urgency" requirement contemplated for such motions.

In *Belisle v. Belisle* (2000), 13 R.F.L. (5th) 262, 2000 CarswellOnt 4735, [2000] O.J. No. 4744 (Ont. S.C.J.), the court refused the mother permission to move with the child to another town. The mother intended to cohabit with her male friend, in what was still an untested relationship. The child had developed stable support systems within his current community, having had the same babysitter for 4 years and having strong ties with the father's extended family. There was no evidence that the new arrangement would be equally supportive and the move would not favour the children's best interests. This case was not decided under the *Divorce Act*.

Where the father's objection to the custodial mother's proposed relocation to a near-by community was largely an attempt to control the mother's life, the court refused the husband's application prohibiting the move: *Biamonte v. Biamonte* (1998), 36 R.F.L. (4th) 349 (Ont. Gen. Div.)

In *Allen v. Allen* (1998), 38 R.F.L. (4th) 96, 1998 CarswellOnt 1818, [1998] O.J. No. 1853 (Ont. Gen. Div.), the court allowed the custodial mother's application to vary the terms of a consent custody order which prohibited her from moving the children more than 20 kilometres away. The wife's fiancée, with whom the wife and children lived, was being transferred. The move was justified financially and the children's best interests would be served by remaining with their mother rather than transferring custody to the father.

In *Schioler v. Schioler* (1997), 34 R.F.L. (4th) 31, 1997 CarswellMan 567, 124 Man. R. (2d) 139 (Man. Q.B.), the court allowed the mother's application varying a joint custody award to a sole custody award in her favour, allowing her to move with the children to another province. The mother was currently unemployed and the proposed move would allow her to begin a new job and thus be a positive role model for the children. In addition, the father had unilaterally reduced his contact with the children and tended to put his own needs before theirs.

In *Chambers v. Chambers* (1997), 34 R.F.L. (4th) 86, 1997 CarswellOnt 4272, 43 O.T.C. 272 (Ont. Gen. Div.), the court refused the father's application varying custody from the custodial mother to himself. Although the mother's planned move to a new city constituted a change in circumstances, it was not designed to frustrate the father's access. The child's relationship with the mother was a positive one and, in the circumstances, a joint custody order was appropriate.

Where the mother removed the children from Alberta to live in Ontario, without notice to the father as required under the mother's custody order, the children were ordered returned to Alberta and joint custody awarded. The children required a strong male role model and their continued residence in Alberta primarily with the mother, was therefore in their best interests. Despite the animosity which existed between the parties, the children's interests favoured joint custody: *P. (T.M.A.) v. P. (F.A.)* (1995), 14 R.F.L. (4th) 290, 30 Alta. L.R. (3d) 317, 1995 CarswellaLTA 205 (Q.B.).

Where in response to the custodial mother's plan to move to another municipality the father himself sought custody, the court declined the mother's request to proceed with the move pending the outcome of the trial. The court was not prepared to make an interim decision which could possibly defeat the father's custody claim: *Delaquis v. Delaquis* (1995), 17 R.F.L. (4th) 459, 104 Man. R. (2d) 258, 1995 CarswellMan 441 (Q.B.).

The court has jurisdiction to prevent a unilateral move by one of two joint custodial parents, even within the province, if the move would adversely affect the quality of custody and access and would not be in the children's best interests: *Smok v. Smok* (1994), 8 R.F.L. (4th) 59, 1994 CarswellAlta 392 (Alta. Q.B.).

In *Hollett v. Collins-Hollet* (1992), 102 Nfld. & P.E.I.R. 145, 323 A.P.R. 145, 1992 CarswellNfld 123 (Nfld. T.D.), the father's application for a change of custody from the mother to himself was allowed in light of the mother's plan to move to another town seven hours drive from her current home. The move was not in the children's best interests as it would remove them in the middle of the school year from the only environment they had ever known. The move was also not a career advancement for the wife and, in order for her to advance, yet another move would be required.

In *Fairchild (Ashe) v. Ashe* (1991), 103 N.S.R. (2d) 231, 282 A.P.R. 231, 1991 CarswellNS 121 (T.D.), the court refused the husband's application for a variation of custody after the custodial mother planned to move with her son from Nova Scotia to Ontario because of her new husband's career. The husband had custody of the parties' daughter and, as he had never encouraged their relationship with the wife, it was likely he would pursue the same course with the son. Further there was no evidence that the transfer would unduly interfere with the husband's access.

In *Caldwell v. Caldwell* (1991), 77 Man. R. (2d) 159, 1991 CarswellMan 399 (Q.B.), the court refused the husband's application that the parties' joint custody arrangement be varied to grant him sole custody. Although the mother, who had primary care of the children, was moving with them from Manitoba to Ontario, the move was only one hour by car and the children's best interests would not be served by a change in custody.

In *Hultman v. Hultman* (1990), 71 Man. R. (3d) 171, 1990 CarswellMan 434 (Q.B.), the court refused the wife's request for a variation of a joint custody term prohibiting the wife from removing the children from Manitoba. The wife wished to move to Ontario to be closer to her boyfriend which would have resulted in the children's loss of contact with their father and a disruptive third change of the children's residence.

Where the wife had wrongfully removed the children from Ontario to British Columbia in order to frustrate the husband's access, the husband's application for the return of the children to Ontario was dismissed. Although a full custody hearing should be conducted in Ontario, it was not in the children's best interests to forcibly remove them from the mother's custody without such a hearing: *Staranowicz v. Staranowicz* (1990), 30 R.F.L. (3d) 185, 1990 CarswellOnt 323 (Ont. Gen. Div.); additional reasons at (1990), 30 R.F.L. (3d) 185 at 190 (Ont. Gen. Div.).

Where the parties' decree *nisi* incorporated a joint custody agreement and the mother unilaterally decided to move with the children from Edmonton to Ottawa, the court allowed the husband's application to vary the decree and transfer custody to him. The mother's proposed move was a sufficient change in circumstances to invoke the court's jurisdiction under s. 17(5) of the *Divorce Act* and, as she failed to prove that the move was in the children's best interests, the variation was justified: *Jones v. Jaworski* (1989), 18 R.F.L. (3d) 385, 93 A.R. 378 (Q.B.).

Where the mother planned to move with the three and one half-year-old child from Montreal to Italy, custody was ordered transferred from the mother to the father. The mother's decision put the child's well-being at risk by removing him from a familiar environment where his interests would be better served: *Droit de la famille — 1185*, [1988] R.D.F. 260 (C.S. Qué.).

Mere change of a child's residence by the custodial parent does not affect the custodial parent's right to custody. Where an agreement exists which does not prohibit removal of children by the custodial parent but which contains specific terms of access, generally, the parties will be taken as having intended that the children continue to reside where access can be exercised without undue inconvenience. Where the children are removed in such a case the issue is whether the custodial parent unreasonably interfered with the other parent's access: *Wainwright v. Wainwright* (1987), 10 R.F.L. (3d) 387, 81 N.S.R. (2d) 413, 203 A.P.R. 413, 1987 CarswellNS 56 (T.D.); affirmed (1988), 1988 CarswellNS 52, 85 N.S.R. (2d) 280, 216 A.P.R. 280, 15 R.F.L. (3d) 174 (C.A.); leave to appeal refused (1989), 93 N.S.R. (2d) 270n (S.C.C.).

In *Smok v. Smok* (1994), 8 R.F.L. (4th) 59, 1994 CarswellAlta 392 (Alta. Q.B.), the court refused to vary the joint custody provision of the parties' separation agreement to allow the mother, who had primary care and control of the children, to move them to a community 6 hours away from where the husband resided. No material change in circumstances was cited in justification of the move.

Where the court incorporated the joint custody provisions of the parties' separation agreement into the decree *nisi* but not another provision prohibiting the child's removal from the province, the father could not rely on either the decree or the agreement in his application to prevent the mother from taking the child to live in Florida. Furthermore, it was in the child's best interests that his mobility not be limited: *LeBlanc v. Holmes* (1993), 141 N.B.R. (2d) 382, 361 A.P.R. 382, 1993 CarswellNB 260 (Q.B.).

Parental and child mobility rights are governed by the best interests of the child. In the case of a young child, who particularly benefits from frequent access visits with the non-custodial parent. The custodial parent's application to remove the child to another jurisdiction may be refused where such access rights would be hampered: *Brigante v. Brigante* (1991), 32 R.F.L. (3d) 299, 1991 CarswellOnt 265 (Ont. U.F.C.).

In *Taylor v. Taylor* (1995), 20 R.F.L. (4th) 18, [1996] N.W.T.R. 187, 1995 CarswellNWT 36, [1995] N.W.T.J. No. 82 (S.C.), the court refused the father's application for an order restraining the wife from moving with the children to another jurisdiction. As it was, the father did not live in the same municipality as the rest of his family and accordingly his access would be no further complicated by the move. Furthermore, the move could result in an improvement in the family's circumstances.

In *Cox v. Harvey* (2000), 13 R.F.L. (5th) 48, 196 Nfld. & P.E.I.R. 306, 589 A.P.R. 306, 2000 CarswellNfld 326, [2000] N.J. No. 313 (Nfld. U.F.C.), the court refused the mother's application to have the parties' joint custody arrangement varied transferring the child's principal residence from the father's home to the mother's. The father was resident in Newfoundland but proposed, for career reasons, to relocate to Ontario, thereby affecting the New Brunswick resident mother's access. The father and his new spouse were the de facto family unit for the child. There was no improper motive behind the father's decision to relocate and the child's best interests, in the short term at least, would be best served by leaving her in the care of her father.

Where the wife proposed to move with the children from Ontario to live with her boyfriend in Nova Scotia, an order was issued requiring that the children remain in Ontario. As the children had no relationship with the boyfriend and had a good relationship with both their father and grandparents in Ontario, their best interests would not be served by the proposed move: *Colley v. Colley* (1991), 31 R.F.L. (3d) 281, 1991 CarswellOnt 245 (Ont. U.F.C.).

Where the mother had breached the parties' joint custody agreement by unilaterally removing the child to another city, it was recommended that the father be granted custody on a variation application. The fact that the mother had left her employment, changed her residence and was less willing to cooperate with the husband constituted a sufficient change in circumstances: *Smith v. Smith* (1987), 7 R.F.L. (3d) 206, 1987 CarswellNS 70 (N.S. Fam. Ct.). See also *Reynders v. Quirk* (1989), 94 N.S.R. (2d) 82, 247 A.P.R. 82, 1989 CarswellNS 368 (Fam. Ct.): *Bennett v. Drouillard* (1988), 15 R.F.L. (3d) 353, 1988 CarswellOnt 271 (Ont. Fam. Ct.).

Divorce Act, 1968

The fact that the custodial mother had remarried and planned to move to another country with the children was held to be insufficient grounds on which to disturb the custody arrangements in *Chesko v. Chesko* (1985), 43 R.F.L. (2d) 341 (Sask. C.A.).

The fact that the custodial parent has removed the child from the jurisdiction of the court which first made the custody order does not amount to a change of circumstances justifying a transfer of custody to the other parent: *MacDonald (Ferguson) v. Ferguson* (1982), 30 R.F.L. (2d) 374 (P.E.I. C.A.).

17§75 — Change in circumstances — remarriage of non-custodial parent

Divorce Act, 1968

Where at the time of the divorce the mother was unemployed, pregnant and living common law with the result that custody was awarded to the father, the mother's subsequent remarriage to a man of some substance was considered a sufficient change of circumstances to justify a variation of the decree *nisi* granting custody to her: *Burnett v. Peterson* (1977), 18 N.B.R. 196 (C.A.).

In *Hewlin v. Hewlin* (1981), 30 Nfld. & P.E.I.R. 340, 84 A.P.R. 340 (Nfld. T.D.), at trial of the divorce, the husband was heavily in debt and had no facilities to care for the children, and therefore custody was awarded to the wife. The husband subsequently stabilized his situation, acquired a common-law wife and applied to vary the decree *nisi* to award custody to himself. Although the father could provide an excellent home and showed a higher degree of sophistication than the mother, there was no evidence that the children had been neglected or mistreated by their mother. In addition the children had been in the sole custody of their mother during most of their young lives and their father had played very little part in their upbringing. Therefore, the welfare of the children demanded that they remain with their mother.

In *Ploughman v. Ploughman* (1974), 5 Nfld. & P.E.I.R. 431 (Nfld. T.D.), custody of the children had, upon divorce, been awarded to the father due to the greater security and stability which he was able to offer. However, the mother's subsequent remarriage into comfortable circumstances combined with the facts of the father's financial reverses and new living arrangement with another woman and her children amounted to a sufficient change in circumstances to justify a variation of the custody provisions in the mother's favour.

17§76 — Change in circumstances — parents' health affecting children

Divorce Act, 1985

In *Lapierre v. Lapierre* (1991), 34 R.F.L. (3d) 129 (Sask. Q.B.), the court allowed the husband's application for variation of custody and care of the parties' two children, which was ordered transferred from the wife to the husband, despite the children's contrary wishes. As the mother suffered from a mood disorder and was turning the children, aged seven and ten, against their father, the change was in their best interests.

Where the wife's anxiety adjustment disorder rendered continuation of the parties' joint custody unworkable, the court allowed the husband's application for a variation of the custody order and he was awarded sole custody: *Turner v. Turner* (1991), 102 N.S.R. (2d) 316, 279 A.P.R. 316 (T.D.).

In *Negard v. Negard* (1991), 121 A.R. 279 (Q.B.), custody of the parties' five-year-old child was changed from the mother to the father on his application for variation. The mother had earlier voluntarily placed the child in the father's care where she had prospered. The mother had emotional and financial problems and planned to take evening courses, which would have reduced the time available for the child.

Where in the exercise of his joint custody rights the father subjected the mother to emotional and psychological abuse, the court allowed the wife's application for sole custody with specified access to the father. The new order would reduce the friction between the parties and would be in the children's best interests: *Shaw v. Shaw* (1991), 38 R.F.L. (3d) 32 (Man. Q.B.).

Where during the two-and-a-half years that he had been in his father's custody the parties' son exhibited behavioural problems and had done badly in school, the court granted the mother's application for a change in custody. The father was not able adequately to provide for the emotional and personal needs of the boy, whereas the mother was enjoying a stable home life: *Carter v. Yablonski* (1989), 75 Sask. R. 269 (Q.B.).

Where the husband had been granted custody largely because of the wife's extreme religious beliefs, her subsequent application for interim custody after the husband had been injured was also dismissed. Interim custody was awarded to the husband's brother as concerns about the wife's religious beliefs continued: *Mosley v. Mosley* (1990), 25 R.F.L. (3d) 110, 102 A.R. 293 (Q.B.).

Where one and one-half years after the decree *nisi*, the parties' 15-year-old son expressed the wish to live with his mother rather than the custodial father, the mother's application to vary the custody provisions of the decree *nisi* was allowed. The father had continued to be abusive towards the mother and the child's emotional needs would be better satisfied by the mother: *Cook v. Cook* (1988), 72 Nfld. & P.E.I.R. 123, 223 A.P.R. 123 (Nfld. T.D.).

In *Demchuk v. Demchuk* (1988), 13 R.F.L. (3d) 348, 84 A.R. 206 (Q.B.), the court allowed the mother's application to vary a joint custody order changing the children's residence from the father's home to her own. The children's best interests required such a change given the father's failure to meet their needs, his refusal to respect the mother's joint custody rights and the emotional and scholastic difficulties which the children experienced as a result.

In *McGivery v. McGivery* (1987), 83 N.B.R. (2d) 138, 212 A.P.R. 138 (Q.B.), the court allowed the husband's application to vary custody and transferred the children to his care, citing their best interests. The children had been happy while living with their father during a one-year temporary custody agreement between the parties which had been brought about because of the wife's work-related mental health problems and the fact that she could not offer a stable environment.

Divorce Act, 1968

In *Yeates v. Yeates* (1982), 52 N.S.R. (2d) 662, 106 A.P.R. 662 (T.D.), the joint custody provisions of the decree *nisi* were varied to grant sole custody of the 10-year-old child to the mother. Although both parties were capable of being custodial parents, the mother had proven to be more perceptive and understanding than the father. The fact that she was younger than the father, a better disciplinarian and better organized favoured her marginally over the father as the more desirable custodian.

In a divorce petition presented to the court, the sole issue appeared to be one of access to the child by the father. During the course of the trial, the parties entered into an agreement that the wife should have custody of the child with the issue of access to be litigated. As a term of the agreement, both parties agreed to attend for a psychiatric examination if so ordered. A decree *nisi* was granted, incorporating an order of custody to the wife. The matter or access was to be returnable before the court after psychiatric examinations. A decree absolute was subsequently granted. Thereafter, the examinations were held, and a report forwarded to the court by a psychiatrist expressing concern as to the mother's mental health, and setting out the views, firstly, that the mother not be permitted to remove the child from the country without the father's consent and secondly, advocating a re-opening of the issue of custody if the mother refused the father access. In the interim, however, the mother took the child to Portugal in anticipation of an adverse report. On the father's application it was held that the decree *nisi* should be varied and custody awarded to the father: *Lebre v. Lebre*, 13 R.F.L. 174, [1973] 2 O.R. 408, 34 D.L.R. (3d) 32 (H.C.).

17§77 — Change in circumstances — conduct affecting children

Divorce Act, 1985

Where the father had become convinced that the mother had been abusing the child, but no real evidence of such evidence existed, the court upheld on appeal an order terminating the existing joint custody order had substituting a sole custody order in the mother's favour. As the parties were no longer able to cooperate, the best interests of the child favoured the sole custody order: *Lucken v. Hopkins* (1994), 8 R.F.L. (4th) 226 (B.C. C.A.).

In *Armstrong v. Khan* (1997), 33 R.F.L. (4th) 438 (Ont. Gen. Div.), the court allowed the mother's application for an order varying the joint-custody arrangement and granting the mother sole custody. The father had physically, emotionally and verbally abused the child to the extend that the child suffered post-traumatic stress syndrome. The child's behaviour would likely further deteriorate if the father was allowed even supervised access.

The fact that the custodial mother maintained a vegetarian lifestyle was not a ground which supported the father's claim for a transfer of custody where the children were in good health and there was no evidence of risk: *Desilets v. Piwowar* (1996), 183 A.R. 313 (Q.B.).

Where the father acted outrageously during access visits with the children and was unable to discuss children-related issues with the wife in a reasonable manner, their consent joint custody award was set aside in favour of a sole custody award in the wife's favour: *Ducas v. Varkony* (1995), 16 R.F.L. (4th) 91, 104 Man. R. (2d) 110 (Q.B.).

Where the wife was frequently absent from home, had one lover who was bordering on alcoholism and another with whom she frequently argued, the court affirmed on appeal a variation order whereby custody of the parties' child was transferred from the wife to the husband. As the husband had entered into a stable relationship and could offer the child a good education, the child's best interest would be served in the husband's care: *C. (M.) v. B. (H.)* (1989), 35 Q.A.C. 90.

In *R. (J.) v. I. (A.)* (1987), 60 Sask. R. 81 (Q.B.); affirmed (1988), 13 R.F.L. (3d) 44, 61 Sask. R. 225 (C.A.), the decree *nisi* was varied and custody of the children was transferred from the husband to the wife based upon evidence that the father was sexually abusing one of the children. Testimony of a social worker and a police officer indicated that some sort of sexual abuse had been occurring and the court admitted into evidence statements made by the children to the social worker concerning such abuse.

Where the mother had alleged sexual abuse of the children at the hands of the father and had clandestinely removed them from the province in breach of a custody order, the court refused the husband's application for an order that mother and children be apprehended and that custody be transferred to him. As the children were not in danger, the order was not in the children's best interests. It was preferable that the mother be served with a notice of the custody proceeding so that the court could benefit from both parties' evidence: *K. (J.E.) v. K. (C.)* (1991), 85 D.L.R. (4th) 284 (Ont. Gen. Div.).

Divorce Act, 1968

In *Peachey v. Peachey* (1986), 49 Sask. R. 47 (Q.B.), a custody order was varied to remove the parties' child from the mother's care as a result of abuse of the child by the mother's common-law spouse. Although the common-law spouse was no longer residing with the mother, she had expressed her desire to reunite with him and the court could not be sure that he would not return.

In *McCormick v. McCormick* (1983), 50 N.B.R. (2d) 222, 131 A.P.R. 222 (Q.B.), the husband, on an application to vary the decree *nisi*, was granted custody of the parties' five-year-old child. Subsequent to the divorce, the custodial mother had commenced to live with a man who had both a drinking problem and a criminal record, with the result that the environment created was no longer in the child's best interests.

Where custody of the children was awarded to the father who subsequently boarded them out to third parties, the court granted the mother's application for variance whereby custody was awarded to her. The court found that the father's actions in depriving the children of the continuous presence of both parents amounted to a material change in circumstances justifying a variation in the children's best interests: *Re Storey* (1976), 26 R.F.L. 339, 14 N.B.R. (2d) 66 (Q.B.).

Where since the divorce the custodial mother had had illicit relationships, had practised wife swapping and had indulged in fornication, the court granted custody of the child to the father upon his application for a variation to the decree *nisi*: *Ducharme v. Ducharme* (1972), 7 N.S.R. (2d) 326 (T.D.).

Where, after a custody award in her favour, the mother began to engage in prostitution, an order was made transferring custody to the father: *Mosure v. Mosure* (1986), 4 R.F.L. (3d) 253 (B.C. S.C.).

17§78 — Change in circumstances — denial of access

Divorce Act, 1985

In *Giles v. Giles* (1995), 17 R.F.L. (4th) 139, 174 A.R. 201, 102 W.A.C. 201 (C.A.), an order removing the father's access rights and barring him from bringing further applications concerning the children for a one-year period was upheld on appeal. The children's lives had been seriously disrupted as a result of the turmoil continuing in the parent's relationship and a period of tranquility to restore stability to their lives was justified.

Where the custodial mother had at one time thwarted the husband's access rights, but over time had come around to the extent that the father was enjoying regular access, an order transferring custody from the mother to the father was reversed on appeal. The trial judge had largely based his decision on the premise that the father was more likely to encourage access by the non-custodial parent. Given the mother's recent behaviour, it could no longer be said that she would not be supportive of the father's access rights: *Kubel v. Kubel* (1995), 15 R.F.L. (4th) 356, 169 A.R. 295, 97 W.A.C. 295 (C.A.).

The unwillingness of a parent to facilitate access is an important factor in considering whether there has been a change in circumstances sufficient to vary a custody order. However, even when such a change in circumstances is established, custody should be varied only if it is in the child's best interests to do so: *Rose v. Rose* (1989), 22 R.F.L. (3d) 72, 98 A.R. 42 (Q.B.).

Where, during the parties' joint custody arrangement, the father, who had the day to day care of the children, repeatedly thwarted the mother's access rights, the court allowed the mother's application for sole custody. The mother was preferable as custodial parent, as she encouraged the children in their relationship with their father, and psychiatric assessment of the children indicated that closer contact with their mother would prove beneficial: *Roman v. Roman* (1989), 100 N.B.R. (2d) 432, 252 A.P.R. 432 (Q.B.).

Where the custodial mother had denied the father's access rights and had interfered with his relationship with his child, his application to vary the decree *nisi* and to grant custody to him was allowed. As the father was willing to allow the mother access and to encourage the child's relationship with her, the variation was the only way to ensure the child's contact with both parents: *Tremblay v. Tremblay*, 10 R.F.L. (3d) 166, 54 Alta. L.R. (2d) 283, [1987] 6 W.W.R. 742, 82 A.R. 24 (Q.B.).

Divorce Act, 1968

The evidence to be adduced in support of a variation application should be limited to the changed circumstances of the parties subsequent to the latest order of the court. This is not to say that cross-examination should be limited to recent events if reference to earlier facts is necessary to determine the credibility of any witnesses, but it must be assumed that the order of the court was in accordance with the law if it has not been previously set aside. In an application to vary custody, once the evidence of the changed circumstances has been received, however, the court must be guided in making its decision by the well-established principles of law relating to custody applications: *Wesson v. Wesson* (1973), 10 R.F.L. 193, 11 N.S.R. (2d) 652, 5 A.P.R. 652 (T.D.).

In *Elliott v. Elliott*, 30 R.F.L. 339, [1977] 2 W.W.R. 758 (B.C. S.C.), custody of three infant children was granted to the respondent mother by order of the Supreme Court made in September. In the following January the parties signed a separation agreement purporting to nullify the court order and give custody to the father. In an action for divorce the court reserved judgment on the respondent's application for custody and in a memorandum to counsel the judge stated he would not vary the order previously made unless he had seen the order and had been given details as to how it came about. He further stated it was not proper procedure to vary a custody order by consent, and the proper way to vary was to go back to the court which had originally made the order.

17§79 — Practice

Divorce Act, 1985

Where the father had brought a succession of unsuccessful applications for variation of access and had not satisfied any of the numerous cost awards against him as he was bankrupt, he was prohibited from bringing further motions without first obtaining leave of the court in *Kerton v. Kerton* (1997), 33 R.F.L. (4th) 285 (Ont. Gen. Div.).

In *O'Leary v. O'Leary* (1993), 112 Nfld. & P.E.I.R. 347, 350 A.P.R. 347 (Nfld. T.D.), the court refused the husband's application for the return of lump sum support paid by him pursuant to an order of a different judge of the same court. The husband was attempting to use variation procedures for the purposes of appeal.

A custody order or variation should be varied on the merits and not simply on default. Accordingly, where the applicant's affidavit in support of the variation was deficient and where the respondent failed to appear, the court refused the application in *Hoppe v. Hoppe* (1990), 91 Sask. R. 193 (Q.B.).

Where the father had refused to return the child to the custodial mother after an access visit and had brought an application for custody, the child was ordered returned to the mother. The status quo had been determined by the earlier custody order, which continued in full force until varied: *Moggey v. Moggey* (1990), 28 R.F.L. (3d) 416 (Sask. Q.B.).

Where the mother brought a motion to strike the father's pleadings in an action to vary access on the ground that the father had disregarded numerous cost awards against him, the motion was dismissed. As the father had not yet filed any pleadings, the motion was found to be premature: *Kerton v. Kerton* (1997), 33 R.F.L. (4th) 285 (Ont. Gen. Div.).

An order varying custody should not be made solely on the basis of affidavit evidence of a 12-year-old child: *Leblue v. Leblue* (1997), 33 R.F.L. (4th) 118, 209 A.R. 227, 160 W.A.C. 227 (C.A.).

A judge is not required to make a finding of a change in the "conditions, means, needs or other circumstances of the child" before ordering a psychological assessment of a child in an application to vary custody: *Tucker v. Tucker* (1998), 41 R.F.L. (4th) 404, 65 Alta. L.R. (3d) 213, [1999] 4 W.W.R. 461, 165 D.L.R. (4th) 103, 219 A.R. 383, 179 W.A.C. 383 (C.A.).

Divorce Act, 1968

Where the Supreme Court of Canada restored the trial judgment in custody proceedings, it was held that the mother, in her application to vary that trial judgment, was entitled to introduce evidence of changed circumstances dating from the trial judgment and not merely from the date of the appeal: *Novic v. Novic* (1984), 37 R.F.L. (2d) 133, 1 O.A.C. 395 (C.A.); leave to appeal refused (1984), 55 N.R. 319 (S.C.C.).

17§80 — Variation of access orders — general

Divorce Act, 1985

Note that pursuant to s. 17(9), where a court varies a custody order, it must follow the principle that a child should have as much contact with each parent as is in the child's best interests and if the court is considering changing custody, it must take into account that person's willingness to bring about such contact.

In *H. (E.A.) v. G. (T.D.)* (1995), 18 R.F.L. (4th) 21, 146 N.S.R. (2d) 254, 422 A.P.R. 254 (C.A.), the trial judge's failure to consider evidence of a child abuse specialist who recommended the discontinuation of the father's access rights was one reason supporting the termination of those rights on appeal.

To alter an order for access, a material change in circumstances must have occurred that affected the best interests of the child: *Cairns v. Cairns* (1995), 10 R.F.L. (4th) 234 (N.B. C.A.); affirming (1994), 3 R.F.L. (4th) 397, 145 N.B.R. (2d) 866, 372 A.P.R. 86 (Q.B.).

In *Gunn v. Gunn* (1994), 10 R.F.L. (4th) 197 (Man. C.A.), the court, on its own initiative, varied the terms of the father's access order, which appeared to be in the best interest of no one.

In determining whether to terminate a father's access order, the court is entitled to take into account the effect that continued access would have on the custodial mother. This factor could be particularly persuasive where the mother's well-founded fear of the father could have a negative impact on the children: *Abdo v. Abdo* (1993), 50 R.F.L. (3d) 171, 126 N.S.R. (2d) 1, 352 A.P.R. 1, 109 D.L.R. (4th) 78 (C.A.).

In *F. (R.J.) v. F. (K.E.)* (1997), 33 R.F.L. (4th) 241 (C.A.), the fact that the trial judge had considered facts which had occurred prior to the divorce did not affect the validity of his findings in a much later application to vary access. As the trial judge in the divorce proceedings had not made any findings of relevance on the issues of custody and access, it was necessary for the judge in the variation proceeding to consider all of the facts of the case.

Section 17(5) of the *Divorce Act, 1985*, which permits variation of custody orders, also includes access orders: *Winkler v. Winkler*, 15 R.F.L. (3d) 337, [1988] 6 W.W.R. 241 (Man. C.A.).

Access is not to be suspended simply because the non-custodial parent is delinquent in meeting support obligations. As the sole criterion on an access application is the best interests of the children, access and support should not be tied together: *H. (F.V.) v. O. (D.A.)* (1988), 16 R.F.L. (3d) 430 (N.B. C.A.).

Where the custodial father's parenting style was somewhat rigid, the court granted the mother's application for increased access in an effort to better balance the father's influence: *Burggraaf v. Burggraaf* (1998), 40 R.F.L. (4th) 26 (Ont. Gen. Div.).

Where the father brought an application to vary the terms of an interim supervised access order, the application was dismissed. As it had only been 3 months since the interim order had been made, the matter was best left to the trial judge: *Kerton v. Kerton* (1997), 33 R.F.L. (4th) 285 (Ont. Gen. Div.).

In *Coulson v. Farmer* (1999), 50 R.F.L. (4th) 345 (Ont. Gen. Div.), the court rejected the father's counter-petition in which he sought increased access to the parties' child. The access sought by the father would be tantamount to joint custody and the court had previously, in awarding custody to the mother, determining that joint custody was not workable given the parties' inflexible and uncompromising attitudes. The father's counter-petition was intended more as an application to vary custody, which could not serve as an indirect route to appeal the initial custody order.

In *B. (B.J.A.) v. R. (K.J.)* (1996), 21 R.F.L. (4th) 401 (Ont. Gen. Div.), the court dismissed the mother's application to remove the father's access to the parties' three-year-old daughter based on allegations that the father had sexually abused the child. The mother's evidence based upon alleged statements of the daughter, the mother's observations of her and unsubstantiated statements attributed to the father's former girlfriend, was insufficient to justify a change in the order.

Where the custodial mother had informally allowed for changes in the father's access rights to accommodate the different circumstances resulting from her remarriage, she could not argue that there had been no changes in circumstances when the father formally sought to increase his access rights: *Belisle v. Poole* (1994), 2 R.F.L. (4th) 165, 111 D.L.R. (4th) 717 (Ont. Gen. Div.).

A mother's anger with the father is not a justification for cancellation of his access rights, nor are his occasional verbal and physical outbursts resulting from her attempts to frustrate his rights: *L. (T.D.) v. L. (L.R.)* (1994), 4 R.F.L. (4th) 103, 114 D.L.R. (4th) 709 (Ont. Gen. Div.).

Where the custodial mother had allowed the father access visits in addition to those required under their divorce decree, but later returned to the specified access schedule, the cessation of the additional access could not be relied upon by the father as a "material change in circumstances" justifying a variation of the access order. The father knew that the additional access would not be permanent when the original access order was issued: *Hamilton v. Hamilton* (1992), 43 R.F.L. (3d) 13 (Alta. Q.B.).

It is appropriate to deny an access parent increased access where he or she has not been exercising rights on a consistent basis: *Farkas v. Farkas* (1990), 85 Sask. R. 265 (Q.B.).

Divorce Act, 1968

When adjudicating upon an application to vary the access provisions contained in a decree *nisi*, the trial judge is not bound by the report of a Family Court judge, who took the evidence of the parties in relation to the application: *Armstrong v. Armstrong* (1984), 38 R.F.L. (2d) 264 (N.S. C.A.).

While the court would normally be more reluctant to interfere with the access provisions of the decree *nisi* which are based on an agreement between the parties, this principle cannot be applied to a case where both parties feel the change should be made in the decree *nisi* incorporating that agreement: *Milbury v. Milbury* (1978), 2 R.F.L. (2d) 301 (Ont. C.A.).

Where subsequent to the divorce the father had given up drinking and had abandoned his former disreputable life style, the court favourably entertained his application for more liberal access rights: *Tocco v. Tocco* (1977), 4 R.F.L. (2d) 174 (Ont. C.A.).

A direction in the decree *nisi* that no application for varying access rights should be made until the expiration of one year is invalid as being contrary to the express provisions of s. 11(2) [now s. 17(1)] of the *Divorce Act*: *Heikel v. Heikel* (1970), 1 R.F.L. 326, 73 W.W.R. 84, 12 D.L.R. (3d) 311 (Alta. C.A.).

"Clearly there has been a change here. The wife, who was the respondent in the previous divorce action, has since the divorce remarried and also, since that time, has acquired a home; both of these factors, in my opinion, are sufficient to permit me to review the access order that was previously made": per Stratton J. in *Craig v. Craig* (1975), 26 R.F.L. 123, 13 N.B.R. (2d) 644 (Q.B.).

Where the father had unduly interfered with the mother's exercise of her custodial rights, the court granted them for a period of time and thereafter specifying the father's access periods with particularity: *Wentzell v. Wentzell* (1970), 3 R.F.L. 122 (Sask. Q.B.).

In *Rutherford v. Rutherford* (1986), 4 R.F.L. (3d) 457 (B.C. S.C.), the court refused the mother's application to terminate the husband's access rights but ordered supervised access based upon her claim that such visits were disturbing to the child. It was unclear which of the parents was actually causing the problem but, if the child was adversely affected in the future, access could be terminated regardless of the source of the difficulty, or custody changed.

17§81 — Change in circumstances — child's move away from the vicinity of the non-custodial parent

No paragraph 17§81.

17§82 — Change in circumstances — access destructive to child

Divorce Act, 1985

In *Lidkea v. Jarrell* (1999), 49 R.F.L. (4th) 324 (Ont. C.A.), an order suspending the father's access to the parties' 11-year-old child was upheld on appeal. As the child did not wish to see the father, who did not take the child's wishes seriously, forced access would not be in the child's best interest.

In *Gorgichuk v. Gorgichuk* (1999), 50 R.F.L. (4th) 395, 180 Sask. R. 126, 205 W.A.C. 126 (C.A.); affirming (1997), 154 Sask. R. 273 (Q.B.), the father's access to his son was found to have been properly terminated after the father had sex in the backseat of his car while the son was sitting in the front seat. The father's actions were clearly improper and it would be harmful to force the son to see him.

Where the father's discipline of his nine-year-old daughter during access visits was found to constitute a violation of her sexual integrity, his access rights were removed in an appeal brought by the mother. The severity of the discipline and its abusive nature was in total disregard of the child's best interests, the father being aware of the child's fragile psyche. The fact that the parties' young son was present during the events and that the episodes adversely affected him was another factor relevant to the discontinuation of access: *H. (E.A.) v. G. (T.D.)* (1995), 18 R.F.L. (4th) 21, 146 N.S.R. (2d) 254, 422 A.P.R. 254 (C.A.).

In *Simmchen v. Potter* (1991), 33 R.F.L. (3d) 430, 119 N.B.R. (2d) 325, 300 A.P.R. 325 (Q.B.); affirmed (1992), 39 R.F.L. (3d) 149, 120 N.B.R. (2d) 447, 302 A.P.R. 447 (C.A.), the court refused to reduce the father's access rights although an expert report recommended such a reduction, based upon the finding that the child experienced no positive benefits from the visits. Access should not be terminated in the absence of danger to the child, which was not the case at hand. Furthermore, the report failed to address the issue of the effect on the child of lack of contact with the father and his family.

In *Starko v. Starko* (1992), 129 A.R. 225 (Q.B.), the court allowed the custodial husband's application for termination of the wife's access rights. The wife's intense resentment toward the husband and his new partner and her continued litigation of access matters had resulted in the child suffering stress, anxiety and other emotional problems. Any potential loss to the child resulting from loss of contact with his mother was not as great as the debilitating stress he was experiencing.

Where the wife suffered from a severe personality disorder which rendered her unable to benefit the children during access visits, and in fact was destructive to them, her access rights were removed and she was prohibited from seeking access for a one-year period: *Smith v. Smith* (1991), 34 R.F.L. (3d) 367, 117 N.B.R. (2d) 81, 295 A.P.R. 81 (Q.B.).

Where the mother suffered from severe paranoia and an abnormal hatred of the husband, the custodial father's application for a restriction of the mother's generous access rights was allowed: *MacDonald v. MacDonald* (1989), 100 N.B.R. (2d) 121, 252 A.P.R. 121 (Q.B.).

17§83 — Change in circumstances — change in schedule

Divorce Act, 1985

Where the mother's access visits disrupted the child's school activities, the court allowed the custodial father's appeal and varied the timing of the mother's access: *Rice v. Rice* (1996), 19 R.F.L. (4th) 26, 137 Sask. R. 285, 107 W.A.C. 285 (C.A.).

In *Meloche v. Kules* (1997), 35 R.F.L. (4th) 297, 35 O.R. (3d) 688 (Gen. Div.), the court refused the mother's application to reduce the father's access time to the child. As the child was now in residence at school during the week, the mother sought the variation to increase her own time available to spend time with the child. However, the mother was still free to visit the child at school and the fact that the child was no longer at home with the mother did not justify a reduction in the father's access.

In *Mikkelsen v. Mikkelsen* (1989), 23 R.F.L. (3d) 428 (Ont. H.C.), the father, whose religion required that he be "master in his own home," was inflexible in exercising his specified access rights to his 12-year-old daughter to the extent that it frequently interfered with her extra-curricular activities. The mother's application to vary access was allowed and a flexible access schedule adopted on the basis that, although the child's wishes do not govern access, the opinions of an intelligent 12-year-old were relevant.

Where due to a change in the father's working hours he could not exercise his access at the time specified in the decree *nisi*, the decree was varied to allow him access on his day off: *Doucet v. Doucet* (1986), 76 N.B.R. (2d) 466, 192 A.P.R. 446 (Q.B.).

Where the parties could not agree as to the meaning of "reasonable access" as contained in the decree *nisi*, the word "reasonable" was removed from the access order and replaced with a fixed access schedule: *Hood v. MacDonald* (1989), 91 N.S.R. (2d) 264, 233 A.P.R. 264 (Fam. Ct.).

Where the mother had insisted on exercising her access rights every weekend so that the father and the children could not spend any free time together, the mother's access was altered to every second weekend. The access arrangements had not been in the children's best interests: *Dupont v. Dupont* (1993), 47 R.F.L. (3d) 273 (B.C. S.C.).

17§84 — Change in circumstances — ageing of child

Divorce Act, 1985

In *Elliott v. Loewen* (1993), 44 R.F.L. (3d) 445 (Man. C.A.), the appellant appealed part of an order which varied the access provisions of a previous consent order. By the terms of the consent order, the parties had agreed that the father would have supervised access to the 18-month-old child for a minimum of eight hours a week. Pursuant to the variation order, the father would have unsupervised access to the child who was then three-year-old for a greater period of time that the previous order permitted.

The appellate court was of the opinion that the motions judge was entitled to take judicial notice of the fact that the needs of a three-year-old child in relation to his father are different from the needs of a child who is 18 months old and that the father's desire to develop a realistic parent/child relationship for the benefit of the child could not be fulfilled with the continuation of supervised access in the appellant's home. However, the variation order did not address the best interests of the child and consequently the appellate court shortened the access time to one four-hour period on the weekend and one two-hour period during the week to take account of the child's regular routine.

17§85 — Variation sought by grandparent

Where a grandparent was not a party in the original divorce, that grandparent lacks standing to seek a variation of a custody order made in the divorce. Section 17 of the *Divorce Act* does not contemplate new proceedings with new parties under the guise of a variation application: *Lowey v. Rhame* (1995), 16 R.F.L. (4th) 400, 136 Sask. R. 1 (Q.B.).

17§86 — Change of child's surname

Where a custodial mother remarries, the changing of a child's surname from that of her biological father should never be based on convenience but rather on the child's best interests. A child's name is not to be automatically changed to conform with that of a new parent: *Herniman v. Woltz* (1996), 22 R.F.L. (4th) 232 (Ont. Gen. Div.).

17§87 — Variation of access conditions

In *Dancak v. Dancak* (1998), 38 R.F.L. (4th) 227 (B.C. S.C.), the fact that the children occasionally missed academic tutoring classes and soccer games during the father's access period was found not to be a sufficient basis for altering those access periods.

Where the father's manic-depression stabilized after beginning treatment with lithium, the court allowed his application to remove the supervision requirement from his access rights: *Chancey v. Chancey* (1994), 7 R.F.L. (4th) 96 (S.C.).

17.1 Variation order by affidavit, etc. — Where both former spouses are ordinarily resident in different provinces, a court of competent jurisdiction may, in accordance with any applicable rules of the court, make a variation order pursuant to subsection 17(1) on the basis of the submissions of the former spouses, whether presented orally before the court or by means of affidavits or any means of telecommunication, if both former spouses consent thereto.

1993, c. 8, s. 2

17.1 — Variation order by affidavit

Section 17.1 provides for a variation proceeding where both former spouses are ordinarily resident in different provinces. A court may make a variation order under s. 17.1 based on the submissions of the former spouses. These submissions may be made orally before the court or subject to the consent of both former spouses by means of affidavits or any means of telecommunication.

17.1§1 — General

There is no requirement that a parties' consent to a proceeding under s. 17.1 of the *Divorce Act* be in writing or be expressed in any formal way. Consent can be inferred from the parties' actions: *Attrill v. Green* (1994), 7 R.F.L. (4th) 176 (Alta. Q.B.).

Variation of a support order is provisional only where the respondent is ordinarily resident in another province and has not accepted the jurisdiction of the court, or where both spouses have not consented to the application of s. 17.1 of the *Divorce Act.* A final variation is not available even where the respondent is served with the application: *Martell v. Height* (1993), 45 R.F.L. (3d) 344 (Sask. Q.B.).

Provisional Orders

18. (1) Definitions — In this section and section 19,

"Attorney General", in respect of a province, means

(a) for Yukon, the member of the Executive Council of Yukon designated by the Commissioner of Yukon,

(b) for the Northwest Territories, the member of the Council of the Northwest Territories designated by the Commissioner of the Northwest Territories,

(b.1) for Nunavut, the member of the Executive Council of Nunavut designated by the Commissioner of Nunavut, and

(c) for the other provinces, the Attorney General of the province,

and includes any person authorized in writing by the member or Attorney General to act for the member or Attorney General in the performance of a function under this section or section 19;

"provisional order" means an order made pursuant to subsection (2).

(2) Provisional order — Notwithstanding paragraph 5(1)(a) and subsection 17(1), where an application is made to a court in a province for a variation order in respect of a support order and

(a) the respondent in the application is ordinarily resident in another province, and has not accepted the jurisdiction of the court, or both former spouses have not consented to the application of section 17.1 in respect of the matter, and

(b) in the circumstances of the case, the court is satisfied that the issues can be adequately determined by proceeding under this section and section 19, the court shall make a variation order with or without notice to and in the absence of the respondent, but such order is provisional only and has no legal effect until it is confirmed in a proceeding under section 19 and, where so confirmed, it has legal effect in accordance with the terms of the order confirming it.

(3) Transmission — Where a court in a province makes a provisional order, it shall send to the Attorney General for the province

(a) three copies of the provisional order certified by a judge or officer of the court;

(b) a certified or sworn document setting out or summarizing the evidence given to the court; and

(c) a statement giving any available information respecting the identification, location, income and assets of the respondent.

(4) Idem — On receipt of the documents referred to in subsection (3), the Attorney General shall send the documents to the Attorney General for the province in which the respondent is ordinarily resident.

(5) Further evidence — Where, during a proceeding under section 19, a court in a province remits the matter back for further evidence to the court that made the provisional order, the court that made the order shall, after giving notice to the applicant, receive further evidence.

(6) Transmission — Where evidence is received under subsection (5), the court that received the evidence shall forward to the court that remitted the matter back a certified or sworn document setting out or summarizing the evidence, together with such recommendations as the court that received the evidence considers appropriate.

1993, c. 8, s. 2; 1993, c. 28, s. 78 (Sched. III, item 43); 1997, c. 1, s. 6; 2002, c. 7, s. 159

18 — Provisional orders

With the passage of the *Divorce Act, 1985*, there is a mechanism (provisional orders), for obtaining a variation where the parties are not ordinarily resident in the same province. A "provisional order" is defined in s. 18(1) as meaning "an order made pursuant to subsection (2)." Section 18(2) provides that where an application is made in one province for a variation of a support order, and the respondent is ordinarily resident in another province, and the court is satisfied that the issues can be decided properly under s. 18 (provisional orders) and s. 19 (confirmation of provisional orders), the court may make a variation order. This order can be made without notice and in the absence of the respondent. However, the variation order is only provisional and has no legal effect until it is confirmed under s. 19. When it is confirmed its effect is according to the terms of the order confirming it.

Section 18 sets out the way in which the order is transmitted to the other province: ss. 18(3) and (4), and the procedure for obtaining further evidence from the court that made the provisional order: ss. 18(5) and (6).

Cases under the provisional *Reciprocal Enforcement of Maintenance Orders Acts* may be of assistance in interpreting this section.

The effect of the amendment in s. 18(2) is that s. 18(2) applies notwithstanding s. 5(1) and s. 17(1). Section 5(1) sets out the jurisdiction of the court in variation proceedings. The previous legislation made no mention of s. 5(1).

The amended s. 18(2) has made several additions to s. 18(2)(a). According to s. 18(2)(a), where the respondent is ordinarily resident in another province and has not consented to the court taking jurisdiction, the court of the province may make a variation order that is provisional only.

The amended s. 18(2) requires the court to make a provisional variation order in these circumstances because the mandatory "shall" is used instead of the discretionary "may".

Cases decided under s. 18(2) before it was amended should be read with caution.

18§1 — Jurisdiction

Divorce Act, 1985

Under ss. 17.1 and 18(2) of the *Divorce Act*, an order varying a foreign judgment is provisional unless the foreign party accepts the jurisdiction of the court. Filing of affidavits in the proceeding and appearance by counsel on the foreigner's behalf are evidence of acceptance of the court's jurisdiction: *Snider v. Kennedy* (1994), 118 Sask. R. 178 (Q.B.).

A court has no jurisdiction to transfer proceedings to vary a support order to another province under the *Divorce Act, 1985*. Nor can a court of competent jurisdiction make a provisional order on a variation application and remit it to another court for confirmation where notice has been given. A party has the right to ask a court in the province where he or she resides to vary a support order, made in another province, on a final basis: *Maximitch v. Maximitch* (1987), 8 R.F.L. (3d) 54 (Man. Q.B.).

A Family Court judge lacks authority to grant a provisional variation order where a respondent has been duly notified of the application to vary: *Munson v. Munson* (1990), 101 N.S.R. (2d) 83, 275 A.P.R. 83 (Fam. Ct.).

In determining the fairness of a request for final variation order pursuant to s. 17 of the *Divorce Act*, as opposed to a provisional variation order pursuant to s. 18, in a different jurisdiction, the relevant factors are: the relative abilities of the two parties to respond in the other jurisdiction, including their financial capacity; the reason why one party is no longer living in the jurisdiction in which the original order was made; the passage of time since the original order; and the balance of convenience: *Gartner v. Gartner* (1993), 146 A.R. 84 (Q.B.).

19. (1) Transmission — On receipt of any documents sent pursuant to subsection 18(4), the Attorney General for the province in which the respondent is ordinarily resident shall send the documents to a court in the province.

(2) Procedure — Subject to subsection (3), where documents have been sent to a court pursuant to subsection (1), the court shall serve on the respondent a copy of the documents and a notice of a hearing respecting confirmation of the provisional order and shall proceed with the hearing, in the absence of the applicant, taking into consideration the certified or sworn document setting out or summarizing the evidence given to the court that made the provisional order.

(3) Return to Attorney General — Where documents have been sent to a court pursuant to subsection (1) and the respondent apparently is outside the province and is not likely to return, the court shall send the documents to the Attorney General for that province, together with any available information respecting the location and circumstances of the respondent.

(4) Idem — On receipt of any documents and information sent pursuant to subsection (3), the Attorney General shall send the documents and information to the Attorney General for the province of the court that made the provisional order.

(5) Right of respondent — In a proceeding under this section, the respondent may raise any matter that might have been raised before the court that made the provisional order.

(6) Further evidence — Where, in a proceeding under this section, the respondent satisfies the court that for the purpose of taking further evidence or for any other purpose it is necessary to remit the matter back to the court that made the provisional order, the court may so remit the matter and adjourn the proceeding for that purpose.

(7) Order of confirmation or refusal — Subject to subsection (7.1), at the conclusion of a proceeding under this section, the court shall make an order

(a) confirming the provisional order without variation;

(b) confirming the provisional order with variation; or

(c) refusing confirmation of the provisional order.

(7.1) Guidelines apply — A court making an order under subsection (7) in respect of a child support order shall do so in accordance with the applicable guidelines.

(8) Further evidence — The court, before making an order confirming the provisional order with variation or an order refusing confirmation of the provisional order, shall decide whether to remit the matter back for further evidence to the court that made the provisional order.

(9) Interim order for support of children — Where a court remits a matter pursuant to this section in relation to a child support order, the court may, pending the making of an order under subsection (7), make an interim order in accordance with the applicable guidelines requiring a spouse to pay for the support of any or all children of the marriage.

(9.1) Interim order for support of spouse — Where a court remits a matter pursuant to this section in relation to a spousal support order, the court may make an interim order requiring a spouse to secure or pay, or to secure and pay, such lump sum or periodic sums, or such lump sum and periodic sums, as the court thinks reasonable for the support of the other spouse, pending the making of an order under subsection (7).

(10) Terms and conditions — The court may make an order under subsection (9) or (9.1) for a definite or indefinite period or until a specified event occurs, and may impose terms, conditions or restrictions in connection with the order as it thinks fit and just.

(11) Provisions applicable — Subsection 17(4), (4.1) and (6) to (7) apply, with such modifications as the circumstances require, in respect of an order made under subsection (9) or (9.1) as if it were a variation order referred to in those subsections.

(12) Report and filing — On making an order under subsection (7), the court in a province shall

(a) send a copy of the order, certified by a judge or officer of the court, to the Attorney General for that province, to the court that made the provisional order and, where that court is not the court that made the support order in respect of which the provisional order was made, to the court that made the support order;

(b) where an order is made confirming the provisional order with or without variation, file the order in the court; and

(c) where an order is made confirming the provisional order with variation or refusing confirmation of the provisional order, give written reasons to the Attorney General for that province and to the court that made the provisional order.

1993, c. 8, s. 4; 1997, c. 1, s. 7

19 — Orders of confirmation

Once a provisional order, made pursuant to s. 18(2), is transmitted to the Attorney General for the province in which the respondent is ordinarily resident, the Attorney General sends the documents to a court in that province: s. 19(1). Section 19 sets out the procedure for making orders of confirmation: s. 19(2), and returning the documents to the Attorney General where the respondent is not in the province and is not likely to return: ss. 19(3) and (4).

In s. 19(2), the procedure for transmission of documents was changed in 1993 so that the court must serve on the respondent and on the applicant a notice of hearing respecting confirmation of the provisional order. Under the repealed section, only the respondent was served. Also in s. 19(2), the discretionary "may" was changed to the mandatory "shall", thus requiring the court to make an order either confirming the provisional order with or without variation or refusing confirmation of the provisional order: s. 25(3).

Section 19 provides that the respondent may raise any issue that might have been raised before the court that made the provisional order, and if the respondent satisfies the court that further evidence is needed, or for any other purpose it is necessary to remit the matter back to the court that made the provisional order, the court may send the matter to the court in the other province and adjourn the proceeding for that purpose: s. 19(6).

There are several types of orders that the court under s. 19 may make. These orders are either an order confirming the provisional order without variation, or an order confirming the provisional order with variation, or an order refusing confirmation of the provisional order: s. 19(7).

Since the 1997 amendments, in cases where the other spouse is out of the jurisdiction, any provisional order for child support must be made according to the federal guidelines, any order confirming a provisional order must be according to the federal guidelines: *Divorce Act*, s. 19(7.1) and (9) to (11).

Before the court makes an order confirming the provisional order with variation or an order refusing confirmation of the provisional order, it is required by the Act to direct itself to the question of whether to remit the matter back for further evidence to the court that made the provisional order: s. 19(8).

Section 19 provides that the court in which the respondent ordinarily resides may make an interim child support order in the province (s. 19(9)) or an interim spousal support order (19(9.1)) with terms and conditions (s. 19(10)) prior to an order being made under

s. 19(7). Further, the section outlines the procedure once an order under s. 19(7) is made: s. 19(12).

Cases decided before the 1993 and 1997 amendments should be read with caution.

Cases under the provincial *Reciprocal Enforcement of Maintenance Orders Act* may be of assistance in interpreting this new provision in the *Divorce Act*.

19§1 — Confirmation — general

Divorce Act, 1985

Where the parties obtained a divorce order in Saskatchewan and the husband later took up residence in British Columbia and obtained a "provisional" order varying the child-support provision of the divorce order, the fact that the Saskatchewan court refused to confirm the order was irrelevant. As the husband was resident in British Columbia and the wife had accepted the jurisdiction of the court there, the decision of the B.C. court was final and did not require confirmation: *Jamieson v. Jamieson* (1997), 29 R.F.L. (4th) 366, [1997] 7 W.W.R. 590 (Sask. Q.B.).

In proceedings under the *Divorce Act* to confirm a provisional support order, the court should take into account the evidence of both parties and should, if necessary, deal with issues of credibility: *Kyler v. Kyler* (1992), 42 R.F.L. (3d) 315, 95 D.L.R. (4th) 90 (Sask. Q.B.).

Where the court accepted the wife's evidence that her ex-husband had quit his job because he was dissatisfied with it and wished to move closer to his girlfriend, the court refused to confirm a provisional order reducing the quantum of child support payable by him: *Kyler v. Kyler*, above.

Where a provisional order varying child support was obtained by the husband based upon inadmissible and contradictory evidence at the pre-trial conference, the court refused to confirm the order. The husband was, however, at liberty to bring a new application dealing with the issues in a proper manner: *Harder v. Harder* (1992), 40 R.F.L. (3d) 108, 101 Sask. R. 27 (Q.B.).

On a confirmation hearing, the confirming court is not to sit in appeal from the court which made the original order. To vary the original order, the confirming court must be satisfied that there has been a change in the conditions, means, needs or other circumstances of the former spouse or child: *Griffiths v. Griffiths* (1991), 109 N.S.R. (2d) 186, 297 A.P.R. 186 (T.D.).

In proceedings under s. 19 of the *Divorce Act* to confirm an extra-provincial provisional support order, the question of entitlement to support is governed by the interpretation of the *Divorce Act* prevailing in the province where the dependent resides: *Kaine v. Kaine* (1990), 27 R.F.L. (3d) 356 (Sask. Q.B.).

In *Watters v. Watters* (1989), 78 Nfld. & P.E.I.R. 339, 244 A.P.R. 339, the Prince Edward Island Trial Division refused to confirm a provisional order of the Nova Scotia Trial Division which substantially increased the amount of child support payable by the husband. The order bore no realistic relationship to the husband's financial capacity to pay.

20. (1) Definition of court — In this section, **"court"**, in respect of a province, has the meaning assigned by subsection 2(1) and includes such other court having jurisdiction in the province as is designated by the Lieutenant Governor in Council of the province as a court for the purposes of this section.

(2) **Legal effect throughout Canada** — Subject to subsection 18(2), an order made under any of sections 15.1 to 17 or subsection 19(7), (9) or (9.1) has legal effect throughout Canada.

(3) **Enforcement** — An order that has legal effect throughout Canada pursuant to subsection (2) may be

(a) registered in any court in a province and enforced in like manner as an order of that court; or

(b) enforced in a province in any other manner provided for by the laws of that province, including its laws respecting reciprocal enforcement between the province and a jurisdiction outside Canada.

(4) **Variation of orders** — Notwithstanding subsection (3), a court may only vary an order that has legal effect throughout Canada pursuant to subsection (2) in accordance with this Act.

1997, c. 1, s. 8

20 — Enforcement

See also Wilton and Miyauchi, *Enforcement of Family Law Orders and Agreements*.

Section 20(2) provides that all orders for corollary relief, except provisional orders made pursuant to s. 18(2), have legal effect throughout Canada. This national effect enables such an order to be enforced in any province regardless of where it originated.

Under the former Act, the superior court of a province had exclusive jurisdiction to grant orders for corollary relief and, pursuant to s. 15, those orders could be registered only in the superior court of other provinces. The uncertainty that existed with respect to whether an order could then be enforced in a court other than the superior court has been resolved by s. 20(1) of the new Act which defines "court" for the purposes of s. 20.

Section 20(1) incorporates the definition of "court" contained in s. 2(1) and expands on it so as to include such other court in the province as is designated by the Lieutenant Governor in Council as a court for the purposes of the section. This section thus contemplates the designation of courts presided over by provincially-appointed judges to exercise enforcement powers resulting in quicker and less expensive enforcement procedures.

Section 20(3) provides that an order for corollary relief may be registered in any court in a province and may be enforced in like manner as an order of that court (s. 20(3)(a)) or in any other manner provided for by the laws of that province, including its reciprocal enforcement laws between the province and a jurisdiction outside Canada: (s. 20(3)(b)). This recognition of alternative means of enforcing support, custody and access orders means that defaulting spouses or former spouses will be subject to an existing enforcement legislation in force in the province.

By virtue of s. 35, the enforcement provisions of s. 20 also apply to interim and final orders for corollary relief made under the *Divorce Act, 1970*.

20§1 — Children outside the jurisdiction

"Sections 14 and 15 [now s. 20] provide that any order I make as to custody has effect throughout Canada and may be registered in any other superior court in Canada and enforced in like manner as an order of that court. It is, therefore, immaterial that the two children are not within the Province of Manitoba as my order will be effective anywhere in Canada": per Bastin J., quoted from the trial judgment in *Whyte v. Whyte* (1969), 69 W.W.R. 536 at 542, 7 D.L.R. (3d) 7 (Man. C.A.).

"By section 15 [now s. 20(3)] of the Act, an order made ... is registrable and enforceable in other provinces; and thus a great stumbling block to the making of an order under the ordinary law is removed. This being the case, I award the custody of the children of the marriage dissolved in this case to their mother resident in Saskatchewan": per Tyrwhitt-Drake L.J.S.C. in *Niccolls v. Niccolls* (1969), 68 W.W.R. 307 at 310, 4 D.L.R. (3d) 209 (B.C. S.C.).

"[An interim custody order may be made under the Act] where the party against whom it is sought to enforce the order is beyond the provincial boundaries. It seems to me that this is consistent with the sort of problem that is endeavoured to be dealt with in s. 5(2) [now s. 3(2) and (3)] of the Act, where petitions may be pending in more than one province": per Arnup J.A. in *Johnson v. Johnson*, 6 R.F.L. 171 at 175, [1972] 1 O.R. 212 (C.A.).

20§2 — "Court ... designated by Lieutenant Governor in Council"

Section 20(3) of the *Divorce Act*, 1985, which allows orders for corollary relief to be registered "in any court in a province", does not include the Federal Court by reason of the definition of "court" in s. 2; *Young v. Hubbert* (1987), 8 R.F.L. (3d) 453, (sub nom. *Young v. Hubbert (Topp)*) [1988] 1 F.C. 354, 15 F.T.R. 56 (T.D.).

As the Nova Scotia Family Court has been designated as a "court" under s. 20 of the *Divorce Act*, it has the jurisdiction to enforce an order for support made under the Act anywhere in Canada in the same manner as it enforces its own orders; imprisonment orders made under the former *Divorce Act* may be enforced as if they had been made under the present Act: *Re LeBlanc* (1986), 77 N.S.R. (2d) 49, 191 A.P.R. 49, (sub nom. *LeBlanc v. Nova Scotia (A.G.)*) 32 D.L.R. (4th) 696 (T.D.).

20§3 — "Enforced in a province in any other manner provided by the laws of that province"

The primary responsibility for the enforcement of orders rests with the provincial government: s. 96(14), *Constitution Act, 1867*. Therefore even though a support order originates under federal legislation, the provinces have the authority to enforce the order.

In *Toker v. Holm* (1987), 8 R.F.L. (3d) 75, 50 Man. R. (2d) 162 (Q.B.), it was held that the enforcement provisions of Part V of the *Family Maintenance Act*, C.C.S.M., c. F20, were established for enforcement of court orders, not the enforcement of laws. Accordingly, the province was not exceeding its powers by providing a mechanism for the enforcement of orders pronounced in accordance with federal legislation, but made or registered in the courts which were within the provincial domain.

In *Geddes v. Geddes* (1983), 51 A.R. 399 (Q.B.), the court granted the wife's application for enforcement of maintenance arrears although at the time of the divorce hearing the wife had agreed to abandon her claim for maintenance and the award was made by the trial judge on his own accord. The court lacked jurisdiction to accede to the husband's request to strike the maintenance provision as the husband's proper remedy was either an appeal from the decree *nisi* or an application to vary the maintenance provisions.

Thus, the *Support and Custody Orders Enforcement Act*, S.O. 1985, c. 6 ("S.C.O.E.A.") applies to orders for corollary relief of support made under the *Divorce Act, 1985*. When the support order is made in Ontario, it must comply with s. 3(3) of the S.C.O.E.A.: *Montague v. Montague* (1987), 11 R.F.L. (3d) 281, 61 O.R. (2d) 781 (U.F.C.).

20.1 (1) Assignment of order — A support order may be assigned to

(a) any minister of the Crown for Canada designated by the Governor in Council;

(b) any minister of the Crown for a province, or any agency in a province, designated by the Lieutenant Governor in Council of the province;

(c) any member of the Legislative Assembly of Yukon, or any agency in Yukon, designated by the Commissioner of Yukon;

(d) any member of the Council of the Northwest Territories, or any agency in the Northwest Territories, designated by the Commissioner of the Northwest Territories; or

(e) any member of the Legislative Assembly of Nunavut, or any agency in Nunavut, designated by the Commissioner of Nunavut.

(2) Rights — A minister, member or agency referred to in subsection (1) to whom an order is assigned is entitled to the payments due under the order, and has the same right to be notified of, and to participate in, proceedings under this Act to vary, rescind, suspend or enforce the order as the person who would otherwise be entitled to the payments

1993, c. 28, s. 78 (Sched. III, item 43.1) [As enacted by 1998, c. 15, s. 23.]; 1997, c. 1, s. 9; 2002, c. 7, s. 160

20.1 — General

Since the 1997 amendments, spousal or child support orders that are corollary to divorce may be assigned to a federal or provincial ministry or agency: *Divorce Act*, s. 20.1.

Appeals

21. (1) Appeal to appellate court — Subject to subsections (2) and (3), an appeal lies to the appellate court from any judgment or order, whether final or interim, rendered or made by a court under this Act.

(2) Restriction on divorce appeals — No appeal lies from a judgment granting a divorce on or after the day on which the divorce takes effect.

(3) Restriction on order appeals — No appeal lies from an order made under this Act more than thirty days after the day on which the order was made.

(4) Extension — An appellate court or a judge thereof may, on special grounds, either before or after the expiration of the time fixed by subsection (3) for instituting an appeal, by order extend that time.

(5) Powers of appellate court — The appellate court may

(a) dismiss the appeal; or

(b) allow the appeal and

(i) render the judgment or make the order that ought to have been rendered or made, including such order or such further or other order as it deems just, or

(ii) order a new hearing where it deems it necessary to do so to correct a substantial wrong or miscarriage of justice.

(6) Procedure on appeals — Except as otherwise provided by this Act or the rules or regulations, an appeal under this section shall be asserted, heard and decided according to the ordinary procedure governing appeals to the appellate court from the court rendering the judgment or making the order being appealed.

21 — Recognition of foreign divorces

To maintain consistency with s. 3(1) which confers jurisdiction on Canadian courts in divorce proceedings, s. 22(1) provides that a divorce granted by a foreign court will be recognized if either former spouse was ordinarily resident in that foreign country for at least one year immediately preceding the institution of proceedings.

Section 22(2) provides that foreign divorces granted on the basis of the independent domicile of the wife will be recognized for all purposes of determining the marital status in Canada of any person [s. 6(2) of old Act].

The common law rules of recognition of foreign divorces have been preserved by s. 20(3) [s. 6(2) of old Act].

21§1 — Appeals — general

Divorce Act, 1985

The appropriate test for determining a reasonable apprehension of judicial bias is whether a reasonable and informed person, with knowledge of all relevant circumstances, viewing the matter realistically and practically, would conclude that a judge's conduct gave rise to a reasonable apprehension of bias: *Miglin v. Miglin*, 34 R.F.L. (5th) 255, 2003 CarswellOnt 1374, 2003 CarswellOnt 1375, [2003] S.C.J. No. 21, 2003 SCC 24, 224 D.L.R. (4th) 193, 171 O.A.C. 201, 302 N.R. 201 (S.C.C.); affirming 198 D.L.R. (4th) 385, [2001] O.J. No. 1510, 144 O.A.C. 155, (sub nom. *M. (L.S.) v. M. (E.J.)*) 16 R.F.L. (5th) 185, 53 O.R. (3d) 641, 2001 CarswellOnt 1404 (Ont. C.A.).

Where the court misapprehends facts which do not affect the central part of its finding, the misapprehensions of evidence are not sufficiently palpable and important and do not have a sufficiently decisive effect so as to justify appellate intervention: *Marinangeli v. Marinangeli* (2003), 2003 CarswellOnt 2691, [2003] O.J. No. 2819, 38 R.F.L. (5th) 307, 174 O.A.C. 76, 228 D.L.R. (4th) 376 (Ont. C.A.). The trial judge had misapprehended the dates that gains from options were realized shortly after Minutes were signed and understood that the cashing in of those options resulted in his income significantly increasing and not modestly increasing, as he had represented.

In *Halpern v. Toronto (City)* (2003), 37 R.F.L. (5th) 130, 2003 CarswellOnt 652, (sub nom. *Halpern v. Canada (Attorney General)*) 169 O.A.C. 172 (Ont. C.A. [In Chambers]), standing was granted to the Coalition of Liberal Rabbis for Same-Sex Marriage to intervene in an appeal dealing with the same-sex marriage issue. Although the coalition had only recently been formed and was not an incorporated entity, it had a unique perspective and could make a useful contribution to the resolution of the issues without causing injustice to the immediate parties.

It is desirable in family law cases that courts give reasons and not conclusory reasons in order to provide public confidence in the administration of the justice system, give the losing party the reasons for having lost, and make the right of appeal meaningful: *Young v. Young*, 2003 CarswellOnt 63 (C.A.).

When the trial judge had excessively interfered with the presentation of the husband's case in his application to vary spousal support provisions contained in the parties' separation agreement, an appeal from the dismissal of his case was allowed. Although some of the judge's questions were valid for the sake of clarification, many were not: *Ravka v. Ravka* (2002), 35 R.F.L. (5th) 176, 2002 CarswellOnt 3081, 165 O.A.C. 44 (Ont. C.A.); reversing (2001), 18 R.F.L. (5th) 155, 2001 CarswellOnt 1642 (Ont. S.C.J.).

In *Amlani v. Hirani*, 13 R.F.L. (5th) 1, 194 D.L.R. (4th) 543, 2000 BCSC 1653, 2000 CarswellBC 2663 (B.C. S.C.), the court refused the husband's application for an order for divorce and the adjournment of all claims for corollary relief. The husband subsequently brought the same application before a different judge, disputing the policy grounds upon which his first application had been dismissed. As the husband's second application was tantamount to an appeal from the first, the court lacked jurisdiction to entertain it.

Where the wife's lawyer had ostensible authority to settle issues on the wife's behalf, the wife could not later attack on appeal the summary judgment which contained the terms of the settlement. Given the lawyer's ostensible authority, it was not necessary for the appeal court to determine the extent of the lawyer's actual authority: *Achenbach v. Achenbach* (1995), 17 R.F.L. (4th) 50, 107 Man. R. (2d) 45, 109 W.A.C. 45, 1995 CarswellMan 435, [1995] M.J. No. 619 (C.A.).

Where the wife had technically complied with the rules, but did not serve the husband with notice that the divorce and corollary relief proceedings were going to final judgment without his having been represented, the court allowed his appeal and ordered a rehearing of the corollary relief issues: *Christianson v. Christiansen* (May 24, 1994), Doc. Edmonton Appeal 9203-0590-AC (Alta. C.A.).

Where, after dismissal of the wife's application for a variation of child support, the Supreme Court of Canada released a judgment which was pertinent to the issues involved, the appellate court was entitled to consider the case afresh: *Hodgert v. Hodgert* (1993), 47 R.F.L. (3d) 216 (Alta. C.A.).

A consent judgment dealing with corollary relief can only be set aside by a fresh action and not by appeal: *Shannon v. Shannon* (1992), 40 R.F.L. (3d) 178 (N.B. C.A.).

Section 17(2) of the *Divorce Act, 1968*, which empowered an appellate court to pronounce the judgment that ought to have been pronounced, does not confer on the appellate court a broad discretion to review discretionary decisions. An appellate court should only interfere with a trial judge's decision where it is persuaded the lower court made a material error: *Pelech v. Pelech*, 7 R.F.L. (3d) 225, [1987] 4 W.W.R. 481, 14 B.C.L.R. (2d) 145 (S.C.C.).

A provincial Court of Appeal has no jurisdiction to issue interpretation directives to lower courts or to decide theoretical questions regarding freedom of religion in custody cases: *B. (G.) v. B. (M.)* (1988), 19 R.F.L. (3d) 283 (Que. C.A.).

"The principles upon which an appellate court is justified in interfering with the exercise of the discretion of a primary tribunal are well known and have been stated in many cases. Shortly, they are — (1) if the primary Judge has acted upon a wrong principle of law; (2) if irrelevant considerations have been taken into account and have affected the decision; (3) if relevant considerations are ignored or not adequately weighed and have affected the decision; (4) if the appellate court is clearly satisfied that the order of the primary Judge has caused an injustice, i.e. that the order is one which is unreasonable or plainly unjust, and (5) the appellate court has no right to substitute its own discretion for that entrusted to the primary Judge": per MacDonald J.A. in *Keddy v. Keddy* (1974), 8 N.S.R. (2d) 158 at 166–167, 45 D.L.R. (3d) 609 (C.A.).

The rule that a judgment or order, once perfected, may not, except by way of appeal, be reviewed or altered is subject to a number of exceptions, and such an order may be varied or set aside if the justice of the case requires it: *Mariline Ltd. v. Mercure* (1970), [1971] 1 W.W.R. 500, 17 D.L.R. (3d) 356 (Man. Q.B.).

A trial judgment should not be overturned where the judge has not been shown to have erred in law, overlooked or misinterpreted material facts, or, generally, to have been clearly wrong: *Webster v. Webster* (1978), 25 N.S.R. (2d) 33, 36 A.P.R. 33 (C.A.).

"In this instance, the trial Judge made no express findings as to credibility and if we are to conclude what view he took of the facts we can only do so by inference from what he has said": per Arnup J.A., dismissing the appeal in the absence of evidence that the trial judge was clearly wrong, in *Spiotte v. Spiotte* (1973), 12 R.F.L. 226 at 226 (Ont. C.A.).

"In the adversary system under which we practise, a trial in the first instance is carried on before a single judge whose responsibility it is inter alia to hear the evidence, to weigh the evidence and to examine the demeanour of the witnesses produced before him. In my opinion, it is not the prerogative of the Appeal Court to interfere with or to substitute its opinion for that of the trial judge unless, of course, it can be said that he did not make full judicial use of the opportunity given to him — but not to this Court — of seeing and hearing the parties — an opportunity denied to an appellate court. It was for this reason that I repeatedly requested the appellant's counsel to point out the flaws or defects in the judgment of the trial Judge at the hearing": per Tweedy J. in *Rennie v. Rennie* (1973), 11 R.F.L. 278 at 281, 38 D.L.R. (3d) 401 (P.E.I. S.C.).

Findings of fact made at trial are not to be reversed on appeal unless it can be established that the trial judge made some palpable and overriding error which affected his assessment of the facts: *Frenette v. Frenette* (1976), 30 R.F.L. 163 (P.E.I. C.A.).

"The trial Judge had the opportunity of seeing both parties, hearing their evidence, and observing their demeanour. He has made a specific finding on credibility, and it has not been shown that he was in definite error in so doing. Accepting these findings, as I think I must, dismissal of this portion of the appeal must follow": per Maguire J.A. in *Powell v. Powell* (1971), 5 R.F.L. 194 at 195–196 (Sask. C.A.).

"The record of the proceedings satisfies me that the trial proceeded in such an unsatisfactory manner that the decision of the learned trial Judge cannot stand. However, to order a new trial would be an injustice to the appellant, if the evidence adduced was such that the petition should have been granted. This is an appeal in which the evidence must be scrutinized by this Court and, if satisfied on such evidence that the petition should have been granted, then the Court should grant the petition in accordance with the powers conferred on it by s. 17(2)(b)(i) [now s. 21 (5)(b)(i)] of the Divorce Act ... I am satisfied that, had the learned trial Judge given proper consideration to all of the evidence, which lent credence to the admission of adultery by the respondent husband, he would have found that such adultery was proved. In my view, the evidence was such as to establish this fact.

The appeal will therefore be allowed": per Culliton C.J.S. in *Morice v. Morice*, 8 R.F.L. 283 at 284–286, [1972] 4 W.W.R. 480, 26 D.L.R. (3D) 375 (Sask. C.A.).

"Counsel for the respondent submitted that the awards [of corollary relief] having been made in the exercise of judicial discretion under s. 11 [now s. 15] of the *Divorce Act*, this court should not interfere unless it were shown that the trial Judge erred in principle or that the amount awarded is wholly erroneous. In my opinion the function and duty of this court in such an appeal is not so limited. Subsection (2) of s. 17 [now s. 21(5)] ... makes it necessary for the Court of Appeal to consider all of the circumstances and make a decision which it deems just. In doing this the court should, no doubt, give due weight to the findings and views of the trial Judge who has the great advantage of seeing and hearing the witnesses. I think this opinion is supported by the statement made by Laskin C.J.C. in *Nash v. Nash* (1974), 16 R.F.L. 295 at 301, 47 D.L.R. (3d) 558 (Can.), that, 's. 17 [now s. 21] of the *Divorce Act* gives the widest powers to the Court of Appeal'. *Vide*: the judgment of this court delivered by the Chief Justice in *Piller v. Piller* (1975), 17 R.F.L. 252": per McFarlane J. in *Lazenby v. Lazenby*, 18 R.F.L. 393 at 394, [1975] W.W.D. 88 (B.C. C.A.).

"In approaching the question of whether the order made below is appropriate, this court has an independent discretion. It need not be shown before we can intervene that the trial judge proceeded on some wrong principle or failed to take into consideration factors that he should have, or took into consideration factors which were not appropriate: see *Piller v. Piller* (1975), 54 D.L.R. (3d) 150 at 153–4, [1975] 4 W.W.R. 342 at 345, 17 R.F.L. 252. I therefore approach this problem as if the court was hearing the matter anew. The fact that I differ in the result does not necessarily mean that [the trial judge] was wrong. It simply means that reasonable men may differ in their view of what is appropriate": per Farris C.J.B.C. in *Carmichael v. Carmichael* (1976), 27 R.F.L. 325 at 329, 69 D.L.R. (3d) 297 (B.C. C.A.).

"With respect, I agree with [the approach of Farris C.J.B.C. in *Piller v. Piller*, 17 R.F.L. 252, [1975] 4 W.W.R. 342, 54 D.L.R. (3d) 150 (B.C. C.A.)] and reject the contention of counsel for the respondent that the [appellate] court's function in the present case rests upon a similar footing as when hearing an appeal from a discretionary order on procedural matters or when reviewing an assessment of damages. In my view, the court has the right and the duty to review the record before it and to exercise an independent discretion within the framework of s. 11 [now ss. 15 to 17] of the Divorce Act. In so doing, regard must be had for the conclusions of the trial judge, and in the present case his findings of fact are accepted": per Hall J.A. in *Guberman v. Guberman*, 27 R.F.L. 15 at 18, [1977] 2 W.W.R. 1 (Man. C.A.).

"The Court has come to the conclusion that it ought not to entertain the appellant's appeal until either the arrears owing by him are paid or we are satisfied that he cannot pay them. Accordingly, the appeal will be adjourned sine die to permit the appellant to fulfil one or the other of those conditions": per Gale C.J.O. in *Parkinson v. Parkinson*, 11 R.F.L. 128 at 128, [1973] 3 O.R. 293, 36 D.L.R. (3d) 521 (C.A.).

The fact that the appellant is in arrears under the original order is not grounds for the court for refusing to hear the appeal: *Bodnar v. Bodnar*, 10 R.F.L. 360, [1972] 6 W.W.R. 618 (B.C. S.C.), dealing with an appeal from a maintenance order made by a provincial court judge.

The appeal court may direct that its order regarding quantum of maintenance shall operate retroactively and in substitution for the order of the trial judge: *Chegwin v. Chegwin*

(1976), 28 R.F.L. 28 (Man. C.A.), dealing with an application under the *Wives' and Children's Maintenance Act*, R.S.M. 1970, c. W170.

"It is common ground that the order of the Court of Appeal is retroactive and speaks from the trial of the action": per Pennell J. in *MacDougall v. MacDougall*, [1971] 1 O.R. 770 at 772 (H.C.).

Where the husband was advised by the wife that the divorce was not proceeding and the trial took place without further notice to him, the Court of Appeal granted him the right to defend the action, with regard to the maintenance claim only: *Bell v. Bell* (1973), 10 R.F.L. 196 (Ont. C.A.).

21§2 — Appeals — practice

Interim Orders

The appeal provisions of the *Divorce Act* prevail over the provisions of the *Saskatchewan Court of Appeal Act*. Accordingly, leave to appeal is not necessary to appeal an interim support order in a divorce action: *Kotelmach v. Mattison* (1987), 11 R.F.L. (3d) 56 (Sask. C.A.).

Where decisions differed regarding the necessity of leave to appeal from an interim support order, the issue was referred to a full panel of the Divisional Court for resolution in *Pollak v. Pollak* (1993), 48 R.F.L. (3d) 56 (Ont. Gen. Div.).

Although s. 21(1) of the *Divorce Act* provides for an absolute right of appeal from final or interim orders under the Act, s. 21(6) specifies that appeals under s. 21 are to be "asserted, heard, and decided according to the ordinary rules applicable to appellate courts", which generally require leave in the case of interim orders. Although the provisions appear to be inconsistent, an ordinary reading leads to the conclusion that leave to appeal is required in the case of interim orders: *Potts v. Potts* (1993), 47 R.F.L. (3d) 82, 13 O.R. (3d) 284, 63 O.A.C. 175 (Div. Ct.).

Procedure

Where the trial judge had failed to apportion a support award between child and spousal support, the appellate court determined the apportionment rather than refer the issue back to the trial judge: *Forbes v. Forbes* (1995), 18 R.F.L. (4th) 182, 1995 CarswellSask 400 (Sask. C.A.).

In British Columbia, an appeal from a master's order under the *Divorce Act, 1985* is properly brought to the Supreme Court of British Columbia. The order should not, however, be disturbed unless the Master was clearly wrong: *Carr v. Carr* (1993), 46 R.F.L. (3d) 326 (B.C. S.C.).

In Ontario, an appeal from the granting of divorce lies to the Court of Appeal. An appeal regarding interlocutory corollary relief lies to the Divisional Court. An appeal concerning both divorce and corollary relief issues, whether interim or final, lies to the Court of Appeal: *Colletta v. Colletta* (1992), 42 R.F.L. (3d) 227, 10 O.R. (3d) 464, 57 O.A.C. 283, 95 D.L.R. (4th) 298 (C.A.).

In British Columbia, a single justice of appeal has no jurisdiction to set aside a "desk order" divorce, even where the parties consent: *Khera v. Khera* (1990), 25 R.F.L. (3d) 82 (B.C. C.A.).

Section 21 (6) of the *Divorce Act, 1985*, which provides that the ordinary procedure for appeals is to apply to appeals under the Act, should not be interpreted as restricting the right to appeal conferred by s. 21(1). All appeals against judgments rendered under the *Divorce Act* are as of right, and not subject to the permission required under the *Quebec Code of Civil Procedure*: *K. (H.) v. S. (D.)* (1988), 18 R.F.L. (3d) 66 (Que. C.A.).

An appeal from an interlocutory order in a family law proceeding should be heard expeditiously. In Ontario, such appeals lend themselves to being heard by a single judge of the Divisional Court in order to avoid delay, as provided in s. 20 of Ontario's *Courts of Justice Act*, R.S.O. 1990, c. C.43: *Bajzat v. Bajzat* (1991), 35 R.F.L. (3d) 59, 52 O.A.C. 25 (Div. Ct.); additional reasons at (September 30, 1991), Doc. 075D (Ont. Div. Ct.).

Effective Date of Order

Upon a successful appeal to the Court of Appeal from a support order, the decision of the Court of Appeal replaces the judgment of the lower court and the effective date of any change is effective as of the date of the lower court order. However, where an injustice would result from the application of this general rule, the appellate court has the jurisdiction to specify a different date upon which its decision is to take effect: *Preweda v. Preweda* (1993), 48 R.F.L. (3d) 190, 88 Man. R. (2d) 2, 51 W.A.C. 2 (C.A.).

Divorce Act, 1968

"Notwithstanding the appeal of a decree nisi, the court does not lose jurisdiction to vary the decree nisi pursuant to s. 11(2) [now s. 17(1)] of the Divorce Act": per Lieff J. in *Seeman v. Seeman* (1976), 28 R.F.L. 275 at 280, 13 O.R. (2d) 414, 71 D.L.R. (3d) 204 (H.C.).

In *Tanenbaum v. Tanenbaum* (1976), 26 R.F.L. 83, 14 O.R. (2d) 208 (C.A.), although the trial judge granted a decree *nisi*, he did not specifically provide for the wife's maintenance. Subsequent to the decree absolute, the wife obtained an order directing an inquiry regarding her entitlement to maintenance. The husband appealed the order to the Court of Appeal where it was determined that as the order was interlocutory in nature, the court was without jurisdiction.

"The Court was informed that, at some time prior to the hearing of the appeal, the family home had been sold, and the appellant had taken up residence in Regina. This is subsequent to the trial and cannot be taken into consideration in determining the rights or obligations of each party as at the time of trial. The disposal of the proceeds of sale may give rise to a change in circumstances, warranting an application to the Court to review the amount of maintenance payments": per Maguire J.A. in *Powell v. Powell* (1971), 5 R.F.L. 194 at 196 (Sask. C.A.).

"A request to defer the hearing of an appeal even when made at such a late date, might, in a case in which the custody of an infant was not involved, have been entertained more favourably by the Court. But because it is not in the interest of the infant that there be delay in the decision of the appeal, the application for deferment was rejected": per Kelly J.A. in *Burke v. Burke* (1974), 17 R.F.L. 95 at 95 (Ont. C.A.).

"The awarding of costs is within the exercise of the trial judge's discretion and before an appeal will be allowed in relation to an award of costs it must be demonstrated that he was wrong in exercising his judgment as he did": per Gale C.J.O. in *Kalesky v. Kalesky* (1974), 17 R.F.L. 321 at 322, 5 O.R. (2d) 546, 51 D.L.R. (3d) 30 (C.A.).

21§2A — Appeals — jurisdiction

In *Rothgiesser v. Rothgiesser* (2000), 2 R.F.L. (5th) 266, 2000 CarswellOnt 50, 183 D.L.R. (4th) 310, 46 O.R. (3d) 577, 128 O.A.C. 302 (Ont. C.A.), the court held that an Ontario court does not have jurisdiction to make a spousal support order where the parties have been divorced in a foreign jurisdiction. Jurisdiction cannot be conferred on the Ontario court by the consent of the parties. The common law has clearly established that "parties cannot empower a court with the authority to make a determination where it otherwise has no authority to do so or its authority is limited by statute". An Ontario court does not have jurisdiction to vary a spousal support obligation if the spousal support order was not made pursuant to a Canadian divorce. A Canadian court does not have jurisdiction to vary a foreign support order. Jurisdiction to vary a foreign spousal support order is derived from provincial legislation regarding the enforcement of support orders. In Ontario, the appropriate legislation is the *Reciprocal Enforcement of Support Orders Act*. In this case, no application to vary an order pursuant to the provisions of that act had been made.

In *Gordon v. Solmon* (1995), 16 R.F.L. (4th) 403 (Ont. C.A.), the court dismissed the wife's application, in the context of the husband's appeal of child support, for an order requiring the husband to pay child support and to make payments to creditors on the wife's behalf. A single judge of the Court was without jurisdiction to make the order sought, which could only be granted upon a motion to vary the trial judgment.

An award of costs in matrimonial proceedings should not be disturbed by an appellate court unless the trial judge had proceeded on a wrong principle: *Hauff v. Hauff* (1994), 5 R.F.L. (4th) 419, 95 Man. R. (2d) 83, 70 W.A.C. 83 (C.A.).

21§3 — Appeals — extending time to appeal

Divorce Act, 1985

An order granting the petitioner's application to vary an unappealed final divorce judgment in respect of child support was pronounced in chambers in *Berro v. Berro*, 2001 CarswellAlta 860, 2001 ABCA 157, 286 A.R. 124, 253 W.A.C. 124, 9 C.P.C. (5th) 226, 93 Alta. L.R. (3d) 230 (Alta. C.A.). The order was formally entered in written form almost a month later. A divorce proceeding is defined as one in which either or both spouses seek a divorce alone or (*inter alia*) together with a child support order, as in this case. The order in question was made under the *Divorce Act*. Section 21(3) of the *Divorce Act* applies to "an order made under this Act" and according to that section it provides that time runs from the pronouncement of the order and the time to appeal expired 30 days after pronouncement. In this case the appeal was filed two weeks late and was consequently out of time. The court dismissed the cross-motion for an extension of time, as there was no evidence of several matters necessary for such a time extension, namely,

> "(a) intent to appeal formed within the time for appeal;
>
> (b) a proper explanation for not appealing in time;
>
> (c) merit to the appeal;
>
> (d) an explanation for the delay in seeking the time extension".

In *Wood v. Wood*, 13 R.F.L. (5th) 216, 203 Sask. R. 82, 240 W.A.C. 82, 2001 SKCA 2, 2001 CarswellSask 88 (Sask. C.A. [In Chambers]), the father's application to extend the time for appealing a child support order was allowed. There appeared to be a fundamental misunderstanding about the father's income which rendered the trial decision questionable. The father had intended to appeal within the allotted time but had failed to do so largely because of misunderstandings by his counsel. Furthermore, the mother would not be prejudiced by the granting of the extension.

In *Orser v. Grant* (2000), 12 R.F.L. (5th) 184, 2000 CarswellOnt 4927 (Ont. Div. Ct.), the court refused the father's application to extend the time for appeal from a child support order. The father had originally brought the appeal in the wrong court but, even after learning of the error, delayed further in launching the appeal in the appropriate court. The father could provide no real justification for the delay and, although he was representing himself, he was a well-educated and sophisticated litigant.

In *Cross v. Cross* (1997), 33 R.F.L. (4th) 387 (B.C. C.A. [In Chambers]), the court refused the father's application for an extension of time to allow him to appeal from an order varying the parties' joint-custody award to one of sole custody in the mother's favour. The parties had not demonstrated the level of agreement required to make joint custody workable and as the child was starting school she required a more stable routine.

Section 21(4) of the *Divorce Act* provides for an extension of the time to appeal with respect to orders made under the Act. The provision does not apply to the divorce decree itself but to corollary orders issued on the same occasion. Any one judge is competent to extend the time period to appeal such orders: *Droit de la famille — 943*, [1991] R.D.F. 105 (C.A. Qué.).

A court should extend the time for appeal from a support order if there is no prejudice to the respondent and the appeal is not frivolous or hopeless: *Levesque v. Levesque* (1992), 41 R.F.L. (3d) 96 (Alta. C.A.).

In *Edgerton v. Edgerton* (1992), 57 O.A.C. 85 (C.A.), the court granted the wife's application for an extension of the time limit for appealing from the divorce judgment. The wife had appeared at trial without counsel and the support order obtained was questionable. As the wife was unable after trial to retain and instruct counsel immediately because of psychiatric problems, the extension was warranted.

In *Droit de la famille — 1054*, [1986] R.D.F. 596 (Qué. C.A.), the court dismissed the husband's application under s. 21(3) of the *Divorce Act* for an order to extend the time for appealing from a provisional maintenance order. Although the husband claimed that he was changing lawyers, there was no indication provided of what steps he had taken to bring about the change.

In *Forbes v. Forbes* (1994), 5 R.F.L. (4th) 79 (B.C. C.A.); additional reasons at (1994), 49 B.C.A.C 236, 80 W.A.C. 236 (C.A.) the court allowed the wife's appeal from her spousal and child support awards launched 15 months after the date of the order. Although it was unclear who was responsible for the delay, the effluxion of time and the emerging issue of support for the older son, who had been living away from the wife for most of the time since the judgment was pronounced, warranted a re-examination of support by the court below using up-to-date evidence.

Divorce Act, 1968

In *Re Belliveau*, 6 R.F.L. 1 at 1, [1972] 1 O.R. 849, 24 D.L.R. (3d) 393 (C.A.), the court held that the fact that the husband had been denied legal aid at the trial of his wife's divorce petition, did not constitute sufficient grounds to interfere with the decree *nisi*. Per Aylesworth J.A.: "In the matter of Frank L. Belliveau we have before us an application from him for leave to extend the time within which he might appeal from a decree nisi granted to his wife. ... Obviously, that application is markedly late. It has no real, effective material in support of it. No real grounds for interfering with the decree nisi are shown, even in arguable form which, of course, would be a condition precedent to this Court at this late date granting an extension of time within which to appeal. In brief, this application has no merit."

"It may be noted that the wife changed her solicitor soon after the decree nisi had been pronounced. The new solicitor was instructed to appeal. For that purpose he felt a need to obtain a copy of the learned trial Judge's reasons for judgment. In the meantime he deferred filing a notice of appeal. By the time he was ready to file an appropriate notice of appeal the time for appealing had elapsed. Looking at the case as a whole I have reached the conclusion that an extension of time is here warranted and that the appeal should be allowed": per Freedman C.J.M. in *Wur v. Wur* (1974), 17 R.F.L. 251 at 251–252 (Man. C.A.).

"I think a fair and liberal interpretation of the intent and effect of the restrictive provision is fully warranted in circumstances such as those we have under consideration in this case. I would therefore hold that this Court has power to grant an extension of time for bringing the proposed appeal [from an order varying the terms of a decree *nisi* with respect to corollary relief]": *per* Allen J.A. in *Duzs v. Duzs*, 10 R.F.L. 113, [1973] 3 W.W.R. 394, 35 D.L.R. (3d) 310 (Alta. C.A.).

"There are, of course, very good grounds why, after a decree absolute has been made, the court should not extend the time for appealing from a decree nisi. The decree absolute affects the status of the parties. There may be remarriage; there may, indeed, be children of a new marriage; and one can readily see why the Parliament of Canada restricted the right of a court of appeal to extend the time for appealing from the granting of a decree nisi to doing so before the divorce has been made absolute. Here, the applicant does not wish to affect the status of the parties, but he does wish to appeal to the Court from the corollary relief granted by the order. ... In my view, a liberal interpretation of the restrictive provisions is to the advantage of the subject and, if reasonable, should be applied": per McGillivray C.J.A. in *Magnusson v. Magnusson*, 21 R.F.L. 204 at 207–208, [1976] 2 W.W.R. 277, 65 D.L.R. (3d) 699 (Alta. C.A.).

"We are inclined to view that, although for many purposes a decree or judgment is not fully effective until entered, for the purposes of calculating the time within which an appeal should be brought the crucial date is the date of the pronouncing of the decree. But we believe that the same result as that at which our brother Guy arrived [that the time began to run upon entry of the decree] can be achieved by resort to our powers under s. 17(4) [now s. 21(4)] of the Divorce Act. In our view this is eminently a case in which the petitioner should be allowed her day in this Court. We think that in the circumstances of this case there are indeed special grounds for extending the time within which an appeal may be brought. We accordingly extended that time until today": per Freedman C.J.M. in *Reid v. Reid*, 9 R.F.L. 259 at 260, [1973] 3 W.W.R. 479, 35 D.L.R (3d) 252 (Man. C.A.). See also *Gullison v. Gullison* (1974), 7 N.B.R. (2d) 22 (C.A.); *Webster v. Webster* (1978), 25 N.S.R. (2d) 33, 36 A.P.R. 33 (C.A.).

"We are well aware of the decision of another panel of this court in *Reid v. Reid*, [1973] 3 W.W.R. 479, 9 R.F.L. 259, as well as the decision of the Alberta Appellate Division in *Duzs v. Duzs*, [1973] 3 W.W.R. 394, 10 R.F.L. 113, 35 D.L.R. (3d) 310 (Alta. C.A.), wherein a distinction was made between an appeal pertaining to a decree *nisi* and an appeal with respect to corollary relief after the decree *nisi* has become absolute. We are of the view that the *Divorce Act*, by s. 17 [now s. 21], is specific in that in questions of decree *nisi* a notice of appeal must be filed not later than 15 days [now 30 days] after the pronouncement of the judgment or the making of the order being appealed from. That is so even if it causes difficulty in those jurisdictions such as this one where time for appeal normally runs from the date of entry and not from the date of pronouncement. However, in matters pertaining to corollary relief time runs from the date of entry. A trial judge always has the privilege to vary his decision until the moment of entry so that variations in the order can and sometimes do occur at the very last minute. An appellate tribunal should only be requested to review that which is firmly established by a written order of the lower court. On that basis, and on the further basis that in this court the deputy registrar, in the performance of his duties, refused to accept the notice of appeal when tendered, we at the hearing of this case extended the time for the filing of notice of appeal to the date of hearing. We indicated that written reasons would follow. In the future, with respect to corollary relief under the *Divorce Act* time to appeal in this jurisdiction shall run from the date of entry of the judgment in the lower court": per Monnin J.A. in *Baird v. Baird*, [1977] 5 W.W.R. 72 at 74–75 (Man. C.A.).

21§3A — Appeals — grounds for divorce

Where the parties' divorce had been granted unopposed, but was based upon a misleading statement in the husband's affidavit as to when the parties finally separated, the wife's appeal was allowed and the decree set aside: *Anderson v. Anderson* (1991), 117 A.R. 181, 2 W.A.C. 181 (C.A.).

In *Ash v. Ash* (1994), 8 R.F.L. (4th) 461, 99 B.C.L.R. (2d) 328, 52 B.C.A.C. 56, 86 W.A.C. 56 (C.A.), the court refused the wife's appeal from the divorce granted to the husband which had been based upon one year's separation. The wife acknowledged that the allegations supporting the husband's petition were true but challenged it on the basis of her own personal religious convictions that she could not remarry absent a decree based upon the husband's misconduct. The wife could not supply any reason why she had not herself petitioned on the basis of marital misconduct and her convictions were her personal ones and not those of any established religion.

21§4 — Appeals — cruelty

Where the parties had been separated for the requisite time in order to obtain a divorce, the appellant wife's raising of an issue of cruelty resulted in unnecessarily prolonging the trial, but did not make it more difficult: *Liedtke v. Liedtke* (1999), 1 R.F.L. (5th) 379, 1999 CarswellBC 1244, [1999] B.C.J. No. 1358, 125 B.C.A.C. 218, 204 W.A.C. 218, 1999 BCCA 364 (B.C. C.A.). On appeal, the court reduced the level of costs awarded against the appelant.

"I am, with respect, totally and completely unable to agree with the learned trial Judge that the appellant was not entitled to a decree of divorce [on the grounds of cruelty]. The persistent course of conduct consisting of the totality of the acts particularized in the petition pursued by the respondent towards his wife, the appellant, over a period of time was of such a character as to be sufficient to warrant a compelling inference that it either caused the appellant to have an ulcer or activated a dormant one which necessitated surgery for its removal. ... In my judgment, with respect to the opinion of the learned trial Judge below, there was in this case no question whatsoever but that the respondent did treat the appellant with cruelty of both a physical and mental nature of such a kind as to render continued cohabitation with him in future intolerable. It follows that the judgment given in the Court below must be set aside and that his appeal succeeds and a decree of divorce should issue to the appellant": per Branca J.A. in *Edwards v. Edwards*, 12 R.F.L. 35 at 44–45, [1973] 1 W.W.R. 82, 30 D.L.R. (3d) 629 (B.C. C.A.). See also *Pongor v. Pongor* (1976), 27 R.F.L. 109 (Ont. C.A.).

"It will be simpler to deal with the appeal by the husband from the granting of the decree nisi to the wife on her cross-petition [alleging cruelty] before dealing with the refusal of the husband's petition. The learned trial judge set out the test laid down by the Ontario Court of Appeal in *Knoll v. Knoll*, 1 R.F.L. 141, [1970] 2 O.R. 169 at 177, 10 D.L.R. (3d) 199. This quotation had been approved by this Division in *Feldman v. Feldman* (1970), 75 W.W.R. 715, 2 R.F.L. 173, 14 D.L.R. (3d) 222. Also in *Feldman v. Feldman*, McDermid J.A. speaking for the court, stated at p. 719: 'A litigant who seeks to upset the finding of cruelty of a trial judge has a more than usual uphill struggle. Lord Oaksey said in *King v. King*, [1953] A.C. 124, [1952] 2 All E.R. 584 at 598, "Divorce petitions on the ground of cruelty are, as has been said, cases in which it is especially important that the findings of the judge should not be interfered with" ...' In my opinion there were facts found by the learned trial judge which could constitute 'mental cruelty' within the meaning of s. 3(d) [now s. 8(2)(b)(ii)] of the Divorce Act, ... The learned trial judge held that it was intolerable for the wife to live with the husband. It therefore follows that the appeal from the award of decree of divorce to the wife must be dismissed": per Moir J.A. in *Krause v. Krause*, 23 R.F.L. 219 at 222, [1976] 2 W.W.R. 622, 64 D.L.R. (3d) 352 (Alta. C.A.).

"'Cruelty' is a question of fact to be determined after considering all the circumstances. The question is: 'Does this conduct by this man towards this woman in the particular circumstances amount to cruelty?' ... In view of the findings of fact which are supported by the evidence and the finding of credibility in favour of the plaintiff, this court would not be justified in interfering with the conclusion of the trial Judge that the conduct of the husband amounted to cruelty": per Evans J.A. in *Casselman v. Posluns* (1974), 3 O.R. (2d) 132 at 135, 44 D.L.R. (3d) 652 (C.A.).

"By his reasons the trial Judge stated that the evidence as presented did not justify the decree of divorce on the grounds of mental and physical cruelty. This Court, with all respect, reaches a contrary conclusion, namely that there is sufficient evidence in the testimony of the petitioner, as well as in that of the medical witness, to justify a finding of cruelty both physical and mental, on the part of the respondent": per McGillivray J.A. in *Reddigan v. Reddigan* (1972), 9 R.F.L. 322 at 322 (Ont. C.A.).

"The respondent argued that there was no evidence before the learned trial judge which would justify his finding of mental cruelty. We need not review the evidence in detail. The learned trial judge referred to the constant hostility between the parties, to constant fights in the home, and to the fact that the respondent showed sustained fits of temper. It is sufficient for us to say that there was some evidence capable of supporting the finding. It is not for us to review the adequacy of the evidence to support his conclusion or to consider whether we would necessarily have agreed with him if we had been the finders of fact": per MacKeigan C.J.N.S. in *MacNeil v. MacNeil* (1975), 25 R.F.L. 82 at 83, 13 N.S.R. (2d) 118, 9 A.P.R. 118 (C.A.).

21§5 — Appeals — support

Divorce Act, 1985

General Principles

In *Boston v. Boston*, 17 R.F.L. (5th) 4, 2001 CarswellOnt 2432, 2001 CarswellOnt 2433, [2001] S.C.J. No. 45, 2001 SCC 43, 201 D.L.R. (4th) 1, 271 N.R. 248, 149 O.A.C. 50, 28 C.C.P.B. 17, [2001] 2 S.C.R. 413 (S.C.C.), the main question for determination was whether pension income should be available for spousal support where the capitalized value of the pension had been included in the spouses' division of property. In disposing of the appeal, the Supreme Court of Canada found that the spousal support order varied by the motions court judge to $590 per month was not an error in principle, a significant misapprehension of the evidence, nor clearly wrong. On the other hand, the Court of Appeal was in error in finding that the decision was "outside the realm of reasonableness". In the result the appeal was allowed, and the judgment of the motions' judge reinstated with the further order that the monthly amount be indexed and arrears of support, if any, be paid.

In *Hickey v. Hickey* (1999), 46 R.F.L. (4th) 1, [1999] S.C.J. No. 9, 1999 CarswellMan 254, 1999 CarswellMan 255, 172 D.L.R. (4th) 577, 240 N.R. 312, [1999] 8 W.W.R. 485, 138 Man. R. (2d) 40, 202 W.A.C. 40, [1999] 2 S.C.R. 518 (S.C.C.), at paragraph 11, Madam Justice L'Heureux-Dube wrote, "Our Court has often emphasized the rule that appeal courts should not overturn support orders unless the reasons disclose an error in principle, a significant misapprehension of the evidence, or unless the award is clearly wrong".

In *Hillier v. Hillier* (2005), 12 R.F.L. (6th) 318, 2005 CarswellBC 295, 2005 BCCA 86 (B.C. C.A.), the court allowed the wife's appeal from an order dismissing her application for increased spousal support. While the trial judge acknowledged an increase child support, it was not referenced in regards to the wife's spousal support.

In *Ramantanis v. Ramantanis* (2004), 8 R.F.L. (6th) 326, 187 Man. R. (2d) 190, 330 W.A.C. 190, 2004 CarswellMan 371, 2004 MBCA 122 (C.A.), the court struck on appeal a lump sum spousal support order which had been awarded to the wife. The "extraordinary circumstances" required to justify such an award simply did not exist in this case.

In *Watts v. Willie* (2004), 8 R.F.L. (6th) 456, 247 D.L.R. (4th) 54, 206 B.C.A.C. 192, 33 W.A.C. 192, 2004 CarswellBC 2795, 2004 BCCA 600 (C.A.), the court dismissed the father's appeal from a child support order requiring him to contribute both to the periodic support and "extraordinary" education expenses of his adult child. The father's concerns about contributing both to ongoing support and extraordinary expenses could be adequately addressed through the parties' periodic review of the child's costs.

In appeals from spousal support orders, significant deference must be given to the trial judge who had the benefit of hearing the parties directly: *Cook v. Cook*, 48 R.F.L. (5th) 268, 2003 CarswellNS 425, [2003] N.S.J. No. 449, 2003 NSCA 131, 219 N.S.R. (2d) 170, 692 A.P.R. 170 (N.S. C.A.); affirming 204 N.S.R. (2d) 167, 639 A.P.R. 167, 27 R.F.L. (5th) 12, 2002 CarswellNS 198, 2002 NSSC 124 (N.S. S.C.).

Where the trial judge had set the amount of the wife's spousal support at a level that he considered sufficient to meet her needs without removing any incentive for her to make efforts to become self- sufficient, her appeal from the award was dismissed in *O. (E.M.) v. O. (W.R.)*, 37 R.F.L. (5th) 401, 2003 CarswellBC 660, 2003 BCCA 191, 181 B.C.A.C. 49, 298 W.A.C. 49 (B.C. C.A.).

The Court of Appeal in *Nahatchewitz v. Nahatchewitz* (1999), 1 R.F.L. (5th) 395, 123 O.A.C. 319, 178 D.L.R. (4th) 496 (C.A.) upheld the award of $15,000 in lump sum spousal support following the reasoning in *Hickey v. Hickey* (1999), 46 R.F.L. (4th) 1, [1999] 2 S.C.R. 518, 172 D.L.R. (4th) 577, 240 N.R. 312, [1999] 8 W.W.R. 485, 138 Man. R. (2d) 40, 202 W.A.C. 40, [1999] S.C.J. No. 9 (S.C.C.) that great deference must be given to trial judges in matters of support. Unless there is an error in principle, the significant misapprehension of the evidence, or unless the award is clearly wrong, it should stand. In this case the trial judge considered all the circumstances of the case including the husband's Undertaking of Assistance given to Immigration Canada.

Following *Hickey v. Hickey* (1999), 172 D.L.R. (4th) 577, 46 R.F.L. (4th) 1, [1999] 2 S.C.R. 518, 240 N.R. 312, [1999] 8 W.W.R. 485, 138 Man. R. (2d) 40, 202 W.A.C. 40, [1999] S.C.J. No. 9 (S.C.C.), the court in *Thornett v. Thornett* (1999), 1 R.F.L. (5th) 171, 127 B.C.A.C. 61, 207 W.A.C. 61 (C.A.) was of the opinion that a support order should only be overturned if the decision disclosed an error in principle, a significant misapprehension of the evidence, or unless the award was clearly wrong. In the *Thornett* case, the court held that in regard to the support issue, the decision was clearly wrong. The trial judge had overlooked the fact that he had reduced the estimated expenses of the wife by $1,000 a month from $4,600 to $3,600. The payment of $2,600 after tax requires a pre-tax amount of $3,500 according to the tax table but the trial judge in reaching his $3,600 figure had taken the gross amount of the wife's imputed income and not the net, after tax amount. Consequently, the appellate court reduced the amount of support payable from $5,000 to $4,000 a month.

The scope of an appellate court's review in an appeal from an award of lump sum support is the same as that of any other review of an order for child or spousal support. Absent a material error on the part of the trial judge, an appellate court does not have an independent discretion to decide the lump sum issue afresh: *Gilman v. Gilman* (1995), 18 R.F.L. (4th) 73, 170 N.B.R. (2d) 21, 435 A.P.R. 21, 1995 CarswellNB 238, 9 C.C.P.B. 237 (C.A.).

An order for spousal support will not be disturbed on appeal where the trial judge's findings are supported by the evidence and there is no palpable and overriding error which affected the judge's assessment of the facts: *Henderson v. Sharma-Henderson* (1994), 7 R.F.L. (4th) 317 (Ont. C.A.); affirming (1993), 47 R.F.L. (3d) 388 (Ont. Gen. Div.).

An appeal court should not retry child support cases even if another judge might have come to a different conclusion. Where the trial judge was entitled to reach a certain conclusion, such decision should not be disturbed in the absence of any error: *Thomas v. Thomas* (1998), 40 R.F.L. (4th) 438, 1998 CarswellBC 1040 (B.C. C.A.).

An appeal from a child support order should not be treated as an opportunity to retry the case. The appellate court should interfere with an order if the trial judge erred in fact or law: *Vincent v. Vincent* (1995), 15 R.F.L. (4th) 273, 132 Nfld. & P.E.I.R. 181, 410 A.P.R. 181, 1995 CarswellNfld 32 (Nfld. C.A.).

Error in Principle

The Supreme Court of Canada found that the Court of Appeal had erred in finding that the term "inappropriate" in the *Federal Child Support Guidelines* meant "inadequate" rather than "unsuitable": *Francis v. Baker*, 50 R.F.L. (4th) 228, [1999] S.C.J. No. 52, 1999 CarswellOnt 2734, 1999 CarswellOnt 2948, [1999] 3 S.C.R. 250, 177 D.L.R. (4th)

1, 246 N.R. 45, 125 O.A.C. 201 (S.C.C.). Consequently, courts have a discretion to increase or decrease the amount of child support set out in the *Guidelines*.

In *Francis v. Baker* (1999), 50 R.F.L. (4th) 228, [1999] S.C.J. No. 52, 1999 CarswellOnt 2734, 1999 CarswellOnt 2948, [1999] 3 S.C.R. 250, 177 D.L.R. (4th) 1, 246 N.R. 45, 125 O.A.C. 201 (S.C.C.), Bastarache J., writing for the court, rejected the argument that the trial judge had abused her discretion on the basis of the large size of the award, in granting the Table Amount of child support. The court would not accept that there was an onus on custodial parents to justify the appropriateness of the *Guidelines* awards for child support where non-custodial parents had income over $150,000.

In the Supreme Court of Canada decision in *B. (G.) v. G. (L.)* (1995), 15 R.F.L. (4th) 201, the wife's appeal was allowed. The trial judge had found that at the time the parties signed their agreement, the appellant was "seeing" a third party and that it was foreseeable that they would co-habit. On the basis of this finding that they might co-habit, there was no material change in circumstances when they did subsequently co-habit. The Court of Appeal had no basis in fact or law to overturn this conclusion.

In *Adams v. Adams*, 35 R.F.L. (5th) 245, 2003 CarswellNB 55, 2003 CarswellNB 56, [2003] N.B.J. No. 41, 2003 NBCA 10, 256 N.B.R. (2d) 136, 670 A.P.R. 136 (N.B. C.A.), the court increased the wife's spousal support on appeal. The trial judge had not sufficiently taken into account the fact that the wife's standard of living had declined since separation while the husband's had remained the same. Also insufficient weight had been given to the fact that the wife was denied access at the present time to the husband's pension, the most valuable marital asset.

In *R. v. R.* (2002), 2002 CarswellOnt 902, 24 R.F.L. (5th) 96, 211 D.L.R. (4th) 403 (Ont. C.A.), the court granted the appeal as, in its opinion, the trial judge committed two material errors in determining that child support under s. 4 was inappropriate. The trial judge had determined the quantum of child support on the basis of the parties' lifestyle and pattern of expenditure during their cohabitation and had therefore not taken into account the significant increase in the father's income after the parties' separation. In addition, the trial judge had not considered whether or not the options in the mother's proposed budget were reasonable, considering the increase in the father's income.

The Ontario Court of Appeal found in *Tremblay v. Tremblay* (1999), 1 R.F.L. (5th) 177, 1999 CarswellOnt 2070, 122 O.A.C. 368 (Ont. C.A.) that the trial court had erred in placing the onus upon the payee/wife to show cause why support should not be continued after two and one half years from the divorce judgment. The marriage had lasted approximately 17 years, during which time, the wife had been a traditional homemaker and mother. She had little education and had only earned small amounts from occasional babysitting.

In *Comrie v. Comrie* (2001), 17 R.F.L. (5th) 271, 2001 CarswellSask 130, [2001] 7 W.W.R. 294, 2001 SKCA 33, 197 D.L.R. (4th) 223, 203 Sask. R. 164, 240 W.A.C. 164 (Sask. C.A.), the appellant appealed against a lower court decision dismissing his application to rescind the spousal maintenance provisions in a consent judgment. The court considered whether or not the trial court had erred in rejecting evidence of the negotiations held before the consent judgment in order to determine the various factors and objectives the parties had considered in determining child and spousal support. In allowing the appeal, the court concluded that the rejected evidence was admissible to decide the core issue in the proceeding.

The British Columbia Court of Appeal in *Stroud v. Stroud* (1996), 20 R.F.L. (4th) 392, 1996 CarswellBC 723, 22 B.C.L.R. (3d) 183, 75 B.C.A.C. 48, 123 W.A.C. 48 dismissed an appeal from an order varying spousal support. At the time of the divorce, the parties consented to a support order. Subsequently, the husband's employer forced him into retirement. In the consent order there had been no provision for the termination of support upon the husband's retirement. The appellate court was of the opinion that the chambers judge, when considering the wife's support, did not err in taking into account that the consent order did not contain any review or termination provisions. The husband's retirement was foreseeable and had been within the contemplation of the parties when they considered the husband's pension. In addition, it was appropriate for the judge when deciding the correct variation order to consider the difference in the means of the parties, which included both income and assets.

Given the length of the parties' marriage, and the wife's needs at the time the order for support was made in the divorce proceedings, the trial judge erred in placing the onus upon her to show cause why support should be continued after two and one-half years from the divorce judgment: *Tremblay v. Tremblay* (1999), 1 R.F.L. (5th) 177, 1999 CarswellOnt 2070, 122 O.A.C. 368 (Ont. C.A.). The parties had been married for 17 years and the wife, who had a grade 10 education, had been a traditional homemaker and mother. She wished to attend community college and upgrade her skills.

In *Montalbetti v. Montalbetti* (2000), 10 R.F.L. (5th) 377, 2000 BCCA 504, 143 B.C.A.C.140, 235 W.A.C.140, 2000 CarswellBC 1902, [2000] B.C.J. No. 1834 (Man. C.A.), the court found on appeal that the trial judge had erred in departing from the *Guidelines* Table Amount where the father had not claimed undue hardship.

Misapprehension of Evidence

In *Francis v. Baker* (1999), 50 R.F.L. (4th) 228, [1999] S.C.J. No. 52, 1999 CarswellOnt 2734, 1999 CarswellOnt 2948, [1999] 3 S.C.R. 250, 177 D.L.R. (4th) 1, 246 N.R. 45, 125 O.A.C. 201 (S.C.C.), the court rejected the appellant's argument to the trial judge's exercise of discretion. The court was of the opinion that the trial judge had not erred in awarding the respondent discretionary expenses above the figures listed in her budget. The Supreme Court of Canada found that there was a proper evidentiary foundation for the award.

The Ontario Court of Appeal in *Stranghi v. Stanghi* (2001), 19 R.F.L. (5th) 392, 2001 CarswellOnt 1726 dismissed the husband's appeal for variation of his spousal support obligations, finding that the trial judge had not misapprehended the evidence. The trial judge's conclusion that the husband was working and was capable of working in a supervisory capacity had an evidentiary basis. The filed reports did not necessarily lead to the conclusion that the husband was unemployed and unemployable.

Where the trial judge had failed, on an application to vary child support, to consider the father's income, the mother's income, the child's needs and the issue of extraordinary expenses, the mother's appeal was allowed and the matter was referred back to the trial court: *Brown v. Simon*, 4 R.F.L. (5th) 50, 134 B.C.A.C. 318, 219 W.A.C. 318, 2000 CarswellBC 135, 2000 BCCA 43 (B.C. C.A.). An appellate court will not interfere with the decision of a chambers judge setting support unless the judge made a material error including a significant misapprehension of evidence: *Robson v. Robson* (1996), 20 R.F.L. (4th) 123, 178 A.R.278, 1993 CarswellNS 41, 122 N.S.R. (2d) 181, 338 A.P.R. 181 (C.A.).

In *Jamieson v. Jamieson* (1995), 14 R.F.L. (4th) 354, 163 N.B.R. (2d) 178, 1995 CarswellNB 34, [1995] N.B.J. No. 342, 419 A.P.R. 178 (C.A.), the court allowed the custodial mother's appeal from an order reducing the quantity of child support payable. Not only had the trial judge made a number of significant errors in his appreciation of the facts but also the order departed so significantly from the usual range of awards in similar circumstances as to amount to a serious error in principle.

Where the trial judge had based a support award upon his misapprehension of the husband's income, which was in reality higher than was found at trial, the wife's appeal was allowed and child support increased: *Matthews v. Matthews* (1991), 34 R.F.L. (3d) 201, 104 N.S.R. (2d) 140, 283 A.P.R. 140, 1991 CarswellNS 60 (C.A.).

Award Clearly Wrong

"Clearly wrong" is not defined in *Black's Law Dictionary*. However, "clearly erroneous" is defined in *Black's Law Dictionary (Revised Fourth Edition)* as "Findings when based upon substantial error in proceedings or misapplication of law or when unsupported by substantial evidence or contrary to clear weight of evidence or induced by erroneous view of the law"(cites omitted).

In *MacIsaac v. MacIsaac* (1996), 21 R.F.L. (4th) 358, 1996 CarswellNS 177, [1996] N.S.J. No. 185, 150 N.S.R. (2d) 321, 436 A.P.R. 321 (N.S. C.A.); reversing in part on other grounds (1995), 149 N.S.R. (2d) 354, 416 A.P.R. 354, 1995 CarswellNS 491 (N.S. S.C.), the court refused, on appeal, to increase the quantum of the wife's spousal support even though it fell short of the trial judge's own calculation of the wife's needs. While the appellate court expressed grave concerns as to the adequacy of the award, taking into account the wife's capital position, it could not conclude that the order was so clearly wrong as to constitute a reversible error.

Fresh Evidence

In an appeal from a child support order, evidence that was available but not put before the court at the time of the original adjudication, will not be admitted as "fresh evidence": *Slade v. Slade* (2001), 13 R.F.L. (5th) 187, 195 D.L.R. (4th) 108, 197 Nfld. & P.E.I.R. 4, 591 A.P.R. 4, 2001 NFCA 2, 2000 CarswellNfld 12, [2001] N.J. No. 5 (Nfld. C.A.).

Where the father had lost his job before a judgment was entered requiring him to pay monthly child support of $2,000, his appeal from the order was successful and the amount dropped to $600. The reduction was justified in light of the fresh evidence as to his financial circumstances which had been adduced on appeal: *Forbes v. Forbes* (1997), 33 R.F.L. (4th) 251, 1997 CarswellBC 90, 86 B.C.A.C. 212, 142 W.A.C. 212 (B.C. C.A.).

In *Wright v. Wright* (1996), 21 R.F.L. (4th) 201, [1996] 4 W.W.R. 1, 141 Sask. R. 44, 114 W.A.C. 44 (C.A.), the court agreed to admit fresh evidence in the father's appeal from a child support order. As the parties wished to resolve the issues expeditiously and as some time had passed since the date of the original order it was best to consider the evidence in the appeal rather than require the father to initiate a separate variation proceeding.

In *Inkumsah-Cosper v. Cosper* (1995), 14 R.F.L. (4th) 152, 141 N.S.R. (2d) 344 (C.A.), the court refused the wife's application to appeal from a consent order dealing with corollary relief issues. The wife's claim that she had been pressured into making the agreement was insufficient justification to allow the introduction of fresh evidence. If the wife had a remedy, it would potentially be against her solicitor.

Where the trial judge's assessment of spousal and child support is based upon mathematical confusion over the husband's net income, the appellate court is obliged to admit fresh evidence to clear up the confusion: *Escaravage v. Escaravage* (1995), 14 R.F.L. (4th) 256, 59 B.C.A.C. 113 (C.A.).

In order to introduce new evidence on an appeal from a support order, the applicant must establish that the evidence was not discoverable before the end of the trial and that the evidence was practically conclusive of an issue in the action: *Mullin v. Mullin* (1992), 102 Nfld. & P.E.I.R. 306, 323 A.P.R. 306 (P.E.I. C.A.).

The husband's application to introduce fresh evidence on an appeal from a spousal support order was dismissed in light of the finding that the evidence could have been obtained at the time of the trial with reasonable diligence: *Henderson v. Sharma-Henderson* (1994), 7 R.F.L. (4th) 317 (Ont. C.A.); affirming (1993), 47 R.F.L. (3d) 388 (Ont. Gen. Div.).

A Court, in a family law matter, may admit fresh evidence on appeal, even if such evidence was available at the time of trial, if its absence would lead to a long term injustice to the applicant: *Cheng v. Cheng* (1994), 4 R.F.L. (4th) 442, 46 B.C.A.C. 63, 75 W.A.C. 63.

In *Shabaga v. Shabaga* (1992), 43 R.F.L. (3d) 220, 75 B.C.L.R. (2d) 128 (C.A.), the court allowed the husband's application to introduce fresh evidence in an appeal from an order dismissing a variation of spousal support. Although the evidence was available at the time of the original hearing, the court held that the rule restricting fresh evidence on appeal should be given a more elastic approach in the content of matrimonial proceedings.

In *Swift v. Swift* (1992), 44 R.F.L. (3d) 250, 61 O.A.C. 225 (Div. Ct.), the court refused, on the wife's appeal from a dismissal of her application for increased support, to allow fresh evidence concerning her health problems and her husband's improved means. The evidence relating to her health had been available at the time of trial and that relating to her husband's improved finances was properly the subject of a variation application.

Where the father had not made full financial disclosure at trial he was not allowed to adduce fresh financial evidence on his appeal from the dismissal of his application for reduced child support. The evidence would have been available at trial had the husband applied due diligence: *Edwards (Pereira) v. Edwards* (1994), 5 R.F.L. (4th) 321 (N.S. C.A.); affirming (1994), 126 N.S.R. (2d) 341, 352 A.P.R. 341 (S.C.); additional reasons at (1994), 127 N.S.R. (2d) 379, 355 A.P.R. 379 (S.C.).

Divorce Act, 1968

"To permit the appellant to adduce additional evidence in this case [an appeal from a lump sum maintenance award] would have the virtual effect of giving the appellant a new trial. Moreover, the appellant, in his submissions to the court, did not specify the exact nature of, or the source from which, he would likely produce the additional evidence he proposes to adduce to allow the court to consider whether such evidence might have affected the result reached by the learned trial judge. Even then it falls to this appellant to show that the evidence he proposes was improperly withheld or is fresh evidence discovered since trial which could not have been discovered with reasonable diligence before trial. This onus has not been discharged": per Haddad J.A. in *Schubert v. Schubert* (1978), 6 Alta. L.R. (2d) 364, 10 A.R. 305 at 312 (C.A.).

In *Berry v. Murray* (1982), 30 R.F.L. (2d) 308 (B.C. C.A.), the court, on an appeal from an award of maintenance, refused to allow the introduction of evidence concerning matters transpiring subsequent to the original order. Per Taggart J.A. at p. 309: "The more we hear material relating to events that have transpired since the trial of the matter, the more we become a court asked to vary the order of the trial judge. I think in all the circumstances it is inappropriate in this case to do so."

"Counsel for the respondent (complainant) [in an affiliation proceeding] takes the position that in order for new evidence to be introduced, the appellant must meet the test laid down by the courts on the basis of which either a new trial will be ordered after judgment or such new evidence will be entertained directly by an appellate court. Counsel referred me to many cases where the test is spelled out. It is most succinctly stated by Patterson J. in the case of: '*Beneficial Finance Co. v. Reardon* (1963), 48 M.P.R. 396, 40 D.L.R. (2d) 54 at 67 (N.S. C.A.) I take it to be undisputed law that before an application for a new trial can be entertained on the grounds of newly discovered evidence, it must be shown (1) that at the time of the trial the appellant was not aware of the evidence, and (2) that such evidence could not have been discovered by the appellant by the exercise of reasonable diligence, and (3) if such evidence was adduced, it would be practically conclusive'": per Hughes J. in *Vindevoghel v. Florek*, 28 R.F.L. 242 at 243, [1976] 5 W.W.R. 178 (Sask. Q.B.).

Generally, on an appeal from a support order, the appellate court should not assume original evidence and entertain fresh evidence on the support issue. In the absence of an error on the part of the trial judge, evidence of events occurring subsequent to the order is properly introduced only in a variation application. The appellate court should only admit fresh evidence if satisfied that the trial judge had committed an error and if the appellate court is able to deal with the issue to save time and expense: *Grohmann v. Grohmann* (1991), 37 R.F.L. (3d) 73, 62 B.C.L.R. (2d) 264, 1991 CarswellBC 321, [1991] B.C.J. No. 3820, 86 D.L.R. (4th) 741, 5 B.C.A.C. 277, 11 W.A.C. 277 (B.C. C.A.); affirming (1990), 67 D.L.R. (4th) 597, 1990 CarswellBC 886.

Facts, which occurred after the making of a support order, cannot properly be taken into account in an appeal from that order. Such facts can only be properly considered in a variation application: *Trainor v. Trainor* (1989), 23 R.F.L. (3d) 39, 80 Sask. R. 1 (C.A.).

Financial Disclosure

Where the husband had apparently failed, at the time of the original child support order, to make full financial disclosure, the court allowed the mother's appeal from the order and remitted the matter to the trial court for reconsideration. In the interests of justice, the wife ought to be given the opportunity to substantiate the husband's inadequate disclosure and argue her case for a retroactive support order: *Yiannitsopoulos v. Patseas* (1997), 28 R.F.L. (4th) 246, 1997 CarswellBC 996, [1997] B.C.J. No. 1128, 92 B.C.A.C. 98, 150 W.A.C. 98, 34 B.C.L.R. (3d) 175, [1997] 7 W.W.R. 220 (B.C. C.A.).

In *Hauff v. Hauff* (1994), 5 R.F.L. (4th) 419, 95 Man. R. (2d) 83, 1994 CarswellMan 40, 70 W.A.C. 83 (C.A.), the husband's failure at trial to make full financial disclosure disentitled him from the benefit of any discretion which the Court may have exercised in his favour on his appeal from a spousal support award.

Where the husband's evidence concerning his income was found, on appeal, to be unreliable and vague, the court allowed the wife's appeal from an order denying her support and directed that the matter be remitted to the trial judge: *Robinson v. Robinson* (1993), 45 R.F.L. (3d) 341, 1993 CarswellNS 41, 122 N.S.R. (2d) 181, 338 A.P.R. 181 (N.S. C.A.).

Where the trial judge had fixed the spousal support payable by the husband after specifically finding that the husband had not made a full and frank disclosure of his financial affairs, the appellate court dismissed the husband's appeal from the quantum of the award. Although the award was generous given the husband's stated income, his conduct at trial had disentitled him from any discretion the court might exercise in his favour: *Hauff v. Hauff* (1994), 5 R.F.L. (4th) 419, 95 Man. R. (2d) 83, 1994 CarswellMan 40, 70 W.A.C. 83 (C.A.).

In *Rust v. Rust*, 42 R.F.L. (5th) 161, 2003 CarswellSask 410, 2003 SKCA 55, 232 Sask. R. 242, 294 W.A.C. 242 (Sask. C.A.); varying 220 Sask. R. 174, 2002 CarswellSask 408, 2002 SKQB 243 (Sask. Q.B.), the court allowed the wife's appeal and substituted a periodic support award in her favour in substitution of the lump sum awarded at trial. The trial judge had calculated his estimation of how long it would likely take for the wife to become self-sufficient and had determined the lump sum accordingly. In such circumstances, periodic support was the preferable route.

Lump Sum Awards

Where the trial judge awarded the wife compensatory support in circumstances which properly supported lump sum support, the appellate court substituted a lump sum award even though the wife had not originally claimed it: *Droit de la famille — 2590*, [1997] R.D.F. 22, 1997 CarswellQue 5 (C.A. Qué.).

In *Wilson v. Wilson* (1997), 27 R.F.L. (4th) 131, 90 B.C.A.C. 152, 147 W.A.C. 152, 1996 CarswellBC 2823, 31 B.C.L.R. (3d) 332 (C.A.), an award of lump sum support in the wife's favour was substituted for the periodic support ordered at trial. The wife's continuing need for support would largely be eliminated if she had the funds available to purchase the husband's share of the matrimonial home. Furthermore, the husband had failed to pay periodic support that had been earlier awarded.

In *Porcari v. Porcari* (1997), 34 R.F.L. (4th) 156, 1997 CarswellOnt 5181 (Ont. C.A.), the court allowed the husband's appeal from an order requiring him to pay lump sum child support. Without the sale of the matrimonial home, in which the wife and children continued to reside, the husband was without funds to satisfy the order. Furthermore the husband had not attempted to avoid his duty to his children and the fact that he was unable to earn an adequate living did not justify the lump sum.

In *Toth v. Toth* (1995), 17 R.F.L. (4th) 55, 13 B.C.L.R. (3d) 1, 64 B.C.A.C. 81, 1995 CarswellBC 932, [1995] B.C.J. No. 1993, 105 W.A.C. 81 (C.A.), the lump sum award to the wife in the form of the husband's interest in the family home was reversed on appeal. The house constituted a family asset and was more appropriately dealt with by way of reapportionment under the provincial matrimonial property legislation.

In *Lee v. Lee* (1995), 18 R.F.L. (4th) 277, 107 Man. R. (2d) 212, 1995 CarswellMan 499, 109 W.A.C. 212 (C.A.), the court allowed the husband's appeal from the wife's $25,000 lump sum spousal support award and reduced it to $4,000. The trial judge had not properly assessed the husband's assets and failed to consider the impact of the order on the husband's monthly income and the tax consequences resulting from the collapse of part of his retirement fund. The husband, who had suffered multiple heart attacks, required the interest from the fund to live.

Appeals from a lump sum award are not to be encouraged. In large part, a lump sum is a question of mechanics of how to collect maintenance, and the trial judge is in the best position to assess such mechanics: *Stricker v. Stricker* (1994), 4 R.F.L. (4th) 29, 1994 CarswellAlta 377 (Alta. C.A.); additional reasons at (1994), 4 R.F.L. (4th) 29 at 31 (Alta. C.A.).

A lump sum award made at trial was quashed on appeal where it appeared that the trial judge had substantially over-estimated both the value of the husband's assets and his annual income: *Lacasse c. Grenon* (6 janvier 1992), C.A. Montréal500-09-000384-917 (C.A. Qué.)).

In *F. (H.) v. F. (E.)* (1993), 110 D.L.R. (4th) 219, 1993 CarswellNB 436, 143 N.B.R. (2d) 189, 366 A.P.R. 189 (N.B. C.A.), the court allowed the husband's appeal from a lump sum support order of $20,000 made in his wife's favour. The husband was unemployed and had only his unemployment insurance benefits available to him to meet his own needs. Given the husband's limited and uncertain means, a lump sum award was inappropriate.

Where the father had a history of avoiding his ongoing child support responsibilities, his appeal from an award of lump sum child support was dismissed: *Stricker v. Stricker* (1994), 4 R.F.L. (4th) 29, 1994 CarswellAlta 377 (Alta. C.A.); additional reasons at (1994), 4 R.F.L. (4th) 29 at 31 (Alta. C.A.). Where the wife's limited term support award had been predicated upon her receipt of a substantial property award, her appeal was allowed and an additional lump sum ordered where payment of the property award had been delayed: *Cunningham v. Cunningham* (1990), 24 R.F.L. (3d) 254, 42 B.C.L.R. (2d) 214, 1990 CarswellBC 4 (B.C. C.A.); additional reasons at (1990), 26 R.F.L. (3d) 337, 46 B.C.L.R. (2d) 212, 1990 CarswellBC 123 (B.C. C.A.); varied on reconsideration (1990), 30 R.F.L. (3d) 159, 51 B.C.L.R. (2d) 332, 1990 CarswellBC 269 (B.C. C.A.).

In *Tatlock v. Tatlock* (1994), 2 R.F.L. (4th) 251, 88 B.C.L.R. (2d) 197, 111 D.L.R. (4th) 577, 40 B.C.A.C. 289, 65 W.A.C. 289, 1994 CarswellBC 116, [1994] B.C.J. No. 403 (C.A.), the court rejected the wife's appeal from the periodic and lump sum support awarded to her. Although the wife maintained that the quantum of support awarded to her would allow only a minimum standard of living, she had neglected to consider the investment income which could result from the lump sum.

Limited Term Awards

In *Messer v. Messer* (1996), 22 R.F.L. (4th) 8, 1996 CarswellSask 131, 141 Sask. R. 163, 114 W.A.C. 163 (Sask. C.A.); reversing (1993), 47 R.F.L. (3d) 4, 108 Sask. R. 155, 1993 CarswellSask 51, [1993] S.J. No. 255 (Sask. Q.B.), the court struck a 4-year limitation on the wife's spousal support award. Given that the husband's annual income was $100,000 and the wife's $6,000, the limitation was inappropriate given the income discrepancy upon the dissolution of the parties' 22-year marriage.

In *MacIsaac v. MacIsaac* (1996), 21 R.F.L. (4th) 358, 1996 CarswellNS 177, [1996] N.S.J. No. 185, 150 N.S.R. (2d) 321, 436 A.P.R. 321 (N.S. C.A.); reversing in part on other grounds (1995), 149 N.S.R. (2d) 354, 416 A.P.R. 354, 1995 CarswellNS 491 (N.S. S.C.), the court removed on appeal, the 2-year limitation placed upon the wife's spousal support payments. After the collapse of the parties' 25-year traditional marriage it was unreasonable to expect that the wife would be employed within 2 years. The limitation had inappropriately emphasized self-sufficiency to the exclusion of other support objectives.

In *Hopkinson v. Hopkinson* (1997), 34 R.F.L. (4th) 137, 43 B.C.L.R. (3d) 232, 1997 CarswellBC 2760, 101 B.C.A.C. 41, 164 W.A.C. 41 (B.C. C.A.), the court refused the wife's appeal from the time limitation placed upon her spousal support award. As she had already obtained employment and a degree of self-sufficiency, the limitation was warranted.

In *Poohkay v. Poohkay* (1997), 30 R.F.L. (4th) 9, 1997 CarswellAlta 604, 200 A.R. 211, 146 W.A.C. 211 (Alta. C.A.); additional reasons at (1997), 1997 CarswellAlta 987, 33 R.F.L. (4th) 140 (Alta. C.A.), the wife successfully appealed from an order dismissing her application for a lifting of the time limitation on her spousal support order. At the time of the original order, the parties had not anticipated the extent to which the mother's duties as a custodial parent would interfere with her educational upgrading efforts. Had the parties known that their assumptions were incorrect at the time the original order was made, a different order would likely have resulted. As the wife would likely be able to enter the workforce in the near future, a lump sum award was preferable to an indefinite periodic one.

Where it was not clear that the wife, given her child-rearing responsibilities, would be able to achieve self-sufficiency within the 7-year limitation of her spousal support, the limitation was removed on appeal subject to a review in 5 years' time: *Metzner v. Metzner* (1997), 28 R.F.L. (4th) 166, 1997 CarswellBC 648, [1997] B.C.J. No. 904, 91 B.C.A.C. 241, 148 W.A.C. 241, 34 B.C.L.R. (3d) 314 (B.C. C.A.).)

In *Donald v. Donald* (1991), 33 R.F.L. (3d) 196, 103 N.S.R. (2d) 322, 282 A.P.R. 322, 81 D.L.R. (4th) 48, 1991 CarswellNS 58 (N.S. C.A.) the court on appeal removed a 5-year limitation placed on the wife's support award. The wife was 47 years old and as she had been out of the workforce for most of the parties' 23-year marriage, it was unrealistic to expect that she would ever become totally self-sufficient.

In *Houle v. Houle* (1994), 9 R.F.L. (4th) 408, 1994 CarswellBC 492, 98 B.C.L.R. (2d) 355, 52 B.C.A.C. 5, 86 W.A.C. 5 (B.C. C.A.), the court allowed the wife's appeal from an order reducing her spousal support and providing for its expiration. Although the wife had earlier acknowledged her responsibility to seek self-sufficiency, the chambers judge had not given sufficient consideration to the evidence supporting the wife's claim that her depression had hampered her efforts.

Where the wife had given up some economic advantages during the parties' six-year marriage, but had also benefited economically in other ways, the court denied her appeal from an order limiting her periodic support entitlement to six months. As the wife was free to again pursue her pre-marriage career, she had not suffered any great economic disadvantage as a result of the marriage: *Grohmann v. Grohmann* (1991), 37 R.F.L. (3d) 73, 62 B.C.L.R. (2d) 264, 1991 CarswellBC 321, [1991] B.C.J. No. 3820, 86 D.L.R. (4th) 741, 5 B.C.A.C. 277, 11 W.A.C. 277 (B.C. C.A.); affirming (1990), 67 D.L.R. (4th) 597, 1990 CarswellBC 886 (B.C. S.C.).

In *P. (M.) c. G. (N.)* (1989), 33 Q.A.C. 279, the wife's appeal from her six-month support award was dismissed. Although the 42-year-old wife was barely surviving financially on part-time work, she was capable of earning a living, her health being good and the children being grown up. Her financial problems could not be connected to the marriage, given the fact that she had worked for most of the last 10 years.

Miscellaneous

In *Tauber v. Tauber* (2000), 6 R.F.L. (5th) 442, 2000 CarswellOnt 2019, [2000] O.J. No. 2133, 48 O.R. (3d) 577, 187 D.L.R. (4th) 1, 133 O.A.C. 66 (Ont. C.A.); additional reasons at (2000), 2000 CarswellOnt 3097, 8 R.F.L. (5th) 441, 190 D.L.R. (4th) 509, 51 O.R. (3d) 81 (Ont. C.A.), the husband appealed with respect to child support among other matters, as the law had changed from the time of trial to the time of appeal. The case went to trial after the Ontario Court of Appeal rendered its decision in *Francis v. Baker* (1998), 34 R.F.L. (4th) 317, 1998 CarswellOnt 931, [1998] O.J. No. 924, 157 D.L.R. (4th) 1, 107 O.A.C. 161, 38 O.R. (3d) 481 (Eng.), (sub nom. *Francis c. Baker)* 38 O.R. (3d) 509 (Fr.) (Ont. C.A.), and before the Supreme Court of Canada decision in *Francis v. Baker* (1999), 50 R.F.L. (4th) 228, [1999] S.C.J. No. 52, 1999 CarswellOnt 2734, 1999 CarswellOnt 2948, [1999] 3 S.C.R. 250, 177 D.L.R. (4th) 1, 246 N.R. 45, 125 O.A.C. 201 (S.C.C.). The trial judge was of the opinion that he was required to order at least the amount of child support set out in the Table. However, in light of the Supreme Court of Canada decision in *Francis v. Baker*, the court may order child support where a payor is earning over $150,000 if the Table Amount is "inappropriate". The Appellate Court was of the opinion, that it was not in a position to undertake the de novo review needed to do justice to the parties and to the child and ordered a new trial on the issue of child support.

Where the trial judge ordered combined child and spousal support of $1,400 and only $894 for the following month, without explaining the reasons for the change, the wife's appeal from the order was allowed. As there was no evidence available upon which to adjust the award, the issue was remitted to trial for determination: *M. (S.A.J.) v. M. (D.D.)* (1999), 45 R.F.L. (4th) 301, 134 Man. R. (2d) 242, 193 W.A.C. 242, 1999 CarswellMan 149, [1999] M.J. No. 118 (C.A.); reversing (1998), 40 R.F.L. 40 (4th) 95, 127 Man.R. (2d) 78, 1998 CarswellMan 178, [1998] M.J. No. 173 (Q.B.).

The appellate court upheld the trial judge's ruling that the wife was not entitled to spousal support where the appellant had precipitously shut down her profitable company which would have provided her with compensation to meet her needs and she had failed to look for new employment: *Westworth v. Westworth* (1999), 1 R.F.L. (5th) 186, 1999 Carswell-Alta 922, [1999] A.J. No. 1189, 250 A.R. 47, 213 W.A.C. 47 (Alta. C.A.). The appeal was allowed in part on another issue.

Where the Federal Child Support Guidelines were not yet in force when a child support order was made, they should not be considered in any appeal from that order: *Prince v. Prince* (1997), 35 R.F.L. (4th) 328, 163 N.S.R. (2d) 28, 487 A.P.R. 28 (C.A.).

In *Munro v. Munro* (1997), 33 R.F.L. (4th) 464 (Ont. C.A.), the wife's spousal support awarded upon dissolution of the parties' 18-year marriage was reduced on appeal. Although the length of the marriage and the fact that the wife had been primary caregiver to the husband's children entitled her to support, the quantum awarded at trial was too high given the impact of an equalization payment upon the parties' incomes.

Where in the course of proceedings to enforce child support arrears the court forgave a portion of the arrears and reduced ongoing child support, an appeal by the payee mother was allowed. The father had not brought an application for variation and the only matter properly before the court was the enforcement proceeding: *Chislett v. Chislett* (1997), 33 R.F.L. (4th) 377 (N.S. C.A.).

Where the trial judge substituted the parties' agreement whereby the custodial mother waived child support with an order requiring the father to pay support, the father's appeal was allowed. The order of the judge did not reflect the full obligation of both parents to provide for support of the child and rather than unilaterally imposing an order, he should have given the parties themselves the opportunity to arrive at their own arrangement: *Arbeau v. Arbeau* (1997), 30 R.F.L. (4th) 192 (N.B. C.A.).

In *Luke v. Luke* (1997), 29 R.F.L. (4th) 319 (Man. C.A.), the husband's appeal from the wife's spousal support award was allowed and her monthly support reduced from $800 to $200. Although the wife had been economically disadvantaged by the marriage breakdown, she was employed and the quantum awarded at trial was an excessive attempt to compensate her for her diminished standard of living.

Where the husband had paid off the accumulated marital debts, supported the wife and child and had been required to pay support of more than half his net earnings, his appeal from the spousal support award was allowed. On the evidence, the husband had borne a disproportionately large share of the family's financial burdens since the date of separation: *Krentz v. Krentz* (1997), 28 R.F.L. (4th) 183 (Man. C.A.).

Where the wife had suffered severe injuries in a motor vehicle accident occurring six months prior to the parties' separation, her award of indefinite support was upheld on appeal. Although the wife's injury was not casually connected to the marriage, it was found to fall within "other circumstances" as contemplated by s. 15(5) of the *Divorce Act*: *Parsons v. Parsons* (1996), 27 R.F.L. (4th) 11 (Man. C.A.); affirming (1996), 22 R.F.L. (4th) 444, 111 Man. R. (2d) 169 (Q.B.). In *Messer v. Messer* (1996), 26 R.F.L. (4th) 352 (Sask. Q.B.); reversed in part (1997), 33 R.F.L. (4th) 426 (Sask. C.A.), the court upheld the wife's entitlement to unlimited time support upon the dissolution of the parties' 30-year traditional marriage. However, as the trial judge had failed to consider both the actual circumstances of each party as well as the effect of an earlier capital distribution, the wife's award was substantially reduced.

In *Miranda v. Miranda* (1996), 26 R.F.L. (4th) 323, 27 B.C.L.R. (3d) 357, 83 B.C.A.C. 275, 136 W.A.C. 275 (C.A.), the court, on appeal, allowed the husband's application to set aside a default spousal support award ordered against him. The husband had failed to respond originally because of his depressed mental state and his lack of fluency in English. However, the application was allowed only on the basis that the order made on reconsideration was to be effective as of the date of the original order.

In *Purcell v. Purcell* (1996), 26 R.F.L. (4th) 267 (Ont. C.A.); varying (1995), 11 R.F.L. (4th) 181 (Ont. Gen. Div.); additional reasons at (1995), 11 R.F.L. (4th) 181 at 200 (Ont. Gen. Div.), the court reduced, on appeal, the quantum of spousal support payable by the wife to the husband. Although the husband's unemployment was in part due to the marriage, the original spousal support order did not give him the incentive to become self-sufficient, nor did it adequately apportion between the parties the financial obligation of child care.

In *Hussey v. Hussey* (1996), 26 R.F.L. (4th) 248 (Alta. C.A.), the court reduced, on appeal, the substantial child support payable by the father. The father's income could not support the award and the trial court had given insufficient weight to expenses of the father which it found to be legitimate.

In *Bostrom v. Bostrom* (1996), 26 R.F.L. (4th) 120, 83 B.C.A.C. 113, 136 W.A.C. 113 (B.C. C.A.), the court upheld a child support order in the father's favour despite the father's claim that the quantum was inadequate. The father had chosen early retirement and part-time work after losing his job at age 59. The trial judge properly attributed to him the ability to earn higher income in setting the support payable. The husband could not shun his responsibilities to his children and actively choose semi-retirement while these family obligations were outstanding.

On an appeal from an order reducing child support where there is no record or agreement as to the chambers judge's reasons, the proper approach is to consider the application afresh: *Cherry v. Cherry* (1996), 22 R.F.L. (4th) 432, 76 B.C.A.C. 202, 125 W.A.C. 202, 24 B.C.L.R. (3d) 158 (C.A.).

Where the wife had done nothing towards her own self-sufficiency or to provide financial support for her children, although she was capable of doing so, the court allowed the husband's appeal from her spousal support award and reduced it from $700 monthly to $400: *Al-Maghazachi v. Dueck* (1995), 17 R.F.L. (4th) 132, 107 Man. R. (2d) 47, 109 W.A.C. 47 (C.A.).

In *Northrup v. Northrup* (1995), 16 R.F.L. (4th) 321 (N.B. C.A.), the court rejected the payor husband's appeal from a child support order brought on the basis that the trial judge had disregarded the husband's need for club memberships and expensive clothing as a result of his employment. The separation had lowered the standard of living for the entire family and the modest circumstances of the children required that the order be upheld.

Where the quantum of spousal awarded at trial is clearly inadequate given the appropriate statutory factors, an appellate court is justified in intervening: *Waterman v. Waterman* (1995), 16 R.F.L. (4th) 10, 133 Nfld. & P.E.I.R. 310, 413 A.P.R. 310 (Nfld. C.A.).

An order requiring the husband to pay a notional amount of child support monthly, which amount would be automatically added to arrears, was struck on appeal. Arrears can accrue only where there has been a failure to meet a current obligation: *Marchak v. Fleury* (1995), 15 R.F.L. (4th) 458, 102 Man. R. (2d) 121 (C.A.).

The fact that a custodial parent may benefit from a child support order through a sharing of common expenses is not a reason to reduce that support order on appeal: *Vincent v. Vincent* (1995), 15 R.F.L. (4th) 273, 132 Nfld. & P.E.I.R. 181, 410 A.P.R. 181, 1995 CarswellNfld 32 (Nfld. C.A.).

A consent order whereby a spouse waives a right to support in exchange for certain pension payments on the part of the other spouse cannot be put aside because that other spouse fails to perform his or her obligations. A consent order may only be set aside if the underlying agreement is invalid or so tainted in its formation as to justify setting it or part of it aside: *McCowan v. McCowan* (1995), 14 R.F.L. (4th) 325, 24 O.R. (3d) 707, 84 O.A.C. 125, 1995 CarswellOnt 435.

In *Muirhead v. Muirhead* (1995), 14 R.F.L. (4th) 276, 6 B.C.L.R. (3d) 229, 59 B.C.A.C. 144 (C.A.), an award of compensatory maintenance made in the wife's favour at trial was overturned on appeal. The trial judge had failed to take into account all of the factors specified in the *Divorce Act*.

In *Ell v. Ell* (1995), 131 Sask. R. 228 (C.A.); affirming (1993), 112 Sask. R. 1 (Q.B.), a lump sum and periodic support award made in the wife's favour was upheld on appeal. The parties' marriage had been a traditional one and the wife was inhibited from becoming self-sufficient because of physical and emotional problems.

In *Willick v. Willick*, [1994] 3 S.C.R. 670, 6 R.F.L. (4th) 161, 125 Sask. R. 81, 81 W.A.C. 81, 173 N.R. 321, 119 D.L.R. (4th) 405, the appeal of a child support order was allowed and support was increased based on the substantial increase in the income of the non-custodial parent.

In *Wallberg v. Wallberg* (1994), 8 R.F.L. (4th) 372 (B.C. C.A.), the court increased on appeal the quantum of spousal support confirmed by the trial judge on the basis of a registrar's report. Although the husband had two sources of income, the registrar had determined his ability to pay through reference to only one, based on the husband's statement that he intended to discontinue a business in the future. Given that the business existed as of the date of the hearing, the income from it should have been taken into account and the trial judge should have exercised his independent discretion in setting the quantum of support.

In *Lasalle v. Lasalle* (1994), 7 R.F.L. (4th) 100 (Alta. C.A.), the court rejected the husband's argument that the wife had benefited from the marriage as a ground for reversing her spousal support award on appeal. Although she had developed some skills during the marriage, it was still likely that her child care responsibilities had inhibited the development of any career she might have developed.

Where 15 months had elapsed from the date of a child and spousal support order and the hearing of the wife's appeal from the order, the appellate court order the matter remitted to the lower court for reconsideration. Given the passage of time and a change in circumstances relating to the eldest child, a new hearing using up-to-date evidence was best: *Forbes v. Forbes* (1994), 5 R.F.L. (4th) 79 (B.C. C.A.); additional reasons at (1994), 49 B.C.A.C. 236, 30 W.A.C. 236 (C.A.).

Where the trial judge had awarded the wife spousal and child support in excess of that claimed by her and the appellate court could not determine whether the appropriate amendments to pleadings had been made, the husband's appeal was allowed and a new trial ordered: *Buttoo v. Buttoo* (1994), 4 R.F.L. (4th) 36 (Ont. C.A.).

In *Floyd v. Floyd* (1994), 2 R.F.L. (4th) 403, 146 N.B.R. (2d) 51, 374 A.P.R. 51 (C.A.), the court allowed the wife's appeal from a fixed term spousal support award and made the order reviewable after a specified time. The award had been premised upon the wife receiving a sizable amount upon disposition of family property. As the disposition was not certain and the wife was unable to find full time employment, the limitation was properly deleted. In *Audley v. Audley* (1993), 50 R.F.L. (3d) 274, 84 B.C.L.R. (2d) 390, 36 B.C.A.C. 127, 58 W.A.C. 127 (C.A.), the court refused on the wife's appeal to interfere with the quantum of child and spousal support awarded to her at trial. Although the quantum appeared low, the trial judge had not erred in his consideration of the parties' means and needs.

Where the payor husband had unilaterally decided to pay the quantum of support which he felt was reasonable, contrary to the terms of an existing support order, the court refused to entertain his appeal from that order: *Elensky v. Elenskaya* (1993), 50 R.F.L. (3d) 231 (B.C. C.A.).

Where the resources available to the parties will not allow them both to maintain their pre-divorce lifestyle, the court will not interfere on appeal with a support order which attempts to share the resources equitably between the parties: *Laurence v. Laurence* (1993), 50 R.F.L. (3d) 26, 85 B.C.L.R. (2d) 378, 33 B.C.A.C. 81, 54 W.A.C. 81 (C.A.).

In *Robinson v. Robinson* (1993), 45 R.F.L. (3d) 341, 1993 CarswellNS 41, 122 N.S.R. (2d) 181, 338 A.P.R. 181 (N.S. C.A.); reversing in part (1992), 111 N.S.R. (2d) 301, 303 A.P.R. 301 (T.D.), the court, on appeal, reversed the trial judge's refusal of the wife's support claim and remitted the issue to the trial judge. The husband's evidence regarding his income was so patently unreliable and vague that the finding that the wife was not entitled to support was arbitrary.

In *C. (P.) c. L. (B.)* (16 décembre 1993), no. C.A. Montréal 500-09-001376-938 (C.A. Qué.), the court allowed the mother's appeal from an order significantly lowering the quantum of child support she received. The decrease had been based partly on the husband's assertion that his income had decreased dramatically after his payment of a sizeable debt. However, the wife's evidence established that the debt had existed at the time of the original support order. Also, the trial judge's assertion that the wife should have been earning more money by this stage was not reasonable considering the on-going economic recession.

In *Giorno v. Giorno* (1992), 39 R.F.L. (3d) 345, 110 N.S.R. (2d) 87, 299 A.P.R. 87, 1992 CarswellNS 63 (C.A.), the court allowed the husband's appeal from a spousal award and reduced the amount he was required to pay. The trial judge had calculated the husband's ability to pay on his previous year's salary which had included a large portion of overtime. As at the time of trial the husband's overtime had been cancelled, only his current income should have been taken into account.

Where the wife was involved in a common-law relationship, and, as a result, had no immediate needs, a spousal support order made in her favour was deleted on appeal. The wife's argument that she wished to protect her support rights should she find herself alone in the future was not sufficient to justify the award: *Desgreniers c. Roy* (7 janvier 1992), C.A. Montréal500-09-000701-912 (C.A. Qué.).

In *Desmarchais c. Bédard* (26 mars 1992), C.A. Montréal 500-09-000337-907 (C.A. Qué.), the 2-year limitation placed on the wife's support order was removed on appeal. The 50-year-old wife had worked very little throughout the parties' lengthy traditional marriage and it was unreasonable to expect her to achieve self-sufficiency within a 2-year period.

In an appeal from a support order it is not the function of the appellate court to re-examine all of the evidence: *Avery c. Menard* (24 mars 1992), C.A. Montréal 500-09-001760-909 (C.A. Qué.).

In Manitoba, the time for filing a notice of appeal with respect to corollary relief orders under the Divorce Act begins to run from the date of entry of the order and not from the date of pronouncement: *Harvey v. Harvey* (1989), 23 R.F.L. (3d) 53, 60 Man. R. (2d) 302 (C.A.).

An appellate court should not retry factual issues in an appeal from an order for support. Nevertheless, appellate intervention may be justified if it will bring the matter to an end: *Quigley v. Fontaine (Quigley)* (1987), 10 R.F.L. (3d) 160 (B.C. C.A.). See also *Fraser v. Fraser* (1987), 10 R.F.L. (3d) 264 (B.C. C.A.).

21§5A — Appeals — variation of support

Divorce Act, 1985

Where the trial judge had allowed the husband's application for a downward variation of child support, absent full financial disclosure by the husband, the variation was struck on appeal. Absence of full disclosure was unfair to the wife as it prevented her from making a full response to the husband's application: *Terry v. Francis* (2004), 11 R.F.L. (6th) 159, 2004 CarswellNS 398, 227 N.S.R. (2d) 99, 720 A.P.R. 99, 2004 NSCA 118 (C.A.).

In *MacDonald v. MacDonald* (2004), 10 R.F.L. (6th) 88, 2004 CarswellNS 522, 229 N.S.R. (2d) 52, 725 A.P.R. 52, 2004 NSCA 153 (C.A.), the court, on appeal, struck a time limitation in the wife's spousal support order that had been imposed in the husband's variation application. The motions judge had focused on the issue of self-sufficiency alone to the virtual exclusion of every other factor specified in the *Divorce Act.* Furthermore, the judge had misapprehended the evidence in several important respects.

In *Llewellyn v. Llewellyn*, 26 R.F.L. (5th) 389, 2002 CarswellBC 529, 2002 BCCA 182, 99 B.C.L.R. (3d) 361, 212 D.L.R. (4th) 153 (B.C. C.A.), the court, on appeal, reduced the amount payable by the husband to discharge the child support arrears owed by him. Payment of the amount set by trial would effectively preclude his exercise of access to his children, who lived some distance away.

In *Rothgiesser v. Rothgiesser* (2000), 2 R.F.L. (5th) 266, 2000 CarswellOnt 50, 183 D.L.R. (4th) 310, 46 O.R. (3d) 577, 128 O.A.C. 302 (Ont. C.A.), the court held that an Ontario court does not have jurisdiction to vary a spousal support obligation if the spousal support order was not made pursuant to a Canadian divorce. It does not have jurisdiction to vary a foreign support order. Jurisdiction to vary a foreign spousal support order is derived from provincial legislation regarding the enforcement of support orders. In Ontario, the appropriate legislation is the *Reciprocal Enforcement of Support Orders Act.* In this case, no application to vary an order pursuant to the provisions of that act had been made.

An Ontario court does not have jurisdiction to vary a final Manitoba order under s. 17 of the *Divorce Act* where the parties are not former spouses: *Brooks v. Brooks* (1998), 39 R.F.L. (4th) 187, 1998 CarswellOnt 3097, 111 O.A.C. 177, 163 D.L.R. (4th) 715, 22 C.P.C. (4th) 209, 41 O.R. (3d) 191 (Ont. C.A.). The British Columbia Court of Appeal was of the opinion in *Stroud v. Stroud* (1996), 20 R.F.L. (4th) 392, 1996 CarswellBC 723, 22 B.C.L.R. (3d) 183, 75 B.C.A.C. 48, 123 W.A.C. 48 that the trial judge did not err in considering the parties' agreement, as embodied in a consent order, as well as the gulf in the parties' means, where deciding the appropriate variation order.

See also *M. (L.S.) v. M. (E.J.)* (2001), 198 D.L.R. (4th) 385, 2001 CarswellOnt 1404, [2001] O.J. No. 1510, 144 O.A.C. 155, 16 R.F.L. (5th) 185, 53 O.R. (3d) 641 (Ont. C.A.); leave to appeal allowed (2001), 2001 CarswellOnt 3484, 2001 CarswellOnt 3485, [2001] S.C.C.A. No. 328, 283 N.R. 395 (note), 157 O.A.C. 400 (note) (Ont. C.A.), at 15 §147. (This case is also known as *Miglin v. Miglin*).

The Ontario Court of Appeal in *Stranghi v. Stanghi* (2001), 19 R.F.L. (5th) 392, 2001 CarswellOnt 1726, dismissed the husband's appeal for variation of his spousal support obligations, finding that the trial judge had not misapprehended the evidence. The trial judge's conclusion that the husband was working and was capable of working in a supervisory capacity had an evidentiary basis. The filed reports did not necessarily lead to the conclusion that the husband was unemployed and unemployable.

In *Francis v. Baker* (1998), (1998), 34 R.F.L. (4th) 317, 1998 CarswellOnt 931, [1998] O.J. No. 924, 157 D.L.R. (4th) 1, 107 O.A.C. 161, 38 O.R. (3d) 481 (Eng.), (sub nom. *Francis c. Baker)* 38 O.R. (3d) 509 (Fr.) (Ont. C.A.); appeal dismissed on other grounds 50 R.F.L. (4th) 228, [1999] S.C.J. No. 52, 1999 CarswellOnt 2734, 1999 CarswellOnt 2948, [1999] 3 S.C.R. 250, 177 D.L.R. (4th) 1, 246 N.R. 45, 125 O.A.C. 201 (S.C.C.), the award of lump sum support of $500,000 was upheld on appeal, as the court was of the opinion that it was fully supported on the evidence. It would appear that the trial judge had found a material change in circumstances justifying a variation because of the great increase in the husband's annual income. The court would not deny the wife her spousal support because the litigation had proceeded extremely slowly.

Where the evidentiary record on an appeal from a child support variation proceeding was sparse in respect of a number of crucial matters before the Court of Appeal, the matter was remitted back to the chambers judge for viva voce evidence. The record was so inadequate that the Court was unable to assess questions before it: *Bradley v. Zaba* (1996), 18 R.F.L. (4th) 1, 137 Sask. R. 295, 107 W.A.C. 295 (C.A.).

The parties were married in 1974, separated in 1988 and were divorced in September 1990. They had one child, born in January 1986. The husband had remarried and was living with his new family in a home purchased by his present spouse. She was supporting the family, since his counseling practice did not produce any significant income. The husband had debts of $40,000, including arrears of $7,530 on the child support payments of $325 per month he had agreed to on separation. The wife had remained in the matrimonial home with the child. They were presently being supported by her father. The trial Judge referred to the husband's debts and lack of income and then ordered that the arrears of maintenance be reduced to $3,000. In granting the wife's appeal, the court found the husband had not demonstrated that he was unable to earn more in some other line of work. There was no reason why he should be relieved of the obligation to which he had agreed: *Stewart v. Stewart* (1994), 2 R.F.L. (4th) 53, 41 B.C.A.C. 213, 66 W.A.C. 213 (C.A.).

Where the motions judge added a cost of living and salary adjustment clause which was neither requested by counsel nor put to counsel for their consideration, the clause was set side on appeal in *Zarrillo v. Kidd* (1994), 10 R.F.L. (4th) 42 (Man. C.A.). There was no reference to the governing statute in this decision.

In *Oyen v. Oyen* (1994), 9 R.F.L. (4th) 454 (B.C. C.A.), at page 459, the court held that "the test to be applied by a court of appeal sitting on appeal from an order made under the *Divorce Act*, 1985, is whether the judgment under appeal discloses "material error", including a misapprehension of the evidence; whether the trial judge erred in principle; or whether the award was otherwise "clearly wrong." In applying this test, the court must consider s. 17 of the *Divorce Act*, 1985, which provides the principles to be applied by a court on an application for variation of maintenance. In the *Oyen* decision, the court found that the chambers judge had not erred in awarding the wife a lump sum of $10,000 for child support, reflecting the fact that there had been a material change in circumstances from the date of the original order which warranted an increase in maintenance but, the chambers judge did err in failing to order increased support for the future. This error amounted to a material error justifying interference by the appellate court. The chambers judge also failed to take into consideration the overall change in the condition, means, and needs of the parties in refusing to order increased child maintenance.

In *MacNeil v. MacIsaac* (1994), 3 R.F.L. (4th) 71 (N.S. C.A.), the appellant appealed from an order which varied an existing corollary relief judgment by requiring the appellant to pay the respondent maintenance of $100 per month and provided a formula by which the maintenance would be increased if the appellant's gross monthly income from all sources became larger. The appeal was dismissed and an application for leave to appeal to the Supreme Court of Canada was refused at (1995) 10 R.F.L. (4th) 187.

In *Wundele v. Wundele* (1994), 8 R.F.L. (4th) 325 (B.C. C.A.), the appellate court restored the original order for child support in the amount of $200 for each of three children, stating that it would be an error in principle to grant relief to a shirking parent who, since separation had lost his job but who did not give any of the proceeds of his pension to his wife to help with their children.

The function of appellate courts is to flesh out broad statutory grants of "discretion" with guidelines: *Levesque v. Levesque* (1994), 4 R.F.L. (4th) 375, [1994] 8 W.W.R. 589, 20 Alta. L.R. (3d) 429 (C.A.); additional reasons at (1995), 165 A.R. 319, 89 W.A.C. 319 (C.A.).

Where the wife's limited term support order was based on an assumption that she would complete a nursing course, the removal of the limitation upon her failure to complete the course was upheld on appeal. The wife's changed circumstances, had they existed at the time of the original order, would have resulted in a different support order: *Therrien-Cliche v. Cliche* (1997), 30 R.F.L. (4th) 97 (Ont. C.A.).

Where a Motions judge had placed too much emphasis on the results of the wife's attempts to achieve self-sufficiency, the time limit imposed on her spousal support order was struck on appeal in *Carroll v. Carroll* (1997), 32 R.F.L. (4th) 231 (Ont. C.A.).

In *Willick v. Willick*, *supra*, the appeal of a child support order was allowed and support was increased based on the substantial increase in the income of the non-custodial parent.

In *Fullerton v. Fullerton* (1999), 49 R.F.L. (4th) 255, 1999 CarswellBC 1438, [1999] B.C.J. No. 1489 (B.C. C.A.), the court refused the mother's appeal from a judgment in which the trial judge refused to vary the child support provisions contained in the parties' settlement agreement. It was within the trial judge's discretion not to order a variance and the decision was not so clearly wrong as to amount to injustice.

An appellate court does not have an "independent discretion" to decide afresh the question of maintenance: *Moge v. Moge*, [1992] 3 S.C.R. 813 at 832, approving the comments of Morden J.A. in *Harrington v. Harrington* (1981), 22 R.F.L. (2d) 40 (Ont. C.A.), and followed in *Martin v. Martin* (1994), 10 R.F.L. (4th) 51 (N.S. C.A.). There was no reference to the governing statute in this latter decision.

An appellate court should only intervene in the decision of a trial court, if there has been a material error in principle, a significant misapprehension of the evidence or an award which is clearly wrong: *Willick v. Willick* (1994), 6 R.F.L. (4th) 161, 173 N.R. 321, 125 Sask. R. 81, 81 W.A.C. 81, 119 D.L.R. (4th) 405, [1994] 3 S.C.R. 670 (S.C.C.).

On an appeal from an order varying child support, the appellate court is entitled to reconsider the matter on its merits where the trial judge below did not give reasons for the variation. However, the trial decision should not be disturbed unless it exceeds "the generous ambit within which reasonable disagreement is possible": *Bock v. Muir* (1990), 27 R.F.L. (3d) 384 (Ont. Div. Ct.).

In *Gardonia v. Russo* (April 16, 1992), C.A. Montréal 500-09-001563-915 (Que. C.A.), the court allowed the wife's appeal from an order reducing the quantum of child support payable by the husband. Although the husband's income had fallen from $55,000 to $32,000 annually, the trial judge had failed to adequately consider the fact that the husband's second wife had an annual income of $25,000 and that she failed to contribute adequately to household expenses.

The quantum of a rehabilitative fund and periodic support are matters within the trial judge's discretion which should not be disturbed by an appellate court absent evidence of an improper exercise of this discretion: *Osmond v. Osmond* (1990), 26 R.F.L. (3d) 1, 96 N.S.R. (2d) 19, 253 A.P.R. 19, 67 D.L.R. (4th) 719 (C.A.).

Where a party seeks variation of a maintenance order on the grounds of a change in circumstances, the trial court is the proper forum for such a hearing. The launching of an appeal does not preclude the trial court from passing upon a change of circumstances to determine whether an award should be varied: *Gresham v. Gresham* (1988), 14 R.F.L. (3d) 446 (Sask. C.A.).

In *Hubick v. Hubick*, 10 R.F.L. (3d) 196, 55 Alta. L.R. (2d) 224, [1988] 1 W.W.R. 129, 82 A.R. 321 (C.A.), the court allowed the husband's appeal from a judgment dismissing his request for the rescission of support arrears. The trial judge had erred in placing too much emphasis on the general policy of ensuring all court orders are respected and had disregarded other factors.

In *F. (R.G.) c. G. (L.)* (1989), 34 Q.A.C. 183, the husband's application for a reduction of child support payable by him was allowed on appeal in light of the fact that he had lost his job and was forced to seek public assistance.

In *Ball c. Rhéaume* (26 mars 1992), C.A. Montréal 500-09-000660-910 (C.A. Qué.), the court allowed the wife's appeal from an order refusing an upward variation of child support. Although the parties had previously agreed to lower support when the wife had remarried, she had subsequently divorced again and it was proper that the husband contribute more towards the children's needs.

Where the husband had obtained a reduction in the support payable by him through a false affidavit misrepresenting his income, the original support order was restored on appeal: *Manolescu v. Manolescu* (1990), 26 R.F.L. (3d) 41 (B.C. C.A.).

A limitation placed on the wife's support entitlement in the course of variation proceedings was removed on appeal. Given the wife's age of 59, her deteriorating health and total lack of job skills, the limitation was inappropriate: *Colp (Silmarie) v. Colp* (1994), 1 R.F.L. (4th) 161, (sub nom. *Colp v. Colp)* 128 N.S.R. (2d) 132, 359 A.P.R. 132, 111 D.L.R. (4th) 252 (C.A.).

In *Droit de la famille — 707*, [1989] R.D.F. 614, (sub nom. D. (C.) v. B. (M.)), 30 Q.A.C. 120 (C.A.), the court dismissed the husband's appeal from an order refusing the termination of spousal support where the appeal hearing occurred after the husband's death. Given the death, the main ground of appeal had no object. Where the court, upon the father's application for variation of the child support payable by him, had rejected his evidence on grounds of credibility, his subsequent appeal was dismissed. The credibility of a witness was within the exclusive province of the trial judge and there was no other ground on which to base the appeal: *Westcott v. Marson* (May 11, 1994), Doc. C.A. 02975 (N.S. C.A.), summarized at [1994] W.D.F.L. 1013.

21§5B — Appeals — interim support

The discretion of a chambers judge in awarding interim child and spousal support will not be disturbed on appeal unless an obvious error had to be corrected and the matter could not go immediately to trial: *Rust v. Rust*, 27 R.F.L. (5th) 179, 2002 CarswellSask 243, 2002 SKCA 50 (Sask. C.A.).

Appeals from interim spousal support orders should generally not be encouraged as they easily lead to a delay in resolving the real issues involved in the divorce: *Vauclair v. Vauclair* (1998), 39 R.F.L. (4th) 124, 126 Man. R. (2d) 136, 167 W.A.C. 136, 1998 CarswellMan 119 (C.A.).

Where it was clear that payment of an interim spousal and child support order would require a contribution by the payor husband's parents, the husband's appeal from the order was allowed and the quantum payable reduced: *Penner v. Penner* (1998), 38 R.F.L.

(4th) 25, 212 A.R. 217, 168 W.A.C. 217, 1998 CarswellAlta 169, [1998] A.J. No. 218 (C.A.).

Where the interim child support order required the husband to pay substantially more than called for in the parties' separation agreement, the husband's appeal from the order was allowed and support reduced to the agreed upon amount. The parties had had independent legal advice when negotiating the agreement which should not have been disregarded. The interim order had actually led to the delay of the trial and the amount of support should accordingly be reduced: *Orth v. Orth* (1998), 36 R.F.L. (4th) 274, 168 Sask. R. 1, 173 W.A.C. 1, 1998 CarswellSask 73, [1998] S.J. No. 58 (C.A.).

Appeals from interim support orders should be discouraged. The proper remedy is to proceed as expeditiously as possible to trial: *Webster v. Lusty* (1992), 44 R.F.L. (3d) 56, 83 Man. R. (2d) 193, 36 W.A.C. 193 (C.A.).

Where an appeal by the wife of her interim support award after a long delay would only lead to further delay of the trial, the appeal was dismissed: *Langevin v. Langevin* (1995), 10 R.F.L. (4th) 229 (Alta. C.A.).

The awarding of interim support involves a substantial amount of discretion on the part of a chambers judge and an appeal court ought not to substitute its opinion for that of a chambers judge: *Gillespie v. Gillespie* (1988), 14 R.F.L. (3d) 450 (B.C.C.A.).

Appeals from interlocutory orders should be discouraged, particularly time-limited interim custody and access orders, where the intent is to grant interim relief only pending a hearing before the trial judge: *Hickey v. Hickey* (February 1, 1994), Doc. C.A. 02936 (N.S. C.A.); affirming (1993), 123 N.S.R. (2d) 437, 340 A.P.R. 437 (S.C.).

An appeal court is very reluctant to interfere with a judge's exercise of discretion to award or withhold interim support. Parties should be encouraged to have the matter tried as expeditiously as possible: *Foss v. Foss* (1991), 31 R.F.L. (3d) 367 (Sask. C.A.).

An appeal from an interlocutory order involving the exercise of discretion, as is the case with an interim support order, should generally be heard as an appeal rather than as a rehearing on the merits. However, where no reasons are given to support the interlocutory order, the matter must be heard *de novo*: *Fisher v. Fisher* (1990), 28 R.F.L. (3d) 324 (Ont. H.C.).

The court will not interfere with a discretionary order, such as an interim support order, unless the wrong principles of law had been applied or a patent injustice would have resulted: *Toulany v. Toulany* (1990), 99 N.S.R. (2d) 250, 270 A.P.R. 250 (C.A.).

Generally, appeal courts should not interfere with interim support orders, except where the order clearly does not meet the child's needs: *Bacon v. Bacon* (1991), 33 R.F.L. (3d) 170 (Sask. C.A.).

An appeal court should vary an interim support order only if it is clearly wrong or if serious or substantial injustice or prejudice would result: *Clancey v. Clancey* (1989), 22 R.F.L. (3d) 70, 91 N.S.R. (2d) 171, 233 A.P.R. 171 (C.A.). See also *MacIver v. MacIver* (1989), 21 R.F.L. (3d) 91 (Man. C.A.), where a similar principle was found to be applicable to interim custody orders.

An appellate court is justified in reducing an interim support order where, based upon the evidence, the amount awarded is significantly greater than the amount needed: *Muttart v. Muttart* (1991), 33 R.F.L. (3d) 439 (Sask. C.A.).

Where the quantum of the wife's interim support order was based upon events which, in the end, did not come about, the court allowed the husband's appeal from the order and cancelled arrears owing: *Martin v. Martin* (1993), 50 R.F.L. (3d) 77 (Sask. C.A.).

As a general rule, an appeal court will not interfere with an award for interim support, even if the quantum seems generous considering the payor's ability to pay and the trial cannot be heard for several months: *Carr v. Carr* (1989), 19 R.F.L. (3d) 281 (Man. C.A.).

An appeal from an interim support order should be prosecuted expeditiously. Where there is an unexplained delay in an appeal from an interim child support order and the court is therefore unable to fairly assess the current needs of the children, an appeal of an order refusing interim support may be dismissed: *Chutter v. Chutter* (1990), 26 R.F.L. (3d) 463 (B.C. C.A.).

Where the husband's standard of living could not possibly have been supported by the income the husband declared to the court, his appeal from an interim support award, based upon his allegations that he could not afford to pay, was dismissed: *Droit de la famille — 923* (November 7, 1990), Doc. No. C.A. Quebec 200-09-00697-877 (C.A. Que.).

In *Resch v. Resch* (1995), 12 R.F.L. (4th) 410, 102 Man. R. (2d) 7 (C.A.), the wife's interim support award of $2,000 monthly was upheld on appeal although the husband's monthly income had been reduced to $2,700. Although the award appeared to be large in respect of the husband's earnings and the wife's needs, the judge had properly taken into account factors such as the parties pre-separation lifestyle, the duration of the marriage, the wife's employment situation, the husband's continuing lifestyle and his company's financial situation.

There is no requirement that a party seeking to appeal an interim support order obtain leave to appeal under provincial civil procedure rules. Section 21(1) of the *Divorce Act* permits appeal without leave and prevails over any provincial rules: *Farden v. Farden* (1996), 141 Sask. R. 178, 114 W.A.C. 178 (C.A.).

The *Divorce Act* does not specifically vest power in the court to make interim orders which have the effect of varying the amount of maintenance ordered in a decree *nisi*: Laing v. Laing (1982), 30 R.F.L. (2d) 292 (Sask. Q.B.).

An order for interim maintenance cannot survive beyond the hearing of the petition. Therefore, a portion of the order providing that "provisional execution of the judgment is ordered notwithstanding appeal" can relate to an appeal of the interim order only and not to an appeal of the dismissal of the petition itself: *Doyle v. Doyle* (1975), 19 R.F.L. 335, 7 Nfld. & P.E.I.R. 341, 3 A.P.R. 341 (Nfld. T.D.).

The Court of Appeal has the power to grant interim alimony pending an appeal even to a wife who has been held disentitled to alimony at trial. This jurisdiction may be exercised by a judge of the Court of Appeal in chambers: *Kaye v. Kaye (No. 3)* (1975), 22 R.F.L. 240, 8 O.R. (2d) 94, 57 D.L.R. (3d) 190 (C.A.).

Local Masters of the High Court do not have normal jurisdiction to award interim alimony when an appeal from the trial on the question of alimony is pending before the Court of Appeal. The Court of Appeal has exclusive power over cases before it unless there be express authority granted to another court or officer: *Boyd v. Boyd* (1972), 9 R.F.L. 272 at 273, [1972] 3 O.R. 765 (H.C.).

The Master has jurisdiction to grant interim alimony pending an appeal in an alimony action and pending a reference as to quantum of alimony by the Court of Appeal: *MacDougall v. MacDougall*, [1971] 1 O.R. 770 (H.C.).

21§5C — Appeals — access

In *Gordon v. Goertz* (1996), 19 R.F.L. (4th) 177, [1996] 2 S.C.R. 27, 1996 CarswellSask 199, [1996] S.C.J. No. 52, 1996 CarswellSask 199F, [1996] 5 W.W.R. 457, 196 N.R. 321, 134 D.L.R. (4th) 321, 141 Sask. R. 241, 114 W.A.C. 241, (sub nom. *Goertz c. Gordon)* [1996] R.D.F. 209 (S.C.C.), the court varied the access order and permitted access to be exercised in Canada, in addition to Australia, the country to which the child was moving. The court found that there was no support in the evidence for restricting access to Australia. She would have more time with her father, keep up her relationships with friends and her extended family.

In *Wodehouse v. Woodhouse* (1995), 20 R.F.L. (4th) 337, 1996 CarswellOnt 1906, [1996] O.J. No. 1975, 136 D.L.R. (4th) 577, 91 O.A.C. 91, 29 O.R. (3d) 417 (Ont. C.A.); leave to appeal refused (1997), [1996] S.C.C.A. No. 402, 99 O.A.C. 80 (note), 209 N.R. 80 (note) (S.C.C.), the appellant mother claimed that the trial judge had overemphasized the assessor's evidence. She was of the view that the assessor had a preconceived opinion that frequent access with the father was the most important factor in determining the best interests of the children. She argued that if the trial judge had given the proper weight to the mother's position and the assessor's evidence, he would have permitted the mother to change the children's residence to Scotland. The appellate court found that the trial judge's reasons, taken as a whole, did not indicate any error. The trial judge acknowledged the value of the children being with a happy custodial parent, but was of the opinion that this factor did not outweigh the detriment that a move would cause. He decided that the best interests of the children would be served by allowing them to maintain their relationship with their father and their community in Ontario.

Where an 11-year-old child did not want to visit with her father, the children's lawyer had recommended the suspension of access. The trial judge suspended access and the appellate court upheld the ruling on appeal: *Lidkea v. Jarrell* (1999), 49 R.F.L. (4th) 324 (Ont. C.A.).

Where the judge did not specifically refer to "changes in circumstances" in making a variation order relating to access, the order was upheld on appeal given that there had been an abundance of evidence supporting changed circumstances: *F. (R.J.) v. F. (K.E.)* (1997), 33 R.F.L. (4th) 241 (Alta. C.A.).

An appellate court should not substitute its discretion for that of the trial judge in establishing the terms of a specified access order: *Lancaster v. Lancaster* (1992), 38 R.F.L. (3d) 373, 109 N.S.R. (2d) 88, 297 A.P.R. 88 (C.A.).

The fact that a motions judge did not give reasons when making an order terminating a father's access rights does not lead to an inference that he failed to consider material relevant to the issue: *Punzo v. Punzo* (1996), 21 R.F.L. (4th) 7, 89 O.A.C. 270.

Where the court terminated a father's access rights after an investigation by the Official Guardian, the court dismissed the father's appeal based upon the grounds that the chambers judge should have directed a trial of the issue on his own motion. In absence of an attempt by the father to cross-examine key witnesses or to seek an order directing a trial as an independent assessment, the trial judge had not erred: *Punzo v. Punzo* (1996), 21 R.F.L. (4th) 7, 89 O.A.C. 270.

In *Al-Maghazachi v. Dueck* (1995), 17 R.F.L. (4th) 132, 107 Man. R. (2d) 47 (C.A.), the wife's appeal from an order granting the husband access to the children was dismissed. The order which set stringent access terms under the supervision of a professional adequately balanced the wife's concerns for the children's safety with parental rights and the children's best interests.

An order barring a father from exercising his access rights should not be disturbed on appeal if made in the child's best interests and absent any error on the part of the trial judge. This is so even if alternative orders were available to the trial judge: *Gazdeczka v. Gazdeczka* (1989), 23 R.F.L. (3d) 200 (B.C. C.A.); leave to appeal to S.C.C. refused (1990), 25 R.F.L. (3d) xxxvii (note) (S.C.C.).

Where the children of the marriage aged 17, 15 and 11 had not seen their father in a number of years and expressly did not wish to, an order granting access to the father was reversed on appeal: *Strobridge v. Strobridge* (1994), 4 R.F.L. (4th) 169, 18 O.R. (3d) 753, 115 D.L.R. (4th) 489 (C.A.); reversing in part (1992), 42 R.F.L. (3d) 154, 95 D.L.R. (4th) 503, 10 O.R. (3d) 540 (Gen. Div.).

In *G. (E.W.) v. Z. (G.B.)* (1994), 8 R.F.L. (4th) 249 (B.C. C.A.), the court refused leave to appeal an order dismissing the husband's application for reinstatement of his access rights. The application had been refused on the basis that the husband had unilaterally ceased to pay child support. The husband based the appeal on the ground that he would resume support in exchange for supervised access. Leave was refused on the basis that the court should not be placed in a position of bargaining with litigants regarding how and when compliance with a court order will occur.

In *Dhaliwal v. Beloud* (1994), 7 R.F.L. (4th) 346 (B.C. C.A.), the court refused the mother's application for leave to appeal from an interim access order in the father's favour. As the trial had already been set up, the issues were best left to the trial judge after hearing testimony under oath.

21§6 — Appeals — custody

Divorce Act

In *Gordon v. Goertz*, 19 R.F.L. (4th) 177, [1996] 2 S.C.R. 27, 1996 CarswellSask 199, [1996] S.C.J. No. 52, 1996 CarswellSask 199F, [1996] 5 W.W.R. 457, 196 N.R. 321, 134 D.L.R. (4th) 321, 141 Sask. R. 241, 114 W.A.C. 241, (sub nom. *Goertz c. Gordon*) [1996] R.D.F. 209, the Supreme Court of Canada considered the issue of whether or not the trial and appeal courts erred in permitting a child to move away from her home in Saskatchewan to Australia with her mother, the custodial parent. The non-custodial parent who had exercised access regularly when the child was in Saskatchewan had been ordered to exercise access only in Australia once the child had moved there. The court held that where a parent applies for a variation of a custody order, there is no legal presumption in favour of the custodial parent, although the custodial parent's views are entitled to great respect. The only real test is the best interests of the child.

At the Supreme Court of Canada, the court was of the opinion that where, as in this case, the custody order sets out terms of access based on the assumption that the child's principal residence would be near the access parent, the relocation of the custodial parent and the child could not have been within the reasonable contemplation of the judge who issued the original permanent custody order. The move constituted a material change and the trial judge was required to make a fresh inquiry as to the best interests of the child.

Where, as in this case, the judge did not do so, it was appropriate that the Supreme Court of Canada should review the decision.

Madam Justice McLachlin held that the fact the child had been in her mother's custody for several years, that the reasons for granting the mother custody in the first place had not substantially changed, and that a change in custody would probably be difficult for the child, were reasons for granting custody to the mother. On the other hand, the move had greatly diminished the child's contact with her father, her extended family and her community in Canada. However, the fact that the father has the means to visit the child in Australia had helped to reduce the detrimental effect of the move on his relationship with her.

The Supreme Court of Canada ruled that the trial judge did not err in continuing the mother's custody of the child, even though she intended to move to Australia. However, the court could see no reason to restrict the father's access to Australia. Access in Canada would permit the child to maintain contact with friends and family. Thus the court affirmed the custody order and allowed the appeal in part, to permit the father to exercise access in Canada.

In *Ladisa v. Ladisa* (2005), 11 R.F.L. (6th) 50, 2005 CarswellOnt 268, 193 O.A.C. 336, [2005] O.J. No. 276 (C.A.), the court dismissed the mother's appeal of a joint custody order. The trial judge had properly considered the parties' history of co-parenting while they were married and the strong ties the children had to both parents.

An appellate court will interfere with a custody order only in cases of an error in principle or a clear factual error in a matter of significance: *Haider v. Malach* (1999), 48 R.F.L. (4th) 314, 177 Sask. R. 285, 199 W.A.C. 285, [1999] S.J. No. 315, 1999 CarswellSask 310 (C.A.); leave to appeal refused [1999] S.C.C.A. No. 374, 249 N.R. 398 (note), 189 Sask. R. 319 (note) (S.C.C.).

Where the trial judge had awarded custody of the child to the mother after finding that the father had convinced the child that he had been sexually assaulted by the mother, the father's appeal from the order was dismissed. The trial judge had properly concluded that the father's actions constituted a grave breach of parental responsibility, precluding him from the custodial role: *B. (S.L.) v. A. (G.)* (2004), 9 R.F.L. (6th) 35, 2004 CarswellAlta 1514, 2004 ABCA 366 (C.A.).

An appellate court should not overturn a custody order in the absence of a material error, a misapprehension of evidence or an error of law. Omissions in reasons for judgement amount to a material error, if they give rise to the reasonable belief that the trial judge must have forgotten, ignored or misconstrued evidence in a way that affects his conclusions: *Segal v. Segal* (2002), 26 R.F.L. (5th) 433, 2002 CarswellOnt 2228 (Ont. C.A.).

In an appeal from a custody matter, finding of fact should not be disturbed in the absence of a palpable and overriding error: *Myketiak v. Myketiak* (2001), 13 R.F.L. (5th) 431, 2001 CarswellSask 84, 2001 SKCA 17, 203 Sask. R. 90, 240 W.A.C. 90 (Sask. C.A.); affirming (1999), 185 Sask. R. 231, 1999 CarswellSask 693 (Sask. Q.B.).

In *Nunweiler v. Nunweiler* (2000), 5 R.F.L. (5th) 442, 186 D.L.R. (4th) 323, 78 B.C.L.R. (3d) 1, [2000] 8 W.W.R. 30, 2000 CarswellBC 958, [2000] B.C.J. No. 935, 2000 B.C.C.A. 300, 137 B.C.A.C. 1, 223 W.A.C. 1 (B.C. C.A.), a condition whereby the mother would lose custody of the child if she did not relocate to 20 miles of the city in which the father was resident was struck on appeal. The mother's move away, which frustrated the father's access, appeared to be based on sound financial reasons and not merely to frustrate the father's rights. The trial judge had focused more on the father's economic interests and insufficiently on the mother's financial situation and the probable impact of the change on the child.

In *P. (M.) c. L. (G.)* (1995), 18 R.F.L. (4e) 185, 1995 CarswellQue 188, (sub nom. *P. (M.) v. L.B. (G.))* 130 D.L.R. (4e) 382, (sub nom. *P. (M.) v. L.B. (G.))* [1995] 4 R.C.S. 592, (sub nom. *P. (M.) v. B. (G.L.))* 190 N.R. 182 (C.S.C.), the custodial parent violated a mobility clause in an agreement and moved outside the jurisdiction. The father's application for a change in custody was unsuccessful originally but the Court of Appeal granted him custody. The mother and child could not be found. At the Supreme Court of Canada, the only evidence before the court was of the mother's conduct and the father's evidence. Consequently, the court upheld the Court of Appeal decision and dismissed the mother's appeal.

In an application by a custodial parent to relocate with the child to another jurisdiction, the best interests of the child should be assessed from a perspective of the child. The proper test is whether there is any reason to believe that the move would not be in the best interests of the child: *Benoit v. Reid* (1995), 18 R.F.L. (4th) 136, 131 D.L.R. (4th) 346, 171 N.B.R. (2d) 161, 437 A.P.R. 161, 1995 CarswellNB 239, (sub nom. *J.B. v. M.D.R.)* [1995] N.B.J. No. 553 (N.B. C.A.). It is not a bar to an application for variation that an original order was made by consent.

Where the mother had been granted interm sole custody after difficulties arose in the joint custody arrangement when the mother began a new relationship, the husband's appeal was allowed and joint custody restored. There was no evidence justifying the disturbance of the *status quo* given that the parties' difficulties in dealing with one another was not adversely affecting the child: *Kiesman v. Lesperance* (1995), 17 R.F.L. (4th) 227, 107 Man. R. (2d) 231 (C.A.).

In *Marshall v. Marshall* (1998), 42 R.F.L. (4th) 180, 168 N.S.R. (2d) 48, 505 A.P.R. 48, 1998 CarswellNS 183, [1998] N.S.J. No. 172 (C.A.), the court allowed the father's appeal from an order granting the mother exclusive custody of the children. The father had not been represented by counsel at trial and did not appreciate the consequences when the trial judge had unilaterally changed an interlocutory application into a trial resulting in a final rather than an interim custody order.

In family matters involving support orders, any decision of the Court of Appeal not in accord with a lower court order is deemed to have been "made" as of the date of the order of the lower court: *Dennis v. Wilson* (1998), 42 R.F.L. (4th) 131, 115 O.A.C. 370, 1998 CarswellOnt 4478. An appeal court should only intervene in a custody case if the trial judge erred in principle or overlooked or disregarded material evidence: *Antoniuk v. Antoniuk* (1989), 22 R.F.L. (3d) 334 (Sask. C.A.).

Where the trial judge in custody proceedings has considered all the evidence and based his or her decision on the child's best interests, an appellate court should not intervene: *Levy v. Levy* (1994), 3 R.F.L. (4th) 281 (N.B. C.A.).

The determining factor in a custody dispute is the child's best interests. In the absence of evidence of an error in principle, an appeal court should not interfere with a trial judge's exercise of discretion in custody matters: *Hamonic v. Hamonic* (1990), 29 R.F.L. (3d) 16, 86 Sask. R. 250 (C.A.).

In *Bainton-Howe v. Bainton-Howe* (1995), 11 R.F.L. (4th) 89 (Alta. C.A.), a condition restricting the mother's access rights unless she underwent counselling for her tendency to be deceitful was removed on appeal. As there was no evidence that her acknowledged acts of deceit had any adverse effect on her parenting ability, the condition was not warranted.

In custody judgments, it is not required that the trial judge discuss extensively the expert evidence which was presented, and the failure to do so does not justify appellate intervention: *Bartesko v. Bartesko* (1990), 31 R.F.L. (3d) 213 (B.C. C.A.).

Where the trial judge had awarded joint custody despite ongoing animosity between the parties, sole custody was awarded to the mother on appeal. Expert evidence did not support the assumption that the parties' relationship would improve over time: *Stewart v. Stewart* (1994), 2 R.F.L. (4th) 53, 41 B.C.A.C. 213, 66 W.A.C. 213 (C.A.).

In *S. (B.A.) v. S. (M.S.)* (1991), 35 R.F.L. (3d) 400, 50 O.A.C. 267 (C.A.), the appellate court cited the trial judge's disregard of the tender years doctrine as one of the factors in reversing a decision whereby the father had been awarded custody of the parties' four-year-old child.

Where the custodial mother had remarried and divorced twice since divorcing the father and had moved to two different provinces the court nevertheless allowed the mother's appeal from an order changing custody to the father. There was insufficient evidence of a material change in circumstances to justify changing the custody order: *Baynes v. Baynes* (1990), 26 R.F.L. (3d) 34 (B.C. C.A.).

An appellant who complies with the Rules is entitled to pursue an appeal from a custody order, although success may appear unlikely. It is only when an appeal is clearly moot or hopeless that it will be summarily dismissed on that ground alone: *Starko v. Starko* (1991), 33 R.F.L. (3d) 277, 117 A.R. 159, 2 W.A.C. 159 (C.A.).

Where the wife had limited financial resources, the husband's application for security for costs on the wife's appeal of a custody order was dismissed as inappropriate: *Starko v. Starko* (1990), 29 R.F.L. (3d) 29 (Alta. C.A.).

On an appeal from a custody order, where the appellant did not oppose the other parent's claim in the court below, and cannot show that he or she was deprived of a fair hearing or that the order was not in the child's best interests, the appeal should be dismissed: *Kellington v. Kellington* (1991), 36 R.F.L. (3d) 118 (B.C. C.A.). Where the child's social worker had improperly played the role of both investigator and therapist in substantiating the child's allegations that the father had sexually abused her, the trial judge's findings of sexual misconduct could not be allowed to stand. However, as the child was afraid of the father, the sole custody award in the mother's favour was not disturbed on appeal: *T. (M.) v. T. (J.)* (1997), 33 R.F.L. (4th) 430 (Ont. Gen. Div.).

Divorce Act, 1968

A custody order should not be disturbed on appeal unless the appellant can show a manifest error on the part of the trial judge: *Margison v. Margison* (1977), 18 N.B.R. (2d) 238 (C.A.). "The law is well settled that a Court of Appeal should not interfere with an order of custody made by a trial Judge, unless it can be said that he did not make full judicial use of the opportunity given to him of seeing and hearing the parties — an opportunity denied to an appellate court. Or, to put it another way, an appellate court should not, in the absence of impelling reasons, interfere with the considered judgment of a trial Judge in custody cases": per Culliton C.J.S. in *Tew v. Tew* (1972), 5 R.F.L. 10 at 11 (Sask. C.A.).

In a custody matter, the decision of a trial judge, who has the advantage of hearing and seeing the parties, should not be overturned on appeal without the most impelling reasons: *Blanchette v. Blanchette* (1977), 1 A.R. 75 (C.A.).

In *Gazdeczka v. Gazdeczka* (1982), 30 R.F.L. (2d) 428 (B.C.C.A.), affirming 28 B.C.L.R. 69 (S.C.), the husband's appeal from an order awarding custody to the wife was dismissed in absence of any evidence that the trial judge had not made full judicial use of the opportunity of seeing and hearing the parties.

"In questions of custody the welfare of the infant is of paramount importance and an appellate court ought not to lightly interfere with the order of a trial judge who has the advantage of hearing the parties and the witnesses unless he has acted on some wrong principle or disregarded material evidence: vide *Zaremba v. Zaremba* (1968), 66 W.W.R. 372 (Sask. C.A.). While this is admittedly a difficult case to sort out and decide, this court should not interfere with the findings of the learned trial judge": per Woods J.A. in *Wakaluk v. Wakaluk* (1976), 25 R.F.L. 292 at 293 (Sask. C.A.).

"[The] exercise of a judge's discretion in custody proceedings should not be interfered with unless the judge acted on a wrong principle or disregarded any material evidence or failed to give any weight or any sufficient weight to any relevant consideration": per Cooper J.A. in *MacDonald v. Lee* (1970), 2 R.F.L. 360 at 365, 2 N.S.R. (2d) 301 (C.A.). See also *Nieforth v. Nieforth* (1974), 11 N.S.R. (2d) 10, 5 A.P.R. 10 (C.A.).

"There is a heavy burden on a trial Judge in a custody issue and his decision should not be replaced by that of an appellate tribunal unless there has been error in principle or misapprehension of the evidence by the trial Judge. In this case the trial Judge correctly stated that the paramount consideration was the welfare and happiness of the children. He reviewed a number of factors which might have tipped the balance in favour of one parent or the other without reaching any conclusion, but expressed the view that the children would be well cared for by either parent. He then returned to the ultimate question of the welfare and happiness of the children and decided that the final determination must depend upon who, as between [the appellant's girlfriend] and the respondent, must bear the main burden of their upbringing. In my opinion, in so doing he not only misdirected himself as to the proper question he had to decide but he misapprehended the evidence on a very important matter. . . . In view of the error of the trial Judge it is necessary for this Court to consider to whom the custody of the children should be granted": per Brooke J.A. in *Ellam v. Ellam* (1975), 21 R.F.L. 357 at 359-360 (Ont. C.A.).

"At the hearing of this appeal the appellant presented evidence . . . of matters that have occurred since the date of the decision appealed from. From the evidence two facts appear which I regard as important. The first is that without notice to or consent of the appellant, the boy was taken by the respondent in September 1973 to India and he has been there since that time. The second is that the boy is being properly cared for there by the respondent and his niece and is well and happy. When this evidence is considered, together with the fact that the boy lived in the same village in India from mid-1967 to mid-1968, I must ask myself what would be the effect on him to order now that custody be restored to the appellant who resides here. In my opinion, even assuming such an order could be made practically effective, it would involve at least grave danger of causing harm to the child. I would, therefore, dismiss the appeal as to custody": per McFarlane J.A. in *Hayre v. Hayre* (1975), 21 R.F.L. 191 at 192-193 (B.C. C.A.).

21§6A — Appeals — interim custody

In *Gamble v. Dyck-Gamble* (2000), 5 R.F.L. (5th) 323, 145 Man. R. (2d) 145, 218 W.A.C. 145, 2000 CarswellMan 134 (Man. C.A.), the Court refused both the appeal and cross-appeal from an interim order granting the custodial mother the temporary right to relocate the children to another province. The trial was pending and rather than pursue the appeal from the interim order — with its attendant costs and potential disruption for the children — quick movement to trial was preferable.

It is particularly important in custody matters that the decision of the trial judge should not be disturbed unless that judge clearly acted on some wrong principle or disregarded material evidence. This principle is even more important when interim custody is in issue: it is generally not in the best interests of children to disturb their status quo when it might be changed again at the next step of the divorce process: *Lancaster v. Lancaster* (1992), 38 R.F.L. (3d) 373, 109 N.S.R. (2d) 88, 297 A.P.R. 88 (C.A.).

A court in one province does not have jurisdiction pursuant to the *Divorce Act* to vary an interim custody order made in another province, where the parties were not former spouses: *Brooks v. Brooks* (1998), 39 R.F.L. (4th) 187, 1998 CarswellOnt 3097, 111 O.A.C. 177, 163 D.L.R. (4th) 715, 22 C.P.C. (4th) 209, 41 O.R. (3d) 191 (Ont. C.A.).

In *Lueck v. Green* (1993), 44 R.F.L. (3d) 206 (Y.T. C.A.), the court refused the father's appeal from an interim custody order whereby de facto custody of two of the parties' children had been transferred from the father to the mother. The children were already with their mother and settled. Furthermore, any credibility issues arising from the affidavit evidence presented at the hearing could not be settled through *viva voce* evidence at trial.

In *Trueman v. Nicholson* (1995), 15 R.F.L. (4th) 320, 32 Alta. L.R. (3d) 297, 169 A.R. 391 (C.A.) the mother's award of interim child custody was affirmed on appeal despite her plans to move with the child from Alberta to Connecticut. However, as a condition of the order, the mother was required to provide a written undertaking that she would return with the child to Alberta for the custody trial and that she would not raise any objections to the jurisdiction of the Alberta courts to determine the issue nor seek adjournments of the trial unless the father did something to frustrate the pre-trial process.

21§6B — Stay pending appeal

In *Tauber v. Tauber* (1999), 49 R.F.L. (4th) 429, 43 O.R. (3d) 53 (Ont. C.A. [In Chambers], the court allowed the father's application for a partial stay pending his appeal from a $17,000 monthly child support order. There were serious issues concerning the correctness of the precedent upon which the trial judge relied and, once paid, there was little likelihood that the father could recover the support payments if the appeal was successful. Accordingly, the father was, pending appeal, ordered to pay $11,000 monthly and to place the $6,000 balance into a trust account. Where the husband lost his job after an order was made requiring him to pay increased spousal support, a stay of the order was granted pending his appeal of it. The appeal had some merit and to dismiss the application for a stay would deprive the husband of his right to have the matter determined by the Court of Appeal: *Forbes v. Forbes* (1996), 22 R.F.L. (4th) 182 (B.C. C.A.).

It is appropriate to stay an order of spousal support pending an appeal from the order where the trial judge clearly acted on wrong principles without calculating the monetary results to both parties and both parties were, in the interim, able to take care of themselves. A stay is particularly appropriate where the appeal may ultimately result in no support being awarded: *Munro v. Munro* (1995), 17 R.F.L. (4th) 362, 84 O.A.C. 399, 25 O.R. (3d) 598 (C.A.).

Where a spouse has been found in contempt for not complying with the terms of a spousal support order, an appeal from the dismissal of the spouse's application to have the support order varied has no bearing on the finding of contempt. Accordingly, in such cases, an order staying committal pending the appeal is not appropriate: *Estrien v. Estrien* (1995), 10 R.F.L. (4th) 321, 79 O.A.C. 307 (C.A.).

In *Winkler v. Winkler* (1990), 27 R.F.L. (3d) 445, 71 D.L.R. (4th) 1, 66 Man. R. (2d) 285 (C.A.) an appeal was allowed from an order staying the wife's application for custody, access and support after her failure to pay an earlier cost order. The court should be cautious in granting stays in custody, access or support litigation, particularly so where it involves making financial considerations paramount to the children's interests.

A stay of a support order pending an appeal from that order should be made only on the clearest of evidence and in the most unusual circumstances: *Armstrong v. Armstrong* (1992), 40 R.F.L. (3d) 438, 55 O.A.C. 205 (C.A.).

Generally, an order for support should not be stayed pending an appeal. There are strong policy reasons for the enforcement, pending appeal, of support orders made at trial. Where a trial judge has heard all of the evidence and has made a decision, the dependants, and in particular children, should not be deprived pending appeal except on the clearest evidence and in the most unusual circumstances: *Armstrong v. Armstrong* (1992), 40 R.F.L. (3d) 438, 55 O.A.C. 205 (C.A.).

No stay of a trial judge's order regarding child and spousal support should be ordered pending appeal unless the moving party establishes undue prejudice or irreparable harm: *Zenner v. Zenner* (1991), 32 R.F.L. (3d) 11 (P.E.I. C.A.).

In *Pierce v. Pierce* (1994), 48 B.C.A.C. 130, 78 W.A.C. 130, the court allowed the husband's application for a stay of an interim support order requiring the husband to pay $5,000 monthly to the wife. Prior to separation, the husband had paid that amount to the wife as the operation's manager of his business. As that working relationship had come to an end with the parties' separation, the continuation of the payment was significantly more than merely maintaining the *status quo*.

In *Levesque v. Levesque* (1992), 41 R.F.L. (3d) 96 (Alta. C.A.), the court refused to order a stay pending the husband's appeal from a child support order. Although the appeal was based on the husband's inability to pay, he could, by rearranging his finances, manage the payments until the appeal was heard. Furthermore, if the appeal was allowed, the wife could set off any overpayment against future payments.

Generally, a court ought not to grant a stay of a custody order pending appeal where the stay effectively decides and concludes the issue on appeal: *Pankovic v. Pankovic* (1988), 15 R.F.L. (3d) 326 (B.C.C.A.).

Where the parties had shared joint custody of the child for two years prior to an order awarding sole custody to the wife, the court refused the husband's application for a stay of the order pending appeal. The trial judge had found that joint custody was not working and any return to joint custody, even on an interim basis, could prove stressful for the child: *Wigmore v. Wigmore* (1989), 24 R.F.L. (3d) 191 (Ont. C.A.).

In *Martini v. Martini* (1987), 8 R.F.L. (3d) 191 (B.C. C.A.), the mother's application for a stay of a custody order pending appeal was refused. If granted the child would be removed from his father's home and transferred to a new school which would not be in his best interests.

21§6C — Stay of appeal

In *Morris v. Morris* (1998), 39 R.F.L. (4th) 121, 1998 CarswellBC 835 (B.C. C.A.), the court refused the husband's application to dismiss an appeal from a consent order launched by the wife, but did grant a stay pending determination of the utility of the appeal. The wife had taken no steps after filing the notice of appeal and the stay placed the onus upon her to take further steps once the situation was clarified.

In *Benoit v. Reid* (1995), 17 R.F.L. (4th) 152, 168 N.B.R. (2d) 68 (C.A.), the court granted the husband's application for a stay of the wife's appeal from an order prohibiting her from removing the children from the jurisdiction. The wife had moved the child despite the order, had been found in contempt, and could not be allowed to proceed until she had purged her contempt.

21§7 — Appeals — Supreme Court of Canada

In *Chartier v. Chartier* (1997), 35 R.F.L. (4th) 255, 16 C.P.C. (4th) 277, [1998] 5 W.W.R. 424, 154 D.L.R. (4th) 442, 123 Man. R. (2d) 127, 159 W.A.C. 127 (C.A.), the wife was granted leave to appeal to the Supreme Court of Canada from a judgment (reported at 29 R.F.L. (4th) 96, 118 Man. R. (2d) 152, 149 W.A.C. 152, 154 D.L.R. (4th) 431, [1997] 8 W.W.R. 348 (Man. C.A.); reversing in part (1996), 111 Man. R. (2d) 27 (Man. Q.B.)) which found that the husband could unilaterally withdraw from an *in loco parentis* relationship with the wife's child. The issue was of national consequence, particularly given that the Manitoba Court of Appeal's approach to issues relating to the interpretation of "child of the marriage" differed from that adopted by other provincial courts of appeal. The carefully reasoned judgment at trial was reversed by the court of appeal without any indication of the reasons which led to that decision. The result is that on the appeal to [the Supreme Court of Canada] we do not have the benefit of knowing why the Appellate Division concluded that the judgment at trial was in error. The trial judge made findings of fact on the contested issues which, in my opinion, are amply supported by the evidence. In a case such as this, involving domestic discord brought about by a sudden reversion of the wife to the religion of her youth after 12 years of tranquil marriage, during which the wife shared her husband's religion and during which children were born who were being reared in that religion, there is considerable advantage in being able to observe the demeanour of the spouses in the witness box as well as to hear their evidence: per Laskin C.J.C., in allowing the appeal and restoring the trial judgment, in *Retzer v. Retzer*, 19 R.F.L. 365 at 366, [1975] 2 S.C.R. 881, 4 N.R. 159, 52 D.L.R. (3d) 159.

It is appropriate for a trial judge to take into account a party's continued employment when fixing the quantum of support, even if the parties have chosen a termination method of pension valuation whereby the pension was valued as though the husband terminated employment in 1988 and for support purposes, the court recognized that the husband was still employed in 1993: *Best v. Best* (1999), 49 R.F.L. (4th) 1, 174 D.L.R. (4th) 235, 242 N.R. 1, 123 O.A.C. 1, [1999] 2 S.C.R. 868, 1999 CarswellOnt 1995, 1999 CarswellOnt 1996 (S.C.C.).

In *P. (M.) c. L. (G.)* (1995), 18 R.F.L. (4th) 185, 1995 CarswellQue 188, (sub nom. *P. (M.) v. L.B. (G.))* 130 D.L.R. (4th) 382, (sub nom. *P. (M.) v. L.B. (G.))* [1995] 4 R.C.S. 592, (sub nom. *P. (M.) v. B. (G.L.))* 190 N.R. 182 (C.S.C.), the custodial parent violated a mobility clause in an agreement and moved outside the jurisdiction. The father's application for a change in custody was unsuccessful originally but on appeal, the Court of Appeal granted him custody. The mother and child could not be found. At the Supreme Court of Canada, the only evidence before the court was of the mother's conduct and the father's evidence. Consequently, the court upheld the Court of Appeal decision and dismissed the mother's appeal.

An order for interim support pending an appeal to the Supreme Court of Canada on a support issue will only be made in exceptional circumstances: *B. (G.) c. G. (L.)* (1994), 165 N.R. 237, 61 Q.A.C. 179 (C.S.C.).

"Due weight has to be given to the inestimable advantage of a trial judge who in considering a custody application, has seen the parties, observed them and thus obtained an opportunity to evaluate the character of the husband and wife. . .": per de Grandpré J., dealing with an application under the *Infants Act*, R.S.O. 1970, c. 222, in *Talsky v. Talsky*, 21 R.F.L. 27 at 28, [1976] 2 S.C.R. 292, 7 N.R. 246, 62 D.L.R. (3d) 267.

21§8 — Appeals — procedural grounds

Where the wife had personally served the husband with the petition for divorce in contravention of R. 57.10(2) of the *Nova Scotia Civil Procedure Rules* the court nevertheless dismissed the husband's appeal from the divorce and corollary relief judgments. The court had, under R. 2.01, the jurisdiction to cure the defect which, in this case was appropriate. Although well aware of the proceedings, the husband took no action and allowed the action to go through uncontested. His disagreement with the child support order could be properly addressed through an application to vary: *Hill v. Hill* (1997), 34 R.F.L. (4th) 18 (N.S. C.A.).

In *Druet v. Druet*, 35 R.F.L. (5th) 54, 2002 CarswellNB 431, 2002 CarswellNB 432, 2002 NBCA 88, 253 N.B.R. (2d) 317, 660 A.P.R. 317 (N.B. C.A.); affirming 239 N.B.R. (2d) 241, 619 A.P.R. 241, 2001 CarswellNB 230, 2001 NBQB 79 (N.B. Q.B.), it was found that the wife's failure to support her spousal support claim by way of counter-petition was a procedural error that did not render her claim a nullity. Despite the fact that her claim had been made only in the form of her "answer" to the husband's petition did not affect the trial judge's jurisdiction to make the order.

General

21.1 (1) Definition of "spouse" — In this section, **"spouse"** has the meaning assigned by subsection 2(1) and includes a former spouse.

(2) Affidavit re removal of barriers to religious remarriage — In any proceedings under this Act, a spouse (in this section referred to as the "deponent") may serve on the other spouse and file with the court an affidavit indicating

(a) that the other spouse is the spouse of the deponent;

(b) the date and place of the marriage, and the official character of the person who solemnized the marriage;

(c) the nature of any barriers to the remarriage of the deponent within the deponent's religion the removal of which is within the other spouse's control;

(d) where there are any barriers to the remarriage of the other spouse within the other spouse's religion the removal of which is within the deponent's control, that the deponent

(i) has removed those barriers, and the date and circumstances of that removal, or

(ii) has signified a willingness to remove those barriers, and the date and circumstances of that signification;

(e) that the deponent has, in writing, requested the other spouse to remove all of the barriers to the remarriage of the deponent within the deponent's religion the removal of which is within the other spouse's control;

(f) the date of the request described in paragraph (e); and

(g) that the other spouse, despite the request described in paragraph (e), has failed to remove all of the barriers referred to in that paragraph.

(3) Powers of court where barriers not removed — Where a spouse who has been served with an affidavit under subsection (2) does not

(a) within fifteen days after that affidavit is filed with the court or within such longer period as the court allows, serve on the deponent and file with the court an affidavit indicating that all of the barriers referred to in paragraph (2)(e) have been removed, and

(b) satisfy the court, in any additional manner that the court may require, that all of the barriers referred to in paragraph (2)(e) have been removed,

the court may, subject to any terms that the court considers appropriate,

(c) dismiss any application filed by that spouse under this Act, and

(d) strike out any other pleadings and affidavits filed by that spouse under this Act.

(4) Special case — Without limiting the generality of the court's discretion under subsection (3), the court may refuse to exercise its powers under paragraphs (3)(c) and (d) where a spouse who has been served with an affidavit under subsection (2)

(a) within fifteen days after that affidavit is filed with the court or within such longer period as the court allows, serves on the deponent and files with the court an affidavit indicating genuine grounds of a religious or conscientious nature for refusing to remove the barriers referred to in paragraph (2)(e); and

(b) satisfies the court, in any additional manner that the court may require, that the spouse has genuine grounds of a religious or conscientious nature for refusing to remove the barriers referred to in paragraph (2)(e).

(5) Affidavits — For the purposes of this section, an affidavit filed with the court by a spouse must, in order to be valid, indicate the date on which it was served on the other spouse.

(6) Where section does not apply — This section does not apply where the power to remove the barrier to religious remarriage lies with a religious body or official.

1990, c. 18, s. 2

21.1 — General

This section was enacted S.C. 1990, c. 18, s. 2.

Note that the barriers to remarriage discussed in s. 21.1 are only those barriers that the parties themselves can remove. The barriers discussed are not those which are solely within the control of the religious authorities to remove.

22. (1) **Recognition of foreign divorce** — A divorce granted, on or after the coming into force of this Act, pursuant to a law of a country or subdivision of a country other than Canada by a tribunal or other authority having jurisdiction to do so shall be recognized for all purposes of determining the marital status in Canada of any person, if either former spouse was ordinarily resident in that country or subdivision for at least one year immediately preceding the commencement of proceedings for the divorce.

(2) **Idem** — A divorce granted, after July 1, 1968, pursuant to a law of a country or subdivision of a country other than Canada by a tribunal or other authority having jurisdiction to do so, on the basis of the domicile of the wife in that country or subdivision determined as if she were unmarried and, if she was a minor, as if she had attained the age of majority, shall be recognized for all purposes of determining the marital status in Canada of any person.

(3) **Other recognition rules preserved** — Nothing in this section abrogates or derogates from any other rule of law respecting the recognition of divorces granted otherwise than under this Act.

22§1 — Presumption of validity

In an *obiter* remark in *Janes v. Pardo* (2002), 24 R.F.L. (5th) 44, 2002 CarswellNfld 16, 208 Nfld. P.E.I.R. 350, 624 A.P.R. 350 (Nfld. T.D.), the court was of the opinion that considering the presumption of the validity of a foreign divorce and modern day attitudes towards divorce, less stringent laws regarding divorce and the increased mobility of people, it should only be in the rarest of cases that foreign divorces are not recognized as valid. The rare cases would include those involving jurisdictional fraud. The concerns for situations where parties change residence so as to facilitate divorce no longer appear as serious as previously, except where the changes are intended to avoid responsibilities upon the breakdown of the marriage, such as responsibility for support or the division of matrimonial property.

The presumption of the validity of a marriage and that of the validity of a foreign divorce decree simply impose a duty upon the party against whom they operate to adduce some evidence in rebuttal. Once evidence has been led on each issue, the presumptions disappear: *Powell v. Cockburn*, 22 R.F.L. 155, [1977] 2 S.C.R. 218, 68 D.L.R. (3d) 700, 8 N.R. 215. See also *Bate v. Bate* (1978), 1 R.F.L. (2d) 298 (Ont. H.C.).

Where divorce proceedings take place before 1968, the provisions of s. 6 (now s. 22(2) and (3)), of the *Divorce Act* cannot be relied on: *Clarkson v. Clarkson*, 1978 CarswellMan 127, 86 D.L.R. (3d) 694 (Man. Q.B.).

22§2 — Invalidity of foreign divorces — standard of proof

The standard of proof required to establish the invalidity of a foreign divorce decree is proof on the balance of probabilities: *Abbruscato v. Abbruscato* (1974), 12 R.F.L. 257 (Ont. Prov. Ct.). See also *Powell v. Cockburn*, 22 R.F.L. 155, [1977] 2 S.C.R. 218, 68 D.L.R. (3d) 700, 8 N.R. 215.

22§3 — Recognition of religious divorces

Where the validity of a religious divorce is recognized by the law of the domicile of the petitioner, such a divorce should similarly be recognized in Canada: *Lozinko v. Bazylok (Lozinko)* (1977), 27 R.F.L. 141 (Ont. H.C.).

A decree of divorce pronounced by a Jewish rabbi is not effective to dissolve the marriage of the parties who are domiciled in Canada: *Favor v. Favor* (1972), 5 R.F.L. 197 (B.C. S.C.).

22§4 — Denial of natural justice in foreign proceedings

"I do not regard the service by publication of the petition in the divorce case in West Germany as something that invalidated the proceedings there. In my view it did not constitute a denial of natural justice. Even under Canadian law such a form of substituted service can occur": per Freedman C.J.M. in *Holub v. Holub*, 26 R.F.L. 263 at 264, [1976] 5 W.W.R. 527, 71 D.L.R. (3d) 698 (Man. C.A.).

"In Mendes Da Costa, Studies in Canadian Family Law (1972), vol. 2 at p. 967, the author makes the following observations [referring to the recognition of foreign divorces on the *Indyka* principle]: 'This is subject to the existing requirement that a decree should not be obtained by fraud, should not involve grave injustice, should not offend against the forum's concept of substantial justice, or that there should otherwise be a denial of natural justice'": per Lerner J. in *Rowland v. Rowland* (1974), 13 R.F.L. 311 at 325, 2 O.R. (2d) 161, 42 D.L.R. (3d) 205 (H.C.).

22§4A — Real and substantial connection with foreign jurisdiction

In *El Qaoud v. Orabi* (2005), 12 R.F.L. (6th) 296, 2005 CarswellNS 86, 2005 NSCA 28 (N.S. C.A.), the court, on appeal, upheld a judgement refusing to recognize the validity of the husband's Jordanian divorce decree. The parties had been married in Kuwait several years before becoming landed immigrants in Canada. The husband had visited Jordan for three days to obtain the divorce. As neither party had been resident in Jordan for one year prior to the divorce and neither had been domiciled there or had any real or substantial connection to Jordan, the divorce could not be recognized under s. 22 of the *Divorce Act*, R.S.C. 1985, c. 3 (2nd Supp.).

In *Janes v. Pardo* (2002), 24 R.F.L. (5th) 44, 2002 CarswellNfld 16, 208 Nfld. P.E.I.R. 350, 624 A.P.R. 350 (Nfld. T.D.), the parties were married in New Mexico and separated less than 2 years later. The husband applied for a divorce in a Newfoundland court and at about the same time the wife applied for and eventually obtained a divorce in a Montana court. There was no evidence before the Newfoundland court as to whether or not either party was ordinarily resident in Montara for at least one year immediately before the divorce proceedings were initiated in that state. The husband sought a ruling from recognized. The husband had divorced before the case of *Indyka v. Indyka* (1969), 1 A.C. 33, [1967] 2 All E.R. 689 (H.L.) which articulated the "substantial connection" rule and, it was argued, that rule did not operate retrospectively to affect the recognition of validity of the husband's 1957 divorce. The court was of the opinion that in England and Canada, the courts have given both retrospective and prospective effect to judicial decisions. Canadian courts have specifically applied *Indyka* to recognize foreign divorce decress prior to 1967. In these cases there is no mention that the courts are making a retrospective application to the common law and it may be that the courts assumed that the retrospective principle is so basic and inherent in law that it could be applied without comment.

The court held that the trial judge was correct to apply the *Indyka* rule to determine that the husband's divorce was valid as there existed a "real and substantial connection" within the meaning of *Indyka* between the petitioner (wife) and the husband as well and the state of California, the jurisdiction in which the divorce was granted.

See also *Casterton, Re*, 1978 CarswellOnt 366, 23 O.R. (2d) 24, 13 C.P.C. 192, 94 D.L.R. (3d) 290 (Ont. H.C.), where the former wife obtained a divorce in England in 1950 when, at the time of the divorce, a foreign divorce was only recognized if the husband were domiciled in the granting jurisdiction at the commencement of the divorce proceedings. In this case, the husband was domiciled in Canada both before and at the time of the commencement of the divorce. The court applied *Indyka* retrospectively and found that the wife who was at all time resident in the United Kingdom had a real and substantial connection with the High Court Justice which granted the decree.

In *Singh v. Mohammed* (1986), 41 Man. R. (2d) 235 (Q.B.), the court refused to recognize the husband's Oklahoma divorce where his connection with that state was a one month stay with relatives during a period of unemployment. The husband was found not to have been domiciled in Oklahoma.

Similarly, the court did not recognize a divorce obtained in Nevada in *Bate v. Bate* (1978), 1 R.F.L. (2d) 298, 1978 CarswellOnt 218 (Ont. H.C.), as there was no "real and substantial connection" between the petitioner and the granting state, Nevada. The petitioner went to Nevada for the sole purpose of obtaining a divorce and while there, was not permanently employed. She did not try to obtain a work or a sponsor and did not take out American citizenship. The court stated that in the case law a "real and substantial connection" has been shown by many diverse factors from residence, employment, nationality, citizenship and holding of property.

22§5 — Foreign divorces obtained by fraud

If a foreign court granting a divorce decree has been fraudulently misled into believing the jurisdictional facts are such as to give it jurisdiction, when in truth they are not, this will be a ground for refusal of the domestic court to recognize the decree. If, however, the fraud goes to the merits of the petition, domestic courts will not pay heed to it, as the substantive grounds upon which the decree is granted have never been of concern to the recognizing court. In cases involving fraud as to jurisdiction, it is open to a third party to impeach the foreign decree in the domestic court: *Powell v. Cockburn*, 22 R.F.L. 155, [1977] 2 S.C.R. 218, 68 D.L.R. (3d) 700, 8 N.R. 215.

22§6 — Preclusion from denying validity

"The present case stands, therefore, as one where the wife's formal submission to the foreign court [in Nevada] was not followed by any act or conduct in reliance upon it [the foreign decree] nor was there any acceptance by her of benefits under it. The Court of Appeal stated in its reasons that she 'in subsequent years, relying on that decree, held herself out to have been, and must be presumed to have wished to be considered as having been divorced from, and therefore no longer the wife of Dr. Downton'. Counsel for the respondent was unable to support this assertion before the Court. There was certainly no affirmative evidence to support it; there is only the fact of a previous separation and the fact that Dr. Downton brought a second wife back with him after the foreign divorce. I am unable to agree, therefore, that the appellant is precluded from denying the validity of the foreign divorce decree in Newfoundland and from insisting on her status as the lawful widow of the deceased": per Laskin J. dealing with an application under the *Family Relief Act*, S.N. 1962, c. 56 [now R.S.N. 1970, c. 124], in *Downton v. Royal Trust Co.*, 15 R.F.L. 43 at 55, [1973] S.C.R. 437, 3 Nfld. & P.E.I.R. 576, 34 D.L.R. (3d) 403.

Although in some instances, a spouse may be estopped from denying the validity of a foreign divorce, neither spouse is precluded from disputing the validity of their marriage. Thus a respondent husband who had married the applicant wife, after having obtained a divorce from his first wife which would not be recognized in Ontario, was not estopped in an application brought under the *Deserted Wives' and Children's Maintenance Act* from impugning that divorce and his subsequent marriage: *Reid v. Reid*, 6 R.F.L. 124, [1972] 1 O.R. 554, 23 D.L.R. (3d) 538 (Co. Ct.).

Where the plaintiff had herself obtained an invalid divorce in California, she was not later precluded from claiming widow's share under the *Dependants' Relief Act*, R.S.O. 1970, c. 126, with respect to the estate of her deceased Ontario-domiciled husband for the following reasons: (1) she received no pecuniary benefit from the divorce; (2) although she did rely on the divorce to the extent that she held herself out to be an unmarried woman, this was understandable since for 30 years after the divorce, she believed herself to be divorced and the law did not require her to go under her previous married name; (3) in the circumstances where Jones [the "husband"] himself acknowledged the invalidity of the Californian divorce, it would not be equitable for the court to insist on the contrary on his behalf or on behalf of those claiming through him. The pecuniary gifts she received from Jones after the divorce were received on the understanding that she was his wife, not that she was not; (4) the length of time that the plaintiff waited before impugning the divorce would not preclude her from doing so in the instant case having regard to: (a) her belief for 30 years that she was divorced, (b) her consideration for the feelings of the defendant Jones [the deceased's second "wife"], (c) the adverse reaction to doing so by Jones, and (d) his assurances that she would be looked after; and (5) no distinction should be drawn between the person who invokes the foreign jurisdiction and one who merely submits to it. Both participated one actively, one passively. Jones set the stage for a judgment of divorce by default: *Re Jones* (1974), 19 R.F.L. 289, 6 O.R. (2d) 11, 51 D.L.R. (3d) 655 (H.C.).

"I can readily find it inequitable to permit a man to go through a form of marriage with a woman, live with her for eight years and then deny the marriage. But in my view there are other very important considerations which militate against the application of the preclusion doctrine in this instance. The parties here have deliberately chosen to obtain a foreign divorce and enter into a marriage ceremony in a foreign state when the most cursory examination of the law would have shown the invalidity of both. Public policy cannot permit either party to claim any benefit from these invalid acts. It is one thing to say that a person cannot resort to a foreign divorce jurisdiction and then claim a benefit as if no divorce had been effected. It is quite another thing to say she can resort to a foreign divorce court patently without jurisdiction and then successfully claim a benefit by reason of a subsequent marriage; and this must be so even though her partner in that subsequent marriage was a knowing party to both transactions. Our laws of marriage and divorce must guide us all and cannot be ignored with impunity": per Grange J., dealing with an action for alimony, in *Fromovitz v. Fromovitz* (1978), 2 R.F.L. (2d) 145 at 155, 16 O.R. (2d) 751, 79 D.L.R. (3d) 148 (H.C.). See also *Re Jones* (1974), 19 R.F.L. 289, 6 O.R. (2d) 11, 51 D.L.R. (3d) 655 (H.C.); *Reid v. Reid*, 6 R.F.L. 124, [1972] 1 O.R. 554, 23 D.L.R. (3d) 538 (Co Ct.).

23. (1) Provincial laws of evidence — Subject to this or any other Act of Parliament, the laws of evidence of the province in which any proceedings under this Act are taken, including the laws of proof of service of any document, apply to such proceedings.

(2) Presumption — For the purposes of this section, where any proceedings are transferred to the Federal Court under subsection 3(3) or 5(3), the proceedings shall be deemed to have been taken in the province specified in the direction of the Court to be the province with which both spouses or former spouses, as the case may be, are or have been most substantially connected.

2002, c. 8, s. 183(1)(i)

23§1 — Standard of proof

"It is now settled that the standard of proof required in a divorce action ... is the standard required in civil actions where the preponderance of probabilities determines the issues. ... [I]t is sufficient if the circumstances are such as would lead the guarded discretion of a reasonable or just man to that conclusion": per Dubinsky J. citing Power on Divorce, 2nd ed., p. 425 in *Shaw v. Shaw* (1971), 4 R.F.L. 392 at 393, 7 N.S.R. (2d) 77 (T.D.). See also *Thompson v. Thompson* (1978), 29 R.F.L. 302 (P.E.I. S.C.); and *Coates v. Coates* (1974), 16 R.F.L. 117, 8 N.B.R. (2d) 1 (Q.B.).

"The standard of proof in divorce actions is the same as in other civil actions, that is, the court must be satisfied that adultery has been committed, based on a preponderance of probability, or, as it has been otherwise put, on such preponderance of evidence as to show that the conclusion sought is the most probable of the possible views of the acts": per Bull J.A. in *Adolph v. Adolph* (1964), 51 W.W.R. 42 at 44 (B.C. C.A.). See also *Kraft v. Kraft* (1969), 8 D.L.R. (3d) 744 (B.C. S.C.).

23§2 — Evidence — presumptions

"There would seem to be some confusion as to the legal effect of presumptions. In the case before us, there are three presumptions which may be relevant: (i) the presumption of the validity of the marriage ...; (ii) the presumption of validity of a foreign divorce decree ...; and (iii) the presumption in favour of the domicile of origin. ... Strictly speaking, they do not conflict or cancel each other out, nor do they give added probative value. Their only effect is to impose a duty on the party against whom they operate to adduce some evidence. ... They may, as in the present case, impose an alternating duty to produce evidence which shifts from one party to the other, a process which Wigmore describes as 'successive presumptions'": per Dickson J. in *Powell v. Cockburn*, 22 R.F.L. 155 at 161, [1977] 2 S.C.R. 218, 8 N.R. 215, 68 D.L.R. (3d) 700.

"The onus is then on the respondent to rebut the presumption of legitimacy, both children having been conceived and born in wedlock. Such rebuttal evidence must be: "strong, distinct, satisfactory, and conclusive" ... inconsistent with any logical conclusion other than that of illegitimacy': *Comeau v. Gauthier* (1970), 3 R.F.L. 55 at 57, 59 (Ont.); 'unquestionably decisive': *Minaker v. Minaker* (1971), 4 R.F.L. 48 at 49 (Man.); 'The highest degree of improbability, if it falls short of impossibility, will not suffice': *Re G.* (1974), 14 R.F.L. 201 at 203, 1 O.R. (2d) 318, 40 D.L.R. (3d) 198": per Gravely Prov. J. in *Johnston v. Johnston* (1975), 23 R.F.L. 367 at 369, 10 O.R. (2d) 249 (Prov. Ct.). See also *L. v. P.* (1978), 27 N.S.R. (2d) 283, 41 A.P.R. 283 (T.D.).

"The presumption of legitimacy in the case of a child born to a married woman is, of course, one of the strangest presumptions known to the law: it can only be rebutted by evidence that is unquestionably decisive to the contrary. This being so it is necessary to scrutinize closely and weigh carefully evidence tending to bastardize issue of a married woman, particularly when, as in the instant case, assess on the part of the husband and sexual relations were admitted for the period in which, in the course of nature, the child was conceived": per Schultz J.A. in *Wikstrom v. Children's Aid Society of Winnipeg*, 16 W.W.R. 577 at 582, 63 Man. R. 272, [1955] 5 D.L.R. 45 (C.A.).

23§2A — Evidence — striking petition

Evidence adduced on discovery is not to be used on a motion to strike a divorce petition as disclosing no reasonable cause of action. In such an application, the allegations of fact contained in the petition are to be assumed as true: *Murphy v. Murphy* (1987), 15 C.P.C. (2d) 225, 78 N.B.R. (2d) 279, 198 A.P.R. 279 (Q.B.).

23§3 — Proof of marriage

"These days it is normally convenient to prove births, deaths and marriages by production of a certificate. Mrs. Porteous might simply have produced a certificate which the person solemnizing the marriage ordinarily gives to those being married: alternatively she might have produced an authenticated extract from the marriage records of the state of Minnesota. Failure to produce evidence from the register of marriages in respect of a marriage of known date and place may not be fatal to Mrs. Porteous's case ... but in the absence of a certificate of satisfactory explanation for non-production the reference to a marriage contained in a delayed certificate of birth can carry little or no weight. An alternative manner of making out her case would have been to adduce facts supportive of a presumptive marriage at the critical time, i.e., prior to her birth. If persons live together as man and wife for such length of time in such circumstances as to have acquired local repute as married, a presumption that they are legally married may arise, which can only be displaced by cogent evidence to the contrary": per Dickson J. in *Porteous v. Dorn*, 17 R.F.L. 144 at 146, [1975] 2 S.C.R. 37, 2 N.R. 501, [1974] 6 W.W.R. 176, 45 D.L.R. (3d) 596. See also *Smith v. Goulet* (1974), 19 R.F.L. 45, 5 O.R. (2d) 337, 50 D.L.R. (3d) 321 (C.A.).

"The evidence of Sammy N. Kerba, a solicitor qualified both in Egypt and in Ontario, persuades me that this was a form of marriage recognized in Egypt where it was celebrated, and that it is a valid marriage under Egyptian law. Exhibit 5 is said to be a translation of a certificate of marriage, and this is sworn by Mr. Kerba to be a valid document under the Egyptian law. Both parties acknowledge the marriage and while the document referred to does not of itself prove the marriage in a manner satisfactory to our procedure, I accept the evidence of both parties that the marriage did in fact take place and the evidence of Mr. Kerba that if it took place as described in the certificate it is a valid marriage": per Osler J. in *El-Sohemy v. El-Sohemy* (1978), 3 R.F.L. (2d) 184 at 186, 21 O.R. (2d) 35, 89 D.L.R. (3d) 145 (H.C.).

"Documentary evidence of a marriage is not a requisite of proof. Statutory presumptions arising from certificates of registration greatly facilitate proof of marriage and are now the customary method used, but they do not displace proof by oral evidence": per Trainor L.J.S.C. in *Uppal v. Uppal* (1977), 2 R.F.L. (2d) 287 at 288 (B.C. S.C.).

"Where a man and woman have cohabited for such a length of time and in such circumstances as to have acquired the reputation of being man and wife, a lawful marriage between them will generally be presumed, although there may be no positive evidence of any marriage having taken place and the presumption can be rebutted only by strong and weighty evidence to the contrary. ... Where there is evidence of a ceremony of marriage having been gone through, followed by the cohabitation of the parties, everything for the validity of the marriage will be presumed, in the absence of decisive evidence to the contrary": per Goodman J. in *Lozinko v. Bazylok (Lozinko)* (1976), 27 R.F.L. 141 at 151 (Ont. H.C.).

"In March 1942 [the petitioner] married one Endra Becsei in her native town and they lived together for some ten weeks, until he was conscripted for forced labour by the German army and sent off with other unfortunates into Russian territory. She never saw him again. ... His death has not been strictly proved before me. I do not consider, however, that the mere possibility of his survival can displace the presumption of regularity and validity which operates in favour of the marriage between the parties on 31st July, 1969 in British Columbia": per McIntyre J. in *Favor v. Favor* (1971), 5 R.F.L. 197 at 197 (B.C. S.C.). See also *Re Spears* (1970), 15 D.L.R. (3d) 494 at 502 (N.S. Co. Ct.); *Re Karnenas* (1978), 3 R.F.L. (2d) 213 at 218 (Ont. Surr. Ct.).

23§4 — Hearsay evidence

"Where a 4½-year-old child is concerned, it is impossible to determine the effect of custody and access upon her without listening to some hearsay. As I indicated during the course of the evidence, however, I have disregarded such evidence where its tendency is to prove the truth of what [the child] is supposed to have said, and I have considered only the significance of the fact that she has said it. I bear in mind too that each side may be expected to have and I believe has remembered or emphasized only those things said by [the child] which tend to advance their respective causes": per Spencer L.J.S.C. in *Pierce v. Pierce*, [1977] 5 W.W.R. 572 at 574 (B.C. S.C.).

23§5 — Proof of paternity

Sections 4 to 7 of the *Children's Law Reform Act*, S.O. 1977, c. 41, do not create within themselves an exclusive means for the determination of paternity. Many courts in Ontario may in the course of various proceedings confirm or make a finding of paternity: *Z v. Z.* (1978), 2 R.F.L. (2d) 297, 20 O.R. (2d) 653 (Prov. Ct.). See also *Re B and B* (1977), 17 O.R. (2d) 332, 80 D.L.R. (3d) 266 (C.A.).

"It is the well-known practice of the Courts in Nova Scotia [in paternity matters] to act upon the evidence of the mother alone if it is believed by the magistrate": per Currie J. in *L. v. P.* (1978), 27 N.S.R. (2d) 283 at 288, 41 A.P.R. 283 (T.D.).

See also *Ganase v. Assick* (1976), 28 R.F.L. 240 at 241 (Ont. Prov. Ct.); *Panaccione v., McNab* (1976), 28 R.F.L. 182 (Ont. Prov. Ct.).

23§6 — Blood tests

In *C. (M.) v. C. (L.A.)* (1990), 24 R.F.L. (3d) 322, 42 B.C.L.R. (2d) 379, [1990] 3 W.W.R. 263, 66 D.L.R. (4th) 421 (C.A.), an appeal from a decision dismissing the husband's application for an order directing tissue typing tests to determine paternity in divorce proceedings, the court ordered that the respondent mother and child should submit to blood tests. An order for tests under the British Columbia rules was discretionary. It is in the interest of justice that the court should have the best possible evidence before it, and consequently, the tests should be performed.

"[There] is no authority for a Judge of the Court of Queen's Bench or any other Court to order that a blood test be taken of an adult without his or her consent or, in the case of a child, without the consent of the mother. The right of privacy is fundamental to any free society and should not be infringed upon by any court in the absence of clear and unequivocal statutory authority. That right must prevail even in the face of a cogent argument that blood test results may be valuable evidence in paternity proceedings. The best evidence rule ought to be pursued with vigour but it cannot be allowed to infringe upon the right of privacy in the absence of a clear expression of legislative will. In the present case, the mother refuses consent to a blood test for herself and her child, and in the absence of statutory authority of the kind mentioned, there is no jurisdiction to order that such a test be done and no adverse consequences should result from the refusal of the mother to give her consent": per Hall J.A. in *J. v. N.*, 28 R.F.L. 234 at 236, [1976] 5 W.W.R. 211, 69 D.L.R. (3d) 347 (Man. C.A.). See also *Panaccione v. McNab* (1976), 28 R.F.L. 182 at 185–186 (Ont. Prov. Ct.); *Dollighan v. Dollighan* (1978), 3 R.F.L. (2d) 210 (Ont. Co. Ct.).

"[Where] a court is asked to decide the issue of paternity, it should have before it the best evidence available and that should include expert scientific evidence by means of a blood test. When one of the parties is prepared to submit to such a test, whereas the other refuses to do so, then I am of the view that the court can, and indeed should, make the appropriate inferences from such refusal": per Karswick Prov. J. in *Panaccione v. McNab* (1976), 28 R.F.L. 182 at 185–186 (Ont. Prov. Ct.).

Landsteiner blood group tests may exclude a man from having fathered a child where ordinary tests show his blood type to be compatible with paternity, though not conclusive: *Dollighan v. Dollighan* (1978), 3 R.F.L. (2d) 210 (Ont. Co. Ct.).

23§7 — *Res judicata*

"My conclusion is that in the present case, since the definition of cruelty and the evidence required to establish it in this action for divorce are different from those which applied in the prior proceedings for judicial separation, it cannot be said that in the prior case the same question, right or fact was determined. In such circumstances it is my view that the doctrine of res judicata does not apply, and certainly should not be given effect prior to the submission of evidence": per Smith C.J.M. in *Galbraith v. Galbraith* (1969), 1 R.F.L. 77 at 82, 69 W.W.R. 390, 5 D.L.R. (3d) 543 (Man. C.A.).

"[W]hile a judgment for divorce is surely a judgment *in rem* (and so conclusive evidence against the whole world) it is the judgment itself that bears this characteristic and not the grounds upon which it might have been based. The grounds found to justify the judgment raised an estoppel *inter partes* only. ... It follows that the admissibility of the judgments granted in the *Darcie* action has nothing to do with the principle of *res judicata*. Even if it did, it would not be binding on the Court or relieve the Court from its statutory duty of determining whether or not a decree of divorce should be granted in this case": per Misener Co. Ct. J. in *McGregor v. McGregor* (1977), 20 O.R. (2d) 680 at 685, 88 D.L.R. (2d) 419 (H.C.).

"Referring back to the present case, it is a matter of court record that adultery has been established, in *Richards v. Richards and Coles* [unreported], as between Richards and Coles. That same adultery is the issue in *Coles v. Coles and Richards* here. I therefore accept the proven record in *Richards v. Richards* as establishing the fact of adultery between Richards and Coles and hence the proof required in the present case, and find that the petitioner herein is, consequently, entitled to the decree sought": per McQuaid J. in *Coles v. Coles* (1977), 4 R.F.L. (2d) 277 at 280 (P.E.I. S.C.).

A finding of adultery under the *Deserted Wives' and Children's Maintenance Act*, R.S.S. 1965, c. 341, may be used only under that Act: *Moch v. Moch*, 20 R.F.L. 305, [1975] 4 W.W.R. 525 (Sask. Q.B.).

A decree for divorce on the grounds of adultery as between petitioner A and respondents B and C, is *res inter alios acta* and is not admissible in evidence, and has no probative value in a hearing for divorce on the grounds of adultery brought by petitioner D, against respondents B and C: *Meshwa v. Meshwa* (1970), 2 R.F.L. 234, 75 W.W.R. 459, 13 D.L.R. (3d) 502 (B.C. S.C.), following *Lingor v. Lingor* (1954), 13 W.W.R. 446 (B.C. S.C.).

"To summarize, the divorce court must not merely ratify the judgment granting the action for separation from bed and board. The latter judgment may only be invoked to explain why the parties have lived separate and, insofar as corollary relief is concerned, the reasons for the judgment may only constitute certain elements of evidence": per Fournier J. in *Desmeules v. Bolduc*, 4 R.F.L. 76 at 82–83, [1971] Que. S.C. 151.

"A judgment for divorce on the grounds of adultery between A and B makes the issue of adultery res judicata. It is a judgment in rem; that is to say, one that is good not only between the parties and their privies, but good as against the world and this is so because it is a judgment affecting status": per Ferguson J. in *Love v. Love*, 1 R.F.L. 193 at 194, [1969] 1 O.R. 291, 2 D.L.R. (3d) 273 (H.C.).

23§8 — Evidence from previous proceedings

In an affiliation proceeding the mother sought to introduce as corroborative evidence that evidence given by a witness (since disappeared) in a divorce action in which the father was the respondent and which related to his wish to have the mother procure an abortion of the child in question. It was held the document was admissible as it satisfied the following four requirements: (1) the party against whom the evidence was tendered was a party in the judicial proceeding from which that evidence arose; (2) there was an identity of issue in the two proceedings, namely, sexual intercourse; (3) the father in the divorce proceeding had a full opportunity for cross-examination; and (4) there was proof that the witness whose evidence was presented in transcript form was unavailable: *Serediuk v. Kogan*, 28 R.F.L 237, [1976] 5 W.W.R. 571 (Man. C.A.). See also *Smith v. Goulet* (1974), 19 R.F.L. 45, 5 O.R. (2d) 337, 50 D.L.R. (3d) 321 (C.A.).

In *Van Ginkel v. Van Ginkel* (1975), 20 R.F.L. 359 at 361 (Man. Q.B.), the court rejected the petitioner's attempt to have transcripts from the trial of his first divorce petition, which had not been successful, accepted as evidence at the trial of a subsequent petition. Per Dewar C.J.Q.B.: "While the parties to both proceedings are the same, the issues are not. In her answer to the second petition the respondent has denied that the petitioner is domiciled in Canada. This places the matter of jurisdiction in issue. According to the pleadings in the first proceeding, residence but not domicile was an issue. Whereas in the first proceedings the petition indicates that the petitioner was relying on his own residence qualifications to invoke jurisdiction, he now relies on the residence qualifications of the respondent. These two differences suggest that there have been changes in the circumstances of the petitioner during the 17-month period between the dates of presentation of the respective petitions and these changes have resulted in a new and substantial issue. There being no dispute as to domicile in the first trial, it cannot be said that there was a full opportunity of cross-examination."

"Counsel for the petitioner has cited a number of authorities in support of his contention that the evidence in The Children of *Unmarried Parents Act* case [an affiliation proceeding] is admissible in proof of the respondent's adultery, but, upon analysis, I am afraid they are all against him. Halsbury, The Laws of England, 3rd ed., and Phipson on Evidence, 11th ed. (1970), each contain a succinct summary of the conditions of admissibility at common law of testimony taken in former proceedings. These are: (1) That the proceedings are between the same parties or their privies; (2) That the same issues are involved; (3) That the party against whom the evidence is tendered had on the former occasion a full opportunity of cross-examination; and (4) That the witness is incapable of being called on the second trial": per McLellan L.J.S.C. in *Harvey v. Harvey* (1974), 26 R.F.L. 342 at 343–344, 16 N.S.R. (2d) 350, 53 D.L.R. (3D) 728 (T.D.). See also *Re Soroka Estate* (1975), 25 R.F.L. 169, 10 O.R. (2d) 638, 64 D.L.R. (3d) 234 (H.C.).

23§9 — Fresh evidence on appeal

Divorce Act, 1985

In *Scott v. Scott* (2004), 10 R.F.L. (6th) 135, 2004 CarswellNB 587, 2004 CarswellNB 588, 2004 NBCA 99, [2004] N.B.J. No. 468 (C.A.), the wife's unsupported evidence concerning her medical condition and her resulting inability to work regularly was considered sufficient to establish those facts in the husband's application to terminate her support. Her evidence alone was, however, found insufficient to establish her adult child's medical disability.

In *Wright v. Wright* (1996), 21 R.F.L. (4th) 201, [1996] 4.W.W.R. 1, 141 Sask. R. 44, 114 W.A.C. 44 (C.A.), the court agreed to admit fresh evidence on the father's appeal from a child support order. As the parties wished to resolve the issues expeditiously and as some time had passed since the date of the original order it was best to consider the evidence in the appeal rather than require the father to initiate a separate variation proceeding.

In *Kowalewich v. Kowalewich*, 19 R.F.L. (5th) 354, 2001 CarswellBC 1404, 2001 BCCA 452 (B.C. C.A.), the court allowed the husband's appeal from the dismissal of his application to vary downward both the spousal and child support payable by him. A new hearing was ordered and new evidence produced by the husband including financial statements, income tax summaries and medical reports, was to be considered. None of this evidence had been available to the husband at the time of his original application.

In *Inkumsah-Cosper v. Cosper* (1995), 14 R.F.L. (4th) 152, 141 N.S.R. (2d) 344, 403 A.P.R. 344 (C.A.), the court refused the wife's application to appeal from a consent order dealing with corollary relief issues. The wife's claim that she had been pressured into making the agreement was insufficient justification to allow the introduction of fresh evidence. If the wife had a remedy, it would potentially be against her solicitor.

Where the trial judge's assessment of spousal and child support is based upon mathematical confusion over the husband's net income, the appellate court is obliged to admit fresh evidence to clear up the confusion: *Escaravage v. Escaravage* (1995), 14 R.F.L. (4th) 256, 59 B.C.A.C. 113, 98 W.A.C. 113 (C.A.).

In order to introduce new evidence on an appeal from a support order, the applicant must establish that the evidence was not discoverable before the end of the trial and that the evidence was practically conclusive of an issue in the action: *Mullin v. Mullin* (1992), 102 Nfld. & P.E.I.R. 306, 323 A.P.R. 306 (P.E.I. C.A.).

The husband's application to introduce fresh evidence on an appeal from a spousal support order was dismissed in light of the finding that the evidence could have been obtained at the time of the trial with reasonable diligence: *Henderson v. Sharma-Henderson* (1994), 7 R.F.L. (4th) 317 (Ont. C.A.); affirming (1993), 47 R.F.L. (3d) 388 (Ont. Gen. Div.).

A Court, in a family law matter, may admit fresh evidence on appeal, even if such evidence was available at the time of trial, if its absence would lead to a long term injustice to the applicant: *Cheng v. Cheng* (1994), 4 R.F.L. (4th) 442, 46 B.C.A.C. 63, 75 W.A.C. 63 (C.A.).

In *Shabaga v. Shabaga* (1992), 43 R.F.L. (3d) 220, 75 B.C.L.R. (2d) 128 (C.A.), the court allowed the husband's application to introduce fresh evidence in an appeal from an order dismissing a variation of spousal support. Although the evidence was available at the time of the original hearing, the court held that the rule restricting fresh evidence on appeal should be given a more elastic approach in the content of matrimonial proceedings.

In *Swift v. Swift* (1992), 44 R.F.L. (3d) 250, 61 O.A.C. 225 (Div. Ct.), the court refused, on the wife's appeal from a dismissal of her application for increased support, to allow fresh evidence concerning her health problems and her husband's improved means. The evidence relating to her health had been available at the time of trial and that relating to her husband's improved finances was properly the subject of a variation application.

Where the father had not made full financial disclosure at trial he was not allowed to adduced fresh financial evidence on his appeal from the dismissal of his application for reduced child support. The evidence would have been available at trial had the husband applied due diligence: *Edwards (Pereira) v. Edwards* (1994), 5 R.F.L. (4th) 321 (N.S. C.A.); affirming (1993), 126 N.S.R. (2d) 341, 352 A.P.R. 341 (S.C.); additional reasons at (1994), 127 N.S.R. (2d) 379, 355 A.P.R. 379 (S.C.).

23§10 — Privilege

In *Bartkowski v. Bartkowski*, 37 R.F.L. (5th) 242, 2003 CarswellBC 712, 2003 BCSC 490 (B.C. S.C. [In Chambers]), the court refused to admit into evidence at the parties' child support proceedings "without prejudice" documents that were exchanged between the parties during earlier settlement negotiations. The communications were clearly "without prejudice" and the attempt to introduce them into evidence was unforgivable.

Divorce Act, 1985

Only in the rarest of circumstances in family matters should privilege for pre-action and pre-trial discussions not be allowed. The parties and their representatives must be assured that all negotiations can be comprehensive and without prejudice should issues proceed to trial. The filing as an exhibit by one spouse of a letter from that spouse's lawyer inviting the other spouse to negotiate does not breach privilege: *Lozano v. Lozano* (1991), 35 R.F.L. (3d) 218 (Ont. Master).

Divorce Act, 1968

"The law in Ontario in respect to privilege attaching to communications made 'without prejudice' is set out in the headnote to the case of *Pirie v. Wyld* (1886), 11 O.R. 422 (C.A.)., to the following effect: 'All communications expressed to be written without prejudice and fairly made for the purpose of expressing the writer's views on the matter of litigation or dispute, as well as overtures for settlement or compromise, and which are not made with some other object in view and wrong motives, are not admissible in evidence'. At pp. 427–28 Cameron C.J. said: 'The authorities seem, though not very numerous, to be clear upon the first point, that letters written or communications made without prejudice, or offers made for the sake of buying peace, or to effect a compromise, are inadmissible in evidence. It seemingly being considered against public policy as having tendency to promote litigation, and to prevent amicable settlements. The language used in the cases is sufficiently wide to cover all communications made under the words 'without prejudice'. The cases in which the rejection of such letters or communications has taken place have generally contained some offer of settlement.' It is clear from the foregoing that the communication may be oral as well as written, so long as the purpose of it is made for settling an existing dispute. ... It is not necessary that the words 'without prejudice' be expressed; it is sufficient if they may be implied. ... There have been cases in England where the courts have held in matrimonial matters that where the parties have consulted a probation officer it follows litigation is imminent and communication with him by the parties leading to reconciliation are privileged. ... If communications between husband and wife through the medium of a third party are privileged, a fortiori, the communications between husband and wife directly are privileged": per Master McBride in *Hillesheim v. Hillesheim* (1974), 19 R.F.L. 42 at 43–44, 6 O.R. (2d) 647 (Master).

The court has a discretion not to admit medical records relating to venereal disease on the ground of public policy. There is, however, no common law doctor-patient privilege against disclosing this evidence: *Carter v. Carter* (1974), 19 R.F.L. 363, 6 O.R. (2d) 603, 53 D.L.R. (3d) 491 (H.C.).

"[I] think it is inimical to a fair trial to force a psychiatrist to disclose the things he has heard from a patient, and, in addition to that, I think it rather shocking that one profession should attempt to dictate the ethics of another, which the courts are doing when they see fit to state what a doctor will say and what he will not": per Steward J. in *Dembie v. Dembie* (1963), 21 R.F.L. 46 at 50 (Ont. H.C.).

Where the wife during the course of an application for interim custody sought to introduce into evidence a psychologist's report which had been prepared during an earlier mediation attempt, it was held that the report was inadmissible. The mediation had been carried out for the purpose of settling issues that were the subject of pending litigation and the information obtained by the psychologist was therefore privileged on the basis that the parties had been engaged in "without prejudice" negotiations: *Porter v. Porter* (1983), 32 R.F.L. (2d) 413, 40 O.R. (2d) 417 (U.F.C.).

23§11 — Counsel as potential witness

Where the wife intended to call the husband's counsel as a witness in the matter involving the determination of the existence of a valid separation agreement, the husband's counsel was ordered disqualified from acting for the husband. On appeal, the disqualification was reversed. The counsel was intended to give evidence concerning the husband's credibility and it was held that such issues should be resolved in the usual evidentiary manner. There was no basis justifying the calling of counsel as a witness: *Hutchinson v. Hutchinson*, 25 R.F.L. (5th) 289, 2002 CarswellMan 111, 2002 MBCA 36, 163 Man. R. (2d) 249, 269 W.A.C. 249 (Man. C.A.).

Where the husband's counsel filed his own affidavit in the husband's application for variation of custody, access and support the court granted the wife's motion to have the counsel removed as solicitor of record. The counsel's affidavit outlined the husband's knowledge at the time the parties' domestic contract was executed, which was an issue relevant to the proceedings. As there was a real likelihood that the counsel would be called as a witness, there was a possibility of a real conflict arising. The factors justifying the removal outweighed the impact on the husband of having to change counsel: *Leopold v. Leopold* (1999), 45 R.F.L. (4th) 362 (Ont. Gen. Div.); reversed (1999), 48 R.F.L. (4th) 388 (Ont. C.A.).

Conversations between a lawyer and his client regarding the client's state of mind when executing a separation agreement is privileged and not admissable in an application to vary the support provisions contained in the agreement. Neither the fact that the lawyer might have relevant evidence to give on a variation motion, nor the fact that the client husband had no recall of his contemplated future circumstances when he executed the agreement, rendered the communication with the lawyer compellable evidence. Accordingly, an order removing the lawyer as solicitor of record was reversed on the husband's appeal: *Leopold v. Leopold* (1999), 48 R.F.L. (4th) 388 (Ont. C.A.); reversing (1999), 45 R.F.L. (4th) 362 (Ont. Gen. Div.).

24. Proof of signature or office — A document offered in a proceeding under this Act that purports to be certified or sworn by a judge or an officer of a court shall, unless the contrary is proved, be proof of the appointment, signature or authority of the judge or officer and, in the case of a document purporting to be sworn, of the appointment, signature or authority of the person before whom the document purports to be sworn.

25. (1) Definition of "competent authority" — In this section, **"competent authority"**, in respect of a court, or appellate court, in a province means the body, person or group of persons ordinarily competent under the laws of that province to make rules regulating the practice and procedure in that court.

(2) Rules — Subject to subsection (3), the competent authority may make rules applicable to any proceedings under this Act in a court, or appellate court, in a province, including, without limiting the generality of the foregoing, rules

(a) regulating the practice and procedure in the court, including the addition of persons as parties to the proceedings;

(b) respecting the conduct and disposition of any proceedings under this Act without an oral hearing;

(b.1) respecting the application of section 17.1 in respect of proceedings for a variation order;

(c) regulating the sittings of the court;

(d) respecting the fixing and awarding of costs;

(e) prescribing and regulating the duties of officers of the court;

(f) respecting the transfer of proceedings under this Act to or from the court; and

(g) prescribing and regulating any other matter considered expedient to attain the ends of justice and carry into effect the purposes and provisions of this Act.

(3) Exercise of power — The power to make rules for a court or appellate court conferred by subsection (2) on a competent authority shall be exercised in the like manner and subject to the like terms and conditions, if any, as the power to make rules for that court conferred on that authority by the laws of the province.

(4) Not statutory instruments — Rules made pursuant to this section by a competent authority that is not a judicial or quasi-judicial body shall be deemed not to be statutory instruments within the meaning and for the purposes of the *Statutory Instruments Act*.

1993, c. 8, s. 5

25 — Provincial rules

The rule-making authority formerly set out in s. 19(1) of the old Act has been extended by s. 25(2). Pursuant to s. 25(2)(b), the competent authority in a province is empowered to make rules respecting the conduct and disposition of any proceedings under the Act without the necessity of an oral hearing. The provinces are thereby authorized to promulgate their own rules prescribing certain circumstances in which a court may accept affidavit evidence in lieu of holding an oral hearing.

This section was amended March 25, 1993 at s. 25(2)(b.1) so that the "competent authority" (*i.e.*, the provincial rules committee) may make rules in regard to variation proceedings (which are based on submissions of former spouses) to allow the submissions to be presented orally before the court or, if both spouses consent, by affidavit.

25§1 — Desk divorces

Application for divorce without appearance by parties are authorized by s. 25 of the *Divorce Act, 1985*. In such divorces, called "desk divorces":

1. A party may plead for relief for his or herself but not for the other party.

2. A court can deal with the respondent's access to the child if the petitioner has claimed custody.

3. Proof of service of the petition is necessary for a desk divorce.

4. A counter-petition may not proceed as a desk divorce until the petition is disposed of and the respondent by counter-petition noted in default.

5. A petitioner need not include in the form of judgment all of the relief to which he or she is entitled or indeed has requested in the petition.

6. The formal judgment may not include corollary relief not claimed in the petition, even where judgment is by consent.

7. Similarly, the formal judgment may not include corollary relief not pleaded, even though the parties have executed minutes of settlement on that point.

8. The material in support must allow the court to decide if reasonable arrangements for child support have been made.

9. Orders in the formal judgment should be in the normal form for court orders and should not contain agreements between the parties, acknowledgments of certain states of affairs or legal propositions.

10. Generally, orders for retroactive support for income tax purposes will not be made in desk divorces. The proper procedure is to apply in chambers, or go to trial to obtain a *nunc pro tunc* order or to apply for a declaration under s. 60.1(3) of the *Income Tax Act: Reshke v. Reshke* (1989), 19 R.F.L. (3d) 156, 65 Alta. L.R. (2d) 249, [1989] 4 W.W.R. 75, 95 A.R. 12 (Q.B.).

In *W. (V.L.) v. W. (V.)*, 36 R.F.L. (5th) 237, 2003 CarswellBC 426, 2003 BCSC 242 (B.C. S.C.), the court refused the husband's application for a "desk divorce" even though the wife did not oppose it. The parties had executed a separation agreement and the husband sought to include orders dismissing any claim which either party may have, inter alia, under the spousal support provisions of the *Divorce Act* "as if heard upon merits at trial". As a separation agreement would not be a bar to a spousal support claim, it was too risky to include provisions barring all future access to the courts.

In Nova Scotia, it is incumbent upon a petitioner to serve a notice of hearing upon the respondent prior to proceeding to obtain the decree as an undefended action under r. 57.15 of the Nova Scotia Civil Procedure Rules. In absence of such notice, the decree is properly set aside on appeal: *Bignell v. Bignell* (1995), 17 R.F.L. (4th) 415, 147 N.S.R. (2d) 311, 426 A.P.R. 311 (C.A.).

In *Anderson v. Anderson* (1995), 10 R.F.L. (4th) 227 (N.S. C.A.), the wife's judgment for divorce, which had proceeded as uncontested when no answer had been filed by the husband, was set aside on appeal. The matter had not been set down within 30 days of the husband's default, in contravention of r. 57.15 of the Nova Scotia Civil Procedure Rules.

A summary judgment for divorce should not be granted where prejudice resulting to the respondent spouse has not been dealt with through corollary relief. In such a case, the issues of the divorce and corollary relief should not be split: *Colletta v. Colletta* (1992), 42 R.F.L. (3d) 227, 10 O.R. (3d) 464, 57 O.A.C. 283, 95 D.L.R. (4th) 298 (C.A.).

A summary judgment for divorce cannot be issued where support issues are in dispute: *Buwalda v. Buwalda* (1996), 22 R.F.L. (4th) 61, 183 A.R. 225 (Q.B.).

Once an answer has been filed to a divorce petition, in the absence of either consent or summary judgment, the action must be tried: *Brock v. Brock* (1995), 166 A.R. 319 (Q.B.).

Where the wife opposed the granting of a summary divorce on the basis that it would result in adverse tax consequences for her, the divorce was nevertheless granted. Corollary relief had been severed from the actual divorce and any tax problems could be resolved through an appropriate support order: *McIntosh v. McIntosh* (1993), 49 R.F.L. (3d) 20 (Ont. Gen. Div.).

Although the court has the power to grant a summary judgment for divorce even where an answer has not been filed, that power should be used cautiously where the parties do not agree to the severance of the divorce from the corollary relief. Summary judgment will be denied in a situation where it would possibly make the respondent spouse's corollary relief claims more difficult: *Zimmerman v. Zimmerman* (1992), 41 R.F.L. (3d) 291, 129 A.R. 392 (Q.B.).

For further technical aspects relating to desk divorces see *Schofield v. Schofield* (1989), 19 R.F.L. (3d) 165, 65 Alta. L.R. (2d) 258, [1989] 4 W.W.R. 84 (Q.B.).

A divorce judgment entered in the absence of an answer or counter-petition is a default judgment which may be varied or set aside on such terms as the court sees fit: *Piwniuk v. Piwniuk* (1992), [1993] 3 W.W.R. 242, 6 Alta. L.R. (3d) 372, 136 A.R. 157 (Q.B.).

In *Burns v. Burns* (1988), 89 N.S.R. (2d) 226, 227 A.P.R. 226 (T.D.), the court refused the husband's application to proceed with the divorce as an uncontested proceeding. As no affidavits acknowledging service of the petition on the wife nor service of the answer and counter-petition on the husband were contained in the court file, the application could not be granted.

25§2 — Representation at proceedings

In *Williams v. Williams* (1999), 50 R.F.L.(4th) 446, 179 Nfld. & P.E.I.R. 283, 546 A.P.R. 283 (Nfld. C.A.), the court refused the husband's appeal from a judgement of divorce and corollary relief that had been made in his absence. On the day prior to the scheduled hearing the husband, who was in Australia, faxed a letter requesting that a court-appointed counsel be made available in his absence. The trial judge was nevertheless justified in proceeding without an adjournment given the lateness of the request and the lack of evidence both that the husband had attempted to secure counsel and that he was unable to afford one.

Individuals who apply for a divorce may represent themselves or be represented by a lawyer. An individual seeking to be represented by an agent who is not a lawyer must first obtain leave of the Court: *Karach v. Karach* (1995), 35 Alta. L.R. (3d) 311, [1996] 3 W.W.R. 297, 177 A.R. 100 (Q.B.).

25§3 — Summary judgment for divorce

An application to strike a family law application by summary judgment should be granted where the subject application is obviously unsustainable. It is an error for a judge to delve too far into the merit of the application, and to make findings of a fact and legal conclusions based upon them: *Mabey v. Mabey*, 12 R.F.L. (6th) 403, 2005 CarswellNS 72, [2005] N.S.J. No. 71, 2005 NSCA 35, 230 N.S.R. (2d) 272, 729 A.P.R. 272 (N.S. C.A.).

An application for summary judgement for divorce can properly be refused out of concern to possible prejudice to both spouses with respect to property division under provincial legislation. Such possible prejudice is a legitimate concern even when it relates to relief that cannot be given under the *Divorce Act*: *Potter v. Potter* (1999), 48 R.F.L. (4th) 450, 232 A.R. 191, 195 W.A.C. 191 (C.A.).

On a motion for summary judgement for divorce, the test is not whether a party can possibly succeed at trial, but whether a party's case is so doubtful that it does not deserve consideration by a trier of fact. In determining whether a genuine issue for trial exists, a motions judge must decide whether the eventiary record establishes that the moving party is capable of proving its claim: *Coulson v. Farmer* (1999), 50 R.F.L. (4th) 345 (Ont. Gen. Div.).

In *Kraft v. Kraft* (1999), 48 R.F.L. (4th) 132, 121 O.A.C. 331 (C.A.), the wife was successful in an appeal from the dismissal of her application to set aside the husband's default judgement for divorce and corollary relief. The wife had purposefully concealed her whereabouts so that the husband was forced to obtain an order for substituted service on the parties' son who continued to live in the matrimonial home. In the wife's subsequent application to have judgement set aside, the son filed an affidavit denying recollecting of having been served and asserting that he had never advised his mother of the pending action. Furthermore, the wife raised issues concerning the property aspects of the judgement which warranted further investigation by the court.

An application for summary judgment for divorce may be denied where it is likely that issues relating to corollary relief will not be dealt with reasonably if severed from the divorce: *Jones v. Jones* (1998), 40 R.F.L. (4th) 292 (Sask. Q.B.).

In *Buwalda v. Buwalda* (1996), 22 R.F.L. (4th) 61, 183 A.R. 225 (Alta. Q.B.) the husband's application for summary judgment in divorce proceedings was dismissed. Issues of support could not be resolved as they were entangled with other property division issues. As neither party had initiated a proceeding for property division, the corollary support issues could not be determined in a summary manner.

25§4 — Discovery in divorce matters

The inherent right of parties to be present during cross-examination on examination for discovery of the other party is not strictly applicable to matrimonial disputes because of their emotional and stressful nature: *Lautenschlager v. Lautenschlager* (1997), 29 R.F.L. (4th) 316, 12 C.P.C. (4th) 188 (Ont. Gen. Div.).

25§5 — Publication bans

The fact that embarrassment may result to one or both parties in the context of their matrimonial litigation does not, in itself, justify a publication ban: *T. (H.) v. T. (C.)* (2004), 10 R.F.L. (6th) 191, 2004 CarswellNun 7, 2004 NUCJ 02 (C.J.).

25.1 (1) Agreements with provinces — With the approval of the Governor in Council, the Minister of Justice may, on behalf of the Government of Canada, enter into an agreement with a province authorizing a provincial child support service designated in the agreement to

(a) assist courts in the province in the determination of the amount of child support; and

(b) recalculate, at regular intervals, in accordance with the applicable guidelines, the amount of child support orders on the basis of updated income information.

(2) Effect of recalculation — Subject to subsection (5), the amount of a child support order as recalculated pursuant to this section shall for all purposes be deemed to be the amount payable under the child support order.

(3) Liability — The former spouse against whom a child support order was made becomes liable to pay the amount as recalculated pursuant to this section thirty-one days after both former spouses to whom the order relates are notified of the recalculation in the manner provided for in the agreement authorizing the recalculation.

(4) Right to vary — Where either or both former spouses to whom a child support order relates do not agree with the amount of the order as recalculated pursuant to this section, either former spouse may, within thirty days after both former spouses are notified of the recalculation in the manner provided for in the agreement authorizing the recalculation, apply to a court of competent jurisdiction for an order under subsection 17(1).

(5) Effect of application — Where an application is made under subsection (4), the operation of subsection (3) is suspended pending the determination of the application, and the child support order continues in effect.

(6) Withdrawal of application — Where an application made under subsection (4) is withdrawn before the determination of the application, the former spouse against whom the order was made becomes liable to pay the amount as recalculated pursuant to this section on the day on which the former spouse would have become liable had the application not been made.

1997, c. 1, s. 10

25.1 — General

The federal and provincial government may enter into an agreement authorizing an agency. Provincial Child Support Service is to assist the court in determining the amount of child support and, in light of new income information, recalculating the amount "at regular intervals." An order may be issued in the recalculated amount, subject to the right of the parties to apply within 30 days to vary the order as recalculated: *Divorce Act*, s. 25.1

26. (1) Regulations — The Governor in Council may make regulations for carrying the purposes and provisions of this Act into effect and, without limiting the generality of the foregoing, may make regulations

(a) respecting the establishment and operation of a central registry of divorce proceedings in Canada; and

(b) providing for uniformity in the rules made pursuant to section 25.

(2) Regulations prevail — Any regulations made pursuant to subsection (1) to provide for uniformity in the rules prevail over those rules.

26 — Federal regulations

Under s. 19(1) of the former Act, the regulation-making power of the Governor in Council was limited to the making of regulations required to assure uniformity in the rules of court made under the Act. Section 26(1) of the new Act expands this discretionary power to make regulations by also authorizing the Governor in Council to make regulations for carrying the purposes and provisions of the Act into effect.

26.1 (1) Guidelines — The Governor in Council may establish guidelines respecting the making of orders for child support, including, but without limiting the generality of the foregoing, guidelines

(a) respecting the way in which the amount of an order for child support is to be determined;

(b) respecting the circumstances in which discretion may be exercised in the making of an order for child support;

(c) authorizing a court to require that the amount payable under an order for child support be paid in periodic payments, in a lump sum or in a lump sum and periodic payments;

(d) authorizing a court to require that the amount payable under an order for child support be paid or secured, or paid and secured, in the manner specified in the order;

(e) respecting the circumstances that give rise to the making of a variation order in respect of a child support order;

(f) respecting the determination of income for the purposes of the application of the guidelines;

(g) authorizing a court to impute income for the purposes of the application of the guidelines; and

(h) respecting the production of income information and providing for sanctions when that information is not provided.

(2) The guidelines shall be based on the principle that spouses have a joint financial obligation to maintain the children of the marriage in accordance with their relative abilities to contribute to the performance of that obligation.

(3) Definition of "order for child support" — In subsection (1) **"order for child support"** means

(a) an order or interim order made under section 15.1;

(b) a variation order in respect of a child support order; or

(c) an order or an interim order made under section 19.

1997, c. 1, s. 11

26.1 — General

The authority for creating guidelines is contained in section 26.1 of the Act. This section provides that the Governor in Council may approve or establish guidelines that prescribe the way the amount is determined, the circumstances in which discretion may be exercised, the authority for payment of the amount by lump sum or periodic payments, or both, the recalculation of the amount, the determination and imputing of income, and the production of income information.

This provision in the Act contemplates comprehensive guidelines, published by regulation, which go far beyond the setting of a table of amounts selected according to the payor's income and the number of children. The federal guidelines live up to this expectation.

The guidelines do more than present a system and method for determining child support amounts. Almost as important is the codification of a procedure for determining income by making specific adjustments to taxable income; by identifying the documents and information needed for the process; and by compelling the production of the documents and information not only for the original determination, but also, upon request, on an annual basis with an eye to an annual review and variation of the amount.

27. (1) Fees — The Governor in Council may, by order, authorize the Minister of Justice to prescribe a fee to be paid by any person to whom a service is provided under this Act or the regulations.

(2) Agreements — The Minister of Justice may, with the approval of the Governor in Council, enter into an agreement with the government of any province respecting the collection and remittance of any fees prescribed pursuant to subsection (1).

28. Review and report — The Minister of Justice shall undertake a comprehensive review of the provisions and operation of the Federal Child Support Guidelines and the determination of child support under this Act and shall cause a report on the review to be laid before each House of Parliament within five years after the coming into force of this section.

1997, c. 1, s. 12

29. [Repealed 1997, c. 1, s. 12.]

30. [Repealed 1997, c. 1, s. 12.]

31. [Repealed 1997, c. 1, s. 12.]

Transitional Provisions

32. Proceedings based on facts arising before commencement of Act — Proceedings may be commenced under this Act notwithstanding that the material facts or circumstances giving rise to the proceedings or to jurisdiction over the proceedings occurred wholly or partly before the day on which this Act comes into force.

Divorce Act, R.S. 1970, c. D-8

33. Proceedings commenced before commencement of Act — Proceedings commenced under the *Divorce Act*, chapter D-8 of the Revised Statutes of Canada, 1970, before the day on which this Act comes into force and not finally disposed of before that day shall be dealt with and disposed of in accordance with that Act as it read immediately before that day, as though it had not been repealed.

1997, c. 1, s. 13

33§1 — General

With respect to proceedings commenced under the *Divorce Act, 1968*, the regulations and procedure under that Act continue to apply to such proceedings: *Vail v. Vail Estate* (1988), 14 R.F.L. (3d) 215 (Ont. C.A.).

Where the plaintiff commenced divorce proceedings in 1987 under the old *Divorce Act* and the defendant cross-petitioned, the court later refused the defendant's motion to dismiss on the procedural ground that the action should have been brought under the new Act. The content was more important than the form, and the fact that the defendant had cross-petitioned removed the right to raise a procedural defect as a reason for dismissal: *Droit de la famille — 1211* (1988), [1989] R.D.F. 122 (C.S. Qué.).

In *Hicks v. Hicks* (1987), 9 R.F.L. (3d) 306 (Sask. Q.B.), the wife, who had petitioned under the former legislation on the grounds of cruelty, was permitted to amend her petition under the new legislation to add the additional ground of marriage breakdown by separation for one year. Section 34 [now s. 33] of the new Act was found not to bar the amendment.

34. (1) Variation and enforcement of orders previously made — Subject to subsection (1.1), any order made under subsection 11(1) of the *Divorce Act*, chapter D-8 of the Revised Statutes of Canada, 1970, including any order made pursuant to section 33 of this Act, and any order to the like effect made corollary to a decree of divorce granted in Canada before July 2, 1968 or granted on or after that day pursuant to subsection 22(2) of that Act may be varied, rescinded, suspended or enforced in accordance with sections 17 to 20, other than subsection 17(10), of this Act as if

(a) the order were a support order or custody order, as the case may be; and

(b) in subsections 17(4), (4.1) and (5), the words **"or the last order made under subsection 11(2) of the *Divorce Act*, chapter D-8 of the Revised Statutes of Canada, 1970, varying that order"** were added immediately before the words **"or the last variation order made in respect of that order"**.

(1.1) Combined orders — Where an application is made under subsection 17(1) to vary an order referred to in subsection (1) that provides a single amount of money for the combined support of one or more children and a former spouse, the court shall rescind the order and treat the application as an application for a child support order and an application for a spousal support order.

(2) Enforcement of interim orders — Any order made under section 10 of the *Divorce Act*, chapter D-8 of the Revised Statutes of Canada, 1970, including any order made pursuant to section 33 of this Act, may be enforced in accordance with section 20 of this Act as if it were an order made under subsection 15.1(1) or 15.2(1) or section 16 of this Act, as the case may be.

(3) Assignment of orders previously made — Any order for the maintenance of a spouse or child of the marriage made under section 10 or 11 of the *Divorce Act*, chapter D-8 of the Revised Statutes of Canada, 1970, including any order made pursuant to section 33 of this Act, and any order to the like effect made corollary to a decree of divorce granted in Canada before July 2, 1968 or granted on or after that day pursuant to subsection 22(2) of that Act may be assigned to any minister, member or agency designated pursuant to section 20.1

1997, c. 1, s. 14

35. Procedural laws continued — The rules and regulations made under the *Divorce Act*, chapter D-8 of the Revised Statutes of Canada, 1970, and the provisions of any other law or of any rule, regulation or other instrument made thereunder respecting any matter in relation to which rules may be made under subsection 25(2) that were in force in Canada or any province immediately before the day on which this Act comes into force and that are not inconsistent with this Act continue in force as though made or enacted by or under this Act until they are repealed or altered by rules or regulations made under this Act or are, by virtue of the making of rules or regulations under this Act, rendered inconsistent with those rules or regulations.

Divorce Act, R.S. 1985, c. 3 (2nd Supp.)

35.1 (1) Variation and enforcement of support orders previously made — Subject to subsection (2), any support order made under this Act before the coming into force of this section may be varied, rescinded, suspended or enforced in accordance with sections 17 to 20 as if the support order were a child support order or a spousal support order, as the case may be.

(2) Combined orders — Where an application is made under subsection 17(1) to vary a support order made under this Act before the coming into force of this section that provides for the combined support of one or more children and a former spouse, the court shall rescind the order and treat the application as an application for a child support order and an application for a spousal support order.

(3) Assignment of orders previously made — Any support order made under this Act before the coming into force of this section may be assigned to any minister, member or agency designated pursuant to section 20.1.

1997, c. 1, s. 15

Commencement

36. Commencement — This Act shall come into force on a day to be fixed by proclamation.

This Act was proclaimed in force June 1, 1986.

CAN. REG. 97-175 — FEDERAL CHILD SUPPORT GUIDELINES

made under the *Divorce Act*

SOR/97-175, as am. SOR/97-563; SOR/99-136; SOR/2000-337; SOR/2000-390 (Fr.); SOR/2001-292; SOR/2005-400; SOR/2007-59.

OBJECTIVES

1. Objectives — The objectives of these Guidelines are

(a) to establish a fair standard of support for children that ensures that they continue to benefit from the financial means of both spouses after separation;

(b) to reduce conflict and tension between spouses by making the calculation of child support orders more objective;

(c) to improve the efficiency of the legal process by giving courts and spouses guidance in setting the levels of child support orders and encouraging settlement; and

(d) to ensure consistent treatment of spouses and children who are in similar circumstances.

INTERPRETATION

2. (1) Definitions — The definitions in this subsection apply in these Guidelines.

"Act" means the *Divorce Act*.

"child" means a child of the marriage.

"income" means the annual income determined under sections 15 to 20.

"order assignee" means a minister, member or agency referred to in subsection 20.1(1) of the Act to whom a child support order is assigned in accordance with that subsection.

"spouse" has the meaning assigned by subsection 2(1) of the Act, and includes a former spouse.

"table" means a federal child support table set out in Schedule I.

"universal child care benefit" means a benefit provided under section 4 of the *Universal Child Care Benefit Act*.

(2) Income Tax Act — Words and expressions that are used in sections 15 to 21 and that are not defined in this section have the meanings assigned to them under the *Income Tax Act*.

(3) Most current information — Where, for the purposes of these Guidelines, any amount is determined on the basis of specified information, the most current information must be used.

(4) Application of Guidelines — In addition to child support orders, these Guidelines apply, with such modifications as the circumstances require, to

(a) interim orders under subsections 15.1(2) and 19(9) of the Act;

(b) orders varying a child support order;

(c) orders referred to in subsection 19(7) of the Act; and

(d) recalculations under paragraph 25.1(1)(b) of the Act.

(5) Recalculations — For greater certainty, the provisions of these Guidelines that confer a discretionary power on a court do not apply to recalculations under paragraph 25.1(1)(b) of the Act by a provincial child support service.

SOR/2007-59, s. 1

Amount of Child Support

3. (1) Presumptive rule — Unless otherwise provided under these Guidelines, the amount of a child support order for children under the age of majority is

(a) the amount set out in the applicable table, according to the number of children under the age of majority to whom the order relates and the income of the spouse against whom the order is sought; and

(b) the amount, if any, determined under section 7.

(2) Child the age of majority or over — Unless otherwise provided under these Guidelines, where a child to whom a child support order relates is the age of majority or over, the amount of the child support order is

(a) the amount determined by applying these Guidelines as if the child were under the age of majority; or

(b) if the court considers that approach to be inappropriate, the amount that it considers appropriate, having regard to the condition, means, needs and other circumstances of the child and the financial ability of each spouse to contribute to the support of the child.

(3) Applicable table — The applicable table is

(a) if the spouse against whom an order is sought resides in Canada

(i) the table for the province in which that spouse ordinarily resides at the time the application for the child support order, or for a variation order in respect of a child support order, is made or the amount is to be recalculated under section 25.1 of the Act,

(ii) where the court is satisfied that the province in which that spouse ordinarily resides has changed since the time described in subparagraph (i), the table for the province in which the spouse ordinarily resides at the time of determining the amount of support, or

(iii) where the court is satisfied that, in the near future after determination of the amount of support, that spouse will ordinarily reside in a given province other than the province in which the spouse ordinarily resides at the time of that determination, the table for the given province; and

(b) if the spouse against whom an order is sought resides outside of Canada, or if the residence of that spouse is unknown, the table for the province where the other spouse ordinarily resides at the time the application for the child support order or for a variation order in respect of a child support order is made or the amount is to be recalculated under section 25.1 of the Act.

SOR/97-563, s. 1

4. Incomes over $150,000 — Where the income of the spouse against whom a child support order is sought is over $150,000, the amount of a child support order is

(a) the amount determined under section 3; or

(b) if the court considers that amount to be inappropriate,

(i) in respect of the first $150,000 of the spouse's income, the amount set out in the applicable table for the number of children under the age of majority to whom the order relates;

(ii) in respect of the balance of the spouse's income, the amount that the court considers appropriate, having regard to the condition, means, needs and other circumstances of the children who are entitled to support and the financial ability of each spouse to contribute to the support of the children; and

(iii) the amount, if any, determined under section 7.

5. Spouse in place of a parent — Where the spouse against whom a child support order is sought stands in the place of a parent for a child, the amount of a child support order is, in respect of that spouse, such amount as the court considers appropriate, having regard to these Guidelines and any other parent's legal duty to support the child.

6. Medical and dental insurance — In making a child support order, where medical or dental insurance coverage for the child is available to either spouse through his or her employer or otherwise at a reasonable rate, the court may order that coverage be acquired or continued.

7. (1) Special or extraordinary expenses — In a child support order the court may, on either spouse's request, provide for an amount to cover all or any portion of the following expenses, which expenses may be estimated, taking into account the necessity of the expense in relation to the child's best interests and the reasonableness of the expense in relation to the means of the spouses and those of the child and to the family's spending pattern prior to the separation:

(a) child care expenses incurred as a result of the custodial parent's employment, illness, disability or education or training for employment;

(b) that portion of the medical and dental insurance premiums attributable to the child;

(c) health-related expenses that exceed insurance reimbursement by at least $100 annually, including orthodontic treatment, professional counselling provided by a psychologist, social worker, psychiatrist or any other person, physiotherapy, occupational therapy, speech therapy and prescription drugs, hearing aids, glasses and contact lenses;

(d) extraordinary expenses for primary or secondary school education or for any other educational programs that meet the child's particular needs;

(e) expenses for post-secondary education; and

(f) extraordinary expenses for extracurricular activities.

(1.1) Definition of "extraordinary expenses" — For the purposes of paragraphs (1)(d) and (f), the term **"extraordinary expenses"** means

(a) expenses that exceed those that the spouse requesting an amount for the extraordinary expenses can reasonably cover, taking into account that spouse's income and the amount that the spouse would receive under the applicable table or, where the court has determined that the table amount is inappropriate, the amount that the court has otherwise determined is appropriate; or

(b) where paragraph (a) is not applicable, expenses that the court considers are extraordinary taking into account

(i) the amount of the expense in relation to the income of the spouse requesting the amount, including the amount that the spouse would receive under the applicable table or, where the court has determined that the table amount is inappropriate, the amount that the court has otherwise determined is appropriate,

(ii) the nature and number of the educational programs and extracurricular activities,

(iii) any special needs and talents of the child or children,

(iv) the overall cost of the programs and activities, and

(v) any other similar factor that the court considers relevant.

(2) Sharing of expense — The guiding principle in determining the amount of an expense referred to in subsection (1) is that the expense is shared by the spouses in proportion to their respective incomes after deducting from the expense, the contribution, if any, from the child.

(3) Subsidies, tax deductions, etc. — Subject to subsection (4), in determining the amount of an expense referred to in subsection (1), the court must take into account any subsidies, benefits or income tax deductions or credits relating to the expense, and any eligibility to claim a subsidy, benefit or income tax deduction or credit relating to the expense.

(4) Universal child care benefit — In determining the amount of an expense referred to in subsection (1), the court shall not take into account any universal child care benefit or any eligibility to claim that benefit.

SOR/2000-337, s. 1; SOR/2005-400, s. 1; SOR/2007-59, s. 2

8. Split custody — Where each spouse has custody of one or more children, the amount of a child support order is the difference between the amount that each spouse would otherwise pay if a child support order were sought against each of the spouses.

9. Shared custody — Where a spouse exercises a right of access to, or has physical custody of, a child for not less than 40 per cent of the time over the course of a year, the amount of the child support order must be determined by taking into account

(a) the amounts set out in the applicable tables for each of the spouses;

(b) the increased costs of shared custody arrangements; and

(c) the conditions, means, needs and other circumstances of each spouse and of any child for whom support is sought.

10. (1) Undue hardship — On either spouse's application, a court may award an amount of child support that is different from the amount determined under any of sections 3 to 5, 8 or 9 if the court finds that the spouse making the request, or a child in respect of whom the request is made, would otherwise suffer undue hardship.

(2) Circumstances that may cause undue hardship — Circumstances that may cause a spouse or child to suffer undue hardship include the following:

(a) the spouse has responsibility for an unusually high level of debts reasonably incurred to support the spouses and their children prior to the separation or to earn a living;

(b) the spouse has unusually high expenses in relation to exercising access to a child;

(c) the spouse has a legal duty under a judgment, order or written separation agreement to support any person;

(d) the spouse has a legal duty to support a child, other than a child of the marriage, who is

(i) under the age of majority, or

(ii) the age of majority or over but is unable, by reason of illness, disability or other cause, to obtain the necessaries of life; and

(e) the spouse has a legal duty to support any person who is unable to obtain the necessaries of life due to an illness or disability.

(3) Standards of living must be considered — Despite a determination of undue hardship under subsection (1), an application under that subsection must be denied by the court if it is of the opinion that the household of the spouse who claims undue hardship would, after determining the amount of child support under any of sections 3 to 5, 8 or 9, have a higher standard of living than the household of the other spouse.

(4) Standards of living test — In comparing standards of living for the purpose of subsection (3), the court may use the comparison of household standards of living test set out in Schedule II.

(5) Reasonable time — Where the court awards a different amount of child support under subsection (1), it may specify, in the child support order, a reasonable time for the satisfaction of any obligation arising from circumstances that cause undue hardship and the amount payable at the end of that time.

(6) Reasons — Where the court makes a child support order in a different amount under this section, it must record its reasons for doing so.

ELEMENTS OF A CHILD SUPPORT ORDER

11. Form of payments — The court may require in a child support order that the amount payable under the order be paid in periodic payments, in a lump sum or in a lump sum and periodic payments.

12. Security — The court may require in the child support order that the amount payable under the order be paid or secured, or paid and secured, in the manner specified in the order.

13. Information to be specified in order — A child support must include the following information:

(a) the name and birth date of each child to whom the order relates;

(b) the income of any spouse whose income is used to determine the amount of the child support order;

(c) the amount determined under paragraph 3(1)(a) for the number of children to whom the order relates;

(d) the amount determined under paragraph 3(2)(b) for a child the age of majority or over;

(e) the particulars of any expense described in subsection 7(1), the child to whom the expense relates, and the amount of the expense or, where that amount cannot be determined, the proportion to be paid in relation to the expense; and

(f) the date on which the lump sum or first payment is payable and the day of the month or other time period on which all subsequent payments are to be made.

VARIATION OF CHILD SUPPORT ORDERS

14. Circumstances for variation — For the purposes of subsection 17(4) of the Act, any one of the following constitutes a change of circumstances that gives rise to the making of a variation order in respect of a child support order:

(a) in the case where the amount of child support includes a determination made in accordance with the applicable table, any change in circumstances that would result in a different child support order or any provision thereof;

(b) in the case where the amount of child support does not include a determination made in accordance with a table, any change in the condition, means, needs or other circumstances of either spouse or of any child who is entitled to support; and

(c) in the case of an order made before May 1, 1997, the coming into force of section 15.1 of the Act, enacted by section 2 of chapter 1 of the Statutes of Canada, (1997).

SOR/97-563, s. 2; SOR/2000-337, s. 2

INCOME

15. (1) Determination of annual income — Subject to subsection (2), a spouse's annual income is determined by the court in accordance with sections 16 to 20.

(2) **Agreement** — Where both spouses agree in writing on the annual income of a spouse, the court may consider that amount to be the spouse's income for the purposes of these Guidelines if the court thinks that the amount is reasonable having regard to the income information provided under section 21.

16. **Calculation of annual income** — Subject to sections 17 to 20, a spouse's annual income is determined using the sources of income set out under the heading "Total income" in the T1 General form issued by the Canada Revenue Agency and is adjusted in accordance with Schedule III.

SOR/2000-337, s. 3; SOR/2007-59, s. 4(a)

17. (1) **Pattern of income** — If the court is of the opinion that the determination of a spouse's annual income under section 16 would not be the fairest determination of that income, the court may have regard to the spouse's income over the last three years and determine an amount that is fair and reasonable in light of any pattern of income, fluctuation in income or receipt of non-recurring amount during those years.

(2) **Non-recurring losses** — Where a spouse has incurred a non-recurring capital or business investment loss, the court may, if it is of the opinion that the determination of the spouse's annual income under section 16 would not provide the fairest determination of the annual income, choose not to apply sections 6 and 7 of Schedule III, and adjust the amount of the loss, including related expenses and carrying charges and interest expenses, to arrive at such amount as the court considers appropriate.

SOR/2000-337, s. 4

18. (1) **Shareholder, director or officer** — Where a spouse is a shareholder, director or officer of a corporation and the court is of the opinion that the amount of the spouse's annual income as determined under section 16 does not fairly reflect all the money available to the spouse for the payment of child support, the court may consider the situations described in section 17 and determine the spouse's annual income to include

(a) all or part of the pre-tax income of the corporation, and of any corporation that is related to that corporation, for the most recent taxation year; or

(b) an amount commensurate with the services that the spouse provides to the corporation, provided that the amount does not exceed the corporation's pre-tax income.

(2) **Adjustment to corporation's pre-tax income** — In determining the pre-tax income of a corporation for the purposes of subsection (1), all amounts paid by the corporation as salaries, wages or management fees, or other payments or benefits, to or on behalf of persons with whom the corporation does not deal at arm's length must be added to the pre-tax income, unless the spouse establishes that the payments were reasonable in the circumstances.

19. (1) **Imputing income** — The court may impute such amount of income to a spouse as it considers appropriate in the circumstances, which circumstances include the following:

(a) the spouse is intentionally under-employed or unemployed, other than where the under-employment or unemployment is required by the needs of a child of the marriage or any child under the age of majority or by the reasonable educational or health needs of the spouse;

(b) the spouse is exempt from paying federal or provincial income tax;

(c) the spouse lives in a country that has effective rates of income tax that are significantly lower than those in Canada;

(d) it appears that income has been diverted which would affect the level of child support to be determined under these Guidelines;

(e) the spouse's property is not reasonably utilized to generate income;

(f) the spouse has failed to provide income information when under a legal obligation to do so;

(g) the spouse unreasonably deducts expenses from income;

(h) the spouse derives a significant portion of income from dividends, capital gains or other sources that are taxed at a lower rate than employment or business income or that are exempt from tax; and

(i) the spouse is a beneficiary under a trust and is or will be in receipt of income or other benefits from the trust.

(2) Reasonableness of Expenses — For the purpose of paragraph (1)(g), the reasonableness of an expense deduction is not solely governed by whether the deduction is permitted under the *Income Tax Act*.

SOR/2000-337, s. 5

20. (1) Non-resident — Subject to subsection (2), where a spouse is a non-resident of Canada, the spouse's annual income is determined as though the spouse were a resident of Canada.

(2) Non-resident taxed at higher rates — Where a spouse is a non-resident of Canada and resides in a country that has effective rates of income tax that are significantly higher than those applicable in the province in which the other spouse ordinarily resides, the spouse's annual income is the amount that the court determines to be appropriate taking those rates into consideration.

SOR/2005-400, s. 2

INCOME INFORMATION

21. (1) Obligation of applicant — A spouse who is applying for a child support order and whose income information is necessary to determine the amount of the order must include the following with the application:

(a) a copy of every personal income tax return filed by the spouse for each of the three most recent taxation years;

(b) a copy of every notice of assessment and re-assessment issued to the spouse for each of the three most recent taxation years;

(c) where the spouse is an employee, the most recent statement of earnings indicating the total earnings paid in the year to date, including overtime or, where such a statement is not provided by the employer, a letter from the spouse's employer setting out that information including the spouse's rate of annual salary or remuneration;

(d) where the spouse is self-employed, for the three most recent taxation years

(i) the financial statements of the spouse's business or professional practice, other than a partnership, and

(ii) a statement showing a breakdown of all salaries, wages, management fees or other payments or benefits paid to, or on behalf of, persons or corporations with whom the spouse does not deal at arm's length;

(e) where the spouse is a partner in a partnership, confirmation of the spouse's income and draw from, and capital in, the partnership for its three most recent taxation years;

(f) where the spouse controls a corporation, for its three most recent taxation years

(i) the financial statements of the corporation and its subsidiaries, and

(ii) a statement showing a breakdown of all salaries, wages, management fees or other payments or benefits paid to, or on behalf of, persons or corporations with whom the corporation, and every related corporation, does not deal at arm's length;

(g) where the spouse is a beneficiary under a trust, a copy of the trust settlement agreement and copies of the trust's three most recent financial statements; and

(h) in addition to any income information that must be included under paragraphs (c) to (g), where the spouse receives income from employment insurance, social assistance, a pension, workers compensation, disability payments or any other source, the most recent statement of income indicating the total amount of income from the applicable source during the current year, or if such a statement is not provided, a letter from the appropriate authority stating the required information.

(2) **Obligation of respondent** — A spouse who is served with an application for a child support order and whose income information is necessary to determine the amount of the order, must, within 30 days after the application is served if the spouse resides in Canada or the United States or within 60 days if the spouse resides elsewhere, or such other time limit as the court specifies, provide the court, as well as the other spouse or the order assignee, as the case may be, with the documents referred to in subsection (1).

(3) **Special expenses or undue hardship** — Where, in the course of proceedings in respect of an application for a child support order, a spouse requests an amount to cover expenses referred to in subsection 7(1) or pleads undue hardship, the spouse who would be receiving the amount of child support must, within 30 days after the amount is sought or undue hardship is pleaded if the spouse resides in Canada or the United States or within 60 days if the spouse resides elsewhere, or such other time limit as the court specifies, provide the court and the other spouse with the documents referred to in subsection (1).

(4) **Income over $150,000** — Where, in the course of proceedings in respect of an application for a child support order, it is established that the income of the spouse who would be paying the amount of child support is greater than $150,000, the other spouse must, within 30 days after the income is established to be greater than $150,000 if the other spouse resides in Canada or the United States or within 60 days if the other spouse

resides elsewhere, or such other time limit as the court specifies, provide the court and the spouse with the documents referred to in subsection (1).

(5) Making of rules not precluded — Nothing in this section precludes the making of rules by a competent authority, within the meaning of section 25 of the Act, respecting the disclosure of income information that is considered necessary for the purposes of the determination of an amount of a child support order.

SOR/2000-337, s. 6

22. (1) Failure to comply — Where a spouse fails to comply with section 21, the other spouse may apply

(a) to have the application for a child support order set down for a hearing, or move for judgment; or

(b) for an order requiring the spouse who failed to comply to provide the court, as well as the other spouse or order assignee, as the case may be, with the required documents.

(2) Costs of the proceedings — Where a court makes an order under paragraph (1)(a) or (b), the court may award costs in favour of the other spouse up to an amount that fully compensates the other spouse for all costs incurred in the proceedings.

23. Adverse inference — Where the court proceeds to a hearing on the basis of an application under paragraph 22(1)(a), the court may draw an adverse inference against the spouse who failed to comply and impute income to that spouse in such amount as it considers appropriate.

24. Failure to comply with court order — Where a spouse fails to comply with an order issued on the basis of an application under paragraph 22(1)(b), the court may

(a) strike out any of the spouse's pleadings;

(b) make a contempt order against the spouse;

(c) proceed to a bearing, in the course of which it may draw an adverse inference against the spouse and impute income to that spouse in such amount as it considers appropriate; and

(d) award costs in favour of the other spouse up to an amount that fully compensates the other spouse for all costs incurred in the proceedings.

25. (1) Continuing obligation to provide income information — Every spouse against whom a child support order has been made must, on the written request of the other spouse or the order assignee, not more than once a year after the making of the order and as long as the child is a child within the meaning of these Guidelines, provide that other spouse or the order assignee with

(a) the documents referred to in subsection 21(1) for any of the three most recent taxation years for which the spouse has not previously provided the documents;

(b) as applicable, any current information, in writing, about the status of any expenses included in the order pursuant to subsection 7(1); and

(c) as applicable, any current information, in writing, about the circumstances relied on by the court in a determination of undue hardship.

(2) **Below minimum income** — Where a court has determined that the spouse against whom a child support order is sought does not have to pay child support because his or her income level is below the minimum amount required for application of the tables, that spouse must, on the written request of the other spouse, not more than once a year after the determination and as long as the child is a child within the meaning of these Guidelines, provide the other spouse with the documents referred to in subsection 21(1) for any of the three most recent taxation years for which the spouse has not previously provided the documents.

(3) **Obligation of receiving spouse** — Where the income information of the spouse in favour of whom a child support order is made is used to determine the amount of the order, the spouse must, not more than once a year after the making of the order and as long as the child is a child within the meaning of these Guidelines, on the written request of the other spouse, provide the other spouse with the documents and information referred to in subsection (1).

(4) **Information requests** — Where a spouse or an order assignee requests information from the other spouse under any of subsections (1) to (3) and the income information of the requesting spouse is used to determine the amount of the child support order, the requesting spouse or order assignee must include the documents and information referred to in subsection (1) with the request.

(5) **Time limit** — A spouse who receives a request made under any of subsections (1) to (3) must provide the required documents within 30 days after the request's receipt if the spouse resides in Canada or the United States and within 60 days after the request's receipt if the spouse resides elsewhere.

(6) **Deemed receipt** — A request made under any of subsections (1) to (3) is deemed to have been received 10 days after it is sent.

(7) **Failure to comply** — A court may, on application by either spouse or an order assignee, where the other spouse has failed to comply with any of subsections (1) to (3)

(a) consider the other spouse to be in contempt of court and award costs in favour of the applicant up to an amount that fully compensates the applicant for all costs incurred in the proceedings; or

(b) make an order requiring the other spouse to provide the required documents to the court, as well as to the spouse or order assignee, as the case may be.

(8) **Unenforceable provision** — A provision in a judgment, order or agreement purporting to limit a spouse's obligation to provide documents under this section is unenforceable.

SOR/97-563, s. 3

26. **Provincial child support services** — A spouse or an order assignee may appoint a provincial child support service to act on their behalf for the purposes of requesting and receiving income information under any of subsections 25(1) to (3), as well as for the purposes of an application under subsection 25(7).

COMING INTO FORCE

27. Coming into force — These Guidelines come into force on May 1, 1997.

SCHEDULE I

(Subsection 2(1))

Federal Child Support Tables

Notes:

1. The federal child support tables set out the amount of monthly child support payments for each province on the basis of the annual income of the spouse ordered to pay child support (the "support payer") and the number of children for whom a table amount is payable. Refer to these Guidelines to determine whether special measures apply.

2. There is a threshold level of income below which no amount of child support is payable. Child support amounts are specified for incomes up to $150,000 per year. Refer to section 4 of these Guidelines to determine the amount of child support payments for support payers with annual incomes over $150,000.

3. Income is set out in the tables in intervals of $1,000. Monthly amounts are determined by adding the applicable basic amount and the amount calculated by multiplying the applicable percentage by the portion of the income that exceeds the lower amount within that interval of income.

Example:

Province: British Columbia

Number of children: 2

Annual income of support payer: $33,760

Basic amount: $515

Percentage: 1.39%

Lower amount of the income interval: $33,000

The amount of monthly child support is calculated as follows:

$515 + [1.39% × ($33,760-$33,000)]

$515 + [1.39/100 × $760]

$515 + [0.0139 × $760]

$515 + $10.56 = $525.56

4. There are separate tables for each province. The amounts vary from one province to another because of differences in provincial income tax rates. The tables are in the following order:

(a) Ontario;

(b) Quebec;

(c) Nova Scotia;

(d) New Brunswick;

(e) Manitoba;

(f) British Columbia;

(g) Prince Edward Island;

(h) Saskatchewan;

(i) Alberta;

(j) Newfoundland and Labrador;

(k) Yukon;

(l) Northwest Territories; and

(m) Nunavut

5. The amounts in the tables are based on economic studies of average spending on children in families at different income levels in Canada. They are calculated on the basis that child support payments are no longer taxable in the hands of the receiving parent and no longer deductible by the paying parent. They are calculated using a mathematical formula and generated by a computer program.

6. The formula referred to in note 5 sets support amounts to reflect average expenditures on children by a spouse with a particular number of children and level of income. The calculation is based on the support payer's income. The formula uses the basic personal amount for non-refundable tax credits to recognize personal expenses, and takes other federal and provincial income taxes and credits into account. Federal Child Tax benefits and Goods and Services Tax credits for children are excluded from the calculation. At lower income levels, the formula sets the amounts to take into account the combined impact of taxes and child support payments on the support payer's limited disposable income.

Federal Child Support Tables/ Tables fédérales de pensions alimentaires pour enfants

Province: Ontario
No. Of Children/ Nbre d'enfants: One/Un

Income/Revenu ($)		Monthly Award/ Paiement mensuel ($)		
From/De	**To/À**	**Basic Amount/ Montant de base**	**Plus (%)**	**Of Income Over/Du revenu dépassant**
0	*7999*	0		
8000	*8999*	0	0.95	8000
9000	*9999*	9	1.89	9000
10000	*10999*	28	1.89	10000
11000	*11999*	47	1.89	11000
12000	*12999*	66	1.89	12000
13000	*13999*	85	1.89	13000
14000	*14999*	104	1.89	14000
15000	*15999*	123	1.68	15000
16000	*16999*	140	0.81	16000
17000	*17999*	148	0.81	17000
18000	*18999*	156	0.81	18000
19000	*19999*	164	0.81	19000
20000	*20999*	172	0.77	20000
21000	*21999*	180	0.77	21000
22000	*22999*	188	0.77	22000
23000	*23999*	195	0.77	23000
24000	*24999*	203	0.77	24000
25000	*25999*	211	1.13	25000
26000	*26999*	222	1.20	26000
27000	*27999*	234	1.20	27000
28000	*28999*	246	1.20	28000
29000	*29999*	258	1.16	29000
30000	*30999*	270	1.13	30000
31000	*31999*	281	1.13	31000
32000	*32999*	293	1.13	32000
33000	*33999*	304	1.17	33000
34000	*34999*	316	0.94	34000
35000	*35999*	325	0.81	35000
36000	*36999*	333	0.82	36000
37000	*37999*	341	0.84	37000
38000	*38999*	350	0.86	38000
39000	*39999*	358	0.90	39000
40000	*40999*	367	0.93	40000

Federal Child Support Tables/ Tables fédérales de pensions alimentaires pour enfants

Province: Ontario
No. Of Children/ Nbre d'enfants: One/Un

Income/Revenu ($)		Monthly Award/ Paiement mensuel ($)		
From/De	**To/À**	**Basic Amount/ Montant de base**	**Plus (%)**	**Of Income Over/Du revenu dépassant**
41000	*41999*	377	0.96	41000
42000	*42999*	386	0.96	42000
43000	*43999*	396	0.96	43000
44000	*44999*	405	0.96	44000
45000	*45999*	415	0.96	45000
46000	*46999*	425	0.96	46000
47000	*47999*	434	0.96	47000
48000	*48999*	444	0.85	48000
49000	*49999*	452	0.96	49000
50000	*50999*	462	0.96	50000
51000	*51999*	471	0.96	51000
52000	*52999*	481	0.96	52000
53000	*53999*	490	0.96	53000
54000	*54999*	500	0.96	54000
55000	*55999*	510	0.96	55000
56000	*56999*	519	0.96	56000
57000	*57999*	529	0.96	57000
58000	*58999*	538	0.96	58000
59000	*59999*	548	0.96	59000
60000	*60999*	557	0.91	60000
61000	*61999*	566	0.87	61000
62000	*62999*	575	0.87	62000
63000	*63999*	584	0.87	63000
64000	*64999*	592	0.87	64000
65000	*65999*	601	0.93	65000
66000	*66999*	610	0.92	66000
67000	*67999*	620	0.90	67000
68000	*68999*	629	0.90	68000
69000	*69999*	638	0.90	69000
70000	*70999*	647	0.77	70000
71000	*71999*	654	0.65	71000
72000	*72999*	661	0.54	72000
73000	*73999*	666	0.65	73000
74000	*74999*	673	0.74	74000

Federal Child Support Tables/ Tables fédérales de pensions alimentaires pour enfants

Province: Ontario
No. Of Children/ Nbre d'enfants: One/Un

Income/Revenu ($)		Monthly Award/ Paiement mensuel ($)		
From/De	To/À	Basic Amount/ Montant de base	Plus (%)	Of Income Over/Du revenu dépassant
75000	*75999*	680	0.79	75000
76000	*76999*	688	0.79	76000
77000	*77999*	696	0.79	77000
78000	*78999*	704	0.79	78000
79000	*79999*	712	0.79	79000
80000	*80999*	719	0.79	80000
81000	*81999*	727	0.79	81000
82000	*82999*	735	0.79	82000
83000	*83999*	743	0.79	83000
84000	*84999*	751	0.79	84000
85000	*85999*	759	0.79	85000
86000	*86999*	767	0.79	86000
87000	*87999*	774	0.79	87000
88000	*88999*	782	0.79	88000
89000	*89999*	790	0.79	89000
90000	*90999*	798	0.79	90000
91000	*91999*	806	0.79	91000
92000	*92999*	814	0.79	92000
93000	*93999*	822	0.79	93000
94000	*94999*	829	0.79	94000
95000	*95999*	837	0.79	95000
96000	*96999*	845	0.79	96000
97000	*97999*	853	0.79	97000
98000	*98999*	861	0.79	98000
99000	*99999*	869	0.79	99000
100000	*100999*	877	0.79	100000
101000	*101999*	884	0.79	101000
102000	*102999*	892	0.79	102000
103000	*103999*	900	0.79	103000
104000	*104999*	908	0.79	104000
105000	*105999*	916	0.79	105000
106000	*106999*	924	0.79	106000
107000	*107999*	932	0.79	107000
108000	*108999*	939	0.79	108000
109000	*109999*	947	0.79	109000

Federal Child Support Tables/ Tables fédérales de pensions alimentaires pour enfants

Province: Ontario
No. Of Children/ Nbre d'enfants: One/Un

Income/Revenu ($)		Monthly Award/ Paiement mensuel ($)		
From/De	To/À	Basic Amount/ Montant de base	Plus (%)	Of Income Over/Du revenu dépassant
110000	*110999*	955	0.79	110000
111000	*111999*	963	0.79	111000
112000	*112999*	971	0.79	112000
113000	*113999*	979	0.78	113000
114000	*114999*	987	0.74	114000
115000	*115999*	994	0.74	115000
116000	*116999*	1001	0.74	116000
117000	*117999*	1009	0.74	117000
118000	*118999*	1016	0.74	118000
119000	*119999*	1024	0.74	119000
120000	*120999*	1031	0.74	120000
121000	*121999*	1039	0.74	121000
122000	*122999*	1046	0.74	122000
123000	*123999*	1053	0.74	123000
124000	*124999*	1061	0.74	124000
125000	*125999*	1068	0.74	125000
126000	*126999*	1076	0.74	126000
127000	*127999*	1083	0.74	127000
128000	*128999*	1091	0.74	128000
129000	*129999*	1098	0.74	129000
130000	*130999*	1106	0.74	130000
131000	*131999*	1113	0.74	131000
132000	*132999*	1120	0.74	132000
133000	*133999*	1128	0.74	133000
134000	*134999*	1135	0.74	134000
135000	*135999*	1143	0.74	135000
136000	*136999*	1150	0.74	136000
137000	*137999*	1158	0.74	137000
138000	*138999*	1165	0.74	138000
139000	*139999*	1173	0.74	139000
140000	*140999*	1180	0.74	140000
141000	*141999*	1187	0.74	141000
142000	*142999*	1195	0.74	142000
143000	*143999*	1202	0.74	143000
144000	*144999*	1210	0.74	144000

Federal Child Support Tables/ Tables fédérales de pensions alimentaires pour enfants

Province: Ontario No. Of Children/ Nbre d'enfants: One/Un

Income/Revenu ($)		Monthly Award/ Paiement mensuel ($)		
From/De	To/À	Basic Amount/ Montant de base	Plus (%)	Of Income Over/Du revenu dépassant
145000	*145999*	1217	0.74	145000
146000	*146999*	1225	0.74	146000
147000	*147999*	1232	0.74	147000
148000	*148999*	1240	0.74	148000
149000	*149999*	1247	0.74	149000
150000	*or greater/ ou plus*	1254	0.74	150000

Federal Child Support Tables/ Tables fédérales de pensions alimentaires pour enfants

Province: Ontario No. Of Children/ Nbre d'enfants: Two/Deux

Income/Revenu ($)		Monthly Award/ Paiement mensuel ($)		
From/De	To/À	Basic Amount/ Montant de base	Plus (%)	Of Income Over/Du revenu dépassant
0	*7999*	0		
8000	*8999*	0	1.75	8000
9000	*9999*	17	4.34	9000
10000	*10999*	61	4.34	10000
11000	*11999*	104	4.20	11000
12000	*12999*	146	3.73	12000
13000	*13999*	184	3.65	13000
14000	*14999*	220	2.21	14000
15000	*15999*	242	1.04	15000
16000	*16999*	253	1.39	16000
17000	*17999*	267	1.39	17000
18000	*18999*	281	1.39	18000
19000	*19999*	294	1.39	19000

Federal Child Support Tables/ Tables fédérales de pensions alimentaires pour enfants

Province: Ontario No. Of Children/ Nbre d'enfants: Two/Deux

Income/Revenu ($)		Monthly Award/ Paiement mensuel ($)		
From/De	To/À	Basic Amount/ Montant de base	Plus (%)	Of Income Over/Du revenu dépassant
20000	*20999*	308	1.33	20000
21000	*21999*	322	1.33	21000
22000	*22999*	335	1.33	22000
23000	*23999*	348	1.33	23000
24000	*24999*	362	1.33	24000
25000	*25999*	375	1.39	25000
26000	*26999*	389	1.39	26000
27000	*27999*	403	1.39	27000
28000	*28999*	417	1.39	28000
29000	*29999*	431	1.33	29000
30000	*30999*	444	1.29	30000
31000	*31999*	457	1.54	31000
32000	*32999*	472	1.63	32000
33000	*33999*	488	1.65	33000
34000	*34999*	505	1.66	34000
35000	*35999*	521	1.54	35000
36000	*36999*	537	1.55	36000
37000	*37999*	552	1.58	37000
38000	*38999*	568	1.61	38000
39000	*39999*	584	1.68	39000
40000	*40999*	601	1.72	40000
41000	*41999*	618	1.75	41000
42000	*42999*	636	1.49	42000
43000	*43999*	651	1.49	43000
44000	*44999*	665	1.49	44000
45000	*45999*	680	1.49	45000
46000	*46999*	695	1.49	46000
47000	*47999*	710	1.49	47000
48000	*48999*	725	1.33	48000
49000	*49999*	738	1.49	49000
50000	*50999*	753	1.49	50000
51000	*51999*	768	1.49	51000
52000	*52999*	783	1.49	52000
53000	*53999*	798	1.49	53000
54000	*54999*	813	1.49	54000

Federal Child Support Tables/ Tables fédérales de pensions alimentaires pour enfants

Province: Ontario No. Of Children/ Nbre d'enfants: Two/Deux

Income/Revenu ($)		Monthly Award/ Paiement mensuel ($)		
From/De	To/À	Basic Amount/ Montant de base	Plus (%)	Of Income Over/Du revenu dépassant
55000	55999	827	1.49	55000
56000	56999	842	1.49	56000
57000	57999	857	1.49	57000
58000	58999	872	1.49	58000
59000	59999	887	1.49	59000
60000	60999	902	1.44	60000
61000	61999	916	1.39	61000
62000	62999	930	1.39	62000
63000	63999	944	1.39	63000
64000	64999	958	1.39	64000
65000	65999	972	1.45	65000
66000	66999	986	1.44	66000
67000	67999	1001	1.40	67000
68000	68999	1015	1.40	68000
69000	69999	1029	1.40	69000
70000	70999	1043	1.24	70000
71000	71999	1055	1.10	71000
72000	72999	1066	0.94	72000
73000	73999	1075	1.10	73000
74000	74999	1086	1.18	74000
75000	75999	1098	1.22	75000
76000	76999	1110	1.22	76000
77000	77999	1122	1.22	77000
78000	78999	1135	1.22	78000
79000	79999	1147	1.22	79000
80000	80999	1159	1.22	80000
81000	81999	1171	1.22	81000
82000	82999	1184	1.22	82000
83000	83999	1196	1.22	83000
84000	84999	1208	1.22	84000
85000	85999	1220	1.22	85000
86000	86999	1232	1.22	86000
87000	87999	1245	1.22	87000
88000	88999	1257	1.22	88000
89000	89999	1269	1.22	89000

Federal Child Support Tables/ Tables fédérales de pensions alimentaires pour enfants

Province: Ontario No. Of Children/ Nbre d'enfants: Two/Deux

Income/Revenu ($)		Monthly Award/ Paiement mensuel ($)		
From/De	To/À	Basic Amount/ Montant de base	Plus (%)	Of Income Over/Du revenu dépassant
90000	90999	1281	1.22	90000
91000	91999	1294	1.22	91000
92000	92999	1306	1.22	92000
93000	93999	1318	1.22	93000
94000	94999	1330	1.22	94000
95000	95999	1343	1.22	95000
96000	96999	1355	1.22	96000
97000	97999	1367	1.22	97000
98000	98999	1379	1.22	98000
99000	99999	1391	1.22	99000
100000	100999	1404	1.22	100000
101000	101999	1416	1.22	101000
102000	102999	1428	1.22	102000
103000	103999	1440	1.22	103000
104000	104999	1453	1.22	104000
105000	105999	1465	1.22	105000
106000	106999	1477	1.22	106000
107000	107999	1489	1.22	107000
108000	108999	1501	1.22	108000
109000	109999	1514	1.22	109000
110000	110999	1526	1.22	110000
111000	111999	1538	1.22	111000
112000	112999	1550	1.22	112000
113000	113999	1563	1.21	113000
114000	114999	1575	1.16	114000
115000	115999	1586	1.16	115000
116000	116999	1598	1.16	116000
117000	117999	1609	1.16	117000
118000	118999	1621	1.16	118000
119000	119999	1633	1.16	119000
120000	120999	1644	1.16	120000
121000	121999	1656	1.16	121000
122000	122999	1667	1.16	122000
123000	123999	1679	1.16	123000
124000	124999	1690	1.16	124000

Federal Child Support Tables/ Tables fédérales de pensions alimentaires pour enfants

Province: Ontario No. Of Children/ Nbre d'enfants: Two/Deux

Income/Revenu ($)		Monthly Award/ Paiement mensuel ($)		
From/De	To/À	Basic Amount/ Montant de base	Plus (%)	Of Income Over/Du revenu dépassant
125000	*125999*	1702	1.16	125000
126000	*126999*	1714	1.16	126000
127000	*127999*	1725	1.16	127000
128000	*128999*	1737	1.16	128000
129000	*129999*	1748	1.16	129000
130000	*130999*	1760	1.16	130000
131000	*131999*	1772	1.16	131000
132000	*132999*	1783	1.16	132000
133000	*133999*	1795	1.16	133000
134000	*134999*	1806	1.16	134000
135000	*135999*	1818	1.16	135000
136000	*136999*	1829	1.16	136000
137000	*137999*	1841	1.16	137000
138000	*138999*	1853	1.16	138000
139000	*139999*	1864	1.16	139000
140000	*140999*	1876	1.16	140000
141000	*141999*	1887	1.16	141000
142000	*142999*	1899	1.16	142000
143000	*143999*	1910	1.16	143000
144000	*144999*	1922	1.16	144000
145000	*145999*	1934	1.16	145000
146000	*146999*	1945	1.16	146000
147000	*147999*	1957	1.16	147000
148000	*148999*	1968	1.16	148000
149000	*149999*	1980	1.16	149000

Federal Child Support Tables/ Tables fédérales de pensions alimentaires pour enfants

Province: Ontario No. Of Children/ Nbre d'enfants: Two/Deux

Income/Revenu ($)		Monthly Award/ Paiement mensuel ($)		
From/De	To/À	Basic Amount/ Montant de base	Plus (%)	Of Income Over/Du revenu dépassant
150000	*or greater/ ou plus*	1992	1.16	150000

Federal Child Support Tables/ Tables fédérales de pensions alimentaires pour enfants

Province: Ontario No. Of Children/ Nbre d'enfants: Three/Trois

Income/Revenu ($)		Monthly Award/ Paiement mensuel ($)		
From/De	To/À	Basic Amount/ Montant de base	Plus (%)	Of Income Over/Du revenu dépassant
0	*7999*	0		
8000	*8999*	0	1.88	8000
9000	*9999*	19	4.68	9000
10000	*10999*	66	4.68	10000
11000	*11999*	112	4.52	11000
12000	*12999*	158	4.02	12000
13000	*13999*	198	3.93	13000
14000	*14999*	237	3.90	14000
15000	*15999*	276	4.21	15000
16000	*16999*	318	4.23	16000
17000	*17999*	361	1.95	17000
18000	*18999*	380	1.86	18000
19000	*19999*	399	1.86	19000
20000	*20999*	417	1.78	20000
21000	*21999*	435	1.78	21000
22000	*22999*	453	1.78	22000
23000	*23999*	470	1.78	23000
24000	*24999*	488	1.78	24000

Federal Child Support Tables/ Tables fédérales de pensions alimentaires pour enfants

Province: Ontario No. Of Children/ Nbre d'enfants: Three/Trois

Income/Revenu ($)		Monthly Award/ Paiement mensuel ($)		
From/De	To/À	Basic Amount/ Montant de base	Plus (%)	Of Income Over/Du revenu dépassant
25000	*25999*	506	1.86	25000
26000	*26999*	525	1.86	26000
27000	*27999*	543	1.86	27000
28000	*28999*	562	1.86	28000
29000	*29999*	580	1.77	29000
30000	*30999*	598	1.72	30000
31000	*31999*	615	1.72	31000
32000	*32999*	632	1.72	32000
33000	*33999*	650	1.61	33000
34000	*34999*	666	1.55	34000
35000	*35999*	681	1.41	35000
36000	*36999*	695	1.88	36000
37000	*37999*	714	1.92	37000
38000	*38999*	733	1.96	38000
39000	*39999*	753	2.05	39000
40000	*40999*	773	2.11	40000
41000	*41999*	795	2.17	41000
42000	*42999*	816	2.17	42000
43000	*43999*	838	2.17	43000
44000	*44999*	860	2.17	44000
45000	*45999*	881	2.17	45000
46000	*46999*	903	2.17	46000
47000	*47999*	925	2.17	47000
48000	*48999*	946	1.96	48000
49000	*49999*	966	2.02	49000
50000	*50999*	986	1.91	50000
51000	*51999*	1005	1.91	51000
52000	*52999*	1024	1.91	52000
53000	*53999*	1043	1.91	53000
54000	*54999*	1063	1.91	54000
55000	*55999*	1082	1.91	55000
56000	*56999*	1101	1.91	56000
57000	*57999*	1120	1.91	57000
58000	*58999*	1139	1.91	58000
59000	*59999*	1158	1.91	59000

Federal Child Support Tables/ Tables fédérales de pensions alimentaires pour enfants

Province: Ontario No. Of Children/ Nbre d'enfants: Three/Trois

Income/Revenu ($)		Monthly Award/ Paiement mensuel ($)		
From/De	To/À	Basic Amount/ Montant de base	Plus (%)	Of Income Over/Du revenu dépassant
60000	*60999*	1177	1.86	60000
61000	*61999*	1196	1.81	61000
62000	*62999*	1214	1.81	62000
63000	*63999*	1232	1.81	63000
64000	*64999*	1250	1.81	64000
65000	*65999*	1268	1.86	65000
66000	*66999*	1287	1.85	66000
67000	*67999*	1305	1.79	67000
68000	*68999*	1323	1.79	68000
69000	*69999*	1341	1.79	69000
70000	*70999*	1359	1.61	70000
71000	*71999*	1375	1.46	71000
72000	*72999*	1390	1.25	72000
73000	*73999*	1402	1.46	73000
74000	*74999*	1417	1.53	74000
75000	*75999*	1432	1.57	75000
76000	*76999*	1448	1.57	76000
77000	*77999*	1464	1.57	77000
78000	*78999*	1479	1.57	78000
79000	*79999*	1495	1.57	79000
80000	*80999*	1511	1.57	80000
81000	*81999*	1527	1.57	81000
82000	*82999*	1542	1.57	82000
83000	*83999*	1558	1.57	83000
84000	*84999*	1574	1.57	84000
85000	*85999*	1590	1.57	85000
86000	*86999*	1605	1.57	86000
87000	*87999*	1621	1.57	87000
88000	*88999*	1637	1.57	88000
89000	*89999*	1652	1.57	89000
90000	*90999*	1668	1.57	90000
91000	*91999*	1684	1.57	91000
92000	*92999*	1700	1.57	92000
93000	*93999*	1715	1.57	93000
94000	*94999*	1731	1.57	94000

Federal Child Support Tables/ Tables fédérales de pensions alimentaires pour enfants

Province: Ontario No. Of Children/ N^bre d'enfants: Three/Trois

Income/Revenu ($)		Monthly Award/ Paiement mensuel ($)		
From/De	To/À	Basic Amount/ Montant de base	Plus (%)	Of Income Over/Du revenu dépassant
95000	*95999*	1747	1.57	95000
96000	*96999*	1762	1.57	96000
97000	*97999*	1778	1.57	97000
98000	*98999*	1794	1.57	98000
99000	*99999*	1810	1.57	99000
100000	*100999*	1825	1.57	100000
101000	*101999*	1841	1.57	101000
102000	*102999*	1857	1.57	102000
103000	*103999*	1872	1.57	103000
104000	*104999*	1888	1.57	104000
105000	*105999*	1904	1.57	105000
106000	*106999*	1920	1.57	106000
107000	*107999*	1935	1.57	107000
108000	*108999*	1951	1.57	108000
109000	*109999*	1967	1.57	109000
110000	*110999*	1983	1.57	110000
111000	*111999*	1998	1.57	111000
112000	*112999*	2014	1.57	112000
113000	*113999*	2030	1.56	113000
114000	*114999*	2045	1.49	114000
115000	*115999*	2060	1.49	115000
116000	*116999*	2075	1.49	116000
117000	*117999*	2090	1.49	117000
118000	*118999*	2105	1.49	118000
119000	*119999*	2120	1.49	119000
120000	*120999*	2135	1.49	120000
121000	*121999*	2149	1.49	121000
122000	*122999*	2164	1.49	122000

Federal Child Support Tables/ Tables fédérales de pensions alimentaires pour enfants

Province: Ontario No. Of Children/ N^bre d'enfants: Three/Trois

Income/Revenu ($)		Monthly Award/ Paiement mensuel ($)		
From/De	To/À	Basic Amount/ Montant de base	Plus (%)	Of Income Over/Du revenu dépassant
123000	*123999*	2179	1.49	123000
124000	*124999*	2194	1.49	124000
125000	*125999*	2209	1.49	125000
126000	*126999*	2224	1.49	126000
127000	*127999*	2239	1.49	127000
128000	*128999*	2254	1.49	128000
129000	*129999*	2269	1.49	129000
130000	*130999*	2283	1.49	130000
131000	*131999*	2298	1.49	131000
132000	*132999*	2313	1.49	132000
133000	*133999*	2328	1.49	133000
134000	*134999*	2343	1.49	134000
135000	*135999*	2358	1.49	135000
136000	*136999*	2373	1.49	136000
137000	*137999*	2388	1.49	137000
138000	*138999*	2403	1.49	138000
139000	*139999*	2417	1.49	139000
140000	*140999*	2432	1.49	140000
141000	*141999*	2447	1.49	141000
142000	*142999*	2462	1.49	142000
143000	*143999*	2477	1.49	143000
144000	*144999*	2492	1.49	144000
145000	*145999*	2507	1.49	145000
146000	*146999*	2522	1.49	146000
147000	*147999*	2536	1.49	147000
148000	*148999*	2551	1.49	148000
149000	*149999*	2566	1.49	149000

Federal Child Support Tables/ Tables fédérales de pensions alimentaires pour enfants

Province: Ontario No. Of Children/ Nbre d'enfants: Three/Trois

Income/Revenu ($)		Monthly Award/ Paiement mensuel ($)		
From/De	To/À	Basic Amount/ Montant de base	Plus (%)	Of Income Over/Du revenu dépassant
150000	*or greater/ ou plus*	2581	1.49	150000

Federal Child Support Tables/ Tables fédérales de pensions alimentaires pour enfants

Province: Ontario No. Of Children/ Nbre d'enfants: Four/Quatre

Income/Revenu ($)		Monthly Award/ Paiement mensuel ($)		
From/De	To/À	Basic Amount/ Montant de base	Plus (%)	Of Income Over/Du revenu dépassant
0	*7999*	0		
8000	*8999*	0	2.01	8000
9000	*9999*	20	5.01	9000
10000	*10999*	70	5.01	10000
11000	*11999*	120	4.84	11000
12000	*12999*	169	4.31	12000
13000	*13999*	212	4.22	13000
14000	*14999*	254	4.18	14000
15000	*15999*	296	4.51	15000
16000	*16999*	341	4.53	16000
17000	*17999*	386	4.53	17000
18000	*18999*	432	4.53	18000
19000	*19999*	477	2.92	19000
20000	*20999*	506	2.14	20000
21000	*21999*	528	2.14	21000
22000	*22999*	549	2.14	22000
23000	*23999*	570	2.14	23000
24000	*24999*	592	2.14	24000
25000	*25999*	613	2.24	25000
26000	*26999*	636	2.24	26000
27000	*27999*	658	2.24	27000
28000	*28999*	680	2.24	28000
29000	*29999*	703	2.14	29000
30000	*30999*	724	2.08	30000
31000	*31999*	745	2.08	31000
32000	*32999*	766	2.08	32000
33000	*33999*	786	1.96	33000
34000	*34999*	806	1.90	34000
35000	*35999*	825	1.70	35000
36000	*36999*	842	1.72	36000
37000	*37999*	859	1.76	37000
38000	*38999*	877	1.81	38000
39000	*39999*	895	1.97	39000
40000	*40999*	915	2.42	40000
41000	*41999*	939	2.49	41000
42000	*42999*	964	2.49	42000
43000	*43999*	989	2.49	43000
44000	*44999*	1014	2.49	44000
45000	*45999*	1039	2.49	45000
46000	*46999*	1064	2.49	46000
47000	*47999*	1088	2.49	47000
48000	*48999*	1113	2.25	48000
49000	*49999*	1136	2.49	49000
50000	*50999*	1161	2.49	50000
51000	*51999*	1186	2.49	51000
52000	*52999*	1211	2.49	52000
53000	*53999*	1235	2.49	53000
54000	*54999*	1260	2.49	54000
55000	*55999*	1285	2.49	55000
56000	*56999*	1310	2.47	56000
57000	*57999*	1335	2.26	57000
58000	*58999*	1358	2.26	58000
59000	*59999*	1380	2.26	59000

Federal Child Support Tables/ Tables fédérales de pensions alimentaires pour enfants

Province: Ontario
No. Of Children/ Nbre d'enfants: Four/Quatre

Income/Revenu ($)		Monthly Award/ Paiement mensuel ($)		
From/De	To/À	Basic Amount/ Montant de base	Plus (%)	Of Income Over/Du revenu dépassant
60000	*60999*	1403	2.21	60000
61000	*61999*	1425	2.15	61000
62000	*62999*	1446	2.15	62000
63000	*63999*	1468	2.15	63000
64000	*64999*	1489	2.15	64000
65000	*65999*	1511	2.20	65000
66000	*66999*	1533	2.18	66000
67000	*67999*	1555	2.12	67000
68000	*68999*	1576	2.12	68000
69000	*69999*	1597	2.12	69000
70000	*70999*	1618	1.91	70000
71000	*71999*	1637	1.76	71000
72000	*72999*	1655	1.51	72000
73000	*73999*	1670	1.76	73000
74000	*74999*	1688	1.82	74000
75000	*75999*	1706	1.86	75000
76000	*76999*	1724	1.86	76000
77000	*77999*	1743	1.86	77000
78000	*78999*	1762	1.86	78000
79000	*79999*	1780	1.86	79000
80000	*80999*	1799	1.86	80000
81000	*81999*	1817	1.86	81000
82000	*82999*	1836	1.86	82000
83000	*83999*	1855	1.86	83000
84000	*84999*	1873	1.86	84000
85000	*85999*	1892	1.86	85000
86000	*86999*	1910	1.86	86000
87000	*87999*	1929	1.86	87000
88000	*88999*	1947	1.86	88000
89000	*89999*	1966	1.86	89000
90000	*90999*	1985	1.86	90000
91000	*91999*	2003	1.86	91000
92000	*92999*	2022	1.86	92000
93000	*93999*	2040	1.86	93000
94000	*94999*	2059	1.86	94000

Federal Child Support Tables/ Tables fédérales de pensions alimentaires pour enfants

Province: Ontario
No. Of Children/ Nbre d'enfants: Four/Quatre

Income/Revenu ($)		Monthly Award/ Paiement mensuel ($)		
From/De	To/À	Basic Amount/ Montant de base	Plus (%)	Of Income Over/Du revenu dépassant
95000	*95999*	2077	1.86	95000
96000	*96999*	2096	1.86	96000
97000	*97999*	2115	1.86	97000
98000	*98999*	2133	1.86	98000
99000	*99999*	2152	1.86	99000
100000	*100999*	2170	1.86	100000
101000	*101999*	2189	1.86	101000
102000	*102999*	2207	1.86	102000
103000	*103999*	2226	1.86	103000
104000	*104999*	2245	1.86	104000
105000	*105999*	2263	1.86	105000
106000	*106999*	2282	1.86	106000
107000	*107999*	2300	1.86	107000
108000	*108999*	2319	1.86	108000
109000	*109999*	2338	1.86	109000
110000	*110999*	2356	1.86	110000
111000	*111999*	2375	1.86	111000
112000	*112999*	2393	1.86	112000
113000	*113999*	2412	1.84	113000
114000	*114999*	2430	1.76	114000
115000	*115999*	2448	1.76	115000
116000	*116999*	2465	1.76	116000
117000	*117999*	2483	1.76	117000
118000	*118999*	2501	1.76	118000
119000	*119999*	2518	1.76	119000
120000	*120999*	2536	1.76	120000
121000	*121999*	2553	1.76	121000
122000	*122999*	2571	1.76	122000
123000	*123999*	2589	1.76	123000
124000	*124999*	2606	1.76	124000
125000	*125999*	2624	1.76	125000
126000	*126999*	2641	1.76	126000
127000	*127999*	2659	1.76	127000
128000	*128999*	2677	1.76	128000
129000	*129999*	2694	1.76	129000

Federal Child Support Tables/ Tables fédérales de pensions alimentaires pour enfants

Province: Ontario
No. Of Children/ Nbre d'enfants: Four/Quatre

Income/Revenu ($)		Monthly Award/ Paiement mensuel ($)		
From/De	To/À	Basic Amount/ Montant de base	Plus (%)	Of Income Over/Du revenu dépassant
130000	*130999*	2712	1.76	130000
131000	*131999*	2729	1.76	131000
132000	*132999*	2747	1.76	132000
133000	*133999*	2764	1.76	133000
134000	*134999*	2782	1.76	134000
135000	*135999*	2800	1.76	135000
136000	*136999*	2817	1.76	136000
137000	*137999*	2835	1.76	137000
138000	*138999*	2852	1.76	138000
139000	*139999*	2870	1.76	139000
140000	*140999*	2888	1.76	140000
141000	*141999*	2905	1.76	141000
142000	*142999*	2923	1.76	142000
143000	*143999*	2940	1.76	143000
144000	*144999*	2958	1.76	144000
145000	*145999*	2976	1.76	145000
146000	*146999*	2993	1.76	146000
147000	*147999*	3011	1.76	147000
148000	*148999*	3028	1.76	148000
149000	*149999*	3046	1.76	149000

Federal Child Support Tables/ Tables fédérales de pensions alimentaires pour enfants

Province: Ontario
No. Of Children/ Nbre d'enfants: Four/Quatre

Income/Revenu ($)		Monthly Award/ Paiement mensuel ($)		
From/De	To/À	Basic Amount/ Montant de base	Plus (%)	Of Income Over/Du revenu dépassant
150000	*or greater/ ou plus*	3064	1.76	150000

Federal Child Support Tables/ Tables fédérales de pensions alimentaires pour enfants

Province: Ontario
No. Of Children/ Nbre d'enfants: Five/Cinq

Income/Revenu ($)		Monthly Award/ Paiement mensuel ($)		
From/De	To/À	Basic Amount/ Montant de base	Plus (%)	Of Income Over/Du revenu dépassant
0	*7999*	0		
8000	*8999*	0	2.01	8000
9000	*9999*	20	5.01	9000
10000	*10999*	70	5.01	10000
11000	*11999*	120	4.84	11000
12000	*12999*	169	4.31	12000
13000	*13999*	212	4.22	13000
14000	*14999*	254	4.18	14000
15000	*15999*	296	4.51	15000
16000	*16999*	341	4.53	16000
17000	*17999*	386	4.53	17000
18000	*18999*	432	4.53	18000
19000	*19999*	477	4.53	19000
20000	*20999*	522	4.35	20000
21000	*21999*	566	4.35	21000
22000	*22999*	609	4.35	22000
23000	*23999*	653	2.55	23000
24000	*24999*	678	2.45	24000

Federal Child Support Tables/ Tables fédérales de pensions alimentaires pour enfants

Province: Ontario
No. Of Children/ Nbre d'enfants: Five/Cinq

Income/Revenu ($)		Monthly Award/ Paiement mensuel ($)		
From/De	To/À	Basic Amount/ Montant de base	Plus (%)	Of Income Over/Du revenu dépassant
25000	*25999*	703	2.56	25000
26000	*26999*	728	2.56	26000
27000	*27999*	754	2.56	27000
28000	*28999*	779	2.56	28000
29000	*29999*	805	2.44	29000
30000	*30999*	829	2.37	30000
31000	*31999*	853	2.37	31000
32000	*32999*	877	2.37	32000
33000	*33999*	900	2.26	33000
34000	*34999*	923	2.18	34000
35000	*35999*	945	1.97	35000
36000	*36999*	965	1.99	36000
37000	*37999*	984	2.04	37000
38000	*38999*	1005	2.09	38000
39000	*39999*	1026	2.20	39000
40000	*40999*	1048	2.27	40000
41000	*41999*	1070	2.34	41000
42000	*42999*	1094	2.34	42000
43000	*43999*	1117	2.49	43000
44000	*44999*	1142	2.76	44000
45000	*45999*	1170	2.76	45000
46000	*46999*	1197	2.76	46000
47000	*47999*	1225	2.76	47000
48000	*48999*	1253	2.48	48000
49000	*49999*	1277	2.76	49000
50000	*50999*	1305	2.76	50000
51000	*51999*	1333	2.76	51000
52000	*52999*	1360	2.76	52000
53000	*53999*	1388	2.76	53000
54000	*54999*	1415	2.76	54000
55000	*55999*	1443	2.76	55000
56000	*56999*	1471	2.76	56000
57000	*57999*	1498	2.76	57000
58000	*58999*	1526	2.76	58000
59000	*59999*	1554	2.76	59000
60000	*60999*	1581	2.71	60000
61000	*61999*	1608	2.65	61000
62000	*62999*	1635	2.65	62000
63000	*63999*	1661	2.65	63000
64000	*64999*	1688	2.53	64000
65000	*65999*	1713	2.48	65000
66000	*66999*	1738	2.46	66000
67000	*67999*	1763	2.39	67000
68000	*68999*	1786	2.39	68000
69000	*69999*	1810	2.39	69000
70000	*70999*	1834	2.16	70000
71000	*71999*	1856	2.00	71000
72000	*72999*	1876	1.73	72000
73000	*73999*	1893	2.00	73000
74000	*74999*	1913	2.06	74000
75000	*75999*	1934	2.10	75000
76000	*76999*	1955	2.10	76000
77000	*77999*	1976	2.10	77000
78000	*78999*	1997	2.10	78000
79000	*79999*	2018	2.10	79000
80000	*80999*	2039	2.10	80000
81000	*81999*	2060	2.10	81000
82000	*82999*	2081	2.10	82000
83000	*83999*	2102	2.10	83000
84000	*84999*	2122	2.10	84000
85000	*85999*	2143	2.10	85000
86000	*86999*	2164	2.10	86000
87000	*87999*	2185	2.10	87000
88000	*88999*	2206	2.10	88000
89000	*89999*	2227	2.10	89000
90000	*90999*	2248	2.10	90000
91000	*91999*	2269	2.10	91000
92000	*92999*	2290	2.10	92000
93000	*93999*	2311	2.10	93000
94000	*94999*	2332	2.10	94000

Federal Child Support Tables/ Tables fédérales de pensions alimentaires pour enfants

Province: Ontario
No. Of Children/ Nbre d'enfants: Five/Cinq

Income/Revenu ($)		Monthly Award/ Paiement mensuel ($)		
From/De	To/À	Basic Amount/ Montant de base	Plus (%)	Of Income Over/Du revenu dépassant
95000	95999	2353	2.10	95000
96000	96999	2374	2.10	96000
97000	97999	2395	2.10	97000
98000	98999	2416	2.10	98000
99000	99999	2437	2.10	99000
100000	100999	2458	2.10	100000
101000	101999	2479	2.10	101000
102000	102999	2500	2.10	102000
103000	103999	2521	2.10	103000
104000	104999	2542	2.10	104000
105000	105999	2563	2.10	105000
106000	106999	2584	2.10	106000
107000	107999	2605	2.10	107000
108000	108999	2626	2.10	108000
109000	109999	2646	2.10	109000
110000	110999	2667	2.10	110000
111000	111999	2688	2.10	111000
112000	112999	2709	2.10	112000
113000	113999	2730	2.07	113000
114000	114999	2751	1.98	114000
115000	115999	2771	1.98	115000
116000	116999	2791	1.98	116000
117000	117999	2811	1.98	117000
118000	118999	2830	1.98	118000
119000	119999	2850	1.98	119000
120000	120999	2870	1.98	120000
121000	121999	2890	1.98	121000
122000	122999	2910	1.98	122000

Federal Child Support Tables/ Tables fédérales de pensions alimentaires pour enfants

Province: Ontario
No. Of Children/ Nbre d'enfants: Five/Cinq

Income/Revenu ($)		Monthly Award/ Paiement mensuel ($)		
From/De	To/À	Basic Amount/ Montant de base	Plus (%)	Of Income Over/Du revenu dépassant
123000	123999	2930	1.98	123000
124000	124999	2950	1.98	124000
125000	125999	2969	1.98	125000
126000	126999	2989	1.98	126000
127000	127999	3009	1.98	127000
128000	128999	3029	1.98	128000
129000	129999	3049	1.98	129000
130000	130999	3069	1.98	130000
131000	131999	3088	1.98	131000
132000	132999	3108	1.98	132000
133000	133999	3128	1.98	133000
134000	134999	3148	1.98	134000
135000	135999	3168	1.98	135000
136000	136999	3188	1.98	136000
137000	137999	3208	1.98	137000
138000	138999	3227	1.98	138000
139000	139999	3247	1.98	139000
140000	140999	3267	1.98	140000
141000	141999	3287	1.98	141000
142000	142999	3307	1.98	142000
143000	143999	3327	1.98	143000
144000	144999	3347	1.98	144000
145000	145999	3366	1.98	145000
146000	146999	3386	1.98	146000
147000	147999	3406	1.98	147000
148000	148999	3426	1.98	148000
149000	149999	3446	1.98	149000

Federal Child Support Tables/ Tables fédérales de pensions alimentaires pour enfants

Province: Ontario
No. Of Children/ Nbre d'enfants: Five/Cinq

Income/Revenu ($)		Monthly Award/ Paiement mensuel ($)		
From/De	To/À	Basic Amount/ Montant de base	Plus (%)	Of Income Over/Du revenu dépassant
150000	*or greater/ ou plus*	3466	1.98	150000

Federal Child Support Tables/ Tables fédérales de pensions alimentaires pour enfants

Province: Ontario
No. Of Children/ Nbre d'enfants: Six or more/ Six ou plus

Income/Revenu ($)		Monthly Award/ Paiement mensuel ($)		
From/De	To/À	Basic Amount/ Montant de base	Plus (%)	Of Income Over/Du revenu dépassant
0	*7999*	0		
8000	*8999*	0	2.01	8000
9000	*9999*	20	5.01	9000
10000	*10999*	70	5.01	10000
11000	*11999*	120	4.84	11000
12000	*12999*	169	4.31	12000
13000	*13999*	212	4.22	13000
14000	*14999*	254	4.18	14000
15000	*15999*	296	4.51	15000
16000	*16999*	341	4.53	16000
17000	*17999*	386	4.53	17000
18000	*18999*	432	4.53	18000
19000	*19999*	477	4.53	19000
20000	*20999*	522	4.35	20000
21000	*21999*	566	4.35	21000
22000	*22999*	609	4.35	22000
23000	*23999*	653	4.35	23000
24000	*24999*	696	4.35	24000

Federal Child Support Tables/ Tables fédérales de pensions alimentaires pour enfants

Province: Ontario
No. Of Children/ Nbre d'enfants: Six or more/ Six ou plus

Income/Revenu ($)		Monthly Award/ Paiement mensuel ($)		
From/De	To/À	Basic Amount/ Montant de base	Plus (%)	Of Income Over/Du revenu dépassant
25000	*25999*	740	4.53	25000
26000	*26999*	785	4.53	26000
27000	*27999*	830	3.27	27000
28000	*28999*	863	2.83	28000
29000	*29999*	891	2.70	29000
30000	*30999*	918	2.62	30000
31000	*31999*	945	2.62	31000
32000	*32999*	971	2.62	32000
33000	*33999*	997	2.50	33000
34000	*34999*	1022	2.43	34000
35000	*35999*	1046	2.19	35000
36000	*36999*	1068	2.21	36000
37000	*37999*	1090	2.27	37000
38000	*38999*	1113	2.33	38000
39000	*39999*	1136	2.45	39000
40000	*40999*	1161	2.52	40000
41000	*41999*	1186	2.60	41000
42000	*42999*	1212	2.60	42000
43000	*43999*	1238	2.60	43000
44000	*44999*	1264	2.60	44000
45000	*45999*	1290	2.60	45000
46000	*46999*	1316	2.60	46000
47000	*47999*	1342	2.84	47000
48000	*48999*	1370	2.69	48000
49000	*49999*	1397	2.99	49000
50000	*50999*	1427	2.99	50000
51000	*51999*	1457	2.99	51000
52000	*52999*	1487	2.99	52000
53000	*53999*	1517	2.99	53000
54000	*54999*	1547	2.99	54000
55000	*55999*	1577	2.99	55000
56000	*56999*	1607	2.99	56000
57000	*57999*	1637	2.99	57000
58000	*58999*	1666	2.99	58000
59000	*59999*	1696	2.99	59000

Federal Child Support Tables/ Tables fédérales de pensions alimentaires pour enfants

Province: Ontario
No. Of Children/ Nbre d'enfants: Six or more/ Six ou plus

Income/Revenu ($) From/De	Income/Revenu ($) To/À	Monthly Award/Paiement mensuel ($) Basic Amount/Montant de base	Plus (%)	Of Income Over/Du revenu dépassant
60000	*60999*	1726	2.93	60000
61000	*61999*	1756	2.88	61000
62000	*62999*	1784	2.88	62000
63000	*63999*	1813	2.88	63000
64000	*64999*	1842	2.88	64000
65000	*65999*	1871	2.95	65000
66000	*66999*	1900	2.94	66000
67000	*67999*	1930	2.91	67000
68000	*68999*	1959	2.91	68000
69000	*69999*	1988	2.91	69000
70000	*70999*	2017	2.39	70000
71000	*71999*	2041	2.21	71000
72000	*72999*	2063	1.91	72000
73000	*73999*	2082	2.21	73000
74000	*74999*	2104	2.27	74000
75000	*75999*	2127	2.30	75000
76000	*76999*	2150	2.30	76000
77000	*77999*	2173	2.30	77000
78000	*78999*	2196	2.30	78000
79000	*79999*	2219	2.30	79000
80000	*80999*	2242	2.30	80000
81000	*81999*	2265	2.30	81000
82000	*82999*	2288	2.30	82000
83000	*83999*	2311	2.30	83000
84000	*84999*	2334	2.30	84000
85000	*85999*	2356	2.30	85000
86000	*86999*	2379	2.30	86000
87000	*87999*	2402	2.30	87000
88000	*88999*	2425	2.30	88000
89000	*89999*	2448	2.30	89000
90000	*90999*	2471	2.30	90000
91000	*91999*	2494	2.30	91000
92000	*92999*	2517	2.30	92000
93000	*93999*	2540	2.30	93000
94000	*94999*	2563	2.30	94000

Federal Child Support Tables/ Tables fédérales de pensions alimentaires pour enfants

Province: Ontario
No. Of Children/ Nbre d'enfants: Six or more/ Six ou plus

Income/Revenu ($) From/De	Income/Revenu ($) To/À	Monthly Award/Paiement mensuel ($) Basic Amount/Montant de base	Plus (%)	Of Income Over/Du revenu dépassant
95000	*95999*	2586	2.30	95000
96000	*96999*	2609	2.30	96000
97000	*97999*	2632	2.30	97000
98000	*98999*	2655	2.30	98000
99000	*99999*	2678	2.30	99000
100000	*100999*	2701	2.30	100000
101000	*101999*	2724	2.30	101000
102000	*102999*	2747	2.30	102000
103000	*103999*	2770	2.30	103000
104000	*104999*	2793	2.30	104000
105000	*105999*	2816	2.30	105000
106000	*106999*	2839	2.30	106000
107000	*107999*	2862	2.30	107000
108000	*108999*	2885	2.30	108000
109000	*109999*	2908	2.30	109000
110000	*110999*	2931	2.30	110000
111000	*111999*	2954	2.30	111000
112000	*112999*	2977	2.30	112000
113000	*113999*	3000	2.27	113000
114000	*114999*	3023	2.18	114000
115000	*115999*	3044	2.18	115000
116000	*116999*	3066	2.18	116000
117000	*117999*	3088	2.18	117000
118000	*118999*	3110	2.18	118000
119000	*119999*	3131	2.18	119000
120000	*120999*	3153	2.18	120000
121000	*121999*	3175	2.18	121000
122000	*122999*	3197	2.18	122000
123000	*123999*	3218	2.18	123000
124000	*124999*	3240	2.18	124000
125000	*125999*	3262	2.18	125000
126000	*126999*	3284	2.18	126000
127000	*127999*	3305	2.18	127000
128000	*128999*	3327	2.18	128000
129000	*129999*	3349	2.18	129000

Federal Child Support Tables/ Tables fédérales de pensions alimentaires pour enfants

Province: Ontario
No. Of Children/ Nbre d'enfants: Six or more/ Six ou plus

Income/Revenu ($)		Monthly Award/ Paiement mensuel ($)		
From/De	To/À	Basic Amount/ Montant de base	Plus (%)	Of Income Over/Du revenu dépassant
130000	*130999*	3371	2.18	130000
131000	*131999*	3392	2.18	131000
132000	*132999*	3414	2.18	132000
133000	*133999*	3436	2.18	133000
134000	*134999*	3458	2.18	134000
135000	*135999*	3479	2.18	135000
136000	*136999*	3501	2.18	136000
137000	*137999*	3523	2.18	137000
138000	*138999*	3545	2.18	138000
139000	*139999*	3566	2.18	139000
140000	*140999*	3588	2.18	140000
141000	*141999*	3610	2.18	141000
142000	*142999*	3632	2.18	142000
143000	*143999*	3653	2.18	143000
144000	*144999*	3675	2.18	144000
145000	*145999*	3697	2.18	145000
146000	*146999*	3719	2.18	146000
147000	*147999*	3740	2.18	147000
148000	*148999*	3762	2.18	148000
149000	*149999*	3784	2.18	149000

Federal Child Support Tables/ Tables fédérales de pensions alimentaires pour enfants

Province: Ontario
No. Of Children/ Nbre d'enfants: Six or more/ Six ou plus

Income/Revenu ($)		Monthly Award/ Paiement mensuel ($)		
From/De	To/À	Basic Amount/ Montant de base	Plus (%)	Of Income Over/Du revenu dépassant
150000	*or greater/ ou plus*	3806	2.18	150000

Federal Child Support Tables/ Tables fédérales de pensions alimentaires pour enfants

Province: Quebec/Québec
No. Of Children/ Nbre d'enfants: ONE/UN

Income/Revenu ($)		Monthly Award/ Paiement mensuel ($)		
From/De	To/À	Basic Amount/ Montant de base	Plus (%)	Of Income Over/Du revenu dépassant
0	*7999*	0		
8000	*8999*	0	1.53	8000
9000	*9999*	15	1.91	9000
10000	*10999*	34	1.91	10000
11000	*11999*	53	1.91	11000
12000	*12999*	73	1.91	12000
13000	*13999*	92	1.91	13000
14000	*14999*	111	1.91	14000
15000	*15999*	130	1.91	15000
16000	*16999*	149	0.34	16000
17000	*17999*	152	0.34	17000
18000	*18999*	156	0.34	18000
19000	*19999*	159	0.34	19000
20000	*20999*	163	0.34	20000
21000	*21999*	166	0.34	21000
22000	*22999*	170	0.34	22000
23000	*23999*	173	0.34	23000
24000	*24999*	176	0.34	24000

Federal Child Support Tables/ Tables fédérales de pensions alimentaires pour enfants

Province: Quebec/Québec
No. Of Children/ Nbre d'enfants: ONE/UN

Income/Revenu ($) From/De	To/À	Monthly Award/ Paiement mensuel ($) Basic Amount/ Montant de base	Plus (%)	Of Income Over/Du revenu dépassant
25000	*25999*	180	0.60	25000
26000	*26999*	186	0.90	26000
27000	*27999*	195	0.89	27000
28000	*28999*	204	0.86	28000
29000	*29999*	212	0.82	29000
30000	*30999*	220	0.79	30000
31000	*31999*	228	0.79	31000
32000	*32999*	236	0.79	32000
33000	*33999*	244	0.79	33000
34000	*34999*	252	0.79	34000
35000	*35999*	260	0.76	35000
36000	*36999*	268	0.83	36000
37000	*37999*	276	0.88	37000
38000	*38999*	285	0.88	38000
39000	*39999*	294	0.90	39000
40000	*40999*	303	0.93	40000
41000	*41999*	312	0.96	41000
42000	*42999*	321	0.96	42000
43000	*43999*	331	0.96	43000
44000	*44999*	341	0.96	44000
45000	*45999*	350	0.96	45000
46000	*46999*	360	0.96	46000
47000	*47999*	369	0.96	47000
48000	*48999*	379	0.96	48000
49000	*49999*	389	0.96	49000
50000	*50999*	398	0.96	50000
51000	*51999*	408	0.96	51000
52000	*52999*	417	0.96	52000
53000	*53999*	427	0.96	53000
54000	*54999*	437	0.96	54000
55000	*55999*	446	0.92	55000
56000	*56999*	455	0.90	56000
57000	*57999*	464	0.90	57000
58000	*58999*	474	0.90	58000
59000	*59999*	483	0.90	59000

Federal Child Support Tables/ Tables fédérales de pensions alimentaires pour enfants

Province: Quebec/Québec
No. Of Children/ Nbre d'enfants: ONE/UN

Income/Revenu ($) From/De	To/À	Monthly Award/ Paiement mensuel ($) Basic Amount/ Montant de base	Plus (%)	Of Income Over/Du revenu dépassant
60000	*60999*	492	0.90	60000
61000	*61999*	501	0.90	61000
62000	*62999*	510	0.90	62000
63000	*63999*	519	0.90	63000
64000	*64999*	528	0.90	64000
65000	*65999*	537	0.90	65000
66000	*66999*	546	0.90	66000
67000	*67999*	555	0.85	67000
68000	*68999*	563	0.80	68000
69000	*69999*	571	0.80	69000
70000	*70999*	579	0.75	70000
71000	*71999*	587	0.75	71000
72000	*72999*	595	0.75	72000
73000	*73999*	602	0.75	73000
74000	*74999*	610	0.75	74000
75000	*75999*	617	0.75	75000
76000	*76999*	625	0.75	76000
77000	*77999*	632	0.75	77000
78000	*78999*	640	0.75	78000
79000	*79999*	647	0.75	79000
80000	*80999*	655	0.75	80000
81000	*81999*	662	0.75	81000
82000	*82999*	670	0.75	82000
83000	*83999*	677	0.75	83000
84000	*84999*	685	0.75	84000
85000	*85999*	693	0.75	85000
86000	*86999*	700	0.75	86000
87000	*87999*	708	0.75	87000
88000	*88999*	715	0.75	88000
89000	*89999*	723	0.75	89000
90000	*90999*	730	0.75	90000
91000	*91999*	738	0.75	91000
92000	*92999*	745	0.75	92000
93000	*93999*	753	0.75	93000
94000	*94999*	760	0.75	94000

Federal Child Support Tables/ Tables fédérales de pensions alimentaires pour enfants

Province: Quebec/Québec No. Of Children/ Nbre d'enfants: ONE/UN

Income/Revenu ($)		Monthly Award/ Paiement mensuel ($)		
From/De	To/À	Basic Amount/ Montant de base	Plus (%)	Of Income Over/Du revenu dépassant
95000	*95999*	768	0.75	95000
96000	*96999*	776	0.75	96000
97000	*97999*	783	0.75	97000
98000	*98999*	791	0.75	98000
99000	*99999*	798	0.75	99000
100000	*100999*	806	0.75	100000
101000	*101999*	813	0.75	101000
102000	*102999*	821	0.75	102000
103000	*103999*	828	0.75	103000
104000	*104999*	836	0.75	104000
105000	*105999*	843	0.75	105000
106000	*106999*	851	0.75	106000
107000	*107999*	858	0.75	107000
108000	*108999*	866	0.75	108000
109000	*109999*	874	0.75	109000
110000	*110999*	881	0.75	110000
111000	*111999*	889	0.75	111000
112000	*112999*	896	0.75	112000
113000	*113999*	904	0.75	113000
114000	*114999*	911	0.72	114000
115000	*115999*	918	0.72	115000
116000	*116999*	926	0.72	116000
117000	*117999*	933	0.72	117000
118000	*118999*	940	0.72	118000
119000	*119999*	947	0.72	119000
120000	*120999*	954	0.72	120000
121000	*121999*	962	0.72	121000
122000	*122999*	969	0.72	122000

Federal Child Support Tables/ Tables fédérales de pensions alimentaires pour enfants

Province: Quebec/Québec No. Of Children/ Nbre d'enfants: ONE/UN

Income/Revenu ($)		Monthly Award/ Paiement mensuel ($)		
From/De	To/À	Basic Amount/ Montant de base	Plus (%)	Of Income Over/Du revenu dépassant
123000	*123999*	976	0.72	123000
124000	*124999*	983	0.72	124000
125000	*125999*	990	0.72	125000
126000	*126999*	997	0.72	126000
127000	*127999*	1005	0.72	127000
128000	*128999*	1012	0.72	128000
129000	*129999*	1019	0.72	129000
130000	*130999*	1026	0.72	130000
131000	*131999*	1033	0.72	131000
132000	*132999*	1041	0.72	132000
133000	*133999*	1048	0.72	133000
134000	*134999*	1055	0.72	134000
135000	*135999*	1062	0.72	135000
136000	*136999*	1069	0.72	136000
137000	*137999*	1077	0.72	137000
138000	*138999*	1084	0.72	138000
139000	*139999*	1091	0.72	139000
140000	*140999*	1098	0.72	140000
141000	*141999*	1105	0.72	141000
142000	*142999*	1113	0.72	142000
143000	*143999*	1120	0.72	143000
144000	*144999*	1127	0.72	144000
145000	*145999*	1134	0.72	145000
146000	*146999*	1141	0.72	146000
147000	*147999*	1149	0.72	147000
148000	*148999*	1156	0.72	148000
149000	*149999*	1163	0.72	149000

Federal Child Support Tables/ Tables fédérales de pensions alimentaires pour enfants

Province: Quebec/Québec No. Of Children/ Nbre d'enfants: ONE/UN

Income/Revenu ($)		Monthly Award/ Paiement mensuel ($)		
From/De	To/À	Basic Amount/ Montant de base	Plus (%)	Of Income Over/Du revenu dépassant
150000	*or greater/ ou plus*	1170	0.72	150000

Federal Child Support Tables/ Tables fédérales de pensions alimentaires pour enfants

Province: Quebec/Québec No. Of Children/ Nbrem d'enfants: Two/Deux

Income/Revenu ($)		Monthly Award/ Paiement mensuel ($)		
From/De	To/À	Basic Amount/ Montant de base	Plus (%)	Of Income Over/Du revenu dépassant
0	*7999*	0		
8000	*8999*	0	3.30	8000
9000	*9999*	33	4.48	9000
10000	*10999*	78	4.48	10000
11000	*11999*	123	4.48	11000
12000	*12999*	167	4.38	12000
13000	*13999*	211	3.53	13000
14000	*14999*	246	1.17	14000
15000	*15999*	258	0.62	15000
16000	*16999*	264	0.90	16000
17000	*17999*	273	0.90	17000
18000	*18999*	282	0.90	18000
19000	*19999*	291	0.90	19000
20000	*20999*	300	0.90	20000
21000	*21999*	309	0.90	21000
22000	*22999*	318	0.90	22000
23000	*23999*	327	0.90	23000
24000	*24999*	337	0.90	24000

Federal Child Support Tables/ Tables fédérales de pensions alimentaires pour enfants

Province: Quebec/Québec No. Of Children/ Nbrem d'enfants: Two/Deux

Income/Revenu ($)		Monthly Award/ Paiement mensuel ($)		
From/De	To/À	Basic Amount/ Montant de base	Plus (%)	Of Income Over/Du revenu dépassant
25000	*25999*	346	0.90	25000
26000	*26999*	355	0.90	26000
27000	*27999*	364	0.74	27000
28000	*28999*	371	1.02	28000
29000	*29999*	381	1.20	29000
30000	*30999*	393	1.16	30000
31000	*31999*	405	1.16	31000
32000	*32999*	417	1.16	32000
33000	*33999*	428	1.16	33000
34000	*34999*	440	1.16	34000
35000	*35999*	452	1.12	35000
36000	*36999*	463	1.22	36000
37000	*37999*	475	1.29	37000
38000	*38999*	488	1.29	38000
39000	*39999*	501	1.33	39000
40000	*40999*	514	1.38	40000
41000	*41999*	528	1.42	41000
42000	*42999*	542	1.42	42000
43000	*43999*	556	1.42	43000
44000	*44999*	571	1.42	44000
45000	*45999*	585	1.42	45000
46000	*46999*	599	1.42	46000
47000	*47999*	613	1.42	47000
48000	*48999*	628	1.42	48000
49000	*49999*	642	1.42	49000
50000	*50999*	656	1.42	50000
51000	*51999*	670	1.42	51000
52000	*52999*	685	1.42	52000
53000	*53999*	699	1.42	53000
54000	*54999*	713	1.42	54000
55000	*55999*	727	1.36	55000
56000	*56999*	741	1.34	56000
57000	*57999*	754	1.34	57000
58000	*58999*	768	1.34	58000
59000	*59999*	781	1.34	59000

Federal Child Support Tables/ Tables fédérales de pensions alimentaires pour enfants

Province: Quebec/Québec No. Of Children/ Nbrem d'enfants: Two/Deux

Income/Revenu ($)		Monthly Award/ Paiement mensuel ($)		
From/De	To/À	Basic Amount/ Montant de base	Plus (%)	Of Income Over/Du revenu dépassant
60000	*60999*	794	1.34	60000
61000	*61999*	808	1.34	61000
62000	*62999*	821	1.34	62000
63000	*63999*	835	1.34	63000
64000	*64999*	848	1.34	64000
65000	*65999*	861	1.34	65000
66000	*66999*	875	1.34	66000
67000	*67999*	888	1.29	67000
68000	*68999*	901	1.25	68000
69000	*69999*	913	1.25	69000
70000	*70999*	926	1.17	70000
71000	*71999*	938	1.17	71000
72000	*72999*	949	1.17	72000
73000	*73999*	961	1.17	73000
74000	*74999*	973	1.17	74000
75000	*75999*	985	1.17	75000
76000	*76999*	996	1.17	76000
77000	*77999*	1008	1.17	77000
78000	*78999*	1020	1.17	78000
79000	*79999*	1031	1.17	79000
80000	*80999*	1043	1.17	80000
81000	*81999*	1055	1.17	81000
82000	*82999*	1067	1.17	82000
83000	*83999*	1078	1.17	83000
84000	*84999*	1090	1.17	84000
85000	*85999*	1102	1.17	85000
86000	*86999*	1114	1.17	86000
87000	*87999*	1125	1.17	87000
88000	*88999*	1137	1.17	88000
89000	*89999*	1149	1.17	89000
90000	*90999*	1160	1.17	90000
91000	*91999*	1172	1.17	91000
92000	*92999*	1184	1.17	92000
93000	*93999*	1196	1.17	93000
94000	*94999*	1207	1.17	94000

Federal Child Support Tables/ Tables fédérales de pensions alimentaires pour enfants

Province: Quebec/Québec No. Of Children/ Nbrem d'enfants: Two/Deux

Income/Revenu ($)		Monthly Award/ Paiement mensuel ($)		
From/De	To/À	Basic Amount/ Montant de base	Plus (%)	Of Income Over/Du revenu dépassant
95000	*95999*	1219	1.17	95000
96000	*96999*	1231	1.17	96000
97000	*97999*	1243	1.17	97000
98000	*98999*	1254	1.17	98000
99000	*99999*	1266	1.17	99000
100000	*100999*	1278	1.17	100000
101000	*101999*	1289	1.17	101000
102000	*102999*	1301	1.17	102000
103000	*103999*	1313	1.17	103000
104000	*104999*	1325	1.17	104000
105000	*105999*	1336	1.17	105000
106000	*106999*	1348	1.17	106000
107000	*107999*	1360	1.17	107000
108000	*108999*	1372	1.17	108000
109000	*109999*	1383	1.17	109000
110000	*110999*	1395	1.17	110000
111000	*111999*	1407	1.17	111000
112000	*112999*	1418	1.17	112000
113000	*113999*	1430	1.16	113000
114000	*114999*	1442	1.12	114000
115000	*115999*	1453	1.12	115000
116000	*116999*	1464	1.12	116000
117000	*117999*	1475	1.12	117000
118000	*118999*	1487	1.12	118000
119000	*119999*	1498	1.12	119000
120000	*120999*	1509	1.12	120000
121000	*121999*	1520	1.12	121000
122000	*122999*	1531	1.12	122000
123000	*123999*	1543	1.12	123000
124000	*124999*	1554	1.12	124000
125000	*125999*	1565	1.12	125000
126000	*126999*	1576	1.12	126000
127000	*127999*	1587	1.12	127000
128000	*128999*	1598	1.12	128000
129000	*129999*	1610	1.12	129000

Federal Child Support Tables/ Tables fédérales de pensions alimentaires pour enfants

Province: Quebec/Québec
No. Of Children/ Nbrem d'enfants: Two/Deux

Income/Revenu ($)		Monthly Award/ Paiement mensuel ($)		
From/De	To/À	Basic Amount/ Montant de base	Plus (%)	Of Income Over/Du revenu dépassant
130000	*130999*	1621	1.12	130000
131000	*131999*	1632	1.12	131000
132000	*132999*	1643	1.12	132000
133000	*133999*	1654	1.12	133000
134000	*134999*	1666	1.12	134000
135000	*135999*	1677	1.12	135000
136000	*136999*	1688	1.12	136000
137000	*137999*	1699	1.12	137000
138000	*138999*	1710	1.12	138000
139000	*139999*	1722	1.12	139000
140000	*140999*	1733	1.12	140000
141000	*141999*	1744	1.12	141000
142000	*142999*	1755	1.12	142000
143000	*143999*	1766	1.12	143000
144000	*144999*	1777	1.12	144000
145000	*145999*	1789	1.12	145000
146000	*146999*	1800	1.12	146000
147000	*147999*	1811	1.12	147000
148000	*148999*	1822	1.12	148000
149000	*149999*	1833	1.12	149000

Federal Child Support Tables/ Tables fédérales de pensions alimentaires pour enfants

Province: Quebec/Québec
No. Of Children/ Nbrem d'enfants: Two/Deux

Income/Revenu ($)		Monthly Award/ Paiement mensuel ($)		
From/De	To/À	Basic Amount/ Montant de base	Plus (%)	Of Income Over/Du revenu dépassant
150000	*or greater/ ou plus*	1845	1.12	150000

Federal Child Support Tables/ Tables fédérales de pensions alimentaires pour enfants

Province: Quebec/Québec
No. Of Children/ Nbre d'enfants: Three/Trois

Income/Revenu ($)		Monthly Award/ Paiement mensuel ($)		
From/De	To/À	Basic Amount/ Montant de base	Plus (%)	Of Income Over/Du revenu dépassant
0	*7999*	0		
8000	*8999*	0	3.56	8000
9000	*9999*	36	4.82	9000
10000	*10999*	84	4.82	10000
11000	*11999*	132	4.82	11000
12000	*12999*	180	4.72	12000
13000	*13999*	227	3.80	13000
14000	*14999*	265	3.77	14000
15000	*15999*	303	3.77	15000
16000	*16999*	341	2.93	16000
17000	*17999*	370	1.35	17000
18000	*18999*	384	1.35	18000
19000	*19999*	397	1.35	19000
20000	*20999*	411	1.35	20000
21000	*21999*	424	1.35	21000
22000	*22999*	438	1.35	22000
23000	*23999*	451	1.35	23000
24000	*24999*	465	1.35	24000

Federal Child Support Tables/ Tables fédérales de pensions alimentaires pour enfants

Province: Quebec/Québec
No. Of Children/ Nbre d'enfants: Three/Trois

Income/Revenu ($)		Monthly Award/ Paiement mensuel ($)		
From/De	To/À	Basic Amount/ Montant de base	Plus (%)	Of Income Over/Du revenu dépassant
25000	*25999*	478	1.35	25000
26000	*26999*	492	1.35	26000
27000	*27999*	505	1.18	27000
28000	*28999*	517	0.88	28000
29000	*29999*	526	0.79	29000
30000	*30999*	534	1.27	30000
31000	*31999*	546	1.46	31000
32000	*32999*	561	1.46	32000
33000	*33999*	576	1.46	33000
34000	*34999*	590	1.46	34000
35000	*35999*	605	1.40	35000
36000	*36999*	619	1.53	36000
37000	*37999*	634	1.63	37000
38000	*38999*	650	1.63	38000
39000	*39999*	667	1.68	39000
40000	*40999*	683	1.74	40000
41000	*41999*	701	1.80	41000
42000	*42999*	719	1.80	42000
43000	*43999*	737	1.80	43000
44000	*44999*	755	1.80	44000
45000	*45999*	773	1.80	45000
46000	*46999*	791	1.80	46000
47000	*47999*	809	1.80	47000
48000	*48999*	826	1.80	48000
49000	*49999*	844	1.80	49000
50000	*50999*	862	1.80	50000
51000	*51999*	880	1.80	51000
52000	*52999*	898	1.80	52000
53000	*53999*	916	1.80	53000
54000	*54999*	934	1.80	54000
55000	*55999*	952	1.72	55000
56000	*56999*	969	1.68	56000
57000	*57999*	986	1.68	57000
58000	*58999*	1003	1.68	58000
59000	*59999*	1020	1.68	59000

Federal Child Support Tables/ Tables fédérales de pensions alimentaires pour enfants

Province: Quebec/Québec
No. Of Children/ Nbre d'enfants: Three/Trois

Income/Revenu ($)		Monthly Award/ Paiement mensuel ($)		
From/De	To/À	Basic Amount/ Montant de base	Plus (%)	Of Income Over/Du revenu dépassant
60000	*60999*	1037	1.68	60000
61000	*61999*	1054	1.68	61000
62000	*62999*	1070	1.68	62000
63000	*63999*	1087	1.68	63000
64000	*64999*	1104	1.68	64000
65000	*65999*	1121	1.68	65000
66000	*66999*	1138	1.68	66000
67000	*67999*	1155	1.64	67000
68000	*68999*	1171	1.60	68000
69000	*69999*	1187	1.60	69000
70000	*70999*	1203	1.51	70000
71000	*71999*	1218	1.51	71000
72000	*72999*	1233	1.51	72000
73000	*73999*	1248	1.51	73000
74000	*74999*	1263	1.51	74000
75000	*75999*	1278	1.51	75000
76000	*76999*	1293	1.51	76000
77000	*77999*	1309	1.51	77000
78000	*78999*	1324	1.51	78000
79000	*79999*	1339	1.51	79000
80000	*80999*	1354	1.51	80000
81000	*81999*	1369	1.51	81000
82000	*82999*	1384	1.51	82000
83000	*83999*	1399	1.51	83000
84000	*84999*	1414	1.51	84000
85000	*85999*	1429	1.51	85000
86000	*86999*	1444	1.51	86000
87000	*87999*	1459	1.51	87000
88000	*88999*	1474	1.51	88000
89000	*89999*	1490	1.51	89000
90000	*90999*	1505	1.51	90000
91000	*91999*	1520	1.51	91000
92000	*92999*	1535	1.51	92000
93000	*93999*	1550	1.51	93000
94000	*94999*	1565	1.51	94000

Federal Child Support Tables/ Tables fédérales de pensions alimentaires pour enfants

Province: Quebec/Québec No. Of Children/ Nbre d'enfants: Three/Trois

Income/Revenu ($)		Monthly Award/ Paiement mensuel ($)		
From/De	To/À	Basic Amount/ Montant de base	Plus (%)	Of Income Over/Du revenu dépassant
95000	*95999*	1580	1.51	95000
96000	*96999*	1595	1.51	96000
97000	*97999*	1610	1.51	97000
98000	*98999*	1625	1.51	98000
99000	*99999*	1640	1.51	99000
100000	*100999*	1655	1.51	100000
101000	*101999*	1670	1.51	101000
102000	*102999*	1686	1.51	102000
103000	*103999*	1701	1.51	103000
104000	*104999*	1716	1.51	104000
105000	*105999*	1731	1.51	105000
106000	*106999*	1746	1.51	106000
107000	*107999*	1761	1.51	107000
108000	*108999*	1776	1.51	108000
109000	*109999*	1791	1.51	109000
110000	*110999*	1806	1.51	110000
111000	*111999*	1821	1.51	111000
112000	*112999*	1836	1.51	112000
113000	*113999*	1851	1.49	113000
114000	*114999*	1866	1.44	114000
115000	*115999*	1881	1.44	115000
116000	*116999*	1895	1.44	116000
117000	*117999*	1910	1.44	117000
118000	*118999*	1924	1.44	118000
119000	*119999*	1938	1.44	119000
120000	*120999*	1953	1.44	120000
121000	*121999*	1967	1.44	121000
122000	*122999*	1981	1.44	122000

Federal Child Support Tables/ Tables fédérales de pensions alimentaires pour enfants

Province: Quebec/Québec No. Of Children/ Nbre d'enfants: Three/Trois

Income/Revenu ($)		Monthly Award/ Paiement mensuel ($)		
From/De	To/À	Basic Amount/ Montant de base	Plus (%)	Of Income Over/Du revenu dépassant
123000	*123999*	1996	1.44	123000
124000	*124999*	2010	1.44	124000
125000	*125999*	2025	1.44	125000
126000	*126999*	2039	1.44	126000
127000	*127999*	2053	1.44	127000
128000	*128999*	2068	1.44	128000
129000	*129999*	2082	1.44	129000
130000	*130999*	2097	1.44	130000
131000	*131999*	2111	1.44	131000
132000	*132999*	2125	1.44	132000
133000	*133999*	2140	1.44	133000
134000	*134999*	2154	1.44	134000
135000	*135999*	2168	1.44	135000
136000	*136999*	2183	1.44	136000
137000	*137999*	2197	1.44	137000
138000	*138999*	2212	1.44	138000
139000	*139999*	2226	1.44	139000
140000	*140999*	2240	1.44	140000
141000	*141999*	2255	1.44	141000
142000	*142999*	2269	1.44	142000
143000	*143999*	2284	1.44	143000
144000	*144999*	2298	1.44	144000
145000	*145999*	2312	1.44	145000
146000	*146999*	2327	1.44	146000
147000	*147999*	2341	1.44	147000
148000	*148999*	2355	1.44	148000
149000	*149999*	2370	1.44	149000

Federal Child Support Tables/ Tables fédérales de pensions alimentaires pour enfants

Province: Quebec/Québec
No. Of Children/ Nbre d'enfants: Three/Trois

Income/Revenu ($)		Monthly Award/ Paiement mensuel ($)		
From/De	To/À	Basic Amount/ Montant de base	Plus (%)	Of Income Over/Du revenu dépassant
150000	*or greater/ ou plus*	2384	1.44	150000

Federal Child Support Tables/ Tables fédérales de pensions alimentaires pour enfants

Province: Quebec/Québec
No. Of Children/ Nbre d'enfants: Four/Quatre

Income/Revenu ($)		Monthly Award/ Paiement mensuel ($)		
From/De	To/À	Basic Amount/ Montant de base	Plus (%)	Of Income Over/Du revenu dépassant
0	*7999*	0		
8000	*8999*	0	3.81	8000
9000	*9999*	38	5.16	9000
10000	*10999*	90	5.16	10000
11000	*11999*	141	5.16	11000
12000	*12999*	193	5.06	12000
13000	*13999*	244	4.07	13000
14000	*14999*	284	4.04	14000
15000	*15999*	325	4.04	15000
16000	*16999*	365	4.04	16000
17000	*17999*	406	4.04	17000
18000	*18999*	446	3.76	18000
19000	*19999*	484	1.72	19000
20000	*20999*	501	1.72	20000
21000	*21999*	518	1.72	21000
22000	*22999*	535	1.72	22000
23000	*23999*	552	1.72	23000
24000	*24999*	569	1.72	24000

Federal Child Support Tables/ Tables fédérales de pensions alimentaires pour enfants

Province: Quebec/Québec
No. Of Children/ Nbre d'enfants: Four/Quatre

Income/Revenu ($)		Monthly Award/ Paiement mensuel ($)		
From/De	To/À	Basic Amount/ Montant de base	Plus (%)	Of Income Over/Du revenu dépassant
25000	*25999*	587	1.72	25000
26000	*26999*	604	1.72	26000
27000	*27999*	621	1.53	27000
28000	*28999*	636	1.21	28000
29000	*29999*	648	1.11	29000
30000	*30999*	660	1.05	30000
31000	*31999*	670	1.05	31000
32000	*32999*	681	1.55	32000
33000	*33999*	696	1.71	33000
34000	*34999*	713	1.71	34000
35000	*35999*	730	1.64	35000
36000	*36999*	747	1.78	36000
37000	*37999*	764	1.90	37000
38000	*38999*	783	1.90	38000
39000	*39999*	802	1.96	39000
40000	*40999*	822	2.03	40000
41000	*41999*	842	2.10	41000
42000	*42999*	863	2.10	42000
43000	*43999*	884	2.10	43000
44000	*44999*	905	2.10	44000
45000	*45999*	926	2.10	45000
46000	*46999*	947	2.10	46000
47000	*47999*	968	2.10	47000
48000	*48999*	989	2.10	48000
49000	*49999*	1010	2.10	49000
50000	*50999*	1031	2.10	50000
51000	*51999*	1052	2.10	51000
52000	*52999*	1073	2.10	52000
53000	*53999*	1094	2.10	53000
54000	*54999*	1115	2.10	54000
55000	*55999*	1136	2.00	55000
56000	*56999*	1156	1.97	56000
57000	*57999*	1176	1.97	57000
58000	*58999*	1196	1.97	58000
59000	*59999*	1215	1.97	59000

Federal Child Support Tables/ Tables fédérales de pensions alimentaires pour enfants

Province: Quebec/Québec
No. Of Children/ Nbre d'enfants: Four/Quatre

Income/Revenu ($)		Monthly Award/ Paiement mensuel ($)		
From/De	To/À	Basic Amount/ Montant de base	Plus (%)	Of Income Over/Du revenu dépassant
60000	*60999*	1235	1.97	60000
61000	*61999*	1255	1.97	61000
62000	*62999*	1274	1.97	62000
63000	*63999*	1294	1.97	63000
64000	*64999*	1314	1.97	64000
65000	*65999*	1333	1.97	65000
66000	*66999*	1353	1.97	66000
67000	*67999*	1373	1.93	67000
68000	*68999*	1392	1.89	68000
69000	*69999*	1411	1.89	69000
70000	*70999*	1430	1.78	70000
71000	*71999*	1448	1.78	71000
72000	*72999*	1465	1.78	72000
73000	*73999*	1483	1.78	73000
74000	*74999*	1501	1.78	74000
75000	*75999*	1519	1.78	75000
76000	*76999*	1537	1.78	76000
77000	*77999*	1554	1.78	77000
78000	*78999*	1572	1.78	78000
79000	*79999*	1590	1.78	79000
80000	*80999*	1608	1.78	80000
81000	*81999*	1626	1.78	81000
82000	*82999*	1644	1.78	82000
83000	*83999*	1661	1.78	83000
84000	*84999*	1679	1.78	84000
85000	*85999*	1697	1.78	85000
86000	*86999*	1715	1.78	86000
87000	*87999*	1733	1.78	87000
88000	*88999*	1751	1.78	88000
89000	*89999*	1768	1.78	89000
90000	*90999*	1786	1.78	90000
91000	*91999*	1804	1.78	91000
92000	*92999*	1822	1.78	92000
93000	*93999*	1840	1.78	93000
94000	*94999*	1857	1.78	94000

Federal Child Support Tables/ Tables fédérales de pensions alimentaires pour enfants

Province: Quebec/Québec
No. Of Children/ Nbre d'enfants: Four/Quatre

Income/Revenu ($)		Monthly Award/ Paiement mensuel ($)		
From/De	To/À	Basic Amount/ Montant de base	Plus (%)	Of Income Over/Du revenu dépassant
95000	*95999*	1875	1.78	95000
96000	*96999*	1893	1.78	96000
97000	*97999*	1911	1.78	97000
98000	*98999*	1929	1.78	98000
99000	*99999*	1947	1.78	99000
100000	*100999*	1964	1.78	100000
101000	*101999*	1982	1.78	101000
102000	*102999*	2000	1.78	102000
103000	*103999*	2018	1.78	103000
104000	*104999*	2036	1.78	104000
105000	*105999*	2054	1.78	105000
106000	*106999*	2071	1.78	106000
107000	*107999*	2089	1.78	107000
108000	*108999*	2107	1.78	108000
109000	*109999*	2125	1.78	109000
110000	*110999*	2143	1.78	110000
111000	*111999*	2160	1.78	111000
112000	*112999*	2178	1.78	112000
113000	*113999*	2196	1.77	113000
114000	*114999*	2214	1.70	114000
115000	*115999*	2231	1.70	115000
116000	*116999*	2248	1.70	116000
117000	*117999*	2265	1.70	117000
118000	*118999*	2282	1.70	118000
119000	*119999*	2299	1.70	119000
120000	*120999*	2316	1.70	120000
121000	*121999*	2333	1.70	121000
122000	*122999*	2350	1.70	122000
123000	*123999*	2367	1.70	123000
124000	*124999*	2384	1.70	124000
125000	*125999*	2401	1.70	125000
126000	*126999*	2418	1.70	126000
127000	*127999*	2435	1.70	127000
128000	*128999*	2452	1.70	128000
129000	*129999*	2469	1.70	129000

Federal Child Support Tables/ Tables fédérales de pensions alimentaires pour enfants | **Province: Quebec/Québec No. Of Children/ Nbre d'enfants: Four/Quatre**

Income/Revenu ($)		Monthly Award/ Paiement mensuel ($)		
From/De	To/À	Basic Amount/ Montant de base	Plus (%)	Of Income Over/Du revenu dépassant
130000	*130999*	2486	1.70	130000
131000	*131999*	2503	1.70	131000
132000	*132999*	2520	1.70	132000
133000	*133999*	2537	1.70	133000
134000	*134999*	2554	1.70	134000
135000	*135999*	2571	1.70	135000
136000	*136999*	2588	1.70	136000
137000	*137999*	2605	1.70	137000
138000	*138999*	2622	1.70	138000
139000	*139999*	2639	1.70	139000
140000	*140999*	2656	1.70	140000
141000	*141999*	2673	1.70	141000
142000	*142999*	2690	1.70	142000
143000	*143999*	2707	1.70	143000
144000	*144999*	2724	1.70	144000
145000	*145999*	2741	1.70	145000
146000	*146999*	2758	1.70	146000
147000	*147999*	2775	1.70	147000
148000	*148999*	2792	1.70	148000
149000	*149999*	2809	1.70	149000
150000	*or greater/ ou plus*	2826	1.70	150000

Federal Child Support Tables/ Tables fédérales de pensions alimentaires pour enfants | **Province: Quebec/Québec No. Of Children/ Nbre d'enfants: Five/Cinq**

Income/Revenu ($)		Monthly Award/ Paiement mensuel ($)		
From/De	To/À	Basic Amount/ Montant de base	Plus (%)	Of Income Over/Du revenu dépassant
0	*7999*	0		
8000	*8999*	0	3.81	8000
9000	*9999*	38	5.16	9000
10000	*10999*	90	5.16	10000
11000	*11999*	141	5.16	11000
12000	*12999*	193	5.06	12000
13000	*13999*	244	4.07	13000
14000	*14999*	284	4.04	14000
15000	*15999*	325	4.04	15000
16000	*16999*	365	4.04	16000
17000	*17999*	406	4.04	17000
18000	*18999*	446	4.04	18000
19000	*19999*	486	4.04	19000
20000	*20999*	527	4.04	20000
21000	*21999*	567	4.04	21000
22000	*22999*	608	2.91	22000
23000	*23999*	637	2.02	23000
24000	*24999*	657	2.02	24000

Federal Child Support Tables/ Tables fédérales de pensions alimentaires pour enfants

Province: Quebec/Québec
No. Of Children/ Nbre d'enfants: Five/Cinq

Income/Revenu ($)		Monthly Award/ Paiement mensuel ($)		
From/De	To/À	Basic Amount/ Montant de base	Plus (%)	Of Income Over/Du revenu dépassant
25000	*25999*	677	2.02	25000
26000	*26999*	697	2.02	26000
27000	*27999*	718	1.83	27000
28000	*28999*	736	1.49	28000
29000	*29999*	751	1.37	29000
30000	*30999*	764	1.31	30000
31000	*31999*	778	1.31	31000
32000	*32999*	791	1.31	32000
33000	*33999*	804	1.31	33000
34000	*34999*	817	1.79	34000
35000	*35999*	835	1.83	35000
36000	*36999*	853	2.00	36000
37000	*37999*	873	2.13	37000
38000	*38999*	894	2.13	38000
39000	*39999*	916	2.19	39000
40000	*40999*	937	2.27	40000
41000	*41999*	960	2.35	41000
42000	*42999*	984	2.35	42000
43000	*43999*	1007	2.35	43000
44000	*44999*	1031	2.35	44000
45000	*45999*	1054	2.35	45000
46000	*46999*	1078	2.35	46000
47000	*47999*	1101	2.35	47000
48000	*48999*	1125	2.35	48000
49000	*49999*	1148	2.35	49000
50000	*50999*	1172	2.35	50000
51000	*51999*	1195	2.35	51000
52000	*52999*	1219	2.35	52000
53000	*53999*	1242	2.35	53000
54000	*54999*	1266	2.35	54000
55000	*55999*	1289	2.25	55000
56000	*56999*	1312	2.20	56000
57000	*57999*	1334	2.20	57000
58000	*58999*	1356	2.20	58000
59000	*59999*	1378	2.20	59000

Federal Child Support Tables/ Tables fédérales de pensions alimentaires pour enfants

Province: Quebec/Québec
No. Of Children/ Nbre d'enfants: Five/Cinq

Income/Revenu ($)		Monthly Award/ Paiement mensuel ($)		
From/De	To/À	Basic Amount/ Montant de base	Plus (%)	Of Income Over/Du revenu dépassant
60000	*60999*	1400	2.20	60000
61000	*61999*	1422	2.20	61000
62000	*62999*	1444	2.20	62000
63000	*63999*	1466	2.20	63000
64000	*64999*	1488	2.20	64000
65000	*65999*	1510	2.20	65000
66000	*66999*	1532	2.20	66000
67000	*67999*	1554	2.17	67000
68000	*68999*	1576	2.13	68000
69000	*69999*	1597	2.13	69000
70000	*70999*	1619	2.01	70000
71000	*71999*	1639	2.01	71000
72000	*72999*	1659	2.01	72000
73000	*73999*	1679	2.01	73000
74000	*74999*	1699	2.01	74000
75000	*75999*	1719	2.01	75000
76000	*76999*	1739	2.01	76000
77000	*77999*	1759	2.01	77000
78000	*78999*	1780	2.01	78000
79000	*79999*	1800	2.01	79000
80000	*80999*	1820	2.01	80000
81000	*81999*	1840	2.01	81000
82000	*82999*	1860	2.01	82000
83000	*83999*	1880	2.01	83000
84000	*84999*	1900	2.01	84000
85000	*85999*	1920	2.01	85000
86000	*86999*	1940	2.01	86000
87000	*87999*	1961	2.01	87000
88000	*88999*	1981	2.01	88000
89000	*89999*	2001	2.01	89000
90000	*90999*	2021	2.01	90000
91000	*91999*	2041	2.01	91000
92000	*92999*	2061	2.01	92000
93000	*93999*	2081	2.01	93000
94000	*94999*	2101	2.01	94000

Federal Child Support Tables/ Tables fédérales de pensions alimentaires pour enfants — **Province: Quebec/Québec** — **No. Of Children/ Nbre d'enfants: Five/Cinq**

Income/Revenu ($)		Monthly Award/ Paiement mensuel ($)		
From/De	To/À	Basic Amount/ Montant de base	Plus (%)	Of Income Over/Du revenu dépassant
95000	*95999*	2121	2.01	95000
96000	*96999*	2141	2.01	96000
97000	*97999*	2162	2.01	97000
98000	*98999*	2182	2.01	98000
99000	*99999*	2202	2.01	99000
100000	*100999*	2222	2.01	100000
101000	*101999*	2242	2.01	101000
102000	*102999*	2262	2.01	102000
103000	*103999*	2282	2.01	103000
104000	*104999*	2302	2.01	104000
105000	*105999*	2322	2.01	105000
106000	*106999*	2343	2.01	106000
107000	*107999*	2363	2.01	107000
108000	*108999*	2383	2.01	108000
109000	*109999*	2403	2.01	109000
110000	*110999*	2423	2.01	110000
111000	*111999*	2443	2.01	111000
112000	*112999*	2463	2.01	112000
113000	*113999*	2483	1.99	113000
114000	*114999*	2503	1.92	114000
115000	*115999*	2522	1.92	115000
116000	*116999*	2542	1.92	116000
117000	*117999*	2561	1.92	117000
118000	*118999*	2580	1.92	118000
119000	*119999*	2599	1.92	119000
120000	*120999*	2618	1.92	120000
121000	*121999*	2637	1.92	121000
122000	*122999*	2657	1.92	122000

Federal Child Support Tables/ Tables fédérales de pensions alimentaires pour enfants — **Province: Quebec/Québec** — **No. Of Children/ Nbre d'enfants: Five/Cinq**

Income/Revenu ($)		Monthly Award/ Paiement mensuel ($)		
From/De	To/À	Basic Amount/ Montant de base	Plus (%)	Of Income Over/Du revenu dépassant
123000	*123999*	2676	1.92	123000
124000	*124999*	2695	1.92	124000
125000	*125999*	2714	1.92	125000
126000	*126999*	2733	1.92	126000
127000	*127999*	2753	1.92	127000
128000	*128999*	2772	1.92	128000
129000	*129999*	2791	1.92	129000
130000	*130999*	2810	1.92	130000
131000	*131999*	2829	1.92	131000
132000	*132999*	2848	1.92	132000
133000	*133999*	2868	1.92	133000
134000	*134999*	2887	1.92	134000
135000	*135999*	2906	1.92	135000
136000	*136999*	2925	1.92	136000
137000	*137999*	2944	1.92	137000
138000	*138999*	2964	1.92	138000
139000	*139999*	2983	1.92	139000
140000	*140999*	3002	1.92	140000
141000	*141999*	3021	1.92	141000
142000	*142999*	3040	1.92	142000
143000	*143999*	3059	1.92	143000
144000	*144999*	3079	1.92	144000
145000	*145999*	3098	1.92	145000
146000	*146999*	3117	1.92	146000
147000	*147999*	3136	1.92	147000
148000	*148999*	3155	1.92	148000
149000	*149999*	3175	1.92	149000

Federal Child Support Tables/ Tables fédérales de pensions alimentaires pour enfants

Province: Quebec/Québec
No. Of Children/ Nbre d'enfants: Five/Cinq

Income/Revenu ($)		Monthly Award/ Paiement mensuel ($)		
From/De	To/À	Basic Amount/ Montant de base	Plus (%)	Of Income Over/Du revenu dépassant
150000	*or greater/ ou plus*	3194	1.92	150000

Federal Child Support Tables/ Tables fédérales de pensions alimentaires pour enfants

Province: Quebec/Québec
No. Of Children/ Nbre d'enfants: Six or more/ Six ou plus

Income/Revenu ($)		Monthly Award/ Paiement mensuel ($)		
From/De	To/À	Basic Amount/ Montant de base	Plus (%)	Of Income Over/Du revenu dépassant
0	*7999*	0		
8000	*8999*	0	3.81	8000
9000	*9999*	38	5.16	9000
10000	*10999*	90	5.16	10000
11000	*11999*	141	5.16	11000
12000	*12999*	193	5.06	12000
13000	*13999*	244	4.07	13000
14000	*14999*	284	4.04	14000
15000	*15999*	325	4.04	15000
16000	*16999*	365	4.04	16000
17000	*17999*	406	4.04	17000
18000	*18999*	446	4.04	18000
19000	*19999*	486	4.04	19000
20000	*20999*	527	4.04	20000
21000	*21999*	567	4.04	21000
22000	*22999*	608	4.04	22000
23000	*23999*	648	4.04	23000
24000	*24999*	688	4.04	24000

Federal Child Support Tables/ Tables fédérales de pensions alimentaires pour enfants

Province: Quebec/Québec
No. Of Children/ Nbre d'enfants: Six or more/ Six ou plus

Income/Revenu ($)		Monthly Award/ Paiement mensuel ($)		
From/De	To/À	Basic Amount/ Montant de base	Plus (%)	Of Income Over/Du revenu dépassant
25000	*25999*	729	4.04	25000
26000	*26999*	769	3.01	26000
27000	*27999*	799	2.08	27000
28000	*28999*	820	1.73	28000
29000	*29999*	837	1.60	29000
30000	*30999*	853	1.52	30000
31000	*31999*	869	1.52	31000
32000	*32999*	884	1.52	32000
33000	*33999*	899	1.52	33000
34000	*34999*	914	1.52	34000
35000	*35999*	929	1.50	35000
36000	*36999*	944	2.03	36000
37000	*37999*	965	2.32	37000
38000	*38999*	988	2.32	38000
39000	*39999*	1011	2.39	39000
40000	*40999*	1035	2.48	40000
41000	*41999*	1060	2.57	41000
42000	*42999*	1086	2.57	42000
43000	*43999*	1111	2.57	43000
44000	*44999*	1137	2.57	44000
45000	*45999*	1163	2.57	45000
46000	*46999*	1188	2.57	46000
47000	*47999*	1214	2.57	47000
48000	*48999*	1240	2.57	48000
49000	*49999*	1265	2.57	49000
50000	*50999*	1291	2.57	50000
51000	*51999*	1317	2.57	51000
52000	*52999*	1342	2.57	52000
53000	*53999*	1368	2.57	53000
54000	*54999*	1394	2.57	54000
55000	*55999*	1419	2.45	55000
56000	*56999*	1444	2.40	56000
57000	*57999*	1468	2.40	57000
58000	*58999*	1492	2.40	58000
59000	*59999*	1516	2.40	59000

Federal Child Support Tables/ Tables fédérales de pensions alimentaires pour enfants

Province: Quebec/Québec
No. Of Children/ Nbre d'enfants: Six or more/ Six ou plus

Income/Revenu ($)		Monthly Award/ Paiement mensuel ($)		
From/De	To/À	Basic Amount/ Montant de base	Plus (%)	Of Income Over/Du revenu dépassant
60000	*60999*	1540	2.40	60000
61000	*61999*	1564	2.40	61000
62000	*62999*	1588	2.40	62000
63000	*63999*	1612	2.40	63000
64000	*64999*	1636	2.40	64000
65000	*65999*	1660	2.40	65000
66000	*66999*	1684	2.40	66000
67000	*67999*	1708	2.37	67000
68000	*68999*	1732	2.34	68000
69000	*69999*	1755	2.34	69000
70000	*70999*	1779	2.20	70000
71000	*71999*	1801	2.20	71000
72000	*72999*	1823	2.20	72000
73000	*73999*	1845	2.20	73000
74000	*74999*	1867	2.20	74000
75000	*75999*	1889	2.20	75000
76000	*76999*	1911	2.20	76000
77000	*77999*	1933	2.20	77000
78000	*78999*	1955	2.20	78000
79000	*79999*	1977	2.20	79000
80000	*80999*	1999	2.20	80000
81000	*81999*	2021	2.20	81000
82000	*82999*	2043	2.20	82000
83000	*83999*	2065	2.20	83000
84000	*84999*	2087	2.20	84000
85000	*85999*	2109	2.20	85000
86000	*86999*	2131	2.20	86000
87000	*87999*	2153	2.20	87000
88000	*88999*	2175	2.20	88000
89000	*89999*	2197	2.20	89000
90000	*90999*	2219	2.20	90000
91000	*91999*	2241	2.20	91000
92000	*92999*	2263	2.20	92000
93000	*93999*	2286	2.20	93000
94000	*94999*	2308	2.20	94000

Federal Child Support Tables/ Tables fédérales de pensions alimentaires pour enfants

Province: Quebec/Québec
No. Of Children/ Nbre d'enfants: Six or more/ Six ou plus

Income/Revenu ($)		Monthly Award/ Paiement mensuel ($)		
From/De	To/À	Basic Amount/ Montant de base	Plus (%)	Of Income Over/Du revenu dépassant
95000	*95999*	2330	2.20	95000
96000	*96999*	2352	2.20	96000
97000	*97999*	2374	2.20	97000
98000	*98999*	2396	2.20	98000
99000	*99999*	2418	2.20	99000
100000	*100999*	2440	2.20	100000
101000	*101999*	2462	2.20	101000
102000	*102999*	2484	2.20	102000
103000	*103999*	2506	2.20	103000
104000	*104999*	2528	2.20	104000
105000	*105999*	2550	2.20	105000
106000	*106999*	2572	2.20	106000
107000	*107999*	2594	2.20	107000
108000	*108999*	2616	2.20	108000
109000	*109999*	2638	2.20	109000
110000	*110999*	2660	2.20	110000
111000	*111999*	2682	2.20	111000
112000	*112999*	2704	2.20	112000
113000	*113999*	2726	2.18	113000
114000	*114999*	2748	2.10	114000
115000	*115999*	2769	2.10	115000
116000	*116999*	2790	2.10	116000
117000	*117999*	2811	2.10	117000
118000	*118999*	2832	2.10	118000
119000	*119999*	2853	2.10	119000
120000	*120999*	2874	2.10	120000
121000	*121999*	2895	2.10	121000
122000	*122999*	2916	2.10	122000
123000	*123999*	2937	2.10	123000
124000	*124999*	2958	2.10	124000
125000	*125999*	2979	2.10	125000
126000	*126999*	3000	2.10	126000
127000	*127999*	3021	2.10	127000
128000	*128999*	3042	2.10	128000
129000	*129999*	3064	2.10	129000

Federal Child Support Tables/ Tables fédérales de pensions alimentaires pour enfants

Province: Quebec/Québec No. Of Children/ Nbre d'enfants: Six or more/ Six ou plus

Income/Revenu ($)		Monthly Award/ Paiement mensuel ($)		
From/De	To/À	Basic Amount/ Montant de base	Plus (%)	Of Income Over/Du revenu dépassant
130000	*130999*	3085	2.10	130000
131000	*131999*	3106	2.10	131000
132000	*132999*	3127	2.10	132000
133000	*133999*	3148	2.10	133000
134000	*134999*	3169	2.10	134000
135000	*135999*	3190	2.10	135000
136000	*136999*	3211	2.10	136000
137000	*137999*	3232	2.10	137000
138000	*138999*	3253	2.10	138000
139000	*139999*	3274	2.10	139000
140000	*140999*	3295	2.10	140000
141000	*141999*	3316	2.10	141000
142000	*142999*	3337	2.10	142000
143000	*143999*	3358	2.10	143000
144000	*144999*	3379	2.10	144000
145000	*145999*	3400	2.10	145000
146000	*146999*	3421	2.10	146000
147000	*147999*	3442	2.10	147000
148000	*148999*	3463	2.10	148000
149000	*149999*	3484	2.10	149000

Federal Child Support Tables/ Tables fédérales de pensions alimentaires pour enfants

Province: Quebec/Québec No. Of Children/ Nbre d'enfants: Six or more/ Six ou plus

Income/Revenu ($)		Monthly Award/ Paiement mensuel ($)		
From/De	To/À	Basic Amount/ Montant de base	Plus (%)	Of Income Over/Du revenu dépassant
150000	*or greater/ ou plus*	3505	2.10	150000

Federal Child Support Tables/ Tables fédérales de pensions alimentaires pour enfants

Province: Nova Scotia/Nouvelle-Écosse No. Of Children/ Nbre d'enfants: One/Un

Income/Revenu ($)		Monthly Award/ Paiement mensuel ($)		
From/De	To/À	Basic Amount/ Montant de base	Plus (%)	Of Income Over/Du revenu dépassant
0	*7999*	0		
8000	*8999*	0	0.93	8000
9000	*9999*	9	1.86	9000
10000	*10999*	28	1.86	10000
11000	*11999*	46	1.86	11000
12000	*12999*	65	1.86	12000
13000	*13999*	84	1.86	13000
14000	*14999*	102	1.86	14000
15000	*15999*	121	1.86	15000
16000	*16999*	139	0.45	16000
17000	*17999*	144	0.45	17000
18000	*18999*	148	0.45	18000
19000	*19999*	153	0.88	19000
20000	*20999*	161	0.90	20000
21000	*21999*	170	1.15	21000
22000	*22999*	182	1.15	22000
23000	*23999*	193	1.15	23000
24000	*24999*	205	1.15	24000

Federal Child Support Tables/ Tables fédérales de pensions alimentaires pour enfants

Province: Nova Scotia/Nouvelle-Écosse No. Of Children/ Nbre d'enfants: One/Un

Income/Revenu ($)		Monthly Award/ Paiement mensuel ($)		
From/De	To/À	Basic Amount/ Montant de base	Plus (%)	Of Income Over/Du revenu dépassant
25000	*25999*	216	1.15	25000
26000	*26999*	228	1.15	26000
27000	*27999*	239	0.97	27000
28000	*28999*	249	0.97	28000
29000	*29999*	259	0.89	29000
30000	*30999*	268	0.82	30000
31000	*31999*	276	0.82	31000
32000	*32999*	284	0.82	32000
33000	*33999*	292	0.82	33000
34000	*34999*	300	0.82	34000
35000	*35999*	308	0.74	35000
36000	*36999*	316	0.78	36000
37000	*37999*	324	0.80	37000
38000	*38999*	332	0.80	38000
39000	*39999*	340	0.82	39000
40000	*40999*	348	0.85	40000
41000	*41999*	356	0.88	41000
42000	*42999*	365	0.88	42000
43000	*43999*	374	0.88	43000
44000	*44999*	383	0.88	44000
45000	*45999*	391	0.88	45000
46000	*46999*	400	0.88	46000
47000	*47999*	409	0.88	47000
48000	*48999*	418	0.88	48000
49000	*49999*	426	0.88	49000
50000	*50999*	435	0.88	50000
51000	*51999*	444	0.88	51000
52000	*52999*	453	0.88	52000
53000	*53999*	462	0.88	53000
54000	*54999*	470	0.88	54000
55000	*55999*	479	0.88	55000
56000	*56999*	488	0.88	56000
57000	*57999*	497	0.88	57000
58000	*58999*	505	0.88	58000
59000	*59999*	514	0.86	59000
60000	*60999*	523	0.85	60000
61000	*61999*	531	0.85	61000
62000	*62999*	540	0.85	62000
63000	*63999*	548	0.85	63000
64000	*64999*	557	0.85	64000
65000	*65999*	565	0.85	65000
66000	*66999*	574	0.85	66000
67000	*67999*	582	0.85	67000
68000	*68999*	591	0.85	68000
69000	*69999*	599	0.85	69000
70000	*70999*	608	0.80	70000
71000	*71999*	616	0.80	71000
72000	*72999*	624	0.80	72000
73000	*73999*	632	0.80	73000
74000	*74999*	640	0.80	74000
75000	*75999*	648	0.80	75000
76000	*76999*	656	0.80	76000
77000	*77999*	664	0.80	77000
78000	*78999*	671	0.80	78000
79000	*79999*	679	0.80	79000
80000	*80999*	687	0.80	80000
81000	*81999*	695	0.80	81000
82000	*82999*	703	0.73	82000
83000	*83999*	711	0.72	83000
84000	*84999*	718	0.72	84000
85000	*85999*	725	0.75	85000
86000	*86999*	732	0.77	86000
87000	*87999*	740	0.77	87000
88000	*88999*	748	0.77	88000
89000	*89999*	756	0.77	89000
90000	*90999*	763	0.77	90000
91000	*91999*	771	0.77	91000
92000	*92999*	779	0.77	92000
93000	*93999*	787	0.76	93000
94000	*94999*	794	0.76	94000

Federal Child Support Tables/ Tables fédérales de pensions alimentaires pour enfants

Province: Nova Scotia/Nouvelle-Écosse No. Of Children/ Nbre d'enfants: One/Un

Income/Revenu ($)		Monthly Award/ Paiement mensuel ($)		
From/De	To/À	Basic Amount/ Montant de base	Plus (%)	Of Income Over/Du revenu dépassant
95000	*95999*	802	0.76	95000
96000	*96999*	809	0.76	96000
97000	*97999*	817	0.76	97000
98000	*98999*	825	0.76	98000
99000	*99999*	832	0.76	99000
100000	*100999*	840	0.76	100000
101000	*101999*	847	0.76	101000
102000	*102999*	855	0.76	102000
103000	*103999*	863	0.76	103000
104000	*104999*	870	0.76	104000
105000	*105999*	878	0.76	105000
106000	*106999*	885	0.76	106000
107000	*107999*	893	0.76	107000
108000	*108999*	901	0.76	108000
109000	*109999*	908	0.76	109000
110000	*110999*	916	0.76	110000
111000	*111999*	923	0.76	111000
112000	*112999*	931	0.76	112000
113000	*113999*	939	0.75	113000
114000	*114999*	946	0.72	114000
115000	*115999*	953	0.72	115000
116000	*116999*	961	0.72	116000
117000	*117999*	968	0.72	117000
118000	*118999*	975	0.72	118000
119000	*119999*	982	0.72	119000
120000	*120999*	989	0.72	120000
121000	*121999*	996	0.72	121000
122000	*122999*	1004	0.72	122000

Federal Child Support Tables/ Tables fédérales de pensions alimentaires pour enfants

Province: Nova Scotia/Nouvelle-Écosse No. Of Children/ Nbre d'enfants: One/Un

Income/Revenu ($)		Monthly Award/ Paiement mensuel ($)		
From/De	To/À	Basic Amount/ Montant de base	Plus (%)	Of Income Over/Du revenu dépassant
123000	*123999*	1011	0.72	123000
124000	*124999*	1018	0.72	124000
125000	*125999*	1025	0.72	125000
126000	*126999*	1032	0.72	126000
127000	*127999*	1040	0.72	127000
128000	*128999*	1047	0.72	128000
129000	*129999*	1054	0.72	129000
130000	*130999*	1061	0.72	130000
131000	*131999*	1068	0.72	131000
132000	*132999*	1076	0.72	132000
133000	*133999*	1083	0.72	133000
134000	*134999*	1090	0.72	134000
135000	*135999*	1097	0.72	135000
136000	*136999*	1104	0.72	136000
137000	*137999*	1111	0.72	137000
138000	*138999*	1119	0.72	138000
139000	*139999*	1126	0.72	139000
140000	*140999*	1133	0.72	140000
141000	*141999*	1140	0.72	141000
142000	*142999*	1147	0.72	142000
143000	*143999*	1155	0.72	143000
144000	*144999*	1162	0.72	144000
145000	*145999*	1169	0.72	145000
146000	*146999*	1176	0.72	146000
147000	*147999*	1183	0.72	147000
148000	*148999*	1191	0.72	148000
149000	*149999*	1198	0.72	149000

Federal Child Support Tables/ Tables fédérales de pensions alimentaires pour enfants — **Province: Nova Scotia/Nouvelle-Écosse** — **No. Of Children/ Nbre d'enfants: One/Un**

Income/Revenu ($)		Monthly Award/ Paiement mensuel ($)		
From/De	To/À	Basic Amount/ Montant de base	Plus (%)	Of Income Over/Du revenu dépassant
150000	*or greater/ ou plus*	1205	0.72	150000

Federal Child Support Tables/ Tables fédérales de pensions alimentaires pour enfants — **Province: Nova Scotia/Nouvelle-Écosse** — **No. Of Children/ Nbre d'enfants: Two/Deux**

Income/Revenu ($)		Monthly Award/ Paiement mensuel ($)		
From/De	To/À	Basic Amount/ Montant de base	Plus (%)	Of Income Over/Du revenu dépassant
0	*7999*	0		
8000	*8999*	0	1.75	8000
9000	*9999*	17	4.34	9000
10000	*10999*	61	4.34	10000
11000	*11999*	104	4.01	11000
12000	*12999*	144	3.90	12000
13000	*13999*	183	3.82	13000
14000	*14999*	222	2.37	14000
15000	*15999*	245	0.66	15000
16000	*16999*	252	1.00	16000
17000	*17999*	262	1.00	17000
18000	*18999*	272	1.00	18000
19000	*19999*	282	1.00	19000
20000	*20999*	292	1.28	20000
21000	*21999*	305	1.67	21000
22000	*22999*	321	1.67	22000
23000	*23999*	338	1.67	23000
24000	*24999*	355	1.67	24000

Federal Child Support Tables/ Tables fédérales de pensions alimentaires pour enfants — **Province: Nova Scotia/Nouvelle-Écosse** — **No. Of Children/ Nbre d'enfants: Two/Deux**

Income/Revenu ($)		Monthly Award/ Paiement mensuel ($)		
From/De	To/À	Basic Amount/ Montant de base	Plus (%)	Of Income Over/Du revenu dépassant
25000	*25999*	371	1.67	25000
26000	*26999*	388	1.67	26000
27000	*27999*	405	1.67	27000
28000	*28999*	421	1.67	28000
29000	*29999*	438	1.54	29000
30000	*30999*	453	1.32	30000
31000	*31999*	467	1.27	31000
32000	*32999*	479	1.27	32000
33000	*33999*	492	1.27	33000
34000	*34999*	505	1.27	34000
35000	*35999*	517	1.14	35000
36000	*36999*	529	1.22	36000
37000	*37999*	541	1.25	37000
38000	*38999*	554	1.25	38000
39000	*39999*	566	1.28	39000
40000	*40999*	579	1.32	40000
41000	*41999*	592	1.36	41000
42000	*42999*	606	1.36	42000
43000	*43999*	619	1.36	43000
44000	*44999*	633	1.36	44000
45000	*45999*	647	1.36	45000
46000	*46999*	660	1.36	46000
47000	*47999*	674	1.36	47000
48000	*48999*	687	1.36	48000
49000	*49999*	701	1.36	49000
50000	*50999*	715	1.36	50000
51000	*51999*	728	1.36	51000
52000	*52999*	742	1.36	52000
53000	*53999*	756	1.36	53000
54000	*54999*	769	1.36	54000
55000	*55999*	783	1.36	55000
56000	*56999*	796	1.36	56000
57000	*57999*	810	1.36	57000
58000	*58999*	824	1.36	58000
59000	*59999*	837	1.33	59000

Federal Child Support Tables/ Tables fédérales de pensions alimentaires pour enfants

Province: Nova Scotia/Nouvelle-Écosse
No. Of Children/ Nbre d'enfants: Two/Deux

Income/Revenu ($)		Monthly Award/ Paiement mensuel ($)		
From/De	**To/À**	**Basic Amount/ Montant de base**	**Plus (%)**	**Of Income Over/Du revenu dépassant**
60000	*60999*	851	1.33	60000
61000	*61999*	864	1.33	61000
62000	*62999*	877	1.33	62000
63000	*63999*	890	1.33	63000
64000	*64999*	904	1.33	64000
65000	*65999*	917	1.33	65000
66000	*66999*	930	1.33	66000
67000	*67999*	943	1.33	67000
68000	*68999*	957	1.33	68000
69000	*69999*	970	1.33	69000
70000	*70999*	983	1.24	70000
71000	*71999*	996	1.24	71000
72000	*72999*	1008	1.24	72000
73000	*73999*	1020	1.24	73000
74000	*74999*	1033	1.24	74000
75000	*75999*	1045	1.24	75000
76000	*76999*	1057	1.24	76000
77000	*77999*	1070	1.24	77000
78000	*78999*	1082	1.24	78000
79000	*79999*	1095	1.24	79000
80000	*80999*	1107	1.24	80000
81000	*81999*	1119	1.24	81000
82000	*82999*	1132	1.17	82000
83000	*83999*	1143	1.15	83000
84000	*84999*	1155	1.15	84000
85000	*85999*	1166	1.18	85000
86000	*86999*	1178	1.20	86000
87000	*87999*	1190	1.20	87000
88000	*88999*	1202	1.20	88000
89000	*89999*	1214	1.20	89000
90000	*90999*	1226	1.20	90000
91000	*91999*	1238	1.20	91000
92000	*92999*	1250	1.20	92000
93000	*93999*	1262	1.18	93000
94000	*94999*	1274	1.18	94000

Federal Child Support Tables/ Tables fédérales de pensions alimentaires pour enfants

Province: Nova Scotia/Nouvelle-Écosse
No. Of Children/ Nbre d'enfants: Two/Deux

Income/Revenu ($)		Monthly Award/ Paiement mensuel ($)		
From/De	**To/À**	**Basic Amount/ Montant de base**	**Plus (%)**	**Of Income Over/Du revenu dépassant**
95000	*95999*	1286	1.18	95000
96000	*96999*	1298	1.18	96000
97000	*97999*	1310	1.18	97000
98000	*98999*	1322	1.18	98000
99000	*99999*	1333	1.18	99000
100000	*100999*	1345	1.18	100000
101000	*101999*	1357	1.18	101000
102000	*102999*	1369	1.18	102000
103000	*103999*	1381	1.18	103000
104000	*104999*	1393	1.18	104000
105000	*105999*	1404	1.18	105000
106000	*106999*	1416	1.18	106000
107000	*107999*	1428	1.18	107000
108000	*108999*	1440	1.18	108000
109000	*109999*	1452	1.18	109000
110000	*110999*	1464	1.18	110000
111000	*111999*	1475	1.18	111000
112000	*112999*	1487	1.18	112000
113000	*113999*	1499	1.17	113000
114000	*114999*	1511	1.12	114000
115000	*115999*	1522	1.12	115000
116000	*116999*	1533	1.12	116000
117000	*117999*	1544	1.12	117000
118000	*118999*	1555	1.12	118000
119000	*119999*	1567	1.12	119000
120000	*120999*	1578	1.12	120000
121000	*121999*	1589	1.12	121000
122000	*122999*	1600	1.12	122000
123000	*123999*	1611	1.12	123000
124000	*124999*	1623	1.12	124000
125000	*125999*	1634	1.12	125000
126000	*126999*	1645	1.12	126000
127000	*127999*	1656	1.12	127000
128000	*128999*	1667	1.12	128000
129000	*129999*	1678	1.12	129000

Federal Child Support Tables/ Tables fédérales de pensions alimentaires pour enfants		**Province: Nova Scotia/Nouvelle-Écosse No. Of Children/ Nbre d'enfants: Two/Deux**		
Income/Revenu ($)		**Monthly Award/ Paiement mensuel ($)**		
From/De	**To/À**	**Basic Amount/ Montant de base**	**Plus (%)**	**Of Income Over/Du revenu dépassant**
130000	*130999*	1690	1.12	130000
131000	*131999*	1701	1.12	131000
132000	*132999*	1712	1.12	132000
133000	*133999*	1723	1.12	133000
134000	*134999*	1734	1.12	134000
135000	*135999*	1746	1.12	135000
136000	*136999*	1757	1.12	136000
137000	*137999*	1768	1.12	137000
138000	*138999*	1779	1.12	138000
139000	*139999*	1790	1.12	139000
140000	*140999*	1801	1.12	140000
141000	*141999*	1813	1.12	141000
142000	*142999*	1824	1.12	142000
143000	*143999*	1835	1.12	143000
144000	*144999*	1846	1.12	144000
145000	*145999*	1857	1.12	145000
146000	*146999*	1869	1.12	146000
147000	*147999*	1880	1.12	147000
148000	*148999*	1891	1.12	148000
149000	*149999*	1902	1.12	149000
150000	*or greater/ ou plus*	1913	1.12	150000

Federal Child Support Tables/ Tables fédérales de pensions alimentaires pour enfants		**Province: Nova Scotia/Nouvelle-Écosse No. Of Children/ Nbre d'enfants: Three/Trois**		
Income/Revenu ($)		**Monthly Award/ Paiement mensuel ($)**		
From/De	**To/À**	**Basic Amount/ Montant de base**	**Plus (%)**	**Of Income Over/Du revenu dépassant**
0	*7999*	0		
8000	*8999*	0	1.88	8000
9000	*9999*	19	4.68	9000
10000	*10999*	66	4.68	10000
11000	*11999*	112	4.32	11000
12000	*12999*	156	4.20	12000
13000	*13999*	198	4.11	13000
14000	*14999*	239	4.08	14000
15000	*15999*	280	3.79	15000
16000	*16999*	317	3.79	16000
17000	*17999*	355	1.55	17000
18000	*18999*	371	1.44	18000
19000	*19999*	385	1.44	19000
20000	*20999*	400	1.44	20000
21000	*21999*	414	1.88	21000
22000	*22999*	433	2.08	22000
23000	*23999*	454	2.08	23000
24000	*24999*	475	2.08	24000

Federal Child Support Tables/ Tables fédérales de pensions alimentaires pour enfants

Province: Nova Scotia/Nouvelle-Écosse No. Of Children/ Nbre d'enfants: Three/Trois

Income/Revenu ($)		Monthly Award/ Paiement mensuel ($)		
From/De	To/À	Basic Amount/ Montant de base	Plus (%)	Of Income Over/Du revenu dépassant
25000	*25999*	495	2.08	25000
26000	*26999*	516	2.08	26000
27000	*27999*	537	2.08	27000
28000	*28999*	558	2.08	28000
29000	*29999*	579	1.93	29000
30000	*30999*	598	1.77	30000
31000	*31999*	616	1.77	31000
32000	*32999*	633	1.77	32000
33000	*33999*	651	1.72	33000
34000	*34999*	668	1.63	34000
35000	*35999*	685	1.47	35000
36000	*36999*	699	1.57	36000
37000	*37999*	715	1.61	37000
38000	*38999*	731	1.61	38000
39000	*39999*	747	1.65	39000
40000	*40999*	764	1.70	40000
41000	*41999*	781	1.75	41000
42000	*42999*	798	1.75	42000
43000	*43999*	816	1.75	43000
44000	*44999*	833	1.75	44000
45000	*45999*	851	1.75	45000
46000	*46999*	868	1.75	46000
47000	*47999*	886	1.75	47000
48000	*48999*	903	1.75	48000
49000	*49999*	921	1.75	49000
50000	*50999*	938	1.75	50000
51000	*51999*	956	1.75	51000
52000	*52999*	973	1.75	52000
53000	*53999*	991	1.75	53000
54000	*54999*	1008	1.75	54000
55000	*55999*	1026	1.75	55000
56000	*56999*	1043	1.75	56000
57000	*57999*	1061	1.75	57000
58000	*58999*	1078	1.75	58000
59000	*59999*	1096	1.71	59000

Federal Child Support Tables/ Tables fédérales de pensions alimentaires pour enfants

Province: Nova Scotia/Nouvelle-Écosse No. Of Children/ Nbre d'enfants: Three/Trois

Income/Revenu ($)		Monthly Award/ Paiement mensuel ($)		
From/De	To/À	Basic Amount/ Montant de base	Plus (%)	Of Income Over/Du revenu dépassant
60000	*60999*	1113	1.70	60000
61000	*61999*	1130	1.70	61000
62000	*62999*	1147	1.70	62000
63000	*63999*	1164	1.70	63000
64000	*64999*	1181	1.70	64000
65000	*65999*	1198	1.70	65000
66000	*66999*	1215	1.70	66000
67000	*67999*	1232	1.70	67000
68000	*68999*	1249	1.70	68000
69000	*69999*	1266	1.70	69000
70000	*70999*	1283	1.59	70000
71000	*71999*	1299	1.59	71000
72000	*72999*	1315	1.59	72000
73000	*73999*	1331	1.59	73000
74000	*74999*	1347	1.59	74000
75000	*75999*	1363	1.59	75000
76000	*76999*	1379	1.59	76000
77000	*77999*	1395	1.59	77000
78000	*78999*	1411	1.59	78000
79000	*79999*	1427	1.59	79000
80000	*80999*	1443	1.59	80000
81000	*81999*	1459	1.59	81000
82000	*82999*	1475	1.52	82000
83000	*83999*	1490	1.50	83000
84000	*84999*	1505	1.50	84000
85000	*85999*	1520	1.53	85000
86000	*86999*	1535	1.55	86000
87000	*87999*	1550	1.55	87000
88000	*88999*	1566	1.55	88000
89000	*89999*	1581	1.55	89000
90000	*90999*	1597	1.55	90000
91000	*91999*	1612	1.55	91000
92000	*92999*	1628	1.55	92000
93000	*93999*	1643	1.52	93000
94000	*94999*	1658	1.52	94000

Federal Child Support Tables/ Tables fédérales de pensions alimentaires pour enfants

Province: Nova Scotia/Nouvelle-Écosse No. Of Children/ Nbre d'enfants: Three/Trois

Income/Revenu ($)		Monthly Award/ Paiement mensuel ($)		
From/De	To/À	Basic Amount/ Montant de base	Plus (%)	Of Income Over/Du revenu dépassant
95000	*95999*	1674	1.52	95000
96000	*96999*	1689	1.52	96000
97000	*97999*	1704	1.52	97000
98000	*98999*	1719	1.52	98000
99000	*99999*	1734	1.52	99000
100000	*100999*	1750	1.52	100000
101000	*101999*	1765	1.52	101000
102000	*102999*	1780	1.52	102000
103000	*103999*	1795	1.52	103000
104000	*104999*	1810	1.52	104000
105000	*105999*	1826	1.52	105000
106000	*106999*	1841	1.52	106000
107000	*107999*	1856	1.52	107000
108000	*108999*	1871	1.52	108000
109000	*109999*	1887	1.52	109000
110000	*110999*	1902	1.52	110000
111000	*111999*	1917	1.52	111000
112000	*112999*	1932	1.52	112000
113000	*113999*	1947	1.50	113000
114000	*114999*	1962	1.44	114000
115000	*115999*	1977	1.44	115000
116000	*116999*	1991	1.44	116000
117000	*117999*	2006	1.44	117000
118000	*118999*	2020	1.44	118000
119000	*119999*	2034	1.44	119000
120000	*120999*	2049	1.44	120000
121000	*121999*	2063	1.44	121000
122000	*122999*	2077	1.44	122000

Federal Child Support Tables/ Tables fédérales de pensions alimentaires pour enfants

Province: Nova Scotia/Nouvelle-Écosse No. Of Children/ Nbre d'enfants: Three/Trois

Income/Revenu ($)		Monthly Award/ Paiement mensuel ($)		
From/De	To/À	Basic Amount/ Montant de base	Plus (%)	Of Income Over/Du revenu dépassant
123000	*123999*	2092	1.44	123000
124000	*124999*	2106	1.44	124000
125000	*125999*	2121	1.44	125000
126000	*126999*	2135	1.44	126000
127000	*127999*	2149	1.44	127000
128000	*128999*	2164	1.44	128000
129000	*129999*	2178	1.44	129000
130000	*130999*	2192	1.44	130000
131000	*131999*	2207	1.44	131000
132000	*132999*	2221	1.44	132000
133000	*133999*	2236	1.44	133000
134000	*134999*	2250	1.44	134000
135000	*135999*	2264	1.44	135000
136000	*136999*	2279	1.44	136000
137000	*137999*	2293	1.44	137000
138000	*138999*	2307	1.44	138000
139000	*139999*	2322	1.44	139000
140000	*140999*	2336	1.44	140000
141000	*141999*	2351	1.44	141000
142000	*142999*	2365	1.44	142000
143000	*143999*	2379	1.44	143000
144000	*144999*	2394	1.44	144000
145000	*145999*	2408	1.44	145000
146000	*146999*	2422	1.44	146000
147000	*147999*	2437	1.44	147000
148000	*148999*	2451	1.44	148000
149000	*149999*	2466	1.44	149000

Federal Child Support Tables/ Tables fédérales de pensions alimentaires pour enfants

Province: Nova Scotia/Nouvelle-Écosse
No. Of Children/ Nbre d'enfants: Three/Trois

Income/Revenu ($)		Monthly Award/ Paiement mensuel ($)		
From/De	**To/À**	**Basic Amount/ Montant de base**	**Plus (%)**	**Of Income Over/Du revenu dépassant**
150000	*or greater/ ou plus*	2480	1.44	150000

Federal Child Support Tables/ Tables fédérales de pensions alimentaires pour enfants

Province: Nova Scotia/Nouvelle-Écosse
No. Of Children/ Nbre d'enfants: Four/Quatre

Income/Revenu ($)		Monthly Award/ Paiement mensuel ($)		
From/De	**To/À**	**Basic Amount/ Montant de base**	**Plus (%)**	**Of Income Over/Du revenu dépassant**
0	*7999*	0		
8000	*8999*	0	2.01	8000
9000	*9999*	20	5.01	9000
10000	*10999*	70	5.01	10000
11000	*11999*	120	4.63	11000
12000	*12999*	167	4.50	12000
13000	*13999*	212	4.41	13000
14000	*14999*	256	4.37	14000
15000	*15999*	299	4.06	15000
16000	*16999*	340	4.06	16000
17000	*17999*	381	4.06	17000
18000	*18999*	421	4.06	18000
19000	*19999*	462	2.59	19000
20000	*20999*	488	1.80	20000
21000	*21999*	506	2.09	21000
22000	*22999*	527	2.16	22000
23000	*23999*	548	2.42	23000
24000	*24999*	573	2.42	24000
25000	*25999*	597	2.42	25000
26000	*26999*	621	2.42	26000
27000	*27999*	645	2.42	27000
28000	*28999*	670	2.42	28000
29000	*29999*	694	2.24	29000
30000	*30999*	716	2.06	30000
31000	*31999*	737	2.06	31000
32000	*32999*	757	2.06	32000
33000	*33999*	778	2.06	33000
34000	*34999*	799	2.06	34000
35000	*35999*	819	1.87	35000
36000	*36999*	838	1.97	36000
37000	*37999*	857	1.90	37000
38000	*38999*	876	1.90	38000
39000	*39999*	895	1.95	39000
40000	*40999*	915	2.01	40000
41000	*41999*	935	2.07	41000
42000	*42999*	956	2.07	42000
43000	*43999*	976	2.07	43000
44000	*44999*	997	2.07	44000
45000	*45999*	1018	2.07	45000
46000	*46999*	1038	2.07	46000
47000	*47999*	1059	2.07	47000
48000	*48999*	1080	2.07	48000
49000	*49999*	1101	2.07	49000
50000	*50999*	1121	2.07	50000
51000	*51999*	1142	2.07	51000
52000	*52999*	1163	2.07	52000
53000	*53999*	1183	2.07	53000
54000	*54999*	1204	2.07	54000
55000	*55999*	1225	2.07	55000
56000	*56999*	1245	2.07	56000
57000	*57999*	1266	2.07	57000
58000	*58999*	1287	2.07	58000
59000	*59999*	1308	2.02	59000

Federal Child Support Tables/ Tables fédérales de pensions alimentaires pour enfants — **Province: Nova Scotia/Nouvelle-Écosse No. Of Children/ Nbre d'enfants: Four/Quatre**

Income/Revenu ($)		Monthly Award/ Paiement mensuel ($)		
From/De	To/À	Basic Amount/ Montant de base	Plus (%)	Of Income Over/Du revenu dépassant
60000	*60999*	1328	2.01	60000
61000	*61999*	1348	2.01	61000
62000	*62999*	1368	2.01	62000
63000	*63999*	1388	2.01	63000
64000	*64999*	1408	2.01	64000
65000	*65999*	1428	2.01	65000
66000	*66999*	1449	2.01	66000
67000	*67999*	1469	2.01	67000
68000	*68999*	1489	2.01	68000
69000	*69999*	1509	2.01	69000
70000	*70999*	1529	1.88	70000
71000	*71999*	1548	1.88	71000
72000	*72999*	1567	1.88	72000
73000	*73999*	1586	1.88	73000
74000	*74999*	1604	1.88	74000
75000	*75999*	1623	1.88	75000
76000	*76999*	1642	1.88	76000
77000	*77999*	1661	1.88	77000
78000	*78999*	1680	1.88	78000
79000	*79999*	1698	1.88	79000
80000	*80999*	1717	1.88	80000
81000	*81999*	1736	1.88	81000
82000	*82999*	1755	1.81	82000
83000	*83999*	1773	1.79	83000
84000	*84999*	1791	1.79	84000
85000	*85999*	1809	1.81	85000
86000	*86999*	1827	1.83	86000
87000	*87999*	1845	1.83	87000
88000	*88999*	1863	1.83	88000
89000	*89999*	1882	1.83	89000
90000	*90999*	1900	1.83	90000
91000	*91999*	1918	1.83	91000
92000	*92999*	1936	1.83	92000
93000	*93999*	1955	1.80	93000
94000	*94999*	1973	1.80	94000

Federal Child Support Tables/ Tables fédérales de pensions alimentaires pour enfants — **Province: Nova Scotia/Nouvelle-Écosse No. Of Children/ Nbre d'enfants: Four/Quatre**

Income/Revenu ($)		Monthly Award/ Paiement mensuel ($)		
From/De	To/À	Basic Amount/ Montant de base	Plus (%)	Of Income Over/Du revenu dépassant
95000	*95999*	1991	1.80	95000
96000	*96999*	2009	1.80	96000
97000	*97999*	2027	1.80	97000
98000	*98999*	2045	1.80	98000
99000	*99999*	2063	1.80	99000
100000	*100999*	2081	1.80	100000
101000	*101999*	2099	1.80	101000
102000	*102999*	2116	1.80	102000
103000	*103999*	2134	1.80	103000
104000	*104999*	2152	1.80	104000
105000	*105999*	2170	1.80	105000
106000	*106999*	2188	1.80	106000
107000	*107999*	2206	1.80	107000
108000	*108999*	2224	1.80	108000
109000	*109999*	2242	1.80	109000
110000	*110999*	2260	1.80	110000
111000	*111999*	2278	1.80	111000
112000	*112999*	2296	1.80	112000
113000	*113999*	2314	1.78	113000
114000	*114999*	2332	1.70	114000
115000	*115999*	2349	1.70	115000
116000	*116999*	2366	1.70	116000
117000	*117999*	2383	1.70	117000
118000	*118999*	2400	1.70	118000
119000	*119999*	2417	1.70	119000
120000	*120999*	2434	1.70	120000
121000	*121999*	2451	1.70	121000
122000	*122999*	2468	1.70	122000
123000	*123999*	2485	1.70	123000
124000	*124999*	2502	1.70	124000
125000	*125999*	2519	1.70	125000
126000	*126999*	2536	1.70	126000
127000	*127999*	2553	1.70	127000
128000	*128999*	2570	1.70	128000
129000	*129999*	2587	1.70	129000

Federal Child Support Tables/ Tables fédérales de pensions alimentaires pour enfants

Province: Nova Scotia/Nouvelle-Écosse No. Of Children/ Nbre d'enfants: Four/Quatre

Income/Revenu ($)		Monthly Award/ Paiement mensuel ($)		
From/De	To/À	Basic Amount/ Montant de base	Plus (%)	Of Income Over/Du revenu dépassant
130000	*130999*	2604	1.70	130000
131000	*131999*	2621	1.70	131000
132000	*132999*	2638	1.70	132000
133000	*133999*	2655	1.70	133000
134000	*134999*	2672	1.70	134000
135000	*135999*	2689	1.70	135000
136000	*136999*	2706	1.70	136000
137000	*137999*	2723	1.70	137000
138000	*138999*	2740	1.70	138000
139000	*139999*	2757	1.70	139000
140000	*140999*	2774	1.70	140000
141000	*141999*	2791	1.70	141000
142000	*142999*	2808	1.70	142000
143000	*143999*	2825	1.70	143000
144000	*144999*	2842	1.70	144000
145000	*145999*	2859	1.70	145000
146000	*146999*	2876	1.70	146000
147000	*147999*	2893	1.70	147000
148000	*148999*	2910	1.70	148000
149000	*149999*	2927	1.70	149000

Federal Child Support Tables/ Tables fédérales de pensions alimentaires pour enfants

Province: Nova Scotia/Nouvelle-Écosse No. Of Children/ Nbre d'enfants: Four/Quatre

Income/Revenu ($)		Monthly Award/ Paiement mensuel ($)		
From/De	To/À	Basic Amount/ Montant de base	Plus (%)	Of Income Over/Du revenu dépassant
150000	*or greater/ ou plus*	2944	1.70	150000

Federal Child Support Tables/ Tables fédérales de pensions alimentaires pour enfants

Province: Nova Scotia/Nouvelle-Écosse No. Of Children/ Nbre d'enfants: Five/Cinq

Income/Revenu ($)		Monthly Award/ Paiement mensuel ($)		
From/De	To/À	Basic Amount/ Montant de base	Plus (%)	Of Income Over/Du revenu dépassant
0	*7999*	0		
8000	*8999*	0	2.01	8000
9000	*9999*	20	5.01	9000
10000	*10999*	70	5.01	10000
11000	*11999*	120	4.63	11000
12000	*12999*	167	4.50	12000
13000	*13999*	212	4.41	13000
14000	*14999*	256	4.37	14000
15000	*15999*	299	4.06	15000
16000	*16999*	340	4.06	16000
17000	*17999*	381	4.06	17000
18000	*18999*	421	4.06	18000
19000	*19999*	462	4.06	19000
20000	*20999*	503	4.06	20000
21000	*21999*	543	4.37	21000
22000	*22999*	587	4.35	22000
23000	*23999*	630	2.40	23000
24000	*24999*	655	2.69	24000

Federal Child Support Tables/ Tables fédérales de pensions alimentaires pour enfants — **Province: Nova Scotia/Nouvelle-Écosse No. Of Children/ N^bre d'enfants: Five/Cinq**

Income/Revenu ($)		Monthly Award/ Paiement mensuel ($)		
From/De	To/À	Basic Amount/ Montant de base	Plus (%)	Of Income Over/Du revenu dépassant
25000	*25999*	681	2.71	25000
26000	*26999*	709	2.71	26000
27000	*27999*	736	2.71	27000
28000	*28999*	763	2.71	28000
29000	*29999*	790	2.50	29000
30000	*30999*	815	2.29	30000
31000	*31999*	838	2.29	31000
32000	*32999*	861	2.29	32000
33000	*33999*	884	2.29	33000
34000	*34999*	907	2.29	34000
35000	*35999*	929	2.08	35000
36000	*36999*	950	2.21	36000
37000	*37999*	972	2.26	37000
38000	*38999*	995	2.26	38000
39000	*39999*	1017	2.31	39000
40000	*40999*	1041	2.29	40000
41000	*41999*	1064	2.34	41000
42000	*42999*	1087	2.34	42000
43000	*43999*	1110	2.34	43000
44000	*44999*	1134	2.34	44000
45000	*45999*	1157	2.34	45000
46000	*46999*	1180	2.34	46000
47000	*47999*	1204	2.34	47000
48000	*48999*	1227	2.34	48000
49000	*49999*	1250	2.34	49000
50000	*50999*	1274	2.34	50000
51000	*51999*	1297	2.34	51000
52000	*52999*	1320	2.34	52000
53000	*53999*	1344	2.34	53000
54000	*54999*	1367	2.34	54000
55000	*55999*	1390	2.34	55000
56000	*56999*	1414	2.34	56000
57000	*57999*	1437	2.34	57000
58000	*58999*	1460	2.34	58000
59000	*59999*	1484	2.28	59000

Federal Child Support Tables/ Tables fédérales de pensions alimentaires pour enfants — **Province: Nova Scotia/Nouvelle-Écosse No. Of Children/ N^bre d'enfants: Five/Cinq**

Income/Revenu ($)		Monthly Award/ Paiement mensuel ($)		
From/De	To/À	Basic Amount/ Montant de base	Plus (%)	Of Income Over/Du revenu dépassant
60000	*60999*	1507	2.27	60000
61000	*61999*	1529	2.27	61000
62000	*62999*	1552	2.27	62000
63000	*63999*	1575	2.27	63000
64000	*64999*	1598	2.27	64000
65000	*65999*	1620	2.27	65000
66000	*66999*	1643	2.27	66000
67000	*67999*	1666	2.27	67000
68000	*68999*	1688	2.27	68000
69000	*69999*	1711	2.27	69000
70000	*70999*	1734	2.12	70000
71000	*71999*	1755	2.12	71000
72000	*72999*	1776	2.12	72000
73000	*73999*	1798	2.12	73000
74000	*74999*	1819	2.12	74000
75000	*75999*	1840	2.12	75000
76000	*76999*	1861	2.12	76000
77000	*77999*	1882	2.12	77000
78000	*78999*	1904	2.12	78000
79000	*79999*	1925	2.12	79000
80000	*80999*	1946	2.12	80000
81000	*81999*	1967	2.12	81000
82000	*82999*	1989	2.04	82000
83000	*83999*	2009	2.02	83000
84000	*84999*	2029	2.02	84000
85000	*85999*	2050	2.04	85000
86000	*86999*	2070	2.06	86000
87000	*87999*	2091	2.06	87000
88000	*88999*	2111	2.06	88000
89000	*89999*	2132	2.06	89000
90000	*90999*	2152	2.06	90000
91000	*91999*	2173	2.06	91000
92000	*92999*	2194	2.06	92000
93000	*93999*	2214	2.03	93000
94000	*94999*	2235	2.03	94000

Federal Child Support Tables/ Tables fédérales de pensions alimentaires pour enfants

Province: Nova Scotia/Nouvelle-Écosse
No. Of Children/ Nbre d'enfants: Five/Cinq

Income/Revenu ($)		Monthly Award/ Paiement mensuel ($)		
From/De	To/À	Basic Amount/ Montant de base	Plus (%)	Of Income Over/Du revenu dépassant
95000	*95999*	2255	2.03	95000
96000	*96999*	2275	2.03	96000
97000	*97999*	2295	2.03	97000
98000	*98999*	2316	2.03	98000
99000	*99999*	2336	2.03	99000
100000	*100999*	2356	2.03	100000
101000	*101999*	2377	2.03	101000
102000	*102999*	2397	2.03	102000
103000	*103999*	2417	2.03	103000
104000	*104999*	2437	2.03	104000
105000	*105999*	2458	2.03	105000
106000	*106999*	2478	2.03	106000
107000	*107999*	2498	2.03	107000
108000	*108999*	2518	2.03	108000
109000	*109999*	2539	2.03	109000
110000	*110999*	2559	2.03	110000
111000	*111999*	2579	2.03	111000
112000	*112999*	2600	2.03	112000
113000	*113999*	2620	2.01	113000
114000	*114999*	2640	1.92	114000
115000	*115999*	2659	1.92	115000
116000	*116999*	2678	1.92	116000
117000	*117999*	2697	1.92	117000
118000	*118999*	2717	1.92	118000
119000	*119999*	2736	1.92	119000
120000	*120999*	2755	1.92	120000
121000	*121999*	2774	1.92	121000
122000	*122999*	2793	1.92	122000

Federal Child Support Tables/ Tables fédérales de pensions alimentaires pour enfants

Province: Nova Scotia/Nouvelle-Écosse
No. Of Children/ Nbre d'enfants: Five/Cinq

Income/Revenu ($)		Monthly Award/ Paiement mensuel ($)		
From/De	To/À	Basic Amount/ Montant de base	Plus (%)	Of Income Over/Du revenu dépassant
123000	*123999*	2812	1.92	123000
124000	*124999*	2832	1.92	124000
125000	*125999*	2851	1.92	125000
126000	*126999*	2870	1.92	126000
127000	*127999*	2889	1.92	127000
128000	*128999*	2908	1.92	128000
129000	*129999*	2927	1.92	129000
130000	*130999*	2947	1.92	130000
131000	*131999*	2966	1.92	131000
132000	*132999*	2985	1.92	132000
133000	*133999*	3004	1.92	133000
134000	*134999*	3023	1.92	134000
135000	*135999*	3042	1.92	135000
136000	*136999*	3062	1.92	136000
137000	*137999*	3081	1.92	137000
138000	*138999*	3100	1.92	138000
139000	*139999*	3119	1.92	139000
140000	*140999*	3138	1.92	140000
141000	*141999*	3157	1.92	141000
142000	*142999*	3177	1.92	142000
143000	*143999*	3196	1.92	143000
144000	*144999*	3215	1.92	144000
145000	*145999*	3234	1.92	145000
146000	*146999*	3253	1.92	146000
147000	*147999*	3272	1.92	147000
148000	*148999*	3292	1.92	148000
149000	*149999*	3311	1.92	149000

Federal Child Support Tables/ Tables fédérales de pensions alimentaires pour enfants

Province: Nova Scotia/Nouvelle-Écosse No. Of Children/ Nbre d'enfants: Five/Cinq

Income/Revenu ($)		Monthly Award/ Paiement mensuel ($)		
From/De	To/À	Basic Amount/ Montant de base	Plus (%)	Of Income Over/Du revenu dépassant
150000	*or greater/ ou plus*	3330	1.92	150000

Federal Child Support Tables/ Tables fédérales de pensions alimentaires pour enfants

Province: Nova Scotia/Nouvelle-Écosse No. Of Children/ Nbre d'enfants: Six or more/Six ou plus

Income/Revenu ($)		Monthly Award/ Paiement mensuel ($)		
From/De	To/À	Basic Amount/ Montant de base	Plus (%)	Of Income Over/Du revenu dépassant
0	*7999*	0		
8000	*8999*	0	2.01	8000
9000	*9999*	20	5.01	9000
10000	*10999*	70	5.01	10000
11000	*11999*	120	4.63	11000
12000	*12999*	167	4.50	12000
13000	*13999*	212	4.41	13000
14000	*14999*	256	4.37	14000
15000	*15999*	299	4.06	15000
16000	*16999*	340	4.06	16000
17000	*17999*	381	4.06	17000
18000	*18999*	421	4.06	18000
19000	*19999*	462	4.06	19000
20000	*20999*	503	4.06	20000
21000	*21999*	543	4.37	21000
22000	*22999*	587	4.37	22000
23000	*23999*	631	4.37	23000
24000	*24999*	674	4.37	24000
25000	*25999*	718	4.37	25000
26000	*26999*	762	4.37	26000
27000	*27999*	806	3.58	27000
28000	*28999*	841	2.95	28000
29000	*29999*	871	2.72	29000
30000	*30999*	898	2.50	30000
31000	*31999*	923	2.50	31000
32000	*32999*	948	2.50	32000
33000	*33999*	973	2.50	33000
34000	*34999*	998	2.50	34000
35000	*35999*	1023	2.26	35000
36000	*36999*	1045	2.40	36000
37000	*37999*	1069	2.45	37000
38000	*38999*	1094	2.45	38000
39000	*39999*	1119	2.52	39000
40000	*40999*	1144	2.59	40000
41000	*41999*	1170	2.67	41000
42000	*42999*	1196	2.67	42000
43000	*43999*	1223	2.61	43000
44000	*44999*	1249	2.56	44000
45000	*45999*	1275	2.56	45000
46000	*46999*	1300	2.56	46000
47000	*47999*	1326	2.56	47000
48000	*48999*	1351	2.56	48000
49000	*49999*	1377	2.56	49000
50000	*50999*	1403	2.56	50000
51000	*51999*	1428	2.56	51000
52000	*52999*	1454	2.56	52000
53000	*53999*	1479	2.56	53000
54000	*54999*	1505	2.56	54000
55000	*55999*	1531	2.56	55000
56000	*56999*	1556	2.56	56000
57000	*57999*	1582	2.56	57000
58000	*58999*	1607	2.56	58000
59000	*59999*	1633	2.50	59000

Federal Child Support Tables/ Tables fédérales de pensions alimentaires pour enfants

Province: Nova Scotia/Nouvelle-Écosse
No. Of Children/ Nbre d'enfants: Six or more/Six ou plus

Income/Revenu ($)		Monthly Award/ Paiement mensuel ($)		
From/De	**To/À**	**Basic Amount/ Montant de base**	**Plus (%)**	**Of Income Over/Du revenu dépassant**
60000	*60999*	1658	2.49	60000
61000	*61999*	1683	2.49	61000
62000	*62999*	1708	2.49	62000
63000	*63999*	1733	2.49	63000
64000	*64999*	1758	2.49	64000
65000	*65999*	1783	2.49	65000
66000	*66999*	1807	2.49	66000
67000	*67999*	1832	2.49	67000
68000	*68999*	1857	2.49	68000
69000	*69999*	1882	2.49	69000
70000	*70999*	1907	2.33	70000
71000	*71999*	1930	2.33	71000
72000	*72999*	1954	2.33	72000
73000	*73999*	1977	2.33	73000
74000	*74999*	2000	2.33	74000
75000	*75999*	2023	2.33	75000
76000	*76999*	2047	2.33	76000
77000	*77999*	2070	2.33	77000
78000	*78999*	2093	2.33	78000
79000	*79999*	2117	2.33	79000
80000	*80999*	2140	2.33	80000
81000	*81999*	2163	2.33	81000
82000	*82999*	2186	2.25	82000
83000	*83999*	2209	2.22	83000
84000	*84999*	2231	2.22	84000
85000	*85999*	2253	2.24	85000
86000	*86999*	2276	2.26	86000
87000	*87999*	2298	2.26	87000
88000	*88999*	2321	2.26	88000
89000	*89999*	2344	2.26	89000
90000	*90999*	2366	2.26	90000
91000	*91999*	2389	2.26	91000
92000	*92999*	2411	2.26	92000
93000	*93999*	2434	2.23	93000
94000	*94999*	2456	2.22	94000

Federal Child Support Tables/ Tables fédérales de pensions alimentaires pour enfants

Province: Nova Scotia/Nouvelle-Écosse
No. Of Children/ Nbre d'enfants: Six or more/Six ou plus

Income/Revenu ($)		Monthly Award/ Paiement mensuel ($)		
From/De	**To/À**	**Basic Amount/ Montant de base**	**Plus (%)**	**Of Income Over/Du revenu dépassant**
95000	*95999*	2478	2.22	95000
96000	*96999*	2501	2.22	96000
97000	*97999*	2523	2.22	97000
98000	*98999*	2545	2.22	98000
99000	*99999*	2567	2.22	99000
100000	*100999*	2590	2.22	100000
101000	*101999*	2612	2.22	101000
102000	*102999*	2634	2.22	102000
103000	*103999*	2656	2.22	103000
104000	*104999*	2678	2.22	104000
105000	*105999*	2701	2.22	105000
106000	*106999*	2723	2.22	106000
107000	*107999*	2745	2.22	107000
108000	*108999*	2767	2.22	108000
109000	*109999*	2790	2.22	109000
110000	*110999*	2812	2.22	110000
111000	*111999*	2834	2.22	111000
112000	*112999*	2856	2.22	112000
113000	*113999*	2879	2.20	113000
114000	*114999*	2900	2.10	114000
115000	*115999*	2922	2.10	115000
116000	*116999*	2943	2.10	116000
117000	*117999*	2964	2.10	117000
118000	*118999*	2985	2.10	118000
119000	*119999*	3006	2.10	119000
120000	*120999*	3027	2.10	120000
121000	*121999*	3048	2.10	121000
122000	*122999*	3069	2.10	122000
123000	*123999*	3090	2.10	123000
124000	*124999*	3111	2.10	124000
125000	*125999*	3132	2.10	125000
126000	*126999*	3153	2.10	126000
127000	*127999*	3174	2.10	127000
128000	*128999*	3195	2.10	128000
129000	*129999*	3216	2.10	129000

Federal Child Support Tables/ Tables fédérales de pensions alimentaires pour enfants

Province: Nova Scotia/Nouvelle-Écosse No. Of Children/ Nbre d'enfants: Six or more/Six ou plus

Income/Revenu ($)		Monthly Award/ Paiement mensuel ($)		
From/De	To/À	Basic Amount/ Montant de base	Plus (%)	Of Income Over/Du revenu dépassant
130000	*130999*	3237	2.10	130000
131000	*131999*	3258	2.10	131000
132000	*132999*	3279	2.10	132000
133000	*133999*	3300	2.10	133000
134000	*134999*	3321	2.10	134000
135000	*135999*	3342	2.10	135000
136000	*136999*	3363	2.10	136000
137000	*137999*	3384	2.10	137000
138000	*138999*	3405	2.10	138000
139000	*139999*	3426	2.10	139000
140000	*140999*	3447	2.10	140000
141000	*141999*	3468	2.10	141000
142000	*142999*	3489	2.10	142000
143000	*143999*	3510	2.10	143000
144000	*144999*	3531	2.10	144000
145000	*145999*	3552	2.10	145000
146000	*146999*	3573	2.10	146000
147000	*147999*	3594	2.10	147000
148000	*148999*	3615	2.10	148000
149000	*149999*	3636	2.10	149000

Federal Child Support Tables/ Tables fédérales de pensions alimentaires pour enfants

Province: Nova Scotia/Nouvelle-Écosse No. Of Children/ Nbre d'enfants: Six or more/Six ou plus

Income/Revenu ($)		Monthly Award/ Paiement mensuel ($)		
From/De	To/À	Basic Amount/ Montant de base	Plus (%)	Of Income Over/Du revenu dépassant
150000	*or greater/ ou plus*	3657	2.10	150000

Federal Child Support Tables/ Tables fédérales de pensions alimentaires pour enfants

Province: New Brunswick/ Nouveau-Brunswick No. Of Children/ Nbre d'enfants: One/Un

Income/Revenu ($)		Monthly Award/ Paiement mensuel ($)		
From/De	To/À	Basic Amount/ Montant de base	Plus (%)	Of Income Over/Du revenu dépassant
0	*7999*	0		
8000	*8999*	0	0.93	8000
9000	*9999*	9	1.87	9000
10000	*10999*	28	1.87	10000
11000	*11999*	47	1.87	11000
12000	*12999*	65	1.87	12000
13000	*13999*	84	1.87	13000
14000	*14999*	103	1.87	14000
15000	*15999*	121	1.87	15000
16000	*16999*	140	0.40	16000
17000	*17999*	144	0.40	17000
18000	*18999*	148	0.40	18000
19000	*19999*	152	0.40	19000
20000	*20999*	156	0.49	20000
21000	*21999*	161	0.96	21000
22000	*22999*	171	1.13	22000
23000	*23999*	182	1.13	23000
24000	*24999*	193	1.13	24000

Federal Child Support Tables/ Tables fédérales de pensions alimentaires pour enfants

Province: New Brunswick/ Nouveau-Brunswick
No. Of Children/ Nbre d'enfants: One/Un

Income/Revenu ($)		Monthly Award/ Paiement mensuel ($)		
From/De	To/À	Basic Amount/ Montant de base	Plus (%)	Of Income Over/Du revenu dépassant
25000	*25999*	205	1.13	25000
26000	*26999*	216	1.13	26000
27000	*27999*	227	1.13	27000
28000	*28999*	239	1.13	28000
29000	*29999*	250	1.09	29000
30000	*30999*	261	1.05	30000
31000	*31999*	272	0.89	31000
32000	*32999*	280	0.83	32000
33000	*33999*	289	0.82	33000
34000	*34999*	297	0.82	34000
35000	*35999*	305	0.74	35000
36000	*36999*	313	0.79	36000
37000	*37999*	320	0.81	37000
38000	*38999*	329	0.81	38000
39000	*39999*	337	0.83	39000
40000	*40999*	345	0.85	40000
41000	*41999*	353	0.88	41000
42000	*42999*	362	0.88	42000
43000	*43999*	371	0.88	43000
44000	*44999*	380	0.88	44000
45000	*45999*	388	0.88	45000
46000	*46999*	397	0.88	46000
47000	*47999*	406	0.88	47000
48000	*48999*	415	0.88	48000
49000	*49999*	424	0.88	49000
50000	*50999*	432	0.88	50000
51000	*51999*	441	0.88	51000
52000	*52999*	450	0.88	52000
53000	*53999*	459	0.88	53000
54000	*54999*	467	0.88	54000
55000	*55999*	476	0.88	55000
56000	*56999*	485	0.88	56000
57000	*57999*	494	0.88	57000
58000	*58999*	503	0.88	58000
59000	*59999*	511	0.88	59000

Federal Child Support Tables/ Tables fédérales de pensions alimentaires pour enfants

Province: New Brunswick/ Nouveau-Brunswick
No. Of Children/ Nbre d'enfants: One/Un

Income/Revenu ($)		Monthly Award/ Paiement mensuel ($)		
From/De	To/À	Basic Amount/ Montant de base	Plus (%)	Of Income Over/Du revenu dépassant
60000	*60999*	520	0.88	60000
61000	*61999*	529	0.88	61000
62000	*62999*	538	0.88	62000
63000	*63999*	546	0.88	63000
64000	*64999*	555	0.86	64000
65000	*65999*	564	0.85	65000
66000	*66999*	572	0.85	66000
67000	*67999*	581	0.85	67000
68000	*68999*	589	0.85	68000
69000	*69999*	598	0.85	69000
70000	*70999*	606	0.80	70000
71000	*71999*	614	0.80	71000
72000	*72999*	622	0.80	72000
73000	*73999*	630	0.80	73000
74000	*74999*	638	0.80	74000
75000	*75999*	646	0.80	75000
76000	*76999*	654	0.80	76000
77000	*77999*	662	0.80	77000
78000	*78999*	670	0.80	78000
79000	*79999*	678	0.80	79000
80000	*80999*	686	0.80	80000
81000	*81999*	694	0.80	81000
82000	*82999*	702	0.80	82000
83000	*83999*	710	0.80	83000
84000	*84999*	718	0.80	84000
85000	*85999*	726	0.80	85000
86000	*86999*	734	0.80	86000
87000	*87999*	742	0.80	87000
88000	*88999*	750	0.80	88000
89000	*89999*	758	0.80	89000
90000	*90999*	766	0.80	90000
91000	*91999*	774	0.80	91000
92000	*92999*	782	0.80	92000
93000	*93999*	790	0.80	93000
94000	*94999*	798	0.80	94000

Federal Child Support Tables/ Tables fédérales de pensions alimentaires pour enfants — **Province: New Brunswick/ Nouveau-Brunswick** — **No. Of Children/ Nbre d'enfants: One/Un**

Income/Revenu ($)		Monthly Award/ Paiement mensuel ($)		
From/De	To/À	Basic Amount/ Montant de base	Plus (%)	Of Income Over/Du revenu dépassant
95000	*95999*	806	0.80	95000
96000	*96999*	814	0.80	96000
97000	*97999*	822	0.80	97000
98000	*98999*	830	0.80	98000
99000	*99999*	838	0.80	99000
100000	*100999*	846	0.80	100000
101000	*101999*	854	0.80	101000
102000	*102999*	862	0.80	102000
103000	*103999*	870	0.80	103000
104000	*104999*	878	0.79	104000
105000	*105999*	886	0.78	105000
106000	*106999*	894	0.78	106000
107000	*107999*	901	0.78	107000
108000	*108999*	909	0.78	108000
109000	*109999*	917	0.78	109000
110000	*110999*	925	0.78	110000
111000	*111999*	933	0.78	111000
112000	*112999*	940	0.78	112000
113000	*113999*	948	0.77	113000
114000	*114999*	956	0.74	114000
115000	*115999*	963	0.74	115000
116000	*116999*	971	0.74	116000
117000	*117999*	978	0.74	117000
118000	*118999*	985	0.74	118000
119000	*119999*	993	0.74	119000
120000	*120999*	1000	0.74	120000
121000	*121999*	1008	0.74	121000
122000	*122999*	1015	0.74	122000

Federal Child Support Tables/ Tables fédérales de pensions alimentaires pour enfants — **Province: New Brunswick/ Nouveau-Brunswick** — **No. Of Children/ Nbre d'enfants: One/Un**

Income/Revenu ($)		Monthly Award/ Paiement mensuel ($)		
From/De	To/À	Basic Amount/ Montant de base	Plus (%)	Of Income Over/Du revenu dépassant
123000	*123999*	1022	0.74	123000
124000	*124999*	1030	0.74	124000
125000	*125999*	1037	0.74	125000
126000	*126999*	1045	0.74	126000
127000	*127999*	1052	0.74	127000
128000	*128999*	1059	0.74	128000
129000	*129999*	1067	0.74	129000
130000	*130999*	1074	0.74	130000
131000	*131999*	1081	0.74	131000
132000	*132999*	1089	0.74	132000
133000	*133999*	1096	0.74	133000
134000	*134999*	1104	0.74	134000
135000	*135999*	1111	0.74	135000
136000	*136999*	1118	0.74	136000
137000	*137999*	1126	0.74	137000
138000	*138999*	1133	0.74	138000
139000	*139999*	1141	0.74	139000
140000	*140999*	1148	0.74	140000
141000	*141999*	1155	0.74	141000
142000	*142999*	1163	0.74	142000
143000	*143999*	1170	0.74	143000
144000	*144999*	1177	0.74	144000
145000	*145999*	1185	0.74	145000
146000	*146999*	1192	0.74	146000
147000	*147999*	1200	0.74	147000
148000	*148999*	1207	0.74	148000
149000	*149999*	1214	0.74	149000

Federal Child Support Tables/ Tables fédérales de pensions alimentaires pour enfants

Province: New Brunswick/ Nouveau-Brunswick
No. Of Children/ Nbre d'enfants: One/Un

Income/Revenu ($)		Monthly Award/ Paiement mensuel ($)		
From/De	To/À	Basic Amount/ Montant de base	Plus (%)	Of Income Over/Du revenu dépassant
150000	*or greater/ ou plus*	1222	0.74	150000

Federal Child Support Tables/ Tables fédérales de pensions alimentaires pour enfants

Province: New Brunswick/ Nouveau-Brunswick
No. Of Children/ Nbre d'enfants: Two/Deux

Income/Revenu ($)		Monthly Award/ Paiement mensuel ($)		
From/De	To/À	Basic Amount/ Montant de base	Plus (%)	Of Income Over/Du revenu dépassant
0	*7999*	0		
8000	*8999*	0	1.75	8000
9000	*9999*	17	4.34	9000
10000	*10999*	61	4.34	10000
11000	*11999*	104	4.34	11000
12000	*12999*	148	4.33	12000
13000	*13999*	191	3.50	13000
14000	*14999*	226	2.05	14000
15000	*15999*	247	0.62	15000
16000	*16999*	253	0.95	16000
17000	*17999*	262	0.95	17000
18000	*18999*	272	0.95	18000
19000	*19999*	281	0.95	19000
20000	*20999*	291	1.03	20000
21000	*21999*	301	1.47	21000
22000	*22999*	316	1.65	22000
23000	*23999*	332	1.65	23000
24000	*24999*	349	1.65	24000

Federal Child Support Tables/ Tables fédérales de pensions alimentaires pour enfants

Province: New Brunswick/ Nouveau-Brunswick
No. Of Children/ Nbre d'enfants: Two/Deux

Income/Revenu ($)		Monthly Award/ Paiement mensuel ($)		
From/De	To/À	Basic Amount/ Montant de base	Plus (%)	Of Income Over/Du revenu dépassant
25000	*25999*	365	1.65	25000
26000	*26999*	382	1.65	26000
27000	*27999*	398	1.65	27000
28000	*28999*	415	1.65	28000
29000	*29999*	431	1.58	29000
30000	*30999*	447	1.53	30000
31000	*31999*	462	1.39	31000
32000	*32999*	476	1.30	32000
33000	*33999*	489	1.28	33000
34000	*34999*	502	1.28	34000
35000	*35999*	515	1.15	35000
36000	*36999*	526	1.22	36000
37000	*37999*	538	1.25	37000
38000	*38999*	551	1.25	38000
39000	*39999*	563	1.29	39000
40000	*40999*	576	1.33	40000
41000	*41999*	590	1.37	41000
42000	*42999*	603	1.37	42000
43000	*43999*	617	1.36	43000
44000	*44999*	631	1.37	44000
45000	*45999*	644	1.37	45000
46000	*46999*	658	1.37	46000
47000	*47999*	672	1.37	47000
48000	*48999*	685	1.37	48000
49000	*49999*	699	1.36	49000
50000	*50999*	712	1.37	50000
51000	*51999*	726	1.37	51000
52000	*52999*	740	1.37	52000
53000	*53999*	753	1.36	53000
54000	*54999*	767	1.37	54000
55000	*55999*	781	1.37	55000
56000	*56999*	794	1.37	56000
57000	*57999*	808	1.37	57000
58000	*58999*	822	1.36	58000
59000	*59999*	835	1.37	59000

Federal Child Support Tables/ Tables fédérales de pensions alimentaires pour enfants

Province: New Brunswick/ Nouveau-Brunswick
No. Of Children/ Nbre d'enfants: Two/Deux

Income/Revenu ($)		Monthly Award/ Paiement mensuel ($)		
From/De	To/À	Basic Amount/ Montant de base	Plus (%)	Of Income Over/Du revenu dépassant
60000	*60999*	849	1.37	60000
61000	*61999*	863	1.37	61000
62000	*62999*	876	1.37	62000
63000	*63999*	890	1.37	63000
64000	*64999*	904	1.34	64000
65000	*65999*	917	1.33	65000
66000	*66999*	930	1.33	66000
67000	*67999*	944	1.33	67000
68000	*68999*	957	1.33	68000
69000	*69999*	970	1.33	69000
70000	*70999*	983	1.24	70000
71000	*71999*	996	1.24	71000
72000	*72999*	1008	1.24	72000
73000	*73999*	1021	1.24	73000
74000	*74999*	1033	1.24	74000
75000	*75999*	1045	1.24	75000
76000	*76999*	1058	1.24	76000
77000	*77999*	1070	1.24	77000
78000	*78999*	1083	1.24	78000
79000	*79999*	1095	1.24	79000
80000	*80999*	1108	1.24	80000
81000	*81999*	1120	1.24	81000
82000	*82999*	1132	1.24	82000
83000	*83999*	1145	1.24	83000
84000	*84999*	1157	1.24	84000
85000	*85999*	1170	1.24	85000
86000	*86999*	1182	1.24	86000
87000	*87999*	1194	1.24	87000
88000	*88999*	1207	1.24	88000
89000	*89999*	1219	1.24	89000
90000	*90999*	1232	1.24	90000
91000	*91999*	1244	1.24	91000
92000	*92999*	1257	1.24	92000
93000	*93999*	1269	1.24	93000
94000	*94999*	1281	1.24	94000

Federal Child Support Tables/ Tables fédérales de pensions alimentaires pour enfants

Province: New Brunswick/ Nouveau-Brunswick
No. Of Children/ Nbre d'enfants: Two/Deux

Income/Revenu ($)		Monthly Award/ Paiement mensuel ($)		
From/De	To/À	Basic Amount/ Montant de base	Plus (%)	Of Income Over/Du revenu dépassant
95000	*95999*	1294	1.24	95000
96000	*96999*	1306	1.24	96000
97000	*97999*	1319	1.24	97000
98000	*98999*	1331	1.24	98000
99000	*99999*	1344	1.24	99000
100000	*100999*	1356	1.24	100000
101000	*101999*	1368	1.24	101000
102000	*102999*	1381	1.24	102000
103000	*103999*	1393	1.24	103000
104000	*104999*	1406	1.23	104000
105000	*105999*	1418	1.21	105000
106000	*106999*	1430	1.21	106000
107000	*107999*	1442	1.21	107000
108000	*108999*	1454	1.21	108000
109000	*109999*	1466	1.21	109000
110000	*110999*	1479	1.21	110000
111000	*111999*	1491	1.21	111000
112000	*112999*	1503	1.21	112000
113000	*113999*	1515	1.20	113000
114000	*114999*	1527	1.15	114000
115000	*115999*	1538	1.15	115000
116000	*116999*	1550	1.15	116000
117000	*117999*	1561	1.15	117000
118000	*118999*	1573	1.15	118000
119000	*119999*	1584	1.15	119000
120000	*120999*	1596	1.15	120000
121000	*121999*	1607	1.15	121000
122000	*122999*	1619	1.15	122000
123000	*123999*	1630	1.15	123000
124000	*124999*	1642	1.15	124000
125000	*125999*	1653	1.15	125000
126000	*126999*	1665	1.15	126000
127000	*127999*	1676	1.15	127000
128000	*128999*	1688	1.15	128000
129000	*129999*	1699	1.15	129000

Federal Child Support Tables/ Tables fédérales de pensions alimentaires pour enfants

Province: New Brunswick/ Nouveau-Brunswick No. Of Children/ Nbre d'enfants: Two/Deux

Income/Revenu ($)		Monthly Award/ Paiement mensuel ($)		
From/De	To/À	Basic Amount/ Montant de base	Plus (%)	Of Income Over/Du revenu dépassant
130000	*130999*	1711	1.15	130000
131000	*131999*	1722	1.15	131000
132000	*132999*	1734	1.15	132000
133000	*133999*	1745	1.15	133000
134000	*134999*	1757	1.15	134000
135000	*135999*	1768	1.15	135000
136000	*136999*	1780	1.15	136000
137000	*137999*	1791	1.15	137000
138000	*138999*	1803	1.15	138000
139000	*139999*	1814	1.15	139000
140000	*140999*	1826	1.15	140000
141000	*141999*	1837	1.15	141000
142000	*142999*	1849	1.15	142000
143000	*143999*	1860	1.15	143000
144000	*144999*	1872	1.15	144000
145000	*145999*	1883	1.15	145000
146000	*146999*	1895	1.15	146000
147000	*147999*	1906	1.15	147000
148000	*148999*	1918	1.15	148000
149000	*149999*	1929	1.15	149000

Federal Child Support Tables/ Tables fédérales de pensions alimentaires pour enfants

Province: New Brunswick/ Nouveau-Brunswick No. Of Children/ Nbre d'enfants: Two/Deux

Income/Revenu ($)		Monthly Award/ Paiement mensuel ($)		
From/De	To/À	Basic Amount/ Montant de base	Plus (%)	Of Income Over/Du revenu dépassant
150000	*or greater/ ou plus*	1940	1.15	150000

Federal Child Support Tables/ Tables fédérales de pensions alimentaires pour enfants

Province: New Brunswick/ Nouveau-Brunswick No. Of Children/ Nbre d'enfants: Three/Trios

Income/Revenu ($)		Monthly Award/ Paiement mensuel ($)		
From/De	To/À	Basic Amount/ Montant de base	Plus (%)	Of Income Over/Du revenu dépassant
0	*7999*	0		
8000	*8999*	0	1.88	8000
9000	*9999*	19	4.68	9000
10000	*10999*	66	4.68	10000
11000	*11999*	112	4.68	11000
12000	*12999*	159	4.66	12000
13000	*13999*	206	3.77	13000
14000	*14999*	243	3.74	14000
15000	*15999*	281	3.74	15000
16000	*16999*	318	3.74	16000
17000	*17999*	356	1.50	17000
18000	*18999*	371	1.39	18000
19000	*19999*	385	1.39	19000
20000	*20999*	399	1.46	20000
21000	*21999*	413	1.87	21000
22000	*22999*	432	2.06	22000
23000	*23999*	453	2.06	23000
24000	*24999*	473	2.06	24000

Federal Child Support Tables/ Tables fédérales de pensions alimentaires pour enfants

Province: New Brunswick/ Nouveau-Brunswick
No. Of Children/ Nbre d'enfants: Three/Trios

Income/Revenu ($)		Monthly Award/ Paiement mensuel ($)		
From/De	To/À	Basic Amount/ Montant de base	Plus (%)	Of Income Over/Du revenu dépassant
25000	*25999*	494	2.06	25000
26000	*26999*	514	2.06	26000
27000	*27999*	535	2.06	27000
28000	*28999*	556	2.06	28000
29000	*29999*	576	1.97	29000
30000	*30999*	596	1.91	30000
31000	*31999*	615	1.78	31000
32000	*32999*	633	1.67	32000
33000	*33999*	650	1.64	33000
34000	*34999*	666	1.64	34000
35000	*35999*	682	1.48	35000
36000	*36999*	697	1.57	36000
37000	*37999*	713	1.61	37000
38000	*38999*	729	1.61	38000
39000	*39999*	745	1.65	39000
40000	*40999*	762	1.70	40000
41000	*41999*	779	1.76	41000
42000	*42999*	796	1.76	42000
43000	*43999*	814	1.76	43000
44000	*44999*	831	1.76	44000
45000	*45999*	849	1.75	45000
46000	*46999*	866	1.76	46000
47000	*47999*	884	1.76	47000
48000	*48999*	901	1.76	48000
49000	*49999*	919	1.76	49000
50000	*50999*	937	1.76	50000
51000	*51999*	954	1.76	51000
52000	*52999*	972	1.76	52000
53000	*53999*	989	1.76	53000
54000	*54999*	1007	1.75	54000
55000	*55999*	1024	1.76	55000
56000	*56999*	1042	1.76	56000
57000	*57999*	1059	1.75	57000
58000	*58999*	1077	1.76	58000
59000	*59999*	1095	1.75	59000

Federal Child Support Tables/ Tables fédérales de pensions alimentaires pour enfants

Province: New Brunswick/ Nouveau-Brunswick
No. Of Children/ Nbre d'enfants: Three/Trios

Income/Revenu ($)		Monthly Award/ Paiement mensuel ($)		
From/De	To/À	Basic Amount/ Montant de base	Plus (%)	Of Income Over/Du revenu dépassant
60000	*60999*	1112	1.76	60000
61000	*61999*	1130	1.76	61000
62000	*62999*	1147	1.75	62000
63000	*63999*	1165	1.76	63000
64000	*64999*	1182	1.72	64000
65000	*65999*	1200	1.71	65000
66000	*66999*	1217	1.71	66000
67000	*67999*	1234	1.71	67000
68000	*68999*	1251	1.71	68000
69000	*69999*	1268	1.71	69000
70000	*70999*	1285	1.60	70000
71000	*71999*	1301	1.60	71000
72000	*72999*	1317	1.60	72000
73000	*73999*	1333	1.60	73000
74000	*74999*	1349	1.60	74000
75000	*75999*	1365	1.60	75000
76000	*76999*	1381	1.60	76000
77000	*77999*	1397	1.60	77000
78000	*78999*	1413	1.60	78000
79000	*79999*	1429	1.60	79000
80000	*80999*	1445	1.60	80000
81000	*81999*	1461	1.60	81000
82000	*82999*	1476	1.60	82000
83000	*83999*	1492	1.60	83000
84000	*84999*	1508	1.60	84000
85000	*85999*	1524	1.60	85000
86000	*86999*	1540	1.60	86000
87000	*87999*	1556	1.60	87000
88000	*88999*	1572	1.60	88000
89000	*89999*	1588	1.60	89000
90000	*90999*	1604	1.60	90000
91000	*91999*	1620	1.60	91000
92000	*92999*	1636	1.60	92000
93000	*93999*	1652	1.60	93000
94000	*94999*	1668	1.60	94000

Federal Child Support Tables/ Tables fédérales de pensions alimentaires pour enfants

Province: New Brunswick/ Nouveau-Brunswick
No. Of Children/ Nbre d'enfants: Three/Trios

Income/Revenu ($)		Monthly Award/ Paiement mensuel ($)		
From/De	To/À	Basic Amount/ Montant de base	Plus (%)	Of Income Over/Du revenu dépassant
95000	*95999*	1684	1.60	95000
96000	*96999*	1700	1.60	96000
97000	*97999*	1716	1.60	97000
98000	*98999*	1732	1.60	98000
99000	*99999*	1748	1.60	99000
100000	*100999*	1764	1.60	100000
101000	*101999*	1780	1.60	101000
102000	*102999*	1796	1.60	102000
103000	*103999*	1812	1.60	103000
104000	*104999*	1828	1.58	104000
105000	*105999*	1844	1.56	105000
106000	*106999*	1859	1.56	106000
107000	*107999*	1875	1.56	107000
108000	*108999*	1890	1.56	108000
109000	*109999*	1906	1.56	109000
110000	*110999*	1922	1.56	110000
111000	*111999*	1937	1.56	111000
112000	*112999*	1953	1.56	112000
113000	*113999*	1968	1.54	113000
114000	*114999*	1984	1.48	114000
115000	*115999*	1999	1.48	115000
116000	*116999*	2013	1.48	116000
117000	*117999*	2028	1.48	117000
118000	*118999*	2043	1.48	118000
119000	*119999*	2058	1.48	119000
120000	*120999*	2072	1.48	120000
121000	*121999*	2087	1.48	121000
122000	*122999*	2102	1.48	122000

Federal Child Support Tables/ Tables fédérales de pensions alimentaires pour enfants

Province: New Brunswick/ Nouveau-Brunswick
No. Of Children/ Nbre d'enfants: Three/Trios

Income/Revenu ($)		Monthly Award/ Paiement mensuel ($)		
From/De	To/À	Basic Amount/ Montant de base	Plus (%)	Of Income Over/Du revenu dépassant
123000	*123999*	2117	1.48	123000
124000	*124999*	2132	1.48	124000
125000	*125999*	2146	1.48	125000
126000	*126999*	2161	1.48	126000
127000	*127999*	2176	1.48	127000
128000	*128999*	2191	1.48	128000
129000	*129999*	2205	1.48	129000
130000	*130999*	2220	1.48	130000
131000	*131999*	2235	1.48	131000
132000	*132999*	2250	1.48	132000
133000	*133999*	2264	1.48	133000
134000	*134999*	2279	1.48	134000
135000	*135999*	2294	1.48	135000
136000	*136999*	2309	1.48	136000
137000	*137999*	2323	1.48	137000
138000	*138999*	2338	1.48	138000
139000	*139999*	2353	1.48	139000
140000	*140999*	2368	1.48	140000
141000	*141999*	2383	1.48	141000
142000	*142999*	2397	1.48	142000
143000	*143999*	2412	1.48	143000
144000	*144999*	2427	1.48	144000
145000	*145999*	2442	1.48	145000
146000	*146999*	2456	1.48	146000
147000	*147999*	2471	1.48	147000
148000	*148999*	2486	1.48	148000
149000	*149999*	2501	1.48	149000

Federal Child Support Tables/ Tables fédérales de pensions alimentaires pour enfants

Province: New Brunswick/ Nouveau-Brunswick No. Of Children/ Nbre d'enfants: Three/Trios

Income/Revenu ($)		Monthly Award/ Paiement mensuel ($)		
From/De	To/À	Basic Amount/ Montant de base	Plus (%)	Of Income Over/Du revenu dépassant
150000	*or greater/ ou plus*	2515	1.48	150000

Federal Child Support Tables/ Tables fédérales de pensions alimentaires pour enfants

Province: New Brunswick/ Nouveau-Brunswick No. Of Children/ Nbre d'enfants: Four/Quatre

Income/Revenu ($)		Monthly Award/ Paiement mensuel ($)		
From/De	To/À	Basic Amount/ Montant de base	Plus (%)	Of Income Over/Du revenu dépassant
0	*7999*	0		
8000	*8999*	0	2.01	8000
9000	*9999*	20	5.01	9000
10000	*10999*	70	5.01	10000
11000	*11999*	120	5.01	11000
12000	*12999*	170	5.00	12000
13000	*13999*	220	4.04	13000
14000	*14999*	261	4.01	14000
15000	*15999*	301	4.01	15000
16000	*16999*	341	4.01	16000
17000	*17999*	381	4.01	17000
18000	*18999*	421	4.01	18000
19000	*19999*	461	2.55	19000
20000	*20999*	487	1.82	20000
21000	*21999*	505	2.19	21000
22000	*22999*	527	2.40	22000
23000	*23999*	551	2.40	23000
24000	*24999*	575	2.40	24000

Federal Child Support Tables/ Tables fédérales de pensions alimentaires pour enfants

Province: New Brunswick/ Nouveau-Brunswick No. Of Children/ Nbre d'enfants: Four/Quatre

Income/Revenu ($)		Monthly Award/ Paiement mensuel ($)		
From/De	To/À	Basic Amount/ Montant de base	Plus (%)	Of Income Over/Du revenu dépassant
25000	*25999*	599	2.40	25000
26000	*26999*	623	2.40	26000
27000	*27999*	647	2.40	27000
28000	*28999*	671	2.40	28000
29000	*29999*	695	2.29	29000
30000	*30999*	718	2.22	30000
31000	*31999*	740	2.11	31000
32000	*32999*	761	1.97	32000
33000	*33999*	781	1.94	33000
34000	*34999*	800	1.94	34000
35000	*35999*	819	1.75	35000
36000	*36999*	837	1.86	36000
37000	*37999*	855	1.91	37000
38000	*38999*	875	1.91	38000
39000	*39999*	894	1.95	39000
40000	*40999*	913	2.01	40000
41000	*41999*	933	2.07	41000
42000	*42999*	954	2.07	42000
43000	*43999*	975	2.07	43000
44000	*44999*	995	2.07	44000
45000	*45999*	1016	2.07	45000
46000	*46999*	1037	2.07	46000
47000	*47999*	1058	2.07	47000
48000	*48999*	1078	2.07	48000
49000	*49999*	1099	2.07	49000
50000	*50999*	1120	2.07	50000
51000	*51999*	1141	2.07	51000
52000	*52999*	1161	2.07	52000
53000	*53999*	1182	2.07	53000
54000	*54999*	1203	2.07	54000
55000	*55999*	1224	2.07	55000
56000	*56999*	1244	2.07	56000
57000	*57999*	1265	2.07	57000
58000	*58999*	1286	2.07	58000
59000	*59999*	1307	2.07	59000

Federal Child Support Tables/ Tables fédérales de pensions alimentaires pour enfants

Province: New Brunswick/ Nouveau-Brunswick
No. Of Children/ Nbre d'enfants: Four/Quatre

Income/Revenu ($)		Monthly Award/ Paiement mensuel ($)		
From/De	To/À	Basic Amount/ Montant de base	Plus (%)	Of Income Over/Du revenu dépassant
60000	*60999*	1327	2.07	60000
61000	*61999*	1348	2.07	61000
62000	*62999*	1369	2.07	62000
63000	*63999*	1390	2.07	63000
64000	*64999*	1410	2.04	64000
65000	*65999*	1431	2.02	65000
66000	*66999*	1451	2.02	66000
67000	*67999*	1471	2.02	67000
68000	*68999*	1491	2.02	68000
69000	*69999*	1511	2.02	69000
70000	*70999*	1532	1.89	70000
71000	*71999*	1550	1.89	71000
72000	*72999*	1569	1.89	72000
73000	*73999*	1588	1.89	73000
74000	*74999*	1607	1.89	74000
75000	*75999*	1626	1.89	75000
76000	*76999*	1645	1.89	76000
77000	*77999*	1664	1.89	77000
78000	*78999*	1683	1.89	78000
79000	*79999*	1701	1.89	79000
80000	*80999*	1720	1.89	80000
81000	*81999*	1739	1.89	81000
82000	*82999*	1758	1.89	82000
83000	*83999*	1777	1.89	83000
84000	*84999*	1796	1.89	84000
85000	*85999*	1815	1.89	85000
86000	*86999*	1834	1.89	86000
87000	*87999*	1852	1.89	87000
88000	*88999*	1871	1.89	88000
89000	*89999*	1890	1.89	89000
90000	*90999*	1909	1.89	90000
91000	*91999*	1928	1.89	91000
92000	*92999*	1947	1.89	92000
93000	*93999*	1966	1.89	93000
94000	*94999*	1984	1.89	94000

Federal Child Support Tables/ Tables fédérales de pensions alimentaires pour enfants

Province: New Brunswick/ Nouveau-Brunswick
No. Of Children/ Nbre d'enfants: Four/Quatre

Income/Revenu ($)		Monthly Award/ Paiement mensuel ($)		
From/De	To/À	Basic Amount/ Montant de base	Plus (%)	Of Income Over/Du revenu dépassant
95000	*95999*	2003	1.89	95000
96000	*96999*	2022	1.89	96000
97000	*97999*	2041	1.89	97000
98000	*98999*	2060	1.89	98000
99000	*99999*	2079	1.89	99000
100000	*100999*	2098	1.89	100000
101000	*101999*	2117	1.89	101000
102000	*102999*	2135	1.89	102000
103000	*103999*	2154	1.89	103000
104000	*104999*	2173	1.87	104000
105000	*105999*	2192	1.84	105000
106000	*106999*	2210	1.84	106000
107000	*107999*	2229	1.84	107000
108000	*108999*	2247	1.84	108000
109000	*109999*	2266	1.84	109000
110000	*110999*	2284	1.84	110000
111000	*111999*	2303	1.84	111000
112000	*112999*	2321	1.84	112000
113000	*113999*	2339	1.82	113000
114000	*114999*	2358	1.75	114000
115000	*115999*	2375	1.75	115000
116000	*116999*	2393	1.75	116000
117000	*117999*	2410	1.75	117000
118000	*118999*	2427	1.75	118000
119000	*119999*	2445	1.75	119000
120000	*120999*	2462	1.75	120000
121000	*121999*	2480	1.75	121000
122000	*122999*	2497	1.75	122000
123000	*123999*	2515	1.75	123000
124000	*124999*	2532	1.75	124000
125000	*125999*	2550	1.75	125000
126000	*126999*	2567	1.75	126000
127000	*127999*	2584	1.75	127000
128000	*128999*	2602	1.75	128000
129000	*129999*	2619	1.75	129000

Federal Child Support Tables/ Tables fédérales de pensions alimentaires pour enfants

Province: New Brunswick/ Nouveau-Brunswick No. Of Children/ Nbre d'enfants: Four/Quatre

Income/Revenu ($)		Monthly Award/ Paiement mensuel ($)		
From/De	To/À	Basic Amount/ Montant de base	Plus (%)	Of Income Over/Du revenu dépassant
130000	*130999*	2637	1.75	130000
131000	*131999*	2654	1.75	131000
132000	*132999*	2672	1.75	132000
133000	*133999*	2689	1.75	133000
134000	*134999*	2707	1.75	134000
135000	*135999*	2724	1.75	135000
136000	*136999*	2742	1.75	136000
137000	*137999*	2759	1.75	137000
138000	*138999*	2776	1.75	138000
139000	*139999*	2794	1.75	139000
140000	*140999*	2811	1.75	140000
141000	*141999*	2829	1.75	141000
142000	*142999*	2846	1.75	142000
143000	*143999*	2864	1.75	143000
144000	*144999*	2881	1.75	144000
145000	*145999*	2899	1.75	145000
146000	*146999*	2916	1.75	146000
147000	*147999*	2934	1.75	147000
148000	*148999*	2951	1.75	148000
149000	*149999*	2968	1.75	149000
150000	*or greater/ ou plus*	2986	1.75	150000

Federal Child Support Tables/ Tables fédérales de pensions alimentaires pour enfants

Province: New Brunswick/ Nouveau-Brunswick No. Of Children/ Nbre d'enfants: Five/Cinq

Income/Revenu ($)		Monthly Award/ Paiement mensuel ($)		
From/De	To/À	Basic Amount/ Montant de base	Plus (%)	Of Income Over/Du revenu dépassant
0	*7999*	0		
8000	*8999*	0	2.01	8000
9000	*9999*	20	5.01	9000
10000	*10999*	70	5.01	10000
11000	*11999*	120	5.01	11000
12000	*12999*	170	5.00	12000
13000	*13999*	220	4.04	13000
14000	*14999*	261	4.01	14000
15000	*15999*	301	4.01	15000
16000	*16999*	341	4.01	16000
17000	*17999*	381	4.01	17000
18000	*18999*	421	4.01	18000
19000	*19999*	461	4.01	19000
20000	*20999*	502	4.01	20000
21000	*21999*	542	4.10	21000
22000	*22999*	583	4.32	22000
23000	*23999*	626	3.38	23000
24000	*24999*	660	2.68	24000

Federal Child Support Tables/ Tables fédérales de pensions alimentaires pour enfants

Province: New Brunswick/ Nouveau-Brunswick
No. Of Children/ Nbre d'enfants: Five/Cinq

Income/Revenu ($)		Monthly Award/ Paiement mensuel ($)		
From/De	To/À	Basic Amount/ Montant de base	Plus (%)	Of Income Over/Du revenu dépassant
25000	*25999*	686	2.68	25000
26000	*26999*	713	2.68	26000
27000	*27999*	740	2.68	27000
28000	*28999*	767	2.68	28000
29000	*29999*	794	2.56	29000
30000	*30999*	819	2.48	30000
31000	*31999*	844	2.38	31000
32000	*32999*	868	2.22	32000
33000	*33999*	890	2.19	33000
34000	*34999*	912	2.19	34000
35000	*35999*	934	1.97	35000
36000	*36999*	953	2.10	36000
37000	*37999*	974	2.15	37000
38000	*38999*	996	2.15	38000
39000	*39999*	1017	2.20	39000
40000	*40999*	1039	2.27	40000
41000	*41999*	1062	2.34	41000
42000	*42999*	1086	2.34	42000
43000	*43999*	1109	2.34	43000
44000	*44999*	1132	2.34	44000
45000	*45999*	1156	2.34	45000
46000	*46999*	1179	2.34	46000
47000	*47999*	1203	2.34	47000
48000	*48999*	1226	2.34	48000
49000	*49999*	1249	2.34	49000
50000	*50999*	1273	2.34	50000
51000	*51999*	1296	2.34	51000
52000	*52999*	1320	2.34	52000
53000	*53999*	1343	2.34	53000
54000	*54999*	1366	2.34	54000
55000	*55999*	1390	2.34	55000
56000	*56999*	1413	2.34	56000
57000	*57999*	1437	2.34	57000
58000	*58999*	1460	2.34	58000
59000	*59999*	1483	2.34	59000

Federal Child Support Tables/ Tables fédérales de pensions alimentaires pour enfants

Province: New Brunswick/ Nouveau-Brunswick
No. Of Children/ Nbre d'enfants: Five/Cinq

Income/Revenu ($)		Monthly Award/ Paiement mensuel ($)		
From/De	To/À	Basic Amount/ Montant de base	Plus (%)	Of Income Over/Du revenu dépassant
60000	*60999*	1507	2.34	60000
61000	*61999*	1530	2.34	61000
62000	*62999*	1554	2.34	62000
63000	*63999*	1577	2.34	63000
64000	*64999*	1600	2.30	64000
65000	*65999*	1623	2.28	65000
66000	*66999*	1646	2.28	66000
67000	*67999*	1669	2.28	67000
68000	*68999*	1692	2.28	68000
69000	*69999*	1714	2.28	69000
70000	*70999*	1737	2.13	70000
71000	*71999*	1758	2.13	71000
72000	*72999*	1780	2.13	72000
73000	*73999*	1801	2.13	73000
74000	*74999*	1822	2.13	74000
75000	*75999*	1844	2.13	75000
76000	*76999*	1865	2.13	76000
77000	*77999*	1886	2.13	77000
78000	*78999*	1907	2.13	78000
79000	*79999*	1929	2.13	79000
80000	*80999*	1950	2.13	80000
81000	*81999*	1971	2.13	81000
82000	*82999*	1993	2.13	82000
83000	*83999*	2014	2.13	83000
84000	*84999*	2035	2.13	84000
85000	*85999*	2056	2.13	85000
86000	*86999*	2078	2.13	86000
87000	*87999*	2099	2.13	87000
88000	*88999*	2120	2.13	88000
89000	*89999*	2142	2.13	89000
90000	*90999*	2163	2.13	90000
91000	*91999*	2184	2.13	91000
92000	*92999*	2206	2.13	92000
93000	*93999*	2227	2.13	93000
94000	*94999*	2248	2.13	94000

Federal Child Support Tables/ Tables fédérales de pensions alimentaires pour enfants

Province: New Brunswick/ Nouveau-Brunswick No. Of Children/ N^bre d'enfants: Five/Cinq

Income/Revenu ($)		Monthly Award/ Paiement mensuel ($)		
From/De	To/À	Basic Amount/ Montant de base	Plus (%)	Of Income Over/Du revenu dépassant
95000	*95999*	2269	2.13	95000
96000	*96999*	2291	2.13	96000
97000	*97999*	2312	2.13	97000
98000	*98999*	2333	2.13	98000
99000	*99999*	2355	2.13	99000
100000	*100999*	2376	2.13	100000
101000	*101999*	2397	2.13	101000
102000	*102999*	2418	2.13	102000
103000	*103999*	2440	2.13	103000
104000	*104999*	2461	2.11	104000
105000	*105999*	2482	2.08	105000
106000	*106999*	2503	2.08	106000
107000	*107999*	2524	2.08	107000
108000	*108999*	2545	2.08	108000
109000	*109999*	2565	2.08	109000
110000	*110999*	2586	2.08	110000
111000	*111999*	2607	2.08	111000
112000	*112999*	2628	2.08	112000
113000	*113999*	2649	2.06	113000
114000	*114999*	2669	1.97	114000
115000	*115999*	2689	1.97	115000
116000	*116999*	2708	1.97	116000
117000	*117999*	2728	1.97	117000
118000	*118999*	2748	1.97	118000
119000	*119999*	2768	1.97	119000
120000	*120999*	2787	1.97	120000
121000	*121999*	2807	1.97	121000
122000	*122999*	2827	1.97	122000

Federal Child Support Tables/ Tables fédérales de pensions alimentaires pour enfants

Province: New Brunswick/ Nouveau-Brunswick No. Of Children/ N^bre d'enfants: Five/Cinq

Income/Revenu ($)		Monthly Award/ Paiement mensuel ($)		
From/De	To/À	Basic Amount/ Montant de base	Plus (%)	Of Income Over/Du revenu dépassant
123000	*123999*	2846	1.97	123000
124000	*124999*	2866	1.97	124000
125000	*125999*	2886	1.97	125000
126000	*126999*	2905	1.97	126000
127000	*127999*	2925	1.97	127000
128000	*128999*	2945	1.97	128000
129000	*129999*	2964	1.97	129000
130000	*130999*	2984	1.97	130000
131000	*131999*	3004	1.97	131000
132000	*132999*	3023	1.97	132000
133000	*133999*	3043	1.97	133000
134000	*134999*	3063	1.97	134000
135000	*135999*	3083	1.97	135000
136000	*136999*	3102	1.97	136000
137000	*137999*	3122	1.97	137000
138000	*138999*	3142	1.97	138000
139000	*139999*	3161	1.97	139000
140000	*140999*	3181	1.97	140000
141000	*141999*	3201	1.97	141000
142000	*142999*	3220	1.97	142000
143000	*143999*	3240	1.97	143000
144000	*144999*	3260	1.97	144000
145000	*145999*	3279	1.97	145000
146000	*146999*	3299	1.97	146000
147000	*147999*	3319	1.97	147000
148000	*148999*	3339	1.97	148000
149000	*149999*	3358	1.97	149000

Federal Child Support Tables/ Tables fédérales de pensions alimentaires pour enfants

Province: New Brunswick/ Nouveau-Brunswick
No. Of Children/ Nbre d'enfants: Five/Cinq

Income/Revenu ($)		Monthly Award/ Paiement mensuel ($)		
From/De	**To/À**	**Basic Amount/ Montant de base**	**Plus (%)**	**Of Income Over/Du revenu dépassant**
150000	*or greater/ ou plus*	3378	1.97	150000

Federal Child Support Tables/ Tables fédérales de pensions alimentaires pour enfants

Province: New Brunswick/ Nouveau-Brunswick
No. Of Children/ Nbre d'enfants: Six or more/Six ou plus

Income/Revenu ($)		Monthly Award/ Paiement mensuel ($)		
From/De	**To/À**	**Basic Amount/ Montant de base**	**Plus (%)**	**Of Income Over/Du revenu dépassant**
0	*7999*	0		
8000	*8999*	0	2.01	8000
9000	*9999*	20	5.01	9000
10000	*10999*	70	5.01	10000
11000	*11999*	120	5.01	11000
12000	*12999*	170	5.00	12000
13000	*13999*	220	4.04	13000
14000	*14999*	261	4.01	14000
15000	*15999*	301	4.01	15000
16000	*16999*	341	4.01	16000
17000	*17999*	381	4.01	17000
18000	*18999*	421	4.01	18000
19000	*19999*	461	4.01	19000
20000	*20999*	502	4.01	20000
21000	*21999*	542	4.10	21000
22000	*22999*	583	4.32	22000
23000	*23999*	626	4.32	23000
24000	*24999*	669	4.32	24000

Federal Child Support Tables/ Tables fédérales de pensions alimentaires pour enfants

Province: New Brunswick/ Nouveau-Brunswick
No. Of Children/ Nbre d'enfants: Six or more/Six ou plus

Income/Revenu ($)		Monthly Award/ Paiement mensuel ($)		
From/De	**To/À**	**Basic Amount/ Montant de base**	**Plus (%)**	**Of Income Over/Du revenu dépassant**
25000	*25999*	712	4.32	25000
26000	*26999*	756	4.32	26000
27000	*27999*	799	4.32	27000
28000	*28999*	842	3.51	28000
29000	*29999*	877	2.79	29000
30000	*30999*	905	2.70	30000
31000	*31999*	932	2.61	31000
32000	*32999*	958	2.44	32000
33000	*33999*	982	2.40	33000
34000	*34999*	1006	2.40	34000
35000	*35999*	1030	2.16	35000
36000	*36999*	1052	2.30	36000
37000	*37999*	1075	2.36	37000
38000	*38999*	1099	2.36	38000
39000	*39999*	1122	2.42	39000
40000	*40999*	1146	2.49	40000
41000	*41999*	1171	2.57	41000
42000	*42999*	1197	2.56	42000
43000	*43999*	1222	2.57	43000
44000	*44999*	1248	2.57	44000
45000	*45999*	1274	2.56	45000
46000	*46999*	1299	2.57	46000
47000	*47999*	1325	2.56	47000
48000	*48999*	1351	2.56	48000
49000	*49999*	1376	2.57	49000
50000	*50999*	1402	2.57	50000
51000	*51999*	1428	2.56	51000
52000	*52999*	1453	2.56	52000
53000	*53999*	1479	2.57	53000
54000	*54999*	1505	2.56	54000
55000	*55999*	1530	2.57	55000
56000	*56999*	1556	2.56	56000
57000	*57999*	1582	2.56	57000
58000	*58999*	1607	2.57	58000
59000	*59999*	1633	2.56	59000

Federal Child Support Tables/ Tables fédérales de pensions alimentaires pour enfants

Province: New Brunswick/ Nouveau-Brunswick
No. Of Children/ Nbre d'enfants: Six or more/Six ou plus

Income/Revenu ($)		Monthly Award/ Paiement mensuel ($)		
From/De	To/À	Basic Amount/ Montant de base	Plus (%)	Of Income Over/Du revenu dépassant
60000	*60999*	1659	2.57	60000
61000	*61999*	1684	2.57	61000
62000	*62999*	1710	2.57	62000
63000	*63999*	1735	2.56	63000
64000	*64999*	1761	2.52	64000
65000	*65999*	1786	2.50	65000
66000	*66999*	1811	2.50	66000
67000	*67999*	1836	2.50	67000
68000	*68999*	1861	2.50	68000
69000	*69999*	1886	2.50	69000
70000	*70999*	1911	2.33	70000
71000	*71999*	1934	2.33	71000
72000	*72999*	1958	2.33	72000
73000	*73999*	1981	2.33	73000
74000	*74999*	2004	2.33	74000
75000	*75999*	2028	2.33	75000
76000	*76999*	2051	2.33	76000
77000	*77999*	2074	2.33	77000
78000	*78999*	2098	2.33	78000
79000	*79999*	2121	2.33	79000
80000	*80999*	2144	2.33	80000
81000	*81999*	2168	2.33	81000
82000	*82999*	2191	2.33	82000
83000	*83999*	2214	2.33	83000
84000	*84999*	2238	2.33	84000
85000	*85999*	2261	2.33	85000
86000	*86999*	2284	2.33	86000
87000	*87999*	2308	2.33	87000
88000	*88999*	2331	2.33	88000
89000	*89999*	2354	2.33	89000
90000	*90999*	2378	2.33	90000
91000	*91999*	2401	2.33	91000
92000	*92999*	2425	2.33	92000
93000	*93999*	2448	2.33	93000
94000	*94999*	2471	2.33	94000

Federal Child Support Tables/ Tables fédérales de pensions alimentaires pour enfants

Province: New Brunswick/ Nouveau-Brunswick
No. Of Children/ Nbre d'enfants: Six or more/Six ou plus

Income/Revenu ($)		Monthly Award/ Paiement mensuel ($)		
From/De	To/À	Basic Amount/ Montant de base	Plus (%)	Of Income Over/Du revenu dépassant
95000	*95999*	2495	2.33	95000
96000	*96999*	2518	2.33	96000
97000	*97999*	2541	2.33	97000
98000	*98999*	2565	2.33	98000
99000	*99999*	2588	2.33	99000
100000	*100999*	2611	2.33	100000
101000	*101999*	2635	2.33	101000
102000	*102999*	2658	2.33	102000
103000	*103999*	2681	2.33	103000
104000	*104999*	2705	2.32	104000
105000	*105999*	2728	2.28	105000
106000	*106999*	2750	2.28	106000
107000	*107999*	2773	2.28	107000
108000	*108999*	2796	2.28	108000
109000	*109999*	2819	2.28	109000
110000	*110999*	2842	2.28	110000
111000	*111999*	2864	2.28	111000
112000	*112999*	2887	2.28	112000
113000	*113999*	2910	2.26	113000
114000	*114999*	2933	2.16	114000
115000	*115999*	2954	2.16	115000
116000	*116999*	2976	2.16	116000
117000	*117999*	2997	2.16	117000
118000	*118999*	3019	2.16	118000
119000	*119999*	3041	2.16	119000
120000	*120999*	3062	2.16	120000
121000	*121999*	3084	2.16	121000
122000	*122999*	3105	2.16	122000
123000	*123999*	3127	2.16	123000
124000	*124999*	3148	2.16	124000
125000	*125999*	3170	2.16	125000
126000	*126999*	3192	2.16	126000
127000	*127999*	3213	2.16	127000
128000	*128999*	3235	2.16	128000
129000	*129999*	3256	2.16	129000

Federal Child Support Tables/ Tables fédérales de pensions alimentaires pour enfants — **Province: New Brunswick/ Nouveau-Brunswick** — **No. Of Children/ Nbre d'enfants: Six or more/Six ou plus**

Income/Revenu ($)		Monthly Award/ Paiement mensuel ($)		
From/De	To/À	Basic Amount/ Montant de base	Plus (%)	Of Income Over/Du revenu dépassant
130000	*130999*	3278	2.16	130000
131000	*131999*	3300	2.16	131000
132000	*132999*	3321	2.16	132000
133000	*133999*	3343	2.16	133000
134000	*134999*	3364	2.16	134000
135000	*135999*	3386	2.16	135000
136000	*136999*	3407	2.16	136000
137000	*137999*	3429	2.16	137000
138000	*138999*	3451	2.16	138000
139000	*139999*	3472	2.16	139000
140000	*140999*	3494	2.16	140000
141000	*141999*	3515	2.16	141000
142000	*142999*	3537	2.16	142000
143000	*143999*	3559	2.16	143000
144000	*144999*	3580	2.16	144000
145000	*145999*	3602	2.16	145000
146000	*146999*	3623	2.16	146000
147000	*147999*	3645	2.16	147000
148000	*148999*	3666	2.16	148000
149000	*149999*	3688	2.16	149000
150000	*or greater/ ou plus*	3710	2.16	150000

Federal Child Support Tables/ Tables fédérales de pensions alimentaires pour enfants — **Province: Manitoba** — **No. Of Children/ Nbre d'enfants: One/Un**

Income/Revenu ($)		Monthly Award/ Paiement mensuel ($)		
From/De	To/À	Basic Amount/ Montant de base	Plus (%)	Of Income Over/Du revenu dépassant
0	*7999*	0		
8000	*8999*	0	0.93	8000
9000	*9999*	9	1.55	9000
10000	*10999*	25	1.55	10000
11000	*11999*	40	1.55	11000
12000	*12999*	56	1.55	12000
13000	*13999*	72	1.55	13000
14000	*14999*	87	1.55	14000
15000	*15999*	103	1.55	15000
16000	*16999*	118	0.53	16000
17000	*17999*	123	0.66	17000
18000	*18999*	130	0.92	18000
19000	*19999*	139	0.97	19000
20000	*20999*	149	0.97	20000
21000	*21999*	158	0.97	21000
22000	*22999*	168	0.99	22000
23000	*23999*	178	1.01	23000
24000	*24999*	188	1.01	24000

Federal Child Support Tables/ Tables fédérales de pensions alimentaires pour enfants

Province: Manitoba No. Of Children/ Nbre d'enfants: One/Un

Income/Revenu ($)		Monthly Award/ Paiement mensuel ($)		
From/De	To/À	Basic Amount/ Montant de base	Plus (%)	Of Income Over/Du revenu dépassant
25000	*25999*	198	1.01	25000
26000	*26999*	208	1.01	26000
27000	*27999*	219	1.01	27000
28000	*28999*	229	1.01	28000
29000	*29999*	239	0.97	29000
30000	*30999*	249	0.93	30000
31000	*31999*	258	0.90	31000
32000	*32999*	267	0.90	32000
33000	*33999*	276	0.90	33000
34000	*34999*	285	0.90	34000
35000	*35999*	294	0.82	35000
36000	*36999*	302	0.87	36000
37000	*37999*	311	0.89	37000
38000	*38999*	320	0.85	38000
39000	*39999*	328	0.87	39000
40000	*40999*	337	0.90	40000
41000	*41999*	346	0.92	41000
42000	*42999*	355	0.92	42000
43000	*43999*	364	0.92	43000
44000	*44999*	374	0.92	44000
45000	*45999*	383	0.89	45000
46000	*46999*	392	0.89	46000
47000	*47999*	401	0.89	47000
48000	*48999*	410	0.89	48000
49000	*49999*	418	0.89	49000
50000	*50999*	427	0.89	50000
51000	*51999*	436	0.89	51000
52000	*52999*	445	0.89	52000
53000	*53999*	454	0.89	53000
54000	*54999*	463	0.89	54000
55000	*55999*	472	0.89	55000
56000	*56999*	481	0.89	56000
57000	*57999*	490	0.89	57000
58000	*58999*	498	0.89	58000
59000	*59999*	507	0.89	59000

Federal Child Support Tables/ Tables fédérales de pensions alimentaires pour enfants

Province: Manitoba No. Of Children/ Nbre d'enfants: One/Un

Income/Revenu ($)		Monthly Award/ Paiement mensuel ($)		
From/De	To/À	Basic Amount/ Montant de base	Plus (%)	Of Income Over/Du revenu dépassant
60000	*60999*	516	0.89	60000
61000	*61999*	525	0.89	61000
62000	*62999*	534	0.89	62000
63000	*63999*	543	0.89	63000
64000	*64999*	552	0.89	64000
65000	*65999*	561	0.84	65000
66000	*66999*	569	0.84	66000
67000	*67999*	578	0.84	67000
68000	*68999*	586	0.84	68000
69000	*69999*	594	0.84	69000
70000	*70999*	603	0.79	70000
71000	*71999*	611	0.79	71000
72000	*72999*	619	0.79	72000
73000	*73999*	626	0.79	73000
74000	*74999*	634	0.79	74000
75000	*75999*	642	0.79	75000
76000	*76999*	650	0.79	76000
77000	*77999*	658	0.79	77000
78000	*78999*	666	0.79	78000
79000	*79999*	674	0.79	79000
80000	*80999*	681	0.79	80000
81000	*81999*	689	0.79	81000
82000	*82999*	697	0.79	82000
83000	*83999*	705	0.79	83000
84000	*84999*	713	0.79	84000
85000	*85999*	721	0.79	85000
86000	*86999*	729	0.79	86000
87000	*87999*	736	0.79	87000
88000	*88999*	744	0.79	88000
89000	*89999*	752	0.79	89000
90000	*90999*	760	0.79	90000
91000	*91999*	768	0.79	91000
92000	*92999*	776	0.79	92000
93000	*93999*	784	0.79	93000
94000	*94999*	791	0.79	94000

Federal Child Support Tables/ Tables fédérales de pensions alimentaires pour enfants

Province: Manitoba No. Of Children/ Nbre d'enfants: One/Un

Income/Revenu ($)		Monthly Award/ Paiement mensuel ($)		
From/De	To/À	Basic Amount/ Montant de base	Plus (%)	Of Income Over/Du revenu dépassant
95000	*95999*	799	0.79	95000
96000	*96999*	807	0.79	96000
97000	*97999*	815	0.79	97000
98000	*98999*	823	0.79	98000
99000	*99999*	831	0.79	99000
100000	*100999*	839	0.79	100000
101000	*101999*	846	0.79	101000
102000	*102999*	854	0.79	102000
103000	*103999*	862	0.79	103000
104000	*104999*	870	0.79	104000
105000	*105999*	878	0.79	105000
106000	*106999*	886	0.79	106000
107000	*107999*	894	0.79	107000
108000	*108999*	902	0.79	108000
109000	*109999*	909	0.79	109000
110000	*110999*	917	0.79	110000
111000	*111999*	925	0.79	111000
112000	*112999*	933	0.79	112000
113000	*113999*	941	0.78	113000
114000	*114999*	949	0.74	114000
115000	*115999*	956	0.74	115000
116000	*116999*	963	0.74	116000
117000	*117999*	971	0.74	117000
118000	*118999*	978	0.74	118000
119000	*119999*	986	0.74	119000
120000	*120999*	993	0.74	120000
121000	*121999*	1001	0.74	121000
122000	*122999*	1008	0.74	122000

Federal Child Support Tables/ Tables fédérales de pensions alimentaires pour enfants

Province: Manitoba No. Of Children/ Nbre d'enfants: One/Un

Income/Revenu ($)		Monthly Award/ Paiement mensuel ($)		
From/De	To/À	Basic Amount/ Montant de base	Plus (%)	Of Income Over/Du revenu dépassant
123000	*123999*	1016	0.74	123000
124000	*124999*	1023	0.74	124000
125000	*125999*	1030	0.74	125000
126000	*126999*	1038	0.74	126000
127000	*127999*	1045	0.74	127000
128000	*128999*	1053	0.74	128000
129000	*129999*	1060	0.74	129000
130000	*130999*	1068	0.74	130000
131000	*131999*	1075	0.74	131000
132000	*132999*	1083	0.74	132000
133000	*133999*	1090	0.74	133000
134000	*134999*	1097	0.74	134000
135000	*135999*	1105	0.74	135000
136000	*136999*	1112	0.74	136000
137000	*137999*	1120	0.74	137000
138000	*138999*	1127	0.74	138000
139000	*139999*	1135	0.74	139000
140000	*140999*	1142	0.74	140000
141000	*141999*	1150	0.74	141000
142000	*142999*	1157	0.74	142000
143000	*143999*	1164	0.74	143000
144000	*144999*	1172	0.74	144000
145000	*145999*	1179	0.74	145000
146000	*146999*	1187	0.74	146000
147000	*147999*	1194	0.74	147000
148000	*148999*	1202	0.74	148000
149000	*149999*	1209	0.74	149000

Federal Child Support Tables/ Tables fédérales de pensions alimentaires pour enfants

Province: Manitoba No. Of Children/ Nbre d'enfants: One/Un

Income/Revenu ($)		Monthly Award/ Paiement mensuel ($)		
From/De	To/À	Basic Amount/ Montant de base	Plus (%)	Of Income Over/Du revenu dépassant
150000	*or greater/ ou plus*	1217	0.74	150000

Federal Child Support Tables/ Tables fédérales de pensions alimentaires pour enfants

Province: Manitoba No. Of Children/ Nbre d'enfants: Two/Deux

Income/Revenu ($)		Monthly Award/ Paiement mensuel ($)		
From/De	To/À	Basic Amount/ Montant de base	Plus (%)	Of Income Over/Du revenu dépassant
0	*7999*	0		
8000	*8999*	0	2.29	8000
9000	*9999*	23	3.88	9000
10000	*10999*	62	3.69	10000
11000	*11999*	98	3.69	11000
12000	*12999*	135	3.69	12000
13000	*13999*	172	3.61	13000
14000	*14999*	208	1.41	14000
15000	*15999*	222	0.75	15000
16000	*16999*	230	1.08	16000
17000	*17999*	241	1.08	17000
18000	*18999*	252	1.08	18000
19000	*19999*	262	1.14	19000
20000	*20999*	274	1.35	20000
21000	*21999*	287	1.48	21000
22000	*22999*	302	1.51	22000
23000	*23999*	317	1.53	23000
24000	*24999*	332	1.53	24000

Federal Child Support Tables/ Tables fédérales de pensions alimentaires pour enfants

Province: Manitoba No. Of Children/ Nbre d'enfants: Two/Deux

Income/Revenu ($)		Monthly Award/ Paiement mensuel ($)		
From/De	To/À	Basic Amount/ Montant de base	Plus (%)	Of Income Over/Du revenu dépassant
25000	*25999*	348	1.53	25000
26000	*26999*	363	1.53	26000
27000	*27999*	378	1.53	27000
28000	*28999*	394	1.53	28000
29000	*29999*	409	1.46	29000
30000	*30999*	424	1.39	30000
31000	*31999*	438	1.36	31000
32000	*32999*	451	1.36	32000
33000	*33999*	465	1.36	33000
34000	*34999*	478	1.36	34000
35000	*35999*	492	1.23	35000
36000	*36999*	504	1.30	36000
37000	*37999*	517	1.33	37000
38000	*38999*	530	1.33	38000
39000	*39999*	544	1.37	39000
40000	*40999*	558	1.39	40000
41000	*41999*	571	1.41	41000
42000	*42999*	586	1.41	42000
43000	*43999*	600	1.41	43000
44000	*44999*	614	1.41	44000
45000	*45999*	628	1.41	45000
46000	*46999*	642	1.41	46000
47000	*47999*	656	1.41	47000
48000	*48999*	670	1.41	48000
49000	*49999*	684	1.41	49000
50000	*50999*	699	1.41	50000
51000	*51999*	713	1.41	51000
52000	*52999*	727	1.41	52000
53000	*53999*	741	1.41	53000
54000	*54999*	755	1.41	54000
55000	*55999*	769	1.41	55000
56000	*56999*	783	1.41	56000
57000	*57999*	798	1.41	57000
58000	*58999*	812	1.41	58000
59000	*59999*	826	1.41	59000

Federal Child Support Tables/ Tables fédérales de pensions alimentaires pour enfants

Province: Manitoba No. Of Children/ Nbre d'enfants: Two/Deux

Income/Revenu ($)		Monthly Award/ Paiement mensuel ($)		
From/De	To/À	Basic Amount/ Montant de base	Plus (%)	Of Income Over/Du revenu dépassant
60000	*60999*	840	1.41	60000
61000	*61999*	854	1.41	61000
62000	*62999*	868	1.41	62000
63000	*63999*	882	1.41	63000
64000	*64999*	897	1.41	64000
65000	*65999*	911	1.34	65000
66000	*66999*	924	1.34	66000
67000	*67999*	937	1.34	67000
68000	*68999*	951	1.34	68000
69000	*69999*	964	1.34	69000
70000	*70999*	978	1.25	70000
71000	*71999*	990	1.25	71000
72000	*72999*	1003	1.25	72000
73000	*73999*	1015	1.25	73000
74000	*74999*	1028	1.25	74000
75000	*75999*	1040	1.22	75000
76000	*76999*	1053	1.22	76000
77000	*77999*	1065	1.22	77000
78000	*78999*	1077	1.22	78000
79000	*79999*	1089	1.22	79000
80000	*80999*	1101	1.22	80000
81000	*81999*	1114	1.22	81000
82000	*82999*	1126	1.22	82000
83000	*83999*	1138	1.22	83000
84000	*84999*	1150	1.22	84000
85000	*85999*	1163	1.22	85000
86000	*86999*	1175	1.22	86000
87000	*87999*	1187	1.22	87000
88000	*88999*	1199	1.22	88000
89000	*89999*	1212	1.22	89000
90000	*90999*	1224	1.22	90000
91000	*91999*	1236	1.22	91000
92000	*92999*	1248	1.22	92000
93000	*93999*	1260	1.22	93000
94000	*94999*	1273	1.22	94000

Federal Child Support Tables/ Tables fédérales de pensions alimentaires pour enfants

Province: Manitoba No. Of Children/ Nbre d'enfants: Two/Deux

Income/Revenu ($)		Monthly Award/ Paiement mensuel ($)		
From/De	To/À	Basic Amount/ Montant de base	Plus (%)	Of Income Over/Du revenu dépassant
95000	*95999*	1285	1.22	95000
96000	*96999*	1297	1.22	96000
97000	*97999*	1309	1.22	97000
98000	*98999*	1322	1.22	98000
99000	*99999*	1334	1.22	99000
100000	*100999*	1346	1.22	100000
101000	*101999*	1358	1.22	101000
102000	*102999*	1371	1.22	102000
103000	*103999*	1383	1.22	103000
104000	*104999*	1395	1.22	104000
105000	*105999*	1407	1.22	105000
106000	*106999*	1419	1.22	106000
107000	*107999*	1432	1.22	107000
108000	*108999*	1444	1.22	108000
109000	*109999*	1456	1.22	109000
110000	*110999*	1468	1.22	110000
111000	*111999*	1481	1.22	111000
112000	*112999*	1493	1.22	112000
113000	*113999*	1505	1.21	113000
114000	*114999*	1517	1.16	114000
115000	*115999*	1529	1.16	115000
116000	*116999*	1540	1.16	116000
117000	*117999*	1552	1.16	117000
118000	*118999*	1563	1.16	118000
119000	*119999*	1575	1.16	119000
120000	*120999*	1587	1.16	120000
121000	*121999*	1598	1.16	121000
122000	*122999*	1610	1.16	122000
123000	*123999*	1621	1.16	123000
124000	*124999*	1633	1.16	124000
125000	*125999*	1645	1.16	125000
126000	*126999*	1656	1.16	126000
127000	*127999*	1668	1.16	127000
128000	*128999*	1679	1.16	128000
129000	*129999*	1691	1.16	129000

Federal Child Support Tables/ Tables fédérales de pensions alimentaires pour enfants

Province: Manitoba No. Of Children/ Nbre d'enfants: Two/Deux

Income/Revenu ($)		Monthly Award/ Paiement mensuel ($)		
From/De	**To/À**	**Basic Amount/ Montant de base**	**Plus (%)**	**Of Income Over/Du revenu dépassant**
130000	*130999*	1702	1.16	130000
131000	*131999*	1714	1.16	131000
132000	*132999*	1726	1.16	132000
133000	*133999*	1737	1.16	133000
134000	*134999*	1749	1.16	134000
135000	*135999*	1760	1.16	135000
136000	*136999*	1772	1.16	136000
137000	*137999*	1783	1.16	137000
138000	*138999*	1795	1.16	138000
139000	*139999*	1807	1.16	139000
140000	*140999*	1818	1.16	140000
141000	*141999*	1830	1.16	141000
142000	*142999*	1841	1.16	142000
143000	*143999*	1853	1.16	143000
144000	*144999*	1865	1.16	144000
145000	*145999*	1876	1.16	145000
146000	*146999*	1888	1.16	146000
147000	*147999*	1899	1.16	147000
148000	*148999*	1911	1.16	148000
149000	*149999*	1922	1.16	149000

Federal Child Support Tables/ Tables fédérales de pensions alimentaires pour enfants

Province: Manitoba No. Of Children/ Nbre d'enfants: Two/Deux

Income/Revenu ($)		Monthly Award/ Paiement mensuel ($)		
From/De	**To/À**	**Basic Amount/ Montant de base**	**Plus (%)**	**Of Income Over/Du revenu dépassant**
150000	*or greater/ ou plus*	1934	1.16	150000

Federal Child Support Tables/ Tables fédérales de pensions alimentaires pour enfants

Province: Manitoba No. Of Children/ Nbre d'enfants: Three/Trois

Income/Revenu ($)		Monthly Award/ Paiement mensuel ($)		
From/De	**To/À**	**Basic Amount/ Montant de base**	**Plus (%)**	**Of Income Over/Du revenu dépassant**
0	*7999*	0		
8000	*8999*	0	2.46	8000
9000	*9999*	25	4.17	9000
10000	*10999*	66	3.97	10000
11000	*11999*	106	3.97	11000
12000	*12999*	146	3.97	12000
13000	*13999*	185	3.88	13000
14000	*14999*	224	3.85	14000
15000	*15999*	263	3.85	15000
16000	*16999*	301	3.32	16000
17000	*17999*	334	1.52	17000
18000	*18999*	350	1.52	18000
19000	*19999*	365	1.58	19000
20000	*20999*	381	1.58	20000
21000	*21999*	397	1.58	21000
22000	*22999*	412	1.61	22000
23000	*23999*	428	1.93	23000
24000	*24999*	448	1.95	24000

Federal Child Support Tables/ Tables fédérales de pensions alimentaires pour enfants

Province: Manitoba
No. Of Children/ Nbre d'enfants: Three/Trois

Income/Revenu ($)		Monthly Award/ Paiement mensuel ($)		
From/De	**To/À**	**Basic Amount/ Montant de base**	**Plus (%)**	**Of Income Over/Du revenu dépassant**
25000	*25999*	467	1.95	25000
26000	*26999*	487	1.95	26000
27000	*27999*	506	1.95	27000
28000	*28999*	526	1.95	28000
29000	*29999*	545	1.86	29000
30000	*30999*	564	1.77	30000
31000	*31999*	581	1.72	31000
32000	*32999*	598	1.72	32000
33000	*33999*	616	1.72	33000
34000	*34999*	633	1.72	34000
35000	*35999*	650	1.56	35000
36000	*36999*	666	1.65	36000
37000	*37999*	682	1.69	37000
38000	*38999*	699	1.69	38000
39000	*39999*	716	1.73	39000
40000	*40999*	733	1.78	40000
41000	*41999*	751	1.83	41000
42000	*42999*	770	1.83	42000
43000	*43999*	788	1.81	43000
44000	*44999*	806	1.81	44000
45000	*45999*	824	1.81	45000
46000	*46999*	842	1.81	46000
47000	*47999*	860	1.81	47000
48000	*48999*	878	1.81	48000
49000	*49999*	896	1.81	49000
50000	*50999*	914	1.81	50000
51000	*51999*	932	1.81	51000
52000	*52999*	950	1.81	52000
53000	*53999*	968	1.81	53000
54000	*54999*	986	1.81	54000
55000	*55999*	1005	1.81	55000
56000	*56999*	1023	1.81	56000
57000	*57999*	1041	1.81	57000
58000	*58999*	1059	1.81	58000
59000	*59999*	1077	1.81	59000

Federal Child Support Tables/ Tables fédérales de pensions alimentaires pour enfants

Province: Manitoba
No. Of Children/ Nbre d'enfants: Three/Trois

Income/Revenu ($)		Monthly Award/ Paiement mensuel ($)		
From/De	**To/À**	**Basic Amount/ Montant de base**	**Plus (%)**	**Of Income Over/Du revenu dépassant**
60000	*60999*	1095	1.81	60000
61000	*61999*	1113	1.81	61000
62000	*62999*	1131	1.81	62000
63000	*63999*	1149	1.81	63000
64000	*64999*	1167	1.81	64000
65000	*65999*	1185	1.71	65000
66000	*66999*	1202	1.71	66000
67000	*67999*	1219	1.71	67000
68000	*68999*	1236	1.71	68000
69000	*69999*	1254	1.71	69000
70000	*70999*	1271	1.60	70000
71000	*71999*	1287	1.60	71000
72000	*72999*	1303	1.60	72000
73000	*73999*	1319	1.60	73000
74000	*74999*	1335	1.60	74000
75000	*75999*	1351	1.60	75000
76000	*76999*	1367	1.60	76000
77000	*77999*	1383	1.60	77000
78000	*78999*	1399	1.60	78000
79000	*79999*	1415	1.60	79000
80000	*80999*	1431	1.60	80000
81000	*81999*	1447	1.60	81000
82000	*82999*	1463	1.60	82000
83000	*83999*	1479	1.60	83000
84000	*84999*	1495	1.60	84000
85000	*85999*	1511	1.60	85000
86000	*86999*	1527	1.60	86000
87000	*87999*	1543	1.60	87000
88000	*88999*	1559	1.60	88000
89000	*89999*	1575	1.60	89000
90000	*90999*	1591	1.60	90000
91000	*91999*	1607	1.60	91000
92000	*92999*	1623	1.60	92000
93000	*93999*	1639	1.60	93000
94000	*94999*	1655	1.60	94000

Federal Child Support Tables/ Tables fédérales de pensions alimentaires pour enfants

Province: Manitoba No. Of Children/ Nbre d'enfants: Three/Trois

Income/Revenu ($)		Monthly Award/ Paiement mensuel ($)		
From/De	To/À	Basic Amount/ Montant de base	Plus (%)	Of Income Over/Du revenu dépassant
95000	*95999*	1671	1.60	95000
96000	*96999*	1687	1.60	96000
97000	*97999*	1703	1.60	97000
98000	*98999*	1719	1.60	98000
99000	*99999*	1735	1.60	99000
100000	*100999*	1751	1.60	100000
101000	*101999*	1767	1.60	101000
102000	*102999*	1783	1.60	102000
103000	*103999*	1799	1.60	103000
104000	*104999*	1815	1.60	104000
105000	*105999*	1831	1.57	105000
106000	*106999*	1846	1.57	106000
107000	*107999*	1862	1.57	107000
108000	*108999*	1878	1.57	108000
109000	*109999*	1894	1.57	109000
110000	*110999*	1909	1.57	110000
111000	*111999*	1925	1.57	111000
112000	*112999*	1941	1.57	112000
113000	*113999*	1956	1.56	113000
114000	*114999*	1972	1.49	114000
115000	*115999*	1987	1.49	115000
116000	*116999*	2002	1.49	116000
117000	*117999*	2017	1.49	117000
118000	*118999*	2032	1.49	118000
119000	*119999*	2046	1.49	119000
120000	*120999*	2061	1.49	120000
121000	*121999*	2076	1.49	121000
122000	*122999*	2091	1.49	122000

Federal Child Support Tables/ Tables fédérales de pensions alimentaires pour enfants

Province: Manitoba No. Of Children/ Nbre d'enfants: Three/Trois

Income/Revenu ($)		Monthly Award/ Paiement mensuel ($)		
From/De	To/À	Basic Amount/ Montant de base	Plus (%)	Of Income Over/Du revenu dépassant
123000	*123999*	2106	1.49	123000
124000	*124999*	2121	1.49	124000
125000	*125999*	2136	1.49	125000
126000	*126999*	2151	1.49	126000
127000	*127999*	2166	1.49	127000
128000	*128999*	2180	1.49	128000
129000	*129999*	2195	1.49	129000
130000	*130999*	2210	1.49	130000
131000	*131999*	2225	1.49	131000
132000	*132999*	2240	1.49	132000
133000	*133999*	2255	1.49	133000
134000	*134999*	2270	1.49	134000
135000	*135999*	2285	1.49	135000
136000	*136999*	2300	1.49	136000
137000	*137999*	2314	1.49	137000
138000	*138999*	2329	1.49	138000
139000	*139999*	2344	1.49	139000
140000	*140999*	2359	1.49	140000
141000	*141999*	2374	1.49	141000
142000	*142999*	2389	1.49	142000
143000	*143999*	2404	1.49	143000
144000	*144999*	2419	1.49	144000
145000	*145999*	2434	1.49	145000
146000	*146999*	2448	1.49	146000
147000	*147999*	2463	1.49	147000
148000	*148999*	2478	1.49	148000
149000	*149999*	2493	1.49	149000

Federal Child Support Tables/ Tables fédérales de pensions alimentaires pour enfants

Province: Manitoba No. Of Children/ Nbre d'enfants: Three/Trois

Income/Revenu ($)		Monthly Award/ Paiement mensuel ($)		
From/De	**To/À**	**Basic Amount/ Montant de base**	**Plus (%)**	**Of Income Over/Du revenu dépassant**
150000	*or greater/ ou plus*	2508	1.49	150000

Federal Child Support Tables/ Tables fédérales de pensions alimentaires pour enfants

Province: Manitoba No. Of Children/ Nbre d'enfants: Four/Quatre

Income/Revenu ($)		Monthly Award/ Paiement mensuel ($)		
From/De	**To/À**	**Basic Amount/ Montant de base**	**Plus (%)**	**Of Income Over/Du revenu dépassant**
0	*7999*	0		
8000	*8999*	0	2.64	8000
9000	*9999*	26	4.47	9000
10000	*10999*	71	4.25	10000
11000	*11999*	114	4.25	11000
12000	*12999*	156	4.25	12000
13000	*13999*	199	4.16	13000
14000	*14999*	240	4.13	14000
15000	*15999*	282	4.13	15000
16000	*16999*	323	4.13	16000
17000	*17999*	364	4.13	17000
18000	*18999*	405	4.13	18000
19000	*19999*	447	2.17	19000
20000	*20999*	468	1.94	20000
21000	*21999*	488	1.94	21000
22000	*22999*	507	1.97	22000
23000	*23999*	527	2.00	23000
24000	*24999*	547	2.00	24000

Federal Child Support Tables/ Tables fédérales de pensions alimentaires pour enfants

Province: Manitoba No. Of Children/ Nbre d'enfants: Four/Quatre

Income/Revenu ($)		Monthly Award/ Paiement mensuel ($)		
From/De	**To/À**	**Basic Amount/ Montant de base**	**Plus (%)**	**Of Income Over/Du revenu dépassant**
25000	*25999*	567	2.07	25000
26000	*26999*	588	2.28	26000
27000	*27999*	611	2.28	27000
28000	*28999*	633	2.28	28000
29000	*29999*	656	2.18	29000
30000	*30999*	678	2.07	30000
31000	*31999*	699	2.02	31000
32000	*32999*	719	2.02	32000
33000	*33999*	739	2.02	33000
34000	*34999*	759	2.02	34000
35000	*35999*	780	1.83	35000
36000	*36999*	798	1.94	36000
37000	*37999*	817	1.99	37000
38000	*38999*	837	1.99	38000
39000	*39999*	857	2.03	39000
40000	*40999*	877	2.09	40000
41000	*41999*	898	2.15	41000
42000	*42999*	920	2.15	42000
43000	*43999*	941	2.15	43000
44000	*44999*	963	2.15	44000
45000	*45999*	984	2.14	45000
46000	*46999*	1006	2.13	46000
47000	*47999*	1027	2.13	47000
48000	*48999*	1048	2.13	48000
49000	*49999*	1069	2.13	49000
50000	*50999*	1091	2.13	50000
51000	*51999*	1112	2.13	51000
52000	*52999*	1133	2.13	52000
53000	*53999*	1154	2.13	53000
54000	*54999*	1176	2.13	54000
55000	*55999*	1197	2.13	55000
56000	*56999*	1218	2.13	56000
57000	*57999*	1240	2.13	57000
58000	*58999*	1261	2.13	58000
59000	*59999*	1282	2.13	59000

Federal Child Support Tables/ Tables fédérales de pensions alimentaires pour enfants — **Province: Manitoba No. Of Children/ Nbre d'enfants: Four/Quatre**

Income/Revenu ($)		Monthly Award/ Paiement mensuel ($)		
From/De	To/À	Basic Amount/ Montant de base	Plus (%)	Of Income Over/Du revenu dépassant
60000	*60999*	1303	2.13	60000
61000	*61999*	1325	2.13	61000
62000	*62999*	1346	2.13	62000
63000	*63999*	1367	2.13	63000
64000	*64999*	1388	2.13	64000
65000	*65999*	1410	2.01	65000
66000	*66999*	1430	2.01	66000
67000	*67999*	1450	2.01	67000
68000	*68999*	1470	2.01	68000
69000	*69999*	1490	2.01	69000
70000	*70999*	1510	1.88	70000
71000	*71999*	1529	1.88	71000
72000	*72999*	1548	1.88	72000
73000	*73999*	1567	1.88	73000
74000	*74999*	1586	1.88	74000
75000	*75999*	1604	1.88	75000
76000	*76999*	1623	1.88	76000
77000	*77999*	1642	1.88	77000
78000	*78999*	1661	1.88	78000
79000	*79999*	1680	1.88	79000
80000	*80999*	1699	1.88	80000
81000	*81999*	1717	1.88	81000
82000	*82999*	1736	1.88	82000
83000	*83999*	1755	1.88	83000
84000	*84999*	1774	1.88	84000
85000	*85999*	1793	1.88	85000
86000	*86999*	1812	1.88	86000
87000	*87999*	1830	1.88	87000
88000	*88999*	1849	1.88	88000
89000	*89999*	1868	1.88	89000
90000	*90999*	1887	1.88	90000
91000	*91999*	1906	1.88	91000
92000	*92999*	1925	1.88	92000
93000	*93999*	1943	1.88	93000
94000	*94999*	1962	1.88	94000

Federal Child Support Tables/ Tables fédérales de pensions alimentaires pour enfants — **Province: Manitoba No. Of Children/ Nbre d'enfants: Four/Quatre**

Income/Revenu ($)		Monthly Award/ Paiement mensuel ($)		
From/De	To/À	Basic Amount/ Montant de base	Plus (%)	Of Income Over/Du revenu dépassant
95000	*95999*	1981	1.88	95000
96000	*96999*	2000	1.88	96000
97000	*97999*	2019	1.88	97000
98000	*98999*	2038	1.88	98000
99000	*99999*	2056	1.88	99000
100000	*100999*	2075	1.88	100000
101000	*101999*	2094	1.88	101000
102000	*102999*	2113	1.88	102000
103000	*103999*	2132	1.88	103000
104000	*104999*	2151	1.88	104000
105000	*105999*	2169	1.88	105000
106000	*106999*	2188	1.88	106000
107000	*107999*	2207	1.88	107000
108000	*108999*	2226	1.88	108000
109000	*109999*	2245	1.88	109000
110000	*110999*	2264	1.88	110000
111000	*111999*	2282	1.88	111000
112000	*112999*	2301	1.88	112000
113000	*113999*	2320	1.86	113000
114000	*114999*	2339	1.78	114000
115000	*115999*	2357	1.78	115000
116000	*116999*	2375	1.78	116000
117000	*117999*	2392	1.78	117000
118000	*118999*	2410	1.78	118000
119000	*119999*	2428	1.78	119000
120000	*120999*	2446	1.78	120000
121000	*121999*	2464	1.78	121000
122000	*122999*	2482	1.78	122000
123000	*123999*	2499	1.78	123000
124000	*124999*	2517	1.78	124000
125000	*125999*	2535	1.78	125000
126000	*126999*	2553	1.78	126000
127000	*127999*	2571	1.78	127000
128000	*128999*	2589	1.78	128000
129000	*129999*	2607	1.78	129000

Federal Child Support Tables/ Tables fédérales de pensions alimentaires pour enfants

Province: Manitoba No. Of Children/ Nbre d'enfants: Four/Quatre

Income/Revenu ($)		Monthly Award/ Paiement mensuel ($)		
From/De	To/À	Basic Amount/ Montant de base	Plus (%)	Of Income Over/Du revenu dépassant
130000	*130999*	2624	1.78	130000
131000	*131999*	2642	1.78	131000
132000	*132999*	2660	1.78	132000
133000	*133999*	2678	1.78	133000
134000	*134999*	2696	1.78	134000
135000	*135999*	2714	1.76	135000
136000	*136999*	2731	1.76	136000
137000	*137999*	2749	1.76	137000
138000	*138999*	2766	1.76	138000
139000	*139999*	2784	1.76	139000
140000	*140999*	2802	1.76	140000
141000	*141999*	2819	1.76	141000
142000	*142999*	2837	1.76	142000
143000	*143999*	2854	1.76	143000
144000	*144999*	2872	1.76	144000
145000	*145999*	2890	1.76	145000
146000	*146999*	2907	1.76	146000
147000	*147999*	2925	1.76	147000
148000	*148999*	2942	1.76	148000
149000	*149999*	2960	1.76	149000

Federal Child Support Tables/ Tables fédérales de pensions alimentaires pour enfants

Province: Manitoba No. Of Children/ Nbre d'enfants: Four/Quatre

Income/Revenu ($)		Monthly Award/ Paiement mensuel ($)		
From/De	To/À	Basic Amount/ Montant de base	Plus (%)	Of Income Over/Du revenu dépassant
150000	*or greater/ ou plus*	2978	1.76	150000

Federal Child Support Tables/ Tables fédérales de pensions alimentaires pour enfants

Province: Manitoba No. Of Children/ Nbre d'enfants: Five/Cinq

Income/Revenu ($)		Monthly Award/ Paiement mensuel ($)		
From/De	To/À	Basic Amount/ Montant de base	Plus (%)	Of Income Over/Du revenu dépassant
0	*7999*	0		
8000	*8999*	0	2.64	8000
9000	*9999*	26	4.47	9000
10000	*10999*	71	4.25	10000
11000	*11999*	114	4.25	11000
12000	*12999*	156	4.25	12000
13000	*13999*	199	4.16	13000
14000	*14999*	240	4.13	14000
15000	*15999*	282	4.13	15000
16000	*16999*	323	4.13	16000
17000	*17999*	364	4.13	17000
18000	*18999*	405	4.13	18000
19000	*19999*	447	4.19	19000
20000	*20999*	489	4.19	20000
21000	*21999*	530	4.19	21000
22000	*22999*	572	3.68	22000
23000	*23999*	609	2.31	23000
24000	*24999*	632	2.31	24000

Federal Child Support Tables/ Tables fédérales de pensions alimentaires pour enfants

Province: Manitoba No. Of Children/ Nbre d'enfants: Five/Cinq

Income/Revenu ($)		Monthly Award/ Paiement mensuel ($)		
From/De	To/À	Basic Amount/ Montant de base	Plus (%)	Of Income Over/Du revenu dépassant
25000	*25999*	655	2.31	25000
26000	*26999*	678	2.31	26000
27000	*27999*	701	2.31	27000
28000	*28999*	725	2.45	28000
29000	*29999*	749	2.45	29000
30000	*30999*	774	2.33	30000
31000	*31999*	797	2.27	31000
32000	*32999*	819	2.27	32000
33000	*33999*	842	2.27	33000
34000	*34999*	865	2.27	34000
35000	*35999*	887	2.05	35000
36000	*36999*	908	2.18	36000
37000	*37999*	930	2.23	37000
38000	*38999*	952	2.23	38000
39000	*39999*	974	2.28	39000
40000	*40999*	997	2.35	40000
41000	*41999*	1021	2.42	41000
42000	*42999*	1045	2.42	42000
43000	*43999*	1069	2.42	43000
44000	*44999*	1093	2.42	44000
45000	*45999*	1117	2.42	45000
46000	*46999*	1141	2.42	46000
47000	*47999*	1166	2.42	47000
48000	*48999*	1190	2.39	48000
49000	*49999*	1214	2.39	49000
50000	*50999*	1238	2.39	50000
51000	*51999*	1262	2.39	51000
52000	*52999*	1286	2.39	52000
53000	*53999*	1309	2.39	53000
54000	*54999*	1333	2.39	54000
55000	*55999*	1357	2.39	55000
56000	*56999*	1381	2.39	56000
57000	*57999*	1405	2.39	57000
58000	*58999*	1429	2.39	58000
59000	*59999*	1453	2.39	59000

Federal Child Support Tables/ Tables fédérales de pensions alimentaires pour enfants

Province: Manitoba No. Of Children/ Nbre d'enfants: Five/Cinq

Income/Revenu ($)		Monthly Award/ Paiement mensuel ($)		
From/De	To/À	Basic Amount/ Montant de base	Plus (%)	Of Income Over/Du revenu dépassant
60000	*60999*	1477	2.39	60000
61000	*61999*	1501	2.39	61000
62000	*62999*	1525	2.39	62000
63000	*63999*	1549	2.39	63000
64000	*64999*	1573	2.39	64000
65000	*65999*	1597	2.27	65000
66000	*66999*	1619	2.27	66000
67000	*67999*	1642	2.27	67000
68000	*68999*	1665	2.27	68000
69000	*69999*	1687	2.27	69000
70000	*70999*	1710	2.12	70000
71000	*71999*	1731	2.12	71000
72000	*72999*	1752	2.12	72000
73000	*73999*	1774	2.12	73000
74000	*74999*	1795	2.12	74000
75000	*75999*	1816	2.12	75000
76000	*76999*	1837	2.12	76000
77000	*77999*	1858	2.12	77000
78000	*78999*	1880	2.12	78000
79000	*79999*	1901	2.12	79000
80000	*80999*	1922	2.12	80000
81000	*81999*	1943	2.12	81000
82000	*82999*	1964	2.12	82000
83000	*83999*	1986	2.12	83000
84000	*84999*	2007	2.12	84000
85000	*85999*	2028	2.12	85000
86000	*86999*	2049	2.12	86000
87000	*87999*	2070	2.12	87000
88000	*88999*	2092	2.12	88000
89000	*89999*	2113	2.12	89000
90000	*90999*	2134	2.12	90000
91000	*91999*	2155	2.12	91000
92000	*92999*	2176	2.12	92000
93000	*93999*	2198	2.12	93000
94000	*94999*	2219	2.12	94000

Federal Child Support Tables/ Tables fédérales de pensions alimentaires pour enfants

Province: Manitoba No. Of Children/ Nbre d'enfants: Five/Cinq

Income/Revenu ($)		Monthly Award/ Paiement mensuel ($)		
From/De	To/À	Basic Amount/ Montant de base	Plus (%)	Of Income Over/Du revenu dépassant
95000	*95999*	2240	2.12	95000
96000	*96999*	2261	2.12	96000
97000	*97999*	2282	2.12	97000
98000	*98999*	2304	2.12	98000
99000	*99999*	2325	2.12	99000
100000	*100999*	2346	2.12	100000
101000	*101999*	2367	2.12	101000
102000	*102999*	2388	2.12	102000
103000	*103999*	2409	2.12	103000
104000	*104999*	2431	2.12	104000
105000	*105999*	2452	2.12	105000
106000	*106999*	2473	2.12	106000
107000	*107999*	2494	2.12	107000
108000	*108999*	2515	2.12	108000
109000	*109999*	2537	2.12	109000
110000	*110999*	2558	2.12	110000
111000	*111999*	2579	2.12	111000
112000	*112999*	2600	2.12	112000
113000	*113999*	2621	2.10	113000
114000	*114999*	2642	2.01	114000
115000	*115999*	2662	2.01	115000
116000	*116999*	2683	2.01	116000
117000	*117999*	2703	2.01	117000
118000	*118999*	2723	2.01	118000
119000	*119999*	2743	2.01	119000
120000	*120999*	2763	2.01	120000
121000	*121999*	2783	2.01	121000
122000	*122999*	2803	2.01	122000

Federal Child Support Tables/ Tables fédérales de pensions alimentaires pour enfants

Province: Manitoba No. Of Children/ Nbre d'enfants: Five/Cinq

Income/Revenu ($)		Monthly Award/ Paiement mensuel ($)		
From/De	To/À	Basic Amount/ Montant de base	Plus (%)	Of Income Over/Du revenu dépassant
123000	*123999*	2823	2.01	123000
124000	*124999*	2843	2.01	124000
125000	*125999*	2863	2.01	125000
126000	*126999*	2883	2.01	126000
127000	*127999*	2903	2.01	127000
128000	*128999*	2924	2.01	128000
129000	*129999*	2944	2.01	129000
130000	*130999*	2964	2.01	130000
131000	*131999*	2984	2.01	131000
132000	*132999*	3004	2.01	132000
133000	*133999*	3024	2.01	133000
134000	*134999*	3044	2.01	134000
135000	*135999*	3064	2.01	135000
136000	*136999*	3084	2.01	136000
137000	*137999*	3104	2.01	137000
138000	*138999*	3124	2.01	138000
139000	*139999*	3144	2.01	139000
140000	*140999*	3165	2.01	140000
141000	*141999*	3185	2.01	141000
142000	*142999*	3205	2.01	142000
143000	*143999*	3225	2.01	143000
144000	*144999*	3245	2.01	144000
145000	*145999*	3265	2.01	145000
146000	*146999*	3285	2.01	146000
147000	*147999*	3305	2.01	147000
148000	*148999*	3325	2.01	148000
149000	*149999*	3345	2.01	149000

Federal Child Support Tables/ Tables fédérales de pensions alimentaires pour enfants

Province: Manitoba
No. Of Children/ Nbre d'enfants: Five/Cinq

Income/Revenu ($)		Monthly Award/ Paiement mensuel ($)		
From/De	**To/À**	**Basic Amount/ Montant de base**	**Plus (%)**	**Of Income Over/Du revenu dépassant**
150000	*or greater/ ou plus*	3365	2.01	150000

Federal Child Support Tables/ Tables fédérales de pensions alimentaires pour enfants

Province: Manitoba
No. Of Children/ Nbre d'enfants: Six or more/ Six ou plus

Income/Revenu ($)		Monthly Award/ Paiement mensuel ($)		
From/De	**To/À**	**Basic Amount/ Montant de base**	**Plus (%)**	**Of Income Over/Du revenu dépassant**
0	*7999*	0		
8000	*8999*	0	2.64	8000
9000	*9999*	26	4.47	9000
10000	*10999*	71	4.25	10000
11000	*11999*	114	4.25	11000
12000	*12999*	156	4.25	12000
13000	*13999*	199	4.16	13000
14000	*14999*	240	4.13	14000
15000	*15999*	282	4.13	15000
16000	*16999*	323	4.13	16000
17000	*17999*	364	4.13	17000
18000	*18999*	405	4.13	18000
19000	*19999*	447	4.19	19000
20000	*20999*	489	4.19	20000
21000	*21999*	530	4.19	21000
22000	*22999*	572	4.22	22000
23000	*23999*	615	4.25	23000
24000	*24999*	657	4.25	24000

Federal Child Support Tables/ Tables fédérales de pensions alimentaires pour enfants

Province: Manitoba
No. Of Children/ Nbre d'enfants: Six or more/ Six ou plus

Income/Revenu ($)		Monthly Award/ Paiement mensuel ($)		
From/De	**To/À**	**Basic Amount/ Montant de base**	**Plus (%)**	**Of Income Over/Du revenu dépassant**
25000	*25999*	700	4.25	25000
26000	*26999*	742	3.92	26000
27000	*27999*	781	2.57	27000
28000	*28999*	807	2.57	28000
29000	*29999*	833	2.44	29000
30000	*30999*	857	2.28	30000
31000	*31999*	880	2.47	31000
32000	*32999*	905	2.48	32000
33000	*33999*	929	2.48	33000
34000	*34999*	954	2.48	34000
35000	*35999*	979	2.24	35000
36000	*36999*	1001	2.38	36000
37000	*37999*	1025	2.44	37000
38000	*38999*	1049	2.44	38000
39000	*39999*	1074	2.49	39000
40000	*40999*	1099	2.57	40000
41000	*41999*	1124	2.64	41000
42000	*42999*	1151	2.64	42000
43000	*43999*	1177	2.64	43000
44000	*44999*	1204	2.64	44000
45000	*45999*	1230	2.64	45000
46000	*46999*	1256	2.64	46000
47000	*47999*	1283	2.64	47000
48000	*48999*	1309	2.64	48000
49000	*49999*	1336	2.64	49000
50000	*50999*	1362	2.63	50000
51000	*51999*	1388	2.62	51000
52000	*52999*	1414	2.62	52000
53000	*53999*	1441	2.62	53000
54000	*54999*	1467	2.62	54000
55000	*55999*	1493	2.62	55000
56000	*56999*	1519	2.62	56000
57000	*57999*	1545	2.62	57000
58000	*58999*	1572	2.62	58000
59000	*59999*	1598	2.62	59000

Federal Child Support Tables/ Tables fédérales de pensions alimentaires pour enfants

Province: Manitoba
No. Of Children/ Nbre d'enfants: Six or more/ Six ou plus

Income/Revenu ($)		Monthly Award/ Paiement mensuel ($)		
From/De	To/À	Basic Amount/ Montant de base	Plus (%)	Of Income Over/Du revenu dépassant
60000	*60999*	1624	2.62	60000
61000	*61999*	1650	2.62	61000
62000	*62999*	1676	2.62	62000
63000	*63999*	1703	2.62	63000
64000	*64999*	1729	2.62	64000
65000	*65999*	1755	2.48	65000
66000	*66999*	1780	2.48	66000
67000	*67999*	1805	2.48	67000
68000	*68999*	1829	2.48	68000
69000	*69999*	1854	2.48	69000
70000	*70999*	1879	2.32	70000
71000	*71999*	1902	2.32	71000
72000	*72999*	1925	2.32	72000
73000	*73999*	1949	2.32	73000
74000	*74999*	1972	2.32	74000
75000	*75999*	1995	2.32	75000
76000	*76999*	2018	2.32	76000
77000	*77999*	2041	2.32	77000
78000	*78999*	2065	2.32	78000
79000	*79999*	2088	2.32	79000
80000	*80999*	2111	2.32	80000
81000	*81999*	2134	2.32	81000
82000	*82999*	2157	2.32	82000
83000	*83999*	2181	2.32	83000
84000	*84999*	2204	2.32	84000
85000	*85999*	2227	2.32	85000
86000	*86999*	2250	2.32	86000
87000	*87999*	2273	2.32	87000
88000	*88999*	2297	2.32	88000
89000	*89999*	2320	2.32	89000
90000	*90999*	2343	2.32	90000
91000	*91999*	2366	2.32	91000
92000	*92999*	2389	2.32	92000
93000	*93999*	2413	2.32	93000
94000	*94999*	2436	2.32	94000

Federal Child Support Tables/ Tables fédérales de pensions alimentaires pour enfants

Province: Manitoba
No. Of Children/ Nbre d'enfants: Six or more/ Six ou plus

Income/Revenu ($)		Monthly Award/ Paiement mensuel ($)		
From/De	To/À	Basic Amount/ Montant de base	Plus (%)	Of Income Over/Du revenu dépassant
95000	*95999*	2459	2.32	95000
96000	*96999*	2482	2.32	96000
97000	*97999*	2505	2.32	97000
98000	*98999*	2528	2.32	98000
99000	*99999*	2552	2.32	99000
100000	*100999*	2575	2.32	100000
101000	*101999*	2598	2.32	101000
102000	*102999*	2621	2.32	102000
103000	*103999*	2644	2.32	103000
104000	*104999*	2668	2.32	104000
105000	*105999*	2691	2.32	105000
106000	*106999*	2714	2.32	106000
107000	*107999*	2737	2.32	107000
108000	*108999*	2760	2.32	108000
109000	*109999*	2784	2.32	109000
110000	*110999*	2807	2.32	110000
111000	*111999*	2830	2.32	111000
112000	*112999*	2853	2.32	112000
113000	*113999*	2876	2.30	113000
114000	*114999*	2899	2.20	114000
115000	*115999*	2921	2.20	115000
116000	*116999*	2943	2.20	116000
117000	*117999*	2965	2.20	117000
118000	*118999*	2987	2.20	118000
119000	*119999*	3009	2.20	119000
120000	*120999*	3031	2.20	120000
121000	*121999*	3053	2.20	121000
122000	*122999*	3075	2.20	122000
123000	*123999*	3097	2.20	123000
124000	*124999*	3119	2.20	124000
125000	*125999*	3141	2.20	125000
126000	*126999*	3163	2.20	126000
127000	*127999*	3185	2.20	127000
128000	*128999*	3207	2.20	128000
129000	*129999*	3229	2.20	129000

Federal Child Support Tables/ Tables fédérales de pensions alimentaires pour enfants

Province: Manitoba
No. Of Children/ Nbre d'enfants: Six or more/ Six ou plus

Income/Revenu ($)		Monthly Award/ Paiement mensuel ($)		
From/De	To/À	Basic Amount/ Montant de base	Plus (%)	Of Income Over/Du revenu dépassant
130000	*130999*	3251	2.20	130000
131000	*131999*	3273	2.20	131000
132000	*132999*	3295	2.20	132000
133000	*133999*	3317	2.20	133000
134000	*134999*	3339	2.20	134000
135000	*135999*	3361	2.20	135000
136000	*136999*	3383	2.20	136000
137000	*137999*	3405	2.20	137000
138000	*138999*	3427	2.20	138000
139000	*139999*	3449	2.20	139000
140000	*140999*	3471	2.20	140000
141000	*141999*	3493	2.20	141000
142000	*142999*	3515	2.20	142000
143000	*143999*	3537	2.20	143000
144000	*144999*	3559	2.20	144000
145000	*145999*	3581	2.20	145000
146000	*146999*	3602	2.20	146000
147000	*147999*	3624	2.20	147000
148000	*148999*	3646	2.20	148000
149000	*149999*	3668	2.20	149000

Federal Child Support Tables/ Tables fédérales de pensions alimentaires pour enfants

Province: Manitoba
No. Of Children/ Nbre d'enfants: Six or more/ Six ou plus

Income/Revenu ($)		Monthly Award/ Paiement mensuel ($)		
From/De	To/À	Basic Amount/ Montant de base	Plus (%)	Of Income Over/Du revenu dépassant
150000	*or greater/ ou plus*	3690	2.20	150000

Federal Child Support Tables/ Tables fédérales de pensions alimentaires pour enfants

Province: British Columbia/ Colombie-Britannique
No. Of Children/ Nbre d'enfants: One/Un

Income/Revenu ($)		Monthly Award/ Paiement mensuel ($)		
From/De	To/À	Basic Amount/ Montant de base	Plus (%)	Of Income Over/Du revenu dépassant
0	*7999*	0		
8000	*8999*	0	0.96	8000
9000	*9999*	10	1.92	9000
10000	*10999*	29	1.92	10000
11000	*11999*	48	1.92	11000
12000	*12999*	67	1.92	12000
13000	*13999*	87	1.92	13000
14000	*14999*	106	1.92	14000
15000	*15999*	125	1.70	15000
16000	*16999*	142	0.82	16000
17000	*17999*	150	0.98	17000
18000	*18999*	160	0.99	18000
19000	*19999*	170	1.01	19000
20000	*20999*	180	1.01	20000
21000	*21999*	190	1.01	21000
22000	*22999*	200	1.01	22000
23000	*23999*	210	1.01	23000
24000	*24999*	220	1.01	24000

Federal Child Support Tables/ Tables fédérales de pensions alimentaires pour enfants

Province: British Columbia/ Colombie-Britannique
No. Of Children/ N^bre d'enfants: One/Un

Income/Revenu ($)		Monthly Award/ Paiement mensuel ($)		
From/De	**To/À**	**Basic Amount/ Montant de base**	**Plus (%)**	**Of Income Over/Du revenu dépassant**
25000	*25999*	230	1.01	25000
26000	*26999*	240	1.01	26000
27000	*27999*	251	1.01	27000
28000	*28999*	261	1.01	28000
29000	*29999*	271	0.96	29000
30000	*30999*	280	0.94	30000
31000	*31999*	290	0.94	31000
32000	*32999*	299	0.92	32000
33000	*33999*	308	0.90	33000
34000	*34999*	317	0.90	34000
35000	*35999*	326	0.81	35000
36000	*36999*	334	0.86	36000
37000	*37999*	343	0.88	37000
38000	*38999*	352	0.88	38000
39000	*39999*	361	0.90	39000
40000	*40999*	370	0.93	40000
41000	*41999*	379	0.96	41000
42000	*42999*	388	0.96	42000
43000	*43999*	398	0.96	43000
44000	*44999*	408	0.96	44000
45000	*45999*	417	0.96	45000
46000	*46999*	427	0.96	46000
47000	*47999*	436	0.96	47000
48000	*48999*	446	0.96	48000
49000	*49999*	455	0.96	49000
50000	*50999*	465	0.96	50000
51000	*51999*	474	0.96	51000
52000	*52999*	484	0.96	52000
53000	*53999*	494	0.96	53000
54000	*54999*	503	0.96	54000
55000	*55999*	513	0.96	55000
56000	*56999*	522	0.96	56000
57000	*57999*	532	0.96	57000
58000	*58999*	541	0.96	58000
59000	*59999*	551	0.96	59000

Federal Child Support Tables/ Tables fédérales de pensions alimentaires pour enfants

Province: British Columbia/ Colombie-Britannique
No. Of Children/ N^bre d'enfants: One/Un

Income/Revenu ($)		Monthly Award/ Paiement mensuel ($)		
From/De	**To/À**	**Basic Amount/ Montant de base**	**Plus (%)**	**Of Income Over/Du revenu dépassant**
60000	*60999*	561	0.96	60000
61000	*61999*	570	0.96	61000
62000	*62999*	580	0.96	62000
63000	*63999*	589	0.96	63000
64000	*64999*	599	0.95	64000
65000	*65999*	608	0.92	65000
66000	*66999*	618	0.92	66000
67000	*67999*	627	0.92	67000
68000	*68999*	636	0.92	68000
69000	*69999*	645	0.92	69000
70000	*70999*	654	0.87	70000
71000	*71999*	663	0.87	71000
72000	*72999*	672	0.87	72000
73000	*73999*	680	0.87	73000
74000	*74999*	689	0.85	74000
75000	*75999*	698	0.84	75000
76000	*76999*	706	0.84	76000
77000	*77999*	714	0.84	77000
78000	*78999*	723	0.84	78000
79000	*79999*	731	0.84	79000
80000	*80999*	739	0.84	80000
81000	*81999*	748	0.84	81000
82000	*82999*	756	0.84	82000
83000	*83999*	765	0.84	83000
84000	*84999*	773	0.84	84000
85000	*85999*	781	0.84	85000
86000	*86999*	790	0.84	86000
87000	*87999*	798	0.84	87000
88000	*88999*	806	0.84	88000
89000	*89999*	815	0.84	89000
90000	*90999*	823	0.83	90000
91000	*91999*	831	0.82	91000
92000	*92999*	840	0.82	92000
93000	*93999*	848	0.82	93000
94000	*94999*	856	0.82	94000

Federal Child Support Tables/ Tables fédérales de pensions alimentaires pour enfants

Province: British Columbia/ Colombie-Britannique
No. Of Children/ Nbre d'enfants: One/Un

Income/Revenu ($)		Monthly Award/ Paiement mensuel ($)		
From/De	To/À	Basic Amount/ Montant de base	Plus (%)	Of Income Over/Du revenu dépassant
95000	*95999*	864	0.82	95000
96000	*96999*	873	0.82	96000
97000	*97999*	881	0.82	97000
98000	*98999*	889	0.82	98000
99000	*99999*	897	0.82	99000
100000	*100999*	906	0.82	100000
101000	*101999*	914	0.82	101000
102000	*102999*	922	0.82	102000
103000	*103999*	930	0.82	103000
104000	*104999*	939	0.82	104000
105000	*105999*	947	0.82	105000
106000	*106999*	955	0.82	106000
107000	*107999*	963	0.82	107000
108000	*108999*	971	0.82	108000
109000	*109999*	980	0.82	109000
110000	*110999*	988	0.82	110000
111000	*111999*	996	0.82	111000
112000	*112999*	1004	0.82	112000
113000	*113999*	1013	0.82	113000
114000	*114999*	1021	0.78	114000
115000	*115999*	1029	0.78	115000
116000	*116999*	1036	0.78	116000
117000	*117999*	1044	0.78	117000
118000	*118999*	1052	0.78	118000
119000	*119999*	1060	0.78	119000
120000	*120999*	1068	0.78	120000
121000	*121999*	1076	0.78	121000
122000	*122999*	1083	0.78	122000

Federal Child Support Tables/ Tables fédérales de pensions alimentaires pour enfants

Province: British Columbia/ Colombie-Britannique
No. Of Children/ Nbre d'enfants: One/Un

Income/Revenu ($)		Monthly Award/ Paiement mensuel ($)		
From/De	To/À	Basic Amount/ Montant de base	Plus (%)	Of Income Over/Du revenu dépassant
123000	*123999*	1091	0.78	123000
124000	*124999*	1099	0.78	124000
125000	*125999*	1107	0.78	125000
126000	*126999*	1115	0.78	126000
127000	*127999*	1122	0.78	127000
128000	*128999*	1130	0.78	128000
129000	*129999*	1138	0.78	129000
130000	*130999*	1146	0.78	130000
131000	*131999*	1154	0.78	131000
132000	*132999*	1162	0.78	132000
133000	*133999*	1169	0.78	133000
134000	*134999*	1177	0.78	134000
135000	*135999*	1185	0.78	135000
136000	*136999*	1193	0.78	136000
137000	*137999*	1201	0.78	137000
138000	*138999*	1208	0.78	138000
139000	*139999*	1216	0.78	139000
140000	*140999*	1224	0.78	140000
141000	*141999*	1232	0.78	141000
142000	*142999*	1240	0.78	142000
143000	*143999*	1248	0.78	143000
144000	*144999*	1255	0.78	144000
145000	*145999*	1263	0.78	145000
146000	*146999*	1271	0.78	146000
147000	*147999*	1279	0.78	147000
148000	*148999*	1287	0.78	148000
149000	*149999*	1294	0.78	149000

Federal Child Support Tables/ Tables fédérales de pensions alimentaires pour enfants

Province: British Columbia/ Colombie-Britannique
No. Of Children/ Nbre d'enfants: One/Un

Income/Revenu ($)		Monthly Award/ Paiement mensuel ($)		
From/De	To/À	Basic Amount/ Montant de base	Plus (%)	Of Income Over/Du revenu dépassant
150000	*or greater/ ou plus*	1302	0.78	150000

Federal Child Support Tables/ Tables fédérales de pensions alimentaires pour enfants

Province: British Columbia/ Colombie-Britannique
No. Of Children/ Nbre d'enfants: Two/Deux

Income/Revenu ($)		Monthly Award/ Paiement mensuel ($)		
From/De	To/À	Basic Amount/ Montant de base	Plus (%)	Of Income Over/Du revenu dépassant
0	*7999*	0		
8000	*8999*	0	2.14	8000
9000	*9999*	21	4.04	9000
10000	*10999*	62	4.04	10000
11000	*11999*	102	4.04	11000
12000	*12999*	143	4.04	12000
13000	*13999*	183	3.96	13000
14000	*14999*	223	2.27	14000
15000	*15999*	245	1.01	15000
16000	*16999*	255	1.38	16000
17000	*17999*	269	1.52	17000
18000	*18999*	284	1.53	18000
19000	*19999*	300	1.57	19000
20000	*20999*	315	1.57	20000
21000	*21999*	331	1.57	21000
22000	*22999*	347	1.57	22000
23000	*23999*	362	1.57	23000
24000	*24999*	378	1.57	24000

Federal Child Support Tables/ Tables fédérales de pensions alimentaires pour enfants

Province: British Columbia/ Colombie-Britannique
No. Of Children/ Nbre d'enfants: Two/Deux

Income/Revenu ($)		Monthly Award/ Paiement mensuel ($)		
From/De	To/À	Basic Amount/ Montant de base	Plus (%)	Of Income Over/Du revenu dépassant
25000	*25999*	394	1.57	25000
26000	*26999*	409	1.57	26000
27000	*27999*	425	1.57	27000
28000	*28999*	441	1.57	28000
29000	*29999*	457	1.50	29000
30000	*30999*	472	1.46	30000
31000	*31999*	486	1.46	31000
32000	*32999*	501	1.42	32000
33000	*33999*	515	1.39	33000
34000	*34999*	529	1.39	34000
35000	*35999*	543	1.27	35000
36000	*36999*	555	1.34	36000
37000	*37999*	569	1.37	37000
38000	*38999*	583	1.37	38000
39000	*39999*	596	1.40	39000
40000	*40999*	610	1.45	40000
41000	*41999*	625	1.49	41000
42000	*42999*	640	1.49	42000
43000	*43999*	655	1.49	43000
44000	*44999*	669	1.49	44000
45000	*45999*	684	1.49	45000
46000	*46999*	699	1.49	46000
47000	*47999*	714	1.49	47000
48000	*48999*	729	1.49	48000
49000	*49999*	744	1.49	49000
50000	*50999*	759	1.49	50000
51000	*51999*	774	1.49	51000
52000	*52999*	788	1.49	52000
53000	*53999*	803	1.49	53000
54000	*54999*	818	1.49	54000
55000	*55999*	833	1.49	55000
56000	*56999*	848	1.49	56000
57000	*57999*	863	1.49	57000
58000	*58999*	878	1.49	58000
59000	*59999*	893	1.49	59000

Federal Child Support Tables/ Tables fédérales de pensions alimentaires pour enfants

Province: British Columbia/ Colombie-Britannique
No. Of Children/ Nbre d'enfants: Two/Deux

Income/Revenu ($)		Monthly Award/ Paiement mensuel ($)		
From/De	To/À	Basic Amount/ Montant de base	Plus (%)	Of Income Over/Du revenu dépassant
60000	*60999*	907	1.49	60000
61000	*61999*	922	1.49	61000
62000	*62999*	937	1.49	62000
63000	*63999*	952	1.49	63000
64000	*64999*	967	1.48	64000
65000	*65999*	982	1.43	65000
66000	*66999*	996	1.43	66000
67000	*67999*	1010	1.43	67000
68000	*68999*	1025	1.43	68000
69000	*69999*	1039	1.43	69000
70000	*70999*	1053	1.35	70000
71000	*71999*	1067	1.35	71000
72000	*72999*	1080	1.35	72000
73000	*73999*	1094	1.35	73000
74000	*74999*	1107	1.33	74000
75000	*75999*	1120	1.30	75000
76000	*76999*	1133	1.30	76000
77000	*77999*	1147	1.30	77000
78000	*78999*	1160	1.30	78000
79000	*79999*	1173	1.30	79000
80000	*80999*	1186	1.30	80000
81000	*81999*	1199	1.30	81000
82000	*82999*	1212	1.30	82000
83000	*83999*	1225	1.30	83000
84000	*84999*	1238	1.30	84000
85000	*85999*	1251	1.30	85000
86000	*86999*	1264	1.30	86000
87000	*87999*	1277	1.30	87000
88000	*88999*	1290	1.30	88000
89000	*89999*	1303	1.30	89000
90000	*90999*	1316	1.29	90000
91000	*91999*	1329	1.28	91000
92000	*92999*	1342	1.28	92000
93000	*93999*	1354	1.28	93000
94000	*94999*	1367	1.28	94000

Federal Child Support Tables/ Tables fédérales de pensions alimentaires pour enfants

Province: British Columbia/ Colombie-Britannique
No. Of Children/ Nbre d'enfants: Two/Deux

Income/Revenu ($)		Monthly Award/ Paiement mensuel ($)		
From/De	To/À	Basic Amount/ Montant de base	Plus (%)	Of Income Over/Du revenu dépassant
95000	*95999*	1380	1.28	95000
96000	*96999*	1393	1.28	96000
97000	*97999*	1406	1.28	97000
98000	*98999*	1418	1.28	98000
99000	*99999*	1431	1.28	99000
100000	*100999*	1444	1.28	100000
101000	*101999*	1457	1.28	101000
102000	*102999*	1470	1.28	102000
103000	*103999*	1483	1.28	103000
104000	*104999*	1495	1.28	104000
105000	*105999*	1508	1.28	105000
106000	*106999*	1521	1.28	106000
107000	*107999*	1534	1.28	107000
108000	*108999*	1547	1.28	108000
109000	*109999*	1559	1.28	109000
110000	*110999*	1572	1.28	110000
111000	*111999*	1585	1.28	111000
112000	*112999*	1598	1.28	112000
113000	*113999*	1611	1.27	113000
114000	*114999*	1623	1.22	114000
115000	*115999*	1636	1.22	115000
116000	*116999*	1648	1.22	116000
117000	*117999*	1660	1.22	117000
118000	*118999*	1672	1.22	118000
119000	*119999*	1684	1.22	119000
120000	*120999*	1696	1.22	120000
121000	*121999*	1708	1.22	121000
122000	*122999*	1721	1.22	122000
123000	*123999*	1733	1.22	123000
124000	*124999*	1745	1.22	124000
125000	*125999*	1757	1.22	125000
126000	*126999*	1769	1.22	126000
127000	*127999*	1781	1.22	127000
128000	*128999*	1794	1.22	128000
129000	*129999*	1806	1.22	129000

Federal Child Support Tables/ Tables fédérales de pensions alimentaires pour enfants

Province: British Columbia/ Colombie-Britannique No. Of Children/ Nbre d'enfants: Two/Deux

Income/Revenu ($)		Monthly Award/ Paiement mensuel ($)		
From/De	To/À	Basic Amount/ Montant de base	Plus (%)	Of Income Over/Du revenu dépassant
130000	*130999*	1818	1.22	130000
131000	*131999*	1830	1.22	131000
132000	*132999*	1842	1.22	132000
133000	*133999*	1854	1.22	133000
134000	*134999*	1867	1.22	134000
135000	*135999*	1879	1.22	135000
136000	*136999*	1891	1.22	136000
137000	*137999*	1903	1.22	137000
138000	*138999*	1915	1.22	138000
139000	*139999*	1927	1.22	139000
140000	*140999*	1940	1.22	140000
141000	*141999*	1952	1.22	141000
142000	*142999*	1964	1.22	142000
143000	*143999*	1976	1.22	143000
144000	*144999*	1988	1.22	144000
145000	*145999*	2000	1.22	145000
146000	*146999*	2013	1.22	146000
147000	*147999*	2025	1.22	147000
148000	*148999*	2037	1.22	148000
149000	*149999*	2049	1.22	149000

Federal Child Support Tables/ Tables fédérales de pensions alimentaires pour enfants

Province: British Columbia/ Colombie-Britannique No. Of Children/ Nbre d'enfants: Two/Deux

Income/Revenu ($)		Monthly Award/ Paiement mensuel ($)		
From/De	To/À	Basic Amount/ Montant de base	Plus (%)	Of Income Over/Du revenu dépassant
150000	*or greater/ ou plus*	2061	1.22	150000

Federal Child Support Tables/ Tables fédérales de pensions alimentaires pour enfants

Province: British Columbia/ Colombie-Britannique No. Of Children/ Nbre d'enfants: Three/Trois

Income/Revenu ($)		Monthly Award/ Paiement mensuel ($)		
From/De	To/À	Basic Amount/ Montant de base	Plus (%)	Of Income Over/Du revenu dépassant
0	*7999*	0		
8000	*8999*	0	2.31	8000
9000	*9999*	23	4.35	9000
10000	*10999*	67	4.35	10000
11000	*11999*	110	4.35	11000
12000	*12999*	154	4.35	12000
13000	*13999*	197	4.26	13000
14000	*14999*	240	4.23	14000
15000	*15999*	282	4.12	15000
16000	*16999*	323	4.12	16000
17000	*17999*	364	1.96	17000
18000	*18999*	384	1.97	18000
19000	*19999*	404	2.02	19000
20000	*20999*	424	2.02	20000
21000	*21999*	444	2.02	21000
22000	*22999*	464	2.02	22000
23000	*23999*	484	2.02	23000
24000	*24999*	504	2.02	24000

Federal Child Support Tables/ Tables fédérales de pensions alimentaires pour enfants — **Province: British Columbia/ Colombie-Britannique** — **No. Of Children/ Nbre d'enfants: Three/Trois**

Income/Revenu ($)		Monthly Award/ Paiement mensuel ($)		
From/De	To/À	Basic Amount/ Montant de base	Plus (%)	Of Income Over/Du revenu dépassant
25000	*25999*	525	2.02	25000
26000	*26999*	545	2.02	26000
27000	*27999*	565	2.02	27000
28000	*28999*	585	2.02	28000
29000	*29999*	605	1.93	29000
30000	*30999*	624	1.88	30000
31000	*31999*	643	1.88	31000
32000	*32999*	662	1.83	32000
33000	*33999*	680	1.79	33000
34000	*34999*	698	1.79	34000
35000	*35999*	716	1.63	35000
36000	*36999*	732	1.72	36000
37000	*37999*	750	1.76	37000
38000	*38999*	767	1.76	38000
39000	*39999*	785	1.81	39000
40000	*40999*	803	1.86	40000
41000	*41999*	821	1.91	41000
42000	*42999*	841	1.91	42000
43000	*43999*	860	1.91	43000
44000	*44999*	879	1.91	44000
45000	*45999*	898	1.91	45000
46000	*46999*	917	1.91	46000
47000	*47999*	936	1.91	47000
48000	*48999*	955	1.91	48000
49000	*49999*	974	1.91	49000
50000	*50999*	994	1.91	50000
51000	*51999*	1013	1.91	51000
52000	*52999*	1032	1.91	52000
53000	*53999*	1051	1.91	53000
54000	*54999*	1070	1.91	54000
55000	*55999*	1089	1.91	55000
56000	*56999*	1108	1.91	56000
57000	*57999*	1127	1.91	57000
58000	*58999*	1147	1.91	58000
59000	*59999*	1166	1.91	59000

Federal Child Support Tables/ Tables fédérales de pensions alimentaires pour enfants — **Province: British Columbia/ Colombie-Britannique** — **No. Of Children/ Nbre d'enfants: Three/Trois**

Income/Revenu ($)		Monthly Award/ Paiement mensuel ($)		
From/De	To/À	Basic Amount/ Montant de base	Plus (%)	Of Income Over/Du revenu dépassant
60000	*60999*	1185	1.91	60000
61000	*61999*	1204	1.91	61000
62000	*62999*	1223	1.91	62000
63000	*63999*	1242	1.91	63000
64000	*64999*	1261	1.91	64000
65000	*65999*	1280	1.84	65000
66000	*66999*	1299	1.84	66000
67000	*67999*	1317	1.84	67000
68000	*68999*	1336	1.84	68000
69000	*69999*	1354	1.84	69000
70000	*70999*	1373	1.73	70000
71000	*71999*	1390	1.73	71000
72000	*72999*	1407	1.73	72000
73000	*73999*	1424	1.73	73000
74000	*74999*	1442	1.71	74000
75000	*75999*	1459	1.68	75000
76000	*76999*	1476	1.68	76000
77000	*77999*	1492	1.68	77000
78000	*78999*	1509	1.68	78000
79000	*79999*	1526	1.68	79000
80000	*80999*	1543	1.68	80000
81000	*81999*	1559	1.68	81000
82000	*82999*	1576	1.68	82000
83000	*83999*	1593	1.68	83000
84000	*84999*	1610	1.68	84000
85000	*85999*	1626	1.68	85000
86000	*86999*	1643	1.68	86000
87000	*87999*	1660	1.68	87000
88000	*88999*	1677	1.67	88000
89000	*89999*	1693	1.68	89000
90000	*90999*	1710	1.66	90000
91000	*91999*	1727	1.65	91000
92000	*92999*	1743	1.65	92000
93000	*93999*	1760	1.65	93000
94000	*94999*	1776	1.65	94000

Federal Child Support Tables/ Tables fédérales de pensions alimentaires pour enfants

Province: British Columbia/ Colombie-Britannique
No. Of Children/ Nbre d'enfants: Three/Trois

Income/Revenu ($)		Monthly Award/ Paiement mensuel ($)		
From/De	**To/À**	**Basic Amount/ Montant de base**	**Plus (%)**	**Of Income Over/Du revenu dépassant**
95000	*95999*	1793	1.65	95000
96000	*96999*	1809	1.65	96000
97000	*97999*	1826	1.65	97000
98000	*98999*	1842	1.65	98000
99000	*99999*	1858	1.65	99000
100000	*100999*	1875	1.65	100000
101000	*101999*	1891	1.65	101000
102000	*102999*	1908	1.65	102000
103000	*103999*	1924	1.65	103000
104000	*104999*	1941	1.65	104000
105000	*105999*	1957	1.65	105000
106000	*106999*	1974	1.65	106000
107000	*107999*	1990	1.65	107000
108000	*108999*	2007	1.65	108000
109000	*109999*	2023	1.65	109000
110000	*110999*	2040	1.65	110000
111000	*111999*	2056	1.65	111000
112000	*112999*	2073	1.65	112000
113000	*113999*	2089	1.63	113000
114000	*114999*	2105	1.56	114000
115000	*115999*	2121	1.56	115000
116000	*116999*	2137	1.56	116000
117000	*117999*	2152	1.56	117000
118000	*118999*	2168	1.56	118000
119000	*119999*	2184	1.56	119000
120000	*120999*	2199	1.56	120000
121000	*121999*	2215	1.56	121000
122000	*122999*	2230	1.56	122000

Federal Child Support Tables/ Tables fédérales de pensions alimentaires pour enfants

Province: British Columbia/ Colombie-Britannique
No. Of Children/ Nbre d'enfants: Three/Trois

Income/Revenu ($)		Monthly Award/ Paiement mensuel ($)		
From/De	**To/À**	**Basic Amount/ Montant de base**	**Plus (%)**	**Of Income Over/Du revenu dépassant**
123000	*123999*	2246	1.56	123000
124000	*124999*	2262	1.56	124000
125000	*125999*	2277	1.56	125000
126000	*126999*	2293	1.56	126000
127000	*127999*	2309	1.56	127000
128000	*128999*	2324	1.56	128000
129000	*129999*	2340	1.56	129000
130000	*130999*	2356	1.56	130000
131000	*131999*	2371	1.56	131000
132000	*132999*	2387	1.56	132000
133000	*133999*	2403	1.56	133000
134000	*134999*	2418	1.56	134000
135000	*135999*	2434	1.56	135000
136000	*136999*	2449	1.56	136000
137000	*137999*	2465	1.56	137000
138000	*138999*	2481	1.56	138000
139000	*139999*	2496	1.56	139000
140000	*140999*	2512	1.56	140000
141000	*141999*	2528	1.56	141000
142000	*142999*	2543	1.56	142000
143000	*143999*	2559	1.56	143000
144000	*144999*	2575	1.56	144000
145000	*145999*	2590	1.56	145000
146000	*146999*	2606	1.56	146000
147000	*147999*	2621	1.56	147000
148000	*148999*	2637	1.56	148000
149000	*149999*	2653	1.56	149000

Federal Child Support Tables/ Tables fédérales de pensions alimentaires pour enfants

Province: British Columbia/ Colombie-Britannique
No. Of Children/ Nbre d'enfants: Three/Trois

Income/Revenu ($)		Monthly Award/ Paiement mensuel ($)		
From/De	To/À	Basic Amount/ Montant de base	Plus (%)	Of Income Over/Du revenu dépassant
150000	*or greater/ ou plus*	2668	1.56	150000

Federal Child Support Tables/ Tables fédérales de pensions alimentaires pour enfants

Province: British Columbia/ Colombie-Britannique
No. Of Children/ Nbre d'enfants: Four/Quatre

Income/Revenu ($)		Monthly Award/ Paiement mensuel ($)		
From/De	To/À	Basic Amount/ Montant de base	Plus (%)	Of Income Over/Du revenu dépassant
0	*7999*	0		
8000	*8999*	0	2.47	8000
9000	*9999*	25	4.66	9000
10000	*10999*	71	4.66	10000
11000	*11999*	118	4.66	11000
12000	*12999*	165	4.66	12000
13000	*13999*	211	4.57	13000
14000	*14999*	257	4.53	14000
15000	*15999*	302	4.41	15000
16000	*16999*	346	4.41	16000
17000	*17999*	390	4.41	17000
18000	*18999*	434	4.44	18000
19000	*19999*	479	3.36	19000
20000	*20999*	512	2.38	20000
21000	*21999*	536	2.38	21000
22000	*22999*	560	2.38	22000
23000	*23999*	584	2.38	23000
24000	*24999*	608	2.38	24000

Federal Child Support Tables/ Tables fédérales de pensions alimentaires pour enfants

Province: British Columbia/ Colombie-Britannique
No. Of Children/ Nbre d'enfants: Four/Quatre

Income/Revenu ($)		Monthly Award/ Paiement mensuel ($)		
From/De	To/À	Basic Amount/ Montant de base	Plus (%)	Of Income Over/Du revenu dépassant
25000	*25999*	632	2.38	25000
26000	*26999*	655	2.38	26000
27000	*27999*	679	2.38	27000
28000	*28999*	703	2.38	28000
29000	*29999*	727	2.28	29000
30000	*30999*	750	2.22	30000
31000	*31999*	772	2.22	31000
32000	*32999*	794	2.16	32000
33000	*33999*	816	2.12	33000
34000	*34999*	837	2.12	34000
35000	*35999*	858	1.92	35000
36000	*36999*	877	2.04	36000
37000	*37999*	897	2.08	37000
38000	*38999*	918	2.08	38000
39000	*39999*	939	2.13	39000
40000	*40999*	960	2.20	40000
41000	*41999*	982	2.26	41000
42000	*42999*	1005	2.26	42000
43000	*43999*	1028	2.26	43000
44000	*44999*	1050	2.26	44000
45000	*45999*	1073	2.26	45000
46000	*46999*	1095	2.26	46000
47000	*47999*	1118	2.26	47000
48000	*48999*	1141	2.26	48000
49000	*49999*	1163	2.26	49000
50000	*50999*	1186	2.26	50000
51000	*51999*	1208	2.26	51000
52000	*52999*	1231	2.26	52000
53000	*53999*	1254	2.26	53000
54000	*54999*	1276	2.26	54000
55000	*55999*	1299	2.26	55000
56000	*56999*	1321	2.26	56000
57000	*57999*	1344	2.26	57000
58000	*58999*	1367	2.26	58000
59000	*59999*	1389	2.26	59000

Federal Child Support Tables/ Tables fédérales de pensions alimentaires pour enfants		**Province: British Columbia/ Colombie-Britannique No. Of Children/ Nbre d'enfants: Four/Quatre**		
Income/Revenu ($)		**Monthly Award/ Paiement mensuel ($)**		
From/De	**To/À**	**Basic Amount/ Montant de base**	**Plus (%)**	**Of Income Over/Du revenu dépassant**
60000	*60999*	1412	2.26	60000
61000	*61999*	1434	2.26	61000
62000	*62999*	1457	2.26	62000
63000	*63999*	1480	2.26	63000
64000	*64999*	1502	2.26	64000
65000	*65999*	1525	2.18	65000
66000	*66999*	1547	2.18	66000
67000	*67999*	1568	2.18	67000
68000	*68999*	1590	2.18	68000
69000	*69999*	1612	2.18	69000
70000	*70999*	1634	2.05	70000
71000	*71999*	1654	2.05	71000
72000	*72999*	1675	2.05	72000
73000	*73999*	1695	2.05	73000
74000	*74999*	1715	2.02	74000
75000	*75999*	1736	1.98	75000
76000	*76999*	1755	1.98	76000
77000	*77999*	1775	1.98	77000
78000	*78999*	1795	1.98	78000
79000	*79999*	1815	1.98	79000
80000	*80999*	1835	1.98	80000
81000	*81999*	1854	1.98	81000
82000	*82999*	1874	1.98	82000
83000	*83999*	1894	1.98	83000
84000	*84999*	1914	1.98	84000
85000	*85999*	1934	1.98	85000
86000	*86999*	1953	1.98	86000
87000	*87999*	1973	1.98	87000
88000	*88999*	1993	1.98	88000
89000	*89999*	2013	1.98	89000
90000	*90999*	2033	1.97	90000
91000	*91999*	2052	1.95	91000
92000	*92999*	2072	1.95	92000
93000	*93999*	2091	1.95	93000
94000	*94999*	2111	1.95	94000

Federal Child Support Tables/ Tables fédérales de pensions alimentaires pour enfants		**Province: British Columbia/ Colombie-Britannique No. Of Children/ Nbre d'enfants: Four/Quatre**		
Income/Revenu ($)		**Monthly Award/ Paiement mensuel ($)**		
From/De	**To/À**	**Basic Amount/ Montant de base**	**Plus (%)**	**Of Income Over/Du revenu dépassant**
95000	*95999*	2130	1.95	95000
96000	*96999*	2150	1.95	96000
97000	*97999*	2169	1.95	97000
98000	*98999*	2188	1.95	98000
99000	*99999*	2208	1.95	99000
100000	*100999*	2227	1.95	100000
101000	*101999*	2247	1.95	101000
102000	*102999*	2266	1.95	102000
103000	*103999*	2286	1.95	103000
104000	*104999*	2305	1.95	104000
105000	*105999*	2325	1.95	105000
106000	*106999*	2344	1.95	106000
107000	*107999*	2364	1.95	107000
108000	*108999*	2383	1.95	108000
109000	*109999*	2403	1.95	109000
110000	*110999*	2422	1.95	110000
111000	*111999*	2442	1.95	111000
112000	*112999*	2461	1.95	112000
113000	*113999*	2480	1.93	113000
114000	*114999*	2500	1.85	114000
115000	*115999*	2518	1.85	115000
116000	*116999*	2537	1.85	116000
117000	*117999*	2555	1.85	117000
118000	*118999*	2574	1.85	118000
119000	*119999*	2592	1.85	119000
120000	*120999*	2611	1.85	120000
121000	*121999*	2629	1.85	121000
122000	*122999*	2648	1.85	122000
123000	*123999*	2666	1.85	123000
124000	*124999*	2685	1.85	124000
125000	*125999*	2703	1.85	125000
126000	*126999*	2722	1.85	126000
127000	*127999*	2740	1.85	127000
128000	*128999*	2759	1.85	128000
129000	*129999*	2777	1.85	129000

Federal Child Support Tables/ Tables fédérales de pensions alimentaires pour enfants

Province: British Columbia/ Colombie-Britannique
No. Of Children/ Nbre d'enfants: Four/Quatre

Income/Revenu ($)		Monthly Award/ Paiement mensuel ($)		
From/De	To/À	Basic Amount/ Montant de base	Plus (%)	Of Income Over/Du revenu dépassant
130000	*130999*	2795	1.85	130000
131000	*131999*	2814	1.85	131000
132000	*132999*	2832	1.85	132000
133000	*133999*	2851	1.85	133000
134000	*134999*	2869	1.85	134000
135000	*135999*	2888	1.85	135000
136000	*136999*	2906	1.85	136000
137000	*137999*	2925	1.85	137000
138000	*138999*	2943	1.85	138000
139000	*139999*	2962	1.85	139000
140000	*140999*	2980	1.85	140000
141000	*141999*	2999	1.85	141000
142000	*142999*	3017	1.85	142000
143000	*143999*	3036	1.85	143000
144000	*144999*	3054	1.85	144000
145000	*145999*	3073	1.85	145000
146000	*146999*	3091	1.85	146000
147000	*147999*	3110	1.85	147000
148000	*148999*	3128	1.85	148000
149000	*149999*	3147	1.85	149000
150000	*or greater/ ou plus*	3165	1.85	150000

Federal Child Support Tables/ Tables fédérales de pensions alimentaires pour enfants

Province: British Columbia/ Colombie-Britannique
No. Of Children/ Nbre d'enfants: Five/Cinq

Income/Revenu ($)		Monthly Award/ Paiement mensuel ($)		
From/De	To/À	Basic Amount/ Montant de base	Plus (%)	Of Income Over/Du revenu dépassant
0	*7999*	0		
8000	*8999*	0	2.47	8000
9000	*9999*	25	4.66	9000
10000	*10999*	71	4.66	10000
11000	*11999*	118	4.66	11000
12000	*12999*	165	4.66	12000
13000	*13999*	211	4.57	13000
14000	*14999*	257	4.53	14000
15000	*15999*	302	4.41	15000
16000	*16999*	346	4.41	16000
17000	*17999*	390	4.41	17000
18000	*18999*	434	4.44	18000
19000	*19999*	479	4.53	19000
20000	*20999*	524	4.53	20000
21000	*21999*	569	4.53	21000
22000	*22999*	615	4.53	22000
23000	*23999*	660	3.36	23000
24000	*24999*	694	2.69	24000

Federal Child Support Tables/ Tables fédérales de pensions alimentaires pour enfants

Province: British Columbia/ Colombie-Britannique
No. Of Children/ Nbre d'enfants: Five/Cinq

Income/Revenu ($)		Monthly Award/ Paiement mensuel ($)		
From/De	To/À	Basic Amount/ Montant de base	Plus (%)	Of Income Over/Du revenu dépassant
25000	*25999*	721	2.69	25000
26000	*26999*	748	2.69	26000
27000	*27999*	774	2.69	27000
28000	*28999*	801	2.69	28000
29000	*29999*	828	2.57	29000
30000	*30999*	854	2.50	30000
31000	*31999*	879	2.50	31000
32000	*32999*	904	2.44	32000
33000	*33999*	928	2.39	33000
34000	*34999*	952	2.39	34000
35000	*35999*	976	2.17	35000
36000	*36999*	998	2.30	36000
37000	*37999*	1021	2.35	37000
38000	*38999*	1044	2.35	38000
39000	*39999*	1068	2.41	39000
40000	*40999*	1092	2.48	40000
41000	*41999*	1117	2.55	41000
42000	*42999*	1142	2.55	42000
43000	*43999*	1168	2.55	43000
44000	*44999*	1193	2.55	44000
45000	*45999*	1219	2.55	45000
46000	*46999*	1244	2.55	46000
47000	*47999*	1270	2.55	47000
48000	*48999*	1295	2.55	48000
49000	*49999*	1321	2.55	49000
50000	*50999*	1346	2.55	50000
51000	*51999*	1372	2.55	51000
52000	*52999*	1397	2.55	52000
53000	*53999*	1423	2.55	53000
54000	*54999*	1448	2.55	54000
55000	*55999*	1474	2.55	55000
56000	*56999*	1499	2.55	56000
57000	*57999*	1525	2.55	57000
58000	*58999*	1550	2.55	58000
59000	*59999*	1576	2.55	59000

Federal Child Support Tables/ Tables fédérales de pensions alimentaires pour enfants

Province: British Columbia/ Colombie-Britannique
No. Of Children/ Nbre d'enfants: Five/Cinq

Income/Revenu ($)		Monthly Award/ Paiement mensuel ($)		
From/De	To/À	Basic Amount/ Montant de base	Plus (%)	Of Income Over/Du revenu dépassant
60000	*60999*	1601	2.55	60000
61000	*61999*	1627	2.55	61000
62000	*62999*	1652	2.55	62000
63000	*63999*	1678	2.55	63000
64000	*64999*	1703	2.54	64000
65000	*65999*	1728	2.46	65000
66000	*66999*	1753	2.46	66000
67000	*67999*	1778	2.46	67000
68000	*68999*	1802	2.46	68000
69000	*69999*	1827	2.46	69000
70000	*70999*	1851	2.31	70000
71000	*71999*	1874	2.31	71000
72000	*72999*	1897	2.31	72000
73000	*73999*	1920	2.31	73000
74000	*74999*	1944	2.27	74000
75000	*75999*	1966	2.23	75000
76000	*76999*	1989	2.23	76000
77000	*77999*	2011	2.23	77000
78000	*78999*	2033	2.23	78000
79000	*79999*	2056	2.23	79000
80000	*80999*	2078	2.23	80000
81000	*81999*	2100	2.23	81000
82000	*82999*	2123	2.23	82000
83000	*83999*	2145	2.23	83000
84000	*84999*	2167	2.23	84000
85000	*85999*	2190	2.23	85000
86000	*86999*	2212	2.23	86000
87000	*87999*	2234	2.23	87000
88000	*88999*	2257	2.23	88000
89000	*89999*	2279	2.23	89000
90000	*90999*	2301	2.22	90000
91000	*91999*	2323	2.20	91000
92000	*92999*	2345	2.20	92000
93000	*93999*	2367	2.20	93000
94000	*94999*	2389	2.20	94000

Federal Child Support Tables/ Tables fédérales de pensions alimentaires pour enfants

Province: British Columbia/ Colombie-Britannique
No. Of Children/ Nbre d'enfants: Five/Cinq

Income/Revenu ($)		Monthly Award/ Paiement mensuel ($)		
From/De	To/À	Basic Amount/ Montant de base	Plus (%)	Of Income Over/Du revenu dépassant
95000	*95999*	2411	2.20	95000
96000	*96999*	2433	2.20	96000
97000	*97999*	2455	2.20	97000
98000	*98999*	2477	2.20	98000
99000	*99999*	2499	2.20	99000
100000	*100999*	2521	2.20	100000
101000	*101999*	2543	2.20	101000
102000	*102999*	2565	2.20	102000
103000	*103999*	2587	2.20	103000
104000	*104999*	2609	2.20	104000
105000	*105999*	2631	2.20	105000
106000	*106999*	2653	2.20	106000
107000	*107999*	2675	2.20	107000
108000	*108999*	2697	2.20	108000
109000	*109999*	2719	2.20	109000
110000	*110999*	2741	2.20	110000
111000	*111999*	2763	2.20	111000
112000	*112999*	2785	2.20	112000
113000	*113999*	2807	2.17	113000
114000	*114999*	2828	2.09	114000
115000	*115999*	2849	2.09	115000
116000	*116999*	2870	2.09	116000
117000	*117999*	2891	2.09	117000
118000	*118999*	2912	2.09	118000
119000	*119999*	2933	2.09	119000
120000	*120999*	2954	2.09	120000
121000	*121999*	2974	2.09	121000
122000	*122999*	2995	2.09	122000

Federal Child Support Tables/ Tables fédérales de pensions alimentaires pour enfants

Province: British Columbia/ Colombie-Britannique
No. Of Children/ Nbre d'enfants: Five/Cinq

Income/Revenu ($)		Monthly Award/ Paiement mensuel ($)		
From/De	To/À	Basic Amount/ Montant de base	Plus (%)	Of Income Over/Du revenu dépassant
123000	*123999*	3016	2.09	123000
124000	*124999*	3037	2.09	124000
125000	*125999*	3058	2.09	125000
126000	*126999*	3079	2.09	126000
127000	*127999*	3099	2.09	127000
128000	*128999*	3120	2.09	128000
129000	*129999*	3141	2.09	129000
130000	*130999*	3162	2.09	130000
131000	*131999*	3183	2.09	131000
132000	*132999*	3204	2.09	132000
133000	*133999*	3225	2.09	133000
134000	*134999*	3245	2.09	134000
135000	*135999*	3266	2.09	135000
136000	*136999*	3287	2.09	136000
137000	*137999*	3308	2.09	137000
138000	*138999*	3329	2.09	138000
139000	*139999*	3350	2.09	139000
140000	*140999*	3371	2.09	140000
141000	*141999*	3391	2.09	141000
142000	*142999*	3412	2.09	142000
143000	*143999*	3433	2.09	143000
144000	*144999*	3454	2.09	144000
145000	*145999*	3475	2.09	145000
146000	*146999*	3496	2.09	146000
147000	*147999*	3517	2.09	147000
148000	*148999*	3537	2.09	148000
149000	*149999*	3558	2.09	149000

Federal Child Support Tables/ Tables fédérales de pensions alimentaires pour enfants

Province: British Columbia/ Colombie-Britannique
No. Of Children/ Nbre d'enfants: Five/Cinq

Income/Revenu ($)		Monthly Award/ Paiement mensuel ($)		
From/De	To/À	Basic Amount/ Montant de base	Plus (%)	Of Income Over/Du revenu dépassant
150000	*or greater/ ou plus*	3579	2.09	150000

Federal Child Support Tables/ Tables fédérales de pensions alimentaires pour enfants

Province: British Columbia/ Colombie-Britannique
No. Of Children/ Nbre d'enfants: Six or more/Six ou plus

Income/Revenu ($)		Monthly Award/ Paiement mensuel ($)		
From/De	To/À	Basic Amount/ Montant de base	Plus (%)	Of Income Over/Du revenu dépassant
0	*7999*	0		
8000	*8999*	0	2.47	8000
9000	*9999*	25	4.66	9000
10000	*10999*	71	4.66	10000
11000	*11999*	118	4.66	11000
12000	*12999*	165	4.66	12000
13000	*13999*	211	4.57	13000
14000	*14999*	257	4.53	14000
15000	*15999*	302	4.41	15000
16000	*16999*	346	4.41	16000
17000	*17999*	390	4.41	17000
18000	*18999*	434	4.44	18000
19000	*19999*	479	4.53	19000
20000	*20999*	524	4.53	20000
21000	*21999*	569	4.53	21000
22000	*22999*	615	4.53	22000
23000	*23999*	660	4.53	23000
24000	*24999*	706	4.53	24000

Federal Child Support Tables/ Tables fédérales de pensions alimentaires pour enfants

Province: British Columbia/ Colombie-Britannique
No. Of Children/ Nbre d'enfants: Six or more/Six ou plus

Income/Revenu ($)		Monthly Award/ Paiement mensuel ($)		
From/De	To/À	Basic Amount/ Montant de base	Plus (%)	Of Income Over/Du revenu dépassant
25000	*25999*	751	4.53	25000
26000	*26999*	796	4.53	26000
27000	*27999*	842	4.29	27000
28000	*28999*	884	2.95	28000
29000	*29999*	914	2.82	29000
30000	*30999*	942	2.74	30000
31000	*31999*	969	2.74	31000
32000	*32999*	997	2.68	32000
33000	*33999*	1024	2.62	33000
34000	*34999*	1050	2.62	34000
35000	*35999*	1076	2.38	35000
36000	*36999*	1100	2.52	36000
37000	*37999*	1125	2.58	37000
38000	*38999*	1151	2.58	38000
39000	*39999*	1176	2.64	39000
40000	*40999*	1203	2.72	40000
41000	*41999*	1230	2.80	41000
42000	*42999*	1258	2.80	42000
43000	*43999*	1286	2.80	43000
44000	*44999*	1314	2.80	44000
45000	*45999*	1342	2.80	45000
46000	*46999*	1370	2.80	46000
47000	*47999*	1398	2.80	47000
48000	*48999*	1426	2.80	48000
49000	*49999*	1454	2.80	49000
50000	*50999*	1482	2.80	50000
51000	*51999*	1510	2.80	51000
52000	*52999*	1538	2.80	52000
53000	*53999*	1565	2.80	53000
54000	*54999*	1593	2.80	54000
55000	*55999*	1621	2.80	55000
56000	*56999*	1649	2.80	56000
57000	*57999*	1677	2.80	57000
58000	*58999*	1705	2.80	58000
59000	*59999*	1733	2.80	59000

Federal Child Support Tables/ Tables fédérales de pensions alimentaires pour enfants

Province: British Columbia/ Colombie-Britannique
No. Of Children/ Nbre d'enfants: Six or more/Six ou plus

Income/Revenu ($)		Monthly Award/ Paiement mensuel ($)		
From/De	To/À	Basic Amount/ Montant de base	Plus (%)	Of Income Over/Du revenu dépassant
60000	*60999*	1761	2.80	60000
61000	*61999*	1789	2.80	61000
62000	*62999*	1817	2.80	62000
63000	*63999*	1845	2.80	63000
64000	*64999*	1873	2.79	64000
65000	*65999*	1901	2.69	65000
66000	*66999*	1928	2.69	66000
67000	*67999*	1955	2.69	67000
68000	*68999*	1982	2.69	68000
69000	*69999*	2008	2.69	69000
70000	*70999*	2035	2.53	70000
71000	*71999*	2061	2.53	71000
72000	*72999*	2086	2.53	72000
73000	*73999*	2111	2.53	73000
74000	*74999*	2137	2.49	74000
75000	*75999*	2162	2.45	75000
76000	*76999*	2186	2.45	76000
77000	*77999*	2210	2.45	77000
78000	*78999*	2235	2.45	78000
79000	*79999*	2259	2.45	79000
80000	*80999*	2284	2.45	80000
81000	*81999*	2308	2.45	81000
82000	*82999*	2333	2.45	82000
83000	*83999*	2357	2.45	83000
84000	*84999*	2382	2.45	84000
85000	*85999*	2406	2.45	85000
86000	*86999*	2431	2.45	86000
87000	*87999*	2455	2.45	87000
88000	*88999*	2480	2.45	88000
89000	*89999*	2504	2.45	89000
90000	*90999*	2529	2.43	90000
91000	*91999*	2553	2.41	91000
92000	*92999*	2577	2.41	92000
93000	*93999*	2601	2.41	93000
94000	*94999*	2625	2.41	94000

Federal Child Support Tables/ Tables fédérales de pensions alimentaires pour enfants

Province: British Columbia/ Colombie-Britannique
No. Of Children/ Nbre d'enfants: Six or more/Six ou plus

Income/Revenu ($)		Monthly Award/ Paiement mensuel ($)		
From/De	To/À	Basic Amount/ Montant de base	Plus (%)	Of Income Over/Du revenu dépassant
95000	*95999*	2649	2.41	95000
96000	*96999*	2673	2.41	96000
97000	*97999*	2697	2.41	97000
98000	*98999*	2722	2.41	98000
99000	*99999*	2746	2.41	99000
100000	*100999*	2770	2.41	100000
101000	*101999*	2794	2.41	101000
102000	*102999*	2818	2.41	102000
103000	*103999*	2842	2.41	103000
104000	*104999*	2866	2.41	104000
105000	*105999*	2890	2.41	105000
106000	*106999*	2914	2.41	106000
107000	*107999*	2938	2.41	107000
108000	*108999*	2962	2.41	108000
109000	*109999*	2986	2.41	109000
110000	*110999*	3010	2.41	110000
111000	*111999*	3035	2.41	111000
112000	*112999*	3059	2.41	112000
113000	*113999*	3083	2.38	113000
114000	*114999*	3107	2.29	114000
115000	*115999*	3129	2.29	115000
116000	*116999*	3152	2.29	116000
117000	*117999*	3175	2.29	117000
118000	*118999*	3198	2.29	118000
119000	*119999*	3221	2.29	119000
120000	*120999*	3244	2.29	120000
121000	*121999*	3267	2.29	121000
122000	*122999*	3289	2.29	122000
123000	*123999*	3312	2.29	123000
124000	*124999*	3335	2.29	124000
125000	*125999*	3358	2.29	125000
126000	*126999*	3381	2.29	126000
127000	*127999*	3404	2.29	127000
128000	*128999*	3427	2.29	128000
129000	*129999*	3449	2.29	129000

Federal Child Support Tables/ Tables fédérales de pensions alimentaires pour enfants

Province: British Columbia/ Colombie-Britannique
No. Of Children/ Nbre d'enfants: Six or more/Six ou plus

Income/Revenu ($)		Monthly Award/ Paiement mensuel ($)		
From/De	To/À	Basic Amount/ Montant de base	Plus (%)	Of Income Over/Du revenu dépassant
130000	*130999*	3472	2.29	130000
131000	*131999*	3495	2.29	131000
132000	*132999*	3518	2.29	132000
133000	*133999*	3541	2.29	133000
134000	*134999*	3564	2.29	134000
135000	*135999*	3587	2.29	135000
136000	*136999*	3609	2.29	136000
137000	*137999*	3632	2.29	137000
138000	*138999*	3655	2.29	138000
139000	*139999*	3678	2.29	139000
140000	*140999*	3701	2.29	140000
141000	*141999*	3724	2.29	141000
142000	*142999*	3747	2.29	142000
143000	*143999*	3769	2.29	143000
144000	*144999*	3792	2.29	144000
145000	*145999*	3815	2.29	145000
146000	*146999*	3838	2.29	146000
147000	*147999*	3861	2.29	147000
148000	*148999*	3884	2.29	148000
149000	*149999*	3907	2.29	149000

Federal Child Support Tables/ Tables fédérales de pensions alimentaires pour enfants

Province: British Columbia/ Colombie-Britannique
No. Of Children/ Nbre d'enfants: Six or more/Six ou plus

Income/Revenu ($)		Monthly Award/ Paiement mensuel ($)		
From/De	To/À	Basic Amount/ Montant de base	Plus (%)	Of Income Over/Du revenu dépassant
150000	*or greater/ ou plus*	3929	2.29	150000

Federal Child Support Tables/ Tables fédérales de pensions alimentaires pour enfants

Province: Prince Edward Island/ Île-du-Prince-Édouard
No. Of Children/ Nbre d'enfants: One/Un

Income/Revenu ($)		Monthly Award/ Paiement mensuel ($)		
From/De	To/À	Basic Amount/ Montant de base	Plus (%)	Of Income Over/Du revenu dépassant
0	*7999*	0		
8000	*8999*	0	0.89	8000
9000	*9999*	9	1.78	9000
10000	*10999*	27	1.78	10000
11000	*11999*	45	1.78	11000
12000	*12999*	62	1.78	12000
13000	*13999*	80	1.78	13000
14000	*14999*	98	1.78	14000
15000	*15999*	116	1.78	15000
16000	*16999*	134	0.40	16000
17000	*17999*	138	0.40	17000
18000	*18999*	142	0.77	18000
19000	*19999*	149	0.89	19000
20000	*20999*	158	1.13	20000
21000	*21999*	170	1.13	21000
22000	*22999*	181	1.13	22000
23000	*23999*	192	1.13	23000
24000	*24999*	204	1.13	24000

Federal Child Support Tables/ Tables fédérales de pensions alimentaires pour enfants

Province: Prince Edward Island/ Île-du-Prince-Édouard
No. Of Children/ Nbre d'enfants: One/Un

Income/Revenu ($)		Monthly Award/ Paiement mensuel ($)		
From/De	To/À	Basic Amount/ Montant de base	Plus (%)	Of Income Over/Du revenu dépassant
25000	*25999*	215	0.96	25000
26000	*26999*	225	0.96	26000
27000	*27999*	234	0.96	27000
28000	*28999*	244	0.96	28000
29000	*29999*	253	0.92	29000
30000	*30999*	263	0.88	30000
31000	*31999*	271	0.83	31000
32000	*32999*	280	0.83	32000
33000	*33999*	288	0.83	33000
34000	*34999*	296	0.83	34000
35000	*35999*	305	0.75	35000
36000	*36999*	312	0.80	36000
37000	*37999*	320	0.82	37000
38000	*38999*	328	0.82	38000
39000	*39999*	337	0.84	39000
40000	*40999*	345	0.87	40000
41000	*41999*	354	0.89	41000
42000	*42999*	363	0.89	42000
43000	*43999*	372	0.89	43000
44000	*44999*	380	0.89	44000
45000	*45999*	389	0.89	45000
46000	*46999*	398	0.89	46000
47000	*47999*	407	0.89	47000
48000	*48999*	416	0.89	48000
49000	*49999*	425	0.89	49000
50000	*50999*	434	0.89	50000
51000	*51999*	443	0.89	51000
52000	*52999*	452	0.89	52000
53000	*53999*	461	0.87	53000
54000	*54999*	469	0.82	54000
55000	*55999*	478	0.82	55000
56000	*56999*	486	0.82	56000
57000	*57999*	494	0.82	57000
58000	*58999*	502	0.86	58000
59000	*59999*	511	0.87	59000

Federal Child Support Tables/ Tables fédérales de pensions alimentaires pour enfants

Province: Prince Edward Island/ Île-du-Prince-Édouard
No. Of Children/ Nbre d'enfants: One/Un

Income/Revenu ($)		Monthly Award/ Paiement mensuel ($)		
From/De	To/À	Basic Amount/ Montant de base	Plus (%)	Of Income Over/Du revenu dépassant
60000	*60999*	520	0.87	60000
61000	*61999*	528	0.85	61000
62000	*62999*	537	0.83	62000
63000	*63999*	545	0.83	63000
64000	*64999*	554	0.83	64000
65000	*65999*	562	0.83	65000
66000	*66999*	570	0.83	66000
67000	*67999*	578	0.83	67000
68000	*68999*	587	0.83	68000
69000	*69999*	595	0.83	69000
70000	*70999*	603	0.77	70000
71000	*71999*	611	0.77	71000
72000	*72999*	619	0.77	72000
73000	*73999*	626	0.77	73000
74000	*74999*	634	0.77	74000
75000	*75999*	642	0.77	75000
76000	*76999*	650	0.77	76000
77000	*77999*	657	0.77	77000
78000	*78999*	665	0.77	78000
79000	*79999*	673	0.77	79000
80000	*80999*	681	0.77	80000
81000	*81999*	688	0.77	81000
82000	*82999*	696	0.77	82000
83000	*83999*	704	0.77	83000
84000	*84999*	711	0.77	84000
85000	*85999*	719	0.77	85000
86000	*86999*	727	0.77	86000
87000	*87999*	735	0.77	87000
88000	*88999*	742	0.77	88000
89000	*89999*	750	0.77	89000
90000	*90999*	758	0.77	90000
91000	*91999*	765	0.77	91000
92000	*92999*	773	0.77	92000
93000	*93999*	781	0.77	93000
94000	*94999*	789	0.77	94000

Federal Child Support Tables/ Tables fédérales de pensions alimentaires pour enfants

Province: Prince Edward Island/ Île-du-Prince-Édouard
No. Of Children/ Nbre d'enfants: One/Un

Income/Revenu ($)		Monthly Award/ Paiement mensuel ($)		
From/De	To/À	Basic Amount/ Montant de base	Plus (%)	Of Income Over/Du revenu dépassant
95000	*95999*	796	0.77	95000
96000	*96999*	804	0.77	96000
97000	*97999*	812	0.77	97000
98000	*98999*	820	0.77	98000
99000	*99999*	827	0.77	99000
100000	*100999*	835	0.77	100000
101000	*101999*	843	0.77	101000
102000	*102999*	850	0.77	102000
103000	*103999*	858	0.77	103000
104000	*104999*	866	0.77	104000
105000	*105999*	874	0.77	105000
106000	*106999*	881	0.77	106000
107000	*107999*	889	0.77	107000
108000	*108999*	897	0.77	108000
109000	*109999*	905	0.77	109000
110000	*110999*	912	0.77	110000
111000	*111999*	920	0.77	111000
112000	*112999*	928	0.77	112000
113000	*113999*	935	0.76	113000
114000	*114999*	943	0.73	114000
115000	*115999*	950	0.73	115000
116000	*116999*	958	0.73	116000
117000	*117999*	965	0.73	117000
118000	*118999*	972	0.73	118000
119000	*119999*	980	0.73	119000
120000	*120999*	987	0.73	120000
121000	*121999*	994	0.73	121000
122000	*122999*	1002	0.73	122000

Federal Child Support Tables/ Tables fédérales de pensions alimentaires pour enfants

Province: Prince Edward Island/ Île-du-Prince-Édouard
No. Of Children/ Nbre d'enfants: One/Un

Income/Revenu ($)		Monthly Award/ Paiement mensuel ($)		
From/De	To/À	Basic Amount/ Montant de base	Plus (%)	Of Income Over/Du revenu dépassant
123000	*123999*	1009	0.73	123000
124000	*124999*	1016	0.73	124000
125000	*125999*	1024	0.73	125000
126000	*126999*	1031	0.73	126000
127000	*127999*	1038	0.73	127000
128000	*128999*	1045	0.73	128000
129000	*129999*	1053	0.73	129000
130000	*130999*	1060	0.73	130000
131000	*131999*	1067	0.73	131000
132000	*132999*	1075	0.73	132000
133000	*133999*	1082	0.73	133000
134000	*134999*	1089	0.73	134000
135000	*135999*	1097	0.73	135000
136000	*136999*	1104	0.73	136000
137000	*137999*	1111	0.73	137000
138000	*138999*	1119	0.73	138000
139000	*139999*	1126	0.73	139000
140000	*140999*	1133	0.73	140000
141000	*141999*	1140	0.73	141000
142000	*142999*	1148	0.73	142000
143000	*143999*	1155	0.73	143000
144000	*144999*	1162	0.73	144000
145000	*145999*	1170	0.73	145000
146000	*146999*	1177	0.73	146000
147000	*147999*	1184	0.73	147000
148000	*148999*	1192	0.73	148000
149000	*149999*	1199	0.73	149000

Federal Child Support Tables/ Tables fédérales de pensions alimentaires pour enfants

Province: Prince Edward Island/ Île-du-Prince-Édouard
No. Of Children/ Nbre d'enfants: One/Un

Income/Revenu ($)		Monthly Award/ Paiement mensuel ($)		
From/De	To/À	Basic Amount/ Montant de base	Plus (%)	Of Income Over/Du revenu dépassant
150000	*or greater/ ou plus*	1206	0.73	150000

Federal Child Support Tables/ Tables fédérales de pensions alimentaires pour enfants

Province: Prince Edward Island/ Île-du-Prince-Édouard
No. Of Children/ Nbre d'enfants: Two/Deux

Income/Revenu ($)		Monthly Award/ Paiement mensuel ($)		
From/De	To/À	Basic Amount/ Montant de base	Plus (%)	Of Income Over/Du revenu dépassant
0	*7999*	0		
8000	*8999*	0	1.75	8000
9000	*9999*	17	4.34	9000
10000	*10999*	61	4.11	10000
11000	*11999*	102	3.85	11000
12000	*12999*	140	3.85	12000
13000	*13999*	179	3.77	13000
14000	*14999*	217	2.33	14000
15000	*15999*	240	0.61	15000
16000	*16999*	246	0.95	16000
17000	*17999*	256	0.95	17000
18000	*18999*	265	0.95	18000
19000	*19999*	275	1.10	19000
20000	*20999*	285	1.65	20000
21000	*21999*	302	1.65	21000
22000	*22999*	318	1.65	22000
23000	*23999*	335	1.65	23000
24000	*24999*	351	1.65	24000

Federal Child Support Tables/ Tables fédérales de pensions alimentaires pour enfants

Province: Prince Edward Island/ Île-du-Prince-Édouard
No. Of Children/ Nbre d'enfants: Two/Deux

Income/Revenu ($)		Monthly Award/ Paiement mensuel ($)		
From/De	To/À	Basic Amount/ Montant de base	Plus (%)	Of Income Over/Du revenu dépassant
25000	*25999*	368	1.65	25000
26000	*26999*	384	1.65	26000
27000	*27999*	401	1.65	27000
28000	*28999*	417	1.65	28000
29000	*29999*	434	1.42	29000
30000	*30999*	448	1.36	30000
31000	*31999*	462	1.30	31000
32000	*32999*	474	1.30	32000
33000	*33999*	487	1.30	33000
34000	*34999*	500	1.30	34000
35000	*35999*	513	1.17	35000
36000	*36999*	525	1.25	36000
37000	*37999*	538	1.28	37000
38000	*38999*	550	1.28	38000
39000	*39999*	563	1.31	39000
40000	*40999*	576	1.35	40000
41000	*41999*	590	1.39	41000
42000	*42999*	604	1.39	42000
43000	*43999*	617	1.39	43000
44000	*44999*	631	1.39	44000
45000	*45999*	645	1.39	45000
46000	*46999*	659	1.39	46000
47000	*47999*	673	1.39	47000
48000	*48999*	687	1.39	48000
49000	*49999*	701	1.39	49000
50000	*50999*	714	1.39	50000
51000	*51999*	728	1.39	51000
52000	*52999*	742	1.39	52000
53000	*53999*	756	1.37	53000
54000	*54999*	770	1.31	54000
55000	*55999*	783	1.31	55000
56000	*56999*	796	1.31	56000
57000	*57999*	809	1.31	57000
58000	*58999*	822	1.35	58000
59000	*59999*	836	1.36	59000

Federal Child Support Tables/ Tables fédérales de pensions alimentaires pour enfants

Province: Prince Edward Island/ Île-du-Prince-Édouard
No. Of Children/ Nbre d'enfants: Two/Deux

Income/Revenu ($)		Monthly Award/ Paiement mensuel ($)		
From/De	To/À	Basic Amount/ Montant de base	Plus (%)	Of Income Over/Du revenu dépassant
60000	*60999*	849	1.36	60000
61000	*61999*	863	1.32	61000
62000	*62999*	876	1.29	62000
63000	*63999*	889	1.29	63000
64000	*64999*	902	1.29	64000
65000	*65999*	915	1.29	65000
66000	*66999*	928	1.29	66000
67000	*67999*	941	1.29	67000
68000	*68999*	954	1.29	68000
69000	*69999*	966	1.29	69000
70000	*70999*	979	1.20	70000
71000	*71999*	991	1.20	71000
72000	*72999*	1003	1.20	72000
73000	*73999*	1015	1.20	73000
74000	*74999*	1027	1.20	74000
75000	*75999*	1039	1.20	75000
76000	*76999*	1051	1.20	76000
77000	*77999*	1063	1.20	77000
78000	*78999*	1075	1.20	78000
79000	*79999*	1087	1.20	79000
80000	*80999*	1099	1.20	80000
81000	*81999*	1111	1.20	81000
82000	*82999*	1124	1.20	82000
83000	*83999*	1136	1.20	83000
84000	*84999*	1148	1.20	84000
85000	*85999*	1160	1.20	85000
86000	*86999*	1172	1.20	86000
87000	*87999*	1184	1.20	87000
88000	*88999*	1196	1.20	88000
89000	*89999*	1208	1.20	89000
90000	*90999*	1220	1.20	90000
91000	*91999*	1232	1.20	91000
92000	*92999*	1244	1.20	92000
93000	*93999*	1256	1.20	93000
94000	*94999*	1268	1.20	94000

Federal Child Support Tables/ Tables fédérales de pensions alimentaires pour enfants

Province: Prince Edward Island/ Île-du-Prince-Édouard
No. Of Children/ Nbre d'enfants: Two/Deux

Income/Revenu ($)		Monthly Award/ Paiement mensuel ($)		
From/De	To/À	Basic Amount/ Montant de base	Plus (%)	Of Income Over/Du revenu dépassant
95000	*95999*	1280	1.20	95000
96000	*96999*	1292	1.20	96000
97000	*97999*	1304	1.20	97000
98000	*98999*	1316	1.20	98000
99000	*99999*	1328	1.20	99000
100000	*100999*	1340	1.20	100000
101000	*101999*	1352	1.20	101000
102000	*102999*	1364	1.20	102000
103000	*103999*	1376	1.20	103000
104000	*104999*	1388	1.20	104000
105000	*105999*	1400	1.20	105000
106000	*106999*	1412	1.20	106000
107000	*107999*	1424	1.20	107000
108000	*108999*	1436	1.20	108000
109000	*109999*	1448	1.20	109000
110000	*110999*	1460	1.20	110000
111000	*111999*	1472	1.20	111000
112000	*112999*	1484	1.20	112000
113000	*113999*	1496	1.19	113000
114000	*114999*	1508	1.14	114000
115000	*115999*	1519	1.14	115000
116000	*116999*	1531	1.14	116000
117000	*117999*	1542	1.14	117000
118000	*118999*	1553	1.14	118000
119000	*119999*	1565	1.14	119000
120000	*120999*	1576	1.14	120000
121000	*121999*	1588	1.14	121000
122000	*122999*	1599	1.14	122000
123000	*123999*	1610	1.14	123000
124000	*124999*	1622	1.14	124000
125000	*125999*	1633	1.14	125000
126000	*126999*	1644	1.14	126000
127000	*127999*	1656	1.14	127000
128000	*128999*	1667	1.14	128000
129000	*129999*	1679	1.14	129000

Federal Child Support Tables/ Tables fédérales de pensions alimentaires pour enfants

Province: Prince Edward Island/ Île-du-Prince-Édouard
No. Of Children/ Nbre d'enfants: Two/Deux

Income/Revenu ($)		Monthly Award/ Paiement mensuel ($)		
From/De	To/À	Basic Amount/ Montant de base	Plus (%)	Of Income Over/Du revenu dépassant
130000	*130999*	1690	1.14	130000
131000	*131999*	1701	1.14	131000
132000	*132999*	1713	1.14	132000
133000	*133999*	1724	1.14	133000
134000	*134999*	1735	1.14	134000
135000	*135999*	1747	1.14	135000
136000	*136999*	1758	1.14	136000
137000	*137999*	1770	1.14	137000
138000	*138999*	1781	1.14	138000
139000	*139999*	1792	1.14	139000
140000	*140999*	1804	1.14	140000
141000	*141999*	1815	1.14	141000
142000	*142999*	1826	1.14	142000
143000	*143999*	1838	1.14	143000
144000	*144999*	1849	1.14	144000
145000	*145999*	1860	1.14	145000
146000	*146999*	1872	1.14	146000
147000	*147999*	1883	1.14	147000
148000	*148999*	1895	1.14	148000
149000	*149999*	1906	1.14	149000

Federal Child Support Tables/ Tables fédérales de pensions alimentaires pour enfants

Province: Prince Edward Island/ Île-du-Prince-Édouard
No. Of Children/ Nbre d'enfants: Two/Deux

Income/Revenu ($)		Monthly Award/ Paiement mensuel ($)		
From/De	To/À	Basic Amount/ Montant de base	Plus (%)	Of Income Over/Du revenu dépassant
150000	*or greater/ ou plus*	1917	1.14	150000

Federal Child Support Tables/ Tables fédérales de pensions alimentaires pour enfants

Province: Prince Edward Island/ Île-du-Prince-Édouard
No. Of Children/ Nbre d'enfants: Three/Trois

Income/Revenu ($)		Monthly Award/ Paiement mensuel ($)		
From/De	To/À	Basic Amount/ Montant de base	Plus (%)	Of Income Over/Du revenu dépassant
0	*7999*	0		
8000	*8999*	0	1.88	8000
9000	*9999*	19	4.68	9000
10000	*10999*	66	4.42	10000
11000	*11999*	110	4.15	11000
12000	*12999*	151	4.15	12000
13000	*13999*	193	4.06	13000
14000	*14999*	233	4.03	14000
15000	*15999*	274	3.74	15000
16000	*16999*	311	3.74	16000
17000	*17999*	348	1.53	17000
18000	*18999*	364	1.39	18000
19000	*19999*	377	1.39	19000
20000	*20999*	391	1.66	20000
21000	*21999*	408	2.03	21000
22000	*22999*	428	2.06	22000
23000	*23999*	449	2.06	23000
24000	*24999*	469	2.06	24000

Federal Child Support Tables/ Tables fédérales de pensions alimentaires pour enfants

Province: Prince Edward Island/ Île-du-Prince-Édouard
No. Of Children/ N^bre^ d'enfants: Three/Trois

Income/Revenu ($)		Monthly Award/ Paiement mensuel ($)		
From/De	**To/À**	**Basic Amount/ Montant de base**	**Plus (%)**	**Of Income Over/Du revenu dépassant**
25000	*25999*	490	2.06	25000
26000	*26999*	511	2.06	26000
27000	*27999*	531	2.06	27000
28000	*28999*	552	2.06	28000
29000	*29999*	572	1.97	29000
30000	*30999*	592	1.89	30000
31000	*31999*	611	1.81	31000
32000	*32999*	629	1.81	32000
33000	*33999*	647	1.67	33000
34000	*34999*	664	1.67	34000
35000	*35999*	680	1.51	35000
36000	*36999*	695	1.60	36000
37000	*37999*	711	1.64	37000
38000	*38999*	728	1.64	38000
39000	*39999*	744	1.68	39000
40000	*40999*	761	1.73	40000
41000	*41999*	778	1.78	41000
42000	*42999*	796	1.78	42000
43000	*43999*	814	1.78	43000
44000	*44999*	832	1.78	44000
45000	*45999*	850	1.78	45000
46000	*46999*	868	1.78	46000
47000	*47999*	885	1.78	47000
48000	*48999*	903	1.78	48000
49000	*49999*	921	1.78	49000
50000	*50999*	939	1.78	50000
51000	*51999*	957	1.78	51000
52000	*52999*	975	1.78	52000
53000	*53999*	992	1.76	53000
54000	*54999*	1010	1.71	54000
55000	*55999*	1027	1.71	55000
56000	*56999*	1044	1.71	56000
57000	*57999*	1061	1.71	57000
58000	*58999*	1078	1.74	58000
59000	*59999*	1096	1.74	59000

Federal Child Support Tables/ Tables fédérales de pensions alimentaires pour enfants

Province: Prince Edward Island/ Île-du-Prince-Édouard
No. Of Children/ N^bre^ d'enfants: Three/Trois

Income/Revenu ($)		Monthly Award/ Paiement mensuel ($)		
From/De	**To/À**	**Basic Amount/ Montant de base**	**Plus (%)**	**Of Income Over/Du revenu dépassant**
60000	*60999*	1113	1.75	60000
61000	*61999*	1131	1.70	61000
62000	*62999*	1148	1.66	62000
63000	*63999*	1164	1.66	63000
64000	*64999*	1181	1.66	64000
65000	*65999*	1197	1.66	65000
66000	*66999*	1214	1.66	66000
67000	*67999*	1230	1.66	67000
68000	*68999*	1247	1.66	68000
69000	*69999*	1264	1.66	69000
70000	*70999*	1280	1.55	70000
71000	*71999*	1296	1.55	71000
72000	*72999*	1311	1.55	72000
73000	*73999*	1326	1.55	73000
74000	*74999*	1342	1.55	74000
75000	*75999*	1357	1.55	75000
76000	*76999*	1373	1.55	76000
77000	*77999*	1388	1.55	77000
78000	*78999*	1404	1.55	78000
79000	*79999*	1419	1.55	79000
80000	*80999*	1435	1.55	80000
81000	*81999*	1450	1.55	81000
82000	*82999*	1466	1.55	82000
83000	*83999*	1481	1.55	83000
84000	*84999*	1496	1.55	84000
85000	*85999*	1512	1.55	85000
86000	*86999*	1527	1.55	86000
87000	*87999*	1543	1.55	87000
88000	*88999*	1558	1.55	88000
89000	*89999*	1574	1.55	89000
90000	*90999*	1589	1.55	90000
91000	*91999*	1605	1.55	91000
92000	*92999*	1620	1.55	92000
93000	*93999*	1636	1.55	93000
94000	*94999*	1651	1.55	94000

Federal Child Support Tables/ Tables fédérales de pensions alimentaires pour enfants

Province: Prince Edward Island/ Île-du-Prince-Édouard
No. Of Children/ Nbre d'enfants: Three/Trois

Income/Revenu ($)		Monthly Award/ Paiement mensuel ($)		
From/De	To/À	Basic Amount/ Montant de base	Plus (%)	Of Income Over/Du revenu dépassant
95000	*95999*	1666	1.55	95000
96000	*96999*	1682	1.55	96000
97000	*97999*	1697	1.55	97000
98000	*98999*	1713	1.55	98000
99000	*99999*	1728	1.55	99000
100000	*100999*	1744	1.55	100000
101000	*101999*	1759	1.55	101000
102000	*102999*	1775	1.55	102000
103000	*103999*	1790	1.55	103000
104000	*104999*	1806	1.55	104000
105000	*105999*	1821	1.55	105000
106000	*106999*	1836	1.55	106000
107000	*107999*	1852	1.55	107000
108000	*108999*	1867	1.55	108000
109000	*109999*	1883	1.55	109000
110000	*110999*	1898	1.55	110000
111000	*111999*	1914	1.55	111000
112000	*112999*	1929	1.55	112000
113000	*113999*	1945	1.53	113000
114000	*114999*	1960	1.46	114000
115000	*115999*	1974	1.46	115000
116000	*116999*	1989	1.46	116000
117000	*117999*	2004	1.46	117000
118000	*118999*	2018	1.46	118000
119000	*119999*	2033	1.46	119000
120000	*120999*	2048	1.46	120000
121000	*121999*	2062	1.46	121000
122000	*122999*	2077	1.46	122000

Federal Child Support Tables/ Tables fédérales de pensions alimentaires pour enfants

Province: Prince Edward Island/ Île-du-Prince-Édouard
No. Of Children/ Nbre d'enfants: Three/Trois

Income/Revenu ($)		Monthly Award/ Paiement mensuel ($)		
From/De	To/À	Basic Amount/ Montant de base	Plus (%)	Of Income Over/Du revenu dépassant
123000	*123999*	2091	1.46	123000
124000	*124999*	2106	1.46	124000
125000	*125999*	2121	1.46	125000
126000	*126999*	2135	1.46	126000
127000	*127999*	2150	1.46	127000
128000	*128999*	2165	1.46	128000
129000	*129999*	2179	1.46	129000
130000	*130999*	2194	1.46	130000
131000	*131999*	2208	1.46	131000
132000	*132999*	2223	1.46	132000
133000	*133999*	2238	1.46	133000
134000	*134999*	2252	1.46	134000
135000	*135999*	2267	1.46	135000
136000	*136999*	2281	1.46	136000
137000	*137999*	2296	1.46	137000
138000	*138999*	2311	1.46	138000
139000	*139999*	2325	1.46	139000
140000	*140999*	2340	1.46	140000
141000	*141999*	2355	1.46	141000
142000	*142999*	2369	1.46	142000
143000	*143999*	2384	1.46	143000
144000	*144999*	2398	1.46	144000
145000	*145999*	2413	1.46	145000
146000	*146999*	2428	1.46	146000
147000	*147999*	2442	1.46	147000
148000	*148999*	2457	1.46	148000
149000	*149999*	2472	1.46	149000

Federal Child Support Tables/ Tables fédérales de pensions alimentaires pour enfants

Province: Prince Edward Island/ Île-du-Prince-Édouard
No. Of Children/ Nbre d'enfants: Three/Trois

Income/Revenu ($)		Monthly Award/ Paiement mensuel ($)		
From/De	To/À	Basic Amount/ Montant de base	Plus (%)	Of Income Over/Du revenu dépassant
150000	or greater/ ou plus	2486	1.46	150000

Federal Child Support Tables/ Tables fédérales de pensions alimentaires pour enfants

Province: Prince Edward Island/ Île-du-Prince-Édouard
No. Of Children/ Nbre d'enfants: Four/Quatre

Income/Revenu ($)		Monthly Award/ Paiement mensuel ($)		
From/De	To/À	Basic Amount/ Montant de base	Plus (%)	Of Income Over/Du revenu dépassant
0	7999	0		
8000	8999	0	2.01	8000
9000	9999	20	5.01	9000
10000	10999	70	4.74	10000
11000	11999	118	4.44	11000
12000	12999	162	4.44	12000
13000	13999	206	4.35	13000
14000	14999	250	4.32	14000
15000	15999	293	4.00	15000
16000	16999	333	4.00	16000
17000	17999	373	4.00	17000
18000	18999	413	4.00	18000
19000	19999	453	2.60	19000
20000	20999	479	2.04	20000
21000	21999	500	2.04	21000
22000	22999	520	2.22	22000
23000	23999	542	2.39	23000
24000	24999	566	2.39	24000

Federal Child Support Tables/ Tables fédérales de pensions alimentaires pour enfants

Province: Prince Edward Island/ Île-du-Prince-Édouard
No. Of Children/ Nbre d'enfants: Four/Quatre

Income/Revenu ($)		Monthly Award/ Paiement mensuel ($)		
From/De	To/À	Basic Amount/ Montant de base	Plus (%)	Of Income Over/Du revenu dépassant
25000	25999	590	2.39	25000
26000	26999	614	2.39	26000
27000	27999	638	2.39	27000
28000	28999	662	2.39	28000
29000	29999	686	2.29	29000
30000	30999	709	2.20	30000
31000	31999	731	2.10	31000
32000	32999	752	2.10	32000
33000	33999	773	2.10	33000
34000	34999	794	2.10	34000
35000	35999	815	1.91	35000
36000	36999	834	2.02	36000
37000	37999	854	1.94	37000
38000	38999	873	1.94	38000
39000	39999	893	1.99	39000
40000	40999	912	2.05	40000
41000	41999	933	2.11	41000
42000	42999	954	2.11	42000
43000	43999	975	2.11	43000
44000	44999	996	2.11	44000
45000	45999	1017	2.11	45000
46000	46999	1038	2.11	46000
47000	47999	1059	2.11	47000
48000	48999	1080	2.11	48000
49000	49999	1101	2.11	49000
50000	50999	1123	2.11	50000
51000	51999	1144	2.11	51000
52000	52999	1165	2.11	52000
53000	53999	1186	2.08	53000
54000	54999	1207	2.03	54000
55000	55999	1227	2.03	55000
56000	56999	1247	2.03	56000
57000	57999	1267	2.03	57000
58000	58999	1288	2.06	58000
59000	59999	1308	2.06	59000

Federal Child Support Tables/ Tables fédérales de pensions alimentaires pour enfants

Province: Prince Edward Island/ Île-du-Prince-Édouard
No. Of Children/ Nbre d'enfants: Four/Quatre

Income/Revenu ($)		Monthly Award/ Paiement mensuel ($)		
From/De	To/À	Basic Amount/ Montant de base	Plus (%)	Of Income Over/Du revenu dépassant
60000	*60999*	1329	2.06	60000
61000	*61999*	1350	2.01	61000
62000	*62999*	1370	1.96	62000
63000	*63999*	1389	1.96	63000
64000	*64999*	1409	1.96	64000
65000	*65999*	1428	1.96	65000
66000	*66999*	1448	1.96	66000
67000	*67999*	1468	1.96	67000
68000	*68999*	1487	1.96	68000
69000	*69999*	1507	1.96	69000
70000	*70999*	1526	1.83	70000
71000	*71999*	1545	1.83	71000
72000	*72999*	1563	1.83	72000
73000	*73999*	1581	1.83	73000
74000	*74999*	1599	1.83	74000
75000	*75999*	1618	1.83	75000
76000	*76999*	1636	1.83	76000
77000	*77999*	1654	1.83	77000
78000	*78999*	1672	1.83	78000
79000	*79999*	1691	1.83	79000
80000	*80999*	1709	1.83	80000
81000	*81999*	1727	1.83	81000
82000	*82999*	1745	1.83	82000
83000	*83999*	1764	1.83	83000
84000	*84999*	1782	1.83	84000
85000	*85999*	1800	1.83	85000
86000	*86999*	1818	1.83	86000
87000	*87999*	1837	1.83	87000
88000	*88999*	1855	1.83	88000
89000	*89999*	1873	1.83	89000
90000	*90999*	1891	1.83	90000
91000	*91999*	1910	1.83	91000
92000	*92999*	1928	1.83	92000
93000	*93999*	1946	1.83	93000
94000	*94999*	1965	1.83	94000

Federal Child Support Tables/ Tables fédérales de pensions alimentaires pour enfants

Province: Prince Edward Island/ Île-du-Prince-Édouard
No. Of Children/ Nbre d'enfants: Four/Quatre

Income/Revenu ($)		Monthly Award/ Paiement mensuel ($)		
From/De	To/À	Basic Amount/ Montant de base	Plus (%)	Of Income Over/Du revenu dépassant
95000	*95999*	1983	1.83	95000
96000	*96999*	2001	1.83	96000
97000	*97999*	2019	1.83	97000
98000	*98999*	2038	1.83	98000
99000	*99999*	2056	1.83	99000
100000	*100999*	2074	1.83	100000
101000	*101999*	2092	1.83	101000
102000	*102999*	2111	1.83	102000
103000	*103999*	2129	1.83	103000
104000	*104999*	2147	1.83	104000
105000	*105999*	2165	1.83	105000
106000	*106999*	2184	1.83	106000
107000	*107999*	2202	1.83	107000
108000	*108999*	2220	1.83	108000
109000	*109999*	2238	1.83	109000
110000	*110999*	2257	1.83	110000
111000	*111999*	2275	1.83	111000
112000	*112999*	2293	1.83	112000
113000	*113999*	2312	1.81	113000
114000	*114999*	2330	1.73	114000
115000	*115999*	2347	1.73	115000
116000	*116999*	2364	1.73	116000
117000	*117999*	2381	1.73	117000
118000	*118999*	2399	1.73	118000
119000	*119999*	2416	1.73	119000
120000	*120999*	2433	1.73	120000
121000	*121999*	2451	1.73	121000
122000	*122999*	2468	1.73	122000
123000	*123999*	2485	1.73	123000
124000	*124999*	2502	1.73	124000
125000	*125999*	2520	1.73	125000
126000	*126999*	2537	1.73	126000
127000	*127999*	2554	1.73	127000
128000	*128999*	2571	1.73	128000
129000	*129999*	2589	1.73	129000

Federal Child Support Tables/ Tables fédérales de pensions alimentaires pour enfants

Province: Prince Edward Island/ Île-du-Prince-Édouard
No. Of Children/ N^bre d'enfants: Four/Quatre

Income/Revenu ($)		Monthly Award/ Paiement mensuel ($)		
From/De	To/À	Basic Amount/ Montant de base	Plus (%)	Of Income Over/Du revenu dépassant
130000	*130999*	2606	1.73	130000
131000	*131999*	2623	1.73	131000
132000	*132999*	2641	1.73	132000
133000	*133999*	2658	1.73	133000
134000	*134999*	2675	1.73	134000
135000	*135999*	2692	1.73	135000
136000	*136999*	2710	1.73	136000
137000	*137999*	2727	1.73	137000
138000	*138999*	2744	1.73	138000
139000	*139999*	2762	1.73	139000
140000	*140999*	2779	1.73	140000
141000	*141999*	2796	1.73	141000
142000	*142999*	2813	1.73	142000
143000	*143999*	2831	1.73	143000
144000	*144999*	2848	1.73	144000
145000	*145999*	2865	1.73	145000
146000	*146999*	2882	1.73	146000
147000	*147999*	2900	1.73	147000
148000	*148999*	2917	1.73	148000
149000	*149999*	2934	1.73	149000

Federal Child Support Tables/ Tables fédérales de pensions alimentaires pour enfants

Province: Prince Edward Island/ Île-du-Prince-Édouard
No. Of Children/ N^bre d'enfants: Four/Quatre

Income/Revenu ($)		Monthly Award/ Paiement mensuel ($)		
From/De	To/À	Basic Amount/ Montant de base	Plus (%)	Of Income Over/Du revenu dépassant
150000	*or greater/ ou plus*	2952	1.73	150000

Federal Child Support Tables/ Tables fédérales de pensions alimentaires pour enfants

Province: Prince Edward Island/ Île-du-Prince-Édouard
No. Of Children/ N^bre d'enfants: Five/Cinq

Income/Revenu ($)		Monthly Award/ Paiement mensuel ($)		
From/De	To/À	Basic Amount/ Montant de base	Plus (%)	Of Income Over/Du revenu dépassant
0	*7999*	0		
8000	*8999*	0	2.01	8000
9000	*9999*	20	5.01	9000
10000	*10999*	70	4.74	10000
11000	*11999*	118	4.44	11000
12000	*12999*	162	4.44	12000
13000	*13999*	206	4.35	13000
14000	*14999*	250	4.32	14000
15000	*15999*	293	4.00	15000
16000	*16999*	333	4.00	16000
17000	*17999*	373	4.00	17000
18000	*18999*	413	4.00	18000
19000	*19999*	453	4.00	19000
20000	*20999*	493	4.32	20000
21000	*21999*	536	4.32	21000
22000	*22999*	580	4.32	22000
23000	*23999*	623	2.38	23000
24000	*24999*	647	2.67	24000

Federal Child Support Tables/ Tables fédérales de pensions alimentaires pour enfants — **Province: Prince Edward Island/ Île-du-Prince-Édouard** — **No. Of Children/ Nbre d'enfants: Five/Cinq**

Income/Revenu ($)		Monthly Award/ Paiement mensuel ($)		
From/De	To/À	Basic Amount/ Montant de base	Plus (%)	Of Income Over/Du revenu dépassant
25000	*25999*	673	2.67	25000
26000	*26999*	700	2.67	26000
27000	*27999*	727	2.67	27000
28000	*28999*	754	2.67	28000
29000	*29999*	780	2.56	29000
30000	*30999*	806	2.45	30000
31000	*31999*	830	2.34	31000
32000	*32999*	854	2.34	32000
33000	*33999*	877	2.34	33000
34000	*34999*	901	2.34	34000
35000	*35999*	924	2.12	35000
36000	*36999*	945	2.25	36000
37000	*37999*	968	2.30	37000
38000	*38999*	991	2.30	38000
39000	*39999*	1014	2.36	39000
40000	*40999*	1037	2.43	40000
41000	*41999*	1062	2.38	41000
42000	*42999*	1085	2.38	42000
43000	*43999*	1109	2.38	43000
44000	*44999*	1133	2.38	44000
45000	*45999*	1157	2.38	45000
46000	*46999*	1180	2.38	46000
47000	*47999*	1204	2.38	47000
48000	*48999*	1228	2.38	48000
49000	*49999*	1252	2.38	49000
50000	*50999*	1276	2.38	50000
51000	*51999*	1299	2.38	51000
52000	*52999*	1323	2.38	52000
53000	*53999*	1347	2.35	53000
54000	*54999*	1370	2.29	54000
55000	*55999*	1393	2.29	55000
56000	*56999*	1416	2.29	56000
57000	*57999*	1439	2.29	57000
58000	*58999*	1462	2.32	58000
59000	*59999*	1485	2.33	59000

Federal Child Support Tables/ Tables fédérales de pensions alimentaires pour enfants — **Province: Prince Edward Island/ Île-du-Prince-Édouard** — **No. Of Children/ Nbre d'enfants: Five/Cinq**

Income/Revenu ($)		Monthly Award/ Paiement mensuel ($)		
From/De	To/À	Basic Amount/ Montant de base	Plus (%)	Of Income Over/Du revenu dépassant
60000	*60999*	1509	2.33	60000
61000	*61999*	1532	2.27	61000
62000	*62999*	1555	2.21	62000
63000	*63999*	1577	2.21	63000
64000	*64999*	1599	2.21	64000
65000	*65999*	1621	2.21	65000
66000	*66999*	1643	2.21	66000
67000	*67999*	1665	2.21	67000
68000	*68999*	1687	2.21	68000
69000	*69999*	1709	2.21	69000
70000	*70999*	1731	2.06	70000
71000	*71999*	1752	2.06	71000
72000	*72999*	1773	2.06	72000
73000	*73999*	1793	2.06	73000
74000	*74999*	1814	2.06	74000
75000	*75999*	1834	2.06	75000
76000	*76999*	1855	2.06	76000
77000	*77999*	1876	2.06	77000
78000	*78999*	1896	2.06	78000
79000	*79999*	1917	2.06	79000
80000	*80999*	1937	2.06	80000
81000	*81999*	1958	2.06	81000
82000	*82999*	1979	2.06	82000
83000	*83999*	1999	2.06	83000
84000	*84999*	2020	2.06	84000
85000	*85999*	2040	2.06	85000
86000	*86999*	2061	2.06	86000
87000	*87999*	2082	2.06	87000
88000	*88999*	2102	2.06	88000
89000	*89999*	2123	2.06	89000
90000	*90999*	2143	2.06	90000
91000	*91999*	2164	2.06	91000
92000	*92999*	2185	2.06	92000
93000	*93999*	2205	2.06	93000
94000	*94999*	2226	2.06	94000

Federal Child Support Tables/ Tables fédérales de pensions alimentaires pour enfants

Province: Prince Edward Island/ Île-du-Prince-Édouard
No. Of Children/ Nbre d'enfants: Five/Cinq

Income/Revenu ($)		Monthly Award/ Paiement mensuel ($)		
From/De	To/À	Basic Amount/ Montant de base	Plus (%)	Of Income Over/Du revenu dépassant
95000	*95999*	2246	2.06	95000
96000	*96999*	2267	2.06	96000
97000	*97999*	2288	2.06	97000
98000	*98999*	2308	2.06	98000
99000	*99999*	2329	2.06	99000
100000	*100999*	2349	2.06	100000
101000	*101999*	2370	2.06	101000
102000	*102999*	2391	2.06	102000
103000	*103999*	2411	2.06	103000
104000	*104999*	2432	2.06	104000
105000	*105999*	2452	2.06	105000
106000	*106999*	2473	2.06	106000
107000	*107999*	2494	2.06	107000
108000	*108999*	2514	2.06	108000
109000	*109999*	2535	2.06	109000
110000	*110999*	2556	2.06	110000
111000	*111999*	2576	2.06	111000
112000	*112999*	2597	2.06	112000
113000	*113999*	2617	2.04	113000
114000	*114999*	2638	1.95	114000
115000	*115999*	2657	1.95	115000
116000	*116999*	2677	1.95	116000
117000	*117999*	2696	1.95	117000
118000	*118999*	2716	1.95	118000
119000	*119999*	2735	1.95	119000
120000	*120999*	2755	1.95	120000
121000	*121999*	2774	1.95	121000
122000	*122999*	2794	1.95	122000

Federal Child Support Tables/ Tables fédérales de pensions alimentaires pour enfants

Province: Prince Edward Island/ Île-du-Prince-Édouard
No. Of Children/ Nbre d'enfants: Five/Cinq

Income/Revenu ($)		Monthly Award/ Paiement mensuel ($)		
From/De	To/À	Basic Amount/ Montant de base	Plus (%)	Of Income Over/Du revenu dépassant
123000	*123999*	2813	1.95	123000
124000	*124999*	2833	1.95	124000
125000	*125999*	2852	1.95	125000
126000	*126999*	2872	1.95	126000
127000	*127999*	2891	1.95	127000
128000	*128999*	2911	1.95	128000
129000	*129999*	2930	1.95	129000
130000	*130999*	2950	1.95	130000
131000	*131999*	2969	1.95	131000
132000	*132999*	2989	1.95	132000
133000	*133999*	3008	1.95	133000
134000	*134999*	3028	1.95	134000
135000	*135999*	3047	1.95	135000
136000	*136999*	3067	1.95	136000
137000	*137999*	3086	1.95	137000
138000	*138999*	3106	1.95	138000
139000	*139999*	3125	1.95	139000
140000	*140999*	3145	1.95	140000
141000	*141999*	3164	1.95	141000
142000	*142999*	3183	1.95	142000
143000	*143999*	3203	1.95	143000
144000	*144999*	3222	1.95	144000
145000	*145999*	3242	1.95	145000
146000	*146999*	3261	1.95	146000
147000	*147999*	3281	1.95	147000
148000	*148999*	3300	1.95	148000
149000	*149999*	3320	1.95	149000

Federal Child Support Tables/ Tables fédérales de pensions alimentaires pour enfants

Province: Prince Edward Island/ Île-du-Prince-Édouard
No. Of Children/ Nbre d'enfants: Five/Cinq

Income/Revenu ($)		Monthly Award/ Paiement mensuel ($)		
From/De	To/À	Basic Amount/ Montant de base	Plus (%)	Of Income Over/Du revenu dépassant
150000	*or greater/ ou plus*	3339	1.95	150000

Federal Child Support Tables/ Tables fédérales de pensions alimentaires pour enfants

Province: Prince Edward Island/ Île-du-Prince-Édouard
No. Of Children/ Nbre d'enfants: Six or more/Six ou plus

Income/Revenu ($)		Monthly Award/ Paiement mensuel ($)		
From/De	To/À	Basic Amount/ Montant de base	Plus (%)	Of Income Over/Du revenu dépassant
0	*7999*	0		
8000	*8999*	0	2.01	8000
9000	*9999*	20	5.01	9000
10000	*10999*	70	4.74	10000
11000	*11999*	118	4.44	11000
12000	*12999*	162	4.44	12000
13000	*13999*	206	4.35	13000
14000	*14999*	250	4.32	14000
15000	*15999*	293	4.00	15000
16000	*16999*	333	4.00	16000
17000	*17999*	373	4.00	17000
18000	*18999*	413	4.00	18000
19000	*19999*	453	4.00	19000
20000	*20999*	493	4.32	20000
21000	*21999*	536	4.32	21000
22000	*22999*	580	4.32	22000
23000	*23999*	623	4.32	23000
24000	*24999*	666	4.32	24000

Federal Child Support Tables/ Tables fédérales de pensions alimentaires pour enfants

Province: Prince Edward Island/ Île-du-Prince-Édouard
No. Of Children/ Nbre d'enfants: Six or more/Six ou plus

Income/Revenu ($)		Monthly Award/ Paiement mensuel ($)		
From/De	To/À	Basic Amount/ Montant de base	Plus (%)	Of Income Over/Du revenu dépassant
25000	*25999*	709	4.32	25000
26000	*26999*	752	4.32	26000
27000	*27999*	795	3.57	27000
28000	*28999*	831	2.91	28000
29000	*29999*	860	2.78	29000
30000	*30999*	888	2.67	30000
31000	*31999*	915	2.55	31000
32000	*32999*	940	2.55	32000
33000	*33999*	966	2.55	33000
34000	*34999*	991	2.55	34000
35000	*35999*	1017	2.31	35000
36000	*36999*	1040	2.45	36000
37000	*37999*	1064	2.50	37000
38000	*38999*	1089	2.50	38000
39000	*39999*	1114	2.56	39000
40000	*40999*	1140	2.64	40000
41000	*41999*	1166	2.71	41000
42000	*42999*	1193	2.71	42000
43000	*43999*	1220	2.71	43000
44000	*44999*	1248	2.71	44000
45000	*45999*	1275	2.61	45000
46000	*46999*	1301	2.61	46000
47000	*47999*	1327	2.61	47000
48000	*48999*	1353	2.61	48000
49000	*49999*	1379	2.61	49000
50000	*50999*	1405	2.61	50000
51000	*51999*	1431	2.61	51000
52000	*52999*	1457	2.61	52000
53000	*53999*	1483	2.58	53000
54000	*54999*	1509	2.52	54000
55000	*55999*	1534	2.52	55000
56000	*56999*	1559	2.52	56000
57000	*57999*	1585	2.52	57000
58000	*58999*	1610	2.55	58000
59000	*59999*	1635	2.55	59000

Federal Child Support Tables/ Tables fédérales de pensions alimentaires pour enfants

Province: Prince Edward Island/ Île-du-Prince-Édouard
No. Of Children/ Nbre d'enfants: Six or more/Six ou plus

Income/Revenu ($)		Monthly Award/ Paiement mensuel ($)		
From/De	To/À	Basic Amount/ Montant de base	Plus (%)	Of Income Over/Du revenu dépassant
60000	*60999*	1661	2.55	60000
61000	*61999*	1686	2.49	61000
62000	*62999*	1711	2.42	62000
63000	*63999*	1735	2.42	63000
64000	*64999*	1760	2.42	64000
65000	*65999*	1784	2.42	65000
66000	*66999*	1808	2.42	66000
67000	*67999*	1832	2.42	67000
68000	*68999*	1856	2.42	68000
69000	*69999*	1881	2.42	69000
70000	*70999*	1905	2.26	70000
71000	*71999*	1927	2.26	71000
72000	*72999*	1950	2.26	72000
73000	*73999*	1973	2.26	73000
74000	*74999*	1995	2.26	74000
75000	*75999*	2018	2.26	75000
76000	*76999*	2040	2.26	76000
77000	*77999*	2063	2.26	77000
78000	*78999*	2086	2.26	78000
79000	*79999*	2108	2.26	79000
80000	*80999*	2131	2.26	80000
81000	*81999*	2153	2.26	81000
82000	*82999*	2176	2.26	82000
83000	*83999*	2199	2.26	83000
84000	*84999*	2221	2.26	84000
85000	*85999*	2244	2.26	85000
86000	*86999*	2266	2.26	86000
87000	*87999*	2289	2.26	87000
88000	*88999*	2311	2.26	88000
89000	*89999*	2334	2.26	89000
90000	*90999*	2357	2.26	90000
91000	*91999*	2379	2.26	91000
92000	*92999*	2402	2.26	92000
93000	*93999*	2424	2.26	93000
94000	*94999*	2447	2.26	94000

Federal Child Support Tables/ Tables fédérales de pensions alimentaires pour enfants

Province: Prince Edward Island/ Île-du-Prince-Édouard
No. Of Children/ Nbre d'enfants: Six or more/Six ou plus

Income/Revenu ($)		Monthly Award/ Paiement mensuel ($)		
From/De	To/À	Basic Amount/ Montant de base	Plus (%)	Of Income Over/Du revenu dépassant
95000	*95999*	2470	2.26	95000
96000	*96999*	2492	2.26	96000
97000	*97999*	2515	2.26	97000
98000	*98999*	2537	2.26	98000
99000	*99999*	2560	2.26	99000
100000	*100999*	2582	2.26	100000
101000	*101999*	2605	2.26	101000
102000	*102999*	2628	2.26	102000
103000	*103999*	2650	2.26	103000
104000	*104999*	2673	2.26	104000
105000	*105999*	2695	2.26	105000
106000	*106999*	2718	2.26	106000
107000	*107999*	2741	2.26	107000
108000	*108999*	2763	2.26	108000
109000	*109999*	2786	2.26	109000
110000	*110999*	2808	2.26	110000
111000	*111999*	2831	2.26	111000
112000	*112999*	2853	2.26	112000
113000	*113999*	2876	2.23	113000
114000	*114999*	2898	2.14	114000
115000	*115999*	2920	2.14	115000
116000	*116999*	2941	2.14	116000
117000	*117999*	2963	2.14	117000
118000	*118999*	2984	2.14	118000
119000	*119999*	3005	2.14	119000
120000	*120999*	3027	2.14	120000
121000	*121999*	3048	2.14	121000
122000	*122999*	3069	2.14	122000
123000	*123999*	3091	2.14	123000
124000	*124999*	3112	2.14	124000
125000	*125999*	3133	2.14	125000
126000	*126999*	3155	2.14	126000
127000	*127999*	3176	2.14	127000
128000	*128999*	3198	2.14	128000
129000	*129999*	3219	2.14	129000

Federal Child Support Tables/ Tables fédérales de pensions alimentaires pour enfants

Province: Prince Edward Island/ Île-du-Prince-Édouard
No. Of Children/ Nbre d'enfants: Six or more/Six ou plus

Income/Revenu ($)		Monthly Award/ Paiement mensuel ($)		
From/De	To/À	Basic Amount/ Montant de base	Plus (%)	Of Income Over/Du revenu dépassant
130000	*130999*	3240	2.14	130000
131000	*131999*	3262	2.14	131000
132000	*132999*	3283	2.14	132000
133000	*133999*	3304	2.14	133000
134000	*134999*	3326	2.14	134000
135000	*135999*	3347	2.14	135000
136000	*136999*	3368	2.14	136000
137000	*137999*	3390	2.14	137000
138000	*138999*	3411	2.14	138000
139000	*139999*	3433	2.14	139000
140000	*140999*	3454	2.14	140000
141000	*141999*	3475	2.14	141000
142000	*142999*	3497	2.14	142000
143000	*143999*	3518	2.14	143000
144000	*144999*	3539	2.14	144000
145000	*145999*	3561	2.14	145000
146000	*146999*	3582	2.14	146000
147000	*147999*	3604	2.14	147000
148000	*148999*	3625	2.14	148000
149000	*149999*	3646	2.14	149000
150000	*or greater/ ou plus*	3668	2.14	150000

Federal Child Support Tables/ Tables fédérales de pensions alimentaires pour enfants

Province: Saskatchewan
No. Of Children/ Nbre d'enfants: One/Un

Income/Revenu ($)		Monthly Award/ Paiement mensuel ($)		
From/De	To/À	Basic Amount/ Montant de base	Plus (%)	Of Income Over/Du revenu dépassant
0	*7999*	0		
8000	*8999*	0	0.84	8000
9000	*9999*	8	1.67	9000
10000	*10999*	25	1.67	10000
11000	*11999*	42	1.67	11000
12000	*12999*	58	1.67	12000
13000	*13999*	75	1.67	13000
14000	*14999*	92	1.67	14000
15000	*15999*	109	1.56	15000
16000	*16999*	124	0.59	16000
17000	*17999*	130	0.74	17000
18000	*18999*	137	0.94	18000
19000	*19999*	147	0.94	19000
20000	*20999*	156	0.94	20000
21000	*21999*	166	0.94	21000
22000	*22999*	175	0.94	22000
23000	*23999*	185	0.94	23000
24000	*24999*	194	0.94	24000

Federal Child Support Tables/ Tables fédérales de pensions alimentaires pour enfants

Province: Saskatchewan No. Of Children/ Nbre d'enfants: One/Un

Income/Revenu ($)		Monthly Award/ Paiement mensuel ($)		
From/De	To/À	Basic Amount/ Montant de base	Plus (%)	Of Income Over/Du revenu dépassant
25000	*25999*	204	0.94	25000
26000	*26999*	213	0.94	26000
27000	*27999*	222	0.94	27000
28000	*28999*	232	0.94	28000
29000	*29999*	241	0.90	29000
30000	*30999*	250	0.87	30000
31000	*31999*	259	0.87	31000
32000	*32999*	268	0.87	32000
33000	*33999*	276	0.87	33000
34000	*34999*	285	0.87	34000
35000	*35999*	294	0.79	35000
36000	*36999*	302	0.82	36000
37000	*37999*	310	0.83	37000
38000	*38999*	318	0.83	38000
39000	*39999*	327	0.85	39000
40000	*40999*	335	0.88	40000
41000	*41999*	344	0.90	41000
42000	*42999*	353	0.90	42000
43000	*43999*	362	0.90	43000
44000	*44999*	371	0.90	44000
45000	*45999*	380	0.90	45000
46000	*46999*	389	0.90	46000
47000	*47999*	398	0.90	47000
48000	*48999*	407	0.90	48000
49000	*49999*	416	0.90	49000
50000	*50999*	425	0.90	50000
51000	*51999*	434	0.90	51000
52000	*52999*	443	0.90	52000
53000	*53999*	452	0.90	53000
54000	*54999*	461	0.90	54000
55000	*55999*	470	0.90	55000
56000	*56999*	479	0.90	56000
57000	*57999*	488	0.90	57000
58000	*58999*	497	0.90	58000
59000	*59999*	507	0.90	59000

Federal Child Support Tables/ Tables fédérales de pensions alimentaires pour enfants

Province: Saskatchewan No. Of Children/ Nbre d'enfants: One/Un

Income/Revenu ($)		Monthly Award/ Paiement mensuel ($)		
From/De	To/À	Basic Amount/ Montant de base	Plus (%)	Of Income Over/Du revenu dépassant
60000	*60999*	516	0.90	60000
61000	*61999*	525	0.90	61000
62000	*62999*	534	0.90	62000
63000	*63999*	543	0.90	63000
64000	*64999*	552	0.90	64000
65000	*65999*	561	0.90	65000
66000	*66999*	570	0.90	66000
67000	*67999*	579	0.90	67000
68000	*68999*	588	0.90	68000
69000	*69999*	597	0.90	69000
70000	*70999*	606	0.85	70000
71000	*71999*	614	0.85	71000
72000	*72999*	623	0.85	72000
73000	*73999*	631	0.85	73000
74000	*74999*	640	0.85	74000
75000	*75999*	648	0.85	75000
76000	*76999*	657	0.85	76000
77000	*77999*	665	0.85	77000
78000	*78999*	674	0.85	78000
79000	*79999*	682	0.85	79000
80000	*80999*	691	0.85	80000
81000	*81999*	699	0.85	81000
82000	*82999*	707	0.85	82000
83000	*83999*	716	0.85	83000
84000	*84999*	724	0.85	84000
85000	*85999*	733	0.85	85000
86000	*86999*	741	0.85	86000
87000	*87999*	750	0.85	87000
88000	*88999*	758	0.85	88000
89000	*89999*	767	0.85	89000
90000	*90999*	775	0.85	90000
91000	*91999*	784	0.85	91000
92000	*92999*	792	0.85	92000
93000	*93999*	801	0.85	93000
94000	*94999*	809	0.85	94000

Federal Child Support Tables/ Tables fédérales de pensions alimentaires pour enfants

Province: Saskatchewan No. Of Children/ Nbre d'enfants: One/Un

Income/Revenu ($)		Monthly Award/ Paiement mensuel ($)		
From/De	To/À	Basic Amount/ Montant de base	Plus (%)	Of Income Over/Du revenu dépassant
95000	*95999*	818	0.85	95000
96000	*96999*	826	0.85	96000
97000	*97999*	835	0.85	97000
98000	*98999*	843	0.85	98000
99000	*99999*	852	0.85	99000
100000	*100999*	860	0.85	100000
101000	*101999*	868	0.85	101000
102000	*102999*	877	0.85	102000
103000	*103999*	885	0.83	103000
104000	*104999*	894	0.82	104000
105000	*105999*	902	0.82	105000
106000	*106999*	910	0.82	106000
107000	*107999*	918	0.82	107000
108000	*108999*	926	0.82	108000
109000	*109999*	935	0.82	109000
110000	*110999*	943	0.82	110000
111000	*111999*	951	0.82	111000
112000	*112999*	959	0.82	112000
113000	*113999*	967	0.81	113000
114000	*114999*	976	0.78	114000
115000	*115999*	983	0.78	115000
116000	*116999*	991	0.78	116000
117000	*117999*	999	0.78	117000
118000	*118999*	1007	0.78	118000
119000	*119999*	1014	0.78	119000
120000	*120999*	1022	0.78	120000
121000	*121999*	1030	0.78	121000
122000	*122999*	1038	0.78	122000

Federal Child Support Tables/ Tables fédérales de pensions alimentaires pour enfants

Province: Saskatchewan No. Of Children/ Nbre d'enfants: One/Un

Income/Revenu ($)		Monthly Award/ Paiement mensuel ($)		
From/De	To/À	Basic Amount/ Montant de base	Plus (%)	Of Income Over/Du revenu dépassant
123000	*123999*	1046	0.78	123000
124000	*124999*	1053	0.78	124000
125000	*125999*	1061	0.78	125000
126000	*126999*	1069	0.78	126000
127000	*127999*	1077	0.78	127000
128000	*128999*	1084	0.78	128000
129000	*129999*	1092	0.78	129000
130000	*130999*	1100	0.78	130000
131000	*131999*	1108	0.78	131000
132000	*132999*	1116	0.78	132000
133000	*133999*	1123	0.78	133000
134000	*134999*	1131	0.78	134000
135000	*135999*	1139	0.78	135000
136000	*136999*	1147	0.78	136000
137000	*137999*	1154	0.78	137000
138000	*138999*	1162	0.78	138000
139000	*139999*	1170	0.78	139000
140000	*140999*	1178	0.78	140000
141000	*141999*	1186	0.78	141000
142000	*142999*	1193	0.78	142000
143000	*143999*	1201	0.78	143000
144000	*144999*	1209	0.78	144000
145000	*145999*	1217	0.78	145000
146000	*146999*	1224	0.78	146000
147000	*147999*	1232	0.78	147000
148000	*148999*	1240	0.78	148000
149000	*149999*	1248	0.78	149000

Federal Child Support Tables/ Tables fédérales de pensions alimentaires pour enfants

Province: Saskatchewan No. Of Children/ Nbre d'enfants: One/Un

Income/Revenu ($)		Monthly Award/ Paiement mensuel ($)		
From/De	To/À	Basic Amount/ Montant de base	Plus (%)	Of Income Over/Du revenu dépassant
150000	*or greater/ ou plus*	1256	0.78	150000

Federal Child Support Tables/ Tables fédérales de pensions alimentaires pour enfants

Province: Saskatchewan No. Of Children/ Nbre d'enfants: Two/Deux

Income/Revenu ($)		Monthly Award/ Paiement mensuel ($)		
From/De	To/À	Basic Amount/ Montant de base	Plus (%)	Of Income Over/Du revenu dépassant
0	*7999*	0		
8000	*8999*	0	1.58	8000
9000	*9999*	16	3.79	9000
10000	*10999*	54	3.79	10000
11000	*11999*	92	3.79	11000
12000	*12999*	129	3.79	12000
13000	*13999*	167	3.71	13000
14000	*14999*	204	2.31	14000
15000	*15999*	228	0.82	15000
16000	*16999*	236	1.15	16000
17000	*17999*	247	1.15	17000
18000	*18999*	259	1.15	18000
19000	*19999*	270	1.15	19000
20000	*20999*	282	1.36	20000
21000	*21999*	295	1.47	21000
22000	*22999*	310	1.47	22000
23000	*23999*	325	1.47	23000
24000	*24999*	339	1.47	24000

Federal Child Support Tables/ Tables fédérales de pensions alimentaires pour enfants

Province: Saskatchewan No. Of Children/ Nbre d'enfants: Two/Deux

Income/Revenu ($)		Monthly Award/ Paiement mensuel ($)		
From/De	To/À	Basic Amount/ Montant de base	Plus (%)	Of Income Over/Du revenu dépassant
25000	*25999*	354	1.47	25000
26000	*26999*	369	1.47	26000
27000	*27999*	383	1.47	27000
28000	*28999*	398	1.47	28000
29000	*29999*	413	1.40	29000
30000	*30999*	427	1.36	30000
31000	*31999*	440	1.36	31000
32000	*32999*	454	1.36	32000
33000	*33999*	468	1.36	33000
34000	*34999*	481	1.36	34000
35000	*35999*	495	1.23	35000
36000	*36999*	507	1.27	36000
37000	*37999*	520	1.30	37000
38000	*38999*	533	1.30	38000
39000	*39999*	546	1.33	39000
40000	*40999*	559	1.37	40000
41000	*41999*	573	1.40	41000
42000	*42999*	587	1.40	42000
43000	*43999*	601	1.40	43000
44000	*44999*	615	1.40	44000
45000	*45999*	629	1.40	45000
46000	*46999*	643	1.40	46000
47000	*47999*	657	1.40	47000
48000	*48999*	671	1.40	48000
49000	*49999*	685	1.40	49000
50000	*50999*	699	1.40	50000
51000	*51999*	713	1.40	51000
52000	*52999*	727	1.40	52000
53000	*53999*	741	1.40	53000
54000	*54999*	755	1.40	54000
55000	*55999*	769	1.40	55000
56000	*56999*	783	1.40	56000
57000	*57999*	797	1.40	57000
58000	*58999*	811	1.40	58000
59000	*59999*	825	1.40	59000

Federal Child Support Tables/ Tables fédérales de pensions alimentaires pour enfants

Province: Saskatchewan No. Of Children/ Nbre d'enfants: Two/Deux

Income/Revenu ($)		Monthly Award/ Paiement mensuel ($)		
From/De	To/À	Basic Amount/ Montant de base	Plus (%)	Of Income Over/Du revenu dépassant
60000	*60999*	839	1.40	60000
61000	*61999*	853	1.40	61000
62000	*62999*	868	1.40	62000
63000	*63999*	882	1.40	63000
64000	*64999*	896	1.40	64000
65000	*65999*	910	1.40	65000
66000	*66999*	924	1.40	66000
67000	*67999*	938	1.40	67000
68000	*68999*	952	1.40	68000
69000	*69999*	966	1.40	69000
70000	*70999*	980	1.32	70000
71000	*71999*	993	1.32	71000
72000	*72999*	1006	1.32	72000
73000	*73999*	1019	1.32	73000
74000	*74999*	1033	1.32	74000
75000	*75999*	1046	1.32	75000
76000	*76999*	1059	1.32	76000
77000	*77999*	1072	1.32	77000
78000	*78999*	1085	1.32	78000
79000	*79999*	1098	1.32	79000
80000	*80999*	1112	1.32	80000
81000	*81999*	1125	1.32	81000
82000	*82999*	1138	1.32	82000
83000	*83999*	1151	1.32	83000
84000	*84999*	1164	1.32	84000
85000	*85999*	1178	1.32	85000
86000	*86999*	1191	1.32	86000
87000	*87999*	1204	1.32	87000
88000	*88999*	1217	1.32	88000
89000	*89999*	1230	1.32	89000
90000	*90999*	1243	1.32	90000
91000	*91999*	1257	1.32	91000
92000	*92999*	1270	1.32	92000
93000	*93999*	1283	1.32	93000
94000	*94999*	1296	1.32	94000

Federal Child Support Tables/ Tables fédérales de pensions alimentaires pour enfants

Province: Saskatchewan No. Of Children/ Nbre d'enfants: Two/Deux

Income/Revenu ($)		Monthly Award/ Paiement mensuel ($)		
From/De	To/À	Basic Amount/ Montant de base	Plus (%)	Of Income Over/Du revenu dépassant
95000	*95999*	1309	1.32	95000
96000	*96999*	1323	1.32	96000
97000	*97999*	1336	1.32	97000
98000	*98999*	1349	1.32	98000
99000	*99999*	1362	1.32	99000
100000	*100999*	1375	1.32	100000
101000	*101999*	1388	1.32	101000
102000	*102999*	1402	1.32	102000
103000	*103999*	1415	1.29	103000
104000	*104999*	1428	1.27	104000
105000	*105999*	1440	1.27	105000
106000	*106999*	1453	1.27	106000
107000	*107999*	1466	1.27	107000
108000	*108999*	1479	1.27	108000
109000	*109999*	1491	1.27	109000
110000	*110999*	1504	1.27	110000
111000	*111999*	1517	1.27	111000
112000	*112999*	1530	1.27	112000
113000	*113999*	1542	1.26	113000
114000	*114999*	1555	1.21	114000
115000	*115999*	1567	1.21	115000
116000	*116999*	1579	1.21	116000
117000	*117999*	1591	1.21	117000
118000	*118999*	1603	1.21	118000
119000	*119999*	1615	1.21	119000
120000	*120999*	1628	1.21	120000
121000	*121999*	1640	1.21	121000
122000	*122999*	1652	1.21	122000
123000	*123999*	1664	1.21	123000
124000	*124999*	1676	1.21	124000
125000	*125999*	1688	1.21	125000
126000	*126999*	1700	1.21	126000
127000	*127999*	1712	1.21	127000
128000	*128999*	1724	1.21	128000
129000	*129999*	1736	1.21	129000

Federal Child Support Tables/ Tables fédérales de pensions alimentaires pour enfants

Province: Saskatchewan No. Of Children/ Nbre d'enfants: Two/Deux

Income/Revenu ($)		Monthly Award/ Paiement mensuel ($)		
From/De	To/À	Basic Amount/ Montant de base	Plus (%)	Of Income Over/Du revenu dépassant
130000	*130999*	1749	1.21	130000
131000	*131999*	1761	1.21	131000
132000	*132999*	1773	1.21	132000
133000	*133999*	1785	1.21	133000
134000	*134999*	1797	1.21	134000
135000	*135999*	1809	1.21	135000
136000	*136999*	1821	1.21	136000
137000	*137999*	1833	1.21	137000
138000	*138999*	1845	1.21	138000
139000	*139999*	1857	1.21	139000
140000	*140999*	1870	1.21	140000
141000	*141999*	1882	1.21	141000
142000	*142999*	1894	1.21	142000
143000	*143999*	1906	1.21	143000
144000	*144999*	1918	1.21	144000
145000	*145999*	1930	1.21	145000
146000	*146999*	1942	1.21	146000
147000	*147999*	1954	1.21	147000
148000	*148999*	1966	1.21	148000
149000	*149999*	1978	1.21	149000

Federal Child Support Tables/ Tables fédérales de pensions alimentaires pour enfants

Province: Saskatchewan No. Of Children/ Nbre d'enfants: Two/Deux

Income/Revenu ($)		Monthly Award/ Paiement mensuel ($)		
From/De	To/À	Basic Amount/ Montant de base	Plus (%)	Of Income Over/Du revenu dépassant
150000	*or greater/ ou plus*	1991	1.21	150000

Federal Child Support Tables/ Tables fédérales de pensions alimentaires pour enfants

Province: Saskatchewan No. Of Children/ Nbre d'enfants: Three/Trois

Income/Revenu ($)		Monthly Award/Paiement mensuel ($)		
From/De	To/À	Basic Amount/ Montant de base	Plus (%)	Of Income Over/Du revenu dépassant
0	*7999*	0		
8000	*8999*	0	1.70	8000
9000	*9999*	17	4.08	9000
10000	*10999*	58	4.08	10000
11000	*11999*	99	4.08	11000
12000	*12999*	139	4.08	12000
13000	*13999*	180	3.99	13000
14000	*14999*	220	3.96	14000
15000	*15999*	260	3.96	15000
16000	*16999*	299	3.96	16000
17000	*17999*	339	1.79	17000
18000	*18999*	357	1.60	18000
19000	*19999*	373	1.60	19000
20000	*20999*	389	1.60	20000
21000	*21999*	405	1.60	21000
22000	*22999*	421	1.60	22000
23000	*23999*	437	1.85	23000
24000	*24999*	456	1.89	24000

Federal Child Support Tables/ Tables fédérales de pensions alimentaires pour enfants

Province: Saskatchewan No. Of Children/ Nbre d'enfants: Three/Trois

Income/Revenu ($)		Monthly Award/Paiement mensuel ($)		
From/De	To/À	Basic Amount/ Montant de base	Plus (%)	Of Income Over/Du revenu dépassant
25000	*25999*	474	1.89	25000
26000	*26999*	493	1.89	26000
27000	*27999*	512	1.89	27000
28000	*28999*	531	1.89	28000
29000	*29999*	550	1.80	29000
30000	*30999*	568	1.75	30000
31000	*31999*	585	1.75	31000
32000	*32999*	603	1.75	32000
33000	*33999*	620	1.75	33000
34000	*34999*	638	1.75	34000
35000	*35999*	655	1.59	35000
36000	*36999*	671	1.64	36000
37000	*37999*	688	1.67	37000
38000	*38999*	704	1.67	38000
39000	*39999*	721	1.71	39000
40000	*40999*	738	1.76	40000
41000	*41999*	755	1.81	41000
42000	*42999*	774	1.81	42000
43000	*43999*	792	1.81	43000
44000	*44999*	810	1.81	44000
45000	*45999*	828	1.81	45000
46000	*46999*	846	1.81	46000
47000	*47999*	864	1.81	47000
48000	*48999*	882	1.81	48000
49000	*49999*	900	1.81	49000
50000	*50999*	918	1.81	50000
51000	*51999*	936	1.81	51000
52000	*52999*	954	1.81	52000
53000	*53999*	972	1.81	53000
54000	*54999*	990	1.81	54000
55000	*55999*	1008	1.81	55000
56000	*56999*	1026	1.81	56000
57000	*57999*	1044	1.81	57000
58000	*58999*	1062	1.81	58000
59000	*59999*	1080	1.81	59000

Federal Child Support Tables/ Tables fédérales de pensions alimentaires pour enfants

Province: Saskatchewan No. Of Children/ Nbre d'enfants: Three/Trois

Income/Revenu ($)		Monthly Award/Paiement mensuel ($)		
From/De	To/À	Basic Amount/ Montant de base	Plus (%)	Of Income Over/Du revenu dépassant
60000	*60999*	1099	1.81	60000
61000	*61999*	1117	1.81	61000
62000	*62999*	1135	1.81	62000
63000	*63999*	1153	1.81	63000
64000	*64999*	1171	1.81	64000
65000	*65999*	1189	1.81	65000
66000	*66999*	1207	1.81	66000
67000	*67999*	1225	1.81	67000
68000	*68999*	1243	1.81	68000
69000	*69999*	1261	1.81	69000
70000	*70999*	1279	1.69	70000
71000	*71999*	1296	1.69	71000
72000	*72999*	1313	1.69	72000
73000	*73999*	1330	1.69	73000
74000	*74999*	1347	1.69	74000
75000	*75999*	1364	1.69	75000
76000	*76999*	1381	1.69	76000
77000	*77999*	1398	1.69	77000
78000	*78999*	1415	1.69	78000
79000	*79999*	1432	1.69	79000
80000	*80999*	1449	1.69	80000
81000	*81999*	1465	1.69	81000
82000	*82999*	1482	1.69	82000
83000	*83999*	1499	1.69	83000
84000	*84999*	1516	1.69	84000
85000	*85999*	1533	1.69	85000
86000	*86999*	1550	1.69	86000
87000	*87999*	1567	1.69	87000
88000	*88999*	1584	1.69	88000
89000	*89999*	1601	1.69	89000
90000	*90999*	1618	1.69	90000
91000	*91999*	1635	1.69	91000
92000	*92999*	1652	1.69	92000
93000	*93999*	1669	1.69	93000
94000	*94999*	1686	1.69	94000

Federal Child Support Tables/ Tables fédérales de pensions alimentaires pour enfants

Province: Saskatchewan
No. Of Children/ Nbre d'enfants: Three/Trois

Income/Revenu ($)		Monthly Award/Paiement mensuel ($)		
From/De	**To/À**	**Basic Amount/ Montant de base**	**Plus (%)**	**Of Income Over/Du revenu dépassant**
95000	*95999*	1703	1.69	95000
96000	*96999*	1720	1.69	96000
97000	*97999*	1737	1.69	97000
98000	*98999*	1754	1.69	98000
99000	*99999*	1770	1.69	99000
100000	*100999*	1787	1.69	100000
101000	*101999*	1804	1.69	101000
102000	*102999*	1821	1.69	102000
103000	*103999*	1838	1.66	103000
104000	*104999*	1855	1.64	104000
105000	*105999*	1871	1.64	105000
106000	*106999*	1888	1.64	106000
107000	*107999*	1904	1.64	107000
108000	*108999*	1920	1.64	108000
109000	*109999*	1937	1.64	109000
110000	*110999*	1953	1.64	110000
111000	*111999*	1970	1.64	111000
112000	*112999*	1986	1.64	112000
113000	*113999*	2002	1.62	113000
114000	*114999*	2019	1.56	114000
115000	*115999*	2034	1.56	115000
116000	*116999*	2050	1.56	116000
117000	*117999*	2065	1.56	117000
118000	*118999*	2081	1.56	118000
119000	*119999*	2096	1.56	119000
120000	*120999*	2112	1.56	120000
121000	*121999*	2127	1.56	121000
122000	*122999*	2143	1.56	122000

Federal Child Support Tables/ Tables fédérales de pensions alimentaires pour enfants

Province: Saskatchewan
No. Of Children/ Nbre d'enfants: Three/Trois

Income/Revenu ($)		Monthly Award/Paiement mensuel ($)		
From/De	**To/À**	**Basic Amount/ Montant de base**	**Plus (%)**	**Of Income Over/Du revenu dépassant**
123000	*123999*	2159	1.56	123000
124000	*124999*	2174	1.56	124000
125000	*125999*	2190	1.56	125000
126000	*126999*	2205	1.56	126000
127000	*127999*	2221	1.56	127000
128000	*128999*	2236	1.56	128000
129000	*129999*	2252	1.56	129000
130000	*130999*	2267	1.56	130000
131000	*131999*	2283	1.56	131000
132000	*132999*	2299	1.56	132000
133000	*133999*	2314	1.56	133000
134000	*134999*	2330	1.56	134000
135000	*135999*	2345	1.56	135000
136000	*136999*	2361	1.56	136000
137000	*137999*	2376	1.56	137000
138000	*138999*	2392	1.56	138000
139000	*139999*	2407	1.56	139000
140000	*140999*	2423	1.56	140000
141000	*141999*	2439	1.56	141000
142000	*142999*	2454	1.56	142000
143000	*143999*	2470	1.56	143000
144000	*144999*	2485	1.56	144000
145000	*145999*	2501	1.56	145000
146000	*146999*	2516	1.56	146000
147000	*147999*	2532	1.56	147000
148000	*148999*	2547	1.56	148000
149000	*149999*	2563	1.56	149000

Federal Child Support Tables/ Tables fédérales de pensions alimentaires pour enfants

Province: Saskatchewan
No. Of Children/ Nbre d'enfants: Three/Trois

Income/Revenu ($)		Monthly Award/Paiement mensuel ($)		
From/De	To/À	Basic Amount/ Montant de base	Plus (%)	Of Income Over/Du revenu dépassant
150000	*or greater/ ou plus*	2579	1.56	150000

Federal Child Support Tables/ Tables fédérales de pensions alimentaires pour enfants

Province: Saskatchewan
No. Of Children/ Nbre d'enfants: Four/Quatre

Income/Revenu ($)		Monthly Award/ Paiement mensuel ($)		
From/De	To/À	Basic Amount/ Montant de base	Plus (%)	Of Income Over/Du revenu dépassant
0	*7999*	0		
8000	*8999*	0	1.82	8000
9000	*9999*	18	4.37	9000
10000	*10999*	62	4.37	10000
11000	*11999*	106	4.37	11000
12000	*12999*	149	4.37	12000
13000	*13999*	193	4.28	13000
14000	*14999*	236	4.25	14000
15000	*15999*	278	4.25	15000
16000	*16999*	321	4.25	16000
17000	*17999*	363	4.25	17000
18000	*18999*	406	4.25	18000
19000	*19999*	448	2.86	19000
20000	*20999*	477	1.97	20000
21000	*21999*	496	1.97	21000
22000	*22999*	516	1.97	22000
23000	*23999*	536	1.97	23000
24000	*24999*	556	1.97	24000

Federal Child Support Tables/ Tables fédérales de pensions alimentaires pour enfants

Province: Saskatchewan
No. Of Children/ Nbre d'enfants: Four/Quatre

Income/Revenu ($)		Monthly Award/ Paiement mensuel ($)		
From/De	To/À	Basic Amount/ Montant de base	Plus (%)	Of Income Over/Du revenu dépassant
25000	*25999*	575	2.00	25000
26000	*26999*	595	2.23	26000
27000	*27999*	618	2.23	27000
28000	*28999*	640	2.23	28000
29000	*29999*	662	2.13	29000
30000	*30999*	683	2.07	30000
31000	*31999*	704	2.07	31000
32000	*32999*	725	2.07	32000
33000	*33999*	745	2.07	33000
34000	*34999*	766	2.07	34000
35000	*35999*	787	1.87	35000
36000	*36999*	806	1.93	36000
37000	*37999*	825	1.97	37000
38000	*38999*	845	1.97	38000
39000	*39999*	864	2.02	39000
40000	*40999*	884	2.07	40000
41000	*41999*	905	2.13	41000
42000	*42999*	926	2.13	42000
43000	*43999*	948	2.13	43000
44000	*44999*	969	2.13	44000
45000	*45999*	990	2.13	45000
46000	*46999*	1012	2.13	46000
47000	*47999*	1033	2.13	47000
48000	*48999*	1054	2.13	48000
49000	*49999*	1076	2.13	49000
50000	*50999*	1097	2.13	50000
51000	*51999*	1118	2.13	51000
52000	*52999*	1140	2.13	52000
53000	*53999*	1161	2.13	53000
54000	*54999*	1183	2.13	54000
55000	*55999*	1204	2.13	55000
56000	*56999*	1225	2.13	56000
57000	*57999*	1247	2.13	57000
58000	*58999*	1268	2.13	58000
59000	*59999*	1289	2.13	59000

Federal Child Support Tables/ Tables fédérales de pensions alimentaires pour enfants

Province: Saskatchewan
No. Of Children/ N^bre d'enfants: Four/Quatre

Income/Revenu ($)		Monthly Award/ Paiement mensuel ($)		
From/De	**To/À**	**Basic Amount/ Montant de base**	**Plus (%)**	**Of Income Over/Du revenu dépassant**
60000	*60999*	1311	2.13	60000
61000	*61999*	1332	2.13	61000
62000	*62999*	1353	2.13	62000
63000	*63999*	1375	2.13	63000
64000	*64999*	1396	2.13	64000
65000	*65999*	1417	2.13	65000
66000	*66999*	1439	2.13	66000
67000	*67999*	1460	2.13	67000
68000	*68999*	1481	2.13	68000
69000	*69999*	1503	2.13	69000
70000	*70999*	1524	2.00	70000
71000	*71999*	1544	2.00	71000
72000	*72999*	1564	2.00	72000
73000	*73999*	1584	2.00	73000
74000	*74999*	1604	2.00	74000
75000	*75999*	1624	2.00	75000
76000	*76999*	1644	2.00	76000
77000	*77999*	1664	2.00	77000
78000	*78999*	1684	2.00	78000
79000	*79999*	1704	2.00	79000
80000	*80999*	1724	2.00	80000
81000	*81999*	1744	2.00	81000
82000	*82999*	1764	2.00	82000
83000	*83999*	1784	2.00	83000
84000	*84999*	1804	2.00	84000
85000	*85999*	1824	2.00	85000
86000	*86999*	1844	2.00	86000
87000	*87999*	1864	2.00	87000
88000	*88999*	1884	2.00	88000
89000	*89999*	1904	2.00	89000
90000	*90999*	1924	2.00	90000
91000	*91999*	1944	2.00	91000
92000	*92999*	1964	2.00	92000
93000	*93999*	1985	2.00	93000
94000	*94999*	2005	2.00	94000

Federal Child Support Tables/ Tables fédérales de pensions alimentaires pour enfants

Province: Saskatchewan
No. Of Children/ N^bre d'enfants: Four/Quatre

Income/Revenu ($)		Monthly Award/ Paiement mensuel ($)		
From/De	**To/À**	**Basic Amount/ Montant de base**	**Plus (%)**	**Of Income Over/Du revenu dépassant**
95000	*95999*	2025	2.00	95000
96000	*96999*	2045	2.00	96000
97000	*97999*	2065	2.00	97000
98000	*98999*	2085	2.00	98000
99000	*99999*	2105	2.00	99000
100000	*100999*	2125	2.00	100000
101000	*101999*	2145	2.00	101000
102000	*102999*	2165	2.00	102000
103000	*103999*	2185	1.96	103000
104000	*104999*	2204	1.94	104000
105000	*105999*	2224	1.94	105000
106000	*106999*	2243	1.94	106000
107000	*107999*	2262	1.94	107000
108000	*108999*	2282	1.94	108000
109000	*109999*	2301	1.94	109000
110000	*110999*	2321	1.94	110000
111000	*111999*	2340	1.94	111000
112000	*112999*	2359	1.94	112000
113000	*113999*	2379	1.92	113000
114000	*114999*	2398	1.84	114000
115000	*115999*	2416	1.84	115000
116000	*116999*	2435	1.84	116000
117000	*117999*	2453	1.84	117000
118000	*118999*	2471	1.84	118000
119000	*119999*	2490	1.84	119000
120000	*120999*	2508	1.84	120000
121000	*121999*	2527	1.84	121000
122000	*122999*	2545	1.84	122000
123000	*123999*	2563	1.84	123000
124000	*124999*	2582	1.84	124000
125000	*125999*	2600	1.84	125000
126000	*126999*	2618	1.84	126000
127000	*127999*	2637	1.84	127000
128000	*128999*	2655	1.84	128000
129000	*129999*	2674	1.84	129000

Federal Child Support Tables/ Tables fédérales de pensions alimentaires pour enfants

Province: Saskatchewan No. Of Children/ Nbre d'enfants: Four/Quatre

Income/Revenu ($)		Monthly Award/ Paiement mensuel ($)		
From/De	To/À	Basic Amount/ Montant de base	Plus (%)	Of Income Over/Du revenu dépassant
130000	*130999*	2692	1.84	130000
131000	*131999*	2710	1.84	131000
132000	*132999*	2729	1.84	132000
133000	*133999*	2747	1.84	133000
134000	*134999*	2765	1.84	134000
135000	*135999*	2784	1.84	135000
136000	*136999*	2802	1.84	136000
137000	*137999*	2821	1.84	137000
138000	*138999*	2839	1.84	138000
139000	*139999*	2857	1.84	139000
140000	*140999*	2876	1.84	140000
141000	*141999*	2894	1.84	141000
142000	*142999*	2913	1.84	142000
143000	*143999*	2931	1.84	143000
144000	*144999*	2949	1.84	144000
145000	*145999*	2968	1.84	145000
146000	*146999*	2986	1.84	146000
147000	*147999*	3004	1.84	147000
148000	*148999*	3023	1.84	148000
149000	*149999*	3041	1.84	149000
150000	*or greater/ ou plus*	3060	1.84	150000

Federal Child Support Tables/ Tables fédérales de pensions alimentaires pour enfants

Province: Saskatchewan No. Of Children/ Nbre d'enfants: Five/Cinq

Income/Revenu ($)		Monthly Award/ Paiement mensuel ($)		
From/De	To/À	Basic Amount/ Montant de base	Plus (%)	Of Income Over/Du revenu dépassant
0	*7999*	0		
8000	*8999*	0	1.82	8000
9000	*9999*	18	4.37	9000
10000	*10999*	62	4.37	10000
11000	*11999*	106	4.37	11000
12000	*12999*	149	4.37	12000
13000	*13999*	193	4.28	13000
14000	*14999*	236	4.25	14000
15000	*15999*	278	4.25	15000
16000	*16999*	321	4.25	16000
17000	*17999*	363	4.25	17000
18000	*18999*	406	4.25	18000
19000	*19999*	448	4.25	19000
20000	*20999*	491	4.25	20000
21000	*21999*	533	4.25	21000
22000	*22999*	576	4.25	22000
23000	*23999*	618	2.30	23000
24000	*24999*	641	2.28	24000

Federal Child Support Tables/ Tables fédérales de pensions alimentaires pour enfants

Province: Saskatchewan
No. Of Children/ Nbre d'enfants: Five/Cinq

Income/Revenu ($)		Monthly Award/ Paiement mensuel ($)		
From/De	To/À	Basic Amount/ Montant de base	Plus (%)	Of Income Over/Du revenu dépassant
25000	*25999*	664	2.28	25000
26000	*26999*	687	2.28	26000
27000	*27999*	709	2.28	27000
28000	*28999*	732	2.36	28000
29000	*29999*	756	2.40	29000
30000	*30999*	780	2.33	30000
31000	*31999*	803	2.33	31000
32000	*32999*	826	2.33	32000
33000	*33999*	850	2.33	33000
34000	*34999*	873	2.33	34000
35000	*35999*	896	2.11	35000
36000	*36999*	917	2.18	36000
37000	*37999*	939	2.22	37000
38000	*38999*	961	2.22	38000
39000	*39999*	984	2.27	39000
40000	*40999*	1006	2.34	40000
41000	*41999*	1030	2.41	41000
42000	*42999*	1054	2.41	42000
43000	*43999*	1078	2.41	43000
44000	*44999*	1102	2.41	44000
45000	*45999*	1126	2.41	45000
46000	*46999*	1150	2.41	46000
47000	*47999*	1174	2.41	47000
48000	*48999*	1198	2.41	48000
49000	*49999*	1222	2.41	49000
50000	*50999*	1246	2.41	50000
51000	*51999*	1271	2.41	51000
52000	*52999*	1295	2.41	52000
53000	*53999*	1319	2.41	53000
54000	*54999*	1343	2.41	54000
55000	*55999*	1367	2.41	55000
56000	*56999*	1391	2.41	56000
57000	*57999*	1415	2.41	57000
58000	*58999*	1439	2.41	58000
59000	*59999*	1463	2.41	59000
60000	*60999*	1487	2.41	60000
61000	*61999*	1511	2.41	61000
62000	*62999*	1535	2.41	62000
63000	*63999*	1559	2.41	63000
64000	*64999*	1584	2.41	64000
65000	*65999*	1608	2.41	65000
66000	*66999*	1632	2.41	66000
67000	*67999*	1656	2.41	67000
68000	*68999*	1680	2.41	68000
69000	*69999*	1704	2.41	69000
70000	*70999*	1728	2.26	70000
71000	*71999*	1751	2.26	71000
72000	*72999*	1773	2.26	72000
73000	*73999*	1796	2.26	73000
74000	*74999*	1818	2.26	74000
75000	*75999*	1841	2.26	75000
76000	*76999*	1864	2.26	76000
77000	*77999*	1886	2.26	77000
78000	*78999*	1909	2.26	78000
79000	*79999*	1931	2.26	79000
80000	*80999*	1954	2.26	80000
81000	*81999*	1976	2.26	81000
82000	*82999*	1999	2.26	82000
83000	*83999*	2022	2.26	83000
84000	*84999*	2044	2.26	84000
85000	*85999*	2067	2.26	85000
86000	*86999*	2089	2.26	86000
87000	*87999*	2112	2.26	87000
88000	*88999*	2135	2.26	88000
89000	*89999*	2157	2.26	89000
90000	*90999*	2180	2.26	90000
91000	*91999*	2202	2.26	91000
92000	*92999*	2225	2.26	92000
93000	*93999*	2248	2.26	93000
94000	*94999*	2270	2.26	94000

Federal Child Support Tables/ Tables fédérales de pensions alimentaires pour enfants

Province: Saskatchewan No. Of Children/ Nbre d'enfants: Five/Cinq

Income/Revenu ($)		Monthly Award/ Paiement mensuel ($)		
From/De	To/À	Basic Amount/ Montant de base	Plus (%)	Of Income Over/Du revenu dépassant
95000	*95999*	2293	2.26	95000
96000	*96999*	2315	2.26	96000
97000	*97999*	2338	2.26	97000
98000	*98999*	2361	2.26	98000
99000	*99999*	2383	2.26	99000
100000	*100999*	2406	2.26	100000
101000	*101999*	2428	2.26	101000
102000	*102999*	2451	2.26	102000
103000	*103999*	2474	2.21	103000
104000	*104999*	2496	2.19	104000
105000	*105999*	2517	2.19	105000
106000	*106999*	2539	2.19	106000
107000	*107999*	2561	2.19	107000
108000	*108999*	2583	2.19	108000
109000	*109999*	2605	2.19	109000
110000	*110999*	2627	2.19	110000
111000	*111999*	2649	2.19	111000
112000	*112999*	2670	2.19	112000
113000	*113999*	2692	2.16	113000
114000	*114999*	2714	2.07	114000
115000	*115999*	2735	2.07	115000
116000	*116999*	2755	2.07	116000
117000	*117999*	2776	2.07	117000
118000	*118999*	2797	2.07	118000
119000	*119999*	2818	2.07	119000
120000	*120999*	2838	2.07	120000
121000	*121999*	2859	2.07	121000
122000	*122999*	2880	2.07	122000

Federal Child Support Tables/ Tables fédérales de pensions alimentaires pour enfants

Province: Saskatchewan No. Of Children/ Nbre d'enfants: Five/Cinq

Income/Revenu ($)		Monthly Award/ Paiement mensuel ($)		
From/De	To/À	Basic Amount/ Montant de base	Plus (%)	Of Income Over/Du revenu dépassant
123000	*123999*	2901	2.07	123000
124000	*124999*	2921	2.07	124000
125000	*125999*	2942	2.07	125000
126000	*126999*	2963	2.07	126000
127000	*127999*	2984	2.07	127000
128000	*128999*	3004	2.07	128000
129000	*129999*	3025	2.07	129000
130000	*130999*	3046	2.07	130000
131000	*131999*	3066	2.07	131000
132000	*132999*	3087	2.07	132000
133000	*133999*	3108	2.07	133000
134000	*134999*	3129	2.07	134000
135000	*135999*	3149	2.07	135000
136000	*136999*	3170	2.07	136000
137000	*137999*	3191	2.07	137000
138000	*138999*	3212	2.07	138000
139000	*139999*	3232	2.07	139000
140000	*140999*	3253	2.07	140000
141000	*141999*	3274	2.07	141000
142000	*142999*	3295	2.07	142000
143000	*143999*	3315	2.07	143000
144000	*144999*	3336	2.07	144000
145000	*145999*	3357	2.07	145000
146000	*146999*	3378	2.07	146000
147000	*147999*	3398	2.07	147000
148000	*148999*	3419	2.07	148000
149000	*149999*	3440	2.07	149000

Federal Child Support Tables/ Tables fédérales de pensions alimentaires pour enfants

Province: Saskatchewan
No. Of Children/ Nbre d'enfants: Five/Cinq

Income/Revenu ($)		Monthly Award/ Paiement mensuel ($)		
From/De	**To/À**	**Basic Amount/ Montant de base**	**Plus (%)**	**Of Income Over/Du revenu dépassant**
150000	*or greater/ ou plus*	3461	2.07	150000

Federal Child Support Tables/ Tables fédérales de pensions alimentaires pour enfants

Province: Saskatchewan
No. Of Children/ Nbre d'enfants: Six or more/ Six ou plus

Income/Revenu ($)		Monthly Award/ Paiement mensuel ($)		
From/De	**To/À**	**Basic Amount/ Montant de base**	**Plus (%)**	**Of Income Over/Du revenu dépassant**
0	*7999*	0		
8000	*8999*	0	1.82	8000
9000	*9999*	18	4.37	9000
10000	*10999*	62	4.37	10000
11000	*11999*	106	4.37	11000
12000	*12999*	149	4.37	12000
13000	*13999*	193	4.28	13000
14000	*14999*	236	4.25	14000
15000	*15999*	278	4.25	15000
16000	*16999*	321	4.25	16000
17000	*17999*	363	4.25	17000
18000	*18999*	406	4.25	18000
19000	*19999*	448	4.25	19000
20000	*20999*	491	4.25	20000
21000	*21999*	533	4.25	21000
22000	*22999*	576	4.25	22000
23000	*23999*	618	4.25	23000
24000	*24999*	660	4.25	24000

Federal Child Support Tables/ Tables fédérales de pensions alimentaires pour enfants

Province: Saskatchewan
No. Of Children/ Nbre d'enfants: Six or more/ Six ou plus

Income/Revenu ($)		Monthly Award/ Paiement mensuel ($)		
From/De	**To/À**	**Basic Amount/ Montant de base**	**Plus (%)**	**Of Income Over/Du revenu dépassant**
25000	*25999*	703	4.25	25000
26000	*26999*	745	4.25	26000
27000	*27999*	788	2.70	27000
28000	*28999*	815	2.54	28000
29000	*29999*	840	2.41	29000
30000	*30999*	864	2.34	30000
31000	*31999*	888	2.46	31000
32000	*32999*	912	2.56	32000
33000	*33999*	938	2.56	33000
34000	*34999*	963	2.56	34000
35000	*35999*	989	2.32	35000
36000	*36999*	1012	2.39	36000
37000	*37999*	1036	2.43	37000
38000	*38999*	1060	2.43	38000
39000	*39999*	1085	2.49	39000
40000	*40999*	1110	2.57	40000
41000	*41999*	1135	2.64	41000
42000	*42999*	1162	2.64	42000
43000	*43999*	1188	2.64	43000
44000	*44999*	1214	2.64	44000
45000	*45999*	1241	2.64	45000
46000	*46999*	1267	2.64	46000
47000	*47999*	1294	2.64	47000
48000	*48999*	1320	2.64	48000
49000	*49999*	1346	2.64	49000
50000	*50999*	1373	2.64	50000
51000	*51999*	1399	2.64	51000
52000	*52999*	1426	2.64	52000
53000	*53999*	1452	2.64	53000
54000	*54999*	1478	2.64	54000
55000	*55999*	1505	2.64	55000
56000	*56999*	1531	2.64	56000
57000	*57999*	1558	2.64	57000
58000	*58999*	1584	2.64	58000
59000	*59999*	1610	2.64	59000

Federal Child Support Tables/ Tables fédérales de pensions alimentaires pour enfants

Province: Saskatchewan No. Of Children/ Nbre d'enfants: Six or more/ Six ou plus

Income/Revenu ($)		Monthly Award/ Paiement mensuel ($)		
From/De	To/À	Basic Amount/ Montant de base	Plus (%)	Of Income Over/Du revenu dépassant
60000	*60999*	1637	2.64	60000
61000	*61999*	1663	2.64	61000
62000	*62999*	1689	2.64	62000
63000	*63999*	1716	2.64	63000
64000	*64999*	1742	2.64	64000
65000	*65999*	1769	2.64	65000
66000	*66999*	1795	2.64	66000
67000	*67999*	1821	2.64	67000
68000	*68999*	1848	2.64	68000
69000	*69999*	1874	2.64	69000
70000	*70999*	1901	2.48	70000
71000	*71999*	1925	2.48	71000
72000	*72999*	1950	2.48	72000
73000	*73999*	1975	2.48	73000
74000	*74999*	2000	2.48	74000
75000	*75999*	2024	2.48	75000
76000	*76999*	2049	2.48	76000
77000	*77999*	2074	2.48	77000
78000	*78999*	2099	2.48	78000
79000	*79999*	2123	2.48	79000
80000	*80999*	2148	2.48	80000
81000	*81999*	2173	2.48	81000
82000	*82999*	2198	2.48	82000
83000	*83999*	2223	2.48	83000
84000	*84999*	2247	2.48	84000
85000	*85999*	2272	2.48	85000
86000	*86999*	2297	2.48	86000
87000	*87999*	2322	2.48	87000
88000	*88999*	2346	2.48	88000
89000	*89999*	2371	2.48	89000
90000	*90999*	2396	2.48	90000
91000	*91999*	2421	2.48	91000
92000	*92999*	2445	2.48	92000
93000	*93999*	2470	2.48	93000
94000	*94999*	2495	2.48	94000

Federal Child Support Tables/ Tables fédérales de pensions alimentaires pour enfants

Province: Saskatchewan No. Of Children/ Nbre d'enfants: Six or more/ Six ou plus

Income/Revenu ($)		Monthly Award/ Paiement mensuel ($)		
From/De	To/À	Basic Amount/ Montant de base	Plus (%)	Of Income Over/Du revenu dépassant
95000	*95999*	2520	2.48	95000
96000	*96999*	2544	2.48	96000
97000	*97999*	2569	2.48	97000
98000	*98999*	2594	2.48	98000
99000	*99999*	2619	2.48	99000
100000	*100999*	2644	2.48	100000
101000	*101999*	2668	2.48	101000
102000	*102999*	2693	2.48	102000
103000	*103999*	2718	2.42	103000
104000	*104999*	2742	2.40	104000
105000	*105999*	2766	2.40	105000
106000	*106999*	2790	2.40	106000
107000	*107999*	2814	2.40	107000
108000	*108999*	2838	2.40	108000
109000	*109999*	2862	2.40	109000
110000	*110999*	2886	2.40	110000
111000	*111999*	2910	2.40	111000
112000	*112999*	2934	2.40	112000
113000	*113999*	2958	2.37	113000
114000	*114999*	2981	2.27	114000
115000	*115999*	3004	2.27	115000
116000	*116999*	3027	2.27	116000
117000	*117999*	3050	2.27	117000
118000	*118999*	3072	2.27	118000
119000	*119999*	3095	2.27	119000
120000	*120999*	3118	2.27	120000
121000	*121999*	3140	2.27	121000
122000	*122999*	3163	2.27	122000
123000	*123999*	3186	2.27	123000
124000	*124999*	3209	2.27	124000
125000	*125999*	3231	2.27	125000
126000	*126999*	3254	2.27	126000
127000	*127999*	3277	2.27	127000
128000	*128999*	3300	2.27	128000
129000	*129999*	3322	2.27	129000

Federal Child Support Tables/ Tables fédérales de pensions alimentaires pour enfants

Province: Saskatchewan
No. Of Children/ Nbre d'enfants: Six or more/ Six ou plus

Income/Revenu ($)		Monthly Award/ Paiement mensuel ($)		
From/De	To/À	Basic Amount/ Montant de base	Plus (%)	Of Income Over/Du revenu dépassant
130000	*130999*	3345	2.27	130000
131000	*131999*	3368	2.27	131000
132000	*132999*	3391	2.27	132000
133000	*133999*	3413	2.27	133000
134000	*134999*	3436	2.27	134000
135000	*135999*	3459	2.27	135000
136000	*136999*	3481	2.27	136000
137000	*137999*	3504	2.27	137000
138000	*138999*	3527	2.27	138000
139000	*139999*	3550	2.27	139000
140000	*140999*	3572	2.27	140000
141000	*141999*	3595	2.27	141000
142000	*142999*	3618	2.27	142000
143000	*143999*	3641	2.27	143000
144000	*144999*	3663	2.27	144000
145000	*145999*	3686	2.27	145000
146000	*146999*	3709	2.27	146000
147000	*147999*	3732	2.27	147000
148000	*148999*	3754	2.27	148000
149000	*149999*	3777	2.27	149000
150000	*or greater/ ou plus*	3800	2.27	150000

Federal Child Support Tables/ Tables fédérales de pensions alimentaires pour enfants

Province: Alberta
No. Of Children/ Nbre d'enfants: One/Un

Income/Revenu ($)		Monthly Award/ Paiement mensuel ($)		
From/De	To/À	Basic Amount/ Montant de base	Plus (%)	Of Income Over/Du revenu dépassant
0	*7999*	0		
8000	*8999*	0	1.06	8000
9000	*9999*	11	2.11	9000
10000	*10999*	32	2.11	10000
11000	*11999*	53	2.11	11000
12000	*12999*	74	2.11	12000
13000	*13999*	95	2.11	13000
14000	*14999*	116	2.11	14000
15000	*15999*	137	1.97	15000
16000	*16999*	157	0.63	16000
17000	*17999*	163	0.63	17000
18000	*18999*	170	0.63	18000
19000	*19999*	176	0.63	19000
20000	*20999*	182	0.63	20000
21000	*21999*	189	0.63	21000
22000	*22999*	195	0.63	22000
23000	*23999*	201	0.63	23000
24000	*24999*	208	0.63	24000

Federal Child Support Tables/ Tables fédérales de pensions alimentaires pour enfants

Province: Alberta
No. Of Children/ Nbre d'enfants: One/Un

Income/Revenu ($)		Monthly Award/ Paiement mensuel ($)		
From/De	**To/À**	**Basic Amount/ Montant de base**	**Plus (%)**	**Of Income Over/Du revenu dépassant**
25000	*25999*	214	0.63	25000
26000	*26999*	220	0.63	26000
27000	*27999*	227	0.63	27000
28000	*28999*	233	0.63	28000
29000	*29999*	239	0.59	29000
30000	*30999*	245	0.69	30000
31000	*31999*	252	0.89	31000
32000	*32999*	261	0.89	32000
33000	*33999*	270	0.89	33000
34000	*34999*	279	0.89	34000
35000	*35999*	288	0.81	35000
36000	*36999*	296	0.85	36000
37000	*37999*	304	0.87	37000
38000	*38999*	313	0.87	38000
39000	*39999*	322	0.89	39000
40000	*40999*	331	0.92	40000
41000	*41999*	340	0.94	41000
42000	*42999*	349	0.94	42000
43000	*43999*	359	0.94	43000
44000	*44999*	368	0.94	44000
45000	*45999*	378	0.94	45000
46000	*46999*	387	0.94	46000
47000	*47999*	396	0.94	47000
48000	*48999*	406	0.94	48000
49000	*49999*	415	0.94	49000
50000	*50999*	425	0.94	50000
51000	*51999*	434	0.94	51000
52000	*52999*	444	0.94	52000
53000	*53999*	453	0.94	53000
54000	*54999*	463	0.94	54000
55000	*55999*	472	0.94	55000
56000	*56999*	481	0.94	56000
57000	*57999*	491	0.94	57000
58000	*58999*	500	0.94	58000
59000	*59999*	510	0.94	59000

Federal Child Support Tables/ Tables fédérales de pensions alimentaires pour enfants

Province: Alberta
No. Of Children/ Nbre d'enfants: One/Un

Income/Revenu ($)		Monthly Award/ Paiement mensuel ($)		
From/De	**To/À**	**Basic Amount/ Montant de base**	**Plus (%)**	**Of Income Over/Du revenu dépassant**
60000	*60999*	519	0.94	60000
61000	*61999*	529	0.94	61000
62000	*62999*	538	0.94	62000
63000	*63999*	548	0.94	63000
64000	*64999*	557	0.94	64000
65000	*65999*	566	0.94	65000
66000	*66999*	576	0.94	66000
67000	*67999*	585	0.94	67000
68000	*68999*	595	0.94	68000
69000	*69999*	604	0.94	69000
70000	*70999*	614	0.89	70000
71000	*71999*	623	0.89	71000
72000	*72999*	631	0.89	72000
73000	*73999*	640	0.89	73000
74000	*74999*	649	0.89	74000
75000	*75999*	658	0.89	75000
76000	*76999*	667	0.89	76000
77000	*77999*	676	0.89	77000
78000	*78999*	685	0.89	78000
79000	*79999*	694	0.89	79000
80000	*80999*	703	0.89	80000
81000	*81999*	711	0.89	81000
82000	*82999*	720	0.89	82000
83000	*83999*	729	0.89	83000
84000	*84999*	738	0.89	84000
85000	*85999*	747	0.89	85000
86000	*86999*	756	0.89	86000
87000	*87999*	765	0.89	87000
88000	*88999*	774	0.89	88000
89000	*89999*	783	0.89	89000
90000	*90999*	791	0.89	90000
91000	*91999*	800	0.89	91000
92000	*92999*	809	0.89	92000
93000	*93999*	818	0.89	93000
94000	*94999*	827	0.89	94000

Federal Child Support Tables/ Tables fédérales de pensions alimentaires pour enfants

Province: Alberta No. Of Children/ Nbre d'enfants: One/Un

Income/Revenu ($)		Monthly Award/ Paiement mensuel ($)		
From/De	To/À	Basic Amount/ Montant de base	Plus (%)	Of Income Over/Du revenu dépassant
95000	*95999*	836	0.89	95000
96000	*96999*	845	0.89	96000
97000	*97999*	854	0.89	97000
98000	*98999*	863	0.89	98000
99000	*99999*	871	0.89	99000
100000	*100999*	880	0.89	100000
101000	*101999*	889	0.89	101000
102000	*102999*	898	0.89	102000
103000	*103999*	907	0.89	103000
104000	*104999*	916	0.89	104000
105000	*105999*	925	0.89	105000
106000	*106999*	934	0.89	106000
107000	*107999*	943	0.89	107000
108000	*108999*	951	0.89	108000
109000	*109999*	960	0.89	109000
110000	*110999*	969	0.89	110000
111000	*111999*	978	0.89	111000
112000	*112999*	987	0.89	112000
113000	*113999*	996	0.88	113000
114000	*114999*	1005	0.85	114000
115000	*115999*	1013	0.85	115000
116000	*116999*	1022	0.85	116000
117000	*117999*	1030	0.85	117000
118000	*118999*	1039	0.85	118000
119000	*119999*	1047	0.85	119000
120000	*120999*	1056	0.85	120000
121000	*121999*	1064	0.85	121000
122000	*122999*	1072	0.85	122000

Federal Child Support Tables/ Tables fédérales de pensions alimentaires pour enfants

Province: Alberta No. Of Children/ Nbre d'enfants: One/Un

Income/Revenu ($)		Monthly Award/ Paiement mensuel ($)		
From/De	To/À	Basic Amount/ Montant de base	Plus (%)	Of Income Over/Du revenu dépassant
123000	*123999*	1081	0.85	123000
124000	*124999*	1089	0.85	124000
125000	*125999*	1098	0.85	125000
126000	*126999*	1106	0.85	126000
127000	*127999*	1115	0.85	127000
128000	*128999*	1123	0.85	128000
129000	*129999*	1132	0.85	129000
130000	*130999*	1140	0.85	130000
131000	*131999*	1149	0.85	131000
132000	*132999*	1157	0.85	132000
133000	*133999*	1166	0.85	133000
134000	*134999*	1174	0.85	134000
135000	*135999*	1183	0.85	135000
136000	*136999*	1191	0.85	136000
137000	*137999*	1200	0.85	137000
138000	*138999*	1208	0.85	138000
139000	*139999*	1216	0.85	139000
140000	*140999*	1225	0.85	140000
141000	*141999*	1233	0.85	141000
142000	*142999*	1242	0.85	142000
143000	*143999*	1250	0.85	143000
144000	*144999*	1259	0.85	144000
145000	*145999*	1267	0.85	145000
146000	*146999*	1276	0.85	146000
147000	*147999*	1284	0.85	147000
148000	*148999*	1293	0.85	148000
149000	*149999*	1301	0.85	149000

Federal Child Support Tables/ Tables fédérales de pensions alimentaires pour enfants

Province: Alberta No. Of Children/ Nbre d'enfants: One/Un

Income/Revenu ($)		Monthly Award/ Paiement mensuel ($)		
From/De	To/À	Basic Amount/ Montant de base	Plus (%)	Of Income Over/Du revenu dépassant
150000	*or greater/ ou plus*	1310	0.85	150000

Federal Child Support Tables/ Tables fédérales de pensions alimentaires pour enfants

Province: Alberta No. Of Children/ Nbre d'enfants: Two/Deux

Income/Revenu ($)		Monthly Award/ Paiement mensuel ($)		
From/De	To/À	Basic Amount/ Montant de base	Plus (%)	Of Income Over/Du revenu dépassant
0	*7999*	0		
8000	*8999*	0	1.75	8000
9000	*9999*	17	4.34	9000
10000	*10999*	61	4.34	10000
11000	*11999*	104	4.34	11000
12000	*12999*	148	4.34	12000
13000	*13999*	191	4.26	13000
14000	*14999*	234	2.76	14000
15000	*15999*	261	0.97	15000
16000	*16999*	271	1.20	16000
17000	*17999*	283	1.20	17000
18000	*18999*	295	1.20	18000
19000	*19999*	307	1.20	19000
20000	*20999*	319	1.20	20000
21000	*21999*	331	1.20	21000
22000	*22999*	343	1.20	22000
23000	*23999*	355	1.20	23000
24000	*24999*	367	1.20	24000

Federal Child Support Tables/ Tables fédérales de pensions alimentaires pour enfants

Province: Alberta No. Of Children/ Nbre d'enfants: Two/Deux

Income/Revenu ($)		Monthly Award/ Paiement mensuel ($)		
From/De	To/À	Basic Amount/ Montant de base	Plus (%)	Of Income Over/Du revenu dépassant
25000	*25999*	379	1.20	25000
26000	*26999*	391	1.20	26000
27000	*27999*	403	1.20	27000
28000	*28999*	415	1.20	28000
29000	*29999*	427	1.13	29000
30000	*30999*	439	1.20	30000
31000	*31999*	451	1.38	31000
32000	*32999*	464	1.38	32000
33000	*33999*	478	1.38	33000
34000	*34999*	492	1.38	34000
35000	*35999*	506	1.25	35000
36000	*36999*	518	1.33	36000
37000	*37999*	532	1.36	37000
38000	*38999*	545	1.36	38000
39000	*39999*	559	1.39	39000
40000	*40999*	573	1.43	40000
41000	*41999*	587	1.47	41000
42000	*42999*	602	1.47	42000
43000	*43999*	616	1.47	43000
44000	*44999*	631	1.47	44000
45000	*45999*	646	1.47	45000
46000	*46999*	660	1.47	46000
47000	*47999*	675	1.47	47000
48000	*48999*	690	1.47	48000
49000	*49999*	704	1.47	49000
50000	*50999*	719	1.47	50000
51000	*51999*	734	1.47	51000
52000	*52999*	749	1.47	52000
53000	*53999*	763	1.47	53000
54000	*54999*	778	1.47	54000
55000	*55999*	793	1.47	55000
56000	*56999*	807	1.47	56000
57000	*57999*	822	1.47	57000
58000	*58999*	837	1.47	58000
59000	*59999*	851	1.47	59000

Federal Child Support Tables/ Tables fédérales de pensions alimentaires pour enfants

Province: Alberta No. Of Children/ Nbre d'enfants: Two/Deux

Income/Revenu ($)		Monthly Award/ Paiement mensuel ($)		
From/De	To/À	Basic Amount/ Montant de base	Plus (%)	Of Income Over/Du revenu dépassant
60000	60999	866	1.47	60000
61000	61999	881	1.47	61000
62000	62999	895	1.47	62000
63000	63999	910	1.47	63000
64000	64999	925	1.47	64000
65000	65999	940	1.47	65000
66000	66999	954	1.47	66000
67000	67999	969	1.47	67000
68000	68999	984	1.47	68000
69000	69999	998	1.47	69000
70000	70999	1013	1.38	70000
71000	71999	1027	1.38	71000
72000	72999	1041	1.38	72000
73000	73999	1054	1.38	73000
74000	74999	1068	1.38	74000
75000	75999	1082	1.38	75000
76000	76999	1096	1.38	76000
77000	77999	1110	1.38	77000
78000	78999	1124	1.38	78000
79000	79999	1137	1.38	79000
80000	80999	1151	1.38	80000
81000	81999	1165	1.38	81000
82000	82999	1179	1.38	82000
83000	83999	1193	1.38	83000
84000	84999	1207	1.38	84000
85000	85999	1220	1.38	85000
86000	86999	1234	1.38	86000
87000	87999	1248	1.38	87000
88000	88999	1262	1.38	88000
89000	89999	1276	1.38	89000
90000	90999	1290	1.38	90000
91000	91999	1303	1.38	91000
92000	92999	1317	1.38	92000
93000	93999	1331	1.38	93000
94000	94999	1345	1.38	94000

Federal Child Support Tables/ Tables fédérales de pensions alimentaires pour enfants

Province: Alberta No. Of Children/ Nbre d'enfants: Two/Deux

Income/Revenu ($)		Monthly Award/ Paiement mensuel ($)		
From/De	To/À	Basic Amount/ Montant de base	Plus (%)	Of Income Over/Du revenu dépassant
95000	95999	1359	1.38	95000
96000	96999	1372	1.38	96000
97000	97999	1386	1.38	97000
98000	98999	1400	1.38	98000
99000	99999	1414	1.38	99000
100000	100999	1428	1.38	100000
101000	101999	1442	1.38	101000
102000	102999	1455	1.38	102000
103000	103999	1469	1.38	103000
104000	104999	1483	1.38	104000
105000	105999	1497	1.38	105000
106000	106999	1511	1.38	106000
107000	107999	1525	1.38	107000
108000	108999	1538	1.38	108000
109000	109999	1552	1.38	109000
110000	110999	1566	1.38	110000
111000	111999	1580	1.38	111000
112000	112999	1594	1.38	112000
113000	113999	1608	1.37	113000
114000	114999	1621	1.32	114000
115000	115999	1634	1.32	115000
116000	116999	1648	1.32	116000
117000	117999	1661	1.32	117000
118000	118999	1674	1.32	118000
119000	119999	1687	1.32	119000
120000	120999	1700	1.32	120000
121000	121999	1713	1.32	121000
122000	122999	1727	1.32	122000
123000	123999	1740	1.32	123000
124000	124999	1753	1.32	124000
125000	125999	1766	1.32	125000
126000	126999	1779	1.32	126000
127000	127999	1793	1.32	127000
128000	128999	1806	1.32	128000
129000	129999	1819	1.32	129000

Federal Child Support Tables/ Tables fédérales de pensions alimentaires pour enfants

Province: Alberta No. Of Children/ Nbre d'enfants: Two/Deux

Income/Revenu ($)		Monthly Award/ Paiement mensuel ($)		
From/De	**To/À**	**Basic Amount/ Montant de base**	**Plus (%)**	**Of Income Over/Du revenu dépassant**
130000	*130999*	1832	1.32	130000
131000	*131999*	1845	1.32	131000
132000	*132999*	1858	1.32	132000
133000	*133999*	1872	1.32	133000
134000	*134999*	1885	1.32	134000
135000	*135999*	1898	1.32	135000
136000	*136999*	1911	1.32	136000
137000	*137999*	1924	1.32	137000
138000	*138999*	1938	1.32	138000
139000	*139999*	1951	1.32	139000
140000	*140999*	1964	1.32	140000
141000	*141999*	1977	1.32	141000
142000	*142999*	1990	1.32	142000
143000	*143999*	2003	1.32	143000
144000	*144999*	2017	1.32	144000
145000	*145999*	2030	1.32	145000
146000	*146999*	2043	1.32	146000
147000	*147999*	2056	1.32	147000
148000	*148999*	2069	1.32	148000
149000	*149999*	2082	1.32	149000
150000	*or greater/ ou plus*	2096	1.32	150000

Federal Child Support Tables/ Tables fédérales de pensions alimentaires pour enfants

Province: Alberta No. Of Children/ Nbre d'enfants: Three/Trois

Income/Revenu ($)		Monthly Award/ Paiement mensuel ($)		
From/De	**To/À**	**Basic Amount/ Montant de base**	**Plus (%)**	**Of Income Over/Du revenu dépassant**
0	*7999*	0		
8000	*8999*	0	1.88	8000
9000	*9999*	19	4.68	9000
10000	*10999*	66	4.68	10000
11000	*11999*	112	4.68	11000
12000	*12999*	159	4.68	12000
13000	*13999*	206	4.59	13000
14000	*14999*	252	4.56	14000
15000	*15999*	297	4.14	15000
16000	*16999*	339	4.02	16000
17000	*17999*	379	1.65	17000
18000	*18999*	395	1.65	18000
19000	*19999*	412	1.65	19000
20000	*20999*	429	1.65	20000
21000	*21999*	445	1.65	21000
22000	*22999*	462	1.65	22000
23000	*23999*	478	1.65	23000
24000	*24999*	495	1.65	24000

Federal Child Support Tables/ Tables fédérales de pensions alimentaires pour enfants

Province: Alberta
No. Of Children/ Nbre d'enfants: Three/Trois

Income/Revenu ($)		Monthly Award/ Paiement mensuel ($)		
From/De	To/À	Basic Amount/ Montant de base	Plus (%)	Of Income Over/Du revenu dépassant
25000	*25999*	511	1.65	25000
26000	*26999*	528	1.65	26000
27000	*27999*	544	1.65	27000
28000	*28999*	561	1.65	28000
29000	*29999*	577	1.57	29000
30000	*30999*	593	1.61	30000
31000	*31999*	609	1.77	31000
32000	*32999*	627	1.77	32000
33000	*33999*	645	1.77	33000
34000	*34999*	663	1.77	34000
35000	*35999*	680	1.61	35000
36000	*36999*	696	1.71	36000
37000	*37999*	713	1.75	37000
38000	*38999*	731	1.75	38000
39000	*39999*	748	1.79	39000
40000	*40999*	766	1.84	40000
41000	*41999*	785	1.89	41000
42000	*42999*	804	1.89	42000
43000	*43999*	822	1.89	43000
44000	*44999*	841	1.89	44000
45000	*45999*	860	1.89	45000
46000	*46999*	879	1.89	46000
47000	*47999*	898	1.89	47000
48000	*48999*	917	1.89	48000
49000	*49999*	936	1.89	49000
50000	*50999*	955	1.89	50000
51000	*51999*	974	1.89	51000
52000	*52999*	992	1.89	52000
53000	*53999*	1011	1.89	53000
54000	*54999*	1030	1.89	54000
55000	*55999*	1049	1.89	55000
56000	*56999*	1068	1.89	56000
57000	*57999*	1087	1.89	57000
58000	*58999*	1106	1.89	58000
59000	*59999*	1125	1.89	59000

Federal Child Support Tables/ Tables fédérales de pensions alimentaires pour enfants

Province: Alberta
No. Of Children/ Nbre d'enfants: Three/Trois

Income/Revenu ($)		Monthly Award/ Paiement mensuel ($)		
From/De	To/À	Basic Amount/ Montant de base	Plus (%)	Of Income Over/Du revenu dépassant
60000	*60999*	1144	1.89	60000
61000	*61999*	1162	1.89	61000
62000	*62999*	1181	1.89	62000
63000	*63999*	1200	1.89	63000
64000	*64999*	1219	1.89	64000
65000	*65999*	1238	1.89	65000
66000	*66999*	1257	1.89	66000
67000	*67999*	1276	1.89	67000
68000	*68999*	1295	1.89	68000
69000	*69999*	1314	1.89	69000
70000	*70999*	1332	1.78	70000
71000	*71999*	1350	1.78	71000
72000	*72999*	1368	1.78	72000
73000	*73999*	1386	1.78	73000
74000	*74999*	1404	1.78	74000
75000	*75999*	1421	1.78	75000
76000	*76999*	1439	1.78	76000
77000	*77999*	1457	1.78	77000
78000	*78999*	1475	1.78	78000
79000	*79999*	1492	1.78	79000
80000	*80999*	1510	1.78	80000
81000	*81999*	1528	1.78	81000
82000	*82999*	1546	1.78	82000
83000	*83999*	1564	1.78	83000
84000	*84999*	1581	1.78	84000
85000	*85999*	1599	1.78	85000
86000	*86999*	1617	1.78	86000
87000	*87999*	1635	1.78	87000
88000	*88999*	1652	1.78	88000
89000	*89999*	1670	1.78	89000
90000	*90999*	1688	1.78	90000
91000	*91999*	1706	1.78	91000
92000	*92999*	1724	1.78	92000
93000	*93999*	1741	1.78	93000
94000	*94999*	1759	1.78	94000

Federal Child Support Tables/ Tables fédérales de pensions alimentaires pour enfants

Province: Alberta
No. Of Children/ Nbre d'enfants: Three/Trois

Income/Revenu ($)		Monthly Award/ Paiement mensuel ($)		
From/De	To/À	Basic Amount/ Montant de base	Plus (%)	Of Income Over/Du revenu dépassant
95000	*95999*	1777	1.78	95000
96000	*96999*	1795	1.78	96000
97000	*97999*	1812	1.78	97000
98000	*98999*	1830	1.78	98000
99000	*99999*	1848	1.78	99000
100000	*100999*	1866	1.78	100000
101000	*101999*	1884	1.78	101000
102000	*102999*	1901	1.78	102000
103000	*103999*	1919	1.78	103000
104000	*104999*	1937	1.78	104000
105000	*105999*	1955	1.78	105000
106000	*106999*	1972	1.78	106000
107000	*107999*	1990	1.78	107000
108000	*108999*	2008	1.78	108000
109000	*109999*	2026	1.78	109000
110000	*110999*	2044	1.78	110000
111000	*111999*	2061	1.78	111000
112000	*112999*	2079	1.78	112000
113000	*113999*	2097	1.76	113000
114000	*114999*	2114	1.69	114000
115000	*115999*	2131	1.69	115000
116000	*116999*	2148	1.69	116000
117000	*117999*	2165	1.69	117000
118000	*118999*	2182	1.69	118000
119000	*119999*	2199	1.69	119000
120000	*120999*	2216	1.69	120000
121000	*121999*	2233	1.69	121000
122000	*122999*	2250	1.69	122000

Federal Child Support Tables/ Tables fédérales de pensions alimentaires pour enfants

Province: Alberta
No. Of Children/ Nbre d'enfants: Three/Trois

Income/Revenu ($)		Monthly Award/ Paiement mensuel ($)		
From/De	To/À	Basic Amount/ Montant de base	Plus (%)	Of Income Over/Du revenu dépassant
123000	*123999*	2267	1.69	123000
124000	*124999*	2284	1.69	124000
125000	*125999*	2301	1.69	125000
126000	*126999*	2318	1.69	126000
127000	*127999*	2335	1.69	127000
128000	*128999*	2352	1.69	128000
129000	*129999*	2369	1.69	129000
130000	*130999*	2386	1.69	130000
131000	*131999*	2403	1.69	131000
132000	*132999*	2419	1.69	132000
133000	*133999*	2436	1.69	133000
134000	*134999*	2453	1.69	134000
135000	*135999*	2470	1.69	135000
136000	*136999*	2487	1.69	136000
137000	*137999*	2504	1.69	137000
138000	*138999*	2521	1.69	138000
139000	*139999*	2538	1.69	139000
140000	*140999*	2555	1.69	140000
141000	*141999*	2572	1.69	141000
142000	*142999*	2589	1.69	142000
143000	*143999*	2606	1.69	143000
144000	*144999*	2623	1.69	144000
145000	*145999*	2640	1.69	145000
146000	*146999*	2657	1.69	146000
147000	*147999*	2674	1.69	147000
148000	*148999*	2691	1.69	148000
149000	*149999*	2708	1.69	149000

Federal Child Support Tables/ Tables fédérales de pensions alimentaires pour enfants

Province: Alberta No. Of Children/ Nbre d'enfants: Three/Trois

Income/Revenu ($)		Monthly Award/ Paiement mensuel ($)		
From/De	To/À	Basic Amount/ Montant de base	Plus (%)	Of Income Over/Du revenu dépassant
150000	*or greater/ ou plus*	2724	1.69	150000

Federal Child Support Tables/ Tables fédérales de pensions alimentaires pour enfants

Province: Alberta No. Of Children/ Nbre d'enfants: Four/Quatre

Income/Revenu ($)		Monthly Award/ Paiement mensuel ($)		
From/De	To/À	Basic Amount/ Montant de base	Plus (%)	Of Income Over/Du revenu dépassant
0	*7999*	0		
8000	*8999*	0	2.01	8000
9000	*9999*	20	5.01	9000
10000	*10999*	70	5.01	10000
11000	*11999*	120	5.01	11000
12000	*12999*	170	5.01	12000
13000	*13999*	221	4.92	13000
14000	*14999*	270	4.89	14000
15000	*15999*	319	4.43	15000
16000	*16999*	363	4.30	16000
17000	*17999*	406	4.30	17000
18000	*18999*	449	4.30	18000
19000	*19999*	492	2.60	19000
20000	*20999*	518	2.03	20000
21000	*21999*	538	2.03	21000
22000	*22999*	559	2.03	22000
23000	*23999*	579	2.03	23000
24000	*24999*	599	2.03	24000

Federal Child Support Tables/ Tables fédérales de pensions alimentaires pour enfants

Province: Alberta No. Of Children/ Nbre d'enfants: Four/Quatre

Income/Revenu ($)		Monthly Award/ Paiement mensuel ($)		
From/De	To/À	Basic Amount/ Montant de base	Plus (%)	Of Income Over/Du revenu dépassant
25000	*25999*	619	2.03	25000
26000	*26999*	640	2.03	26000
27000	*27999*	660	2.03	27000
28000	*28999*	680	2.03	28000
29000	*29999*	700	1.92	29000
30000	*30999*	720	1.95	30000
31000	*31999*	739	2.10	31000
32000	*32999*	760	2.10	32000
33000	*33999*	781	2.10	33000
34000	*34999*	802	2.10	34000
35000	*35999*	823	1.90	35000
36000	*36999*	842	2.02	36000
37000	*37999*	862	2.06	37000
38000	*38999*	883	2.06	38000
39000	*39999*	904	2.11	39000
40000	*40999*	925	2.17	40000
41000	*41999*	946	2.23	41000
42000	*42999*	969	2.23	42000
43000	*43999*	991	2.23	43000
44000	*44999*	1013	2.23	44000
45000	*45999*	1036	2.23	45000
46000	*46999*	1058	2.23	46000
47000	*47999*	1080	2.23	47000
48000	*48999*	1103	2.23	48000
49000	*49999*	1125	2.23	49000
50000	*50999*	1147	2.23	50000
51000	*51999*	1170	2.23	51000
52000	*52999*	1192	2.23	52000
53000	*53999*	1214	2.23	53000
54000	*54999*	1237	2.23	54000
55000	*55999*	1259	2.23	55000
56000	*56999*	1281	2.23	56000
57000	*57999*	1304	2.23	57000
58000	*58999*	1326	2.23	58000
59000	*59999*	1348	2.23	59000

Federal Child Support Tables/ Tables fédérales de pensions alimentaires pour enfants

Province: Alberta No. Of Children/ Nbre d'enfants: Four/Quatre

Income/Revenu ($)		Monthly Award/ Paiement mensuel ($)		
From/De	To/À	Basic Amount/ Montant de base	Plus (%)	Of Income Over/Du revenu dépassant
60000	*60999*	1371	2.23	60000
61000	*61999*	1393	2.23	61000
62000	*62999*	1415	2.23	62000
63000	*63999*	1438	2.23	63000
64000	*64999*	1460	2.23	64000
65000	*65999*	1482	2.23	65000
66000	*66999*	1504	2.23	66000
67000	*67999*	1527	2.23	67000
68000	*68999*	1549	2.23	68000
69000	*69999*	1571	2.23	69000
70000	*70999*	1594	2.10	70000
71000	*71999*	1615	2.10	71000
72000	*72999*	1636	2.10	72000
73000	*73999*	1657	2.10	73000
74000	*74999*	1678	2.10	74000
75000	*75999*	1699	2.10	75000
76000	*76999*	1720	2.10	76000
77000	*77999*	1741	2.10	77000
78000	*78999*	1762	2.10	78000
79000	*79999*	1783	2.10	79000
80000	*80999*	1804	2.10	80000
81000	*81999*	1825	2.10	81000
82000	*82999*	1846	2.10	82000
83000	*83999*	1867	2.10	83000
84000	*84999*	1888	2.10	84000
85000	*85999*	1909	2.10	85000
86000	*86999*	1930	2.10	86000
87000	*87999*	1951	2.10	87000
88000	*88999*	1972	2.10	88000
89000	*89999*	1993	2.10	89000
90000	*90999*	2014	2.10	90000
91000	*91999*	2035	2.10	91000
92000	*92999*	2056	2.10	92000
93000	*93999*	2077	2.10	93000
94000	*94999*	2098	2.10	94000

Federal Child Support Tables/ Tables fédérales de pensions alimentaires pour enfants

Province: Alberta No. Of Children/ Nbre d'enfants: Four/Quatre

Income/Revenu ($)		Monthly Award/ Paiement mensuel ($)		
From/De	To/À	Basic Amount/ Montant de base	Plus (%)	Of Income Over/Du revenu dépassant
95000	*95999*	2119	2.10	95000
96000	*96999*	2140	2.10	96000
97000	*97999*	2161	2.10	97000
98000	*98999*	2182	2.10	98000
99000	*99999*	2203	2.10	99000
100000	*100999*	2224	2.10	100000
101000	*101999*	2245	2.10	101000
102000	*102999*	2266	2.10	102000
103000	*103999*	2287	2.10	103000
104000	*104999*	2308	2.10	104000
105000	*105999*	2329	2.10	105000
106000	*106999*	2350	2.10	106000
107000	*107999*	2371	2.10	107000
108000	*108999*	2392	2.10	108000
109000	*109999*	2413	2.10	109000
110000	*110999*	2434	2.10	110000
111000	*111999*	2455	2.10	111000
112000	*112999*	2476	2.10	112000
113000	*113999*	2497	2.08	113000
114000	*114999*	2518	2.00	114000
115000	*115999*	2538	2.00	115000
116000	*116999*	2558	2.00	116000
117000	*117999*	2578	2.00	117000
118000	*118999*	2598	2.00	118000
119000	*119999*	2618	2.00	119000
120000	*120999*	2638	2.00	120000
121000	*121999*	2658	2.00	121000
122000	*122999*	2678	2.00	122000
123000	*123999*	2698	2.00	123000
124000	*124999*	2718	2.00	124000
125000	*125999*	2738	2.00	125000
126000	*126999*	2758	2.00	126000
127000	*127999*	2778	2.00	127000
128000	*128999*	2798	2.00	128000
129000	*129999*	2818	2.00	129000

Federal Child Support Tables/ Tables fédérales de pensions alimentaires pour enfants

Province: Alberta
No. Of Children/ Nbre d'enfants: Four/Quatre

Income/Revenu ($)		Monthly Award/ Paiement mensuel ($)		
From/De	To/À	Basic Amount/ Montant de base	Plus (%)	Of Income Over/Du revenu dépassant
130000	*130999*	2838	2.00	130000
131000	*131999*	2858	2.00	131000
132000	*132999*	2878	2.00	132000
133000	*133999*	2899	2.00	133000
134000	*134999*	2919	2.00	134000
135000	*135999*	2939	2.00	135000
136000	*136999*	2959	2.00	136000
137000	*137999*	2979	2.00	137000
138000	*138999*	2999	2.00	138000
139000	*139999*	3019	2.00	139000
140000	*140999*	3039	2.00	140000
141000	*141999*	3059	2.00	141000
142000	*142999*	3079	2.00	142000
143000	*143999*	3099	2.00	143000
144000	*144999*	3119	2.00	144000
145000	*145999*	3139	2.00	145000
146000	*146999*	3159	2.00	146000
147000	*147999*	3179	2.00	147000
148000	*148999*	3199	2.00	148000
149000	*149999*	3219	2.00	149000

Federal Child Support Tables/ Tables fédérales de pensions alimentaires pour enfants

Province: Alberta
No. Of Children/ Nbre d'enfants: Four/Quatre

Income/Revenu ($)		Monthly Award/ Paiement mensuel ($)		
From/De	To/À	Basic Amount/ Montant de base	Plus (%)	Of Income Over/Du revenu dépassant
150000	*or greater/ ou plus*	3239	2.00	150000

Federal Child Support Tables/ Tables fédérales de pensions alimentaires pour enfants

Province: Alberta
No. Of Children/ Nbre d'enfants: Five/Cinq

Income/Revenu ($)		Monthly Award/ Paiement mensuel ($)		
From/De	To/À	Basic Amount/ Montant de base	Plus (%)	Of Income Over/Du revenu dépassant
0	*7999*	0		
8000	*8999*	0	2.01	8000
9000	*9999*	20	5.01	9000
10000	*10999*	70	5.01	10000
11000	*11999*	120	5.01	11000
12000	*12999*	170	5.01	12000
13000	*13999*	221	4.92	13000
14000	*14999*	270	4.89	14000
15000	*15999*	319	4.43	15000
16000	*16999*	363	4.30	16000
17000	*17999*	406	4.30	17000
18000	*18999*	449	4.30	18000
19000	*19999*	492	4.30	19000
20000	*20999*	535	4.30	20000
21000	*21999*	578	4.30	21000
22000	*22999*	621	4.16	22000
23000	*23999*	663	2.34	23000
24000	*24999*	686	2.34	24000

Federal Child Support Tables/ Tables fédérales de pensions alimentaires pour enfants

Province: Alberta No. Of Children/ N^bre d'enfants: Five/Cinq

Income/Revenu ($)		Monthly Award/ Paiement mensuel ($)		
From/De	To/À	Basic Amount/ Montant de base	Plus (%)	Of Income Over/Du revenu dépassant
25000	*25999*	709	2.34	25000
26000	*26999*	733	2.34	26000
27000	*27999*	756	2.34	27000
28000	*28999*	780	2.34	28000
29000	*29999*	803	2.22	29000
30000	*30999*	825	2.23	30000
31000	*31999*	847	2.37	31000
32000	*32999*	871	2.37	32000
33000	*33999*	895	2.37	33000
34000	*34999*	918	2.37	34000
35000	*35999*	942	2.15	35000
36000	*36999*	964	2.28	36000
37000	*37999*	986	2.33	37000
38000	*38999*	1010	2.33	38000
39000	*39999*	1033	2.38	39000
40000	*40999*	1057	2.45	40000
41000	*41999*	1081	2.52	41000
42000	*42999*	1106	2.52	42000
43000	*43999*	1132	2.52	43000
44000	*44999*	1157	2.52	44000
45000	*45999*	1182	2.52	45000
46000	*46999*	1207	2.52	46000
47000	*47999*	1232	2.52	47000
48000	*48999*	1258	2.52	48000
49000	*49999*	1283	2.52	49000
50000	*50999*	1308	2.52	50000
51000	*51999*	1333	2.52	51000
52000	*52999*	1358	2.52	52000
53000	*53999*	1383	2.52	53000
54000	*54999*	1409	2.52	54000
55000	*55999*	1434	2.52	55000
56000	*56999*	1459	2.52	56000
57000	*57999*	1484	2.52	57000
58000	*58999*	1509	2.52	58000
59000	*59999*	1535	2.52	59000

Federal Child Support Tables/ Tables fédérales de pensions alimentaires pour enfants

Province: Alberta No. Of Children/ N^bre d'enfants: Five/Cinq

Income/Revenu ($)		Monthly Award/ Paiement mensuel ($)		
From/De	To/À	Basic Amount/ Montant de base	Plus (%)	Of Income Over/Du revenu dépassant
60000	*60999*	1560	2.52	60000
61000	*61999*	1585	2.52	61000
62000	*62999*	1610	2.52	62000
63000	*63999*	1635	2.52	63000
64000	*64999*	1660	2.52	64000
65000	*65999*	1686	2.52	65000
66000	*66999*	1711	2.52	66000
67000	*67999*	1736	2.52	67000
68000	*68999*	1761	2.52	68000
69000	*69999*	1786	2.52	69000
70000	*70999*	1812	2.37	70000
71000	*71999*	1835	2.37	71000
72000	*72999*	1859	2.37	72000
73000	*73999*	1883	2.37	73000
74000	*74999*	1906	2.37	74000
75000	*75999*	1930	2.37	75000
76000	*76999*	1954	2.37	76000
77000	*77999*	1978	2.37	77000
78000	*78999*	2001	2.37	78000
79000	*79999*	2025	2.37	79000
80000	*80999*	2049	2.37	80000
81000	*81999*	2072	2.37	81000
82000	*82999*	2096	2.37	82000
83000	*83999*	2120	2.37	83000
84000	*84999*	2143	2.37	84000
85000	*85999*	2167	2.37	85000
86000	*86999*	2191	2.37	86000
87000	*87999*	2215	2.37	87000
88000	*88999*	2238	2.37	88000
89000	*89999*	2262	2.37	89000
90000	*90999*	2286	2.37	90000
91000	*91999*	2309	2.37	91000
92000	*92999*	2333	2.37	92000
93000	*93999*	2357	2.37	93000
94000	*94999*	2380	2.37	94000

Federal Child Support Tables/ Tables fédérales de pensions alimentaires pour enfants

Province: Alberta
No. Of Children/ Nbre d'enfants: Five/Cinq

Income/Revenu ($)		Monthly Award/ Paiement mensuel ($)		
From/De	To/À	Basic Amount/ Montant de base	Plus (%)	Of Income Over/Du revenu dépassant
95000	*95999*	2404	2.37	95000
96000	*96999*	2428	2.37	96000
97000	*97999*	2452	2.37	97000
98000	*98999*	2475	2.37	98000
99000	*99999*	2499	2.37	99000
100000	*100999*	2523	2.37	100000
101000	*101999*	2546	2.37	101000
102000	*102999*	2570	2.37	102000
103000	*103999*	2594	2.37	103000
104000	*104999*	2618	2.37	104000
105000	*105999*	2641	2.37	105000
106000	*106999*	2665	2.37	106000
107000	*107999*	2689	2.37	107000
108000	*108999*	2712	2.37	108000
109000	*109999*	2736	2.37	109000
110000	*110999*	2760	2.37	110000
111000	*111999*	2783	2.37	111000
112000	*112999*	2807	2.37	112000
113000	*113999*	2831	2.35	113000
114000	*114999*	2854	2.26	114000
115000	*115999*	2877	2.26	115000
116000	*116999*	2900	2.26	116000
117000	*117999*	2922	2.26	117000
118000	*118999*	2945	2.26	118000
119000	*119999*	2967	2.26	119000
120000	*120999*	2990	2.26	120000
121000	*121999*	3012	2.26	121000
122000	*122999*	3035	2.26	122000

Federal Child Support Tables/ Tables fédérales de pensions alimentaires pour enfants

Province: Alberta
No. Of Children/ Nbre d'enfants: Five/Cinq

Income/Revenu ($)		Monthly Award/ Paiement mensuel ($)		
From/De	To/À	Basic Amount/ Montant de base	Plus (%)	Of Income Over/Du revenu dépassant
123000	*123999*	3058	2.26	123000
124000	*124999*	3080	2.26	124000
125000	*125999*	3103	2.26	125000
126000	*126999*	3125	2.26	126000
127000	*127999*	3148	2.26	127000
128000	*128999*	3171	2.26	128000
129000	*129999*	3193	2.26	129000
130000	*130999*	3216	2.26	130000
131000	*131999*	3238	2.26	131000
132000	*132999*	3261	2.26	132000
133000	*133999*	3284	2.26	133000
134000	*134999*	3306	2.26	134000
135000	*135999*	3329	2.26	135000
136000	*136999*	3351	2.26	136000
137000	*137999*	3374	2.26	137000
138000	*138999*	3397	2.26	138000
139000	*139999*	3419	2.26	139000
140000	*140999*	3442	2.26	140000
141000	*141999*	3464	2.26	141000
142000	*142999*	3487	2.26	142000
143000	*143999*	3510	2.26	143000
144000	*144999*	3532	2.26	144000
145000	*145999*	3555	2.26	145000
146000	*146999*	3577	2.26	146000
147000	*147999*	3600	2.26	147000
148000	*148999*	3622	2.26	148000
149000	*149999*	3645	2.26	149000

Federal Child Support Tables/ Tables fédérales de pensions alimentaires pour enfants — **Province: Alberta** — **No. Of Children/ N^bre d'enfants: Five/Cinq**

Income/Revenu ($)		Monthly Award/ Paiement mensuel ($)		
From/De	To/À	Basic Amount/ Montant de base	Plus (%)	Of Income Over/Du revenu dépassant
150000	*or greater/ ou plus*	3668	2.26	150000

Federal Child Support Tables/ Tables fédérales de pensions alimentaires pour enfants — **Province: Alberta** — **No. Of Children/ N^bre d'enfants: Six or more/ Six ou plus**

Income/Revenu ($)		Monthly Award/ Paiement mensuel ($)		
From/De	To/À	Basic Amount/ Montant de base	Plus (%)	Of Income Over/Du revenu dépassant
0	*7999*	0		
8000	*8999*	0	2.01	8000
9000	*9999*	20	5.01	9000
10000	*10999*	70	5.01	10000
11000	*11999*	120	5.01	11000
12000	*12999*	170	5.01	12000
13000	*13999*	221	4.92	13000
14000	*14999*	270	4.89	14000
15000	*15999*	319	4.43	15000
16000	*16999*	363	4.30	16000
17000	*17999*	406	4.30	17000
18000	*18999*	449	4.30	18000
19000	*19999*	492	4.30	19000
20000	*20999*	535	4.30	20000
21000	*21999*	578	4.30	21000
22000	*22999*	621	4.30	22000
23000	*23999*	664	4.30	23000
24000	*24999*	707	4.30	24000

Federal Child Support Tables/ Tables fédérales de pensions alimentaires pour enfants — **Province: Alberta** — **No. Of Children/ N^bre d'enfants: Six or more/ Six ou plus**

Income/Revenu ($)		Monthly Award/ Paiement mensuel ($)		
From/De	To/À	Basic Amount/ Montant de base	Plus (%)	Of Income Over/Du revenu dépassant
25000	*25999*	750	4.30	25000
26000	*26999*	793	4.30	26000
27000	*27999*	836	2.72	27000
28000	*28999*	864	2.60	28000
29000	*29999*	890	2.47	29000
30000	*30999*	914	2.47	30000
31000	*31999*	939	2.59	31000
32000	*32999*	965	2.59	32000
33000	*33999*	991	2.59	33000
34000	*34999*	1017	2.59	34000
35000	*35999*	1043	2.36	35000
36000	*36999*	1066	2.50	36000
37000	*37999*	1091	2.55	37000
38000	*38999*	1117	2.55	38000
39000	*39999*	1142	2.61	39000
40000	*40999*	1168	2.69	40000
41000	*41999*	1195	2.76	41000
42000	*42999*	1223	2.76	42000
43000	*43999*	1250	2.76	43000
44000	*44999*	1278	2.76	44000
45000	*45999*	1306	2.76	45000
46000	*46999*	1333	2.76	46000
47000	*47999*	1361	2.76	47000
48000	*48999*	1389	2.76	48000
49000	*49999*	1416	2.76	49000
50000	*50999*	1444	2.76	50000
51000	*51999*	1471	2.76	51000
52000	*52999*	1499	2.76	52000
53000	*53999*	1527	2.76	53000
54000	*54999*	1554	2.76	54000
55000	*55999*	1582	2.76	55000
56000	*56999*	1609	2.76	56000
57000	*57999*	1637	2.76	57000
58000	*58999*	1665	2.76	58000
59000	*59999*	1692	2.76	59000

Federal Child Support Tables/ Tables fédérales de pensions alimentaires pour enfants

Province: Alberta
No. Of Children/ Nbre d'enfants: Six or more/ Six ou plus

Income/Revenu ($)		Monthly Award/ Paiement mensuel ($)		
From/De	To/À	Basic Amount/ Montant de base	Plus (%)	Of Income Over/Du revenu dépassant
60000	*60999*	1720	2.76	60000
61000	*61999*	1747	2.76	61000
62000	*62999*	1775	2.76	62000
63000	*63999*	1803	2.76	63000
64000	*64999*	1830	2.76	64000
65000	*65999*	1858	2.76	65000
66000	*66999*	1885	2.76	66000
67000	*67999*	1913	2.76	67000
68000	*68999*	1941	2.76	68000
69000	*69999*	1968	2.76	69000
70000	*70999*	1996	2.60	70000
71000	*71999*	2022	2.60	71000
72000	*72999*	2048	2.60	72000
73000	*73999*	2074	2.60	73000
74000	*74999*	2100	2.60	74000
75000	*75999*	2126	2.60	75000
76000	*76999*	2152	2.60	76000
77000	*77999*	2178	2.60	77000
78000	*78999*	2204	2.60	78000
79000	*79999*	2230	2.60	79000
80000	*80999*	2256	2.60	80000
81000	*81999*	2282	2.60	81000
82000	*82999*	2308	2.60	82000
83000	*83999*	2334	2.60	83000
84000	*84999*	2360	2.60	84000
85000	*85999*	2386	2.60	85000
86000	*86999*	2412	2.60	86000
87000	*87999*	2438	2.60	87000
88000	*88999*	2464	2.60	88000
89000	*89999*	2490	2.60	89000
90000	*90999*	2516	2.60	90000
91000	*91999*	2542	2.60	91000
92000	*92999*	2567	2.60	92000
93000	*93999*	2593	2.60	93000
94000	*94999*	2619	2.60	94000

Federal Child Support Tables/ Tables fédérales de pensions alimentaires pour enfants

Province: Alberta
No. Of Children/ Nbre d'enfants: Six or more/ Six ou plus

Income/Revenu ($)		Monthly Award/ Paiement mensuel ($)		
From/De	To/À	Basic Amount/ Montant de base	Plus (%)	Of Income Over/Du revenu dépassant
95000	*95999*	2645	2.60	95000
96000	*96999*	2671	2.60	96000
97000	*97999*	2697	2.60	97000
98000	*98999*	2723	2.60	98000
99000	*99999*	2749	2.60	99000
100000	*100999*	2775	2.60	100000
101000	*101999*	2801	2.60	101000
102000	*102999*	2827	2.60	102000
103000	*103999*	2853	2.60	103000
104000	*104999*	2879	2.60	104000
105000	*105999*	2905	2.60	105000
106000	*106999*	2931	2.60	106000
107000	*107999*	2957	2.60	107000
108000	*108999*	2983	2.60	108000
109000	*109999*	3009	2.60	109000
110000	*110999*	3035	2.60	110000
111000	*111999*	3061	2.60	111000
112000	*112999*	3087	2.60	112000
113000	*113999*	3113	2.57	113000
114000	*114999*	3139	2.48	114000
115000	*115999*	3164	2.48	115000
116000	*116999*	3188	2.48	116000
117000	*117999*	3213	2.48	117000
118000	*118999*	3238	2.48	118000
119000	*119999*	3263	2.48	119000
120000	*120999*	3287	2.48	120000
121000	*121999*	3312	2.48	121000
122000	*122999*	3337	2.48	122000
123000	*123999*	3362	2.48	123000
124000	*124999*	3387	2.48	124000
125000	*125999*	3411	2.48	125000
126000	*126999*	3436	2.48	126000
127000	*127999*	3461	2.48	127000
128000	*128999*	3486	2.48	128000
129000	*129999*	3510	2.48	129000

Federal Child Support Tables/ Tables fédérales de pensions alimentaires pour enfants

Province: Alberta No. Of Children/ Nbre d'enfants: Six or more/ Six ou plus

Income/Revenu ($)		Monthly Award/ Paiement mensuel ($)		
From/De	To/À	Basic Amount/ Montant de base	Plus (%)	Of Income Over/Du revenu dépassant
130000	*130999*	3535	2.48	130000
131000	*131999*	3560	2.48	131000
132000	*132999*	3585	2.48	132000
133000	*133999*	3609	2.48	133000
134000	*134999*	3634	2.48	134000
135000	*135999*	3659	2.48	135000
136000	*136999*	3684	2.48	136000
137000	*137999*	3708	2.48	137000
138000	*138999*	3733	2.48	138000
139000	*139999*	3758	2.48	139000
140000	*140999*	3783	2.48	140000
141000	*141999*	3808	2.48	141000
142000	*142999*	3832	2.48	142000
143000	*143999*	3857	2.48	143000
144000	*144999*	3882	2.48	144000
145000	*145999*	3907	2.48	145000
146000	*146999*	3931	2.48	146000
147000	*147999*	3956	2.48	147000
148000	*148999*	3981	2.48	148000
149000	*149999*	4006	2.48	149000
150000	*or greater/ ou plus*	4030	2.48	150000

Federal Child Support Tables/ Tables fédérales de pensions alimentaires pour enfants

Province: Newfoundland and Labrador/Terre-Neuve-et-Labrador No. Of Children/ Nbre d'enfants: One/Un

Income/Revenu ($)		Monthly Award/ Paiement mensuel ($)		
From/De	To/À	Basic Amount/ Montant de base	Plus (%)	Of Income Over/Du revenu dépassant
0	*7999*	0		
8000	*8999*	0	0.81	8000
9000	*9999*	8	2.03	9000
10000	*10999*	28	2.03	10000
11000	*11999*	49	2.03	11000
12000	*12999*	69	2.03	12000
13000	*13999*	89	2.03	13000
14000	*14999*	110	1.23	14000
15000	*15999*	122	0.52	15000
16000	*16999*	127	0.95	16000
17000	*17999*	137	0.95	17000
18000	*18999*	146	0.95	18000
19000	*19999*	156	0.95	19000
20000	*20999*	165	0.95	20000
21000	*21999*	175	0.95	21000
22000	*22999*	184	0.95	22000
23000	*23999*	194	0.95	23000
24000	*24999*	203	0.95	24000

Federal Child Support Tables/ Tables fédérales de pensions alimentaires pour enfants

Province: Newfoundland and Labrador/Terre-Neuve-et-Labrador
No. Of Children/ N^bre d'enfants: One/Un

Income/Revenu ($)		Monthly Award/ Paiement mensuel ($)		
From/De	To/À	Basic Amount/ Montant de base	Plus (%)	Of Income Over/Du revenu dépassant
25000	*25999*	213	0.95	25000
26000	*26999*	222	0.95	26000
27000	*27999*	231	0.95	27000
28000	*28999*	241	0.95	28000
29000	*29999*	250	0.87	29000
30000	*30999*	259	0.80	30000
31000	*31999*	267	0.80	31000
32000	*32999*	275	0.80	32000
33000	*33999*	283	0.80	33000
34000	*34999*	291	0.80	34000
35000	*35999*	299	0.72	35000
36000	*36999*	307	0.77	36000
37000	*37999*	314	0.79	37000
38000	*38999*	322	0.79	38000
39000	*39999*	330	0.81	39000
40000	*40999*	338	0.83	40000
41000	*41999*	346	0.86	41000
42000	*42999*	355	0.86	42000
43000	*43999*	364	0.86	43000
44000	*44999*	372	0.86	44000
45000	*45999*	381	0.86	45000
46000	*46999*	389	0.86	46000
47000	*47999*	398	0.86	47000
48000	*48999*	407	0.86	48000
49000	*49999*	415	0.86	49000
50000	*50999*	424	0.86	50000
51000	*51999*	432	0.86	51000
52000	*52999*	441	0.86	52000
53000	*53999*	449	0.86	53000
54000	*54999*	458	0.86	54000
55000	*55999*	467	0.86	55000
56000	*56999*	475	0.86	56000
57000	*57999*	484	0.86	57000
58000	*58999*	492	0.86	58000
59000	*59999*	501	0.84	59000

Federal Child Support Tables/ Tables fédérales de pensions alimentaires pour enfants

Province: Newfoundland and Labrador/Terre-Neuve-et-Labrador
No. Of Children/ N^bre d'enfants: One/Un

Income/Revenu ($)		Monthly Award/ Paiement mensuel ($)		
From/De	To/À	Basic Amount/ Montant de base	Plus (%)	Of Income Over/Du revenu dépassant
60000	*60999*	509	0.77	60000
61000	*61999*	517	0.75	61000
62000	*62999*	525	0.75	62000
63000	*63999*	532	0.77	63000
64000	*64999*	540	0.81	64000
65000	*65999*	548	0.81	65000
66000	*66999*	556	0.81	66000
67000	*67999*	564	0.81	67000
68000	*68999*	572	0.81	68000
69000	*69999*	580	0.81	69000
70000	*70999*	588	0.75	70000
71000	*71999*	596	0.75	71000
72000	*72999*	604	0.75	72000
73000	*73999*	611	0.75	73000
74000	*74999*	619	0.75	74000
75000	*75999*	626	0.75	75000
76000	*76999*	634	0.75	76000
77000	*77999*	641	0.75	77000
78000	*78999*	649	0.75	78000
79000	*79999*	656	0.75	79000
80000	*80999*	664	0.75	80000
81000	*81999*	672	0.75	81000
82000	*82999*	679	0.75	82000
83000	*83999*	687	0.75	83000
84000	*84999*	694	0.75	84000
85000	*85999*	702	0.75	85000
86000	*86999*	709	0.75	86000
87000	*87999*	717	0.75	87000
88000	*88999*	724	0.75	88000
89000	*89999*	732	0.75	89000
90000	*90999*	739	0.75	90000
91000	*91999*	747	0.75	91000
92000	*92999*	755	0.75	92000
93000	*93999*	762	0.75	93000
94000	*94999*	770	0.75	94000

Federal Child Support Tables/ Tables fédérales de pensions alimentaires pour enfants — **Province: Newfoundland and Labrador/Terre-Neuve-et-Labrador No. Of Children/ Nbre d'enfants: One/Un**

Income/Revenu ($)		Monthly Award/ Paiement mensuel ($)		
From/De	To/À	Basic Amount/ Montant de base	Plus (%)	Of Income Over/Du revenu dépassant
95000	*95999*	777	0.75	95000
96000	*96999*	785	0.75	96000
97000	*97999*	792	0.75	97000
98000	*98999*	800	0.75	98000
99000	*99999*	807	0.75	99000
100000	*100999*	815	0.75	100000
101000	*101999*	823	0.75	101000
102000	*102999*	830	0.75	102000
103000	*103999*	838	0.75	103000
104000	*104999*	845	0.75	104000
105000	*105999*	853	0.75	105000
106000	*106999*	860	0.75	106000
107000	*107999*	868	0.75	107000
108000	*108999*	875	0.75	108000
109000	*109999*	883	0.75	109000
110000	*110999*	890	0.75	110000
111000	*111999*	898	0.75	111000
112000	*112999*	906	0.75	112000
113000	*113999*	913	0.75	113000
114000	*114999*	921	0.71	114000
115000	*115999*	928	0.71	115000
116000	*116999*	935	0.71	116000
117000	*117999*	942	0.71	117000
118000	*118999*	949	0.71	118000
119000	*119999*	956	0.71	119000
120000	*120999*	963	0.71	120000
121000	*121999*	971	0.71	121000
122000	*122999*	978	0.71	122000

Federal Child Support Tables/ Tables fédérales de pensions alimentaires pour enfants — **Province: Newfoundland and Labrador/Terre-Neuve-et-Labrador No. Of Children/ Nbre d'enfants: One/Un**

Income/Revenu ($)		Monthly Award/ Paiement mensuel ($)		
From/De	To/À	Basic Amount/ Montant de base	Plus (%)	Of Income Over/Du revenu dépassant
123000	*123999*	985	0.71	123000
124000	*124999*	992	0.71	124000
125000	*125999*	999	0.71	125000
126000	*126999*	1006	0.71	126000
127000	*127999*	1013	0.71	127000
128000	*128999*	1020	0.71	128000
129000	*129999*	1028	0.71	129000
130000	*130999*	1035	0.71	130000
131000	*131999*	1042	0.71	131000
132000	*132999*	1049	0.71	132000
133000	*133999*	1056	0.71	133000
134000	*134999*	1063	0.71	134000
135000	*135999*	1070	0.71	135000
136000	*136999*	1078	0.71	136000
137000	*137999*	1085	0.71	137000
138000	*138999*	1092	0.71	138000
139000	*139999*	1099	0.71	139000
140000	*140999*	1106	0.71	140000
141000	*141999*	1113	0.71	141000
142000	*142999*	1120	0.71	142000
143000	*143999*	1127	0.71	143000
144000	*144999*	1135	0.71	144000
145000	*145999*	1142	0.71	145000
146000	*146999*	1149	0.71	146000
147000	*147999*	1156	0.71	147000
148000	*148999*	1163	0.71	148000
149000	*149999*	1170	0.71	149000

Federal Child Support Tables/ Tables fédérales de pensions alimentaires pour enfants

Province: Newfoundland and Labrador/Terre-Neuve-et-Labrador
No. Of Children/ N^bre d'enfants: One/Un

Income/Revenu ($)		Monthly Award/ Paiement mensuel ($)		
From/De	To/À	Basic Amount/ Montant de base	Plus (%)	Of Income Over/Du revenu dépassant
150000	*or greater/ ou plus*	1177	0.71	150000

Federal Child Support Tables/ Tables fédérales de pensions alimentaires pour enfants

Province: Newfoundland and Labrador/Terre-Neuve-et-Labrador
No. Of Children/ N^bre d'enfants: Two/Deux

Income/Revenu ($)		Monthly Award/ Paiement mensuel ($)		
From/De	To/À	Basic Amount/ Montant de base	Plus (%)	Of Income Over/Du revenu dépassant
0	*7999*	0		
8000	*8999*	0	1.31	8000
9000	*9999*	13	3.81	9000
10000	*10999*	51	3.81	10000
11000	*11999*	89	3.81	11000
12000	*12999*	127	3.81	12000
13000	*13999*	166	3.73	13000
14000	*14999*	203	2.43	14000
15000	*15999*	227	1.05	15000
16000	*16999*	238	1.48	16000
17000	*17999*	252	1.48	17000
18000	*18999*	267	1.48	18000
19000	*19999*	282	1.48	19000
20000	*20999*	297	1.48	20000
21000	*21999*	312	1.48	21000
22000	*22999*	326	1.48	22000
23000	*23999*	341	1.48	23000
24000	*24999*	356	1.48	24000

Federal Child Support Tables/ Tables fédérales de pensions alimentaires pour enfants

Province: Newfoundland and Labrador/Terre-Neuve-et-Labrador
No. Of Children/ N^bre d'enfants: Two/Deux

Income/Revenu ($)		Monthly Award/ Paiement mensuel ($)		
From/De	To/À	Basic Amount/ Montant de base	Plus (%)	Of Income Over/Du revenu dépassant
25000	*25999*	371	1.48	25000
26000	*26999*	385	1.48	26000
27000	*27999*	400	1.48	27000
28000	*28999*	415	1.48	28000
29000	*29999*	430	1.36	29000
30000	*30999*	443	1.25	30000
31000	*31999*	456	1.25	31000
32000	*32999*	468	1.25	32000
33000	*33999*	481	1.25	33000
34000	*34999*	493	1.25	34000
35000	*35999*	506	1.12	35000
36000	*36999*	517	1.20	36000
37000	*37999*	529	1.23	37000
38000	*38999*	541	1.23	38000
39000	*39999*	553	1.26	39000
40000	*40999*	566	1.30	40000
41000	*41999*	579	1.34	41000
42000	*42999*	592	1.34	42000
43000	*43999*	606	1.34	43000
44000	*44999*	619	1.34	44000
45000	*45999*	632	1.34	45000
46000	*46999*	646	1.34	46000
47000	*47999*	659	1.34	47000
48000	*48999*	672	1.34	48000
49000	*49999*	686	1.34	49000
50000	*50999*	699	1.34	50000
51000	*51999*	712	1.34	51000
52000	*52999*	726	1.34	52000
53000	*53999*	739	1.34	53000
54000	*54999*	753	1.34	54000
55000	*55999*	766	1.34	55000
56000	*56999*	779	1.34	56000
57000	*57999*	793	1.34	57000
58000	*58999*	806	1.34	58000
59000	*59999*	819	1.30	59000

Federal Child Support Tables/ Tables fédérales de pensions alimentaires pour enfants **Province: Newfoundland and Labrador/Terre-Neuve-et-Labrador No. Of Children/ Nbre d'enfants: Two/Deux**

Income/Revenu ($)		Monthly Award/ Paiement mensuel ($)		
From/De	To/À	Basic Amount/ Montant de base	Plus (%)	Of Income Over/Du revenu dépassant
60000	*60999*	832	1.23	60000
61000	*61999*	845	1.21	61000
62000	*62999*	857	1.21	62000
63000	*63999*	869	1.22	63000
64000	*64999*	881	1.26	64000
65000	*65999*	894	1.26	65000
66000	*66999*	906	1.26	66000
67000	*67999*	919	1.26	67000
68000	*68999*	932	1.26	68000
69000	*69999*	944	1.26	69000
70000	*70999*	957	1.17	70000
71000	*71999*	968	1.17	71000
72000	*72999*	980	1.17	72000
73000	*73999*	992	1.17	73000
74000	*74999*	1004	1.17	74000
75000	*75999*	1015	1.17	75000
76000	*76999*	1027	1.17	76000
77000	*77999*	1039	1.17	77000
78000	*78999*	1051	1.17	78000
79000	*79999*	1062	1.17	79000
80000	*80999*	1074	1.17	80000
81000	*81999*	1086	1.17	81000
82000	*82999*	1098	1.17	82000
83000	*83999*	1109	1.17	83000
84000	*84999*	1121	1.17	84000
85000	*85999*	1133	1.17	85000
86000	*86999*	1145	1.17	86000
87000	*87999*	1156	1.17	87000
88000	*88999*	1168	1.17	88000
89000	*89999*	1180	1.17	89000
90000	*90999*	1192	1.17	90000
91000	*91999*	1203	1.17	91000
92000	*92999*	1215	1.17	92000
93000	*93999*	1227	1.17	93000
94000	*94999*	1239	1.17	94000

Federal Child Support Tables/ Tables fédérales de pensions alimentaires pour enfants **Province: Newfoundland and Labrador/Terre-Neuve-et-Labrador No. Of Children/ Nbre d'enfants: Two/Deux**

Income/Revenu ($)		Monthly Award/ Paiement mensuel ($)		
From/De	To/À	Basic Amount/ Montant de base	Plus (%)	Of Income Over/Du revenu dépassant
95000	*95999*	1250	1.17	95000
96000	*96999*	1262	1.17	96000
97000	*97999*	1274	1.17	97000
98000	*98999*	1286	1.17	98000
99000	*99999*	1297	1.17	99000
100000	*100999*	1309	1.17	100000
101000	*101999*	1321	1.17	101000
102000	*102999*	1333	1.17	102000
103000	*103999*	1344	1.17	103000
104000	*104999*	1356	1.17	104000
105000	*105999*	1368	1.17	105000
106000	*106999*	1380	1.17	106000
107000	*107999*	1391	1.17	107000
108000	*108999*	1403	1.17	108000
109000	*109999*	1415	1.17	109000
110000	*110999*	1427	1.17	110000
111000	*111999*	1438	1.17	111000
112000	*112999*	1450	1.17	112000
113000	*113999*	1462	1.16	113000
114000	*114999*	1473	1.11	114000
115000	*115999*	1484	1.11	115000
116000	*116999*	1496	1.11	116000
117000	*117999*	1507	1.11	117000
118000	*118999*	1518	1.11	118000
119000	*119999*	1529	1.11	119000
120000	*120999*	1540	1.11	120000
121000	*121999*	1551	1.11	121000
122000	*122999*	1562	1.11	122000
123000	*123999*	1573	1.11	123000
124000	*124999*	1584	1.11	124000
125000	*125999*	1595	1.11	125000
126000	*126999*	1607	1.11	126000
127000	*127999*	1618	1.11	127000
128000	*128999*	1629	1.11	128000
129000	*129999*	1640	1.11	129000

Federal Child Support Tables/ Tables fédérales de pensions alimentaires pour enfants

Province: Newfoundland and Labrador/Terre-Neuve-et-Labrador
No. Of Children/ Nbre d'enfants: Two/Deux

Income/Revenu ($)		Monthly Award/ Paiement mensuel ($)		
From/De	To/À	Basic Amount/ Montant de base	Plus (%)	Of Income Over/Du revenu dépassant
130000	*130999*	1651	1.11	130000
131000	*131999*	1662	1.11	131000
132000	*132999*	1673	1.11	132000
133000	*133999*	1684	1.11	133000
134000	*134999*	1695	1.11	134000
135000	*135999*	1706	1.11	135000
136000	*136999*	1717	1.11	136000
137000	*137999*	1729	1.11	137000
138000	*138999*	1740	1.11	138000
139000	*139999*	1751	1.11	139000
140000	*140999*	1762	1.11	140000
141000	*141999*	1773	1.11	141000
142000	*142999*	1784	1.11	142000
143000	*143999*	1795	1.11	143000
144000	*144999*	1806	1.11	144000
145000	*145999*	1817	1.11	145000
146000	*146999*	1828	1.11	146000
147000	*147999*	1840	1.11	147000
148000	*148999*	1851	1.11	148000
149000	*149999*	1862	1.11	149000

Federal Child Support Tables/ Tables fédérales de pensions alimentaires pour enfants

Province: Newfoundland and Labrador/Terre-Neuve-et-Labrador
No. Of Children/ Nbre d'enfants: Two/Deux

Income/Revenu ($)		Monthly Award/ Paiement mensuel ($)		
From/De	To/À	Basic Amount/ Montant de base	Plus (%)	Of Income Over/Du revenu dépassant
150000	*or greater/ ou plus*	1873	1.11	150000

Federal Child Support Tables/ Tables fédérales de pensions alimentaires pour enfants

Province: Newfoundland and Labrador/Terre-Neuve-et-Labrador
No. Of Children/ Nbre d'enfants: Three/Trois

Income/Revenu ($)		Monthly Award/ Paiement mensuel ($)		
From/De	To/À	Basic Amount/ Montant de base	Plus (%)	Of Income Over/Du revenu dépassant
0	*7999*	0		
8000	*8999*	0	1.41	8000
9000	*9999*	14	4.10	9000
10000	*10999*	55	4.10	10000
11000	*11999*	96	4.10	11000
12000	*12999*	137	4.10	12000
13000	*13999*	178	4.02	13000
14000	*14999*	218	3.99	14000
15000	*15999*	258	3.75	15000
16000	*16999*	296	3.99	16000
17000	*17999*	336	2.85	17000
18000	*18999*	364	1.90	18000
19000	*19999*	383	1.90	19000
20000	*20999*	402	1.90	20000
21000	*21999*	421	1.90	21000
22000	*22999*	440	1.90	22000
23000	*23999*	459	1.90	23000
24000	*24999*	478	1.90	24000

Federal Child Support Tables/ Tables fédérales de pensions alimentaires pour enfants — **Province: Newfoundland and Labrador/Terre-Neuve-et-Labrador** — **No. Of Children/ N^bre d'enfants: Three/Trois**

Income/Revenu ($)		Monthly Award/ Paiement mensuel ($)		
From/De	To/À	Basic Amount/ Montant de base	Plus (%)	Of Income Over/Du revenu dépassant
25000	*25999*	497	1.90	25000
26000	*26999*	516	1.90	26000
27000	*27999*	535	1.90	27000
28000	*28999*	554	1.90	28000
29000	*29999*	573	1.75	29000
30000	*30999*	590	1.60	30000
31000	*31999*	606	1.60	31000
32000	*32999*	623	1.60	32000
33000	*33999*	639	1.60	33000
34000	*34999*	655	1.60	34000
35000	*35999*	671	1.44	35000
36000	*36999*	685	1.54	36000
37000	*37999*	700	1.58	37000
38000	*38999*	716	1.58	38000
39000	*39999*	732	1.62	39000
40000	*40999*	748	1.67	40000
41000	*41999*	765	1.72	41000
42000	*42999*	782	1.72	42000
43000	*43999*	799	1.72	43000
44000	*44999*	816	1.72	44000
45000	*45999*	834	1.72	45000
46000	*46999*	851	1.72	46000
47000	*47999*	868	1.72	47000
48000	*48999*	885	1.72	48000
49000	*49999*	902	1.72	49000
50000	*50999*	919	1.72	50000
51000	*51999*	937	1.72	51000
52000	*52999*	954	1.72	52000
53000	*53999*	971	1.72	53000
54000	*54999*	988	1.72	54000
55000	*55999*	1005	1.72	55000
56000	*56999*	1022	1.72	56000
57000	*57999*	1040	1.72	57000
58000	*58999*	1057	1.72	58000
59000	*59999*	1074	1.68	59000

Federal Child Support Tables/ Tables fédérales de pensions alimentaires pour enfants — **Province: Newfoundland and Labrador/Terre-Neuve-et-Labrador** — **No. Of Children/ N^bre d'enfants: Three/Trois**

Income/Revenu ($)		Monthly Award/ Paiement mensuel ($)		
From/De	To/À	Basic Amount/ Montant de base	Plus (%)	Of Income Over/Du revenu dépassant
60000	*60999*	1091	1.59	60000
61000	*61999*	1107	1.58	61000
62000	*62999*	1122	1.58	62000
63000	*63999*	1138	1.59	63000
64000	*64999*	1154	1.62	64000
65000	*65999*	1170	1.62	65000
66000	*66999*	1187	1.62	66000
67000	*67999*	1203	1.62	67000
68000	*68999*	1219	1.62	68000
69000	*69999*	1235	1.62	69000
70000	*70999*	1251	1.51	70000
71000	*71999*	1266	1.51	71000
72000	*72999*	1282	1.51	72000
73000	*73999*	1297	1.51	73000
74000	*74999*	1312	1.51	74000
75000	*75999*	1327	1.51	75000
76000	*76999*	1342	1.51	76000
77000	*77999*	1357	1.51	77000
78000	*78999*	1372	1.51	78000
79000	*79999*	1387	1.51	79000
80000	*80999*	1402	1.51	80000
81000	*81999*	1417	1.51	81000
82000	*82999*	1433	1.51	82000
83000	*83999*	1448	1.51	83000
84000	*84999*	1463	1.51	84000
85000	*85999*	1478	1.51	85000
86000	*86999*	1493	1.51	86000
87000	*87999*	1508	1.51	87000
88000	*88999*	1523	1.51	88000
89000	*89999*	1538	1.51	89000
90000	*90999*	1553	1.51	90000
91000	*91999*	1568	1.51	91000
92000	*92999*	1584	1.51	92000
93000	*93999*	1599	1.51	93000
94000	*94999*	1614	1.51	94000

Federal Child Support Tables/ Tables fédérales de pensions alimentaires pour enfants

Province: Newfoundland and Labrador/Terre-Neuve-et-Labrador
No. Of Children/ Nbre d'enfants: Three/Trois

Income/Revenu ($)		Monthly Award/ Paiement mensuel ($)		
From/De	To/À	Basic Amount/ Montant de base	Plus (%)	Of Income Over/Du revenu dépassant
95000	*95999*	1629	1.51	95000
96000	*96999*	1644	1.51	96000
97000	*97999*	1659	1.51	97000
98000	*98999*	1674	1.51	98000
99000	*99999*	1689	1.51	99000
100000	*100999*	1704	1.51	100000
101000	*101999*	1719	1.51	101000
102000	*102999*	1735	1.51	102000
103000	*103999*	1750	1.51	103000
104000	*104999*	1765	1.51	104000
105000	*105999*	1780	1.51	105000
106000	*106999*	1795	1.51	106000
107000	*107999*	1810	1.51	107000
108000	*108999*	1825	1.51	108000
109000	*109999*	1840	1.51	109000
110000	*110999*	1855	1.51	110000
111000	*111999*	1870	1.51	111000
112000	*112999*	1886	1.51	112000
113000	*113999*	1901	1.49	113000
114000	*114999*	1916	1.43	114000
115000	*115999*	1930	1.43	115000
116000	*116999*	1944	1.43	116000
117000	*117999*	1958	1.43	117000
118000	*118999*	1973	1.43	118000
119000	*119999*	1987	1.43	119000
120000	*120999*	2001	1.43	120000
121000	*121999*	2015	1.43	121000
122000	*122999*	2030	1.43	122000

Federal Child Support Tables/ Tables fédérales de pensions alimentaires pour enfants

Province: Newfoundland and Labrador/Terre-Neuve-et-Labrador
No. Of Children/ Nbre d'enfants: Three/Trois

Income/Revenu ($)		Monthly Award/ Paiement mensuel ($)		
From/De	To/À	Basic Amount/ Montant de base	Plus (%)	Of Income Over/Du revenu dépassant
123000	*123999*	2044	1.43	123000
124000	*124999*	2058	1.43	124000
125000	*125999*	2073	1.43	125000
126000	*126999*	2087	1.43	126000
127000	*127999*	2101	1.43	127000
128000	*128999*	2115	1.43	128000
129000	*129999*	2130	1.43	129000
130000	*130999*	2144	1.43	130000
131000	*131999*	2158	1.43	131000
132000	*132999*	2172	1.43	132000
133000	*133999*	2187	1.43	133000
134000	*134999*	2201	1.43	134000
135000	*135999*	2215	1.43	135000
136000	*136999*	2229	1.43	136000
137000	*137999*	2244	1.43	137000
138000	*138999*	2258	1.43	138000
139000	*139999*	2272	1.43	139000
140000	*140999*	2287	1.43	140000
141000	*141999*	2301	1.43	141000
142000	*142999*	2315	1.43	142000
143000	*143999*	2329	1.43	143000
144000	*144999*	2344	1.43	144000
145000	*145999*	2358	1.43	145000
146000	*146999*	2372	1.43	146000
147000	*147999*	2386	1.43	147000
148000	*148999*	2401	1.43	148000
149000	*149999*	2415	1.43	149000

Federal Child Support Tables/ Tables fédérales de pensions alimentaires pour enfants

Province: Newfoundland and Labrador/Terre-Neuve-et-Labrador
No. Of Children/ Nbre d'enfants: Three/Trois

Income/Revenu ($)		Monthly Award/ Paiement mensuel ($)		
From/De	**To/À**	**Basic Amount/ Montant de base**	**Plus (%)**	**Of Income Over/Du revenu dépassant**
150000	*or greater/ ou plus*	2429	1.43	150000

Federal Child Support Tables/ Tables fédérales de pensions alimentaires pour enfants

Province: Newfoundland and Labrador/Terre-Neuve-et-Labrador
No. Of Children/ Nbre d'enfants: Four/Quatre

Income/Revenu ($)		Monthly Award Paiement mensuel ($)		
From/De	**To/À**	**Basic Amount/ Montant de base**	**Plus (%)**	**Of Income Over/Du revenu dépassant**
0	*7999*	0		
8000	*8999*	0	1.51	8000
9000	*9999*	15	4.40	9000
10000	*10999*	59	4.40	10000
11000	*11999*	103	4.40	11000
12000	*12999*	147	4.40	12000
13000	*13999*	191	4.30	13000
14000	*14999*	234	4.27	14000
15000	*15999*	277	4.02	15000
16000	*16999*	317	4.27	16000
17000	*17999*	360	4.27	17000
18000	*18999*	402	4.27	18000
19000	*19999*	445	4.27	19000
20000	*20999*	488	2.30	20000
21000	*21999*	511	2.24	21000
22000	*22999*	533	2.24	22000
23000	*23999*	556	2.24	23000
24000	*24999*	578	2.24	24000

Federal Child Support Tables/ Tables fédérales de pensions alimentaires pour enfants

Province: Newfoundland and Labrador/Terre-Neuve-et-Labrador
No. Of Children/ Nbre d'enfants: Four/Quatre

Income/Revenu ($)		Monthly Award Paiement mensuel ($)		
From/De	**To/À**	**Basic Amount/ Montant de base**	**Plus (%)**	**Of Income Over/Du revenu dépassant**
25000	*25999*	600	2.24	25000
26000	*26999*	623	2.24	26000
27000	*27999*	645	2.24	27000
28000	*28999*	668	2.24	28000
29000	*29999*	690	2.06	29000
30000	*30999*	711	1.90	30000
31000	*31999*	730	1.90	31000
32000	*32999*	749	1.90	32000
33000	*33999*	768	1.90	33000
34000	*34999*	787	1.90	34000
35000	*35999*	806	1.70	35000
36000	*36999*	823	1.82	36000
37000	*37999*	841	1.86	37000
38000	*38999*	860	1.86	38000
39000	*39999*	878	1.91	39000
40000	*40999*	897	1.97	40000
41000	*41999*	917	2.03	41000
42000	*42999*	937	2.03	42000
43000	*43999*	958	2.03	43000
44000	*44999*	978	2.03	44000
45000	*45999*	998	2.03	45000
46000	*46999*	1018	2.03	46000
47000	*47999*	1039	2.03	47000
48000	*48999*	1059	2.03	48000
49000	*49999*	1079	2.03	49000
50000	*50999*	1100	2.03	50000
51000	*51999*	1120	2.03	51000
52000	*52999*	1140	2.03	52000
53000	*53999*	1161	2.03	53000
54000	*54999*	1181	2.03	54000
55000	*55999*	1201	2.03	55000
56000	*56999*	1221	2.03	56000
57000	*57999*	1242	2.03	57000
58000	*58999*	1262	2.03	58000
59000	*59999*	1282	1.98	59000

Federal Child Support Tables/ Tables fédérales de pensions alimentaires pour enfants

Province: Newfoundland and Labrador/Terre-Neuve-et-Labrador
No. Of Children/ Nbre d'enfants: Four/Quatre

Income/Revenu ($)		Monthly Award Paiement mensuel ($)		
From/De	To/À	Basic Amount/ Montant de base	Plus (%)	Of Income Over/Du revenu dépassant
60000	*60999*	1302	1.89	60000
61000	*61999*	1321	1.87	61000
62000	*62999*	1340	1.87	62000
63000	*63999*	1359	1.89	63000
64000	*64999*	1377	1.92	64000
65000	*65999*	1397	1.92	65000
66000	*66999*	1416	1.92	66000
67000	*67999*	1435	1.92	67000
68000	*68999*	1454	1.92	68000
69000	*69999*	1473	1.92	69000
70000	*70999*	1492	1.78	70000
71000	*71999*	1510	1.78	71000
72000	*72999*	1528	1.78	72000
73000	*73999*	1546	1.78	73000
74000	*74999*	1564	1.78	74000
75000	*75999*	1582	1.78	75000
76000	*76999*	1599	1.78	76000
77000	*77999*	1617	1.78	77000
78000	*78999*	1635	1.78	78000
79000	*79999*	1653	1.78	79000
80000	*80999*	1671	1.78	80000
81000	*81999*	1689	1.78	81000
82000	*82999*	1707	1.78	82000
83000	*83999*	1724	1.78	83000
84000	*84999*	1742	1.78	84000
85000	*85999*	1760	1.78	85000
86000	*86999*	1778	1.78	86000
87000	*87999*	1796	1.78	87000
88000	*88999*	1814	1.78	88000
89000	*89999*	1831	1.78	89000
90000	*90999*	1849	1.78	90000
91000	*91999*	1867	1.78	91000
92000	*92999*	1885	1.78	92000
93000	*93999*	1903	1.78	93000
94000	*94999*	1921	1.78	94000

Federal Child Support Tables/ Tables fédérales de pensions alimentaires pour enfants

Province: Newfoundland and Labrador/Terre-Neuve-et-Labrador
No. Of Children/ Nbre d'enfants: Four/Quatre

Income/Revenu ($)		Monthly Award Paiement mensuel ($)		
From/De	To/À	Basic Amount/ Montant de base	Plus (%)	Of Income Over/Du revenu dépassant
95000	*95999*	1939	1.78	95000
96000	*96999*	1956	1.78	96000
97000	*97999*	1974	1.78	97000
98000	*98999*	1992	1.78	98000
99000	*99999*	2010	1.78	99000
100000	*100999*	2028	1.78	100000
101000	*101999*	2046	1.78	101000
102000	*102999*	2063	1.78	102000
103000	*103999*	2081	1.78	103000
104000	*104999*	2099	1.78	104000
105000	*105999*	2117	1.78	105000
106000	*106999*	2135	1.78	106000
107000	*107999*	2153	1.78	107000
108000	*108999*	2171	1.78	108000
109000	*109999*	2188	1.78	109000
110000	*110999*	2206	1.78	110000
111000	*111999*	2224	1.78	111000
112000	*112999*	2242	1.78	112000
113000	*113999*	2260	1.77	113000
114000	*114999*	2277	1.69	114000
115000	*115999*	2294	1.69	115000
116000	*116999*	2311	1.69	116000
117000	*117999*	2328	1.69	117000
118000	*118999*	2345	1.69	118000
119000	*119999*	2362	1.69	119000
120000	*120999*	2379	1.69	120000
121000	*121999*	2395	1.69	121000
122000	*122999*	2412	1.69	122000
123000	*123999*	2429	1.69	123000
124000	*124999*	2446	1.69	124000
125000	*125999*	2463	1.69	125000
126000	*126999*	2480	1.69	126000
127000	*127999*	2497	1.69	127000
128000	*128999*	2513	1.69	128000
129000	*129999*	2530	1.69	129000

Federal Child Support Tables/ Tables fédérales de pensions alimentaires pour enfants

Province: Newfoundland and Labrador/Terre-Neuve-et-Labrador
No. Of Children/ Nbre d'enfants: Four/Quatre

Income/Revenu ($)		Monthly Award Paiement mensuel ($)		
From/De	To/À	Basic Amount/ Montant de base	Plus (%)	Of Income Over/Du revenu dépassant
130000	*130999*	2547	1.69	130000
131000	*131999*	2564	1.69	131000
132000	*132999*	2581	1.69	132000
133000	*133999*	2598	1.69	133000
134000	*134999*	2615	1.69	134000
135000	*135999*	2631	1.69	135000
136000	*136999*	2648	1.69	136000
137000	*137999*	2665	1.69	137000
138000	*138999*	2682	1.69	138000
139000	*139999*	2699	1.69	139000
140000	*140999*	2716	1.69	140000
141000	*141999*	2733	1.69	141000
142000	*142999*	2749	1.69	142000
143000	*143999*	2766	1.69	143000
144000	*144999*	2783	1.69	144000
145000	*145999*	2800	1.69	145000
146000	*146999*	2817	1.69	146000
147000	*147999*	2834	1.69	147000
148000	*148999*	2851	1.69	148000
149000	*149999*	2868	1.69	149000

Federal Child Support Tables/ Tables fédérales de pensions alimentaires pour enfants

Province: Newfoundland and Labrador/Terre-Neuve-et-Labrador
No. Of Children/ Nbre d'enfants: Four/Quatre

Income/Revenu ($)		Monthly Award Paiement mensuel ($)		
From/De	To/À	Basic Amount/ Montant de base	Plus (%)	Of Income Over/Du revenu dépassant
150000	*or greater/ ou plus*	2884	1.69	150000

Federal Child Support Tables/ Tables fédérales de pensions alimentaires pour enfants

Province: Newfoundland and Labrador/Terre-Neuve-et-Labrador
No. Of Children/ Nbre d'enfants: Five/Cinq

Income/Revenu ($)		Monthly Award/ Paiement mensuel ($)		
From/De	To/À	Basic Amount/ Montant de base	Plus (%)	Of Income Over/Du revenu dépassant
0	*7999*	0		
8000	*8999*	0	1.51	8000
9000	*9999*	15	4.40	9000
10000	*10999*	59	4.40	10000
11000	*11999*	103	4.40	11000
12000	*12999*	147	4.40	12000
13000	*13999*	191	4.30	13000
14000	*14999*	234	4.27	14000
15000	*15999*	277	4.02	15000
16000	*16999*	317	4.27	16000
17000	*17999*	360	4.27	17000
18000	*18999*	402	4.27	18000
19000	*19999*	445	4.27	19000
20000	*20999*	488	4.27	20000
21000	*21999*	531	4.27	21000
22000	*22999*	573	4.27	22000
23000	*23999*	616	4.27	23000
24000	*24999*	659	2.81	24000

Federal Child Support Tables/Tables fédérales de pensions alimentaires pour enfants

Province: Newfoundland and Labrador/Terre-Neuve-et-Labrador
No. Of Children/Nbre d'enfants: Five/Cinq

Income/Revenu ($)		Monthly Award/Paiement mensuel ($)		
From/De	To/À	Basic Amount/Montant de base	Plus (%)	Of Income Over/Du revenu dépassant
25000	25999	687	2.53	25000
26000	26999	712	2.53	26000
27000	27999	737	2.53	27000
28000	28999	763	2.53	28000
29000	29999	788	2.33	29000
30000	30999	811	2.14	30000
31000	31999	833	2.14	31000
32000	32999	854	2.14	32000
33000	33999	875	2.14	33000
34000	34999	897	2.14	34000
35000	35999	918	1.92	35000
36000	36999	937	2.05	36000
37000	37999	958	2.10	37000
38000	38999	979	2.10	38000
39000	39999	1000	2.16	39000
40000	40999	1022	2.22	40000
41000	41999	1044	2.29	41000
42000	42999	1067	2.29	42000
43000	43999	1090	2.29	43000
44000	44999	1112	2.29	44000
45000	45999	1135	2.29	45000
46000	46999	1158	2.29	46000
47000	47999	1181	2.29	47000
48000	48999	1204	2.29	48000
49000	49999	1227	2.29	49000
50000	50999	1250	2.29	50000
51000	51999	1273	2.29	51000
52000	52999	1296	2.29	52000
53000	53999	1319	2.29	53000
54000	54999	1341	2.29	54000
55000	55999	1364	2.29	55000
56000	56999	1387	2.29	56000
57000	57999	1410	2.29	57000
58000	58999	1433	2.29	58000
59000	59999	1456	2.24	59000

Federal Child Support Tables/Tables fédérales de pensions alimentaires pour enfants

Province: Newfoundland and Labrador/Terre-Neuve-et-Labrador
No. Of Children/Nbre d'enfants: Five/Cinq

Income/Revenu ($)		Monthly Award/Paiement mensuel ($)		
From/De	To/À	Basic Amount/Montant de base	Plus (%)	Of Income Over/Du revenu dépassant
60000	60999	1478	2.14	60000
61000	61999	1500	2.12	61000
62000	62999	1521	2.12	62000
63000	63999	1542	2.13	63000
64000	64999	1564	2.16	64000
65000	65999	1585	2.16	65000
66000	66999	1607	2.16	66000
67000	67999	1628	2.16	67000
68000	68999	1650	2.16	68000
69000	69999	1672	2.16	69000
70000	70999	1693	2.01	70000
71000	71999	1713	2.01	71000
72000	72999	1734	2.01	72000
73000	73999	1754	2.01	73000
74000	74999	1774	2.01	74000
75000	75999	1794	2.01	75000
76000	76999	1814	2.01	76000
77000	77999	1834	2.01	77000
78000	78999	1854	2.01	78000
79000	79999	1874	2.01	79000
80000	80999	1895	2.01	80000
81000	81999	1915	2.01	81000
82000	82999	1935	2.01	82000
83000	83999	1955	2.01	83000
84000	84999	1975	2.01	84000
85000	85999	1995	2.01	85000
86000	86999	2015	2.01	86000
87000	87999	2036	2.01	87000
88000	88999	2056	2.01	88000
89000	89999	2076	2.01	89000
90000	90999	2096	2.01	90000
91000	91999	2116	2.01	91000
92000	92999	2136	2.01	92000
93000	93999	2156	2.01	93000
94000	94999	2176	2.01	94000

Federal Child Support Tables/ Tables fédérales de pensions alimentaires pour enfants — **Province: Newfoundland and Labrador/Terre-Neuve-et-Labrador No. Of Children/ Nbre d'enfants: Five/Cinq**

Income/Revenu ($)		Monthly Award/ Paiement mensuel ($)		
From/De	To/À	Basic Amount/ Montant de base	Plus (%)	Of Income Over/Du revenu dépassant
95000	*95999*	2197	2.01	95000
96000	*96999*	2217	2.01	96000
97000	*97999*	2237	2.01	97000
98000	*98999*	2257	2.01	98000
99000	*99999*	2277	2.01	99000
100000	*100999*	2297	2.01	100000
101000	*101999*	2317	2.01	101000
102000	*102999*	2338	2.01	102000
103000	*103999*	2358	2.01	103000
104000	*104999*	2378	2.01	104000
105000	*105999*	2398	2.01	105000
106000	*106999*	2418	2.01	106000
107000	*107999*	2438	2.01	107000
108000	*108999*	2458	2.01	108000
109000	*109999*	2478	2.01	109000
110000	*110999*	2499	2.01	110000
111000	*111999*	2519	2.01	111000
112000	*112999*	2539	2.01	112000
113000	*113999*	2559	1.99	113000
114000	*114999*	2579	1.90	114000
115000	*115999*	2598	1.90	115000
116000	*116999*	2617	1.90	116000
117000	*117999*	2636	1.90	117000
118000	*118999*	2655	1.90	118000
119000	*119999*	2674	1.90	119000
120000	*120999*	2693	1.90	120000
121000	*121999*	2712	1.90	121000
122000	*122999*	2731	1.90	122000

Federal Child Support Tables/ Tables fédérales de pensions alimentaires pour enfants — **Province: Newfoundland and Labrador/Terre-Neuve-et-Labrador No. Of Children/ Nbre d'enfants: Five/Cinq**

Income/Revenu ($)		Monthly Award/ Paiement mensuel ($)		
From/De	To/À	Basic Amount/ Montant de base	Plus (%)	Of Income Over/Du revenu dépassant
123000	*123999*	2750	1.90	123000
124000	*124999*	2769	1.90	124000
125000	*125999*	2788	1.90	125000
126000	*126999*	2807	1.90	126000
127000	*127999*	2826	1.90	127000
128000	*128999*	2845	1.90	128000
129000	*129999*	2864	1.90	129000
130000	*130999*	2883	1.90	130000
131000	*131999*	2902	1.90	131000
132000	*132999*	2921	1.90	132000
133000	*133999*	2940	1.90	133000
134000	*134999*	2959	1.90	134000
135000	*135999*	2978	1.90	135000
136000	*136999*	2997	1.90	136000
137000	*137999*	3016	1.90	137000
138000	*138999*	3035	1.90	138000
139000	*139999*	3054	1.90	139000
140000	*140999*	3073	1.90	140000
141000	*141999*	3093	1.90	141000
142000	*142999*	3112	1.90	142000
143000	*143999*	3131	1.90	143000
144000	*144999*	3150	1.90	144000
145000	*145999*	3169	1.90	145000
146000	*146999*	3188	1.90	146000
147000	*147999*	3207	1.90	147000
148000	*148999*	3226	1.90	148000
149000	*149999*	3245	1.90	149000

Federal Child Support Tables/ Tables fédérales de pensions alimentaires pour enfants

Province: Newfoundland and Labrador/Terre-Neuve-et-Labrador
No. Of Children/ Nbre d'enfants: Five/Cinq

Income/Revenu ($)		Monthly Award/ Paiement mensuel ($)		
From/De	To/À	Basic Amount/ Montant de base	Plus (%)	Of Income Over/Du revenu dépassant
150000	*or greater/ ou plus*	3264	1.90	150000

Federal Child Support Tables/ Tables fédérales de pensions alimentaires pour enfants

Province: Newfoundland and Labrador/Terre-Neuve-et-Labrador
No. Of Children/ Nbre d'enfants: Six or more/Six ou plus

Income/Revenu ($)		Monthly Award/ Paiement mensuel ($)		
From/De	To/À	Basic Amount/ Montant de base	Plus (%)	Of Income Over/Du revenu dépassant
0	*7999*	0		
8000	*8999*	0	1.51	8000
9000	*9999*	15	4.40	9000
10000	*10999*	59	4.40	10000
11000	*11999*	103	4.40	11000
12000	*12999*	147	4.40	12000
13000	*13999*	191	4.30	13000
14000	*14999*	234	4.27	14000
15000	*15999*	277	4.02	15000
16000	*16999*	317	4.27	16000
17000	*17999*	360	4.27	17000
18000	*18999*	402	4.27	18000
19000	*19999*	445	4.27	19000
20000	*20999*	488	4.27	20000
21000	*21999*	531	4.27	21000
22000	*22999*	573	4.27	22000
23000	*23999*	616	4.27	23000
24000	*24999*	659	4.27	24000

Federal Child Support Tables/ Tables fédérales de pensions alimentaires pour enfants

Province: Newfoundland and Labrador/Terre-Neuve-et-Labrador
No. Of Children/ Nbre d'enfants: Six or more/Six ou plus

Income/Revenu ($)		Monthly Award/ Paiement mensuel ($)		
From/De	To/À	Basic Amount/ Montant de base	Plus (%)	Of Income Over/Du revenu dépassant
25000	*25999*	701	4.27	25000
26000	*26999*	744	4.27	26000
27000	*27999*	787	4.27	27000
28000	*28999*	829	4.12	28000
29000	*29999*	871	2.55	29000
30000	*30999*	896	2.34	30000
31000	*31999*	920	2.34	31000
32000	*32999*	943	2.34	32000
33000	*33999*	967	2.34	33000
34000	*34999*	990	2.34	34000
35000	*35999*	1013	2.11	35000
36000	*36999*	1034	2.25	36000
37000	*37999*	1057	2.30	37000
38000	*38999*	1080	2.30	38000
39000	*39999*	1103	2.36	39000
40000	*40999*	1127	2.44	40000
41000	*41999*	1151	2.51	41000
42000	*42999*	1176	2.51	42000
43000	*43999*	1201	2.51	43000
44000	*44999*	1226	2.51	44000
45000	*45999*	1251	2.51	45000
46000	*46999*	1277	2.51	46000
47000	*47999*	1302	2.51	47000
48000	*48999*	1327	2.51	48000
49000	*49999*	1352	2.51	49000
50000	*50999*	1377	2.51	50000
51000	*51999*	1402	2.51	51000
52000	*52999*	1427	2.51	52000
53000	*53999*	1452	2.51	53000
54000	*54999*	1477	2.51	54000
55000	*55999*	1503	2.51	55000
56000	*56999*	1528	2.51	56000
57000	*57999*	1553	2.51	57000
58000	*58999*	1578	2.51	58000
59000	*59999*	1603	2.45	59000

Federal Child Support Tables/ Tables fédérales de pensions alimentaires pour enfants — **Province: Newfoundland and Labrador/Terre-Neuve-et-Labrador** — **No. Of Children/ Nbre d'enfants: Six or more/Six ou plus**

Income/Revenu ($)		Monthly Award/ Paiement mensuel ($)		
From/De	To/À	Basic Amount/ Montant de base	Plus (%)	Of Income Over/Du revenu dépassant
60000	*60999*	1627	2.35	60000
61000	*61999*	1651	2.33	61000
62000	*62999*	1674	2.33	62000
63000	*63999*	1698	2.34	63000
64000	*64999*	1721	2.37	64000
65000	*65999*	1745	2.37	65000
66000	*66999*	1769	2.37	66000
67000	*67999*	1792	2.37	67000
68000	*68999*	1816	2.37	68000
69000	*69999*	1840	2.37	69000
70000	*70999*	1863	2.21	70000
71000	*71999*	1885	2.21	71000
72000	*72999*	1907	2.21	72000
73000	*73999*	1929	2.21	73000
74000	*74999*	1952	2.21	74000
75000	*75999*	1974	2.21	75000
76000	*76999*	1996	2.21	76000
77000	*77999*	2018	2.21	77000
78000	*78999*	2040	2.21	78000
79000	*79999*	2062	2.21	79000
80000	*80999*	2084	2.21	80000
81000	*81999*	2106	2.21	81000
82000	*82999*	2128	2.21	82000
83000	*83999*	2150	2.21	83000
84000	*84999*	2172	2.21	84000
85000	*85999*	2194	2.21	85000
86000	*86999*	2216	2.21	86000
87000	*87999*	2238	2.21	87000
88000	*88999*	2261	2.21	88000
89000	*89999*	2283	2.21	89000
90000	*90999*	2305	2.21	90000
91000	*91999*	2327	2.21	91000
92000	*92999*	2349	2.21	92000
93000	*93999*	2371	2.21	93000
94000	*94999*	2393	2.21	94000

Federal Child Support Tables/ Tables fédérales de pensions alimentaires pour enfants — **Province: Newfoundland and Labrador/Terre-Neuve-et-Labrador** — **No. Of Children/ Nbre d'enfants: Six or more/Six ou plus**

Income/Revenu ($)		Monthly Award/ Paiement mensuel ($)		
From/De	To/À	Basic Amount/ Montant de base	Plus (%)	Of Income Over/Du revenu dépassant
95000	*95999*	2415	2.21	95000
96000	*96999*	2437	2.21	96000
97000	*97999*	2459	2.21	97000
98000	*98999*	2481	2.21	98000
99000	*99999*	2503	2.21	99000
100000	*100999*	2525	2.21	100000
101000	*101999*	2547	2.21	101000
102000	*102999*	2569	2.21	102000
103000	*103999*	2592	2.21	103000
104000	*104999*	2614	2.21	104000
105000	*105999*	2636	2.21	105000
106000	*106999*	2658	2.21	106000
107000	*107999*	2680	2.21	107000
108000	*108999*	2702	2.21	108000
109000	*109999*	2724	2.21	109000
110000	*110999*	2746	2.21	110000
111000	*111999*	2768	2.21	111000
112000	*112999*	2790	2.21	112000
113000	*113999*	2812	2.18	113000
114000	*114999*	2834	2.09	114000
115000	*115999*	2855	2.09	115000
116000	*116999*	2876	2.09	116000
117000	*117999*	2897	2.09	117000
118000	*118999*	2917	2.09	118000
119000	*119999*	2938	2.09	119000
120000	*120999*	2959	2.09	120000
121000	*121999*	2980	2.09	121000
122000	*122999*	3001	2.09	122000
123000	*123999*	3022	2.09	123000
124000	*124999*	3043	2.09	124000
125000	*125999*	3063	2.09	125000
126000	*126999*	3084	2.09	126000
127000	*127999*	3105	2.09	127000
128000	*128999*	3126	2.09	128000
129000	*129999*	3147	2.09	129000

Federal Child Support Tables/ Tables fédérales de pensions alimentaires pour enfants

Province: Newfoundland and Labrador/Terre-Neuve-et-Labrador No. Of Children/ Nbre d'enfants: Six or more/Six ou plus

Income/Revenu ($)		Monthly Award/ Paiement mensuel ($)		
From/De	To/À	Basic Amount/ Montant de base	Plus (%)	Of Income Over/Du revenu dépassant
130000	*130999*	3168	2.09	130000
131000	*131999*	3189	2.09	131000
132000	*132999*	3209	2.09	132000
133000	*133999*	3230	2.09	133000
134000	*134999*	3251	2.09	134000
135000	*135999*	3272	2.09	135000
136000	*136999*	3293	2.09	136000
137000	*137999*	3314	2.09	137000
138000	*138999*	3334	2.09	138000
139000	*139999*	3355	2.09	139000
140000	*140999*	3376	2.09	140000
141000	*141999*	3397	2.09	141000
142000	*142999*	3418	2.09	142000
143000	*143999*	3439	2.09	143000
144000	*144999*	3460	2.09	144000
145000	*145999*	3480	2.09	145000
146000	*146999*	3501	2.09	146000
147000	*147999*	3522	2.09	147000
148000	*148999*	3543	2.09	148000
149000	*149999*	3564	2.09	149000

Federal Child Support Tables/ Tables fédérales de pensions alimentaires pour enfants

Province: Newfoundland and Labrador/Terre-Neuve-et-Labrador No. Of Children/ Nbre d'enfants: Six or more/Six ou plus

Income/Revenu ($)		Monthly Award/ Paiement mensuel ($)		
From/De	To/À	Basic Amount/ Montant de base	Plus (%)	Of Income Over/Du revenu dépassant
150000	*or greater/ ou plus*	3585	2.09	150000

Federal Child Support Tables/ Tables fédérales de pensions alimentaires pour enfants

Province: Yukon No. Of Children/ Nbre d'enfants: One/Un

Income/Revenu ($)		Monthly Award/ Paiement mensuel ($)		
From/De	To/À	Basic Amount/ Montant de base	Plus (%)	Of Income Over/Du revenu dépassant
0	*7999*	0		
8000	*8999*	0	0.00	8000
9000	*9999*	0	0.00	9000
10000	*10999*	0	0.00	10000
11000	*11999*	0	0.55	11000
12000	*12999*	5	3.94	12000
13000	*13999*	45	3.87	13000
14000	*14999*	84	3.62	14000
15000	*15999*	120	2.98	15000
16000	*16999*	150	0.67	16000
17000	*17999*	156	0.67	17000
18000	*18999*	163	0.67	18000
19000	*19999*	170	0.92	19000
20000	*20999*	179	0.95	20000
21000	*21999*	188	0.95	21000
22000	*22999*	198	0.95	22000
23000	*23999*	207	0.95	23000
24000	*24999*	217	0.95	24000

Federal Child Support Tables/ Tables fédérales de pensions alimentaires pour enfants

Province: Yukon
No. Of Children/ Nbre d'enfants: One/Un

Income/Revenu ($)		Monthly Award/ Paiement mensuel ($)		
From/De	To/À	Basic Amount/ Montant de base	Plus (%)	Of Income Over/Du revenu dépassant
25000	*25999*	227	0.99	25000
26000	*26999*	236	0.99	26000
27000	*27999*	246	0.99	27000
28000	*28999*	256	0.99	28000
29000	*29999*	266	0.95	29000
30000	*30999*	276	0.93	30000
31000	*31999*	285	0.93	31000
32000	*32999*	294	0.93	32000
33000	*33999*	304	0.93	33000
34000	*34999*	313	0.93	34000
35000	*35999*	322	0.81	35000
36000	*36999*	330	0.86	36000
37000	*37999*	339	0.87	37000
38000	*38999*	347	0.87	38000
39000	*39999*	356	0.90	39000
40000	*40999*	365	0.92	40000
41000	*41999*	374	0.95	41000
42000	*42999*	384	0.95	42000
43000	*43999*	393	0.95	43000
44000	*44999*	403	0.95	44000
45000	*45999*	412	0.95	45000
46000	*46999*	422	0.95	46000
47000	*47999*	431	0.95	47000
48000	*48999*	441	0.95	48000
49000	*49999*	450	0.95	49000
50000	*50999*	460	0.95	50000
51000	*51999*	469	0.95	51000
52000	*52999*	479	0.95	52000
53000	*53999*	488	0.95	53000
54000	*54999*	498	0.95	54000
55000	*55999*	507	0.95	55000
56000	*56999*	517	0.95	56000
57000	*57999*	526	0.95	57000
58000	*58999*	536	0.95	58000
59000	*59999*	545	0.95	59000

Federal Child Support Tables/ Tables fédérales de pensions alimentaires pour enfants

Province: Yukon
No. Of Children/ Nbre d'enfants: One/Un

Income/Revenu ($)		Monthly Award/ Paiement mensuel ($)		
From/De	To/À	Basic Amount/ Montant de base	Plus (%)	Of Income Over/Du revenu dépassant
60000	*60999*	555	0.95	60000
61000	*61999*	564	0.95	61000
62000	*62999*	574	0.95	62000
63000	*63999*	583	0.95	63000
64000	*64999*	593	0.95	64000
65000	*65999*	602	0.95	65000
66000	*66999*	612	0.95	66000
67000	*67999*	621	0.95	67000
68000	*68999*	631	0.95	68000
69000	*69999*	640	0.95	69000
70000	*70999*	650	0.87	70000
71000	*71999*	658	0.87	71000
72000	*72999*	667	0.87	72000
73000	*73999*	676	0.87	73000
74000	*74999*	684	0.87	74000
75000	*75999*	693	0.87	75000
76000	*76999*	702	0.87	76000
77000	*77999*	710	0.86	77000
78000	*78999*	719	0.84	78000
79000	*79999*	727	0.84	79000
80000	*80999*	736	0.84	80000
81000	*81999*	744	0.84	81000
82000	*82999*	753	0.86	82000
83000	*83999*	761	0.86	83000
84000	*84999*	770	0.86	84000
85000	*85999*	779	0.86	85000
86000	*86999*	787	0.86	86000
87000	*87999*	796	0.86	87000
88000	*88999*	804	0.86	88000
89000	*89999*	813	0.86	89000
90000	*90999*	822	0.86	90000
91000	*91999*	830	0.86	91000
92000	*92999*	839	0.86	92000
93000	*93999*	847	0.86	93000
94000	*94999*	856	0.86	94000

Federal Child Support Tables/ Tables fédérales de pensions alimentaires pour enfants

Province: Yukon
No. Of Children/ Nbre d'enfants: One/Un

Income/Revenu ($)		Monthly Award/ Paiement mensuel ($)		
From/De	To/À	Basic Amount/ Montant de base	Plus (%)	Of Income Over/Du revenu dépassant
95000	*95999*	865	0.86	95000
96000	*96999*	873	0.86	96000
97000	*97999*	882	0.86	97000
98000	*98999*	890	0.86	98000
99000	*99999*	899	0.86	99000
100000	*100999*	908	0.86	100000
101000	*101999*	916	0.86	101000
102000	*102999*	925	0.86	102000
103000	*103999*	934	0.86	103000
104000	*104999*	942	0.86	104000
105000	*105999*	951	0.86	105000
106000	*106999*	959	0.86	106000
107000	*107999*	968	0.86	107000
108000	*108999*	977	0.86	108000
109000	*109999*	985	0.86	109000
110000	*110999*	994	0.86	110000
111000	*111999*	1002	0.86	111000
112000	*112999*	1011	0.86	112000
113000	*113999*	1020	0.85	113000
114000	*114999*	1028	0.80	114000
115000	*115999*	1036	0.80	115000
116000	*116999*	1044	0.80	116000
117000	*117999*	1052	0.80	117000
118000	*118999*	1060	0.80	118000
119000	*119999*	1068	0.80	119000
120000	*120999*	1076	0.80	120000
121000	*121999*	1084	0.80	121000
122000	*122999*	1092	0.80	122000

Federal Child Support Tables/ Tables fédérales de pensions alimentaires pour enfants

Province: Yukon
No. Of Children/ Nbre d'enfants: One/Un

Income/Revenu ($)		Monthly Award/ Paiement mensuel ($)		
From/De	To/À	Basic Amount/ Montant de base	Plus (%)	Of Income Over/Du revenu dépassant
123000	*123999*	1100	0.80	123000
124000	*124999*	1108	0.80	124000
125000	*125999*	1116	0.80	125000
126000	*126999*	1124	0.80	126000
127000	*127999*	1132	0.80	127000
128000	*128999*	1140	0.80	128000
129000	*129999*	1148	0.80	129000
130000	*130999*	1156	0.80	130000
131000	*131999*	1164	0.80	131000
132000	*132999*	1172	0.80	132000
133000	*133999*	1180	0.80	133000
134000	*134999*	1188	0.80	134000
135000	*135999*	1196	0.80	135000
136000	*136999*	1204	0.80	136000
137000	*137999*	1212	0.80	137000
138000	*138999*	1220	0.80	138000
139000	*139999*	1228	0.80	139000
140000	*140999*	1236	0.80	140000
141000	*141999*	1244	0.80	141000
142000	*142999*	1252	0.80	142000
143000	*143999*	1260	0.80	143000
144000	*144999*	1268	0.80	144000
145000	*145999*	1276	0.80	145000
146000	*146999*	1284	0.80	146000
147000	*147999*	1292	0.80	147000
148000	*148999*	1300	0.80	148000
149000	*149999*	1308	0.80	149000

Federal Child Support Tables/ Tables fédérales de pensions alimentaires pour enfants

Province: Yukon
No. Of Children/ Nbre d'enfants: One/Un

Income/Revenu ($)		Monthly Award/ Paiement mensuel ($)		
From/De	To/À	Basic Amount/ Montant de base	Plus (%)	Of Income Over/Du revenu dépassant
150000	*or greater/ ou plus*	1316	0.80	150000

Federal Child Support Tables/ Tables fédérales de pensions alimentaires pour enfants

Province: Yukon
No. Of Children/ Nbre d'enfants: Two/Deux

Income/Revenu ($)		Monthly Award/ Paiement mensuel ($)		
From/De	To/À	Basic Amount/ Montant de base	Plus (%)	Of Income Over/Du revenu dépassant
0	*7999*	0		
8000	*8999*	0	0.00	8000
9000	*9999*	0	0.00	9000
10000	*10999*	0	0.00	10000
11000	*11999*	0	0.59	11000
12000	*12999*	6	4.27	12000
13000	*13999*	49	4.19	13000
14000	*14999*	91	3.92	14000
15000	*15999*	130	3.72	15000
16000	*16999*	167	3.72	16000
17000	*17999*	204	3.72	17000
18000	*18999*	241	3.72	18000
19000	*19999*	278	3.61	19000
20000	*20999*	315	1.48	20000
21000	*21999*	329	1.48	21000
22000	*22999*	344	1.48	22000
23000	*23999*	359	1.48	23000
24000	*24999*	374	1.48	24000

Federal Child Support Tables/ Tables fédérales de pensions alimentaires pour enfants

Province: Yukon
No. Of Children/ Nbre d'enfants: Two/Deux

Income/Revenu ($)		Monthly Award/ Paiement mensuel ($)		
From/De	To/À	Basic Amount/ Montant de base	Plus (%)	Of Income Over/Du revenu dépassant
25000	*25999*	389	1.55	25000
26000	*26999*	404	1.55	26000
27000	*27999*	420	1.55	27000
28000	*28999*	435	1.55	28000
29000	*29999*	451	1.48	29000
30000	*30999*	465	1.44	30000
31000	*31999*	480	1.44	31000
32000	*32999*	494	1.44	32000
33000	*33999*	509	1.44	33000
34000	*34999*	523	1.44	34000
35000	*35999*	537	1.26	35000
36000	*36999*	550	1.33	36000
37000	*37999*	563	1.36	37000
38000	*38999*	577	1.36	38000
39000	*39999*	590	1.39	39000
40000	*40999*	604	1.43	40000
41000	*41999*	619	1.48	41000
42000	*42999*	633	1.48	42000
43000	*43999*	648	1.48	43000
44000	*44999*	663	1.48	44000
45000	*45999*	678	1.48	45000
46000	*46999*	693	1.48	46000
47000	*47999*	707	1.48	47000
48000	*48999*	722	1.48	48000
49000	*49999*	737	1.48	49000
50000	*50999*	752	1.48	50000
51000	*51999*	766	1.48	51000
52000	*52999*	781	1.48	52000
53000	*53999*	796	1.48	53000
54000	*54999*	811	1.48	54000
55000	*55999*	825	1.48	55000
56000	*56999*	840	1.48	56000
57000	*57999*	855	1.48	57000
58000	*58999*	870	1.48	58000
59000	*59999*	884	1.48	59000

Federal Child Support Tables/ Tables fédérales de pensions alimentaires pour enfants

Province: Yukon
No. Of Children/ Nbre d'enfants: Two/Deux

Income/Revenu ($)		Monthly Award/ Paiement mensuel ($)		
From/De	**To/À**	**Basic Amount/ Montant de base**	**Plus (%)**	**Of Income Over/Du revenu dépassant**
60000	*60999*	899	1.48	60000
61000	*61999*	914	1.48	61000
62000	*62999*	929	1.48	62000
63000	*63999*	943	1.48	63000
64000	*64999*	958	1.48	64000
65000	*65999*	973	1.48	65000
66000	*66999*	988	1.48	66000
67000	*67999*	1002	1.48	67000
68000	*68999*	1017	1.48	68000
69000	*69999*	1032	1.48	69000
70000	*70999*	1047	1.35	70000
71000	*71999*	1060	1.35	71000
72000	*72999*	1074	1.35	72000
73000	*73999*	1087	1.35	73000
74000	*74999*	1101	1.35	74000
75000	*75999*	1114	1.35	75000
76000	*76999*	1128	1.35	76000
77000	*77999*	1141	1.35	77000
78000	*78999*	1155	1.32	78000
79000	*79999*	1168	1.32	79000
80000	*80999*	1181	1.32	80000
81000	*81999*	1195	1.32	81000
82000	*82999*	1208	1.34	82000
83000	*83999*	1221	1.34	83000
84000	*84999*	1235	1.34	84000
85000	*85999*	1248	1.34	85000
86000	*86999*	1261	1.34	86000
87000	*87999*	1275	1.34	87000
88000	*88999*	1288	1.34	88000
89000	*89999*	1301	1.34	89000
90000	*90999*	1315	1.34	90000
91000	*91999*	1328	1.34	91000
92000	*92999*	1342	1.34	92000
93000	*93999*	1355	1.34	93000
94000	*94999*	1368	1.34	94000

Federal Child Support Tables/ Tables fédérales de pensions alimentaires pour enfants

Province: Yukon
No. Of Children/ Nbre d'enfants: Two/Deux

Income/Revenu ($)		Monthly Award/ Paiement mensuel ($)		
From/De	**To/À**	**Basic Amount/ Montant de base**	**Plus (%)**	**Of Income Over/Du revenu dépassant**
95000	*95999*	1382	1.34	95000
96000	*96999*	1395	1.34	96000
97000	*97999*	1409	1.34	97000
98000	*98999*	1422	1.34	98000
99000	*99999*	1435	1.34	99000
100000	*100999*	1449	1.34	100000
101000	*101999*	1462	1.34	101000
102000	*102999*	1476	1.34	102000
103000	*103999*	1489	1.34	103000
104000	*104999*	1502	1.34	104000
105000	*105999*	1516	1.34	105000
106000	*106999*	1529	1.34	106000
107000	*107999*	1543	1.34	107000
108000	*108999*	1556	1.34	108000
109000	*109999*	1569	1.34	109000
110000	*110999*	1583	1.34	110000
111000	*111999*	1596	1.34	111000
112000	*112999*	1609	1.34	112000
113000	*113999*	1623	1.32	113000
114000	*114999*	1636	1.24	114000
115000	*115999*	1649	1.24	115000
116000	*116999*	1661	1.24	116000
117000	*117999*	1673	1.24	117000
118000	*118999*	1686	1.24	118000
119000	*119999*	1698	1.24	119000
120000	*120999*	1711	1.24	120000
121000	*121999*	1723	1.24	121000
122000	*122999*	1736	1.24	122000
123000	*123999*	1748	1.24	123000
124000	*124999*	1761	1.24	124000
125000	*125999*	1773	1.24	125000
126000	*126999*	1785	1.24	126000
127000	*127999*	1798	1.24	127000
128000	*128999*	1810	1.24	128000
129000	*129999*	1823	1.24	129000

Federal Child Support Tables/ Tables fédérales de pensions alimentaires pour enfants

Province: Yukon
No. Of Children/ N^bre d'enfants: Two/Deux

Income/Revenu ($)		Monthly Award/ Paiement mensuel ($)		
From/De	**To/À**	**Basic Amount/ Montant de base**	**Plus (%)**	**Of Income Over/Du revenu dépassant**
130000	*130999*	1835	1.24	130000
131000	*131999*	1848	1.24	131000
132000	*132999*	1860	1.24	132000
133000	*133999*	1873	1.24	133000
134000	*134999*	1885	1.24	134000
135000	*135999*	1897	1.24	135000
136000	*136999*	1910	1.24	136000
137000	*137999*	1922	1.24	137000
138000	*138999*	1935	1.24	138000
139000	*139999*	1947	1.24	139000
140000	*140999*	1960	1.24	140000
141000	*141999*	1972	1.24	141000
142000	*142999*	1985	1.24	142000
143000	*143999*	1997	1.24	143000
144000	*144999*	2009	1.24	144000
145000	*145999*	2022	1.24	145000
146000	*146999*	2034	1.24	146000
147000	*147999*	2047	1.24	147000
148000	*148999*	2059	1.24	148000
149000	*149999*	2072	1.24	149000

Federal Child Support Tables/ Tables fédérales de pensions alimentaires pour enfants

Province: Yukon
No. Of Children/ N^bre d'enfants: Two/Deux

Income/Revenu ($)		Monthly Award/ Paiement mensuel ($)		
From/De	**To/À**	**Basic Amount/ Montant de base**	**Plus (%)**	**Of Income Over/Du revenu dépassant**
150000	*or greater/ ou plus*	2084	1.24	150000

Federal Child Support Tables/ Tables fédérales de pensions alimentaires pour enfants

Province: Yukon
No. Of Children/ N^bre d'enfants: Three/Trois

Income/Revenu ($)		Monthly Award/ Paiement mensuel ($)		
From/De	**To/À**	**Basic Amount/ Montant de base**	**Plus (%)**	**Of Income Over/Du revenu dépassant**
0	*7999*	0		
8000	*8999*	0	0.00	8000
9000	*9999*	O	0.00	9000
10000	*10999*	0	0.00	10000
11000	*11999*	0	0.64	11000
12000	*12999*	6	4.60	12000
13000	*13999*	52	4.51	13000
14000	*14999*	98	4.22	14000
15000	*15999*	140	4.00	15000
16000	*16999*	180	4.00	16000
17000	*17999*	220	4.00	17000
18000	*18999*	260	4.00	18000
19000	*19999*	300	4.00	19000
20000	*20999*	340	4.00	20000
21000	*21999*	380	4.00	21000
22000	*22999*	420	4.00	22000
23000	*23999*	460	3.93	23000
24000	*24999*	499	1.91	24000

Federal Child Support Tables/ Tables fédérales de pensions alimentaires pour enfants

Province: Yukon
No. Of Children/ Nbre d'enfants: Three/Trois

Income/Revenu ($)		Monthly Award/ Paiement mensuel ($)		
From/De	To/À	Basic Amount/ Montant de base	Plus (%)	Of Income Over/Du revenu dépassant
25000	*25999*	518	1.99	25000
26000	*26999*	538	1.99	26000
27000	*27999*	558	1.99	27000
28000	*28999*	578	1.99	28000
29000	*29999*	598	1.90	29000
30000	*30999*	617	1.85	30000
31000	*31999*	636	1.85	31000
32000	*32999*	654	1.85	32000
33000	*33999*	673	1.85	33000
34000	*34999*	691	1.85	34000
35000	*35999*	710	1.61	35000
36000	*36999*	726	1.71	36000
37000	*37999*	743	1.75	37000
38000	*38999*	760	1.75	38000
39000	*39999*	778	1.79	39000
40000	*40999*	796	1.84	40000
41000	*41999*	814	1.90	41000
42000	*42999*	833	1.90	42000
43000	*43999*	852	1.90	43000
44000	*44999*	871	1.90	44000
45000	*45999*	890	1.90	45000
46000	*46999*	909	1.90	46000
47000	*47999*	928	1.90	47000
48000	*48999*	947	1.90	48000
49000	*49999*	966	1.90	49000
50000	*50999*	985	1.90	50000
51000	*51999*	1004	1.90	51000
52000	*52999*	1023	1.90	52000
53000	*53999*	1042	1.90	53000
54000	*54999*	1061	1.90	54000
55000	*55999*	1080	1.90	55000
56000	*56999*	1099	1.90	56000
57000	*57999*	1118	1.90	57000
58000	*58999*	1137	1.90	58000
59000	*59999*	1156	1.90	59000

Federal Child Support Tables/ Tables fédérales de pensions alimentaires pour enfants

Province: Yukon
No. Of Children/ Nbre d'enfants: Three/Trois

Income/Revenu ($)		Monthly Award/ Paiement mensuel ($)		
From/De	To/À	Basic Amount/ Montant de base	Plus (%)	Of Income Over/Du revenu dépassant
60000	*60999*	1175	1.90	60000
61000	*61999*	1194	1.90	61000
62000	*62999*	1213	1.90	62000
63000	*63999*	1232	1.90	63000
64000	*64999*	1251	1.90	64000
65000	*65999*	1270	1.90	65000
66000	*66999*	1289	1.90	66000
67000	*67999*	1308	1.90	67000
68000	*68999*	1327	1.90	68000
69000	*69999*	1346	1.90	69000
70000	*70999*	1365	1.74	70000
71000	*71999*	1382	1.74	71000
72000	*72999*	1399	1.74	72000
73000	*73999*	1417	1.74	73000
74000	*74999*	1434	1.74	74000
75000	*75999*	1451	1.74	75000
76000	*76999*	1469	1.74	76000
77000	*77999*	1486	1.73	77000
78000	*78999*	1503	1.71	78000
79000	*79999*	1521	1.71	79000
80000	*80999*	1538	1.71	80000
81000	*81999*	1555	1.71	81000
82000	*82999*	1572	1.72	82000
83000	*83999*	1589	1.72	83000
84000	*84999*	1606	1.72	84000
85000	*85999*	1623	1.72	85000
86000	*86999*	1641	1.72	86000
87000	*87999*	1658	1.72	87000
88000	*88999*	1675	1.72	88000
89000	*89999*	1692	1.72	89000
90000	*90999*	1709	1.72	90000
91000	*91999*	1727	1.72	91000
92000	*92999*	1744	1.72	92000
93000	*93999*	1761	1.72	93000
94000	*94999*	1778	1.72	94000

Federal Child Support Tables/ Tables fédérales de pensions alimentaires pour enfants

Province: Yukon No. Of Children/ Nbre d'enfants: Three/Trois

Income/Revenu ($)		Monthly Award/ Paiement mensuel ($)		
From/De	To/À	Basic Amount/ Montant de base	Plus (%)	Of Income Over/Du revenu dépassant
95000	*95999*	1796	1.72	95000
96000	*96999*	1813	1.72	96000
97000	*97999*	1830	1.72	97000
98000	*98999*	1847	1.72	98000
99000	*99999*	1864	1.72	99000
100000	*100999*	1882	1.72	100000
101000	*101999*	1899	1.72	101000
102000	*102999*	1916	1.72	102000
103000	*103999*	1933	1.72	103000
104000	*104999*	1951	1.72	104000
105000	*105999*	1968	1.72	105000
106000	*106999*	1985	1.72	106000
107000	*107999*	2002	1.72	107000
108000	*108999*	2019	1.72	108000
109000	*109999*	2037	1.72	109000
110000	*110999*	2054	1.72	110000
111000	*111999*	2071	1.72	111000
112000	*112999*	2088	1.72	112000
113000	*113999*	2106	1.70	113000
114000	*114999*	2122	1.60	114000
115000	*115999*	2138	1.60	115000
116000	*116999*	2154	1.60	116000
117000	*117999*	2170	1.60	117000
118000	*118999*	2186	1.60	118000
119000	*119999*	2203	1.60	119000
120000	*120999*	2219	1.60	120000
121000	*121999*	2235	1.60	121000
122000	*122999*	2251	1.60	122000

Federal Child Support Tables/ Tables fédérales de pensions alimentaires pour enfants

Province: Yukon No. Of Children/ Nbre d'enfants: Three/Trois

Income/Revenu ($)		Monthly Award/ Paiement mensuel ($)		
From/De	To/À	Basic Amount/ Montant de base	Plus (%)	Of Income Over/Du revenu dépassant
123000	*123999*	2267	1.60	123000
124000	*124999*	2283	1.60	124000
125000	*125999*	2299	1.60	125000
126000	*126999*	2315	1.60	126000
127000	*127999*	2331	1.60	127000
128000	*128999*	2347	1.60	128000
129000	*129999*	2363	1.60	129000
130000	*130999*	2379	1.60	130000
131000	*131999*	2395	1.60	131000
132000	*132999*	2411	1.60	132000
133000	*133999*	2427	1.60	133000
134000	*134999*	2443	1.60	134000
135000	*135999*	2459	1.60	135000
136000	*136999*	2475	1.60	136000
137000	*137999*	2491	1.60	137000
138000	*138999*	2507	1.60	138000
139000	*139999*	2523	1.60	139000
140000	*140999*	2539	1.60	140000
141000	*141999*	2555	1.60	141000
142000	*142999*	2571	1.60	142000
143000	*143999*	2587	1.60	143000
144000	*144999*	2603	1.60	144000
145000	*145999*	2619	1.60	145000
146000	*146999*	2635	1.60	146000
147000	*147999*	2651	1.60	147000
148000	*148999*	2667	1.60	148000
149000	*149999*	2683	1.60	149000

Federal Child Support Tables/ Tables fédérales de pensions alimentaires pour enfants

Province: Yukon No. Of Children/ N^bre d'enfants: Three/Trois

Income/Revenu ($)		Monthly Award/ Paiement mensuel ($)		
From/De	To/À	Basic Amount/ Montant de base	Plus (%)	Of Income Over/Du revenu dépassant
150000	*or greater/ ou plus*	2699	1.60	150000

Federal Child Support Tables/ Tables fédérales de pensions alimentaires pour enfants

Province: Yukon No. Of Children/ N^bre d'enfants: Four/Quatre

Income/Revenu ($)		Monthly Award/ Paiement mensuel ($)		
From/De	To/À	Basic Amount/ Montant de base	Plus (%)	Of Income Over/Du revenu dépassant
0	*7999*	0		
8000	*8999*	0	0.00	8000
9000	*9999*	0	0.00	9000
10000	*10999*	0	0.00	10000
11000	*11999*	0	0.69	11000
12000	*12999*	7	4.93	12000
13000	*13999*	56	4.84	13000
14000	*14999*	105	4.52	14000
15000	*15999*	150	4.29	15000
16000	*16999*	193	4.29	16000
17000	*17999*	236	4.29	17000
18000	*18999*	278	4.29	18000
19000	*19999*	321	4.29	19000
20000	*20999*	364	4.29	20000
21000	*21999*	407	4.29	21000
22000	*22999*	450	4.29	22000
23000	*23999*	493	4.29	23000
24000	*24999*	536	4.29	24000
25000	*25999*	579	4.48	25000
26000	*26999*	623	4.48	26000
27000	*27999*	668	2.69	27000
28000	*28999*	695	2.35	28000
29000	*29999*	719	2.25	29000
30000	*30999*	741	2.19	30000
31000	*31999*	763	2.19	31000
32000	*32999*	785	2.19	32000
33000	*33999*	807	2.19	33000
34000	*34999*	829	2.19	34000
35000	*35999*	850	1.91	35000
36000	*36999*	870	2.02	36000
37000	*37999*	890	2.07	37000
38000	*38999*	910	2.07	38000
39000	*39999*	931	2.12	39000
40000	*40999*	952	2.18	40000
41000	*41999*	974	2.24	41000
42000	*42999*	996	2.24	42000
43000	*43999*	1019	2.24	43000
44000	*44999*	1041	2.24	44000
45000	*45999*	1064	2.24	45000
46000	*46999*	1086	2.24	46000
47000	*47999*	1109	2.24	47000
48000	*48999*	1131	2.24	48000
49000	*49999*	1153	2.24	49000
50000	*50999*	1176	2.24	50000
51000	*51999*	1198	2.24	51000
52000	*52999*	1221	2.24	52000
53000	*53999*	1243	2.24	53000
54000	*54999*	1266	2.24	54000
55000	*55999*	1288	2.24	55000
56000	*56999*	1310	2.24	56000
57000	*57999*	1333	2.24	57000
58000	*58999*	1355	2.24	58000
59000	*59999*	1378	2.24	59000

Federal Child Support Tables/ Tables fédérales de pensions alimentaires pour enfants

Province: Yukon No. Of Children/ Nbre d'enfants: Four/Quatre

Income/Revenu ($)		Monthly Award/ Paiement mensuel ($)		
From/De	To/À	Basic Amount/ Montant de base	Plus (%)	Of Income Over/Du revenu dépassant
60000	*60999*	1400	2.24	60000
61000	*61999*	1423	2.24	61000
62000	*62999*	1445	2.24	62000
63000	*63999*	1467	2.24	63000
64000	*64999*	1490	2.24	64000
65000	*65999*	1512	2.24	65000
66000	*66999*	1535	2.24	66000
67000	*67999*	1557	2.24	67000
68000	*68999*	1580	2.24	68000
69000	*69999*	1602	2.24	69000
70000	*70999*	1624	2.05	70000
71000	*71999*	1645	2.05	71000
72000	*72999*	1666	2.05	72000
73000	*73999*	1686	2.05	73000
74000	*74999*	1707	2.05	74000
75000	*75999*	1727	2.05	75000
76000	*76999*	1748	2.05	76000
77000	*77999*	1768	2.05	77000
78000	*78999*	1789	2.02	78000
79000	*79999*	1809	2.02	79000
80000	*80999*	1829	2.02	80000
81000	*81999*	1849	2.02	81000
82000	*82999*	1870	2.03	82000
83000	*83999*	1890	2.03	83000
84000	*84999*	1910	2.03	84000
85000	*85999*	1931	2.03	85000
86000	*86999*	1951	2.03	86000
87000	*87999*	1971	2.03	87000
88000	*88999*	1992	2.03	88000
89000	*89999*	2012	2.03	89000
90000	*90999*	2032	2.03	90000
91000	*91999*	2053	2.03	91000
92000	*92999*	2073	2.03	92000
93000	*93999*	2093	2.03	93000
94000	*94999*	2114	2.03	94000

Federal Child Support Tables/ Tables fédérales de pensions alimentaires pour enfants

Province: Yukon No. Of Children/ Nbre d'enfants: Four/Quatre

Income/Revenu ($)		Monthly Award/ Paiement mensuel ($)		
From/De	To/À	Basic Amount/ Montant de base	Plus (%)	Of Income Over/Du revenu dépassant
95000	*95999*	2134	2.03	95000
96000	*96999*	2154	2.03	96000
97000	*97999*	2175	2.03	97000
98000	*98999*	2195	2.03	98000
99000	*99999*	2215	2.03	99000
100000	*100999*	2236	2.03	100000
101000	*101999*	2256	2.03	101000
102000	*102999*	2277	2.03	102000
103000	*103999*	2297	2.03	103000
104000	*104999*	2317	2.03	104000
105000	*105999*	2338	2.03	105000
106000	*106999*	2358	2.03	106000
107000	*107999*	2378	2.03	107000
108000	*108999*	2399	2.03	108000
109000	*109999*	2419	2.03	109000
110000	*110999*	2439	2.03	110000
111000	*111999*	2460	2.03	111000
112000	*112999*	2480	2.03	112000
113000	*113999*	2500	2.01	113000
114000	*114999*	2520	1.89	114000
115000	*115999*	2539	1.89	115000
116000	*116999*	2558	1.89	116000
117000	*117999*	2577	1.89	117000
118000	*118999*	2596	1.89	118000
119000	*119999*	2615	1.89	119000
120000	*120999*	2634	1.89	120000
121000	*121999*	2653	1.89	121000
122000	*122999*	2672	1.89	122000
123000	*123999*	2691	1.89	123000
124000	*124999*	2710	1.89	124000
125000	*125999*	2728	1.89	125000
126000	*126999*	2747	1.89	126000
127000	*127999*	2766	1.89	127000
128000	*128999*	2785	1.89	128000
129000	*129999*	2804	1.89	129000

Federal Child Support Tables/ Tables fédérales de pensions alimentaires pour enfants

Province: Yukon
No. Of Children/ Nbre d'enfants: Four/Quatre

Income/Revenu ($)		Monthly Award/ Paiement mensuel ($)		
From/De	To/À	Basic Amount/ Montant de base	Plus (%)	Of Income Over/Du revenu dépassant
130000	*130999*	2823	1.89	130000
131000	*131999*	2842	1.89	131000
132000	*132999*	2861	1.89	132000
133000	*133999*	2880	1.89	133000
134000	*134999*	2899	1.89	134000
135000	*135999*	2918	1.89	135000
136000	*136999*	2936	1.89	136000
137000	*137999*	2955	1.89	137000
138000	*138999*	2974	1.89	138000
139000	*139999*	2993	1.89	139000
140000	*140999*	3012	1.89	140000
141000	*141999*	3031	1.89	141000
142000	*142999*	3050	1.89	142000
143000	*143999*	3069	1.89	143000
144000	*144999*	3088	1.89	144000
145000	*145999*	3107	1.89	145000
146000	*146999*	3126	1.89	146000
147000	*147999*	3144	1.89	147000
148000	*148999*	3163	1.89	148000
149000	*149999*	3182	1.89	149000

Federal Child Support Tables/ Tables fédérales de pensions alimentaires pour enfants

Province: Yukon
No. Of Children/ Nbre d'enfants: Four/Quatre

Income/Revenu ($)		Monthly Award/ Paiement mensuel ($)		
From/De	To/À	Basic Amount/ Montant de base	Plus (%)	Of Income Over/Du revenu dépassant
150000	*or greater/ ou plus*	3201	1.89	150000

Federal Child Support Tables/ Tables fédérales de pensions alimentaires pour enfants

Province: Yukon
No. Of Children/ Nbre d'enfants: Five/Cinq

Income/Revenu ($)		Monthly Award/ Paiement mensuel ($)		
From/De	To/À	Basic Amount/ Montant de base	Plus (%)	Of Income Over/Du revenu dépassant
0	*7999*	0		
8000	*8999*	0	0.00	8000
9000	*9999*	0	0.00	9000
10000	*10999*	0	0.00	10000
11000	*11999*	0	0.69	11000
12000	*12999*	7	4.93	12000
13000	*13999*	56	4.84	13000
14000	*14999*	105	4.52	14000
15000	*15999*	150	4.29	15000
16000	*16999*	193	4.29	16000
17000	*17999*	236	4.29	17000
18000	*18999*	278	4.29	18000
19000	*19999*	321	4.29	19000
20000	*20999*	364	4.29	20000
21000	*21999*	407	4.29	21000
22000	*22999*	450	4.29	22000
23000	*23999*	493	4.29	23000
24000	*24999*	536	4.29	24000

Federal Child Support Tables/ Tables fédérales de pensions alimentaires pour enfants

Province: Yukon
No. Of Children/ Nbre d'enfants: Five/Cinq

Income/Revenu ($)		Monthly Award/ Paiement mensuel ($)		
From/De	To/À	Basic Amount/ Montant de base	Plus (%)	Of Income Over/Du revenu dépassant
25000	*25999*	579	4.48	25000
26000	*26999*	623	4.48	26000
27000	*27999*	668	4.48	27000
28000	*28999*	713	4.48	28000
29000	*29999*	758	4.28	29000
30000	*30999*	801	4.16	30000
31000	*31999*	842	4.16	31000
32000	*32999*	884	3.46	32000
33000	*33999*	918	2.47	33000
34000	*34999*	943	2.47	34000
35000	*35999*	968	2.15	35000
36000	*36999*	989	2.28	36000
37000	*37999*	1012	2.33	37000
38000	*38999*	1036	2.33	38000
39000	*39999*	1059	2.39	39000
40000	*40999*	1083	2.46	40000
41000	*41999*	1107	2.53	41000
42000	*42999*	1133	2.53	42000
43000	*43999*	1158	2.53	43000
44000	*44999*	1183	2.53	44000
45000	*45999*	1209	2.53	45000
46000	*46999*	1234	2.53	46000
47000	*47999*	1259	2.53	47000
48000	*48999*	1284	2.53	48000
49000	*49999*	1310	2.53	49000
50000	*50999*	1335	2.53	50000
51000	*51999*	1360	2.53	51000
52000	*52999*	1386	2.53	52000
53000	*53999*	1411	2.53	53000
54000	*54999*	1436	2.53	54000
55000	*55999*	1462	2.53	55000
56000	*56999*	1487	2.53	56000
57000	*57999*	1512	2.53	57000
58000	*58999*	1537	2.53	58000
59000	*59999*	1563	2.53	59000

Federal Child Support Tables/ Tables fédérales de pensions alimentaires pour enfants

Province: Yukon
No. Of Children/ Nbre d'enfants: Five/Cinq

Income/Revenu ($)		Monthly Award/ Paiement mensuel ($)		
From/De	To/À	Basic Amount/ Montant de base	Plus (%)	Of Income Over/Du revenu dépassant
60000	*60999*	1588	2.53	60000
61000	*61999*	1613	2.53	61000
62000	*62999*	1639	2.53	62000
63000	*63999*	1664	2.53	63000
64000	*64999*	1689	2.53	64000
65000	*65999*	1715	2.53	65000
66000	*66999*	1740	2.53	66000
67000	*67999*	1765	2.53	67000
68000	*68999*	1791	2.53	68000
69000	*69999*	1816	2.53	69000
70000	*70999*	1841	2.32	70000
71000	*71999*	1864	2.32	71000
72000	*72999*	1887	2.32	72000
73000	*73999*	1911	2.32	73000
74000	*74999*	1934	2.32	74000
75000	*75999*	1957	2.32	75000
76000	*76999*	1980	2.32	76000
77000	*77999*	2003	2.31	77000
78000	*78999*	2026	2.28	78000
79000	*79999*	2049	2.28	79000
80000	*80999*	2072	2.28	80000
81000	*81999*	2095	2.28	81000
82000	*82999*	2118	2.30	82000
83000	*83999*	2141	2.30	83000
84000	*84999*	2164	2.30	84000
85000	*85999*	2187	2.30	85000
86000	*86999*	2210	2.30	86000
87000	*87999*	2233	2.30	87000
88000	*88999*	2255	2.30	88000
89000	*89999*	2278	2.30	89000
90000	*90999*	2301	2.30	90000
91000	*91999*	2324	2.30	91000
92000	*92999*	2347	2.30	92000
93000	*93999*	2370	2.30	93000
94000	*94999*	2393	2.30	94000

Federal Child Support Tables/ Tables fédérales de pensions alimentaires pour enfants

Province: Yukon
No. Of Children/ Nbre d'enfants: Five/Cinq

Income/Revenu ($)		Monthly Award/ Paiement mensuel ($)		
From/De	To/À	Basic Amount/ Montant de base	Plus (%)	Of Income Over/Du revenu dépassant
95000	*95999*	2416	2.30	95000
96000	*96999*	2439	2.30	96000
97000	*97999*	2462	2.30	97000
98000	*98999*	2485	2.30	98000
99000	*99999*	2508	2.30	99000
100000	*100999*	2531	2.30	100000
101000	*101999*	2554	2.30	101000
102000	*102999*	2577	2.30	102000
103000	*103999*	2600	2.30	103000
104000	*104999*	2623	2.30	104000
105000	*105999*	2646	2.30	105000
106000	*106999*	2669	2.30	106000
107000	*107999*	2692	2.30	107000
108000	*108999*	2715	2.30	108000
109000	*109999*	2738	2.30	109000
110000	*110999*	2761	2.30	110000
111000	*111999*	2784	2.30	111000
112000	*112999*	2806	2.30	112000
113000	*113999*	2829	2.26	113000
114000	*114999*	2852	2.13	114000
115000	*115999*	2873	2.13	115000
116000	*116999*	2895	2.13	116000
117000	*117999*	2916	2.13	117000
118000	*118999*	2937	2.13	118000
119000	*119999*	2959	2.13	119000
120000	*120999*	2980	2.13	120000
121000	*121999*	3001	2.13	121000
122000	*122999*	3023	2.13	122000

Federal Child Support Tables/ Tables fédérales de pensions alimentaires pour enfants

Province: Yukon
No. Of Children/ Nbre d'enfants: Five/Cinq

Income/Revenu ($)		Monthly Award/ Paiement mensuel ($)		
From/De	To/À	Basic Amount/ Montant de base	Plus (%)	Of Income Over/Du revenu dépassant
123000	*123999*	3044	2.13	123000
124000	*124999*	3065	2.13	124000
125000	*125999*	3087	2.13	125000
126000	*126999*	3108	2.13	126000
127000	*127999*	3129	2.13	127000
128000	*128999*	3151	2.13	128000
129000	*129999*	3172	2.13	129000
130000	*130999*	3193	2.13	130000
131000	*131999*	3215	2.13	131000
132000	*132999*	3236	2.13	132000
133000	*133999*	3257	2.13	133000
134000	*134999*	3279	2.13	134000
135000	*135999*	3300	2.13	135000
136000	*136999*	3321	2.13	136000
137000	*137999*	3343	2.13	137000
138000	*138999*	3364	2.13	138000
139000	*139999*	3385	2.13	139000
140000	*140999*	3407	2.13	140000
141000	*141999*	3428	2.13	141000
142000	*142999*	3449	2.13	142000
143000	*143999*	3471	2.13	143000
144000	*144999*	3492	2.13	144000
145000	*145999*	3513	2.13	145000
146000	*146999*	3535	2.13	146000
147000	*147999*	3556	2.13	147000
148000	*148999*	3577	2.13	148000
149000	*149999*	3599	2.13	149000

Federal Child Support Tables/ Tables fédérales de pensions alimentaires pour enfants

Province: Yukon No. Of Children/ Nbre d'enfants: Five/Cinq

Income/Revenu ($)		Monthly Award/ Paiement mensuel ($)		
From/De	To/À	Basic Amount/ Montant de base	Plus (%)	Of Income Over/Du revenu dépassant
150000	*or greater/ ou plus*	3620	2.13	150000

Federal Child Support Tables/ Tables fédérales de pensions alimentaires pour enfants

Province: Yukon No. Of Children/ Nbre d'enfants: Six or more/ Six ou plus

Income/Revenu ($)		Monthly Award/ Paiement mensuel ($)		
From/De	To/À	Basic Amount/ Montant de base	Plus (%)	Of Income Over/Du revenu dépassant
0	*7999*	0		
8000	*8999*	0	0.00	8000
9000	*9999*	0	0.00	9000
10000	*10999*	0	0.00	10000
11000	*11999*	0	0.69	11000
12000	*12999*	7	4.93	12000
13000	*13999*	56	4.84	13000
14000	*14999*	105	4.52	14000
15000	*15999*	150	4.29	15000
16000	*16999*	193	4.29	16000
17000	*17999*	236	4.29	17000
18000	*18999*	278	4.29	18000
19000	*19999*	321	4.29	19000
20000	*20999*	364	4.29	20000
21000	*21999*	407	4.29	21000
22000	*22999*	450	4.29	22000
23000	*23999*	493	4.29	23000
24000	*24999*	536	4.29	24000

Federal Child Support Tables/ Tables fédérales de pensions alimentaires pour enfants

Province: Yukon No. Of Children/ Nbre d'enfants: Six or more/ Six ou plus

Income/Revenu ($)		Monthly Award/ Paiement mensuel ($)		
From/De	To/À	Basic Amount/ Montant de base	Plus (%)	Of Income Over/Du revenu dépassant
25000	*25999*	579	4.48	25000
26000	*26999*	623	4.48	26000
27000	*27999*	668	4.48	27000
28000	*28999*	713	4.48	28000
29000	*29999*	758	4.28	29000
30000	*30999*	801	4.16	30000
31000	*31999*	842	4.16	31000
32000	*32999*	884	4.16	32000
33000	*33999*	925	4.16	33000
34000	*34999*	967	4.16	34000
35000	*35999*	1009	3.63	35000
36000	*36999*	1045	3.85	36000
37000	*37999*	1084	3.94	37000
38000	*38999*	1123	3.94	38000
39000	*39999*	1162	3.08	39000
40000	*40999*	1193	2.70	40000
41000	*41999*	1220	2.77	41000
42000	*42999*	1248	2.77	42000
43000	*43999*	1276	2.77	43000
44000	*44999*	1303	2.77	44000
45000	*45999*	1331	2.77	45000
46000	*46999*	1359	2.77	46000
47000	*47999*	1386	2.77	47000
48000	*48999*	1414	2.77	48000
49000	*49999*	1442	2.77	49000
50000	*50999*	1470	2.77	50000
51000	*51999*	1497	2.77	51000
52000	*52999*	1525	2.77	52000
53000	*53999*	1553	2.77	53000
54000	*54999*	1581	2.77	54000
55000	*55999*	1608	2.77	55000
56000	*56999*	1636	2.77	56000
57000	*57999*	1664	2.77	57000
58000	*58999*	1692	2.77	58000
59000	*59999*	1719	2.77	59000

Federal Child Support Tables/ Tables fédérales de pensions alimentaires pour enfants

Province: Yukon No. Of Children/ Nbre d'enfants: Six or more/ Six ou plus

Income/Revenu ($)		Monthly Award/ Paiement mensuel ($)		
From/De	To/À	Basic Amount/ Montant de base	Plus (%)	Of Income Over/Du revenu dépassant
60000	*60999*	1747	2.77	60000
61000	*61999*	1775	2.77	61000
62000	*62999*	1803	2.77	62000
63000	*63999*	1830	2.77	63000
64000	*64999*	1858	2.77	64000
65000	*65999*	1886	2.77	65000
66000	*66999*	1913	2.77	66000
67000	*67999*	1941	2.77	67000
68000	*68999*	1969	2.77	68000
69000	*69999*	1997	2.77	69000
70000	*70999*	2024	2.54	70000
71000	*71999*	2050	2.54	71000
72000	*72999*	2075	2.54	72000
73000	*73999*	2101	2.54	73000
74000	*74999*	2126	2.54	74000
75000	*75999*	2151	2.54	75000
76000	*76999*	2177	2.54	76000
77000	*77999*	2202	2.53	77000
78000	*78999*	2228	2.50	78000
79000	*79999*	2253	2.50	79000
80000	*80999*	2278	2.50	80000
81000	*81999*	2303	2.50	81000
82000	*82999*	2328	2.52	82000
83000	*83999*	2353	2.52	83000
84000	*84999*	2378	2.52	84000
85000	*85999*	2403	2.52	85000
86000	*86999*	2428	2.52	86000
87000	*87999*	2454	2.52	87000
88000	*88999*	2479	2.52	88000
89000	*89999*	2504	2.52	89000
90000	*90999*	2529	2.52	90000
91000	*91999*	2554	2.52	91000
92000	*92999*	2579	2.52	92000
93000	*93999*	2605	2.52	93000
94000	*94999*	2630	2.52	94000

Federal Child Support Tables/ Tables fédérales de pensions alimentaires pour enfants

Province: Yukon No. Of Children/ Nbre d'enfants: Six or more/ Six ou plus

Income/Revenu ($)		Monthly Award/ Paiement mensuel ($)		
From/De	To/À	Basic Amount/ Montant de base	Plus (%)	Of Income Over/Du revenu dépassant
95000	*95999*	2655	2.52	95000
96000	*96999*	2680	2.52	96000
97000	*97999*	2705	2.52	97000
98000	*98999*	2730	2.52	98000
99000	*99999*	2756	2.52	99000
100000	*100999*	2781	2.52	100000
101000	*101999*	2806	2.52	101000
102000	*102999*	2831	2.52	102000
103000	*103999*	2856	2.52	103000
104000	*104999*	2881	2.52	104000
105000	*105999*	2907	2.52	105000
106000	*106999*	2932	2.52	106000
107000	*107999*	2957	2.52	107000
108000	*108999*	2982	2.52	108000
109000	*109999*	3007	2.52	109000
110000	*110999*	3032	2.52	110000
111000	*111999*	3058	2.52	111000
112000	*112999*	3083	2.52	112000
113000	*113999*	3108	2.48	113000
114000	*114999*	3133	2.34	114000
115000	*115999*	3156	2.34	115000
116000	*116999*	3179	2.34	116000
117000	*117999*	3203	2.34	117000
118000	*118999*	3226	2.34	118000
119000	*119999*	3250	2.34	119000
120000	*120999*	3273	2.34	120000
121000	*121999*	3296	2.34	121000
122000	*122999*	3320	2.34	122000
123000	*123999*	3343	2.34	123000
124000	*124999*	3367	2.34	124000
125000	*125999*	3390	2.34	125000
126000	*126999*	3413	2.34	126000
127000	*127999*	3437	2.34	127000
128000	*128999*	3460	2.34	128000
129000	*129999*	3483	2.34	129000

Federal Child Support Tables/ Tables fédérales de pensions alimentaires pour enfants

Province: Yukon
No. Of Children/ Nbre d'enfants: Six or more/ Six ou plus

Income/Revenu ($)		Monthly Award/ Paiement mensuel ($)		
From/De	To/À	Basic Amount/ Montant de base	Plus (%)	Of Income Over/Du revenu dépassant
130000	*130999*	3507	2.34	130000
131000	*131999*	3530	2.34	131000
132000	*132999*	3554	2.34	132000
133000	*133999*	3577	2.34	133000
134000	*134999*	3600	2.34	134000
135000	*135999*	3624	2.34	135000
136000	*136999*	3647	2.34	136000
137000	*137999*	3671	2.34	137000
138000	*138999*	3694	2.34	138000
139000	*139999*	3717	2.34	139000
140000	*140999*	3741	2.34	140000
141000	*141999*	3764	2.34	141000
142000	*142999*	3788	2.34	142000
143000	*143999*	3811	2.34	143000
144000	*144999*	3834	2.34	144000
145000	*145999*	3858	2.34	145000
146000	*146999*	3881	2.34	146000
147000	*147999*	3904	2.34	147000
148000	*148999*	3928	2.34	148000
149000	*149999*	3951	2.34	149000

Federal Child Support Tables/ Tables fédérales de pensions alimentaires pour enfants

Province: Yukon
No. Of Children/ Nbre d'enfants: Six or more/ Six ou plus

Income/Revenu ($)		Monthly Award/ Paiement mensuel ($)		
From/De	To/À	Basic Amount/ Montant de base	Plus (%)	Of Income Over/Du revenu dépassant
150000	*or greater/ ou plus*	3975	2.34	150000

Federal Child Support Tables/ Tables fédérales de pensions alimentaires pour enfants

Province: Northwest Territories/Territoires du Nord-Ouest
No. Of Children/ Nbre d'enfants: One/Un

Income/Revenu ($)		Monthly Award/ Paiement mensuel ($)		
From/De	To/À	Basic Amount/ Montant de base	Plus (%)	Of Income Over/Du revenu dépassant
0	*7999*	0		
8000	*8999*	0	1.40	8000
9000	*9999*	14	2.00	9000
10000	*10999*	34	2.00	10000
11000	*11999*	54	2.00	11000
12000	*12999*	74	2.00	12000
13000	*13999*	94	2.00	13000
14000	*14999*	114	2.00	14000
15000	*15999*	134	1.75	15000
16000	*16999*	151	0.77	16000
17000	*17999*	159	0.78	17000
18000	*18999*	167	0.78	18000
19000	*19999*	174	0.78	19000
20000	*20999*	182	0.78	20000
21000	*21999*	190	0.78	21000
22000	*22999*	198	0.78	22000
23000	*23999*	206	0.78	23000
24000	*24999*	213	0.93	24000

Federal Child Support Tables/ Tables fédérales de pensions alimentaires pour enfants

Province: Northwest Territories/Territoires du Nord-Ouest
No. Of Children/ Nbre d'enfants: One/Un

Income/Revenu ($)		Monthly Award/ Paiement mensuel ($)		
From/De	**To/À**	**Basic Amount/ Montant de base**	**Plus (%)**	**Of Income Over/Du revenu dépassant**
25000	*25999*	223	1.01	25000
26000	*26999*	233	1.01	26000
27000	*27999*	243	1.01	27000
28000	*28999*	253	1.01	28000
29000	*29999*	263	0.97	29000
30000	*30999*	273	0.94	30000
31000	*31999*	282	0.94	31000
32000	*32999*	292	0.94	32000
33000	*33999*	301	0.91	33000
34000	*34999*	310	0.90	34000
35000	*35999*	319	0.82	35000
36000	*36999*	327	0.87	36000
37000	*37999*	336	0.89	37000
38000	*38999*	345	0.89	38000
39000	*39999*	354	0.91	39000
40000	*40999*	363	0.94	40000
41000	*41999*	372	0.96	41000
42000	*42999*	382	0.96	42000
43000	*43999*	392	0.96	43000
44000	*44999*	401	0.96	44000
45000	*45999*	411	0.96	45000
46000	*46999*	420	0.96	46000
47000	*47999*	430	0.96	47000
48000	*48999*	440	0.96	48000
49000	*49999*	449	0.96	49000
50000	*50999*	459	0.96	50000
51000	*51999*	468	0.96	51000
52000	*52999*	478	0.96	52000
53000	*53999*	488	0.96	53000
54000	*54999*	497	0.96	54000
55000	*55999*	507	0.96	55000
56000	*56999*	516	0.96	56000
57000	*57999*	526	0.96	57000
58000	*58999*	536	0.96	58000
59000	*59999*	545	0.96	59000

Federal Child Support Tables/ Tables fédérales de pensions alimentaires pour enfants

Province: Northwest Territories/Territoires du Nord-Ouest
No. Of Children/ Nbre d'enfants: One/Un

Income/Revenu ($)		Monthly Award/ Paiement mensuel ($)		
From/De	**To/À**	**Basic Amount/ Montant de base**	**Plus (%)**	**Of Income Over/Du revenu dépassant**
60000	*60999*	555	0.96	60000
61000	*61999*	564	0.96	61000
62000	*62999*	574	0.96	62000
63000	*63999*	584	0.96	63000
64000	*64999*	593	0.96	64000
65000	*65999*	603	0.96	65000
66000	*66999*	612	0.93	66000
67000	*67999*	622	0.92	67000
68000	*68999*	631	0.92	68000
69000	*69999*	640	0.92	69000
70000	*70999*	649	0.86	70000
71000	*71999*	658	0.86	71000
72000	*72999*	666	0.86	72000
73000	*73999*	675	0.86	73000
74000	*74999*	684	0.86	74000
75000	*75999*	692	0.86	75000
76000	*76999*	701	0.86	76000
77000	*77999*	710	0.86	77000
78000	*78999*	718	0.86	78000
79000	*79999*	727	0.86	79000
80000	*80999*	735	0.86	80000
81000	*81999*	744	0.86	81000
82000	*82999*	753	0.86	82000
83000	*83999*	761	0.86	83000
84000	*84999*	770	0.86	84000
85000	*85999*	779	0.86	85000
86000	*86999*	787	0.86	86000
87000	*87999*	796	0.86	87000
88000	*88999*	804	0.86	88000
89000	*89999*	813	0.86	89000
90000	*90999*	822	0.86	90000
91000	*91999*	830	0.86	91000
92000	*92999*	839	0.86	92000
93000	*93999*	847	0.86	93000
94000	*94999*	856	0.86	94000

Federal Child Support Tables/Tables fédérales de pensions alimentaires pour enfants

Province: Northwest Territories/Territoires du Nord-Ouest
No. Of Children/Nbre d'enfants: One/Un

Income/Revenu ($)		Monthly Award/Paiement mensuel ($)		
From/De	**To/À**	**Basic Amount/Montant de base**	**Plus (%)**	**Of Income Over/Du revenu dépassant**
95000	*95999*	865	0.86	95000
96000	*96999*	873	0.86	96000
97000	*97999*	882	0.86	97000
98000	*98999*	891	0.86	98000
99000	*99999*	899	0.86	99000
100000	*100999*	908	0.86	100000
101000	*101999*	916	0.86	101000
102000	*102999*	925	0.86	102000
103000	*103999*	934	0.86	103000
104000	*104999*	942	0.86	104000
105000	*105999*	951	0.86	105000
106000	*106999*	960	0.86	106000
107000	*107999*	968	0.86	107000
108000	*108999*	977	0.84	108000
109000	*109999*	985	0.84	109000
110000	*110999*	994	0.84	110000
111000	*111999*	1002	0.84	111000
112000	*112999*	1010	0.84	112000
113000	*113999*	1019	0.83	113000
114000	*114999*	1027	0.80	114000
115000	*115999*	1035	0.80	115000
116000	*116999*	1043	0.80	116000
117000	*117999*	1051	0.80	117000
118000	*118999*	1059	0.80	118000
119000	*119999*	1067	0.80	119000
120000	*120999*	1075	0.80	120000
121000	*121999*	1083	0.80	121000
122000	*122999*	1091	0.80	122000

Federal Child Support Tables/Tables fédérales de pensions alimentaires pour enfants

Province: Northwest Territories/Territoires du Nord-Ouest
No. Of Children/Nbre d'enfants: One/Un

Income/Revenu ($)		Monthly Award/Paiement mensuel ($)		
From/De	**To/À**	**Basic Amount/Montant de base**	**Plus (%)**	**Of Income Over/Du revenu dépassant**
123000	*123999*	1099	0.80	123000
124000	*124999*	1107	0.80	124000
125000	*125999*	1115	0.80	125000
126000	*126999*	1123	0.80	126000
127000	*127999*	1131	0.80	127000
128000	*128999*	1139	0.80	128000
129000	*129999*	1147	0.80	129000
130000	*130999*	1155	0.80	130000
131000	*131999*	1163	0.80	131000
132000	*132999*	1171	0.80	132000
133000	*133999*	1179	0.80	133000
134000	*134999*	1187	0.80	134000
135000	*135999*	1195	0.80	135000
136000	*136999*	1203	0.80	136000
137000	*137999*	1211	0.80	137000
138000	*138999*	1219	0.80	138000
139000	*139999*	1227	0.80	139000
140000	*140999*	1235	0.80	140000
141000	*141999*	1242	0.80	141000
142000	*142999*	1250	0.80	142000
143000	*143999*	1258	0.80	143000
144000	*144999*	1266	0.80	144000
145000	*145999*	1274	0.80	145000
146000	*146999*	1282	0.80	146000
147000	*147999*	1290	0.80	147000
148000	*148999*	1298	0.80	148000
149000	*149999*	1306	0.80	149000

Federal Child Support Tables/ Tables fédérales de pensions alimentaires pour enfants

Province: Northwest Territories/Territoires du Nord-Ouest
No. Of Children/ Nbre d'enfants: One/Un

Income/Revenu ($)		Monthly Award/ Paiement mensuel ($)		
From/De	**To/À**	**Basic Amount/ Montant de base**	**Plus (%)**	**Of Income Over/Du revenu dépassant**
150000	*or greater/ ou plus*	1314	0.80	150000

Federal Child Support Tables/ Tables fédérales de pensions alimentaires pour enfants

Province: Northwest Territories/Territoires du Nord-Ouest
No. Of Children/ Nbre d'enfants: Two/Deux

Income/Revenu ($)		Monthly Award/ Paiement mensuel ($)		
From/De	**To/À**	**Basic Amount/ Montant de base**	**Plus (%)**	**Of Income Over/Du revenu dépassant**
0	*7999*	0		
8000	*8999*	0	3.10	8000
9000	*9999*	31	4.34	9000
10000	*10999*	74	4.34	10000
11000	*11999*	118	4.34	11000
12000	*12999*	161	4.01	12000
13000	*13999*	201	3.90	13000
14000	*14999*	240	1.62	14000
15000	*15999*	257	1.00	15000
16000	*16999*	267	1.35	16000
17000	*17999*	280	1.36	17000
18000	*18999*	294	1.36	18000
19000	*19999*	307	1.36	19000
20000	*20999*	321	1.36	20000
21000	*21999*	335	1.36	21000
22000	*22999*	348	1.36	22000
23000	*23999*	362	1.36	23000
24000	*24999*	376	1.50	24000
25000	*25999*	391	1.57	25000
26000	*26999*	406	1.57	26000
27000	*27999*	422	1.57	27000
28000	*28999*	438	1.57	28000
29000	*29999*	453	1.50	29000
30000	*30999*	468	1.46	30000
31000	*31999*	483	1.46	31000
32000	*32999*	498	1.46	32000
33000	*33999*	512	1.42	33000
34000	*34999*	526	1.40	34000
35000	*35999*	541	1.28	35000
36000	*36999*	553	1.35	36000
37000	*37999*	567	1.38	37000
38000	*38999*	581	1.38	38000
39000	*39999*	595	1.42	39000
40000	*40999*	609	1.46	40000
41000	*41999*	623	1.50	41000
42000	*42999*	638	1.50	42000
43000	*43999*	653	1.50	43000
44000	*44999*	668	1.50	44000
45000	*45999*	683	1.50	45000
46000	*46999*	698	1.50	46000
47000	*47999*	713	1.50	47000
48000	*48999*	728	1.49	48000
49000	*49999*	743	1.49	49000
50000	*50999*	758	1.49	50000
51000	*51999*	773	1.49	51000
52000	*52999*	788	1.49	52000
53000	*53999*	803	1.49	53000
54000	*54999*	818	1.49	54000
55000	*55999*	833	1.49	55000
56000	*56999*	848	1.49	56000
57000	*57999*	862	1.49	57000
58000	*58999*	877	1.49	58000
59000	*59999*	892	1.49	59000

Federal Child Support Tables/ Tables fédérales de pensions alimentaires pour enfants — **Province: Northwest Territories/Territoires du Nord-Ouest** — **No. Of Children/ Nbre d'enfants: Two/Deux**

Income/Revenu ($)		Monthly Award/ Paiement mensuel ($)		
From/De	To/À	Basic Amount/ Montant de base	Plus (%)	Of Income Over/Du revenu dépassant
60000	*60999*	907	1.49	60000
61000	*61999*	922	1.49	61000
62000	*62999*	937	1.49	62000
63000	*63999*	952	1.49	63000
64000	*64999*	967	1.49	64000
65000	*65999*	982	1.49	65000
66000	*66999*	997	1.45	66000
67000	*67999*	1011	1.43	67000
68000	*68999*	1026	1.43	68000
69000	*69999*	1040	1.43	69000
70000	*70999*	1054	1.34	70000
71000	*71999*	1068	1.34	71000
72000	*72999*	1081	1.34	72000
73000	*73999*	1094	1.34	73000
74000	*74999*	1108	1.34	74000
75000	*75999*	1121	1.34	75000
76000	*76999*	1135	1.34	76000
77000	*77999*	1148	1.34	77000
78000	*78999*	1161	1.34	78000
79000	*79999*	1175	1.34	79000
80000	*80999*	1188	1.34	80000
81000	*81999*	1202	1.34	81000
82000	*82999*	1215	1.34	82000
83000	*83999*	1228	1.34	83000
84000	*84999*	1242	1.34	84000
85000	*85999*	1255	1.34	85000
86000	*86999*	1269	1.34	86000
87000	*87999*	1282	1.34	87000
88000	*88999*	1295	1.34	88000
89000	*89999*	1309	1.34	89000
90000	*90999*	1322	1.34	90000
91000	*91999*	1336	1.34	91000
92000	*92999*	1349	1.34	92000
93000	*93999*	1363	1.34	93000
94000	*94999*	1376	1.34	94000

Federal Child Support Tables/ Tables fédérales de pensions alimentaires pour enfants — **Province: Northwest Territories/Territoires du Nord-Ouest** — **No. Of Children/ Nbre d'enfants: Two/Deux**

Income/Revenu ($)		Monthly Award/ Paiement mensuel ($)		
From/De	To/À	Basic Amount/ Montant de base	Plus (%)	Of Income Over/Du revenu dépassant
95000	*95999*	1389	1.34	95000
96000	*96999*	1403	1.34	96000
97000	*97999*	1416	1.34	97000
98000	*98999*	1430	1.34	98000
99000	*99999*	1443	1.34	99000
100000	*100999*	1456	1.34	100000
101000	*101999*	1470	1.34	101000
102000	*102999*	1483	1.34	102000
103000	*103999*	1497	1.34	103000
104000	*104999*	1510	1.34	104000
105000	*105999*	1523	1.34	105000
106000	*106999*	1537	1.34	106000
107000	*107999*	1550	1.34	107000
108000	*108999*	1564	1.31	108000
109000	*109999*	1577	1.31	109000
110000	*110999*	1590	1.31	110000
111000	*111999*	1603	1.31	111000
112000	*112999*	1616	1.31	112000
113000	*113999*	1629	1.29	113000
114000	*114999*	1642	1.24	114000
115000	*115999*	1654	1.24	115000
116000	*116999*	1667	1.24	116000
117000	*117999*	1679	1.24	117000
118000	*118999*	1692	1.24	118000
119000	*119999*	1704	1.24	119000
120000	*120999*	1716	1.24	120000
121000	*121999*	1729	1.24	121000
122000	*122999*	1741	1.24	122000
123000	*123999*	1754	1.24	123000
124000	*124999*	1766	1.24	124000
125000	*125999*	1778	1.24	125000
126000	*126999*	1791	1.24	126000
127000	*127999*	1803	1.24	127000
128000	*128999*	1816	1.24	128000
129000	*129999*	1828	1.24	129000

Federal Child Support Tables/ Tables fédérales de pensions alimentaires pour enfants

Province: Northwest Territories/Territoires du Nord-Ouest
No. Of Children/ Nbre d'enfants: Two/Deux

Income/Revenu ($)		Monthly Award/ Paiement mensuel ($)		
From/De	To/À	Basic Amount/ Montant de base	Plus (%)	Of Income Over/Du revenu dépassant
130000	*130999*	1840	1.24	130000
131000	*131999*	1853	1.24	131000
132000	*132999*	1865	1.24	132000
133000	*133999*	1878	1.24	133000
134000	*134999*	1890	1.24	134000
135000	*135999*	1903	1.24	135000
136000	*136999*	1915	1.24	136000
137000	*137999*	1927	1.24	137000
138000	*138999*	1940	1.24	138000
139000	*139999*	1952	1.24	139000
140000	*140999*	1965	1.24	140000
141000	*141999*	1977	1.24	141000
142000	*142999*	1989	1.24	142000
143000	*143999*	2002	1.24	143000
144000	*144999*	2014	1.24	144000
145000	*145999*	2027	1.24	145000
146000	*146999*	2039	1.24	146000
147000	*147999*	2051	1.24	147000
148000	*148999*	2064	1.24	148000
149000	*149999*	2076	1.24	149000

Federal Child Support Tables/ Tables fédérales de pensions alimentaires pour enfants

Province: Northwest Territories/Territoires du Nord-Ouest
No. Of Children/ Nbre d'enfants: Two/Deux

Income/Revenu ($)		Monthly Award/ Paiement mensuel ($)		
From/De	To/À	Basic Amount/ Montant de base	Plus (%)	Of Income Over/Du revenu dépassant
150000	*or greater/ ou plus*	2089	1.24	150000

Federal Child Support Tables/ Tables fédérales de pensions alimentaires pour enfants

Province: Northwest Territories/Territoires du Nord-Ouest
No. Of Children/ Nbre d'enfants: Three/Trois

Income/Revenu ($)		Monthly Award/ Paiement mensuel ($)		
From/De	To/À	Basic Amount/ Montant de base	Plus (%)	Of Income Over/Du revenu dépassant
0	*7999*	0		
8000	*8999*	0	3.34	8000
9000	*9999*	33	4.68	9000
10000	*10999*	80	4.68	10000
11000	*11999*	127	4.68	11000
12000	*12999*	174	4.32	12000
13000	*13999*	217	4.20	13000
14000	*14999*	259	4.17	14000
15000	*15999*	301	4.17	15000
16000	*16999*	342	3.46	16000
17000	*17999*	377	1.83	17000
18000	*18999*	395	1.83	18000
19000	*19999*	414	1.83	19000
20000	*20999*	432	1.83	20000
21000	*21999*	450	1.83	21000
22000	*22999*	469	1.83	22000
23000	*23999*	487	1.83	23000
24000	*24999*	505	1.96	24000

Federal Child Support Tables/Tables fédérales de pensions alimentaires pour enfants — **Province: Northwest Territories/Territoires du Nord-Ouest** — **No. Of Children/Nbre d'enfants: Three/Trois**

Income/Revenu ($)		Monthly Award/Paiement mensuel ($)		
From/De	To/À	Basic Amount/Montant de base	Plus (%)	Of Income Over/Du revenu dépassant
25000	*25999*	525	2.02	25000
26000	*26999*	545	2.02	26000
27000	*27999*	565	2.02	27000
28000	*28999*	585	2.02	28000
29000	*29999*	606	1.93	29000
30000	*30999*	625	1.88	30000
31000	*31999*	644	1.88	31000
32000	*32999*	663	1.88	32000
33000	*33999*	681	1.82	33000
34000	*34999*	700	1.81	34000
35000	*35999*	718	1.64	35000
36000	*36999*	734	1.74	36000
37000	*37999*	752	1.78	37000
38000	*38999*	769	1.78	38000
39000	*39999*	787	1.82	39000
40000	*40999*	805	1.87	40000
41000	*41999*	824	1.93	41000
42000	*42999*	843	1.93	42000
43000	*43999*	863	1.93	43000
44000	*44999*	882	1.93	44000
45000	*45999*	901	1.93	45000
46000	*46999*	920	1.93	46000
47000	*47999*	940	1.93	47000
48000	*48999*	959	1.92	48000
49000	*49999*	978	1.92	49000
50000	*50999*	997	1.92	50000
51000	*51999*	1017	1.92	51000
52000	*52999*	1036	1.92	52000
53000	*53999*	1055	1.92	53000
54000	*54999*	1074	1.92	54000
55000	*55999*	1093	1.92	55000
56000	*56999*	1112	1.92	56000
57000	*57999*	1132	1.92	57000
58000	*58999*	1151	1.92	58000
59000	*59999*	1170	1.92	59000

Federal Child Support Tables/Tables fédérales de pensions alimentaires pour enfants — **Province: Northwest Territories/Territoires du Nord-Ouest** — **No. Of Children/Nbre d'enfants: Three/Trois**

Income/Revenu ($)		Monthly Award/Paiement mensuel ($)		
From/De	To/À	Basic Amount/Montant de base	Plus (%)	Of Income Over/Du revenu dépassant
60000	*60999*	1189	1.92	60000
61000	*61999*	1208	1.92	61000
62000	*62999*	1228	1.92	62000
63000	*63999*	1247	1.92	63000
64000	*64999*	1266	1.92	64000
65000	*65999*	1285	1.92	65000
66000	*66999*	1304	1.86	66000
67000	*67999*	1323	1.83	67000
68000	*68999*	1341	1.83	68000
69000	*69999*	1360	1.83	69000
70000	*70999*	1378	1.72	70000
71000	*71999*	1395	1.72	71000
72000	*72999*	1413	1.72	72000
73000	*73999*	1430	1.72	73000
74000	*74999*	1447	1.72	74000
75000	*75999*	1464	1.72	75000
76000	*76999*	1482	1.72	76000
77000	*77999*	1499	1.72	77000
78000	*78999*	1516	1.72	78000
79000	*79999*	1533	1.72	79000
80000	*80999*	1550	1.72	80000
81000	*81999*	1568	1.72	81000
82000	*82999*	1585	1.72	82000
83000	*83999*	1602	1.72	83000
84000	*84999*	1619	1.72	84000
85000	*85999*	1637	1.72	85000
86000	*86999*	1654	1.72	86000
87000	*87999*	1671	1.72	87000
88000	*88999*	1688	1.72	88000
89000	*89999*	1706	1.72	89000
90000	*90999*	1723	1.72	90000
91000	*91999*	1740	1.72	91000
92000	*92999*	1757	1.72	92000
93000	*93999*	1775	1.72	93000
94000	*94999*	1792	1.72	94000

Federal Child Support Tables/Tables fédérales de pensions alimentaires pour enfants

Province: Northwest Territories/Territoires du Nord-Ouest
No. Of Children/N^{bre} d'enfants: Three/Trois

Income/Revenu ($)		Monthly Award/Paiement mensuel ($)		
From/De	To/À	Basic Amount/Montant de base	Plus (%)	Of Income Over/Du revenu dépassant
95000	*95999*	1809	1.72	95000
96000	*96999*	1826	1.72	96000
97000	*97999*	1843	1.72	97000
98000	*98999*	1861	1.72	98000
99000	*99999*	1878	1.72	99000
100000	*100999*	1895	1.72	100000
101000	*101999*	1912	1.72	101000
102000	*102999*	1930	1.72	102000
103000	*103999*	1947	1.72	103000
104000	*104999*	1964	1.72	104000
105000	*105999*	1981	1.72	105000
106000	*106999*	1999	1.72	106000
107000	*107999*	2016	1.72	107000
108000	*108999*	2033	1.68	108000
109000	*109999*	2050	1.68	109000
110000	*110999*	2067	1.68	110000
111000	*111999*	2083	1.68	111000
112000	*112999*	2100	1.68	112000
113000	*113999*	2117	1.66	113000
114000	*114999*	2134	1.60	114000
115000	*115999*	2150	1.60	115000
116000	*116999*	2166	1.60	116000
117000	*117999*	2182	1.60	117000
118000	*118999*	2198	1.60	118000
119000	*119999*	2214	1.60	119000
120000	*120999*	2229	1.60	120000
121000	*121999*	2245	1.60	121000
122000	*122999*	2261	1.60	122000

Federal Child Support Tables/Tables fédérales de pensions alimentaires pour enfants

Province: Northwest Territories/Territoires du Nord-Ouest
No. Of Children/N^{bre} d'enfants: Three/Trois

Income/Revenu ($)		Monthly Award/Paiement mensuel ($)		
From/De	To/À	Basic Amount/Montant de base	Plus (%)	Of Income Over/Du revenu dépassant
123000	*123999*	2277	1.60	123000
124000	*124999*	2293	1.60	124000
125000	*125999*	2309	1.60	125000
126000	*126999*	2325	1.60	126000
127000	*127999*	2341	1.60	127000
128000	*128999*	2357	1.60	128000
129000	*129999*	2373	1.60	129000
130000	*130999*	2389	1.60	130000
131000	*131999*	2405	1.60	131000
132000	*132999*	2421	1.60	132000
133000	*133999*	2437	1.60	133000
134000	*134999*	2453	1.60	134000
135000	*135999*	2469	1.60	135000
136000	*136999*	2485	1.60	136000
137000	*137999*	2501	1.60	137000
138000	*138999*	2517	1.60	138000
139000	*139999*	2533	1.60	139000
140000	*140999*	2549	1.60	140000
141000	*141999*	2565	1.60	141000
142000	*142999*	2581	1.60	142000
143000	*143999*	2597	1.60	143000
144000	*144999*	2612	1.60	144000
145000	*145999*	2628	1.60	145000
146000	*146999*	2644	1.60	146000
147000	*147999*	2660	1.60	147000
148000	*148999*	2676	1.60	148000
149000	*149999*	2692	1.60	149000

Federal Child Support Tables/ Tables fédérales de pensions alimentaires pour enfants

Province: Northwest Territories/Territoires du Nord-Ouest No. Of Children/ Nbre d'enfants: Three/Trois

Income/Revenu ($)		Monthly Award/ Paiement mensuel ($)		
From/De	To/À	Basic Amount/ Montant de base	Plus (%)	Of Income Over/Du revenu dépassant
150000	*or greater/ ou plus*	2708	1.60	150000

Federal Child Support Tables/ Tables fédérales de pensions alimentaires pour enfants

Province: Northwest Territories/Territoires du Nord-Ouest No. Of Children/ Nbre d'enfants: Four/Quatre

Income/Revenu ($)		Monthly Award/ Paiement mensuel ($)		
From/De	To/À	Basic Amount/ Montant de base	Plus (%)	Of Income Over/Du revenu dépassant
0	*7999*	0		
8000	*8999*	0	3.58	8000
9000	*9999*	36	5.01	9000
10000	*10999*	86	5.01	10000
11000	*11999*	136	5.01	11000
12000	*12999*	186	4.63	12000
13000	*13999*	232	4.50	13000
14000	*14999*	277	4.47	14000
15000	*15999*	322	4.47	15000
16000	*16999*	367	4.50	16000
17000	*17999*	412	4.55	17000
18000	*18999*	457	4.34	18000
19000	*19999*	501	2.22	19000
20000	*20999*	523	2.22	20000
21000	*21999*	545	2.22	21000
22000	*22999*	567	2.22	22000
23000	*23999*	589	2.22	23000
24000	*24999*	611	2.33	24000

Federal Child Support Tables/ Tables fédérales de pensions alimentaires pour enfants

Province: Northwest Territories/Territoires du Nord-Ouest No. Of Children/ Nbre d'enfants: Four/Quatre

Income/Revenu ($)		Monthly Award/ Paiement mensuel ($)		
From/De	To/À	Basic Amount/ Montant de base	Plus (%)	Of Income Over/Du revenu dépassant
25000	*25999*	635	2.39	25000
26000	*26999*	659	2.39	26000
27000	*27999*	682	2.39	27000
28000	*28999*	706	2.39	28000
29000	*29999*	730	2.28	29000
30000	*30999*	753	2.22	30000
31000	*31999*	775	2.22	31000
32000	*32999*	798	2.22	32000
33000	*33999*	820	2.16	33000
34000	*34999*	841	2.13	34000
35000	*35999*	863	1.94	35000
36000	*36999*	882	2.06	36000
37000	*37999*	903	2.10	37000
38000	*38999*	924	2.10	38000
39000	*39999*	945	2.15	39000
40000	*40999*	966	2.21	40000
41000	*41999*	988	2.28	41000
42000	*42999*	1011	2.28	42000
43000	*43999*	1034	2.28	43000
44000	*44999*	1057	2.28	44000
45000	*45999*	1079	2.28	45000
46000	*46999*	1102	2.28	46000
47000	*47999*	1125	2.28	47000
48000	*48999*	1148	2.27	48000
49000	*49999*	1170	2.27	49000
50000	*50999*	1193	2.27	50000
51000	*51999*	1216	2.27	51000
52000	*52999*	1238	2.27	52000
53000	*53999*	1261	2.27	53000
54000	*54999*	1284	2.27	54000
55000	*55999*	1307	2.27	55000
56000	*56999*	1329	2.27	56000
57000	*57999*	1352	2.27	57000
58000	*58999*	1375	2.27	58000
59000	*59999*	1397	2.27	59000

Federal Child Support Tables/ Tables fédérales de pensions alimentaires pour enfants — **Province: Northwest Territories/Territoires du Nord-Ouest No. Of Children/ Nbre d'enfants: Four/Quatre**

Income/Revenu ($)		Monthly Award/ Paiement mensuel ($)		
From/De	To/À	Basic Amount/ Montant de base	Plus (%)	Of Income Over/Du revenu dépassant
60000	*60999*	1420	2.27	60000
61000	*61999*	1443	2.27	61000
62000	*62999*	1465	2.27	62000
63000	*63999*	1488	2.27	63000
64000	*64999*	1511	2.27	64000
65000	*65999*	1533	2.27	65000
66000	*66999*	1556	2.20	66000
67000	*67999*	1578	2.17	67000
68000	*68999*	1600	2.17	68000
69000	*69999*	1621	2.17	69000
70000	*70999*	1643	2.04	70000
71000	*71999*	1664	2.04	71000
72000	*72999*	1684	2.04	72000
73000	*73999*	1704	2.04	73000
74000	*74999*	1725	2.04	74000
75000	*75999*	1745	2.04	75000
76000	*76999*	1765	2.04	76000
77000	*77999*	1786	2.04	77000
78000	*78999*	1806	2.04	78000
79000	*79999*	1826	2.04	79000
80000	*80999*	1847	2.04	80000
81000	*81999*	1867	2.04	81000
82000	*82999*	1888	2.04	82000
83000	*83999*	1908	2.04	83000
84000	*84999*	1928	2.04	84000
85000	*85999*	1949	2.04	85000
86000	*86999*	1969	2.04	86000
87000	*87999*	1989	2.04	87000
88000	*88999*	2010	2.04	88000
89000	*89999*	2030	2.04	89000
90000	*90999*	2051	2.04	90000
91000	*91999*	2071	2.04	91000
92000	*92999*	2091	2.04	92000
93000	*93999*	2112	2.04	93000
94000	*94999*	2132	2.04	94000

Federal Child Support Tables/ Tables fédérales de pensions alimentaires pour enfants — **Province: Northwest Territories/Territoires du Nord-Ouest No. Of Children/ Nbre d'enfants: Four/Quatre**

Income/Revenu ($)		Monthly Award/ Paiement mensuel ($)		
From/De	To/À	Basic Amount/ Montant de base	Plus (%)	Of Income Over/Du revenu dépassant
95000	*95999*	2152	2.04	95000
96000	*96999*	2173	2.04	96000
97000	*97999*	2193	2.04	97000
98000	*98999*	2213	2.04	98000
99000	*99999*	2234	2.04	99000
100000	*100999*	2254	2.04	100000
101000	*101999*	2275	2.04	101000
102000	*102999*	2295	2.04	102000
103000	*103999*	2315	2.04	103000
104000	*104999*	2336	2.04	104000
105000	*105999*	2356	2.04	105000
106000	*106999*	2376	2.04	106000
107000	*107999*	2397	2.04	107000
108000	*108999*	2417	1.99	108000
109000	*109999*	2437	1.98	109000
110000	*110999*	2457	1.98	110000
111000	*111999*	2477	1.98	111000
112000	*112999*	2497	1.98	112000
113000	*113999*	2516	1.97	113000
114000	*114999*	2536	1.89	114000
115000	*115999*	2555	1.89	115000
116000	*116999*	2574	1.89	116000
117000	*117999*	2593	1.89	117000
118000	*118999*	2612	1.89	118000
119000	*119999*	2630	1.89	119000
120000	*120999*	2649	1.89	120000
121000	*121999*	2668	1.89	121000
122000	*122999*	2687	1.89	122000
123000	*123999*	2706	1.89	123000
124000	*124999*	2725	1.89	124000
125000	*125999*	2744	1.89	125000
126000	*126999*	2762	1.89	126000
127000	*127999*	2781	1.89	127000
128000	*128999*	2800	1.89	128000
129000	*129999*	2819	1.89	129000

Federal Child Support Tables/ Tables fédérales de pensions alimentaires pour enfants

Province: Northwest Territories/Territoires du Nord-Ouest
No. Of Children/ N^bre d'enfants: Four/Quatre

Income/Revenu ($)		Monthly Award/ Paiement mensuel ($)		
From/De	To/À	Basic Amount/ Montant de base	Plus (%)	Of Income Over/Du revenu dépassant
130000	*130999*	2838	1.89	130000
131000	*131999*	2857	1.89	131000
132000	*132999*	2876	1.89	132000
133000	*133999*	2894	1.89	133000
134000	*134999*	2913	1.89	134000
135000	*135999*	2932	1.89	135000
136000	*136999*	2951	1.89	136000
137000	*137999*	2970	1.89	137000
138000	*138999*	2989	1.89	138000
139000	*139999*	3008	1.89	139000
140000	*140999*	3026	1.89	140000
141000	*141999*	3045	1.89	141000
142000	*142999*	3064	1.89	142000
143000	*143999*	3083	1.89	143000
144000	*144999*	3102	1.89	144000
145000	*145999*	3121	1.89	145000
146000	*146999*	3140	1.89	146000
147000	*147999*	3159	1.89	147000
148000	*148999*	3177	1.89	148000
149000	*149999*	3196	1.89	149000
150000	*or greater/ ou plus*	3215	1.89	150000

Federal Child Support Tables/ Tables fédérales de pensions alimentaires pour enfants

Province: Northwest Territories/Territoires du Nord-Ouest
No. Of Children/ N^bre d'enfants: Five/Cinq

Income/Revenu ($)		Monthly Award/ Paiement mensuel ($)		
From/De	To/À	Basic Amount/ Montant de base	Plus (%)	Of Income Over/Du revenu dépassant
0	*7999*	0		
8000	*8999*	0	3.58	8000
9000	*9999*	36	5.01	9000
10000	*10999*	86	5.01	10000
11000	*11999*	136	5.01	11000
12000	*12999*	186	4.63	12000
13000	*13999*	232	4.50	13000
14000	*14999*	277	4.47	14000
15000	*15999*	322	4.47	15000
16000	*16999*	367	4.50	16000
17000	*17999*	412	4.55	17000
18000	*18999*	457	4.55	18000
19000	*19999*	503	4.55	19000
20000	*20999*	548	4.55	20000
21000	*21999*	593	4.55	21000
22000	*22999*	639	3.56	22000
23000	*23999*	675	2.54	23000
24000	*24999*	700	2.64	24000

Federal Child Support Tables/ Tables fédérales de pensions alimentaires pour enfants — **Province: Northwest Territories/Territoires du Nord-Ouest** — **No. Of Children/ Nbre d'enfants: Five/Cinq**

Income/Revenu ($)		Monthly Award/ Paiement mensuel ($)		
From/De	To/À	Basic Amount/ Montant de base	Plus (%)	Of Income Over/Du revenu dépassant
25000	*25999*	726	2.69	25000
26000	*26999*	753	2.69	26000
27000	*27999*	780	2.69	27000
28000	*28999*	807	2.69	28000
29000	*29999*	834	2.58	29000
30000	*30999*	860	2.51	30000
31000	*31999*	885	2.51	31000
32000	*32999*	910	2.51	32000
33000	*33999*	935	2.43	33000
34000	*34999*	959	2.41	34000
35000	*35999*	983	2.19	35000
36000	*36999*	1005	2.32	36000
37000	*37999*	1029	2.37	37000
38000	*38999*	1052	2.37	38000
39000	*39999*	1076	2.43	39000
40000	*40999*	1100	2.50	40000
41000	*41999*	1125	2.57	41000
42000	*42999*	1151	2.57	42000
43000	*43999*	1177	2.57	43000
44000	*44999*	1202	2.57	44000
45000	*45999*	1228	2.57	45000
46000	*46999*	1254	2.57	46000
47000	*47999*	1279	2.57	47000
48000	*48999*	1305	2.56	48000
49000	*49999*	1331	2.56	49000
50000	*50999*	1356	2.56	50000
51000	*51999*	1382	2.56	51000
52000	*52999*	1407	2.56	52000
53000	*53999*	1433	2.56	53000
54000	*54999*	1459	2.56	54000
55000	*55999*	1484	2.56	55000
56000	*56999*	1510	2.56	56000
57000	*57999*	1535	2.56	57000
58000	*58999*	1561	2.56	58000
59000	*59999*	1587	2.56	59000

Federal Child Support Tables/ Tables fédérales de pensions alimentaires pour enfants — **Province: Northwest Territories/Territoires du Nord-Ouest** — **No. Of Children/ Nbre d'enfants: Five/Cinq**

Income/Revenu ($)		Monthly Award/ Paiement mensuel ($)		
From/De	To/À	Basic Amount/ Montant de base	Plus (%)	Of Income Over/Du revenu dépassant
60000	*60999*	1612	2.56	60000
61000	*61999*	1638	2.56	61000
62000	*62999*	1663	2.56	62000
63000	*63999*	1689	2.56	63000
64000	*64999*	1715	2.56	64000
65000	*65999*	1740	2.56	65000
66000	*66999*	1766	2.49	66000
67000	*67999*	1791	2.45	67000
68000	*68999*	1815	2.45	68000
69000	*69999*	1840	2.45	69000
70000	*70999*	1864	2.30	70000
71000	*71999*	1887	2.30	71000
72000	*72999*	1910	2.30	72000
73000	*73999*	1933	2.30	73000
74000	*74999*	1956	2.30	74000
75000	*75999*	1979	2.30	75000
76000	*76999*	2002	2.30	76000
77000	*77999*	2025	2.30	77000
78000	*78999*	2048	2.30	78000
79000	*79999*	2071	2.30	79000
80000	*80999*	2094	2.30	80000
81000	*81999*	2117	2.30	81000
82000	*82999*	2140	2.30	82000
83000	*83999*	2163	2.30	83000
84000	*84999*	2186	2.30	84000
85000	*85999*	2209	2.30	85000
86000	*86999*	2232	2.30	86000
87000	*87999*	2255	2.30	87000
88000	*88999*	2278	2.30	88000
89000	*89999*	2301	2.30	89000
90000	*90999*	2324	2.30	90000
91000	*91999*	2347	2.30	91000
92000	*92999*	2370	2.30	92000
93000	*93999*	2393	2.30	93000
94000	*94999*	2416	2.30	94000

Federal Child Support Tables/ Tables fédérales de pensions alimentaires pour enfants

Province: Northwest Territories/Territoires du Nord-Ouest
No. Of Children/ Nbre d'enfants: Five/Cinq

Income/Revenu ($)		Monthly Award/ Paiement mensuel ($)		
From/De	**To/À**	**Basic Amount/ Montant de base**	**Plus (%)**	**Of Income Over/Du revenu dépassant**
95000	*95999*	2439	2.30	95000
96000	*96999*	2462	2.30	96000
97000	*97999*	2484	2.30	97000
98000	*98999*	2507	2.30	98000
99000	*99999*	2530	2.30	99000
100000	*100999*	2553	2.30	100000
101000	*101999*	2576	2.30	101000
102000	*102999*	2599	2.30	102000
103000	*103999*	2622	2.30	103000
104000	*104999*	2645	2.30	104000
105000	*105999*	2668	2.30	105000
106000	*106999*	2691	2.30	106000
107000	*107999*	2714	2.30	107000
108000	*108999*	2737	2.25	108000
109000	*109999*	2760	2.24	109000
110000	*110999*	2782	2.24	110000
111000	*111999*	2805	2.24	111000
112000	*112999*	2827	2.24	112000
113000	*113999*	2849	2.22	113000
114000	*114999*	2871	2.13	114000
115000	*115999*	2893	2.13	115000
116000	*116999*	2914	2.13	116000
117000	*117999*	2935	2.13	117000
118000	*118999*	2957	2.13	118000
119000	*119999*	2978	2.13	119000
120000	*120999*	2999	2.13	120000
121000	*121999*	3020	2.13	121000
122000	*122999*	3042	2.13	122000

Federal Child Support Tables/ Tables fédérales de pensions alimentaires pour enfants

Province: Northwest Territories/Territoires du Nord-Ouest
No. Of Children/ Nbre d'enfants: Five/Cinq

Income/Revenu ($)		Monthly Award/ Paiement mensuel ($)		
From/De	**To/À**	**Basic Amount/ Montant de base**	**Plus (%)**	**Of Income Over/Du revenu dépassant**
123000	*123999*	3063	2.13	123000
124000	*124999*	3084	2.13	124000
125000	*125999*	3106	2.13	125000
126000	*126999*	3127	2.13	126000
127000	*127999*	3148	2.13	127000
128000	*128999*	3169	2.13	128000
129000	*129999*	3191	2.13	129000
130000	*130999*	3212	2.13	130000
131000	*131999*	3233	2.13	131000
132000	*132999*	3254	2.13	132000
133000	*133999*	3276	2.13	133000
134000	*134999*	3297	2.13	134000
135000	*135999*	3318	2.13	135000
136000	*136999*	3340	2.13	136000
137000	*137999*	3361	2.13	137000
138000	*138999*	3382	2.13	138000
139000	*139999*	3403	2.13	139000
140000	*140999*	3425	2.13	140000
141000	*141999*	3446	2.13	141000
142000	*142999*	3467	2.13	142000
143000	*143999*	3489	2.13	143000
144000	*144999*	3510	2.13	144000
145000	*145999*	3531	2.13	145000
146000	*146999*	3552	2.13	146000
147000	*147999*	3574	2.13	147000
148000	*148999*	3595	2.13	148000
149000	*149999*	3616	2.13	149000

Federal Child Support Tables/ Tables fédérales de pensions alimentaires pour enfants

Province: Northwest Territories/Territoires du Nord-Ouest
No. Of Children/ Nbre d'enfants: Five/Cinq

Income/Revenu ($)		**Monthly Award/ Paiement mensuel ($)**		
From/De	**To/À**	**Basic Amount/ Montant de base**	**Plus (%)**	**Of Income Over/Du revenu dépassant**
150000	*or greater/ ou plus*	3637	2.13	150000

Federal Child Support Tables/ Tables fédérales de pensions alimentaires pour enfants

Province: Northwest Territories/Territoires du Nord-Ouest
No. Of Children/ Nbre d'enfants: Six or more/Six ou plus

Income/Revenu ($)		**Monthly Award/ Paiement mensuel ($)**		
From/De	**To/À**	**Basic Amount/ Montant de base**	**Plus (%)**	**Of Income Over/Du revenu dépassant**
0	*7999*	0		
8000	*8999*	0	3.58	8000
9000	*9999*	36	5.01	9000
10000	*10999*	86	5.01	10000
11000	*11999*	136	5.01	11000
12000	*12999*	186	4.63	12000
13000	*13999*	232	4.50	13000
14000	*14999*	277	4.47	14000
15000	*15999*	322	4.47	15000
16000	*16999*	367	4.50	16000
17000	*17999*	412	4.55	17000
18000	*18999*	457	4.55	18000
19000	*19999*	503	4.55	19000
20000	*20999*	548	4.55	20000
21000	*21999*	593	4.55	21000
22000	*22999*	639	4.55	22000
23000	*23999*	684	4.55	23000
24000	*24999*	730	4.55	24000

Federal Child Support Tables/ Tables fédérales de pensions alimentaires pour enfants

Province: Northwest Territories/Territoires du Nord-Ouest
No. Of Children/ Nbre d'enfants: Six or more/Six ou plus

Income/Revenu ($)		**Monthly Award/ Paiement mensuel ($)**		
From/De	**To/À**	**Basic Amount/ Montant de base**	**Plus (%)**	**Of Income Over/Du revenu dépassant**
25000	*25999*	775	4.55	25000
26000	*26999*	821	4.21	26000
27000	*27999*	863	2.95	27000
28000	*28999*	892	2.95	28000
29000	*29999*	922	2.82	29000
30000	*30999*	950	2.75	30000
31000	*31999*	978	2.75	31000
32000	*32999*	1005	2.75	32000
33000	*33999*	1033	2.67	33000
34000	*34999*	1059	2.64	34000
35000	*35999*	1086	2.40	35000
36000	*36999*	1110	2.34	36000
37000	*37999*	1135	2.60	37000
38000	*38999*	1161	2.60	38000
39000	*39999*	1187	2.66	39000
40000	*40999*	1214	2.74	40000
41000	*41999*	1241	2.82	41000
42000	*42999*	1269	2.82	42000
43000	*43999*	1297	2.82	43000
44000	*44999*	1326	2.82	44000
45000	*45999*	1354	2.82	45000
46000	*46999*	1382	2.82	46000
47000	*47999*	1410	2.82	47000
48000	*48999*	1438	2.81	48000
49000	*49999*	1466	2.81	49000
50000	*50999*	1494	2.81	50000
51000	*51999*	1522	2.81	51000
52000	*52999*	1550	2.81	52000
53000	*53999*	1579	2.81	53000
54000	*54999*	1607	2.81	54000
55000	*55999*	1635	2.81	55000
56000	*56999*	1663	2.81	56000
57000	*57999*	1691	2.81	57000
58000	*58999*	1719	2.81	58000
59000	*59999*	1747	2.81	59000

Federal Child Support Tables/ Tables fédérales de pensions alimentaires pour enfants

Province: Northwest Territories/Territoires du Nord-Ouest No. Of Children/ Nbre d'enfants: Six or more/Six ou plus

Income/Revenu ($)		Monthly Award/ Paiement mensuel ($)		
From/De	To/À	Basic Amount/ Montant de base	Plus (%)	Of Income Over/Du revenu dépassant
60000	*60999*	1775	2.81	60000
61000	*61999*	1803	2.81	61000
62000	*62999*	1831	2.81	62000
63000	*63999*	1859	2.81	63000
64000	*64999*	1887	2.81	64000
65000	*65999*	1915	2.81	65000
66000	*66999*	1943	2.72	66000
67000	*67999*	1970	2.68	67000
68000	*68999*	1997	2.68	68000
69000	*69999*	2024	2.68	69000
70000	*70999*	2051	2.52	70000
71000	*71999*	2076	2.52	71000
72000	*72999*	2101	2.52	72000
73000	*73999*	2126	2.52	73000
74000	*74999*	2152	2.52	74000
75000	*75999*	2177	2.52	75000
76000	*76999*	2202	2.52	76000
77000	*77999*	2227	2.52	77000
78000	*78999*	2252	2.52	78000
79000	*79999*	2278	2.52	79000
80000	*80999*	2303	2.52	80000
81000	*81999*	2328	2.52	81000
82000	*82999*	2353	2.52	82000
83000	*83999*	2378	2.52	83000
84000	*84999*	2404	2.52	84000
85000	*85999*	2429	2.52	85000
86000	*86999*	2454	2.52	86000
87000	*87999*	2479	2.52	87000
88000	*88999*	2504	2.52	88000
89000	*89999*	2530	2.52	89000
90000	*90999*	2555	2.52	90000
91000	*91999*	2580	2.52	91000
92000	*92999*	2605	2.52	92000
93000	*93999*	2630	2.52	93000
94000	*94999*	2655	2.52	94000

Federal Child Support Tables/ Tables fédérales de pensions alimentaires pour enfants

Province: Northwest Territories/Territoires du Nord-Ouest No. Of Children/ Nbre d'enfants: Six or more/Six ou plus

Income/Revenu ($)		Monthly Award/ Paiement mensuel ($)		
From/De	To/À	Basic Amount/ Montant de base	Plus (%)	Of Income Over/Du revenu dépassant
95000	*95999*	2681	2.52	95000
96000	*96999*	2706	2.52	96000
97000	*97999*	2731	2.52	97000
98000	*98999*	2756	2.52	98000
99000	*99999*	2781	2.52	99000
100000	*100999*	2807	2.52	100000
101000	*101999*	2832	2.52	101000
102000	*102999*	2857	2.52	102000
103000	*103999*	2882	2.52	103000
104000	*104999*	2907	2.52	104000
105000	*105999*	2933	2.52	105000
106000	*106999*	2958	2.52	106000
107000	*107999*	2983	2.52	107000
108000	*108999*	3008	2.46	108000
109000	*109999*	3033	2.45	109000
110000	*110999*	3057	2.45	110000
111000	*111999*	3082	2.45	111000
112000	*112999*	3106	2.45	112000
113000	*113999*	3131	2.43	113000
114000	*114999*	3155	2.33	114000
115000	*115999*	3179	2.33	115000
116000	*116999*	3202	2.33	116000
117000	*117999*	3225	2.33	117000
118000	*118999*	3249	2.33	118000
119000	*119999*	3272	2.33	119000
120000	*120999*	3295	2.33	120000
121000	*121999*	3319	2.33	121000
122000	*122999*	3342	2.33	122000
123000	*123999*	3365	2.33	123000
124000	*124999*	3388	2.33	124000
125000	*125999*	3412	2.33	125000
126000	*126999*	3435	2.33	126000
127000	*127999*	3458	2.33	127000
128000	*128999*	3482	2.33	128000
129000	*129999*	3505	2.33	129000

Federal Child Support Tables/Tables fédérales de pensions alimentaires pour enfants — **Province: Northwest Territories/Territoires du Nord-Ouest** — **No. Of Children/N^bre d'enfants: Six or more/Six ou plus**

Income/Revenu ($)		Monthly Award/Paiement mensuel ($)		
From/De	To/À	Basic Amount/Montant de base	Plus (%)	Of Income Over/Du revenu dépassant
130000	*130999*	3528	2.33	130000
131000	*131999*	3552	2.33	131000
132000	*132999*	3575	2.33	132000
133000	*133999*	3598	2.33	133000
134000	*134999*	3622	2.33	134000
135000	*135999*	3645	2.33	135000
136000	*136999*	3668	2.33	136000
137000	*137999*	3692	2.33	137000
138000	*138999*	3715	2.33	138000
139000	*139999*	3738	2.33	139000
140000	*140999*	3762	2.33	140000
141000	*141999*	3785	2.33	141000
142000	*142999*	3808	2.33	142000
143000	*143999*	3832	2.33	143000
144000	*144999*	3855	2.33	144000
145000	*145999*	3878	2.33	145000
146000	*146999*	3902	2.33	146000
147000	*147999*	3925	2.33	147000
148000	*148999*	3948	2.33	148000
149000	*149999*	3972	2.33	149000

Federal Child Support Tables/Tables fédérales de pensions alimentaires pour enfants — **Province: Northwest Territories/Territoires du Nord-Ouest** — **No. Of Children/N^bre d'enfants: Six or more/Six ou plus**

Income/Revenu ($)		Monthly Award/Paiement mensuel ($)		
From/De	To/À	Basic Amount/Montant de base	Plus (%)	Of Income Over/Du revenu dépassant
150000	*or greater/ou plus*	3995	2.33	150000

Federal Child Support Tables/Tables fédérales de pensions alimentaires pour enfants — **Province: Nunavut** — **No. Of Children/N^bre d'enfants: One/Un**

Income/Revenu ($)		Monthly Award/Paiement mensuel ($)		
From/De	To/À	Basic Amount/Montant de base	Plus (%)	Of Income Over/Du revenu dépassant
0	*7999*	0		
8000	*8999*	0	1.44	8000
9000	*9999*	14	2.05	9000
10000	*10999*	35	2.05	10000
11000	*11999*	55	2.05	11000
12000	*12999*	76	2.05	12000
13000	*13999*	96	2.05	13000
14000	*14999*	117	2.05	14000
15000	*15999*	138	1.83	15000
16000	*16999*	156	0.93	16000
17000	*17999*	165	0.93	17000
18000	*18999*	174	0.93	18000
19000	*19999*	184	0.93	19000
20000	*20999*	193	0.93	20000
21000	*21999*	202	0.93	21000
22000	*22999*	211	1.01	22000
23000	*23999*	221	1.05	23000
24000	*24999*	232	1.05	24000

Federal Child Support Tables/ Tables fédérales de pensions alimentaires pour enfants

Province: Nunavut
No. Of Children/ Nbre d'enfants: One/Un

Income/Revenu ($)		Monthly Award/ Paiement mensuel ($)		
From/De	To/À	Basic Amount/ Montant de base	Plus (%)	Of Income Over/Du revenu dépassant
25000	*25999*	243	1.05	25000
26000	*26999*	253	1.05	26000
27000	*27999*	264	1.05	27000
28000	*28999*	274	1.05	28000
29000	*29999*	285	1.01	29000
30000	*30999*	295	0.99	30000
31000	*31999*	305	0.99	31000
32000	*32999*	315	0.99	32000
33000	*33999*	324	0.99	33000
34000	*34999*	334	0.99	34000
35000	*35999*	344	0.86	35000
36000	*36999*	353	0.91	36000
37000	*37999*	362	0.93	37000
38000	*38999*	371	0.93	38000
39000	*39999*	380	0.95	39000
40000	*40999*	390	0.98	40000
41000	*41999*	400	1.01	41000
42000	*42999*	410	1.01	42000
43000	*43999*	420	1.01	43000
44000	*44999*	430	1.01	44000
45000	*45999*	440	1.01	45000
46000	*46999*	450	0.99	46000
47000	*47999*	460	0.99	47000
48000	*48999*	470	0.99	48000
49000	*49999*	480	0.99	49000
50000	*50999*	490	0.99	50000
51000	*51999*	499	0.99	51000
52000	*52999*	509	0.99	52000
53000	*53999*	519	0.99	53000
54000	*54999*	529	0.99	54000
55000	*55999*	539	0.99	55000
56000	*56999*	549	0.99	56000
57000	*57999*	559	0.99	57000
58000	*58999*	568	0.99	58000
59000	*59999*	578	0.99	59000

Federal Child Support Tables/ Tables fédérales de pensions alimentaires pour enfants

Province: Nunavut
No. Of Children/ Nbre d'enfants: One/Un

Income/Revenu ($)		Monthly Award/ Paiement mensuel ($)		
From/De	To/À	Basic Amount/ Montant de base	Plus (%)	Of Income Over/Du revenu dépassant
60000	*60999*	588	0.99	60000
61000	*61999*	598	0.99	61000
62000	*62999*	608	0.99	62000
63000	*63999*	618	0.99	63000
64000	*64999*	628	0.99	64000
65000	*65999*	637	0.99	65000
66000	*66999*	647	0.99	66000
67000	*67999*	657	0.99	67000
68000	*68999*	667	0.99	68000
69000	*69999*	677	0.99	69000
70000	*70999*	687	0.90	70000
71000	*71999*	696	0.90	71000
72000	*72999*	705	0.90	72000
73000	*73999*	714	0.90	73000
74000	*74999*	723	0.90	74000
75000	*75999*	732	0.90	75000
76000	*76999*	741	0.90	76000
77000	*77999*	750	0.90	77000
78000	*78999*	759	0.90	78000
79000	*79999*	768	0.90	79000
80000	*80999*	777	0.90	80000
81000	*81999*	786	0.90	81000
82000	*82999*	795	0.90	82000
83000	*83999*	804	0.90	83000
84000	*84999*	813	0.90	84000
85000	*85999*	822	0.90	85000
86000	*86999*	831	0.90	86000
87000	*87999*	840	0.90	87000
88000	*88999*	849	0.90	88000
89000	*89999*	858	0.90	89000
90000	*90999*	867	0.90	90000
91000	*91999*	876	0.90	91000
92000	*92999*	885	0.90	92000
93000	*93999*	894	0.90	93000
94000	*94999*	903	0.90	94000

Federal Child Support Tables/ Tables fédérales de pensions alimentaires pour enfants — **Province: Nunavut — No. Of Children/ Nbre d'enfants: One/Un**

Income/Revenu ($)		Monthly Award/ Paiement mensuel ($)		
From/De	To/À	Basic Amount/ Montant de base	Plus (%)	Of Income Over/Du revenu dépassant
95000	*95999*	912	0.90	95000
96000	*96999*	922	0.90	96000
97000	*97999*	931	0.90	97000
98000	*98999*	940	0.90	98000
99000	*99999*	949	0.90	99000
100000	*100999*	958	0.90	100000
101000	*101999*	967	0.90	101000
102000	*102999*	976	0.90	102000
103000	*103999*	985	0.90	103000
104000	*104999*	994	0.90	104000
105000	*105999*	1003	0.90	105000
106000	*106999*	1012	0.90	106000
107000	*107999*	1021	0.90	107000
108000	*108999*	1030	0.90	108000
109000	*109999*	1039	0.90	109000
110000	*110999*	1048	0.90	110000
111000	*111999*	1057	0.90	111000
112000	*112999*	1066	0.90	112000
113000	*113999*	1075	0.89	113000
114000	*114999*	1084	0.83	114000
115000	*115999*	1092	0.83	115000
116000	*116999*	1100	0.83	116000
117000	*117999*	1109	0.83	117000
118000	*118999*	1117	0.83	118000
119000	*119999*	1125	0.83	119000
120000	*120999*	1133	0.83	120000
121000	*121999*	1142	0.83	121000
122000	*122999*	1150	0.83	122000

Federal Child Support Tables/ Tables fédérales de pensions alimentaires pour enfants — **Province: Nunavut — No. Of Children/ Nbre d'enfants: One/Un**

Income/Revenu ($)		Monthly Award/ Paiement mensuel ($)		
From/De	To/À	Basic Amount/ Montant de base	Plus (%)	Of Income Over/Du revenu dépassant
123000	*123999*	1158	0.83	123000
124000	*124999*	1166	0.83	124000
125000	*125999*	1175	0.83	125000
126000	*126999*	1183	0.83	126000
127000	*127999*	1191	0.83	127000
128000	*128999*	1200	0.83	128000
129000	*129999*	1208	0.83	129000
130000	*130999*	1216	0.83	130000
131000	*131999*	1224	0.83	131000
132000	*132999*	1233	0.83	132000
133000	*133999*	1241	0.83	133000
134000	*134999*	1249	0.83	134000
135000	*135999*	1257	0.83	135000
136000	*136999*	1266	0.83	136000
137000	*137999*	1274	0.83	137000
138000	*138999*	1282	0.83	138000
139000	*139999*	1290	0.83	139000
140000	*140999*	1299	0.83	140000
141000	*141999*	1307	0.83	141000
142000	*142999*	1315	0.83	142000
143000	*143999*	1324	0.83	143000
144000	*144999*	1332	0.83	144000
145000	*145999*	1340	0.83	145000
146000	*146999*	1348	0.83	146000
147000	*147999*	1357	0.83	147000
148000	*148999*	1365	0.83	148000
149000	*149999*	1373	0.83	149000

Federal Child Support Tables/ Tables fédérales de pensions alimentaires pour enfants

Province: Nunavut
No. Of Children/ Nbre d'enfants: One/Un

Income/Revenu ($)		Monthly Award/ Paiement mensuel ($)		
From/De	To/À	Basic Amount/ Montant de base	Plus (%)	Of Income Over/Du revenu dépassant
150000	*or greater/ ou plus*	1381	0.83	150000

Federal Child Support Tables/ Tables fédérales de pensions alimentaires pour enfants

Province: Nunavut
No. Of Children/ Nbre d'enfants: Two/Deux

Income/Revenu ($)		Monthly Award/ Paiement mensuel ($)		
From/De	To/À	Basic Amount/ Montant de base	Plus (%)	Of Income Over/Du revenu dépassant
0	*7999*	0		
8000	*8999*	0	2.72	8000
9000	*9999*	27	4.45	9000
10000	*10999*	72	4.45	10000
11000	*11999*	116	4.27	11000
12000	*12999*	159	4.22	12000
13000	*13999*	201	4.14	13000
14000	*14999*	243	1.74	14000
15000	*15999*	260	1.19	15000
16000	*16999*	272	1.53	16000
17000	*17999*	287	1.53	17000
18000	*18999*	302	1.53	18000
19000	*19999*	318	1.53	19000
20000	*20999*	333	1.53	20000
21000	*21999*	348	1.53	21000
22000	*22999*	363	1.60	22000
23000	*23999*	379	1.64	23000
24000	*24999*	396	1.64	24000

Federal Child Support Tables/ Tables fédérales de pensions alimentaires pour enfants

Province: Nunavut
No. Of Children/ Nbre d'enfants: Two/Deux

Income/Revenu ($)		Monthly Award/ Paiement mensuel ($)		
From/De	To/À	Basic Amount/ Montant de base	Plus (%)	Of Income Over/Du revenu dépassant
25000	*25999*	412	1.64	25000
26000	*26999*	429	1.64	26000
27000	*27999*	445	1.64	27000
28000	*28999*	461	1.64	28000
29000	*29999*	478	1.57	29000
30000	*30999*	494	1.53	30000
31000	*31999*	509	1.53	31000
32000	*32999*	524	1.53	32000
33000	*33999*	540	1.53	33000
34000	*34999*	555	1.53	34000
35000	*35999*	570	1.34	35000
36000	*36999*	584	1.42	36000
37000	*37999*	598	1.45	37000
38000	*38999*	612	1.45	38000
39000	*39999*	627	1.48	39000
40000	*40999*	642	1.52	40000
41000	*41999*	657	1.57	41000
42000	*42999*	672	1.57	42000
43000	*43999*	688	1.57	43000
44000	*44999*	704	1.57	44000
45000	*45999*	719	1.57	45000
46000	*46999*	735	1.53	46000
47000	*47999*	750	1.53	47000
48000	*48999*	766	1.53	48000
49000	*49999*	781	1.53	49000
50000	*50999*	796	1.53	50000
51000	*51999*	812	1.53	51000
52000	*52999*	827	1.53	52000
53000	*53999*	842	1.53	53000
54000	*54999*	858	1.53	54000
55000	*55999*	873	1.53	55000
56000	*56999*	888	1.53	56000
57000	*57999*	904	1.53	57000
58000	*58999*	919	1.53	58000
59000	*59999*	935	1.53	59000

Federal Child Support Tables/ Tables fédérales de pensions alimentaires pour enfants

Province: Nunavut
No. Of Children/ Nbre d'enfants: Two/Deux

Income/Revenu ($)		Monthly Award/ Paiement mensuel ($)		
From/De	To/À	Basic Amount/ Montant de base	Plus (%)	Of Income Over/Du revenu dépassant
60000	*60999*	950	1.53	60000
61000	*61999*	965	1.53	61000
62000	*62999*	981	1.53	62000
63000	*63999*	996	1.53	63000
64000	*64999*	1011	1.53	64000
65000	*65999*	1027	1.53	65000
66000	*66999*	1042	1.53	66000
67000	*67999*	1057	1.53	67000
68000	*68999*	1073	1.53	68000
69000	*69999*	1088	1.53	69000
70000	*70999*	1103	1.40	70000
71000	*71999*	1117	1.40	71000
72000	*72999*	1131	1.40	72000
73000	*73999*	1145	1.40	73000
74000	*74999*	1159	1.40	74000
75000	*75999*	1173	1.40	75000
76000	*76999*	1187	1.40	76000
77000	*77999*	1202	1.40	77000
78000	*78999*	1216	1.40	78000
79000	*79999*	1230	1.40	79000
80000	*80999*	1244	1.40	80000
81000	*81999*	1258	1.40	81000
82000	*82999*	1272	1.40	82000
83000	*83999*	1286	1.40	83000
84000	*84999*	1300	1.40	84000
85000	*85999*	1314	1.40	85000
86000	*86999*	1328	1.40	86000
87000	*87999*	1342	1.40	87000
88000	*88999*	1356	1.40	88000
89000	*89999*	1370	1.40	89000
90000	*90999*	1384	1.40	90000
91000	*91999*	1398	1.40	91000
92000	*92999*	1412	1.40	92000
93000	*93999*	1426	1.40	93000
94000	*94999*	1440	1.40	94000

Federal Child Support Tables/ Tables fédérales de pensions alimentaires pour enfants

Province: Nunavut
No. Of Children/ Nbre d'enfants: Two/Deux

Income/Revenu ($)		Monthly Award/ Paiement mensuel ($)		
From/De	To/À	Basic Amount/ Montant de base	Plus (%)	Of Income Over/Du revenu dépassant
95000	*95999*	1454	1.40	95000
96000	*96999*	1468	1.40	96000
97000	*97999*	1482	1.40	97000
98000	*98999*	1496	1.40	98000
99000	*99999*	1510	1.40	99000
100000	*100999*	1525	1.40	100000
101000	*101999*	1539	1.40	101000
102000	*102999*	1553	1.40	102000
103000	*103999*	1567	1.40	103000
104000	*104999*	1581	1.40	104000
105000	*105999*	1595	1.40	105000
106000	*106999*	1609	1.40	106000
107000	*107999*	1623	1.40	107000
108000	*108999*	1637	1.40	108000
109000	*109999*	1651	1.40	109000
110000	*110999*	1665	1.40	110000
111000	*111999*	1679	1.40	111000
112000	*112999*	1693	1.40	112000
113000	*113999*	1707	1.38	113000
114000	*114999*	1721	1.29	114000
115000	*115999*	1734	1.29	115000
116000	*116999*	1747	1.29	116000
117000	*117999*	1759	1.29	117000
118000	*118999*	1772	1.29	118000
119000	*119999*	1785	1.29	119000
120000	*120999*	1798	1.29	120000
121000	*121999*	1811	1.29	121000
122000	*122999*	1824	1.29	122000
123000	*123999*	1837	1.29	123000
124000	*124999*	1849	1.29	124000
125000	*125999*	1862	1.29	125000
126000	*126999*	1875	1.29	126000
127000	*127999*	1888	1.29	127000
128000	*128999*	1901	1.29	128000
129000	*129999*	1914	1.29	129000

Federal Child Support Tables/ Tables fédérales de pensions alimentaires pour enfants

Province: Nunavut
No. Of Children/ Nbre d'enfants: Two/Deux

Income/Revenu ($)		Monthly Award/ Paiement mensuel ($)		
From/De	To/À	Basic Amount/ Montant de base	Plus (%)	Of Income Over/Du revenu dépassant
130000	*130999*	1927	1.29	130000
131000	*131999*	1939	1.29	131000
132000	*132999*	1952	1.29	132000
133000	*133999*	1965	1.29	133000
134000	*134999*	1978	1.29	134000
135000	*135999*	1991	1.29	135000
136000	*136999*	2004	1.29	136000
137000	*137999*	2017	1.29	137000
138000	*138999*	2029	1.29	138000
139000	*139999*	2042	1.29	139000
140000	*140999*	2055	1.29	140000
141000	*141999*	2068	1.29	141000
142000	*142999*	2081	1.29	142000
143000	*143999*	2094	1.29	143000
144000	*144999*	2107	1.29	144000
145000	*145999*	2119	1.29	145000
146000	*146999*	2132	1.29	146000
147000	*147999*	2145	1.29	147000
148000	*148999*	2158	1.29	148000
149000	*149999*	2171	1.29	149000
150000	*or greater/ ou plus*	2184	1.29	150000

Federal Child Support Tables/ Tables fédérales de pensions alimentaires pour enfants

Province: Nunavut
No. Of Children/ Nbre d'enfants: Three/Trois

Income/Revenu ($)		Monthly Award/ Paiement mensuel ($)		
From/De	To/À	Basic Amount/ Montant de base	Plus (%)	Of Income Over/Du revenu dépassant
0	*7999*	0		
8000	*8999*	0	2.93	8000
9000	*9999*	29	4.79	9000
10000	*10999*	77	4.79	10000
11000	*11999*	125	4.60	11000
12000	*12999*	171	4.55	12000
13000	*13999*	217	4.46	13000
14000	*14999*	261	4.43	14000
15000	*15999*	306	4.43	15000
16000	*16999*	350	3.48	16000
17000	*17999*	385	2.01	17000
18000	*18999*	405	2.01	18000
19000	*19999*	425	2.01	19000
20000	*20999*	445	2.01	20000
21000	*21999*	465	2.01	21000
22000	*22999*	485	2.07	22000
23000	*23999*	506	2.11	23000
24000	*24999*	527	2.11	24000

Federal Child Support Tables/ Tables fédérales de pensions alimentaires pour enfants

Province: Nunavut
No. Of Children/ Nbre d'enfants: Three/Trois

Income/Revenu ($)		Monthly Award/ Paiement mensuel ($)		
From/De	**To/À**	**Basic Amount/ Montant de base**	**Plus (%)**	**Of Income Over/Du revenu dépassant**
25000	*25999*	548	2.11	25000
26000	*26999*	569	2.11	26000
27000	*27999*	590	2.11	27000
28000	*28999*	611	2.11	28000
29000	*29999*	632	2.02	29000
30000	*30999*	653	1.97	30000
31000	*31999*	672	1.97	31000
32000	*32999*	692	1.97	32000
33000	*33999*	712	1.97	33000
34000	*34999*	731	1.97	34000
35000	*35999*	751	1.72	35000
36000	*36999*	768	1.82	36000
37000	*37999*	787	1.86	37000
38000	*38999*	805	1.86	38000
39000	*39999*	824	1.90	39000
40000	*40999*	843	1.96	40000
41000	*41999*	862	2.01	41000
42000	*42999*	883	2.01	42000
43000	*43999*	903	2.01	43000
44000	*44999*	923	2.01	44000
45000	*45999*	943	2.01	45000
46000	*46999*	963	1.97	46000
47000	*47999*	983	1.97	47000
48000	*48999*	1003	1.97	48000
49000	*49999*	1022	1.97	49000
50000	*50999*	1042	1.97	50000
51000	*51999*	1062	1.97	51000
52000	*52999*	1081	1.97	52000
53000	*53999*	1101	1.97	53000
54000	*54999*	1121	1.97	54000
55000	*55999*	1141	1.97	55000
56000	*56999*	1160	1.97	56000
57000	*57999*	1180	1.97	57000
58000	*58999*	1200	1.97	58000
59000	*59999*	1219	1.97	59000

Federal Child Support Tables/ Tables fédérales de pensions alimentaires pour enfants

Province: Nunavut
No. Of Children/ Nbre d'enfants: Three/Trois

Income/Revenu ($)		Monthly Award/ Paiement mensuel ($)		
From/De	**To/À**	**Basic Amount/ Montant de base**	**Plus (%)**	**Of Income Over/Du revenu dépassant**
60000	*60999*	1239	1.97	60000
61000	*61999*	1259	1.97	61000
62000	*62999*	1279	1.97	62000
63000	*63999*	1298	1.97	63000
64000	*64999*	1318	1.97	64000
65000	*65999*	1338	1.97	65000
66000	*66999*	1358	1.97	66000
67000	*67999*	1377	1.97	67000
68000	*68999*	1397	1.97	68000
69000	*69999*	1417	1.97	69000
70000	*70999*	1436	1.81	70000
71000	*71999*	1454	1.81	71000
72000	*72999*	1473	1.81	72000
73000	*73999*	1491	1.81	73000
74000	*74999*	1509	1.81	74000
75000	*75999*	1527	1.81	75000
76000	*76999*	1545	1.81	76000
77000	*77999*	1563	1.81	77000
78000	*78999*	1581	1.81	78000
79000	*79999*	1599	1.81	79000
80000	*80999*	1617	1.81	80000
81000	*81999*	1635	1.81	81000
82000	*82999*	1653	1.81	82000
83000	*83999*	1671	1.81	83000
84000	*84999*	1689	1.81	84000
85000	*85999*	1707	1.81	85000
86000	*86999*	1725	1.81	86000
87000	*87999*	1743	1.81	87000
88000	*88999*	1761	1.81	88000
89000	*89999*	1779	1.81	89000
90000	*90999*	1798	1.81	90000
91000	*91999*	1816	1.81	91000
92000	*92999*	1834	1.81	92000
93000	*93999*	1852	1.81	93000
94000	*94999*	1870	1.81	94000

Federal Child Support Tables/ Tables fédérales de pensions alimentaires pour enfants

Province: Nunavut No. Of Children/ Nbre d'enfants: Three/Trois

Income/Revenu ($)		Monthly Award/ Paiement mensuel ($)		
From/De	To/À	Basic Amount/ Montant de base	Plus (%)	Of Income Over/Du revenu dépassant
95000	*95999*	1888	1.81	95000
96000	*96999*	1906	1.81	96000
97000	*97999*	1924	1.81	97000
98000	*98999*	1942	1.81	98000
99000	*99999*	1960	1.81	99000
100000	*100999*	1978	1.81	100000
101000	*101999*	1996	1.81	101000
102000	*102999*	2014	1.81	102000
103000	*103999*	2032	1.81	103000
104000	*104999*	2050	1.81	104000
105000	*105999*	2068	1.81	105000
106000	*106999*	2086	1.81	106000
107000	*107999*	2104	1.81	107000
108000	*108999*	2123	1.81	108000
109000	*109999*	2141	1.81	109000
110000	*110999*	2159	1.81	110000
111000	*111999*	2177	1.81	111000
112000	*112999*	2195	1.81	112000
113000	*113999*	2213	1.78	113000
114000	*114999*	2231	1.65	114000
115000	*115999*	2247	1.65	115000
116000	*116999*	2264	1.65	116000
117000	*117999*	2280	1.65	117000
118000	*118999*	2297	1.65	118000
119000	*119999*	2313	1.65	119000
120000	*120999*	2330	1.65	120000
121000	*121999*	2346	1.65	121000
122000	*122999*	2363	1.65	122000

Federal Child Support Tables/ Tables fédérales de pensions alimentaires pour enfants

Province: Nunavut No. Of Children/ Nbre d'enfants: Three/Trois

Income/Revenu ($)		Monthly Award/ Paiement mensuel ($)		
From/De	To/À	Basic Amount/ Montant de base	Plus (%)	Of Income Over/Du revenu dépassant
123000	*123999*	2379	1.65	123000
124000	*124999*	2396	1.65	124000
125000	*125999*	2412	1.65	125000
126000	*126999*	2429	1.65	126000
127000	*127999*	2445	1.65	127000
128000	*128999*	2462	1.65	128000
129000	*129999*	2478	1.65	129000
130000	*130999*	2495	1.65	130000
131000	*131999*	2512	1.65	131000
132000	*132999*	2528	1.65	132000
133000	*133999*	2545	1.65	133000
134000	*134999*	2561	1.65	134000
135000	*135999*	2578	1.65	135000
136000	*136999*	2594	1.65	136000
137000	*137999*	2611	1.65	137000
138000	*138999*	2627	1.65	138000
139000	*139999*	2644	1.65	139000
140000	*140999*	2660	1.65	140000
141000	*141999*	2677	1.65	141000
142000	*142999*	2693	1.65	142000
143000	*143999*	2710	1.65	143000
144000	*144999*	2726	1.65	144000
145000	*145999*	2743	1.65	145000
146000	*146999*	2759	1.65	146000
147000	*147999*	2776	1.65	147000
148000	*148999*	2793	1.65	148000
149000	*149999*	2809	1.65	149000

Federal Child Support Tables/ Tables fédérales de pensions alimentaires pour enfants

Province: Nunavut
No. Of Children/ Nbre d'enfants: Three/Trois

Income/Revenu ($)		Monthly Award/ Paiement mensuel ($)		
From/De	To/À	Basic Amount/ Montant de base	Plus (%)	Of Income Over/Du revenu dépassant
150000	*or greater/ ou plus*	2826	1.65	150000

Federal Child Support Tables/ Tables fédérales de pensions alimentaires pour enfants

Province: Nunavut
No. Of Children/ Nbre d'enfants: Four/Quatre

Income/Revenu ($)		Monthly Award/ Paiement mensuel ($)		
From/De	To/À	Basic Amount/ Montant de base	Plus (%)	Of Income Over/Du revenu dépassant
0	*7999*	0		
8000	*8999*	0	3.14	8000
9000	*9999*	31	5.14	9000
10000	*10999*	83	5.14	10000
11000	*11999*	134	4.92	11000
12000	*12999*	183	4.87	12000
13000	*13999*	232	4.78	13000
14000	*14999*	280	4.75	14000
15000	*15999*	327	4.75	15000
16000	*16999*	375	4.75	16000
17000	*17999*	422	4.75	17000
18000	*18999*	470	4.27	18000
19000	*19999*	513	2.40	19000
20000	*20999*	537	2.40	20000
21000	*21999*	561	2.40	21000
22000	*22999*	585	2.46	22000
23000	*23999*	609	2.49	23000
24000	*24999*	634	2.49	24000

Federal Child Support Tables/ Tables fédérales de pensions alimentaires pour enfants

Province: Nunavut
No. Of Children/ Nbre d'enfants: Four/Quatre

Income/Revenu ($)		Monthly Award/ Paiement mensuel ($)		
From/De	To/À	Basic Amount/ Montant de base	Plus (%)	Of Income Over/Du revenu dépassant
25000	*25999*	659	2.49	25000
26000	*26999*	684	2.49	26000
27000	*27999*	709	2.49	27000
28000	*28999*	734	2.49	28000
29000	*29999*	759	2.39	29000
30000	*30999*	783	2.33	30000
31000	*31999*	806	2.33	31000
32000	*32999*	829	2.33	32000
33000	*33999*	852	2.33	33000
34000	*34999*	876	2.33	34000
35000	*35999*	899	2.04	35000
36000	*36999*	919	2.15	36000
37000	*37999*	941	2.20	37000
38000	*38999*	963	2.20	38000
39000	*39999*	985	2.25	39000
40000	*40999*	1007	2.32	40000
41000	*41999*	1031	2.38	41000
42000	*42999*	1054	2.38	42000
43000	*43999*	1078	2.38	43000
44000	*44999*	1102	2.38	44000
45000	*45999*	1126	2.38	45000
46000	*46999*	1150	2.33	46000
47000	*47999*	1173	2.33	47000
48000	*48999*	1196	2.33	48000
49000	*49999*	1220	2.33	49000
50000	*50999*	1243	2.33	50000
51000	*51999*	1266	2.33	51000
52000	*52999*	1289	2.33	52000
53000	*53999*	1313	2.33	53000
54000	*54999*	1336	2.33	54000
55000	*55999*	1359	2.33	55000
56000	*56999*	1383	2.33	56000
57000	*57999*	1406	2.33	57000
58000	*58999*	1429	2.33	58000
59000	*59999*	1453	2.33	59000

Federal Child Support Tables/ Tables fédérales de pensions alimentaires pour enfants

Province: Nunavut No. Of Children/ Nbre d'enfants: Four/Quatre

Income/Revenu ($)		Monthly Award/ Paiement mensuel ($)		
From/De	To/À	Basic Amount/ Montant de base	Plus (%)	Of Income Over/Du revenu dépassant
60000	*60999*	1476	2.33	60000
61000	*61999*	1499	2.33	61000
62000	*62999*	1523	2.33	62000
63000	*63999*	1546	2.33	63000
64000	*64999*	1569	2.33	64000
65000	*65999*	1592	2.33	65000
66000	*66999*	1616	2.33	66000
67000	*67999*	1639	2.33	67000
68000	*68999*	1662	2.33	68000
69000	*69999*	1686	2.33	69000
70000	*70999*	1709	2.13	70000
71000	*71999*	1730	2.13	71000
72000	*72999*	1752	2.13	72000
73000	*73999*	1773	2.13	73000
74000	*74999*	1794	2.13	74000
75000	*75999*	1816	2.13	75000
76000	*76999*	1837	2.13	76000
77000	*77999*	1858	2.13	77000
78000	*78999*	1880	2.13	78000
79000	*79999*	1901	2.13	79000
80000	*80999*	1922	2.13	80000
81000	*81999*	1944	2.13	81000
82000	*82999*	1965	2.13	82000
83000	*83999*	1986	2.13	83000
84000	*84999*	2008	2.13	84000
85000	*85999*	2029	2.13	85000
86000	*86999*	2050	2.13	86000
87000	*87999*	2072	2.13	87000
88000	*88999*	2093	2.13	88000
89000	*89999*	2114	2.13	89000
90000	*90999*	2136	2.13	90000
91000	*91999*	2157	2.13	91000
92000	*92999*	2178	2.13	92000
93000	*93999*	2200	2.13	93000
94000	*94999*	2221	2.13	94000

Federal Child Support Tables/ Tables fédérales de pensions alimentaires pour enfants

Province: Nunavut No. Of Children/ Nbre d'enfants: Four/Quatre

Income/Revenu ($)		Monthly Award/ Paiement mensuel ($)		
From/De	To/À	Basic Amount/ Montant de base	Plus (%)	Of Income Over/Du revenu dépassant
95000	*95999*	2242	2.13	95000
96000	*96999*	2264	2.13	96000
97000	*97999*	2285	2.13	97000
98000	*98999*	2306	2.13	98000
99000	*99999*	2328	2.13	99000
100000	*100999*	2349	2.13	100000
101000	*101999*	2370	2.13	101000
102000	*102999*	2392	2.13	102000
103000	*103999*	2413	2.13	103000
104000	*104999*	2434	2.13	104000
105000	*105999*	2456	2.13	105000
106000	*106999*	2477	2.13	106000
107000	*107999*	2499	2.13	107000
108000	*108999*	2520	2.13	108000
109000	*109999*	2541	2.13	109000
110000	*110999*	2563	2.13	110000
111000	*111999*	2584	2.13	111000
112000	*112999*	2605	2.13	112000
113000	*113999*	2627	2.10	113000
114000	*114999*	2648	1.95	114000
115000	*115999*	2667	1.95	115000
116000	*116999*	2687	1.95	116000
117000	*117999*	2706	1.95	117000
118000	*118999*	2726	1.95	118000
119000	*119999*	2745	1.95	119000
120000	*120999*	2765	1.95	120000
121000	*121999*	2784	1.95	121000
122000	*122999*	2804	1.95	122000
123000	*123999*	2823	1.95	123000
124000	*124999*	2843	1.95	124000
125000	*125999*	2862	1.95	125000
126000	*126999*	2882	1.95	126000
127000	*127999*	2901	1.95	127000
128000	*128999*	2921	1.95	128000
129000	*129999*	2941	1.95	129000

Federal Child Support Tables/ Tables fédérales de pensions alimentaires pour enfants

Province: Nunavut
No. Of Children/ Nbre d'enfants: Four/Quatre

Income/Revenu ($)		Monthly Award/ Paiement mensuel ($)		
From/De	To/À	Basic Amount/ Montant de base	Plus (%)	Of Income Over/Du revenu dépassant
130000	*130999*	2960	1.95	130000
131000	*131999*	2980	1.95	131000
132000	*132999*	2999	1.95	132000
133000	*133999*	3019	1.95	133000
134000	*134999*	3038	1.95	134000
135000	*135999*	3058	1.95	135000
136000	*136999*	3077	1.95	136000
137000	*137999*	3097	1.95	137000
138000	*138999*	3116	1.95	138000
139000	*139999*	3136	1.95	139000
140000	*140999*	3155	1.95	140000
141000	*141999*	3175	1.95	141000
142000	*142999*	3194	1.95	142000
143000	*143999*	3214	1.95	143000
144000	*144999*	3234	1.95	144000
145000	*145999*	3253	1.95	145000
146000	*146999*	3273	1.95	146000
147000	*147999*	3292	1.95	147000
148000	*148999*	3312	1.95	148000
149000	*149999*	3331	1.95	149000

Federal Child Support Tables/ Tables fédérales de pensions alimentaires pour enfants

Province: Nunavut
No. Of Children/ Nbre d'enfants: Four/Quatre

Income/Revenu ($)		Monthly Award/ Paiement mensuel ($)		
From/De	To/À	Basic Amount/ Montant de base	Plus (%)	Of Income Over/Du revenu dépassant
150000	*or greater/ ou plus*	3351	1.95	150000

Federal Child Support Tables/ Tables fédérales de pensions alimentaires pour enfants

Province: Nunavut
No. Of Children/ Nbre d'enfants: Five/Cinq

Income/Revenu ($)		Monthly Award/ Paiement mensuel ($)		
From/De	To/À	Basic Amount/ Montant de base	Plus (%)	Of Income Over/Du revenu dépassant
0	*7999*	0		
8000	*8999*	0	3.14	8000
9000	*9999*	31	5.14	9000
10000	*10999*	83	5.14	10000
11000	*11999*	134	4.92	11000
12000	*12999*	183	4.87	12000
13000	*13999*	232	4.78	13000
14000	*14999*	280	4.75	14000
15000	*15999*	327	4.75	15000
16000	*16999*	375	4.75	16000
17000	*17999*	422	4.75	17000
18000	*18999*	470	4.75	18000
19000	*19999*	517	4.75	19000
20000	*20999*	565	4.75	20000
21000	*21999*	612	4.75	21000
22000	*22999*	660	3.56	22000
23000	*23999*	695	2.81	23000
24000	*24999*	723	2.81	24000

Federal Child Support Tables/ Tables fédérales de pensions alimentaires pour enfants

Province: Nunavut
No. Of Children/ N^{bre} d'enfants: Five/Cinq

Income/Revenu ($)		Monthly Award/ Paiement mensuel ($)		
From/De	To/À	Basic Amount/ Montant de base	Plus (%)	Of Income Over/Du revenu dépassant
25000	*25999*	752	2.81	25000
26000	*26999*	780	2.81	26000
27000	*27999*	808	2.81	27000
28000	*28999*	836	2.81	28000
29000	*29999*	864	2.70	29000
30000	*30999*	891	2.63	30000
31000	*31999*	917	2.63	31000
32000	*32999*	944	2.63	32000
33000	*33999*	970	2.63	33000
34000	*34999*	996	2.63	34000
35000	*35999*	1022	2.30	35000
36000	*36999*	1045	2.43	36000
37000	*37999*	1070	2.48	37000
38000	*38999*	1094	2.48	38000
39000	*39999*	1119	2.54	39000
40000	*40999*	1145	2.61	40000
41000	*41999*	1171	2.69	41000
42000	*42999*	1198	2.69	42000
43000	*43999*	1224	2.69	43000
44000	*44999*	1251	2.69	44000
45000	*45999*	1278	2.69	45000
46000	*46999*	1305	2.63	46000
47000	*47999*	1331	2.63	47000
48000	*48999*	1358	2.63	48000
49000	*49999*	1384	2.63	49000
50000	*50999*	1410	2.63	50000
51000	*51999*	1437	2.63	51000
52000	*52999*	1463	2.63	52000
53000	*53999*	1489	2.63	53000
54000	*54999*	1515	2.63	54000
55000	*55999*	1542	2.63	55000
56000	*56999*	1568	2.63	56000
57000	*57999*	1594	2.63	57000
58000	*58999*	1621	2.63	58000
59000	*59999*	1647	2.63	59000

Federal Child Support Tables/ Tables fédérales de pensions alimentaires pour enfants

Province: Nunavut
No. Of Children/ N^{bre} d'enfants: Five/Cinq

Income/Revenu ($)		Monthly Award/ Paiement mensuel ($)		
From/De	To/À	Basic Amount/ Montant de base	Plus (%)	Of Income Over/Du revenu dépassant
60000	*60999*	1673	2.63	60000
61000	*61999*	1699	2.63	61000
62000	*62999*	1726	2.63	62000
63000	*63999*	1752	2.63	63000
64000	*64999*	1778	2.63	64000
65000	*65999*	1805	2.63	65000
66000	*66999*	1831	2.63	66000
67000	*67999*	1857	2.63	67000
68000	*68999*	1884	2.63	68000
69000	*69999*	1910	2.63	69000
70000	*70999*	1936	2.41	70000
71000	*71999*	1960	2.41	71000
72000	*72999*	1984	2.41	72000
73000	*73999*	2008	2.41	73000
74000	*74999*	2032	2.41	74000
75000	*75999*	2057	2.41	75000
76000	*76999*	2081	2.41	76000
77000	*77999*	2105	2.41	77000
78000	*78999*	2129	2.41	78000
79000	*79999*	2153	2.41	79000
80000	*80999*	2177	2.41	80000
81000	*81999*	2201	2.41	81000
82000	*82999*	2225	2.41	82000
83000	*83999*	2249	2.41	83000
84000	*84999*	2273	2.41	84000
85000	*85999*	2297	2.41	85000
86000	*86999*	2321	2.41	86000
87000	*87999*	2345	2.41	87000
88000	*88999*	2369	2.41	88000
89000	*89999*	2394	2.41	89000
90000	*90999*	2418	2.41	90000
91000	*91999*	2442	2.41	91000
92000	*92999*	2466	2.41	92000
93000	*93999*	2490	2.41	93000
94000	*94999*	2514	2.41	94000

Federal Child Support Tables/ Tables fédérales de pensions alimentaires pour enfants

Province: Nunavut No. Of Children/ Nbre d'enfants: Five/Cinq

Income/Revenu ($)		Monthly Award/ Paiement mensuel ($)		
From/De	To/À	Basic Amount/ Montant de base	Plus (%)	Of Income Over/Du revenu dépassant
95000	*95999*	2538	2.41	95000
96000	*96999*	2562	2.41	96000
97000	*97999*	2586	2.41	97000
98000	*98999*	2610	2.41	98000
99000	*99999*	2634	2.41	99000
100000	*100999*	2658	2.41	100000
101000	*101999*	2682	2.41	101000
102000	*102999*	2707	2.41	102000
103000	*103999*	2731	2.41	103000
104000	*104999*	2755	2.41	104000
105000	*105999*	2779	2.41	105000
106000	*106999*	2803	2.41	106000
107000	*107999*	2827	2.41	107000
108000	*108999*	2851	2.41	108000
109000	*109999*	2875	2.41	109000
110000	*110999*	2899	2.41	110000
111000	*111999*	2923	2.41	111000
112000	*112999*	2947	2.41	112000
113000	*113999*	2971	2.37	113000
114000	*114999*	2995	2.20	114000
115000	*115999*	3017	2.20	115000
116000	*116999*	3039	2.20	116000
117000	*117999*	3061	2.20	117000
118000	*118999*	3083	2.20	118000
119000	*119999*	3105	2.20	119000
120000	*120999*	3127	2.20	120000
121000	*121999*	3149	2.20	121000
122000	*122999*	3171	2.20	122000

Federal Child Support Tables/ Tables fédérales de pensions alimentaires pour enfants

Province: Nunavut No. Of Children/ Nbre d'enfants: Five/Cinq

Income/Revenu ($)		Monthly Award/ Paiement mensuel ($)		
From/De	To/À	Basic Amount/ Montant de base	Plus (%)	Of Income Over/Du revenu dépassant
123000	*123999*	3193	2.20	123000
124000	*124999*	3215	2.20	124000
125000	*125999*	3237	2.20	125000
126000	*126999*	3259	2.20	126000
127000	*127999*	3282	2.20	127000
128000	*128999*	3304	2.20	128000
129000	*129999*	3326	2.20	129000
130000	*130999*	3348	2.20	130000
131000	*131999*	3370	2.20	131000
132000	*132999*	3392	2.20	132000
133000	*133999*	3414	2.20	133000
134000	*134999*	3436	2.20	134000
135000	*135999*	3458	2.20	135000
136000	*136999*	3480	2.20	136000
137000	*137999*	3502	2.20	137000
138000	*138999*	3524	2.20	138000
139000	*139999*	3546	2.20	139000
140000	*140999*	3568	2.20	140000
141000	*141999*	3590	2.20	141000
142000	*142999*	3612	2.20	142000
143000	*143999*	3634	2.20	143000
144000	*144999*	3656	2.20	144000
145000	*145999*	3678	2.20	145000
146000	*146999*	3700	2.20	146000
147000	*147999*	3722	2.20	147000
148000	*148999*	3744	2.20	148000
149000	*149999*	3766	2.20	149000

Federal Child Support Tables/ Tables fédérales de pensions alimentaires pour enfants

Province: Nunavut
No. Of Children/ Nbre d'enfants: Five/Cinq

Income/Revenu ($)		Monthly Award/ Paiement mensuel ($)		
From/De	To/À	Basic Amount/ Montant de base	Plus (%)	Of Income Over/Du revenu dépassant
150000	*or greater/ ou plus*	3788	2.20	150000

Federal Child Support Tables/ Tables fédérales de pensions alimentaires pour enfants

Province: Nunavut
No. Of Children/ Nbre d'enfants: Six or more/ Six ou plus

Income/Revenu ($)		Monthly Award/ Paiement mensuel ($)		
From/De	To/À	Basic Amount/ Montant de base	Plus (%)	Of Income Over/Du revenu dépassant
0	*7999*	0		
8000	*8999*	0	3.14	8000
9000	*9999*	31	5.14	9000
10000	*10999*	83	5.14	10000
11000	*11999*	134	4.92	11000
12000	*12999*	183	4.87	12000
13000	*13999*	232	4.78	13000
14000	*14999*	280	4.75	14000
15000	*15999*	327	4.75	15000
16000	*16999*	375	4.75	16000
17000	*17999*	422	4.75	17000
18000	*18999*	470	4.75	18000
19000	*19999*	517	4.75	19000
20000	*20999*	565	4.75	20000
21000	*21999*	612	4.75	21000
22000	*22999*	660	4.75	22000
23000	*23999*	707	4.75	23000
24000	*24999*	755	4.75	24000

Federal Child Support Tables/ Tables fédérales de pensions alimentaires pour enfants

Province: Nunavut
No. Of Children/ Nbre d'enfants: Six or more/ Six ou plus

Income/Revenu ($)		Monthly Award/ Paiement mensuel ($)		
From/De	To/À	Basic Amount/ Montant de base	Plus (%)	Of Income Over/Du revenu dépassant
25000	*25999*	802	4.75	25000
26000	*26999*	850	4.19	26000
27000	*27999*	891	3.08	27000
28000	*28999*	922	3.08	28000
29000	*29999*	953	2.96	29000
30000	*30999*	983	2.88	30000
31000	*31999*	1012	2.88	31000
32000	*32999*	1040	2.88	32000
33000	*33999*	1069	2.88	33000
34000	*34999*	1098	2.88	34000
35000	*35999*	1127	2.52	35000
36000	*36999*	1152	2.66	36000
37000	*37999*	1179	2.72	37000
38000	*38999*	1206	2.72	38000
39000	*39999*	1233	2.78	39000
40000	*40999*	1261	2.86	40000
41000	*41999*	1289	2.94	41000
42000	*42999*	1319	2.94	42000
43000	*43999*	1348	2.94	43000
44000	*44999*	1378	2.94	44000
45000	*45999*	1407	2.94	45000
46000	*46999*	1437	2.88	46000
47000	*47999*	1465	2.88	47000
48000	*48999*	1494	2.88	48000
49000	*49999*	1523	2.88	49000
50000	*50999*	1552	2.88	50000
51000	*51999*	1581	2.88	51000
52000	*52999*	1610	2.88	52000
53000	*53999*	1638	2.88	53000
54000	*54999*	1667	2.88	54000
55000	*55999*	1696	2.88	55000
56000	*56999*	1725	2.88	56000
57000	*57999*	1754	2.88	57000
58000	*58999*	1782	2.88	58000
59000	*59999*	1811	2.88	59000

Federal Child Support Tables/ Tables fédérales de pensions alimentaires pour enfants

Province: Nunavut
No. Of Children/ Nbre d'enfants: Six or more/ Six ou plus

Income/Revenu ($)		Monthly Award/ Paiement mensuel ($)		
From/De	To/À	Basic Amount/ Montant de base	Plus (%)	Of Income Over/Du revenu dépassant
60000	*60999*	1840	2.88	60000
61000	*61999*	1869	2.88	61000
62000	*62999*	1898	2.88	62000
63000	*63999*	1927	2.88	63000
64000	*64999*	1955	2.88	64000
65000	*65999*	1984	2.88	65000
66000	*66999*	2013	2.88	66000
67000	*67999*	2042	2.88	67000
68000	*68999*	2071	2.88	68000
69000	*69999*	2100	2.88	69000
70000	*70999*	2128	2.64	70000
71000	*71999*	2155	2.64	71000
72000	*72999*	2181	2.64	72000
73000	*73999*	2208	2.64	73000
74000	*74999*	2234	2.64	74000
75000	*75999*	2260	2.64	75000
76000	*76999*	2287	2.64	76000
77000	*77999*	2313	2.64	77000
78000	*78999*	2339	2.64	78000
79000	*79999*	2366	2.64	79000
80000	*80999*	2392	2.64	80000
81000	*81999*	2419	2.64	81000
82000	*82999*	2445	2.64	82000
83000	*83999*	2471	2.64	83000
84000	*84999*	2498	2.64	84000
85000	*85999*	2524	2.64	85000
86000	*86999*	2551	2.64	86000
87000	*87999*	2577	2.64	87000
88000	*88999*	2603	2.64	88000
89000	*89999*	2630	2.64	89000
90000	*90999*	2656	2.64	90000
91000	*91999*	2683	2.64	91000
92000	*92999*	2709	2.64	92000
93000	*93999*	2735	2.64	93000
94000	*94999*	2762	2.64	94000

Federal Child Support Tables/ Tables fédérales de pensions alimentaires pour enfants

Province: Nunavut
No. Of Children/ Nbre d'enfants: Six or more/ Six ou plus

Income/Revenu ($)		Monthly Award/ Paiement mensuel ($)		
From/De	To/À	Basic Amount/ Montant de base	Plus (%)	Of Income Over/Du revenu dépassant
95000	*95999*	2788	2.64	95000
96000	*96999*	2814	2.64	96000
97000	*97999*	2841	2.64	97000
98000	*98999*	2867	2.64	98000
99000	*99999*	2894	2.64	99000
100000	*100999*	2920	2.64	100000
101000	*101999*	2946	2.64	101000
102000	*102999*	2973	2.64	102000
103000	*103999*	2999	2.64	103000
104000	*104999*	3026	2.64	104000
105000	*105999*	3052	2.64	105000
106000	*106999*	3078	2.64	106000
107000	*107999*	3105	2.64	107000
108000	*108999*	3131	2.64	108000
109000	*109999*	3158	2.64	109000
110000	*110999*	3184	2.64	110000
111000	*111999*	3210	2.64	111000
112000	*112999*	3237	2.64	112000
113000	*113999*	3263	2.60	113000
114000	*114999*	3289	2.42	114000
115000	*115999*	3313	2.42	115000
116000	*116999*	3337	2.42	116000
117000	*117999*	3362	2.42	117000
118000	*118999*	3386	2.42	118000
119000	*119999*	3410	2.42	119000
120000	*120999*	3434	2.42	120000
121000	*121999*	3458	2.42	121000
122000	*122999*	3482	2.42	122000
123000	*123999*	3506	2.42	123000
124000	*124999*	3531	2.42	124000
125000	*125999*	3555	2.42	125000
126000	*126999*	3579	2.42	126000
127000	*127999*	3603	2.42	127000
128000	*128999*	3627	2.42	128000
129000	*129999*	3651	2.42	129000

Federal Child Support Tables/ Tables fédérales de pensions alimentaires pour enfants

Province: Nunavut
No. Of Children/ Nbre d'enfants: Six or more/ Six ou plus

Income/Revenu ($)		Monthly Award/ Paiement mensuel ($)		
From/De	To/À	Basic Amount/ Montant de base	Plus (%)	Of Income Over/Du revenu dépassant
130000	*130999*	3676	2.42	130000
131000	*131999*	3700	2.42	131000
132000	*132999*	3724	2.42	132000
133000	*133999*	3748	2.42	133000
134000	*134999*	3772	2.42	134000
135000	*135999*	3796	2.42	135000
136000	*136999*	3820	2.42	136000
137000	*137999*	3845	2.42	137000
138000	*138999*	3869	2.42	138000
139000	*139999*	3893	2.42	139000
140000	*140999*	3917	2.42	140000
141000	*141999*	3941	2.42	141000
142000	*142999*	3965	2.42	142000
143000	*143999*	3990	2.42	143000
144000	*144999*	4014	2.42	144000
145000	*145999*	4038	2.42	145000
146000	*146999*	4062	2.42	146000
147000	*147999*	4086	2.42	147000
148000	*148999*	4110	2.42	148000
149000	*149999*	4135	2.42	149000
150000	*or greater/ ou plus*	4159	2.42	150000

SOR/97-563, ss. 4–9; SOR/99-136, ss. 1, 2; SOR/2005-400, ss. 3–5

SCHEDULE II

(Subsection 10(4))

COMPARISON OF HOUSEHOLD STANDARDS OF LIVING TEST

1. Definitions — The definitions in this section apply in this Schedule.

"average tax rate" [Repealed SOR/2000-337, s. 7(1).]

"child" means a child of the marriage or a child who

(a) is under the age of majority; or

(b) is the age of majority or over but is unable, by reason of illness, disability or other cause to obtain the necessaries of life.

"household" means a spouse and any of the following persons residing with the spouse

(a) any person who has a legal duty to support the spouse or whom the spouse has a legal duty to support;

(b) any person who shares living expenses with the spouse or from whom the spouse otherwise receives an economic benefit as a result of living with that person, if the court considers it reasonable for that person to be considered part of the household; and

(c) any child whom the spouse or the person described in paragraph (a) or (b) has a legal duty to support.

"taxable income" means the annual taxable income determined using the calculations required to determine "Taxable Income" in the T1 General form issued by the Canada Revenue Agency.

SOR/2007-59, s. 4(b)

2. Test — The comparison of household standards of living test is as follows:

Step 1

Establish the annual income of each person in each household by applying the formula

$$A - B - C$$

where

A is the person's income determined in accordance with sections 15 to 20 of these Guidelines,

B is the federal and provincial taxes payable on the person's taxable income, and

C is the person's source deductions for premiums paid under the *Employment Insurance Act* and contributions made to the *Canada Pension Plan* and the *Quebec Pension Plan.*

Where the information on which to base the income determination is not provided, the court may impute income in the amount it considers appropriate.

Step 2

Adjust the annual income of each person in each household by

(a) deducting the following amounts, calculated on an annual basis:

(i) any amount relied on by the court as a factor that resulted in a determination of undue hardship, except any amount attributable to the support of a member of the household that is not incurred due to a disability or serious illness of that member,

(ii) the amount that would otherwise be payable by the person in respect of a child to whom the order relates, if the pleading of undue hardship was not made,

(A) under the applicable table, or

(B) as is considered by the court to be appropriate, where the court considers the table amount to be inappropriate,

(iii) any amount of support that is paid by the person under a judgment, order or written separation agreement, except

(A) an amount already deducted under subparagraph (i), and

(B) an amount paid by the person in respect of a child to whom the order referred to in subparagraph (ii) relates; and

(b) adding the following amounts, calculated on an annual basis:

(i) any amount that would otherwise be receivable by the person in respect of a child to whom the order relates, if the pleading of undue hardship was not made,

(A) under the applicable table, or

(B) as is considered by the court to be appropriate, where the court considers the table amount to be inappropriate,

(ii) any amount of child support that the person has received for any child under a judgment, order or written separation agreement.

Step 3

Add the amounts of adjusted annual income for all the persons in each household to determine the total household income for each household.

Step 4

Determine the applicable low-income measures amount for each household based on the following:

(Low-income Measures)

Household Size		**Low-income Measures Amount**
One person 1 adult		$10,382
	Two persons	
2 adults		$14,535
1 adult and 1 child		$14,535
	Three persons	
3 adults		$18,688
2 adults and 1 child		$17,649
1 adult and 2 children		$17,649
	Four persons	
4 adults		$22,840
3 adults and 1 child		$21,802
2 adults and 2 children		$20,764
1 adult and 3 children		$20,764
	Five persons	
5 adults		$26,993
4 adults and 1 child		$25,955
3 adults and 2 children		$24,917
2 adults and 3 children		$23,879
1 adult and 4 children		$23,879
	Six persons	
6 adults		$31,145
5 adults and 1 child		$30,108
4 adults and 2 children		$29,070
3 adults and 3 children		$28,031
2 adults and 4 children		$26,993

(Low-income Measures)	
Household Size	**Low-income Measures Amount**
1 adult and 5 children	$26,993
Seven persons	
7 adults	$34,261
6 adults and 1 child	$33,222
5 adults and 2 children	$32,184
4 adults and 3 children	$31,146
3 adults and 4 children	$30,108
2 adults and 5 children	$29,070
1 adult and 6 children	$29,070
Eight persons	
8 adults	$38,413
7 adults and 1 child	$37,375
6 adults and 2 children	$36,337
5 adults and 3 children	$35,299
4 adults and 4 children	$34,261
3 adults and 5 children	$33,222
2 adults and 6 children	$32,184
1 adult and 7 children	$32,184

Step 5

Divide the household income amount (Step 3) by the low-income measures amount (Step 4) to get a household income ratio for each household.

Step 6

Compare the household income ratios. The household that has the higher ratio has the higher standard of living.

SOR/97-563, ss. 10, 11; SOR/2000-337, s. 7; SOR/2005-400, s. 6

SCHEDULE III

(Section 16)

ADJUSTMENTS TO INCOME

1. Employment expenses — Where the spouse is an employee, the spouse's applicable employment expenses described in the following provisions of the *Income Tax Act* are deducted:

(a) [Repealed SOR/2000-337, s. 8(1).]

(b) paragraph 8(1)(d) concerning expenses of teacher's exchange fund contribution;

(c) paragraph 8(1)(e) concerning expenses of railway employees;

(d) paragraph 8(1)(f) concerning sales expenses;

(e) paragraph 8(1)(g) concerning transport employee's expenses;

(f) paragraph 8(1)(h) concerning travel expenses;

(f.1) paragraph 8(1)(h.1) concerning motor vehicle travel expenses;

(g) paragraph 8(1)(i) concerning dues and other expenses of performing duties;

(h) paragraph 8(1)(j) concerning motor vehicle and aircraft costs;

(i) paragraph 8(1)(l.1) concerning *Canada Pension Plan* contributions and *Employment Insurance Act* premiums paid in respect of another employee who acts as an assistant or substitute for the spouse;

(j) paragraph 8(1)(n) concerning salary reimbursement;

(k) paragraph 8(1)(o) concerning forfeited amounts;

(l) paragraph 8(1)(p) concerning musical instrument costs; and

(m) paragraph 8(1)(q) concerning artists' employment expenses.

SOR/97-563, s. 12; SOR/2000-337, s. 8

2. Child support — Deduct any child support received that is included to determine total income in the T1 General form issued by the Canada Revenue Agency.

SOR/97-563, s. 13; SOR/2000-337, s. 9; SOR/2007-59, s. 4(c)

3. Spousal support and universal child care benefit — To calculate income for the purpose of determining an amount under an applicable table, deduct

(a) the spousal support received from the other spouse; and

(b) any universal child care benefit that is included to determine the spouse's total income in the T1 General form issued by the Canada Revenue Agency.

SOR/2007-59, s. 3

3.1 Special or extraordinary expenses — To calculate income for the purpose of determining an amount under section 7 of these Guidelines, deduct the spousal support paid to the other spouse and, as applicable, make the following adjustment in respect of universal child care benefits:

(a) deduct benefits that are included to determine the spouse's total income in the T1 General form issued by the Canada Revenue Agency and that are for a child for whom special or extraordinary expenses are not being requested; or

(b) include benefits that are not included to determine the spouse's total income in the T1 General form issued by the Canada Revenue Agency and that are received by the spouse for a child for whom special or extraordinary expenses are being requested.

SOR/2007-59, s. 3

4. Social assistance — Deduct any amount of social assistance income that is not attributable to the spouse.

SOR/2000-337, s. 10

5. Dividends from taxable Canadian corporations — Replace the taxable amount of dividends from taxable Canadian corporations received by the spouse by the actual amount of those dividends received by the spouse.

6. Capital gains and capital losses — Replace the taxable capital gains realized in a year by the spouse by the actual amount of capital gains realized by the spouse in excess of the spouse's actual capital losses in that year.

7. Business investment losses — Deduct the actual amount of business investment losses suffered by the spouse during the year.

8. Carrying charges — Deduct the spouse's carrying charges and interest expenses that are paid by the spouse and that would be deductible under the *Income Tax Act.*

9. Net self-employment income — Where the spouse's net self-employment income is determined by deducting an amount for salaries, benefits, wages or management fees, or other payments, paid to or on behalf of persons with whom the spouse does not deal at arm's length, include that amount, unless the spouse establishes that the payments were necessary to earn the self-employment income and were reasonable in the circumstances.

10. Additional amount — Where the spouse reports income from self-employment that, in accordance with sections 34.1 and 34.2 of the *Income Tax Act*, includes an additional amount earned in a prior period, deduct the amount earned in the prior period, net of reserves.

SOR/2000-337, s. 11

11. Capital cost allowance for property — Include the spouse's deduction for an allowable capital cost allowance with respect to real property.

12. Partnership income — Where the spouse earns income through a partnership or sole proprietorship, deduct any amount included in income that is properly required by the partnership or sole proprietorship for purposes of capitalization.

SOR/97-563, s. 14

13. (1) Employee stock options — Where the spouse has received, as an employee benefit, options to purchase shares of a Canadian-controlled private corporation, or a publicly traded corporation that is subject to the same tax treatment with reference to stock options as a Canadian-controlled private corporation, and has exercised those options during the year, add the difference between the value of the shares at the time the options are exercised and the amount paid by the spouse for the shares, and any amount paid by the spouse to acquire the options to purchase the shares, to the income for the year in which the options are exercised.

(2) Disposal of shares — If the spouse has disposed of the shares during a year, deduct from the income for that year the difference determined under subsection (1).

SOR/2000-337, s. 12; SOR/2001-292, s. 1

SPOUSAL SUPPORT ADVISORY GUIDELINES

The Spousal Support Advisory Guidelines: A Draft Proposal was published on-line in January 2005 and the full text can be found at:

http://www.justice.gc.ca/en/dept/pub/spousal/project/index.html

Updates with current information are at:

http://www.westlawecarswell.com/familysource/ssagarticles/

The following is an abridgment of the Executive Summary and chapters 1 through 10 of the Advisory Guidelines. Chapter 11, the last chapter, which sets out the authors' conclusion of their proposal, has been omitted. The authors of the guidelines have followed up on their draft with published "updates" and relevant excerpts of the updates have been inserted in appropriate places in the abridgement that follows. The full text of the chapters and the updates should be read for a more complete understanding of their contents. See online addresses, above.

A few general observations must be made at the start. First, the proposal "is truly a *draft* that invites application, experimentation, discussion and feedback with a view to further revisions." Second, "They are informal guidelines that will operate on an *advisory basis only*." Third, they are to be "used to determine the amount and duration of spousal support within the legal framework of the *Divorce Act* and the judicial decisions interpreting its provisions." It is expected that they will be used under provincial/territorial laws, also, except where these laws differ on matters such as the effect of a prior agreement on spousal support. Fourth, and most important, the proposal does not deal with entitlement, "just amount and duration once entitlement has been found."

"There are two basic formulas in the proposal: the *without child support* formula and the *with child support* formula. ... Both formulas use *income sharing* as the method for determining the amount of spousal support, not budgets. The formulas produce *ranges* for the amount and duration of support, not just a single number. The precise number chosen within that range will be a matter for negotiation or adjudication, depending upon the facts of a particular case." (Executive Summary.)

1 — Background — The Current Law of Spousal Support

1.1 — The Legislative Framework

Spousal support, when sought in the context of a divorce, is governed by the federal *Divorce Act*. There are also provincial and territorial laws that govern spousal support outside the divorce context, applying to unmarried couples and to married couples who have separated but are not applying for a divorce. The statutory provisions are an important starting point in understanding the law around spousal support; they provide the framework within which the proposed advisory guidelines will operate. The proposed advisory guidelines do nothing to alter that legislative framework.

Federal and provincial/territorial spousal support legislation in Canada tends to take the form of relatively open-ended provisions incorporating a variety of factors and objectives. Much room is left for judicial discretion in the interpretation and application of the legislation. Judicial interpretations in turn guide lawyers and mediators advising clients negotiating spousal support settlements.

The specific focus of this project has been on developing informal guidelines to assist in the determination of the amount and duration of spousal support under the *Divorce Act.* The current *Divorce Act*, enacted in 1985, attempts to provide guidance for spousal support determinations by setting out, in s. 15.2(6), four objectives for spousal support:

> 15.2 (6) An order ... that provides for the support of a spouse should
>
> (a) recognize any economic advantages or disadvantages to the spouses arising from the marriage or its breakdown;
>
> (b) apportion between the spouses any financial consequences arising from the care of any child of the marriage over and above the obligation apportioned between the spouses pursuant to subsection (8) [i.e. through child support];
>
> (c) relieve any economic hardship of the spouses arising from the breakdown of the marriage; and
>
> (d) in so far as practicable, promote the economic self-sufficiency of each spouse within a reasonable period of time.

In addition, s. 15.2(4) lists certain factors to be taken into account in making support orders for a spouse:

> 15.2 (4) In making an order ... the court shall take into consideration the condition, means, needs and other circumstances of each spouse including
>
> (a) the length of time the spouses cohabited;
>
> (b) the functions performed by the spouse during cohabitation; and
>
> (c) any order, agreement or arrangement relating to support of the spouse or child.

Finally, s. 15.2(5) is more specific, indicating one factor that may *not* be taken into account — spousal misconduct:

> 15.2 (5) In making an order [for spousal support or an interim order] the court shall not take into consideration any misconduct of a spouse in relation to the marriage.

Provincial/territorial support law is governed by distinctive statutory regimes. However, in practice there is much overlap between federal and provincial/territorial support laws. The leading Supreme Court of Canada decisions on spousal support, *Moge* and *Bracklow*, which will be discussed in more detail below, articulated a broad conceptual framework for spousal support that has been relied upon in decisions under both provincial/territorial and federal legislation. Indeed, *Bracklow*, below, which combined claims under both the *Divorce Act* and provincial legislation, made no real distinction between the two.

Given this overlap, it is possible that these advisory guidelines might be used under provincial/territorial support legislation. Any such use would have to take account of the distinctive features of these statutes. In Chapter 4, below, we discuss in more detail some of the specific issues that would arise in the application of the advisory guidelines to support determinations under provincial/territorial spousal support laws. *It is important to keep in mind when reading this document that the advisory guidelines were developed for use under the federal Divorce Act.*

1.2 — Judicial Interpretation

In two important decisions, *Moge v. Moge*, 1992 CarswellMan 143, 1992 CarswellMan 222, [1993] R.D.F. 168, [1993] 1 W.W.R. 481, 99 D.L.R. (4th) 456, [1992] 3 S.C.R. 813, 81 Man. R. (2d) 161, 30 W.A.C. 161, 43 R.F.L. (3d) 345, 145 N.R. 1 (S.C.C.) and *Bracklow v. Bracklow*, 1999 CarswellBC 532, 1999 CarswellBC 533, [1999] S.C.J. No. 14, 169 D.L.R. (4th) 577, 236 N.R. 79, 44 R.F.L. (4th) 1, 120 B.C.A.C. 211, 196 W.A.C. 211, [1999] 1 S.C.R. 420, [1999] 8 W.W.R. 740, 63 B.C.L.R. (3d) 77 (S.C.C.), the Supreme Court of Canada has attempted to clarify the general principles that structure our law of spousal support. These decisions, together with the legislation, constitute the current legal framework for spousal support. Our proposed advisory guidelines do nothing to displace these decisions, but are rather an attempt to develop formulas to better implement the principles these decisions recognize.

The combined effect of these two decisions is a very broad basis for spousal support under the *Divorce Act*. Both *Moge* and *Bracklow* can be seen as responses to, and rejections of, the very limited view of spousal support that had emerged from the Supreme Court of Canada's 1987 *Pelech* trilogy [*Pelech v. Pelech*, 1987 CarswellBC 147, [1987] 1 S.C.R. 801; *Richardson v. Richardson*, 1987 CarswellOnt 963, [1987] 1 S.C.R. 857; and *Caron v. Caron*, 1987 CarswellYukon 8, [1987] 1 S.C.R. 892] which had emphasized the importance of finality and promoting a clean break between divorced spouses. In the wake of *Pelech*, spousal support came to be viewed as a transitional or rehabilitative remedy. Time-limited spousal support orders came to be the norm, even in cases of long, traditional marriages.

In the ground-breaking *Moge* decision in 1992, the Supreme Court of Canada clearly rejected the *Pelech* trilogy and the clean-break model of spousal support. The Court emphasized that all four support objectives in the 1985 *Divorce Act* had to be given weight and that the clean-break model of spousal support unduly emphasized only one of those objectives — the promotion of spousal self-sufficiency after divorce — at the expense of all the others. Former spouses were obligated to make reasonable efforts to maximize their earning capacity and contribute to their own support but the Court recognized that some spouses, despite their best efforts, would not be able to become self-sufficient. In the Court's view, the clean-break model went too far in deeming spouses to be self-sufficient when they were not. In *Moge*, the Court endorsed an expansive compensatory basis for spousal support, portraying its purpose as the equitable distribution between the spouses of the *economic* consequences of the marriage — both its economic advantages and disadvantages. While the Court recognized that many different circumstances could give rise to compensatory claims, the decision focused on the most common situation — that where a spouse has sacrificed labour force participation to care for children, both during the marriage and after marriage breakdown. Under the compensatory approach of *Moge*, spousal support came to be understood primarily as a form of compensation for the loss of economic opportunity — or in the language of the *Divorce Act*, the economic disadvantage — resulting from the roles adopted during the marriage.

The compensatory principle from *Moge* continues to play a significant role in structuring our law of spousal support. However, when lower courts attempted to implement the compensatory principle, which the Supreme Court of Canada had presented at a high level of generality, they ran into some difficulties on both the practical and theoretical fronts.

On the practical front, the compensatory principle is difficult to implement. Establishing a support claim requires, in principle, individualized evidence of earning capacity loss. As the Supreme Court of Canada itself acknowledged in *Moge*, providing this form of expert evidence can be costly. Evidence of earning capacity loss can also be difficult to obtain and somewhat hypothetical, particularly in cases of long marriages where the spouse claiming spousal support had no established career before assuming the role of homemaker. Difficult questions of causation can also arise as to why a spouse remained out of the labour force or chose lowly paid employment. On a practical level, effective implementation of the compensatory principle requires the development of proxy measures of economic loss that will inevitably involve some sacrifice of accuracy and theoretical purity.

After *Moge*, Canadian courts showed no enthusiasm for reliance upon expert economic evidence documenting loss of earning capacity. Instead, "need" — the traditional conceptual anchor of spousal support — became a convenient proxy measure of economic disadvantage. A spouse in economic need was presumed to be suffering economic disadvantage as a result of the marriage; conversely, a spouse not in need was presumed not to have suffered any economic disadvantage as a result of the marriage. The use of need and standard of living as proxy measures for loss of opportunity was expressly endorsed by Bastarache J.A. in *Ross v. Ross* (1995), 1995 CarswellNB 160, 16 R.F.L. (4th) 1, 168 N.B.R. (2d) 147, 430 A.P.R. 147 (N.B C.A.), a New Brunswick case involving a long traditional marriage:

> It is in cases where it is not possible to determine the extent of the economic loss of the disadvantaged spouse that the Court will consider need and standard of living as the primary criteria, together with the ability to pay of the other spouse.

At least in longer marriages, need came to be measured against the marital standard of living, a measure suggested by the Supreme Court of Canada itself in *Moge*:

> As marriage should be regarded as a joint endeavour, the longer the relationship endures, the closer the economic union, the greater will be the presumptive claim to equal standards of living upon its dissolution.

The rule that emerged in many lower court decisions was that the goal of spousal support following longer marriages was to provide the support claimant with a reasonable standard of living judged in light of the marital standard of living. In some cases, as in *Ross*, the principle for long marriages has been expressed as providing similar lifestyles or roughly equivalent standards of living for each of the spouses.

On the theoretical front, the post-*Moge* case law also revealed concerns with the limitations of a pure compensatory analysis that would confine the basis for spousal support to economic loss caused by the roles adopted during the marriage. Some judges shifted the compensatory focus to the economic *advantages* of the marriage in the form of the earning capacity the payor spouse was able to maintain and enhance. Other judges found the compensatory framework itself too restrictive. Compensatory theories narrowed the basis for entitlement. This was something many judges resisted. Some judges read the *Divorce Act* spousal support objectives more broadly, focussing on the section referring to the relief of economic hardship caused by the marriage breakdown. Others read *Moge* as a general directive to ameliorate the post-divorce impoverishment of former spouses. The most serious limitations of a compensatory analysis arose in cases involving ill or disabled spouses, whose economic needs were not related to marital roles and who could not claim spousal support based on losses or gains in earning capacity during the marriage.

The Supreme Court of Canada directly addressed these limitations of the compensatory principle in its 1999 decision in *Bracklow*. In that case the Court ruled that there is also a non-compensatory basis for spousal support under the *Divorce Act* based on "need alone." Thus a former spouse has an obligation to pay spousal support if the other spouse is experiencing economic need at the point of marriage breakdown, even when that need does not arise from the roles adopted during the marriage. The Court based this obligation on a view of marriage as a relationship involving mutual obligations and complex interdependencies that may be difficult to unravel when the marriage breaks down. The Court also spoke of marriage as involving the assumption of basic social obligations, reflecting the view that primary responsibility for support of a needy partner rests upon the family rather than the state. The Court went on to say that the extent of a former spouse's obligation to meet his or her former partner's post-divorce needs would be dependent upon many factors, including the length of the relationship, the way the parties had structured their relationship, ability to pay, and the re-partnering or remarriage of the former spouses.

Bracklow clearly expanded the basis of the spousal support obligation under the *Divorce Act* to include need as well as compensation. However, in the course of doing so the decision increased the level of uncertainty about the nature and extent of the spousal support obligation, well beyond what had existed after *Moge*. The Supreme Court of Canada failed to provide a definition of "need," leaving open the question of whether it meant an inability to provide a basic standard of living or whether it should be assessed in the context of the marital standard of living. After *Bracklow*, many argued that any spouse who experienced a significant decline in standard of living after marriage breakdown was entitled to spousal support.

Even more significantly, *Bracklow* emphasized the highly discretionary, individualized nature of spousal support decisions. The Court was clear that the *Divorce Act* endorses no single theory of spousal support and must retain flexibility to allow judges to respond appropriately to the diverse forms that marital relationships can take. The Court presented spousal support determinations as first and foremost exercises of discretion by trial judges who were required to "balance" the multiple support objectives and factors under the *Divorce Act* and apply them in the context of the facts of particular cases. One of the main messages of *Bracklow* was that there were no rules in spousal support.

1.3 — The Problem of Spousal Support and the Need for Guidelines

The current culture of spousal support is one that emphasizes individualized decision making and an absence of rules. Since the *Bracklow* decision, multiple theories of spousal support compete with each other while, on the ground, spousal support cases are negotiated and argued under an amorphous needs-and-means framework dominated by budgets. "Need" means many different things to different people and many different theories of spousal support can be couched in the language of need. The guidelines project springs from the growing concern expressed by lawyers and judges that the highly discretionary nature of the current law of spousal support has created an unacceptable degree of uncertainty and unpredictability.

. . . . .

[The proposed advisory guidelines] have been developed for the purpose of bringing more certainty and predictability to spousal support determinations. They incorporate the basic principles of compensation and need that the Supreme Court of Canada has identified as the bases for spousal support under the *Divorce Act*. The advisory guidelines attempt to provide a more structured way of implementing those principles through formulas based on income sharing, i.e. formulas based on sharing specified percentages of spousal incomes.

. . . . .

2 — The Guidelines Project

2.1 — The Nature of the Proposed Guidelines: Informal, Voluntary and Advisory

There are many preconceptions about what spousal support guidelines are and how they will work. Any talk of spousal support guidelines immediately brings to mind the *Federal Child Support Guidelines*. ... [T]his comparison should be resisted. The proposed advisory guidelines ... are very different.

Unlike the *Federal Child Support Guidelines*, these *advisory guidelines* do not involve formal legislative reform. They are not being legislated by the federal government. They are intended to be *informal* guidelines that will operate on an *advisory* basis only, within the existing legislative framework.

. . . . .

Government involvement in this process is limited. The federal Department of Justice is supporting the development of the advisory guidelines by providing financial support, communicating information on the project, participating in the discussions with the working group of family law experts, and keeping provincial and territorial governments informed. The project has no provincial/territorial sanction.

... [T]his process for creating and implementing the advisory guidelines is one of working "from the ground up", in contrast to the "from the top down" process of formal legislative reform. ....

2.2 — The Challenges of the Project

2.2.1 — Theory and practice

[T]his project is not directed at a theoretical re-ordering of the law of spousal support. Its aims are practical rather than theoretical — to provide a practical tool to assist family lawyers, mediators and judges who are confronted daily with the dilemma of determining appropriate levels of spousal support. As *Bracklow* has made clear, the *Divorce Act* does not mandate any one model of spousal support. [This was] kept in mind in constructing these guidelines. Reflecting current practice means reflecting a wide range of competing views of spousal support. No one theory or model or ideology or formula can be used. The formulas, described in more detail below, incorporate elements of different theories. In addition, the exceptions recognize alternate or subsidiary models of spousal support. There is no theoretical purity in the guidelines ... — they are the product of much compromise.

But increased consistency and predictability — the goals of the project — do require structure, even if it does not come from theoretical purity. The project is premised on the view that patterns and structure are beginning to emerge in the law, at least in a range of typical cases. But in the current culture of spousal support, these are often not discussed or articulated or openly acknowledged within the family law system. This project has attempted to build upon and facilitate those developments.

2.2.2 — Reflecting current practice, changing current practice

Admittedly, there is a central tension in the project between reflecting practice and changing practice. As informal rules of practice without the force of law, the guidelines must reflect current practice and cannot stray too far from existing results over all. That said, there is also much in current practice that is inconsistent, arbitrary and hard to explain. These advisory guidelines were developed because of their potential to constrain some of these current practices. In building upon current practice the project draws on best practices or emerging trends. The proposed guidelines incorporate and reflect much of the current practice of spousal support while at the same time seeking greater consistency and logic in the results. Inevitably, even if there are some changes to current practice under these guidelines, the changes must be incremental.

The proposed advisory guidelines are not intended to raise the current levels of spousal support over the broad run of cases. Inevitably, greater consistency under the advisory guidelines will mean that some spouses will see higher support awards and others will see lower awards. The guidelines should logically lead to more frequent spousal support awards, as they offer default ranges and reduce the cost of ascertaining support amounts. Some spouses who would give up on seeking spousal support under the current costly and unpredictable discretionary regime will obtain support under the advisory guidelines. ... But it is not the policy or intent of these guidelines to produce bigger support amounts.

2.2.3 — National guidelines and local spousal support cultures

[There is a] problem of squaring national guidelines with local and regional patterns of support. To the extent that local variations reflect higher or lower incomes, guidelines can adjust for that. The ranges provided by the advisory guidelines leave some scope for adjustment towards local patterns and local conditions. There may be some local twists that require further fine-tuning in the next phase. ... [T]he advisory guidelines might lead to some cross-fertilization of ideas amongst regions, as guidelines may force reconsideration of some local practices. During the next discussion phase, one of the challenges will be whether local or regional variations are so significant that the advisory guidelines must explicitly adjust further for such variations.

. . . . .

3 — Why Guidelines? How Will They Work in Practice

In this chapter we deal with the preliminary question that many will be asking: Are spousal support guidelines that utilize mathematical formulas based on income sharing a good idea? We review the advantages and disadvantages of spousal support guidelines focusing on the particular scheme of informal, voluntary and advisory guidelines we are proposing. To illustrate their potential usefulness, we also sketch how these advisory guidelines might work in practice.

3.1 — The Advantages and Disadvantages of Guidelines

In Canadian family law, if you mention guidelines most people think of the *Federal Child Support Guidelines*. They are not guidelines at all — they are really rules. The proposed advisory guidelines are *true guidelines* that are distinguished from the *Federal*

Child Support Guidelines by the descriptor advisory. Not legislated, but informal guides for lawyers and judges. Not binding but adopted voluntarily because of their usefulness as a tool in determining support. Even then, only advisory, a starting point for negotiation and adjudication. Dealing only with amount and duration, not entitlement. Constructed around two different formulas applicable to different marital situations and each offering a range of possible results rather than dictating a specific outcome. Containing broad exceptions that are not exhaustive of the grounds for departure.

Most of the advantages of guidelines are the usual arguments in favour of less discretion in family law generally. If rules are found at one end of the decision-making spectrum and discretion at the other, the current law of spousal support, after *Bracklow*, would be located very close to the discretion end. Advisory guidelines of the kind proposed would move the law back towards the middle ground between these two extremes.

The *advantages* of spousal support advisory guidelines:

(1) *To provide a starting point for negotiations and decisions.* At their best the guidelines will be loosely presumptive, a starting point from which parties will have to give reasons for any departure. The proposed advisory guidelines itemize a series of exceptions that will constrain and rationalize departures from the basic ranges.... [T]he guidelines will establish a starting point, assuming entitlement has been established. They will be most helpful in the typical or common cases that are usually resolved in negotiations.

(2) *To reduce conflict and to encourage settlement.* All other financial matters on family dissolution are now governed by rules — property division, pensions, child support. Spousal support is the last remaining pool of unfettered discretion. It is also typically the last financial issue to be resolved. Spousal support thus becomes the flashpoint for unhappiness with all the other financial rules, as well as for any remaining bitterness between spouses. Guidelines can limit the range of results and constrain the issues and information required, thereby encouraging settlement and damping down some of the conflict between the parties. Any reduction in conflict in family law, especially where children are involved, must be treated as an advantage.

(3) *To reduce the costs and improve the efficiency of the process.* In financial matters, it is ultimately dollars weighed against dollars, i.e. the cost of legal fees and disbursements weighed against the money gained or lost in support or property. Advisory guidelines can provide a starting point from which the parties can each decide whether further negotiation or litigation to push to the limits of the ranges, or beyond, is warranted. Further, published guidelines are even more important where one or both parties are unrepresented.

(4) *To avoid budgets and to simplify the process.* Under the current discretionary regime, expense budgets are required. Much time and trouble is taken, in disclosure and discovery, to particularize expenses — past, present and proposed — with the process often of dubious value in the end. Because guidelines are based on income sharing, there is no need to construct individual budgets. Less information is required and the process is simplified considerably.

(5) *To provide a basic structure for further judicial elaboration.* Advisory guidelines may prove to speed up, or perhaps more accurately, to kick start, the normal process of legal development in an area of judicial discretion. Under the current discretionary law, that process has nearly ground to a halt. Guidelines could give basic structure and shape to the law, with room left for lawyers and courts to adjust,

modify, identify possible new exceptions, etc. By their very existence, guidelines create pressure to give reasons for any departures in negotiations or decisions.

(6) *To create consistency and legitimacy.* Advisory guidelines should create greater consistency in outcomes as well as more open explanations of how those outcomes were reached. In doing so, over time, the amounts and duration of spousal support under the advisory guidelines can develop a legitimacy of their own, as has been the case with child support amounts. Eventually, the outcomes generated by the advisory guidelines will come to be seen as appropriate for many payors and recipients.

Next, the *disadvantages* of guidelines are considered, as compared to the current discretionary regime. In assessing these disadvantages, it is important to remember the nature of these specific advisory guidelines. There is a tendency for critics to assume guidelines will operate like rules, for example, to foreclose arguments based upon the facts of a particular case.

(1) *Too rigid.* Guidelines may be seen to deny individual justice, as their starting premise is average justice, generating reasonable results across a range of typical cases. An individual spouse may be denied a meaningful opportunity to argue why his or her case is unique or exceptional.

(2) *Spousal support is too complicated.* Many think spousal support is just too complicated for any formulaic approach. There are too many legal factors to balance, too many marital facts to be proved, and too many exceptions — marital fact situations that are just too diverse. Implicit in this view is the assumption that there are very few typical or standard fact patterns in spousal support, so few that it is not worth even developing guidelines for those typical fact patterns. Also implicit in this criticism is often an assumption that guidelines will be built around one big formula for all marriages.

(3) *Discretion allows intuitive reasoning.* Some argue that spousal support is a residual remedy; the last financial remedy that can be used flexibly to accomplish global justice in family matters. On this view, there are many factors at work, often intuitively, in reaching a just result, a result that is sometimes hard to explain.

(4) *Regional variations too great.* There are clearly local and regional variations in the amount and duration of spousal support. Some suggest that such variations are so great that any national guidelines would be of limited usefulness.

(5) *Litigation will be foreclosed.* For those who wish to settle, there is no question that guidelines will assist the negotiation process. But what if a party doesn't want to settle but wants to litigate? What if judges turn these guidelines into rules foreclosing arguments in court? That is a risk with any guidelines.

Many of these disadvantages depend upon the structure and operation of the specific set of guidelines involved. In constructing these advisory guidelines the authors have been conscious of many of the potential disadvantages of guidelines and have tried to address them. The advisory guidelines proposed involve more than one formula, ranges for amount and duration, and exceptions and other features that keep them in the middle of the rules-vs.-discretion spectrum.

Given the current state of spousal support law, the advantages of advisory guidelines significantly outweigh the disadvantages. In fact, without such guidelines, it may be impossible to move the law forward at all, based on the experience since *Bracklow*.

. . . . .

3.2 — How These Advisory Guidelines Might Work in Practice

.....

The proposed advisory guidelines will not be legally binding, operating more like persuasive law reform. Initially the advisory guidelines might simply serve as another tool in determining spousal support, a litmus test for support outcomes determined by more traditional methods, another source of arguments in negotiation and adjudication. Over time, as they prove their usefulness, they may become an accepted starting point from which parties will have to give reasons for any departure.

In negotiations, if the advisory guidelines were to suggest a range of $1,000 to $1,500 per month for spousal support, a spouse seeking to have support fixed within that range would argue that the advisory guidelines ought to be used since his or her case is typical. The spouse suggesting an amount outside that range, whether higher or lower, would presumably take the position that his or her case falls within an exception or warrants a departure from the guidelines or even that the guidelines' numbers are just wrong. If both parties are prepared to work within that range, then the usual arguments would be made about why the amount should be fixed at the higher or lower end of that range.

In settlement conferences, the parties might repeat these arguments or the judge might ask the parties whether they have considered the advisory guidelines. The judge might want to know why one or the other party took the view that this case fell outside the range.

Finally, in hearings or trials, the parties might make the same arguments and be faced with the same questions from the Bench. Undoubtedly, different judges will treat the advisory guidelines with varying degrees of practical force, with some applying them more rigorously and others using them more loosely. For the latter, the guidelines will be just another tool, used to test a result obtained by a more conventional needs-and-means analysis of budgets. But some judges might start from the advisory guidelines, resorting to budgets and other individual financial data only to fine-tune the guideline numbers.

.....

4 — The Basic Structure of the Advisory Guidelines

.... This chapter presents a structural overview of the scheme of the advisory guidelines.

.....

The basic concept of income sharing on which the advisory guidelines are constructed will be discussed, followed by a step by step review of the specific components of the advisory guidelines. This review is divided into three main sections. First, the preliminary issues that arise prior to any consideration of the formulas are dealt with — what might be called issues of application. Then the basic structure of the income-sharing formulas for determination of amount and duration of support that are at the heart of the proposed approach will be discussed. The outcomes generated by the formulas are not necessarily determinative, however. The final section deals with the possibilities for restructuring the formula outcomes (by trading off amount against duration), and for departing from the amounts and durations generated by the formulas, through exceptions.

4.1 — Income Sharing

The core concept on which these spousal support advisory guidelines are built is *income sharing*. Budgets will no longer play a primary role in determining spousal support outcomes. Instead the advisory guidelines will look to the incomes of the parties and rely on a mathematical formula to determine the portion of spousal incomes to be shared. Contrary to common perception, *income sharing does not mean equal sharing*. There are many ways of sharing income; it all depends on the formula that is adopted.

Other factors, shown below, are also relevant in determining support outcomes under the proposed advisory guidelines, such as the presence of dependent children or the length of the marriage. But the income levels of the parties, and more specifically the income disparity between them, become the primary determinants of support outcomes. Under the spousal support advisory guidelines, as under the child support guidelines, the precise determination of income, including the imputing of income, will undoubtedly become a much more significant issue than it has in the past.

. . . . .

The *method* of income sharing can be used as a practical and efficient way of implementing many support objectives such as compensation for the economic advantages and disadvantages of the marriage or the recognition of need and economic dependency. Such use of *proxy measures* already exists in spousal support law — think of the prevalent use of standard of living and a needs and means analysis to quantify compensatory support.

The proposed guidelines do not commit to any particular theory of spousal support. As will become clear in the discussion of the different formulas, they aim to accommodate the multiple theories that now inform our law and, to generate results that are in broad conformity with existing patterns in the law.

. . . . .

4.2 — Preliminary Issues — The Applicability of the Advisory Guidelines

4.2.1 — Form and force

Unlike the *Federal Child Support Guidelines*, the proposed spousal support advisory guidelines *will not be legislated*. Following the practice in some American jurisdictions, these are *informal guidelines. They are not legally binding. Their use is completely voluntary*. They will be adopted on a voluntary basis by lawyers and judges to the extent they find them useful, and will operate as a practical tool within *the existing legal framework*. As non-legislated, informal guidelines, these guidelines are *advisory only*. They are intended as a *starting point* for negotiation and adjudication.

Courts and lawyers will certainly be free to order or negotiate spousal support outcomes that differ from those generated by the advisory guidelines. However, the authors hope that the advisory guidelines will have significant voluntary buy-in because of their usefulness — because of the structure and consistency they provide and because they are perceived to generate appropriate outcomes. If so, the advisory guidelines might develop some presumptive force, in the loose sense of the word, such that parties would have to make arguments for departing from the starting point provided by the formulas. The advisory guidelines also explicitly set out a series of exceptions, albeit not exhaustive, providing a structured framework for departures from the formulas.

4.2.2 — Entitlement

The proposed advisory guidelines do *not* deal with entitlement. The informal status of the proposed guidelines means that they must remain subject to the entitlement provisions of the *Divorce Act*, notably ss. 15.2(4) and (6) as interpreted by the courts. Entitlement therefore remains a threshold issue to be determined before the guidelines will be applicable. *On its own, a mere disparity of income that would generate an amount under the advisory guidelines, does not automatically lead to entitlement.*

The advisory guidelines were drafted on the assumption that the current law of spousal support, post-*Bracklow*, offers a very expansive basis for entitlement to spousal support. Effectively any significant income disparity generates an entitlement to some support, leaving amount and duration as the main issues to be determined in spousal support cases. However, the guidelines leave the issue of when an income disparity is significant, in the sense of signaling entitlement, to the courts. It is open to a court to find no entitlement on a particular set of facts, despite income disparity, and these advisory guidelines do not speak to that issue.

The advisory guidelines may, over time, shape understandings of entitlement. But this would be part of the normal evolution of the law in this area, controlled by the courts. It is also possible that the law of entitlement may change over time in other directions, if the Supreme Court of Canada or an appellate court were to decide to narrow or refine *Bracklow*.

4.2.3 — Application to agreements

The advisory guidelines *do not deal with the effect of a prior agreement on spousal support*. This issue, like entitlement, is outside the scope of the advisory guidelines and will continue to be dealt with under the evolving law guided by the Supreme Court of Canada's recent decision in *Miglin v. Miglin*, [2003] 1 S.C.R. 303.

. . . . .

It is expected, however, that the advisory guidelines will play an important role in the *negotiation* of agreements by providing a more structured framework for negotiation and some benchmarks of fairness. One possible effect of the advisory guidelines might thus be a reduction in the number of agreements that are subsequently perceived to be unfair by one of the parties. Another might be that courts will be better able to identify unfair agreements when an agreement is subsequently challenged.

Further discussion of the application of the advisory guidelines in the cases where there are spousal support agreements can be found in Chapter 10.

4.2.4 — Interim orders

The advisory guidelines are intended to apply to interim orders as well as final orders. The authors anticipate, in fact, that they will be particularly valuable at the interim stage, which is now dominated by a needs-and-means analysis — budgets, expenses and deficits that require individualized decision making. In many American jurisdictions, guidelines were developed only for the interim stage.

Any periods of interim support clearly have to be included within the durational limits set by the advisory guidelines. Otherwise, if duration were only to be fixed in final orders, there would be incentives in both directions — for some to drag out proceedings and for others to speed them up — and general inequity.

The advisory guidelines do recognize that the amount may need to be set differently during the interim period while parties are sorting out their financial situation immediately after separation. To accommodate these short-term concerns, the advisory guidelines recognize an exception for compelling financial circumstances in the interim period.

Interim support is dealt with more extensively in Chapter 8.

4.2.5 — Review and variation

The primary application of these advisory guidelines is to *initial determinations* of spousal support at the point of separation or divorce, whether through negotiated agreements or court orders. Ideally a truly comprehensive set of advisory guidelines would apply not only to the initial determination of support but also to subsequent reviews and variations over time. However, these issues have proven the most difficult to reduce to a formula given the uncertainty in the current law concerning the effect of post-separation income changes.

A more modest course was chosen: identifying certain situations where the advisory guidelines will apply on reviews and variations, including increases in the recipient's income and decreases in the payor's income. Others, such as post-separation increases in the payor's income, re-partnering, remarriage and second families, have been left to discretionary determinations under the evolving framework of current law. Developing advisory guidelines to deal with some of these difficult issues may take place at a later stage of the project, after there has been some experience with these proposed advisory guidelines.

The application of the advisory guidelines in the context of review and variation is dealt with more extensively in Chapter 10.

4.2.6 — Application to provincial/territorial law

The proposed advisory guidelines have specifically been developed under the federal *Divorce Act* and are intended for use under that legislation. Provincial/territorial support law is governed by distinct statutory regimes. However, in practice there is much overlap between federal and provincial/territorial support laws.

The broad conceptual framework for spousal support articulated by the Supreme Court of Canada in *Moge* and *Bracklow* has been relied upon under both provincial and federal legislation. Indeed *Bracklow*, which combined claims under the *Divorce Act* and provincial legislation, made no real distinction between the two. Given this overlap, it is possible that the advisory guidelines might be used under provincial/territorial support legislation.

The proposed advisory guidelines are informal and not binding. They will be used only to the extent that lawyers, judges and mediators find them to be a helpful tool in spousal support determinations. Because they establish ranges for amount and duration, the spousal support advisory guidelines offer a fair amount of flexibility to accommodate any distinctive patterns under provincial/territorial law, just as they are able to respond to local variation under the *Divorce Act*. As well, departures from the advisory guidelines are always possible if the results generated by the formulas are inappropriate in the context of provincial/territorial support regimes.

The authors recognize that there are some clear differences between provincial/territorial support laws and the *Divorce Act*. Many provincial/territorial laws have specific provisions governing entitlement that would constrain the operation of the advisory guidelines. However the proposed advisory guidelines only deal with amount and duration, and not entitlement. Also, provincial/territorial statutes often include specific provisions governing the effect of agreements. However, because the advisory guidelines do not deal with the effect of agreements there will be no conflict.

Provincial laws also differ from the *Divorce Act* in their application to unmarried couples but this will not cause any difficulties with respect to the operation of the advisory guidelines. Although we conveniently referred to length of marriage as a relevant factor in the operation of the formulas, they actually rely upon the period of spousal cohabitation (including periods of pre-marital cohabitation), thus providing for easy meshing with provincial/territorial legislation.

It is important to keep in mind when reading this document that the draft advisory guidelines were not specifically developed for the provincial/territorial context; they were developed for use under the *Divorce Act*.

4.2.7 — Application to same-sex marriages

At the time of writing of this Draft Proposal, the *Divorce Act* had not been amended to extend to married same-sex couples the rights to seek divorce and corollary relief. If those amendments are made, the advisory guidelines would have the same application to same-sex couples whose marriages have broken down and who are seeking spousal support under the *Divorce Act*, as they do to opposite-sex married couples. Provincial/territorial support laws, which cover unmarried couples, do apply to same-sex relationships that satisfy the statutory conditions for entitlement.

4.3 — The Formulas

The advisory guidelines are constructed around *two basic income-sharing formulas*, rather than just one formula.

4.3.1 — Categories of marriages: with and without children

The advisory guidelines are structured around a fundamental distinction between marriages where there are no dependent children and those where there are; or more specifically around the distinction between cases where there is no concurrent child support obligation, and those where there is. The result is *two different formulas*.

In cases where there are no dependent children, the *without child support formula* applies. This formula relies heavily upon length of marriage — or more precisely, the length of relationship, including periods of pre-marital cohabitation — to determine both the amount and duration of support. Both amount and duration increase with the length of the relationship. This formula is constructed around the concept of *merger over time* which offers a useful tool for implementing both compensatory and non-compensatory support objectives in cases where there are no dependent children in a way that reflects general patterns in the current law.

Under the basic without child support formula:

- The *amount* of spousal support is 1.5 to 2 percent of the difference between the spouses' gross incomes for each year of marriage.
- *Duration* is .5 to 1 year of support for each year of marriage, with duration becoming indefinite after 20 years.

The *without child support* formula is discussed in detail in Chapter 5.

In cases where there are dependent children, an alternative formula — the *with child support formula* — applies. The distinctive treatment of marriages with dependent children and concurrent child support obligations is justified by both theoretical and practical considerations and is reflected in current case law.

On the theoretical front, marriages with dependent children raise strong compensatory claims based on the economic disadvantages flowing from assumption of primary responsibility for child care, not only during the marriage, *but also after separation*. The authors have identified this aspect of the compensatory principle as it operates in cases involving dependent children as the *parental partnership principle*, and have drawn on this concept in structuring the *with child support* formula.

The parental partnership principle is reflected in s. 15.2(6)(c) of the *Divorce Act*, which specifically directs that a spousal support order should apportion between the spouses any financial consequences arising from the care of any child of the marriage over and above any obligation for the support of any child of the marriage. The *Federal Child Support Guidelines* do not fully take into account the *indirect* costs of child-rearing, leaving such costs to be compensated for by spousal support. For marriages with dependent children, length of marriage is not the most important determinant of support outcomes as compared to post-separation child-care responsibilities.

On the practical front, child support must be calculated first and given priority over spousal support. As well, the differential tax treatment of child and spousal support must be taken into account, complicating the calculations. The *with child support* formula thus works with computer software calculations of net disposable incomes, of the kind often used now by lawyers and judges.

Under the basic with child support formula:

- Spousal support is an *amount* that will leave the recipient spouse with between 40 and 46 percent of the spouses' net incomes *after child support has been taken out.* (We refer to the spouses' net income after child support has been taken out as *Individual Net Disposable Income* or INDI).
- *The approach to duration under this formula is more complex and flexible than under the without child support formula and relies upon both length of marriage and duration of the post-separation child-rearing period.*

The *with child support* formula is discussed in detail in Chapter 6.

4.3.2 — Length of marriage

Under the advisory guidelines length of marriage is a primary determinant of support outcomes in cases *without* dependent children. Under the *without child support* formula the percentage of income sharing is sensitive to and increases with length of the marriage; the same is true of duration of support.

Length of marriage is much less relevant under the *with child support* formula although it still plays some role in determining duration under that formula.

Given the relevance of length of marriage under the advisory guidelines, it is important to clarify its meaning. *While we use the convenient term length of marriage, the more accurate description is the length of the relationship, which includes periods of pre-marital cohabitation, and ends with separation.*

In discussing the development and operation of the advisory guidelines we have sometimes classified marriages according to 3 categories based on length — short (under 5 years); medium (5–19 years); and long (20 years plus). The main value of these categories comes in determining the duration of support, or in thinking about the kinds of circumstances that will call for exceptions to the *without child support* formula.

These categories correspond to those implicitly underlying the current law and outcomes. Current law shows a fair amount of consistency in approach with respect to long and short marriages without dependent children; medium duration marriages without children generate much more uncertainty. Not surprisingly, the development of advisory guidelines for that category of cases proved the most difficult.

4.3.3 — Duration

The proposed advisory guidelines attempt to offer a formula for the determination of the duration as well as the amount of awards. Although judges and lawyers often see amount and duration as distinct issues, they are related; the two elements combined determine the total or global amount of a support award.

The proposed advisory guidelines set out the presumptive conditions for indefinite support. In other cases they establish time limits on the duration of awards. In particular, time limits are a significant feature of the *without child support* formula. They play a less significant, or softer, role under the *with child support* formula.

Time limits are admittedly a problem under the current law in Canada. After *Moge*, time-limited orders became less and less common. After *Bracklow*, some judges have brought back time limits, at least for non-compensatory support orders. While time limits are still frequently negotiated by parties in agreements and consent orders, many courts still frown upon time limits for all but short marriages.

Duration remains highly uncertain under the current law, particularly in medium duration marriages. The issue of duration is often put off to the future, to be dealt with through ongoing reviews and variations. Under current practice, uncertainty about duration can generate low monthly awards, as judges or lawyers fear that any monthly amount ordered or agreed upon could continue for a long time, even indefinitely.

In the authors' view, reasonable time limits are an essential element of spousal support advisory guidelines intended to promote greater certainty, especially if the guidelines generate reasonable monthly amounts. The time limits generated by the formulas are potentially very generous; in marriages of medium duration they can extend for periods of up to 19 years. These time limits are thus very different from the short and arbitrary time limits, typically of between three to five years, that became standard under the clean-break model of spousal support. Once marriages are of any significant length, the time limits under the Guidelines operate in conjunction with generous monthly amounts.

If current law cannot allow the reasonable and potentially quite generous time limits proposed by the advisory guidelines, then the advisory guidelines will have to be re-designed and the amounts generated by the formulas lowered. Amount and duration are interrelated parts of the formulas — they are a package deal. Using one part of the formula without the other would undermine the integrity and coherence of the proposed approach. The advisory guidelines do provide for restructuring, which allows duration to be extended by lowering the amount of support.

4.3.4 — Ranges

The advisory guidelines do not generate a fixed figure for either amount or duration, but instead produce *a range of outcomes* that provide a starting point for negotiation or adjudication. The ranges developed for duration under the *without child support* formula are particularly broad, reflecting the variation and uncertainty in current practice. After some period of experience with the advisory guidelines, some tightening of these may be possible.

Ranges create scope for more individualized decision making, allowing for argument about where a particular case should fall within the range in light of the *Divorce Act*'s multiple support objectives and factors. Ranges can also accommodate some of the variations in current practice, including local variations in spousal support cultures.

4.3.5 — Determining income

Income-sharing schemes work directly off income, as income levels essentially determine the amount of support to be paid. Under these advisory guidelines, the accurate determination of income will become a much more significant issue in spousal support cases than it has in the past, and there will be more incentives to dispute income. However, because these advisory guidelines generate ranges and not specific amounts, absolute precision in the determination of income may not be as crucial as under the *Federal Child Support Guidelines*. Many cases will involve combined claims for child and spousal support, where a precise determination of income is already required for child support purposes.

The starting point for the determination of income under both formulas is the definition of income under the Federal Child Support Guidelines, including the Schedule III adjustments. This is consistent with current practice. In cases involving combined claims for child and spousal support, the payor's income, as determined under the *Federal Child Support Guidelines*, is also the basis for assessing spousal support.

These advisory guidelines do not solve the complex issues of income determination that arise in cases involving self-employment income and other forms of non-employment income. These are difficult cases under the *Federal Child Support Guidelines* and will remain so under these spousal support advisory guidelines. In determining income it may be necessary, as under the *Federal Child Support Guidelines*, to *impute income* in situations where a spouse's actual income does not appropriately reflect his or her earning capacity. In some cases the issue will be imputing income to the payor spouse; on variations and reviews the issue may be imputing income to the recipient spouse if it is established that the he or she has failed to make appropriate efforts towards self-sufficiency.

Imputing income is the appropriate tool under the advisory guidelines to deal with concerns about any disincentives to self-sufficiency created by generous amounts of spousal support, especially at higher income levels. In current practice, self-sufficiency concerns often result in downward adjustments of amount in initial orders. Under these advisory guidelines, the amount of support is determined by spousal incomes and such loose adjustments are not possible. If a spouse is failing to realize his or her earning capacity, income at the appropriate level can be imputed subsequently at the stage of review or variation.

4.3.6 — Net vs. gross income

Existing guideline models vary, using both gross (before tax) and net (after tax) incomes in their income-sharing formulas. Good arguments can be made in favour of each method of calculating income.

Gross income is more readily calculated, without software, and more easily understood by most spouses. Gross income is also consistent with the *Federal Child Support Guidelines*.

Net income figures are more accurate and deal more effectively with the differential tax treatment of child and spousal support and the various tax benefits that accrue when there are children. Computer software, upon which many judges and lawyers have come to rely, also works with net income in calculations of monthly cash flow.

Different methods of calculating income are used under the two formulas:

- The *without child support* formula, which applies in cases where there are no dependent children of the marriage and hence no concurrent child support obligations, utilizes *gross income* in the interests of ease of calculation.
- The *with child support* formula relies upon *net income* calculations.

Both formulas generate a gross amount of spousal support that will be subject to the current deduction/inclusion rules for tax purposes. These advisory guidelines, given their informal status, do nothing to change the current tax treatment of spousal support.

The definitions of income used under each of the formulas are discussed in more detail in Chapters 5 and 6.

4.3.7 — Ceilings and floors

As with the *Federal Child Support Guidelines*, the spousal support advisory guidelines establish ceilings and floors in terms of the income levels to which they are applicable. These advisory guidelines allow more flexibility in amounts over a certain ceiling (as with incomes over $150,000 under the *Federal Child Support Guidelines*) and fix a floor below which spousal support is not payable (like the $7,000 floor under the *Federal Child Support Guidelines*).

As under the *Federal Child Support Guidelines*, we have set both the ceiling and the floor by reference to the annual gross income of the payor. The ceiling has been set at a gross annual income for the payor of $350,000 and the floor at a gross annual income of $20,000.

Ceiling and floors are dealt with more extensively in Chapter 7.

4.4 — After the Formulas Have Been Applied: Issues of Restructuring and Exceptions

Under the advisory guidelines there is still much room for the exercise of discretion to respond to the facts of particular cases. As discussed above, there is considerable room for discretion in the fixing of precise amounts and durations within the ranges generated by the formulas. Here the authors discuss two further opportunities for the exercise of discretion under their proposed approach: one is the ability to restructure the formula outcomes by trading off amount against duration; the other is the possibility of departing from the formula outcomes by relying upon exceptions.

4.4.1 — Restructuring

Although the formulas generate separate figures for amount and duration, the advisory guidelines explicitly recognize that these awards can be restructured by trading off amount against duration. Such tradeoffs are commonly made in separation agreements and consent orders. The advisory guidelines also recognize that judges may adjust amount and duration in a similar way.

In *Bracklow*, the Supreme Court of Canada explicitly recognized that the amount and duration of awards can be configured in different ways to yield awards of similar value (what the Court called quantum). Thus the Court noted that an order for a smaller amount paid out over a long period of time can be equivalent to an order for a higher amount paid out over a shorter period of time.

Restructuring can be used in three ways:

- to *front-end load* awards by increasing the amount beyond the formulas' ranges and shortening duration;
- to *extend duration* beyond the formulas' ranges by lowering the monthly amount; and
- to formulate a *lump sum* payment by combining amount and duration.

It is expected that in many cases where the outcomes generated by the formulas initially appear to be inappropriate, the issue will be resolved through restructuring. When restructuring is relied upon to resolve issues of inappropriate formula outcomes, awards remain consistent with the overall or global amounts generated by the advisory guidelines. Restructuring thus does not involve an exception or departure from the formulas.

Restructuring is dealt with in more detail in both Chapters 5 and 6 in the context of the discussions of the two formulas. Because restructuring will have more application in cases being dealt with under the *without child support* formula the more extensive discussion will be found in Chapter 5.

4.4.2 — Exceptions

The formulas are intended to generate appropriate outcomes in the majority of cases. The authors recognize, however, that there will be cases where the formula outcomes, even after consideration of restructuring, will not generate results consistent with the support objectives and factors under the *Divorce Act*. The formulas are intended to generate appropriate results in a wide range of *typical* cases; exceptions are required for *unusual* cases.

The informal, advisory nature of these guidelines means that the formula outcomes are never binding and departures are always possible on a case by case basis where the formula outcomes are found to be inappropriate. The advisory guidelines do, however, itemize a series of exceptions which, although clearly not exhaustive, are intended to assist lawyers and judges in framing and assessing departures from the formulas. The exceptions create room both for the operation of competing theories of spousal support and for consideration of the particular factual circumstances in individual cases where these may not be sufficiently accommodated by restructuring.

The exceptions include, for example, a compensatory exception that allows for awards of greater value than those generated by the formula in shorter marriages where there have been economic losses as a result of the marriage or contributions to the other spouse's career that are disproportionate to the length of the marriage. The inability to be self-supporting because of illness or disability may also constitute an exception, as may disproportionate responsibility for marital debts or support obligations to children and spouses from prior relationships.

As with restructuring, exceptions are dealt with in more detail in Chapters 5 and 6 in the context of the discussions of the two formulas.

5 — The Without Child Support Formula

The formula defines ranges for the amount and duration of spousal support:

> *Amount* ranges from 1.5 to 2 percent of the difference between the spouses' gross incomes (the *gross income difference*) for each year of marriage (or, more precisely, years of cohabitation), up to a maximum of 50 percent. The range remains fixed for marriages 25 years or longer at 37.5 to 50 percent of income difference.
>
> *Duration* ranges from .5 to 1 year for each year of marriage. However, support will be *indefinite* if the marriage is *20 years or longer* in duration or, if the marriage has lasted 5 years or longer, when the years of marriage and age of the support recipient (at separation) added together total 65 or more (the *rule of 65*).

This formula applies where there are no dependent children and consequently no concurrent child support obligations. The length of marriage is a key factor both with respect to the amount calculated and to the duration of the obligation to pay it.

Marriages for the *without child support* formula are divided into three categories based on length:

1. short (under 5 years);
2. medium (5 to 19 years); and
3. long (20 years plus)

"Merger over time" is the underlying philosophy of this formula. This philosophy recognizes that as a marriage lengthens, the spouses more deeply merge their economic and non-economic lives, resulting in greater claims to the marital standard of living. Support outcomes, therefore, are directly related to the length of the marriage.

5.1 — Basic Structure of the Without Child Support Formula

There are in fact two formulas — one for amount and one for duration. The formulas generate an upper and lower range of values, rather than one fixed value.

There are two crucial factors in the formula:

1. gross income difference between the spouses and
2. the length of the marriage, which, for these purposes, is interpreted to mean the length of the period of cohabitation. (See *Determining the length of the marriage*, s. 5.3.4, below.)

Both amount and duration increase incrementally with increases in the length of the marriage.

The formulas are intended to apply to initial determinations of support at the point of separation or divorce, using the spouses' incomes at the time the support is being determined by a court or negotiated by the parties.

Orders and agreements under the advisory guidelines are subject to variation if there is a change in circumstances. Also, they may include provisions for review.

The following example shows the basic calculations required under the formula.

Example 5.1

Arthur and Ellen have separated after a 20-year marriage and one child. During the marriage Arthur, who had just finished his commerce degree when the two met, worked for a bank, rising through the ranks and eventually becoming a branch manager. He was transferred several times during the course of the marriage. His gross annual income is now $90,000. Ellen worked for a few years early in the marriage as a bank teller, then stayed home until their son was in school full time. She worked part time as a store clerk until he finished high school. Their son is now independent. Ellen now works full time as a receptionist earning $30,000 gross per year. Both Arthur and Ellen are in their mid forties.

Assuming entitlement has been established in this case, here is how support would be determined under the *without child support* formula.

To determine the *amount* of support:

- Determine the *gross income difference* between the parties:

  $90,000 – $30,000 = $60,000

- Determine the *applicable percentage* by multiplying the length of the marriage by 1.5–2:

  1.5 × 20 years = 30 percent

  to

  2 × 20 years = 40 percent

- Apply the applicable percentage to the income difference:

  30 percent × $60,000 = $18,000/year ($1,500/month)

  to

  40 percent × $60,000 = $24,000/year ($2,000/month)

Duration would be indefinite in this case because the length of the marriage was 20 years.

Thus, assuming entitlement, spousal support under the formula would be in the range of $1,500 to $2,000 per month for an indefinite duration, subject to variation and possibly review.

An award of $1,500 per month, at the low end of the range, would leave Ellen with a gross annual income of $48,000 and Arthur with one of $72,000. An award of $2,000 per month, at the high end of the range, would leave Ellen with a gross annual income of $54,000 and Arthur with one of $66,000. We will deal below with the factors that determine the setting of a precise amount within that range.

5.1.1 — The formula for amount

This formula uses gross income figures rather than net, with income defined by reference to the definition of income under the federal *Child Support Guidelines*. The percentages are applied to the *income difference* between the spouses, not to the pool of combined spousal incomes.

The income difference between the spouses operates as a proxy measure of their differential loss of the marital standard of living and, in long marriages where there have been children, of the differential impact of marital roles on the spouses' earning capacities.

The formula for amount does not use a fixed or flat percentage for sharing the income differential. The formula incorporates a durational factor to increase the percentage of income shared as the marriage increases in length. The durational factor is 1.5 to 2 percent of the gross income difference for each year of marriage (cohabitation).

The ranges for amount were developed by first determining the point when maximum sharing would be reached, which was set at 25 years. It is assumed that maximum sharing would involve something close to equalization of incomes, or sharing 50 percent of the gross income difference.

5.1.2 — The formula for duration

The duration of the support obligation increases with the length of marriage. Subject to the special provisions for indefinite support, the formula generates: (1) a minimum duration of half the length of the marriage and (2) a maximum duration of the whole length of the marriage.

This is consistent with the concept of merger over time.

Age of the recipient is a significant factor as it affects his or her ability to become self-supporting.

The ranges for duration under this formula are very broad allowing for adjustment to suit the circumstance.

5.1.2.1 — The problem of time limits

Time limits pose a problem under the current law, particularly in medium-length marriages, although time limits are considered essential to permit the guidelines to generate reasonable monthly awards.

The time limits for the duration of the obligation as determined by the formula are potentially generous; for example, in medium-length marriages, the obligation can extend for up to 19 years.

5.1.2.2 — Indefinite support

The support obligation is indefinite with respect to duration once the marriage has lasted 20 years or longer (the 20-year rule). "Indefinite" means that no time limit is placed on the duration of the support in the initial order. An order for indefinite support does not necessarily mean permanent support, and it certainly does not mean that support will continue indefinitely at the level set by the formula. Where the order is indefinite with respect to duration, it will be subject to any review conditions attached to it and the usual rights to vary, which are not changed by the advisory guidelines.

The formula also provides that indefinite support will be available in cases where the marriage is between five and twenty years, if the years of marriage plus the age of the support recipient at the time of separation equals or exceeds 65 (the rule of 65). The rule of 65 for indefinite support is not available in short marriages under 5 years in length, in light of the assumption in the current law that short marriages generate limited support obligations.

5.2 — Merger over Time and Existing Theories of Spousal Support

The idea that underlies the *without child support* formula and explains income in proportion to the length of the marriage is merger over time; that is, as a marriage lengthens, spouses merge their economic and non-economic lives more deeply. This concept offers an effective way of capturing both the compensatory and non-compensatory spousal support objectives that have been recognized by our law since *Moge* and *Bracklow*. The spousal income difference serves as a convenient and efficient proxy measure for loss of the marital standard of living, replacing the uncertainty and imprecision of budgets.

Merger over time has a significant compensatory component. It tends to satisfy compensatory claims in long marriages for the assumption of primary responsibility for child care, and claims based on earning-capacity loss. The formula will deal also with non-compensatory support claims based on dependency, need, or loss of the marital standard of living where these claims exist, but limits the extent of the obligation according to the length of the marriage.

5.3 — Applying the Formula

5.3.1 — Entitlement a prior issue

Entitlement to support is not determined by the formula, but is an issue to be decided under the *Divorce Act* and applicable case law. The mere existence of an income difference that would generate an amount under the formula does not automatically result in an entitlement to spousal support.

5.3.2 — No minimum income difference fixed

The formula does not fix a minimum income difference before income sharing is permitted. The issue of when an income difference becomes insignificant in terms of entitlement to spousal support has been left to discretionary determinations under current law.

5.3.3 — Determining income under the without child support formula

The calculation of each spouse's gross income is a crucial step under the without child support formula. The calculation follows the definition of income under the Child Support Guidelines, including the Schedule III adjustments. The adjustments, for example, allow a court to impute income where a spouse's actual income does not appropriately reflect his or her earning capacity.

5.3.4 — Determining the length of the marriage

This is in fact the period of time that the parties cohabited including cohabitation before marriage. In determining the length of cohabitation, the simplest approach is to round up or down to the nearest full year. Because the formula generates a range and not a fixed number, addition or subtraction of half a year will likely make little or no difference to the outcome.

5.3.5 — Primary application to initial orders

As under the current law, orders made under the advisory guidelines will be open to variation in the future, based upon a material change in circumstances and may also include provisions for review.

5.4 — Making the Formula Concrete — Some Examples

5.4.1 — A short-marriage example

A short marriage is less than five years in length. Support will always be time-limited in these cases. Since the amounts generated by the formula are small for short marriages, the parties may resort to restructuring more often than spouses in long marriages (and corresponding larger amounts) to convert periodic payments to a lump sum.

The following example illustrates the effect of a short marriage on amount and duration.

Example 5.2

Karl and Beth were married for only four years. They had no children. Beth was 25 when they met and Karl was 30. When they married, Beth was a struggling artist who earned a meagre gross income of $12,000 a year giving art lessons to children. Karl is a music teacher with a gross annual income of $60,000. With Karl's encouragement, Beth stopped working during the marriage to devote herself to her painting.

Entitlement is a threshold issue before the advisory guidelines apply. On these facts, given the disparity in income and Beth's unemployment at the point of marriage breakdown, entitlement is likely to be found.

The conditions for indefinite support do not apply and duration would be calculated on the basis of .5 to 1 year of support for each year of marriage.

To determine the *amount* of support under the formula:

- Determine the *gross income difference* between the parties:

  $60,000 – 0 = $60,000

- Determine the *applicable percentage* by multiplying the length of the marriage by 1.5–2:

  1.5 × 4 years = 6 percent

  to

  2 × 4 years = 8 percent

- Apply the applicable percentage to the income difference:

  6 percent × $60,000 = $3,600/year ($300/month)

  to

  8 percent × $60,000 = $4,800/year ($400/month)

Duration of spousal support = (.5-1) × 4 years of marriage = 2 to 4 years

The result under the without child support formula is support in the range of $300 to $400 per month for a duration of 2 to 4 years.

Using *restructuring*, this modest award could be converted into a lump sum or into a periodic award that would be paid out over a very short time period such as one year.

5.4.2 — A medium-length marriage example

Except where the rule of 65 is applicable (see definition in formula, s. 5, above), the formula generates time limits that vary with the length of the marriage. The ranges for duration are very wide thus able to accommodate diverse circumstances. It is anticipated that there will be a frequent need to rely upon restructuring to adjust the formula outcomes. It is expected that in these situations, there will likely be the greatest resort to exceptions.

Example 5.3

Bob and Susan have been married 10 years. They married in their late twenties and Sue is now 38. Bob is employed as a computer salesman and Sue is a hairdresser. Both worked throughout the marriage. There were no children. Bob's gross annual income is $65,000; Sue's is $25,000.

Entitlement is a threshold issue before the advisory guidelines are applicable. An argument might be made that there is no entitlement to support: Sue is employed full time and could support herself, and there is no compensatory basis for support. However, Sue will suffer a significant drop in standard of living as result of the marriage breakdown and, at an income of $25,000, will likely experience some economic hardship. Current law would suggest an entitlement to at least transitional support on a non-compensatory basis to allow Sue to adjust to a lower standard of living.

The case does not satisfy the conditions for indefinite support. The marriage is under 20 years and the case does not fall within the rule of 65 for indefinite support because Sue's age at separation plus years of marriage is below 65 (38+10=48).

To determine the *amount* of support under the formula:

- Determine the *gross income difference* between the parties:

$$\$65{,}000 - \$25{,}000 = \$40{,}000$$

- Determine the *applicable percentage* by multiplying the length of the marriage by 1.5–2:

$$1.5 \times 10 \text{ years} = 15 \text{ percent}$$

to

$$2 \times 10 \text{ years} = 20 \text{ percent}$$

- Apply the applicable percentage to the income difference:

$$15 \text{ percent} \times \$40{,}000 = \$6{,}000/\text{year } (\$500/\text{month})$$

to

$$20 \text{ percent} \times \$40{,}000 = \$8{,}000/\text{year } (\$667/\text{month})$$

Duration of spousal support = (.5-1) × 10 years of marriage = 5 to 10 years

The result under the formula is support in the range of $500 to $667 per month for a duration of 5 to 10 years.

Consistent with current law, the formula essentially generates modest top-up support for a transitional period to assist Sue in adjusting from the marital standard of living.

An award of $500 per month, at the low end of the range, would leave Sue with a gross annual income of $31,000 and Bob with one of $59,000. An award of $667 per month, at the high end of the range, would leave Sue with a gross annual income of $33,000 and Bob with one of $57,000. In a marriage of this length the formula does not equalize incomes.

(Another example is included in the full text of the proposal.)

5.4.3 — A long-marriage example

In the current case law, there is difficulty in finding consensus on appropriate outcomes in cases of long marriages where there are no children or where both spouses have been fully employed, with or without children. The formula is intended to cover cases of long marriages where there is significant income disparity, but no strong compensatory claim.

Example 5.5

John and Mary were married for 28 years. Theirs was a traditional marriage in which John worked his way up the career ladder and now earns $100,000 gross per year, while Mary stayed home and raised their two children, both of whom are now grown up and on their own. Mary is 50 years of age and has no income. John is 55.

Entitlement to spousal support is clear on these facts and thus the advisory guidelines are applicable. Because the length of the marriage is over 25 years, the maximum range for amount applies — 37.5 to 50 percent of the gross income difference.

To determine the *amount* of support under the formula:

- Determine the *gross income difference* between the parties:

  $100,000 – 0 = $100,000

- The maximum range for amount is 37.5 to 50 percent of the gross income difference
- Apply the applicable percentage to the income difference:

  37.5 percent × $100,000 = $37,500/year ($3,125/month)

  to

  50 percent × $100,000 = $50,000/year ($4,167/month)

Duration is indefinite because the marriage is 20 years or over in length.

The formula results in a range for support of $3,125 to $4,167 per month for an indefinite duration, subject to variation and possibly review.

An award of $3,125 per month, at the low end of the range, would leave Mary with a gross income of $37,500 per year and John with one of $62,500. An award of $4,167 per month, at the high end of the range, would leave both parties with a gross annual income of $50,000. In this case an award at the highest end of the range would not be appropriate given the need to recognize John's costs of earning an income. An award of 50 percent of the gross income difference would actually leave Mary with a higher net income than John.

It would be inappropriate to *impute income* to Mary in an initial order given her long absence from the work, especially if the order is being made near the time of separation. However, at some point in the future, on a variation or review, income may be imputed to Mary, and spousal support re-determined, if evidence establishes that she is not making reasonable efforts to contribute to her own support. The order would also be open to variation over time in response to many other changes in the parties' circumstances, the most likely being John's retirement.

(Another example is included in the full text of the proposal.)

5.5 — Using the Ranges

The *without child support* formula generates ranges for amount and for duration as well, unless the conditions for indefinite support are met. The ranges allow the parties and their counsel, or a court, to make adjustments to take into account the particulars of the individual case in light of the support factors and objectives found in the *Divorce Act.* For example:

1. A strong compensatory claim may be a factor that favours a support award at the higher end of the ranges both for amount and duration, for instance, where economic circumstances are the result of marital roles.
2. Where the recipient has limited income and/or earning capacity, because of age or other circumstances, the recipient's needs may push an award to the higher end of the ranges for amount and duration.
3. Property division may affect where support is fixed within the ranges for amount or duration.
4. Need and limited ability to pay on the part of the payer spouse may pus an award to the lower ends of the ranges.
5. Self-sufficiency incentives may push in different directions.

This list is not exhaustive. The ranges allow room for local and regional differences in support outcomes.

5.6 — Restructuring

Restructuring allows amount and duration to be traded off against each other, as long as the overall value of the restructured award remains within the global or total amount generated by the formula when amount is multiplied by duration.

There are three ways to restructure:

1. to front-end load awards by increasing the amount beyond the formula's range and shortening duration;
2. to extend duration beyond the formula's range by lowering the monthly amount; and
3. to formulate a lump sum payment by combining amount and duration.

Restructuring will have its main application in cases governed by the advisory guidelines with the *without child support* formula. Restructuring can only be used where the formula generates time limits rather than indefinite support.

5.7 — Exceptions

These are only considered after considering adjustment in the ranges for amount and duration and restructuring. (Of course, advisory guidelines, being advisory only, can be ignored, whenever they are considered inappropriate). The more common exceptions are discussed in this section.

5.7.1 — The compensatory exception

Short and medium length marriages — These cases usually concern small amounts of support. Customarily there is a reduced importance of compensatory support. Usually in these cases, the transitional function of non-compensatory support is more important.However, short and medium length marriages can involve large compensatory claims, disproportionate to the length of the marriage, even without children involved. The claims may relate to an economic loss or may involve a restitutionary claim for an economic advantage conferred.

Where a claimant spouse can prove such a disproportionate compensatory claim, it allows for an individualized determination of the amount of spousal support, based on the size and nature of that claim. The formula will not offer much assistance.

5.7.2. — Illness and disability

Many such cases can be accommodated within the formula. The central concern is the recipient's need for long-term or indefinite support. Under the without children child support formula in long-term marriages, there is indefinite support after 20 years of marriage or based upon the rule of 65. In most medium — to — long marriages, the ranges for duration and amount offer considerable scope for the needs of an ill or disabled spouse. In some medium-length marriages, where the formula generates time limits, restructuring may have to be employed. Monthly amounts could be reduced and the duration extended beyond the maximum, especially where spousal support is effectively covering the period until retirement, when the recipient's pension and old age benefits become payable.

The advisory guidelines propose a limited exception for illness and disability cases, as these are the cases that the courts often treat as exceptional.

5.7.3 — Debt payment

Marital debts do not necessarily affect spousal support. In many cases debts are adequately taken into account in property division, reducing the amount of shareable property. When a couple has a negative net worth, then the allocation of the debt payments can have a dramatic impact upon ability to pay. If the payor is required to pay a disproportionate share of the debts, then there may have to be some reduction in support from the amounts generated by the formula. The reduction may only be for a specified period, depending upon the balance remaining to be paid. At the end of that period, support could automatically revert to an amount within the range or, in some cases, a review may be ordered at that time. Where assets exceed debts, there can be little reason for a debt exception, as the party responsible for the debt will usually also hold the corresponding asset or other assets.

Property division

There are no broad or additional exceptions based on property division. The advisory guidelines already accommodate some of the property concerns, including the following:

1. Each spouse is expected to generate reasonable income from his or her assets and income can be imputed where a spouse fails to do so. The income imputed will affect the operation of the formula.

2. Property-related concerns may, in some cases, determine whether support is fixed at the upper or lower ends of the ranges for amount or duration.

3. Many high property cases are also high-income cases, bringing into play the ceiling above which the formula will not necessarily apply.

The advisory guidelines on amount and duration do not change the law from *Boston v. Boston*, [2001] 2 S.C.R. 413, 2001 CarswellOnt 2432, 2001 CarswellOnt 2433, 17 R.F.L.

(5th) 4, 201 D.L.R. (4th) 1, 271 N.R. 248, governing double-dipping, a problem mostly involving pensions.

5.7.4 — Prior support obligations

A move to an income-sharing method of determining spousal support under a formula will require an explicit exception for prior support obligations. The exception could apply to either the payor spouse or the recipient spouse, although the issue comes up most frequently for payors. Usually, the prior support obligation will involve child support but spousal support may also be involved after a longer first marriage and then a shorter second marriage.

Where there are prior support obligations, a spouse's gross income will have to be adjusted to reflect those obligations, before computing the gross income difference and applying the percentage ranges to that difference.

5.7.5 — Interim support

Where there are compelling financial circumstances at the interim stage, an exception can be made. See 8, *INTERIM SUPPORT*, below.

6 — The With Child Support Formula

General

The *with child support* formula for spousal support is used where a child support obligation exists for a child of the marriage. An obligation to a child from a prior marriage or relationship is an exception, and does not come within the ordinary operation of the formula.

Net incomes of the spouses are used because of complications of tax and child benefit issues that must be taken into account.

The *with child support* formula presupposes that the children are in the custody of the spouse receiving the spousal support. Variations on the formula are necessary in cases of shared and split custody.

6.1 — The Rationales for Spousal Support

Spousal support under the "*with child support* formula" is based on the compensatory model. The rationale for using this model is that the spouse having responsibility for the care of the children should be compensated on the separation for foregone careers and missed opportunities during the marriage, and after the separation, for the losses associated with continuing child care. Compensation for continuing child care is supported, and the conventional compensatory approach is broadened, by the parental partnership theory discussed in recent literature and case law. Unlike the conventional compensatory approach, parental partnership looks at not just past loss, but also the continuing economic disadvantage that flows from present and future child-care responsibilities. For shorter marriages with younger children, these present and future responsibilities are more telling. Further, the parental partnership rationale better reflects the reality that many women never acquire a career before marriage, or mould their pre-marital employment in expectation of their primary parental role after marriage.

The direct costs of child-rearing are included in child support ordered under the *Child Support Guidelines*, but the indirect costs have been left to be compensated through spousal support. Principal among these indirect costs is the custodial parent's reduced ability to maximize his or her income because of child-care responsibilities.

6.2 — Background to the Basic Formula

The *with child support* formula differs from the *without child support* formula: First, the *with child support* formula uses the net incomes of the spouses, not their gross incomes. Second, the *with child support* formula divides the pool of combined net income between the two spouses, not just the difference between the spouses' gross incomes. Third, in the *with child support* formula, the upper and lower percentage limits for net income division do not change with the length of the marriage.

The pool of combined net incomes is smaller than a pool of the familiar family net disposable income would be, and is called the individual net disposable income or INDI.

The basic formula applies, without modification, only where the higher income spouse is paying both child and spousal support to the lower income spouse who is also the parent with custody or primary care of the children.

6.3 — The Basic With Child Support Formula

The formula requires the following steps.

(1) Determine the *individual net disposable income (INDI)* of each spouse:

- Guidelines Income *minus* Child Support *minus* Taxes and Deductions = Payor's INDI
- Guidelines Income *minus* Notional Child Support *minus* Taxes and Deductions *plus* Government Benefits and Credits = Recipient's INDI

(2) Add together the individual net disposable incomes. Determine the range of spousal support amounts that would be required to leave the lower income recipient spouse with between 40 and 46 percent of the combined INDI.

6.3.1 — Calculating individual net disposable income

The formula uses the same definition of income as is found in the *Child Support Guidelines* except included in each spouse's income are the government benefits and refundable credits such as the Child Tax Benefit, the National Child Benefit, the GST credit, the refundable medical credit and various provincial benefit and credit schemes.

To arrive at the INDI, first the actual and notional contributions to child support are deducted from income. For the payor this is the table amount plus any contributions to special or extraordinary expenses or any other *Guidelines* amount that is actually payable. For the child support recipient a notional table amount is deducted along with actual special or extraordinary expenses. The notional table amount is the amount that the recipient spouse would be obliged to pay, if she or he were the payor spouse (non-custodial parent) and not the recipient spouse. Second, income taxes and other deductions are subtracted from the incomes of both spouses. Other deductions not already made in the calculation of income under the *Guidelines* would include employment insurance premiums, Canada Pension Plan contributions, and premiums for benefits such as medical or dental insurance, and group life insurance. (The deductions do not include mandatory pension contributions, but the size of the contributions may be used as a factor to justify fixing an amount toward the lower end of the spousal support range.)

6.3.2 — The Basic Formula: Dividing Individual Net Disposable Income

After determining the individual net disposable income (INDI), the next step is to add them together. Then hypothetical spousal support is estimated at different amounts and the calculations are made for each of these amounts until the result leaves the lower income/recipient spouse with between 40 and 46% of the combined pool of individual net disposable income. These calculations are impracticable to do manually and computer software has been developed to perform them automatically.

The range of 40 to 46 percent of INDI was chosen for the formula because it typically covered spousal support outcomes in the middle of the very wide range of outcomes now observed in most of Canada. To capture the middle of the range on a national basis means that some areas will find the upper limit (46 percent) a bit low and other areas will consider even the lower limit (40 percent) at the higher end of their local range. The 46 percent of INDI at the upper end of the proposed formula generates a family net disposable income (a larger pool of net income than INDI) for the recipient spouse of 56 to 58 percent where there are two children. At the lower end of the range, a spousal support amount that leaves the recipient spouse with 40 percent of INDI will typically leave that spouse and the children with more than 50 percent of the family net disposable income.

The length of the marriage does not affect the upper and lower percentages in the *with child support* formula. This is a central departure from the approach used in the *without child support* formula where the length of the marriage has a direct bearing on the percentages.

6.4 — Amounts of Spousal Support: Example of the Basic Formula

The following example will show the range of monthly spousal support generated by the basic formula. To simplify the exposition of the formula's operation, it is assumed that the parents and children live in Ontario. Also, special or extraordinary expenses have not been included.

Example 6.1

Ted and Alice have separated after 11 years together. Ted works at a local manufacturing plant, earning $80,000 gross per year. Alice has been home with the two children, now aged 8 and 10, who continue to reside with her after separation. After the separation, Alice found work, less than full time, earning $20,000 gross per year. Alice's mother provides lunch and after-school care for the children, for nothing, when Alice has to work. Ted will pay the table amount for child support, $1,031 per month. Alice's notional table amount would be $285. There are no s. 7 expenses (if there were, the spousal amounts would be lower).

Under the proposed formula, Ted would pay spousal support in the range of $697 to $1,287 per month.

The amount of spousal support is obviously affected by the *number of children*. If Ted and Alice had only one child, the range would be higher, from $1,048 to $1,593 per month. If the couple had three children, Ted's ability to pay would be reduced, bringing the range down to $391 to $975 monthly. Four children would lower that range even further, down to a range from zero to $530 per month.

(More examples are found in the full text of the proposal.)

6.5 — Fixing an Amount Within the Range

The formula produces a range for the amount of spousal support. In fixing an amount within that range the following factors might be considered. This is not an exhaustive list, but are some of the more prominent factors found in the current discretionary law.

First, *compensatory principles* would suggest that the more the recipient spouse gave up in the paid labour market, the higher one would go within the range. To give a simple example, two tax lawyers marry fresh out of law school, but one stays home with the children and the other pursues a career within a large law firm. Compensatory logic would dictate that something close to the maximum 46 percent would make sense here, as the payor spouse's income is a very good proxy measure of where the recipient spouse would have been. Given the presence of dependent children under this formula, almost every case will have a compensatory element and the lower and higher ends of the range reflect that. What moves a case up or down the range is the relative strength or weakness of the compensatory claim.

Second, *the age, number and needs of the children* will affect placement within the range. A child with special needs will usually demand more time and resources from the care-giving parent, thus reducing that parent's ability to earn in the paid labour market and pushing spousal support towards the upper end. The same will generally be true for the parent with primary care of an infant or toddler, as contrasted to care of an older child or adolescent. Generally speaking, when ability to pay is in issue, the larger the number of children, the less income is left available to pay spousal support. As income levels rise, spousal support can be higher to reflect the fact that more children generally mean more care-giving and more restrictions upon the custodial parent's ability to work outside the home.

Third, *the needs and ability to pay of the payor spouse* will have special importance at the lower end of the income spectrum. For example, at this lower end the amount of any mandatory deduction for pension contributions will likely have to be taken into account in determining ability to pay. Also a concern for lower income payors will be their direct spending on expenses for the children during their time with the children. A lower income payor should be left with sufficient funds to exercise meaningful access to his or her children.

Fourth, *the needs and standard of living of the recipient and the children* will tend to push spousal support awards towards the higher end of the range. Even when spousal support is at the maximum 46 percent of individual net disposable income, a homemaker recipient and the children will be left with a noticeably lower household standard of living (assuming no new partners or children for either spouse). At lower income levels, need will create pressure to move to the higher end of the range, but that will be balanced by the needs of the payor spouse, as mentioned above. By contrast, if the recipient has remarried or re-partnered, then spousal support could be set towards the lower end of the range. Equally, the recipient may have reduced living costs, which might justify support at the lower end.

Fifth, *length of marriage* will still be a factor to help determine where within the range spousal support should be set, but only one of a number of factors. All other things being equal, the longer the marriage, the more likely it is that one might move towards the higher end of the range. But all other things are rarely equal, as a short marriage with very young children and a stay-at-home custodial parent may be a far more compelling case for the maximum amount.

Sixth, *self-sufficiency incentives* might encourage an award at the higher end of the range, where this could mean that a recipient spouse obtains retraining or education, and then remunerative employment and less support in future. Or, as happens under the current case law, a judge might fix an amount at the lower end to encourage the recipient to make greater efforts towards self-sufficiency.

6.6 — Duration under the Basic Formula

The initial order for spousal support under the *with child support* formula is to be indefinite in duration subject to the usual process of review or variation. However, there would be a generally understood outside time limits that would inform the process of review and variation. These outside time limits would combine the factors of length of marriage and length of the remaining child-rearing period, under two different tests for maximum duration. These time limits are generous, with elements of flexibility built in.

For longer marriages a recipient spouse should get the benefit of the time limits based upon length of marriage that might be obtained under the *without child support* formula, as these will typically run well beyond the end of any child-rearing period. More difficult is the situation of the custodial or residential parent who has the care of young children after a shorter marriage. Here an outside time limit has been chosen based on the child-rearing period remaining. Thus, there are two tests for maximum duration under this formula, one for longer marriages and another for shorter marriages.

6.6.1 — The longer-marriage test for duration

The test for the duration of the spousal support obligation in longer marriages is modelled on the test for duration under the *without child support* formula: where the length of the marriage exceeds the number of years remaining for the last or youngest child to finish high school, then the *maximum duration* under the *with child support* formula will be the length of the marriage, subject to the provisions under the *without child support* formula for indefinite support after 20 years of marriage.

This first test will govern for most marriages of 10 years or more, i.e. most medium and long marriages where there are still dependent children at home at the time of the initial order. Where the dependent children are older and by implication the marriage has been longer, the indefinite support provisions that apply where the marriage has lasted 20 years will often take effect.

Example 6.1, above, may be used to explain this test. Ted and Alice cohabited for 11 years during their marriage and are now in their late thirties or early forties, with two children, aged 8 and 10 at separation. The maximum duration under the *without child support* formula would be 11 years. That is longer than the 10 years remaining to the end of high school for the youngest child. The initial support order would be indefinite in form, but it would be expected that the *maximum duration* for spousal support would be 11 years. Reviews and variations in the meantime may have brought support to an end before then, and certainly the amount may have been reduced significantly during this period. But if support is still in pay after 11 years, there would be an expectation, barring exceptional circumstances, that support would be terminated at that point on an application for review or variation.

This test speaks only of *maximum duration*. No *minimum duration*, or lower end of a range, for marriages with dependent children is proposed. This approach to duration is applied under both the longer-marriage and shorter-marriage tests. This different approach to duration in marriages involving dependent children more appropriately reflects the past, present and future demands of child-rearing and the impact of these demands upon the recipient spouse's earning capacities. In the *without child support* formula, the lower end of the range for duration is fixed at one-half year for each year of marriage. That part of the formula would not be imported here, under the longer-marriage test for duration. Practically, most of these cases with children would likely end up at the longer end of the range anyway. Duration shorter than the maximum is possible under both tests, but only through the normal process of review or variation, depending upon the individual income and employment situations of the spouses.

6.6.2 — The shorter-marriage test for duration

The test applicable to shorter marriages will operate where the period of time until the last or youngest child finishes high school is greater than the length of the marriage.

Any initial order for spousal support would likely be indefinite in form, *subject to review*, including any conditions stated in the initial order or agreement concerning training, education or employment. The *date for review* would be tied to the age of the children at the time of the initial order or agreement:

- where the children are of pre-school age, then no later than the month after the last or youngest child commences full-time school; *or*
- where the children are under the age of twelve, then no later than the month after the last or youngest child reaches the age of twelve.

Reviews may be fixed more frequently, or at different intervals, or with more or less stringent conditions, under this approach. The starting premise is that the *with child support* formula generates reasonably generous amounts of spousal support and the flip side should be a clear obligation upon recipient spouses to work towards self-sufficiency or at least the maximum of their earning capacity in the context of their child-care responsibilities.

The *maximum duration* for spousal support under this test would be *the date when the last or youngest child finishes high school*. Relatively few cases will reach this outside time limit and those that do will likely involve reduced amounts of top-up support by that date. Hence, extensions beyond that date should only be granted in *exceptional circumstances*, e.g. some cases involving special needs children. In effect, the maximum duration here would operate like a terminating review order. As with the longer-marriage test for duration, no minimum duration is proposed.

6.7 — Custodial Variations: Shared and Split Custody

The basic *with child support* formula assumes that the recipient of spousal support has custody or primary care of the children. Adjustments need to be made, therefore, in cases where the children are in the shared custody of their parents, and in cases where the children are split between the parents with each parent having custody or primary care one or more of them.

6.7.1 — Shared custody

Where the spouses have *shared custody*, the starting point for the calculation of child support under s. 9(a) of the *Federal Child Support Guidelines* has been the straight set-off of table amounts for the number of children subject to shared custody, based upon current appeal decisions. That amount is then adjusted, usually upwards, but occasionally downwards, based upon s. 9(b) (increased costs of shared custody) and s. 9(c) (other circumstances, including actual spending, assets and debts, etc.).

Under the basic formula, the child support paid from the payor's income is deducted and then that child support amount paid plus a notional amount for child support is deducted from the recipient's income, to obtain individual net disposable income. Shared custody requires some changes to this basic formula.

In making these changes it is understood that a court employing the other elements in s. 9 may make a child support order for more or less than what a straight set-off would produce. However, unless indicated otherwise by the Supreme Court of Canada in the appeal pending before it on the interpretation of s. 9, it will be assumed in adjusting the formula that the payor is paying only the straight set-off amount of child support in a shared custody case.

Shared custody takes for granted that both parents pay expenses for the child while in their care. It is proposed that the full table amount (plus any s. 7 contributions) be deducted from the payor spouse's net disposable income. For the recipient, the notional table amount (plus any contribution to s. 7 expenses) should be deducted. This would be done in the calculation of INDI, even though the child support paid by the payor and received by the recipient would be the straight set-off amount.

Using this method of calculation, it turns out that the spousal support ranges are basically the same in these shared custody situations as in sole custody situations. Shared custody arrangements do not result in any lowering of spousal support. A typical shared custody example can demonstrate this result.

Example 6.4

Peter and Cynthia have separated after nine years together. Peter works as a reporter at the local television station, earning $65,000 gross per year, while his wife Cynthia works for a local arts organization, earning $39,000 gross per year. First, assume their two children, aged 8 and 7, are in the sole or primary custody of Cynthia. Peter's table amount of child support would be $879 per month, Cynthia's $557 per month. Assume no s. 7 expenses. Under our proposed formula, *assuming entitlement*, which may be contested in this case, Peter would pay spousal support to Cynthia in the range of zero to $302 per month. (At zero spousal support, Cynthia would have 42.7 percent of INDI.)

But what if Peter and Cynthia shared custody, say on a week about, 50/50 basis? First, assume Peter only paid the straight set-off amount of child support, i.e. $879 - $557 = $322. We would still deduct from Peter's income the full table amount of $879 and we would still reduce Cynthia's income by her notional table amount of $577, but Cynthia would now be receiving only $322 per month, an amount removed from her income (no longer the full $879 paid in the sole custody setting). The result would be the same range for spousal support as above, zero to $302 per month.

6.7.2 — Split custody

In a *split custody* situation, more significant changes to the basic formula are required. If each parent has one or more children in their primary care or custody, then s. 8 of the *Federal Child Support Guidelines* requires a set-off of table amounts, with each spouse paying the table amount for the number of children in the other spouse's custody. But this means that *each* parent will also be considered to support the child or children in their care directly, out of their remaining income. Thus, in the split custody situation, a notional table amount must be deducted from each parent, not just the recipient but the payor as well. Since there is one child in each household, there are no economies of scale and accordingly larger proportions of their incomes are devoted to child support, leaving a smaller pool of INDI to be divided by way of spousal support. Again, as with shared custody, this would be done in the calculation of INDI, even though the child support paid by the payor and received by the recipient would be the set-off amount directed by the s. 8 formula.

Example 6.5

Take the case of Peter and Cynthia again, and assume that each parent has custody of one child, same incomes, same facts. Peter's one child table amount would be $543 per month, Cynthia's $337 per month. Under s. 8 of the *Federal Child Support Guidelines*, these table amounts would be offset, with Peter paying Cynthia $206 per month. In calculating Peter's individual net disposable income, for spousal support purposes, we would propose to deduct the full one child amount, twice, once for the table amount effectively paid to Cynthia and once for the notional amount spent directly on the child in his care. Similarly, in calculating Cynthia's INDI, we would make a double deduction of her one-child table amount, once for the amount effectively paid to Peter for the child in his care, plus a notional table amount for the child in Cynthia's own care. The actual child support paid by Peter to Cynthia would be $206, the one-child set-off amount under s. 8. Using the split custody formula for spousal support, Peter would pay spousal support to Cynthia in the range of zero to $325 per month. (At zero spousal support, Cynthia would have 41.4 percent of INDI.)

6.8 — A Hybrid Formula for Spousal Support Paid by the Custodial Parent

The basic formula for marriages with dependent children assumes that the higher income spouse pays both child and spousal support to the recipient parent, who also has sole or primary custody of the children. The spousal support to be paid must then adjust for the payor's child support payments. The shared and split custody situations may change the math, but both still involve the higher income spouse paying both child and spousal support to the recipient.

A different formula is required where the higher income spouse paying spousal support is also the parent with sole or primary custody of the children. Now spousal support and child support flow in opposite directions. The *without child support* formula does not apply, however, as it assumes no dependent children. This situation is common enough to warrant a formula to guide the outcome.

The starting point is the *without child support* formula. In this situation the recipient parent does not have the primary care of children and thus more closely resembles the single recipient in the *without child support* formula. The primary rationale for the payment of spousal support in these cases will be merger over time, rather than parental partnership. That said, a number of lower income recipient spouses in this situation will continue to play an important role in their children's lives and any formula must be able to adjust in such cases. The other advantage of the *without child support* formula is ease of calculation, but the formula will have to be modified to back-out child support and to take into account tax implications.

Formula for Spousal Support Paid by Custodial Parent

(1) Reduce the payor spouse's Guidelines income by the *grossed-up notional table amount* for child support (plus a gross-up of any contributions to s. 7 expenses).

(2) If the recipient spouse is paying child support, reduce the recipient's Guidelines income by the *grossed-up amount of child support paid* (table amount plus any s. 7 contributions).

(3) Determine the *adjusted gross income difference* between the spouses and then quantum ranges from 1.5 percent to 2 percent for each year of marriage, up to a maximum of 50.

(4) *Duration* ranges from .5 to 1 year of support for each year of marriage, with the same rules for indefinite support as under the *without child support* formula.

In reducing gross incomes by grossed-up amounts for child support, this formula does the same thing conceptually as the basic *with child support* formula — it establishes the spouses' available incomes after their child support obligations are fulfilled. To gross up the child support will require a calculation of the gross value of the non-taxable child support, using the appropriate marginal tax rate for the payor or recipient spouse.

Example 6.6

Kathleen and Gordon were married for 21 years. They have two children, one a self-supporting university student, and the other a high school student living with Gordon. Gordon is a pharmacist and earns $73,500 gross per year. Kathleen was home with the children and, for years, ran a child care operation at home. Kathleen has done some re-training, but has also has had serious health problems. She has no income at present and cannot pay child support. Assume no s. 7 expenses.

There would be little question of entitlement to spousal support on these facts. First, we would reduce Gordon's income by the notional table amount of child support, $595 per month, grossed up to $936 per month at his marginal tax rate, or $11,232 on an annual basis. Gordon's adjusted or reduced income would thus be $62,268. After a 21-year marriage, Kathleen would receive a range of 31.5 to 42 percent of the adjusted gross income difference of $62,268.

Under our proposed formula, Gordon would pay spousal support in the range of $1,635 to $2,179 per month.Given the length of the marriage (21 years), Kathleen's support would be indefinite, subject to review or variation.

Example 6.7

Matt earns $100,000 gross per year and has custody of two teenage children. Anna earns $30,000 gross per year. The spouses separated after 16 years together. There are no s. 7 expenses.

Assume entitlement to spousal support has been established.

First, Matt's income is reduced by the table amount for two children, $1,240, grossed-up to $2,192 per month or $26,304 annually. Matt's reduced income would thus be $73,696. Anna is required to pay child support at the table amount of $446 per month, grossed-up to $572 monthly or $6,864 annually. Anna's reduced income would be $23,136. After a 16-year marriage, Anna would receive a range of 24 to 32 percent of the adjusted gross income difference of $50,560.

Under our proposed formula, Matt would pay spousal support in a range from $1,011 to $1,348 per month, for a duration of 8 to 16 years.

One *exception* should be made to this custodial payor formula. Where the recipient spouse and non-custodial parent plays an important role in the child's care and upbringing after separation, yet the marriage was shorter and the child is younger, the ranges for amount and duration applied here (from the *without child support* formula) may not allow that spouse to continue to fulfil that parental role. Under this parenting exception, it should be possible to exceed the upper limits on both *amount* and *duration* for that purpose.

6.9 — Restructuring

Restructuring as described earlier under the *without child support* formula has less relevance for marriages with dependent children. Under the basic formula above, many of the recipient spouses with older dependent children will qualify for indefinite support. Further, the maximum duration under the second, shorter marriage, test for duration will be much more uncertain, given the review process and the softer nature of the maximum duration. It will thus be more difficult in these cases to establish the global or total amount of the formula outcome as is required for restructuring.

But there will be some medium-term marriages that will attract the length-of-marriage time limits under the first, longer-marriage test for duration. For these cases, restructuring can have some meaning. In some cases, a recipient spouse may want an amount of support above the upper end of the range for a shorter period of time, e.g. to pursue a more expensive educational program. Or, in others, a recipient parent may want to receive support for a longer period, in an amount reduced below the lower end of the range, e.g. to bridge a period to the availability of pension and retirement income.

Further, restructuring will have some obvious application in the custodial payor situation described immediately above.

6.10 — Exceptions

One of the exceptions that allows a departure from the basic *with child support* formula is the situation governed by the special formula discussed above, where the payor of spousal support is also the custodial parent. Other exceptions do not have a formulaic basis for the departure and are ruled by discretion. Many of these exceptions are the same as those discussed under the *without child support* formula. Some of the most common exceptions will be described here.

6.10.1 — Compensatory exceptions

The scope for a compensatory exception will be eliminated under the *with child support* formula, given the weight given to compensatory considerations in the construction of this formula and the generous maximum durations available under the two tests for duration.

6.10.2 — Illness and disability

This exception operates on duration under the *without child support* formula, mostly where the marriage is of short-to-medium duration. Under the basic *with child support* formula, there will be much less scope for this exception. There are two settings where this exception will operate:

- where restructuring is not sufficient to accommodate the duration concerns raised by illness and disability in cases governed by the longer-marriage test for duration; and
- where the recipient spouse does not play an important role in the child's care and upbringing, perhaps on account of illness or disability, and thus the parenting exception would not apply under the custodial payor formula.

6.10.3 — Debt payments

Where the payor spouse has a disproportionate responsibility for debt payments, some adjustment may be required under the *with child support* formula, as explained in the discussion of the *without child support* formula.

6.10.4 — Prior support obligations

An obligation to pay support for a prior spouse or prior children will require a slightly different adjustment under this formula, which works with net disposable incomes rather than the gross incomes of the *without child support* formula. Usually this exception will apply to the payor spouse. In calculating the payor spouse's individual net disposable income, this exception will require that any amounts of support paid to prior spouses or children be deducted, thereby reducing the size of the pool of individual net disposable income between the current spouses and also reducing the payor's share of that smaller pool. Because net incomes are used under this formula, there is no need to gross up any child support amounts and the software can work out the after-tax value of the gross amount of spousal support.

6.10.5 — Interim support

Where there are compelling financial circumstances at the interim stage, an exception can be made, as is explained in more detail below.

6.11 — The Crossover Between Formulas

There is one last issue to be considered, that of crossover between the formulas. The most frequent crossover situation will be in cases where child support ceases after a medium-to-long marriage, where the children were older or even university-age at the time of the initial order. At this point, either spouse could apply to vary, to bring spousal support under the *without child support* formula. In most cases, it will be the recipient spouse making the application, to obtain an increase in spousal support under the *without child support* formula, once child support is no longer payable and the payor's ability to pay improves as a result. Specific examples of crossover will be considered in the discussion, which deals with variation, review and other topics.

7 — Ceilings and Floors

Where income sharing is the basic principle to determine the amount of spousal support, it is necessary to consider ceilings and floors. The *ceiling* is the income level for the paying spouse above which any formula gives way to discretion. The *floor* is the income level for the payor below which zero support is to be paid. The proposed ceiling is a gross annual income for the payor of $350,000 and the floor is an income of $20,000.

7.1 — Ceilings

There is no absolute ceiling, just an income level above which the standard fixed-percentage-of income formula can be varied, to create a lesser percentage of income above that level. The payor's gross income of $350,000 is the basis for the proposed ceiling. No formula should be applied to divide income received above that amount. The $350,000 figure was chosen because it was considered the highest amount practically possible. The highest amount was chosen in order to maintain the predictability and consistency of the formulas as far as possible up the income spectrum. There was also concern about creating cliffs, that is, points where there are dramatic increases or decreases in support amounts.

With child support formula — The ceiling is complicated by the fact that child support increases as incomes rise above the spousal support ceiling. There are two suggested approaches.

1. The first approach (the "minimum plus" approach) uses the formula to determine the minimum amount for spousal support. A notional calculation is made for spousal support at the $350,000 ceiling, using the child support payable at the ceiling. This would determine the "minimum" spousal support range even though the actual income might be $450,000 or some other amount over $350,000. Assuming the recipient earned no income and there are two children, the formula using the notional calculation would result in a minimum of $8,050 a month (using the Ontario tables). There would be discretion to add to this minimum after taking into account the actual amount of child support being paid.
2. The second approach is one of pure discretion. Again, assuming the recipient earned no income, once the payor's income exceeded the ceiling, there would be no minimum spousal support, only a dollar figure that would take into account the actual amount of child support paid, an amount which can be very large for cases well above the ceiling.

7.2 — Floors

The advisory guidelines provide several methods to adjust for the payor's low income depending on the circumstances.

1. Where the payor has a low income or where there is a modest differential in incomes at lower income levels, a court can decide or the parties can agree that there is no entitlement to support.
2. Where there are dependent children, the formula gives priority to child support, consistent with s. 15.3 of the *Divorce Act*. That priority will often eliminate any ability to pay spousal support at lower income levels, especially at the bottom end of the formula's range.

3. Under the without child support formula, even if there is entitlement, the income differentials may be quite small, producing very small amounts at the lower end of the formula's ranges, particularly in short-and medium- duration marriages.

The proposal directs that no amount of spousal support should be payable until the payor's gross income exceeds $20,000 a year. There is some concern that the $20,000 floor may be too low, creating real hardship for payor spouses and ultimately threatening the credibility of the formulas. There is also concern about a cliff effect for those payors just above the floor. Currently, the cliff effect can be best avoided by an exception for cases where the payor spouse's gross income is more than $20,000 but less than $30,000. For cases within this range, assuming entitlement, consideration should be given to the percentages sought under the applicable formula, the net disposable income left to the payor spouse, and the impact of a spousal support payment upon the work incentives and marginal gains of the payor. Another exception may be called for where the payor's income is below the floor. For example, a potential payor spouse with an income of less than $20,000 may be able to afford to pay spousal support because he or she is living with parents or otherwise has significantly reduced expenses. This example indicates that there should not be an absolute rule about income floors. Another reason for staying away from an absolute income floor for amount is that such a floor would effectively create a rule about entitlement which the guidelines should not do, considering their informal and advisory character.

8 — Interim Support

The advisory guidelines are appropriate for interim support, since there is a need for a quick, easily calculated amount, knowing that more precise adjustments can be made at trial. If the formula is used at the interim stage, it would be unnecessary to perform a traditional needs-and-means analysis, assessed through budgets, current and proposed expenses, etc., except in unusual cases. Also, conflict between the spouses at this stage could be reduced and settlements encouraged.

However, the formulas may not be applicable in all circumstances at the interim stage. It may not be possible to adjust household finances quickly enough to operate fairly within the ranges, and difficulties may arise where marriages are shorter, or incomes are lower, or property has not yet been divided.

Periods of interim spousal support are to be subject to the durational limits fixed by the advisory guidelines under either formula. If these limits were not included, there would be incentives for some spouses to delay proceedings and for others to rush them forward. In addition, differing periods of interim support would produce inequities between spouses. Some would receive support longer than others even though the length of their marriages was the same.

9 — Applying the Advisory Guidelines in Quebec

The advisory guidelines require some modifications for Quebec, principally because Quebec's guidelines for the determination of child support differ in significant ways from the *Federal Child Support Guidelines*. Most of Quebec's guidelines are found in the *Regulation Respecting the Determination of Child Support Payments*. The Regulation is made under the authority of the *Code of Civil Procedure* and the *Civil Code*, both of which also contain provisions governing the determination of child support. These various provisions (or rules) apply to determine child support under the *Civil Code* and under the *Divorce Act.*

9.1 — The Definition of Income

In Quebec, the formulas start with the definition of annual income (revenue annuel) in section 9 of the *Regulation Respecting the Determination of Child Support Payments*. It is a gross income measure.

9.2 — Length of Marriage Under the Without Child Support Formula

Under the *Civil Code* there is no entitlement to spousal support for unmarried cohabitants. Some Quebec judges ignore pre-marital cohabitation, while other judges treat that period as a relevant consideration in determining spousal support in divorce proceedings. These differences in approach will have important consequences for spousal support in the application of the *without child support* formula.

9.3 — Child Support and the With Child Support Formula

Where one party lives outside the province and the federal guidelines apply in a Quebec divorce, no adjustments to the *with child support* formula are necessary. However, the Quebec child support rules apply in most divorce cases, and when these rules apply some changes are needed.

Section 825.13 of the *Quebec Code of Civil Procedure* clearly gives priority to child support over spousal support, in language similar to s. 15.3(1) of the *Divorce Act*. But the Quebec child support rules differ from the federal guidelines in several important respects (e.g. both parents' incomes are taken into account, the floor in higher, there is a $10,000 basic deduction for self-support, and the ceiling for the combined disposable income of the parents is $200,000 annually) and these differences need to be taken into account when applying the *with child support* formula.

The advisory guidelines offer a step-by-step procedure for the application of the *with child support* formula under Quebec law and should be consulted for a detailed understanding of its operation.

10 — Variation, Review, Remarriage, Second Families

The Spousal Support Advisory Guidelines apply on reviews and variations as far as the consensus of the parties and the current case law allow. They apply, for example, where there are increases in the recipient's income, or decreases in the payor's income. Other situations such as post-separation increases in the payor's income, re-partnering, remarriage and second families, are not considered in the formulas and are left to discretionary, case-by-case determinations.

10.1 — Material Changes, Review and Issues of Continuing Entitlement

The advisory guidelines do not and cannot affect the basic legal structure of variation and review. The spouse seeking to vary court-ordered support will still need to prove a material change before the advisory guidelines can be used to determine amount and duration. Also, a review is possible only if a provision for review was included in the initial order and only if any preconditions for review are met.

Where spousal support has been negotiated, the possibilities for reviewing or modifying spousal support will depend on many factors, including the drafting of the agreement and whether or not the agreement has been incorporated into the divorce judgment. Where the agreement has not been incorporated into an order, the effect of subsequent changes in the parties' situation will be governed by the terms of the agreement. If the agreement provides for reviews by the parties at specified times or includes a material change clause, and if the conditions for these are met, the advisory guidelines may apply to determine amount and duration. If the agreement is a final agreement in which spousal support has been waived or time-limited, then the advisory guidelines would have no application.

The advisory guidelines confer no power to override agreements. The *Miglin* case continues to apply on the issue of the effect of a prior agreement on a court's ability to award spousal support. The advisory guidelines would come into play only if a finding were made that the agreement was not determinative and spousal support was to be determined anew by the court.

Where a spousal support agreement has been incorporated into a divorce judgment, the variation provisions of the *Divorce Act* apply, and if the agreement provides for review, and conditions for a variation or review are met, the advisory guidelines may be applicable to determine amount and duration.

10.2 — Applications to Reduce Spousal Support Because of Changes in Income

There are three situations where an application to reduce spousal support because of a change in income might be made:

1. the payor spouse's income goes down;
2. the recipient spouse's income goes up; or
3. the payor spouse applies to reduce or terminate support on the grounds that the recipient spouse ought to have a higher income.

In each of these situations, the advisory guidelines can be used to determine the amount of continuing support if it is found that a variation ought to be made.

10.3 — The Payor's Post-Separation Income Increase

Under the current law, some rough notion of causation is applied to post-separation income increases for the payor, in determining whether the income increase should be reflected in increased spousal support and if so, by how much. The amount of sharing of post-separation increases involves a complex, fact-based decision. The guideline drafters propose one limit in these cases; the upper limit upon any increased spousal support ought to be the numbers generated by the formulas.

10.4 — The Recipient's Reduced Income After Separation

Under the current law, some notion of causation seems to operate here as well requiring another complex, fact-based decision. While a formulaic solution is not possible, the same upper limit may be applied.

10.5 — Crossover Between the Two Formulas

Either spouse may apply to cross over from the *with child support* formula to the *without child support* formula, by way of application to vary or, if so provided in the order or agreement, by way of review. The crossover from one formula to the other will only affect the amount of spousal support, not the duration. Crossover situations will be found mostly in medium-to-long marriages, where the children are older at the time of the initial order or agreement. In a longer marriage, the application to vary by crossing over to the *without child support* formula, will often come from the recipient spouse. Situations where the payor spouse would apply to vary and cross over to the *without child support* formula would be more rare. Usually, these would be cases where the marriage lasted 15 years or less. The payor spouse would argue that the *without child support* formula, where the length of the marriage drives the percentages, provides for a lower range for spousal support than the *with child support* formula and should be applied in place of it.

10.6 — The Payor's Remarriage or Re-partnering

Under the present law, the payor's remarriage or re-partnering is not usually grounds for a reduction in spousal support. There is no need for a formulaic adjustment upon such an event occurring.

10.7 — The Recipient's Remarriage or Re-partnering

Under the current law the recipient's remarriage or re-partnering does have an effect on spousal support, but to what extent is not certain. The cases are fact driven. No formula has been found to accommodate all of the situations that arise. An ability to predict outcomes in extreme cases, which is possible, is not a sufficient basis upon which to construct a formula to make adjustments to the support obligation.

10.8 — Second Families

Second families, or more accurately subsequent children, raise difficult support issues. Generally, the first family is given priority in the case law, except where payment of first-family support would put the second family on social assistance or otherwise into poverty. Where child support is the only issue, the approach is to treat all the payor's children equally. And there is a tendency to reduce the weight to be given to the spousal support obligation, in light of this concern for the equal treatment of children. Since there is no policy in the Federal Child Support Guidelines on this issue, it is impossible to set out a related policy on spousal support in relation to subsequent children. The decision on this issue must be left to a case-by-case determination.

INCOME TAX ACT

An Act Respecting Income Taxes

REVISED STATUTES OF CANADA 1985, c. 1 (5TH SUPPLEMENT), AS AMENDED BY 1994, cc. 7, 8, 13, 21, 28, 29, 38, 41; 1995, cc. 1, 3, 11, 17, 18, 21, 38, 46; 1996, cc. 6, 11, 21, 23; 1997, cc. 10, 12, 25, 26; 1998, cc. 19, 21, 34; 1999, cc. 10, 17, 22, 26, 31; 2000, cc. 9, 12, 14, 19, 30; 2001, cc. 16, 17, 27, 41; 2002, cc. 8, 9; 2003, cc. 15, 19, 28; 2004, cc. 11, 22, 24, 25, 26; 2005, cc. 19, 21, 30, 33, 34, 35, 38, 47 [not in force at date of publication], 49; 2006, cc. 1, 4, 9, 12; 2007, c. 2, 16, 29.

. . . . .

PART I — INCOME TAX

. . . . .

DIVISION B — COMPUTATION OF INCOME

. . . . .

Subdivision d — Other Sources of Income

56. (1) Amounts to be included in income for year — Without restricting the generality of section 3, there shall be included in computing the income of a taxpayer for a taxation year,

(a) **pension benefits, unemployment insurance benefits, etc.** — any amount received by the taxpayer in the year as, on account or in lieu of payment of, or in satisfaction of,

(i) a superannuation or pension benefit including, without limiting the generality of the foregoing,

(A) the amount of any pension, supplement or spouse's or common-law partner's allowance under the *Old Age Security Act* and the amount of any similar payment under a law of a province,

(B) the amount of any benefit under the *Canada Pension Plan* or a provincial pension plan as defined in section 3 of that Act,

(C) the amount of any payment out of or under a prescribed provincial pension plan, and

(C.1) the amount of any payment out of or under a foreign retirement arrangement established under the laws of a country, except to the extent that the amount would not, if the taxpayer were resident in the country, be subject to income taxation in the country,

Proposed Amendment — 56(1)(a)(i)(C.1) — Income inclusion on conversion to Roth IRA

Dept. of Finance press release 1998-129, December 18, 1998: See under 56(12).

but not including

(D) the portion of a benefit received out of or under an employee benefit plan that is required by paragraph 6(1)(g) to be included in computing the taxpayer's income for the year, or would be required to be so included if that paragraph were read without reference to subparagraph 6(1)(g)(ii),

(E) the portion of an amount received out of or under a retirement compensation arrangement that is required by paragraph (x) or (z) to be included in computing the taxpayer's income for the year, and

(F) a benefit received under section 71 of the *Canada Pension Plan* or under a similar provision of a provincial pension plan as defined in section 3 of that Act,

(ii) a retiring allowance, other than an amount received out of or under an employee benefit plan, a retirement compensation arrangement or a salary deferral arrangement,

(iii) a death benefit,

(iv) a benefit under the *Unemployment Insurance Act*, other than a payment relating to a course or program designed to facilitate the re-entry into the labour force of a claimant under that Act, or a benefit under Part I, VIII or VIII.1 of the *Employment Insurance Act*,

(v) a benefit under regulations made under an appropriation Act providing for a scheme of transitional assistance benefits to persons employed in the production of products to which the Canada-United States Agreement on Automotive Products, signed on January 16, 1965 applies, or

(vi) except to the extent otherwise required to be included in computing the taxpayer's income, a prescribed benefit under a government assistance program;

(vii) [Repealed 1994, c. 21, s. 25(1)]

Proposed Addition — 56(1)(a)(vii)

(vii) a benefit under the *Act respecting parental insurance R.S.Q., c. A-29.011*;

Application: Bill C-33 (First Senate Reading June 18, 2007) (Part 2 — technical), subsec. 70(1), will add subpara. 56(1)(a)(vii), applicable to 2006 *et seq.*

Technical Notes: Paragraph 56(1)(a) includes in the income of a taxpayer certain amounts received in a taxation year. This paragraph is amended by adding new subparagraph (vii) to include in the income of a taxpayer the amount of a benefit received under the new Quebec Parental Insurance Plan.

This amendment applies to the 2006 and subsequent taxation years and is consequential to the introduction of the new Quebec Parental Insurance Plan on January 1, 2006.

Dept. of Finance news release 2005-050, July 19, 2005: *Amendments to be Recommended to the* Income Tax Act *With Respect to the Québec Parental Insurance Plan*

The Department of Finance today indicated its intention to recommend amendments to the *Income Tax Act* to provide for the tax treatment of benefits and premiums under the Québec Parental Insurance Plan (QPIP), which is expected to come into force on January 1, 2006.

The QPIP will replace maternity and parental benefits currently provided under the employment insurance (EI) program for eligible Quebec residents. EI premiums for employers and employees in Quebec will be reduced to reflect the fact that Quebec residents will no longer receive maternity and parental benefits under EI. QPIP premiums will be collected directly by the Province of Quebec.

The proposed amendments would ensure that the federal tax treatment of QPIP premiums and benefits is consistent with the federal tax treatment of EI premiums and benefits. Specifically:

- Benefits paid under the QPIP would be included in the calculation of an individual's income [56(1)(a)(iv) — ed.].
- Employees would be eligible for a federal non-refundable tax credit for QPIP premiums paid, to be provided at the same rate as the federal non-refundable tax credit for EI premiums [118.7 — ed.].
- Employers would be able to deduct premiums paid under the plan in the calculation of their income [9(1), and 8(1)(l.1) for individuals — ed.].
- The self-employed would be eligible for a non-refundable tax credit for the employee's share of QPIP premiums [118.7 — ed.] and a tax deduction for the employer's share [9(1) — ed.], where the calculation of these shares is determined by the Province of Quebec.

These amendments would apply to benefits received and premiums paid upon the implementation of the QPIP. It is intended that legislation to implement the proposed amendments be introduced at the earliest opportunity.

For further information, media may contact: David Gamble, Public Affairs and Operations Division, (613) 996-8080.

(a.1) **[death] benefits under CPP/QPP** — where the taxpayer is an estate that arose on or as a consequence of the death of an individual, each benefit received under section 71 of the *Canada Pension Plan*, or under a similar provision of a provincial pension plan as defined in section 3 of that Act, after July 1997 and in the year in respect of the death of the individual;

(a.2) **pension income reallocation** — where the taxpayer is a pension transferee (as defined in subsection 60.03(1)), any amount that is a split-pension amount (as defined in that subsection) in respect of the pension transferee for the taxation year;

(b) **[spousal or child] support** — the total of all amounts each of which is an amount determined by the formula

$$A - (B + C)$$

where

A is the total of all amounts each of which is a support amount received after 1996 and before the end of the year by the taxpayer from a particular person where the taxpayer and the particular person were living separate and apart at the time the amount was received,

B is the total of all amounts each of which is a child support amount that became receivable by the taxpayer from the particular person under an agreement or order on or after its commencement day and before the end of the year in respect of a period that began on or after its commencement day, and

C is the total of all amounts each of which is a support amount received after 1996 by the taxpayer from the particular person and included in the taxpayer's income for a preceding taxation year;

(c) [Repealed 1997, c. 25, s. 8(1)]

(c.1) [Repealed 1994, c. 7, Sch. VIII, s. 17(2)]

(c.2) **reimbursement of support payments** — an amount received by the taxpayer in the year under a decree, order or judgment of a competent tribunal as a reimbursement of an amount deducted under paragraph 60(b) or (c), or under paragraph 60(c.1) as it applies, in computing the taxpayer's income for the year or a preceding taxation year to decrees, orders and judgments made before 1993;

(d) **annuity payments** — any amount received by the taxpayer in the year as an annuity payment other than an amount

(i) otherwise required to be included in computing the taxpayer's income for the year, or

(ii) with respect to an interest in an annuity contract to which subsection 12.2(1) applies (or would apply if the contract had an anniversary day in the year at a time when the taxpayer held the interest);

(d.1) [Repealed 1994, c. 7, Sch. II, s. 32(4)]

(d.2) **idem [annuity payments]** — any amount received out of or under, or as proceeds of disposition of, an annuity the payment for which was

(i) deductible in computing the taxpayer's income because of paragraph 60(l) or because of subsection 146(5.5) of the *Income Tax Act*, Chapter 148 of the Revised Statutes of Canada, 1952,

(ii) made in circumstances to which subsection 146(21) applied, or

(iii) made pursuant to or under a deferred profit sharing plan by a trustee under the plan to purchase the annuity for a beneficiary under the plan;

(e) **disposition of income-averaging annuity contract** — any amount received by the taxpayer in the year as, on account or in lieu of payment of, or in satisfaction of, proceeds of the surrender, cancellation, redemption, sale or other disposition of an income-averaging annuity contract;

(f) **idem** — any amount deemed by subsection 61.1(1) to have been received by the taxpayer in the year as proceeds of the disposition of an income-averaging annuity contract;

(g) **supplementary unemployment benefit plan** — amounts received by the taxpayer in the year from a trustee under a supplementary unemployment benefit plan as provided by section 145;

(h) **registered retirement savings plan, etc. [RRSP or RRIF]** — amounts required by section 146 in respect of a registered retirement savings plan or a registered retirement income fund to be included in computing the taxpayer's income for the year;

(h.1) **Home Buyers' Plan** — amounts required by section 146.01 to be included in computing the taxpayer's income for the year;

(h.2) **Lifelong Learning Plan** — amounts required by section 146.02 to be included in computing the taxpayer's income for the year;

(i) **deferred profit sharing plan** — amounts received by the taxpayer in the year under a deferred profit sharing plan as provided by section 147;

(j) **life insurance policy proceeds** — any amount required by subsection 148(1) or (1.1) to be included in computing the taxpayer's income for the year;

(k) **certain tools of an employee, re proceeds** — all amounts received in the year by a person or partnership (in this paragraph referred to as the "vendor") as consideration for the disposition by the vendor of a property the cost of which was included in computing an amount under paragraph 8(1)(r) or (s) in respect of the vendor or in respect of a person with whom the vendor does not deal at arm's length, to the extent that the total of those amounts received in respect of the disposition in the year and in preceding taxation years exceeds the total of the cost to the vendor of the property immediately before the disposition and all amounts included in respect of the disposition under this paragraph in computing the vendor's income for a preceding taxation year, unless the property was acquired by the vendor in circumstances to which subsection 85(5.1) or subsection 97(5) applied;

(l) **legal expenses [awarded or reimbursed]** — amounts received by the taxpayer in the year as

> (i) legal costs awarded to the taxpayer by a court on an appeal in relation to an assessment of any tax, interest or penalties referred to in paragraph 60(o),
>
> (ii) reimbursement of costs incurred in relation to a decision of the Canada Employment and Immigration Commission, the Canada Employment and Insurance Commission, a board of referees or an umpire under the *Unemployment Insurance Act* or the *Employment Insurance Act*, or
>
> (iii) reimbursement of costs incurred in relation to an assessment or a decision under the *Canada Pension Plan* or a provincial pension plan as defined in section 3 of that Act,

if with respect to that assessment or decision, as the case may be, an amount has been deducted or may be deductible under paragraph 60(o) in computing the taxpayer's income;

(l.1) **idem** — amounts received by the taxpayer in the year as an award or a reimbursement in respect of legal expenses (other than those relating to a division or settlement of property arising out of, or on a breakdown of, a marriage or common-law partnership) paid to collect or establish a right to a retiring allowance or a benefit under a pension fund or plan (other than a benefit under the *Canada Pension Plan* or a provincial pension plan as defined in section 3 of that Act) in respect of employment;

(m) [Repealed 1996, c. 23, s. 172]

Proposed Addition — 56(1)(m)

(m) **bad debt recovered [non-competition agreement]** — any amount received by the taxpayer, or by a person who does not deal at arm's length with the taxpayer, in the year on account of a debt in respect of which a deduction was made under paragraph 60(f) in computing the taxpayer's income for a preceding taxation year;

Application: Bill C-33 (First Senate Reading June 18, 2007) (Part 2 — technical), subsec. 70(2), will add para. 56(1)(m), applicable after October 7, 2003.

Technical Notes: New paragraph 56(1)(m) is added to provide that a taxpayer is required to include in income any amount received in a taxation year on account of a debt in respect of which a bad debt deduction was made under new paragraph 60(f) in computing the taxpayer's income for a preceding taxation year. In other words, if a taxpayer makes a bad debt deduction for an amount receivable in respect of a restrictive covenant that was previously included in computing the taxpayer's income because of new section 56.4 (or new subsection 6(3.1)), and the taxpayer (or a person not dealing at arm's length with the taxpayer) subsequently receives the amount, the amount so received is to be included in computing the taxpayer's income.

(n) **scholarships, bursaries, etc.** — the amount, if any, by which

(i) the total of all amounts (other than amounts described in paragraph (q), amounts received in the course of business, and amounts received in respect of, in the course of or by virtue of an office or employment) received by the taxpayer in the year, each of which is an amount received by the taxpayer as or on account of a scholarship, fellowship or bursary, or a prize for achievement in a field of endeavour ordinarily carried on by the taxpayer (other than a prescribed prize),

exceeds

(ii) the taxpayer's scholarship exemption for the year computed under subsection (3);

Proposed Amendment — Scholarship exemption

Federal budget, Notice of Ways and Means Motion, May 2, 2006: See under 56(3).

(n.1) **apprenticeship incentive grant** — amounts received by the taxpayer in the year under the Apprenticeship Incentive Grant program administered by the Department of Human Resources and Social Development;

(o) **research grants** — the amount, if any, by which any grant received by the taxpayer in the year to enable the taxpayer to carry on research or any similar work exceeds the total of expenses incurred by the taxpayer in the year for the purpose of carrying on the work, other than

(i) personal or living expenses of the taxpayer except travel expenses (including the entire amount expended for meals and lodging) incurred by the taxpayer while away from home in the course of carrying on the work,

(ii) expenses in respect of which the taxpayer has been reimbursed, or

(iii) expenses that are otherwise deductible in computing the taxpayer's income for the year;

(p) **refund of scholarships, bursaries and research grants** — amounts as described in paragraph 60(q) received by the taxpayer in the year from an individual;

(q) **education savings plan payments** — amounts in respect of a registered education savings plan required by section 146.1 to be included in computing the taxpayer's income for the year;

(r) **[government] financial assistance** — amounts received in the year by the taxpayer as

(i) earnings supplements provided under a project sponsored by a government or government agency in Canada to encourage individuals to obtain or keep employment,

(ii) financial assistance under a program established by the Canada Employment Insurance Commission under Part II of the *Employment Insurance Act*, or

(iii) financial assistance under a program that is

(A) established by a government or government agency in Canada or by an organization,

(B) similar to a program established under Part II of that Act, and

(C) the subject of an agreement between the government, government agency or organization and the Canada Employment Insurance Commission because of section 63 of that Act;

Proposed Addition — 56(1)(r)(iv)

(iv) financial assistance provided under a program established by a government, or government agency, in Canada that provides income replacement benefits similar to income replacement benefits provided under a program established under the *Employment Insurance Act*;

Application: Bill C-33 (First Senate Reading June 18, 2007) (Part 2 — technical), subsec. 70(3), will add subpara. 56(1)(r)(iv), applicable to 2003 *et seq*

Technical Notes: Paragraph 56(1)(r) requires that certain amounts received as earnings supplements under government sponsored projects or as financial assistance under programs established by the Canada Employment Insurance Commission or under similar programs established by other government entities or organizations pursuant to agreements with the Commission are to be included in computing the recipient's income.

In recent years, there have been a number of income replacement benefits paid under government programs, usually in response to an unforeseen event, or as bridging benefits payable until another program is implemented. These income replacement benefits are generally paid to individuals who are not eligible for employment insurance (EI) benefits either because they have not worked enough weeks or because they have otherwise exhausted their benefits. However, the benefits paid are generally calculated by reference to the amounts that the individual would receive under the *Employment Insurance Act* if they were eligible for benefits under that Act.

Paragraph 56(1)(r) is amended, for the 2003 and subsequent taxation years, to clarify that income replacement benefits received under government assistance programs that are similar to income replacement payments provided under the *Employment Insurance Act* are to be included in computing the recipient's income.

(s) **grants under prescribed programs** — the amount of any grant received in the year under a prescribed program of the Government of Canada relating to home insulation or energy conversion by

(i) the taxpayer, other than a married taxpayer or a taxpayer who is in a common-law partnership who resided with the taxpayer's spouse or common-law partner at the time the grant was received and whose income for the year is less than the taxpayer's spouse's or common-law partner's income for the year, or

(ii) the spouse or common-law partner of the taxpayer with whom the taxpayer resided at the time the grant was received, if the spouse's or common-law partner's income for the year is less than the taxpayer's income for the year

to the extent that the amount is not required by paragraph 12(1)(u) to be included in computing the taxpayer's or the taxpayer's spouse's or common-law partner's income for the year or a subsequent year;

(t) **registered retirement income fund** — amounts in respect of a registered retirement income fund required by section 146.3 to be included in computing the taxpayer's income for the year;

(u) **social assistance [welfare] payments** — a social assistance payment made on the basis of a means, needs or income test and received in the year by

(i) the taxpayer, other than a married taxpayer or a taxpayer who is in a common-law partnership who resided with the taxpayer's spouse or common-law partner at the time the payment was received and whose income for the year is less than the spouse's or common-law partner's income for the year, or

(ii) the taxpayer's spouse or common-law partner, if the taxpayer resided with the spouse or common-law partner at the time the payment was received and if the spouse's or common-law partner's income for the year is less than the taxpayer's income for the year,

except to the extent that the payment is otherwise required to be included in computing the income for a taxation year of the taxpayer or the taxpayer's spouse or common-law partner;

(v) **workers' compensation** — compensation received under an employees' or workers' compensation law of Canada or a province in respect of an injury, a disability or death;

(w) **salary deferral arrangement** — the total of all amounts each of which is an amount received by the taxpayer as a benefit (other than an amount received by or from a trust governed by a salary deferral arrangement) in the year out of or under a salary deferral arrangement in respect of a person other than the taxpayer except to the extent that the amount, or another amount that may reasonably be considered to relate thereto, has been included in computing the income of that other person for the year or for any preceding taxation year;

(x) **retirement compensation arrangement** — any amount, including a return of contributions, received in the year by the taxpayer or another person, other than an amount required to be included in that other person's income for a taxation year under paragraph 12(1)(n.3), out of or under a retirement compensation arrangement that can reasonably be considered to have been received in respect of an office or employment of the taxpayer;

(y) **idem** — any amount received or that became receivable in the year by the taxpayer as proceeds from the disposition of an interest in a retirement compensation arrangement;

(z) **idem** — the total of all amounts, including a return of contributions, each of which is an amount received in the year by the taxpayer out of or under a retirement compensation arrangement that can reasonably be considered to have been received in respect of an office or employment of a person other than the taxpayer, except to the extent that the amount was required

(i) under paragraph 12(1)(n.3) to be included in computing the taxpayer's income for a taxation year, or

(ii) under paragraph (x) or subsection 70(2) to be included in computing the income for the year of a person resident in Canada other than the taxpayer; and

(aa) **[benefit from registered national arts service organization]** — the value of benefits received or enjoyed by any person in the year in respect of workshops, seminars, training programs and similar development programs because of the taxpayer's membership in a registered national arts service organization.

(1.1) Application of subsec. 12.2(11) — The definitions in subsection 12.2(11) apply to paragraph (1)(d).

(2) Indirect payments — A payment or transfer of property made pursuant to the direction of, or with the concurrence of, a taxpayer to some other person for the benefit of the taxpayer or as a benefit that the taxpayer desired to have conferred on the other person (other than by an assignment of any portion of a retirement pension pursuant to section 65.1 of the *Canada Pension Plan* or a comparable provision of a provincial pension plan as defined in section 3 of that Act or of a prescribed provincial pension plan) shall be included in computing the taxpayer's income to the extent that it would be if the payment or transfer had been made to the taxpayer.

(3) Exemption for scholarships, fellowships, bursaries and prizes — For the purpose of subparagraph (1)(n)(ii), a taxpayer's scholarship exemption for a taxation year is the total of

(a) the total of all amounts each of which is the amount included under subparagraph (1)(n)(i) in computing the taxpayer's income for the taxation year in respect of a scholarship, fellowship or bursary received in connection with the taxpayer's enrolment in an educational program in respect of which an amount may be deducted under subsection 118.6(2) in computing the taxpayer's tax payable under this Part for the taxation year,

(b) the total of all amounts each of which is the lesser of

(i) the amount included under subparagraph (1)(n)(i) in computing the taxpayer's income for the taxation year in respect of a scholarship, fellowship, bursary or prize that is to be used by the taxpayer in the production of a literary, dramatic, musical or artistic work, and

(ii) the total of all amounts each of which is an expense incurred by the taxpayer in the taxation year for the purpose of fulfilling the conditions under which the amount described in subparagraph (i) was received, other than

(A) personal or living expenses of the taxpayer (except expenses in respect of travel, meals and lodging incurred by the taxpayer in the course of fulfilling those conditions and while absent from the taxpayer's usual place of residence for the period to which the scholarship, fellowship, bursary or prize, as the case may be, relates),

(B) expenses for which the taxpayer is entitled to be reimbursed, and

(C) expenses that are otherwise deductible in computing the taxpayer's income, and

(c) the lesser of $500 and the amount by which the total described in subparagraph (1)(n)(i) for the taxation year exceeds the total of the amounts determined under paragraphs (a) and (b).

Proposed Amendment — 56(3)

Federal Budget, Notice of Ways and Means Motion, March 19, 2007: *Elementary and Secondary School Scholarships*

(9) That, for the 2007 and subsequent taxation years, there be excluded from an individual's income for a taxation year the total of all amounts received in the taxation year by the individual on account of scholarships and bursaries in connection with the individual's enrolment in an elementary or secondary school.

Federal Budget, Supplementary Information, March 19, 2007: *Elementary and Secondary School Scholarships*

Scholarships to attend elementary and secondary schools are included in computing the income of the student to the extent that they exceed $500. Budget 2007 proposes to honour the Government's commitment to student academic excellence and choice by fully exempting scholarships and bursaries that are provided to attend elementary and secondary schools.

Example

> Mike received a scholarship in 2007 of $30,000 to study at a high school in Ontario. Under the current system, all of this money except for the first $500 would be taxable, and Mike would owe $3,189 in federal income tax on this scholarship.
>
> In 2007, because of the full exemption on scholarship income, he will not pay any federal income tax on his scholarship.

This measure will apply for the 2007 and subsequent taxation years.

(4) Transfer of rights to income — Where a taxpayer has, at any time before the end of a taxation year, transferred or assigned to a person with whom the taxpayer was not dealing at arm's length the right to an amount (other than any portion of a retirement pension assigned by the taxpayer under section 65.1 of the *Canada Pension Plan* or a comparable provision of a provincial pension plan as defined in section 3 of that Act) that would, if the right had not been so transferred or assigned, be included in computing the taxpayer's income for the taxation year, the part of the amount that relates to the period in the year throughout which the taxpayer is resident in Canada shall be included in computing the taxpayer's income for the year unless the income is from property and the taxpayer has also transferred or assigned the property.

(4.1) Interest free or low interest loans — Where

(a) a particular individual (other than a trust) or a trust in which the particular individual is beneficially interested has, directly or indirectly by means of a trust or by any means whatever, received a loan from or become indebted to

(i) another individual (in this subsection referred to as the "creditor") who

(A) does not deal at arm's length with the particular individual, and

(B) is not a trust, or

(ii) a trust (in this subsection referred to as the "creditor trust") to which another individual (in this subsection referred to as the "original transferor") who

(A) does not deal at arm's length with the particular individual,

(B) was resident in Canada at any time in the period during which the loan or indebtedness is outstanding, and

(C) is not a trust,

has, directly or indirectly by means of a trust or by any means whatever, transferred property, and

(b) it can reasonably be considered that one of the main reasons for making the loan or incurring the indebtedness was to reduce or avoid tax by causing income from

(i) the loaned property,

(ii) property that the loan or indebtedness enabled or assisted the particular individual, or the trust in which the particular individual is beneficially interested, to acquire, or

(iii) property substituted for property referred to in subparagraph (i) or (ii)

to be included in the income of the particular individual,

the following rules apply:

(c) any income of the particular individual for a taxation year from the property referred to in paragraph (b) that relates to the period or periods in the year throughout which the creditor or the creditor trust, as the case may be, was resident in Canada and the particular individual was not dealing at arm's length with the creditor or the original transferor, as the case may be, shall be deemed,

(i) where subparagraph (a)(i) applies, to be income of the creditor for that year and not of the particular individual except to the extent that

(A) section 74.1 applies or would, but for subsection 74.5(3), apply, or

(B) subsection 75(2) applies

to that income, and

(ii) where subparagraph (a)(ii) applies, to be income of the creditor trust for that year and not of the particular individual except to the extent that

(A) subparagraph (i) applies,

(B) section 74.1 applies or would, but for subsection 74.5(3), apply, or

(C) subsection 75(2) applies (otherwise than because of paragraph (d))

to that income; and

(d) where subsection 75(2) applies to any of the property referred to in paragraph (b) and subparagraph (c)(ii) applies to income from the property, subsection 75(2) applies after subparagraph (c)(ii) is applied.

(4.2) Exception — Notwithstanding any other provision of this Act, subsection (4.1) does not apply to any income derived in a particular taxation year where

(a) interest was charged on the loan or indebtedness at a rate equal to or greater than the lesser of

(i) the prescribed rate of interest in effect at the time the loan was made or the indebtedness arose, and

(ii) the rate that would, having regard to all the circumstances, have been agreed on, at the time the loan was made or the indebtedness arose, between parties dealing with each other at arm's length;

(b) the amount of interest that was payable in respect of the particular year in respect of the loan or indebtedness was paid not later than 30 days after the end of the particular year; and

(c) the amount of interest that was payable in respect of each taxation year preceding the particular year in respect of the loan or indebtedness was paid not later than 30 days after the end of each of those preceding taxation years.

(4.3) Repayment of existing indebtedness — For the purposes of subsection (4.1), where at any time a particular property is used to repay, in whole or in part, a loan or indebtedness that enabled or assisted an individual to acquire another property, there shall be included in computing the income from the particular property that proportion of the income or loss, as the case may be, derived after that time from the other property or from property substituted therefor that the amount so repaid is of the cost to the individual of the other property, but for greater certainty nothing in this subsection shall affect the application of subsection (4.1) to any income or loss derived from the other property or from property substituted therefor.

(5) Exception for split income — Subsections (2), (4) and (4.1) do not apply to any amount that is included in computing a specified individual's split income for a taxation year.

(6) [Universal] Child care benefit — There shall be included in computing the income of a taxpayer for a taxation year the total of all amounts each of which is a benefit paid under section 4 of the *Universal Child Care Benefit Act* that is received in the taxation year by

(a) the taxpayer, if

(i) the taxpayer does not have a spouse or common-law partner at the end of the year, or

(ii) the income, for the taxation year, of the person who is the taxpayer's spouse or common-law partner at the end of the taxation year is equal to or greater than the income of the taxpayer for the taxation year; or

(b) the taxpayer's spouse or common-law partner at the end of the taxation year, if the income of the spouse or common-law partner for the taxation year is greater than the taxpayer's income for the taxation year.

(7) [Repealed 1994, c. 7, Sch. VII, s. 1(1)]

(8) CPP/QPP and UCCB amounts for previous years — Notwithstanding subsections (1) and (6), if

(a) one or more amounts are received by an individual (other than a trust) in a taxation year as, on account of, in lieu of payment of or in satisfaction of, any benefit under the *Universal Child Care Benefit Act*, the *Canada Pension Plan* or a provincial pension plan as defined in section 3 of the *Canada Pension Plan*, and

(b) a portion, not less than $300, of the total of those amounts relates to one or more preceding taxation years,

that portion shall, at the option of the individual, not be included in the individual's income.

(9) Meaning of "income for the year" — For the purposes of paragraphs (1)(s) and (u), "income for the year" of a person means the amount that would, but for those paragraphs, paragraphs 60(v.1) and (w) and section 63, be the income of that person for the year.

(10) Severability of retirement compensation arrangement — Where a retirement compensation arrangement is part of a plan or arrangement (in this subsection referred to as the "plan") under which amounts not related to the retirement compensation arrangement are payable or provided, for the purposes of this Act, other than this subsection,

(a) the retirement compensation arrangement shall be deemed to be a separate arrangement independent of other parts of the plan of which it is a part; and

(b) subject to subsection 6(14), amounts paid out of or under the plan shall be deemed to have first been paid out of the retirement compensation arrangement unless a provision in the plan otherwise provides.

(11) Disposition of property by RCA trust — For the purposes of paragraphs (1)(x) and (z), where, at any time in a year, a trust governed by a retirement compensation arrangement

(a) disposes of property to a person for consideration less than the fair market value of the property at the time of the disposition, or for no consideration,

(b) acquires property from a person for consideration greater than the fair market value of the property at the time of the acquisition, or

(c) permits a person to use or enjoy property of the trust for no consideration or for consideration less than the fair market value of such use or enjoyment,

the amount, if any, by which such fair market value differs from the consideration or, if there is no consideration, the amount of the fair market value shall be deemed to be an amount received at that time by the person out of or under the arrangement that can reasonably be considered to have been received in respect of an office or employment of a taxpayer.

(12) [Repealed 1997, c. 25, s. 8(3)]

Proposed Addition — 56(12)

(12) Foreign retirement arrangement — If an amount in respect of a foreign retirement arrangement is, as a result of a transaction, an event or a circumstance, considered to be distributed to an individual under the income tax laws of the country in which the arrangement is established, the amount is, for the purpose of paragraph (1)(a), deemed to be received by the individual as a payment out of the arrangement in the taxation year that includes the time of the transaction, event or circumstance.

Application: Bill C-33 (First Senate Reading June 18, 2007) (Part 2 — technical), subsec. 70(4), will add subsec. 56(12), applicable to 1998 *et seq.* except that, for taxation years that end before 2002, the subsec. is to be read as follows:

(12) For the purpose of paragraph (1)(a),

(a) if an amount in respect of a foreign retirement arrangement is considered, under section 408A(d)(3)(C) of the *Internal Revenue Code of 1986* of the United States (in this subsection referred to as the "Code"), to be distributed to an individual as a result of a conversion of the arrangement after 1998 and before 2002, the amount is deemed to be received by the individual as a payment out of the arrangement in the taxation year that includes the time of the conversion; and

(b) if an individual received an amount as a payment out of or under a foreign retirement arrangement in 1998, or an amount is considered under section 408A(d)(3)(C) of the Code to be distributed to the individual as a result of a conversion of the arrangement in 1998, the individual was resident in Canada at the time of the receipt or conversion and the amount is an amount to which section 408A(d)(3)(A)(iii) of the Code applies,

(i) the amount is deemed not to have been received by the individual, and

(ii) an amount equal to the amount that is included under section 408A(d)(3)(A)(iii) or 408A(d)(3)(E) of the Code in the individual's gross income for a particular taxable year is deemed to be an amount received by the individual, in the taxation year that includes the day on which the particular taxable year begins, as a payment out of the arrangement, where the expressions "gross income" and "taxable year" in this subparagraph have the meanings assigned to those expressions by the Code.

Technical Notes: Clause 56(1)(a)(i)(C.1) generally requires that payments received by a taxpayer from a foreign retirement arrangement (FRA) be included in computing the taxpayer's income as a superannuation or pension benefit. An FRA is defined in subsection 248(1) as a prescribed plan or arrangement. Presently, the only arrangements prescribed to be an FRA under Regulation 6803 are individual retirement accounts and annuities (IRAs) established pursuant to section 408(a), (b) or (h) of the United States' *Internal Revenue Code of 1986* (referred to as the "Code").

New subsection 56(12) is introduced to require Canadian residents who hold IRAs to include in income any amount treated under the Code as a distribution from an IRA, to the extent that the amount is required to be included in income for U.S. tax purposes. New subsection 56(12), among other things, gives effect to a proposal that was announced in Finance Canada News Release 1998-129, dated December 18, 1998.

In certain circumstances, the Code provides that an amount is to be treated as a distribution from an IRA even though no distribution has in fact been made. For example, if an individual converts an IRA into a Roth IRA (which is an individual retirement plan established pursuant to section 408A(b) of the Code) simply by amending the plan terms, section 408A(d)(3)(C) of the Code treats the converted amount as a distribution from the regular IRA and, thus, includible in income for U.S. tax purposes. For Canadian tax purposes, however, the converted amount might not be considered to have been received by the individual and, thus, could escape taxation in Canada. Other circumstances in which the Code treats a distribution to have occurred include borrowing money from an IRA and using an IRA as security for a loan. New subsection 56(12) clarifies that such "deemed" distributions under the Code are to be treated as distributions for Canadian income tax purposes.

More specifically, subsection 56(12) provides that, for the purpose of paragraph 56(1)(a), an individual is deemed to have received an amount as a payment from an FRA where, as a result of a transaction, event or circumstance, the income tax laws of the foreign country in which the FRA is established treats the amount as having been distributed from the FRA to the individual. The taxation year in which the individual is deemed to have received the amount is the taxation year that includes the time of the transaction, event or circumstance.

Subsection 56(12) applies to the 1998 and subsequent taxation years except that, in its application to the 1998 to 2001 taxation years, two modifications are made. First, its application is limited to circumstances involving the conversion of an IRA into a Roth IRA. Second, for conversions of IRAs into Roth IRAs that occurred in 1998, the amount and timing of the income inclusion in Canada will match the amount and timing in the U.S. Under the Code, individuals who converted an IRA into a Roth IRA in 1998 were entitled to spread the income inclusion over a four-year period. Subsection 56(12) provides for the same treatment. However, if an individual became resident in Canada after having converted an IRA into a Roth IRA in 1998, the individual will not be subject to taxation in Canada on any amounts relating to the conversion that remain taxable for U.S. tax purposes.

Dept. of Finance news release 1998-129, December 18, 1998: *Qualified RRSP Investments and IRAs*

Finance Minister Paul Martin today announced that he will propose changes to the *Income Tax Act* and the *Income Tax Regulations* to address two issues that have been recently raised with the Department of Finance, in the context of retirement savings decisions currently being made by individuals.

[First measure now implemented in Reg. 4900(1)(n.1) — ed.]

The second issue deals with individual retirement accounts (IRAs) established under the United States Internal Revenue Code. The Minister announced that he will propose an amendment to the *Income Tax Act* in response to recent changes to the Code relating to IRAs.

The changes to the Code have established a new type of IRA, known as a Roth IRA. Under the Code, contributions to a Roth IRA are not deductible, but investment income accrues tax-free and distributions are generally not taxable. Under certain circumstances, an individual may convert an ordinary IRA into a Roth IRA, but is required to include in computing income for the year of conversion the value of the ordinary IRA at the time of conversion. If the conversion is made in 1998, the income inclusion may be spread out over a four-year period.

The proposed amendment to the Act would affect Canadian residents who convert ordinary IRAs into Roth IRAs. It would require that the individual include in income for Canadian tax purposes any amount that must be included in income for U.S. tax purposes. This would ensure that the conversion amount is taxed in Canada, even where the IRA is converted simply by amending its terms. It would also ensure that the amount and timing of the inclusion in Canada matches the amount and timing in the U.S., thus allowing individuals to maximize the use of U.S. taxes paid on conversion as foreign tax credits in computing Canadian income tax payable.

Mr. Martin noted that the deferral opportunities in the U.S. for Roth IRAs are far more generous than the deferral opportunities in the U.S. for ordinary IRAs and the deferral opportunities in Canada for tax-assisted retirement savings. In particular, contributions can be made to a Roth IRA at any age, and there is no requirement for payments under a Roth IRA to begin by a certain age. Accordingly, there are no plans to provide tax assistance by way of an exemption from or deferral of taxation in Canada on earnings within a Roth IRA.

For further information: Tax Legislation Division, (613) 992-1916; Jean-Michel Catta, Public Affairs and Operations Division, (613) 992-1574.

56.1 (1) Support — For the purposes of paragraph 56(1)(b) and subsection 118(5), where an order or agreement, or any variation thereof, provides for the payment of an amount to a taxpayer or for the benefit of the taxpayer, children in the taxpayer's custody or both the taxpayer and those children, the amount or any part thereof

(a) when payable, is deemed to be payable to and receivable by the taxpayer; and

(b) when paid, is deemed to have been paid to and received by the taxpayer.

(2) Agreement — For the purposes of section 56, this section and subsection 118(5), the amount determined by the formula

$$A - B$$

where

A is the total of all amounts each of which is an amount (other than an amount that is otherwise a support amount) that became payable by a person in a taxation year, under an order of a competent tribunal or under a written agreement, in respect of an expense (other than an expenditure in respect of a self-contained domestic establishment in which the person resides or an expenditure for the acquisition of tangible property that is not an expenditure on account of a medical or education expense or in respect of the acquisition, improvement or maintenance of a self-contained domestic establishment in which the taxpayer described in paragraph (a) or (b) resides) incurred in the year or the preceding taxation year for the maintenance of a taxpayer, children in the taxpayer's custody or both the taxpayer and those children, where the taxpayer is

Proposed Amendment — 56.1(2)A opening words

Application: Bill C-33 (First Senate Reading June 18, 2007) (Part 3 — bijuralism), s. 219, will amend the opening words of the description of A in subsec. 56.1(2) by substituting "tangible property, or for civil law corporeal property," for "tangible property", to come into force on Royal Assent.

Technical Notes: See under 12(4).

(a) the person's spouse or common-law partner or former spouse or common-law partner, or

(b) where the amount became payable under an order made by a competent tribunal in accordance with the laws of a province, an individual who is the parent of a child of whom the person is a legal parent,

and

B is the amount, if any, by which

(a) the total of all amounts each of which is an amount included in the total determined for A in respect of the acquisition or improvement of a self-contained domestic establishment in which the taxpayer resides, including any payment of principal or interest in respect of a loan made or indebtedness incurred to finance, in any manner whatever, such acquisition or improvement

exceeds

(b) the total of all amounts each of which is an amount equal to $1/5$ of the original principal amount of a loan or indebtedness described in paragraph (a),

is, where the order or written agreement, as the case may be, provides that this subsection and subsection 60.1(2) shall apply to any amount paid or payable thereunder, deemed to be an amount payable to and receivable by the taxpayer as an allowance on a periodic basis, and the taxpayer is deemed to have discretion as to the use of that amount.

(3) **Prior payments** — For the purposes of this section and section 56, where a written agreement or order of a competent tribunal made at any time in a taxation year provides that an amount received before that time and in the year or the preceding taxation year is to be considered to have been paid and received thereunder,

(a) the amount is deemed to have been received thereunder; and

(b) the agreement or order is deemed, except for the purpose of this subsection, to have been made on the day on which the first such amount was received, except that, where the agreement or order is made after April 1997 and varies a child support amount payable to the recipient from the last such amount received by the recipient before May 1997, each varied amount of child support received under the agreement or order is deemed to have been receivable under an agreement or order the commencement day of which is the day on which the first payment of the varied amount is required to be made.

(4) **Definitions** — The definitions in this subsection apply in this section and section 56.

"child support amount" means any support amount that is not identified in the agreement or order under which it is receivable as being solely for the support of a recipient who is a spouse or common-law partner or former spouse or common-law partner of the payer or who is a parent of a child of whom the payer is a legal parent.

"commencement day" at any time of an agreement or order means

(a) where the agreement or order is made after April 1997, the day it is made; and

(b) where the agreement or order is made before May 1997, the day, if any, that is after April 1997 and is the earliest of

(i) the day specified as the commencement day of the agreement or order by the payer and recipient under the agreement or order in a joint election filed with the Minister in prescribed form and manner,

(ii) where the agreement or order is varied after April 1997 to change the child support amounts payable to the recipient, the day on which the first payment of the varied amount is required to be made,

(iii) where a subsequent agreement or order is made after April 1997, the effect of which is to change the total child support amounts payable to the recipient by the payer, the commencement day of the first such subsequent agreement or order, and

(iv) the day specified in the agreement or order, or any variation thereof, as the commencement day of the agreement or order for the purposes of this Act.

"support amount" means an amount payable or receivable as an allowance on a periodic basis for the maintenance of the recipient, children of the recipient or both the recipient and children of the recipient, if the recipient has discretion as to the use of the amount, and

(a) the recipient is the spouse or common-law partner or former spouse or common-law partner of the payer, the recipient and payer are living separate and apart because of the breakdown of their marriage or common-law partnership and the amount is receivable under an order of a competent tribunal or under a written agreement; or

(b) the payer is a legal parent of a child of the recipient and the amount is receivable under an order made by a competent tribunal in accordance with the laws of a province.

. . . . .

Subdivision e — Deductions in Computing Income

60. Other deductions — There may be deducted in computing a taxpayer's income for a taxation year such of the following amounts as are applicable:

(a) **capital element of annuity payments** — the capital element of each annuity payment included by virtue of paragraph 56(1)(d) in computing the taxpayer's income for the year, that is to say,

(i) if the annuity was paid under a contract, an amount equal to that part of the payment determined in prescribed manner to have been a return of capital, and

(ii) if the annuity was paid under a will or trust, such part of the payment as can be established by the recipient not to have been paid out of the income of the estate or trust;

(b) **[spousal or child] support** — the total of all amounts each of which is an amount determined by the formula

$$A - (B + C)$$

where

A is the total of all amounts each of which is a support amount paid after 1996 and before the end of the year by the taxpayer to a particular person, where the taxpayer and the particular person were living separate and apart at the time the amount was paid,

B is the total of all amounts each of which is a child support amount that became payable by the taxpayer to the particular person under an agreement or order on or after its commencement day and before the end of the year in respect of a period that began on or after its commencement day, and

C is the total of all amounts each of which is a support amount paid by the taxpayer to the particular person after 1996 and deductible in computing the taxpayer's income for a preceding taxation year;

(c) **pension income reallocation** — where the taxpayer is a pensioner (as defined in subsection 60.03(1)), any amount that is a split-pension amount (as defined in that subsection) in respect of the pensioner for the taxation year;

(c.1) [Repealed]

(c.2) **repayment of support payments** — an amount paid by the taxpayer in the year or one of the 2 preceding taxation years under a decree, order or judgment of a competent tribunal as a repayment of an amount included under paragraph 56(1)(b) or (c), or under paragraph 56(1)(c.1) (as it applies, in computing the taxpayer's income for the year or a preceding taxation year, to decrees, orders and judgments made before 1993) to the extent that it was not so deducted for a preceding taxation year;

(d) **interest on death duties** — an amount equal to annual interest accruing within the taxation year in respect of succession duties, inheritance taxes or estate taxes;

(e) **CPP/QPP contributions on self-employed earnings** — ½ of the lesser of

(i) the total of all amounts each of which is an amount payable by the taxpayer in respect of self-employed earnings for the year as a contribution under the *Canada Pension Plan* or under a provincial pension plan within the meaning assigned by section 3 of that Act, and

(ii) the maximum amount of such contributions payable by the taxpayer for the year under the plan;

(f) [Repealed 1994, c. 7, Sch. II, s. 32(4)]

Proposed Addition — 60(f)

(f) **restrictive covenant — bad debt** — all debts owing to a taxpayer that are established by the taxpayer to have become bad debts in the taxation year and that are in respect of an amount included because of the operation of subsection 6(3.1) or 56.4(2) in computing the taxpayer's income in a preceding taxation year;

Application: Bill C-33 (First Senate Reading June 18, 2007) (Part 2 — technical), subsec. 72(1), will add para. 60(f), applicable after October 7, 2003.

Technical Notes: New paragraph 60(f) provides a taxpayer with a deduction for a bad debt in respect of an amount that was receivable on a restrictive covenant and previously included in computing the taxpayer's income because of new section 56.4 (or new subsection 6(3.1)).

(i) **premium or payment under RRSP or RRIF** — any amount that is deductible under section 146 or subsection 147.3(13.1) in computing the income of the taxpayer for the year;

(j) **transfer of superannuation benefits [to RRSP]** — such part of the total of all amounts each of which is

(i) a superannuation or pension benefit (other than any amount in respect of the benefit that is deducted in computing the taxable income of the taxpayer for a taxation year because of subparagraph 110(1)(f)(i) or a benefit that is part of a series of periodic payments) payable out of or under a pension plan that is not a registered pension plan, attributable to services rendered by the taxpayer or a spouse or common-law partner or former spouse or common-law partner of the taxpayer in a period throughout which that person was not resident in Canada, and included in computing the income of the taxpayer for the year because of subparagraph 56(1)(a)(i), or

(ii) an eligible amount in respect of the taxpayer for the year under section 60.01, subsection 104(27) or (27.1) or paragraph 147(10.2)(d),

as

(iii) is designated by the taxpayer in the taxpayer's return of income under this Part for the year, and

(iv) does not exceed the total of all amounts each of which is an amount paid by the taxpayer in the year or within 60 days after the end of the year

(A) as a contribution to or under a registered pension plan for the taxpayer's benefit, other than the portion thereof deductible under paragraph 8(1)(m) in computing the taxpayer's income for the year, or

(B) as a premium (within the meaning assigned by subsection 146(1)) under a registered retirement savings plan under which the taxpayer is the annuitant (within the meaning assigned by subsection 146(1)), other than the portion thereof designated for a taxation year for the purposes of paragraph (l),

to the extent that the amount was not deducted in computing the taxpayer's income for a preceding taxation year;

(j.02) **payment to registered pension plan [pre-April 1988 agreements]** — an amount equal to the lesser of

(i) the total of

(A) all contributions made in the year by the taxpayer to registered pension plans in respect of eligible service of the taxpayer before 1990 under the plans, where the taxpayer was obliged under the terms of an agreement in writing entered into before March 28, 1988 to make the contributions, and

(B) all amounts each of which is an amount paid in the year by the taxpayer to a registered pension plan as

(I) a repayment under a prescribed statutory provision of an amount received from the plan that was included under subsection 56(1) in computing the taxpayer's income for a taxation year ending before 1990, where the taxpayer was obliged as a consequence of a written election made before March 28, 1988 to make the repayment, or

(II) interest in respect of a repayment referred to in subclause (I),

other than the portion of that total that is deductible under paragraph 8(1)(m) or paragraph (j.03) in computing the taxpayer's income for the year, and

(ii) the total of all amounts each of which is an amount paid out of or under a registered pension plan as part of a series of periodic payments and included under subsection 56(1) in computing the taxpayer's income for the year, other than the portion of that total that can reasonably be considered to have been designated by the taxpayer for the purpose of paragraph (j.2);

(j.03) **repayments of pre-1990 pension benefits** — an amount equal to the lesser of

(i) the total of all amounts each of which is an amount paid in the year or a preceding taxation year by the taxpayer to a registered pension plan that was not deductible in computing the taxpayer's income for a preceding taxation year and that was paid as

(A) a repayment under a prescribed statutory provision of an amount received from the plan that was included under subsection 56(1) in computing the taxpayer's income for a taxation year ending before 1990, or

(B) interest in respect of a repayment referred to in clause (A), and

(ii) the amount, if any, by which $3,500 exceeds the amount deducted under paragraph 8(1)(m) in computing the taxpayer's income for the year;

(j.04) **repayments of post-1989 pension benefits** — the total of all amounts each of which is an amount paid in the year by the taxpayer to a registered pension plan as

(i) a repayment under a prescribed statutory provision of an amount received from the plan that

(A) was included under subsection 56(1) in computing the taxpayer's income for a taxation year ending after 1989, and

(B) can reasonably be considered not to have been designated by the taxpayer for the purpose of paragraph (j.2), or

(ii) interest in respect of a repayment referred to in subparagraph (i),

except to the extent that the total was deductible under paragraph 8(1)(m) in computing the taxpayer's income for the year;

(j.1) **transfer of retiring allowances [to RRSP]** — such part of the total of all amounts each of which is an amount paid to the taxpayer by an employer, or under a retirement compensation arrangement to which the employer has contributed, as a retiring allowance and included in computing the taxpayer's income for the year by virtue of subparagraph 56(1)(a)(ii) or paragraph 56(1)(x) as

(i) is designated by the taxpayer in the taxpayer's return of income under this Part for the year,

(ii) does not exceed the amount, if any, by which the total of

(A) $2,000 multiplied by the number of years before 1996 during which the employee or former employee in respect of whom the payment was made (in this paragraph referred to as the "retiree") was employed by the employer or a person related to the employer, and

(B) $1,500 multiplied by the number by which the number of years before 1989 described in clause (A) exceeds the number that can reasonably be regarded as the equivalent number of years before 1989 in respect of which employer contributions under either a pension plan or a deferred profit sharing plan of the employer or a person related to the employer had vested in the retiree at the time of the payment

exceeds the total of

(C) all amounts deducted under this paragraph in respect of amounts paid before the year in respect of the retiree

(I) by the employer or a person related to the employer, or

(II) under a retirement compensation arrangement to which the employer or a person related to the employer has contributed,

(C.1) all other amounts deducted under this paragraph for the year in respect of amounts paid in the year in respect of the retiree

(I) by a person related to the employer, or

(II) under a retirement compensation arrangement to which a person related to the employer has contributed, and

(D) all amounts deducted under paragraph (t) in computing the retiree's income for the year in respect of a retirement compensation arrangement to which the employer or a person related to the employer has contributed, and

(iii) does not exceed the total of all amounts each of which is an amount paid by the taxpayer in the year or within 60 days after the end of the year in respect of the amount so designated

(A) as a contribution to or under a registered pension plan, other than the portion thereof deductible under paragraph (j) or 8(1)(m) in computing the taxpayer's income for the year, or

(B) as a premium (within the meaning assigned by section 146) under a registered retirement savings plan under which the taxpayer is the annuitant (within the meaning assigned by section 146), other than the portion thereof that has been designated for the purposes of paragraph (j) or (l),

to the extent that it was not deducted in computing the taxpayer's income for a preceding taxation year

and for the purposes of this paragraph, "person related to the employer" includes

(iv) any person whose business was acquired or continued by the employer, and

(v) a previous employer of the retiree whose service therewith is recognized in determining the retiree's pension benefits;

(k) [Repealed under former Act]

(l) **transfer of refund of premium under RRSP [on death]** — the total of all amounts each of which is an amount paid by or on behalf of the taxpayer in the year or within 60 days after the end of the year (or within such longer period after the end of the year as is acceptable to the Minister)

(i) as a premium under a registered retirement savings plan under which the taxpayer is the annuitant,

(ii) to acquire, from a person licensed or otherwise authorized under the laws of Canada or a province to carry on in Canada an annuities business, an annuity

(A) under which the taxpayer is the annuitant

Proposed Amendment — 60(l)(ii)(A)

[Former proposed amendment to 60(l)(ii)(A) is now 60.011 — ed.]

Possible Future Amendment — 60(l)(ii)(A)

Federal budget, Supplementary Information, February 23, 2005: *Registered Retirement Savings Plans and Registered Retirement Income Funds*

Currently, financially-dependent children with mental or physical infirmities are eligible to receive, on a tax-deferred basis, a deceased parent's (or in the case of a child that is financially dependent on a grandparent, the deceased grandparent's) proceeds from a registered retirement savings plan (RRSP) or a registered retirement income fund (RRIF) if the funds are transferred to the child's RRSP or are used to purchase a life annuity. The Committee [Technical Advisory Committee on Tax

Measures for Persons with Disabilities; see under 118.3(1) — ed.] recommended that the Government review these rules in order to allow more flexibility in respect of a deceased's RRSP or RRIF proceeds left to a financially-dependent child or grandchild with a disability and, in particular, that the use of a discretionary trust be permitted in these circumstances. The Government will review the tax rules in this area with a view to providing more flexibility where appropriate.

(I) for the taxpayer's life, or for the lives jointly of the taxpayer and the taxpayer's spouse or common-law partner either without a guaranteed period, or with a guaranteed period that is not greater than 90 years minus the lesser of the age in whole years of the taxpayer and the age in whole years of the taxpayer's spouse or common-law partner at the time the annuity was acquired, or

(II) for a term equal to 90 years minus the age in whole years of the taxpayer or the age in whole years of the taxpayer's spouse or common-law partner, at the time the annuity was acquired, or

(B) under which the taxpayer, or a trust under which the taxpayer is the sole person beneficially interested in amounts payable under the annuity, is the annuitant for a term not exceeding 18 years minus the age in whole years of the taxpayer at the time the annuity was acquired

Proposed Amendment — 60(l)(ii)(B)

(B) under which the taxpayer is the annuitant for a term not exceeding 18 years minus the age in whole years of the taxpayer at the time the annuity was acquired

Application: Bill C-33 (First Senate Reading June 18, 2007) (Part 2 — technical), subsec. 72(2), will amend cl. 60(l)(ii)(B) to read as above, applicable after 1988. (See 60.011.)

Technical Notes: In circumstances where an individual has received (or is deemed to have received) certain taxable lump sum amounts from a registered retirement savings plan, a registered retirement income fund or a registered pension plan, paragraph 60(l) allows the individual to claim an offsetting deduction for qualifying payments (not exceeding the amounts so received) made by or on behalf of the individual.

If the individual is a minor and the taxable amount is received as a consequence of the death of a parent or grandparent on whom the minor was financially dependent, a payment made to acquire an immediate annuity payable for a fixed term not exceeding 18 years minus the age of the minor at the time of acquisition is a qualifying payment for the purpose of paragraph 60(l). Clause 60(l)(ii)(B) requires that the annuitant under the annuity be either the minor or a trust under which the minor is the sole person beneficially interested in amounts payable under the annuity.

Clause 60(l)(ii)(B) is amended to require that the minor be the annuitant under the annuity. This is consequential to the introduction of new section 60.011 which, among other things, allows this requirement in paragraph 60(l) to be disregarded, if the annuitant under the term annuity is a trust under which the minor is the sole person beneficially interested in amounts payable under the annuity. Section 60.011 also provides that, in determining if the minor is the sole person beneficially interested in amounts payable under the annuity, any right of a person to receive an amount from the trust only on or after the death of the minor is to be disregarded. Section 60.011 also introduces a requirement, applicable with respect to annuities acquired after 2005, that the annuity provide for commutation on the death of the minor. (Refer to the explanatory notes to new section 60.011 for further details.)

This amendment applies after 1988, which reflects the effective date of the amendment to paragraph 60(l) allowing a trust to be named as the annuitant.

that does not provide for any payment thereunder except

(C) the single payment by or on behalf of the taxpayer,

(D) annual or more frequent periodic payments

(I) beginning not later than one year after the date of the payment referred to in clause (C), and

(II) each of which is equal to all other such payments or not equal to all other such payments solely because of an adjustment that would, if the annuity were an annuity under a retirement savings plan, be in accordance with subparagraphs 146(3)(b)(iii) to (v), and

(E) payments in full or partial commutation of the annuity and, where the commutation is partial,

(I) equal annual or more frequent periodic payments thereafter, or

(II) annual or more frequent periodic payments thereafter that are not equal solely because of an adjustment that would, if the annuity were an annuity under a retirement savings plan, be in accordance with subparagraphs 146(3)(b)(iii) to (v),

or

(iii) to a carrier as consideration for a registered retirement income fund under which the taxpayer is the annuitant

where that total

(iv) is designated by the taxpayer in the taxpayer's return of income under this Part for the year,

(v) does not exceed the total of

(A) the amount included in computing the taxpayer's income for the year as a refund of premiums out of or under a registered retirement savings plan under which the taxpayer's spouse or common-law partner was the annuitant,

(B) the amount included in computing the taxpayer's income for the year as a refund of premiums out of or under a registered retirement savings plan where the taxpayer was dependent by reason of physical or mental infirmity on the annuitant under the plan,

(B.01) the amount included in computing the taxpayer's income for the year as a payment (other than a payment that is part of a series of periodic payments or that relates to an actuarial surplus) received by the taxpayer out of or under a registered pension plan as a consequence of the death of an individual of whom the taxpayer was a child or grandchild, if the taxpayer was, immediately before the death, financially dependent on the individual for support because of mental or physical infirmity,

(B.1) the least of

(I) the amount paid by or on behalf of the taxpayer to acquire an annuity that would be described in subparagraph (ii) if that subparagraph were read without reference to clause (A) thereof,

(II) the amount (other than any portion of it that is included in the amount determined under clause (B), (B.01) or (B.2)) that is included in computing the taxpayer's income for the year as

1. a payment (other than a payment that is part of a series of periodic payments or that relates to an actuarial surplus) received by the taxpayer out of or under a registered pension plan,

2. a refund of premiums out of or under a registered retirement savings plan, or

3. a designated benefit in respect of a registered retirement income fund (in this clause having the meaning assigned by subsection 146.3(1))

as a consequence of the death of an individual of whom the taxpayer is a child or grandchild, and

(III) the amount, if any, by which the amount determined for the year under subclause (II) in respect of the taxpayer exceeds the amount, if any, by which

1. the total of all designated benefits of the taxpayer for the year in respect of registered retirement income funds

exceeds

2. the total of all amounts that would be eligible amounts of the taxpayer for the year in respect of those funds (within the meaning that would be assigned by subsection 146.3(6.11) if the taxpayer were described in paragraph (b) thereof), and

(B.2) all eligible amounts of the taxpayer for the year in respect of registered retirement income funds (within the meaning assigned by subsection 146.3(6.11)),

and, where the amount is paid by a direct transfer from the issuer of a registered retirement savings plan or a carrier of a registered retirement income fund,

(C) the amount included in computing the taxpayer's income for the year as a consequence of a payment described in subparagraph 146(2)(b)(ii), and

(D) the amount, if any, by which

(I) the amount received by the taxpayer out of or under a registered retirement income fund under which the taxpayer is the annuitant and included because of subsection 146.3(5) in computing the taxpayer's income for the year

exceeds

(II) the amount, if any, by which the minimum amount (within the meaning assigned by subsection 146.3(1)) under the fund for the year exceeds the total of all amounts received out of or under the fund in the year by an individual who was an annuitant under the fund before the taxpayer became the annuitant under the fund and that were included because of subsection 146.3(5) in computing that individual's income for the year, and

(vi) was not deducted in computing the taxpayer's income for a preceding taxation year;

(m.1) **succession duties applicable to certain property** — that proportion of any superannuation or pension benefit, death benefit, benefit under a registered retirement savings plan, benefit under a deferred profit sharing plan or benefit that is a payment under an income-averaging annuity contract, received by the taxpayer in the year, on or after the death of a predecessor, in payment of or on account of property to which the taxpayer is the successor, that

(i) such part of any succession duties payable under a law of a province in respect of the death of the predecessor as may reasonably be regarded as attributable to the property in payment of or on account of which the benefit was so received,

is of

(ii) the value of the property in payment of or on account of which the benefit was so received, as computed for the purposes of the law referred to in subparagraph (i);

(n) **repayment of pension or benefits** — any amount paid by the taxpayer in the year as a repayment (otherwise than because of Part VII of the *Unemployment Insurance Act*, chapter U-1 of the Revised Statutes of Canada, 1985, or of Part VII of the *Employment Insurance Act*) of any of the following amounts to the extent that the amount was included in computing the taxpayer's income, and not deducted in computing the taxpayer's taxable income, for the year or for a preceding taxation year, namely,

(i) a pension described in clause 56(1)(a)(i)(A),

(ii) a benefit described in clause 56(1)(a)(i)(B),

(iii) an amount described in subparagraph 56(1)(a)(ii),

(iv) a benefit described in subparagraph 56(1)(a)(iv),

(v) a benefit described in subparagraph 56(1)(a)(vi), and

Proposed Addition — 60(n)(v.1)

(v.1) a benefit described in subparagraph 56(1)(a)(vii), and

Application: Bill C-33 (First Senate Reading June 18, 2007) (Part 2 — technical), subsec. 72(3), will add subpara. 60(n)(v.1), applicable to 2006 *et seq.*

Technical Notes: Paragraph 60(n) provides a deduction for repayments of certain benefits included in income. This paragraph is amended, consequential to the introduction of the new Quebec Parental Insurance Plan on January 1, 2006, to provide for a deduction for repayments made under that Plan.

(vi) an amount described in paragraph 56(1)(r);

(o) **legal [or other] expenses [of objection or appeal]** — amounts paid by the taxpayer in the year in respect of fees or expenses incurred in preparing, instituting or prosecuting an objection to, or an appeal in relation to,

(i) an assessment of tax, interest or penalties under this Act or an Act of a province that imposes a tax similar to the tax imposed under this Act,

(ii) a decision of the Canada Employment and Immigration Commission, the Canada Employment and Insurance Commission, a board of referees or an umpire under the *Unemployment Insurance Act* or the *Employment Insurance Act*,

(iii) an assessment of any income tax deductible by the taxpayer under section 126 or any interest or penalty with respect thereto, or

(iv) an assessment or a decision made under the *Canada Pension Plan* or a provincial pension plan as defined in section 3 of that Act;

(o.1) **legal expenses** — the amount, if any, by which the lesser of

(i) the total of all legal expenses (other than those relating to a division or settlement of property arising out of, or on a breakdown of, a marriage or common-law partnership) paid by the taxpayer in the year or in any of the 7 preceding taxation years to collect or establish a right to an amount of

(A) a benefit under a pension fund or plan (other than a benefit under the *Canada Pension Plan* or a provincial pension plan as defined in section 3 of that Act) in respect of the employment of the taxpayer or a deceased individual of whom the taxpayer was a dependant, relation or legal representative, or

(B) a retiring allowance of the taxpayer or a deceased individual of whom the taxpayer was a dependant, relation or legal representative, and

(ii) the amount, if any, by which the total of all amounts each of which is

(A) an amount described in clause (i)(A) or (B)

(I) that is received after 1985,

(II) in respect of which legal expenses described in subparagraph (i) were paid, and

(III) that is included in computing the income of the taxpayer for the year or a preceding taxation year, or

(B) an amount included in computing the income of the taxpayer under paragraph 56(1)(l.1) for the year or a preceding taxation year,

exceeds the total of all amounts each of which is an amount deducted under paragraph (j), (j.01), (j.1) or (j.2) in computing the income of the taxpayer for the year or a preceding taxation year, to the extent that the amount may reasonably be considered to have been deductible as a consequence of the receipt of an amount referred to in clause (A),

exceeds

(iii) the portion of the total described in subparagraph (i) in respect of the taxpayer that may reasonably be considered to have been deductible under this paragraph in computing the income of the taxpayer for a preceding taxation year;

(p) **repayment of apprenticeship incentive grant** — the total of all amounts each of which is an amount paid in the taxation year as a repayment under the Apprenticeship Incentive Grant program of an amount that was included because of paragraph 56(1)(n.1) in computing the taxpayer's income for the taxation year or a preceding taxation year;

(q) **refund of income payments** — where the taxpayer is an individual, an amount paid by the taxpayer in the year to a person with whom the taxpayer was dealing at arm's length (in this paragraph referred to as the "payer") if

(i) the amount has been included in computing the income of the taxpayer in a preceding taxation year as an amount described in subparagraph 56(1)(n)(i) or paragraph 56(1)(o) paid to the taxpayer by the payer,

(ii) at the time the amount was paid by the payer to the taxpayer a condition was stipulated for the taxpayer to fulfil,

(iii) as a result of the failure of the taxpayer to fulfil the condition referred to in subparagraph (ii) the taxpayer was required to repay the amount to the payer,

(iv) during the period for which the amount referred to in subparagraph (i) was paid the taxpayer did not provide other than occasional services to the payer as an officer or under a contract of employment, and

(v) the amount was paid to the taxpayer for the purpose of enabling the taxpayer to further the taxpayer's education;

(s) **repayment of policy loan** — the total of all repayments made by the taxpayer in the year in respect of a policy loan (within the meaning assigned by subsection 148(9) made under a life insurance policy, not exceeding the amount, if any, by which

(i) the total of all amounts required by subsection 148(1) to be included in computing the taxpayer's income for the year or a preceding taxation year from a disposition described in paragraph (b) of the definition "disposition" in subsection 148(9) in respect of that policy

exceeds

(ii) the total of all repayments made by the taxpayer in respect of the policy loan that were deductible in computing the taxpayer's income for a preceding taxation year;

(t) **RCA distributions** — where an amount in respect of a particular retirement compensation arrangement is required by paragraph 56(1)(x) or (z) or subsection 70(2) to be included in computing the taxpayer's income for the year, an amount equal to the lesser of

(i) the total of all amounts in respect of the particular arrangement so required to be included in computing the taxpayer's income for the year, and

(ii) the amount, if any, by which the total of all amounts each of which is

(A) an amount (other than an amount deductible under paragraph 8(1)(m.2) or transferred to the particular arrangement under circumstances in which subsection 207.6(7) applies) contributed under the particular arrangement by the taxpayer while it was a retirement compensation arrangement and before the end of the year,

(A.1) an amount transferred in respect of the taxpayer before the end of the year to the particular arrangement from another retirement compensation arrangement under circumstances in which subsection 207.6(7) applies, to the extent that the amount would have been deductible under this paragraph in respect of the other arrangement in computing the taxpayer's income if it had been received by the taxpayer out of the other arrangement,

(B) an amount paid by the taxpayer before the end of the year and at a time when the taxpayer was resident in Canada to acquire an interest in the particular arrangement, or

(C) an amount that was received or became receivable by the taxpayer before the end of the year and at a time when the taxpayer was resident in Canada as proceeds from the disposition of an interest in the particular arrangement,

exceeds the total of all amounts each of which is

(D) an amount deducted under this paragraph or paragraph (u) in respect of the particular arrangement in computing the taxpayer's income for a preceding taxation year, or

(E) an amount transferred in respect of the taxpayer before the end of the year from the particular arrangement to another retirement compensation arrangement under circumstances in which subsection 207.6(7) applies, to the extent that the amount would have been deductible under this paragraph in respect of the particular arrangement in computing the taxpayer's income if it had been received by the taxpayer out of the particular arrangement;

(u) **RCA dispositions** — where an amount in respect of a particular retirement compensation arrangement is required by paragraph 56(1)(y) to be included in computing the taxpayer's income for the year, an amount equal to the lesser of

(i) the total of all amounts in respect of the particular arrangement so required to be included in computing the taxpayer's income for the year, and

(ii) the amount, if any, by which the total of all amounts each of which is

(A) an amount (other than an amount deductible under paragraph 8(1)(m.2) or transferred to the particular arrangement under circumstances in which subsection 207.6(7) applies) contributed under the particular arrangement by the taxpayer while it was a retirement compensation arrangement and before the end of the year,

(A.1) an amount transferred in respect of the taxpayer before the end of the year to the particular arrangement from another retirement compensation arrangement under circumstances in which subsection 207.6(7) applies, to the extent that the amount would have been deductible under paragraph (t) in respect of the other arrangement in computing the taxpayer's income if it had been received by the taxpayer out of the other arrangement, or

(B) an amount paid by the taxpayer before the end of the year and at a time when the taxpayer was resident in Canada to acquire an interest in the particular arrangement

exceeds the total of all amounts each of which is

(C) an amount deducted under paragraph (t) in respect of the particular arrangement in computing the taxpayer's income for the year or a preceding taxation year,

(D) an amount deducted under this paragraph in respect of the particular arrangement in computing the taxpayer's income for a preceding taxation year, or

(E) an amount transferred in respect of the taxpayer before the end of the year from the particular arrangement to another retirement compensation arrangement under circumstances in which subsection 207.6(7) applies, to the extent that the amount would have been deductible under paragraph (t) in respect of the particular arrangement in computing the taxpayer's income if it had been received by the taxpayer out of the particular arrangement;

(v) **contribution to a provincial pension plan** — the least of

(i) the amount, if any, by which

(A) the total of all amounts each of which is a contribution made in the year, or within 60 days after the end of the year, by the taxpayer to the account of the taxpayer, or of the taxpayer's spouse or common-law partner, under a prescribed provincial pension plan

exceeds

(B) the portion of the total described in clause (A) that was deducted in computing the taxpayer's income for the preceding taxation year,

(ii) the prescribed amount for the year in respect of the plan, and

(iii) the amount by which the taxpayer's RRSP deduction limit for the year exceeds the total of the amounts deducted under subsections 146(5) and (5.1) in computing the taxpayer's income for the year;

(v.1) **UI and EI benefit repayment** — any benefit repayment payable by the taxpayer under Part VII of the *Unemployment Insurance Act* or Part VII of the *Employment Insurance Act* on or before April 30 of the following year, to the extent that the amount was not deductible in computing the taxpayer's income for any preceding taxation year;

(w) **tax under Part I.2** — the amount of the taxpayer's tax payable under Part I.2 for the year;

(x) **repayment under *Canada Education Savings Act*** — the total of all amounts each of which is an amount paid by the taxpayer in the year as a repayment, under the *Canada Education Savings Act* or under a program administered pursuant to an agreement entered into under section 12 of that Act, of an amount that was included because of subsection 146.1(7) in computing the taxpayer's income for the year or a preceding taxation year; and

Proposed Amendment — Quebec CESGs

Federal Budget, Notice of Ways and Means Motion and Supplementary Information, March 19, 2007: See under 146.1(1)"contribution".

(y) **repayment of UCCB** — the total of all amounts each of which is an amount paid in the taxation year as a repayment, under the *Universal Child Care Benefit Act*, of a benefit that was included because of subsection 56(6) in computing the taxpayer's income for the taxation year or a preceding taxation year.

Proposed Amendment — Recontribution of income from employees' leave of absence plan

Letter from Dept. of Finance, June 30, 2000: See under 81(1).

. . . . .

60.01 Eligible amount — For the purpose of paragraph 60(j), the amount, if any, by which

(a) the amount of any payment received by a taxpayer in a taxation year out of or under a foreign retirement arrangement and included in computing the taxpayer's income because of clause 56(1)(a)(i)(C.1) (other than any portion thereof that is included in respect of the taxpayer for the year under subparagraph 60(j)(i) or that is part of a series of periodic payments)

exceeds

(b) the portion, if any, of the payment included under paragraph (a) that can reasonably be considered to derive from contributions to the foreign retirement arrangement made by a person other than the taxpayer or the taxpayer's spouse or common-law partner or former spouse or common-law partner,

is an eligible amount in respect of the taxpayer for the year.

. . . . .

60.02 Application of subpara. 60(v)(iii) — Subparagraph 60(v)(iii) is applicable to the 1991 and subsequent taxation years.

60.03 (1) Definitions — The following definitions apply in this section.

"eligible pension income" has the same meaning as in subsection 118(7).

"joint election" in respect of a pensioner and a pension transferee for a taxation year means an election made jointly in prescribed form by the pensioner and the pension transferee and filed with the Minister with both the pensioner's and the pension transferee's returns of income for the taxation year in respect of which the election is made, on or before their respective filing-due dates for the taxation year.

"pensioner" for a taxation year means an individual who

(a) receives eligible pension income in the taxation year; and

(b) is resident in Canada,

(i) if the individual dies in the taxation year, at the time that is immediately before the individual's death, or

(ii) in any other case, at the end of the calendar year in which the taxation year ends.

"pension income" has the meaning assigned by section 118.

"pension transferee" for a taxation year means an individual who

(a) is resident in Canada,

(i) if the individual dies in the taxation year, at the time that is immediately before the individual's death, or

(ii) in any other case, at the end of the calendar year in which the taxation year ends; and

(b) at any time in the taxation year is married to, or in a common-law partnership with, a pensioner and is not, by reason of the breakdown of their marriage or common-law partnership, living separate and apart from the pensioner at the end of the taxation year and for a period of at least 90 days commencing in the taxation year.

"qualified pension income" has the meaning assigned by section 118.

"split-pension amount" for a taxation year is the amount elected by a pensioner and a pension transferee in a joint election for the taxation year not exceeding the amount determined by the formula

$$0.5A \times B/C$$

where

A is the eligible pension income of the pensioner for the taxation year;

B is the number of months in the pensioner's taxation year at any time during which the pensioner was married to, or was in a common-law partnership with, the pension transferee; and

C is the number of months in the pensioner's taxation year.

(2) Effect of pension income split — For the purpose of subsection 118(3), if a pensioner and a pension transferee have made a joint election in a taxation year,

(a) the pensioner is deemed not to have received the portion of the pensioner's pension income or qualified pension income, as the case may be, for the taxation year that is equal to the amount of the pensioner's split-pension amount for that taxation year; and

(b) the pension transferee is deemed to have received the split-pension amount

(i) as pension income, to the extent that the split-pension amount was pension income to the pensioner, and

(ii) as qualified pension income, to the extent that the split-pension amount was qualified pension income to the pensioner.

(3) Limitation — A pensioner may file only one joint election for a particular taxation year.

(4) False declaration — A joint election is invalid if the Minister establishes that a pensioner or a pension transferee has knowingly or under circumstances amounting to gross negligence made a false declaration in the joint election.

60.1 (1) Support — For the purposes of paragraph 60(b) and subsection 118(5), where an order or agreement, or any variation thereof, provides for the payment of an amount by a taxpayer to a person or for the benefit of the person, children in the person's custody or both the person and those children, the amount or any part thereof

(a) when payable, is deemed to be payable to and receivable by that person; and

(b) when paid, is deemed to have been paid to and received by that person.

(2) Agreement — For the purposes of section 60, this section and subsection 118(5), the amount determined by the formula

$$A - B$$

where

A is the total of all amounts each of which is an amount (other than an amount that is otherwise a support amount) that became payable by a taxpayer in a taxation year, under an order of a competent tribunal or under a written agreement, in respect of an expense (other than an expenditure in respect of a self-contained domestic establishment in which the taxpayer resides or an expenditure for the acquisition of tangible property that is not an expenditure on account of a medical or education expense or in respect of the acquisition, improvement or maintenance of a self-contained domestic establishment in which the person described in paragraph (a) or (b) resides) incurred in the year or the preceding taxation year for the maintenance of a person, children in the person's custody or both the person and those children, where the person is

Proposed Amendment — 60.1(2)A opening words

Application: Bill C-33 (First Senate Reading June 18, 2007) (Part 3 — bijuralism), s. 220, will amend the opening words of the description of A in subsec. 60.1(2) by substituting "tangible property, or for civil law corporeal property," for "tangible property", to come into force on Royal Assent.

Technical Notes: See under 12(4).

(a) the taxpayer's spouse or common-law partner or former spouse or common-law partner, or

(b) where the amount became payable under an order made by a competent tribunal in accordance with the laws of a province, an individual who is a parent of a child of whom the taxpayer is a legal parent,

and

B is the amount, if any, by which

(a) the total of all amounts each of which is an amount included in the total determined for A in respect of the acquisition or improvement of a self-contained domestic establishment in which that person resides, including any payment of principal or interest in respect of a loan made or indebtedness incurred to finance, in any manner whatever, such acquisition or improvement

exceeds

(b) the total of all amounts each of which is an amount equal to 1/5 of the original principal amount of a loan or indebtedness described in paragraph (a), is, where the order or written agreement, as the case may be, provides that this subsection and subsection 56.1(2) shall apply to any amount paid or payable thereunder, deemed to be an amount payable by the taxpayer to that person and receivable by that person as an allowance on a periodic basis, and that person is deemed to have discretion as to the use of that amount.

(3) Prior payments — For the purposes of this section and section 60, where a written agreement or order of a competent tribunal made at any time in a taxation year provides that an amount paid before that time and in the year or the preceding taxation year is to be considered to have been paid and received thereunder,

(a) the amount is deemed to have been paid thereunder; and

(b) the agreement or order is deemed, except for the purpose of this subsection, to have been made on the day on which the first such amount was paid, except that, where the agreement or order is made after April 1997 and varies a child support amount payable to the recipient from the last such amount paid to the recipient before May 1997, each varied amount of child support paid under the agreement or order is deemed to have been payable under an agreement or order the commencement day of which is the day on which the first payment of the varied amount is required to be made.

(4) Definitions — The definitions in subsection 56.1(4) apply in this section and section 60.

.....

.....

.....

INDEX

(All references are to sections of the *Divorce Act* and paragraphs of the text unless the abbreviations ITA (referring to the *Income Tax Act*), FCSG (Federal Child Support Guidelines) or SSG (Spousal Support Advisory Guidelines) are used.

A